AMERICA AT THE POLLS

AMERICA AT THE POLLS

A HANDBOOK OF AMERICAN
PRESIDENTIAL ELECTION
STATISTICS 1920-1964

COMPILED AND EDITED BY
RICHARD M. SCAMMON

GOVERNMENTAL AFFAIRS INSTITUTE

UNIVERSITY OF PITTSBURGH PRESS   PITTSBURGH   1965

© GOVERNMENTAL AFFAIRS INSTITUTE 1965

Printed in the United States of America

Library of Congress catalog card number: 65–27801

CONTENTS

PREFACE

AMERICA AT THE POLLS is a statistical history of American Presidential elections in the years since the end of World War I. This volume reveals our country's voting habits in twelve Presidential elections beginning with the general enfranchisement of women and the election of President Harding in 1920, and concluding with President Johnson's victory in 1964. Following the format of the Institute's AMERICA VOTES series, detailed vote figures, percentages and pluralities are presented for every state and every county to provide a comprehensive, authoritative reference volume.

This study has been made possible through the generous financial support of the Maurice and Laura Falk Foundation of Pittsburgh. In accordance with the Foundation's policies, however, responsibility for the material used and for its treatment in AMERICA AT THE POLLS rests with the Institute and its Elections Research Center.

Edward H. Litchfield
Chairman of the Board
Governmental Affairs Institute

Washington, D. C.
October, 1965

INTRODUCTION

Data for this study of Presidential voting have been organized along the lines of the Institute's AMERICA VOTES series. Thus, the first pages give national Presidential voting figures by states for the twelve elections from 1920 through 1964, followed by detailed county-by-county data for each of the states.

As in AMERICA VOTES, state and county figures include total vote, Republican-Democratic-Other breakdown, pluralities, and percentages of total and major vote for Republican and Democratic candidates. Each national table is followed by a brief note listing candidates and their national vote and identifying special characteristics in the state vote. Special aspects of the Electoral College vote are included here and any variations between the plurality figures in these national tables and Republican-Democratic plurality figures in the state sections are listed.

Each state data section is followed by a note page giving the composition of the other vote in detail and indicating any special circumstances of the state vote—canvassing problems, organization of new counties, dual elector tickets, minor party effect on pluralities, and the like. There is an entry for other vote for each of the twelve elections, while the special cases entries are limited to those years for which comments have been required.

Alaska and Hawaii have been carried in all national tables so as to preserve the line relationship of the various states. The District of Columbia, which voted only in the 1964 election, has been listed only once—at the end of the 1964 table. In the state tables, *all* listings include *all* units reporting at any time over the twelve elections included in AMERICA AT THE POLLS. Thus the place of any unit of a state in the 1964 table will be the same as the place of that unit in the 1920 table.

Popular voting for President in America is actually voting for electors and the traditional practice has been to report the popular vote as the vote for the "highest elector"—the elector candidate polling the largest state-wide vote on each of the competing elector tickets. Increasingly American voters may mark their Presidential choice *en bloc,* but some states still require a vote for each individual elector and therefore report varying vote totals for elector candidates. In AMERICA AT THE POLLS the "highest elector" system has been used except for county data for certain of the earlier elections in Michigan and New Jersey, as indicated in the notes for those states.

In some states Presidential candidates have had the support of two or three elector tickets. These tickets have sometimes included the same electors, as in the Liberal party nominations of national Democratic candidates in New York, sometimes not. Where there has been local or national endorsement of candidates, votes for these separate elector tickets have been combined and the make-up of the combined vote detailed in the state note section concerned. In only two situations have voters not been able to ballot for the national Republican or Democratic candidates. In Alabama in 1948 the Democratic elector candidates were pledged to the States Rights nominees rather than to the national Democratic ticket and in 1964 in Alabama the Democratic elector candidates were unpledged. In both circumstances the vote cast for these Democratic elector candidates has been classed as "other".

Over the twelve elections included in this volume most votes have been cast for Republican or Democratic candidates. Those for other nominees have been included in the "other" category even though in particular circumstances they could be regarded as a major part of a national, or at least of a state, contest. In 1924, for example, the Progressive candidates polled close to five million votes and were the effective opposition in a number of states. Since 1948 a number of States Rights or unpledged elector tickets have polled well in certain of the Southern states. For uniformity of treatment, however, AMERICA AT THE POLLS follows the practice of AMERICA VOTES and of earlier studies in combining these votes into a single "other" category.

For some years Democratic candidates have appeared on the Minnesota ballot as Democratic-Farmer-Labor, but the single word "Democratic" is used in this volume; similarly Republican votes in one election in California were canvassed as Republican-Prohibition, but the single word "Republican" is used in AMERICA AT THE POLLS. For the other parties as well, party names have been standardized and a single label used to designate candidates. Thus, in 1924, votes for LaFollette are carried as Progressive, whatever their state label may have been. Similarly, votes in 1936 for Lemke are given as Union and votes in 1948 for Wallace as Progressive. Additional details are supplied in the state note sections to clarify 1952, 1956, and 1960 voting situations involving the use of the same party name by different candidates in different states.

As in the AMERICA VOTES series, plurality figures have been calculated on a Republican-Democratic basis except for the data in the national tables. In a few instances the pluralities given in these national tables differ from the Republican-Democratic pluralities in the individual state tables, and such variations are indicated in the appropriate national note section. State note sections indicate situations in which the Republican-Democratic plurality is not a true plurality. These notes as to minor party candidates winning or running second are not intended to list such situations in detail, but rather to alert the user to this aspect of the printed plurality figures.

Except where otherwise indicated in the state note sections, the data used for AMERICA AT THE POLLS have been drawn from the official state canvass reports covering the twelve Presidential elections from 1920 through 1964. These reports have been supplemented and interpreted by reference to the reports of the Clerk of the House of Representatives, the files of the National Archives, and the data prepared for the various state publications designed on the AMERICA VOTES format. Contemporary almanac and press material has also been consulted, especially for the earlier elections.

The most important sources for interpretation of data, however, have been the two pioneer research studies of Professor Edgar Eugene Robinson. These volumes, THE PRESIDENTIAL VOTE, 1896-1932 and THEY VOTED FOR ROOSEVELT: THE PRESIDENTIAL VOTE, 1932-1944, remain basic reference sources in the field of electoral statistics and a guide to all the research efforts which have followed their publication. While differences will be noted in the data published in AMERICA AT THE POLLS and the figures used in these and other reference studies, these differences will usually be small and stem most often from varying interpretations of the available statistics. Naturally, the responsibility for the particular sets of figures and data interpretations used in this volume is that of the Editor alone.

Since a study of this sort involves the publication of a vast number of figures, it is inevitable that errors will occur. Users are urged to write the Editor as to any they may discover, since supplementary material to AMERICA AT THE POLLS will be published from time to time. This material will include corrective data and results of the Institute's continuing research on Presidential election statistics. Research studies presently planned include greater detail on minor party voting, particularly for those situations in which a minor party vote is included in AMERICA AT THE POLLS only as a state-wide figure, voting in Presidential preference primaries, and voting for President in larger cities.

It would be impossible to list all those to whom acknowledgment is due for assistance in bringing this book to the public. The support of the Falk Foundation has been noted in the Preface, the assistance of the data sources in this Introduction. Officials at the national, state and local level have been helpful beyond the requirements of their offices and scholars in various parts of America have supplied interpretations of data in a number of special situations. Much of the data collection was done by Ellen Perlman and Alice McGillivray, while the design and programming of the computer operation was undertaken by George Lunger and Michael Greenberg, data processing statisticians for the Radio Corporation of America.

To all who have helped in gathering this material and in preparing it for publication must go the gratitude of the Editor and the thanks of all those who will use this study of AMERICA AT THE POLLS.

Richard M. Scammon, Director
Elections Research Center
Governmental Affairs Institute

Washington, D. C.
October, 1965

AMERICA AT THE POLLS

UNITED STATES

PRESIDENT 1920

State	Electoral Vote Rep.	Dem.	Other	Total Vote	Republican	Democratic	Other	Plurality	Total Vote Rep.	Dem.	Major Vote Rep.	Dem.
Alabama		12		233,951	74,719	156,064	3,168	81,345 D	31.9%	66.7%	32.4%	67.6%
Alaska												
Arizona	3			66,803	37,016	29,546	241	7,470 R	55.4%	44.2%	55.6%	44.4%
Arkansas		9		183,871	72,316	106,427	5,128	34,111 D	39.3%	57.9%	40.5%	59.5%
California	13			943,463	624,992	229,191	89,280	395,801 R	66.2%	24.3%	73.2%	26.8%
Colorado	6			292,053	173,248	104,936	13,869	68,312 R	59.3%	35.9%	62.3%	37.7%
Connecticut	7			365,518	229,238	120,721	15,559	108,517 R	62.7%	33.0%	65.5%	34.5%
Delaware	3			94,875	52,858	39,911	2,106	12,947 R	55.7%	42.1%	57.0%	43.0%
Florida		6		145,684	44,853	90,515	10,316	45,662 D	30.8%	62.1%	33.1%	66.9%
Georgia		14		149,558	42,981	106,112	465	63,131 D	28.7%	71.0%	28.8%	71.2%
Hawaii												
Idaho	4			138,281	91,351	46,930		44,421 R	66.1%	33.9%	66.1%	33.9%
Illinois	29			2,094,714	1,420,480	534,395	139,839	886,085 R	67.8%	25.5%	72.7%	27.3%
Indiana	15			1,262,974	696,370	511,364	55,240	185,006 R	55.1%	40.5%	57.7%	42.3%
Iowa	13			894,959	634,674	227,804	32,481	406,870 R	70.9%	25.5%	73.6%	26.4%
Kansas	10			570,243	369,268	185,464	15,511	183,804 R	64.8%	32.5%	66.6%	33.4%
Kentucky		13		918,636	452,480	456,497	9,659	4,017 D	49.3%	49.7%	49.8%	50.2%
Louisiana		10		126,397	38,539	87,519	339	48,980 D	30.5%	69.2%	30.6%	69.4%
Maine	6			197,840	136,355	58,961	2,524	77,394 R	68.9%	29.8%	69.8%	30.2%
Maryland	8			428,443	236,117	180,626	11,700	55,491 R	55.1%	42.2%	56.7%	43.3%
Massachusetts	18			993,718	681,153	276,691	35,874	404,462 R	68.5%	27.8%	71.1%	28.9%
Michigan	15			1,048,411	762,865	233,450	52,096	529,415 R	72.8%	22.3%	76.6%	23.4%
Minnesota	12			735,838	519,421	142,994	73,423	376,427 R	70.6%	19.4%	78.4%	21.6%
Mississippi		10		82,351	11,576	69,136	1,639	57,560 D	14.1%	84.0%	14.3%	85.7%
Missouri	18			1,332,140	727,252	574,699	30,189	152,553 R	54.6%	43.1%	55.9%	44.1%
Montana	4			179,006	109,430	57,372	12,204	52,058 R	61.1%	32.1%	65.6%	34.4%
Nebraska	8			382,743	247,498	119,608	15,637	127,890 R	64.7%	31.3%	67.4%	32.6%
Nevada	3			27,194	15,479	9,851	1,864	5,628 R	56.9%	36.2%	61.1%	38.9%
New Hampshire	4			159,092	95,196	62,662	1,234	32,534 R	59.8%	39.4%	60.3%	39.7%
New Jersey	14			910,251	615,333	258,761	36,157	356,572 R	67.6%	28.4%	70.4%	29.6%
New Mexico	3			105,412	57,634	46,668	1,110	10,966 R	54.7%	44.3%	55.3%	44.7%
New York	45			2,898,513	1,871,167	781,238	246,108	1,089,929 R	64.6%	27.0%	70.5%	29.5%
North Carolina		12		538,649	232,819	305,367	463	72,548 D	43.2%	56.7%	43.3%	56.7%
North Dakota	5			205,786	160,082	37,422	8,282	122,660 R	77.8%	18.2%	81.1%	18.9%
Ohio	24			2,021,653	1,182,022	780,037	59,594	401,985 R	58.5%	38.6%	60.2%	39.8%
Oklahoma	10			485,678	243,840	216,122	25,716	27,718 R	50.2%	44.5%	53.0%	47.0%
Oregon	5			238,522	143,592	80,019	14,911	63,573 R	60.2%	33.5%	64.2%	35.8%
Pennsylvania	38			1,851,248	1,218,215	503,202	129,831	715,013 R	65.8%	27.2%	70.8%	29.2%
Rhode Island	5			167,981	107,463	55,062	5,456	52,401 R	64.0%	32.8%	66.1%	33.9%
South Carolina		9		66,808	2,610	64,170	28	61,560 D	3.9%	96.1%	3.9%	96.1%
South Dakota	5			182,237	110,692	35,938	35,607	74,754 R	60.7%	19.7%	75.5%	24.5%
Tennessee	12			428,036	219,229	206,558	2,249	12,671 R	51.2%	48.3%	51.5%	48.5%
Texas		20		486,109	114,658	287,920	83,531	173,262 D	23.6%	59.2%	28.5%	71.5%
Utah	4			145,828	81,555	56,639	7,634	24,916 R	55.9%	38.8%	59.0%	41.0%
Vermont	4			89,961	68,212	20,919	830	47,293 R	75.8%	23.3%	76.5%	23.5%
Virginia		12		231,000	87,456	141,670	1,874	54,214 D	37.9%	61.3%	38.2%	61.8%
Washington	7			398,715	223,137	84,298	91,280	138,839 R	56.0%	21.1%	72.6%	27.4%
West Virginia	8			509,936	282,007	220,785	7,144	61,222 R	55.3%	43.3%	56.1%	43.9%
Wisconsin	13			701,281	498,576	113,422	89,283	385,154 R	71.1%	16.2%	81.5%	18.5%
Wyoming	3			56,253	35,091	17,429	3,733	17,662 R	62.4%	31.0%	66.8%	33.2%
United States	404	127	-	26,768,613	16,153,115	9,133,092	1,482,406	7,020,023 R	60.3%	34.1%	63.9%	36.1%

The Republican figure in South Carolina includes votes cast for two elector tickets; the figure in Florida is the vote cast for the one elector candidate who ran on both Republican tickets in that state.

All state plurality figures are consistent with the Republican-Democratic pluralities as printed in the individual state sections. In Washington, the total vote for minor party candidates exceeded that for the Democratic candidates, but the Democratic total was greater than that for any one of the minor party nominees.

The full list of candidates for President and Vice-President was:

16,153,115	Warren G. Harding and Calvin Coolidge, <u>Republican</u>.
9,133,092	James M. Cox and Franklin D. Roosevelt, <u>Democratic</u>.
915,490	Eugene V. Debs and Seymour Stedman, <u>Socialist</u>.
265,229	Parley P. Christensen and Max S. Hayes, <u>Farmer-Labor</u>.
189,339	Aaron S. Watkins and D. Leigh Colvin, <u>Prohibition</u>.
48,098	James Ferguson and William J. Hough, <u>American</u>.
30,594	William W. Cox and August Gillhaus, <u>Socialist Labor</u>.
5,833	Robert C. Macauley and Richard C. Barnum, <u>Single Tax</u>.

In addition, 27,309 votes were cast in Texas for a Black-and-Tan Republican elector ticket and 514 scattered votes were reported from various states.

UNITED STATES

PRESIDENT 1924

State	Electoral Vote Rep.	Dem.	Other	Total Vote	Republican	Democratic	Other	Plurality	Percentage Total Vote Rep.	Dem.	Major Vote Rep.	Dem.
Alabama		12		164,563	42,823	113,138	8,602	70,315 D	26.0%	68.8%	27.5%	72.5%
Alaska												
Arizona	3			73,961	30,516	26,235	17,210	4,281 R	41.3%	35.5%	53.8%	46.2%
Arkansas		9		138,540	40,583	84,790	13,167	44,207 D	29.3%	61.2%	32.4%	67.6%
California	13			1,281,778	733,250	105,514	443,014	308,601 R	57.2%	8.2%	87.4%	12.6%
Colorado	6			342,261	195,171	75,238	71,852	119,933 R	57.0%	22.0%	72.2%	27.8%
Connecticut	7			400,396	246,322	110,184	43,890	136,138 R	61.5%	27.5%	69.1%	30.9%
Delaware	3			90,885	52,441	33,445	4,999	18,996 R	57.7%	36.8%	61.1%	38.9%
Florida		6		109,158	30,633	62,083	16,442	31,450 D	28.1%	56.9%	33.0%	67.0%
Georgia		14		166,635	30,300	123,262	13,073	92,962 D	18.2%	74.0%	19.7%	80.3%
Hawaii												
Idaho	4			147,690	69,791	23,951	53,948	15,843 R	47.3%	16.2%	74.5%	25.5%
Illinois	29			2,470,067	1,453,321	576,975	439,771	876,346 R	58.8%	23.4%	71.6%	28.4%
Indiana	15			1,272,390	703,042	492,245	77,103	210,797 R	55.3%	38.7%	58.8%	41.2%
Iowa	13			976,770	537,458	160,382	278,930	263,010 R	55.0%	16.4%	77.0%	23.0%
Kansas	10			662,456	407,671	156,320	98,465	251,351 R	61.5%	23.6%	72.3%	27.7%
Kentucky	13			813,843	396,758	375,593	41,492	21,165 R	48.8%	46.2%	51.4%	48.6%
Louisiana		10		121,951	24,670	93,218	4,063	68,548 D	20.2%	76.4%	20.9%	79.1%
Maine	6			192,192	138,440	41,964	11,788	96,476 R	72.0%	21.8%	76.7%	23.3%
Maryland	8			358,630	162,414	148,072	48,144	14,342 R	45.3%	41.3%	52.3%	47.7%
Massachusetts	18			1,129,837	703,476	280,831	145,530	422,645 R	62.3%	24.9%	71.5%	28.5%
Michigan	15			1,160,419	874,631	152,359	133,429	722,272 R	75.4%	13.1%	85.2%	14.8%
Minnesota	12			822,146	420,759	55,913	345,474	81,567 R	51.2%	6.8%	88.3%	11.7%
Mississippi		10		112,442	8,494	100,474	3,474	91,980 D	7.6%	89.4%	7.8%	92.2%
Missouri	18			1,310,095	648,488	574,962	86,645	73,526 R	49.5%	43.9%	53.0%	47.0%
Montana	4			174,425	74,138	33,805	66,482	8,014 R	42.5%	19.4%	68.7%	31.3%
Nebraska	8			463,559	218,985	137,299	107,275	81,686 R	47.2%	29.6%	61.5%	38.5%
Nevada	3			26,921	11,243	5,909	9,769	1,474 R	41.8%	21.9%	65.5%	34.5%
New Hampshire	4			164,769	98,575	57,201	8,993	41,374 R	59.8%	34.7%	63.3%	36.7%
New Jersey	14			1,088,054	676,277	298,043	113,734	378,234 R	62.2%	27.4%	69.4%	30.6%
New Mexico	3			112,830	54,745	48,542	9,543	6,203 R	48.5%	43.0%	53.0%	47.0%
New York	45			3,263,939	1,820,058	950,796	493,085	869,262 R	55.8%	29.1%	65.7%	34.3%
North Carolina		12		481,608	190,754	284,190	6,664	93,436 D	39.6%	59.0%	40.2%	59.8%
North Dakota	5			199,081	94,931	13,858	90,292	5,009 R	47.7%	7.0%	87.3%	12.7%
Ohio	24			2,016,296	1,176,130	477,887	362,279	698,243 R	58.3%	23.7%	71.1%	28.9%
Oklahoma		10		527,828	225,756	255,798	46,274	30,042 D	42.8%	48.5%	46.9%	53.1%
Oregon	5			279,488	142,579	67,589	69,320	74,176 R	51.0%	24.2%	67.8%	32.2%
Pennsylvania	38			2,144,850	1,401,481	409,192	334,177	992,289 R	65.3%	19.1%	77.4%	22.6%
Rhode Island	5			210,115	125,286	76,606	8,223	48,680 R	59.6%	36.5%	62.1%	37.9%
South Carolina		9		50,755	1,123	49,008	624	47,885 D	2.2%	96.6%	2.2%	97.8%
South Dakota	5			203,868	101,299	27,214	75,355	25,944 R	49.7%	13.3%	78.8%	21.2%
Tennessee		12		301,030	130,831	159,339	10,860	28,508 D	43.5%	52.9%	45.1%	54.9%
Texas		20		657,054	130,794	483,381	42,879	352,587 D	19.9%	73.6%	21.3%	78.7%
Utah	4			156,990	77,327	47,001	32,662	30,326 R	49.3%	29.9%	62.2%	37.8%
Vermont	4			102,917	80,498	16,124	6,295	64,374 R	78.2%	15.7%	83.3%	16.7%
Virginia		12		223,603	73,328	139,717	10,558	66,389 D	32.8%	62.5%	34.4%	65.6%
Washington	7			421,549	220,224	42,842	158,483	69,497 R	52.2%	10.2%	83.7%	16.3%
West Virginia	8			583,662	288,635	257,232	37,795	31,403 R	49.5%	44.1%	52.9%	47.1%
Wisconsin			13	840,827	311,614	68,115	461,098	142,064 P	37.1%	8.1%	82.1%	17.9%
Wyoming	3			79,900	41,858	12,868	25,174	16,684 R	52.4%	16.1%	76.5%	23.5%
United States	382	136	13	29,095,023	15,719,921	8,386,704	4,988,398	7,333,217 R	54.0%	28.8%	65.2%	34.8%

Wisconsin's 13 electoral votes were cast for the Progressive nominees. In several states the Progressive total includes votes cast for two or three elector tickets.

State plurality figures are consistent with the Republican-Democratic pluralities as printed in the individual state sections except in Wisconsin (which the Progressive nominees won) and in the eleven states in which the Progressive candidates ran second.

The full list of candidates for President and Vice-President was:

15,719,921	Calvin Coolidge and Charles G. Dawes, Republican.
8,386,704	John W. Davis and Charles W. Bryan, Democratic.
4,832,532	Robert M. LaFollette and Burton K. Wheeler, Progressive.
56,292	Herman P. Faris and Marie Caroline Brehm, Prohibition.
34,174	Frank T. Johns and Verne L. Reynolds, Socialist Labor.
33,360	William Z. Foster and Benjamin Gitlow, Communist.
24,340	Gilbert O. Nations and Leander L. Pickett, American.
2,948	William J. Wallace and John C. Lincoln, Commonwealth Land.

In addition, 4,752 scattered votes were reported from various states.

UNITED STATES

PRESIDENT 1928

State	Electoral Vote Rep.	Dem.	Other	Total Vote	Republican	Democratic	Other	Plurality	Total Vote Rep.	Dem.	Major Vote Rep.	Dem.
Alabama		12		248,981	120,725	127,796	460	7,071 D	48.5%	51.3%	48.6%	51.4%
Alaska												
Arizona	3			91,254	52,533	38,537	184	13,996 R	57.6%	42.2%	57.7%	42.3%
Arkansas		9		197,726	77,784	119,196	746	41,412 D	39.3%	60.3%	39.5%	60.5%
California	13			1,796,656	1,162,323	614,365	19,968	547,958 R	64.7%	34.2%	65.4%	34.6%
Colorado	6			392,242	253,872	133,131	5,239	120,741 R	64.7%	33.9%	65.6%	34.4%
Connecticut	7			553,118	296,641	252,085	4,392	44,556 R	53.6%	45.6%	54.1%	45.9%
Delaware	3			104,602	68,860	35,354	388	33,506 R	65.8%	33.8%	66.1%	33.9%
Florida	6			252,068	145,860	101,764	4,444	44,096 R	57.9%	40.4%	58.9%	41.1%
Georgia		14		231,592	101,800	129,604	188	27,804 D	44.0%	56.0%	44.0%	56.0%
Hawaii												
Idaho	4			151,541	97,322	52,926	1,293	44,396 R	64.2%	34.9%	64.8%	35.2%
Illinois	29			3,107,489	1,769,141	1,313,817	24,531	455,324 R	56.9%	42.3%	57.4%	42.6%
Indiana	15			1,421,314	848,290	562,691	10,333	285,599 R	59.7%	39.6%	60.1%	39.9%
Iowa	13			1,009,189	623,570	379,011	6,608	244,559 R	61.8%	37.6%	62.2%	37.8%
Kansas	10			713,200	513,672	193,003	6,525	320,669 R	72.0%	27.1%	72.7%	27.3%
Kentucky	13			940,521	558,064	381,070	1,387	176,994 R	59.3%	40.5%	59.4%	40.6%
Louisiana		10		215,833	51,160	164,655	18	113,495 D	23.7%	76.3%	23.7%	76.3%
Maine	6			262,170	179,923	81,179	1,068	98,744 R	68.6%	31.0%	68.9%	31.1%
Maryland	8			528,348	301,479	223,626	3,243	77,853 R	57.1%	42.3%	57.4%	42.6%
Massachusetts		18		1,577,823	775,566	792,758	9,499	17,192 D	49.2%	50.2%	49.5%	50.5%
Michigan	15			1,372,082	965,396	396,762	9,924	568,634 R	70.4%	28.9%	70.9%	29.1%
Minnesota	12			970,976	560,977	396,451	13,548	164,526 R	57.8%	40.8%	58.6%	41.4%
Mississippi		10		151,568	27,030	124,538		97,508 D	17.8%	82.2%	17.8%	82.2%
Missouri	18			1,500,845	834,080	662,684	4,081	171,396 R	55.6%	44.2%	55.7%	44.3%
Montana	4			194,108	113,300	78,578	2,230	34,722 R	58.4%	40.5%	59.0%	41.0%
Nebraska	8			547,128	345,745	197,950	3,433	147,795 R	63.2%	36.2%	63.6%	36.4%
Nevada	3			39,417	18,327	14,090		4,237 R	56.5%	43.5%	56.5%	43.5%
New Hampshire	4			196,757	115,404	80,715	638	34,689 R	58.7%	41.0%	58.8%	41.2%
New Jersey	14			1,549,381	926,050	616,517	6,814	309,533 R	59.8%	39.8%	60.0%	40.0%
New Mexico	3			118,077	69,708	48,211	158	21,497 R	59.0%	40.8%	59.1%	40.9%
New York	45			4,405,626	2,193,344	2,089,863	122,419	103,481 R	49.8%	47.4%	51.2%	48.8%
North Carolina	12			635,150	348,923	286,227		62,696 R	54.9%	45.1%	54.9%	45.1%
North Dakota	5			239,845	131,419	106,648	1,778	24,771 R	54.8%	44.5%	55.2%	44.8%
Ohio	24			2,508,346	1,627,546	864,210	16,590	763,336 R	64.9%	34.5%	65.3%	34.7%
Oklahoma	10			618,427	394,046	219,174	5,207	174,872 R	63.7%	35.4%	64.3%	35.7%
Oregon	5			319,942	205,341	109,223	5,378	96,118 R	64.2%	34.1%	65.3%	34.7%
Pennsylvania	38			3,150,612	2,055,382	1,067,586	27,644	987,796 R	65.2%	33.9%	65.8%	34.2%
Rhode Island		5		237,194	117,522	118,973	699	1,451 D	49.5%	50.2%	49.7%	50.3%
South Carolina		9		68,605	5,858	62,700	47	56,842 D	8.5%	91.4%	8.5%	91.5%
South Dakota	5			261,857	157,603	102,660	1,594	54,943 R	60.2%	39.2%	60.6%	39.4%
Tennessee	12			353,192	195,388	157,143	661	38,245 R	55.3%	44.5%	55.4%	44.6%
Texas	20			717,733	372,324	344,542	867	27,782 R	51.9%	48.0%	51.9%	48.1%
Utah	4			176,603	94,618	80,985	1,000	13,633 R	53.6%	45.9%	53.9%	46.1%
Vermont	4			135,191	90,404	44,440	347	45,964 R	66.9%	32.9%	67.0%	33.0%
Virginia	12			305,364	164,609	140,146	609	24,463 R	53.9%	45.9%	54.0%	46.0%
Washington	7			500,840	335,844	156,772	8,224	179,072 R	67.1%	31.3%	68.2%	31.8%
West Virginia	8			642,752	375,551	263,784	3,417	111,767 R	58.4%	41.0%	58.7%	41.3%
Wisconsin	13			1,016,831	544,205	450,259	22,367	93,946 R	53.5%	44.3%	54.7%	45.3%
Wyoming	3			82,835	52,748	29,299	788	23,449 R	63.7%	35.4%	64.3%	35.7%
United States	444	87	-	36,805,951	21,437,277	15,007,698	360,976	6,429,579 R	58.2%	40.8%	58.8%	41.2%

The Republican figures in Georgia, Mississippi, and South Carolina include votes cast for two or three elector tickets; in Pennsylvania the Communist total includes votes cast for two elector tickets.

All state plurality figures are consistent with the Republican-Democratic pluralities as printed in the individual state sections.

The full list of candidates for President and Vice-President was:

21,437,277	Herbert C. Hoover and Charles Curtis, Republican.
15,007,698	Alfred E. Smith and Joseph T. Robinson, Democratic.
265,583	Norman Thomas and James H. Maurer, Socialist.
46,896	William Z. Foster and Benjamin Gitlow, Communist.
21,586	Verne L. Reynolds and Jeremiah D. Crowley, Socialist Labor.
20,101	William F. Varney and James A. Edgerton, Prohibition.
6,390	Frank E. Webb and L. R. Tillman, Farmer-Labor.

In addition, 420 scattered votes were reported from various states.

UNITED STATES

PRESIDENT 1932

State	Electoral Vote Rep.	Dem.	Other	Total Vote	Republican	Democratic	Other	Plurality	Total Vote Rep.	Dem.	Major Vote Rep.	Dem.
Alabama		11		245,303	34,675	207,910	2,718	173,235 D	14.1%	84.8%	14.3%	85.7%
Alaska												
Arizona		3		118,251	36,104	79,264	2,883	43,160 D	30.5%	67.0%	31.3%	68.7%
Arkansas		9		216,569	27,465	186,829	2,275	159,364 D	12.7%	86.3%	12.8%	87.2%
California		22		2,266,972	847,902	1,324,157	94,913	476,255 D	37.4%	58.4%	39.0%	61.0%
Colorado		6		457,696	189,617	250,877	17,202	61,260 D	41.4%	54.8%	43.0%	57.0%
Connecticut	8			594,183	288,420	281,632	24,131	6,788 R	48.5%	47.4%	50.6%	49.4%
Delaware	3			112,901	57,073	54,319	1,509	2,754 R	50.6%	48.1%	51.2%	48.8%
Florida		7		276,943	69,170	206,307	1,466	137,137 D	25.0%	74.5%	25.1%	74.9%
Georgia		12		255,590	19,863	234,118	1,609	214,255 D	7.8%	91.6%	7.8%	92.2%
Hawaii												
Idaho		4		186,520	71,312	109,479	5,729	38,167 D	38.2%	58.7%	39.4%	60.6%
Illinois		29		3,407,926	1,432,756	1,882,304	92,866	449,548 D	42.0%	55.2%	43.2%	56.8%
Indiana		14		1,576,927	677,184	862,054	37,689	184,870 D	42.9%	54.7%	44.0%	56.0%
Iowa		11		1,036,687	414,433	598,019	24,235	183,586 D	40.0%	57.7%	40.9%	59.1%
Kansas		9		791,978	349,498	424,204	18,276	74,706 D	44.1%	53.6%	45.2%	54.8%
Kentucky		11		983,059	394,716	580,574	7,769	185,858 D	40.2%	59.1%	40.5%	59.5%
Louisiana		10		268,804	18,853	249,418	533	230,565 D	7.0%	92.8%	7.0%	93.0%
Maine	5			298,444	166,631	128,907	2,006	37,724 R	55.8%	43.2%	56.4%	43.6%
Maryland		8		511,054	184,184	314,314	12,556	130,130 D	36.0%	61.5%	36.9%	63.1%
Massachusetts		17		1,580,114	736,959	800,148	43,007	63,189 D	46.6%	50.6%	47.9%	52.1%
Michigan		19		1,664,765	739,894	871,700	53,171	131,806 D	44.4%	52.4%	45.9%	54.1%
Minnesota		11		1,002,843	363,959	600,806	38,078	236,847 D	36.3%	59.9%	37.7%	62.3%
Mississippi		9		146,034	5,180	140,168	686	134,988 D	3.5%	96.0%	3.6%	96.4%
Missouri		15		1,609,894	564,713	1,025,406	19,775	460,693 D	35.1%	63.7%	35.5%	64.5%
Montana		4		216,479	78,078	127,286	11,115	49,208 D	36.1%	58.8%	38.0%	62.0%
Nebraska		7		570,135	201,177	359,082	9,876	157,905 D	35.3%	63.0%	35.9%	64.1%
Nevada		0		41,430	12,674	28,756		16,082 D	30.6%	69.4%	30.6%	69.4%
New Hampshire	4			205,520	103,629	100,680	1,211	2,949 R	50.4%	49.0%	50.7%	49.3%
New Jersey		16		1,630,063	775,684	806,630	47,749	30,946 D	47.6%	49.5%	49.0%	51.0%
New Mexico		3		151,606	54,217	95,089	2,300	40,872 D	35.8%	62.7%	36.3%	63.7%
New York		47		4,688,614	1,937,963	2,534,959	215,692	596,996 D	41.3%	54.1%	43.3%	56.7%
North Carolina		13		711,498	208,344	497,566	5,588	289,222 D	29.3%	69.9%	29.5%	70.5%
North Dakota		4		256,290	71,772	178,350	6,168	106,578 D	28.0%	69.6%	28.7%	71.3%
Ohio		26		2,609,728	1,227,319	1,301,695	80,714	74,376 D	47.0%	49.9%	48.5%	51.5%
Oklahoma		11		704,633	188,165	516,468		328,303 D	26.7%	73.3%	26.7%	73.3%
Oregon		5		368,751	136,019	213,871	18,861	77,852 D	36.9%	58.0%	38.9%	61.1%
Pennsylvania	36			2,859,021	1,453,540	1,295,948	109,533	157,592 R	50.8%	45.3%	52.9%	47.1%
Rhode Island		4		266,170	115,266	146,604	4,300	31,338 D	43.3%	55.1%	44.0%	56.0%
South Carolina		8		104,407	1,978	102,347	82	100,369 D	1.9%	98.0%	1.9%	98.1%
South Dakota		4		288,438	99,212	183,515	5,711	84,303 D	34.4%	63.6%	35.1%	64.9%
Tennessee		11		390,273	126,752	259,473	4,048	132,721 D	32.5%	66.5%	32.8%	67.2%
Texas		23		874,382	98,218	771,109	5,055	672,891 D	11.2%	88.2%	11.3%	88.7%
Utah		4		206,578	84,795	116,750	5,033	31,955 D	41.0%	56.5%	42.1%	57.9%
Vermont	3			136,980	78,984	56,266	1,730	22,718 R	57.7%	41.1%	58.4%	41.6%
Virginia		11		297,942	89,637	203,979	4,326	114,342 D	30.1%	68.5%	30.5%	69.5%
Washington		8		614,814	208,645	353,260	52,909	144,615 D	33.9%	57.5%	37.1%	62.9%
West Virginia		8		743,774	330,731	405,124	7,919	74,393 D	44.5%	54.5%	44.9%	55.1%
Wisconsin		12		1,114,814	347,741	707,410	59,663	359,669 D	31.2%	63.5%	33.0%	67.0%
Wyoming		3		96,962	39,583	54,370	3,009	14,787 D	40.8%	56.1%	42.1%	57.9%
United States	59	472	-	39,758,759	15,760,684	22,829,501	1,168,574	7,068,817 D	39.6%	57.4%	40.8%	59.2%

8

The Republican figure in Mississippi includes votes cast for two elector tickets.

All state plurality figures are consistent with the Republican-Democratic pluralities as printed in the individual state sections.

The full list of candidates for President and Vice-President was:

22,829,501	Franklin D. Roosevelt and John N. Garner, Democratic.
15,760,684	Herbert C. Hoover and Charles Curtis, Republican.
884,649	Norman Thomas and James H. Maurer, Socialist.
103,253	William Z. Foster and James W. Ford, Communist.
81,872	William D. Upshaw and Frank S. Regan, Prohibition.
53,247	William H. Harvey and Frank Hemenway, Liberty.
34,043	Verne L. Reynolds and John W. Aiken, Socialist Labor.
7,431	Jacob S. Coxey and Julius J. Reiter, Farmer-Labor.
1,645	John Zahnd and Florence Garvin, National.
740	James R. Cox and Victor C. Tisdal, Jobless.

In addition, 157 votes were cast for a Jacksonian elector ticket in Texas and 9 in Arizona for an Arizona Progressive Democratic ticket. 1,528 scattered votes were reported from various states.

UNITED STATES

PRESIDENT 1936

State	Electoral Vote Rep.	Dem.	Other	Total Vote	Republican	Democratic	Other	Plurality	Total Vote Rep.	Dem.	Major Vote Rep.	Dem.
Alabama		11		275,744	35,358	238,196	2,190	202,838 D	12.8%	86.4%	12.9%	87.1%
Alaska												
Arizona		3		124,163	33,433	86,722	4,008	53,289 D	26.9%	69.8%	27.8%	72.2%
Arkansas		9		179,431	32,049	146,765	617	114,716 D	17.9%	81.8%	17.9%	82.1%
California		22		2,638,882	836,431	1,766,836	35,615	930,405 D	31.7%	67.0%	32.1%	67.9%
Colorado		6		488,685	181,267	295,021	12,397	113,754 D	37.1%	60.4%	38.1%	61.9%
Connecticut		8		690,723	278,685	382,129	29,909	103,444 D	40.3%	55.3%	42.2%	57.8%
Delaware		3		127,603	57,236	69,702	665	12,466 D	44.9%	54.6%	45.1%	54.9%
Florida		7		327,436	78,248	249,117	71	170,869 D	23.9%	76.1%	23.9%	76.1%
Georgia		12		293,170	36,943	255,363	864	218,420 D	12.6%	87.1%	12.6%	87.4%
Hawaii												
Idaho		4		199,617	66,256	125,683	7,678	59,427 D	33.2%	63.0%	34.5%	65.5%
Illinois		29		3,956,522	1,570,393	2,282,999	103,130	712,606 D	39.7%	57.7%	40.8%	59.2%
Indiana		14		1,650,897	691,570	934,974	24,353	243,404 D	41.9%	56.6%	42.5%	57.5%
Iowa		11		1,142,737	487,977	621,756	33,004	133,779 D	42.7%	54.4%	44.0%	56.0%
Kansas		9		865,507	397,727	464,520	3,260	66,793 D	46.0%	53.7%	46.1%	53.9%
Kentucky		11		926,214	369,702	541,944	14,568	172,242 D	39.9%	58.5%	40.6%	59.4%
Louisiana		10		329,778	36,791	292,894	93	256,103 D	11.2%	88.8%	11.2%	88.8%
Maine	5			304,240	168,823	126,333	9,084	42,490 R	55.5%	41.5%	57.2%	42.8%
Maryland		8		624,896	231,435	389,612	3,849	158,177 D	37.0%	62.3%	37.3%	62.7%
Massachusetts		17		1,840,357	768,613	942,716	129,028	174,103 D	41.8%	51.2%	44.9%	55.1%
Michigan		19		1,805,098	699,733	1,016,794	88,571	317,061 D	38.8%	56.3%	40.8%	59.2%
Minnesota		11		1,129,975	350,461	698,811	80,703	348,350 D	31.0%	61.8%	33.4%	66.6%
Mississippi		9		162,142	4,467	157,333	342	152,866 D	2.8%	97.0%	2.8%	97.2%
Missouri		15		1,828,635	697,891	1,111,043	19,701	413,152 D	38.2%	60.8%	38.6%	61.4%
Montana		4		230,502	63,598	159,690	7,214	96,092 D	27.6%	69.3%	28.5%	71.5%
Nebraska		7		608,023	247,731	347,445	12,847	99,714 D	40.7%	57.1%	41.6%	58.4%
Nevada		3		43,848	11,923	31,925		20,002 D	27.2%	72.8%	27.2%	72.8%
New Hampshire		4		218,114	104,642	108,460	5,012	3,818 D	48.0%	49.7%	49.1%	50.9%
New Jersey		16		1,820,437	720,322	1,083,850	16,265	363,528 D	39.6%	59.5%	39.9%	60.1%
New Mexico		3		169,135	61,727	106,037	1,371	44,310 D	36.5%	62.7%	36.8%	63.2%
New York		47		5,596,398	2,180,670	3,293,222	122,506	1,112,552 D	39.0%	58.8%	39.8%	60.2%
North Carolina		13		839,475	223,294	616,141	40	392,847 D	26.6%	73.4%	26.6%	73.4%
North Dakota		4		273,716	72,751	163,148	37,817	90,397 D	26.6%	59.6%	30.8%	69.2%
Ohio		26		3,012,660	1,127,855	1,747,140	137,665	619,285 D	37.4%	58.0%	39.2%	60.8%
Oklahoma		11		749,740	245,122	501,069	3,549	255,947 D	32.7%	66.8%	32.8%	67.2%
Oregon		5		414,021	122,706	266,733	24,582	144,027 D	29.6%	64.4%	31.5%	68.5%
Pennsylvania		36		4,138,105	1,690,300	2,353,788	94,017	663,488 D	40.8%	56.9%	41.8%	58.2%
Rhode Island		4		310,278	125,031	164,338	20,909	39,307 D	40.3%	53.0%	43.2%	56.8%
South Carolina		8		115,437	1,646	113,791		112,145 D	1.4%	98.6%	1.4%	98.6%
South Dakota		4		296,452	125,977	160,137	10,338	34,160 D	42.5%	54.0%	44.0%	56.0%
Tennessee		11		477,086	147,055	328,083	1,948	181,028 D	30.8%	68.8%	30.9%	69.1%
Texas		23		849,701	104,661	739,952	5,088	635,291 D	12.3%	87.1%	12.4%	87.6%
Utah		4		216,679	64,555	150,248	1,876	85,693 D	29.8%	69.3%	30.1%	69.9%
Vermont	3			143,689	81,023	62,124	542	18,899 R	56.4%	43.2%	56.6%	43.4%
Virginia		11		334,590	98,336	234,980	1,274	136,644 D	29.4%	70.2%	29.5%	70.5%
Washington		8		692,338	206,892	459,579	25,867	252,687 D	29.9%	66.4%	31.0%	69.0%
West Virginia		8		829,945	325,358	502,582	2,005	177,224 D	39.2%	60.6%	39.3%	60.7%
Wisconsin		12		1,258,560	380,828	802,984	74,748	422,156 D	30.3%	63.8%	32.2%	67.8%
Wyoming		3		103,382	38,739	62,624	2,019	23,885 D	37.5%	60.6%	38.2%	61.8%
United States	8	523	-	45,654,763	16,684,231	27,757,333	1,213,199	11,073,102 D	36.5%	60.8%	37.5%	62.5%

The Republican figures in Delaware, Mississippi, and South Carolina include votes cast for two elector tickets. In New York the Democratic figure includes American Labor votes.

All state plurality figures are consistent with the Republican-Democratic pluralities as printed in the individual state sections.

The full list of candidates for President and Vice-President was:

27,757,333	Franklin D. Roosevelt and John N. Garner, Democratic.
16,684,231	Alfred M. Landon and Frank Knox, Republican.
892,267	William Lemke and Thomas C. O'Brien, Union.
187,833	Norman Thomas and George A. Nelson, Socialist.
80,171	Earl Browder and James W. Ford, Communist.
37,677	D. Leigh Colvin and Claude A. Watson, Prohibition.
12,829	John W. Aiken and Emil F. Teichert, Socialist Labor.
1,598	William Dudley Pelley and Willard W. Kemp, Christian.

In addition, 824 scattered votes were reported from various states.

UNITED STATES

PRESIDENT 1940

State	Electoral Vote Rep.	Dem.	Other	Total Vote	Republican	Democratic	Other	Plurality	Percentage Total Vote Rep.	Dem.	Major Vote Rep.	Dem.
Alabama		11		294,219	42,184	250,726	1,309	208,542 D	14.3%	85.2%	14.4%	85.6%
Alaska												
Arizona		3		150,039	54,030	95,267	742	41,237 D	36.0%	63.5%	36.2%	63.8%
Arkansas		9		200,429	42,122	157,213	1,094	115,091 D	21.0%	78.4%	21.1%	78.9%
California		22		3,268,791	1,351,419	1,877,618	39,754	526,199 D	41.3%	57.4%	41.9%	58.1%
Colorado	6			549,004	279,576	265,554	3,874	14,022 R	50.9%	48.4%	51.3%	48.7%
Connecticut		8		781,502	361,819	417,621	2,062	55,802 D	46.3%	53.4%	46.4%	53.6%
Delaware		3		136,374	61,440	74,599	335	13,159 D	45.1%	54.7%	45.2%	54.8%
Florida		7		485,640	126,158	359,334	148	233,176 D	26.0%	74.0%	26.0%	74.0%
Georgia		12		312,686	46,495	265,194	997	218,699 D	14.9%	84.8%	14.9%	85.1%
Hawaii												
Idaho		4		235,168	106,553	127,842	773	21,289 D	45.3%	54.4%	45.5%	54.5%
Illinois		29		4,217,935	2,047,240	2,149,934	20,761	102,694 D	48.5%	51.0%	48.8%	51.2%
Indiana	14			1,782,747	899,466	874,063	9,218	25,403 R	50.5%	49.0%	50.7%	49.3%
Iowa	11			1,215,432	632,370	578,802	4,260	53,568 R	52.0%	47.6%	52.2%	47.8%
Kansas	9			860,297	489,169	364,725	6,403	124,444 R	56.9%	42.4%	57.3%	42.7%
Kentucky		11		970,163	410,384	557,322	2,457	146,938 D	42.3%	57.4%	42.4%	57.6%
Louisiana		10		372,305	52,446	319,751	108	267,305 D	14.1%	85.9%	14.1%	85.9%
Maine	5			320,840	163,951	156,478	411	7,473 R	51.1%	48.8%	51.2%	48.8%
Maryland		8		660,104	269,534	384,546	6,024	115,012 D	40.8%	58.3%	41.2%	58.8%
Massachusetts		17		2,026,993	939,700	1,076,522	10,771	136,822 D	46.4%	53.1%	46.6%	53.4%
Michigan	19			2,085,929	1,039,917	1,032,991	13,021	6,926 R	49.9%	49.5%	50.2%	49.8%
Minnesota		11		1,251,188	596,274	644,196	10,718	47,922 D	47.7%	51.5%	48.1%	51.9%
Mississippi		9		175,824	7,364	168,267	193	160,903 D	4.2%	95.7%	4.2%	95.8%
Missouri		15		1,833,729	871,009	958,476	4,244	87,467 D	47.5%	52.3%	47.6%	52.4%
Montana		4		247,873	99,579	145,698	2,596	46,119 D	40.2%	58.8%	40.6%	59.4%
Nebraska	7			615,878	352,201	263,677		88,524 R	57.2%	42.8%	57.2%	42.8%
Nevada		3		53,174	21,229	31,945		10,716 D	39.9%	60.1%	39.9%	60.1%
New Hampshire		4		235,419	110,127	125,292		15,165 D	46.8%	53.2%	46.8%	53.2%
New Jersey		16		1,972,552	945,475	1,016,808	10,269	71,333 D	47.9%	51.5%	48.2%	51.8%
New Mexico		3		183,258	79,315	103,699	244	24,384 D	43.3%	56.6%	43.3%	56.7%
New York		47		6,301,596	3,027,478	3,251,918	22,200	224,440 D	48.0%	51.6%	48.2%	51.8%
North Carolina		13		822,648	213,633	609,015		395,382 D	26.0%	74.0%	26.0%	74.0%
North Dakota	4			280,775	154,590	124,036	2,149	30,554 R	55.1%	44.2%	55.5%	44.5%
Ohio		26		3,319,912	1,586,773	1,733,139		146,366 D	47.8%	52.2%	47.8%	52.2%
Oklahoma		11		826,212	348,872	474,313	3,027	125,441 D	42.2%	57.4%	42.4%	57.6%
Oregon		5		481,240	219,555	258,415	3,270	38,860 D	45.6%	53.7%	45.9%	54.1%
Pennsylvania		36		4,078,714	1,889,848	2,171,035	17,831	281,187 D	46.3%	53.2%	46.5%	53.5%
Rhode Island		4		321,152	138,654	182,181	317	43,527 D	43.2%	56.7%	43.2%	56.8%
South Carolina		8		99,830	4,360	95,470		91,110 D	4.4%	95.6%	4.4%	95.6%
South Dakota	4			308,427	177,065	131,362		45,703 R	57.4%	42.6%	57.4%	42.6%
Tennessee		11		522,823	169,153	351,601	2,069	182,448 D	32.4%	67.3%	32.5%	67.5%
Texas		23		1,124,437	212,692	909,974	1,771	697,282 D	18.9%	80.9%	18.9%	81.1%
Utah		4		247,819	93,151	154,277	391	61,126 D	37.6%	62.3%	37.6%	62.4%
Vermont	3			143,062	78,371	64,269	422	14,102 R	54.8%	44.9%	54.9%	45.1%
Virginia		11		346,608	109,363	235,961	1,284	126,598 D	31.6%	68.1%	31.7%	68.3%
Washington		8		793,833	322,123	462,145	9,565	140,022 D	40.6%	58.2%	41.1%	58.9%
West Virginia		8		868,076	372,414	495,662		123,248 D	42.9%	57.1%	42.9%	57.1%
Wisconsin		12		1,405,522	679,206	704,821	21,495	25,615 D	48.3%	50.1%	49.1%	50.9%
Wyoming		3		112,240	52,633	59,287	320	6,654 D	46.9%	52.8%	47.0%	53.0%
United States	82	449	-	49,900,418	22,348,480	27,313,041	238,897	4,964,561 D	44.8%	54.7%	45.0%	55.0%

The Republican figures in Connecticut, Georgia, Mississippi and South Carolina include votes cast for two or three elector tickets. In New York the Democratic figure includes American Labor votes.

All state plurality figures are consistent with the Republican-Democratic pluralities as printed in the individual state sections.

The full list of candidates for President and Vice-President was:

27,313,041	Franklin D. Roosevelt and Henry A. Wallace, Democratic.
22,348,480	Wendell Willkie and Charles L. McNary, Republican.
116,410	Norman Thomas and Maynard C. Krueger, Socialist.
58,708	Roger Babson and Edgar V. Moorman, Prohibition.
46,259	Earl Browder and James W. Ford, Communist.
14,892	John W. Aiken and Aaron M. Orange, Socialist Labor.

In addition, 545 votes were cast in North Dakota for the individual candidacy of Alfred Knutson and 2,083 scattered votes were reported from various states.

UNITED STATES

PRESIDENT 1944

State	Electoral Vote Rep.	Dem.	Other	Total Vote	Republican	Democratic	Other	Plurality	Total Vote Rep.	Dem.	Major Vote Rep.	Dem.
Alabama		11		244,743	44,540	198,918	1,285	154,378 D	18.2%	81.3%	18.3%	81.7%
Alaska												
Arizona		4		137,634	56,287	80,926	421	24,639 D	40.9%	58.8%	41.0%	59.0%
Arkansas		9		212,954	63,551	148,965	438	85,414 D	29.8%	70.0%	29.9%	70.1%
California		25		3,520,875	1,512,965	1,988,564	19,346	475,599 D	43.0%	56.5%	43.2%	56.8%
Colorado	6			505,039	268,731	234,331	1,977	34,400 R	53.2%	46.4%	53.4%	46.6%
Connecticut		8		831,990	390,527	435,146	6,317	44,619 D	46.9%	52.3%	47.3%	52.7%
Delaware		3		125,361	56,747	68,166	448	11,419 D	45.3%	54.4%	45.4%	54.6%
Florida		8		482,803	143,215	339,377	211	196,162 D	29.7%	70.3%	29.7%	70.3%
Georgia		12		328,129	59,900	268,187	42	208,287 D	18.3%	81.7%	18.3%	81.7%
Hawaii												
Idaho		4		208,321	100,137	107,399	785	7,262 D	48.1%	51.6%	48.3%	51.7%
Illinois		28		4,036,061	1,939,314	2,079,479	17,268	140,165 D	48.0%	51.5%	48.3%	51.7%
Indiana	13			1,672,091	875,891	781,403	14,797	94,488 R	52.4%	46.7%	52.9%	47.1%
Iowa	10			1,052,599	547,267	499,876	5,456	47,391 R	52.0%	47.5%	52.3%	47.7%
Kansas	8			733,776	442,096	287,458	4,222	154,638 R	60.2%	39.2%	60.6%	39.4%
Kentucky		11		867,924	392,448	472,589	2,887	80,141 D	45.2%	54.5%	45.4%	54.6%
Louisiana		10		349,383	67,750	281,564	69	213,814 D	19.4%	80.6%	19.4%	80.6%
Maine	5			296,400	155,434	140,631	335	14,803 R	52.4%	47.4%	52.5%	47.5%
Maryland		8		608,439	292,949	315,490		22,541 D	48.1%	51.9%	48.1%	51.9%
Massachusetts		16		1,960,665	921,350	1,035,296	4,019	113,946 D	47.0%	52.8%	47.1%	52.9%
Michigan		19		2,205,223	1,084,423	1,106,899	13,901	22,476 D	49.2%	50.2%	49.5%	50.5%
Minnesota		11		1,125,504	527,416	589,864	8,224	62,448 D	46.9%	52.4%	47.2%	52.8%
Mississippi		9		180,234	11,613	168,621		157,008 D	6.4%	93.6%	6.4%	93.6%
Missouri		15		1,571,697	761,175	807,356	3,166	46,181 D	48.4%	51.4%	48.5%	51.5%
Montana		4		207,355	93,163	112,556	1,036	19,393 D	44.9%	54.3%	45.3%	54.7%
Nebraska	6			563,126	329,880	233,246		96,634 R	58.6%	41.4%	58.6%	41.4%
Nevada		3		54,234	24,611	29,623		5,012 D	45.4%	54.6%	45.4%	54.6%
New Hampshire		4		229,625	109,916	119,663	46	9,747 D	47.9%	52.1%	47.9%	52.1%
New Jersey		16		1,963,761	961,335	987,874	14,552	26,539 D	49.0%	50.3%	49.3%	50.7%
New Mexico		4		152,225	70,688	81,389	148	10,701 D	46.4%	53.5%	46.5%	53.5%
New York		47		6,316,790	2,987,647	3,304,238	24,905	316,591 D	47.3%	52.3%	47.5%	52.5%
North Carolina		14		790,554	263,155	527,399		264,244 D	33.3%	66.7%	33.3%	66.7%
North Dakota	4			220,182	118,535	100,144	1,503	18,391 R	53.8%	45.5%	54.2%	45.8%
Ohio	25			3,153,056	1,582,293	1,570,763		11,530 R	50.2%	49.8%	50.2%	49.8%
Oklahoma		10		722,636	319,424	401,549	1,663	82,125 D	44.2%	55.6%	44.3%	55.7%
Oregon		6		480,147	225,365	248,635	6,147	23,270 D	46.9%	51.8%	47.5%	52.5%
Pennsylvania		35		3,794,793	1,835,054	1,940,479	19,260	105,425 D	48.4%	51.1%	48.6%	51.4%
Rhode Island		4		299,276	123,487	175,356	433	51,869 D	41.3%	58.6%	41.3%	58.7%
South Carolina		8		103,382	4,617	90,601	8,164	82,802 D	4.5%	87.6%	4.8%	95.2%
South Dakota	4			232,076	135,365	96,711		38,654 R	58.3%	41.7%	58.3%	41.7%
Tennessee		12		510,692	200,311	308,707	1,674	108,396 D	39.2%	60.4%	39.4%	60.6%
Texas		23		1,150,334	191,423	821,605	137,306	630,182 D	16.6%	71.4%	18.9%	81.1%
Utah		4		248,319	97,891	150,088	340	52,197 D	39.4%	60.4%	39.5%	60.5%
Vermont	3			125,361	71,527	53,820	14	17,707 R	57.1%	42.9%	57.1%	42.9%
Virginia		11		388,485	145,243	242,276	966	97,033 D	37.4%	62.4%	37.5%	62.5%
Washington		8		856,328	361,689	486,774	7,865	125,085 D	42.2%	56.8%	42.6%	57.4%
West Virginia		8		715,596	322,819	392,777		69,958 D	45.1%	54.9%	45.1%	54.9%
Wisconsin	12			1,339,152	674,532	650,413	14,207	24,119 R	50.4%	48.6%	50.9%	49.1%
Wyoming	3			101,340	51,921	49,419		2,502 R	51.2%	48.8%	51.2%	48.8%
United States	99	432	-	47,976,670	22,017,617	25,612,610	346,443	3,594,993 D	45.9%	53.4%	46.2%	53.8%

The Republican figures in Georgia, Mississippi, and South Carolina include votes cast for two elector tickets. The Democratic figure in Mississippi includes votes cast for two elector tickets and in New York includes American Labor and Liberal votes.

State plurality figures are consistent with the Republican-Democratic pluralities as printed in the individual state sections except in South Carolina; in that state a Southern Democratic elector ticket ran in second place ahead of the Republican candidates.

The full list of candidates for President and Vice-President was:

25,612,610	Franklin D. Roosevelt and Harry S. Truman, <u>Democratic</u>.
22,017,617	Thomas E. Dewey and John W. Bricker, <u>Republican</u>.
79,003	Norman Thomas and Darlington Hoopes, <u>Socialist</u>.
74,779	Claude A. Watson and Andrew Johnson, <u>Prohibition</u>.
45,191	Edward A. Teichert and Arla A. Albaugh, <u>Socialist Labor</u>.
1,780	Gerald L. K. Smith and Harry Romer, <u>America First</u>.

In addition, 135,444 votes were cast in Texas for a Texas Regulars elector ticket and 7,799 in South Carolina for a Southern Democratic elector ticket. 2,447 scattered votes were reported from various states.

UNITED STATES

PRESIDENT 1948

State	Electoral Vote Rep.	Dem.	Other	Total Vote	Republican	Democratic	Other	Plurality	Percentage Total Vote Rep.	Dem.	Major Vote Rep.	Dem.
Alabama			11	214,980	40,930		174,050	130,513 SR	19.0%		100.0%	
Alaska												
Arizona		4		177,065	77,597	95,251	4,217	17,654 D	43.8%	53.8%	44.9%	55.1%
Arkansas		9		242,475	50,959	149,659	41,857	98,700 D	21.0%	61.7%	25.4%	74.6%
California		25		4,021,538	1,895,269	1,913,134	213,135	17,865 D	47.1%	47.6%	49.8%	50.2%
Colorado		6		515,237	239,714	267,288	8,235	27,574 D	46.5%	51.9%	47.3%	52.7%
Connecticut	8			883,518	437,754	423,297	22,467	14,457 R	49.5%	47.9%	50.8%	49.2%
Delaware	3			139,073	69,588	67,813	1,672	1,775 R	50.0%	48.8%	50.6%	49.4%
Florida		8		577,643	194,280	281,988	101,375	87,708 D	33.6%	48.8%	40.8%	59.2%
Georgia		12		418,844	76,691	254,646	87,507	169,511 D	18.3%	60.8%	23.1%	76.9%
Hawaii												
Idaho		4		214,816	101,514	107,370	5,932	5,856 D	47.3%	50.0%	48.6%	51.4%
Illinois		28		3,984,046	1,961,103	1,994,715	28,228	33,612 D	49.2%	50.1%	49.6%	50.4%
Indiana	13			1,656,212	821,079	807,831	27,302	13,248 R	49.6%	48.8%	50.4%	49.6%
Iowa		10		1,038,264	494,018	522,380	21,866	28,362 D	47.6%	50.3%	48.6%	51.4%
Kansas	8			788,819	423,039	351,902	13,878	71,137 R	53.6%	44.6%	54.6%	45.4%
Kentucky		11		822,658	341,210	466,756	14,692	125,546 D	41.5%	56.7%	42.2%	57.8%
Louisiana			10	416,336	72,657	136,344	207,335	67,946 SR	17.5%	32.7%	34.8%	65.2%
Maine	5			264,787	150,234	111,916	2,637	38,318 R	56.7%	42.3%	57.3%	42.7%
Maryland	8			596,748	294,814	286,521	15,413	8,293 R	49.4%	48.0%	50.7%	49.3%
Massachusetts		16		2,107,146	909,370	1,151,788	45,988	242,418 D	43.2%	54.7%	44.1%	55.9%
Michigan	19			2,109,609	1,038,595	1,003,448	67,566	35,147 R	49.2%	47.6%	50.9%	49.1%
Minnesota		11		1,212,226	483,617	692,966	35,643	209,349 D	39.9%	57.2%	41.1%	58.9%
Mississippi			9	192,190	5,043	19,384	167,763	148,154 SR	2.6%	10.1%	20.6%	79.4%
Missouri		15		1,578,628	655,039	917,315	6,274	262,276 D	41.5%	58.1%	41.7%	58.3%
Montana		4		224,278	96,770	119,071	8,437	22,301 D	43.1%	53.1%	44.8%	55.2%
Nebraska	6			488,940	264,774	224,165	1	40,609 R	54.2%	45.8%	54.2%	45.8%
Nevada		3		62,117	29,357	31,291	1,469	1,934 D	47.3%	50.4%	48.4%	51.6%
New Hampshire	4			231,440	121,299	107,995	2,146	13,304 R	52.4%	46.7%	52.9%	47.1%
New Jersey	16			1,949,555	981,124	895,455	72,976	85,669 R	50.3%	45.9%	52.3%	47.7%
New Mexico		4		187,063	80,303	105,464	1,296	25,161 D	42.9%	56.4%	43.2%	56.8%
New York	47			6,177,337	2,841,163	2,780,204	555,970	60,959 R	46.0%	45.0%	50.5%	49.5%
North Carolina		14		791,209	258,572	459,070	73,567	200,498 D	32.7%	58.0%	36.0%	64.0%
North Dakota	4			220,716	115,139	95,812	9,765	19,327 R	52.2%	43.4%	54.6%	45.4%
Ohio		25		2,936,071	1,445,684	1,452,791	37,596	7,107 D	49.2%	49.5%	49.9%	50.1%
Oklahoma		10		721,599	268,817	452,782		183,965 D	37.3%	62.7%	37.3%	62.7%
Oregon	6			524,080	260,904	243,147	20,029	17,757 R	49.8%	46.4%	51.8%	48.2%
Pennsylvania	35			3,735,348	1,902,197	1,752,426	80,725	149,771 R	50.9%	46.9%	52.0%	48.0%
Rhode Island		4		327,702	135,787	188,736	3,179	52,949 D	41.4%	57.6%	41.8%	58.2%
South Carolina			8	142,571	5,386	34,423	102,762	68,184 SR	3.8%	24.1%	13.5%	86.5%
South Dakota	4			250,105	129,651	117,653	2,801	11,998 R	51.8%	47.0%	52.4%	47.6%
Tennessee		11	1	550,283	202,914	270,402	76,967	67,488 D	36.9%	49.1%	42.9%	57.1%
Texas		23		1,249,577	303,467	824,235	121,875	520,768 D	24.3%	66.0%	26.9%	73.1%
Utah		4		276,306	124,402	149,151	2,753	24,749 D	45.0%	54.0%	45.5%	54.5%
Vermont	3			123,382	75,926	45,557	1,899	30,369 R	61.5%	36.9%	62.5%	37.5%
Virginia		11		419,256	172,070	200,786	46,400	28,716 D	41.0%	47.9%	46.1%	53.9%
Washington		8		905,058	386,314	476,165	42,579	89,851 D	42.7%	52.6%	44.8%	55.2%
West Virginia		8		748,750	316,251	429,188	3,311	112,937 D	42.2%	57.3%	42.4%	57.6%
Wisconsin		12		1,276,800	590,959	647,310	38,531	56,351 D	46.3%	50.7%	47.7%	52.3%
Wyoming		3		101,425	47,947	52,354	1,124	4,407 D	47.3%	51.6%	47.8%	52.2%
United States	189	303	39	48,793,826	21,991,291	24,179,345	2,623,190	2,188,054 D	45.1%	49.6%	47.6%	52.4%

The electoral votes of Alabama, Louisiana, Mississippi, and South Carolina were cast for the States Rights nominees. In addition, one of the 12 Democratic electors chosen in Tennessee cast his Electoral College vote for the States Rights nominees rather than for the national Democratic candidates.

In Alabama the Democratic electors were pledged to the States Rights candidates. There were no national Democratic electors on the ballot in that state.

The Republican figure in Mississippi includes votes cast for two elector tickets. In New York the Democratic figure includes Liberal votes.

State plurality figures are consistent with the Republican-Democratic pluralities as printed in the individual state sections except in the four states carried by the States Rights candidates (Alabama, Louisiana, Mississippi, and South Carolina) and in Georgia, in which the States Rights nominees ran ahead of the Republican candidates for second place.

The full list of candidates for President and Vice-President was:

24,179,345	Harry S. Truman and Alben W. Barkley, Democratic.
21,991,291	Thomas E. Dewey and Earl Warren, Republican.
1,176,125	Strom Thurmond and Fielding L. Wright, States Rights.
1,157,326	Henry A. Wallace and Glen H. Taylor, Progressive.
139,572	Norman Thomas and Tucker P. Smith, Socialist.
103,900	Claude A. Watson and Dale H. Learn, Prohibition.
29,241	Edward A. Teichert and Stephen Emery, Socialist Labor.
13,614	Farrell Dobbs and Grace Carlson, Socialist Workers.

In addition, 3,412 scattered votes were reported from various states.

UNITED STATES

PRESIDENT 1952

State	Electoral Vote Rep.	Dem.	Other	Total Vote	Republican	Democratic	Other	Plurality	Total Vote Rep.	Dem.	Major Vote Rep.	Dem.
Alabama		11		426,120	149,231	275,075	1,814	125,844 D	35.0%	64.6%	35.2%	64.8%
Alaska												
Arizona	4			260,570	152,042	108,528		43,514 R	58.3%	41.7%	58.3%	41.7%
Arkansas		8		404,800	177,155	226,300	1,345	49,145 D	43.8%	55.9%	43.9%	56.1%
California	32			5,141,849	2,897,310	2,197,548	46,991	699,762 R	56.3%	42.7%	56.9%	43.1%
Colorado	6			630,103	379,782	245,504	4,817	134,278 R	60.3%	39.0%	60.7%	39.3%
Connecticut	8			1,096,911	611,012	481,649	4,250	129,363 R	55.7%	43.9%	55.9%	44.1%
Delaware	3			174,025	90,059	83,315	651	6,744 R	51.8%	47.9%	51.9%	48.1%
Florida	10			989,337	544,036	444,950	351	99,086 R	55.0%	45.0%	55.0%	45.0%
Georgia		12		655,785	198,961	456,823	1	257,862 D	30.3%	69.7%	30.3%	69.7%
Hawaii												
Idaho	4			276,254	180,707	95,081	466	85,626 R	65.4%	34.4%	65.5%	34.5%
Illinois	27			4,481,058	2,457,327	2,013,920	9,811	443,407 R	54.8%	44.9%	55.0%	45.0%
Indiana	13			1,955,049	1,136,259	801,530	17,260	334,729 R	58.1%	41.0%	58.6%	41.4%
Iowa	10			1,268,773	808,906	451,513	8,354	357,393 R	63.8%	35.6%	64.2%	35.8%
Kansas	8			896,166	616,302	273,296	6,568	343,006 R	68.8%	30.5%	69.3%	30.7%
Kentucky		10		993,148	495,029	495,729	2,390	700 D	49.8%	49.9%	50.0%	50.0%
Louisiana		10		651,952	306,925	345,027		38,102 D	47.1%	52.9%	47.1%	52.9%
Maine	5			351,786	232,353	118,806	627	113,547 R	66.0%	33.8%	66.2%	33.8%
Maryland	9			902,074	499,424	395,337	7,313	104,087 R	55.4%	43.8%	55.8%	44.2%
Massachusetts	16			2,383,398	1,292,325	1,083,525	7,548	208,800 R	54.2%	45.5%	54.4%	45.6%
Michigan	20			2,798,592	1,551,529	1,230,657	16,406	320,872 R	55.4%	44.0%	55.8%	44.2%
Minnesota	11			1,379,483	763,211	608,458	7,814	154,753 R	55.3%	44.1%	55.6%	44.4%
Mississippi		8		285,532	112,966	172,566		59,600 D	39.6%	60.4%	39.6%	60.4%
Missouri	13			1,892,062	959,429	929,830	2,803	29,599 R	50.7%	49.1%	50.8%	49.2%
Montana	4			265,037	157,394	106,213	1,430	51,181 R	59.4%	40.1%	59.7%	40.3%
Nebraska	6			609,660	421,603	188,057		233,546 R	69.2%	30.8%	69.2%	30.8%
Nevada	3			82,190	50,502	31,688		18,814 R	61.4%	38.6%	61.4%	38.6%
New Hampshire	4			272,950	166,287	106,663		59,624 R	60.9%	39.1%	60.9%	39.1%
New Jersey	16			2,418,554	1,373,613	1,015,902	29,039	357,711 R	56.8%	42.0%	57.5%	42.5%
New Mexico	4			238,608	132,170	105,661	777	26,509 R	55.4%	44.3%	55.6%	44.4%
New York	45			7,128,239	3,952,813	3,104,601	70,825	848,212 R	55.5%	43.6%	56.0%	44.0%
North Carolina		14		1,210,910	558,107	652,803		94,696 D	46.1%	53.9%	46.1%	53.9%
North Dakota	4			270,127	191,712	76,694	1,721	115,018 R	71.0%	28.4%	71.4%	28.6%
Ohio	25			3,700,758	2,100,391	1,600,367		500,024 R	56.8%	43.2%	56.8%	43.2%
Oklahoma	8			948,984	518,045	430,939		87,106 R	54.6%	45.4%	54.6%	45.4%
Oregon	6			695,059	420,815	270,579	3,665	150,236 R	60.5%	38.9%	60.9%	39.1%
Pennsylvania	32			4,580,969	2,415,789	2,146,269	18,911	269,520 R	52.7%	46.9%	53.0%	47.0%
Rhode Island	4			414,498	210,935	203,293	270	7,642 R	50.9%	49.0%	50.9%	49.1%
South Carolina		8		341,087	168,082	173,004	1	4,922 D	49.3%	50.7%	49.3%	50.7%
South Dakota	4			294,283	203,857	90,426		113,431 R	69.3%	30.7%	69.3%	30.7%
Tennessee	11			892,553	446,147	443,710	2,696	2,437 R	50.0%	49.7%	50.1%	49.9%
Texas	24			2,075,946	1,102,878	969,228	3,840	133,650 R	53.1%	46.7%	53.2%	46.8%
Utah	4			329,554	194,190	135,364		58,826 R	58.9%	41.1%	58.9%	41.1%
Vermont	3			153,557	109,717	43,355	485	66,362 R	71.5%	28.2%	71.7%	28.3%
Virginia	12			619,689	349,037	268,677	1,975	80,360 R	56.3%	43.4%	56.5%	43.5%
Washington	9			1,102,708	599,107	492,845	10,756	106,262 R	54.3%	44.7%	54.9%	45.1%
West Virginia		8		873,548	419,970	453,578		33,608 D	48.1%	51.9%	48.1%	51.9%
Wisconsin	12			1,607,370	979,744	622,175	5,451	357,569 R	61.0%	38.7%	61.2%	38.8%
Wyoming	3			129,253	81,049	47,934	270	33,115 R	62.7%	37.1%	62.8%	37.2%
United States	442	89	-	61,550,918	33,936,234	27,314,992	299,692	6,621,242 R	55.1%	44.4%	55.4%	44.6%

The Republican figure in South Carolina includes votes cast for two elector tickets; in Mississippi the Republican total is the vote cast for an Independent elector ticket "pledged to vote for the nominees of the National Republican Party". In New York the Democratic figure includes Liberal votes.

All state plurality figures are consistent with the Republican-Democratic pluralities as printed in the individual state sections.

The full list of candidates for President and Vice-President was:

33,936,234	Dwight D. Eisenhower and Richard M. Nixon, Republican.
27,314,992	Adlai E. Stevenson and John J. Sparkman, Democratic.
140,023	Vincent Hallinan and Charlotta Bass, Progressive.
72,949	Stuart Hamblen and Enoch A. Holtwick, Prohibition.
30,267	Eric Hass and Stephen Emery, Socialist Labor.
20,203	Darlington Hoopes and Samuel H. Friedman, Socialist.
10,312	Farrell Dobbs and Myra Tanner Weiss, Socialist Workers.
4,203	Henry B. Krajewski and Frank Jenkins, Poor Man's Party.

In addition, 17,205 votes were cast for various elector tickets filed on behalf of General Douglas MacArthur, including Christian Nationalist (with Jack B. Tenney as candidate for Vice-President), Constitution (with Vivien Kellems), and America First (with Senator Harry Flood Byrd). In California, Missouri, and Texas the MacArthur vote was cast for two elector tickets. 4,530 scattered votes were reported from various states.

UNITED STATES

PRESIDENT 1956

State	Electoral Vote Rep.	Dem.	Other	Total Vote	Republican	Democratic	Other	Plurality	Percentage Total Vote Rep.	Dem.	Major Vote Rep.	Dem.
Alabama		10	1	496,861	195,694	280,844	20,323	85,150 D	39.4%	56.5%	41.1%	58.9%
Alaska												
Arizona	4			290,173	176,990	112,880	303	64,110 R	61.0%	38.9%	61.1%	38.9%
Arkansas		8		406,572	186,287	213,277	7,008	26,990 D	45.8%	52.5%	46.6%	53.4%
California	32			5,466,355	3,027,668	2,420,135	18,552	607,533 R	55.4%	44.3%	55.6%	44.4%
Colorado	6			657,074	394,479	257,997	4,598	136,482 R	60.0%	39.3%	60.5%	39.5%
Connecticut	8			1,117,121	711,837	405,079	205	306,758 R	63.7%	36.3%	63.7%	36.3%
Delaware	3			177,988	98,057	79,421	510	18,636 R	55.1%	44.6%	55.3%	44.7%
Florida	10			1,125,762	643,849	480,371	1,542	163,478 R	57.2%	42.7%	57.3%	42.7%
Georgia		12		669,655	222,778	444,688	2,189	221,910 D	33.3%	66.4%	33.4%	66.6%
Hawaii												
Idaho	4			272,989	166,979	105,868	142	61,111 R	61.2%	38.8%	61.2%	38.8%
Illinois	27			4,407,407	2,623,327	1,775,682	8,398	847,645 R	59.5%	40.3%	59.6%	40.4%
Indiana	13			1,974,607	1,182,811	783,908	7,888	398,903 R	59.9%	39.7%	60.1%	39.9%
Iowa	10			1,234,564	729,187	501,858	3,519	227,329 R	59.1%	40.7%	59.2%	40.8%
Kansas	8			866,243	566,878	296,317	3,048	270,561 R	65.4%	34.2%	65.7%	34.3%
Kentucky	10			1,053,805	572,192	476,453	5,160	95,739 R	54.3%	45.2%	54.6%	45.4%
Louisiana	10			617,544	329,047	243,977	44,520	85,070 R	53.3%	39.5%	57.4%	42.6%
Maine	5			351,706	249,238	102,468		146,770 R	70.9%	29.1%	70.9%	29.1%
Maryland	9			932,827	559,738	372,613	476	187,125 R	60.0%	39.9%	60.0%	40.0%
Massachusetts	16			2,348,506	1,393,197	948,190	7,119	445,007 R	59.3%	40.4%	59.5%	40.5%
Michigan	20			3,080,468	1,713,647	1,359,898	6,923	353,749 R	55.6%	44.1%	55.8%	44.2%
Minnesota	11			1,340,005	719,302	617,525	3,178	101,777 R	53.7%	46.1%	53.8%	46.2%
Mississippi		8		248,104	60,685	144,453	42,966	83,768 D	24.5%	58.2%	29.6%	70.4%
Missouri		13		1,832,562	914,289	918,273		3,984 D	49.9%	50.1%	49.9%	50.1%
Montana	4			271,171	154,933	116,238		38,695 R	57.1%	42.9%	57.1%	42.9%
Nebraska	6			577,137	378,108	199,029		179,079 R	65.5%	34.5%	65.5%	34.5%
Nevada	3			96,689	56,049	40,640		15,409 R	58.0%	42.0%	58.0%	42.0%
New Hampshire	4			266,994	176,519	90,364	111	86,155 R	66.1%	33.8%	66.1%	33.9%
New Jersey	16			2,484,312	1,606,942	850,337	27,033	756,605 R	64.7%	34.2%	65.4%	34.6%
New Mexico	4			253,926	146,788	106,098	1,040	40,690 R	57.8%	41.8%	58.0%	42.0%
New York	45			7,095,971	4,345,506	2,747,944	2,521	1,597,562 R	61.2%	38.7%	61.3%	38.7%
North Carolina		14		1,165,592	575,062	590,530		15,468 D	49.3%	50.7%	49.3%	50.7%
North Dakota	4			253,991	156,766	96,742	483	60,024 R	61.7%	38.1%	61.8%	38.2%
Ohio	25			3,702,265	2,262,610	1,439,655		822,955 R	61.1%	38.9%	61.1%	38.9%
Oklahoma	8			859,350	473,769	385,581		88,188 R	55.1%	44.9%	55.1%	44.9%
Oregon	6			736,132	406,393	329,204	535	77,189 R	55.2%	44.7%	55.2%	44.8%
Pennsylvania	32			4,576,503	2,585,252	1,981,769	9,482	603,483 R	56.5%	43.3%	56.6%	43.4%
Rhode Island	4			387,609	225,819	161,790		64,029 R	58.3%	41.7%	58.3%	41.7%
South Carolina		8		300,583	75,700	136,372	88,511	47,863 D	25.2%	45.4%	35.7%	64.3%
South Dakota	4			293,857	171,569	122,288		49,281 R	58.4%	41.6%	58.4%	41.6%
Tennessee	11			939,404	462,288	456,507	20,609	5,781 R	49.2%	48.6%	50.3%	49.7%
Texas	24			1,955,168	1,080,619	859,958	14,591	220,661 R	55.3%	44.0%	55.7%	44.3%
Utah	4			333,995	215,631	118,364		97,267 R	64.6%	35.4%	64.6%	35.4%
Vermont	3			152,978	110,390	42,549	39	67,841 R	72.2%	27.8%	72.2%	27.8%
Virginia	12			697,978	386,459	267,760	43,759	118,699 R	55.4%	38.4%	59.1%	40.9%
Washington	9			1,150,889	620,430	523,002	7,457	97,428 R	53.9%	45.4%	54.3%	45.7%
West Virginia	8			830,831	449,297	381,534		67,763 R	54.1%	45.9%	54.1%	45.9%
Wisconsin	12			1,550,558	954,844	586,768	8,946	368,076 R	61.6%	37.8%	61.9%	38.1%
Wyoming	3			124,127	74,573	49,554		25,019 R	60.1%	39.9%	60.1%	39.9%
United States	457	73	1	62,026,908	35,590,472	26,022,752	413,684	9,567,720 R	57.4%	42.0%	57.8%	42.2%

One of the 11 Democratic electors chosen in Alabama cast his Electoral College vote for Walter B. Jones and Herman Talmadge rather than for the national Democratic candidates.

The Republican figure in Mississippi includes votes cast for two elector tickets. In New York the Democratic figure includes Liberal votes.

State plurality figures are consistent with the Republican-Democratic pluralities as printed in the individual state sections except in South Carolina; in that state an Independent elector ticket ran ahead of the Republican candidates for second place.

The full list of candidates for President and Vice-President was:

35,590,472	Dwight D. Eisenhower and Richard M. Nixon, Republican.
26,022,752	Adlai E. Stevenson and Estes Kefauver, Democratic.
111,178	T. Coleman Andrews and Thomas H. Werdel, States Rights.
44,450	Eric Hass and Georgia Cozzini, Socialist Labor.
41,937	Enoch A. Holtwick and Edwin M. Cooper, Prohibition.
7,797	Farrell Dobbs and Myra Tanner Weiss, Socialist Workers.
2,657	Harry Flood Byrd and William E. Jenner, States Rights.
2,126	Darlington Hoopes and Samuel H. Friedman, Socialist.
1,829	Henry B. Krajewski and Anne Marie Yezo, American Third Party.
8	Gerald L. K. Smith and Charles F. Robertson, Christian Nationalist.

In addition, 196,318 votes were cast in Alabama, Louisiana, Mississippi, and South Carolina for Independent electors or for States Rights elector tickets not officially pledged to any candidate, and 5,384 scattered votes were reported from various states.

UNITED STATES

PRESIDENT 1960

State	Electoral Vote Rep.	Dem.	Other	Total Vote	Republican	Democratic	Other	Plurality	Percentage Total Vote Rep.	Dem.	Major Vote Rep.	Dem.
Alabama		5	6	570,225	237,981	324,050	8,194	86,069 D	41.7%	56.8%	42.3%	57.7%
Alaska	3			60,762	30,953	29,809		1,144 R	50.9%	49.1%	50.9%	49.1%
Arizona	4			398,491	221,241	176,781	469	44,460 R	55.5%	44.4%	55.6%	44.4%
Arkansas		8		428,509	184,508	215,049	28,952	30,541 D	43.1%	50.2%	46.2%	53.8%
California	32			6,506,578	3,259,722	3,224,099	22,757	35,623 R	50.1%	49.6%	50.3%	49.7%
Colorado	6			736,236	402,242	330,629	3,365	71,613 R	54.6%	44.9%	54.9%	45.1%
Connecticut		8		1,222,883	565,813	657,055	15	91,242 D	46.3%	53.7%	46.3%	53.7%
Delaware		3		196,683	96,373	99,590	720	3,217 D	49.0%	50.6%	49.2%	50.8%
Florida	10			1,544,176	795,476	748,700		46,776 R	51.5%	48.5%	51.5%	48.5%
Georgia		12		733,349	274,472	458,638	239	184,166 D	37.4%	62.5%	37.4%	62.6%
Hawaii		3		184,705	92,295	92,410		115 D	50.0%	50.0%	50.0%	50.0%
Idaho	4			300,450	161,597	138,853		22,744 R	53.8%	46.2%	53.8%	46.2%
Illinois		27		4,757,409	2,368,988	2,377,846	10,575	8,858 D	49.8%	50.0%	49.9%	50.1%
Indiana	13			2,135,360	1,175,120	952,358	7,882	222,762 R	55.0%	44.6%	55.2%	44.8%
Iowa	10			1,273,810	722,381	550,565	864	171,816 R	56.7%	43.2%	56.7%	43.3%
Kansas	8			928,825	561,474	363,213	4,138	198,261 R	60.4%	39.1%	60.7%	39.3%
Kentucky	10			1,124,462	602,607	521,855		80,752 R	53.6%	46.4%	53.6%	46.4%
Louisiana		10		807,891	230,980	407,339	169,572	176,359 D	28.6%	50.4%	36.2%	63.8%
Maine	5			421,767	240,608	181,150		59,440 R	57.0%	43.0%	57.0%	43.0%
Maryland		9		1,055,349	489,538	565,808	3	76,270 D	46.4%	53.6%	46.4%	53.6%
Massachusetts		16		2,469,480	976,750	1,487,174	5,556	510,424 D	39.6%	60.2%	39.6%	60.4%
Michigan		20		3,318,097	1,620,428	1,687,269	10,400	66,841 D	48.8%	50.9%	49.0%	51.0%
Minnesota		11		1,541,887	757,915	779,933	4,039	22,018 D	49.2%	50.6%	49.3%	50.7%
Mississippi			8	298,171	73,561	108,362	116,248	7,886 U	24.7%	36.3%	40.4%	59.6%
Missouri		13		1,934,422	962,221	972,201		9,980 D	49.7%	50.3%	49.7%	50.3%
Montana	4			277,579	141,841	134,891	847	6,950 R	51.1%	48.6%	51.3%	48.7%
Nebraska	6			613,095	380,553	232,542		148,011 R	62.1%	37.9%	62.1%	37.9%
Nevada		3		107,267	52,387	54,880		2,493 D	48.8%	51.2%	48.8%	51.2%
New Hampshire	4			295,761	157,989	137,772		20,217 R	53.4%	46.6%	53.4%	46.6%
New Jersey		16		2,773,111	1,363,324	1,385,415	24,372	22,091 D	49.2%	50.0%	49.6%	50.4%
New Mexico		4		311,107	153,733	156,027	1,347	2,294 D	49.4%	50.2%	49.6%	50.4%
New York		45		7,291,079	3,446,419	3,830,085	14,575	383,666 D	47.3%	52.5%	47.4%	52.6%
North Carolina		14		1,368,556	655,420	713,136		57,716 D	47.9%	52.1%	47.9%	52.1%
North Dakota	4			278,431	154,310	123,963	158	30,347 R	55.4%	44.5%	55.5%	44.5%
Ohio	25			4,161,859	2,217,611	1,944,248		273,363 R	53.3%	46.7%	53.3%	46.7%
Oklahoma	7		1	903,150	533,039	370,111		162,928 R	59.0%	41.0%	59.0%	41.0%
Oregon	6			776,421	408,060	367,402	959	40,658 R	52.6%	47.3%	52.6%	47.4%
Pennsylvania		32		5,006,541	2,439,956	2,556,282	10,303	116,326 D	48.7%	51.1%	48.8%	51.2%
Rhode Island		4		405,535	147,502	258,032	1	110,530 D	36.4%	63.6%	36.4%	63.6%
South Carolina		8		386,688	188,558	198,129	1	9,571 D	48.8%	51.2%	48.8%	51.2%
South Dakota	4			306,487	178,417	128,070		50,347 R	58.2%	41.8%	58.2%	41.8%
Tennessee	11			1,051,792	556,577	481,453	13,762	75,124 R	52.9%	45.8%	53.6%	46.4%
Texas		24		2,311,084	1,121,310	1,167,567	22,207	46,257 D	48.5%	50.5%	49.0%	51.0%
Utah	4			374,709	205,361	169,248	100	36,113 R	54.8%	45.2%	54.8%	45.2%
Vermont	3			167,324	98,131	69,186	7	28,945 R	58.6%	41.3%	58.6%	41.4%
Virginia	12			771,449	404,521	362,327	4,601	42,194 R	52.4%	47.0%	52.8%	47.2%
Washington	9			1,241,572	629,273	599,298	13,001	29,975 R	50.7%	48.3%	51.2%	48.8%
West Virginia		8		837,781	395,995	441,786		45,791 D	47.3%	52.7%	47.3%	52.7%
Wisconsin	12			1,729,082	895,175	830,805	3,102	64,370 R	51.8%	48.0%	51.9%	48.1%
Wyoming	3			140,782	77,451	63,331		14,120 R	55.0%	45.0%	55.0%	45.0%
United States	219	303	15	68,838,219	34,108,157	34,226,731	503,331	118,574 D	49.5%	49.7%	49.9%	50.1%

Senator Harry Flood Byrd received 15 votes for President in the Electoral College; these were the votes of 6 of the 11 Democratic electors in Alabama, all 8 unpledged Democratic electors in Mississippi, and one of the 8 Republican electors in Oklahoma. The Alabama and Mississippi electors also cast 14 votes for Senator Strom Thurmond for Vice-President; the single Oklahoma elector voted for Senator Barry M. Goldwater for Vice-President.

In New York the Democratic figure includes Liberal votes.

State plurality figures are consistent with the Republican-Democratic pluralities as printed in the individual state sections except in Mississippi; in that state an unpledged Democratic elector ticket carried the state, with the national Democratic candidates second and the Republican nominees third.

The full list of candidates for President and Vice-President was:

34,226,731	John F. Kennedy and Lyndon B. Johnson, Democratic.
34,108,157	Richard M. Nixon and Henry Cabot Lodge, Republican.
47,522	Eric Hass and Georgia Cozzini, Socialist Labor.
46,203	Rutherford L. Decker and E. Harold Munn, Prohibition.
44,977	Orval E. Faubus and John G. Crommelin, National States Rights.
40,165	Farrell Dobbs and Myra Tanner Weiss, Socialist Workers.
18,162	Charles L. Sullivan and Merritt B. Curtis, Constitution.
8,708	J. Bracken Lee and Kent H. Courtney, Conservative.
4,204	C. Benton Coiner and Edward J. Silverman, Conservative.
1,767	Lar Daly and B. M. Miller, Tax Cut.
1,485	Clennon King and Reginald Carter, Independent Afro-American.
1,401	Merritt B. Curtis and B. M. Miller, Constitution.

In addition, 169,572 votes were cast in Louisiana for Independent electors and 116,248 in Mississippi for an unpledged Democratic elector ticket. 539 votes were cast in Michigan for an Independent American ticket and 2,378 scattered votes were reported from various states.

UNITED STATES

PRESIDENT 1964

State	Electoral Vote Rep.	Dem.	Other	Total Vote	Republican	Democratic	Other	Plurality	Total Vote Rep.	Dem.	Major Vote Rep.	Dem.
Alabama	10			689,818	479,085		210,733	268,353 R	69.5%		100.0%	
Alaska		3		67,259	22,930	44,329		21,399 D	34.1%	65.9%	34.1%	65.9%
Arizona	5			480,770	242,535	237,753	482	4,782 R	50.4%	49.5%	50.5%	49.5%
Arkansas		6		560,426	243,264	314,197	2,965	70,933 D	43.4%	56.1%	43.6%	56.4%
California		40		7,057,586	2,879,108	4,171,877	6,601	1,292,769 D	40.8%	59.1%	40.8%	59.2%
Colorado		6		776,986	296,767	476,024	4,195	179,257 D	38.2%	61.3%	38.4%	61.6%
Connecticut		8		1,218,578	390,996	826,269	1,313	435,273 D	32.1%	67.8%	32.1%	67.9%
Delaware		3		201,320	78,078	122,704	538	44,626 D	38.8%	60.9%	38.9%	61.1%
Florida		14		1,854,481	905,941	948,540		42,599 D	48.9%	51.1%	48.9%	51.1%
Georgia	12			1,139,335	616,584	522,556	195	94,028 R	54.1%	45.9%	54.1%	45.9%
Hawaii		4		207,271	44,022	163,249		119,227 D	21.2%	78.8%	21.2%	78.8%
Idaho		4		292,477	143,557	148,920		5,363 D	49.1%	50.9%	49.1%	50.9%
Illinois		26		4,702,841	1,905,946	2,796,833	62	890,887 D	40.5%	59.5%	40.5%	59.5%
Indiana		13		2,091,606	911,118	1,170,848	9,640	259,730 D	43.6%	56.0%	43.8%	56.2%
Iowa		9		1,184,539	449,148	733,030	2,361	283,882 D	37.9%	61.9%	38.0%	62.0%
Kansas		7		857,901	386,579	464,028	7,294	77,449 D	45.1%	54.1%	45.4%	54.6%
Kentucky		9		1,046,105	372,977	669,659	3,469	296,682 D	35.7%	64.0%	35.8%	64.2%
Louisiana	10			896,293	509,225	387,068		122,157 R	56.8%	43.2%	56.8%	43.2%
Maine		4		380,965	118,701	262,264		143,563 D	31.2%	68.8%	31.2%	68.8%
Maryland		10		1,116,457	385,495	730,912	50	345,417 D	34.5%	65.5%	34.5%	65.5%
Massachusetts		14		2,344,798	549,727	1,786,422	8,649	1,236,695 D	23.4%	76.2%	23.5%	76.5%
Michigan		21		3,203,102	1,060,152	2,136,615	6,335	1,076,463 D	33.1%	66.7%	33.2%	66.8%
Minnesota		10		1,554,462	559,624	991,117	3,721	431,493 D	36.0%	63.8%	36.1%	63.9%
Mississippi	7			409,146	356,528	52,618		303,910 R	87.1%	12.9%	87.1%	12.9%
Missouri		12		1,817,879	653,535	1,164,344		510,809 D	36.0%	64.0%	36.0%	64.0%
Montana		4		278,628	113,032	164,246	1,350	51,214 D	40.6%	58.9%	40.8%	59.2%
Nebraska		5		584,154	276,847	307,307		30,460 D	47.4%	52.6%	47.4%	52.6%
Nevada		3		135,433	56,094	79,339		23,245 D	41.4%	58.6%	41.4%	58.6%
New Hampshire		4		288,093	104,029	184,064		80,035 D	36.1%	63.9%	36.1%	63.9%
New Jersey		17		2,847,663	964,174	1,868,231	15,258	904,057 D	33.9%	65.6%	34.0%	66.0%
New Mexico		4		328,645	132,838	194,015	1,792	61,177 D	40.4%	59.0%	40.6%	59.4%
New York		43		7,166,275	2,243,559	4,913,102	9,614	2,669,543 D	31.3%	68.6%	31.3%	68.7%
North Carolina		13		1,424,983	624,844	800,139		175,295 D	43.8%	56.2%	43.8%	56.2%
North Dakota		4		258,389	108,207	149,784	398	41,577 D	41.9%	58.0%	41.9%	58.1%
Ohio		26		3,969,196	1,470,865	2,498,331		1,027,466 D	37.1%	62.9%	37.1%	62.9%
Oklahoma		8		932,499	412,665	519,834		107,169 D	44.3%	55.7%	44.3%	55.7%
Oregon		6		786,305	282,779	501,017	2,509	218,238 D	36.0%	63.7%	36.1%	63.9%
Pennsylvania		29		4,822,690	1,673,657	3,130,954	18,079	1,457,297 D	34.7%	64.9%	34.8%	65.2%
Rhode Island		4		390,091	74,615	315,463	13	240,848 D	19.1%	80.9%	19.1%	80.9%
South Carolina	8			524,779	309,048	215,723	8	93,325 R	58.9%	41.1%	58.9%	41.1%
South Dakota		4		293,118	130,108	163,010		32,902 D	44.4%	55.6%	44.4%	55.6%
Tennessee		11		1,144,046	508,965	635,047	34	126,082 D	44.5%	55.5%	44.5%	55.5%
Texas		25		2,626,811	958,566	1,663,185	5,060	704,619 D	36.5%	63.3%	36.6%	63.4%
Utah		4		401,413	181,785	219,628		37,843 D	45.3%	54.7%	45.3%	54.7%
Vermont		3		163,089	54,942	108,127	20	53,185 D	33.7%	66.3%	33.7%	66.3%
Virginia		12		1,042,267	481,334	558,038	2,895	76,704 D	46.2%	53.5%	46.3%	53.7%
Washington		9		1,258,374	470,366	779,699	8,309	309,333 D	37.4%	62.0%	37.6%	62.4%
West Virginia		7		792,040	253,953	538,087		284,134 D	32.1%	67.9%	32.1%	67.9%
Wisconsin		12		1,691,815	638,495	1,050,424	2,896	411,929 D	37.7%	62.1%	37.8%	62.2%
Wyoming		3		142,716	61,998	80,718		18,720 D	43.4%	56.6%	43.4%	56.6%
District of Columbia		3		198,597	28,801	169,796		140,995 D	14.5%	85.5%	14.5%	85.5%
United States	52	486	-	70,644,510	27,178,188	43,129,484	336,838	15,951,296 D	38.5%	61.1%	38.7%	61.3%

In New York the Democratic figure includes Liberal votes.

State plurality figures are consistent with the Republican-Democratic pluralities as printed in the individual state sections except in Alabama; in that state the Democratic electors were unpledged and no national Democratic electors appeared on the ballot.

The full list of candidates for President and Vice-President was:

43,129,484	Lyndon B. Johnson and Hubert H. Humphrey, <u>Democratic</u>.
27,178,188	Barry M. Goldwater and William E. Miller, <u>Republican</u>.
45,219	Eric Hass and Henning A. Blomen, <u>Socialist Labor</u>.
32,720	Clifton DeBerry and Edward Shaw, <u>Socialist Workers</u>.
23,267	E. Harold Munn and Mark R. Shaw, <u>Prohibition</u>.
6,953	John Kasper and J. B. Stoner, <u>National States Rights</u>.
5,060	Joseph B. Lightburn and T. C. Billings, <u>Constitution</u>.
19	James Hensley and John O. Hopkins, <u>Universal</u>.

In addition, 210,732 votes were cast in Alabama for an unpledged Democratic elector ticket and 12,868 scattered votes were reported from various states.

ALABAMA

PRESIDENT 1920

County	Total Vote	Republican	Democratic	Other	Rep.-Dem. Plurality	% Total Vote Rep.	% Total Vote Dem.	% Major Vote Rep.	% Major Vote Dem.
AUTAUGA	1,139	210	918	11	708 D	18.4%	80.6%	18.6%	81.4%
BALDWIN	1,937	556	1,230	151	674 D	28.7%	63.5%	31.1%	58.9%
BARBOUR	1,786	203	1,568	15	1,365 D	11.4%	87.8%	11.5%	88.5%
BIBB	2,148	364	1,643	141	1,279 D	16.9%	76.5%	18.1%	81.9%
BLOUNT	7,050	3,465	3,535	50	70 D	49.2%	50.1%	49.5%	50.5%
BULLOCK	880	2	877	1	875 D	0.2%	99.7%	0.2%	99.8%
BUTLER	1,471	153	1,299	19	1,146 D	10.4%	88.3%	10.5%	89.5%
CALHOUN	4,601	1,139	3,423	39	2,284 D	24.8%	74.4%	25.0%	75.0%
CHAMBERS	2,330	322	1,994	14	1,672 D	13.8%	85.6%	13.9%	86.1%
CHEROKEE	3,603	1,576	1,969	58	393 D	43.7%	54.6%	44.5%	55.5%
CHILTON	3,289	2,273	962	54	1,311 R	69.1%	29.2%	70.3%	29.7%
CHOCTAW	1,156	82	1,071	3	989 D	7.1%	92.6%	7.1%	92.9%
CLARKE	1,302	43	1,253	6	1,210 D	3.3%	96.2%	3.3%	96.7%
CLAY	4,301	2,133	2,165	3	32 D	49.6%	50.3%	49.6%	50.4%
CLEBURNE	1,657	971	684	2	287 R	58.6%	41.3%	58.7%	41.3%
COFFEE	2,408	673	1,721	14	1,048 D	27.9%	71.5%	28.1%	71.9%
COLBERT	2,581	650	1,869	62	1,219 D	25.2%	72.4%	25.8%	74.2%
CONECUH	1,564	189	1,375	0	1,186 D	12.1%	87.9%	12.1%	87.9%
COOSA	1,764	741	1,007	16	266 D	42.0%	57.1%	42.4%	57.6%
COVINGTON	2,654	548	2,039	67	1,491 D	20.6%	76.8%	21.2%	78.8%
CRENSHAW	1,729	310	1,411	8	1,101 D	17.9%	81.6%	18.0%	82.0%
CULLMAN	6,101	3,492	2,566	43	926 R	57.2%	42.1%	57.6%	42.4%
DALE	2,175	768	1,386	21	618 D	35.3%	63.7%	35.7%	64.3%
DALLAS	2,780	78	2,702	0	2,624 D	2.8%	97.2%	2.8%	97.2%
DE KALB	8,795	4,852	3,894	49	958 R	55.2%	44.3%	55.5%	44.5%
ELMORE	2,121	353	1,762	6	1,409 D	16.6%	83.1%	16.7%	83.3%
ESCAMBIA	1,637	178	1,455	4	1,277 D	10.9%	88.9%	10.9%	89.1%
ETOWAH	9,238	3,218	5,917	103	2,699 D	34.8%	64.1%	35.2%	64.8%
FAYETTE	3,309	1,865	1,413	31	452 R	56.4%	42.7%	56.9%	43.1%
FRANKLIN	5,089	2,930	2,094	65	836 R	57.6%	41.1%	58.3%	41.7%
GENEVA	2,612	1,088	1,488	36	400 D	41.7%	57.0%	42.2%	57.8%
GREENE	531	10	520	1	510 D	1.9%	97.9%	1.9%	98.1%
HALE	975	18	953	4	935 D	1.8%	97.7%	1.9%	98.1%
HENRY	1,205	489	715	1	226 D	40.6%	59.3%	40.6%	59.4%
HOUSTON	2,656	571	2,045	40	1,474 D	21.5%	77.0%	21.8%	78.2%
JACKSON	4,013	1,483	2,513	17	1,030 D	37.0%	62.6%	37.1%	62.9%
JEFFERSON	32,939	7,124	24,982	833	17,858 D	21.6%	75.8%	22.2%	77.8%
LAMAR	2,220	576	1,628	16	1,052 D	25.9%	73.3%	26.1%	73.9%
LAUDERDALE	3,870	1,164	2,644	62	1,480 D	30.1%	68.3%	30.6%	69.4%
LAWRENCE	1,782	831	935	16	104 D	46.6%	52.5%	47.1%	52.9%
LEE	1,893	155	1,620	118	1,465 D	8.2%	85.6%	8.7%	91.3%
LIMESTONE	2,114	285	1,812	17	1,527 D	13.5%	85.7%	13.6%	86.4%
LOWNDES	733	6	727	0	721 D	0.8%	99.2%	0.8%	99.2%
MACON	759	64	693	2	629 D	8.4%	91.3%	8.5%	91.5%
MADISON	3,340	489	2,822	29	2,333 D	14.6%	84.5%	14.8%	85.2%
MARENGO	1,412	42	1,370	0	1,328 D	3.0%	97.0%	3.0%	97.0%
MARION	4,329	1,865	2,461	3	596 D	43.1%	56.8%	43.1%	56.9%
MARSHALL	7,958	3,879	4,041	38	162 D	48.7%	50.8%	49.0%	51.0%
MOBILE	9,023	2,681	6,171	171	3,490 D	29.7%	68.4%	30.3%	69.7%
MONROE	1,328	20	1,295	13	1,275 D	1.5%	97.5%	1.5%	98.5%
MONTGOMERY	6,775	314	6,411	50	6,097 D	4.6%	94.6%	4.7%	95.3%
MORGAN	5,329	1,201	4,057	71	2,856 D	22.5%	76.1%	22.8%	77.2%
PERRY	1,243	34	1,195	14	1,161 D	2.7%	96.1%	2.8%	97.2%
PICKENS	1,702	263	1,419	20	1,156 D	15.5%	83.4%	15.6%	84.4%
PIKE	1,802	204	1,586	12	1,382 D	11.3%	88.0%	11.4%	88.6%
RANDOLPH	2,479	1,113	1,357	9	244 D	44.9%	54.7%	45.1%	54.9%
RUSSELL	748	29	671	48	642 D	3.9%	89.7%	4.1%	95.9%
ST. CLAIR	4,653	2,561	1,934	158	627 R	55.0%	41.6%	57.0%	43.0%
SHELBY	5,782	3,235	2,523	24	712 R	55.9%	43.6%	56.2%	43.8%
SUMTER	1,106	15	1,088	3	1,073 D	1.4%	98.4%	1.4%	98.6%

PRESIDENT 1924

County	Total Vote	Republican	Democratic	Other	Rep.-Dem. Plurality	% Total Vote Rep.	% Total Vote Dem.	% Major Vote Rep.	% Major Vote Dem.
AUTAUGA	954	146	781	27	635 D	15.3%	81.9%	15.7%	84.3%
BALDWIN	1,978	549	1,023	406	474 D	27.8%	51.7%	34.9%	65.1%
BARBOUR	1,463	78	1,340	45	1,262 D	5.3%	91.6%	5.5%	94.5%
BIBB	1,374	251	875	248	624 D	18.3%	63.7%	22.3%	77.7%
BLOUNT	3,710	1,518	2,083	109	565 D	40.9%	56.1%	42.2%	57.8%
BULLOCK	772	8	763	1	755 D	1.0%	98.8%	1.0%	99.0%
BUTLER	1,260	95	1,050	115	955 D	7.5%	83.3%	8.3%	91.7%
CALHOUN	2,819	766	1,907	146	1,141 D	27.2%	67.7%	28.7%	71.3%
CHAMBERS	2,112	146	1,922	44	1,776 D	6.9%	91.0%	7.1%	92.9%
CHEROKEE	2,276	845	1,380	51	535 D	37.1%	60.6%	38.0%	62.0%
CHILTON	2,524	1,595	848	81	747 R	63.2%	33.6%	65.3%	34.7%
CHOCTAW	1,044	19	1,021	4	1,002 D	1.8%	97.8%	1.8%	98.2%
CLARKE	1,152	78	1,059	15	981 D	6.8%	91.9%	6.9%	93.1%
CLAY	2,667	1,017	1,597	53	580 D	38.1%	59.9%	38.9%	61.1%
CLEBURNE	1,360	696	622	42	74 R	51.2%	45.7%	52.8%	47.2%
COFFEE	1,945	323	1,597	25	1,274 D	16.6%	82.1%	16.8%	83.2%
COLBERT	2,278	576	1,503	199	927 D	25.3%	66.0%	27.7%	72.3%
CONECUH	1,084	92	955	37	863 D	8.5%	88.1%	8.8%	91.2%
COOSA	1,314	508	790	16	282 D	38.7%	60.1%	39.1%	60.9%
COVINGTON	2,068	156	1,776	136	1,620 D	7.5%	85.9%	8.1%	91.9%
CRENSHAW	1,243	117	1,107	19	990 D	9.4%	89.1%	9.6%	90.4%
CULLMAN	3,633	1,639	1,809	185	170 D	45.1%	49.8%	47.5%	52.5%
DALE	1,441	297	1,117	27	820 D	20.6%	77.5%	21.0%	79.0%
DALLAS	1,948	50	1,898	0	1,848 D	2.6%	97.4%	2.6%	97.4%
DE KALB	6,562	3,434	3,003	125	431 R	52.3%	45.8%	53.3%	46.7%
ELMORE	1,333	219	1,088	26	869 D	16.4%	81.6%	16.8%	83.2%
ESCAMBIA	1,420	152	1,217	51	1,065 D	10.7%	85.7%	11.1%	88.9%
ETOWAH	5,017	1,664	3,081	272	1,417 D	33.2%	61.4%	35.1%	64.9%
FAYETTE	2,368	977	1,358	33	381 D	41.3%	57.3%	41.9%	58.1%
FRANKLIN	4,283	2,230	1,985	68	245 R	52.1%	46.3%	52.9%	47.1%
GENEVA	1,713	477	1,191	45	714 D	27.8%	69.5%	28.6%	71.4%
GREENE	415	5	408	2	403 D	1.2%	98.3%	1.2%	98.8%
HALE	885	23	856	6	833 D	2.6%	96.7%	2.6%	97.4%
HENRY	1,035	179	816	40	637 D	17.3%	78.8%	18.0%	82.0%
HOUSTON	2,064	242	1,731	91	1,489 D	11.7%	83.9%	12.3%	87.7%
JACKSON	2,909	885	1,923	101	1,038 D	30.4%	66.1%	31.5%	68.5%
JEFFERSON	23,780	5,678	15,133	2,969	9,455 D	23.9%	63.7%	27.3%	72.7%
LAMAR	1,369	262	1,087	20	825 D	19.1%	79.4%	19.4%	80.6%
LAUDERDALE	3,178	823	2,266	89	1,443 D	25.9%	71.3%	26.6%	73.4%
LAWRENCE	1,472	468	990	14	522 D	31.8%	67.3%	32.1%	67.9%
LEE	1,504	98	1,290	116	1,192 D	6.5%	85.8%	7.1%	92.9%
LIMESTONE	1,620	136	1,415	69	1,279 D	8.4%	87.3%	8.8%	91.2%
LOWNDES	628	5	602	21	597 D	0.8%	95.9%	0.8%	99.2%
MACON	589	48	538	3	490 D	8.1%	91.3%	8.2%	91.8%
MADISON	2,586	368	2,166	52	1,798 D	14.2%	83.8%	14.5%	85.5%
MARENGO	1,263	17	1,243	3	1,226 D	1.3%	98.4%	1.3%	98.7%
MARION	2,598	1,226	1,359	13	133 D	47.2%	52.3%	47.4%	52.6%
MARSHALL	4,433	1,718	2,629	86	911 D	38.8%	59.3%	39.5%	60.5%
MOBILE	6,355	1,814	4,125	416	2,311 D	28.5%	64.9%	30.5%	69.5%
MONROE	1,202	22	1,155	25	1,133 D	1.8%	96.1%	1.9%	98.1%
MONTGOMERY	5,042	233	4,422	387	4,189 D	4.6%	87.7%	5.0%	95.0%
MORGAN	3,139	519	2,247	373	1,728 D	16.5%	71.6%	18.8%	81.2%
PERRY	965	25	928	12	903 D	2.6%	96.2%	2.6%	97.4%
PICKENS	1,195	132	1,045	18	913 D	11.0%	87.4%	11.2%	88.8%
PIKE	1,882	30	1,832	20	1,802 D	1.6%	97.3%	1.6%	98.4%
RANDOLPH	2,001	669	1,307	25	638 D	33.4%	65.3%	33.9%	66.1%
RUSSELL	519	14	474	31	460 D	2.7%	91.3%	2.9%	97.1%
ST. CLAIR	2,828	1,432	1,281	115	151 R	50.6%	45.3%	52.8%	47.2%
SHELBY	3,827	1,753	1,882	192	129 D	45.8%	49.2%	48.2%	51.8%
SUMTER	884	28	837	19	809 D	3.2%	94.7%	3.2%	96.8%

ALABAMA

PRESIDENT 1920

County	Total Vote	Republican	Democratic	Other	Rep.-Dem. Plurality	Percentage Total Vote Rep.	Dem.	Major Vote Rep.	Dem.
TALLADEGA	3,089	931	2,137	21	1,206 D	30.1%	69.2%	30.3%	69.7%
TALLAPOOSA	2,552	269	2,257	26	1,988 D	10.5%	88.4%	10.6%	89.4%
TUSCALOOSA	3,956	491	3,438	27	2,947 D	12.4%	86.9%	12.5%	87.5%
WALKER	9,399	4,488	4,703	208	215 D	47.7%	50.0%	48.8%	51.2%
WASHINGTON	663	85	575	3	490 D	12.8%	86.7%	12.9%	87.1%
WILCOX	1,102	2	1,099	1	1,097 D	0.2%	99.7%	0.2%	99.8%
WINSTON	3,344	2,307	1,037		1,270 R	69.0%	31.0%	69.0%	31.0%
TOTAL	233,951	74,719	156,064	3,168	81,345 D	31.9%	66.7%	32.4%	67.6%

PRESIDENT 1924

County	Total Vote	Republican	Democratic	Other	Rep.-Dem. Plurality	Percentage Total Vote Rep.	Dem.	Major Vote Rep.	Dem.
TALLADEGA	2,412	628	1,730	54	1,102 D	26.0%	71.7%	26.6%	73.4%
TALLAPOOSA	1,720	1	1,713	6	1,712 D	0.1%	99.6%	0.1%	99.9%
TUSCALOOSA	2,754	247	2,363	144	2,116 D	9.0%	85.8%	9.5%	90.5%
WALKER	6,138	2,446	3,351	341	905 D	39.9%	54.6%	42.2%	57.8%
WASHINGTON	678	55	610	13	555 D	8.1%	90.0%	8.3%	91.7%
WILCOX	959	6	938	15	932 D	0.6%	97.8%	0.6%	99.4%
WINSTON	1,796	1,096	650	50	446 R	61.0%	36.2%	62.8%	37.2%
TOTAL	164,563	42,823	113,138	8,602	70,315 D	26.0%	68.8%	27.5%	72.5%

ALABAMA

PRESIDENT 1928

County	Total Vote	Republican	Democratic	Other	Rep.-Dem. Plurality	%Total Rep	%Total Dem	%Major Rep	%Major Dem
AUTAUGA	1,566	683	883		200 D	43.6	56.4	43.6	56.4
BALDWIN	2,719	1,388	1,317	14	71 R	51.0	48.4	51.3	48.4
BARBOUR	2,374	845	1,506	23	661 D	35.6	63.4	35.9	64.1
BIBB	2,199	1,003	1,188	8	185 D	45.6	54.0	45.8	54.2
BLOUNT	3,352	1,745	1,607		138 R	52.1	47.9	52.1	47.9
BULLOCK	948	249	699		450 D	26.3	73.7	26.3	73.7
BUTLER	1,934	699	1,235		536 D	36.1	63.9	36.1	63.9
CALHOUN	4,655	2,537	2,117	1	420 R	54.5	45.5	54.5	45.5
CHAMBERS	2,731	1,732	999		733 R	63.4	36.6	63.4	36.6
CHEROKEE	2,413	1,515	894	4	621 R	62.8	37.0	62.9	37.1
CHILTON	4,593	3,186	1,402	5	1,784 R	69.4	30.5	69.4	30.6
CHOCTAW	1,671	429	1,242		313 D	25.7	74.3	25.7	74.3
CLARKE	2,598	936	1,662		726 D	36.0	64.0	36.0	64.0
CLAY	2,868	1,889	978	1	911 R	65.9	34.1	65.9	34.1
CLEBURNE	1,902	1,108	794		314 R	58.3	41.7	58.3	41.7
COFFEE	2,645	1,036	1,609		573 D	39.2	60.8	39.2	60.8
COLBERT	3,948	1,249	2,596	103	1,347 D	31.6	65.7	32.5	67.5
CONECUH	1,971	1,113	858		255 R	56.5	43.5	56.5	43.5
COOSA	1,778	1,078	699		379 R	60.7	39.3	60.7	39.3
COVINGTON	3,686	1,681	2,000	5	319 D	45.6	54.3	45.7	54.3
CRENSHAW	2,292	978	1,314		336 D	42.7	57.3	42.7	57.3
CULLMAN	4,533	2,959	1,574	1	1,385 R	65.3	34.7	65.3	34.7
DALE	2,234	1,000	1,233	1	233 D	44.8	55.2	44.8	55.2
DALLAS	2,611	705	1,905	1	1,200 D	27.0	73.0	27.0	73.0
DE KALB	9,720	5,761	3,957	2	1,804 R	59.3	40.7	59.3	40.7
ELMORE	3,081	1,770	1,309	2	461 R	57.5	42.5	57.5	42.5
ESCAMBIA	2,832	1,754	1,077	1	677 R	62.0	38.0	62.0	38.0
ETOWAH	6,134	3,612	2,484	38	1,128 R	58.9	40.5	59.3	40.7
FAYETTE	2,818	1,686	1,131	1	555 R	59.8	40.1	59.9	40.1
FRANKLIN	5,222	2,937	2,279	6	658 R	56.3	43.6	56.3	43.7
GENEVA	3,018	1,533	1,485		48 R	50.8	49.2	50.8	49.2
GREENE	640	39	601		562 D	6.1	93.9	6.1	93.9
HALE	1,451	403	1,048		645 D	27.8	72.2	27.8	72.2
HENRY	1,613	796	815	2	19 D	49.4	50.5	49.4	50.6
HOUSTON	4,256	1,963	2,290	3	327 D	46.2	53.8	46.2	53.8
JACKSON	5,247	3,081	2,153	13	928 R	58.7	41.0	58.9	41.1
JEFFERSON	34,907	18,060	16,735	112	1,325 R	51.7	47.9	51.9	48.1
LAMAR	2,216	804	1,412		608 D	36.3	63.7	36.3	63.7
LAUDERDALE	4,174	1,410	2,763	1	1,353 D	33.8	66.2	33.8	66.2
LAWRENCE	2,046	1,008	1,035		27 D	49.3	50.6	49.3	50.7
LEE	2,455	1,016	1,436	3	420 D	41.4	58.5	41.4	58.6
LIMESTONE	2,096	407	1,689		1,282 D	19.4	80.6	19.4	80.6
LOWNDES	883	180	703		523 D	20.4	79.6	20.4	79.6
MACON	877	348	526	3	178 D	39.7	60.0	39.8	60.2
MADISON	5,378	2,695	2,681	2	14 R	50.1	49.9	50.1	49.9
MARENGO	2,650	752	1,898		1,146 D	28.4	71.6	28.4	71.6
MARION	3,029	1,488	1,541		53 D	49.1	50.9	49.1	50.9
MARSHALL	4,844	2,511	2,322	11	189 R	51.8	47.9	52.0	48.0
MOBILE	11,033	5,058	5,965	10	907 D	45.8	54.1	45.9	54.1
MONROE	2,417	1,074	1,343		269 D	44.4	55.6	44.4	55.6
MONTGOMERY	9,464	3,114	6,347	3	3,233 D	32.9	67.1	32.9	67.1
MORGAN	7,460	4,085	3,366	9	719 R	54.8	45.1	54.8	45.2
PERRY	1,702	459	1,242	1	783 D	27.0	73.0	27.0	73.0
PICKENS	1,662	634	1,028		394 D	38.1	61.9	38.1	61.9
PIKE	2,375	552	1,819	4	1,297 D	23.2	76.6	23.3	76.7
RANDOLPH	3,074	1,815	1,257	2	558 R	59.1	40.9	59.1	40.9
RUSSELL	1,197	333	846	18	513 D	27.8	70.7	28.2	71.8
ST. CLAIR	3,896	2,581	1,313	2	1,268 R	66.2	33.7	66.3	33.7
SHELBY	4,203	2,502	1,679	22	823 R	59.5	39.9	59.8	40.2
SUMTER	1,206	191	1,015		824 D	15.8	84.2	15.8	84.2

PRESIDENT 1932

County	Total Vote	Republican	Democratic	Other	Rep.-Dem. Plurality	%Total Rep	%Total Dem	%Major Rep	%Major Dem
AUTAUGA	1,474	138	1,322	14	1,184 D	9.4	89.7	9.5	90.5
BALDWIN	2,731	544	2,098	139	1,554 D	19.6	75.4	20.6	79.4
BARBOUR	2,278	64	2,207	7	2,143 D	2.8	96.9	2.8	97.2
BIBB	1,812	145	1,636	31	1,491 D	8.0	90.3	8.1	91.9
BLOUNT	2,952	582	2,332	48	1,750 D	19.6	78.7	20.0	80.0
BULLOCK	1,017	12	1,004	1	992 D	1.2	98.7	1.2	98.8
BUTLER	2,354	74	2,280	10	2,206 D	3.1	96.4	3.1	96.5
CALHOUN	5,137	684	4,392	31	3,708 D	13.4	86.0	13.5	86.5
CHAMBERS	2,903	342	2,550	11	2,208 D	11.8	87.8	11.8	88.2
CHEROKEE	2,282	359	1,897	26	1,538 D	15.7	83.1	15.9	84.1
CHILTON	3,253	1,532	1,664	57	132 D	47.1	51.2	47.9	52.1
CHOCTAW	1,582	48	1,533	4	1,485 D	3.0	96.9	3.0	97.0
CLARKE	3,050	931	2,103	16	1,172 D	30.5	69.0	30.7	69.3
CLAY	1,822	405	1,403	4	998 D	22.4	77.4	22.4	77.6
COFFEE	2,965	95	2,868	2	2,773 D	3.2	96.7	3.2	96.8
COLBERT	3,244	312	2,908	24	2,596 D	9.7	89.6	9.7	90.3
CONECUH	2,239	114	2,125		2,011 D	5.1	94.9	5.1	94.9
COOSA	1,531	250	1,265	16	1,015 D	16.3	82.6	16.5	83.5
COVINGTON	3,968	99	3,855	14	3,756 D	2.5	97.2	2.5	97.5
CRENSHAW	2,340	127	2,200	13	2,073 D	5.4	94.0	5.5	94.5
CULLMAN	3,954	956	2,910	78	1,954 D	24.3	73.6	24.7	75.3
DALE	2,455	155	2,300		2,145 D	6.3	93.7	6.3	93.7
DALLAS	3,134	93	3,027	14	2,934 D	3.0	96.6	3.0	97.0
DE KALB	7,790	3,496	4,217	77	721 D	44.9	54.1	45.3	54.7
ELMORE	3,641	160	3,198	283	3,038 D	4.4	87.8	4.8	95.2
ESCAMBIA	2,184	157	2,024	3	1,867 D	7.2	92.7	7.2	92.8
ETOWAH	6,322	1,093	5,167	62	4,074 D	17.3	81.7	17.5	82.5
FAYETTE	2,769	733	2,013	23	1,280 D	26.5	72.7	26.7	73.3
FRANKLIN	4,457	1,547	2,876	34	1,329 D	34.7	64.5	35.0	65.0
GENEVA	2,852	270	2,559	23	2,289 D	9.5	89.7	9.5	90.5
GREENE	675	9	665	1	656 D	1.3	98.5	1.3	98.7
HALE	1,348	70	1,275	3	1,205 D	5.2	94.6	5.2	94.8
HENRY	1,787	42	1,741	4	1,699 D	2.4	97.4	2.4	97.6
HOUSTON	4,031	157	3,863	11	3,706 D	3.9	95.8	3.9	96.1
JACKSON	4,056	938	3,110	8	2,172 D	23.1	76.7	23.2	76.8
JEFFERSON	36,541	4,572	31,156	813	26,584 D	12.5	85.3	12.8	87.2
LAMAR	2,473	258	2,207	8	1,949 D	10.4	89.2	10.5	89.5
LAUDERDALE	3,789	432	3,336	21	2,904 D	11.4	88.0	11.5	88.5
LAWRENCE	2,219	299	1,920		1,621 D	13.5	86.5	13.5	86.5
LEE	2,102	103	1,988	11	1,885 D	4.9	94.6	4.9	95.1
LIMESTONE	2,780	107	2,667	6	2,560 D	3.8	95.9	3.9	96.1
LOWNDES	962	18	905	56	849 D	1.6	94.1	1.6	98.4
MACON	5,399	559	4,792	48	4,233 D	10.4	88.6	10.4	89.6
MARENGO	2,197	50	2,097	50	2,047 D	2.3	95.6	2.3	97.7
MARION	2,883	545	2,325	13	1,780 D	18.9	80.6	19.0	81.0
MARSHALL	4,850	914	3,836	100	2,922 D	18.9	79.1	19.1	80.9
MOBILE	11,442	1,705	9,658	79	7,953 D	14.9	84.4	15.0	85.0
MONROE	2,043	66	1,972	5	1,906 D	3.2	96.5	3.2	96.8
MONTGOMERY	10,533	441	10,066	26	9,625 D	4.2	95.6	4.2	95.8
MORGAN	5,744	656	4,986	102	4,330 D	11.4	86.8	11.6	88.4
PERRY	1,454	37	1,382	35	1,345 D	2.5	95.0	2.6	97.4
PICKENS	1,697	128	1,479	90	1,351 D	7.5	87.2	8.0	92.0
PIKE	2,599	52	2,545	2	2,493 D	2.0	97.9	2.0	98.0
RANDOLPH	3,005	767	2,226	12	1,459 D	25.5	74.1	25.6	74.4
RUSSELL	2,037	46	1,984	7	1,938 D	2.3	97.4	2.3	97.7
ST. CLAIR	3,675	1,449	2,185	41	736 D	39.4	59.5	39.9	60.1
SHELBY	3,263	864	2,365	34	1,501 D	26.5	72.5	26.8	73.2
SUMTER	1,319	26	1,293		1,267 D	2.0	98.0	2.0	98.0

ALABAMA

PRESIDENT 1928

County	Total Vote	Republican	Democratic	Other	Rep.-Dem. Plurality	Percentage Total Vote Rep.	Dem.	Major Vote Rep.	Dem.
TALLADEGA	3,308	1,602	1,693	13	91 D	48.4%	51.2%	48.6%	51.4%
TALLAPOOSA	3,107	1,257	1,849	1	592 D	40.5%	59.5%	40.5%	59.5%
TUSCALOOSA	3,981	1,210	2,769	2	1,559 D	30.4%	69.6%	30.4%	69.6%
WALKER	7,863	3,635	4,228		593 D	46.2%	53.8%	46.2%	53.8%
WASHINGTON	1,234	515	718	1	203 D	41.7%	58.2%	41.8%	58.2%
WILCOX	1,246	266	979	1	713 D	21.3%	78.6%	21.4%	78.6%
WINSTON	2,745	2,085	659	1	1,426 R	76.0%	24.0%	76.0%	24.0%
TOTAL	248,981	120,725	127,796	460	7,071 D	48.5%	51.3%	48.6%	51.4%

PRESIDENT 1932

County	Total Vote	Republican	Democratic	Other	Rep.-Dem. Plurality	Percentage Total Vote Rep.	Dem.	Major Vote Rep.	Dem.
TALLADEGA	3,978	617	3,354	7	2,737 D	15.5%	84.3%	15.5%	84.5%
TALLAPOOSA	3,537	138	3,391	8	3,253 D	3.9%	95.9%	3.9%	96.1%
TUSCALOOSA	5,657	302	5,322	33	5,020 D	5.3%	94.1%	5.4%	94.6%
WALKER	6,371	1,583	4,734	54	3,151 D	24.8%	74.3%	25.1%	74.9%
WASHINGTON	1,389	81	1,307	1	1,226 D	5.8%	94.1%	5.8%	94.2%
WILCOX	1,381	23	1,358		1,335 D	1.7%	98.3%	1.7%	98.3%
WINSTON	2,019	1,005	1,006	8	1 D	49.8%	49.8%	50.0%	50.0%
TOTAL	245,303	34,675	207,910	2,718	173,235 D	14.1%	84.8%	14.3%	85.7%

ALABAMA

PRESIDENT 1936

County	Total Vote	Republican	Democratic	Other	Rep.-Dem. Plurality	%TV Rep.	%TV Dem.	%MV Rep.	%MV Dem.
AUTAUGA	1,617	84	1,525	8	1,441 D	5.2%	94.3%	5.2%	94.8%
BALDWIN	2,967	434	2,338	195	1,904 D	14.6%	78.8%	15.7%	84.3%
BARBOUR	2,448	50	2,386	12	2,336 D	2.0%	97.5%	2.1%	97.9%
BIBB	2,066	190	1,868	8	1,678 D	9.2%	90.4%	9.2%	90.8%
BLOUNT	3,564	744	2,788	32	2,044 D	20.9%	78.2%	21.1%	78.9%
BULLOCK	1,194	5	1,188	1	1,183 D	0.4%	99.5%	0.4%	99.6%
BUTLER	2,448	83	2,358	7	2,275 D	3.4%	96.3%	3.4%	96.6%
CALHOUN	4,961	581	4,322	58	3,741 D	11.7%	87.1%	11.8%	88.2%
CHAMBERS	3,742	112	3,626	4	3,514 D	3.0%	96.9%	3.0%	97.0%
CHEROKEE	2,507	374	2,114	19	1,740 D	14.9%	84.3%	15.0%	85.0%
CHILTON	4,055	1,469	2,565	21	1,096 D	36.2%	63.3%	36.4%	63.6%
CHOCTAW	1,581	74	1,507	—	1,433 D	4.7%	95.3%	4.7%	95.3%
CLARKE	2,735	60	2,673	2	2,613 D	2.2%	97.7%	2.2%	97.8%
CLAY	2,978	700	2,138	140	1,438 D	23.5%	71.8%	24.7%	75.3%
CLEBURNE	1,766	543	1,212	11	669 D	30.7%	68.6%	30.9%	69.1%
COFFEE	3,305	110	3,178	17	3,068 D	3.3%	96.2%	3.3%	96.7%
COLBERT	3,628	251	3,365	12	3,114 D	6.9%	92.8%	6.9%	93.1%
CONECUH	2,296	89	2,195	12	2,106 D	3.9%	95.6%	3.9%	96.1%
COOSA	1,617	239	1,346	32	1,107 D	14.8%	83.2%	15.1%	84.9%
COVINGTON	4,447	167	4,265	15	4,098 D	3.8%	95.9%	3.8%	96.1%
CRENSHAW	2,471	96	2,371	4	2,275 D	3.9%	96.0%	3.9%	96.1%
CULLMAN	5,505	1,703	3,781	21	2,078 D	30.9%	68.7%	31.1%	68.9%
DALE	2,599	193	2,404	2	2,211 D	7.4%	92.5%	7.4%	92.6%
DALLAS	3,258	49	3,205	4	3,156 D	1.5%	98.4%	1.5%	98.5%
DE KALB	10,764	4,620	6,121	23	1,501 D	42.9%	56.9%	43.0%	57.0%
ELMORE	4,297	182	3,967	148	3,785 D	4.2%	92.3%	4.4%	95.6%
ESCAMBIA	2,698	103	2,585	10	2,482 D	3.8%	95.8%	3.8%	96.2%
ETOWAH	6,978	1,207	5,739	32	4,532 D	17.3%	82.2%	17.4%	82.6%
FAYETTE	2,999	732	2,244	23	1,512 D	24.4%	74.8%	24.6%	75.4%
FRANKLIN	4,964	1,875	3,059	30	1,184 D	37.8%	61.6%	38.0%	62.0%
GENEVA	2,949	295	2,652	2	2,357 D	10.0%	89.9%	10.0%	90.0%
GREENE	884	20	861	3	841 D	2.3%	97.4%	2.3%	97.7%
HALE	1,654	20	1,626	8	1,606 D	1.2%	98.3%	1.2%	98.8%
HENRY	1,963	35	1,925	3	1,890 D	1.8%	98.1%	1.8%	98.2%
HOUSTON	3,783	230	3,538	15	3,308 D	6.1%	93.5%	6.1%	93.9%
JACKSON	4,383	926	3,450	7	2,524 D	21.1%	78.7%	21.2%	78.8%
JEFFERSON	40,198	3,813	35,982	403	32,169 D	9.5%	89.5%	9.6%	90.4%
LAMAR	2,594	195	2,393	6	2,198 D	7.5%	92.3%	7.5%	92.5%
LAUDERDALE	5,125	390	4,685	50	4,295 D	7.6%	91.4%	7.7%	92.3%
LAWRENCE	2,663	444	2,213	6	1,769 D	16.7%	83.1%	16.7%	83.3%
LEE	2,283	93	2,183	7	2,090 D	4.1%	95.6%	4.1%	95.9%
LIMESTONE	2,990	108	2,861	21	2,753 D	3.6%	95.7%	3.6%	96.4%
LOWNDES	1,217	10	1,205	2	1,195 D	0.8%	99.0%	0.8%	99.2%
MACON	1,185	39	1,146	—	1,107 D	3.3%	96.7%	3.3%	96.7%
MADISON	6,220	514	5,661	45	5,147 D	8.3%	91.0%	8.3%	91.7%
MARENGO	2,321	33	2,287	1	2,254 D	1.4%	98.5%	1.4%	98.6%
MARION	3,609	911	2,655	43	1,744 D	25.2%	73.6%	25.5%	74.5%
MARSHALL	5,152	925	4,208	19	3,283 D	18.0%	81.7%	18.0%	82.0%
MOBILE	12,412	1,072	11,165	175	10,093 D	8.6%	90.0%	8.8%	91.2%
MONROE	2,596	29	2,558	9	2,529 D	1.1%	98.5%	1.1%	98.9%
MONTGOMERY	12,332	223	12,061	48	11,838 D	1.8%	97.8%	1.8%	98.2%
MORGAN	6,058	432	5,597	29	5,165 D	7.1%	92.4%	7.2%	92.8%
PERRY	1,551	24	1,527	—	1,503 D	1.5%	98.4%	1.5%	98.5%
PICKENS	1,781	107	1,665	9	1,558 D	6.0%	93.5%	6.0%	94.0%
PIKE	3,157	55	3,100	2	3,045 D	1.7%	98.2%	1.7%	98.3%
RANDOLPH	3,574	793	2,766	15	1,973 D	22.2%	77.4%	22.3%	77.7%
RUSSELL	2,256	66	2,181	9	2,115 D	2.9%	96.7%	2.9%	97.1%
ST CLAIR	3,880	1,464	2,399	17	935 D	37.7%	61.8%	37.9%	62.1%
SHELBY	3,181	777	2,371	33	1,594 D	24.4%	74.5%	24.7%	75.3%
SUMTER	1,393	24	1,369	—	1,345 D	1.7%	98.3%	1.7%	98.3%

PRESIDENT 1940

County	Total Vote	Republican	Democratic	Other	Rep.-Dem. Plurality	%TV Rep.	%TV Dem.	%MV Rep.	%MV Dem.
AUTAUGA	1,741	99	1,630	12	1,531 D	5.7%	93.6%	5.7%	94.3%
BALDWIN	3,501	617	2,681	203	2,064 D	17.6%	76.6%	18.7%	81.3%
BARBOUR	2,428	90	2,328	10	2,238 D	3.7%	95.9%	3.7%	96.3%
BIBB	2,012	173	1,821	18	1,648 D	8.6%	90.5%	8.7%	91.3%
BLOUNT	3,677	855	2,784	38	1,929 D	23.3%	75.7%	23.5%	76.5%
BULLOCK	1,319	18	1,301	—	1,283 D	1.4%	98.6%	1.4%	98.6%
BUTLER	2,788	52	2,732	4	2,680 D	1.9%	98.0%	1.9%	98.1%
CALHOUN	5,073	645	4,408	20	3,763 D	12.7%	86.9%	12.8%	87.2%
CHAMBERS	4,262	110	4,141	11	4,031 D	2.6%	97.2%	2.6%	97.4%
CHEROKEE	3,010	381	2,617	12	2,236 D	12.7%	86.9%	12.7%	87.3%
CHILTON	4,751	1,995	2,746	10	751 D	42.0%	57.8%	42.1%	57.9%
CHOCTAW	2,096	73	2,023	—	1,950 D	3.5%	96.5%	3.5%	96.5%
CLARKE	3,802	48	3,753	1	3,705 D	1.3%	98.7%	1.3%	98.7%
CLAY	3,023	854	2,153	16	1,299 D	28.3%	71.2%	28.4%	71.6%
CLEBURNE	1,808	434	1,369	5	935 D	24.0%	75.7%	24.1%	75.9%
COFFEE	2,371	145	2,226	—	2,081 D	6.1%	93.9%	6.1%	93.9%
COLBERT	4,371	365	3,998	8	3,633 D	8.4%	91.5%	8.4%	91.6%
CONECUH	2,400	50	2,345	5	2,295 D	2.1%	97.7%	2.1%	97.9%
COOSA	1,677	317	1,347	13	1,030 D	18.9%	80.3%	19.1%	80.9%
COVINGTON	4,824	186	4,635	3	4,449 D	3.9%	96.1%	3.9%	96.1%
CRENSHAW	2,773	84	2,680	9	2,596 D	3.0%	96.6%	3.0%	97.0%
CULLMAN	8,686	3,057	5,603	26	2,546 D	35.2%	64.5%	35.3%	64.7%
DALE	2,922	374	2,543	5	2,169 D	12.8%	87.0%	12.8%	87.2%
DALLAS	3,266	157	3,106	3	2,949 D	4.8%	95.1%	4.8%	95.2%
DE KALB	8,259	2,810	5,432	17	2,622 D	34.0%	65.6%	34.1%	66.1%
ELMORE	4,420	144	4,267	9	4,123 D	3.3%	96.5%	3.3%	96.7%
ESCAMBIA	2,917	137	2,772	8	2,635 D	4.7%	95.0%	4.7%	95.3%
ETOWAH	8,315	1,270	7,012	33	5,742 D	15.3%	84.3%	15.3%	84.7%
FAYETTE	2,848	737	2,091	20	1,354 D	25.9%	73.4%	26.1%	73.9%
FRANKLIN	5,533	1,989	3,523	21	1,534 D	35.9%	63.7%	36.1%	63.9%
GENEVA	2,942	364	2,565	13	2,201 D	12.4%	87.2%	12.4%	87.6%
GREENE	971	77	894	—	817 D	7.9%	92.1%	7.9%	92.1%
HALE	1,723	32	1,691	—	1,659 D	1.9%	98.1%	1.9%	98.1%
HENRY	2,031	69	1,960	2	1,891 D	3.4%	96.5%	3.4%	96.6%
HOUSTON	4,439	483	3,941	15	3,458 D	10.9%	88.8%	10.9%	89.1%
JACKSON	4,772	945	3,818	9	2,873 D	19.8%	80.0%	19.8%	80.2%
JEFFERSON	44,001	6,714	37,110	177	30,396 D	15.3%	84.3%	15.3%	84.7%
LAMAR	2,952	275	2,665	12	2,390 D	9.3%	90.3%	9.4%	90.6%
LAUDERDALE	5,606	507	5,065	34	4,558 D	9.1%	90.3%	9.1%	90.9%
LAWRENCE	2,769	480	2,277	12	1,797 D	17.3%	82.2%	17.4%	82.6%
LEE	2,674	103	2,566	5	2,463 D	3.9%	96.0%	3.9%	96.1%
LIMESTONE	3,045	95	2,941	9	2,846 D	3.1%	96.6%	3.1%	96.9%
LOWNDES	1,145	12	1,132	1	1,120 D	1.0%	98.9%	1.0%	99.0%
MACON	1,301	41	1,259	1	1,218 D	3.2%	96.8%	3.2%	96.8%
MADISON	6,098	566	5,515	17	4,949 D	9.3%	90.4%	9.3%	90.7%
MARENGO	2,356	70	2,284	2	2,214 D	3.0%	96.9%	3.0%	97.0%
MARION	3,811	1,081	2,654	76	1,573 D	28.9%	69.6%	28.9%	71.1%
MARSHALL	5,079	913	4,142	24	3,229 D	18.0%	81.6%	18.1%	81.9%
MOBILE	13,493	1,887	11,480	126	9,593 D	14.1%	85.1%	14.1%	85.9%
MONROE	3,008	40	2,953	15	2,913 D	1.3%	98.2%	1.3%	98.7%
MONTGOMERY	11,573	230	11,311	32	11,081 D	2.0%	97.7%	2.0%	98.0%
MORGAN	5,878	500	5,345	33	4,845 D	8.6%	90.9%	8.6%	91.4%
PERRY	1,551	39	1,509	3	1,470 D	2.5%	97.2%	2.5%	97.5%
PICKENS	1,863	140	1,714	9	1,574 D	7.5%	92.0%	7.6%	92.4%
PIKE	3,178	121	3,049	8	2,928 D	3.8%	95.9%	3.8%	96.2%
RANDOLPH	3,089	670	2,407	12	1,737 D	21.7%	77.9%	21.8%	78.2%
RUSSELL	2,486	48	2,435	3	2,387 D	1.9%	97.9%	1.9%	98.1%
ST CLAIR	4,024	1,540	2,462	22	922 D	38.3%	61.3%	38.5%	61.5%
SHELBY	3,722	938	2,777	7	1,839 D	25.2%	74.6%	25.2%	74.8%
SUMTER	1,451	46	1,404	1	1,358 D	3.2%	96.8%	3.2%	96.8%

ALABAMA

PRESIDENT 1936

County	Total Vote	Republican	Democratic	Other	Rep.-Dem. Plurality	Percentage Total Vote Rep.	Dem.	Major Vote Rep.	Dem.
TALLADEGA	4,391	489	3,751	151	3,262 D	11.1%	85.4%	11.5%	88.5%
TALLAPOOSA	3,772	141	3,625	6	3,484 D	3.7%	96.1%	3.7%	96.3%
TUSCALOOSA	6,393	332	6,029	32	5,697 D	5.2%	94.3%	5.2%	94.8%
WALKER	7,484	1,699	5,697	88	3,998 D	22.7%	76.1%	23.0%	77.0%
WASHINGTON	1,822	72	1,736	14	1,664 D	4.0%	95.3%	4.0%	96.0%
WILCOX	1,377	11	1,365	1	1,354 D	0.8%	99.1%	0.8%	99.2%
WINSTON	2,706	1,428	1,270	8	158 R	52.8%	46.9%	52.9%	47.1%
TOTAL	275,744	35,358	238,196	2,190	202,838 D	12.8%	86.4%	12.9%	87.1%

PRESIDENT 1940

County	Total Vote	Republican	Democratic	Other	Rep.-Dem. Plurality	Percentage Total Vote Rep.	Dem.	Major Vote Rep.	Dem.
TALLADEGA	4,512	534	3,965	13	3,431 D	11.8%	87.9%	11.9%	88.1%
TALLAPOOSA	4,475	139	4,325	11	4,186 D	3.1%	96.6%	3.1%	96.9%
TUSCALOOSA	6,732	426	6,284	22	5,858 D	6.3%	93.3%	6.3%	93.7%
WALKER	7,971	2,007	5,940	24	3,933 D	25.2%	74.5%	25.3%	74.7%
WASHINGTON	1,978	80	1,892	6	1,812 D	4.0%	95.7%	4.1%	95.9%
WILCOX	1,554	20	1,534		1,514 D	1.3%	98.7%	1.3%	98.7%
WINSTON	3,091	1,686	1,394	11	292 R	54.5%	45.1%	54.7%	45.3%
TOTAL	294,219	42,184	250,726	1,309	208,542 D	14.3%	85.2%	14.4%	85.6%

ALABAMA

PRESIDENT 1944

County	Total Vote	Republican	Democratic	Other	Rep.-Dem. Plurality	%Total Vote Rep.	%Total Vote Dem.	%Major Vote Rep.	%Major Vote Dem.
AUTAUGA	1,364	117	1,242	5	1,125 D	8.6%	91.1%	8.6%	91.4%
BALDWIN	2,727	695	2,002	30	1,307 D	25.5%	73.4%	25.8%	74.2%
BARBOUR	2,357	67	2,237	53	2,170 D	2.8%	94.9%	2.9%	97.1%
BIBB	1,546	244	1,287	15	1,043 D	15.8%	83.2%	15.9%	84.1%
BLOUNT	3,145	998	2,134	13	1,136 D	31.7%	67.9%	31.9%	68.1%
BULLOCK	1,080	24	1,056		1,032 D	2.2%	97.8%	2.2%	97.8%
BUTLER	2,000	80	1,915	5	1,835 D	4.0%	95.8%	4.0%	96.0%
CALHOUN	5,030	694	4,308	28	3,614 D	13.8%	85.6%	13.9%	86.1%
CHAMBERS	3,662	194	3,458	10	3,264 D	5.3%	94.7%	5.3%	94.7%
CHEROKEE	2,200	408	1,774	18	1,366 D	18.5%	80.6%	18.7%	81.3%
CHILTON	3,376	1,385	1,984	7	599 D	41.0%	58.8%	41.1%	58.9%
CHOCTAW	1,332	86	1,243	3	1,157 D	6.5%	93.3%	6.5%	93.5%
CLARKE	2,408	142	2,263	3	2,121 D	5.9%	94.0%	5.9%	94.1%
CLAY	2,290	741	1,535	14	794 D	32.4%	67.0%	32.6%	67.4%
CLEBURNE	1,458	504	948	6	444 D	34.6%	65.0%	34.7%	65.3%
COFFEE	2,964	115	2,846	3	2,731 D	3.9%	96.0%	3.9%	96.1%
COLBERT	3,889	496	3,386	7	2,890 D	12.8%	87.1%	12.8%	87.2%
CONECUH	1,640	127	1,498	15	1,371 D	7.7%	92.0%	7.8%	92.2%
COOSA	1,481	394	1,079	8	685 D	26.6%	72.9%	26.7%	73.3%
COVINGTON	3,231	256	2,972	3	2,716 D	7.9%	92.0%	7.9%	92.1%
CRENSHAW	2,105	118	1,980	7	1,862 D	5.6%	94.1%	5.6%	94.4%
CULLMAN	6,145	2,202	3,898	45	1,696 D	35.8%	63.4%	36.1%	63.9%
DALE	2,447	325	2,094	28	1,769 D	13.3%	85.6%	13.4%	86.6%
DALLAS	3,043	149	2,883	11	2,734 D	4.9%	94.4%	4.9%	95.1%
DE KALB	7,002	2,627	4,366	9	1,739 D	37.5%	62.4%	37.6%	62.4%
ELMORE	3,295	184	3,108	3	2,924 D	5.6%	94.3%	5.6%	94.4%
ESCAMBIA	2,355	266	2,077	12	1,811 D	11.3%	88.4%	11.4%	88.6%
ETOWAH	7,521	1,525	5,895	101	4,370 D	20.3%	78.4%	20.6%	79.4%
FAYETTE	2,571	913	1,648	10	735 D	35.5%	64.1%	35.7%	64.3%
FRANKLIN	4,568	1,853	2,709	6	856 D	40.6%	59.3%	40.6%	59.4%
GENEVA	2,404	385	2,004	15	1,619 D	16.0%	83.4%	16.1%	83.9%
GREENE	722	45	676	1	631 D	6.2%	93.6%	6.2%	93.8%
HALE	1,298	33	1,265		1,232 D	2.5%	97.5%	2.5%	97.5%
HENRY	1,683	46	1,635	2	1,589 D	2.7%	97.1%	2.7%	97.3%
HOUSTON	3,648	282	3,349	17	3,067 D	7.7%	91.8%	7.8%	92.2%
JACKSON	4,000	1,026	2,967	7	1,941 D	25.6%	74.2%	25.7%	74.3%
JEFFERSON	38,684	7,409	31,101	174	23,692 D	19.2%	80.4%	19.2%	80.8%
LAMAR	2,352	310	2,125	17	1,815 D	13.3%	86.6%	13.3%	86.7%
LAUDERDALE	4,611	590	4,001	20	3,411 D	12.5%	86.8%	12.9%	87.1%
LAWRENCE	2,463	565	1,893	5	1,328 D	22.5%	76.9%	23.0%	77.0%
LEE	2,151	134	2,011	6	1,877 D	6.2%	93.5%	6.2%	93.8%
LIMESTONE	2,744	129	2,605	10	2,476 D	4.7%	94.9%	4.7%	95.3%
LOWNDES	819	16	802	1	786 D	2.0%	97.9%	2.0%	98.0%
MACON	1,115	82	1,032	1	950 D	7.4%	92.6%	7.4%	92.6%
MADISON	5,421	455	4,951	15	4,496 D	8.4%	91.3%	8.4%	91.6%
MARENGO	1,844	89	1,746	9	1,657 D	4.8%	94.7%	4.9%	95.1%
MARION	3,137	1,260	1,866	11	606 D	40.3%	59.5%	40.3%	59.7%
MARSHALL	4,561	1,200	3,356	5	2,156 D	26.3%	73.6%	26.3%	73.7%
MOBILE	12,423	2,867	9,439	117	6,572 D	23.1%	76.6%	23.3%	76.7%
MONROE	2,041	46	1,991	4	1,945 D	2.3%	97.6%	2.3%	97.7%
MONTGOMERY	9,562	381	9,143	38	8,762 D	4.0%	95.6%	4.0%	96.0%
MORGAN	4,838	664	4,124	50	3,460 D	13.7%	85.2%	13.9%	86.1%
PERRY	1,053	47	1,004	2	957 D	4.5%	95.3%	4.5%	95.5%
PICKENS	1,699	209	1,482	8	1,273 D	12.3%	87.2%	12.4%	87.6%
PIKE	2,480	90	2,328	62	2,238 D	3.6%	93.9%	3.7%	96.3%
RANDOLPH	2,512	702	1,785	25	1,083 D	27.3%	71.1%	28.2%	71.8%
RUSSELL	2,228	115	2,109	4	1,994 D	5.2%	94.7%	5.2%	94.8%
ST CLAIR	2,950	1,117	1,819	14	702 D	37.9%	61.7%	37.9%	62.0%
SHELBY	2,913	945	1,955	13	1,010 D	32.4%	67.1%	32.6%	67.3%
SUMTER	1,131	53	1,075	3	1,022 D	4.7%	95.0%	4.7%	95.3%

PRESIDENT 1948

County	Total Vote	Republican	Democratic	Other	Rep.-Dem. Plurality	%Total Vote Rep.	%Total Vote Dem.	%Major Vote Rep.	%Major Vote Dem.
AUTAUGA	1,286	110		1,176	110 R	8.6%		100.0%	
BALDWIN	3,445	767		2,678	767 R	22.3%		100.0%	
BARBOUR	1,788	101		1,687	101 R	5.6%		100.0%	
BIBB	1,343	123		1,220	123 R	9.2%		100.0%	
BLOUNT	2,563	771		1,792	771 R	30.1%		100.0%	
BULLOCK	809	10		799	10 R	1.2%		100.0%	
BUTLER	1,409	91		1,318	91 R	6.5%		100.0%	
CALHOUN	4,181	856		3,325	856 R	20.5%		100.0%	
CHAMBERS	1,767	218		1,549	218 R	12.3%		100.0%	
CHEROKEE	1,293	217		1,076	217 R	16.8%		100.0%	
CHILTON	3,569	1,584		1,985	1,584 R	44.4%		100.0%	
CHOCTAW	1,457	16		1,441	16 R	1.1%		100.0%	
CLARKE	2,110	47		2,063	47 R	2.2%		100.0%	
CLAY	1,502	387		1,115	387 R	25.8%		100.0%	
CLEBURNE	1,027	317		710	317 R	30.9%		100.0%	
COFFEE	2,152	113		2,039	113 R	5.3%		100.0%	
COLBERT	3,125	488		2,637	488 R	15.6%		100.0%	
CONECUH	1,409	64		1,345	64 R	4.5%		100.0%	
COOSA	1,124	275		849	275 R	24.5%		100.0%	
COVINGTON	2,936	154		2,782	154 R	5.2%		100.0%	
CRENSHAW	1,432	38		1,394	38 R	2.7%		100.0%	
CULLMAN	5,364	1,755		3,609	1,755 R	32.7%		100.0%	
DALE	1,602	230		1,372	230 R	14.4%		100.0%	
DALLAS	2,870	132		2,738	132 R	4.6%		100.0%	
DE KALB	6,333	2,743		3,590	2,743 R	43.3%		100.0%	
ELMORE	2,570	167		2,403	167 R	6.5%		100.0%	
ESCAMBIA	1,882	188		1,694	188 R	10.0%		100.0%	
ETOWAH	7,661	1,615		6,046	1,615 R	21.1%		100.0%	
FAYETTE	1,662	580		1,082	580 R	35.8%		100.0%	
FRANKLIN	5,794	2,555		3,239	2,555 R	44.1%		100.0%	
GENEVA	2,123	286		1,837	286 R	13.5%		100.0%	
GREENE	656	31		625	31 R	4.7%		100.0%	
HALE	1,087	43		1,044	43 R	4.0%		100.0%	
HENRY	1,088	47		1,041	47 R	4.3%		100.0%	
HOUSTON	3,165	426		2,739	426 R	13.5%		100.0%	
JACKSON	2,347	603		1,744	603 R	25.7%		100.0%	
JEFFERSON	37,861	7,261		30,600	7,261 R	19.2%		100.0%	
LAMAR	1,622	180		1,442	180 R	11.1%		100.0%	
LAUDERDALE	3,822	546		3,276	546 R	14.3%		100.0%	
LAWRENCE	1,806	357		1,449	357 R	19.8%		100.0%	
LEE	2,007	258		1,749	258 R	12.9%		100.0%	
LIMESTONE	1,932	112		1,820	112 R	5.7%		100.0%	
LOWNDES	792	13		779	13 R	1.6%		100.0%	
MACON	1,211	110		1,101	110 R	9.1%		100.0%	
MADISON	3,526	466		3,060	466 R	13.2%		100.0%	
MARENGO	1,943	67		1,876	67 R	3.4%		100.0%	
MARION	2,476	813		1,663	813 R	32.8%		100.0%	
MARSHALL	3,387	870		2,517	870 R	25.7%		100.0%	
MOBILE	13,835	2,685		11,150	2,685 R	19.4%		100.0%	
MONROE	1,725	31		1,694	31 R	1.8%		100.0%	
MONTGOMERY	7,204	802		6,402	802 R	11.1%		100.0%	
MORGAN	4,382	512		3,870	512 R	11.7%		100.0%	
PERRY	1,081	30		1,051	30 R	2.8%		100.0%	
PICKENS	1,524	91		1,433	91 R	6.0%		100.0%	
PIKE	1,834	87		1,747	87 R	4.7%		100.0%	
RANDOLPH	1,730	469		1,261	469 R	27.1%		100.0%	
RUSSELL	1,776	94		1,682	94 R	5.3%		100.0%	
ST CLAIR	2,980	1,063		1,917	1,063 R	35.7%		100.0%	
SHELBY	2,820	921		1,899	921 R	32.7%		100.0%	
SUMTER	1,113	52		1,061	52 R	4.7%		100.0%	

ALABAMA

PRESIDENT 1944

County	Total Vote	Republican	Democratic	Other	Rep.-Dem. Plurality	Percentage Total Vote Rep.	Dem.	Major Vote Rep.	Dem.
TALLADEGA	3,806	675	3,102	29	2,427 D	17.7%	81.5%	17.9%	82.1%
TALLAPOOSA	3,469	136	3,326	7	3,190 D	3.9%	95.9%	3.9%	96.1%
TUSCALOOSA	5,573	584	4,939	50	4,355 D	10.5%	88.6%	10.6%	89.4%
WALKER	6,907	2,241	4,619	47	2,378 D	32.4%	66.9%	32.7%	67.3%
WASHINGTON	1,568	115	1,447	6	1,332 D	7.3%	92.3%	7.4%	92.6%
WILCOX	1,241	30	1,209	2	1,179 D	2.4%	97.4%	2.4%	97.6%
WINSTON	2,460	1,538	912	10	626 R	62.5%	37.1%	62.8%	37.2%
TOTAL	244,743	44,540	198,918	1,285	154,378 D	18.2%	81.3%	18.3%	81.7%

PRESIDENT 1948

County	Total Vote	Republican	Democratic	Other	Rep.-Dem. Plurality	Percentage Total Vote Rep.	Dem.	Major Vote Rep.	Dem.
TALLADEGA	3,705	593		3,112	593 R	16.0%		100.0%	
TALLAPOOSA	2,474	156		2,318	156 R	6.3%		100.0%	
TUSCALOOSA	5,455	658		4,797	658 R	12.1%		100.0%	
WALKER	6,028	1,852		4,176	1,852 R	30.7%		100.0%	
WASHINGTON	1,344	31		1,313	31 R	2.3%		100.0%	
WILCOX	1,176	14		1,162	14 R	1.2%		100.0%	
WINSTON	2,468	1,588		880	1,588 R	64.3%		100.0%	
TOTAL	214,980	40,930		174,050	40,930 R	19.0%		100.0%	

ALABAMA

PRESIDENT 1952

County	Total Vote	Republican	Democratic	Other	Rep.-Dem. Plurality	Total Vote Rep. %	Total Vote Dem. %	Major Vote Rep. %	Major Vote Dem. %
AUTAUGA	2,308	787	1,505	16	718 D	34.1	65.2	34.3	65.7
BALDWIN	6,617	3,179	3,386	52	207 D	48.0	51.2	48.4	51.6
BARBOUR	3,050	798	2,250	2	1,452 D	26.2	73.8	26.2	73.8
BIBB	2,769	784	1,971	14	1,187 D	28.3	71.2	28.5	71.5
BLOUNT	4,888	1,720	3,161	7	1,441 D	35.2	64.7	35.2	64.8
BULLOCK	1,360	442	918		476 D	32.5	67.5	32.5	67.5
BUTLER	3,528	1,087	2,440	1	1,353 D	30.8	69.2	30.8	69.2
CALHOUN	11,193	3,064	8,023	106	4,959 D	27.4	71.7	27.6	72.4
CHAMBERS	7,190	990	6,155	45	5,165 D	13.8	85.6	13.9	86.1
CHEROKEE	3,211	539	2,664	8	2,125 D	16.8	83.0	16.8	83.2
CHILTON	4,844	2,563	2,269	12	294 R	52.9	46.8	53.0	47.0
CHOCTAW	2,185	593	1,583	9	990 D	27.1	72.4	27.3	72.5
CLARKE	4,425	1,303	3,121	1	1,818 D	29.4	70.5	29.5	70.5
CLAY	3,164	1,183	1,972	9	789 D	37.4	62.3	37.5	62.5
CLEBURNE	2,354	792	1,557	5	765 D	33.6	66.1	33.7	66.3
COFFEE	4,620	699	3,919	2	3,220 D	15.1	84.8	15.1	84.9
COLBERT	7,308	1,381	5,920	7	4,539 D	18.9	81.0	18.9	81.1
CONECUH	2,458	749	1,678	31	929 D	30.5	68.3	30.9	69.1
COOSA	2,291	788	1,501	2	713 D	34.4	65.5	34.4	65.5
COVINGTON	6,558	1,581	4,956	21	3,375 D	24.1	75.6	24.2	75.8
CRENSHAW	3,032	544	2,485	3	1,941 D	17.9	82.0	18.0	82.0
CULLMAN	8,667	3,391	5,254	22	1,863 D	39.1	60.6	39.2	60.8
DALE	3,763	1,073	2,669	21	1,596 D	28.5	70.9	28.7	71.3
DALLAS	4,632	2,550	2,082		468 R	55.1	44.9	55.1	44.9
DE KALB	9,217	3,997	5,209	11	1,212 D	43.4	56.5	43.4	56.6
ELMORE	5,518	1,315	4,199	4	2,884 D	23.8	76.1	23.8	76.2
ESCAMBIA	4,583	1,187	3,385	11	2,193 D	25.9	73.9	26.0	74.0
ETOWAH	15,697	4,634	10,997	66	6,363 D	29.5	70.1	29.6	70.4
FAYETTE	3,779	1,481	2,287	11	805 D	39.1	60.5	39.3	60.7
FRANKLIN	5,893	2,424	3,461	8	1,037 D	41.1	58.7	41.2	58.8
GENEVA	3,656	950	2,703	3	1,753 D	26.0	73.9	26.0	74.0
GREENE	1,105	430	674	1	244 D	38.9	61.0	38.9	61.1
HALE	1,972	758	1,210	4	452 D	38.4	61.4	38.5	61.5
HENRY	2,392	421	1,966	5	1,545 D	17.5	82.2	17.6	82.4
HOUSTON	6,364	2,517	3,779	68	1,262 D	39.5	59.4	40.0	60.0
JACKSON	4,959	1,272	3,677	10	2,405 D	25.7	74.1	25.7	74.3
JEFFERSON	70,766	32,254	38,111	401	5,857 D	45.5	53.9	45.8	54.2
LAMAR	3,118	605	2,512	1	1,907 D	19.4	80.6	19.4	80.6
LAUDERDALE	9,027	1,910	7,007	20	5,097 D	21.2	78.6	21.2	78.8
LAWRENCE	3,466	809	2,651	6	1,842 D	23.3	76.5	23.4	76.6
LEE	4,434	1,626	2,803	5	1,177 D	36.7	63.2	36.7	63.3
LIMESTONE	4,406	549	3,844	13	3,295 D	12.5	87.2	12.5	87.5
LOWNDES	1,443	631	809	3	178 D	43.7	56.1	43.8	56.2
MACON	2,079	621	1,457	1	836 D	29.9	70.1	29.9	70.1
MADISON	9,920	1,623	8,216	81	6,593 D	16.4	82.8	16.5	83.5
MARENGO	3,152	1,362	1,790		428 D	43.2	56.8	43.2	56.8
MARION	4,348	1,489	2,850	9	1,361 D	34.2	65.5	34.3	65.7
MARSHALL	8,099	2,069	6,011	19	3,942 D	25.5	74.2	25.6	74.4
MOBILE	28,715	14,153	14,473	89	320 D	49.3	50.4	49.4	50.6
MONROE	3,231	637	2,587	7	1,950 D	19.7	80.1	19.7	80.2
MONTGOMERY	17,529	8,102	9,234	193	1,132 D	46.2	52.7	46.7	53.3
MORGAN	9,380	2,335	7,029	16	4,694 D	24.9	74.9	24.9	75.1
PERRY	2,112	756	1,352	4	596 D	35.8	64.0	35.9	64.1
PICKENS	2,442	905	1,519	18	614 D	37.1	62.2	37.3	62.7
PIKE	3,514	965	2,546	3	1,581 D	27.5	72.5	27.5	72.5
RANDOLPH	4,018	1,047	2,964	7	1,917 D	26.1	73.8	26.1	73.9
RUSSELL	4,434	867	3,564	3	2,697 D	19.6	80.4	19.6	80.4
ST CLAIR	3,922	1,590	2,326	6	736 D	40.5	59.3	40.6	59.4
SHELBY	4,636	2,156	2,473	7	317 D	46.5	53.3	46.6	53.4
SUMTER	1,599	702	894	3	192 D	43.9	55.9	44.0	56.0

PRESIDENT 1956

County	Total Vote	Republican	Democratic	Other	Rep.-Dem. Plurality	Total Vote Rep. %	Total Vote Dem. %	Major Vote Rep. %	Major Vote Dem. %
AUTAUGA	2,287	857	1,161	269	304 D	37.5	50.8	42.5	57.5
BALDWIN	8,415	4,293	3,878	244	415 R	51.0	46.1	52.5	47.5
BARBOUR	3,449	777	2,530	142	1,753 D	22.5	73.4	23.5	76.5
BIBB	2,582	1,004	1,471	107	467 D	38.9	57.0	40.6	59.4
BLOUNT	5,922	2,628	3,208	86	580 D	44.4	54.2	45.0	55.0
BULLOCK	1,252	304	812	136	508 D	24.3	64.9	27.2	72.8
BUTLER	3,533	1,324	1,958	251	634 D	37.5	55.4	40.3	59.7
CALHOUN	13,900	4,473	9,069	358	4,596 D	32.2	65.2	33.0	67.0
CHAMBERS	6,737	1,448	5,165	124	3,717 D	21.5	76.7	21.9	78.1
CHEROKEE	3,513	845	2,661	7	1,816 D	24.1	75.7	24.1	75.9
CHILTON	5,148	3,139	1,891	118	1,248 R	61.0	36.7	62.4	37.6
CHOCTAW	1,779	457	1,250	72	793 D	25.7	70.3	26.8	73.2
CLARKE	3,388	1,246	1,962	180	716 D	36.8	57.9	38.8	61.2
CLAY	3,323	1,597	1,677	49	80 D	48.1	50.5	48.8	51.2
CLEBURNE	2,470	1,056	1,407	7	351 D	42.8	57.0	42.9	57.1
COFFEE	5,268	973	4,163	132	3,190 D	18.5	79.0	18.9	81.1
COLBERT	8,637	1,819	7,007	111	5,188 D	20.4	78.4	20.6	79.4
CONECUH	2,754	885	1,687	182	802 D	32.1	61.3	34.4	65.6
COOSA	2,519	1,070	1,411	38	341 D	42.5	56.0	43.1	56.9
COVINGTON	7,490	2,257	4,887	346	2,630 D	30.1	65.2	31.6	68.4
CRENSHAW	2,975	567	2,252	156	1,685 D	19.1	75.7	20.1	79.9
CULLMAN	9,929	4,381	5,510	38	1,129 D	44.1	55.5	44.3	55.7
DALE	3,712	1,284	2,318	110	1,034 D	34.6	62.4	35.6	64.4
DALLAS	5,358	2,324	2,121	913	203 R	43.4	39.6	52.3	47.7
DE KALB	11,468	5,684	5,768	16	84 D	49.6	50.3	49.6	50.4
ELMORE	5,394	1,619	3,353	422	1,734 D	30.0	62.2	32.6	67.4
ESCAMBIA	5,299	1,529	3,437	333	1,908 D	28.9	64.8	30.8	69.2
ETOWAH	19,886	7,198	12,374	314	5,176 D	36.2	62.2	36.8	63.2
FAYETTE	3,928	1,948	1,956	24	8 D	49.6	49.8	49.9	50.1
FRANKLIN	6,769	3,399	3,354	16	45 R	50.2	49.5	50.3	49.7
GENEVA	4,118	1,179	2,841	98	1,662 D	28.6	69.0	29.3	70.7
GREENE	1,044	309	691	44	382 D	29.6	66.2	30.9	69.2
HALE	1,917	504	1,314	99	810 D	26.3	68.5	27.7	72.3
HENRY	2,713	429	2,127	157	1,698 D	15.8	78.4	16.8	83.2
HOUSTON	6,841	2,632	3,630	579	998 D	38.5	53.1	42.0	58.0
JACKSON	6,647	1,868	4,758	21	2,890 D	28.1	71.6	28.2	71.8
JEFFERSON	87,513	43,695	38,604	5,214	5,091 R	49.9	44.1	53.1	46.9
LAMAR	3,399	867	2,501	31	1,634 D	25.5	73.5	25.7	74.3
LAUDERDALE	11,692	2,458	9,150	84	6,692 D	21.0	78.3	21.2	78.8
LAWRENCE	4,185	1,197	2,961	27	1,764 D	28.6	70.8	28.8	71.2
LEE	5,051	1,586	3,302	163	1,716 D	31.4	65.3	32.4	67.6
LIMESTONE	4,750	589	4,145	16	3,556 D	12.4	87.3	12.4	87.6
LOWNDES	1,192	326	623	243	297 D	27.3	52.3	34.4	65.6
MACON	2,193	1,067	1,024	102	43 R	48.7	46.7	51.0	49.0
MADISON	12,150	2,993	9,054	103	6,061 D	24.6	74.5	24.8	75.2
MARENGO	3,052	1,009	1,858	185	849 D	33.1	60.9	35.2	64.8
MARION	5,495	2,536	2,849	110	313 D	46.9	52.0	47.1	52.9
MARSHALL	9,534	3,166	6,329	95	3,163 D	32.3	66.7	32.7	67.3
MOBILE	39,534	20,639	17,163	1,732	3,476 R	52.2	43.4	54.6	45.4
MONROE	2,958	759	2,069	130	1,310 D	25.7	69.9	26.8	73.2
MONTGOMERY	18,841	8,727	6,890	3,224	1,837 R	46.3	36.6	55.9	44.1
MORGAN	10,872	2,974	7,671	227	4,697 D	27.4	70.6	27.9	72.1
PERRY	1,812	974	613	225	361 R	53.8	33.8	61.4	38.6
PICKENS	2,824	993	1,660	171	667 D	35.2	58.8	37.4	62.6
PIKE	3,839	997	2,631	211	1,634 D	26.0	68.5	27.5	72.5
RANDOLPH	4,761	1,584	3,151	26	1,567 D	33.3	66.2	33.5	66.5
RUSSELL	4,479	1,265	3,060	154	1,795 D	28.2	68.3	29.2	70.8
ST CLAIR	4,975	2,441	2,420	114	21 R	49.1	48.6	50.2	49.8
SHELBY	5,581	2,901	2,502	178	399 R	52.0	44.8	53.7	46.3
SUMTER	1,671	578	981	112	403 D	34.6	58.7	37.1	62.9

ALABAMA

PRESIDENT 1952

County	Total Vote	Republican	Democratic	Other	Rep.-Dem. Plurality	Percentage Total Vote Rep.	Dem.	Major Vote Rep.	Dem.
TALLADEGA	8,642	3,588	5,028	26	1,440 D	41.5%	58.2%	41.6%	58.4%
TALLAPOOSA	6,249	1,187	5,055	7	3,868 D	19.0%	80.9%	19.0%	81.0%
TUSCALOOSA	11,720	3,872	7,677	171	3,805 D	33.0%	65.5%	33.5%	66.5%
WALKER	10,432	3,490	6,862	80	3,372 D	33.5%	65.8%	33.7%	66.3%
WASHINGTON	2,607	623	1,977	7	1,354 D	23.9%	75.8%	24.0%	76.0%
WILCOX	1,714	725	988	1	263 D	42.3%	57.6%	42.3%	57.7%
WINSTON	3,416	2,017	1,390	9	627 R	59.0%	40.7%	59.2%	40.8%
TOTAL	426,120	149,231	275,075	1,814	125,844 D	35.0%	64.6%	35.2%	64.8%

PRESIDENT 1956

County	Total Vote	Republican	Democratic	Other	Rep.-Dem. Plurality	Percentage Total Vote Rep.	Dem.	Major Vote Rep.	Dem.
TALLADEGA	9,597	4,197	5,243	157	1,046 D	43.7%	54.6%	44.5%	55.5%
TALLAPOOSA	7,042	1,879	5,070	93	3,191 D	26.7%	72.0%	27.0%	73.0%
TUSCALOOSA	13,798	4,994	8,186	618	3,192 D	36.2%	59.3%	37.9%	62.1%
WALKER	12,919	5,179	7,661	79	2,482 D	40.1%	59.3%	40.3%	59.7%
WASHINGTON	2,569	777	1,705	87	928 D	30.2%	66.4%	31.3%	68.7%
WILCOX	1,474	499	778	197	279 D	33.9%	52.8%	39.1%	60.9%
WINSTON	4,570	2,998	1,570	2	1,428 R	65.6%	34.4%	65.6%	34.4%
TOTAL	496,861	195,694	280,844	20,323	85,150 D	39.4%	56.5%	41.1%	58.9%

ALABAMA

PRESIDENT 1960

County	Total Vote	Republican	Democratic	Other	Rep.-Dem. Plurality	% Total Vote Rep.	% Total Vote Dem.	% Major Vote Rep.	% Major Vote Dem.
AUTAUGA	2,651	1,149	1,413	89	264 D	43.3%	53.3%	44.8%	55.2%
BALDWIN	10,728	4,812	5,729	187	917 D	44.9%	53.4%	45.7%	54.3%
BARBOUR	3,493	1,166	2,290	37	1,124 D	33.4%	65.6%	33.7%	66.3%
BIBB	2,757	1,052	1,701	4	649 D	38.2%	61.7%	38.2%	61.8%
BLOUNT	5,990	2,557	3,414	19	857 D	42.7%	57.0%	42.8%	57.2%
BULLOCK	1,256	412	838	6	426 D	32.8%	66.7%	33.0%	67.0%
BUTLER	4,194	1,231	2,943	20	1,712 D	29.4%	70.2%	29.5%	70.5%
CALHOUN	14,658	4,821	9,619	218	4,798 D	32.9%	65.6%	33.4%	66.6%
CHAMBERS	7,154	1,865	5,172	117	3,307 D	26.1%	72.3%	26.5%	73.5%
CHEROKEE	3,987	872	3,106	9	2,234 D	21.9%	77.9%	21.9%	78.1%
CHILTON	5,041	3,201	1,821	19	1,380 R	63.5%	36.1%	63.7%	36.3%
CHOCTAW	2,148	612	1,439	97	827 D	28.5%	67.0%	29.8%	70.2%
CLARKE	4,259	2,016	2,151	92	135 D	47.3%	50.5%	48.4%	51.6%
CLAY	3,311	1,548	1,740	23	192 D	46.8%	52.5%	47.1%	52.9%
CLEBURNE	2,530	1,008	1,510	12	502 D	39.8%	59.7%	40.0%	60.0%
COFFEE	5,884	1,381	4,480	23	3,099 D	23.5%	76.1%	23.6%	76.4%
COLBERT	10,403	2,815	7,377	211	4,562 D	27.1%	70.9%	27.6%	72.4%
CONECUH	2,667	650	1,917	100	1,267 D	24.4%	71.9%	25.3%	74.7%
COOSA	2,584	1,073	1,492	19	419 D	41.5%	57.7%	41.8%	58.2%
COVINGTON	7,775	2,047	5,686	42	3,639 D	26.3%	73.1%	26.5%	73.5%
CRENSHAW	3,501	573	2,921	7	2,348 D	16.4%	83.4%	16.4%	83.6%
CULLMAN	10,616	4,248	6,346	22	2,098 D	40.0%	59.8%	40.1%	59.9%
DALE	4,351	1,634	2,663	54	1,029 D	37.6%	61.2%	38.0%	62.0%
DALLAS	5,561	2,872	2,455	234	417 R	51.6%	44.1%	53.9%	46.1%
DE KALB	11,464	5,585	5,849	30	264 D	48.7%	51.0%	48.7%	51.2%
ELMORE	5,522	1,919	3,524	79	1,605 D	34.8%	63.8%	35.3%	64.7%
ESCAMBIA	6,096	1,810	4,173	113	2,363 D	29.7%	68.5%	30.3%	69.7%
ETOWAH	21,819	7,128	14,316	375	7,188 D	32.7%	65.6%	33.2%	66.8%
FAYETTE	4,218	1,923	2,278	17	355 D	45.6%	54.0%	45.8%	54.2%
FRANKLIN	7,551	4,069	3,443	39	626 R	53.9%	45.6%	54.2%	45.8%
GENEVA	4,670	1,502	3,157	11	1,655 D	32.2%	67.6%	32.2%	67.8%
GREENE	1,155	381	753	21	372 D	33.0%	65.2%	33.6%	66.4%
HALE	2,123	741	1,369	13	628 D	34.9%	64.5%	35.1%	64.9%
HENRY	2,745	588	2,140	17	1,552 D	21.4%	78.0%	21.6%	78.4%
HOUSTON	8,100	4,055	3,960	85	95 R	50.1%	48.9%	50.6%	49.4%
JACKSON	6,871	2,036	4,789	46	2,753 D	29.6%	69.7%	29.8%	70.2%
JEFFERSON	106,758	60,004	44,681	2,073	15,323 D	56.2%	41.9%	57.3%	42.7%
LAMAR	3,546	964	2,518	64	1,554 D	27.2%	71.0%	27.7%	72.3%
LAUDERDALE	12,347	3,570	6,533	244	2,963 D	28.9%	70.5%	29.5%	70.5%
LAWRENCE	4,315	1,365	2,937	13	1,572 D	31.6%	68.1%	31.7%	68.3%
LEE	6,150	2,301	3,795	54	1,494 D	37.4%	61.7%	37.7%	62.3%
LIMESTONE	5,279	991	4,277	11	3,285 D	18.8%	81.0%	18.8%	81.2%
LOWNDES	1,329	432	884	13	442 D	32.5%	66.5%	32.8%	67.2%
MACON	2,223	877	1,319	27	442 D	39.5%	59.3%	39.9%	60.1%
MADISON	16,506	5,299	11,004	203	5,705 D	32.1%	66.7%	32.5%	67.5%
MARENGO	3,300	1,235	1,915	150	681 D	37.4%	58.0%	39.2%	60.8%
MARION	6,068	2,938	3,103	27	165 D	48.4%	51.1%	48.6%	51.4%
MARSHALL	10,023	3,398	6,606	19	3,203 D	33.9%	65.9%	34.0%	66.0%
MOBILE	55,297	24,608	29,221	1,438	4,613 D	44.5%	52.9%	45.7%	54.3%
MONROE	3,306	989	2,279	38	1,290 D	29.3%	68.9%	30.3%	69.7%
MONTGOMERY	22,311	11,778	10,159	374	1,619 R	52.3%	45.5%	53.7%	46.3%
MORGAN	12,183	4,357	7,776	50	3,419 D	35.1%	63.8%	35.9%	64.1%
PERRY	1,901	744	1,079	78	335 D	39.1%	56.8%	40.8%	59.2%
PICKENS	3,050	1,277	1,926	47	649 D	39.3%	59.3%	39.9%	60.1%
PIKE	4,554	1,006	3,503	25	2,497 D	22.2%	77.3%	22.3%	77.7%
RANDOLPH	4,924	1,697	3,184	43	1,487 D	34.5%	64.7%	34.8%	65.2%
RUSSELL	5,325	1,770	3,494	61	1,724 D	33.2%	65.6%	33.6%	66.4%
ST CLAIR	5,676	2,589	3,062	25	473 D	45.5%	53.9%	45.8%	54.2%
SHELBY	6,470	3,157	3,252	61	95 D	48.8%	50.3%	49.3%	50.7%
SUMTER	1,685	623	986	76	363 D	37.0%	58.5%	38.7%	61.3%

PRESIDENT 1964

County	Total Vote	Republican	Democratic	Other	Rep.-Dem. Plurality	% Total Vote Rep.	% Total Vote Dem.	% Major Vote Rep.	% Major Vote Dem.
AUTAUGA	3,460	2,969		491	2,969 R	85.8%		100.0%	
BALDWIN	13,400	10,870		2,530	10,870 R	81.1%		100.0%	
BARBOUR	4,831	3,853		978	3,853 R	79.8%		100.0%	
BIBB	3,126	2,623		503	2,623 R	83.9%		100.0%	
BLOUNT	6,869	4,442		2,427	4,442 R	64.7%		100.0%	
BULLOCK	2,630	1,516		1,114	1,516 R	57.6%		100.0%	
BUTLER	4,975	4,002		973	4,002 R	80.4%		100.0%	
CALHOUN	16,845	10,635		6,210	10,635 R	63.1%		100.0%	
CHAMBERS	7,187	4,630		2,557	4,630 R	64.4%		100.0%	
CHEROKEE	3,809	1,893		1,916	1,893 R	49.7%		100.0%	
CHILTON	6,847	5,202		1,645	5,202 R	76.0%		100.0%	
CHOCTAW	2,910	2,497		413	2,497 R	85.8%		100.0%	
CLARKE	5,384	4,460		924	4,460 R	82.8%		100.0%	
CLAY	4,014	2,815		1,199	2,815 R	70.1%		100.0%	
CLEBURNE	2,828	2,156		672	2,156 R	76.2%		100.0%	
COFFEE	6,123	4,910		1,213	4,910 R	80.2%		100.0%	
COLBERT	10,840	5,267		5,573	5,267 R	48.6%		100.0%	
CONECUH	3,421	2,782		639	2,782 R	81.3%		100.0%	
COOSA	2,718	1,978		740	1,978 R	72.8%		100.0%	
COVINGTON	9,175	7,554		1,621	7,554 R	82.3%		100.0%	
CRENSHAW	3,824	3,008		816	3,008 R	78.7%		100.0%	
CULLMAN	12,262	7,152		5,110	7,152 R	58.3%		100.0%	
DALE	5,933	4,970		963	4,970 R	83.8%		100.0%	
DALLAS	6,607	5,888		719	5,888 R	89.1%		100.0%	
DE KALB	11,694	6,746		4,948	6,746 R	57.7%		100.0%	
ELMORE	7,596	6,363		1,233	6,363 R	83.8%		100.0%	
ESCAMBIA	7,551	5,623		1,928	5,623 R	74.5%		100.0%	
ETOWAH	21,833	12,894		8,939	12,894 R	59.1%		100.0%	
FAYETTE	4,490	3,203		1,287	3,203 R	71.3%		100.0%	
FRANKLIN	7,135	4,025		3,110	4,025 R	56.4%		100.0%	
GENEVA	5,576	4,502		1,074	4,502 R	80.7%		100.0%	
GREENE	1,711	1,124		587	1,124 R	65.7%		100.0%	
HALE	2,445	1,898		548	1,898 R	77.6%		100.0%	
HENRY	3,485	2,896		589	2,896 R	83.1%		100.0%	
HOUSTON	11,774	10,353		1,421	10,353 R	87.9%		100.0%	
JACKSON	5,875	2,730		3,145	2,730 R	46.5%		100.0%	
JEFFERSON	138,838	100,756		38,082	100,756 R	72.6%		100.0%	
LAMAR	3,775	2,734		1,041	2,734 R	72.4%		100.0%	
LAUDERDALE	12,571	5,978		6,593	5,978 R	47.6%		100.0%	
LAWRENCE	3,617	1,809		1,808	1,809 R	50.0%		100.0%	
LEE	7,516	5,914		1,602	5,914 R	78.7%		100.0%	
LIMESTONE	5,404	2,377		3,027	2,377 R	44.0%		100.0%	
LOWNDES	1,853	1,548		310	1,548 R	83.3%		100.0%	
MACON	4,831	1,858		2,973	1,858 R	38.5%		100.0%	
MADISON	27,495	14,279		13,217	14,279 R	51.9%		100.0%	
MARENGO	4,466	3,677		789	3,677 R	82.3%		100.0%	
MARION	5,713	3,966		1,747	3,966 R	69.4%		100.0%	
MARSHALL	10,143	5,712		4,428	5,712 R	56.3%		100.0%	
MOBILE	69,981	49,493		20,488	49,493 R	70.7%		100.0%	
MONROE	4,756	3,870		886	3,870 R	81.4%		100.0%	
MONTGOMERY	30,497	23,015		7,482	23,015 R	75.5%		100.0%	
MORGAN	12,381	7,013		5,368	7,013 R	56.6%		100.0%	
PERRY	2,566	2,046		520	2,046 R	79.7%		100.0%	
PICKENS	4,162	3,416		746	3,416 R	82.1%		100.0%	
PIKE	5,176	4,373		803	4,373 R	84.5%		100.0%	
RANDOLPH	4,991	3,127		1,864	3,127 R	62.7%		100.0%	
RUSSELL	6,414	4,877		1,537	4,877 R	76.0%		100.0%	
ST CLAIR	6,802	4,813		1,989	4,813 R	70.8%		100.0%	
SHELBY	7,980	6,037		1,943	6,037 R	75.7%		100.0%	
SUMTER	2,058	1,653		405	1,653 R	80.3%		100.0%	

ALABAMA

PRESIDENT 1960

County	Total Vote	Republican	Democratic	Other	Rep.-Dem. Plurality	Percentage			
						Total Vote		Major Vote	
						Rep.	Dem.	Rep.	Dem.
TALLADEGA	10,554	4,723	5,732	99	1,009 D	44.8%	54.3%	45.2%	54.8%
TALLAPOOSA	7,692	2,150	5,494	48	3,344 D	28.0%	71.4%	28.1%	71.9%
TUSCALOOSA	14,190	5,598	8,348	244	2,750 D	39.5%	58.8%	40.1%	59.9%
WALKER	13,651	5,463	8,188		2,725 D	40.0%	60.0%	40.0%	60.0%
WASHINGTON	2,940	792	2,079	69	1,287 D	26.9%	70.7%	27.6%	72.4%
WILCOX	1,581	513	1,061	7	548 D	32.4%	67.1%	32.6%	67.4%
WINSTON	5,108	3,421	1,681	6	1,740 R	67.0%	32.9%	67.1%	32.9%
TOTAL	570,225	237,981	324,050	8,194	86,069 D	41.7%	56.8%	42.3%	57.7%

PRESIDENT 1964

County	Total Vote	Republican	Democratic	Other	Rep.-Dem. Plurality	Percentage			
						Total Vote		Major Vote	
						Rep.	Dem.	Rep.	Dem.
TALLADEGA	12,658	8,946		3,712	8,946 R	70.7%		100.0%	
TALLAPOOSA	7,263	5,530		1,733	5,530 R	76.1%		100.0%	
TUSCALOOSA	19,263	13,227		6,036	13,227 R	68.7%		100.0%	
WALKER	14,692	8,582		6,110	8,582 R	58.4%		100.0%	
WASHINGTON	3,994	2,803		1,191	2,803 R	70.2%		100.0%	
WILCOX	1,946	1,789		157	1,789 R	91.9%		100.0%	
WINSTON	4,829	3,438		1,391	3,438 R	71.2%		100.0%	
TOTAL	689,818	479,085		210,733	479,085 R	69.5%		100.0%	

ALABAMA

OTHER VOTE COMPOSITION:

1920   2,402 Socialist; 766 Prohibition.
1924   8,040 Progressive; 562 Prohibition.
1928   Socialist.
1932   2,030 Socialist; 675 Communist; 13 Prohibition.
1936   719 Prohibition; 678 Communist; 551 Union; 242 Socialist.

1940   700 Prohibition; 509 Communist; 100 Socialist.
1944   1,095 Prohibition; 190 Socialist.
1948   171,443 States Rights; 1,522 Progressive; 1,085 Prohibition.
1952   Prohibition.
1956   Independent.

1960   4,367 National States Rights; 2,106 Prohibition; 1,485 Independent Afro-American;
           236 scattered.
1964   210,732 Unpledged Democratic; 1 scattered.

SPECIAL CASES:

1920   Socialist candidates ran second in one county.
1924   Progressive candidates ran second in several counties.
1932   Communist candidates ran second in one county.
1948   The national Democratic candidates were not represented on the ballot. States
           Rights candidates carried the state and almost all counties.
1956   One Democratic elector voted in the Electoral College for Walter B. Jones and
           Herman Talmadge.

1960   Of the 11 candidates on the Democratic elector ticket, 6 were unpledged. In the
           Electoral College these 6 voted for Senators Harry Flood Byrd and Strom
           Thurmond.
1964   The national Democratic candidates were not represented on the ballot. Un-
           pledged Democratic electors carried several counties.

ALASKA

PRESIDENT 1960

Election District	Total Vote	Republican	Democratic	Other	Rep.-Dem. Plurality	Total Vote Rep.	Total Vote Dem.	Major Vote Rep.	Major Vote Dem.
ELECTION DISTRICT 1	358	147	211		64 D	41.1%	58.9%	41.1%	58.9%
ELECTION DISTRICT 2	3,650	1,898	1,752		146 R	52.0%	48.0%	52.0%	48.0%
ELECTION DISTRICT 3	1,439	760	679		81 R	52.8%	47.2%	52.8%	47.2%
ELECTION DISTRICT 4	2,116	984	1,132		148 D	46.5%	53.5%	46.5%	53.5%
ELECTION DISTRICT 5	3,950	2,031	1,919		112 R	51.4%	48.6%	51.4%	48.6%
ELECTION DISTRICT 6	1,099	461	638		177 D	41.9%	58.1%	41.9%	58.1%
ELECTION DISTRICT 7	542	267	275		8 D	49.3%	50.7%	49.3%	50.7%
ELECTION DISTRICT 8	722	337	385		48 D	46.7%	53.3%	46.7%	53.3%
ELECTION DISTRICT 9	2,008	1,045	963		82 R	52.0%	48.0%	52.0%	48.0%
ELECTION DISTRICT 10	19,708	10,537	9,171		1,366 R	53.5%	46.5%	53.5%	46.5%
ELECTION DISTRICT 11	1,154	539	615		76 D	46.7%	53.3%	46.7%	53.3%
ELECTION DISTRICT 12	1,952	907	1,045		138 D	46.5%	53.5%	46.5%	53.5%
ELECTION DISTRICT 13	1,356	555	801		246 D	40.9%	59.1%	40.9%	59.1%
ELECTION DISTRICT 14	563	161	402		241 D	28.6%	71.4%	28.6%	71.4%
ELECTION DISTRICT 15	817	304	513		209 D	37.2%	62.8%	37.2%	62.8%
ELECTION DISTRICT 16	724	523	201		322 R	72.2%	27.8%	72.2%	27.8%
ELECTION DISTRICT 17	536	295	241		54 R	55.0%	45.0%	55.0%	45.0%
ELECTION DISTRICT 18	861	367	494		127 D	42.6%	57.4%	42.6%	57.4%
ELECTION DISTRICT 19	8,664	4,229	4,435		206 D	48.8%	51.2%	48.8%	51.2%
ELECTION DISTRICT 20	434	178	256		78 D	41.0%	59.0%	41.0%	59.0%
ELECTION DISTRICT 21	429	186	243		57 D	43.4%	56.6%	43.4%	56.6%
ELECTION DISTRICT 22	840	547	293		254 R	65.1%	34.9%	65.1%	34.9%
ELECTION DISTRICT 23	1,693	941	752		189 R	55.6%	44.4%	55.6%	44.4%
ELECTION DISTRICT 24	265	90	175		85 D	34.0%	66.0%	34.0%	66.0%
ABSENTEE	4,882	2,664	2,218		446 R	54.6%	45.4%	54.6%	45.4%
TOTAL	60,762	30,953	29,809		1,144 R	50.9%	49.1%	50.9%	49.1%

PRESIDENT 1964

Election District	Total Vote	Republican	Democratic	Other	Rep.-Dem. Plurality	Total Vote Rep.	Total Vote Dem.	Major Vote Rep.	Major Vote Dem.
ELECTION DISTRICT 1	4,595	1,554	3,041		1,487 D	33.8%	66.2%	33.8%	66.2%
ELECTION DISTRICT 2	1,842	464	1,378		914 D	25.2%	74.8%	25.2%	74.8%
ELECTION DISTRICT 3	2,396	651	1,745		1,094 D	27.2%	72.8%	27.2%	72.8%
ELECTION DISTRICT 4	5,307	1,545	3,762		2,217 D	29.1%	70.9%	29.1%	70.9%
ELECTION DISTRICT 5	1,306	250	1,056		806 D	19.1%	80.9%	19.1%	80.9%
ELECTION DISTRICT 6	1,485	495	990		495 D	33.3%	66.7%	33.3%	66.7%
ELECTION DISTRICT 7	2,205	963	1,242		279 D	43.7%	56.3%	43.7%	56.3%
ELECTION DISTRICT 8	22,588	9,051	13,537		4,486 D	40.1%	59.9%	40.1%	59.9%
ELECTION DISTRICT 9	938	264	674		410 D	28.1%	71.9%	28.1%	71.9%
ELECTION DISTRICT 10	2,627	1,000	1,627		627 D	38.1%	61.9%	38.1%	61.9%
ELECTION DISTRICT 11	1,582	399	1,183		784 D	25.2%	74.8%	25.2%	74.8%
ELECTION DISTRICT 12	855	124	731		607 D	14.5%	85.5%	14.5%	85.5%
ELECTION DISTRICT 13	1,198	267	931		664 D	22.3%	77.7%	22.3%	77.7%
ELECTION DISTRICT 14	1,715	214	1,501		1,287 D	12.5%	87.5%	12.5%	87.5%
ELECTION DISTRICT 15	1,966	600	1,366		766 D	30.5%	69.5%	30.5%	69.5%
ELECTION DISTRICT 16	10,750	4,340	6,410		2,070 D	40.4%	59.6%	40.4%	59.6%
ELECTION DISTRICT 17	1,401	252	1,149		897 D	18.0%	82.0%	18.0%	82.0%
ELECTION DISTRICT 18	1,791	420	1,371		951 D	23.5%	76.5%	23.5%	76.5%
ELECTION DISTRICT 19	712	77	635		558 D	10.8%	89.2%	10.8%	89.2%
TOTAL	67,259	22,930	44,329		21,399 D	34.1%	65.9%	34.1%	65.9%

ALASKA

OTHER VOTE COMPOSITION:

1960
1964

SPECIAL CASES:

The boundaries and designations of Alaska's election districts were altered and the number of districts reduced between the two elections covered in this volume.

ARIZONA

PRESIDENT 1920

County	Total Vote	Republican	Democratic	Other	Rep.-Dem. Plurality	Percentage Total Vote Rep.	Total Vote Dem.	Major Vote Rep.	Major Vote Dem.
APACHE	1,302	679	618	5	61 R	52.2%	47.5%	52.4%	47.6%
COCHISE	9,771	5,341	4,430		911 R	54.7%	45.3%	54.7%	45.3%
COCONINO	2,123	1,342	781		561 R	63.2%	36.8%	63.2%	36.8%
GILA	6,330	3,311	2,894	125	417 R	52.3%	45.7%	53.4%	46.6%
GRAHAM	2,323	1,062	1,261		199 D	45.7%	54.3%	45.7%	54.3%
GREENLEE	2,058	905	1,131	22	226 D	44.0%	55.0%	44.4%	55.6%
MARICOPA	20,161	11,336	8,825		2,511 R	56.2%	43.8%	56.2%	43.8%
MOHAVE	1,791	996	722	73	274 R	55.6%	40.3%	58.0%	42.0%
NAVAJO	2,115	1,078	1,031	6	47 R	51.0%	48.7%	51.1%	48.9%
PIMA	5,847	3,392	2,455		937 R	58.0%	42.0%	58.0%	42.0%
PINAL	2,767	1,493	1,264	10	229 R	54.0%	45.7%	54.2%	45.8%
SANTA CRUZ	1,556	850	706		144 R	54.6%	45.4%	54.6%	45.4%
YAVAPAI	5,876	3,625	2,251		1,374 R	61.7%	38.3%	61.7%	38.3%
YUMA	2,783	1,606	1,177		429 R	57.7%	42.3%	57.7%	42.3%
TOTAL	66,803	37,016	29,546	241	7,470 R	55.4%	44.2%	55.6%	44.4%

PRESIDENT 1924

County	Total Vote	Republican	Democratic	Other	Rep.-Dem. Plurality	Percentage Total Vote Rep.	Total Vote Dem.	Major Vote Rep.	Major Vote Dem.
APACHE	1,278	620	548	110	72 R	48.5%	42.9%	53.1%	46.9%
COCHISE	9,699	3,712	3,496	2,491	216 R	38.3%	36.0%	51.5%	48.5%
COCONINO	2,317	1,045	711	561	334 R	45.1%	30.7%	59.5%	40.5%
GILA	6,348	2,193	2,218	1,937	25 D	34.5%	34.9%	49.7%	50.3%
GRAHAM	2,451	813	1,252	386	439 D	33.2%	51.1%	39.4%	60.6%
GREENLEE	1,348	404	768	176	364 D	30.0%	57.0%	34.5%	65.5%
MARICOPA	23,758	10,611	9,177	3,970	1,434 R	44.7%	38.6%	53.6%	46.5%
MOHAVE	1,942	738	475	729	263 R	38.0%	24.5%	60.8%	39.2%
NAVAJO	2,471	1,060	684	727	376 R	42.9%	27.7%	60.8%	39.2%
PIMA	8,439	3,559	2,594	2,286	965 R	42.2%	30.7%	57.8%	42.2%
PINAL	2,631	1,075	988	568	87 R	40.9%	37.6%	52.1%	47.9%
SANTA CRUZ	1,450	579	673	198	94 D	39.9%	46.4%	46.2%	53.8%
YAVAPAI	6,763	2,827	1,800	2,136	1,027 R	41.8%	26.6%	61.1%	38.9%
YUMA	3,066	1,280	851	935	429 R	41.7%	27.8%	60.1%	39.9%
TOTAL	73,961	30,516	26,235	17,210	4,281 R	41.3%	35.5%	53.8%	46.2%

ARIZONA

PRESIDENT 1928

County	Total Vote	Republican	Democratic	Other	Rep.-Dem. Plurality	Percentage Total Vote Rep.	Total Vote Dem.	Major Vote Rep.	Major Vote Dem.
APACHE	1,628	837	791		46 R	51.4%	48.6%	51.4%	48.6%
COCHISE	10,083	5,776	4,262	45	1,514 R	57.3%	42.3%	57.5%	42.5%
COCONINO	2,901	1,717	1,172	12	545 R	59.2%	40.4%	59.4%	40.6%
GILA	6,790	3,436	3,341	13	95 R	50.6%	49.2%	50.7%	49.3%
GRAHAM	2,861	1,238	1,615	8	377 D	43.3%	56.4%	43.4%	56.6%
GREENLEE	1,628	685	935	8	250 D	42.1%	57.4%	42.3%	57.7%
MARICOPA	32,269	20,089	12,146	34	7,943 R	62.3%	37.6%	62.3%	37.7%
MOHAVE	1,868	1,127	728	13	399 R	60.3%	39.0%	60.8%	39.2%
NAVAJO	2,924	1,608	1,316		292 R	55.0%	45.0%	55.0%	45.0%
PIMA	11,653	6,635	4,976	42	1,659 R	56.9%	42.7%	57.1%	42.9%
PINAL	3,054	1,631	1,419	4	212 R	53.4%	46.5%	53.5%	46.5%
SANTA CRUZ	1,884	919	962	3	43 D	48.8%	51.1%	48.9%	51.1%
YAVAPAI	7,794	4,507	3,285	2	1,222 R	57.8%	42.1%	57.8%	42.2%
YUMA	3,917	2,328	1,589		739 R	59.4%	40.6%	59.4%	40.6%
TOTAL	91,254	52,533	38,537	184	13,996 R	57.6%	42.2%	57.7%	42.3%

PRESIDENT 1932

County	Total Vote	Republican	Democratic	Other	Rep.-Dem. Plurality	Percentage Total Vote Rep.	Total Vote Dem.	Major Vote Rep.	Major Vote Dem.
APACHE	2,034	760	1,271	3	511 D	37.4%	62.5%	37.4%	62.6%
COCHISE	11,216	2,838	7,798	580	4,960 D	25.3%	69.5%	26.7%	73.3%
COCONINO	3,853	1,110	2,689	54	1,579 D	28.8%	69.8%	29.2%	70.8%
GILA	6,718	1,865	4,625	228	2,760 D	27.8%	68.8%	28.7%	71.3%
GRAHAM	3,625	718	2,867	40	2,149 D	19.8%	79.1%	20.0%	80.0%
GREENLEE	1,954	377	1,558	19	1,181 D	19.3%	79.7%	19.5%	80.5%
MARICOPA	44,280	15,086	28,601	593	13,515 D	34.1%	64.6%	34.5%	65.5%
MOHAVE	2,283	537	1,660	86	1,123 D	23.5%	72.7%	24.4%	75.6%
NAVAJO	4,146	1,248	2,602	296	1,354 D	30.1%	62.8%	32.4%	67.6%
PIMA	17,727	6,152	11,061	514	4,909 D	34.7%	62.4%	35.7%	64.3%
PINAL	4,184	1,000	3,137	47	2,137 D	23.9%	75.0%	24.2%	75.8%
SANTA CRUZ	2,260	625	1,606	29	981 D	27.7%	71.1%	28.0%	72.0%
YAVAPAI	9,141	2,626	6,326	189	3,700 D	28.7%	69.2%	29.3%	70.7%
YUMA	4,830	1,162	3,463	205	2,301 D	24.1%	71.7%	25.1%	74.9%
TOTAL	118,251	36,104	79,264	2,883	43,160 D	30.5%	67.0%	31.3%	68.7%

ARIZONA

PRESIDENT 1936

County	Total Vote	Republican	Democratic	Other	Rep.-Dem. Plurality	Percentage Total Vote Rep.	Dem.	Major Vote Rep.	Dem.
APACHE	2,327	638	1,674	15	1,036 D	27.4%	71.9%	27.6%	72.4%
COCHISE	10,499	2,092	8,130	277	6,038 D	19.9%	77.4%	20.5%	79.5%
COCONINO	3,829	1,140	2,578	111	1,438 D	29.8%	67.3%	30.7%	69.3%
GILA	6,568	1,526	4,859	183	3,333 D	23.2%	74.0%	23.9%	76.1%
GRAHAM	4,375	680	3,541	154	2,861 D	15.5%	80.9%	16.1%	83.9%
GREENLEE	1,771	218	1,526	27	1,308 D	12.3%	86.2%	12.5%	87.5%
MARICOPA	47,610	13,671	32,031	1,908	18,360 D	28.7%	67.3%	29.9%	70.1%
MOHAVE	2,529	609	1,814	106	1,205 D	24.1%	71.7%	25.1%	74.9%
NAVAJO	4,142	1,052	3,037	53	1,985 D	25.4%	73.3%	25.7%	74.3%
PIMA	18,590	6,079	12,249	262	6,170 D	32.7%	65.9%	33.2%	66.8%
PINAL	4,868	1,216	3,498	154	2,282 D	25.0%	71.9%	25.8%	74.2%
SANTA CRUZ	2,530	742	1,729	59	987 D	29.3%	68.3%	30.0%	70.0%
YAVAPAI	9,926	2,794	6,628	504	3,834 D	28.1%	66.8%	29.7%	70.3%
YUMA	4,599	976	3,428	195	2,452 D	21.2%	74.5%	22.2%	77.8%
TOTAL	124,163	33,433	86,722	4,008	53,289 D	26.9%	69.8%	27.8%	72.2%

PRESIDENT 1940

County	Total Vote	Republican	Democratic	Other	Rep.-Dem. Plurality	Percentage Total Vote Rep.	Dem.	Major Vote Rep.	Dem.
APACHE	2,898	926	1,969	3	1,043 D	32.0%	67.9%	32.0%	68.0%
COCHISE	11,950	3,170	8,748	32	5,578 D	26.5%	73.2%	26.6%	73.4%
COCONINO	4,951	1,913	3,025	13	1,112 D	38.6%	61.1%	38.7%	61.3%
GILA	8,407	2,624	5,752	31	3,128 D	31.2%	68.4%	31.3%	68.7%
GRAHAM	4,310	1,161	3,130	19	1,969 D	26.9%	72.6%	27.1%	72.9%
GREENLEE	2,803	619	2,175	9	1,556 D	22.1%	77.6%	22.2%	77.8%
MARICOPA	58,079	22,610	35,055	414	12,445 D	38.9%	60.4%	39.2%	60.8%
MOHAVE	3,224	1,198	2,024	2	826 D	37.2%	62.8%	37.2%	62.8%
NAVAJO	4,597	1,533	3,052	12	1,519 D	33.3%	66.4%	33.4%	66.6%
PIMA	23,562	9,445	14,035	82	4,590 D	40.1%	59.6%	40.2%	59.8%
PINAL	6,429	1,996	4,411	22	2,415 D	31.0%	68.6%	31.2%	68.8%
SANTA CRUZ	2,516	978	1,536	2	558 D	38.9%	61.0%	39.1%	61.1%
YAVAPAI	10,282	3,987	6,217	78	2,230 D	38.8%	60.6%	38.9%	60.9%
YUMA	6,031	1,870	4,138	23	2,268 D	31.0%	68.6%	31.1%	68.9%
TOTAL	150,039	54,030	95,267	742	41,237 D	36.0%	63.5%	36.2%	63.8%

ARIZONA

PRESIDENT 1944

County	Total Vote	Republican	Democratic	Other	Rep.-Dem. Plurality	Percentage Total Vote Rep.	Dem.	Major Vote Rep.	Dem.
APACHE	1,968	728	1,238	2	510 D	37.0%	62.9%	37.0%	63.0%
COCHISE	10,319	3,371	6,935	13	3,564 D	32.7%	67.2%	32.7%	67.3%
COCONINO	4,028	1,786	2,236	6	450 D	44.3%	55.5%	44.4%	55.6%
GILA	7,107	2,260	4,818	29	2,558 D	31.8%	67.8%	31.9%	68.1%
GRAHAM	3,549	1,151	2,393	5	1,242 D	32.4%	67.4%	32.5%	67.5%
GREENLEE	2,704	739	1,956	9	1,217 D	27.3%	72.3%	27.4%	72.6%
MARICOPA	57,258	24,853	32,197	208	7,344 D	43.4%	56.2%	43.6%	56.4%
MOHAVE	2,284	974	1,303	7	329 D	42.6%	57.0%	42.8%	57.2%
NAVAJO	4,252	1,579	2,660	13	1,081 D	37.1%	62.6%	37.2%	62.8%
PIMA	23,913	10,850	13,006	57	2,156 D	45.4%	54.4%	45.5%	54.5%
PINAL	4,957	1,909	3,026	22	1,117 D	38.5%	61.0%	38.7%	61.3%
SANTA CRUZ	2,022	727	1,291	4	564 D	36.0%	63.8%	36.0%	64.0%
YAVAPAI	7,960	3,529	4,395	36	866 D	44.3%	55.2%	44.5%	55.5%
YUMA	5,313	1,831	3,472	10	1,641 D	34.5%	65.3%	34.5%	65.5%
TOTAL	137,634	56,287	80,926	421	24,639 D	40.9%	58.8%	41.0%	59.0%

PRESIDENT 1948

County	Total Vote	Republican	Democratic	Other	Rep.-Dem. Plurality	Percentage Total Vote Rep.	Dem.	Major Vote Rep.	Dem.
APACHE	2,455	970	1,480	5	510 D	39.5%	60.3%	39.6%	60.4%
COCHISE	10,370	3,854	6,198	318	2,344 D	37.2%	59.8%	38.3%	61.7%
COCONINO	4,441	2,093	2,309	39	216 D	47.1%	52.0%	47.5%	52.5%
GILA	7,265	2,329	4,780	156	2,451 D	32.1%	65.8%	32.8%	67.2%
GRAHAM	3,386	1,209	2,139	38	930 D	35.7%	63.2%	36.1%	63.9%
GREENLEE	2,961	680	2,069	212	1,389 D	23.0%	69.9%	24.7%	75.3%
MARICOPA	78,992	36,585	40,498	1,909	3,913 D	46.3%	51.3%	47.5%	52.5%
MOHAVE	2,712	1,167	1,499	46	332 D	43.0%	55.3%	43.8%	56.2%
NAVAJO	4,566	1,841	2,669	56	828 D	40.3%	58.5%	40.8%	59.2%
PIMA	35,625	16,968	17,692	965	724 D	47.6%	49.7%	49.0%	51.0%
PINAL	5,887	2,232	3,572	83	1,340 D	37.9%	60.7%	38.5%	61.5%
SANTA CRUZ	2,519	1,058	1,424	37	366 D	42.0%	56.5%	42.6%	57.4%
YAVAPAI	8,922	4,287	4,439	196	152 D	48.0%	49.8%	49.1%	50.9%
YUMA	6,964	2,324	4,483	157	2,159 D	33.4%	64.4%	34.1%	65.9%
TOTAL	177,065	77,597	95,251	4,217	17,654 D	43.8%	53.8%	44.9%	55.1%

ARIZONA

PRESIDENT 1952

County	Total Vote	Republican	Democratic	Other	Rep.-Dem. Plurality	Total Vote %Rep.	Dem.	Major Vote %Rep.	Dem.
APACHE	2,960	1,767	1,193		574 R	59.7%	40.3%	59.7%	40.3%
COCHISE	12,135	6,495	5,640		855 R	53.5%	46.5%	53.5%	46.5%
COCONINO	6,235	3,827	2,408		1,419 R	61.4%	38.6%	61.4%	38.6%
GILA	8,698	3,770	4,928		1,158 D	43.3%	56.7%	43.3%	56.7%
GRAHAM	4,391	2,191	2,200		9 D	49.9%	50.1%	49.9%	50.1%
GREENLEE	4,396	1,377	3,019		1,642 D	31.3%	68.7%	31.3%	68.7%
MARICOPA	127,534	77,249	50,285		26,964 R	60.6%	39.4%	60.6%	39.4%
MOHAVE	2,812	1,746	1,066		680 R	62.1%	37.9%	62.1%	37.9%
NAVAJO	6,071	3,478	2,593		885 R	57.3%	42.7%	57.3%	42.7%
PIMA	53,350	32,113	21,237		10,876 R	60.2%	39.8%	60.2%	39.8%
PINAL	9,507	4,985	4,522		463 R	52.4%	47.6%	52.4%	47.6%
SANTA CRUZ	3,081	1,716	1,365		351 R	55.7%	44.3%	55.7%	44.3%
YAVAPAI	10,195	6,567	3,628		2,939 R	64.4%	35.6%	64.4%	35.6%
YUMA	9,205	4,761	4,444		317 R	51.7%	48.3%	51.7%	48.3%
TOTAL	260,570	152,042	108,528		43,514 R	58.3%	41.7%	58.3%	41.7%

PRESIDENT 1956

County	Total Vote	Republican	Democratic	Other	Rep.-Dem. Plurality	Total Vote %Rep.	Dem.	Major Vote %Rep.	Dem.
APACHE	2,667	1,685	981	1	704 R	63.2%	36.8%	63.2%	36.8%
COCHISE	12,230	6,893	5,328	9	1,565 R	56.4%	43.6%	56.4%	43.6%
COCONINO	6,369	4,044	2,314	11	1,730 R	63.5%	36.3%	63.6%	36.4%
GILA	8,260	4,234	4,026		208 R	51.3%	48.7%	51.3%	48.7%
GRAHAM	4,072	2,384	1,688		696 R	58.5%	41.5%	58.5%	41.5%
GREENLEE	4,495	1,784	2,711		927 D	39.7%	60.3%	39.7%	60.3%
MARICOPA	146,341	92,140	54,010	191	38,130 R	63.0%	36.9%	63.0%	37.0%
MOHAVE	2,497	1,523	968	6	555 R	61.0%	38.8%	61.1%	38.9%
NAVAJO	5,970	3,928	2,033	9	1,895 R	65.8%	34.1%	65.9%	34.1%
PIMA	62,885	39,298	23,536	51	15,762 R	62.5%	37.4%	62.5%	37.5%
PINAL	10,842	5,762	5,063	17	699 R	53.1%	46.7%	53.2%	46.8%
SANTA CRUZ	2,778	1,646	1,131	1	515 R	59.3%	40.7%	59.3%	40.7%
YAVAPAI	9,654	6,339	3,315		3,024 R	65.7%	34.3%	65.7%	34.3%
YUMA	11,113	5,330	5,776	7	446 D	48.0%	52.0%	48.0%	52.0%
TOTAL	290,173	176,990	112,880	303	64,110 R	61.0%	38.9%	61.1%	38.9%

ARIZONA

PRESIDENT 1960

County	Total Vote	Republican	Democratic	Other	Rep.-Dem. Plurality	Total Vote %Rep.	Dem.	Major Vote %Rep.	Dem.
APACHE	3,030	1,568	1,459	3	109 R	51.7%	48.2%	51.8%	48.2%
COCHISE	15,007	7,572	7,419	16	153 R	50.5%	49.4%	50.5%	49.5%
COCONINO	8,944	4,870	4,065	9	805 R	54.4%	45.4%	54.5%	45.5%
GILA	9,065	3,806	5,251	8	1,445 D	42.0%	57.9%	42.0%	58.0%
GRAHAM	4,583	2,491	2,091	1	400 R	54.4%	45.6%	54.4%	45.6%
GREENLEE	4,386	1,313	3,069	4	1,756 D	29.9%	70.0%	30.0%	70.0%
MARICOPA	214,059	127,090	86,834	135	40,256 R	59.4%	40.6%	59.4%	40.6%
MOHAVE	2,952	1,641	1,303	8	338 R	55.6%	44.1%	55.7%	44.3%
NAVAJO	7,151	4,090	3,052	9	1,038 R	57.2%	42.7%	57.3%	42.7%
PIMA	89,144	46,734	42,171	239	4,563 R	52.4%	47.3%	52.6%	47.4%
PINAL	13,684	6,441	7,232	11	791 D	47.1%	52.9%	47.1%	52.9%
SANTA CRUZ	3,135	1,265	1,868	2	603 D	40.4%	59.6%	40.4%	59.6%
YAVAPAI	11,147	6,813	4,325	9	2,488 R	61.1%	38.8%	61.2%	38.8%
YUMA	12,204	5,547	6,642	15	1,095 D	45.5%	54.4%	45.5%	54.5%
TOTAL	398,491	221,241	176,781	469	44,460 R	55.5%	44.4%	55.6%	44.4%

PRESIDENT 1964

County	Total Vote	Republican	Democratic	Other	Rep.-Dem. Plurality	Total Vote %Rep.	Dem.	Major Vote %Rep.	Dem.
APACHE	3,892	1,849	2,042	1	193 D	47.5%	52.5%	47.5%	52.5%
COCHISE	16,697	7,644	9,045	8	1,401 D	45.8%	54.2%	45.8%	54.2%
COCONINO	11,037	5,756	5,270	11	486 R	52.2%	47.7%	52.2%	47.8%
GILA	10,537	3,713	6,821	3	3,108 D	35.2%	64.7%	35.2%	64.8%
GRAHAM	5,438	2,655	2,783		128 D	48.8%	51.2%	48.8%	51.2%
GREENLEE	4,279	1,132	3,147		2,015 D	26.5%	73.5%	26.5%	73.5%
MARICOPA	265,326	143,114	122,042	170	21,072 R	53.9%	46.0%	54.0%	46.0%
MOHAVE	4,339	2,091	2,243	5	152 D	48.2%	51.7%	48.2%	51.8%
NAVAJO	9,649	4,870	4,770	9	100 R	50.4%	49.4%	50.5%	49.5%
PIMA	101,278	46,955	54,120	203	7,165 D	46.4%	53.4%	46.5%	53.5%
PINAL	16,872	6,956	9,911	5	2,955 D	41.2%	58.7%	41.2%	58.8%
SANTA CRUZ	3,460	1,503	1,955	2	452 D	43.4%	56.5%	43.5%	56.5%
YAVAPAI	13,556	7,749	5,747	60	2,002 R	57.2%	42.4%	57.4%	42.6%
YUMA	14,410	6,548	7,857	5	1,309 D	45.4%	54.5%	45.5%	54.5%
TOTAL	480,770	242,535	237,753	482	4,782 R	50.4%	49.5%	50.5%	49.5%

ARIZONA

OTHER VOTE COMPOSITION:

1920	222 Socialist; 15 Farmer-Labor; 4 Prohibition.
1924	Progressive.
1928	Communist.
1932	2,618 Socialist; 256 Communist; 9 Arizona Progressive Democratic.
1936	3,307 Union; 384 Prohibition; 317 Socialist.
1940	Prohibition.
1944	Prohibition.
1948	3,310 Progressive; 786 Prohibition; 121 Socialist Labor.
1952	
1956	States Rights.
1960	Socialist Labor.
1964	Socialist Labor.

SPECIAL CASES:

1924	Progressive candidates ran second in several counties.
1932	Though there were Arizona Progressive Democratic nominees for some offices, the party had no candidates for President, Vice-President, or elector. Nevertheless, 9 Arizona Progressive Democratic elector votes were reported in the state canvass.

ARKANSAS

PRESIDENT 1920

County	Total Vote	Republican	Democratic	Other	Rep.-Dem. Plurality	Total Vote Rep.	Total Vote Dem.	Major Vote Rep.	Major Vote Dem.
ARKANSAS	2,387	1,199	1,156	32	43 R	50.2%	48.4%	50.9%	49.1%
ASHLEY	2,069	725	1,312	32	587 D	35.0%	63.4%	35.6%	64.4%
BAXTER	1,261	484	707	70	223 D	38.4%	56.1%	40.6%	59.4%
BENTON	4,870	1,916	2,838	116	922 D	39.3%	58.3%	40.3%	59.7%
BOONE	1,817	647	1,106	64	459 D	35.6%	60.9%	36.9%	63.1%
BRADLEY	1,757	540	1,146	71	606 D	30.7%	65.2%	32.0%	68.0%
CALHOUN	1,139	337	736	66	399 D	29.6%	64.6%	31.4%	68.6%
CARROLL	2,747	1,338	1,344	65	6 D	48.7%	48.9%	49.9%	50.1%
CHICOT	1,386	489	887	10	398 D	35.3%	64.0%	35.5%	64.5%
CLARK	2,546	1,020	1,507	19	487 D	40.1%	59.2%	40.4%	59.6%
CLAY	3,492	1,536	1,775	181	239 D	44.0%	50.8%	46.4%	53.6%
CLEBURNE	1,206	459	678	69	219 D	38.1%	56.2%	40.4%	59.6%
CLEVELAND	1,299	475	809	15	334 D	36.6%	62.3%	37.0%	63.0%
COLUMBIA	2,926	857	2,052	17	1,195 D	29.3%	70.1%	29.5%	70.5%
CONWAY	3,071	1,243	1,791	37	548 D	40.5%	58.3%	41.0%	59.0%
CRAIGHEAD	3,241	1,058	2,079	104	1,021 D	32.6%	64.1%	33.7%	66.3%
CRAWFORD	3,398	1,497	1,861	40	364 D	44.1%	54.8%	44.6%	55.4%
CRITTENDEN	1,080	167	905	8	738 D	15.5%	83.8%	15.6%	84.4%
CROSS	1,344	457	845	42	388 D	34.0%	62.9%	35.1%	64.9%
DALLAS	1,821	659	1,140	22	481 D	36.2%	62.6%	36.6%	63.4%
DESHA	1,314	360	931	23	571 D	27.4%	70.9%	27.9%	72.1%
DREW	2,198	773	1,397	28	624 D	35.2%	63.6%	35.6%	64.4%
FAULKNER	3,251	1,148	1,971	132	823 D	35.3%	60.6%	36.8%	63.2%
FRANKLIN	2,392	769	1,502	121	733 D	32.1%	62.8%	33.8%	66.1%
FULTON	1,283	502	763	18	261 D	39.1%	59.5%	39.7%	60.3%
GARLAND	3,131	1,423	1,619	89	196 D	45.4%	51.7%	46.8%	53.2%
GRANT	865	230	619	16	389 D	26.6%	71.6%	27.1%	72.9%
GREENE	3,017	1,072	1,865	80	793 D	35.5%	61.8%	36.5%	63.5%
HEMPSTEAD	4,018	1,754	2,239	25	485 D	43.7%	55.7%	43.9%	56.1%
HOT SPRING	2,024	910	1,061	53	151 D	45.0%	52.4%	46.2%	53.8%
HOWARD	2,688	1,208	1,452	28	244 D	44.9%	54.0%	45.4%	54.6%
INDEPENDENCE	2,710	1,077	1,546	87	469 D	39.7%	57.0%	41.1%	58.9%
IZARD	1,352	485	841	26	356 D	35.9%	62.2%	36.6%	63.4%
JACKSON	2,804	1,131	1,575	98	444 D	40.3%	56.2%	41.8%	58.2%
JEFFERSON	3,783	1,048	2,670	65	1,622 D	27.7%	70.6%	28.2%	71.8%
JOHNSON	2,755	996	1,579	180	583 D	36.2%	57.3%	38.7%	61.3%
LAFAYETTE	1,460	500	954	6	454 D	34.2%	65.4%	34.4%	65.6%
LAWRENCE	2,434	699	1,686	49	987 D	28.7%	69.3%	29.3%	70.7%
LEE	1,500	354	1,108	38	754 D	23.6%	73.9%	24.2%	75.8%
LINCOLN	1,885	988	888	9	100 R	52.4%	47.1%	52.7%	47.3%
LITTLE RIVER	1,521	618	853	50	235 D	40.6%	56.1%	42.0%	58.0%
LOGAN	3,779	1,871	1,840	68	31 R	49.5%	48.7%	50.4%	49.5%
LONOKE	2,481	697	1,711	73	1,014 D	28.1%	69.0%	28.9%	71.1%
MADISON	3,230	1,715	1,463	52	252 R	53.1%	45.3%	54.0%	46.0%
MARION	1,297	371	744	182	373 D	28.6%	57.4%	33.3%	66.7%
MILLER	2,466	836	1,545	85	709 D	33.9%	62.7%	35.1%	64.9%
MISSISSIPPI	2,980	1,050	1,809	121	759 D	35.2%	60.7%	36.7%	63.3%
MONROE	1,776	912	834	30	78 R	51.4%	47.0%	52.2%	47.8%
MONTGOMERY	1,119	615	430	74	185 R	55.0%	38.4%	58.9%	41.1%
NEVADA	2,551	1,292	1,220	39	72 R	50.6%	47.8%	51.4%	48.6%
NEWTON	1,374	828	486	60	342 R	60.3%	35.4%	63.0%	37.0%
OUACHITA	2,474	1,141	1,307	26	166 D	46.1%	52.8%	46.6%	53.4%
PERRY	1,367	592	738	37	146 D	43.3%	54.0%	44.5%	55.5%
PHILLIPS	2,842	868	1,965	9	1,097 D	30.5%	69.1%	30.6%	69.4%
PIKE	1,817	921	849	47	72 R	50.7%	46.7%	52.0%	48.0%
POINSETT	1,922	633	1,201	88	568 D	32.9%	62.5%	34.5%	65.5%
POLK	2,535	1,173	1,208	154	35 D	46.3%	47.7%	49.3%	50.7%
POPE	3,271	1,142	2,082	69	962 D	34.2%	63.7%	35.0%	65.0%
PRAIRIE	1,845	842	962	41	120 D	45.6%	52.1%	46.7%	53.3%
PULASKI	10,367	3,711	6,506	150	2,795 D	35.8%	62.8%	36.3%	63.7%

PRESIDENT 1924

County	Total Vote	Republican	Democratic	Other	Rep.-Dem. Plurality	Total Vote Rep.	Total Vote Dem.	Major Vote Rep.	Major Vote Dem.
ARKANSAS	1,350	488	772	90	284 D	36.1%	57.2%	38.7%	61.3%
ASHLEY	1,649	506	1,048	95	542 D	30.7%	63.6%	32.6%	67.4%
BAXTER	1,103	301	640	162	339 D	27.3%	58.0%	32.0%	68.0%
BENTON	4,573	1,694	2,313	566	619 D	37.0%	50.6%	42.3%	57.7%
BOONE	2,499	937	1,350	212	413 D	37.5%	54.0%	41.0%	59.0%
BRADLEY	1,555	453	1,002	100	549 D	29.1%	64.4%	31.1%	68.9%
CALHOUN	745	150	553	42	403 D	20.1%	74.2%	21.3%	78.7%
CARROLL	2,524	969	1,421	134	452 D	38.4%	56.3%	40.5%	59.5%
CHICOT	1,050	325	708	17	383 D	31.0%	67.4%	31.5%	68.5%
CLARK	1,910	483	1,223	204	740 D	25.3%	64.0%	28.3%	71.7%
CLAY	2,720	1,084	1,429	207	345 D	39.9%	52.5%	43.1%	56.9%
CLEBURNE	900	238	569	93	331 D	26.4%	63.2%	29.5%	70.5%
CLEVELAND	818	174	613	31	439 D	21.3%	74.9%	22.1%	77.9%
COLUMBIA	1,795	350	1,382	63	1,032 D	19.5%	77.0%	20.2%	79.8%
CONWAY	1,560	526	909	125	383 D	33.7%	58.3%	36.7%	63.3%
CRAIGHEAD	2,794	812	1,711	271	899 D	29.1%	61.2%	32.2%	67.8%
CRAWFORD	2,910	996	1,445	469	449 D	34.2%	49.7%	40.8%	59.2%
CRITTENDEN	874	77	777	20	700 D	8.8%	88.9%	9.0%	91.0%
CROSS	911	192	625	94	433 D	21.1%	68.6%	23.5%	76.5%
DALLAS	1,503	401	1,068	34	667 D	26.7%	71.1%	27.3%	72.7%
DESHA	970	209	540	221	331 D	21.5%	55.7%	27.9%	72.1%
DREW	1,603	563	1,018	22	455 D	35.1%	63.5%	35.6%	64.4%
FAULKNER	2,132	536	1,436	160	900 D	25.1%	67.4%	27.2%	72.8%
FRANKLIN	1,831	422	1,188	221	766 D	23.0%	64.9%	26.2%	73.8%
FULTON	1,007	292	678	37	386 D	29.0%	67.3%	30.1%	69.9%
GARLAND	2,837	1,064	1,501	272	437 D	37.5%	52.9%	41.5%	58.5%
GRANT	858	133	628	97	495 D	15.5%	73.2%	17.5%	82.5%
GREENE	1,935	456	1,148	331	692 D	23.6%	59.3%	28.4%	71.6%
HEMPSTEAD	2,354	715	1,459	180	744 D	30.4%	62.0%	32.9%	67.1%
HOT SPRING	1,340	392	793	155	401 D	29.3%	59.2%	33.1%	66.9%
HOWARD	1,462	338	954	170	616 D	23.1%	65.3%	26.2%	73.8%
INDEPENDENCE	2,042	534	1,313	195	779 D	26.2%	64.3%	28.9%	71.1%
IZARD	1,000	241	728	31	487 D	24.1%	72.8%	24.8%	75.1%
JACKSON	1,541	392	1,069	80	677 D	25.4%	69.4%	26.8%	73.2%
JEFFERSON	3,172	707	1,950	515	1,243 D	22.3%	61.5%	26.6%	73.4%
JOHNSON	1,572	311	1,029	232	718 D	19.8%	65.5%	23.2%	76.8%
LAFAYETTE	1,215	298	788	129	490 D	24.5%	64.9%	27.4%	72.6%
LAWRENCE	1,126	261	689	176	428 D	23.2%	61.2%	27.5%	72.5%
LEE	1,703	596	1,103	4	507 D	35.0%	64.8%	35.1%	64.9%
LINCOLN	738	170	563	5	393 D	23.0%	76.3%	23.2%	76.8%
LITTLE RIVER	868	276	546	46	270 D	31.8%	62.9%	33.6%	66.4%
LOGAN	2,923	937	1,457	529	520 D	32.1%	49.8%	39.1%	60.9%
LONOKE	1,345	321	962	62	641 D	23.9%	71.5%	25.0%	75.0%
MADISON	2,696	1,263	1,335	98	72 D	46.8%	49.5%	48.6%	51.4%
MARION	1,308	282	825	201	543 D	21.6%	63.1%	25.5%	74.5%
MILLER	2,297	397	1,460	440	1,063 D	17.3%	63.6%	21.4%	78.6%
MISSISSIPPI	2,828	703	2,039	86	1,336 D	24.9%	72.1%	25.6%	74.4%
MONROE	1,269	330	838	101	508 D	26.0%	66.0%	28.3%	71.7%
MONTGOMERY	882	360	431	91	71 D	40.8%	48.9%	45.5%	54.5%
NEVADA	1,291	386	719	186	333 D	29.9%	55.7%	34.9%	65.1%
NEWTON	944	578	298	68	280 R	61.2%	31.6%	66.0%	34.0%
OUACHITA	2,312	952	1,318	42	366 D	41.2%	57.0%	41.9%	58.1%
PERRY	790	260	386	144	126 D	32.9%	48.9%	40.2%	59.8%
PHILLIPS	2,310	454	1,785	71	1,331 D	19.7%	77.3%	20.3%	79.7%
PIKE	1,184	378	732	74	354 D	31.9%	61.8%	34.1%	65.9%
POINSETT	1,723	393	1,182	148	789 D	22.8%	68.6%	25.0%	75.0%
POLK	1,594	502	863	229	361 D	31.5%	54.1%	36.8%	63.2%
POPE	2,256	479	1,581	196	1,102 D	21.2%	70.1%	23.3%	76.7%
PRAIRIE	1,181	386	730	65	344 D	32.7%	61.8%	34.6%	65.4%
PULASKI	9,622	2,729	5,706	1,187	2,977 D	28.4%	59.3%	32.4%	67.6%

ARKANSAS

PRESIDENT 1920

County	Total Vote	Republican	Democratic	Other	Rep.-Dem. Plurality	Percentage Total Vote Rep.	Dem.	Major Vote Rep.	Dem.
RANDOLPH	2,092	652	1,412	28	760 D	31.2%	67.5%	31.6%	68.4%
ST. FRANCIS	2,212	903	1,252	57	349 D	40.8%	56.6%	41.9%	58.1%
SALINE	1,670	403	1,206	61	803 D	24.1%	72.2%	25.0%	75.0%
SCOTT	1,602	751	771	80	20 D	46.9%	48.1%	49.3%	50.7%
SEARCY	1,760	1,070	594	96	476 R	60.8%	33.8%	64.3%	35.7%
SEBASTIAN	7,586	3,492	3,852	242	360 D	46.0%	50.8%	47.5%	52.5%
SEVIER	1,997	599	1,236	162	637 D	30.0%	61.9%	32.6%	67.4%
SHARP	1,514	400	995	119	595 D	26.4%	65.7%	28.7%	71.3%
STONE	935	367	516	52	149 D	39.3%	55.2%	41.6%	58.4%
UNION	2,316	493	1,763	60	1,270 D	21.3%	76.1%	21.9%	78.1%
VAN BUREN	1,902	1,388	440	74	948 R	73.0%	23.1%	75.9%	24.1%
WASHINGTON	4,879	2,118	2,637	124	519 D	43.4%	54.0%	44.5%	55.5%
WHITE	3,593	1,359	2,086	148	727 D	37.8%	58.1%	39.4%	60.6%
WOODRUFF	2,032	943	1,049	40	106 D	46.4%	51.6%	47.3%	52.7%
YELL	3,046	1,042	1,925	79	883 D	34.2%	63.2%	35.1%	64.9%
TOTAL	183,871	72,316	106,427	5,128	34,111 D	39.3%	57.9%	40.5%	59.5%

PRESIDENT 1924

County	Total Vote	Republican	Democratic	Other	Rep.-Dem. Plurality	Percentage Total Vote Rep.	Dem.	Major Vote Rep.	Dem.
RANDOLPH	1,208	389	772	47	383 D	32.2%	63.9%	33.5%	66.5%
ST. FRANCIS	1,467	433	972	62	539 D	29.5%	66.3%	30.8%	69.2%
SALINE	1,055	144	770	141	626 D	13.6%	73.0%	15.8%	84.2%
SCOTT	1,128	375	607	146	232 D	33.2%	53.8%	38.2%	61.8%
SEARCY	1,321	797	415	109	382 R	60.3%	31.4%	65.8%	34.2%
SEBASTIAN	5,992	1,985	3,148	859	1,163 D	33.1%	52.5%	38.7%	61.3%
SEVIER	1,477	270	931	276	661 D	18.3%	63.0%	22.5%	77.5%
SHARP	995	210	729	56	519 D	21.1%	73.3%	22.4%	77.6%
STONE	650	210	386	54	176 D	32.3%	59.4%	35.2%	64.8%
UNION	2,673	450	1,967	256	1,517 D	16.8%	73.6%	18.6%	81.4%
VAN BUREN	1,444	435	922	87	487 D	30.1%	63.9%	32.1%	67.9%
WASHINGTON	4,083	1,466	2,281	336	815 D	35.9%	55.9%	39.1%	60.9%
WHITE	2,452	679	1,488	285	809 D	27.7%	60.7%	31.3%	68.7%
WOODRUFF	1,047	254	762	31	508 D	24.3%	72.8%	25.0%	75.0%
YELL	1,744	334	1,314	96	980 D	19.2%	75.3%	20.3%	79.7%
TOTAL	138,540	40,563	84,790	13,167	44,207 D	29.3%	61.2%	32.4%	67.6%

ARKANSAS

PRESIDENT 1928

County	Total Vote	Republican	Democratic	Other	Rep.-Dem. Plurality	% Total Vote Rep.	% Total Vote Dem.	% Major Vote Rep.	% Major Vote Dem.
ARKANSAS	2,545	1,046	1,491	8	445 D	41.1%	58.6%	41.2%	58.8%
ASHLEY	2,182	786	1,393	3	607 D	36.0%	63.8%	36.1%	63.9%
BAXTER	1,180	504	665	11	161 D	42.7%	56.4%	43.1%	56.9%
BENTON	5,669	3,248	2,348	73	900 R	57.3%	41.4%	58.0%	42.0%
BOONE	3,264	1,543	1,708	13	165 D	47.3%	52.3%	47.5%	52.5%
BRADLEY	1,934	447	1,487		1,040 D	23.1%	76.9%	23.1%	76.9%
CALHOUN	1,033	262	765	6	503 D	25.4%	74.1%	25.5%	74.5%
CARROLL	3,312	1,757	1,540	15	217 R	53.0%	46.5%	53.3%	46.7%
CHICOT	1,468	445	1,021	2	576 D	30.3%	69.6%	30.4%	69.6%
CLARK	2,736	913	1,817	6	904 D	33.4%	66.4%	33.4%	66.6%
CLAY	2,708	1,254	1,435	19	181 D	46.3%	53.0%	46.6%	53.4%
CLEBURNE	1,442	574	856	12	282 D	39.8%	59.4%	40.1%	59.9%
CLEVELAND	1,167	476	690	1	214 D	40.8%	59.2%	40.8%	59.2%
COLUMBIA	2,370	617	1,752	1	1,135 D	26.0%	73.9%	26.0%	74.0%
CONWAY	2,182	665	1,514	3	849 D	30.5%	69.4%	30.5%	69.5%
CRAIGHEAD	4,118	1,958	2,132	28	174 D	47.5%	51.8%	47.9%	52.1%
CRAWFORD	3,302	1,559	1,743		184 D	47.2%	52.8%	47.2%	52.8%
CRITTENDEN	1,940	304	1,635	1	1,331 D	15.7%	84.3%	15.7%	84.3%
CROSS	1,610	324	1,282	4	958 D	20.1%	79.6%	20.2%	79.8%
DALLAS	1,537	503	1,030	4	527 D	32.7%	67.0%	32.8%	67.2%
DESHA	1,415	331	1,082	2	751 D	23.4%	76.5%	23.5%	76.5%
DREW	1,956	500	1,452	4	952 D	25.6%	74.2%	25.6%	74.4%
FAULKNER	3,664	992	2,659	13	1,667 D	27.1%	72.6%	27.2%	72.8%
FRANKLIN	2,119	774	1,329	16	555 D	36.5%	62.7%	36.8%	63.2%
FULTON	1,622	686	934	2	248 D	42.3%	57.6%	42.3%	57.7%
GARLAND	5,558	2,720	2,823	15	103 D	48.9%	50.8%	49.1%	50.9%
GRANT	1,486	439	1,045	2	606 D	29.5%	70.3%	29.6%	70.4%
GREENE	2,450	1,011	1,426	13	415 D	41.3%	58.2%	41.5%	58.5%
HEMPSTEAD	2,929	886	2,038	5	1,152 D	30.2%	69.6%	30.3%	69.7%
HOT SPRING	2,130	1,126	999	5	127 R	52.9%	46.9%	53.0%	47.0%
HOWARD	1,827	763	1,055	9	292 D	41.8%	57.7%	42.0%	58.0%
INDEPENDENCE	2,668	1,150	1,511	7	361 D	43.1%	56.6%	43.2%	56.8%
IZARD	1,602	696	902	4	206 D	43.4%	56.3%	43.6%	56.4%
JACKSON	2,234	698	1,527	9	829 D	31.2%	68.4%	31.4%	68.6%
JEFFERSON	4,450	1,830	2,611	9	781 D	41.1%	58.7%	41.2%	58.8%
JOHNSON	2,074	766	1,292	16	526 D	36.9%	62.3%	37.2%	62.8%
LAFAYETTE	1,427	435	991	1	556 D	30.5%	69.4%	30.5%	69.5%
LAWRENCE	1,983	774	1,204	5	430 D	39.0%	60.7%	39.1%	60.9%
LEE	1,195	149	1,046		897 D	12.5%	87.5%	12.5%	87.5%
LINCOLN	1,021	151	869	1	718 D	14.8%	85.1%	14.8%	85.2%
LITTLE RIVER	1,375	457	916	2	459 D	33.2%	66.6%	33.3%	66.7%
LOGAN	3,430	1,455	1,967	8	512 D	42.4%	57.3%	42.5%	57.5%
LONOKE	2,536	676	1,857	3	1,181 D	26.7%	73.2%	26.7%	73.3%
MADISON	4,500	2,760	1,717	23	1,043 R	61.3%	38.2%	61.6%	38.4%
MARION	1,173	436	731	6	295 D	37.1%	62.3%	37.4%	62.6%
MILLER	2,911	1,150	1,752	9	602 D	39.5%	60.2%	39.6%	60.4%
MISSISSIPPI	5,799	1,324	4,451	24	3,127 D	22.8%	76.8%	22.9%	77.1%
MONROE	1,263	411	851	1	440 D	32.5%	67.4%	32.6%	67.4%
MONTGOMERY	1,715	976	726	13	250 R	56.9%	42.3%	57.3%	42.7%
NEVADA	2,192	946	1,242	4	296 D	43.2%	56.7%	43.2%	56.8%
NEWTON	1,857	1,316	533	8	783 R	70.9%	28.7%	71.2%	28.8%
OUACHITA	2,633	1,051	1,582		531 D	39.9%	60.1%	39.9%	60.1%
PERRY	1,113	474	636	3	162 D	42.6%	57.1%	42.7%	57.3%
PHILLIPS	2,552	487	2,061	4	1,574 D	19.1%	80.8%	19.1%	80.9%
PIKE	1,483	698	779	6	81 D	47.1%	52.5%	47.3%	52.7%
POINSETT	3,518	1,182	2,324	12	1,142 D	33.6%	66.1%	33.7%	66.3%
POLK	1,916	1,022	870	24	152 R	53.3%	45.4%	54.0%	46.0%
POPE	4,317	1,559	2,735	23	1,176 D	36.1%	63.4%	36.3%	63.7%
PRAIRIE	1,621	613	1,000	8	387 D	37.8%	61.7%	38.0%	62.0%
PULASKI	14,124	4,880	9,215	29	4,335 D	34.6%	65.2%	34.6%	65.4%

PRESIDENT 1932

County	Total Vote	Republican	Democratic	Other	Rep.-Dem. Plurality	% Total Vote Rep.	% Total Vote Dem.	% Major Vote Rep.	% Major Vote Dem.
ARKANSAS	3,395	494	2,867	34	2,373 D	14.6%	84.4%	14.7%	85.3%
ASHLEY	2,733	188	2,537	8	2,349 D	6.9%	92.8%	6.9%	93.1%
BAXTER	1,254	194	1,039	21	845 D	15.5%	82.9%	15.7%	84.3%
BENTON	5,198	1,275	3,775	148	2,500 D	24.5%	72.6%	25.2%	74.8%
BOONE	3,385	697	2,644	44	1,947 D	20.6%	78.1%	20.9%	79.1%
BRADLEY	2,117	125	1,985	7	1,860 D	5.9%	93.8%	5.9%	94.1%
CALHOUN	1,302	59	1,235	8	1,176 D	4.5%	94.9%	4.6%	95.4%
CARROLL	2,941	758	2,150	33	1,392 D	25.8%	73.1%	26.1%	73.9%
CHICOT	1,780	98	1,680	2	1,582 D	5.5%	94.4%	5.5%	94.5%
CLARK	3,235	183	3,037	15	2,854 D	5.7%	93.9%	5.7%	94.3%
CLAY	2,306	397	1,891	18	1,494 D	17.2%	82.0%	17.4%	82.6%
CLEBURNE	1,982	204	1,750	28	1,546 D	10.3%	88.3%	10.4%	89.6%
CLEVELAND	1,534	92	1,440	2	1,348 D	6.0%	93.9%	6.0%	94.0%
COLUMBIA	2,515	85	2,420	10	2,335 D	3.4%	96.2%	3.4%	96.6%
CONWAY	2,835	285	2,530	20	2,245 D	10.1%	89.2%	10.1%	89.9%
CRAIGHEAD	5,066	606	4,412	48	3,806 D	12.0%	87.1%	12.1%	87.9%
CRAWFORD	3,824	809	2,962	53	2,153 D	21.2%	77.5%	21.5%	78.5%
CRITTENDEN	2,454	37	2,411	6	2,374 D	1.5%	98.2%	1.5%	98.5%
CROSS	2,164	87	2,066	11	1,979 D	4.0%	95.5%	4.0%	96.0%
DALLAS	2,296	150	2,139	7	1,989 D	6.5%	93.2%	6.6%	93.4%
DESHA	1,639	81	1,549	9	1,468 D	4.9%	94.5%	5.0%	95.0%
DREW	1,969	198	1,760	11	1,562 D	10.1%	89.4%	10.1%	89.9%
FAULKNER	3,243	437	2,749	57	2,312 D	13.5%	84.8%	13.7%	86.3%
FRANKLIN	2,235	275	1,896	64	1,621 D	12.3%	84.8%	12.7%	87.3%
FULTON	1,473	237	1,235	1	998 D	16.1%	83.8%	16.1%	83.9%
GARLAND	5,086	833	4,252	1	3,419 D	16.4%	83.6%	16.4%	83.6%
GRANT	1,685	55	1,626	4	1,571 D	3.3%	96.5%	3.3%	96.7%
GREENE	3,584	274	3,277	33	3,003 D	7.6%	91.4%	7.7%	92.3%
HEMPSTEAD	3,159	317	2,840	2	2,523 D	10.0%	89.9%	10.0%	90.0%
HOT SPRING	2,806	237	2,542	27	2,305 D	8.4%	90.6%	8.5%	91.5%
HOWARD	1,871	165	1,703	3	1,538 D	8.8%	91.0%	8.8%	91.2%
INDEPENDENCE	2,811	371	2,427	13	2,056 D	13.2%	86.3%	13.3%	86.7%
IZARD	1,439	200	1,227	12	1,027 D	13.9%	85.3%	14.0%	86.0%
JACKSON	2,723	193	2,521	9	2,328 D	7.1%	92.6%	7.1%	92.9%
JEFFERSON	2,990	419	2,548	23	2,129 D	14.0%	85.2%	14.1%	85.9%
JOHNSON	1,908	284	1,557	67	1,273 D	14.9%	81.6%	15.4%	84.6%
LAFAYETTE	1,652	151	1,495	6	1,344 D	9.1%	90.5%	9.5%	90.5%
LAWRENCE	3,413	293	3,056	64	2,763 D	8.6%	89.5%	8.7%	91.3%
LEE	1,678	39	1,635	4	1,596 D	2.3%	97.4%	2.3%	97.7%
LINCOLN	1,351	49	1,301	1	1,252 D	3.6%	96.3%	3.6%	96.4%
LITTLE RIVER	1,524	118	1,399	7	1,281 D	7.7%	91.8%	7.8%	92.2%
LOGAN	3,174	645	2,493	36	1,848 D	20.3%	78.5%	20.6%	79.4%
LONOKE	3,138	175	2,951	12	2,776 D	5.6%	94.0%	5.6%	94.4%
MADISON	5,095	2,197	2,803	95	606 D	43.1%	55.0%	43.9%	56.1%
MARION	1,599	235	1,282	82	1,047 D	14.7%	80.2%	15.5%	84.5%
MILLER	4,233	322	3,876	35	3,554 D	7.6%	91.6%	7.7%	92.3%
MISSISSIPPI	6,203	364	5,776	63	5,412 D	5.9%	93.1%	5.9%	94.1%
MONROE	1,935	170	1,753	12	1,583 D	8.8%	90.6%	8.8%	91.2%
MONTGOMERY	1,739	211	1,495	33	1,284 D	12.1%	86.0%	12.4%	87.6%
NEVADA	2,564	197	2,358	9	2,161 D	7.7%	92.0%	7.7%	92.3%
NEWTON	1,510	540	941	29	401 D	35.8%	62.3%	36.5%	63.5%
OUACHITA	3,557	432	3,118	7	2,686 D	12.1%	87.7%	12.2%	87.8%
PERRY	1,474	123	1,347	4	1,224 D	8.3%	91.4%	8.4%	91.6%
PHILLIPS	3,144	142	2,976	26	2,834 D	4.5%	94.7%	4.5%	95.4%
PIKE	1,659	176	1,480	3	1,304 D	10.6%	89.2%	10.6%	89.4%
POINSETT	4,636	252	4,312	72	4,060 D	5.4%	93.0%	5.5%	94.5%
POLK	1,874	223	1,568	83	1,345 D	11.9%	83.7%	12.5%	87.5%
POPE	2,702	280	2,391	31	2,111 D	10.4%	88.5%	10.5%	89.5%
PRAIRIE	1,911	158	1,743	10	1,585 D	8.3%	91.2%	8.3%	91.7%
PULASKI	16,440	2,281	14,049	110	11,768 D	13.9%	85.5%	14.0%	86.0%

ARKANSAS

PRESIDENT 1928

County	Total Vote	Republican	Democratic	Other	Rep.-Dem. Plurality	Percentage Total Vote Rep.	Dem.	Major Vote Rep.	Dem.
RANDOLPH	2,311	776	1,527	8	751 D	33.6%	66.1%	33.7%	66.3%
ST FRANCIS	2,002	617	1,376	9	759 D	30.8%	68.7%	31.0%	69.0%
SALINE	1,786	520	1,261	5	741 D	29.1%	70.6%	29.2%	70.8%
SCOTT	1,475	573	891	11	318 D	38.8%	60.4%	39.1%	60.9%
SEARCY	2,046	1,425	606	15	819 R	69.6%	29.6%	70.2%	29.8%
SEBASTIAN	6,684	3,465	3,186	33	279 R	51.8%	47.7%	52.1%	47.9%
SEVIER	1,783	524	1,259		735 D	29.4%	70.6%	29.4%	70.6%
SHARP	1,310	501	808	1	307 D	38.2%	61.7%	38.3%	61.7%
STONE	1,144	499	628	17	129 D	43.6%	54.9%	44.3%	55.7%
UNION	4,748	1,612	3,128	8	1,516 D	34.0%	65.9%	34.0%	66.0%
VAN BUREN	2,537	994	1,539	4	545 D	39.2%	60.7%	39.2%	60.8%
WASHINGTON	5,567	3,132	2,395	40	737 R	56.3%	43.0%	56.7%	43.3%
WHITE	4,279	1,957	2,299	23	342 D	45.7%	53.7%	46.0%	54.0%
WOODRUFF	1,617	452	1,163	2	711 D	28.0%	71.9%	28.0%	72.0%
YELL	2,901	802	2,086	13	1,284 D	27.6%	71.9%	27.8%	72.2%
TOTAL	197,726	77,784	119,196	746	41,412 D	39.3%	60.3%	39.5%	60.5%

PRESIDENT 1932

County	Total Vote	Republican	Democratic	Other	Rep.-Dem. Plurality	Percentage Total Vote Rep.	Dem.	Major Vote Rep.	Dem.
RANDOLPH	2,243	206	2,021	16	1,815 D	9.2%	90.1%	9.3%	90.7%
ST FRANCIS	2,367	130	2,191	46	2,061 D	5.5%	92.6%	5.6%	94.4%
SALINE	2,129	107	1,990	32	1,883 D	5.0%	93.5%	5.1%	94.9%
SCOTT	1,312	174	1,042	96	868 D	13.3%	79.4%	14.3%	85.7%
SEARCY	1,808	846	947	15	101 D	46.8%	52.4%	47.2%	52.8%
SEBASTIAN	6,260	1,268	4,937	55	3,669 D	20.3%	78.9%	20.4%	79.6%
SEVIER	2,193	162	2,009	22	1,847 D	7.4%	91.6%	7.5%	92.5%
SHARP	1,484	142	1,334	8	1,192 D	9.6%	89.9%	9.6%	90.4%
STONE	1,390	261	1,100	29	839 D	18.8%	79.1%	19.2%	80.8%
UNION	5,738	245	5,429	64	5,184 D	4.3%	94.6%	4.3%	95.7%
VAN BUREN	1,890	413	1,456	21	1,043 D	21.9%	77.0%	22.1%	77.9%
WASHINGTON	6,596	1,502	4,971	123	3,469 D	22.8%	75.4%	23.2%	76.8%
WHITE	3,705	430	3,251	24	2,821 D	11.6%	87.7%	11.7%	88.3%
WOODRUFF	2,022	135	1,864	23	1,729 D	6.7%	92.2%	6.8%	93.2%
YELL	2,290	272	2,010	8	1,738 D	11.9%	87.8%	11.9%	88.1%
TOTAL	216,569	27,465	186,829	2,275	159,364 D	12.7%	86.3%	12.8%	87.2%

ARKANSAS

PRESIDENT 1936

County	Total Vote	Republican	Democratic	Other	Rep.-Dem. Plurality	% Total Vote Rep.	% Total Vote Dem.	% Major Vote Rep.	% Major Vote Dem.
ARKANSAS	2,357	341	2,008	8	1,667 D	14.5%	85.2%	14.5%	85.5%
ASHLEY	1,477	95	1,382		1,287 D	6.4%	93.6%	6.4%	93.6%
BAXTER	1,155	375	773	7	398 D	32.5%	66.9%	32.7%	67.3%
BENTON	4,114	1,672	2,418	24	746 D	40.6%	58.8%	40.9%	59.1%
BOONE	3,448	1,052	2,386	10	1,334 D	30.5%	69.2%	30.6%	69.4%
BRADLEY	1,637	65	1,571	1	1,506 D	4.0%	96.0%	4.0%	96.0%
CALHOUN	735	30	704	1	674 D	4.1%	95.8%	4.1%	95.9%
CARROLL	2,595	940	1,649	6	709 D	36.2%	63.5%	36.3%	63.7%
CHICOT	1,221	75	1,145	1	1,070 D	6.1%	93.8%	6.1%	93.9%
CLARK	2,163	193	1,962	8	1,769 D	8.9%	90.7%	9.0%	91.0%
CLAY	2,579	795	1,778	6	983 D	30.8%	68.9%	30.9%	69.1%
CLEBURNE	1,271	336	927	8	591 D	26.4%	72.9%	26.6%	73.4%
CLEVELAND	1,136	45	1,088	3	1,043 D	4.0%	95.8%	4.0%	96.0%
COLUMBIA	1,911	64	1,847		1,783 D	3.3%	96.7%	3.3%	96.7%
CONWAY	2,320	305	2,013	2	1,708 D	13.1%	86.8%	13.2%	86.8%
CRAIGHEAD	4,066	710	3,335	21	2,625 D	17.5%	82.0%	17.6%	82.4%
CRAWFORD	2,672	697	1,963	12	1,266 D	26.1%	73.5%	26.2%	73.8%
CRITTENDEN	1,880	22	1,858		1,836 D	1.2%	98.8%	1.2%	98.8%
CROSS	1,797	133	1,644	20	1,511 D	7.4%	91.5%	7.5%	92.5%
DALLAS	1,536	103	1,433		1,330 D	6.7%	93.3%	6.7%	93.3%
DESHA	1,468	55	1,411	2	1,356 D	3.7%	96.1%	3.8%	96.2%
DREW	1,301	70	1,229	2	1,159 D	5.4%	94.5%	5.4%	94.6%
FAULKNER	3,044	511	2,521	12	2,010 D	16.8%	82.8%	16.9%	83.1%
FRANKLIN	2,247	345	1,890	12	1,545 D	15.4%	84.1%	15.4%	84.6%
FULTON	1,386	437	946	13	509 D	31.5%	68.3%	31.6%	68.4%
GARLAND	4,183	1,217	2,931	35	1,714 D	29.1%	70.1%	29.3%	70.7%
GRANT	1,126	147	978	1	831 D	13.1%	86.9%	13.1%	86.9%
GREENE	2,229	412	1,811	6	1,399 D	18.5%	81.2%	18.5%	81.5%
HEMPSTEAD	2,623	190	2,431	2	2,241 D	7.2%	92.7%	7.2%	92.8%
HOT SPRING	2,033	444	1,581	8	1,137 D	21.8%	77.8%	21.9%	78.1%
HOWARD	1,717	275	1,437	5	1,162 D	16.0%	83.7%	16.1%	83.9%
INDEPENDENCE	2,792	685	2,101	6	1,416 D	24.5%	75.3%	24.6%	75.4%
IZARD	1,766	416	1,350		934 D	23.6%	76.4%	23.6%	76.4%
JACKSON	2,479	327	2,151	1	1,824 D	13.2%	86.8%	13.2%	86.8%
JEFFERSON	3,645	224	3,414	7	3,190 D	6.1%	93.7%	6.2%	93.8%
JOHNSON	1,772	318	1,432	22	1,114 D	17.9%	80.8%	18.2%	81.8%
LAFAYETTE	1,382	100	1,279	3	1,179 D	7.2%	92.5%	7.3%	92.7%
LAWRENCE	2,703	457	2,230	16	1,773 D	16.9%	82.5%	17.0%	83.0%
LEE	1,325	66	1,257	2	1,191 D	5.0%	94.9%	5.0%	95.0%
LINCOLN	952	39	913		874 D	4.1%	95.9%	4.1%	95.9%
LITTLE RIVER	1,255	192	1,056	7	864 D	15.3%	84.1%	15.4%	84.6%
LOGAN	3,440	770	2,663	7	1,893 D	22.4%	77.4%	22.4%	77.6%
LONOKE	3,047	310	2,735	2	2,425 D	10.2%	89.8%	10.2%	89.8%
MADISON	3,167	1,484	1,679	4	195 D	46.9%	53.0%	46.9%	53.1%
MARION	1,440	435	989	16	554 D	30.2%	68.7%	30.5%	69.5%
MILLER	3,021	323	2,689	9	2,366 D	10.7%	89.0%	10.7%	89.3%
MISSISSIPPI	5,147	303	4,835	9	4,532 D	5.9%	93.9%	5.9%	94.1%
MONROE	1,187	82	1,102	3	1,020 D	6.9%	92.8%	6.9%	93.1%
MONTGOMERY	1,519	465	1,034	20	569 D	30.6%	68.1%	31.0%	69.0%
NEVADA	1,461	204	1,252	5	1,048 D	14.0%	85.7%	14.0%	86.0%
NEWTON	1,991	1,053	938		115 R	52.9%	47.1%	52.9%	47.1%
OUACHITA	3,070	262	2,808		2,546 D	8.5%	91.5%	8.5%	91.5%
PERRY	1,148	249	899		650 D	21.7%	78.3%	21.7%	78.3%
PHILLIPS	2,363	94	2,259	10	2,165 D	4.0%	95.6%	4.0%	96.0%
PIKE	1,278	283	994	1	711 D	22.1%	77.8%	22.2%	77.8%
POINSETT	4,049	563	3,457	29	2,894 D	13.9%	85.4%	14.0%	86.0%
POLK	1,735	537	1,170	28	633 D	31.0%	67.4%	31.5%	68.5%
POPE	3,030	348	2,678	4	2,330 D	11.5%	88.4%	11.5%	88.5%
PRAIRIE	1,606	282	1,321	3	1,039 D	17.6%	82.3%	17.6%	82.4%
PULASKI	12,830	1,320	11,482	28	10,162 D	10.3%	89.5%	10.3%	89.7%

PRESIDENT 1940

County	Total Vote	Republican	Democratic	Other	Rep.-Dem. Plurality	% Total Vote Rep.	% Total Vote Dem.	% Major Vote Rep.	% Major Vote Dem.
ARKANSAS	3,132	742	2,345	45	1,603 D	23.7%	74.9%	24.0%	76.0%
ASHLEY	2,023	184	1,835	4	1,651 D	9.1%	90.7%	9.1%	90.9%
BAXTER	1,355	489	859	7	370 D	36.1%	63.4%	36.3%	63.7%
BENTON	4,473	1,962	2,442	69	480 D	43.9%	54.6%	44.6%	55.4%
BOONE	2,869	786	2,054	29	1,268 D	27.4%	71.6%	27.7%	72.3%
BRADLEY	2,066	123	1,939	4	1,816 D	6.0%	93.9%	6.0%	94.0%
CALHOUN	862	44	818		774 D	5.1%	94.9%	5.1%	94.9%
CARROLL	2,687	1,081	1,604	2	523 D	40.2%	59.7%	40.3%	59.7%
CHICOT	1,755	161	1,592	2	1,431 D	9.2%	90.7%	9.2%	90.8%
CLARK	2,327	311	2,008	8	1,697 D	13.4%	86.3%	13.4%	86.6%
CLAY	2,779	1,029	1,676	74	647 D	37.0%	60.3%	38.0%	62.0%
CLEBURNE	1,218	374	834	10	460 D	30.7%	68.5%	31.0%	69.0%
CLEVELAND	1,048	58	989	1	931 D	5.5%	94.4%	5.5%	94.5%
COLUMBIA	2,422	149	2,270	3	2,121 D	6.2%	93.7%	6.2%	93.8%
CONWAY	2,340	272	2,067	1	1,795 D	11.6%	88.3%	11.6%	88.4%
CRAIGHEAD	4,262	935	3,300	27	2,365 D	21.9%	77.4%	22.1%	77.9%
CRAWFORD	2,318	691	1,581	46	890 D	29.8%	68.2%	30.4%	69.6%
CRITTENDEN	2,040	72	1,966	2	1,894 D	3.5%	96.4%	3.5%	96.5%
CROSS	2,035	285	1,746	4	1,461 D	14.0%	85.8%	14.0%	86.0%
DALLAS	1,467	118	1,295	54	1,177 D	8.0%	88.3%	8.4%	91.6%
DESHA	1,526	146	1,370	10	1,224 D	9.6%	89.8%	9.6%	90.4%
DREW	1,511	152	1,329	30	1,177 D	10.1%	88.0%	10.3%	89.7%
FAULKNER	3,066	519	2,535	12	2,016 D	16.9%	82.7%	17.0%	83.0%
FRANKLIN	1,922	319	1,601	2	1,282 D	16.6%	83.3%	16.6%	83.4%
FULTON	1,183	333	838	12	505 D	28.1%	70.8%	28.4%	71.6%
GARLAND	4,772	1,424	3,335	13	1,911 D	29.8%	69.9%	29.9%	70.1%
GRANT	1,203	160	1,043		883 D	13.3%	86.7%	13.3%	86.7%
GREENE	2,735	510	2,220	5	1,710 D	18.6%	81.2%	18.7%	81.3%
HEMPSTEAD	3,229	415	2,814		2,399 D	12.9%	87.1%	12.9%	87.1%
HOT SPRING	2,217	482	1,730	5	1,248 D	21.7%	78.0%	21.8%	78.2%
HOWARD	1,973	419	1,540	14	1,121 D	21.2%	78.1%	21.4%	78.6%
INDEPENDENCE	3,220	928	2,276	16	1,348 D	28.8%	70.7%	29.0%	71.0%
IZARD	1,426	366	1,058	2	692 D	25.7%	74.2%	25.7%	74.3%
JACKSON	2,628	382	2,223	23	1,841 D	14.5%	84.6%	14.7%	85.3%
JEFFERSON	4,429	587	3,829	13	3,242 D	13.3%	86.5%	13.3%	86.7%
JOHNSON	1,756	318	1,429	9	1,111 D	18.1%	81.4%	18.2%	81.8%
LAFAYETTE	1,536	159	1,352	25	1,193 D	10.4%	88.0%	10.5%	89.5%
LAWRENCE	3,360	852	2,484	24	1,632 D	25.4%	73.9%	25.5%	74.5%
LEE	1,212	109	1,100	3	991 D	9.0%	90.8%	9.0%	91.0%
LINCOLN	1,025	199	816	10	617 D	9.7%	89.4%	9.8%	90.2%
LITTLE RIVER	1,392	276	1,104	12	828 D	19.8%	79.3%	20.0%	80.0%
LOGAN	3,896	1,065	2,831		1,766 D	27.3%	72.7%	27.3%	72.7%
LONOKE	2,225	323	1,899	3	1,576 D	14.5%	85.3%	14.5%	85.5%
MADISON	4,308	2,107	2,196	5	89 D	48.9%	51.0%	49.0%	51.0%
MARION	1,201	320	864	17	544 D	26.6%	71.9%	27.0%	73.0%
MILLER	3,599	563	3,019	17	2,456 D	15.6%	83.9%	15.7%	84.3%
MISSISSIPPI	5,891	616	5,257	18	4,641 D	10.5%	89.2%	10.5%	89.5%
MONROE	1,624	128	1,494	2	1,366 D	7.9%	92.0%	7.9%	92.1%
MONTGOMERY	1,417	400	1,012	5	612 D	28.2%	71.4%	28.3%	71.7%
NEVADA	1,630	224	1,399	7	1,175 D	13.7%	85.8%	13.8%	86.2%
NEWTON	2,618	1,392	1,202	24	190 R	53.2%	45.9%	53.7%	46.3%
OUACHITA	3,240	284	2,951	5	2,667 D	8.8%	91.1%	8.8%	91.2%
PERRY	990	206	783	1	577 D	20.8%	79.1%	20.8%	79.2%
PHILLIPS	2,480	245	2,235		1,990 D	9.9%	90.1%	9.9%	90.1%
PIKE	1,409	424	974	11	550 D	30.1%	69.1%	30.3%	69.7%
POINSETT	4,817	670	4,138	9	3,468 D	13.9%	85.9%	13.9%	86.1%
POLK	1,858	585	1,255	18	670 D	31.5%	67.5%	31.8%	68.2%
POPE	4,561	770	3,765	26	2,995 D	16.9%	82.5%	17.0%	83.0%
PRAIRIE	1,408	336	1,069	3	733 D	23.9%	75.9%	23.9%	76.1%
PULASKI	17,230	2,955	14,219	56	11,264 D	17.2%	82.5%	17.2%	82.8%

ARKANSAS

PRESIDENT 1936

County	Total Vote	Republican	Democratic	Other	Rep.-Dem. Plurality	Percentage Total Vote Rep.	Dem.	Major Vote Rep.	Dem.
RANDOLPH	2,110	414	1,693	3	1,279 D	19.6%	80.2%	19.6%	80.4%
ST. FRANCIS	2,046	94	1,938	14	1,844 D	4.6%	94.7%	4.6%	95.4%
SALINE	1,903	359	1,520	24	1,161 D	18.9%	79.9%	19.1%	80.9%
SCOTT	1,502	363	1,137	2	774 D	24.2%	75.7%	24.2%	75.8%
SEARCY	1,778	1,010	767	1	243 R	56.8%	43.1%	56.8%	43.2%
SEBASTIAN	5,720	1,161	4,539	20	3,378 D	20.3%	79.4%	20.4%	79.6%
SEVIER	1,500	289	1,200	11	911 D	19.3%	80.0%	19.4%	80.6%
SHARP	1,235	289	934	12	645 D	23.4%	75.6%	23.6%	76.4%
STONE	772	248	521	3	273 D	32.1%	67.5%	32.2%	67.8%
UNION	4,408	254	4,141	13	3,887 D	5.8%	93.9%	5.8%	94.2%
VAN BUREN	1,969	541	1,422	6	881 D	27.5%	72.2%	27.6%	72.4%
WASHINGTON	4,977	1,579	3,378	20	1,799 D	31.7%	67.9%	31.9%	68.1%
WHITE	3,045	535	2,503	7	1,968 D	17.6%	82.2%	17.6%	82.4%
WOODRUFF	1,739	253	1,473	13	1,220 D	14.5%	84.7%	14.7%	85.3%
YELL	2,700	318	2,382		2,064 D	11.8%	88.2%	11.8%	88.2%
TOTAL	179,431	32,049	146,765	617	114,716 D	17.9%	81.8%	17.9%	82.1%

PRESIDENT 1940

County	Total Vote	Republican	Democratic	Other	Rep.-Dem. Plurality	Percentage Total Vote Rep.	Dem.	Major Vote Rep.	Dem.
RANDOLPH	2,179	474	1,687	18	1,213 D	21.8%	77.4%	21.9%	78.1%
ST. FRANCIS	1,894	192	1,671	31	1,479 D	10.1%	88.2%	10.3%	89.7%
SALINE	2,251	274	1,963	14	1,689 D	12.2%	87.2%	12.2%	87.8%
SCOTT	1,353	353	992	8	639 D	26.1%	73.3%	26.2%	73.8%
SEARCY	2,278	1,292	982	4	310 R	56.7%	43.1%	56.8%	43.2%
SEBASTIAN	7,246	1,968	5,249	29	3,281 D	27.2%	72.4%	27.3%	72.7%
SEVIER	1,675	293	1,374	8	1,081 D	17.5%	82.0%	17.6%	82.4%
SHARP	1,537	433	1,099	5	666 D	28.2%	71.5%	28.3%	71.7%
STONE	1,057	406	644	7	238 D	38.4%	60.9%	38.7%	61.3%
UNION	5,345	489	4,842	14	4,353 D	9.1%	90.6%	9.2%	90.8%
VAN BUREN	1,470	402	1,068		666 D	27.3%	72.7%	27.3%	72.7%
WASHINGTON	4,750	1,819	2,873	58	1,054 D	38.3%	60.5%	38.8%	61.2%
WHITE	4,245	876	3,345	24	2,469 D	20.6%	78.8%	20.8%	79.2%
WOODRUFF	1,481	193	1,280	8	1,087 D	13.0%	86.4%	13.1%	86.9%
YELL	2,467	224	2,236	7	2,012 D	9.1%	90.6%	9.1%	90.9%
TOTAL	200,429	42,122	157,213	1,094	115,091 D	21.0%	78.4%	21.1%	78.9%

ARKANSAS

PRESIDENT 1944

County	Total Vote	Republican	Democratic	Other	Rep.-Dem. Plurality	%Total Rep.	%Total Dem.	%Major Rep.	%Major Dem.
ARKANSAS	2,751	1,031	1,711	9	680 D	37.5	62.2	37.6	62.4
ASHLEY	2,460	285	2,169	6	1,884 D	11.6	88.2	11.6	88.4
BAXTER	1,372	572	796	4	224 D	41.7	58.0	41.8	58.2
BENTON	6,175	3,305	2,861	9	444 R	53.5	46.3	53.6	46.4
BOONE	3,481	1,349	2,132		783 D	38.8	61.2	38.8	61.2
BRADLEY	1,877	162	1,710	5	1,548 D	8.6	91.1	8.7	91.3
CALHOUN	1,028	122	906		784 D	11.9	88.1	11.9	88.1
CARROLL	2,640	1,176	1,464		288 D	44.5	55.5	44.5	55.5
CHICOT	1,826	270	1,552	4	1,282 D	14.8	85.0	14.8	85.2
CLARK	2,621	637	1,981	3	1,344 D	24.3	75.6	24.3	75.7
CLAY	3,361	1,422	1,934	5	512 D	42.3	57.5	42.4	57.6
CLEBURNE	1,437	582	839	16	257 D	40.5	58.4	41.0	59.0
CLEVELAND	1,110	150	960		810 D	13.5	86.5	13.5	86.5
COLUMBIA	2,543	394	2,145	4	1,751 D	15.5	84.3	15.5	84.5
CONWAY	2,221	639	1,579	3	940 D	28.8	71.1	28.8	71.2
CRAIGHEAD	5,074	1,474	3,582	18	2,108 D	29.1	70.6	29.2	70.8
CRAWFORD	2,862	1,141	1,702	19	561 D	39.9	59.5	40.2	59.9
CRITTENDEN	1,920	372	1,548		1,176 D	19.4	80.6	19.4	80.6
CROSS	2,182	452	1,724	6	1,272 D	20.7	79.0	20.9	79.2
DALLAS	1,507	266	1,238	3	972 D	17.7	82.1	17.7	82.3
DESHA	1,362	186	1,175	1	989 D	13.7	86.3	13.7	86.3
DREW	1,691	320	1,370	1	1,050 D	18.9	81.0	18.9	81.1
FAULKNER	3,239	897	2,332	10	1,435 D	27.7	72.0	27.8	72.2
FRANKLIN	1,647	457	1,188	2	731 D	27.7	72.1	27.8	72.2
FULTON	1,187	525	660	2	135 D	44.2	55.6	44.3	55.7
GARLAND	5,669	2,069	3,596	4	1,527 D	36.5	63.4	36.5	63.5
GRANT	1,422	334	1,088		754 D	23.5	76.5	23.5	76.5
GREENE	3,501	928	2,565	8	1,637 D	26.5	73.3	26.6	73.4
HEMPSTEAD	2,789	624	2,157	8	1,533 D	22.4	77.3	22.4	77.6
HOT SPRING	2,510	853	1,646	11	793 D	34.0	65.6	34.1	65.9
HOWARD	2,118	576	1,538	4	962 D	27.2	72.6	27.2	72.8
INDEPENDENCE	2,980	1,192	1,779	9	587 D	40.0	59.7	40.1	59.9
IZARD	1,259	402	853	4	451 D	31.9	67.8	32.0	68.0
JACKSON	2,732	414	2,318		1,904 D	15.2	84.8	15.2	84.8
JEFFERSON	5,676	1,578	4,095	3	2,517 D	27.8	72.1	27.8	72.2
JOHNSON	1,911	593	1,311	7	718 D	31.0	68.6	31.1	68.9
LAFAYETTE	1,327	177	1,150		973 D	13.3	86.7	13.3	86.7
LAWRENCE	2,740	927	1,810	3	883 D	33.8	66.1	33.9	66.1
LEE	1,396	275	1,118	3	843 D	19.7	80.1	19.7	80.3
LINCOLN	1,175	141	1,034		893 D	12.0	88.0	12.0	88.0
LITTLE RIVER	1,289	326	961	2	635 D	25.3	74.6	25.3	74.7
LOGAN	3,555	1,279	2,269	7	990 D	36.0	63.8	36.0	64.0
LONOKE	2,763	697	2,064	2	1,367 D	25.2	74.7	25.2	74.8
MADISON	3,908	2,120	1,788		332 R	54.2	45.7	54.2	45.8
MARION	1,268	414	842	12	428 D	32.6	66.4	33.0	67.0
MILLER	3,851	972	2,873	6	1,901 D	25.2	74.6	25.3	74.7
MISSISSIPPI	5,235	1,292	3,938	5	2,646 D	24.7	75.2	24.7	75.3
MONROE	1,606	291	1,311	4	1,020 D	18.1	81.6	18.1	81.8
MONTGOMERY	924	349	573	2	224 D	37.8	62.0	37.9	62.1
NEVADA	1,771	415	1,353	3	938 D	23.4	76.4	23.5	76.5
NEWTON	1,650	934	710	6	224 R	56.6	43.0	56.8	43.2
OUACHITA	3,628	473	3,154	1	2,681 D	13.0	86.9	13.0	87.0
PERRY	995	285	710		425 D	28.6	71.4	28.6	71.4
PHILLIPS	2,548	501	2,046	1	1,545 D	19.7	80.3	19.7	80.3
PIKE	1,292	405	877	10	472 D	31.3	67.9	31.6	68.4
POINSETT	2,818	311	2,506	1	2,195 D	11.0	88.9	11.0	89.0
POLK	1,773	764	999	10	235 D	43.1	56.3	43.3	56.7
POPE	2,861	805	2,048	8	1,243 D	28.1	71.6	28.2	71.8
PRAIRIE	1,585	465	1,117	3	652 D	29.3	70.5	29.4	70.6
PULASKI	22,589	6,069	16,470	50	10,401 D	26.9	72.9	26.9	73.1

PRESIDENT 1948

County	Total Vote	Republican	Democratic	Other	Rep.-Dem. Plurality	%Total Rep.	%Total Dem.	%Major Rep.	%Major Dem.
ARKANSAS	3,356	737	1,781	838	1,044 D	22.0	53.1	29.3	70.7
ASHLEY	2,408	197	1,844	367	1,647 D	8.2	76.6	9.7	90.3
BAXTER	1,760	553	1,098	109	545 D	31.4	62.4	33.5	66.5
BENTON	6,513	2,911	3,281	321	370 D	44.7	50.4	47.0	53.0
BOONE	4,995	1,499	3,190	306	1,691 D	30.0	63.9	32.0	68.0
BRADLEY	2,187	213	1,426	548	1,213 D	9.7	65.2	13.0	87.0
CALHOUN	918	45	768	105	723 D	4.9	83.7	5.5	94.5
CARROLL	3,688	1,525	2,032	131	507 D	41.4	55.1	42.9	57.1
CHICOT	1,762	203	952	607	749 D	11.5	54.0	17.6	82.4
CLARK	2,509	383	1,750	376	1,367 D	15.3	69.7	18.0	82.0
CLAY	3,091	878	2,069	144	1,191 D	28.4	66.9	29.8	70.2
CLEBURNE	1,447	312	1,061	74	749 D	21.6	73.3	22.7	77.3
CLEVELAND	1,006	79	679	248	600 D	7.9	67.5	10.4	89.6
COLUMBIA	2,981	217	1,788	976	1,571 D	7.3	60.0	10.8	89.2
CONWAY	2,454	425	1,771	258	1,346 D	17.3	72.2	19.4	80.6
CRAIGHEAD	5,110	759	3,238	1,113	2,479 D	14.9	63.4	19.0	81.0
CRAWFORD	2,952	1,002	1,730	220	728 D	33.9	58.6	36.7	63.3
CRITTENDEN	2,392	137	594	1,661	457 D	5.7	24.8	18.7	81.3
CROSS	2,265	213	1,100	952	887 D	9.4	48.6	16.2	83.8
DALLAS	1,702	152	1,174	376	1,022 D	8.9	69.0	11.5	88.5
DESHA	3,033	233	2,122	678	1,889 D	7.7	70.0	9.9	90.1
DREW	2,027	182	1,204	641	1,022 D	9.0	59.4	13.1	86.9
FAULKNER	3,597	626	2,653	318	2,027 D	17.4	73.8	19.1	80.9
FRANKLIN	2,092	391	1,591	110	1,200 D	18.7	76.1	19.7	80.3
FULTON	1,227	339	850	38	511 D	27.6	69.3	28.5	71.5
GARLAND	7,154	2,286	3,764	1,104	1,478 D	32.0	52.6	37.8	62.2
GRANT	1,235	121	883	231	762 D	9.8	71.5	12.1	87.9
GREENE	3,390	502	2,657	231	2,155 D	14.8	78.4	15.9	84.1
HEMPSTEAD	3,069	386	1,683	1,000	1,297 D	12.6	54.8	18.7	81.3
HOT SPRING	2,764	555	1,932	277	1,377 D	20.1	69.9	22.3	77.7
HOWARD	1,652	199	1,250	203	1,051 D	12.0	75.7	13.7	86.3
INDEPENDENCE	3,541	855	2,340	346	1,485 D	24.1	66.1	26.8	73.2
IZARD	1,566	240	1,283	43	1,043 D	15.3	81.9	15.8	84.2
JACKSON	3,270	338	2,696	236	2,358 D	10.3	82.4	11.1	88.9
JEFFERSON	8,214	1,176	5,086	1,952	3,910 D	14.3	61.9	18.8	81.2
JOHNSON	2,249	523	1,565	161	1,042 D	23.3	69.6	25.0	75.0
LAFAYETTE	1,424	113	700	611	587 D	7.9	49.2	13.9	86.1
LAWRENCE	2,672	497	2,001	174	1,504 D	18.6	74.9	19.9	80.1
LEE	1,491	95	528	868	433 D	6.4	35.4	15.2	84.8
LINCOLN	1,681	378	1,108	195	730 D	22.5	65.9	25.4	74.6
LITTLE RIVER	1,524	169	900	455	731 D	11.1	59.1	15.8	84.2
LOGAN	3,192	902	2,130	160	1,228 D	28.3	66.7	29.7	70.3
LONOKE	2,991	383	2,045	563	1,662 D	12.8	68.4	15.6	84.4
MADISON	4,297	2,201	2,041	55	160 R	51.2	47.5	51.9	48.1
MARION	1,561	381	1,133	47	752 D	24.4	72.6	25.2	74.8
MILLER	4,579	488	2,850	1,241	2,362 D	10.7	62.2	14.6	85.4
MISSISSIPPI	6,335	771	3,763	1,801	2,992 D	12.2	59.4	17.0	83.0
MONROE	2,350	299	1,431	620	1,132 D	12.7	60.9	17.3	82.7
MONTGOMERY	1,243	236	935	72	699 D	19.0	75.2	20.2	79.8
NEVADA	1,772	202	1,140	430	938 D	11.4	64.3	15.1	84.9
NEWTON	1,748	879	848	21	31 R	50.3	48.5	50.9	49.1
OUACHITA	4,818	476	3,315	1,027	2,839 D	9.9	68.8	12.6	87.4
PERRY	1,091	201	731	159	530 D	18.4	67.0	21.6	78.4
PHILLIPS	3,099	351	1,018	1,730	667 D	11.3	32.8	25.6	74.4
PIKE	1,351	256	997	98	741 D	18.9	73.8	20.4	79.6
POINSETT	3,702	435	2,415	852	1,980 D	11.8	65.2	15.3	84.7
POLK	2,140	554	1,417	169	863 D	25.9	66.2	28.1	71.9
POPE	3,716	764	2,525	427	1,761 D	20.6	67.9	23.2	76.8
PRAIRIE	1,678	260	1,020	398	760 D	15.5	60.8	20.3	79.7
PULASKI	24,639	5,910	13,120	5,609	7,210 D	24.0	53.2	31.1	68.9

ARKANSAS

PRESIDENT 1944

County	Total Vote	Republican	Democratic	Other	Rep.-Dem. Plurality	Total Vote Rep.	Total Vote Dem.	Major Vote Rep.	Major Vote Dem.
RANDOLPH	2,049	529	1,514	6	985 D	25.8%	73.9%	25.9%	74.1%
ST FRANCIS	2,108	446	1,654	8	1,208 D	21.2%	78.5%	21.2%	78.8%
SALINE	3,217	643	2,556	18	1,913 D	20.0%	79.5%	20.1%	79.9%
SCOTT	1,246	348	898		550 D	27.9%	72.1%	27.9%	72.1%
SEARCY	2,307	1,409	891	7	518 R	61.1%	38.6%	61.3%	38.7%
SEBASTIAN	9,467	3,452	6,008	7	2,556 D	36.5%	63.5%	36.5%	63.5%
SEVIER	1,746	389	1,356	1	967 D	22.3%	77.7%	22.3%	77.7%
SHARP	1,893	664	1,217	12	553 D	35.1%	64.3%	35.3%	64.7%
STONE	1,154	549	592	13	43 D	47.6%	51.3%	48.1%	51.9%
UNION	5,459	833	4,624	2	3,791 D	15.3%	84.7%	15.3%	84.7%
VAN BUREN	1,747	655	1,090	2	435 D	37.5%	62.4%	37.5%	62.5%
WASHINGTON	6,201	3,084	3,089	28	5 D	49.7%	49.8%	50.0%	50.0%
WHITE	3,878	1,346	2,532		1,186 D	34.7%	65.3%	34.7%	65.3%
WOODRUFF	1,662	279	1,377	6	1,098 D	16.8%	82.9%	16.8%	83.2%
YELL	2,132	489	1,642	1	1,153 D	22.9%	77.0%	22.9%	77.1%
TOTAL	212,954	63,551	148,965	438	85,414 D	29.8%	70.0%	29.9%	70.1%

PRESIDENT 1948

County	Total Vote	Republican	Democratic	Other	Rep.-Dem. Plurality	Total Vote Rep.	Total Vote Dem.	Major Vote Rep.	Major Vote Dem.
RANDOLPH	2,633	377	2,139	117	1,762 D	14.3%	81.2%	15.0%	85.0%
ST FRANCIS	2,155	178	1,011	966	833 D	8.3%	46.9%	15.0%	85.0%
SALINE	2,868	390	2,070	408	1,680 D	13.6%	72.2%	15.9%	84.1%
SCOTT	1,408	260	1,093	55	833 D	18.5%	77.6%	19.2%	80.8%
SEARCY	2,326	1,064	1,205	57	141 D	45.7%	51.8%	46.9%	53.1%
SEBASTIAN	8,848	2,928	5,075	845	2,147 D	33.1%	57.4%	36.6%	63.4%
SEVIER	1,837	267	1,314	256	1,047 D	14.5%	71.5%	16.9%	83.1%
SHARP	1,453	295	1,078	80	783 D	20.3%	74.2%	21.5%	78.5%
STONE	1,919	644	1,186	89	542 D	33.6%	61.8%	35.2%	64.8%
UNION	8,339	1,039	5,588	1,712	4,549 D	12.5%	67.0%	15.7%	84.3%
VAN BUREN	2,070	617	1,324	129	707 D	29.8%	64.0%	31.8%	68.2%
WASHINGTON	7,074	2,859	3,493	722	634 D	40.4%	49.4%	45.0%	55.0%
WHITE	4,625	833	3,193	599	2,360 D	18.0%	69.0%	20.7%	79.3%
WOODRUFF	1,829	207	1,008	614	801 D	11.3%	55.1%	17.0%	83.0%
YELL	2,421	408	1,866	147	1,458 D	16.9%	77.1%	17.9%	82.1%
TOTAL	242,475	51,959	149,659	41,857	98,700 D	21.0%	61.7%	25.4%	74.6%

ARKANSAS

PRESIDENT 1952

County	Total Vote	Republican	Democratic	Other	Rep.-Dem. Plurality	Tot. Rep. %	Tot. Dem. %	Maj. Rep. %	Maj. Dem. %
ARKANSAS	5,358	2,697	2,648	13	49 R	50.3%	49.4%	50.5%	49.5%
ASHLEY	4,729	1,249	3,471	9	2,222 D	26.4%	73.4%	26.5%	73.5%
BAXTER	2,793	1,387	1,388	18	1 D	49.7%	49.7%	50.0%	50.0%
BENTON	11,500	7,916	3,558	26	4,358 R	68.8%	30.9%	69.0%	31.0%
BOONE	6,155	3,361	2,786	8	575 R	54.6%	45.3%	54.7%	45.3%
BRADLEY	3,297	869	2,417	11	1,548 D	26.4%	73.3%	26.4%	73.6%
CALHOUN	1,607	272	1,332	3	1,060 D	16.9%	82.9%	17.0%	83.0%
CARROLL	4,258	2,752	1,493	13	1,259 R	64.6%	35.1%	64.8%	35.2%
CHICOT	3,663	1,191	2,458	14	1,267 D	32.5%	67.1%	32.6%	67.4%
CLARK	4,647	1,679	2,963	5	1,284 D	36.1%	63.8%	36.2%	63.8%
CLAY	4,408	2,105	2,277	26	172 D	47.8%	51.7%	48.0%	52.0%
CLEBURNE	1,971	918	1,045	8	127 D	46.6%	53.0%	46.8%	53.2%
CLEVELAND	1,728	477	1,248	3	771 D	27.6%	72.2%	27.7%	72.3%
COLUMBIA	5,299	1,931	3,359	9	1,428 D	36.4%	63.4%	36.5%	63.5%
CONWAY	5,317	2,133	3,174	10	1,041 D	40.1%	59.7%	40.2%	59.8%
CRAIGHEAD	10,202	4,199	5,975	28	1,776 D	41.2%	58.6%	41.3%	58.7%
CRAWFORD	5,269	2,782	2,477	10	305 R	52.8%	47.0%	52.9%	47.1%
CRITTENDEN	4,884	1,885	2,982	17	1,097 D	38.6%	61.1%	38.7%	61.3%
CROSS	3,817	1,461	2,344	12	883 D	38.3%	61.4%	38.4%	61.6%
DALLAS	2,944	737	2,202	5	1,465 D	25.0%	74.8%	25.1%	74.9%
DESHA	4,192	1,037	3,150	5	2,113 D	24.7%	75.1%	24.8%	75.2%
DREW	3,306	1,040	2,261	5	1,221 D	31.5%	68.4%	31.5%	68.5%
FAULKNER	5,470	1,995	3,461	14	1,466 D	36.5%	63.3%	36.6%	63.4%
FRANKLIN	2,982	1,215	1,762	5	547 D	40.7%	59.1%	40.8%	59.2%
FULTON	1,938	890	1,048		158 D	45.9%	54.1%	45.9%	54.1%
GARLAND	13,065	7,848	5,165	52	2,683 R	60.1%	39.5%	60.3%	39.7%
GRANT	2,135	637	1,487	11	850 D	29.8%	69.6%	30.0%	70.0%
GREENE	5,458	1,875	3,571	12	1,696 D	34.4%	65.4%	34.4%	65.6%
HEMPSTEAD	4,901	2,115	2,771	15	656 D	43.2%	56.5%	43.3%	56.7%
HOT SPRING	5,331	1,842	3,474	15	1,632 D	34.6%	65.2%	34.7%	65.3%
HOWARD	2,443	944	1,492	7	548 D	38.6%	61.1%	38.8%	61.2%
INDEPENDENCE	5,003	2,499	2,485	19	14 R	50.0%	49.7%	50.1%	49.9%
IZARD	1,715	629	1,085	1	456 D	36.7%	63.3%	36.7%	63.3%
JACKSON	5,917	1,516	4,401		2,885 D	25.6%	74.4%	25.6%	74.4%
JEFFERSON	14,252	5,925	8,300	27	2,375 D	41.6%	58.2%	41.7%	58.3%
JOHNSON	3,765	1,728	2,021	16	293 D	45.9%	53.7%	46.1%	53.9%
LAFAYETTE	2,386	733	1,637	16	904 D	30.7%	68.6%	30.9%	69.1%
LAWRENCE	3,844	1,570	2,206	68	636 D	40.8%	57.4%	41.6%	58.4%
LEE	2,988	1,054	1,923	11	869 D	35.3%	64.4%	35.4%	64.6%
LINCOLN	2,472	595	1,871	6	1,276 D	24.1%	75.7%	24.1%	75.9%
LITTLE RIVER	2,308	783	1,522	3	739 D	33.9%	65.9%	34.0%	66.0%
LOGAN	4,689	2,103	2,567	19	464 D	44.8%	54.7%	45.0%	55.0%
LONOKE	5,094	1,570	3,517	7	1,947 D	30.8%	69.0%	30.9%	69.1%
MADISON	4,987	2,868	2,110	9	758 R	57.5%	42.3%	57.6%	42.4%
MARION	1,960	844	1,099	17	255 D	43.1%	56.1%	43.4%	56.6%
MILLER	8,509	3,137	5,337	35	2,200 D	36.9%	62.7%	37.0%	63.0%
MISSISSIPPI	11,567	4,586	6,968	13	2,382 D	39.6%	60.2%	39.7%	60.3%
MONROE	2,781	947	1,834		887 D	34.1%	65.9%	34.1%	65.9%
MONTGOMERY	1,630	815	807	8	8 R	50.0%	49.5%	50.2%	49.8%
NEVADA	3,014	1,037	1,972	5	935 D	34.4%	65.4%	34.5%	65.5%
NEWTON	2,838	1,728	1,107	3	621 R	60.9%	39.0%	61.0%	39.0%
OUACHITA	8,136	2,171	5,936	29	3,765 D	26.7%	73.0%	26.8%	73.2%
PERRY	1,310	502	802	6	300 D	38.3%	61.2%	38.5%	61.5%
PHILLIPS	6,340	2,592	3,741	7	1,149 D	40.9%	59.0%	40.9%	59.1%
PIKE	1,938	742	1,163	33	421 D	38.3%	60.0%	39.0%	61.0%
POINSETT	6,321	2,010	4,303	8	2,293 D	31.8%	68.1%	31.8%	68.2%
POLK	3,141	1,756	1,379	6	377 R	55.9%	43.9%	56.0%	44.0%
POPE	5,266	2,226	3,036	4	810 D	42.3%	57.7%	42.3%	57.7%
PRAIRIE	2,541	871	1,664	6	793 D	34.3%	65.5%	34.4%	65.6%
PULASKI	48,286	23,460	24,448	378	988 D	48.6%	50.6%	49.0%	51.0%

PRESIDENT 1956

County	Total Vote	Republican	Democratic	Other	Rep.-Dem. Plurality	Tot. Rep. %	Tot. Dem. %	Maj. Rep. %	Maj. Dem. %
ARKANSAS	5,635	2,826	2,736	73	90 R	50.2%	48.6%	50.8%	49.2%
ASHLEY	4,270	1,183	2,820	267	1,637 D	27.7%	66.0%	29.6%	70.4%
BAXTER	3,192	1,721	1,451	20	270 R	53.9%	45.5%	54.3%	45.7%
BENTON	10,305	6,500	3,744	61	2,756 R	63.1%	36.3%	63.5%	36.5%
BOONE	6,006	3,153	2,829	24	324 R	52.5%	47.1%	52.7%	47.3%
BRADLEY	4,426	1,361	3,010	55	1,649 D	30.8%	68.0%	31.1%	68.9%
CALHOUN	1,762	445	1,303	14	858 D	25.3%	74.0%	25.5%	74.5%
CARROLL	4,080	2,310	1,651	119	659 R	56.6%	40.5%	58.3%	41.7%
CHICOT	3,455	1,043	2,273	139	1,230 D	30.2%	65.8%	31.5%	68.5%
CLARK	4,840	1,973	2,809	58	836 D	40.8%	58.0%	41.3%	58.7%
CLAY	4,113	1,711	2,368	34	657 D	41.6%	57.6%	41.9%	58.1%
CLEBURNE	2,048	947	1,094	7	147 D	46.2%	53.4%	46.4%	53.6%
CLEVELAND	1,592	423	1,149	20	726 D	26.6%	72.2%	26.9%	73.1%
COLUMBIA	5,394	2,342	2,845	207	503 D	43.4%	52.7%	45.2%	54.8%
CONWAY	4,281	1,636	2,618	27	982 D	38.2%	61.2%	38.5%	61.5%
CRAIGHEAD	10,060	4,035	5,876	149	1,841 D	40.1%	58.4%	40.7%	59.3%
CRAWFORD	5,843	3,090	2,723	30	367 R	52.9%	46.6%	53.2%	46.8%
CRITTENDEN	4,873	2,476	2,120	277	356 R	50.8%	43.5%	53.9%	46.1%
CROSS	3,417	1,176	2,165	76	989 D	34.4%	63.4%	35.2%	64.8%
DALLAS	2,762	984	1,726	52	742 D	35.6%	62.5%	36.3%	63.7%
DESHA	4,191	1,204	2,935	52	1,731 D	28.7%	70.0%	29.1%	70.9%
DREW	3,586	1,265	2,234	87	969 D	35.3%	62.3%	36.2%	63.8%
FAULKNER	5,860	2,399	3,428	33	1,029 D	40.9%	58.5%	41.2%	58.8%
FRANKLIN	2,771	1,137	1,614	20	477 D	41.0%	58.2%	41.3%	58.7%
FULTON	1,771	799	958	14	159 D	45.1%	54.1%	45.5%	54.5%
GARLAND	15,076	9,427	5,437	212	3,990 R	62.5%	36.1%	63.4%	36.6%
GRANT	2,139	818	1,272	49	454 D	38.2%	59.5%	39.1%	60.9%
GREENE	5,389	1,898	3,454	37	1,556 D	35.2%	64.1%	35.5%	64.5%
HEMPSTEAD	4,997	2,227	2,694	76	467 D	44.6%	53.9%	45.3%	54.7%
HOT SPRING	6,502	2,923	3,525	54	602 D	45.0%	54.2%	45.3%	54.7%
HOWARD	2,785	1,329	1,428	28	99 D	47.7%	51.3%	48.2%	51.8%
INDEPENDENCE	4,683	2,333	2,316	34	17 R	49.8%	49.5%	50.2%	49.8%
IZARD	1,716	511	1,200	5	689 D	29.8%	69.9%	29.9%	70.1%
JACKSON	5,061	1,323	3,699	39	2,376 D	26.1%	73.1%	26.3%	73.7%
JEFFERSON	12,558	5,743	6,426	389	683 D	45.7%	51.2%	47.2%	52.8%
JOHNSON	3,245	1,520	1,697	28	177 D	46.8%	52.3%	47.2%	52.8%
LAFAYETTE	2,280	836	1,348	96	512 D	36.7%	59.1%	38.3%	61.7%
LAWRENCE	3,948	1,584	2,303	61	719 D	40.1%	58.3%	40.8%	59.2%
LEE	2,814	974	1,719	121	745 D	34.6%	61.1%	36.2%	63.8%
LINCOLN	2,405	767	1,616	22	849 D	31.9%	67.2%	32.2%	67.8%
LITTLE RIVER	2,198	828	1,308	62	480 D	37.7%	59.5%	38.8%	61.2%
LOGAN	4,412	2,081	2,307	24	226 D	47.2%	52.3%	47.4%	52.6%
LONOKE	5,336	1,932	3,234	170	1,302 D	36.2%	60.6%	37.4%	62.6%
MADISON	4,716	2,525	2,186	5	339 R	53.5%	46.4%	53.6%	46.4%
MARION	1,922	857	1,061	4	204 D	44.6%	55.2%	44.7%	55.3%
MILLER	9,987	4,307	5,402	278	1,095 D	43.1%	54.1%	44.4%	55.6%
MISSISSIPPI	10,955	4,269	6,428	258	2,159 D	39.0%	58.7%	39.9%	60.1%
MONROE	2,634	1,099	1,460	75	361 D	41.7%	55.4%	42.9%	57.1%
MONTGOMERY	1,829	965	846	18	119 R	52.8%	46.3%	53.3%	46.7%
NEVADA	2,943	1,039	1,871	33	832 D	35.3%	63.6%	35.7%	64.3%
NEWTON	2,316	1,481	832	3	649 R	63.9%	35.9%	64.0%	36.0%
OUACHITA	8,129	2,819	5,188	122	2,369 D	34.7%	63.8%	35.2%	64.8%
PERRY	1,304	572	719	13	147 D	43.9%	55.1%	44.3%	55.7%
PHILLIPS	6,940	2,826	3,917	197	1,091 D	40.7%	56.4%	41.9%	58.1%
PIKE	1,903	905	985	13	80 D	47.6%	51.8%	47.9%	52.1%
POINSETT	6,006	2,117	3,817	72	1,700 D	35.2%	63.6%	35.7%	64.3%
POLK	3,143	1,832	1,287	24	545 R	58.3%	40.9%	58.7%	41.3%
POPE	5,045	2,267	2,753	25	486 D	44.9%	54.6%	45.2%	54.8%
PRAIRIE	2,440	917	1,504	19	587 D	37.6%	61.6%	37.9%	62.1%
PULASKI	50,301	25,702	23,372	1,227	2,330 R	51.1%	46.5%	52.4%	47.6%

ARKANSAS

PRESIDENT 1952

County	Total Vote	Republican	Democratic	Other	Rep.-Dem. Plurality	Percentage Total Vote Rep.	Dem.	Major Vote Rep.	Dem.
RANDOLPH	3,254	1,302	1,941	11	639 D	40.0%	59.6%	40.1%	59.9%
ST FRANCIS	4,259	1,792	2,466	1	674 D	42.1%	57.9%	42.1%	57.9%
SALINE	5,863	1,766	4,045	52	2,279 D	30.1%	69.0%	30.4%	69.6%
SCOTT	2,101	893	1,197	11	304 D	42.5%	57.0%	42.7%	57.3%
SEARCY	3,004	1,996	1,007	1	989 R	66.4%	33.5%	66.5%	33.5%
SEBASTIAN	17,944	10,114	7,802	28	2,312 R	56.4%	43.5%	56.5%	43.5%
SEVIER	2,805	1,130	1,673	2	543 D	40.3%	59.6%	40.3%	59.7%
SHARP	1,697	655	1,039	3	384 D	38.5%	61.2%	38.7%	61.3%
STONE	1,274	700	573	1	127 R	54.9%	45.0%	55.0%	45.0%
UNION	12,810	5,266	7,515	29	2,249 D	41.1%	58.7%	41.2%	58.8%
VAN BUREN	3,102	1,530	1,559	13	29 D	49.3%	50.3%	49.5%	50.5%
WASHINGTON	13,611	8,650	4,923	38	3,727 R	63.5%	36.2%	63.7%	36.3%
WHITE	7,070	2,884	4,179	7	1,295 D	40.8%	59.1%	40.8%	59.2%
WOODRUFF	2,839	818	2,017	4	1,199 D	28.8%	71.0%	28.9%	71.1%
YELL	3,144	1,243	1,884	17	641 D	39.5%	59.9%	39.8%	60.2%
TOTAL	404,800	177,155	226,300	1,345	49,145 D	43.8%	55.9%	43.9%	56.1%

PRESIDENT 1956

County	Total Vote	Republican	Democratic	Other	Rep.-Dem. Plurality	Percentage Total Vote Rep.	Dem.	Major Vote Rep.	Dem.
RANDOLPH	2,893	1,117	1,763	13	646 D	38.6%	60.9%	38.8%	61.2%
ST FRANCIS	4,199	1,864	2,114	201	230 D	44.9%	50.3%	47.1%	52.9%
SALINE	6,378	2,603	3,705	70	1,102 D	40.8%	58.1%	41.3%	58.7%
SCOTT	2,899	1,637	1,248	14	389 R	56.5%	43.0%	56.7%	43.3%
SEARCY	3,374	2,441	909	24	1,532 R	72.3%	26.9%	72.9%	27.1%
SEBASTIAN	17,841	10,234	7,489	118	2,745 R	57.4%	42.0%	57.7%	42.3%
SEVIER	2,678	1,159	1,500	19	341 D	43.3%	56.0%	43.6%	56.4%
SHARP	1,600	645	927	28	282 D	40.3%	57.9%	41.0%	59.0%
STONE	1,411	651	756	4	105 D	46.1%	53.6%	46.3%	53.7%
UNION	12,726	5,059	7,055	612	1,996 D	39.8%	55.4%	41.8%	58.2%
VAN BUREN	2,642	1,296	1,331	15	35 D	49.1%	50.4%	49.3%	50.7%
WASHINGTON	12,623	7,683	4,857	83	2,826 R	60.9%	38.5%	61.3%	38.7%
WHITE	8,750	3,813	4,895	42	1,082 D	43.6%	55.9%	43.8%	56.2%
WOODRUFF	2,675	992	1,630	53	638 D	37.1%	60.9%	37.8%	62.2%
YELL	3,393	1,361	2,008	4	627 D	40.7%	59.2%	40.7%	59.3%
TOTAL	406,572	186,287	213,277	7,008	26,990 D	45.8%	52.5%	46.6%	53.4%

ARKANSAS

PRESIDENT 1960

County	Total Vote	Republican	Democratic	Other	Rep.-Dem. Plurality	% Total Vote Rep.	% Total Vote Dem.	% Major Vote Rep.	% Major Vote Dem.
ARKANSAS	5,318	2,043	2,789	486	746 D	38.4%	52.4%	42.3%	57.7%
ASHLEY	5,026	1,288	3,118	620	1,830 D	25.6%	62.0%	29.2%	70.8%
BAXTER	3,879	2,108	1,694	77	414 R	54.3%	43.7%	55.4%	44.6%
BENTON	11,590	7,832	3,619	139	4,213 R	67.6%	31.2%	68.4%	31.6%
BOONE	6,233	3,388	2,774	71	614 R	54.4%	44.5%	55.0%	45.0%
BRADLEY	4,210	873	2,960	377	2,087 D	20.7%	70.3%	22.8%	77.2%
CALHOUN	1,598	295	1,151	152	856 D	18.5%	72.0%	20.4%	79.6%
CARROLL	3,965	2,615	1,301	49	1,314 R	66.0%	32.8%	66.8%	33.2%
CHICOT	3,051	979	1,803	269	824 D	32.1%	59.1%	35.2%	64.8%
CLARK	5,083	1,357	3,295	431	1,938 D	26.7%	64.8%	29.2%	70.8%
CLAY	4,568	2,543	1,908	117	635 R	55.7%	41.8%	57.1%	42.9%
CLEBURNE	2,282	1,026	1,144	112	118 D	45.0%	50.1%	47.3%	52.7%
CLEVELAND	1,715	290	1,216	209	926 D	16.9%	70.9%	19.3%	80.7%
COLUMBIA	5,605	2,372	2,427	806	55 D	42.3%	43.3%	49.4%	50.6%
CONWAY	4,796	1,685	2,900	211	1,215 D	35.1%	60.5%	36.8%	63.2%
CRAIGHEAD	10,738	5,258	4,898	582	360 R	49.0%	45.6%	51.8%	48.2%
CRAWFORD	5,907	3,373	2,430	104	943 R	57.1%	41.1%	58.1%	41.9%
CRITTENDEN	5,128	2,234	2,679	215	445 D	43.6%	52.2%	45.5%	54.5%
CROSS	3,615	1,287	2,088	240	801 D	35.6%	57.8%	38.1%	61.9%
DALLAS	2,615	659	1,639	317	980 D	25.2%	62.7%	28.7%	71.3%
DESHA	3,936	1,063	2,502	371	1,439 D	27.0%	63.6%	29.8%	70.2%
DREW	3,372	889	2,107	376	1,218 D	26.4%	62.5%	29.7%	70.3%
FAULKNER	6,609	2,426	3,820	363	1,394 D	36.7%	57.8%	38.8%	61.2%
FRANKLIN	3,751	1,631	2,025	95	394 D	43.5%	54.0%	44.6%	55.4%
FULTON	1,849	1,127	703	19	424 R	61.0%	38.0%	61.6%	38.4%
GARLAND	13,944	7,204	6,333	407	871 R	51.7%	45.4%	53.2%	46.8%
GRANT	2,269	563	1,394	312	831 D	24.8%	61.4%	28.8%	71.2%
GREENE	5,569	2,658	2,774	137	116 D	47.7%	49.8%	48.9%	51.1%
HEMPSTEAD	4,759	1,948	2,596	215	648 D	40.9%	54.5%	42.9%	57.1%
HOT SPRING	5,854	1,732	3,454	668	1,722 D	29.6%	59.0%	33.4%	66.6%
HOWARD	2,735	1,225	1,366	144	141 D	44.8%	49.9%	47.3%	52.7%
INDEPENDENCE	5,289	2,639	2,487	163	152 R	49.9%	47.0%	51.5%	48.5%
IZARD	2,248	808	1,340	100	532 D	35.9%	59.4%	37.6%	62.4%
JACKSON	5,159	1,986	2,860	313	874 D	38.5%	55.4%	41.0%	59.0%
JEFFERSON	15,235	4,889	8,442	1,904	3,553 D	31.8%	55.4%	36.4%	63.6%
JOHNSON	3,523	1,490	1,938	95	448 D	42.3%	55.0%	43.5%	56.5%
LAFAYETTE	2,325	713	1,286	326	573 D	30.7%	55.3%	35.7%	64.3%
LAWRENCE	4,065	1,800	2,074	191	274 D	44.3%	51.0%	46.5%	53.5%
LEE	2,701	1,034	1,409	258	375 D	38.3%	52.2%	42.3%	57.7%
LINCOLN	2,646	626	1,780	240	1,154 D	23.7%	67.3%	26.0%	74.0%
LITTLE RIVER	2,323	692	1,514	117	822 D	29.8%	65.2%	31.4%	68.6%
LOGAN	4,764	2,014	2,636	114	622 D	42.3%	55.3%	43.3%	56.7%
LONOKE	5,348	2,560	2,691	97	131 D	47.9%	50.3%	48.8%	51.2%
MADISON	4,201	2,445	1,702	54	743 R	58.2%	40.5%	59.0%	41.0%
MARION	2,008	1,016	968	24	48 R	50.6%	48.2%	51.2%	48.8%
MILLER	8,117	3,113	4,550	454	1,437 D	38.4%	56.1%	40.6%	59.4%
MISSISSIPPI	10,585	4,983	5,138	464	155 D	47.1%	48.5%	49.2%	50.8%
MONROE	3,068	833	1,856	379	1,023 D	27.2%	60.5%	31.0%	69.0%
MONTGOMERY	1,677	836	788	53	48 R	49.9%	47.0%	51.5%	48.5%
NEVADA	2,751	937	1,605	209	668 D	34.1%	58.3%	36.9%	63.1%
NEWTON	2,687	1,814	844	29	970 R	67.5%	31.4%	68.2%	31.8%
OUACHITA	8,192	2,439	5,169	584	2,730 D	29.8%	63.1%	32.1%	67.9%
PERRY	1,385	501	789	95	288 D	36.2%	57.0%	38.8%	61.2%
PHILLIPS	6,677	2,168	4,105	404	1,937 D	32.5%	61.5%	34.6%	65.4%
PIKE	2,102	1,013	997	92	16 R	48.2%	47.4%	50.4%	49.6%
POINSETT	5,444	2,430	2,817	197	387 D	44.6%	51.7%	46.3%	53.7%
POLK	3,632	1,882	1,635	115	247 R	51.8%	45.0%	53.5%	46.5%
POPE	5,589	2,573	2,760	256	187 D	46.0%	49.4%	48.2%	51.8%
PRAIRIE	2,636	734	1,680	222	946 D	27.8%	63.7%	30.4%	69.6%
PULASKI	55,788	22,146	26,034	7,608	3,888 D	39.7%	46.7%	46.0%	54.0%

PRESIDENT 1964

County	Total Vote	Republican	Democratic	Other	Rep.-Dem. Plurality	% Total Vote Rep.	% Total Vote Dem.	% Major Vote Rep.	% Major Vote Dem.
ARKANSAS	6,990	3,769	3,200	21	569 R	53.9%	45.8%	54.1%	45.9%
ASHLEY	6,710	3,742	2,901	67	841 R	55.8%	43.2%	56.3%	43.7%
BAXTER	4,891	1,986	2,900	5	914 D	40.6%	59.3%	40.6%	59.4%
BENTON	11,662	5,977	5,655	30	322 R	51.3%	48.5%	51.4%	48.6%
BOONE	6,646	2,857	3,770	19	913 D	43.0%	56.7%	43.1%	56.9%
BRADLEY	4,102	1,852	2,229	21	377 D	45.1%	54.3%	45.4%	54.6%
CALHOUN	2,322	889	1,409	24	520 D	38.3%	60.7%	38.7%	61.3%
CARROLL	4,110	2,105	2,005	0	100 R	51.2%	48.8%	51.2%	48.8%
CHICOT	4,903	1,972	2,916	15	944 D	40.2%	59.5%	40.3%	59.7%
CLARK	6,037	1,884	4,127	26	2,243 D	31.2%	68.4%	31.3%	68.7%
CLAY	5,321	1,999	3,280	42	1,281 D	37.6%	61.6%	37.9%	62.1%
CLEBURNE	3,875	1,221	2,645	9	1,424 D	31.5%	68.3%	31.6%	68.4%
CLEVELAND	2,165	1,026	1,121	18	95 D	47.4%	51.8%	47.8%	52.2%
COLUMBIA	7,533	4,009	3,485	39	524 R	53.2%	46.3%	53.5%	46.5%
CONWAY	6,602	2,378	4,205	19	1,827 D	36.0%	63.7%	36.1%	63.9%
CRAIGHEAD	13,541	5,163	8,334	44	3,171 D	38.1%	61.5%	38.3%	61.7%
CRAWFORD	6,852	3,293	3,537	21	243 D	48.1%	51.6%	48.2%	51.8%
CRITTENDEN	8,302	4,065	4,168	69	103 D	49.0%	50.2%	49.4%	50.6%
CROSS	4,580	2,147	2,421	12	274 D	46.9%	52.9%	47.0%	53.0%
DALLAS	3,447	1,625	1,779	43	154 D	47.1%	51.6%	47.7%	52.3%
DESHA	5,236	1,930	3,294	12	1,364 D	36.9%	62.9%	36.9%	63.1%
DREW	4,121	2,109	1,980	32	129 R	51.2%	48.0%	51.6%	48.4%
FAULKNER	9,417	3,259	6,116	42	2,857 D	34.6%	64.9%	34.8%	65.2%
FRANKLIN	4,298	1,580	2,685	33	1,105 D	36.8%	62.5%	37.0%	63.0%
FULTON	2,557	846	1,704	7	858 D	33.1%	66.6%	33.2%	66.8%
GARLAND	21,629	9,952	11,591	86	1,639 D	46.0%	53.6%	46.2%	53.8%
GRANT	3,047	1,308	1,678	61	370 D	42.9%	55.1%	43.8%	56.2%
GREENE	7,037	2,271	4,742	24	2,471 D	32.3%	67.4%	32.4%	67.6%
HEMPSTEAD	5,891	2,493	3,355	43	862 D	42.3%	57.0%	42.6%	57.4%
HOT SPRING	7,522	2,911	4,543	68	1,632 D	38.7%	60.4%	39.1%	60.9%
HOWARD	3,063	1,649	1,320	94	329 R	53.8%	43.1%	55.5%	44.5%
INDEPENDENCE	6,960	2,470	4,455	35	1,985 D	35.5%	64.0%	35.7%	64.3%
IZARD	2,486	726	1,736	24	1,010 D	29.2%	69.8%	29.5%	70.5%
JACKSON	6,828	2,141	4,651	36	2,510 D	31.4%	68.1%	31.5%	68.5%
JEFFERSON	22,969	9,968	12,872	129	2,904 D	43.4%	56.0%	43.6%	56.4%
JOHNSON	4,683	1,535	3,127	21	1,592 D	32.8%	66.8%	32.9%	67.1%
LAFAYETTE	2,967	1,476	1,484	7	8 D	49.7%	50.0%	49.9%	50.1%
LAWRENCE	5,538	2,013	3,498	27	1,485 D	36.3%	63.2%	36.5%	63.5%
LEE	4,011	1,668	2,335	8	667 D	41.6%	58.2%	41.7%	58.3%
LINCOLN	3,882	1,410	2,468	4	1,058 D	36.3%	63.6%	36.4%	63.6%
LITTLE RIVER	3,194	1,141	2,040	13	899 D	35.7%	63.9%	35.9%	64.1%
LOGAN	5,896	2,265	3,604	27	1,339 D	38.4%	61.1%	38.6%	61.4%
LONOKE	7,477	3,636	3,818	23	182 D	48.6%	51.1%	48.8%	51.2%
MADISON	4,726	1,997	2,715	14	718 D	42.3%	57.4%	42.4%	57.6%
MARION	2,759	1,088	1,661	10	573 D	39.4%	60.2%	39.6%	60.4%
MILLER	9,492	4,253	5,190	49	937 D	44.8%	54.7%	45.0%	55.0%
MISSISSIPPI	14,911	6,213	8,678	20	2,465 D	41.7%	58.2%	41.7%	58.3%
MONROE	4,237	1,968	2,258	11	290 D	46.4%	53.3%	46.6%	53.4%
MONTGOMERY	2,202	832	1,358	12	526 D	37.8%	61.7%	38.0%	62.0%
NEVADA	3,625	1,406	2,190	29	784 D	38.8%	60.4%	39.1%	60.9%
NEWTON	2,769	1,357	1,374	38	17 D	49.0%	49.6%	49.7%	50.3%
OUACHITA	10,698	3,572	7,056	70	3,484 D	33.6%	66.0%	33.6%	66.4%
PERRY	2,387	1,048	1,320	19	272 D	43.9%	55.3%	44.3%	55.7%
PHILLIPS	9,790	3,963	5,818	9	1,855 D	40.5%	59.4%	40.5%	59.5%
PIKE	2,787	1,241	1,531	15	290 D	44.5%	54.9%	44.8%	55.2%
POINSETT	8,679	3,031	5,635	13	2,604 D	34.9%	64.9%	35.0%	65.0%
POLK	4,608	2,022	2,575	11	553 D	43.9%	55.9%	44.0%	56.0%
POPE	7,780	2,651	4,972	157	2,321 D	34.1%	63.9%	34.8%	65.2%
PRAIRIE	3,310	1,476	1,812	22	336 D	44.6%	54.7%	44.9%	55.1%
PULASKI	79,289	38,312	40,535	442	2,223 D	48.3%	51.1%	48.6%	51.4%

ARKANSAS

PRESIDENT 1960

County	Total Vote	Republican	Democratic	Other	Rep.-Dem. Plurality	Total Vote Rep.	Dem.	Major Vote Rep.	Dem.
RANDOLPH	3,278	1,620	1,556	102	64 R	49.4%	47.5%	51.0%	49.0%
ST FRANCIS	4,518	1,786	2,432	300	645 D	39.5%	53.8%	42.3%	57.7%
SALINE	6,791	2,195	3,898	698	1,703 D	32.3%	57.4%	36.0%	64.0%
SCOTT	2,264	1,137	1,116	11	21 R	50.2%	49.3%	50.5%	49.5%
SEARCY	3,351	2,297	1,022	32	1,275 R	68.5%	30.5%	69.2%	30.8%
SEBASTIAN	20,696	11,744	8,726	226	3,018 R	56.7%	42.2%	57.4%	42.6%
SEVIER	2,835	1,141	1,580	114	439 D	40.2%	55.7%	41.9%	58.1%
SHARP	1,786	911	807	68	104 R	51.0%	45.2%	53.0%	47.0%
STONE	1,943	959	897	87	62 R	49.4%	46.2%	51.7%	48.3%
UNION	13,565	5,631	6,500	1,434	869 D	41.5%	47.9%	46.4%	53.6%
VAN BUREN	2,267	1,009	1,158	100	149 D	44.5%	51.1%	46.6%	53.4%
WASHINGTON	15,679	10,088	5,391	200	4,697 R	64.3%	34.4%	65.2%	34.8%
WHITE	9,834	3,985	5,244	605	1,259 D	40.5%	53.3%	43.2%	56.8%
WOODRUFF	2,535	667	1,613	255	946 D	26.3%	63.6%	29.3%	70.7%
YELL	3,433	1,303	2,008	122	705 D	38.0%	58.5%	39.4%	60.6%
TOTAL	428,509	184,508	215,049	28,952	30,541 D	43.1%	50.2%	46.2%	53.8%

PRESIDENT 1964

County	Total Vote	Republican	Democratic	Other	Rep.-Dem. Plurality	Total Vote Rep.	Dem.	Major Vote Rep.	Dem.
RANDOLPH	4,009	1,312	2,680	17	1,368 D	32.7%	66.8%	32.9%	67.1%
ST FRANCIS	7,038	3,377	3,651	10	274 D	48.0%	51.9%	48.1%	51.9%
SALINE	9,313	3,628	5,605	80	1,977 D	39.0%	60.2%	39.3%	60.7%
SCOTT	2,964	1,121	1,838	5	717 D	37.8%	62.0%	37.9%	62.1%
SEARCY	3,163	1,649	1,508	6	141 R	52.1%	47.7%	52.2%	47.8%
SEBASTIAN	23,493	13,110	10,299	84	2,811 R	55.8%	43.8%	56.0%	44.0%
SEVIER	3,383	1,249	2,123	11	874 D	36.9%	62.8%	37.0%	63.0%
SHARP	3,047	1,215	1,810	22	595 D	39.9%	59.4%	40.2%	59.8%
STONE	2,340	942	1,374	24	432 D	40.3%	58.7%	40.7%	59.3%
UNION	15,580	8,472	6,948	160	1,524 R	54.4%	44.6%	54.9%	45.1%
VAN BUREN	3,352	1,270	2,054	28	784 D	37.9%	61.3%	38.2%	61.8%
WASHINGTON	17,070	6,856	10,166	48	3,310 D	40.2%	59.6%	40.3%	59.7%
WHITE	11,684	5,023	6,566	95	1,543 D	43.0%	56.2%	43.3%	56.7%
WOODRUFF	3,693	1,366	2,307	20	941 D	37.0%	62.5%	37.2%	62.8%
YELL	4,948	1,527	3,407	14	1,880 D	30.9%	68.9%	30.9%	69.1%
TOTAL	560,426	243,264	314,197	2,965	70,933 D	43.4%	56.1%	43.6%	56.4%

ARKANSAS

OTHER VOTE COMPOSITION:

1920	Socialist.
1924	Progressive.
1928	429 Socialist; 317 Communist.
1932	1,166 Socialist; 952 Liberty; 157 Communist.
1936	446 Socialist; 167 Communist; 4 Union.
1940	793 Prohibition; 301 Socialist.
1944	Socialist.
1948	40,068 States Rights; 1,037 Socialist; 751 Progressive; 1 Prohibition.
1952	886 Prohibition; 458 Christian Nationalist (MacArthur); 1 Socialist Labor.
1956	States Rights.
1960	National States Rights.
1964	National States Rights.

SPECIAL CASES:

State canvass reports for 1920 and 1924 are unavailable; data for both these elections have been taken from Edgar Eugene Robinson's studies, with the addition of unofficial figures for Logan county in 1920.

1924	Progressive candidates ran second in several counties.
1948	States Rights candidates carried several counties and ran second in a number of others.

CALIFORNIA

PRESIDENT 1920

County	Total Vote	Republican	Democratic	Other	Rep-Dem. Plurality	Total Vote Rep.	Dem.	Major Vote Rep.	Dem.
ALAMEDA	105,889	73,177	21,468	11,244	51,709 R	69.1%	20.3%	77.3%	22.7%
ALPINE	70	64	6		58 R	91.4%	8.6%	91.4%	8.6%
AMADOR	2,105	1,350	639	116	711 R	64.1%	30.4%	67.9%	32.1%
BUTTE	8,234	5,409	2,262	563	3,147 R	65.7%	27.5%	70.5%	29.5%
CALAVERAS	2,314	1,480	641	193	839 R	64.0%	27.7%	69.8%	30.2%
COLUSA	2,686	1,645	907	134	738 R	61.2%	33.8%	64.5%	35.5%
CONTRA COSTA	14,182	9,041	3,483	1,658	5,558 R	63.7%	24.6%	72.2%	27.8%
DEL NORTE	952	596	279	77	317 R	62.6%	29.3%	68.1%	31.9%
EL DORADO	2,542	1,636	726	180	910 R	64.4%	28.6%	69.3%	30.7%
FRESNO	25,413	14,621	9,613	2,179	5,008 R	55.4%	36.4%	60.3%	39.7%
GLENN	2,985	1,916	902	167	1,014 R	64.2%	30.2%	68.0%	32.0%
HUMBOLDT	9,340	6,528	1,778	1,034	4,750 R	69.9%	19.0%	78.6%	21.4%
IMPERIAL	7,284	4,699	2,022	563	2,677 R	64.5%	27.8%	69.9%	30.1%
INYO	2,089	1,195	682	212	513 R	57.2%	32.6%	63.7%	36.3%
KERN	14,444	7,079	6,095	1,270	984 R	49.0%	42.2%	53.7%	46.3%
KINGS	4,707	2,806	1,604	297	1,202 R	59.6%	34.1%	63.6%	36.4%
LAKE	1,735	993	571	171	422 R	57.2%	32.9%	63.5%	36.5%
LASSEN	2,389	1,582	643	164	939 R	66.2%	26.9%	71.1%	28.9%
LOS ANGELES	257,264	178,117	55,661	23,486	122,456 R	69.2%	21.6%	76.2%	23.8%
MADERA	3,208	1,779	1,145	284	634 R	55.5%	35.7%	60.8%	39.2%
MARIN	7,813	5,375	1,688	750	3,637 R	68.8%	21.6%	76.1%	23.9%
MARIPOSA	874	484	320	70	154 R	55.4%	36.6%	60.2%	39.8%
MENDOCINO	6,749	4,443	1,789	517	2,654 R	65.8%	26.5%	71.3%	28.7%
MERCED	5,488	3,457	1,537	494	1,920 R	63.0%	28.0%	69.2%	30.8%
MODOC	1,585	992	535	58	457 R	62.6%	33.8%	65.0%	35.0%
MONO	251	170	56	25	114 R	67.7%	22.3%	75.2%	24.8%
MONTEREY	7,109	4,817	1,771	521	3,046 R	67.8%	24.9%	73.1%	26.9%
NAPA	6,266	4,448	1,444	374	3,034 R	71.0%	23.0%	75.5%	24.5%
NEVADA	3,163	2,055	747	361	1,308 R	65.0%	23.6%	73.3%	26.7%
ORANGE	17,893	12,797	3,502	1,594	9,295 R	71.5%	19.6%	78.5%	21.5%
PLACER	4,869	2,894	1,559	416	1,335 R	59.4%	32.0%	65.0%	35.0%
PLUMAS	1,562	999	403	160	596 R	64.0%	25.8%	71.3%	28.7%
RIVERSIDE	13,118	9,124	2,798	1,196	6,326 R	69.6%	21.3%	76.5%	23.5%
SACRAMENTO	24,100	15,634	7,150	1,316	8,484 R	64.9%	29.7%	68.6%	31.4%
SAN BENITO	3,023	1,965	900	158	1,065 R	65.0%	29.8%	68.6%	31.4%
SAN BERNARDINO	19,921	12,518	5,620	1,783	6,898 R	62.8%	28.2%	69.0%	31.0%
SAN DIEGO	31,087	19,826	8,478	2,783	11,348 R	63.8%	27.3%	70.0%	30.0%
SAN FRANCISCO	147,421	96,105	32,637	18,679	63,468 R	65.2%	22.1%	74.5%	25.5%
SAN JOAQUIN	19,698	12,003	6,487	1,208	5,516 R	60.9%	32.9%	64.9%	35.1%
SAN LUIS OBISPO	6,673	4,123	1,606	944	2,517 R	61.8%	24.1%	72.0%	28.0%
SAN MATEO	10,217	7,205	1,958	1,054	5,247 R	70.5%	19.2%	78.6%	21.4%
SANTA BARBARA	10,339	6,970	2,586	783	4,384 R	67.5%	25.0%	72.9%	27.1%
SANTA CLARA	26,732	19,565	6,485	682	13,080 R	66.1%	22.6%	75.1%	24.9%
SANTA CRUZ	7,974	5,285	1,957	732	3,328 R	66.3%	24.5%	73.0%	27.0%
SHASTA	3,396	2,108	1,028	260	1,080 R	62.1%	30.3%	67.2%	32.8%
SIERRA	701	506	158	37	348 R	72.2%	22.5%	76.2%	23.8%
SISKIYOU	4,844	2,909	1,502	433	1,407 R	60.0%	31.0%	65.9%	34.1%
SOLANO	10,965	7,102	2,954	909	4,148 R	64.8%	26.9%	70.6%	29.4%
SONOMA	16,512	10,377	4,070	1,065	6,307 R	62.9%	25.2%	71.8%	28.2%
STANISLAUS	11,423	7,038	3,055	1,330	3,983 R	61.6%	26.7%	69.7%	30.3%
SUTTER	2,648	1,862	636	150	1,226 R	70.3%	24.0%	74.5%	25.5%
TEHAMA	3,983	2,462	1,079	442	1,383 R	61.8%	27.1%	69.5%	30.5%
TRINITY	989	622	285	82	337 R	62.9%	28.8%	68.6%	31.4%
TULARE	14,914	9,136	4,837	941	4,299 R	61.3%	32.4%	65.4%	34.6%
TUOLUMNE	2,164	1,285	659	220	626 R	59.4%	30.5%	66.1%	33.9%
VENTURA	6,883	5,231	1,305	347	3,926 R	76.0%	19.0%	80.0%	20.0%
YOLO	5,448	3,375	1,787	286	1,588 R	61.9%	32.8%	65.4%	34.6%
YUBA	2,846	2,012	696	138	1,316 R	70.7%	24.5%	74.3%	25.7%
TOTAL	943,463	624,992	229,191	89,280	395,801 R	66.2%	24.3%	73.2%	26.8%

PRESIDENT 1924

County	Total Vote	Republican	Democratic	Other	Rep-Dem. Plurality	Total Vote Rep.	Dem.	Major Vote Rep.	Dem.
ALAMEDA	132,490	81,454	8,020	43,016	73,434 R	61.5%	6.1%	91.0%	9.0%
ALPINE	59	52	5	2	47 R	88.1%	8.5%	91.2%	8.8%
AMADOR	1,847	719	316	812	403 R	38.9%	17.1%	69.5%	30.5%
BUTTE	10,372	4,382	1,299	4,691	3,083 R	42.2%	12.5%	77.1%	22.9%
CALAVERAS	2,211	872	333	1,006	539 R	39.4%	15.1%	72.4%	27.6%
COLUSA	2,571	1,127	495	949	632 R	43.8%	19.3%	69.5%	30.5%
CONTRA COSTA	16,573	9,061	1,114	6,398	7,947 R	54.7%	6.7%	89.1%	10.9%
DEL NORTE	1,007	530	122	355	408 R	52.6%	12.1%	81.3%	18.7%
EL DORADO	2,991	852	361	1,778	491 R	28.5%	12.1%	70.2%	29.8%
FRESNO	35,527	15,635	4,610	15,282	11,025 R	44.0%	13.0%	77.2%	22.8%
GLENN	3,220	1,444	367	1,409	1,077 R	44.8%	11.4%	79.7%	20.3%
HUMBOLDT	11,922	6,767	845	4,298	5,922 R	56.8%	7.1%	88.9%	11.1%
IMPERIAL	6,872	3,455	759	2,658	2,696 R	50.3%	11.0%	82.0%	18.0%
INYO	1,999	950	256	793	694 R	47.5%	12.8%	78.8%	21.2%
KERN	18,763	8,646	3,159	6,958	5,487 R	46.1%	16.8%	73.2%	26.8%
KINGS	5,624	2,812	1,109	1,703	1,703 R	50.0%	19.7%	71.7%	28.3%
LAKE	1,769	795	261	713	534 R	44.9%	14.8%	75.3%	24.7%
LASSEN	2,629	1,072	356	1,201	716 R	40.8%	13.5%	75.1%	24.9%
LOS ANGELES	457,457	299,675	33,554	124,228	266,121 R	65.5%	7.3%	89.9%	10.1%
MADERA	3,558	1,518	450	1,590	1,068 R	42.7%	12.6%	77.1%	22.9%
MARIN	10,800	5,780	656	4,364	5,124 R	53.5%	6.1%	89.8%	10.2%
MARIPOSA	855	344	168	343	176 R	40.2%	19.6%	67.2%	32.8%
MENDOCINO	6,137	3,465	739	1,933	2,726 R	56.5%	12.0%	82.4%	17.6%
MERCED	6,749	3,573	710	2,466	2,863 R	52.9%	10.5%	83.4%	16.6%
MODOC	1,672	731	374	567	357 R	43.7%	22.4%	66.2%	33.8%
MONO	310	166	45	99	121 R	53.5%	14.5%	78.7%	21.3%
MONTEREY	7,768	4,744	886	2,138	3,858 R	61.1%	11.4%	84.3%	15.7%
NAPA	6,576	3,605	670	2,301	2,935 R	54.8%	10.2%	84.3%	15.7%
NEVADA	3,583	1,513	307	1,763	1,206 R	42.2%	8.6%	83.1%	16.9%
ORANGE	29,566	19,913	2,565	7,088	17,348 R	67.4%	8.7%	88.6%	11.4%
PLACER	5,984	2,192	390	3,402	1,802 R	36.6%	6.5%	84.9%	15.1%
PLUMAS	1,713	564	182	967	382 R	32.9%	10.6%	75.6%	24.4%
RIVERSIDE	15,516	9,601	1,318	4,579	8,301 R	62.0%	8.5%	87.9%	12.1%
SACRAMENTO	32,617	13,400	2,285	16,932	11,115 R	41.1%	7.0%	85.4%	14.6%
SAN BENITO	2,695	1,443	361	891	1,082 R	53.5%	13.4%	80.0%	20.0%
SAN BERNARDINO	28,061	15,974	2,634	9,453	13,340 R	56.9%	9.4%	85.8%	14.2%
SAN DIEGO	46,391	22,726	2,944	20,721	19,782 R	49.0%	6.3%	88.5%	11.5%
SAN FRANCISCO	153,920	73,494	9,811	70,615	63,683 R	47.7%	6.4%	88.2%	11.8%
SAN JOAQUIN	22,607	11,056	2,397	9,154	8,659 R	48.9%	10.6%	82.2%	17.8%
SAN LUIS OBISPO	7,761	3,804	731	3,226	3,073 R	49.0%	9.4%	83.9%	16.1%
SAN MATEO	14,702	8,126	771	5,805	7,355 R	55.3%	5.2%	91.3%	8.7%
SANTA BARBARA	13,318	8,615	1,242	3,461	7,373 R	64.7%	9.3%	87.4%	12.6%
SANTA CLARA	34,568	20,056	2,560	11,952	17,496 R	58.0%	7.4%	88.7%	11.3%
SANTA CRUZ	8,879	5,402	801	2,676	4,601 R	60.8%	9.0%	87.1%	12.9%
SHASTA	4,651	1,951	598	2,102	1,353 R	41.9%	12.9%	76.5%	23.5%
SIERRA	709	276	73	360	203 R	38.9%	10.3%	79.1%	20.9%
SISKIYOU	6,005	2,437	584	2,984	1,853 R	40.6%	9.6%	80.7%	19.3%
SOLANO	9,962	4,782	957	4,223	3,825 R	48.0%	9.6%	83.3%	16.7%
SONOMA	17,028	9,535	1,767	5,726	7,768 R	56.0%	10.4%	84.4%	15.6%
STANISLAUS	13,312	7,569	1,274	4,469	6,295 R	56.9%	9.6%	85.6%	14.4%
SUTTER	3,239	1,617	367	1,255	1,250 R	49.9%	11.3%	81.5%	18.5%
TEHAMA	4,227	1,943	486	1,798	1,457 R	46.0%	11.5%	80.0%	20.0%
TRINITY	921	336	154	431	182 R	36.5%	16.7%	68.6%	31.4%
TULARE	18,674	9,484	3,425	5,765	6,059 R	50.8%	18.3%	73.5%	26.5%
TUOLUMNE	2,991	1,287	357	1,347	930 R	43.0%	11.9%	78.3%	21.7%
VENTURA	8,755	5,705	911	2,139	4,794 R	65.2%	10.4%	86.2%	13.8%
YOLO	5,447	2,470	797	2,180	1,673 R	45.3%	14.6%	75.6%	24.4%
YUBA	3,660	1,735	426	1,499	1,309 R	47.4%	11.6%	80.3%	19.7%
TOTAL	1,281,778	733,250	105,514	443,014	627,736 R	57.2%	8.2%	87.4%	12.6%

CALIFORNIA

PRESIDENT 1928

County	Total Vote	Republican	Democratic	Other	Rep.-Dem. Plurality	% Total Rep.	% Total Dem.	% Major Rep.	% Major Dem.
ALAMEDA	181,194	118,539	60,875	1,780	57,664 R	65.4%	33.6%	66.1%	33.9%
ALPINE	52	49	3	—	46 R	94.2%	5.8%	94.2%	5.8%
AMADOR	2,244	990	1,246	8	256 D	44.1%	55.5%	44.3%	55.7%
BUTTE	10,432	6,306	3,946	180	2,360 R	60.4%	37.8%	61.5%	38.5%
CALAVERAS	2,336	1,262	1,066	18	196 R	53.8%	45.4%	54.2%	45.8%
COLUSA	3,112	1,752	1,338	22	414 R	56.3%	43.0%	56.7%	43.3%
CONTRA COSTA	22,349	13,495	8,573	281	4,922 R	60.4%	38.4%	61.2%	38.8%
DEL NORTE	1,380	771	599	10	172 R	55.9%	43.4%	56.3%	43.7%
EL DORADO	2,775	1,228	1,516	31	288 D	44.3%	54.6%	44.8%	55.2%
FRESNO	38,098	20,687	16,884	527	3,803 R	54.3%	44.3%	55.1%	44.9%
GLENN	3,792	2,466	1,297	29	1,169 R	65.0%	34.2%	65.5%	34.5%
HUMBOLDT	13,135	9,162	3,726	247	5,436 R	69.8%	28.4%	71.1%	28.9%
IMPERIAL	8,012	5,417	2,486	109	2,931 R	67.6%	31.0%	68.5%	31.5%
INYO	2,102	1,206	861	35	345 R	57.4%	41.0%	58.3%	41.7%
KERN	23,445	14,692	8,541	212	6,151 R	62.7%	36.4%	63.2%	36.8%
KINGS	5,721	2,947	2,701	73	246 R	51.5%	47.2%	52.2%	47.8%
LAKE	2,784	1,820	926	38	894 R	65.4%	33.3%	66.3%	33.7%
LASSEN	3,721	2,111	1,597	13	514 R	56.7%	42.9%	56.9%	43.1%
LOS ANGELES	731,301	513,526	209,945	7,830	303,581 R	70.2%	28.7%	71.0%	29.0%
MADERA	4,289	2,354	1,896	39	458 R	54.9%	44.2%	55.4%	44.6%
MARIN	13,688	7,862	5,686	140	2,176 R	57.4%	41.5%	58.0%	42.0%
MARIPOSA	1,192	656	517	19	139 R	55.0%	43.4%	55.9%	44.1%
MENDOCINO	7,588	4,699	2,628	150	2,182 R	63.4%	34.4%	64.7%	35.3%
MERCED	7,718	4,644	2,970	104	1,674 R	60.2%	38.5%	61.0%	39.0%
MODOC	1,660	942	711	7	231 R	56.7%	42.8%	57.0%	43.0%
MONO	356	220	127	9	93 R	61.8%	35.7%	63.4%	36.6%
MONTEREY	11,452	7,228	4,138	86	3,090 R	63.1%	36.1%	63.6%	36.4%
NAPA	8,175	4,699	3,422	54	1,277 R	57.5%	41.9%	57.9%	42.1%
NEVADA	4,179	2,173	1,959	47	214 R	52.0%	46.9%	52.6%	47.4%
ORANGE	38,527	30,572	7,611	344	22,961 R	79.4%	19.8%	80.1%	19.9%
PLACER	7,450	3,669	3,685	96	16 D	49.2%	49.5%	49.9%	50.1%
PLUMAS	2,075	947	1,079	49	132 D	45.6%	52.0%	46.7%	53.3%
RIVERSIDE	22,581	17,600	4,769	212	12,831 R	77.9%	21.1%	78.7%	21.3%
SACRAMENTO	40,849	20,762	19,684	403	1,078 R	50.8%	48.2%	51.3%	48.7%
SAN BENITO	3,348	1,971	1,366	11	605 R	58.9%	40.8%	59.1%	40.9%
SAN BERNARDINO	39,112	29,229	9,436	447	19,793 R	74.7%	24.1%	75.6%	24.4%
SAN DIEGO	71,151	47,769	22,749	633	25,020 R	67.1%	32.0%	67.7%	32.3%
SAN FRANCISCO	195,468	95,987	96,632	2,849	645 D	49.1%	49.4%	49.8%	50.2%
SAN JOAQUIN	27,326	16,695	10,343	288	6,352 R	61.1%	37.9%	61.7%	38.3%
SAN LUIS OBISPO	8,920	5,425	3,336	159	2,089 R	60.8%	37.4%	61.9%	38.1%
SAN MATEO	24,392	14,360	9,755	277	4,605 R	58.9%	40.0%	59.5%	40.5%
SANTA BARBARA	16,799	11,666	4,954	179	6,712 R	69.4%	29.5%	70.2%	29.8%
SANTA CLARA	49,694	31,710	17,589	395	14,121 R	63.8%	35.4%	64.3%	35.7%
SANTA CRUZ	12,075	8,275	3,688	112	4,587 R	68.5%	30.5%	69.2%	30.8%
SHASTA	4,408	2,301	2,025	82	276 R	52.2%	45.9%	53.2%	46.8%
SIERRA	887	457	420	10	37 R	51.5%	47.4%	52.1%	47.9%
SISKIYOU	6,772	3,758	2,916	98	842 R	55.5%	43.1%	56.3%	43.7%
SOLANO	13,497	7,061	6,278	158	783 R	52.3%	46.5%	52.9%	47.1%
SONOMA	21,591	12,891	8,506	194	4,385 R	59.7%	39.4%	60.2%	39.8%
STANISLAUS	16,019	10,753	5,063	203	5,690 R	67.1%	31.6%	68.0%	32.0%
SUTTER	4,148	2,239	1,875	34	364 R	54.0%	45.2%	54.4%	45.6%
TEHAMA	5,174	3,393	1,650	131	1,743 R	65.6%	31.9%	67.3%	32.7%
TRINITY	915	447	433	35	14 R	48.9%	47.3%	50.8%	49.2%
TULARE	18,910	12,057	6,635	218	5,422 R	63.8%	35.1%	64.5%	35.5%
TUOLUMNE	3,159	1,731	1,360	68	371 R	54.8%	43.1%	56.0%	44.0%
VENTURA	12,851	9,017	3,717	117	5,300 R	70.2%	28.9%	70.8%	29.2%
YOLO	6,224	3,545	2,641	38	904 R	57.0%	42.4%	57.3%	42.7%
YUBA	4,042	2,022	1,990	30	32 R	50.0%	49.2%	50.4%	49.6%
TOTAL	1,796,656	1,162,323	614,365	19,968	547,958 R	64.7%	34.2%	65.4%	34.6%

PRESIDENT 1932

County	Total Vote	Republican	Democratic	Other	Rep.-Dem. Plurality	% Total Rep.	% Total Dem.	% Major Rep.	% Major Dem.
ALAMEDA	204,344	89,303	106,388	8,653	17,085 D	43.7%	52.1%	45.6%	54.4%
ALPINE	112	53	56	3	3 D	47.3%	50.0%	48.6%	51.4%
AMADOR	3,244	822	2,367	55	1,545 D	25.3%	73.0%	25.8%	74.2%
BUTTE	14,832	4,322	9,645	865	5,323 D	29.1%	65.0%	30.9%	69.1%
CALAVERAS	2,599	754	1,744	101	990 D	29.0%	67.1%	30.2%	69.8%
COLUSA	3,982	1,095	2,752	135	1,657 D	27.5%	69.1%	28.5%	71.5%
CONTRA COSTA	29,192	10,907	17,218	1,067	6,311 D	37.4%	59.0%	38.8%	61.2%
DEL NORTE	2,059	637	1,319	103	682 D	30.9%	64.1%	32.6%	67.4%
EL DORADO	4,135	956	3,034	145	2,078 D	23.1%	73.4%	24.0%	76.0%
FRESNO	46,537	12,134	32,528	1,875	20,394 D	26.1%	69.9%	27.2%	72.8%
GLENN	4,569	1,432	2,973	164	1,541 D	31.3%	65.1%	32.5%	67.5%
HUMBOLDT	16,073	6,795	8,723	555	1,928 D	42.3%	54.3%	43.8%	56.2%
IMPERIAL	13,039	3,783	8,772	484	4,989 D	29.0%	67.3%	30.1%	69.9%
INYO	2,258	698	1,459	101	761 D	30.9%	64.6%	32.4%	67.6%
KERN	27,920	7,011	19,634	1,275	12,623 D	25.1%	70.3%	26.3%	73.7%
KINGS	7,518	2,009	5,191	318	3,182 D	26.7%	69.0%	27.9%	72.1%
LAKE	3,744	1,301	2,344	99	1,043 D	34.7%	62.6%	35.7%	64.3%
LASSEN	4,340	1,167	3,056	117	1,889 D	26.9%	70.4%	27.6%	72.4%
LOS ANGELES	969,148	373,738	554,476	40,934	180,738 D	38.6%	57.2%	40.3%	59.7%
MADERA	4,928	1,243	3,457	228	2,214 D	25.2%	70.2%	26.4%	73.6%
MARIN	16,993	6,480	9,764	749	3,284 D	38.1%	57.5%	39.9%	60.1%
MARIPOSA	2,038	560	1,386	92	826 D	27.5%	68.0%	28.8%	71.2%
MENDOCINO	9,551	3,365	5,867	319	2,502 D	35.2%	61.4%	36.4%	63.6%
MERCED	10,734	2,920	7,202	612	4,282 D	27.2%	67.1%	28.8%	71.2%
MODOC	2,386	655	1,643	88	988 D	27.5%	68.9%	28.5%	71.5%
MONO	581	199	374	8	175 D	34.3%	64.4%	34.7%	65.3%
MONTEREY	15,750	6,200	8,942	608	2,742 D	39.4%	56.8%	40.9%	59.1%
NAPA	9,524	3,521	5,745	258	2,224 D	37.0%	60.3%	38.0%	62.0%
NEVADA	5,596	1,842	3,544	210	1,702 D	32.9%	63.3%	34.2%	65.8%
ORANGE	49,274	22,623	23,835	2,816	1,212 D	45.9%	48.4%	48.7%	51.3%
PLACER	8,683	2,242	6,200	241	3,958 D	25.8%	71.4%	26.6%	73.4%
PLUMAS	2,684	582	2,035	67	1,453 D	21.7%	75.8%	22.2%	77.8%
RIVERSIDE	28,112	14,112	12,755	1,245	1,357 D	50.2%	45.4%	52.5%	47.5%
SACRAMENTO	52,465	14,553	36,370	1,542	21,817 D	27.7%	69.3%	28.6%	71.4%
SAN BENITO	3,744	1,269	2,283	192	1,014 D	33.9%	61.0%	35.7%	64.3%
SAN BERNARDINO	49,548	22,094	24,889	2,565	2,795 D	44.6%	50.2%	47.0%	53.0%
SAN DIEGO	85,150	35,305	45,622	4,223	10,317 D	41.5%	53.6%	43.6%	56.4%
SAN FRANCISCO	222,828	70,152	144,236	8,440	74,084 D	31.5%	64.7%	32.7%	67.3%
SAN JOAQUIN	34,622	11,145	21,929	1,548	10,784 D	32.2%	63.3%	33.7%	66.3%
SAN LUIS OBISPO	12,062	3,449	7,933	680	4,484 D	28.6%	65.8%	30.3%	69.7%
SAN MATEO	33,879	13,442	19,094	1,343	5,652 D	39.7%	56.4%	41.3%	58.7%
SANTA BARBARA	23,291	8,864	13,373	1,054	4,509 D	38.1%	57.4%	39.9%	60.1%
SANTA CLARA	57,525	27,353	28,272	1,900	919 D	47.5%	49.1%	50.5%	49.5%
SANTA CRUZ	14,990	6,005	8,246	739	2,241 D	40.1%	55.0%	42.1%	57.9%
SHASTA	5,782	1,382	4,170	230	2,788 D	23.9%	72.1%	24.9%	75.1%
SIERRA	1,147	292	796	59	504 D	25.5%	69.4%	26.8%	73.2%
SISKIYOU	9,184	2,458	6,367	359	3,909 D	26.8%	69.3%	27.9%	72.1%
SOLANO	14,461	4,382	9,712	367	5,330 D	30.3%	67.2%	31.1%	68.9%
SONOMA	25,657	9,161	15,686	810	6,525 D	35.7%	61.1%	36.9%	63.1%
STANISLAUS	21,042	7,614	12,336	1,092	4,722 D	36.2%	58.6%	38.2%	61.8%
SUTTER	5,407	1,392	3,807	208	2,415 D	25.7%	70.4%	26.8%	73.2%
TEHAMA	5,851	2,001	3,534	316	1,533 D	34.2%	60.4%	36.2%	63.8%
TRINITY	1,508	318	1,101	89	783 D	21.1%	73.0%	22.4%	77.6%
TULARE	24,999	8,066	15,631	1,302	7,565 D	32.3%	62.5%	34.0%	66.0%
TUOLUMNE	3,794	1,145	2,521	128	1,376 D	30.2%	66.4%	31.2%	68.8%
VENTURA	18,535	6,908	10,903	724	3,999 D	37.3%	58.8%	38.8%	61.2%
YOLO	8,529	2,515	5,780	234	3,265 D	29.5%	67.8%	30.3%	69.7%
YUBA	4,493	1,176	3,138	179	1,962 D	26.2%	69.8%	27.3%	72.7%
TOTAL	2,266,972	847,902	1,324,157	94,913	476,255 D	37.4%	58.4%	39.0%	61.0%

CALIFORNIA

PRESIDENT 1936

County	Total Vote	Republican	Democratic	Other	Rep.–Dem. Plurality	Total Vote Rep.	Total Vote Dem.	Major Vote Rep.	Major Vote Dem.
ALAMEDA	234,686	82,352	149,323	3,011	66,971 D	35.1%	63.6%	35.5%	64.5%
ALPINE	159	74	85	—	11 D	46.5%	53.5%	46.5%	53.5%
AMADOR	3,323	777	2,506	40	1,729 D	23.4%	75.4%	23.7%	76.3%
BUTTE	15,928	5,103	10,490	335	5,387 D	32.0%	65.9%	32.7%	67.3%
CALAVERAS	3,534	960	2,520	54	1,560 D	27.2%	71.3%	27.6%	72.4%
COLUSA	4,213	1,186	2,965	62	1,779 D	28.2%	70.4%	28.6%	71.4%
CONTRA COSTA	35,975	9,504	26,107	364	16,603 D	26.4%	72.3%	27.0%	73.0%
DEL NORTE	2,174	853	1,292	29	439 D	39.2%	59.4%	39.8%	60.2%
EL DORADO	5,312	1,228	4,019	65	2,791 D	23.1%	75.7%	23.4%	76.6%
FRESNO	55,126	11,545	42,859	722	31,314 D	20.9%	77.7%	21.2%	78.8%
GLENN	4,984	1,620	3,288	76	1,668 D	32.5%	66.0%	33.0%	67.0%
HUMBOLDT	18,925	6,808	11,909	208	5,101 D	36.0%	62.9%	36.4%	63.6%
IMPERIAL	12,444	4,771	7,560	113	2,789 D	38.3%	60.8%	38.7%	61.3%
INYO	2,501	912	1,560	29	648 D	36.5%	62.4%	36.9%	63.1%
KERN	34,479	8,345	25,726	408	17,381 D	24.2%	74.6%	24.5%	75.5%
KINGS	9,404	2,226	7,062	116	4,836 D	23.7%	75.1%	24.0%	76.0%
LAKE	3,687	1,797	1,837	53	40 D	48.7%	49.8%	49.4%	50.6%
LASSEN	5,276	1,035	4,193	48	3,158 D	19.6%	79.5%	19.8%	80.2%
LOS ANGELES	1,130,415	357,401	757,351	15,663	399,950 D	31.6%	67.0%	32.0%	68.0%
MADERA	5,134	1,387	4,646	101	3,259 D	22.6%	75.7%	23.0%	77.0%
MARIN	18,572	6,211	12,152	209	5,941 D	33.4%	65.4%	33.8%	66.2%
MARIPOSA	2,563	621	1,907	35	1,286 D	24.2%	74.4%	24.6%	75.4%
MENDOCINO	10,266	3,670	6,432	164	2,762 D	35.7%	62.7%	36.3%	63.7%
MERCED	12,868	3,230	9,208	230	5,978 D	25.1%	71.5%	25.6%	74.0%
MODOC	2,851	968	1,828	35	860 D	34.2%	64.6%	34.6%	65.4%
MONO	707	241	458	8	217 D	34.1%	64.8%	34.5%	65.5%
MONTEREY	20,067	7,565	12,267	235	4,702 D	37.7%	61.1%	38.2%	61.9%
NAPA	10,390	3,973	6,210	147	2,297 D	38.2%	60.3%	38.6%	61.2%
NEVADA	7,131	1,913	5,128	90	3,215 D	25.8%	71.9%	26.2%	72.8%
ORANGE	54,251	23,494	29,836	921	6,342 D	43.3%	55.0%	44.1%	55.9%
PLACER	10,388	2,321	7,959	108	5,638 D	22.3%	76.6%	22.6%	77.4%
PLUMAS	3,435	680	2,707	48	2,027 D	19.8%	78.8%	20.1%	79.9%
RIVERSIDE	34,107	16,674	17,011	422	337 D	48.9%	49.9%	49.5%	50.5%
SACRAMENTO	60,184	12,119	47,265	800	35,146 D	20.1%	78.5%	20.4%	79.6%
SAN BENITO	4,142	1,515	2,565	62	1,050 D	36.6%	61.9%	37.1%	62.9%
SAN BERNARDINO	57,016	22,219	33,955	842	11,736 D	39.0%	59.6%	39.6%	60.4%
SAN DIEGO	101,854	35,686	64,628	1,540	28,942 D	35.0%	63.5%	35.6%	64.4%
SAN FRANCISCO	265,001	65,436	196,197	3,368	130,761 D	24.7%	74.0%	25.0%	75.0%
SAN JOAQUIN	39,723	10,172	29,078	473	18,906 D	25.6%	73.2%	25.9%	74.1%
SAN LUIS OBISPO	12,906	4,812	7,889	205	3,077 D	37.3%	61.1%	37.9%	62.1%
SAN MATEO	41,248	13,650	27,087	511	13,437 D	33.1%	65.7%	33.5%	66.5%
SANTA BARBARA	26,045	9,728	15,923	394	6,195 D	37.4%	61.1%	37.9%	62.1%
SANTA CLARA	65,576	26,498	38,346	732	11,848 D	40.4%	58.5%	40.9%	59.1%
SANTA CRUZ	17,908	8,260	9,326	322	1,066 D	46.1%	52.1%	47.0%	53.0%
SHASTA	7,510	2,159	5,236	115	3,077 D	28.7%	69.7%	29.2%	70.8%
SIERRA	1,507	340	1,152	15	812 D	22.6%	76.4%	22.8%	77.2%
SISKIYOU	9,909	2,919	6,865	125	3,946 D	29.5%	69.3%	29.9%	70.2%
SOLANO	17,244	3,603	13,459	182	9,856 D	20.9%	78.1%	21.1%	78.9%
SONOMA	28,706	11,185	17,273	248	6,088 D	39.0%	60.2%	39.3%	60.7%
STANISLAUS	24,302	8,613	15,341	348	6,728 D	35.4%	63.1%	36.0%	64.0%
SUTTER	5,738	1,613	4,019	106	2,436 D	28.1%	70.0%	28.6%	71.4%
TEHAMA	6,178	2,376	3,687	115	1,311 D	38.5%	59.7%	39.2%	60.8%
TRINITY	2,122	655	1,424	43	769 D	30.9%	67.1%	31.5%	68.5%
TULARE	28,015	8,624	18,956	435	10,332 D	30.8%	67.7%	31.3%	68.7%
TUOLUMNE	4,542	1,199	3,303	40	2,104 D	26.4%	72.7%	26.6%	73.4%
VENTURA	21,198	7,579	13,384	235	5,805 D	35.8%	63.1%	36.2%	63.8%
YOLO	8,692	2,594	5,992	106	3,398 D	29.8%	68.9%	30.2%	69.8%
YUBA	5,561	1,332	4,125	104	2,793 D	24.0%	74.2%	24.4%	75.6%
TOTAL	2,638,882	836,431	1,766,836	35,615	930,405 D	31.7%	67.0%	32.1%	67.9%

PRESIDENT 1940

County	Total Vote	Republican	Democratic	Other	Rep.–Dem. Plurality	Total Vote Rep.	Total Vote Dem.	Major Vote Rep.	Major Vote Dem.
ALAMEDA	268,496	116,961	148,224	3,311	31,263 D	43.6%	55.2%	44.1%	55.9%
ALPINE	188	125	62	1	63 R	66.5%	33.0%	66.8%	33.2%
AMADOR	4,176	1,372	2,762	42	1,390 D	32.9%	66.1%	33.2%	66.8%
BUTTE	18,372	7,433	10,684	255	3,251 D	40.5%	58.2%	41.0%	59.0%
CALAVERAS	4,083	1,649	2,405	29	756 D	40.4%	58.9%	40.7%	59.3%
COLUSA	4,464	1,774	2,655	35	881 D	39.7%	59.5%	40.1%	59.9%
CONTRA COSTA	50,040	18,627	30,900	513	12,273 D	37.2%	61.8%	37.6%	62.4%
DEL NORTE	2,302	1,233	1,034	35	199 R	53.6%	44.9%	54.4%	45.6%
EL DORADO	6,237	2,019	4,144	74	2,125 D	32.4%	66.4%	32.8%	67.2%
FRESNO	70,750	21,079	48,866	805	27,787 D	29.8%	69.1%	30.1%	69.9%
GLENN	5,631	2,473	3,095	63	622 D	43.9%	55.0%	44.4%	55.6%
HUMBOLDT	22,024	9,470	12,329	225	2,859 D	43.0%	54.5%	43.4%	53.0%
IMPERIAL	14,712	6,854	7,728	130	874 D	46.6%	52.5%	47.0%	53.0%
INYO	3,330	1,483	1,820	27	337 D	44.5%	54.7%	44.9%	55.1%
KERN	52,126	19,445	32,202	479	12,757 D	37.3%	61.8%	37.6%	62.4%
KINGS	12,320	3,911	8,307	102	4,396 D	31.7%	67.4%	32.0%	68.0%
LAKE	4,151	2,215	1,897	39	318 R	53.4%	45.7%	53.9%	46.1%
LASSEN	6,313	1,902	4,367	44	2,465 D	30.1%	69.2%	30.3%	69.7%
LOS ANGELES	1,415,269	574,266	822,718	18,285	248,452 D	40.6%	58.1%	41.1%	58.9%
MADERA	8,503	2,653	5,749	101	3,096 D	31.2%	67.6%	31.6%	68.4%
MARIN	22,640	10,974	11,365	301	391 D	48.5%	50.2%	49.1%	50.9%
MARIPOSA	3,003	1,035	1,935	33	900 D	34.5%	64.4%	34.8%	65.2%
MENDOCINO	12,569	5,345	7,055	169	1,710 D	42.5%	56.1%	42.8%	56.9%
MERCED	16,784	6,101	10,501	182	4,400 D	36.4%	62.6%	36.7%	63.3%
MODOC	3,630	1,371	2,232	27	861 D	37.8%	61.5%	38.1%	61.9%
MONO	995	459	523	13	64 D	46.1%	52.6%	46.7%	53.3%
MONTEREY	26,853	11,853	14,758	242	2,905 D	44.0%	55.0%	44.5%	55.6%
NAPA	12,853	5,924	6,771	158	847 D	46.1%	52.7%	46.7%	53.3%
NEVADA	8,759	2,863	5,782	114	2,919 D	32.7%	66.0%	33.1%	66.9%
ORANGE	64,997	36,070	28,236	691	7,834 R	55.5%	43.4%	56.1%	43.9%
PLACER	12,436	3,887	8,402	147	4,515 D	31.3%	67.6%	31.6%	68.4%
PLUMAS	4,740	1,270	3,418	52	2,148 D	26.8%	72.1%	27.1%	72.9%
RIVERSIDE	42,380	21,779	20,003	598	1,776 R	51.4%	47.2%	52.1%	47.9%
SACRAMENTO	75,416	23,201	51,351	864	28,150 D	30.8%	68.1%	31.1%	68.9%
SAN BENITO	4,883	2,407	2,441	35	34 D	49.3%	50.0%	49.6%	50.4%
SAN BERNARDINO	68,878	30,511	37,520	847	7,009 D	44.3%	54.5%	44.8%	55.2%
SAN DIEGO	128,110	55,434	71,188	1,488	15,754 D	43.3%	55.6%	43.8%	56.2%
SAN FRANCISCO	311,878	122,449	185,607	3,822	63,158 D	39.3%	59.5%	39.7%	60.3%
SAN JOAQUIN	50,498	23,403	26,536	559	3,133 D	46.3%	52.5%	46.9%	53.1%
SAN LUIS OBISPO	15,920	7,204	8,499	217	1,295 D	45.3%	53.4%	45.9%	54.1%
SAN MATEO	56,951	26,539	29,831	581	3,292 D	46.6%	52.4%	47.1%	52.9%
SANTA BARBARA	31,678	14,107	17,237	334	3,130 D	44.5%	54.4%	45.0%	55.0%
SANTA CLARA	81,496	40,100	40,449	947	349 D	49.2%	49.6%	49.8%	50.2%
SANTA CRUZ	22,486	11,453	10,683	350	770 R	50.9%	47.5%	51.7%	48.3%
SHASTA	12,733	3,909	8,662	162	4,753 D	30.7%	68.0%	31.1%	68.9%
SIERRA	1,578	511	1,057	10	546 D	32.4%	67.0%	32.6%	67.4%
SISKIYOU	12,212	4,387	7,714	111	3,327 D	35.9%	63.2%	36.3%	63.7%
SOLANO	21,323	6,081	15,054	188	8,973 D	28.5%	70.6%	28.8%	71.2%
SONOMA	32,379	15,230	16,819	330	1,589 D	47.0%	52.0%	47.5%	52.5%
STANISLAUS	31,745	14,803	16,494	448	1,691 D	46.6%	52.0%	47.3%	52.7%
SUTTER	7,345	3,089	4,195	61	1,106 D	42.1%	57.1%	42.4%	57.6%
TEHAMA	6,628	2,913	3,618	97	705 D	43.9%	54.6%	44.6%	55.4%
TRINITY	2,242	780	1,431	31	651 D	34.8%	63.8%	35.3%	64.7%
TULARE	35,971	15,414	20,129	428	4,715 D	42.9%	56.0%	43.4%	56.6%
TUOLUMNE	5,624	2,004	3,541	79	1,537 D	35.6%	63.0%	36.1%	63.9%
VENTURA	26,634	11,225	15,182	227	3,957 D	42.1%	57.0%	42.5%	57.5%
YOLO	10,854	4,373	6,380	101	2,007 D	40.3%	58.8%	40.7%	59.3%
YUBA	7,217	2,471	4,660	86	2,189 D	34.2%	64.6%	34.7%	65.3%
TOTAL	3,268,791	1,351,419	1,877,618	39,754	526,199 D	41.3%	57.4%	41.9%	58.1%

CALIFORNIA

PRESIDENT 1944

County	Total Vote	Republican	Democratic	Other	Rep.-Dem. Plurality	Total Vote Rep.	Total Vote Dem.	Major Vote Rep.	Major Vote Dem.
ALAMEDA	293,987	122,982	169,631	1,374	46,649 D	41.8%	57.7%	42.0%	58.0%
ALPINE	143	98	45		53 R	68.5%	31.5%	68.5%	31.5%
AMADOR	3,203	1,191	1,976	36	785 D	37.2%	61.7%	37.6%	62.4%
BUTTE	16,768	7,852	8,811	105	959 D	46.8%	52.5%	47.1%	52.9%
CALAVERAS	3,369	1,455	1,893	21	438 D	43.2%	56.2%	43.5%	56.5%
COLUSA	3,679	1,579	2,090	10	511 D	42.9%	56.8%	43.0%	57.0%
CONTRA COSTA	74,785	26,816	47,831	138	21,015 D	35.8%	64.0%	35.9%	64.1%
DEL NORTE	1,830	1,011	818	1	193 R	55.2%	44.7%	55.3%	44.7%
EL DORADO	5,031	1,990	3,016	25	1,026 D	39.6%	59.9%	39.8%	60.2%
FRESNO	63,862	22,668	40,769	425	18,101 D	35.5%	63.8%	35.7%	64.3%
GLENN	4,884	2,409	2,452	23	43 D	49.3%	50.2%	49.6%	50.4%
HUMBOLDT	21,260	9,127	12,083	50	2,956 D	42.9%	56.8%	43.0%	57.0%
IMPERIAL	11,112	5,979	5,085	48	894 R	53.8%	45.8%	54.0%	46.0%
INYO	3,355	1,699	1,647	9	52 R	50.6%	49.1%	50.8%	49.2%
KERN	47,161	20,730	26,205	226	5,475 D	44.0%	55.6%	44.2%	55.8%
KINGS	10,134	3,468	6,591	75	3,123 D	34.2%	65.0%	34.5%	65.5%
LAKE	3,746	2,059	1,671	16	388 R	55.0%	44.6%	55.2%	44.8%
LASSEN	5,589	1,896	3,678	15	1,782 D	34.0%	65.8%	34.0%	66.0%
LOS ANGELES	1,561,564	666,441	886,252	8,871	219,811 D	42.7%	56.8%	42.9%	57.1%
MADERA	7,190	2,865	4,276	49	1,411 D	39.8%	59.5%	40.1%	59.9%
MARIN	27,896	13,304	14,516	76	1,212 D	47.7%	52.0%	47.8%	52.2%
MARIPOSA	2,185	965	1,203	17	238 D	44.2%	55.1%	44.5%	55.5%
MENDOCINO	10,143	4,655	5,452	36	797 D	45.9%	53.8%	46.1%	53.9%
MERCED	15,779	6,518	9,192	69	2,674 D	41.3%	58.3%	41.5%	58.5%
MODOC	2,837	1,288	1,540	9	252 D	45.4%	54.3%	45.5%	54.5%
MONO	621	378	242	1	136 R	60.9%	39.0%	61.0%	39.0%
MONTEREY	26,728	12,246	14,342	140	2,096 D	45.8%	53.7%	46.1%	53.9%
NAPA	14,936	7,092	7,748	96	656 D	47.5%	51.9%	47.8%	52.2%
NEVADA	5,961	2,648	3,266	47	618 D	44.4%	54.8%	44.8%	55.2%
ORANGE	67,450	38,394	28,649	407	9,745 R	56.9%	42.5%	57.3%	42.7%
PLACER	11,409	4,196	7,149	64	2,953 D	36.8%	62.7%	36.8%	63.0%
PLUMAS	3,759	1,126	2,625	8	1,499 D	30.0%	69.8%	30.0%	70.0%
RIVERSIDE	42,953	23,168	19,439	346	3,729 R	54.4%	45.3%	54.6%	45.4%
SACRAMENTO	74,218	24,611	49,204	403	24,593 D	33.2%	66.3%	33.3%	66.7%
SAN BENITO	4,267	2,253	1,998	16	255 R	52.8%	46.8%	53.0%	47.0%
SAN BERNARDINO	73,260	34,084	38,530	646	4,446 D	46.5%	52.6%	46.9%	53.1%
SAN DIEGO	166,764	75,746	89,959	1,059	14,213 D	45.4%	53.9%	45.7%	54.3%
SAN FRANCISCO	344,731	134,163	208,609	1,959	74,446 D	38.9%	60.5%	39.1%	60.9%
SAN JOAQUIN	51,588	24,357	27,074	157	2,717 D	47.2%	52.5%	47.4%	52.6%
SAN LUIS OBISPO	15,936	7,793	8,068	75	275 D	48.9%	50.6%	49.1%	50.9%
SAN MATEO	68,342	33,590	34,594	158	1,004 D	49.1%	50.6%	49.3%	50.7%
SANTA BARBARA	29,457	13,647	15,721	89	2,074 D	46.3%	53.4%	46.5%	53.5%
SANTA CLARA	83,777	39,410	43,869	499	4,460 D	47.0%	52.4%	47.3%	52.7%
SANTA CRUZ	20,637	11,102	9,357	178	1,745 R	53.8%	45.3%	54.3%	45.7%
SHASTA	9,843	4,023	5,798	22	1,775 D	40.9%	58.9%	41.0%	59.0%
SIERRA	1,110	443	662	5	219 D	39.9%	59.6%	40.1%	59.9%
SISKIYOU	10,323	4,351	5,914	58	1,563 D	42.1%	57.3%	42.1%	57.9%
SOLANO	34,801	10,361	24,335	105	13,974 D	29.8%	69.9%	29.9%	70.1%
SONOMA	32,369	10,309	15,949	111	3,360 D	50.4%	49.3%	50.6%	49.4%
STANISLAUS	30,271	14,297	15,537	437	1,240 D	47.2%	51.3%	47.9%	52.1%
SUTTER	6,223	3,111	3,083	29	28 R	50.0%	49.5%	50.2%	49.8%
TEHAMA	6,074	2,903	3,130	41	227 D	47.8%	51.5%	48.1%	51.9%
TRINITY	1,343	567	770	6	203 D	42.2%	57.3%	42.4%	57.6%
TULARE	32,464	16,005	16,221	238	216 D	49.3%	50.0%	49.7%	50.3%
TUOLUMNE	4,462	1,864	2,566	32	702 D	41.8%	57.5%	42.1%	57.9%
VENTURA	27,544	11,071	16,342	131	5,271 D	40.2%	59.3%	40.4%	59.6%
YOLO	10,116	4,233	5,837	46	1,604 D	41.8%	57.7%	41.8%	58.0%
YUBA	5,646	2,379	3,254	13	875 D	42.1%	57.6%	42.2%	57.8%
TOTAL	3,520,875	1,512,965	1,988,564	19,346	475,599 D	43.0%	56.5%	43.2%	56.8%

PRESIDENT 1948

County	Total Vote	Republican	Democratic	Other	Rep.-Dem. Plurality	Total Vote Rep.	Total Vote Dem.	Major Vote Rep.	Major Vote Dem.
ALAMEDA	323,331	150,588	154,549	18,194	3,961 D	46.6%	47.8%	49.4%	50.6%
ALPINE	138	106	25	7	81 R	76.8%	18.1%	80.9%	19.1%
AMADOR	4,063	1,578	2,334	151	756 D	38.8%	57.4%	40.3%	59.7%
BUTTE	22,181	10,948	10,133	1,100	815 D	49.4%	45.7%	51.9%	48.1%
CALAVERAS	4,037	1,888	1,995	154	107 D	46.8%	49.4%	48.6%	51.4%
COLUSA	3,901	1,803	2,020	78	217 D	46.2%	51.8%	47.2%	52.8%
CONTRA COSTA	91,376	36,998	50,277	4,141	13,319 D	40.4%	55.0%	42.4%	57.6%
DEL NORTE	2,840	1,541	1,172	127	369 R	54.3%	41.3%	56.8%	43.2%
EL DORADO	6,724	2,894	3,493	337	599 D	43.0%	51.9%	45.3%	54.7%
FRESNO	81,665	30,379	47,762	3,524	17,383 D	37.2%	58.5%	38.9%	61.1%
GLENN	5,528	2,819	2,578	131	241 R	51.0%	46.6%	52.2%	47.8%
HUMBOLDT	23,266	10,979	11,268	1,019	289 D	47.2%	48.4%	49.4%	50.6%
IMPERIAL	11,610	6,217	5,301	292	916 R	52.5%	44.9%	54.0%	46.0%
INYO	3,827	2,135	1,539	153	596 R	55.8%	40.2%	58.1%	41.9%
KERN	58,611	24,464	33,029	1,318	8,565 D	41.6%	56.2%	42.6%	57.4%
KINGS	11,521	4,289	6,909	323	2,620 D	37.2%	60.0%	38.3%	61.7%
LAKE	5,333	3,054	1,999	280	1,055 R	57.3%	37.5%	60.4%	39.6%
LASSEN	5,773	1,960	3,632	181	1,672 D	34.0%	62.9%	35.1%	64.9%
LOS ANGELES	1,729,082	804,232	812,690	112,160	8,458 D	46.5%	47.0%	49.7%	50.3%
MADERA	8,982	3,416	5,226	340	1,810 D	38.0%	58.2%	39.5%	60.5%
MARIN	32,855	18,747	12,540	1,568	6,207 R	57.1%	38.2%	59.9%	40.1%
MARIPOSA	2,467	1,378	983	106	395 R	55.9%	39.8%	58.4%	41.6%
MENDOCINO	12,603	6,368	5,553	682	815 R	50.5%	44.1%	53.4%	46.6%
MERCED	18,124	7,321	9,959	444	2,238 D	40.5%	54.9%	53.7%	46.3%
MODOC	3,180	1,480	1,607	93	127 D	46.5%	50.5%	47.9%	52.1%
MONO	835	541	255	39	286 R	64.8%	30.5%	68.0%	32.0%
MONTEREY	34,063	17,233	15,704	1,126	1,529 R	50.6%	46.1%	52.3%	47.7%
NAPA	16,516	8,724	7,207	585	1,517 R	52.3%	43.6%	54.8%	45.2%
NEVADA	8,326	3,917	3,914	495	3 R	47.0%	47.0%	50.0%	50.0%
ORANGE	79,814	48,587	29,018	2,209	19,569 R	60.9%	36.4%	62.6%	37.4%
PLACER	15,109	5,570	8,837	702	3,267 D	36.9%	58.5%	38.7%	61.3%
PLUMAS	5,058	1,657	3,125	276	1,468 D	32.8%	61.8%	34.7%	65.3%
RIVERSIDE	57,864	32,059	23,305	2,350	8,904 R	55.7%	40.3%	57.9%	42.0%
SACRAMENTO	92,842	35,074	54,197	3,571	19,123 D	37.8%	58.4%	39.3%	60.7%
SAN BENITO	4,987	2,775	2,096	116	679 R	55.6%	42.0%	57.0%	43.0%
SAN BERNARDINO	95,838	46,552	45,691	3,577	879 R	48.6%	47.7%	49.5%	50.5%
SAN DIEGO	205,459	101,552	98,217	5,690	3,335 R	50.5%	47.8%	50.8%	49.2%
SAN FRANCISCO	350,709	160,135	167,726	22,848	7,591 D	45.7%	47.8%	48.8%	51.2%
SAN JOAQUIN	59,361	29,135	27,908	2,318	1,227 R	49.1%	47.0%	51.1%	48.9%
SAN LUIS OBISPO	19,304	10,325	8,135	844	2,190 R	53.5%	42.1%	55.9%	44.1%
SAN MATEO	86,272	48,909	34,215	3,148	14,694 R	56.7%	39.7%	58.8%	41.2%
SANTA BARBARA	34,400	19,950	13,085	1,317	6,913 R	58.1%	38.0%	60.4%	39.6%
SANTA CLARA	99,502	52,982	41,905	4,615	11,077 R	53.2%	42.1%	55.8%	44.2%
SANTA CRUZ	26,690	15,395	9,862	1,433	5,533 R	57.7%	37.0%	61.0%	39.0%
SHASTA	12,623	5,010	7,177	436	2,167 D	39.7%	56.9%	41.1%	58.9%
SIERRA	1,258	546	660	52	114 D	43.4%	52.5%	45.3%	54.7%
SISKIYOU	12,498	5,315	6,749	434	1,434 D	42.5%	54.0%	44.1%	55.9%
SOLANO	36,624	12,345	23,257	1,022	10,912 D	33.7%	63.5%	34.7%	65.3%
SONOMA	39,984	22,077	16,026	1,881	6,051 R	55.2%	40.1%	57.9%	42.1%
STANISLAUS	38,371	18,564	18,350	1,457	214 R	48.4%	47.8%	50.3%	49.7%
SUTTER	7,458	3,913	3,362	183	551 R	52.5%	45.1%	53.8%	46.2%
TEHAMA	6,530	3,348	2,920	262	428 R	51.3%	44.7%	53.4%	46.6%
TRINITY	2,163	975	1,053	135	78 D	45.1%	48.7%	48.1%	51.9%
TULARE	39,192	18,414	19,681	1,097	1,267 D	47.0%	50.2%	48.3%	51.7%
TUOLUMNE	5,474	2,639	2,561	274	78 R	48.2%	46.8%	50.8%	49.2%
VENTURA	33,049	13,930	18,100	1,019	4,170 D	42.1%	54.8%	43.5%	56.5%
YOLO	12,684	5,560	6,655	469	1,095 D	43.8%	52.5%	45.5%	54.5%
YUBA	7,263	3,403	3,608	252	205 D	46.9%	49.7%	48.5%	51.5%
TOTAL	4,021,538	1,895,269	1,913,134	213,135	17,865 D	47.1%	47.6%	49.8%	50.2%

CALIFORNIA

PRESIDENT 1952

County	Total Vote	Republican	Democratic	Other	Rep.-Dem. Plurality	Tot% Rep.	Tot% Dem.	Maj% Rep.	Maj% Dem.
ALAMEDA	369,776	192,941	173,853	2,982	19,088 R	52.2%	47.0%	52.6%	47.4%
ALPINE	148	129	19		110 R	87.2%	12.8%	87.2%	12.8%
AMADOR	4,416	2,303	2,070	43	233 R	52.2%	46.9%	52.7%	47.3%
BUTTE	29,133	18,390	10,491	252	7,899 R	63.1%	36.0%	63.7%	36.3%
CALAVERAS	4,824	2,942	1,838	44	1,104 R	61.0%	38.1%	61.5%	38.5%
COLUSA	4,513	2,678	1,818	17	860 R	59.3%	40.3%	59.6%	40.4%
CONTRA COSTA	137,281	67,453	69,060	768	1,607 D	49.1%	50.3%	49.4%	50.6%
DEL NORTE	4,384	2,757	1,578	49	1,179 R	62.9%	36.0%	63.6%	36.4%
EL DORADO	8,073	4,828	3,152	93	1,676 R	59.8%	39.0%	60.5%	39.5%
FRESNO	107,376	52,025	54,541	810	2,516 D	48.5%	50.8%	48.8%	51.2%
GLENN	6,600	4,224	2,342	34	1,882 R	64.0%	35.5%	64.3%	35.7%
HUMBOLDT	31,687	18,913	12,490	284	6,423 R	59.7%	39.4%	60.2%	39.8%
IMPERIAL	16,903	10,462	6,333	108	4,129 R	61.9%	37.5%	62.3%	37.7%
INYO	5,162	3,549	1,585	28	1,964 R	68.8%	30.7%	69.1%	30.9%
KERN	81,332	44,600	36,151	581	8,449 R	54.8%	44.4%	55.2%	44.8%
KINGS	15,083	7,336	7,639	108	303 D	48.6%	50.6%	49.0%	51.0%
LAKE	6,087	4,113	1,911	63	2,202 R	67.6%	31.4%	68.3%	31.7%
LASSEN	7,262	3,119	4,104	39	985 D	42.9%	56.5%	43.2%	56.8%
LOS ANGELES	2,201,212	1,226,971	950,093	24,148	276,878 R	55.7%	43.2%	56.4%	43.6%
MADERA	12,091	5,933	6,042	116	109 D	49.1%	50.0%	49.5%	50.5%
MARIN	44,278	29,574	14,236	468	15,333 R	56.3%	32.2%	67.5%	32.5%
MARIPOSA	2,946	1,941	969	36	972 R	65.9%	32.9%	66.7%	33.3%
MENDOCINO	17,157	10,388	6,580	189	3,808 R	60.5%	38.4%	61.2%	38.8%
MERCED	24,395	12,865	11,316	214	1,549 R	52.7%	46.4%	53.2%	46.8%
MODOC	4,047	2,475	1,548	24	927 R	61.2%	38.3%	61.5%	38.5%
MONO	982	754	220	8	534 R	76.3%	22.4%	77.4%	22.6%
MONTEREY	46,451	28,786	17,411	254	11,375 R	62.0%	37.5%	62.3%	37.7%
NAPA	21,747	13,273	8,316	158	4,957 R	61.0%	38.2%	61.5%	38.5%
NEVADA	9,818	6,252	3,476	90	2,776 R	63.7%	35.4%	64.3%	35.7%
ORANGE	110,904	77,548	32,530	826	45,018 R	69.9%	29.3%	70.4%	29.6%
PLACER	18,153	9,104	8,887	162	217 R	50.2%	49.0%	50.6%	49.4%
PLUMAS	5,721	2,491	3,174	56	683 D	43.5%	55.5%	44.0%	56.0%
RIVERSIDE	75,641	48,874	26,016	759	22,858 R	64.6%	34.4%	65.2%	34.7%
SACRAMENTO	131,641	63,788	67,053	800	3,265 D	48.5%	50.9%	48.8%	51.2%
SAN BENITO	5,415	3,503	1,891	21	1,612 R	64.7%	34.9%	64.9%	35.1%
SAN BERNARDINO	129,631	73,921	54,615	1,095	19,306 R	57.0%	42.1%	57.5%	42.5%
SAN DIEGO	278,751	175,281	101,880	1,590	73,401 R	62.9%	36.5%	63.2%	36.8%
SAN FRANCISCO	359,949	188,531	167,282	4,136	21,249 R	52.4%	46.5%	53.0%	47.0%
SAN JOAQUIN	79,107	44,033	34,510	564	9,523 R	55.7%	43.6%	56.1%	43.9%
SAN LUIS OBISPO	25,691	16,733	8,761	197	7,972 R	65.1%	34.1%	65.6%	34.4%
SAN MATEO	139,222	87,780	50,802	640	36,978 R	63.1%	36.5%	63.3%	36.7%
SANTA BARBARA	44,943	29,984	14,793	166	15,191 R	66.7%	32.9%	67.0%	33.0%
SANTA CLARA	147,807	87,554	59,350	903	28,204 R	59.2%	40.2%	59.6%	40.4%
SANTA CRUZ	34,361	22,910	11,080	371	11,830 R	66.7%	32.2%	67.4%	32.6%
SHASTA	17,013	9,507	7,386	120	2,121 R	55.9%	43.4%	56.3%	43.7%
SIERRA	1,363	723	632	8	91 R	53.0%	46.4%	53.4%	46.6%
SISKIYOU	14,684	8,195	6,346	143	1,849 R	55.8%	43.2%	56.4%	43.6%
SOLANO	44,238	18,456	25,569	213	7,113 D	41.7%	57.8%	41.9%	58.1%
SONOMA	51,717	34,088	17,046	583	17,042 R	65.9%	33.0%	66.7%	33.3%
STANISLAUS	50,913	28,090	22,271	552	5,819 R	55.2%	43.7%	55.8%	44.2%
SUTTER	10,071	6,780	3,250	41	3,530 R	67.3%	32.3%	67.6%	32.4%
TEHAMA	8,465	5,436	2,993	76	2,483 R	64.2%	34.9%	64.6%	35.3%
TRINITY	2,674	1,526	1,120	28	406 R	57.1%	41.9%	57.7%	42.3%
TULARE	50,827	28,602	21,603	422	7,199 R	56.6%	42.5%	57.1%	42.9%
TUOLUMNE	6,402	3,753	2,593	56	1,160 R	58.6%	40.5%	59.1%	40.9%
VENTURA	45,137	23,392	21,489	256	1,903 R	51.8%	47.6%	52.1%	47.9%
YOLO	16,999	8,967	7,895	137	1,072 R	52.8%	46.4%	53.2%	46.4%
YUBA	9,237	5,586	3,589	62	1,997 R	60.5%	38.9%	60.9%	39.1%
TOTAL	5,141,849	2,897,310	2,197,548	46,991	699,762 R	56.3%	42.7%	56.9%	43.1%

PRESIDENT 1956

County	Total Vote	Republican	Democratic	Other	Rep.-Dem. Plurality	Tot% Rep.	Tot% Dem.	Maj% Rep.	Maj% Dem.
ALAMEDA	368,131	192,911	174,033	1,187	18,878 R	52.4%	47.3%	52.6%	47.4%
ALPINE	143	114	29		85 R	79.7%	20.3%	79.7%	20.3%
AMADOR	4,325	2,126	2,181	18	55 D	49.2%	50.4%	49.4%	50.6%
BUTTE	31,462	18,382	12,933	147	5,449 R	58.4%	41.1%	58.7%	41.3%
CALAVERAS	4,909	2,843	2,049	17	794 R	57.9%	41.7%	58.1%	41.9%
COLUSA	4,648	2,474	2,171	3	303 R	53.2%	46.7%	53.3%	46.7%
CONTRA COSTA	147,051	74,971	71,733	347	3,238 R	51.0%	48.8%	51.1%	48.9%
DEL NORTE	5,487	2,918	2,552	17	366 R	53.2%	46.5%	53.8%	46.2%
EL DORADO	8,607	4,613	3,957	37	656 R	53.6%	46.0%	53.8%	46.2%
FRESNO	119,115	51,611	67,234	270	15,623 D	43.3%	56.4%	43.4%	56.6%
GLENN	6,665	3,463	3,192	10	271 R	52.0%	47.9%	52.0%	48.0%
HUMBOLDT	36,177	19,019	17,025	133	1,994 R	52.6%	47.1%	52.8%	47.2%
IMPERIAL	18,781	10,526	8,197	58	2,329 R	56.0%	43.6%	56.2%	43.8%
INYO	5,324	3,524	1,782	18	1,742 R	66.2%	33.5%	66.4%	33.6%
KERN	90,875	46,220	43,533	322	2,687 R	51.3%	48.3%	51.5%	48.5%
KINGS	14,652	6,195	8,417	40	2,222 D	42.3%	57.4%	42.4%	57.6%
LAKE	6,282	4,073	2,185	24	1,888 R	64.8%	34.8%	65.1%	34.9%
LASSEN	5,963	2,533	3,412	18	879 D	42.5%	57.2%	42.6%	57.4%
LOS ANGELES	2,275,424	1,260,206	1,007,887	7,331	252,319 R	55.4%	44.3%	55.6%	44.4%
MADERA	12,439	5,239	7,162	38	1,923 D	42.1%	57.6%	42.2%	57.8%
MARIN	51,244	33,792	17,301	151	16,491 R	65.9%	33.8%	66.1%	33.9%
MARIPOSA	2,615	1,577	1,031	7	546 R	60.3%	39.4%	60.5%	39.5%
MENDOCINO	18,137	10,327	7,767	43	2,560 R	56.9%	42.8%	57.1%	42.9%
MERCED	24,852	11,430	13,366	56	1,936 D	46.0%	53.8%	46.1%	53.9%
MODOC	3,723	1,981	1,729	13	252 R	53.2%	46.4%	53.4%	46.6%
MONO	912	673	237	2	436 R	73.8%	26.0%	74.0%	26.0%
MONTEREY	49,573	29,514	19,932	127	9,582 R	59.5%	40.3%	59.7%	40.3%
NAPA	24,333	13,610	10,623	100	2,987 R	55.9%	43.7%	56.2%	43.8%
NEVADA	9,173	5,475	3,667	31	1,808 R	59.7%	40.0%	59.9%	40.1%
ORANGE	169,879	113,510	54,895	1,474	58,615 R	66.8%	32.3%	67.4%	32.6%
PLACER	19,739	9,059	10,611	69	1,552 D	45.9%	53.8%	46.1%	53.9%
PLUMAS	5,415	2,267	3,127	21	860 D	41.9%	57.7%	42.5%	57.5%
RIVERSIDE	91,329	56,766	34,098	465	22,668 R	62.2%	37.3%	62.5%	37.5%
SACRAMENTO	150,080	67,686	82,134	260	14,448 D	45.1%	54.7%	45.2%	54.8%
SAN BENITO	5,463	3,252	2,201	10	1,051 R	59.5%	40.3%	59.6%	40.4%
SAN BERNARDINO	151,650	86,263	64,946	441	21,317 R	56.9%	42.8%	57.0%	43.0%
SAN DIEGO	303,576	195,742	106,716	1,118	89,026 R	64.5%	35.2%	64.7%	35.3%
SAN FRANCISCO	336,998	173,648	161,766	1,584	11,882 R	51.5%	48.0%	51.8%	48.2%
SAN JOAQUIN	81,600	44,491	36,941	168	7,550 R	54.5%	45.3%	54.6%	45.4%
SAN LUIS OBISPO	27,748	16,223	11,407	118	4,816 R	58.5%	41.1%	58.7%	41.3%
SAN MATEO	163,903	100,049	63,637	217	36,412 R	61.0%	38.8%	61.1%	38.9%
SANTA BARBARA	48,484	31,294	16,925	265	14,369 R	64.5%	34.9%	64.5%	35.1%
SANTA CLARA	178,818	105,657	72,528	633	33,129 R	59.1%	40.6%	59.3%	40.7%
SANTA CRUZ	34,774	22,109	12,574	93	9,535 R	63.6%	36.2%	63.7%	36.3%
SHASTA	20,149	8,833	11,239	77	2,406 D	43.8%	55.8%	44.0%	56.0%
SIERRA	1,262	638	620	4	18 R	50.6%	49.1%	50.7%	49.3%
SISKIYOU	13,741	6,841	6,837	63	4 R	49.8%	49.8%	50.0%	50.0%
SOLANO	42,663	17,865	24,903	95	7,038 D	41.7%	58.1%	41.8%	58.2%
SONOMA	54,361	33,659	20,616	86	13,043 R	61.9%	37.9%	62.0%	38.0%
STANISLAUS	54,927	26,695	28,040	192	1,345 D	48.6%	51.0%	48.8%	51.2%
SUTTER	10,077	6,327	3,673	77	2,654 R	62.8%	36.4%	63.3%	36.7%
TEHAMA	9,042	4,866	4,143	33	723 R	53.8%	45.8%	54.0%	46.0%
TRINITY	2,870	1,447	1,406	17	41 R	50.4%	49.0%	50.7%	49.3%
TULARE	49,618	26,051	23,407	160	2,644 R	52.5%	47.2%	52.7%	47.3%
TUOLUMNE	6,943	3,619	3,310	14	309 R	52.1%	47.7%	52.2%	47.8%
VENTURA	52,767	26,342	26,276	149	66 R	49.9%	49.8%	50.1%	49.9%
YOLO	19,479	9,347	10,075	57	728 D	48.0%	51.7%	48.1%	51.9%
YUBA	8,576	4,782	3,767	27	1,015 R	55.8%	43.9%	55.9%	44.1%
TOTAL	5,466,355	3,027,668	2,420,135	18,552	607,533 R	55.4%	44.3%	55.6%	44.4%

CALIFORNIA

PRESIDENT 1960

County	Total Vote	Republican	Democratic	Other	Rep.-Dem. Plurality		% Total Vote Rep.	% Total Vote Dem.	% Major Vote Rep.	% Major Vote Dem.
ALAMEDA	402,000	183,354	217,172	1,474	33,818	D	45.6	54.0	45.8	54.2
ALPINE	172	132	40		92	R	76.7	23.3	76.7	23.3
AMADOR	4,887	2,175	2,690	22	515	D	44.5	55.0	44.7	55.3
BUTTE	36,175	20,638	15,163	174	5,475	R	57.0	41.9	57.9	42.1
CALAVERAS	5,361	2,820	2,509	32	311	R	52.6	46.8	52.9	47.1
COLUSA	4,861	2,497	2,348	16	149	R	51.4	48.3	51.5	48.5
CONTRA COSTA	177,123	82,922	93,622	579	10,700	D	46.8	52.9	47.0	53.0
DEL NORTE	6,294	3,024	3,225	45	201	D	48.0	51.2	48.4	51.6
EL DORADO	12,337	6,065	6,175	97	110	D	49.2	50.0	49.6	50.4
FRESNO	130,702	57,930	72,164	608	14,234	D	44.3	55.2	44.5	55.5
GLENN	7,356	3,911	3,410	35	501	R	53.2	46.4	53.4	46.6
HUMBOLDT	38,691	18,074	20,391	226	2,317	D	46.7	52.7	47.0	53.0
IMPERIAL	19,806	10,606	9,119	81	1,487	R	53.5	46.2	53.8	46.2
INYO	5,420	2,962	2,443	15	519	R	54.6	45.1	54.8	45.2
KERN	104,705	52,800	51,440	465	1,360	R	50.4	49.1	50.7	49.3
KINGS	16,522	6,991	9,439	92	2,448	D	42.3	57.1	42.6	57.4
LAKE	7,109	4,176	2,897	36	1,279	R	58.7	40.8	59.0	41.0
LASSEN	5,877	2,365	3,472	40	1,107	D	40.2	59.1	40.5	59.5
LOS ANGELES	2,634,499	1,302,661	1,323,818	8,020	21,157	D	49.4	50.2	49.6	50.4
MADERA	14,057	5,869	8,126	62	2,257	D	41.8	57.8	41.9	58.1
MARIN	65,665	37,620	27,888	157	9,732	R	57.3	42.5	57.4	42.6
MARIPOSA	2,963	1,599	1,338	26	261	R	54.0	45.4	54.4	45.6
MENDOCINO	18,871	9,301	9,476	94	175	D	49.3	50.2	49.5	50.5
MERCED	27,646	11,990	15,545	111	3,555	D	43.4	56.2	43.6	56.4
MODOC	3,550	1,839	1,691	20	148	R	51.8	47.6	52.1	47.9
MONO	1,375	912	457	6	455	R	66.3	33.2	66.6	33.4
MONTEREY	59,413	33,428	25,805	180	7,623	R	56.3	43.4	56.4	43.6
NAPA	28,778	15,125	13,499	154	1,626	R	52.6	46.9	52.8	47.2
NEVADA	10,141	5,419	4,633	89	786	R	53.4	45.7	53.9	46.1
ORANGE	287,599	174,891	112,007	701	62,884	R	60.8	38.9	61.0	39.0
PLACER	23,863	10,439	13,304	120	2,865	D	43.7	55.8	44.0	56.0
PLUMAS	5,378	2,015	3,333	30	1,318	D	37.5	62.0	37.7	62.3
RIVERSIDE	117,276	65,855	50,877	544	14,978	R	56.2	43.4	56.4	43.6
SACRAMENTO	194,756	84,252	109,695	809	25,443	D	43.3	56.3	43.4	56.6
SAN BENITO	5,945	3,056	2,876	13	180	R	51.4	48.4	51.5	48.5
SAN BERNARDINO	191,313	99,481	90,888	944	8,593	R	52.0	47.5	52.3	47.7
SAN DIEGO	395,421	223,056	171,259	1,106	51,797	R	56.4	43.3	56.6	43.4
SAN FRANCISCO	342,219	143,001	197,734	1,484	54,733	D	41.8	57.8	42.0	58.0
SAN JOAQUIN	91,657	48,441	42,855	361	5,586	R	52.9	46.9	53.1	46.9
SAN LUIS OBISPO	33,055	17,862	14,975	218	2,887	R	54.0	45.3	54.4	45.6
SAN MATEO	202,252	104,570	97,154	528	7,416	R	51.7	48.0	51.8	48.2
SANTA BARBARA	68,402	38,605	29,609	188	8,996	R	56.7	43.0	56.9	43.1
SANTA CLARA	250,092	131,735	117,667	690	14,068	R	52.7	47.0	52.8	47.2
SANTA CRUZ	41,704	24,858	16,659	187	8,199	R	59.6	39.9	59.9	40.1
SHASTA	24,301	9,462	14,691	148	5,229	D	38.9	60.5	39.2	60.8
SIERRA	1,231	576	647	8	71	D	46.8	52.6	47.1	52.9
SISKIYOU	14,620	6,279	8,245	96	1,966	D	42.9	56.4	43.2	56.4
SOLANO	45,869	18,751	26,977	141	8,226	D	40.9	58.8	41.0	59.0
SONOMA	64,032	34,641	29,147	244	5,494	R	54.1	45.5	54.4	45.7
STANISLAUS	60,890	30,213	30,302	375	89	D	49.6	49.8	49.9	50.1
SUTTER	11,954	7,520	4,379	55	3,141	R	62.9	36.6	63.2	36.8
TEHAMA	11,052	5,520	5,483	47	39	R	50.0	49.6	50.2	49.8
TRINITY	3,698	1,418	2,262	18	844	D	38.3	61.2	38.5	61.5
TULARE	54,582	29,456	24,887	239	4,569	R	54.0	45.6	54.2	45.8
TUOLUMNE	7,516	3,691	3,781	44	90	D	49.1	50.3	49.4	50.6
VENTURA	70,723	35,074	35,334	315	260	D	49.6	50.0	49.8	50.2
YOLO	22,589	10,104	12,395	90	2,291	D	44.7	54.9	44.9	55.1
YUBA	10,233	5,293	4,882	58	411	R	51.7	47.7	52.0	48.0
TOTAL	6,506,578	3,259,722	3,224,099	22,757	35,623	R	50.1	49.6	50.3	49.7

PRESIDENT 1964

County	Total Vote	Republican	Democratic	Other	Rep.-Dem. Plurality		% Total Vote Rep.	% Total Vote Dem.	% Major Vote Rep.	% Major Vote Dem.
ALAMEDA	427,340	142,998	283,833	509	140,835	D	33.5	66.4	33.5	66.5
ALPINE	215	124	91		33	R	57.7	42.3	57.7	42.3
AMADOR	5,098	1,682	3,410	6	1,728	D	33.0	66.9	33.0	67.0
BUTTE	40,419	19,574	20,831	14	1,257	D	48.4	51.5	48.4	51.6
CALAVERAS	5,397	2,244	3,145	8	901	D	41.6	58.3	41.6	58.4
COLUSA	4,606	1,811	2,790	5	979	D	39.3	60.6	39.4	60.6
CONTRA COSTA	178,245	65,011	113,071	163	48,060	D	36.5	63.4	36.5	63.5
DEL NORTE	5,727	2,075	3,652		1,577	D	36.2	63.8	36.2	63.8
EL DORADO	14,610	5,775	8,810	25	3,035	D	39.5	60.3	39.6	60.4
FRESNO	136,308	46,792	89,375	141	42,583	D	34.3	65.6	34.4	65.6
GLENN	7,290	3,351	3,937	2	586	D	46.0	54.0	46.0	54.0
HUMBOLDT	38,499	12,909	25,515	75	12,606	D	33.5	66.3	33.5	66.4
IMPERIAL	21,492	10,330	11,143	19	813	D	48.1	51.8	48.1	51.9
INYO	5,915	2,751	3,161	3	410	D	46.5	53.4	46.5	53.5
KERN	109,308	45,014	64,174	120	19,160	D	41.2	58.7	41.2	58.8
KINGS	18,840	5,753	13,073	14	7,320	D	30.5	69.4	30.6	69.4
LAKE	8,302	3,616	4,680	6	1,064	D	43.6	56.4	43.6	56.4
LASSEN	6,201	2,124	4,072	5	1,948	D	34.3	65.7	34.3	65.7
LOS ANGELES	2,730,918	1,161,067	1,566,300	1,551	407,233	D	42.5	57.3	42.5	57.5
MADERA	13,862	4,461	9,391	10	4,930	D	32.2	67.7	32.2	67.8
MARIN	75,364	28,682	46,462	220	17,780	D	38.1	61.7	38.2	61.8
MARIPOSA	2,968	1,264	1,704		440	D	42.6	57.4	42.6	57.4
MENDOCINO	18,227	6,324	11,869	36	5,547	D	34.7	65.1	34.8	65.2
MERCED	28,269	8,814	19,431	24	10,617	D	31.2	68.7	31.2	68.8
MODOC	3,358	1,386	1,972		586	D	41.3	58.7	41.3	58.7
MONO	1,516	850	666		184	R	56.1	43.9	56.1	43.9
MONTEREY	64,844	24,579	40,093	172	15,514	D	37.9	61.8	38.0	62.0
NAPA	31,210	11,567	19,580	63	8,013	D	37.1	62.7	37.1	62.9
NEVADA	11,318	4,899	6,397	22	1,498	D	43.3	56.5	43.4	56.7
ORANGE	401,165	224,196	176,539	430	47,657	R	55.9	44.0	55.9	44.1
PLACER	27,676	9,389	18,256	31	8,867	D	34.0	66.0	34.0	66.0
PLUMAS	5,713	1,686	4,019	8	2,333	D	29.5	70.4	29.5	70.4
RIVERSIDE	141,788	61,165	80,528	95	19,363	D	43.1	56.8	43.2	56.8
SACRAMENTO	323,908	92,994	230,758	156	137,764	D	28.7	71.2	28.7	71.3
SAN BENITO	6,237	2,444	3,779	14	1,335	D	39.2	60.6	39.3	60.7
SAN BERNARDINO	215,400	92,145	123,012	243	30,867	D	42.8	57.1	42.8	57.2
SAN DIEGO	426,286	214,445	211,808	33	2,637	R	50.3	49.7	50.3	49.7
SAN FRANCISCO	320,527	117,420	202,249	858	84,829	D	36.6	63.1	36.7	63.3
SAN JOAQUIN	95,586	36,546	59,210	83	22,664	D	38.2	61.8	38.2	61.8
SAN LUIS OBISPO	37,186	14,906	22,252	28	7,346	D	40.1	59.9	40.1	59.9
SAN MATEO	219,191	77,916	140,978	297	63,062	D	35.5	64.3	35.5	64.4
SANTA BARBARA	86,486	38,020	48,381	85	10,361	D	44.0	55.9	44.0	56.0
SANTA CLARA	320,527	117,836	202,714	858	84,878	D	36.6	63.3	36.7	63.3
SANTA CRUZ	45,644	18,836	26,714	94	7,878	D	41.3	58.5	41.4	58.6
SHASTA	28,350	9,178	19,142	30	9,964	D	32.4	67.5	32.4	67.6
SIERRA	1,241	413	828		415	D	33.3	66.7	33.3	66.7
SISKIYOU	14,335	5,186	9,126	23	3,940	D	36.2	63.6	36.2	63.7
SOLANO	50,240	15,263	34,930	47	19,667	D	30.4	69.5	30.4	69.6
SONOMA	72,136	27,677	44,354	105	16,677	D	38.4	61.5	38.4	61.6
STANISLAUS	65,128	21,973	43,078	77	21,105	D	33.7	66.1	33.8	66.2
SUTTER	14,044	7,241	6,787	16	454	R	51.6	48.3	51.6	48.4
TEHAMA	11,467	4,529	6,928	10	2,399	D	39.5	60.4	39.5	60.5
TRINITY	3,439	1,252	2,175	12	923	D	36.4	63.2	36.5	63.5
TULARE	56,552	22,527	33,974	51	11,447	D	39.9	60.0	39.9	60.1
TUOLUMNE	7,820	2,861	4,939	20	2,078	D	36.6	63.1	36.7	63.3
VENTURA	98,238	40,264	57,805	169	17,541	D	41.0	58.8	41.1	58.9
YOLO	26,274	7,976	18,266	32	10,290	D	30.4	69.5	30.4	69.6
YUBA	11,739	4,964	6,766	9	1,802	D	42.3	57.6	42.3	57.7
TOTAL	7,057,586	2,879,108	4,171,877	6,601	1,292,769	D	40.8	59.1	40.8	59.2

CALIFORNIA

OTHER VOTE COMPOSITION:

1920   64,076 Socialist; 25,204 Prohibition.
1924   424,649 Progressive; 18,365 Prohibition.
1928   19,595 Socialist; 373 scattered.
1932   63,299 Socialist; 20,637 Prohibition; 9,827 Liberty; 1,023 Communist; 127 scattered.
1936   12,917 Prohibition; 11,331 Socialist; 10,877 Communist; 490 scattered.

1940   16,506 Socialist; 13,586 Communist; 9,400 Prohibition; 262 scattered.
1944   14,770 Prohibition; 2,515 Socialist; 180 Socialist Labor; 1,881 scattered.
1948   190,381 Progressive; 16,926 Prohibition; 3,459 Socialist; 1,228 States Rights; 195 Socialist Labor; 133 Socialist Workers; 813 scattered.
1952   24,106 Progressive; 15,653 Prohibition; 3,504 Christian Nationalist-Constitution (MacArthur); 273 Socialist Labor; 206 Socialist; 3,249 scattered.
1956   11,119 Prohibition; 6,087 States Rights; 300 Socialist Labor; 123 Socialist, 96 Socialist Workers; 8 Christian Nationalist; 819 scattered.

1960   21,706 Prohibition; 1,051 Socialist Labor.
1964   489 Socialist Labor; 378 Socialist Workers; 305 Prohibition; 19 Universal; 5,410 scattered.

SPECIAL CASES:

1924   Progressive candidates carried several counties and ran second in almost all others.
1952   MacArthur total includes 3,326 Christian Nationalist and 178 Constitution votes.

COLORADO

PRESIDENT 1920

County	Total Vote	Republican	Democratic	Other	Rep.-Dem. Plurality	%Total Rep.	%Total Dem.	%Major Rep.	%Major Dem.
ADAMS	4,360	2,510	1,633	217	877 R	57.6%	37.5%	60.6%	39.4%
ALAMOSA	2,084	1,081	949	54	132 R	51.9%	45.5%	53.3%	46.7%
ARAPAHOE	4,900	2,930	1,752	218	1,178 R	59.8%	35.8%	62.6%	37.4%
ARCHULETA	1,109	700	379	30	321 R	63.1%	34.2%	64.9%	35.1%
BACA	2,555	1,615	695	245	920 R	63.2%	27.2%	69.9%	30.1%
BENT	2,611	1,584	937	90	647 R	60.7%	35.9%	62.8%	37.2%
BOULDER	11,148	6,456	4,200	492	2,256 R	57.9%	37.7%	60.6%	39.4%
CHAFFEE	2,837	1,501	1,233	103	268 R	52.9%	43.5%	54.9%	45.1%
CHEYENNE	1,301	840	358	103	482 R	64.6%	27.5%	70.1%	29.9%
CLEAR CREEK	1,312	765	518	29	247 R	58.3%	39.5%	59.6%	40.4%
CONEJOS	2,512	1,595	886	31	709 R	63.5%	35.3%	64.3%	35.7%
COSTILLA	1,571	778	750	43	28 R	49.5%	47.7%	50.9%	49.1%
CROWLEY	2,223	1,348	792	83	556 R	60.6%	35.6%	63.0%	37.0%
CUSTER	885	560	289	36	271 R	63.3%	32.7%	66.0%	34.0%
DELTA	4,603	2,596	1,750	257	846 R	56.4%	38.0%	59.7%	40.3%
DENVER	70,258	43,581	22,839	3,838	20,742 R	62.0%	32.5%	65.6%	34.4%
DOLORES	408	197	153	58	44 R	48.3%	37.5%	56.3%	43.7%
DOUGLAS	1,544	948	561	35	387 R	61.4%	36.3%	62.8%	37.2%
EAGLE	1,549	854	649	46	205 R	55.1%	41.9%	56.8%	43.2%
ELBERT	2,493	1,654	673	166	981 R	66.3%	27.0%	71.1%	28.9%
EL PASO	15,189	9,535	5,073	581	4,462 R	62.8%	33.4%	65.3%	34.7%
FREMONT	5,676	3,027	2,339	310	688 R	53.3%	41.2%	56.4%	43.6%
GARFIELD	3,520	1,912	1,489	119	423 R	54.3%	42.3%	56.2%	43.8%
GILPIN	621	416	189	16	227 R	67.0%	30.4%	68.8%	31.2%
GRAND	1,236	649	553	34	96 R	52.5%	44.7%	54.0%	46.0%
GUNNISON	2,223	1,055	1,022	146	33 R	47.5%	46.0%	50.8%	49.2%
HINSDALE	252	149	67	36	82 R	59.1%	26.6%	69.0%	31.0%
HUERFANO	4,938	2,539	2,291	108	248 R	51.4%	46.4%	52.6%	47.4%
JACKSON	527	402	113	12	289 R	76.3%	21.4%	78.1%	21.9%
JEFFERSON	5,840	3,593	1,941	306	1,652 R	61.5%	33.2%	64.9%	35.1%
KIOWA	1,449	864	521	64	343 R	59.6%	36.0%	62.4%	37.6%
KIT CARSON	2,859	1,872	796	191	1,076 R	65.5%	27.8%	70.2%	29.8%
LAKE	2,421	1,287	992	142	295 R	53.2%	41.0%	56.5%	43.5%
LA PLATA	3,365	1,711	1,445	209	266 R	50.8%	42.9%	54.2%	45.8%
LARIMER	8,528	5,487	2,708	333	2,779 R	64.3%	31.6%	67.0%	33.0%
LAS ANIMAS	9,196	4,707	4,167	322	540 R	51.2%	45.3%	53.0%	47.0%
LINCOLN	2,963	1,815	1,013	135	802 R	61.3%	34.2%	64.2%	35.8%
LOGAN	5,230	3,123	1,893	214	1,230 R	59.7%	36.2%	62.3%	37.7%
MESA	7,271	3,621	3,138	512	483 R	49.8%	43.2%	53.6%	46.4%
MINERAL	371	183	146	42	37 R	49.3%	39.4%	55.6%	44.4%
MOFFAT	1,978	1,294	589	95	705 R	65.4%	29.8%	68.7%	31.3%
MONTEZUMA	1,793	936	727	130	209 R	52.2%	40.5%	56.3%	43.7%
MONTROSE	4,058	2,225	1,522	311	703 R	54.8%	37.5%	59.4%	40.6%
MORGAN	4,420	3,114	1,105	201	2,009 R	70.5%	25.0%	73.0%	26.2%
OTERO	6,876	3,846	2,727	303	1,119 R	55.9%	39.7%	58.5%	41.5%
OURAY	1,195	735	402	58	333 R	61.5%	33.6%	64.6%	35.4%
PARK	878	511	320	47	191 R	58.2%	36.4%	61.5%	38.5%
PHILLIPS	1,783	1,191	480	112	711 R	66.8%	26.9%	71.3%	28.7%
PITKIN	968	478	417	73	61 R	49.4%	43.1%	53.4%	46.6%
PROWERS	4,077	2,650	1,247	180	1,403 R	65.0%	30.6%	68.0%	32.0%
PUEBLO	18,109	9,621	7,863	625	1,758 R	53.1%	43.4%	55.0%	45.0%
RIO BLANCO	1,274	793	455	26	338 R	62.2%	35.7%	63.5%	36.5%
RIO GRANDE	2,721	1,660	985	76	675 R	61.0%	36.2%	62.8%	37.2%
ROUTT	3,224	1,854	1,224	146	630 R	57.5%	38.0%	60.2%	39.8%
SAGUACHE	1,981	1,195	717	69	478 R	60.3%	36.2%	62.5%	37.5%
SAN JUAN	654	330	290	34	40 R	50.5%	44.3%	53.2%	46.8%
SAN MIGUEL	1,709	928	688	93	240 R	54.3%	40.3%	57.4%	42.6%
SEDGWICK	1,254	819	372	63	447 R	65.3%	29.7%	68.8%	31.2%
SUMMIT	830	418	388	24	30 R	50.4%	46.7%	51.9%	48.1%
TELLER	2,681	1,552	1,010	119	542 R	57.9%	37.7%	60.6%	39.4%

PRESIDENT 1924

County	Total Vote	Republican	Democratic	Other	Rep.-Dem. Plurality	%Total Rep.	%Total Dem.	%Major Rep.	%Major Dem.
ADAMS	5,203	2,931	1,209	1,063	1,722 R	56.3%	23.2%	70.8%	29.2%
ALAMOSA	2,486	1,009	625	852	384 R	40.6%	25.1%	61.8%	38.2%
ARAPAHOE	6,643	4,267	1,209	1,167	3,058 R	64.2%	18.2%	77.9%	22.1%
ARCHULETA	1,046	451	269	326	182 R	43.1%	25.8%	62.6%	37.4%
BACA	2,533	1,174	653	706	521 R	46.3%	25.8%	64.3%	35.7%
BENT	2,791	1,511	804	476	707 R	54.1%	28.8%	65.3%	34.7%
BOULDER	12,927	7,595	3,273	2,059	4,322 R	58.8%	25.3%	69.9%	30.1%
CHAFFEE	3,078	1,336	612	1,130	724 R	43.4%	19.9%	68.6%	31.4%
CHEYENNE	1,571	875	236	460	639 R	55.7%	15.0%	78.8%	21.2%
CLEAR CREEK	1,167	722	284	161	438 R	61.9%	24.3%	71.8%	28.2%
CONEJOS	2,626	1,475	995	156	480 R	56.2%	37.9%	59.7%	40.3%
COSTILLA	1,561	755	665	141	90 R	48.4%	42.6%	53.2%	46.8%
CROWLEY	2,164	1,087	667	410	420 R	50.2%	30.8%	62.0%	38.0%
CUSTER	966	429	281	256	148 R	44.4%	29.1%	60.4%	39.6%
DELTA	5,063	2,752	1,345	966	1,407 R	54.4%	26.6%	67.2%	32.8%
DENVER	93,123	59,077	15,764	18,282	43,313 R	63.4%	16.9%	78.9%	21.1%
DOLORES	446	95	157	194	62 D	21.3%	35.2%	37.7%	62.3%
DOUGLAS	1,572	870	383	319	487 R	55.3%	24.4%	69.4%	30.6%
EAGLE	1,625	722	431	472	291 R	44.4%	26.5%	62.6%	37.4%
ELBERT	2,598	1,428	506	664	922 R	55.0%	19.5%	73.8%	26.2%
EL PASO	18,344	10,215	4,140	3,989	6,075 R	55.7%	22.6%	71.2%	28.8%
FREMONT	7,252	4,433	1,550	1,269	2,883 R	61.1%	21.4%	74.1%	25.9%
GARFIELD	3,772	1,934	917	921	1,017 R	51.3%	24.3%	67.8%	32.2%
GILPIN	659	361	161	137	200 R	54.8%	24.4%	69.2%	30.8%
GRAND	1,254	681	308	265	373 R	54.3%	24.6%	68.9%	31.1%
GUNNISON	2,510	1,122	598	790	524 R	44.7%	23.8%	65.2%	34.8%
HINSDALE	276	138	79	59	59 R	50.0%	28.6%	63.6%	36.4%
HUERFANO	5,672	2,784	1,219	1,669	1,565 R	49.1%	21.5%	69.5%	30.5%
JACKSON	585	394	111	80	283 R	67.4%	19.0%	78.0%	22.0%
JEFFERSON	7,645	4,869	1,271	1,505	3,598 R	63.7%	16.6%	79.3%	20.7%
KIOWA	1,695	805	431	459	374 R	47.5%	25.4%	65.1%	34.9%
KIT CARSON	3,501	2,108	720	673	1,388 R	60.2%	20.6%	74.5%	25.5%
LAKE	2,337	1,005	613	719	392 R	43.0%	26.3%	62.1%	37.9%
LA PLATA	4,182	1,469	1,516	1,197	47 D	35.1%	36.3%	49.2%	50.8%
LARIMER	9,809	6,538	1,970	1,301	4,568 R	66.7%	20.1%	76.8%	23.2%
LAS ANIMAS	11,706	5,698	2,758	3,250	2,940 R	48.7%	23.6%	67.4%	32.6%
LINCOLN	3,002	1,642	634	726	1,008 R	54.7%	21.1%	72.1%	27.9%
LOGAN	5,581	3,103	946	1,532	2,157 R	55.6%	17.0%	76.6%	23.4%
MESA	8,902	4,053	2,388	2,461	1,665 R	45.5%	26.8%	62.9%	37.1%
MINERAL	326	150	101	75	49 R	46.0%	31.0%	59.8%	40.2%
MOFFAT	1,990	1,009	647	334	362 R	50.7%	32.5%	60.9%	39.1%
MONTEZUMA	2,033	703	721	609	18 D	34.6%	35.5%	49.4%	50.6%
MONTROSE	4,533	2,077	1,239	1,217	838 R	45.8%	27.3%	62.6%	37.4%
MORGAN	4,745	3,321	757	667	2,564 R	70.0%	16.0%	81.4%	18.6%
OTERO	7,930	4,694	1,938	1,298	2,756 R	59.2%	24.4%	71.1%	28.9%
OURAY	1,093	484	256	353	228 R	44.3%	23.4%	65.4%	34.6%
PARK	1,176	660	316	200	344 R	56.1%	26.9%	67.6%	32.4%
PHILLIPS	2,169	1,076	397	696	679 R	49.6%	18.3%	73.0%	27.0%
PITKIN	935	442	204	289	238 R	47.3%	21.8%	68.4%	31.6%
PROWERS	4,330	2,564	1,042	724	1,522 R	59.2%	24.1%	71.1%	28.9%
PUEBLO	20,009	10,577	4,917	4,515	5,660 R	52.9%	24.6%	68.3%	31.7%
RIO BLANCO	1,259	766	407	86	359 R	60.8%	32.3%	65.3%	34.7%
RIO GRANDE	2,938	1,572	922	444	650 R	53.5%	31.4%	63.0%	37.0%
ROUTT	3,405	1,822	1,116	467	706 R	53.5%	32.8%	62.0%	38.0%
SAGUACHE	2,066	1,205	591	270	614 R	58.3%	28.6%	67.1%	32.9%
SAN JUAN	548	218	206	124	12 R	39.8%	37.6%	51.4%	48.6%
SAN MIGUEL	1,552	677	567	308	110 R	43.6%	36.5%	54.4%	45.6%
SEDGWICK	1,499	779	372	348	407 R	52.0%	24.8%	67.7%	32.3%
SUMMIT	745	354	241	150	113 R	47.5%	32.3%	59.5%	40.5%
TELLER	2,630	1,283	592	755	691 R	48.4%	22.5%	68.4%	31.6%

COLORADO

PRESIDENT 1920

County	Total Vote	Republican	Democratic	Other	Rep.-Dem. Plurality	Percentage Total Vote Rep.	Dem.	Major Vote Rep.	Dem.
WASHINGTON	3,337	2,117	1,060	160	1,057 R	63.4%	31.8%	66.6%	33.4%
WELD	16,100	10,268	5,202	630	5,066 R	63.8%	32.3%	66.4%	33.6%
YUMA	4,215	2,673	1,254	288	1,419 R	63.4%	29.8%	68.1%	31.9%
TOTAL	292,053	173,248	104,936	13,869	68,312 R	59.3%	35.9%	62.3%	37.7%

PRESIDENT 1924

County	Total Vote	Republican	Democratic	Other	Rep.-Dem. Plurality	Percentage Total Vote Rep.	Dem.	Major Vote Rep.	Dem.
WASHINGTON	3,411	1,851	720	840	1,131 R	54.3%	21.1%	72.0%	28.0%
WELD	16,250	10,185	3,406	2,659	6,779 R	62.7%	21.0%	74.9%	25.1%
YUMA	4,816	2,789	865	1,162	1,924 R	57.9%	18.0%	76.3%	23.7%
TOTAL	342,261	195,171	75,238	71,852	119,933 R	57.0%	22.0%	72.2%	27.8%

COLORADO

PRESIDENT 1928

County	Total Vote	Republican	Democratic	Other	Rep.-Dem. Plurality	%Total Vote Rep.	%Total Vote Dem.	%Major Vote Rep.	%Major Vote Dem.
ADAMS	6,388	4,031	2,265	92	1,766 R	63.1%	35.5%	64.0%	36.0%
ALAMOSA	3,021	1,759	1,239	23	520 R	58.2%	41.0%	58.7%	41.3%
ARAPAHOE	8,659	6,086	2,463	110	3,623 R	70.3%	28.4%	71.2%	28.8%
ARCHULETA	1,080	610	447	23	163 R	56.5%	41.4%	57.7%	42.3%
BACA	2,686	2,108	524	54	1,584 R	78.5%	19.5%	80.1%	19.9%
BENT	2,713	1,957	741	15	1,216 R	72.1%	27.3%	72.5%	27.5%
BOULDER	14,015	9,457	4,363	195	5,094 R	67.5%	31.1%	68.4%	31.6%
CHAFFEE	3,160	1,880	1,230	50	650 R	59.5%	38.9%	60.5%	39.5%
CHEYENNE	1,480	945	500	35	445 R	63.9%	33.8%	65.4%	34.6%
CLEAR CREEK	1,294	790	481	23	309 R	61.1%	37.2%	62.2%	37.8%
CONEJOS	3,234	1,463	1,692	79	229 D	45.2%	52.3%	46.4%	53.6%
COSTILLA	1,760	657	1,070	33	413 D	37.3%	60.8%	38.0%	62.0%
CROWLEY	1,900	1,243	635	22	608 R	65.4%	33.4%	66.2%	33.8%
CUSTER	1,019	600	389	30	211 R	58.9%	38.2%	60.7%	39.3%
DELTA	5,542	3,731	1,672	139	2,059 R	67.3%	30.2%	69.1%	30.9%
DENVER	116,002	73,543	41,238	1,221	32,305 R	63.4%	35.5%	64.1%	35.9%
DOLORES	692	387	278	27	109 R	55.9%	40.2%	58.2%	41.8%
DOUGLAS	1,723	1,107	603	13	504 R	64.2%	35.0%	64.7%	35.3%
EAGLE	1,605	1,014	570	21	444 R	63.2%	35.5%	64.0%	36.0%
ELBERT	2,708	1,933	738	37	1,195 R	71.4%	27.3%	72.4%	27.6%
EL PASO	21,578	16,243	5,069	266	11,174 R	75.3%	23.5%	76.2%	23.8%
FREMONT	7,799	5,365	2,352	82	3,013 R	68.8%	30.2%	69.5%	30.5%
GARFIELD	4,056	2,435	1,562	59	873 R	60.0%	38.5%	60.9%	39.1%
GILPIN	542	299	236	7	63 R	55.2%	43.5%	55.9%	44.1%
GRAND	1,239	770	451	18	319 R	62.1%	36.4%	63.1%	36.9%
GUNNISON	2,637	1,456	1,135	46	321 R	55.2%	43.0%	56.2%	43.8%
HINSDALE	238	128	106	4	22 R	53.8%	44.5%	54.7%	45.3%
HUERFANO	6,633	3,260	3,343	30	83 D	49.1%	50.4%	49.4%	50.6%
JACKSON	666	401	249	16	152 R	60.2%	37.4%	61.7%	38.3%
JEFFERSON	9,775	6,754	2,880	141	3,874 R	69.1%	29.5%	70.1%	29.9%
KIOWA	1,515	1,024	458	33	566 R	67.6%	30.2%	69.1%	30.9%
KIT CARSON	3,690	2,486	1,137	67	1,349 R	67.4%	30.8%	68.6%	31.4%
LAKE	2,469	990	1,449	30	459 D	40.1%	58.7%	40.6%	59.4%
LA PLATA	4,762	2,837	1,872	53	965 R	59.6%	39.3%	60.2%	39.8%
LARIMER	11,578	8,213	3,203	162	5,010 R	70.9%	27.7%	71.9%	28.1%
LAS ANIMAS	11,995	5,367	6,459	169	1,092 D	44.7%	53.8%	45.4%	54.6%
LINCOLN	3,053	2,110	888	55	1,222 R	69.1%	29.1%	70.4%	29.6%
LOGAN	6,086	4,377	1,620	89	2,757 R	71.9%	26.6%	73.0%	27.0%
MESA	9,802	6,446	3,223	133	3,223 R	65.8%	32.9%	66.7%	33.3%
MINERAL	350	144	187	19	43 D	41.1%	53.4%	43.5%	56.5%
MOFFAT	2,085	1,346	710	29	636 R	64.6%	34.1%	65.5%	34.5%
MONTEZUMA	2,150	1,341	772	37	569 R	62.4%	35.9%	63.5%	36.5%
MONTROSE	4,271	2,873	1,297	101	1,576 R	67.3%	30.4%	68.9%	31.1%
MORGAN	5,515	4,197	1,242	76	2,955 R	76.1%	22.5%	77.2%	22.8%
OTERO	7,730	5,788	1,876	66	3,912 R	74.9%	24.3%	75.5%	24.5%
OURAY	1,039	535	479	25	56 R	51.5%	46.1%	52.8%	47.2%
PARK	1,178	740	419	19	321 R	62.8%	35.6%	63.8%	36.2%
PHILLIPS	2,210	1,440	705	65	735 R	65.2%	31.9%	67.1%	32.9%
PITKIN	952	485	454	13	31 R	50.9%	47.7%	51.7%	48.3%
PROWERS	4,515	3,228	1,216	71	2,012 R	71.5%	26.9%	72.6%	27.4%
PUEBLO	23,673	15,541	7,881	251	7,660 R	65.6%	33.3%	66.4%	33.6%
RIO BLANCO	1,313	860	429	24	431 R	65.5%	32.7%	66.7%	33.3%
RIO GRANDE	3,520	2,254	1,226	40	1,028 R	64.0%	34.8%	64.8%	35.2%
ROUTT	4,017	2,304	1,645	68	659 R	57.4%	41.0%	58.3%	41.7%
SAGUACHE	2,381	1,491	854	36	637 R	62.6%	35.9%	63.6%	36.4%
SAN JUAN	746	277	436	33	159 D	37.1%	58.4%	38.8%	61.2%
SAN MIGUEL	1,313	721	554	38	167 R	54.9%	42.2%	56.5%	43.5%
SEDGWICK	1,847	1,247	580	20	667 R	67.5%	31.4%	68.3%	31.7%
SUMMIT	681	362	306	13	56 R	53.2%	44.9%	54.2%	45.8%
TELLER	2,275	1,184	1,037	54	147 R	52.0%	45.6%	53.3%	46.7%

PRESIDENT 1932

County	Total Vote	Republican	Democratic	Other	Rep.-Dem. Plurality	%Total Vote Rep.	%Total Vote Dem.	%Major Vote Rep.	%Major Vote Dem.
ADAMS	7,665	2,812	4,554	299	1,742 D	36.7%	59.4%	38.2%	61.8%
ALAMOSA	3,534	1,306	2,141	87	835 D	37.0%	60.6%	37.9%	62.1%
ARAPAHOE	10,642	4,287	5,796	559	1,509 D	40.3%	54.5%	42.5%	57.5%
ARCHULETA	1,410	462	928	20	466 D	32.8%	65.8%	33.2%	66.8%
BACA	3,965	1,349	2,247	369	898 D	34.0%	56.7%	37.5%	62.5%
BENT	3,353	1,327	1,948	78	621 D	39.6%	58.1%	40.5%	59.5%
BOULDER	16,707	7,487	8,412	808	925 D	44.8%	50.4%	47.1%	52.9%
CHAFFEE	3,628	1,061	2,393	174	1,332 D	29.2%	66.0%	30.7%	69.3%
CHEYENNE	1,893	746	1,042	105	296 D	39.4%	55.0%	41.7%	58.3%
CLEAR CREEK	1,564	597	939	28	342 D	38.2%	60.0%	38.9%	61.1%
CONEJOS	3,851	1,190	2,641	20	1,451 D	30.9%	68.6%	31.1%	68.9%
COSTILLA	2,215	707	1,475	33	768 D	31.9%	66.6%	32.4%	67.6%
CROWLEY	2,117	811	1,266	40	455 D	38.3%	59.8%	39.0%	61.0%
CUSTER	1,199	413	729	57	316 D	34.4%	60.8%	36.2%	63.8%
DELTA	6,327	2,341	3,467	519	1,126 D	37.0%	54.8%	40.3%	59.7%
DENVER	136,558	59,372	72,868	4,318	13,496 D	43.5%	53.4%	44.9%	55.1%
DOLORES	691	183	464	44	281 D	26.5%	67.1%	28.3%	71.7%
DOUGLAS	1,946	836	1,061	49	225 D	43.0%	54.5%	44.1%	55.9%
EAGLE	2,106	712	1,348	46	636 D	33.8%	64.0%	34.6%	65.4%
ELBERT	3,074	1,277	1,649	148	372 D	41.5%	53.6%	43.6%	56.4%
EL PASO	24,350	12,017	11,353	980	664 R	49.4%	46.6%	51.4%	48.6%
FREMONT	8,029	3,294	4,295	440	1,001 D	41.0%	53.5%	43.4%	56.6%
GARFIELD	4,810	1,734	2,946	130	1,212 D	36.0%	61.2%	37.1%	62.9%
GILPIN	835	271	539	25	268 D	32.5%	64.6%	33.5%	66.5%
GRAND	1,395	598	771	26	173 D	42.9%	55.3%	43.7%	56.3%
GUNNISON	2,916	985	1,807	124	822 D	33.8%	62.0%	35.3%	64.7%
HINSDALE	246	94	138	14	44 D	38.2%	56.1%	40.5%	59.5%
HUERFANO	6,744	2,490	4,159	95	1,669 D	36.9%	61.7%	37.4%	62.6%
JACKSON	822	390	415	17	25 D	47.4%	50.5%	48.4%	51.6%
JEFFERSON	12,048	5,522	6,023	503	501 D	45.8%	50.0%	47.8%	52.2%
KIOWA	1,968	769	1,113	86	344 D	39.1%	56.6%	40.9%	59.1%
KIT CARSON	4,313	1,835	2,289	189	454 D	42.5%	53.1%	44.5%	55.5%
LAKE	2,296	801	1,436	59	635 D	34.9%	62.5%	35.8%	64.2%
LA PLATA	5,517	2,124	3,156	237	1,032 D	38.5%	57.2%	40.2%	59.8%
LARIMER	14,118	7,040	6,494	584	546 R	49.9%	46.0%	52.0%	48.0%
LAS ANIMAS	12,877	3,651	8,964	262	5,313 D	28.4%	69.6%	28.9%	71.1%
LINCOLN	3,556	1,453	1,979	124	526 D	41.1%	55.6%	42.3%	57.7%
LOGAN	6,947	3,157	3,641	149	484 D	45.4%	52.4%	46.4%	53.6%
MESA	11,807	4,388	6,682	737	2,294 D	37.2%	56.6%	39.6%	60.4%
MINERAL	379	112	210	57	98 D	29.6%	55.4%	34.8%	65.2%
MOFFAT	2,407	880	1,388	139	508 D	36.6%	57.7%	38.8%	61.2%
MONTEZUMA	2,786	887	1,779	120	892 D	31.8%	63.9%	33.3%	66.7%
MONTROSE	4,858	1,992	2,516	350	524 D	41.0%	51.8%	44.2%	55.8%
MORGAN	6,765	3,370	3,181	214	189 R	49.8%	47.0%	51.4%	48.6%
OTERO	9,287	3,974	5,107	206	1,133 D	42.8%	55.0%	43.8%	56.2%
OURAY	1,152	398	706	48	308 D	34.5%	61.3%	36.1%	63.9%
PARK	1,735	577	1,057	101	480 D	33.3%	60.9%	35.3%	64.7%
PHILLIPS	2,592	903	1,453	236	550 D	34.8%	56.1%	38.3%	61.7%
PITKIN	1,012	239	727	46	488 D	23.6%	71.8%	24.7%	75.3%
PROWERS	5,726	2,568	3,020	138	452 D	44.8%	52.7%	45.9%	54.1%
PUEBLO	26,354	10,414	15,325	615	4,911 D	39.5%	58.2%	40.5%	59.5%
RIO BLANCO	1,545	687	826	32	139 D	44.5%	53.5%	45.4%	54.6%
RIO GRANDE	4,258	1,557	2,539	162	982 D	36.6%	59.6%	38.0%	62.0%
ROUTT	3,916	1,075	2,643	198	1,568 D	27.5%	67.5%	28.9%	71.1%
SAGUACHE	2,458	931	1,427	100	496 D	37.9%	58.1%	39.5%	60.5%
SAN JUAN	713	160	544	9	384 D	22.4%	76.3%	22.7%	77.3%
SAN MIGUEL	1,288	383	862	43	479 D	29.7%	66.9%	30.8%	69.2%
SEDGWICK	2,261	884	1,288	89	404 D	39.1%	57.0%	40.7%	59.3%
SUMMIT	644	224	397	23	173 D	34.8%	61.6%	36.1%	63.9%
TELLER	2,489	752	1,534	203	782 D	30.2%	61.6%	32.9%	67.1%

COLORADO

PRESIDENT 1928

| County | Total Vote | Republican | Democratic | Other | Rep.-Dem. Plurality | Percentage | | | |
| | | | | | | Total Vote | | Major Vote | |
						Rep.	Dem.	Rep.	Dem.
WASHINGTON	3,046	2,132	851	63	1,281 R	70.0%	27.9%	71.5%	28.5%
WELD	19,717	13,719	5,762	236	7,957 R	69.6%	29.2%	70.4%	29.6%
YUMA	4,924	3,401	1,383	140	2,018 R	69.1%	28.1%	71.1%	28.9%
TOTAL	392,242	253,872	133,131	5,239	120,741 R	64.7%	33.9%	65.6%	34.4%

PRESIDENT 1932

| County | Total Vote | Republican | Democratic | Other | Rep.-Dem. Plurality | Percentage | | | |
| | | | | | | Total Vote | | Major Vote | |
						Rep.	Dem.	Rep.	Dem.
WASHINGTON	3,913	1,385	2,378	150	993 D	35.4%	60.8%	36.8%	63.2%
WELD	22,945	10,754	11,182	1,009	428 D	46.9%	48.7%	49.0%	51.0%
YUMA	5,701	2,129	3,220	352	1,091 D	37.3%	56.5%	39.8%	60.2%
TOTAL	457,696	189,617	250,877	17,202	61,260 D	41.4%	54.8%	43.0%	57.0%

COLORADO

PRESIDENT 1936

County	Total Vote	Republican	Democratic	Other	Rep.-Dem. Plurality	TV Rep.	TV Dem.	MV Rep.	MV Dem.
ADAMS	8,151	3,124	4,865	162	1,741 D	38.3%	59.7%	39.1%	60.9%
ALAMOSA	3,999	1,188	2,754	57	1,566 D	29.7%	68.9%	30.1%	69.9%
ARAPAHOE	11,171	4,272	6,489	410	2,217 D	38.2%	58.1%	39.7%	60.3%
ARCHULETA	1,533	541	761	31	220 D	40.6%	57.1%	41.6%	58.4%
BACA	3,264	1,288	1,797	179	509 D	39.5%	55.1%	41.8%	58.2%
BENT	3,181	1,299	1,821	61	522 D	40.8%	57.2%	41.6%	58.4%
BOULDER	17,501	7,244	9,788	469	2,544 D	41.4%	55.9%	42.5%	57.5%
CHAFFEE	3,664	1,069	2,447	148	1,378 D	29.2%	66.8%	30.4%	69.6%
CHEYENNE	1,710	767	903	40	136 D	44.9%	52.8%	45.9%	54.1%
CLEAR CREEK	2,076	720	1,340	16	620 D	34.7%	64.5%	35.0%	65.0%
CONEJOS	3,710	1,305	2,347	58	1,042 D	35.2%	63.3%	35.7%	64.3%
COSTILLA	2,504	930	1,518	56	588 D	37.1%	60.6%	38.0%	62.0%
CROWLEY	2,134	920	1,163	51	243 D	43.1%	54.5%	44.2%	55.6%
CUSTER	1,220	526	674	20	148 D	43.1%	55.2%	43.8%	56.2%
DELTA	6,468	2,661	3,230	577	569 D	41.1%	49.9%	45.2%	54.8%
DENVER	152,492	50,743	99,263	2,486	48,520 D	33.3%	65.1%	33.8%	66.2%
DOLORES	582	225	323	34	98 D	38.7%	55.5%	41.1%	58.9%
DOUGLAS	1,968	895	1,044	29	149 D	45.5%	53.0%	46.2%	53.8%
EAGLE	2,347	776	1,541	30	765 D	33.1%	65.7%	33.5%	66.5%
ELBERT	2,776	1,374	1,319	83	55 R	49.5%	47.5%	51.0%	49.0%
EL PASO	27,537	10,965	15,652	920	4,687 D	39.8%	56.8%	41.2%	58.8%
FREMONT	8,461	3,631	4,471	359	840 D	42.9%	52.8%	44.8%	55.2%
GARFIELD	4,528	1,945	2,406	177	461 D	43.0%	53.1%	44.7%	55.3%
GILPIN	1,077	321	736	20	415 D	29.8%	68.3%	30.4%	69.6%
GRAND	1,568	714	846	8	132 D	45.5%	54.0%	45.8%	54.2%
GUNNISON	3,215	978	2,179	58	1,201 D	30.4%	67.8%	31.0%	69.0%
HINSDALE	270	129	137	4	8 D	47.8%	50.7%	48.5%	51.5%
HUERFANO	7,136	2,299	4,793	44	2,494 D	32.2%	67.2%	32.4%	67.6%
JACKSON	886	419	433	34	14 D	47.3%	48.9%	49.2%	50.8%
JEFFERSON	12,825	5,271	7,283	271	2,012 D	41.1%	56.8%	42.0%	58.0%
KIOWA	1,732	772	918	42	146 D	44.6%	53.0%	45.7%	54.3%
KIT CARSON	3,901	1,980	1,730	191	250 R	50.8%	44.3%	53.4%	46.6%
LAKE	2,823	650	2,146	27	1,496 D	23.0%	76.0%	23.2%	76.8%
LA PLATA	5,579	2,354	3,040	185	686 D	42.2%	54.5%	43.6%	56.4%
LARIMER	15,221	7,243	7,521	457	278 D	47.6%	49.4%	49.1%	50.9%
LAS ANIMAS	13,612	3,333	10,220	59	6,887 D	24.5%	75.1%	24.6%	75.4%
LINCOLN	3,163	1,440	1,660	83	240 D	44.4%	52.5%	46.1%	53.9%
LOGAN	7,360	3,136	4,070	154	934 D	42.6%	55.3%	43.5%	56.5%
MESA	12,399	3,654	7,824	921	4,170 D	29.5%	63.1%	31.8%	68.2%
MINERAL	417	126	285	6	159 D	30.2%	68.3%	30.7%	69.3%
MOFFAT	2,264	954	1,090	220	136 D	42.1%	48.1%	46.7%	53.3%
MONTEZUMA	2,795	1,087	1,579	129	492 D	38.9%	56.5%	40.8%	59.2%
MONTROSE	5,425	2,248	2,938	239	690 D	41.4%	54.2%	43.3%	56.7%
MORGAN	6,481	3,058	3,146	277	88 D	47.2%	48.5%	49.3%	50.7%
OTERO	9,772	3,859	5,775	138	1,916 D	39.5%	59.1%	40.1%	59.9%
OURAY	1,116	428	677	11	249 D	38.4%	60.7%	38.7%	61.3%
PARK	2,110	746	1,336	28	590 D	35.4%	63.3%	35.8%	64.2%
PHILLIPS	2,603	941	1,602	60	661 D	36.2%	61.5%	37.0%	63.0%
PITKIN	1,017	305	659	53	354 D	30.0%	64.8%	31.6%	68.4%
PROWERS	5,539	2,432	2,896	211	464 D	43.9%	52.3%	45.6%	54.4%
PUEBLO	29,224	10,071	18,660	493	8,589 D	34.5%	63.9%	35.1%	64.9%
RIO BLANCO	1,488	830	587	71	243 R	55.8%	39.4%	58.6%	41.4%
RIO GRANDE	4,524	1,884	2,574	66	690 D	41.6%	56.9%	42.3%	57.7%
ROUTT	4,575	1,541	2,817	217	1,276 D	33.7%	61.6%	35.4%	64.6%
SAGUACHE	2,446	1,071	1,321	54	250 D	43.8%	54.0%	44.8%	55.2%
SAN JUAN	830	196	622	12	426 D	23.6%	74.9%	24.0%	76.0%
SAN MIGUEL	1,348	433	860	55	427 D	32.1%	63.8%	33.5%	66.5%
SEDGWICK	2,408	977	1,358	73	381 D	40.6%	56.4%	41.8%	58.2%
SUMMIT	769	268	496	5	228 D	34.9%	64.5%	35.1%	64.9%
TELLER	3,368	940	2,349	79	1,409 D	27.9%	69.7%	28.6%	71.4%

PRESIDENT 1940

County	Total Vote	Republican	Democratic	Other	Rep.-Dem. Plurality	TV Rep.	TV Dem.	MV Rep.	MV Dem.
ADAMS	9,503	4,767	4,674	62	93 R	50.2%	49.2%	50.5%	49.5%
ALAMOSA	4,733	2,243	2,467	23	224 D	47.4%	52.1%	47.6%	52.4%
ARAPAHOE	15,696	7,988	7,571	137	417 R	50.9%	48.2%	51.3%	48.7%
ARCHULETA	1,618	869	744	5	125 R	53.7%	46.0%	53.9%	46.1%
BACA	2,772	1,567	1,167	38	400 R	56.5%	42.1%	57.3%	42.7%
BENT	3,675	1,899	1,759	17	140 R	51.7%	47.9%	51.9%	48.1%
BOULDER	19,776	10,525	9,039	212	1,486 R	53.2%	45.7%	53.8%	46.2%
CHAFFEE	4,121	1,933	2,153	35	220 D	46.9%	52.2%	47.3%	52.7%
CHEYENNE	1,681	915	758	8	157 R	54.4%	45.1%	54.7%	45.3%
CLEAR CREEK	2,306	1,018	1,281	7	263 D	44.1%	55.6%	44.3%	55.7%
CONEJOS	4,526	2,028	2,481	17	453 D	44.8%	54.8%	45.0%	55.0%
COSTILLA	2,845	1,121	1,698	26	577 D	39.4%	59.7%	39.8%	60.2%
CROWLEY	2,281	1,419	850	12	569 R	62.2%	37.3%	62.5%	37.5%
CUSTER	1,194	685	495	14	190 R	57.1%	41.5%	58.1%	41.9%
DELTA	7,315	4,175	3,044	96	1,131 R	57.1%	41.6%	57.8%	42.2%
DENVER	173,371	81,328	90,938	1,105	9,610 D	46.9%	52.5%	47.2%	52.8%
DOLORES	873	478	379	16	99 R	54.8%	43.4%	55.8%	44.2%
DOUGLAS	2,108	1,298	801	9	497 R	61.6%	38.0%	61.8%	38.2%
EAGLE	2,564	1,077	1,474	13	397 D	42.0%	57.5%	42.2%	57.8%
ELBERT	2,700	1,756	934	10	822 R	65.0%	34.6%	65.3%	34.7%
EL PASO	30,315	16,766	13,320	229	3,446 R	55.3%	43.9%	55.7%	44.3%
FREMONT	9,394	5,150	4,186	58	964 R	54.8%	44.6%	55.2%	44.8%
GARFIELD	5,061	2,694	2,131	26	753 R	54.8%	42.6%	57.5%	42.5%
GILPIN	849	413	431	5	18 D	48.6%	50.8%	48.9%	51.1%
GRAND	1,946	1,074	863	9	211 R	55.2%	44.3%	55.4%	44.6%
GUNNISON	3,351	1,556	1,771	24	215 D	46.4%	52.8%	46.8%	53.2%
HINSDALE	255	150	103	2	47 R	58.8%	40.4%	59.3%	40.7%
HUERFANO	6,736	2,738	3,974	24	1,236 D	40.6%	59.0%	40.8%	59.2%
JACKSON	888	526	357	5	169 R	59.2%	40.2%	59.6%	40.4%
JEFFERSON	16,625	8,780	7,745	100	1,035 R	52.8%	46.6%	53.1%	46.9%
KIOWA	1,594	986	598	10	388 R	61.9%	37.5%	62.2%	37.8%
KIT CARSON	3,612	2,481	1,100	31	1,381 R	68.7%	30.5%	69.3%	30.7%
LAKE	3,481	1,403	2,063	15	660 D	40.3%	59.3%	40.5%	59.5%
LA PLATA	6,745	3,871	2,835	39	1,036 R	57.4%	42.0%	57.7%	42.3%
LARIMER	17,248	10,720	6,402	126	4,318 R	62.2%	37.1%	62.6%	37.4%
LAS ANIMAS	13,675	4,859	8,766	50	3,907 D	35.5%	64.1%	35.7%	64.3%
LINCOLN	2,988	1,780	1,185	23	595 R	59.6%	39.7%	60.0%	40.0%
LOGAN	7,515	4,613	2,819	83	1,794 R	61.4%	37.5%	62.1%	37.9%
MESA	14,912	7,049	7,694	169	645 D	47.3%	51.6%	47.8%	52.2%
MINERAL	508	229	273	6	44 D	45.1%	53.7%	45.6%	54.4%
MOFFAT	2,627	1,556	1,056	15	500 R	59.2%	40.2%	59.6%	40.4%
MONTEZUMA	3,904	2,313	1,573	18	740 R	59.2%	40.3%	59.5%	40.5%
MONTROSE	6,855	3,744	3,013	98	731 R	54.6%	44.0%	55.4%	44.6%
MORGAN	7,238	4,654	2,527	57	2,127 R	64.3%	34.9%	64.8%	35.2%
OTERO	10,088	5,459	4,567	62	892 R	54.1%	45.3%	54.4%	45.6%
OURAY	1,199	589	606	4	17 D	49.1%	50.5%	49.3%	50.7%
PARK	1,861	986	869	6	117 R	53.0%	46.7%	53.2%	46.8%
PHILLIPS	2,151	1,168	919	64	249 R	54.3%	42.7%	56.0%	44.0%
PITKIN	998	484	503	11	19 D	48.5%	50.4%	49.0%	51.0%
PROWERS	5,477	3,115	2,309	53	806 R	56.9%	42.2%	57.4%	42.6%
PUEBLO	33,115	14,185	18,805	125	4,620 D	42.8%	56.8%	43.0%	57.0%
RIO BLANCO	1,559	1,021	530	8	491 R	65.5%	34.0%	65.8%	34.2%
RIO GRANDE	5,357	3,075	2,242	40	833 R	57.4%	41.9%	57.8%	42.1%
ROUTT	5,019	2,212	2,775	32	563 D	44.1%	55.3%	44.4%	55.6%
SAGUACHE	2,631	1,462	1,142	27	320 R	55.6%	43.4%	55.6%	43.9%
SAN JUAN	834	452	378	4	74 R	54.2%	45.3%	54.5%	45.5%
SAN MIGUEL	1,587	729	851	7	122 D	45.9%	53.6%	46.1%	53.9%
SEDGWICK	2,419	1,448	959	12	489 R	59.9%	39.6%	60.2%	39.8%
SUMMIT	1,024	479	540	5	61 D	46.8%	52.7%	47.0%	53.0%
TELLER	3,372	1,268	2,084	20	816 D	37.6%	61.8%	37.8%	62.2%

COLORADO

PRESIDENT 1936

County	Total Vote	Republican	Democratic	Other	Rep.-Dem. Plurality	Percentage Total Vote Rep.	Dem.	Major Vote Rep.	Dem.
WASHINGTON	3,886	1,723	2,071	92	348 D	44.3%	53.3%	45.4%	54.6%
WELD	23,296	9,606	12,993	697	3,387 D	41.2%	55.8%	42.5%	57.5%
YUMA	5,440	2,462	2,878	100	416 D	45.3%	52.9%	46.1%	53.9%
TOTAL	438,685	181,267	295,021	12,397	113,754 D	37.1%	60.4%	38.1%	61.9%

PRESIDENT 1940

County	Total Vote	Republican	Democratic	Other	Rep.-Dem. Plurality	Percentage Total Vote Rep.	Dem.	Major Vote Rep.	Dem.
WASHINGTON	3,816	2,390	1,403	23	987 R	62.6%	36.8%	63.0%	37.0%
WELD	27,039	16,129	10,653	227	5,476 R	59.7%	39.4%	60.2%	39.8%
YUMA	5,508	3,531	1,917	60	1,614 R	64.1%	34.8%	64.8%	35.2%
TOTAL	549,004	279,576	265,554	3,874	14,022 R	50.9%	48.4%	51.3%	48.7%

COLORADO

PRESIDENT 1944

County	Total Vote	Republican	Democratic	Other	Rep.-Dem. Plurality	% Total Vote Rep.	% Total Vote Dem.	% Major Vote Rep.	% Major Vote Dem.
ADAMS	9,063	4,933	4,101	29	832 R	54.4	45.2	54.6	45.4
ALAMOSA	3,749	1,933	1,806	10	127 R	51.6	48.2	51.7	48.3
ARAPAHOE	16,611	9,057	7,485	69	1,572 R	54.5	45.1	54.8	45.2
ARCHULETA	1,030	602	427	1	175 R	58.4	41.5	58.5	41.5
BACA	2,469	1,528	941		587 R	61.9	38.1	61.9	38.1
BENT	3,021	1,556	1,456	9	100 R	51.5	48.2	51.7	48.3
BOULDER	17,610	10,054	7,442	114	2,612 R	57.1	42.3	57.5	42.5
CHAFFEE	3,430	1,675	1,731	24	56 D	48.8	50.5	49.2	50.8
CHEYENNE	1,521	923	594	4	329 R	60.7	39.1	60.8	39.2
CLEAR CREEK	1,438	795	636	7	159 R	55.3	44.2	55.6	44.4
CONEJOS	3,768	1,740	2,028		288 D	46.2	53.8	46.2	53.8
COSTILLA	2,416	896	1,515	5	619 D	37.1	62.7	37.2	62.8
CROWLEY	1,929	1,214	710	5	504 R	62.9	36.8	63.1	36.9
CUSTER	943	601	333	9	268 R	63.7	35.3	64.3	35.7
DELTA	5,838	3,462	2,351	25	1,111 R	59.3	40.3	59.6	40.4
DENVER	177,091	86,331	90,001	759	3,670 D	48.7	50.8	49.0	51.0
DOLORES	729	429	300		129 R	58.8	41.2	58.8	41.2
DOUGLAS	1,857	1,214	638	5	576 R	65.4	34.4	65.6	34.4
EAGLE	1,879	922	952	5	30 D	49.1	50.7	49.2	50.8
ELBERT	2,044	1,413	628	3	785 R	69.1	30.7	69.2	30.8
EL PASO	28,186	16,392	11,679	115	4,713 R	58.2	41.4	58.4	41.6
FREMONT	8,166	4,953	3,180	33	1,773 R	60.7	38.9	60.9	39.1
GARFIELD	4,464	2,588	1,865	11	723 R	58.0	41.8	58.1	41.9
GILPIN	487	272	213	2	59 R	55.9	43.7	56.1	43.9
GRAND	1,524	968	554	2	414 R	63.5	36.4	63.6	36.4
GUNNISON	2,637	1,221	1,411	5	190 D	46.3	53.5	46.4	53.6
HINSDALE	185	124	61		63 R	67.0	33.0	67.0	33.0
HUERFANO	5,427	2,119	3,290	18	1,171 D	39.0	60.6	39.2	60.8
JACKSON	715	463	252		211 R	64.8	35.2	64.8	35.2
JEFFERSON	17,160	9,815	7,277	68	2,538 R	57.2	42.4	57.4	42.6
KIOWA	1,498	970	522	6	448 R	64.8	34.8	65.0	35.0
KIT CARSON	3,419	2,471	937	11	1,534 R	72.3	27.4	72.5	27.5
LAKE	2,937	1,236	1,687	14	451 D	42.1	57.4	42.3	57.7
LA PLATA	5,069	3,023	2,031	15	992 R	59.6	40.1	59.8	40.2
LARIMER	15,144	9,914	5,172	58	4,742 R	65.5	34.2	65.7	34.3
LAS ANIMAS	11,034	4,179	6,800	55	2,621 D	37.9	61.6	38.1	61.9
LINCOLN	2,839	1,689	1,147	3	542 R	59.5	40.4	59.6	40.4
LOGAN	6,487	3,998	2,471	18	1,527 R	61.6	38.1	61.8	38.2
MESA	13,598	6,653	6,870	75	217 D	48.9	50.5	49.2	50.8
MINERAL	322	170	150	2	20 R	52.8	46.6	53.1	46.9
MOFFAT	2,374	1,445	923	6	522 R	60.9	38.9	61.0	39.0
MONTEZUMA	2,825	1,610	1,207	8	403 R	57.0	42.7	57.2	42.8
MONTROSE	5,237	2,952	2,258	27	694 R	56.4	43.1	56.7	43.3
MORGAN	6,026	4,166	1,839	21	2,327 R	69.1	30.5	69.4	30.6
OTERO	8,816	5,002	3,791	23	1,211 R	56.7	43.0	56.9	43.1
OURAY	807	503	303	1	200 R	62.3	37.5	62.4	37.6
PARK	1,102	670	426	6	244 R	60.8	38.7	61.1	38.9
PHILLIPS	2,233	1,455	761	17	694 R	65.2	34.1	65.7	34.3
PITKIN	724	368	355	1	13 R	50.8	49.0	50.9	49.1
PROWERS	4,762	2,796	1,948	18	848 R	58.7	40.9	58.9	41.1
PUEBLO	32,983	13,848	19,039	96	5,191 D	42.0	57.7	42.1	57.9
RIO BLANCO	1,337	881	451	5	430 R	65.9	33.7	66.1	33.9
RIO GRANDE	3,900	2,567	1,325	8	1,242 R	65.8	34.0	66.0	34.0
ROUTT	3,831	1,869	1,940	22	71 D	48.8	50.6	49.1	50.9
SAGUACHE	1,938	1,204	729	5	475 R	62.1	37.6	62.3	37.7
SAN JUAN	587	328	258	1	70 R	55.9	44.0	56.0	44.0
SAN MIGUEL	1,173	536	630	7	94 D	45.7	53.7	46.0	54.0
SEDGWICK	1,799	1,228	568	3	660 R	68.3	31.6	68.4	31.6
SUMMIT	566	326	237	3	89 R	57.6	41.9	57.9	42.1
TELLER	1,650	829	808	13	21 R	50.2	49.0	50.6	49.4

PRESIDENT 1948

County	Total Vote	Republican	Democratic	Other	Rep.-Dem. Plurality	% Total Vote Rep.	% Total Vote Dem.	% Major Vote Rep.	% Major Vote Dem.
ADAMS	10,791	4,419	6,240	132	1,821 D	41.0	57.8	41.5	58.5
ALAMOSA	4,374	1,950	2,395	29	445 D	44.6	54.8	44.9	55.1
ARAPAHOE	15,080	6,962	7,943	175	981 D	46.2	52.7	46.7	53.3
ARCHULETA	1,084	479	597	8	118 D	44.2	55.1	44.5	55.5
BACA	2,652	1,260	1,368	24	108 D	47.5	51.6	47.9	52.1
BENT	2,984	1,296	1,658	30	362 D	43.4	55.6	43.9	56.1
BOULDER	19,839	10,335	8,792	712	1,543 R	52.1	44.3	54.0	46.0
CHAFFEE	3,580	1,476	2,065	39	589 D	41.2	57.7	41.7	58.3
CHEYENNE	1,386	713	657	16	56 R	51.4	47.4	52.0	48.0
CLEAR CREEK	1,664	836	810	18	26 R	50.2	48.7	50.8	49.2
CONEJOS	3,827	1,532	2,236	59	704 D	40.0	58.4	40.7	59.3
COSTILLA	2,532	921	1,563	48	642 D	36.4	61.7	37.1	62.9
CROWLEY	2,040	1,027	1,004	9	23 R	50.3	49.2	50.6	49.4
CUSTER	943	547	384	12	163 R	58.0	40.7	58.8	41.2
DELTA	6,469	3,158	3,171	140	13 D	48.8	49.0	49.9	50.1
DENVER	169,067	76,364	89,489	3,214	13,125 D	45.2	52.9	46.0	54.0
DOLORES	797	352	435	10	83 D	44.2	54.6	44.7	55.3
DOUGLAS	1,756	979	767	10	212 R	55.8	43.7	56.1	43.9
EAGLE	1,806	738	1,008	60	270 D	40.9	55.8	42.3	57.7
ELBERT	2,049	1,155	873	21	282 R	56.4	42.6	57.0	43.0
EL PASO	28,419	15,705	12,291	423	3,414 R	55.3	43.2	56.1	43.9
FREMONT	8,627	4,421	4,077	129	344 R	51.2	47.3	52.0	48.0
GARFIELD	4,922	2,416	2,364	142	52 R	49.1	48.0	50.5	49.5
GILPIN	611	302	296	13	6 R	49.4	48.4	50.5	49.5
GRAND	1,562	777	763	22	14 R	49.7	48.8	50.5	49.5
GUNNISON	2,494	1,103	1,326	65	223 D	44.2	53.2	45.4	54.6
HINSDALE	208	133	75		58 R	63.9	36.1	63.9	36.1
HUERFANO	5,410	1,841	3,448	121	1,607 D	34.0	63.7	34.8	65.2
JACKSON	618	327	291		36 R	52.9	47.1	52.9	47.1
JEFFERSON	19,308	9,903	9,145	260	758 R	51.3	47.4	52.0	48.0
KIOWA	1,431	758	659	14	99 R	53.0	46.1	53.5	46.5
KIT CARSON	3,181	1,873	1,281	27	592 R	58.9	40.3	59.4	40.6
LAKE	2,502	838	1,581	83	743 D	33.5	63.2	34.6	65.4
LA PLATA	5,360	2,735	2,536	89	199 R	51.0	47.3	51.9	48.1
LARIMER	17,029	9,813	7,062	154	2,751 R	57.6	41.5	58.2	41.8
LAS ANIMAS	11,210	3,452	7,586	172	4,134 D	30.8	67.7	31.3	68.7
LINCOLN	2,516	1,271	1,231	14	40 R	50.5	48.9	50.8	49.2
LOGAN	6,448	3,223	3,179	46	44 R	50.0	49.3	50.3	49.7
MESA	15,185	6,586	8,401	198	1,815 D	43.4	55.3	43.9	56.1
MINERAL	335	144	190	1	46 D	43.0	56.7	43.1	56.9
MOFFAT	2,391	1,261	1,101	29	160 R	52.7	46.0	53.4	46.6
MONTEZUMA	3,313	1,630	1,653	30	23 D	49.2	49.9	49.6	50.4
MONTROSE	5,116	2,473	2,544	99	71 D	48.3	49.7	49.3	50.7
MORGAN	6,382	3,417	2,912	53	505 R	53.5	45.6	54.0	46.0
OTERO	9,032	4,311	4,640	81	329 D	47.7	51.4	48.2	51.8
OURAY	1,045	574	461	10	113 R	54.9	44.1	55.5	44.5
PARK	1,152	637	505	10	132 R	55.3	43.8	55.8	44.2
PHILLIPS	2,049	1,076	932	41	144 R	52.5	45.5	53.6	46.4
PITKIN	751	319	409	23	90 D	42.5	54.5	43.8	56.2
PROWERS	5,047	2,505	2,497	45	8 R	49.6	49.5	50.1	49.9
PUEBLO	35,041	12,756	21,637	648	8,881 D	36.4	61.7	37.1	62.9
RIO BLANCO	1,751	981	752	18	229 R	56.0	42.9	56.6	43.4
RIO GRANDE	3,876	2,049	1,814	13	235 R	52.9	46.8	53.0	47.0
ROUTT	3,651	1,492	2,088	71	596 D	40.9	57.2	41.7	58.3
SAGUACHE	1,937	914	1,009	14	95 D	47.2	52.1	47.5	52.5
SAN JUAN	700	329	348	23	19 D	47.0	49.7	48.6	51.4
SAN MIGUEL	1,079	451	613	15	162 D	41.8	56.8	42.4	57.6
SEDGWICK	1,867	1,020	834	13	186 R	54.6	44.7	55.0	45.0
SUMMIT	675	292	378	5	86 D	43.3	56.0	43.6	56.4
TELLER	1,547	748	779	20	31 D	48.4	50.4	49.0	51.0

COLORADO

PRESIDENT 1944

County	Total Vote	Republican	Democratic	Other	Rep.-Dem. Plurality	Percentage Total Vote Rep.	Dem.	Major Vote Rep.	Dem.
WASHINGTON	3,328	2,259	1,058	11	1,201 R	57.9%	31.8%	68.1%	31.9%
WELD	23,086	14,546	8,459	81	6,087 R	53.0%	36.6%	63.2%	36.8%
YUMA	4,221	2,847	1,374		1,473 R	57.4%	32.6%	67.4%	32.6%
TOTAL	505,039	268,731	234,331	1,977	34,400 R	53.2%	46.4%	53.4%	46.6%

PRESIDENT 1948

County	Total Vote	Republican	Democratic	Other	Rep.-Dem. Plurality	Percentage Total Vote Rep.	Dem.	Major Vote Rep.	Dem.
WASHINGTON	2,958	1,636	1,304	18	332 R	55.3%	44.1%	55.6%	44.4%
WELD	23,639	12,446	10,934	259	1,512 R	52.7%	46.3%	53.2%	46.8%
YUMA	4,213	2,277	1,907	29	370 R	54.0%	45.3%	54.4%	45.6%
TOTAL	515,237	239,714	267,288	8,235	27,574 D	46.5%	51.9%	47.3%	52.7%

COLORADO

PRESIDENT 1952

County	Total Vote	Republican	Democratic	Other	Rep.-Dem. Plurality	Total Vote Rep.	Total Vote Dem.	Major Vote Rep.	Major Vote Dem.
ADAMS	16,387	8,995	7,321	71	1,674 R	54.9%	44.7%	55.1%	44.9%
ALAMOSA	4,391	2,728	1,626	37	1,102 R	62.1%	37.0%	62.7%	37.3%
ARAPAHOE	25,534	15,402	9,843	289	5,559 R	60.3%	38.5%	61.0%	39.0%
ARCHULETA	1,070	691	377	2	314 R	64.6%	35.2%	64.7%	35.3%
BACA	3,236	2,122	1,094	20	1,028 R	65.6%	33.8%	66.0%	34.0%
BENT	3,283	1,950	1,317	16	633 R	59.4%	40.1%	59.7%	40.3%
BOULDER	23,079	15,069	7,767	243	7,302 R	65.3%	33.7%	66.0%	34.0%
CHAFFEE	3,829	2,171	1,643	15	528 R	56.7%	42.9%	56.9%	43.1%
CHEYENNE	1,522	1,004	515	3	489 R	66.0%	33.8%	66.1%	33.9%
CLEAR CREEK	1,691	1,145	540	6	605 R	67.7%	31.9%	68.0%	32.0%
CONEJOS	3,902	2,194	1,610	98	584 R	56.2%	41.3%	57.7%	42.3%
COSTILLA	2,447	1,070	1,369	8	299 D	43.7%	55.9%	43.9%	56.1%
CROWLEY	2,281	1,546	726	9	820 R	67.8%	31.8%	68.0%	32.0%
CUSTER	899	662	231	6	431 R	73.6%	25.7%	74.1%	25.9%
DELTA	7,441	4,986	2,389	66	2,597 R	67.0%	32.1%	67.6%	32.4%
DENVER	213,563	119,792	92,237	1,534	27,555 R	56.1%	43.2%	56.5%	43.5%
DOLORES	871	542	323	6	219 R	62.2%	37.1%	62.7%	37.3%
DOUGLAS	2,068	1,427	637	4	790 R	69.0%	30.8%	69.1%	30.9%
EAGLE	2,313	1,242	1,058	13	184 R	53.7%	45.7%	54.0%	46.0%
ELBERT	2,176	1,579	586	11	993 R	72.6%	26.9%	72.9%	27.1%
EL PASO	36,778	25,272	11,203	303	14,069 R	68.7%	30.5%	69.3%	30.7%
FREMONT	9,199	5,964	3,176	59	2,788 R	64.8%	34.5%	65.3%	34.7%
GARFIELD	5,719	3,914	1,777	28	2,137 R	68.4%	31.1%	68.8%	31.2%
GILPIN	591	357	228	6	129 R	60.4%	38.6%	61.0%	39.0%
GRAND	1,895	1,333	554	8	779 R	70.3%	29.2%	70.6%	29.4%
GUNNISON	2,578	1,533	1,045		488 R	59.5%	40.5%	59.5%	40.5%
HINSDALE	208	154	54		100 R	74.0%	26.0%	74.0%	26.0%
HUERFANO	4,968	2,178	2,773	17	595 D	43.8%	55.8%	44.0%	56.0%
JACKSON	886	579	305	2	274 R	65.3%	34.4%	65.5%	34.5%
JEFFERSON	31,674	19,971	11,509	194	8,462 R	63.1%	36.3%	63.4%	36.6%
KIOWA	1,478	1,047	412	19	635 R	70.8%	27.9%	71.8%	28.2%
KIT CARSON	3,535	2,511	998	26	1,513 R	71.0%	28.2%	71.6%	28.4%
LAKE	2,897	1,303	1,585	9	282 D	45.0%	54.7%	45.1%	54.9%
LA PLATA	6,701	4,425	2,210	66	2,215 R	66.0%	33.0%	66.7%	33.3%
LARIMER	19,860	14,484	5,266	110	9,218 R	72.9%	26.5%	73.3%	26.7%
LAS ANIMAS	10,964	4,467	6,446	51	1,979 D	40.7%	58.8%	40.9%	59.1%
LINCOLN	2,773	1,843	927	43	916 R	66.5%	33.4%	66.5%	33.5%
LOGAN	7,739	5,237	2,459	43	2,778 R	67.7%	31.8%	68.0%	32.0%
MESA	18,845	11,883	6,883	79	5,000 R	63.1%	36.5%	63.3%	36.7%
MINERAL	308	209	98	1	111 R	67.9%	31.8%	68.1%	31.9%
MOFFAT	2,741	1,922	808	11	1,114 R	70.1%	29.5%	70.4%	29.6%
MONTEZUMA	3,626	2,466	1,127	33	1,339 R	68.0%	31.1%	68.6%	31.4%
MONTROSE	6,371	4,279	2,037	55	2,242 R	67.2%	32.0%	67.7%	32.3%
MORGAN	7,714	5,371	2,297	46	3,074 R	69.6%	29.8%	70.0%	30.0%
OTERO	10,307	6,552	3,721	34	2,831 R	63.6%	36.1%	63.8%	36.2%
OURAY	1,127	697	413	17	284 R	61.8%	36.6%	62.8%	37.2%
PARK	1,125	775	343	7	432 R	68.9%	30.5%	69.3%	30.7%
PHILLIPS	2,466	1,670	789	7	881 R	67.7%	32.0%	67.9%	32.1%
PITKIN	867	556	309	2	247 R	64.1%	35.6%	64.3%	35.7%
PROWERS	6,108	3,978	2,087	43	1,891 R	65.1%	34.2%	65.6%	34.4%
PUEBLO	41,659	20,333	20,613	713	280 D	48.8%	49.5%	49.7%	50.3%
RIO BLANCO	2,257	1,612	633	12	979 R	71.4%	28.0%	71.8%	28.2%
RIO GRANDE	4,566	3,201	1,350	15	1,851 R	70.1%	29.6%	70.3%	29.7%
ROUTT	3,739	2,143	1,575	21	568 R	57.3%	42.1%	57.6%	42.4%
SAGUACHE	2,065	1,344	714	7	630 R	65.1%	34.6%	65.3%	34.7%
SAN JUAN	761	432	327	2	105 R	56.8%	43.0%	56.9%	43.1%
SAN MIGUEL	1,185	654	524	7	130 R	55.2%	44.2%	55.5%	44.5%
SEDGWICK	2,223	1,528	686	9	842 R	68.7%	30.9%	69.0%	31.0%
SUMMIT	714	442	271	1	171 R	61.9%	38.0%	62.0%	38.0%
TELLER	1,631	1,042	572	17	470 R	63.9%	35.1%	64.6%	35.4%

PRESIDENT 1956

County	Total Vote	Republican	Democratic	Other	Rep.-Dem. Plurality	Total Vote Rep.	Total Vote Dem.	Major Vote Rep.	Major Vote Dem.
ADAMS	24,463	12,778	11,470	215	1,308 R	52.2%	46.9%	52.7%	47.3%
ALAMOSA	3,918	2,442	1,465	11	977 R	62.3%	37.4%	62.5%	37.5%
ARAPAHOE	31,243	19,716	11,351	176	8,365 R	63.1%	36.3%	63.5%	36.5%
ARCHULETA	1,060	635	423	2	212 R	59.9%	39.9%	60.0%	40.0%
BACA	2,876	1,715	1,150	11	565 R	59.6%	40.0%	59.9%	40.1%
BENT	3,001	1,718	1,283		435 R	57.2%	42.8%	57.2%	42.8%
BOULDER	25,039	16,748	8,149	142	8,599 R	66.9%	32.5%	67.3%	32.7%
CHAFFEE	3,587	2,284	1,303		981 R	63.7%	36.3%	63.7%	36.3%
CHEYENNE	1,329	820	507	2	313 R	61.7%	38.1%	61.8%	38.2%
CLEAR CREEK	1,500	973	520	7	453 R	64.9%	34.7%	65.2%	34.8%
CONEJOS	3,371	1,884	1,471	16	413 R	55.9%	43.6%	56.2%	43.8%
COSTILLA	2,254	958	1,256	40	298 D	42.5%	55.7%	43.3%	56.7%
CROWLEY	1,966	1,220	745	1	475 R	62.1%	37.9%	62.1%	37.9%
CUSTER	799	534	264	1	270 R	66.6%	33.1%	66.9%	33.1%
DELTA	7,002	4,531	2,458	13	2,073 R	64.7%	35.1%	64.8%	35.2%
DENVER	217,121	121,402	93,812	1,907	27,590 R	55.9%	43.2%	56.4%	43.6%
DOLORES	901	544	354	3	190 R	60.4%	39.3%	60.6%	39.4%
DOUGLAS	2,215	1,508	697	10	811 R	68.1%	31.5%	68.4%	31.6%
EAGLE	2,012	1,154	852	6	302 R	57.4%	42.3%	57.5%	42.5%
ELBERT	2,000	1,295	702	3	593 R	64.8%	35.1%	64.8%	35.2%
EL PASO	39,666	27,282	11,879	505	15,403 R	68.8%	29.9%	69.7%	30.3%
FREMONT	8,962	6,040	2,896	26	3,144 R	67.4%	32.3%	67.6%	32.4%
GARFIELD	5,297	3,332	1,953	12	1,379 R	62.9%	36.9%	63.0%	37.0%
GILPIN	639	394	244	1	150 R	61.7%	38.2%	61.8%	38.2%
GRAND	1,737	1,239	496	2	743 R	71.3%	28.6%	71.4%	28.6%
GUNNISON	2,247	1,400	846	1	554 R	62.3%	37.7%	62.3%	37.7%
HINSDALE	202	155	47		108 R	76.7%	23.3%	76.7%	23.3%
HUERFANO	4,365	2,091	2,262	12	171 D	47.9%	51.8%	48.0%	52.0%
JACKSON	892	594	297	1	297 R	66.6%	33.3%	66.7%	33.3%
JEFFERSON	39,865	25,398	14,270	197	11,128 R	63.7%	35.8%	64.0%	36.0%
KIOWA	1,253	810	443		367 R	64.6%	35.4%	64.6%	35.4%
KIT CARSON	3,161	2,243	911	7	1,332 R	71.0%	28.8%	71.1%	28.9%
LAKE	2,793	1,433	1,355	5	78 R	51.3%	48.5%	51.4%	48.6%
LA PLATA	7,140	4,770	2,366	4	2,404 R	66.8%	33.1%	66.8%	33.2%
LARIMER	20,015	14,364	5,612	39	8,752 R	71.8%	28.0%	71.9%	28.1%
LAS ANIMAS	10,414	5,290	5,099	25	191 R	50.8%	49.0%	50.9%	49.1%
LINCOLN	2,617	1,603	1,012	20	591 R	61.3%	38.7%	61.3%	38.7%
LOGAN	8,060	5,199	2,841	60	2,358 R	64.5%	35.2%	64.7%	35.3%
MESA	20,496	12,869	7,567	60	5,302 R	62.7%	36.9%	63.0%	37.0%
MINERAL	268	168	99	1	69 R	62.7%	36.9%	62.9%	37.1%
MOFFAT	2,561	1,762	797	2	965 R	68.8%	31.1%	68.9%	31.1%
MONTEZUMA	3,919	2,492	1,402	25	1,090 R	63.6%	35.8%	63.6%	36.0%
MONTROSE	6,534	4,054	2,461	19	1,593 R	62.0%	37.7%	62.2%	37.8%
MORGAN	8,298	5,325	2,956	17	2,369 R	64.2%	35.6%	64.3%	35.7%
OTERO	9,693	5,964	3,722	7	2,242 R	61.5%	38.4%	61.6%	38.4%
OURAY	962	634	322	6	312 R	65.9%	33.5%	66.3%	33.7%
PARK	1,013	715	297	1	418 R	70.6%	29.3%	70.7%	29.3%
PHILLIPS	2,423	1,535	887	1	648 R	63.4%	36.6%	63.4%	36.6%
PITKIN	885	550	334	1	216 R	62.1%	37.7%	62.2%	37.8%
PROWERS	5,815	3,550	2,460	5	890 R	57.6%	42.3%	57.7%	42.3%
PUEBLO	44,814	23,454	20,433	927	3,021 R	52.3%	45.6%	53.4%	46.6%
RIO BLANCO	2,229	1,593	635	1	958 R	71.5%	28.5%	71.5%	28.5%
RIO GRANDE	4,264	2,816	1,441	7	1,375 R	66.0%	33.8%	66.1%	33.9%
ROUTT	3,147	1,811	1,330	6	481 R	57.5%	42.3%	57.7%	42.3%
SAGUACHE	1,980	1,149	823	8	326 R	58.0%	41.6%	58.3%	41.7%
SAN JUAN	555	324	231		93 R	58.4%	41.6%	58.4%	41.6%
SAN MIGUEL	1,120	648	469	3	179 R	57.9%	41.9%	58.4%	42.0%
SEDGWICK	2,099	1,334	760	5	574 R	63.6%	36.2%	63.7%	36.3%
SUMMIT	664	429	235		194 R	64.6%	35.4%	64.6%	35.4%
TELLER	1,471	977	494		483 R	66.4%	33.6%	66.4%	33.6%

COLORADO

PRESIDENT 1952

County	Total Vote	Republican	Democratic	Other	Rep.-Dem. Plurality	Percentage Total Vote Rep.	Dem.	Major Vote Rep.	Dem.
WASHINGTON	3,443	2,398	1,009	36	1,389 R	69.6%	29.3%	70.4%	29.6%
WELD	27,096	18,002	8,890	204	9,112 R	66.4%	32.8%	66.9%	33.1%
YUMA	4,733	3,404	1,292	37	2,112 R	71.9%	27.3%	72.5%	27.5%
TOTAL	630,103	379,782	245,504	4,817	134,278 R	60.3%	39.0%	60.7%	39.3%

PRESIDENT 1956

County	Total Vote	Republican	Democratic	Other	Rep.-Dem. Plurality	Percentage Total Vote Rep.	Dem.	Major Vote Rep.	Dem.
WASHINGTON	3,098	2,020	1,067	11	953 R	65.2%	34.4%	65.4%	34.6%
WELD	27,455	17,228	10,170	57	7,058 R	62.7%	37.0%	62.9%	37.1%
YUMA	4,329	2,782	1,544	3	1,238 R	64.3%	35.7%	64.3%	35.7%
TOTAL	657,074	394,479	257,997	4,598	136,482 R	60.0%	39.3%	60.5%	39.5%

COLORADO

PRESIDENT 1960

County	Total Vote	Republican	Democratic	Other	Rep.-Dem. Plurality	Total Vote Rep.	Total Vote Dem.	Major Vote Rep.	Major Vote Dem.
ADAMS	39,798	18,452	21,168	178	2,716 D	46.4%	53.2%	46.6%	53.4%
ALAMOSA	4,086	2,271	1,811	4	460 R	55.6%	44.3%	55.6%	44.4%
ARAPAHOE	43,916	26,379	17,400	137	8,979 R	60.1%	39.6%	60.3%	39.7%
ARCHULETA	1,057	489	567		78 D	46.3%	53.6%	46.3%	53.7%
BACA	2,772	1,815	952	5	863 R	65.5%	34.3%	65.6%	34.4%
BENT	2,904	1,671	1,228	5	443 R	57.5%	42.3%	57.6%	42.4%
BOULDER	32,197	19,791	12,276	130	7,515 R	61.4%	38.1%	61.7%	38.3%
CHAFFEE	4,016	2,094	1,918	4	176 R	52.1%	47.8%	52.2%	47.8%
CHEYENNE	1,227	806	419	2	387 R	65.7%	34.1%	65.8%	34.2%
CLEAR CREEK	1,652	964	688		276 R	58.4%	41.6%	58.4%	41.6%
CONEJOS	3,523	1,367	2,069	87	702 D	38.8%	58.7%	39.8%	60.2%
COSTILLA	2,001	637	1,351	13	714 D	31.8%	67.5%	32.0%	68.0%
CROWLEY	1,805	1,099	705	1	394 R	60.9%	39.0%	60.9%	39.1%
CUSTER	823	509	314		195 R	61.8%	38.2%	61.8%	38.2%
DELTA	7,343	4,644	2,689	10	1,955 R	63.2%	36.6%	63.3%	36.7%
DENVER	220,701	109,446	109,637	1,618	191 D	49.6%	49.7%	50.0%	50.0%
DOLORES	862	476	386		90 R	55.2%	44.8%	55.2%	44.8%
DOUGLAS	2,313	1,490	823		667 R	64.4%	35.6%	64.4%	35.6%
EAGLE	1,871	989	880	2	109 R	52.9%	47.0%	52.9%	47.1%
ELBERT	1,928	1,240	686	2	554 R	64.3%	35.6%	64.4%	35.6%
EL PASO	48,704	31,625	17,018	61	14,607 R	64.9%	34.9%	65.0%	35.0%
FREMONT	9,454	5,690	3,730	34	1,960 R	60.2%	39.4%	60.4%	39.6%
GARFIELD	5,539	3,215	2,313	11	902 R	58.0%	41.8%	58.2%	41.8%
GILPIN	538	315	223		92 R	58.6%	41.4%	58.6%	41.4%
GRAND	1,763	1,104	657	2	447 R	62.6%	37.3%	62.7%	37.3%
GUNNISON	2,343	1,296	1,044	3	252 R	55.3%	44.6%	55.4%	44.6%
HINSDALE	220	138	82		56 R	62.7%	37.3%	62.7%	37.3%
HUERFANO	4,053	1,367	2,673	13	1,306 D	33.7%	66.0%	33.8%	66.2%
JACKSON	865	504	360	1	144 R	58.3%	41.6%	58.3%	41.7%
JEFFERSON	57,204	34,105	22,962	137	11,143 R	59.6%	40.1%	59.8%	40.2%
KIOWA	1,364	865	498	1	367 R	63.4%	36.5%	63.5%	36.5%
KIT CARSON	3,361	2,248	1,103	10	1,145 R	66.9%	32.8%	67.1%	32.9%
LAKE	2,803	954	1,842	7	888 D	34.0%	65.7%	34.1%	65.9%
LA PLATA	8,111	4,772	3,329	10	1,443 R	58.8%	41.0%	58.9%	41.1%
LARIMER	23,255	15,671	7,550	34	8,121 R	67.4%	32.5%	67.5%	32.5%
LAS ANIMAS	9,722	2,989	6,704	29	3,715 D	30.7%	69.0%	30.8%	69.2%
LINCOLN	2,542	1,498	1,041	5	457 R	58.9%	41.0%	59.0%	41.0%
LOGAN	8,341	5,002	3,334	5	1,668 R	60.0%	40.0%	60.0%	40.0%
MESA	22,431	13,015	9,072	45	3,943 R	58.0%	40.4%	58.9%	41.1%
MINERAL	305	146	158	1	12 D	47.9%	51.8%	48.0%	52.0%
MOFFAT	2,957	1,754	1,200	3	554 R	59.3%	40.6%	59.4%	40.6%
MONTEZUMA	4,900	2,778	2,115	7	663 R	56.7%	43.2%	56.8%	43.2%
MONTROSE	6,925	4,040	2,861	24	1,179 R	58.3%	41.3%	58.5%	41.5%
MORGAN	8,111	5,092	3,151	16	1,941 R	61.7%	38.2%	61.8%	38.3%
OTERO	10,229	6,015	4,199	15	1,816 R	58.8%	41.0%	58.9%	41.1%
OURAY	940	508	432		76 R	54.0%	46.0%	54.0%	46.0%
PARK	1,082	642	438	2	204 R	59.3%	40.5%	59.4%	40.6%
PHILLIPS	2,318	1,455	862	1	593 R	62.8%	37.2%	62.8%	37.3%
PITKIN	1,167	679	488		191 R	58.2%	41.8%	58.2%	41.8%
PROWERS	6,030	3,567	2,457	6	1,110 R	59.2%	40.8%	59.2%	40.8%
PUEBLO	48,582	20,579	27,421	582	6,842 D	42.4%	56.4%	42.9%	57.1%
RIO BLANCO	2,188	1,391	794	3	597 R	63.6%	36.3%	63.7%	36.3%
RIO GRANDE	4,312	2,524	1,782	6	742 R	58.5%	41.3%	58.6%	41.4%
ROUTT	3,067	1,651	1,414	2	237 R	53.8%	46.1%	53.9%	46.1%
SAGUACHE	1,949	956	984	9	28 D	49.1%	50.5%	49.3%	50.7%
SAN JUAN	482	218	261	3	43 D	45.2%	54.1%	45.5%	54.5%
SAN MIGUEL	1,139	525	612	2	87 D	46.1%	53.7%	46.2%	53.8%
SEDGWICK	2,003	1,230	769	4	461 R	61.4%	38.4%	61.5%	38.5%
SUMMIT	827	424	400	3	24 R	51.3%	48.4%	51.5%	48.5%
TELLER	1,349	723	622	4	101 R	53.6%	46.1%	53.8%	46.2%

PRESIDENT 1964

County	Total Vote	Republican	Democratic	Other	Rep.-Dem. Plurality	Total Vote Rep.	Total Vote Dem.	Major Vote Rep.	Major Vote Dem.
ADAMS	51,454	15,652	35,498	304	19,846 D	30.4%	69.0%	30.6%	69.4%
ALAMOSA	3,976	1,488	2,481	7	993 D	37.4%	62.4%	37.5%	62.5%
ARAPAHOE	51,358	23,071	27,940	347	4,869 D	44.9%	54.4%	45.2%	54.8%
ARCHULETA	1,008	370	632		262 D	36.7%	62.7%	36.9%	63.1%
BACA	2,618	1,241	1,366	11	125 D	47.4%	52.2%	47.6%	52.4%
BENT	2,696	937	1,737	22	800 D	34.8%	64.4%	35.0%	65.0%
BOULDER	40,330	17,373	22,737	220	5,364 D	43.1%	56.3%	43.3%	56.5%
CHAFFEE	3,951	1,476	2,463	12	987 D	37.4%	62.3%	37.5%	62.5%
CHEYENNE	1,283	545	735	3	190 D	42.5%	57.4%	42.6%	57.4%
CLEAR CREEK	1,767	676	1,086	5	410 D	38.3%	61.5%	38.4%	61.6%
CONEJOS	3,076	1,031	2,033	12	1,002 D	33.5%	66.1%	33.6%	66.4%
COSTILLA	1,589	299	1,284	6	985 D	18.8%	80.8%	18.9%	81.1%
CROWLEY	1,663	690	967	6	277 D	41.5%	58.1%	41.6%	58.4%
CUSTER	767	358	406	3	48 D	46.7%	52.9%	46.9%	53.1%
DELTA	6,826	2,883	3,927	16	1,044 D	42.2%	57.5%	42.3%	57.7%
DENVER	218,288	73,279	143,480	1,529	70,201 D	33.6%	65.7%	33.8%	66.2%
DOLORES	818	322	496		174 D	39.4%	60.6%	39.4%	60.6%
DOUGLAS	2,791	1,336	1,442	13	106 D	47.9%	51.7%	48.1%	51.9%
EAGLE	1,945	644	1,299	2	655 D	33.1%	66.8%	33.1%	66.9%
ELBERT	1,785	924	857	4	67 R	51.8%	48.0%	51.9%	48.1%
EL PASO	51,807	23,822	27,844	141	4,022 D	46.0%	53.7%	46.1%	53.9%
FREMONT	9,088	3,875	5,181	32	1,306 D	42.6%	57.0%	42.8%	57.2%
GARFIELD	5,488	2,282	3,196	10	914 D	41.6%	58.2%	41.7%	58.3%
GILPIN	600	233	363	4	130 D	38.8%	60.5%	39.1%	60.9%
GRAND	1,724	814	902	8	88 D	47.2%	52.3%	47.4%	52.6%
GUNNISON	2,443	903	1,540		637 D	37.0%	63.0%	37.0%	63.0%
HINSDALE	201	107	94		13 R	53.2%	46.8%	53.2%	46.8%
HUERFANO	3,634	895	2,734	5	1,839 D	24.6%	75.2%	24.7%	75.3%
JACKSON	741	354	384	3	30 D	47.8%	51.8%	48.0%	52.0%
JEFFERSON	76,812	33,398	43,162	252	9,764 D	43.5%	56.2%	43.6%	56.4%
KIOWA	1,280	579	701		122 D	45.2%	54.8%	45.2%	54.8%
KIT CARSON	3,233	1,316	1,906	11	590 D	40.7%	59.0%	40.8%	59.2%
LAKE	3,051	681	2,362	8	1,681 D	22.3%	77.4%	22.4%	77.6%
LA PLATA	8,007	3,550	4,442	15	892 D	44.3%	55.5%	44.4%	55.6%
LARIMER	24,585	11,636	12,776	173	1,140 D	47.3%	52.0%	47.7%	52.3%
LAS ANIMAS	8,453	1,833	6,591	29	4,758 D	21.7%	78.0%	21.8%	78.6%
LINCOLN	2,439	1,104	1,327	8	223 D	45.3%	54.4%	45.4%	54.6%
LOGAN	7,731	3,497	4,222	12	725 D	45.2%	54.6%	45.3%	54.7%
MESA	21,082	8,317	12,716	49	4,399 D	39.5%	60.3%	39.5%	60.5%
MINERAL	296	89	204	3	115 D	30.1%	68.9%	30.4%	69.6%
MOFFAT	3,103	1,438	1,657	8	219 D	46.3%	53.4%	46.5%	53.5%
MONTEZUMA	4,738	2,035	2,686	17	651 D	43.0%	56.7%	43.1%	56.9%
MONTROSE	6,709	2,678	4,009	22	1,331 D	39.9%	59.8%	40.0%	59.8%
MORGAN	7,520	3,228	4,271	21	1,043 D	42.9%	56.8%	43.0%	57.0%
OTERO	9,636	3,605	5,999	32	2,394 D	37.4%	62.3%	37.5%	62.5%
OURAY	820	358	456	6	98 D	43.7%	55.6%	44.0%	56.0%
PARK	1,009	493	515	1	22 D	48.9%	51.0%	48.9%	51.1%
PHILLIPS	2,260	1,012	1,243	5	231 D	44.8%	55.0%	44.8%	55.0%
PITKIN	1,504	540	959	6	418 D	35.9%	63.7%	36.0%	64.0%
PROWERS	5,822	2,044	3,759	19	1,715 D	35.1%	64.6%	35.2%	64.8%
PUEBLO	48,536	13,103	34,933	500	21,830 D	27.0%	72.0%	27.3%	72.7%
RIO BLANCO	2,152	1,015	1,134	3	119 D	47.2%	52.7%	47.2%	52.8%
RIO GRANDE	3,867	1,699	2,161	7	462 D	43.9%	55.9%	44.0%	56.0%
ROUTT	2,964	1,095	1,853	16	758 D	36.9%	62.5%	37.1%	62.9%
SAGUACHE	1,725	622	1,099	4	477 D	36.1%	63.7%	36.1%	63.9%
SAN JUAN	407	129	278		149 D	31.7%	68.3%	31.7%	68.3%
SAN MIGUEL	970	332	636	2	304 D	34.2%	65.6%	34.3%	65.7%
SEDGWICK	1,839	895	942	2	47 D	48.7%	51.2%	48.7%	51.3%
SUMMIT	828	344	483	1	139 D	41.5%	58.3%	41.6%	58.4%
TELLER	1,264	577	685	2	108 D	45.6%	54.2%	45.7%	54.3%

COLORADO

PRESIDENT 1960

County	Total Vote	Republican	Democratic	Other	Rep.-Dem. Plurality	Percentage Total Vote Rep.	Dem.	Major Vote Rep.	Dem.
WASHINGTON	3,022	1,979	1,039	4	940 R	65.5%	34.4%	65.6%	34.4%
WELD	28,790	17,558	11,179	53	6,379 R	51.0%	38.8%	61.1%	38.9%
YUMA	4,305	2,806	1,489	10	1,317 R	55.2%	34.6%	65.3%	34.7%
TOTAL	736,236	402,242	330,629	3,365	71,613 R	54.6%	44.9%	54.9%	45.1%

PRESIDENT 1964

County	Total Vote	Republican	Democratic	Other	Rep.-Dem. Plurality	Percentage Total Vote Rep.	Dem.	Major Vote Rep.	Dem.
WASHINGTON	2,779	1,434	1,341	4	93 R	51.6%	48.3%	51.7%	48.3%
WELD	29,679	12,204	17,268	207	5,064 D	41.1%	58.2%	41.4%	58.6%
YUMA	4,171	2,007	2,145	19	138 D	48.1%	51.4%	48.3%	51.7%
TOTAL	776,986	296,767	476,024	4,195	179,257 D	38.2%	61.3%	38.4%	61.6%

COLORADO

OTHER VOTE COMPOSITION:

1920 8,046 Socialist; 3,016 Farmer-Labor; 2,807 Prohibition.
1924 69,946 Progressive; 966 Prohibition; 562 Communist; 378 Socialist Labor.
1928 3,472 Socialist; 1,092 Farmer-Labor; 675 Communist.
1932 13,591 Socialist; 1,928 Prohibition; 787 Communist; 469 Farmer-Labor; 427 Socialist Labor.
1936 9,962 Union; 1,594 Socialist; 497 Communist; 344 Socialist Labor.

1940 1,899 Socialist; 1,597 Prohibition; 378 Communist.
1944 Socialist.
1948 6,115 Progressive; 1,678 Socialist; 228 Socialist Workers; 214 Socialist Labor.
1952 2,181 Constitution (MacArthur); 1,919 Progressive; 365 Socialist; 352 Socialist Labor.
1956 3,308 Socialist Labor; 759 States Rights; 531 Socialist.

1960 2,803 Socialist Labor; 562 Socialist Workers.
1964 2,537 Socialist Workers; 1,356 Prohibition; 302 Socialist Labor.

SPECIAL CASES:

1924 Progressive total includes 57,368 LaFollette-Wheeler and 12,578 Farmer-Labor-and-LaFollette votes. This combined vote carried one county and was second in others.

CONNECTICUT

PRESIDENT 1920

County	Total Vote	Republican	Democratic	Other	Rep.-Dem. Plurality	Total Vote Rep.	Total Vote Dem.	Major Vote Rep.	Major Vote Dem.
FAIRFIELD	83,113	55,251	24,761	3,101	30,490 R	66.5%	29.8%	69.1%	30.9%
HARTFORD	88,979	54,046	30,287	4,646	23,759 R	60.7%	34.0%	64.1%	35.9%
LITCHFIELD	21,847	14,405	6,938	504	7,457 R	65.9%	31.8%	67.5%	32.5%
MIDDLESEX	12,948	8,447	4,170	331	4,277 R	65.2%	32.2%	66.9%	33.1%
NEW HAVEN	109,474	65,938	37,977	5,559	27,951 R	60.2%	34.7%	63.5%	36.5%
NEW LONDON	27,520	17,422	9,209	889	8,213 R	63.3%	33.5%	65.4%	34.6%
TOLLAND	7,765	5,135	2,308	322	2,827 R	66.1%	29.7%	69.0%	31.0%
WINDHAM	13,872	8,554	5,071	207	3,553 R	62.0%	36.6%	62.9%	37.1%
TOTAL	365,518	229,238	120,721	15,559	108,517 R	62.7%	33.0%	65.5%	34.5%

PRESIDENT 1924

County	Total Vote	Republican	Democratic	Other	Rep.-Dem. Plurality	Total Vote Rep.	Total Vote Dem.	Major Vote Rep.	Major Vote Dem.
FAIRFIELD	87,647	58,041	18,815	10,791	39,226 R	66.2%	21.5%	75.5%	24.5%
HARTFORD	99,142	61,381	28,139	9,622	33,242 R	61.9%	28.4%	68.6%	31.4%
LITCHFIELD	25,273	15,499	6,645	3,129	8,854 R	61.3%	26.3%	70.0%	30.0%
MIDDLESEX	14,387	9,383	4,009	995	5,374 R	65.2%	27.9%	70.1%	29.9%
NEW HAVEN	120,519	69,164	36,247	15,108	32,917 R	57.4%	30.1%	65.6%	34.4%
NEW LONDON	29,206	18,205	8,615	2,386	9,590 R	62.3%	29.5%	67.9%	32.1%
TOLLAND	8,285	5,161	2,239	885	2,922 R	62.3%	27.0%	69.7%	30.3%
WINDHAM	15,937	9,488	5,475	974	4,013 R	59.5%	34.4%	63.4%	36.6%
TOTAL	400,396	246,322	110,184	43,890	136,138 R	61.5%	27.5%	69.1%	30.9%

CONNECTICUT

PRESIDENT 1928

County	Total Vote	Republican	Democratic	Other	Rep.-Dem. Plurality	Total Vote Rep.	Total Vote Dem.	Major Vote Rep.	Major Vote Dem.
FAIRFIELD	127,948	71,410	55,491	1,047	15,919 R	55.8%	43.4%	56.3%	43.7%
HARTFORD	142,955	75,997	65,789	1,169	10,208 R	53.2%	46.0%	53.6%	46.4%
LITCHFIELD	30,061	19,157	10,766	138	8,391 R	63.7%	35.8%	64.0%	36.0%
MIDDLESEX	18,700	11,205	7,380	115	3,825 R	59.9%	39.5%	60.3%	39.7%
NEW HAVEN	165,048	80,952	82,657	1,439	1,705 D	49.0%	50.1%	49.5%	50.5%
NEW LONDON	37,969	21,378	16,299	292	5,079 R	56.3%	42.9%	56.7%	43.3%
TOLLAND	10,884	6,502	4,256	126	2,246 R	59.7%	39.1%	60.4%	39.6%
WINDHAM	19,553	10,040	9,447	66	593 R	51.3%	48.3%	51.5%	48.5%
TOTAL	553,118	296,641	252,085	4,392	44,556 R	53.6%	45.6%	54.1%	45.9%

PRESIDENT 1932

County	Total Vote	Republican	Democratic	Other	Rep.-Dem. Plurality	Total Vote Rep.	Total Vote Dem.	Major Vote Rep.	Major Vote Dem.
FAIRFIELD	144,697	72,238	64,367	8,092	7,871 R	49.9%	44.5%	52.9%	47.1%
HARTFORD	150,153	72,611	72,322	5,220	289 R	48.4%	48.2%	50.1%	49.9%
LITCHFIELD	32,811	18,682	13,469	660	5,213 R	56.9%	41.1%	58.1%	41.9%
MIDDLESEX	20,400	10,770	9,286	344	1,484 R	52.8%	45.5%	53.7%	46.3%
NEW HAVEN	174,141	79,019	86,826	8,296	7,807 D	45.4%	49.9%	47.6%	52.4%
NEW LONDON	40,155	19,721	19,576	858	145 R	49.1%	48.8%	50.2%	49.8%
TOLLAND	11,297	5,857	4,985	455	872 R	51.8%	44.1%	54.0%	46.0%
WINDHAM	20,559	9,522	10,801	206	1,279 D	46.4%	52.6%	46.9%	53.1%
TOTAL	594,183	288,420	281,632	24,131	6,788 R	48.5%	47.4%	50.6%	49.4%

CONNECTICUT

PRESIDENT 1936

County	Total Vote	Republican	Democratic	Other	Rep.-Dem. Plurality	Total Vote Rep.	Total Vote Dem.	Major Vote Rep.	Major Vote Dem.
FAIRFIELD	163,263	67,846	87,329	8,088	19,483 D	41.6%	53.5%	43.7%	56.3%
HARTFORD	176,318	65,652	103,450	7,216	37,798 D	37.2%	58.7%	38.8%	61.2%
LITCHFIELD	37,193	18,850	17,468	875	1,382 R	50.7%	47.0%	51.9%	48.1%
MIDDLESEX	23,578	10,925	12,294	359	1,369 D	46.3%	52.1%	47.1%	52.9%
NEW HAVEN	204,611	76,614	117,308	10,689	40,694 D	37.4%	57.3%	39.5%	60.5%
NEW LONDON	47,703	21,367	24,999	1,337	3,632 D	44.8%	52.4%	46.1%	53.9%
TOLLAND	13,129	5,965	6,676	488	711 D	45.4%	50.8%	47.2%	52.8%
WINDHAM	24,928	11,466	12,605	857	1,139 D	46.0%	50.6%	47.6%	52.4%
TOTAL	690,723	278,685	382,129	29,909	103,444 D	40.3%	55.3%	42.2%	57.8%

PRESIDENT 1940

County	Total Vote	Republican	Democratic	Other	Rep.-Dem. Plurality	Total Vote Rep.	Total Vote Dem.	Major Vote Rep.	Major Vote Dem.
FAIRFIELD	185,707	91,190	93,688	829	2,498 D	49.1%	50.4%	49.3%	50.7%
HARTFORD	202,953	88,155	114,336	462	26,181 D	43.4%	56.3%	43.5%	56.5%
LITCHFIELD	42,542	22,956	19,537	49	3,419 R	54.0%	45.9%	54.0%	46.0%
MIDDLESEX	26,530	13,447	13,044	39	403 R	50.7%	49.2%	50.8%	49.2%
NEW HAVEN	229,689	103,100	126,072	517	22,972 D	44.9%	54.9%	45.0%	55.0%
NEW LONDON	51,773	23,389	28,286	98	4,897 D	45.2%	54.6%	45.3%	54.7%
TOLLAND	15,197	7,503	7,669	25	166 D	49.4%	50.5%	49.5%	50.5%
WINDHAM	27,111	12,079	14,989	43	2,910 D	44.6%	55.3%	44.6%	55.4%
TOTAL	781,502	361,819	417,621	2,062	55,802 D	46.3%	53.4%	46.4%	53.6%

CONNECTICUT

PRESIDENT 1944

County	Total Vote	Republican	Democratic	Other	Rep.-Dem. Plurality	Total Vote Rep.	Total Vote Dem.	Major Vote Rep.	Major Vote Dem.
FAIRFIELD	205,297	103,693	99,181	2,423	4,512 R	50.5%	48.3%	51.1%	48.9%
HARTFORD	224,218	95,224	127,841	1,153	32,617 D	42.5%	57.0%	42.7%	57.3%
LITCHFIELD	43,479	24,019	19,212	248	4,807 R	55.2%	44.2%	55.6%	44.4%
MIDDLESEX	28,042	14,315	13,551	176	764 R	51.0%	48.3%	51.4%	48.6%
NEW HAVEN	234,144	108,883	123,450	1,811	14,567 D	46.5%	52.7%	46.9%	53.1%
NEW LONDON	53,742	24,153	29,304	285	5,151 D	44.9%	54.5%	45.2%	54.8%
TOLLAND	16,046	8,208	7,721	117	487 R	51.2%	48.1%	51.5%	48.5%
WINDHAM	27,022	12,032	14,886	104	2,854 D	44.5%	55.1%	44.7%	55.3%
TOTAL	831,990	390,527	435,146	6,317	44,619 D	46.9%	52.3%	47.3%	52.7%

PRESIDENT 1948

County	Total Vote	Republican	Democratic	Other	Rep.-Dem. Plurality	Total Vote Rep.	Total Vote Dem.	Major Vote Rep.	Major Vote Dem.
FAIRFIELD	217,072	118,636	90,767	7,669	27,869 R	54.7%	41.8%	56.7%	43.3%
HARTFORD	235,293	105,262	124,874	5,157	19,612 D	44.7%	53.1%	45.7%	54.3%
LITCHFIELD	46,299	26,848	18,628	823	8,220 R	58.0%	40.2%	59.0%	41.0%
MIDDLESEX	31,265	16,119	14,609	537	1,510 R	51.6%	46.7%	52.5%	47.5%
NEW HAVEN	248,993	120,769	121,591	6,633	822 D	48.5%	48.8%	49.8%	50.2%
NEW LONDON	57,814	27,416	29,425	973	2,009 D	47.4%	50.9%	48.2%	51.8%
TOLLAND	17,329	9,012	7,970	347	1,042 R	52.0%	46.0%	53.1%	46.9%
WINDHAM	29,453	13,692	15,433	328	1,741 D	46.5%	52.4%	47.0%	53.0%
TOTAL	883,518	437,754	423,297	22,467	14,457 R	49.5%	47.9%	50.8%	49.2%

PRESIDENT 1952

County	Total Vote	Republican	Democratic	Other	Rep.-Dem. Plurality	Total Vote Rep.	Total Vote Dem.	Major Vote Rep.	Major Vote Dem.
FAIRFIELD	275,495	167,278	106,403	1,814	60,875 R	60.7%	38.6%	61.1%	38.9%
HARTFORD	297,715	150,332	146,551	832	3,781 R	50.5%	49.2%	50.6%	49.4%
LITCHFIELD	56,005	35,735	20,163	107	15,572 R	63.8%	36.0%	63.9%	36.1%
MIDDLESEX	37,953	22,157	15,722	74	6,435 R	58.4%	41.4%	58.5%	41.5%
NEW HAVEN	303,542	165,917	136,476	1,149	29,441 R	54.7%	45.0%	54.9%	45.1%
NEW LONDON	69,670	38,148	31,374	148	6,774 R	54.8%	45.0%	54.9%	45.1%
TOLLAND	22,943	13,466	9,445	52	4,041 R	58.8%	41.1%	58.8%	41.2%
WINDHAM	33,588	17,979	15,535	74	2,444 R	53.5%	46.3%	53.6%	46.4%
TOTAL	1,096,911	611,012	481,649	4,250	129,363 R	55.7%	43.9%	55.9%	44.1%

PRESIDENT 1956

County	Total Vote	Republican	Democratic	Other	Rep.-Dem. Plurality	Total Vote Rep.	Total Vote Dem.	Major Vote Rep.	Major Vote Dem.
FAIRFIELD	284,847	199,841	84,890	116	114,951 R	70.2%	29.8%	70.2%	29.8%
HARTFORD	302,842	175,894	126,923	25	48,971 R	58.1%	41.9%	58.1%	41.9%
LITCHFIELD	57,261	40,029	17,226	6	22,803 R	69.9%	30.1%	69.9%	30.1%
MIDDLESEX	39,355	25,496	13,851	8	11,645 R	64.8%	35.2%	64.8%	35.2%
NEW HAVEN	303,459	191,215	112,208	36	79,007 R	63.0%	37.0%	63.0%	37.0%
NEW LONDON	70,781	43,453	27,317	11	16,136 R	61.4%	38.6%	61.4%	38.6%
TOLLAND	24,992	15,880	9,111	1	6,769 R	63.5%	36.5%	63.5%	36.5%
WINDHAM	33,584	20,029	13,553	2	6,476 R	59.6%	40.4%	59.6%	40.4%
TOTAL	1,117,121	711,837	405,079	205	306,758 R	63.7%	36.3%	63.7%	36.3%

PRESIDENT 1960

County	Total Vote	Republican	Democratic	Other	Rep.-Dem. Plurality	Total Vote Rep.	Total Vote Dem.	Major Vote Rep.	Major Vote Dem.
FAIRFIELD	314,226	167,778	146,442	6	21,336 R	53.4%	46.6%	53.4%	46.6%
HARTFORD	331,864	136,459	195,403	2	58,944 D	41.1%	58.9%	41.1%	58.9%
LITCHFIELD	63,108	34,043	29,062	3	4,981 R	53.9%	46.1%	53.9%	46.1%
MIDDLESEX	44,204	22,045	22,158	1	113 D	49.9%	50.1%	49.9%	50.1%
NEW HAVEN	325,539	136,852	188,685	2	51,833 D	42.0%	58.0%	42.0%	58.0%
NEW LONDON	78,696	38,070	40,625	1	2,555 D	48.4%	51.6%	48.4%	51.6%
TOLLAND	29,961	15,386	14,575		811 R	51.4%	48.6%	51.4%	48.6%
WINDHAM	35,285	15,180	20,105		4,925 D	43.0%	57.0%	43.0%	57.0%
TOTAL	1,222,883	565,813	657,055	15	91,242 D	46.3%	53.7%	46.3%	53.7%

PRESIDENT 1964

County	Total Vote	Republican	Democratic	Other	Rep.-Dem. Plurality	Total Vote Rep.	Total Vote Dem.	Major Vote Rep.	Major Vote Dem.
FAIRFIELD	320,619	125,576	194,782	261	69,206 D	39.2%	60.8%	39.2%	60.8%
HARTFORD	329,504	88,811	240,071	622	151,260 D	27.0%	72.9%	27.0%	73.0%
LITCHFIELD	61,068	20,834	40,172	62	19,338 D	34.1%	65.8%	34.2%	65.8%
MIDDLESEX	45,285	14,697	30,517	71	15,820 D	32.5%	67.4%	32.5%	67.5%
NEW HAVEN	316,570	97,656	218,743	171	121,087 D	30.8%	69.1%	30.9%	69.1%
NEW LONDON	78,991	24,391	54,551	49	30,160 D	30.9%	69.1%	30.9%	69.1%
TOLLAND	32,204	9,951	22,195	58	12,244 D	30.9%	68.9%	30.9%	69.0%
WINDHAM	34,337	9,080	25,238	19	16,158 D	26.4%	73.5%	26.5%	73.5%
TOTAL	1,218,578	390,996	826,269	1,313	435,273 D	32.1%	67.8%	32.1%	67.9%

CONNECTICUT

OTHER VOTE COMPOSITION:

1920	10,350 Socialist; 1,947 Farmer-Labor; 1,771 Prohibition; 1,491 Socialist Labor.
1924	42,416 Progressive; 1,373 Socialist Labor; 101 scattered.
1928	3,029 Socialist; 738 Communist; 625 Socialist Labor.
1932	20,480 Socialist; 2,287 Socialist Labor; 1,364 Communist.
1936	21,805 Union; 5,683 Socialist; 1,228 Socialist Labor; 1,193 Communist.
1940	1,091 Communist; 971 Socialist Labor.
1944	5,097 Socialist; 1,220 Socialist Labor.
1948	13,713 Progressive; 6,964 Socialist; 1,184 Socialist Labor; 606 Socialist Workers.
1952	2,244 Socialist; 1,466 Progressive; 535 Socialist Labor; 5 scattered.
1956	Scattered.
1960	Scattered.
1964	Scattered.

SPECIAL CASES:

1940	Republican total includes 361,021 Republican and 798 Union votes.

DELAWARE

PRESIDENT 1920

County	Total Vote	Republican	Democratic	Other	Rep.-Dem. Plurality	Percentage Total Vote Rep.	Dem.	Major Vote Rep.	Dem.
KENT	13,889	6,511	7,211	167	700 D	46.9%	51.9%	47.4%	52.6%
NEW CASTLE	62,791	36,600	24,252	1,939	12,348 R	58.3%	38.6%	60.1%	39.9%
SUSSEX	18,195	9,747	8,448		1,299 R	53.6%	46.4%	53.6%	46.4%
TOTAL	94,875	52,858	39,911	2,106	12,947 R	55.7%	42.1%	57.0%	43.0%

PRESIDENT 1924

County	Total Vote	Republican	Democratic	Other	Rep.-Dem. Plurality	Percentage Total Vote Rep.	Dem.	Major Vote Rep.	Dem.
KENT	14,021	6,894	6,935	192	41 D	49.2%	49.5%	49.9%	50.1%
NEW CASTLE	57,851	35,427	17,842	4,582	17,585 R	61.2%	30.8%	66.5%	33.5%
SUSSEX	19,013	10,120	8,668	225	1,452 R	53.2%	45.6%	53.9%	46.1%
TOTAL	90,885	52,441	33,445	4,999	18,996 R	57.7%	36.8%	61.1%	38.9%

PRESIDENT 1928

County	Total Vote	Republican	Democratic	Other	Rep.-Dem. Plurality	Percentage Total Vote Rep.	Dem.	Major Vote Rep.	Dem.
KENT	14,089	8,335	5,727	27	2,608 R	59.2%	40.6%	59.3%	40.7%
NEW CASTLE	70,412	47,641	22,464	307	25,177 R	67.7%	31.9%	68.0%	32.0%
SUSSEX	20,101	12,884	7,163	54	5,721 R	64.1%	35.6%	64.3%	35.7%
TOTAL	104,602	68,860	35,354	388	33,506 R	65.8%	33.8%	66.1%	33.9%

PRESIDENT 1932

County	Total Vote	Republican	Democratic	Other	Rep.-Dem. Plurality	Percentage Total Vote Rep.	Dem.	Major Vote Rep.	Dem.
KENT	15,490	6,597	8,829	64	2,232 D	42.6%	57.0%	42.8%	57.2%
NEW CASTLE	74,109	39,844	32,872	1,393	6,972 R	53.8%	44.4%	54.8%	45.2%
SUSSEX	23,302	10,632	12,618	52	1,986 D	45.6%	54.1%	45.7%	54.3%
TOTAL	112,901	57,073	54,319	1,509	2,754 R	50.6%	48.1%	51.2%	48.8%

PRESIDENT 1936

County	Total Vote	Republican	Democratic	Other	Rep.-Dem. Plurality	Percentage Total Vote Rep.	Dem.	Major Vote Rep.	Dem.
KENT	17,005	7,389	9,588	28	2,199 D	43.5%	56.4%	43.5%	56.5%
NEW CASTLE	85,766	37,851	47,315	600	9,464 D	44.1%	55.2%	44.4%	55.6%
SUSSEX	24,832	11,996	12,799	37	803 D	48.3%	51.5%	48.4%	51.6%
TOTAL	127,603	57,236	69,702	665	12,466 D	44.9%	54.6%	45.1%	54.9%

PRESIDENT 1940

County	Total Vote	Republican	Democratic	Other	Rep.-Dem. Plurality	Percentage Total Vote Rep.	Dem.	Major Vote Rep.	Dem.
KENT	17,353	8,079	9,226	48	1,147 D	46.6%	53.2%	46.7%	53.3%
NEW CASTLE	93,936	41,508	52,167	261	10,659 D	44.2%	55.2%	44.3%	55.6%
SUSSEX	25,085	11,853	13,206	26	1,353 D	47.3%	52.6%	47.3%	52.7%
TOTAL	136,374	61,440	74,599	335	13,159 D	45.1%	54.7%	45.2%	54.8%

DELAWARE

PRESIDENT 1944

County	Total Vote	Republican	Democratic	Other	Rep.-Dem. Plurality	Percentage Total Vote Rep.	Dem.	Major Vote Rep.	Dem.
KENT	15,026	7,069	7,900	57	831 D	47.0%	52.6%	47.2%	52.8%
NEW CASTLE	87,689	37,783	49,588	318	11,805 D	43.1%	56.5%	43.2%	56.8%
SUSSEX	22,646	11,895	10,678	73	1,217 R	52.5%	47.2%	52.7%	47.3%
TOTAL	125,361	56,747	68,166	448	11,419 D	45.3%	54.4%	45.4%	54.6%

PRESIDENT 1948

County	Total Vote	Republican	Democratic	Other	Rep.-Dem. Plurality	Percentage Total Vote Rep.	Dem.	Major Vote Rep.	Dem.
KENT	16,790	8,501	8,174	115	327 R	50.6%	48.7%	51.0%	49.0%
NEW CASTLE	97,001	47,451	48,117	1,433	666 D	48.9%	49.6%	49.7%	50.3%
SUSSEX	25,282	13,636	11,522	124	2,114 R	53.9%	45.6%	54.2%	45.8%
TOTAL	139,073	69,588	67,813	1,672	1,775 R	50.0%	48.8%	50.6%	49.4%

PRESIDENT 1952

County	Total Vote	Republican	Democratic	Other	Rep.-Dem. Plurality	Percentage Total Vote Rep.	Dem.	Major Vote Rep.	Dem.
KENT	20,108	10,144	9,874	90	270 R	50.4%	49.1%	50.7%	49.3%
NEW CASTLE	121,396	62,658	58,387	351	4,271 R	51.6%	48.1%	51.8%	48.2%
SUSSEX	32,521	17,257	15,054	210	2,203 R	53.1%	46.3%	53.4%	46.6%
TOTAL	174,025	90,059	83,315	651	6,744 R	51.8%	47.9%	51.9%	48.1%

PRESIDENT 1956

County	Total Vote	Republican	Democratic	Other	Rep.-Dem. Plurality	Percentage Total Vote Rep.	Dem.	Major Vote Rep.	Dem.
KENT	19,745	10,303	9,319	123	984 R	52.2%	47.2%	52.5%	47.5%
NEW CASTLE	127,813	71,133	56,405	275	14,728 R	55.7%	44.1%	55.8%	44.2%
SUSSEX	30,430	16,621	13,697	112	2,924 R	54.6%	45.0%	54.8%	45.2%
TOTAL	177,988	98,057	79,421	510	18,636 R	55.1%	44.6%	55.3%	44.7%

PRESIDENT 1960

County	Total Vote	Republican	Democratic	Other	Rep.-Dem. Plurality	Percentage Total Vote Rep.	Dem.	Major Vote Rep.	Dem.
KENT	21,616	10,697	10,754	165	57 D	49.5%	49.8%	49.9%	50.1%
NEW CASTLE	142,974	69,284	73,364	326	4,080 D	48.5%	51.3%	48.6%	51.4%
SUSSEX	32,093	16,392	15,472	229	920 R	51.1%	48.2%	51.4%	48.6%
TOTAL	196,683	96,373	99,590	720	3,217 D	49.0%	50.6%	49.2%	50.8%

PRESIDENT 1964

County	Total Vote	Republican	Democratic	Other	Rep.-Dem. Plurality	Percentage Total Vote Rep.	Dem.	Major Vote Rep.	Dem.
KENT	22,054	9,006	12,981	67	3,975 D	40.8%	58.9%	41.0%	59.0%
NEW CASTLE	146,893	54,767	91,752	374	36,985 D	37.3%	62.5%	37.4%	62.6%
SUSSEX	32,373	14,305	17,971	97	3,666 D	44.2%	55.5%	44.3%	55.7%
TOTAL	201,320	78,078	122,704	538	44,626 D	38.8%	60.9%	38.9%	61.1%

DELAWARE

OTHER VOTE COMPOSITION:

1920	988 Socialist; 986 Prohibition; 93 Farmer-Labor; 39 Single Tax.
1924	4,979 Progressive; 20 Commonwealth Land.
1928	329 Socialist; 59 Communist.
1932	1,376 Socialist; 133 Communist.
1936	442 Union; 172 Socialist; 51 Communist.
1940	220 Prohibition; 115 Socialist.
1944	294 Prohibition; 154 Socialist.
1948	1,050 Progressive; 343 Prohibition; 250 Socialist; 29 Socialist Labor.
1952	242 Socialist Labor; 234 Prohibition; 155 Progressive; 20 Socialist.
1956	400 Prohibition; 110 Socialist Labor.
1960	354 National States Rights; 284 Prohibition; 82 Socialist Labor.
1964	425 Prohibition; 113 Socialist Labor.

SPECIAL CASES:

1936	Republican total includes 54,014 Republican and 3,222 Independent Republican votes.

FLORIDA

PRESIDENT 1920

County	Total Vote	Republican	Democratic	Other	Rep.-Dem. Plurality	Total Vote Rep.	Total Vote Dem.	Major Vote Rep.	Major Vote Dem.
ALACHUA	4,564	1,119	3,310	135	2,191 D	24.5%	72.5%	25.3%	74.7%
BAKER	508	115	346	47	231 D	22.6%	68.1%	24.9%	75.1%
BAY	1,490	551	818	121	267 D	37.0%	54.9%	40.2%	59.8%
BRADFORD	1,610	248	1,269	93	1,021 D	15.4%	78.8%	16.3%	83.7%
BREVARD	1,677	659	894	124	235 D	39.3%	53.3%	42.4%	57.6%
BROWARD	999	442	415	142	27 R	44.2%	41.5%	51.6%	48.4%
CALHOUN	1,098	99	861	138	762 D	9.0%	78.4%	10.3%	89.7%
CHARLOTTE									
CITRUS	788	94	651	43	557 D	11.9%	82.6%	12.6%	87.4%
CLAY	1,123	486	558	79	72 D	43.3%	49.7%	46.6%	53.4%
COLLIER									
COLUMBIA	1,543	162	1,248	133	1,086 D	10.5%	80.9%	11.5%	88.5%
DADE	8,078	3,077	4,288	713	1,211 D	38.1%	53.1%	41.8%	58.2%
DE SOTO	3,844	1,077	2,496	271	1,419 D	28.0%	64.9%	30.1%	69.9%
DIXIE									
DUVAL	21,257	6,628	13,650	979	7,022 D	31.2%	64.2%	32.7%	67.3%
ESCAMBIA	5,345	1,227	3,485	633	2,258 D	23.0%	65.2%	26.0%	74.0%
FLAGLER	374	74	206	94	132 D	19.8%	55.1%	26.4%	73.6%
FRANKLIN	946	276	587	83	311 D	29.2%	62.1%	32.0%	68.0%
GADSDEN	1,988	38	1,922	28	1,884 D	1.9%	96.7%	1.9%	98.1%
GILCHRIST									
GLADES									
GULF									
HAMILTON	949	151	706	92	555 D	15.9%	74.4%	17.6%	82.4%
HARDEE									
HENDRY									
HERNANDO	818	132	622	64	490 D	16.1%	76.0%	17.5%	82.5%
HIGHLANDS									
HILLSBOROUGH	12,349	3,772	6,976	1,601	3,204 D	30.5%	56.5%	35.1%	64.9%
HOLMES	1,600	537	869	194	332 D	33.6%	54.3%	38.2%	61.8%
INDIAN RIVER									
JACKSON	3,104	508	2,443	153	1,935 D	16.4%	78.7%	17.2%	82.8%
JEFFERSON	1,046	239	754	53	515 D	22.8%	72.1%	24.1%	75.9%
LAFAYETTE	714	69	618	27	549 D	9.7%	86.6%	10.0%	90.0%
LAKE	2,540	734	1,720	86	986 D	28.9%	67.7%	29.9%	70.1%
LEE	1,694	626	938	130	312 D	37.0%	55.4%	40.0%	60.0%
LEON	1,968	452	1,412	104	960 D	23.0%	71.7%	24.2%	75.8%
LEVY	1,278	377	882	19	505 D	29.5%	69.0%	29.9%	70.1%
LIBERTY	454	5	416	33	411 D	1.1%	91.6%	1.2%	98.8%
MADISON	986	30	920	36	890 D	3.0%	93.3%	3.2%	96.8%
MANATEE	2,867	884	1,790	193	906 D	30.8%	62.4%	33.1%	66.9%
MARION	3,902	1,232	2,436	234	1,204 D	31.6%	62.4%	33.6%	66.4%
MARTIN									
MONROE	1,747	510	979	258	469 D	29.2%	56.0%	34.3%	65.7%
NASSAU	1,248	281	900	67	619 D	22.5%	72.1%	23.8%	76.2%
OKALOOSA	1,003	411	568	24	157 D	41.0%	56.6%	42.0%	58.0%
OKEECHOBEE	364	58	237	69	179 D	15.9%	65.1%	19.7%	80.3%
ORANGE	3,668	1,447	2,035	186	588 D	39.4%	55.5%	41.6%	58.4%
OSCEOLA	1,871	1,035	728	108	307 R	55.3%	38.9%	58.7%	41.3%
PALM BEACH	3,886	1,892	1,488	506	404 R	48.7%	38.3%	56.0%	44.0%
PASCO	1,884	630	1,166	88	536 D	33.4%	61.9%	35.1%	64.9%
PINELLAS	5,819	2,529	2,848	442	319 D	43.5%	48.9%	47.0%	53.0%
POLK	5,949	1,782	3,918	249	2,136 D	30.0%	65.9%	31.3%	68.7%
PUTNAM	2,915	1,181	1,557	177	376 D	40.5%	53.4%	43.1%	56.9%
ST JOHNS	3,215	1,221	1,810	184	589 D	38.0%	56.3%	40.3%	59.7%
ST LUCIE	1,997	707	1,167	123	460 D	35.4%	58.4%	37.7%	62.3%
SANTA ROSA	1,153	333	813	7	480 D	28.9%	70.5%	29.1%	70.9%
SARASOTA									
SEMINOLE	2,376	767	1,485	124	718 D	32.3%	62.5%	34.1%	65.9%
SUMTER	1,155	219	921	15	702 D	19.0%	79.7%	19.2%	80.8%

PRESIDENT 1924

County	Total Vote	Republican	Democratic	Other	Rep.-Dem. Plurality	Total Vote Rep.	Total Vote Dem.	Major Vote Rep.	Major Vote Dem.
ALACHUA	2,794	528	1,995	271	1,467 D	18.9%	71.4%	20.9%	79.1%
BAKER	379	124	215	40	91 D	32.7%	56.7%	36.6%	63.4%
BAY	1,248	318	838	92	520 D	25.5%	67.1%	27.5%	72.5%
BRADFORD	660	94	539	27	445 D	14.2%	81.7%	14.8%	85.2%
BREVARD	1,505	515	872	118	357 D	34.2%	57.9%	37.1%	62.9%
BROWARD	982	407	421	154	14 D	41.4%	42.9%	49.2%	50.8%
CALHOUN	519	56	406	57	350 D	10.8%	78.2%	12.1%	87.9%
CHARLOTTE	535	167	321	47	154 D	31.2%	60.0%	34.2%	65.8%
CITRUS	505	30	423	52	393 D	5.9%	83.8%	6.6%	93.4%
CLAY	593	171	339	83	168 D	28.8%	57.2%	33.5%	66.5%
COLLIER	180	15	148	17	133 D	8.3%	82.6%	9.2%	90.8%
COLUMBIA	951	85	776	90	691 D	8.9%	81.6%	9.9%	90.1%
DADE	10,583	2,753	3,474	4,356	721 D	26.0%	32.8%	44.2%	55.8%
DE SOTO	685	230	411	44	181 D	25.1%	70.1%	35.9%	64.1%
DIXIE	273	14	257	2	243 D	5.1%	94.1%	5.2%	94.8%
DUVAL	11,376	3,291	5,908	2,177	2,617 D	28.9%	51.9%	35.8%	64.2%
ESCAMBIA	4,342	1,274	2,290	778	1,016 D	29.3%	52.7%	35.7%	64.3%
FLAGLER	372	75	202	95	127 D	20.2%	54.3%	27.1%	72.9%
FRANKLIN	545	109	417	19	308 D	20.0%	76.5%	20.7%	79.3%
GADSDEN	802	47	681	74	634 D	5.9%	84.9%	6.5%	93.5%
GILCHRIST									
GLADES	347	83	212	52	129 D	23.9%	61.1%	28.1%	71.9%
GULF									
HAMILTON	822	143	619	60	476 D	17.4%	75.3%	18.8%	81.2%
HARDEE	1,165	264	795	106	531 D	22.7%	68.2%	24.9%	75.1%
HENDRY	172	21	132	19	111 D	12.2%	76.7%	13.7%	86.3%
HERNANDO	401	59	300	42	241 D	14.7%	74.8%	16.4%	83.6%
HIGHLANDS	794	265	457	72	192 D	33.4%	57.6%	36.7%	63.3%
HILLSBOROUGH	7,180	1,585	4,470	1,125	2,885 D	22.1%	62.3%	26.2%	73.8%
HOLMES	1,177	377	658	142	281 D	32.0%	55.9%	36.4%	63.6%
INDIAN RIVER									
JACKSON	2,193	320	1,771	102	1,451 D	14.6%	80.8%	15.3%	84.7%
JEFFERSON	681	66	566	49	500 D	9.7%	83.1%	10.4%	89.6%
LAFAYETTE	406	33	358	15	325 D	8.1%	88.2%	8.4%	91.6%
LAKE	2,600	948	1,381	271	433 D	36.5%	53.1%	40.7%	59.3%
LEE	1,622	552	845	225	293 D	34.0%	52.1%	39.5%	60.5%
LEON	1,110	92	947	71	855 D	8.3%	85.3%	8.9%	91.1%
LEVY	816	214	524	78	310 D	26.2%	64.2%	29.0%	71.0%
LIBERTY	224	18	193	13	175 D	8.0%	86.2%	8.5%	91.5%
MADISON	593	23	538	32	515 D	3.9%	90.7%	4.1%	95.9%
MANATEE	1,933	629	1,064	240	435 D	32.5%	55.0%	37.2%	62.8%
MARION	2,081	359	1,528	194	1,169 D	17.3%	73.4%	19.0%	81.0%
MARTIN									
MONROE	1,232	262	835	135	573 D	21.3%	67.8%	23.9%	76.1%
NASSAU	765	106	617	42	511 D	13.9%	80.7%	14.7%	85.3%
OKALOOSA	953	183	642	128	459 D	19.2%	67.4%	22.2%	77.8%
OKEECHOBEE	272	57	182	33	125 D	21.0%	66.9%	23.8%	76.2%
ORANGE	4,108	1,653	1,883	572	230 D	40.2%	45.8%	46.7%	53.3%
OSCEOLA	1,761	589	884	288	295 D	33.4%	50.2%	40.0%	60.0%
PALM BEACH	3,741	1,726	1,543	472	183 R	46.1%	41.2%	52.8%	47.2%
PASCO	1,456	472	780	204	308 D	32.4%	53.6%	37.7%	62.3%
PINELLAS	6,043	2,872	2,633	538	239 R	47.5%	43.6%	52.2%	47.8%
POLK	5,295	1,530	3,070	696	1,540 D	28.9%	58.0%	33.3%	66.7%
PUTNAM	1,634	574	889	171	315 D	35.1%	54.4%	39.2%	60.8%
ST JOHNS	1,884	517	1,023	344	506 D	27.4%	54.3%	33.6%	66.4%
ST LUCIE	1,418	524	722	172	198 D	37.0%	50.9%	42.1%	57.9%
SANTA ROSA	981	229	693	59	464 D	23.3%	70.6%	24.8%	75.2%
SARASOTA	462	187	204	71	17 D	40.5%	44.2%	47.8%	52.2%
SEMINOLE	1,586	372	945	269	573 D	23.5%	59.6%	28.2%	71.8%
SUMTER	678	108	481	89	373 D	15.9%	70.9%	18.3%	81.7%

FLORIDA

PRESIDENT 1920

County	Total Vote	Republican	Democratic	Other	Rep.-Dem. Plurality	Percentage			
						Total Vote		Major Vote	
						Rep.	Dem.	Rep.	Dem.
SUWANNEE	2,048	382	1,486	180	1,104 D	18.7%	72.6%	20.4%	79.6%
TAYLOR	722	128	563	31	435 D	17.7%	78.0%	18.5%	81.5%
UNION									
VOLUSIA	5,266	2,175	2,763	328	588 D	41.3%	52.5%	44.0%	56.0%
WAKULLA	668	119	530	19	411 D	17.8%	79.3%	18.3%	81.7%
WALTON	2,019	619	1,297	103	678 D	30.7%	64.2%	32.3%	67.7%
WASHINGTON	1,210	307	750	153	443 D	25.4%	62.0%	29.0%	71.0%
TOTAL	145,684	44,853	90,515	10,316	45,662 D	30.8%	62.1%	33.1%	66.9%

PRESIDENT 1924

County	Total Vote	Republican	Democratic	Other	Rep.-Dem. Plurality	Percentage			
						Total Vote		Major Vote	
						Rep.	Dem.	Rep.	Dem.
SUWANNEE	1,168	111	977	80	866 D	9.5%	83.6%	10.2%	89.8%
TAYLOR	608	100	476	32	376 D	16.4%	78.3%	17.4%	82.6%
UNION	348	16	322	10	306 D	4.6%	92.5%	4.7%	95.3%
VOLUSIA	3,995	1,631	2,042	322	411 D	40.8%	51.1%	44.4%	55.6%
WAKULLA	389	34	332	23	298 D	8.7%	85.3%	9.3%	90.7%
WALTON	1,172	220	825	127	605 D	18.8%	70.4%	21.1%	78.9%
WASHINGTON	832	206	562	64	356 D	24.8%	67.5%	26.8%	73.2%
TOTAL	109,158	30,633	62,083	16,442	31,450 D	28.1%	56.9%	33.0%	67.0%

FLORIDA

PRESIDENT 1928

County	Total Vote	Republican	Democratic	Other	Rep.-Dem. Plurality	Total Vote Rep.	Total Vote Dem.	Major Vote Rep.	Major Vote Dem.
ALACHUA	4,008	1,824	1,965	219	141 D	45.5%	49.0%	48.1%	51.9%
BAKER	934	676	242	16	434 R	72.4%	25.9%	73.6%	26.4%
BAY	2,200	974	1,190	36	216 D	44.3%	54.1%	45.0%	55.0%
BRADFORD	1,221	534	679	8	145 D	43.7%	55.6%	44.0%	56.0%
BREVARD	2,946	1,830	1,063	53	767 R	62.1%	36.1%	63.3%	36.7%
BROWARD	4,540	2,889	1,564	87	1,325 R	63.6%	34.4%	64.9%	35.1%
CALHOUN	1,168	409	727	32	318 D	35.0%	62.2%	36.0%	64.0%
CHARLOTTE	1,064	593	441	30	152 R	55.7%	41.4%	57.4%	42.6%
CITRUS	1,337	505	816	16	311 D	37.8%	61.0%	38.2%	61.8%
CLAY	1,510	1,088	394	28	694 R	72.1%	26.1%	73.4%	26.6%
COLLIER	408	151	256	1	105 D	37.0%	62.7%	37.1%	62.9%
COLUMBIA	1,716	418	1,276	22	858 D	24.4%	74.4%	24.7%	75.3%
DADE	26,368	15,860	10,136	372	5,724 R	60.1%	38.4%	61.0%	39.0%
DE SOTO	2,158	1,382	748	28	634 R	64.0%	34.7%	64.9%	35.1%
DIXIE	805	463	342		121 R	57.5%	42.5%	57.5%	42.5%
DUVAL	26,689	16,919	9,316	454	7,603 R	63.4%	34.9%	64.5%	35.5%
ESCAMBIA	8,333	4,443	3,772	118	671 R	53.3%	45.3%	54.1%	45.9%
FLAGLER	559	325	219	15	106 R	58.1%	39.2%	59.7%	40.3%
FRANKLIN	754	334	417	3	83 D	44.3%	55.3%	44.5%	55.5%
GADSDEN	1,551	346	1,184	21	838 D	22.3%	76.3%	22.6%	77.4%
GILCHRIST	550	125	392	33	267 D	22.7%	71.3%	24.2%	75.8%
GLADES	616	331	281	4	50 R	53.7%	45.6%	54.1%	45.9%
GULF	446	156	275	15	119 D	35.0%	61.7%	36.2%	63.8%
HAMILTON	992	167	741	84	574 D	16.8%	74.7%	18.4%	81.6%
HARDEE	2,979	2,087	826	66	1,261 R	70.1%	27.7%	71.6%	28.4%
HENDRY	622	337	266	19	71 R	54.2%	42.8%	55.9%	44.1%
HERNANDO	1,383	661	701	21	40 D	47.8%	50.7%	48.5%	51.5%
HIGHLANDS	2,094	1,393	669	32	724 R	66.5%	31.9%	67.6%	32.4%
HILLSBOROUGH	22,088	11,703	9,993	392	1,710 R	53.0%	45.2%	53.9%	46.1%
HOLMES	3,036	2,260	735	41	1,525 R	74.4%	24.2%	75.5%	24.5%
INDIAN RIVER	1,523	847	657	19	190 R	55.6%	43.1%	56.3%	43.7%
JACKSON	3,946	1,398	2,516	32	1,118 D	35.4%	63.8%	35.7%	64.3%
JEFFERSON	1,162	235	919	5	684 D	20.2%	79.1%	20.4%	79.6%
LAFAYETTE	575	135	435	5	300 D	23.5%	75.7%	23.7%	76.3%
LAKE	4,969	3,383	1,474	112	1,909 R	68.1%	29.7%	69.7%	30.3%
LEE	3,258	2,058	1,154	46	904 R	63.2%	35.4%	64.1%	35.9%
LEON	2,549	630	1,888	31	1,258 D	24.7%	74.1%	25.0%	75.0%
LEVY	1,538	711	797	30	86 D	46.2%	51.8%	47.1%	52.9%
LIBERTY	375	147	226	2	79 D	39.2%	60.3%	39.4%	60.6%
MADISON	1,035	266	769		503 D	25.7%	74.3%	25.7%	74.3%
MANATEE	4,235	2,705	1,462	58	1,243 R	63.9%	34.8%	64.8%	35.2%
MARION	3,873	1,927	1,863	83	64 R	49.8%	48.1%	50.8%	49.2%
MARTIN	3,211	1,703	1,074	434	629 R	53.0%	33.4%	61.3%	38.7%
MONROE	3,092	1,142	1,899	51	757 D	36.9%	61.4%	37.6%	62.4%
NASSAU	1,325	863	445	17	418 R	65.1%	33.6%	66.0%	34.0%
OKALOOSA	1,905	1,385	503	17	882 R	72.7%	26.4%	73.4%	26.6%
OKEECHOBEE	954	657	287	10	370 R	68.9%	30.1%	69.6%	30.4%
ORANGE	9,315	6,524	2,616	175	3,908 R	70.0%	28.1%	71.4%	28.6%
OSCEOLA	2,921	1,760	1,127	34	633 R	60.3%	38.6%	61.0%	39.0%
PALM BEACH	8,248	5,298	2,652	298	2,645 R	64.2%	32.2%	66.6%	33.4%
PASCO	2,932	1,591	1,308	33	283 R	54.3%	44.6%	54.9%	45.1%
PINELLAS	14,151	10,545	3,439	167	7,105 R	74.5%	24.3%	75.4%	24.6%
POLK	12,386	7,460	4,576	350	2,884 R	60.2%	36.9%	62.0%	38.0%
PUTNAM	3,341	2,105	1,156	80	949 R	63.0%	34.6%	64.6%	35.4%
ST JOHNS	5,291	1,939	3,307	45	1,363 D	36.6%	62.5%	37.0%	63.0%
ST LUCIE	1,759	983	741	35	242 R	55.9%	42.1%	57.0%	43.0%
SANTA ROSA	2,201	1,628	541	32	1,087 R	74.1%	24.6%	75.1%	24.9%
SARASOTA	2,839	1,603	1,181	55	422 R	56.5%	41.6%	57.6%	42.4%
SEMINOLE	3,036	1,788	1,187	61	601 R	58.9%	39.1%	60.1%	39.9%
SUMTER	2,072	1,152	909	11	243 R	55.5%	43.9%	55.9%	44.1%

PRESIDENT 1932

County	Total Vote	Republican	Democratic	Other	Rep.-Dem. Plurality	Total Vote Rep.	Total Vote Dem.	Major Vote Rep.	Major Vote Dem.
ALACHUA	4,489	983	3,506		2,523 D	21.9%	78.1%	21.9%	78.1%
BAKER	1,365	87	1,278		1,191 D	6.4%	93.6%	6.4%	93.6%
BAY	3,121	429	2,692		2,263 D	13.7%	86.3%	13.7%	86.3%
BRADFORD	1,527	210	1,317		1,107 D	13.8%	86.2%	13.8%	86.2%
BREVARD	2,808	956	1,852		896 D	34.0%	66.0%	34.0%	66.0%
BROWARD	5,010	1,717	3,293		1,576 D	34.3%	65.7%	34.3%	65.7%
CALHOUN	1,460	129	1,331		1,202 D	8.8%	91.2%	8.8%	91.2%
CHARLOTTE	1,350	396	954		558 D	29.3%	70.7%	29.3%	70.7%
CITRUS	1,356	147	1,209		1,062 D	10.8%	89.2%	10.8%	89.2%
CLAY	1,641	556	1,085		729 D	30.2%	69.8%	30.2%	69.8%
COLLIER	461	37	424		387 D	8.0%	92.0%	8.0%	92.0%
COLUMBIA	2,671	174	2,497		2,323 D	6.5%	93.5%	6.5%	93.5%
DADE	27,064	9,244	17,820		8,576 D	34.2%	65.8%	34.2%	65.8%
DE SOTO	2,130	506	1,624		1,118 D	23.8%	76.2%	23.8%	76.2%
DIXIE	1,151	55	1,096		1,041 D	4.8%	95.2%	4.8%	95.2%
DUVAL	25,134	6,096	19,038		12,942 D	24.3%	75.7%	24.3%	75.7%
ESCAMBIA	7,840	1,658	6,182		4,524 D	21.1%	78.9%	21.1%	78.9%
FLAGLER	569	94	475		381 D	16.5%	83.5%	16.5%	83.5%
FRANKLIN	1,057	99	958		859 D	9.4%	90.6%	9.4%	90.6%
GADSDEN	1,970	105	1,865		1,760 D	5.3%	94.7%	5.3%	94.7%
GILCHRIST	871	57	814		757 D	6.5%	93.5%	6.5%	93.5%
GLADES	676	148	528		380 D	21.9%	78.1%	21.9%	78.1%
GULF	678	30	648		618 D	4.4%	95.6%	4.4%	95.6%
HAMILTON	1,271	110	1,161		1,051 D	8.7%	91.3%	8.7%	91.3%
HARDEE	3,051	566	2,485		1,919 D	18.6%	81.4%	18.6%	81.4%
HENDRY	846	163	683		520 D	19.3%	80.7%	19.3%	80.7%
HERNANDO	1,355	258	1,097		839 D	19.0%	81.0%	19.0%	81.0%
HIGHLANDS	2,376	851	1,525		674 D	35.8%	64.2%	35.8%	64.2%
HILLSBOROUGH	23,854	4,711	19,143		14,432 D	19.7%	80.3%	19.7%	80.3%
HOLMES	3,130	429	2,701		2,272 D	13.7%	86.3%	13.7%	86.3%
INDIAN RIVER	1,754	446	1,308		862 D	25.4%	74.6%	25.4%	74.6%
JACKSON	5,431	599	4,832		4,233 D	11.0%	89.0%	11.0%	89.0%
JEFFERSON	1,499	81	1,418		1,337 D	5.4%	94.6%	5.4%	94.6%
LAFAYETTE	956	27	929		902 D	2.8%	97.2%	2.8%	97.2%
LAKE	4,937	1,867	3,070		1,203 D	37.8%	62.2%	37.8%	62.2%
LEE	3,530	973	2,557		1,584 D	27.6%	72.4%	27.6%	72.4%
LEON	3,202	252	2,950		2,698 D	7.9%	92.1%	7.9%	92.1%
LEVY	1,744	123	1,621		1,498 D	7.1%	92.9%	7.1%	92.9%
LIBERTY	713	31	682		651 D	4.3%	95.7%	4.3%	95.7%
MADISON	1,823	221	1,602		1,381 D	12.1%	87.9%	12.1%	87.9%
MANATEE	4,174	1,280	2,894		1,614 D	30.7%	69.3%	30.7%	69.3%
MARION	4,170	962	3,208		2,246 D	23.1%	76.9%	23.1%	76.9%
MARTIN	1,204	379	825		446 D	31.5%	68.5%	31.5%	68.5%
MONROE	3,174	336	2,838		2,502 D	10.6%	89.4%	10.6%	89.4%
NASSAU	1,502	296	1,206		910 D	19.7%	80.3%	19.7%	80.3%
OKALOOSA	2,369	232	2,137		1,905 D	9.8%	90.2%	9.8%	90.2%
OKEECHOBEE	892	90	802		712 D	10.1%	89.9%	10.1%	89.9%
ORANGE	8,399	3,522	4,877		1,355 D	41.9%	58.1%	41.9%	58.1%
OSCEOLA	2,562	906	1,656		750 D	35.4%	64.6%	35.4%	64.6%
PALM BEACH	11,740	4,006	7,734		3,728 D	34.1%	65.9%	34.1%	65.9%
PASCO	3,310	806	2,504		1,698 D	24.4%	75.6%	24.4%	75.6%
PINELLAS	16,694	7,024	9,670		2,646 D	42.1%	57.9%	42.1%	57.9%
POLK	12,953	3,490	9,463		5,973 D	26.9%	73.1%	26.9%	73.1%
PUTNAM	3,220	911	2,309		1,398 D	28.3%	71.7%	28.3%	71.7%
ST JOHNS	4,609	1,265	3,344		2,079 D	27.4%	72.6%	27.4%	72.6%
ST LUCIE	1,992	390	1,602		1,212 D	19.6%	80.4%	19.6%	80.4%
SANTA ROSA	3,121	315	2,806		2,491 D	10.1%	89.9%	10.1%	89.9%
SARASOTA	2,579	667	1,912		1,245 D	25.9%	74.1%	25.9%	74.1%
SEMINOLE	3,090	948	2,142		1,194 D	30.7%	69.3%	30.7%	69.3%
SUMTER	2,414	276	2,138		1,862 D	11.4%	88.6%	11.4%	88.6%

FLORIDA

PRESIDENT 1928

County	Total Vote	Republican	Democratic	Other	Rep.-Dem. Plurality	Percentage Total Vote Rep.	Total Vote Dem.	Major Vote Rep.	Major Vote Dem.
SUWANNEE	1,913	606	1,286	21	680 D	31.7%	67.2%	32.0%	68.0%
TAYLOR	1,222	465	739	18	274 D	38.1%	60.5%	38.6%	61.4%
UNION	689	177	503	9	326 D	25.7%	73.0%	26.0%	74.0%
VOLUSIA	9,808	6,648	3,043	117	3,605 R	67.8%	31.0%	68.6%	31.4%
WAKULLA	542	66	470	6	404 D	12.2%	86.7%	12.3%	87.7%
WALTON	2,404	1,475	908	21	567 R	61.4%	37.8%	61.9%	38.1%
WASHINGTON	2,398	1,672	671	55	1,001 R	69.7%	28.0%	71.4%	28.6%
TOTAL	252,068	145,860	101,764	4,444	44,096 R	57.9%	40.4%	58.9%	41.1%

PRESIDENT 1932

County	Total Vote	Republican	Democratic	Other	Rep.-Dem. Plurality	Percentage Total Vote Rep.	Total Vote Dem.	Major Vote Rep.	Major Vote Dem.
SUWANNEE	2,286	163	2,123		1,960 D	7.1%	92.9%	7.1%	92.9%
TAYLOR	1,577	130	1,447		1,317 D	8.2%	91.8%	8.2%	91.8%
UNION	957	60	897		837 D	6.3%	93.7%	6.3%	93.7%
VOLUSIA	11,811	4,425	7,386		2,961 D	37.5%	62.5%	37.5%	62.5%
WAKULLA	1,056	20	1,036		1,016 D	1.9%	98.1%	1.9%	98.1%
WALTON	2,782	305	2,477		2,172 D	11.0%	89.0%	11.0%	89.0%
WASHINGTON	2,769	345	2,424		2,079 D	12.5%	87.5%	12.5%	87.5%
TOTAL	276,943	69,170	206,307	1,466	137,137 D	25.0%	74.5%	25.1%	74.9%

FLORIDA

PRESIDENT 1936

County	Total Vote	Republican	Democratic	Other	Rep.-Dem. Plurality	Total Vote Rep.	Total Vote Dem.	Major Vote Rep.	Major Vote Dem.
ALACHUA	5,678	890	4,788		3,898 D	15.7%	84.3%	15.7%	84.3%
BAKER	1,671	116	1,555		1,439 D	6.9%	93.1%	6.9%	93.1%
BAY	3,743	541	3,202		2,661 D	14.5%	85.5%	14.5%	85.5%
BRADFORD	1,787	293	1,494		1,201 D	16.4%	83.6%	16.4%	83.6%
BREVARD	3,447	1,147	2,300		1,153 D	33.3%	66.7%	33.3%	66.7%
BROWARD	6,291	1,906	4,385		2,479 D	30.3%	69.7%	30.3%	69.7%
CALHOUN	1,224	181	1,043		862 D	14.8%	85.2%	14.8%	85.2%
CHARLOTTE	1,330	548	782		234 D	41.2%	58.8%	41.2%	58.8%
CITRUS	1,525	159	1,366		1,207 D	10.4%	89.6%	10.4%	89.6%
CLAY	1,813	562	1,251		689 D	31.0%	69.0%	31.0%	69.0%
COLLIER	990	88	902		814 D	8.9%	91.1%	8.9%	91.1%
COLUMBIA	2,979	196	2,783		2,587 D	6.6%	93.4%	6.6%	93.4%
DADE	38,323	10,295	28,007	21	17,712 D	26.9%	73.1%	26.0%	74.0%
DE SOTO	2,154	560	1,594		1,034 D	26.0%	74.0%	26.0%	74.0%
DIXIE	1,234	64	1,170		1,106 D	5.2%	94.8%	5.2%	94.8%
DUVAL	31,357	5,368	25,989		20,621 D	17.1%	82.9%	17.1%	82.9%
ESCAMBIA	10,705	1,567	9,138		7,571 D	14.6%	85.4%	14.6%	85.4%
FLAGLER	613	106	507		401 D	17.3%	82.7%	17.3%	82.7%
FRANKLIN	1,538	125	1,413		1,288 D	8.1%	91.9%	8.1%	91.9%
GADSDEN	2,770	198	2,572		2,374 D	7.1%	92.9%	7.1%	92.9%
GILCHRIST	892	56	836		780 D	6.3%	93.7%	6.3%	93.7%
GLADES	758	235	523		288 D	31.0%	69.0%	31.0%	69.0%
GULF	915	71	844		773 D	7.8%	92.2%	7.8%	92.2%
HAMILTON	1,627	73	1,554		1,481 D	4.5%	95.5%	4.5%	95.5%
HARDEE	2,986	844	2,142		1,298 D	28.3%	71.7%	26.3%	71.7%
HENDRY	975	234	741		507 D	24.0%	76.0%	24.0%	76.0%
HERNANDO	1,428	313	1,115		802 D	21.9%	78.1%	21.9%	78.1%
HIGHLANDS	2,752	842	1,898		1,056 D	30.6%	69.0%	30.6%	69.4%
HILLSBOROUGH	25,563	5,361	20,202	12	14,841 D	21.0%	79.0%	21.0%	79.0%
HOLMES	3,985	772	3,213		2,441 D	19.4%	80.6%	19.4%	80.6%
INDIAN RIVER	1,802	532	1,270		738 D	29.5%	70.5%	29.5%	70.5%
JACKSON	4,108	351	3,757		3,406 D	8.5%	91.5%	8.5%	91.5%
JEFFERSON	1,370	127	1,243		1,116 D	9.3%	90.7%	9.3%	90.7%
LAFAYETTE	1,364	80	1,284		1,204 D	6.9%	93.1%	6.9%	93.1%
LAKE	6,080	2,034	4,045	1	2,011 D	33.5%	66.5%	33.5%	66.5%
LEE	3,688	1,137	2,549	2	1,412 D	30.8%	69.1%	30.8%	69.2%
LEON	4,047	277	3,770		3,493 D	6.8%	93.2%	6.8%	93.2%
LEVY	2,186	183	2,003		1,820 D	8.4%	91.6%	8.4%	91.6%
LIBERTY	864	64	800		736 D	7.4%	92.6%	7.4%	92.6%
MADISON	2,462	184	2,278		2,094 D	7.5%	92.5%	7.5%	92.5%
MANATEE	4,942	1,455	3,487		2,032 D	29.4%	70.6%	29.4%	70.6%
MARION	5,424	760	4,664		3,904 D	14.0%	86.0%	14.0%	86.0%
MARTIN	1,105	327	778		451 D	29.6%	70.4%	29.6%	70.4%
MONROE	2,887	282	2,605		2,323 D	9.8%	90.2%	9.8%	90.2%
NASSAU	1,337	242	1,095		853 D	18.1%	81.9%	18.1%	81.9%
OKALOOSA	2,890	457	2,433		1,976 D	15.8%	84.2%	15.8%	84.2%
OKEECHOBEE	841	186	655		469 D	22.1%	77.9%	22.1%	77.9%
ORANGE	11,717	4,394	7,314	9	2,920 D	37.5%	62.4%	37.5%	62.5%
OSCEOLA	2,723	1,101	1,622		521 D	40.4%	59.6%	40.4%	59.6%
PALM BEACH	14,117	4,478	9,635	4	5,157 D	31.7%	68.3%	31.7%	68.3%
PASCO	3,388	1,159	2,229		1,870 D	34.2%	65.8%	34.2%	65.8%
PINELLAS	20,265	8,183	12,072	10	3,889 D	40.4%	59.6%	40.4%	59.6%
POLK	14,614	4,164	10,441		5,277 D	28.5%	71.4%	28.5%	71.5%
PUTNAM	3,684	975	2,709		1,734 D	26.5%	73.5%	26.5%	73.5%
ST JOHNS	4,496	1,085	3,411		2,326 D	24.1%	75.9%	24.1%	75.9%
ST LUCIE	2,443	497	1,946		1,449 D	20.3%	79.7%	20.3%	79.7%
SANTA ROSA	3,678	744	2,934		2,190 D	20.2%	79.8%	20.2%	79.8%
SARASOTA	3,473	1,055	2,418		1,363 D	30.4%	69.6%	30.4%	69.6%
SEMINOLE	3,477	897	2,580		1,683 D	25.8%	74.2%	25.8%	74.2%
SUMTER	2,458	734	1,724		990 D	29.9%	70.1%	29.9%	70.1%

PRESIDENT 1940

County	Total Vote	Republican	Democratic	Other	Rep.-Dem. Plurality	Total Vote Rep.	Total Vote Dem.	Major Vote Rep.	Major Vote Dem.
ALACHUA	8,086	1,372	6,714		5,342 D	17.0%	83.0%	17.0%	83.0%
BAKER	1,466	114	1,352		1,238 D	7.8%	92.2%	7.8%	92.2%
BAY	5,837	684	5,153		4,469 D	11.7%	88.3%	11.7%	88.3%
BRADFORD	1,849	261	1,588		1,327 D	14.1%	85.9%	14.1%	85.9%
BREVARD	4,979	1,984	2,995		1,011 D	39.8%	60.2%	39.8%	60.2%
BROWARD	10,410	3,988	6,422		2,434 D	38.3%	61.7%	38.3%	61.7%
CALHOUN	1,893	171	1,722		1,551 D	9.0%	91.0%	9.0%	91.0%
CHARLOTTE	1,317	407	910		503 D	30.9%	69.1%	30.9%	69.1%
CITRUS	1,755	194	1,561		1,367 D	11.1%	88.9%	11.1%	88.9%
CLAY	1,986	498	1,488		990 D	25.1%	74.9%	25.1%	74.9%
COLLIER	965	156	809		653 D	16.2%	83.8%	16.2%	83.8%
COLUMBIA	3,331	443	2,888		2,445 D	13.3%	86.7%	13.3%	86.7%
DADE	77,145	25,224	51,921		26,697 D	32.7%	67.3%	32.7%	67.3%
DE SOTO	2,414	526	1,888		1,362 D	21.8%	78.2%	21.8%	78.2%
DIXIE	1,504	84	1,420		1,336 D	5.6%	94.4%	5.6%	94.4%
DUVAL	50,180	9,177	41,003		31,826 D	18.3%	81.7%	18.3%	81.7%
ESCAMBIA	18,450	2,249	16,201		13,952 D	12.2%	87.8%	12.2%	87.8%
FLAGLER	689	136	553		417 D	19.7%	80.3%	19.7%	80.3%
FRANKLIN	1,502	102	1,400		1,298 D	6.8%	93.2%	6.8%	93.2%
GADSDEN	3,635	417	3,218		2,801 D	11.5%	88.5%	11.5%	88.5%
GILCHRIST	1,099	88	1,011		923 D	8.0%	92.0%	8.0%	92.0%
GLADES	644	180	464		284 D	28.0%	72.0%	28.0%	72.0%
GULF	1,747	105	1,642		1,537 D	6.0%	94.0%	6.0%	94.0%
HAMILTON	1,609	185	1,424		1,239 D	11.5%	88.5%	11.5%	88.5%
HARDEE	3,253	694	2,559		1,865 D	21.3%	78.7%	21.3%	78.7%
HENDRY	1,357	317	1,040		723 D	23.4%	76.6%	23.4%	76.6%
HERNANDO	1,532	381	1,151		770 D	24.9%	75.1%	24.9%	75.1%
HIGHLANDS	3,093	878	2,215		1,337 D	28.4%	71.6%	28.4%	71.6%
HILLSBOROUGH	38,543	7,805	30,738		22,933 D	20.3%	79.7%	20.3%	79.7%
HOLMES	3,571	887	2,684		1,797 D	24.8%	75.2%	24.8%	75.2%
INDIAN RIVER	2,391	904	1,487		583 D	37.8%	62.2%	37.8%	62.2%
JACKSON	6,473	866	5,607		4,741 D	13.4%	86.6%	13.4%	86.6%
JEFFERSON	1,627	215	1,412		1,197 D	13.2%	86.8%	13.2%	86.8%
LAFAYETTE	1,212	122	1,090		968 D	10.1%	89.9%	10.1%	89.9%
LAKE	7,981	2,659	5,322		2,663 D	33.3%	66.7%	33.3%	66.7%
LEE	5,153	1,622	3,531		1,909 D	31.5%	68.5%	31.5%	68.5%
LEON	6,042	583	5,459		4,876 D	9.6%	90.4%	9.6%	90.4%
LEVY	2,793	266	2,527		2,261 D	9.5%	90.5%	9.5%	90.5%
LIBERTY	1,066	119	947		828 D	11.2%	88.8%	11.2%	88.8%
MADISON	2,861	440	2,421		1,981 D	15.4%	84.6%	15.4%	84.6%
MANATEE	7,114	1,983	5,131		3,148 D	27.9%	72.1%	27.9%	72.1%
MARION	7,424	1,297	6,127		4,830 D	17.5%	82.5%	17.5%	82.5%
MARTIN	1,614	596	1,018		422 D	36.9%	63.1%	36.9%	63.1%
MONROE	4,565	463	4,102		3,639 D	10.1%	89.9%	10.1%	89.9%
NASSAU	2,309	421	1,888		1,467 D	18.2%	81.8%	18.2%	81.8%
OKALOOSA	3,693	690	3,003		2,313 D	18.7%	81.3%	18.7%	81.3%
OKEECHOBEE	944	122	822		700 D	12.9%	87.1%	12.9%	87.1%
ORANGE	21,019	8,198	12,821		4,623 D	39.0%	61.0%	39.0%	61.0%
OSCEOLA	3,443	1,428	2,015		587 D	41.5%	58.5%	41.5%	58.5%
PALM BEACH	19,255	7,371	11,884		4,513 D	38.3%	61.7%	38.3%	61.7%
PASCO	4,453	1,362	3,091		1,729 D	30.6%	69.4%	30.6%	69.4%
PINELLAS	32,268	13,327	18,941		5,614 D	41.3%	58.7%	41.3%	58.7%
POLK	23,254	5,564	17,690		12,126 D	23.9%	76.1%	23.9%	76.1%
PUTNAM	4,485	1,008	3,477		2,469 D	22.5%	77.5%	22.5%	77.5%
ST JOHNS	5,425	1,303	4,122		2,819 D	24.0%	76.0%	24.0%	76.0%
ST LUCIE	3,131	962	2,169		1,207 D	30.7%	69.3%	30.7%	69.3%
SANTA ROSA	3,556	656	2,910		2,254 D	18.4%	81.6%	18.4%	81.6%
SARASOTA	5,445	1,672	3,773		2,101 D	30.7%	69.3%	30.7%	69.3%
SEMINOLE	4,519	1,369	3,150		1,781 D	30.3%	69.7%	30.3%	69.7%
SUMTER	2,635	253	2,382		2,129 D	9.6%	90.4%	9.6%	90.4%

FLORIDA

PRESIDENT 1936

County	Total Vote	Republican	Democratic	Other	Rep.-Dem. Plurality	Percentage			
						Total Vote		Major Vote	
						Rep.	Dem.	Rep.	Dem.
SUWANNEE	3,065	202	2,863		2,661 D	6.6%	93.4%	6.6%	93.4%
TAYLOR	2,024	127	1,897		1,770 D	6.3%	93.7%	6.3%	93.7%
UNION	1,178	89	1,089		1,000 D	7.6%	92.4%	7.6%	92.4%
VOLUSIA	12,858	4,934	7,924		2,990 D	38.4%	61.6%	38.4%	61.6%
WAKULLA	1,462	45	1,417		1,372 D	3.1%	96.9%	3.1%	96.9%
WALTON	3,288	510	2,778		2,268 D	15.5%	84.5%	15.5%	84.5%
WASHINGTON	2,778	486	2,289	3	1,803 D	17.5%	82.4%	17.5%	82.5%
TOTAL	327,436	78,248	249,117	71	170,869 D	23.9%	76.1%	23.9%	76.1%

PRESIDENT 1940

County	Total Vote	Republican	Democratic	Other	Rep.-Dem. Plurality	Percentage			
						Total Vote		Major Vote	
						Rep.	Dem.	Rep.	Dem.
SUWANNEE	3,267	401	2,866		2,465 D	12.3%	87.7%	12.3%	87.7%
TAYLOR	2,697	198	2,499		2,301 D	7.3%	92.7%	7.3%	92.7%
UNION	1,119	95	1,024		929 D	8.5%	91.5%	8.5%	91.5%
VOLUSIA	16,533	6,509	10,024		3,515 D	39.4%	60.6%	39.4%	60.6%
WAKULLA	1,406	70	1,336		1,266 D	5.0%	95.0%	5.0%	95.0%
WALTON	3,911	694	3,217		2,523 D	17.7%	82.3%	17.7%	82.3%
WASHINGTON	2,558	643	1,915		1,272 D	25.1%	74.9%	25.1%	74.9%
TOTAL	485,640	126,158	359,334	148	233,176 D	26.0%	74.0%	26.0%	74.0%

FLORIDA

PRESIDENT 1944

County	Total Vote	Republican	Democratic	Other	Rep.-Dem. Plurality	Total Vote Rep.	Total Vote Dem.	Major Vote Rep.	Major Vote Dem.
ALACHUA	7,445	1,690	5,755		4,065 D	22.7%	77.3%	22.7%	77.3%
BAKER	1,264	127	1,137		1,010 D	10.0%	90.0%	10.0%	90.0%
BAY	7,443	1,126	6,317		5,191 D	15.1%	84.9%	15.1%	84.9%
BRADFORD	2,130	355	1,775		1,420 D	16.7%	83.3%	16.7%	83.3%
BREVARD	4,420	1,769	2,651		882 D	40.0%	60.0%	40.0%	60.0%
BROWARD	11,766	5,583	6,183		600 D	47.5%	52.5%	47.5%	52.5%
CALHOUN	1,711	207	1,504		1,297 D	12.1%	87.9%	12.1%	87.9%
CHARLOTTE	1,193	404	789		285 D	33.9%	66.1%	33.9%	66.1%
CITRUS	1,592	264	1,328		1,064 D	16.6%	83.4%	16.6%	83.4%
CLAY	1,771	520	1,251		731 D	29.4%	70.6%	29.4%	70.6%
COLLIER	820	180	640		460 D	22.0%	78.0%	22.0%	78.0%
COLUMBIA	3,004	537	2,467		1,930 D	17.9%	82.1%	17.9%	82.1%
DADE	90,457	30,357	60,100		29,743 D	33.6%	66.4%	33.6%	66.4%
DE SOTO	2,265	543	1,722		1,179 D	24.0%	76.0%	24.0%	76.0%
DIXIE	1,188	84	1,104		1,020 D	7.1%	92.9%	7.1%	92.9%
DUVAL	49,087	12,220	36,867		24,647 D	24.9%	75.1%	24.9%	75.1%
ESCAMBIA	19,431	3,191	16,240		13,049 D	16.4%	83.6%	16.4%	83.6%
FLAGLER	515	114	401		287 D	22.1%	77.9%	22.1%	77.9%
FRANKLIN	1,278	102	1,176		1,074 D	8.0%	92.0%	8.0%	92.0%
GADSDEN	3,036	462	2,574		2,112 D	15.2%	84.8%	15.2%	84.8%
GILCHRIST	943	81	862		781 D	8.6%	91.4%	8.6%	91.4%
GLADES	537	164	373		209 D	30.5%	69.5%	30.5%	69.5%
GULF	1,350	83	1,267		1,184 D	6.1%	93.9%	6.1%	93.9%
HAMILTON	1,462	262	1,200		938 D	17.9%	82.1%	17.9%	82.1%
HARDEE	2,864	708	2,156		1,448 D	24.7%	75.3%	24.7%	75.3%
HENDRY	1,280	347	933		586 D	27.1%	72.9%	27.1%	72.9%
HERNANDO	1,348	346	1,002		656 D	25.7%	74.3%	25.7%	74.3%
HIGHLANDS	2,987	874	2,113		1,239 D	29.3%	70.7%	29.3%	70.7%
HILLSBOROUGH	41,398	10,252	31,146		20,894 D	24.8%	75.2%	24.8%	75.2%
HOLMES	3,560	908	2,652		1,744 D	25.5%	74.5%	25.5%	74.5%
INDIAN RIVER	2,051	759	1,292		533 D	37.0%	63.0%	37.0%	63.0%
JACKSON	5,584	951	4,633		3,682 D	17.0%	83.0%	17.0%	83.0%
JEFFERSON	1,259	188	1,071		883 D	14.9%	85.1%	14.9%	85.1%
LAFAYETTE	965	140	825		685 D	14.5%	85.5%	14.5%	85.5%
LAKE	7,016	2,693	4,323		1,630 D	38.4%	61.6%	38.4%	61.6%
LEE	5,218	1,865	3,353		1,488 D	35.7%	64.3%	35.7%	64.3%
LEON	5,340	835	4,505		3,670 D	15.6%	84.4%	15.6%	84.4%
LEVY	2,332	225	2,107		1,882 D	9.6%	90.4%	9.6%	90.4%
LIBERTY	664	38	626		588 D	5.7%	94.3%	5.7%	94.3%
MADISON	2,207	293	1,914		1,621 D	13.3%	86.7%	13.3%	86.7%
MANATEE	6,762	2,218	4,544		2,326 D	32.8%	67.2%	32.8%	67.2%
MARION	7,239	1,642	5,597		3,955 D	22.7%	77.3%	22.7%	77.3%
MARTIN	1,490	530	960		430 D	35.6%	64.4%	35.6%	64.4%
MONROE	4,448	566	3,882		3,316 D	12.7%	87.3%	12.7%	87.3%
NASSAU	2,419	527	1,892		1,365 D	21.8%	78.2%	21.8%	78.2%
OKALOOSA	3,503	626	2,877		2,251 D	17.9%	82.1%	17.9%	82.1%
OKEECHOBEE	872	119	753		634 D	13.6%	86.4%	13.6%	86.4%
ORANGE	20,834	8,826	12,008		3,182 D	42.4%	57.6%	42.4%	57.6%
OSCEOLA	3,163	1,400	1,763		363 D	44.3%	55.7%	44.3%	55.7%
PALM BEACH	18,721	7,628	11,093		3,465 D	40.7%	59.3%	40.7%	59.3%
PASCO	3,875	1,352	2,523		1,171 D	34.9%	65.1%	34.9%	65.1%
PINELLAS	33,914	14,340	19,574		5,234 D	42.3%	57.7%	42.3%	57.7%
POLK	18,302	5,150	13,152		8,002 D	28.1%	71.9%	28.1%	71.9%
PUTNAM	4,089	1,163	2,926		1,763 D	28.4%	71.6%	28.4%	71.6%
ST JOHNS	5,346	1,582	3,764		2,182 D	29.6%	70.4%	29.6%	70.4%
ST LUCIE	3,049	920	2,129		1,209 D	30.2%	69.8%	30.2%	69.8%
SANTA ROSA	3,469	862	2,607		1,745 D	24.8%	75.2%	24.8%	75.2%
SARASOTA	5,552	2,109	3,443		1,334 D	38.0%	62.0%	38.0%	62.0%
SEMINOLE	4,292	1,352	2,940		1,588 D	31.5%	68.5%	31.5%	68.5%
SUMTER	2,114	276	1,838		1,562 D	13.1%	86.9%	13.1%	86.9%

PRESIDENT 1948

County	Total Vote	Republican	Democratic	Other	Rep.-Dem. Plurality	Total Vote Rep.	Total Vote Dem.	Major Vote Rep.	Major Vote Dem.
ALACHUA	10,182	2,403	3,745	4,034	1,342 D	23.6%	36.8%	39.1%	60.9%
BAKER	1,176	112	849	215	737 D	9.5%	72.2%	11.7%	88.3%
BAY	7,312	928	5,168	1,216	4,240 D	12.7%	70.7%	15.2%	84.8%
BRADFORD	2,190	357	1,228	605	871 D	16.3%	56.1%	22.5%	77.5%
BREVARD	5,564	2,315	2,348	901	33 D	41.6%	42.2%	49.6%	50.4%
BROWARD	19,551	9,933	7,096	2,492	2,837 R	50.9%	36.4%	58.3%	41.7%
CALHOUN	1,794	128	1,404	262	1,276 D	7.1%	78.3%	8.4%	91.6%
CHARLOTTE	1,268	559	520	189	39 R	44.1%	41.0%	51.8%	48.2%
CITRUS	1,652	461	940	251	479 D	27.9%	56.9%	32.9%	67.1%
CLAY	2,772	722	1,544	476	822 D	26.3%	56.3%	31.9%	68.1%
COLLIER	880	247	362	271	115 D	28.1%	41.1%	40.6%	59.4%
COLUMBIA	3,332	553	1,797	982	1,244 D	16.6%	53.9%	23.5%	76.5%
DADE	115,512	41,301	59,681	10,530	18,380 D	37.0%	53.5%	40.9%	59.1%
DE SOTO	2,082	569	1,157	356	588 D	27.3%	55.6%	33.0%	67.0%
DIXIE	1,271	111	862	298	751 D	8.7%	67.8%	11.4%	88.6%
DUVAL	59,695	15,379	28,567	15,749	13,188 D	25.8%	47.9%	35.0%	65.0%
ESCAMBIA	22,156	3,267	13,982	4,907	10,715 D	14.7%	63.1%	18.9%	81.1%
FLAGLER	648	154	153	341	1 R	23.8%	23.6%	50.2%	49.8%
FRANKLIN	1,062	130	635	297	505 D	12.2%	59.8%	17.0%	83.0%
GADSDEN	2,832	376	1,427	999	1,051 D	13.4%	50.9%	20.9%	79.1%
GILCHRIST	1,051	46	884	131	838 D	4.3%	83.3%	4.9%	95.1%
GLADES	555	150	274	131	124 D	27.0%	49.4%	35.4%	64.6%
GULF	1,579	146	1,219	214	1,073 D	9.2%	77.2%	10.7%	89.3%
HAMILTON	1,612	202	1,071	339	869 D	12.5%	66.4%	15.9%	84.1%
HARDEE	2,857	689	1,871	297	1,182 D	24.1%	65.5%	26.9%	73.1%
HENDRY	1,297	340	699	258	359 D	26.2%	53.9%	32.7%	67.3%
HERNANDO	1,672	441	825	406	384 D	26.4%	49.3%	34.8%	65.2%
HIGHLANDS	4,260	1,471	2,257	532	786 D	34.5%	53.0%	39.5%	60.5%
HILLSBOROUGH	41,286	13,529	18,854	8,903	5,325 D	32.8%	45.7%	41.8%	58.2%
HOLMES	3,196	492	1,799	905	1,307 D	15.4%	56.3%	21.5%	78.5%
INDIAN RIVER	2,448	1,134	1,055	259	79 R	46.3%	43.1%	51.8%	48.2%
JACKSON	5,750	648	3,169	1,933	2,521 D	11.3%	55.1%	17.0%	83.0%
JEFFERSON	1,323	153	700	470	547 D	11.6%	52.9%	17.9%	82.1%
LAFAYETTE	1,145	52	975	118	923 D	4.5%	85.2%	5.1%	94.9%
LAKE	8,279	3,579	3,474	1,226	105 R	43.2%	42.0%	50.7%	49.3%
LEE	5,797	2,276	1,883	1,638	393 R	39.3%	32.5%	54.7%	45.3%
LEON	6,161	1,149	3,607	1,405	2,458 D	18.6%	58.5%	24.2%	75.8%
LEVY	2,023	225	1,128	670	903 D	11.1%	55.8%	16.6%	83.4%
LIBERTY	849	30	737	82	707 D	3.5%	86.8%	3.8%	96.1%
MADISON	2,300	207	1,189	904	982 D	9.0%	51.7%	14.8%	85.2%
MANATEE	7,610	3,371	2,766	1,473	605 R	44.3%	36.3%	54.9%	45.1%
MARION	8,156	1,829	4,650	1,677	2,821 D	22.4%	57.0%	28.2%	71.8%
MARTIN	2,114	948	815	351	133 R	44.8%	38.6%	53.8%	46.2%
MONROE	4,503	548	3,759	196	3,211 D	12.2%	83.5%	12.7%	87.3%
NASSAU	2,755	540	1,558	697	978 D	19.6%	55.1%	26.2%	73.8%
OKALOOSA	4,007	486	2,519	1,002	2,033 D	12.1%	62.9%	16.2%	83.8%
OKEECHOBEE	1,048	179	784	85	605 D	17.1%	74.8%	18.6%	81.4%
ORANGE	25,652	11,971	10,063	3,618	1,908 R	46.7%	39.2%	54.3%	45.7%
OSCEOLA	3,532	1,575	1,577	380	2 D	44.6%	44.6%	50.0%	50.0%
PALM BEACH	24,115	10,996	9,408	3,711	1,588 R	45.6%	39.0%	53.9%	46.1%
PASCO	4,881	1,839	2,375	667	536 D	37.7%	48.7%	43.6%	56.4%
PINELLAS	44,524	24,900	15,724	3,900	9,176 R	55.9%	35.3%	61.3%	38.7%
POLK	22,892	7,692	12,034	3,166	4,342 D	33.6%	52.6%	39.0%	61.0%
PUTNAM	4,835	1,435	1,947	1,453	512 D	29.7%	40.3%	42.4%	57.6%
ST JOHNS	6,305	1,840	1,994	2,471	154 D	29.2%	31.6%	48.0%	52.0%
ST LUCIE	4,440	1,689	1,704	1,047	15 D	38.0%	38.4%	49.8%	50.2%
SANTA ROSA	3,524	549	2,316	659	1,767 D	15.6%	65.7%	19.2%	80.8%
SARASOTA	7,125	3,559	2,302	1,264	1,257 R	50.0%	32.3%	60.7%	39.3%
SEMINOLE	5,007	1,665	2,261	1,081	596 D	33.3%	45.2%	42.4%	57.6%
SUMTER	2,152	251	1,411	490	1,160 D	11.7%	65.6%	15.1%	84.9%

FLORIDA

PRESIDENT 1944

County	Total Vote	Republican	Democratic	Other	Rep.-Dem. Plurality	Percentage Total Vote Rep.	Dem.	Major Vote Rep.	Dem.
SUWANNEE	3,009	483	2,526		2,043 D	16.1%	83.9%	16.1%	83.9%
TAYLOR	1,993	165	1,828		1,663 D	8.3%	91.7%	8.3%	91.7%
UNION	1,007	102	905		803 D	10.1%	89.9%	10.1%	89.9%
VOLUSIA	14,394	6,161	8,233		2,072 D	42.8%	57.2%	42.8%	57.2%
WAKULLA	1,091	73	1,018		945 D	6.7%	93.3%	6.7%	93.3%
WALTON	3,258	689	2,569		1,880 D	21.1%	78.9%	21.1%	78.9%
WASHINGTON	2,206	507	1,699		1,192 D	23.0%	77.0%	23.0%	77.0%
TOTAL	482,803	143,215	339,377	211	196,162 D	29.7%	70.3%	29.7%	70.3%

PRESIDENT 1948

County	Total Vote	Republican	Democratic	Other	Rep.-Dem. Plurality	Percentage Total Vote Rep.	Dem.	Major Vote Rep.	Dem.
SUWANNEE	4,235	398	3,033	804	2,635 D	9.4%	71.6%	11.6%	88.4%
TAYLOR	1,999	216	1,354	429	1,138 D	10.8%	67.7%	13.8%	86.2%
UNION	874	55	594	225	539 D	6.3%	68.0%	8.5%	91.5%
VOLUSIA	19,678	7,764	9,202	2,712	1,438 D	39.5%	46.8%	45.8%	54.2%
WAKULLA	1,379	72	997	310	925 D	5.2%	72.3%	6.7%	93.3%
WALTON	3,799	652	2,366	781	1,714 D	17.2%	62.3%	21.6%	78.4%
WASHINGTON	2,211	297	1,380	534	1,083 D	13.4%	62.4%	17.7%	82.3%
TOTAL	577,643	194,280	281,988	101,375	87,708 D	33.6%	48.8%	40.8%	59.2%

FLORIDA

PRESIDENT 1952

County	Total Vote	Republican	Democratic	Other	Rep.-Dem. Plurality		Total Vote % Rep.	Dem.	Major Vote % Rep.	Dem.
ALACHUA	14,422	8,432	5,990		2,442	R	58.5%	41.5%	58.5%	41.5%
BAKER	1,901	419	1,482		1,063	D	22.0%	78.0%	22.0%	78.0%
BAY	13,601	4,812	8,789		3,977	D	35.4%	64.6%	35.4%	64.6%
BRADFORD	3,288	976	2,312		1,336	D	29.7%	70.3%	29.7%	70.3%
BREVARD	10,913	6,756	4,157		2,599	R	61.9%	38.1%	61.9%	38.1%
BROWARD	38,360	26,506	11,854		14,652	R	69.1%	30.9%	69.1%	30.9%
CALHOUN	2,417	590	1,827		1,237	D	24.4%	75.6%	24.4%	75.6%
CHARLOTTE	1,929	1,134	795		339	R	58.8%	41.2%	58.8%	41.2%
CITRUS	2,610	1,249	1,361		112	D	47.9%	52.1%	47.9%	52.1%
CLAY	4,312	2,116	2,196		80	D	49.1%	50.9%	49.1%	50.9%
COLLIER	2,190	1,086	1,104		18	D	49.6%	50.4%	49.6%	50.4%
COLUMBIA	5,270	2,041	3,229		1,188	D	38.7%	61.3%	38.7%	61.3%
DADE	215,196	122,174	93,022		29,152	R	56.8%	43.2%	56.8%	43.2%
DE SOTO	3,048	1,256	1,792		536	D	41.2%	58.8%	41.2%	58.8%
DIXIE	1,264	440	824		384	D	34.8%	65.2%	34.8%	65.2%
DUVAL	104,295	50,346	53,949		3,603	D	48.3%	51.7%	48.3%	51.7%
ESCAMBIA	32,671	12,176	20,495		8,319	D	37.3%	62.7%	37.3%	62.7%
FLAGLER	998	512	486		26	R	51.3%	48.7%	51.3%	48.7%
FRANKLIN	1,849	611	1,238		627	D	33.0%	67.0%	33.0%	67.0%
GADSDEN	4,541	1,835	2,706		871	D	40.4%	59.6%	40.4%	59.6%
GILCHRIST	1,187	195	992		797	D	16.4%	83.6%	16.4%	83.6%
GLADES	665	264	401		137	D	39.7%	60.3%	39.7%	60.3%
GULF	2,259	490	1,769		1,279	D	21.7%	78.3%	21.7%	78.3%
HAMILTON	2,110	658	1,452		794	D	31.2%	68.8%	31.2%	68.8%
HARDEE	3,871	1,802	2,069		267	D	46.5%	53.4%	46.5%	53.4%
HENDRY	1,970	918	1,052		134	D	46.6%	53.4%	46.6%	53.4%
HERNANDO	2,383	1,279	1,104		175	R	53.7%	46.3%	53.7%	46.3%
HIGHLANDS	5,688	2,952	2,736		216	R	51.9%	48.1%	51.9%	48.1%
HILLSBOROUGH	69,568	36,316	33,252		3,064	R	52.2%	47.8%	52.2%	47.8%
HOLMES	4,446	1,230	3,216		1,986	D	27.7%	72.3%	27.7%	72.3%
INDIAN RIVER	4,633	3,055	1,578		1,477	R	65.9%	34.1%	65.9%	34.1%
JACKSON	8,120	2,398	5,722		3,324	D	29.5%	70.5%	29.5%	70.5%
JEFFERSON	1,836	665	1,171		506	D	36.2%	63.8%	36.2%	63.8%
LAFAYETTE	1,250	269	981		712	D	21.5%	78.5%	21.5%	78.5%
LAKE	12,929	9,132	3,797		5,335	R	70.6%	29.4%	70.6%	29.4%
LEE	9,356	5,528	3,828		1,700	R	59.1%	40.9%	59.1%	40.9%
LEON	13,604	5,604	8,000		2,396	D	41.2%	58.8%	41.2%	58.8%
LEVY	3,076	1,066	2,010		944	D	34.7%	65.3%	34.7%	65.3%
LIBERTY	1,274	237	1,037		800	D	18.6%	81.4%	18.6%	81.4%
MADISON	2,834	1,209	1,625		416	D	42.7%	57.3%	42.7%	57.3%
MANATEE	13,638	9,055	4,583		4,472	R	66.4%	33.6%	66.4%	33.6%
MARION	11,988	6,134	5,854		280	R	51.2%	48.8%	51.2%	48.8%
MARTIN	3,570	2,308	1,262		1,046	R	64.6%	35.4%	64.6%	35.4%
MONROE	7,884	2,943	4,941		1,998	D	37.3%	62.7%	37.3%	62.7%
NASSAU	4,241	1,731	2,510		779	D	40.8%	59.2%	40.8%	59.2%
OKALOOSA	7,730	2,355	5,375		3,020	D	30.5%	69.5%	30.5%	69.5%
OKEECHOBEE	1,420	539	881		342	D	38.0%	62.0%	38.0%	62.0%
ORANGE	41,954	29,813	12,141		17,672	R	71.1%	28.9%	71.1%	28.9%
OSCEOLA	5,033	3,133	1,900		1,233	R	62.2%	37.8%	62.2%	37.8%
PALM BEACH	42,318	28,595	13,723		14,872	R	67.6%	32.4%	67.6%	32.4%
PASCO	8,111	4,562	3,549		1,013	R	56.2%	43.8%	56.2%	43.8%
PINELLAS	78,056	55,691	22,365		33,326	R	71.3%	28.7%	71.3%	28.7%
POLK	40,430	20,874	19,556		1,313	R	51.6%	48.4%	51.6%	48.4%
PUTNAM	7,291	3,766	3,525		241	R	51.7%	48.3%	51.7%	48.3%
ST JOHNS	9,068	4,702	4,366		336	R	51.9%	48.1%	51.9%	48.1%
ST LUCIE	7,449	4,667	2,782		1,885	R	62.7%	37.3%	62.7%	37.3%
SANTA ROSA	6,119	1,744	4,375		2,631	D	28.5%	71.5%	28.5%	71.5%
SARASOTA	13,483	9,538	3,945		5,593	R	70.7%	29.3%	70.7%	29.3%
SEMINOLE	7,803	4,683	3,120		1,563	R	60.0%	40.0%	60.0%	40.0%
SUMTER	3,331	1,054	2,277		1,223	D	31.6%	68.4%	31.6%	68.4%

PRESIDENT 1956

County	Total Vote	Republican	Democratic	Other	Rep.-Dem. Plurality		Total Vote % Rep.	Dem.	Major Vote % Rep.	Dem.
ALACHUA	14,846	7,939	6,889	18	1,050	R	53.5%	46.4%	53.5%	46.5%
BAKER	1,811	366	1,443	2	1,077	D	20.2%	79.7%	20.2%	79.8%
BAY	13,653	4,971	8,645	37	3,674	D	36.4%	63.3%	36.5%	63.5%
BRADFORD	3,540	1,203	2,328	9	1,125	D	34.0%	65.8%	34.1%	65.9%
BREVARD	13,932	10,004	3,928		6,076	R	71.8%	28.2%	71.8%	28.2%
BROWARD	60,289	43,552	16,561	176	26,991	R	72.2%	27.5%	72.5%	27.5%
CALHOUN	2,255	554	1,701		1,147	D	24.6%	75.4%	24.6%	75.4%
CHARLOTTE	2,518	1,589	929		660	R	63.1%	36.9%	63.1%	36.9%
CITRUS	3,117	1,570	1,527	20	43	R	50.4%	49.0%	50.7%	49.3%
CLAY	4,420	2,372	2,048		324	R	53.7%	46.3%	53.7%	46.3%
COLLIER	3,238	1,934	1,304		630	R	59.7%	40.3%	59.7%	40.3%
COLUMBIA	5,095	1,841	3,246	8	1,405	D	36.1%	63.7%	36.2%	63.8%
DADE	236,522	130,938	105,559	25	25,379	R	55.4%	44.6%	55.4%	44.6%
DE SOTO	2,549	1,234	1,315		81	D	48.4%	51.6%	48.4%	51.6%
DIXIE	1,278	370	904	4	534	D	29.0%	70.7%	29.0%	71.0%
DUVAL	106,772	53,481	53,127	164	354	R	50.1%	49.8%	50.2%	49.8%
ESCAMBIA	35,558	13,227	22,320	11	9,093	D	37.2%	62.8%	37.2%	62.8%
FLAGLER	1,204	498	690	16	192	D	41.4%	57.3%	41.9%	58.1%
FRANKLIN	1,529	571	958		387	D	37.3%	62.7%	37.3%	62.7%
GADSDEN	3,607	1,321	2,262	24	941	D	36.6%	62.7%	36.9%	63.1%
GILCHRIST	1,062	137	925		788	D	12.9%	87.1%	12.9%	87.1%
GLADES	648	309	339		30	D	47.7%	52.3%	47.7%	52.3%
GULF	2,363	570	1,793		1,223	D	24.1%	75.9%	24.1%	75.9%
HAMILTON	1,960	464	1,493	3	1,029	D	23.7%	76.2%	23.7%	76.3%
HARDEE	3,479	1,589	1,890		301	D	45.7%	54.3%	45.7%	54.3%
HENDRY	2,076	1,071	1,003	2	68	R	51.6%	48.3%	51.6%	48.4%
HERNANDO	2,788	1,295	1,435	58	140	D	46.5%	51.5%	47.4%	52.6%
HIGHLANDS	5,776	3,480	2,296		1,184	R	60.2%	39.8%	60.2%	39.8%
HILLSBOROUGH	80,599	41,889	38,610	100	3,279	R	52.0%	47.9%	52.0%	48.0%
HOLMES	3,552	1,036	2,516		1,480	D	29.2%	70.8%	29.2%	70.8%
INDIAN RIVER	5,758	4,059	1,699		2,360	R	70.5%	29.5%	70.5%	29.5%
JACKSON	8,516	2,543	5,973		3,430	D	29.9%	70.1%	29.9%	70.1%
JEFFERSON	1,241	187	1,054		867	D	15.1%	84.9%	15.1%	84.9%
LAFAYETTE	1,201	540	661		121	D	45.0%	55.0%	45.0%	55.0%
LAKE	15,372	10,888	4,326	158	6,562	R	70.8%	28.1%	71.6%	28.4%
LEE	12,085	7,565	4,520		3,045	R	62.6%	37.4%	62.6%	37.4%
LEON	13,922	6,828	7,022	72	194	D	49.0%	50.4%	49.3%	50.7%
LEVY	2,770	934	1,821	15	887	D	33.7%	65.7%	33.9%	66.1%
LIBERTY	1,112	238	870	4	632	D	21.4%	78.2%	21.5%	78.5%
MADISON	3,089	1,017	2,064	8	1,047	D	32.9%	66.8%	33.0%	67.0%
MANATEE	17,362	11,904	5,394	64	6,510	R	68.6%	31.1%	68.8%	31.2%
MARION	12,499	6,362	6,114	23	248	R	50.9%	48.9%	51.0%	49.0%
MARTIN	4,387	2,997	1,387	3	1,610	R	68.3%	31.6%	68.4%	31.6%
MONROE	7,668	3,337	4,327	4	990	D	43.5%	56.4%	43.5%	56.5%
NASSAU	4,497	1,717	2,765	15	1,048	D	38.2%	61.5%	38.3%	61.7%
OKALOOSA	8,536	2,788	5,748		2,960	D	32.7%	67.3%	32.7%	67.3%
OKEECHOBEE	1,410	575	835		260	D	40.8%	59.2%	40.8%	59.2%
ORANGE	52,066	37,482	14,532	52	22,950	R	72.0%	27.9%	72.1%	27.9%
OSCEOLA	5,527	3,602	1,923	2	1,679	R	65.2%	34.8%	65.2%	34.8%
PALM BEACH	50,147	35,746	14,321	80	21,425	R	71.3%	28.6%	71.4%	28.6%
PASCO	9,742	5,501	4,181	60	1,320	R	56.5%	42.9%	56.8%	43.2%
PINELLAS	102,532	74,314	28,113	105	46,201	R	72.5%	27.4%	72.6%	27.4%
POLK	42,332	23,682	18,626	24	5,056	R	55.9%	44.0%	56.0%	44.0%
PUTNAM	7,485	3,232	4,212	41	980	D	43.2%	56.3%	43.4%	56.6%
ST JOHNS	9,073	5,104	3,940	29	1,164	R	56.3%	43.4%	56.4%	43.6%
ST LUCIE	8,192	5,435	2,731	26	2,704	R	66.3%	33.3%	66.6%	33.4%
SANTA ROSA	6,053	1,909	4,144		2,235	D	31.5%	68.5%	31.5%	68.5%
SARASOTA	19,003	13,937	5,052	14	8,885	R	73.3%	26.6%	73.4%	26.6%
SEMINOLE	8,977	5,841	3,125	11	2,716	R	65.1%	34.8%	65.1%	34.9%
SUMTER	3,390	1,061	2,329		1,268	D	31.3%	68.7%	31.3%	68.7%

FLORIDA

PRESIDENT 1952

County	Total Vote	Republican	Democratic	Other	Rep.-Dem. Plurality	Percentage Total Vote Rep.	Dem.	Percentage Major Vote Rep.	Dem.
SUWANNEE	4,438	1,611	2,827		1,216 D	36.3%	63.7%	36.3%	63.7%
TAYLOR	2,531	744	1,787		1,043 D	29.4%	70.6%	29.4%	70.6%
UNION	1,236	268	968		700 D	21.7%	78.3%	21.7%	78.3%
VOLUSIA	31,725	19,815	11,910		7,905 R	62.5%	37.5%	62.5%	37.5%
WAKULLA	1,547	375	1,172		797 D	24.2%	75.8%	24.2%	75.8%
WALTON	5,095	1,502	3,593		2,091 D	29.5%	70.5%	29.5%	70.5%
WASHINGTON	3,363	1,100	2,263		1,163 D	32.7%	67.3%	32.7%	67.3%
TOTAL	989,337	544,036	444,950	351	99,086 R	55.0%	45.0%	55.0%	45.0%

PRESIDENT 1956

County	Total Vote	Republican	Democratic	Other	Rep.-Dem. Plurality	Percentage Total Vote Rep.	Dem.	Percentage Major Vote Rep.	Dem.
SUWANNEE	4,209	1,046	3,163		2,117 D	24.9%	75.1%	24.9%	75.1%
TAYLOR	2,721	776	1,945		1,169 D	28.5%	71.5%	28.5%	71.5%
UNION	1,176	218	958		740 D	18.5%	81.5%	18.5%	81.5%
VOLUSIA	39,614	25,103	14,489	22	10,614 D	63.4%	36.6%	63.4%	36.6%
WAKULLA	1,467	393	1,074		681 D	26.8%	73.2%	26.8%	73.2%
WALTON	4,831	1,606	3,225		1,619 D	33.2%	66.8%	33.2%	66.8%
WASHINGTON	3,208	1,027	2,164	17	1,137 D	32.0%	67.5%	32.2%	67.8%
TOTAL	1,125,762	643,849	480,371	1,542	163,478 R	57.2%	42.7%	57.3%	42.7%

FLORIDA

PRESIDENT 1960

County	Total Vote	Republican	Democratic	Other	Rep.-Dem. Plurality	Total Vote Rep.	Total Vote Dem.	Major Vote Rep.	Major Vote Dem.
ALACHUA	19,351	10,072	9,279		793 R	52.0%	48.0%	52.0%	48.0%
BAKER	1,867	398	1,469		1,071 D	21.3%	78.7%	21.3%	78.7%
BAY	16,014	5,435	10,579		5,144 D	33.9%	66.1%	33.9%	66.1%
BRADFORD	3,666	1,131	2,535		1,404 D	30.9%	69.1%	30.9%	69.1%
BREVARD	28,654	17,585	11,069		6,515 R	61.4%	38.6%	61.4%	38.6%
BROWARD	116,105	68,294	47,811		20,483 R	58.8%	41.2%	58.8%	41.2%
CALHOUN	2,228	634	1,594		960 D	28.5%	71.5%	28.5%	71.5%
CHARLOTTE	4,967	3,026	1,941		1,085 R	60.9%	39.1%	60.9%	39.1%
CITRUS	3,591	1,861	1,730		131 R	51.8%	48.2%	51.8%	48.2%
CLAY	5,243	2,515	2,728		213 D	48.0%	52.0%	48.0%	52.0%
COLLIER	4,458	2,708	1,750		958 R	60.7%	39.3%	60.7%	39.3%
COLUMBIA	5,789	2,094	3,695		1,601 D	36.2%	63.8%	36.2%	63.8%
DADE	317,620	134,506	183,114		48,608 D	42.3%	57.7%	42.3%	57.7%
DE SOTO	3,367	1,687	1,680		7 R	50.1%	49.9%	50.1%	49.9%
DIXIE	1,368	392	976		584 D	28.7%	71.3%	28.7%	71.3%
DUVAL	129,164	59,073	70,091		11,018 D	45.7%	54.3%	45.7%	54.3%
ESCAMBIA	46,213	17,925	28,288		10,363 D	38.8%	61.2%	38.8%	61.2%
FLAGLER	1,359	426	933		507 D	31.3%	68.7%	31.3%	68.7%
FRANKLIN	2,258	764	1,494		730 D	33.8%	66.2%	33.8%	66.2%
GADSDEN	4,353	2,010	2,343		333 D	46.2%	53.8%	46.2%	53.8%
GILCHRIST	1,111	277	834		557 D	24.9%	75.1%	24.9%	75.1%
GLADES	708	314	394		80 D	44.4%	55.6%	44.4%	55.6%
GULF	3,005	657	2,348		1,691 D	21.9%	78.1%	21.9%	78.1%
HAMILTON	1,987	656	1,331		675 D	33.0%	67.0%	33.0%	67.0%
HARDEE	3,701	1,960	1,741		219 R	53.0%	47.0%	53.0%	47.0%
HENDRY	2,350	1,043	1,307		264 D	44.4%	55.6%	44.4%	55.6%
HERNANDO	3,769	1,809	1,960		151 D	48.0%	52.0%	48.0%	52.0%
HIGHLANDS	7,491	4,369	3,122		1,247 R	58.3%	41.7%	58.3%	41.7%
HILLSBOROUGH	111,127	48,887	62,240		13,353 D	44.0%	56.0%	44.0%	56.0%
HOLMES	3,605	1,235	2,370		1,135 D	34.3%	65.7%	34.3%	65.7%
INDIAN RIVER	7,626	4,656	2,970		1,686 R	61.1%	38.9%	61.1%	38.9%
JACKSON	3,845	2,851	5,994		3,143 D	32.2%	67.8%	32.2%	67.8%
JEFFERSON	1,729	600	1,129		529 D	34.7%	65.3%	34.7%	65.3%
LAFAYETTE	1,090	297	793		496 D	27.2%	72.8%	27.2%	72.8%
LAKE	17,915	12,979	4,936		8,043 R	72.4%	27.6%	72.4%	27.6%
LEE	15,851	10,357	5,494		4,863 R	65.3%	34.7%	65.3%	34.7%
LEON	19,512	9,079	10,433		1,354 D	46.5%	53.5%	46.5%	53.5%
LEVY	2,999	996	2,003		1,007 D	33.2%	66.8%	33.2%	66.8%
LIBERTY	1,105	243	862		619 D	22.0%	78.0%	22.0%	78.0%
MADISON	3,236	1,152	2,084		932 D	35.6%	64.4%	35.6%	64.4%
MANATEE	25,276	16,462	8,814		7,648 R	65.1%	34.9%	65.1%	34.9%
MARION	14,249	7,043	7,206		163 D	49.4%	50.6%	49.4%	50.6%
MARTIN	6,365	3,701	2,664		1,037 R	58.1%	41.9%	58.1%	41.9%
MONROE	10,388	3,416	6,972		3,556 D	32.9%	67.1%	32.9%	67.1%
NASSAU	4,948	1,666	3,282		1,616 D	33.7%	66.3%	33.7%	66.3%
OKALOOSA	12,948	4,685	8,263		3,578 D	36.2%	63.8%	36.2%	63.8%
OKEECHOBEE	1,756	631	1,125		494 D	35.9%	64.1%	35.9%	64.1%
ORANGE	67,973	48,244	19,729		28,515 R	71.0%	29.0%	71.0%	29.0%
OSCEOLA	6,869	4,691	2,178		2,513 R	68.3%	31.7%	68.3%	31.7%
PALM BEACH	75,208	45,337	29,871		15,466 R	60.3%	39.7%	60.3%	39.7%
PASCO	13,020	7,188	5,832		1,356 R	55.2%	44.8%	55.2%	44.8%
PINELLAS	159,833	101,779	58,054		43,725 R	63.7%	36.3%	63.7%	36.3%
POLK	55,164	31,618	23,546		8,072 R	57.3%	42.7%	57.3%	42.7%
PUTNAM	8,695	4,236	4,459		223 D	48.7%	51.3%	48.7%	51.3%
ST JOHNS	9,708	4,125	5,583		1,458 D	42.5%	57.5%	42.5%	57.5%
ST LUCIE	11,714	6,354	5,360		994 R	54.2%	45.8%	54.2%	45.8%
SANTA ROSA	7,737	2,777	4,960		2,183 D	35.9%	64.1%	35.9%	64.1%
SARASOTA	28,282	19,995	8,287		11,708 R	70.7%	29.3%	70.7%	29.3%
SEMINOLE	13,827	8,936	4,891		4,045 R	64.6%	35.4%	64.6%	35.4%
SUMTER	3,399	1,120	2,279		1,159 D	33.0%	67.0%	33.0%	67.0%

PRESIDENT 1964

County	Total Vote	Republican	Democratic	Other	Rep.-Dem. Plurality	Total Vote Rep.	Total Vote Dem.	Major Vote Rep.	Major Vote Dem.
ALACHUA	24,634	11,151	13,483		2,332 D	45.3%	54.7%	45.3%	54.7%
BAKER	2,258	1,121	1,137		16 D	49.6%	50.4%	49.6%	50.4%
BAY	20,695	12,849	7,846		5,003 R	62.1%	37.9%	62.1%	37.9%
BRADFORD	4,307	1,987	2,320		333 D	46.1%	53.9%	46.1%	53.9%
BREVARD	49,384	24,551	24,833		282 D	49.7%	50.3%	49.7%	50.3%
BROWARD	153,670	85,264	68,406		16,858 R	55.5%	44.5%	55.5%	44.5%
CALHOUN	2,773	1,793	980		813 R	64.7%	35.3%	64.7%	35.3%
CHARLOTTE	8,994	4,163	4,831		668 D	46.3%	53.7%	46.3%	53.7%
CITRUS	4,850	2,329	2,521		192 D	48.0%	52.0%	48.0%	52.0%
CLAY	6,919	3,805	3,114		691 R	55.0%	45.0%	55.0%	45.0%
COLLIER	6,458	3,581	2,877		704 R	55.5%	44.5%	55.5%	44.5%
COLUMBIA	7,394	4,145	3,249		896 R	56.1%	43.9%	56.1%	43.9%
DADE	326,421	117,480	208,941		91,461 D	36.0%	64.0%	36.0%	64.0%
DE SOTO	3,763	1,986	1,777		209 R	52.8%	47.2%	52.8%	47.2%
DIXIE	1,831	908	923		15 D	49.6%	50.4%	49.6%	50.4%
DUVAL	160,481	81,116	79,365		1,751 R	50.5%	49.5%	50.5%	49.5%
ESCAMBIA	57,785	32,414	25,371		7,043 R	56.1%	43.9%	56.1%	43.9%
FLAGLER	1,658	718	940		222 D	43.3%	56.7%	43.3%	56.7%
FRANKLIN	2,785	1,419	1,366		53 R	51.0%	49.0%	51.0%	49.0%
GADSDEN	9,763	5,207	4,556		651 R	53.3%	46.7%	53.3%	46.7%
GILCHRIST	1,251	540	711		171 D	43.2%	56.8%	43.2%	56.8%
GLADES	982	541	441		100 R	55.1%	44.9%	55.1%	44.9%
GULF	3,660	2,001	1,659		342 R	54.7%	45.3%	54.7%	45.3%
HAMILTON	2,460	1,158	1,302		144 D	47.1%	52.9%	47.1%	52.9%
HARDEE	4,229	2,321	1,908		413 R	54.9%	45.1%	54.9%	45.1%
HENDRY	3,002	1,650	1,352		298 R	55.0%	45.0%	55.0%	45.0%
HERNANDO	4,657	2,337	2,320		17 R	50.2%	49.8%	50.2%	49.8%
HIGHLANDS	8,980	4,747	4,233		514 R	52.9%	47.1%	52.9%	47.1%
HILLSBOROUGH	122,905	50,616	71,289		20,673 D	41.5%	58.5%	41.5%	58.5%
HOLMES	2,418	1,225	1,193		2,032 R	73.0%	27.0%	73.0%	27.0%
INDIAN RIVER	11,313	6,191	5,122		1,069 R	54.7%	45.3%	54.7%	45.3%
JACKSON	11,453	7,064	4,386		2,678 R	61.7%	38.3%	61.7%	38.3%
JEFFERSON	1,193	648	545		103 R	54.3%	45.7%	54.3%	45.7%
LAFAYETTE	1,193	648	545		103 R	54.3%	45.7%	54.3%	45.7%
LAKE	20,670	12,897	7,773		5,124 R	62.4%	37.6%	62.4%	37.6%
LEE	23,090	12,886	10,204		2,682 R	55.8%	44.2%	55.8%	44.2%
LEON	26,108	15,181	10,927		4,254 R	58.1%	41.9%	58.1%	41.9%
LEVY	3,566	1,580	1,986		406 D	44.3%	55.7%	44.3%	55.7%
LIBERTY	1,287	910	377		533 R	70.7%	29.3%	70.7%	29.3%
MADISON	4,943	2,822	2,121		701 R	57.1%	42.9%	57.1%	42.9%
MANATEE	30,221	17,147	13,074		4,073 R	56.7%	43.3%	56.7%	43.3%
MARION	19,991	10,879	9,112		1,767 R	54.4%	45.6%	54.4%	45.6%
MARTIN	7,913	4,292	3,621		671 R	54.2%	45.8%	54.2%	45.8%
MONROE	13,778	4,842	8,936		4,094 D	35.1%	64.9%	35.1%	64.9%
NASSAU	5,915	3,134	2,781		353 R	53.0%	47.0%	53.0%	47.0%
OKALOOSA	17,851	9,961	7,890		2,071 R	55.8%	44.2%	55.8%	44.2%
OKEECHOBEE	2,332	1,316	1,016		300 R	56.4%	43.6%	56.4%	43.6%
ORANGE	87,132	48,684	38,248		10,636 R	56.1%	43.9%	56.1%	43.9%
OSCEOLA	8,047	4,516	3,531		985 R	56.1%	43.9%	56.1%	43.9%
PALM BEACH	93,450	49,614	43,836		5,778 R	53.1%	46.9%	53.1%	46.9%
PASCO	15,741	7,606	8,135		529 D	48.3%	51.7%	48.3%	51.7%
PINELLAS	178,795	80,414	98,381		17,967 D	45.0%	55.0%	45.0%	55.0%
POLK	65,261	35,906	29,355		6,551 R	55.0%	45.0%	55.0%	45.0%
PUTNAM	10,067	5,072	4,995		77 R	50.4%	49.6%	50.4%	49.6%
ST JOHNS	11,807	7,450	4,357		3,093 R	63.1%	36.9%	63.1%	36.9%
ST LUCIE	14,952	7,204	7,748		544 D	48.2%	51.8%	48.2%	51.8%
SANTA ROSA	9,553	5,983	3,570		2,413 R	62.6%	37.4%	62.6%	37.4%
SARASOTA	35,854	21,917	13,937		7,980 R	61.1%	38.9%	61.1%	38.9%
SEMINOLE	19,203	10,078	9,125		953 R	52.5%	47.5%	52.5%	47.5%
SUMTER	3,890	1,631	2,259		628 D	41.9%	58.1%	41.9%	58.1%

FLORIDA

PRESIDENT 1960

County	Total Vote	Republican	Democratic	Other	Rep.-Dem. Plurality	Percentage Total Vote Rep.	Dem.	Major Vote Rep.	Dem.
SUWANNEE	4,325	1,536	2,789		1,253 D	35.5%	64.5%	35.5%	64.5%
TAYLOR	3,120	1,212	1,908		696 D	38.8%	61.2%	38.8%	61.2%
UNION	1,252	311	941		630 D	24.8%	75.2%	24.8%	75.2%
VOLUSIA	51,744	28,367	23,377		4,990 R	54.8%	45.2%	54.8%	45.2%
WAKULLA	1,525	379	1,146		767 D	24.9%	75.1%	24.9%	75.1%
WALTON	5,126	1,484	3,642		2,158 D	29.0%	71.0%	29.0%	71.0%
WASHINGTON	3,328	1,230	2,098		868 D	37.0%	63.0%	37.0%	63.0%
TOTAL	1,544,176	795,476	748,700		46,776 R	51.5%	48.5%	51.5%	48.5%

PRESIDENT 1964

County	Total Vote	Republican	Democratic	Other	Rep.-Dem. Plurality	Percentage Total Vote Rep.	Dem.	Major Vote Rep.	Dem.
SUWANNEE	5,395	3,002	2,393		609 R	55.6%	44.4%	55.6%	44.4%
TAYLOR	4,369	2,661	1,708		953 R	60.9%	39.1%	60.9%	39.1%
UNION	1,450	710	740		30 D	49.0%	51.0%	49.0%	51.0%
VOLUSIA	59,889	24,988	34,901		9,913 D	41.7%	58.3%	41.7%	58.3%
WAKULLA	2,023	1,270	753		517 R	62.8%	37.2%	62.8%	37.2%
WALTON	6,202	3,753	2,449		1,304 R	60.5%	39.5%	60.5%	39.5%
WASHINGTON	4,225	2,725	1,500		1,225 R	64.5%	35.5%	64.5%	35.5%
TOTAL	1,854,481	905,941	948,540		42,599 D	48.9%	51.1%	48.9%	51.1%

FLORIDA

OTHER VOTE COMPOSITION:

1920	5,189 Socialist; 5,127 Prohibition.
1924	8,625 Progressive; 5,498 Prohibition; 2,319 American.
1928	2,284 Socialist; 2,160 Communist.
1932	775 Socialist; 691 scattered. Votes reported as state-wide totals, not by counties.
1936	Scattered.
1940	Scattered; reported as a state-wide total, not by counties.
1944	Scattered; reported as a state-wide total, not by counties.
1948	89,755 States Rights; 11,620 Progressive.
1952	Scattered; reported as a state-wide total, not by counties.
1956	Scattered.
1960	
1964	

SPECIAL CASES:

1920   The Republican vote is the vote cast for the single elector candidate who ran on both the regular Republican and the White Republican elector tickets. Variations in canvassed figures for individual electors placed the Prohibition vote second in two counties.

1924   Progressive candidates ran second in several counties; variations in canvassed figures for individual electors placed the Prohibition vote second in one county. Charlotte, Dixie, Glades, Hardee, Highlands, Sarasota, and Union counties organized in 1921; Collier and Hendry counties organized in 1923.

1928   Gulf, Indian River, and Martin counties organized in 1925; Gilchrist county organized in 1926.

1948   States Rights candidates carried several counties and ran second in a number of others.

GEORGIA

PRESIDENT 1920

County	Total Vote	Republican	Democratic	Other	Rep.-Dem. Plurality	% Total Vote Rep.	% Total Vote Dem.	% Major Vote Rep.	% Major Vote Dem.
APPLING	509	196	313		117 D	38.5%	61.5%	38.5%	61.5%
ATKINSON	572	119	453		334 D	20.8%	79.2%	20.8%	79.2%
BACON	526	219	307		88 D	41.6%	58.4%	41.6%	58.4%
BAKER	221	80	141		61 D	36.2%	63.8%	36.2%	63.8%
BALDWIN	646	92	554		462 D	14.2%	85.8%	14.2%	85.8%
BANKS	821	342	479		137 D	41.7%	58.3%	41.7%	58.3%
BARROW	1,143	412	731		319 D	36.0%	64.0%	36.0%	64.0%
BARTOW	1,676	754	922		168 D	45.0%	55.0%	45.0%	55.0%
BEN HILL	775	232	543		311 D	29.9%	70.1%	29.9%	70.1%
BERRIEN	681	58	623		565 D	8.5%	91.5%	8.5%	91.5%
BIBB	2,488	458	2,030		1,572 D	18.4%	81.6%	18.4%	81.6%
BLECKLEY	262		262		262 D		100.0%		100.0%
BRANTLEY									
BROOKS	673	76	597		521 D	11.3%	88.7%	11.3%	88.7%
BRYAN	196	21	175		154 D	10.7%	89.3%	10.7%	89.3%
BULLOCH	1,346	248	1,098		850 D	18.4%	81.6%	18.4%	81.6%
BURKE	426	39	387		348 D	9.2%	90.8%	9.2%	90.8%
BUTTS	643	141	502		361 D	21.9%	78.1%	21.9%	78.1%
CALHOUN	454	5	449		444 D	1.1%	98.9%	1.1%	98.9%
CAMDEN	166	14	152		138 D	8.4%	91.6%	8.4%	91.6%
CAMPBELL	370	107	263		156 D	28.9%	71.1%	28.9%	71.1%
CANDLER	741	68	673		605 D	9.2%	90.8%	9.2%	90.8%
CARROLL	2,859	1,227	1,632		405 D	42.9%	57.1%	42.9%	57.1%
CATOOSA	88	33	55		22 D	37.5%	62.5%	37.5%	62.5%
CHARLTON	185	28	157		129 D	15.1%	84.9%	15.1%	84.9%
CHATHAM	5,238	995	4,243		3,248 D	19.0%	81.0%	19.0%	81.0%
CHATTAHOOCHEE	92	5	87		82 D	5.4%	94.6%	5.4%	94.6%
CHATTOOGA	1,401	514	887		373 D	36.7%	63.3%	36.7%	63.3%
CHEROKEE	1,682	1,138	544		594 R	67.7%	32.3%	67.7%	32.3%
CLARKE	1,636	217	1,419		1,202 D	13.3%	86.7%	13.3%	86.7%
CLAY	293	63	230		167 D	21.5%	78.5%	21.5%	78.5%
CLAYTON	509	34	475		441 D	6.7%	93.3%	6.7%	93.3%
CLINCH	371	77	294		217 D	20.8%	79.2%	20.8%	79.2%
COBB	2,303	1,095	1,208		113 D	47.5%	52.5%	47.5%	52.5%
COFFEE	656	230	426		196 D	35.1%	64.9%	35.1%	64.9%
COLQUITT	1,291	523	768		245 D	40.5%	59.5%	40.5%	59.5%
COLUMBIA	476		476		476 D		100.0%		100.0%
COOK	563	303	260		43 R	53.8%	46.2%	53.8%	46.2%
COWETA	1,263	169	1,094		925 D	13.4%	86.6%	13.4%	86.6%
CRAWFORD	300	65	235		170 D	21.7%	78.3%	21.7%	78.3%
CRISP	648	83	565		482 D	12.8%	87.2%	12.8%	87.2%
DADE	608	114	494		380 D	18.8%	81.2%	18.8%	81.2%
DAWSON	608	354	254		100 R	58.2%	41.8%	58.2%	41.8%
DECATUR	1,282	300	982		682 D	23.4%	76.6%	23.4%	76.6%
DE KALB	2,650	803	1,847		1,044 D	30.3%	69.7%	30.3%	69.7%
DODGE	804	177	627		450 D	22.0%	78.0%	22.0%	78.0%
DOOLY	583	39	544		505 D	6.7%	93.3%	6.7%	93.3%
DOUGHERTY	726	105	621		516 D	14.5%	85.5%	14.5%	85.5%
DOUGLAS	902	475	427		48 R	52.7%	47.3%	52.7%	47.3%
EARLY	415	34	381		347 D	8.2%	91.8%	8.2%	91.8%
ECHOLS	448	16	432		416 D	3.6%	96.4%	3.6%	96.4%
EFFINGHAM	844	118	726		608 D	14.0%	86.0%	14.0%	86.0%
ELBERT	1,634	190	1,444		1,254 D	11.6%	88.4%	11.6%	88.4%
EMANUEL	1,434	187	1,247		1,060 D	13.0%	87.0%	13.0%	87.0%
EVANS									
FANNIN	1,632	1,083	549		534 R	66.4%	33.6%	66.4%	33.6%
FAYETTE	311	80	231		151 D	25.7%	74.3%	25.7%	74.3%
FLOYD	2,590	667	1,923		1,256 D	25.8%	74.2%	25.8%	74.2%
FORSYTH	1,554	741	813		72 D	47.7%	52.3%	47.7%	52.3%
FRANKLIN	1,336	447	889		442 D	33.5%	66.5%	33.5%	66.5%

PRESIDENT 1924

County	Total Vote	Republican	Democratic	Other	Rep.-Dem. Plurality	% Total Vote Rep.	% Total Vote Dem.	% Major Vote Rep.	% Major Vote Dem.
APPLING	257	44	212	1	168 D	17.1%	82.5%	17.2%	82.8%
ATKINSON	436	25	394	17	369 D	5.7%	90.4%	6.0%	94.0%
BACON	1,055	79	961	15	882 D	7.5%	91.1%	7.6%	92.4%
BAKER	273	21	245	7	224 D	7.7%	89.7%	7.9%	92.1%
BALDWIN	984	107	826	51	719 D	10.9%	83.9%	11.5%	88.5%
BANKS	393	86	291	16	205 D	21.9%	74.0%	22.8%	77.2%
BARROW	762	88	501	173	413 D	11.5%	65.7%	14.9%	85.1%
BARTOW	1,393	482	846	65	364 D	34.6%	60.7%	36.3%	63.7%
BEN HILL	847	150	507	190	357 D	17.7%	59.9%	22.8%	77.2%
BERRIEN	432	13	409	10	396 D	3.0%	94.7%	3.1%	96.9%
BIBB	4,385	455	3,647	283	3,192 D	10.4%	83.2%	11.1%	88.9%
BLECKLEY	405	21	367	17	346 D	5.2%	90.6%	5.4%	94.6%
BRANTLEY	279	9	238	32	229 D	3.2%	85.3%	3.6%	96.4%
BROOKS	1,321	128	1,179	14	1,051 D	9.7%	89.3%	9.8%	90.2%
BRYAN	208	9	196	3	187 D	4.3%	94.2%	4.4%	95.6%
BULLOCH	1,052	37	989	26	952 D	3.5%	94.0%	3.6%	96.4%
BURKE	541	76	449	16	373 D	14.0%	83.0%	14.5%	85.5%
BUTTS	581	50	493	38	443 D	8.6%	84.9%	9.2%	90.8%
CALHOUN	412	66	343	3	277 D	16.0%	83.3%	16.1%	83.9%
CAMDEN	175	1	172	2	171 D	0.6%	98.3%	0.6%	99.4%
CAMPBELL	508	18	477	13	459 D	3.5%	93.9%	3.6%	96.4%
CANDLER	269	14	241	14	227 D	5.2%	89.6%	5.5%	94.5%
CARROLL	2,538	526	1,784	228	1,258 D	20.7%	70.3%	22.8%	77.2%
CATOOSA	932	242	661	29	419 D	26.0%	70.9%	26.8%	73.2%
CHARLTON	178	20	151	7	131 D	11.2%	84.8%	11.7%	88.3%
CHATHAM	8,815	1,800	6,158	857	4,358 D	20.4%	69.9%	22.6%	77.4%
CHATTAHOOCHEE	227	14	208	5	194 D	6.2%	91.6%	6.3%	93.7%
CHATTOOGA	2,061	412	1,615	34	1,203 D	20.0%	78.4%	20.3%	79.7%
CHEROKEE	1,503	601	848	54	247 D	40.0%	56.4%	41.5%	58.5%
CLARKE	1,860	267	1,530	63	1,263 D	14.4%	82.3%	14.9%	85.1%
CLAY	331	51	246	34	195 D	15.4%	74.3%	17.2%	82.8%
CLAYTON	394	46	273	75	227 D	11.7%	69.3%	14.4%	85.6%
CLINCH	265	13	235	17	222 D	4.9%	88.7%	5.2%	94.8%
COBB	1,910	362	1,360	188	998 D	19.0%	71.2%	21.0%	79.0%
COFFEE	650	62	510	78	448 D	9.5%	78.5%	10.8%	89.2%
COLQUITT	1,922	205	1,572	145	1,367 D	10.7%	81.8%	11.5%	88.5%
COLUMBIA	300	47	213	40	166 D	15.7%	71.0%	18.1%	81.9%
COOK	581	44	502	35	458 D	7.6%	86.4%	8.1%	91.9%
COWETA	1,117	67	1,010	40	943 D	6.0%	90.4%	6.2%	93.8%
CRAWFORD	374	7	352	15	345 D	1.9%	94.1%	1.9%	98.1%
CRISP	476	21	439	16	418 D	4.4%	92.2%	4.6%	95.4%
DADE	741	119	563	59	444 D	16.1%	76.0%	17.4%	82.6%
DAWSON	546	264	279	3	15 D	48.4%	51.1%	48.6%	51.4%
DECATUR	922	151	637	134	486 D	16.4%	69.1%	19.2%	80.8%
DE KALB	3,241	590	2,277	374	1,687 D	18.2%	70.3%	20.6%	79.4%
DODGE	1,754	91	1,654	9	1,563 D	5.2%	94.3%	5.2%	94.8%
DOOLY	637	45	590	2	545 D	7.1%	92.6%	7.1%	92.9%
DOUGHERTY	1,314	167	1,065	82	898 D	12.7%	81.1%	13.6%	86.4%
DOUGLAS	575	86	355	134	269 D	15.0%	61.7%	19.5%	80.5%
EARLY	435	22	351	62	329 D	5.1%	80.7%	5.9%	94.1%
ECHOLS	495	11	482	2	471 D	2.2%	97.4%	2.2%	97.8%
EFFINGHAM	406	39	337	30	298 D	9.6%	83.0%	10.4%	89.6%
ELBERT	1,287	72	1,024	191	952 D	5.6%	79.6%	6.6%	93.4%
EMANUEL	774	39	710	25	671 D	5.0%	91.7%	5.2%	94.8%
EVANS	824	21	790	13	769 D	2.5%	95.9%	2.6%	97.4%
FANNIN	2,732	1,650	1,079	3	571 R	60.4%	39.5%	60.5%	39.5%
FAYETTE	323	24	257	42	233 D	7.4%	79.6%	8.5%	91.5%
FLOYD	2,604	470	1,922	212	1,452 D	18.0%	73.8%	19.6%	80.4%
FORSYTH	1,030	298	715	17	417 D	28.9%	69.4%	29.4%	70.6%
FRANKLIN	843	109	618	116	509 D	12.9%	73.3%	15.0%	85.0%

GEORGIA

PRESIDENT 1920

County	Total Vote	Republican	Democratic	Other	Rep.-Dem. Plurality	Total Vote Rep.	Total Vote Dem.	Major Vote Rep.	Major Vote Dem.
FULTON	9,971	3,336	6,635		3,299 D	33.5%	66.5%	33.5%	66.5%
GILMER	1,208	662	546		115 R	54.8%	45.2%	54.8%	45.2%
GLASCOCK	315	83	232		149 D	26.3%	73.7%	26.3%	73.7%
GLYNN	554	132	422		290 D	23.8%	76.2%	23.8%	76.2%
GORDON	1,642	929	713		216 R	56.6%	43.4%	56.6%	43.4%
GRADY	1,119	232	887		655 D	20.7%	79.3%	20.7%	79.3%
GREENE	859	178	681		503 D	20.7%	79.3%	20.7%	79.3%
GWINNETT	2,785	1,140	1,645		505 D	40.9%	59.1%	40.9%	59.1%
HABERSHAM	1,129	626	503		123 R	55.4%	44.6%	55.4%	44.6%
HALL	2,327	852	1,475		623 D	36.5%	63.4%	36.6%	63.4%
HANCOCK	551	53	498		445 D	9.6%	90.4%	9.6%	90.4%
HARALSON	1,546	1,108	438		670 R	71.7%	28.3%	71.7%	28.3%
HARRIS	407	9	398		389 D	2.2%	97.8%	2.2%	97.8%
HART	1,017	323	694		371 D	31.8%	68.2%	31.8%	68.2%
HEARD	475	14	461		447 D	2.9%	97.1%	2.9%	97.1%
HENRY	608		608		608 D		100.0%		100.0%
HOUSTON	762	39	723		684 D	5.1%	94.9%	5.1%	94.9%
IRWIN	639	114	525		411 D	17.8%	82.2%	17.8%	82.2%
JACKSON	1,403	334	1,069		735 D	23.8%	76.2%	23.8%	76.2%
JASPER	471	42	429		387 D	8.9%	91.1%	8.9%	91.1%
JEFF DAVIS	563	303	260		43 R	53.8%	46.2%	53.8%	46.2%
JEFFERSON	919	82	837		755 D	8.9%	91.1%	8.9%	91.1%
JENKINS	380	49	331		282 D	12.9%	87.1%	12.9%	87.1%
JOHNSON	380	74	306		232 D	19.5%	80.5%	19.5%	80.5%
JONES	118	31	87		55 D	26.3%	73.7%	26.3%	73.7%
LAMAR	1,517	350	1,167		817 D	23.1%	76.9%	23.1%	76.9%
LANIER	270	19	251		232 D	7.0%	93.0%	7.0%	93.0%
LAURENS	478	175	303		128 D	36.6%	63.4%	36.6%	63.4%
LEE									
LIBERTY									
LINCOLN	512	3	509		506 D	0.6%	99.4%	0.6%	99.4%
LONG									
LOWNDES	1,528	220	1,308		1,088 D	14.4%	85.6%	14.4%	85.6%
LUMPKIN	360	205	155		50 R	56.9%	43.1%	56.9%	43.1%
MCDUFFIE	491	109	382		273 D	22.2%	77.8%	22.2%	77.8%
MCINTOSH	158	39	119		80 D	24.7%	75.3%	24.7%	75.3%
MACON	551	68	483		415 D	12.3%	87.7%	12.3%	87.7%
MADISON	974	281	693		412 D	28.9%	71.1%	28.9%	71.1%
MARION	416	180	236		56 D	43.3%	56.7%	43.3%	56.7%
MERIWETHER	1,245	186	1,059		873 D	14.9%	85.1%	14.9%	85.1%
MILLER	185	30	155		125 D	16.2%	83.8%	16.2%	83.8%
MILTON	509	231	278		47 R	45.4%	54.6%	45.4%	54.6%
MITCHELL	1,074	144	930		786 D	13.4%	86.6%	13.4%	86.6%
MONROE	920	83	837		754 D	9.0%	91.0%	9.0%	91.0%
MONTGOMERY	317	148	169		21 D	46.7%	53.3%	46.7%	53.3%
MORGAN	626	176	450		274 D	28.1%	71.9%	28.1%	71.9%
MURRAY	1,579	851	728		123 R	53.9%	46.1%	53.9%	46.1%
MUSCOGEE	1,473	101	1,372		1,271 D	6.9%	93.1%	6.9%	93.1%
NEWTON	1,102	349	753		404 D	31.7%	68.3%	31.7%	68.3%
OCONEE	449	108	341		233 D	24.1%	75.9%	24.1%	75.9%
OGLETHORPE	886	42	844		802 D	4.7%	95.3%	4.7%	95.3%
PAULDING	1,294	954	340		614 R	73.7%	26.3%	73.7%	26.3%
PEACH									
PICKENS	1,267	830	437		393 R	65.5%	34.5%	65.5%	34.5%
PIERCE	529	122	407		285 D	23.1%	76.9%	23.1%	76.9%
PIKE	1,557	280	1,277		997 D	18.0%	82.0%	18.0%	82.0%
POLK	1,662	1,004	658		346 R	60.4%	39.6%	60.4%	39.6%
PULASKI	395	57	338		281 D	14.4%	85.6%	14.4%	85.6%
PUTNAM	425	5	420		415 D	1.2%	98.8%	1.2%	98.8%
QUITMAN	139	4	135		131 D	2.9%	97.1%	2.9%	97.1%

PRESIDENT 1924

County	Total Vote	Republican	Democratic	Other	Rep.-Dem. Plurality	Total Vote Rep.	Total Vote Dem.	Major Vote Rep.	Major Vote Dem.
FULTON	12,638	3,229	7,830	1,579	4,601 D	25.5%	62.0%	29.2%	70.8%
GILMER	1,688	912	776	68	136 R	54.0%	46.0%	54.0%	46.0%
GLASCOCK	205	26	111	68	85 D	12.7%	54.1%	19.0%	81.0%
GLYNN	970	283	612	75	329 D	29.2%	63.1%	31.6%	68.4%
GORDON	1,340	397	875	68	478 D	29.6%	65.3%	31.2%	68.8%
GRADY	1,574	100	1,449	25	1,349 D	6.4%	92.1%	6.5%	93.5%
GREENE	781	77	558	146	481 D	9.9%	71.4%	12.1%	87.9%
GWINNETT	1,334	207	1,011	116	804 D	15.5%	75.8%	17.0%	83.0%
HABERSHAM	1,192	322	808	62	486 D	27.0%	67.8%	28.5%	71.5%
HALL	1,863	290	1,398	175	1,108 D	15.6%	75.0%	17.2%	82.8%
HANCOCK	308	22	272	14	250 D	7.1%	88.3%	7.5%	92.5%
HARALSON	1,235	667	447	121	220 R	54.0%	36.2%	59.9%	40.1%
HARRIS	517	20	457	40	437 D	3.9%	88.4%	4.2%	95.8%
HART	1,117	65	857	195	792 D	5.8%	76.7%	7.0%	93.0%
HEARD	369	35	327	7	292 D	9.5%	88.6%	9.7%	90.3%
HENRY	714	53	594	67	541 D	7.4%	83.2%	8.2%	91.8%
HOUSTON	1,709	75	1,611	23	1,536 D	4.4%	94.3%	4.4%	95.6%
IRWIN	324	35	268	21	233 D	10.8%	82.7%	11.6%	88.4%
JACKSON	1,214	142	993	79	851 D	11.7%	81.8%	12.5%	87.5%
JASPER	525	68	448	9	380 D	13.0%	85.3%	13.2%	86.8%
JEFF DAVIS	167	39	122	6	83 D	23.4%	73.1%	24.2%	75.8%
JEFFERSON	682	103	502	77	399 D	15.1%	73.6%	17.0%	83.0%
JENKINS	240	16	200	24	184 D	6.7%	83.3%	7.4%	92.6%
JOHNSON	1,368	194	1,058	116	864 D	14.2%	77.3%	15.5%	84.5%
JONES	443	26	414	3	388 D	5.9%	93.5%	5.9%	94.1%
LAMAR	664	38	594	32	556 D	5.7%	89.5%	6.0%	94.0%
LANIER	403	46	356	1	310 D	11.4%	88.3%	11.4%	88.6%
LAURENS	1,299	121	1,127	51	1,006 D	9.3%	86.8%	9.7%	90.3%
LEE	245	23	211	11	188 D	9.4%	86.1%	9.7%	90.3%
LIBERTY	415	39	334	43	295 D	9.4%	80.3%	10.5%	89.5%
LINCOLN	1,264	121	847	296	726 D	9.6%	67.0%	12.5%	87.5%
LONG	564	19	499	46	480 D	3.4%	88.5%	3.7%	96.3%
LOWNDES	1,211	57	1,095	59	1,038 D	4.7%	90.4%	4.9%	95.1%
LUMPKIN	478	111	357	10	246 D	23.2%	74.7%	23.7%	76.3%
MCDUFFIE	560	37	267	256	230 D	6.6%	47.7%	12.2%	87.8%
MCINTOSH	173	44	127	2	83 D	25.4%	73.4%	25.7%	74.3%
MACON	750	52	649	49	597 D	6.9%	86.5%	7.4%	92.6%
MADISON	686	121	504	61	383 D	17.6%	73.5%	19.4%	80.6%
MARION	321	31	272	18	241 D	9.7%	84.7%	10.2%	89.8%
MERIWETHER	1,331	103	886	342	783 D	7.7%	66.6%	10.4%	89.6%
MILLER	183	45	126	12	81 D	24.6%	68.9%	26.3%	73.7%
MILTON	328	53	224	51	171 D	16.2%	68.3%	19.1%	80.9%
MITCHELL	838	51	736	51	685 D	6.1%	87.8%	6.5%	93.5%
MONROE	767	64	672	31	608 D	8.3%	87.6%	8.7%	91.3%
MONTGOMERY	453	87	353	13	266 D	19.2%	77.9%	19.8%	80.2%
MORGAN	768	126	598	44	472 D	16.4%	77.9%	17.4%	82.6%
MURRAY	1,531	648	818	65	170 D	42.3%	53.4%	44.2%	55.8%
MUSCOGEE	2,415	218	2,067	130	1,849 D	9.0%	85.6%	9.5%	90.5%
NEWTON	950	139	716	95	577 D	14.6%	75.4%	16.3%	83.7%
OCONEE	387	46	279	62	233 D	11.9%	72.1%	14.2%	85.8%
OGLETHORPE	1,965	129	1,748	88	1,619 D	6.6%	89.0%	6.9%	93.1%
PAULDING	923	378	419	126	41 D	41.0%	45.4%	47.4%	52.6%
PEACH									
PICKENS	1,907	1,149	754	4	395 R	60.3%	39.5%	60.4%	39.6%
PIERCE	501	83	397	21	314 D	16.6%	79.2%	17.3%	82.7%
PIKE	1,008	41	895	72	854 D	4.1%	88.8%	4.4%	95.6%
POLK	1,441	481	803	157	322 R	33.4%	55.7%	37.5%	62.5%
PULASKI	492	29	442	21	413 D	5.9%	89.8%	6.2%	93.8%
PUTNAM	468	7	457	4	450 D	1.5%	97.6%	1.5%	98.5%
QUITMAN	150	8	138	4	130 D	5.3%	92.0%	5.5%	94.5%

GEORGIA

PRESIDENT 1920

County	Total Vote	Republican	Democratic	Other	Rep.-Dem. Plurality	Total Vote Rep.	Total Vote Dem.	Major Vote Rep.	Major Vote Dem.
RABUN	459	147	312		165 D	32.0%	68.0%	32.0%	68.0%
RANDOLPH	585	51	534		483 D	8.7%	91.3%	8.7%	91.3%
RICHMOND	3,167	511	2,656		2,145 D	16.1%	83.9%	16.1%	83.9%
ROCKDALE	689	201	488		287 D	29.2%	70.8%	29.2%	70.8%
SCHLEY	288	53	235		182 D	18.4%	81.6%	18.4%	81.6%
SCREVEN	899	260	639		379 D	28.9%	71.1%	28.9%	71.1%
SEMINOLE	1,011	181	830		649 D	17.9%	82.1%	17.9%	82.1%
SPALDING	667	252	415		163 D	37.8%	62.2%	37.8%	62.2%
STEPHENS	375	31	344		313 D	8.3%	91.7%	8.3%	91.7%
STEWART									
SUMTER	1,372	296	1,076		780 D	21.6%	78.4%	21.6%	78.4%
TALBOT	422	43	379		336 D	10.2%	89.8%	10.2%	89.8%
TALIAFERRO	342	12	330		318 D	3.5%	96.5%	3.5%	96.5%
TATTNALL	748	301	447		146 D	40.2%	59.8%	40.2%	59.8%
TAYLOR	702	211	491		280 D	30.1%	69.9%	30.1%	69.9%
TELFAIR	1,106	37	1,069		1,032 D	3.3%	96.7%	3.3%	96.7%
TERRELL	548	48	500		452 D	8.8%	91.2%	8.8%	91.2%
THOMAS	1,298	168	1,130		962 D	12.9%	87.1%	12.9%	87.1%
TIFT	730	154	576		422 D	21.1%	78.9%	21.1%	78.9%
TOOMBS	643	246	397		151 D	38.3%	61.7%	38.3%	61.7%
TOWNS	654	398	256		142 R	60.9%	39.1%	60.9%	39.1%
TREUTLEN	370	107	263		156 D	28.9%	71.1%	28.9%	71.1%
TROUP	1,793	342	1,451		1,109 D	19.1%	80.9%	19.1%	80.9%
TURNER	575	182	393		211 D	31.7%	68.3%	31.7%	68.3%
TWIGGS	317	44	273		229 D	13.9%	86.1%	13.9%	86.1%
UNION	1,031	562	469		93 R	54.5%	45.5%	54.5%	45.5%
UPSON	1,127	170	957		787 D	15.1%	84.9%	15.1%	84.9%
WALKER	2,416	1,069	1,347		278 D	44.2%	55.8%	44.2%	55.8%
WALTON	1,312	123	1,189		1,066 D	9.4%	90.6%	9.4%	90.6%
WARE	1,116	215	901		686 D	19.3%	80.7%	19.3%	80.7%
WARREN	485	83	402		319 D	17.1%	82.9%	17.1%	82.9%
WASHINGTON	1,252	118	1,134		1,016 D	9.4%	90.6%	9.4%	90.6%
WAYNE	432	25	407		382 D	5.8%	94.2%	5.8%	94.2%
WEBSTER	209	24	185		161 D	11.5%	88.5%	11.5%	88.5%
WHEELER	451	101	350		249 D	22.4%	77.6%	22.4%	77.6%
WHITE	473	264	209		55 R	55.8%	44.2%	55.8%	44.2%
WHITFIELD	1,835	1,073	762		311 R	58.5%	41.5%	58.5%	41.5%
WILCOX	587	106	481		375 D	18.1%	81.9%	18.1%	81.9%
WILKES	888	12	876		864 D	1.4%	98.6%	1.4%	98.6%
WILKINSON	293	37	256		219 D	12.6%	87.4%	12.6%	87.4%
WORTH	840	214	626		412 D	25.5%	74.5%	25.5%	74.5%
TOTAL	149,558	42,981	106,112	465	63,131 D	28.7%	71.0%	28.8%	71.2%

PRESIDENT 1924

County	Total Vote	Republican	Democratic	Other	Rep.-Dem. Plurality	Total Vote Rep.	Total Vote Dem.	Major Vote Rep.	Major Vote Dem.
RABUN	593	117	454	22	337 D	19.7%	76.6%	20.5%	79.5%
RANDOLPH	656	88	518	50	430 D	13.4%	79.0%	14.5%	85.5%
RICHMOND	3,844	1,296	2,169	379	873 D	33.7%	56.4%	37.4%	62.6%
ROCKDALE	434	24	382	28	358 D	5.5%	88.0%	5.9%	94.1%
SCHLEY	281	12	266	3	254 D	4.3%	94.7%	4.3%	95.7%
SCREVEN	1,145	288	821	36	533 D	25.2%	71.7%	26.0%	74.0%
SEMINOLE	245	24	201	20	177 D	9.8%	82.0%	10.7%	89.3%
SPALDING	1,420	75	1,257	88	1,182 D	5.3%	88.5%	5.6%	94.4%
STEPHENS	599	40	523	36	483 D	6.7%	87.3%	7.1%	92.9%
STEWART	465	24	408	33	384 D	5.2%	87.7%	5.6%	94.4%
SUMTER	1,462	124	1,225	113	1,101 D	8.5%	83.8%	9.2%	90.8%
TALBOT	526	33	491	2	458 D	6.3%	93.3%	6.3%	93.7%
TALIAFERRO	293	4	228	61	224 D	1.4%	77.8%	1.7%	98.3%
TATTNALL	1,315	66	1,100	149	1,034 D	5.0%	83.7%	5.7%	94.3%
TAYLOR	486	96	370	20	274 D	19.8%	76.1%	20.6%	79.4%
TELFAIR	1,757	264	1,382	111	1,118 D	15.0%	78.7%	16.0%	84.0%
TERRELL	696	45	630	21	585 D	6.5%	90.5%	6.7%	93.3%
THOMAS	1,463	115	1,280	68	1,165 D	7.9%	87.5%	8.2%	91.8%
TIFT	595	33	522	40	489 D	5.5%	87.7%	5.7%	94.3%
TOOMBS	378	32	314	32	282 D	8.5%	83.1%	9.2%	90.8%
TOWNS	1,372	765	604	3	161 R	55.8%	44.0%	55.9%	44.1%
TREUTLEN	252	27	222	3	195 D	10.7%	88.1%	10.8%	89.2%
TROUP	1,684	165	1,422	97	1,257 D	9.8%	84.4%	10.4%	89.6%
TURNER	536	166	338	32	172 D	31.0%	63.1%	32.9%	67.1%
TWIGGS	486	39	417	30	378 D	8.0%	85.8%	8.6%	91.4%
UNION	1,567	719	793	55	74 D	45.9%	50.6%	47.6%	52.4%
UPSON	581	37	484	60	447 D	6.4%	83.3%	7.1%	92.9%
WALKER	2,672	878	1,740	54	862 D	32.9%	65.1%	33.5%	66.5%
WALTON	1,025	90	873	62	783 D	8.8%	85.2%	9.3%	90.7%
WARE	1,996	216	1,497	283	1,281 D	10.8%	75.0%	12.6%	87.4%
WARREN	387	36	253	98	217 D	9.3%	65.4%	12.5%	87.5%
WASHINGTON	965	130	758	77	628 D	13.5%	78.5%	14.6%	85.4%
WAYNE	503	33	409	61	376 D	6.6%	81.3%	7.5%	92.5%
WEBSTER	160	10	140	10	130 D	6.2%	87.5%	6.7%	93.3%
WHEELER	869		772	97	772 D		88.8%		100.0%
WHITE	650	158	476	16	318 D	24.3%	73.2%	24.9%	75.1%
WHITFIELD	1,996	668	1,236	92	568 D	33.5%	61.9%	35.1%	64.9%
WILCOX	490	21	431	38	410 D	4.3%	88.0%	4.6%	95.4%
WILKES	1,075	44	836	195	792 D	4.1%	77.8%	5.0%	95.0%
WILKINSON	353	56	284	13	228 D	15.9%	80.5%	16.5%	83.5%
WORTH	731	40	616	75	576 D	5.5%	84.3%	6.1%	93.9%
TOTAL	166,635	30,300	123,262	13,073	92,962 D	18.2%	74.0%	19.7%	80.3%

GEORGIA

PRESIDENT 1928

County	Total Vote	Republican	Democratic	Other	Rep.-Dem. Plurality	Total Vote Rep.	Total Vote Dem.	Major Vote Rep.	Major Vote Dem.
APPLING	994	579	415		164 R	58.2%	41.8%	58.2%	41.8%
ATKINSON	471	121	350		229 D	25.7%	74.3%	25.7%	74.3%
BACON	508	203	305		102 D	40.0%	60.0%	40.0%	60.0%
BAKER	561	99	462		363 D	17.6%	82.4%	17.6%	82.4%
BALDWIN	982	270	712		442 D	27.5%	72.5%	27.5%	72.5%
BANKS	785	363	422		59 D	46.2%	53.8%	46.2%	53.8%
BARROW	1,163	684	479		205 R	58.8%	41.2%	58.8%	41.2%
BARTOW	1,668	838	830		8 R	50.2%	49.8%	50.2%	49.8%
BEN HILL	1,466	460	1,006		546 D	31.4%	68.6%	31.4%	68.6%
BERRIEN	840	105	735		630 D	12.5%	87.5%	12.5%	87.5%
BIBB	4,367	2,078	2,289		211 D	47.6%	52.4%	47.6%	52.4%
BLECKLEY	712	71	641		570 D	10.0%	90.0%	10.0%	90.0%
BRANTLEY	338	172	166		6 R	50.9%	49.1%	50.9%	49.1%
BROOKS	962	192	770		578 D	20.0%	80.0%	20.0%	80.0%
BRYAN	370	151	219		68 D	40.8%	59.2%	40.8%	59.2%
BULLOCH	1,645	387	1,258		871 D	23.5%	76.5%	23.5%	76.5%
BURKE	947	260	687		427 D	27.5%	72.5%	27.5%	72.5%
BUTTS	994	148	846		698 D	14.9%	85.1%	14.9%	85.1%
CALHOUN	662	91	571		480 D	13.7%	86.3%	13.7%	86.3%
CAMDEN	541	267	274		7 D	49.4%	50.6%	49.4%	50.6%
CAMPBELL	752	327	425		98 D	43.5%	56.5%	43.5%	56.5%
CANDLER	544	133	411		278 D	24.4%	75.6%	24.4%	75.6%
CARROLL	4,025	2,112	1,913		199 R	52.5%	47.5%	52.5%	47.5%
CATOOSA	1,167	605	562		43 R	51.8%	48.2%	51.8%	48.2%
CHARLTON	575	160	415		255 D	27.8%	72.2%	27.8%	72.2%
CHATHAM	10,822	5,288	5,534		246 D	48.9%	51.1%	48.9%	51.1%
CHATTAHOOCHEE	159	18	141		123 D	11.3%	88.7%	11.3%	88.7%
CHATTOOGA	2,016	1,096	920		176 R	54.4%	45.6%	54.4%	45.6%
CHEROKEE	2,260	1,679	581		1,098 R	74.3%	25.7%	74.3%	25.7%
CLARKE	2,131	724	1,407		683 D	34.0%	66.0%	34.0%	66.0%
CLAY	461	56	405		349 D	12.1%	87.9%	12.1%	87.9%
CLAYTON	1,231	619	612		7 R	50.3%	49.7%	50.3%	49.7%
CLINCH	860	143	717		574 D	16.6%	83.4%	16.6%	83.4%
COBB	3,137	1,711	1,426		285 R	54.5%	45.5%	54.5%	45.5%
COFFEE	1,767	591	1,176		585 D	33.4%	66.6%	33.4%	66.6%
COLQUITT	1,766	796	970		174 D	45.1%	54.9%	45.1%	54.9%
COLUMBIA	513	234	279		45 D	45.6%	54.4%	45.6%	54.4%
COOK	926	237	689		452 D	25.6%	74.4%	25.6%	74.4%
COWETA	1,885	229	1,656		1,427 D	12.1%	87.9%	12.1%	87.9%
CRAWFORD	406	48	358		310 D	11.8%	88.2%	11.8%	88.2%
CRISP	925	402	523		121 D	43.5%	56.5%	43.5%	56.5%
DADE	781	328	453		125 D	42.0%	58.0%	42.0%	58.0%
DAWSON	622	290	332		42 D	46.6%	53.4%	46.6%	53.4%
DECATUR	1,890	1,156	734		422 R	61.2%	38.8%	61.2%	38.8%
DE KALB	4,671	2,378	2,293		85 R	50.9%	49.1%	50.9%	49.1%
DODGE	950	273	677		404 D	28.7%	71.3%	28.7%	71.3%
DOOLY	900	156	744		588 D	17.3%	82.7%	17.3%	82.7%
DOUGHERTY	1,361	379	982		603 D	27.8%	72.2%	27.8%	72.2%
DOUGLAS	1,058	606	452		154 R	57.3%	42.7%	57.3%	42.7%
EARLY	905	231	674		443 D	25.5%	74.5%	25.5%	74.5%
ECHOLS	343	29	314		285 D	8.5%	91.5%	8.5%	91.5%
EFFINGHAM	790	627	163		464 R	79.4%	20.6%	79.4%	20.6%
ELBERT	1,983	931	1,052		121 D	46.9%	53.1%	46.9%	53.1%
EMANUEL	1,431	355	1,076		721 D	24.8%	75.2%	24.8%	75.2%
EVANS	681	192	489		297 D	28.2%	71.8%	28.2%	71.8%
FANNIN	2,541	1,730	811		919 R	68.1%	31.9%	68.1%	31.9%
FAYETTE	557	190	367		177 D	34.1%	65.9%	34.1%	65.9%
FLOYD	3,224	1,730	1,494		236 R	53.7%	46.3%	53.7%	46.3%
FORSYTH	1,221	934	287		647 R	76.5%	23.5%	76.5%	23.5%
FRANKLIN	1,571	801	770		31 R	51.0%	49.0%	51.0%	49.0%

PRESIDENT 1932

County	Total Vote	Republican	Democratic	Other	Rep.-Dem. Plurality	Total Vote Rep.	Total Vote Dem.	Major Vote Rep.	Major Vote Dem.
APPLING	665	64	601		537 D	9.6%	90.4%	9.6%	90.4%
ATKINSON	793	41	747	5	706 D	5.2%	94.2%	5.2%	94.8%
BACON	528	11	515	2	504 D	2.1%	97.5%	2.1%	97.9%
BAKER	652	2	647	3	645 D	0.3%	99.2%	0.3%	99.7%
BALDWIN	854	45	801	8	756 D	5.3%	93.8%	5.3%	94.7%
BANKS	1,361	58	1,283	20	1,225 D	4.3%	94.3%	4.3%	95.7%
BARROW	1,145	23	1,111	11	1,088 D	2.0%	97.0%	2.0%	98.0%
BARTOW	1,677	121	1,546	10	1,425 D	7.2%	92.2%	7.3%	92.7%
BEN HILL	1,116	85	1,026	5	941 D	7.6%	91.9%	7.7%	92.3%
BERRIEN	1,485	19	1,447	19	1,428 D	1.3%	97.4%	1.3%	98.7%
BIBB	4,808	405	4,372	31	3,967 D	8.4%	90.9%	8.5%	91.5%
BLECKLEY	1,376	37	1,338	1	1,301 D	2.7%	97.2%	2.7%	97.3%
BRANTLEY	717	22	693	2	671 D	3.1%	96.7%	3.1%	96.9%
BROOKS	1,506	75	1,426	5	1,351 D	5.0%	94.7%	5.0%	95.0%
BRYAN	373	17	353	3	336 D	4.6%	94.6%	4.6%	95.4%
BULLOCH	2,231	17	2,203	11	2,186 D	0.8%	98.7%	0.8%	99.2%
BURKE	522	18	498	6	480 D	3.4%	95.4%	3.5%	96.5%
BUTTS	1,725	21	1,693	11	1,672 D	1.2%	98.1%	1.2%	98.8%
CALHOUN	497	10	483	4	473 D	2.0%	97.2%	2.0%	98.0%
CAMDEN	469	49	417	3	368 D	10.4%	88.9%	10.5%	89.5%
CAMPBELL	490	13	476	1	463 D	2.7%	97.1%	2.7%	97.3%
CANDLER									
CARROLL	3,546	284	3,232	30	2,948 D	8.0%	91.1%	8.1%	91.9%
CATOOSA	1,117	123	985	9	862 D	11.0%	88.2%	11.1%	88.9%
CHARLTON	363	32	330	1	298 D	8.8%	90.9%	8.8%	91.2%
CHATHAM	9,744	1,669	8,020	55	6,351 D	17.1%	82.3%	17.2%	82.8%
CHATTAHOOCHEE	187	1	186		185 D	0.5%	99.5%	0.5%	99.5%
CHATTOOGA	2,411	188	2,200	23	2,012 D	7.8%	91.2%	7.9%	92.1%
CHEROKEE	2,059	314	1,727	18	1,413 D	15.3%	83.9%	15.4%	84.6%
CLARKE	2,164	159	1,992	13	1,833 D	7.3%	92.1%	7.4%	92.6%
CLAY	448	12	433	3	421 D	2.7%	96.7%	2.7%	97.3%
CLAYTON	1,403	35	1,361	7	1,326 D	2.5%	97.0%	2.5%	97.5%
CLINCH	474	11	461	2	450 D	2.3%	97.3%	2.3%	97.7%
COBB	3,321	218	3,079	24	2,861 D	6.6%	92.7%	6.6%	93.4%
COFFEE	1,702	29	1,652	21	1,623 D	1.7%	97.1%	1.7%	98.3%
COLQUITT	3,652	101	3,534	17	3,433 D	2.8%	96.8%	2.8%	97.2%
COLUMBIA	539	11	517	11	506 D	2.0%	95.9%	2.0%	98.0%
COOK	1,440	25	1,408	7	1,383 D	1.7%	97.8%	1.7%	98.3%
COWETA	2,185	46	2,137	6	2,091 D	2.1%	97.8%	2.1%	97.9%
CRAWFORD	281	9	272		263 D	3.2%	96.8%	3.2%	96.8%
CRISP	740	10	725	5	715 D	1.4%	98.0%	1.4%	98.6%
DADE	887	103	770	14	667 D	11.6%	86.8%	11.8%	88.2%
DAWSON	676	105	567	4	462 D	15.5%	83.9%	15.6%	84.4%
DECATUR	1,257	65	1,169	23	1,104 D	5.2%	93.0%	5.3%	94.7%
DE KALB	6,039	633	5,323	83	4,690 D	10.5%	88.1%	10.6%	89.4%
DODGE	2,843	33	2,809	1	2,776 D	1.2%	98.8%	1.2%	98.8%
DOOLY	1,151	8	1,139	4	1,131 D	0.7%	99.0%	0.7%	99.3%
DOUGHERTY	2,111	95	2,012	4	1,917 D	4.5%	95.3%	4.5%	95.5%
DOUGLAS	1,087	57	1,013	17	956 D	5.2%	93.2%	5.3%	94.7%
EARLY	1,152	19	1,131	2	1,112 D	1.6%	98.2%	1.7%	98.3%
ECHOLS	419	5	414		409 D	1.2%	98.8%	1.2%	98.8%
EFFINGHAM	610	90	518	2	428 D	14.8%	84.9%	14.8%	85.2%
ELBERT	2,119	77	2,023	19	1,946 D	3.6%	95.5%	3.7%	96.3%
EMANUEL	2,457	33	2,420	4	2,387 D	1.3%	98.5%	1.3%	98.7%
EVANS	576	21	548	7	527 D	3.6%	95.1%	3.7%	96.3%
FANNIN	3,342	1,967	1,375	1	592 R	58.9%	41.1%	58.9%	41.1%
FAYETTE	753	6	746	1	740 D	0.8%	99.1%	0.8%	99.2%
FLOYD	4,672	300	4,342	30	4,042 D	6.4%	92.9%	6.5%	93.5%
FORSYTH	1,750	117	1,627	6	1,510 D	6.7%	93.0%	6.7%	93.3%
FRANKLIN	1,461	78	1,361	22	1,283 D	5.3%	93.2%	5.4%	94.6%

GEORGIA

PRESIDENT 1928

County	Total Vote	Republican	Democratic	Other	Rep.-Dem. Plurality	% Total Vote Rep.	% Total Vote Dem.	% Major Vote Rep.	% Major Vote Dem.
FULTON	18,240	9,368	8,872		496 R	51.4%	48.6%	51.4%	48.6%
GILMER	1,541	1,012	529		483 R	65.7%	34.3%	65.7%	34.3%
GLASCOCK	348	225	123		102 R	64.7%	35.3%	64.7%	35.3%
GLYNN	1,348	799	549		250 R	59.3%	40.7%	59.3%	40.7%
GORDON	1,779	1,039	740		299 R	58.4%	41.6%	58.4%	41.6%
GRADY	1,611	439	1,172		733 D	27.3%	72.7%	27.3%	72.7%
GREENE	872	245	627		382 D	28.1%	71.9%	28.1%	71.9%
GWINNETT	2,032	1,062	970		92 R	52.3%	47.7%	52.3%	47.7%
HABERSHAM	2,509	1,404	1,105		299 R	56.0%	44.0%	56.0%	44.0%
HALL	3,096	1,573	1,523		50 R	50.8%	49.2%	50.8%	49.2%
HANCOCK	670	118	552		434 D	17.6%	82.4%	17.6%	82.4%
HARALSON	2,237	1,547	690		857 R	69.2%	30.8%	69.2%	30.8%
HARRIS	695	144	551		407 D	20.7%	79.3%	20.7%	79.3%
HART	1,522	603	919		316 D	39.6%	60.4%	39.6%	60.4%
HEARD	883	390	493		103 D	44.2%	55.8%	44.2%	55.8%
HENRY	1,123	360	763		403 D	32.1%	67.9%	32.1%	67.9%
HOUSTON	415	92	323		231 D	22.2%	77.8%	22.2%	77.8%
IRWIN	1,079	162	917		755 D	15.0%	85.0%	15.0%	85.0%
JACKSON	1,677	818	859		41 D	48.8%	51.2%	48.8%	51.2%
JASPER	772	140	632		492 D	18.1%	81.9%	18.1%	81.9%
JEFF DAVIS	495	180	315		135 D	36.4%	63.6%	36.4%	63.6%
JEFFERSON	1,855	1,057	798		259 R	57.0%	43.0%	57.0%	43.0%
JENKINS	741	332	409		77 D	44.8%	55.2%	44.8%	55.2%
JOHNSON	916	284	632		348 D	31.0%	69.0%	31.0%	69.0%
JONES	514	100	414		314 D	19.5%	80.5%	19.5%	80.5%
LAMAR	798	126	672		546 D	15.8%	84.2%	15.8%	84.2%
LANIER	441	138	303		165 D	31.3%	68.7%	31.3%	68.7%
LAURENS	2,457	470	1,987		1,517 D	19.1%	80.9%	19.1%	80.9%
LEE	332	45	287		242 D	13.6%	86.4%	13.6%	86.4%
LIBERTY	404	203	201		2 R	50.2%	49.8%	50.2%	49.8%
LINCOLN	858	413	445		32 D	48.1%	51.9%	48.1%	51.9%
LONG	567	401	166		235 R	70.7%	29.3%	70.7%	29.3%
LOWNDES	2,009	596	1,413		817 D	29.7%	70.3%	29.7%	70.3%
LUMPKIN	941	381	560		179 D	40.5%	59.5%	40.5%	59.5%
MCDUFFIE	685	381	304		77 R	55.6%	44.4%	55.6%	44.4%
MCINTOSH	321	180	141		39 R	56.1%	43.9%	56.1%	43.9%
MACON	1,077	258	819		561 D	24.0%	76.0%	24.0%	76.0%
MADISON	1,328	527	801		274 D	39.7%	60.3%	39.7%	60.3%
MARION	479	114	365		251 D	23.8%	76.2%	23.8%	76.2%
MERIWETHER	1,802	287	1,515		1,228 D	15.9%	84.1%	15.9%	84.1%
MILLER	423	101	322		221 D	23.9%	76.1%	23.9%	76.1%
MILTON	627	444	183		261 R	70.8%	29.2%	70.8%	29.2%
MITCHELL	1,501	143	1,358		1,215 D	9.5%	90.5%	9.5%	90.5%
MONROE	1,130	329	801		472 D	29.1%	70.9%	29.1%	70.9%
MONTGOMERY	435	98	337		239 D	22.5%	77.5%	22.5%	77.5%
MORGAN	1,011	208	803		595 D	20.6%	79.4%	20.6%	79.4%
MURRAY	2,088	1,106	982		124 R	53.0%	47.0%	53.0%	47.0%
MUSCOGEE	3,672	1,574	2,098		524 D	42.9%	57.1%	42.9%	57.1%
NEWTON	1,571	698	873		175 D	44.4%	55.6%	44.4%	55.6%
OCONEE	644	300	344		44 D	46.6%	53.4%	46.6%	53.4%
OGLETHORPE	1,018	205	813		608 D	20.1%	79.9%	20.1%	79.9%
PAULDING	1,991	1,301	690		611 R	65.3%	34.7%	65.3%	34.7%
PEACH	780	208	572		364 D	26.7%	73.3%	26.7%	73.3%
PICKENS	1,862	1,319	543		776 R	70.8%	29.2%	70.8%	29.2%
PIERCE	808	285	523		238 D	35.3%	64.7%	35.3%	64.7%
PIKE	952	238	714		476 D	25.0%	75.0%	25.0%	75.0%
POLK	2,348	1,462	886		576 R	62.3%	37.7%	62.3%	37.7%
PULASKI	744	105	639		534 D	14.1%	85.9%	14.1%	85.9%
PUTNAM	739	57	682		625 D	7.7%	92.3%	7.7%	92.3%
QUITMAN	215	41	174		133 D	19.1%	80.9%	19.1%	80.9%

PRESIDENT 1932

County	Total Vote	Republican	Democratic	Other	Rep.-Dem. Plurality	% Total Vote Rep.	% Total Vote Dem.	% Major Vote Rep.	% Major Vote Dem.
FULTON	22,453	2,063	20,137	253	18,074 D	9.2%	89.7%	9.3%	90.7%
GILMER	1,826	616	1,210		594 D	33.7%	66.3%	33.7%	66.3%
GLASCOCK	400	7	393		386 D	1.8%	98.2%	1.8%	98.2%
GLYNN	1,452	186	1,262	4	1,076 D	12.8%	86.9%	12.8%	87.2%
GORDON	1,848	122	1,708	18	1,586 D	6.6%	92.4%	6.7%	93.3%
GRADY	2,254	60	2,184	10	2,124 D	2.7%	96.9%	2.7%	97.3%
GREENE	972	52	918	2	866 D	5.3%	94.4%	5.4%	94.6%
GWINNETT	2,708	91	2,616	1	2,525 D	3.4%	96.6%	3.4%	96.6%
HABERSHAM	1,947	225	1,693	29	1,468 D	11.6%	87.0%	11.7%	88.3%
HALL	2,780	120	2,649	11	2,529 D	4.3%	95.3%	4.3%	95.7%
HANCOCK	551	18	529	4	511 D	3.3%	96.0%	3.3%	96.7%
HARALSON	1,501	223	1,278		1,055 D	14.9%	85.1%	14.9%	85.1%
HARRIS	875	21	851	3	830 D	2.4%	97.1%	2.4%	97.6%
HART	1,274	12	1,261	1	1,249 D	0.9%	99.0%	0.9%	99.1%
HEARD	1,016	24	989	3	965 D	2.4%	97.3%	2.4%	97.6%
HENRY	1,532	21	1,496	15	1,475 D	1.4%	97.7%	1.4%	98.6%
HOUSTON	487	27	460		433 D	5.5%	94.5%	5.5%	94.5%
IRWIN	1,439	22	1,416	1	1,394 D	1.5%	98.4%	1.5%	98.5%
JACKSON	1,485	80	1,389	16	1,309 D	5.4%	93.5%	5.4%	94.6%
JASPER	790	14	773	3	759 D	1.8%	97.8%	1.8%	98.2%
JEFF DAVIS	1,182	50	1,129	3	1,079 D	4.1%	95.7%	4.1%	95.9%
JEFFERSON	1,536	65	1,454	17	1,389 D	4.2%	94.7%	4.3%	95.7%
JENKINS	530	20	510		490 D	3.8%	96.2%	3.8%	96.2%
JOHNSON	1,340	18	1,314	8	1,296 D	1.3%	98.1%	1.4%	98.6%
JONES	556		553	3	553 D		99.5%		100.0%
LAMAR	754	33	714	7	681 D	4.4%	94.7%	4.4%	95.6%
LANIER	217	3	211	3	208 D	1.4%	97.2%	1.4%	98.6%
LAURENS	2,227	38	2,188	1	2,150 D	1.7%	97.9%	1.7%	98.3%
LEE	258	6	252		246 D	2.3%	97.1%	2.3%	97.7%
LIBERTY	308	18	289	1	271 D	5.8%	93.8%	5.9%	94.1%
LINCOLN	664	3	660	1	657 D	0.5%	99.4%	0.5%	99.5%
LONG	449	14	430	5	416 D	3.1%	95.8%	3.2%	96.8%
LOWNDES	1,944	97	1,840	7	1,743 D	5.0%	94.7%	5.0%	95.0%
LUMPKIN	1,005	81	924		843 D	8.1%	91.9%	8.1%	91.9%
MCDUFFIE	604	29	568	7	539 D	4.8%	94.0%	4.9%	95.1%
MCINTOSH	290	19	271		252 D	6.6%	93.4%	6.6%	93.4%
MACON	1,497	55	1,438	4	1,383 D	3.7%	96.1%	3.7%	96.3%
MADISON	2,170	38	2,124	8	2,086 D	1.8%	97.9%	1.8%	98.2%
MARION	479	24	455		431 D	5.0%	95.0%	5.0%	95.0%
MERIWETHER	2,662	53	2,604	5	2,551 D	2.0%	97.8%	2.0%	98.0%
MILLER	396		392	4	392 D		99.0%		100.0%
MILTON	2,117	15	2,097	5	2,082 D	0.7%	99.1%	0.7%	99.3%
MITCHELL	1,246	45	1,200	1	1,155 D	3.6%	96.3%	3.6%	96.4%
MONROE									
MONTGOMERY	893	17	868	8	851 D	1.9%	97.2%	1.9%	98.1%
MORGAN	1,006	74	923	9	849 D	7.4%	91.7%	7.4%	92.6%
MURRAY	2,233	350	1,874	9	1,524 D	15.7%	83.9%	15.7%	84.3%
MUSCOGEE	3,667	230	3,413	24	3,183 D	6.3%	93.1%	6.3%	93.7%
NEWTON	1,727	45	1,672	10	1,627 D	2.6%	96.8%	2.6%	97.4%
OCONEE	718	39	664	15	625 D	5.4%	92.5%	5.5%	94.5%
OGLETHORPE	1,276	34	1,240	2	1,206 D	2.7%	97.2%	2.7%	97.3%
PAULDING	2,228	276	1,914	38	1,638 D	12.4%	85.9%	12.6%	87.4%
PEACH	656	56	595	5	539 D	8.5%	90.7%	8.6%	91.4%
PICKENS	2,215	743	1,472		729 D	33.5%	66.5%	33.5%	66.5%
PIERCE	1,129	29	1,094	6	1,065 D	2.6%	96.9%	2.6%	97.4%
PIKE	1,064	33	1,021	10	988 D	3.1%	96.0%	3.1%	96.9%
POLK	2,381	211	2,170		1,959 D	8.9%	91.1%	8.9%	91.1%
PULASKI	987	14	973		959 D	1.4%	98.6%	1.4%	98.6%
PUTNAM	806	33	770	3	737 D	4.1%	95.5%	4.1%	95.9%
QUITMAN	243		239	4	239 D		98.4%		100.0%

GEORGIA

PRESIDENT 1928

County	Total Vote	Republican	Democratic	Other	Rep.-Dem. Plurality	TV Rep.	TV Dem.	MV Rep.	MV Dem.
RABUN	896	306	590		284 D	34.2%	65.8%	34.2%	65.8%
RANDOLPH	980	177	803		626 D	18.1%	81.9%	18.1%	81.9%
RICHMOND	7,190	5,104	2,086		3,018 R	71.0%	29.0%	71.0%	29.0%
ROCKDALE	628	156	472		316 D	24.8%	75.2%	24.8%	75.2%
SCHLEY	405	77	328		251 D	19.0%	81.0%	19.0%	81.0%
SCREVEN	1,006	706	300		406 R	70.2%	29.8%	70.2%	29.8%
SEMINOLE	481	110	371		261 D	22.9%	77.1%	22.9%	77.1%
SPALDING	2,146	412	1,734		1,322 D	19.2%	80.8%	19.2%	80.8%
STEPHENS	708	270	438		168 D	38.1%	61.9%	38.1%	61.9%
STEWART	820	88	732		644 D	10.7%	89.3%	10.7%	89.3%
SUMTER	1,531	294	1,237		943 D	19.2%	80.8%	19.2%	80.8%
TALBOT	610	74	536		452 D	12.1%	87.9%	12.1%	87.9%
TALIAFERRO	504	58	446		388 D	11.5%	88.5%	11.5%	88.5%
TATTNALL	1,251	791	460		331 R	63.2%	36.8%	63.2%	36.8%
TAYLOR	943	353	590		237 D	37.4%	62.6%	37.4%	62.6%
TELFAIR	2,389	332	2,057		1,725 D	13.9%	86.1%	13.9%	86.1%
TERRELL	1,013	116	897		781 D	11.5%	88.5%	11.5%	88.5%
THOMAS	2,054	814	1,240		426 D	39.6%	60.4%	39.6%	60.4%
TIFT	1,247	511	736		225 D	41.0%	59.0%	41.0%	59.0%
TOOMBS	1,166	551	615		64 D	47.3%	52.7%	47.3%	52.7%
TOWNS	1,374	857	517		340 R	62.4%	37.6%	62.4%	37.6%
TREUTLEN	456	64	392		328 D	14.3%	86.0%	14.0%	86.0%
TROUP	2,524	967	1,557		590 D	38.3%	61.7%	38.3%	61.7%
TURNER	854	526	328		198 R	61.5%	38.4%	61.6%	38.4%
TWIGGS	645	74	571		497 D	11.5%	88.5%	11.5%	88.5%
UNION	3,496	2,873	623		2,250 R	82.2%	17.8%	82.2%	17.8%
UPSON	942	221	721		500 D	23.5%	76.5%	23.5%	76.5%
WALKER	2,839	1,786	1,053		733 R	62.9%	37.1%	62.9%	37.1%
WALTON	1,559	424	1,135		711 D	27.2%	72.8%	27.2%	72.8%
WARE	2,755	1,339	1,416		77 D	48.6%	51.4%	48.6%	51.4%
WARREN	502	255	247		8 R	50.8%	49.2%	50.8%	49.2%
WASHINGTON	1,614	472	1,142		670 D	29.2%	70.8%	29.2%	70.8%
WAYNE	901	413	488		75 D	45.8%	54.2%	45.8%	54.2%
WEBSTER	235	61	174		113 D	26.0%	74.0%	26.0%	74.0%
WHEELER	413	101	312		211 D	24.5%	75.5%	24.5%	75.5%
WHITE	842	568	274		294 R	67.5%	32.5%	67.5%	32.5%
WHITFIELD	2,804	1,650	1,154		496 R	58.8%	41.2%	58.8%	41.2%
WILCOX	675	216	459		243 D	32.0%	68.0%	32.0%	68.0%
WILKES	1,545	798	747		51 R	51.7%	48.3%	51.7%	48.3%
WILKINSON	714	227	487		260 D	31.8%	68.2%	31.8%	68.2%
WORTH	1,262	310	952		642 D	24.5%	75.4%	24.6%	75.4%
TOTAL	231,592	101,800	129,604	188	27,804 D	44.0%	56.0%	44.0%	56.0%

PRESIDENT 1932

County	Total Vote	Republican	Democratic	Other	Rep.-Dem. Plurality	TV Rep.	TV Dem.	MV Rep.	MV Dem.
RABUN	979	78	893	8	815 D	8.0%	91.2%	8.0%	92.0%
RANDOLPH	1,383	31	1,344	8	1,313 D	2.2%	97.2%	2.3%	97.7%
RICHMOND	5,694	738	4,873	83	4,135 D	13.0%	85.6%	13.2%	86.8%
ROCKDALE	483	18	461	4	443 D	3.7%	95.4%	3.8%	96.2%
SCHLEY	408	8	398	2	390 D	2.0%	97.5%	2.0%	98.0%
SCREVEN	557	46	508	3	462 D	8.3%	91.2%	8.3%	91.7%
SEMINOLE	806	20	776	10	756 D	2.5%	96.3%	2.5%	97.6%
SPALDING	2,251	54	2,185	12	2,131 D	2.4%	97.1%	2.4%	97.6%
STEPHENS	1,052	18	1,026	8	1,008 D	1.7%	97.5%	1.7%	98.3%
STEWART	606	15	588	3	573 D	2.5%	97.0%	2.5%	97.5%
SUMTER	1,692	57	1,619	16	1,562 D	3.4%	95.7%	3.4%	96.6%
TALBOT	960	45	912	3	867 D	4.7%	95.0%	4.7%	95.3%
TALIAFERRO	506	3	503		500 D	0.6%	99.4%	0.6%	99.4%
TATTNALL	2,176	37	2,133	6	2,096 D	1.7%	98.0%	1.7%	98.3%
TAYLOR	732	44	685	3	641 D	6.0%	93.6%	6.0%	94.0%
TELFAIR	797	45	746	6	701 D	5.6%	93.6%	5.7%	94.3%
TERRELL	1,027	24	1,000	3	976 D	2.3%	97.4%	2.3%	97.7%
THOMAS	2,710	90	2,607	13	2,517 D	3.3%	96.2%	3.3%	96.7%
TIFT	1,466	65	1,394	7	1,329 D	4.4%	95.1%	4.5%	95.5%
TOOMBS	1,936	54	1,868	14	1,814 D	2.8%	96.5%	2.8%	97.2%
TOWNS	1,532	790	742		48 R	51.6%	48.4%	51.6%	48.4%
TREUTLEN	885	36	849		813 D	4.1%	95.9%	4.1%	95.9%
TROUP	2,454	81	2,371	2	2,290 D	3.3%	96.6%	3.3%	96.7%
TURNER	977	59	909	9	850 D	6.0%	93.0%	6.1%	93.9%
TWIGGS	664	15	646	3	631 D	2.3%	97.3%	2.3%	97.7%
UNION	2,154	810	1,344		534 D	37.6%	62.4%	37.6%	62.4%
UPSON	1,684	20	1,660	4	1,640 D	1.2%	98.6%	1.2%	98.8%
WALKER	2,691	405	2,255	31	1,850 D	15.1%	83.8%	15.1%	84.8%
WALTON	2,172	36	2,136		2,100 D	1.7%	98.3%	1.7%	98.3%
WARE	2,723	205	2,504	14	2,299 D	7.5%	92.0%	7.6%	92.4%
WARREN	697	18	676	3	658 D	2.6%	97.0%	2.6%	97.4%
WASHINGTON	1,941	18	1,923		1,905 D	0.9%	99.3%	0.5%	99.5%
WAYNE	1,111	60	1,044	7	984 D	5.4%	94.0%	5.4%	94.6%
WEBSTER	240	5	235		230 D	2.1%	97.9%	2.1%	97.9%
WHEELER	1,157	29	1,127	1	1,098 D	2.5%	97.4%	2.5%	97.5%
WHITE	991	53	936	2	883 D	5.3%	94.5%	5.4%	94.6%
WHITFIELD	2,912	483	2,384	45	1,901 D	16.8%	81.9%	16.8%	83.2%
WILCOX	645	25	619	1	594 D	3.9%	96.0%	3.9%	96.1%
WILKES	1,224	42	1,172	10	1,130 D	3.4%	95.8%	3.5%	96.5%
WILKINSON	726		726		726 D		100.0%		100.0%
WORTH	2,310	38	2,269	3	2,231 D	1.6%	98.2%	1.6%	98.4%
TOTAL	255,590	19,863	234,118	1,609	214,255 D	7.8%	91.6%	7.8%	92.2%

GEORGIA

PRESIDENT 1936

County	Total Vote	Republican	Democratic	Other	Rep.-Dem. Plurality	Total Vote Rep.	Total Vote Dem.	Major Vote Rep.	Major Vote Dem.
APPLING	1,457	140	1,309	8	1,169 D	9.6%	89.8%	9.7%	90.3%
ATKINSON	987	29	958		929 D	2.9%	97.1%	2.9%	97.1%
BACON	991	62	929		867 D	6.3%	93.7%	6.3%	93.7%
BAKER	613	13	599	1	586 D	2.1%	97.7%	2.1%	97.9%
BALDWIN	926	113	811	2	698 D	12.2%	87.6%	12.2%	87.8%
BANKS	822	181	641		460 D	22.0%	78.0%	22.0%	78.0%
BARROW	1,355	172	1,181	2	1,009 D	12.7%	87.2%	12.7%	87.3%
BARTOW	2,680	444	2,228	8	1,784 D	16.6%	83.1%	16.6%	83.4%
BEN HILL	1,294	146	1,147	1	1,001 D	11.3%	88.6%	11.3%	88.7%
BERRIEN	1,753	53	1,700		1,647 D	3.0%	97.0%	3.0%	97.0%
BIBB	6,197	452	5,722	23	5,270 D	7.3%	92.3%	7.3%	92.7%
BLECKLEY	720	69	649	2	580 D	9.6%	90.1%	9.6%	90.4%
BRANTLEY	572	40	527	5	487 D	7.0%	92.1%	7.1%	92.9%
BROOKS	1,377	94	1,277	6	1,183 D	6.8%	92.7%	6.9%	93.1%
BRYAN	699	63	632	4	569 D	9.0%	90.4%	9.1%	90.9%
BULLOCH	2,049	66	1,978	5	1,912 D	3.2%	96.5%	3.2%	96.8%
BURKE	1,094	51	1,040	3	989 D	4.7%	95.1%	4.7%	95.3%
BUTTS	853	28	820	5	792 D	3.3%	96.1%	3.3%	96.7%
CALHOUN	793	14	777	2	763 D	1.8%	98.0%	1.8%	98.2%
CAMDEN	571	53	515	3	462 D	9.3%	90.2%	9.3%	90.7%
CAMPBELL									
CANDLER	1,075	80	992	3	912 D	7.4%	92.3%	7.5%	92.5%
CARROLL	4,374	653	3,717	4	3,064 D	14.9%	85.0%	14.9%	85.1%
CATOOSA	1,239	218	1,018	3	800 D	17.6%	82.2%	17.6%	82.4%
CHARLTON	497	28	468	1	440 D	5.6%	94.2%	5.6%	94.4%
CHATHAM	11,270	1,227	10,019	24	8,792 D	10.9%	88.9%	10.9%	89.1%
CHATTAHOOCHEE	226	20	206		186 D	8.8%	91.2%	8.8%	91.2%
CHATTOOGA	3,232	231	2,999	2	2,768 D	7.1%	92.8%	7.2%	92.8%
CHEROKEE	2,060	842	1,211	7	369 D	40.9%	58.6%	41.0%	59.0%
CLARKE	2,796	160	2,632	4	2,472 D	5.7%	94.1%	5.7%	94.3%
CLAY	499	13	484	2	471 D	2.6%	97.0%	2.6%	97.4%
CLAYTON	1,530	175	1,352	3	1,177 D	11.4%	88.4%	11.5%	88.5%
CLINCH	1,075	71	1,002	2	931 D	6.6%	93.4%	6.6%	93.4%
COBB	3,515	707	2,802	6	2,095 D	20.1%	79.7%	20.1%	79.9%
COFFEE	1,819	116	1,702	1	1,586 D	6.4%	93.6%	6.4%	93.6%
COLQUITT	2,901	448	2,449	4	2,001 D	15.4%	84.4%	15.5%	84.5%
COLUMBIA	700	34	659	7	625 D	4.9%	94.1%	4.9%	95.1%
COOK	1,816	117	1,697	2	1,580 D	6.4%	93.4%	6.4%	93.6%
COWETA	2,336	73	2,260	3	2,187 D	3.1%	96.7%	3.1%	96.9%
CRAWFORD	437	22	413	2	391 D	5.0%	94.5%	5.1%	94.9%
CRISP	1,110	79	1,029	2	950 D	7.1%	92.7%	7.1%	92.9%
DADE	985	127	857	1	730 D	12.9%	87.0%	12.9%	87.1%
DAWSON	699	322	377		55 D	46.1%	53.9%	46.1%	53.9%
DECATUR	2,053	79	1,965	9	1,886 D	3.8%	95.4%	4.5%	95.5%
DE KALB	8,560	1,137	7,391	32	6,254 D	13.3%	86.3%	13.3%	86.7%
DODGE	1,336	71	1,259	6	1,188 D	5.3%	94.2%	5.3%	94.7%
DOOLY	1,380	41	1,336	3	1,295 D	3.0%	96.7%	3.0%	97.0%
DOUGHERTY	2,716	122	2,591	3	2,469 D	4.5%	95.4%	4.5%	95.5%
DOUGLAS	1,255	237	1,015	3	778 D	18.9%	80.9%	18.9%	81.1%
EARLY	1,157	46	1,107	4	1,061 D	4.0%	95.7%	4.0%	96.0%
ECHOLS	331	30	300	1	270 D	9.1%	90.6%	9.1%	90.9%
EFFINGHAM	755	142	612	1	470 D	18.8%	81.1%	18.8%	81.2%
ELBERT	2,232	438	1,772	22	1,334 D	19.6%	79.4%	19.6%	80.2%
EMANUEL	2,081	125	1,943	13	1,818 D	6.0%	93.4%	6.0%	94.0%
EVANS	771	35	733	3	698 D	4.5%	95.1%	4.6%	95.4%
FANNIN	3,430	1,890	1,540		350 R	55.1%	44.9%	55.1%	44.9%
FAYETTE	819	70	748	1	678 D	8.5%	91.3%	8.6%	91.4%
FLOYD	6,119	612	5,499	8	4,887 D	10.0%	89.9%	10.0%	90.0%
FORSYTH	1,331	551	780		229 D	41.4%	58.6%	41.4%	58.6%
FRANKLIN	1,869	238	1,621	10	1,383 D	12.7%	86.7%	12.8%	87.2%

PRESIDENT 1940

County	Total Vote	Republican	Democratic	Other	Rep.-Dem. Plurality	Total Vote Rep.	Total Vote Dem.	Major Vote Rep.	Major Vote Dem.
APPLING	1,842	312	1,514	16	1,202 D	16.9%	82.2%	17.1%	82.9%
ATKINSON	770	66	703	1	637 D	8.6%	91.3%	8.6%	91.4%
BACON	923	97	821	5	724 D	10.5%	88.9%	10.6%	89.4%
BAKER	588	30	557	1	527 D	5.1%	94.7%	5.1%	94.9%
BALDWIN	1,520	203	1,313	4	1,110 D	13.4%	86.4%	13.4%	86.6%
BANKS	838	164	668	6	504 D	19.6%	79.7%	19.7%	80.3%
BARROW	1,839	219	1,615	5	1,396 D	11.9%	87.8%	11.9%	88.1%
BARTOW	2,060	318	1,734	8	1,416 D	15.4%	84.2%	15.5%	84.5%
BEN HILL	1,392	181	1,206	5	1,025 D	13.0%	86.6%	13.0%	87.0%
BERRIEN	1,180	23	1,156	1	1,133 D	1.9%	98.0%	2.0%	98.0%
BIBB	8,137	1,371	6,729	37	5,358 D	16.8%	82.7%	16.9%	83.1%
BLECKLEY	888	100	785	3	685 D	11.3%	88.4%	11.3%	88.7%
BRANTLEY	1,030	67	960	3	893 D	6.5%	93.2%	6.5%	93.5%
BROOKS	1,552	248	1,300	4	1,052 D	16.0%	83.9%	16.0%	84.0%
BRYAN	925	49	874	2	825 D	5.3%	94.5%	5.3%	94.7%
BULLOCH	2,210	141	2,063	6	1,922 D	6.4%	93.3%	6.4%	93.6%
BURKE	1,077	42	1,029	6	987 D	3.9%	95.5%	3.9%	96.1%
BUTTS	1,101	87	1,012	2	925 D	7.9%	91.9%	7.9%	92.1%
CALHOUN	643	33	610		577 D	5.1%	94.9%	5.1%	94.9%
CAMDEN	625	60	564	1	504 D	9.6%	90.2%	9.6%	90.4%
CAMPBELL									
CANDLER	813	63	748	2	685 D	7.7%	92.0%	7.8%	92.2%
CARROLL	4,432	616	3,808	8	3,192 D	13.9%	85.9%	13.9%	86.1%
CATOOSA	1,689	249	1,440		1,191 D	14.7%	85.3%	14.7%	85.3%
CHARLTON	622	60	562		502 D	9.6%	90.4%	9.6%	90.4%
CHATHAM	12,052	1,985	10,048	19	8,063 D	16.5%	83.4%	16.5%	83.5%
CHATTAHOOCHEE	224	20	204		184 D	8.9%	91.1%	8.9%	91.1%
CHATTOOGA	2,697	273	2,413	11	2,140 D	10.1%	89.5%	10.2%	89.8%
CHEROKEE	2,582	1,017	1,552	13	535 D	39.4%	60.1%	39.6%	60.4%
CLARKE	3,150	246	2,894	10	2,648 D	7.8%	91.9%	7.8%	92.2%
CLAY	523	33	488	2	455 D	6.3%	93.3%	6.3%	93.7%
CLAYTON	1,545	161	1,382	2	1,221 D	10.4%	89.4%	10.4%	89.6%
CLINCH	1,112	63	1,049		986 D	5.7%	94.3%	5.7%	94.3%
COBB	5,448	992	4,447	9	3,455 D	18.2%	81.6%	18.2%	81.8%
COFFEE	1,694	128	1,561	5	1,433 D	7.6%	92.1%	7.6%	92.4%
COLQUITT	2,361	525	1,819	17	1,294 D	22.2%	77.0%	22.4%	77.6%
COLUMBIA	677	46	627	4	581 D	6.8%	92.6%	6.8%	93.2%
COOK	1,084	143	941		798 D	13.2%	86.8%	13.2%	86.8%
COWETA	2,957	103	2,846	8	2,743 D	3.5%	96.2%	3.5%	96.5%
CRAWFORD	437	74	362	1	288 D	16.9%	82.8%	17.0%	83.0%
CRISP	1,182	129	1,049	4	920 D	10.9%	88.7%	11.0%	89.0%
DADE	1,133	151	982		831 D	13.3%	86.7%	13.3%	86.7%
DAWSON	763	276	484	3	208 D	36.2%	63.4%	36.3%	63.7%
DECATUR	2,000	217	1,781	2	1,564 D	10.8%	89.0%	10.9%	89.1%
DE KALB	10,988	2,081	8,862	45	6,781 D	18.9%	80.7%	19.0%	81.0%
DODGE	1,456	171	1,280	5	1,109 D	11.7%	87.9%	11.8%	88.2%
DOOLY	1,337	124	1,209	4	1,085 D	9.3%	90.4%	9.3%	90.7%
DOUGHERTY	2,356	180	2,175	1	1,995 D	7.6%	92.3%	7.6%	92.3%
DOUGLAS	1,033	195	833	5	638 D	18.9%	80.6%	19.0%	81.0%
EARLY	1,857	104	1,751	2	1,647 D	5.6%	94.3%	5.6%	94.4%
ECHOLS	460	18	441	1	423 D	3.9%	95.9%	3.9%	96.1%
EFFINGHAM	860	227	633		406 D	26.4%	73.6%	26.4%	73.6%
ELBERT	2,429	357	2,052	20	1,695 D	14.7%	84.5%	14.8%	85.2%
EMANUEL	1,511	81	1,428	2	1,347 D	5.4%	94.5%	5.4%	94.6%
EVANS	1,520	112	1,399	9	1,287 D	7.4%	92.0%	7.4%	92.6%
FANNIN	4,027	2,256	1,771		485 R	56.0%	44.0%	56.0%	44.0%
FAYETTE	621	44	577		533 D	7.1%	92.9%	7.1%	92.9%
FLOYD	6,461	912	5,528	21	4,616 D	14.1%	85.6%	14.2%	85.8%
FORSYTH	2,012	634	1,378		744 D	31.5%	68.5%	31.5%	68.5%
FRANKLIN	1,822	222	1,579	21	1,357 D	12.2%	86.7%	12.3%	87.7%

GEORGIA

County	1936 Total Vote	Republican	Democratic	Other	Rep.-Dem. Plurality	TV % Rep.	TV % Dem.	MV % Rep.	MV % Dem.	1940 Total Vote	Republican	Democratic	Other	Rep.-Dem. Plurality	TV % Rep.	TV % Dem.	MV % Rep.	MV % Dem.
FULTON	30,829	3,552	27,183	94	23,631 D	11.5%	88.2%	11.6%	88.4%	37,466	6,033	31,311	122	25,278 D	16.1%	83.6%	16.2%	83.8%
GILMER	2,175	1,047	1,128		81 D	48.1%	51.9%	48.1%	51.9%	1,521	653	865	3	212 D	42.9%	56.9%	43.0%	57.0%
GLASCOCK	440	68	369	3	301 D	15.5%	83.9%	15.6%	84.4%	410	76	332	2	256 D	18.5%	81.0%	18.6%	81.4%
GLYNN	2,188	260	1,925	3	1,665 D	11.9%	88.0%	11.9%	88.0%	2,295	274	2,014	7	1,740 D	11.9%	87.8%	12.0%	88.0%
GORDON	2,537	504	2,026	7	1,522 D	19.9%	79.9%	19.9%	80.1%	2,159	527	1,623	9	1,096 D	24.4%	75.2%	24.5%	75.5%
GRADY	1,829	163	1,659	7	1,496 D	8.9%	90.7%	8.9%	91.1%	1,697	224	1,461	12	1,237 D	13.2%	86.1%	13.3%	86.7%
GREENE	1,444	86	1,348	10	1,262 D	6.0%	93.4%	6.0%	94.0%	1,658	148	1,497	13	1,349 D	8.9%	90.3%	9.0%	91.0%
GWINNETT	2,926	541	2,382	3	1,841 D	18.5%	81.4%	18.5%	81.5%	4,771	728	4,023	20	3,295 D	15.3%	84.3%	15.3%	84.7%
HABERSHAM	2,328	424	1,884	20	1,460 D	18.2%	80.9%	18.4%	81.5%	2,328	421	1,880	9	1,419 D	18.5%	80.8%	18.6%	81.4%
HALL	3,181	444	2,731	6	2,287 D	14.0%	85.9%	14.0%	86.0%	3,482	513	2,943	26	2,430 D	14.7%	84.5%	14.8%	85.2%
HANCOCK	570	57	504	9	447 D	10.0%	88.4%	10.2%	89.8%	655	153	501	1	348 D	23.4%	76.5%	23.4%	76.6%
HARALSON	2,438	787	1,643	8	856 D	32.3%	67.4%	32.4%	67.6%	1,858	457	1,397	4	940 D	24.6%	75.2%	24.4%	75.6%
HARRIS	1,008	54	953	1	899 D	5.4%	94.5%	5.4%	94.6%	993	71	914	8	843 D	7.2%	92.0%	7.2%	92.8%
HART	1,741	222	1,514	5	1,292 D	12.8%	87.0%	12.8%	87.2%	1,441	97	1,328	16	1,231 D	6.7%	92.1%	6.8%	93.2%
HEARD	883	155	725	3	570 D	17.5%	82.1%	17.5%	82.4%	870	221	647	2	426 D	25.4%	74.4%	25.5%	74.5%
HENRY	1,482	116	1,362	4	1,246 D	7.8%	91.9%	7.8%	92.2%	1,654	101	1,551	2	1,450 D	6.1%	93.8%	6.1%	93.9%
HOUSTON	833	37	796		759 D	4.4%	95.6%	4.4%	95.6%	772	149	622	1	473 D	19.3%	80.6%	19.3%	80.7%
IRWIN	1,141	110	1,025	6	915 D	9.6%	89.8%	9.7%	90.3%	1,162	197	962	3	765 D	17.0%	82.8%	17.0%	83.0%
JACKSON	2,638	187	2,447	4	2,260 D	7.1%	92.8%	7.1%	92.9%	1,771	166	1,599	6	1,433 D	9.4%	90.3%	9.4%	90.6%
JASPER	956	33	923		890 D	3.5%	96.5%	3.5%	96.5%	763	72	689	2	617 D	9.4%	90.3%	9.5%	90.5%
JEFF DAVIS	724	93	631		538 D	12.8%	87.2%	12.8%	87.2%	799	101	696	2	595 D	12.6%	87.1%	12.7%	87.3%
JEFFERSON	1,418	168	1,238	12	1,070 D	11.8%	87.3%	11.9%	88.1%	1,246	171	1,068	7	897 D	13.7%	85.7%	13.8%	86.2%
JENKINS	912	32	880		848 D	3.5%	96.5%	3.5%	96.5%	1,011	69	940	2	871 D	6.8%	93.0%	6.8%	93.2%
JOHNSON	2,205	334	1,861	10	1,527 D	15.1%	84.4%	15.2%	84.8%	2,704	306	2,386	12	2,080 D	11.3%	88.2%	11.4%	88.6%
JONES	531	23	508		485 D	4.3%	95.7%	4.3%	95.7%	715	101	613	1	512 D	14.1%	85.7%	14.1%	85.9%
LAMAR	909	69	839		770 D	7.6%	92.3%	7.6%	92.4%	959	85	869	5	784 D	8.9%	90.6%	8.9%	91.1%
LANIER	835	30	800	5	770 D	3.6%	95.8%	3.6%	96.4%	625	16	607	2	591 D	2.6%	97.1%	2.6%	97.4%
LAURENS	2,931	304	2,620	7	2,316 D	10.4%	89.4%	10.4%	89.6%	2,755	435	2,316	4	1,881 D	15.8%	84.1%	15.8%	84.2%
LEE	492	1	490	1	489 D	0.2%	99.6%	0.2%	99.6%	435	17	416	2	399 D	3.9%	95.6%	3.9%	96.1%
LIBERTY	421	49	369	3	320 D	11.6%	87.6%	11.7%	88.3%	510	102	407	1	305 D	20.0%	79.8%	20.0%	80.0%
LINCOLN	666	88	561	17	473 D	13.2%	84.2%	13.6%	86.4%	538	67	466	5	399 D	12.5%	86.6%	12.6%	87.4%
LONG	359	51	305	3	254 D	14.2%	85.0%	14.3%	85.7%	397	76	319	2	243 D	19.1%	80.4%	19.2%	80.8%
LOWNDES	3,266	130	3,099	37	2,969 D	4.0%	94.9%	4.0%	96.0%	2,822	260	2,551	11	2,291 D	9.2%	90.4%	9.2%	90.8%
LUMPKIN	777	160	617		457 D	20.5%	79.4%	20.6%	79.4%	1,067	165	899	3	734 D	15.5%	84.3%	15.5%	84.5%
MCDUFFIE	809	98	705	6	607 D	12.1%	87.1%	12.2%	87.8%	1,041	75	959	7	884 D	7.2%	92.1%	7.3%	92.7%
MCINTOSH	361	53	308		255 D	14.7%	85.3%	14.7%	85.3%	574	106	468	4	362 D	18.5%	81.5%	18.5%	81.5%
MACON	1,053	92	958	3	865 D	8.7%	91.0%	8.8%	91.2%	928	72	852	4	780 D	7.8%	91.8%	7.8%	92.2%
MADISON	2,098	393	1,697	8	1,304 D	18.7%	80.9%	18.8%	81.2%	1,359	185	1,160	14	975 D	13.6%	85.4%	13.8%	86.2%
MARION	483	62	420	1	358 D	12.8%	87.0%	12.9%	87.1%	683	77	605	1	528 D	11.3%	88.6%	11.3%	88.7%
MERIWETHER	2,577	138	2,438	1	2,300 D	5.4%	94.6%	5.4%	94.6%	2,908	174	2,726	8	2,552 D	6.0%	93.7%	6.0%	94.0%
MILLER	690	36	653	1	617 D	5.2%	94.6%	5.2%	94.8%	825	50	775		725 D	6.1%	93.9%	6.1%	93.9%
MILTON	2,381	79	2,297	5	2,218 D	3.3%	96.5%	3.3%	96.7%	2,286	155	2,131		1,976 D	6.8%	93.2%	6.8%	93.2%
MITCHELL	1,431	147	1,277	7	1,130 D	10.3%	89.2%	10.3%	89.7%	1,069	49	1,014	6	965 D	4.6%	94.9%	4.6%	95.4%
MONROE	1,034	81	945	8	864 D	7.8%	91.4%	7.9%	92.1%	767	75	686	6	611 D	9.8%	89.4%	9.9%	90.1%
MONTGOMERY																		
MORGAN	1,169	37	1,130	2	1,093 D	3.2%	96.7%	3.2%	96.8%	508	24	484		460 D	4.7%	95.3%	4.7%	95.3%
MURRAY	2,404	806	1,597	1	791 D	33.5%	66.4%	33.5%	66.5%	1,946	545	1,399	2	854 D	28.0%	71.9%	28.0%	72.0%
MUSCOGEE	5,471	455	5,009	7	4,554 D	8.3%	91.6%	8.3%	91.7%	6,101	702	5,392	7	4,690 D	11.5%	88.4%	11.5%	88.5%
NEWTON	2,126	123	1,994	9	1,871 D	5.8%	93.8%	5.8%	94.2%	1,611	95	1,512	4	1,417 D	5.9%	93.9%	5.9%	94.1%
OCONEE	659	173	483	3	310 D	26.3%	73.3%	26.4%	73.6%	817	177	635	5	458 D	21.7%	77.6%	21.8%	78.2%
OGLETHORPE	964	115	845	4	730 D	11.9%	87.7%	12.0%	88.0%	950	131	818	1	687 D	13.8%	86.1%	13.8%	86.2%
PAULDING	2,034	645	1,386	3	741 D	31.7%	68.1%	31.8%	68.2%	2,435	770	1,653	12	883 D	31.6%	67.9%	31.8%	68.2%
PEACH	829	49	767	13	718 D	5.9%	92.5%	6.0%	94.0%	899	155	738	6	583 D	17.4%	82.6%	17.4%	82.6%
PICKENS	2,276	1,053	1,223		170 D	46.3%	53.7%	46.3%	53.7%	2,020	884	1,124	12	240 D	43.8%	55.6%	44.0%	56.0%
PIERCE	1,549	45	1,494	10	1,449 D	2.9%	96.4%	2.9%	97.1%	1,030	84	943	3	859 D	8.2%	91.6%	8.2%	91.8%
PIKE	1,062	149	910	3	761 D	14.0%	85.7%	14.1%	85.9%	1,038	209	829		620 D	20.1%	79.9%	20.1%	79.9%
POLK	3,147	389	2,754	4	2,365 D	12.4%	87.5%	12.4%	87.6%	3,104	401	2,693	10	2,292 D	12.9%	86.8%	13.0%	87.0%
PULASKI	854	38	808	8	770 D	4.4%	94.6%	4.5%	95.5%	520	38	478	4	440 D	7.3%	91.9%	7.4%	92.6%
PUTNAM	755	51	703	1	652 D	6.8%	93.1%	6.8%	93.2%	792	61	730	1	669 D	7.7%	92.2%	7.7%	92.3%
QUITMAN	374	19	355		336 D	5.1%	94.9%	5.1%	94.9%	343	19	324		305 D	5.5%	94.5%	5.5%	94.5%

PRESIDENT 1936   PRESIDENT 1940

GEORGIA

PRESIDENT 1936

County	Total Vote	Republican	Democratic	Other	Rep.-Dem. Plurality	Percentage Total Vote Rep.	Total Vote Dem.	Major Vote Rep.	Major Vote Dem.
RABUN	1,111	162	948	1	786 D	14.6%	85.3%	14.6%	85.4%
RANDOLPH	1,287	74	1,208	5	1,134 D	5.7%	93.9%	5.8%	94.2%
RICHMOND	7,810	551	7,239	20	6,688 D	7.1%	92.7%	7.1%	92.9%
ROCKDALE	911	73	837	1	764 D	8.0%	91.9%	8.0%	92.0%
SCHLEY	462	43	419	—	376 D	9.3%	90.7%	9.3%	90.7%
SCREVEN	1,009	61	933	15	872 D	6.0%	92.5%	6.1%	93.9%
SEMINOLE	843	82	761	—	679 D	9.7%	90.3%	9.7%	90.3%
SPALDING	2,500	36	2,457	7	2,421 D	1.4%	98.3%	1.4%	98.6%
STEPHENS	1,212	68	1,142	2	1,074 D	5.6%	94.2%	5.6%	94.4%
STEWART	681	49	628	4	579 D	7.2%	92.2%	7.2%	92.8%
SUMTER	1,934	58	1,870	6	1,812 D	3.0%	96.7%	3.0%	97.0%
TALBOT	843	41	796	6	755 D	4.9%	94.4%	4.9%	95.1%
TALIAFERRO	573	14	552	7	538 D	2.4%	96.3%	2.5%	97.5%
TATTNALL	1,272	214	1,047	11	833 D	16.8%	82.3%	17.0%	83.0%
TAYLOR	921	147	771	3	624 D	16.0%	83.7%	16.0%	84.0%
TELFAIR	1,279	121	1,158	—	1,037 D	9.5%	90.5%	9.5%	90.5%
TERRELL	1,399	61	1,336	2	1,275 D	4.4%	95.5%	4.4%	95.6%
THOMAS	2,645	222	2,409	14	2,187 D	8.4%	91.1%	8.4%	91.6%
TIFT	1,798	161	1,627	10	1,466 D	9.0%	90.5%	9.0%	91.0%
TOOMBS	1,083	78	1,001	4	923 D	7.2%	92.4%	7.2%	92.8%
TOWNS	1,495	732	763	—	31 D	49.0%	51.0%	49.0%	51.0%
TREUTLEN	936	23	912	1	889 D	2.5%	97.4%	2.5%	97.5%
TROUP	2,898	167	2,728	3	2,561 D	5.8%	94.1%	5.8%	94.2%
TURNER	1,048	188	860	—	672 D	17.9%	82.1%	17.9%	82.1%
TWIGGS	549	57	491	1	434 D	10.4%	89.4%	10.4%	89.6%
UNION	1,931	783	1,148	—	365 D	40.5%	59.5%	40.5%	59.5%
UPSON	1,610	138	1,471	1	1,333 D	8.6%	91.4%	8.6%	91.4%
WALKER	2,776	458	2,313	5	1,855 D	16.5%	83.3%	16.5%	83.5%
WALTON	2,086	132	1,952	2	1,820 D	6.3%	93.6%	6.3%	93.7%
WARE	2,827	256	2,566	5	2,310 D	9.1%	90.8%	9.1%	90.9%
WARREN	682	129	545	8	416 D	18.9%	79.9%	18.9%	80.9%
WASHINGTON	1,441	149	1,286	6	1,137 D	10.3%	89.2%	10.4%	89.6%
WAYNE	899	105	788	6	683 D	11.7%	87.7%	11.8%	88.2%
WEBSTER	351	40	310	1	270 D	11.4%	88.3%	11.4%	88.6%
WHEELER	689	94	594	1	500 D	13.6%	86.2%	13.7%	86.3%
WHITE	760	161	599	—	438 D	21.2%	78.8%	21.2%	78.8%
WHITFIELD	3,367	877	2,481	9	1,604 D	26.0%	73.7%	26.1%	73.9%
WILCOX	1,263	195	1,066	2	871 D	15.4%	84.4%	15.5%	84.5%
WILKES	1,122	78	1,031	13	953 D	7.0%	91.9%	7.0%	93.0%
WILKINSON	818	118	695	5	577 D	14.4%	85.0%	14.5%	85.5%
WORTH	1,257	132	1,124	1	992 D	10.5%	89.4%	10.5%	89.5%
TOTAL	293,170	36,943	255,363	864	218,420 D	12.6%	87.1%	12.6%	87.4%

PRESIDENT 1940

County	Total Vote	Republican	Democratic	Other	Rep.-Dem. Plurality	Percentage Total Vote Rep.	Total Vote Dem.	Major Vote Rep.	Major Vote Dem.
RABUN	1,043	82	958	3	876 D	7.9%	91.9%	7.9%	92.1%
RANDOLPH	1,443	143	1,298	2	1,155 D	9.9%	90.0%	9.9%	90.1%
RICHMOND	6,508	641	5,855	12	5,214 D	9.8%	90.0%	9.9%	90.1%
ROCKDALE	1,380	86	1,291	3	1,205 D	6.2%	93.6%	6.2%	93.8%
SCHLEY	542	69	471	2	402 D	12.7%	86.9%	12.8%	87.2%
SCREVEN	1,279	100	1,174	5	1,074 D	7.8%	91.8%	7.8%	92.2%
SEMINOLE	946	58	884	4	826 D	6.1%	93.4%	6.2%	93.8%
SPALDING	3,223	197	3,022	4	2,825 D	6.1%	93.8%	6.1%	93.9%
STEPHENS	1,182	90	1,084	8	994 D	7.6%	91.7%	7.7%	92.3%
STEWART	652	52	600	—	548 D	8.0%	92.0%	8.0%	92.0%
SUMTER	1,692	118	1,561	13	1,443 D	7.0%	92.3%	7.0%	93.0%
TALBOT	706	49	656	1	607 D	6.9%	92.9%	7.0%	93.0%
TALIAFERRO	526	19	507	—	488 D	3.6%	96.4%	3.6%	96.4%
TATTNALL	1,674	421	1,246	7	825 D	25.2%	74.4%	25.3%	74.7%
TAYLOR	1,011	213	796	2	583 D	21.1%	78.7%	21.1%	78.9%
TELFAIR	1,508	104	1,391	13	1,287 D	6.9%	92.2%	7.0%	93.0%
TERRELL	1,040	—	1,040	—	1,040 D	0.0%	100.0%	0.0%	100.0%
THOMAS	2,448	371	2,072	5	1,701 D	15.2%	84.6%	15.2%	84.8%
TIFT	1,711	226	1,463	22	1,237 D	13.2%	85.5%	13.4%	86.6%
TOOMBS	1,195	134	1,061	—	927 D	11.2%	88.8%	11.2%	88.8%
TOWNS	1,724	830	894	—	64 D	48.1%	51.9%	48.1%	51.9%
TREUTLEN	1,222	38	1,184	—	1,146 D	3.1%	96.9%	3.1%	96.9%
TROUP	3,477	288	3,176	13	2,888 D	8.3%	91.3%	8.3%	91.7%
TURNER	1,147	351	791	5	440 D	30.6%	69.0%	30.7%	69.3%
TWIGGS	814	91	723	—	632 D	11.2%	88.8%	11.2%	88.8%
UNION	1,509	557	950	2	393 D	36.9%	63.0%	37.0%	63.0%
UPSON	2,394	159	2,235	—	2,076 D	6.6%	93.4%	6.6%	93.4%
WALKER	3,424	558	2,859	7	2,301 D	16.3%	83.5%	16.3%	83.7%
WALTON	2,288	104	2,179	5	2,075 D	4.5%	95.2%	4.6%	95.4%
WARE	2,986	308	2,672	6	2,364 D	10.3%	89.5%	10.3%	89.7%
WARREN	703	95	606	2	511 D	13.5%	86.2%	13.6%	86.4%
WASHINGTON	1,374	253	1,112	9	859 D	18.4%	80.9%	18.5%	81.5%
WAYNE	1,725	179	1,542	4	1,363 D	10.4%	89.4%	10.4%	89.6%
WEBSTER	330	50	280	—	230 D	15.2%	84.8%	15.2%	84.8%
WHEELER	615	117	495	3	378 D	19.0%	80.5%	19.1%	80.9%
WHITE	865	111	754	—	643 D	12.8%	87.2%	12.8%	87.2%
WHITFIELD	4,157	991	3,162	4	2,171 D	23.8%	76.0%	23.9%	76.1%
WILCOX	1,017	118	890	9	772 D	11.6%	87.5%	11.7%	88.3%
WILKES	1,152	123	1,022	7	899 D	10.7%	88.7%	10.7%	89.3%
WILKINSON	1,054	147	906	1	759 D	13.9%	85.0%	14.0%	86.0%
WORTH	1,129	190	936	3	746 D	16.8%	82.9%	16.9%	83.1%
TOTAL	312,686	46,495	265,194	997	218,699 D	14.9%	84.8%	14.9%	85.1%

GEORGIA

PRESIDENT 1944

County	Total Vote	Republican	Democratic	Other	Rep-Dem Plurality	% Total Vote Rep.	% Total Vote Dem.	% Major Vote Rep.	% Major Vote Dem.
APPLING	1,705	387	1,318		931 D	22.7%	77.3%	22.7%	77.3%
ATKINSON	856	90	766		676 D	10.5%	89.5%	10.5%	89.5%
BACON	983	220	763		543 D	22.4%	77.6%	22.4%	77.6%
BAKER	509	31	478		447 D	6.1%	93.9%	6.1%	93.9%
BALDWIN	1,614	307	1,307		1,000 D	19.0%	81.0%	19.0%	81.0%
BANKS	619	129	490		365 D	20.3%	79.7%	20.3%	79.7%
BARROW	1,770	257	1,513		1,256 D	14.5%	85.5%	14.5%	85.5%
BARTOW	2,421	506	1,915		1,409 D	20.9%	79.1%	20.9%	79.1%
BEN HILL	1,237	190	1,046	1	856 D	15.4%	84.6%	15.4%	84.6%
BERRIEN	1,698	217	1,481		1,264 D	12.8%	87.2%	12.8%	87.2%
BIBB	7,236	1,884	5,352		3,468 D	26.0%	74.0%	26.0%	74.0%
BLECKLEY	1,028	213	815		602 D	20.7%	79.3%	20.7%	79.3%
BRANTLEY	664	124	540		416 D	18.7%	81.3%	18.7%	81.3%
BROOKS	1,660	279	1,381		1,102 D	16.8%	83.2%	16.8%	83.2%
BRYAN	778	90	688		598 D	11.6%	88.4%	11.6%	88.4%
BULLOCH	2,195	274	1,921		1,647 D	12.5%	87.5%	12.5%	87.5%
BURKE	1,062	153	909		756 D	14.4%	85.6%	14.4%	85.6%
BUTTS	1,415	85	1,330		1,245 D	6.0%	94.0%	6.0%	94.0%
CALHOUN	773	37	736		699 D	4.8%	95.2%	4.8%	95.2%
CAMDEN	632	76	556		480 D	12.0%	88.0%	12.0%	88.0%
CANDLER	791	138	653		515 D	17.4%	82.6%	17.4%	82.6%
CARROLL	4,035	704	3,331		2,627 D	17.4%	82.6%	17.4%	82.6%
CATOOSA	1,848	395	1,453		1,058 D	21.4%	78.6%	21.4%	78.6%
CHARLTON	551	89	462		373 D	16.2%	83.8%	16.2%	83.8%
CHATHAM	10,783	2,058	8,725		6,667 D	19.1%	80.9%	19.1%	80.9%
CHATTAHOOCHEE	119	19	100		81 D	16.0%	84.0%	16.0%	84.0%
CHATTOOGA	2,782	287	2,495		2,208 D	10.3%	89.7%	10.3%	89.7%
CHEROKEE	2,407	1,059	1,348		289 D	44.0%	56.0%	44.0%	56.0%
CLARKE	3,386	274	3,112		2,838 D	8.1%	91.9%	8.1%	91.9%
CLAY	477	35	442		407 D	7.3%	92.7%	7.3%	92.7%
CLAYTON	2,074	245	1,828	1	1,583 D	11.8%	88.1%	11.8%	88.2%
CLINCH	646	64	582		518 D	9.9%	90.1%	9.9%	90.1%
COBB	6,349	1,349	5,000		3,651 D	21.2%	78.8%	21.2%	78.8%
COFFEE	1,991	366	1,625		1,259 D	18.4%	81.6%	18.4%	81.6%
COLQUITT	3,004	696	2,308		1,612 D	23.2%	76.8%	23.2%	76.8%
COLUMBIA	580	72	508		436 D	12.4%	87.6%	12.4%	87.6%
COOK	1,359	204	1,155		951 D	15.0%	85.0%	15.0%	85.0%
COWETA	2,779	130	2,649		2,519 D	4.7%	95.3%	4.7%	95.3%
CRAWFORD	525	149	375	1	226 D	28.4%	71.6%	28.4%	71.6%
CRISP	1,416	217	1,199		982 D	15.3%	84.7%	15.3%	84.7%
DADE	1,112	169	943		774 D	15.2%	84.8%	15.2%	84.8%
DAWSON	811	342	469		127 D	42.2%	57.8%	42.2%	57.8%
DECATUR	1,900	294	1,606		1,312 D	15.5%	84.5%	15.5%	84.5%
DE KALB	14,625	2,555	12,069	1	9,514 D	17.5%	82.5%	17.5%	82.5%
DODGE	1,674	237	1,437		1,200 D	14.2%	85.8%	14.2%	85.8%
DOOLY	932	87	845		758 D	9.3%	90.7%	9.3%	90.7%
DOUGHERTY	3,537	338	3,199		2,861 D	9.6%	90.4%	9.6%	90.4%
DOUGLAS	1,108	280	828		548 D	25.3%	74.7%	25.3%	74.7%
EARLY	1,830	77	1,753		1,676 D	4.2%	95.8%	4.2%	95.8%
ECHOLS	508	42	466		424 D	8.3%	91.7%	8.3%	91.7%
EFFINGHAM	798	365	433		68 D	45.7%	54.3%	45.7%	54.3%
ELBERT	1,934	370	1,564		1,194 D	19.1%	80.9%	19.1%	80.9%
EMANUEL	1,953	317	1,635	1	1,318 D	16.2%	83.7%	16.2%	83.8%
EVANS	874	117	756	1	639 D	13.4%	86.5%	13.4%	86.6%
FANNIN	3,278	1,980	1,298		682 R	60.4%	39.6%	60.4%	39.6%
FAYETTE	880	98	782		684 D	11.1%	88.9%	11.1%	88.9%
FLOYD	5,887	1,123	4,764		3,641 D	19.1%	80.9%	19.1%	80.9%
FORSYTH	1,742	695	1,047		352 D	39.9%	60.1%	39.9%	60.1%
FRANKLIN	1,705	328	1,377		1,049 D	19.2%	80.8%	19.2%	80.8%

PRESIDENT 1948

County	Total Vote	Republican	Democratic	Other	Rep-Dem Plurality	% Total Vote Rep.	% Total Vote Dem.	% Major Vote Rep.	% Major Vote Dem.
APPLING	3,207	289	2,268	650	1,979 D	9.0%	70.7%	11.3%	88.7%
ATKINSON	1,120	65	938	116	872 D	5.9%	83.8%	6.6%	93.4%
BACON	1,235	104	785	346	681 D	8.4%	63.6%	11.7%	88.3%
BAKER	283	7	218	58	211 D	2.5%	77.0%	3.1%	96.9%
BALDWIN	2,095	559	1,132	404	573 D	26.7%	54.0%	33.1%	66.9%
BANKS	598	38	533	27	495 D	6.4%	89.1%	6.7%	93.3%
BARROW	2,053	155	1,554	344	1,399 D	7.5%	75.7%	9.1%	90.9%
BARTOW	3,068	440	2,384	244	1,944 D	14.3%	77.7%	15.6%	84.4%
BEN HILL	1,896	223	1,438	235	1,215 D	11.8%	75.8%	13.4%	86.6%
BERRIEN	2,127	107	1,772	248	1,665 D	5.0%	83.3%	5.7%	94.3%
BIBB	14,077	3,043	7,011	4,023	3,968 D	21.6%	49.8%	30.3%	69.7%
BLECKLEY	854	79	544	231	465 D	9.2%	63.7%	11.7%	85.4%
BRANTLEY	766	79	463	224	384 D	10.3%	60.4%	14.6%	85.4%
BROOKS	1,677	188	975	514	787 D	11.2%	58.1%	16.2%	83.8%
BRYAN	1,759	135	1,147	477	1,012 D	7.7%	65.2%	10.5%	89.5%
BULLOCH	2,953	276	2,036	641	1,760 D	9.3%	68.9%	11.9%	88.1%
BURKE	1,496	107	357	1,032	250 D	7.2%	23.9%	23.1%	76.9%
BUTTS	1,168	61	987	120	926 D	5.2%	84.5%	5.8%	94.2%
CALHOUN	514	36	399	79	363 D	7.0%	77.6%	8.3%	91.7%
CAMDEN	1,085	208	552	325	344 D	19.2%	50.9%	27.4%	72.6%
CANDLER	1,007	125	589	293	464 D	12.4%	58.5%	17.5%	82.5%
CARROLL	3,671	526	2,671	474	2,145 D	14.3%	72.8%	16.5%	83.5%
CATOOSA	1,538	268	1,051	219	783 D	17.4%	68.3%	20.3%	79.7%
CHARLTON	558	70	339	159	269 D	12.3%	59.7%	17.1%	82.9%
CHATHAM	23,897	5,966	10,864	7,067	4,898 D	25.0%	45.5%	35.4%	64.6%
CHATTAHOOCHEE	116	1	46	69	45 D	0.9%	39.7%	2.1%	97.9%
CHATTOOGA	3,950	362	3,396	192	3,034 D	9.2%	86.0%	9.6%	90.4%
CHEROKEE	2,153	631	1,267	255	636 D	29.3%	58.8%	33.2%	66.8%
CLARKE	4,317	707	3,095	515	2,388 D	16.4%	71.7%	18.6%	81.4%
CLAY	367	39	295	33	256 D	10.6%	80.4%	11.7%	88.3%
CLAYTON	3,296	339	2,192	765	1,853 D	10.3%	66.5%	13.4%	86.6%
CLINCH	1,744	168	1,283	293	1,115 D	9.6%	73.6%	11.6%	88.4%
COBB	7,098	1,524	4,766	808	3,242 D	21.5%	67.1%	24.2%	75.8%
COFFEE	4,144	309	3,168	667	2,859 D	7.5%	76.4%	8.9%	91.1%
COLQUITT	3,465	537	2,255	673	1,718 D	15.5%	65.1%	19.2%	80.8%
COLUMBIA	1,060	59	164	837	105 D	5.6%	15.5%	26.5%	73.5%
COOK	1,574	123	1,192	259	1,069 D	7.8%	75.7%	9.4%	90.6%
COWETA	2,649	219	2,214	216	1,995 D	8.3%	83.6%	9.0%	91.0%
CRAWFORD	710	64	389	257	325 D	9.0%	54.8%	14.1%	85.9%
CRISP	1,973	221	1,225	527	1,004 D	11.2%	62.1%	15.3%	84.7%
DADE	2,026	338	1,488	200	1,150 D	16.7%	73.4%	18.5%	81.5%
DAWSON	1,488	786	660	42	126 R	52.8%	44.4%	54.4%	45.6%
DECATUR	2,272	296	1,209	767	913 D	13.0%	53.2%	19.7%	80.3%
DE KALB	19,521	5,758	10,826	2,937	5,068 D	29.5%	55.5%	34.7%	65.3%
DODGE	2,473	210	1,725	538	1,515 D	8.5%	69.8%	10.9%	89.1%
DOOLY	652	22	577	53	555 D	3.4%	88.5%	3.7%	96.3%
DOUGHERTY	3,921	614	2,517	790	1,903 D	15.7%	64.2%	19.6%	80.4%
DOUGLAS	3,346	1,019	1,336	991	317 D	30.5%	39.9%	43.3%	56.7%
EARLY	1,353	94	1,110	149	1,016 D	6.9%	82.0%	7.8%	92.2%
ECHOLS	623	32	332	259	300 D	5.1%	53.3%	8.8%	91.2%
EFFINGHAM	1,293	160	347	786	187 D	12.4%	26.8%	31.6%	68.4%
ELBERT	2,123	152	1,617	354	1,465 D	7.2%	76.2%	8.6%	91.4%
EMANUEL	2,398	241	1,436	721	1,195 D	10.1%	59.9%	14.4%	85.6%
EVANS	1,402	118	953	331	835 D	8.4%	68.0%	11.0%	89.0%
FANNIN	4,870	2,789	1,998	83	791 R	57.3%	41.0%	58.3%	41.7%
FAYETTE	1,144	54	825	265	771 D	4.7%	72.1%	6.1%	93.9%
FLOYD	7,611	1,689	5,247	675	3,558 D	22.1%	68.9%	24.4%	75.6%
FORSYTH	2,662	573	1,813	276	1,240 D	21.5%	68.1%	24.0%	76.0%
FRANKLIN	1,329	138	1,036	155	898 D	10.4%	78.0%	11.8%	88.2%

GEORGIA

PRESIDENT 1944

County	Total Vote	Republican	Democratic	Other	Rep.-Dem. Plurality	Total Vote Rep.	Total Vote Dem.	Major Vote Rep.	Major Vote Dem.
FULTON	44,848	7,687	37,161		29,474 D	17.1%	82.9%	17.1%	82.9%
GILMER	1,677	793	884		91 D	47.3%	52.7%	47.3%	52.7%
GLASCOCK	479	161	318		157 D	33.6%	66.4%	33.6%	66.4%
GLYNN	2,380	385	1,995		1,610 D	16.2%	83.8%	16.2%	83.8%
GORDON	2,075	617	1,457	1	840 D	29.7%	70.2%	29.7%	70.3%
GRADY	1,884	223	1,661		1,438 D	11.8%	88.2%	11.8%	88.2%
GREENE	1,394	144	1,246	4	1,102 D	10.3%	89.4%	10.4%	89.6%
GWINNETT	4,052	713	3,339		2,666 D	17.6%	82.4%	17.6%	82.4%
HABERSHAM	2,346	504	1,842		1,338 D	21.5%	78.5%	21.5%	78.5%
HALL	3,863	796	3,066	1	2,270 D	20.6%	79.4%	20.6%	79.4%
HANCOCK	489	109	380		271 D	22.3%	77.7%	22.3%	77.7%
HARALSON	2,159	911	1,248		337 D	42.2%	57.8%	42.2%	57.8%
HARRIS	972	79	893		814 D	8.1%	91.9%	8.1%	91.9%
HART	1,344	183	1,161		978 D	13.6%	86.4%	13.6%	86.4%
HEARD	742	185	557		372 D	24.9%	75.1%	24.9%	75.1%
HENRY	1,613	152	1,461		1,309 D	9.4%	90.6%	9.4%	90.6%
HOUSTON	725	190	535		345 D	26.2%	73.8%	26.9%	73.1%
IRWIN	1,121	259	862		603 D	23.1%	76.9%	23.1%	76.9%
JACKSON	1,975	221	1,754		1,533 D	11.2%	88.8%	11.2%	88.8%
JASPER	863	86	777		691 D	10.0%	90.0%	10.0%	90.0%
JEFF DAVIS	857	120	737		617 D	14.0%	86.0%	14.0%	86.0%
JEFFERSON	1,317	274	1,043		769 D	20.8%	79.2%	20.8%	79.2%
JENKINS	799	101	698		597 D	12.6%	87.4%	12.6%	87.4%
JOHNSON	1,282	304	978		674 D	23.7%	76.3%	23.7%	76.3%
JONES	859	196	661	2	465 D	22.8%	76.9%	22.9%	77.1%
LAMAR	1,158	143	1,015		872 D	12.3%	87.7%	12.3%	87.7%
LANIER	665	40	625		585 D	6.0%	94.0%	6.0%	94.0%
LAURENS	3,042	498	2,544		2,046 D	16.4%	83.6%	16.4%	83.6%
LEE	474	27	447		420 D	5.7%	94.3%	5.7%	94.3%
LIBERTY	603	122	481		359 D	20.2%	79.8%	20.2%	79.8%
LINCOLN	609	165	444		279 D	27.1%	72.9%	27.1%	72.9%
LONG	447	129	318		189 D	28.9%	71.1%	28.9%	71.1%
LOWNDES	2,493	401	2,092		1,691 D	16.1%	83.9%	16.1%	83.9%
LUMPKIN	1,108	212	896		684 D	19.1%	80.9%	19.1%	80.9%
MCDUFFIE	982	187	795		608 D	19.0%	81.0%	19.0%	81.0%
MCINTOSH	558	149	406	3	257 D	26.7%	72.8%	26.8%	73.2%
MACON	1,057	168	889		721 D	15.9%	84.1%	15.9%	84.1%
MADISON	1,502	265	1,235	2	970 D	17.6%	82.2%	17.7%	82.3%
MARION	571	70	501		431 D	12.3%	87.7%	12.3%	87.7%
MERIWETHER	2,376	189	2,187		1,998 D	8.0%	92.0%	8.0%	92.0%
MILLER	868	59	809		750 D	6.8%	93.2%	6.8%	93.2%
MILTON									
MITCHELL	2,405	226	2,179		1,953 D	9.4%	90.6%	9.4%	90.6%
MONROE	1,542	410	1,132		722 D	26.6%	73.4%	26.6%	73.4%
MONTGOMERY	670	94	575	1	481 D	14.0%	85.8%	14.1%	85.9%
MORGAN	1,221	51	1,166	4	1,115 D	4.2%	95.5%	4.2%	95.8%
MURRAY	2,046	671	1,375		704 D	32.8%	67.2%	32.8%	67.2%
MUSCOGEE	7,842	1,344	6,498		5,154 D	17.1%	82.9%	17.1%	82.9%
NEWTON	2,145	123	2,022		1,899 D	5.7%	94.3%	5.7%	94.3%
OCONEE	765	195	570		375 D	25.5%	74.5%	25.5%	74.5%
OGLETHORPE	1,095	173	922		749 D	15.8%	84.2%	15.8%	84.2%
PAULDING	2,033	775	1,355	3	580 D	36.3%	63.6%	36.4%	63.6%
PEACH	1,155	236	919		683 D	20.4%	79.6%	20.4%	79.6%
PICKENS	1,575	795	780		15 R	50.5%	49.5%	50.5%	49.5%
PIERCE	1,234	165	1,069		904 D	13.4%	86.6%	13.4%	86.6%
PIKE	875	133	742		609 D	15.2%	84.8%	15.2%	84.8%
POLK	3,161	463	2,698		2,235 D	14.6%	85.4%	14.6%	85.4%
PULASKI	647	55	592		537 D	8.5%	91.5%	8.5%	91.5%
PUTNAM	775	74	701		627 D	9.5%	90.5%	9.5%	90.5%
QUITMAN	371	16	355		339 D	4.3%	95.7%	4.3%	95.7%

PRESIDENT 1948

County	Total Vote	Republican	Democratic	Other	Rep.-Dem. Plurality	Total Vote Rep.	Total Vote Dem.	Major Vote Rep.	Major Vote Dem.
FULTON	51,054	14,976	29,318	6,760	14,342 D	29.3%	57.4%	33.8%	66.2%
GILMER	2,540	1,203	1,275	62	72 D	47.4%	50.2%	48.5%	51.5%
GLASCOCK	504	13	123	368	110 D	2.6%	24.4%	9.6%	90.4%
GLYNN	4,580	1,090	2,444	1,046	1,354 D	23.8%	53.4%	30.8%	69.2%
GORDON	2,065	377	1,523	165	1,146 D	18.3%	73.8%	19.8%	80.2%
GRADY	2,180	244	1,516	420	1,272 D	11.2%	69.5%	13.9%	86.1%
GREENE	1,590	92	1,213	285	1,121 D	5.8%	76.3%	7.0%	93.0%
GWINNETT	3,727	413	2,832	482	2,419 D	11.1%	76.0%	12.7%	87.3%
HABERSHAM	2,071	368	1,477	226	1,109 D	17.8%	71.3%	19.9%	80.1%
HALL	4,159	606	3,093	460	2,487 D	14.6%	74.4%	16.4%	83.6%
HANCOCK	772	111	441	220	330 D	14.4%	57.1%	20.1%	79.9%
HARALSON	3,563	831	2,263	469	1,432 D	23.3%	63.5%	26.9%	73.1%
HARRIS	1,137	138	759	240	621 D	12.1%	66.8%	15.4%	84.6%
HART	1,530	78	1,363	89	1,285 D	5.1%	89.1%	5.4%	94.6%
HEARD	800	77	670	53	593 D	9.6%	83.8%	10.3%	89.7%
HENRY	1,846	229	1,400	217	1,171 D	12.4%	75.8%	14.1%	85.9%
HOUSTON	2,072	204	1,437	431	1,233 D	9.8%	69.4%	12.4%	87.6%
IRWIN	1,355	146	946	263	800 D	10.8%	69.8%	13.4%	86.6%
JACKSON	2,222	145	1,866	211	1,721 D	6.5%	84.0%	7.2%	92.8%
JASPER	865	87	562	216	475 D	10.1%	65.0%	13.4%	86.6%
JEFF DAVIS	905	70	611	224	541 D	7.7%	67.5%	10.3%	89.7%
JEFFERSON	1,716	137	544	1,035	407 D	8.0%	31.7%	20.1%	79.9%
JENKINS	969	98	595	276	497 D	10.1%	61.4%	14.1%	85.9%
JOHNSON	1,256	67	685	504	618 D	5.3%	54.5%	8.9%	91.1%
JONES	1,114	103	588	423	485 D	9.2%	52.8%	14.9%	85.1%
LAMAR	1,269	164	909	196	745 D	12.9%	71.6%	15.3%	84.1%
LANIER	680	92	486	102	394 D	13.5%	71.5%	15.9%	84.1%
LAURENS	3,804	268	2,325	1,211	2,057 D	7.0%	61.1%	10.3%	89.7%
LEE	468	36	215	217	179 D	7.7%	45.9%	14.3%	85.7%
LIBERTY	1,212	121	820	271	699 D	10.0%	67.7%	12.9%	87.1%
LINCOLN	729	32	99	598	67 D	4.4%	13.6%	24.4%	75.6%
LONG	513	25	337	151	312 D	4.9%	65.7%	6.9%	93.1%
LOWNDES	3,958	634	1,867	1,457	1,233 D	16.0%	47.2%	25.3%	74.7%
LUMPKIN	739	142	547	50	405 D	19.2%	74.0%	20.6%	79.4%
MCDUFFIE	1,500	51	182	1,267	131 D	3.4%	12.1%	21.9%	78.1%
MCINTOSH	870	233	425	212	192 D	26.8%	48.9%	35.4%	64.6%
MACON	1,182	127	675	380	548 D	10.7%	57.1%	15.8%	84.2%
MADISON	1,439	62	1,160	217	1,098 D	4.3%	80.6%	5.1%	94.9%
MARION	541	45	283	213	238 D	8.3%	52.3%	13.7%	86.3%
MERIWETHER	2,409	204	1,967	238	1,763 D	8.5%	81.7%	9.4%	90.6%
MILLER	861	32	723	106	691 D	3.7%	84.0%	4.2%	95.8%
MILTON									
MITCHELL	2,067	152	1,453	462	1,301 D	7.4%	70.3%	9.5%	90.5%
MONROE	1,420	169	881	370	712 D	11.9%	62.0%	16.1%	83.9%
MONTGOMERY	1,693	117	1,048	528	931 D	6.9%	61.9%	10.0%	90.0%
MORGAN	1,406	115	1,147	144	1,032 D	8.2%	81.6%	9.1%	90.9%
MURRAY	2,424	616	1,653	155	1,037 D	25.4%	68.2%	27.1%	72.9%
MUSCOGEE	10,203	2,443	5,920	1,840	3,477 D	23.9%	58.0%	29.2%	70.8%
NEWTON	2,500	243	2,113	144	1,870 D	9.7%	84.5%	10.3%	89.7%
OCONEE	935	94	579	262	485 D	10.1%	61.9%	14.0%	86.0%
OGLETHORPE	1,118	62	819	237	757 D	5.5%	73.3%	7.0%	93.0%
PAULDING	1,456	333	981	142	648 D	22.9%	67.4%	25.3%	74.7%
PEACH	1,193	166	642	385	476 D	13.9%	53.8%	20.5%	79.5%
PICKENS	2,722	1,255	1,239	228	16 R	46.1%	45.5%	50.3%	49.7%
PIERCE	1,514	108	908	498	800 D	7.1%	60.0%	10.6%	89.4%
PIKE	472	72	256	144	184 D	15.3%	54.2%	22.0%	78.0%
POLK	3,706	491	2,918	297	2,427 D	13.2%	78.7%	14.4%	85.6%
PULASKI	794	64	567	163	503 D	8.1%	71.4%	10.1%	89.9%
PUTNAM	854	110	609	135	499 D	12.9%	71.3%	15.3%	84.7%
QUITMAN	361	19	246	96	227 D	5.3%	68.1%	7.2%	92.8%

GEORGIA

PRESIDENT 1944

County	Total Vote	Republican	Democratic	Other	Rep.-Dem. Plurality	Total Vote Rep.	Total Vote Dem.	Major Vote Rep.	Major Vote Dem.
RABUN	1,432	185	1,247		1,062 D	12.9%	87.1%	12.9%	87.1%
RANDOLPH	1,265	106	1,159		1,053 D	8.4%	91.6%	8.4%	91.6%
RICHMOND	8,070	1,152	6,918		5,756 D	14.3%	85.7%	14.3%	85.7%
ROCKDALE	1,042	96	946		850 D	9.2%	90.8%	9.2%	90.8%
SCHLEY	366	37	329		292 D	10.1%	89.9%	10.1%	89.9%
SCREVEN	1,092	197	895		698 D	18.0%	82.0%	18.0%	82.0%
SEMINOLE	1,159	83	1,076		993 D	7.2%	92.8%	7.2%	92.8%
SPALDING	3,023	217	2,805	1	2,538 D	7.2%	92.8%	7.2%	92.8%
STEPHENS	1,370	212	1,158		946 D	15.5%	84.5%	15.5%	84.5%
STEWART	675	78	597		519 D	11.6%	88.4%	11.6%	88.4%
SUMTER	1,744	194	1,550		1,356 D	11.1%	88.9%	11.1%	88.9%
TALBOT	877	45	832		787 D	5.1%	94.9%	5.1%	94.9%
TALIAFERRO	395	6	389		383 D	1.5%	98.5%	1.5%	98.5%
TATTNALL	1,709	494	1,215		721 D	28.9%	71.1%	28.9%	71.1%
TAYLOR	1,042	269	773		504 D	25.8%	74.2%	25.8%	74.2%
TELFAIR	1,361	174	1,187		1,013 D	12.8%	87.2%	12.8%	87.2%
TERRELL	1,688	49	1,639		1,590 D	2.9%	97.1%	2.9%	97.1%
THOMAS	2,305	557	1,747	1	1,190 D	24.2%	75.8%	24.2%	75.8%
TIFT	2,026	396	1,630		1,234 D	19.5%	80.5%	19.5%	80.5%
TOOMBS	2,062	237	1,825		1,588 D	11.5%	88.5%	11.5%	88.5%
TOWNS	1,811	674	1,137		463 D	37.2%	62.8%	37.2%	62.8%
TREUTLEN	947	54	893		839 D	5.7%	94.3%	5.7%	94.3%
TROUP	3,575	342	3,233		2,891 D	9.6%	90.4%	9.6%	90.4%
TURNER	1,132	334	797	1	463 D	29.5%	70.5%	29.5%	70.5%
TWIGGS	627	170	457		287 D	27.1%	72.9%	27.1%	72.9%
UNION	2,048	760	1,288		528 D	37.1%	62.9%	37.1%	62.9%
UPSON	2,605	243	2,362		2,119 D	9.3%	90.7%	9.3%	90.7%
WALKER	3,519	765	2,753	1	1,988 D	21.7%	78.3%	21.7%	78.3%
WALTON	2,218	172	2,046		1,874 D	7.8%	92.2%	7.8%	92.2%
WARE	2,767	459	2,306	2	1,847 D	16.6%	83.4%	16.6%	83.4%
WARREN	603	152	449	2	297 D	25.2%	74.5%	25.3%	74.7%
WASHINGTON	1,445	351	1,094		743 D	24.3%	75.7%	24.3%	75.7%
WAYNE	1,230	252	978		726 D	20.5%	79.5%	20.5%	79.5%
WEBSTER	349	65	284		219 D	18.6%	81.4%	18.6%	81.4%
WHEELER	668	151	517		366 D	22.6%	77.4%	22.6%	77.4%
WHITE	869	161	706	2	545 D	18.5%	81.2%	18.6%	81.4%
WHITFIELD	3,859	1,032	2,827		1,795 D	26.7%	73.3%	26.7%	73.3%
WILCOX	1,570	206	1,364		1,158 D	13.1%	86.9%	13.1%	86.9%
WILKES	1,105	159	946		787 D	14.4%	85.6%	14.4%	85.6%
WILKINSON	1,034	271	763		492 D	26.2%	73.8%	26.2%	73.8%
WORTH	1,314	218	1,096		878 D	16.6%	83.4%	16.6%	83.4%
TOTAL	328,129	59,900	268,187	42	208,287 D	18.3%	81.7%	18.3%	81.7%

PRESIDENT 1948

County	Total Vote	Republican	Democratic	Other	Rep.-Dem. Plurality	Total Vote Rep.	Total Vote Dem.	Major Vote Rep.	Major Vote Dem.
RABUN	969	165	747	57	582 D	17.0%	77.1%	18.1%	81.9%
RANDOLPH	970	134	575	261	441 D	13.8%	59.3%	18.9%	81.1%
RICHMOND	12,846	1,528	2,450	8,868	922 D	11.9%	19.1%	38.4%	61.6%
ROCKDALE	1,481	126	1,209	146	1,083 D	8.5%	81.6%	9.4%	90.6%
SCHLEY	375	43	257	75	214 D	11.5%	68.5%	14.3%	85.7%
SCREVEN	1,513	172	838	503	666 D	11.4%	55.4%	17.0%	83.0%
SEMINOLE	899	105	722	72	617 D	11.7%	80.3%	12.7%	87.3%
SPALDING	4,625	506	3,441	679	2,935 D	10.9%	74.4%	12.8%	87.2%
STEPHENS	1,323	278	912	133	634 D	21.0%	68.9%	23.4%	76.6%
STEWART	588	46	276	266	230 D	7.8%	46.9%	14.3%	85.7%
SUMTER	2,144	256	1,018	870	762 D	11.9%	47.5%	20.1%	79.9%
TALBOT	812	92	582	138	490 D	11.3%	71.7%	13.6%	86.4%
TALIAFERRO	599	21	504	74	483 D	3.5%	84.1%	4.0%	96.0%
TATTNALL	1,864	216	1,071	577	855 D	11.6%	57.5%	16.8%	83.2%
TAYLOR	1,101	99	638	364	539 D	9.0%	57.9%	13.4%	86.6%
TELFAIR	1,127	75	712	340	637 D	6.7%	63.2%	9.5%	90.5%
TERRELL	951	100	608	243	508 D	10.5%	63.9%	14.1%	85.9%
THOMAS	3,667	925	1,429	1,313	504 D	25.2%	39.0%	39.3%	60.7%
TIFT	4,644	637	3,158	849	2,521 D	13.7%	68.0%	16.8%	83.2%
TOOMBS	2,016	193	1,161	662	968 D	9.6%	57.6%	14.3%	85.7%
TOWNS	824	302	516	6	214 D	36.7%	62.6%	36.9%	63.1%
TREUTLEN	673	26	413	234	387 D	3.9%	61.4%	5.9%	94.1%
TROUP	5,169	536	3,896	737	3,360 D	10.4%	75.4%	12.1%	87.9%
TURNER	1,143	147	774	222	627 D	12.9%	67.7%	16.0%	84.0%
TWIGGS	815	52	359	404	307 D	6.4%	44.0%	12.7%	87.3%
UNION	2,778	1,274	1,420	84	146 D	45.9%	51.1%	47.3%	52.7%
UPSON	2,993	262	2,432	299	2,170 D	8.8%	81.3%	9.7%	90.3%
WALKER	4,895	980	3,418	497	2,438 D	20.0%	69.8%	22.3%	77.7%
WALTON	2,871	164	2,440	267	2,276 D	5.7%	85.0%	6.3%	93.7%
WARE	4,650	655	2,611	1,384	1,956 D	14.1%	56.2%	20.1%	79.9%
WARREN	814	33	256	525	223 D	4.1%	31.4%	11.4%	88.6%
WASHINGTON	1,379	204	1,169	6	965 D	14.9%	84.8%	14.9%	85.1%
WAYNE	1,752	190	1,277	285	1,087 D	10.8%	72.9%	13.0%	87.0%
WEBSTER	314	79	118	117	39 D	25.4%	37.6%	40.1%	59.9%
WHEELER	885	39	560	286	521 D	4.4%	63.3%	6.5%	93.5%
WHITE	630	59	497	74	438 D	9.4%	78.9%	10.6%	89.4%
WHITFIELD	5,391	1,249	3,419	723	2,170 D	23.2%	63.4%	26.8%	73.2%
WILCOX	1,115	75	791	249	716 D	6.9%	70.9%	8.7%	91.3%
WILKES	1,212	95	771	346	676 D	7.8%	63.6%	11.0%	89.0%
WILKINSON	1,099	96	501	502	405 D	8.7%	45.6%	16.1%	83.9%
WORTH	1,504	124	1,159	221	1,035 D	8.2%	77.1%	9.7%	90.3%
TOTAL	418,844	76,691	254,646	87,507	177,955 D	18.3%	60.8%	23.1%	76.9%

GEORGIA

PRESIDENT 1952

County	Total Vote	Republican	Democratic	Other	Rep.-Dem. Plurality	Total Vote Rep.	Total Vote Dem.	Major Vote Rep.	Major Vote Dem.
APPLING	2,892	713	2,179		1,466 D	24.7%	75.3%	24.7%	75.3%
ATKINSON	1,754	194	1,560		1,366 D	11.1%	88.9%	11.1%	88.9%
BACON	2,055	543	1,512		969 D	26.4%	73.6%	26.4%	73.6%
BAKER	1,160	155	1,005		850 D	13.4%	86.6%	13.4%	86.6%
BALDWIN	3,341	1,023	2,318		1,295 D	30.6%	69.4%	30.6%	69.4%
BANKS	1,459	204	1,255		1,051 D	14.0%	86.0%	14.0%	86.0%
BARROW	2,603	236	2,367		2,131 D	9.1%	90.9%	9.1%	90.9%
BARTOW	5,156	1,183	3,973		2,790 D	22.9%	77.1%	22.9%	77.1%
BEN HILL	2,745	697	2,048		1,351 D	25.4%	74.6%	25.4%	74.6%
BERRIEN	2,551	364	2,187		1,823 D	14.3%	85.7%	14.3%	85.7%
BIBB	20,808	6,121	14,687		8,566 D	29.4%	70.6%	29.4%	70.6%
BLECKLEY	1,704	187	1,517		1,330 D	11.0%	89.0%	11.0%	89.0%
BRANTLEY	1,358	276	1,082		806 D	20.3%	79.7%	20.3%	79.7%
BROOKS	2,666	800	1,866		1,066 D	30.0%	70.0%	30.0%	70.0%
BRYAN	1,302	331	971		640 D	25.4%	74.6%	25.4%	74.6%
BULLOCH	4,528	909	3,619		2,710 D	20.1%	79.9%	20.1%	79.9%
BURKE	2,092	932	1,160		228 D	44.6%	55.4%	44.6%	55.4%
BUTTS	2,099	189	1,910		1,721 D	9.0%	91.0%	9.0%	91.0%
CALHOUN	957	147	810		663 D	15.4%	84.6%	15.4%	84.6%
CAMDEN	1,904	619	1,285		666 D	32.5%	67.5%	32.5%	67.5%
CAMPBELL	1,870	422	1,448		1,026 D	22.6%	77.4%	22.6%	77.4%
CARROLL	6,401	1,194	5,207		4,013 D	18.7%	81.3%	18.7%	81.3%
CATOOSA	3,598	1,371	2,227		856 D	38.1%	61.9%	38.1%	61.9%
CHARLTON	1,103	288	815		527 D	26.1%	73.9%	26.1%	73.9%
CHATHAM	29,902	15,532	14,370		1,162 D	51.9%	48.1%	51.9%	48.1%
CHATTAHOOCHEE	189	73	116		43 D	38.6%	61.4%	38.6%	61.4%
CHATTOOGA	4,387	771	3,616		2,845 D	17.6%	82.4%	17.6%	82.4%
CHEROKEE	4,070	1,618	2,452		834 D	39.8%	60.2%	39.8%	60.2%
CLARKE	6,492	1,588	4,904		3,316 D	24.5%	75.5%	24.5%	75.5%
CLAY	657	176	481		305 D	26.8%	73.2%	26.8%	73.2%
CLAYTON	5,288	1,230	4,058		2,828 D	23.3%	76.7%	23.3%	76.7%
CLINCH	1,518	350	1,168		818 D	23.1%	76.9%	23.1%	76.9%
COBB	14,545	4,163	10,168		6,019 D	29.0%	71.0%	29.0%	71.0%
COFFEE	4,370	1,078	3,292		2,214 D	24.7%	75.3%	24.7%	75.3%
COLQUITT	5,928	1,411	4,517		3,106 D	23.8%	76.2%	23.8%	76.2%
COLUMBIA	1,379	530	849		319 D	38.4%	61.6%	38.4%	61.6%
COOK	2,742	395	2,347		1,952 D	14.4%	85.6%	14.4%	85.6%
COWETA	4,489	652	3,837		3,185 D	14.5%	85.5%	14.5%	85.5%
CRAWFORD	1,093	145	948		803 D	13.3%	86.7%	13.3%	86.7%
CRISP	3,065	949	2,116		1,167 D	31.0%	69.0%	31.0%	69.0%
DADE	1,982	686	1,296		610 D	34.6%	65.4%	34.6%	65.4%
DAWSON	1,240	470	770		300 D	37.9%	62.1%	37.9%	62.1%
DECATUR	3,582	1,001	2,581		1,580 D	27.9%	72.1%	27.9%	72.1%
DE KALB	36,453	15,588	20,865		5,277 D	42.8%	57.2%	42.8%	57.2%
DODGE	3,899	454	3,445		2,991 D	11.6%	88.4%	11.6%	88.4%
DOOLY	1,961	197	1,764		1,567 D	10.0%	90.0%	10.0%	90.0%
DOUGHERTY	6,970	2,535	4,435		1,900 D	36.4%	63.6%	36.4%	63.6%
DOUGLAS	2,747	645	2,102		1,457 D	23.5%	76.5%	23.5%	76.5%
EARLY	2,110	307	1,803		1,496 D	14.5%	85.5%	14.5%	85.5%
ECHOLS	626	94	532		438 D	15.0%	85.0%	15.0%	85.0%
EFFINGHAM	1,629	829	800		29 R	50.9%	49.1%	50.9%	49.1%
ELBERT	3,831	552	3,279		2,727 D	14.4%	85.6%	14.4%	85.6%
EMANUEL	3,303	661	2,642		1,981 D	20.0%	80.0%	20.0%	80.0%
EVANS	1,657	433	1,224		791 D	26.1%	73.9%	26.1%	73.9%
FANNIN	4,817	2,904	1,913		991 R	60.3%	39.7%	60.3%	39.7%
FAYETTE	1,409	195	1,214		1,019 D	13.8%	86.2%	13.8%	86.2%
FLOYD	13,009	4,532	8,477		3,945 D	34.8%	65.2%	34.8%	65.2%
FORSYTH	1,927	536	1,391		855 D	27.8%	72.2%	27.8%	72.2%
FRANKLIN	3,275	373	2,902		2,529 D	11.4%	88.6%	11.4%	88.6%

PRESIDENT 1956

County	Total Vote	Republican	Democratic	Other	Rep.-Dem. Plurality	Total Vote Rep.	Total Vote Dem.	Major Vote Rep.	Major Vote Dem.
APPLING	2,369	506	1,719	144	1,213 D	21.4%	72.6%	22.7%	77.3%
ATKINSON	1,841	122	1,719		1,597 D	6.6%	93.4%	6.6%	93.4%
BACON	2,839	394	2,445		2,051 D	13.9%	86.1%	13.9%	86.1%
BAKER	815	32	783		751 D	3.9%	96.1%	3.9%	96.1%
BALDWIN	3,361	1,080	2,275	6	1,195 D	32.1%	67.7%	32.2%	67.8%
BANKS	1,179	187	990	2	803 D	15.9%	84.0%	15.9%	84.1%
BARROW	2,708	442	2,266		1,824 D	16.3%	83.7%	16.3%	83.7%
BARTOW	5,176	1,536	3,640		2,104 D	29.7%	70.3%	29.7%	70.3%
BEN HILL	2,708	554	2,150	4	1,596 D	20.5%	79.4%	20.5%	79.5%
BERRIEN	2,571	167	2,403	1	2,236 D	6.5%	93.5%	6.5%	93.5%
BIBB	22,750	7,368	15,382		8,014 D	32.4%	67.6%	32.4%	67.6%
BLECKLEY	1,673	136	1,537		1,401 D	8.1%	91.9%	8.1%	91.9%
BRANTLEY	1,436	228	1,208		980 D	15.9%	84.1%	15.9%	84.1%
BROOKS	2,487	534	1,936	17	1,402 D	21.5%	77.8%	21.6%	78.4%
BRYAN	1,576	331	1,242	3	911 D	21.0%	78.8%	21.0%	79.0%
BULLOCH	4,315	901	3,414		2,513 D	20.9%	79.1%	20.9%	79.1%
BURKE	2,049	721	1,300	28	579 D	35.2%	63.4%	35.7%	64.3%
BUTTS	2,208	323	1,885		1,562 D	14.6%	85.4%	14.6%	85.4%
CALHOUN	1,206	107	1,094	5	987 D	8.9%	90.7%	8.9%	91.1%
CAMDEN	2,194	1,014	1,178	2	164 D	46.2%	53.7%	46.3%	53.7%
CAMPBELL	1,318	308	996	14	688 D	23.4%	75.6%	23.6%	76.4%
CARROLL	6,567	1,712	4,855		3,143 D	26.1%	73.9%	26.1%	73.9%
CATOOSA	3,583	1,336	2,163	84	827 D	37.3%	60.4%	38.2%	61.8%
CHARLTON	954	204	750		546 D	21.4%	78.6%	21.4%	78.6%
CHATHAM	26,099	16,512	9,587		6,925 R	63.3%	36.7%	63.3%	36.7%
CHATTAHOOCHEE	150	43	107		64 D	28.7%	71.3%	28.7%	71.3%
CHATTOOGA	5,506	1,682	3,823	1	2,141 D	30.6%	69.4%	30.6%	69.4%
CHEROKEE	3,939	1,829	2,110		281 D	46.4%	53.6%	46.4%	53.6%
CLARKE	6,371	2,107	4,257	7	2,150 D	33.1%	66.8%	33.1%	66.9%
CLAY	499	103	390	6	287 D	20.6%	78.2%	20.9%	79.1%
CLAYTON	7,115	1,593	5,522		3,929 D	22.4%	77.6%	22.4%	77.6%
CLINCH	2,097	518	1,579		1,061 D	24.7%	75.3%	24.7%	75.3%
COBB	18,510	6,798	11,696	16	4,898 D	36.7%	63.2%	36.8%	63.2%
COFFEE	3,774	574	3,199	1	2,625 D	15.2%	84.8%	15.2%	84.8%
COLQUITT	5,765	1,336	4,412	17	3,076 D	23.2%	76.5%	23.3%	76.8%
COLUMBIA	1,329	463	866	1	403 D	34.8%	65.2%	34.8%	65.4%
COOK	2,346	245	2,100	1	1,855 D	10.4%	89.5%	10.4%	89.6%
COWETA	3,855	850	3,003	2	2,153 D	22.1%	77.9%	22.3%	77.7%
CRAWFORD	893	109	779	5	670 D	12.2%	87.2%	12.3%	87.7%
CRISP	3,366	835	2,526	5	1,691 D	24.8%	75.0%	24.8%	75.2%
DADE	1,586	723	863		140 D	45.6%	54.4%	45.6%	54.4%
DAWSON	1,334	613	721		108 D	46.0%	54.0%	46.0%	54.0%
DECATUR	4,761	1,062	3,699		2,637 D	22.3%	77.7%	22.3%	77.7%
DE KALB	46,341	15,979	30,336	26	14,357 D	34.5%	65.5%	34.5%	65.5%
DODGE	4,219	738	3,479	2	2,741 D	17.5%	82.4%	17.5%	82.5%
DOOLY	2,025	174	1,851		1,677 D	8.6%	91.4%	8.6%	91.4%
DOUGHERTY	7,513	3,248	4,126	139	878 D	43.2%	54.9%	44.0%	56.0%
DOUGLAS	3,112	1,001	2,111		1,110 D	32.2%	67.8%	32.2%	68.0%
EARLY	2,014	193	1,818	3	1,625 D	9.6%	90.3%	9.6%	90.4%
ECHOLS	666	134	530	2	396 D	20.1%	79.6%	20.2%	79.8%
EFFINGHAM	1,369	637	611	121	26 R	46.5%	44.6%	51.0%	49.0%
ELBERT	4,085	447	3,635	3	3,188 D	10.9%	89.0%	11.0%	89.0%
EMANUEL	3,052	679	2,373		1,694 D	22.2%	77.8%	22.2%	77.8%
EVANS	1,513	356	1,154	3	798 D	23.5%	76.3%	23.6%	76.4%
FANNIN	5,466	3,521	1,945		1,576 R	64.4%	35.6%	64.4%	35.6%
FAYETTE	1,446	138	1,308		1,170 D	9.5%	90.5%	9.5%	90.5%
FLOYD	12,588	5,955	6,633		678 D	47.3%	52.7%	47.3%	52.7%
FORSYTH	3,129	1,131	1,998		867 D	36.1%	63.9%	36.1%	63.9%
FRANKLIN	3,225	253	2,968	4	2,715 D	7.8%	92.0%	7.9%	92.1%

GEORGIA

PRESIDENT 1952

County	Total Vote	Republican	Democratic	Other	Rep.-Dem. Plurality	% Total Vote Rep.	% Total Vote Dem.	% Major Vote Rep.	% Major Vote Dem.
FULTON	87,656	35,197	52,459		17,262 D	40.2%	59.8%	40.2%	59.8%
GILMER	2,683	1,324	1,359		35 D	49.3%	50.7%	49.3%	50.7%
GLASCOCK	614	233	381		148 D	37.9%	62.1%	37.9%	62.1%
GLYNN	5,923	2,575	3,348		773 D	43.5%	56.5%	43.5%	56.5%
GORDON	3,083	880	2,203		1,323 D	28.5%	71.5%	28.5%	71.5%
GRADY	3,425	643	2,782		2,139 D	18.8%	81.2%	18.8%	81.2%
GREENE	2,720	397	2,323		1,926 D	14.6%	85.4%	14.6%	85.4%
GWINNETT	7,041	1,015	6,026		5,011 D	14.4%	85.6%	14.4%	85.6%
HABERSHAM	3,568	921	2,647		1,726 D	25.8%	74.2%	25.8%	74.2%
HALL	7,966	1,845	6,121		4,276 D	23.2%	76.8%	23.2%	76.8%
HANCOCK	1,512	267	1,245		978 D	17.7%	82.3%	17.7%	82.3%
HARALSON	3,547	1,264	2,283		1,019 D	35.6%	64.4%	35.6%	64.4%
HARRIS	1,918	544	1,374		830 D	28.4%	71.6%	28.4%	71.6%
HART	3,448	204	3,244		3,040 D	5.9%	94.1%	5.9%	94.1%
HEARD	1,373	184	1,189		1,005 D	13.4%	86.6%	13.4%	86.6%
HENRY	3,142	553	2,589		2,036 D	17.6%	82.4%	17.6%	82.4%
HOUSTON	3,300	511	2,789		2,278 D	15.5%	84.5%	15.5%	84.5%
IRWIN	1,991	516	1,475		959 D	25.9%	74.1%	25.9%	74.1%
JACKSON	3,750	409	3,341		2,932 D	10.9%	89.1%	10.9%	89.1%
JASPER	1,333	228	1,105		877 D	17.1%	82.9%	17.1%	82.9%
JEFF DAVIS	1,690	367	1,323		956 D	21.7%	78.3%	21.7%	78.3%
JEFFERSON	2,220	744	1,476		732 D	33.5%	66.5%	33.5%	66.5%
JENKINS	1,534	368	1,166		798 D	24.0%	76.0%	24.0%	76.0%
JOHNSON	2,152	344	1,808		1,464 D	16.0%	84.0%	16.0%	84.0%
JONES	1,705	278	1,427		1,149 D	16.3%	83.7%	16.3%	83.7%
LAMAR	1,981	429	1,552		1,123 D	21.7%	78.3%	21.7%	78.3%
LANIER	1,015	170	845		675 D	16.7%	83.3%	16.7%	83.3%
LAURENS	6,047	1,046	5,001		3,955 D	17.3%	82.7%	17.3%	82.7%
LEE	595	205	390		185 D	34.5%	65.5%	34.5%	65.5%
LIBERTY	1,965	517	1,448		931 D	26.3%	73.7%	26.3%	73.7%
LINCOLN	971	327	644		317 D	33.7%	66.3%	33.7%	66.3%
LONG	1,111	420	691		271 D	37.8%	62.2%	37.8%	62.2%
LOWNDES	5,324	2,079	3,245		1,166 D	39.0%	61.0%	39.0%	61.0%
LUMPKIN	1,367	370	997		627 D	27.1%	72.9%	27.1%	72.9%
MCDUFFIE	2,105	933	1,172		239 D	44.3%	55.7%	44.3%	55.7%
MCINTOSH	1,227	503	724		221 D	41.0%	59.0%	41.0%	59.0%
MACON	1,791	319	1,472		1,153 D	17.8%	82.2%	17.8%	82.2%
MADISON	2,124	225	1,899		1,674 D	10.6%	89.4%	10.6%	89.4%
MARION	833	182	651		469 D	21.8%	78.2%	21.8%	78.2%
MERIWETHER	4,082	531	3,551		3,020 D	13.0%	87.0%	13.0%	87.0%
MILLER	1,840	223	1,617		1,394 D	12.1%	87.9%	12.1%	87.9%
MILTON									
MITCHELL	3,655	601	3,054		2,453 D	16.4%	83.6%	16.4%	83.6%
MONROE	2,907	501	2,406		1,905 D	17.2%	82.8%	17.2%	82.8%
MONTGOMERY	2,048	290	1,758		1,468 D	14.2%	85.8%	14.2%	85.8%
MORGAN	1,896	247	1,649		1,402 D	13.0%	87.0%	13.0%	87.0%
MURRAY	2,596	756	1,840		1,084 D	29.1%	70.9%	29.1%	70.9%
MUSCOGEE	19,034	7,814	11,220		3,406 D	41.1%	58.9%	41.1%	58.9%
NEWTON	3,960	431	3,529		3,098 D	10.9%	89.1%	10.9%	89.1%
OCONEE	1,519	337	1,182		845 D	22.2%	77.8%	22.2%	77.8%
OGLETHORPE	1,669	208	1,461		1,253 D	12.5%	87.5%	12.5%	87.5%
PAULDING	2,940	788	2,152		1,364 D	26.8%	73.2%	26.8%	73.2%
PEACH	1,898	374	1,524		1,150 D	19.7%	80.3%	19.7%	80.3%
PICKENS	2,640	1,328	1,312		16 R	50.3%	49.7%	50.3%	49.7%
PIERCE	2,495	592	1,903		1,311 D	23.7%	76.3%	23.7%	76.3%
PIKE	1,534	286	1,248		962 D	18.6%	81.4%	18.6%	81.4%
POLK	5,746	1,299	4,447		3,148 D	22.6%	77.4%	22.6%	77.4%
PULASKI	1,737	165	1,572		1,407 D	9.5%	90.5%	9.5%	90.5%
PUTNAM	1,501	250	1,251		1,001 D	16.7%	83.3%	16.7%	83.3%
QUITMAN	425	93	332		239 D	21.9%	78.1%	21.9%	78.1%

PRESIDENT 1956

County	Total Vote	Republican	Democratic	Other	Rep.-Dem. Plurality	% Total Vote Rep.	% Total Vote Dem.	% Major Vote Rep.	% Major Vote Dem.
FULTON	93,219	40,966	52,062	191	11,096 D	43.9%	55.8%	44.0%	56.0%
GILMER	3,134	1,857	1,275	2	582 R	59.3%	40.7%	59.3%	40.7%
GLASCOCK	425	110	314	1	204 D	25.9%	73.9%	25.9%	74.1%
GLYNN	6,169	3,098	3,071		27 D	50.2%	49.8%	50.2%	49.8%
GORDON	3,003	1,025	1,972	6	947 D	34.1%	65.7%	34.2%	65.8%
GRADY	3,193	496	2,697		2,201 D	15.5%	84.5%	15.5%	84.5%
GREENE	2,555	541	2,012	2	1,471 D	21.2%	78.7%	21.2%	78.8%
GWINNETT	7,130	1,443	5,687		4,244 D	20.2%	79.8%	20.2%	79.8%
HABERSHAM	3,131	855	2,276		1,421 D	27.3%	72.7%	27.3%	72.7%
HALL	8,741	2,752	5,989		3,237 D	31.5%	68.5%	31.5%	68.5%
HANCOCK	1,214	354	860		506 D	29.2%	70.8%	29.2%	70.8%
HARALSON	4,690	2,218	2,472		254 D	47.3%	52.7%	47.3%	52.7%
HARRIS	1,901	563	1,328	10	765 D	29.6%	69.9%	29.8%	70.2%
HART	2,133	117	2,016		1,899 D	5.5%	94.5%	5.5%	94.5%
HEARD	1,300	194	1,106		912 D	14.9%	85.1%	14.9%	85.1%
HENRY	3,484	848	2,636		1,788 D	24.3%	75.7%	24.3%	75.7%
HOUSTON	5,551	1,060	4,483	8	3,423 D	19.1%	80.8%	19.1%	80.9%
IRWIN	1,866	312	1,554		1,242 D	16.7%	83.3%	16.7%	83.3%
JACKSON	3,547	438	3,100	9	2,662 D	12.3%	87.4%	12.4%	87.6%
JASPER	1,250	288	962		674 D	23.0%	77.0%	23.0%	77.0%
JEFF DAVIS	1,907	247	1,656	4	1,409 D	13.0%	86.8%	13.0%	87.0%
JEFFERSON	1,883	515	1,356	12	841 D	27.3%	72.0%	27.5%	72.5%
JENKINS	1,272	261	1,000	11	739 D	20.5%	78.6%	20.7%	79.3%
JOHNSON	1,869	179	1,607	83	1,428 D	9.6%	86.0%	10.0%	90.0%
JONES	1,596	382	1,208	6	826 D	23.9%	75.7%	24.0%	76.0%
LAMAR	2,086	555	1,531		976 D	26.6%	73.4%	26.6%	73.4%
LANIER	1,044	152	890	2	738 D	14.6%	85.2%	14.6%	85.4%
LAURENS	6,274	1,189	5,085		3,896 D	19.0%	81.0%	19.0%	81.0%
LEE	620	79	532	9	453 D	12.7%	85.8%	12.9%	87.1%
LIBERTY	1,859	967	892		75 R	52.0%	48.0%	52.0%	48.0%
LINCOLN	851	155	696		541 D	18.2%	81.8%	18.2%	81.8%
LONG	1,476	281	1,195		914 D	19.0%	81.0%	19.0%	81.0%
LOWNDES	6,087	2,135	3,936	16	1,801 D	35.1%	64.7%	35.2%	64.8%
LUMPKIN	1,179	486	693		207 D	41.2%	58.8%	41.2%	58.8%
MCDUFFIE	1,690	649	1,039	2	390 D	38.4%	61.5%	38.4%	61.6%
MCINTOSH	1,510	886	624		262 R	58.7%	41.3%	58.7%	41.3%
MACON	2,354	363	1,984	7	1,621 D	15.4%	84.3%	15.5%	84.5%
MADISON	2,383	161	2,222		2,061 D	6.8%	93.2%	6.8%	93.2%
MARION	776	158	618		460 D	20.4%	79.6%	20.4%	79.6%
MERIWETHER	3,736	592	3,137	7	2,545 D	15.8%	84.0%	15.9%	84.1%
MILLER	2,004	441	1,563		1,122 D	22.0%	78.0%	22.0%	78.0%
MILTON									
MITCHELL	3,131	382	2,735	14	2,353 D	12.2%	87.4%	12.3%	87.7%
MONROE	2,051	506	1,545		1,039 D	24.7%	75.3%	24.7%	75.3%
MONTGOMERY	1,325	271	1,052	2	781 D	20.5%	79.4%	20.5%	79.5%
MORGAN	1,738	246	1,492		1,246 D	14.2%	85.8%	14.2%	85.8%
MURRAY	2,963	1,144	1,819		675 D	38.6%	61.4%	38.6%	61.4%
MUSCOGEE	15,523	7,676	7,660	187	16 R	49.4%	49.3%	50.0%	50.0%
NEWTON	3,764	532	3,232		2,700 D	14.1%	85.9%	14.1%	85.9%
OCONEE	1,478	314	1,159	5	845 D	21.2%	78.4%	21.3%	78.7%
OGLETHORPE	1,572	167	1,404	1	1,237 D	10.6%	89.3%	10.6%	89.4%
PAULDING	2,539	940	1,599		659 D	37.0%	63.0%	37.0%	63.0%
PEACH	2,005	461	1,541	3	1,080 D	23.0%	76.9%	23.0%	77.0%
PICKENS	3,577	2,341	1,236		1,105 R	65.4%	34.6%	65.4%	34.6%
PIERCE	2,152	386	1,766		1,380 D	17.9%	82.1%	17.9%	82.1%
PIKE	1,277	210	1,067		857 D	16.4%	83.6%	16.4%	83.6%
POLK	6,601	2,098	4,502	1	2,404 D	31.8%	68.2%	31.8%	68.2%
PULASKI	1,593	171	1,422		1,251 D	10.7%	89.3%	10.7%	89.3%
PUTNAM	1,361	268	1,093		825 D	19.7%	80.3%	19.7%	80.3%
QUITMAN	386	31	355	1	324 D	8.0%	92.0%	8.0%	92.0%

GEORGIA

PRESIDENT 1952

County	Total Vote	Republican	Democratic	Other	Rep.-Dem. Plurality	Percentage Total Vote Rep.	Dem.	Major Vote Rep.	Dem.
RABUN	1,769	449	1,320		871 D	25.4%	74.6%	25.4%	74.6%
RANDOLPH	1,926	507	1,419		912 D	26.3%	73.7%	26.3%	73.7%
RICHMOND	17,931	9,347	8,584		763 R	52.1%	47.9%	52.1%	47.9%
ROCKDALE	1,986	321	1,665		1,344 D	16.2%	83.8%	16.2%	83.8%
SCHLEY	584	148	436		288 D	25.3%	74.7%	25.3%	74.7%
SCREVEN	2,276	692	1,584		892 D	30.4%	69.6%	30.4%	69.6%
SEMINOLE	1,302	176	1,126		950 D	13.5%	86.5%	13.5%	86.5%
SPALDING	6,545	1,249	5,296		4,047 D	19.1%	80.9%	19.1%	80.9%
STEPHENS	4,200	661	3,539		2,878 D	15.7%	84.3%	15.7%	84.3%
STEWART	1,127	311	816		505 D	27.6%	72.4%	27.6%	72.4%
SUMTER	3,523	1,068	2,455		1,387 D	30.3%	69.7%	30.3%	69.7%
TALBOT	853	175	678		503 D	20.5%	79.5%	20.5%	79.5%
TALIAFERRO	976	103	873		770 D	10.6%	89.4%	10.6%	89.4%
TATTNALL	3,547	1,114	2,433		1,319 D	31.4%	68.6%	31.4%	68.6%
TAYLOR	1,956	277	1,679		1,402 D	14.2%	85.8%	14.2%	85.8%
TELFAIR	2,938	243	2,695		2,452 D	8.3%	91.7%	8.3%	91.7%
TERRELL	1,744	369	1,375		1,006 D	21.2%	78.8%	21.2%	78.8%
THOMAS	6,244	2,273	3,971		1,698 D	36.4%	63.6%	36.4%	63.6%
TIFT	4,272	1,318	2,954		1,636 D	30.9%	69.1%	30.9%	69.1%
TOOMBS	3,364	723	2,641		1,918 D	21.5%	78.5%	21.5%	78.5%
TOWNS	2,094	983	1,111		128 D	46.9%	53.1%	46.9%	53.1%
TREUTLEN	1,517	101	1,416		1,315 D	6.7%	93.3%	6.7%	93.3%
TROUP	9,017	1,887	7,130		5,243 D	20.9%	79.1%	20.9%	79.1%
TURNER	1,759	402	1,357		955 D	22.9%	77.1%	22.9%	77.1%
TWIGGS	1,271	191	1,080		889 D	15.0%	85.0%	15.0%	85.0%
UNION	2,690	1,330	1,360		30 D	49.4%	50.6%	49.4%	50.6%
UPSON	4,485	648	3,837		3,189 D	14.4%	85.6%	14.4%	85.6%
WALKER	7,232	2,866	4,366		1,500 D	39.6%	60.4%	39.6%	60.4%
WALTON	3,996	324	3,672		3,348 D	8.1%	91.9%	8.1%	91.9%
WARE	8,045	2,418	5,627		3,209 D	30.1%	69.9%	30.1%	69.9%
WARREN	1,067	374	693		319 D	35.1%	64.9%	35.1%	64.9%
WASHINGTON	3,176	795	2,381		1,586 D	25.0%	75.0%	25.0%	75.0%
WAYNE	2,761	832	1,929		1,097 D	30.1%	69.9%	30.1%	69.9%
WEBSTER	473	138	335		197 D	29.2%	70.8%	29.2%	70.8%
WHEELER	1,541	261	1,280		1,019 D	16.9%	83.1%	16.9%	83.1%
WHITE	1,421	282	1,139		857 D	19.8%	80.2%	19.8%	80.2%
WHITFIELD	7,456	2,795	4,661		1,866 D	37.5%	62.5%	37.5%	62.5%
WILCOX	2,179	301	1,878		1,577 D	13.8%	86.2%	13.8%	86.2%
WILKES	1,786	286	1,500		1,214 D	16.0%	84.0%	16.0%	84.0%
WILKINSON	2,007	378	1,629		1,251 D	18.8%	81.2%	18.8%	81.2%
WORTH	2,430	444	1,986		1,542 D	18.3%	81.7%	18.3%	81.7%
TOTAL	655,785	198,961	456,823	1	257,862 D	30.3%	69.7%	30.3%	69.7%

PRESIDENT 1956

County	Total Vote	Republican	Democratic	Other	Rep.-Dem. Plurality	Percentage Total Vote Rep.	Dem.	Major Vote Rep.	Dem.
RABUN	1,808	413	1,391	4	978 D	22.8%	76.9%	22.9%	77.1%
RANDOLPH	2,129	547	1,582		1,035 D	25.7%	74.3%	25.7%	74.3%
RICHMOND	17,365	10,251	6,819	295	3,432 R	59.0%	39.3%	60.1%	39.9%
ROCKDALE	2,263	484	1,779		1,295 D	21.4%	78.6%	21.4%	78.6%
SCHLEY	565	117	441	7	324 D	21.0%	78.1%	21.0%	79.0%
SCREVEN	1,865	521	1,332	12	811 D	27.9%	71.4%	28.1%	71.9%
SEMINOLE	1,474	129	1,343	2	1,214 D	8.8%	91.1%	8.8%	91.2%
SPALDING	6,329	1,458	4,853	18	3,395 D	23.0%	76.7%	23.0%	76.9%
STEPHENS	3,279	684	2,595		1,911 D	20.9%	79.1%	20.9%	79.1%
STEWART	939	235	692	12	457 D	25.0%	73.7%	25.4%	74.6%
SUMTER	3,234	730	2,149	355	1,419 D	22.6%	66.5%	25.4%	74.6%
TALBOT	848	136	710	2	574 D	16.0%	83.7%	16.1%	83.9%
TALIAFERRO	759	160	599		439 D	21.1%	78.9%	21.1%	78.9%
TATTNALL	2,321	440	1,881		1,441 D	19.0%	81.0%	19.0%	81.0%
TAYLOR	1,642	276	1,359	7	1,083 D	16.8%	82.8%	16.9%	83.1%
TELFAIR	2,359	284	2,075		1,791 D	12.0%	88.0%	12.0%	88.0%
TERRELL	1,508	203	1,301	4	1,098 D	13.5%	86.3%	13.5%	86.5%
THOMAS	5,762	2,240	3,522		1,282 D	38.9%	61.1%	38.9%	61.1%
TIFT	4,083	960	3,123		2,163 D	23.5%	76.5%	23.5%	76.5%
TOOMBS	2,963	565	2,397	1	1,832 D	19.1%	80.9%	19.1%	80.9%
TOWNS	1,981	1,096	885		211 R	55.3%	44.7%	55.3%	44.7%
TREUTLEN	1,077	117	960		843 D	10.9%	89.1%	10.9%	89.1%
TROUP	8,386	2,214	6,162	10	3,948 D	26.4%	73.5%	26.4%	73.6%
TURNER	1,752	354	1,398		1,044 D	20.2%	79.8%	20.2%	79.8%
TWIGGS	1,164	158	1,002	4	844 D	13.6%	86.1%	13.6%	86.4%
UNION	2,746	1,360	1,386		26 D	49.5%	50.5%	49.5%	50.5%
UPSON	4,134	712	3,422		2,710 D	17.2%	82.8%	17.2%	82.8%
WALKER	7,368	3,552	3,693	123	141 D	48.2%	50.1%	49.0%	51.0%
WALTON	3,744	470	3,271	3	2,801 D	12.6%	87.4%	12.6%	87.4%
WARE	8,164	2,276	5,888		3,612 D	27.9%	72.1%	27.9%	72.1%
WARREN	853	152	675	26	523 D	17.8%	79.1%	18.4%	81.6%
WASHINGTON	3,135	602	2,530	3	1,928 D	19.2%	80.7%	19.2%	80.8%
WAYNE	3,034	950	2,084		1,134 D	31.3%	68.7%	31.3%	68.7%
WEBSTER	346	51	295		244 D	14.7%	85.3%	14.7%	85.3%
WHEELER	1,143	150	993		843 D	13.1%	86.9%	13.1%	86.9%
WHITE	1,569	469	1,100		631 D	29.9%	70.1%	29.9%	70.1%
WHITFIELD	8,469	4,205	4,264		59 D	49.7%	50.3%	49.7%	50.3%
WILCOX	1,918	232	1,686		1,454 D	12.1%	87.9%	12.1%	87.9%
WILKES	2,039	305	1,714	20	1,409 D	15.0%	84.1%	15.1%	84.9%
WILKINSON	1,694	393	1,299	2	906 D	23.2%	76.7%	23.2%	76.8%
WORTH	2,375	293	2,078	4	1,785 D	12.3%	87.5%	12.4%	87.6%
TOTAL	669,655	222,778	444,688	2,189	221,910 D	33.3%	66.4%	33.4%	66.6%

GEORGIA

PRESIDENT 1960

County	Total Vote	Republican	Democratic	Other	Rep.-Dem. Plurality	Total Vote Rep.	Total Vote Dem.	Major Vote Rep.	Major Vote Dem.
APPLING	2,690	717	1,973		1,256 D	26.7%	73.3%	26.7%	73.3%
ATKINSON	1,537	239	1,298		1,059 D	15.5%	84.5%	15.5%	84.5%
BACON	1,747	579	1,168		589 D	33.1%	66.9%	33.1%	66.9%
BAKER	786	66	720		654 D	8.4%	91.6%	8.4%	91.6%
BALDWIN	3,526	1,264	2,262		998 D	35.8%	64.2%	35.8%	64.2%
BANKS	1,391	221	1,170		949 D	15.9%	84.1%	15.9%	84.1%
BARROW	3,336	577	2,759		2,182 D	17.3%	82.7%	17.3%	82.7%
BARTOW	4,837	1,292	3,545		2,253 D	26.7%	73.3%	26.7%	73.3%
BEN HILL	2,439	558	1,881		1,323 D	22.9%	77.1%	22.9%	77.1%
BERRIEN	3,155	368	2,787		2,419 D	11.7%	88.3%	11.7%	88.3%
BIBB	24,910	10,523	14,387		3,864 D	42.2%	57.8%	42.2%	57.8%
BLECKLEY	2,384	633	1,751		1,118 D	26.5%	73.4%	26.5%	73.4%
BRANTLEY	1,677	344	1,333		989 D	20.5%	79.5%	20.5%	79.5%
BROOKS	2,265	765	1,500		735 D	33.3%	66.2%	33.8%	66.2%
BRYAN	1,751	428	1,323		895 D	24.4%	75.6%	24.4%	75.6%
BULLOCH	4,879	1,506	3,373		1,867 D	30.9%	69.1%	30.9%	69.1%
BURKE	2,189	1,027	1,162		135 D	46.9%	53.1%	46.9%	53.1%
BUTTS	2,055	382	1,673		1,291 D	18.5%	81.4%	18.6%	81.4%
CALHOUN	934	131	803		672 D	14.0%	86.0%	14.0%	86.0%
CAMDEN	2,271	950	1,321		371 D	41.8%	58.2%	41.8%	58.2%
CAMPBELL									
CANDLER	1,376	433	943		510 D	31.5%	68.5%	31.5%	68.5%
CARROLL	6,427	1,729	4,698		2,969 D	26.9%	73.1%	26.9%	73.1%
CATOOSA	4,188	2,074	2,114		40 D	49.5%	50.5%	49.5%	50.5%
CHARLTON	1,022	289	733		444 D	28.3%	71.7%	28.3%	71.7%
CHATHAM	34,175	17,935	16,240		1,695 R	52.5%	47.5%	52.5%	47.5%
CHATTAHOOCHEE	256	66	190		124 D	25.8%	74.2%	25.8%	74.2%
CHATTOOGA	5,282	1,596	3,686		2,090 D	30.2%	69.8%	30.2%	69.8%
CHEROKEE	5,418	2,341	3,077		736 D	43.2%	56.8%	43.2%	56.8%
CLARKE	7,062	2,250	4,812		2,562 D	31.9%	68.1%	31.9%	68.1%
CLAY	612	84	528		444 D	13.7%	86.3%	13.7%	86.3%
CLAYTON	8,845	2,953	5,892		2,939 D	33.4%	66.6%	33.4%	66.6%
CLINCH	1,295	397	898		501 D	30.7%	69.3%	30.7%	69.3%
COBB	21,146	8,240	12,906		4,666 D	39.0%	61.0%	39.0%	61.0%
COFFEE	4,363	987	3,376		2,389 D	22.6%	77.4%	22.6%	77.4%
COLQUITT	6,082	1,685	4,397		2,712 D	27.7%	72.3%	27.7%	72.3%
COLUMBIA	2,345	1,155	1,190		35 D	49.3%	50.7%	49.3%	50.7%
COOK	2,334	399	1,935		1,536 D	17.1%	82.9%	17.1%	82.9%
COWETA	5,014	1,159	3,855		2,696 D	23.1%	76.9%	23.1%	76.9%
CRAWFORD	1,000	203	797		594 D	20.3%	79.7%	20.3%	79.7%
CRISP	3,328	963	2,365		1,402 D	28.9%	71.1%	28.9%	71.1%
DADE	1,852	909	943		34 D	49.1%	50.9%	49.1%	50.9%
DAWSON	1,317	401	916		515 D	30.4%	69.6%	30.4%	69.6%
DECATUR	3,698	918	2,780		1,862 D	24.8%	75.2%	24.8%	75.2%
DE KALB	48,162	24,046	24,116		70 D	49.9%	50.1%	49.9%	50.1%
DODGE	4,764	1,134	3,630		2,496 D	23.8%	76.2%	23.8%	76.2%
DOOLY	1,953	220	1,733		1,513 D	11.3%	88.7%	11.3%	88.7%
DOUGHERTY	8,845	4,323	4,522		199 D	48.9%	51.1%	48.9%	51.1%
DOUGLAS	3,712	1,136	2,576		1,440 D	30.6%	69.4%	30.6%	69.4%
EARLY	2,158	254	1,904		1,650 D	11.8%	88.2%	11.8%	88.2%
ECHOLS	365	108	257		149 D	29.6%	70.4%	29.6%	70.4%
EFFINGHAM	1,765	885	880		5 R	50.1%	49.9%	50.1%	49.9%
ELBERT	4,281	609	3,672		3,063 D	14.2%	85.8%	14.2%	85.8%
EMANUEL	3,633	1,120	2,513		1,393 D	30.8%	69.2%	30.8%	69.2%
EVANS	1,636	567	1,069		502 D	34.7%	65.3%	34.7%	65.3%
FANNIN	4,601	3,022	1,579		1,443 R	65.7%	34.3%	65.7%	34.3%
FAYETTE	1,557	359	1,198		839 D	23.1%	76.9%	23.1%	76.9%
FLOYD	13,458	6,108	7,350		1,242 D	45.4%	54.6%	45.4%	54.6%
FORSYTH	3,150	841	2,309		1,468 D	26.7%	73.3%	26.7%	73.3%
FRANKLIN	3,517	308	3,209		2,901 D	8.8%	91.2%	8.8%	91.2%

PRESIDENT 1964

County	Total Vote	Republican	Democratic	Other	Rep.-Dem. Plurality	Total Vote Rep.	Total Vote Dem.	Major Vote Rep.	Major Vote Dem.
APPLING	4,159	2,597	1,562		1,035 R	62.4%	37.6%	62.4%	37.6%
ATKINSON	1,969	1,157	811	1	346 R	58.8%	41.2%	58.8%	41.2%
BACON	3,315	2,136	1,179		957 R	64.4%	35.6%	64.4%	35.6%
BAKER	1,515	914	600	1	314 R	60.3%	39.6%	60.4%	39.6%
BALDWIN	6,170	3,430	2,740		690 R	55.6%	44.4%	55.6%	44.4%
BANKS	1,806	548	1,258		710 D	30.3%	69.7%	30.3%	69.7%
BARROW	4,593	2,316	2,277		39 R	50.4%	49.6%	50.4%	49.6%
BARTOW	7,448	2,813	4,635		1,822 D	37.8%	62.2%	37.8%	62.2%
BEN HILL	3,613	2,089	1,523		566 R	57.8%	42.2%	57.8%	42.2%
BERRIEN	6,731	4,073	2,658	1	1,415 R	60.5%	39.5%	60.5%	39.5%
BIBB	43,472	25,641	17,831		7,810 R	59.0%	41.0%	59.0%	41.0%
BLECKLEY	3,556	2,578	978		1,600 R	72.5%	27.5%	72.5%	27.5%
BRANTLEY	2,140	1,231	909		322 R	57.5%	42.5%	57.5%	42.5%
BROOKS	3,370	2,342	1,027	1	1,315 R	69.5%	30.5%	69.5%	30.5%
BRYAN	2,290	1,433	857		576 R	62.6%	37.4%	62.6%	37.4%
BULLOCH	7,543	4,823	2,720		2,103 R	63.9%	36.1%	63.9%	36.1%
BURKE	4,242	3,034	1,208		1,826 R	71.5%	28.5%	71.5%	28.5%
BUTTS	2,795	1,261	1,534		273 D	45.1%	54.9%	45.1%	54.9%
CALHOUN	1,355	1,066	289		777 R	78.7%	21.3%	78.7%	21.3%
CAMDEN	3,495	1,802	1,693		109 R	51.6%	48.4%	51.6%	48.4%
CAMPBELL									
CANDLER	2,505	1,710	795		915 R	68.3%	31.7%	68.3%	31.7%
CARROLL	9,780	4,984	4,794		190 R	51.0%	49.0%	51.0%	49.0%
CATOOSA	7,071	4,143	2,922	6	1,221 R	58.6%	41.3%	58.6%	41.4%
CHARLTON	1,753	1,179	574		605 R	67.3%	32.7%	67.3%	32.7%
CHATHAM	56,318	33,141	23,176	1	9,965 R	58.8%	41.2%	58.8%	41.2%
CHATTAHOOCHEE	437	246	191		55 R	56.3%	43.7%	56.3%	43.7%
CHATTOOGA	5,465	1,476	3,986	3	2,510 D	27.0%	72.9%	27.0%	73.0%
CHEROKEE	6,587	3,398	3,189		209 R	51.6%	48.4%	51.6%	48.4%
CLARKE	12,394	4,875	7,519		2,644 D	39.3%	60.7%	39.3%	60.7%
CLAY	906	544	360	2	184 R	60.0%	39.7%	60.2%	39.8%
CLAYTON	16,397	10,488	5,869	10	4,619 R	64.1%	35.9%	64.1%	35.9%
CLINCH	1,790	1,084	706		378 R	60.6%	39.4%	60.6%	39.4%
COBB	37,511	20,863	16,647	1	4,216 R	55.6%	44.4%	55.6%	44.4%
COFFEE	7,111	4,392	2,719		1,673 R	61.8%	38.2%	61.8%	38.2%
COLQUITT	9,060	6,493	2,563	4	3,930 R	71.7%	28.3%	71.7%	28.3%
COLUMBIA	4,003	2,575	1,428		1,147 R	64.3%	35.7%	64.3%	35.7%
COOK	3,395	2,058	1,337		721 R	60.6%	39.4%	60.6%	39.4%
COWETA	7,368	3,656	3,712		56 D	49.6%	50.4%	49.6%	50.4%
CRAWFORD	1,680	957	723		234 R	57.0%	43.0%	57.0%	43.0%
CRISP	5,093	3,337	1,756		1,581 R	65.5%	34.5%	65.5%	34.5%
DADE	2,608	1,378	1,227	3	151 R	52.8%	47.1%	52.8%	47.1%
DAWSON	1,571	639	932		293 D	40.7%	59.3%	40.7%	59.3%
DECATUR	7,072	5,060	2,011	1	3,049 R	71.5%	28.4%	71.6%	28.4%
DE KALB	86,602	49,448	37,154		12,294 R	57.1%	42.9%	57.1%	42.9%
DODGE	5,661	3,285	2,376		909 R	58.0%	42.0%	58.0%	42.0%
DOOLY	3,133	1,662	1,471		191 R	53.0%	47.0%	53.0%	47.0%
DOUGHERTY	18,024	12,776	5,248		7,528 R	70.9%	29.1%	70.9%	29.1%
DOUGLAS	5,816	3,315	2,501		814 R	57.0%	43.0%	57.0%	43.0%
EARLY	3,169	2,398	771		1,627 R	75.7%	24.3%	75.7%	24.3%
ECHOLS	583	399	184		215 R	68.4%	31.6%	68.4%	31.6%
EFFINGHAM	3,356	2,676	680		1,996 R	79.7%	20.3%	79.7%	20.3%
ELBERT	5,059	1,887	3,172		1,285 D	37.3%	62.7%	37.3%	62.7%
EMANUEL	5,590	3,311	2,279		1,032 R	59.2%	40.8%	59.2%	40.8%
EVANS	2,371	1,572	799		773 R	66.3%	33.7%	66.3%	33.7%
FANNIN	6,268	3,433	2,834	1	599 R	54.8%	45.2%	54.8%	45.2%
FAYETTE	2,249	1,349	896	4	453 R	60.0%	39.8%	60.1%	39.9%
FLOYD	18,636	9,849	8,750	37	1,099 R	52.8%	47.0%	53.0%	47.0%
FORSYTH	3,154	1,849	1,305	1	544 R	59.2%	40.8%	59.2%	40.8%
FRANKLIN	3,624	864	2,758	2	1,894 D	23.8%	76.1%	23.9%	76.1%

GEORGIA

PRESIDENT 1960

County	Total Vote	Republican	Democratic	Other	Rep.-Dem. Plurality	% Total Vote Rep.	% Total Vote Dem.	% Major Vote Rep.	% Major Vote Dem.
FULTON	109,743	53,940	55,803		1,863 D	49.2%	50.8%	49.2%	50.8%
GILMER	3,322	1,850	1,472		378 R	55.7%	44.3%	55.7%	44.3%
GLASCOCK	479	180	299		119 D	37.6%	62.4%	37.6%	62.4%
GLYNN	6,510	2,926	3,584		658 D	44.9%	55.1%	44.9%	55.1%
GORDON	3,301	1,148	2,153		1,005 D	34.8%	65.2%	34.8%	65.2%
GRADY	3,133	592	2,541		1,949 D	18.9%	81.1%	18.9%	81.1%
GREENE	2,307	328	1,979		1,651 D	14.2%	85.8%	14.2%	85.8%
GWINNETT	8,815	2,336	6,479		4,143 D	26.5%	73.5%	26.5%	73.5%
HABERSHAM	3,425	895	2,530		1,635 D	26.1%	73.9%	26.1%	73.9%
HALL	9,206	2,903	6,303		3,400 D	31.5%	68.5%	31.5%	68.5%
HANCOCK	1,066	286	780		494 D	26.8%	73.2%	26.8%	73.2%
HARALSON	4,652	1,869	2,783		914 D	40.2%	59.8%	40.2%	59.8%
HARRIS	2,097	735	1,362		627 D	35.1%	64.9%	35.1%	64.9%
HART	4,238	275	3,963		3,688 D	6.5%	93.5%	6.5%	93.5%
HEARD	1,405	181	1,224		1,043 D	12.9%	87.1%	12.9%	87.1%
HENRY	3,998	1,041	2,957		1,916 D	26.0%	74.0%	26.0%	74.0%
HOUSTON	5,790	1,757	4,033		2,276 D	30.3%	69.7%	30.3%	69.7%
IRWIN	1,977	352	1,625		1,273 D	17.8%	82.2%	17.8%	82.2%
JACKSON	4,125	472	3,653		3,181 D	11.4%	88.6%	11.4%	88.6%
JASPER	1,220	271	949		678 D	22.2%	77.8%	22.2%	77.8%
JEFF DAVIS	1,227	402	825		423 D	32.8%	67.2%	32.8%	67.2%
JEFFERSON	2,256	986	1,270		284 D	43.7%	56.3%	43.7%	56.3%
JENKINS	1,667	313	1,354		1,041 D	18.8%	81.2%	18.8%	81.2%
JOHNSON	1,786	488	1,298		810 D	27.3%	72.7%	27.3%	72.7%
JONES	1,904	489	1,415		926 D	25.7%	74.3%	25.7%	74.3%
LAMAR	1,842	479	1,363		884 D	26.0%	74.0%	26.0%	74.0%
LANIER	1,247	198	1,049		851 D	15.9%	84.1%	15.9%	84.1%
LAURENS	6,532	1,884	4,648		2,764 D	28.8%	71.2%	28.8%	71.2%
LEE	595	191	404		213 D	32.1%	67.9%	32.1%	67.9%
LIBERTY	2,519	929	1,590		661 D	36.9%	63.1%	36.9%	63.1%
LINCOLN	866	197	669		472 D	22.7%	77.3%	22.7%	77.3%
LONG	1,176	898	278		620 R	76.4%	23.6%	76.4%	23.6%
LOWNDES	6,513	2,908	3,605		697 D	44.6%	55.4%	44.6%	55.4%
LUMPKIN	1,370	495	875		380 D	36.1%	63.9%	36.1%	63.9%
McDUFFIE	2,118	1,039	1,079		40 D	49.1%	50.9%	49.1%	50.9%
McINTOSH	1,245	451	794		343 D	36.2%	63.8%	36.2%	63.8%
MACON	1,926	438	1,488		1,050 D	22.7%	77.3%	22.7%	77.3%
MADISON	2,623	205	2,418		2,213 D	7.8%	92.2%	7.8%	92.2%
MARION	799	154	645		491 D	19.3%	80.7%	19.3%	80.7%
MERIWETHER	3,806	706	3,100		2,394 D	18.5%	81.5%	18.5%	81.5%
MILLER	1,178	62	1,116		1,054 D	5.3%	94.7%	5.3%	94.7%
MILTON									
MITCHELL	3,694	430	3,264		2,834 D	11.6%	88.4%	11.6%	88.4%
MONROE	2,223	581	1,642		1,061 D	26.1%	73.9%	26.1%	73.9%
MONTGOMERY	1,832	381	1,451		1,070 D	20.8%	79.2%	20.8%	79.2%
MORGAN	1,861	373	1,488		1,115 D	20.0%	80.0%	20.0%	80.0%
MURRAY	2,801	925	1,876		951 D	33.0%	67.0%	33.0%	67.0%
MUSCOGEE	18,131	9,578	8,553		1,025 R	52.8%	47.2%	52.8%	47.2%
NEWTON	3,893	708	3,185		2,477 D	18.2%	81.8%	18.2%	81.8%
OCONEE	1,515	297	1,218		921 D	19.6%	80.4%	19.6%	80.4%
OGLETHORPE	1,548	142	1,406		1,264 D	9.2%	90.8%	9.2%	90.8%
PAULDING	3,208	812	2,396		1,584 D	25.3%	74.7%	25.3%	74.7%
PEACH	2,061	628	1,433		805 D	30.5%	69.5%	30.5%	69.5%
PICKENS	3,416	1,943	1,473		470 R	56.9%	43.1%	56.9%	43.1%
PIERCE	1,993	544	1,449		905 D	27.3%	72.7%	27.3%	72.7%
PIKE	1,283	255	1,028		773 D	19.9%	80.1%	19.9%	80.1%
POLK	6,097	1,746	4,351		2,605 D	28.6%	71.4%	28.6%	71.4%
PULASKI	1,490	334	1,156		822 D	22.4%	77.6%	22.4%	77.6%
PUTNAM	1,409	305	1,104		799 D	21.6%	78.4%	21.6%	78.4%
QUITMAN	455	67	388		321 D	14.7%	85.3%	14.7%	85.3%

PRESIDENT 1964

County	Total Vote	Republican	Democratic	Other	Rep.-Dem. Plurality	% Total Vote Rep.	% Total Vote Dem.	% Major Vote Rep.	% Major Vote Dem.
FULTON	166,756	73,205	93,540	11	20,335 D	43.9%	56.1%	43.9%	56.1%
GILMER	4,326	2,167	2,159		8 R	50.1%	49.9%	50.1%	49.9%
GLASCOCK	970	836	134		702 R	86.2%	13.8%	86.2%	13.8%
GLYNN	13,057	7,341	5,712	4	1,629 R	56.2%	43.7%	56.2%	43.8%
GORDON	5,577	2,317	3,260		943 D	41.5%	58.5%	41.5%	58.5%
GRADY	4,870	2,983	1,887		1,096 R	61.3%	38.7%	61.3%	38.7%
GREENE	3,791	2,698	1,093		1,605 R	71.2%	28.8%	71.2%	28.8%
GWINNETT	13,531	6,823	6,705	3	118 R	50.4%	49.6%	50.4%	49.6%
HABERSHAM	5,009	1,595	3,412	2	1,817 D	31.8%	68.1%	31.9%	68.1%
HALL	12,310	4,296	8,003	11	3,707 D	34.9%	65.0%	34.9%	65.1%
HANCOCK	1,999	925	1,074		149 D	46.3%	53.7%	46.3%	53.7%
HARALSON	5,317	3,129	2,186	2	943 R	58.8%	41.1%	58.9%	41.1%
HARRIS	3,106	2,166	940		1,226 R	69.7%	30.3%	69.7%	30.3%
HART	4,318	1,166	3,142	10	1,976 D	27.0%	72.8%	27.1%	72.9%
HEARD	1,869	807	1,061	1	254 D	43.2%	56.8%	43.2%	56.8%
HENRY	6,709	3,125	3,583	1	458 D	46.6%	53.4%	46.6%	53.4%
HOUSTON	10,791	6,532	4,258	1	2,274 R	60.5%	39.5%	60.5%	39.5%
IRWIN	2,757	2,017	740		1,277 R	73.2%	26.8%	73.2%	26.8%
JACKSON	5,617	1,664	3,953		2,289 D	29.6%	70.4%	29.6%	70.4%
JASPER	1,923	1,075	848		227 R	55.9%	44.1%	55.9%	44.1%
JEFF DAVIS	2,620	1,875	745		1,130 R	71.6%	28.4%	71.6%	28.4%
JEFFERSON	4,205	2,950	1,253	2	1,697 R	70.2%	29.8%	70.2%	29.8%
JENKINS	2,417	1,509	908		601 R	62.4%	37.6%	62.4%	37.6%
JOHNSON	2,622	1,940	682		1,258 R	74.0%	26.0%	74.0%	26.0%
JONES	3,185	1,805	1,380		425 R	56.7%	43.3%	56.7%	43.3%
LAMAR	3,121	1,570	1,548	3	22 R	50.3%	49.6%	50.4%	49.6%
LANIER	1,380	719	661		58 R	52.1%	47.9%	52.1%	47.9%
LAURENS	9,287	5,457	3,828	2	1,629 R	58.8%	41.2%	58.8%	41.2%
LEE	1,285	1,041	244		797 R	81.0%	19.0%	81.0%	19.0%
LIBERTY	3,670	1,458	2,212		754 D	39.7%	60.3%	39.7%	60.3%
LINCOLN	1,296	943	353		590 R	72.8%	27.2%	72.8%	27.2%
LONG	1,582	246	1,336		1,090 D	15.5%	84.5%	15.5%	84.5%
LOWNDES	11,175	6,811	4,363	1	2,448 R	60.9%	39.0%	60.9%	39.1%
LUMPKIN	2,045	855	1,189	1	334 D	41.8%	58.1%	41.8%	58.2%
McDUFFIE	3,781	2,657	1,124		1,533 R	70.3%	29.7%	70.3%	29.7%
McINTOSH	1,988	795	1,193		398 D	40.0%	60.0%	40.0%	60.0%
MACON	2,799	1,723	1,076		647 R	61.6%	38.4%	61.6%	38.4%
MADISON	3,531	1,190	2,341		1,151 D	33.7%	66.3%	33.7%	66.3%
MARION	1,085	719	365	1	354 R	66.3%	33.7%	66.3%	33.7%
MERIWETHER	4,674	2,250	2,423	1	173 D	48.1%	51.8%	48.1%	51.9%
MILLER	1,932	1,658	274		1,384 R	85.8%	14.2%	85.8%	14.2%
MILTON									
MITCHELL	4,462	3,265	1,197		2,068 R	73.2%	26.8%	73.2%	26.8%
MONROE	3,244	1,665	1,578	1	87 R	51.3%	48.6%	51.3%	48.7%
MONTGOMERY	2,287	1,409	878		531 R	61.6%	38.4%	61.6%	38.4%
MORGAN	3,139	1,485	1,654		169 D	47.3%	52.7%	47.3%	52.7%
MURRAY	3,495	1,064	2,426	5	1,362 D	30.4%	69.4%	30.5%	69.5%
MUSCOGEE	33,474	21,025	12,446	3	8,579 R	62.8%	37.2%	62.8%	37.2%
NEWTON	6,298	2,678	3,620		942 D	42.5%	57.5%	42.5%	57.5%
OCONEE	2,314	1,241	1,073		168 R	53.6%	46.4%	53.6%	46.4%
OGLETHORPE	1,990	1,126	864		262 R	56.6%	43.4%	56.6%	43.4%
PAULDING	4,427	1,914	2,513		599 D	43.2%	56.8%	43.2%	56.8%
PEACH	3,556	1,970	1,585	1	385 R	55.4%	44.6%	55.4%	44.6%
PICKENS	3,885	1,955	1,930		25 R	50.3%	49.7%	50.3%	49.7%
PIERCE	2,963	1,981	982		999 R	66.9%	33.1%	66.9%	33.1%
PIKE	2,010	1,064	946		118 R	52.9%	47.1%	52.9%	47.1%
POLK	7,840	3,282	4,555	3	1,273 D	41.9%	58.1%	41.9%	58.1%
PULASKI	2,726	1,768	953	5	815 R	64.9%	35.0%	65.0%	35.0%
PUTNAM	2,214	1,196	1,018		178 R	54.0%	46.0%	54.0%	46.0%
QUITMAN	607	377	230		147 R	62.1%	37.9%	62.1%	37.9%

GEORGIA

PRESIDENT 1960

County	Total Vote	Republican	Democratic	Other	Rep.-Dem. Plurality	Total Vote Rep.	Total Vote Dem.	Major Vote Rep.	Major Vote Dem.
RABUN	2,016	464	1,552		1,088 D	23.0%	77.0%	23.0%	77.0%
RANDOLPH	1,893	457	1,436		979 D	24.1%	75.9%	24.1%	75.9%
RICHMOND	21,846	11,978	9,868		2,110 R	54.8%	45.2%	54.8%	45.2%
ROCKDALE	2,261	496	1,765		1,269 D	21.9%	78.1%	21.9%	78.1%
SCHLEY	605	138	467		329 D	22.8%	77.2%	22.8%	77.2%
SCREVEN	2,447	957	1,490		533 D	39.1%	60.9%	39.1%	60.9%
SEMINOLE	1,656	77	1,579		1,502 D	4.6%	95.4%	4.6%	95.4%
SPALDING	6,179	1,753	4,426		2,673 D	23.4%	71.6%	28.4%	71.6%
STEPHENS	3,902	815	3,087		2,272 D	20.9%	79.1%	20.9%	79.1%
STEWART	948	302	646		344 D	31.9%	68.1%	31.9%	68.1%
SUMTER	3,236	962	2,274		1,312 D	29.7%	70.3%	29.7%	70.3%
TALBOT	978	207	771		564 D	21.2%	78.8%	21.2%	78.8%
TALIAFERRO	803	148	655		507 D	18.4%	81.6%	18.4%	81.6%
TATTNALL	2,777	869	1,908		1,039 D	31.3%	68.7%	31.3%	68.7%
TAYLOR	1,566	365	1,201		836 D	23.3%	76.7%	23.3%	76.7%
TELFAIR	3,713	791	2,922		2,131 D	21.3%	78.7%	21.3%	78.7%
TERRELL	1,637	285	1,352		1,067 D	17.4%	82.6%	17.4%	82.6%
THOMAS	5,511	2,285	3,226		941 D	41.5%	58.5%	41.5%	58.5%
TIFT	4,387	1,423	2,964		1,541 D	32.4%	67.6%	32.4%	67.6%
TOOMBS	3,247	1,038	2,209		1,171 D	32.0%	68.0%	32.0%	68.0%
TOWNS	2,324	1,272	1,052		220 R	54.7%	45.3%	54.7%	45.3%
TREUTLEN	1,143	216	927		711 D	18.9%	81.1%	18.9%	81.1%
TROUP	8,553	2,808	5,745		2,937 D	32.8%	67.2%	32.8%	67.2%
TURNER	1,873	328	1,545		1,217 D	17.5%	82.5%	17.5%	82.5%
TWIGGS	1,108	263	845		582 D	23.7%	76.3%	23.7%	76.3%
UNION	2,722	1,537	1,185		352 R	56.5%	43.5%	56.5%	43.5%
UPSON	4,263	1,001	3,262		2,261 D	23.5%	76.5%	23.5%	76.5%
WALKER	8,593	4,027	4,566		539 D	46.9%	53.1%	46.9%	53.1%
WALTON	3,498	403	3,095		2,692 D	11.5%	88.5%	11.5%	88.5%
WARE	7,334	2,235	5,099		2,864 D	30.5%	69.5%	30.5%	69.5%
WARREN	846	375	471		96 D	44.3%	55.7%	44.3%	55.7%
WASHINGTON	2,960	956	2,004		1,048 D	32.3%	67.7%	32.3%	67.7%
WAYNE	4,246	1,387	2,862		1,475 D	32.6%	67.4%	32.6%	67.4%
WEBSTER	374	77	297		220 D	20.6%	79.4%	20.6%	79.4%
WHEELER	1,196	226	970		744 D	18.9%	81.1%	18.9%	81.1%
WHITE	2,446	662	1,784		1,122 D	27.1%	72.9%	27.1%	72.9%
WHITFIELD	7,752	4,148	3,604		544 R	53.5%	46.5%	53.5%	46.5%
WILCOX	2,020	306	1,714		1,408 D	15.1%	84.9%	15.1%	84.9%
WILKES	2,181	395	1,786		1,391 D	18.1%	81.9%	18.1%	81.9%
WILKINSON	1,955	631	1,324		693 D	32.3%	67.7%	32.3%	67.7%
WORTH	2,448	338	2,110		1,772 D	13.8%	86.2%	13.8%	86.2%
TOTAL	733,349	274,472	458,638	239	184,166 D	37.4%	62.5%	37.4%	62.6%

PRESIDENT 1964

County	Total Vote	Republican	Democratic	Other	Rep.-Dem. Plurality	Total Vote Rep.	Total Vote Dem.	Major Vote Rep.	Major Vote Dem.
RABUN	2,347	551	1,796		1,245 D	23.5%	76.5%	23.5%	76.5%
RANDOLPH	2,621	1,656	962	3	694 R	63.2%	36.7%	63.3%	36.7%
RICHMOND	35,029	21,481	13,545	3	7,936 R	61.3%	38.7%	61.3%	38.7%
ROCKDALE	3,475	1,503	1,972		469 D	43.3%	56.7%	43.3%	56.7%
SCHLEY	954	577	377		200 R	60.5%	39.5%	60.5%	39.5%
SCREVEN	3,736	2,260	1,446		814 R	61.0%	39.0%	61.0%	39.0%
SEMINOLE	1,721	1,294	427		867 R	75.2%	24.8%	75.2%	24.8%
SPALDING	10,229	4,763	5,466		703 D	46.6%	53.4%	46.6%	53.4%
STEPHENS	4,854	1,371	3,483		2,112 D	28.2%	71.8%	28.2%	71.8%
STEWART	1,413	1,037	373	3	664 R	73.4%	26.4%	73.5%	26.5%
SUMTER	5,501	3,774	1,727		2,047 R	68.6%	31.4%	68.6%	31.4%
TALBOT	1,336	679	627		52 R	52.0%	48.0%	52.0%	48.0%
TALIAFERRO	955	337	628		291 D	34.9%	65.1%	34.9%	65.1%
TATTNALL	4,912	3,264	1,648		1,616 R	66.4%	33.6%	66.4%	33.6%
TAYLOR	2,470	1,372	1,097	1	275 R	55.5%	44.4%	55.6%	44.4%
TELFAIR	3,736	1,914	1,872		42 R	50.6%	49.4%	50.6%	49.4%
TERRELL	2,490	1,921	569		1,352 R	77.1%	22.9%	77.1%	22.9%
THOMAS	9,553	6,306	3,257		3,049 R	65.9%	34.1%	65.9%	34.1%
TIFT	6,936	4,650	2,286		2,364 R	67.0%	33.0%	67.0%	33.0%
TOOMBS	5,228	3,543	1,685		1,858 R	67.8%	32.2%	67.8%	32.2%
TOWNS	2,432	1,140	1,289	3	149 D	46.9%	53.0%	46.9%	53.1%
TREUTLEN	2,054	722	1,331	1	609 D	35.2%	64.8%	35.2%	64.8%
TROUP	11,309	5,277	6,032		755 D	46.7%	53.3%	46.7%	53.3%
TURNER	2,391	1,672	719		953 R	69.9%	30.1%	69.9%	30.1%
TWIGGS	1,964	1,178	786		392 R	60.0%	40.0%	60.0%	40.0%
UNION	3,608	1,473	2,135		662 D	40.8%	59.2%	40.8%	59.2%
UPSON	6,384	3,103	3,275	6	172 D	48.6%	51.3%	48.7%	51.3%
WALKER	11,401	5,939	5,454	8	485 R	52.1%	47.8%	52.1%	47.8%
WALTON	5,226	2,874	2,350	2	524 R	55.0%	45.0%	55.0%	45.0%
WARE	10,137	4,948	5,189		241 D	48.8%	51.2%	48.8%	51.2%
WARREN	1,454	1,070	384		686 R	73.6%	26.4%	73.6%	26.4%
WASHINGTON	4,127	2,296	1,830	1	466 R	55.6%	44.3%	55.6%	44.4%
WAYNE	5,801	3,619	2,182		1,437 R	62.4%	37.6%	62.4%	37.6%
WEBSTER	601	457	144		313 R	76.0%	24.0%	76.0%	24.0%
WHEELER	1,829	849	980		131 D	46.4%	53.6%	46.4%	53.6%
WHITE	2,363	840	1,520	3	680 D	35.5%	64.3%	35.6%	64.3%
WHITFIELD	11,880	4,546	7,330	4	2,784 D	38.3%	61.7%	38.3%	61.7%
WILCOX	2,694	1,794	900		894 R	66.6%	33.4%	66.6%	33.4%
WILKES	3,089	1,652	1,437		215 R	53.5%	46.5%	53.5%	46.5%
WILKINSON	3,135	2,172	963		1,209 R	69.3%	30.7%	69.3%	30.7%
WORTH	4,019	3,157	862		2,295 R	78.6%	21.4%	78.6%	21.4%
TOTAL	1,139,335	616,584	522,556	195	94,028 R	54.1%	45.9%	54.1%	45.9%

GEORGIA

OTHER VOTE COMPOSITION:

1920   Socialist; reported as a state-wide total, not by counties.
1924   12,687 Progressive; 231 Prohibition; 155 American. The county-by-county fig-
        ures include only the Progressive vote; the state-wide total also includes the
        Prohibition and American vote.
1928   124 Socialist; 64 Communist. Votes reported as state-wide totals, not by
        counties.
1932   1,125 Prohibition; 461 Socialist; 23 Communist.
1936   660 Prohibition; 136 Union; 68 Socialist.

1940   983 Prohibition; 14 scattered.
1944   36 Prohibition; 6 Socialist.
1948   85,135 States Rights; 1,636 Progressive; 732 Prohibition; 3 Socialist; 1 scattered.
1952   Scattered.
1956   2,096 States Rights; 93 scattered.

1960   Scattered; reported as a state-wide total, not by counties.
1964   Scattered.

SPECIAL CASES:

1920   No returns canvassed for Echols county.
1924   Progressive candidates ran second in a number of counties. Brantley, Lamar,
        Lanier, Long, and Seminole counties organized in 1921.
1928   Republican total includes 65,423 Republican and 36,377 anti-Smith votes. Peach
        county organized in 1925.
1932   Prohibition or Socialist candidates ran second in several counties in which there
        was no Republican vote and in one county in which the Republican vote was two.
        Campbell and Milton counties merged with Fulton County prior to this election.
1940   Republican total includes 23,934 Republican and 22,561 Independent Democratic
        votes.

1944   Republican total includes 56,527 Republican and 3,373 Independent Democratic
        votes.
1948   States Rights candidates carried several counties and ran second in a number of
        others.

HAWAII

PRESIDENT 1960

County	Total Vote	Republican	Democratic	Other	Rep.-Dem. Plurality	Percentage			
						Total Vote		Major Vote	
						Rep.	Dem.	Rep.	Dem.
HAWAII	23,808	12,251	11,557		694 R	51.5%	48.5%	51.5%	48.5%
HONOLULU	134,456	65,541	68,915		3,374 D	48.7%	51.3%	48.7%	51.3%
KAUAI	10,291	5,655	4,636		1,019 R	55.0%	45.0%	55.0%	45.0%
MAUI	16,150	8,848	7,302		1,546 R	54.8%	45.2%	54.8%	45.2%
TOTAL	184,705	92,295	92,410		115 D	50.0%	50.0%	50.0%	50.0%

PRESIDENT 1964

County	Total Vote	Republican	Democratic	Other	Rep.-Dem. Plurality	Percentage			
						Total Vote		Major Vote	
						Rep.	Dem.	Rep.	Dem.
HAWAII	24,973	4,962	20,011		15,049 D	19.9%	80.1%	19.9%	80.1%
HONOLULU	155,395	33,536	121,859		88,323 D	21.6%	78.4%	21.6%	78.4%
KAUAI	10,684	1,971	8,713		6,742 D	18.4%	81.6%	18.4%	81.6%
MAUI	16,259	3,553	12,666		9,113 D	21.9%	78.1%	21.9%	78.1%
TOTAL	207,271	44,022	163,249		119,227 D	21.2%	78.8%	21.2%	78.8%

HAWAII

OTHER VOTE COMPOSITION:

1960
1964

SPECIAL CASES:

The vote of Kalawao county, an area of 14 square miles on Molokai Island consisting entirely of the Kalaupapa Hansen's disease settlement, is included with the Maui county vote.

IDAHO

PRESIDENT 1920

County	Total Vote	Republican	Democratic	Other	Rep.-Dem. Plurality	Total Vote Rep.	Total Vote Dem.	Major Vote Rep.	Major Vote Dem.
ADA	12,730	8,535	4,195		4,340 R	67.0%	33.0%	67.0%	33.0%
ADAMS	1,118	721	397		324 R	64.5%	35.5%	64.5%	35.5%
BANNOCK	7,909	4,908	3,001		1,907 R	62.1%	37.9%	62.1%	37.9%
BEAR LAKE	3,022	1,845	1,177		658 R	61.1%	38.9%	61.1%	38.9%
BENEWAH	2,186	1,390	796		594 R	63.6%	36.4%	63.6%	36.4%
BINGHAM	4,544	3,355	1,189		2,156 R	73.8%	26.2%	73.8%	26.2%
BLAINE	1,786	1,222	564		658 R	68.4%	31.6%	68.4%	31.6%
BOISE	991	613	378		235 R	61.9%	38.1%	61.9%	38.1%
BONNER	3,829	2,272	1,557		715 R	59.3%	40.7%	59.3%	40.7%
BONNEVILLE	4,882	3,440	1,442		1,998 R	70.5%	29.5%	70.5%	29.5%
BOUNDARY	1,430	904	526		378 R	63.2%	36.8%	63.2%	36.8%
BUTTE	999	680	319		361 R	68.1%	31.9%	68.1%	31.9%
CAMAS	681	406	275		131 R	59.6%	40.4%	59.6%	40.4%
CANYON	9,139	5,754	3,385		2,369 R	63.0%	37.0%	63.0%	37.0%
CARIBOU	750	568	182		386 R	75.7%	24.3%	75.7%	24.3%
CASSIA	3,928	2,741	1,187		1,554 R	69.8%	30.2%	69.8%	30.2%
CLARK	793	611	182		429 R	77.0%	23.0%	77.0%	23.0%
CLEARWATER	1,509	1,021	488		533 R	67.7%	32.3%	67.7%	32.3%
CUSTER	1,237	844	393		451 R	68.2%	31.8%	68.2%	31.8%
ELMORE	1,972	1,103	869		234 R	55.9%	44.1%	55.9%	44.1%
FRANKLIN	2,539	1,630	909		721 R	64.2%	35.8%	64.2%	35.8%
FREMONT	3,118	2,040	1,078		962 R	65.4%	34.6%	65.4%	34.6%
GEM	2,268	1,433	835		598 R	63.2%	36.8%	63.2%	36.8%
GOODING	2,703	1,913	790		1,123 R	70.8%	29.2%	70.8%	29.2%
IDAHO	3,637	2,501	1,136		1,365 R	68.8%	31.2%	68.8%	31.2%
JEFFERSON	2,578	1,831	747		1,084 R	71.0%	29.0%	71.0%	29.0%
JEROME	2,591	1,803	788		1,015 R	69.6%	30.4%	69.6%	30.4%
KOOTENAI	5,481	3,640	1,841		1,799 R	66.4%	33.6%	66.4%	33.6%
LATAH	5,559	3,991	1,568		2,423 R	71.8%	28.2%	71.8%	28.2%
LEMHI	2,034	1,333	701		632 R	65.5%	34.5%	65.5%	34.5%
LEWIS	1,808	1,089	719		370 R	60.2%	39.8%	60.2%	39.8%
LINCOLN	1,207	781	426		355 R	64.7%	35.3%	64.7%	35.3%
MADISON	2,913	1,932	981		951 R	66.3%	33.7%	66.3%	33.7%
MINIDOKA	2,735	1,629	1,106		523 R	59.6%	40.4%	59.6%	40.4%
NEZ PERCE	4,396	2,840	1,556		1,284 R	64.6%	35.4%	64.6%	35.4%
ONEIDA	2,275	1,519	756		763 R	66.8%	33.2%	66.8%	33.2%
OWYHEE	1,540	1,022	518		504 R	66.4%	33.6%	66.4%	33.6%
PAYETTE	2,515	1,727	788		939 R	68.7%	31.3%	68.7%	31.3%
POWER	1,754	1,188	566		622 R	67.7%	32.3%	67.7%	32.3%
SHOSHONE	4,926	3,194	1,732		1,462 R	64.8%	35.2%	64.8%	35.2%
TETON	1,345	932	413		519 R	69.3%	30.7%	69.3%	30.7%
TWIN FALLS	8,893	6,011	2,882		3,129 R	67.6%	32.4%	67.6%	32.4%
VALLEY	843	519	324		195 R	61.6%	38.4%	61.6%	38.4%
WASHINGTON	3,188	1,920	1,268		652 R	60.2%	39.8%	60.2%	39.8%
TOTAL	138,281	91,351	46,930		44,421 R	66.1%	33.9%	66.1%	33.9%

PRESIDENT 1924

County	Total Vote	Republican	Democratic	Other	Rep.-Dem. Plurality	Total Vote Rep.	Total Vote Dem.	Major Vote Rep.	Major Vote Dem.
ADA	13,189	7,181	2,253	3,755	4,928 R	54.4%	17.1%	76.1%	23.9%
ADAMS	971	419	195	357	224 R	43.2%	20.1%	68.2%	31.8%
BANNOCK	10,027	4,521	1,598	3,908	2,923 R	45.1%	15.9%	73.9%	26.1%
BEAR LAKE	2,956	1,607	873	476	734 R	54.4%	29.5%	64.8%	35.2%
BENEWAH	2,449	1,154	310	985	844 R	47.1%	12.7%	78.8%	21.2%
BINGHAM	5,013	2,683	689	1,641	1,994 R	53.5%	13.7%	79.6%	20.4%
BLAINE	1,780	774	527	479	247 R	43.5%	29.6%	59.5%	40.5%
BOISE	874	379	189	306	190 R	43.4%	21.6%	66.7%	33.3%
BONNER	4,222	1,707	529	1,986	1,178 R	40.4%	12.5%	76.3%	23.7%
BONNEVILLE	5,332	2,865	425	2,042	2,440 R	53.7%	8.0%	87.1%	12.9%
BOUNDARY	1,771	839	240	692	599 R	47.4%	13.6%	77.8%	22.2%
BUTTE	879	404	192	283	212 R	46.0%	21.8%	67.8%	32.2%
CAMAS	625	215	110	300	105 R	34.4%	17.6%	66.2%	33.8%
CANYON	9,943	3,821	964	5,158	2,857 R	38.4%	9.7%	79.9%	20.1%
CARIBOU	855	507	142	207	365 R	59.2%	16.6%	78.1%	21.9%
CASSIA	3,888	2,038	519	1,331	1,519 R	52.4%	13.3%	79.7%	20.3%
CLARK	709	494	43	172	451 R	69.7%	6.1%	92.0%	8.0%
CLEARWATER	1,975	937	318	720	619 R	47.4%	16.1%	74.7%	25.3%
CUSTER	1,256	584	385	287	199 R	46.5%	30.7%	60.3%	39.7%
ELMORE	2,064	785	375	904	410 R	38.0%	18.2%	67.7%	32.3%
FRANKLIN	2,615	1,360	536	719	824 R	52.0%	20.5%	71.7%	28.3%
FREMONT	3,662	1,660	527	1,475	1,133 R	45.3%	14.4%	75.9%	24.1%
GEM	2,583	1,068	376	1,139	692 R	41.3%	14.6%	74.0%	26.0%
GOODING	2,465	1,101	418	946	683 R	44.7%	17.0%	72.5%	27.5%
IDAHO	3,543	1,355	768	1,420	587 R	38.2%	21.7%	63.8%	36.2%
JEFFERSON	2,767	1,391	297	1,079	1,094 R	50.3%	10.7%	82.4%	17.6%
JEROME	2,358	1,107	362	889	745 R	46.9%	15.4%	75.4%	24.6%
KOOTENAI	7,274	3,272	756	3,246	2,516 R	45.0%	10.4%	81.2%	18.8%
LATAH	5,795	3,028	835	1,932	2,193 R	52.3%	14.4%	78.4%	21.6%
LEMHI	1,926	1,096	434	396	662 R	56.9%	22.5%	71.6%	28.4%
LEWIS	1,998	646	590	762	56 R	32.3%	29.5%	52.3%	47.7%
LINCOLN	1,272	690	156	426	534 R	54.2%	12.3%	81.6%	18.4%
MADISON	2,728	1,418	693	617	725 R	52.0%	25.4%	67.2%	32.8%
MINIDOKA	2,612	1,043	198	1,371	845 R	39.9%	7.6%	84.0%	16.0%
NEZ PERCE	5,283	2,244	1,199	1,840	1,045 R	42.5%	22.7%	65.2%	34.8%
ONEIDA	2,149	939	463	747	476 R	43.7%	21.5%	67.0%	33.0%
OWYHEE	1,536	562	305	669	257 R	36.6%	19.9%	64.8%	35.4%
PAYETTE	2,416	1,145	389	882	756 R	47.4%	16.1%	74.6%	25.4%
POWER	1,744	757	307	680	450 R	43.4%	17.6%	71.1%	28.9%
SHOSHONE	5,927	3,035	825	2,067	2,210 R	51.2%	13.9%	78.6%	21.4%
TETON	1,182	664	180	338	484 R	56.2%	15.2%	78.7%	21.3%
TWIN FALLS	9,046	4,637	1,630	2,779	3,007 R	51.3%	18.0%	74.0%	26.0%
VALLEY	1,198	486	214	498	272 R	40.6%	17.9%	69.4%	30.6%
WASHINGTON	2,832	1,173	617	1,042	556 R	41.4%	21.8%	65.5%	34.5%
TOTAL	147,690	69,791	23,951	53,948	45,840 R	47.3%	16.2%	74.5%	25.5%

IDAHO

PRESIDENT 1928

County	Total Vote	Republican	Democratic	Other	Rep.-Dem. Plurality	Total Vote Rep.	Total Vote Dem.	Major Vote Rep.	Major Vote Dem.
ADA	14,308	10,279	3,921	108	6,358 R	71.8%	27.4%	72.4%	27.6%
ADAMS	905	521	374	10	147 R	57.6%	41.3%	58.2%	41.8%
BANNOCK	9,953	5,297	4,602	54	695 R	53.2%	46.2%	53.5%	46.5%
BEAR LAKE	2,955	1,802	1,146	7	656 R	61.0%	38.8%	61.1%	38.9%
BENEWAH	2,338	1,343	958	37	385 R	57.4%	41.0%	58.4%	41.6%
BINGHAM	5,035	3,236	1,778	21	1,458 R	64.3%	35.3%	64.5%	35.5%
BLAINE	1,634	849	780	5	69 R	52.0%	47.7%	52.1%	47.9%
BOISE	919	521	389	9	132 R	56.7%	42.3%	57.3%	42.7%
BONNER	4,524	2,861	1,603	60	1,258 R	63.2%	35.4%	64.1%	35.9%
BONNEVILLE	5,336	3,218	2,110	8	1,108 R	60.3%	39.5%	60.4%	39.6%
BOUNDARY	1,646	1,015	607	24	408 R	61.7%	36.9%	62.6%	37.4%
BUTTE	797	493	301	3	192 R	61.9%	37.8%	62.1%	37.9%
CAMAS	653	413	230	10	183 R	63.2%	35.2%	64.2%	35.8%
CANYON	9,619	7,293	2,187	139	5,106 R	75.8%	22.7%	76.9%	23.1%
CARIBOU	766	471	291	4	180 R	61.5%	38.0%	61.8%	38.2%
CASSIA	3,402	2,388	994	20	1,394 R	70.2%	29.2%	70.6%	29.4%
CLARK	518	388	129	1	259 R	74.9%	24.9%	75.0%	25.0%
CLEARWATER	2,074	1,195	852	27	343 R	57.6%	41.1%	58.4%	41.6%
CUSTER	1,171	647	516	8	131 R	55.3%	44.1%	55.6%	44.4%
ELMORE	1,877	1,125	739	13	386 R	59.9%	39.4%	60.4%	39.6%
FRANKLIN	2,926	1,718	1,193	15	525 R	58.7%	40.8%	59.0%	41.0%
FREMONT	3,619	1,674	1,933	12	259 D	46.3%	53.4%	46.4%	53.6%
GEM	2,332	1,656	646	30	1,010 R	71.0%	27.7%	71.9%	28.1%
GOODING	2,689	1,852	821	16	1,031 R	68.9%	30.5%	69.3%	30.7%
IDAHO	3,812	2,099	1,676	37	423 R	55.1%	44.0%	55.6%	44.4%
JEFFERSON	3,028	1,671	1,350	7	321 R	55.2%	44.6%	55.3%	44.7%
JEROME	2,831	2,050	759	22	1,291 R	72.4%	26.8%	72.9%	27.1%
KOOTENAI	7,114	4,973	2,020	121	2,953 R	69.9%	28.4%	71.1%	28.9%
LATAH	6,225	4,472	1,681	72	2,791 R	71.8%	27.0%	72.7%	27.3%
LEMHI	1,994	1,139	837	18	302 R	57.1%	42.0%	57.6%	42.4%
LEWIS	1,964	1,146	793	25	353 R	58.4%	40.4%	59.1%	40.9%
LINCOLN	1,227	865	358	4	507 R	70.5%	29.2%	70.7%	29.3%
MADISON	2,900	1,670	1,228	2	442 R	57.6%	42.3%	57.7%	42.3%
MINIDOKA	2,996	1,832	1,132	32	700 R	61.1%	37.8%	61.8%	38.2%
NEZ PERCE	6,644	4,054	2,535	55	1,519 R	61.0%	38.2%	61.5%	38.5%
ONEIDA	2,211	1,184	1,020	7	164 R	53.6%	46.1%	53.7%	46.3%
OWYHEE	1,476	918	533	25	385 R	62.2%	36.1%	63.3%	36.7%
PAYETTE	2,890	2,203	621	66	1,582 R	76.2%	21.5%	78.0%	22.0%
POWER	1,508	852	653	3	199 R	56.5%	43.3%	56.6%	43.4%
SHOSHONE	6,117	3,648	2,430	39	1,218 R	59.6%	39.7%	60.0%	40.0%
TETON	1,103	753	348	2	405 R	68.3%	31.6%	68.4%	31.6%
TWIN FALLS	9,338	6,791	2,471	76	4,320 R	72.7%	26.5%	73.3%	26.7%
VALLEY	1,195	774	407	14	367 R	64.8%	34.1%	65.5%	34.5%
WASHINGTON	2,972	1,973	974	25	999 R	66.4%	32.8%	66.9%	33.1%
TOTAL	151,541	97,322	52,926	1,293	44,396 R	64.2%	34.9%	64.8%	35.2%

PRESIDENT 1932

County	Total Vote	Republican	Democratic	Other	Rep.-Dem. Plurality	Total Vote Rep.	Total Vote Dem.	Major Vote Rep.	Major Vote Dem.
ADA	17,529	8,062	8,836	631	774 D	46.0%	50.4%	47.7%	52.3%
ADAMS	1,242	318	854	70	536 D	25.6%	68.8%	27.1%	72.9%
BANNOCK	12,932	4,549	8,271	112	3,722 D	35.2%	64.0%	35.5%	64.5%
BEAR LAKE	3,509	1,785	1,721	64	64 R	50.9%	49.0%	50.9%	49.1%
BENEWAH	2,720	979	1,602	139	623 D	36.0%	58.9%	37.9%	62.1%
BINGHAM	6,810	2,897	3,802	111	905 D	42.5%	55.8%	43.2%	56.8%
BLAINE	1,846	696	1,133	17	437 D	37.7%	61.4%	38.1%	61.9%
BOISE	1,059	342	679	38	337 D	32.3%	64.1%	33.5%	66.5%
BONNER	5,794	1,951	3,695	148	1,744 D	33.7%	63.8%	34.6%	65.4%
BONNEVILLE	7,190	2,759	4,298	133	1,539 D	38.4%	59.8%	39.1%	60.9%
BOUNDARY	2,290	765	1,451	74	686 D	33.4%	63.4%	34.5%	65.5%
BUTTE	981	395	581	5	186 D	40.3%	59.2%	40.5%	59.5%
CAMAS	690	234	441	15	207 D	33.9%	63.9%	34.7%	65.3%
CANYON	13,074	5,085	6,940	1,049	1,855 D	38.9%	53.1%	42.3%	57.7%
CARIBOU	908	397	499	12	102 D	43.7%	55.0%	44.3%	55.7%
CASSIA	4,666	2,025	2,598	43	573 D	43.4%	55.7%	43.8%	56.2%
CLARK	602	276	325	1	49 D	45.8%	54.0%	45.9%	54.1%
CLEARWATER	2,553	822	1,699	32	877 D	32.2%	66.5%	32.6%	67.4%
CUSTER	1,306	443	839	24	396 D	33.9%	64.2%	34.6%	65.4%
ELMORE	2,489	797	1,615	77	818 D	32.0%	64.9%	33.0%	67.0%
FRANKLIN	3,637	1,760	1,871	6	111 D	48.4%	51.4%	48.5%	51.5%
FREMONT	4,340	1,509	2,830	1	1,321 D	34.8%	65.2%	34.8%	65.2%
GEM	3,261	898	2,007	356	1,109 D	27.5%	61.5%	30.9%	69.1%
GOODING	3,540	1,451	1,911	178	460 D	41.0%	54.0%	43.2%	56.8%
IDAHO	4,196	1,089	3,005	102	1,916 D	26.0%	71.6%	26.6%	73.4%
JEFFERSON	3,729	1,174	2,501	54	1,327 D	31.5%	67.1%	31.9%	68.1%
JEROME	3,682	1,396	2,219	67	823 D	37.9%	60.3%	38.6%	61.4%
KOOTENAI	8,269	2,820	4,743	706	1,923 D	34.1%	57.4%	37.3%	62.7%
LATAH	6,763	3,091	3,554	118	463 D	45.7%	52.6%	46.5%	53.5%
LEMHI	2,167	793	1,332	42	539 D	36.6%	61.5%	37.3%	62.7%
LEWIS	1,957	526	1,390	41	864 D	26.9%	71.0%	27.5%	72.5%
LINCOLN	1,589	692	869	28	177 D	43.5%	54.7%	44.3%	55.7%
MADISON	3,400	1,265	2,112	23	847 D	37.2%	62.1%	37.5%	62.5%
MINIDOKA	3,363	1,126	2,164	73	1,038 D	33.5%	64.3%	34.2%	65.8%
NEZ PERCE	7,416	2,215	5,077	124	2,862 D	29.9%	68.5%	30.4%	69.6%
ONEIDA	2,512	1,045	1,449	18	404 D	41.6%	57.7%	41.9%	58.1%
OWYHEE	1,614	587	959	68	372 D	36.4%	59.4%	38.0%	62.0%
PAYETTE	3,596	1,538	1,836	222	298 D	42.8%	51.1%	45.6%	54.4%
POWER	1,726	593	1,126	7	533 D	34.4%	65.1%	34.5%	65.5%
SHOSHONE	7,354	2,907	4,347	100	1,440 D	39.5%	59.1%	40.1%	59.9%
TETON	1,539	672	860	7	188 D	43.7%	55.9%	43.9%	56.1%
TWIN FALLS	11,717	4,926	6,395	396	1,469 D	42.0%	54.6%	43.5%	55.5%
VALLEY	1,460	447	921	92	474 D	30.6%	63.1%	32.5%	67.5%
WASHINGTON	3,503	1,215	2,122	166	907 D	34.7%	60.6%	36.4%	63.6%
TOTAL	186,520	71,312	109,479	5,729	38,167 D	38.2%	58.7%	39.4%	60.6%

IDAHO

PRESIDENT 1936

County	Total Vote	Republican	Democratic	Other	Rep.-Dem. Plurality	Total Vote Rep.	Total Vote Dem.	Major Vote Rep.	Major Vote Dem.
ADA	20,574	7,581	12,027	966	4,446 D	36.8%	58.5%	38.7%	61.3%
ADAMS	1,296	434	770	92	336 D	33.5%	59.4%	36.0%	64.0%
BANNOCK	13,393	3,830	9,443	120	5,613 D	28.6%	70.5%	28.9%	71.1%
BEAR LAKE	3,486	1,404	2,078	4	674 D	40.3%	59.6%	40.3%	59.7%
BENEWAH	2,901	897	1,906	98	1,009 D	31.9%	65.7%	32.0%	68.0%
BINGHAM	6,753	2,354	4,215	184	1,861 D	34.9%	62.4%	35.8%	64.2%
BLAINE	2,107	735	1,361	11	626 D	34.9%	64.6%	35.1%	64.9%
BOISE	1,190	368	780	42	412 D	31.9%	65.5%	32.1%	67.9%
BONNER	5,993	2,016	3,521	456	1,505 D	33.6%	58.8%	36.4%	63.6%
BONNEVILLE	7,787	2,213	5,439	135	3,226 D	28.4%	69.8%	28.9%	71.1%
BOUNDARY	2,162	732	1,304	126	572 D	33.9%	60.3%	36.0%	64.0%
BUTTE	869	312	546	11	234 D	35.9%	62.8%	36.4%	63.6%
CAMAS	731	274	442	15	168 D	37.5%	60.5%	38.3%	61.6%
CANYON	14,547	4,910	8,290	1,347	3,380 D	33.8%	57.0%	37.2%	62.8%
CARIBOU	962	321	640	1	319 D	33.4%	66.5%	33.4%	66.6%
CASSIA	4,797	1,629	3,100	68	1,471 D	34.0%	64.6%	34.4%	65.6%
CLARK	580	304	272	4	32 R	52.4%	46.9%	52.8%	47.2%
CLEARWATER	2,926	812	1,959	155	1,147 D	27.8%	67.0%	29.3%	70.7%
CUSTER	1,421	530	875	16	345 D	37.3%	61.6%	37.7%	62.3%
ELMORE	2,380	688	1,567	125	879 D	28.9%	65.8%	30.5%	69.5%
FRANKLIN	3,670	1,396	2,255	19	859 D	38.0%	61.4%	38.2%	61.8%
FREMONT	4,366	1,423	2,904	39	1,481 D	32.6%	66.5%	32.9%	67.1%
GEM	3,568	879	2,468	221	1,589 D	24.6%	69.2%	26.3%	73.7%
GOODING	3,705	1,505	2,100	100	595 D	40.6%	56.7%	41.7%	58.3%
IDAHO	4,929	1,535	3,104	290	1,569 D	31.1%	63.0%	33.4%	66.6%
JEFFERSON	3,864	1,037	2,776	51	1,739 D	26.8%	71.8%	27.2%	72.8%
JEROME	3,778	1,297	2,374	107	1,077 D	34.3%	62.8%	35.3%	64.7%
KOOTENAI	8,999	2,586	5,752	661	3,166 D	28.7%	63.9%	31.0%	69.0%
LATAH	7,458	2,838	4,359	261	1,521 D	38.1%	58.4%	39.4%	60.6%
LEMHI	2,666	943	1,648	75	705 D	35.4%	61.8%	36.4%	63.6%
LEWIS	2,168	507	1,612	49	1,105 D	23.4%	74.4%	23.9%	76.1%
LINCOLN	1,721	766	916	39	150 D	44.5%	53.2%	45.5%	54.5%
MADISON	3,592	1,114	2,455	23	1,341 D	31.0%	68.3%	31.2%	68.8%
MINIDOKA	3,097	948	2,095	54	1,147 D	30.6%	67.6%	31.2%	68.8%
NEZ PERCE	7,985	1,988	5,705	292	3,717 D	24.9%	71.4%	25.8%	74.2%
ONEIDA	2,638	955	1,673	10	718 D	36.2%	63.4%	36.3%	63.7%
OWYHEE	1,728	500	1,106	122	506 D	28.9%	64.0%	31.1%	68.9%
PAYETTE	3,663	1,524	1,677	462	153 D	41.6%	45.8%	47.6%	52.4%
POWER	1,812	708	1,075	29	367 D	39.1%	59.3%	39.7%	60.3%
SHOSHONE	7,582	2,146	5,377	59	3,231 D	28.3%	70.9%	28.5%	71.5%
TETON	1,409	542	834	33	292 D	38.5%	59.2%	39.4%	60.6%
TWIN FALLS	12,828	4,966	7,476	386	2,510 D	38.7%	58.3%	39.9%	60.1%
VALLEY	1,980	575	1,260	145	685 D	29.0%	63.6%	31.3%	68.7%
WASHINGTON	3,556	1,234	2,147	175	913 D	34.7%	61.4%	35.5%	63.5%
TOTAL	199,617	66,256	125,683	7,678	59,427 D	33.2%	63.0%	34.5%	65.5%

PRESIDENT 1940

County	Total Vote	Republican	Democratic	Other	Rep.-Dem. Plurality	Total Vote Rep.	Total Vote Dem.	Major Vote Rep.	Major Vote Dem.
ADA	25,293	12,861	12,381	51	480 R	50.8%	49.0%	51.0%	49.0%
ADAMS	1,711	779	929	3	150 D	45.5%	54.3%	45.6%	54.4%
BANNOCK	15,913	5,419	10,493	1	5,074 D	34.1%	65.9%	34.1%	65.9%
BEAR LAKE	3,787	1,761	2,026		265 D	46.5%	53.5%	46.5%	53.5%
BENEWAH	3,250	1,304	1,924	22	620 D	40.1%	59.2%	40.4%	59.6%
BINGHAM	7,488	3,662	3,815	11	153 D	48.9%	50.9%	49.0%	51.0%
BLAINE	2,687	1,124	1,559	4	435 D	41.8%	58.0%	41.9%	58.1%
BOISE	1,167	489	677	1	188 D	41.9%	58.0%	41.9%	58.1%
BONNER	6,940	3,072	3,834	34	762 D	44.3%	55.2%	44.5%	55.5%
BONNEVILLE	9,900	3,999	5,891	10	1,892 D	40.4%	59.5%	40.4%	59.6%
BOUNDARY	2,684	1,221	1,393	70	172 D	45.5%	51.9%	46.7%	53.3%
BUTTE	871	423	448		25 D	48.6%	51.4%	48.6%	51.4%
CAMAS	743	367	381		14 D	49.1%	50.9%	49.1%	50.9%
CANYON	17,473	8,776	8,639	63	137 R	50.2%	49.4%	50.4%	49.6%
CARIBOU	1,049	390	658	1	268 D	37.2%	62.7%	37.2%	62.8%
CASSIA	5,689	2,748	2,930	11	182 D	48.3%	51.5%	48.4%	51.6%
CLARK	611	399	212		187 R	65.3%	34.7%	65.3%	34.7%
CLEARWATER	3,429	1,128	2,284	17	1,156 D	32.9%	66.6%	33.1%	66.9%
CUSTER	1,659	760	894	5	134 D	45.8%	53.9%	45.9%	54.1%
ELMORE	2,713	1,077	1,632	4	555 D	39.7%	60.2%	39.8%	60.2%
FRANKLIN	4,227	2,069	2,158		89 D	48.9%	51.1%	48.9%	51.1%
FREMONT	4,554	1,996	2,556	2	560 D	43.8%	56.1%	43.8%	56.2%
GEM	4,132	1,462	2,666	4	1,204 D	35.4%	64.5%	35.4%	64.6%
GOODING	4,275	1,919	2,352	4	433 D	44.9%	55.0%	45.1%	54.9%
IDAHO	5,545	2,641	2,888	16	247 D	47.6%	52.1%	47.8%	52.2%
JEFFERSON	4,364	1,717	2,631	16	914 D	39.3%	60.3%	39.5%	60.5%
JEROME	4,408	2,520	1,881	7	639 R	57.2%	42.7%	57.3%	42.7%
KOOTENAI	10,462	4,333	5,997	132	1,664 D	41.4%	57.3%	41.9%	58.1%
LATAH	8,500	3,971	4,494	35	523 D	46.7%	52.9%	46.9%	53.1%
LEMHI	3,077	1,412	1,664	1	252 D	45.9%	54.1%	45.9%	54.1%
LEWIS	2,198	729	1,462	7	733 D	33.2%	66.5%	33.3%	66.7%
LINCOLN	1,902	1,009	886	7	123 R	53.0%	46.6%	53.2%	46.8%
MADISON	3,851	1,632	2,218	1	586 D	42.4%	57.6%	42.4%	57.6%
MINIDOKA	3,974	1,979	1,982	13	3 D	49.8%	49.9%	50.0%	50.0%
NEZ PERCE	9,413	3,409	5,963	41	2,554 D	36.2%	63.3%	36.4%	63.6%
ONEIDA	2,584	1,140	1,440	4	300 D	44.1%	55.8%	44.2%	55.8%
OWYHEE	2,205	1,031	1,160	14	129 D	46.8%	52.6%	47.1%	52.9%
PAYETTE	4,364	2,554	1,790	20	764 R	58.5%	41.0%	58.8%	41.2%
POWER	1,885	951	931	3	20 R	50.5%	49.4%	50.5%	49.5%
SHOSHONE	10,172	3,525	6,565	82	3,040 D	34.7%	64.5%	34.9%	65.1%
TETON	1,511	667	844		177 D	44.1%	55.9%	44.1%	55.9%
TWIN FALLS	16,351	9,031	7,286	34	1,745 R	55.2%	44.6%	55.3%	44.7%
VALLEY	1,943	761	1,165	17	404 D	39.2%	60.0%	39.5%	60.5%
WASHINGTON	4,204	1,903	2,296	5	393 D	45.3%	54.6%	45.3%	54.7%
TOTAL	235,168	106,553	127,842	773	21,289 D	45.3%	54.4%	45.5%	54.5%

IDAHO

PRESIDENT 1944

County	Total Vote	Republican	Democratic	Other	Rep.-Dem. Plurality	Total Vote Rep.	Total Vote Dem.	Major Vote Rep.	Major Vote Dem.
ADA	24,144	13,410	10,667	67	2,743 R	55.5%	44.2%	55.7%	44.3%
ADAMS	1,364	642	721	1	79 D	47.1%	52.9%	47.1%	52.9%
BANNOCK	15,105	5,413	9,681	11	4,268 D	35.8%	64.1%	35.9%	64.1%
BEAR LAKE	3,347	1,613	1,732	2	119 D	48.2%	51.7%	48.2%	51.8%
BENEWAH	2,643	1,173	1,446	24	273 D	44.4%	54.7%	44.8%	55.2%
BINGHAM	6,658	3,223	3,428	7	205 D	48.4%	51.5%	48.5%	51.5%
BLAINE	1,916	874	1,037	5	163 D	45.6%	54.1%	45.7%	54.3%
BOISE	1,031	464	564	3	100 D	45.0%	54.7%	45.1%	54.9%
BONNER	6,063	2,924	3,116	23	192 D	48.2%	51.4%	48.4%	51.6%
BONNEVILLE	8,999	4,048	4,935	16	887 D	45.0%	54.8%	45.1%	54.9%
BOUNDARY	2,160	1,064	1,053	43	11 R	49.3%	48.8%	50.3%	49.7%
BUTTE	849	431	416	2	15 R	50.8%	49.0%	50.9%	49.1%
CAMAS	618	301	317		16 D	48.7%	51.3%	48.7%	51.3%
CANYON	16,762	9,215	7,306	241	1,909 R	55.0%	43.6%	55.8%	44.2%
CARIBOU	978	462	516		54 D	47.2%	52.8%	47.2%	52.8%
CASSIA	4,896	2,563	2,325	8	238 R	52.3%	47.5%	52.4%	47.6%
CLARK	499	317	180	2	137 R	63.5%	36.1%	63.8%	36.2%
CLEARWATER	2,626	865	1,744	17	879 D	32.9%	66.4%	33.2%	66.8%
CUSTER	1,178	565	613		48 D	48.0%	52.0%	48.0%	52.0%
ELMORE	2,667	1,030	1,627	10	597 D	38.6%	61.0%	38.8%	61.2%
FRANKLIN	3,925	1,950	1,971	4	21 D	49.7%	50.2%	49.7%	50.3%
FREMONT	3,871	1,755	2,116	36	361 D	45.3%	54.7%	45.3%	54.7%
GEM	3,265	1,363	1,866	8	503 D	41.7%	57.2%	41.9%	58.1%
GOODING	3,716	2,049	1,659	8	390 R	55.1%	44.6%	55.3%	44.7%
IDAHO	4,063	1,977	2,071	15	94 D	48.7%	51.0%	48.8%	51.2%
JEFFERSON	3,665	1,458	2,198	9	740 D	39.8%	60.0%	39.9%	60.1%
JEROME	3,898	2,157	1,741		416 R	55.3%	44.7%	55.3%	44.7%
KOOTENAI	10,222	4,388	5,792	42	1,404 D	42.9%	56.7%	43.1%	56.9%
LATAH	7,083	3,526	3,514	43	12 R	49.8%	49.6%	50.1%	49.9%
LEMHI	2,040	1,048	988	4	60 R	51.4%	48.4%	51.5%	48.5%
LEWIS	1,811	589	1,222		633 D	32.5%	67.5%	32.5%	67.5%
LINCOLN	1,720	934	784	2	150 R	54.3%	45.6%	54.4%	45.6%
MADISON	3,458	1,527	1,927	4	400 D	44.2%	55.8%	44.2%	55.8%
MINIDOKA	3,424	1,781	1,635	8	146 R	52.0%	47.8%	52.1%	47.9%
NEZ PERCE	8,649	3,159	5,453	37	2,294 D	36.5%	63.0%	36.7%	63.3%
ONEIDA	2,163	935	1,227	1	292 D	43.2%	56.7%	43.2%	56.8%
OWYHEE	1,819	983	824	12	159 R	54.0%	45.3%	54.4%	45.6%
PAYETTE	3,885	2,485	1,382	18	1,103 R	64.0%	35.5%	64.3%	35.7%
POWER	1,696	895	801		94 R	52.8%	47.2%	52.8%	47.2%
SHOSHONE	8,463	3,162	5,290	11	2,128 D	37.4%	62.5%	37.4%	62.6%
TETON	1,193	552	641		89 D	46.3%	53.7%	46.3%	53.7%
TWIN FALLS	14,116	7,946	6,128	42	1,818 R	56.3%	43.4%	56.5%	43.5%
VALLEY	1,819	919	896	4	23 R	50.5%	49.3%	50.6%	49.4%
WASHINGTON	3,854	2,002	1,849	3	153 R	51.9%	48.0%	52.0%	48.0%
TOTAL	208,321	100,137	107,399	785	7,262 D	48.1%	51.6%	48.3%	51.7%

PRESIDENT 1948

County	Total Vote	Republican	Democratic	Other	Rep.-Dem. Plurality	Total Vote Rep.	Total Vote Dem.	Major Vote Rep.	Major Vote Dem.
ADA	26,705	14,972	11,253	480	3,719 R	56.1%	42.1%	57.1%	42.9%
ADAMS	1,274	603	647	24	44 D	47.3%	50.8%	48.2%	51.8%
BANNOCK	15,560	5,580	9,679	301	4,099 D	35.9%	62.2%	36.6%	63.4%
BEAR LAKE	3,280	1,590	1,664	26	74 D	48.5%	50.7%	48.9%	51.1%
BENEWAH	2,731	1,038	1,590	103	552 D	38.0%	58.2%	39.5%	60.5%
BINGHAM	6,448	3,162	3,197	89	35 D	49.0%	49.6%	49.7%	50.3%
BLAINE	2,152	945	1,182	35	237 D	43.7%	54.7%	44.4%	55.6%
BOISE	940	437	479	24	42 D	46.5%	51.0%	47.7%	52.3%
BONNER	5,867	2,666	2,916	285	250 D	45.4%	49.7%	47.8%	52.2%
BONNEVILLE	10,001	4,499	5,382	120	883 D	45.0%	53.8%	45.5%	54.5%
BOUNDARY	2,099	910	1,029	160	119 D	43.4%	49.0%	46.9%	53.1%
BUTTE	846	412	426	8	14 D	48.7%	50.4%	49.2%	50.8%
CAMAS	575	289	278	8	11 R	50.3%	48.3%	51.0%	49.0%
CANYON	18,363	9,700	7,903	760	1,797 R	52.8%	43.0%	55.1%	44.9%
CARIBOU	930	447	475	8	28 D	48.1%	51.1%	48.5%	51.5%
CASSIA	4,671	2,424	2,178	69	246 R	51.9%	46.6%	52.7%	47.3%
CLARK	432	262	165	5	97 R	60.6%	38.2%	61.4%	38.6%
CLEARWATER	2,549	820	1,571	158	751 D	32.2%	61.6%	34.3%	65.7%
CUSTER	1,257	612	625	20	13 D	48.7%	49.7%	49.5%	50.5%
ELMORE	2,503	854	1,589	60	735 D	34.1%	63.5%	35.0%	65.0%
FRANKLIN	3,813	2,028	1,763	22	265 R	53.2%	46.2%	53.5%	46.5%
FREMONT	3,811	1,777	2,014	20	237 D	46.6%	52.8%	46.9%	53.1%
GEM	3,426	1,585	1,724	117	139 D	46.3%	50.3%	47.9%	52.1%
GOODING	4,015	2,111	1,844	60	267 R	52.6%	45.9%	53.4%	46.6%
IDAHO	4,218	1,790	2,300	128	510 D	42.4%	54.5%	43.8%	56.2%
JEFFERSON	3,568	1,490	2,017	61	527 D	41.8%	56.5%	42.5%	57.5%
JEROME	4,305	2,128	2,124	53	4 R	49.4%	49.3%	50.0%	50.0%
KOOTENAI	10,262	4,265	5,284	713	1,019 D	41.6%	51.5%	44.7%	55.3%
LATAH	7,889	3,805	3,810	274	5 D	48.2%	48.3%	50.0%	50.0%
LEMHI	1,938	1,037	864	37	173 R	53.5%	44.6%	54.6%	45.4%
LEWIS	1,763	487	1,224	52	737 D	27.6%	69.4%	28.5%	71.5%
LINCOLN	1,617	851	748	18	103 R	52.6%	46.3%	53.2%	46.8%
MADISON	3,647	1,602	2,024	21	422 D	43.9%	55.5%	44.2%	55.8%
MINIDOKA	3,432	1,654	1,668	110	14 D	48.2%	48.6%	49.8%	50.2%
NEZ PERCE	9,322	3,168	5,747	407	2,579 D	34.0%	61.6%	35.5%	64.5%
ONEIDA	1,982	962	1,008	12	46 D	48.5%	50.9%	48.8%	51.2%
OWYHEE	1,937	969	925	43	44 R	50.0%	47.8%	51.2%	48.8%
PAYETTE	4,081	2,430	1,568	83	862 R	59.5%	38.4%	60.5%	39.2%
POWER	1,681	875	795	11	80 R	52.1%	47.3%	52.4%	47.6%
SHOSHONE	8,261	3,200	4,472	589	1,272 D	38.7%	54.1%	41.7%	58.3%
TETON	1,272	593	672	7	79 D	46.6%	52.8%	46.9%	53.1%
TWIN FALLS	14,061	7,833	6,019	209	1,814 R	55.7%	42.8%	56.5%	43.5%
VALLEY	1,841	939	828	74	111 R	51.0%	45.0%	53.1%	46.9%
WASHINGTON	3,481	1,713	1,700	68	13 R	49.2%	48.8%	50.2%	49.8%
TOTAL	214,816	101,514	107,370	5,932	5,856 D	47.3%	50.0%	48.6%	51.4%

IDAHO

PRESIDENT 1952

County	Total Vote	Republican	Democratic	Other	Rep.-Dem. Plurality	Total Vote Rep. %	Total Vote Dem. %	Major Vote Rep. %	Major Vote Dem. %
ADA	37,736	27,415	10,281	40	17,134 R	72.5%	27.2%	72.7%	27.3%
ADAMS	1,452	933	517	2	416 R	64.3%	35.6%	64.3%	35.7%
BANNOCK	19,662	10,864	8,771	27	2,093 R	55.3%	44.6%	55.3%	44.7%
BEAR LAKE	3,574	2,300	1,274	—	1,026 R	64.4%	35.6%	64.4%	35.6%
BENEWAH	3,011	1,568	1,436	7	132 R	52.1%	47.7%	52.2%	47.8%
BINGHAM	9,143	6,114	3,024	5	3,090 R	66.9%	33.1%	66.9%	33.1%
BLAINE	2,642	1,609	1,033	—	576 R	60.9%	39.1%	60.9%	39.1%
BOISE	970	655	309	6	346 R	67.5%	31.9%	67.9%	32.1%
BONNER	7,645	4,309	3,293	43	1,016 R	56.4%	43.1%	56.7%	43.3%
BONNEVILLE	14,993	10,252	4,737	4	5,515 R	68.4%	31.6%	68.4%	31.6%
BOUNDARY	2,691	1,641	1,040	10	601 R	61.0%	38.6%	61.2%	38.8%
BUTTE	1,389	916	473	—	443 R	65.9%	34.1%	65.9%	34.1%
CAMAS	650	425	224	1	201 R	65.5%	34.4%	65.5%	34.5%
CANYON	23,942	17,065	6,810	67	10,255 R	71.3%	28.4%	71.5%	28.5%
CARIBOU	2,598	1,788	809	1	979 R	68.8%	31.1%	68.8%	31.2%
CASSIA	6,159	4,481	1,676	2	2,805 R	72.8%	27.2%	72.8%	27.2%
CLARK	508	382	126	—	256 R	75.2%	24.8%	75.2%	24.8%
CLEARWATER	3,327	1,494	1,826	7	332 D	44.9%	54.9%	45.0%	55.0%
CUSTER	1,517	1,058	452	7	606 R	69.7%	29.8%	70.1%	29.9%
ELMORE	3,143	1,653	1,484	6	169 R	52.6%	47.2%	52.7%	47.3%
FRANKLIN	4,436	3,252	1,181	3	2,071 R	73.3%	26.6%	73.4%	26.6%
FREMONT	4,213	2,710	1,500	3	1,210 R	64.3%	35.6%	64.3%	35.7%
GEM	4,128	2,568	1,555	5	1,013 R	62.2%	37.7%	62.3%	37.7%
GOODING	4,860	3,452	1,404	4	2,048 R	71.0%	28.9%	71.1%	28.9%
IDAHO	5,330	3,054	2,269	7	785 R	57.3%	42.6%	57.4%	42.6%
JEFFERSON	4,446	2,970	1,474	2	1,496 R	66.8%	33.2%	66.8%	33.2%
JEROME	5,130	3,807	1,318	5	2,489 R	74.2%	25.7%	74.3%	25.7%
KOOTENAI	12,774	7,272	5,414	88	1,858 R	56.9%	42.4%	57.3%	42.7%
LATAH	8,702	5,440	3,254	8	2,186 R	62.5%	37.4%	62.6%	37.4%
LEMHI	2,950	2,100	848	2	1,252 R	71.2%	28.7%	71.2%	28.8%
LEWIS	2,280	1,004	1,276	—	272 D	44.0%	56.0%	44.0%	56.0%
LINCOLN	1,945	1,383	562	—	821 R	71.1%	28.9%	71.1%	28.9%
MADISON	4,106	2,756	1,348	2	1,408 R	67.1%	32.8%	67.2%	32.8%
MINIDOKA	4,381	3,128	1,253	—	1,875 R	71.4%	28.6%	71.4%	28.5%
NEZ PERCE	11,231	5,659	5,552	20	107 R	50.4%	49.4%	50.5%	49.5%
ONEIDA	2,287	1,547	739	1	808 R	67.6%	32.3%	67.7%	32.3%
OWYHEE	2,575	1,813	759	3	1,054 R	70.4%	29.5%	70.5%	29.5%
PAYETTE	5,439	3,936	1,491	12	2,445 R	72.4%	27.4%	72.5%	27.5%
POWER	1,911	1,308	603	—	705 R	68.4%	31.5%	68.4%	31.6%
SHOSHONE	9,862	5,119	4,684	59	435 R	51.9%	47.5%	52.2%	47.8%
TETON	1,455	964	491	—	473 R	66.3%	33.7%	66.3%	33.7%
TWIN FALLS	19,023	14,471	4,548	4	9,923 R	76.1%	23.9%	76.1%	23.9%
VALLEY	2,008	1,456	552	—	904 R	72.5%	27.5%	72.5%	27.5%
WASHINGTON	4,030	2,616	1,411	3	1,205 R	64.9%	35.0%	65.0%	35.0%
TOTAL	276,254	180,707	95,081	466	85,626 R	65.4%	34.4%	65.5%	34.5%

PRESIDENT 1956

County	Total Vote	Republican	Democratic	Other	Rep.-Dem. Plurality	Total Vote Rep. %	Total Vote Dem. %	Major Vote Rep. %	Major Vote Dem. %
ADA	37,750	26,387	11,328	35	15,059 R	69.9%	30.0%	70.0%	30.0%
ADAMS	1,584	842	542	—	300 R	60.8%	39.2%	60.8%	39.2%
BANNOCK	19,584	10,476	9,101	7	1,375 R	53.5%	46.5%	53.5%	46.5%
BEAR LAKE	3,399	2,181	1,218	—	963 R	64.2%	35.8%	64.2%	35.8%
BENEWAH	2,903	1,460	1,442	1	18 R	50.3%	49.7%	50.3%	49.7%
BINGHAM	9,265	5,853	3,412	—	2,441 R	63.2%	36.8%	63.2%	36.8%
BLAINE	2,367	1,384	978	5	406 R	58.5%	41.3%	58.6%	41.4%
BOISE	855	570	285	—	285 R	66.7%	33.3%	66.7%	33.3%
BONNER	7,464	3,937	3,514	13	423 R	52.7%	47.1%	52.8%	47.2%
BONNEVILLE	16,778	11,099	5,676	3	5,423 R	66.2%	33.8%	66.2%	33.8%
BOUNDARY	2,571	1,419	1,150	2	269 R	55.2%	44.7%	55.2%	44.8%
BUTTE	1,443	774	669	—	105 R	53.6%	46.4%	53.6%	46.4%
CAMAS	603	337	266	—	71 R	55.9%	44.1%	55.9%	44.1%
CANYON	23,052	15,483	7,540	29	7,943 R	67.2%	32.7%	67.3%	32.7%
CARIBOU	2,618	1,668	950	—	718 R	63.7%	36.3%	63.7%	36.3%
CASSIA	5,733	3,944	1,789	—	2,155 R	68.8%	31.2%	68.8%	31.2%
CLARK	469	318	151	—	167 R	67.8%	32.2%	67.8%	32.2%
CLEARWATER	3,532	1,508	2,024	—	516 D	42.7%	57.3%	42.7%	57.3%
CUSTER	1,344	811	533	—	278 R	60.3%	39.7%	60.3%	39.7%
ELMORE	3,609	1,849	1,759	1	90 R	51.2%	48.7%	51.2%	48.8%
FRANKLIN	3,976	2,795	1,181	—	1,614 R	70.3%	29.7%	70.3%	29.7%
FREMONT	4,048	2,513	1,535	—	978 R	62.1%	37.9%	62.1%	37.9%
GEM	4,164	2,445	1,717	2	728 R	58.7%	41.2%	58.7%	41.3%
GOODING	4,620	2,835	1,783	2	1,052 R	61.4%	38.6%	61.4%	38.6%
IDAHO	5,263	2,703	2,546	14	157 R	51.2%	48.4%	51.5%	48.5%
JEFFERSON	4,571	2,748	1,823	—	925 R	60.1%	39.9%	60.1%	39.9%
JEROME	4,832	3,127	1,705	—	1,422 R	64.7%	35.3%	64.7%	35.3%
KOOTENAI	13,502	7,330	6,149	23	1,181 R	54.3%	45.5%	54.4%	45.6%
LATAH	8,706	5,024	3,682	—	1,342 R	57.7%	42.3%	57.7%	42.3%
LEMHI	2,832	1,794	1,038	—	756 R	63.3%	36.7%	63.3%	36.7%
LEWIS	2,125	833	1,292	—	459 D	39.2%	60.8%	39.2%	60.8%
LINCOLN	1,729	1,069	660	—	409 R	61.8%	38.2%	61.8%	38.2%
MADISON	3,961	2,538	1,423	—	1,115 R	64.1%	35.9%	64.1%	35.9%
MINIDOKA	4,646	2,954	1,692	—	1,262 R	63.6%	36.4%	63.6%	36.4%
NEZ PERCE	12,083	5,635	6,448	—	813 D	46.6%	53.4%	46.6%	53.4%
ONEIDA	2,062	1,324	738	—	586 R	64.2%	35.8%	64.2%	35.8%
OWYHEE	2,332	1,468	864	—	604 R	63.0%	37.0%	63.0%	37.0%
PAYETTE	5,114	3,342	1,767	5	1,575 R	65.4%	34.6%	65.4%	34.6%
POWER	1,877	1,108	769	—	339 R	59.0%	41.0%	59.0%	41.0%
SHOSHONE	9,046	4,598	4,448	—	150 R	50.8%	49.2%	50.8%	49.2%
TETON	1,293	842	451	—	391 R	65.1%	34.9%	65.1%	34.9%
TWIN FALLS	17,763	12,097	5,666	—	6,431 R	68.1%	31.9%	68.1%	31.9%
VALLEY	1,796	1,285	511	—	774 R	71.5%	28.5%	71.5%	28.5%
WASHINGTON	3,925	2,272	1,653	—	619 R	57.9%	42.1%	57.9%	42.1%
TOTAL	272,989	166,979	105,868	142	61,111 R	61.2%	38.8%	61.2%	38.8%

IDAHO

PRESIDENT 1960

County	Total Vote	Republican	Democratic	Other	Rep.-Dem. Plurality	Total Vote Rep.	Total Vote Dem.	Major Vote Rep.	Major Vote Dem.
ADA	44,720	27,703	17,017		10,686 R	61.9%	38.1%	61.9%	38.1%
ADAMS	1,523	799	724		75 R	52.5%	47.5%	52.5%	47.5%
BANNOCK	21,743	9,157	12,586		3,429 D	42.1%	57.9%	42.1%	57.9%
BEAR LAKE	3,526	1,963	1,563		400 R	55.7%	44.3%	55.7%	44.3%
BENEWAH	3,030	1,274	1,756		482 D	42.0%	58.0%	42.0%	58.0%
BINGHAM	10,777	5,934	4,843		1,091 R	55.1%	44.9%	55.1%	44.9%
BLAINE	2,468	1,216	1,252		36 D	49.3%	50.7%	49.3%	50.7%
BOISE	888	456	432		24 R	51.4%	48.6%	51.4%	48.6%
BONNER	7,639	3,575	4,064		489 D	46.8%	53.2%	46.8%	53.2%
BONNEVILLE	19,956	11,111	8,845		2,266 R	55.7%	44.3%	55.7%	44.3%
BOUNDARY	2,738	1,237	1,501		264 D	45.2%	54.8%	45.2%	54.8%
BUTTE	1,681	680	1,001		321 D	40.5%	59.5%	40.5%	59.5%
CAMAS	606	284	322		38 D	46.9%	53.1%	46.9%	53.1%
CANYON	25,546	15,865	9,681		6,184 R	62.1%	37.9%	62.1%	37.9%
CARIBOU	2,837	1,544	1,293		251 R	54.4%	45.6%	54.4%	45.6%
CASSIA	6,742	4,297	2,445		1,852 R	63.7%	36.3%	63.7%	36.3%
CLARK	459	283	176		107 R	61.7%	38.3%	61.7%	38.3%
CLEARWATER	3,600	1,193	2,407		1,214 D	33.1%	66.9%	33.1%	66.9%
CUSTER	1,489	651	838		187 D	43.7%	56.3%	43.7%	56.3%
ELMORE	4,666	2,226	2,440		214 D	47.7%	52.3%	47.7%	52.3%
FRANKLIN	3,985	2,633	1,352		1,281 R	66.1%	33.9%	66.1%	33.9%
FREMONT	4,117	2,230	1,887		343 R	54.2%	45.8%	54.2%	45.8%
GEM	4,404	2,428	1,976		452 R	55.1%	44.9%	55.1%	44.9%
GOODING	4,528	2,523	2,005		518 R	55.7%	44.3%	55.7%	44.3%
IDAHO	5,504	2,248	3,256		1,008 D	40.8%	59.2%	40.8%	59.2%
JEFFERSON	4,999	2,625	2,374		251 R	52.5%	47.5%	52.5%	47.5%
JEROME	5,182	3,031	2,151		880 R	58.5%	41.5%	58.5%	41.5%
KOOTENAI	14,448	6,704	7,744		1,040 D	46.4%	53.6%	46.4%	53.6%
LATAH	9,425	4,789	4,636		153 R	50.8%	49.2%	50.8%	49.2%
LEMHI	2,638	1,355	1,283		72 R	51.4%	48.6%	51.4%	48.6%
LEWIS	2,213	781	1,432		651 D	35.3%	64.7%	35.3%	64.7%
LINCOLN	1,753	970	783		187 R	55.3%	44.7%	55.3%	44.7%
MADISON	4,052	2,374	1,678		696 R	58.6%	41.4%	58.6%	41.4%
MINIDOKA	5,827	3,360	2,467		893 R	57.7%	42.3%	57.7%	42.3%
NEZ PERCE	13,147	5,203	7,944		2,741 D	39.6%	60.4%	39.6%	60.4%
ONEIDA	1,910	1,111	799		312 R	58.2%	41.8%	58.2%	41.8%
OWYHEE	2,629	1,500	1,129		371 R	57.1%	42.9%	57.1%	42.9%
PAYETTE	5,605	3,472	2,133		1,339 R	61.9%	38.1%	61.9%	38.1%
POWER	2,025	1,065	960		105 R	52.6%	47.4%	52.6%	47.4%
SHOSHONE	8,433	3,432	5,001		1,569 D	40.7%	59.3%	40.7%	59.3%
TETON	1,283	714	569		145 R	55.7%	44.3%	55.7%	44.3%
TWIN FALLS	19,584	12,171	7,413		4,758 R	62.1%	37.9%	62.1%	37.9%
VALLEY	2,095	1,179	916		263 R	56.3%	43.7%	56.3%	43.7%
WASHINGTON	4,030	2,251	1,779		472 R	55.9%	44.1%	55.9%	44.1%
TOTAL	300,450	161,597	138,853		22,744 R	53.8%	46.2%	53.8%	46.2%

PRESIDENT 1964

County	Total Vote	Republican	Democratic	Other	Rep.-Dem. Plurality	Total Vote Rep.	Total Vote Dem.	Major Vote Rep.	Major Vote Dem.
ADA	45,043	25,404	19,639		5,765 R	56.4%	43.6%	56.4%	43.6%
ADAMS	1,439	689	750		61 D	47.9%	52.1%	47.9%	52.1%
BANNOCK	21,308	7,825	13,483		5,658 D	36.7%	63.3%	36.7%	63.3%
BEAR LAKE	3,266	1,409	1,857		448 D	43.1%	56.9%	43.1%	56.9%
BENEWAH	2,777	981	1,796		815 D	35.3%	64.7%	35.3%	64.7%
BINGHAM	10,595	5,364	5,231		133 R	50.6%	49.4%	50.6%	49.4%
BLAINE	2,454	1,161	1,293		132 D	47.3%	52.7%	47.3%	52.7%
BOISE	864	414	450		36 D	47.9%	52.1%	47.9%	52.1%
BONNER	7,303	2,975	4,328		1,353 D	40.7%	59.3%	40.7%	59.3%
BONNEVILLE	20,373	10,736	9,637		1,099 R	52.7%	47.3%	52.7%	47.3%
BOUNDARY	2,483	1,065	1,418		353 D	42.9%	57.1%	42.9%	57.1%
BUTTE	1,497	649	848		199 D	43.4%	56.6%	43.4%	56.6%
CAMAS	574	316	258		58 R	55.1%	44.9%	55.1%	44.9%
CANYON	24,067	13,466	10,601		2,865 R	56.0%	44.0%	56.0%	44.0%
CARIBOU	2,725	1,303	1,422		119 D	47.8%	52.2%	47.8%	52.2%
CASSIA	6,617	4,009	2,608		1,401 R	60.6%	39.4%	60.6%	39.4%
CLARK	448	262	186		76 R	58.5%	41.5%	58.5%	41.5%
CLEARWATER	3,213	767	2,446		1,679 D	23.9%	76.1%	23.9%	76.1%
CUSTER	1,434	720	714		6 R	50.2%	49.8%	50.2%	49.8%
ELMORE	4,167	1,857	2,310		453 D	44.6%	55.4%	44.6%	55.4%
FRANKLIN	3,983	2,400	1,583		817 R	60.3%	39.7%	60.3%	39.7%
FREMONT	3,915	1,945	1,970		25 D	49.7%	50.3%	49.7%	50.3%
GEM	4,307	1,979	2,328		349 D	45.9%	54.1%	45.9%	54.1%
GOODING	4,375	2,527	1,848		679 R	57.8%	42.2%	57.8%	42.2%
IDAHO	5,178	1,990	3,188		1,198 D	38.4%	61.6%	38.4%	61.6%
JEFFERSON	4,801	2,740	2,061		679 R	57.1%	42.9%	57.1%	42.9%
JEROME	4,941	3,113	1,828		1,285 R	63.0%	37.0%	63.0%	37.0%
KOOTENAI	14,311	6,096	8,215		2,119 D	42.6%	57.4%	42.6%	57.4%
LATAH	8,724	3,475	5,249		1,774 D	39.8%	60.2%	39.8%	60.2%
LEMHI	2,563	1,496	1,067		429 R	58.4%	41.6%	58.4%	41.6%
LEWIS	2,044	487	1,557		1,070 D	23.8%	76.2%	23.8%	76.2%
LINCOLN	1,586	969	617		352 R	61.1%	38.9%	61.1%	38.9%
MADISON	4,050	2,101	1,949		152 R	51.9%	48.1%	51.9%	48.1%
MINIDOKA	5,938	3,111	2,827		284 R	52.4%	47.6%	52.4%	47.6%
NEZ PERCE	13,157	3,912	9,245		5,333 D	29.7%	70.3%	29.7%	70.3%
ONEIDA	1,879	1,111	768		343 R	59.1%	40.9%	59.1%	40.9%
OWYHEE	2,384	1,216	1,168		48 R	51.0%	49.0%	51.0%	49.0%
PAYETTE	5,272	2,764	2,508		256 R	52.4%	47.6%	52.4%	47.6%
POWER	2,127	966	1,161		195 D	45.4%	54.6%	45.4%	54.6%
SHOSHONE	8,078	2,884	5,194		2,310 D	35.7%	64.3%	35.7%	64.3%
TETON	1,273	675	598		77 R	53.0%	47.0%	53.0%	47.0%
TWIN FALLS	19,156	11,518	7,638		3,880 R	60.1%	39.9%	60.1%	39.9%
VALLEY	2,106	980	1,126		146 D	46.5%	53.5%	46.5%	53.5%
WASHINGTON	3,682	1,730	1,952		222 D	47.0%	53.0%	47.0%	53.0%
TOTAL	292,477	143,557	148,920		5,363 D	49.1%	50.9%	49.1%	50.9%

IDAHO

OTHER VOTE COMPOSITION:

1920	
1924	Progressive.
1928	Socialist.
1932	4,712 Liberty; 526 Socialist; 491 Communist.
1936	Union.
1940	497 Socialist; 276 Communist.
1944	503 Prohibition; 282 Socialist.
1948	4,972 Progressive; 628 Prohibition; 332 Socialist.
1952	443 Progressive; 23 scattered.
1956	126 States Rights; 16 scattered.
1960	
1964	

SPECIAL CASES:

1924   Progressive candidates carried several counties and ran second in many others.

ILLINOIS

PRESIDENT 1920

County	Total Vote	Republican	Democratic	Other	Rep.-Dem. Plurality	Total Vote Rep.	Total Vote Dem.	Major Vote Rep.	Major Vote Dem.
ADAMS	22,521	12,852	7,222	2,447	5,630 R	57.1%	32.1%	64.0%	36.0%
ALEXANDER	8,539	5,287	3,167	85	2,120 R	61.9%	37.1%	62.5%	37.5%
BOND	5,663	3,662	1,533	468	2,129 R	64.7%	27.1%	70.5%	29.5%
BOONE	6,025	5,386	496	143	4,890 R	89.4%	8.2%	91.6%	8.4%
BROWN	3,527	1,590	1,866	71	276 D	45.1%	52.9%	46.0%	54.0%
BUREAU	13,302	9,968	2,354	980	7,614 R	74.9%	17.7%	80.9%	19.1%
CALHOUN	2,109	1,367	703	39	664 R	64.8%	33.3%	66.0%	34.0%
CARROLL	5,994	5,194	606	194	4,588 R	86.7%	10.1%	89.6%	10.4%
CASS	7,318	3,956	2,861	501	1,095 R	54.1%	39.1%	58.0%	42.0%
CHAMPAIGN	21,681	15,573	5,247	861	10,326 R	71.8%	24.2%	74.8%	25.2%
CHRISTIAN	14,285	7,535	5,398	1,352	2,137 R	52.7%	37.8%	58.3%	41.7%
CLARK	9,597	5,312	4,181	104	1,131 R	55.4%	43.6%	56.0%	44.0%
CLAY	6,149	3,683	2,358	108	1,325 R	59.9%	38.3%	61.0%	39.0%
CLINTON	7,164	4,564	1,661	939	2,903 R	63.7%	23.2%	73.3%	26.7%
COLES	14,574	8,563	5,811	200	2,752 R	58.8%	39.9%	59.6%	40.4%
COOK	893,137	635,197	197,499	60,441	437,698 R	71.1%	22.1%	76.3%	23.7%
CRAWFORD	9,430	5,188	4,092	150	1,096 R	55.0%	43.4%	55.9%	44.1%
CUMBERLAND	5,320	3,095	2,162	63	933 R	58.2%	40.6%	58.9%	41.1%
DE KALB	12,361	10,374	1,700	287	8,674 R	83.9%	13.8%	85.9%	14.1%
DE WITT	8,242	5,001	3,079	162	1,922 R	60.7%	37.4%	61.9%	38.1%
DOUGLAS	7,491	4,885	2,308	298	2,577 R	65.2%	30.8%	67.9%	32.1%
DU PAGE	14,976	12,280	2,084	612	10,196 R	82.0%	13.9%	85.5%	14.5%
EDGAR	12,667	6,750	5,694	223	1,056 R	53.3%	45.0%	54.2%	45.8%
EDWARDS	3,790	3,002	742	46	2,260 R	79.2%	19.6%	80.2%	19.8%
EFFINGHAM	7,267	4,176	2,985	106	1,191 R	57.5%	41.1%	58.3%	41.7%
FAYETTE	9,846	5,758	3,824	264	1,934 R	58.5%	38.8%	60.1%	39.9%
FORD	6,062	4,995	958	109	4,037 R	82.4%	15.8%	84.2%	15.8%
FRANKLIN	14,886	7,608	4,894	2,384	2,714 R	51.1%	32.9%	60.8%	39.1%
FULTON	16,072	9,523	5,293	1,256	4,230 R	59.3%	32.9%	64.3%	35.7%
GALLATIN	4,373	2,184	2,000	189	184 R	49.9%	45.7%	52.2%	47.8%
GREENE	7,683	3,685	3,776	222	91 D	48.0%	49.1%	49.4%	50.6%
GRUNDY	5,805	4,647	803	355	3,844 R	80.1%	13.8%	85.3%	14.7%
HAMILTON	5,886	3,220	2,591	75	629 R	54.7%	44.0%	55.4%	44.6%
HANCOCK	12,778	7,379	5,125	274	2,254 R	57.7%	40.1%	59.0%	41.0%
HARDIN	2,527	1,555	943	29	612 R	61.5%	37.3%	62.2%	37.8%
HENDERSON	3,584	2,747	740	97	2,007 R	76.6%	20.6%	78.8%	21.2%
HENRY	15,677	12,379	2,530	768	9,849 R	79.0%	16.1%	83.0%	17.0%
IROQUOIS	11,809	9,186	2,429	194	6,757 R	77.8%	20.6%	79.1%	20.9%
JACKSON	13,347	8,003	4,575	769	3,428 R	60.0%	34.3%	63.6%	36.4%
JASPER	6,351	3,279	2,971	101	308 R	51.6%	46.8%	52.5%	47.5%
JEFFERSON	10,660	5,711	4,772	177	939 R	53.6%	44.8%	54.5%	45.5%
JERSEY	4,962	2,873	1,999	90	874 R	57.9%	40.3%	59.0%	41.0%
JO DAVIESS	7,997	6,098	1,604	295	4,494 R	76.3%	20.1%	79.2%	20.8%
JOHNSON	4,191	2,972	1,137	82	1,835 R	70.9%	27.1%	72.3%	27.7%
KANE	32,398	26,832	4,323	1,243	22,509 R	82.8%	13.3%	86.1%	13.9%
KANKAKEE	16,201	12,853	2,828	520	10,025 R	79.3%	17.5%	82.0%	18.0%
KENDALL	3,931	3,459	439	33	3,020 R	88.0%	11.2%	88.7%	11.3%
KNOX	17,005	12,559	2,852	1,594	9,707 R	73.9%	16.8%	81.5%	18.5%
LAKE	19,096	15,712	2,321	1,063	13,391 R	82.3%	12.2%	87.1%	12.9%
LA SALLE	32,434	23,751	6,626	2,057	17,125 R	73.2%	20.4%	78.2%	21.8%
LAWRENCE	8,714	4,720	3,707	287	1,013 R	54.2%	42.5%	56.0%	44.0%
LEE	9,646	7,615	1,715	316	5,900 R	78.9%	17.8%	81.6%	18.4%
LIVINGSTON	13,874	10,382	3,101	391	7,281 R	74.8%	22.4%	77.0%	23.0%
LOGAN	10,738	6,957	3,232	549	3,725 R	64.8%	30.1%	68.3%	31.7%
MCDONOUGH	11,430	7,221	3,930	279	3,291 R	63.2%	34.4%	64.8%	35.2%
MCHENRY	11,616	9,885	1,536	195	8,349 R	85.1%	13.2%	86.6%	13.4%
MCLEAN	25,555	16,680	6,411	2,464	10,269 R	65.3%	25.1%	72.2%	27.8%
MACON	25,257	16,486	7,917	854	8,569 R	65.3%	31.3%	67.6%	32.4%
MACOUPIN	19,470	8,700	5,936	4,834	2,764 R	44.7%	30.5%	59.4%	40.6%
MADISON	33,292	19,249	10,149	3,894	9,100 R	57.8%	30.5%	65.5%	34.5%

PRESIDENT 1924

County	Total Vote	Republican	Democratic	Other	Rep.-Dem. Plurality	Total Vote Rep.	Total Vote Dem.	Major Vote Rep.	Major Vote Dem.
ADAMS	24,404	9,985	8,628	5,791	1,357 R	40.9%	35.4%	53.6%	46.4%
ALEXANDER	7,685	4,465	2,639	581	1,826 R	58.1%	34.3%	62.9%	37.1%
BOND	6,407	3,644	2,143	620	1,501 R	56.9%	33.4%	63.0%	37.0%
BOONE	6,464	4,872	348	1,244	4,524 R	75.4%	5.4%	93.3%	6.7%
BROWN	3,946	1,637	2,149	160	512 D	41.5%	54.5%	43.2%	56.8%
BUREAU	15,663	9,457	1,995	4,211	7,462 R	60.4%	12.7%	82.6%	17.4%
CALHOUN	2,361	1,136	1,115	110	21 R	48.1%	47.2%	50.5%	49.5%
CARROLL	7,482	4,559	603	2,320	3,956 R	60.9%	8.1%	88.3%	11.7%
CASS	7,613	3,139	2,909	1,565	230 R	41.2%	38.2%	51.9%	48.1%
CHAMPAIGN	22,677	14,244	5,221	3,212	9,023 R	62.8%	23.0%	73.2%	26.8%
CHRISTIAN	16,056	7,398	5,826	2,832	1,572 R	46.1%	36.3%	55.9%	44.1%
CLARK	9,218	4,731	4,203	284	528 R	51.5%	45.5%	53.0%	47.0%
CLAY	6,919	3,432	2,987	500	445 R	49.6%	43.2%	53.5%	46.5%
CLINTON	7,942	2,358	1,693	3,891	665 R	29.7%	21.3%	58.2%	41.8%
COLES	15,194	8,342	5,544	1,308	2,798 R	54.9%	36.5%	60.1%	39.9%
COOK	1,113,652	688,973	226,141	198,538	462,832 R	61.9%	20.3%	75.3%	24.7%
CRAWFORD	9,425	4,830	4,223	372	607 R	51.2%	44.8%	53.4%	46.6%
CUMBERLAND	5,281	2,698	2,384	199	314 R	51.1%	45.1%	53.1%	46.9%
DE KALB	13,744	10,500	1,540	1,704	8,960 R	76.4%	11.2%	87.2%	12.8%
DE WITT	8,802	5,173	2,752	877	2,421 R	58.8%	31.3%	65.3%	34.7%
DOUGLAS	7,270	4,046	2,315	909	1,731 R	55.7%	31.8%	63.6%	36.4%
DU PAGE	23,233	16,917	1,893	4,423	15,024 R	72.8%	8.1%	89.9%	10.1%
EDGAR	12,037	6,297	5,222	518	1,075 R	52.3%	43.4%	54.7%	45.3%
EDWARDS	3,952	2,750	1,047	155	1,703 R	69.6%	26.5%	72.4%	27.6%
EFFINGHAM	8,063	3,159	3,814	1,090	655 D	39.2%	47.3%	45.3%	54.7%
FAYETTE	10,344	5,010	4,668	666	342 R	48.4%	45.1%	51.8%	48.2%
FORD	6,624	4,672	1,093	859	3,579 R	70.5%	16.5%	81.0%	19.0%
FRANKLIN	17,121	6,779	5,791	4,551	988 R	39.6%	33.8%	53.9%	46.1%
FULTON	17,921	8,664	5,011	4,246	3,653 R	48.3%	28.0%	63.4%	36.6%
GALLATIN	4,576	1,792	2,385	399	593 D	39.2%	52.1%	42.9%	57.1%
GREENE	8,878	3,527	4,648	703	1,121 D	39.7%	52.4%	43.1%	56.9%
GRUNDY	6,780	4,337	742	1,701	3,595 R	64.0%	10.9%	85.4%	14.6%
HAMILTON	6,041	2,659	3,168	214	509 D	44.0%	52.4%	45.6%	54.4%
HANCOCK	12,885	6,678	5,189	1,018	1,489 R	51.8%	40.3%	56.3%	43.7%
HARDIN	2,809	1,378	1,358	73	20 R	49.1%	48.3%	50.4%	49.6%
HENDERSON	3,951	2,879	803	269	2,076 R	72.9%	20.3%	78.2%	21.8%
HENRY	18,179	13,159	1,944	3,076	11,215 R	72.4%	10.7%	87.1%	12.9%
IROQUOIS	11,702	7,498	2,303	1,901	5,195 R	64.1%	19.7%	76.5%	23.5%
JACKSON	13,030	6,424	4,707	1,899	1,717 R	49.1%	36.1%	57.7%	42.3%
JASPER	6,397	3,030	3,144	223	114 D	47.4%	49.1%	49.1%	50.9%
JEFFERSON	12,130	5,406	6,258	466	852 D	44.6%	51.6%	46.3%	53.7%
JERSEY	5,536	2,460	2,723	353	263 D	44.4%	49.2%	47.5%	52.5%
JO DAVIESS	9,659	4,864	1,477	3,318	3,387 R	50.4%	15.3%	76.7%	23.3%
JOHNSON	4,073	2,468	1,408	197	1,060 R	60.6%	34.6%	63.7%	36.3%
KANE	42,858	32,717	3,517	6,624	29,200 R	76.3%	8.2%	90.3%	9.7%
KANKAKEE	18,471	12,462	2,488	3,521	9,974 R	67.5%	13.5%	83.4%	16.6%
KENDALL	4,409	3,513	432	464	3,081 R	79.7%	9.8%	89.0%	11.0%
KNOX	19,680	12,968	2,617	4,095	10,351 R	65.9%	13.3%	83.2%	16.8%
LAKE	24,150	18,229	2,008	3,913	16,221 R	75.5%	8.3%	90.1%	9.9%
LA SALLE	35,417	21,417	6,216	7,784	15,201 R	60.5%	17.6%	77.5%	22.5%
LAWRENCE	8,945	4,607	4,103	235	504 R	51.5%	45.9%	52.9%	47.1%
LEE	12,057	8,363	2,367	1,327	5,996 R	69.4%	19.6%	77.9%	22.1%
LIVINGSTON	15,025	9,695	2,911	2,419	6,784 R	64.5%	19.4%	76.9%	23.1%
LOGAN	12,356	7,063	3,708	1,585	3,355 R	57.2%	30.0%	65.6%	34.4%
MCDONOUGH	12,306	7,505	4,016	785	3,489 R	61.0%	32.6%	65.1%	34.9%
MCHENRY	13,015	8,751	1,372	2,892	7,379 R	67.2%	10.5%	86.4%	13.6%
MCLEAN	29,582	16,550	6,826	6,206	9,724 R	55.9%	23.1%	70.8%	29.2%
MACON	27,331	16,458	6,670	4,203	9,788 R	60.2%	24.4%	71.2%	28.8%
MACOUPIN	21,841	8,571	6,134	7,136	2,437 R	39.2%	28.1%	58.3%	41.7%
MADISON	41,851	19,926	12,863	9,062	7,063 R	47.6%	30.7%	60.8%	39.2%

ILLINOIS

PRESIDENT 1920

County	Total Vote	Republican	Democratic	Other	Rep.-Dem. Plurality	Percentage Total Vote Rep.	Percentage Total Vote Dem.	Percentage Major Vote Rep.	Percentage Major Vote Dem.
MARION	12,715	6,620	4,351	1,744	2,269 R	52.1%	34.2%	60.3%	39.7%
MARSHALL	5,523	3,734	1,568	221	2,166 R	67.6%	28.4%	70.4%	29.6%
MASON	6,579	3,842	2,595	142	1,247 R	58.4%	39.4%	59.7%	40.3%
MASSAC	4,496	3,731	688	77	3,043 R	83.0%	15.3%	84.4%	15.6%
MENARD	4,869	2,882	1,864	123	1,018 R	59.2%	38.3%	60.7%	39.3%
MERCER	7,416	5,531	1,574	311	3,957 R	74.6%	21.2%	77.8%	22.2%
MONROE	4,215	2,955	932	328	2,023 R	70.1%	22.1%	76.0%	24.0%
MONTGOMERY	14,039	7,429	4,756	1,854	2,673 R	52.9%	33.9%	61.0%	39.0%
MORGAN	12,993	8,169	4,447	377	3,722 R	62.9%	34.2%	64.8%	35.2%
MOULTRIE	5,881	3,279	2,513	89	766 R	55.3%	42.7%	56.6%	43.4%
OGLE	11,233	9,322	1,720	191	7,602 R	83.0%	15.3%	84.4%	15.6%
PEORIA	37,182	24,541	9,453	3,188	15,088 R	66.0%	25.4%	72.2%	27.8%
PERRY	7,864	4,598	2,478	788	2,120 R	58.5%	31.5%	65.0%	35.0%
PIATT	6,284	4,283	1,903	98	2,380 R	68.2%	30.3%	69.2%	30.8%
PIKE	10,280	5,564	4,279	437	1,285 R	54.1%	41.6%	56.5%	43.5%
POPE	3,211	2,486	687	38	1,799 R	77.4%	21.4%	78.3%	21.7%
PULASKI	6,368	4,002	2,276	90	1,726 R	62.8%	35.7%	63.7%	36.3%
PUTNAM	2,192	1,623	362	207	1,261 R	74.0%	16.5%	81.8%	18.2%
RANDOLPH	9,882	6,180	3,181	521	2,999 R	62.5%	32.2%	66.0%	34.0%
RICHLAND	5,304	3,026	2,174	104	852 R	57.1%	41.0%	58.2%	41.8%
ROCK ISLAND	30,719	21,908	5,208	3,603	16,700 R	71.3%	17.0%	80.8%	19.2%
ST. CLAIR	42,231	21,681	14,032	6,518	7,649 R	51.3%	33.2%	60.7%	39.3%
SALINE	12,692	6,722	3,500	2,470	3,222 R	53.0%	27.6%	65.8%	34.2%
SANGAMON	36,723	21,820	11,000	3,903	10,820 R	59.4%	30.0%	66.5%	33.5%
SCHUYLER	5,199	2,800	2,258	141	542 R	53.9%	43.4%	55.4%	44.6%
SCOTT	3,971	2,075	1,786	110	289 R	52.3%	45.0%	53.7%	46.3%
SHELBY	11,776	6,351	5,113	312	1,238 R	53.9%	43.4%	55.4%	44.6%
STARK	3,456	2,750	661	45	2,089 R	79.6%	19.1%	80.6%	19.4%
STEPHENSON	12,821	9,570	2,772	479	6,798 R	74.6%	21.6%	77.5%	22.5%
TAZEWELL	12,250	7,679	3,640	931	4,039 R	62.7%	29.7%	67.8%	32.2%
UNION	6,847	3,119	3,660	68	541 D	45.6%	53.5%	46.0%	54.0%
VERMILION	29,439	18,175	8,634	2,630	9,541 R	61.7%	29.3%	67.8%	32.2%
WABASH	5,479	2,871	2,514	94	357 R	52.4%	45.9%	53.3%	46.7%
WARREN	9,090	6,309	2,236	545	4,073 R	69.4%	24.6%	73.8%	26.2%
WASHINGTON	6,386	4,519	1,102	765	3,417 R	70.8%	17.3%	80.4%	19.6%
WAYNE	8,113	4,908	3,137	68	1,771 R	60.5%	38.7%	61.0%	39.0%
WHITE	8,772	4,494	4,148	130	346 R	51.2%	47.3%	52.0%	48.0%
WHITESIDE	13,363	10,923	1,927	513	8,996 R	81.7%	14.4%	85.0%	15.0%
WILL	28,474	21,746	5,410	1,318	16,336 R	76.4%	19.0%	80.1%	19.9%
WILLIAMSON	17,834	10,118	4,728	2,988	5,390 R	56.7%	26.5%	68.2%	31.8%
WINNEBAGO	25,134	19,913	3,355	1,866	15,558 R	79.2%	13.3%	85.6%	14.4%
WOODFORD	7,137	4,929	1,977	231	2,952 R	69.1%	27.7%	71.4%	28.6%
TOTAL	2,094,714	1,420,480	534,395	139,839	885,085 R	67.8%	25.5%	72.7%	27.3%

PRESIDENT 1924

County	Total Vote	Republican	Democratic	Other	Rep.-Dem. Plurality	Percentage Total Vote Rep.	Percentage Total Vote Dem.	Percentage Major Vote Rep.	Percentage Major Vote Dem.
MARION	13,381	5,889	4,768	2,724	1,121 R	44.0%	35.6%	55.3%	44.7%
MARSHALL	6,465	3,776	1,836	853	1,940 R	58.4%	28.4%	67.3%	32.7%
MASON	6,580	3,522	2,536	622	986 R	52.7%	38.0%	58.1%	41.9%
MASSAC	4,517	3,227	920	370	2,307 R	71.4%	20.4%	77.8%	22.2%
MENARD	5,217	2,931	1,954	332	977 R	56.2%	37.5%	60.0%	40.0%
MERCER	8,225	5,618	1,699	908	3,919 R	68.3%	20.7%	76.8%	23.2%
MONROE	4,943	2,390	1,369	1,184	1,021 R	48.4%	27.7%	63.6%	36.4%
MONTGOMERY	16,975	8,022	5,922	3,331	2,400 R	47.3%	33.1%	58.8%	41.2%
MORGAN	14,844	8,223	5,721	900	2,502 R	55.4%	38.5%	59.0%	41.0%
MOULTRIE	5,652	3,001	2,403	248	598 R	53.1%	42.5%	55.5%	44.5%
OGLE	11,799	8,449	1,591	1,759	6,858 R	71.6%	13.5%	84.2%	15.8%
PEORIA	43,412	25,243	6,343	11,526	18,900 R	58.6%	14.7%	79.9%	20.1%
PERRY	9,289	3,693	3,007	2,589	686 R	39.8%	32.4%	55.1%	44.9%
PIATT	5,907	3,799	1,733	375	2,066 R	64.3%	29.3%	68.7%	31.3%
PIKE	10,943	4,989	5,424	530	435 D	45.6%	49.6%	47.9%	52.1%
POPE	3,249	2,161	978	110	1,183 R	66.5%	30.1%	68.8%	31.2%
PULASKI	5,449	3,355	1,700	394	1,655 R	61.6%	31.2%	66.4%	33.6%
PUTNAM	2,218	1,364	260	594	1,104 R	61.5%	11.7%	84.0%	16.0%
RANDOLPH	10,680	4,527	3,734	2,619	793 R	41.6%	34.3%	54.8%	45.2%
RICHLAND	6,155	3,082	2,749	324	333 R	50.1%	44.7%	52.9%	47.1%
ROCK ISLAND	35,647	20,563	3,631	11,453	16,932 R	57.7%	10.2%	85.0%	15.0%
ST. CLAIR	50,994	23,380	14,921	12,693	8,459 R	45.8%	29.3%	61.0%	39.0%
SALINE	12,937	6,084	4,037	2,816	2,047 R	47.0%	31.2%	60.1%	39.9%
SANGAMON	45,446	23,443	12,640	9,363	10,803 R	51.6%	27.8%	65.0%	35.0%
SCHUYLER	5,906	2,729	2,860	317	131 D	46.2%	48.4%	48.8%	51.2%
SCOTT	4,411	2,227	1,994	190	233 R	50.5%	45.2%	52.8%	47.2%
SHELBY	11,646	5,605	5,265	776	340 R	48.1%	45.2%	51.6%	48.4%
STARK	3,796	2,698	784	314	1,914 R	71.1%	20.7%	77.5%	22.5%
STEPHENSON	16,216	8,638	2,452	5,126	6,186 R	53.3%	15.1%	77.9%	22.1%
TAZEWELL	14,370	7,488	3,375	3,507	4,113 R	52.1%	23.5%	68.9%	31.1%
UNION	6,586	2,579	3,783	224	1,204 D	39.2%	57.4%	40.5%	59.5%
VERMILION	32,615	17,822	6,424	8,369	11,398 R	54.6%	19.7%	73.5%	26.5%
WABASH	5,621	2,564	2,442	615	122 R	45.6%	43.4%	51.2%	48.8%
WARREN	10,623	6,912	2,440	1,271	4,472 R	65.1%	23.0%	73.9%	26.1%
WASHINGTON	6,103	3,444	1,717	942	1,727 R	56.4%	28.1%	66.7%	33.3%
WAYNE	9,368	4,937	4,247	184	690 R	52.7%	45.3%	53.8%	46.2%
WHITE	8,454	3,780	4,377	297	597 D	44.7%	51.8%	46.3%	53.7%
WHITESIDE	15,576	11,532	1,957	2,087	9,575 R	74.0%	12.6%	85.5%	14.5%
WILL	35,505	22,780	4,707	8,018	18,073 R	64.2%	13.3%	82.9%	17.1%
WILLIAMSON	20,689	9,366	6,117	5,206	3,249 R	45.3%	29.6%	60.5%	39.5%
WINNEBAGO	30,814	21,978	2,228	6,608	19,750 R	71.3%	7.2%	90.8%	9.2%
WOODFORD	7,464	4,290	1,828	1,346	2,462 R	57.5%	24.5%	70.1%	29.9%
TOTAL	2,470,067	1,453,321	576,975	439,771	876,346 R	58.8%	23.4%	71.6%	28.4%

ILLINOIS

PRESIDENT 1928

County	Total Vote	Republican	Democratic	Other	Rep.-Dem. Plurality	Total Vote Rep.	Total Vote Dem.	Major Vote Rep.	Major Vote Dem.
ADAMS	29,093	15,590	13,215	288	2,375 R	53.6%	45.4%	54.1%	45.9%
ALEXANDER	9,252	5,666	3,558	28	2,108 R	61.2%	38.5%	61.4%	38.6%
BOND	6,494	4,160	2,298	36	1,862 R	64.1%	35.4%	64.4%	35.6%
BOONE	7,369	5,965	1,371	33	4,594 R	80.9%	18.6%	81.3%	18.7%
BROWN	4,165	2,289	1,867	9	422 R	55.0%	44.8%	55.1%	44.9%
BUREAU	18,133	11,557	6,486	90	5,071 R	63.7%	35.8%	64.1%	35.9%
CALHOUN	3,178	1,594	1,551	33	43 R	50.2%	48.8%	50.7%	49.3%
CARROLL	8,118	6,197	1,876	45	4,321 R	76.3%	23.1%	76.8%	23.2%
CASS	7,494	4,009	3,461	24	548 R	53.5%	46.2%	53.7%	46.3%
CHAMPAIGN	28,550	19,494	8,915	141	10,579 R	68.3%	31.2%	68.6%	31.4%
CHRISTIAN	17,431	9,896	7,345	190	2,551 R	56.8%	42.1%	57.4%	42.6%
CLARK	9,288	5,632	3,621	35	2,011 R	60.6%	38.9%	60.9%	39.1%
CLAY	6,940	4,522	2,418		2,104 R	65.2%	34.8%	65.2%	34.8%
CLINTON	9,852	3,031	6,774	47	3,743 D	30.8%	68.8%	30.9%	69.1%
COLES	16,607	11,479	5,071	57	6,408 R	69.1%	30.5%	69.4%	30.6%
COOK	1,540,171	812,063	716,283	11,825	95,780 R	52.7%	46.5%	53.1%	46.9%
CRAWFORD	9,522	5,989	3,495	38	2,494 R	62.9%	36.7%	63.1%	36.9%
CUMBERLAND	5,143	3,242	1,873	28	1,369 R	63.0%	36.4%	63.4%	36.6%
DE KALB	15,503	11,501	3,940	62	7,561 R	74.2%	25.4%	74.5%	25.5%
DE WITT	8,790	6,100	2,631	59	3,469 R	69.4%	29.9%	69.9%	30.1%
DOUGLAS	7,171	4,890	2,239	42	2,651 R	68.2%	31.2%	68.6%	31.4%
DU PAGE	38,712	28,016	10,479	217	17,537 R	72.4%	27.1%	72.8%	27.2%
EDGAR	12,886	7,509	5,325	52	2,184 R	58.3%	41.3%	58.5%	41.5%
EDWARDS	3,826	2,861	950	15	1,911 R	74.8%	24.8%	75.1%	24.9%
EFFINGHAM	8,214	3,882	4,239	93	357 D	47.3%	51.6%	47.8%	52.2%
FAYETTE	10,616	6,545	3,998	73	2,547 R	61.7%	37.7%	62.1%	37.9%
FORD	6,793	4,668	2,098	27	2,570 R	68.7%	30.9%	69.0%	31.0%
FRANKLIN	21,622	9,900	11,369	353	1,469 D	45.8%	52.6%	46.5%	53.5%
FULTON	17,680	10,600	6,591	489	4,009 R	60.0%	37.3%	61.7%	38.3%
GALLATIN	4,373	2,002	2,343	28	341 D	45.8%	53.6%	46.1%	53.9%
GREENE	8,421	4,299	4,076	46	223 R	51.1%	48.4%	51.3%	48.7%
GRUNDY	8,329	5,126	3,174	29	1,952 R	61.5%	38.1%	61.8%	38.2%
HAMILTON	6,412	3,275	3,037	100	238 R	51.1%	47.4%	51.9%	48.1%
HANCOCK	13,290	7,795	5,447	48	2,348 R	58.7%	41.0%	58.9%	41.1%
HARDIN	2,732	1,758	933	41	825 R	64.3%	34.2%	65.3%	34.7%
HENDERSON	3,790	2,695	1,065	30	1,630 R	71.1%	28.1%	71.7%	28.3%
HENRY	20,707	14,866	5,858	183	8,808 R	70.7%	28.3%	71.5%	28.5%
IROQUOIS	13,923	8,453	5,421	49	3,032 R	60.7%	38.9%	60.9%	39.1%
JACKSON	15,102	9,180	5,836	86	3,344 R	60.8%	38.6%	61.1%	38.9%
JASPER	6,272	3,201	3,055	16	146 R	51.0%	48.7%	51.2%	48.8%
JEFFERSON	13,301	7,326	5,905	70	1,421 R	55.1%	44.4%	55.4%	44.6%
JERSEY	5,480	2,993	2,473	14	520 R	54.6%	45.1%	54.8%	45.2%
JO DAVIESS	10,283	6,333	3,856	94	2,477 R	61.6%	37.5%	62.2%	37.8%
JOHNSON	4,091	2,892	1,163	36	1,729 R	70.7%	28.4%	71.3%	28.7%
KANE	54,673	38,236	16,184	253	22,052 R	70.0%	29.6%	70.3%	29.7%
KANKAKEE	22,279	11,905	10,247	127	1,658 R	53.4%	46.0%	53.7%	46.3%
KENDALL	4,752	3,569	1,154	29	2,415 R	75.1%	24.3%	75.5%	24.5%
KNOX	22,330	16,151	5,993	186	10,158 R	72.3%	26.8%	72.9%	27.1%
LAKE	39,587	26,814	12,252	521	14,562 R	67.7%	30.9%	68.6%	31.4%
LA SALLE	45,228	24,039	20,807	382	3,232 R	53.2%	46.0%	53.6%	46.4%
LAWRENCE	9,726	5,851	3,806	69	2,045 R	60.2%	39.1%	60.6%	39.4%
LEE	13,760	9,238	4,476	46	4,762 R	67.1%	32.5%	67.4%	32.6%
LIVINGSTON	16,992	11,161	5,737	94	5,424 R	65.7%	33.8%	66.0%	34.0%
LOGAN	12,725	7,631	5,019	75	2,612 R	60.0%	39.4%	60.3%	39.7%
MCDONOUGH	13,138	8,953	4,104	81	4,849 R	68.1%	31.2%	68.6%	31.4%
MCHENRY	16,319	10,661	5,596	62	5,065 R	65.3%	34.3%	65.6%	34.4%
MCLEAN	31,789	20,780	10,742	267	10,038 R	65.4%	33.8%	65.9%	34.1%
MACON	34,654	24,492	9,932	230	14,560 R	70.7%	28.7%	71.1%	28.9%
MACOUPIN	22,438	10,699	11,290	449	591 D	47.7%	50.3%	48.7%	51.3%
MADISON	52,406	28,028	23,658	720	4,370 R	53.5%	45.1%	54.2%	45.8%

PRESIDENT 1932

County	Total Vote	Republican	Democratic	Other	Rep.-Dem. Plurality	Total Vote Rep.	Total Vote Dem.	Major Vote Rep.	Major Vote Dem.
ADAMS	31,669	10,134	21,098	437	10,964 D	32.0%	66.6%	32.4%	67.6%
ALEXANDER	10,533	4,729	5,653	151	924 D	44.9%	53.7%	45.5%	54.5%
BOND	6,958	3,171	3,630	157	459 D	45.6%	52.2%	46.6%	53.4%
BOONE	7,575	5,244	2,239	92	3,005 R	69.2%	29.6%	70.1%	29.9%
BROWN	3,993	1,148	2,822	23	1,674 D	28.8%	70.7%	28.9%	71.1%
BUREAU	19,280	8,721	10,309	250	1,588 D	45.2%	53.5%	45.8%	54.2%
CALHOUN	3,504	1,239	2,229	36	990 D	35.4%	63.6%	35.7%	64.3%
CARROLL	8,495	4,571	3,812	112	759 D	53.8%	44.9%	54.5%	45.5%
CASS	8,507	2,745	5,669	93	2,924 D	32.3%	66.6%	32.6%	67.4%
CHAMPAIGN	31,070	13,995	16,474	601	2,479 D	45.0%	53.0%	45.9%	54.1%
CHRISTIAN	18,242	6,096	11,515	631	5,419 D	33.4%	63.1%	34.6%	65.4%
CLARK	9,881	4,148	5,659	74	1,511 D	42.0%	57.3%	42.3%	57.7%
CLAY	8,064	3,373	4,565	126	1,192 D	41.8%	56.6%	42.5%	57.5%
CLINTON	10,466	2,548	7,756	162	5,188 D	24.3%	73.9%	24.8%	75.2%
COLES	18,559	7,313	11,081	165	3,768 D	39.4%	59.7%	39.8%	60.2%
COOK	1,664,232	690,146	919,231	54,855	229,085 D	41.5%	55.2%	42.9%	57.1%
CRAWFORD	10,800	4,550	6,081	169	1,531 D	42.1%	56.3%	42.8%	57.2%
CUMBERLAND	5,324	2,166	3,128	30	962 D	40.7%	58.8%	40.9%	59.1%
DE KALB	16,594	9,356	6,923	315	2,433 R	56.4%	41.7%	57.5%	42.5%
DE WITT	9,673	4,207	5,339	127	1,132 D	43.5%	55.2%	44.1%	55.9%
DOUGLAS	8,236	3,108	4,954	174	1,846 D	37.7%	60.2%	38.6%	61.4%
DU PAGE	45,809	25,758	18,547	1,504	7,211 D	56.2%	40.5%	58.1%	41.9%
EDGAR	13,836	5,953	7,745	138	1,792 D	43.0%	56.0%	43.5%	56.5%
EDWARDS	4,216	2,203	1,956	57	247 D	52.3%	46.4%	53.0%	47.0%
EFFINGHAM	9,569	2,933	6,503	133	3,570 D	30.7%	68.0%	31.1%	68.9%
FAYETTE	12,360	5,122	7,053	185	1,931 D	41.4%	57.1%	42.1%	57.9%
FORD	7,616	3,342	4,175	99	833 D	43.9%	54.8%	44.5%	55.5%
FRANKLIN	23,290	7,560	14,754	976	7,194 D	32.5%	63.3%	33.9%	66.1%
FULTON	20,611	7,579	12,144	888	4,565 D	36.8%	58.9%	38.4%	61.6%
GALLATIN	4,813	1,279	3,469	65	2,190 D	26.6%	72.1%	26.9%	73.1%
GREENE	9,335	2,857	6,347	131	3,490 D	30.6%	68.0%	31.0%	69.0%
GRUNDY	9,315	4,491	4,755	69	264 D	48.2%	51.0%	48.6%	51.4%
HAMILTON	6,617	2,513	4,059	45	1,546 D	38.0%	61.3%	38.2%	61.8%
HANCOCK	13,734	4,789	8,808	137	4,019 D	34.9%	64.1%	35.2%	64.8%
HARDIN	3,223	1,559	1,610	54	51 D	48.4%	50.0%	49.2%	50.8%
HENDERSON	4,266	1,815	2,372	79	557 D	42.5%	55.6%	43.3%	56.7%
HENRY	22,199	11,376	10,122	701	1,254 D	51.2%	45.6%	52.9%	47.1%
IROQUOIS	15,898	6,303	9,434	161	3,131 D	39.6%	59.3%	40.1%	59.9%
JACKSON	17,715	7,636	9,730	349	2,094 D	43.1%	54.9%	44.0%	56.0%
JASPER	6,726	2,300	4,390	36	2,090 D	34.2%	65.3%	34.4%	65.6%
JEFFERSON	15,005	5,333	9,495	177	4,162 D	35.5%	63.3%	36.0%	64.0%
JERSEY	6,069	2,157	3,807	105	1,650 D	35.5%	62.7%	36.2%	63.8%
JO DAVIESS	10,177	4,520	5,497	160	977 D	44.4%	54.0%	45.1%	54.9%
JOHNSON	4,861	2,424	2,387	50	37 R	49.9%	49.1%	50.4%	49.6%
KANE	58,656	32,934	24,638	1,084	8,296 D	56.1%	42.0%	57.2%	42.8%
KANKAKEE	24,792	10,873	13,555	364	2,682 D	43.9%	54.7%	44.5%	55.5%
KENDALL	5,209	2,749	2,398	62	351 R	52.8%	46.0%	53.4%	46.6%
KNOX	24,918	12,244	12,282	392	38 D	49.1%	49.3%	49.9%	50.1%
LAKE	47,122	23,994	21,139	1,989	2,855 D	50.9%	44.9%	53.2%	46.8%
LA SALLE	47,587	19,179	27,500	908	8,321 D	40.3%	57.8%	41.1%	58.9%
LAWRENCE	10,441	4,194	6,100	147	1,906 D	40.2%	58.4%	40.7%	59.3%
LEE	15,161	7,802	7,182	177	620 R	51.5%	47.4%	52.1%	47.9%
LIVINGSTON	18,589	8,403	10,024	162	1,621 D	45.2%	53.9%	45.6%	54.4%
LOGAN	14,116	5,850	8,119	147	2,269 D	41.4%	57.5%	41.9%	58.1%
MCDONOUGH	14,105	6,329	7,608	168	1,279 D	44.9%	53.9%	45.4%	54.6%
MCHENRY	18,594	9,880	8,260	454	1,620 R	53.1%	44.4%	54.5%	45.5%
MCLEAN	35,871	15,450	19,535	886	4,085 D	43.1%	54.5%	44.2%	55.8%
MACON	39,346	17,068	21,638	640	4,570 D	43.4%	55.0%	43.8%	56.2%
MACOUPIN	23,640	7,031	14,810	1,799	7,779 D	29.7%	62.6%	32.2%	67.8%
MADISON	57,238	19,774	35,211	2,253	15,437 D	34.5%	61.5%	36.0%	64.0%

ILLINOIS

PRESIDENT 1928

County	Total Vote	Republican	Democratic	Other	Rep.-Dem. Plurality	Total Vote Rep.	Total Vote Dem.	Major Vote Rep.	Major Vote Dem.
MARION	15,052	9,110	5,823	119	3,287 R	60.5%	38.7%	61.0%	39.0%
MARSHALL	6,865	4,029	2,828	8	1,201 R	58.7%	41.2%	58.8%	41.2%
MASON	7,221	3,956	3,246	19	711 R	54.8%	45.0%	54.9%	45.1%
MASSAC	4,673	3,405	1,241	27	2,164 R	72.9%	26.6%	73.3%	26.7%
MENARD	5,025	3,243	1,742	40	1,501 R	64.5%	34.7%	65.1%	34.9%
MERCER	8,073	5,699	2,316	58	3,383 R	70.6%	28.7%	71.1%	28.9%
MONROE	5,665	2,721	2,934	10	213 D	48.0%	51.8%	48.1%	51.9%
MONTGOMERY	16,575	8,999	7,392	184	1,607 R	54.3%	44.6%	54.9%	45.1%
MORGAN	16,046	10,192	5,805	49	4,387 R	63.5%	36.2%	63.7%	36.3%
MOULTRIE	5,488	3,310	2,168	10	1,142 R	60.3%	39.5%	60.4%	39.6%
OGLE	12,546	9,808	2,691	47	7,117 R	78.2%	21.4%	78.5%	21.5%
PEORIA	54,913	31,024	23,150	739	7,874 R	56.5%	42.2%	57.3%	42.2%
PERRY	9,766	4,636	5,029	101	393 D	47.5%	51.5%	48.0%	52.0%
PIATT	6,557	4,565	1,959	33	2,606 R	69.6%	29.9%	70.0%	30.0%
PIKE	10,836	6,705	4,008	123	2,697 R	61.9%	37.0%	62.6%	37.4%
POPE	2,706	2,004	679	23	1,325 R	74.1%	25.1%	74.7%	25.3%
PULASKI	5,092	3,319	1,726	47	1,593 R	65.2%	33.9%	65.6%	34.2%
PUTNAM	2,270	1,387	869	14	518 R	61.1%	38.3%	61.5%	38.5%
RANDOLPH	12,093	5,739	6,251	103	512 D	47.5%	51.7%	47.9%	52.1%
RICHLAND	6,623	4,042	2,550	31	1,492 R	61.0%	38.5%	61.3%	38.7%
ROCK ISLAND	41,776	27,246	14,334	196	12,912 R	65.2%	34.3%	65.5%	34.5%
ST CLAIR	68,037	31,026	36,374	637	5,348 D	45.6%	53.5%	46.0%	54.0%
SALINE	13,083	7,525	6,337	121	1,188 R	53.8%	45.3%	54.3%	45.7%
SANGAMON	53,271	31,957	21,026	288	10,931 R	60.0%	39.5%	60.3%	39.7%
SCHUYLER	5,576	3,011	2,542	23	469 R	54.0%	45.6%	54.2%	45.8%
SCOTT	4,338	2,601	1,730	7	871 R	60.0%	39.9%	60.1%	39.9%
SHELBY	11,528	7,214	4,071	243	3,143 R	62.6%	35.3%	63.9%	36.1%
STARK	4,293	2,966	1,306	21	1,660 R	69.1%	30.4%	69.4%	30.6%
STEPHENSON	17,643	11,992	5,579	72	6,413 R	68.0%	31.6%	68.2%	31.8%
TAZEWELL	16,586	9,409	6,910	267	2,499 R	56.7%	41.7%	57.7%	42.3%
UNION	7,530	3,352	4,149	29	797 D	44.5%	55.1%	44.7%	55.3%
VERMILION	34,717	21,616	12,728	373	8,888 R	62.3%	36.7%	62.9%	37.1%
WABASH	6,369	2,373	3,955	41	1,582 D	37.3%	62.1%	37.5%	62.5%
WARREN	10,753	7,915	2,681	157	5,234 R	73.6%	24.9%	74.7%	25.3%
WASHINGTON	6,508	3,638	2,848	22	790 R	55.9%	43.8%	56.1%	43.9%
WAYNE	8,364	5,189	3,108	67	2,081 R	62.0%	37.2%	62.5%	37.5%
WHITE	7,879	4,177	3,666	36	511 R	53.0%	46.5%	53.3%	46.7%
WHITESIDE	17,728	13,580	4,079	69	9,501 R	76.6%	23.0%	76.9%	23.1%
WILL	47,405	26,081	20,877	447	5,204 R	55.0%	44.0%	55.5%	44.5%
WILLIAMSON	21,309	10,913	10,139	257	774 R	51.2%	47.6%	51.8%	48.2%
WINNEBAGO	41,372	33,258	7,684	430	25,574 R	80.4%	18.6%	81.2%	18.8%
WOODFORD	8,524	5,140	3,311	73	1,829 R	60.3%	38.8%	60.8%	39.2%
TOTAL	3,107,489	1,769,141	1,313,817	24,531	455,324 R	56.9%	42.3%	57.4%	42.6%

PRESIDENT 1932

County	Total Vote	Republican	Democratic	Other	Rep.-Dem. Plurality	Total Vote Rep.	Total Vote Dem.	Major Vote Rep.	Major Vote Dem.
MARION	17,380	6,276	10,791	313	4,515 D	36.1%	62.1%	36.8%	63.2%
MARSHALL	7,345	3,166	4,133	46	967 D	43.1%	56.3%	43.4%	56.6%
MASON	8,300	2,551	5,681	68	3,130 D	30.7%	68.4%	31.0%	69.0%
MASSAC	5,525	2,851	2,593	81	258 R	51.6%	46.9%	52.4%	47.6%
MENARD	5,823	2,327	3,453	43	1,126 D	40.0%	59.3%	40.3%	59.7%
MERCER	8,835	4,436	4,309	90	127 R	50.2%	48.8%	50.7%	49.3%
MONROE	6,259	2,186	3,993	80	1,807 D	34.9%	63.8%	35.4%	64.6%
MONTGOMERY	17,126	5,945	10,456	725	4,511 D	34.7%	61.1%	36.2%	63.8%
MORGAN	18,130	7,787	10,170	173	2,383 D	43.0%	56.1%	43.4%	56.6%
MOULTRIE	6,646	2,353	4,219	74	1,866 D	35.4%	63.5%	35.8%	64.2%
OGLE	13,912	8,224	5,416	272	2,808 R	59.1%	38.9%	60.3%	39.7%
PEORIA	63,716	25,166	37,605	945	12,439 D	39.5%	59.0%	40.1%	59.9%
PERRY	11,502	3,778	7,400	324	3,622 D	32.8%	64.3%	33.8%	66.2%
PIATT	7,643	3,179	4,200	64	1,021 D	42.7%	56.4%	43.1%	56.9%
PIKE	12,452	4,181	8,013	258	3,832 D	33.6%	64.4%	34.3%	65.7%
POPE	3,732	2,011	1,697	24	314 R	53.9%	45.5%	54.2%	45.8%
PULASKI	6,726	3,225	3,446	55	221 D	47.9%	51.2%	48.3%	51.7%
PUTNAM	2,651	1,050	1,554	47	504 D	39.6%	58.6%	40.3%	59.7%
RANDOLPH	13,647	4,747	8,634	266	3,887 D	34.8%	63.3%	35.5%	64.5%
RICHLAND	7,182	2,765	4,318	99	1,553 D	38.5%	60.1%	39.0%	61.0%
ROCK ISLAND	46,549	21,205	24,676	668	3,471 D	45.6%	53.0%	46.2%	53.8%
ST CLAIR	72,571	22,744	47,305	2,522	24,561 D	31.3%	65.2%	32.5%	67.5%
SALINE	16,673	6,294	9,725	454	3,431 D	38.2%	59.0%	39.3%	60.7%
SANGAMON	60,643	26,856	32,745	1,042	5,889 D	44.3%	54.0%	45.1%	54.9%
SCHUYLER	5,930	2,075	3,782	73	1,707 D	35.0%	63.8%	35.4%	64.6%
SCOTT	4,804	1,740	3,012	52	1,272 D	36.2%	62.7%	36.6%	63.4%
SHELBY	12,569	4,657	8,093	219	3,436 D	35.7%	62.4%	36.5%	63.5%
STARK	4,533	2,119	2,369	45	250 D	46.7%	52.3%	47.2%	52.8%
STEPHENSON	20,198	8,963	10,728	507	1,765 D	44.4%	53.1%	45.5%	54.5%
TAZEWELL	21,055	7,260	13,591	204	6,331 D	34.5%	64.5%	34.8%	65.2%
UNION	9,085	2,859	6,157	69	3,298 D	31.5%	67.8%	31.7%	68.3%
VERMILION	40,677	15,643	24,032	1,002	8,389 D	38.5%	59.1%	39.4%	60.6%
WABASH	6,695	2,309	4,280	106	1,971 D	34.5%	63.9%	35.0%	65.0%
WARREN	11,258	5,498	5,610	150	112 D	48.8%	49.8%	49.5%	50.5%
WASHINGTON	7,926	3,076	4,696	154	1,620 D	38.8%	59.2%	39.6%	60.4%
WAYNE	9,656	4,097	5,488	71	1,391 D	42.4%	56.8%	42.7%	57.3%
WHITE	9,298	3,320	5,909	69	2,589 D	35.7%	63.6%	36.0%	64.0%
WHITESIDE	18,626	11,388	7,010	228	4,378 R	61.1%	37.6%	61.9%	38.1%
WILL	52,266	25,173	25,798	1,295	625 D	48.2%	49.4%	49.4%	50.6%
WILLIAMSON	22,265	8,714	12,961	590	4,247 D	39.1%	58.2%	40.2%	59.8%
WINNEBAGO	46,625	26,632	17,707	2,286	8,925 R	57.1%	38.0%	60.1%	39.9%
WOODFORD	9,192	3,866	5,244	82	1,378 D	42.1%	57.0%	42.4%	57.6%
TOTAL	3,407,926	1,432,756	1,882,304	92,866	449,548 D	42.0%	55.2%	43.2%	56.8%

ILLINOIS

PRESIDENT 1936

County	Total Vote	Republican	Democratic	Other	Rep.-Dem. Plurality	%TV Rep.	%TV Dem.	%MV Rep.	%MV Dem.
ADAMS	33,473	13,114	18,857	1,502	5,743 D	39.2	56.3	41.0	59.0
ALEXANDER	12,653	5,553	6,972	128	1,419 D	43.9	55.1	44.3	55.7
BOND	7,836	4,046	3,541	249	505 R	51.6	45.2	53.3	46.7
BOONE	8,022	5,375	2,383	264	2,992 R	67.0	29.7	69.3	30.7
BROWN	4,549	1,591	2,873	85	1,282 D	35.0	63.2	35.6	64.4
BUREAU	20,322	10,462	9,516	344	946 R	51.5	46.8	52.4	47.6
CALHOUN	4,112	1,883	2,058	161	175 D	45.9	50.0	47.8	52.2
CARROLL	9,328	4,886	4,368	74	518 R	52.4	46.8	52.8	47.2
CASS	9,090	3,209	5,786	95	2,577 D	35.3	63.7	35.7	64.3
CHAMPAIGN	34,535	15,808	18,203	524	2,395 D	45.8	52.7	46.5	53.5
CHRISTIAN	20,521	8,145	11,400	976	3,255 D	39.7	55.6	41.7	58.3
CLARK	11,314	5,426	5,836	52	410 D	48.0	51.6	48.2	51.8
CLAY	9,384	4,528	4,752	104	224 D	48.3	50.6	48.8	51.2
CLINTON	11,145	3,653	5,355	2,137	1,702 D	32.8	48.0	40.6	59.4
COLES	20,868	8,800	11,931	137	3,131 D	42.2	57.2	42.4	57.6
COOK	2,009,457	701,206	1,253,164	55,087	551,958 D	34.9	62.4	35.9	64.1
CRAWFORD	12,059	5,823	6,164	112	341 D	48.3	51.1	48.6	51.4
CUMBERLAND	6,356	3,016	3,290	50	274 D	47.5	51.8	47.8	52.2
DE KALB	18,275	9,826	7,899	550	1,927 R	53.8	43.2	55.4	44.6
DE WITT	10,280	4,544	5,676	60	1,132 D	44.2	55.2	44.5	55.5
DOUGLAS	9,694	4,606	5,029	59	423 D	47.5	51.9	47.8	52.2
DU PAGE	51,632	28,380	21,684	1,568	6,696 R	55.0	42.0	56.7	43.3
EDGAR	14,898	6,929	7,822	147	893 D	46.5	52.5	47.0	53.0
EDWARDS	5,100	2,813	2,211	76	602 R	55.2	43.4	56.0	44.0
EFFINGHAM	10,583	4,293	6,030	260	1,737 D	40.6	57.0	41.6	58.4
FAYETTE	13,371	6,419	6,824	128	405 D	48.0	51.0	48.5	51.5
FORD	8,410	4,524	3,715	171	809 R	53.8	44.2	54.9	45.1
FRANKLIN	26,625	10,708	15,254	663	4,546 D	40.2	57.3	41.2	58.8
FULTON	23,422	10,130	12,864	428	2,734 D	43.2	54.9	44.1	55.9
GALLATIN	5,774	2,004	3,701	69	1,697 D	34.7	64.1	35.1	64.9
GREENE	10,544	3,916	6,510	118	2,594 D	37.1	61.7	37.6	62.4
GRUNDY	10,185	5,360	4,481	344	879 R	52.6	44.0	54.4	45.5
HAMILTON	7,535	3,321	4,152	62	831 D	44.1	55.1	44.4	55.6
HANCOCK	15,507	7,383	7,726	398	343 D	47.6	49.8	48.9	51.1
HARDIN	4,011	2,008	1,984	19	24 R	50.1	49.5	50.3	49.7
HENDERSON	5,220	2,663	2,496	61	167 R	51.0	47.8	51.6	48.4
HENRY	24,094	11,953	11,490	651	463 R	49.6	47.7	51.0	49.0
IROQUOIS	17,173	7,908	8,654	611	746 D	46.0	50.4	47.7	52.3
JACKSON	20,546	10,363	9,971	212	392 R	50.4	48.5	51.0	49.0
JASPER	7,502	3,221	4,149	132	928 D	42.9	55.3	43.7	56.3
JEFFERSON	17,668	7,290	10,240	138	2,950 D	41.3	58.0	41.6	58.4
JERSEY	7,061	3,023	3,955	83	932 D	42.8	56.0	43.3	56.7
JO DAVIESS	10,950	5,619	5,079	252	540 R	51.3	46.4	52.5	47.5
JOHNSON	6,050	3,537	2,497	16	1,040 R	58.5	41.3	58.6	41.4
KANE	63,729	33,491	28,187	2,051	5,304 R	52.6	44.2	54.3	45.7
KANKAKEE	26,538	10,935	13,162	2,441	2,227 D	41.2	49.6	45.4	54.6
KENDALL	5,720	3,138	2,374	208	764 R	54.9	41.5	56.9	43.1
KNOX	29,124	14,712	13,697	715	1,015 R	50.5	47.0	51.8	48.2
LAKE	53,675	27,548	24,524	1,603	3,024 R	51.3	45.7	52.9	47.1
LA SALLE	51,201	22,240	26,926	2,035	4,686 D	43.4	52.6	45.2	54.8
LAWRENCE	11,398	5,060	6,168	170	1,108 D	44.4	54.1	45.1	54.9
LEE	16,232	8,914	6,845	473	2,069 R	54.9	42.2	56.6	43.4
LIVINGSTON	20,334	10,801	9,190	343	1,611 R	53.1	45.2	54.0	46.0
LOGAN	15,087	7,019	7,886	182	867 D	46.5	52.3	47.1	52.9
MCDONOUGH	16,012	8,723	7,138	151	1,585 R	54.5	44.6	55.0	45.0
MCHENRY	19,866	12,031	6,893	942	5,138 R	60.6	34.7	63.6	36.4
MCLEAN	39,132	16,826	21,508	798	4,682 D	43.0	55.0	43.9	56.1
MACON	43,486	15,585	27,360	541	11,775 D	35.8	62.9	36.3	63.7
MACOUPIN	25,851	9,502	14,896	1,453	5,394 D	36.8	57.6	38.9	61.1
MADISON	65,686	22,073	42,172	1,441	20,099 D	33.6	64.2	34.4	65.6

PRESIDENT 1940

County	Total Vote	Republican	Democratic	Other	Rep.-Dem. Plurality	%TV Rep.	%TV Dem.	%MV Rep.	%MV Dem.
ADAMS	36,333	18,480	17,361	492	1,119 R	50.9	47.8	51.6	48.4
ALEXANDER	12,988	6,260	6,591	137	331 D	48.2	50.7	48.7	51.3
BOND	8,285	4,754	3,376	155	1,378 R	57.4	40.7	58.5	41.5
BOONE	8,632	6,330	2,277	25	4,053 R	73.3	26.4	73.5	26.5
BROWN	4,648	2,101	2,478	69	377 D	45.2	53.3	45.9	54.1
BUREAU	21,607	13,258	8,274	75	4,984 R	61.4	38.3	61.6	38.4
CALHOUN	4,158	2,516	1,625	17	891 R	60.5	39.1	60.8	39.2
CARROLL	10,013	6,398	3,592	23	2,806 R	63.9	35.9	64.0	36.0
CASS	9,416	4,490	4,854	72	364 D	47.7	51.6	48.1	51.9
CHAMPAIGN	38,144	20,314	17,563	267	2,751 R	53.3	46.0	53.6	46.4
CHRISTIAN	21,862	10,255	11,457	150	1,202 D	46.9	52.4	47.2	52.8
CLARK	10,836	5,976	4,807	53	1,169 R	55.1	44.4	55.4	44.6
CLAY	10,222	5,185	4,934	103	251 R	50.7	48.3	51.2	48.8
CLINTON	12,230	7,582	4,558	90	3,024 R	62.0	37.3	62.5	37.5
COLES	22,014	10,528	11,409	77	881 D	47.8	51.8	48.0	52.0
COOK	2,114,807	938,454	1,168,141	8,212	229,687 D	44.4	55.2	44.5	55.5
CRAWFORD	12,805	7,036	5,703	66	1,333 R	54.9	44.5	55.2	44.8
CUMBERLAND	6,451	3,330	3,091	30	239 R	51.6	47.9	51.9	48.1
DE KALB	19,668	12,577	6,989	102	5,588 R	63.9	35.5	64.3	35.7
DE WITT	10,574	5,477	5,052	45	425 R	51.8	47.8	52.0	48.0
DOUGLAS	10,031	5,451	4,513	67	938 R	54.3	45.0	54.7	45.3
DU PAGE	60,049	40,746	18,923	380	21,823 R	67.9	31.5	68.3	31.7
EDGAR	14,780	7,985	6,713	82	1,272 R	54.0	45.4	54.5	45.5
EDWARDS	5,182	3,361	1,770	51	1,591 R	64.9	34.2	65.5	34.5
EFFINGHAM	12,006	5,941	5,988	77	47 D	49.5	49.9	49.8	50.2
FAYETTE	14,915	7,486	7,286	143	200 R	50.2	48.9	50.7	49.3
FORD	8,862	5,770	3,062	30	2,708 R	65.1	34.6	65.3	34.7
FRANKLIN	28,660	12,936	15,523	201	2,587 D	45.1	54.2	45.5	54.5
FULTON	25,228	12,816	12,198	214	618 R	50.8	48.4	51.2	48.8
GALLATIN	5,929	2,588	3,293	48	705 D	43.6	55.5	44.0	56.0
GREENE	10,925	4,840	6,015	70	1,175 D	44.3	55.1	44.6	55.4
GRUNDY	10,741	6,593	4,105	43	2,488 R	61.4	38.2	61.6	38.4
HAMILTON	7,748	4,005	3,691	52	314 R	51.7	47.6	52.0	48.0
HANCOCK	15,961	9,108	6,688	165	2,420 R	57.1	41.9	57.7	42.3
HARDIN	4,333	2,333	1,974	26	359 R	53.8	45.6	54.2	45.8
HENDERSON	5,281	3,264	1,977	40	1,287 R	61.8	37.4	62.3	37.7
HENRY	25,648	14,971	10,481	196	4,490 R	58.4	40.9	58.8	41.2
IROQUOIS	18,191	11,047	7,036	108	4,011 R	60.7	38.7	61.1	38.9
JACKSON	21,708	11,980	9,600	128	2,380 R	55.2	44.2	55.5	44.5
JASPER	7,815	4,082	3,689	44	393 R	52.2	47.2	52.5	47.5
JEFFERSON	19,715	8,692	10,887	136	2,195 D	44.1	55.2	44.4	55.6
JERSEY	7,694	3,958	3,692	44	266 R	51.4	48.0	51.7	48.3
JO DAVIESS	11,192	7,290	3,869	33	3,421 R	65.1	34.6	65.3	34.7
JOHNSON	6,094	3,827	2,254	13	1,573 R	62.8	37.0	62.9	37.1
KANE	67,914	41,949	25,676	289	16,273 R	61.8	37.8	62.0	38.0
KANKAKEE	29,838	15,998	13,716	124	2,282 R	53.6	46.0	53.8	46.2
KENDALL	6,196	4,200	1,978	18	2,222 R	67.8	31.9	68.0	32.0
KNOX	30,224	17,459	12,597	168	4,862 R	57.8	41.7	58.1	41.9
LAKE	63,461	38,242	24,965	254	13,277 R	60.3	39.3	60.5	39.5
LA SALLE	55,399	25,296	29,704	399	4,408 D	45.7	53.6	46.0	54.0
LAWRENCE	11,833	6,061	5,625	147	436 R	51.2	47.5	51.9	48.1
LEE	17,285	11,228	6,005	52	5,223 R	65.0	34.7	65.2	34.8
LIVINGSTON	21,686	13,909	7,722	55	6,187 R	64.1	35.6	64.3	35.7
LOGAN	15,725	8,929	6,753	43	2,176 R	56.8	42.9	56.9	43.1
MCDONOUGH	16,217	10,326	5,783	108	4,543 R	63.7	35.7	64.1	35.9
MCHENRY	22,795	16,480	6,170	145	10,310 R	72.3	27.1	72.8	27.2
MCLEAN	40,166	21,865	18,024	277	3,841 R	54.4	44.9	54.8	45.2
MACON	47,864	19,998	27,589	277	7,591 D	41.8	57.6	42.0	58.0
MACOUPIN	27,610	13,000	14,356	254	1,356 D	47.1	52.0	47.5	52.5
MADISON	75,929	30,445	44,803	681	14,358 D	40.1	59.0	40.5	59.5

ILLINOIS

PRESIDENT 1936

County	Total Vote	Republican	Democratic	Other	Rep.-Dem. Plurality	% Total Vote Rep.	% Total Vote Dem.	% Major Vote Rep.	% Major Vote Dem.
MARION	19,446	8,321	10,820	305	2,499 D	42.8%	55.6%	43.5%	56.5%
MARSHALL	7,760	3,544	4,149	67	605 D	45.7%	53.5%	46.1%	53.9%
MASON	8,731	3,395	5,278	58	1,883 D	38.9%	60.5%	39.1%	60.9%
MASSAC	5,983	3,894	3,039	50	855 R	58.8%	43.5%	56.2%	43.8%
MENARD	6,277	3,067	3,152	58	85 D	48.9%	50.2%	49.3%	50.7%
MERCER	9,884	5,028	4,751	105	277 R	50.9%	48.1%	51.4%	48.6%
MONROE	6,850	3,226	3,477	147	251 D	47.1%	50.8%	48.1%	51.9%
MONTGOMERY	18,964	8,140	10,132	692	1,992 D	42.9%	53.4%	44.5%	55.5%
MORGAN	18,811	8,844	9,800	167	956 D	47.0%	52.1%	47.4%	52.6%
MOULTRIE	7,249	3,074	4,110	65	1,036 D	42.4%	56.7%	42.8%	57.2%
OGLE	15,546	9,576	5,776	194	3,800 R	61.6%	37.2%	62.4%	37.6%
PEORIA	74,865	25,425	48,063	1,377	22,638 D	34.0%	64.2%	34.6%	65.4%
PERRY	12,768	5,482	7,043	243	1,561 D	42.9%	55.2%	43.8%	56.2%
PIATT	8,061	3,931	4,084	46	153 D	48.8%	50.7%	49.0%	51.0%
PIKE	13,974	5,589	8,187	198	2,598 D	40.0%	58.6%	40.6%	59.4%
POPE	4,548	2,787	1,728	33	1,059 R	61.3%	38.0%	61.7%	38.3%
PULASKI	7,645	3,774	3,804	67	30 D	49.4%	49.8%	49.8%	50.2%
PUTNAM	2,901	1,435	1,437	29	2 D	49.5%	49.5%	50.0%	50.0%
RANDOLPH	15,701	7,057	8,247	397	1,190 D	44.9%	52.5%	46.1%	53.9%
RICHLAND	8,492	4,040	4,268	184	228 D	47.6%	50.3%	48.6%	51.4%
ROCK ISLAND	53,027	19,487	32,741	799	13,254 D	36.7%	61.7%	37.3%	62.7%
ST CLAIR	83,762	26,684	54,238	2,840	27,554 D	31.9%	64.8%	33.0%	67.0%
SALINE	19,616	9,055	10,253	308	1,198 D	46.2%	52.3%	46.9%	53.1%
SANGAMON	63,670	29,562	32,281	1,827	2,719 D	46.4%	50.7%	47.8%	52.2%
SCHUYLER	6,957	3,029	3,885	43	856 D	43.5%	55.8%	43.8%	56.2%
SCOTT	5,138	2,165	2,945	28	780 D	42.1%	57.3%	42.4%	57.6%
SHELBY	14,201	5,795	8,186	220	2,391 D	40.8%	57.6%	41.4%	58.6%
STARK	4,958	2,696	2,220	42	476 R	54.4%	44.8%	54.8%	45.2%
STEPHENSON	21,342	9,943	10,567	832	624 D	46.6%	49.5%	48.5%	51.5%
TAZEWELL	24,774	7,946	16,487	341	8,541 D	32.1%	66.5%	32.5%	67.5%
UNION	10,461	4,165	6,260	36	2,095 D	39.8%	59.8%	40.0%	60.0%
VERMILION	44,156	18,350	25,016	790	6,666 D	41.6%	56.7%	42.3%	57.7%
WABASH	7,224	2,860	4,214	150	1,354 D	39.6%	58.3%	40.4%	59.6%
WARREN	12,465	6,919	5,409	137	1,510 R	55.5%	43.4%	56.1%	43.9%
WASHINGTON	8,868	4,540	4,119	209	421 R	51.2%	46.4%	52.4%	47.6%
WAYNE	11,330	5,528	5,752	50	224 D	48.8%	50.8%	49.0%	51.0%
WHITE	10,909	4,322	6,511	76	2,189 D	39.6%	59.7%	39.9%	60.1%
WHITESIDE	21,243	12,666	7,982	595	4,684 R	59.6%	37.6%	61.3%	38.7%
WILL	55,314	25,028	28,135	2,151	3,107 D	45.2%	50.9%	47.1%	52.9%
WILLIAMSON	27,334	12,319	14,663	352	2,344 D	45.1%	53.6%	45.7%	54.3%
WINNEBAGO	53,989	24,997	27,200	1,792	2,203 D	46.3%	50.4%	47.9%	52.1%
WOODFORD	10,093	4,845	5,122	126	277 D	48.0%	50.7%	48.6%	51.4%
TOTAL	3,956,522	1,570,393	2,282,999	103,130	712,606 D	39.7%	57.7%	40.8%	59.2%

PRESIDENT 1940

County	Total Vote	Republican	Democratic	Other	Rep.-Dem. Plurality	% Total Vote Rep.	% Total Vote Dem.	% Major Vote Rep.	% Major Vote Dem.
MARION	24,476	10,461	13,807	208	3,346 D	42.7%	56.4%	43.1%	56.9%
MARSHALL	7,910	4,527	4,343	40	1,184 R	57.2%	42.3%	57.5%	42.5%
MASON	8,998	4,541	4,416	41	125 R	50.5%	49.1%	50.7%	49.3%
MASSAC	7,574	4,722	2,813	39	1,909 R	62.3%	37.1%	62.7%	37.3%
MENARD	6,458	3,531	2,894	33	637 R	54.7%	44.8%	55.0%	45.0%
MERCER	10,204	6,336	3,830	38	2,506 R	62.1%	37.5%	62.3%	37.7%
MONROE	7,602	4,754	2,826	22	1,928 R	62.5%	37.2%	62.7%	37.3%
MONTGOMERY	20,325	10,497	9,654	174	843 R	51.6%	47.5%	52.1%	47.9%
MORGAN	19,283	10,137	9,082	64	1,055 R	52.6%	47.1%	52.7%	47.3%
MOULTRIE	7,373	3,636	3,696	41	60 D	49.3%	50.1%	49.6%	50.4%
OGLE	16,742	11,838	4,833	71	7,005 R	70.7%	28.9%	71.0%	29.0%
PEORIA	77,221	34,911	42,009	301	7,098 D	45.2%	54.4%	45.4%	54.6%
PERRY	13,837	7,243	6,539	55	704 R	52.3%	47.3%	52.6%	47.4%
PIATT	8,159	4,564	3,564	31	1,000 R	55.9%	43.7%	56.2%	43.8%
PIKE	14,441	6,619	7,676	146	1,057 D	45.8%	53.2%	46.3%	53.7%
POPE	4,430	2,914	1,499	17	1,415 R	65.8%	33.8%	66.0%	34.0%
PULASKI	8,085	4,589	3,456	40	1,133 R	56.8%	42.7%	57.0%	43.0%
PUTNAM	2,985	1,778	1,195	12	583 R	59.6%	40.0%	59.8%	40.2%
RANDOLPH	17,215	9,333	7,802	80	1,531 R	54.2%	45.3%	54.5%	45.5%
RICHLAND	9,446	5,022	4,335	89	687 R	53.2%	45.9%	53.7%	46.3%
ROCK ISLAND	61,101	25,629	35,240	232	9,611 D	41.9%	57.7%	42.1%	57.9%
ST CLAIR	89,891	35,998	53,482	411	17,484 D	40.0%	59.5%	40.2%	59.8%
SALINE	21,377	10,567	10,692	118	125 D	49.4%	50.0%	49.7%	50.3%
SANGAMON	67,628	35,464	31,943	221	3,521 R	52.4%	47.2%	52.6%	47.4%
SCHUYLER	6,803	3,318	3,404	81	86 D	48.8%	50.0%	49.4%	50.6%
SCOTT	5,099	2,585	2,492	22	93 R	50.7%	48.9%	50.9%	49.1%
SHELBY	15,197	7,250	7,704	243	454 D	47.7%	50.7%	48.5%	51.5%
STARK	5,225	3,393	1,818	14	1,575 R	64.9%	34.8%	65.1%	34.9%
STEPHENSON	23,045	14,040	8,911	94	5,129 R	60.9%	38.7%	61.2%	38.8%
TAZEWELL	30,159	12,419	17,624	116	5,205 D	41.2%	58.4%	41.3%	58.7%
UNION	10,800	4,915	5,804	81	889 D	45.5%	53.7%	45.9%	54.1%
VERMILION	46,242	23,059	22,891	292	168 R	49.9%	49.5%	50.2%	49.8%
WABASH	7,965	3,659	4,187	119	528 D	45.9%	52.6%	46.6%	53.4%
WARREN	12,735	7,790	4,878	67	2,912 R	61.2%	38.3%	61.5%	38.5%
WASHINGTON	9,222	5,701	3,479	42	2,222 R	61.8%	37.7%	62.1%	37.9%
WAYNE	12,192	6,556	5,569	67	987 R	53.8%	45.7%	54.1%	45.9%
WHITE	11,493	5,459	5,909	125	450 D	47.5%	51.4%	48.0%	52.0%
WHITESIDE	23,242	15,752	7,356	134	8,396 R	67.8%	31.6%	68.2%	31.8%
WILL	61,946	32,291	29,442	213	2,849 R	52.1%	47.5%	52.3%	47.7%
WILLIAMSON	29,217	14,433	14,645	139	212 D	49.4%	50.1%	49.6%	50.4%
WINNEBAGO	59,127	30,683	28,061	383	2,622 R	51.9%	47.5%	52.2%	47.8%
WOODFORD	10,942	6,575	4,314	53	2,261 R	60.1%	39.4%	60.4%	39.6%
TOTAL	4,217,935	2,047,240	2,149,934	20,761	102,694 D	48.5%	51.0%	48.8%	51.2%

ILLINOIS

PRESIDENT 1944

County	Total Vote	Republican	Democratic	Other	Rep.-Dem. Plurality	Rep. % (Total)	Dem. % (Total)	Rep. % (Major)	Dem. % (Major)
ADAMS	29,439	15,564	13,733	142	1,831 R	52.9%	46.6%	53.1%	46.9%
ALEXANDER	9,637	4,792	4,767	78	25 R	49.7%	49.5%	50.1%	49.9%
BOND	6,708	3,907	2,607	194	1,300 R	58.2%	38.9%	60.0%	40.0%
BOONE	7,800	5,708	2,074	18	3,634 R	73.2%	26.6%	73.3%	26.7%
BROWN	3,607	1,738	1,849	20	111 D	48.2%	51.3%	48.5%	51.5%
BUREAU	18,829	11,802	6,976	51	4,826 R	62.7%	37.0%	62.9%	37.1%
CALHOUN	3,241	1,956	1,271	14	685 R	60.4%	39.2%	60.6%	39.4%
CARROLL	8,962	6,101	2,843	18	3,258 R	68.1%	31.7%	68.2%	31.8%
CASS	7,585	3,641	3,909	35	268 D	48.0%	51.5%	48.2%	51.8%
CHAMPAIGN	32,954	18,935	13,842	177	5,093 R	57.5%	42.0%	57.8%	42.2%
CHRISTIAN	18,437	8,995	9,360	82	365 D	48.8%	50.8%	49.0%	51.0%
CLARK	9,044	5,373	3,619	52	1,754 R	59.4%	40.0%	59.8%	40.2%
CLAY	8,110	4,484	3,531	95	953 R	55.3%	43.5%	55.9%	44.1%
CLINTON	10,750	6,753	3,944	53	2,809 R	62.8%	36.7%	63.1%	36.9%
COLES	18,463	9,473	8,936	54	537 R	51.3%	48.4%	51.5%	48.5%
COOK	2,206,191	924,659	1,275,367	6,165	350,708 D	41.9%	57.8%	42.0%	58.0%
CRAWFORD	10,617	6,056	4,482	79	1,574 R	57.0%	42.2%	57.5%	42.5%
CUMBERLAND	5,106	2,700	2,391	15	309 R	52.9%	46.8%	53.0%	47.0%
DE KALB	18,210	12,157	6,004	49	6,153 R	66.8%	33.0%	66.9%	33.1%
DE WITT	8,357	4,630	3,658	69	972 R	55.4%	43.8%	55.9%	44.1%
DOUGLAS	8,035	4,684	3,323	28	1,361 R	58.3%	41.4%	58.5%	41.5%
DU PAGE	60,775	41,890	18,711	174	23,179 R	68.9%	30.8%	69.1%	30.9%
EDGAR	12,069	6,961	5,054	54	1,907 R	57.7%	41.9%	58.0%	42.0%
EDWARDS	4,250	3,016	1,197	37	1,819 R	71.0%	28.2%	71.6%	28.4%
EFFINGHAM	10,119	5,441	4,587	91	854 R	53.8%	45.3%	54.3%	45.7%
FAYETTE	11,887	6,332	5,435	120	897 R	53.3%	45.7%	53.8%	46.2%
FORD	7,605	5,317	2,270	18	3,047 R	69.9%	29.8%	70.1%	29.9%
FRANKLIN	23,213	11,377	11,663	173	286 D	49.0%	50.2%	49.4%	50.6%
FULTON	20,229	11,117	8,946	166	2,171 R	55.0%	44.2%	55.4%	44.6%
GALLATIN	4,295	2,073	2,175	47	102 D	48.3%	50.6%	48.8%	51.2%
GREENE	8,574	4,261	4,268	45	7 D	49.7%	49.8%	50.0%	50.0%
GRUNDY	9,876	6,310	3,544	22	2,766 R	63.9%	35.9%	64.0%	36.0%
HAMILTON	6,551	3,582	2,914	55	668 R	54.7%	44.5%	55.1%	44.9%
HANCOCK	13,378	7,972	5,338	68	2,634 R	59.5%	39.9%	59.9%	40.1%
HARDIN	3,438	2,037	1,370	31	667 R	59.2%	39.8%	59.8%	40.2%
HENDERSON	4,255	2,695	1,550	10	1,145 R	63.3%	36.4%	63.5%	36.5%
HENRY	22,761	13,539	9,130	92	4,409 R	59.5%	40.1%	59.7%	40.3%
IROQUOIS	15,648	10,389	5,168	91	5,221 R	66.4%	33.0%	66.6%	33.4%
JACKSON	16,791	10,002	6,735	54	3,267 R	59.6%	40.1%	59.8%	40.2%
JASPER	6,624	3,453	3,142	29	311 R	52.1%	47.4%	52.4%	47.6%
JEFFERSON	16,551	7,916	8,496	139	580 D	47.8%	51.3%	48.2%	51.8%
JERSEY	6,486	3,546	2,910	30	636 R	54.7%	44.9%	54.9%	45.1%
JO DAVIESS	9,797	6,465	3,298	34	3,167 R	66.0%	33.7%	66.2%	33.8%
JOHNSON	4,833	3,298	1,522	13	1,776 R	68.2%	31.5%	68.4%	31.6%
KANE	62,236	38,689	23,362	185	15,327 R	62.2%	37.5%	62.4%	37.6%
KANKAKEE	26,688	15,256	11,342	90	3,914 R	57.2%	42.5%	57.4%	42.6%
KENDALL	5,701	4,022	1,673	6	2,349 R	70.5%	29.3%	70.6%	29.4%
KNOX	26,160	15,964	10,070	126	5,894 R	61.0%	38.5%	61.3%	38.7%
LAKE	61,310	35,674	25,453	183	10,221 R	58.2%	41.5%	58.4%	41.6%
LA SALLE	51,878	28,179	21,489	2,210	6,690 R	54.3%	41.4%	56.7%	43.3%
LAWRENCE	9,305	5,191	4,003	111	1,188 R	55.8%	43.0%	56.5%	43.5%
LEE	15,317	10,397	4,889	21	5,498 R	67.9%	31.9%	68.0%	32.0%
LIVINGSTON	18,719	12,436	6,231	52	6,205 R	66.4%	33.3%	66.6%	33.4%
LOGAN	12,852	7,955	4,868	29	3,087 R	61.9%	37.9%	62.0%	38.0%
MCDONOUGH	13,616	9,028	4,497	91	4,531 R	66.3%	33.0%	66.8%	33.2%
MCHENRY	21,299	15,666	5,567	66	10,099 R	73.6%	26.1%	73.8%	26.2%
MCLEAN	33,562	19,366	14,011	185	5,355 R	57.7%	41.7%	58.0%	42.0%
MACON	42,569	19,608	22,808	153	3,200 D	46.1%	53.5%	46.2%	53.8%
MACOUPIN	23,683	11,572	11,951	160	379 D	48.9%	50.5%	49.2%	50.8%
MADISON	68,872	28,399	40,114	359	11,715 D	41.2%	58.2%	41.5%	58.5%

PRESIDENT 1948

County	Total Vote	Republican	Democratic	Other	Rep.-Dem. Plurality	Rep. % (Total)	Dem. % (Total)	Rep. % (Major)	Dem. % (Major)
ADAMS	29,441	14,329	14,960	152	631 D	48.7%	50.8%	48.9%	51.1%
ALEXANDER	9,298	4,561	4,641	96	80 D	49.1%	49.9%	49.6%	50.4%
BOND	6,483	3,438	2,837	208	601 R	53.0%	43.6%	54.6%	45.4%
BOONE	6,882	4,916	1,941	25	2,975 R	71.4%	28.2%	71.7%	28.3%
BROWN	3,389	1,562	1,805	22	243 D	46.1%	53.3%	46.4%	53.6%
BUREAU	17,748	11,207	6,463	78	4,744 R	63.1%	36.4%	63.4%	36.6%
CALHOUN	2,923	1,526	1,377	20	149 R	52.2%	47.1%	52.6%	47.4%
CARROLL	8,189	5,318	2,809	62	2,509 R	64.9%	34.3%	65.4%	34.6%
CASS	7,217	3,391	3,776	50	385 D	47.0%	52.3%	47.3%	52.7%
CHAMPAIGN	31,465	19,156	11,572	737	7,584 R	60.9%	36.8%	62.3%	37.7%
CHRISTIAN	17,062	7,576	9,366	120	1,790 D	44.4%	54.9%	44.7%	55.3%
CLARK	8,303	4,477	3,714	112	763 D	53.9%	44.7%	54.7%	45.3%
CLAY	7,108	3,782	3,160	166	622 R	53.2%	44.5%	54.5%	45.5%
CLINTON	9,963	5,128	4,773	62	355 R	51.5%	47.9%	51.8%	48.2%
COLES	17,084	8,638	8,393	53	245 R	50.6%	49.1%	50.7%	49.3%
COOK	2,245,899	1,015,800	1,216,636	13,463	200,836 D	45.2%	54.2%	45.5%	54.5%
CRAWFORD	9,364	5,111	4,150	103	961 R	54.6%	44.3%	55.2%	44.8%
CUMBERLAND	4,832	2,451	2,353	98	98 R	50.7%	48.7%	51.0%	49.0%
DE KALB	16,567	11,380	5,082	105	6,298 R	68.7%	30.7%	69.1%	30.9%
DE WITT	7,513	4,178	3,290	45	888 R	55.6%	43.8%	55.9%	44.1%
DOUGLAS	7,129	4,181	2,893	55	1,288 R	58.6%	40.6%	59.1%	40.9%
DU PAGE	62,258	45,794	15,528	916	30,266 R	73.6%	24.9%	74.7%	25.3%
EDGAR	11,470	6,282	5,121	67	1,161 R	54.8%	44.6%	55.1%	44.9%
EDWARDS	3,770	2,491	1,206	73	1,285 R	66.1%	32.0%	67.4%	32.6%
EFFINGHAM	9,859	4,823	4,940	96	117 D	48.9%	50.1%	49.4%	50.6%
FAYETTE	11,608	5,717	5,771	120	54 D	49.3%	49.7%	49.8%	50.2%
FORD	7,015	4,903	2,079	33	2,824 R	69.9%	29.6%	70.2%	29.8%
FRANKLIN	21,444	9,407	11,750	287	2,343 D	43.9%	54.8%	44.5%	55.5%
FULTON	17,933	9,504	8,226	203	1,278 R	53.0%	45.9%	53.6%	46.4%
GALLATIN	4,200	1,789	2,385	26	596 D	42.6%	56.8%	42.9%	57.1%
GREENE	7,727	3,639	4,035	53	396 D	47.1%	52.2%	47.4%	52.6%
GRUNDY	9,240	5,954	3,255	31	2,699 R	64.4%	35.2%	64.7%	35.3%
HAMILTON	5,669	2,887	2,750	32	137 R	50.9%	48.5%	51.2%	48.8%
HANCOCK	12,779	7,098	5,559	122	1,539 R	55.5%	43.5%	56.1%	43.9%
HARDIN	3,087	1,713	1,358	16	355 R	55.5%	44.0%	55.8%	44.2%
HENDERSON	3,838	2,336	1,465	37	871 R	60.9%	38.2%	61.5%	38.5%
HENRY	21,011	12,363	8,489	159	3,874 R	58.8%	40.4%	59.3%	40.7%
IROQUOIS	14,001	9,051	4,823	127	4,228 R	64.6%	34.4%	65.2%	34.8%
JACKSON	15,408	8,288	6,939	181	1,349 R	53.8%	45.0%	54.4%	45.6%
JASPER	5,943	2,957	2,936	50	21 R	49.8%	49.4%	50.2%	49.8%
JEFFERSON	16,321	7,393	8,928	—	1,535 D	45.3%	54.7%	45.3%	54.7%
JERSEY	6,139	3,021	3,092	26	71 D	49.2%	50.4%	49.4%	50.6%
JO DAVIESS	8,570	5,299	3,210	61	2,079 R	61.8%	37.5%	62.2%	37.8%
JOHNSON	4,309	2,778	1,510	21	1,268 R	64.5%	35.0%	64.8%	35.0%
KANE	60,992	39,284	21,176	532	18,108 R	64.4%	34.7%	65.0%	35.0%
KANKAKEE	27,201	15,699	11,305	197	4,394 R	57.7%	41.6%	58.1%	41.9%
KENDALL	5,469	3,925	1,517	27	2,408 R	71.8%	27.7%	72.1%	27.9%
KNOX	24,952	15,016	9,772	164	5,244 R	60.2%	39.2%	60.6%	39.4%
LAKE	62,368	39,456	22,192	720	17,264 R	63.3%	35.6%	64.0%	36.0%
LA SALLE	44,440	24,453	19,666	321	4,787 R	55.0%	44.3%	55.4%	44.6%
LAWRENCE	9,057	4,472	4,391	194	81 R	49.4%	48.5%	50.5%	49.5%
LEE	13,441	9,001	4,368	72	4,633 R	67.0%	32.5%	67.3%	32.7%
LIVINGSTON	16,876	11,184	5,618	74	5,566 R	66.3%	33.3%	66.6%	33.4%
LOGAN	12,312	7,431	4,832	49	2,599 R	60.4%	39.2%	60.6%	39.4%
MCDONOUGH	12,373	8,058	4,206	109	3,852 R	65.1%	34.0%	65.7%	34.3%
MCHENRY	20,949	15,387	5,459	103	9,928 R	73.4%	26.1%	73.8%	26.2%
MCLEAN	31,517	18,430	12,904	183	5,526 R	58.5%	40.9%	58.8%	41.2%
MACON	40,456	18,719	21,487	250	2,768 D	46.3%	53.1%	46.6%	53.4%
MACOUPIN	22,298	10,198	11,742	358	1,544 D	45.7%	52.7%	46.5%	53.5%
MADISON	66,306	25,059	40,897	350	15,838 D	37.8%	61.7%	38.0%	62.0%

ILLINOIS

PRESIDENT 1944

County	Total Vote	Republican	Democratic	Other	Rep.-Dem. Plurality	Total Vote % Rep.	Total Vote % Dem.	Major Vote % Rep.	Major Vote % Dem.
MARION	19,640	9,408	10,079	153	671 D	47.9%	51.3%	48.3%	51.7%
MARSHALL	6,801	4,195	2,596	10	1,599 R	61.7%	38.2%	61.8%	38.2%
MASON	7,262	3,959	3,282	21	677 R	54.5%	45.2%	54.7%	45.3%
MASSAC	5,648	3,814	1,758	76	2,056 R	67.5%	31.1%	68.4%	31.6%
MENARD	4,926	3,013	1,888	25	1,125 R	61.2%	38.3%	61.5%	38.5%
MERCER	8,978	5,667	3,277	34	2,390 R	63.1%	36.5%	63.4%	36.6%
MONROE	6,109	4,032	2,068	9	1,964 R	66.0%	33.9%	66.1%	33.9%
MONTGOMERY	17,045	8,989	7,855	201	1,134 R	52.7%	46.1%	53.4%	46.6%
MORGAN	15,930	8,923	6,965	42	1,958 R	56.0%	43.7%	56.2%	43.8%
MOULTRIE	6,079	3,180	2,853	46	327 R	52.3%	46.9%	52.7%	47.3%
OGLE	14,712	10,680	3,951	81	6,729 R	72.6%	26.9%	73.0%	27.0%
PEORIA	67,251	34,171	32,837	243	1,334 R	50.8%	48.8%	51.0%	49.0%
PERRY	10,946	6,236	4,677	33	1,559 R	57.0%	42.7%	57.1%	42.9%
PIATT	6,588	3,912	2,641	35	1,271 R	59.4%	40.1%	59.7%	40.3%
PIKE	11,532	5,633	5,833	66	200 D	48.8%	50.6%	49.1%	50.9%
POPE	3,158	2,305	813	40	1,492 R	73.0%	25.7%	73.9%	26.1%
PULASKI	5,598	3,248	2,311	39	937 R	58.0%	41.3%	58.4%	41.6%
PUTNAM	2,396	1,521	865	10	656 R	63.5%	36.1%	63.7%	36.3%
RANDOLPH	13,756	7,518	6,199	39	1,319 R	54.7%	45.1%	54.8%	45.2%
RICHLAND	7,514	4,577	2,858	79	1,719 R	60.9%	38.0%	61.6%	38.4%
ROCK ISLAND	54,262	23,980	30,102	180	6,122 D	44.2%	55.5%	44.3%	55.7%
ST CLAIR	82,209	33,557	48,325	327	14,768 D	40.8%	58.8%	41.0%	59.0%
SALINE	16,539	9,083	7,351	105	1,732 R	54.9%	44.4%	55.1%	44.9%
SANGAMON	61,745	32,871	28,713	161	4,158 R	53.2%	46.5%	53.4%	46.6%
SCHUYLER	5,405	2,801	2,555	49	246 R	51.8%	47.3%	52.3%	47.7%
SCOTT	4,058	2,185	1,864	9	321 R	53.8%	45.9%	54.0%	46.0%
SHELBY	12,243	6,201	5,919	123	282 R	50.6%	48.3%	51.2%	48.8%
STARK	4,458	3,050	1,401	7	1,649 R	68.4%	31.4%	68.5%	31.5%
STEPHENSON	19,821	11,948	7,755	118	4,193 R	60.3%	39.1%	60.6%	39.4%
TAZEWELL	27,039	12,531	14,412	96	1,881 D	46.3%	53.3%	46.5%	53.5%
UNION	8,527	4,114	4,367	46	253 D	48.2%	51.2%	48.5%	51.5%
VERMILION	39,454	20,794	18,387	273	2,407 R	52.7%	46.6%	53.1%	46.9%
WABASH	6,603	3,496	3,026	81	470 R	52.9%	45.8%	53.6%	46.4%
WARREN	11,050	7,085	3,926	39	3,159 R	64.1%	35.5%	64.4%	35.7%
WASHINGTON	8,186	5,428	2,723	35	2,705 R	66.3%	33.3%	66.6%	33.4%
WAYNE	9,763	5,683	4,019	61	1,664 R	58.6%	41.2%	58.6%	41.4%
WHITE	10,052	5,139	4,822	91	317 R	51.1%	48.0%	51.6%	48.4%
WHITESIDE	19,888	14,162	5,555	171	8,607 R	71.2%	27.9%	71.8%	28.2%
WILL	57,453	30,058	27,085	310	2,973 R	52.3%	47.1%	52.8%	47.4%
WILLIAMSON	22,671	12,594	9,974	103	2,620 R	55.8%	44.0%	55.8%	44.2%
WINNEBAGO	58,945	30,837	27,831	277	3,006 R	52.3%	47.2%	52.6%	47.4%
WOODFORD	9,787	6,237	3,514	36	2,723 R	63.7%	35.9%	64.0%	36.0%
TOTAL	4,036,061	1,939,314	2,079,479	17,268	140,165 D	48.0%	51.5%	48.3%	51.7%

PRESIDENT 1948

County	Total Vote	Republican	Democratic	Other	Rep.-Dem. Plurality	Total Vote % Rep.	Total Vote % Dem.	Major Vote % Rep.	Major Vote % Dem.
MARION	16,884	7,798	8,878	208	1,080 D	46.2%	52.6%	46.8%	53.2%
MARSHALL	6,318	3,785	2,514	19	1,271 R	59.9%	39.8%	60.1%	39.9%
MASON	7,074	3,525	3,503	46	22 R	49.8%	49.5%	50.2%	49.8%
MASSAC	5,125	3,201	1,842	82	1,359 R	62.5%	35.9%	63.5%	36.5%
MENARD	4,968	2,899	2,043	26	856 R	58.4%	41.1%	58.7%	41.3%
MERCER	8,420	5,267	3,117	36	2,150 R	62.6%	37.0%	62.8%	37.2%
MONROE	5,432	3,403	2,026	3	1,377 R	62.6%	37.3%	62.7%	37.3%
MONTGOMERY	16,455	8,348	7,902	205	446 R	50.7%	48.0%	51.4%	48.6%
MORGAN	15,255	8,398	6,798	59	1,600 R	55.1%	44.6%	55.3%	44.7%
MOULTRIE	6,161	3,043	3,037	81	6 R	49.4%	49.3%	50.0%	50.0%
OGLE	13,373	9,519	3,796	63	5,723 R	71.2%	28.4%	71.5%	28.5%
PEORIA	66,352	35,018	31,026	308	3,992 R	52.8%	46.8%	53.0%	47.0%
PERRY	10,226	5,109	5,043	74	66 R	50.0%	49.3%	50.3%	49.7%
PIATT	6,064	3,646	2,361	57	1,285 R	60.1%	38.9%	60.7%	39.3%
PIKE	10,494	4,722	5,674	98	952 D	45.0%	54.1%	45.4%	54.6%
POPE	2,696	1,764	916	16	848 R	65.4%	34.0%	65.8%	34.2%
PULASKI	5,033	2,658	2,344	31	314 R	52.8%	46.6%	53.1%	46.9%
PUTNAM	2,336	1,405	905	26	500 R	60.1%	38.7%	60.8%	39.2%
RANDOLPH	13,781	6,867	6,852	62	15 R	49.8%	49.7%	50.1%	49.9%
RICHLAND	6,413	3,884	2,438	91	1,446 R	60.6%	38.0%	61.4%	38.6%
ROCK ISLAND	47,211	22,192	24,542	477	2,350 D	47.0%	52.0%	47.5%	52.5%
ST CLAIR	85,617	30,883	54,260	474	23,377 D	36.1%	63.4%	36.3%	63.7%
SALINE	15,485	7,676	7,718	91	42 D	49.6%	49.8%	49.8%	50.1%
SANGAMON	63,273	33,714	29,196	363	4,518 R	53.3%	46.1%	53.6%	46.4%
SCHUYLER	5,074	2,519	2,464	91	55 R	49.6%	48.6%	50.6%	49.4%
SCOTT	3,588	1,840	1,735	13	105 R	51.3%	48.4%	51.5%	48.5%
SHELBY	11,029	5,282	5,589	158	307 D	47.9%	50.7%	48.6%	51.4%
STARK	3,707	2,537	1,163	7	1,374 R	68.4%	31.4%	68.6%	31.4%
STEPHENSON	18,122	10,564	7,409	149	3,155 R	58.3%	40.9%	58.8%	41.2%
TAZEWELL	26,778	12,504	14,131	143	1,627 D	46.7%	52.8%	46.9%	53.1%
UNION	8,398	3,864	4,479	55	615 D	46.0%	53.3%	46.3%	53.7%
VERMILION	35,646	18,994	16,173	479	2,821 R	53.3%	45.4%	54.0%	46.0%
WABASH	5,898	2,916	2,857	125	59 R	49.4%	48.4%	50.5%	49.5%
WARREN	10,179	6,738	3,367	74	3,371 R	66.2%	33.1%	66.7%	33.3%
WASHINGTON	7,330	4,544	2,737	49	1,807 R	62.0%	37.3%	62.4%	37.6%
WAYNE	9,114	4,984	4,070	60	914 R	54.7%	44.7%	55.0%	45.0%
WHITE	9,338	4,498	4,761	79	263 D	48.2%	51.0%	48.6%	51.4%
WHITESIDE	18,375	12,922	5,299	154	7,623 R	70.3%	28.8%	70.9%	29.1%
WILL	55,628	28,601	26,430	597	2,171 R	51.4%	47.5%	52.0%	48.0%
WILLIAMSON	20,357	10,386	9,841	130	545 R	51.0%	48.3%	51.3%	48.7%
WINNEBAGO	57,313	29,537	27,145	631	2,392 R	51.5%	47.4%	52.1%	47.9%
WOODFORD	9,275	5,784	3,446	46	2,338 R	62.4%	37.1%	62.7%	37.3%
TOTAL	3,984,045	1,961,103	1,994,715	28,228	33,612 D	49.2%	50.1%	49.6%	50.4%

ILLINOIS

PRESIDENT 1952

County	Total Vote	Republican	Democratic	Other	Rep.-Dem. Plurality	Total Vote Rep.	Total Vote Dem.	Major Vote Rep.	Major Vote Dem.
ADAMS	32,974	19,652	13,301	21	6,351 R	59.6%	40.3%	59.6%	40.4%
ALEXANDER	9,553	5,219	4,305	29	914 R	54.6%	45.1%	54.8%	45.2%
BOND	7,359	4,565	2,776	18	1,789 R	62.0%	37.7%	62.2%	37.8%
BOONE	8,932	6,628	2,287	17	4,341 R	74.2%	25.6%	74.3%	25.7%
BROWN	3,699	2,137	1,557	5	580 R	57.8%	42.1%	57.9%	42.1%
BUREAU	20,498	14,300	6,173	25	8,127 R	69.8%	30.1%	69.8%	30.2%
CALHOUN	3,371	1,915	1,454	2	461 R	56.8%	43.1%	56.8%	43.2%
CARROLL	9,576	6,978	2,584	14	4,394 R	72.9%	27.0%	73.0%	27.0%
CASS	7,565	4,152	3,405	8	747 R	54.9%	45.0%	54.9%	45.1%
CHAMPAIGN	41,251	27,188	13,951	112	13,237 R	65.9%	33.8%	66.1%	33.9%
CHRISTIAN	19,767	9,906	9,844	17	62 R	50.1%	49.8%	50.2%	49.8%
CLARK	9,326	5,700	3,621	5	2,079 R	61.1%	38.8%	61.2%	38.8%
CLAY	8,701	5,254	3,432	15	1,822 R	60.4%	39.4%	60.5%	39.5%
CLINTON	11,620	6,760	4,853	7	1,907 R	58.1%	41.8%	58.2%	41.8%
COLES	20,556	12,660	7,876	20	4,784 R	61.6%	38.3%	61.6%	38.4%
COOK	2,367,939	1,188,973	1,172,454	6,512	16,519 R	50.2%	49.5%	50.3%	49.7%
CRAWFORD	10,724	6,768	3,887	9	2,821 R	63.1%	36.8%	63.3%	36.8%
CUMBERLAND	5,514	3,302	2,200	12	1,102 R	59.9%	39.9%	60.0%	40.0%
DE KALB	19,947	14,807	5,110	30	9,697 R	74.2%	25.6%	74.3%	25.7%
DE WITT	8,436	5,212	3,221	3	1,991 R	61.8%	38.2%	61.8%	38.2%
DOUGLAS	8,241	5,530	2,706	5	2,824 R	67.1%	32.8%	67.1%	32.9%
DU PAGE	93,840	71,134	22,489	217	48,645 R	75.8%	24.0%	76.0%	24.0%
EDGAR	12,891	8,323	4,558	10	3,765 R	64.6%	35.4%	64.6%	35.4%
EDWARDS	4,669	3,502	1,162	5	2,340 R	75.0%	24.9%	75.1%	24.9%
EFFINGHAM	11,300	6,530	4,745	25	1,785 R	57.8%	42.0%	57.9%	42.1%
FAYETTE	12,339	7,028	5,299	12	1,729 R	57.0%	42.9%	57.0%	43.0%
FORD	8,345	6,216	2,121	8	4,095 R	74.5%	25.4%	74.6%	25.4%
FRANKLIN	23,766	11,723	11,981	62	258 D	49.3%	50.4%	49.5%	50.5%
FULTON	21,760	13,302	8,414	44	4,888 R	61.1%	38.7%	61.3%	38.7%
GALLATIN	4,461	2,300	2,153	8	147 R	51.6%	48.3%	51.7%	48.3%
GREENE	9,132	5,019	4,106	7	913 R	55.0%	45.0%	55.0%	45.0%
GRUNDY	10,478	7,347	3,118	13	4,229 R	70.1%	29.7%	70.2%	29.8%
HAMILTON	6,717	4,047	2,662	8	1,385 R	60.3%	39.6%	60.3%	39.7%
HANCOCK	13,881	9,181	4,681	19	4,500 R	66.1%	33.7%	66.2%	33.8%
HARDIN	3,553	1,984	1,563	6	421 R	55.8%	44.0%	55.9%	44.1%
HENDERSON	4,303	2,839	1,458	6	1,381 R	66.0%	33.9%	66.1%	33.9%
HENRY	24,892	16,301	8,558	33	7,743 R	65.5%	34.4%	65.6%	34.4%
IROQUOIS	17,107	12,456	4,634	17	7,822 R	72.8%	27.1%	72.9%	27.0%
JACKSON	17,674	10,193	7,457	24	2,736 R	57.7%	42.2%	57.8%	42.2%
JASPER	6,491	3,753	2,728	10	1,025 R	57.8%	42.0%	57.8%	42.1%
JEFFERSON	18,558	9,841	8,698	19	1,143 R	53.0%	46.9%	53.1%	46.9%
JERSEY	7,461	4,031	3,424	6	607 R	54.0%	45.9%	54.1%	45.9%
JO DAVIESS	10,003	7,132	2,858	13	4,274 R	71.3%	28.6%	71.4%	28.6%
JOHNSON	4,947	3,327	1,614	6	1,713 R	67.3%	32.6%	67.3%	32.7%
KANE	74,955	50,801	24,058	96	26,743 R	67.8%	32.1%	67.9%	32.1%
KANKAKEE	33,005	20,279	12,636	90	7,643 R	61.4%	38.3%	61.6%	38.4%
KENDALL	6,461	4,982	1,476	3	3,506 R	77.1%	22.8%	77.2%	22.8%
KNOX	28,940	18,569	10,354	17	8,215 R	64.2%	35.8%	64.2%	35.8%
LAKE	87,427	54,929	32,353	145	22,576 R	62.8%	37.0%	63.1%	37.1%
LA SALLE	54,277	32,857	21,321	99	11,536 R	60.5%	39.3%	60.6%	39.4%
LAWRENCE	10,086	6,207	3,875	4	2,332 R	61.5%	38.4%	61.6%	38.4%
LEE	16,651	11,941	4,700	10	7,241 R	71.8%	28.2%	72.0%	28.0%
LIVINGSTON	19,727	14,095	5,612	20	8,483 R	71.5%	28.4%	71.8%	28.2%
LOGAN	14,229	9,162	5,048	19	4,114 R	64.4%	35.5%	64.5%	35.5%
MCDONOUGH	14,053	10,126	3,922	5	6,204 R	72.1%	27.9%	72.1%	27.9%
MCHENRY	28,257	20,975	7,218	64	13,757 R	74.2%	25.5%	74.4%	25.6%
MCLEAN	37,826	24,494	13,296	36	11,198 R	64.8%	35.2%	64.8%	35.2%
MACON	48,066	25,744	22,277	45	3,467 R	53.6%	46.3%	53.6%	46.4%
MACOUPIN	25,348	12,336	12,944	68	608 D	48.7%	51.1%	48.8%	51.2%
MADISON	87,039	36,206	50,734	99	14,528 D	41.6%	58.3%	41.6%	58.4%

PRESIDENT 1956

County	Total Vote	Republican	Democratic	Other	Rep.-Dem. Plurality	Total Vote Rep.	Total Vote Dem.	Major Vote Rep.	Major Vote Dem.
ADAMS	31,003	19,569	11,402	32	8,167 R	63.1%	36.8%	63.2%	36.8%
ALEXANDER	8,613	4,425	4,167	21	258 R	51.4%	48.4%	51.5%	48.5%
BOND	7,187	4,342	2,834	11	1,508 R	60.4%	39.4%	60.5%	39.5%
BOONE	8,602	6,706	1,890	6	4,816 R	78.0%	22.0%	78.0%	22.0%
BROWN	3,775	2,026	1,748	1	278 R	53.7%	46.3%	53.7%	46.3%
BUREAU	19,711	13,909	5,781	21	8,128 R	70.6%	29.3%	70.6%	29.4%
CALHOUN	3,391	1,892	1,498	1	394 R	55.8%	44.2%	55.8%	44.2%
CARROLL	9,211	6,503	2,693	15	3,810 R	70.6%	29.2%	70.7%	29.3%
CASS	7,504	4,125	3,368	11	757 R	55.0%	44.9%	55.1%	44.9%
CHAMPAIGN	42,040	28,190	13,799	51	14,391 R	67.1%	32.8%	67.1%	32.9%
CHRISTIAN	19,434	10,282	9,093	59	1,189 R	52.9%	46.8%	53.1%	46.9%
CLARK	8,974	5,451	3,519	4	1,932 R	60.7%	39.2%	60.8%	39.2%
CLAY	8,648	5,079	3,553	16	1,526 R	58.7%	41.1%	58.7%	41.2%
CLINTON	11,627	7,378	4,242	7	3,136 R	63.5%	36.5%	63.5%	36.5%
COLES	20,015	12,436	7,569	10	4,867 R	62.1%	37.8%	62.2%	37.8%
COOK	2,276,844	1,293,223	977,821	5,800	315,402 R	56.8%	42.9%	56.9%	43.1%
CRAWFORD	10,662	6,747	3,906	9	2,841 R	63.3%	36.6%	63.3%	36.7%
CUMBERLAND	5,512	3,235	2,272	5	963 R	58.7%	41.2%	58.7%	41.3%
DE KALB	19,930	15,078	4,826	25	10,252 R	75.7%	24.2%	75.8%	24.2%
DE WITT	8,404	5,307	3,083	14	2,224 R	63.1%	36.6%	63.2%	36.8%
DOUGLAS	8,339	5,559	2,774	6	2,785 R	66.7%	33.3%	66.7%	33.3%
DU PAGE	115,144	91,834	23,103	207	68,731 R	79.8%	20.1%	79.9%	20.1%
EDGAR	12,309	7,942	4,362	8	3,580 R	64.5%	35.4%	64.5%	35.5%
EDWARDS	4,550	3,339	1,210	1	2,129 R	73.4%	26.6%	73.4%	26.6%
EFFINGHAM	11,380	6,904	4,455	21	2,449 R	60.7%	39.1%	60.8%	39.2%
FAYETTE	11,658	6,739	4,914	5	1,825 R	57.8%	42.2%	57.8%	42.2%
FORD	8,182	6,027	2,152	3	3,875 R	73.7%	26.3%	73.7%	26.3%
FRANKLIN	23,069	11,761	11,308	—	453 R	51.0%	49.0%	51.0%	49.0%
FULTON	21,125	12,375	8,702	48	3,673 R	58.6%	41.2%	58.7%	41.3%
GALLATIN	4,415	2,179	2,230	6	51 D	49.4%	50.5%	49.4%	50.6%
GREENE	8,646	4,718	3,909	19	809 R	54.6%	45.2%	54.7%	45.3%
GRUNDY	10,261	7,640	2,618	3	5,022 R	74.5%	25.5%	74.5%	25.5%
HAMILTON	6,364	3,675	2,685	4	990 R	57.7%	42.2%	57.8%	42.2%
HANCOCK	13,297	8,431	4,854	12	3,577 R	63.4%	36.5%	63.5%	36.5%
HARDIN	3,371	1,919	1,444	8	475 R	56.9%	42.8%	57.1%	42.9%
HENDERSON	4,215	2,743	1,469	3	1,274 R	65.1%	34.9%	65.1%	34.9%
HENRY	24,284	15,896	8,349	39	7,547 R	65.5%	34.4%	65.5%	34.4%
IROQUOIS	16,609	12,104	4,487	18	7,617 R	72.9%	27.0%	72.9%	27.0%
JACKSON	17,927	10,526	7,391	10	3,135 R	58.7%	41.2%	58.7%	41.2%
JASPER	6,002	3,107	2,895	—	212 R	51.8%	48.2%	51.8%	48.2%
JEFFERSON	17,727	9,637	8,090	5	1,547 R	54.4%	45.6%	54.4%	45.6%
JERSEY	7,640	4,220	3,415	18	805 R	55.2%	44.7%	55.3%	44.7%
JO DAVIESS	9,686	6,762	2,906	2	3,856 R	69.8%	30.0%	69.9%	30.1%
JOHNSON	4,524	2,973	1,549	59	1,424 R	65.7%	34.2%	65.7%	34.3%
KANE	76,916	56,009	20,848	59	35,161 R	72.8%	27.1%	72.9%	27.1%
KANKAKEE	33,128	21,993	11,088	47	10,905 R	66.4%	33.5%	66.5%	33.5%
KENDALL	6,471	5,057	1,407	7	3,650 R	78.1%	21.7%	78.2%	21.8%
KNOX	28,251	18,656	9,558	37	9,098 R	66.0%	33.8%	66.1%	33.9%
LAKE	99,189	66,781	32,279	129	34,502 R	67.3%	32.5%	67.4%	32.6%
LA SALLE	51,862	33,461	18,318	83	15,143 R	64.5%	35.3%	64.6%	35.4%
LAWRENCE	9,862	6,104	3,751	7	2,353 R	61.9%	38.0%	61.9%	38.1%
LEE	16,189	11,653	4,531	5	7,122 R	72.0%	28.0%	72.0%	28.0%
LIVINGSTON	19,143	13,939	5,197	—	8,742 R	72.8%	27.1%	72.8%	27.1%
LOGAN	14,396	9,589	4,793	14	4,796 R	66.6%	33.3%	66.6%	33.3%
MCDONOUGH	13,605	9,725	3,872	8	5,853 R	71.5%	28.4%	71.5%	28.5%
MCHENRY	31,798	24,912	6,820	66	18,092 R	78.3%	21.4%	78.5%	21.5%
MCLEAN	38,111	25,758	12,332	21	13,426 R	67.5%	32.3%	67.6%	32.4%
MACON	50,771	27,673	23,066	32	4,607 R	54.5%	45.4%	54.5%	45.5%
MACOUPIN	24,627	12,290	12,303	34	13 D	49.9%	49.9%	50.0%	50.0%
MADISON	87,398	39,413	47,897	88	8,484 D	45.1%	54.8%	45.1%	54.9%

ILLINOIS

PRESIDENT 1952

County	Total Vote	Republican	Democratic	Other	Rep-Dem. Plurality	Total Vote Rep.	Total Vote Dem.	Major Vote Rep.	Major Vote Dem.
MARION	20,140	10,804	9,317	19	1,487 R	53.6%	46.3%	53.7%	46.3%
MARSHALL	7,201	4,850	2,343	8	2,507 R	67.4%	32.5%	67.4%	32.6%
MASON	8,047	4,982	3,061	4	1,921 R	61.9%	38.0%	61.9%	38.1%
MASSAC	6,930	4,212	2,711	7	1,501 R	60.8%	39.1%	60.8%	39.2%
MENARD	5,256	3,307	1,946	3	1,361 R	62.9%	37.0%	63.0%	37.0%
MERCER	9,097	6,416	2,679	2	3,737 R	70.5%	29.4%	70.5%	29.5%
MONROE	6,959	4,528	2,430	1	2,098 R	65.1%	34.9%	65.1%	34.9%
MONTGOMERY	18,225	10,014	8,195	16	1,819 R	55.0%	45.0%	55.0%	45.0%
MORGAN	17,046	10,405	6,637	4	3,768 R	61.0%	38.9%	61.1%	38.9%
MOULTRIE	6,563	3,880	2,675	8	1,205 R	59.1%	40.8%	59.2%	40.8%
OGLE	17,163	13,351	3,796	16	9,555 R	77.8%	22.1%	77.9%	22.1%
PEORIA	83,339	49,245	33,955	139	15,290 R	59.1%	40.7%	59.2%	40.8%
PERRY	11,923	6,580	5,340	3	1,240 R	55.2%	44.8%	55.2%	44.8%
PIATT	6,932	4,701	2,220	11	2,481 R	67.8%	32.0%	67.9%	32.1%
PIKE	11,611	6,382	5,219	10	1,163 R	55.0%	44.9%	55.0%	45.0%
POPE	2,883	1,947	933	3	1,014 R	67.5%	32.4%	67.6%	32.4%
PULASKI	5,854	3,447	2,397	10	1,050 R	58.9%	40.9%	59.0%	41.0%
PUTNAM	2,703	1,691	1,010	2	681 R	62.6%	37.4%	62.6%	37.4%
RANDOLPH	15,438	8,427	6,998	13	1,429 R	54.6%	45.3%	54.6%	45.4%
RICHLAND	8,139	5,569	2,565	5	3,004 R	68.4%	31.5%	68.5%	31.5%
ROCK ISLAND	60,912	32,933	27,879	100	5,054 R	54.1%	45.8%	54.2%	45.8%
ST. CLAIR	100,503	39,713	60,311	479	20,598 D	39.5%	60.0%	39.7%	60.3%
SALINE	17,006	9,206	7,771	29	1,435 R	54.1%	45.7%	54.2%	45.8%
SANGAMON	72,968	39,392	33,526	50	5,866 R	54.0%	45.9%	54.0%	46.0%
SCHUYLER	5,375	3,295	2,076	4	1,219 R	61.3%	38.6%	61.3%	38.7%
SCOTT	3,807	2,298	1,506	3	792 R	60.4%	39.6%	60.4%	39.6%
SHELBY	12,469	7,189	5,268	12	1,921 R	57.7%	42.2%	57.7%	42.3%
STARK	4,500	3,398	1,100	2	2,298 R	75.5%	24.4%	75.5%	24.5%
STEPHENSON	21,086	14,446	6,605	35	7,841 R	68.5%	31.3%	68.6%	31.4%
TAZEWELL	37,653	20,763	16,862	28	3,901 R	55.1%	44.8%	55.2%	44.8%
UNION	8,963	4,658	4,296	9	362 R	52.0%	47.9%	52.0%	48.0%
VERMILION	44,226	25,367	18,771	88	6,596 R	57.4%	42.4%	57.5%	42.5%
WABASH	6,917	4,246	2,661	10	1,585 R	61.4%	38.5%	61.5%	38.5%
WARREN	11,004	8,020	2,973	11	5,047 R	72.9%	27.0%	73.0%	27.0%
WASHINGTON	8,381	5,546	2,824	11	2,722 R	66.2%	33.7%	66.3%	33.7%
WAYNE	10,418	6,495	3,911	12	2,584 R	62.3%	37.5%	62.4%	37.6%
WHITE	10,431	6,141	4,284	6	1,857 R	58.9%	41.1%	58.9%	41.1%
WHITESIDE	23,599	17,294	6,238	67	11,056 R	73.3%	26.4%	73.5%	26.5%
WILL	58,392	38,533	29,749	110	8,784 R	56.3%	43.5%	56.4%	43.6%
WILLIAMSON	24,223	13,348	10,838	37	2,510 R	55.1%	44.7%	55.2%	44.8%
WINNEBAGO	75,004	43,468	31,409	127	12,059 R	58.0%	41.9%	58.1%	41.9%
WOODFORD	11,308	8,022	3,273	13	4,749 R	70.9%	28.9%	71.0%	29.0%
TOTAL	4,481,058	2,457,327	2,013,920	9,811	443,407 R	54.8%	44.9%	55.0%	45.0%

PRESIDENT 1956

County	Total Vote	Republican	Democratic	Other	Rep-Dem. Plurality	Total Vote Rep.	Total Vote Dem.	Major Vote Rep.	Major Vote Dem.
MARION	19,385	10,813	8,551	21	2,262 R	55.8%	44.1%	55.8%	44.2%
MARSHALL	7,014	4,764	2,245	5	2,519 R	67.9%	32.0%	68.0%	32.0%
MASON	7,889	4,677	3,199	13	1,478 R	59.3%	40.6%	59.4%	40.6%
MASSAC	6,629	4,265	2,359	5	1,906 R	64.3%	35.6%	64.4%	35.6%
MENARD	5,025	3,188	1,833	4	1,355 R	63.4%	36.5%	63.5%	36.5%
MERCER	8,708	5,732	2,969	7	2,763 R	65.8%	34.1%	65.9%	34.1%
MONROE	7,364	4,715	2,648	1	2,067 R	64.0%	36.0%	64.0%	36.0%
MONTGOMERY	17,645	9,945	7,692	8	2,253 R	56.4%	43.6%	56.4%	43.6%
MORGAN	16,600	10,262	6,327	11	3,935 R	61.8%	38.1%	61.9%	38.1%
MOULTRIE	6,515	3,756	2,751	8	1,005 R	57.7%	42.2%	57.7%	42.3%
OGLE	16,870	13,194	3,660	16	9,534 R	78.2%	21.7%	78.3%	21.7%
PEORIA	81,141	50,888	30,145	108	20,743 R	62.7%	37.2%	62.8%	37.2%
PERRY	11,414	6,513	4,901	1	1,612 R	57.1%	42.9%	57.1%	42.9%
PIATT	6,979	4,622	2,356	1	2,266 R	66.2%	33.8%	66.2%	33.8%
PIKE	11,318	5,920	5,382	16	538 R	52.3%	47.6%	52.4%	47.6%
POPE	2,765	1,842	922	1	920 R	66.6%	33.3%	66.6%	33.4%
PULASKI	5,227	2,966	2,246	15	720 R	56.7%	43.0%	56.9%	43.1%
PUTNAM	2,641	1,724	913	4	811 R	65.3%	34.6%	65.4%	34.6%
RANDOLPH	15,221	8,439	6,778	4	1,661 R	55.4%	44.5%	55.5%	44.5%
RICHLAND	7,794	5,304	2,485	5	2,819 R	68.1%	31.9%	68.1%	31.9%
ROCK ISLAND	60,605	31,342	29,145	118	2,197 R	51.7%	48.1%	51.8%	48.2%
ST. CLAIR	97,106	41,528	55,295	283	13,767 D	42.8%	56.9%	42.8%	57.1%
SALINE	15,726	8,481	7,245	20	1,266 R	54.0%	45.9%	54.0%	46.0%
SANGAMON	71,935	42,951	28,949	35	14,002 R	59.7%	40.2%	59.7%	40.3%
SCHUYLER	5,270	3,068	2,189	13	879 R	58.2%	41.5%	58.4%	41.6%
SCOTT	3,731	2,303	1,478	1	825 R	60.9%	39.1%	60.9%	39.1%
SHELBY	12,425	7,075	5,337	13	1,738 R	56.9%	43.0%	57.0%	43.0%
STARK	4,351	3,241	1,118	2	2,123 R	74.3%	25.6%	74.4%	25.6%
STEPHENSON	20,614	14,245	6,349	20	7,896 R	69.1%	30.8%	69.2%	30.8%
TAZEWELL	39,970	23,690	16,230	50	7,460 R	59.3%	40.6%	59.3%	40.7%
UNION	8,559	4,204	4,359	6	155 D	49.1%	50.9%	49.1%	50.9%
VERMILION	44,535	26,534	17,991	60	8,543 R	59.5%	40.4%	59.6%	40.4%
WABASH	7,146	4,425	2,713	8	1,712 R	61.9%	38.0%	62.0%	38.0%
WARREN	10,582	7,580	2,996	6	4,584 R	71.6%	28.3%	71.7%	28.3%
WASHINGTON	8,135	5,299	2,820	16	2,479 R	65.1%	34.7%	65.3%	34.7%
WAYNE	10,242	6,286	3,942	14	2,344 R	61.4%	38.5%	61.5%	38.5%
WHITE	10,917	6,128	4,778	11	1,350 R	56.2%	43.8%	56.2%	43.9%
WHITESIDE	23,784	17,589	6,158	37	11,431 R	74.0%	25.9%	74.1%	25.9%
WILL	70,916	45,688	25,188	100	20,440 R	64.3%	35.5%	64.4%	35.6%
WILLIAMSON	23,810	13,438	10,345	27	3,093 R	56.4%	43.4%	56.5%	43.5%
WINNEBAGO	77,484	48,332	29,063	89	19,269 R	62.4%	37.5%	62.4%	37.6%
WOODFORD	11,783	8,505	3,257	21	5,248 R	72.2%	27.6%	72.3%	27.7%
TOTAL	4,407,407	2,623,327	1,775,682	8,398	847,645 R	59.5%	40.3%	59.6%	40.4%

ILLINOIS

PRESIDENT 1960

County	Total Vote	Republican	Democratic	Other	Rep.-Dem. Plurality	% Total Vote Rep.	% Total Vote Dem.	% Major Vote Rep.	% Major Vote Dem.
ADAMS	33,529	18,674	14,827	28	3,847 R	55.7%	44.2%	55.7%	44.3%
ALEXANDER	8,638	4,143	4,477	18	334 D	48.0%	51.8%	48.1%	51.9%
BOND	7,162	4,297	2,856	9	1,441 R	60.0%	39.9%	60.1%	39.9%
BOONE	9,162	6,552	2,605	5	3,947 R	71.5%	28.4%	71.6%	28.4%
BROWN	3,740	1,889	1,849	2	40 R	50.5%	49.4%	50.5%	49.5%
BUREAU	20,407	12,597	7,786	24	4,811 R	61.7%	38.2%	61.8%	38.2%
CALHOUN	3,267	1,654	1,608	5	46 R	50.6%	49.2%	50.7%	49.3%
CARROLL	9,418	6,282	3,097	39	3,185 R	66.7%	32.9%	67.0%	33.0%
CASS	7,715	4,015	3,692	8	323 R	52.0%	47.9%	52.1%	47.9%
CHAMPAIGN	45,441	27,793	17,115	533	10,678 R	61.2%	37.7%	61.9%	38.1%
CHRISTIAN	19,485	9,263	10,207	15	944 D	47.5%	52.4%	47.6%	52.4%
CLARK	9,273	5,319	3,949	5	1,370 R	57.4%	42.6%	57.4%	42.6%
CLAY	8,538	5,134	3,394	10	1,740 R	60.1%	39.8%	60.2%	39.8%
CLINTON	11,903	5,709	6,188	6	479 D	48.0%	52.0%	48.0%	52.0%
COLES	20,814	12,166	8,629	19	3,537 R	58.5%	41.5%	58.5%	41.5%
COOK	2,445,269	1,059,607	1,378,343	7,319	318,736 D	43.3%	56.4%	43.5%	56.5%
CRAWFORD	11,058	6,809	4,245	4	2,564 R	61.6%	38.4%	61.6%	38.4%
CUMBERLAND	5,500	3,020	2,475	5	545 R	54.9%	45.0%	55.0%	45.0%
DE KALB	22,388	15,586	6,783	19	8,803 R	69.6%	30.3%	69.7%	30.3%
DE WITT	8,689	5,074	3,607	8	1,467 R	58.4%	41.5%	58.4%	41.6%
DOUGLAS	9,299	5,761	3,532	6	2,229 R	62.0%	38.0%	62.0%	38.0%
DU PAGE	145,445	101,014	44,263	168	56,751 R	69.5%	30.4%	69.5%	30.5%
EDGAR	12,376	7,348	5,024	4	2,324 R	59.4%	40.6%	59.5%	40.6%
EDWARDS	4,745	3,291	1,446	8	1,845 R	69.4%	30.5%	69.5%	30.5%
EFFINGHAM	12,092	6,410	5,676	6	734 R	53.0%	46.9%	53.0%	47.0%
FAYETTE	11,504	6,586	4,907	11	1,679 R	57.2%	42.7%	57.3%	42.7%
FORD	8,478	5,779	2,698	1	3,081 R	68.2%	31.8%	68.2%	31.8%
FRANKLIN	23,266	11,861	11,368	37	493 R	51.0%	48.9%	51.1%	48.9%
FULTON	22,251	11,999	10,194	58	1,805 R	53.9%	45.8%	54.1%	45.9%
GALLATIN	4,570	2,179	2,386	5	207 D	47.7%	52.2%	47.7%	52.3%
GREENE	8,344	4,487	3,847	10	640 R	53.8%	46.1%	53.8%	46.2%
GRUNDY	11,228	6,948	4,276	4	2,672 R	61.9%	38.1%	61.9%	38.1%
HAMILTON	6,454	3,804	2,639	11	1,165 R	58.9%	40.9%	59.0%	41.0%
HANCOCK	12,990	8,036	4,947	7	3,089 R	61.9%	38.1%	61.9%	38.1%
HARDIN	3,413	1,944	1,465	4	479 R	57.0%	42.9%	57.0%	43.0%
HENDERSON	4,273	2,572	1,697	4	875 R	60.2%	39.7%	60.2%	39.8%
HENRY	24,690	14,297	10,372	21	3,925 R	57.9%	42.0%	58.0%	42.0%
IROQUOIS	17,213	11,376	5,821	16	5,555 R	66.1%	33.8%	66.1%	33.8%
JACKSON	19,112	10,568	8,527	17	2,041 R	55.3%	44.6%	55.3%	44.7%
JASPER	6,421	3,393	3,027	1	366 R	52.8%	47.1%	52.9%	47.1%
JEFFERSON	17,625	9,841	7,784		2,057 R	55.8%	44.2%	55.8%	44.2%
JERSEY	8,343	4,247	4,087	9	160 R	50.9%	49.0%	51.0%	49.0%
JO DAVIESS	10,417	6,111	4,293	13	1,818 R	58.7%	41.2%	58.7%	41.3%
JOHNSON	4,197	2,778	1,413	6	1,365 R	66.2%	33.7%	66.3%	33.7%
KANE	86,761	55,389	31,279	93	24,110 R	63.8%	36.1%	63.9%	36.1%
KANKAKEE	37,452	20,311	17,115	26	3,196 R	54.2%	45.7%	54.3%	45.7%
KENDALL	8,228	5,975	2,242	11	3,733 R	72.6%	27.2%	72.7%	27.3%
KNOX	29,850	17,938	11,889	23	6,049 R	60.1%	39.8%	60.1%	39.8%
LAKE	114,899	67,809	46,941	149	20,868 R	59.0%	40.9%	59.1%	40.9%
LA SALLE	55,125	27,552	27,532	41	20 R	50.0%	49.9%	50.0%	50.0%
LAWRENCE	9,800	6,120	3,667	13	2,453 R	62.4%	37.4%	62.5%	37.5%
LEE	16,739	10,835	5,896	8	4,939 R	64.7%	35.2%	64.8%	35.2%
LIVINGSTON	19,783	13,139	6,642	2	6,497 R	66.4%	33.5%	66.4%	33.6%
LOGAN	15,090	9,383	5,691	16	3,692 R	62.2%	37.7%	62.2%	37.8%
MCDONOUGH	13,893	9,363	4,520	10	4,843 R	67.4%	32.5%	67.4%	32.6%
MCHENRY	38,508	25,787	12,659	62	13,128 R	67.0%	32.9%	67.1%	32.9%
MCLEAN	38,761	24,758	13,971	32	10,787 R	63.9%	36.0%	63.9%	36.1%
MACON	53,288	27,151	26,029	108	1,122 R	50.9%	48.8%	51.0%	48.9%
MACOUPIN	24,896	11,731	13,120	45	1,389 D	47.1%	52.7%	47.2%	52.8%
MADISON	97,904	42,984	54,787	133	11,803 D	43.9%	56.0%	44.0%	56.0%

PRESIDENT 1964

County	Total Vote	Republican	Democratic	Other	Rep.-Dem. Plurality	% Total Vote Rep.	% Total Vote Dem.	% Major Vote Rep.	% Major Vote Dem.
ADAMS	32,314	13,993	18,321		4,328 D	43.3%	56.7%	43.3%	56.7%
ALEXANDER	7,658	2,895	4,763		1,868 D	37.8%	62.2%	37.8%	62.2%
BOND	6,873	3,058	3,815		757 D	44.5%	55.5%	44.5%	55.5%
BOONE	8,747	5,053	3,694		1,359 R	57.8%	42.2%	57.8%	42.2%
BROWN	3,438	1,355	2,083		728 D	39.4%	60.6%	39.4%	60.6%
BUREAU	18,638	9,552	9,086		466 R	51.3%	48.7%	51.3%	48.7%
CALHOUN	3,093	1,288	1,805		517 D	41.6%	58.4%	41.6%	58.4%
CARROLL	8,549	4,487	4,062		425 R	52.5%	47.5%	52.5%	47.5%
CASS	7,260	2,836	4,424		1,588 D	39.1%	60.9%	39.1%	60.9%
CHAMPAIGN	47,802	22,010	25,792		3,782 D	46.0%	54.0%	46.0%	54.0%
CHRISTIAN	18,051	6,153	11,898		5,745 D	34.1%	65.9%	34.1%	65.9%
CLARK	8,867	4,403	4,464		61 D	49.7%	50.3%	49.7%	50.3%
CLAY	8,216	3,665	4,551		886 D	44.6%	55.4%	44.6%	55.4%
CLINTON	12,031	4,692	7,339		2,647 D	39.0%	61.0%	39.0%	61.0%
COLES	20,255	8,878	11,377		2,499 D	43.8%	56.2%	43.8%	56.2%
COOK	2,432,899	895,718	1,537,181		641,463 D	36.8%	63.2%	36.8%	63.2%
CRAWFORD	10,458	4,834	5,624		790 D	46.2%	53.8%	46.2%	53.8%
CUMBERLAND	5,307	2,251	3,056		805 D	42.4%	57.6%	42.4%	57.6%
DE KALB	22,049	11,791	10,257		1,534 R	53.5%	46.5%	53.5%	46.5%
DE WITT	7,976	3,605	4,371		766 D	45.2%	54.8%	45.2%	54.8%
DOUGLAS	8,918	4,223	4,695		472 D	47.4%	52.6%	47.4%	52.6%
DU PAGE	165,100	98,871	66,229	1	32,642 R	59.9%	40.1%	59.9%	40.1%
EDGAR	11,793	5,827	5,966		139 D	49.4%	50.6%	49.4%	50.6%
EDWARDS	4,253	2,262	1,991		271 R	53.2%	46.8%	53.2%	46.8%
EFFINGHAM	11,826	5,044	6,782		1,738 D	42.7%	57.3%	42.7%	57.3%
FAYETTE	10,787	4,492	6,295		1,803 D	41.6%	58.4%	41.6%	58.4%
FORD	8,077	4,650	3,427		1,223 R	57.6%	42.4%	57.6%	42.4%
FRANKLIN	21,201	7,620	13,581		5,961 D	35.9%	64.1%	35.9%	64.1%
FULTON	20,815	7,785	13,030		5,245 D	37.4%	62.6%	37.4%	62.6%
GALLATIN	4,239	1,394	2,845		1,451 D	32.9%	67.1%	32.9%	67.1%
GREENE	7,909	3,128	4,781		1,653 D	39.5%	60.5%	39.5%	60.5%
GRUNDY	10,768	5,522	5,246		276 R	51.3%	48.7%	51.3%	48.7%
HAMILTON	5,694	2,561	3,133		572 D	45.0%	55.0%	45.0%	55.0%
HANCOCK	11,756	5,557	6,199		642 D	47.3%	52.7%	47.3%	52.7%
HARDIN	2,963	1,324	1,639		315 D	44.7%	55.3%	44.7%	55.3%
HENDERSON	4,134	1,863	2,271		408 D	45.1%	54.9%	45.1%	54.9%
HENRY	22,729	10,644	12,085		1,441 D	46.8%	53.2%	46.8%	53.2%
IROQUOIS	16,452	9,423	7,029		2,394 R	57.3%	42.7%	57.3%	42.7%
JACKSON	19,178	7,013	12,165		5,152 D	36.6%	63.4%	36.6%	63.4%
JASPER	6,020	2,614	3,406		792 D	43.4%	56.6%	43.4%	56.6%
JEFFERSON	15,901	6,248	9,653		3,405 D	39.3%	60.7%	39.3%	60.7%
JERSEY	6,977	3,041	3,936		895 D	43.6%	56.4%	43.6%	56.4%
JO DAVIESS	9,425	4,607	4,818		211 D	48.9%	51.1%	48.9%	51.1%
JOHNSON	3,987	2,217	1,770		447 R	55.6%	44.4%	55.6%	44.4%
KANE	87,094	46,391	40,703		5,688 R	53.3%	46.7%	53.3%	46.7%
KANKAKEE	36,874	16,082	20,792		4,710 D	43.6%	56.4%	43.6%	56.4%
KENDALL	9,140	5,710	3,430		2,280 R	62.5%	37.5%	62.5%	37.5%
KNOX	27,850	12,850	15,000		2,150 D	46.1%	53.9%	46.1%	53.9%
LAKE	120,667	58,216	62,785	42	4,569 D	48.4%	51.6%	48.4%	51.6%
LA SALLE	52,139	21,216	30,923		9,707 D	40.7%	59.3%	40.7%	59.3%
LAWRENCE	9,312	4,176	5,136		960 D	44.8%	55.2%	44.8%	55.2%
LEE	15,760	8,445	7,315		1,130 R	53.6%	46.4%	53.6%	46.4%
LIVINGSTON	18,715	10,239	8,476		1,763 R	54.7%	45.3%	54.7%	45.3%
LOGAN	14,517	6,805	7,712		907 D	46.9%	53.1%	46.9%	53.1%
MCDONOUGH	13,051	6,907	6,144		763 R	52.9%	47.1%	52.9%	47.1%
MCHENRY	40,517	22,503	18,014		4,489 R	55.5%	44.5%	55.5%	44.5%
MCLEAN	38,670	19,120	19,550		430 D	49.4%	50.6%	49.4%	50.6%
MACON	53,002	17,957	35,045		17,088 D	33.9%	66.1%	33.9%	66.1%
MACOUPIN	23,657	8,430	15,227		6,797 D	35.6%	64.4%	35.6%	64.4%
MADISON	95,124	30,009	65,115		35,106 D	31.5%	68.5%	31.5%	68.5%

ILLINOIS

PRESIDENT 1960

County	Total Vote	Republican	Democratic	Other	Rep-Dem Plurality	Total Vote Rep.	Total Vote Dem.	Major Vote Rep.	Major Vote Dem.
MARION	20,250	11,121	9,116	13	2,005 R	54.9%	45.0%	55.0%	45.0%
MARSHALL	7,138	4,150	2,981	7	1,169 R	58.1%	41.8%	58.2%	41.8%
MASON	8,180	4,337	3,824	19	513 R	53.0%	46.7%	53.1%	46.9%
MASSAC	7,171	4,521	2,644	6	1,877 R	63.0%	36.9%	63.1%	36.9%
MENARD	5,193	3,120	2,068	5	1,052 R	60.1%	39.8%	60.1%	39.9%
MERCER	9,061	5,582	3,476	3	2,106 R	61.6%	38.4%	61.6%	38.4%
MONROE	8,133	4,731	3,398	4	1,333 R	58.2%	41.8%	58.2%	41.8%
MONTGOMERY	18,007	9,178	8,815	14	363 R	51.0%	49.0%	51.0%	49.0%
MORGAN	17,062	9,791	7,259	12	2,532 R	57.4%	42.5%	57.4%	42.6%
MOULTRIE	6,831	3,752	3,079		673 R	54.9%	45.1%	54.9%	45.1%
OGLE	18,025	13,226	4,792	7	6,434 R	73.4%	26.6%	73.4%	26.6%
PEORIA	84,676	45,529	39,061	86	6,468 R	53.8%	46.1%	53.8%	46.2%
PERRY	11,672	6,608	4,958	6	1,750 R	57.5%	42.5%	57.5%	42.5%
PIATT	7,399	4,506	2,889	4	1,617 R	60.9%	39.0%	60.9%	39.1%
PIKE	11,436	5,965	5,461	10	504 R	52.2%	47.8%	52.2%	47.8%
POPE	2,665	1,689	971	5	718 R	63.4%	36.4%	63.5%	36.5%
PULASKI	4,961	2,621	2,322	18	299 R	53.0%	46.8%	53.0%	46.8%
PUTNAM	2,619	1,457	1,160	2	297 R	55.6%	44.3%	55.7%	44.3%
RANDOLPH	15,347	7,988	7,344	15	644 R	52.0%	47.9%	52.1%	47.9%
RICHLAND	8,353	5,329	3,015	9	2,314 R	63.8%	36.1%	63.9%	36.1%
ROCK ISLAND	56,454	32,534	33,812	108	1,278 D	49.0%	50.9%	49.0%	51.0%
ST CLAIR	109,751	42,046	67,367	338	25,321 D	38.3%	61.4%	38.4%	61.6%
SALINE	15,707	8,853	6,835	19	2,018 R	56.4%	43.5%	56.4%	43.6%
SANGAMON	77,335	41,483	35,793	59	5,690 R	53.6%	46.3%	53.7%	46.3%
SCHUYLER	5,164	3,047	2,115	2	932 R	59.0%	41.0%	59.0%	41.0%
SCOTT	3,814	2,267	1,543	4	724 R	59.4%	40.5%	59.5%	40.5%
SHELBY	12,603	6,872	5,720	11	1,152 R	54.5%	45.4%	54.6%	45.4%
STARK	4,314	2,925	1,383	6	1,542 R	67.8%	32.1%	67.9%	32.1%
STEPHENSON	21,995	13,872	8,055	68	5,817 R	63.1%	36.6%	63.3%	36.7%
TAZEWELL	44,526	23,967	20,521	38	3,446 R	53.8%	46.1%	53.9%	46.1%
UNION	8,763	4,432	4,321	10	111 R	50.6%	49.3%	50.6%	49.4%
VERMILION	46,342	26,571	19,702	69	6,869 R	57.3%	42.5%	57.4%	42.6%
WABASH	7,278	4,261	3,013	4	1,248 R	58.5%	41.4%	58.6%	41.4%
WARREN	11,066	7,221	3,835	10	3,386 R	65.3%	34.6%	65.3%	34.7%
WASHINGTON	8,157	5,053	3,093	11	1,960 R	61.9%	37.9%	62.0%	38.0%
WAYNE	10,615	6,652	3,954	9	2,698 R	62.7%	37.2%	62.7%	37.3%
WHITE	10,577	5,810	4,756	11	1,054 R	54.9%	44.9%	55.0%	45.0%
WHITESIDE	26,592	17,434	9,112	46	8,322 R	65.5%	34.3%	65.6%	34.3%
WILL	83,712	42,575	41,056	81	1,519 R	50.9%	49.0%	50.9%	49.1%
WILLIAMSON	25,096	13,732	11,335	29	2,397 R	54.7%	45.2%	54.8%	45.2%
WINNEBAGO	89,741	49,541	40,090	110	9,451 R	55.2%	44.7%	55.3%	44.7%
WOODFORD	12,509	8,101	4,401	7	3,700 R	64.8%	35.2%	64.8%	35.2%
TOTAL	4,757,409	2,368,988	2,377,846	10,575	8,858 D	49.8%	50.0%	49.9%	50.1%

PRESIDENT 1964

County	Total Vote	Republican	Democratic	Other	Rep-Dem Plurality	Total Vote Rep.	Total Vote Dem.	Major Vote Rep.	Major Vote Dem.
MARION	19,423	7,060	12,363		5,303 D	36.3%	63.7%	36.3%	63.7%
MARSHALL	6,770	3,209	3,561		352 D	47.4%	52.6%	47.4%	52.6%
MASON	7,690	2,833	4,857		2,024 D	36.8%	63.2%	36.8%	63.2%
MASSAC	6,474	3,078	3,396		318 D	47.5%	52.5%	47.5%	52.5%
MENARD	4,813	2,322	2,491		169 D	48.2%	51.8%	48.2%	51.8%
MERCER	8,630	4,220	4,410		190 D	48.9%	51.1%	48.9%	51.1%
MONROE	8,541	3,936	4,605		669 D	46.1%	53.9%	46.1%	53.9%
MONTGOMERY	17,006	6,425	10,581		4,156 D	37.8%	62.2%	37.8%	62.2%
MORGAN	16,475	7,240	9,235		1,995 D	43.9%	56.1%	43.9%	56.1%
MOULTRIE	6,226	2,493	3,733		1,240 D	40.0%	60.0%	40.0%	60.0%
OGLE	17,347	10,430	6,917		3,513 R	60.1%	39.9%	60.1%	39.9%
PEORIA	80,687	33,327	47,360		14,033 D	41.3%	58.7%	41.3%	58.7%
PERRY	10,926	4,287	6,639		2,352 D	39.2%	60.8%	39.2%	60.8%
PIATT	7,038	3,141	3,897		756 D	44.6%	55.4%	44.6%	55.4%
PIKE	10,689	4,113	6,576		2,463 D	38.5%	61.5%	38.5%	61.5%
POPE	2,446	1,329	1,117		212 R	54.3%	45.7%	54.3%	45.7%
PULASKI	5,048	1,716	3,332	16	1,616 D	34.0%	66.0%	34.0%	66.0%
PUTNAM	2,490	1,131	1,359		228 D	45.4%	54.6%	45.4%	54.6%
RANDOLPH	15,002	5,803	9,199		3,396 D	38.7%	61.3%	38.7%	61.3%
RICHLAND	8,140	3,901	4,239		338 D	47.9%	52.1%	47.9%	52.1%
ROCK ISLAND	65,473	23,714	41,759		18,045 D	36.2%	63.8%	36.2%	63.8%
ST CLAIR	102,231	28,226	74,005		45,779 D	27.6%	72.4%	27.6%	72.4%
SALINE	14,028	5,691	8,337		2,646 D	40.6%	59.4%	40.6%	59.4%
SANGAMON	76,166	33,077	43,073		9,996 D	43.4%	56.6%	43.4%	56.6%
SCHUYLER	4,921	2,417	2,504		87 D	49.1%	50.9%	49.1%	50.9%
SCOTT	3,579	1,627	1,952		325 D	45.5%	54.5%	45.5%	54.5%
SHELBY	11,369	4,281	7,088		2,807 D	37.7%	62.3%	37.7%	62.3%
STARK	3,893	2,117	1,776		341 R	54.4%	45.6%	54.4%	45.6%
STEPHENSON	20,106	9,252	10,854		1,602 D	46.0%	54.0%	46.0%	54.0%
TAZEWELL	45,731	17,170	28,561		11,391 D	37.5%	62.5%	37.5%	62.5%
UNION	8,350	3,142	5,208		2,066 D	37.6%	62.4%	37.6%	62.4%
VERMILION	44,271	19,506	24,765		5,259 D	44.1%	55.9%	44.1%	55.9%
WABASH	6,626	2,905	3,721		816 D	43.8%	56.2%	43.8%	56.2%
WARREN	9,931	5,588	4,670	3	588 R	52.9%	47.0%	53.0%	47.0%
WASHINGTON	7,510	3,840	3,670		170 R	51.1%	48.9%	51.1%	48.9%
WAYNE	9,943	4,745	5,198		453 D	47.7%	52.3%	47.7%	52.3%
WHITE	9,963	4,000	5,963		1,963 D	40.1%	59.9%	40.1%	59.9%
WHITESIDE	25,476	12,940	12,536		404 R	50.8%	49.2%	50.8%	49.2%
WILL	88,282	38,619	49,663		11,044 D	43.7%	56.3%	43.7%	56.3%
WILLIAMSON	23,743	9,130	14,613		5,483 D	38.5%	61.5%	38.5%	61.5%
WINNEBAGO	88,754	39,920	48,834		8,914 D	45.0%	55.0%	45.0%	55.0%
WOODFORD	12,162	6,248	5,914		334 R	51.4%	48.6%	51.4%	48.6%
TOTAL	4,702,841	1,905,946	2,796,833	62	890,887 D	40.5%	59.5%	40.5%	59.5%

ILLINOIS

OTHER VOTE COMPOSITION:

1920   74,747 Socialist; 49,630 Farmer-Labor; 11,216 Prohibition; 3,471 Socialist Labor; 775 Single Tax.

1924   432,027 Progressive; 2,622 Communist; 2,367 Prohibition; 2,334 Socialist Labor; 421 Commonwealth Land.

1928   19,138 Socialist; 3,581 Communist; 1,812 Socialist Labor.

1932   67,258 Socialist; 15,582 Communist; 6,388 Prohibition; 3,638 Socialist Labor.

1936   89,439 Union; 7,530 Socialist; 3,439 Prohibition; 1,921 Socialist Labor; 801 Communist.

1940   10,914 Socialist; 9,190 Prohibition; 657 scattered.

1944   9,677 Socialist Labor; 7,411 Prohibition; 180 Socialist. The Socialist vote is not included in the county-by-county figures; it is reported only as a part of the state-wide total.

1948   11,959 Prohibition; 11,522 Socialist; 3,118 Socialist Labor; 1,629 scattered.

1952   9,363 Socialist Labor; 448 scattered.

1956   8,342 Socialist Labor; 56 scattered.

1960   10,560 Socialist Labor; 15 scattered.

1964   Scattered.

SPECIAL CASES:

1924   Progressive candidates carried one county and ran second in others.

INDIANA

PRESIDENT 1920

County	Total Vote	Republican	Democratic	Other	Rep.-Dem. Plurality	Total Vote Rep.	Total Vote Dem.	Major Vote Rep.	Major Vote Dem.
ADAMS	7,998	4,144	3,653	201	491 R	51.8%	45.7%	53.1%	46.9%
ALLEN	42,177	24,208	13,804	4,165	10,404 R	57.4%	32.7%	63.7%	36.3%
BARTHOLOMEW	12,210	6,585	5,420	205	1,165 R	53.9%	44.4%	54.9%	45.1%
BENTON	6,081	3,900	2,098	83	1,802 R	64.1%	34.5%	65.0%	35.0%
BLACKFORD	6,073	3,145	2,555	373	590 R	51.8%	42.1%	55.2%	44.8%
BOONE	13,058	6,650	6,178	230	472 R	50.9%	47.3%	51.8%	48.2%
BROWN	2,144	788	1,316	40	528 D	36.8%	61.4%	37.5%	62.5%
CARROLL	9,284	5,006	4,186	92	820 R	53.9%	45.1%	54.5%	45.5%
CASS	18,314	9,545	8,194	575	1,351 R	52.1%	44.7%	53.8%	46.2%
CLARK	13,357	6,466	6,729	162	253 D	48.4%	50.4%	49.0%	51.0%
CLAY	12,716	6,129	5,612	975	517 R	48.2%	44.1%	52.2%	47.8%
CLINTON	14,717	7,739	6,721	257	1,018 R	52.6%	45.7%	53.5%	46.5%
CRAWFORD	4,669	2,290	2,213	166	77 R	49.0%	47.4%	50.9%	49.1%
DAVIESS	12,633	6,748	5,587	298	1,161 R	53.4%	44.2%	54.7%	45.3%
DEARBORN	10,183	5,159	4,884	140	275 R	50.7%	48.0%	51.4%	48.6%
DECATUR	9,566	5,516	3,896	154	1,620 R	57.7%	40.7%	58.6%	41.4%
DE KALB	11,560	6,514	4,750	296	1,764 R	56.3%	41.1%	57.8%	42.2%
DELAWARE	24,030	14,845	8,329	856	6,516 R	61.8%	34.7%	64.1%	35.9%
DUBOIS	9,095	3,738	4,238	1,119	500 D	41.1%	46.6%	46.9%	53.1%
ELKHART	20,461	12,297	5,770	2,394	6,527 R	60.1%	28.2%	68.1%	31.9%
FAYETTE	8,738	4,742	3,768	228	974 R	54.3%	43.1%	55.7%	44.3%
FLOYD	15,447	7,669	7,391	387	278 R	49.6%	47.8%	50.9%	49.1%
FOUNTAIN	9,647	5,218	4,088	341	1,130 R	54.1%	42.4%	56.1%	43.9%
FRANKLIN	6,893	3,137	3,671	85	534 D	45.5%	53.3%	46.1%	53.9%
FULTON	8,554	4,618	3,602	334	1,016 R	54.0%	42.1%	56.2%	43.8%
GIBSON	14,610	7,498	6,384	728	1,114 R	51.3%	43.7%	54.0%	46.0%
GRANT	22,405	12,349	7,900	2,156	4,449 R	55.1%	35.3%	61.0%	39.0%
GREENE	15,388	7,486	6,335	1,567	1,151 R	48.6%	41.2%	54.2%	45.8%
HAMILTON	12,527	7,897	4,280	350	3,617 R	63.0%	34.2%	64.9%	35.1%
HANCOCK	9,579	4,422	4,958	199	536 D	46.2%	51.8%	47.1%	52.9%
HARRISON	8,301	4,271	3,898	132	373 R	51.5%	47.0%	52.3%	47.7%
HENDRICKS	10,630	6,293	4,192	145	2,101 R	59.2%	39.4%	60.0%	40.0%
HENRY	15,328	8,742	5,824	762	2,918 R	57.0%	38.0%	60.0%	40.0%
HOWARD	17,730	10,379	5,767	1,584	4,612 R	58.5%	32.5%	64.3%	35.7%
HUNTINGTON	15,093	8,100	6,506	487	1,594 R	53.7%	43.1%	55.5%	44.5%
JACKSON	10,552	5,069	5,319	164	250 D	48.0%	50.4%	48.8%	51.2%
JASPER	5,895	3,942	1,872	81	2,070 R	66.9%	31.8%	67.8%	32.2%
JAY	11,414	6,089	4,759	566	1,330 R	53.3%	41.7%	56.1%	43.9%
JEFFERSON	9,880	5,732	4,000	148	1,732 R	58.0%	40.5%	58.9%	41.1%
JENNINGS	6,117	3,404	2,603	110	801 R	55.6%	42.6%	56.7%	43.3%
JOHNSON	10,722	4,863	5,452	407	589 D	45.4%	50.8%	47.1%	52.9%
KNOX	19,479	10,011	8,052	1,416	1,959 R	51.4%	41.3%	55.4%	44.6%
KOSCIUSKO	13,504	8,326	4,836	342	3,490 R	61.7%	35.8%	63.3%	36.7%
LAGRANGE	5,663	3,852	1,687	124	2,165 R	68.0%	29.8%	69.5%	30.5%
LAKE	38,028	26,296	7,136	4,596	19,160 R	69.2%	18.8%	78.7%	21.3%
LA PORTE	17,238	11,204	5,459	575	5,745 R	65.0%	31.7%	67.2%	32.8%
LAWRENCE	11,708	6,808	4,709	191	2,099 R	58.1%	40.2%	59.1%	40.9%
MADISON	31,562	15,704	13,325	2,533	2,379 R	49.8%	42.2%	54.1%	45.9%
MARION	145,571	79,957	61,460	4,154	18,497 R	54.9%	42.2%	56.5%	43.5%
MARSHALL	10,642	5,708	4,631	303	1,077 R	53.6%	43.5%	55.2%	44.8%
MARTIN	5,255	2,747	2,443	65	304 R	52.3%	46.5%	52.9%	47.1%
MIAMI	14,124	7,336	6,259	529	1,077 R	51.9%	44.3%	54.0%	46.0%
MONROE	10,500	5,633	4,751	116	882 R	53.6%	45.2%	54.2%	45.8%
MONTGOMERY	16,135	8,792	7,159	184	1,633 R	54.5%	44.4%	55.1%	44.9%
MORGAN	10,069	5,634	4,254	181	1,380 R	55.9%	42.2%	57.0%	43.0%
NEWTON	4,861	3,129	1,664	68	1,465 R	64.4%	34.2%	65.3%	34.7%
NOBLE	11,213	6,820	4,148	245	2,672 R	60.8%	37.0%	62.2%	37.8%
OHIO	2,312	1,177	1,097	38	80 R	50.9%	47.4%	51.8%	48.2%
ORANGE	8,029	4,726	3,222	81	1,504 R	58.9%	40.1%	59.5%	40.5%
OWEN	6,094	2,997	2,948	149	49 R	49.2%	48.4%	50.4%	49.6%

PRESIDENT 1924

County	Total Vote	Republican	Democratic	Other	Rep.-Dem. Plurality	Total Vote Rep.	Total Vote Dem.	Major Vote Rep.	Major Vote Dem.
ADAMS	8,055	3,330	4,300	425	970 D	41.3%	53.4%	43.6%	56.4%
ALLEN	46,573	25,207	17,244	4,122	7,963 R	54.1%	37.0%	59.4%	40.6%
BARTHOLOMEW	11,668	6,606	4,760	302	1,846 R	56.6%	40.8%	58.1%	41.9%
BENTON	5,590	3,250	2,104	236	1,146 R	58.1%	37.6%	60.7%	39.3%
BLACKFORD	6,953	3,553	3,094	306	459 R	51.1%	44.5%	53.5%	46.5%
BOONE	11,900	6,256	5,466	178	790 R	52.6%	45.9%	53.4%	46.6%
BROWN	2,047	756	1,229	62	473 D	36.9%	60.0%	38.1%	61.9%
CARROLL	8,489	4,543	3,660	286	883 R	53.5%	43.1%	55.4%	44.6%
CASS	17,783	9,939	5,276	2,568	4,663 R	55.9%	29.7%	65.3%	34.7%
CLARK	11,498	5,944	5,218	336	726 R	51.7%	45.4%	53.3%	46.7%
CLAY	12,189	5,955	5,349	885	606 R	48.9%	43.9%	52.7%	47.3%
CLINTON	13,862	7,469	6,070	323	1,399 R	53.9%	43.8%	55.2%	44.8%
CRAWFORD	4,450	1,917	2,384	149	467 D	43.1%	53.6%	44.6%	55.4%
DAVIESS	12,500	6,427	5,558	515	869 R	51.4%	44.5%	53.6%	46.4%
DEARBORN	9,536	4,588	4,330	618	258 R	48.1%	45.4%	51.4%	48.6%
DECATUR	9,269	4,907	4,092	270	815 R	52.9%	44.1%	54.5%	45.5%
DE KALB	11,154	6,093	4,133	928	1,960 R	54.6%	37.1%	59.6%	40.4%
DELAWARE	23,340	14,411	7,830	1,099	6,581 R	61.7%	33.5%	64.8%	35.2%
DUBOIS	8,870	2,708	5,651	511	2,943 D	30.5%	63.7%	32.4%	67.6%
ELKHART	20,304	13,096	4,729	2,479	8,367 R	64.5%	23.3%	73.5%	26.5%
FAYETTE	8,501	5,284	2,940	277	2,344 R	62.2%	34.6%	64.3%	35.7%
FLOYD	14,479	6,733	6,971	775	238 D	46.5%	48.1%	49.1%	50.9%
FOUNTAIN	9,353	4,796	4,282	275	514 R	51.3%	45.8%	52.8%	47.2%
FRANKLIN	7,418	3,296	3,915	207	619 D	44.4%	52.8%	45.7%	54.3%
FULTON	7,796	4,329	3,244	223	1,085 R	55.5%	41.6%	57.2%	42.8%
GIBSON	14,308	7,100	6,149	1,059	951 R	49.6%	43.0%	53.6%	46.4%
GRANT	20,276	11,173	7,086	2,017	4,087 R	55.1%	34.9%	61.2%	38.8%
GREENE	14,521	6,670	5,966	1,885	704 R	45.9%	41.1%	52.8%	47.2%
HAMILTON	11,498	7,463	3,785	250	3,678 R	64.9%	32.9%	66.3%	33.7%
HANCOCK	8,595	4,063	4,364	168	301 D	47.3%	50.8%	48.2%	51.8%
HARRISON	8,064	3,896	4,005	163	109 D	48.3%	49.7%	49.3%	50.7%
HENDRICKS	9,449	5,766	3,489	194	2,277 R	61.0%	36.9%	62.3%	37.7%
HENRY	14,461	8,800	5,376	285	3,424 R	60.9%	37.2%	62.1%	37.9%
HOWARD	17,383	10,438	5,451	1,494	4,987 R	60.0%	31.4%	65.7%	34.3%
HUNTINGTON	14,462	7,437	5,506	1,519	1,931 R	51.4%	38.1%	57.5%	42.5%
JACKSON	10,057	4,187	5,332	538	1,145 D	41.6%	53.0%	44.0%	56.0%
JASPER	5,716	3,679	1,744	293	1,935 R	64.4%	30.5%	67.8%	32.2%
JAY	10,890	5,753	4,812	325	941 R	52.8%	44.2%	54.5%	45.5%
JEFFERSON	9,355	5,192	3,914	249	1,278 R	55.5%	41.8%	57.0%	43.0%
JENNINGS	6,444	3,506	2,730	208	776 R	54.4%	42.4%	56.2%	43.8%
JOHNSON	9,757	4,954	4,699	104	255 R	50.8%	48.2%	51.3%	48.7%
KNOX	19,168	8,493	8,603	2,072	110 D	44.3%	44.9%	49.7%	50.3%
KOSCIUSKO	13,690	8,819	4,384	487	4,435 R	64.4%	32.0%	66.8%	33.2%
LAGRANGE	4,864	3,081	1,566	217	1,515 R	63.3%	32.2%	66.3%	33.7%
LAKE	47,968	30,990	10,918	6,060	20,072 R	64.6%	22.8%	73.9%	26.1%
LA PORTE	18,943	11,597	5,214	2,132	6,383 R	61.2%	27.5%	69.0%	31.0%
LAWRENCE	12,254	7,438	4,414	402	3,024 R	60.7%	36.0%	62.8%	37.2%
MADISON	32,003	15,637	12,061	4,305	3,576 R	48.9%	37.7%	56.5%	43.5%
MARION	160,880	95,135	59,498	6,247	35,637 R	59.1%	37.0%	61.5%	38.5%
MARSHALL	10,050	5,354	4,277	419	1,077 R	53.3%	42.6%	55.6%	44.4%
MARTIN	5,281	2,470	2,669	142	199 D	46.8%	50.5%	48.1%	51.9%
MIAMI	13,199	6,796	4,976	1,427	1,820 R	51.5%	37.7%	57.7%	42.3%
MONROE	11,312	6,247	4,689	376	1,558 R	55.2%	41.5%	57.1%	42.9%
MONTGOMERY	14,295	8,366	5,708	221	2,658 R	58.5%	39.9%	59.4%	40.6%
MORGAN	9,586	5,328	4,042	216	1,286 R	55.6%	42.2%	56.9%	43.1%
NEWTON	4,481	2,705	1,523	253	1,182 R	60.4%	34.0%	64.0%	36.0%
NOBLE	10,397	5,793	4,163	441	1,630 R	55.7%	40.0%	58.2%	41.8%
OHIO	2,105	989	1,058	58	69 D	47.0%	50.3%	48.3%	51.7%
ORANGE	8,098	4,538	3,374	186	1,164 R	56.0%	41.7%	57.4%	42.6%
OWEN	5,541	2,627	2,670	244	43 D	47.4%	48.2%	49.6%	50.4%

INDIANA

PRESIDENT 1920

County	Total Vote	Republican	Democratic	Other	Rep.-Dem. Plurality	Total Vote Rep.	Total Vote Dem.	Major Vote Rep.	Major Vote Dem.
PARKE	8,888	4,989	3,543	356	1,446 R	56.1%	39.9%	58.5%	41.5%
PERRY	7,465	3,864	3,560	41	304 R	51.8%	47.7%	52.0%	48.0%
PIKE	7,863	4,069	3,067	727	1,002 R	51.7%	39.0%	57.0%	43.0%
PORTER	7,664	5,570	1,671	423	3,899 R	72.7%	21.8%	76.9%	23.1%
POSEY	9,658	4,802	4,695	161	107 R	49.7%	48.6%	50.6%	49.4%
PULASKI	5,085	2,740	2,228	117	512 R	53.9%	43.8%	55.2%	44.8%
PUTNAM	10,746	5,140	5,417	189	277 D	47.8%	50.4%	48.7%	51.3%
RANDOLPH	13,439	8,773	4,198	468	4,575 R	65.3%	31.2%	67.6%	32.4%
RIPLEY	9,452	5,372	3,976	104	1,396 R	56.8%	42.1%	57.5%	42.5%
RUSH	10,803	6,113	4,513	177	1,600 R	56.6%	41.8%	57.5%	42.5%
ST JOSEPH	31,305	17,675	12,355	1,275	5,320 R	56.5%	39.5%	58.9%	41.1%
SCOTT	3,597	1,709	1,848	40	139 D	47.5%	51.4%	48.0%	52.0%
SHELBY	13,437	6,336	6,845	256	509 D	47.2%	50.9%	48.1%	51.9%
SPENCER	9,240	5,270	3,855	115	1,415 R	57.0%	41.7%	57.8%	42.2%
STARKE	4,264	2,683	1,467	114	1,216 R	62.9%	34.4%	64.7%	35.3%
STEUBEN	6,848	4,963	1,676	209	3,287 R	72.5%	24.5%	74.8%	25.2%
SULLIVAN	12,991	5,376	6,160	1,455	784 D	41.4%	47.4%	46.6%	53.4%
SWITZERLAND	5,038	2,525	2,412	101	113 R	50.1%	47.9%	51.1%	48.9%
TIPPECANOE	20,639	12,730	7,562	347	5,168 R	61.7%	36.6%	62.7%	37.3%
TIPTON	8,472	4,357	3,956	159	401 R	51.4%	46.7%	52.4%	47.6%
UNION	3,403	1,984	1,375	44	609 R	58.3%	40.4%	59.1%	40.9%
VANDERBURGH	36,946	19,357	13,904	3,685	5,453 R	52.4%	37.6%	58.2%	41.8%
VERMILLION	9,439	4,916	3,218	1,305	1,698 R	52.1%	34.1%	60.4%	39.6%
VIGO	37,114	18,668	15,739	2,707	2,929 R	50.3%	42.4%	54.3%	45.7%
WABASH	13,290	8,018	4,827	445	3,191 R	60.3%	36.3%	62.4%	37.6%
WARREN	4,707	3,337	1,311	59	2,026 R	70.9%	27.9%	71.8%	28.2%
WARRICK	9,033	4,675	3,915	443	760 R	51.8%	43.3%	54.4%	45.5%
WASHINGTON	7,913	3,708	4,157	48	449 D	46.9%	52.5%	47.1%	52.9%
WAYNE	21,221	12,631	8,015	575	4,616 R	59.5%	37.8%	61.2%	38.8%
WELLS	9,305	4,430	4,653	222	223 D	47.6%	50.0%	48.8%	51.2%
WHITE	8,317	4,871	3,375	71	1,496 R	58.6%	40.6%	59.1%	40.9%
WHITLEY	8,629	4,550	3,929	170	601 R	52.5%	45.5%	53.6%	46.4%
TOTAL	1,262,974	696,370	511,364	55,240	185,006 R	55.1%	40.5%	57.7%	42.3%

PRESIDENT 1924

County	Total Vote	Republican	Democratic	Other	Rep.-Dem. Plurality	Total Vote Rep.	Total Vote Dem.	Major Vote Rep.	Major Vote Dem.
PARKE	8,249	4,877	2,898	474	1,979 R	59.1%	35.1%	62.7%	37.3%
PERRY	7,314	3,240	3,895	179	655 D	44.3%	53.3%	45.4%	54.6%
PIKE	7,965	3,885	3,604	476	281 R	48.8%	45.2%	51.9%	48.1%
PORTER	8,284	5,613	1,640	1,031	3,973 R	67.8%	19.8%	77.4%	22.6%
POSEY	8,548	4,173	4,115	260	58 R	48.8%	48.1%	50.3%	49.7%
PULASKI	4,952	2,725	1,953	274	772 R	55.0%	39.4%	58.3%	41.7%
PUTNAM	10,032	4,930	4,759	343	171 R	49.1%	47.4%	50.9%	49.1%
RANDOLPH	11,539	7,397	3,768	374	3,629 R	64.1%	32.7%	66.3%	33.7%
RIPLEY	9,576	4,694	4,257	625	437 R	49.0%	44.5%	52.4%	47.6%
RUSH	9,521	5,958	3,415	148	2,543 R	62.6%	35.9%	63.6%	36.4%
ST JOSEPH	41,082	23,682	15,056	2,344	8,626 R	57.6%	36.6%	61.1%	38.9%
SCOTT	3,436	1,532	1,824	80	292 D	44.6%	53.1%	45.6%	54.4%
SHELBY	12,936	6,664	5,976	296	688 R	51.5%	46.2%	52.7%	47.3%
SPENCER	9,045	4,395	4,409	241	14 D	48.6%	48.7%	49.9%	50.1%
STARKE	4,394	2,329	1,555	510	774 R	53.0%	35.4%	60.0%	40.0%
STEUBEN	5,905	4,046	1,610	249	2,436 R	68.5%	27.3%	71.5%	28.5%
SULLIVAN	12,053	5,139	5,213	1,701	74 D	42.6%	43.3%	49.6%	50.4%
SWITZERLAND	4,858	2,346	2,414	98	68 D	48.3%	49.7%	49.3%	50.7%
TIPPECANOE	20,823	12,161	7,619	1,043	4,542 R	58.4%	36.6%	61.5%	38.5%
TIPTON	8,150	4,183	3,660	307	523 R	51.3%	44.9%	53.3%	46.7%
UNION	3,245	1,907	1,284	54	623 R	58.8%	39.6%	59.8%	40.2%
VANDERBURGH	46,856	25,907	17,186	3,763	8,721 R	55.3%	36.7%	60.1%	39.9%
VERMILLION	9,135	4,489	2,779	1,867	1,710 R	49.1%	30.4%	61.8%	38.2%
VIGO	37,059	19,545	12,999	4,515	6,546 R	52.7%	35.1%	60.1%	39.9%
WABASH	12,040	7,277	4,054	709	3,223 R	60.4%	33.7%	64.2%	35.8%
WARREN	4,357	3,035	1,150	172	1,885 R	69.7%	26.4%	72.5%	27.5%
WARRICK	8,617	4,437	3,797	383	640 R	51.5%	44.1%	53.9%	46.1%
WASHINGTON	7,502	3,479	3,942	81	463 D	46.4%	52.5%	46.9%	53.1%
WAYNE	19,225	11,487	6,211	1,527	5,276 R	59.8%	32.3%	64.9%	35.1%
WELLS	8,754	3,932	4,537	285	605 D	44.9%	51.8%	46.4%	53.6%
WHITE	7,940	4,475	3,138	327	1,337 R	56.4%	39.5%	58.8%	41.2%
WHITLEY	8,060	4,420	3,484	156	936 R	54.8%	43.2%	55.9%	44.1%
TOTAL	1,272,390	703,042	492,245	77,103	210,797 R	55.3%	38.7%	58.8%	41.2%

INDIANA

PRESIDENT 1928

County	Total Vote	Republican	Democratic	Other	Rep.-Dem. Plurality	%Total Rep.	%Total Dem.	%Major Rep.	%Major Dem.
ADAMS	8,139	4,045	4,066	28	21 D	49.7	50.0	49.9	50.1
ALLEN	60,720	34,234	26,292	194	7,942 R	56.4	43.3	56.6	43.4
BARTHOLOMEW	11,752	6,788	4,881	83	1,907 R	57.8	41.5	58.2	41.8
BENTON	5,756	3,360	2,368	28	992 R	58.4	41.1	58.7	41.3
BLACKFORD	6,541	3,882	2,576	83	1,306 R	59.3	39.4	60.1	39.9
BOONE	11,147	6,556	4,500	91	2,056 R	58.8	40.4	59.3	40.7
BROWN	1,977	959	999	19	40 D	48.5	50.5	49.0	51.0
CARROLL	8,028	4,780	3,182	66	1,598 R	59.5	39.6	60.0	40.0
CASS	17,163	10,522	6,522	119	4,000 R	61.3	38.0	61.7	38.3
CLARK	14,285	8,056	6,193	36	1,863 R	56.4	43.4	56.5	43.5
CLAY	12,641	7,103	5,358	180	1,745 R	56.2	42.4	57.0	43.0
CLINTON	13,610	7,606	5,895	109	1,711 R	55.9	43.3	56.3	43.7
CRAWFORD	4,656	2,672	1,933	51	739 R	57.4	41.5	58.0	42.0
DAVIESS	12,543	7,116	5,324	103	1,792 R	56.7	42.4	57.2	42.8
DEARBORN	10,829	6,334	4,459	36	1,875 R	58.5	41.2	58.7	41.3
DECATUR	9,246	5,400	3,791	55	1,609 R	58.4	41.0	58.8	41.2
DE KALB	11,514	7,373	4,077	64	3,296 R	64.0	35.4	64.4	35.6
DELAWARE	27,770	19,102	8,532	136	10,570 R	68.8	30.7	69.1	30.9
DUBOIS	9,384	3,301	6,044	39	2,743 D	35.2	64.4	35.3	64.7
ELKHART	27,924	20,876	6,900	148	13,976 R	74.8	24.7	75.2	24.8
FAYETTE	9,379	5,874	3,455	50	2,419 R	62.6	36.8	63.0	37.0
FLOYD	17,902	10,471	7,327	104	3,144 R	58.5	40.9	58.8	41.2
FOUNTAIN	8,921	4,960	3,894	67	1,066 R	55.6	43.6	56.0	44.0
FRANKLIN	7,260	3,426	3,817	17	391 D	47.2	52.6	47.3	52.7
FULTON	7,574	4,627	2,881	66	1,746 R	61.1	38.0	61.6	38.4
GIBSON	14,259	8,137	5,882	240	2,255 R	57.1	41.3	58.0	42.0
GRANT	22,216	14,659	7,273	284	7,386 R	66.0	32.7	66.8	33.2
GREENE	14,291	8,262	5,761	268	2,501 R	57.8	40.3	58.8	41.1
HAMILTON	11,645	7,960	3,611	74	4,349 R	68.4	31.0	68.8	31.2
HANCOCK	8,476	4,788	3,626	62	1,162 R	56.5	42.8	56.9	43.1
HARRISON	8,158	4,440	3,664	54	776 R	54.4	44.9	54.8	45.2
HENDRICKS	9,190	5,954	3,181	55	2,773 R	64.8	34.6	65.2	34.8
HENRY	15,324	10,502	4,554	268	5,948 R	68.5	29.7	69.8	30.2
HOWARD	18,885	12,632	5,930	323	6,702 R	66.9	31.4	68.1	31.9
HUNTINGTON	14,136	8,323	5,678	135	2,645 R	58.9	40.2	59.4	40.6
JACKSON	10,347	5,151	5,130	66	21 R	49.8	49.6	50.1	49.9
JASPER	5,636	3,700	1,915	21	1,785 R	65.6	34.0	65.9	34.1
JAY	10,844	5,998	4,759	87	1,239 R	55.3	43.9	55.8	44.2
JEFFERSON	9,251	5,295	3,906	50	1,389 R	57.2	42.2	57.5	42.5
JENNINGS	6,098	3,705	2,369	24	1,336 R	60.8	38.8	61.0	39.0
JOHNSON	10,152	5,513	4,548	91	965 R	54.3	44.8	54.8	45.2
KNOX	20,104	10,035	9,837	232	198 R	49.9	48.9	50.5	49.5
KOSCIUSKO	12,620	7,973	4,537	110	3,436 R	63.2	36.0	63.7	36.3
LAGRANGE	4,924	3,171	1,720	33	1,451 R	64.4	34.9	64.8	35.2
LAKE	81,719	48,768	32,321	630	16,447 R	59.7	39.6	60.1	39.9
LA PORTE	24,075	14,763	9,254	58	5,509 R	61.3	38.4	61.5	38.5
LAWRENCE	14,329	9,844	4,428	57	5,416 R	68.7	30.9	69.0	31.0
MADISON	35,814	23,083	12,496	235	10,587 R	64.5	34.9	64.9	35.1
MARION	184,100	109,630	73,309	1,161	36,321 R	59.5	39.8	59.9	40.1
MARSHALL	11,185	6,738	4,377	70	2,361 R	60.2	39.1	60.6	39.4
MARTIN	4,722	2,450	2,245	27	205 R	51.9	47.5	52.2	47.8
MIAMI	14,052	8,318	5,592	142	2,726 R	59.2	39.8	59.8	40.2
MONROE	13,259	8,883	4,317	59	4,566 R	67.0	32.6	67.3	32.7
MONTGOMERY	13,915	8,863	4,960	92	3,903 R	63.7	35.6	64.1	35.9
MORGAN	9,460	5,464	3,933	63	1,531 R	57.8	41.6	58.1	41.9
NEWTON	4,735	3,053	1,649	33	1,404 R	64.5	34.8	64.9	35.1
NOBLE	10,605	6,338	4,207	60	2,131 R	59.8	39.7	60.1	39.9
OHIO	2,154	1,230	911	13	319 R	57.1	42.3	57.4	42.6
ORANGE	8,234	5,086	3,112	36	1,974 R	61.8	37.8	62.0	38.0
OWEN	5,517	3,036	2,420	61	616 R	55.0	43.9	55.6	44.4

PRESIDENT 1932

County	Total Vote	Republican	Democratic	Other	Rep.-Dem. Plurality	%Total Rep.	%Total Dem.	%Major Rep.	%Major Dem.
ADAMS	8,913	2,910	5,892	111	2,982 D	32.6	66.1	33.1	66.9
ALLEN	66,562	27,065	38,447	1,050	11,382 D	40.7	57.8	41.3	58.7
BARTHOLOMEW	13,938	6,015	7,533	390	1,518 D	43.2	54.0	44.4	55.6
BENTON	5,983	2,433	3,496	54	1,063 D	40.7	58.4	41.0	59.0
BLACKFORD	7,130	2,890	4,088	152	1,198 D	40.5	57.3	41.4	58.6
BOONE	12,440	5,309	6,900	231	1,591 D	42.7	55.5	43.5	56.5
BROWN	2,527	790	1,676	61	886 D	31.3	66.3	32.0	68.0
CARROLL	8,799	3,853	4,866	80	1,013 D	43.8	55.3	44.5	55.5
CASS	19,248	7,980	10,987	281	3,007 D	41.5	57.1	42.1	57.9
CLARK	15,522	5,881	9,501	140	3,620 D	37.9	61.2	38.2	61.8
CLAY	13,818	5,343	8,151	324	2,808 D	38.7	59.0	39.6	60.4
CLINTON	14,776	6,288	8,314	174	2,026 D	42.6	56.3	43.1	56.9
CRAWFORD	5,528	2,175	3,272	81	1,097 D	39.3	59.2	39.9	60.1
DAVIESS	12,889	5,838	6,772	279	934 D	45.3	52.5	46.3	53.7
DEARBORN	11,275	4,716	6,429	130	1,713 D	41.8	57.0	42.3	57.7
DECATUR	10,198	4,646	5,437	115	791 D	45.6	53.3	46.1	53.9
DE KALB	12,981	5,590	7,235	156	1,645 D	43.1	55.7	43.6	56.4
DELAWARE	31,245	16,012	14,346	887	1,666 R	51.2	45.9	52.7	47.3
DUBOIS	9,996	2,357	7,547	92	5,190 D	23.6	75.5	23.8	76.2
ELKHART	29,566	13,826	14,885	855	1,059 D	46.8	50.3	48.2	51.8
FAYETTE	10,154	4,867	5,148	139	281 D	47.9	50.7	48.6	51.4
FLOYD	18,153	7,333	10,497	323	3,164 D	40.4	57.8	41.1	58.9
FOUNTAIN	9,950	4,162	5,665	123	1,503 D	41.8	56.9	42.4	57.6
FRANKLIN	7,459	2,687	4,704	68	2,017 D	36.0	63.1	36.4	63.6
FULTON	8,722	3,787	4,794	141	1,007 D	43.4	55.0	44.1	55.9
GIBSON	15,863	6,237	9,162	464	2,925 D	39.3	57.8	40.5	59.5
GRANT	25,961	11,398	13,390	1,173	1,992 D	43.9	51.6	46.0	54.0
GREENE	15,593	6,845	8,845	277	2,000 D	43.9	55.5	44.8	55.2
HAMILTON	13,376	7,100	5,999	277	1,101 R	53.1	44.8	54.2	45.8
HANCOCK	10,081	4,055	5,836	190	1,781 D	40.2	57.9	41.0	59.0
HARRISON	8,864	3,553	5,128	123	1,575 D	40.4	58.2	40.9	59.1
HENDRICKS	10,817	5,317	5,293	207	24 R	49.2	48.9	50.5	49.5
HENRY	17,319	8,430	8,255	634	175 R	48.7	47.7	50.5	49.5
HOWARD	20,744	9,257	10,541	946	1,284 D	44.6	50.8	46.8	53.2
HUNTINGTON	15,821	6,791	8,697	333	1,906 D	42.9	55.0	43.8	56.2
JACKSON	12,086	3,996	7,882	208	3,886 D	33.1	65.2	33.6	66.4
JASPER	6,504	2,897	3,538	69	641 D	44.5	54.4	45.0	55.0
JAY	11,711	5,018	6,693		1,675 D	42.8	57.2	42.9	57.1
JEFFERSON	10,164	4,670	5,305	189	635 D	45.9	52.2	46.8	53.3
JENNINGS	6,717	3,020	3,603	94	583 D	45.0	53.6	45.6	54.4
JOHNSON	11,718	4,593	6,940	185	2,347 D	39.2	59.2	39.8	60.2
KNOX	21,140	6,590	14,084	466	7,494 D	31.2	66.6	31.9	68.1
KOSCIUSKO	14,791	7,063	7,475	253	412 D	47.8	50.5	48.6	51.4
LAGRANGE	5,820	2,461	3,261	98	800 D	42.3	56.0	43.0	57.0
LAKE	91,492	42,596	46,060	2,836	3,464 D	46.6	50.3	48.0	52.0
LA PORTE	25,995	10,739	14,890	366	4,151 D	41.3	57.3	41.9	58.1
LAWRENCE	16,741	8,314	8,215	212	99 R	49.7	49.1	50.3	49.7
MADISON	41,860	18,803	22,069	988	3,266 D	44.9	52.7	46.0	54.0
MARION	212,664	98,256	106,661	7,747	8,405 D	46.2	50.2	47.9	52.1
MARSHALL	12,407	4,943	7,212	252	2,269 D	39.8	58.1	40.7	59.3
MARTIN	5,225	2,106	3,072	47	966 D	40.3	58.8	40.7	59.3
MIAMI	15,191	5,987	8,892	312	2,905 D	39.4	58.5	40.2	59.8
MONROE	16,497	7,759	8,478	260	719 D	47.0	51.4	47.8	52.2
MONTGOMERY	14,704	6,417	8,077	210	1,660 D	43.6	54.9	44.3	55.7
MORGAN	10,795	4,825	5,775	195	950 D	44.7	53.5	45.5	54.5
NEWTON	5,102	2,380	2,654	68	274 D	46.6	52.0	47.3	52.7
NOBLE	11,968	5,304	6,538	126	1,234 D	44.3	54.6	44.8	55.2
OHIO	2,305	997	1,288	20	291 D	43.3	55.9	43.6	56.4
ORANGE	9,487	4,561	4,844	82	283 D	48.1	51.1	48.5	51.5
OWEN	6,236	2,423	3,639	174	1,216 D	38.9	58.4	40.0	60.0

INDIANA

PRESIDENT 1928

County	Total Vote	Republican	Democratic	Other	Rep.-Dem. Plurality	% Total Vote Rep.	% Total Vote Dem.	% Major Vote Rep.	% Major Vote Dem.
PARKE	7,981	4,729	3,165	87	1,564 R	59.3%	39.7%	59.9%	40.1%
PERRY	7,561	3,772	3,782	7	10 D	49.9%	50.0%	49.9%	50.1%
PIKE	7,673	4,190	3,409	74	781 R	54.6%	44.4%	55.1%	44.9%
PORTER	10,090	7,107	2,921	62	4,186 R	70.4%	28.9%	70.9%	29.1%
POSEY	8,487	4,396	4,052	39	344 R	51.8%	47.7%	52.0%	48.0%
PULASKI	4,852	2,738	2,040	74	698 R	56.4%	42.0%	57.3%	42.7%
PUTNAM	9,603	5,351	4,177	75	1,174 R	55.7%	43.5%	56.2%	43.8%
RANDOLPH	11,733	8,368	3,264	101	5,104 R	71.3%	27.8%	71.9%	28.1%
RIPLEY	9,476	5,059	4,387	30	672 R	53.4%	46.3%	53.6%	46.4%
RUSH	9,711	6,640	2,996	75	3,644 R	68.4%	30.9%	68.9%	31.1%
ST JOSEPH	64,006	36,844	26,846	316	9,998 R	57.6%	41.9%	57.8%	42.2%
SCOTT	3,263	1,719	1,527	17	192 R	52.7%	46.8%	53.0%	47.0%
SHELBY	13,389	7,516	5,790	83	1,726 R	56.1%	43.2%	56.5%	43.5%
SPENCER	8,844	4,672	4,152	20	520 R	52.8%	46.9%	52.9%	47.1%
STARKE	4,813	2,759	2,016	38	743 R	57.3%	41.9%	57.8%	42.2%
STEUBEN	6,216	4,435	1,730	51	2,705 R	71.3%	27.8%	71.9%	28.1%
SULLIVAN	12,134	6,199	5,642	293	557 R	51.1%	46.5%	52.4%	47.6%
SWITZERLAND	4,464	2,617	1,805	42	812 R	58.6%	40.4%	59.2%	40.8%
TIPPECANOE	23,978	15,165	8,720	93	6,445 R	63.2%	36.4%	63.5%	36.5%
TIPTON	8,050	4,774	3,186	90	1,588 R	59.3%	39.6%	60.0%	40.0%
UNION	3,184	2,101	1,069	14	1,032 R	66.0%	33.6%	66.3%	33.7%
VANDERBURGH	48,905	29,067	19,646	192	9,421 R	59.4%	40.2%	59.7%	40.3%
VERMILLION	10,100	5,192	4,793	115	399 R	51.4%	47.5%	52.0%	48.0%
VIGO	41,968	22,962	18,509	497	4,453 R	54.7%	44.1%	55.4%	44.6%
WABASH	12,508	8,537	3,872	99	4,665 R	68.3%	31.0%	68.8%	31.2%
WARREN	3,856	2,644	1,188	24	1,456 R	68.6%	30.8%	69.0%	31.0%
WARRICK	8,505	4,603	3,744	158	859 R	54.1%	44.0%	55.1%	44.9%
WASHINGTON	7,381	3,835	3,518	28	317 R	52.0%	47.7%	52.2%	47.8%
WAYNE	23,601	15,936	7,547	118	8,389 R	67.5%	32.0%	67.9%	32.1%
WELLS	8,465	4,142	4,246	77	104 D	48.9%	50.2%	49.4%	50.6%
WHITE	7,556	4,534	2,980	42	1,554 R	60.0%	39.4%	60.3%	39.7%
WHITLEY	7,869	4,519	3,294	56	1,225 R	57.4%	41.9%	57.8%	42.2%
TOTAL	1,421,314	848,290	562,691	10,333	285,599 R	59.7%	39.6%	60.1%	39.9%

PRESIDENT 1932

County	Total Vote	Republican	Democratic	Other	Rep.-Dem. Plurality	% Total Vote Rep.	% Total Vote Dem.	% Major Vote Rep.	% Major Vote Dem.
PARKE	8,864	3,926	4,703	235	777 D	44.3%	53.1%	45.5%	54.5%
PERRY	8,357	3,253	5,053	51	1,800 D	38.9%	60.5%	39.2%	60.8%
PIKE	7,931	3,193	4,547	191	1,354 D	40.3%	57.3%	41.3%	58.7%
PORTER	11,382	5,631	5,542	209	89 R	49.5%	48.7%	50.4%	49.6%
POSEY	8,644	2,876	5,641	127	2,765 D	33.3%	65.3%	33.8%	66.2%
PULASKI	5,641	2,226	3,286	129	1,060 D	39.5%	58.3%	40.4%	59.6%
PUTNAM	10,968	4,438	6,168	362	1,730 D	40.5%	56.2%	41.8%	58.2%
RANDOLPH	13,166	6,509	6,223	434	286 R	49.4%	47.3%	51.1%	48.9%
RIPLEY	10,348	4,240	5,987	121	1,747 D	41.0%	57.9%	41.5%	58.5%
RUSH	10,290	5,094	5,056	140	38 R	49.5%	49.1%	50.2%	49.8%
ST JOSEPH	68,563	28,198	38,026	2,339	9,828 D	41.1%	55.5%	42.6%	57.4%
SCOTT	4,008	1,722	2,240	46	518 D	43.0%	55.9%	43.5%	56.5%
SHELBY	14,219	5,410	8,552	257	3,142 D	38.0%	60.1%	38.7%	61.3%
SPENCER	9,503	4,014	5,422	67	1,408 D	42.2%	57.1%	42.5%	57.5%
STARKE	6,010	2,449	3,420	141	971 D	40.7%	56.9%	41.7%	58.3%
STEUBEN	7,428	3,594	3,717	117	123 D	48.4%	50.0%	49.2%	50.8%
SULLIVAN	12,477	3,667	7,835	975	4,168 D	29.4%	62.8%	31.9%	68.1%
SWITZERLAND	5,035	1,953	2,981	101	1,028 D	38.8%	59.2%	39.6%	60.4%
TIPPECANOE	25,663	11,818	13,609	236	1,791 D	46.1%	53.0%	46.5%	53.5%
TIPTON	8,723	3,680	4,898	145	1,218 D	42.2%	56.2%	42.9%	57.1%
UNION	3,289	1,658	1,587	44	71 R	50.4%	48.3%	51.1%	48.9%
VANDERBURGH	49,752	16,873	31,828	1,051	14,955 D	33.9%	64.0%	34.6%	65.4%
VERMILLION	10,872	4,115	6,390	367	2,275 D	37.8%	58.8%	39.2%	60.8%
VIGO	45,187	18,310	25,886	991	7,576 D	40.5%	57.3%	41.4%	58.6%
WABASH	13,476	6,652	6,553	271	99 R	49.4%	48.6%	50.4%	49.6%
WARREN	4,544	2,223	2,256	65	33 D	48.9%	49.6%	49.6%	50.4%
WARRICK	9,086	3,429	5,409	248	1,980 D	37.7%	59.5%	38.8%	61.2%
WASHINGTON	8,181	3,316	4,809	56	1,493 D	40.5%	58.8%	40.8%	59.2%
WAYNE	26,506	12,683	13,287	536	604 D	47.8%	50.1%	48.8%	51.2%
WELLS	9,528	3,073	6,236	219	3,163 D	32.3%	65.4%	33.0%	67.0%
WHITE	8,592	3,484	4,976	132	1,492 D	40.5%	57.9%	41.2%	58.8%
WHITLEY	8,853	3,471	5,058	324	1,587 D	39.2%	57.1%	40.7%	59.3%
TOTAL	1,576,927	677,184	862,054	37,689	184,870 D	42.9%	54.7%	44.0%	56.0%

INDIANA

PRESIDENT 1936

County	Total Vote	Republican	Democratic	Other	Rep.-Dem. Plurality	% Total Rep.	% Total Dem.	% Major Rep.	% Major Dem.
ADAMS	9,208	3,249	5,822	137	2,573 D	35.3	63.2	35.8	64.2
ALLEN	66,146	24,765	39,151	2,230	14,386 D	37.4	59.2	38.7	61.3
BARTHOLOMEW	15,107	6,484	8,536	87	2,052 D	42.9	56.5	43.2	56.8
BENTON	6,331	2,989	3,211	131	222 D	47.2	50.7	48.2	51.8
BLACKFORD	7,145	2,845	4,217	83	1,372 D	39.8	59.0	40.3	59.7
BOONE	12,593	5,739	6,775	79	1,036 D	45.6	53.8	45.9	54.1
BROWN	2,844	1,244	1,585	15	341 D	43.7	55.7	44.0	56.0
CARROLL	9,167	4,426	4,676	65	250 D	48.3	51.0	48.6	51.4
CASS	19,422	8,528	10,475	419	1,947 D	43.9	53.9	44.9	55.1
CLARK	15,896	5,536	10,116	244	4,580 D	34.8	63.6	35.4	64.6
CLAY	14,683	6,335	8,235	113	1,900 D	43.1	56.1	43.5	56.5
CLINTON	15,730	7,265	8,340	125	1,075 D	46.2	53.0	46.6	53.4
CRAWFORD	5,519	2,589	2,919	11	330 D	46.9	52.9	47.0	53.0
DAVIESS	13,470	6,459	6,848	163	389 D	48.0	50.8	48.5	51.5
DEARBORN	11,256	4,669	6,366	221	1,697 D	41.5	56.6	42.3	57.7
DECATUR	10,107	5,126	4,887	94	239 R	50.7	48.4	51.2	48.8
DE KALB	13,027	5,848	6,970	209	1,122 D	44.9	53.5	45.6	54.4
DELAWARE	33,527	14,207	19,048	272	4,841 D	42.4	56.8	42.7	57.3
DUBOIS	10,359	3,011	6,927	421	3,916 D	29.1	66.9	30.3	69.7
ELKHART	30,371	14,896	14,473	1,002	423 R	49.0	47.7	50.7	49.3
FAYETTE	10,922	5,067	5,756	99	689 D	46.4	52.7	46.8	53.2
FLOYD	18,121	6,976	10,654	491	3,678 D	38.5	58.8	39.6	60.4
FOUNTAIN	10,316	4,663	5,617	36	954 D	45.2	54.4	45.4	54.6
FRANKLIN	7,164	2,952	3,891	321	939 D	41.2	54.3	43.1	56.9
FULTON	9,004	4,541	4,322	141	219 R	50.4	48.0	51.2	48.8
GIBSON	16,710	7,078	9,392	240	2,314 D	42.4	56.2	43.0	57.0
GRANT	26,260	11,774	13,655	831	1,881 D	44.8	52.0	46.3	53.7
GREENE	17,344	9,730	7,460	154	2,270 R	56.1	43.0	56.6	43.4
HAMILTON	12,870	7,323	5,396	151	1,927 R	56.9	41.9	57.6	42.4
HANCOCK	10,180	4,174	5,962	44	1,788 D	41.0	58.6	41.2	58.8
HARRISON	8,986	3,885	5,025	76	1,140 D	43.2	55.9	43.6	56.4
HENDRICKS	11,097	5,776	5,237	84	539 R	52.1	47.2	52.4	47.6
HENRY	19,420	9,099	10,172	149	1,073 D	46.9	52.4	47.2	52.8
HOWARD	22,336	9,534	12,288	524	2,754 D	42.7	55.0	43.7	56.3
HUNTINGTON	15,697	7,024	8,361	312	1,337 D	44.7	53.3	45.7	54.3
JACKSON	13,037	4,951	8,018	68	3,067 D	38.0	61.5	38.2	61.8
JASPER	6,721	3,109	3,540	72	431 D	46.3	52.7	46.8	53.2
JAY	11,967	5,233	6,535	199	1,302 D	43.7	54.6	44.5	55.5
JEFFERSON	10,207	5,320	4,805	82	515 R	52.1	47.1	52.5	47.5
JENNINGS	6,823	3,594	3,157	72	437 R	52.7	46.3	53.2	46.8
JOHNSON	12,329	5,315	6,934	80	1,619 D	43.1	56.2	43.4	56.6
KNOX	22,400	8,589	13,669	142	5,080 D	38.3	61.0	38.6	61.4
KOSCIUSKO	15,179	8,182	6,890	107	1,292 R	53.9	45.4	54.3	45.7
LAGRANGE	6,042	3,125	2,821	96	304 R	51.7	46.7	52.6	47.4
LAKE	103,750	33,689	68,551	1,510	34,862 D	32.5	66.1	33.0	67.0
LA PORTE	27,392	11,722	15,359	311	3,637 D	42.8	56.1	43.3	56.7
LAWRENCE	18,178	9,982	8,062	134	1,920 R	54.9	44.4	55.3	44.7
MADISON	44,495	16,644	27,347	504	10,703 D	37.4	61.5	37.8	62.2
MARION	216,550	87,798	124,961	3,791	37,163 D	40.5	57.7	41.3	58.7
MARSHALL	12,971	6,118	6,651	202	533 D	47.2	51.3	47.9	52.1
MARTIN	5,546	2,583	2,923	40	340 D	46.6	52.7	46.9	53.1
MIAMI	15,122	6,747	8,173	202	1,426 D	44.6	54.0	45.2	54.8
MONROE	18,110	8,842	9,220	48	378 D	48.8	50.9	49.0	51.0
MONTGOMERY	15,549	7,369	8,053	127	684 D	47.4	51.8	47.8	52.2
MORGAN	11,328	5,793	5,451	84	342 R	51.1	48.1	51.5	48.5
NEWTON	5,408	2,937	2,430	41	507 R	54.3	44.9	54.7	45.3
NOBLE	11,936	5,760	5,990	186	230 D	48.3	50.2	49.0	51.0
OHIO	2,384	1,022	1,362	—	340 D	42.9	57.1	42.9	57.1
ORANGE	9,692	5,106	4,549	37	557 R	52.7	46.9	52.9	47.1
OWEN	6,648	3,091	3,498	59	407 D	46.5	52.6	46.9	53.1

PRESIDENT 1940

County	Total Vote	Republican	Democratic	Other	Rep.-Dem. Plurality	% Total Rep.	% Total Dem.	% Major Rep.	% Major Dem.
ADAMS	9,730	5,247	4,382	101	865 R	53.9	45.0	54.5	45.5
ALLEN	70,709	40,430	29,967	312	10,463 R	57.2	42.4	57.4	42.6
BARTHOLOMEW	16,155	7,890	8,180	86	290 D	48.8	50.6	49.1	50.9
BENTON	6,384	3,675	2,689	20	986 R	57.6	42.1	57.7	42.3
BLACKFORD	7,530	3,352	4,095	83	743 D	44.5	54.4	45.0	55.0
BOONE	13,267	7,066	6,152	49	914 R	53.3	46.4	53.5	46.5
BROWN	3,160	1,477	1,662	21	185 D	46.7	52.6	47.1	52.9
CARROLL	9,273	5,012	4,214	47	798 R	54.0	45.5	54.3	45.7
CASS	20,385	10,057	10,268	61	211 D	49.3	50.4	49.5	50.5
CLARK	15,104	6,044	9,015	45	2,971 D	40.0	59.7	40.1	59.9
CLAY	15,114	7,768	7,255	91	513 R	51.4	48.0	51.7	48.3
CLINTON	16,444	8,610	7,732	102	878 R	52.4	47.0	52.7	47.3
CRAWFORD	5,529	2,652	2,836	41	184 D	48.0	51.3	48.3	51.7
DAVIESS	14,057	7,615	6,401	59	1,214 R	54.2	45.5	54.3	45.7
DEARBORN	11,987	5,908	6,038	41	130 D	49.3	50.4	49.5	50.5
DECATUR	10,547	6,087	4,417	43	1,670 R	57.7	41.9	57.9	42.1
DE KALB	13,422	7,676	5,690	60	1,986 R	57.2	42.4	57.4	42.6
DELAWARE	38,691	17,616	20,836	239	3,220 D	45.5	53.9	45.8	54.2
DUBOIS	10,745	4,729	5,992	24	1,263 D	44.0	55.8	44.1	55.9
ELKHART	33,715	19,735	13,620	361	6,115 R	58.5	40.4	59.2	40.8
FAYETTE	11,147	5,567	5,542	38	25 R	49.9	49.7	50.1	49.9
FLOYD	18,944	8,056	10,799	89	2,743 D	42.5	57.0	42.7	57.3
FOUNTAIN	10,572	4,783	5,771	18	988 D	45.2	54.6	45.3	54.7
FRANKLIN	7,539	4,381	3,142	16	1,239 R	58.1	41.7	58.2	41.8
FULTON	9,672	5,532	3,879	61	1,653 R	57.2	40.1	58.8	41.2
GIBSON	17,223	8,326	8,709	188	383 D	48.3	50.6	48.9	51.1
GRANT	28,779	15,187	13,257	335	1,930 R	52.8	46.1	53.4	46.6
GREENE	17,889	9,071	8,718	100	353 R	50.7	48.7	51.0	49.0
HAMILTON	13,797	8,931	4,791	75	4,140 R	64.7	34.7	65.1	34.9
HANCOCK	10,785	5,283	5,417	85	134 D	49.0	50.2	49.4	50.6
HARRISON	9,439	4,650	4,725	64	75 D	49.3	50.1	49.6	50.4
HENDRICKS	11,710	6,782	4,883	45	1,899 R	57.9	41.7	58.1	41.9
HENRY	20,853	11,051	9,623	179	1,428 R	53.0	46.1	53.5	46.5
HOWARD	24,793	11,855	12,655	283	800 D	47.8	51.0	48.4	51.6
HUNTINGTON	16,497	9,110	7,220	167	1,890 R	55.2	43.8	55.8	44.2
JACKSON	13,917	6,281	7,557	79	1,276 D	45.1	54.3	45.4	54.6
JASPER	7,241	4,462	2,751	28	1,711 R	61.6	38.0	61.9	38.1
JAY	13,149	6,478	6,554	117	76 D	49.3	49.8	49.7	50.3
JEFFERSON	10,676	5,957	4,688	31	1,269 R	55.8	43.9	56.0	44.0
JENNINGS	6,939	3,921	2,988	30	933 R	56.5	43.1	56.7	43.3
JOHNSON	12,857	6,451	6,350	56	101 R	50.2	49.4	50.4	49.6
KNOX	23,590	11,211	12,265	114	1,054 D	47.5	52.0	47.8	52.2
KOSCIUSKO	15,760	9,879	5,768	113	4,111 R	62.7	36.6	63.1	36.9
LAGRANGE	5,882	3,731	2,124	27	1,607 R	63.4	36.1	63.7	36.3
LAKE	118,330	45,898	71,985	447	26,087 D	38.8	60.8	38.9	61.1
LA PORTE	29,593	15,771	13,732	90	2,039 R	53.3	46.4	53.5	46.5
LAWRENCE	17,308	10,717	6,553	38	4,164 R	61.9	37.9	62.1	37.9
MADISON	48,754	22,382	26,111	261	3,729 D	45.9	53.6	46.2	53.8
MARION	247,539	124,845	121,907	787	2,938 R	50.4	49.2	50.6	49.4
MARSHALL	13,681	7,718	5,852	111	1,866 R	56.4	42.8	56.9	43.1
MARTIN	5,554	2,902	2,638	14	264 R	52.3	47.5	52.4	47.6
MIAMI	15,575	8,227	7,252	96	975 R	52.8	46.6	53.1	46.9
MONROE	18,499	10,311	8,117	71	2,194 R	55.7	43.9	56.0	44.0
MONTGOMERY	15,616	8,554	6,994	68	1,560 R	54.8	44.8	55.0	45.0
MORGAN	11,564	6,613	4,895	56	1,718 R	57.2	42.3	57.5	42.5
NEWTON	5,674	3,536	2,116	22	1,420 R	62.3	37.3	62.6	37.4
NOBLE	12,517	7,443	5,014	60	2,429 R	59.5	40.1	59.7	40.3
OHIO	2,404	1,186	1,210	8	24 D	49.3	50.3	49.5	50.5
ORANGE	9,553	5,519	4,003	31	1,516 R	57.8	41.9	58.0	42.0
OWEN	6,868	3,709	3,121	38	588 R	54.0	45.4	54.3	45.7

INDIANA

PRESIDENT 1936

County	Total Vote	Republican	Democratic	Other	Rep.-Dem. Plurality	Total Vote Rep.	Total Vote Dem.	Major Vote Rep.	Major Vote Dem.
PARKE	9,542	4,665	4,811	66	146 D	48.9%	50.4%	49.2%	50.8%
PERRY	8,619	3,619	4,752	248	1,133 D	42.0%	55.1%	43.2%	56.8%
PIKE	8,882	3,885	4,952	45	1,067 D	43.7%	55.8%	44.0%	56.0%
PORTER	11,936	6,278	5,560	98	718 R	52.6%	46.6%	53.0%	47.0%
POSEY	8,888	3,088	5,630	170	2,542 D	34.7%	63.3%	35.4%	64.6%
PULASKI	6,120	2,780	3,274	66	494 D	45.4%	53.5%	45.9%	54.1%
PUTNAM	11,207	4,961	6,177	69	1,216 D	44.3%	55.1%	44.5%	55.5%
RANDOLPH	13,283	6,682	6,487	114	195 R	50.3%	48.8%	50.7%	49.3%
RIPLEY	11,698	4,919	5,546	233	627 D	46.0%	51.8%	47.0%	53.0%
RUSH	11,500	5,457	5,999	44	542 D	47.5%	52.2%	47.6%	52.4%
ST JOSEPH	70,339	25,807	43,131	1,401	17,324 D	36.7%	61.3%	37.4%	62.6%
SCOTT	4,746	2,034	2,696	16	662 D	42.9%	56.8%	43.0%	57.0%
SHELBY	14,717	6,026	8,552	139	2,526 D	40.9%	58.1%	41.3%	58.7%
SPENCER	9,676	4,567	4,966	143	399 D	47.2%	51.3%	47.9%	52.1%
STARKE	6,032	2,846	3,143	43	297 D	47.2%	52.1%	47.5%	52.5%
STEUBEN	7,545	3,998	3,402	145	596 R	53.0%	45.1%	54.0%	46.0%
SULLIVAN	15,154	4,685	10,203	266	5,518 D	30.9%	67.3%	31.5%	68.5%
SWITZERLAND	5,066	2,212	2,840	14	628 D	43.7%	56.1%	43.8%	56.2%
TIPPECANOE	26,122	13,081	12,732	309	349 R	50.1%	48.7%	50.7%	49.3%
TIPTON	8,739	3,842	4,796	101	954 D	44.0%	54.9%	44.5%	55.5%
UNION	3,313	1,630	1,662	21	32 D	49.2%	50.2%	49.5%	50.5%
VANDERBURGH	57,085	14,725	41,490	870	26,765 D	25.8%	72.7%	26.2%	73.8%
VERMILLION	11,635	4,320	7,188	127	2,868 D	37.1%	61.8%	37.5%	62.5%
VIGO	50,738	17,278	33,018	442	15,740 D	34.1%	65.1%	34.4%	65.6%
WABASH	13,623	7,223	6,200	200	1,023 R	53.0%	45.5%	53.8%	46.2%
WARREN	5,045	2,780	2,242	23	538 R	55.1%	44.4%	55.4%	44.6%
WARRICK	9,429	3,968	5,343	118	1,375 D	42.1%	56.7%	42.6%	57.4%
WASHINGTON	8,482	3,690	4,766	26	1,076 D	43.5%	56.4%	43.6%	56.4%
WAYNE	26,373	12,126	13,696	551	1,570 D	46.0%	51.9%	47.0%	53.0%
WELLS	9,854	3,606	6,189	59	2,583 D	36.6%	62.8%	36.8%	63.2%
WHITE	9,250	4,245	4,863	142	618 D	45.9%	52.6%	46.6%	53.4%
WHITLEY	9,150	3,959	5,115	76	1,156 D	43.3%	55.9%	43.6%	56.4%
*TOTAL	1,650,897	691,570	934,974	24,353	243,404 D	41.9%	56.6%	42.5%	57.5%

PRESIDENT 1940

County	Total Vote	Republican	Democratic	Other	Rep.-Dem. Plurality	Total Vote Rep.	Total Vote Dem.	Major Vote Rep.	Major Vote Dem.
PARKE	9,683	5,242	4,384	57	858 R	54.1%	45.3%	54.5%	45.5%
PERRY	8,978	4,489	4,475	14	14 R	50.0%	49.8%	50.1%	49.9%
PIKE	9,177	4,672	4,449	56	223 R	50.9%	48.5%	51.2%	48.8%
PORTER	14,161	8,270	5,840	51	2,430 R	58.4%	41.2%	58.6%	41.4%
POSEY	9,593	4,514	5,022	57	508 D	47.1%	52.4%	47.3%	52.7%
PULASKI	6,588	3,472	3,021	95	451 R	52.7%	45.9%	53.5%	46.5%
PUTNAM	11,901	5,832	6,020	49	188 D	49.0%	50.6%	49.2%	50.8%
RANDOLPH	14,046	8,033	5,787	226	2,246 R	57.2%	41.2%	58.1%	41.9%
RIPLEY	10,933	6,061	4,834	38	1,227 R	55.4%	44.2%	55.6%	44.4%
RUSH	10,807	6,486	4,282	39	2,204 R	60.0%	39.6%	60.2%	39.8%
ST JOSEPH	82,158	36,164	45,620	374	9,456 D	44.0%	55.5%	44.2%	55.8%
SCOTT	4,972	2,285	2,668	19	383 D	46.0%	53.7%	46.1%	53.9%
SHELBY	15,348	7,216	8,015	117	799 D	47.0%	52.2%	47.4%	52.6%
SPENCER	9,889	5,667	4,180	42	1,487 R	57.3%	42.3%	57.6%	42.4%
STARKE	6,412	3,473	2,917	22	556 R	54.2%	45.5%	54.4%	45.6%
STEUBEN	7,620	5,056	2,524	40	2,532 R	66.4%	33.1%	66.7%	33.3%
SULLIVAN	15,289	6,471	8,667	151	2,196 D	42.3%	56.7%	42.7%	57.3%
SWITZERLAND	4,966	2,285	2,659	22	374 D	46.0%	53.5%	46.2%	53.8%
TIPPECANOE	28,350	16,148	12,129	73	4,019 R	57.0%	42.8%	57.1%	42.9%
TIPTON	8,978	4,749	4,173	56	576 R	52.9%	46.5%	53.2%	46.8%
UNION	3,443	2,009	1,415	19	594 R	58.4%	41.1%	58.7%	41.3%
VANDERBURGH	67,267	28,417	38,567	283	10,150 D	42.2%	57.3%	42.4%	57.6%
VERMILLION	11,973	5,716	6,174	83	458 D	47.7%	51.6%	48.1%	51.9%
VIGO	52,684	23,177	29,308	199	6,131 D	44.0%	55.6%	44.1%	55.9%
WABASH	14,327	8,755	5,431	141	3,324 R	61.1%	37.9%	61.7%	38.3%
WARREN	4,940	2,999	1,927	14	1,072 R	60.7%	39.0%	60.9%	39.1%
WARRICK	10,517	5,456	5,019	42	437 R	51.9%	47.7%	52.1%	47.9%
WASHINGTON	8,716	4,216	4,471	29	255 D	48.4%	51.3%	48.5%	51.5%
WAYNE	29,370	15,058	14,139	173	919 R	51.3%	48.1%	51.6%	48.4%
WELLS	10,257	4,898	5,236	123	338 D	47.8%	51.0%	48.3%	51.7%
WHITE	9,409	5,189	4,176	44	1,013 R	55.1%	44.4%	55.4%	44.6%
WHITLEY	9,561	5,100	4,404	57	696 R	53.3%	46.1%	53.7%	46.3%
	1,782,747	899,466	874,063	9,218	25,403 R	50.5%	49.0%	50.7%	49.3%

INDIANA

PRESIDENT 1944

County	Total Vote	Republican	Democratic	Other	Rep.-Dem. Plurality		Total Vote Rep.	Dem.	Major Vote Rep.	Dem.
ADAMS	9,601	5,648	3,804	149	1,844	R	58.8%	39.6%	59.8%	40.2%
ALLEN	72,709	41,907	30,445	357	11,462	R	57.6%	41.9%	57.9%	42.1%
BARTHOLOMEW	15,080	7,689	7,139	252	550	R	51.0%	47.3%	51.9%	48.1%
BENTON	5,713	3,621	2,065	27	1,556	R	63.4%	36.1%	63.7%	36.3%
BLACKFORD	6,439	3,079	3,207	153	128	D	47.8%	49.8%	49.0%	51.0%
BOONE	12,185	6,823	5,292	70	1,531	R	56.0%	43.4%	56.3%	43.7%
BROWN	2,571	1,174	1,352	45	178	D	45.7%	52.6%	46.5%	53.5%
CARROLL	8,505	4,872	3,578	55	1,294	R	57.3%	42.1%	57.7%	42.3%
CASS	18,506	9,788	8,615	103	1,173	R	52.9%	46.6%	53.2%	46.8%
CLARK	17,081	7,241	9,778	62	2,537	D	42.4%	57.2%	42.5%	57.5%
CLAY	12,553	6,688	5,721	144	967	R	53.3%	45.6%	53.9%	46.1%
CLINTON	14,605	8,087	6,381	137	1,706	R	55.4%	43.7%	55.9%	44.1%
CRAWFORD	4,927	2,488	2,335	104	153	R	50.5%	47.4%	51.6%	48.4%
DAVIESS	13,052	7,458	5,523	71	1,935	R	57.1%	42.3%	57.5%	42.5%
DEARBORN	10,691	5,487	5,157	47	330	R	51.3%	48.2%	51.6%	48.4%
DECATUR	9,003	5,479	3,471	53	2,008	R	60.9%	38.6%	61.2%	38.8%
DE KALB	12,387	7,479	4,810	98	2,669	R	60.4%	38.8%	60.9%	39.1%
DELAWARE	36,575	17,340	18,780	455	1,440	D	47.4%	51.3%	48.0%	52.0%
DUBOIS	10,162	4,855	5,273	34	418	D	47.8%	51.9%	47.9%	52.1%
ELKHART	34,208	20,659	12,991	558	7,668	R	60.4%	38.0%	61.4%	38.6%
FAYETTE	10,938	5,603	5,299	36	304	R	51.2%	48.4%	51.4%	48.6%
FLOYD	19,071	8,410	10,541	120	2,131	D	44.1%	55.3%	44.8%	55.2%
FOUNTAIN	9,625	5,557	4,022	46	1,535	R	57.7%	41.8%	58.0%	42.0%
FRANKLIN	6,346	3,796	2,530	20	1,266	R	59.8%	39.9%	60.0%	40.0%
FULTON	8,469	5,190	3,201	78	1,989	R	61.3%	37.8%	61.9%	38.1%
GIBSON	15,525	7,895	7,462	168	433	R	50.9%	48.1%	51.4%	48.6%
GRANT	26,379	14,527	11,031	821	3,496	R	55.1%	41.8%	56.8%	43.2%
GREENE	15,086	8,213	6,744	129	1,469	R	54.4%	44.7%	54.9%	45.1%
HAMILTON	12,560	8,297	4,101	162	4,196	R	66.1%	32.7%	66.9%	33.1%
HANCOCK	9,938	5,139	4,652	147	487	R	51.7%	46.8%	52.5%	47.5%
HARRISON	8,786	4,397	4,285	104	112	R	50.0%	48.8%	50.6%	49.4%
HENDRICKS	11,039	6,673	4,297	69	2,376	R	60.4%	38.9%	60.8%	39.2%
HENRY	17,296	10,583	6,297	416	4,286	R	61.2%	36.4%	62.7%	37.3%
HOWARD	23,265	11,515	11,224	526	291	R	49.5%	48.2%	50.6%	49.4%
HUNTINGTON	15,166	8,668	6,128	370	2,540	R	57.2%	40.4%	58.6%	41.4%
JACKSON	12,426	6,321	5,982	123	339	R	50.9%	48.1%	51.4%	48.6%
JASPER	6,550	4,364	2,168	18	2,196	R	66.6%	33.1%	66.8%	33.2%
JAY	11,629	6,207	5,166	256	1,041	R	53.4%	44.4%	54.6%	45.4%
JEFFERSON	10,234	5,748	4,376	110	1,372	R	56.2%	42.8%	56.8%	43.2%
JENNINGS	6,219	3,643	2,537	39	1,106	R	58.6%	40.8%	58.9%	41.1%
JOHNSON	11,673	6,194	5,426	123	768	R	53.1%	46.5%	53.3%	46.7%
KNOX	20,463	10,023	10,297	143	274	D	49.0%	50.3%	49.3%	50.7%
KOSCIUSKO	14,708	9,200	5,246	262	3,954	R	62.5%	35.6%	63.7%	36.3%
LAGRANGE	5,095	3,501	1,539	55	1,962	R	68.7%	30.2%	69.5%	30.5%
LAKE	123,950	48,147	75,066	737	26,919	D	38.8%	60.6%	39.1%	60.9%
LA PORTE	30,568	16,543	13,896	129	2,647	R	54.1%	45.5%	54.3%	45.7%
LAWRENCE	14,515	9,200	5,246	69	3,954	R	63.4%	36.1%	63.7%	36.3%
MADISON	46,383	21,381	24,488	514	3,107	D	46.1%	52.8%	46.6%	53.4%
MARION	223,837	116,421	106,382	1,034	10,039	R	52.0%	47.5%	52.3%	47.7%
MARSHALL	13,736	8,225	5,254	257	2,971	R	59.9%	38.2%	61.0%	39.0%
MARTIN	4,997	2,467	2,515	15	48	D	49.4%	50.3%	49.5%	50.5%
MIAMI	14,777	8,207	6,379	191	1,828	R	55.5%	43.2%	55.8%	43.7%
MONROE	16,125	8,993	6,809	323	2,184	R	55.8%	42.2%	56.9%	43.1%
MONTGOMERY	13,999	8,319	5,620	60	2,699	R	59.4%	40.1%	59.7%	40.3%
MORGAN	10,348	6,115	4,156	77	1,959	R	59.1%	40.2%	59.5%	40.5%
NEWTON	5,004	3,398	1,583	23	1,815	R	67.9%	31.6%	68.2%	31.8%
NOBLE	11,448	7,200	4,174	74	3,026	R	62.9%	36.5%	63.3%	36.7%
OHIO	2,184	1,126	1,043	15	83	R	51.6%	47.8%	51.9%	48.1%
ORANGE	7,966	4,784	3,130	52	1,654	R	60.1%	39.3%	60.4%	39.6%
OWEN	5,975	3,318	2,602	55	716	R	55.5%	43.5%	56.0%	44.0%

PRESIDENT 1948

County	Total Vote	Republican	Democratic	Other	Rep.-Dem. Plurality		Total Vote Rep.	Dem.	Major Vote Rep.	Dem.
ADAMS	9,645	4,832	4,640	173	192	R	50.1%	48.1%	51.0%	49.0%
ALLEN	69,436	37,494	31,239	703	6,255	R	54.0%	45.0%	54.6%	45.4%
BARTHOLOMEW	16,012	7,804	7,960	248	156	D	48.7%	49.7%	49.5%	50.5%
BENTON	5,570	3,224	2,317	29	907	R	57.9%	41.6%	58.2%	41.8%
BLACKFORD	6,641	2,840	3,611	190	771	D	42.8%	54.4%	44.0%	56.0%
BOONE	11,586	6,450	5,037	99	1,413	R	55.7%	43.5%	56.2%	43.8%
BROWN	2,629	1,092	1,459	78	367	D	41.5%	55.5%	42.8%	57.2%
CARROLL	8,514	4,597	3,845	72	752	R	54.0%	45.2%	54.5%	45.5%
CASS	19,385	9,105	10,086	194	981	D	47.0%	52.0%	47.4%	52.6%
CLARK	18,153	7,001	10,953	199	3,952	D	38.6%	60.3%	39.0%	61.0%
CLAY	11,905	5,654	5,965	286	311	D	47.5%	50.1%	48.7%	51.3%
CLINTON	14,921	7,762	7,001	158	761	R	52.0%	46.9%	52.6%	47.4%
CRAWFORD	5,167	2,427	2,625	115	198	D	47.0%	50.8%	48.0%	52.0%
DAVIESS	13,044	7,030	5,867	147	1,163	R	53.9%	45.0%	54.5%	45.5%
DEARBORN	11,462	5,353	6,040	69	687	D	46.7%	52.7%	47.0%	53.0%
DECATUR	9,065	5,163	3,808	95	1,355	R	56.9%	42.0%	57.6%	42.4%
DE KALB	12,552	6,941	5,439	272	1,502	R	54.9%	43.3%	56.1%	43.9%
DELAWARE	33,525	15,662	17,060	803	1,398	D	46.7%	50.9%	47.9%	52.1%
DUBOIS	10,928	4,295	6,564	69	2,269	D	39.3%	60.1%	39.6%	60.4%
ELKHART	33,517	18,999	13,703	815	5,296	R	56.7%	40.9%	58.1%	41.9%
FAYETTE	11,338	5,399	5,876	63	477	D	47.6%	51.8%	47.9%	52.1%
FLOYD	19,121	8,367	10,593	161	2,226	D	43.8%	55.4%	44.1%	55.9%
FOUNTAIN	9,471	5,186	4,215	70	971	R	54.8%	44.5%	55.2%	44.8%
FRANKLIN	6,468	3,566	2,860	42	706	R	55.1%	44.2%	55.5%	44.5%
FULTON	8,398	4,930	3,233	235	1,697	R	58.7%	38.5%	60.4%	39.6%
GIBSON	15,709	7,431	7,988	290	557	D	47.3%	50.8%	48.2%	51.8%
GRANT	26,115	13,138	12,212	765	926	R	50.3%	46.8%	51.8%	48.2%
GREENE	15,463	7,453	7,709	301	256	D	48.2%	49.9%	49.2%	50.8%
HAMILTON	12,107	7,521	4,384	202	3,137	R	62.1%	36.2%	63.2%	36.8%
HANCOCK	9,826	4,721	4,948	157	227	D	48.0%	50.4%	48.8%	51.2%
HARRISON	8,751	4,104	4,465	182	361	D	46.9%	51.0%	47.9%	53.1%
HENDRICKS	10,682	6,327	4,280	75	2,047	R	59.2%	40.1%	59.6%	40.4%
HENRY	19,421	10,487	8,523	411	1,964	R	54.0%	43.9%	55.1%	44.9%
HOWARD	24,362	10,874	12,937	551	2,063	D	44.6%	53.1%	45.7%	54.3%
HUNTINGTON	15,723	8,178	7,202	343	976	R	52.0%	45.8%	53.2%	46.8%
JACKSON	13,471	6,062	7,258	151	1,196	D	45.0%	53.9%	45.5%	54.5%
JASPER	6,603	4,330	2,216	67	2,104	R	65.6%	33.6%	66.1%	33.9%
JAY	9,942	5,635	5,520	287	115	R	49.2%	48.8%	50.5%	49.5%
JEFFERSON	9,604	5,166	4,302	136	864	R	53.8%	44.8%	54.6%	45.4%
JENNINGS	6,636	3,485	3,084	67	401	R	52.5%	46.5%	53.1%	46.9%
JOHNSON	12,454	6,151	6,216	87	65	D	49.4%	49.9%	49.7%	50.3%
KNOX	21,182	9,250	11,650	282	2,400	D	43.7%	55.0%	44.3%	55.7%
KOSCIUSKO	14,855	9,327	5,102	426	4,225	R	62.8%	34.3%	64.6%	35.4%
LAGRANGE	4,867	3,106	1,628	133	1,478	R	63.8%	33.4%	65.6%	34.4%
LAKE	132,595	51,413	77,025	4,157	25,612	D	38.8%	58.1%	40.0%	60.0%
LA PORTE	29,859	15,661	13,923	275	1,738	R	52.4%	46.6%	52.9%	47.1%
LAWRENCE	14,869	8,643	6,131	95	2,512	R	58.1%	41.2%	58.5%	41.5%
MADISON	43,948	18,917	24,439	592	5,522	D	43.0%	55.6%	43.6%	56.4%
MARION	204,013	103,603	97,915	2,495	5,688	R	50.8%	48.0%	51.4%	48.6%
MARSHALL	13,819	7,873	5,661	285	2,212	R	57.0%	41.0%	58.2%	41.8%
MARTIN	5,073	2,230	2,788	55	558	D	44.0%	55.0%	44.4%	55.6%
MIAMI	13,863	7,083	6,538	242	545	R	51.1%	47.2%	52.0%	48.0%
MONROE	17,532	9,579	7,375	578	2,204	R	54.6%	42.1%	56.5%	43.5%
MONTGOMERY	13,537	7,890	5,492	155	2,398	R	58.3%	40.6%	59.0%	41.0%
MORGAN	10,297	5,677	4,428	192	1,249	R	55.1%	43.0%	56.2%	43.8%
NEWTON	4,845	3,312	1,483	50	1,829	R	68.4%	30.6%	69.1%	30.9%
NOBLE	11,344	6,503	4,676	165	1,827	R	57.3%	41.2%	58.2%	41.8%
OHIO	2,215	1,031	1,173	11	142	D	46.5%	53.0%	46.8%	53.2%
ORANGE	8,021	4,574	3,359	88	1,215	R	57.0%	41.9%	57.7%	42.3%
OWEN	5,870	3,002	2,738	130	264	R	51.1%	46.6%	52.3%	47.7%

INDIANA

PRESIDENT 1944

County	Total Vote	Republican	Democratic	Other	Rep.-Dem. Plurality	Total Vote Rep.	Total Vote Dem.	Major Vote Rep.	Major Vote Dem.
PARKE	8,048	4,751	3,241	56	1,510 R	59.0%	40.3%	59.4%	40.6%
PERRY	8,102	4,087	3,996	19	91 R	50.4%	49.3%	50.6%	49.4%
PIKE	7,886	4,267	3,513	106	754 R	54.1%	44.5%	54.8%	45.2%
PORTER	14,146	8,561	5,528	57	3,033 R	60.5%	39.1%	60.8%	39.2%
POSEY	8,619	4,374	4,183	62	191 R	50.7%	48.5%	51.1%	48.9%
PULASKI	5,826	3,206	2,509	111	697 R	55.0%	43.1%	56.1%	43.9%
PUTNAM	10,283	5,386	4,857	40	529 R	52.4%	47.2%	52.6%	47.4%
RANDOLPH	12,758	7,805	4,590	363	3,215 R	61.2%	36.0%	63.0%	37.0%
RIPLEY	9,544	5,642	3,835	67	1,807 R	59.1%	40.2%	59.5%	40.5%
RUSH	9,821	5,853	3,891	77	1,962 R	59.6%	39.6%	60.1%	39.9%
ST JOSEPH	87,589	39,875	47,149	565	7,274 D	45.5%	53.8%	45.8%	54.2%
SCOTT	5,054	2,379	2,621	54	242 D	47.1%	51.9%	47.6%	52.4%
SHELBY	13,733	6,816	6,798	119	18 R	49.6%	49.5%	50.1%	49.9%
SPENCER	8,686	4,986	3,647	53	1,339 R	57.4%	42.0%	57.8%	42.2%
STARKE	6,415	3,574	2,791	50	783 R	55.7%	43.5%	56.2%	43.8%
STEUBEN	6,618	4,739	1,837	42	2,902 R	71.6%	27.8%	72.1%	27.9%
SULLIVAN	12,397	5,855	6,420	122	565 D	47.2%	51.8%	47.7%	52.3%
SWITZERLAND	4,267	2,019	2,191	57	172 D	47.3%	51.3%	48.0%	52.0%
TIPPECANOE	26,212	15,888	10,229	95	5,659 R	60.6%	39.0%	60.8%	39.2%
TIPTON	7,843	4,296	3,427	120	869 R	54.8%	43.7%	55.6%	44.4%
UNION	3,169	1,998	1,154	17	844 R	63.0%	36.4%	63.4%	36.6%
VANDERBURGH	65,462	30,684	34,440	338	3,756 D	46.9%	52.6%	47.1%	52.9%
VERMILLION	9,963	4,998	4,912	53	86 R	50.2%	49.3%	50.4%	49.6%
VIGO	46,223	21,493	24,649	81	3,156 D	46.5%	53.3%	46.6%	53.4%
WABASH	13,415	8,357	4,665	393	3,692 R	62.3%	34.8%	64.2%	35.8%
WARREN	4,434	2,870	1,555	9	1,315 R	64.7%	35.1%	64.9%	35.1%
WARRICK	9,166	5,042	4,049	75	993 R	55.0%	44.2%	55.5%	44.5%
WASHINGTON	8,015	4,033	3,940	42	93 R	50.3%	49.2%	50.6%	49.4%
WAYNE	28,059	15,295	12,432	332	2,863 R	54.5%	44.3%	55.2%	44.8%
WELLS	9,410	4,708	4,475	227	233 R	50.0%	47.6%	51.3%	48.7%
WHITE	8,650	5,039	3,570	41	1,469 R	58.3%	41.3%	58.5%	41.5%
WHITLEY	9,427	5,268	4,079	80	1,189 R	55.9%	43.3%	56.4%	43.6%
TOTAL	1,672,091	875,891	781,403	14,797	94,488 R	52.4%	46.7%	52.9%	47.1%

PRESIDENT 1948

County	Total Vote	Republican	Democratic	Other	Rep.-Dem. Plurality	Total Vote Rep.	Total Vote Dem.	Major Vote Rep.	Major Vote Dem.
PARKE	8,112	4,326	3,681	105	645 R	53.3%	45.4%	54.0%	46.0%
PERRY	8,354	3,761	4,569	24	808 D	45.0%	54.7%	45.2%	54.8%
PIKE	7,452	3,696	3,596	160	100 R	49.6%	48.3%	50.7%	49.3%
PORTER	14,318	8,907	5,161	250	3,746 R	62.2%	36.0%	63.3%	36.7%
POSEY	8,731	3,879	4,729	123	850 D	44.4%	54.2%	45.1%	54.9%
PULASKI	5,992	3,039	2,736	217	303 R	50.7%	45.7%	52.6%	47.4%
PUTNAM	9,963	5,072	4,814	77	258 R	50.9%	48.3%	51.3%	48.7%
RANDOLPH	12,287	7,122	4,655	510	2,467 R	58.0%	37.9%	60.5%	39.5%
RIPLEY	9,961	5,313	4,574	74	739 R	53.3%	45.9%	53.7%	46.3%
RUSH	9,321	5,362	3,814	145	1,548 R	57.5%	40.9%	58.4%	41.6%
ST JOSEPH	90,846	39,593	49,866	1,387	10,273 D	43.6%	54.9%	44.3%	55.7%
SCOTT	5,635	2,429	3,128	78	699 D	43.1%	55.5%	43.7%	56.3%
SHELBY	13,324	6,068	6,992	264	924 D	45.5%	52.5%	46.5%	53.5%
SPENCER	8,726	4,496	4,163	67	333 R	51.5%	47.7%	51.9%	48.1%
STARKE	6,960	3,518	3,312	130	206 R	50.5%	47.6%	51.5%	48.5%
STEUBEN	6,452	4,341	1,996	115	2,345 R	67.3%	30.9%	68.5%	31.5%
SULLIVAN	11,801	4,824	6,705	272	1,881 D	40.9%	56.8%	41.8%	58.1%
SWITZERLAND	4,247	1,839	2,375	33	536 D	43.3%	55.9%	43.6%	56.4%
TIPPECANOE	28,107	17,034	10,825	248	6,209 R	60.6%	38.5%	61.1%	38.9%
TIPTON	8,210	4,169	3,925	116	244 R	50.8%	47.8%	51.5%	48.5%
UNION	2,939	1,859	1,049	31	810 R	63.3%	35.7%	63.9%	36.1%
VANDERBURGH	60,956	27,584	32,640	732	5,056 D	45.3%	53.5%	45.8%	54.2%
VERMILLION	10,404	4,685	5,426	293	741 D	45.0%	52.2%	46.3%	53.7%
VIGO	45,564	19,049	25,906	609	6,857 D	41.8%	56.9%	42.4%	57.6%
WABASH	13,245	8,149	4,692	404	3,457 R	61.5%	35.4%	63.5%	36.5%
WARREN	3,869	2,444	1,391	34	1,053 R	63.2%	36.0%	63.7%	36.3%
WARRICK	9,440	4,602	4,750	88	148 D	48.8%	50.3%	49.2%	50.8%
WASHINGTON	7,757	3,660	4,033	64	373 D	47.2%	52.0%	47.6%	52.4%
WAYNE	26,716	15,445	10,749	522	4,696 R	57.8%	40.2%	59.0%	41.0%
WELLS	9,094	4,288	4,726	80	438 D	47.2%	52.0%	47.6%	52.4%
WHITE	8,813	4,911	3,849	53	1,062 R	55.7%	43.7%	56.1%	43.9%
WHITLEY	9,089	4,715	4,240	134	475 R	51.9%	46.6%	52.7%	47.3%
TOTAL	1,656,212	821,079	807,831	27,302	13,248 R	49.6%	48.8%	50.4%	49.6%

INDIANA

PRESIDENT 1952

County	Total Vote	Republican	Democratic	Other	Rep.-Dem. Plurality	Total Vote Rep.	Total Vote Dem.	Major Vote Rep.	Major Vote Dem.
ADAMS	10,408	6,204	3,744	460	2,460 R	59.6%	36.0%	62.4%	37.6%
ALLEN	82,941	54,877	27,506	558	27,371 R	66.2%	33.2%	66.6%	33.4%
BARTHOLOMEW	19,502	11,462	7,844	196	3,618 R	58.8%	40.2%	59.4%	40.6%
BENTON	5,957	4,125	1,815	17	2,310 R	69.2%	30.5%	69.4%	30.6%
BLACKFORD	7,066	3,759	3,144	163	615 R	53.2%	44.5%	54.5%	45.5%
BOONE	13,673	8,619	4,986	68	3,633 R	63.0%	36.5%	63.4%	36.6%
BROWN	2,964	1,517	1,414	33	103 R	51.2%	47.7%	51.8%	48.2%
CARROLL	9,178	5,902	3,208	68	2,694 R	64.3%	35.0%	64.8%	35.2%
CASS	21,385	12,296	7,982	107	4,314 R	60.3%	39.2%	60.6%	39.4%
CLARK	23,025	11,190	11,703	132	513 D	48.6%	50.8%	48.9%	51.1%
CLAY	13,351	7,118	6,078	155	1,040 R	53.3%	45.5%	53.9%	46.1%
CLINTON	16,724	10,057	6,469	198	3,588 R	60.1%	38.7%	60.9%	39.1%
CRAWFORD	5,304	2,750	2,457	97	293 R	51.8%	46.3%	52.8%	47.2%
DAVIESS	13,676	8,328	5,247	101	3,081 R	60.9%	38.4%	61.3%	38.7%
DEARBORN	12,934	7,091	5,810	33	1,281 R	54.8%	44.9%	55.0%	45.0%
DECATUR	9,961	6,490	3,393	78	3,097 R	65.2%	34.1%	65.7%	34.3%
DE KALB	13,476	8,713	4,347	416	4,366 R	64.7%	32.3%	66.7%	33.3%
DELAWARE	43,590	24,272	18,733	585	5,539 R	55.7%	43.0%	56.4%	43.6%
DUBOIS	12,227	6,538	5,658	31	880 R	53.5%	46.3%	53.6%	46.4%
ELKHART	38,108	25,277	12,002	829	13,275 R	66.3%	31.5%	67.8%	32.2%
FAYETTE	12,270	7,000	5,178	92	1,822 R	57.0%	42.2%	57.5%	42.5%
FLOYD	22,139	11,608	10,368	163	1,240 R	52.4%	46.8%	52.8%	47.2%
FOUNTAIN	10,119	6,208	3,871	40	2,337 R	61.3%	38.2%	61.6%	38.4%
FRANKLIN	7,230	4,630	2,548	52	2,082 R	64.0%	35.2%	64.5%	35.5%
FULTON	9,175	6,247	2,799	129	3,448 R	68.1%	30.5%	69.1%	30.9%
GIBSON	16,986	9,171	7,617	198	1,554 R	54.0%	44.8%	54.6%	45.4%
GRANT	27,923	16,678	10,646	599	6,032 R	59.7%	38.1%	61.0%	39.0%
GREENE	16,189	8,620	7,417	152	1,203 R	53.2%	45.8%	53.8%	46.2%
HAMILTON	15,560	10,843	4,564	153	6,279 R	69.7%	29.3%	70.4%	29.6%
HANCOCK	11,619	6,964	4,539	116	2,425 R	59.9%	39.1%	60.5%	39.5%
HARRISON	9,454	5,069	4,213	172	856 R	53.6%	44.6%	54.6%	45.4%
HENDRICKS	14,586	9,712	4,793	81	4,919 R	66.6%	32.9%	67.0%	33.0%
HENRY	22,882	14,184	8,378	320	5,806 R	62.0%	36.6%	62.9%	37.1%
HOWARD	28,517	15,212	12,938	367	2,274 R	53.3%	45.4%	54.0%	46.0%
HUNTINGTON	16,953	10,508	6,114	331	4,394 R	62.0%	36.1%	63.2%	36.8%
JACKSON	14,630	8,067	6,460	103	1,607 R	55.1%	44.2%	55.5%	44.5%
JASPER	7,692	5,556	2,102	34	3,454 R	72.2%	27.3%	72.6%	27.4%
JAY	12,331	7,270	4,764	297	2,506 R	59.0%	38.6%	60.4%	39.6%
JEFFERSON	10,473	6,169	4,251	53	1,918 R	59.0%	40.6%	59.2%	40.8%
JENNINGS	7,286	4,460	2,777	49	1,683 R	61.2%	38.1%	61.6%	38.4%
JOHNSON	15,082	9,119	5,909	54	3,210 R	60.5%	39.2%	60.7%	39.3%
KNOX	22,316	12,786	9,384	146	3,402 R	57.3%	42.1%	57.7%	42.3%
KOSCIUSKO	16,710	11,521	4,677	512	6,844 R	68.9%	28.0%	71.1%	28.9%
LAGRANGE	5,555	3,822	1,604	129	2,218 R	68.8%	28.9%	70.4%	29.6%
LAKE	165,845	74,073	90,721	1,051	16,648 D	44.7%	54.7%	44.9%	55.1%
LA PORTE	37,733	22,576	15,011	146	7,565 R	59.8%	39.8%	60.1%	39.9%
LAWRENCE	17,475	11,296	6,044	135	5,252 R	64.6%	34.6%	65.1%	34.9%
MADISON	54,334	28,730	25,125	519	3,605 R	52.8%	46.2%	53.3%	46.7%
MARION	271,939	164,466	106,387	1,086	58,079 R	60.5%	39.1%	60.7%	39.3%
MARSHALL	15,828	9,990	5,538	300	4,452 R	63.1%	35.0%	64.3%	35.7%
MARTIN	5,332	2,757	2,546	29	211 R	51.7%	47.7%	52.0%	48.0%
MIAMI	15,694	9,254	6,264	176	2,990 R	59.0%	39.9%	59.6%	40.4%
MONROE	19,925	12,072	7,745	108	4,327 R	60.6%	38.9%	60.9%	39.1%
MONTGOMERY	16,041	10,569	5,386	86	5,183 R	65.9%	33.6%	66.2%	33.8%
MORGAN	13,072	8,222	4,755	95	3,467 R	62.9%	36.4%	63.4%	36.6%
NEWTON	5,561	4,159	1,373	29	2,786 R	74.8%	24.7%	75.2%	24.8%
NOBLE	12,544	8,203	4,151	190	4,052 R	65.4%	33.1%	66.4%	33.6%
OHIO	2,348	1,219	1,119	10	100 R	51.9%	47.7%	52.1%	47.9%
ORANGE	8,898	5,551	3,272	75	2,279 R	62.4%	36.8%	62.9%	37.1%
OWEN	6,361	3,713	2,577	71	1,136 R	58.4%	40.5%	59.0%	41.0%

PRESIDENT 1956

County	Total Vote	Republican	Democratic	Other	Rep.-Dem. Plurality	Total Vote Rep.	Total Vote Dem.	Major Vote Rep.	Major Vote Dem.
ADAMS	10,708	7,079	3,520	109	3,559 R	66.1%	32.9%	66.8%	33.2%
ALLEN	83,844	58,210	25,444	190	32,766 R	69.4%	30.3%	69.6%	30.4%
BARTHOLOMEW	20,453	12,227	8,134	92	4,093 R	59.8%	39.8%	60.1%	39.9%
BENTON	5,974	4,004	1,961	9	2,043 R	67.0%	32.8%	67.1%	32.9%
BLACKFORD	7,071	3,855	3,152	64	703 R	54.5%	44.6%	55.0%	45.0%
BOONE	13,926	8,573	5,318	35	3,255 R	61.6%	38.2%	61.7%	38.3%
BROWN	3,219	1,649	1,555	15	94 R	51.2%	48.3%	51.5%	48.5%
CARROLL	9,086	5,748	3,312	26	2,436 R	63.4%	36.5%	63.4%	36.6%
CASS	20,299	12,624	7,594	81	5,030 R	62.2%	37.4%	62.4%	37.6%
CLARK	24,433	12,483	11,871	79	612 R	51.1%	48.6%	51.3%	48.7%
CLAY	13,061	7,302	5,720	39	1,582 R	55.9%	43.8%	56.1%	43.9%
CLINTON	16,032	9,690	6,268	74	3,422 R	60.4%	39.1%	60.7%	39.3%
CRAWFORD	5,185	2,694	2,433	58	261 R	52.0%	46.9%	52.5%	47.5%
DAVIESS	13,707	8,608	5,057	42	3,551 R	62.8%	36.9%	63.0%	37.0%
DEARBORN	12,746	7,189	5,535	22	1,654 R	56.4%	43.4%	56.5%	43.5%
DECATUR	9,851	6,390	3,427	34	2,963 R	64.9%	34.8%	65.1%	34.9%
DE KALB	13,575	9,061	4,435	79	4,626 R	66.7%	32.7%	67.1%	32.9%
DELAWARE	45,827	24,792	20,818	217	3,974 R	54.1%	45.4%	54.4%	45.6%
DUBOIS	12,139	6,942	5,177	20	1,765 R	57.2%	42.6%	57.3%	42.7%
ELKHART	40,677	28,088	12,363	226	15,725 R	69.1%	30.4%	69.4%	30.6%
FAYETTE	11,862	6,673	5,156	33	1,517 R	56.3%	43.5%	56.4%	43.6%
FLOYD	18,865	10,410	8,378	77	2,032 R	55.2%	44.4%	55.4%	44.6%
FOUNTAIN	10,230	6,456	3,751	23	2,705 R	63.1%	36.7%	63.3%	36.7%
FRANKLIN	7,259	4,429	2,573	26	1,856 R	63.0%	36.6%	63.3%	36.7%
FULTON	9,259	6,258	2,945	56	3,313 R	67.6%	31.8%	68.0%	32.0%
GIBSON	16,653	9,256	7,318	79	1,938 R	55.6%	43.9%	55.8%	44.2%
GRANT	27,206	17,548	9,455	203	8,093 R	64.5%	34.8%	65.0%	35.0%
GREENE	15,969	8,722	7,186	61	1,536 R	54.6%	45.0%	54.8%	45.2%
HAMILTON	16,271	11,220	4,974	77	6,246 R	69.0%	30.6%	69.3%	30.7%
HANCOCK	11,617	6,962	4,600	55	2,362 R	59.9%	39.6%	60.2%	39.8%
HARRISON	9,648	5,299	4,266	83	1,033 R	54.9%	44.2%	55.4%	44.6%
HENDRICKS	16,129	10,578	5,521	30	5,057 R	65.6%	34.2%	65.7%	34.3%
HENRY	22,418	13,750	8,502	166	5,248 R	61.3%	37.9%	61.8%	38.2%
HOWARD	29,581	17,234	12,159	188	5,075 R	58.3%	41.1%	58.6%	41.4%
HUNTINGTON	17,184	11,024	6,027	133	4,997 R	64.2%	35.1%	64.7%	35.3%
JACKSON	14,617	8,375	6,185	57	2,190 R	57.3%	42.3%	57.5%	42.5%
JASPER	7,399	5,374	2,004	21	3,370 R	72.6%	27.1%	72.8%	27.2%
JAY	11,454	6,767	4,571	116	2,196 R	59.1%	39.9%	59.7%	40.3%
JEFFERSON	11,004	6,632	4,344	28	2,288 R	60.3%	39.5%	60.4%	39.6%
JENNINGS	7,414	4,502	2,879	33	1,623 R	60.7%	38.8%	61.0%	39.0%
JOHNSON	16,291	10,125	6,125	41	4,000 R	62.2%	37.6%	62.3%	37.7%
KNOX	21,801	13,047	8,691	63	4,356 R	59.8%	39.9%	60.0%	40.0%
KOSCIUSKO	17,824	12,777	4,904	143	7,873 R	71.7%	27.5%	72.3%	27.7%
LAGRANGE	5,414	3,815	1,562	37	2,253 R	70.5%	28.9%	71.0%	29.0%
LAKE	178,460	92,803	85,000	657	7,803 R	52.0%	47.6%	52.2%	47.8%
LA PORTE	39,142	24,622	14,417	103	10,205 R	62.9%	36.8%	63.1%	36.9%
LAWRENCE	17,346	11,090	6,197	59	4,893 R	63.9%	35.7%	64.2%	35.8%
MADISON	55,943	30,329	25,408	206	4,921 R	54.2%	45.4%	54.4%	45.6%
MARION	262,347	162,566	99,102	679	63,464 R	62.0%	37.8%	62.1%	37.9%
MARSHALL	15,982	10,504	5,398	80	5,106 R	65.7%	33.8%	66.1%	33.9%
MARTIN	5,296	2,946	2,343	7	603 R	55.6%	44.2%	55.7%	44.3%
MIAMI	15,372	9,574	5,724	74	3,850 R	62.3%	37.2%	62.5%	37.4%
MONROE	21,015	13,223	7,732	60	5,491 R	62.9%	36.8%	63.1%	36.9%
MONTGOMERY	15,927	10,418	5,443	66	4,975 R	65.4%	34.2%	65.7%	34.3%
MORGAN	13,103	8,318	4,735	50	3,583 R	63.5%	36.1%	63.7%	36.3%
NEWTON	5,222	3,890	1,316	16	2,574 R	74.5%	25.2%	74.7%	25.3%
NOBLE	12,267	8,175	4,028	64	4,147 R	66.6%	32.8%	67.0%	33.0%
OHIO	2,331	1,237	1,087	7	150 R	53.0%	46.6%	53.2%	46.8%
ORANGE	9,221	5,751	3,438	32	2,313 R	62.4%	37.3%	62.6%	37.4%
OWEN	6,301	3,685	2,581	35	1,104 R	58.5%	41.0%	58.8%	41.2%

INDIANA

PRESIDENT 1952

County	Total Vote	Republican	Democratic	Other	Rep.-Dem. Plurality	Total Vote Rep.	Total Vote Dem.	Major Vote Rep.	Major Vote Dem.
PARKE	8,690	5,069	3,574	47	1,495 R	58.3%	41.1%	58.6%	41.4%
PERRY	8,832	4,816	4,001	15	815 R	54.5%	45.3%	54.6%	45.4%
PIKE	7,838	4,253	3,478	107	775 R	54.3%	44.4%	55.0%	45.0%
PORTER	19,190	13,194	5,909	87	7,285 R	68.8%	30.8%	69.1%	30.9%
POSEY	9,187	5,293	3,835	59	1,458 R	57.6%	41.7%	58.0%	42.0%
PULASKI	6,387	4,030	2,244	113	1,786 R	63.1%	35.1%	64.2%	35.8%
PUTNAM	11,118	6,632	4,446	40	2,186 R	59.7%	40.0%	59.9%	40.1%
RANDOLPH	13,986	9,150	4,461	375	4,689 R	65.4%	31.9%	67.2%	32.8%
RIPLEY	10,725	6,650	4,031	44	2,619 R	62.0%	37.6%	62.3%	37.7%
RUSH	10,353	6,918	3,348	87	3,570 R	66.8%	32.3%	67.4%	32.6%
ST JOSEPH	107,632	53,537	53,269	826	268 R	49.7%	49.5%	50.1%	49.9%
SCOTT	5,959	2,984	2,931	44	53 R	50.1%	49.2%	50.4%	49.6%
SHELBY	15,671	8,961	6,552	158	2,409 R	57.2%	41.8%	57.8%	42.2%
SPENCER	8,941	5,497	3,401	43	2,096 R	61.5%	38.0%	61.8%	38.2%
STARKE	8,196	4,871	3,274	51	1,597 R	59.4%	39.9%	59.8%	40.2%
STEUBEN	7,288	5,322	1,886	80	3,436 R	73.0%	25.9%	73.8%	26.2%
SULLIVAN	12,988	5,929	6,964	95	1,035 D	45.6%	53.6%	46.0%	54.0%
SWITZERLAND	4,275	2,070	2,167	38	97 D	48.4%	50.7%	48.9%	51.1%
TIPPECANOE	33,246	23,447	9,678	121	13,769 R	70.5%	29.1%	70.8%	29.2%
TIPTON	8,745	5,299	3,362	84	1,937 R	60.6%	38.4%	61.2%	38.8%
UNION	3,211	2,159	1,029	23	1,130 R	67.2%	32.0%	67.7%	32.3%
VANDERBURGH	72,187	42,010	29,718	459	12,292 R	58.2%	41.2%	58.6%	41.4%
VERMILLION	11,043	5,283	5,708	52	425 D	47.8%	51.7%	48.1%	51.9%
VIGO	51,878	25,806	25,841	231	35 D	49.7%	49.8%	50.0%	50.1%
WABASH	14,690	9,980	4,395	315	5,585 R	67.9%	29.9%	69.4%	30.6%
WARREN	4,548	3,191	1,332	25	1,859 R	70.2%	29.3%	70.6%	29.4%
WARRICK	10,762	6,064	4,639	59	1,425 R	56.3%	43.1%	56.6%	43.3%
WASHINGTON	8,745	4,849	3,844	52	1,005 R	55.4%	44.0%	55.8%	44.2%
WAYNE	32,180	20,068	11,819	293	8,249 R	62.4%	36.7%	62.9%	37.1%
WELLS	9,633	5,380	3,963	290	1,417 R	55.8%	41.1%	57.6%	42.4%
WHITE	10,052	6,795	3,211	46	3,584 R	67.6%	31.9%	67.9%	32.1%
WHITLEY	9,776	5,893	3,755	128	2,138 R	60.3%	38.4%	61.1%	38.9%
TOTAL	1,955,049	1,136,259	801,530	17,260	334,729 R	58.1%	41.0%	58.6%	41.4%

PRESIDENT 1956

County	Total Vote	Republican	Democratic	Other	Rep.-Dem. Plurality	Total Vote Rep.	Total Vote Dem.	Major Vote Rep.	Major Vote Dem.
PARKE	8,604	5,080	3,502	22	1,578 R	59.0%	40.7%	59.2%	40.8%
PERRY	8,993	4,946	4,037	10	909 R	55.0%	44.9%	55.1%	44.9%
PIKE	8,015	4,596	3,353	66	1,243 R	57.3%	41.8%	57.8%	42.2%
PORTER	20,589	14,970	5,574	45	9,396 R	72.7%	27.1%	72.9%	27.1%
POSEY	9,724	5,780	3,919	25	1,861 R	59.4%	40.3%	59.6%	40.4%
PULASKI	6,633	4,117	2,424	92	1,693 R	62.1%	36.5%	62.9%	37.1%
PUTNAM	11,280	6,684	4,572	24	2,112 R	59.3%	40.5%	59.4%	40.6%
RANDOLPH	13,873	9,020	4,701	152	4,319 R	65.0%	33.9%	65.7%	34.3%
RIPLEY	10,633	6,577	4,026	30	2,551 R	61.9%	37.9%	62.0%	38.0%
RUSH	9,587	6,202	3,346	39	2,856 R	64.7%	34.9%	65.0%	35.0%
ST JOSEPH	112,472	57,827	54,152	493	3,675 R	51.4%	48.1%	51.6%	48.4%
SCOTT	6,156	3,117	3,011	28	106 R	50.6%	48.9%	50.9%	49.1%
SHELBY	15,811	9,170	6,561	80	2,609 R	58.0%	41.5%	58.3%	41.7%
SPENCER	8,960	5,404	3,530	26	1,874 R	60.3%	39.4%	60.5%	39.5%
STARKE	8,447	5,063	3,349	35	1,714 R	59.9%	39.6%	59.9%	39.8%
STEUBEN	7,739	5,538	2,171	30	3,367 R	71.6%	28.1%	71.8%	28.2%
SULLIVAN	11,946	5,829	6,048	69	219 D	48.8%	50.6%	49.1%	50.9%
SWITZERLAND	4,209	2,074	2,114	21	40 D	49.3%	50.2%	49.5%	50.5%
TIPPECANOE	33,843	23,776	9,995	72	13,781 R	70.3%	29.5%	70.4%	29.6%
TIPTON	8,305	4,939	3,320	46	1,619 R	59.5%	40.0%	59.8%	40.2%
UNION	3,192	2,026	1,157	9	869 R	63.5%	36.2%	63.7%	36.3%
VANDERBURGH	73,619	42,462	30,860	297	11,602 R	57.7%	41.9%	57.9%	42.1%
VERMILLION	10,533	5,352	5,149	32	203 R	50.8%	48.9%	51.0%	49.0%
VIGO	50,068	25,253	24,680	135	573 R	50.4%	49.3%	50.6%	49.4%
WABASH	14,496	10,318	4,085	93	6,233 R	71.2%	28.2%	71.6%	28.4%
WARREN	4,406	2,979	1,408	19	1,571 R	67.6%	32.0%	67.9%	32.1%
WARRICK	10,987	6,286	4,668	33	1,618 R	57.2%	42.5%	57.4%	42.6%
WASHINGTON	8,739	4,864	3,849	26	1,015 R	55.7%	44.0%	55.8%	44.2%
WAYNE	32,638	20,157	12,337	144	7,820 R	61.8%	37.8%	62.0%	38.0%
WELLS	9,778	5,703	3,984	91	1,719 R	58.3%	40.7%	58.9%	41.1%
WHITE	9,949	6,708	3,219	22	3,489 R	67.4%	32.4%	67.6%	32.4%
WHITLEY	10,157	6,422	3,688	47	2,734 R	63.2%	36.3%	63.5%	36.5%
TOTAL	1,974,607	1,182,811	783,908	7,888	398,903 R	59.9%	39.7%	60.1%	39.9%

INDIANA

PRESIDENT 1960

County	Total Vote	Republican	Democratic	Other	Rep.-Dem. Plurality	Total Vote % Rep.	Total Vote % Dem.	Major Vote % Rep.	Major Vote % Dem.
ADAMS	11,409	6,972	4,338	99	2,634 R	61.1%	38.0%	61.6%	38.4%
ALLEN	99,618	60,103	39,235	280	20,868 R	60.3%	39.4%	60.5%	39.5%
BARTHOLOMEW	23,026	13,606	9,290	130	4,316 R	59.1%	41.3%	59.4%	40.6%
BENTON	6,032	3,626	2,399	7	1,227 R	60.1%	39.8%	60.2%	39.8%
BLACKFORD	7,009	3,738	3,228	43	510 R	53.3%	45.1%	53.7%	46.3%
BOONE	14,416	8,979	5,377	60	3,582 R	62.3%	37.3%	62.5%	37.5%
BROWN	3,244	1,679	1,533	32	146 R	51.8%	47.3%	52.3%	47.7%
CARROLL	8,744	5,411	3,299	34	2,112 R	61.9%	37.7%	62.1%	37.9%
CASS	19,577	11,392	8,091	94	3,301 R	58.2%	41.3%	58.5%	41.5%
CLARK	27,304	12,803	14,431	70	1,628 D	46.9%	52.9%	47.0%	53.0%
CLAY	12,834	7,434	5,342	58	2,092 R	57.9%	41.6%	58.2%	41.8%
CLINTON	16,217	9,620	6,533	64	3,087 R	59.3%	40.3%	59.6%	40.4%
CRAWFORD	5,255	2,915	2,305	35	610 R	55.5%	43.9%	55.8%	44.2%
DAVIESS	13,763	8,285	5,433	45	2,852 R	60.2%	39.5%	60.4%	39.6%
DEARBORN	13,854	7,619	6,216	19	1,403 R	55.0%	44.9%	55.1%	44.9%
DECATUR	10,370	6,240	4,080	50	2,160 R	60.2%	39.3%	60.5%	39.5%
DE KALB	14,295	8,957	5,277	61	3,630 R	62.7%	36.9%	62.9%	37.1%
DELAWARE	49,610	26,167	23,266	177	2,901 R	52.7%	46.9%	52.9%	47.1%
DUBOIS	13,353	5,117	8,214	22	3,097 D	38.3%	61.5%	38.5%	61.6%
ELKHART	44,693	28,056	16,264	373	11,792 R	62.8%	36.4%	63.3%	36.7%
FAYETTE	12,023	6,729	5,246	48	1,483 R	56.0%	43.6%	56.2%	43.8%
FLOYD	24,037	11,629	12,346	62	717 D	48.4%	51.4%	48.5%	51.5%
FOUNTAIN	10,429	6,123	4,277	29	1,846 R	58.7%	41.0%	58.9%	41.1%
FRANKLIN	7,645	4,108	3,523	14	585 R	53.7%	46.1%	53.8%	46.2%
FULTON	9,133	6,038	3,047	48	2,991 R	66.1%	33.4%	66.5%	33.5%
GIBSON	16,399	8,838	7,479	82	1,359 R	53.9%	45.6%	54.2%	45.8%
GRANT	32,841	19,021	13,642	178	5,379 R	57.9%	41.5%	58.2%	41.8%
GREENE	15,239	8,810	6,325	104	2,485 R	57.8%	41.5%	58.2%	41.8%
HAMILTON	18,984	13,409	5,511	64	7,898 R	70.6%	29.0%	70.9%	29.1%
HANCOCK	12,528	7,543	4,930	55	2,613 R	60.2%	39.4%	60.5%	39.5%
HARRISON	9,989	5,374	4,566	49	808 R	53.8%	45.7%	54.1%	45.9%
HENDRICKS	19,066	12,490	6,481	95	6,009 R	65.5%	34.0%	65.8%	34.2%
HENRY	23,530	13,752	9,629	149	4,123 R	58.4%	40.9%	58.8%	41.0%
HOWARD	31,502	17,938	13,415	149	4,523 R	57.2%	42.6%	57.2%	42.6%
HUNTINGTON	17,930	10,658	7,163	109	3,495 R	59.4%	39.9%	59.8%	40.2%
JACKSON	14,861	8,213	6,582	66	1,631 R	55.3%	44.3%	55.5%	44.5%
JASPER	8,339	5,364	2,959	16	2,405 R	64.3%	35.5%	64.4%	35.6%
JAY	11,492	6,519	4,899	74	1,620 R	56.7%	42.6%	57.1%	42.9%
JEFFERSON	11,492	6,333	5,119	40	1,214 R	55.1%	44.5%	55.3%	44.7%
JENNINGS	7,908	4,478	3,403	27	1,075 R	56.6%	43.0%	56.8%	43.2%
JOHNSON	19,919	12,426	7,400	93	5,026 R	62.4%	37.2%	62.7%	37.3%
KNOX	21,516	11,490	9,918	108	1,572 R	53.4%	46.1%	53.7%	46.3%
KOSCIUSKO	19,591	13,539	5,839	213	7,700 R	69.1%	29.8%	69.9%	30.1%
LAGRANGE	6,422	4,433	1,965	24	2,468 R	69.0%	30.6%	70.0%	30.7%
LAKE	211,358	78,278	132,554	526	54,276 D	37.0%	62.7%	37.1%	62.9%
LA PORTE	43,140	22,738	20,317	85	2,421 R	52.7%	47.1%	52.8%	47.2%
LAWRENCE	18,182	11,119	6,977	86	4,142 R	61.2%	38.4%	61.4%	38.6%
MADISON	59,445	31,098	28,154	193	2,944 R	52.3%	47.4%	52.5%	47.5%
MARION	288,206	166,202	121,336	668	44,866 R	57.7%	42.1%	57.8%	42.2%
MARSHALL	16,744	10,460	6,210	74	4,250 R	62.5%	37.1%	62.7%	37.3%
MARTIN	5,346	2,756	2,585	5	171 R	51.6%	48.4%	51.6%	48.4%
MIAMI	15,131	8,844	6,191	96	2,653 R	58.4%	40.9%	58.8%	41.2%
MONROE	22,184	14,513	7,535	136	6,978 R	65.4%	34.0%	65.8%	34.2%
MONTGOMERY	16,511	10,957	5,477	77	5,480 R	66.4%	33.2%	66.7%	33.3%
MORGAN	14,860	9,416	5,375	69	4,041 R	63.4%	36.2%	63.7%	36.3%
NEWTON	5,401	3,517	1,870	14	1,647 R	65.1%	34.6%	65.3%	34.7%
NOBLE	13,387	8,069	5,264	54	2,805 R	60.3%	39.3%	60.5%	39.5%
OHIO	2,336	1,314	1,015	7	299 R	56.2%	43.5%	56.4%	43.6%
ORANGE	9,442	5,589	3,818	35	1,771 R	59.2%	40.4%	59.4%	40.6%
OWEN	6,128	3,700	2,379	49	1,321 R	60.4%	38.8%	60.9%	39.1%

PRESIDENT 1964

County	Total Vote	Republican	Democratic	Other	Rep.-Dem. Plurality	Total Vote % Rep.	Total Vote % Dem.	Major Vote % Rep.	Major Vote % Dem.
ADAMS	10,973	4,230	6,637	106	2,407 D	38.5%	60.5%	38.9%	61.1%
ALLEN	100,353	49,284	50,706	363	1,422 D	49.1%	50.5%	49.3%	50.7%
BARTHOLOMEW	24,090	11,026	12,940	124	1,914 D	45.8%	53.7%	46.0%	54.0%
BENTON	5,831	2,886	2,940	5	54 D	49.5%	50.4%	49.5%	50.5%
BLACKFORD	6,829	2,552	4,210	67	1,658 D	37.4%	61.6%	37.7%	62.3%
BOONE	14,181	7,419	6,716	46	703 R	52.3%	47.4%	52.5%	47.5%
BROWN	3,544	1,390	2,135	19	745 D	39.2%	60.2%	39.4%	60.6%
CARROLL	8,714	3,896	4,789	29	893 D	44.7%	55.0%	44.9%	55.1%
CASS	18,978	7,705	11,148	95	3,443 D	40.8%	58.7%	41.0%	59.0%
CLARK	25,256	7,701	17,330	125	9,629 D	30.6%	68.9%	30.8%	69.2%
CLAY	12,026	5,412	6,528	86	1,116 D	45.0%	54.3%	45.3%	54.7%
CLINTON	15,582	7,157	8,353	72	1,196 D	45.9%	53.6%	46.1%	53.9%
CRAWFORD	4,380	1,828	2,514	38	686 D	41.7%	57.4%	42.1%	57.9%
DAVIESS	12,895	6,319	6,528	48	209 D	49.0%	50.6%	49.2%	50.8%
DEARBORN	13,198	5,473	7,699	26	2,226 D	41.5%	58.3%	41.6%	58.4%
DECATUR	10,315	4,702	5,564	49	862 D	45.6%	53.9%	45.8%	54.2%
DE KALB	13,889	6,210	7,559	120	1,349 D	44.7%	54.4%	45.1%	54.8%
DELAWARE	48,678	20,022	28,469	187	8,447 D	41.1%	58.5%	41.3%	58.7%
DUBOIS	13,939	3,800	10,114	25	6,314 D	27.3%	72.6%	27.3%	72.7%
ELKHART	41,914	19,870	21,679	365	1,809 D	47.4%	51.7%	47.8%	52.2%
FAYETTE	11,393	4,637	6,713	43	2,076 D	40.7%	58.9%	40.9%	59.1%
FLOYD	23,638	7,834	15,656	148	7,822 D	33.1%	66.2%	33.4%	66.6%
FOUNTAIN	10,278	4,666	5,574	38	908 D	45.4%	54.2%	45.6%	54.4%
FRANKLIN	6,995	2,956	4,021	18	1,065 D	42.3%	57.5%	42.5%	57.7%
FULTON	8,313	4,410	4,374	34	36 R	50.0%	49.6%	50.2%	49.8%
GIBSON	16,458	5,865	10,507	86	4,642 D	35.6%	63.8%	35.8%	64.2%
GRANT	32,494	14,688	17,574	232	2,886 D	45.2%	54.1%	45.6%	54.4%
GREENE	14,570	5,919	8,574	77	2,655 D	40.6%	58.8%	40.8%	59.2%
HAMILTON	19,681	12,060	7,553	68	4,507 R	61.3%	38.4%	61.5%	38.5%
HANCOCK	12,993	6,370	6,573	50	203 D	49.0%	50.6%	49.2%	50.8%
HARRISON	9,708	3,671	5,949	88	2,278 D	37.8%	61.3%	38.2%	61.8%
HENDRICKS	20,405	11,497	8,857	51	2,640 R	56.3%	43.4%	56.5%	43.5%
HENRY	22,697	10,184	12,374	139	2,190 D	44.9%	54.5%	45.1%	54.9%
HOWARD	30,941	12,897	17,809	235	4,912 D	41.7%	57.6%	42.0%	58.0%
HUNTINGTON	16,844	7,438	9,308	98	1,870 D	44.2%	55.3%	44.4%	55.6%
JACKSON	14,971	6,285	8,572	114	2,287 D	42.0%	57.3%	42.3%	57.7%
JASPER	8,516	4,497	3,995	24	502 R	52.8%	46.9%	53.0%	47.0%
JAY	11,318	4,439	6,781	98	2,342 D	39.2%	59.9%	39.6%	60.4%
JEFFERSON	11,586	4,808	6,694	84	1,886 D	41.5%	57.8%	41.8%	58.2%
JENNINGS	7,811	3,469	4,307	35	838 D	44.4%	55.1%	44.6%	55.4%
JOHNSON	20,663	11,472	10,099	92	1,373 R	50.7%	48.9%	50.9%	49.1%
KNOX	20,411	7,612	12,678	121	5,066 D	37.3%	62.1%	37.5%	62.5%
KOSCIUSKO	19,388	10,488	8,759	141	1,729 R	54.1%	45.2%	54.5%	45.5%
LAGRANGE	5,640	2,785	2,818	37	33 D	49.4%	50.0%	49.7%	50.3%
LAKE	209,523	73,722	134,978	823	61,256 D	35.2%	64.4%	35.3%	64.7%
LA PORTE	38,594	16,270	22,220	104	5,950 D	42.2%	57.6%	42.3%	57.7%
LAWRENCE	16,956	8,186	8,677	93	491 D	48.3%	51.2%	48.5%	51.5%
MADISON	57,729	24,171	33,325	233	9,154 D	41.9%	57.7%	42.0%	58.0%
MARION	296,381	143,015	152,418	948	9,403 D	48.3%	51.4%	48.4%	51.6%
MARSHALL	16,415	7,895	8,397	123	502 D	48.1%	51.2%	48.5%	51.5%
MARTIN	5,146	2,000	3,137	9	1,137 D	38.9%	60.9%	38.9%	61.1%
MIAMI	14,060	6,270	7,667	123	1,397 D	44.6%	54.5%	45.0%	55.0%
MONROE	22,372	10,309	11,918	145	1,609 D	46.1%	53.3%	46.4%	53.6%
MONTGOMERY	15,930	7,823	8,042	65	219 D	49.1%	50.5%	49.3%	50.7%
MORGAN	15,428	8,347	7,011	70	1,336 R	54.1%	45.4%	54.3%	45.7%
NEWTON	5,340	2,780	2,547	13	233 R	52.1%	47.7%	52.2%	47.8%
NOBLE	13,363	5,682	7,621	60	1,939 D	42.5%	57.0%	42.7%	57.3%
OHIO	2,308	905	1,397	6	492 D	39.2%	60.5%	39.3%	60.7%
ORANGE	8,710	4,187	4,490	33	303 D	48.1%	51.5%	48.3%	51.7%
OWEN	6,160	2,788	3,339	33	551 D	45.3%	54.2%	45.5%	54.5%

INDIANA

PRESIDENT 1960

County	Total Vote	Republican	Democratic	Other	Rep.-Dem. Plurality	Total Vote Rep.	Total Vote Dem.	Major Vote Rep.	Major Vote Dem.
PARKE	8,046	4,662	3,361	23	1,301 R	57.9%	41.8%	58.1%	41.9%
PERRY	9,308	4,372	4,920	16	548 D	47.0%	52.9%	47.1%	52.9%
PIKE	7,716	4,606	3,046	64	1,560 R	59.7%	39.5%	60.2%	39.8%
PORTER	26,474	15,666	10,733	75	4,933 R	59.2%	40.5%	59.3%	40.7%
POSEY	9,857	5,369	4,457	31	912 R	54.5%	45.2%	54.6%	45.4%
PULASKI	6,771	3,905	2,746	120	1,159 R	57.7%	40.6%	58.7%	41.3%
PUTNAM	11,423	6,583	4,798	42	1,785 R	57.6%	42.0%	57.8%	42.2%
RANDOLPH	14,677	9,528	5,035	114	4,493 R	64.9%	34.3%	65.4%	34.6%
RIPLEY	10,818	6,053	4,730	35	1,323 R	56.0%	43.7%	56.1%	43.9%
RUSH	9,782	6,215	3,516	51	2,699 R	63.5%	35.9%	63.9%	36.1%
ST JOSEPH	117,499	53,621	63,553	325	9,932 D	45.6%	54.1%	45.8%	54.2%
SCOTT	6,301	3,213	3,064	24	149 R	51.0%	48.6%	51.2%	48.8%
SHELBY	16,602	9,421	7,111	70	2,310 R	56.7%	42.8%	57.0%	43.0%
SPENCER	9,373	5,050	4,303	20	747 R	53.9%	45.9%	54.0%	46.0%
STARKE	8,619	4,592	3,995	32	597 R	53.3%	46.4%	53.5%	46.5%
STEUBEN	8,079	5,464	2,588	27	2,876 R	67.6%	32.0%	67.9%	32.1%
SULLIVAN	12,060	6,012	5,975	73	37 R	49.9%	49.5%	50.2%	49.8%
SWITZERLAND	3,905	1,929	1,955	21	26 D	49.4%	50.1%	49.7%	50.3%
TIPPECANOE	38,668	24,572	14,041	55	10,531 R	63.5%	36.3%	63.6%	36.4%
TIPTON	8,223	4,924	3,299		1,625 R	59.9%	40.1%	59.9%	40.1%
UNION	3,275	2,087	1,180	8	907 R	63.7%	36.0%	63.9%	36.1%
VANDERBURGH	77,635	41,068	36,330	237	4,738 R	52.9%	46.8%	53.1%	46.9%
VERMILLION	10,227	4,798	5,391	38	593 D	46.9%	52.7%	47.1%	52.9%
VIGO	50,178	24,940	25,105	133	165 D	49.7%	50.0%	49.8%	50.2%
WABASH	15,297	10,420	4,788	89	5,632 R	68.1%	31.3%	68.5%	31.5%
WARREN	4,464	2,870	1,574	20	1,296 R	64.3%	35.3%	64.6%	35.4%
WARRICK	11,554	6,482	5,042	30	1,440 R	56.1%	43.6%	56.2%	43.8%
WASHINGTON	8,913	5,057	3,821	35	1,236 R	56.7%	42.9%	57.0%	43.0%
WAYNE	32,580	19,764	12,721	95	7,043 R	60.7%	39.0%	60.8%	39.2%
WELLS	10,242	6,034	4,128	80	1,906 R	58.9%	40.3%	59.4%	40.6%
WHITE	10,612	6,678	3,914	20	2,764 R	62.9%	36.9%	63.0%	37.0%
WHITLEY	10,943	6,621	4,266	56	2,355 R	60.5%	39.0%	60.8%	39.2%
TOTAL	2,135,360	1,175,120	952,358	7,882	222,762 R	55.0%	44.6%	55.2%	44.8%

PRESIDENT 1964

County	Total Vote	Republican	Democratic	Other	Rep.-Dem. Plurality	Total Vote Rep.	Total Vote Dem.	Major Vote Rep.	Major Vote Dem.
PARKE	7,621	3,570	4,034	17	464 D	46.8%	52.9%	46.9%	53.1%
PERRY	9,341	3,090	6,226	25	3,136 D	33.1%	66.7%	33.2%	66.8%
PIKE	7,272	2,703	4,519	50	1,816 D	37.2%	62.1%	37.4%	62.6%
PORTER	27,607	14,480	12,975	152	1,505 R	52.5%	47.0%	52.7%	47.3%
POSEY	9,770	3,573	6,164	33	2,591 D	36.6%	63.1%	36.7%	63.3%
PULASKI	6,634	3,202	3,408	24	206 D	48.3%	51.4%	48.4%	51.6%
PUTNAM	11,630	5,331	6,275	24	944 D	45.8%	54.0%	45.9%	54.1%
RANDOLPH	13,506	6,551	6,804	151	253 D	48.5%	50.4%	49.1%	50.9%
RIPLEY	10,552	4,587	5,933	32	1,346 D	43.5%	56.2%	43.6%	56.4%
RUSH	9,025	4,507	4,450	68	57 R	49.9%	49.3%	50.3%	49.7%
ST JOSEPH	106,346	39,872	65,844	630	25,972 D	37.5%	61.9%	37.7%	62.3%
SCOTT	6,203	1,992	4,205	6	2,213 D	32.1%	67.8%	32.1%	67.9%
SHELBY	16,455	7,310	9,078	67	1,768 D	44.4%	55.2%	44.6%	55.4%
SPENCER	8,834	3,980	4,834	20	854 D	45.1%	54.7%	45.2%	54.8%
STARKE	8,321	3,466	4,838	17	1,372 D	41.7%	58.1%	41.7%	58.3%
STEUBEN	8,105	4,075	3,999	31	76 R	50.3%	49.3%	50.5%	49.5%
SULLIVAN	11,260	3,867	7,351	42	3,484 D	34.3%	65.3%	34.5%	65.5%
SWITZERLAND	3,640	1,390	2,231	19	841 D	38.2%	61.3%	38.4%	61.6%
TIPPECANOE	39,372	19,036	20,257	79	1,221 D	48.3%	51.5%	48.4%	51.6%
TIPTON	8,316	3,863	4,410	43	547 D	46.5%	53.0%	46.7%	53.3%
UNION	3,005	1,531	1,463	11	68 R	50.9%	48.7%	51.1%	48.9%
VANDERBURGH	73,407	27,231	45,796	380	18,565 D	37.1%	62.4%	37.3%	62.7%
VERMILLION	9,382	3,397	5,957	28	2,560 D	36.2%	63.5%	36.3%	63.7%
VIGO	46,751	19,001	27,606	144	8,605 D	40.6%	59.0%	40.8%	59.2%
WABASH	14,535	6,905	7,485	145	580 D	47.5%	51.5%	48.0%	52.0%
WARREN	4,425	2,154	2,261	10	107 D	48.7%	51.1%	48.8%	51.2%
WARRICK	11,640	4,376	7,222	42	2,846 D	37.6%	62.0%	37.7%	62.3%
WASHINGTON	8,573	3,598	4,943	32	1,345 D	42.0%	57.7%	42.1%	57.9%
WAYNE	30,724	15,342	15,269	113	73 R	49.9%	49.7%	50.1%	49.9%
WELLS	10,055	4,018	5,945	92	1,927 D	40.0%	59.1%	40.3%	59.7%
WHITE	10,455	5,015	5,407	33	392 D	48.0%	51.7%	48.1%	51.9%
WHITLEY	10,747	4,896	5,798	53	902 D	45.6%	53.9%	45.8%	54.2%
TOTAL	2,091,606	911,118	1,170,848	9,640	259,730 D	43.6%	56.0%	43.8%	56.2%

INDIANA

OTHER VOTE COMPOSITION:

1920   24,713 Socialist; 16,499 Farmer-Labor; 13,462 Prohibition; 566 Single Tax.

1924   71,700 Progressive; 4,416 Prohibition; 987 Communist.

1928   5,496 Prohibition; 3,871 Socialist; 645 Socialist Labor; 321 Communist.

1932   21,388 Socialist; 10,399 Prohibition; 2,187 Communist; 2,070 Socialist Labor;
1,645 National. The National vote represents the total of the highest elector,
though the published county-by-county figures include only 1,615 National
votes; the state total for other votes is thus 30 above the sum of the
counties.

1936   19,407 Union; 3,856 Socialist; 1,090 Communist.

1940   6,437 Prohibition; 2,075 Socialist; 706 Socialist Labor.

1944   12,574 Prohibition; 2,223 Socialist.

1948   14,711 Prohibition; 9,649 Progressive; 2,179 Socialist; 763 Socialist Labor.

1952   15,335 Prohibition; 1,085 Progressive; 840 Socialist Labor.

1956   6,554 Prohibition; 1,334 Socialist Labor.

1960   6,746 Prohibition; 1,136 Socialist Labor.

1964   8,266 Prohibition; 1,374 Socialist Labor.

IOWA

PRESIDENT 1920

County	Total Vote	Republican	Democratic	Other	Rep.-Dem. Plurality	Total Vote Rep.	Total Vote Dem.	Major Vote Rep.	Major Vote Dem.
ADAIR	5,563	4,133	1,358	72	2,775 R	74.3%	24.4%	75.3%	24.7%
ADAMS	4,557	2,845	1,670	42	1,175 R	62.4%	36.6%	63.0%	37.0%
ALLAMAKEE	7,090	5,192	1,833	65	3,359 R	73.2%	25.9%	73.9%	26.1%
APPANOOSE	9,743	6,382	2,952	409	3,430 R	65.5%	30.3%	68.4%	31.6%
AUDUBON	4,378	2,963	1,405	10	1,558 R	67.7%	32.1%	67.8%	32.2%
BENTON	9,207	6,539	2,343	325	4,196 R	71.0%	25.4%	73.6%	26.4%
BLACK HAWK	22,101	16,920	4,000	1,181	12,920 R	76.6%	18.1%	80.9%	19.1%
BOONE	9,980	7,093	2,240	647	4,853 R	71.1%	22.4%	76.0%	24.0%
BREMER	7,269	6,287	902	80	5,385 R	86.5%	12.4%	87.5%	12.5%
BUCHANAN	7,997	6,334	1,600	63	4,734 R	79.2%	20.0%	79.8%	20.2%
BUENA VISTA	6,270	4,927	1,204	139	3,723 R	78.6%	19.2%	80.4%	19.6%
BUTLER	6,806	5,900	830	76	5,070 R	86.7%	12.2%	87.7%	12.3%
CALHOUN	6,858	5,277	1,479	102	3,798 R	76.9%	21.6%	78.1%	21.9%
CARROLL	8,671	6,320	2,174	177	4,146 R	72.9%	25.1%	74.4%	25.6%
CASS	8,382	6,558	1,668	156	4,890 R	78.2%	19.9%	79.7%	20.3%
CEDAR	7,315	5,697	1,420	198	4,277 R	77.9%	19.4%	80.0%	20.0%
CERRO GORDO	10,951	8,293	2,302	356	5,991 R	75.7%	21.0%	78.3%	21.7%
CHEROKEE	5,849	4,544	1,211	94	3,333 R	77.7%	20.7%	79.0%	21.0%
CHICKASAW	6,744	4,517	1,211	1,016	3,306 R	67.0%	18.0%	78.9%	21.1%
CLARKE	4,450	3,150	1,257	43	1,893 R	70.8%	28.2%	71.5%	28.5%
CLAY	5,585	4,471	1,001	113	3,470 R	80.1%	17.9%	81.7%	18.3%
CLAYTON	8,706	6,747	1,808	151	4,939 R	77.5%	20.8%	78.9%	21.1%
CLINTON	17,536	11,746	3,153	2,637	8,593 R	67.0%	18.0%	78.8%	21.2%
CRAWFORD	7,972	5,473	2,151	348	3,322 R	68.7%	27.0%	71.8%	28.2%
DALLAS	9,454	6,677	2,577	200	4,100 R	70.6%	27.3%	72.2%	27.8%
DAVIS	5,535	3,117	2,353	65	764 R	56.3%	42.5%	57.0%	43.0%
DECATUR	6,845	4,187	2,592	66	1,595 R	61.2%	37.9%	61.8%	38.2%
DELAWARE	7,088	5,880	1,111	97	4,769 R	83.0%	15.7%	84.1%	15.9%
DES MOINES	12,997	8,287	3,449	1,261	4,838 R	63.8%	26.5%	70.6%	29.4%
DICKINSON	4,101	3,298	760	43	2,538 R	80.4%	18.5%	81.3%	18.7%
DUBUQUE	21,000	12,436	7,636	928	4,800 R	59.2%	36.4%	62.0%	38.0%
EMMET	4,421	3,360	991	70	2,369 R	76.0%	22.4%	77.2%	22.8%
FAYETTE	10,444	8,265	1,941	238	6,324 R	79.1%	18.6%	81.0%	19.0%
FLOYD	7,197	6,106	933	158	5,173 R	84.8%	13.0%	86.7%	13.3%
FRANKLIN	5,109	4,397	601	111	3,796 R	86.1%	11.8%	88.0%	12.0%
FREMONT	6,364	3,776	2,524	64	1,252 R	59.3%	39.7%	59.9%	40.1%
GREENE	6,460	5,102	1,303	55	3,799 R	79.0%	20.2%	79.7%	20.3%
GRUNDY	5,432	4,662	714	56	3,948 R	85.8%	13.1%	86.7%	13.3%
GUTHRIE	7,099	5,338	1,647	114	3,691 R	75.2%	23.2%	76.4%	23.6%
HAMILTON	7,148	5,924	1,126	98	4,798 R	82.9%	15.8%	84.0%	16.0%
HANCOCK	4,474	3,617	725	132	2,892 R	80.8%	16.2%	83.3%	16.7%
HARDIN	7,915	6,646	1,076	193	5,570 R	84.0%	13.6%	86.1%	13.9%
HARRISON	9,742	6,254	3,352	136	2,902 R	64.2%	34.4%	65.1%	34.9%
HENRY	7,306	5,254	1,939	113	3,315 R	71.9%	26.5%	73.0%	27.0%
HOWARD	5,418	3,601	1,717	100	1,884 R	66.5%	31.7%	67.7%	32.3%
HUMBOLDT	4,319	3,577	681	61	2,896 R	82.8%	15.8%	84.0%	16.0%
IDA	4,684	3,547	1,090	47	2,457 R	75.7%	23.3%	76.5%	23.5%
IOWA	6,997	4,892	2,019	86	2,873 R	69.9%	28.9%	70.8%	29.2%
JACKSON	7,005	4,763	1,954	288	2,809 R	68.0%	27.9%	70.9%	29.1%
JASPER	11,029	7,417	3,390	222	4,027 R	67.2%	30.7%	68.6%	31.4%
JEFFERSON	6,108	4,558	1,450	100	3,108 R	74.6%	23.7%	75.9%	24.1%
JOHNSON	10,923	5,696	5,032	195	664 R	52.1%	46.1%	53.1%	46.9%
JONES	8,461	5,962	2,436	63	3,526 R	70.5%	28.8%	71.0%	29.0%
KEOKUK	9,135	6,207	2,800	128	3,407 R	67.9%	30.7%	68.9%	31.1%
KOSSUTH	7,769	6,018	1,682	69	4,336 R	77.5%	21.6%	78.2%	21.8%
LEE	16,322	10,763	5,177	382	5,586 R	65.9%	31.7%	67.5%	32.5%
LINN	27,818	20,036	6,932	850	13,104 R	72.0%	24.9%	74.3%	25.7%
LOUISA	5,594	4,560	932	102	3,628 R	81.5%	16.7%	83.0%	17.0%
LUCAS	5,506	3,775	1,463	268	2,312 R	68.6%	26.6%	72.1%	27.9%
LYON	4,459	3,633	729	97	2,904 R	81.5%	16.3%	83.3%	16.7%

PRESIDENT 1924

County	Total Vote	Republican	Democratic	Other	Rep.-Dem. Plurality	Total Vote Rep.	Total Vote Dem.	Major Vote Rep.	Major Vote Dem.
ADAIR	6,006	4,043	688	1,275	3,355 R	67.3%	11.5%	85.5%	14.5%
ADAMS	4,691	2,547	897	1,247	1,650 R	54.3%	19.1%	74.0%	26.0%
ALLAMAKEE	7,154	2,755	1,289	3,110	1,466 R	38.5%	18.0%	68.1%	31.9%
APPANOOSE	11,175	6,421	2,032	2,722	4,389 R	57.5%	18.2%	76.0%	24.0%
AUDUBON	4,592	2,475	965	1,152	1,510 R	53.9%	21.0%	71.9%	28.1%
BENTON	9,102	5,314	1,459	2,329	3,855 R	58.4%	16.0%	78.5%	21.5%
BLACK HAWK	24,191	15,813	2,981	5,397	12,832 R	65.4%	12.3%	84.1%	15.9%
BOONE	10,635	4,980	702	4,953	4,278 R	46.8%	6.6%	87.6%	12.4%
BREMER	7,302	3,532	911	2,859	2,621 R	48.4%	12.5%	79.5%	20.5%
BUCHANAN	8,648	5,459	1,780	1,409	3,679 R	63.1%	20.6%	75.4%	24.6%
BUENA VISTA	7,266	3,812	683	2,771	3,129 R	52.5%	9.4%	84.8%	15.2%
BUTLER	6,411	3,823	667	1,921	3,156 R	59.6%	10.4%	85.1%	14.9%
CALHOUN	6,601	3,529	714	2,358	2,815 R	53.5%	10.8%	83.2%	16.8%
CARROLL	8,308	3,590	1,994	2,724	1,596 R	43.2%	24.0%	64.3%	35.7%
CASS	8,308	5,721	1,099	1,488	4,622 R	68.9%	13.2%	83.9%	16.1%
CEDAR	7,613	4,625	1,478	1,510	3,147 R	60.8%	19.4%	75.8%	24.2%
CERRO GORDO	14,269	8,410	1,345	4,514	7,065 R	58.9%	9.4%	86.2%	13.8%
CHEROKEE	6,172	3,240	904	2,028	2,336 R	52.5%	14.6%	78.2%	21.8%
CHICKASAW	7,340	3,416	1,736	2,188	1,680 R	46.5%	23.6%	66.3%	33.7%
CLARKE	4,860	2,554	743	1,563	1,811 R	52.6%	15.3%	77.5%	22.5%
CLAY	5,780	3,549	378	1,853	3,171 R	61.4%	6.5%	90.4%	9.6%
CLAYTON	10,038	4,168	1,556	4,314	2,612 R	41.5%	15.5%	72.8%	27.2%
CLINTON	19,636	10,359	3,811	5,466	6,548 R	52.8%	19.4%	73.1%	26.9%
CRAWFORD	7,775	2,882	1,255	3,638	1,627 R	37.1%	16.1%	69.7%	30.3%
DALLAS	10,251	6,359	933	2,959	5,426 R	62.0%	9.1%	87.2%	12.8%
DAVIS	5,748	2,804	1,802	1,142	1,002 R	48.8%	31.4%	60.9%	39.1%
DECATUR	6,831	3,221	1,693	1,917	1,528 R	47.2%	24.8%	65.5%	34.5%
DELAWARE	7,630	4,938	1,146	1,546	3,792 R	64.7%	15.0%	81.2%	18.8%
DES MOINES	14,739	7,995	2,616	4,128	5,379 R	54.2%	17.7%	75.3%	24.7%
DICKINSON	4,419	2,967	435	1,017	2,532 R	67.1%	9.8%	87.2%	12.8%
DUBUQUE	24,566	8,280	5,718	10,568	2,562 R	33.7%	23.3%	59.2%	40.8%
EMMET	5,133	2,739	407	1,987	2,332 R	53.4%	7.9%	87.1%	12.9%
FAYETTE	11,880	5,974	1,272	4,634	4,702 R	50.3%	10.7%	82.4%	17.6%
FLOYD	7,589	5,012	529	2,048	4,483 R	66.0%	7.0%	90.5%	9.5%
FRANKLIN	5,128	3,064	360	1,704	2,704 R	59.8%	7.0%	89.5%	10.5%
FREMONT	6,220	3,313	2,525	382	788 R	53.3%	40.6%	56.7%	43.3%
GREENE	6,886	4,599	790	1,497	3,809 R	66.8%	11.5%	85.3%	14.7%
GRUNDY	5,738	3,322	615	1,801	2,707 R	57.9%	10.7%	84.4%	15.6%
GUTHRIE	7,181	4,314	840	2,027	3,474 R	60.1%	11.7%	83.7%	16.3%
HAMILTON	7,239	4,401	490	2,348	3,911 R	60.8%	6.8%	90.0%	10.0%
HANCOCK	5,338	3,183	550	1,605	2,633 R	59.6%	10.3%	85.3%	14.7%
HARDIN	7,833	4,714	634	2,485	4,080 R	60.2%	8.1%	88.1%	11.9%
HARRISON	9,955	5,062	3,179	1,714	1,883 R	50.9%	31.9%	61.4%	38.6%
HENRY	7,293	4,536	1,344	1,413	3,192 R	62.2%	18.4%	77.1%	22.9%
HOWARD	5,975	2,850	1,604	1,521	1,246 R	47.7%	26.8%	64.0%	36.0%
HUMBOLDT	4,754	2,841	370	1,543	2,471 R	59.8%	7.8%	88.5%	11.5%
IDA	4,674	2,033	685	1,956	1,348 R	43.5%	14.7%	74.8%	25.2%
IOWA	6,813	3,549	1,458	1,806	2,091 R	52.1%	21.4%	70.9%	29.1%
JACKSON	8,325	4,218	2,352	1,755	1,866 R	50.7%	28.3%	64.2%	35.8%
JASPER	11,543	6,565	1,214	3,764	5,351 R	56.9%	10.5%	84.4%	15.6%
JEFFERSON	6,590	4,062	1,249	1,279	2,813 R	61.6%	19.0%	76.5%	23.5%
JOHNSON	12,864	5,741	4,570	2,553	1,171 R	44.6%	35.5%	55.7%	44.3%
JONES	7,918	4,524	2,212	1,182	2,312 R	57.1%	27.9%	67.2%	32.8%
KEOKUK	9,329	4,795	2,568	1,966	2,227 R	51.4%	27.5%	65.1%	34.9%
KOSSUTH	8,737	3,806	1,369	3,562	2,437 R	43.6%	15.7%	73.5%	26.5%
LEE	18,350	9,999	4,903	3,448	5,096 R	54.5%	26.7%	67.1%	32.9%
LINN	34,647	22,371	5,941	6,335	16,430 R	64.6%	17.1%	79.0%	21.0%
LOUISA	4,540	2,952	643	945	2,309 R	65.0%	14.2%	82.1%	17.9%
LUCAS	6,242	3,288	824	2,130	2,464 R	52.7%	13.2%	80.0%	20.0%
LYON	4,725	2,082	481	2,162	1,601 R	44.1%	10.2%	81.2%	18.8%

IOWA

PRESIDENT 1920

County	Total Vote	Republican	Democratic	Other	Rep.-Dem. Plurality	Total Vote Rep.	Total Vote Dem.	Major Vote Rep.	Major Vote Dem.
MADISON	6,487	4,465	1,899	123	2,566 R	68.8%	29.3%	70.2%	29.8%
MAHASKA	10,440	6,739	3,339	362	3,480 R	64.5%	32.0%	66.9%	33.1%
MARION	9,599	5,435	3,861	303	1,574 R	56.6%	40.2%	58.5%	41.5%
MARSHALL	11,800	9,334	2,166	300	7,168 R	79.1%	18.4%	81.2%	18.8%
MILLS	5,338	3,683	1,592	63	2,091 R	69.0%	29.8%	69.8%	30.2%
MITCHELL	5,332	4,476	773	83	3,703 R	83.9%	14.5%	85.3%	14.7%
MONONA	6,575	4,569	1,960	46	2,609 R	69.5%	29.8%	70.0%	30.0%
MONROE	7,352	4,500	2,081	771	2,419 R	61.2%	28.3%	68.4%	31.6%
MONTGOMERY	6,510	4,980	1,404	126	3,576 R	76.5%	21.6%	78.0%	22.0%
MUSCATINE	11,544	8,115	2,293	1,136	5,822 R	70.3%	19.9%	78.0%	22.0%
O'BRIEN	6,714	5,137	1,468	109	3,669 R	76.5%	21.9%	77.8%	22.2%
OSCEOLA	3,541	2,717	754	70	1,963 R	76.7%	21.3%	78.3%	21.7%
PAGE	9,131	6,949	1,931	251	5,018 R	76.1%	21.1%	78.3%	21.7%
PALO ALTO	5,466	3,904	1,467	95	2,437 R	71.4%	25.8%	73.2%	27.3%
PLYMOUTH	7,996	6,090	1,801	105	4,289 R	76.2%	22.5%	77.2%	22.8%
POCAHONTAS	5,774	4,046	1,639	89	2,407 R	70.1%	28.4%	71.2%	28.8%
POLK	53,986	36,073	16,281	1,632	19,792 R	66.8%	30.2%	68.9%	31.1%
POTTAWATTAMIE	20,887	13,506	6,659	722	6,847 R	64.7%	31.9%	67.0%	33.0%
POWESHIEK	8,130	5,806	2,125	199	3,681 R	71.4%	26.1%	73.2%	26.8%
RINGGOLD	5,095	3,702	1,327	66	2,375 R	72.7%	26.0%	73.6%	26.4%
SAC	6,334	4,984	1,268	82	3,716 R	78.7%	20.0%	79.7%	20.3%
SCOTT	27,631	16,233	5,473	5,925	10,760 R	58.7%	19.8%	74.8%	25.2%
SHELBY	6,550	4,621	1,882	47	2,739 R	70.5%	28.7%	71.1%	28.9%
SIOUX	7,653	6,068	1,510	75	4,558 R	79.3%	19.7%	80.1%	19.9%
STORY	10,784	8,713	1,909	162	6,804 R	80.8%	17.7%	82.0%	18.0%
TAMA	9,073	6,352	2,552	169	3,800 R	70.0%	28.1%	71.3%	28.7%
TAYLOR	6,901	4,997	1,757	147	3,240 R	72.4%	25.5%	74.0%	26.0%
UNION	6,805	4,466	2,228	111	2,238 R	65.6%	32.7%	66.7%	33.3%
VAN BUREN	6,086	4,321	1,682	83	2,639 R	71.0%	27.6%	72.0%	28.0%
WAPELLO	14,537	9,884	4,131	522	5,753 R	68.0%	28.4%	70.5%	29.5%
WARREN	7,548	5,323	2,066	159	3,257 R	70.5%	27.4%	72.0%	28.0%
WASHINGTON	8,177	5,813	2,257	107	3,556 R	71.1%	27.6%	72.0%	28.0%
WAYNE	6,773	4,234	2,434	105	1,800 R	62.5%	35.9%	63.5%	36.5%
WEBSTER	12,988	8,312	2,804	1,872	5,508 R	64.0%	21.6%	74.8%	25.2%
WINNEBAGO	4,514	3,931	469	114	3,462 R	87.1%	10.4%	89.3%	10.7%
WINNESHIEK	8,797	6,684	1,933	180	4,751 R	76.0%	22.0%	77.6%	22.4%
WOODBURY	28,362	17,603	9,815	944	7,788 R	62.1%	34.6%	64.2%	35.8%
WORTH	4,009	3,401	516	92	2,885 R	84.8%	12.9%	86.8%	13.2%
WRIGHT	7,082	5,739	1,205	138	4,534 R	81.0%	17.0%	82.6%	17.4%
TOTAL	894,959	634,674	227,804	32,481	406,870 R	70.9%	25.5%	73.6%	26.4%

PRESIDENT 1924

County	Total Vote	Republican	Democratic	Other	Rep.-Dem. Plurality	Total Vote Rep.	Total Vote Dem.	Major Vote Rep.	Major Vote Dem.
MADISON	6,888	4,191	1,367	1,330	2,824 R	60.8%	19.8%	75.4%	24.6%
MAHASKA	10,492	5,810	1,673	3,010	4,137 R	55.4%	15.9%	77.6%	22.4%
MARION	10,599	5,058	2,383	3,154	2,675 R	47.7%	22.5%	68.0%	32.0%
MARSHALL	11,110	9,010	1,516	2,584	7,494 R	68.7%	11.6%	85.6%	14.4%
MILLS	5,825	3,348	1,750	727	1,598 R	57.5%	30.0%	65.7%	34.3%
MITCHELL	6,150	2,892	400	2,858	2,492 R	47.0%	6.5%	87.8%	12.2%
MONONA	6,268	3,195	1,271	1,802	1,924 R	51.0%	20.3%	71.5%	28.5%
MONROE	8,000	4,098	1,388	2,514	2,710 R	51.2%	17.4%	74.7%	25.3%
MONTGOMERY	7,154	4,617	805	1,732	3,812 R	64.5%	11.3%	85.2%	14.8%
MUSCATINE	11,785	7,731	1,963	2,091	5,768 R	65.6%	16.7%	79.8%	20.2%
O'BRIEN	7,128	4,172	756	2,200	3,416 R	58.5%	10.6%	84.7%	15.3%
OSCEOLA	3,716	1,876	386	1,454	1,490 R	50.5%	10.4%	82.9%	17.1%
PAGE	9,177	6,023	1,643	1,511	4,380 R	65.6%	17.9%	78.6%	21.4%
PALO ALTO	5,929	2,943	593	2,393	2,350 R	49.6%	10.0%	83.2%	16.8%
PLYMOUTH	9,036	3,803	1,605	3,628	2,198 R	42.1%	17.8%	70.3%	29.7%
POCAHONTAS	6,290	2,537	819	2,934	1,718 R	40.3%	13.0%	75.6%	24.4%
POLK	59,723	37,491	6,665	15,567	30,826 R	62.8%	11.2%	84.9%	15.1%
POTTAWATTAMIE	25,322	13,380	5,305	6,637	8,075 R	52.8%	21.0%	71.6%	28.4%
POWESHIEK	8,221	5,414	1,428	2,379	2,986 R	53.7%	17.4%	75.6%	24.4%
RINGGOLD	5,186	3,147	882	1,157	2,265 R	60.7%	17.0%	78.1%	21.9%
SAC	6,533	3,970	674	1,889	3,296 R	60.8%	10.3%	85.5%	14.5%
SCOTT	30,194	18,360	4,347	7,487	14,013 R	60.8%	14.4%	80.9%	19.1%
SHELBY	6,750	3,252	2,297	1,201	955 R	48.2%	34.0%	58.6%	41.4%
SIOUX	8,416	4,960	900	2,556	4,060 R	58.9%	10.7%	84.6%	15.4%
STORY	10,780	6,916	1,310	2,554	5,606 R	64.2%	12.2%	84.1%	15.9%
TAMA	9,360	5,177	2,180	2,003	2,997 R	55.3%	23.3%	70.4%	29.6%
TAYLOR	6,971	4,254	1,138	1,579	3,116 R	61.0%	16.3%	78.9%	21.1%
UNION	7,841	4,250	1,168	2,425	3,084 R	54.2%	14.9%	78.5%	21.5%
VAN BUREN	5,964	3,623	1,209	1,132	2,414 R	60.7%	20.3%	75.0%	25.0%
WAPELLO	17,307	9,870	3,039	4,398	6,831 R	57.0%	17.6%	76.5%	23.5%
WARREN	7,536	4,683	1,274	1,579	3,409 R	62.1%	16.9%	78.6%	21.4%
WASHINGTON	8,371	5,053	1,868	1,450	3,185 R	60.4%	22.3%	73.0%	27.0%
WAYNE	6,634	3,322	1,826	1,486	1,496 R	50.1%	27.5%	64.5%	35.5%
WEBSTER	13,996	6,641	2,076	5,279	4,565 R	47.4%	14.4%	76.2%	23.8%
WINNEBAGO	5,167	2,445	225	2,497	2,220 R	47.3%	4.4%	91.6%	8.4%
WINNESHIEK	9,427	4,154	1,510	3,763	2,644 R	44.1%	16.0%	73.3%	26.7%
WOODBURY	35,034	16,639	5,676	12,719	10,963 R	47.5%	16.2%	74.6%	25.4%
WORTH	4,589	2,340	180	2,069	2,160 R	51.0%	3.9%	92.9%	7.1%
WRIGHT	7,531	4,323	501	2,707	3,822 R	57.4%	6.7%	89.6%	10.4%
TOTAL	976,770	537,458	160,382	278,930	377,076 R	55.0%	16.4%	77.0%	23.0%

IOWA

PRESIDENT 1928

County	Total Vote	Republican	Democratic	Other	Rep.-Dem. Plurality	Total Vote Rep.	Total Vote Dem.	Major Vote Rep.	Major Vote Dem.
ADAIR	6,030	4,176	1,854		2,322 R	69.3%	30.7%	69.3%	30.7%
ADAMS	4,437	2,958	1,479		1,479 R	66.7%	33.3%	66.7%	33.3%
ALLAMAKEE	8,012	4,785	3,227		1,558 R	59.7%	40.3%	59.7%	40.3%
APPANOOSE	10,204	6,864	3,340		3,524 R	67.3%	32.7%	67.3%	32.7%
AUDUBON	4,704	2,340	2,364		24 D	49.7%	50.3%	49.7%	50.3%
BENTON	8,976	5,669	3,307		2,362 R	63.2%	36.8%	63.2%	36.8%
BLACK HAWK	27,876	19,409	8,467		10,942 R	69.6%	30.4%	69.6%	30.4%
BOONE	10,570	7,521	3,049		4,472 R	71.2%	28.8%	71.2%	28.8%
BREMER	7,025	3,879	3,146		733 R	55.2%	44.8%	55.2%	44.8%
BUCHANAN	8,984	5,885	3,099		2,786 R	65.5%	34.5%	65.5%	34.5%
BUENA VISTA	7,696	5,087	2,609		2,478 R	66.1%	33.9%	66.1%	33.9%
BUTLER	6,665	4,789	1,876		2,913 R	71.9%	28.1%	71.9%	28.1%
CALHOUN	6,817	4,136	2,681		1,455 R	60.7%	39.3%	60.7%	39.3%
CARROLL	10,148	4,014	6,134		2,120 D	39.6%	60.4%	39.6%	60.4%
CASS	8,760	6,120	2,640		3,480 R	69.9%	30.1%	69.9%	30.1%
CEDAR	7,373	4,856	2,517		2,339 R	65.9%	34.1%	65.9%	34.1%
CERRO GORDO	14,490	9,582	4,908		4,674 R	66.1%	33.9%	66.1%	33.9%
CHEROKEE	6,610	3,909	2,701		1,208 R	59.1%	40.9%	59.1%	40.9%
CHICKASAW	7,377	3,712	3,665		47 R	50.3%	49.7%	50.3%	49.7%
CLARKE	4,422	2,780	1,642		1,138 R	62.9%	37.1%	62.9%	37.1%
CLAY	6,050	3,986	2,064		1,922 R	65.9%	34.1%	65.9%	34.1%
CLAYTON	11,005	6,774	4,231		2,543 R	61.6%	38.4%	61.6%	38.4%
CLINTON	20,938	12,295	8,643		3,652 R	58.7%	41.3%	58.7%	41.3%
CRAWFORD	7,931	3,436	4,495		1,059 D	43.3%	56.7%	43.3%	56.7%
DALLAS	10,402	7,294	3,108		4,186 R	70.1%	29.9%	70.1%	29.9%
DAVIS	5,656	3,097	2,559		538 R	54.8%	45.2%	54.8%	45.2%
DECATUR	6,617	3,942	2,675		1,267 R	59.6%	40.4%	59.6%	40.4%
DELAWARE	8,433	5,390	3,043		2,347 R	63.9%	36.1%	63.9%	36.1%
DES MOINES	16,125	10,547	5,578		4,969 R	65.4%	34.6%	65.4%	34.6%
DICKINSON	4,296	3,045	1,251		1,794 R	70.9%	29.1%	70.9%	29.1%
DUBUQUE	29,181	9,744	19,437		9,693 D	33.4%	66.6%	33.4%	66.6%
EMMET	4,590	3,218	1,372		1,846 R	70.1%	29.9%	70.1%	29.9%
FAYETTE	12,399	8,338	4,061		4,277 R	67.2%	32.8%	67.2%	32.8%
FLOYD	7,749	5,675	2,074		3,601 R	73.2%	26.8%	73.2%	26.8%
FRANKLIN	5,112	3,424	1,688		1,736 R	67.0%	33.0%	67.0%	33.0%
FREMONT	6,419	3,597	2,822		775 R	56.0%	44.0%	56.0%	44.0%
GREENE	6,306	4,299	2,007		2,292 R	68.2%	31.8%	68.2%	31.8%
GRUNDY	5,291	3,671	1,620		2,051 R	69.4%	30.6%	69.4%	30.6%
GUTHRIE	7,007	4,772	2,235		2,537 R	68.1%	31.9%	68.1%	31.9%
HAMILTON	7,146	4,171	2,975		1,196 R	58.4%	41.6%	58.4%	41.6%
HANCOCK	5,047	3,114	1,933		1,181 R	61.7%	38.3%	61.7%	38.3%
HARDIN	8,104	5,731	2,373		3,358 R	70.7%	29.3%	70.7%	29.3%
HARRISON	10,011	5,605	4,406		1,199 R	56.0%	44.0%	56.0%	44.0%
HENRY	7,213	5,160	2,053		3,107 R	71.5%	28.5%	71.5%	28.5%
HOWARD	6,568	3,375	3,193		182 R	51.4%	48.6%	51.4%	48.6%
HUMBOLDT	4,507	2,828	1,679		1,149 R	62.7%	37.3%	62.7%	37.3%
IDA	4,658	2,486	2,172		314 R	53.4%	46.6%	53.4%	46.6%
IOWA	7,166	4,091	3,075		1,016 R	57.1%	42.9%	57.1%	42.9%
JACKSON	8,469	4,740	3,729		1,011 R	56.0%	44.0%	56.0%	44.0%
JASPER	13,001	9,144	3,857		5,287 R	70.3%	29.7%	70.3%	29.7%
JEFFERSON	7,078	4,919	2,159		2,760 R	69.5%	30.5%	69.5%	30.5%
JOHNSON	14,469	7,288	7,181		107 R	50.4%	49.6%	50.4%	49.6%
JONES	8,066	5,090	2,976		2,114 R	63.1%	36.9%	63.1%	36.9%
KEOKUK	9,076	5,304	3,772		1,532 R	58.4%	41.6%	58.4%	41.6%
KOSSUTH	9,614	4,878	4,736		142 R	50.7%	49.3%	50.7%	49.3%
LEE	19,430	11,645	7,785		3,860 R	59.9%	40.1%	59.9%	40.1%
LINN	37,167	25,452	11,715		13,737 R	68.5%	31.5%	68.5%	31.5%
LOUISA	4,732	3,275	1,457		1,818 R	69.2%	30.8%	69.2%	30.8%
LUCAS	5,699	3,811	1,888		1,923 R	66.9%	33.1%	66.9%	33.1%
LYON	4,802	3,170	1,632		1,538 R	66.0%	34.0%	66.0%	34.0%

PRESIDENT 1932

County	Total Vote	Republican	Democratic	Other	Rep.-Dem. Plurality	Total Vote Rep.	Total Vote Dem.	Major Vote Rep.	Major Vote Dem.
ADAIR	4,949	2,305	2,607	37	302 D	46.6%	52.7%	46.9%	53.1%
ADAMS	3,939	1,795	2,097	47	302 D	45.6%	53.2%	46.1%	53.9%
ALLAMAKEE	7,848	3,009	4,783	56	1,774 D	38.3%	60.9%	38.6%	61.4%
APPANOOSE	10,017	4,229	5,519	269	1,290 D	42.2%	55.1%	43.4%	56.6%
AUDUBON	4,633	1,604	2,986	43	1,382 D	34.6%	64.5%	34.9%	65.1%
BENTON	9,819	3,424	6,070	325	2,646 D	34.9%	61.8%	36.1%	63.9%
BLACK HAWK	29,765	14,746	14,660	359	86 R	49.5%	49.3%	50.1%	49.9%
BOONE	9,722	3,694	5,293	735	1,599 D	38.0%	54.4%	41.1%	58.9%
BREMER	7,994	2,520	5,411	63	2,891 D	31.5%	67.7%	31.8%	68.2%
BUCHANAN	9,500	4,401	5,004	95	603 D	46.3%	52.7%	46.8%	53.2%
BUENA VISTA	8,210	3,162	4,835	213	1,673 D	38.5%	58.9%	39.5%	60.5%
BUTLER	7,116	3,012	4,028	76	1,016 D	42.3%	56.6%	42.8%	57.2%
CALHOUN	6,977	2,404	4,368	205	1,964 D	34.5%	62.6%	35.5%	64.5%
CARROLL	9,499	2,265	7,174	60	4,909 D	23.8%	75.5%	24.0%	76.0%
CASS	8,645	4,215	4,339	91	124 D	48.8%	50.2%	49.3%	50.7%
CEDAR	8,068	3,277	4,718	73	1,441 D	40.6%	58.5%	41.0%	59.0%
CERRO GORDO	16,218	7,317	8,752	149	1,435 D	45.1%	54.0%	45.5%	54.5%
CHEROKEE	7,382	2,570	4,701	111	2,131 D	34.8%	63.7%	35.3%	64.7%
CHICKASAW	7,676	2,585	5,047	44	2,462 D	33.7%	65.8%	33.9%	66.1%
CLARKE	4,030	1,608	2,342	80	734 D	39.9%	58.1%	40.7%	59.3%
CLAY	6,769	2,599	3,944	226	1,345 D	38.4%	58.3%	39.7%	60.3%
CLAYTON	11,134	3,725	7,347	62	3,622 D	33.5%	66.0%	33.6%	66.4%
CLINTON	21,880	9,085	12,587	208	3,502 D	41.5%	57.5%	41.9%	58.1%
CRAWFORD	8,942	2,334	6,084	524	3,750 D	26.1%	68.0%	27.7%	72.3%
DALLAS	9,611	4,516	4,887	208	371 D	47.0%	50.8%	48.0%	52.0%
DAVIS	5,195	1,757	3,351	87	1,594 D	33.8%	64.5%	34.4%	65.6%
DECATUR	5,830	2,148	3,591	91	1,443 D	36.8%	61.6%	37.4%	62.6%
DELAWARE	8,754	4,088	4,559	107	471 D	46.7%	52.1%	47.3%	52.7%
DES MOINES	15,675	5,590	9,395	690	3,805 D	35.7%	59.9%	37.3%	62.7%
DICKINSON	4,706	2,074	2,500	132	426 D	44.1%	53.1%	45.3%	54.7%
DUBUQUE	26,999	6,747	19,210	1,042	12,463 D	25.0%	71.2%	26.0%	74.0%
EMMET	4,709	2,129	2,486	94	357 D	45.2%	52.8%	46.1%	53.9%
FAYETTE	13,022	5,166	7,690	166	2,524 D	39.7%	59.1%	40.2%	59.8%
FLOYD	8,781	4,083	4,563	135	480 D	46.5%	52.0%	47.2%	52.8%
FRANKLIN	6,110	2,013	3,782	315	1,769 D	32.9%	61.9%	34.7%	65.3%
FREMONT	6,989	2,339	4,585	65	2,246 D	33.5%	65.6%	33.8%	66.2%
GREENE	5,278	2,360	2,747	171	387 D	44.7%	52.0%	46.2%	53.8%
GRUNDY	6,134	2,419	3,661	54	1,242 D	39.4%	59.7%	39.8%	60.2%
GUTHRIE	5,812	2,637	3,099	76	462 D	45.4%	53.3%	46.0%	54.0%
HAMILTON	7,624	2,330	5,191	103	2,861 D	30.6%	68.1%	31.0%	69.0%
HANCOCK	6,254	2,355	3,822	77	1,467 D	37.7%	61.1%	38.1%	61.9%
HARDIN	9,246	3,523	5,022	701	1,499 D	38.1%	54.3%	41.2%	58.8%
HARRISON	11,008	3,513	7,427	68	3,914 D	31.9%	67.5%	32.1%	67.9%
HENRY	8,074	3,398	4,518	158	1,120 D	42.1%	55.9%	42.9%	57.1%
HOWARD	6,658	2,426	4,176	56	1,750 D	36.4%	62.7%	36.7%	63.3%
HUMBOLDT	4,889	2,028	2,804	57	776 D	41.5%	57.4%	42.0%	58.0%
IDA	5,187	1,452	3,661	74	2,209 D	28.0%	70.6%	28.4%	71.6%
IOWA	7,499	2,628	4,376	495	1,748 D	35.0%	58.4%	37.5%	62.5%
JACKSON	8,499	2,892	5,094	513	2,202 D	34.0%	59.9%	36.2%	63.8%
JASPER	12,401	5,399	6,781	221	1,382 D	43.5%	54.7%	44.3%	55.7%
JEFFERSON	7,110	2,955	4,056	99	1,101 D	41.6%	57.0%	42.1%	57.9%
JOHNSON	14,483	5,484	8,764	235	3,280 D	37.9%	60.5%	38.5%	61.5%
JONES	8,501	3,500	4,952	49	1,452 D	41.2%	58.3%	41.4%	58.6%
KEOKUK	9,369	3,442	5,839	88	2,397 D	36.7%	62.3%	37.1%	62.9%
KOSSUTH	10,148	3,075	6,925	148	3,850 D	30.3%	68.2%	30.8%	69.2%
LEE	17,902	7,084	10,624	194	3,540 D	39.6%	59.3%	40.0%	60.0%
LINN	36,915	18,733	17,693	489	1,040 R	50.7%	47.9%	51.4%	48.6%
LOUISA	4,989	2,045	2,856	88	811 D	41.0%	57.2%	41.7%	58.3%
LUCAS	5,699	2,381	3,434	161	1,053 D	39.8%	60.9%	40.9%	59.1%
LYON	5,297	1,684	3,543	70	1,859 D	31.8%	66.9%	32.2%	67.8%

IOWA

PRESIDENT 1928

County	Total Vote	Republican	Democratic	Other	Rep.-Dem. Plurality	Total Vote Rep.	Total Vote Dem.	Major Vote Rep.	Major Vote Dem.
MADISON	6,542	4,364	2,178		2,186 R	66.7%	33.3%	66.7%	33.3%
MAHASKA	10,568	7,368	3,200		4,168 R	69.7%	30.3%	69.7%	30.3%
MARION	10,338	6,225	4,113		2,112 R	60.2%	39.8%	60.2%	39.8%
MARSHALL	12,710	9,326	3,384		5,942 R	73.4%	26.6%	73.4%	26.6%
MILLS	5,608	3,429	2,179		1,250 R	61.1%	38.9%	61.1%	38.9%
MITCHELL	5,842	3,534	2,308		1,226 R	60.5%	39.5%	60.5%	39.5%
MONONA	6,581	3,745	2,836		909 R	56.9%	43.1%	56.9%	43.1%
MONROE	6,879	4,060	2,819		1,241 R	59.0%	41.0%	59.0%	41.0%
MONTGOMERY	7,234	5,155	2,079		3,076 R	71.3%	28.7%	71.3%	28.7%
MUSCATINE	12,659	8,604	4,055		4,549 R	68.0%	32.0%	68.0%	32.0%
O'BRIEN	7,242	4,845	2,397		2,448 R	66.9%	33.1%	66.9%	33.1%
OSCEOLA	3,652	2,085	1,567		518 R	57.1%	42.9%	57.1%	42.9%
PAGE	9,659	7,181	2,478		4,703 R	74.3%	25.7%	74.3%	25.7%
PALO ALTO	6,306	3,463	2,843		620 R	54.9%	45.1%	54.9%	45.1%
PLYMOUTH	9,863	4,848	5,015		167 D	49.2%	50.8%	49.2%	50.8%
POCAHONTAS	6,146	3,322	2,824		498 R	54.1%	45.9%	54.1%	45.9%
POLK	62,015	42,290	19,725		22,565 R	68.2%	31.8%	68.2%	31.8%
POTTAWATTAMIE	24,259	14,354	9,905		4,449 R	59.2%	40.8%	59.2%	40.8%
POWESHIEK	7,999	5,212	2,787		2,425 R	65.1%	34.8%	65.2%	34.8%
RINGGOLD	5,246	3,674	1,572		2,102 R	70.0%	30.0%	70.0%	30.0%
SAC	6,875	4,461	2,414		2,047 R	64.9%	35.1%	64.9%	35.1%
SCOTT	29,916	16,974	12,942		4,032 R	56.7%	43.3%	56.7%	43.3%
SHELBY	7,063	3,459	3,604		145 D	49.0%	51.0%	49.0%	51.0%
SIOUX	9,217	6,378	2,839		3,539 R	69.2%	30.8%	69.2%	30.8%
STORY	11,749	9,035	2,714		6,321 R	76.9%	23.1%	76.9%	23.1%
TAMA	10,387	5,589	4,798		791 R	53.8%	46.2%	53.8%	46.2%
TAYLOR	6,774	4,700	2,074		2,626 R	69.4%	30.6%	69.4%	30.5%
UNION	8,083	5,432	2,651		2,781 R	67.2%	32.8%	67.2%	32.8%
VAN BUREN	5,848	3,904	1,944		1,960 R	66.8%	33.2%	66.8%	33.2%
WAPELLO	17,379	11,586	5,793		5,793 R	66.7%	33.3%	66.7%	33.3%
WARREN	7,533	5,294	2,239		3,055 R	70.3%	29.7%	70.3%	29.7%
WASHINGTON	8,702	5,948	2,754		3,194 R	68.4%	31.6%	68.4%	31.5%
WAYNE	6,490	3,911	2,579		1,332 R	60.3%	39.7%	60.3%	39.7%
WEBSTER	15,022	8,525	6,497		2,028 R	56.8%	43.2%	56.8%	43.2%
WINNEBAGO	4,654	3,386	1,268		2,118 R	72.8%	27.2%	72.8%	27.2%
WINNESHIEK	9,619	5,084	4,535		549 R	52.9%	47.1%	52.9%	47.1%
WOODBURY	37,418	20,587	16,831		3,756 R	55.0%	45.0%	55.0%	45.0%
WORTH	4,231	2,921	1,310		1,611 R	69.0%	31.0%	69.0%	31.0%
WRIGHT	7,567	5,020	2,547		2,473 R	66.3%	33.7%	66.3%	33.7%
TOTAL	1,009,189	623,570	379,011	6,608	244,559 R	61.8%	37.6%	62.2%	37.8%

PRESIDENT 1932

County	Total Vote	Republican	Democratic	Other	Rep.-Dem. Plurality	Total Vote Rep.	Total Vote Dem.	Major Vote Rep.	Major Vote Dem.
MADISON	5,655	2,563	2,923	69	260 D	47.1%	51.7%	47.7%	52.3%
MAHASKA	10,713	4,555	5,586	472	931 D	43.5%	52.1%	45.5%	54.5%
MARION	11,034	3,595	7,067	272	3,372 D	33.5%	64.0%	34.3%	65.7%
MARSHALL	13,483	6,504	6,385	494	219 R	49.0%	47.4%	50.8%	49.2%
MILLS	6,356	2,420	3,861	75	1,441 D	38.1%	60.7%	38.5%	61.5%
MITCHELL	6,549	2,527	3,940	82	1,413 D	38.6%	60.2%	39.1%	60.9%
MONONA	7,812	2,181	5,537	94	3,356 D	27.9%	70.9%	28.3%	71.7%
MONROE	6,426	2,458	3,716	252	1,258 D	38.3%	57.8%	39.8%	60.2%
MONTGOMERY	7,401	3,507	3,760	134	253 D	47.4%	50.8%	48.3%	51.7%
MUSCATINE	12,917	6,160	6,423	334	263 D	47.7%	49.7%	49.0%	51.0%
O'BRIEN	7,848	3,213	4,503	132	1,290 D	40.9%	57.4%	41.6%	58.4%
OSCEOLA	3,829	1,190	2,590	49	1,400 D	31.1%	67.6%	31.5%	68.5%
PAGE	9,507	4,512	4,863	132	351 D	47.5%	51.2%	48.1%	51.9%
PALO ALTO	6,568	2,378	4,094	96	1,716 D	36.2%	62.3%	36.7%	63.3%
PLYMOUTH	10,563	2,888	7,565	110	4,677 D	27.3%	71.6%	27.6%	72.4%
POCAHONTAS	6,321	1,800	4,245	276	2,445 D	28.5%	67.2%	29.8%	70.2%
POLK	68,672	34,023	31,517	3,132	2,506 R	49.5%	45.9%	51.9%	48.1%
POTTAWATTAMIE	26,616	9,565	16,674	377	7,109 D	35.9%	62.6%	36.5%	63.5%
POWESHIEK	8,355	3,490	4,649	216	1,159 D	41.8%	55.6%	42.9%	57.1%
RINGGOLD	4,823	2,082	2,480	61	398 D	45.0%	53.6%	45.6%	54.4%
SAC	7,369	3,131	4,165	73	1,034 D	42.5%	56.5%	42.9%	57.1%
SCOTT	32,455	14,218	16,887	1,350	2,669 D	43.8%	52.0%	45.7%	54.3%
SHELBY	7,550	2,478	4,940	122	2,462 D	32.9%	65.5%	33.4%	66.6%
SIOUX	10,202	3,943	6,170	89	2,227 D	38.6%	60.5%	39.0%	61.0%
STORY	12,992	6,735	5,638	619	1,097 R	51.8%	43.4%	54.4%	45.6%
TAMA	10,920	4,051	6,704	165	2,653 D	37.1%	61.4%	37.7%	62.3%
TAYLOR	5,924	2,570	3,159	95	489 D	45.8%	53.3%	45.8%	54.2%
UNION	7,083	3,043	3,967	73	924 D	43.0%	56.0%	43.4%	56.6%
VAN BUREN	5,581	2,375	3,135	71	760 D	42.5%	56.2%	43.1%	56.9%
WAPELLO	17,076	7,256	9,504	316	2,248 D	42.5%	55.7%	43.3%	56.7%
WARREN	7,408	3,725	3,542	141	183 R	50.3%	47.8%	51.3%	48.7%
WASHINGTON	8,595	3,889	4,554	152	665 D	45.2%	53.0%	46.1%	53.9%
WAYNE	6,328	2,311	3,896	121	1,585 D	36.5%	61.6%	37.2%	62.8%
WEBSTER	15,022	5,243	8,957	917	3,714 D	34.7%	59.3%	36.9%	63.1%
WINNEBAGO	5,499	2,012	3,281	206	1,269 D	36.6%	59.7%	38.0%	62.0%
WINNESHIEK	10,333	3,348	6,823	162	3,475 D	32.4%	66.0%	32.9%	67.1%
WOODBURY	39,922	12,764	26,397	761	13,633 D	32.0%	66.1%	32.6%	67.4%
WORTH	4,395	1,590	2,640	65	950 D	38.0%	60.1%	39.0%	61.0%
WRIGHT	8,334	3,262	4,922	150	1,660 D	39.1%	59.1%	39.9%	60.1%
TOTAL	1,036,687	414,433	598,019	24,235	183,586 D	40.0%	57.7%	40.9%	59.1%

IOWA

PRESIDENT 1936

County	Total Vote	Republican	Democratic	Other	Rep.-Dem. Plurality	% Total Vote Rep.	% Total Vote Dem.	% Major Vote Rep.	% Major Vote Dem.
ADAIR	6,763	3,436	3,243	84	193 R	50.8%	48.0%	51.4%	48.6%
ADAMS	5,268	2,953	2,249	66	704 R	56.1%	42.7%	56.8%	43.2%
ALLAMAKEE	8,763	4,053	4,327	383	274 D	46.3%	49.4%	48.4%	51.6%
APPANOOSE	12,203	5,511	6,599	93	1,088 D	45.2%	54.1%	45.5%	54.5%
AUDUBON	5,839	2,344	3,448	47	1,104 D	40.1%	59.1%	40.5%	59.5%
BENTON	9,934	4,144	5,606	184	1,462 D	41.7%	56.4%	42.5%	57.5%
BLACK HAWK	31,681	13,666	16,793	1,222	3,127 D	43.1%	53.0%	44.9%	55.1%
BOONE	11,629	4,110	7,080	439	2,970 D	35.3%	60.9%	36.7%	63.3%
BREMER	8,470	3,220	5,058	192	1,838 D	38.0%	59.7%	38.9%	61.1%
BUCHANAN	9,894	4,734	5,025	135	291 D	47.8%	50.8%	48.5%	51.5%
BUENA VISTA	8,785	3,334	5,287	164	1,953 D	38.0%	60.2%	38.7%	61.3%
BUTLER	7,551	3,604	3,786	161	182 D	47.7%	50.1%	48.8%	51.2%
CALHOUN	7,699	3,027	4,544	128	1,517 D	39.3%	59.0%	40.0%	60.0%
CARROLL	10,503	3,259	6,285	959	3,026 D	31.0%	59.8%	34.1%	65.9%
CASS	9,962	5,622	4,284	56	1,338 R	56.4%	43.0%	56.8%	43.2%
CEDAR	8,235	3,686	4,385	164	699 D	44.8%	53.2%	45.7%	54.3%
CERRO GORDO	17,794	7,599	9,694	501	2,095 D	42.7%	54.5%	43.9%	56.1%
CHEROKEE	7,845	2,902	4,716	227	1,814 D	37.0%	60.1%	38.1%	61.9%
CHICKASAW	7,866	3,143	4,458	265	1,315 D	40.0%	56.7%	41.3%	58.7%
CLARKE	5,263	2,571	2,613	79	42 D	48.9%	49.6%	49.6%	50.4%
CLAY	7,586	2,774	4,691	121	1,917 D	36.6%	61.8%	37.2%	62.8%
CLAYTON	12,236	5,017	6,731	488	1,714 D	41.0%	55.0%	42.7%	57.3%
CLINTON	23,042	10,016	12,269	757	2,253 D	43.5%	53.2%	44.9%	55.1%
CRAWFORD	9,502	3,514	5,720	268	2,206 D	37.0%	60.2%	38.1%	61.9%
DALLAS	11,973	5,442	6,341	190	899 D	45.5%	53.0%	46.2%	53.8%
DAVIS	6,313	2,815	3,463	35	648 D	44.6%	54.9%	44.8%	55.2%
DECATUR	7,494	3,327	4,131	36	804 D	44.4%	55.1%	44.6%	55.4%
DELAWARE	9,046	4,483	4,350	213	133 R	49.6%	48.1%	50.8%	49.2%
DES MOINES	15,705	6,763	7,011	1,931	248 D	43.1%	44.6%	49.1%	50.9%
DICKINSON	5,791	2,322	3,399	70	1,077 D	40.1%	58.7%	40.6%	59.4%
DUBUQUE	27,378	8,275	16,291	2,812	8,016 D	30.2%	59.5%	33.7%	66.3%
EMMET	5,645	2,362	3,158	125	796 D	41.8%	55.9%	42.8%	57.2%
FAYETTE	13,397	5,891	7,210	296	1,319 D	44.0%	53.8%	45.0%	55.0%
FLOYD	9,031	4,267	4,242	522	25 R	47.2%	47.0%	50.1%	49.9%
FRANKLIN	6,705	2,530	3,993	182	1,463 D	37.7%	59.6%	38.8%	61.2%
FREMONT	7,617	3,291	4,301	25	1,010 D	43.2%	56.5%	43.3%	56.7%
GREENE	7,559	3,384	3,961	214	577 D	44.8%	52.4%	46.1%	53.9%
GRUNDY	6,703	2,656	3,918	129	1,262 D	39.6%	58.5%	40.4%	59.6%
GUTHRIE	8,070	4,155	3,542	373	613 R	51.5%	43.9%	54.0%	46.0%
HAMILTON	8,758	3,174	5,432	152	2,258 D	36.2%	62.0%	36.9%	63.1%
HANCOCK	6,629	2,585	3,930	114	1,345 D	39.0%	59.3%	39.7%	60.3%
HARDIN	9,933	4,306	5,429	198	1,123 D	43.4%	54.7%	44.2%	55.8%
HARRISON	11,678	5,314	6,206	158	892 D	45.5%	53.1%	46.1%	53.9%
HENRY	8,271	4,480	3,542	249	938 R	54.2%	42.8%	55.8%	44.2%
HOWARD	7,098	2,947	3,861	290	914 D	41.5%	54.4%	43.3%	56.7%
HUMBOLDT	5,797	2,262	3,420	115	1,158 D	39.0%	59.0%	39.8%	60.2%
IDA	5,333	1,834	3,397	102	1,563 D	34.4%	63.7%	35.1%	64.9%
IOWA	7,712	3,360	4,163	189	803 D	43.6%	54.0%	44.7%	55.3%
JACKSON	8,823	3,581	4,889	353	1,308 D	40.6%	55.4%	42.3%	57.7%
JASPER	14,395	5,875	8,315	205	2,440 D	40.8%	57.8%	41.4%	58.6%
JEFFERSON	7,941	4,037	3,690	214	347 R	50.8%	46.5%	52.2%	47.8%
JOHNSON	14,743	5,629	8,794	320	3,165 D	38.2%	59.6%	39.0%	61.0%
JONES	9,356	4,141	5,052	163	911 D	44.3%	54.0%	45.0%	55.0%
KEOKUK	9,878	4,491	5,162	225	671 D	45.5%	52.3%	46.5%	53.5%
KOSSUTH	11,863	3,569	8,071	223	4,502 D	30.1%	68.0%	30.7%	69.3%
LEE	19,317	8,955	9,630	732	675 D	46.4%	49.9%	48.2%	51.8%
LINN	39,806	19,129	19,724	953	595 D	48.1%	49.6%	49.2%	50.8%
LOUISA	5,615	2,655	2,859	101	204 D	47.3%	50.9%	48.2%	51.8%
LUCAS	7,382	3,414	3,773	195	359 D	46.2%	51.1%	47.5%	52.5%
LYON	5,944	2,264	3,590	90	1,326 D	38.1%	60.4%	38.7%	61.3%

PRESIDENT 1940

County	Total Vote	Republican	Democratic	Other	Rep.-Dem. Plurality	% Total Vote Rep.	% Total Vote Dem.	% Major Vote Rep.	% Major Vote Dem.
ADAIR	6,648	3,907	2,734	7	1,173 R	58.8%	41.1%	58.8%	41.2%
ADAMS	5,292	3,182	2,088	22	1,094 R	60.1%	39.5%	60.4%	39.6%
ALLAMAKEE	9,122	5,840	3,258	24	2,582 R	64.0%	35.7%	64.2%	35.8%
APPANOOSE	12,202	6,032	6,069	101	37 D	49.4%	49.7%	49.8%	50.2%
AUDUBON	5,875	2,632	3,236	7	604 D	44.8%	55.1%	44.9%	55.1%
BENTON	10,693	5,298	5,363	32	65 D	49.5%	50.2%	49.7%	50.3%
BLACK HAWK	34,532	17,132	17,305	95	173 D	49.6%	50.1%	49.7%	50.3%
BOONE	12,469	5,227	7,168	74	1,941 D	41.9%	57.5%	42.2%	57.8%
BREMER	8,495	5,374	3,103	18	2,271 R	63.3%	36.5%	63.4%	36.6%
BUCHANAN	10,309	5,630	4,649	30	981 R	54.6%	45.1%	54.8%	45.2%
BUENA VISTA	9,399	4,576	4,784	39	208 D	48.7%	50.9%	48.9%	51.1%
BUTLER	7,628	4,848	2,760	20	2,088 R	63.6%	36.2%	63.7%	36.3%
CALHOUN	8,161	3,792	4,344	25	552 D	46.5%	53.2%	46.6%	53.4%
CARROLL	10,923	5,376	5,526	21	150 D	49.2%	50.6%	49.3%	50.7%
CASS	10,172	6,377	3,763	32	2,614 R	62.7%	37.0%	62.9%	37.1%
CEDAR	8,840	5,521	3,293	26	2,228 R	62.5%	37.3%	62.6%	37.4%
CERRO GORDO	20,612	9,728	10,839	45	1,111 D	47.2%	52.6%	47.3%	52.7%
CHEROKEE	8,332	4,458	3,855	19	603 R	53.5%	46.3%	53.6%	46.4%
CHICKASAW	8,423	4,440	3,981	2	459 R	52.7%	47.3%	52.7%	47.3%
CLARKE	5,510	2,962	2,513	35	449 R	53.8%	45.6%	54.1%	45.9%
CLAY	8,025	3,673	4,328	24	655 D	45.8%	53.9%	45.9%	54.1%
CLAYTON	12,434	7,443	4,973	18	2,470 R	59.9%	40.0%	59.9%	40.1%
CLINTON	22,449	12,177	10,251	50	1,926 R	54.2%	45.7%	54.3%	45.7%
CRAWFORD	9,449	5,284	4,130	35	1,154 R	55.9%	43.7%	56.1%	43.9%
DALLAS	12,628	6,218	6,279	131	61 D	49.2%	49.7%	49.8%	50.2%
DAVIS	6,377	2,975	3,374	28	399 D	46.7%	52.9%	46.9%	53.1%
DECATUR	7,448	3,494	3,938	16	444 D	46.9%	52.9%	47.0%	53.0%
DELAWARE	9,176	6,175	2,985	16	3,190 R	67.3%	32.5%	67.4%	32.6%
DES MOINES	17,625	10,988	6,578	59	4,410 R	62.3%	37.3%	62.5%	37.4%
DICKINSON	5,742	2,736	2,985	21	249 D	47.6%	52.0%	47.8%	52.2%
DUBUQUE	28,441	14,590	13,805	46	785 R	51.3%	48.5%	51.4%	48.5%
EMMET	6,197	3,053	3,097	47	44 D	49.3%	50.0%	49.6%	50.4%
FAYETTE	14,342	8,237	6,066	39	2,171 R	57.4%	42.3%	57.6%	42.4%
FLOYD	10,031	5,829	4,167	35	1,662 R	58.1%	41.5%	58.3%	41.7%
FRANKLIN	7,310	3,623	3,540	147	83 R	49.6%	48.4%	50.6%	49.4%
FREMONT	7,764	3,825	3,914	25	89 D	49.3%	50.4%	49.4%	50.6%
GREENE	7,506	3,920	3,566	20	354 R	52.2%	47.5%	52.4%	47.6%
GRUNDY	6,674	3,908	2,745	21	1,163 R	58.6%	41.1%	58.7%	41.3%
GUTHRIE	8,255	4,733	3,489	33	1,244 R	57.3%	42.3%	57.6%	42.4%
HAMILTON	9,501	4,183	5,279	39	1,096 D	44.0%	55.6%	44.2%	55.8%
HANCOCK	7,173	3,632	3,514	27	118 R	50.6%	49.0%	50.8%	49.2%
HARDIN	10,491	5,692	4,764	35	928 R	54.3%	45.4%	54.4%	45.6%
HARRISON	11,428	6,094	5,317	17	777 R	53.3%	46.5%	53.4%	46.6%
HENRY	8,749	5,893	2,837	19	3,056 R	67.3%	32.4%	67.5%	32.5%
HOWARD	7,405	3,714	3,675	16	39 R	50.2%	49.6%	50.3%	49.7%
HUMBOLDT	6,143	2,853	3,268	22	415 D	46.4%	53.2%	46.6%	53.4%
IDA	5,487	3,166	2,306	15	860 R	57.7%	42.0%	57.9%	42.1%
IOWA	8,488	4,696	3,649	143	1,047 R	55.3%	43.0%	56.3%	43.7%
JACKSON	9,661	5,417	4,218	26	1,199 R	56.1%	43.7%	56.2%	43.8%
JASPER	15,421	7,240	8,129	52	889 D	46.9%	52.7%	47.1%	52.9%
JEFFERSON	8,336	4,891	3,402	43	1,489 R	58.7%	40.8%	59.0%	41.0%
JOHNSON	16,278	7,206	9,017	55	1,811 D	44.3%	55.4%	44.4%	55.6%
JONES	9,929	5,630	4,273	26	1,357 R	56.7%	43.0%	56.9%	43.1%
KEOKUK	9,988	5,394	4,552	42	842 R	54.0%	45.6%	54.2%	45.8%
KOSSUTH	12,165	5,639	6,502	24	863 D	46.4%	53.4%	46.4%	53.6%
LEE	19,766	10,616	9,117	33	1,499 R	53.7%	46.1%	53.8%	46.2%
LINN	43,235	23,581	19,531	123	4,050 R	54.5%	45.2%	54.7%	45.3%
LOUISA	5,627	3,330	2,247	50	1,083 R	59.2%	39.9%	59.7%	40.3%
LUCAS	7,149	3,806	3,255	88	551 R	53.2%	45.5%	53.9%	46.1%
LYON	6,540	3,880	2,648	12	1,232 R	59.3%	40.5%	59.4%	40.6%

IOWA

PRESIDENT 1936

County	Total Vote	Republican	Democratic	Other	Rep.-Dem. Plurality	Total Vote Rep.	Total Vote Dem.	Major Vote Rep.	Major Vote Dem.
MADISON	7,609	4,188	3,365	56	823 R	55.0%	44.2%	55.4%	44.6%
MAHASKA	11,726	5,270	6,094	362	824 D	44.9%	52.0%	46.4%	53.6%
MARION	11,986	4,975	6,745	266	1,770 D	41.5%	56.3%	42.4%	57.6%
MARSHALL	14,008	7,377	6,297	334	1,080 R	52.7%	45.0%	53.9%	46.1%
MILLS	7,075	3,424	3,610	41	186 D	48.4%	51.0%	48.7%	51.3%
MITCHELL	6,603	2,765	3,610	228	845 D	41.9%	54.7%	43.4%	56.6%
MONONA	8,500	3,008	5,346	146	2,338 D	35.4%	62.9%	36.0%	64.0%
MONROE	7,461	3,001	4,205	255	1,204 D	40.2%	56.4%	41.6%	58.4%
MONTGOMERY	8,386	4,395	3,920	71	475 R	52.4%	46.7%	52.9%	47.1%
MUSCATINE	13,313	6,332	6,593	388	261 D	47.6%	49.5%	49.0%	51.0%
O'BRIEN	8,612	3,350	5,139	123	1,789 D	38.9%	59.7%	39.5%	60.5%
OSCEOLA	4,453	1,539	2,812	102	1,273 D	34.6%	63.1%	35.4%	64.6%
PAGE	11,323	6,624	4,646	53	1,978 R	58.5%	41.0%	58.8%	41.2%
PALO ALTO	7,333	2,613	4,515	205	1,902 D	35.6%	61.6%	36.7%	63.3%
PLYMOUTH	11,445	4,133	5,994	1,318	1,861 D	36.1%	52.4%	40.8%	59.2%
POCAHONTAS	6,819	2,277	4,357	185	2,080 D	33.4%	63.9%	34.3%	65.7%
POLK	79,460	33,819	44,274	1,367	10,455 D	42.6%	55.7%	43.3%	56.7%
POTTAWATTAMIE	28,913	12,223	16,259	431	4,036 D	42.3%	56.2%	42.9%	57.1%
POWESHIEK	8,996	4,037	4,745	214	708 D	44.9%	52.7%	46.0%	54.0%
RINGGOLD	5,995	3,316	2,615	64	701 R	55.3%	43.6%	55.9%	44.1%
SAC	8,023	3,437	4,472	114	1,035 D	42.8%	55.7%	43.5%	56.5%
SCOTT	34,145	12,691	20,737	717	8,046 D	37.2%	60.7%	38.0%	62.0%
SHELBY	8,231	3,490	4,264	477	774 D	42.4%	51.8%	45.0%	55.0%
SIOUX	10,669	4,543	5,553	573	1,010 D	42.6%	52.0%	45.0%	55.0%
STORY	13,588	6,358	6,933	297	575 D	46.8%	51.0%	47.8%	52.2%
TAMA	11,522	4,737	6,625	160	1,888 D	41.1%	57.5%	41.7%	58.3%
TAYLOR	7,545	4,145	3,337	63	808 R	54.9%	44.2%	55.4%	44.6%
UNION	8,699	4,647	3,938	114	709 R	53.4%	45.3%	54.1%	45.9%
VAN BUREN	6,422	3,535	2,804	83	731 R	55.0%	43.7%	55.8%	44.2%
WAPELLO	18,512	7,647	10,578	287	2,931 D	41.3%	57.1%	42.0%	58.0%
WARREN	8,805	4,642	4,011	152	631 R	52.7%	45.5%	53.6%	46.4%
WASHINGTON	9,118	4,619	4,379	120	240 R	50.7%	48.0%	51.3%	48.7%
WAYNE	7,452	3,609	3,778	65	169 D	48.4%	50.7%	48.8%	51.2%
WEBSTER	17,174	6,494	9,885	795	3,391 D	37.8%	57.6%	39.6%	60.4%
WINNEBAGO	5,927	2,592	3,133	202	541 D	43.7%	52.9%	45.3%	54.7%
WINNESHIEK	11,181	4,489	5,980	712	1,491 D	40.1%	53.5%	42.9%	57.1%
WOODBURY	43,002	14,157	26,847	1,998	12,690 D	32.9%	62.4%	34.5%	65.5%
WORTH	4,984	1,964	2,976	44	1,012 D	39.4%	59.7%	39.8%	60.2%
WRIGHT	8,710	3,311	5,177	222	1,866 D	38.0%	59.4%	39.0%	61.0%
TOTAL	1,142,737	487,977	621,756	33,004	133,779 D	42.7%	54.4%	44.0%	56.0%

PRESIDENT 1940

County	Total Vote	Republican	Democratic	Other	Rep.-Dem. Plurality	Total Vote Rep.	Total Vote Dem.	Major Vote Rep.	Major Vote Dem.
MADISON	7,600	4,477	3,094	29	1,383 R	58.9%	40.7%	59.1%	40.9%
MAHASKA	11,977	6,123	5,757	97	366 R	51.1%	48.1%	51.5%	48.5%
MARION	12,753	5,763	6,915	75	1,152 D	45.2%	54.2%	45.5%	54.5%
MARSHALL	15,065	8,503	6,497	65	2,006 R	56.4%	43.1%	56.7%	43.3%
MILLS	6,749	3,873	2,862	14	1,011 R	57.4%	42.4%	57.5%	42.5%
MITCHELL	6,987	3,947	3,025	15	922 R	56.5%	43.3%	56.6%	43.4%
MONONA	8,990	4,192	4,783	15	591 D	46.6%	53.2%	46.7%	53.3%
MONROE	7,336	3,270	3,994	72	724 D	44.6%	54.4%	45.0%	55.0%
MONTGOMERY	8,220	4,848	3,332	40	1,516 R	59.0%	40.5%	59.3%	40.7%
MUSCATINE	14,421	8,543	5,825	53	2,718 R	59.2%	40.4%	59.5%	40.5%
O'BRIEN	8,931	4,760	4,133	38	627 R	53.3%	46.3%	53.5%	46.5%
OSCEOLA	4,742	2,425	2,288	29	137 R	51.1%	48.2%	51.5%	48.5%
PAGE	11,566	7,407	4,102	57	3,305 R	64.0%	35.5%	64.4%	35.6%
PALO ALTO	7,822	3,322	4,482	18	1,160 D	42.5%	57.3%	42.6%	57.4%
PLYMOUTH	11,579	7,725	3,831	23	3,894 R	66.7%	33.1%	66.8%	33.2%
POCAHONTAS	7,121	2,985	4,118	18	1,133 D	41.9%	57.8%	42.0%	58.0%
POLK	93,193	41,245	51,647	301	10,402 D	44.3%	55.4%	44.4%	55.6%
POTTAWATTAMIE	31,188	15,929	15,221	38	708 R	51.1%	48.8%	51.1%	48.9%
POWESHIEK	9,611	4,773	4,794	44	21 D	49.7%	49.9%	49.9%	50.1%
RINGGOLD	5,894	3,507	2,374	13	1,133 R	59.5%	40.3%	59.6%	40.4%
SAC	8,121	4,358	3,754	9	604 R	53.7%	46.2%	53.7%	46.3%
SCOTT	39,630	18,504	20,996	130	2,492 D	46.7%	53.0%	46.8%	53.2%
SHELBY	8,460	4,613	3,811	36	802 R	54.5%	45.0%	54.8%	45.2%
SIOUX	11,750	7,585	4,144	21	3,441 R	64.6%	35.3%	64.7%	35.3%
STORY	15,070	7,853	7,152	65	701 R	52.1%	47.5%	52.3%	47.7%
TAMA	11,893	5,865	5,996	32	131 D	49.3%	50.4%	49.4%	50.6%
TAYLOR	7,421	4,420	2,976	25	1,444 R	59.6%	40.1%	59.8%	40.2%
UNION	8,668	5,421	3,229	18	2,192 R	62.5%	37.3%	62.7%	37.3%
VAN BUREN	6,550	4,108	2,416	26	1,692 R	62.7%	36.9%	63.0%	37.0%
WAPELLO	21,006	9,039	11,880	87	2,841 D	43.0%	56.6%	43.2%	56.8%
WARREN	8,923	5,016	3,856	51	1,160 R	56.2%	43.2%	56.5%	43.5%
WASHINGTON	9,721	5,649	4,030	42	1,619 R	58.1%	41.5%	58.4%	41.6%
WAYNE	7,401	3,748	3,625	28	123 R	50.6%	49.0%	50.8%	49.2%
WEBSTER	18,366	7,583	10,731	52	3,148 D	41.3%	58.4%	41.4%	58.6%
WINNEBAGO	6,388	3,308	3,051	29	257 R	51.8%	47.8%	52.0%	48.0%
WINNESHIEK	11,637	6,208	5,405	24	803 R	53.3%	46.4%	53.5%	46.5%
WOODBURY	47,378	22,632	24,457	89	1,825 D	48.2%	51.6%	48.3%	51.7%
WORTH	5,455	2,434	3,007	14	573 D	44.6%	55.1%	44.7%	55.3%
WRIGHT	9,350	4,443	4,871	36	428 D	47.5%	52.1%	47.7%	52.3%
TOTAL	1,215,432	632,370	578,802	4,260	53,568 R	52.0%	47.6%	52.2%	47.8%

IOWA

PRESIDENT 1944

County	Total Vote	Republican	Democratic	Other	Rep.-Dem. Plurality	%TV Rep.	%TV Dem.	%MV Rep.	%MV Dem.
ADAIR	5,743	3,428	2,297	18	1,131 R	59.7	40.0	59.9	40.1
ADAMS	4,413	2,540	1,868	5	672 R	57.6	42.3	57.6	42.4
ALLAMAKEE	7,929	5,017	2,893	19	2,124 R	63.3	36.5	63.4	36.6
APPANOOSE	10,020	4,928	5,015	77	87 D	49.2	50.0	49.6	50.4
AUDUBON	5,447	2,346	3,094	7	748 D	43.1	56.8	43.1	56.9
BENTON	9,039	4,378	4,619	42	241 D	48.4	51.1	48.7	51.3
BLACK HAWK	32,434	15,687	16,593	154	906 D	48.4	51.2	48.6	51.4
BOONE	11,003	4,868	6,062	73	1,194 D	44.2	55.1	44.5	55.5
BREMER	7,642	4,861	2,764	17	2,097 R	63.6	36.2	63.8	36.2
BUCHANAN	8,508	4,653	3,841	14	812 R	54.7	45.1	54.8	45.2
BUENA VISTA	8,309	3,993	4,277	39	284 D	48.1	51.5	48.3	51.7
BUTLER	6,431	4,182	2,225	24	1,957 R	65.0	34.6	65.3	34.7
CALHOUN	6,946	3,375	3,544	27	169 D	48.6	51.0	48.8	51.2
CARROLL	9,659	4,833	4,799	27	34 R	50.0	49.7	50.2	49.8
CASS	8,561	5,610	2,928	23	2,682 R	65.5	34.2	65.7	34.3
CEDAR	7,307	4,673	2,610	24	2,063 R	64.0	35.7	64.2	35.8
CERRO GORDO	17,459	8,311	9,088	60	777 D	47.6	52.0	47.8	52.2
CHEROKEE	6,949	3,723	3,197	29	526 R	53.6	46.0	53.8	46.2
CHICKASAW	6,929	3,575	3,328	26	247 R	51.6	48.0	51.8	48.2
CLARKE	4,584	2,603	1,946	35	657 R	56.8	42.5	57.2	42.8
CLAY	6,724	3,055	3,639	30	584 D	45.4	54.1	45.6	54.4
CLAYTON	10,163	5,855	4,259	49	1,596 R	57.6	41.9	57.9	42.1
CLINTON	19,624	11,533	8,028	63	3,505 R	58.8	40.9	59.0	41.0
CRAWFORD	7,509	4,242	3,218	49	1,024 R	56.5	42.9	56.9	43.1
DALLAS	10,864	5,413	5,316	135	97 R	49.8	48.9	50.5	49.5
DAVIS	5,318	2,559	2,727	32	168 D	48.1	51.3	48.4	51.6
DECATUR	6,268	2,934	3,316	18	382 D	46.8	52.9	46.9	53.1
DELAWARE	7,682	5,164	2,498	20	2,666 R	67.2	32.5	67.4	32.6
DES MOINES	17,177	9,488	7,543	146	1,945 R	55.2	43.9	55.7	44.3
DICKINSON	4,627	2,133	2,473	21	340 D	46.1	53.4	46.3	53.7
DUBUQUE	25,458	12,502	12,867	89	365 D	49.1	50.5	49.3	50.7
EMMET	5,286	2,668	2,577	41	91 R	50.5	48.8	50.9	49.1
FAYETTE	11,846	6,693	5,105	48	1,588 R	56.5	43.1	56.7	43.3
FLOYD	8,731	5,248	3,446	37	1,802 R	60.1	39.5	60.4	39.6
FRANKLIN	6,062	3,150	2,851	61	299 R	52.0	47.0	52.5	47.5
FREMONT	5,877	3,113	2,747	17	366 R	53.0	46.7	53.1	46.9
GREENE	6,263	3,437	2,797	29	640 R	54.9	44.7	55.1	44.9
GRUNDY	5,834	3,625	2,191	18	1,434 R	62.1	37.6	62.3	37.7
GUTHRIE	6,977	4,042	2,899	36	1,143 R	57.9	41.6	58.2	41.8
HAMILTON	8,180	3,837	4,302	41	465 D	46.9	52.6	47.1	52.9
HANCOCK	6,003	3,114	2,855	34	259 R	51.9	47.6	52.2	47.8
HARDIN	9,094	5,059	3,975	60	1,084 R	55.6	43.7	56.0	44.0
HARRISON	9,309	5,059	4,201	49	858 R	54.3	45.1	54.6	45.4
HENRY	7,998	5,208	2,741	49	2,467 R	65.1	34.3	65.5	34.5
HOWARD	6,114	2,961	3,132	21	171 D	48.4	51.2	48.6	51.4
HUMBOLDT	5,290	2,525	2,749	16	224 D	47.7	52.0	47.9	52.1
IDA	4,601	2,640	1,943	18	697 R	57.4	42.2	57.6	42.4
IOWA	7,340	3,959	3,119	262	840 R	53.9	42.5	55.9	44.1
JACKSON	7,886	4,341	3,537	88	804 R	55.0	44.9	55.1	44.9
JASPER	13,479	6,413	6,978	88	565 D	47.6	51.8	47.9	52.1
JEFFERSON	7,344	4,335	2,926	83	1,409 R	59.0	39.8	59.7	40.3
JOHNSON	14,897	6,396	8,434	67	2,038 D	42.9	56.6	43.1	56.9
JONES	8,032	4,453	3,563	16	890 R	55.4	44.4	55.5	44.5
KEOKUK	8,606	4,644	3,900	62	744 R	54.0	45.3	54.4	45.6
KOSSUTH	10,433	4,918	5,488	27	570 D	47.1	52.6	47.3	52.7
LEE	17,736	9,406	8,252	78	1,154 R	53.0	46.5	53.3	46.7
LINN	42,562	21,293	21,123	146	170 R	50.0	49.6	50.2	49.8
LOUISA	4,679	2,745	1,894	40	851 R	58.7	40.5	59.2	40.8
LUCAS	5,713	3,139	2,526	48	613 R	54.9	44.2	55.3	44.7
LYON	5,042	3,065	1,970	7	1,095 R	60.8	39.1	60.9	39.1

PRESIDENT 1948

County	Total Vote	Republican	Democratic	Other	Rep.-Dem. Plurality	%TV Rep.	%TV Dem.	%MV Rep.	%MV Dem.
ADAIR	5,523	2,879	2,567	77	312 R	52.1	46.5	52.9	47.1
ADAMS	4,012	2,142	1,817	53	325 R	53.4	45.3	54.1	45.9
ALLAMAKEE	7,726	4,474	3,172	80	1,302 R	57.9	41.1	58.5	41.5
APPANOOSE	9,296	4,078	4,998	220	920 D	43.9	53.8	44.9	55.1
AUDUBON	5,153	2,177	2,840	136	663 D	42.2	55.1	43.4	56.6
BENTON	8,367	3,770	4,209	388	439 D	45.1	50.3	47.2	52.8
BLACK HAWK	36,230	16,041	19,603	586	3,562 D	44.3	54.1	45.0	55.0
BOONE	10,222	4,183	5,541	498	1,358 D	40.9	54.2	43.0	57.0
BREMER	7,433	3,837	3,502	94	335 R	51.6	47.1	52.3	47.7
BUCHANAN	8,523	4,310	4,127	86	183 R	50.6	48.4	51.1	48.9
BUENA VISTA	8,493	3,959	4,340	194	381 D	46.6	51.1	47.7	52.3
BUTLER	6,513	3,380	3,008	125	372 R	51.9	46.2	52.9	47.1
CALHOUN	6,398	3,083	3,164	151	81 D	48.2	49.5	49.4	50.6
CARROLL	9,786	3,974	5,711	101	1,737 D	40.6	58.4	41.0	59.0
CASS	8,559	5,106	3,372	81	1,734 R	59.7	39.4	60.2	39.8
CEDAR	7,016	3,957	2,958	101	999 R	56.4	42.2	57.2	42.8
CERRO GORDO	17,592	7,840	9,544	208	1,704 D	44.6	54.3	45.1	54.9
CHEROKEE	7,144	3,318	3,739	87	421 D	46.4	52.3	47.0	53.0
CHICKASAW	7,589	3,449	4,071	69	622 D	45.4	53.6	45.9	54.1
CLARKE	4,379	2,195	2,101	83	94 R	50.1	48.0	51.1	48.9
CLAY	6,961	3,036	3,649	276	613 D	43.6	52.4	45.4	54.6
CLAYTON	10,111	5,151	4,857	103	294 R	50.9	48.0	51.5	48.5
CLINTON	18,665	9,859	8,534	272	1,325 R	52.8	45.7	53.6	46.4
CRAWFORD	7,485	3,267	3,983	235	716 D	43.6	53.2	45.1	54.9
DALLAS	10,819	4,810	5,661	348	851 D	44.5	52.3	45.9	54.1
DAVIS	5,305	2,276	2,982	47	706 D	42.9	56.2	43.3	56.7
DECATUR	5,803	2,547	3,172	84	625 D	43.9	54.7	44.5	55.5
DELAWARE	7,498	4,555	2,876	67	1,679 R	60.7	38.4	61.3	38.7
DES MOINES	16,729	7,621	8,792	316	1,171 D	45.6	52.6	46.4	53.6
DICKINSON	4,766	2,304	2,324	138	20 D	48.3	48.8	49.8	50.2
DUBUQUE	25,913	10,111	15,521	281	5,410 D	39.0	59.9	39.4	60.6
EMMET	5,313	2,464	2,752	97	288 D	46.4	51.8	47.2	52.8
FAYETTE	11,760	6,296	5,303	161	993 R	53.5	45.1	54.3	45.7
FLOYD	10,648	4,644	5,839	165	1,195 D	43.6	54.8	44.3	55.7
FRANKLIN	6,021	2,716	2,871	434	155 D	45.1	47.7	48.6	51.4
FREMONT	5,378	2,698	2,637	43	61 R	50.2	49.0	50.6	49.4
GREENE	6,290	3,059	2,946	285	113 R	48.6	46.8	50.9	49.1
GRUNDY	5,647	3,154	2,344	149	810 R	55.9	41.5	57.4	42.6
GUTHRIE	6,891	3,389	3,392	110	3 D	49.2	49.2	50.0	50.0
HAMILTON	7,345	3,535	3,613	197	78 D	48.1	49.2	49.5	50.5
HANCOCK	6,051	2,802	3,096	153	294 D	46.3	51.2	47.5	52.5
HARDIN	8,854	4,553	4,023	278	530 R	51.4	45.4	53.1	46.9
HARRISON	9,016	4,341	4,608	67	267 D	48.1	51.1	48.5	51.5
HENRY	7,805	4,620	3,042	143	1,578 R	59.2	39.0	60.3	39.7
HOWARD	6,090	2,630	3,378	82	748 D	43.2	55.5	43.8	56.2
HUMBOLDT	5,432	2,498	2,855	79	357 D	46.0	52.6	46.7	53.3
IDA	4,698	2,257	2,365	76	108 D	48.0	50.3	48.8	51.2
IOWA	6,978	3,659	3,030	289	629 R	52.4	43.4	54.7	45.3
JACKSON	7,005	3,597	3,263	145	334 R	51.3	46.6	52.4	47.6
JASPER	12,786	5,710	6,684	392	974 D	44.7	52.3	46.1	53.9
JEFFERSON	7,088	3,906	3,033	149	873 R	55.1	42.8	56.3	43.7
JOHNSON	16,303	7,139	8,611	553	1,472 D	43.8	52.8	45.3	54.7
JONES	8,322	4,290	3,915	117	375 R	51.6	47.0	52.3	47.7
KEOKUK	8,475	4,201	4,118	156	83 R	49.6	48.6	50.5	49.5
KOSSUTH	10,353	4,186	6,039	128	1,853 D	40.4	58.3	40.9	59.1
LEE	17,212	7,801	9,201	210	1,400 D	45.3	53.5	45.9	54.1
LINN	43,098	20,881	20,995	1,222	114 D	48.5	48.7	49.9	50.1
LOUISA	4,429	2,420	1,945	64	475 R	54.6	43.9	55.4	44.6
LUCAS	5,475	2,656	2,697	122	41 D	48.5	49.3	49.6	50.4
LYON	4,740	2,500	2,174	66	326 R	52.7	45.9	53.5	46.5

IOWA

PRESIDENT 1944

County	Total Vote	Republican	Democratic	Other	Rep.-Dem. Plurality	Total Vote Rep.	Total Vote Dem.	Major Vote Rep.	Major Vote Dem.
MADISON	5,313	3,737	2,550	26	1,187 R	55.2%	40.4%	59.4%	40.6%
MAHASKA	10,072	5,123	4,652	297	471 R	50.9%	46.2%	52.4%	47.6%
MARION	11,338	4,874	6,365	99	1,491 D	43.0%	56.6%	43.4%	56.6%
MARSHALL	13,157	7,325	5,598	234	1,727 R	55.7%	42.5%	56.7%	43.3%
MILLS	5,421	3,288	2,106	27	1,182 R	60.7%	38.8%	61.0%	39.0%
MITCHELL	6,132	3,406	2,696	30	710 R	55.5%	44.0%	55.8%	44.2%
MONONA	7,366	3,583	3,761	22	178 D	48.6%	51.1%	48.8%	51.2%
MONROE	5,929	2,625	3,258	46	633 D	44.3%	55.0%	44.6%	55.4%
MONTGOMERY	6,783	4,165	2,572	46	1,593 R	61.4%	37.9%	61.8%	38.2%
MUSCATINE	11,963	7,104	4,801	58	2,303 R	59.4%	40.1%	59.7%	40.3%
O'BRIEN	7,201	4,033	3,138	30	895 R	56.0%	43.6%	56.2%	43.8%
OSCEOLA	3,798	2,100	1,689	9	411 R	55.3%	44.5%	55.4%	44.6%
PAGE	9,682	6,300	3,297	85	3,003 R	65.1%	34.1%	65.6%	34.4%
PALO ALTO	6,533	2,772	3,726	35	954 D	42.4%	57.0%	42.7%	57.3%
PLYMOUTH	9,076	6,085	2,970	21	3,115 R	67.0%	32.7%	67.2%	32.8%
POCAHONTAS	6,199	2,600	3,577	22	977 D	41.9%	57.7%	42.1%	57.9%
POLK	83,118	36,629	46,072	417	9,443 D	44.1%	55.4%	44.3%	55.7%
POTTAWATTAMIE	25,818	14,007	11,752	59	2,255 R	54.3%	45.5%	54.4%	45.6%
POWESHIEK	8,461	4,186	4,234	41	48 D	49.5%	50.0%	49.7%	50.3%
RINGGOLD	4,662	2,767	1,867	28	900 R	59.4%	40.0%	59.7%	40.3%
SAC	7,030	3,770	3,223	37	547 R	53.6%	45.8%	53.9%	46.1%
SCOTT	37,081	18,015	18,962	104	947 D	48.6%	51.1%	48.7%	51.3%
SHELBY	6,933	3,873	2,978	82	895 R	55.9%	43.0%	56.5%	43.5%
SIOUX	9,940	6,552	3,369	19	3,183 R	65.9%	33.9%	66.0%	34.0%
STORY	13,818	7,163	6,554	101	609 R	51.8%	47.4%	52.2%	47.8%
TAMA	10,567	5,249	5,286	32	37 D	49.7%	50.0%	49.8%	50.2%
TAYLOR	6,200	3,804	2,376	20	1,428 R	61.4%	38.3%	61.5%	38.5%
UNION	7,450	4,566	2,861	23	1,705 R	61.3%	38.4%	61.5%	38.5%
VAN BUREN	5,122	3,095	1,997	30	1,398 R	60.4%	39.0%	60.8%	39.2%
WAPELLO	19,089	8,244	10,732	113	2,488 D	43.2%	56.2%	43.4%	56.6%
WARREN	7,641	4,266	3,319	56	947 R	55.8%	43.4%	56.2%	43.8%
WASHINGTON	8,763	5,308	3,423	32	1,885 R	60.6%	39.1%	60.8%	39.2%
WAYNE	6,158	3,098	3,025	35	73 R	50.3%	49.1%	50.6%	49.4%
WEBSTER	16,468	6,935	9,477	56	2,542 D	42.1%	57.5%	42.3%	57.7%
WINNEBAGO	5,480	2,808	2,654	18	154 R	51.2%	48.4%	51.4%	48.6%
WINNESHIEK	9,893	5,318	4,557	18	761 R	53.8%	46.1%	53.9%	46.1%
WOODBURY	39,096	18,544	20,448	104	1,904 D	47.4%	52.3%	47.6%	52.4%
WORTH	4,725	2,086	2,629	10	543 D	44.1%	55.6%	44.2%	55.8%
WRIGHT	8,183	3,916	4,232	35	316 D	47.9%	51.7%	48.1%	51.9%
TOTAL	1,052,599	547,267	499,876	5,456	47,391 R	52.0%	47.5%	52.3%	47.7%

PRESIDENT 1948

County	Total Vote	Republican	Democratic	Other	Rep.-Dem. Plurality	Total Vote Rep.	Total Vote Dem.	Major Vote Rep.	Major Vote Dem.
MADISON	6,123	3,207	2,827	89	380 R	52.4%	46.2%	53.1%	46.9%
MAHASKA	9,030	4,238	4,327	465	89 D	46.9%	47.9%	49.5%	50.5%
MARION	10,870	4,312	6,300	258	1,988 D	39.7%	58.0%	40.6%	59.4%
MARSHALL	12,833	6,698	5,602	533	1,096 R	52.2%	43.7%	54.5%	45.5%
MILLS	5,107	2,921	2,155	31	766 R	57.2%	42.2%	57.5%	42.5%
MITCHELL	6,119	3,021	2,873	225	148 R	49.4%	47.0%	51.3%	48.7%
MONONA	7,346	3,179	4,098	69	919 D	43.3%	55.8%	43.7%	56.3%
MONROE	5,926	2,371	3,445	110	1,074 D	40.0%	58.1%	40.8%	59.2%
MONTGOMERY	6,910	4,084	2,751	75	1,333 R	59.1%	39.8%	59.8%	40.2%
MUSCATINE	11,615	5,003	5,466	146	537 D	51.7%	47.1%	52.3%	47.7%
O'BRIEN	7,326	3,697	3,421	208	276 R	50.5%	46.7%	51.9%	48.1%
OSCEOLA	3,939	1,772	2,123	44	351 D	45.0%	53.9%	45.5%	54.5%
PAGE	9,374	5,638	3,567	169	2,071 R	60.1%	38.1%	61.2%	38.8%
PALO ALTO	6,601	2,594	3,858	149	1,264 D	39.3%	58.4%	40.2%	59.8%
PLYMOUTH	9,416	5,002	4,339	75	663 R	53.1%	46.1%	53.5%	46.5%
POCAHONTAS	6,051	2,397	3,500	154	1,103 D	39.6%	57.8%	40.6%	59.4%
POLK	81,379	33,742	45,289	2,348	11,547 D	41.5%	55.7%	42.7%	57.3%
POTTAWATTAMIE	24,095	12,384	11,430	281	954 R	51.4%	47.4%	52.0%	48.0%
POWESHIEK	8,385	3,888	4,324	173	436 D	46.4%	51.6%	47.3%	52.7%
RINGGOLD	4,459	2,487	1,922	50	565 R	55.8%	43.1%	56.4%	43.6%
SAC	7,363	3,505	3,699	159	194 D	47.6%	50.2%	48.7%	51.3%
SCOTT	34,081	16,841	16,661	578	181 R	49.4%	48.9%	50.3%	49.7%
SHELBY	6,935	3,301	3,499	135	198 D	47.6%	50.5%	48.5%	51.5%
SIOUX	9,811	5,597	4,042	162	1,555 R	57.1%	41.2%	58.1%	41.9%
STORY	15,251	8,307	6,152	792	2,155 R	54.5%	40.3%	57.5%	42.5%
TAMA	10,028	4,763	5,115	150	352 D	47.5%	51.0%	48.2%	51.8%
TAYLOR	5,698	3,244	2,402	52	842 R	56.9%	42.2%	57.5%	42.5%
UNION	7,414	4,138	3,218	58	920 R	55.8%	43.4%	56.3%	43.7%
VAN BUREN	4,698	2,702	1,917	69	785 R	57.6%	40.9%	58.5%	41.5%
WAPELLO	18,976	7,875	10,841	260	2,966 D	41.5%	57.1%	42.1%	57.9%
WARREN	7,605	3,876	3,481	248	395 R	51.0%	45.8%	52.7%	47.3%
WASHINGTON	8,245	4,680	3,485	80	1,195 R	56.8%	42.3%	57.3%	42.7%
WAYNE	6,123	2,738	3,314	71	576 D	44.7%	54.1%	45.2%	54.8%
WEBSTER	17,066	6,951	9,508	607	2,557 D	40.7%	55.7%	42.2%	57.8%
WINNEBAGO	5,451	2,636	2,626	189	10 R	48.4%	48.2%	50.1%	49.9%
WINNESHIEK	9,663	4,594	4,905	164	311 D	47.5%	50.8%	48.4%	51.6%
WOODBURY	39,084	16,655	22,056	373	5,401 D	42.6%	56.4%	43.0%	57.0%
WORTH	4,637	1,878	2,623	136	745 D	40.5%	56.6%	41.7%	58.3%
WRIGHT	7,800	3,810	3,866	124	56 D	48.8%	49.6%	49.6%	50.4%
TOTAL	1,038,264	494,018	522,380	21,866	28,362 D	47.6%	50.3%	48.6%	51.4%

IOWA

PRESIDENT 1952

County	Total Vote	Republican	Democratic	Other	Rep.-Dem. Plurality	Tot. Rep.	Tot. Dem.	Maj. Rep.	Maj. Dem.
ADAIR	6,326	4,497	1,817	12	2,680 R	71.1%	28.7%	71.2%	28.8%
ADAMS	4,531	3,129	1,383	19	1,746 R	69.1%	30.5%	69.3%	30.7%
ALLAMAKEE	8,438	6,087	2,341	10	3,746 R	72.1%	27.7%	72.2%	27.8%
APPANOOSE	9,804	5,429	4,276	99	1,153 R	55.4%	43.6%	55.9%	44.1%
AUDUBON	5,829	3,605	2,220	4	1,385 R	61.8%	38.1%	61.9%	38.1%
BENTON	10,689	6,316	3,831	542	2,485 R	59.1%	35.8%	62.2%	37.8%
BLACK HAWK	46,234	28,671	17,360	203	11,311 R	62.0%	37.5%	62.3%	37.7%
BOONE	12,947	7,901	4,896	150	3,005 R	61.0%	37.8%	61.7%	38.3%
BREMER	9,183	6,806	2,363	14	4,443 R	74.1%	25.7%	74.2%	25.8%
BUCHANAN	9,484	6,431	3,019	34	3,412 R	67.8%	31.8%	68.1%	31.9%
BUENA VISTA	10,813	7,539	3,254	20	4,285 R	69.7%	30.1%	69.9%	30.1%
BUTLER	8,210	6,360	1,836	14	4,524 R	77.5%	22.4%	77.6%	22.4%
CALHOUN	7,966	5,391	2,411	164	2,980 R	67.7%	30.3%	69.1%	30.9%
CARROLL	11,628	7,473	4,139	16	3,334 R	64.3%	35.6%	64.4%	35.6%
CASS	9,727	7,355	2,349	23	5,006 R	75.6%	24.1%	75.8%	24.2%
CEDAR	8,640	6,176	2,447	17	3,729 R	71.5%	28.3%	71.6%	28.4%
CERRO GORDO	21,608	13,207	8,354	47	4,853 R	61.1%	38.7%	61.3%	38.7%
CHEROKEE	8,541	6,018	2,502	21	3,516 R	70.5%	29.3%	70.6%	29.4%
CHICKASAW	7,949	5,022	2,921	6	2,101 R	63.2%	36.7%	63.2%	36.8%
CLARKE	4,894	3,215	1,653	26	1,562 R	65.7%	33.8%	66.0%	34.0%
CLAY	8,641	6,271	2,258	112	4,013 R	72.6%	26.1%	73.5%	26.5%
CLAYTON	11,408	7,669	3,730	9	3,939 R	67.2%	32.7%	67.3%	32.7%
CLINTON	23,385	15,372	7,975	38	7,397 R	65.7%	34.1%	65.8%	34.2%
CRAWFORD	8,868	5,646	3,107	115	2,539 R	63.7%	35.0%	64.5%	35.5%
DALLAS	12,610	8,008	4,501	101	3,507 R	63.5%	35.7%	64.0%	36.0%
DAVIS	5,495	3,195	2,283	17	912 R	58.1%	41.5%	58.3%	41.7%
DECATUR	6,168	3,621	2,521	26	1,100 R	58.7%	40.9%	59.0%	41.0%
DELAWARE	8,810	6,449	2,351	10	4,098 R	73.2%	26.7%	73.3%	26.7%
DES MOINES	20,957	12,182	8,686	89	3,496 R	58.1%	41.4%	58.4%	41.6%
DICKINSON	6,194	4,401	1,748	45	2,653 R	71.1%	28.2%	71.6%	28.4%
DUBUQUE	32,845	18,075	14,542	228	3,533 R	55.0%	44.3%	55.4%	44.6%
EMMET	6,904	3,935	2,947	22	988 R	57.0%	42.7%	57.2%	42.8%
FAYETTE	13,589	9,152	4,403	34	4,749 R	67.3%	32.4%	67.5%	32.5%
FLOYD	10,054	7,042	2,999	13	4,043 R	70.0%	29.8%	70.1%	29.9%
FRANKLIN	7,470	5,432	1,941	97	3,491 R	72.7%	26.0%	73.7%	26.3%
FREMONT	5,894	3,802	2,085	7	1,717 R	64.5%	35.4%	64.6%	35.4%
GREENE	7,725	5,378	2,228	119	3,150 R	69.6%	28.8%	70.7%	29.3%
GRUNDY	7,156	5,652	1,483	21	4,169 R	79.0%	20.7%	79.2%	20.8%
GUTHRIE	7,671	5,377	2,281	13	3,096 R	70.1%	29.7%	70.2%	29.8%
HAMILTON	9,828	7,006	2,788	34	4,218 R	71.3%	28.4%	71.5%	28.5%
HANCOCK	7,178	5,115	2,053	10	3,062 R	71.3%	28.6%	71.4%	28.6%
HARDIN	11,132	7,880	3,205	47	4,675 R	70.8%	28.8%	71.1%	28.9%
HARRISON	9,366	5,972	3,370	24	2,602 R	63.8%	36.0%	63.9%	36.1%
HENRY	8,931	6,424	2,438	69	3,986 R	71.9%	27.3%	72.5%	27.5%
HOWARD	6,881	4,305	2,564	12	1,741 R	62.6%	37.3%	62.7%	37.3%
HUMBOLDT	6,674	4,534	2,124	16	2,410 R	67.9%	31.8%	68.1%	31.9%
IDA	5,418	3,800	1,603	15	2,197 R	70.1%	29.6%	70.3%	29.7%
IOWA	8,362	5,625	2,514	223	3,111 R	67.3%	30.1%	69.1%	30.9%
JACKSON	9,127	5,867	3,074	186	2,793 R	64.3%	33.7%	65.6%	34.4%
JASPER	16,465	9,610	6,756	99	2,854 R	58.4%	41.0%	58.7%	41.3%
JEFFERSON	8,149	5,630	2,470	49	3,160 R	69.1%	30.3%	69.5%	30.5%
JOHNSON	19,350	11,231	8,067	52	3,164 R	58.0%	41.7%	58.2%	41.8%
JONES	9,073	6,070	2,991	12	3,079 R	66.9%	33.0%	67.0%	33.0%
KEOKUK	8,897	5,712	3,135	50	2,577 R	64.2%	35.2%	64.6%	35.4%
KOSSUTH	12,105	7,765	4,330	10	3,435 R	64.2%	35.8%	64.2%	35.8%
LEE	20,969	12,289	8,625	55	3,664 R	58.6%	41.1%	58.8%	41.2%
LINN	53,441	31,383	21,818	240	9,565 R	58.7%	40.8%	59.0%	41.0%
LOUISA	5,369	3,675	1,673	21	2,002 R	68.5%	31.2%	68.7%	31.3%
LUCAS	6,215	3,921	2,217	77	1,704 R	63.1%	35.7%	63.9%	36.1%
LYON	6,226	4,893	1,324	9	3,569 R	78.6%	21.3%	78.7%	21.3%

PRESIDENT 1956

County	Total Vote	Republican	Democratic	Other	Rep.-Dem. Plurality	Tot. Rep.	Tot. Dem.	Maj. Rep.	Maj. Dem.
ADAIR	5,791	3,426	2,362	3	1,064 R	59.2%	40.8%	59.2%	40.8%
ADAMS	4,020	2,248	1,756	16	492 R	55.9%	43.7%	56.1%	43.9%
ALLAMAKEE	7,824	5,182	2,622	20	2,560 R	66.2%	33.5%	66.4%	33.6%
APPANOOSE	9,054	4,980	4,064	10	916 R	55.0%	44.9%	55.1%	44.9%
AUDUBON	5,664	3,057	2,585	2	472 R	54.0%	45.6%	54.2%	45.8%
BENTON	10,006	5,634	3,946	426	1,688 R	56.3%	39.4%	58.8%	41.2%
BLACK HAWK	48,719	28,250	20,403	66	7,847 R	58.0%	41.9%	58.1%	41.9%
BOONE	12,564	6,740	5,815	9	925 R	53.6%	46.3%	53.7%	46.3%
BREMER	8,831	5,930	2,892	9	3,038 R	67.2%	32.7%	67.2%	32.8%
BUCHANAN	9,035	5,512	3,513	10	1,999 R	61.0%	38.9%	61.1%	38.9%
BUENA VISTA	10,563	6,470	4,083	10	2,387 R	61.3%	38.7%	61.3%	38.7%
BUTLER	7,961	5,669	2,289	3	3,380 R	71.2%	28.8%	71.2%	28.8%
CALHOUN	7,669	4,409	2,972	288	1,437 R	57.5%	38.8%	59.7%	40.3%
CARROLL	10,913	5,816	5,085	12	731 R	53.3%	46.6%	53.4%	46.6%
CASS	8,930	6,103	2,818	9	3,285 R	68.3%	31.6%	68.4%	31.6%
CEDAR	8,258	5,344	2,912	2	2,432 R	64.7%	35.3%	64.7%	35.3%
CERRO GORDO	21,841	12,449	9,362	30	3,087 R	57.0%	42.9%	57.1%	42.9%
CHEROKEE	8,079	4,821	3,254	4	1,567 R	59.7%	40.3%	59.7%	40.3%
CHICKASAW	7,495	4,205	3,275	15	930 R	56.1%	43.7%	56.2%	43.8%
CLARKE	4,397	2,462	1,929	6	533 R	56.0%	43.9%	56.1%	43.9%
CLAY	8,190	5,107	2,970	113	2,137 R	62.4%	36.3%	63.2%	36.8%
CLAYTON	10,926	6,529	4,384	13	2,145 R	59.8%	40.1%	59.8%	40.2%
CLINTON	23,208	14,765	8,394	49	6,371 R	63.6%	36.2%	63.8%	36.2%
CRAWFORD	8,374	4,608	3,749	17	859 R	55.0%	44.8%	55.1%	44.9%
DALLAS	11,806	6,619	5,185	2	1,434 R	56.1%	43.9%	56.1%	43.9%
DAVIS	5,129	2,661	2,458	10	203 R	51.9%	47.9%	52.0%	48.0%
DECATUR	5,725	2,912	2,806	7	106 R	50.9%	49.0%	50.9%	49.1%
DELAWARE	8,369	5,732	2,621	16	3,111 R	68.5%	31.3%	68.6%	31.4%
DES MOINES	19,958	11,152	8,781	25	2,371 R	55.9%	44.0%	55.9%	44.1%
DICKINSON	6,157	3,641	2,498	18	1,143 R	59.1%	40.6%	59.3%	40.7%
DUBUQUE	31,247	17,923	13,174	150	4,749 R	57.4%	42.2%	57.6%	42.4%
EMMET	6,584	4,193	2,386	5	1,807 R	63.7%	36.2%	63.7%	36.3%
FAYETTE	12,866	7,914	4,935	17	2,979 R	61.5%	38.4%	61.6%	38.4%
FLOYD	9,927	6,172	3,739	16	2,433 R	62.2%	37.7%	62.3%	37.7%
FRANKLIN	7,084	4,563	2,513	8	2,050 R	64.4%	35.5%	64.5%	35.5%
FREMONT	5,511	3,241	2,254	16	987 R	58.8%	40.9%	59.0%	41.0%
GREENE	7,162	4,255	2,802	105	1,453 R	59.4%	39.1%	60.3%	39.7%
GRUNDY	6,827	4,915	1,908	4	3,007 R	72.0%	28.0%	72.0%	28.0%
GUTHRIE	7,270	4,283	2,981	6	1,302 R	58.9%	41.0%	59.0%	41.0%
HAMILTON	9,514	5,667	3,829	18	1,838 R	59.6%	40.2%	59.7%	40.3%
HANCOCK	7,114	4,305	2,803	6	1,502 R	60.5%	39.4%	60.6%	39.4%
HARDIN	10,432	6,642	3,775	15	2,867 R	63.7%	36.2%	63.8%	36.2%
HARRISON	8,935	5,209	3,709	17	1,500 R	58.3%	41.5%	58.4%	41.6%
HENRY	8,495	5,818	2,667	10	3,151 R	68.5%	31.4%	68.6%	31.4%
HOWARD	6,605	3,491	3,106	8	385 R	52.9%	47.0%	52.9%	47.1%
HUMBOLDT	6,507	3,747	2,756	4	991 R	57.6%	42.4%	57.6%	42.4%
IDA	5,310	3,226	2,083	1	1,143 R	60.8%	39.2%	60.8%	39.2%
IOWA	7,777	4,875	2,753	149	2,122 R	62.7%	35.4%	63.9%	36.1%
JACKSON	8,905	5,575	3,181	149	2,394 R	62.6%	35.7%	63.7%	36.3%
JASPER	16,428	9,310	7,098	20	2,212 R	56.7%	43.2%	56.7%	43.3%
JEFFERSON	7,659	4,807	2,845	7	1,962 R	62.8%	37.1%	62.8%	37.2%
JOHNSON	20,076	11,298	8,767	11	2,531 R	56.3%	43.7%	56.3%	43.7%
JONES	8,967	5,605	3,352	10	2,253 R	62.5%	37.4%	62.6%	37.4%
KEOKUK	8,338	4,680	3,649	9	1,031 R	56.1%	43.8%	56.2%	43.8%
KOSSUTH	12,204	6,680	5,514	10	1,166 R	54.7%	45.2%	54.8%	45.2%
LEE	19,829	11,571	8,226	32	3,345 R	58.4%	41.5%	58.4%	41.6%
LINN	55,116	33,402	21,667	47	11,735 R	60.6%	39.3%	60.7%	39.3%
LOUISA	5,048	3,184	1,858	6	1,326 R	63.1%	36.8%	63.1%	36.9%
LUCAS	5,832	3,397	2,431	4	966 R	58.3%	41.7%	58.3%	41.7%
LYON	6,150	4,356	1,790	4	2,566 R	70.8%	29.1%	70.9%	29.1%

IOWA

PRESIDENT 1952

County	Total Vote	Republican	Democratic	Other	Rep.-Dem. Plurality		Total Vote Rep.	Total Vote Dem.	Major Vote Rep.	Major Vote Dem.
MADISON	7,149	4,967	2,131	51	2,835	R	59.5%	29.8%	70.0%	30.0%
MAHASKA	11,523	7,369	3,745	409	3,624	R	64.0%	32.5%	66.3%	33.7%
MARION	12,516	7,165	5,196	155	1,969	R	57.2%	41.5%	58.0%	42.0%
MARSHALL	16,890	11,135	5,314	441	5,821	R	65.9%	31.5%	67.7%	32.3%
MILLS	5,834	4,028	1,792	14	2,236	R	69.0%	30.7%	69.2%	30.8%
MITCHELL	7,237	5,050	2,175	12	2,875	R	69.3%	30.1%	69.9%	30.1%
MONONA	7,784	4,849	2,918	17	1,931	R	62.3%	37.5%	62.4%	37.6%
MONROE	6,042	3,219	2,785	38	434	R	53.3%	46.1%	53.6%	46.4%
MONTGOMERY	8,334	6,074	2,235	25	3,839	R	72.9%	26.8%	73.1%	26.9%
MUSCATINE	15,196	9,361	5,772	63	3,589	R	61.5%	38.0%	61.9%	38.1%
O'BRIEN	9,360	7,130	2,192	38	4,938	R	76.2%	23.4%	76.5%	23.5%
OSCEOLA	4,981	3,573	1,396	12	2,177	R	71.7%	28.0%	71.9%	28.1%
PAGE	11,553	8,840	2,669	44	6,171	R	76.5%	23.1%	76.8%	23.2%
PALO ALTO	7,597	4,595	2,993	9	1,602	R	60.5%	39.4%	60.6%	39.4%
PLYMOUTH	10,957	8,140	2,768	49	5,372	R	74.3%	25.3%	74.6%	25.4%
POCAHONTAS	7,245	4,472	2,517	256	1,955	R	61.7%	34.7%	64.0%	36.0%
POLK	112,783	60,934	50,867	982	10,067	R	54.0%	45.1%	54.5%	45.5%
POTTAWATTAMIE	30,854	18,894	11,897	63	6,997	R	61.2%	38.6%	61.4%	38.6%
POWESHIEK	9,498	6,105	3,318	75	2,787	R	64.3%	34.9%	64.8%	35.2%
RINGGOLD	4,871	3,442	1,408	21	2,034	R	70.7%	28.9%	71.0%	29.0%
SAC	8,894	6,417	2,451	26	3,966	R	72.1%	27.6%	72.4%	27.6%
SCOTT	48,026	29,719	17,807	500	11,912	R	61.9%	37.1%	62.5%	37.5%
SHELBY	7,939	5,135	2,762	42	2,373	R	64.7%	34.8%	65.0%	35.0%
SIOUX	12,349	10,275	2,050	24	8,225	R	83.2%	16.6%	83.4%	16.6%
STORY	19,296	13,857	5,299	140	8,558	R	71.8%	27.5%	72.3%	27.7%
TAMA	11,154	7,061	4,076	17	2,985	R	63.3%	36.5%	63.4%	36.6%
TAYLOR	6,423	4,608	1,784	31	2,824	R	71.7%	27.8%	72.1%	27.9%
UNION	8,332	5,742	2,566	24	3,176	R	68.9%	30.8%	69.1%	30.9%
VAN BUREN	5,480	3,870	1,577	33	2,293	R	70.6%	28.8%	71.0%	29.0%
WAPELLO	22,150	11,571	10,449	130	1,122	R	52.2%	47.2%	52.5%	47.5%
WARREN	9,017	5,911	3,042	64	2,869	R	65.6%	33.7%	66.0%	34.0%
WASHINGTON	9,585	6,946	2,604	35	4,342	R	72.5%	27.2%	72.7%	27.3%
WAYNE	6,525	3,995	2,497	33	1,498	R	61.2%	38.3%	61.5%	38.5%
WEBSTER	21,385	12,336	8,681	368	3,655	R	57.7%	40.6%	58.7%	41.3%
WINNEBAGO	6,499	4,574	1,905	20	2,669	R	70.4%	29.3%	70.6%	29.4%
WINNESHIEK	10,736	7,154	3,560	22	3,594	R	66.6%	33.2%	66.8%	33.2%
WOODBURY	47,151	27,518	19,474	159	8,044	R	58.4%	41.3%	58.6%	41.4%
WORTH	5,404	3,315	2,075	14	1,240	R	61.3%	38.4%	61.5%	38.5%
WRIGHT	9,783	6,566	3,186	31	3,380	R	67.1%	32.6%	67.3%	32.6%
TOTAL	1,268,773	808,906	451,513	8,354	357,393	R	63.8%	35.6%	64.2%	35.8%

PRESIDENT 1956

County	Total Vote	Republican	Democratic	Other	Rep.-Dem. Plurality		Total Vote Rep.	Total Vote Dem.	Major Vote Rep.	Major Vote Dem.
MADISON	6,544	3,883	2,652	9	1,231	R	59.3%	40.5%	59.4%	40.6%
MAHASKA	11,034	6,864	3,965	205	2,899	R	62.2%	35.9%	63.4%	36.6%
MARION	12,168	6,830	5,316	22	1,514	R	56.1%	43.7%	56.2%	43.8%
MARSHALL	16,425	10,305	5,755	365	4,550	R	62.7%	35.0%	64.2%	35.8%
MILLS	5,454	3,539	1,897	18	1,642	R	64.9%	34.8%	65.1%	34.9%
MITCHELL	6,812	4,175	2,630	7	1,545	R	61.3%	38.6%	61.4%	38.6%
MONONA	7,345	3,854	3,477	14	377	R	52.5%	47.3%	52.6%	47.4%
MONROE	5,512	2,984	2,616	12	368	R	53.2%	46.6%	53.3%	46.7%
MONTGOMERY	7,643	5,027	2,597	19	2,430	R	65.2%	34.0%	65.9%	34.1%
MUSCATINE	14,298	8,552	5,718	28	2,834	R	59.8%	40.0%	59.9%	40.1%
O'BRIEN	9,118	6,138	2,970	10	3,168	R	67.3%	32.6%	67.4%	32.6%
OSCEOLA	4,772	2,986	1,779	7	1,207	R	62.6%	37.3%	62.7%	37.3%
PAGE	10,397	7,380	3,001	16	4,379	R	71.0%	28.9%	71.1%	28.9%
PALO ALTO	7,421	3,795	3,624	2	171	R	51.1%	48.8%	51.2%	48.8%
PLYMOUTH	10,748	7,246	3,502		3,744	R	67.4%	32.6%	67.4%	32.6%
POCAHONTAS	6,818	3,606	3,201	11	405	R	52.9%	46.9%	53.0%	47.0%
POLK	115,491	62,392	53,025	74	9,367	R	54.0%	45.9%	54.1%	45.9%
POTTAWATTAMIE	30,468	17,632	12,731	105	4,901	R	57.9%	41.8%	58.1%	41.9%
POWESHIEK	8,749	5,145	3,602	2	1,543	R	58.8%	41.2%	58.8%	41.2%
RINGGOLD	4,490	2,713	1,775	2	938	R	60.4%	39.5%	60.5%	39.5%
SAC	8,125	4,874	3,248	3	1,626	R	60.0%	40.0%	60.0%	40.0%
SCOTT	47,104	27,965	18,969	170	8,996	R	59.4%	40.3%	59.6%	40.4%
SHELBY	7,793	4,425	3,300	68	1,125	R	56.8%	42.3%	57.3%	42.7%
SIOUX	12,328	9,651	2,666	11	6,985	R	78.3%	21.6%	78.4%	21.6%
STORY	19,640	13,264	6,352	24	6,912	R	67.5%	32.3%	67.6%	32.4%
TAMA	10,773	5,952	4,795	26	1,157	R	55.2%	44.5%	55.4%	44.6%
TAYLOR	5,978	3,533	2,436	9	1,097	R	59.1%	40.7%	59.2%	40.8%
UNION	7,501	4,666	2,828	7	1,838	R	62.2%	37.7%	62.3%	37.7%
VAN BUREN	5,068	3,233	1,833	2	1,400	R	63.8%	36.2%	63.8%	36.2%
WAPELLO	21,381	10,401	10,960	20	559	D	48.6%	51.3%	48.7%	51.3%
WARREN	9,174	5,430	3,729	15	1,701	R	59.2%	40.6%	59.3%	40.7%
WASHINGTON	8,876	5,844	3,022	10	2,822	R	65.8%	34.0%	65.9%	34.1%
WAYNE	5,897	3,340	2,553	4	787	R	56.6%	43.3%	56.7%	43.3%
WEBSTER	21,049	11,097	9,901	51	1,196	R	52.7%	47.0%	52.8%	47.2%
WINNEBAGO	6,453	3,926	2,521	6	1,405	R	60.8%	39.1%	60.9%	39.1%
WINNESHIEK	10,460	6,192	4,251	17	1,941	R	59.2%	40.6%	59.3%	40.7%
WOODBURY	45,445	25,399	19,997	49	5,402	R	55.9%	44.0%	55.9%	44.1%
WORTH	5,167	2,700	2,465	2	235	R	52.3%	47.7%	52.3%	47.7%
WRIGHT	9,390	5,512	3,865	13	1,647	R	58.7%	41.2%	58.8%	41.2%
TOTAL	1,234,564	729,187	501,858	3,519	227,329	R	59.1%	40.7%	59.2%	40.8%

IOWA

PRESIDENT 1960

County	Total Vote	Republican	Democratic	Other	Rep.-Dem. Plurality	%TV Rep.	%TV Dem.	%MV Rep.	%MV Dem.
ADAIR	5,630	3,383	2,245	2	1,138 R	60.1	39.9	60.1	39.9
ADAMS	3,828	2,185	1,643		542 R	57.1	42.9	57.1	42.9
ALLAMAKEE	7,916	4,970	2,933	13	2,037 R	62.8	37.1	62.9	37.1
APPANOOSE	8,480	5,040	3,422	18	1,618 R	59.4	40.4	59.6	40.4
AUDUBON	5,532	2,935	2,595	2	340 R	53.1	46.9	53.1	46.9
BENTON	10,601	5,972	4,620	9	1,352 R	56.3	43.6	56.4	43.6
BLACK HAWK	52,551	28,435	24,078	38	4,357 R	54.1	45.8	54.1	45.9
BOONE	12,527	6,761	5,759	7	1,002 R	54.0	46.0	54.0	46.0
BREMER	9,742	6,504	3,234	4	3,270 R	66.8	33.2	66.8	33.2
BUCHANAN	9,433	5,179	4,251	3	928 R	54.9	45.1	54.9	45.1
BUENA VISTA	9,996	6,351	3,637	8	2,714 R	63.5	36.4	63.6	36.4
BUTLER	7,616	5,345	2,268	3	3,077 R	70.2	29.8	70.2	29.8
CALHOUN	7,595	4,465	3,123	7	1,362 R	59.0	41.0	59.1	41.0
CARROLL	11,721	4,648	7,064	9	2,416 D	39.7	60.3	39.7	60.3
CASS	9,354	6,290	3,059	5	3,231 R	67.2	32.7	67.3	32.7
CEDAR	8,425	5,217	3,203	5	2,014 R	61.9	38.0	62.0	38.0
CERRO GORDO	22,889	12,830	10,044	15	2,786 R	56.1	43.9	56.1	43.9
CHEROKEE	8,106	4,791	3,309	6	1,482 R	59.1	40.8	59.1	40.9
CHICKASAW	7,889	3,822	4,063	4	241 D	48.4	51.5	48.5	51.5
CLARKE	4,550	2,631	1,906	13	725 R	57.8	41.9	58.0	42.0
CLAY	8,604	5,165	3,437	2	1,728 R	60.0	39.9	60.0	40.0
CLAYTON	11,057	6,441	4,612	4	1,829 R	58.3	41.7	58.3	41.7
CLINTON	24,330	13,797	10,508	25	3,289 R	56.7	43.2	56.8	43.2
CRAWFORD	8,518	4,791	3,720	7	1,071 R	56.2	43.7	56.3	43.7
DALLAS	12,176	6,566	5,597	13	969 R	53.9	46.0	54.0	46.0
DAVIS	4,949	2,641	2,303	5	338 R	53.4	46.5	53.4	46.6
DECATUR	5,457	3,039	2,411	7	628 R	55.7	44.2	55.8	44.2
DELAWARE	8,703	5,015	3,687	1	1,327 R	57.6	42.4	57.6	42.4
DES MOINES	20,591	10,678	9,872	41	806 R	51.9	47.9	52.0	48.0
DICKINSON	6,273	3,575	2,696	2	879 R	57.0	43.0	57.0	43.0
DUBUQUE	34,766	12,740	22,007	19	9,267 D	36.6	63.3	36.7	63.3
EMMET	6,853	4,284	2,563	6	1,721 R	62.5	37.4	62.6	37.4
FAYETTE	13,611	8,330	5,256	25	3,074 R	61.2	38.6	61.3	38.7
FLOYD	9,746	5,774	3,970	2	1,804 R	59.2	40.7	59.3	40.7
FRANKLIN	6,996	4,514	2,476	6	2,038 R	64.5	35.4	64.6	35.4
FREMONT	5,336	3,027	2,307	2	720 R	56.7	43.2	56.8	43.3
GREENE	6,954	4,063	2,874	17	1,184 R	58.4	41.3	58.6	41.4
GRUNDY	7,166	4,989	2,174	3	2,815 R	69.6	30.3	69.6	30.4
GUTHRIE	6,949	4,046	2,896	7	1,150 R	58.2	41.7	58.3	41.7
HAMILTON	9,174	5,265	3,905	4	1,360 R	57.4	42.6	57.4	42.6
HANCOCK	6,937	4,179	2,757	1	1,422 R	60.2	39.7	60.3	39.7
HARDIN	10,330	6,438	3,888	4	2,550 R	62.3	37.6	62.3	37.7
HARRISON	8,562	4,940	3,618	4	1,322 R	57.7	42.2	57.7	42.3
HENRY	7,930	5,084	2,839	7	2,245 R	64.1	35.8	64.2	35.8
HOWARD	6,784	3,378	3,406		28 D	49.8	50.2	49.8	50.2
HUMBOLDT	6,243	3,537	2,706		831 R	56.7	43.3	56.7	43.3
IDA	5,241	3,290	1,949	2	1,341 R	62.8	37.2	62.8	37.2
IOWA	7,790	4,944	2,828	18	2,116 R	63.5	36.3	63.6	36.4
JACKSON	9,434	5,084	4,345	5	739 R	53.9	46.1	53.9	46.1
JASPER	16,585	9,332	7,242	11	2,090 R	56.3	43.7	56.3	43.7
JEFFERSON	7,722	4,942	2,780	18	2,162 R	64.0	36.0	64.0	36.0
JOHNSON	21,508	10,927	10,563	18	364 R	50.8	49.1	50.8	49.2
JONES	9,469	5,541	3,924	4	1,617 R	58.5	41.4	58.5	41.5
KEOKUK	8,115	4,697	3,408	10	1,289 R	57.9	42.0	58.0	42.0
KOSSUTH	12,084	6,278	5,806		472 R	52.0	48.0	52.0	48.0
LEE	20,701	10,765	9,936		829 R	52.0	48.0	52.0	48.0
LINN	61,839	34,200	27,614	25	6,586 R	55.3	44.7	55.3	44.7
LOUISA	5,004	3,036	1,966	2	1,070 R	60.7	39.3	60.7	39.3
LUCAS	5,865	3,512	2,344	9	1,168 R	59.9	40.0	60.0	40.0
LYON	6,676	4,917	1,752	7	3,165 R	73.7	26.2	73.7	26.3

PRESIDENT 1964

County	Total Vote	Republican	Democratic	Other	Rep.-Dem. Plurality	%TV Rep.	%TV Dem.	%MV Rep.	%MV Dem.
ADAIR	4,812	1,953	2,851	8	898 D	40.6	59.2	40.7	59.3
ADAMS	3,263	1,321	1,941	1	620 D	40.5	59.5	40.5	59.5
ALLAMAKEE	7,200	3,691	3,504	5	187 R	51.3	48.7	51.3	48.7
APPANOOSE	7,856	2,872	4,960	24	2,088 D	36.6	63.1	36.7	63.3
AUDUBON	4,885	1,871	3,011	3	1,140 D	38.3	61.6	38.3	61.7
BENTON	10,084	3,453	6,614	17	3,161 D	34.2	65.6	34.3	65.7
BLACK HAWK	50,516	19,744	30,716	56	10,972 D	39.1	60.8	39.1	60.9
BOONE	11,335	3,543	7,699	93	4,156 D	31.5	67.9	31.5	68.5
BREMER	8,939	3,880	5,045	14	1,165 D	43.4	56.4	43.5	56.5
BUCHANAN	8,823	3,187	5,621	15	2,434 D	36.1	63.7	36.2	63.8
BUENA VISTA	8,997	3,747	5,245	5	1,498 D	41.6	58.3	41.7	58.3
BUTLER	6,832	3,462	3,370		92 D	50.7	49.3	50.7	49.3
CALHOUN	6,837	2,422	4,407	8	1,985 D	35.4	64.5	35.5	64.5
CARROLL	10,207	2,387	7,807	13	5,420 D	23.4	76.5	23.4	76.6
CASS	8,198	4,182	4,006	10	176 R	51.0	48.9	51.1	48.9
CEDAR	7,735	3,106	4,617	12	1,511 D	40.2	59.7	40.2	59.8
CERRO GORDO	21,071	7,884	13,156	31	5,272 D	37.4	62.4	37.5	62.5
CHEROKEE	7,525	3,180	4,336	9	1,156 D	42.3	57.6	42.3	57.7
CHICKASAW	7,182	2,632	4,545	5	1,913 D	36.7	63.3	36.7	63.3
CLARKE	4,212	1,546	2,659	7	1,113 D	36.8	63.1	36.8	63.2
CLAY	7,749	2,999	4,631	119	1,632 D	38.7	59.8	39.3	60.7
CLAYTON	9,550	3,923	5,624	3	1,701 D	41.1	58.9	41.1	58.9
CLINTON	22,533	8,219	14,267	47	6,048 D	36.5	63.3	36.6	63.3
CRAWFORD	8,037	2,999	5,024	14	2,025 D	37.3	62.5	37.4	62.6
DALLAS	11,262	3,763	7,447	52	3,684 D	33.4	66.1	33.6	66.4
DAVIS	4,402	1,424	2,966	12	1,542 D	32.4	67.4	32.4	67.6
DECATUR	4,885	1,542	3,331	12	1,789 D	31.6	68.2	31.6	68.4
DELAWARE	8,065	3,427	4,623	15	1,196 D	42.5	57.3	42.6	57.4
DES MOINES	19,762	5,830	13,894	38	8,064 D	29.5	70.3	29.6	70.4
DICKINSON	5,938	2,443	3,490	5	1,047 D	41.1	58.8	41.2	58.8
DUBUQUE	33,823	10,104	23,695	24	13,591 D	29.9	70.1	29.9	70.1
EMMET	6,103	2,611	3,487	5	876 D	42.8	57.1	42.8	57.2
FAYETTE	12,482	5,567	6,900	15	1,333 D	44.6	55.3	44.7	55.3
FLOYD	9,043	3,721	5,317	5	1,596 D	41.2	58.8	41.2	58.8
FRANKLIN	6,061	2,452	3,582	27	1,130 D	40.5	59.1	40.6	59.4
FREMONT	4,761	2,044	2,703	14	659 D	42.9	56.8	43.1	56.9
GREENE	5,986	2,141	3,828	17	1,687 D	35.8	63.9	35.9	64.1
GRUNDY	6,808	3,215	3,582	11	367 D	47.2	52.6	47.3	52.7
GUTHRIE	6,146	2,169	3,962	15	1,793 D	35.3	64.6	35.4	64.6
HAMILTON	8,332	3,127	5,195	10	2,068 D	37.5	62.3	37.6	62.4
HANCOCK	6,133	2,269	3,857	7	1,588 D	37.0	62.9	37.0	63.0
HARDIN	9,304	3,828	5,459	17	1,631 D	41.2	58.6	41.2	58.8
HARRISON	7,787	3,203	4,575	9	1,372 D	41.1	58.8	41.2	58.8
HENRY	7,482	3,247	4,223	12	976 D	43.4	56.4	43.5	56.5
HOWARD	6,211	2,360	3,841	10	1,481 D	38.0	61.8	38.1	61.9
HUMBOLDT	5,630	2,250	3,376	4	1,126 D	40.0	59.9	40.0	60.0
IDA	4,884	1,977	2,905	2	928 D	40.5	59.5	40.5	59.5
IOWA	7,102	2,828	4,261	13	1,433 D	39.8	60.0	39.9	60.1
JACKSON	8,205	3,066	5,130	9	2,064 D	37.4	62.5	37.4	62.6
JASPER	15,561	5,321	10,216	24	4,895 D	34.2	65.6	34.2	65.8
JEFFERSON	6,916	2,755	4,135	26	1,380 D	39.8	59.8	40.0	60.0
JOHNSON	21,608	6,860	14,717	41	7,857 D	31.7	68.1	31.8	68.2
JONES	8,672	3,154	5,511	7	2,357 D	36.4	63.5	36.4	63.6
KEOKUK	7,404	2,597	4,790	17	2,193 D	35.1	64.7	35.2	64.8
KOSSUTH	10,674	3,776	6,893	5	3,117 D	35.4	64.6	35.4	64.6
LEE	18,582	6,321	12,244	17	5,923 D	34.0	65.9	34.0	66.0
LINN	62,029	21,845	40,106	78	18,261 D	35.2	64.7	35.4	64.6
LOUISA	4,481	1,835	2,624	12	779 D	41.2	58.6	41.3	58.7
LUCAS	5,260	1,935	3,310	15	1,375 D	36.8	62.9	36.9	63.1
LYON	5,935	3,185	2,747	3	438 R	53.7	46.3	53.7	46.3

IOWA

PRESIDENT 1960

County	Total Vote	Republican	Democratic	Other	Rep.-Dem. Plurality	Total Vote Rep.	Total Vote Dem.	Major Vote Rep.	Major Vote Dem.
MADISON	6,529	3,804	2,722	3	1,082 R	58.3%	41.7%	58.3%	41.7%
MAHASKA	10,901	7,129	3,746	26	3,383 R	65.4%	34.4%	65.6%	34.4%
MARION	12,008	7,444	4,547	17	2,897 R	62.0%	37.9%	62.1%	37.9%
MARSHALL	17,042	10,265	6,761	16	3,504 R	60.2%	39.7%	60.3%	39.7%
MILLS	5,256	3,436	1,820		1,616 R	65.4%	34.6%	65.4%	34.6%
MITCHELL	6,798	3,915	2,873	10	1,042 R	57.6%	42.3%	57.7%	42.3%
MONONA	7,070	3,863	3,207		656 R	54.6%	45.4%	54.6%	45.4%
MONROE	5,391	2,922	2,459	10	463 R	54.2%	45.6%	54.3%	45.7%
MONTGOMERY	7,630	4,974	2,655	1	2,319 R	65.2%	34.8%	65.2%	34.8%
MUSCATINE	14,698	8,555	6,135	8	2,420 R	58.2%	41.7%	58.2%	41.8%
O'BRIEN	9,480	6,509	2,967	4	3,542 R	68.7%	31.3%	68.7%	31.3%
OSCEOLA	4,782	2,965	1,814	3	1,151 R	62.0%	37.9%	62.0%	38.0%
PAGE	10,172	7,089	3,075	8	4,014 R	69.7%	30.2%	69.7%	30.3%
PALO ALTO	7,249	3,551	3,695	3	144 D	49.3%	51.0%	49.0%	51.0%
PLYMOUTH	11,103	6,432	4,671		1,761 R	57.9%	42.1%	57.9%	42.1%
POCAHONTAS	6,859	3,445	3,408	6	37 R	50.2%	49.7%	50.3%	49.7%
POLK	119,234	64,077	55,091	66	8,986 R	53.7%	46.2%	53.8%	46.2%
POTTAWATTAMIE	33,261	19,223	14,025	13	5,198 R	57.8%	42.2%	57.8%	42.2%
POWESHIEK	8,904	5,232	3,671	1	1,561 R	58.8%	41.2%	58.8%	41.2%
RINGGOLD	4,321	2,538	1,781	2	757 R	58.7%	41.2%	58.8%	41.2%
SAC	7,904	4,850	3,054		1,796 R	61.4%	38.6%	61.4%	38.6%
SCOTT	50,671	27,617	23,004	50	4,613 R	54.6%	45.4%	54.6%	45.4%
SHELBY	7,644	4,210	3,427	7	783 R	55.1%	44.8%	55.1%	44.8%
SIOUX	12,934	10,284	2,643	7	7,641 R	79.6%	20.4%	79.5%	20.4%
STORY	21,004	13,708	7,281	15	6,427 R	65.3%	34.7%	65.3%	34.7%
TAMA	10,486	5,535	4,950	1	585 R	52.8%	47.2%	52.8%	47.2%
TAYLOR	5,581	3,452	2,126	3	1,326 R	61.9%	38.1%	61.9%	38.1%
UNION	7,142	4,417	2,720	5	1,697 R	61.8%	38.1%	61.9%	38.1%
VAN BUREN	4,894	3,129	1,760	5	1,369 R	63.9%	36.0%	64.0%	36.0%
WAPELLO	22,167	11,036	11,116	15	80 D	49.8%	50.1%	49.8%	50.2%
WARREN	10,149	6,013	4,136		1,877 R	59.2%	40.8%	59.2%	40.8%
WASHINGTON	9,089	5,861	3,222	6	2,639 R	64.5%	35.4%	64.5%	35.5%
WAYNE	5,715	3,401	2,307	7	1,094 R	59.5%	40.4%	59.6%	40.4%
WEBSTER	21,435	10,741	10,680	14	61 R	50.1%	49.8%	50.1%	49.9%
WINNEBAGO	6,549	4,082	2,463	4	1,619 R	62.3%	37.6%	62.4%	37.6%
WINNESHIEK	10,530	5,737	4,786	7	951 R	54.5%	45.5%	54.5%	45.5%
WOODBURY	48,744	26,832	21,906	6	4,926 R	55.0%	44.9%	55.1%	44.9%
WORTH	5,048	2,740	2,303	5	437 R	54.3%	45.6%	54.3%	45.7%
WRIGHT	9,560	5,386	4,159	15	1,227 R	56.3%	43.5%	56.4%	43.6%
TOTAL	1,273,810	722,381	550,565	864	171,816 R	56.7%	43.2%	56.7%	43.3%

PRESIDENT 1964

County	Total Vote	Republican	Democratic	Other	Rep.-Dem. Plurality	Total Vote Rep.	Total Vote Dem.	Major Vote Rep.	Major Vote Dem.
MADISON	5,780	2,250	3,518	12	1,268 D	38.9%	60.9%	39.0%	61.0%
MAHASKA	10,205	3,787	6,396	22	2,609 D	37.1%	62.7%	37.2%	62.8%
MARION	11,842	3,903	7,911	28	4,008 D	33.0%	66.8%	33.0%	67.0%
MARSHALL	16,176	6,323	9,815	38	3,492 D	39.1%	60.7%	39.2%	60.8%
MILLS	4,689	2,424	2,463	2	39 D	49.6%	50.4%	49.6%	50.4%
MITCHELL	6,373	2,489	3,868	16	1,379 D	39.1%	60.7%	39.2%	60.8%
MONONA	6,187	2,208	3,971	8	1,763 D	35.7%	64.2%	35.7%	64.3%
MONROE	4,791	1,588	3,186	17	1,598 D	33.1%	66.5%	33.3%	66.7%
MONTGOMERY	6,601	3,101	3,489	11	388 D	47.0%	52.9%	47.1%	52.9%
MUSCATINE	13,577	5,547	8,020	10	2,473 D	40.9%	59.1%	40.9%	59.1%
O'BRIEN	8,637	4,336	4,295	6	41 R	50.2%	49.7%	50.2%	49.8%
OSCEOLA	4,301	1,798	2,498	5	700 D	41.8%	58.1%	41.9%	58.1%
PAGE	9,209	4,775	4,402	32	373 R	51.9%	47.8%	52.0%	48.0%
PALO ALTO	6,547	2,206	4,441		2,235 D	33.2%	66.8%	33.2%	66.8%
PLYMOUTH	10,613	4,920	5,691	2	771 D	46.4%	53.6%	46.4%	53.6%
POCAHONTAS	6,072	2,079	3,988	5	1,909 D	34.2%	65.7%	34.3%	65.7%
POLK	111,953	37,280	74,194	479	36,914 D	33.3%	66.3%	33.4%	66.6%
POTTAWATTAMIE	31,799	14,208	17,569	22	3,361 D	44.7%	55.3%	44.7%	55.3%
POWESHIEK	8,334	3,109	5,213	12	2,104 D	37.3%	62.6%	37.4%	62.6%
RINGGOLD	3,840	1,571	2,260	9	689 D	40.9%	58.9%	41.0%	59.1%
SAC	7,302	2,937	4,358	7	1,421 D	40.2%	59.7%	40.3%	59.7%
SCOTT	51,098	19,488	31,526	84	12,038 D	38.1%	61.7%	38.2%	61.8%
SHELBY	7,137	2,928	4,148	61	1,220 D	41.0%	58.1%	41.4%	58.5%
SIOUX	12,323	8,078	4,233	12	3,845 R	65.6%	34.4%	65.6%	34.4%
STORY	20,610	8,188	12,329	93	4,141 D	39.7%	59.8%	39.9%	60.1%
TAMA	9,608	3,543	6,057	8	2,514 D	36.9%	63.0%	36.9%	63.1%
TAYLOR	4,942	2,162	2,780		618 D	43.7%	56.3%	43.7%	56.3%
UNION	6,263	2,502	3,751	10	1,249 D	39.9%	59.9%	40.0%	60.0%
VAN BUREN	4,257	1,700	2,555	2	855 D	39.9%	60.0%	40.0%	60.0%
WAPELLO	19,546	5,524	13,971	51	8,447 D	28.3%	71.5%	28.3%	71.7%
WARREN	10,351	3,679	6,639	33	2,960 D	35.5%	64.1%	35.7%	64.3%
WASHINGTON	7,919	3,315	4,587	17	1,272 D	41.9%	57.9%	42.0%	58.0%
WAYNE	5,062	1,994	3,062	6	1,068 D	39.4%	60.5%	39.4%	60.6%
WEBSTER	19,635	6,576	13,005	54	6,429 D	33.5%	66.2%	33.6%	66.4%
WINNEBAGO	6,017	2,331	3,677	9	1,346 D	38.7%	61.1%	38.8%	61.2%
WINNESHIEK	9,759	3,941	5,811	7	1,870 D	40.4%	59.5%	40.4%	59.6%
WOODBURY	44,218	17,347	26,841	30	9,494 D	39.2%	60.7%	39.3%	60.7%
WORTH	4,723	1,777	2,936	10	1,159 D	37.6%	62.2%	37.7%	62.3%
WRIGHT	7,836	2,831	4,998	17	2,167 D	36.1%	63.8%	36.2%	63.8%
TOTAL	1,184,539	449,148	733,030	2,361	283,882 D	37.9%	61.9%	38.0%	62.0%

IOWA

OTHER VOTE COMPOSITION:

1920 16,981 Socialist; 10,321 Farmer-Labor; 4,197 Prohibition; 982 Socialist Labor.

1924 274,448 Progressive; 4,037 Communist; 445 scattered. The county-by-county figures include only the Progressive vote; the state-wide total also includes the Communist and scattered vote.

1928 3,088 Farmer-Labor; 2,960 Socialist; 328 Communist; 230 Socialist Labor; 2 scattered. Votes reported as state-wide totals, not by counties.

1932 20,467 Socialist; 2,111 Prohibition; 1,094 Farmer-Labor; 559 Communist; 4 scattered.

1936 29,687 Union; 1,373 Socialist; 1,182 Prohibition; 506 Communist; 252 Socialist Labor; 4 scattered.

1940 2,284 Prohibition; 1,524 Communist; 452 Socialist Labor.

1944 3,752 Prohibition; 1,511 Socialist; 193 Socialist Labor.

1948 12,125 Progressive; 4,274 Socialist Labor; 3,382 Prohibition; 1,829 Socialist; 256 Socialist Workers.

1952 5,085 Progressive; 2,882 Prohibition; 219 Socialist; 139 Socialist Labor; 29 scattered.

1956 3,202 States Rights; 192 Socialist; 125 Socialist Labor.

1960 634 Socialist Workers; 230 Socialist Labor.

1964 1,902 Prohibition; 182 Socialist Labor; 159 Socialist Workers; 118 scattered.

SPECIAL CASES:

1924 Progressive candidates carried several counties and ran second in many others.

KANSAS

PRESIDENT 1920

County	Total Vote	Republican	Democratic	Other	Rep-Dem Plurality	% Total Rep.	% Total Dem.	% Major Rep.	% Major Dem.
ALLEN	7,522	5,091	2,272	159	2,819 R	67.7%	30.2%	69.1%	30.9%
ANDERSON	4,884	3,068	1,708	108	1,360 R	62.8%	35.0%	64.2%	35.8%
ATCHISON	9,031	5,872	3,082	77	2,790 R	65.0%	34.1%	65.6%	34.4%
BARBER	3,612	2,400	1,098	114	1,302 R	66.4%	30.4%	68.6%	31.4%
BARTON	5,806	3,993	1,688	125	2,305 R	68.8%	29.1%	70.3%	29.7%
BOURBON	8,051	4,194	3,632	225	562 R	52.1%	45.1%	53.6%	46.4%
BROWN	7,262	5,249	1,937	76	3,312 R	72.3%	26.7%	73.0%	27.0%
BUTLER	11,264	6,821	4,112	331	2,709 R	60.6%	36.5%	62.4%	37.6%
CHASE	2,622	1,659	904	59	755 R	63.3%	34.5%	64.7%	35.3%
CHAUTAUQUA	3,702	2,539	936	227	1,603 R	68.6%	25.3%	73.1%	26.9%
CHEROKEE	9,790	5,466	3,832	492	1,634 R	55.8%	39.1%	58.8%	41.2%
CHEYENNE	1,710	1,079	471	160	608 R	63.1%	27.5%	69.6%	30.4%
CLARK	1,588	923	610	55	313 R	58.1%	38.4%	60.2%	39.8%
CLAY	4,844	3,521	1,155	168	2,366 R	72.7%	23.8%	75.3%	24.7%
CLOUD	5,858	4,090	1,534	234	2,556 R	69.8%	26.2%	72.7%	27.3%
COFFEY	5,249	3,370	1,785	94	1,585 R	64.2%	34.0%	65.4%	34.6%
COMANCHE	1,778	1,121	612	45	509 R	63.0%	34.4%	64.7%	35.3%
COWLEY	12,414	7,352	4,733	329	2,619 R	59.2%	38.1%	60.8%	39.2%
CRAWFORD	14,553	7,957	5,362	1,234	2,595 R	54.7%	36.8%	59.7%	40.3%
DECATUR	2,809	1,448	1,221	140	227 R	51.5%	43.5%	54.3%	45.7%
DICKINSON	8,337	5,761	2,387	189	3,374 R	69.1%	28.6%	70.7%	29.3%
DONIPHAN	4,406	3,369	978	59	2,391 R	76.5%	22.2%	77.5%	22.5%
DOUGLAS	8,557	6,266	2,197	94	4,069 R	73.2%	25.7%	74.0%	26.0%
EDWARDS	2,540	1,782	681	77	1,101 R	70.2%	26.8%	72.4%	27.6%
ELK	3,452	2,253	1,110	89	1,143 R	65.3%	32.2%	67.0%	33.0%
ELLIS	3,173	2,385	740	48	1,645 R	75.2%	23.3%	76.3%	23.7%
ELLSWORTH	3,451	2,264	1,090	97	1,174 R	65.6%	31.6%	67.5%	32.5%
FINNEY	2,281	1,573	619	89	954 R	69.0%	27.1%	71.8%	28.2%
FORD	5,339	3,505	1,679	155	1,826 R	65.6%	31.4%	67.6%	36.2%
FRANKLIN	8,005	5,216	2,606	183	2,610 R	65.2%	32.6%	66.7%	33.3%
GEARY	3,456	2,404	962	90	1,442 R	69.6%	27.8%	71.4%	28.6%
GOVE	1,268	950	285	33	665 R	74.9%	22.5%	76.9%	23.1%
GRAHAM	2,588	1,658	762	168	896 R	64.1%	29.4%	68.5%	31.5%
GRANT	460	339	108	13	231 R	73.7%	23.5%	75.8%	24.2%
GRAY	1,547	962	507	78	455 R	62.2%	32.8%	65.5%	34.5%
GREELEY	393	273	93	27	180 R	69.5%	23.7%	74.6%	25.4%
GREENWOOD	5,007	3,422	1,478	107	1,944 R	68.3%	29.5%	69.8%	30.2%
HAMILTON	1,025	591	371	63	220 R	57.7%	36.2%	61.4%	38.6%
HARPER	4,206	2,593	1,486	127	1,107 R	61.7%	35.3%	63.6%	36.4%
HARVEY	7,060	4,454	2,457	149	1,997 R	63.1%	34.8%	64.4%	35.6%
HASKELL	638	444	150	44	294 R	69.6%	23.5%	74.7%	25.3%
HODGEMAN	1,289	945	306	38	639 R	73.3%	23.7%	75.5%	24.5%
JACKSON	5,346	3,753	1,562	31	2,191 R	70.2%	29.2%	70.6%	29.4%
JEFFERSON	5,029	3,463	1,535	31	1,928 R	68.8%	30.5%	69.3%	30.7%
JEWELL	5,940	3,925	1,899	116	2,026 R	66.1%	32.0%	67.4%	32.6%
JOHNSON	6,729	4,325	2,303	101	2,022 R	64.3%	34.2%	65.3%	34.7%
KEARNY	968	617	266	85	351 R	63.7%	27.5%	69.9%	30.1%
KINGMAN	4,460	2,818	1,557	85	1,261 R	63.2%	34.9%	64.4%	35.6%
KIOWA	2,030	1,411	587	32	824 R	69.5%	28.9%	70.6%	29.4%
LABETTE	11,384	6,596	4,328	460	2,268 R	57.9%	38.0%	60.4%	39.6%
LANE	1,026	656	298	72	358 R	63.9%	29.0%	68.8%	31.2%
LEAVENWORTH	10,524	6,846	3,409	269	3,437 R	65.1%	32.4%	66.8%	33.2%
LINCOLN	3,306	2,298	935	73	1,363 R	69.5%	28.3%	71.1%	28.9%
LINN	5,075	3,189	1,764	122	1,425 R	62.8%	34.8%	64.4%	35.6%
LOGAN	1,138	781	312	45	469 R	68.6%	27.4%	71.5%	28.5%
LYON	8,990	5,492	3,303	195	2,189 R	61.1%	36.7%	62.5%	37.6%
MCPHERSON	7,007	4,870	1,926	211	2,944 R	69.5%	27.5%	71.7%	28.3%
MARION	5,834	3,840	1,713	281	2,127 R	65.8%	29.4%	69.2%	30.8%
MARSHALL	7,984	5,706	2,026	252	3,680 R	71.5%	25.4%	73.8%	26.2%
MEADE	1,742	1,236	483	23	753 R	71.0%	27.7%	71.9%	28.1%

PRESIDENT 1924

County	Total Vote	Republican	Democratic	Other	Rep-Dem Plurality	% Total Rep.	% Total Dem.	% Major Rep.	% Major Dem.
ALLEN	8,723	6,101	2,181	441	3,920 R	69.9%	25.0%	73.7%	26.3%
ANDERSON	5,085	3,101	1,421	563	1,680 R	61.0%	27.9%	68.6%	31.4%
ATCHISON	9,785	6,246	2,199	1,341	4,047 R	63.8%	22.5%	74.0%	26.0%
BARBER	3,808	2,218	909	681	1,309 R	58.2%	23.9%	70.9%	29.1%
BARTON	7,274	4,109	1,605	1,560	2,504 R	56.5%	22.1%	71.9%	28.1%
BOURBON	8,598	4,210	2,850	1,538	1,360 R	49.0%	33.1%	59.6%	40.4%
BROWN	8,191	5,647	1,866	678	3,781 R	68.9%	22.8%	75.2%	24.8%
BUTLER	12,716	7,367	3,642	1,707	3,725 R	57.9%	28.6%	66.9%	33.1%
CHASE	2,910	1,822	758	330	1,064 R	62.6%	26.0%	70.6%	29.4%
CHAUTAUQUA	4,066	2,439	1,087	540	1,352 R	60.0%	26.7%	69.2%	30.8%
CHEROKEE	10,278	5,437	3,071	1,770	2,366 R	52.9%	29.9%	63.9%	36.1%
CHEYENNE	2,221	1,119	485	617	634 R	50.4%	21.8%	69.8%	30.2%
CLARK	1,638	969	410	259	559 R	59.2%	25.0%	70.3%	29.7%
CLAY	5,986	3,767	1,417	802	2,350 R	62.9%	23.7%	72.7%	27.3%
CLOUD	6,939	4,342	1,238	1,359	3,104 R	62.6%	17.8%	77.8%	22.2%
COFFEY	5,686	3,552	1,631	503	1,921 R	62.5%	28.7%	68.5%	31.5%
COMANCHE	1,741	1,049	432	260	617 R	60.3%	24.8%	70.8%	29.2%
COWLEY	14,577	8,529	3,161	2,887	5,368 R	58.5%	21.7%	73.0%	27.0%
CRAWFORD	18,005	9,663	4,060	4,282	5,603 R	53.7%	22.5%	72.5%	27.5%
DECATUR	3,457	1,621	1,218	618	403 R	46.9%	35.2%	57.1%	42.9%
DICKINSON	9,566	6,178	1,690	1,698	4,488 R	64.6%	17.7%	78.5%	21.5%
DONIPHAN	5,206	3,789	1,072	345	2,717 R	72.8%	20.6%	77.9%	22.1%
DOUGLAS	10,700	8,052	1,922	726	6,130 R	75.3%	18.0%	80.7%	19.3%
EDWARDS	2,880	1,929	548	403	1,381 R	67.0%	19.0%	77.9%	22.1%
ELK	3,802	2,443	1,104	255	1,339 R	64.3%	29.0%	68.9%	31.1%
ELLIS	3,802	1,763	842	1,197	921 R	46.4%	22.1%	67.7%	32.3%
ELLSWORTH	3,890	2,286	950	654	1,336 R	58.8%	24.4%	70.6%	29.4%
FINNEY	2,843	1,753	614	476	1,139 R	61.7%	21.6%	74.1%	25.9%
FORD	5,948	3,449	1,551	948	1,898 R	58.0%	26.1%	69.0%	31.0%
FRANKLIN	8,960	6,008	2,324	628	3,684 R	67.1%	25.9%	72.1%	27.9%
GEARY	4,037	2,678	723	636	1,955 R	66.3%	17.9%	78.7%	21.3%
GOVE	1,787	1,211	400	176	811 R	67.7%	22.4%	75.2%	24.8%
GRAHAM	3,033	1,631	629	773	1,002 R	53.8%	20.7%	72.2%	27.8%
GRANT	684	459	148	77	311 R	67.1%	21.6%	75.6%	24.4%
GRAY	1,616	959	463	194	496 R	59.3%	28.7%	67.4%	32.6%
GREELEY	556	357	75	124	282 R	64.2%	13.5%	82.6%	17.4%
GREENWOOD	6,532	4,181	1,795	556	2,386 R	64.0%	27.5%	70.0%	30.0%
HAMILTON	1,167	610	307	250	303 R	52.3%	26.3%	66.5%	33.5%
HARPER	4,262	2,280	1,321	681	959 R	53.2%	30.9%	63.3%	36.7%
HARVEY	7,630	4,499	1,744	1,387	2,755 R	59.0%	22.9%	72.1%	27.9%
HASKELL	757	493	167	97	326 R	65.1%	22.1%	74.7%	25.3%
HODGEMAN	1,462	899	367	216	532 R	60.7%	24.8%	71.0%	29.0%
JACKSON	6,177	4,391	1,419	367	2,972 R	71.1%	23.0%	75.6%	24.4%
JEFFERSON	6,082	4,422	1,320	340	3,102 R	72.7%	21.7%	77.0%	23.0%
JEWELL	6,698	4,342	1,861	495	2,481 R	64.8%	27.8%	70.0%	30.0%
JOHNSON	9,224	6,102	2,519	603	3,583 R	66.2%	27.3%	70.8%	29.2%
KEARNY	1,103	635	199	269	436 R	57.6%	18.0%	76.1%	23.9%
KINGMAN	4,447	2,416	1,077	954	1,339 R	54.3%	24.2%	69.2%	30.8%
KIOWA	2,199	1,541	498	160	1,043 R	70.1%	22.6%	75.6%	24.4%
LABETTE	11,933	6,593	2,971	2,369	3,622 R	55.3%	24.9%	68.9%	31.1%
LANE	1,173	693	281	199	412 R	59.1%	24.0%	71.1%	28.9%
LEAVENWORTH	13,856	9,429	2,982	1,445	6,447 R	68.0%	21.5%	76.0%	24.0%
LINCOLN	3,833	2,277	615	941	1,662 R	59.1%	16.0%	78.7%	21.3%
LINN	5,458	3,161	1,683	614	1,478 R	57.9%	30.8%	65.3%	34.7%
LOGAN	1,475	942	286	247	656 R	63.9%	19.4%	76.7%	23.3%
LYON	10,974	6,290	2,750	1,934	3,540 R	57.3%	25.1%	69.6%	30.4%
MCPHERSON	7,771	5,128	1,530	1,113	3,598 R	66.0%	19.7%	77.0%	23.0%
MARION	7,109	4,008	1,520	1,581	2,488 R	56.4%	21.4%	72.5%	27.5%
MARSHALL	9,317	5,809	2,369	1,139	3,440 R	62.3%	25.4%	71.0%	29.0%
MEADE	1,927	1,290	472	165	818 R	66.9%	24.5%	73.2%	26.8%

KANSAS

PRESIDENT 1920

County	Total Vote	Republican	Democratic	Other	Rep.-Dem. Plurality	Total Vote Rep.	Total Vote Dem.	Major Vote Rep.	Major Vote Dem.
MIAMI	6,664	4,060	2,450	154	1,610 R	60.9%	36.8%	62.4%	37.6%
MITCHELL	4,845	3,310	1,409	126	1,901 R	68.3%	29.1%	70.1%	29.9%
MONTGOMERY	16,145	10,044	5,657	444	4,387 R	62.2%	35.0%	64.0%	36.0%
MORRIS	4,534	3,001	1,467	66	1,534 R	66.2%	32.4%	67.2%	32.8%
MORTON	1,073	783	266	24	517 R	73.0%	24.8%	74.6%	25.4%
NEMAHA	6,437	4,655	1,731	51	2,924 R	72.3%	26.9%	72.9%	27.1%
NEOSHO	8,467	5,150	3,195	122	1,955 R	60.8%	37.7%	61.7%	38.3%
NESS	2,005	1,402	492	111	910 R	69.9%	24.5%	74.0%	26.0%
NORTON	3,507	2,288	1,082	137	1,206 R	65.2%	30.9%	67.9%	32.1%
OSAGE	7,177	4,507	2,414	256	2,093 R	62.8%	33.6%	65.1%	34.9%
OSBORNE	4,110	3,060	980	70	2,080 R	74.5%	23.8%	75.7%	24.3%
OTTAWA	3,991	2,512	1,358	121	1,154 R	62.9%	34.0%	64.9%	35.1%
PAWNEE	3,326	2,128	1,138	60	990 R	64.0%	34.2%	65.2%	34.8%
PHILLIPS	4,172	2,862	1,230	80	1,632 R	68.6%	29.5%	69.9%	30.1%
POTTAWATOMIE	5,823	4,481	1,293	49	3,188 R	77.0%	22.2%	77.6%	22.4%
PRATT	4,243	2,722	1,433	88	1,289 R	64.2%	33.8%	65.5%	34.5%
RAWLINS	1,907	1,236	495	176	741 R	64.8%	26.0%	71.4%	28.6%
RENO	14,375	9,649	4,385	341	5,264 R	67.1%	30.5%	68.8%	31.2%
REPUBLIC	5,440	3,661	1,672	107	1,989 R	67.3%	30.7%	68.6%	31.4%
RICE	5,289	3,651	1,532	106	2,119 R	69.0%	29.0%	70.4%	29.6%
RILEY	6,626	4,875	1,610	141	3,265 R	73.6%	24.3%	75.2%	24.8%
ROOKS	3,064	2,143	843	78	1,300 R	69.9%	27.5%	71.8%	28.2%
RUSH	2,747	2,017	605	125	1,412 R	73.4%	22.0%	76.9%	23.1%
RUSSELL	3,198	2,407	724	67	1,683 R	75.3%	22.6%	76.9%	23.1%
SALINE	8,622	5,554	2,808	260	2,746 R	64.4%	32.6%	66.4%	33.6%
SCOTT	1,078	636	379	63	257 R	59.0%	35.2%	62.7%	37.3%
SEDGWICK	28,134	16,642	10,998	494	5,644 R	59.2%	39.1%	60.2%	39.8%
SEWARD	2,097	1,290	722	85	568 R	61.5%	34.4%	64.1%	35.9%
SHAWNEE	22,349	14,814	7,217	318	7,597 R	66.3%	32.3%	67.2%	32.8%
SHERIDAN	1,715	1,194	477	44	717 R	69.6%	27.8%	71.5%	28.5%
SHERMAN	1,962	1,066	789	107	277 R	54.3%	40.2%	57.5%	42.5%
SMITH	4,918	3,251	1,535	132	1,716 R	66.1%	31.2%	67.9%	32.1%
STAFFORD	3,968	2,779	1,057	132	1,722 R	70.0%	26.6%	72.4%	27.6%
STANTON	368	269	89	10	180 R	73.1%	24.2%	75.1%	24.9%
STEVENS	1,261	876	346	39	530 R	69.5%	27.4%	71.7%	28.3%
SUMNER	9,638	5,830	3,454	354	2,376 R	60.5%	35.8%	62.8%	37.2%
THOMAS	1,917	1,046	747	124	299 R	54.6%	39.0%	58.3%	41.7%
TREGO	1,731	1,299	395	37	904 R	75.0%	22.8%	76.7%	23.3%
WABAUNSEE	3,683	2,859	782	42	2,077 R	77.6%	21.2%	78.5%	21.5%
WALLACE	898	632	203	63	429 R	70.4%	22.6%	75.7%	24.3%
WASHINGTON	5,772	4,390	1,287	95	3,103 R	76.1%	22.3%	77.3%	22.7%
WICHITA	571	422	127	22	295 R	73.9%	22.2%	76.9%	23.1%
WILSON	6,076	4,024	1,768	284	2,256 R	66.2%	29.1%	69.5%	30.5%
WOODSON	3,279	2,253	944	82	1,309 R	68.7%	28.8%	70.5%	29.5%
WYANDOTTE	33,702	19,294	13,737	671	5,557 R	57.2%	40.8%	58.4%	41.6%
TOTAL	570,243	369,268	185,464	15,511	183,804 R	64.8%	32.5%	66.6%	33.4%

PRESIDENT 1924

County	Total Vote	Republican	Democratic	Other	Rep.-Dem. Plurality	Total Vote Rep.	Total Vote Dem.	Major Vote Rep.	Major Vote Dem.
MIAMI	7,753	4,788	1,994	971	2,794 R	61.8%	25.7%	70.6%	29.4%
MITCHELL	5,287	3,161	1,470	656	1,691 R	59.8%	27.8%	68.3%	31.7%
MONTGOMERY	17,163	11,160	4,178	1,825	6,982 R	65.0%	24.3%	72.8%	27.2%
MORRIS	4,774	3,089	1,040	645	2,049 R	64.7%	21.8%	74.8%	25.2%
MORTON	1,216	669	286	261	383 R	55.0%	23.5%	70.1%	29.9%
NEMAHA	6,799	4,096	1,846	857	2,250 R	60.2%	27.2%	68.9%	31.1%
NEOSHO	8,699	5,106	2,274	1,319	2,832 R	58.7%	26.1%	69.2%	30.8%
NESS	2,520	1,629	541	350	1,088 R	64.6%	21.5%	75.1%	24.9%
NORTON	4,682	2,778	1,261	643	1,517 R	59.3%	26.9%	68.8%	31.2%
OSAGE	7,843	4,957	2,050	836	2,907 R	63.2%	26.1%	70.7%	29.3%
OSBORNE	4,658	3,333	905	420	2,428 R	71.6%	19.4%	78.6%	21.4%
OTTAWA	4,108	2,475	854	779	1,621 R	60.2%	20.8%	74.3%	25.7%
PAWNEE	3,849	2,407	1,111	331	1,296 R	62.5%	28.9%	68.4%	31.6%
PHILLIPS	4,815	2,647	1,376	792	1,271 R	55.0%	28.6%	65.8%	34.2%
POTTAWATOMIE	6,356	4,340	1,471	545	2,869 R	68.3%	23.1%	74.7%	25.3%
PRATT	4,815	2,762	1,205	848	1,557 R	57.4%	25.0%	69.6%	30.4%
RAWLINS	2,649	1,213	742	694	471 R	45.8%	28.0%	62.0%	38.0%
RENO	15,851	10,339	3,675	1,837	6,664 R	65.2%	23.2%	73.8%	26.2%
REPUBLIC	6,122	3,671	1,616	835	2,055 R	60.0%	26.4%	69.4%	30.6%
RICE	5,720	3,920	1,303	497	2,617 R	68.5%	22.8%	75.1%	24.9%
RILEY	7,790	5,455	1,646	689	3,809 R	70.0%	21.1%	76.8%	23.2%
ROOKS	3,699	2,442	930	327	1,512 R	66.0%	25.1%	72.4%	27.6%
RUSH	3,109	1,780	787	542	993 R	57.3%	25.3%	69.3%	30.7%
RUSSELL	4,101	2,637	687	777	1,950 R	64.3%	16.8%	79.3%	20.7%
SALINE	10,505	6,534	1,966	2,005	4,568 R	62.2%	18.7%	76.9%	23.1%
SCOTT	1,443	734	445	264	289 R	50.9%	30.8%	62.3%	37.7%
SEDGWICK	36,943	21,144	8,712	7,087	12,432 R	57.2%	23.6%	70.8%	29.2%
SEWARD	2,277	1,184	676	417	508 R	52.0%	29.7%	63.7%	36.3%
SHAWNEE	27,878	20,132	5,099	2,647	15,033 R	72.2%	18.3%	79.8%	20.2%
SHERIDAN	2,233	1,320	542	371	778 R	59.1%	24.3%	70.9%	29.1%
SHERMAN	2,445	1,122	528	795	594 R	45.9%	21.6%	68.0%	32.0%
SMITH	5,637	3,226	1,634	777	1,592 R	57.2%	29.0%	66.4%	33.6%
STAFFORD	4,520	3,100	957	463	2,143 R	68.6%	21.2%	76.4%	23.6%
STANTON	607	379	158	70	221 R	62.4%	26.0%	70.6%	29.4%
STEVENS	1,372	913	302	157	611 R	66.5%	22.0%	75.1%	24.9%
SUMNER	10,108	5,552	2,556	2,000	2,996 R	54.9%	25.3%	68.5%	31.5%
THOMAS	2,735	1,436	822	477	614 R	52.5%	30.1%	63.6%	36.4%
TREGO	1,928	1,121	399	408	722 R	58.1%	20.7%	73.8%	26.2%
WABAUNSEE	4,161	2,742	633	786	2,109 R	65.9%	15.2%	81.8%	18.8%
WALLACE	1,123	603	171	349	432 R	53.7%	15.2%	77.9%	22.1%
WASHINGTON	6,756	4,120	1,528	1,108	2,592 R	61.0%	22.6%	72.9%	27.1%
WICHITA	769	482	147	140	335 R	62.7%	19.1%	76.6%	23.4%
WILSON	7,071	4,596	1,736	739	2,860 R	65.0%	24.6%	72.6%	27.4%
WOODSON	3,818	2,412	1,026	380	1,386 R	63.2%	26.9%	70.2%	29.8%
WYANDOTTE	40,148	23,881	8,913	7,354	14,968 R	59.5%	22.2%	72.8%	27.2%
TOTAL	662,456	407,671	156,320	98,465	251,351 R	61.5%	23.6%	72.3%	27.7%

KANSAS

PRESIDENT 1928 / PRESIDENT 1932

County	1928 Total Vote	1928 Republican	1928 Democratic	1928 Other	1928 Rep.-Dem. Plurality	1928 %TV Rep.	1928 %TV Dem.	1928 %MV Rep.	1928 %MV Dem.	1932 Total Vote	1932 Republican	1932 Democratic	1932 Other	1932 Rep.-Dem. Plurality	1932 %TV Rep.	1932 %TV Dem.	1932 %MV Rep.	1932 %MV Dem.
ALLEN	8,550	6,695	1,803	52	4,892 R	78.3%	21.1%	78.8%	21.2%	8,935	4,510	4,249	177	261 R	50.5%	47.5%	51.5%	48.5%
ANDERSON	5,485	3,562	1,874	49	1,688 R	64.9%	34.2%	65.5%	34.5%	6,075	2,408	3,580	88	1,172 D	39.6%	58.9%	40.2%	59.8%
ATCHISON	10,440	6,647	3,756	37	2,891 R	63.7%	36.0%	63.9%	36.1%	10,575	4,778	5,640	157	862 D	45.2%	53.3%	45.9%	54.1%
BARBER	3,904	2,984	871	49	2,113 R	76.4%	22.3%	77.4%	22.6%	4,088	1,671	2,321	96	650 D	40.9%	56.8%	41.9%	58.1%
BARTON	7,767	4,966	2,777	24	2,189 R	63.9%	35.8%	64.1%	35.9%	8,238	3,365	4,776	97	1,411 D	40.8%	58.0%	41.3%	58.7%
BOURBON	9,556	7,251	2,223	82	5,028 R	75.9%	23.3%	76.5%	23.5%	10,035	4,277	5,577	181	1,300 D	42.6%	55.6%	43.4%	56.6%
BROWN	8,717	6,692	2,005	20	4,687 R	76.8%	23.0%	76.9%	23.1%	8,669	5,005	3,604	60	1,401 R	57.7%	41.6%	58.1%	41.9%
BUTLER	12,802	10,168	2,533	101	7,635 R	79.4%	19.8%	80.1%	19.9%	13,994	6,116	7,447	431	1,331 D	43.7%	53.2%	45.1%	54.9%
CHASE	2,856	2,079	739	38	1,340 R	72.8%	25.9%	73.8%	26.2%	3,231	1,485	1,703	43	218 D	46.0%	52.7%	46.6%	53.4%
CHAUTAUQUA	4,348	3,303	944	101	2,359 R	76.0%	21.7%	77.8%	22.2%	4,360	1,893	2,263	204	370 D	43.4%	51.9%	45.5%	54.5%
CHEROKEE	11,296	7,478	3,442	376	4,036 R	66.2%	30.5%	68.5%	31.5%	11,880	4,045	7,442	393	3,397 D	34.0%	62.6%	35.2%	64.8%
CHEYENNE	2,106	1,466	586	54	880 R	69.6%	27.8%	71.4%	28.6%	2,829	979	1,716	134	737 D	34.6%	60.7%	36.3%	63.7%
CLARK	1,810	1,383	419	8	964 R	76.4%	23.1%	76.7%	23.3%	2,106	938	1,152	16	214 D	44.5%	54.7%	44.9%	55.1%
CLAY	6,044	4,457	1,515	72	2,942 R	73.7%	25.1%	74.6%	25.4%	6,591	3,115	3,289	187	174 D	47.3%	49.9%	48.6%	51.4%
CLOUD	7,745	5,286	2,376	83	2,910 R	68.3%	30.7%	69.0%	31.0%	7,812	3,120	4,457	235	1,337 D	39.9%	57.1%	41.2%	58.8%
COFFEY	5,883	4,342	1,514	27	2,828 R	73.8%	25.7%	74.1%	25.9%	6,184	2,707	3,389	88	682 D	43.8%	54.8%	44.4%	55.6%
COMANCHE	1,943	1,554	385	4	1,169 R	80.0%	19.8%	80.1%	19.9%	2,152	945	1,175	32	230 D	43.9%	54.6%	44.6%	55.4%
COWLEY	15,721	12,701	2,818	202	9,883 R	80.8%	17.9%	81.8%	18.2%	17,126	7,657	8,681	788	1,024 D	44.7%	50.7%	46.9%	53.1%
CRAWFORD	17,642	10,992	6,351	299	4,641 R	62.3%	36.0%	63.4%	36.6%	18,401	6,684	10,994	523	4,110 D	37.4%	59.7%	38.5%	61.5%
DECATUR	3,478	2,314	1,129	35	1,185 R	66.5%	32.5%	67.2%	32.8%	3,969	1,439	2,422	108	983 D	36.3%	61.0%	37.3%	62.7%
DICKINSON	10,070	7,798	2,246	66	5,512 R	77.0%	22.3%	77.5%	22.5%	10,849	5,320	5,339	190	19 D	49.0%	49.2%	49.9%	50.1%
DONIPHAN	5,509	4,002	1,496	11	2,506 R	72.6%	27.2%	72.8%	27.3%	5,349	2,748	2,532	69	216 R	51.4%	47.3%	52.0%	48.0%
DOUGLAS	11,292	8,887	2,297	108	6,590 R	78.7%	20.3%	79.5%	20.5%	12,521	7,346	4,833	342	2,513 R	58.7%	38.6%	60.3%	39.7%
EDWARDS	2,959	2,171	768	20	1,403 R	73.4%	26.0%	73.9%	26.1%	3,198	1,420	1,693	85	273 D	44.4%	52.9%	45.6%	54.4%
ELK	3,880	3,007	831	42	2,176 R	77.5%	21.4%	78.3%	21.7%	4,057	1,746	2,239	72	493 D	43.0%	55.2%	43.8%	56.2%
ELLIS	5,075	1,700	3,364	11	1,664 D	33.5%	66.3%	33.6%	66.4%	5,970	1,465	4,449	56	2,984 D	24.5%	74.5%	24.8%	75.2%
ELLSWORTH	4,068	2,450	1,588	30	862 R	60.2%	39.0%	60.7%	39.3%	4,598	1,607	2,928	63	1,321 D	34.9%	63.7%	35.4%	64.6%
FINNEY	3,174	2,433	709	32	1,724 R	76.7%	22.3%	77.4%	22.6%	4,500	2,116	2,300	84	184 D	47.0%	51.1%	47.9%	52.1%
FORD	6,835	4,893	1,870	72	3,023 R	71.6%	27.4%	72.3%	27.7%	8,015	3,335	4,442	238	1,107 D	41.6%	55.4%	42.9%	57.1%
FRANKLIN	9,370	7,346	1,951	73	5,395 R	78.4%	20.8%	79.0%	21.0%	9,742	4,887	4,690	165	197 R	50.2%	48.1%	51.0%	49.0%
GEARY	3,971	2,746	1,203	22	1,543 R	69.2%	30.3%	69.5%	30.5%	4,783	1,957	2,705	121	748 D	40.9%	56.6%	42.0%	58.0%
GOVE	2,072	1,470	590	12	880 R	70.9%	28.5%	71.4%	28.6%	2,280	1,043	1,186	51	143 D	45.7%	52.0%	46.8%	53.2%
GRAHAM	2,970	1,832	1,087	51	745 R	61.7%	36.6%	62.8%	37.2%	3,464	1,284	2,082	98	798 D	37.1%	60.1%	38.1%	61.9%
GRANT	831	635	185	11	450 R	76.4%	22.3%	77.4%	22.6%	1,172	395	737	40	342 D	33.7%	62.9%	34.9%	65.1%
GRAY	1,918	1,294	606	18	688 R	67.5%	31.6%	68.1%	31.9%	2,317	910	1,348	59	438 D	39.3%	58.2%	40.3%	59.7%
GREELEY	561	439	121	1	318 R	78.3%	21.6%	78.4%	21.6%	842	359	440	43	81 D	42.6%	52.3%	44.9%	55.1%
GREENWOOD	7,466	5,863	1,554	49	4,309 R	78.5%	20.8%	79.0%	21.0%	7,747	3,592	4,002	153	410 D	46.4%	51.7%	47.3%	52.7%
HAMILTON	1,226	839	363	24	476 R	68.4%	29.6%	69.8%	30.2%	1,775	651	1,021	103	370 D	36.7%	57.5%	38.9%	61.1%
HARPER	4,768	3,712	1,005	51	2,707 R	77.9%	21.1%	78.7%	21.3%	5,145	2,116	2,860	169	744 D	41.1%	55.6%	42.5%	57.5%
HARVEY	8,155	6,330	1,748	77	4,582 R	77.6%	21.4%	78.4%	21.6%	8,507	4,192	4,091	224	101 R	49.3%	48.1%	50.6%	49.4%
HASKELL	880	646	222	12	424 R	73.4%	25.2%	74.4%	25.6%	1,126	456	639	31	183 D	40.5%	56.7%	41.6%	58.4%
HODGEMAN	1,661	1,122	528	11	594 R	67.5%	31.8%	68.0%	32.0%	1,859	847	988	24	141 D	45.6%	53.1%	46.2%	53.8%
JACKSON	6,453	4,811	1,602	40	3,209 R	74.6%	24.8%	75.0%	25.0%	6,799	3,271	3,442	86	171 D	48.1%	50.6%	48.7%	51.3%
JEFFERSON	6,433	4,810	1,601	22	3,209 R	74.8%	24.9%	75.0%	25.0%	6,271	2,974	3,185	112	211 D	47.4%	50.8%	48.3%	51.7%
JEWELL	5,960	4,583	1,289	88	3,294 R	76.9%	21.6%	78.0%	22.0%	6,896	3,324	3,367	205	43 D	48.2%	48.8%	49.7%	50.3%
JOHNSON	11,627	8,185	3,373	69	4,812 R	70.4%	29.0%	70.8%	29.2%	13,096	6,487	6,485	124	2 R	49.5%	49.5%	50.0%	50.0%
KEARNY	1,106	854	229	23	625 R	77.2%	20.7%	78.9%	21.1%	1,359	529	771	59	242 D	38.9%	56.7%	40.7%	59.3%
KINGMAN	4,721	3,287	1,408	26	1,879 R	69.6%	29.8%	70.0%	30.0%	5,065	1,923	3,050	92	1,127 D	38.0%	60.2%	38.7%	61.3%
KIOWA	2,350	1,929	406	15	1,523 R	82.1%	17.3%	82.6%	17.4%	2,500	1,306	1,159	35	147 R	52.2%	46.4%	53.0%	47.0%
LABETTE	12,191	9,048	2,969	174	6,079 R	74.2%	24.4%	75.3%	24.7%	13,755	5,794	7,667	294	1,873 D	42.1%	55.7%	43.0%	57.0%
LANE	1,338	954	364	20	590 R	71.3%	27.2%	72.4%	27.6%	1,567	672	866	29	194 D	42.9%	55.3%	43.7%	56.3%
LEAVENWORTH	15,056	8,472	6,539	45	1,933 R	56.3%	43.4%	56.4%	43.6%	16,114	6,484	9,507	123	3,023 D	40.2%	59.0%	40.5%	59.5%
LINCOLN	3,631	2,655	953	23	1,702 R	73.1%	26.2%	73.6%	26.4%	4,051	1,653	2,297	101	644 D	40.8%	56.7%	41.8%	58.2%
LINN	5,627	4,231	1,328	68	2,903 R	75.2%	23.6%	76.1%	23.9%	5,953	2,647	3,216	90	569 D	44.5%	54.0%	45.1%	54.9%
LOGAN	1,488	1,066	405	17	661 R	71.6%	27.2%	72.5%	27.5%	1,959	867	1,025	67	158 D	44.3%	52.3%	45.8%	54.2%
LYON	11,595	8,753	2,761	81	5,992 R	75.5%	23.8%	76.0%	24.0%	12,755	6,044	6,365	347	321 D	47.4%	49.9%	48.7%	51.3%
MCPHERSON	7,789	6,230	1,457	102	4,773 R	80.0%	18.7%	81.0%	19.0%	9,377	4,098	5,003	276	905 D	43.7%	53.4%	45.0%	55.0%
MARION	7,410	5,446	1,938	26	3,508 R	73.5%	26.2%	73.8%	26.2%	7,715	3,220	4,366	129	1,146 D	41.7%	56.6%	42.4%	57.6%
MARSHALL	10,316	6,918	3,329	69	3,589 R	67.1%	32.3%	67.5%	32.5%	10,544	4,455	5,970	119	1,515 D	42.3%	56.6%	42.7%	57.3%
MEADE	2,336	1,709	618	9	1,091 R	73.2%	26.5%	73.4%	26.6%	2,521	1,248	1,231	42	17 R	49.5%	48.8%	50.3%	49.7%

KANSAS

PRESIDENT 1928

County	Total Vote	Republican	Democratic	Other	Rep-Dem Plurality	Total Vote Rep.	Dem.	Major Vote Rep.	Dem.
MIAMI	8,157	5,931	2,148	78	3,783 R	72.7%	26.3%	73.4%	26.6%
MITCHELL	5,164	3,245	1,855	64	1,390 R	62.8%	35.9%	63.6%	36.4%
MONTGOMERY	18,760	14,316	4,205	239	10,111 R	76.3%	22.4%	77.3%	22.7%
MORRIS	4,815	3,830	929	56	2,901 R	79.5%	19.3%	80.5%	19.5%
MORTON	1,282	1,010	259	13	751 R	78.8%	20.2%	79.6%	20.4%
NEMAHA	7,592	4,639	2,919	34	1,720 R	61.1%	38.4%	61.4%	38.6%
NEOSHO	9,136	6,603	2,459	74	4,144 R	72.3%	26.9%	72.9%	27.1%
NESS	2,878	2,058	784	36	1,274 R	71.5%	27.2%	72.4%	27.6%
NORTON	4,548	3,365	1,087	96	2,278 R	74.0%	23.9%	75.6%	24.4%
OSAGE	8,056	5,900	2,058	98	3,842 R	73.2%	25.5%	74.1%	25.9%
OSBORNE	4,528	3,683	821	24	2,862 R	81.3%	18.1%	81.8%	18.2%
OTTAWA	4,354	3,158	1,131	65	2,027 R	72.5%	26.0%	73.6%	26.4%
PAWNEE	3,763	2,829	918	16	1,911 R	75.2%	24.4%	75.5%	24.5%
PHILLIPS	4,595	3,206	1,332	57	1,874 R	69.8%	29.0%	70.6%	29.4%
POTTAWATOMIE	6,816	4,451	2,341	24	2,110 R	65.3%	34.3%	65.5%	34.5%
PRATT	5,032	4,055	934	43	3,121 R	80.6%	18.6%	81.3%	18.7%
RAWLINS	2,887	1,668	1,164	55	504 R	57.8%	40.3%	58.9%	41.1%
RENO	16,868	12,872	3,843	153	9,029 R	77.0%	22.8%	77.0%	23.0%
REPUBLIC	6,341	4,324	1,956	61	2,368 R	68.2%	30.8%	68.9%	31.1%
RICE	5,835	4,321	1,462	52	2,859 R	74.1%	25.1%	74.7%	25.3%
RILEY	8,461	6,592	1,791	78	4,801 R	77.9%	21.2%	78.6%	21.4%
ROOKS	3,652	2,583	1,044	25	1,539 R	70.7%	28.6%	71.2%	28.8%
RUSH	3,307	1,985	1,296	26	689 R	60.0%	39.2%	60.5%	39.5%
RUSSELL	4,180	2,782	1,366	32	1,416 R	66.6%	32.7%	67.1%	32.9%
SALINE	11,056	7,872	3,108	76	4,764 R	71.2%	28.1%	71.7%	28.3%
SCOTT	1,347	886	450	11	436 R	65.8%	33.4%	66.3%	33.7%
SEDGWICK	43,186	32,132	10,649	405	21,483 R	74.4%	24.7%	75.1%	24.9%
SEWARD	2,433	1,873	538	22	1,335 R	77.0%	22.1%	77.5%	22.5%
SHAWNEE	32,336	24,723	7,433	180	17,290 R	76.5%	23.0%	76.9%	23.1%
SHERIDAN	2,396	1,450	930	16	520 R	60.5%	38.8%	60.9%	39.1%
SHERMAN	2,718	2,028	630	60	1,398 R	74.6%	23.2%	76.3%	23.7%
SMITH	5,409	4,021	1,338	50	2,683 R	74.3%	24.7%	75.0%	25.0%
STAFFORD	4,355	3,278	1,025	52	2,253 R	75.3%	23.5%	76.2%	23.8%
STANTON	664	497	164	3	333 R	74.8%	24.7%	75.2%	24.8%
STEVENS	1,443	1,133	300	10	833 R	78.5%	20.8%	79.1%	20.9%
SUMNER	11,240	8,951	2,108	181	6,843 R	79.6%	18.8%	80.9%	19.1%
THOMAS	2,771	1,828	899	44	929 R	66.0%	32.4%	67.0%	33.0%
TREGO	2,354	1,359	982	13	377 R	57.7%	41.7%	58.1%	41.9%
WABAUNSEE	4,311	3,099	1,189	23	1,910 R	71.9%	27.6%	72.3%	27.7%
WALLACE	1,115	738	356	21	382 R	66.2%	31.9%	67.5%	32.5%
WASHINGTON	7,097	4,781	2,267	49	2,514 R	67.4%	31.9%	67.8%	32.2%
WICHITA	845	464	370	11	94 R	54.9%	43.8%	55.6%	44.4%
WILSON	7,141	5,603	1,465	73	4,138 R	78.5%	20.5%	79.3%	20.7%
WOODSON	3,767	2,885	855	27	2,030 R	76.6%	22.7%	77.1%	22.9%
WYANDOTTE	49,978	32,829	16,884	265	15,945 R	65.7%	33.8%	66.0%	34.0%
TOTAL	713,200	513,672	193,003	6,525	320,669 R	72.0%	27.1%	72.7%	27.3%

PRESIDENT 1932

County	Total Vote Rep.	Dem.	Major Vote Rep.	Dem.	Rep-Dem Plurality	Other	Democratic	Republican	Total Vote
MIAMI	43.0%	55.6%	43.6%	56.4%	1,072 D	114	4,739	3,667	8,520
MITCHELL	42.7%	54.2%	44.1%	55.9%	674 D	181	3,176	2,502	5,859
MONTGOMERY	49.0%	48.9%	50.0%	50.0%	17 R	440	9,941	9,958	20,339
MORRIS	49.7%	47.5%	51.1%	48.9%	114 R	146	2,452	2,566	5,164
MORTON	34.6%	61.0%	36.2%	63.8%	472 D	79	1,093	621	1,793
NEMAHA	40.6%	58.7%	40.9%	59.1%	1,411 D	55	4,578	3,167	7,800
NEOSHO	42.9%	56.4%	42.9%	57.1%	1,404 D	137	5,616	4,212	9,965
NESS	42.6%	53.6%	44.3%	55.7%	363 D	123	1,772	1,409	3,304
NORTON	44.2%	52.6%	45.6%	54.4%	433 D	168	2,705	2,272	5,145
OSAGE	45.4%	51.4%	46.9%	53.1%	492 D	259	4,199	3,707	8,165
OSBORNE	51.9%	45.4%	53.4%	46.6%	324 R	133	2,231	2,555	4,919
OTTAWA	41.3%	54.9%	42.9%	57.1%	621 D	170	2,505	1,884	4,559
PAWNEE	42.5%	55.2%	43.5%	56.5%	562 D	103	2,451	1,889	4,443
PHILLIPS	40.6%	56.4%	41.9%	58.1%	842 D	155	3,007	2,165	5,327
POTTAWATOMIE	45.5%	53.2%	46.1%	53.9%	571 D	97	3,910	3,339	7,346
PRATT	40.2%	57.6%	41.1%	58.9%	942 D	121	3,109	2,167	5,397
RAWLINS	31.1%	65.6%	32.2%	67.8%	1,181 D	114	2,245	1,064	3,423
RENO	47.3%	49.3%	49.0%	51.0%	379 D	647	9,351	8,972	18,970
REPUBLIC	38.6%	59.6%	39.3%	60.7%	1,450 D	127	4,105	2,655	6,887
RICE	49.3%	48.2%	50.6%	49.4%	70 R	154	3,037	3,107	6,298
RILEY	54.7%	42.0%	56.5%	43.5%	1,236 R	327	4,101	5,337	9,765
ROOKS	46.4%	51.6%	47.4%	52.6%	224 D	88	2,229	2,005	4,322
RUSH	38.0%	60.3%	38.6%	61.4%	842 D	66	2,275	1,433	3,774
RUSSELL	39.0%	58.8%	39.9%	60.1%	918 D	103	2,723	1,805	4,631
SALINE	41.2%	55.7%	42.5%	57.5%	1,853 D	389	7,118	5,265	12,772
SCOTT	34.0%	62.5%	35.3%	64.7%	497 D	61	1,092	595	1,748
SEDGWICK	41.5%	55.8%	42.6%	57.4%	7,529 D	1,435	29,344	21,815	52,594
SEWARD	42.6%	53.0%	45.1%	54.9%	279 D	99	1,576	1,297	2,972
SHAWNEE	53.4%	44.3%	54.6%	45.4%	3,376 R	823	16,471	19,847	37,141
SHERIDAN	32.4%	65.5%	33.1%	66.9%	895 D	56	1,773	878	2,707
SHERMAN	32.2%	61.1%	34.5%	65.5%	998 D	232	2,110	1,112	3,454
SMITH	46.5%	51.1%	47.6%	52.4%	285 D	144	3,155	2,870	6,169
STAFFORD	41.2%	56.2%	42.3%	57.7%	706 D	122	2,651	1,945	4,718
STANTON	40.2%	58.4%	40.8%	59.2%	186 D	14	598	412	1,024
STEVENS	31.1%	65.9%	32.1%	67.9%	647 D	57	1,225	578	1,860
SUMNER	42.4%	54.7%	43.7%	56.3%	1,427 D	340	6,353	4,926	11,619
THOMAS	33.7%	61.2%	35.5%	64.5%	945 D	177	2,103	1,158	3,438
TREGO	33.8%	64.4%	34.4%	65.6%	833 D	50	1,751	918	2,719
WABAUNSEE	47.4%	50.7%	48.3%	51.7%	161 D	93	2,465	2,304	4,862
WALLACE	40.3%	54.6%	42.4%	57.6%	200 D	71	761	561	1,393
WASHINGTON	43.4%	55.3%	44.0%	56.0%	910 D	95	4,234	3,324	7,653
WICHITA	32.9%	64.3%	33.9%	66.1%	357 D	32	732	375	1,139
WILSON	44.9%	52.5%	46.1%	53.9%	579 D	193	4,001	3,422	7,616
WOODSON	45.2%	52.0%	46.5%	53.5%	277 D	117	2,119	1,842	4,078
WYANDOTTE	43.3%	55.5%	43.8%	56.2%	7,158 D	721	32,629	25,471	58,821
TOTAL	44.1%	53.6%	45.2%	54.8%	74,706 D	18,276	424,204	349,498	791,978

KANSAS

PRESIDENT 1936

County	Total Vote	Republican	Democratic	Other	Rep.-Dem. Plurality	%Total Rep.	%Total Dem.	%Major Rep.	%Major Dem.
ALLEN	9,945	6,071	3,869	5	2,202 R	61.0%	38.9%	61.1%	38.9%
ANDERSON	6,318	3,452	2,767	99	685 R	54.6%	43.8%	55.5%	44.5%
ATCHISON	11,160	5,312	5,817	31	505 D	47.6%	52.1%	47.7%	52.3%
BARBER	4,608	1,816	2,774	18	958 D	39.4%	60.2%	39.6%	60.4%
BARTON	9,517	3,534	5,978	5	2,444 D	37.1%	62.8%	37.2%	62.8%
BOURBON	11,120	5,402	5,714	4	312 D	48.6%	51.4%	48.6%	51.4%
BROWN	9,320	5,814	3,495	11	2,319 R	62.4%	37.5%	62.5%	37.5%
BUTLER	15,514	6,204	9,283	27	3,079 D	40.0%	59.8%	40.1%	59.9%
CHASE	3,325	1,610	1,706	9	96 D	48.4%	51.3%	48.6%	51.4%
CHAUTAUQUA	4,599	2,506	2,080	13	426 R	54.5%	45.2%	54.6%	45.4%
CHEROKEE	13,408	5,445	7,894	69	2,449 D	40.6%	58.9%	40.8%	59.2%
CHEYENNE	2,925	1,241	1,673	11	432 D	42.4%	57.2%	42.6%	57.4%
CLARK	2,358	899	1,457	2	558 D	38.1%	61.8%	38.2%	61.8%
CLAY	6,987	3,525	3,441	21	84 R	50.5%	49.2%	50.6%	49.4%
CLOUD	8,785	4,208	4,546	31	338 D	47.9%	51.7%	48.1%	51.9%
COFFEY	6,578	3,900	2,662	16	1,238 R	59.3%	40.5%	59.4%	40.6%
COMANCHE	2,363	932	1,428	3	496 D	39.4%	60.4%	39.5%	60.5%
COWLEY	19,255	8,378	10,805	72	2,427 D	43.5%	56.1%	43.7%	56.3%
CRAWFORD	21,636	8,596	12,974	66	4,378 D	39.7%	60.0%	39.9%	60.1%
DECATUR	4,104	1,727	2,362	15	635 D	42.1%	57.5%	42.2%	57.8%
DICKINSON	11,283	5,936	5,313	34	623 R	52.6%	47.0%	52.8%	47.2%
DONIPHAN	6,559	3,791	2,749	19	1,042 R	57.8%	41.9%	58.0%	42.0%
DOUGLAS	13,379	8,324	4,961	94	3,363 R	62.2%	37.1%	62.7%	37.3%
EDWARDS	3,383	1,394	1,986	3	592 D	41.2%	58.7%	41.2%	58.8%
ELK	4,423	2,355	2,059	9	296 R	53.2%	46.5%	53.4%	46.6%
ELLIS	6,469	1,622	4,834	13	3,212 D	25.1%	74.7%	25.1%	74.9%
ELLSWORTH	5,055	2,058	2,990	7	932 D	40.7%	59.1%	40.8%	59.2%
FINNEY	4,557	1,863	2,682	12	819 D	40.9%	58.9%	41.0%	59.0%
FORD	8,730	3,378	5,335	17	1,957 D	38.7%	61.1%	38.8%	61.2%
FRANKLIN	10,538	6,007	4,503	28	1,504 R	57.0%	42.7%	57.2%	42.8%
GEARY	5,367	2,382	2,973	12	591 D	44.4%	55.4%	44.5%	55.5%
GOVE	2,222	1,107	1,090	25	17 R	49.8%	49.1%	50.4%	49.6%
GRAHAM	3,202	1,462	1,734	6	272 D	45.7%	54.2%	45.7%	54.3%
GRANT	1,092	476	616	-	140 D	43.6%	56.4%	43.6%	56.4%
GRAY	2,225	764	1,459	2	695 D	34.3%	65.6%	34.4%	65.6%
GREELEY	785	396	388	1	8 R	50.4%	49.4%	50.5%	49.5%
GREENWOOD	8,345	4,146	4,176	23	30 D	49.7%	50.0%	49.8%	50.2%
HAMILTON	1,616	720	885	11	165 D	44.6%	54.8%	44.9%	55.1%
HARPER	5,854	2,441	3,391	22	950 D	41.7%	57.9%	41.9%	58.1%
HARVEY	9,841	4,456	5,357	28	901 D	45.3%	54.4%	45.4%	54.6%
HASKELL	1,069	442	626	1	184 D	41.3%	58.6%	41.4%	58.6%
HODGEMAN	1,946	781	1,162	3	381 D	40.1%	59.7%	40.2%	59.8%
JACKSON	6,959	3,680	3,265	14	415 R	52.9%	46.9%	53.0%	47.0%
JEFFERSON	6,841	3,711	3,105	25	606 R	54.2%	45.4%	54.4%	45.6%
JEWELL	6,664	3,849	2,780	35	1,069 R	57.8%	41.7%	58.1%	41.9%
JOHNSON	14,554	8,399	6,108	47	2,291 R	57.7%	42.0%	57.9%	42.1%
KEARNY	1,313	586	716	11	130 D	44.6%	54.5%	45.0%	55.0%
KINGMAN	5,732	2,014	3,705	13	1,591 D	35.1%	64.6%	35.2%	64.8%
KIOWA	2,705	1,280	1,417	8	137 D	47.3%	52.4%	47.5%	52.5%
LABETTE	14,716	6,610	8,050	56	1,440 D	44.9%	54.7%	45.1%	54.9%
LANE	1,558	682	853	23	171 D	43.8%	54.7%	44.4%	55.6%
LEAVENWORTH	16,601	8,532	7,996	73	536 R	51.4%	48.1%	51.6%	48.4%
LINCOLN	4,220	2,001	2,209	10	208 D	47.4%	52.3%	47.5%	52.5%
LINN	6,587	2,682	3,872	33	1,190 D	40.7%	58.8%	40.9%	59.1%
LOGAN	1,867	955	908	4	47 R	51.2%	48.6%	51.3%	48.7%
LYON	13,423	6,005	7,340	78	1,335 D	44.7%	54.7%	45.0%	55.0%
MCPHERSON	11,044	4,744	6,256	44	1,512 D	43.0%	56.6%	43.1%	56.9%
MARION	8,426	4,185	4,207	34	22 D	49.7%	49.9%	49.9%	50.1%
MARSHALL	11,190	5,929	5,238	23	591 R	53.0%	46.8%	53.1%	46.9%
MEADE	2,615	1,218	1,394	3	176 D	46.6%	53.3%	46.6%	53.4%

PRESIDENT 1940

County	Total Vote	Republican	Democratic	Other	Rep.-Dem. Plurality	%Total Rep.	%Total Dem.	%Major Rep.	%Major Dem.
ALLEN	9,600	6,376	3,178	46	3,198 R	66.4%	33.1%	66.7%	33.3%
ANDERSON	6,033	3,886	2,114	33	1,772 R	64.4%	35.0%	64.8%	35.2%
ATCHISON	10,560	5,921	4,557	82	1,364 R	56.1%	43.2%	56.5%	43.5%
BARBER	4,521	2,389	2,074	58	315 R	52.8%	45.9%	53.5%	46.5%
BARTON	11,043	6,011	4,982	50	1,029 R	54.4%	45.1%	54.7%	45.3%
BOURBON	10,727	5,751	4,898	78	853 R	53.6%	45.7%	54.0%	46.0%
BROWN	8,684	6,008	2,633	43	3,375 R	69.2%	30.3%	69.5%	30.5%
BUTLER	15,360	7,619	7,615	126	4 R	49.6%	49.6%	50.0%	50.0%
CHASE	3,238	1,871	1,344	23	527 R	57.8%	41.5%	58.2%	41.8%
CHAUTAUQUA	4,606	2,888	1,679	39	1,209 R	62.7%	36.5%	63.2%	36.8%
CHEROKEE	13,396	6,600	6,670	126	70 D	49.3%	49.8%	49.7%	50.3%
CHEYENNE	2,744	1,760	971	13	789 R	64.1%	35.4%	64.4%	35.6%
CLARK	2,167	1,072	1,079	16	7 D	49.5%	49.8%	49.8%	50.2%
CLAY	6,836	4,699	2,067	70	2,632 R	68.7%	30.2%	69.5%	30.5%
CLOUD	8,728	5,275	3,327	126	1,948 R	60.4%	38.1%	61.3%	38.7%
COFFEY	6,480	4,164	2,272	44	1,892 R	64.3%	35.1%	64.7%	35.3%
COMANCHE	2,222	1,322	880	20	442 R	59.5%	39.6%	60.0%	40.0%
COWLEY	17,935	9,684	8,115	136	1,569 R	54.0%	45.2%	54.4%	45.6%
CRAWFORD	21,275	10,143	11,002	130	859 D	47.7%	51.7%	48.0%	52.0%
DECATUR	3,593	2,018	1,546	29	472 R	56.2%	43.0%	56.6%	43.4%
DICKINSON	10,958	6,931	3,957	70	2,974 R	63.3%	36.1%	63.7%	36.3%
DONIPHAN	6,210	4,204	1,986	20	2,218 R	67.7%	32.0%	67.9%	32.1%
DOUGLAS	13,014	9,146	3,727	141	5,419 R	70.3%	28.6%	71.0%	29.0%
EDWARDS	3,136	1,886	1,219	31	667 R	60.1%	38.9%	60.7%	39.3%
ELK	4,283	2,774	1,478	31	1,296 R	64.8%	34.5%	65.2%	34.8%
ELLIS	6,946	3,622	3,299	25	323 R	52.1%	47.5%	52.3%	47.7%
ELLSWORTH	4,910	2,658	2,237	15	421 R	54.1%	45.6%	54.3%	45.7%
FINNEY	4,110	2,059	2,027	24	32 R	50.1%	49.3%	50.4%	49.6%
FORD	8,382	4,356	3,954	72	402 R	51.9%	47.2%	52.4%	47.6%
FRANKLIN	10,020	6,393	3,542	85	2,851 R	63.8%	35.3%	64.3%	35.7%
GEARY	5,394	2,840	2,504	50	336 R	52.7%	46.4%	53.1%	46.9%
GOVE	2,039	1,352	659	28	693 R	66.3%	32.3%	67.2%	32.8%
GRAHAM	2,959	1,804	1,135	20	669 R	61.0%	38.4%	61.4%	38.6%
GRANT	1,006	614	382	10	232 R	61.0%	38.0%	61.6%	38.4%
GRAY	2,036	1,056	962	18	94 R	51.9%	47.2%	52.3%	47.7%
GREELEY	770	497	268	5	229 R	64.5%	34.8%	65.0%	35.0%
GREENWOOD	8,109	4,893	3,160	56	1,733 R	60.3%	39.0%	60.8%	39.2%
HAMILTON	1,377	798	569	10	229 R	58.0%	41.3%	58.4%	41.6%
HARPER	5,751	3,205	2,478	68	727 R	55.7%	43.1%	56.4%	43.6%
HARVEY	9,759	5,539	4,087	133	1,452 R	56.8%	41.9%	57.5%	42.5%
HASKELL	1,038	607	425	6	182 R	58.5%	40.9%	58.8%	41.2%
HODGEMAN	1,794	1,092	690	12	402 R	60.9%	38.5%	61.3%	38.7%
JACKSON	6,737	4,306	2,397	34	1,909 R	63.9%	35.6%	64.2%	35.8%
JEFFERSON	6,580	4,330	2,212	38	2,118 R	65.8%	33.6%	66.2%	33.8%
JEWELL	6,415	4,591	1,719	105	2,872 R	71.6%	26.8%	72.8%	27.2%
JOHNSON	16,142	10,326	5,770	46	4,556 R	64.0%	35.7%	64.2%	35.8%
KEARNY	1,243	721	519	3	202 R	58.0%	41.8%	58.1%	41.9%
KINGMAN	5,645	3,068	2,528	49	540 R	54.3%	44.8%	54.8%	45.2%
KIOWA	2,451	1,571	844	36	727 R	64.1%	34.4%	65.1%	34.9%
LABETTE	15,157	8,210	6,860	87	1,350 R	54.2%	45.3%	54.5%	45.5%
LANE	1,461	888	557	16	331 R	60.8%	38.1%	61.5%	38.5%
LEAVENWORTH	14,598	8,503	6,053	42	2,450 R	58.2%	41.5%	58.4%	41.6%
LINCOLN	4,169	2,822	1,301	46	1,521 R	67.7%	31.2%	68.4%	31.6%
LINN	6,187	4,086	2,067	34	2,019 R	66.0%	33.4%	66.4%	33.6%
LOGAN	1,797	1,201	584	12	617 R	66.8%	32.5%	67.3%	32.7%
LYON	13,219	6,918	6,170	131	748 R	52.3%	46.7%	52.9%	47.1%
MCPHERSON	11,176	6,732	4,240	204	2,492 R	60.2%	37.9%	61.4%	38.6%
MARION	8,547	5,764	2,724	59	3,040 R	67.4%	31.9%	67.9%	32.1%
MARSHALL	10,931	7,286	3,588	57	3,698 R	66.7%	32.8%	67.0%	33.0%
MEADE	2,647	1,618	970	59	648 R	61.1%	36.6%	62.5%	37.5%

KANSAS

PRESIDENT 1936

County	Total Vote	Republican	Democratic	Other	Rep.-Dem. Plurality	% Total Vote Rep.	% Total Vote Dem.	% Major Vote Rep.	% Major Vote Dem.
MIAMI	9,291	4,676	4,601	14	75 R	50.3%	49.5%	50.4%	49.6%
MITCHELL	6,111	2,781	3,289	41	508 D	45.5%	53.8%	45.8%	54.2%
MONTGOMERY	23,167	11,565	11,535	67	30 R	49.9%	49.9%	50.1%	49.9%
MORRIS	5,575	2,751	2,805	19	54 D	49.3%	50.3%	49.5%	50.5%
MORTON	1,521	636	876	9	240 D	41.8%	57.6%	42.1%	57.9%
NEMAHA	8,172	3,903	4,175	94	272 D	47.8%	51.1%	48.3%	51.7%
NEOSHO	11,428	5,777	5,611	40	166 R	50.6%	49.1%	50.7%	49.3%
NESS	3,332	1,302	2,002	18	700 D	39.2%	60.3%	39.4%	60.6%
NORTON	5,160	2,829	2,307	24	522 R	54.8%	44.7%	55.1%	44.9%
OSAGE	8,486	4,232	4,224	30	8 R	49.9%	49.8%	50.0%	50.0%
OSBORNE	4,978	2,765	2,200	13	565 R	55.5%	44.2%	55.7%	44.3%
OTTAWA	5,033	2,230	2,785	18	555 D	44.3%	55.3%	44.5%	55.5%
PAWNEE	4,576	1,753	2,814	9	1,061 D	38.3%	61.5%	38.4%	61.6%
PHILLIPS	5,358	3,193	2,154	11	1,039 R	59.6%	40.0%	59.7%	40.3%
POTTAWATOMIE	7,398	3,977	3,284	137	693 R	53.8%	44.4%	54.8%	45.2%
PRATT	5,827	1,946	3,871	10	1,925 D	33.4%	66.4%	33.5%	66.5%
RAWLINS	3,404	1,364	2,029	11	665 D	40.1%	59.6%	40.2%	59.8%
RENO	22,896	8,607	14,203	86	5,596 D	37.6%	62.0%	37.7%	62.3%
REPUBLIC	7,280	3,830	3,427	23	403 R	52.6%	47.1%	52.8%	47.2%
RICE	8,245	3,318	4,905	22	1,587 D	40.2%	59.5%	40.4%	59.6%
RILEY	10,278	6,077	4,104	97	1,973 R	59.1%	39.9%	59.7%	40.3%
ROOKS	4,385	2,150	2,235		85 D	49.0%	51.0%	49.0%	51.0%
RUSH	4,219	1,733	2,482	4	749 D	41.1%	58.8%	41.1%	58.9%
RUSSELL	5,984	2,241	3,736	7	1,495 D	37.4%	62.4%	37.5%	62.5%
SALINE	13,983	6,061	7,872	50	1,811 D	43.3%	56.3%	43.5%	56.5%
SCOTT	1,724	625	1,096	3	471 D	36.3%	63.6%	36.3%	63.7%
SEDGWICK	61,353	21,654	39,503	196	17,849 D	35.3%	64.4%	35.6%	64.4%
SEWARD	3,109	1,108	1,997	4	889 D	35.6%	64.2%	35.7%	64.3%
SHAWNEE	42,888	19,785	22,942	161	3,157 D	46.1%	53.5%	46.3%	53.7%
SHERIDAN	2,501	1,007	1,442	52	435 D	40.3%	57.7%	41.1%	58.9%
SHERMAN	3,029	1,159	1,814	56	655 D	38.3%	59.9%	39.0%	61.0%
SMITH	6,156	3,292	2,847	17	445 R	53.5%	46.2%	53.6%	46.4%
STAFFORD	5,171	1,939	3,212	20	1,273 D	37.5%	62.1%	37.6%	62.4%
STANTON	770	311	458	1	147 D	40.4%	59.5%	40.4%	59.6%
STEVENS	1,730	701	1,023	6	322 D	40.5%	59.1%	40.7%	59.3%
SUMNER	12,939	4,946	7,966	27	3,020 D	38.2%	61.6%	38.3%	61.7%
THOMAS	3,388	1,200	2,168	20	968 D	35.4%	64.0%	35.6%	64.4%
TREGO	2,811	1,012	1,783	16	771 D	36.0%	63.4%	36.2%	63.8%
WABAUNSEE	5,059	2,809	2,235	15	574 R	55.5%	44.2%	55.7%	44.3%
WALLACE	1,161	658	492	11	166 R	56.7%	42.4%	57.2%	42.8%
WASHINGTON	8,192	4,809	3,355	28	1,454 R	58.7%	41.0%	58.9%	41.1%
WICHITA	1,091	448	637	6	189 D	41.1%	58.4%	41.4%	58.7%
WILSON	8,687	4,829	3,816	42	1,013 R	55.6%	43.9%	55.9%	44.1%
WOODSON	4,277	2,374	1,884	19	490 R	55.5%	44.0%	55.9%	44.4%
WYANDOTTE	64,596	26,239	38,101	256	11,862 D	40.6%	59.0%	40.8%	59.2%
TOTAL	865,507	397,727	464,520	3,260	66,793 D	46.0%	53.7%	46.1%	53.9%

PRESIDENT 1940

County	Total Vote	Republican	Democratic	Other	Rep.-Dem. Plurality	% Total Vote Rep.	% Total Vote Dem.	% Major Vote Rep.	% Major Vote Dem.
MIAMI	9,121	5,178	3,900	43	1,278 R	56.8%	42.8%	57.0%	43.0%
MITCHELL	5,792	3,681	2,060	51	1,621 R	63.6%	35.6%	64.1%	35.9%
MONTGOMERY	23,894	13,782	9,999	114	3,782 R	57.7%	41.8%	58.0%	42.0%
MORRIS	5,315	3,276	1,992	47	1,284 R	61.6%	37.5%	62.2%	37.8%
MORTON	1,154	643	503	8	140 R	55.7%	43.6%	56.1%	43.9%
NEMAHA	7,889	5,178	2,679	32	2,499 R	65.6%	34.0%	65.9%	34.1%
NEOSHO	11,031	6,556	4,419	56	2,137 R	59.4%	40.1%	59.7%	40.3%
NESS	3,112	1,826	1,230	56	596 R	58.7%	39.5%	59.8%	40.2%
NORTON	4,859	3,415	1,338	66	2,037 R	70.3%	28.4%	71.2%	28.8%
OSAGE	8,247	4,991	3,186	70	1,805 R	60.5%	38.6%	61.0%	39.0%
OSBORNE	4,995	3,424	1,488	83	1,936 R	68.5%	29.8%	69.7%	30.3%
OTTAWA	4,925	2,810	2,065	50	745 R	57.1%	41.9%	57.6%	42.4%
PAWNEE	4,587	2,329	2,216	42	113 R	50.8%	48.3%	51.2%	48.8%
PHILLIPS	5,290	3,676	1,563	51	2,113 R	69.5%	29.5%	70.2%	29.8%
POTTAWATOMIE	7,299	5,045	2,226	28	2,819 R	69.1%	30.5%	69.4%	30.6%
PRATT	5,867	2,930	2,870	67	60 R	49.9%	48.9%	50.5%	49.5%
RAWLINS	3,030	1,758	1,247	25	511 R	58.0%	41.2%	58.5%	41.5%
RENO	23,208	12,448	10,543	217	1,905 R	53.6%	45.4%	54.1%	45.9%
REPUBLIC	7,003	4,450	2,511	42	1,939 R	63.5%	35.9%	63.9%	36.1%
RICE	8,483	4,792	3,635	56	1,157 R	56.5%	42.9%	56.9%	43.1%
RILEY	10,818	7,420	3,293	105	4,127 R	68.6%	30.4%	69.3%	30.7%
ROOKS	4,273	2,590	1,650	33	940 R	60.6%	38.6%	61.1%	38.9%
RUSH	4,001	2,394	1,588	19	806 R	59.8%	39.7%	60.1%	39.9%
RUSSELL	6,342	3,714	2,579	49	1,135 R	58.6%	40.7%	59.0%	41.0%
SALINE	14,581	7,975	6,514	92	1,461 R	54.7%	44.7%	55.0%	45.0%
SCOTT	1,726	988	717	21	271 R	57.2%	41.5%	57.9%	42.1%
SEDGWICK	66,926	32,160	34,219	547	2,059 D	48.1%	51.1%	48.4%	51.6%
SEWARD	3,027	1,503	1,474	50	29 R	49.7%	48.7%	50.5%	49.5%
SHAWNEE	43,454	23,882	19,375	197	4,507 R	55.0%	44.6%	55.2%	44.8%
SHERIDAN	2,404	1,492	903	9	589 R	62.1%	37.6%	62.3%	37.7%
SHERMAN	3,008	1,569	1,399	40	170 R	52.2%	46.5%	52.9%	47.1%
SMITH	5,535	3,630	1,855	50	1,775 R	65.6%	33.5%	66.2%	33.8%
STAFFORD	5,357	2,795	2,509	53	286 R	52.2%	46.8%	52.7%	47.3%
STANTON	692	378	301	13	77 R	54.6%	43.5%	55.7%	44.3%
STEVENS	1,546	851	674	21	177 R	55.0%	43.6%	55.8%	44.2%
SUMNER	12,698	6,585	5,988	125	597 R	51.9%	47.2%	52.4%	47.6%
THOMAS	3,175	1,721	1,423	31	298 R	54.2%	44.8%	54.7%	45.3%
TREGO	2,728	1,571	1,140	17	431 R	57.6%	41.8%	57.9%	42.1%
WABAUNSEE	4,727	3,481	1,212	34	2,269 R	73.6%	25.6%	74.2%	25.8%
WALLACE	1,127	756	361	10	395 R	67.1%	32.0%	67.7%	32.3%
WASHINGTON	7,903	5,792	2,061	50	3,731 R	73.3%	26.1%	73.8%	26.2%
WICHITA	1,090	644	433	13	211 R	59.1%	39.8%	59.8%	40.2%
WILSON	8,209	5,288	2,859	62	2,429 R	64.4%	34.8%	64.9%	35.1%
WOODSON	4,065	2,637	1,398	30	1,239 R	64.9%	34.4%	65.4%	34.6%
WYANDOTTE	66,643	28,152	38,239	252	10,087 D	42.2%	57.4%	42.4%	57.6%
TOTAL	860,297	489,169	364,725	6,403	124,444 R	56.9%	42.4%	57.3%	42.7%

KANSAS

PRESIDENT 1944

County	Total Vote	Republican	Democratic	Other	Rep.-Dem. Plurality	Total Vote Rep.	Total Vote Dem.	Major Vote Rep.	Major Vote Dem.
ALLEN	7,340	5,032	2,262	46	2,770 R	68.6%	30.8%	69.0%	31.0%
ANDERSON	4,716	3,060	1,649	7	1,411 R	64.9%	35.0%	65.0%	35.0%
ATCHISON	8,076	4,731	3,325	20	1,406 R	58.6%	41.2%	58.7%	41.3%
BARBER	3,672	2,140	1,501	31	639 R	58.3%	40.9%	58.8%	41.2%
BARTON	9,345	5,547	3,761	37	1,786 R	59.4%	40.2%	59.6%	40.4%
BOURBON	8,451	4,790	3,622	39	1,168 R	56.7%	42.9%	56.9%	43.1%
BROWN	6,779	4,947	1,817	15	3,130 R	73.0%	26.8%	73.1%	26.9%
BUTLER	13,203	7,064	6,084	55	980 R	53.5%	46.1%	53.7%	46.3%
CHASE	2,517	1,510	998	9	512 R	60.0%	39.7%	60.2%	39.8%
CHAUTAUQUA	3,421	2,305	1,106	10	1,199 R	67.4%	32.3%	67.6%	32.4%
CHEROKEE	9,988	5,458	4,468	62	990 R	54.6%	44.7%	55.0%	45.0%
CHEYENNE	2,368	1,610	736	22	874 R	68.0%	31.1%	68.6%	31.4%
CLARK	1,706	950	741	15	209 R	55.7%	43.4%	56.2%	43.8%
CLAY	5,551	4,101	1,391	59	2,710 R	74.0%	25.1%	74.7%	25.3%
CLOUD	6,875	4,377	2,391	107	1,986 R	63.7%	34.8%	64.7%	35.3%
COFFEY	5,144	3,461	1,660	23	1,801 R	67.3%	32.3%	67.6%	32.4%
COMANCHE	1,705	1,048	642	15	406 R	61.5%	37.7%	62.0%	38.0%
COWLEY	15,220	8,453	6,577	90	1,876 R	55.9%	43.5%	56.2%	43.8%
CRAWFORD	17,311	9,017	8,211	83	806 R	52.1%	47.4%	52.3%	47.7%
DECATUR	2,934	1,758	1,159	17	599 R	59.9%	39.5%	60.3%	39.7%
DICKINSON	9,446	6,227	3,190	29	3,037 R	65.9%	33.8%	66.1%	33.9%
DONIPHAN	4,491	3,230	1,261	—	1,969 R	71.9%	28.1%	71.9%	28.1%
DOUGLAS	12,189	8,224	3,886	79	4,338 R	67.5%	31.9%	67.9%	32.1%
EDWARDS	2,564	1,669	876	19	793 R	65.1%	34.2%	65.6%	34.4%
ELK	3,246	2,283	954	9	1,329 R	70.3%	29.4%	70.5%	29.5%
ELLIS	5,603	3,369	2,218	16	1,151 R	60.1%	39.6%	60.3%	39.7%
ELLSWORTH	3,974	2,290	1,678	6	612 R	57.6%	42.2%	57.7%	42.3%
FINNEY	4,065	2,366	1,667	32	699 R	58.2%	41.0%	58.7%	41.3%
FORD	7,181	4,110	2,994	77	1,116 R	57.2%	41.7%	57.9%	42.1%
FRANKLIN	8,310	5,375	2,880	55	2,495 R	64.7%	34.7%	65.1%	34.9%
GEARY	4,973	2,833	2,107	33	726 R	57.0%	42.4%	57.3%	42.7%
GOVE	1,562	1,125	420	17	705 R	72.0%	26.9%	72.8%	27.2%
GRAHAM	2,482	1,651	814	17	837 R	66.5%	32.8%	67.0%	33.0%
GRANT	853	566	282	5	284 R	66.4%	33.1%	66.7%	33.3%
GRAY	1,854	1,057	775	22	282 R	57.0%	41.8%	57.7%	42.3%
GREELEY	600	378	215	7	163 R	63.0%	35.8%	63.7%	36.3%
GREENWOOD	6,187	3,959	2,187	41	1,772 R	64.0%	35.3%	64.4%	35.6%
HAMILTON	1,275	795	471	9	324 R	62.4%	36.9%	62.8%	37.2%
HARPER	4,468	2,849	1,573	46	1,276 R	63.8%	35.2%	64.4%	35.6%
HARVEY	8,703	5,339	3,300	64	2,039 R	61.3%	37.9%	61.8%	38.2%
HASKELL	868	520	342	6	178 R	59.9%	39.4%	60.3%	39.7%
HODGEMAN	1,481	982	490	25	492 R	66.3%	33.1%	66.7%	33.3%
JACKSON	5,257	3,665	1,567	25	2,098 R	69.7%	29.8%	70.0%	30.0%
JEFFERSON	5,098	3,504	1,575	19	1,929 R	68.7%	30.9%	69.0%	31.0%
JEWELL	5,059	3,754	1,216	89	2,538 R	74.2%	24.0%	75.5%	24.5%
JOHNSON	17,773	11,951	5,771	51	6,180 R	67.2%	32.5%	67.4%	32.6%
KEARNY	980	612	365	3	247 R	62.4%	37.2%	62.6%	37.4%
KINGMAN	4,435	2,827	1,579	29	1,248 R	63.7%	35.6%	64.2%	35.8%
KIOWA	2,125	1,479	618	28	861 R	69.5%	29.1%	70.5%	29.5%
LABETTE	12,926	7,480	5,398	48	2,082 R	57.9%	41.8%	58.1%	41.9%
LANE	1,173	773	388	12	385 R	65.9%	33.1%	66.6%	33.4%
LEAVENWORTH	12,438	7,282	5,097	59	2,185 R	58.5%	41.0%	58.8%	41.2%
LINCOLN	3,339	2,405	910	24	1,495 R	72.0%	27.3%	72.5%	27.5%
LINN	4,647	3,185	1,442	20	1,743 R	68.5%	31.0%	68.8%	31.2%
LOGAN	1,518	1,107	406	5	701 R	72.3%	26.8%	73.2%	26.8%
LYON	10,799	5,710	4,984	105	726 R	52.9%	46.2%	53.4%	46.6%
MCPHERSON	9,372	5,840	3,321	211	2,519 R	62.3%	35.4%	63.7%	36.3%
MARION	7,185	5,219	1,925	41	3,294 R	72.5%	26.8%	73.1%	26.9%
MARSHALL	8,886	6,184	2,681	21	3,503 R	69.5%	30.2%	69.8%	30.2%
MEADE	2,087	1,424	631	32	793 R	68.2%	30.2%	69.3%	30.7%

PRESIDENT 1948

County	Total Vote	Republican	Democratic	Other	Rep.-Dem. Plurality	Total Vote Rep.	Total Vote Dem.	Major Vote Rep.	Major Vote Dem.
ALLEN	7,685	4,704	2,891	90	1,813 R	61.2%	37.6%	61.9%	38.1%
ANDERSON	4,902	2,787	2,071	44	716 R	56.9%	42.2%	57.4%	42.6%
ATCHISON	8,113	4,141	3,910	62	231 R	51.0%	48.2%	51.4%	48.6%
BARBER	3,953	2,013	1,891	49	122 R	50.9%	47.8%	51.6%	48.4%
BARTON	11,610	6,191	5,307	112	884 R	53.4%	45.8%	53.8%	46.2%
BOURBON	8,215	4,225	3,879	111	346 R	51.4%	47.2%	52.1%	47.9%
BROWN	6,646	4,518	2,060	68	2,458 R	68.0%	31.0%	68.7%	31.3%
BUTLER	12,952	6,551	6,269	132	282 R	50.6%	48.4%	51.1%	48.9%
CHASE	2,430	1,432	961	37	471 R	58.9%	39.5%	59.8%	40.2%
CHAUTAUQUA	3,244	1,925	1,261	58	664 R	59.3%	38.9%	60.4%	39.6%
CHEROKEE	9,653	4,616	4,854	183	238 D	47.8%	50.2%	48.7%	51.3%
CHEYENNE	2,278	1,219	978	81	241 R	53.5%	42.9%	55.5%	44.5%
CLARK	1,807	999	777	31	222 R	55.3%	43.0%	56.2%	43.8%
CLAY	5,711	3,763	1,804	144	1,959 R	65.9%	31.6%	67.6%	32.4%
CLOUD	7,155	4,018	2,891	246	1,127 R	56.2%	40.4%	58.2%	41.8%
COFFEY	4,812	2,945	1,796	71	1,149 R	61.2%	37.3%	62.1%	37.9%
COMANCHE	1,740	1,077	650	13	427 R	61.9%	37.4%	62.4%	37.6%
COWLEY	15,541	8,102	7,042	397	1,060 R	52.1%	45.3%	53.5%	46.5%
CRAWFORD	17,815	8,229	9,005	581	776 D	46.2%	50.5%	47.7%	52.3%
DECATUR	3,005	1,545	1,402	58	143 R	51.4%	46.7%	52.4%	47.6%
DICKINSON	9,867	5,918	3,815	134	2,103 R	60.0%	38.7%	60.8%	39.2%
DONIPHAN	4,369	2,785	1,555	29	1,230 R	63.7%	35.6%	64.2%	35.8%
DOUGLAS	14,454	9,287	4,778	389	4,509 R	64.2%	33.1%	66.0%	34.0%
EDWARDS	2,798	1,627	1,083	88	544 R	58.1%	38.7%	60.0%	40.0%
ELK	3,075	1,962	1,087	26	875 R	63.8%	35.3%	64.3%	35.7%
ELLIS	6,606	2,676	3,863	67	1,187 D	40.5%	58.5%	40.9%	59.1%
ELLSWORTH	4,079	2,155	1,879	45	276 R	52.8%	46.1%	53.4%	46.6%
FINNEY	5,015	2,508	2,367	140	141 R	50.0%	47.2%	51.4%	48.6%
FORD	8,662	4,089	4,396	177	307 D	47.2%	50.8%	48.2%	51.8%
FRANKLIN	8,834	5,145	3,467	222	1,678 R	58.2%	39.2%	59.7%	40.3%
GEARY	5,760	2,864	2,810	86	54 R	49.7%	48.8%	50.5%	49.5%
GOVE	1,792	1,030	719	43	311 R	57.5%	40.1%	58.9%	41.1%
GRAHAM	2,328	1,380	913	35	467 R	59.3%	39.2%	60.2%	39.8%
GRANT	1,391	742	625	24	117 R	53.3%	44.9%	54.3%	45.7%
GRAY	1,928	1,035	869	24	166 R	53.7%	45.1%	54.4%	45.6%
GREELEY	733	391	326	16	65 R	53.3%	44.5%	54.5%	45.5%
GREENWOOD	6,200	3,553	2,574	73	979 R	57.3%	41.5%	58.0%	42.0%
HAMILTON	1,479	749	722	8	27 R	50.6%	48.8%	50.9%	49.1%
HARPER	4,560	2,702	1,752	106	950 R	59.3%	38.4%	60.7%	39.3%
HARVEY	9,130	5,270	3,615	245	1,655 R	57.7%	39.6%	59.3%	40.7%
HASKELL	1,083	592	466	25	126 R	54.7%	43.0%	56.0%	44.0%
HODGEMAN	1,555	945	590	20	355 R	60.8%	37.9%	61.6%	38.4%
JACKSON	5,165	3,166	1,958	41	1,208 R	61.3%	37.9%	61.8%	38.2%
JEFFERSON	5,058	2,986	2,010	62	976 R	59.0%	39.7%	59.8%	40.2%
JEWELL	4,975	3,143	1,574	258	1,569 R	63.2%	31.6%	66.6%	33.4%
JOHNSON	23,378	14,191	8,982	205	5,209 R	60.7%	38.4%	61.2%	38.8%
KEARNY	1,242	676	541	25	135 R	54.4%	43.5%	55.5%	44.5%
KINGMAN	4,724	2,640	2,008	76	632 R	55.9%	42.5%	56.8%	43.2%
KIOWA	2,104	1,258	722	124	536 R	59.8%	34.3%	63.5%	36.5%
LABETTE	12,565	6,298	6,113	154	185 R	50.1%	48.7%	50.7%	49.3%
LANE	1,328	764	525	39	239 R	57.5%	39.5%	59.3%	40.7%
LEAVENWORTH	13,317	6,474	6,740	103	266 D	48.6%	50.6%	49.0%	51.0%
LINCOLN	3,318	2,181	1,094	43	1,087 R	65.7%	33.0%	66.6%	33.4%
LINN	4,354	2,632	1,673	49	959 R	60.5%	38.4%	61.1%	38.8%
LOGAN	1,734	1,105	579	50	526 R	63.7%	33.4%	65.6%	34.4%
LYON	11,876	5,941	5,708	227	233 R	50.0%	48.1%	51.0%	49.0%
MCPHERSON	10,344	5,952	3,879	513	2,073 R	57.5%	37.5%	60.5%	39.5%
MARION	7,285	4,724	2,421	140	2,303 R	64.8%	33.2%	66.1%	33.9%
MARSHALL	8,329	5,122	3,148	59	1,974 R	61.5%	37.8%	61.9%	38.1%
MEADE	2,336	1,406	834	96	572 R	60.2%	35.7%	62.8%	37.2%

KANSAS

PRESIDENT 1944

County	Total Vote	Republican	Democratic	Other	Rep.-Dem. Plurality	%TV Rep.	%TV Dem.	%MV Rep.	%MV Dem.
MIAMI	7,552	4,326	3,217	9	1,109 R	57.3%	42.6%	57.4%	42.6%
MITCHELL	4,857	3,238	1,579	40	1,659 R	66.7%	32.5%	67.2%	32.8%
MONTGOMERY	18,844	11,738	7,063	43	4,675 R	62.3%	37.5%	62.4%	37.6%
MORRIS	4,231	2,628	1,584	19	1,044 R	62.1%	37.4%	62.4%	37.6%
MORTON	987	617	367	3	250 R	62.5%	37.2%	62.7%	37.3%
NEMAHA	6,437	4,277	2,149	11	2,128 R	66.4%	33.4%	66.6%	33.4%
NEOSHO	8,679	5,420	3,233	26	2,187 R	62.4%	37.3%	62.6%	37.4%
NESS	2,666	1,745	876	45	869 R	65.5%	32.9%	66.6%	33.4%
NORTON	4,078	2,890	1,159	29	1,731 R	70.9%	28.4%	71.4%	28.6%
OSAGE	6,377	4,107	2,212	58	1,895 R	64.4%	34.7%	65.0%	35.0%
OSBORNE	3,953	2,827	1,078	48	1,749 R	71.5%	27.3%	72.4%	27.6%
OTTAWA	3,847	2,428	1,378	41	1,050 R	63.1%	35.8%	63.8%	36.2%
PAWNEE	3,806	2,057	1,727	22	330 R	54.0%	45.4%	54.4%	45.6%
PHILLIPS	4,197	3,053	1,098	46	1,955 R	72.7%	26.2%	73.5%	26.5%
POTTAWATOMIE	5,819	4,074	1,727	18	2,347 R	70.0%	29.7%	70.2%	29.8%
PRATT	5,029	2,658	2,334	37	324 R	52.9%	46.4%	53.2%	46.8%
RAWLINS	2,542	1,569	955	18	614 R	61.7%	37.6%	62.2%	37.8%
RENO	18,743	11,004	7,604	135	3,400 R	58.7%	40.6%	59.1%	40.9%
REPUBLIC	5,715	3,802	1,891	22	1,911 R	66.5%	33.1%	66.8%	33.2%
RICE	6,584	4,024	2,505	55	1,519 R	61.1%	38.0%	61.6%	38.4%
RILEY	9,244	6,511	2,659	74	3,852 R	70.4%	28.8%	71.0%	29.0%
ROOKS	3,549	2,361	1,166	22	1,195 R	66.5%	32.9%	66.9%	33.1%
RUSH	3,283	2,193	1,076	14	1,117 R	66.8%	32.8%	67.1%	32.9%
RUSSELL	4,950	3,344	1,583	23	1,761 R	67.6%	32.0%	67.9%	32.1%
SALINE	12,723	7,571	5,097	55	2,474 R	59.5%	40.1%	59.8%	40.2%
SCOTT	1,482	903	565	14	338 R	60.9%	38.1%	61.5%	38.5%
SEDGWICK	73,698	38,896	34,442	360	4,454 R	52.8%	46.7%	53.0%	47.0%
SEWARD	2,949	1,590	1,342	17	248 R	53.9%	45.5%	54.2%	45.8%
SHAWNEE	36,247	21,396	14,678	173	6,718 R	59.0%	40.5%	59.3%	40.7%
SHERIDAN	2,007	1,342	658	7	684 R	66.9%	32.8%	67.1%	32.9%
SHERMAN	2,677	1,608	1,021	48	587 R	60.1%	38.1%	61.2%	38.8%
SMITH	4,693	3,282	1,377	34	1,905 R	69.9%	29.3%	70.4%	29.6%
STAFFORD	4,432	2,493	1,908	31	585 R	56.2%	43.1%	56.6%	43.4%
STANTON	645	398	240	7	158 R	61.7%	37.2%	62.4%	37.6%
STEVENS	1,176	760	414	2	346 R	64.6%	35.2%	64.7%	35.3%
SUMNER	10,594	6,343	4,187	64	2,156 R	59.9%	39.5%	60.2%	39.8%
THOMAS	2,758	1,631	1,097	30	534 R	59.1%	39.8%	59.8%	40.2%
TREGO	2,354	1,459	883	12	576 R	62.0%	37.5%	62.3%	37.7%
WABAUNSEE	3,738	2,839	873	26	1,966 R	75.9%	23.3%	76.5%	23.5%
WALLACE	1,017	720	292	5	428 R	70.8%	28.7%	71.1%	28.9%
WASHINGTON	6,536	5,040	1,455	41	3,585 R	77.1%	22.3%	77.6%	22.4%
WICHITA	939	604	329	6	275 R	64.3%	35.0%	64.7%	35.3%
WILSON	6,195	4,248	1,912	35	2,336 R	68.6%	30.9%	69.0%	31.0%
WOODSON	3,318	2,308	999	11	1,309 R	69.6%	30.1%	69.8%	30.2%
WYANDOTTE	59,945	26,817	32,914	214	6,097 D	44.7%	54.9%	44.9%	55.1%
TOTAL	733,776	442,096	287,458	4,222	154,638 R	60.2%	39.2%	60.6%	39.4%

PRESIDENT 1948

County	Total Vote	Republican	Democratic	Other	Rep.-Dem. Plurality	%TV Rep.	%TV Dem.	%MV Rep.	%MV Dem.
MIAMI	7,388	3,650	3,660	78	10 D	49.4%	49.5%	49.9%	50.1%
MITCHELL	4,823	2,998	1,750	75	1,248 R	62.2%	36.3%	63.1%	36.9%
MONTGOMERY	19,444	10,636	8,621	187	2,015 R	54.7%	44.3%	55.2%	44.8%
MORRIS	4,047	2,285	1,701	61	584 R	56.5%	42.0%	57.3%	42.7%
MORTON	1,186	624	545	17	79 R	52.6%	46.0%	53.4%	46.6%
NEMAHA	6,371	3,529	2,810	32	719 R	55.4%	44.1%	55.7%	44.3%
NEOSHO	8,947	5,072	3,770	105	1,302 R	56.7%	42.1%	57.4%	42.6%
NESS	2,907	1,689	1,130	88	559 R	58.1%	38.9%	59.9%	40.1%
NORTON	4,036	2,461	1,414	161	1,047 R	61.0%	35.0%	63.5%	36.5%
OSAGE	6,254	3,474	2,659	121	815 R	55.5%	42.5%	56.6%	43.4%
OSBORNE	4,140	2,603	1,420	117	1,183 R	62.9%	34.3%	64.7%	35.3%
OTTAWA	3,734	2,203	1,424	107	779 R	59.0%	38.1%	60.7%	39.3%
PAWNEE	4,235	2,221	1,945	69	276 R	52.4%	45.9%	53.3%	46.7%
PHILLIPS	4,094	2,715	1,223	156	1,492 R	66.3%	29.9%	68.9%	31.1%
POTTAWATOMIE	5,921	3,709	2,167	45	1,542 R	62.6%	36.6%	63.1%	36.9%
PRATT	5,731	2,878	2,751	102	127 R	50.2%	48.0%	51.1%	48.9%
RAWLINS	2,522	1,389	1,095	38	294 R	55.1%	43.4%	55.9%	44.1%
RENO	21,567	11,187	9,957	423	1,230 R	51.9%	46.2%	52.9%	47.1%
REPUBLIC	5,586	3,375	2,109	102	1,266 R	60.4%	37.8%	61.5%	38.5%
RICE	6,882	4,002	2,752	128	1,250 R	58.2%	40.0%	59.3%	40.7%
RILEY	13,567	9,227	4,052	288	5,175 R	68.0%	29.9%	69.5%	30.5%
ROOKS	3,882	2,197	1,636	49	561 R	56.6%	42.1%	57.3%	42.7%
RUSH	3,262	1,840	1,360	62	480 R	56.4%	41.7%	57.5%	42.5%
RUSSELL	5,512	3,113	2,343	56	770 R	56.5%	42.5%	57.1%	42.9%
SALINE	14,920	7,928	6,798	194	1,130 R	53.1%	45.6%	53.8%	46.2%
SCOTT	1,829	1,040	739	50	301 R	56.9%	40.4%	58.5%	41.5%
SEDGWICK	79,029	39,165	38,621	1,243	544 R	49.6%	48.9%	50.3%	49.7%
SEWARD	3,517	1,889	1,614	14	275 R	53.7%	45.9%	53.9%	46.1%
SHAWNEE	44,808	23,673	20,346	789	3,327 R	52.8%	45.4%	53.8%	46.2%
SHERIDAN	2,082	1,097	966	19	131 R	52.7%	46.4%	53.2%	46.8%
SHERMAN	2,760	1,380	1,289	91	91 R	50.0%	46.7%	51.7%	48.3%
SMITH	4,456	2,760	1,590	106	1,170 R	61.9%	35.7%	63.4%	36.6%
STAFFORD	4,453	2,304	2,049	100	255 R	51.7%	46.0%	52.9%	47.1%
STANTON	720	407	300	13	107 R	56.5%	41.7%	57.6%	42.4%
STEVENS	1,521	822	666	33	156 R	54.0%	43.8%	55.2%	44.8%
SUMNER	10,685	5,922	4,571	192	1,351 R	55.4%	42.8%	56.4%	43.6%
THOMAS	3,030	1,497	1,476	57	21 R	49.4%	48.7%	50.4%	49.6%
TREGO	2,387	1,237	1,117	33	120 R	51.8%	46.8%	52.5%	47.5%
WABAUNSEE	3,648	2,437	1,162	49	1,275 R	66.8%	31.9%	67.7%	32.3%
WALLACE	1,094	637	439	18	198 R	58.2%	40.1%	59.2%	40.8%
WASHINGTON	5,883	3,894	1,894	95	2,000 R	66.2%	32.2%	67.3%	32.7%
WICHITA	1,077	606	443	28	163 R	56.3%	41.1%	57.8%	42.2%
WILSON	6,506	3,868	2,538	100	1,330 R	59.5%	39.0%	60.4%	39.6%
WOODSON	3,191	1,997	1,145	49	852 R	62.6%	35.9%	63.6%	36.4%
WYANDOTTE	66,788	24,398	41,366	1,024	16,968 D	36.5%	61.9%	37.1%	62.9%
TOTAL	788,819	423,039	351,902	13,878	71,137 R	53.6%	44.6%	54.6%	45.4%

KANSAS

PRESIDENT 1952

County	Total Vote	Republican	Democratic	Other	Rep.-Dem. Plurality	Total Vote Rep.	Total Vote Dem.	Major Vote Rep.	Major Vote Dem.
ALLEN	8,236	6,045	2,160	31	3,885 R	73.4%	26.2%	73.7%	26.3%
ANDERSON	5,018	3,672	1,333	13	2,339 R	73.2%	26.6%	73.4%	26.6%
ATCHISON	9,296	6,004	3,283	9	2,721 R	64.6%	35.3%	64.6%	35.4%
BARBER	4,145	3,071	1,028	46	2,043 R	74.1%	24.8%	74.9%	25.1%
BARTON	13,319	9,380	3,847	92	5,533 R	70.4%	28.9%	70.9%	29.1%
BOURBON	8,864	5,785	3,023	56	2,762 R	65.3%	34.1%	65.7%	34.3%
BROWN	7,491	6,031	1,440	20	4,591 R	80.5%	19.3%	80.7%	19.3%
BUTLER	15,651	10,179	5,359	113	4,820 R	65.0%	34.2%	65.5%	34.5%
CHASE	2,334	1,815	513	6	1,302 R	77.8%	22.0%	78.0%	22.0%
CHAUTAUQUA	3,400	2,542	837	21	1,705 R	74.8%	24.6%	75.2%	24.8%
CHEROKEE	10,914	6,261	4,597	56	1,664 R	57.4%	42.1%	57.7%	42.3%
CHEYENNE	2,532	1,915	597	20	1,318 R	75.6%	23.6%	76.2%	23.8%
CLARK	1,924	1,410	479	35	931 R	73.3%	24.9%	74.6%	25.4%
CLAY	5,961	5,059	831	71	4,228 R	84.9%	13.9%	85.9%	14.1%
CLOUD	7,417	5,580	1,793	44	3,787 R	75.2%	24.2%	75.7%	24.3%
COFFEY	4,989	3,731	1,239	19	2,492 R	74.8%	24.8%	75.1%	24.9%
COMANCHE	1,827	1,443	374	10	1,069 R	79.0%	20.5%	79.4%	20.6%
COWLEY	16,812	11,454	5,242	116	6,212 R	68.1%	31.2%	68.6%	31.4%
CRAWFORD	19,074	10,646	8,350	78	2,296 R	55.8%	43.8%	56.0%	44.0%
DECATUR	3,288	2,451	821	16	1,630 R	74.5%	25.0%	74.9%	25.1%
DICKINSON	10,967	8,969	1,967	31	7,002 R	81.8%	17.9%	82.0%	18.0%
DONIPHAN	4,902	3,711	1,175	16	2,536 R	75.7%	24.0%	75.9%	24.0%
DOUGLAS	14,924	11,095	3,765	64	7,330 R	74.3%	25.2%	74.7%	25.3%
EDWARDS	2,869	2,192	647	30	1,545 R	76.4%	22.6%	76.8%	23.2%
ELK	3,116	2,380	717	19	1,663 R	76.4%	23.0%	76.8%	23.2%
ELLIS	7,413	4,882	2,528	3	2,354 R	65.9%	34.1%	65.9%	34.1%
ELLSWORTH	4,311	3,219	1,068	24	2,151 R	74.7%	24.8%	75.1%	24.9%
FINNEY	5,932	4,290	1,597	45	2,693 R	72.3%	26.9%	72.9%	27.1%
FORD	9,221	6,359	2,748	114	3,611 R	69.0%	29.8%	69.8%	30.2%
FRANKLIN	9,584	6,983	2,532	69	4,451 R	72.9%	26.4%	73.4%	26.6%
GEARY	6,116	4,314	1,750	52	2,564 R	70.5%	28.6%	71.1%	28.9%
GOVE	1,916	1,453	453	10	1,000 R	75.8%	23.6%	76.2%	23.8%
GRAHAM	2,560	1,859	686	15	1,173 R	72.6%	26.8%	73.0%	27.0%
GRANT	1,798	1,277	502	19	775 R	71.0%	27.9%	71.8%	28.2%
GRAY	2,061	1,515	537	9	978 R	73.5%	26.1%	73.8%	26.2%
GREELEY	917	725	181	11	544 R	79.1%	19.7%	80.0%	20.0%
GREENWOOD	6,749	4,974	1,743	32	3,231 R	73.7%	25.8%	74.1%	25.9%
HAMILTON	1,663	1,209	437	17	772 R	72.7%	26.3%	73.5%	26.5%
HARPER	4,547	3,575	927	45	2,648 R	78.6%	20.4%	79.4%	20.6%
HARVEY	10,095	7,154	2,726	215	4,428 R	70.9%	27.0%	72.4%	27.6%
HASKELL	1,171	870	283	18	587 R	74.3%	24.2%	75.5%	24.5%
HODGEMAN	1,740	1,330	392	18	938 R	76.4%	22.5%	77.2%	22.8%
JACKSON	5,527	4,161	1,358	26	2,803 R	75.3%	24.6%	75.4%	24.6%
JEFFERSON	5,417	3,980	1,411	26	2,569 R	73.5%	26.2%	73.8%	26.2%
JEWELL	5,147	4,162	885	100	3,277 R	80.9%	17.2%	82.5%	17.5%
JOHNSON	40,163	29,103	10,990	70	18,113 R	72.5%	27.4%	72.6%	27.4%
KEARNY	1,390	1,012	362	16	650 R	72.8%	26.0%	73.4%	26.6%
KINGMAN	4,992	3,820	1,096	76	2,724 R	76.5%	22.0%	77.7%	22.3%
KIOWA	2,338	1,838	432	68	1,406 R	78.6%	18.5%	81.0%	19.0%
LABETTE	13,913	8,624	5,219	70	3,405 R	62.0%	37.5%	62.3%	37.7%
LANE	1,467	1,142	311	14	831 R	77.8%	21.2%	78.6%	21.4%
LEAVENWORTH	14,783	9,046	5,698	39	3,348 R	61.2%	38.5%	61.6%	38.6%
LINCOLN	3,357	2,841	507	9	2,334 R	84.6%	15.1%	84.9%	15.1%
LINN	4,767	3,527	1,220	20	2,307 R	74.0%	25.6%	74.3%	25.7%
LOGAN	1,931	1,544	369	18	1,175 R	80.0%	19.1%	80.7%	19.3%
LYON	12,568	8,544	3,944	80	4,600 R	68.0%	31.4%	68.4%	31.6%
MCPHERSON	10,798	8,053	2,371	374	5,682 R	74.6%	22.0%	77.3%	22.7%
MARION	7,767	6,228	1,361	178	4,867 R	80.2%	17.5%	82.1%	17.9%
MARSHALL	9,092	6,851	2,215	26	4,636 R	75.4%	24.4%	75.6%	24.4%
MEADE	2,680	2,061	568	51	1,493 R	76.9%	21.2%	78.4%	21.6%

PRESIDENT 1956

County	Total Vote	Republican	Democratic	Other	Rep.-Dem. Plurality	Total Vote Rep.	Total Vote Dem.	Major Vote Rep.	Major Vote Dem.
ALLEN	7,508	5,342	2,143	23	3,199 R	71.2%	28.5%	71.4%	28.6%
ANDERSON	4,463	3,080	1,369	14	1,711 R	69.0%	30.7%	69.2%	30.8%
ATCHISON	8,751	5,608	3,134	10	2,474 R	64.1%	35.8%	64.2%	35.8%
BARBER	3,949	2,698	1,241	10	1,457 R	68.3%	31.4%	68.5%	31.5%
BARTON	13,062	8,644	4,378	41	4,266 R	66.2%	33.5%	66.4%	33.6%
BOURBON	8,504	5,306	3,151	47	2,155 R	62.4%	37.1%	62.7%	37.3%
BROWN	6,677	5,138	1,519	20	3,619 R	77.0%	22.8%	77.2%	22.8%
BUTLER	15,794	9,591	6,158	45	3,433 R	60.7%	39.0%	60.9%	39.1%
CHASE	2,086	1,553	529	4	1,024 R	74.4%	25.4%	74.6%	25.4%
CHAUTAUQUA	3,077	2,180	887	10	1,293 R	70.8%	28.8%	71.1%	28.9%
CHEROKEE	9,975	5,824	4,112	39	1,712 R	58.4%	41.2%	58.6%	41.4%
CHEYENNE	2,150	1,479	663	8	816 R	68.8%	30.8%	69.0%	31.0%
CLARK	1,780	1,243	529	8	714 R	69.8%	29.7%	70.1%	29.9%
CLAY	5,461	4,378	1,034	49	3,344 R	80.2%	18.9%	80.9%	19.1%
CLOUD	6,509	4,466	2,008	35	2,458 R	68.6%	30.8%	69.0%	31.0%
COFFEY	4,549	3,286	1,247	16	2,039 R	72.2%	27.4%	72.5%	27.5%
COMANCHE	1,710	1,238	461	11	777 R	72.4%	27.0%	72.9%	27.1%
COWLEY	10,533	6,734	3,753	46	2,981 R	63.9%	35.6%	64.2%	35.8%
CRAWFORD	17,437	9,578	7,799	60	1,779 R	54.9%	44.7%	55.1%	44.9%
DECATUR	2,957	2,028	920	9	1,108 R	68.6%	31.1%	68.8%	31.2%
DICKINSON	9,908	7,422	2,452	34	4,970 R	74.9%	24.7%	75.2%	24.8%
DONIPHAN	4,339	3,130	1,197	12	1,933 R	72.1%	27.6%	72.3%	27.6%
DOUGLAS	15,351	11,029	4,283	39	6,746 R	71.8%	27.9%	72.0%	28.0%
EDWARDS	2,597	1,816	771	10	1,045 R	69.9%	29.7%	70.2%	29.8%
ELK	2,731	1,909	812	10	1,097 R	69.9%	29.7%	70.2%	29.8%
ELLIS	7,528	4,466	3,058	4	1,408 R	59.3%	40.6%	59.4%	40.6%
ELLSWORTH	3,889	2,524	1,351	14	1,173 R	64.9%	34.7%	65.1%	34.9%
FINNEY	5,348	3,576	1,752	20	1,824 R	66.8%	32.6%	67.1%	32.8%
FORD	8,320	5,561	2,710	49	2,851 R	66.8%	32.6%	67.2%	32.8%
FRANKLIN	9,181	6,557	2,591	33	3,966 R	71.4%	28.2%	71.7%	28.3%
GEARY	6,123	4,013	2,078	32	1,935 R	65.5%	33.9%	65.9%	34.1%
GOVE	1,819	1,315	492	12	823 R	72.3%	27.0%	72.8%	27.2%
GRAHAM	2,411	1,676	725	11	951 R	69.5%	30.1%	69.8%	30.2%
GRANT	1,523	1,058	459	6	599 R	69.5%	30.1%	69.7%	30.3%
GRAY	1,914	1,278	627	9	651 R	66.8%	32.8%	67.1%	32.9%
GREELEY	777	599	174	4	425 R	77.1%	22.4%	77.5%	22.5%
GREENWOOD	5,948	4,164	1,763	21	2,401 R	70.0%	29.6%	70.3%	29.7%
HAMILTON	1,426	865	552	9	313 R	60.7%	38.7%	61.0%	39.0%
HARPER	4,445	3,111	1,311	23	1,800 R	70.0%	29.5%	70.4%	29.5%
HARVEY	10,494	7,367	3,084	43	4,283 R	70.2%	29.4%	70.5%	29.5%
HASKELL	1,176	829	341	6	488 R	70.5%	29.0%	70.9%	29.1%
HODGEMAN	1,554	1,113	435	6	678 R	71.6%	28.0%	71.9%	28.1%
JACKSON	4,887	3,469	1,356	62	2,113 R	71.0%	27.7%	71.9%	28.0%
JEFFERSON	5,235	3,677	1,536	22	2,141 R	70.2%	29.3%	70.5%	29.5%
JEWELL	4,496	3,395	1,034	67	2,361 R	75.5%	23.0%	76.7%	23.3%
JOHNSON	49,733	35,511	14,185	37	21,326 R	71.4%	28.5%	71.5%	28.5%
KEARNY	1,275	854	418	3	436 R	67.0%	32.8%	67.1%	32.9%
KINGMAN	4,670	3,226	1,428	16	1,798 R	69.1%	30.6%	69.3%	30.7%
KIOWA	2,254	1,717	517	20	1,200 R	76.2%	22.9%	76.9%	23.1%
LABETTE	12,936	7,677	5,202	57	2,475 R	59.3%	40.2%	59.6%	40.4%
LANE	1,376	992	380	4	612 R	72.1%	27.6%	72.3%	27.6%
LEAVENWORTH	14,339	8,826	5,480	33	3,346 R	61.6%	38.2%	61.7%	38.3%
LINCOLN	2,912	2,219	681	12	1,538 R	76.2%	23.4%	76.5%	23.5%
LINN	4,175	2,991	1,177	7	1,814 R	71.6%	28.2%	71.8%	28.2%
LOGAN	1,829	1,328	493	8	835 R	72.6%	27.0%	72.9%	27.1%
LYON	11,911	8,021	3,831	59	4,190 R	67.3%	32.2%	67.7%	32.3%
MCPHERSON	10,198	7,521	2,603	74	4,918 R	73.7%	25.5%	74.3%	25.7%
MARION	6,998	5,318	1,644	36	3,674 R	76.0%	23.5%	76.4%	23.6%
MARSHALL	8,179	5,664	2,487	28	3,177 R	69.3%	30.4%	69.5%	30.5%
MEADE	2,315	1,720	575	20	1,145 R	74.3%	24.8%	74.9%	25.1%

KANSAS

PRESIDENT 1952

County	Total Vote	Republican	Democratic	Other	Rep.-Dem. Plurality	Total Vote Rep.	Total Vote Dem.	Major Vote Rep.	Major Vote Dem.
MIAMI	9,022	5,623	3,374	25	2,249 R	62.3%	37.4%	62.5%	37.5%
MITCHELL	5,146	4,167	961	18	3,206 R	81.0%	18.7%	81.3%	18.7%
MONTGOMERY	22,070	14,261	7,679	130	6,582 R	64.6%	34.8%	65.0%	35.0%
MORRIS	4,403	3,263	1,124	16	2,139 R	74.1%	25.5%	74.4%	25.6%
MORTON	1,277	893	362	22	531 R	69.9%	28.3%	71.2%	28.8%
NEMAHA	6,812	5,175	1,618	19	3,557 R	76.0%	23.8%	76.2%	23.8%
NEOSHO	9,614	6,595	2,987	32	3,608 R	68.6%	31.1%	68.8%	31.2%
NESS	3,000	2,288	664	48	1,624 R	76.3%	22.1%	77.5%	22.5%
NORTON	4,631	3,530	1,047	54	2,483 R	76.2%	22.6%	77.1%	22.9%
OSAGE	6,666	4,589	2,036	41	2,553 R	68.8%	30.5%	69.3%	30.7%
OSBORNE	4,403	3,577	754	72	2,823 R	81.2%	17.1%	82.6%	17.4%
OTTAWA	3,755	2,916	801	38	2,115 R	77.7%	21.3%	78.5%	21.5%
PAWNEE	4,824	3,431	1,340	53	2,091 R	71.1%	27.8%	71.9%	28.1%
PHILLIPS	4,631	3,713	884	34	2,829 R	80.2%	19.1%	80.8%	19.2%
POTTAWATOMIE	6,343	4,944	1,387	12	3,557 R	77.9%	21.9%	78.1%	21.9%
PRATT	5,805	3,998	1,743	64	2,255 R	68.9%	30.0%	69.6%	30.4%
RAWLINS	2,796	2,120	670	6	1,450 R	75.8%	24.0%	76.0%	24.0%
RENO	22,983	15,762	6,555	666	9,207 R	68.6%	28.5%	70.6%	29.4%
REPUBLIC	5,961	4,573	1,358	30	3,215 R	76.7%	22.8%	77.1%	22.9%
RICE	7,478	5,572	1,832	74	3,740 R	74.5%	24.5%	75.3%	24.7%
RILEY	12,201	9,799	2,352	50	7,447 R	80.3%	19.3%	80.6%	19.4%
ROOKS	4,482	3,331	1,105	46	2,226 R	74.3%	24.7%	75.1%	24.9%
RUSH	3,510	2,650	843	17	1,807 R	75.5%	24.0%	75.9%	24.1%
RUSSELL	6,333	4,813	1,499	21	3,314 R	76.0%	23.7%	76.3%	23.7%
SALINE	16,409	12,326	4,003	80	8,323 R	75.1%	24.4%	75.5%	24.5%
SCOTT	2,146	1,681	443	22	1,238 R	78.3%	20.6%	79.1%	20.9%
SEDGWICK	106,788	70,983	34,926	879	36,057 R	66.5%	32.7%	67.0%	33.0%
SEWARD	4,308	3,136	1,146	26	1,990 R	72.8%	26.6%	73.2%	26.8%
SHAWNEE	51,067	33,201	17,651	215	15,550 R	65.0%	34.6%	65.3%	34.7%
SHERIDAN	2,140	1,581	555	4	1,026 R	73.9%	25.9%	74.0%	26.0%
SHERMAN	3,413	2,403	941	69	1,462 R	70.4%	27.6%	71.9%	28.1%
SMITH	4,660	3,623	986	51	2,637 R	77.7%	21.2%	78.6%	21.4%
STAFFORD	4,436	3,162	1,174	100	1,988 R	71.3%	26.5%	72.9%	27.1%
STANTON	890	664	215	11	449 R	74.6%	24.2%	75.5%	24.5%
STEVENS	1,918	1,480	423	15	1,057 R	77.2%	22.1%	77.8%	22.2%
SUMNER	11,797	8,134	3,567	96	4,567 R	68.9%	30.2%	69.5%	30.5%
THOMAS	3,585	2,490	1,069	26	1,421 R	69.5%	29.8%	70.0%	30.0%
TREGO	2,533	1,915	608	10	1,307 R	75.6%	24.0%	75.9%	24.1%
WABAUNSEE	3,927	3,182	736	9	2,446 R	81.0%	18.7%	81.2%	18.8%
WALLACE	1,199	945	249	5	696 R	78.8%	20.8%	79.1%	20.9%
WASHINGTON	6,309	5,135	1,148	26	3,987 R	81.4%	18.2%	81.7%	18.3%
WICHITA	1,199	910	276	13	634 R	75.9%	23.0%	76.7%	24.1%
WILSON	7,078	5,180	1,845	53	3,335 R	73.2%	26.1%	73.7%	26.3%
WOODSON	3,400	2,594	786	20	1,808 R	76.3%	23.1%	76.7%	23.3%
WYANDOTTE	73,657	34,648	38,751	258	4,103 D	47.0%	52.6%	47.2%	52.8%
TOTAL	896,166	616,302	273,296	6,568	343,006 R	68.8%	30.5%	69.3%	30.7%

PRESIDENT 1956

County	Total Vote	Republican	Democratic	Other	Rep.-Dem. Plurality	Total Vote Rep.	Total Vote Dem.	Major Vote Rep.	Major Vote Dem.
MIAMI	8,484	5,031	3,428	25	1,603 R	59.3%	40.4%	59.5%	40.5%
MITCHELL	4,432	3,198	1,214	20	1,984 R	72.2%	27.4%	72.5%	27.5%
MONTGOMERY	20,598	13,262	7,265	81	5,987 R	64.3%	35.3%	64.6%	35.4%
MORRIS	3,905	2,677	1,208	20	1,469 R	68.6%	30.9%	68.9%	31.1%
MORTON	1,257	814	436	7	378 R	64.8%	34.7%	65.1%	34.9%
NEMAHA	6,251	4,195	2,038	18	2,157 R	67.1%	32.6%	67.3%	32.7%
NEOSHO	8,920	5,886	3,005	29	2,881 R	66.0%	33.8%	66.2%	33.8%
NESS	2,650	1,876	758	16	1,118 R	70.8%	28.6%	71.2%	28.8%
NORTON	4,264	3,052	1,194	18	1,858 R	71.6%	28.0%	71.9%	28.1%
OSAGE	6,147	4,136	1,979	32	2,157 R	67.3%	32.2%	67.6%	32.4%
OSBORNE	3,999	2,948	1,023	28	1,925 R	73.7%	25.6%	74.2%	25.8%
OTTAWA	3,385	2,329	1,037	19	1,292 R	68.8%	30.6%	69.2%	30.8%
PAWNEE	4,375	2,788	1,567	20	1,221 R	63.7%	35.8%	64.0%	36.0%
PHILLIPS	4,129	3,117	985	27	2,132 R	75.5%	23.9%	76.0%	24.0%
POTTAWATOMIE	5,782	4,335	1,422	25	2,913 R	75.0%	24.6%	75.3%	24.7%
PRATT	5,610	3,620	1,956	34	1,664 R	64.5%	34.9%	64.9%	35.1%
RAWLINS	2,387	1,668	711	8	957 R	69.9%	29.8%	70.1%	29.9%
RENO	22,620	15,057	7,461	102	7,596 R	66.6%	33.0%	66.9%	33.1%
REPUBLIC	5,266	3,621	1,613	32	2,008 R	68.8%	30.6%	69.2%	30.8%
RICE	6,581	4,638	1,926	17	2,712 R	70.5%	29.3%	70.7%	29.3%
RILEY	12,213	9,385	2,784	44	6,601 R	76.8%	22.8%	77.1%	22.9%
ROOKS	4,316	3,059	1,238	19	1,821 R	70.9%	28.7%	71.2%	28.8%
RUSH	3,094	2,007	1,080	7	927 R	64.9%	34.9%	65.0%	35.0%
RUSSELL	5,461	3,920	1,528	13	2,392 R	71.8%	28.0%	72.0%	28.0%
SALINE	16,117	11,172	4,908	37	6,264 R	69.3%	30.5%	69.5%	30.5%
SCOTT	1,832	1,376	451	5	925 R	75.1%	24.6%	75.3%	24.7%
SEDGWICK	118,360	72,292	45,732	336	26,560 R	61.1%	38.6%	61.3%	38.7%
SEWARD	4,066	2,885	1,162	19	1,723 R	71.0%	28.6%	71.3%	28.7%
SHAWNEE	49,075	32,647	16,298	130	16,349 R	66.5%	33.2%	66.7%	33.3%
SHERIDAN	1,964	1,324	633	7	691 R	67.4%	32.2%	67.7%	32.3%
SHERMAN	2,809	1,825	962	22	863 R	65.0%	34.2%	65.5%	34.5%
SMITH	4,307	3,142	1,139	26	2,003 R	73.0%	26.4%	73.4%	26.6%
STAFFORD	3,990	2,728	1,242	20	1,486 R	68.4%	31.1%	68.7%	31.3%
STANTON	782	549	226	7	323 R	70.2%	28.9%	70.8%	29.2%
STEVENS	1,845	1,273	565	7	708 R	69.0%	30.6%	69.3%	30.7%
SUMNER	11,158	7,024	4,088	46	2,936 R	63.0%	36.6%	63.2%	36.8%
THOMAS	3,042	1,888	1,138	16	750 R	62.1%	37.4%	62.4%	37.6%
TREGO	2,403	1,668	726	9	942 R	69.4%	30.2%	69.7%	30.3%
WABAUNSEE	3,458	2,650	802	6	1,848 R	76.6%	23.2%	76.8%	23.2%
WALLACE	941	684	251	6	433 R	72.7%	26.7%	73.2%	26.8%
WASHINGTON	5,641	4,220	1,389	32	2,831 R	74.8%	24.6%	75.2%	24.8%
WICHITA	1,061	747	312	2	435 R	70.4%	29.4%	70.5%	29.5%
WILSON	6,167	4,502	1,645	20	2,857 R	73.0%	26.7%	73.2%	26.8%
WOODSON	3,063	2,171	870	22	1,301 R	70.9%	28.4%	71.4%	28.6%
WYANDOTTE	72,632	34,604	37,842	186	3,238 D	47.6%	52.1%	47.8%	52.2%
TOTAL	866,243	566,878	296,317	3,048	270,561 R	65.4%	34.2%	65.7%	34.3%

KANSAS

PRESIDENT 1960

County	Total Vote	Republican	Democratic	Other	Rep.-Dem. Plurality	%Total Rep.	%Total Dem.	%Major Rep.	%Major Dem.
ALLEN	7,508	4,947	2,540	21	2,407 R	65.9%	33.8%	66.1%	33.9%
ANDERSON	4,274	2,665	1,589	20	1,076 R	62.4%	37.2%	62.6%	37.4%
ATCHISON	9,160	4,793	4,336	31	457 R	52.3%	47.3%	52.5%	47.5%
BARBER	4,066	2,703	1,347	16	1,356 R	66.5%	33.1%	66.7%	33.3%
BARTON	13,665	7,599	6,036	30	1,563 R	55.6%	44.2%	55.7%	44.3%
BOURBON	8,031	5,062	2,928	41	2,134 R	63.0%	36.5%	63.4%	36.6%
BROWN	6,515	4,707	1,773	35	2,934 R	72.2%	27.2%	72.6%	27.4%
BUTLER	17,232	10,059	7,112	61	2,947 R	58.4%	41.3%	58.6%	41.4%
CHASE	1,992	1,276	708	8	568 R	64.1%	35.5%	64.3%	35.7%
CHAUTAUQUA	3,062	2,160	885	17	1,275 R	70.5%	28.9%	70.9%	29.1%
CHEROKEE	10,192	5,753	4,366	73	1,387 R	55.4%	42.8%	56.0%	43.1%
CHEYENNE	2,271	1,622	636	13	986 R	71.4%	28.0%	71.8%	28.2%
CLARK	1,830	1,286	538	6	748 R	70.3%	29.4%	70.5%	29.5%
CLAY	5,226	3,937	1,246	43	2,691 R	75.3%	23.8%	76.0%	24.0%
CLOUD	6,677	4,045	2,607	25	1,438 R	60.6%	39.0%	60.8%	39.2%
COFFEY	4,197	2,925	1,263	9	1,662 R	69.7%	30.1%	69.8%	30.2%
COMANCHE	1,652	1,187	460	5	727 R	71.9%	27.9%	72.1%	27.9%
COWLEY	16,580	10,276	6,205	99	4,071 R	62.0%	37.4%	62.3%	37.6%
CRAWFORD	17,777	9,383	8,325	69	1,058 R	52.8%	46.8%	52.9%	47.0%
DECATUR	2,892	1,846	1,038	8	808 R	63.8%	35.9%	64.0%	36.0%
DICKINSON	10,055	6,956	3,054	45	3,902 R	69.2%	30.4%	69.5%	30.5%
DONIPHAN	4,277	2,882	1,383	12	1,499 R	67.4%	32.3%	67.6%	32.4%
DOUGLAS	17,065	11,337	5,690	38	5,647 R	66.4%	33.3%	66.6%	33.4%
EDWARDS	2,584	1,588	986	10	602 R	61.5%	38.2%	61.7%	38.3%
ELK	2,673	1,830	823	20	1,007 R	68.5%	30.8%	69.0%	31.0%
ELLIS	8,977	3,156	5,815	6	2,659 D	35.2%	64.8%	35.2%	64.8%
ELLSWORTH	3,687	2,189	1,488	10	701 R	59.4%	40.4%	59.5%	40.5%
FINNEY	6,240	3,720	2,490	30	1,230 R	59.6%	39.9%	59.9%	40.1%
FORD	9,017	5,200	3,792	25	1,408 R	57.7%	42.1%	57.8%	42.2%
FRANKLIN	9,029	6,158	2,824	47	3,334 R	68.2%	31.3%	68.6%	31.4%
GEARY	6,183	3,789	2,365	29	1,424 R	61.3%	38.3%	61.6%	38.4%
GOVE	1,907	1,065	828	14	237 R	55.8%	43.4%	56.3%	43.7%
GRAHAM	2,497	1,572	918	7	654 R	63.0%	36.8%	63.1%	36.9%
GRANT	1,942	1,235	702	5	533 R	63.6%	36.1%	63.8%	36.2%
GRAY	1,899	1,150	744	5	406 R	60.6%	39.2%	60.7%	39.3%
GREELEY	914	645	262	7	383 R	70.6%	28.7%	71.1%	28.9%
GREENWOOD	5,571	3,758	1,804	9	1,954 R	67.5%	32.4%	67.6%	32.4%
HAMILTON	1,481	885	591	5	294 R	59.8%	39.9%	60.0%	40.0%
HARPER	4,622	3,158	1,439	25	1,719 R	68.3%	31.1%	68.7%	31.3%
HARVEY	11,404	7,798	3,537	69	4,261 R	68.4%	31.0%	68.8%	31.2%
HASKELL	1,328	853	471	4	382 R	64.2%	35.5%	64.4%	35.6%
HODGEMAN	1,507	926	570	11	356 R	61.4%	37.8%	61.9%	38.1%
JACKSON	4,861	3,279	1,567	15	1,712 R	67.5%	32.2%	67.7%	32.3%
JEFFERSON	5,101	3,353	1,739	9	1,614 R	65.7%	34.1%	65.8%	34.2%
JEWELL	4,033	2,914	1,095	24	1,819 R	72.3%	27.2%	72.7%	27.3%
JOHNSON	65,033	43,026	21,914	93	21,112 R	66.2%	33.7%	66.3%	33.7%
KEARNY	1,362	846	513	3	333 R	62.1%	37.7%	62.3%	37.7%
KINGMAN	4,662	2,904	1,735	23	1,169 R	62.3%	37.2%	62.6%	37.4%
KIOWA	2,229	1,662	555	12	1,107 R	74.6%	24.9%	75.0%	25.0%
LABETTE	12,807	7,491	5,248	68	2,243 R	58.5%	41.0%	58.8%	41.2%
LANE	1,379	902	462	15	440 R	65.4%	33.5%	66.1%	33.9%
LEAVENWORTH	14,832	7,870	6,926	36	944 R	53.1%	46.7%	53.2%	46.8%
LINCOLN	2,884	2,052	822	10	1,230 R	71.2%	28.5%	71.4%	28.6%
LINN	4,024	2,824	1,176	24	1,648 R	70.2%	29.2%	70.6%	29.4%
LOGAN	1,906	1,243	651	12	592 R	65.2%	34.2%	65.6%	34.4%
LYON	12,266	7,470	4,755	41	2,715 R	60.9%	38.8%	61.1%	38.9%
MCPHERSON	10,759	7,920	2,774	65	5,146 R	73.6%	25.8%	74.1%	25.9%
MARION	7,172	5,250	1,904	18	3,346 R	73.2%	26.5%	73.4%	26.6%
MARSHALL	7,891	4,932	2,931	28	2,001 R	62.5%	37.1%	62.7%	37.3%
MEADE	2,591	1,826	754	11	1,072 R	70.5%	29.1%	70.8%	29.2%

PRESIDENT 1964

County	Total Vote	Republican	Democratic	Other	Rep.-Dem. Plurality	%Total Rep.	%Total Dem.	%Major Rep.	%Major Dem.
ALLEN	6,252	2,841	3,369	42	528 D	45.4%	53.9%	45.7%	54.3%
ANDERSON	3,780	1,692	2,058	30	366 D	44.8%	54.4%	45.1%	54.9%
ATCHISON	8,229	3,147	5,037	45	1,890 D	38.2%	61.2%	38.5%	61.5%
BARBER	3,624	1,758	1,845	21	87 D	48.5%	50.9%	48.8%	51.2%
BARTON	12,221	4,826	7,340	55	2,514 D	39.5%	60.1%	39.7%	60.3%
BOURBON	7,323	3,290	3,980	53	690 D	44.9%	54.3%	45.3%	54.7%
BROWN	5,636	3,213	2,386	37	827 R	57.0%	42.3%	57.4%	42.6%
BUTLER	15,552	6,364	9,061	107	2,697 D	41.0%	58.3%	41.3%	58.7%
CHASE	1,793	902	886	5	16 R	50.3%	49.4%	50.4%	49.6%
CHAUTAUQUA	2,640	1,463	1,163	14	300 R	55.4%	44.1%	55.7%	44.3%
CHEROKEE	9,497	3,730	5,720	47	1,990 D	39.3%	60.2%	39.5%	60.5%
CHEYENNE	2,040	1,147	886	7	261 R	56.2%	43.4%	56.4%	43.6%
CLARK	1,665	777	881	7	104 D	46.7%	52.9%	46.9%	53.1%
CLAY	4,873	3,030	1,806	37	1,224 R	62.2%	37.1%	62.7%	37.3%
CLOUD	6,043	2,680	3,314	49	634 D	44.3%	54.8%	44.7%	55.3%
COFFEY	3,606	1,998	1,594	14	404 R	55.4%	44.2%	55.6%	44.4%
COMANCHE	1,524	694	818	12	124 D	45.5%	53.7%	45.9%	54.1%
COWLEY	14,797	7,092	7,591	114	499 D	47.9%	51.3%	48.3%	51.7%
CRAWFORD	16,644	6,286	10,282	76	3,996 D	37.8%	61.8%	37.9%	62.1%
DECATUR	2,712	1,382	1,314	16	68 R	51.0%	48.5%	51.3%	48.7%
DICKINSON	8,847	4,704	4,070	73	634 R	53.2%	46.0%	53.6%	46.4%
DONIPHAN	3,824	1,952	1,856	16	96 R	51.0%	48.5%	51.3%	48.7%
DOUGLAS	17,353	7,825	9,416	112	1,591 D	45.1%	54.3%	45.4%	54.6%
EDWARDS	2,373	932	1,427	14	495 D	39.3%	60.1%	39.5%	60.5%
ELK	2,273	1,267	994	12	273 R	55.7%	43.7%	56.0%	44.0%
ELLIS	8,020	2,440	5,553	27	3,113 D	30.4%	69.2%	30.5%	69.5%
ELLSWORTH	3,537	1,406	2,118	13	712 D	39.8%	59.9%	39.9%	60.1%
FINNEY	5,883	2,201	3,639	43	1,438 D	37.4%	61.9%	37.7%	62.3%
FORD	8,761	3,481	5,221	59	1,740 D	39.7%	59.6%	40.0%	60.0%
FRANKLIN	8,221	3,725	4,410	86	685 D	45.3%	53.6%	45.8%	54.2%
GEARY	5,745	2,259	3,419	67	1,160 D	39.3%	59.5%	39.8%	60.2%
GOVE	1,813	774	1,022	17	248 D	42.7%	56.4%	43.1%	56.9%
GRAHAM	2,408	1,194	1,193	21	1 R	49.6%	49.5%	50.0%	50.0%
GRANT	1,775	727	1,023	25	296 D	41.0%	57.6%	41.5%	58.5%
GRAY	1,793	643	1,136	14	493 D	35.9%	63.4%	36.1%	63.9%
GREELEY	865	388	469	9	81 D	44.8%	54.2%	45.3%	54.7%
GREENWOOD	4,801	2,717	2,048	36	669 R	56.6%	42.7%	57.0%	43.0%
HAMILTON	1,421	685	726	10	41 D	48.2%	51.1%	48.5%	51.5%
HARPER	3,810	1,969	1,813	28	156 R	51.7%	47.6%	52.1%	47.9%
HARVEY	10,415	4,979	5,306	130	327 D	47.8%	50.9%	48.4%	51.6%
HASKELL	1,409	570	820	19	250 D	40.5%	58.2%	41.0%	59.0%
HODGEMAN	1,434	607	821	6	214 D	42.3%	57.3%	42.5%	57.5%
JACKSON	4,336	2,334	1,971	31	363 R	53.8%	45.5%	54.2%	45.8%
JEFFERSON	4,485	2,380	2,066	39	314 R	53.1%	46.1%	53.5%	46.5%
JEWELL	3,535	1,895	1,601	39	294 R	53.6%	45.3%	54.2%	45.8%
JOHNSON	69,179	37,672	31,213	294	6,459 R	54.5%	45.1%	54.7%	45.3%
KEARNY	1,315	563	737	15	174 D	42.8%	56.0%	43.3%	56.7%
KINGMAN	4,175	1,917	2,226	32	309 D	46.3%	53.3%	46.3%	53.7%
KIOWA	2,130	1,135	970	25	165 R	53.3%	45.5%	53.9%	46.1%
LABETTE	11,062	4,761	6,208	93	1,447 D	43.0%	56.1%	43.4%	56.6%
LANE	1,370	586	773	11	187 D	42.8%	56.4%	43.1%	56.9%
LEAVENWORTH	13,089	5,544	7,479	66	1,935 D	42.3%	57.1%	42.6%	57.4%
LINCOLN	2,703	1,373	1,316	14	57 R	50.8%	48.7%	51.1%	48.9%
LINN	3,679	1,939	1,725	15	214 R	52.7%	46.9%	52.9%	47.1%
LOGAN	1,941	967	957	17	10 R	49.8%	49.3%	50.3%	49.7%
LYON	11,462	5,184	6,197	81	1,013 D	45.2%	54.1%	45.5%	54.5%
MCPHERSON	9,826	4,483	5,173	170	690 D	45.6%	52.6%	46.4%	53.6%
MARION	6,341	3,481	2,792	68	689 R	54.9%	44.0%	55.5%	44.5%
MARSHALL	6,822	3,432	3,334	56	98 R	50.3%	48.9%	50.7%	49.3%
MEADE	2,492	1,290	1,179	23	111 R	51.8%	47.3%	52.2%	47.8%

KANSAS

PRESIDENT 1960

County	Total Vote	Republican	Democratic	Other	Rep.-Dem. Plurality	Total Vote Rep.	Total Vote Dem.	Major Vote Rep.	Major Vote Dem.
MIAMI	8,396	4,857	3,505	34	1,352 R	57.8%	41.7%	58.1%	41.9%
MITCHELL	4,497	2,779	1,692	26	1,087 R	61.8%	37.6%	62.2%	37.8%
MONTGOMERY	20,638	12,536	7,938	164	4,598 R	60.7%	38.5%	61.2%	38.8%
MORRIS	3,580	2,413	1,148	19	1,265 R	67.4%	32.1%	67.8%	32.2%
MORTON	1,513	918	586	9	332 R	60.7%	38.7%	61.0%	39.0%
NEMAHA	6,267	3,360	2,884	23	476 R	53.6%	46.0%	53.8%	46.2%
NEOSHO	9,371	5,877	3,451	43	2,426 R	62.7%	36.8%	63.0%	37.0%
NESS	2,655	1,683	960	12	723 R	63.4%	36.2%	63.7%	36.3%
NORTON	4,089	2,781	1,300	8	1,481 R	68.0%	31.8%	68.1%	31.9%
OSAGE	6,061	3,880	2,150	31	1,730 R	64.0%	35.5%	64.3%	35.7%
OSBORNE	3,903	2,731	1,152	20	1,579 R	70.0%	29.5%	70.3%	29.7%
OTTAWA	3,278	2,190	1,072	16	1,118 R	66.8%	32.7%	67.1%	32.9%
PAWNEE	4,489	2,618	1,853	18	765 R	58.3%	41.3%	58.6%	41.4%
PHILLIPS	4,145	3,123	1,004	18	2,119 R	75.3%	24.2%	75.7%	24.3%
POTTAWATOMIE	5,804	3,666	2,125	13	1,541 R	63.2%	36.6%	63.3%	36.7%
PRATT	5,506	3,501	1,968	37	1,533 R	63.6%	35.7%	64.0%	36.0%
RAWLINS	2,527	1,560	951	16	609 R	61.7%	37.6%	62.1%	37.9%
RENO	24,339	14,655	9,557	127	5,098 R	60.2%	39.3%	60.5%	39.5%
REPUBLIC	5,117	3,358	1,724	35	1,634 R	65.6%	33.7%	66.1%	33.9%
RICE	6,680	4,329	2,328	23	2,001 R	64.8%	34.9%	65.0%	35.0%
RILEY	12,600	9,068	3,482	50	5,586 R	72.0%	27.6%	72.3%	27.7%
ROOKS	4,490	2,840	1,639	11	1,201 R	63.3%	36.5%	63.4%	36.5%
RUSH	3,097	1,668	1,418	11	250 R	53.9%	45.8%	54.1%	45.9%
RUSSELL	5,501	3,607	1,870	24	1,737 R	65.6%	34.0%	65.9%	34.1%
SALINE	17,568	11,023	6,495	50	4,528 R	62.7%	37.0%	62.9%	37.1%
SCOTT	2,124	1,514	598	12	916 R	71.3%	28.2%	71.7%	28.3%
SEDGWICK	133,084	73,501	58,887	696	14,614 R	55.2%	44.2%	55.5%	44.5%
SEWARD	5,642	3,974	1,654	14	2,320 R	70.4%	29.3%	70.6%	29.4%
SHAWNEE	55,749	33,803	21,799	147	12,004 R	60.6%	39.1%	60.6%	39.2%
SHERIDAN	2,016	1,047	954	15	93 R	51.9%	47.3%	52.3%	47.7%
SHERMAN	3,119	2,030	1,074	15	956 R	65.1%	34.4%	65.4%	34.6%
SMITH	4,192	3,013	1,157	22	1,856 R	71.9%	27.6%	72.3%	27.7%
STAFFORD	3,862	2,531	1,305	26	1,226 R	65.5%	33.8%	66.0%	34.0%
STANTON	954	627	323	4	304 R	65.7%	33.9%	66.0%	34.0%
STEVENS	2,044	1,405	630	9	775 R	68.7%	30.8%	69.0%	31.0%
SUMNER	11,736	7,219	4,462	55	2,757 R	61.5%	38.0%	61.8%	38.2%
THOMAS	3,384	2,081	1,285	18	796 R	61.5%	38.0%	61.8%	38.2%
TREGO	2,309	1,426	875	8	551 R	61.8%	37.9%	62.0%	38.0%
WABAUNSEE	3,331	2,351	969	11	1,382 R	70.6%	29.1%	70.8%	29.2%
WALLACE	1,066	727	339		388 R	68.2%	31.8%	68.2%	31.8%
WASHINGTON	5,444	3,707	1,706	31	2,001 R	68.1%	31.3%	68.5%	31.5%
WICHITA	1,262	702	554	6	148 R	55.6%	43.9%	55.9%	44.1%
WILSON	6,394	4,333	2,034	27	2,299 R	67.8%	31.8%	68.1%	31.9%
WOODSON	2,751	1,853	888	10	965 R	67.4%	32.3%	67.6%	32.4%
WYANDOTTE	76,801	34,764	41,433	604	6,669 D	45.3%	53.9%	45.6%	54.4%
TOTAL	928,825	561,474	363,213	4,138	198,261 R	60.4%	39.1%	60.7%	39.3%

PRESIDENT 1964

County	Total Vote	Republican	Democratic	Other	Rep.-Dem. Plurality	Total Vote Rep.	Total Vote Dem.	Major Vote Rep.	Major Vote Dem.
MIAMI	7,570	2,907	4,620	43	1,713 D	38.4%	61.0%	38.6%	61.4%
MITCHELL	3,880	1,951	1,898	31	53 D	50.3%	48.9%	50.7%	49.3%
MONTGOMERY	17,416	8,437	8,853	126	416 D	48.4%	50.8%	48.8%	51.2%
MORRIS	3,323	1,683	1,605	35	78 D	50.6%	48.3%	51.2%	48.8%
MORTON	1,561	609	938	14	329 D	39.0%	60.1%	39.4%	60.6%
NEMAHA	5,683	2,391	3,260	32	869 D	42.1%	57.4%	42.3%	57.7%
NEOSHO	8,296	3,458	4,795	43	1,337 D	41.7%	57.8%	41.9%	58.1%
NESS	2,615	1,034	1,562	19	528 D	39.5%	59.7%	39.8%	60.2%
NORTON	3,736	2,245	1,449	42	796 R	60.1%	38.8%	60.8%	39.2%
OSAGE	5,460	2,681	2,737	42	56 D	49.1%	50.1%	49.5%	50.5%
OSBORNE	3,401	1,700	1,659	42	41 R	50.0%	48.8%	50.6%	49.4%
OTTAWA	3,052	1,491	1,535	26	44 D	48.9%	50.3%	49.3%	50.7%
PAWNEE	4,074	1,468	2,577	29	1,109 D	36.0%	63.3%	36.3%	63.7%
PHILLIPS	4,000	2,164	1,804	32	360 R	54.1%	45.1%	54.5%	45.5%
POTTAWATOMIE	5,070	2,606	2,432	32	174 R	51.4%	48.0%	51.7%	48.3%
PRATT	5,129	2,493	2,594	42	101 D	48.6%	50.6%	49.0%	51.0%
RAWLINS	2,261	1,292	959	10	333 R	57.1%	42.4%	57.4%	42.6%
RENO	23,973	8,829	14,936	208	6,107 D	36.8%	62.3%	37.2%	62.6%
REPUBLIC	4,674	2,414	2,222	38	192 R	51.6%	47.5%	52.1%	47.9%
RICE	6,098	2,390	3,665	43	1,275 D	39.2%	60.1%	39.5%	60.5%
RILEY	12,137	6,396	5,597	144	799 R	52.7%	46.1%	53.3%	46.7%
ROOKS	3,924	1,985	1,923	16	62 R	50.6%	49.0%	50.8%	49.2%
RUSH	2,901	1,098	1,778	25	680 D	37.8%	61.3%	38.2%	61.8%
RUSSELL	4,977	2,435	2,505	37	70 D	48.9%	50.3%	49.3%	50.7%
SALINE	16,357	6,533	9,725	99	3,192 D	39.9%	59.5%	40.2%	59.8%
SCOTT	2,177	1,143	1,016	18	127 R	52.5%	46.7%	52.9%	47.1%
SEDGWICK	120,181	52,592	66,372	1,217	13,780 D	43.8%	55.2%	44.2%	55.8%
SEWARD	5,462	2,910	2,520	32	390 R	53.3%	46.1%	53.6%	46.4%
SHAWNEE	56,625	25,736	30,626	263	4,890 D	45.4%	54.1%	45.7%	54.3%
SHERIDAN	1,847	808	1,028	11	220 D	43.7%	55.7%	44.0%	56.0%
SHERMAN	3,010	1,463	1,522	25	59 D	48.6%	50.6%	49.0%	51.0%
SMITH	3,871	2,026	1,809	36	217 R	52.3%	46.7%	52.8%	47.2%
STAFFORD	3,641	1,516	2,087	38	571 D	41.6%	57.3%	41.9%	57.9%
STANTON	970	459	500	11	41 D	47.3%	51.5%	47.9%	52.1%
STEVENS	2,020	992	1,006	22	14 D	49.1%	49.8%	49.6%	50.4%
SUMNER	10,450	4,760	5,574	116	814 D	45.6%	53.3%	46.1%	53.9%
THOMAS	3,348	1,528	1,793	27	265 D	45.6%	53.6%	46.0%	54.0%
TREGO	2,162	974	1,177	11	203 D	45.1%	54.4%	45.3%	54.7%
WABAUNSEE	3,152	1,839	1,287	26	552 R	58.3%	40.8%	58.8%	41.2%
WALLACE	1,018	516	496	6	20 R	50.7%	48.7%	51.0%	49.0%
WASHINGTON	4,705	2,654	2,015	36	639 R	56.4%	42.8%	56.8%	43.2%
WICHITA	1,197	529	662	6	133 D	44.2%	55.3%	44.4%	55.6%
WILSON	5,556	2,919	2,592	45	327 R	52.5%	46.7%	53.0%	47.0%
WOODSON	2,431	1,279	1,128	24	151 R	52.6%	46.4%	53.1%	46.9%
WYANDOTTE	65,351	20,553	43,442	1,356	22,889 D	31.5%	66.5%	32.1%	67.9%
TOTAL	857,901	386,579	464,028	7,294	77,449 D	45.1%	54.1%	45.4%	54.6%

KANSAS

OTHER VOTE COMPOSITION:

1920   Socialist.
1924   98,461 Progressive; 4 scattered.
1928   6,205 Socialist; 320 Communist.
1932   Socialist.
1936   2,766 Socialist; 494 Union. State-wide total includes 18 absentee Socialist
        votes cast outside the state and not reported by counties.

1940   4,056 Prohibition; 2,347 Socialist.
1944   2,609 Prohibition; 1,613 Socialist.
1948   6,468 Prohibition; 4,603 Progressive; 2,807 Socialist.
1952   6,038 Prohibition; 530 Socialist.
1956   Prohibition.

1960   Prohibition.
1964   5,393 Prohibition; 1,901 Socialist Labor.

SPECIAL CASES:

1924   Progressive candidates ran second in several counties.

KENTUCKY

PRESIDENT 1920

County	Total Vote	Republican	Democratic	Other	Rep.-Dem. Plurality	% Total Vote Rep.	% Total Vote Dem.	% Major Vote Rep.	% Major Vote Dem.
ADAIR	6,265	3,526	2,725	14	801 R	56.3%	43.5%	56.4%	43.6%
ALLEN	5,770	3,476	2,255	39	1,221 R	60.2%	39.1%	60.7%	39.3%
ANDERSON	4,330	1,819	2,499	12	680 D	42.0%	57.7%	42.1%	57.9%
BALLARD	5,213	1,107	3,987	119	2,880 D	21.2%	76.5%	21.7%	78.3%
BARREN	9,531	3,972	5,499	60	1,527 D	41.7%	57.7%	41.9%	58.1%
BATH	4,459	1,997	2,440	22	443 D	44.8%	54.7%	45.0%	55.0%
BELL	9,014	6,691	2,277	46	4,414 R	74.2%	25.3%	74.6%	25.4%
BOONE	4,480	973	3,472	35	2,499 D	21.7%	77.5%	21.9%	78.1%
BOURBON	9,524	4,029	5,452	43	1,423 D	42.3%	57.2%	42.5%	57.5%
BOYD	11,563	6,334	5,103	126	1,231 R	54.8%	44.1%	55.4%	44.6%
BOYLE	7,342	3,205	4,099	38	894 D	43.7%	55.8%	43.9%	56.1%
BRACKEN	4,468	1,791	2,621	56	830 D	40.1%	58.7%	40.6%	59.4%
BREATHITT	5,232	2,464	2,737	31	273 D	47.1%	52.3%	47.4%	52.6%
BRECKINRIDGE	8,099	4,368	3,702	29	666 D	53.9%	45.7%	54.1%	45.9%
BULLITT	3,954	1,393	2,548	13	1,155 D	35.2%	64.4%	35.3%	64.7%
BUTLER	5,466	4,097	1,356	13	2,741 R	75.0%	24.8%	75.1%	24.9%
CALDWELL	5,792	2,958	2,746	88	212 R	51.1%	47.4%	51.9%	48.1%
CALLOWAY	6,284	1,520	4,574	190	3,054 D	24.2%	72.8%	24.9%	75.1%
CAMPBELL	23,976	12,210	10,597	1,169	1,613 R	50.9%	44.2%	53.5%	46.5%
CARLISLE	3,442	688	2,688	66	2,000 D	20.0%	78.1%	20.4%	79.6%
CARROLL	4,141	906	3,209	26	2,303 D	21.9%	77.5%	22.0%	78.0%
CARTER	7,414	4,595	2,757	62	1,838 R	62.0%	37.2%	62.5%	37.5%
CASEY	5,533	3,543	1,951	39	1,592 R	64.0%	35.3%	64.5%	35.5%
CHRISTIAN	16,057	8,743	7,209	105	1,534 R	54.5%	44.9%	54.8%	45.2%
CLARK	7,987	3,105	4,846	36	1,741 D	38.9%	60.7%	39.1%	60.9%
CLAY	5,008	4,015	960	33	3,055 R	80.2%	19.2%	80.7%	19.3%
CLINTON	2,798	2,356	431	11	1,925 R	84.2%	15.4%	84.5%	15.5%
CRITTENDEN	5,311	3,149	2,138	24	1,011 R	59.3%	40.3%	59.6%	40.4%
CUMBERLAND	3,324	2,380	931	13	1,449 R	71.6%	28.0%	71.9%	28.1%
DAVIESS	17,359	7,584	9,669	106	2,085 D	43.7%	55.7%	44.0%	56.0%
EDMONSON	3,535	2,348	1,171	16	1,177 R	66.4%	33.1%	66.7%	33.3%
ELLIOTT	2,637	860	1,764	13	904 D	32.6%	66.9%	32.8%	67.2%
ESTILL	4,387	2,552	1,823	12	729 R	58.2%	41.6%	58.3%	41.7%
FAYETTE	24,139	11,032	12,926	181	1,894 D	45.7%	53.5%	46.0%	54.0%
FLEMING	6,474	2,960	3,488	26	528 D	45.7%	53.9%	45.9%	54.1%
FLOYD	6,468	2,825	3,597	46	772 D	43.7%	55.6%	44.0%	56.0%
FRANKLIN	8,609	2,710	5,878	21	3,168 D	31.5%	68.3%	31.6%	68.4%
FULTON	5,239	1,365	3,843	31	2,478 D	26.1%	73.4%	26.2%	73.8%
GALLATIN	2,327	536	1,782	9	1,246 D	23.0%	76.6%	23.1%	76.9%
GARRARD	5,469	2,994	2,434	41	560 R	54.7%	44.5%	55.2%	44.8%
GRANT	4,337	1,613	2,686	38	1,073 D	37.2%	61.9%	37.5%	62.5%
GRAVES	12,500	3,241	9,018	241	5,777 D	25.9%	72.1%	26.4%	73.6%
GRAYSON	7,049	4,174	2,830	45	1,344 R	59.2%	40.1%	59.6%	40.4%
GREEN	4,050	2,310	1,723	17	587 R	57.0%	42.5%	57.3%	42.7%
GREENUP	5,963	3,111	2,754	98	357 R	52.2%	46.2%	53.0%	47.0%
HANCOCK	2,879	1,446	1,384	49	62 R	50.2%	48.1%	51.1%	48.9%
HARDIN	8,782	3,334	5,382	66	2,048 D	38.0%	61.3%	38.3%	61.7%
HARLAN	9,351	7,493	1,805	53	5,688 R	80.1%	19.3%	80.6%	19.4%
HARRISON	7,239	2,378	4,804	57	2,426 D	32.8%	66.4%	33.1%	66.9%
HART	6,313	3,264	2,972	77	292 R	51.7%	47.1%	52.3%	47.7%
HENDERSON	11,718	4,161	7,272	285	3,111 D	35.5%	62.1%	36.4%	63.6%
HENRY	6,897	2,208	4,640	49	2,432 D	32.0%	67.3%	32.2%	67.8%
HICKMAN	3,934	866	3,045	23	2,179 D	22.0%	77.4%	22.1%	77.9%
HOPKINS	14,836	6,732	7,829	275	1,097 D	45.4%	52.8%	46.2%	53.8%
JACKSON	3,444	3,174	260	10	2,914 R	92.2%	7.5%	92.4%	7.6%
JEFFERSON	125,549	68,202	56,046	1,301	12,156 R	54.3%	44.6%	54.9%	45.1%
JESSAMINE	5,689	2,349	3,206	134	857 D	41.3%	56.4%	42.3%	57.7%
JOHNSON	6,137	4,373	1,714	50	2,659 R	71.3%	27.9%	71.8%	28.2%
KENTON	28,730	11,411	16,300	1,019	4,889 D	39.7%	56.7%	41.2%	58.8%
KNOTT	3,108	802	2,295	11	1,493 D	25.8%	73.8%	25.9%	74.1%

PRESIDENT 1924

County	Total Vote	Republican	Democratic	Other	Rep.-Dem. Plurality	% Total Vote Rep.	% Total Vote Dem.	% Major Vote Rep.	% Major Vote Dem.
ADAIR	5,032	2,725	2,269	38	456 R	54.2%	45.1%	54.6%	45.4%
ALLEN	5,501	3,092	2,373	36	719 R	56.2%	43.1%	56.6%	43.4%
ANDERSON	3,541	1,398	2,089	54	691 D	39.5%	59.0%	40.1%	59.9%
BALLARD	3,983	751	3,128	104	2,377 D	18.9%	78.5%	19.4%	80.6%
BARREN	7,965	3,431	4,449	85	1,018 D	43.1%	55.9%	43.5%	56.5%
BATH	3,839	1,723	2,095	21	372 D	44.9%	54.6%	45.1%	54.9%
BELL	7,896	5,371	2,166	359	3,205 R	68.0%	27.4%	71.3%	28.7%
BOONE	3,515	1,173	2,204	138	1,031 D	33.4%	62.7%	34.7%	65.3%
BOURBON	7,831	3,679	4,034	118	355 D	47.0%	51.5%	47.7%	52.3%
BOYD	10,893	6,042	4,079	772	1,963 R	55.5%	37.4%	59.7%	40.3%
BOYLE	6,200	2,656	3,197	347	541 D	42.8%	51.6%	45.4%	54.6%
BRACKEN	3,413	1,749	1,485	179	264 R	51.2%	43.5%	54.1%	45.9%
BREATHITT	4,544	1,708	2,826	10	1,118 D	37.6%	62.2%	37.7%	62.3%
BRECKINRIDGE	7,162	3,814	3,230	118	584 R	53.3%	45.1%	54.1%	45.9%
BULLITT	2,859	942	1,789	128	847 D	32.9%	62.6%	34.5%	65.5%
BUTLER	3,831	2,597	1,177	57	1,420 R	67.8%	30.7%	68.8%	31.2%
CALDWELL	4,832	2,475	2,183	174	292 R	51.2%	45.2%	53.1%	46.9%
CALLOWAY	4,882	936	3,790	156	2,854 D	19.2%	77.6%	19.8%	80.2%
CAMPBELL	24,849	12,242	5,564	7,043	6,678 R	49.3%	22.4%	68.8%	31.2%
CARLISLE	2,758	467	2,250	41	1,783 D	16.9%	81.6%	17.2%	82.8%
CARROLL	3,561	1,298	2,243	20	945 D	36.5%	63.0%	36.7%	63.3%
CARTER	7,213	4,414	2,552	247	1,862 R	61.2%	35.4%	63.4%	36.6%
CASEY	4,920	3,090	1,797	33	1,293 R	62.8%	36.5%	63.2%	36.8%
CHRISTIAN	13,850	7,150	6,585	115	565 R	51.6%	47.5%	52.1%	47.9%
CLARK	6,612	2,686	3,857	69	1,171 D	40.6%	58.3%	41.1%	58.9%
CLAY	4,815	3,551	1,144	120	2,407 R	73.7%	23.8%	75.6%	24.4%
CLINTON	2,607	2,047	543	17	1,504 R	78.5%	20.8%	79.0%	21.0%
CRITTENDEN	4,421	2,486	1,869	66	617 R	56.2%	42.3%	57.1%	42.9%
CUMBERLAND	3,049	2,113	918	18	1,195 R	69.3%	30.1%	69.7%	30.3%
DAVIESS	15,510	7,202	8,116	192	914 D	46.4%	52.3%	47.0%	53.0%
EDMONSON	3,188	2,005	1,183		822 R	62.9%	37.1%	62.9%	37.1%
ELLIOTT	2,324	591	1,702	31	1,111 D	25.4%	73.2%	25.8%	74.2%
ESTILL	4,343	2,071	2,052	220	19 R	47.7%	47.2%	50.2%	49.8%
FAYETTE	22,396	11,632	10,433	331	1,199 R	51.9%	46.6%	52.7%	47.3%
FLEMING	5,180	2,543	2,590	47	47 D	49.1%	50.0%	49.5%	50.5%
FLOYD	8,484	3,685	4,220	579	535 D	43.4%	49.7%	46.6%	53.4%
FRANKLIN	7,591	2,811	4,678	102	1,867 D	37.0%	61.6%	37.5%	62.5%
FULTON	4,292	891	3,336	65	2,445 D	20.8%	77.7%	21.1%	78.9%
GALLATIN	1,779	749	1,007	23	258 D	42.1%	56.6%	42.7%	57.3%
GARRARD	4,728	2,575	2,126	27	449 R	54.5%	45.0%	54.8%	45.2%
GRANT	3,579	1,424	1,923	232	499 D	39.8%	53.7%	42.5%	57.5%
GRAVES	9,813	2,279	7,266	268	4,987 D	23.2%	74.0%	23.9%	76.1%
GRAYSON	6,068	3,149	2,858	61	291 R	51.9%	47.1%	52.4%	47.6%
GREEN	3,470	1,909	1,548	13	361 R	55.0%	44.6%	55.2%	44.8%
GREENUP	5,286	2,490	1,932	864	558 R	47.1%	36.5%	56.3%	43.7%
HANCOCK	2,706	1,313	1,323	70	10 D	48.5%	48.9%	49.8%	50.2%
HARDIN	7,175	2,712	4,296	167	1,584 D	37.8%	59.9%	38.7%	61.3%
HARLAN	13,206	9,632	2,133	1,441	7,499 R	72.9%	16.2%	81.9%	18.1%
HARRISON	6,153	2,129	3,924	100	1,795 D	34.6%	63.8%	35.2%	64.8%
HART	5,642	2,687	2,862	93	175 D	47.6%	50.7%	48.4%	51.6%
HENDERSON	9,060	4,828	4,046	186	782 R	53.3%	44.7%	54.4%	45.6%
HENRY	5,656	1,910	3,706	40	1,796 D	33.8%	65.5%	34.0%	66.0%
HICKMAN	2,901	614	2,270	17	1,656 D	21.2%	78.2%	21.3%	78.7%
HOPKINS	11,793	5,231	5,864	698	633 D	44.4%	49.7%	47.1%	52.9%
JACKSON	3,046	2,686	284	76	2,402 R	88.2%	9.3%	90.4%	9.6%
JEFFERSON	117,293	61,475	50,409	5,409	11,066 R	52.4%	43.0%	54.9%	45.1%
JESSAMINE	4,764	2,144	2,470	150	326 D	45.0%	51.8%	46.5%	53.5%
JOHNSON	4,938	3,025	1,480	433	1,545 R	61.3%	30.0%	67.1%	32.9%
KENTON	30,446	13,444	7,948	9,054	5,496 R	44.2%	26.1%	62.8%	37.2%
KNOTT	3,173	866	2,286	21	1,420 D	27.3%	72.0%	27.5%	72.5%

KENTUCKY

PRESIDENT 1920

County	Total Vote	Republican	Democratic	Other	Rep.-Dem. Plurality	Total Vote Rep.	Total Vote Dem.	Major Vote Rep.	Major Vote Dem.
KNOX	6,818	5,228	1,534	56	3,694 R	76.7%	22.5%	77.3%	22.7%
LARUE	4,211	1,838	2,361	12	523 D	43.6%	56.1%	43.8%	56.2%
LAUREL	5,909	4,252	1,621	36	2,631 R	72.1%	27.4%	72.4%	27.6%
LAWRENCE	5,433	2,849	2,558	26	291 R	52.4%	47.1%	52.7%	47.3%
LEE	3,116	1,856	1,246	14	610 R	59.5%	40.0%	59.8%	40.2%
LESLIE	2,734	2,576	142	16	2,434 R	94.2%	5.2%	94.8%	5.2%
LETCHER	6,301	4,317	1,960	24	2,357 R	68.5%	31.1%	68.8%	31.2%
LEWIS	5,827	4,186	1,550	91	2,636 R	71.8%	26.6%	73.0%	27.0%
LINCOLN	7,566	3,710	3,787	69	77 D	49.0%	50.1%	49.5%	50.5%
LIVINGSTON	3,784	1,790	1,933	61	143 D	47.3%	51.1%	48.1%	51.9%
LOGAN	10,125	3,948	6,111	66	2,163 D	39.0%	60.4%	39.2%	60.8%
LYON	3,282	1,275	1,968	39	693 D	38.3%	60.0%	39.3%	60.7%
MCCRACKEN	14,880	6,085	8,496	299	2,411 D	40.9%	57.1%	41.7%	58.3%
MCCREARY	3,439	2,889	525	25	2,364 R	84.0%	15.3%	84.6%	15.4%
MCLEAN	5,221	2,408	2,754	59	346 D	46.1%	52.7%	46.6%	53.4%
MADISON	11,739	6,012	5,647	80	365 R	51.2%	48.1%	51.6%	48.4%
MAGOFFIN	3,715	2,347	1,352	16	995 R	63.2%	36.4%	63.4%	36.6%
MARION	6,258	2,431	3,807	20	1,376 D	38.3%	60.8%	39.0%	61.0%
MARSHALL	5,492	1,883	3,569	40	1,686 D	34.3%	65.0%	35.0%	65.0%
MARTIN	2,077	1,726	330	21	1,396 R	83.1%	15.9%	83.9%	16.1%
MASON	8,476	3,743	4,691	42	948 D	44.2%	55.3%	44.4%	55.6%
MEADE	3,693	1,468	2,195	30	727 D	39.8%	59.4%	40.1%	59.9%
MENIFEE	1,746	581	1,149	16	568 D	33.3%	65.8%	33.6%	66.4%
MERCER	6,446	2,786	3,623	33	837 D	43.3%	56.2%	43.5%	56.5%
METCALFE	3,259	1,809	1,442	8	367 R	55.5%	44.2%	55.6%	44.4%
MONROE	4,549	3,426	1,108	15	2,318 R	75.3%	24.4%	75.6%	24.4%
MONTGOMERY	5,260	2,163	3,069	28	906 D	41.1%	58.3%	41.3%	58.7%
MORGAN	5,166	1,802	3,347	17	1,545 D	34.9%	64.8%	35.0%	65.0%
MUHLENBERG	11,753	6,667	4,824	262	1,843 R	56.7%	41.0%	58.0%	42.0%
NELSON	8,033	2,945	5,061	27	2,116 D	36.7%	63.0%	36.8%	63.2%
NICHOLAS	4,494	1,496	2,953	45	1,457 D	33.3%	65.7%	33.6%	66.4%
OHIO	9,571	5,371	4,011	189	1,360 R	56.1%	41.9%	57.2%	42.8%
OLDHAM	3,684	1,014	2,655	15	1,641 D	27.5%	72.1%	27.6%	72.4%
OWEN	5,689	1,049	4,623	17	3,574 D	18.4%	81.3%	18.5%	81.5%
OWSLEY	2,180	1,914	257	9	1,657 R	87.8%	11.8%	88.2%	11.8%
PENDLETON	4,752	2,105	2,598	49	493 D	44.3%	54.7%	44.8%	55.2%
PERRY	6,573	4,345	2,203	25	2,142 R	66.1%	33.5%	66.4%	33.6%
PIKE	13,622	7,911	5,619	92	2,292 R	58.1%	41.2%	58.5%	41.5%
POWELL	1,884	835	1,038	11	203 D	44.3%	55.1%	44.5%	55.5%
PULASKI	11,059	7,262	3,749	48	3,513 R	65.7%	33.9%	66.0%	34.0%
ROBERTSON	1,570	623	940	7	317 D	39.7%	59.9%	39.9%	60.1%
ROCKCASTLE	5,018	3,561	1,438	19	2,123 R	71.0%	28.7%	71.2%	28.8%
ROWAN	2,847	1,564	1,264	19	300 R	54.9%	44.4%	55.3%	44.7%
RUSSELL	3,751	2,587	1,157	7	1,430 R	69.0%	30.8%	69.1%	30.9%
SCOTT	7,679	2,661	4,993	25	2,332 D	34.7%	65.0%	34.8%	65.2%
SHELBY	8,879	3,402	5,446	31	2,044 D	38.3%	61.3%	38.4%	61.6%
SIMPSON	4,907	1,680	3,206	21	1,526 D	34.2%	65.3%	34.4%	65.6%
SPENCER	3,253	1,102	2,135	16	1,033 D	33.9%	65.6%	34.0%	66.0%
TAYLOR	4,898	2,493	2,380	25	113 R	50.9%	48.6%	51.2%	48.8%
TODD	6,010	2,663	3,292	55	629 D	44.3%	54.8%	44.7%	55.3%
TRIGG	5,548	2,420	3,056	72	636 D	43.6%	55.1%	44.2%	55.8%
TRIMBLE	2,434	361	2,057	16	1,696 D	14.8%	84.5%	14.9%	85.1%
UNION	6,947	1,943	4,919	85	2,976 D	28.0%	70.8%	28.3%	71.7%
WARREN	12,599	5,474	7,010	115	1,536 D	43.4%	55.6%	43.8%	56.2%
WASHINGTON	5,502	2,892	2,600	10	292 R	52.6%	47.3%	52.7%	47.3%
WAYNE	4,849	2,992	1,827	30	1,165 R	61.7%	37.7%	62.1%	37.9%
WEBSTER	8,415	3,554	4,831	30	1,277 D	42.2%	57.4%	42.4%	57.6%
WHITLEY	8,819	7,235	1,556	28	5,679 R	82.0%	17.6%	82.3%	17.7%
WOLFE	2,432	939	1,476	17	537 D	38.6%	60.7%	38.9%	61.1%
WOODFORD	5,542	2,218	3,299	25	1,081 D	40.0%	59.5%	40.2%	59.8%
TOTAL	918,636	452,480	455,497	9,659	4,017 D	49.3%	49.7%	49.8%	50.2%

PRESIDENT 1924

County	Total Vote	Republican	Democratic	Other	Rep.-Dem. Plurality	Total Vote Rep.	Total Vote Dem.	Major Vote Rep.	Major Vote Dem.
KNOX	5,638	3,761	1,587	290	2,174 R	66.7%	28.1%	70.3%	29.7%
LARUE	3,390	1,368	1,993	29	625 D	40.4%	58.8%	40.7%	59.3%
LAUREL	4,880	3,211	1,451	218	1,760 R	65.8%	29.7%	68.9%	31.1%
LAWRENCE	5,040	2,509	2,445	86	64 R	49.8%	48.5%	50.6%	49.4%
LEE	2,708	1,319	1,348	41	29 D	48.7%	49.8%	49.5%	50.5%
LESLIE	2,291	2,035	223	33	1,812 R	88.8%	9.7%	90.1%	9.9%
LETCHER	5,711	3,112	1,912	687	1,200 R	54.5%	33.5%	61.9%	38.1%
LEWIS	4,642	3,002	1,445	195	1,557 R	64.7%	31.1%	67.5%	32.5%
LINCOLN	6,356	3,002	3,100	254	98 D	47.2%	48.8%	49.2%	50.8%
LIVINGSTON	3,085	1,250	1,768	67	518 D	40.5%	57.3%	41.4%	58.6%
LOGAN	8,637	3,686	4,772	179	1,086 D	42.7%	55.3%	43.6%	56.4%
LYON	2,716	976	1,696	44	720 D	35.9%	62.4%	36.5%	63.5%
MCCRACKEN	12,256	4,956	6,028	1,274	1,072 D	40.4%	49.2%	45.1%	54.9%
MCCREARY	3,056	2,283	533	240	1,750 R	74.7%	17.4%	81.1%	18.9%
MCLEAN	4,239	1,638	2,284	117	446 D	43.4%	53.9%	44.6%	55.4%
MADISON	10,269	5,253	4,895	121	358 R	51.2%	47.7%	51.8%	48.2%
MAGOFFIN	3,961	2,182	1,757	22	425 R	55.1%	44.4%	55.4%	44.6%
MARION	5,107	1,956	3,055	96	1,099 D	38.3%	59.8%	39.0%	61.0%
MARSHALL	3,993	1,175	2,752	66	1,577 D	29.4%	68.9%	29.9%	70.1%
MARTIN	2,042	1,481	364	197	1,117 R	72.5%	17.8%	80.3%	19.7%
MASON	7,021	3,372	3,525	124	153 D	48.0%	50.2%	48.9%	51.1%
MEADE	2,931	1,082	1,802	47	720 D	36.9%	61.5%	37.5%	62.5%
MENIFEE	1,339	445	873	21	428 D	33.2%	65.2%	33.8%	66.2%
MERCER	5,267	2,510	2,698	59	188 D	47.7%	51.2%	48.2%	51.8%
METCALFE	2,708	1,430	1,262	16	168 R	52.8%	46.6%	53.1%	46.9%
MONROE	3,442	2,434	970	38	1,464 R	70.7%	28.2%	71.5%	28.5%
MONTGOMERY	4,340	1,942	2,347	51	405 D	44.7%	54.1%	45.3%	54.7%
MORGAN	5,131	1,792	3,311	28	1,519 D	34.9%	64.5%	35.1%	64.9%
MUHLENBERG	10,471	5,210	4,379	882	831 R	49.8%	41.8%	54.3%	45.7%
NELSON	6,008	2,066	3,863	79	1,797 D	34.4%	64.3%	34.8%	65.2%
NICHOLAS	3,610	1,333	2,235	42	902 D	36.9%	61.9%	37.4%	62.6%
OHIO	9,067	4,909	3,817	341	1,092 R	54.1%	42.1%	56.3%	43.7%
OLDHAM	2,888	899	1,954	35	1,055 D	31.1%	67.6%	31.5%	68.5%
OWEN	4,107	914	3,155	38	2,241 D	22.3%	76.8%	22.5%	77.5%
OWSLEY	1,759	1,409	323	27	1,086 R	80.1%	18.4%	81.4%	18.6%
PENDLETON	4,290	2,117	2,028	145	89 R	49.3%	47.3%	51.1%	48.9%
PERRY	7,324	4,307	2,658	359	1,649 R	58.8%	36.3%	61.8%	38.2%
PIKE	13,471	6,990	5,835	646	1,155 R	51.9%	43.3%	54.5%	45.5%
POWELL	1,689	724	939	26	215 D	42.9%	55.6%	43.5%	56.5%
PULASKI	10,298	6,464	3,158	676	3,306 R	62.8%	30.7%	67.2%	32.8%
ROBERTSON	1,177	485	680	12	195 D	41.2%	57.8%	41.6%	58.4%
ROCKCASTLE	4,061	2,679	1,277	105	1,402 R	66.0%	31.4%	67.7%	32.3%
ROWAN	2,453	1,305	1,092	56	213 R	53.2%	44.5%	54.4%	45.6%
RUSSELL	3,506	2,258	1,224	24	1,034 R	64.4%	34.9%	64.8%	35.2%
SCOTT	6,188	2,315	3,805	68	1,490 D	37.4%	61.5%	37.8%	62.2%
SHELBY	7,100	2,936	4,092	72	1,156 D	41.4%	57.6%	41.8%	58.2%
SIMPSON	4,025	1,285	2,688	52	1,403 D	31.9%	66.8%	32.3%	67.7%
SPENCER	2,273	943	1,320	10	377 D	41.5%	58.1%	41.7%	58.3%
TAYLOR	4,312	2,227	2,052	33	175 R	51.6%	47.6%	52.0%	48.0%
TODD	4,673	1,935	2,679	59	744 D	41.4%	57.3%	41.9%	58.1%
TRIGG	4,769	2,108	2,625	36	517 D	44.2%	55.0%	44.5%	55.5%
TRIMBLE	2,028	335	1,676	17	1,341 D	16.5%	82.6%	16.7%	83.3%
UNION	5,537	1,768	3,493	276	1,725 D	31.9%	63.1%	33.6%	66.4%
WARREN	12,705	5,568	7,005	132	1,437 D	43.8%	55.1%	44.3%	55.7%
WASHINGTON	4,519	2,268	2,238	13	30 R	50.2%	49.5%	50.3%	49.7%
WAYNE	4,446	2,397	2,020	29	377 R	53.9%	45.4%	54.3%	45.7%
WEBSTER	6,680	3,160	3,449	71	289 D	47.3%	51.6%	47.8%	52.2%
WHITLEY	6,857	4,676	1,413	768	3,263 R	68.2%	20.6%	76.8%	23.2%
WOLFE	2,435	821	1,597	17	776 D	33.7%	65.6%	34.0%	66.0%
WOODFORD	4,562	2,077	2,472	13	395 D	45.5%	54.2%	45.7%	54.3%
TOTAL	813,843	396,758	375,593	41,492	21,165 R	48.8%	46.2%	51.4%	48.6%

KENTUCKY

PRESIDENT 1928

County	Total Vote	Republican	Democratic	Other	Rep.-Dem. Plurality	Total Vote Rep.	Total Vote Dem.	Major Vote Rep.	Major Vote Dem.
ADAIR	5,588	3,856	1,732		2,124 R	69.0%	31.0%	69.0%	31.0%
ALLEN	5,815	4,253	1,562		2,691 R	73.1%	26.9%	73.1%	26.9%
ANDERSON	3,578	1,859	1,718	1	141 R	52.0%	48.0%	52.0%	48.0%
BALLARD	3,839	940	2,896	3	1,956 D	24.5%	75.4%	24.5%	75.5%
BARREN	8,636	5,101	3,530	5	1,571 R	59.1%	40.9%	59.1%	40.9%
BATH	4,061	2,223	1,830	8	393 R	54.7%	45.1%	54.8%	45.2%
BELL	9,145	6,570	2,551	24	4,019 R	71.8%	27.9%	72.0%	28.0%
BOONE	4,466	2,604	1,855	7	749 R	58.3%	41.5%	58.4%	41.6%
BOURBON	7,734	4,512	3,218	4	1,294 R	58.3%	41.6%	58.4%	41.6%
BOYD	13,736	9,118	4,611	7	4,507 R	66.4%	33.6%	66.4%	33.6%
BOYLE	6,512	3,517	2,992	3	525 R	54.0%	45.9%	54.0%	46.0%
BRACKEN	4,030	2,820	1,201	9	1,619 R	70.0%	29.8%	70.1%	29.9%
BREATHITT	5,326	2,309	3,017		708 D	43.4%	56.6%	43.4%	56.6%
BRECKINRIDGE	7,773	4,783	2,987	3	1,796 R	61.5%	38.4%	61.6%	38.4%
BULLITT	3,554	1,793	1,758	3	35 R	50.5%	49.5%	50.5%	49.5%
BUTLER	3,963	3,272	684	7	2,588 R	82.6%	17.3%	82.7%	17.3%
CALDWELL	4,560	2,855	1,695	10	1,160 R	62.6%	37.2%	62.7%	37.3%
CALLOWAY	5,002	1,557	3,431	14	1,874 D	31.1%	68.6%	31.2%	68.8%
CAMPBELL	31,920	17,317	14,508	95	2,809 R	54.3%	45.5%	54.4%	45.6%
CARLISLE	2,783	787	1,994	2	1,207 D	28.3%	71.6%	28.3%	71.7%
CARROLL	3,515	1,649	1,863	3	214 D	46.9%	53.0%	47.0%	53.0%
CARTER	7,773	5,342	2,392	39	2,950 R	68.7%	30.8%	69.1%	30.9%
CASEY	5,330	3,805	1,519	6	2,286 R	71.4%	28.5%	71.5%	28.5%
CHRISTIAN	12,771	7,069	5,702		1,367 R	55.4%	44.6%	55.4%	44.6%
CLARK	6,955	3,495	3,460		35 R	50.3%	49.7%	50.3%	49.7%
CLAY	5,104	4,439	651	14	3,788 R	87.0%	12.8%	87.2%	12.8%
CLINTON	2,905	2,580	325		2,255 R	88.8%	11.1%	88.8%	11.2%
CRITTENDEN	4,382	3,000	1,376	6	1,624 R	68.5%	31.4%	68.6%	31.4%
CUMBERLAND	3,132	2,593	538	1	2,055 R	82.8%	17.2%	82.9%	17.2%
DAVIESS	16,243	8,896	7,332	15	1,564 R	54.8%	45.1%	54.8%	45.2%
EDMONSON	4,186	3,104	1,076	6	2,028 R	74.2%	25.7%	74.3%	25.7%
ELLIOTT	1,918	601	1,317		716 D	31.3%	68.7%	31.3%	68.7%
ESTILL	5,532	3,641	1,886	5	1,755 R	65.9%	34.1%	65.9%	34.1%
FAYETTE	26,092	16,988	9,065	39	7,923 R	65.1%	34.7%	65.2%	34.8%
FLEMING	5,888	3,798	2,086	4	1,712 R	64.5%	35.4%	64.5%	35.5%
FLOYD	10,830	5,109	5,721		612 D	47.2%	52.8%	47.2%	52.8%
FRANKLIN	7,345	3,485	3,853	7	368 D	47.4%	52.5%	47.5%	52.5%
FULTON	4,503	1,366	3,132	5	1,766 D	30.4%	69.6%	30.4%	69.6%
GALLATIN	1,835	1,010	823	2	187 R	55.0%	44.9%	55.1%	44.9%
GARRARD	4,591	2,862	1,729		1,133 R	62.3%	37.7%	62.3%	37.7%
GRANT	4,116	2,448	1,662	6	786 R	59.5%	40.4%	59.6%	40.4%
GRAVES	9,484	3,223	6,237	24	3,014 D	34.0%	65.9%	34.1%	65.9%
GRAYSON	6,242	3,937	2,295	10	1,642 R	63.1%	36.8%	63.2%	36.8%
GREEN	4,096	2,824	1,272		1,552 R	68.9%	31.1%	68.9%	31.1%
GREENUP	6,845	4,410	2,435		1,975 R	64.4%	35.6%	64.4%	35.6%
HANCOCK	2,767	1,614	1,151	2	463 R	58.3%	41.6%	58.4%	41.6%
HARDIN	7,848	4,624	3,210	14	1,414 R	58.9%	41.0%	59.0%	41.0%
HARLAN	16,246	12,251	3,958	37	8,293 R	75.4%	24.4%	75.6%	24.4%
HARRISON	6,078	2,909	3,164	5	255 D	47.9%	52.1%	47.9%	52.1%
HART	5,833	3,480	2,339	14	1,141 R	59.7%	40.1%	59.8%	40.2%
HENDERSON	9,544	5,443	4,068	33	1,375 R	57.0%	42.6%	57.2%	42.8%
HENRY	5,270	2,334	2,929	7	595 D	44.3%	55.6%	44.3%	55.7%
HICKMAN	2,936	767	2,163	6	1,396 D	26.1%	73.7%	26.2%	73.8%
HOPKINS	13,000	6,330	6,640	30	310 D	48.7%	51.1%	48.8%	51.2%
JACKSON	3,680	3,552	123	5	3,429 R	96.5%	3.3%	96.5%	3.3%
JEFFERSON	162,613	97,803	64,472	338	33,331 R	60.1%	39.6%	60.3%	39.7%
JESSAMINE	5,152	2,857	2,295		562 R	55.5%	44.5%	55.5%	44.5%
JOHNSON	7,217	5,339	1,869	9	3,470 R	74.0%	25.9%	74.1%	25.9%
KENTON	39,208	21,043	18,165		2,878 R	53.7%	46.3%	53.7%	46.3%
KNOTT	3,826	1,004	2,822		1,818 D	26.2%	73.8%	26.2%	73.8%

PRESIDENT 1932

County	Total Vote	Republican	Democratic	Other	Rep.-Dem. Plurality	Total Vote Rep.	Total Vote Dem.	Major Vote Rep.	Major Vote Dem.
ADAIR	6,347	3,084	3,251	12	167 D	48.6%	51.2%	48.7%	51.3%
ALLEN	6,368	3,219	3,116	33	103 R	50.5%	48.9%	50.8%	49.2%
ANDERSON	3,634	1,184	2,415	35	1,231 D	32.6%	66.5%	32.9%	67.1%
BALLARD	4,584	572	3,987	25	3,415 D	12.5%	87.0%	12.5%	87.5%
BARREN	10,181	3,622	6,518	41	2,896 D	35.6%	64.0%	35.7%	64.3%
BATH	4,505	1,576	2,909	20	1,333 D	35.0%	64.6%	35.1%	64.9%
BELL	10,213	4,695	5,440	78	745 D	46.0%	53.3%	46.3%	53.7%
BOONE	4,923	1,355	3,536	32	2,181 D	27.5%	71.8%	27.7%	72.3%
BOURBON	7,604	2,820	4,759	25	1,939 D	37.1%	62.6%	37.2%	62.8%
BOYD	15,343	6,853	8,315	175	1,462 D	44.7%	54.2%	45.2%	54.8%
BOYLE	6,711	2,208	4,473	30	2,265 D	32.9%	66.7%	33.0%	67.0%
BRACKEN	3,921	1,471	2,407	43	936 D	37.5%	61.4%	37.5%	62.1%
BREATHITT	5,902	1,371	4,524	7	3,153 D	23.2%	76.7%	23.3%	76.7%
BRECKINRIDGE	7,085	3,237	3,814	34	577 D	45.7%	53.7%	45.9%	54.1%
BULLITT	4,014	1,088	2,918	8	1,830 D	27.1%	72.7%	27.2%	72.8%
BUTLER	4,331	2,586	1,736	9	850 R	59.7%	40.1%	59.8%	40.2%
CALDWELL	5,039	2,020	2,971	48	951 D	40.1%	59.0%	40.5%	59.5%
CALLOWAY	7,184	813	6,335	36	5,522 D	11.3%	88.0%	11.4%	88.6%
CAMPBELL	30,208	11,665	17,776	767	6,111 D	38.6%	58.8%	39.6%	60.4%
CARLISLE	3,253	402	2,840	11	2,438 D	12.4%	87.3%	12.4%	87.6%
CARROLL	3,795	761	3,015	19	2,254 D	20.1%	79.4%	20.2%	79.8%
CARTER	9,020	4,376	4,565	79	189 D	48.5%	50.6%	48.9%	51.1%
CASEY	6,516	3,840	2,651	25	1,189 R	59.2%	40.7%	59.2%	40.8%
CHRISTIAN	12,920	5,235	7,618	67	2,383 D	40.5%	59.0%	40.7%	59.3%
CLARK	6,936	1,981	4,920	35	2,939 D	28.6%	70.9%	28.7%	71.3%
CLAY	5,620	3,474	2,133	13	1,341 R	61.8%	38.0%	62.0%	38.0%
CLINTON	3,330	2,422	908		1,514 R	72.7%	27.3%	72.7%	27.3%
CRITTENDEN	4,320	2,185	2,119	16	66 R	50.6%	49.1%	50.8%	49.2%
CUMBERLAND	3,615	2,369	1,235	11	1,134 R	65.5%	34.2%	65.7%	34.3%
DAVIESS	15,685	5,059	10,527	99	5,468 D	32.3%	67.1%	32.5%	67.5%
EDMONSON	4,499	2,690	1,796	13	894 R	59.8%	39.9%	60.0%	40.0%
ELLIOTT	2,532	382	2,150		1,768 D	15.1%	84.9%	15.1%	84.9%
ESTILL	6,136	2,963	3,150	23	187 D	48.3%	51.3%	48.5%	51.5%
FAYETTE	27,869	11,847	15,765	257	3,918 D	42.5%	56.6%	42.9%	57.1%
FLEMING	6,124	2,638	3,442	44	804 D	43.1%	56.2%	43.4%	56.6%
FLOYD	11,986	3,415	8,537	34	5,122 D	28.5%	71.2%	28.6%	71.4%
FRANKLIN	8,404	2,034	6,331	39	4,297 D	24.2%	75.3%	24.3%	75.7%
FULTON	4,845	837	3,985	23	3,148 D	17.3%	82.2%	17.4%	82.6%
GALLATIN	2,163	365	1,792	6	1,427 D	16.9%	82.8%	16.9%	83.1%
GARRARD	4,859	2,276	2,582	1	306 D	46.8%	53.1%	46.9%	53.1%
GRANT	4,592	1,407	3,148	37	1,741 D	30.6%	68.6%	30.9%	69.1%
GRAVES	11,764	1,813	9,888	51	8,063 D	15.5%	84.1%	15.6%	84.4%
GRAYSON	7,624	3,721	3,872	31	151 D	48.8%	50.8%	49.0%	51.0%
GREEN	4,563	2,281	2,277	25	4 R	49.8%	49.9%	50.0%	50.0%
GREENUP	8,492	3,422	4,963	107	1,541 D	40.3%	58.4%	40.8%	59.2%
HANCOCK	2,826	1,174	1,623	29	449 D	41.5%	57.4%	42.0%	58.0%
HARDIN	8,920	2,801	6,047	72	3,246 D	31.4%	67.8%	31.7%	68.3%
HARLAN	20,254	11,118	9,091	45	2,027 R	54.9%	44.9%	55.0%	45.0%
HARRISON	6,790	1,833	4,909	48	3,076 D	27.0%	72.3%	27.2%	72.8%
HART	6,642	2,601	4,008	33	1,407 D	39.2%	60.3%	39.4%	60.6%
HENDERSON	8,881	2,485	6,100	296	3,615 D	28.0%	68.7%	28.9%	71.1%
HENRY	5,987	1,643	4,303	41	2,660 D	27.4%	71.9%	27.6%	72.4%
HICKMAN	3,789	446	3,327	16	2,881 D	11.8%	87.8%	11.8%	88.2%
HOPKINS	13,085	3,817	9,158	110	5,341 D	29.2%	70.0%	29.4%	70.6%
JACKSON	3,416	2,879	529	8	2,350 R	84.3%	15.5%	84.5%	15.5%
JEFFERSON	141,096	67,137	72,402	1,557	5,265 D	47.6%	51.3%	48.1%	51.9%
JESSAMINE	4,595	1,710	2,873	12	1,163 D	37.2%	62.5%	37.3%	62.7%
JOHNSON	8,025	4,871	3,134	20	1,737 R	60.7%	39.1%	60.8%	39.2%
KENTON	34,263	11,202	22,311	750	11,109 D	32.7%	65.1%	33.4%	66.6%
KNOTT	5,190	747	4,443		3,696 D	14.4%	85.6%	14.4%	85.6%

KENTUCKY

PRESIDENT 1928

County	Total Vote	Republican	Democratic	Other	Rep.-Dem. Plurality	% Total Vote Rep.	% Total Vote Dem.	% Major Vote Rep.	% Major Vote Dem.
KNOX	7,432	5,928	1,497	7	4,431 R	79.8%	20.1%	79.8%	20.2%
LARUE	3,625	1,892	1,727	6	165 R	52.2%	47.6%	52.3%	47.7%
LAUREL	6,052	4,906	1,141	5	3,765 R	81.1%	18.9%	81.1%	18.9%
LAWRENCE	5,499	3,277	2,217	5	1,060 R	59.5%	40.3%	59.6%	40.4%
LEE	3,137	2,005	1,131	1	874 R	63.9%	36.1%	63.9%	36.1%
LESLIE	2,969	2,806	159	4	2,647 R	94.5%	5.4%	94.6%	5.4%
LETCHER	8,918	5,400	3,502	16	1,898 R	60.6%	39.3%	60.7%	39.3%
LEWIS	5,203	4,077	1,120	6	2,957 R	78.4%	21.5%	78.4%	21.6%
LINCOLN	5,227	3,903	1,314	10	2,589 R	74.7%	25.1%	74.8%	25.2%
LIVINGSTON	2,989	1,767	1,217	5	550 R	59.1%	40.7%	59.2%	40.8%
LOGAN	8,708	4,858	3,843	7	1,015 R	55.8%	44.1%	55.8%	44.2%
LYON	2,509	1,215	1,286	8	71 D	48.4%	51.3%	48.6%	51.4%
MCCRACKEN	12,943	7,368	5,535	40	1,833 R	56.9%	42.8%	57.1%	42.9%
MCCREARY	4,065	3,622	435	8	3,187 R	89.1%	10.7%	89.3%	10.7%
MCLEAN	4,147	2,408	1,728	11	680 R	58.1%	41.7%	58.2%	41.8%
MADISON	11,090	6,325	4,736	29	1,589 R	57.0%	42.7%	57.2%	42.8%
MAGOFFIN	4,622	2,816	1,806	—	1,010 R	60.9%	39.1%	60.9%	39.1%
MARION	5,863	2,395	3,461	7	1,066 D	40.8%	59.0%	40.9%	59.1%
MARSHALL	3,925	1,879	2,036	10	157 D	47.9%	51.9%	48.0%	52.0%
MARTIN	2,081	1,674	404	3	1,270 R	80.4%	19.4%	80.6%	19.4%
MASON	8,382	5,012	3,364	6	1,648 R	59.8%	40.1%	59.8%	40.2%
MEADE	3,317	1,610	1,700	7	90 D	48.5%	51.3%	48.6%	51.4%
MENIFEE	1,457	732	725	—	7 R	50.2%	49.8%	50.2%	49.8%
MERCER	5,606	3,462	2,140	4	1,322 R	61.8%	38.2%	61.8%	38.2%
METCALFE	3,458	2,314	1,144	—	1,170 R	66.9%	33.1%	66.9%	33.1%
MONROE	3,979	3,127	843	9	2,284 R	78.6%	21.2%	78.8%	21.2%
MONTGOMERY	4,699	2,742	1,938	19	804 R	58.4%	41.2%	58.6%	41.4%
MORGAN	4,600	2,025	2,575	—	550 D	44.0%	56.0%	44.0%	56.0%
MUHLENBERG	11,830	6,651	5,130	49	1,521 R	56.2%	43.3%	56.4%	43.5%
NELSON	6,960	2,926	4,031	3	1,105 D	42.0%	57.9%	42.1%	57.9%
NICHOLAS	3,707	1,867	1,836	4	31 R	50.4%	49.5%	50.4%	49.6%
OHIO	8,514	5,690	2,784	40	2,906 R	66.8%	32.7%	67.1%	32.9%
OLDHAM	2,969	1,604	1,359	6	245 R	54.0%	45.8%	54.1%	45.9%
OWEN	4,135	1,573	2,552	10	979 D	38.0%	61.7%	38.1%	61.9%
OWSLEY	2,353	2,107	241	5	1,866 R	89.5%	10.2%	89.7%	10.3%
PENDLETON	4,768	3,196	1,567	5	1,629 R	67.0%	32.9%	67.1%	32.9%
PERRY	9,927	6,099	3,814	14	2,285 R	61.4%	38.4%	61.5%	38.5%
PIKE	17,335	9,386	7,930	19	1,456 R	54.1%	45.7%	54.2%	45.8%
POWELL	1,892	1,160	732	—	428 R	61.3%	38.7%	61.3%	38.7%
PULASKI	11,857	9,348	2,494	15	6,854 R	78.8%	21.0%	78.9%	21.1%
ROBERTSON	1,382	742	640	—	102 R	53.7%	46.3%	53.7%	46.3%
ROCKCASTLE	4,766	3,858	908	—	2,950 R	80.9%	19.1%	80.9%	19.1%
ROWAN	3,032	1,857	1,170	5	687 R	61.2%	38.6%	61.3%	38.7%
RUSSELL	3,860	3,028	823	9	2,205 R	78.4%	21.3%	78.6%	21.4%
SCOTT	6,043	3,192	2,843	8	349 R	52.8%	47.0%	52.9%	47.1%
SHELBY	7,165	3,933	3,232	—	701 R	54.9%	45.1%	54.9%	45.1%
SIMPSON	4,125	1,635	2,490	—	855 D	39.6%	60.4%	39.6%	60.4%
SPENCER	2,516	1,565	947	4	618 R	62.2%	37.6%	62.3%	37.7%
TAYLOR	4,841	3,149	1,684	8	1,465 R	65.0%	34.8%	65.2%	34.8%
TODD	4,915	2,496	2,416	3	80 R	50.8%	49.2%	50.8%	49.2%
TRIGG	4,381	2,346	2,031	4	315 R	53.5%	46.4%	53.6%	46.4%
TRIMBLE	1,897	573	1,317	7	744 D	30.2%	69.4%	30.3%	69.7%
UNION	6,243	2,350	3,884	9	1,534 D	37.6%	62.2%	37.7%	62.3%
WARREN	13,024	7,931	5,092	1	2,839 R	60.9%	39.1%	60.9%	39.1%
WASHINGTON	5,204	2,933	2,266	5	667 R	56.4%	43.5%	56.4%	43.6%
WAYNE	4,542	2,907	1,635	—	1,272 R	64.0%	36.0%	64.0%	36.0%
WEBSTER	7,127	3,527	3,591	9	64 D	49.5%	50.4%	49.6%	50.4%
WHITLEY	9,680	8,060	1,610	10	6,450 R	83.3%	16.6%	83.4%	16.6%
WOLFE	2,626	1,270	1,356	—	86 D	48.4%	51.6%	48.4%	51.6%
WOODFORD	4,551	2,490	2,056	5	434 R	54.7%	45.2%	54.8%	45.2%
TOTAL	940,521	558,064	381,070	1,387	176,994 R	59.3%	40.5%	59.4%	40.6%

PRESIDENT 1932

County	Total Vote	Republican	Democratic	Other	Rep.-Dem. Plurality	% Total Vote Rep.	% Total Vote Dem.	% Major Vote Rep.	% Major Vote Dem.
KNOX	7,938	4,513	3,375	50	1,138 R	56.9%	42.5%	57.2%	42.8%
LARUE	3,899	1,235	2,650	14	1,415 D	31.7%	68.0%	31.8%	68.2%
LAUREL	8,430	4,827	3,569	34	1,258 R	57.3%	42.3%	57.5%	42.5%
LAWRENCE	6,494	2,766	3,701	27	935 D	42.6%	57.0%	42.8%	57.2%
LEE	3,607	1,628	1,970	9	342 D	45.2%	54.7%	45.2%	54.8%
LESLIE	3,387	2,810	569	8	2,241 R	83.0%	16.8%	83.2%	16.8%
LETCHER	9,975	4,732	5,190	53	458 D	47.4%	52.0%	47.7%	52.3%
LEWIS	5,748	3,212	2,488	48	724 R	55.9%	43.3%	56.4%	43.6%
LINCOLN	7,695	3,063	4,574	58	1,511 D	39.8%	59.4%	40.1%	59.9%
LIVINGSTON	3,312	1,070	2,231	11	1,161 D	32.3%	67.4%	32.4%	67.6%
LOGAN	9,917	2,778	7,072	67	4,294 D	28.0%	71.3%	28.2%	71.8%
LYON	2,979	873	2,099	7	1,226 D	29.3%	70.5%	29.4%	70.6%
MCCRACKEN	12,499	3,140	9,188	171	6,048 D	25.1%	73.5%	25.5%	74.5%
MCCREARY	4,576	3,360	1,194	22	2,166 R	73.4%	26.1%	73.8%	26.2%
MCLEAN	4,224	1,412	2,771	41	1,359 D	33.4%	65.6%	33.8%	66.2%
MADISON	12,884	5,811	6,957	116	1,146 D	45.1%	54.0%	45.5%	54.5%
MAGOFFIN	5,395	2,661	2,721	13	60 D	49.3%	50.4%	49.4%	50.6%
MARION	6,021	1,571	4,427	23	2,856 D	26.1%	73.5%	26.2%	73.8%
MARSHALL	5,129	863	4,246	20	3,383 D	16.8%	82.8%	16.9%	83.1%
MARTIN	2,559	1,774	770	15	1,004 R	69.3%	30.1%	69.7%	30.3%
MASON	8,334	3,213	5,065	56	1,852 D	38.6%	60.8%	38.8%	61.2%
MEADE	3,564	1,050	2,488	26	1,438 D	29.5%	69.8%	29.7%	70.3%
MENIFEE	1,910	474	1,425	11	951 D	24.8%	74.6%	25.0%	75.0%
MERCER	5,745	1,950	3,759	36	1,809 D	33.9%	65.4%	34.2%	65.8%
METCALFE	3,730	1,729	1,985	16	256 D	46.4%	53.2%	46.6%	53.4%
MONROE	4,190	2,559	1,610	11	939 R	61.1%	38.7%	61.2%	38.8%
MONTGOMERY	4,338	1,515	2,810	13	1,295 D	34.9%	64.8%	35.0%	65.0%
MORGAN	5,584	1,435	4,137	12	2,702 D	25.7%	74.1%	25.7%	74.3%
MUHLENBERG	11,630	4,349	7,162	119	2,813 D	37.4%	61.6%	37.8%	62.2%
NELSON	7,401	2,100	5,272	29	3,172 D	28.4%	71.2%	28.5%	71.5%
NICHOLAS	3,988	1,219	2,728	41	1,509 D	30.6%	68.4%	30.9%	69.1%
OHIO	9,934	4,880	4,870	184	10 R	49.1%	49.0%	50.1%	49.9%
OLDHAM	3,233	888	2,319	26	1,431 D	27.5%	71.7%	27.7%	72.3%
OWEN	4,960	658	4,240	62	3,582 D	13.3%	85.5%	13.4%	86.6%
OWSLEY	2,510	1,985	520	5	1,465 R	79.1%	20.7%	79.2%	20.8%
PENDLETON	4,620	1,812	2,745	63	933 D	39.2%	59.4%	39.8%	60.2%
PERRY	11,655	5,240	6,393	22	1,153 D	45.0%	54.9%	45.0%	55.0%
PIKE	20,674	7,914	12,686	74	4,772 D	38.3%	61.4%	38.4%	61.6%
POWELL	2,135	826	1,300	9	474 D	38.7%	60.9%	38.9%	61.1%
PULASKI	11,861	6,905	4,931	25	1,974 R	58.2%	41.6%	58.3%	41.7%
ROBERTSON	1,604	538	1,056	10	518 D	33.5%	65.8%	33.8%	66.2%
ROCKCASTLE	5,564	3,577	1,976	11	1,601 R	64.3%	35.5%	64.4%	35.6%
ROWAN	4,490	1,622	2,844	24	1,222 D	36.1%	63.3%	36.3%	63.7%
RUSSELL	4,216	2,490	1,699	27	791 R	59.1%	40.3%	59.4%	40.6%
SCOTT	6,551	1,943	4,572	36	2,629 D	29.7%	69.8%	29.8%	70.2%
SHELBY	7,325	2,108	5,180	37	3,072 D	28.8%	70.7%	28.9%	71.1%
SIMPSON	4,827	1,203	3,603	21	2,400 D	24.9%	74.6%	25.0%	75.0%
SPENCER	2,515	736	1,773	6	1,037 D	29.3%	70.5%	29.3%	70.7%
TAYLOR	5,454	2,592	2,823	39	231 D	47.5%	51.8%	47.9%	52.1%
TODD	5,556	1,562	3,966	28	2,404 D	28.1%	71.4%	28.3%	71.7%
TRIGG	5,078	1,452	3,611	15	2,159 D	28.6%	71.1%	28.7%	71.3%
TRIMBLE	2,354	257	2,083	14	1,826 D	10.9%	88.5%	11.0%	89.0%
UNION	5,991	1,063	4,892	36	3,829 D	17.7%	81.7%	17.9%	82.1%
WARREN	13,578	4,569	8,932	77	4,363 D	33.7%	65.8%	33.8%	66.2%
WASHINGTON	5,203	2,340	2,841	22	501 D	45.0%	54.6%	45.2%	54.8%
WAYNE	5,646	2,682	2,929	35	247 D	47.5%	51.9%	47.8%	52.2%
WEBSTER	7,138	2,257	4,833	48	2,576 D	31.6%	67.7%	31.8%	68.2%
WHITLEY	9,820	6,186	3,576	58	2,610 R	63.0%	36.4%	63.4%	36.6%
WOLFE	3,232	909	2,321	2	1,412 D	28.1%	71.8%	28.1%	71.9%
WOODFORD	4,918	1,720	3,180	18	1,460 D	35.0%	64.7%	35.1%	64.9%
TOTAL	983,059	394,716	580,574	7,769	185,858 D	40.2%	59.1%	40.5%	59.5%

KENTUCKY

PRESIDENT 1936

County	Total Vote	Republican	Democratic	Other	Rep-Dem Plurality	T.V. Rep.	T.V. Dem.	M.V. Rep.	M.V. Dem.
ADAIR	6,050	3,371	2,669	10	702 R	55.7%	44.1%	55.8%	44.2%
ALLEN	5,505	3,070	2,422	13	648 R	55.8%	44.0%	55.9%	44.1%
ANDERSON	3,825	1,360	2,454	11	1,094 D	35.6%	64.2%	35.7%	64.3%
BALLARD	4,303	773	3,523	7	2,750 D	18.0%	81.9%	18.0%	82.0%
BARREN	8,513	3,352	5,137	24	1,785 D	39.4%	60.3%	39.5%	60.5%
BATH	4,530	1,725	2,795	10	1,070 D	38.1%	61.7%	38.2%	61.8%
BELL	10,461	4,573	5,853	35	1,280 D	43.7%	56.0%	43.9%	56.1%
BOONE	3,915	1,042	2,785	88	1,743 D	26.6%	71.1%	27.2%	72.8%
BOURBON	6,364	2,471	3,872	21	1,401 D	38.8%	60.8%	39.0%	61.0%
BOYD	16,492	6,650	9,762	80	3,112 D	40.3%	59.2%	40.5%	59.5%
BOYLE	6,606	2,431	4,148	27	1,717 D	36.8%	62.8%	37.0%	63.0%
BRACKEN	3,444	1,436	1,956	52	520 D	41.7%	56.8%	42.3%	57.7%
BREATHITT	5,781	1,790	3,980	11	2,190 D	31.0%	68.8%	31.0%	69.0%
BRECKINRIDGE	6,225	2,898	3,233	94	335 D	46.6%	51.9%	47.3%	52.7%
BULLITT	3,136	647	2,474	15	1,827 D	20.6%	78.9%	20.7%	79.3%
BUTLER	3,835	2,594	1,237	4	1,357 R	67.6%	32.3%	67.7%	32.3%
CALDWELL	4,848	2,121	2,699	28	578 D	43.8%	55.6%	44.0%	56.0%
CALLOWAY	6,472	939	5,523	10	4,584 D	14.5%	85.3%	14.5%	85.5%
CAMPBELL	30,194	10,327	16,780	3,087	6,453 D	34.2%	55.6%	38.1%	61.9%
CARLISLE	2,600	420	2,150	30	1,730 D	16.2%	82.7%	16.3%	83.7%
CARROLL	3,547	794	2,718	35	1,924 D	22.4%	76.6%	22.6%	77.4%
CARTER	7,810	4,372	3,403	35	969 R	56.0%	43.6%	56.2%	43.8%
CASEY	5,536	3,588	1,925	23	1,663 R	64.8%	34.8%	65.1%	34.9%
CHRISTIAN	12,030	5,370	6,660		1,290 D	44.6%	55.4%	44.6%	55.4%
CLARK	6,659	2,246	4,396	17	2,150 D	33.7%	66.2%	33.8%	66.2%
CLAY	5,659	4,087	1,572		2,515 R	72.2%	27.8%	72.2%	27.8%
CLINTON	2,848	2,147	701		1,446 R	75.4%	24.6%	75.4%	24.6%
CRITTENDEN	3,065	2,441	1,926	8	515 R	55.8%	44.0%	55.9%	44.1%
CUMBERLAND		2,127	935	3	1,192 R	69.5%	30.5%	69.5%	30.5%
DAVIESS	15,347	4,636	9,957	754	5,321 D	30.2%	64.9%	31.8%	68.2%
EDMONSON	3,860	2,526	1,329	5	1,197 R	65.4%	34.4%	65.5%	34.5%
ELLIOTT	2,019	480	1,539		1,059 D	23.8%	76.2%	23.8%	76.2%
ESTILL	5,590	2,931	2,646	13	285 R	52.4%	47.3%	52.6%	47.3%
FAYETTE	26,175	11,544	14,428	203	2,884 D	44.1%	55.1%	44.1%	55.9%
FLEMING	5,649	2,749	2,879	21	130 D	48.7%	51.0%	48.8%	51.2%
FLOYD	11,337	3,375	7,962		4,587 D	29.8%	70.2%	29.8%	70.2%
FRANKLIN	8,258	2,010	6,222	26	4,212 D	24.3%	75.3%	24.4%	75.6%
FULTON	4,526	782	3,727	17	2,945 D	17.3%	82.3%	17.3%	82.7%
GALLATIN	1,875	404	1,456	15	1,052 D	21.5%	77.7%	21.7%	78.3%
GARRARD	4,535	2,252	2,276	7	24 D	49.7%	50.2%	49.7%	50.3%
GRANT	3,939	1,353	2,560	26	1,207 D	34.3%	65.0%	34.6%	65.4%
GRAVES	11,065	1,692	9,231	142	7,539 D	15.3%	83.4%	15.5%	84.5%
GRAYSON	5,603	2,907	2,676	20	231 R	51.9%	47.7%	52.1%	47.9%
GREEN	4,312	2,336	1,970	6	366 R	54.2%	45.7%	54.3%	45.6%
GREENUP	8,659	3,973	4,686		713 D	45.9%	54.1%	45.9%	54.1%
HANCOCK	2,422	1,087	1,317	18	230 D	44.9%	54.4%	45.2%	54.8%
HARDIN	6,814	2,284	4,480	50	2,196 D	33.5%	65.7%	33.8%	66.2%
HARLAN	18,570	7,510	11,060		3,550 D	40.4%	59.6%	40.4%	59.6%
HARRISON	6,149	1,756	4,378	15	2,622 D	28.6%	71.2%	28.6%	71.4%
HART	6,511	3,147	3,341	23	194 D	48.3%	51.3%	48.5%	51.5%
HENDERSON	8,833	1,811	6,835	187	5,024 D	20.5%	77.4%	20.9%	79.1%
HENRY	5,065	1,516	3,545	4	2,029 D	29.9%	70.0%	30.0%	70.0%
HICKMAN	2,952	385	2,548	19	2,163 D	13.0%	86.3%	13.1%	86.9%
HOPKINS	11,838	3,602	8,193	43	4,591 D	30.4%	69.2%	30.5%	69.5%
JACKSON	3,863	3,440	420	3	3,020 R	89.1%	10.9%	89.1%	10.9%
JEFFERSON	142,369	53,043	85,748	3,578	32,705 D	37.3%	60.2%	38.2%	61.8%
JESSAMINE	4,902	2,066	2,813	23	747 D	42.1%	57.4%	42.3%	57.7%
JOHNSON	7,429	4,305	3,106	18	1,199 R	57.9%	41.8%	58.1%	41.9%
KENTON	34,666	8,885	21,879	3,902	12,994 D	25.6%	63.1%	28.9%	71.1%
KNOTT	4,353	865	3,488		2,623 D	19.9%	80.1%	19.9%	80.1%

PRESIDENT 1940

County	Total Vote	Republican	Democratic	Other	Rep-Dem Plurality	T.V. Rep.	T.V. Dem.	M.V. Rep.	M.V. Dem.
ADAIR	6,398	3,674	2,711	13	963 R	57.4%	42.4%	57.5%	42.5%
ALLEN	5,289	3,232	2,036	21	1,196 R	61.1%	38.5%	61.4%	38.6%
ANDERSON	3,769	1,224	2,515	10	1,271 D	33.0%	66.7%	33.1%	66.9%
BALLARD	3,971	758	3,212	1	2,454 D	19.1%	80.9%	19.1%	80.9%
BARREN	8,132	3,233	4,888	11	1,655 D	39.8%	60.1%	39.8%	60.2%
BATH	4,176	1,636	2,528	12	892 D	39.2%	60.5%	39.3%	60.7%
BELL	10,899	4,962	5,910	27	948 D	45.5%	54.2%	45.6%	54.4%
BOONE	3,888	1,357	2,518	13	1,161 D	34.9%	64.8%	35.0%	65.0%
BOURBON	6,931	2,673	4,254	4	1,581 D	38.6%	61.4%	38.6%	61.4%
BOYD	17,265	7,322	9,868	75	2,546 D	42.4%	57.2%	42.6%	57.4%
BOYLE	6,349	2,257	4,081	11	1,824 D	35.5%	64.3%	35.6%	64.4%
BRACKEN	3,521	1,551	1,961	9	410 D	44.0%	55.7%	44.2%	55.8%
BREATHITT	5,590	1,602	3,977	11	2,375 D	28.7%	71.1%	28.7%	71.3%
BRECKINRIDGE	6,591	3,258	3,296	37	38 D	49.4%	50.0%	49.7%	50.3%
BULLITT	3,207	813	2,388	6	1,575 D	25.4%	74.5%	25.4%	74.6%
BUTLER	4,624	3,163	1,455	6	1,708 R	68.4%	31.5%	68.5%	31.5%
CALDWELL	5,130	2,246	2,858	26	612 D	43.8%	55.7%	44.0%	56.0%
CALLOWAY	6,698	896	5,793	9	4,897 D	13.4%	86.5%	13.4%	86.6%
CAMPBELL	29,820	14,916	14,801	103	115 R	50.0%	49.6%	50.2%	49.8%
CARLISLE	2,878	500	2,366	12	1,866 D	17.4%	82.2%	17.4%	82.6%
CARROLL	3,730	804	2,915	11	2,111 D	21.6%	78.2%	21.6%	78.4%
CARTER	7,946	4,520	3,403	23	1,117 R	56.9%	43.6%	57.0%	43.0%
CASEY	5,753	3,874	1,862	17	2,012 R	67.3%	32.4%	67.5%	32.5%
CHRISTIAN	12,181	5,566	6,599	16	1,033 D	45.7%	54.2%	45.8%	54.2%
CLARK	6,125	2,136	3,970	19	1,834 D	34.9%	64.8%	35.0%	65.0%
CLAY	6,027	4,395	1,632		2,763 R	72.9%	27.1%	72.9%	27.1%
CLINTON	3,328	2,573	755		1,818 R	77.3%	22.7%	77.3%	22.7%
CRITTENDEN	4,472	2,624	1,834	14	790 R	58.7%	41.0%	58.9%	41.1%
CUMBERLAND		2,533	872	4	1,661 R	74.3%	25.6%	74.4%	25.6%
DAVIESS	15,026	5,633	9,344	49	3,711 D	37.5%	62.2%	37.6%	62.4%
EDMONSON	3,934	2,589	1,332	13	1,257 R	65.8%	33.9%	66.0%	34.0%
ELLIOTT	2,647	634	2,013		1,379 D	24.0%	76.0%	24.0%	76.0%
ESTILL	5,486	2,889	2,587	10	302 R	52.6%	47.2%	52.8%	47.2%
FAYETTE	28,432	12,514	15,834	84	3,320 D	44.0%	55.7%	44.1%	55.9%
FLEMING	5,868	2,855	2,999	14	144 D	48.7%	51.1%	48.8%	51.2%
FLOYD	12,811	3,711	9,100		5,389 D	29.0%	71.0%	29.0%	71.0%
FRANKLIN	8,897	1,927	6,956	14	5,029 D	21.7%	78.2%	21.7%	78.3%
FULTON	4,392	791	3,592	9	2,801 D	18.0%	81.8%	18.0%	82.0%
GALLATIN	1,972	495	1,473	4	978 D	25.1%	74.7%	25.2%	74.8%
GARRARD	4,318	2,148	2,162	8	14 D	49.7%	50.1%	49.7%	50.2%
GRANT	4,269	1,535	2,729	5	1,194 D	36.0%	63.9%	36.0%	64.0%
GRAVES	11,935	2,122	9,786	27	7,664 D	17.8%	82.0%	17.8%	82.2%
GRAYSON	5,861	3,156	2,678	27	478 R	53.8%	45.7%	54.1%	45.9%
GREEN	4,508	2,497	1,993	18	504 R	55.4%	44.2%	55.6%	44.4%
GREENUP	8,825	4,059	4,742	24	683 D	45.9%	53.7%	46.0%	53.9%
HANCOCK	2,764	1,424	1,338	2	86 R	51.5%	48.4%	51.6%	48.4%
HARDIN	7,090	2,351	4,718	21	2,367 D	33.2%	66.5%	33.3%	66.7%
HARLAN	16,483	5,859	10,582	42	4,723 D	35.5%	64.2%	35.6%	64.4%
HARRISON	5,954	1,707	4,228	19	2,521 D	28.7%	71.0%	28.8%	71.2%
HART	6,155	2,866	3,280		414 D	46.6%	53.3%	46.6%	53.4%
HENDERSON	9,211	2,455	6,727	29	4,272 D	26.7%	73.0%	26.7%	73.3%
HENRY	5,329	1,445	3,862	22	2,417 D	27.1%	72.5%	27.2%	72.8%
HICKMAN	3,255	490	2,758	7	2,268 D	15.1%	84.7%	15.1%	84.9%
HOPKINS	12,609	3,884	8,695	30	4,811 D	30.8%	69.0%	30.9%	69.1%
JACKSON	4,200	3,722	465	13	3,257 R	88.6%	11.1%	88.9%	11.1%
JEFFERSON	161,218	66,052	94,710	456	28,658 D	41.0%	58.7%	41.1%	58.9%
JESSAMINE	4,692	1,837	2,813	40	978 D	39.2%	60.0%	39.3%	60.5%
JOHNSON	8,094	5,042	3,042	10	2,000 R	62.3%	37.6%	62.4%	37.6%
KENTON	32,482	13,147	19,261	74	6,114 D	40.5%	59.3%	40.6%	59.4%
KNOTT	5,193	759	4,434		3,675 D	14.6%	85.4%	14.6%	85.4%

KENTUCKY

PRESIDENT 1936

County	Total Vote	Republican	Democratic	Other	Rep.-Dem. Plurality	Total Vote Rep.	Total Vote Dem.	Major Vote Rep.	Major Vote Dem.
KNOX	8,345	4,921	3,419	5	1,502 R	59.0%	41.0%	59.0%	41.0%
LARUE	3,467	1,151	2,305	11	1,154 D	33.2%	66.5%	33.3%	66.7%
LAUREL	7,487	4,798	2,677	12	2,121 R	64.1%	35.8%	64.2%	35.8%
LAWRENCE	6,128	2,944	3,175	9	231 D	48.0%	51.8%	48.1%	51.9%
LEE	3,254	1,812	1,440	2	372 R	55.7%	44.3%	55.7%	44.3%
LESLIE	3,337	2,716	618	3	2,098 R	81.4%	18.5%	81.5%	18.5%
LETCHER	10,122	3,871	6,240	11	2,369 D	38.3%	61.6%	38.3%	61.7%
LEWIS	5,257	3,255	1,985	17	1,270 R	61.9%	37.8%	62.1%	37.9%
LINCOLN	5,826	3,211	2,575	40	364 D	47.0%	52.4%	45.8%	54.2%
LIVINGSTON	2,947	1,039	1,897	11	858 D	35.3%	64.4%	35.4%	64.6%
LOGAN	6,745	1,812	4,912	21	3,100 D	26.9%	72.8%	26.9%	73.1%
LYON	2,799	929	1,861	9	932 D	33.2%	66.5%	33.3%	66.7%
MCCRACKEN	13,829	3,160	10,557	112	7,397 D	22.9%	76.3%	23.0%	77.0%
MCCREARY	4,069	2,953	1,105	11	1,848 R	72.8%	27.2%	72.8%	27.2%
MCLEAN	3,879	1,338	2,496	45	1,158 D	34.5%	64.3%	34.9%	65.1%
MADISON	12,376	6,034	6,259	83	225 D	48.8%	50.6%	49.1%	50.9%
MAGOFFIN	5,137	2,577	2,554	6	23 R	50.2%	49.7%	50.2%	49.8%
MARION	5,146	1,567	3,526	53	1,959 D	30.5%	68.5%	30.8%	69.2%
MARSHALL	4,624	1,141	3,472	11	2,331 D	24.7%	75.1%	24.7%	75.3%
MARTIN	2,855	2,037	817	1	1,220 R	71.3%	28.6%	71.4%	28.6%
MASON	7,967	3,317	4,503	147	1,186 D	41.6%	56.5%	42.4%	57.6%
MEADE	2,967	785	2,102	80	1,317 D	26.5%	70.8%	27.2%	72.8%
MENIFEE	1,686	559	1,123	4	564 D	33.2%	66.6%	33.2%	66.8%
MERCER	5,846	2,161	3,659	26	1,498 D	37.0%	62.6%	37.1%	62.9%
METCALFE	3,530	1,777	1,748	5	29 R	50.3%	49.5%	50.4%	49.6%
MONROE	3,706	2,345	1,352	9	993 R	63.3%	36.5%	63.4%	36.6%
MONTGOMERY	4,267	1,649	2,594	24	945 D	38.0%	60.8%	38.9%	61.1%
MORGAN	4,531	1,269	3,256	6	1,987 D	28.0%	71.9%	28.0%	72.0%
MUHLENBERG	10,628	4,168	6,385	75	2,217 D	39.2%	60.1%	39.5%	60.5%
NELSON	6,358	1,913	4,234	211	2,321 D	30.1%	66.6%	31.1%	68.9%
NICHOLAS	3,620	1,277	2,325	18	1,048 D	35.3%	64.2%	35.5%	64.5%
OHIO	8,589	4,532	4,030	27	502 R	52.8%	46.9%	52.9%	47.1%
OLDHAM	2,794	760	2,020	14	1,260 D	27.2%	72.3%	27.3%	72.7%
OWEN	4,065	661	3,392	12	2,731 D	16.3%	83.4%	16.3%	83.7%
OWSLEY	2,738	2,273	464	1	1,809 R	83.0%	16.9%	83.0%	17.0%
PENDLETON	4,311	1,837	2,432	42	595 D	42.6%	56.4%	43.0%	57.0%
PERRY	11,359	4,595	6,753	11	2,158 D	40.5%	59.5%	40.5%	59.5%
PIKE	19,603	8,210	11,382	11	3,172 D	41.9%	58.1%	41.9%	58.1%
POWELL	2,197	998	1,185	14	187 D	45.4%	53.9%	45.7%	54.3%
PULASKI	12,305	7,570	4,711	24	2,859 R	61.5%	38.3%	61.6%	38.4%
ROBERTSON	1,403	498	897	8	399 D	35.7%	63.9%	35.7%	64.3%
ROCKCASTLE	5,443	3,875	1,568		2,307 R	71.2%	28.8%	71.2%	28.8%
ROWAN	3,684	1,687	1,989	8	302 D	45.9%	54.0%	45.9%	54.1%
RUSSELL	3,942	2,688	1,235	19	1,453 R	68.2%	31.3%	68.5%	31.5%
SCOTT	5,838	1,861	3,966	11	2,105 D	31.9%	67.9%	31.9%	68.1%
SHELBY	6,317	1,898	4,384	35	2,486 D	30.0%	69.4%	30.2%	69.8%
SIMPSON	4,280	1,240	3,027	13	1,787 D	29.0%	70.7%	29.1%	70.9%
SPENCER	2,294	638	1,647	9	1,009 D	27.8%	71.8%	27.9%	72.1%
TAYLOR	5,491	2,738	2,732	21	6 R	49.8%	49.7%	50.1%	49.9%
TODD	4,176	1,178	2,987	11	1,809 D	28.2%	71.5%	28.3%	71.7%
TRIGG	4,468	1,521	2,928	19	1,407 D	34.0%	65.5%	34.2%	65.8%
TRIMBLE	1,948	271	1,659	18	1,388 D	13.9%	85.2%	14.0%	86.0%
UNION	5,785	965	4,713	107	3,748 D	16.7%	81.5%	17.0%	83.0%
WARREN	12,514	4,347	8,113	54	3,766 D	34.7%	64.8%	34.9%	65.1%
WASHINGTON	4,943	2,391	2,516	36	125 D	48.4%	50.9%	48.7%	51.3%
WAYNE	5,480	2,924	2,546	10	378 R	53.4%	46.5%	53.5%	46.5%
WEBSTER	6,792	1,983	4,788	21	2,805 D	29.2%	70.5%	29.3%	70.7%
WHITLEY	8,920	5,733	3,175	12	2,558 R	64.3%	35.6%	64.4%	35.6%
WOLFE	2,549	972	1,577		605 D	38.1%	61.9%	38.1%	61.9%
WOODFORD	4,138	1,558	2,574	6	1,016 D	37.7%	62.2%	37.7%	62.3%
TOTAL	926,214	369,702	541,944	14,568	172,242 D	39.9%	58.5%	40.6%	59.4%

PRESIDENT 1940

County	Total Vote	Republican	Democratic	Other	Rep.-Dem. Plurality	Total Vote Rep.	Total Vote Dem.	Major Vote Rep.	Major Vote Dem.
KNOX	8,330	5,003	3,319	8	1,684 R	60.1%	39.8%	60.1%	39.9%
LARUE	3,781	1,309	2,463	9	1,154 D	34.6%	65.5%	34.7%	65.3%
LAUREL	8,060	5,180	2,860	20	2,320 R	64.3%	35.5%	64.4%	35.6%
LAWRENCE	6,252	3,055	3,178	19	123 D	48.9%	50.8%	49.0%	51.0%
LEE	3,495	1,866	1,622	7	244 R	53.4%	46.4%	53.5%	46.5%
LESLIE	3,921	3,292	626	3	2,666 R	84.0%	16.0%	84.0%	16.0%
LETCHER	10,579	4,433	6,127	19	1,694 D	41.9%	57.9%	42.0%	58.0%
LEWIS	5,249	3,371	1,878		1,493 R	64.2%	35.8%	64.2%	35.8%
LINCOLN	6,783	3,090	3,657	36	567 D	45.6%	53.9%	45.8%	54.2%
LIVINGSTON	3,213	1,184	2,013	16	829 D	36.9%	62.7%	37.0%	63.0%
LOGAN	8,908	2,268	6,631	9	4,363 D	25.5%	74.4%	25.5%	74.5%
LYON	2,917	921	1,979	17	1,058 D	31.6%	67.8%	31.8%	68.2%
MCCRACKEN	15,168	3,554	11,562	52	8,008 D	23.4%	76.2%	23.5%	76.5%
MCCREARY	4,429	3,154	1,265	10	1,924 R	71.6%	28.2%	71.8%	28.2%
MCLEAN	4,417	1,698	2,709	10	1,011 D	38.4%	61.3%	38.5%	61.5%
MADISON	12,340	5,789	6,484	67	695 D	46.9%	52.5%	47.2%	52.8%
MAGOFFIN	5,481	2,668	2,812	1	144 D	48.7%	51.3%	48.7%	51.3%
MARION	5,264	1,763	3,482	19	1,719 D	33.5%	66.1%	33.6%	66.4%
MARSHALL	4,662	1,100	3,549	13	2,449 D	23.7%	76.1%	23.7%	76.3%
MARTIN	3,102	2,275	826	1	1,449 R	73.3%	26.6%	73.4%	26.6%
MASON	8,117	3,704	4,386	27	682 D	45.6%	54.0%	45.8%	54.2%
MEADE	3,121	995	2,114	12	1,119 D	31.9%	67.7%	32.0%	68.0%
MENIFEE	1,692	511	1,176	5	665 D	30.2%	69.4%	30.3%	69.7%
MERCER	5,470	1,845	3,606	19	1,761 D	33.7%	65.9%	33.8%	66.2%
METCALFE	4,044	2,206	1,826	12	380 R	54.7%	45.2%	54.7%	45.3%
MONROE	4,722	3,321	1,390	11	1,931 R	70.3%	29.4%	70.5%	29.5%
MONTGOMERY	4,439	1,671	2,755	13	1,084 D	37.6%	62.1%	37.8%	62.2%
MORGAN	5,657	1,509	4,148	28	2,639 D	26.7%	73.3%	26.7%	73.3%
MUHLENBERG	10,500	5,332	5,140	28	192 R	50.8%	49.0%	50.9%	49.1%
NELSON	6,310	2,109	4,193	8	2,084 D	33.4%	66.5%	33.5%	66.5%
NICHOLAS	3,345	1,207	2,124	14	917 D	36.1%	63.5%	36.2%	63.8%
OHIO	8,204	4,451	3,729	24	722 R	54.3%	45.4%	54.4%	45.6%
OLDHAM	2,841	848	1,983	10	1,135 D	29.8%	69.8%	30.0%	70.0%
OWEN	4,231	569	3,655	7	3,086 D	13.4%	86.4%	13.5%	86.5%
OWSLEY	3,266	2,672	591	3	2,081 R	81.8%	18.1%	81.9%	18.1%
PENDLETON	4,208	2,029	2,165	14	136 D	48.2%	51.4%	48.4%	51.6%
PERRY	11,563	4,693	6,852	18	2,159 D	40.6%	59.2%	40.6%	59.4%
PIKE	21,161	8,985	12,160	16	3,175 D	42.5%	57.5%	42.5%	57.5%
POWELL	2,270	989	1,266	15	277 D	43.6%	55.8%	43.9%	56.1%
PULASKI	13,468	8,533	4,896	39	3,637 R	63.4%	36.4%	63.5%	36.5%
ROBERTSON	1,414	578	829	7	251 D	40.9%	58.6%	41.1%	58.9%
ROCKCASTLE	5,194	3,536	1,652	6	1,884 R	68.1%	31.8%	68.2%	31.8%
ROWAN	4,240	1,944	2,294	2	350 D	45.8%	54.1%	45.9%	54.1%
RUSSELL	4,334	3,069	1,250	15	1,819 R	70.8%	28.8%	71.1%	28.9%
SCOTT	5,849	1,795	4,039	15	2,244 D	30.7%	69.1%	30.7%	69.2%
SHELBY	6,702	1,861	4,823	18	2,962 D	27.8%	72.0%	27.8%	72.2%
SIMPSON	3,945	987	2,950	8	1,963 D	25.0%	74.7%	25.1%	74.9%
SPENCER	2,300	567	1,728	5	1,161 D	24.7%	75.1%	24.7%	75.3%
TAYLOR	5,606	2,792	2,790	24	2 R	49.8%	49.8%	50.0%	50.0%
TODD	4,792	1,436	3,337	19	1,901 D	30.0%	69.6%	30.1%	69.9%
TRIGG	4,388	1,494	2,883	11	1,389 D	34.0%	65.7%	34.1%	65.9%
TRIMBLE	2,155	242	1,909	4	1,667 D	11.2%	88.6%	11.3%	88.7%
UNION	5,474	1,111	4,355	8	3,244 D	20.3%	79.5%	20.3%	79.7%
WARREN	11,800	4,195	7,569	36	3,374 D	35.6%	64.1%	35.7%	64.3%
WASHINGTON	4,976	2,362	2,612	2	250 D	47.5%	52.4%	47.5%	52.5%
WAYNE	5,702	3,177	2,519	6	658 R	55.7%	44.2%	55.8%	44.2%
WEBSTER	6,321	2,107	4,197	17	2,090 D	33.3%	66.4%	33.4%	66.6%
WHITLEY	10,596	6,502	4,078	16	2,424 R	61.4%	38.5%	61.9%	38.5%
WOLFE	3,273	1,032	2,205	36	1,173 D	31.9%	68.1%	31.9%	68.1%
WOODFORD	4,151	1,514	2,630	7	1,116 D	36.5%	63.4%	36.5%	63.5%
TOTAL	970,163	410,384	557,322	2,457	146,938 D	42.3%	57.4%	42.4%	57.6%

KENTUCKY

PRESIDENT 1944

County	Total Vote	Republican	Democratic	Other	Rep.-Dem. Plurality	% Total Vote Rep.	% Total Vote Dem.	% Major Vote Rep.	% Major Vote Dem.
ADAIR	5,847	3,414	2,411	22	1,003 R	58.4%	41.2%	58.6%	41.4%
ALLEN	4,886	3,120	1,742	24	1,378 R	63.9%	35.7%	64.2%	35.8%
ANDERSON	3,579	1,409	2,148	22	739 D	39.4%	60.0%	39.6%	60.4%
BALLARD	3,491	637	2,845	9	2,208 D	18.2%	81.5%	18.3%	81.7%
BARREN	7,701	3,262	4,439		1,177 D	42.4%	57.6%	42.4%	57.6%
BATH	3,773	1,581	2,184	8	603 D	41.9%	57.9%	42.0%	58.0%
BELL	9,474	4,822	4,616	36	206 R	50.9%	48.7%	51.1%	48.9%
BOONE	3,921	1,457	2,451	13	994 D	37.2%	62.5%	37.3%	62.7%
BOURBON	5,803	1,957	3,828	18	1,871 D	33.7%	66.0%	33.8%	66.2%
BOYD	15,040	6,868	8,130	42	1,262 D	45.7%	54.0%	45.8%	54.2%
BOYLE	5,719	2,195	3,490	34	1,295 D	38.4%	61.0%	38.6%	61.4%
BRACKEN	3,417	1,483	1,915	19	432 D	43.4%	56.0%	43.6%	56.4%
BREATHITT	4,183	1,230	2,922	31	1,692 D	29.4%	69.9%	29.6%	70.4%
BRECKINRIDGE	6,218	3,292	2,889	37	403 R	52.9%	46.5%	53.3%	46.7%
BULLITT	2,976	876	2,092	8	1,216 D	29.4%	70.3%	29.5%	70.5%
BUTLER	4,514	3,354	1,153	7	2,201 R	74.3%	25.5%	74.4%	25.6%
CALDWELL	4,696	2,242	2,444	10	202 R	47.7%	52.0%	47.8%	52.2%
CALLOWAY	6,026	1,121	4,888	17	3,767 D	18.6%	81.1%	18.7%	81.3%
CAMPBELL	26,670	13,647	12,959	64	688 R	51.2%	48.5%	51.3%	48.7%
CARLISLE	2,568	505	2,057	6	1,552 D	19.7%	80.1%	19.7%	80.3%
CARROLL	3,428	755	2,662	11	1,907 D	22.0%	77.7%	22.1%	77.9%
CARTER	6,860	4,117	2,733	10	1,384 R	60.0%	39.8%	60.1%	39.9%
CASEY	5,409	3,869	1,520	20	2,349 R	71.5%	28.1%	71.8%	28.2%
CHRISTIAN	10,801	4,506	6,260	35	1,754 D	41.7%	58.0%	41.9%	58.1%
CLARK	5,564	1,929	3,608	27	1,679 D	34.7%	64.8%	34.8%	65.2%
CLAY	5,495	4,307	1,185	3	3,122 R	78.4%	21.6%	78.4%	21.6%
CLINTON	3,185	2,618	564	3	2,054 R	82.2%	17.7%	82.3%	17.7%
CRITTENDEN	4,259	2,690	1,544	25	1,146 R	63.2%	36.3%	63.5%	36.5%
CUMBERLAND	3,346	2,619	717	10	1,902 R	78.3%	21.4%	78.5%	21.5%
DAVIESS	14,355	6,135	8,143	77	2,008 D	42.7%	56.7%	43.0%	57.0%
EDMONSON	3,458	2,433	1,016	9	1,417 R	70.4%	29.4%	70.5%	29.5%
ELLIOTT	2,235	514	1,721		1,207 D	23.0%	77.0%	23.0%	77.0%
ESTILL	4,517	2,493	2,000	24	493 R	55.2%	44.3%	55.5%	44.5%
FAYETTE	24,598	10,857	13,567	174	2,710 D	44.1%	55.2%	44.5%	55.5%
FLEMING	5,292	2,666	2,612	14	54 R	50.4%	49.4%	50.5%	49.5%
FLOYD	10,926	3,197	7,729		4,532 D	29.3%	70.7%	29.3%	70.7%
FRANKLIN	8,448	2,050	6,356	42	4,306 D	24.3%	75.2%	24.4%	75.6%
FULTON	3,640	654	2,973	13	2,319 D	18.0%	81.7%	18.0%	82.0%
GALLATIN	1,888	516	1,360	12	844 D	27.3%	72.0%	27.5%	72.5%
GARRARD	3,820	2,042	1,764	14	278 R	53.5%	46.2%	53.7%	46.3%
GRANT	4,047	1,621	2,413	13	792 D	40.1%	59.6%	40.2%	59.8%
GRAVES	10,238	2,172	8,057	9	5,885 D	21.2%	78.7%	21.2%	78.8%
GRAYSON	6,085	3,629	2,436	20	1,193 R	59.6%	40.0%	59.8%	40.2%
GREEN	4,219	2,379	1,809	31	570 R	56.4%	42.9%	56.6%	43.2%
GREENUP	7,542	3,718	3,821	3	103 D	49.3%	50.7%	49.3%	50.7%
HANCOCK	2,509	1,365	1,129	15	236 R	54.4%	45.0%	54.7%	45.3%
HARDIN	7,294	2,831	4,436	27	1,605 D	38.8%	60.8%	39.0%	61.0%
HARLAN	13,838	5,815	8,000	23	2,185 D	42.0%	57.8%	42.1%	57.9%
HARRISON	5,192	1,466	3,706	20	2,240 D	28.2%	71.4%	28.3%	71.7%
HART	6,162	3,014	3,138	10	124 D	48.9%	50.9%	49.0%	51.0%
HENDERSON	8,595	2,683	5,887	25	3,204 D	31.2%	68.5%	31.3%	68.7%
HENRY	5,063	1,497	3,548	18	2,051 D	29.5%	70.1%	29.6%	70.3%
HICKMAN	2,602	588	2,005	9	1,417 D	22.6%	77.1%	22.7%	77.3%
HOPKINS	11,174	3,795	7,352	27	3,557 D	34.0%	65.6%	34.0%	66.0%
JACKSON	3,908	3,578	328	2	3,250 R	91.6%	8.4%	91.6%	8.4%
JEFFERSON	141,621	60,905	80,236	480	19,331 D	43.0%	56.7%	43.2%	56.8%
JESSAMINE	4,248	1,790	2,426	32	636 D	42.1%	57.1%	42.5%	57.5%
JOHNSON	6,874	4,642	2,222	10	2,420 R	67.5%	32.3%	67.6%	32.4%
KENTON	30,236	12,654	17,524	58	4,870 D	41.9%	58.0%	41.9%	58.1%
KNOTT	4,670	803	3,867		3,064 D	17.2%	82.8%	17.2%	82.8%

PRESIDENT 1948

County	Total Vote	Republican	Democratic	Other	Rep.-Dem. Plurality	% Total Vote Rep.	% Total Vote Dem.	% Major Vote Rep.	% Major Vote Dem.
ADAIR	5,036	2,839	2,144	53	695 R	56.4%	42.6%	57.0%	43.0%
ALLEN	3,985	2,280	1,605	100	675 R	57.2%	40.3%	58.7%	41.3%
ANDERSON	3,154	971	2,135	48	1,164 D	30.8%	67.7%	31.3%	68.7%
BALLARD	3,195	454	2,702	39	2,248 D	14.2%	84.6%	14.4%	85.6%
BARREN	6,715	2,437	4,095	183	1,658 D	36.3%	61.0%	37.3%	62.7%
BATH	3,591	1,276	2,287	28	1,011 D	35.5%	63.7%	35.8%	64.2%
BELL	10,124	4,327	5,708	89	1,381 D	42.7%	56.4%	43.1%	56.9%
BOONE	3,523	1,151	2,320	52	1,169 D	32.7%	65.9%	33.2%	66.8%
BOURBON	5,302	1,610	3,562	130	1,952 D	30.4%	67.2%	31.1%	68.9%
BOYD	15,844	6,707	9,006	131	2,299 D	42.3%	56.8%	42.7%	57.3%
BOYLE	5,336	1,897	3,338	101	1,441 D	35.6%	62.6%	36.2%	63.8%
BRACKEN	3,134	1,239	1,863	32	624 D	39.5%	59.4%	39.9%	60.1%
BREATHITT	4,264	957	3,295	12	2,338 D	22.4%	77.3%	22.5%	77.5%
BRECKINRIDGE	5,110	2,407	2,623	80	216 D	47.1%	51.3%	47.9%	52.1%
BULLITT	2,385	673	1,681	31	1,008 D	28.2%	70.5%	28.6%	71.4%
BUTLER	3,658	2,494	1,105	59	1,389 R	68.2%	30.2%	69.3%	30.7%
CALDWELL	3,985	1,626	2,210	149	584 D	40.8%	55.5%	42.4%	57.6%
CALLOWAY	5,668	681	4,896	91	4,215 D	12.0%	86.4%	12.2%	87.8%
CAMPBELL	25,231	11,851	13,008	372	1,157 D	47.0%	51.6%	47.7%	52.3%
CARLISLE	2,199	279	1,899	21	1,620 D	12.7%	86.4%	12.8%	87.2%
CARROLL	3,345	639	2,626	80	1,987 D	19.1%	78.5%	19.6%	80.4%
CARTER	6,577	3,472	3,082	23	390 R	52.8%	46.9%	53.0%	47.0%
CASEY	4,911	3,380	1,495	36	1,885 R	68.8%	30.4%	69.3%	30.7%
CHRISTIAN	9,502	3,242	5,582	678	2,340 D	34.1%	58.7%	36.7%	63.3%
CLARK	4,908	1,508	3,292	108	1,784 D	30.7%	67.1%	31.4%	68.6%
CLAY	4,676	3,142	1,468	66	1,674 R	67.2%	31.4%	68.2%	31.8%
CLINTON	3,048	2,295	709	44	1,586 R	75.3%	23.3%	76.4%	23.6%
CRITTENDEN	3,461	1,927	1,497	37	430 R	55.7%	43.3%	56.3%	43.7%
CUMBERLAND	2,775	1,947	794	34	1,153 R	70.2%	28.6%	71.0%	29.0%
DAVIESS	13,727	4,873	8,682	172	3,809 D	35.5%	63.2%	35.9%	64.1%
EDMONSON	3,048	1,984	1,031	33	953 R	65.1%	33.8%	65.8%	34.2%
ELLIOTT	2,512	410	2,095	7	1,685 D	16.3%	83.4%	16.4%	83.6%
ESTILL	4,045	2,056	1,937	52	119 R	50.8%	47.9%	51.5%	48.5%
FAYETTE	25,155	10,959	13,202	994	2,243 D	43.0%	52.5%	45.4%	54.6%
FLEMING	4,852	2,088	2,722	42	634 D	43.0%	56.1%	43.4%	56.6%
FLOYD	12,016	3,127	8,823	66	5,696 D	26.0%	73.4%	26.2%	73.8%
FRANKLIN	8,822	1,962	6,679	181	4,717 D	22.2%	75.7%	22.7%	77.3%
FULTON	3,110	450	2,497	163	2,047 D	14.5%	80.3%	15.3%	84.7%
GALLATIN	1,731	342	1,381	8	1,039 D	19.8%	79.8%	19.8%	80.2%
GARRARD	3,656	1,890	1,725	41	165 R	51.7%	47.2%	52.3%	47.7%
GRANT	3,803	1,154	2,633	16	1,479 D	30.3%	69.2%	30.5%	69.5%
GRAVES	10,276	1,442	8,682	152	7,240 D	14.0%	84.5%	14.2%	85.8%
GRAYSON	5,092	2,880	2,174	38	706 R	56.6%	42.7%	57.0%	43.0%
GREEN	3,860	2,186	1,628	46	558 R	56.6%	42.2%	57.3%	42.7%
GREENUP	7,406	3,168	4,186	52	1,018 D	42.8%	56.5%	43.1%	56.9%
HANCOCK	2,147	985	1,146	16	161 D	45.9%	53.4%	46.2%	53.8%
HARDIN	6,447	2,297	3,990	160	1,693 D	35.6%	61.9%	36.5%	63.5%
HARLAN	13,710	4,402	9,158	150	4,756 D	32.1%	66.8%	32.5%	67.5%
HARRISON	4,802	1,224	3,494	84	2,270 D	25.5%	72.8%	25.8%	74.1%
HART	4,865	2,311	2,495	59	184 D	47.5%	51.3%	48.1%	51.9%
HENDERSON	7,646	1,904	5,499	243	3,595 D	24.9%	71.9%	25.7%	74.3%
HENRY	4,640	1,193	3,398	49	2,205 D	25.7%	73.2%	26.0%	74.0%
HICKMAN	2,564	326	2,143	95	1,817 D	12.7%	83.6%	13.2%	86.8%
HOPKINS	9,366	2,608	6,149	609	3,541 D	27.8%	65.7%	29.8%	70.2%
JACKSON	3,222	2,781	429	12	2,352 R	86.3%	13.3%	86.6%	13.4%
JEFFERSON	143,629	69,645	70,756	3,228	1,111 D	48.5%	49.3%	49.6%	50.4%
JESSAMINE	3,878	1,414	2,301	163	887 D	36.5%	59.3%	38.1%	61.9%
JOHNSON	6,392	3,993	2,378	21	1,615 R	62.5%	37.2%	62.7%	37.3%
KENTON	30,200	10,771	18,918	511	8,147 D	35.7%	62.6%	36.3%	63.7%
KNOTT	5,414	754	4,660		3,906 D	13.9%	86.1%	13.9%	86.1%

KENTUCKY

PRESIDENT 1944

County	Total Vote	Republican	Democratic	Other	Rep.-Dem. Plurality	Total Vote Rep. %	Total Vote Dem. %	Major Vote Rep. %	Major Vote Dem. %
KNOX	7,570	5,178	2,385	7	2,793 R	68.4%	31.5%	68.5%	31.5%
LARUE	3,641	1,550	2,065	26	515 D	42.6%	56.7%	42.9%	57.1%
LAUREL	7,160	5,051	2,104	5	2,947 R	70.5%	29.4%	70.6%	29.4%
LAWRENCE	5,135	2,715	2,408	12	307 R	52.9%	46.9%	53.0%	47.0%
LEE	2,550	1,468	1,072	10	396 R	57.6%	42.0%	57.8%	42.2%
LESLIE	3,178	2,679	499	16	2,180 R	84.3%	15.7%	84.3%	15.7%
LETCHER	8,670	4,055	4,599	16	544 D	46.8%	53.0%	46.9%	53.1%
LEWIS	4,717	3,275	1,434	8	1,841 R	69.4%	30.4%	69.5%	30.5%
LINCOLN	5,922	2,793	3,087	42	294 D	47.2%	52.1%	47.5%	52.5%
LIVINGSTON	2,892	1,202	1,686	4	484 D	41.6%	58.3%	41.6%	58.4%
LOGAN	7,339	2,211	5,110	18	2,899 D	30.1%	69.6%	30.2%	69.8%
LYON	2,679	924	1,743	12	819 D	34.5%	65.1%	34.6%	65.4%
MCCRACKEN	15,120	4,190	10,846	84	6,656 D	27.7%	71.7%	27.9%	72.1%
MCCREARY	4,301	3,419	880	2	2,539 R	79.5%	20.5%	79.5%	20.5%
MCLEAN	3,997	1,752	2,222	23	470 D	43.8%	55.6%	44.1%	55.9%
MADISON	11,307	5,468	5,769	70	301 D	48.4%	51.0%	48.7%	51.3%
MAGOFFIN	4,166	2,135	2,031	—	104 R	51.2%	48.8%	51.2%	48.8%
MARION	4,694	1,673	2,996	25	1,323 D	35.6%	63.8%	35.8%	64.2%
MARSHALL	4,274	1,316	2,947	11	1,631 D	30.8%	69.0%	30.9%	69.1%
MARTIN	2,639	2,067	571	1	1,496 R	78.3%	21.6%	78.4%	21.6%
MASON	7,105	3,256	3,810	39	554 D	45.8%	53.6%	46.1%	53.9%
MEADE	2,880	1,040	1,828	12	788 D	36.1%	63.5%	36.3%	63.7%
MENIFEE	1,547	568	976	3	408 D	36.7%	63.1%	36.9%	63.1%
MERCER	5,146	2,039	3,086	21	1,047 D	39.6%	60.0%	39.8%	60.2%
METCALFE	4,012	2,306	1,694	12	612 R	57.5%	42.2%	57.6%	42.4%
MONROE	4,749	3,648	1,101	8	2,547 R	76.8%	23.2%	76.8%	23.2%
MONTGOMERY	3,823	1,481	2,334	5	853 D	38.7%	61.1%	38.8%	61.2%
MORGAN	4,464	1,217	3,242	5	2,025 D	27.3%	72.6%	27.3%	72.7%
MUHLENBERG	8,304	4,618	3,657	29	961 R	55.6%	44.0%	55.8%	44.2%
NELSON	5,811	2,136	3,648	27	1,512 D	36.8%	62.8%	36.9%	63.1%
NICHOLAS	2,885	1,059	1,813	13	754 D	36.7%	62.8%	36.9%	63.1%
OHIO	7,657	4,494	3,131	32	1,363 R	58.7%	40.9%	58.9%	41.1%
OLDHAM	2,947	1,021	1,908	18	887 D	34.6%	64.7%	34.8%	65.1%
OWEN	3,800	627	3,157	16	2,530 D	16.5%	83.1%	16.6%	83.4%
OWSLEY	2,361	2,033	325	3	1,708 R	86.1%	13.8%	86.2%	13.8%
PENDLETON	4,090	1,977	2,096	17	119 D	48.3%	51.2%	48.5%	51.5%
PERRY	9,862	4,333	5,527	2	1,194 D	43.9%	56.0%	44.0%	56.1%
PIKE	17,897	8,092	9,757	48	1,665 D	45.2%	54.5%	45.3%	54.7%
POWELL	1,931	902	1,023	6	121 D	46.7%	53.0%	46.9%	53.1%
PULASKI	12,328	8,318	3,934	76	4,384 R	67.5%	31.9%	67.9%	32.1%
ROBERTSON	1,413	556	855	2	299 D	39.3%	60.5%	39.4%	60.6%
ROCKCASTLE	5,136	3,802	1,327	7	2,475 R	74.0%	25.8%	74.1%	25.9%
ROWAN	3,774	1,815	1,944	15	129 D	48.1%	51.5%	48.3%	51.7%
RUSSELL	4,219	3,019	1,185	15	1,834 R	71.6%	28.1%	71.8%	28.2%
SCOTT	5,248	1,589	3,627	32	2,038 D	30.3%	69.1%	30.5%	69.5%
SHELBY	6,446	1,997	4,415	34	2,418 D	31.0%	68.5%	31.2%	68.9%
SIMPSON	3,850	1,012	2,821	17	1,809 D	26.4%	73.3%	26.4%	73.6%
SPENCER	2,096	646	1,443	7	797 D	30.9%	68.8%	30.9%	69.1%
TAYLOR	5,136	2,622	2,475	39	147 R	51.1%	48.2%	51.4%	48.6%
TODD	4,374	1,363	2,990	21	1,627 D	31.2%	68.4%	31.3%	68.7%
TRIGG	3,857	1,332	2,511	14	1,179 D	34.5%	65.1%	34.7%	65.3%
TRIMBLE	2,210	264	1,916	30	1,652 D	11.9%	86.7%	12.1%	87.9%
UNION	4,436	935	3,489	12	2,554 D	21.1%	78.7%	21.1%	78.9%
WARREN	12,509	4,944	7,528	37	2,584 D	39.5%	60.2%	39.6%	60.4%
WASHINGTON	4,654	2,353	2,283	18	70 R	50.5%	49.1%	50.8%	49.2%
WAYNE	5,070	3,048	2,022	25	1,026 R	60.1%	39.9%	60.1%	39.9%
WEBSTER	5,189	1,840	3,324	25	1,484 D	35.5%	64.1%	35.6%	64.4%
WHITLEY	8,731	6,378	2,352	1	4,026 R	73.1%	26.9%	73.1%	26.9%
WOLFE	2,341	889	1,450	2	561 D	38.0%	61.9%	38.0%	62.0%
WOODFORD	3,542	1,374	2,154	14	780 D	38.8%	60.8%	38.9%	61.1%
TOTAL	867,924	392,448	472,589	2,887	80,141 D	45.2%	54.5%	45.4%	54.6%

PRESIDENT 1948

County	Total Vote	Republican	Democratic	Other	Rep.-Dem. Plurality	Total Vote Rep. %	Total Vote Dem. %	Major Vote Rep. %	Major Vote Dem. %
KNOX	7,123	4,241	2,814	68	1,427 R	59.5%	39.5%	60.1%	39.9%
LARUE	3,205	1,277	1,864	65	587 D	39.8%	58.1%	40.7%	59.3%
LAUREL	6,326	4,107	2,187	32	1,920 R	64.9%	34.6%	65.3%	34.7%
LAWRENCE	4,521	2,117	2,372	32	255 D	46.8%	52.5%	47.2%	52.8%
LEE	2,317	1,233	1,058	26	175 R	53.2%	45.7%	53.8%	46.2%
LESLIE	3,211	2,397	783	31	1,614 R	74.6%	24.4%	75.4%	24.6%
LETCHER	8,324	3,560	4,741	23	1,181 D	42.8%	57.0%	42.9%	57.1%
LEWIS	4,172	2,708	1,449	15	1,259 R	64.9%	34.7%	65.1%	34.9%
LINCOLN	5,614	2,593	2,920	101	327 D	46.2%	52.0%	47.0%	53.0%
LIVINGSTON	2,311	671	1,622	18	951 D	29.0%	70.2%	29.3%	70.7%
LOGAN	5,865	1,352	4,355	158	3,003 D	23.1%	74.3%	23.7%	76.3%
LYON	2,155	582	1,505	68	923 D	27.0%	69.8%	27.9%	72.1%
MCCRACKEN	14,754	3,251	11,183	320	7,932 D	22.0%	75.8%	22.5%	77.5%
MCCREARY	3,978	3,031	933	14	2,098 R	76.2%	23.5%	76.5%	23.5%
MCLEAN	3,272	1,112	2,104	56	992 D	34.0%	64.3%	34.6%	65.4%
MADISON	10,156	4,619	5,344	193	725 D	45.5%	52.6%	46.4%	53.6%
MAGOFFIN	4,135	1,882	2,253	—	371 D	45.5%	54.5%	45.5%	54.5%
MARION	4,225	1,171	3,008	46	1,837 D	27.7%	71.2%	28.0%	72.0%
MARSHALL	3,673	711	2,942	20	2,231 D	19.4%	80.1%	19.5%	80.5%
MARTIN	2,898	1,964	911	23	1,053 R	67.8%	31.4%	68.3%	31.7%
MASON	6,208	2,519	3,620	69	1,101 D	40.6%	58.3%	41.0%	59.0%
MEADE	2,725	774	1,915	37	1,141 D	28.4%	70.3%	28.8%	71.2%
MENIFEE	1,564	435	1,112	17	677 D	27.8%	71.1%	28.1%	71.9%
MERCER	4,363	1,599	2,682	82	1,083 D	36.6%	61.5%	37.4%	62.6%
METCALFE	3,346	1,640	1,683	23	43 D	49.0%	50.3%	49.4%	50.6%
MONROE	4,097	2,812	1,249	36	1,563 R	68.6%	30.5%	69.2%	30.8%
MONTGOMERY	3,960	1,083	2,731	146	1,648 D	27.3%	69.0%	28.4%	71.6%
MORGAN	4,487	987	3,488	12	2,501 D	22.0%	77.7%	22.1%	77.9%
MUHLENBERG	8,031	3,478	4,426	127	948 D	43.3%	55.1%	44.0%	56.0%
NELSON	5,336	1,715	3,556	65	1,841 D	32.1%	66.6%	32.5%	67.5%
NICHOLAS	2,742	815	1,885	42	1,070 D	29.7%	68.7%	30.2%	69.8%
OHIO	6,106	3,300	2,721	85	579 R	54.0%	44.6%	54.8%	45.2%
OLDHAM	2,829	1,036	1,703	90	667 D	36.6%	60.2%	37.8%	62.2%
OWEN	3,583	504	3,056	23	2,552 D	14.1%	85.3%	14.2%	85.8%
OWSLEY	2,161	1,718	437	6	1,281 R	79.5%	20.2%	79.7%	20.3%
PENDLETON	3,374	1,373	1,958	43	585 D	40.7%	58.0%	41.2%	58.8%
PERRY	9,453	3,755	5,614	84	1,859 D	39.7%	59.4%	40.1%	59.9%
PIKE	19,642	8,097	11,423	122	3,326 D	41.2%	58.2%	41.5%	58.5%
POWELL	1,713	728	975	10	247 D	42.5%	56.9%	42.7%	57.3%
PULASKI	11,510	7,549	3,844	117	3,705 R	65.6%	33.4%	66.3%	33.7%
ROBERTSON	1,314	442	864	8	422 D	33.6%	65.8%	33.8%	66.2%
ROCKCASTLE	4,564	3,236	1,309	19	1,927 R	70.9%	28.7%	71.2%	28.8%
ROWAN	3,622	1,502	2,097	23	595 D	41.5%	57.9%	41.7%	58.3%
RUSSELL	3,613	2,404	1,191	18	1,213 R	66.5%	33.0%	66.9%	33.1%
SCOTT	5,014	1,352	3,548	114	2,196 D	27.0%	70.8%	27.6%	72.4%
SHELBY	5,622	1,626	3,840	156	2,214 D	28.9%	68.3%	29.7%	70.3%
SIMPSON	3,619	762	2,752	105	1,990 D	21.1%	76.0%	21.7%	78.3%
SPENCER	1,812	493	1,298	21	805 D	27.2%	71.6%	27.5%	72.5%
TAYLOR	4,581	2,087	2,415	79	328 D	45.6%	52.7%	46.4%	53.6%
TODD	3,900	827	2,929	144	2,102 D	21.2%	75.1%	22.0%	78.0%
TRIGG	3,383	816	2,485	82	1,669 D	24.1%	73.5%	24.7%	75.3%
TRIMBLE	1,968	194	1,746	28	1,552 D	9.9%	88.7%	10.0%	90.0%
UNION	4,406	744	3,607	55	2,863 D	16.9%	81.9%	17.1%	82.9%
WARREN	11,189	3,919	6,768	502	2,849 D	35.0%	60.5%	36.7%	63.3%
WASHINGTON	3,962	1,813	2,121	28	308 D	45.8%	53.5%	46.1%	53.9%
WAYNE	4,548	2,480	2,029	39	451 R	54.5%	44.6%	55.0%	45.0%
WEBSTER	4,459	1,087	3,288	84	2,201 D	24.4%	73.7%	24.8%	75.2%
WHITLEY	8,653	5,611	2,932	110	2,679 R	64.8%	33.9%	65.7%	34.3%
WOLFE	2,733	813	1,918	2	1,105 D	29.7%	70.2%	29.8%	70.2%
WOODFORD	3,555	1,229	2,175	151	946 D	34.6%	61.2%	36.1%	63.9%
TOTAL	822,658	341,210	466,756	14,692	125,546 D	41.5%	56.7%	42.2%	57.8%

KENTUCKY

PRESIDENT 1952

County	Total Vote	Republican	Democratic	Other	Rep.-Dem. Plurality	Total Vote %Rep	Total Vote %Dem	Major Vote %Rep	Major Vote %Dem
ADAIR	5,927	3,737	2,184	6	1,553 R	63.1%	36.8%	63.1%	36.9%
ALLEN	4,717	2,946	1,750	21	1,196 R	62.5%	37.1%	62.7%	37.3%
ANDERSON	3,607	1,445	2,153	9	708 D	40.1%	59.7%	40.2%	59.8%
BALLARD	3,767	851	2,910	6	2,059 D	22.6%	77.2%	22.6%	77.4%
BARREN	8,365	3,743	4,618	4	875 D	44.7%	55.2%	44.8%	55.2%
BATH	4,142	1,737	2,400	5	663 D	41.9%	57.9%	42.0%	58.0%
BELL	11,761	6,461	5,276	24	1,185 R	54.9%	44.9%	55.0%	45.0%
BOONE	4,946	2,309	2,620	17	311 D	46.7%	53.0%	46.8%	53.2%
BOURBON	5,570	2,229	3,339	2	1,110 D	40.0%	59.9%	40.0%	60.0%
BOYD	20,720	10,426	10,245	49	181 R	50.3%	49.4%	50.4%	49.6%
BOYLE	6,763	2,969	3,771	23	802 D	43.9%	55.7%	44.1%	55.9%
BRACKEN	3,444	1,690	1,753	1	63 D	49.1%	50.9%	49.1%	50.9%
BREATHITT	4,764	1,381	3,383	0	2,002 D	29.0%	71.0%	29.0%	71.0%
BRECKINRIDGE	5,922	3,078	2,828	16	250 R	52.0%	47.8%	52.1%	47.9%
BULLITT	3,418	1,292	2,121	5	829 D	37.8%	62.1%	37.9%	62.1%
BUTLER	4,165	2,996	1,157	12	1,839 R	71.9%	27.8%	72.1%	27.9%
CALDWELL	4,650	2,507	2,133	10	374 R	53.9%	45.9%	54.0%	46.0%
CALLOWAY	7,275	1,829	5,434	12	3,605 D	25.1%	74.7%	25.2%	74.8%
CAMPBELL	30,716	17,705	12,976	35	4,729 R	57.6%	42.2%	57.7%	42.3%
CARLISLE	2,524	656	1,867	1	1,211 D	26.0%	74.0%	26.0%	74.0%
CARROLL	3,632	1,019	2,605	8	1,586 D	28.1%	71.7%	28.1%	71.9%
CARTER	7,262	4,221	3,019	22	1,202 R	58.1%	41.6%	58.3%	41.7%
CASEY	5,366	3,831	1,522	13	2,309 R	71.4%	28.4%	71.6%	28.4%
CHRISTIAN	11,672	4,858	6,787	27	1,929 D	41.6%	58.1%	41.7%	58.3%
CLARK	6,212	2,592	3,620	0	1,028 D	41.7%	58.1%	41.7%	58.3%
CLAY	5,544	4,161	1,365	18	2,796 R	75.1%	24.6%	75.3%	24.7%
CLINTON	3,546	2,856	678	12	2,178 R	80.5%	19.1%	80.8%	19.2%
CRITTENDEN	3,914	2,471	1,427	16	1,044 R	63.1%	36.5%	63.4%	36.6%
CUMBERLAND	3,349	2,426	909	14	1,517 R	72.4%	27.1%	72.7%	27.3%
DAVIESS	18,010	10,462	7,522	26	2,940 R	58.1%	41.8%	58.2%	41.8%
EDMONSON	3,273	2,279	992	2	1,287 R	69.6%	30.3%	69.7%	30.3%
ELLIOTT	2,703	629	2,074	0	1,445 D	23.3%	76.7%	23.3%	76.7%
ESTILL	4,550	2,630	1,900	20	730 R	57.8%	41.8%	58.1%	41.9%
FAYETTE	31,789	17,376	14,275	138	3,101 R	54.7%	44.9%	54.9%	45.1%
FLEMING	5,050	2,592	2,446	12	146 R	51.3%	48.4%	51.4%	48.6%
FLOYD	13,189	4,238	8,940	11	4,702 D	32.1%	67.8%	32.2%	67.8%
FRANKLIN	10,411	3,097	7,309	5	4,212 D	29.7%	70.2%	29.8%	70.2%
FULTON	3,942	1,266	2,673	3	1,407 D	32.1%	67.8%	32.1%	67.9%
GALLATIN	1,851	465	1,383	3	918 D	25.1%	74.7%	25.2%	74.8%
GARRARD	4,331	2,398	1,927	6	471 R	55.4%	44.5%	55.4%	44.6%
GRANT	4,161	1,609	2,545	7	936 D	38.7%	61.1%	38.7%	61.3%
GRAVES	12,530	2,925	9,592	13	6,667 D	23.3%	76.6%	23.4%	76.6%
GRAYSON	6,362	4,011	2,341	10	1,670 R	63.0%	36.8%	63.1%	36.9%
GREEN	4,641	2,773	1,857	11	916 R	59.8%	40.0%	59.9%	40.1%
GREENUP	9,078	4,354	4,716	8	362 D	48.0%	51.9%	48.0%	52.0%
HANCOCK	2,525	1,341	1,177	7	164 R	53.1%	46.6%	53.3%	46.7%
HARDIN	8,558	3,914	4,599	45	685 D	45.7%	53.7%	46.0%	54.0%
HARLAN	17,330	7,284	10,025	21	2,741 D	42.0%	57.8%	42.1%	57.9%
HARRISON	5,240	1,866	3,367	7	1,501 D	35.6%	64.3%	35.7%	64.3%
HART	5,903	2,934	2,952	17	18 D	49.7%	50.0%	49.8%	50.2%
HENDERSON	10,893	4,929	5,913	51	984 D	45.2%	54.3%	45.5%	54.5%
HENRY	5,062	1,584	3,468	10	1,884 D	31.3%	68.5%	31.4%	68.6%
HICKMAN	2,865	871	1,988	6	1,117 D	30.4%	69.4%	30.5%	69.5%
HOPKINS	11,469	4,285	7,157	27	2,872 D	37.4%	62.4%	37.4%	62.6%
JACKSON	3,578	3,104	471	3	2,633 R	86.8%	13.2%	86.8%	13.2%
JEFFERSON	181,447	99,069	81,642	736	17,427 R	54.6%	45.0%	54.8%	45.2%
JESSAMINE	4,792	2,193	2,578	21	385 D	45.8%	53.8%	46.0%	54.0%
JOHNSON	7,856	5,199	2,654	3	2,545 R	66.2%	33.8%	66.2%	33.8%
KENTON	38,709	19,200	19,457	52	257 D	49.6%	50.3%	49.7%	50.3%
KNOTT	5,582	1,124	4,437	21	3,313 D	20.1%	79.5%	20.2%	79.8%

PRESIDENT 1956

County	Total Vote	Republican	Democratic	Other	Rep.-Dem. Plurality	Total Vote %Rep	Total Vote %Dem	Major Vote %Rep	Major Vote %Dem
ADAIR	6,651	4,157	2,491	3	1,666 R	62.5%	37.5%	62.5%	37.5%
ALLEN	5,193	3,200	1,975	18	1,225 R	61.6%	38.0%	61.8%	38.2%
ANDERSON	3,973	1,878	2,089	6	211 D	47.3%	52.5%	47.3%	52.7%
BALLARD	3,936	838	3,088	10	2,250 D	21.3%	78.5%	21.3%	78.7%
BARREN	9,414	4,206	5,206	2	1,000 D	44.7%	55.3%	44.7%	55.3%
BATH	4,125	1,889	2,221	15	332 D	45.8%	53.8%	46.0%	54.0%
BELL	11,319	6,824	4,477	18	2,347 R	60.3%	39.6%	60.4%	39.6%
BOONE	6,090	3,139	2,933	18	206 R	51.5%	48.2%	51.7%	48.3%
BOURBON	5,790	2,475	3,263	52	788 D	42.7%	56.4%	43.1%	56.9%
BOYD	20,082	11,502	8,546	34	2,956 R	57.3%	42.6%	57.4%	42.6%
BOYLE	6,880	3,427	3,436	17	9 D	49.8%	49.9%	49.9%	50.1%
BRACKEN	3,276	1,754	1,515	7	239 R	53.5%	46.2%	53.7%	46.3%
BREATHITT	5,673	2,423	3,246	4	823 D	42.7%	57.2%	42.7%	57.3%
BRECKINRIDGE	6,651	3,764	2,867	20	917 R	56.4%	43.0%	56.9%	43.1%
BULLITT	4,290	2,007	2,279	4	272 D	46.8%	53.1%	46.8%	53.2%
BUTLER	4,513	3,303	1,202	8	2,101 R	73.2%	26.6%	73.3%	26.7%
CALDWELL	5,124	2,681	2,417	26	264 R	52.3%	47.2%	52.6%	47.4%
CALLOWAY	8,460	2,292	6,152	16	3,860 D	27.1%	72.7%	27.1%	72.9%
CAMPBELL	29,171	18,617	10,359	195	8,258 R	63.8%	35.5%	64.2%	35.8%
CARLISLE	2,676	608	2,063	5	1,455 D	22.7%	77.1%	22.8%	77.2%
CARROLL	3,316	1,130	2,169	17	1,039 D	34.1%	65.4%	34.3%	65.7%
CARTER	8,258	5,127	3,112	19	2,015 R	62.1%	37.7%	62.2%	37.8%
CASEY	5,749	4,167	1,570	12	2,597 R	72.5%	27.3%	72.6%	27.4%
CHRISTIAN	11,495	4,963	6,487	45	1,524 D	43.2%	56.4%	43.3%	56.7%
CLARK	6,663	3,030	3,609	24	579 D	45.5%	54.2%	45.6%	54.4%
CLAY	5,928	4,897	1,027	4	3,870 R	82.5%	17.3%	82.7%	17.3%
CLINTON	4,147	3,396	747	4	2,649 R	81.9%	18.0%	82.0%	18.0%
CRITTENDEN	4,068	2,548	1,494	26	1,054 R	62.6%	36.7%	63.0%	37.0%
CUMBERLAND	3,601	2,584	1,000	17	1,584 R	71.8%	27.8%	72.1%	27.9%
DAVIESS	18,373	11,491	6,674	208	4,817 R	62.5%	36.3%	63.3%	36.7%
EDMONSON	3,897	2,800	1,092	5	1,708 R	71.9%	28.0%	71.9%	28.1%
ELLIOTT	3,176	1,033	2,143	0	1,110 D	32.5%	67.5%	32.5%	67.5%
ESTILL	4,868	2,946	1,912	10	1,034 R	60.5%	39.3%	60.6%	39.4%
FAYETTE	35,683	21,904	13,547	232	8,357 R	61.4%	38.0%	61.8%	38.2%
FLEMING	5,280	2,744	2,519	17	225 R	52.0%	47.7%	52.1%	47.9%
FLOYD	14,088	6,166	7,907	15	1,741 D	43.8%	56.1%	43.8%	56.1%
FRANKLIN	10,553	4,047	6,412	94	2,365 D	38.3%	60.8%	38.7%	61.3%
FULTON	4,128	1,147	2,953	28	1,806 D	27.8%	71.5%	28.0%	72.0%
GALLATIN	1,771	547	1,223	1	676 D	30.9%	69.1%	30.9%	69.1%
GARRARD	4,133	2,311	1,798	24	513 R	55.9%	43.5%	56.2%	43.8%
GRANT	3,996	1,680	2,300	16	620 D	42.0%	57.6%	42.2%	57.8%
GRAVES	13,815	3,711	10,090	14	6,379 D	26.9%	73.0%	26.9%	73.1%
GRAYSON	6,592	4,565	2,021	6	2,544 R	69.3%	30.7%	69.3%	30.7%
GREEN	4,689	2,951	1,726	12	1,225 R	62.9%	36.8%	63.1%	36.9%
GREENUP	10,538	5,464	5,045	29	419 R	51.9%	47.9%	52.0%	48.0%
HANCOCK	2,346	1,317	1,022	7	295 R	56.1%	43.6%	56.3%	43.7%
HARDIN	9,430	5,050	4,325	55	725 R	53.6%	45.9%	53.9%	46.1%
HARLAN	15,761	8,820	6,915	26	1,905 R	56.0%	43.9%	56.1%	43.9%
HARRISON	5,657	2,128	3,515	14	1,387 D	37.6%	62.1%	37.7%	62.3%
HART	6,506	3,288	3,207	11	69 R	50.4%	49.3%	50.5%	49.5%
HENDERSON	10,838	5,085	5,501	252	416 D	46.9%	50.8%	48.0%	52.0%
HENRY	4,838	1,670	3,157	11	1,487 D	34.5%	65.3%	34.6%	65.4%
HICKMAN	3,163	785	2,367	11	1,582 D	24.8%	74.8%	24.9%	75.1%
HOPKINS	11,917	5,300	6,535	82	1,235 D	44.5%	54.8%	44.8%	55.2%
JACKSON	4,471	3,950	501	20	3,449 R	88.3%	11.2%	88.7%	11.3%
JEFFERSON	203,917	119,262	83,483	1,172	35,779 R	58.5%	40.9%	58.8%	41.2%
JESSAMINE	4,553	2,340	2,072	141	268 R	51.4%	45.5%	53.0%	47.0%
JOHNSON	8,165	5,802	2,356	7	3,446 R	71.1%	28.9%	71.1%	28.9%
KENTON	36,070	20,895	14,923	252	5,972 R	57.9%	41.4%	58.3%	41.7%
KNOTT	5,712	1,715	3,987	10	2,272 D	30.0%	69.8%	30.1%	69.9%

KENTUCKY

PRESIDENT 1952

County	Total Vote	Republican	Democratic	Other	Rep.-Dem. Plurality	Total Vote Rep.	Total Vote Dem.	Major Vote Rep.	Major Vote Dem.
KNOX	8,253	5,470	2,766	17	2,704 R	66.3%	33.5%	66.4%	33.6%
LARUE	3,862	1,701	2,161		460 D	44.0%	56.0%	44.0%	56.0%
LAUREL	8,051	5,776	2,263	12	3,513 R	71.7%	28.1%	71.8%	28.2%
LAWRENCE	5,302	2,696	2,597	9	99 R	50.8%	49.0%	50.9%	49.1%
LEE	2,678	1,572	1,100	6	472 R	58.7%	41.1%	58.8%	41.2%
LESLIE	3,959	3,239	705	15	2,534 R	81.8%	17.9%	82.1%	17.9%
LETCHER	9,786	4,689	5,097		408 D	47.9%	52.1%	47.9%	52.1%
LEWIS	4,888	3,317	1,556	15	1,761 R	67.9%	31.9%	68.1%	31.9%
LINCOLN	6,114	3,186	2,910	18	276 R	52.1%	47.6%	52.3%	47.7%
LIVINGSTON	2,657	1,102	1,554	1	452 D	41.5%	58.5%	41.5%	58.5%
LOGAN	7,690	2,758	4,917	15	2,159 D	35.9%	63.9%	35.9%	64.1%
LYON	2,158	746	1,404	8	658 D	34.6%	65.1%	34.7%	65.3%
McCRACKEN	18,375	6,051	12,302	22	6,251 D	32.9%	66.9%	33.0%	67.0%
McCREARY	4,309	3,360	937	12	2,423 R	78.0%	21.7%	78.2%	21.8%
McLEAN	3,763	1,791	1,961	11	170 D	47.6%	52.1%	47.7%	52.3%
MADISON	11,815	5,886	5,901	28	15 D	49.8%	49.9%	49.9%	50.1%
MAGOFFIN	4,342	2,093	2,243	6	150 D	48.2%	51.7%	48.3%	51.7%
MARION	5,429	2,262	3,159	8	897 D	41.7%	58.2%	41.7%	58.3%
MARSHALL	4,934	1,474	3,445	15	1,971 D	29.9%	69.8%	30.0%	70.0%
MARTIN	3,815	2,641	1,174		1,467 R	69.2%	30.8%	69.2%	30.8%
MASON	7,228	3,606	3,614	8	8 D	49.9%	50.0%	49.9%	50.1%
MEADE	3,310	1,265	2,040	5	775 D	38.2%	61.6%	38.3%	61.7%
MENIFEE	1,863	638	1,219	6	581 D	34.2%	65.4%	34.4%	65.6%
MERCER	5,312	2,545	2,740	27	195 D	47.9%	51.6%	48.2%	51.8%
METCALFE	4,037	2,176	1,848	13	328 R	53.9%	45.8%	54.1%	45.9%
MONROE	4,759	3,675	1,084		2,591 R	77.2%	22.8%	77.2%	22.8%
MONTGOMERY	4,648	1,981	2,653	14	672 D	42.6%	57.1%	42.7%	57.3%
MORGAN	4,476	1,311	3,161	4	1,850 D	29.3%	70.6%	29.3%	70.7%
MUHLENBERG	9,812	4,761	5,037	14	276 D	48.5%	51.3%	48.6%	51.4%
NELSON	6,494	3,064	3,417	13	353 D	47.2%	52.6%	47.3%	52.7%
NICHOLAS	2,979	1,156	1,819	4	663 D	38.8%	61.1%	38.9%	61.1%
OHIO	7,142	4,428	2,700	14	1,728 R	62.0%	37.8%	62.1%	37.9%
OLDHAM	3,476	1,723	1,735	18	12 D	49.6%	49.9%	49.8%	50.2%
OWEN	4,000	819	3,174	7	2,355 D	20.5%	79.4%	20.5%	79.5%
OWSLEY	2,387	1,954	419	14	1,535 R	81.9%	17.6%	82.3%	17.7%
PENDLETON	3,892	1,895	1,993	4	98 D	48.7%	51.2%	48.7%	51.3%
PERRY	10,762	5,210	5,538	14	328 D	48.4%	51.5%	48.5%	51.5%
PIKE	22,576	9,778	12,761	37	2,983 D	43.3%	56.5%	43.4%	56.6%
POWELL	2,213	992	1,218	3	226 D	44.8%	55.0%	44.9%	55.1%
PULASKI	13,707	9,651	4,032	24	5,619 R	70.4%	29.4%	70.5%	29.5%
ROBERTSON	1,451	623	827	1	204 D	42.9%	57.0%	42.9%	57.0%
ROCKCASTLE	4,842	3,503	1,326	13	2,177 R	72.5%	27.4%	72.5%	27.5%
ROWAN	4,216	1,985	2,220	11	235 D	47.1%	52.7%	47.2%	52.8%
RUSSELL	4,095	2,913	1,171	11	1,742 R	71.1%	28.6%	71.3%	28.7%
SCOTT	5,261	2,077	3,171	13	1,094 D	39.5%	60.3%	39.6%	60.4%
SHELBY	6,562	2,474	4,076	12	1,602 D	37.7%	62.1%	37.8%	62.2%
SIMPSON	4,040	1,310	2,724	6	1,414 D	32.4%	67.4%	32.5%	67.5%
SPENCER	2,007	723	1,283	1	560 D	36.0%	63.9%	36.0%	64.0%
TAYLOR	5,592	3,126	2,439	27	687 R	55.9%	43.6%	56.1%	43.8%
TODD	4,416	1,401	2,995	20	1,594 D	31.7%	67.8%	31.9%	68.1%
TRIGG	3,725	1,134	2,585	6	1,451 D	30.4%	69.4%	30.5%	69.5%
TRIMBLE	2,240	370	1,855	15	1,485 D	16.5%	82.8%	16.6%	83.4%
UNION	5,422	1,967	3,445	10	1,478 D	36.3%	63.5%	36.3%	63.7%
WARREN	14,407	7,267	7,106	34	161 R	50.4%	49.3%	50.6%	49.4%
WASHINGTON	4,415	2,290	2,114	11	176 R	51.9%	47.9%	52.0%	48.0%
WAYNE	5,861	3,396	2,461	4	935 R	57.9%	42.0%	58.0%	42.0%
WEBSTER	5,386	1,858	3,516	12	1,658 D	34.5%	65.3%	34.6%	65.4%
WHITLEY	10,011	7,030	2,958	23	4,072 R	70.2%	29.5%	70.4%	29.6%
WOLFE	2,435	876	1,557	2	681 D	36.0%	63.9%	36.0%	64.0%
WOODFORD	4,171	1,845	2,319	7	474 D	44.2%	55.6%	44.3%	55.7%
TOTAL	993,148	495,029	495,729	2,390	700 D	49.8%	49.9%	50.0%	50.0%

PRESIDENT 1956

County	Total Vote	Republican	Democratic	Other	Rep.-Dem. Plurality	Total Vote Rep.	Total Vote Dem.	Major Vote Rep.	Major Vote Dem.
KNOX	8,882	6,341	2,539	2	3,802 R	71.4%	28.6%	71.4%	28.6%
LARUE	4,259	2,387	1,859	13	528 R	56.0%	43.6%	56.2%	43.8%
LAUREL	8,916	6,586	2,316	14	4,270 R	73.9%	26.0%	74.0%	26.0%
LAWRENCE	5,438	2,932	2,495	11	437 R	53.9%	45.9%	54.0%	46.0%
LEE	2,716	1,774	938	4	836 R	65.3%	34.5%	65.4%	34.6%
LESLIE	4,315	3,770	531	14	3,239 R	87.4%	12.3%	87.7%	12.3%
LETCHER	9,904	5,741	4,133	30	1,608 R	58.0%	41.7%	58.1%	41.9%
LEWIS	4,927	3,333	1,585	9	1,748 R	67.6%	32.2%	67.8%	32.2%
LINCOLN	6,510	3,535	2,953	22	582 R	54.3%	45.4%	54.5%	45.5%
LIVINGSTON	3,046	1,247	1,795	4	548 D	40.9%	58.9%	41.0%	59.0%
LOGAN	8,174	2,855	5,299	20	2,444 D	34.9%	64.8%	35.0%	65.0%
LYON	2,535	989	1,527	19	538 D	39.0%	60.2%	39.3%	60.7%
McCRACKEN	21,258	7,076	14,103	79	7,027 D	33.3%	66.3%	33.4%	66.6%
McCREARY	4,630	3,812	814	4	2,998 R	82.3%	17.6%	82.4%	17.6%
McLEAN	3,870	1,886	1,965	19	79 D	48.7%	50.8%	49.0%	51.0%
MADISON	11,710	5,955	5,670	85	285 R	50.9%	48.4%	51.2%	48.8%
MAGOFFIN	4,509	2,343	2,162	4	181 R	52.0%	47.9%	52.0%	48.0%
MARION	5,892	2,945	2,927	20	18 R	50.0%	49.7%	50.2%	49.8%
MARSHALL	6,382	2,015	4,358	9	2,343 D	31.6%	68.3%	31.6%	68.4%
MARTIN	3,653	2,927	694	12	2,233 R	80.6%	19.1%	80.8%	19.2%
MASON	7,490	3,880	3,572	38	308 R	51.8%	47.7%	52.1%	47.9%
MEADE	3,692	1,670	2,016	6	346 D	45.2%	54.6%	45.3%	54.7%
MENIFEE	1,985	799	1,185	1	386 D	40.3%	59.7%	40.3%	59.7%
MERCER	5,952	3,168	2,767	17	401 R	53.2%	46.5%	53.4%	46.6%
METCALFE	4,438	2,412	2,014	12	398 R	54.3%	45.4%	54.5%	45.5%
MONROE	5,014	3,759	1,256	19	2,504 R	75.0%	25.0%	75.0%	25.0%
MONTGOMERY	4,895	2,220	2,656	6	436 D	45.4%	54.3%	45.5%	54.5%
MORGAN	5,043	1,878	3,164	38	1,286 D	37.2%	62.7%	37.2%	62.8%
MUHLENBERG	10,113	5,323	4,752	18	571 R	52.6%	47.0%	52.8%	47.2%
NELSON	7,365	4,107	3,240	18	867 R	55.8%	44.0%	55.9%	44.1%
NICHOLAS	2,695	999	1,667	29	668 D	37.1%	61.9%	37.5%	62.5%
OHIO	7,649	4,901	2,726	22	2,175 R	64.1%	35.6%	64.3%	35.7%
OLDHAM	3,909	2,128	1,769	12	359 R	54.4%	45.3%	54.6%	45.4%
OWEN	3,791	857	2,928	6	2,071 D	22.6%	77.2%	22.6%	77.4%
OWSLEY	2,347	2,013	331	3	1,682 R	85.8%	14.1%	85.9%	14.1%
PENDLETON	4,174	2,273	1,889	12	384 R	54.5%	45.3%	54.6%	45.4%
PERRY	11,161	6,591	4,545	25	2,046 R	59.1%	40.7%	59.2%	40.8%
PIKE	23,185	11,678	11,466	41	212 R	50.5%	49.5%	50.5%	49.5%
POWELL	2,685	1,339	1,343	3	4 D	49.9%	50.0%	49.9%	50.1%
PULASKI	14,572	10,636	3,899	37	6,737 R	73.0%	26.8%	73.2%	26.8%
ROBERTSON	1,412	617	793	2	176 D	43.7%	56.2%	43.8%	56.2%
ROCKCASTLE	5,112	3,787	1,313	12	2,474 R	74.1%	25.7%	74.3%	25.7%
ROWAN	4,857	2,470	2,380	7	90 R	50.8%	49.0%	50.9%	49.1%
RUSSELL	4,358	3,065	1,284	9	1,781 R	70.3%	29.5%	70.5%	29.5%
SCOTT	4,848	1,940	2,860	48	920 D	40.0%	59.0%	40.4%	59.6%
SHELBY	6,799	2,768	4,017	14	1,249 D	40.7%	59.1%	40.8%	59.2%
SIMPSON	4,350	1,454	2,879	17	1,425 D	33.4%	66.2%	33.6%	66.4%
SPENCER	2,127	896	1,214	17	318 D	42.3%	57.5%	42.5%	57.5%
TAYLOR	6,342	3,892	2,433	17	1,459 R	61.4%	38.4%	61.5%	38.5%
TODD	4,585	1,480	3,087	18	1,607 D	32.3%	67.3%	32.4%	67.6%
TRIGG	3,855	1,329	2,517	9	1,188 D	34.5%	65.3%	34.6%	65.4%
TRIMBLE	2,310	506	1,792	12	1,286 D	21.9%	77.6%	22.0%	78.0%
UNION	5,193	1,956	2,863	374	907 D	37.7%	55.1%	40.6%	59.4%
WARREN	15,310	8,123	7,143	44	980 R	53.1%	46.7%	53.2%	46.8%
WASHINGTON	4,637	2,536	2,084	17	452 R	54.7%	44.9%	54.9%	45.1%
WAYNE	5,902	3,609	2,263	30	1,346 R	61.1%	38.3%	61.5%	38.5%
WEBSTER	5,253	1,948	3,050	255	1,102 D	37.1%	58.1%	39.0%	61.0%
WHITLEY	10,438	7,759	2,656	23	5,103 R	74.3%	25.4%	74.5%	25.5%
WOLFE	2,742	1,059	1,683		624 D	38.6%	61.4%	38.6%	61.4%
WOODFORD	4,257	2,170	2,027	60	143 R	51.0%	47.6%	51.7%	48.3%
TOTAL	1,053,805	572,192	476,453	5,160	95,739 R	54.3%	45.2%	54.6%	45.4%

KENTUCKY

PRESIDENT 1960

County	Total Vote	Republican	Democratic	Other	Rep.-Dem. Plurality	%Total Rep.	%Total Dem.	%Major Rep.	%Major Dem.
ADAIR	6,890	4,621	2,269		2,352 R	67.1%	32.9%	67.1%	32.9%
ALLEN	5,073	3,410	1,663		1,747 R	67.2%	32.8%	67.2%	32.8%
ANDERSON	4,071	2,033	2,038		5 D	49.9%	50.1%	49.9%	50.1%
BALLARD	3,867	1,121	2,746		1,625 D	29.0%	71.0%	29.0%	71.0%
BARREN	10,133	5,187	4,946		241 R	51.2%	48.8%	51.2%	48.8%
BATH	3,954	1,888	2,066		178 D	47.7%	52.3%	47.7%	52.3%
BELL	11,986	6,805	5,181		1,624 R	56.8%	43.2%	56.8%	43.2%
BOONE	7,800	4,835	2,965		1,870 R	62.0%	38.0%	62.0%	38.0%
BOURBON	5,535	2,379	3,156		777 D	43.0%	57.0%	43.0%	57.0%
BOYD	20,399	11,305	9,094		2,211 R	55.4%	44.6%	55.4%	44.6%
BOYLE	6,932	3,624	3,308		316 R	52.3%	47.7%	52.3%	47.7%
BRACKEN	3,328	2,002	1,326		676 R	60.2%	39.8%	60.2%	39.8%
BREATHITT	5,303	1,996	3,307		1,311 D	37.6%	62.4%	37.6%	62.4%
BRECKINRIDGE	7,115	3,979	3,136		843 R	55.9%	44.1%	55.9%	44.1%
BULLITT	5,120	2,683	2,437		246 R	52.4%	47.6%	52.4%	47.6%
BUTLER	4,648	3,656	992		2,664 R	78.7%	21.3%	78.7%	21.3%
CALDWELL	5,579	3,442	2,137		1,305 R	61.7%	38.3%	61.7%	38.3%
CALLOWAY	8,049	3,356	4,693		1,337 D	41.7%	58.3%	41.7%	58.3%
CAMPBELL	32,078	17,388	14,690		2,698 R	54.2%	45.8%	54.2%	45.8%
CARLISLE	2,748	978	1,770		792 D	35.6%	64.4%	35.6%	64.4%
CARROLL	3,360	1,135	2,225		1,090 D	33.8%	66.2%	33.8%	66.2%
CARTER	8,435	4,956	3,479		1,477 R	58.8%	41.2%	58.8%	41.2%
CASEY	6,224	4,811	1,413		3,398 R	77.3%	22.7%	77.3%	22.7%
CHRISTIAN	12,125	5,251	6,874		1,623 D	43.3%	56.7%	43.3%	56.7%
CLARK	6,341	3,317	3,024		293 R	52.3%	47.7%	52.3%	47.7%
CLAY	6,303	4,922	1,381		3,541 R	78.1%	21.9%	78.1%	21.9%
CLINTON	4,190	3,524	666		2,858 R	84.1%	15.9%	84.1%	15.9%
CRITTENDEN	4,089	2,770	1,319		1,451 R	67.7%	32.3%	67.7%	32.3%
CUMBERLAND	3,537	2,697	840		1,857 R	76.3%	23.7%	76.3%	23.7%
DAVIESS	23,231	13,385	9,846		3,539 R	57.6%	42.4%	57.6%	42.4%
EDMONSON	3,960	2,884	1,076		1,808 R	72.8%	27.2%	72.8%	27.2%
ELLIOTT	2,523	789	1,734		945 D	31.3%	68.7%	31.3%	68.7%
ESTILL	4,993	3,238	1,755		1,483 R	64.9%	35.1%	64.9%	35.1%
FAYETTE	41,647	25,169	16,478		8,691 R	60.4%	39.6%	60.4%	39.6%
FLEMING	4,993	2,777	2,216		561 R	55.6%	44.4%	55.6%	44.4%
FLOYD	14,886	5,010	9,876		4,866 D	33.7%	66.3%	33.7%	66.3%
FRANKLIN	11,794	4,742	7,052		2,310 D	40.2%	59.8%	40.2%	59.8%
FULTON	4,275	1,567	2,708		1,141 D	36.7%	63.3%	36.7%	63.3%
GALLATIN	1,784	756	1,028		272 D	42.4%	57.6%	42.4%	57.6%
GARRARD	4,539	2,759	1,780		979 R	60.8%	39.2%	60.8%	39.2%
GRANT	4,062	2,163	1,899		264 R	53.2%	46.8%	53.2%	46.8%
GRAVES	12,543	4,854	7,689		2,835 D	38.7%	61.3%	38.7%	61.3%
GRAYSON	7,162	4,807	2,355		2,452 R	67.1%	32.9%	67.1%	32.9%
GREEN	5,186	3,606	1,580		2,026 R	69.5%	30.5%	69.5%	30.5%
GREENUP	11,346	6,101	5,245		856 R	53.8%	46.2%	53.8%	46.2%
HANCOCK	2,506	1,488	1,018		470 R	59.4%	40.6%	59.4%	40.6%
HARDIN	11,332	6,191	5,141		1,050 R	54.6%	45.4%	54.6%	45.4%
HARLAN	16,596	7,485	9,211		1,726 D	44.8%	55.2%	44.8%	55.2%
HARRISON	5,787	2,306	3,481		1,175 D	39.8%	60.2%	39.8%	60.2%
HART	6,739	3,610	3,129		481 R	53.6%	46.4%	53.6%	46.4%
HENDERSON	10,867	5,302	5,565		263 D	48.8%	51.2%	48.8%	51.2%
HENRY	4,683	1,714	2,969		1,255 D	36.6%	63.4%	36.6%	63.4%
HICKMAN	3,144	968	2,176		1,208 D	30.8%	69.2%	30.8%	69.2%
HOPKINS	12,010	5,574	6,436		862 D	46.4%	53.6%	46.4%	53.6%
JACKSON	4,342	3,923	419		3,504 R	90.4%	9.6%	90.4%	9.6%
JEFFERSON	235,755	118,575	117,180		1,395 R	50.3%	49.7%	50.3%	49.7%
JESSAMINE	4,809	2,787	2,022		765 R	58.0%	42.0%	58.0%	42.0%
JOHNSON	7,939	5,317	2,622		2,695 R	67.0%	33.0%	67.0%	33.0%
KENTON	41,323	21,857	19,466		2,391 R	52.9%	47.1%	52.9%	47.1%
KNOTT	5,369	1,412	3,957		2,545 D	26.3%	73.7%	26.3%	73.7%

PRESIDENT 1964

County	Total Vote	Republican	Democratic	Other	Rep.-Dem. Plurality	%Total Rep.	%Total Dem.	%Major Rep.	%Major Dem.
ADAIR	5,927	3,052	2,854	21	198 R	51.5%	48.2%	51.7%	48.3%
ALLEN	4,342	2,309	2,023	10	286 R	53.2%	46.5%	53.3%	46.7%
ANDERSON	3,586	1,085	2,491	10	1,406 D	30.3%	69.5%	30.3%	69.7%
BALLARD	3,409	519	2,867	23	2,348 D	15.2%	84.1%	15.3%	84.7%
BARREN	9,380	2,936	6,420	24	3,484 D	31.3%	68.4%	31.4%	68.6%
BATH	3,587	1,009	2,571	7	1,562 D	28.1%	71.7%	28.2%	71.8%
BELL	11,227	4,185	6,979	63	2,794 D	37.3%	62.2%	37.5%	62.5%
BOONE	8,522	3,430	5,077	15	1,647 D	40.2%	59.6%	40.3%	59.7%
BOURBON	5,316	1,222	4,068	26	2,846 D	23.0%	76.5%	23.1%	76.9%
BOYD	18,437	6,941	11,436	60	4,495 D	37.6%	62.0%	37.8%	62.2%
BOYLE	6,962	1,972	4,976	14	3,004 D	28.3%	71.5%	28.4%	71.6%
BRACKEN	2,819	861	1,958		1,097 D	30.5%	69.5%	30.5%	69.5%
BREATHITT	5,383	669	4,714		4,045 D	12.4%	87.6%	12.4%	87.6%
BRECKINRIDGE	5,911	2,167	3,733	11	1,566 D	36.7%	63.2%	36.7%	63.3%
BULLITT	5,330	1,417	3,900	13	2,483 D	26.6%	73.2%	26.7%	73.3%
BUTLER	3,992	2,429	1,555	8	874 R	60.8%	39.0%	61.0%	39.0%
CALDWELL	4,598	1,738	2,831	29	1,093 D	37.8%	61.6%	38.0%	62.0%
CALLOWAY	8,886	1,576	7,290	20	5,714 D	17.7%	82.0%	17.8%	82.2%
CAMPBELL	28,264	12,209	16,012	43	3,803 D	43.2%	56.7%	43.3%	56.7%
CARLISLE	1,853	282	1,565	6	1,283 D	15.2%	84.5%	15.3%	84.7%
CARROLL	3,105	491	2,592	22	2,101 D	15.8%	83.5%	15.9%	84.1%
CARTER	6,987	2,821	4,136	30	1,315 D	40.4%	59.2%	40.5%	59.5%
CASEY	5,356	3,457	1,875	24	1,582 R	64.5%	35.0%	64.8%	35.2%
CHRISTIAN	12,630	3,882	8,727	21	4,845 D	30.7%	69.1%	30.8%	69.2%
CLARK	6,237	2,019	4,205	13	2,186 D	32.4%	67.4%	32.4%	67.6%
CLAY	6,343	3,223	3,098	22	125 R	50.8%	48.8%	51.0%	49.0%
CLINTON	3,369	2,351	994	24	1,357 R	69.8%	29.5%	70.3%	29.7%
CRITTENDEN	3,497	1,863	1,627	7	236 R	53.3%	46.5%	53.4%	46.6%
CUMBERLAND	3,164	1,794	1,348	22	446 R	56.7%	42.6%	57.1%	42.9%
DAVIESS	23,755	8,350	15,253	152	6,903 D	35.1%	64.2%	35.4%	64.6%
EDMONSON	2,647	1,603	1,022	22	581 R	60.6%	38.6%	61.1%	38.9%
ELLIOTT	2,351	323	2,026	2	1,703 D	13.7%	86.2%	13.8%	86.2%
ESTILL	4,102	1,996	2,105	1	109 D	48.7%	51.3%	48.7%	51.3%
FAYETTE	44,192	18,739	25,317	136	6,578 D	42.4%	57.3%	42.7%	57.3%
FLEMING	4,352	1,668	2,678	6	1,010 D	38.3%	61.5%	38.4%	61.6%
FLOYD	14,041	2,352	11,644	45	9,292 D	16.8%	82.9%	16.8%	83.2%
FRANKLIN	12,494	2,320	10,130	44	7,810 D	18.6%	81.1%	18.6%	81.4%
FULTON	3,672	1,169	2,493	10	1,324 D	31.8%	67.9%	31.9%	68.1%
GALLATIN	1,517	267	1,246	4	979 D	17.6%	82.1%	17.6%	82.4%
GARRARD	3,935	1,828	2,092	15	264 D	46.5%	53.2%	46.6%	53.4%
GRANT	3,545	1,068	2,461	16	1,393 D	30.1%	69.4%	30.3%	69.7%
GRAVES	12,390	2,389	9,958	43	7,569 D	19.3%	80.4%	19.3%	80.7%
GRAYSON	5,894	2,974	2,920		54 R	50.5%	49.5%	50.5%	49.5%
GREEN	4,286	2,110	2,160	16	50 D	49.2%	50.4%	49.4%	50.6%
GREENUP	10,764	4,045	6,680	39	2,635 D	37.6%	62.1%	37.7%	62.3%
HANCOCK	2,190	756	1,423	11	667 D	34.5%	65.0%	34.7%	65.3%
HARDIN	11,264	3,744	7,460	60	3,716 D	33.2%	66.2%	33.4%	66.6%
HARLAN	13,428	4,025	9,394	9	5,369 D	30.0%	70.0%	30.0%	70.0%
HARRISON	5,246	1,054	4,179	13	3,125 D	20.1%	79.7%	20.1%	79.9%
HART	5,295	1,961	3,313	21	1,352 D	37.0%	62.6%	37.2%	62.8%
HENDERSON	10,785	2,734	8,022	29	5,288 D	25.4%	74.4%	25.4%	74.6%
HENRY	4,363	838	3,521	4	2,683 D	19.2%	80.7%	19.2%	80.8%
HICKMAN	2,774	613	2,149	12	1,536 D	22.1%	77.5%	22.2%	77.8%
HOPKINS	11,297	3,328	7,954	15	4,626 D	29.5%	70.4%	29.5%	70.5%
JACKSON	3,597	2,654	920	23	1,734 R	73.8%	25.6%	74.3%	25.7%
JEFFERSON	227,823	80,951	146,023	849	65,072 D	35.5%	64.1%	35.7%	64.3%
JESSAMINE	6,205	3,075	3,053	77	22 R	49.6%	49.2%	50.2%	49.8%
JOHNSON	4,482	1,968	2,485	29	517 D	43.9%	55.4%	44.2%	55.8%
KENTON	38,795	15,630	23,103	62	7,473 D	40.3%	59.6%	40.4%	59.6%
KNOTT	5,230	482	4,739	9	4,257 D	9.2%	90.6%	9.2%	90.8%

KENTUCKY

PRESIDENT 1960

County	Total Vote	Republican	Democratic	Other	Rep.-Dem. Plurality	Total Vote Rep.	Total Vote Dem.	Major Vote Rep.	Major Vote Dem.
KNOX	8,770	5,814	2,956		2,858 R	66.3%	33.7%	66.3%	33.7%
LARUE	4,381	2,668	1,713		955 R	60.9%	39.1%	60.9%	39.1%
LAUREL	9,794	7,485	2,309		5,176 R	76.4%	23.6%	76.4%	23.6%
LAWRENCE	5,540	3,030	2,510		520 R	54.7%	45.3%	54.7%	45.3%
LEE	2,970	2,012	958		1,054 R	67.7%	32.3%	67.7%	32.3%
LESLIE	4,689	3,894	795		3,099 R	83.0%	17.0%	83.0%	17.0%
LETCHER	8,666	4,408	4,258		150 R	50.9%	49.1%	50.9%	49.1%
LEWIS	5,498	3,816	1,682		2,134 R	69.4%	30.6%	69.4%	30.6%
LINCOLN	6,128	3,747	2,381		1,366 R	61.1%	38.9%	61.1%	38.9%
LIVINGSTON	3,157	1,639	1,518		121 R	51.9%	48.1%	51.9%	48.1%
LOGAN	8,836	4,117	4,719		602 D	46.6%	53.4%	46.6%	53.4%
LYON	2,403	1,024	1,379		355 D	42.6%	57.4%	42.6%	57.4%
MCCRACKEN	22,228	9,689	12,539		2,850 D	43.6%	56.4%	43.6%	56.4%
MCCREARY	4,595	3,671	924		2,747 R	79.9%	20.1%	79.9%	20.1%
MCLEAN	3,985	2,269	1,716		553 R	56.9%	43.1%	56.9%	43.1%
MADISON	12,313	6,692	5,621		1,071 R	54.3%	45.7%	54.3%	45.7%
MAGOFFIN	5,207	2,736	2,471		265 R	52.5%	47.5%	52.5%	47.5%
MARION	6,495	2,203	4,292		2,089 D	33.9%	66.1%	33.9%	66.1%
MARSHALL	6,872	3,388	3,484		96 D	49.3%	50.7%	49.3%	50.7%
MARTIN	3,925	2,809	1,116		1,693 R	71.6%	28.4%	71.6%	28.4%
MASON	7,487	4,334	3,153		1,181 R	57.9%	42.1%	57.9%	42.1%
MEADE	4,211	1,826	2,385		559 D	43.4%	56.6%	43.4%	56.6%
MENIFEE	1,806	817	989		172 D	45.2%	54.8%	45.2%	54.8%
MERCER	6,282	3,569	2,713		856 R	56.8%	43.2%	56.8%	43.2%
METCALFE	3,699	2,146	1,553		593 R	58.0%	42.0%	58.0%	42.0%
MONROE	5,307	4,337	970		3,367 R	81.7%	18.3%	81.7%	18.3%
MONTGOMERY	5,080	2,451	2,629		178 D	48.2%	51.8%	48.2%	51.8%
MORGAN	4,628	1,718	2,910		1,192 D	37.1%	62.9%	37.1%	62.9%
MUHLENBERG	10,395	5,968	4,427		1,541 R	57.4%	42.6%	57.4%	42.6%
NELSON	7,734	3,021	4,713		1,692 D	39.1%	60.9%	39.1%	60.9%
NICHOLAS	2,513	1,058	1,455		397 D	42.1%	57.9%	42.1%	57.9%
OHIO	7,650	5,230	2,420		2,810 R	68.4%	31.6%	68.4%	31.6%
OLDHAM	4,181	2,221	1,960		261 R	53.1%	46.9%	53.1%	46.9%
OWEN	3,658	1,212	2,446		1,234 D	33.1%	66.9%	33.1%	66.9%
OWSLEY	2,515	2,169	346		1,823 R	86.2%	13.8%	86.2%	13.8%
PENDLETON	3,884	2,387	1,497		890 R	61.5%	38.5%	61.5%	38.5%
PERRY	10,725	5,754	4,971		783 R	53.7%	46.3%	53.7%	46.3%
PIKE	22,995	9,956	13,039		3,083 D	43.3%	56.7%	43.3%	56.7%
POWELL	2,630	1,508	1,122		386 R	57.3%	42.7%	57.3%	42.7%
PULASKI	14,996	11,899	3,097		8,802 R	79.3%	20.7%	79.3%	20.7%
ROBERTSON	1,246	594	652		58 D	47.7%	52.3%	47.7%	52.3%
ROCKCASTLE	5,123	3,982	1,141		2,841 R	77.7%	22.3%	77.7%	22.3%
ROWAN	4,970	2,558	2,412		146 R	51.5%	48.5%	51.5%	48.5%
RUSSELL	4,866	3,636	1,230		2,406 R	74.7%	25.3%	74.7%	25.3%
SCOTT	4,798	2,200	2,598		398 D	45.9%	54.1%	45.9%	54.1%
SHELBY	6,756	2,934	3,822		888 D	43.4%	56.6%	43.4%	56.6%
SIMPSON	4,569	1,927	2,642		715 D	42.2%	57.8%	42.2%	57.8%
SPENCER	2,182	1,134	1,048		86 R	52.0%	48.0%	52.0%	48.0%
TAYLOR	6,855	4,669	2,186		2,483 R	68.1%	31.9%	68.1%	31.9%
TODD	4,673	1,846	2,827		981 D	39.5%	60.5%	39.5%	60.5%
TRIGG	3,911	1,500	2,411		911 D	38.4%	61.6%	38.4%	61.6%
TRIMBLE	2,330	743	1,587		844 D	31.9%	68.1%	31.9%	68.1%
UNION	5,246	1,789	3,457		1,668 D	34.1%	65.9%	34.1%	65.9%
WARREN	16,531	9,074	7,457		1,617 R	54.9%	45.1%	54.9%	45.1%
WASHINGTON	5,023	2,632	2,391		241 R	52.4%	47.6%	52.4%	47.6%
WAYNE	5,937	3,973	1,964		2,009 R	66.9%	33.1%	66.9%	33.1%
WEBSTER	5,677	2,498	3,179		681 D	44.0%	56.0%	44.0%	56.0%
WHITLEY	10,514	7,553	2,961		4,592 R	71.8%	28.2%	71.8%	28.2%
WOLFE	2,813	1,259	1,554		295 D	44.8%	55.2%	44.8%	55.2%
WOODFORD	4,177	2,227	1,950		277 R	53.3%	46.7%	53.3%	46.7%
TOTAL	1,124,462	602,607	521,855		80,752 R	53.6%	46.4%	53.6%	46.4%

PRESIDENT 1964

County	Total Vote	Republican	Democratic	Other	Rep.-Dem. Plurality	Total Vote Rep.	Total Vote Dem.	Major Vote Rep.	Major Vote Dem.
KNOX	7,770	3,583	4,150	37	567 D	46.1%	53.4%	46.3%	53.7%
LARUE	3,957	1,195	2,742	20	1,547 D	30.2%	69.3%	30.4%	69.6%
LAUREL	8,665	5,008	3,633	24	1,375 R	57.8%	41.9%	58.0%	42.0%
LAWRENCE	4,455	1,745	2,703	7	958 D	39.2%	60.7%	39.2%	60.8%
LEE	2,543	1,162	1,376	5	214 D	45.7%	54.1%	45.8%	54.2%
LESLIE	3,774	1,971	1,795	8	176 R	52.2%	47.6%	52.3%	47.7%
LETCHER	8,063	2,632	5,420	11	2,788 D	32.6%	67.2%	32.7%	67.3%
LEWIS	4,294	2,230	2,047	17	183 R	51.9%	47.7%	52.1%	47.9%
LINCOLN	5,277	1,958	3,307	12	1,349 D	37.1%	62.7%	37.2%	62.8%
LIVINGSTON	2,979	821	2,147	11	1,326 D	27.6%	72.1%	27.7%	72.3%
LOGAN	8,494	2,232	6,234	28	4,002 D	26.3%	73.4%	26.4%	73.6%
LYON	2,006	583	1,412	11	829 D	29.1%	70.4%	29.2%	70.8%
MCCRACKEN	20,808	4,543	16,178	87	11,635 D	21.9%	77.7%	21.9%	78.1%
MCCREARY	3,683	2,230	1,428	25	802 R	60.5%	38.8%	61.0%	39.0%
MCLEAN	3,755	1,173	2,576	6	1,403 D	31.2%	68.6%	31.3%	68.7%
MADISON	11,200	4,266	6,877	57	2,611 D	38.1%	61.4%	38.3%	61.7%
MAGOFFIN	3,853	1,327	2,498	28	1,171 D	34.4%	64.8%	34.7%	65.3%
MARION	5,344	1,074	4,265	5	3,191 D	20.1%	79.8%	20.1%	79.9%
MARSHALL	7,668	1,679	5,968	21	4,289 D	21.9%	77.8%	22.0%	78.0%
MARTIN	3,306	1,567	1,694	45	127 D	47.4%	51.2%	48.1%	51.9%
MASON	6,952	2,437	4,502	13	2,065 D	35.1%	64.8%	35.1%	64.9%
MEADE	4,136	1,055	3,076	5	2,021 D	25.5%	74.4%	25.5%	74.5%
MENIFEE	1,401	318	1,076	7	758 D	22.7%	76.8%	22.8%	77.2%
MERCER	5,317	1,732	3,564	21	1,832 D	32.5%	67.0%	32.7%	67.3%
METCALFE	3,306	1,277	1,967	8	690 D	39.3%	60.5%	39.4%	60.6%
MONROE	5,010	3,293	1,713	4	1,580 R	65.7%	34.2%	65.8%	34.2%
MONTGOMERY	4,563	1,540	3,039	48	1,499 D	33.6%	66.4%	33.7%	66.4%
MORGAN	3,867	546	3,293	20	2,747 D	14.1%	84.7%	14.2%	85.8%
MUHLENBERG	9,741	3,300	6,421	20	3,121 D	33.9%	65.9%	33.9%	66.1%
NELSON	7,296	1,683	5,586	27	3,903 D	23.1%	76.6%	23.2%	76.8%
NICHOLAS	2,378	621	1,742	15	1,121 D	26.1%	73.3%	26.3%	73.7%
OHIO	6,287	2,979	3,303	5	324 D	47.4%	52.5%	47.4%	52.6%
OLDHAM	3,684	1,256	2,622	6	1,366 D	32.3%	67.5%	32.4%	67.6%
OWEN	3,389	405	2,980	4	2,575 D	12.0%	87.9%	12.0%	88.0%
OWSLEY	1,744	1,167	571	6	596 R	66.9%	32.7%	67.1%	32.9%
PENDLETON	3,815	1,313	2,495	7	1,182 D	34.4%	65.4%	34.5%	65.5%
PERRY	9,947	3,211	6,728	8	3,517 D	32.3%	67.6%	32.3%	67.7%
PIKE	21,253	7,078	14,140	35	7,062 D	33.4%	66.5%	33.4%	66.6%
POWELL	2,625	993	1,622	10	629 D	37.8%	61.8%	38.0%	62.0%
PULASKI	13,278	7,383	5,840	55	1,543 R	55.6%	44.0%	55.8%	44.2%
ROBERTSON	1,119	383	734	2	351 D	34.2%	65.6%	34.3%	65.7%
ROCKCASTLE	4,476	2,829	1,631	16	1,198 R	63.2%	36.4%	63.4%	36.6%
ROWAN	4,396	1,554	2,824	18	1,270 D	35.4%	64.2%	35.5%	64.5%
RUSSELL	4,273	2,521	1,729	23	792 R	59.0%	40.5%	59.3%	40.7%
SCOTT	4,639	1,330	3,289	20	1,959 D	28.7%	70.9%	28.8%	71.2%
SHELBY	6,333	1,384	4,933	16	3,549 D	21.9%	77.9%	21.9%	78.1%
SIMPSON	4,144	967	3,168	9	2,201 D	23.3%	76.4%	23.4%	76.6%
SPENCER	1,954	525	1,422	7	897 D	26.9%	72.8%	27.0%	73.0%
TAYLOR	5,709	2,594	3,082	33	488 D	45.4%	54.0%	45.5%	54.5%
TODD	4,091	1,339	2,738	14	1,399 D	32.7%	66.9%	32.8%	67.2%
TRIGG	3,714	912	2,790	12	1,878 D	24.6%	75.1%	24.6%	75.4%
TRIMBLE	2,178	292	1,881	5	1,589 D	13.4%	86.4%	13.4%	86.6%
UNION	5,181	1,220	3,934	27	2,714 D	23.5%	75.9%	23.7%	76.3%
WARREN	15,831	5,915	9,887	29	3,972 D	37.4%	62.5%	37.4%	62.6%
WASHINGTON	4,351	1,561	2,790		1,229 D	35.9%	64.1%	35.9%	64.1%
WAYNE	5,144	2,389	2,737	18	348 D	46.4%	53.2%	46.6%	53.4%
WEBSTER	4,954	1,217	3,741	6	2,524 D	24.5%	75.4%	24.5%	75.5%
WHITLEY	9,559	4,779	4,782	38	3 D	49.8%	50.0%	50.0%	50.0%
WOLFE	2,597	562	2,018	17	1,456 D	21.6%	77.7%	21.8%	78.2%
WOODFORD	4,213	1,215	2,974	24	1,759 D	28.8%	70.6%	29.0%	71.0%
TOTAL	1,046,105	372,977	669,659	3,469	296,682 D	35.7%	64.0%	35.8%	64.2%

KENTUCKY

OTHER VOTE COMPOSITION:

1920	6,409 Socialist; 3,250 Prohibition.
1924	38,465 Progressive; 1,501 Socialist Labor; 1,300 American; 226 Commonwealth Land.
1928	783 Socialist; 316 Socialist Labor; 288 Communist.
1932	3,853 Socialist; 2,252 Prohibition; 1,393 Socialist Labor; 271 Communist.
1936	12,501 Union; 939 Prohibition; 627 Socialist; 294 Socialist Labor; 207 Communist.
1940	1,443 Prohibition; 1,014 Socialist.
1944	2,023 Prohibition; 535 Socialist; 329 Socialist Labor.
1948	10,411 States Rights; 1,567 Progressive; 1,284 Socialist; 1,245 Prohibition; 185 Socialist Labor.
1952	1,161 Prohibition; 893 Socialist Labor; 336 Progressive.
1956	2,657 States Rights (Byrd); 2,145 Prohibition; 358 Socialist Labor.
1960	
1964	National States Rights.

SPECIAL CASES:

1924	Progressive candidates ran second in two counties.

LOUISIANA

PRESIDENT 1920

Parish	Total Vote	Republican	Democratic	Other	Rep-Dem Plurality	%Total Vote Rep.	%Total Vote Dem.	%Major Vote Rep.	%Major Vote Dem.
ACADIA	2,205	1,141	1,058	6	83 R	51.7%	48.0%	51.9%	48.1%
ALLEN	1,250	242	1,008		766 D	19.4%	80.6%	19.4%	80.6%
ASCENSION	1,118	496	622		126 D	44.4%	55.6%	44.4%	55.6%
ASSUMPTION	927	725	202		523 R	78.2%	21.8%	78.2%	21.8%
AVOYELLES	2,146	724	1,422		698 D	33.7%	66.3%	33.7%	66.3%
BEAUREGARD	1,362	202	1,146	14	944 D	14.8%	84.1%	15.0%	85.0%
BIENVILLE	1,704	257	1,419	28	1,162 D	15.1%	83.3%	15.3%	84.7%
BOSSIER	775	44	731		687 D	5.7%	94.3%	5.7%	94.3%
CADDO	4,665	401	4,264		3,863 D	8.6%	91.4%	8.6%	91.4%
CALCASIEU	2,976	483	2,480	13	1,997 D	16.2%	83.3%	16.3%	83.7%
CALDWELL	667	128	539		411 D	19.2%	80.8%	19.2%	80.8%
CAMERON	157	11	146		135 D	7.0%	93.0%	7.0%	93.0%
CATAHOULA	693	176	517		341 D	25.4%	74.6%	25.4%	74.6%
CLAIBORNE	1,264	48	1,216		1,168 D	3.8%	96.2%	3.8%	96.2%
CONCORDIA	392	12	380		368 D	3.1%	96.9%	3.1%	96.9%
DE SOTO	1,275	56	1,219		1,163 D	4.4%	95.6%	4.4%	95.6%
EAST BATON ROUGE	2,778	442	2,336		1,894 D	15.9%	84.1%	15.9%	84.1%
EAST CARROLL	255	8	247		239 D	3.1%	96.9%	3.1%	96.9%
EAST FELICIANA	559	30	529		499 D	5.4%	94.6%	5.4%	94.6%
EVANGELINE	1,129	587	542		45 R	52.0%	48.0%	52.0%	48.0%
FRANKLIN	1,071	173	898		725 D	16.2%	83.8%	16.2%	83.8%
GRANT	783	109	674		565 D	13.9%	86.1%	13.9%	86.1%
IBERIA	1,713	1,275	438		837 R	74.4%	25.6%	74.4%	25.6%
IBERVILLE	850	465	385		80 R	54.7%	45.3%	54.7%	45.3%
JACKSON	1,395	166	1,229		1,063 D	11.9%	88.1%	11.9%	88.1%
JEFFERSON	1,430	192	1,238		1,046 D	13.4%	86.6%	13.4%	86.6%
JEFFERSON DAVIS	1,623	895	728		167 R	55.1%	44.9%	55.1%	44.9%
LAFAYETTE	1,868	1,045	823		222 R	55.9%	44.1%	55.9%	44.1%
LAFOURCHE	1,381	1,044	337		707 R	75.6%	24.4%	75.6%	24.4%
LA SALLE	694	109	570	15	461 D	15.7%	82.1%	16.1%	83.9%
LINCOLN	1,172	183	989		806 D	15.6%	84.4%	15.6%	84.4%
LIVINGSTON	893	218	674	1	456 D	24.4%	75.5%	24.4%	75.6%
MADISON	335	4	331		327 D	1.2%	98.8%	1.2%	98.8%
MOREHOUSE	660	38	622		584 D	5.8%	94.2%	5.8%	94.2%
NATCHITOCHES	1,798	203	1,595		1,392 D	11.3%	88.7%	11.3%	88.7%
ORLEANS	50,543	17,819	32,724		14,905 D	35.3%	64.7%	35.3%	64.7%
OUACHITA	1,646	164	1,481	1	1,317 D	10.0%	90.0%	10.0%	90.0%
PLAQUEMINES	469	124	329	16	205 D	26.4%	70.1%	27.4%	72.6%
POINTE COUPEE	550	143	407		264 D	26.0%	74.0%	26.0%	74.0%
RAPIDES	3,211	445	2,765	1	2,320 D	13.9%	86.1%	13.9%	86.1%
RED RIVER	953	187	766		579 D	19.6%	80.4%	19.6%	80.4%
RICHLAND	714	50	664		514 D	7.0%	93.0%	7.0%	93.0%
SABINE	1,356	111	1,245		1,134 D	8.2%	91.8%	8.2%	91.8%
ST BERNARD	414	56	358		302 D	13.5%	86.5%	13.5%	86.5%
ST CHARLES	275	92	183		91 D	33.5%	66.5%	33.5%	66.5%
ST HELENA	402	36	366		330 D	9.0%	91.0%	9.0%	91.0%
ST JAMES	875	533	342		191 R	60.9%	39.1%	60.9%	39.1%
ST JOHN THE BAPTIST	489	250	239		11 R	51.1%	48.9%	51.1%	48.9%
ST LANDRY	1,959	942	1,017		75 D	48.1%	51.9%	48.1%	51.9%
ST MARTIN	738	419	319		100 R	56.8%	43.2%	56.8%	43.2%
ST MARY	1,327	788	539		249 R	59.4%	40.6%	59.4%	40.6%
ST TAMMANY	1,243	276	967		691 D	22.2%	77.8%	22.2%	77.8%
TANGIPAHOA	1,941	440	1,501		1,061 D	22.7%	77.3%	22.7%	77.3%
TENSAS	258	15	243		228 D	5.8%	94.2%	5.8%	94.2%
TERREBONNE	1,190	713	477		236 R	59.9%	40.1%	59.9%	40.1%
UNION	1,319	98	1,221		1,123 D	7.4%	92.6%	7.4%	92.6%
VERMILION	1,970	1,420	549	1	871 R	72.1%	27.9%	72.1%	27.9%
VERNON	1,348	205	1,143		938 D	15.2%	84.8%	15.2%	84.8%
WASHINGTON	1,259	165	1,094		929 D	13.1%	86.9%	13.1%	86.9%
WEBSTER	1,121	112	1,009		897 D	10.0%	90.0%	10.0%	90.0%

PRESIDENT 1924

Parish	Total Vote	Republican	Democratic	Other	Rep-Dem Plurality	%Total Vote Rep.	%Total Vote Dem.	%Major Vote Rep.	%Major Vote Dem.
ACADIA	2,288	691	1,481	116	790 D	30.2%	64.7%	31.8%	68.2%
ALLEN	1,422	410	1,012		602 D	28.8%	71.2%	28.8%	71.2%
ASCENSION	956	277	679		402 D	29.0%	71.0%	29.0%	71.0%
ASSUMPTION	906	601	305		296 R	66.3%	33.7%	66.3%	33.7%
AVOYELLES	1,324	314	1,010		696 D	23.7%	76.3%	23.7%	76.3%
BEAUREGARD	1,427	235	1,191	1	956 D	16.5%	83.5%	16.5%	83.5%
BIENVILLE	844	67	774	3	707 D	7.9%	91.7%	8.0%	92.0%
BOSSIER	822	48	751	23	703 D	5.8%	91.4%	6.0%	94.0%
CADDO	5,990	1,062	4,517	411	3,455 D	17.7%	75.4%	19.0%	81.0%
CALCASIEU	3,656	1,129	2,494	33	1,365 D	30.9%	68.2%	31.2%	68.8%
CALDWELL	523	77	442	4	365 D	14.7%	84.5%	14.8%	85.2%
CAMERON	373	20	353		333 D	5.4%	94.6%	5.4%	94.6%
CATAHOULA	296	78	218		140 D	26.4%	73.6%	26.4%	73.6%
CLAIBORNE	1,306	54	1,252		1,198 D	4.1%	95.9%	4.1%	95.9%
CONCORDIA	365	46	319		273 D	12.6%	87.4%	12.6%	87.4%
DE SOTO	1,275	118	1,146	11	1,028 D	9.3%	89.9%	9.3%	90.7%
EAST BATON ROUGE	3,394	611	2,764	19	2,153 D	18.0%	81.4%	18.1%	79.6%
EAST CARROLL	348	71	277		206 D	20.4%	79.6%	20.4%	79.6%
EAST FELICIANA	529	25	504		479 D	4.7%	95.3%	4.7%	95.3%
EVANGELINE	757	153	603	1	450 D	20.2%	79.7%	20.2%	79.8%
FRANKLIN	830	143	687		544 D	17.2%	82.8%	17.2%	82.8%
GRANT	762	167	595		428 D	21.9%	78.1%	21.9%	78.1%
IBERIA	1,419	679	740		61 D	47.9%	52.1%	47.9%	52.1%
IBERVILLE	954	391	556	7	165 D	41.3%	58.3%	41.3%	58.7%
JACKSON	770	88	682		594 D	11.4%	88.6%	11.4%	88.6%
JEFFERSON	2,175	296	1,663	216	1,367 D	13.6%	76.5%	15.1%	84.9%
JEFFERSON DAVIS	1,856	883	973		90 D	47.6%	52.4%	47.6%	52.4%
LAFAYETTE	1,833	531	978	324	447 D	29.0%	53.4%	35.2%	52.4%
LAFOURCHE	1,299	611	678		67 D	47.0%	52.4%	47.4%	52.6%
LA SALLE	559	102	456	11	354 D	17.9%	80.1%	18.3%	81.7%
LINCOLN	1,156	157	1,005		848 D	13.5%	86.2%	13.5%	86.5%
LIVINGSTON	757	110	657	4	547 D	14.3%	85.7%	14.3%	85.7%
MADISON	287	13	274		261 D	4.5%	95.5%	4.5%	95.5%
MOREHOUSE	723	141	582		441 D	19.5%	80.5%	19.5%	80.5%
NATCHITOCHES	1,346	200	1,132	14	932 D	14.9%	84.1%	15.0%	85.0%
ORLEANS	47,791	7,865	37,785	2,141	29,920 D	16.5%	79.1%	17.2%	82.8%
OUACHITA	2,108	480	1,542	86	1,062 D	22.8%	73.1%	23.7%	76.3%
PLAQUEMINES	571	119	432	20	313 D	20.8%	75.7%	21.6%	78.4%
POINTE COUPEE	528	146	369	13	223 D	27.7%	69.9%	28.3%	71.7%
RAPIDES	3,220	1,022	2,159	109	1,137 D	31.1%	65.6%	32.1%	67.9%
RED RIVER	647	34	579	34	545 D	5.3%	89.5%	5.5%	94.5%
RICHLAND	794	116	678		562 D	14.6%	85.4%	14.6%	85.4%
SABINE	1,403	217	1,176	10	959 D	15.5%	83.8%	15.6%	84.4%
ST BERNARD	539	13	526		513 D	2.4%	97.6%	2.4%	97.6%
ST CHARLES	620	132	488		356 D	21.3%	78.7%	21.3%	78.7%
ST HELENA	203	18	185		167 D	8.9%	91.1%	8.9%	91.1%
ST JAMES	896	278	615	3	337 D	31.0%	68.6%	31.1%	68.4%
ST JOHN THE BAPTIST	530	194	336		142 D	36.6%	63.4%	36.6%	63.4%
ST LANDRY	1,711	357	1,354		997 D	20.9%	79.1%	20.9%	79.1%
ST MARTIN	656	172	461	23	289 D	26.2%	70.3%	27.2%	72.8%
ST MARY	1,300	633	639	28	6 D	48.7%	49.2%	49.8%	50.2%
ST TAMMANY	1,311	269	969	73	700 D	20.5%	73.9%	21.7%	78.3%
TANGIPAHOA	2,105	479	1,626		1,147 D	22.8%	77.3%	22.8%	77.2%
TENSAS	359	21	338		317 D	5.8%	94.2%	5.8%	94.2%
TERREBONNE	897	415	482		67 D	46.3%	53.7%	46.3%	53.7%
UNION	883	7	875	1	868 D	0.8%	99.1%	0.8%	99.2%
VERMILION	1,014	416	598		182 D	41.0%	59.0%	41.0%	59.0%
VERNON	1,547	142	1,372	33	1,230 D	9.2%	88.7%	9.4%	90.6%
WASHINGTON	1,646	179	1,278	189	1,099 D	10.9%	77.6%	12.3%	87.7%
WEBSTER	1,033	52	929	52	877 D	5.0%	89.9%	5.3%	94.7%

LOUISIANA

PRESIDENT 1920

Parish	Total Vote	Republican	Democratic	Other	Rep.-Dem. Plurality	Percentage Total Vote Rep.	Dem.	Major Vote Rep.	Dem.
WEST BATON ROUGE	527	175	352		177 D	33.2%	66.8%	33.2%	66.8%
WEST CARROLL	470	104	346	20	242 D	22.1%	73.6%	23.1%	76.9%
WEST FELICIANA	390	34	356		322 D	8.7%	91.3%	8.7%	91.3%
WINN	1,477	291	963	223	672 D	19.7%	65.2%	23.2%	76.8%
TOTAL	126,397	38,539	87,519	339	48,980 D	30.5%	69.2%	30.6%	69.4%

PRESIDENT 1924

Parish	Total Vote	Republican	Democratic	Other	Rep.-Dem. Plurality	Percentage Total Vote Rep.	Dem.	Major Vote Rep.	Dem.
WEST BATON ROUGE	324	92	191	41	99 D	28.4%	59.0%	32.5%	67.5%
WEST CARROLL	419	68	342	9	274 D	16.2%	81.6%	16.6%	83.4%
WEST FELICIANA	362	15	347		332 D	4.1%	95.9%	4.1%	95.9%
WINN	917	120	797		677 D	13.1%	86.9%	13.1%	86.9%
TOTAL	121,951	24,670	93,218	4,063	68,548 D	20.2%	76.4%	20.9%	79.1%

LOUISIANA

PRESIDENT 1928

Parish	Total Vote	Republican	Democratic	Other	Rep.-Dem. Plurality	Total Vote Rep.	Total Vote Dem.	Major Vote Rep.	Major Vote Dem.
ACADIA	4,704	1,071	3,633		2,562 D	22.8%	77.2%	22.8%	77.2%
ALLEN	2,033	725	1,308		583 D	35.7%	64.3%	35.7%	64.3%
ASCENSION	1,838	436	1,402		966 D	23.7%	76.3%	23.7%	76.3%
ASSUMPTION	1,255	307	948		641 D	24.5%	75.5%	24.5%	75.5%
AVOYELLES	3,315	419	2,896		2,477 D	12.6%	87.4%	12.6%	87.4%
BEAUREGARD	1,981	468	1,513		1,045 D	23.6%	76.4%	23.6%	76.4%
BIENVILLE	1,668	367	1,301		934 D	22.0%	78.0%	22.0%	78.0%
BOSSIER	1,412	225	1,187		962 D	15.9%	84.1%	15.9%	84.1%
CADDO	10,599	3,665	6,934		3,269 D	34.6%	65.4%	34.6%	65.4%
CALCASIEU	5,532	1,997	3,532	3	1,535 D	36.1%	63.8%	36.1%	63.9%
CALDWELL	1,090	288	802		514 D	26.4%	73.6%	26.4%	73.6%
CAMERON	431	41	390		349 D	9.5%	90.5%	9.5%	90.5%
CATAHOULA	1,051	341	710		369 D	32.4%	67.6%	32.4%	67.6%
CLAIBORNE	1,809	249	1,560		1,311 D	13.8%	86.2%	13.8%	86.2%
CONCORDIA	724	133	591		458 D	18.4%	81.6%	18.4%	81.6%
DE SOTO	1,964	517	1,445	2	928 D	26.3%	73.6%	26.4%	73.6%
EAST BATON ROUGE	7,570	2,995	4,575		1,580 D	39.6%	60.4%	39.6%	60.4%
EAST CARROLL	566	130	436		306 D	23.0%	77.0%	23.0%	77.0%
EAST FELICIANA	782	160	622		462 D	20.5%	79.5%	20.5%	79.5%
EVANGELINE	2,173	300	1,873		1,573 D	13.8%	86.2%	13.8%	86.2%
FRANKLIN	1,633	492	1,141		649 D	30.1%	69.9%	30.1%	69.9%
GRANT	1,528	505	1,023		518 D	33.0%	67.0%	33.0%	67.0%
IBERIA	2,974	413	2,561		2,148 D	13.9%	86.1%	13.9%	86.1%
IBERVILLE	1,908	278	1,630		1,352 D	14.6%	85.4%	14.6%	85.4%
JACKSON	907		907		907 D	0.0%	100.0%	0.0%	100.0%
JEFFERSON	6,068	742	5,326		4,584 D	12.2%	87.8%	12.2%	87.8%
JEFFERSON DAVIS	2,823	1,120	1,703		583 D	39.7%	60.3%	39.7%	60.3%
LAFAYETTE	3,789	592	3,197		2,605 D	15.6%	84.4%	15.6%	84.4%
LAFOURCHE	2,237	243	1,994		1,751 D	10.9%	89.1%	10.9%	89.1%
LA SALLE	1,331	450	881		431 D	33.8%	66.2%	33.8%	66.2%
LINCOLN	1,711	670	1,041		371 D	39.2%	60.8%	39.2%	60.8%
LIVINGSTON	2,022	975	1,047		72 D	48.2%	51.8%	48.2%	51.8%
MADISON	469	151	318		167 D	32.2%	67.8%	32.2%	67.8%
MOREHOUSE	1,180	340	840		500 D	28.8%	71.2%	28.8%	71.2%
NATCHITOCHES	2,625	526	2,099		1,573 D	20.0%	80.0%	20.0%	80.0%
ORLEANS	70,343	14,424	55,919		41,495 D	20.5%	79.5%	20.5%	79.5%
OUACHITA	4,119	1,380	2,739		1,359 D	33.5%	66.5%	33.5%	66.5%
PLAQUEMINES	1,154	98	1,056		958 D	8.5%	91.5%	8.5%	91.5%
POINTE COUPEE	1,432	102	1,330		1,228 D	7.1%	92.9%	7.1%	92.9%
RAPIDES	6,964	2,494	4,470		1,976 D	35.8%	64.2%	35.8%	64.2%
RED RIVER	1,219	317	891	11	574 D	26.0%	73.1%	26.2%	73.8%
RICHLAND	1,325	242	1,083		841 D	18.3%	81.7%	18.3%	81.7%
SABINE	2,149	735	1,414		679 D	34.2%	65.8%	34.2%	65.8%
ST BERNARD	2,436	77	2,359		2,282 D	3.2%	96.8%	3.2%	96.8%
ST CHARLES	1,224	108	1,116		1,008 D	8.8%	91.2%	8.8%	91.2%
ST HELENA	754	145	609		464 D	19.2%	80.8%	19.2%	80.8%
ST JAMES	1,614	128	1,486		1,358 D	7.9%	92.1%	7.9%	92.1%
ST JOHN THE BAPTIST	1,089	118	971		853 D	10.8%	89.2%	10.8%	89.2%
ST LANDRY	4,112	718	3,394		2,676 D	17.5%	82.5%	17.5%	82.5%
ST MARTIN	2,134	242	1,892		1,650 D	11.3%	88.7%	11.3%	88.7%
ST MARY	2,359	605	1,754		1,149 D	25.6%	74.4%	25.6%	74.4%
ST TAMMANY	2,756	945	1,811		866 D	34.3%	65.7%	34.3%	65.7%
TANGIPAHOA	4,249	1,415	2,834		1,419 D	33.3%	66.7%	33.3%	66.7%
TENSAS	446	96	350		254 D	21.5%	78.5%	21.5%	78.5%
TERREBONNE	1,910	268	1,642		1,374 D	14.0%	86.0%	14.0%	86.0%
UNION	1,509	422	1,085	2	663 D	28.0%	71.9%	28.0%	72.0%
VERMILION	3,031	451	2,580		2,129 D	14.9%	85.1%	14.9%	85.1%
VERNON	2,691	500	2,191		1,691 D	18.6%	81.4%	18.6%	81.4%
WASHINGTON	3,548	1,528	2,020		492 D	43.1%	56.9%	43.1%	56.9%
WEBSTER	1,786	356	1,430		1,074 D	19.9%	80.1%	19.9%	80.1%

PRESIDENT 1932

Parish	Total Vote	Republican	Democratic	Other	Rep.-Dem. Plurality	Total Vote Rep.	Total Vote Dem.	Major Vote Rep.	Major Vote Dem.
ACADIA	3,934	351	3,583		3,232 D	8.9%	91.1%	8.9%	91.1%
ALLEN	2,209	130	2,075	4	1,945 D	5.9%	93.9%	5.9%	94.1%
ASCENSION	2,079	279	1,800		1,521 D	13.4%	86.6%	13.4%	86.6%
ASSUMPTION	1,924	386	1,538		1,152 D	20.1%	79.9%	20.1%	79.9%
AVOYELLES	3,278	130	3,148		3,018 D	4.0%	96.0%	4.0%	96.0%
BEAUREGARD	2,465	146	2,319		2,173 D	5.9%	94.1%	5.9%	94.1%
BIENVILLE	2,713	41	2,671	1	2,630 D	1.5%	98.5%	1.5%	98.5%
BOSSIER	2,247	56	2,191		2,135 D	2.5%	97.5%	2.5%	97.5%
CADDO	13,553	1,309	12,159	85	10,850 D	9.7%	89.7%	9.7%	90.3%
CALCASIEU	6,805	678	6,105	22	5,427 D	10.0%	89.7%	10.0%	90.0%
CALDWELL	1,541	86	1,448	7	1,362 D	5.6%	94.0%	5.6%	94.4%
CAMERON	948	10	938		928 D	1.1%	98.9%	1.1%	98.9%
CATAHOULA	1,369	29	1,340		1,311 D	2.1%	97.9%	2.1%	97.9%
CLAIBORNE	2,826	61	2,765		2,704 D	2.2%	97.8%	2.2%	97.8%
CONCORDIA	1,019	20	999		979 D	2.0%	98.0%	2.0%	98.0%
DE SOTO	2,505	87	2,416	2	2,329 D	3.5%	96.4%	3.5%	96.5%
EAST BATON ROUGE	7,441	1,045	6,363	33	5,318 D	14.0%	85.5%	14.1%	85.9%
EAST CARROLL	775	24	751		727 D	3.1%	96.9%	3.1%	96.9%
EAST FELICIANA	1,243	65	1,178		1,113 D	5.2%	94.8%	5.2%	94.8%
EVANGELINE	3,167	52	3,115		3,063 D	1.6%	98.4%	1.6%	98.4%
FRANKLIN	3,010	78	2,930	2	2,852 D	2.6%	97.3%	2.6%	97.4%
GRANT	2,048	81	1,966	1	1,885 D	4.0%	96.0%	4.0%	96.0%
IBERIA	3,210	798	2,412		1,614 D	24.9%	75.1%	24.9%	75.1%
IBERVILLE	1,738	430	1,308		878 D	24.7%	75.3%	24.7%	75.3%
JACKSON	1,782	34	1,748		1,714 D	1.9%	98.1%	1.9%	98.1%
JEFFERSON	7,875	466	7,395	14	6,929 D	5.9%	93.9%	5.9%	94.1%
JEFFERSON DAVIS	2,824	512	2,308	4	1,796 D	18.1%	81.7%	18.2%	81.8%
LAFAYETTE	4,312	291	4,019	2	3,728 D	6.7%	93.2%	6.8%	93.2%
LAFOURCHE	2,988	364	2,623	1	2,259 D	12.2%	87.8%	12.2%	87.8%
LA SALLE	1,856	117	1,738	1	1,621 D	6.3%	93.6%	6.3%	93.7%
LINCOLN	2,071	163	1,908		1,745 D	7.9%	92.1%	7.9%	92.1%
LIVINGSTON	2,042	89	1,953		1,864 D	4.4%	95.6%	4.4%	95.6%
MADISON	615	67	548		481 D	10.9%	89.1%	10.9%	89.1%
MOREHOUSE	2,097	83	2,014		1,931 D	4.0%	96.0%	4.0%	96.0%
NATCHITOCHES	3,633	173	3,458	2	3,285 D	4.8%	95.2%	4.8%	95.2%
ORLEANS	90,850	5,407	85,288	165	79,881 D	6.0%	93.9%	6.0%	94.0%
OUACHITA	6,427	423	5,968	36	5,545 D	6.6%	92.9%	6.6%	93.4%
PLAQUEMINES	1,956	38	1,918		1,880 D	1.9%	98.1%	1.9%	98.1%
POINTE COUPEE	1,092	65	1,027		962 D	6.0%	94.0%	6.0%	94.0%
RAPIDES	8,258	680	7,578		6,898 D	8.2%	91.8%	8.2%	91.8%
RED RIVER	1,689	24	1,661	4	1,637 D	1.4%	98.3%	1.4%	98.6%
RICHLAND	1,820	46	1,773	1	1,727 D	2.5%	97.4%	2.5%	97.5%
SABINE	3,128	110	3,008	10	2,898 D	3.5%	96.2%	3.5%	96.5%
ST BERNARD	1,631	106	1,525		1,419 D	6.5%	93.5%	6.5%	93.5%
ST CHARLES	1,519	86	1,429	4	1,343 D	5.7%	94.1%	5.7%	94.3%
ST HELENA	988	26	962		936 D	2.6%	97.4%	2.6%	97.4%
ST JAMES	1,955	240	1,715		1,475 D	12.3%	87.7%	12.3%	87.7%
ST JOHN THE BAPTIST	1,004	176	799	29	623 D	17.5%	79.6%	18.1%	81.9%
ST LANDRY	4,063	297	3,766		3,469 D	7.3%	92.7%	7.3%	92.7%
ST MARTIN	1,527	107	1,420		1,313 D	7.0%	93.0%	7.0%	93.0%
ST MARY	2,545	473	2,072		1,599 D	18.6%	81.4%	18.6%	81.4%
ST TAMMANY	3,389	178	3,206	5	3,028 D	5.3%	94.6%	5.3%	94.7%
TANGIPAHOA	4,862	455	4,404	3	3,949 D	9.4%	90.6%	9.4%	90.6%
TENSAS	665	29	635	1	606 D	4.4%	95.5%	4.4%	95.6%
TERREBONNE	2,341	215	2,126		1,911 D	9.2%	90.8%	9.2%	90.8%
UNION	2,343	58	2,285		2,227 D	2.5%	97.5%	2.5%	97.5%
VERMILION	3,214	269	2,945		2,676 D	8.4%	91.6%	8.4%	91.6%
VERNON	2,969	46	2,868	55	2,822 D	1.5%	96.6%	1.5%	98.4%
WASHINGTON	4,281	283	3,997	1	3,714 D	6.6%	93.4%	6.6%	93.4%
WEBSTER	3,093	73	3,020		2,947 D	2.4%	97.6%	2.4%	97.6%

LOUISIANA

PRESIDENT 1928

Parish	Total Vote	Republican	Democratic	Other	Rep.-Dem. Plurality	Percentage			
						Total Vote		Major Vote	
						Rep.	Dem.	Rep.	Dem.
WEST BATON ROUGE	686	78	608		530 D	11.4%	88.6%	11.4%	88.6%
WEST CARROLL	887	214	673		459 D	24.1%	75.9%	24.1%	75.9%
WEST FELICIANA	511	90	421		331 D	17.6%	82.4%	17.6%	82.4%
WINN	1,694	533	1,161		628 D	31.5%	68.5%	31.5%	68.5%
TOTAL	215,833	51,160	164,655	18	113,495 D	23.7%	76.3%	23.7%	76.3%

PRESIDENT 1932

Parish	Total Vote	Republican	Democratic	Other	Rep.-Dem. Plurality	Percentage			
						Total Vote		Major Vote	
						Rep.	Dem.	Rep.	Dem.
WEST BATON ROUGE	689	96	593		497 D	13.9%	86.1%	13.9%	86.1%
WEST CARROLL	1,502	31	1,471		1,440 D	2.1%	97.9%	2.1%	97.9%
WEST FELICIANA	606	49	557		508 D	8.1%	91.9%	8.1%	91.9%
WINN	2,246	36	2,172	38	2,136 D	1.6%	96.7%	1.6%	98.4%
TOTAL	268,804	18,853	249,418	533	230,565 D	7.0%	92.8%	7.0%	93.0%

LOUISIANA

PRESIDENT 1936

Parish	Total Vote	Republican	Democratic	Other	Rep-Dem Plurality	% Total Vote Rep.	% Total Vote Dem.	% Major Vote Rep.	% Major Vote Dem.
ACADIA	4,945	441	4,504		4,063 D	8.9%	91.1%	8.9%	91.1%
ALLEN	2,531	324	2,207		1,863 D	12.8%	87.2%	12.8%	87.2%
ASCENSION	2,710	350	2,359		2,009 D	12.9%	87.0%	12.9%	87.1%
ASSUMPTION	1,823	1,111	712	1	399 R	60.9%	39.1%	60.9%	39.1%
AVOYELLES	4,860	452	4,408		3,956 D	9.3%	90.7%	9.3%	90.7%
BEAUREGARD	2,730	549	2,181		1,632 D	20.1%	79.9%	20.1%	79.9%
BIENVILLE	2,807	213	2,593	1	2,380 D	7.6%	92.4%	7.6%	92.4%
BOSSIER	2,170	193	1,975	2	1,782 D	8.9%	91.0%	8.9%	91.1%
CADDO	13,857	1,697	12,156	4	10,459 D	12.2%	87.7%	12.3%	87.7%
CALCASIEU	7,309	1,037	6,259	13	5,222 D	14.2%	85.6%	14.2%	85.8%
CALDWELL	1,606	235	1,371		1,136 D	14.6%	85.4%	14.6%	85.4%
CAMERON	1,083	16	1,067		1,051 D	1.5%	98.5%	1.5%	98.5%
CATAHOULA	1,461	98	1,363		1,265 D	6.7%	93.3%	6.7%	93.3%
CLAIBORNE	2,711	146	2,563	2	2,417 D	5.4%	94.5%	5.4%	94.6%
CONCORDIA	1,211	58	1,152	1	1,094 D	4.8%	95.1%	4.8%	95.2%
DE SOTO	2,430	93	2,337		2,244 D	3.8%	96.2%	3.8%	96.2%
EAST BATON ROUGE	10,980	1,069	9,911		8,842 D	9.7%	90.3%	9.7%	90.3%
EAST CARROLL	906	95	811		716 D	10.5%	89.5%	10.5%	89.5%
EAST FELICIANA	1,159	102	1,057		955 D	8.8%	91.2%	8.8%	91.2%
EVANGELINE	3,815	331	3,484		3,153 D	8.7%	91.3%	8.7%	91.3%
FRANKLIN	3,187	231	2,948	8	2,717 D	7.2%	92.5%	7.3%	92.7%
GRANT	2,358	511	1,847		1,336 D	21.7%	78.3%	21.7%	78.3%
IBERIA	3,829	1,234	2,595		1,361 D	32.2%	67.8%	32.2%	67.8%
IBERVILLE	2,216	263	1,953		1,690 D	11.9%	88.1%	11.9%	88.1%
JACKSON	1,976	169	1,807		1,638 D	8.6%	91.4%	8.6%	91.4%
JEFFERSON	9,767	705	9,056	6	8,351 D	7.2%	92.7%	7.2%	92.8%
JEFFERSON DAVIS	3,175	608	2,567		1,959 D	19.1%	80.9%	19.1%	80.9%
LAFAYETTE	4,876	306	4,570		4,264 D	6.3%	93.7%	6.3%	93.7%
LAFOURCHE	3,827	1,630	2,195	2	565 D	42.6%	57.4%	42.6%	57.4%
LA SALLE	1,899	256	1,643		1,387 D	13.5%	86.5%	13.5%	86.5%
LINCOLN	2,356	201	2,154	1	1,953 D	8.5%	91.4%	8.5%	91.5%
LIVINGSTON	2,910	496	2,414		1,918 D	17.0%	83.0%	17.0%	83.0%
MADISON	1,156	71	1,085		1,014 D	6.1%	93.9%	6.1%	93.9%
MOREHOUSE	2,688	172	2,512	2	2,340 D	6.4%	93.5%	6.4%	93.6%
NATCHITOCHES	3,978	502	3,476		2,974 D	12.6%	87.4%	12.6%	87.4%
ORLEANS	118,282	10,254	108,012	16	97,758 D	8.7%	91.3%	8.7%	91.3%
OUACHITA	8,748	1,113	7,635		6,522 D	12.7%	87.3%	12.7%	87.3%
PLAQUEMINES	2,303	94	2,115		2,021 D	4.1%	95.9%	4.1%	95.9%
POINTE COUPEE	1,535	116	1,419		1,303 D	7.6%	92.4%	7.6%	92.4%
RAPIDES	9,274	1,257	8,017		6,760 D	13.6%	86.4%	13.6%	86.4%
RED RIVER	1,773	132	1,641		1,509 D	7.4%	92.6%	7.4%	92.6%
RICHLAND	2,594	165	2,425	4	2,260 D	6.4%	93.5%	6.4%	93.6%
SABINE	2,865	417	2,447	1	2,030 D	14.6%	85.4%	14.6%	85.4%
ST BERNARD	2,294	25	2,269		2,244 D	1.1%	98.9%	1.1%	98.9%
ST CHARLES	1,599	96	1,503		1,407 D	6.0%	94.0%	6.0%	94.0%
ST HELENA	1,301	102	1,199		1,097 D	7.8%	92.2%	7.8%	92.2%
ST JAMES	1,834	259	1,575		1,316 D	14.1%	85.9%	14.1%	85.9%
ST JOHN THE BAPTIST	2,004	262	1,742		1,480 D	13.1%	86.9%	13.1%	86.9%
ST LANDRY	6,080	441	5,639		5,198 D	7.3%	92.7%	7.3%	92.7%
ST MARTIN	2,738	100	2,638		2,538 D	3.7%	96.3%	3.7%	96.3%
ST MARY	2,429	487	1,942		1,455 D	20.0%	80.0%	20.0%	80.0%
ST TAMMANY	4,071	594	3,477		2,883 D	14.6%	85.4%	14.6%	85.4%
TANGIPAHOA	6,000	1,374	4,624	2	3,250 D	22.9%	77.1%	22.9%	77.1%
TENSAS	835	23	812		789 D	2.8%	97.2%	2.8%	97.2%
TERREBONNE	2,420	526	1,894		1,368 D	21.7%	78.3%	21.7%	78.3%
UNION	2,050	272	1,778		1,506 D	13.3%	86.7%	13.3%	86.7%
VERMILION	4,652	496	4,141	15	3,645 D	10.7%	89.0%	10.7%	89.3%
VERNON	3,764	928	2,831	5	1,903 D	24.7%	75.2%	24.7%	75.3%
WASHINGTON	6,017	350	5,667		5,317 D	5.8%	94.2%	5.8%	94.2%
WEBSTER	3,106	301	2,799	6	2,498 D	9.7%	90.1%	9.7%	90.3%

PRESIDENT 1940

Parish	Total Vote	Republican	Democratic	Other	Rep-Dem Plurality	% Total Vote Rep.	% Total Vote Dem.	% Major Vote Rep.	% Major Vote Dem.
ACADIA	5,779	719	5,058	2	4,339 D	12.4%	87.5%	12.4%	87.6%
ALLEN	2,869	277	2,592		2,315 D	9.7%	90.3%	9.7%	90.3%
ASCENSION	2,836	385	2,451		2,066 D	13.6%	86.4%	13.6%	86.4%
ASSUMPTION	2,481	722	1,759		1,037 D	29.1%	70.9%	29.1%	70.9%
AVOYELLES	5,066	183	4,883		4,700 D	3.6%	96.4%	3.6%	96.4%
BEAUREGARD	3,205	528	2,677		2,149 D	16.5%	83.5%	16.5%	83.5%
BIENVILLE	3,246	362	2,883	1	2,521 D	11.2%	88.8%	11.2%	88.8%
BOSSIER	3,340	275	3,045	20	2,770 D	8.3%	91.1%	8.3%	91.7%
CADDO	20,345	3,124	17,192	29	14,068 D	15.4%	84.5%	15.4%	84.6%
CALCASIEU	8,429	1,425	6,993	11	5,568 D	16.9%	83.0%	16.9%	83.1%
CALDWELL	1,986	318	1,668		1,350 D	16.0%	84.0%	16.0%	84.0%
CAMERON	1,223	48	1,175		1,127 D	3.9%	96.1%	3.9%	96.1%
CATAHOULA	1,646	134	1,512		1,378 D	8.1%	91.9%	8.1%	91.9%
CLAIBORNE	3,236	187	3,049		2,862 D	5.8%	94.2%	5.8%	94.2%
CONCORDIA	1,292	119	1,173		1,054 D	9.2%	90.8%	9.2%	90.8%
DE SOTO	3,083	211	2,872		2,661 D	6.8%	93.2%	6.8%	93.2%
EAST BATON ROUGE	15,065	1,762	13,303		11,541 D	11.7%	88.3%	11.7%	88.3%
EAST CARROLL	1,295	270	1,025		755 D	20.8%	79.2%	20.8%	79.2%
EAST FELICIANA	1,223	164	1,059		895 D	13.4%	86.6%	13.4%	86.6%
EVANGELINE	3,789	220	3,569		3,349 D	5.8%	94.2%	5.8%	94.2%
FRANKLIN	3,451	292	3,159		2,867 D	8.5%	91.5%	8.5%	91.5%
GRANT	2,766	232	2,534		2,302 D	8.4%	91.6%	8.4%	91.6%
IBERIA	5,797	1,706	4,091		2,385 D	29.4%	70.6%	29.4%	70.6%
IBERVILLE	3,001	496	2,505		2,009 D	16.5%	83.5%	16.5%	83.5%
JACKSON	3,014	280	2,734		2,454 D	9.3%	90.7%	9.3%	90.7%
JEFFERSON	9,316	982	8,334		7,352 D	10.5%	89.5%	10.5%	89.5%
JEFFERSON DAVIS	3,585	1,054	2,531		1,477 D	29.4%	70.6%	29.4%	70.6%
LAFAYETTE	8,173	1,850	6,323		4,473 D	23.2%	77.4%	23.2%	76.8%
LAFOURCHE	4,596	1,065	3,531		2,466 D	23.2%	76.8%	23.2%	76.8%
LA SALLE	2,307	258	2,039	10	1,781 D	11.2%	88.4%	11.2%	88.8%
LINCOLN	3,418	449	2,969		2,520 D	13.1%	86.9%	13.1%	86.9%
LIVINGSTON	3,223	252	2,971		2,719 D	7.8%	92.2%	7.8%	92.2%
MADISON	1,199	182	1,017		835 D	15.2%	84.8%	15.2%	84.8%
MOREHOUSE	2,639	222	2,417		2,195 D	8.4%	91.6%	8.4%	91.6%
NATCHITOCHES	4,503	684	3,824		3,140 D	15.2%	84.8%	15.2%	84.8%
ORLEANS	114,364	16,406	97,930	28	81,524 D	14.3%	85.6%	14.3%	85.7%
OUACHITA	10,015	1,509	8,506		6,997 D	15.1%	84.9%	15.1%	84.9%
PLAQUEMINES	2,083	204	1,879		1,675 D	9.3%	90.7%	9.3%	90.7%
POINTE COUPEE	2,124	247	1,877		1,630 D	11.6%	88.4%	11.6%	88.4%
RAPIDES	9,969	869	9,100		8,231 D	8.7%	91.3%	8.7%	91.3%
RED RIVER	2,123	231	1,892		1,661 D	10.9%	89.1%	10.9%	89.1%
RICHLAND	2,727	310	2,417		2,107 D	11.4%	88.6%	11.4%	88.6%
SABINE	3,614	588	3,026		2,438 D	16.3%	83.7%	16.3%	83.7%
ST BERNARD	1,825	110	1,715		1,605 D	6.0%	94.0%	6.0%	94.0%
ST CHARLES	1,703	153	1,550		1,397 D	9.0%	91.0%	9.0%	91.0%
ST HELENA	1,087	80	1,007		927 D	7.4%	92.6%	7.4%	92.6%
ST JAMES	1,969	506	1,463		957 D	25.7%	74.3%	25.7%	74.3%
ST JOHN THE BAPTIST	1,477	285	1,192		907 D	19.3%	80.7%	19.3%	80.7%
ST LANDRY	6,919	561	6,358		5,797 D	8.1%	91.9%	8.1%	91.9%
ST MARTIN	3,854	602	3,252		2,650 D	15.6%	84.4%	15.6%	84.4%
ST MARY	4,425	739	3,686		2,947 D	16.7%	83.3%	16.7%	83.3%
ST TAMMANY	5,143	668	4,475		3,807 D	13.0%	87.0%	13.0%	87.0%
TANGIPAHOA	7,187	1,284	5,900	3	4,616 D	17.9%	82.1%	17.9%	82.1%
TENSAS	1,052	95	957		862 D	9.0%	91.0%	9.0%	91.0%
TERREBONNE	3,818	601	3,217		2,616 D	15.7%	84.3%	15.7%	84.3%
UNION	3,213	371	2,842		2,471 D	11.5%	88.5%	11.5%	88.5%
VERMILION	7,590	2,621	4,969		2,348 D	34.5%	65.5%	34.5%	65.5%
VERNON	3,750	311	3,439		3,128 D	8.3%	91.7%	8.3%	91.7%
WASHINGTON	6,376	314	6,062		5,748 D	4.9%	95.1%	4.9%	95.1%
WEBSTER	4,113	332	3,777	4	3,445 D	8.1%	91.9%	8.1%	91.9%

LOUISIANA

PRESIDENT 1936

Parish	Total Vote	Republican	Democratic	Other	Rep.-Dem. Plurality	Percentage			
						Total Vote		Major Vote	
						Rep.	Dem.	Rep.	Dem.
WEST BATON ROUGE	949	80	868	1	788 D	8.4%	91.5%	8.4%	91.6%
WEST CARROLL	1,672	232	1,440		1,208 D	13.9%	86.1%	13.9%	86.1%
WEST FELICIANA	640	76	564		488 D	11.9%	88.1%	11.9%	88.1%
WINN	2,647	254	2,393		2,139 D	9.6%	90.4%	9.6%	90.4%
TOTAL	329,778	36,791	292,894	93	256,103 D	11.2%	88.8%	11.2%	88.8%

PRESIDENT 1940

Parish	Total Vote	Republican	Democratic	Other	Rep.-Dem. Plurality	Percentage			
						Total Vote		Major Vote	
						Rep.	Dem.	Rep.	Dem.
WEST BATON ROUGE	1,326	141	1,185		1,044 D	10.6%	89.4%	10.6%	89.4%
WEST CARROLL	2,238	362	1,876		1,514 D	16.2%	83.8%	16.2%	83.8%
WEST FELICIANA	760	127	633		506 D	16.7%	83.3%	16.7%	83.3%
WINN	2,934	382	2,552		2,170 D	13.0%	87.0%	13.0%	87.0%
TOTAL	372,305	52,446	319,751	108	267,305 D	14.1%	85.9%	14.1%	85.9%

LOUISIANA

PRESIDENT 1944

Parish	Total Vote	Republican	Democratic	Other	Rep.-Dem. Plurality	%TV Rep.	%TV Dem.	%MV Rep.	%MV Dem.
ACADIA	5,462	1,023	4,439		3,416 D	18.7%	81.3%	18.7%	81.3%
ALLEN	2,541	336	2,205		1,869 D	13.2%	86.8%	13.2%	86.8%
ASCENSION	2,655	364	2,291		1,927 D	13.7%	86.3%	13.7%	86.3%
ASSUMPTION	1,845	426	1,419		993 D	23.1%	76.9%	23.1%	76.9%
AVOYELLES	4,095	306	3,789		3,483 D	7.5%	92.5%	7.5%	92.5%
BEAUREGARD	2,985	759	2,226		1,467 D	25.4%	74.6%	25.4%	74.6%
BIENVILLE	2,506	705	1,801		1,096 D	28.1%	71.9%	28.1%	71.9%
BOSSIER	3,053	622	2,430	1	1,808 D	20.4%	79.6%	20.4%	79.6%
CADDO	18,810	5,885	12,896	29	7,011 D	31.3%	68.6%	31.3%	68.7%
CALCASIEU	9,728	1,867	7,861		5,994 D	19.2%	80.8%	19.2%	80.8%
CALDWELL	1,647	505	1,142		637 D	30.7%	69.3%	30.7%	69.3%
CAMERON	1,111	86	1,025		939 D	7.7%	92.3%	7.7%	92.3%
CATAHOULA	1,499	291	1,208		917 D	19.4%	80.6%	19.4%	80.6%
CLAIBORNE	2,844	578	2,266		1,688 D	20.3%	79.7%	20.3%	79.7%
CONCORDIA	1,175	201	974		773 D	17.1%	82.9%	17.1%	82.9%
DE SOTO	2,396	538	1,858		1,320 D	22.5%	77.5%	22.5%	77.5%
EAST BATON ROUGE	17,782	3,025	14,757		11,732 D	17.0%	83.0%	17.0%	83.0%
EAST CARROLL	1,282	357	925		568 D	27.8%	72.2%	27.8%	72.2%
EAST FELICIANA	1,089	220	869		649 D	20.2%	79.8%	20.2%	79.8%
EVANGELINE	3,304	275	3,029		2,754 D	8.3%	91.7%	8.3%	91.7%
FRANKLIN	3,073	597	2,476		1,879 D	19.4%	80.6%	19.4%	80.6%
GRANT	2,495	556	1,939		1,383 D	22.3%	77.7%	22.3%	77.7%
IBERIA	4,802	1,141	3,661		2,520 D	23.8%	76.2%	23.8%	76.2%
IBERVILLE	2,697	432	2,265		1,833 D	16.0%	84.0%	16.0%	84.0%
JACKSON	2,257	414	1,840	3	1,426 D	18.3%	81.5%	18.4%	81.6%
JEFFERSON	12,050	1,782	10,268		8,486 D	14.8%	85.2%	14.8%	85.2%
JEFFERSON DAVIS	3,485	1,156	2,329		1,173 D	33.2%	66.6%	33.2%	66.6%
LAFAYETTE	5,543	742	4,801		4,059 D	13.4%	86.6%	13.4%	86.6%
LAFOURCHE	5,855	875	4,980		4,105 D	14.9%	85.1%	14.9%	85.1%
LA SALLE	2,548	504	2,018	26	1,514 D	19.8%	79.2%	20.0%	80.0%
LINCOLN	2,737	1,032	1,705		673 D	37.7%	62.3%	37.7%	62.3%
LIVINGSTON	2,803	343	2,460		2,117 D	12.2%	87.8%	12.2%	87.8%
MADISON	1,102	338	764		426 D	30.7%	69.3%	30.7%	69.3%
MOREHOUSE	2,337	478	1,859		1,381 D	20.5%	79.5%	20.5%	79.5%
NATCHITOCHES	3,644	1,105	2,536	3	1,431 D	30.3%	69.6%	30.3%	69.7%
ORLEANS	110,608	20,190	90,411	7	70,221 D	18.3%	81.7%	18.3%	81.7%
OUACHITA	8,956	2,627	6,329		3,702 D	29.3%	70.7%	29.3%	70.7%
PLAQUEMINES	2,090	335	1,755		1,420 D	16.0%	84.0%	16.0%	84.0%
POINTE COUPEE	1,707	271	1,436		1,165 D	15.9%	84.1%	15.9%	84.1%
RAPIDES	10,844	1,712	9,132		7,420 D	15.8%	84.2%	15.8%	84.2%
RED RIVER	1,384	409	975		566 D	29.6%	70.4%	29.6%	70.4%
RICHLAND	2,575	488	2,087		1,599 D	19.0%	81.0%	19.0%	81.0%
SABINE	3,087	1,039	2,048		1,009 D	33.7%	66.3%	33.7%	66.3%
ST BERNARD	2,124	80	2,044		1,964 D	3.8%	96.2%	3.8%	96.2%
ST CHARLES	2,119	174	1,945		1,771 D	8.2%	91.8%	8.2%	91.8%
ST HELENA	791	108	683		575 D	13.7%	86.3%	13.7%	86.3%
ST JAMES	1,652	265	1,387		1,122 D	16.0%	84.0%	16.0%	84.0%
ST JOHN THE BAPTIST	1,519	195	1,324		1,129 D	12.8%	87.2%	12.8%	87.2%
ST LANDRY	5,207	784	4,423		3,639 D	15.1%	84.9%	15.1%	84.9%
ST MARTIN	2,537	153	2,384		2,231 D	6.0%	94.0%	6.0%	94.0%
ST MARY	4,129	538	3,591		3,053 D	13.0%	87.0%	13.0%	87.0%
ST TAMMANY	4,153	703	3,450		2,747 D	16.9%	83.1%	16.9%	83.1%
TANGIPAHOA	5,991	1,572	4,419		2,847 D	26.2%	73.8%	26.2%	73.8%
TENSAS	798	160	638		478 D	20.1%	79.9%	20.1%	79.9%
TERREBONNE	4,089	550	3,539		2,989 D	13.5%	86.5%	13.5%	86.5%
UNION	2,568	803	1,765		962 D	31.3%	68.7%	31.3%	68.7%
VERMILLION	5,360	676	4,684		4,008 D	12.6%	87.4%	12.6%	87.4%
VERNON	4,097	1,022	3,075		2,053 D	24.9%	75.1%	24.9%	75.1%
WASHINGTON	5,216	406	4,810		4,404 D	7.8%	92.2%	7.8%	92.2%
WEBSTER	4,554	899	3,655		2,756 D	19.7%	80.3%	19.7%	80.3%

PRESIDENT 1948

Parish	Total Vote	Republican	Democratic	Other	Rep.-Dem. Plurality	%TV Rep.	%TV Dem.	%MV Rep.	%MV Dem.
ACADIA	6,678	784	2,382	3,512	1,598 D	11.7%	35.7%	24.8%	75.2%
ALLEN	3,219	241	1,996	982	1,755 D	7.5%	62.0%	10.8%	89.2%
ASCENSION	2,983	433	1,126	1,424	693 D	14.5%	37.7%	27.8%	72.2%
ASSUMPTION	1,834	469	362	1,003	107 R	25.6%	19.7%	56.4%	43.6%
AVOYELLES	7,105	285	1,356	5,464	1,071 D	4.0%	19.1%	17.4%	82.6%
BEAUREGARD	3,473	449	1,653	1,371	1,204 D	12.9%	47.6%	21.4%	78.6%
BIENVILLE	2,977	191	421	2,365	230 D	6.4%	14.1%	31.2%	68.8%
BOSSIER	3,876	338	1,147	2,391	809 D	8.7%	29.6%	22.8%	77.2%
CADDO	22,117	4,777	5,985	11,355	1,208 D	21.6%	27.1%	44.4%	55.6%
CALCASIEU	12,438	1,940	7,074	3,424	5,134 D	15.6%	56.9%	21.5%	78.5%
CALDWELL	1,748	151	777	820	626 D	8.6%	44.5%	16.3%	83.7%
CAMERON	1,123	87	742	294	655 D	7.7%	66.1%	10.5%	89.5%
CATAHOULA	1,666	86	515	1,065	429 D	5.2%	30.6%	9.5%	85.5%
CLAIBORNE	2,786	265	457	2,064	192 D	9.5%	16.4%	36.7%	63.3%
CONCORDIA	1,567	98	329	1,140	231 D	6.3%	21.0%	23.0%	77.0%
DE SOTO	2,778	270	617	1,891	347 D	9.7%	22.2%	30.4%	69.6%
EAST BATON ROUGE	21,464	4,585	8,560	8,319	3,975 D	21.4%	39.9%	34.9%	65.1%
EAST CARROLL	1,104	116	323	665	207 D	10.5%	29.3%	26.4%	73.6%
EAST FELICIANA	1,234	127	267	840	140 D	10.5%	21.6%	32.2%	67.8%
EVANGELINE	5,773	206	1,149	4,418	943 D	3.6%	19.9%	15.2%	84.8%
FRANKLIN	3,885	149	1,857	1,879	1,708 D	3.8%	47.8%	7.4%	92.6%
GRANT	2,840	273	1,120	1,447	847 D	9.6%	39.4%	19.6%	80.4%
IBERIA	6,157	2,910	1,015	2,232	1,895 R	47.3%	16.5%	74.1%	25.9%
IBERVILLE	3,067	506	1,697	864	1,191 D	16.5%	55.3%	23.0%	77.0%
JACKSON	2,289	169	713	1,407	544 D	7.4%	31.1%	19.2%	80.8%
JEFFERSON	16,168	2,620	4,654	8,894	2,034 D	16.2%	28.8%	36.0%	64.0%
JEFFERSON DAVIS	3,641	793	1,717	1,131	924 D	21.8%	47.2%	31.6%	68.4%
LAFAYETTE	7,599	2,068	1,787	3,744	281 R	27.2%	23.5%	53.6%	46.4%
LAFOURCHE	5,913	1,247	1,586	3,080	339 D	21.1%	26.8%	44.0%	56.0%
LA SALLE	2,751	266	716	1,769	450 D	9.7%	26.0%	27.1%	72.9%
LINCOLN	3,201	353	625	2,223	272 D	11.0%	19.5%	36.1%	63.9%
LIVINGSTON	3,471	264	1,841	1,366	1,577 D	7.6%	53.0%	12.5%	87.5%
MADISON	1,366	127	197	1,042	70 D	9.3%	14.4%	39.2%	60.8%
MOREHOUSE	2,814	242	1,177	1,395	935 D	8.6%	41.8%	17.1%	82.9%
NATCHITOCHES	5,352	763	1,692	2,897	929 D	14.3%	31.6%	31.1%	68.9%
ORLEANS	123,785	29,442	41,900	52,443	12,458 D	23.8%	33.8%	41.3%	58.7%
OUACHITA	10,802	1,729	4,213	4,860	2,484 D	16.0%	39.0%	29.1%	70.9%
PLAQUEMINES	2,774	90	77	2,607	13 R	3.2%	2.8%	53.9%	46.1%
POINTE COUPEE	1,979	198	402	1,379	204 D	10.0%	20.3%	33.0%	67.0%
RAPIDES	13,060	1,707	4,730	6,623	3,023 D	13.1%	36.2%	26.5%	73.5%
RED RIVER	2,106	113	452	1,541	339 D	5.4%	21.5%	20.0%	80.0%
RICHLAND	2,535	119	960	1,456	841 D	4.7%	37.9%	11.0%	89.0%
SABINE	4,126	469	1,405	2,252	936 D	11.4%	34.1%	25.0%	75.0%
ST BERNARD	2,445	107	91	2,247	16 R	4.4%	3.7%	54.0%	46.0%
ST CHARLES	2,410	286	914	1,210	628 D	11.9%	37.9%	23.8%	76.2%
ST HELENA	1,191	59	469	663	410 D	5.0%	39.4%	11.2%	88.8%
ST JAMES	2,117	453	859	805	406 D	21.4%	40.6%	34.5%	65.5%
ST JOHN THE BAPTIST	1,880	379	799	702	420 D	20.2%	42.5%	32.2%	67.8%
ST LANDRY	7,747	829	1,779	5,139	950 D	10.7%	22.9%	31.8%	68.2%
ST MARTIN	3,824	688	307	2,829	381 R	18.0%	8.0%	69.1%	30.9%
ST MARY	3,503	824	918	1,761	94 D	23.5%	26.2%	47.3%	52.7%
ST TAMMANY	5,041	790	1,184	3,087	394 D	15.7%	23.1%	40.4%	59.6%
TANGIPAHOA	7,408	1,287	2,184	3,937	897 D	17.4%	29.5%	37.1%	62.9%
TENSAS	1,045	72	239	734	167 D	6.9%	22.9%	23.2%	76.8%
TERREBONNE	4,334	1,048	1,262	2,024	214 D	24.2%	29.1%	45.4%	54.6%
UNION	2,856	259	724	1,873	465 D	9.1%	25.4%	26.3%	73.7%
VERMILLION	6,261	1,212	1,806	3,243	594 D	19.4%	28.8%	40.2%	59.8%
VERNON	4,582	296	1,939	2,347	1,643 D	6.5%	42.3%	13.2%	86.8%
WASHINGTON	7,801	371	3,267	4,163	2,896 D	4.8%	41.9%	10.2%	89.8%
WEBSTER	5,291	455	1,933	2,903	1,478 D	8.6%	36.5%	19.1%	80.9%

LOUISIANA

PRESIDENT 1944

Parish	Total Vote	Republican	Democratic	Other	Rep.-Dem. Plurality	Percentage Total Vote Rep.	Dem.	Major Vote Rep.	Dem.
WEST BATON ROUGE	1,132	87	1,045		958 D	7.7%	92.3%	7.7%	92.3%
WEST CARROLL	1,971	581	1,390		809 D	29.5%	70.5%	29.5%	70.5%
WEST FELICIANA	604	178	426		248 D	29.5%	70.5%	29.5%	70.5%
WINN	2,284	881	1,403		522 D	38.6%	61.4%	38.6%	61.4%
TOTAL	349,383	67,750	281,564	69	213,814 D	19.4%	80.6%	19.4%	80.6%

PRESIDENT 1948

Parish	Total Vote	Republican	Democratic	Other	Rep.-Dem. Plurality	Percentage Total Vote Rep.	Dem.	Major Vote Rep.	Dem.
WEST BATON ROUGE	1,167	141	557	469	416 D	12.1%	47.7%	20.2%	79.8%
WEST CARROLL	2,297	151	921	1,225	770 D	6.6%	40.1%	14.1%	85.9%
WEST FELICIANA	582	102	101	379	1 R	17.5%	17.4%	50.2%	49.8%
WINN	2,930	333	940	1,657	607 D	11.4%	32.1%	26.2%	73.8%
TOTAL	416,336	72,657	136,344	207,335	63,687 D	17.5%	32.7%	34.8%	65.2%

LOUISIANA

PRESIDENT 1952

Parish	Total Vote	Republican	Democratic	Other	Rep-Dem Plurality	Total Vote Rep.	Total Vote Dem.	Major Vote Rep.	Major Vote Dem.
ACADIA	10,030	4,167	5,863		1,696 D	41.5%	58.5%	41.5%	58.5%
ALLEN	5,215	1,461	3,754		2,293 D	28.0%	72.0%	28.0%	72.0%
ASCENSION	5,380	1,787	3,593		1,806 D	33.2%	66.8%	33.2%	66.8%
ASSUMPTION	2,857	1,210	1,647		437 D	42.4%	57.6%	42.4%	57.6%
AVOYELLES	6,884	2,479	4,405		1,926 D	36.0%	64.0%	36.0%	64.0%
BEAUREGARD	1,785	789	996		207 D	44.2%	55.8%	44.2%	55.8%
BIENVILLE	3,740	1,986	1,754		232 R	53.1%	46.9%	53.1%	46.9%
BOSSIER	6,360	3,677	2,683		994 R	57.8%	42.2%	57.8%	42.2%
CADDO	42,404	27,850	14,554		13,296 R	65.7%	34.3%	65.7%	34.3%
CALCASIEU	26,916	11,102	15,814		4,712 D	41.2%	58.8%	41.2%	58.8%
CALDWELL	2,123	961	1,162		201 D	45.3%	54.7%	45.3%	54.7%
CAMERON	1,689	684	1,005		321 D	40.5%	59.5%	40.5%	59.5%
CATAHOULA	2,220	884	1,336		452 D	39.8%	60.2%	39.8%	60.2%
CLAIBORNE	4,326	2,796	1,530		1,266 R	64.6%	35.4%	64.6%	35.4%
CONCORDIA	2,362	1,110	1,252		142 D	47.0%	53.0%	47.0%	53.0%
DE SOTO	3,981	2,303	1,678		625 R	57.8%	42.2%	57.8%	42.2%
EAST BATON ROUGE	42,798	19,693	23,105		3,412 D	46.0%	54.0%	46.0%	54.0%
EAST CARROLL	1,675	757	918		161 D	45.2%	54.8%	45.2%	54.8%
EAST FELICIANA	1,895	876	1,019		143 D	46.2%	53.8%	46.2%	53.8%
EVANGELINE	5,843	2,445	3,398		953 D	41.8%	58.2%	41.8%	58.2%
FRANKLIN	4,447	1,614	2,833		1,219 D	36.3%	63.7%	36.3%	63.7%
GRANT	4,089	1,443	2,646		1,203 D	35.3%	64.7%	35.3%	64.7%
IBERIA	9,709	5,669	4,040		1,629 R	58.4%	41.6%	58.4%	41.6%
IBERVILLE	5,207	1,710	3,497		1,787 D	32.8%	67.2%	32.8%	67.2%
JACKSON	4,431	1,614	2,817		1,203 D	36.4%	63.6%	36.4%	63.6%
JEFFERSON	36,455	17,090	19,365		2,275 D	46.9%	53.1%	46.9%	53.1%
JEFFERSON DAVIS	7,031	3,447	3,584		137 D	49.0%	51.0%	49.0%	51.0%
LAFAYETTE	12,913	6,470	6,443		27 R	50.1%	49.9%	50.1%	49.9%
LAFOURCHE	9,135	3,739	5,396		1,657 D	40.9%	59.1%	40.9%	59.1%
LA SALLE	3,693	1,692	2,001		309 D	45.8%	54.2%	45.8%	54.2%
LINCOLN	5,083	3,074	2,009		1,065 R	60.5%	39.5%	60.5%	39.5%
LIVINGSTON	5,014	1,436	3,578		2,142 D	28.6%	71.4%	28.6%	71.4%
MADISON	1,948	1,253	695		558 R	64.3%	35.7%	64.3%	35.7%
MOREHOUSE	5,573	2,567	3,006		439 D	46.1%	53.9%	46.1%	53.9%
NATCHITOCHES	6,980	3,104	3,876		772 D	44.5%	55.5%	44.5%	55.5%
ORLEANS	175,571	85,572	89,999		4,127 D	48.7%	51.3%	48.7%	51.3%
OUACHITA	18,617	8,842	9,775		933 D	47.5%	52.5%	47.5%	52.5%
PLAQUEMINES	3,625	3,370	255		3,115 R	93.0%	7.0%	93.0%	7.0%
POINTE COUPEE	2,559	1,174	1,385		211 D	45.9%	54.1%	45.9%	54.1%
RAPIDES	23,325	9,749	13,576		3,827 D	41.8%	58.2%	41.8%	58.2%
RED RIVER	2,596	774	1,822		1,048 D	29.8%	70.2%	29.8%	70.2%
RICHLAND	4,144	1,645	2,499		854 D	39.7%	60.3%	39.7%	60.3%
SABINE	5,321	2,039	3,282		1,243 D	38.3%	61.7%	38.3%	61.7%
ST BERNARD	4,384	2,267	2,117		150 R	51.7%	48.3%	51.7%	48.3%
ST CHARLES	3,765	1,086	2,679		1,593 D	28.8%	71.2%	28.8%	71.2%
ST HELENA	1,481	586	895		309 D	39.6%	60.4%	39.6%	60.4%
ST JAMES	3,518	1,353	2,165		812 D	38.5%	61.5%	38.5%	61.5%
ST JOHN THE BAPTIST	2,786	654	2,132		1,478 D	23.5%	76.5%	23.5%	76.5%
ST LANDRY	10,064	5,303	4,761		542 R	52.7%	47.3%	52.7%	47.3%
ST MARTIN	3,566	1,554	2,012		458 D	43.6%	56.4%	43.6%	56.4%
ST MARY	8,666	4,417	4,249		168 R	51.0%	49.0%	51.0%	49.0%
ST TAMMANY	8,063	3,598	4,465		867 D	44.6%	55.4%	44.6%	55.4%
TANGIPAHOA	11,016	5,166	5,850		684 D	46.9%	53.1%	46.9%	53.1%
TENSAS	1,391	703	688		15 R	50.5%	49.5%	50.5%	49.5%
TERREBONNE	8,100	3,848	4,252		404 D	47.5%	52.5%	47.5%	52.5%
UNION	3,949	1,894	2,055		161 D	48.0%	52.0%	48.0%	52.0%
VERMILION	9,129	3,868	5,261		1,393 D	42.4%	57.6%	42.4%	57.6%
VERNON	5,962	2,130	3,832		1,702 D	35.7%	64.3%	35.7%	64.3%
WASHINGTON	9,852	2,432	7,420		4,988 D	24.7%	75.3%	24.7%	75.3%
WEBSTER	7,986	3,442	4,544		1,102 D	43.1%	56.9%	43.1%	56.9%

PRESIDENT 1956

Parish	Total Vote	Republican	Democratic	Other	Rep-Dem Plurality	Total Vote Rep.	Total Vote Dem.	Major Vote Rep.	Major Vote Dem.
ACADIA	10,517	4,204	6,122	191	1,918 D	40.0%	58.2%	40.7%	59.3%
ALLEN	4,893	2,469	2,284	140	185 R	50.5%	46.7%	51.9%	48.1%
ASCENSION	4,535	1,853	2,606	76	753 D	40.9%	57.5%	41.6%	58.4%
ASSUMPTION	3,096	1,708	1,282	106	426 R	55.2%	41.4%	57.1%	42.9%
AVOYELLES	7,319	3,255	3,628	436	373 D	44.5%	49.6%	47.3%	52.7%
BEAUREGARD	5,146	2,711	2,276	159	435 R	52.7%	44.2%	54.4%	45.6%
BIENVILLE	3,100	1,515	815	770	700 R	48.9%	26.3%	65.0%	35.0%
BOSSIER	6,345	3,107	1,954	1,284	1,153 R	49.0%	30.8%	61.4%	38.6%
CADDO	38,849	23,432	10,780	4,637	12,652 R	60.3%	27.7%	68.5%	31.5%
CALCASIEU	26,733	13,760	12,255	718	1,505 R	51.5%	45.8%	52.9%	47.1%
CALDWELL	1,669	587	468	614	119 R	35.2%	28.0%	55.6%	44.4%
CAMERON	1,360	547	794	19	247 D	40.2%	58.4%	40.8%	59.2%
CATAHOULA	1,802	845	707	250	138 R	46.9%	39.2%	54.4%	45.6%
CLAIBORNE	3,886	2,084	810	992	1,274 R	53.6%	20.8%	72.0%	28.0%
CONCORDIA	2,116	841	699	576	142 R	39.7%	33.0%	54.6%	45.4%
DE SOTO	3,771	2,011	1,206	554	805 R	53.3%	32.0%	62.5%	37.5%
EAST BATON ROUGE	42,331	24,018	17,072	1,241	6,946 R	56.7%	40.3%	58.5%	41.5%
EAST CARROLL	1,347	415	545	387	130 D	30.8%	40.5%	43.2%	56.8%
EAST FELICIANA	2,425	912	1,304	219	392 D	37.5%	53.8%	41.2%	58.8%
EVANGELINE	5,680	2,170	3,336	174	1,166 D	38.2%	58.7%	39.4%	60.6%
FRANKLIN	3,457	1,130	1,352	975	222 D	32.7%	39.1%	45.5%	54.5%
GRANT	3,539	1,630	1,542	367	88 R	46.1%	43.6%	51.4%	48.6%
IBERIA	10,615	6,733	3,544	338	3,189 R	63.4%	33.4%	65.5%	34.5%
IBERVILLE	3,924	1,843	2,018	63	175 D	47.0%	51.4%	47.7%	52.3%
JACKSON	2,862	1,553	916	393	637 R	54.3%	32.0%	62.9%	37.1%
JEFFERSON	42,499	24,324	16,577	1,598	7,747 R	57.2%	39.0%	59.5%	40.5%
JEFFERSON DAVIS	6,626	4,170	2,346	110	1,824 R	62.9%	35.4%	64.0%	36.0%
LAFAYETTE	11,753	6,711	4,695	347	2,016 R	57.1%	39.9%	58.8%	41.2%
LAFOURCHE	9,528	5,741	3,466	321	2,275 R	60.3%	36.4%	62.4%	37.6%
LA SALLE	3,062	1,885	951	226	934 R	61.6%	31.1%	66.5%	33.5%
LINCOLN	4,520	2,676	1,014	830	1,662 R	59.2%	22.4%	72.5%	27.5%
LIVINGSTON	4,372	1,628	2,571	173	943 D	37.2%	58.8%	38.8%	61.2%
MADISON	1,692	461	276	955	185 R	27.2%	16.3%	62.6%	37.4%
MOREHOUSE	5,182	1,850	1,512	1,820	338 R	35.7%	29.2%	55.0%	45.0%
NATCHITOCHES	5,770	3,203	2,028	539	1,175 R	55.5%	35.1%	61.2%	38.8%
ORLEANS	164,634	93,082	64,958	6,594	28,124 R	56.5%	39.5%	58.9%	41.1%
OUACHITA	15,158	7,094	4,372	3,692	2,722 R	46.8%	28.8%	61.9%	38.1%
PLAQUEMINES	3,692	2,998	534	160	2,464 R	81.2%	14.5%	84.9%	15.1%
POINTE COUPEE	2,958	1,542	1,332	84	210 R	52.1%	45.2%	53.7%	46.3%
RAPIDES	16,911	9,105	5,961	1,845	3,144 R	53.8%	35.2%	60.4%	39.6%
RED RIVER	1,788	661	803	324	142 D	37.0%	44.9%	45.2%	54.8%
RICHLAND	3,557	1,063	1,094	1,400	31 D	29.9%	30.8%	49.3%	50.7%
SABINE	4,134	2,086	1,800	248	286 R	50.5%	43.5%	53.7%	46.3%
ST BERNARD	7,217	3,648	3,283	286	365 R	50.5%	45.5%	52.6%	47.4%
ST CHARLES	4,177	2,417	1,671	89	746 R	57.9%	40.0%	59.1%	40.9%
ST HELENA	1,689	545	997	147	452 D	32.3%	59.0%	35.3%	64.7%
ST JAMES	3,759	1,849	1,832	78	17 R	49.2%	48.7%	50.2%	49.8%
ST JOHN THE BAPTIST	2,714	1,372	1,278	64	94 R	50.6%	47.1%	51.8%	48.2%
ST LANDRY	9,970	5,141	4,435	394	706 R	51.6%	44.5%	53.7%	46.3%
ST MARTIN	3,780	1,615	2,069	96	454 D	42.7%	54.7%	43.8%	56.2%
ST MARY	6,653	4,097	2,395	171	1,702 R	61.5%	35.9%	63.1%	36.9%
ST TAMMANY	7,639	3,965	3,373	301	592 R	51.9%	44.2%	54.5%	45.5%
TANGIPAHOA	11,135	5,788	4,831	566	957 R	51.7%	43.6%	54.5%	45.5%
TENSAS	1,026	359	324	343	35 R	35.0%	31.6%	52.6%	47.4%
TERREBONNE	7,684	4,983	2,460	241	2,523 R	64.8%	32.0%	66.9%	33.1%
UNION	3,418	1,384	878	1,156	506 R	40.5%	25.7%	61.2%	38.8%
VERMILION	8,695	3,877	4,564	254	687 D	44.6%	52.5%	45.9%	54.1%
VERNON	4,762	2,372	2,158	232	214 R	49.8%	45.3%	52.4%	47.6%
WASHINGTON	8,047	3,081	4,658	308	1,577 D	38.3%	57.9%	39.8%	60.2%
WEBSTER	6,733	3,280	2,352	1,101	928 R	48.7%	34.9%	58.2%	41.8%

LOUISIANA

PRESIDENT 1952

Parish	Total Vote	Republican	Democratic	Other	Rep.-Dem. Plurality	Percentage — Total Vote Rep.	Dem.	Major Vote Rep.	Dem.
WEST BATON ROUGE	1,984	704	1,280		576 D	35.5%	64.5%	35.5%	64.5%
WEST CARROLL	3,438	1,398	2,040		642 D	40.7%	59.3%	40.7%	59.3%
WEST FELICIANA	782	503	279		224 R	64.3%	35.7%	64.3%	35.7%
WINN	4,121	1,915	2,206		291 D	46.5%	53.5%	46.5%	53.5%
TOTAL	651,952	306,925	345,027		38,102 D	47.1%	52.9%	47.1%	52.9%

PRESIDENT 1956

Parish	Total Vote	Republican	Democratic	Other	Rep.-Dem. Plurality	Percentage — Total Vote Rep.	Dem.	Major Vote Rep.	Dem.
WEST BATON ROUGE	2,314	1,035	1,208	71	173 D	44.7%	52.2%	46.1%	53.9%
WEST CARROLL	2,622	658	875	1,089	217 D	25.1%	33.4%	42.9%	57.1%
WEST FELICIANA	784	442	296	46	146 R	56.4%	37.8%	59.9%	40.1%
WINN	3,503	1,736	1,225	542	511 R	49.6%	35.0%	58.6%	41.4%
TOTAL	617,544	329,047	243,977	44,520	85,070 R	53.3%	39.5%	57.4%	42.6%

LOUISIANA

PRESIDENT 1960

Parish	Total Vote	Republican	Democratic	Other	Rep.-Dem. Plurality	TV Rep.	TV Dem.	MV Rep.	MV Dem.
ACADIA	15,084	2,616	11,440	1,028	8,824 D	17.3%	75.8%	18.6%	81.4%
ALLEN	5,215	1,676	3,719	820	2,043 D	27.0%	59.8%	31.1%	68.9%
ASCENSION	7,610	1,012	5,689	909	4,677 D	13.3%	74.8%	15.1%	84.9%
ASSUMPTION	4,211	766	3,019	426	2,253 D	18.2%	71.7%	20.2%	79.8%
AVOYELLES	10,035	1,270	7,625	1,140	6,355 D	12.7%	76.0%	14.3%	85.7%
BEAUREGARD	5,965	2,432	2,903	630	471 D	40.8%	48.7%	45.6%	54.4%
BIENVILLE	3,548	1,230	625	1,693	605 R	34.7%	17.6%	66.3%	33.7%
BOSSIER	8,720	3,429	2,198	3,093	1,231 R	39.3%	25.2%	60.9%	39.1%
CADDO	46,301	25,139	11,481	9,681	13,658 R	54.3%	24.8%	68.6%	31.4%
CALCASIEU	37,627	10,243	24,233	3,151	13,990 D	27.2%	64.4%	29.7%	70.3%
CALDWELL	2,041	716	694	631	22 R	35.1%	34.0%	50.8%	49.2%
CAMERON	2,340	322	1,944	74	1,622 D	13.8%	83.1%	14.2%	85.8%
CATAHOULA	2,132	971	558	603	413 R	45.5%	26.2%	63.5%	36.5%
CLAIBORNE	3,854	1,336	558	2,029	647 R	34.7%	12.7%	73.2%	26.8%
CONCORDIA	3,331	1,009	768	1,554	241 R	30.3%	23.1%	56.8%	43.2%
DE SOTO	4,439	1,603	1,183	1,653	420 R	36.1%	26.7%	57.5%	42.5%
EAST BATON ROUGE	56,435	17,749	26,326	12,360	8,577 D	31.4%	46.6%	40.3%	59.7%
EAST CARROLL	1,524	448	364	712	84 R	29.4%	23.9%	55.2%	44.8%
EAST FELICIANA	1,927	313	475	1,139	162 D	16.2%	24.6%	39.7%	60.3%
EVANGELINE	9,764	1,105	7,865	794	6,760 D	11.3%	80.6%	12.3%	87.7%
FRANKLIN	4,039	1,336	1,213	1,490	123 R	33.1%	30.0%	52.4%	47.6%
GRANT	3,882	1,254	1,219	1,409	35 R	32.3%	31.4%	50.7%	49.3%
IBERIA	15,470	3,551	9,235	2,684	5,684 D	23.0%	59.7%	27.8%	72.2%
IBERVILLE	6,309	1,000	4,558	751	3,558 D	15.9%	72.2%	18.0%	82.0%
JACKSON	4,100	1,799	1,398	903	401 R	43.9%	34.1%	56.3%	43.7%
JEFFERSON	62,638	17,215	32,119	13,304	14,904 D	27.5%	51.3%	34.9%	65.1%
JEFFERSON DAVIS	8,712	2,251	5,904	557	3,653 D	25.8%	67.8%	27.6%	72.4%
LAFAYETTE	22,684	6,047	14,132	2,505	8,085 D	25.7%	62.3%	30.0%	70.0%
LAFOURCHE	16,055	2,930	12,244	881	9,314 D	13.2%	76.3%	19.3%	80.7%
LA SALLE	3,842	2,123	843	876	1,280 R	55.3%	21.9%	71.6%	28.4%
LINCOLN	5,109	2,766	1,051	1,292	1,715 R	54.1%	20.6%	72.5%	27.5%
LIVINGSTON	6,628	954	2,881	2,793	1,927 D	14.4%	43.5%	24.9%	75.1%
MADISON	1,888	629	235	1,024	394 R	33.3%	12.4%	72.6%	27.4%
MOREHOUSE	4,780	2,551	1,085	1,144	1,466 R	53.4%	22.7%	70.2%	29.8%
NATCHITOCHES	7,060	2,562	2,781	1,717	219 D	36.3%	39.4%	48.0%	52.0%
ORLEANS	175,767	47,111	87,242	41,414	40,131 D	26.8%	49.6%	35.1%	64.9%
OUACHITA	19,291	10,525	5,202	3,564	5,323 R	54.6%	27.0%	66.9%	33.1%
PLAQUEMINES	5,146	712	1,087	3,347	375 D	13.8%	21.1%	39.6%	60.4%
POINTE COUPEE	4,574	674	2,953	485	2,279 D	14.6%	64.5%	18.6%	81.4%
RAPIDES	23,782	8,155	9,651	5,976	1,496 D	34.3%	40.6%	45.8%	54.2%
RED RIVER	1,917	406	377	1,134	29 R	21.2%	19.7%	51.9%	48.1%
RICHLAND	3,869	1,378	996	1,495	382 R	35.6%	25.6%	58.0%	42.0%
SABINE	5,889	2,419	2,412	1,058	7 R	41.1%	41.0%	50.1%	49.9%
ST BERNARD	10,949	1,431	4,660	4,858	3,229 D	13.1%	42.6%	23.5%	76.5%
ST CHARLES	6,602	1,377	4,708	517	3,331 D	20.9%	71.3%	22.6%	77.4%
ST HELENA	1,809	296	678	835	382 D	16.4%	37.5%	30.4%	69.6%
ST JAMES	5,314	620	4,362	332	3,742 D	11.7%	82.1%	12.4%	87.6%
ST JOHN THE BAPTIST	4,720	488	3,782	450	3,294 D	10.3%	80.1%	11.4%	88.6%
ST LANDRY	20,262	3,083	14,625	2,554	11,542 D	15.2%	72.2%	17.4%	82.6%
ST MARTIN	7,063	858	5,506	699	4,648 D	12.1%	78.0%	13.5%	86.5%
ST MARY	10,832	2,992	6,671	1,169	3,679 D	27.6%	61.6%	31.0%	69.0%
ST TAMMANY	11,063	2,850	5,179	3,034	2,329 D	25.8%	46.8%	35.5%	64.5%
TANGIPAHOA	14,351	3,285	6,648	4,418	3,363 D	22.5%	46.3%	33.1%	66.9%
TENSAS	1,208	510	247	451	263 R	42.2%	20.4%	67.4%	32.6%
TERREBONNE	13,210	3,126	8,992	1,092	5,866 D	23.7%	68.1%	25.8%	74.2%
UNION	4,063	2,017	1,034	1,012	983 R	49.6%	25.4%	66.1%	33.9%
VERMILION	14,595	2,170	11,257	1,168	9,087 D	14.5%	77.1%	16.2%	83.8%
VERNON	6,160	1,991	3,145	1,024	1,154 D	32.3%	51.1%	38.8%	61.2%
WASHINGTON	11,400	1,847	5,678	3,875	3,831 D	16.2%	49.8%	24.5%	75.5%
WEBSTER	7,667	3,139	1,273	3,255	1,866 R	40.9%	16.6%	71.1%	28.9%

PRESIDENT 1964

Parish	Total Vote	Republican	Democratic	Other	Rep.-Dem. Plurality	TV Rep.	TV Dem.	MV Rep.	MV Dem.
ACADIA	15,169	6,706	9,463		2,757 D	41.5%	58.5%	41.5%	58.5%
ALLEN	5,491	2,704	3,787		1,083 D	41.7%	58.3%	41.7%	58.3%
ASCENSION	8,076	3,197	4,879		1,682 D	39.6%	60.4%	39.6%	60.4%
ASSUMPTION	5,168	2,112	3,056		944 D	40.9%	59.1%	40.9%	59.1%
AVOYELLES	9,976	4,874	5,102		228 D	48.9%	51.1%	48.9%	51.1%
BEAUREGARD	6,398	3,349	3,049		300 R	52.3%	47.7%	52.3%	47.7%
BIENVILLE	4,595	3,740	855		2,885 R	81.4%	18.6%	81.4%	18.6%
BOSSIER	11,759	9,822	1,937		7,885 R	83.5%	16.5%	83.5%	16.5%
CADDO	52,355	42,197	10,158		32,039 R	80.6%	19.4%	80.6%	19.4%
CALCASIEU	40,331	17,046	23,285		6,239 D	42.3%	57.7%	42.3%	57.7%
CALDWELL	3,143	2,534	609		1,925 R	80.6%	19.4%	80.6%	19.4%
CAMERON	2,447	871	1,576		705 D	35.6%	64.4%	35.6%	64.4%
CATAHOULA	2,947	2,387	560		1,827 R	81.0%	19.0%	81.0%	19.0%
CLAIBORNE	4,399	3,917	482		3,435 R	89.0%	11.0%	89.0%	11.0%
CONCORDIA	4,831	4,022	809		3,213 R	83.3%	16.7%	83.3%	16.7%
DE SOTO	5,208	3,954	1,254		2,700 R	75.9%	24.1%	75.9%	24.1%
EAST BATON ROUGE	63,116	36,964	26,152		10,812 R	58.6%	41.4%	58.6%	41.4%
EAST CARROLL	1,749	1,486	263		1,223 R	85.0%	15.0%	85.0%	15.0%
EAST FELICIANA	2,386	1,900	486		1,414 R	79.6%	20.4%	79.6%	20.4%
EVANGELINE	10,138	3,975	6,163		2,188 D	39.2%	60.8%	39.2%	60.8%
FRANKLIN	6,229	5,470	759		4,711 R	87.8%	12.2%	87.8%	12.2%
GRANT	4,746	3,292	1,454		1,838 R	69.4%	30.6%	69.4%	30.6%
IBERIA	16,337	8,196	8,141		55 R	50.2%	49.8%	50.2%	49.8%
IBERVILLE	7,877	3,432	4,445		1,013 D	43.6%	56.4%	43.6%	56.4%
JACKSON	6,073	4,521	1,552		2,969 R	74.4%	25.6%	74.4%	25.6%
JEFFERSON	68,965	37,161	31,804		5,357 R	53.9%	46.1%	53.9%	46.1%
JEFFERSON DAVIS	8,639	3,673	4,966		1,293 D	42.5%	57.5%	42.5%	57.5%
LAFAYETTE	26,885	12,398	14,487		2,089 D	46.1%	53.9%	46.1%	53.9%
LAFOURCHE	18,209	6,164	12,045		5,881 D	33.9%	66.1%	33.9%	66.1%
LA SALLE	5,183	4,319	864		3,455 R	83.3%	16.7%	83.3%	16.7%
LINCOLN	7,480	5,766	1,714		4,052 R	77.1%	22.9%	77.1%	22.9%
LIVINGSTON	9,017	5,508	3,509		1,999 R	61.1%	38.9%	61.1%	38.9%
MADISON	2,478	2,061	417		1,644 R	83.2%	16.8%	83.2%	16.8%
MOREHOUSE	7,113	6,222	891		5,331 R	87.5%	12.5%	87.5%	12.5%
NATCHITOCHES	8,500	5,525	2,975		2,550 R	65.0%	35.0%	65.0%	35.0%
ORLEANS	165,094	81,049	82,045		996 D	49.7%	50.3%	49.7%	50.3%
OUACHITA	25,198	21,024	4,174		16,850 R	83.4%	16.6%	83.4%	16.6%
PLAQUEMINES	5,679	4,904	775		4,129 R	86.4%	13.6%	86.4%	13.6%
POINTE COUPEE	4,574	2,327	2,247		80 R	50.9%	49.1%	50.9%	49.1%
RAPIDES	28,114	18,122	9,992		8,130 R	64.5%	35.5%	64.5%	35.5%
RED RIVER	2,559	2,235	334		1,901 R	87.0%	13.0%	87.0%	13.0%
RICHLAND	5,245	4,498	747		3,751 R	85.8%	14.2%	85.8%	14.2%
SABINE	6,246	4,165	2,081		2,084 R	66.7%	33.3%	66.7%	33.3%
ST BERNARD	14,220	8,055	6,175		1,880 R	56.6%	43.4%	56.6%	43.4%
ST CHARLES	7,800	2,715	5,085		2,370 D	34.8%	65.2%	34.8%	65.2%
ST HELENA	2,025	1,319	706		613 R	65.1%	34.9%	65.1%	34.9%
ST JAMES	5,681	1,467	4,214		2,747 D	25.8%	74.2%	25.8%	74.2%
ST JOHN THE BAPTIST	5,652	1,694	3,958		2,264 D	30.0%	70.0%	30.0%	70.0%
ST LANDRY	22,727	10,920	11,807		887 D	48.0%	52.0%	48.0%	52.0%
ST MARTIN	7,468	2,793	4,675		1,882 D	37.4%	62.6%	37.4%	62.6%
ST MARY	12,857	5,530	7,327		1,797 D	43.0%	57.0%	43.0%	57.0%
ST TAMMANY	14,577	7,883	6,694		1,189 R	54.1%	45.9%	54.1%	45.9%
TANGIPAHOA	16,841	9,732	7,109		2,623 R	57.8%	42.2%	57.8%	42.2%
TENSAS	1,847	1,655	192		1,463 R	89.6%	10.4%	89.6%	10.4%
TERREBONNE	15,306	6,729	8,577		1,848 D	44.0%	56.0%	44.0%	56.0%
UNION	5,689	4,534	1,155		3,379 R	79.7%	20.3%	79.7%	20.3%
VERMILION	14,188	4,984	9,204		4,220 D	35.1%	64.9%	35.1%	64.9%
VERNON	7,260	3,696	3,564		132 R	50.9%	49.1%	50.9%	49.1%
WASHINGTON	12,263	7,438	4,825		2,613 R	60.7%	39.3%	60.7%	39.3%
WEBSTER	9,932	8,177	1,755		6,422 R	82.3%	17.7%	82.3%	17.7%

LOUISIANA

PRESIDENT 1960

Parish	Total Vote	Republican	Democratic	Other	Rep.-Dem. Plurality	Percentage			
						Total Vote		Major Vote	
						Rep.	Dem.	Rep.	Dem.
WEST BATON ROUGE	3,141	390	2,315	436	1,925 D	12.4%	73.7%	14.4%	85.6%
WEST CARROLL	2,423	742	784	897	42 D	30.6%	32.4%	48.6%	51.4%
WEST FELICIANA	891	196	271	424	75 D	22.0%	30.4%	42.0%	58.0%
WINN	4,096	1,839	1,108	1,149	731 R	44.9%	27.1%	62.4%	37.6%
TOTAL	807,891	230,980	407,339	169,572	176,359 D	28.6%	50.4%	36.2%	63.8%

PRESIDENT 1964

Parish	Total Vote	Republican	Democratic	Other	Rep.-Dem. Plurality	Percentage			
						Total Vote		Major Vote	
						Rep.	Dem.	Rep.	Dem.
WEST BATON ROUGE	3,727	1,835	1,892		57 D	49.2%	50.8%	49.2%	50.8%
WEST CARROLL	3,412	3,017	395		2,622 R	88.4%	11.6%	88.4%	11.6%
WEST FELICIANA	1,120	897	223		674 R	80.1%	19.9%	80.1%	19.9%
WINN	5,559	4,366	1,193		3,173 R	78.5%	21.5%	78.5%	21.5%
TOTAL	896,293	509,225	387,068		122,157 R	56.8%	43.2%	56.8%	43.2%

LOUISIANA

OTHER VOTE COMPOSITION:

1920   Scattered.
1924   Scattered.
1928   Scattered.
1932   Scattered.
1936   Scattered.

1940   Scattered.
1944   Scattered.
1948   204,290 States Rights; 3,035 Progressive; 10 scattered.
1952
1956   Unpledged States Rights.

1960   Independent.
1964

SPECIAL CASES:

1924   A number of the scattered votes were write-ins for LaFollette, but the division of the scattered votes among individuals was not reported.

1948   States Rights candidates carried the state, leading or running second in all parishes.

1956   Unpledged States Rights electors carried several parishes and ran second in others.

1960   Independent electors carried a number of parishes and ran second in others.

MAINE

PRESIDENT 1920

County	Total Vote	Republican	Democratic	Other	Rep.-Dem. Plurality	Total Vote Rep.	Total Vote Dem.	Major Vote Rep.	Major Vote Dem.
ANDROSCOGGIN	15,724	9,565	5,757	402	3,808 R	60.8%	36.6%	62.4%	37.6%
AROOSTOOK	12,648	11,191	1,407	50	9,784 R	88.5%	11.1%	88.8%	11.2%
CUMBERLAND	35,585	24,623	10,484	478	14,139 R	69.2%	29.5%	70.1%	29.9%
FRANKLIN	5,526	3,820	1,668	38	2,152 R	69.1%	30.2%	69.6%	30.4%
HANCOCK	7,818	5,604	2,154	60	3,450 R	71.7%	27.6%	72.2%	27.8%
KENNEBEC	17,973	12,333	5,466	174	6,867 R	68.6%	30.4%	69.3%	30.7%
KNOX	8,183	4,979	2,971	233	2,008 R	60.8%	36.3%	62.6%	37.4%
LINCOLN	4,983	3,668	1,256	59	2,412 R	73.6%	25.2%	74.5%	25.5%
OXFORD	11,304	7,301	3,906	97	3,395 R	64.6%	34.6%	65.1%	34.9%
PENOBSCOT	20,398	14,145	6,110	143	8,035 R	69.3%	30.0%	69.8%	30.2%
PISCATAQUIS	5,886	4,049	1,788	49	2,261 R	68.8%	30.4%	69.4%	30.6%
SAGADAHOC	5,642	3,857	1,709	76	2,148 R	68.3%	30.3%	69.3%	30.7%
SOMERSET	9,592	6,533	2,770	289	3,763 R	68.1%	28.9%	70.2%	29.8%
WALDO	6,128	4,383	1,666	79	2,717 R	71.5%	27.2%	72.5%	27.5%
WASHINGTON	9,870	6,768	2,997	105	3,771 R	68.6%	30.4%	69.3%	30.7%
YORK	20,580	13,536	6,852	192	6,684 R	65.8%	33.3%	66.4%	33.6%
TOTAL	197,840	136,355	58,961	2,524	77,394 R	68.9%	29.8%	69.8%	30.2%

PRESIDENT 1924

County	Total Vote	Republican	Democratic	Other	Rep.-Dem. Plurality	Total Vote Rep.	Total Vote Dem.	Major Vote Rep.	Major Vote Dem.
ANDROSCOGGIN	16,187	9,680	4,733	1,774	4,947 R	59.8%	29.2%	67.2%	32.8%
AROOSTOOK	11,707	9,554	1,510	643	8,044 R	81.6%	12.9%	86.4%	13.6%
CUMBERLAND	35,719	26,187	7,078	2,454	19,109 R	73.3%	19.8%	78.7%	21.3%
FRANKLIN	4,681	3,389	1,123	169	2,266 R	72.4%	24.0%	75.1%	24.9%
HANCOCK	7,075	5,474	1,392	209	4,082 R	77.4%	19.7%	79.7%	20.3%
KENNEBEC	18,159	13,122	4,184	853	8,938 R	72.0%	23.0%	75.8%	24.2%
KNOX	7,028	4,919	1,770	339	3,149 R	70.0%	25.2%	73.5%	26.5%
LINCOLN	4,280	3,311	878	91	2,433 R	77.4%	20.5%	79.0%	21.0%
OXFORD	10,103	7,062	2,563	478	4,499 R	69.9%	25.4%	73.4%	26.6%
PENOBSCOT	20,128	15,081	3,618	1,429	11,463 R	74.9%	18.0%	80.7%	19.3%
PISCATAQUIS	5,308	4,031	974	303	3,057 R	75.9%	18.3%	80.5%	19.5%
SAGADAHOC	4,802	3,518	1,084	200	2,434 R	73.3%	22.6%	76.4%	23.6%
SOMERSET	9,285	6,855	1,822	608	5,033 R	73.8%	19.6%	79.0%	21.0%
WALDO	5,281	4,003	1,125	153	2,878 R	75.8%	21.3%	78.1%	21.9%
WASHINGTON	8,621	6,010	2,106	505	3,904 R	69.7%	24.4%	74.1%	25.9%
YORK	23,828	16,244	6,004	1,580	10,240 R	68.2%	25.2%	73.0%	27.0%
TOTAL	192,192	138,440	41,964	11,788	96,476 R	72.0%	21.8%	76.7%	23.3%

MAINE

PRESIDENT 1928

County	Total Vote	Republican	Democratic	Other	Rep.-Dem. Plurality	Total Vote Rep.	Total Vote Dem.	Major Vote Rep.	Major Vote Dem.
ANDROSCOGGIN	22,854	11,790	10,940	124	850 R	51.6%	47.9%	51.9%	48.1%
AROOSTOOK	20,357	14,545	5,771	41	8,774 R	71.4%	28.3%	71.6%	28.4%
CUMBERLAND	48,995	33,190	15,648	157	17,542 R	67.7%	31.9%	68.0%	32.0%
FRANKLIN	6,432	4,923	1,487	22	3,436 R	76.5%	23.1%	76.8%	23.2%
HANCOCK	9,946	8,140	1,773	33	6,367 R	81.8%	17.8%	82.1%	17.9%
KENNEBEC	23,859	15,541	8,226	92	7,315 R	65.1%	34.5%	65.4%	34.6%
KNOX	9,080	6,660	2,332	88	4,328 R	73.3%	25.7%	74.1%	25.9%
LINCOLN	5,669	4,470	1,181	18	3,289 R	78.8%	20.8%	79.1%	20.9%
OXFORD	13,490	9,409	4,015	66	5,394 R	69.7%	29.8%	70.1%	29.9%
PENOBSCOT	30,960	21,750	9,114	96	12,636 R	70.3%	29.4%	70.5%	29.5%
PISCATAQUIS	6,161	4,792	1,353	16	3,439 R	77.8%	22.0%	78.0%	22.0%
SAGADAHOC	6,208	4,605	1,583	20	3,022 R	74.2%	25.5%	74.4%	25.6%
SOMERSET	11,406	8,055	3,251	100	4,804 R	70.6%	28.5%	71.2%	28.8%
WALDO	6,294	4,851	1,402	41	3,449 R	77.1%	22.3%	77.6%	22.4%
WASHINGTON	11,639	8,531	3,073	35	5,458 R	73.3%	26.4%	73.5%	26.5%
YORK	28,820	18,671	10,030	119	8,641 R	64.8%	34.8%	65.1%	34.9%
TOTAL	262,170	179,923	81,179	1,068	98,744 R	68.6%	31.0%	68.9%	31.1%

PRESIDENT 1932

County	Total Vote	Republican	Democratic	Other	Rep.-Dem. Plurality	Total Vote Rep.	Total Vote Dem.	Major Vote Rep.	Major Vote Dem.
ANDROSCOGGIN	24,562	9,838	14,441	283	4,603 D	40.1%	58.8%	40.5%	59.5%
AROOSTOOK	23,631	14,054	9,409	168	4,645 R	59.5%	39.8%	59.9%	40.1%
CUMBERLAND	54,033	32,864	20,655	514	12,209 R	60.8%	38.2%	61.4%	38.6%
FRANKLIN	7,733	4,521	3,171	41	1,350 R	58.5%	41.0%	58.8%	41.2%
HANCOCK	12,396	7,942	4,369	85	3,573 R	64.1%	35.2%	64.5%	35.5%
KENNEBEC	26,797	14,451	12,110	236	2,341 R	53.9%	45.2%	54.4%	45.6%
KNOX	11,159	6,169	4,765	225	1,404 R	55.3%	42.7%	56.4%	43.6%
LINCOLN	7,309	4,666	2,602	41	2,064 R	63.8%	35.6%	64.2%	35.8%
OXFORD	15,673	8,264	7,179	230	1,085 R	52.7%	45.8%	53.5%	46.5%
PENOBSCOT	32,317	18,987	13,058	272	5,929 R	58.8%	40.4%	59.3%	40.7%
PISCATAQUIS	7,099	4,198	2,849	52	1,349 R	59.1%	40.1%	59.6%	40.4%
SAGADAHOC	7,037	4,220	2,763	54	1,457 R	60.0%	39.3%	60.4%	39.6%
SOMERSET	13,461	7,144	6,040	277	1,104 R	53.1%	44.9%	54.2%	45.8%
WALDO	8,467	4,505	3,907	55	598 R	53.2%	46.1%	53.6%	46.4%
WASHINGTON	14,451	7,507	6,829	115	678 R	51.9%	47.3%	52.4%	47.6%
YORK	32,319	17,301	14,760	258	2,541 R	53.5%	45.7%	54.0%	46.0%
TOTAL	298,444	166,631	128,907	2,906	37,724 R	55.8%	43.2%	56.4%	43.6%

MAINE

PRESIDENT 1936

County	Total Vote	Republican	Democratic	Other	Rep.-Dem. Plurality	Total Vote Rep.	Total Vote Dem.	Major Vote Rep.	Major Vote Dem.
ANDROSCOGGIN	27,477	10,480	16,657	340	6,177 D	38.1%	60.6%	38.6%	61.4%
AROOSTOOK	22,736	14,708	7,704	324	7,004 R	64.7%	33.9%	65.6%	34.4%
CUMBERLAND	54,030	30,021	22,895	1,114	7,126 R	55.6%	42.4%	56.7%	43.3%
FRANKLIN	7,928	4,957	2,859	112	2,098 R	62.5%	36.1%	63.4%	36.6%
HANCOCK	12,700	9,151	3,315	234	5,836 R	72.1%	26.1%	73.4%	26.6%
KENNEBEC	27,081	14,987	11,268	826	3,719 R	55.3%	41.6%	57.1%	42.9%
KNOX	10,879	6,567	3,991	321	2,576 R	60.4%	36.7%	62.2%	37.8%
LINCOLN	7,232	5,252	1,850	130	3,402 R	72.6%	25.6%	74.0%	26.0%
OXFORD	15,366	8,778	5,836	752	2,942 R	57.1%	38.0%	60.1%	39.9%
PENOBSCOT	31,368	19,077	9,732	2,559	9,345 R	60.8%	31.0%	65.2%	33.8%
PISCATAQUIS	7,295	4,057	3,051	187	1,006 R	55.6%	41.8%	57.1%	42.9%
SAGADAHOC	7,130	3,707	3,273	150	434 R	52.0%	45.9%	53.1%	46.9%
SOMERSET	13,281	7,558	5,282	441	2,276 R	56.9%	39.8%	58.9%	41.1%
WALDO	8,172	5,309	2,678	185	2,631 R	65.0%	32.8%	66.5%	33.5%
WASHINGTON	14,495	6,387	7,925	183	1,538 D	44.1%	54.7%	44.6%	55.4%
YORK	37,070	17,827	18,017	1,226	190 D	48.1%	48.6%	49.7%	50.3%
TOTAL	304,240	168,823	126,333	9,084	42,490 R	55.5%	41.5%	57.2%	42.8%

PRESIDENT 1940

County	Total Vote	Republican	Democratic	Other	Rep.-Dem. Plurality	Total Vote Rep.	Total Vote Dem.	Major Vote Rep.	Major Vote Dem.
ANDROSCOGGIN	29,707	10,394	19,273	40	8,879 D	35.0%	64.9%	35.0%	65.0%
AROOSTOOK	23,804	13,888	9,877	39	4,011 R	58.3%	41.5%	58.4%	41.6%
CUMBERLAND	56,782	29,795	26,911	76	2,884 R	52.5%	47.4%	52.5%	47.5%
FRANKLIN	7,779	4,548	3,224	7	1,324 R	58.5%	41.4%	58.5%	41.5%
HANCOCK	12,807	8,539	4,255	13	4,224 R	66.4%	33.5%	66.5%	33.6%
KENNEBEC	30,765	14,877	15,861	27	984 D	48.4%	51.6%	48.4%	51.6%
KNOX	10,747	6,530	4,197	20	2,333 R	60.8%	39.1%	60.9%	39.1%
LINCOLN	7,664	5,244	2,415	25	2,829 R	68.4%	31.5%	68.5%	31.5%
OXFORD	16,183	8,656	7,502	25	1,154 R	53.5%	46.4%	53.6%	46.4%
PENOBSCOT	33,471	18,674	14,757	40	3,917 R	55.8%	44.1%	55.9%	44.1%
PISCATAQUIS	7,312	3,806	3,499	7	307 R	52.1%	47.9%	52.1%	47.9%
SAGADAHOC	8,092	3,504	4,575	13	1,071 D	43.3%	56.5%	43.4%	56.6%
SOMERSET	14,088	7,526	6,534	28	992 R	53.4%	46.4%	53.5%	46.5%
WALDO	8,398	5,170	3,214	14	1,956 R	61.6%	38.3%	61.7%	38.3%
WASHINGTON	14,326	6,253	8,048	25	1,795 D	43.6%	56.2%	43.7%	56.3%
YORK	38,855	16,547	22,276	32	5,729 D	42.6%	57.3%	42.6%	57.4%
TOTAL	320,841	163,951	156,478	411	7,473 R	51.1%	48.8%	51.2%	48.8%

MAINE

PRESIDENT 1944

County	Total Vote	Republican	Democratic	Other	Rep.-Dem. Plurality	Total Vote Rep.	Total Vote Dem.	Major Vote Rep.	Major Vote Dem.
ANDROSCOGGIN	30,039	10,927	19,078	34	8,151 D	36.4%	63.5%	36.4%	63.6%
AROOSTOOK	19,717	11,678	8,017	22	3,661 R	59.2%	40.7%	59.3%	40.7%
CUMBERLAND	56,278	29,349	26,857	72	2,492 R	52.2%	47.7%	52.2%	47.8%
FRANKLIN	6,777	4,127	2,646	4	1,481 R	60.9%	39.0%	60.9%	39.1%
HANCOCK	10,396	7,143	3,241	12	3,902 R	68.7%	31.2%	68.8%	31.2%
KENNEBEC	28,430	14,335	14,070	25	265 R	50.4%	49.5%	50.5%	49.5%
KNOX	9,363	5,590	3,758	15	1,832 R	59.7%	40.1%	59.8%	40.2%
LINCOLN	7,030	4,919	2,102	9	2,817 R	70.0%	29.9%	70.0%	29.9%
OXFORD	14,442	8,053	6,377	12	1,676 R	55.8%	44.2%	55.8%	44.2%
PENOBSCOT	30,264	16,934	13,292	38	3,642 R	56.0%	43.9%	56.0%	44.0%
PISCATAQUIS	6,494	3,536	2,957	1	579 R	54.5%	45.5%	54.5%	45.5%
SAGADAHOC	7,889	3,883	4,003	3	120 D	49.2%	50.7%	49.2%	50.8%
SOMERSET	12,523	7,167	5,331	25	1,836 R	57.2%	42.6%	57.3%	42.7%
WALDO	6,104	4,291	1,807	6	2,484 R	70.3%	29.6%	70.4%	29.6%
WASHINGTON	11,107	5,380	5,709	18	329 D	48.4%	51.4%	48.5%	51.5%
YORK	39,547	18,122	21,386	39	3,264 D	45.8%	54.1%	45.9%	54.1%
TOTAL	296,400	155,434	140,631	335	14,803 R	52.4%	47.4%	52.5%	47.5%

PRESIDENT 1948

County	Total Vote	Republican	Democratic	Other	Rep.-Dem. Plurality	Total Vote Rep.	Total Vote Dem.	Major Vote Rep.	Major Vote Dem.
ANDROSCOGGIN	29,165	11,443	17,405	317	5,962 D	39.2%	59.7%	39.7%	60.3%
AROOSTOOK	16,740	9,489	7,183	68	2,276 R	56.5%	42.9%	56.8%	43.2%
CUMBERLAND	49,885	30,284	18,913	688	11,371 R	60.7%	37.9%	61.6%	38.4%
FRANKLIN	5,920	3,741	2,135	44	1,606 R	63.2%	36.1%	63.7%	36.3%
HANCOCK	8,830	6,863	1,878	89	4,985 R	77.7%	21.3%	78.5%	21.5%
KENNEBEC	25,260	13,923	11,163	174	2,760 R	55.1%	44.2%	55.5%	44.5%
KNOX	7,395	5,374	1,924	97	3,450 R	72.7%	26.0%	73.6%	26.4%
LINCOLN	5,893	4,743	1,095	55	3,648 R	80.5%	18.6%	81.2%	18.8%
OXFORD	12,782	7,444	5,183	155	2,261 R	58.2%	40.5%	59.0%	41.0%
PENOBSCOT	27,315	16,367	10,705	243	5,662 R	59.9%	39.2%	60.5%	39.5%
PISCATAQUIS	5,438	3,227	2,181	30	1,046 R	59.3%	40.1%	59.7%	40.3%
SAGADAHOC	6,371	3,745	2,556	70	1,189 R	58.8%	40.1%	59.4%	40.6%
SOMERSET	10,418	6,301	4,034	83	2,267 R	60.5%	38.7%	61.0%	39.0%
WALDO	5,890	4,371	1,469	50	2,902 R	74.2%	24.9%	74.8%	25.2%
WASHINGTON	8,748	5,130	3,538	80	1,592 R	58.6%	40.4%	59.2%	40.8%
YORK	38,737	17,819	20,554	364	2,735 D	46.0%	53.1%	46.4%	53.6%
TOTAL	264,787	150,234	111,916	2,637	38,318 R	56.7%	42.3%	57.3%	42.7%

MAINE

PRESIDENT 1952

County	Total Vote	Republican	Democratic	Other	Rep.-Dem. Plurality	Total Vote Rep.	Total Vote Dem.	Major Vote Rep.	Major Vote Dem.
ANDROSCOGGIN	35,676	18,049	17,560	67	489 R	50.6%	49.2%	50.7%	49.3%
AROOSTOOK	24,476	16,851	7,561	64	9,290 R	68.8%	30.9%	69.0%	31.0%
CUMBERLAND	67,898	46,957	20,831	110	26,126 R	69.2%	30.6%	69.3%	30.7%
FRANKLIN	8,036	5,885	2,137	14	3,748 R	73.2%	26.6%	73.4%	26.6%
HANCOCK	12,734	10,596	2,111	27	8,485 R	83.2%	16.6%	83.4%	16.6%
KENNEBEC	33,351	21,207	12,113	31	9,094 R	63.6%	36.3%	63.6%	36.4%
KNOX	11,227	8,793	2,414	20	6,379 R	78.3%	21.5%	78.5%	21.5%
LINCOLN	8,074	6,766	1,299	9	5,467 R	83.8%	16.1%	83.9%	16.1%
OXFORD	17,375	11,575	5,757	43	5,818 R	66.6%	33.1%	66.6%	33.3%
PENOBSCOT	35,885	24,614	11,222	49	13,392 R	68.6%	31.3%	68.7%	31.3%
PISCATAQUIS	6,923	4,652	2,261	10	2,391 R	67.2%	32.7%	67.3%	32.7%
SAGADAHOC	8,668	5,799	2,850	19	2,949 R	66.9%	32.9%	67.0%	33.0%
SOMERSET	14,649	9,805	4,815	29	4,990 R	66.9%	32.9%	67.1%	32.9%
WALDO	7,925	6,363	1,545	17	4,818 R	80.3%	19.5%	80.5%	19.5%
WASHINGTON	11,225	7,396	3,806	23	3,590 R	65.9%	33.9%	66.0%	34.0%
YORK	47,664	27,045	20,524	95	6,521 R	56.7%	43.1%	56.9%	43.1%
TOTAL	351,786	232,353	118,806	627	113,547 R	66.0%	33.8%	66.2%	33.8%

PRESIDENT 1956

County	Total Vote	Republican	Democratic	Other	Rep.-Dem. Plurality	Total Vote Rep.	Total Vote Dem.	Major Vote Rep.	Major Vote Dem.
ANDROSCOGGIN	36,227	20,385	15,842		4,543 R	56.3%	43.7%	56.3%	43.7%
AROOSTOOK	22,090	16,001	6,089		9,912 R	72.4%	27.6%	72.4%	27.6%
CUMBERLAND	69,134	49,696	19,438		30,258 R	71.9%	28.1%	71.9%	28.1%
FRANKLIN	7,987	6,307	1,680		4,627 R	79.0%	21.0%	79.0%	21.0%
HANCOCK	13,020	11,316	1,704		9,612 R	86.9%	13.1%	86.9%	13.1%
KENNEBEC	34,511	23,028	11,483		11,545 R	66.7%	33.3%	66.7%	33.3%
KNOX	10,903	8,866	2,037		6,829 R	81.3%	18.7%	81.3%	18.7%
LINCOLN	8,355	7,191	1,164		6,027 R	86.1%	13.9%	86.1%	13.9%
OXFORD	17,260	12,607	4,653		7,954 R	73.0%	27.0%	73.0%	27.0%
PENOBSCOT	36,374	27,806	8,568		19,238 R	76.4%	23.6%	76.4%	23.6%
PISCATAQUIS	6,877	5,336	1,541		3,795 R	77.6%	22.4%	77.6%	22.4%
SAGADAHOC	8,502	6,201	2,301		3,900 R	72.9%	27.1%	72.9%	27.1%
SOMERSET	14,590	10,471	4,119		6,352 R	71.8%	28.2%	71.8%	28.2%
WALDO	7,974	6,590	1,384		5,206 R	82.6%	17.4%	82.6%	17.4%
WASHINGTON	10,736	8,181	2,555		5,626 R	76.2%	23.8%	76.2%	23.8%
YORK	47,166	29,256	17,910		11,346 R	62.0%	38.0%	62.0%	38.0%
TOTAL	351,706	249,238	102,468		146,770 R	70.9%	29.1%	70.9%	29.1%

MAINE

PRESIDENT 1960

County	Total Vote	Republican	Democratic	Other	Rep.-Dem. Plurality	Total Vote Rep.	Total Vote Dem.	Major Vote Rep.	Major Vote Dem.
ANDROSCOGGIN	40,751	14,654	26,097		11,443 D	36.0%	64.0%	36.0%	64.0%
AROOSTOOK	33,497	18,698	14,799		3,899 R	55.8%	44.2%	55.8%	44.2%
CUMBERLAND	80,824	47,271	33,553		13,718 R	58.5%	41.5%	58.5%	41.5%
FRANKLIN	9,440	6,136	3,304		2,832 R	65.0%	35.0%	65.0%	35.0%
HANCOCK	15,482	12,119	3,363		8,756 R	78.3%	21.7%	78.3%	21.7%
KENNEBEC	39,951	21,699	18,252		3,447 R	54.3%	45.7%	54.3%	45.7%
KNOX	12,899	9,083	3,816		5,267 R	70.4%	29.6%	70.4%	29.6%
LINCOLN	9,899	7,562	2,337		5,225 R	76.4%	23.6%	76.4%	23.6%
OXFORD	20,666	11,715	8,951		2,764 R	56.7%	43.3%	56.7%	43.3%
PENOBSCOT	47,634	28,459	19,175		9,284 R	59.7%	40.3%	59.7%	40.3%
PISCATAQUIS	7,818	4,959	2,859		2,100 R	63.4%	36.6%	63.4%	36.6%
SAGADAHOC	10,351	6,386	3,965		2,421 R	61.7%	38.3%	61.7%	38.3%
SOMERSET	17,098	10,142	6,956		3,186 R	59.3%	40.7%	59.3%	40.7%
WALDO	9,689	6,844	2,845		3,999 R	70.6%	29.4%	70.6%	29.4%
WASHINGTON	13,834	9,118	4,716		4,402 R	65.9%	34.1%	65.9%	34.1%
YORK	51,934	25,763	26,171		408 D	49.6%	50.4%	49.6%	50.4%
TOTAL	421,767	240,608	181,159		59,449 R	57.0%	43.0%	57.0%	43.0%

PRESIDENT 1964

County	Total Vote	Republican	Democratic	Other	Rep.-Dem. Plurality	Total Vote Rep.	Total Vote Dem.	Major Vote Rep.	Major Vote Dem.
ANDROSCOGGIN	37,521	7,441	30,080		22,639 D	19.8%	80.2%	19.8%	80.2%
AROOSTOOK	27,546	9,994	17,552		7,558 D	36.3%	63.7%	36.3%	63.7%
CUMBERLAND	73,209	22,365	50,844		28,479 D	30.5%	69.5%	30.5%	69.5%
FRANKLIN	8,671	2,887	5,784		2,897 D	33.3%	66.7%	33.3%	66.7%
HANCOCK	13,719	6,304	7,415		1,111 D	46.0%	54.0%	46.0%	54.0%
KENNEBEC	36,120	11,307	24,813		13,506 D	31.3%	68.7%	31.3%	68.7%
KNOX	11,426	4,404	7,022		2,618 D	38.5%	61.5%	38.5%	61.5%
LINCOLN	9,083	3,984	5,099		1,115 D	43.9%	56.1%	43.9%	56.1%
OXFORD	18,956	5,340	13,616		8,276 D	28.2%	71.8%	28.2%	71.8%
PENOBSCOT	43,215	14,449	28,766		14,317 D	33.4%	66.6%	33.4%	66.6%
PISCATAQUIS	7,254	2,473	4,781		2,308 D	34.1%	65.9%	34.1%	65.9%
SAGADAHOC	9,739	2,733	7,006		4,273 D	28.1%	71.9%	28.1%	71.9%
SOMERSET	15,235	4,541	10,694		6,153 D	29.8%	70.2%	29.8%	70.2%
WALDO	8,721	3,324	5,397		2,073 D	38.1%	61.9%	38.1%	61.9%
WASHINGTON	13,128	3,816	9,312		5,496 D	29.1%	70.9%	29.1%	70.9%
YORK	47,422	13,339	34,083		20,744 D	28.1%	71.9%	28.1%	71.9%
TOTAL	380,965	118,701	262,264		143,563 D	31.2%	68.8%	31.2%	68.8%

MAINE

OTHER VOTE COMPOSITION:

1920	2,214 Socialist; 310 Single Tax.
1924	11,382 Progressive; 406 Socialist Labor.
1928	Socialist.
1932	2,489 Socialist; 255 Socialist Labor; 162 Communist.
1936	7,581 Union; 783 Socialist; 334 Prohibition; 257 Communist; 129 Socialist Labor.
1940	Communist.
1944	Socialist Labor.
1948	1,884 Progressive; 547 Socialist; 206 Socialist Labor.
1952	332 Progressive; 156 Socialist Labor; 138 Socialist; 1 scattered.
1956	
1960	
1964	

MARYLAND

PRESIDENT 1920

County	Total Vote	Republican	Democratic	Other	Rep.-Dem. Plurality	Percentage Total Vote Rep.	Dem.	Major Vote Rep.	Dem.
ALLEGANY	16,726	9,595	5,643	1,488	3,952 R	57.4%	33.7%	63.0%	37.0%
ANNE ARUNDEL	11,370	6,199	5,053	118	1,146 R	54.5%	44.4%	55.1%	44.9%
BALTIMORE	22,183	12,432	9,365	386	3,067 R	56.0%	42.2%	57.0%	43.0%
BALTIMORE CITY	220,146	125,526	86,748	7,872	38,778 R	57.0%	39.4%	59.1%	40.9%
CALVERT	3,001	1,741	1,230	30	511 R	58.0%	41.0%	58.6%	41.4%
CAROLINE	5,990	2,929	3,012	49	83 D	48.9%	50.3%	49.3%	50.7%
CARROLL	10,125	5,784	4,273	68	1,511 R	57.1%	42.2%	57.5%	42.5%
CECIL	6,957	3,435	3,468	54	33 D	49.4%	49.8%	49.8%	50.2%
CHARLES	4,270	2,585	1,642	43	943 R	60.5%	38.5%	61.2%	38.8%
DORCHESTER	8,210	4,218	3,950	42	268 R	51.4%	48.1%	51.6%	48.4%
FREDERICK	17,518	9,559	7,747	212	1,812 R	54.6%	44.2%	55.2%	44.8%
GARRETT	3,993	2,805	1,070	118	1,735 R	70.2%	26.8%	72.4%	27.6%
HARFORD	8,374	4,175	4,134	65	41 R	49.9%	49.4%	50.2%	49.8%
HOWARD	5,068	2,608	2,397	63	211 R	51.5%	47.3%	52.1%	47.9%
KENT	5,886	2,838	3,034	14	196 D	48.2%	51.5%	48.3%	51.7%
MONTGOMERY	12,402	5,948	6,277	177	329 D	48.0%	50.6%	48.7%	51.3%
PRINCE GEORGES	11,663	6,628	4,857	178	1,771 R	56.8%	41.6%	57.7%	42.3%
QUEEN ANNES	5,762	2,157	3,519	86	1,362 D	37.4%	61.1%	38.0%	62.0%
ST MARYS	4,094	2,175	1,861	58	314 R	53.1%	45.5%	53.9%	46.1%
SOMERSET	6,354	3,658	2,634	62	1,024 R	57.6%	41.5%	58.1%	41.9%
TALBOT	6,200	3,050	3,130	20	80 D	49.2%	50.5%	49.4%	50.6%
WASHINGTON	15,995	8,757	6,852	386	1,905 R	54.7%	42.8%	56.1%	43.9%
WICOMICO	9,309	4,225	5,054	30	829 D	45.4%	54.3%	45.5%	54.5%
WORCESTER	6,847	3,090	3,676	81	586 D	45.1%	53.7%	45.7%	54.3%
TOTAL	428,443	236,117	180,626	11,700	55,491 R	55.1%	42.2%	56.7%	43.3%

PRESIDENT 1924

County	Total Vote	Republican	Democratic	Other	Rep.-Dem. Plurality	Percentage Total Vote Rep.	Dem.	Major Vote Rep.	Dem.
ALLEGANY	16,370	9,042	4,442	2,886	4,600 R	55.2%	27.1%	67.1%	32.9%
ANNE ARUNDEL	8,255	3,670	3,766	819	96 D	44.5%	45.6%	49.4%	50.6%
BALTIMORE	21,661	9,363	9,424	2,854	41 D	43.3%	43.5%	49.9%	50.1%
BALTIMORE CITY	163,252	69,588	60,222	33,442	9,366 R	42.6%	36.9%	53.6%	46.4%
CALVERT	2,893	1,564	1,242	87	322 R	54.1%	42.9%	55.7%	44.3%
CAROLINE	4,888	2,210	2,493	185	283 D	45.2%	51.0%	47.0%	53.0%
CARROLL	10,263	5,301	4,616	346	685 R	51.7%	45.0%	53.5%	46.5%
CECIL	6,266	3,156	2,863	247	293 R	50.4%	45.7%	52.4%	47.6%
CHARLES	3,914	2,215	1,491	208	724 R	56.6%	38.1%	59.8%	40.2%
DORCHESTER	6,612	3,356	3,047	209	309 R	50.8%	46.1%	52.4%	47.6%
FREDERICK	17,106	8,441	7,740	925	701 R	49.3%	45.2%	52.2%	47.8%
GARRETT	4,198	2,594	1,226	378	1,368 R	61.8%	29.2%	67.9%	32.1%
HARFORD	7,758	3,545	3,841	372	296 D	45.7%	49.5%	48.0%	52.0%
HOWARD	5,169	1,989	2,786	394	797 D	38.5%	53.9%	41.7%	58.3%
KENT	4,749	2,019	2,628	102	609 D	42.5%	55.3%	43.4%	56.6%
MONTGOMERY	12,894	5,675	6,639	580	964 D	44.0%	51.5%	46.1%	53.9%
PRINCE GEORGES	12,490	5,868	5,088	1,534	780 R	47.0%	40.7%	53.6%	46.4%
QUEEN ANNES	4,908	1,656	3,155	97	1,499 D	33.7%	64.3%	34.4%	65.6%
ST MARYS	3,703	1,653	1,949	101	296 D	44.6%	52.6%	45.9%	54.1%
SOMERSET	6,310	3,230	2,903	177	327 R	51.2%	46.0%	52.7%	47.3%
TALBOT	5,488	2,451	2,859	178	408 D	44.7%	52.1%	46.2%	53.8%
WASHINGTON	15,106	7,460	5,964	1,682	1,496 R	49.4%	39.5%	55.6%	44.4%
WICOMICO	8,635	3,744	4,620	271	876 D	43.4%	53.5%	44.8%	55.2%
WORCESTER	5,742	2,604	3,068	70	464 D	45.4%	53.4%	45.9%	54.1%
TOTAL	358,630	162,414	148,072	48,144	14,342 R	45.3%	41.3%	52.3%	47.7%

MARYLAND

PRESIDENT 1928

County	Total Vote	Republican	Democratic	Other	Rep.-Dem. Plurality	Total Vote Rep.	Total Vote Dem.	Major Vote Rep.	Major Vote Dem.
ALLEGANY	28,703	19,443	9,026	234	10,417 R	67.7%	31.4%	68.3%	31.7%
ANNE ARUNDEL	16,486	10,145	6,259	82	3,886 R	61.5%	38.0%	61.8%	38.2%
BALTIMORE	39,701	23,889	15,632	180	8,257 R	60.2%	39.4%	60.4%	39.6%
BALTIMORE CITY	263,058	135,182	126,106	1,770	9,076 R	51.4%	47.9%	51.7%	48.3%
CALVERT	3,262	2,085	1,144	33	941 R	63.9%	35.1%	64.6%	35.4%
CAROLINE	5,322	3,270	2,030	22	1,240 R	61.4%	38.1%	61.7%	38.3%
CARROLL	12,419	8,644	3,731	44	4,913 R	69.6%	30.0%	69.9%	30.1%
CECIL	7,962	5,706	2,201	55	3,505 R	71.7%	27.6%	72.2%	27.8%
CHARLES	4,391	2,522	1,860	9	662 R	57.4%	42.4%	57.6%	42.4%
DORCHESTER	8,535	6,333	2,180	22	4,153 R	74.2%	25.5%	74.4%	25.6%
FREDERICK	20,089	12,569	7,406	114	5,163 R	62.6%	36.9%	62.9%	37.1%
GARRETT	5,577	4,371	1,168	38	3,203 R	78.4%	20.9%	78.9%	21.1%
HARFORD	10,040	6,479	3,506	55	2,973 R	64.5%	34.9%	64.9%	35.1%
HOWARD	6,417	3,296	3,088	33	208 R	51.4%	48.1%	51.6%	48.4%
KENT	5,257	2,777	2,450	30	327 R	52.8%	46.6%	53.1%	46.9%
MONTGOMERY	16,139	9,318	6,739	82	2,579 R	57.7%	41.8%	58.0%	42.0%
PRINCE GEORGES	16,562	9,782	6,658	122	3,124 R	59.1%	40.2%	59.5%	40.5%
QUEEN ANNES	5,389	2,666	2,700	23	34 D	49.5%	50.1%	49.7%	50.3%
ST MARYS	4,733	1,609	3,006	118	1,397 D	34.0%	63.5%	34.9%	65.1%
SOMERSET	7,395	5,071	2,277	47	2,794 R	68.6%	30.8%	69.0%	31.0%
TALBOT	6,443	3,990	2,432	21	1,558 R	61.9%	37.7%	62.1%	37.9%
WASHINGTON	18,301	12,404	5,816	81	6,588 R	67.8%	31.8%	68.1%	31.9%
WICOMICO	10,033	5,923	4,095	15	1,828 R	59.0%	40.8%	59.1%	40.9%
WORCESTER	6,134	4,005	2,116	13	1,889 R	65.3%	34.5%	65.4%	34.6%
TOTAL	528,348	301,479	223,626	3,243	77,853 R	57.1%	42.3%	57.4%	42.6%

PRESIDENT 1932

County	Total Vote	Republican	Democratic	Other	Rep.-Dem. Plurality	Total Vote Rep.	Total Vote Dem.	Major Vote Rep.	Major Vote Dem.
ALLEGANY	26,322	12,911	12,033	1,378	878 R	49.1%	45.7%	51.8%	48.2%
ANNE ARUNDEL	15,933	5,778	9,761	394	3,983 D	36.3%	61.3%	37.2%	62.8%
BALTIMORE	39,494	13,938	24,626	930	10,688 D	35.3%	62.4%	36.1%	63.9%
BALTIMORE CITY	247,232	78,954	160,309	7,969	81,355 D	31.9%	64.8%	33.0%	67.0%
CALVERT	3,577	1,838	1,696	43	142 R	51.4%	47.4%	52.0%	48.0%
CAROLINE	5,671	1,998	3,651	22	1,653 D	35.2%	64.4%	35.4%	64.6%
CARROLL	12,306	5,732	6,482	92	750 D	46.6%	52.7%	46.9%	53.1%
CECIL	7,959	3,569	4,282	108	713 D	44.8%	53.8%	45.5%	54.5%
CHARLES	4,371	1,851	2,473	47	622 D	42.3%	56.6%	42.8%	57.2%
DORCHESTER	8,052	3,466	4,547	39	1,081 D	43.0%	56.5%	43.3%	56.7%
FREDERICK	18,024	7,144	10,686	194	3,542 D	39.6%	59.3%	40.1%	59.9%
GARRETT	5,443	3,048	2,232	163	816 R	56.0%	41.0%	57.7%	42.3%
HARFORD	10,134	3,954	6,073	107	2,119 D	39.0%	59.9%	39.4%	60.6%
HOWARD	6,190	1,970	4,161	59	2,191 D	31.8%	67.2%	32.1%	67.9%
KENT	3,854	1,468	2,370	16	902 D	38.1%	61.5%	38.2%	61.8%
MONTGOMERY	15,763	5,698	9,882	183	4,184 D	36.1%	62.7%	36.6%	63.4%
PRINCE GEORGES	18,556	6,696	11,580	280	4,884 D	36.1%	62.4%	36.6%	63.4%
QUEEN ANNES	5,294	1,583	3,683	28	2,100 D	29.9%	69.6%	30.1%	69.9%
ST MARYS	4,300	1,322	2,885	93	1,563 D	30.7%	67.1%	31.4%	68.6%
SOMERSET	8,545	3,675	4,811	59	1,136 D	43.0%	56.3%	43.3%	56.7%
TALBOT	6,950	2,672	4,233	45	1,561 D	38.4%	60.9%	38.7%	61.3%
WASHINGTON	20,527	8,929	11,370	228	2,441 D	43.5%	55.4%	44.0%	56.0%
WICOMICO	10,755	3,812	6,895	48	3,083 D	35.4%	64.1%	35.6%	64.4%
WORCESTER	5,802	2,178	3,593	31	1,415 D	37.5%	61.9%	37.7%	62.3%
TOTAL	511,054	184,184	314,314	12,556	130,130 D	36.0%	61.5%	36.9%	63.1%

MARYLAND

PRESIDENT 1936

County	Total Vote	Republican	Democratic	Other	Rep.-Dem. Plurality	Total Vote Rep.	Total Vote Dem.	Major Vote Rep.	Major Vote Dem.
ALLEGANY	31,203	11,191	19,721	291	8,530 D	35.9%	63.2%	36.2%	63.8%
ANNE ARUNDEL	20,033	8,478	11,413	142	2,935 D	42.3%	57.0%	42.6%	57.4%
BALTIMORE	47,576	18,893	28,367	316	9,474 D	39.7%	59.6%	40.0%	60.0%
BALTIMORE CITY	310,294	97,667	210,668	1,959	113,001 D	31.5%	67.9%	31.7%	68.3%
CALVERT	3,979	2,082	1,872	25	210 R	52.3%	47.0%	52.7%	47.3%
CAROLINE	6,206	2,611	3,579	16	968 D	42.1%	57.7%	42.2%	57.8%
CARROLL	13,957	7,383	6,496	78	887 R	52.9%	46.5%	53.2%	46.8%
CECIL	8,582	3,617	4,914	51	1,297 D	42.1%	57.3%	42.4%	57.6%
CHARLES	5,284	2,623	2,597	64	26 R	49.6%	49.1%	50.2%	49.8%
DORCHESTER	9,039	3,735	5,293	11	1,558 D	41.3%	58.6%	41.4%	58.6%
FREDERICK	20,286	9,500	10,722	64	1,222 D	46.8%	52.9%	47.0%	53.0%
GARRETT	7,373	4,057	3,252	64	805 R	55.0%	44.1%	55.5%	44.5%
HARFORD	11,531	5,327	6,165	39	838 D	46.2%	53.5%	46.4%	53.6%
HOWARD	6,825	2,638	4,138	49	1,500 D	38.7%	60.6%	38.9%	61.1%
KENT	5,507	2,543	2,931	33	388 D	46.2%	53.2%	46.5%	53.5%
MONTGOMERY	23,532	10,133	13,246	153	3,113 D	43.1%	56.3%	43.3%	56.7%
PRINCE GEORGES	23,295	8,107	15,087	101	6,980 D	34.8%	64.8%	35.0%	65.0%
QUEEN ANNES	5,503	1,946	3,548	9	1,602 D	35.4%	64.5%	35.4%	64.6%
ST MARYS	5,239	2,286	2,829	124	543 D	43.6%	54.0%	44.7%	55.3%
SOMERSET	8,958	4,770	4,116	72	654 R	53.2%	45.9%	53.7%	46.3%
TALBOT	7,365	3,578	3,768	19	190 D	48.6%	51.2%	48.7%	51.3%
WASHINGTON	24,718	10,619	14,050	49	3,431 D	43.0%	56.8%	43.0%	57.0%
WICOMICO	11,913	4,545	7,273	95	2,728 D	38.2%	61.1%	38.5%	61.5%
WORCESTER	6,698	3,106	3,567	25	461 D	46.4%	53.3%	46.5%	53.5%
TOTAL	624,896	231,435	389,612	3,849	158,177 D	37.0%	62.3%	37.3%	62.7%

PRESIDENT 1940

County	Total Vote	Republican	Democratic	Other	Rep.-Dem. Plurality	Total Vote Rep.	Total Vote Dem.	Major Vote Rep.	Major Vote Dem.
ALLEGANY	33,448	14,804	18,456	188	3,652 D	44.3%	55.2%	44.5%	55.5%
ANNE ARUNDEL	22,405	9,204	13,116	85	3,912 D	41.1%	58.5%	41.2%	58.8%
BALTIMORE	57,198	26,652	30,360	186	3,708 D	46.6%	53.1%	46.7%	53.3%
BALTIMORE CITY	315,996	112,364	199,715	3,917	87,351 D	35.6%	63.2%	36.0%	64.0%
CALVERT	4,246	2,067	2,149	30	82 D	48.7%	50.6%	49.0%	51.0%
CAROLINE	6,401	3,087	3,284	30	197 D	48.2%	51.3%	48.5%	51.5%
CARROLL	14,178	8,300	5,833	45	2,467 R	58.5%	41.1%	58.7%	41.3%
CECIL	9,288	3,878	5,360	50	1,482 D	41.8%	57.7%	42.0%	58.0%
CHARLES	5,464	2,716	2,692	56	24 R	49.7%	49.3%	50.2%	49.8%
DORCHESTER	10,128	3,953	6,088	87	2,135 D	39.0%	60.1%	39.4%	60.6%
FREDERICK	21,833	10,485	11,255	93	770 D	48.0%	51.6%	48.2%	51.8%
GARRETT	7,230	4,387	2,805	38	1,582 R	60.7%	38.8%	61.0%	39.0%
HARFORD	12,060	6,501	5,500	59	1,001 R	53.9%	45.6%	54.2%	45.8%
HOWARD	7,069	3,082	3,957	30	875 D	43.6%	56.0%	43.8%	56.2%
KENT	5,681	2,639	3,014	28	375 D	46.5%	53.1%	46.7%	53.3%
MONTGOMERY	29,521	13,831	15,177	513	1,346 D	46.9%	51.4%	47.7%	52.3%
PRINCE GEORGES	26,251	9,523	16,592	136	7,069 D	36.3%	63.2%	36.5%	63.5%
QUEEN ANNES	6,126	2,508	3,581	37	1,073 D	40.9%	58.5%	41.2%	58.8%
ST MARYS	5,205	2,301	2,860	44	559 D	44.2%	54.9%	44.6%	55.4%
SOMERSET	8,390	3,954	4,352	84	398 D	47.1%	51.9%	47.6%	52.4%
TALBOT	8,106	4,368	3,689	49	679 R	53.9%	45.5%	54.2%	45.8%
WASHINGTON	25,262	11,054	14,125	83	3,071 D	43.8%	55.9%	43.9%	56.1%
WICOMICO	12,012	4,741	7,198	73	2,457 D	39.5%	59.9%	39.7%	60.3%
WORCESTER	6,606	3,135	3,388	83	253 D	47.5%	51.3%	48.1%	51.9%
TOTAL	660,104	269,534	384,546	6,024	115,012 D	40.8%	58.3%	41.2%	58.8%

MARYLAND

PRESIDENT 1944

County	Total Vote	Republican	Democratic	Other	Rep.-Dem. Plurality	Total Vote Rep.	Total Vote Dem.	Major Vote Rep.	Major Vote Dem.
ALLEGANY	30,934	15,589	15,345		244 R	50.4%	49.6%	50.4%	49.6%
ANNE ARUNDEL	21,129	10,860	10,269		591 R	51.4%	48.6%	51.4%	48.6%
BALTIMORE	60,322	34,047	26,275		7,772 R	56.4%	43.6%	56.4%	43.6%
BALTIMORE CITY	276,310	112,817	163,493		50,676 D	40.8%	59.2%	40.8%	59.2%
CALVERT	3,733	2,184	1,549		635 R	58.5%	41.5%	58.5%	41.5%
CAROLINE	5,133	3,073	2,060		1,013 R	59.9%	40.1%	59.9%	40.1%
CARROLL	13,482	8,999	4,483		4,516 R	66.7%	33.3%	66.7%	33.3%
CECIL	8,342	3,680	4,662		982 D	44.1%	55.9%	44.1%	55.9%
CHARLES	4,630	2,755	1,875		880 R	59.5%	40.5%	59.5%	40.5%
DORCHESTER	9,005	4,241	4,764		523 D	47.1%	52.9%	47.1%	52.9%
FREDERICK	19,895	11,367	8,528		2,839 R	57.1%	42.9%	57.1%	42.9%
GARRETT	6,123	4,162	1,961		2,201 R	68.0%	32.0%	68.0%	32.0%
HARFORD	11,590	6,751	4,839		1,912 R	58.2%	41.8%	58.2%	41.8%
HOWARD	6,484	3,344	3,140		204 R	51.6%	48.4%	51.6%	48.4%
KENT	4,805	2,351	2,454		103 D	48.9%	51.1%	48.9%	51.1%
MONTGOMERY	35,724	20,400	15,324		5,076 R	57.1%	42.9%	57.1%	42.9%
PRINCE GEORGES	27,756	13,750	14,006		256 D	49.5%	50.5%	49.5%	50.5%
QUEEN ANNES	5,146	2,119	3,027		908 D	41.2%	58.8%	41.2%	58.8%
ST MARYS	4,564	2,673	1,891		782 R	58.6%	41.4%	58.6%	41.4%
SOMERSET	6,915	3,790	3,125		665 R	54.8%	45.2%	54.8%	45.2%
TALBOT	6,480	3,712	2,768		944 R	57.3%	42.7%	57.3%	42.7%
WASHINGTON	23,592	12,227	11,365		862 R	51.8%	48.2%	51.8%	48.2%
WICOMICO	10,714	5,040	5,674		634 D	47.0%	53.0%	47.0%	53.0%
WORCESTER	5,631	3,018	2,613		405 R	53.6%	46.4%	53.6%	46.4%
TOTAL	603,439	292,949	315,490		22,541 D	48.1%	51.9%	48.1%	51.9%

PRESIDENT 1948

County	Total Vote	Republican	Democratic	Other	Rep.-Dem. Plurality	Total Vote Rep.	Total Vote Dem.	Major Vote Rep.	Major Vote Dem.
ALLEGANY	29,348	14,375	14,398	575	23 D	49.0%	49.1%	50.0%	50.0%
ANNE ARUNDEL	20,475	10,973	8,713	789	2,260 R	53.6%	42.6%	55.7%	44.3%
BALTIMORE	74,715	41,846	31,883	986	9,963 R	56.0%	42.7%	56.8%	43.2%
BALTIMORE CITY	255,363	110,879	134,615	9,869	23,736 D	43.4%	52.7%	45.2%	54.8%
CALVERT	3,820	1,919	1,851	50	68 R	50.2%	48.5%	50.9%	49.1%
CAROLINE	5,223	2,746	2,430	47	316 R	52.6%	46.5%	53.1%	46.9%
CARROLL	12,333	8,003	4,226	104	3,777 R	64.9%	34.3%	65.4%	34.6%
CECIL	8,237	3,866	4,323	48	457 D	46.9%	52.5%	47.2%	52.8%
CHARLES	4,684	2,703	1,878	103	825 R	57.7%	40.1%	59.0%	41.0%
DORCHESTER	8,389	3,751	4,507	131	756 D	44.7%	53.7%	45.4%	54.6%
FREDERICK	17,197	9,934	7,142	121	2,792 R	57.8%	41.5%	58.2%	41.8%
GARRETT	5,498	3,536	1,909	53	1,627 R	64.3%	34.7%	64.9%	35.1%
HARFORD	11,834	6,168	5,494	172	674 R	52.1%	46.4%	52.9%	47.1%
HOWARD	6,028	3,113	2,725	190	388 R	51.6%	45.2%	53.3%	46.7%
KENT	5,048	2,489	2,524	35	35 D	49.3%	50.0%	49.7%	50.3%
MONTGOMERY	38,407	23,174	14,336	897	8,838 R	60.3%	37.3%	61.8%	38.2%
PRINCE GEORGES	30,164	14,718	14,874	572	156 D	48.8%	49.3%	49.7%	50.3%
QUEEN ANNES	4,766	2,038	2,660	88	622 D	42.6%	55.6%	43.4%	56.6%
ST MARYS	4,641	2,247	2,293	101	46 D	48.4%	49.4%	49.5%	50.5%
SOMERSET	6,307	3,129	3,112	66	17 R	49.6%	49.3%	50.1%	49.9%
TALBOT	6,001	3,585	2,344	72	1,241 R	59.7%	39.1%	60.5%	39.5%
WASHINGTON	22,645	11,887	10,588	170	1,299 R	52.5%	46.8%	52.9%	47.1%
WICOMICO	10,571	5,062	5,415	94	353 D	47.9%	51.2%	48.3%	51.7%
WORCESTER	5,034	2,673	2,281	80	392 R	53.1%	45.3%	54.0%	46.0%
TOTAL	596,748	294,814	286,521	15,413	8,293 R	49.4%	48.0%	50.7%	49.3%

MARYLAND

PRESIDENT 1952

County	Total Vote	Republican	Democratic	Other	Rep.-Dem. Plurality	Percentage Total Vote Rep.	Dem.	Major Vote Rep.	Dem.
ALLEGANY	33,762	19,186	14,529	47	4,657 R	56.8%	43.0%	56.9%	43.1%
ANNE ARUNDEL	38,300	23,273	14,739	288	8,534 R	60.8%	38.5%	61.2%	38.8%
BALTIMORE	130,858	81,898	48,476	484	33,422 R	62.6%	37.0%	62.8%	37.2%
BALTIMORE CITY	349,858	166,605	178,469	4,784	11,864 D	47.6%	51.0%	48.3%	51.7%
CALVERT	5,012	2,769	2,209	34	560 R	55.2%	44.1%	55.6%	44.4%
CAROLINE	6,899	4,155	2,733	11	1,422 R	60.2%	39.6%	60.3%	39.7%
CARROLL	16,522	11,563	4,934	25	6,629 R	70.0%	29.9%	70.1%	29.9%
CECIL	12,098	6,482	5,590	26	892 R	53.6%	46.2%	53.7%	46.3%
CHARLES	7,721	4,334	3,338	49	996 R	56.1%	43.2%	56.5%	43.5%
DORCHESTER	10,499	5,524	4,823	152	701 R	52.6%	45.9%	53.4%	46.6%
FREDERICK	22,451	14,562	7,851	38	6,711 R	64.9%	35.0%	65.0%	35.0%
GARRETT	7,279	4,980	2,281	18	2,699 R	68.4%	31.3%	68.6%	31.4%
HARFORD	17,659	10,770	6,809	80	3,961 R	61.0%	38.6%	61.3%	38.7%
HOWARD	9,302	5,497	3,693	112	1,804 R	59.1%	39.7%	59.8%	40.2%
KENT	6,171	3,656	2,504	11	1,152 R	59.2%	40.6%	59.4%	40.6%
MONTGOMERY	76,653	47,805	28,381	467	19,424 R	62.4%	37.0%	62.7%	37.3%
PRINCE GEORGES	67,602	38,060	29,119	423	8,941 R	56.3%	43.1%	56.7%	43.3%
QUEEN ANNES	6,265	3,170	3,058	37	112 R	50.6%	48.8%	50.9%	49.1%
ST.MARYS	7,891	4,270	3,588	33	682 R	54.1%	45.5%	54.3%	45.7%
SOMERSET	8,103	4,113	3,951	39	162 R	50.8%	48.8%	51.0%	49.0%
TALBOT	8,395	5,357	3,019	19	2,338 R	63.8%	36.0%	64.0%	36.0%
WASHINGTON	30,394	17,653	12,657	84	4,996 R	58.1%	41.6%	58.2%	41.8%
WICOMICO	14,965	9,061	5,878	26	3,183 R	60.5%	39.3%	60.7%	39.3%
WORCESTER	7,415	4,681	2,708	26	1,973 R	63.1%	36.5%	63.4%	36.6%
TOTAL	902,074	499,424	395,337	7,313	104,087 R	55.4%	43.8%	55.8%	44.2%

PRESIDENT 1956

County	Total Vote	Republican	Democratic	Other	Rep.-Dem. Plurality	Percentage Total Vote Rep.	Dem.	Major Vote Rep.	Dem.
ALLEGANY	31,014	20,239	10,775		9,464 R	65.3%	34.7%	65.3%	34.7%
ANNE ARUNDEL	44,696	28,622	15,888	186	12,734 R	64.0%	35.5%	64.3%	35.7%
BALTIMORE	152,386	104,021	48,270	95	55,751 R	68.3%	31.7%	68.3%	31.7%
BALTIMORE CITY	318,847	178,244	140,603		37,641 R	55.9%	44.1%	55.9%	44.1%
CALVERT	4,756	2,764	1,966	26	798 R	58.1%	41.3%	58.4%	41.6%
CAROLINE	6,912	4,208	2,702	2	1,506 R	60.9%	39.1%	60.9%	39.1%
CARROLL	16,183	11,749	4,423	11	7,326 R	72.6%	27.3%	72.7%	27.3%
CECIL	12,153	7,217	4,936		2,281 R	59.4%	40.6%	59.4%	40.6%
CHARLES	9,019	5,088	3,931		1,157 R	56.4%	43.6%	56.4%	43.6%
DORCHESTER	9,556	5,809	3,733	14	2,076 R	60.8%	39.1%	60.9%	39.1%
FREDERICK	22,010	14,387	7,619	4	6,768 R	65.4%	34.6%	65.4%	34.6%
GARRETT	7,600	5,555	2,045		3,510 R	73.1%	26.9%	73.1%	26.9%
HARFORD	19,245	12,657	6,588		6,069 R	65.8%	34.2%	65.8%	34.2%
HOWARD	10,182	6,534	3,599	49	2,935 R	64.2%	35.3%	64.5%	35.5%
KENT	6,125	3,747	2,378		1,369 R	61.2%	38.8%	61.2%	38.8%
MONTGOMERY	99,107	56,501	42,606		13,895 R	57.0%	43.0%	57.0%	43.0%
PRINCE GEORGES	79,955	40,654	39,280	21	1,374 R	50.8%	49.1%	50.9%	49.1%
QUEEN ANNES	5,962	3,321	2,641		680 R	55.7%	44.3%	55.7%	44.3%
ST.MARYS	7,784	4,336	3,443	5	893 R	55.7%	44.2%	55.9%	44.3%
SOMERSET	7,801	4,770	3,031		1,739 R	61.1%	38.9%	61.1%	38.9%
TALBOT	8,810	6,018	2,735	57	3,283 R	68.3%	31.0%	68.8%	31.2%
WASHINGTON	31,023	19,455	11,562	6	7,893 R	62.7%	37.3%	62.7%	37.3%
WICOMICO	14,666	9,377	5,289		4,088 R	63.9%	36.1%	63.9%	36.1%
WORCESTER	7,035	4,465	2,570		1,895 R	63.5%	36.5%	63.5%	36.5%
TOTAL	932,827	559,738	372,613	476	187,125 R	60.0%	39.9%	60.0%	40.0%

MARYLAND

PRESIDENT 1960

County	Total Vote	Republican	Democratic	Other	Rep.-Dem. Plurality	Percentage — Total Vote Rep.	Dem.	Major Vote Rep.	Dem.
ALLEGANY	34,190	20,489	13,701		6,788 R	59.9%	40.1%	59.9%	40.1%
ANNE ARUNDEL	56,658	30,595	26,063		4,532 R	54.0%	46.0%	54.0%	46.0%
BALTIMORE	190,423	96,027	94,396		1,631 R	50.4%	49.6%	50.4%	49.6%
BALTIMORE CITY	317,457	114,705	202,752		88,047 D	36.1%	63.9%	36.1%	63.9%
CALVERT	4,708	2,173	2,535		362 D	46.2%	53.8%	46.2%	53.8%
CAROLINE	7,079	3,698	3,381		317 R	52.2%	47.8%	52.2%	47.8%
CARROLL	17,208	11,445	5,763		5,682 R	66.5%	33.5%	66.5%	33.5%
CECIL	13,433	7,368	6,065		1,303 R	54.8%	45.2%	54.8%	45.2%
CHARLES	10,042	4,560	5,482		922 D	45.4%	54.6%	45.4%	54.6%
DORCHESTER	9,590	4,626	4,964		338 D	48.2%	51.8%	48.2%	51.8%
FREDERICK	23,319	13,408	9,910	1	3,498 R	57.5%	42.5%	57.5%	42.5%
GARRETT	7,414	5,057	2,357		2,700 R	68.2%	31.8%	68.2%	31.8%
HARFORD	21,383	12,090	9,293		2,797 R	56.5%	43.5%	56.6%	43.4%
HOWARD	12,465	7,051	5,412	2	1,639 R	56.6%	43.4%	56.6%	43.4%
KENT	6,343	3,264	3,079		185 R	51.5%	48.5%	51.5%	48.5%
MONTGOMERY	128,704	62,679	66,025		3,346 D	48.7%	51.3%	48.7%	51.3%
PRINCE GEORGES	106,830	44,817	62,013		17,196 D	42.0%	58.0%	42.0%	58.0%
QUEEN ANNES	6,032	2,906	3,126		220 D	48.2%	51.8%	48.2%	51.8%
ST MARYS	8,832	3,080	5,752		2,672 D	34.9%	65.1%	34.9%	65.1%
SOMERSET	7,978	4,030	3,948		82 R	50.5%	49.5%	50.5%	49.5%
TALBOT	8,457	4,995	3,462		1,533 R	59.1%	40.9%	59.1%	40.9%
WASHINGTON	33,460	17,828	15,632		2,196 R	53.3%	46.7%	53.3%	46.7%
WICOMICO	16,021	8,671	7,350		1,321 R	54.1%	45.9%	54.1%	45.9%
WORCESTER	7,323	3,976	3,347		629 R	54.3%	45.7%	54.3%	45.7%
TOTAL	1,055,349	489,538	565,808	3	76,270 D	46.4%	53.6%	46.4%	53.6%

PRESIDENT 1964

County	Total Vote	Republican	Democratic	Other	Rep.-Dem. Plurality	Percentage — Total Vote Rep.	Dem.	Major Vote Rep.	Dem.
ALLEGANY	32,809	12,384	20,425		8,041 D	37.7%	62.3%	37.7%	62.3%
ANNE ARUNDEL	64,706	26,725	37,981	50	11,256 D	41.3%	58.7%	41.3%	58.7%
BALTIMORE	195,073	77,870	117,153		39,283 D	39.9%	60.1%	39.9%	60.1%
BALTIMORE CITY	316,805	76,089	240,716		164,627 D	24.0%	76.0%	24.0%	76.0%
CALVERT	5,100	1,765	3,335		1,570 D	34.6%	65.4%	34.6%	65.4%
CAROLINE	6,406	2,696	3,710		1,014 D	42.1%	57.9%	42.1%	57.9%
CARROLL	16,783	8,332	8,451		119 D	49.6%	50.4%	49.6%	50.4%
CECIL	13,184	5,330	7,854		2,524 D	40.4%	59.6%	40.4%	59.6%
CHARLES	10,001	3,455	6,546		3,091 D	34.5%	65.5%	34.5%	65.5%
DORCHESTER	9,891	5,327	4,564		763 R	53.9%	46.1%	53.9%	46.1%
FREDERICK	23,812	9,264	14,548		5,284 D	38.9%	61.1%	38.9%	61.1%
GARRETT	7,139	3,624	3,515		109 R	50.8%	49.2%	50.8%	49.2%
HARFORD	23,518	9,968	13,550		3,582 D	42.4%	57.6%	42.4%	57.6%
HOWARD	15,018	6,833	8,185		1,352 D	45.5%	54.5%	45.5%	54.5%
KENT	6,121	2,008	4,113		2,105 D	32.8%	67.2%	32.8%	67.2%
MONTGOMERY	155,667	52,554	103,113		50,559 D	33.8%	66.2%	33.8%	66.2%
PRINCE GEORGES	128,219	46,413	81,806		35,393 D	36.2%	63.8%	36.2%	63.8%
QUEEN ANNES	6,007	1,955	4,052		2,097 D	32.5%	67.5%	32.5%	67.5%
ST MARYS	8,709	2,878	5,831		2,953 D	33.0%	67.0%	33.0%	67.0%
SOMERSET	7,682	3,155	4,527		1,372 D	41.1%	58.9%	41.1%	58.9%
TALBOT	8,364	3,693	4,671		978 D	44.2%	55.8%	44.2%	55.8%
WASHINGTON	32,614	12,756	19,858		7,102 D	39.1%	60.9%	39.1%	60.9%
WICOMICO	16,143	7,448	8,695		1,247 D	46.1%	53.9%	46.1%	53.9%
WORCESTER	6,686	2,973	3,713		740 D	44.5%	55.5%	44.5%	55.5%
TOTAL	1,116,457	385,495	730,912	50	345,417 D	34.5%	65.5%	34.5%	65.5%

MARYLAND

OTHER VOTE COMPOSITION:

1920	8,876 Socialist; 1,645 Farmer-Labor; 1,178 Socialist Labor; 1 scattered.
1924	47,157 Progressive; 987 Socialist Labor.
1928	1,701 Socialist; 906 Socialist Labor; 636 Communist.
1932	10,489 Socialist; 1,036 Socialist Labor; 1,031 Communist.
1936	1,629 Socialist; 1,305 Socialist Labor; 915 Communist.
1940	4,093 Socialist; 1,274 Communist; 657 Socialist Labor.
1944	
1948	9,983 Progressive; 2,941 Socialist; 2,489 States Rights.
1952	Progressive.
1956	Scattered.
1960	Scattered.
1964	Scattered.

MASSACHUSETTS

PRESIDENT 1920

County	Total Vote	Republican	Democratic	Other	Rep.-Dem. Plurality	Total Vote Rep.	Total Vote Dem.	Major Vote Rep.	Major Vote Dem.
BARNSTABLE	7,562	6,383	1,125	54	5,253 R	84.4%	14.9%	85.0%	15.0%
BERKSHIRE	31,910	20,138	10,956	816	9,182 R	63.1%	34.3%	64.8%	35.2%
BRISTOL	77,032	56,734	17,719	2,579	39,015 R	73.6%	23.0%	76.2%	23.8%
DUKES	1,168	1,013	150	5	863 R	86.7%	12.8%	87.1%	12.9%
ESSEX	132,264	95,057	30,560	6,647	64,497 R	71.9%	23.1%	75.7%	24.3%
FRANKLIN	12,757	9,931	2,542	284	7,389 R	77.8%	19.9%	79.6%	20.4%
HAMPDEN	67,820	46,741	19,156	1,923	27,585 R	68.9%	28.2%	70.9%	29.1%
HAMPSHIRE	18,793	13,174	5,305	314	7,869 R	70.1%	28.2%	71.3%	28.7%
MIDDLESEX	224,078	156,636	61,661	5,781	94,975 R	69.9%	27.5%	71.8%	28.2%
NANTUCKET	816	608	205	3	403 R	74.5%	25.1%	74.8%	25.2%
NORFOLK	69,385	51,826	15,720	1,839	36,106 R	74.7%	22.7%	76.7%	23.3%
PLYMOUTH	45,663	33,582	9,373	2,708	24,209 R	73.5%	20.5%	78.2%	21.8%
SUFFOLK	186,098	108,089	67,552	10,457	40,537 R	58.1%	36.3%	61.5%	38.5%
WORCESTER	118,372	81,241	34,667	2,464	46,574 R	68.6%	29.3%	70.1%	29.9%
TOTAL	993,718	681,153	276,691	35,874	404,462 R	68.5%	27.8%	71.1%	28.9%

PRESIDENT 1924

County	Total Vote	Republican	Democratic	Other	Rep.-Dem. Plurality	Total Vote Rep.	Total Vote Dem.	Major Vote Rep.	Major Vote Dem.
BARNSTABLE	8,577	7,333	881	363	6,452 R	85.5%	10.3%	89.3%	10.7%
BERKSHIRE	34,571	21,106	9,712	3,753	11,394 R	61.1%	28.1%	68.5%	31.5%
BRISTOL	88,980	58,929	19,802	10,249	39,127 R	66.2%	22.3%	74.8%	25.2%
DUKES	1,360	1,182	108	70	1,074 R	86.9%	7.9%	91.6%	8.4%
ESSEX	139,550	92,918	25,635	20,997	67,283 R	66.6%	18.4%	78.4%	21.6%
FRANKLIN	14,717	11,350	2,089	1,278	9,261 R	77.1%	14.2%	84.5%	15.5%
HAMPDEN	77,515	46,489	19,079	11,947	27,410 R	60.0%	24.6%	70.9%	29.1%
HAMPSHIRE	21,014	13,918	5,037	2,059	8,881 R	66.2%	24.0%	73.4%	26.6%
MIDDLESEX	255,235	162,530	64,544	28,161	97,986 R	63.7%	25.3%	71.6%	28.4%
NANTUCKET	889	708	167	14	541 R	79.6%	18.8%	80.9%	19.1%
NORFOLK	81,505	57,948	15,041	8,516	42,907 R	71.1%	18.5%	79.4%	20.6%
PLYMOUTH	50,355	34,728	8,863	6,764	25,865 R	69.0%	17.6%	79.7%	20.3%
SUFFOLK	221,993	104,658	78,702	38,633	25,956 R	47.1%	35.5%	57.1%	42.9%
WORCESTER	133,576	89,679	31,171	12,726	58,508 R	67.1%	23.3%	74.2%	25.8%
TOTAL	1,129,837	703,476	280,831	145,530	422,645 R	62.3%	24.9%	71.5%	28.5%

MASSACHUSETTS

PRESIDENT 1928

County	Total Vote	Republican	Democratic	Other	Rep.-Dem. Plurality	Total Vote Rep.	Total Vote Dem.	Major Vote Rep.	Major Vote Dem.
BARNSTABLE	12,845	9,886	2,899	60	6,987 R	77.0%	22.6%	77.3%	22.7%
BERKSHIRE	48,174	23,855	24,075	244	220 D	49.5%	50.0%	49.8%	50.2%
BRISTOL	115,755	55,205	59,257	1,293	4,052 D	47.7%	51.2%	48.2%	51.8%
DUKES	1,958	1,487	470	1	1,017 R	75.9%	24.0%	76.0%	24.0%
ESSEX	192,810	102,008	89,508	1,294	12,500 R	52.9%	46.4%	53.3%	46.7%
FRANKLIN	20,324	14,333	5,842	149	8,491 R	70.5%	28.7%	71.0%	29.0%
HAMPDEN	118,822	56,063	62,056	703	5,993 D	47.2%	52.2%	47.5%	52.5%
HAMPSHIRE	27,051	14,101	12,695	255	1,406 R	52.1%	46.9%	52.6%	47.4%
MIDDLESEX	363,841	189,189	173,339	1,313	15,850 R	52.0%	47.6%	52.2%	47.8%
NANTUCKET	1,261	865	395	1	470 R	68.6%	31.3%	68.7%	31.3%
NORFOLK	121,076	73,530	47,057	489	26,473 R	60.7%	38.9%	61.0%	39.0%
PLYMOUTH	66,766	41,362	24,887	517	16,475 R	62.0%	37.3%	62.4%	37.6%
SUFFOLK	306,130	99,392	204,603	2,135	105,211 D	32.5%	66.8%	32.7%	67.3%
WORCESTER	181,010	94,290	85,675	1,045	8,615 R	52.1%	47.3%	52.4%	47.6%
TOTAL	1,577,823	775,566	792,758	9,499	17,192 D	49.2%	50.2%	49.5%	50.5%

PRESIDENT 1932

County	Total Vote	Republican	Democratic	Other	Rep.-Dem. Plurality	Total Vote Rep.	Total Vote Dem.	Major Vote Rep.	Major Vote Dem.
BARNSTABLE	13,527	9,476	3,829	222	5,647 R	70.1%	28.3%	71.2%	28.8%
BERKSHIRE	48,220	23,186	23,252	1,782	66 D	48.1%	48.2%	49.9%	50.1%
BRISTOL	116,675	50,846	62,474	3,355	11,628 D	43.6%	53.5%	44.9%	55.1%
DUKES	1,933	1,330	583	20	747 R	68.8%	30.2%	69.5%	30.5%
ESSEX	193,018	95,277	91,787	5,954	3,490 R	49.4%	47.6%	50.9%	49.1%
FRANKLIN	19,748	13,040	6,248	460	6,792 R	66.0%	31.6%	67.6%	32.4%
HAMPDEN	123,629	55,032	63,189	5,408	8,157 D	44.5%	51.1%	46.6%	53.4%
HAMPSHIRE	26,869	13,241	12,332	1,296	909 R	49.3%	45.9%	51.8%	48.2%
MIDDLESEX	365,751	184,486	174,257	7,008	10,229 R	50.4%	47.6%	51.4%	48.6%
NANTUCKET	1,380	812	561	7	251 R	58.8%	40.7%	59.1%	40.9%
NORFOLK	127,146	75,232	49,121	2,793	26,111 R	59.2%	38.6%	60.5%	39.5%
PLYMOUTH	65,744	37,729	26,137	1,878	11,592 R	57.4%	39.8%	59.1%	40.9%
SUFFOLK	296,072	88,737	198,792	8,543	110,055 D	30.0%	67.1%	30.9%	69.1%
WORCESTER	180,402	88,535	87,586	4,281	949 R	49.1%	48.6%	50.3%	49.7%
TOTAL	1,580,114	736,959	800,148	43,007	63,189 D	46.6%	50.6%	47.9%	52.1%

MASSACHUSETTS

PRESIDENT 1936

County	Total Vote	Republican	Democratic	Other	Rep.-Dem. Plurality	Total Vote Rep.	Total Vote Dem.	Major Vote Rep.	Major Vote Dem.
BARNSTABLE	16,485	11,337	4,751	397	6,586 R	68.8%	28.8%	70.5%	29.5%
BERKSHIRE	53,568	22,607	29,087	1,874	6,480 D	42.2%	54.3%	43.7%	56.3%
BRISTOL	141,145	49,754	80,805	10,586	31,051 D	35.3%	57.2%	38.1%	61.9%
DUKES	2,615	1,655	931	29	724 R	63.3%	35.6%	64.0%	36.0%
ESSEX	222,999	97,310	106,078	19,611	8,768 D	43.6%	47.6%	47.8%	52.2%
FRANKLIN	23,721	13,756	9,324	641	4,432 R	58.0%	39.3%	59.6%	40.4%
HAMPDEN	140,180	51,288	80,164	8,728	28,876 D	36.6%	57.2%	39.0%	61.0%
HAMPSHIRE	30,906	14,012	15,412	1,482	1,400 D	45.3%	49.9%	47.6%	52.4%
MIDDLESEX	419,520	199,704	189,512	30,304	10,192 R	47.6%	45.2%	51.3%	48.7%
NANTUCKET	1,544	969	548	27	421 R	62.8%	35.5%	63.9%	36.1%
NORFOLK	148,890	82,545	57,770	8,575	24,775 R	55.4%	38.8%	58.8%	41.2%
PLYMOUTH	78,010	41,942	30,466	5,602	11,476 R	53.8%	39.1%	57.9%	42.1%
SUFFOLK	350,010	96,418	223,732	29,860	127,314 D	27.5%	63.9%	30.1%	69.9%
WORCESTER	210,764	85,316	114,136	11,312	28,820 D	40.5%	54.2%	42.8%	57.2%
TOTAL	1,840,357	768,613	942,716	129,028	174,103 D	41.8%	51.2%	44.9%	55.1%

PRESIDENT 1940

County	Total Vote	Republican	Democratic	Other	Rep.-Dem. Plurality	Total Vote Rep.	Total Vote Dem.	Major Vote Rep.	Major Vote Dem.
BARNSTABLE	18,118	12,659	5,351	108	7,308 R	69.9%	29.5%	70.3%	29.7%
BERKSHIRE	58,880	25,973	32,620	287	6,647 D	44.1%	55.4%	44.3%	55.7%
BRISTOL	158,391	60,643	97,571	677	37,428 D	38.0%	61.6%	38.1%	61.9%
DUKES	2,670	1,643	1,014	13	629 R	61.5%	38.0%	61.8%	38.2%
ESSEX	243,735	116,134	125,998	1,603	9,864 D	47.6%	51.7%	48.0%	52.0%
FRANKLIN	23,728	14,137	9,472	119	4,665 R	59.6%	39.9%	59.9%	40.1%
HAMPDEN	154,796	64,502	89,477	817	24,975 D	41.7%	57.8%	41.9%	58.1%
HAMPSHIRE	33,715	15,651	17,823	241	2,172 D	46.4%	52.9%	46.8%	53.2%
MIDDLESEX	463,437	242,658	218,663	2,116	23,995 R	52.4%	47.2%	52.6%	47.4%
NANTUCKET	1,647	1,015	624	8	391 R	61.6%	37.9%	61.9%	38.1%
NORFOLK	166,017	97,525	67,654	838	29,871 R	58.7%	40.8%	59.0%	41.0%
PLYMOUTH	83,606	48,517	34,481	508	14,136 R	58.2%	41.2%	58.5%	41.5%
SUFFOLK	384,108	138,575	243,233	2,337	104,658 D	36.5%	63.3%	36.3%	63.7%
WORCESTER	234,108	100,468	132,541	1,099	32,073 D	42.9%	56.6%	43.1%	56.9%
TOTAL	2,026,993	939,700	1,076,522	10,771	136,822 D	46.4%	53.1%	46.6%	53.4%

MASSACHUSETTS

PRESIDENT 1944

County	Total Vote	Republican	Democratic	Other	Rep.-Dem. Plurality	Total Vote Rep.	Total Vote Dem.	Major Vote Rep.	Major Vote Dem.
BARNSTABLE	16,525	11,543	4,938	44	6,605 R	69.9%	29.9%	70.0%	30.0%
BERKSHIRE	56,227	24,830	31,212	185	6,382 D	44.2%	55.5%	44.3%	55.7%
BRISTOL	151,692	60,880	90,529	283	29,649 D	40.1%	59.7%	40.2%	59.8%
DUKES	2,234	1,372	861	1	511 R	61.4%	38.5%	61.4%	38.6%
ESSEX	235,756	111,958	118,228	570	6,270 D	48.5%	51.2%	48.6%	51.4%
FRANKLIN	22,703	13,252	9,400	51	3,852 R	58.4%	41.4%	58.5%	41.5%
HAMPDEN	155,486	63,293	91,819	374	28,526 D	40.7%	59.1%	40.8%	59.2%
HAMPSHIRE	32,680	14,907	17,676	97	2,769 D	45.6%	54.1%	45.8%	54.2%
MIDDLESEX	447,080	236,102	210,253	725	25,849 R	52.8%	47.0%	52.9%	47.1%
NANTUCKET	1,349	779	569	1	210 R	57.7%	42.2%	57.8%	42.2%
NORFOLK	167,479	97,490	69,606	383	27,884 R	58.2%	41.6%	58.3%	41.7%
PLYMOUTH	79,709	47,245	32,290	174	14,955 R	59.3%	40.5%	59.4%	40.6%
SUFFOLK	374,487	139,285	234,475	727	95,190 D	37.2%	62.6%	37.3%	62.7%
WORCESTER	222,258	98,414	123,440	404	25,026 D	44.3%	55.5%	44.4%	55.6%
TOTAL	1,960,665	921,350	1,035,296	4,019	113,946 D	47.0%	52.8%	47.1%	52.9%

PRESIDENT 1948

County	Total Vote	Republican	Democratic	Other	Rep.-Dem. Plurality	Total Vote Rep.	Total Vote Dem.	Major Vote Rep.	Major Vote Dem.
BARNSTABLE	19,490	14,633	4,616	241	10,017 R	75.1%	23.7%	76.0%	24.0%
BERKSHIRE	59,267	27,482	30,668	1,117	3,186 D	46.4%	51.7%	47.3%	52.7%
BRISTOL	172,551	63,216	106,741	2,594	43,525 D	36.6%	61.9%	37.2%	62.8%
DUKES	2,484	1,731	720	33	1,011 R	69.7%	29.0%	70.6%	29.4%
ESSEX	246,371	108,894	132,016	5,461	23,122 D	44.2%	53.6%	45.2%	54.8%
FRANKLIN	24,373	14,919	9,231	223	5,688 R	61.2%	37.9%	61.8%	38.2%
HAMPDEN	167,720	70,256	94,609	2,855	24,353 D	41.9%	56.4%	42.6%	57.4%
HAMPSHIRE	35,833	17,331	18,012	490	681 D	48.4%	50.3%	49.0%	51.0%
MIDDLESEX	485,908	228,262	248,240	9,406	19,978 D	47.0%	51.1%	47.9%	52.1%
NANTUCKET	1,442	1,013	409	20	604 R	70.2%	28.4%	71.2%	28.8%
NORFOLK	176,737	100,280	72,327	4,130	27,953 R	56.7%	40.9%	58.1%	41.9%
PLYMOUTH	85,146	48,925	34,765	1,456	14,160 R	57.5%	40.8%	58.5%	41.5%
SUFFOLK	385,067	105,671	265,611	13,785	159,940 D	27.4%	69.0%	28.5%	71.5%
WORCESTER	244,757	106,757	133,823	4,177	27,066 D	43.6%	54.7%	44.4%	55.6%
TOTAL	2,107,146	909,370	1,151,788	45,988	242,418 D	43.2%	54.7%	44.1%	55.9%

MASSACHUSETTS

PRESIDENT 1952

County	Total Vote	Republican	Democratic	Other	Rep.-Dem. Plurality	Percentage Total Vote Rep.	Dem.	Percentage Major Vote Rep.	Dem.
BARNSTABLE	25,971	20,943	4,984	44	15,959 R	80.6%	19.2%	80.8%	19.2%
BERKSHIRE	68,441	38,413	29,785	243	8,628 R	56.1%	43.5%	56.3%	43.7%
BRISTOL	192,011	98,105	93,444	462	4,661 R	51.1%	48.7%	51.2%	48.8%
DUKES	3,198	2,432	760	6	1,672 R	76.0%	23.8%	76.2%	23.8%
ESSEX	280,409	156,030	123,334	1,045	32,696 R	55.6%	44.0%	55.9%	44.1%
FRANKLIN	28,268	19,489	8,729	50	10,760 R	68.9%	30.9%	69.1%	30.9%
HAMPDEN	190,193	98,641	90,936	616	7,705 R	51.9%	47.8%	52.0%	48.0%
HAMPSHIRE	41,486	24,141	17,247	98	6,894 R	58.2%	41.6%	58.3%	41.7%
MIDDLESEX	554,605	316,069	236,910	1,626	79,159 R	57.0%	42.7%	57.2%	42.8%
NANTUCKET	1,897	1,490	405	2	1,085 R	78.5%	21.3%	78.6%	21.4%
NORFOLK	215,361	140,409	74,321	631	65,088 R	65.2%	34.5%	65.4%	34.6%
PLYMOUTH	101,042	67,922	32,815	305	35,107 R	67.2%	32.5%	67.4%	32.6%
SUFFOLK	404,879	162,147	240,957	1,775	78,810 D	40.0%	59.5%	40.2%	59.8%
WORCESTER	275,637	146,094	128,898	645	17,196 R	53.0%	46.8%	53.1%	46.9%
TOTAL	2,383,398	1,292,325	1,083,525	7,548	203,600 R	54.2%	45.5%	54.4%	45.6%

PRESIDENT 1956

County	Total Vote	Republican	Democratic	Other	Rep.-Dem. Plurality	Percentage Total Vote Rep.	Dem.	Percentage Major Vote Rep.	Dem.
BARNSTABLE	28,202	23,472	4,672	58	18,800 R	83.2%	16.6%	83.4%	16.6%
BERKSHIRE	66,973	41,355	25,361	257	15,994 R	61.7%	37.9%	62.0%	38.0%
BRISTOL	189,365	109,542	79,357	466	30,185 R	57.8%	41.9%	58.0%	42.0%
DUKES	3,160	2,618	541	1	2,077 R	82.8%	17.1%	82.9%	17.1%
ESSEX	276,453	166,115	109,671	667	56,444 R	60.1%	39.7%	60.2%	39.8%
FRANKLIN	27,436	19,779	7,574	83	12,205 R	72.1%	27.6%	72.3%	27.7%
HAMPDEN	187,367	104,689	81,743	935	22,946 R	55.9%	43.6%	56.2%	43.8%
HAMPSHIRE	42,554	26,361	16,119	84	10,242 R	61.9%	37.9%	62.1%	37.9%
MIDDLESEX	551,373	343,125	216,668	1,580	126,457 R	61.1%	38.6%	61.3%	38.7%
NANTUCKET	1,900	1,582	317	1	1,265 R	83.3%	16.7%	83.3%	16.7%
NORFOLK	229,996	152,747	76,656	593	76,091 R	66.4%	33.3%	66.6%	33.4%
PLYMOUTH	106,161	75,575	30,377	209	45,198 R	71.2%	28.6%	71.3%	28.7%
SUFFOLK	355,686	162,836	191,245	1,605	28,409 D	45.8%	53.8%	46.0%	54.0%
WORCESTER	271,870	163,401	107,889	580	55,512 R	60.1%	39.7%	60.2%	39.8%
TOTAL	2,348,506	1,393,197	948,190	7,119	445,007 R	59.3%	40.4%	59.5%	40.5%

MASSACHUSETTS

PRESIDENT 1960

County	Total Vote	Republican	Democratic	Other	Rep.-Dem. Plurality	Percentage Total Vote Rep.	Dem.	Percentage Major Vote Rep.	Dem.
BARNSTABLE	33,372	20,900	12,423	49	8,477 R	62.6%	37.2%	62.7%	37.3%
BERKSHIRE	68,629	27,335	41,132	162	13,797 D	39.8%	59.9%	39.9%	60.1%
BRISTOL	194,722	64,290	130,049	383	65,759 D	33.0%	66.8%	33.1%	66.9%
DUKES	3,286	1,998	1,282	6	716 R	60.8%	39.0%	60.9%	39.1%
ESSEX	295,081	126,599	167,875	607	41,276 D	42.9%	56.9%	43.0%	57.0%
FRANKLIN	28,011	15,682	12,282	47	3,400 R	56.0%	43.8%	56.1%	43.9%
HAMPDEN	193,828	72,054	121,061	713	49,007 D	37.2%	62.5%	37.3%	62.7%
HAMPSHIRE	45,096	19,346	25,667	83	6,321 D	42.9%	56.9%	43.0%	57.0%
MIDDLESEX	603,516	246,126	356,130	1,260	110,004 D	40.8%	59.0%	40.9%	59.1%
NANTUCKET	1,919	1,219	698	2	521 R	63.5%	36.4%	63.6%	35.4%
NORFOLK	257,721	121,744	135,474	503	13,730 D	47.2%	52.6%	47.3%	52.7%
PLYMOUTH	118,349	60,977	57,175	197	3,802 R	51.5%	48.3%	51.6%	48.4%
SUFFOLK	339,617	85,750	252,823	1,044	167,073 D	25.2%	74.4%	25.3%	74.7%
WORCESTER	286,333	112,730	173,103	500	60,373 D	39.4%	60.5%	39.4%	60.6%
TOTAL	2,469,480	976,750	1,487,174	5,556	510,424 D	39.6%	60.2%	39.6%	60.4%

PRESIDENT 1964

County	Total Vote	Republican	Democratic	Other	Rep.-Dem. Plurality	Percentage Total Vote Rep.	Dem.	Percentage Major Vote Rep.	Dem.
BARNSTABLE	35,355	15,133	20,101	121	4,968 D	42.8%	56.9%	42.9%	57.1%
BERKSHIRE	64,331	15,160	48,839	332	33,679 D	23.6%	75.9%	23.7%	76.3%
BRISTOL	185,636	39,230	146,885	521	107,655 D	21.0%	78.7%	21.1%	78.9%
DUKES	3,214	1,015	2,187	12	1,172 D	31.6%	68.0%	31.7%	68.3%
ESSEX	282,945	71,653	210,135	1,157	138,482 D	25.3%	74.3%	25.4%	74.6%
FRANKLIN	25,624	8,344	17,106	174	8,762 D	32.6%	66.8%	32.8%	67.2%
HAMPDEN	178,219	44,299	133,085	835	88,786 D	24.9%	74.7%	25.0%	75.0%
HAMPSHIRE	43,645	11,385	32,058	202	20,673 D	26.1%	73.5%	26.2%	73.8%
MIDDLESEX	576,810	134,729	439,790	2,291	305,061 D	23.4%	76.2%	23.5%	76.5%
NANTUCKET	1,787	587	1,197	3	610 D	32.8%	67.0%	32.9%	67.1%
NORFOLK	256,012	68,612	186,488	912	117,876 D	26.8%	72.8%	26.9%	73.1%
PLYMOUTH	120,335	37,941	82,007	387	44,066 D	31.5%	68.1%	31.6%	68.4%
SUFFOLK	298,263	40,251	257,161	842	216,910 D	13.5%	86.2%	13.5%	86.5%
WORCESTER	271,631	61,388	209,383	860	147,995 D	22.6%	77.1%	22.7%	77.3%
TOTAL	2,344,798	549,727	1,786,422	8,649	1,236,695 D	23.4%	76.2%	23.5%	76.5%

MASSACHUSETTS

OTHER VOTE COMPOSITION:

1920   32,267 Socialist; 3,583 Socialist Labor; 24 scattered.
1924   141,225 Progressive; 2,635 Communist; 1,668 Socialist Labor; 2 scattered.
1928   6,262 Socialist; 2,461 Communist; 772 Socialist Labor; 4 scattered.
1932   34,305 Socialist; 4,821 Communist; 2,668 Socialist Labor; 1,142 Prohibition; 71
          scattered.
1936   118,639 Union; 5,111 Socialist; 2,930 Communist; 1,305 Socialist Labor; 1,032
          Prohibition; 11 scattered.

1940   4,091 Socialist; 3,806 Communist; 1,492 Socialist Labor; 1,370 Prohibition; 12
          scattered.
1944   2,780 Socialist Labor; 973 Prohibition; 266 scattered.
1948   38,157 Progressive; 5,535 Socialist Labor; 1,663 Prohibition; 633 scattered.
1952   4,636 Progressive; 1,957 Socialist Labor; 886 Prohibition; 69 scattered.
1956   5,573 Socialist Labor; 1,205 Prohibition; 341 scattered.

1960   3,892 Socialist Labor; 1,633 Prohibition; 31 scattered.
1964   4,755 Socialist Labor; 3,735 Prohibition; 159 scattered.

MICHIGAN

PRESIDENT 1920

County	Total Vote	Republican	Democratic	Other	Rep.-Dem. Plurality	% Total Vote Rep.	% Total Vote Dem.	% Major Vote Rep.	% Major Vote Dem.
ALCONA	1,375	1,043	264	68	779 R	75.9	19.2	79.8	20.2
ALGER	1,911	1,263	468	180	795 R	66.1	24.5	73.0	27.0
ALLEGAN	10,311	7,825	2,154	332	5,671 R	75.9	20.9	78.4	21.6
ALPENA	5,470	3,467	1,893	110	1,574 R	63.4	34.6	64.7	35.3
ANTRIM	2,915	2,260	518	137	1,742 R	77.5	17.8	81.4	18.6
ARENAC	2,292	1,521	669	102	852 R	66.4	29.2	69.5	30.5
BARAGA	1,832	1,368	304	160	1,064 R	74.7	16.6	81.8	18.2
BARRY	7,291	5,154	1,874	263	3,280 R	70.7	25.7	73.3	26.7
BAY	21,460	13,933	7,011	516	6,922 R	64.9	32.7	66.5	33.5
BENZIE	2,111	1,520	422	169	1,098 R	72.0	20.0	78.3	21.7
BERRIEN	21,265	15,748	4,855	662	10,893 R	74.1	22.8	76.4	23.6
BRANCH	8,181	5,704	2,181	296	3,523 R	69.7	26.7	72.3	27.7
CALHOUN	24,193	16,722	6,291	1,180	10,431 R	69.1	26.0	72.7	27.3
CASS	6,058	4,498	1,286	274	3,212 R	74.2	21.2	77.8	22.2
CHARLEVOIX	3,995	3,079	704	212	2,375 R	77.1	17.6	81.4	18.6
CHEBOYGAN	3,895	2,472	1,281	142	1,191 R	63.5	32.9	65.9	34.1
CHIPPEWA	6,364	4,732	1,266	366	3,466 R	74.4	19.9	78.9	21.1
CLARE	2,398	1,762	511	125	1,251 R	73.5	21.3	77.5	22.5
CLINTON	7,628	6,019	1,464	145	4,555 R	78.9	19.2	80.4	19.6
CRAWFORD	1,127	726	361	40	365 R	64.4	32.0	66.8	33.2
DELTA	7,550	4,938	1,985	627	2,953 R	65.4	26.3	71.3	28.7
DICKINSON	4,617	3,539	580	498	2,959 R	76.7	12.6	85.9	14.1
EATON	10,344	7,343	2,727	274	4,616 R	71.0	26.4	72.9	27.1
EMMET	4,441	3,059	1,070	312	1,989 R	68.9	24.1	74.1	25.9
GENESEE	32,873	24,543	7,408	922	17,135 R	74.7	22.5	76.8	23.2
GLADWIN	2,144	1,687	313	144	1,374 R	78.7	14.6	84.4	15.6
GOGEBIC	6,882	5,486	823	573	4,663 R	79.7	12.0	87.0	13.0
GRAND TRAVERSE	5,478	4,056	1,158	264	2,898 R	74.0	21.1	77.8	22.2
GRATIOT	8,498	6,578	1,846	74	4,732 R	77.4	21.7	78.1	21.9
HILLSDALE	9,406	6,690	2,467	249	4,223 R	71.1	26.2	73.1	26.9
HOUGHTON	18,625	14,938	3,088	599	11,850 R	80.2	16.6	82.9	17.1
HURON	10,117	8,354	1,581	182	6,773 R	82.6	15.6	84.1	15.9
INGHAM	25,460	18,554	7,061	982	11,376 R	69.6	26.7	72.0	27.2
IONIA	11,802	7,977	3,395	430	4,582 R	67.6	28.8	70.1	29.9
IOSCO	2,624	2,013	548	63	1,465 R	76.7	20.9	78.6	21.4
IRON	4,245	3,515	497	233	3,018 R	82.8	11.7	87.6	12.4
ISABELLA	6,894	5,089	1,627	178	3,462 R	73.8	23.6	75.8	24.2
JACKSON	24,534	15,922	7,789	823	8,133 R	64.9	31.7	67.2	32.8
KALAMAZOO	23,584	13,765	5,271	1,348	8,494 R	67.5	25.9	72.3	27.7
KALKASKA	1,216	890	224	102	656 R	73.2	18.4	79.9	20.1
KENT	58,175	40,802	14,763	2,610	26,039 R	70.1	25.4	73.4	26.6
KEWEENAW	1,441	1,272	89	80	1,183 R	88.3	6.3	93.5	6.5
LAKE	1,238	926	261	51	665 R	74.8	21.1	78.0	22.0
LAPEER	7,026	5,523	1,298	205	4,225 R	78.6	18.5	81.0	19.0
LEELANAU	2,621	2,156	406	59	1,750 R	82.3	15.5	84.2	15.8
LENAWEE	17,379	11,973	5,095	311	6,878 R	68.9	29.3	70.1	29.9
LIVINGSTON	7,237	4,639	2,437	161	2,202 R	64.1	33.7	65.6	34.4
LUCE	925	708	187	30	521 R	76.5	20.2	79.1	20.9
MACKINAC	2,680	1,685	932	63	753 R	62.9	34.8	64.4	35.6
MACOMB	13,161	9,735	3,023	403	6,712 R	74.0	23.0	76.3	23.7
MANISTEE	4,570	2,179	2,184	207	5 D	47.7	47.8	49.9	50.1
MARQUETTE	13,103	9,233	3,012	858	6,221 R	70.5	23.0	75.4	24.6
MASON	5,263	3,652	1,338	273	2,314 R	69.4	25.4	73.2	26.8
MECOSTA	5,258	3,932	1,145	181	2,787 R	74.8	21.8	77.4	22.6
MENOMINEE	6,967	5,045	1,560	362	3,485 R	72.4	22.4	76.4	23.6
MIDLAND	5,217	4,115	959	143	3,156 R	78.9	18.4	81.1	18.9
MISSAUKEE	2,184	1,801	345	38	1,456 R	82.5	15.8	83.9	16.1
MONROE	14,096	8,646	5,224	226	3,422 R	61.3	37.1	62.3	37.7
MONTCALM	8,598	6,644	1,695	259	4,949 R	77.3	19.7	79.7	20.3
MONTMORENCY	1,101	832	199	70	633 R	75.6	18.1	80.7	19.3

PRESIDENT 1924

County	Total Vote	Republican	Democratic	Other	Rep.-Dem. Plurality	% Total Vote Rep.	% Total Vote Dem.	% Major Vote Rep.	% Major Vote Dem.
ALCONA	1,420	1,027	184	209	843 R	72.3	13.0	84.8	15.2
ALGER	2,440	1,623	228	589	1,395 R	66.5	9.3	87.7	12.3
ALLEGAN	11,872	9,417	1,562	893	7,855 R	79.3	13.2	85.8	14.2
ALPENA	6,107	4,628	948	531	3,680 R	75.8	15.5	83.0	17.0
ANTRIM	2,925	2,246	371	308	1,875 R	76.8	12.7	85.8	14.2
ARENAC	2,615	1,767	575	273	1,192 R	67.6	22.0	75.4	24.6
BARAGA	2,386	1,714	208	464	1,506 R	71.8	8.7	89.2	10.8
BARRY	7,958	5,656	2,046	296	3,610 R	70.7	25.6	73.4	26.6
BAY	22,951	14,861	5,881	2,209	8,980 R	64.8	25.6	71.6	28.4
BENZIE	2,603	1,922	198	483	1,724 R	73.8	7.6	90.7	9.3
BERRIEN	24,497	15,612	4,445	4,440	11,167 R	63.7	18.1	77.8	22.2
BRANCH	9,302	6,016	2,253	1,033	3,763 R	64.7	24.2	72.8	27.2
CALHOUN	25,262	18,165	4,020	3,077	14,145 R	71.9	15.9	81.9	18.1
CASS	7,584	4,545	2,328	711	2,217 R	59.9	30.7	66.1	33.9
CHARLEVOIX	4,201	3,346	406	449	2,940 R	79.6	9.7	89.2	10.8
CHEBOYGAN	4,182	2,683	994	505	1,689 R	64.2	23.8	73.0	27.0
CHIPPEWA	7,029	5,443	516	1,070	4,927 R	77.4	7.3	91.3	8.7
CLARE	2,472	1,920	358	194	1,562 R	77.7	14.5	84.3	15.7
CLINTON	8,641	6,637	1,359	645	5,278 R	76.8	15.7	83.0	17.0
CRAWFORD	1,152	840	163	149	677 R	72.9	14.1	83.7	16.3
DELTA	9,554	4,761	463	4,330	4,298 R	49.8	4.8	91.1	8.9
DICKINSON	6,609	4,538	400	1,671	4,138 R	68.7	6.1	91.9	8.1
EATON	11,175	8,232	2,462	481	5,770 R	73.7	22.0	77.0	23.0
EMMET	4,362	3,020	773	569	2,247 R	69.2	17.7	79.6	20.4
GENESEE	40,878	34,264	4,225	2,389	30,039 R	83.8	10.3	89.0	11.0
GLADWIN	2,435	1,908	255	272	1,653 R	78.4	10.5	88.2	11.8
GOGEBIC	7,707	5,128	487	2,092	4,641 R	66.5	6.3	91.3	8.7
GRAND TRAVERSE	5,358	4,011	558	789	3,453 R	74.9	10.4	87.8	12.2
GRATIOT	8,832	6,720	1,839	273	4,881 R	76.1	20.8	78.5	21.5
HILLSDALE	9,578	6,556	1,980	1,042	4,576 R	68.4	20.7	76.8	23.2
HOUGHTON	16,662	13,833	1,045	1,784	12,788 R	83.0	6.3	93.0	7.0
HURON	10,898	8,843	988	1,067	7,855 R	81.1	9.1	90.0	10.0
INGHAM	34,505	28,505	4,814	1,686	23,191 R	81.2	14.0	85.3	14.7
IONIA	12,979	9,502	2,821	656	6,681 R	73.2	21.7	77.1	22.9
IOSCO	2,398	1,713	304	381	1,409 R	71.4	12.7	84.9	15.1
IRON	4,307	2,802	247	1,258	2,555 R	65.1	5.7	91.9	8.1
ISABELLA	6,805	5,245	1,208	352	4,037 R	77.1	17.8	81.3	18.7
JACKSON	28,390	19,640	5,639	3,111	14,001 R	69.2	19.9	77.7	22.3
KALAMAZOO	24,500	18,451	3,587	2,462	14,864 R	75.3	14.6	83.7	16.3
KALKASKA	1,371	966	205	200	761 R	70.5	15.0	82.5	17.5
KENT	59,008	45,207	7,982	5,819	37,225 R	76.6	13.5	85.0	15.0
KEWEENAW	1,559	1,421	50	88	1,371 R	91.1	3.2	96.6	3.4
LAKE	1,554	1,069	313	172	756 R	68.8	20.1	77.4	22.6
LAPEER	7,558	6,297	929	332	5,368 R	83.3	12.3	87.1	12.9
LEELANAU	2,378	1,792	301	285	1,491 R	75.4	12.7	85.6	14.4
LENAWEE	18,388	13,358	3,950	1,080	9,408 R	72.6	21.5	77.2	22.8
LIVINGSTON	7,252	4,886	2,037	329	2,849 R	67.4	28.1	70.6	29.4
LUCE	1,054	850	112	92	738 R	80.6	10.6	88.4	11.6
MACKINAC	3,111	1,606	998	507	608 R	51.6	32.1	61.7	38.3
MACOMB	15,933	11,147	3,191	1,595	7,956 R	70.0	20.0	77.7	22.3
MANISTEE	6,371	3,701	1,314	1,356	2,387 R	58.1	20.6	73.8	26.2
MARQUETTE	13,820	9,771	845	3,204	8,926 R	70.7	6.1	92.0	8.0
MASON	5,310	3,567	815	928	2,752 R	67.2	15.3	81.4	18.6
MECOSTA	5,047	3,884	794	369	3,090 R	77.0	15.7	83.0	17.0
MENOMINEE	7,764	4,142	1,055	2,567	3,087 R	53.3	13.6	79.7	20.3
MIDLAND	5,063	4,004	625	434	3,379 R	79.1	12.3	86.5	13.5
MISSAUKEE	2,025	1,723	208	94	1,515 R	85.1	10.3	89.2	10.8
MONROE	15,383	8,940	4,981	1,462	3,959 R	58.1	32.4	64.2	35.8
MONTCALM	8,791	6,942	1,396	453	5,546 R	79.0	15.9	83.3	16.7
MONTMORENCY	1,170	748	140	282	608 R	63.9	12.0	84.2	15.8

MICHIGAN

PRESIDENT 1920

County	Total Vote	Republican	Democratic	Other	Rep.-Dem. Plurality	Percentage Total Vote Rep.	Dem.	Major Vote Rep.	Dem.
MUSKEGON	15,877	11,702	3,468	707	8,234 R	73.7%	21.8%	77.1%	22.9%
NEWAYGO	5,307	4,188	929	190	3,259 R	78.9%	17.5%	81.8%	18.2%
OAKLAND	27,220	19,321	6,421	1,478	12,900 R	71.0%	23.6%	75.1%	24.9%
OCEANA	4,541	3,535	785	221	2,750 R	77.8%	17.3%	81.8%	18.2%
OGEMAW	2,233	1,687	444	102	1,243 R	75.5%	19.9%	79.2%	20.8%
ONTONAGON	2,920	1,977	657	286	1,320 R	67.7%	22.5%	75.1%	24.9%
OSCEOLA	4,457	3,603	769	85	2,834 R	80.8%	17.3%	82.4%	17.6%
OSCODA	524	439	75	10	364 R	83.8%	14.3%	85.4%	14.6%
OTSEGO	1,365	874	466	25	408 R	64.0%	34.1%	65.2%	34.8%
OTTAWA	13,370	10,528	2,391	451	8,137 R	78.7%	17.9%	81.5%	18.5%
PRESQUE ISLE	3,123	2,522	525	76	1,997 R	80.8%	16.8%	82.8%	17.2%
ROSCOMMON	866	652	182	32	470 R	75.3%	21.0%	78.2%	21.8%
SAGINAW	29,932	20,425	8,494	1,013	11,931 R	68.2%	28.4%	70.6%	29.4%
ST CLAIR	19,879	14,938	4,566	375	10,372 R	75.1%	23.0%	76.6%	23.4%
ST JOSEPH	9,063	6,035	2,725	303	3,310 R	66.6%	30.1%	68.9%	31.1%
SANILAC	8,571	7,256	1,146	169	6,110 R	84.7%	13.4%	86.4%	13.6%
SCHOOLCRAFT	2,490	1,776	428	286	1,348 R	71.3%	17.2%	80.6%	19.4%
SHIAWASSEE	10,287	7,194	2,595	498	4,599 R	69.9%	25.2%	73.5%	26.5%
TUSCOLA	8,809	7,282	1,269	258	6,013 R	82.7%	14.4%	85.2%	14.8%
VAN BUREN	9,192	6,904	1,988	300	4,916 R	75.1%	21.6%	77.6%	22.4%
WASHTENAW	18,912	14,082	4,468	362	9,614 R	74.5%	23.6%	75.9%	24.1%
WAYNE	294,943	220,482	51,773	22,688	168,709 R	74.8%	17.6%	81.0%	19.0%
WEXFORD	4,664	3,406	1,095	163	2,311 R	73.0%	23.5%	75.7%	24.3%
TOTAL	1,048,411	762,865	233,450	52,096	529,415 R	72.8%	22.3%	76.6%	23.4%

PRESIDENT 1924

County	Total Vote	Republican	Democratic	Other	Rep.-Dem. Plurality	Percentage Total Vote Rep.	Dem.	Major Vote Rep.	Dem.
MUSKEGON	18,206	14,422	1,462	2,322	12,960 R	79.2%	8.0%	90.8%	9.2%
NEWAYGO	5,356	4,243	720	393	3,523 R	79.2%	13.4%	85.5%	14.5%
OAKLAND	35,196	28,603	4,105	2,488	24,498 R	81.3%	11.7%	87.4%	12.6%
OCEANA	4,450	3,335	650	465	2,685 R	74.9%	14.6%	83.7%	16.3%
OGEMAW	2,161	1,714	258	189	1,456 R	79.3%	11.9%	86.9%	13.1%
ONTONAGON	3,149	2,249	417	483	1,832 R	71.4%	13.2%	84.4%	15.6%
OSCEOLA	3,921	3,050	566	305	2,484 R	77.8%	14.4%	84.3%	15.7%
OSCODA	473	389	52	32	337 R	82.2%	11.0%	88.2%	11.8%
OTSEGO	1,550	1,144	249	157	895 R	73.8%	16.1%	82.1%	17.9%
OTTAWA	14,880	11,688	1,871	1,321	9,817 R	78.5%	12.6%	86.2%	13.8%
PRESQUE ISLE	3,432	2,315	431	686	1,884 R	67.5%	12.6%	84.3%	15.7%
ROSCOMMON	695	484	99	112	385 R	69.6%	14.2%	83.0%	17.0%
SAGINAW	34,738	23,618	6,206	4,914	17,412 R	68.0%	17.9%	79.2%	20.8%
ST CLAIR	22,780	17,435	3,600	1,745	13,835 R	76.5%	15.8%	82.9%	17.1%
ST JOSEPH	10,137	6,633	2,649	855	3,984 R	65.4%	26.1%	71.5%	28.5%
SANILAC	9,188	7,767	983	438	6,784 R	84.5%	10.7%	88.8%	11.2%
SCHOOLCRAFT	2,470	1,515	190	765	1,325 R	61.3%	7.7%	88.9%	11.1%
SHIAWASSEE	12,313	8,987	1,738	1,588	7,249 R	73.0%	14.1%	83.8%	16.2%
TUSCOLA	9,319	7,490	1,076	753	6,414 R	80.4%	11.5%	87.4%	12.6%
VAN BUREN	10,320	7,384	1,646	1,290	5,738 R	71.6%	15.9%	81.8%	18.2%
WASHTENAW	19,830	14,326	3,603	1,901	10,723 R	72.2%	18.2%	79.9%	20.1%
WAYNE	335,336	268,653	23,817	42,866	244,836 R	80.1%	7.1%	91.9%	8.1%
WEXFORD	5,068	3,926	592	550	3,334 R	77.5%	11.7%	86.9%	13.1%
TOTAL	1,160,419	874,631	152,359	133,429	722,272 R	75.4%	13.1%	85.2%	14.8%

MICHIGAN

PRESIDENT 1928

County	Total Vote	Republican	Democratic	Other	Rep.-Dem. Plurality	Total Vote Rep.	Total Vote Dem.	Major Vote Rep.	Major Vote Dem.
ALCONA	1,458	1,149	302	7	847 R	78.8%	20.7%	79.2%	20.8%
ALGER	2,906	1,716	1,053	137	563 R	59.1%	36.2%	62.0%	38.0%
ALLEGAN	13,217	10,792	2,358	67	8,434 R	81.7%	17.8%	82.1%	17.9%
ALPENA	5,466	3,467	1,984	15	1,483 R	63.4%	36.3%	63.6%	36.4%
ANTRIM	3,263	2,756	484	23	2,272 R	84.5%	14.8%	85.1%	14.9%
ARENAC	2,375	1,612	749	14	863 R	67.9%	31.5%	68.3%	31.7%
BARAGA	3,375	2,203	1,046	126	1,157 R	65.3%	31.0%	67.8%	32.2%
BARRY	7,561	6,044	1,459	58	4,585 R	79.9%	19.4%	80.6%	19.4%
BAY	21,941	12,467	9,395	79	3,072 R	56.8%	42.9%	57.0%	43.0%
BENZIE	2,194	1,849	321	24	1,528 R	84.3%	14.6%	85.2%	14.8%
BERRIEN	27,791	19,064	8,555	172	10,509 R	68.6%	30.8%	69.0%	31.0%
BRANCH	9,150	6,818	2,266	66	4,552 R	74.5%	24.8%	75.1%	24.9%
CALHOUN	30,321	24,379	5,769	173	18,610 R	80.4%	19.0%	80.8%	19.1%
CASS	8,143	5,720	2,346	77	3,374 R	70.2%	28.8%	70.9%	29.1%
CHARLEVOIX	4,363	3,489	842	32	2,647 R	80.0%	19.3%	80.6%	19.4%
CHEBOYGAN	4,546	2,743	1,784	19	959 R	60.3%	39.2%	60.6%	39.4%
CHIPPEWA	7,755	5,326	2,355	74	2,971 R	68.7%	30.4%	69.3%	30.7%
CLARE	2,324	1,920	381	23	1,539 R	82.6%	16.4%	83.4%	16.6%
CLINTON	8,210	6,161	2,013	36	4,148 R	75.0%	24.5%	75.4%	24.6%
CRAWFORD	1,017	776	237	4	539 R	76.3%	23.3%	76.6%	23.4%
DELTA	10,930	5,420	5,419	91	1 R	49.6%	49.6%	50.0%	50.0%
DICKINSON	10,509	5,840	4,626	43	1,214 R	55.6%	44.0%	55.8%	44.2%
EATON	10,836	8,493	2,285	58	6,228 R	78.4%	21.1%	78.8%	21.2%
EMMET	4,882	3,679	1,166	37	2,513 R	75.4%	23.9%	75.9%	24.1%
GENESEE	53,853	42,743	10,910	200	31,833 R	79.4%	20.3%	79.7%	20.3%
GLADWIN	2,143	1,795	341	7	1,454 R	83.8%	15.9%	84.0%	16.0%
GOGEBIC	9,362	6,061	3,134	167	2,927 R	64.7%	33.5%	65.9%	34.1%
GRAND TRAVERSE	5,940	4,429	1,489	22	2,940 R	74.6%	25.1%	74.8%	25.2%
GRATIOT	10,741	8,823	1,854	64	6,969 R	82.1%	17.3%	82.6%	17.4%
HILLSDALE	10,226	8,282	1,893	51	6,389 R	81.0%	18.5%	81.4%	18.6%
HOUGHTON	18,042	11,240	6,573	229	4,667 R	62.3%	36.4%	63.1%	36.9%
HURON	10,875	7,046	3,797	32	3,249 R	64.8%	34.9%	65.0%	35.0%
INGHAM	37,243	29,383	7,654	206	21,729 R	78.9%	20.6%	79.3%	20.7%
IONIA	12,643	9,471	3,089	83	6,382 R	74.9%	24.4%	75.4%	24.6%
IOSCO	2,439	1,873	552	14	1,321 R	76.8%	22.6%	77.2%	22.8%
IRON	6,415	4,103	2,262	50	1,841 R	64.0%	35.3%	64.5%	35.5%
ISABELLA	6,736	4,926	1,762	48	3,164 R	73.1%	26.2%	73.7%	26.3%
JACKSON	32,693	25,080	7,462	151	17,618 R	76.7%	22.8%	77.1%	22.9%
KALAMAZOO	29,630	23,626	5,946	258	17,680 R	79.7%	19.9%	80.1%	20.1%
KALKASKA	1,168	988	160	20	828 R	84.6%	13.7%	86.1%	13.9%
KENT	75,310	56,573	18,229	508	38,344 R	75.1%	24.2%	75.6%	24.4%
KEWEENAW	1,704	1,305	360	39	945 R	76.6%	21.1%	78.4%	21.6%
LAKE	1,570	1,147	409	14	738 R	73.1%	26.1%	73.7%	26.3%
LAPEER	7,867	6,514	1,312	41	5,202 R	82.8%	16.7%	83.2%	16.8%
LEELANAU	2,437	1,521	903	13	618 R	62.4%	37.1%	62.7%	37.3%
LENAWEE	19,227	14,794	4,321	112	10,473 R	76.9%	22.5%	77.4%	22.6%
LIVINGSTON	7,741	5,642	2,075	24	3,557 R	72.9%	26.8%	73.1%	26.9%
LUCE	1,827	1,466	350	11	1,116 R	80.2%	19.2%	80.7%	19.3%
MACKINAC	3,243	1,879	1,355	9	524 R	57.9%	41.9%	58.1%	41.9%
MACOMB	20,299	12,845	7,363	91	5,482 R	63.3%	36.3%	63.6%	36.4%
MANISTEE	6,799	4,129	2,624	46	1,505 R	60.7%	38.6%	61.1%	38.9%
MARQUETTE	15,811	10,879	4,716	216	6,153 R	68.8%	29.8%	69.8%	30.2%
MASON	5,936	4,318	1,567	51	2,751 R	72.7%	26.4%	73.4%	26.6%
MECOSTA	5,463	4,422	1,004	37	3,418 R	80.9%	18.4%	81.5%	18.5%
MENOMINEE	8,507	4,255	4,198	54	57 R	50.0%	49.3%	50.3%	49.7%
MIDLAND	5,538	4,555	964	19	3,591 R	82.2%	17.4%	82.5%	17.5%
MISSAUKEE	2,014	1,756	247	11	1,509 R	87.2%	12.3%	87.7%	12.3%
MONROE	17,507	10,202	7,242	63	2,950 R	58.3%	41.4%	58.5%	41.5%
MONTCALM	9,318	7,691	1,572	55	6,119 R	82.5%	16.9%	83.0%	17.0%
MONTMORENCY	1,064	787	270	7	517 R	74.0%	25.4%	74.5%	25.5%

PRESIDENT 1932

County	Total Vote	Republican	Democratic	Other	Rep.-Dem. Plurality	Total Vote Rep.	Total Vote Dem.	Major Vote Rep.	Major Vote Dem.
ALCONA	1,842	881	884	77	3 D	47.8%	48.0%	49.9%	50.1%
ALGER	3,690	1,354	2,111	225	757 D	36.7%	57.2%	39.1%	60.9%
ALLEGAN	16,082	8,705	7,030	347	1,675 R	54.1%	43.7%	55.3%	44.7%
ALPENA	7,006	3,222	3,562	222	340 D	46.0%	50.8%	47.5%	52.5%
ANTRIM	4,158	2,308	1,686	164	622 R	55.5%	40.5%	57.8%	42.2%
ARENAC	3,666	1,471	2,086	109	615 D	40.1%	56.9%	41.4%	58.6%
BARAGA	4,086	1,917	2,016	153	99 D	46.9%	49.3%	48.7%	51.3%
BARRY	9,258	4,556	4,416	286	140 R	49.2%	47.7%	50.8%	49.2%
BAY	25,092	9,816	14,708	568	4,892 D	39.1%	58.6%	40.0%	60.0%
BENZIE	3,176	1,595	1,432	149	163 R	50.2%	45.1%	52.7%	47.3%
BERRIEN	33,264	14,123	18,447	694	4,324 D	42.5%	55.5%	43.4%	56.6%
BRANCH	10,640	4,663	5,685	292	1,022 D	43.8%	53.4%	45.1%	54.9%
CALHOUN	33,563	16,255	16,281	1,027	26 D	48.4%	48.5%	50.0%	50.0%
CASS	9,636	3,994	5,349	293	1,355 D	41.4%	55.5%	42.7%	57.3%
CHARLEVOIX	5,291	2,623	2,344	324	279 R	49.6%	44.3%	52.8%	47.2%
CHEBOYGAN	5,811	2,309	3,431	71	1,122 D	39.7%	59.0%	40.2%	59.8%
CHIPPEWA	9,665	5,252	4,221	192	1,031 R	54.3%	43.7%	55.4%	44.6%
CLARE	3,324	1,474	1,741	109	267 D	44.3%	52.4%	45.8%	54.2%
CLINTON	9,853	4,647	5,098	108	451 D	47.2%	51.7%	47.7%	52.3%
CRAWFORD	1,337	559	755	23	196 D	41.8%	56.5%	43.4%	57.5%
DELTA	12,251	4,386	7,363	536	2,977 D	35.7%	59.9%	37.3%	62.7%
DICKINSON	12,031	5,120	6,482	429	1,362 D	42.6%	53.9%	44.1%	55.9%
EATON	13,172	5,840	6,887	445	1,047 D	44.3%	52.3%	45.9%	54.1%
EMMET	6,275	2,890	3,110	275	220 D	46.1%	49.6%	48.2%	51.8%
GENESEE	67,267	28,231	36,860	2,176	8,629 D	42.0%	54.8%	43.4%	56.6%
GLADWIN	3,142	1,378	1,661	103	283 D	43.9%	52.9%	45.3%	54.7%
GOGEBIC	11,521	5,379	5,531	611	152 D	46.7%	48.0%	49.3%	50.7%
GRAND TRAVERSE	7,531	3,442	3,907	182	465 D	45.7%	51.9%	46.8%	53.2%
GRATIOT	11,538	5,123	6,124	291	1,001 D	44.4%	53.1%	45.5%	54.5%
HILLSDALE	11,867	5,879	5,696	292	183 R	49.5%	48.0%	50.8%	49.2%
HOUGHTON	20,780	12,308	7,838	634	4,470 R	59.2%	37.7%	61.1%	38.9%
HURON	11,690	5,707	5,770	213	63 D	48.8%	49.4%	49.7%	50.3%
INGHAM	44,545	21,044	22,370	1,131	1,326 D	47.2%	50.2%	48.5%	51.5%
IONIA	15,100	6,074	8,695	331	2,621 D	40.2%	57.6%	41.1%	58.9%
IOSCO	3,186	1,581	1,500	105	81 R	49.6%	47.1%	51.3%	48.7%
IRON	8,116	4,347	3,416	353	931 R	53.6%	42.1%	56.0%	44.0%
ISABELLA	8,645	4,211	4,272	162	61 D	48.7%	49.4%	49.6%	50.4%
JACKSON	33,730	16,150	16,584	996	434 D	47.9%	49.2%	49.3%	50.7%
KALAMAZOO	33,785	18,584	13,974	1,227	4,610 R	55.0%	41.4%	57.1%	42.9%
KALKASKA	1,485	705	649	131	56 R	47.5%	43.7%	52.1%	47.9%
KENT	86,723	42,186	41,601	2,936	585 R	48.6%	48.0%	50.3%	49.7%
KEWEENAW	2,007	1,454	527	26	927 R	72.4%	26.3%	73.4%	26.6%
LAKE	2,312	991	1,241	80	250 D	42.9%	53.7%	44.4%	55.6%
LAPEER	9,412	4,882	4,315	215	567 R	51.9%	45.8%	53.1%	46.9%
LEELANAU	3,313	1,527	1,746	40	219 D	46.1%	52.7%	46.7%	53.3%
LENAWEE	21,607	10,912	10,420	275	492 R	50.5%	48.2%	51.2%	48.8%
LIVINGSTON	9,357	4,534	4,684	139	150 D	48.5%	50.1%	49.2%	50.8%
LUCE	2,235	1,259	928	48	331 R	56.3%	41.5%	57.6%	42.4%
MACKINAC	4,109	1,504	2,578	27	1,074 D	36.6%	62.7%	36.8%	63.2%
MACOMB	25,984	8,649	16,539	796	7,890 D	33.3%	63.7%	34.3%	65.7%
MANISTEE	8,115	3,256	4,475	384	1,219 D	40.1%	55.1%	42.1%	57.9%
MARQUETTE	17,629	9,810	7,221	598	2,589 R	55.6%	41.0%	57.6%	42.4%
MASON	7,292	3,098	3,854	340	756 D	42.5%	52.9%	44.6%	55.4%
MECOSTA	6,635	3,336	3,152	147	184 R	50.3%	47.5%	51.4%	48.6%
MENOMINEE	9,473	3,374	5,782	317	2,408 D	35.6%	61.0%	36.9%	63.1%
MIDLAND	7,489	3,791	3,553	145	238 R	50.6%	47.4%	51.6%	48.4%
MISSAUKEE	2,789	1,439	1,282	68	157 R	51.6%	46.0%	52.9%	47.1%
MONROE	20,010	7,255	12,417	338	5,162 D	36.3%	62.1%	36.9%	63.1%
MONTCALM	11,403	5,704	5,166	533	538 R	50.0%	45.3%	52.5%	47.5%
MONTMORENCY	1,564	595	903	66	308 D	38.0%	57.7%	39.7%	60.3%

MICHIGAN

PRESIDENT 1928

County	Total Vote	Republican	Democratic	Other	Rep.-Dem. Plurality	Percentage Total Vote Rep.	Dem.	Major Vote Rep.	Dem.
MUSKEGON	22,281	16,997	5,158	126	11,839 R	76.3%	23.1%	76.7%	23.3%
NEWAYGO	5,465	4,552	888	25	3,664 R	83.3%	16.2%	83.7%	16.3%
OAKLAND	55,618	45,343	10,011	264	35,332 R	81.5%	18.0%	81.9%	18.1%
OCEANA	4,469	3,555	871	43	2,684 R	79.5%	19.5%	80.3%	19.7%
OGEMAW	2,221	1,630	579	12	1,051 R	73.4%	26.1%	73.8%	26.2%
ONTONAGON	4,013	2,394	1,353	266	1,041 R	59.7%	33.7%	63.9%	36.1%
OSCEOLA	4,527	3,923	582	22	3,341 R	86.7%	12.9%	87.1%	12.9%
OSCODA	551	476	73	2	403 R	86.4%	13.2%	86.7%	13.3%
OTSEGO	1,531	1,049	476	6	573 R	68.5%	31.1%	68.8%	31.2%
OTTAWA	18,035	15,417	2,524	94	12,893 R	85.5%	14.0%	85.9%	14.1%
PRESQUE ISLE	3,041	1,992	1,029	20	963 R	65.5%	33.8%	65.9%	34.1%
ROSCOMMON	1,023	780	236	7	544 R	76.2%	23.1%	76.8%	23.2%
SAGINAW	34,242	22,467	11,555	220	10,912 R	65.6%	33.7%	66.0%	34.0%
ST CLAIR	25,399	18,177	7,151	71	11,026 R	71.6%	28.2%	71.8%	28.2%
ST JOSEPH	11,546	8,781	2,698	67	6,083 R	76.1%	23.4%	76.5%	23.5%
SANILAC	9,668	7,888	1,736	44	6,152 R	81.6%	18.0%	82.0%	18.0%
SCHOOLCRAFT	2,733	1,826	877	30	949 R	66.8%	32.1%	67.6%	32.4%
SHIAWASSEE	12,407	9,851	2,496	60	7,355 R	79.4%	20.1%	79.8%	20.2%
TUSCOLA	9,703	8,188	1,464	51	6,724 R	84.4%	15.1%	84.8%	15.2%
VAN BUREN	12,050	9,325	2,643	82	6,682 R	77.4%	21.9%	77.9%	22.1%
WASHTENAW	25,093	19,676	5,308	109	14,368 R	78.4%	21.2%	78.8%	21.2%
WAYNE	426,718	265,852	157,047	3,819	108,805 R	62.3%	36.8%	62.9%	37.1%
WEXFORD	5,708	4,825	853	30	3,972 R	84.5%	14.9%	85.0%	15.0%
TOTAL	1,372,082	965,396	396,762	9,924	568,634 R	70.4%	28.9%	70.9%	29.1%

PRESIDENT 1932

Total Vote	Republican	Democratic	Other	Rep.-Dem. Plurality	Percentage Total Vote Rep.	Dem.	Major Vote Rep.	Dem.
26,265	11,971	13,497	797	1,526 D	45.6%	51.4%	47.0%	53.0%
6,953	3,458	3,275	220	183 R	49.7%	47.1%	51.4%	48.6%
67,928	32,462	33,135	2,331	673 D	47.8%	48.8%	49.5%	50.5%
5,707	2,481	3,051	175	570 D	43.5%	53.5%	44.8%	55.2%
3,204	1,472	1,645	87	173 D	45.9%	51.3%	47.2%	52.8%
5,023	2,287	2,337	399	50 D	45.5%	46.5%	49.5%	50.5%
5,381	2,969	2,321	91	648 R	55.2%	43.1%	56.1%	43.9%
775	410	349	16	61 R	52.9%	45.0%	54.0%	46.0%
2,493	1,006	1,377	110	371 D	40.4%	55.2%	42.2%	57.8%
20,700	12,076	7,981	643	4,095 R	58.3%	38.6%	60.2%	39.8%
3,865	1,560	2,217	88	657 D	40.4%	57.4%	41.3%	58.7%
1,410	601	757	52	156 D	42.6%	53.7%	44.3%	55.7%
41,414	17,794	22,643	977	4,849 D	43.0%	54.7%	44.0%	56.0%
28,041	14,883	12,776	382	2,107 R	53.1%	45.6%	53.8%	46.2%
12,852	5,626	6,917	309	1,291 D	43.8%	53.8%	44.9%	55.1%
11,205	6,860	4,077	268	2,783 R	61.2%	36.4%	62.7%	37.3%
3,511	1,722	1,660	129	62 R	49.0%	47.3%	50.9%	49.1%
14,936	6,600	8,002	334	1,402 D	44.2%	53.6%	45.2%	54.8%
11,367	6,110	5,077	180	1,033 R	53.8%	44.7%	54.6%	45.4%
14,641	6,954	7,223	464	269 D	47.5%	49.3%	49.1%	50.9%
29,100	15,368	12,552	1,180	2,816 R	52.8%	43.1%	55.0%	45.0%
543,601	212,678	310,686	20,237	98,008 D	39.1%	57.2%	40.6%	59.4%
6,804	3,425	3,251	128	174 R	50.3%	47.8%	51.3%	48.7%
1,664,765	739,894	871,700	53,171	131,806 D	44.4%	52.4%	45.9%	54.1%

MICHIGAN

PRESIDENT 1936

County	Total Vote	Republican	Democratic	Other	Rep.-Dem. Plurality	Total Vote % Rep.	Total Vote % Dem.	Major Vote % Rep.	Major Vote % Dem.
ALCONA	2,410	1,276	919	215	357 R	52.9%	38.1%	58.1%	41.9%
ALGER	4,209	1,291	2,824	94	1,533 D	30.7%	67.1%	31.4%	68.6%
ALLEGAN	16,106	9,247	5,922	937	3,325 R	57.4%	36.8%	61.0%	39.0%
ALPENA	7,076	3,536	3,231	309	305 R	50.0%	45.7%	52.3%	47.7%
ANTRIM	4,608	2,391	2,032	185	359 R	51.9%	44.1%	54.1%	45.9%
ARENAC	3,460	1,505	1,761	194	256 D	43.5%	50.9%	46.1%	53.9%
BARAGA	4,335	2,035	2,218	82	183 D	46.9%	51.2%	47.8%	52.2%
BARRY	9,255	4,950	3,880	425	1,070 R	53.5%	41.9%	56.1%	43.9%
BAY	24,885	8,729	13,789	2,367	5,050 D	35.1%	55.4%	38.8%	61.2%
BENZIE	3,658	1,742	1,686	230	56 R	47.6%	46.1%	50.8%	49.2%
BERRIEN	37,125	15,321	20,822	982	5,501 D	41.3%	56.1%	42.4%	57.6%
BRANCH	11,375	5,528	5,425	422	103 R	48.6%	47.7%	50.5%	49.5%
CALHOUN	36,153	15,667	20,231	1,255	4,564 D	43.3%	56.0%	43.6%	56.4%
CASS	10,345	4,525	5,114	706	589 D	43.7%	49.4%	47.0%	53.0%
CHARLEVOIX	5,722	2,814	2,669	239	145 R	49.2%	46.6%	51.3%	48.7%
CHEBOYGAN	6,009	2,584	3,016	409	432 D	43.0%	50.2%	46.1%	53.9%
CHIPPEWA	10,398	4,901	5,259	238	358 D	47.1%	50.6%	48.2%	51.8%
CLARE	3,708	1,979	1,494	235	485 R	53.4%	40.3%	57.0%	43.0%
CLINTON	9,823	4,915	4,296	612	619 R	50.0%	43.7%	53.4%	46.6%
CRAWFORD	1,493	580	876	37	296 D	38.8%	58.7%	39.8%	60.2%
DELTA	13,791	4,527	8,954	310	4,427 D	32.8%	64.9%	33.6%	66.4%
DICKINSON	12,934	4,563	7,952	419	3,389 D	35.3%	61.5%	36.5%	63.5%
EATON	14,031	6,649	6,780	602	131 D	47.4%	48.3%	49.5%	50.5%
EMMET	6,489	2,893	3,075	521	182 D	44.6%	47.4%	48.5%	51.5%
GENESEE	73,931	21,097	49,891	2,943	28,794 D	28.5%	67.5%	29.7%	70.3%
GLADWIN	3,343	1,645	1,533	165	112 R	49.2%	45.9%	51.8%	48.2%
GOGEBIC	13,257	4,649	8,461	147	3,812 D	35.1%	63.8%	35.5%	64.5%
GRAND TRAVERSE	7,980	3,676	3,827	477	151 D	46.1%	48.0%	49.0%	51.0%
GRATIOT	11,298	5,322	5,457	519	135 D	47.1%	48.3%	49.4%	50.6%
HILLSDALE	12,217	6,723	5,023	471	1,700 R	55.0%	41.1%	57.2%	42.8%
HOUGHTON	21,206	9,345	11,642	219	2,297 D	44.1%	54.9%	44.5%	55.5%
HURON	11,207	5,240	3,949	2,018	1,291 R	46.8%	35.2%	57.0%	43.0%
INGHAM	48,313	19,434	27,086	1,793	7,652 D	40.2%	56.1%	41.8%	58.2%
IONIA	14,782	6,487	7,140	1,155	653 D	43.9%	48.3%	47.6%	52.4%
IOSCO	3,475	1,768	1,547	160	221 R	50.9%	44.5%	53.3%	46.7%
IRON	9,130	3,834	5,216	80	1,382 D	42.0%	57.1%	42.4%	57.6%
ISABELLA	8,658	4,051	3,871	736	180 R	46.8%	44.7%	51.1%	48.9%
JACKSON	36,486	16,350	19,288	848	2,938 D	44.8%	52.9%	45.9%	54.1%
KALAMAZOO	37,380	17,824	17,870	1,686	46 D	47.7%	47.8%	49.9%	50.1%
KALKASKA	1,870	855	952	63	97 D	45.7%	50.9%	47.3%	52.7%
KENT	85,304	36,633	44,823	3,848	8,190 D	42.9%	52.5%	45.0%	55.0%
KEWEENAW	2,154	1,070	1,060	24	10 R	49.7%	49.2%	50.2%	49.8%
LAKE	2,493	1,091	1,337	65	246 D	43.8%	53.6%	44.9%	55.1%
LAPEER	9,364	5,081	3,868	415	1,213 R	54.3%	41.3%	56.8%	43.2%
LEELANAU	3,405	1,692	1,542	171	150 R	49.7%	45.3%	52.3%	47.7%
LENAWEE	21,435	12,154	8,299	982	3,855 R	56.7%	38.7%	59.4%	40.6%
LIVINGSTON	9,563	5,117	4,117	329	1,000 R	53.5%	43.1%	55.4%	44.6%
LUCE	2,515	1,199	1,297	19	98 D	47.7%	51.6%	48.0%	52.0%
MACKINAC	4,346	1,984	2,286	76	302 D	45.7%	52.6%	46.5%	53.5%
MACOMB	29,299	9,383	17,593	2,323	8,210 D	32.0%	60.0%	34.8%	65.2%
MANISTEE	8,350	3,509	4,542	299	1,033 D	42.0%	54.4%	43.6%	56.4%
MARQUETTE	19,844	7,607	11,994	243	4,387 D	38.3%	60.4%	38.8%	61.2%
MASON	8,190	3,224	4,598	368	1,374 D	39.4%	56.1%	41.2%	58.8%
MECOSTA	6,341	3,176	2,621	544	555 R	50.1%	41.3%	54.8%	45.2%
MENOMINEE	10,546	3,556	6,447	543	2,891 D	33.7%	61.1%	35.5%	64.5%
MIDLAND	7,957	3,829	3,751	377	78 R	48.1%	47.1%	50.5%	49.5%
MISSAUKEE	3,163	1,730	1,385	48	345 R	54.7%	43.8%	55.5%	44.5%
MONROE	21,284	8,330	11,075	1,879	2,745 D	39.1%	52.0%	42.9%	57.1%
MONTCALM	10,925	5,031	4,950	944	81 R	46.1%	45.3%	50.4%	49.6%
MONTMORENCY	1,798	792	958	48	166 D	44.0%	53.3%	45.3%	54.7%

PRESIDENT 1940

County	Total Vote	Republican	Democratic	Other	Rep.-Dem. Plurality	Total Vote % Rep.	Total Vote % Dem.	Major Vote % Rep.	Major Vote % Dem.
ALCONA	2,501	1,648	847	6	801 R	65.9%	33.9%	66.1%	33.9%
ALGER	4,675	1,629	2,984	62	1,355 D	34.8%	63.8%	35.3%	64.7%
ALLEGAN	17,792	12,347	5,385	60	6,962 R	69.4%	30.3%	69.6%	30.4%
ALPENA	8,432	4,822	3,597	13	1,225 R	57.2%	42.7%	57.3%	42.7%
ANTRIM	4,553	3,027	1,497	29	1,530 R	66.5%	32.9%	66.9%	33.1%
ARENAC	3,807	2,293	1,499	15	794 R	60.2%	39.4%	60.5%	39.5%
BARAGA	4,697	2,512	2,152	33	360 R	53.5%	45.8%	53.9%	46.1%
BARRY	10,025	6,872	3,091	62	3,781 R	68.5%	30.8%	69.0%	31.0%
BAY	29,585	14,618	14,902	67	284 D	49.4%	50.4%	49.5%	50.5%
BENZIE	3,765	2,320	1,429	16	891 R	61.6%	38.0%	61.9%	38.1%
BERRIEN	39,947	22,778	16,961	208	5,817 R	57.0%	42.5%	57.3%	42.7%
BRANCH	11,764	7,400	4,318	46	3,082 R	62.9%	36.7%	63.2%	36.8%
CALHOUN	40,610	21,633	18,682	295	2,951 R	53.3%	46.0%	53.7%	46.3%
CASS	11,268	6,868	4,340	60	2,528 R	61.0%	38.5%	61.3%	38.7%
CHARLEVOIX	5,736	3,522	2,163	51	1,359 R	61.4%	37.7%	62.0%	38.0%
CHEBOYGAN	6,523	3,646	2,856	21	790 R	55.9%	43.8%	56.1%	43.9%
CHIPPEWA	11,353	5,851	5,473	29	378 R	51.5%	48.2%	51.7%	48.3%
CLARE	4,300	3,004	1,277	19	1,727 R	69.9%	29.7%	70.2%	29.8%
CLINTON	11,081	8,311	2,745	25	5,566 R	75.0%	24.8%	75.2%	24.8%
CRAWFORD	1,662	873	777	12	96 R	52.5%	46.8%	52.9%	47.1%
DELTA	15,101	6,218	8,802	81	2,584 D	41.2%	58.3%	41.4%	58.6%
DICKINSON	13,389	5,953	7,347	89	1,394 D	44.4%	54.9%	44.8%	55.2%
EATON	15,594	9,864	5,645	85	4,219 R	63.3%	36.2%	63.6%	36.4%
EMMET	7,071	4,216	2,831	24	1,385 R	59.6%	40.0%	59.8%	40.2%
GENESEE	89,283	38,495	50,300	488	11,805 D	43.1%	56.3%	43.4%	56.6%
GLADWIN	4,044	2,741	1,294	9	1,447 R	67.8%	32.0%	67.9%	32.1%
GOGEBIC	15,734	6,431	9,104	199	2,673 D	40.9%	57.9%	41.4%	58.5%
GRAND TRAVERSE	8,745	5,621	3,094	30	2,527 R	64.3%	35.4%	64.5%	35.5%
GRATIOT	12,551	8,661	3,825	65	4,836 R	69.0%	30.5%	69.4%	30.6%
HILLSDALE	13,007	9,398	3,538	71	5,860 R	72.3%	27.2%	72.6%	27.4%
HOUGHTON	21,926	11,030	10,815	81	215 R	50.3%	49.3%	50.5%	49.5%
HURON	13,258	10,570	2,654	34	7,916 R	79.7%	20.0%	79.9%	20.1%
INGHAM	57,382	32,565	24,375	442	8,190 R	56.8%	42.5%	57.2%	42.8%
IONIA	14,916	9,439	5,399	78	4,040 R	63.3%	36.2%	63.6%	36.4%
IOSCO	3,825	2,504	1,303	18	1,201 R	65.5%	34.1%	65.8%	34.2%
IRON	9,661	4,766	4,808	87	42 D	49.3%	49.8%	49.8%	50.2%
ISABELLA	9,891	7,019	2,828	44	4,191 R	71.0%	28.6%	71.3%	28.7%
JACKSON	39,941	24,558	15,170	213	9,388 R	61.5%	38.0%	61.8%	38.2%
KALAMAZOO	43,622	25,596	17,733	293	7,863 R	58.7%	40.7%	59.1%	40.9%
KALKASKA	1,885	1,155	718	12	437 R	61.3%	38.1%	61.7%	38.3%
KENT	102,076	53,131	48,196	749	4,935 R	52.1%	47.2%	52.4%	47.6%
KEWEENAW	2,060	1,080	967	13	113 R	52.4%	46.9%	52.8%	47.2%
LAKE	2,495	1,413	1,070	12	343 R	56.6%	42.9%	56.9%	43.1%
LAPEER	11,044	7,714	3,299	31	4,415 R	69.8%	29.9%	70.0%	30.0%
LEELANAU	3,639	2,405	1,223	11	1,182 R	66.1%	33.6%	66.3%	33.7%
LENAWEE	24,156	16,963	7,132	71	9,831 R	70.2%	29.5%	70.4%	29.6%
LIVINGSTON	10,356	7,068	3,254	34	3,814 R	68.3%	31.4%	68.5%	31.5%
LUCE	2,617	1,542	1,069	6	473 R	58.9%	40.8%	59.1%	40.9%
MACKINAC	4,679	2,591	2,075	13	516 R	55.4%	44.3%	55.5%	44.5%
MACOMB	39,054	17,848	21,003	203	3,155 D	45.7%	53.8%	45.9%	54.1%
MANISTEE	8,892	4,630	4,242	20	388 R	52.1%	47.7%	52.2%	47.8%
MARQUETTE	21,982	9,034	12,854	94	3,820 D	41.1%	58.5%	41.3%	58.7%
MASON	8,763	4,874	3,836	53	1,038 R	55.6%	43.8%	56.0%	44.0%
MECOSTA	6,932	4,759	2,153	20	2,606 R	68.7%	31.1%	68.9%	31.1%
MENOMINEE	11,208	5,409	5,727	72	318 D	48.3%	51.1%	48.6%	51.4%
MIDLAND	10,157	6,269	3,834	54	2,435 R	61.7%	37.7%	62.1%	37.9%
MISSAUKEE	3,223	2,154	1,037	32	1,117 R	66.8%	32.2%	67.5%	32.5%
MONROE	23,945	13,517	10,368	60	3,149 R	56.5%	43.3%	56.6%	43.4%
MONTCALM	11,855	7,633	4,119	103	3,514 R	64.4%	34.7%	65.0%	35.0%
MONTMORENCY	1,966	1,189	768	9	421 R	60.5%	39.1%	60.8%	39.2%

MICHIGAN

PRESIDENT 1936

County	Total Vote	Republican	Democratic	Other	Rep.-Dem. Plurality	Percentage Total Vote Rep.	Dem.	Major Vote Rep.	Dem.
MUSKEGON	27,133	9,366	17,252	515	7,886 D	34.5%	63.6%	35.2%	64.8%
NEWAYGO	7,644	3,930	3,288	426	642 R	51.4%	43.0%	54.4%	45.6%
OAKLAND	73,997	30,071	40,329	3,597	10,258 D	40.6%	54.5%	42.7%	57.3%
OCEANA	5,861	2,663	2,902	296	239 D	45.4%	49.5%	47.9%	52.1%
OGEMAW	3,605	1,631	1,774	200	143 D	45.2%	49.2%	47.9%	52.1%
ONTONAGON	5,563	2,162	3,233	168	1,071 D	38.9%	58.1%	40.1%	59.9%
OSCEOLA	5,520	3,107	1,992	421	1,115 R	56.3%	36.1%	60.9%	39.1%
OSCODA	956	456	492	8	36 D	47.7%	51.5%	48.1%	51.9%
OTSEGO	2,447	1,102	1,280	65	178 D	45.0%	52.3%	46.3%	53.7%
OTTAWA	21,645	11,114	9,579	952	1,535 R	51.3%	44.3%	53.7%	46.3%
PRESQUE ISLE	4,605	1,621	2,905	79	1,284 D	35.2%	63.1%	35.8%	64.2%
ROSCOMMON	1,684	836	782	66	54 R	49.6%	46.4%	51.7%	48.3%
SAGINAW	41,410	15,527	22,592	3,291	7,065 D	37.5%	54.6%	40.7%	59.3%
ST CLAIR	27,782	12,760	12,663	2,359	97 R	45.9%	45.6%	50.2%	49.8%
ST JOSEPH	13,809	7,160	6,048	601	1,112 R	51.9%	43.8%	54.2%	45.8%
SANILAC	11,036	6,975	3,285	776	3,690 R	63.2%	29.8%	68.0%	32.0%
SCHOOLCRAFT	3,885	1,430	2,333	122	903 D	36.8%	60.1%	38.0%	62.0%
SHIAWASSEE	13,878	6,017	6,666	1,195	649 D	43.4%	48.0%	47.4%	52.6%
TUSCOLA	11,037	6,188	3,743	1,106	2,445 R	56.1%	33.9%	62.3%	37.7%
VAN BUREN	16,655	9,110	6,720	825	2,390 R	54.7%	40.3%	57.5%	42.5%
WASHTENAW	29,510	14,986	13,589	935	1,397 R	50.8%	46.0%	52.4%	47.6%
WAYNE	626,120	190,732	404,055	31,333	213,323 D	30.5%	64.5%	32.1%	67.9%
WEXFORD	7,109	3,153	3,771	185	618 D	44.4%	53.0%	45.5%	54.5%
TOTAL	1,805,098	699,733	1,016,794	88,571	317,061 D	38.8%	56.3%	40.8%	59.2%

PRESIDENT 1940

County	Total Vote	Republican	Democratic	Other	Rep.-Dem. Plurality	Percentage Total Vote Rep.	Dem.	Major Vote Rep.	Dem.
MUSKEGON	34,424	14,957	19,257	210	4,300 D	43.4%	55.9%	43.7%	56.3%
NEWAYGO	8,145	5,418	2,693	34	2,725 R	66.5%	33.1%	66.8%	33.2%
OAKLAND	96,623	49,002	47,022	599	1,980 R	50.7%	48.7%	51.0%	49.0%
OCEANA	6,127	3,711	2,379	37	1,332 R	60.6%	38.8%	60.9%	39.1%
OGEMAW	3,739	2,447	1,278	14	1,169 R	65.4%	34.2%	65.7%	34.3%
ONTONAGON	6,116	2,880	3,103	133	223 D	47.1%	50.7%	48.1%	51.9%
OSCEOLA	5,789	4,217	1,555	17	2,662 R	72.8%	26.9%	73.1%	26.9%
OSCODA	1,073	661	409	3	252 R	61.6%	38.1%	61.8%	38.2%
OTSEGO	2,480	1,353	1,119	8	234 R	54.6%	45.1%	54.7%	45.3%
OTTAWA	24,784	15,462	9,152	170	6,310 R	62.4%	36.9%	62.8%	37.2%
PRESQUE ISLE	5,160	2,552	2,595	13	43 D	49.5%	50.3%	49.6%	50.4%
ROSCOMMON	2,118	1,360	739	19	621 R	64.2%	34.9%	64.6%	35.2%
SAGINAW	49,753	27,042	22,490	221	4,552 R	54.4%	45.2%	54.6%	45.4%
ST CLAIR	30,976	18,635	12,259	82	6,376 R	60.2%	39.6%	60.3%	39.7%
ST JOSEPH	15,115	10,025	5,045	45	4,980 R	66.3%	33.4%	66.5%	33.5%
SANILAC	12,527	10,289	2,195	43	8,094 R	82.1%	17.5%	82.4%	17.6%
SCHOOLCRAFT	4,334	2,003	2,320	11	317 D	46.2%	53.5%	46.3%	53.7%
SHIAWASSEE	15,804	9,995	5,727	82	4,268 R	63.2%	36.2%	63.6%	36.4%
TUSCOLA	13,448	10,146	3,257	45	6,889 R	75.4%	24.2%	75.7%	24.3%
VAN BUREN	17,297	11,571	5,625	101	5,946 R	66.9%	32.5%	67.3%	32.7%
WASHTENAW	33,719	21,664	11,802	253	9,862 R	64.2%	35.0%	64.7%	35.3%
WAYNE	732,569	275,974	451,003	5,592	175,029 D	37.7%	61.6%	38.0%	62.0%
WEXFORD	7,326	4,322	2,947	57	1,375 R	59.0%	40.2%	59.5%	40.5%
TOTAL	2,085,929	1,039,917	1,032,991	13,021	6,926 R	49.9%	49.5%	50.2%	49.8%

MICHIGAN

PRESIDENT 1944

County	Total Vote	Republican	Democratic	Other	Rep.-Dem. Plurality	% Total Vote Rep.	% Total Vote Dem.	% Major Vote Rep.	% Major Vote Dem.
ALCONA	2,230	1,503	716	11	787 R	67.4%	32.1%	67.7%	32.3%
ALGER	4,036	1,504	2,519	13	1,015 D	37.3%	62.4%	37.4%	62.6%
ALLEGAN	16,878	12,327	4,480	71	7,847 R	73.3%	26.5%	73.3%	26.7%
ALPENA	7,327	4,453	2,856	18	1,597 R	60.8%	39.0%	60.9%	39.1%
ANTRIM	3,681	2,626	1,206	49	1,420 R	67.7%	31.1%	68.5%	31.5%
ARENAC	3,271	1,978	1,280	13	698 R	60.5%	39.1%	60.7%	39.3%
BARAGA	3,714	1,829	1,874	11	45 D	49.2%	50.5%	49.4%	50.6%
BARRY	10,203	7,057	3,010	136	4,047 R	69.2%	29.5%	70.1%	29.9%
BAY	31,204	15,459	15,602	143	143 D	49.5%	50.0%	49.8%	50.2%
BENZIE	3,142	2,026	1,084	32	942 R	64.5%	34.5%	65.1%	34.9%
BERRIEN	40,934	24,832	15,886	216	8,946 R	60.7%	38.8%	61.0%	39.0%
BRANCH	10,609	7,155	3,406	48	3,749 R	67.4%	32.1%	67.7%	32.3%
CALHOUN	37,693	20,664	16,611	418	4,053 R	54.8%	44.1%	55.4%	44.6%
CASS	10,051	6,566	3,417	68	3,149 R	65.3%	34.0%	65.8%	34.2%
CHARLEVOIX	4,974	3,039	1,893	42	1,146 R	61.1%	38.1%	61.6%	38.4%
CHEBOYGAN	5,116	2,943	2,141	32	802 R	57.5%	41.8%	57.9%	42.1%
CHIPPEWA	9,725	5,335	4,344	46	991 R	54.9%	44.7%	55.1%	44.9%
CLARE	3,735	2,636	1,078	21	1,558 R	70.6%	28.9%	71.0%	29.0%
CLINTON	10,984	8,422	2,533	29	5,889 R	76.7%	23.1%	76.9%	23.1%
CRAWFORD	1,355	797	550	8	247 R	58.8%	40.6%	59.2%	40.8%
DELTA	12,644	5,213	7,375	56	2,162 D	41.2%	58.3%	41.4%	58.6%
DICKINSON	11,842	4,987	6,740	115	1,753 D	42.1%	56.9%	42.5%	57.5%
EATON	15,140	9,975	5,049	116	4,926 R	65.9%	33.3%	66.4%	33.6%
EMMET	5,782	3,538	2,206	38	1,332 R	61.2%	38.2%	61.6%	38.4%
GENESEE	94,116	41,145	52,444	527	11,299 D	43.7%	55.7%	44.0%	56.0%
GLADWIN	3,464	2,457	985	22	1,472 R	70.9%	28.4%	71.4%	28.6%
GOGEBIC	13,268	5,283	7,938	47	2,655 D	39.8%	59.8%	40.0%	60.0%
GRAND TRAVERSE	8,075	5,413	2,607	55	2,806 R	67.0%	32.3%	67.5%	32.5%
GRATIOT	11,244	7,987	3,153	97	4,827 R	71.0%	28.1%	71.7%	28.3%
HILLSDALE	12,598	9,364	3,153	81	6,211 R	74.3%	25.0%	74.8%	25.2%
HOUGHTON	19,238	9,110	10,066	62	956 D	47.4%	52.3%	47.5%	52.5%
HURON	11,898	9,538	2,301	59	7,237 R	80.2%	19.3%	80.6%	19.4%
INGHAM	58,313	34,255	23,655	403	10,600 R	58.7%	40.6%	59.2%	40.8%
IONIA	13,914	9,331	4,437	146	4,894 R	67.1%	31.9%	67.8%	32.2%
IOSCO	3,479	2,340	1,127	12	1,213 R	57.3%	32.4%	67.5%	32.5%
IRON	8,546	3,945	4,537	64	592 D	46.2%	53.1%	46.5%	53.5%
ISABELLA	8,949	6,356	2,522	71	3,834 R	71.0%	28.2%	71.6%	28.4%
JACKSON	37,100	22,992	13,859	249	9,133 R	62.0%	37.4%	62.4%	37.6%
KALAMAZOO	41,654	24,974	16,223	457	8,751 R	60.0%	38.9%	60.6%	39.4%
KALKASKA	1,412	992	409	11	583 R	70.3%	29.0%	70.8%	29.2%
KENT	99,116	54,163	43,679	1,274	10,484 R	54.6%	44.1%	55.4%	44.6%
KEWEENAW	1,837	866	965	6	99 D	47.1%	52.5%	47.3%	52.7%
LAKE	1,946	1,145	794	7	351 R	58.8%	40.8%	59.1%	40.9%
LAPEER	10,821	7,769	3,002	50	4,767 R	71.8%	27.7%	72.1%	27.9%
LEELANAU	3,023	2,063	944	16	1,119 R	68.2%	31.2%	68.6%	31.4%
LENAWEE	23,243	16,382	6,750	111	9,632 R	70.5%	29.0%	70.8%	29.2%
LIVINGSTON	10,391	7,417	2,910	64	4,507 R	71.4%	28.0%	71.8%	28.2%
LUCE	1,993	1,195	790	8	405 R	60.0%	39.6%	60.2%	39.8%
MACKINAC	3,776	2,268	1,488	20	780 R	60.1%	39.4%	60.4%	39.6%
MACOMB	45,135	21,305	23,506	324	2,201 D	47.2%	52.1%	47.5%	52.5%
MANISTEE	7,530	4,095	3,398	37	697 R	54.4%	45.1%	54.7%	45.3%
MARQUETTE	19,944	8,163	11,707	74	3,544 D	40.9%	58.7%	41.1%	58.9%
MASON	7,630	4,446	3,137	47	1,309 R	58.3%	41.1%	58.6%	41.4%
MECOSTA	5,995	4,217	1,708	70	2,509 R	70.3%	28.5%	71.2%	28.8%
MENOMINEE	9,573	4,869	4,632	72	237 R	50.9%	48.4%	51.2%	48.8%
MIDLAND	10,482	6,850	3,569	63	3,281 R	65.4%	34.0%	65.7%	34.3%
MISSAUKEE	2,763	1,979	759	25	1,220 R	71.6%	27.5%	72.3%	27.7%
MONROE	23,836	13,478	10,275	83	3,203 R	56.5%	43.1%	56.7%	43.3%
MONTCALM	10,790	7,525	3,168	97	4,357 R	70.4%	29.4%	70.4%	29.6%
MONTMORENCY	1,586	1,034	541	11	493 R	65.2%	34.1%	65.7%	34.3%

PRESIDENT 1948

County	Total Vote	Republican	Democratic	Other	Rep.-Dem. Plurality	% Total Vote Rep.	% Total Vote Dem.	% Major Vote Rep.	% Major Vote Dem.
ALCONA	2,168	1,425	708	35	717 R	65.7%	32.7%	66.8%	33.2%
ALGER	3,983	1,702	2,009	272	307 D	42.7%	50.4%	45.9%	54.1%
ALLEGAN	15,424	10,439	4,594	391	5,845 R	67.7%	29.8%	69.4%	30.6%
ALPENA	7,452	4,313	2,743	96	1,570 R	60.3%	38.4%	61.1%	38.9%
ANTRIM	3,849	2,588	1,129	132	1,459 R	67.2%	29.3%	69.6%	30.4%
ARENAC	3,041	1,790	1,203	48	587 R	58.9%	39.6%	59.8%	40.2%
BARAGA	3,748	1,878	1,656	214	222 R	50.1%	44.2%	53.1%	46.9%
BARRY	8,768	5,677	2,726	365	2,951 R	64.7%	31.1%	67.6%	32.4%
BAY	27,997	13,321	14,349	327	1,028 D	47.6%	51.3%	48.1%	51.9%
BENZIE	3,089	2,013	964	112	1,049 R	65.2%	31.2%	67.6%	32.4%
BERRIEN	37,361	22,003	14,516	842	7,487 R	58.9%	38.9%	60.3%	39.7%
BRANCH	10,027	6,323	3,405	299	2,918 R	63.1%	34.0%	65.0%	35.0%
CALHOUN	35,096	19,285	15,077	734	4,208 R	54.9%	43.0%	56.1%	43.9%
CASS	9,032	5,615	3,201	216	2,414 R	62.2%	35.4%	63.7%	36.3%
CHARLEVOIX	4,695	2,911	1,847	137	1,064 R	59.5%	37.7%	61.2%	38.8%
CHEBOYGAN	5,109	3,184	1,842	83	1,342 R	62.3%	36.1%	63.4%	36.6%
CHIPPEWA	9,331	4,977	3,860	494	1,117 R	53.3%	41.4%	56.3%	43.7%
CLARE	3,605	2,512	1,197	96	1,315 R	66.0%	31.5%	67.7%	32.3%
CLINTON	10,191	7,510	2,523	158	4,987 R	73.7%	24.8%	74.8%	25.1%
CRAWFORD	1,328	849	455	24	394 R	63.9%	34.3%	65.1%	34.9%
DELTA	12,633	5,414	6,943	276	1,529 D	42.9%	55.0%	43.8%	56.2%
DICKINSON	11,209	4,417	6,295	497	1,878 D	39.1%	55.7%	41.2%	58.8%
EATON	13,320	8,637	4,273	410	4,373 R	64.8%	32.0%	66.9%	33.1%
EMMET	5,621	3,565	1,922	134	1,643 R	63.4%	34.2%	65.0%	35.0%
GENESEE	86,228	38,270	45,032	2,926	6,762 D	44.4%	52.2%	45.9%	54.1%
GLADWIN	3,104	2,062	963	79	1,099 R	66.4%	31.0%	68.2%	31.8%
GOGEBIC	12,569	5,204	6,722	643	1,518 D	41.4%	53.5%	43.6%	56.4%
GRAND TRAVERSE	8,015	5,473	2,365	177	3,108 R	68.3%	29.5%	70.2%	30.2%
GRATIOT	10,760	7,035	2,659	333	4,376 R	70.2%	26.5%	72.6%	27.4%
HILLSDALE	10,760	7,232	3,095	433	4,137 R	67.2%	28.8%	70.0%	30.0%
HOUGHTON	17,471	9,541	6,925	1,005	2,616 R	54.6%	39.6%	57.9%	42.1%
HURON	10,648	7,978	2,562	108	5,416 R	74.9%	24.1%	75.7%	24.3%
INGHAM	52,575	31,868	19,366	1,341	12,502 R	60.6%	36.8%	62.2%	37.8%
IONIA	12,731	7,868	4,450	311	4,450 R	62.6%	35.0%	64.2%	35.8%
IOSCO	3,772	2,599	1,115	58	1,484 R	68.9%	29.6%	70.0%	30.0%
IRON	8,212	3,659	4,125	428	466 D	44.6%	50.2%	47.0%	53.0%
ISABELLA	8,158	5,485	2,487	186	2,998 R	67.2%	30.5%	68.8%	31.2%
JACKSON	35,037	21,449	12,809	779	8,640 R	61.2%	36.6%	62.6%	37.4%
KALAMAZOO	41,517	23,799	16,393	1,325	7,406 R	57.3%	39.5%	59.2%	40.8%
KALKASKA	1,277	837	400	40	437 R	65.5%	31.3%	67.7%	32.3%
KENT	98,776	53,669	43,205	1,902	10,464 R	54.3%	43.7%	55.4%	44.6%
KEWEENAW	1,625	814	647	164	167 R	50.1%	39.8%	55.7%	44.3%
LAKE	2,490	1,348	1,077	65	271 R	54.1%	43.3%	55.6%	44.4%
LAPEER	13,298	8,358	4,668	272	3,690 R	62.9%	35.1%	64.2%	35.8%
LEELANAU	2,794	1,928	835	31	1,093 R	69.0%	29.9%	69.8%	30.2%
LENAWEE	21,291	14,369	6,529	393	7,840 R	67.5%	30.7%	68.8%	31.2%
LIVINGSTON	10,379	7,368	2,813	198	4,555 R	71.0%	27.1%	72.4%	27.6%
LUCE	1,887	1,273	570	44	703 R	67.5%	30.2%	69.1%	30.9%
MACKINAC	3,362	2,268	1,044	42	1,044 R	60.4%	33.8%	65.7%	34.3%
MACOMB	47,660	21,205	25,265	1,190	4,060 D	44.5%	53.0%	45.6%	54.4%
MANISTEE	7,399	3,913	3,339	147	574 R	52.9%	45.1%	54.0%	46.0%
MARQUETTE	19,064	8,591	10,003	470	1,412 D	45.1%	52.5%	46.2%	53.8%
MASON	7,407	4,147	2,988	272	1,159 R	56.0%	40.3%	58.1%	41.9%
MECOSTA	5,557	3,803	1,572	182	2,231 R	68.4%	28.3%	70.8%	29.2%
MENOMINEE	9,667	4,420	5,094	153	674 D	45.7%	52.7%	46.5%	53.5%
MIDLAND	9,156	5,811	3,204	181	2,607 R	63.2%	34.8%	64.5%	35.5%
MISSAUKEE	2,554	1,742	750	62	992 R	68.2%	29.4%	69.9%	30.1%
MONROE	21,824	11,070	10,434	320	636 R	50.7%	47.8%	51.5%	48.5%
MONTCALM	9,335	6,081	2,999	255	3,082 R	65.1%	32.1%	67.0%	33.0%
MONTMORENCY	1,644	1,054	553	37	501 R	64.1%	33.6%	65.6%	34.4%

MICHIGAN

PRESIDENT 1944

County	Total Vote	Republican	Democratic	Other	Rep.-Dem. Plurality	Total Vote Rep.	Total Vote Dem.	Major Vote Rep.	Major Vote Dem.
MUSKEGON	36,786	16,536	19,963	287	3,427 D	45.0%	54.3%	45.3%	54.7%
NEWAYGO	7,434	5,250	2,156	28	3,094 R	70.6%	29.0%	70.9%	29.1%
OAKLAND	115,813	59,627	55,272	914	4,355 R	51.5%	47.7%	51.9%	48.1%
OCEANA	5,335	3,534	1,738	63	1,796 R	66.2%	32.6%	67.0%	33.0%
OGEMAW	3,363	2,339	1,006	18	1,333 R	69.6%	29.9%	69.9%	30.1%
ONTONAGON	5,061	2,433	2,611	17	178 D	48.1%	51.6%	48.2%	51.8%
OSCEOLA	5,178	3,787	1,338	53	2,449 R	73.1%	25.8%	73.9%	26.1%
OSCODA	950	615	332	3	283 R	64.7%	34.9%	64.9%	35.1%
OTSEGO	2,182	1,259	912	11	347 R	57.7%	41.8%	58.0%	42.0%
OTTAWA	25,786	17,077	8,511	198	8,566 R	66.2%	33.0%	66.7%	33.3%
PRESQUE ISLE	4,314	2,209	2,092	13	117 R	51.2%	48.5%	51.4%	48.6%
ROSCOMMON	1,789	1,292	484	13	808 R	72.2%	27.1%	72.7%	27.3%
SAGINAW	48,402	27,289	20,383	730	6,906 R	56.4%	42.1%	57.2%	42.8%
ST CLAIR	31,123	19,175	11,813	135	7,362 R	61.6%	38.0%	61.9%	38.1%
ST JOSEPH	14,089	9,785	4,235	69	5,550 R	69.5%	30.1%	69.8%	30.2%
SANILAC	11,587	9,512	2,015	60	7,497 R	82.1%	17.4%	82.5%	17.5%
SCHOOLCRAFT	3,447	1,704	1,724	19	20 D	49.4%	50.0%	49.7%	50.3%
SHIAWASSEE	16,957	11,601	5,292	64	6,309 R	68.4%	31.2%	68.7%	31.3%
TUSCOLA	12,787	9,789	2,938	60	6,851 R	76.6%	23.0%	76.9%	23.1%
VAN BUREN	16,037	10,951	5,002	84	5,949 R	68.3%	31.2%	68.6%	31.4%
WASHTENAW	39,906	24,740	14,922	244	9,818 R	62.0%	37.4%	62.4%	37.6%
WAYNE	875,093	316,270	554,670	4,153	238,400 D	36.1%	63.4%	36.3%	63.7%
WEXFORD	6,656	4,074	2,489	93	1,585 R	61.2%	37.4%	62.1%	37.9%
TOTAL	2,205,223	1,084,423	1,106,899	13,901	22,476 D	49.2%	50.2%	49.5%	50.5%

PRESIDENT 1948

County	Total Vote	Republican	Democratic	Other	Rep.-Dem. Plurality	Total Vote Rep.	Total Vote Dem.	Major Vote Rep.	Major Vote Dem.
MUSKEGON	37,107	15,382	20,631	1,094	5,249 D	41.5%	55.6%	42.7%	57.3%
NEWAYGO	6,566	4,394	2,027	145	2,367 R	66.9%	30.9%	68.4%	31.6%
OAKLAND	116,866	62,516	51,491	2,859	11,025 R	53.5%	44.1%	54.8%	45.2%
OCEANA	4,899	2,943	1,714	242	1,229 R	60.1%	35.0%	63.2%	36.8%
OGEMAW	3,187	2,062	1,038	87	1,024 R	64.7%	32.6%	66.5%	33.5%
ONTONAGON	5,104	2,561	2,163	380	398 R	50.2%	42.4%	54.2%	45.8%
OSCEOLA	4,555	3,122	1,276	157	1,846 R	68.5%	28.0%	71.0%	29.0%
OSCODA	1,089	785	285	19	500 R	72.1%	26.2%	73.4%	26.6%
OTSEGO	2,320	1,392	888	40	504 R	60.0%	38.3%	61.1%	38.9%
OTTAWA	25,288	16,028	8,789	471	7,239 R	63.4%	34.8%	64.6%	35.4%
PRESQUE ISLE	4,165	2,271	1,872	22	399 R	54.5%	44.9%	54.8%	45.2%
ROSCOMMON	2,781	2,055	687	39	1,368 R	73.9%	24.7%	74.9%	25.1%
SAGINAW	40,733	22,923	16,995	815	5,928 R	56.3%	41.7%	57.4%	42.6%
ST CLAIR	28,942	17,883	10,647	412	7,236 R	61.8%	36.8%	62.7%	37.3%
ST JOSEPH	12,436	8,166	3,928	342	4,238 R	65.7%	31.6%	67.5%	32.5%
SANILAC	10,606	8,237	2,167	202	6,070 R	77.7%	20.4%	79.2%	20.8%
SCHOOLCRAFT	3,447	1,713	1,651	83	62 R	49.7%	47.9%	50.9%	49.1%
SHIAWASSEE	15,496	10,377	4,852	267	5,525 R	67.0%	31.3%	68.1%	31.9%
TUSCOLA	11,041	8,125	2,676	240	5,449 R	73.6%	24.2%	75.2%	24.8%
VAN BUREN	14,004	9,511	4,082	411	5,429 R	67.9%	29.1%	70.0%	30.0%
WASHTENAW	38,567	24,588	12,721	1,258	11,867 R	63.8%	33.0%	65.9%	34.1%
WAYNE	846,106	321,773	489,654	34,679	167,881 D	38.0%	57.9%	39.7%	60.3%
WEXFORD	6,717	3,833	2,635	249	1,198 R	57.1%	39.2%	59.3%	40.7%
TOTAL	2,109,609	1,038,595	1,003,448	67,566	35,147 R	49.2%	47.6%	50.9%	49.1%

MICHIGAN

PRESIDENT 1952

County	Total Vote	Republican	Democratic	Other	Rep.-Dem. Plurality	Total Vote Rep.	Total Vote Dem.	Major Vote Rep.	Major Vote Dem.
ALCONA	2,215	1,441	766	8	675 R	65.1%	34.5%	65.3%	34.7%
ALGER	4,159	2,066	2,058	35	8 R	49.7%	49.5%	50.1%	49.9%
ALLEGAN	21,338	15,663	5,437	238	10,226 R	73.4%	25.5%	74.2%	25.8%
ALPENA	9,421	6,248	3,134	39	3,114 R	66.3%	33.3%	66.6%	33.4%
ANTRIM	4,618	3,533	1,046	39	2,487 R	76.5%	22.7%	77.2%	22.8%
ARENAC	4,064	2,753	1,290	21	1,463 R	67.7%	31.7%	68.1%	31.9%
BARAGA	3,671	2,103	1,540	28	563 R	57.3%	42.0%	57.7%	42.3%
BARRY	12,287	8,933	3,230	124	5,703 R	72.7%	26.3%	73.4%	26.6%
BAY	34,396	20,087	14,113	196	5,974 R	58.4%	41.0%	58.7%	41.3%
BENZIE	3,768	2,752	980	36	1,772 R	73.0%	26.0%	73.7%	26.3%
BERRIEN	52,320	32,932	19,088	300	13,844 R	62.9%	36.5%	63.3%	36.7%
BRANCH	12,884	9,215	3,564	105	5,651 R	71.5%	27.7%	72.1%	27.9%
CALHOUN	51,447	31,941	19,171	335	12,770 R	62.1%	37.3%	62.5%	37.5%
CASS	13,072	8,479	4,500	93	3,979 R	64.9%	34.4%	65.3%	34.7%
CHARLEVOIX	5,722	3,895	1,778	49	2,117 R	68.1%	31.1%	68.7%	31.3%
CHEBOYGAN	6,309	4,385	1,900	24	2,485 R	69.5%	30.1%	69.8%	30.2%
CHIPPEWA	11,389	7,075	4,257	57	2,818 R	62.1%	37.4%	62.4%	37.6%
CLARE	4,630	3,529	1,059	42	2,470 R	76.2%	22.9%	76.9%	23.1%
CLINTON	13,566	10,510	2,977	79	7,533 R	77.5%	21.9%	77.9%	22.1%
CRAWFORD	1,835	1,331	490	14	841 R	72.5%	26.7%	73.1%	26.9%
DELTA	14,458	7,488	6,921	49	567 R	51.8%	47.9%	52.0%	48.0%
DICKINSON	11,811	6,045	5,710	56	335 R	51.2%	48.3%	51.4%	48.6%
EATON	19,018	13,723	5,170	125	8,553 R	72.6%	27.2%	73.2%	26.8%
EMMET	7,014	5,113	1,871	30	3,242 R	72.9%	26.7%	73.3%	26.7%
GENESEE	119,712	62,220	56,753	739	5,467 R	52.0%	47.4%	52.3%	47.7%
GLADWIN	3,996	3,031	936	29	2,095 R	75.9%	23.4%	76.4%	23.6%
GOGEBIC	13,051	6,195	6,803	53	608 D	47.5%	52.1%	47.7%	52.3%
GRAND TRAVERSE	11,711	9,034	2,639	38	6,395 R	77.1%	22.5%	77.4%	22.6%
GRATIOT	13,021	10,034	2,887	100	7,147 R	77.0%	22.2%	77.4%	22.3%
HILLSDALE	14,143	10,680	3,340	123	7,340 R	75.5%	23.6%	76.2%	23.8%
HOUGHTON	17,733	10,563	7,100	70	3,463 R	59.5%	40.0%	59.8%	40.2%
HURON	13,089	10,639	2,421	29	8,218 R	81.3%	18.5%	81.5%	18.5%
INGHAM	76,161	51,503	24,125	533	27,378 R	67.5%	31.7%	68.1%	31.9%
IONIA	15,819	10,970	4,722	127	6,248 R	69.3%	29.9%	69.9%	30.1%
IOSCO	5,059	3,772	1,274	13	2,498 R	74.5%	25.2%	74.8%	25.2%
IRON	9,216	4,564	4,597	55	33 D	49.5%	49.9%	49.8%	50.2%
ISABELLA	11,180	8,222	2,881	77	5,341 R	73.5%	25.8%	74.1%	25.9%
JACKSON	48,105	32,810	15,065	230	17,745 R	68.2%	31.3%	68.5%	31.5%
KALAMAZOO	58,185	38,847	18,967	371	19,880 R	66.8%	32.6%	67.2%	32.8%
KALKASKA	1,823	1,326	483	14	843 R	72.7%	26.5%	73.3%	26.7%
KENT	128,315	79,647	47,221	1,447	32,426 R	62.1%	36.8%	62.8%	37.2%
KEWEENAW	1,559	801	747	11	54 R	51.4%	47.9%	51.7%	48.3%
LAKE	2,696	1,549	1,127	20	422 R	57.5%	41.8%	57.9%	42.1%
LAPEER	13,656	9,940	3,644	72	6,296 R	72.8%	26.7%	73.2%	26.8%
LEELANAU	3,934	2,926	999	9	1,927 R	74.4%	25.4%	74.5%	25.5%
LENAWEE	27,549	20,035	7,397	117	12,638 R	72.7%	26.9%	73.0%	27.0%
LIVINGSTON	12,955	9,790	3,086	79	6,704 R	75.6%	23.8%	76.0%	24.0%
LUCE	2,159	1,603	553	3	1,050 R	74.2%	25.6%	74.4%	25.6%
MACKINAC	4,354	3,058	1,285	11	1,773 R	70.2%	29.5%	70.4%	29.6%
MACOMB	74,364	37,474	36,544	346	930 R	50.4%	49.1%	50.6%	49.4%
MANISTEE	8,376	5,235	3,114	27	2,121 R	62.5%	37.2%	62.7%	37.3%
MARQUETTE	21,655	11,618	9,949	88	1,669 R	53.7%	45.9%	53.9%	46.1%
MASON	9,558	6,179	3,298	81	2,881 R	64.6%	34.5%	65.2%	34.8%
MECOSTA	7,102	5,436	1,587	79	3,849 R	76.5%	22.3%	77.4%	22.6%
MENOMINEE	11,068	6,147	4,884	37	1,263 R	55.5%	44.1%	55.5%	44.3%
MIDLAND	14,570	10,508	3,945	117	6,563 R	72.1%	27.1%	72.7%	27.3%
MISSAUKEE	3,156	2,525	600	31	1,925 R	80.0%	19.0%	80.6%	19.2%
MONROE	30,074	17,159	12,758	157	4,401 R	57.1%	42.4%	57.4%	42.6%
MONTCALM	13,926	9,946	3,844	136	6,102 R	71.4%	27.6%	72.1%	27.9%
MONTMORENCY	2,015	1,449	544	22	905 R	71.9%	27.0%	72.7%	27.3%

PRESIDENT 1956

County	Total Vote	Republican	Democratic	Other	Rep.-Dem. Plurality	Total Vote Rep.	Total Vote Dem.	Major Vote Rep.	Major Vote Dem.
ALCONA	2,784	1,991	788	5	1,203 R	71.5%	28.3%	71.6%	28.4%
ALGER	4,193	2,070	2,105	18	35 D	49.4%	50.2%	49.6%	50.4%
ALLEGAN	22,177	16,509	5,617	51	10,892 R	74.4%	25.3%	74.6%	25.4%
ALPENA	10,177	7,142	3,033	2	4,109 R	70.2%	29.8%	70.2%	29.8%
ANTRIM	5,008	3,623	1,376	9	2,247 R	72.3%	27.5%	72.5%	27.5%
ARENAC	4,155	2,631	1,520	4	1,111 R	63.3%	36.6%	63.4%	36.6%
BARAGA	3,545	1,968	1,574	3	394 R	55.5%	44.4%	55.6%	44.4%
BARRY	13,329	9,359	3,907	63	5,452 R	70.2%	29.3%	70.5%	29.5%
BAY	38,948	23,519	15,301	128	8,218 R	60.4%	39.3%	60.6%	39.4%
BENZIE	3,661	2,620	1,046	15	1,574 R	71.5%	28.4%	71.5%	28.5%
BERRIEN	54,045	35,397	18,454	194	16,943 R	65.5%	34.1%	65.7%	34.3%
BRANCH	12,744	8,856	3,827	61	5,029 R	69.5%	30.0%	69.8%	30.2%
CALHOUN	52,643	32,284	20,184	175	12,100 R	61.3%	38.3%	61.5%	38.5%
CASS	13,788	8,899	4,842	47	4,057 R	64.5%	35.1%	64.8%	35.2%
CHARLEVOIX	5,874	3,924	1,935	15	1,989 R	66.8%	32.9%	67.0%	33.0%
CHEBOYGAN	6,296	4,379	1,910	7	2,469 R	69.6%	30.3%	69.6%	30.4%
CHIPPEWA	11,117	6,997	4,106	14	2,891 R	62.9%	37.1%	62.9%	37.1%
CLARE	4,928	3,721	1,194	13	2,527 R	75.5%	24.2%	75.7%	24.3%
CLINTON	14,474	10,770	3,673	31	7,097 R	74.4%	25.4%	74.6%	25.4%
CRAWFORD	1,930	1,380	547	3	833 R	71.5%	28.3%	71.6%	28.4%
DELTA	14,300	7,766	6,489	45	1,277 R	54.3%	45.4%	54.5%	45.5%
DICKINSON	11,330	6,200	5,113	17	1,087 R	54.7%	45.1%	54.8%	45.2%
EATON	19,850	13,762	6,053	35	7,709 R	69.3%	30.5%	69.5%	30.5%
EMMET	6,695	4,764	1,903	28	2,861 R	71.2%	28.4%	71.5%	28.5%
GENESEE	138,474	75,461	62,808	235	12,653 R	54.5%	45.4%	54.6%	45.4%
GLADWIN	4,248	3,121	1,117	10	2,004 R	73.5%	26.3%	73.6%	26.4%
GOGEBIC	13,032	6,865	6,142	25	723 R	52.7%	47.1%	52.8%	47.2%
GRAND TRAVERSE	12,388	9,102	3,256	30	5,846 R	73.5%	26.3%	73.7%	26.3%
GRATIOT	13,630	10,319	3,267	44	7,052 R	75.7%	24.0%	76.0%	24.0%
HILLSDALE	13,805	10,311	3,428	67	6,883 R	74.7%	24.8%	75.0%	25.0%
HOUGHTON	16,511	9,620	6,866	25	2,754 R	58.3%	41.6%	58.4%	41.6%
HURON	13,704	10,493	3,192	19	7,301 R	76.6%	23.3%	76.7%	23.3%
INGHAM	82,554	55,211	27,323	120	27,888 R	66.8%	33.1%	66.9%	33.1%
IONIA	15,999	11,001	4,952	46	6,049 R	68.8%	31.0%	69.0%	31.0%
IOSCO	6,048	4,385	1,660	3	2,725 R	72.5%	27.4%	72.5%	27.5%
IRON	9,458	4,955	4,490	13	465 R	52.4%	47.5%	52.5%	47.5%
ISABELLA	11,621	8,415	3,183	23	5,232 R	72.4%	27.4%	72.6%	27.4%
JACKSON	51,079	35,453	15,479	147	19,974 R	69.4%	30.3%	69.6%	30.4%
KALAMAZOO	61,433	43,305	17,808	320	25,497 R	70.5%	29.0%	70.9%	29.1%
KALKASKA	2,088	1,443	636	9	807 R	69.1%	30.5%	69.4%	30.6%
KENT	144,482	94,969	48,871	642	46,098 R	65.7%	33.8%	66.0%	34.0%
KEWEENAW	1,523	834	689	0	145 R	54.8%	45.2%	54.8%	45.2%
LAKE	2,699	1,614	1,083	2	531 R	59.8%	40.1%	59.8%	40.2%
LAPEER	14,459	10,527	3,913	19	6,614 R	72.8%	27.1%	72.9%	27.1%
LEELANAU	4,278	2,987	1,287	4	1,700 R	69.8%	30.1%	69.9%	30.1%
LENAWEE	29,031	21,100	7,845	74	13,243 R	72.7%	27.1%	72.8%	27.2%
LIVINGSTON	14,205	10,315	3,845	45	6,470 R	72.6%	27.2%	72.8%	27.3%
LUCE	2,390	1,734	651	5	1,083 R	72.6%	27.2%	72.7%	27.3%
MACKINAC	4,623	3,279	1,540	4	1,739 R	68.0%	31.9%	68.0%	32.0%
MACOMB	121,419	58,337	62,816	266	4,479 D	48.0%	51.7%	48.2%	51.8%
MANISTEE	8,336	5,313	3,014	9	2,299 R	63.7%	36.2%	63.8%	36.2%
MARQUETTE	22,084	12,504	9,543	37	2,961 R	56.6%	43.2%	56.7%	43.3%
MASON	9,428	6,142	3,274	12	2,868 R	65.1%	34.7%	65.2%	34.8%
MECOSTA	7,279	5,492	1,768	19	3,724 R	75.4%	24.3%	75.6%	24.4%
MENOMINEE	10,757	6,137	4,610	10	1,527 R	57.1%	42.9%	57.1%	42.9%
MIDLAND	17,662	13,207	4,422	33	8,785 R	74.8%	25.0%	74.9%	25.1%
MISSAUKEE	3,168	2,433	727	8	1,706 R	76.8%	22.9%	77.0%	23.0%
MONROE	33,305	18,782	14,414	109	4,368 R	56.4%	43.3%	56.6%	43.3%
MONTCALM	13,981	9,759	4,189	33	5,570 R	69.8%	30.0%	70.0%	30.0%
MONTMORENCY	1,996	1,385	608	3	777 R	69.4%	30.5%	69.5%	30.5%

MICHIGAN

PRESIDENT 1952

County	Total Vote	Republican	Democratic	Other	Rep.-Dem. Plurality	Percentage Total Vote Rep.	Dem.	Major Vote Rep.	Dem.
MUSKEGON	50,446	25,967	23,826	653	2,141 R	51.5%	47.2%	52.1%	47.9%
NEWAYGO	9,351	6,715	2,541	95	4,174 R	71.8%	27.2%	72.5%	27.5%
OAKLAND	190,179	115,503	73,871	805	41,632 R	60.7%	38.8%	61.0%	39.0%
OCEANA	6,622	4,704	1,799	119	2,905 R	71.0%	27.2%	72.3%	27.7%
OGEMAW	4,036	2,983	1,030	23	1,953 R	73.9%	25.5%	74.3%	25.7%
ONTONAGON	5,159	2,961	2,134	64	827 R	57.4%	41.4%	58.1%	41.9%
OSCEOLA	5,842	4,607	1,160	75	3,447 R	78.9%	19.9%	79.9%	20.1%
OSCODA	1,297	1,047	246	4	801 R	80.7%	19.0%	81.0%	19.0%
OTSEGO	2,818	1,941	865	12	1,076 R	68.9%	30.7%	69.2%	30.8%
OTTAWA	30,657	22,328	7,835	494	14,493 R	72.8%	25.6%	74.0%	26.0%
PRESQUE ISLE	4,822	2,982	1,825	15	1,157 R	61.8%	37.8%	62.0%	38.0%
ROSCOMMON	3,239	2,547	676	16	1,871 R	78.6%	20.9%	79.0%	21.0%
SAGINAW	60,100	38,604	20,983	513	17,621 R	64.2%	34.9%	64.8%	35.2%
ST CLAIR	40,256	27,894	12,268	94	15,626 R	69.3%	30.5%	69.5%	30.5%
ST JOSEPH	16,887	12,191	4,509	187	7,682 R	72.2%	26.7%	73.0%	27.0%
SANILAC	13,557	11,181	2,298	78	8,883 R	82.5%	17.0%	83.0%	17.0%
SCHOOLCRAFT	4,052	2,352	1,692	8	660 R	58.0%	41.8%	58.2%	41.8%
SHIAWASSEE	19,824	13,562	6,056	206	7,506 R	68.4%	30.5%	69.1%	30.9%
TUSCOLA	15,119	11,788	3,251	80	8,537 R	78.0%	21.5%	78.4%	21.6%
VAN BUREN	18,659	13,231	5,309	119	7,922 R	70.9%	28.5%	71.4%	28.6%
WASHTENAW	53,759	35,826	17,671	262	18,155 R	66.6%	32.9%	67.0%	33.0%
WAYNE	1,083,381	456,371	622,236	4,774	165,865 D	42.1%	57.4%	42.3%	57.7%
WEXFORD	8,073	5,569	2,407	97	3,162 R	69.0%	29.8%	69.8%	30.2%
TOTAL	2,798,592	1,551,529	1,230,657	16,406	320,872 R	55.4%	44.0%	55.8%	44.2%

PRESIDENT 1956

County	Total Vote	Republican	Democratic	Other	Rep.-Dem. Plurality	Percentage Total Vote Rep.	Dem.	Major Vote Rep.	Dem.
MUSKEGON	56,246	30,395	25,679	172	4,716 R	54.0%	45.7%	54.2%	45.8%
NEWAYGO	9,916	7,088	2,808	20	4,280 R	71.5%	28.3%	71.6%	28.4%
OAKLAND	253,418	152,990	99,901	527	53,089 R	60.4%	39.4%	60.5%	39.5%
OCEANA	6,372	4,479	1,868	25	2,611 R	70.3%	29.3%	70.6%	29.4%
OGEMAW	4,237	2,931	1,300	6	1,631 R	69.2%	30.7%	69.3%	30.7%
ONTONAGON	5,155	2,976	2,175	4	801 R	57.7%	42.2%	57.8%	42.2%
OSCEOLA	5,811	4,549	1,236	26	3,313 R	78.3%	21.3%	78.6%	21.4%
OSCODA	1,338	1,044	294		750 R	78.0%	22.0%	78.0%	22.0%
OTSEGO	3,028	1,930	1,095	3	835 R	63.7%	36.2%	63.8%	36.2%
OTTAWA	38,200	28,611	9,459	130	19,152 R	74.9%	24.8%	75.2%	24.8%
PRESQUE ISLE	4,978	3,058	1,917	3	1,141 R	61.4%	38.5%	61.5%	38.5%
ROSCOMMON	3,509	2,674	827	8	1,847 R	76.2%	23.6%	76.4%	23.6%
SAGINAW	69,361	43,470	25,681	210	17,789 R	62.7%	37.0%	62.9%	37.1%
ST CLAIR	41,920	29,116	12,753	51	16,363 R	69.5%	30.4%	69.5%	30.5%
ST JOSEPH	16,634	12,328	4,242	64	8,086 R	74.1%	25.5%	74.4%	25.6%
SANILAC	14,066	11,095	2,954	17	8,141 R	78.9%	21.0%	79.0%	21.0%
SCHOOLCRAFT	4,177	2,453	1,723	1	730 R	58.7%	41.2%	58.7%	41.3%
SHIAWASSEE	21,551	14,600	6,873	78	7,727 R	67.7%	31.9%	68.0%	32.0%
TUSCOLA	15,935	12,052	3,864	19	8,188 R	75.6%	24.2%	75.7%	24.3%
VAN BUREN	19,063	13,291	5,678	94	7,613 R	69.7%	29.8%	70.1%	29.9%
WASHTENAW	58,176	38,911	19,124	141	19,787 R	66.9%	32.9%	67.0%	33.0%
WAYNE	1,148,245	481,783	664,618	1,844	182,835 D	42.0%	57.9%	42.0%	58.0%
WEXFORD	7,683	5,052	2,604	27	2,448 R	65.8%	33.9%	66.0%	34.0%
TOTAL	3,080,468	1,713,647	1,359,898	6,923	353,749 R	55.6%	44.1%	55.8%	44.2%

PRESIDENT 1960

County	Total Vote	Republican	Democratic	Other	Rep.-Dem. Plurality	Total Vote Rep.	Total Vote Dem.	Major Vote Rep.	Major Vote Dem.
ALCONA	3,099	2,053	1,038	8	1,015 R	66.2%	33.5%	66.4%	33.6%
ALGER	3,990	1,663	2,321	6	658 D	41.7%	58.2%	41.7%	58.3%
ALLEGAN	23,472	16,660	6,752	60	9,908 R	71.0%	28.8%	71.2%	28.3%
ALPENA	11,653	6,573	5,071	9	1,502 R	56.4%	43.5%	56.4%	43.5%
ANTRIM	5,052	3,398	1,647	7	1,751 R	67.3%	32.6%	67.4%	32.5%
ARENAC	4,250	2,352	1,888	10	464 R	55.3%	44.4%	55.5%	44.5%
BARAGA	3,836	1,861	1,964	11	103 D	48.5%	51.2%	48.7%	51.3%
BARRY	13,767	9,298	4,406	63	4,892 R	67.5%	32.0%	67.8%	32.2%
BAY	44,011	20,909	22,998	104	2,089 D	47.5%	52.3%	47.6%	52.4%
BENZIE	3,795	2,484	1,306	5	1,178 R	65.5%	34.4%	65.5%	34.5%
BERRIEN	61,506	37,425	23,837	244	13,588 R	60.8%	38.8%	61.1%	38.9%
BRANCH	13,587	8,752	4,759	76	3,993 R	64.4%	35.0%	64.8%	35.2%
CALHOUN	55,793	32,080	23,511	202	8,569 R	57.5%	42.1%	57.7%	42.3%
CASS	15,117	8,585	6,468	64	2,117 R	56.8%	42.8%	57.0%	43.0%
CHARLEVOIX	6,419	3,987	2,422	10	1,565 R	62.1%	37.7%	62.4%	37.6%
CHEBOYGAN	6,796	3,817	2,977	22	840 R	56.2%	43.8%	56.3%	43.7%
CHIPPEWA	11,751	6,490	5,239	22	1,251 R	55.2%	44.6%	55.3%	44.7%
CLARE	5,130	3,516	1,507	7	2,009 R	70.5%	29.4%	70.6%	29.4%
CLINTON	15,072	10,227	4,822	23	5,405 R	67.9%	32.0%	68.0%	32.0%
CRAWFORD	2,251	1,464	783	4	681 R	65.0%	34.8%	65.2%	34.8%
DELTA	14,413	6,460	7,924	29	1,464 D	44.3%	55.0%	44.9%	55.1%
DICKINSON	11,995	5,336	6,645	14	1,309 D	44.4%	55.4%	44.5%	55.5%
EATON	21,149	14,163	6,912	74	7,251 R	67.3%	32.7%	67.2%	32.8%
EMMET	7,198	4,574	2,602	22	1,972 R	63.5%	36.1%	63.7%	36.3%
GENESEE	147,457	74,940	72,059	458	2,881 R	50.8%	48.9%	51.0%	49.0%
GLADWIN	4,712	3,282	1,424	6	1,858 R	69.7%	30.2%	69.7%	30.3%
GOGEBIC	12,659	5,429	7,200	30	1,771 D	42.8%	56.9%	43.0%	57.0%
GRAND TRAVERSE	13,540	8,618	4,886	36	3,732 R	63.6%	36.1%	63.8%	36.2%
GRATIOT	13,734	9,854	3,859	21	5,995 R	71.7%	28.1%	71.9%	28.1%
HILLSDALE	14,340	10,208	4,069	63	6,139 R	71.2%	28.4%	71.5%	28.5%
HOUGHTON	15,822	7,767	8,021	34	254 D	49.1%	50.7%	49.2%	50.8%
HURON	15,386	9,592	5,775	19	3,817 R	62.3%	37.5%	62.4%	37.6%
INGHAM	86,907	54,655	32,043	209	22,612 R	62.6%	36.9%	63.0%	37.0%
IONIA	16,834	10,405	6,377	52	4,028 R	61.8%	37.9%	62.0%	38.0%
IOSCO	6,866	4,308	2,549	9	1,759 R	62.7%	37.1%	62.8%	37.2%
IRON	9,165	3,919	5,232	14	1,313 D	42.8%	57.1%	42.8%	57.2%
ISABELLA	12,335	7,880	4,431	24	3,449 R	63.9%	35.9%	64.0%	36.0%
JACKSON	67,434	42,800	24,286	348	18,514 R	63.5%	36.0%	63.8%	36.2%
KALAMAZOO	55,779	34,660	20,995	124	13,665 R	62.1%	37.6%	62.3%	37.7%
KALKASKA	2,039	1,341	693	5	648 R	65.8%	34.0%	65.9%	34.1%
KENT	157,296	95,477	61,313	506	34,164 R	60.7%	39.0%	60.9%	39.1%
KEWEENAW	1,343	684	655	4	29 R	50.9%	48.8%	51.1%	48.9%
LAKE	2,757	1,441	1,313	3	128 R	52.3%	47.6%	52.3%	47.7%
LAPEER	15,567	10,450	5,099	18	5,351 R	67.1%	32.8%	67.2%	32.8%
LEELANAU	4,556	2,730	1,810	6	920 R	60.1%	39.8%	60.1%	39.9%
LENAWEE	30,719	19,859	10,785	75	9,074 R	64.6%	35.1%	64.8%	35.2%
LIVINGSTON	15,987	10,340	5,608	39	4,732 R	64.7%	35.1%	64.8%	35.2%
LUCE	2,362	1,534	828		706 R	64.9%	35.0%	64.9%	35.1%
MACKINAC	5,117	3,064	2,042	11	1,022 R	59.9%	39.9%	60.0%	40.0%
MACOMB	168,195	61,989	105,681	525	43,692 D	36.9%	62.8%	37.0%	63.0%
MANISTEE	8,999	4,867	4,122	10	745 R	54.1%	45.8%	54.1%	45.9%
MARQUETTE	21,917	10,690	11,177	50	487 D	48.8%	51.0%	48.9%	51.1%
MASON	10,326	6,011	4,305	10	1,706 R	58.2%	41.7%	58.3%	41.7%
MECOSTA	7,703	5,306	2,380	17	2,926 R	68.9%	30.9%	69.0%	31.0%
MENOMINEE	10,938	5,064	5,857	17	793 D	46.3%	53.5%	46.4%	53.6%
MIDLAND	21,071	14,235	6,815	21	7,420 R	67.6%	32.3%	67.6%	32.4%
MISSAUKEE	3,171	2,531	627	13	1,904 R	79.8%	19.8%	80.1%	19.9%
MONROE	38,423	18,607	19,684	132	1,077 D	48.4%	51.2%	48.6%	51.4%
MONTCALM	14,892	10,085	4,767	40	5,318 R	67.7%	32.0%	67.9%	32.1%
MONTMORENCY	2,453	1,565	866	2	699 R	64.3%	35.6%	64.4%	35.6%

PRESIDENT 1964

County	Total Vote	Republican	Democratic	Other	Rep.-Dem. Plurality	Total Vote Rep.	Total Vote Dem.	Major Vote Rep.	Major Vote Dem.
ALCONA	2,815	1,199	1,611	5	412 D	42.6%	57.2%	42.7%	57.3%
ALGER	3,755	1,010	2,743	2	1,733 D	26.9%	73.0%	26.9%	73.1%
ALLEGAN	23,194	11,223	11,934	37	711 D	48.4%	51.5%	48.5%	51.5%
ALPENA	11,472	3,954	7,508	10	3,554 D	34.5%	65.4%	34.5%	65.5%
ANTRIM	4,863	2,172	2,684	7	512 D	44.7%	55.2%	44.7%	55.3%
ARENAC	3,852	1,413	2,436	3	1,023 D	36.7%	63.2%	36.7%	63.3%
BARAGA	3,736	1,160	2,568	8	1,408 D	31.0%	68.7%	31.0%	68.9%
BARRY	13,650	5,509	8,102	39	2,593 D	40.4%	59.4%	40.5%	59.5%
BAY	41,706	11,896	29,754	56	17,858 D	28.5%	71.3%	28.6%	71.4%
BENZIE	3,662	1,674	1,983	5	309 D	45.7%	54.2%	45.8%	54.2%
BERRIEN	60,162	26,387	33,653	122	7,266 D	43.9%	55.9%	43.9%	56.1%
BRANCH	13,034	5,110	7,858	66	2,748 D	39.2%	60.3%	39.4%	60.6%
CALHOUN	52,025	18,987	32,939	99	13,952 D	36.5%	63.3%	36.6%	63.4%
CASS	14,742	5,925	8,789	28	2,864 D	40.2%	59.6%	40.3%	59.7%
CHARLEVOIX	6,428	2,664	3,757	7	1,093 D	41.4%	58.4%	41.5%	58.5%
CHEBOYGAN	6,381	2,342	4,028	11	1,686 D	36.7%	63.1%	36.8%	63.2%
CHIPPEWA	10,658	4,098	6,537	23	2,439 D	38.4%	61.3%	38.5%	61.5%
CLARE	5,197	2,268	2,927	12	669 D	43.5%	56.3%	43.5%	56.5%
CLINTON	14,837	5,891	8,932	14	3,041 D	39.7%	60.2%	39.7%	60.3%
CRAWFORD	2,160	696	1,464		768 D	32.2%	67.8%	32.2%	67.8%
DELTA	14,507	4,434	10,046	27	5,612 D	30.6%	69.2%	30.6%	69.4%
DICKINSON	11,297	3,365	7,921	11	4,556 D	29.8%	70.1%	29.8%	70.2%
EATON	21,555	8,919	12,590	46	3,671 D	41.4%	58.4%	41.5%	58.5%
EMMET	6,937	2,731	4,197	9	1,466 D	39.4%	60.5%	39.5%	60.5%
GENESEE	148,878	48,311	100,346	221	52,035 D	32.5%	67.4%	32.5%	67.5%
GLADWIN	4,683	1,941	2,725	17	784 D	41.4%	58.2%	41.6%	58.4%
GOGEBIC	11,319	3,350	7,945	24	4,595 D	29.6%	70.2%	29.7%	70.3%
GRAND TRAVERSE	13,693	6,198	7,475	20	1,277 D	45.3%	54.6%	45.3%	54.7%
GRATIOT	12,778	5,369	7,383	26	2,014 D	42.0%	57.8%	42.1%	57.9%
HILLSDALE	13,090	6,420	6,564	106	144 D	49.0%	50.1%	49.4%	50.6%
HOUGHTON	14,791	5,024	9,761	6	4,737 D	34.0%	66.0%	34.0%	66.0%
HURON	13,626	6,263	7,349	14	1,086 D	46.0%	53.9%	46.0%	54.0%
INGHAM	86,829	32,965	53,685	179	20,720 D	38.0%	61.8%	38.0%	62.0%
IONIA	16,113	5,698	10,362	53	4,664 D	35.4%	64.3%	35.5%	64.5%
IOSCO	7,044	2,704	4,336	4	1,632 D	38.4%	61.6%	38.4%	61.6%
IRON	8,423	2,399	6,011	13	3,612 D	28.5%	71.4%	28.5%	71.5%
ISABELLA	11,727	4,672	7,040	15	2,368 D	39.9%	60.0%	39.9%	60.1%
JACKSON	49,247	20,940	28,219	88	7,279 D	42.5%	57.3%	42.6%	57.4%
KALAMAZOO	68,014	27,100	40,789	215	13,689 D	39.8%	59.9%	40.0%	60.0%
KALKASKA	2,084	861	1,220	3	359 D	41.3%	58.5%	41.4%	58.6%
KENT	153,959	66,830	86,860	269	20,030 D	43.4%	56.4%	43.5%	56.5%
KEWEENAW	1,235	374	860	1	486 D	30.3%	69.6%	30.3%	69.7%
LAKE	2,770	791	1,978	1	1,187 D	28.6%	71.4%	28.6%	71.4%
LAPEER	14,624	6,012	8,595	17	2,583 D	41.1%	58.8%	41.2%	58.8%
LEELANAU	4,451	2,074	2,369	8	295 D	46.6%	53.2%	46.7%	53.3%
LENAWEE	28,260	11,385	16,815	60	5,430 D	40.3%	59.5%	40.4%	59.6%
LIVINGSTON	16,441	5,723	9,698	20	2,975 D	40.9%	59.0%	40.9%	59.1%
LUCE	2,331	871	1,459	1	588 D	37.4%	62.6%	37.4%	62.6%
MACKINAC	4,717	1,967	2,748	2	781 D	41.7%	58.3%	41.7%	58.3%
MACOMB	176,521	44,684	131,450	387	86,766 D	25.3%	74.5%	25.4%	74.6%
MANISTEE	8,444	2,918	5,520	6	2,602 D	34.6%	65.4%	34.6%	65.4%
MARQUETTE	20,696	6,615	14,045	36	7,430 D	32.0%	67.9%	32.0%	68.0%
MASON	9,846	3,842	5,993	11	2,151 D	39.0%	60.9%	39.1%	60.9%
MECOSTA	7,667	3,454	4,214	9	760 D	45.0%	54.9%	45.0%	55.0%
MENOMINEE	10,682	3,545	7,119	18	3,574 D	33.2%	66.6%	33.2%	66.8%
MIDLAND	21,555	9,020	12,587	48	3,567 D	41.7%	58.1%	41.7%	58.3%
MISSAUKEE	3,075	1,786	1,288		498 R	58.1%	41.9%	58.1%	41.9%
MONROE	38,111	11,499	26,528	84	15,029 D	30.2%	69.6%	30.2%	69.8%
MONTCALM	14,177	5,181	8,970	26	3,789 D	36.5%	63.3%	36.6%	63.4%
MONTMORENCY	2,256	863	1,369	4	506 D	38.6%	61.2%	38.7%	61.3%

MICHIGAN

PRESIDENT 1960

County	Total Vote	Republican	Democratic	Other	Rep.-Dem. Plurality	Total Vote Rep.	Total Vote Dem.	Major Vote Rep.	Major Vote Dem.
MUSKEGON	61,661	32,667	28,755	239	3,912 R	53.0%	46.6%	53.2%	46.8%
NEWAYGO	10,872	7,453	3,404	15	4,049 R	68.6%	31.3%	68.6%	31.4%
OAKLAND	298,562	162,026	135,531	1,005	26,495 R	54.3%	45.4%	54.5%	45.5%
OCEANA	7,082	4,418	2,651	13	1,767 R	62.4%	37.4%	62.5%	37.5%
OGEMAW	4,542	2,664	1,867	11	797 R	58.7%	41.1%	58.8%	41.2%
ONTONAGON	5,175	2,620	2,553	2	67 R	50.6%	49.3%	50.6%	49.4%
OSCEOLA	5,865	4,477	1,378	10	3,099 R	76.3%	23.5%	76.5%	23.5%
OSCODA	1,634	1,174	458	2	716 R	71.8%	28.0%	71.9%	28.1%
OTSEGO	3,469	1,944	1,521	4	423 R	56.0%	43.8%	56.1%	43.9%
OTTAWA	43,423	32,678	10,617	128	22,061 R	75.3%	24.5%	75.5%	24.5%
PRESQUE ISLE	5,602	2,950	2,649	3	301 R	52.7%	47.3%	52.7%	47.3%
ROSCOMMON	3,962	2,731	1,226	5	1,505 R	68.9%	30.9%	69.0%	31.0%
SAGINAW	74,272	41,351	32,715	206	8,636 R	55.7%	44.0%	55.8%	44.2%
ST CLAIR	45,774	27,366	18,332	76	9,034 R	59.8%	40.0%	59.9%	40.1%
ST JOSEPH	17,847	12,337	5,445	65	6,892 R	69.1%	30.5%	69.4%	30.6%
SANILAC	15,185	11,005	4,153	27	6,852 R	72.5%	27.3%	72.6%	27.4%
SCHOOLCRAFT	4,298	2,183	2,107	8	76 R	50.8%	49.0%	50.9%	49.1%
SHIAWASSEE	22,604	13,757	8,773	74	4,984 R	60.9%	38.8%	61.1%	38.9%
TUSCOLA	17,308	11,931	5,357	20	6,574 R	68.9%	31.0%	69.0%	31.0%
VAN BUREN	20,096	12,903	7,082	111	5,821 R	64.2%	35.2%	64.6%	35.4%
WASHTENAW	64,986	39,632	25,129	225	14,503 R	61.0%	38.7%	61.2%	38.8%
WAYNE	1,171,909	394,485	773,327	4,097	378,842 D	33.7%	66.0%	33.8%	66.2%
WEXFORD	8,096	5,262	2,807	27	2,455 R	65.0%	34.7%	65.2%	34.8%
TOTAL	3,318,097	1,620,428	1,687,269	10,400	66,841 D	48.8%	50.9%	49.0%	51.0%

PRESIDENT 1964

County	Total Vote	Republican	Democratic	Other	Rep.-Dem. Plurality	Total Vote Rep.	Total Vote Dem.	Major Vote Rep.	Major Vote Dem.
MUSKEGON	59,034	22,146	36,769	119	14,623 D	37.5%	62.3%	37.6%	62.4%
NEWAYGO	10,399	4,931	5,457	11	526 D	47.4%	52.5%	47.5%	52.5%
OAKLAND	297,508	114,025	182,797	686	68,772 D	38.3%	61.4%	38.4%	61.6%
OCEANA	6,743	2,958	3,773	12	815 D	43.9%	56.0%	43.9%	56.1%
OGEMAW	4,425	1,609	2,812	4	1,203 D	36.4%	63.5%	36.4%	63.6%
ONTONAGON	5,150	1,658	3,485	7	1,827 D	32.2%	67.7%	32.2%	67.8%
OSCEOLA	5,690	2,779	2,891	20	112 D	48.8%	50.8%	49.0%	51.0%
OSCODA	1,721	784	930	7	146 D	45.6%	54.0%	45.7%	54.3%
OTSEGO	3,462	1,214	2,245	3	1,031 D	35.1%	64.8%	35.1%	54.9%
OTTAWA	44,735	24,512	20,151	72	4,361 R	54.8%	45.0%	54.9%	45.1%
PRESQUE ISLE	5,337	1,770	3,565	2	1,795 D	33.2%	66.8%	33.2%	66.8%
ROSCOMMON	4,074	1,722	2,345	7	623 D	42.3%	57.6%	42.3%	57.7%
SAGINAW	73,582	28,146	45,309	127	17,163 D	38.3%	61.6%	38.3%	61.7%
ST CLAIR	41,735	17,011	24,662	62	7,651 D	40.8%	59.1%	40.8%	59.2%
ST JOSEPH	16,623	7,307	9,284	32	1,977 D	44.0%	55.9%	44.0%	56.0%
SANILAC	13,874	7,590	6,266	18	1,324 R	54.7%	45.2%	54.8%	45.2%
SCHOOLCRAFT	4,076	1,397	2,675	4	1,278 D	34.3%	65.6%	34.3%	65.7%
SHIAWASSEE	21,503	7,786	13,676	41	5,890 D	36.2%	63.6%	36.2%	63.7%
TUSCOLA	16,905	7,509	9,374	22	1,865 D	44.4%	55.5%	44.5%	55.5%
VAN BUREN	19,504	8,120	11,336	48	3,216 D	41.6%	58.1%	41.7%	58.3%
WASHTENAW	67,890	25,595	42,089	206	16,494 D	37.7%	62.0%	37.8%	62.2%
WAYNE	1,094,724	260,901	831,674	2,149	570,773 D	23.8%	76.0%	23.9%	76.1%
WEXFORD	7,446	3,016	4,414	16	1,398 D	40.5%	59.3%	40.6%	59.4%
TOTAL	3,203,102	1,060,152	2,136,615	6,335	1,076,463 D	33.1%	66.7%	33.2%	66.8%

MICHIGAN

OTHER VOTE COMPOSITION:

1920   28,947 Socialist; 10,480 Farmer-Labor; 9,646 Prohibition; 2,539 Socialist Labor;
        484 Single Tax.
1924   122,014 Progressive; 6,085 Prohibition; 5,330 Socialist Labor.
1928   3,516 Socialist; 2,881 Communist; 2,728 Prohibition; 799 Socialist Labor.
1932   39,205 Socialist; 9,318 Communist; 2,893 Prohibition; 1,401 Socialist Labor; 217
        Liberty; 137 Farmer-Labor.
1936   75,795 Union; 8,208 Socialist; 3,384 Communist; 600 Socialist Labor; 579 Prohi-
        bition; 5 scattered.

1940   7,593 Socialist; 2,834 Communist; 1,795 Prohibition; 795 Socialist Labor; 4
        scattered.
1944   6,503 Prohibition; 4,598 Socialist; 1,530 America First; 1,264 Socialist Labor;
        6 scattered.
1948   46,515 Progressive; 13,052 Prohibition; 6,063 Socialist; 1,263 Socialist Labor;
        672 Socialist Workers; 1 scattered.
1952   10,331 Prohibition; 3,922 Progressive; 1,495 Socialist Labor; 655 Socialist
        Workers; 3 scattered.
1956   Prohibition.

1960   4,347 Socialist Workers; 2,029 Prohibition; 1,767 Tax Cut; 1,718 Socialist Labor;
        539 Independent American.
1964   3,817 Socialist Workers; 1,704 Socialist Labor; 669 Prohibition; 145 scattered.

SPECIAL CASES:

1920   The state totals are for the highest elector for each party, but the individual
        county figures are the average elector vote, as reported by the state can-
        vass. Adding the individual county figures will thus produce slightly
        smaller totals than those on the state total line.
1924   Progressive candidates ran second in a number of counties.
1960   Though there were Independent American nominees for some offices, the party
        had no candidates for President, Vice-President, or elector. Nevertheless,
        539 Independent American elector votes were reported in the state canvass.

MINNESOTA

PRESIDENT 1920

County	Total Vote	Republican	Democratic	Other	Rep.-Dem. Plurality	% Total Vote Rep.	% Total Vote Dem.	% Major Vote Rep.	% Major Vote Dem.
AITKIN	4,181	2,933	613	635	2,320 R	70.2	14.7	82.7	17.3
ANOKA	4,859	3,505	865	489	2,640 R	72.1	17.8	80.2	19.8
BECKER	6,349	4,811	901	637	3,910 R	75.8	14.2	84.2	15.8
BELTRAMI	7,375	4,518	1,427	1,430	3,091 R	61.3	19.3	76.0	24.0
BENTON	3,704	2,920	554	230	2,366 R	78.8	15.0	84.1	15.9
BIG STONE	3,090	2,415	451	224	1,964 R	78.2	14.6	84.3	15.7
BLUE EARTH	11,251	8,894	1,974	383	6,920 R	79.1	17.5	81.8	18.2
BROWN	7,240	5,841	796	603	5,045 R	80.7	11.0	88.0	12.0
CARLTON	4,764	2,833	1,152	779	1,681 R	59.5	24.2	71.1	28.9
CARVER	5,810	5,073	562	175	4,511 R	87.3	9.7	90.0	10.0
CASS	4,598	3,242	710	646	2,532 R	70.5	15.4	82.0	18.0
CHIPPEWA	5,064	3,532	960	572	2,572 R	69.7	19.0	78.6	21.4
CHISAGO	5,450	4,361	484	605	3,877 R	80.0	8.9	90.0	10.0
CLAY	6,771	4,943	1,335	493	3,608 R	73.0	19.7	78.7	21.3
CLEARWATER	2,528	1,788	340	400	1,448 R	70.7	13.4	84.0	16.0
COOK	641	467	98	76	369 R	72.9	15.3	82.7	17.3
COTTONWOOD	4,500	3,882	451	167	3,431 R	86.3	10.0	89.6	10.4
CROW WING	7,481	5,262	1,077	1,142	4,185 R	70.3	14.4	83.0	17.0
DAKOTA	8,086	5,373	2,190	523	3,183 R	66.4	27.1	71.0	29.0
DODGE	4,060	3,386	516	158	2,870 R	83.4	12.7	86.8	13.2
DOUGLAS	6,696	4,428	733	1,535	3,695 R	66.1	10.9	85.8	14.2
FARIBAULT	7,775	6,687	869	219	5,818 R	86.0	11.2	88.5	11.5
FILLMORE	8,544	7,341	899	304	6,442 R	85.9	10.5	89.1	10.9
FREEBORN	8,263	6,772	1,131	360	5,641 R	82.0	13.7	85.7	14.3
GOODHUE	10,968	9,330	1,118	520	8,212 R	85.1	10.2	89.3	10.7
GRANT	3,202	2,427	533	242	1,894 R	75.8	16.6	82.0	18.0
HENNEPIN	140,169	90,517	28,911	20,741	61,606 R	64.6	20.6	75.8	24.2
HOUSTON	4,787	4,101	598	88	3,503 R	85.7	12.5	87.3	12.7
HUBBARD	3,031	2,238	453	340	1,785 R	73.8	14.9	83.2	16.8
ISANTI	4,450	3,007	405	1,038	2,602 R	67.6	9.1	88.1	11.9
ITASCA	6,813	3,973	1,930	910	2,043 R	58.3	28.3	67.3	32.7
JACKSON	5,158	4,313	715	130	3,598 R	83.6	13.9	85.8	14.2
KANABEC	3,219	2,436	332	451	2,104 R	75.7	10.3	88.0	12.0
KANDIYOHI	7,474	4,759	1,282	1,433	3,477 R	63.7	17.2	78.8	21.2
KITTSON	3,329	2,485	599	245	1,886 R	74.6	18.0	80.6	19.4
KOOCHICHING	3,230	1,786	859	585	927 R	55.3	26.6	67.5	32.5
LAC QUI PARLE	5,127	4,219	653	255	3,566 R	82.3	12.7	86.6	13.4
LAKE	2,419	990	594	835	396 R	40.9	24.6	62.5	37.5
LAKE OF THE WOODS									
LE SUEUR	6,130	4,059	1,853	218	2,206 R	66.2	30.2	68.7	31.3
LINCOLN	3,384	2,548	673	163	1,875 R	75.3	19.9	79.1	20.9
LYON	6,229	4,557	1,232	440	3,325 R	73.2	19.8	78.7	21.3
MCLEOD	6,996	5,430	1,139	427	4,291 R	77.6	16.3	82.7	17.3
MAHNOMEN	1,995	1,076	215	204	861 R	72.0	14.4	83.3	16.7
MARSHALL	6,283	4,738	885	660	3,853 R	75.4	14.1	84.3	15.7
MARTIN	6,554	5,142	1,221	191	3,921 R	78.5	18.6	80.8	19.2
MEEKER	5,986	4,693	878	415	3,815 R	78.4	14.7	84.2	15.8
MILLE LACS	4,812	3,571	526	765	2,995 R	73.2	10.9	87.0	13.0
MORRISON	6,924	5,371	1,131	422	4,240 R	77.5	16.3	82.6	17.4
MOWER	7,725	6,339	1,061	325	5,278 R	82.1	13.7	85.7	14.3
MURRAY	4,131	3,270	698	163	2,572 R	79.2	16.9	82.4	17.6
NICOLLET	4,931	4,115	556	260	3,559 R	83.5	11.3	88.1	11.9
NOBLES	5,550	4,420	982	148	3,438 R	79.6	17.7	81.8	18.2
NORMAN	4,653	3,451	481	721	2,970 R	74.2	10.3	87.8	12.2
OLMSTED	9,245	7,130	1,756	359	5,374 R	77.1	19.0	80.2	19.8
OTTER TAIL	14,119	11,084	1,741	1,294	9,343 R	78.5	12.3	86.4	13.6
PENNINGTON	3,802	2,320	768	714	1,552 R	60.7	20.1	75.1	24.9
PINE	5,804	3,879	1,127	798	2,752 R	66.8	19.4	77.5	22.5
PIPESTONE	3,888	3,106	490	292	2,616 R	79.9	12.6	86.4	13.6
POLK	11,800	8,197	2,111	1,492	6,086 R	69.5	17.9	79.5	20.5

PRESIDENT 1924

County	Total Vote	Republican	Democratic	Other	Rep.-Dem. Plurality	% Total Vote Rep.	% Total Vote Dem.	% Major Vote Rep.	% Major Vote Dem.
AITKIN	5,068	2,720	212	2,136	2,508 R	53.7	4.2	92.8	7.2
ANOKA	5,505	3,146	458	1,901	2,688 R	57.1	8.3	87.3	12.7
BECKER	6,452	2,936	429	3,087	2,507 R	45.5	6.6	87.3	12.7
BELTRAMI	6,404	2,960	323	3,121	2,637 R	46.2	5.0	90.2	9.8
BENTON	3,888	1,629	572	1,687	1,057 R	41.9	14.7	74.0	26.0
BIG STONE	3,303	1,524	260	1,519	1,264 R	46.1	7.9	85.4	14.6
BLUE EARTH	12,295	6,773	1,123	4,399	5,650 R	55.1	9.1	85.8	14.2
BROWN	7,076	2,255	270	4,551	1,985 R	31.9	3.8	89.3	10.7
CARLTON	6,314	3,142	303	2,869	2,839 R	49.8	4.8	91.2	8.8
CARVER	5,508	2,214	358	2,936	1,856 R	40.2	6.5	86.1	13.9
CASS	5,173	2,800	270	2,103	2,530 R	54.1	5.2	91.2	8.8
CHIPPEWA	5,060	2,140	140	2,780	2,000 R	42.3	2.7	93.9	6.1
CHISAGO	5,072	2,678	135	2,259	2,543 R	52.8	2.7	95.2	4.8
CLAY	6,916	3,081	439	3,396	2,642 R	44.5	6.3	87.5	12.5
CLEARWATER	2,717	1,020	86	1,611	934 R	37.5	3.2	92.2	7.8
COOK	693	471	29	193	442 R	68.0	4.2	94.2	5.8
COTTONWOOD	4,776	2,722	217	1,837	2,505 R	57.0	4.5	92.6	7.4
CROW WING	8,449	4,230	417	3,802	3,813 R	50.1	4.9	91.0	9.0
DAKOTA	9,284	3,931	929	4,424	3,002 R	42.3	10.0	80.9	19.1
DODGE	4,329	2,856	215	1,258	2,641 R	66.0	5.0	93.0	7.0
DOUGLAS	6,192	2,424	315	3,453	2,109 R	39.1	5.1	88.5	11.5
FARIBAULT	8,057	4,682	578	2,797	4,104 R	58.1	7.2	89.0	11.0
FILLMORE	8,845	5,550	460	2,835	5,090 R	62.7	5.2	92.3	7.7
FREEBORN	9,630	6,139	480	3,011	5,659 R	63.7	5.0	92.7	7.3
GOODHUE	11,599	6,849	615	4,135	6,234 R	59.0	5.3	91.8	8.2
GRANT	3,402	1,674	118	1,610	1,556 R	49.2	3.5	93.4	6.6
HENNEPIN	171,337	101,120	10,806	59,411	90,314 R	59.0	6.3	90.3	9.7
HOUSTON	5,192	2,782	402	2,008	2,380 R	53.6	7.7	87.4	12.6
HUBBARD	3,259	1,884	191	1,184	1,693 R	57.8	5.9	90.8	9.2
ISANTI	4,016	1,588	79	2,349	1,509 R	39.5	2.0	95.3	4.7
ITASCA	8,255	4,961	496	2,798	4,465 R	60.1	6.0	90.9	9.1
JACKSON	5,637	2,760	407	2,470	2,353 R	49.0	7.2	87.1	12.9
KANABEC	3,168	1,507	128	1,533	1,379 R	47.6	4.0	92.2	7.8
KANDIYOHI	8,022	3,222	222	4,578	3,000 R	40.2	2.8	93.6	6.4
KITTSON	3,109	1,333	249	1,527	1,084 R	42.9	8.0	84.3	15.7
KOOCHICHING	4,105	1,536	222	2,347	1,314 R	37.4	5.4	87.4	12.6
LAC QUI PARLE	5,473	2,860	106	2,507	2,754 R	52.3	1.9	96.4	3.6
LAKE	2,683	1,251	60	1,372	1,191 R	46.6	2.2	95.4	4.6
LAKE OF THE WOODS	1,646	703	92	851	611 R	42.7	5.6	88.4	11.6
LE SUEUR	6,481	2,475	1,199	2,807	1,276 R	38.2	18.5	67.4	32.6
LINCOLN	3,450	1,657	252	1,541	1,405 R	48.0	7.3	86.8	13.2
LYON	6,553	3,519	334	2,700	3,185 R	53.7	5.1	91.3	8.7
MCLEOD	6,329	2,841	563	2,925	2,278 R	44.9	8.9	83.5	16.5
MAHNOMEN	1,867	629	122	1,116	507 R	33.7	6.5	83.8	16.2
MARSHALL	5,246	2,100	290	2,856	1,810 R	40.0	5.5	87.9	12.1
MARTIN	7,535	4,238	751	2,546	3,487 R	56.2	10.0	84.9	15.1
MEEKER	6,064	2,757	365	2,942	2,392 R	45.5	6.0	88.3	11.7
MILLE LACS	4,946	2,413	167	2,366	2,246 R	48.8	3.4	93.5	6.5
MORRISON	7,514	3,128	769	3,617	2,359 R	41.6	10.2	80.3	19.7
MOWER	9,088	5,061	564	3,463	4,497 R	55.7	6.2	90.0	10.0
MURRAY	4,441	2,034	334	2,073	1,700 R	45.8	7.5	85.9	14.1
NICOLLET	5,031	2,518	287	2,226	2,231 R	50.0	5.7	89.8	10.2
NOBLES	6,150	2,835	421	2,894	2,414 R	46.1	6.8	87.1	12.9
NORMAN	4,363	1,997	171	2,195	1,826 R	45.8	3.9	92.1	7.9
OLMSTED	10,127	5,722	857	3,548	4,865 R	56.5	8.5	87.0	13.0
OTTER TAIL	13,629	7,557	568	5,504	6,989 R	55.4	4.2	93.0	7.0
PENNINGTON	3,609	1,126	146	2,337	980 R	31.2	4.0	88.5	11.5
PINE	6,438	2,706	469	3,263	2,237 R	42.0	7.3	85.2	14.8
PIPESTONE	4,290	2,066	219	2,005	1,847 R	48.2	5.1	90.4	9.6
POLK	11,440	5,027	663	5,750	4,364 R	43.9	5.8	88.3	11.7

MINNESOTA

PRESIDENT 1920

County	Total Vote	Republican	Democratic	Other	Rep.-Dem. Plurality	Total Vote Rep.	Total Vote Dem.	Major Vote Rep.	Major Vote Dem.
POPE	4,540	3,466	709	365	2,757 R	76.3%	15.6%	83.0%	17.0%
RAMSEY	68,587	40,204	21,110	7,273	19,094 R	58.6%	30.8%	65.6%	34.4%
RED LAKE	2,097	1,308	558	231	750 R	62.4%	26.6%	70.1%	29.9%
REDWOOD	6,728	5,589	880	259	4,709 R	83.1%	13.1%	86.4%	13.6%
RENVILLE	8,141	5,995	1,283	863	4,712 R	73.6%	15.8%	82.4%	17.6%
RICE	8,715	6,500	2,040	175	4,460 R	74.6%	23.4%	76.1%	23.9%
ROCK	3,692	3,121	442	129	2,679 R	84.5%	12.0%	87.6%	12.4%
ROSEAU	3,722	2,387	500	835	1,887 R	64.1%	13.4%	82.7%	17.3%
ST LOUIS	49,115	27,987	14,767	6,361	13,220 R	57.0%	30.1%	65.5%	34.5%
SCOTT	4,372	3,015	1,253	104	1,762 R	69.0%	28.7%	70.6%	29.4%
SHERBURNE	3,225	2,747	307	171	2,440 R	85.2%	9.5%	89.9%	10.1%
SIBLEY	4,885	4,198	502	185	3,696 R	85.9%	10.3%	89.3%	10.7%
STEARNS	15,714	13,566	1,616	532	11,950 R	86.3%	10.3%	89.4%	10.6%
STEELE	5,550	4,243	1,167	140	3,076 R	76.5%	21.0%	78.4%	21.6%
STEVENS	2,930	2,339	457	134	1,882 R	79.8%	15.6%	83.7%	16.3%
SWIFT	5,060	3,553	985	522	2,568 R	70.2%	19.5%	78.3%	21.7%
TODD	7,662	5,448	1,464	750	3,984 R	71.1%	19.1%	78.8%	21.2%
TRAVERSE	2,403	1,759	550	94	1,209 R	73.2%	22.9%	76.2%	23.8%
WABASHA	6,364	4,907	1,275	182	3,632 R	77.1%	20.0%	79.4%	20.6%
WADENA	3,487	2,635	503	349	2,132 R	75.5%	14.4%	84.0%	16.0%
WASECA	5,051	3,626	1,257	168	2,369 R	71.3%	24.9%	74.3%	25.7%
WASHINGTON	7,819	5,852	1,558	409	4,294 R	74.3%	19.9%	79.0%	21.0%
WATONWAN	4,312	3,510	647	155	2,863 R	81.4%	15.0%	84.4%	15.6%
WILKIN	2,801	2,106	561	134	1,545 R	75.2%	20.0%	79.0%	21.0%
WINONA	11,300	7,688	2,896	516	4,992 R	68.0%	25.6%	73.1%	26.9%
WRIGHT	8,820	7,013	1,299	508	5,714 R	79.5%	14.7%	84.4%	15.6%
YELLOW MEDICINE	5,829	4,225	814	790	3,411 R	72.5%	14.0%	83.8%	16.2%
TOTAL	735,838	519,421	142,994	73,423	376,427 R	70.6%	19.4%	78.4%	21.6%

PRESIDENT 1924

County	Total Vote	Republican	Democratic	Other	Rep.-Dem. Plurality	Total Vote Rep.	Total Vote Dem.	Major Vote Rep.	Major Vote Dem.
POPE	4,531	2,079	151	2,301	1,928 R	45.9%	3.3%	93.2%	6.8%
RAMSEY	83,019	39,566	8,407	35,046	31,159 R	47.7%	10.1%	82.5%	17.5%
RED LAKE	1,827	643	213	971	430 R	35.2%	11.7%	75.1%	24.9%
REDWOOD	6,597	3,342	443	2,812	2,899 R	50.7%	6.7%	88.3%	11.7%
RENVILLE	7,981	3,405	641	3,935	2,764 R	42.7%	8.0%	84.2%	15.8%
RICE	9,603	5,883	1,199	2,521	4,684 R	61.3%	12.5%	83.1%	16.9%
ROCK	3,973	2,065	261	1,647	1,804 R	52.0%	6.6%	88.8%	11.2%
ROSEAU	3,334	1,300	148	1,886	1,152 R	39.0%	4.4%	89.8%	10.2%
ST LOUIS	64,623	37,033	2,577	25,013	34,456 R	57.3%	4.0%	93.5%	6.5%
SCOTT	4,520	1,324	829	2,367	495 R	29.3%	18.3%	61.5%	38.5%
SHERBURNE	3,081	1,961	180	940	1,781 R	63.6%	5.8%	91.6%	8.4%
SIBLEY	5,060	1,749	341	2,970	1,408 R	34.6%	6.7%	83.7%	16.3%
STEARNS	17,314	6,469	1,354	9,491	5,115 R	37.4%	7.8%	82.7%	17.3%
STEELE	6,047	3,598	796	1,653	2,802 R	59.5%	13.2%	81.9%	18.1%
STEVENS	3,170	1,553	238	1,379	1,315 R	49.0%	7.5%	86.7%	13.3%
SWIFT	4,922	1,654	334	2,934	1,320 R	33.6%	6.8%	83.2%	16.8%
TODD	8,379	4,441	557	3,381	3,884 R	53.0%	6.6%	88.9%	11.1%
TRAVERSE	2,548	1,002	202	1,344	800 R	39.3%	7.9%	83.2%	16.8%
WABASHA	6,307	2,834	644	2,829	2,190 R	44.9%	10.2%	81.5%	18.5%
WADENA	3,465	1,900	182	1,383	1,718 R	54.8%	5.3%	91.3%	8.7%
WASECA	5,605	2,081	442	3,082	1,639 R	37.1%	7.9%	82.5%	17.5%
WASHINGTON	8,553	4,482	699	3,372	3,783 R	52.4%	8.2%	86.5%	13.5%
WATONWAN	4,288	2,297	279	1,712	2,018 R	53.6%	6.5%	89.2%	10.8%
WILKIN	2,845	1,342	245	1,258	1,097 R	47.2%	8.6%	84.6%	15.4%
WINONA	13,026	5,670	1,111	6,245	4,559 R	43.5%	8.5%	83.6%	16.4%
WRIGHT	9,151	4,349	567	4,235	3,782 R	47.5%	6.2%	88.5%	11.5%
YELLOW MEDICINE	5,887	2,278	151	3,458	2,127 R	38.7%	2.6%	93.8%	6.2%
TOTAL	822,146	420,759	55,913	345,474	364,846 R	51.2%	6.8%	88.3%	11.7%

MINNESOTA

PRESIDENT 1928

County	Total Vote	Republican	Democratic	Other	Rep.-Dem. Plurality	Total Vote Rep.	Total Vote Dem.	Major Vote Rep.	Major Vote Dem.
AITKIN	5,636	3,951	1,428	257	2,523 R	70.1%	25.3%	73.5%	26.5%
ANOKA	6,462	3,816	2,571	75	1,245 R	59.1%	39.8%	59.7%	40.3%
BECKER	7,703	4,273	3,253	177	1,020 R	55.5%	42.2%	56.8%	43.2%
BELTRAMI	6,522	4,062	2,221	239	1,841 R	62.3%	34.1%	64.7%	35.3%
BENTON	5,126	2,373	2,732	21	359 D	46.3%	53.3%	46.5%	53.5%
BIG STONE	3,799	1,641	2,133	25	492 D	43.2%	56.1%	43.5%	56.5%
BLUE EARTH	13,376	8,120	5,177	79	2,943 R	60.7%	38.7%	61.1%	38.9%
BROWN	9,016	3,611	5,341	64	1,730 D	40.1%	59.2%	40.3%	59.7%
CARLTON	7,158	4,582	2,138	438	2,444 R	64.0%	29.9%	68.2%	31.8%
CARVER	6,901	3,983	2,885	33	1,098 R	57.7%	41.8%	58.0%	42.0%
CASS	5,642	3,781	1,747	114	2,034 R	67.0%	31.0%	68.4%	31.6%
CHIPPEWA	5,651	3,547	2,032	72	1,515 R	62.8%	36.0%	63.6%	36.4%
CHISAGO	5,582	4,215	1,297	70	2,918 R	75.5%	23.2%	76.5%	23.5%
CLAY	8,272	5,057	3,128	87	1,929 R	61.1%	37.8%	61.8%	38.2%
CLEARWATER	3,163	1,898	1,189	76	709 R	60.0%	37.6%	61.5%	38.5%
COOK	839	609	219	11	390 R	72.6%	26.1%	73.6%	26.4%
COTTONWOOD	5,048	3,405	1,604	39	1,801 R	67.9%	31.8%	68.0%	32.0%
CROW WING	9,483	6,436	2,851	196	3,585 R	67.9%	30.1%	69.3%	30.7%
DAKOTA	13,323	6,019	7,215	89	1,196 D	45.2%	54.2%	45.5%	54.5%
DODGE	4,791	3,569	1,196	26	2,373 R	74.5%	25.0%	74.9%	25.1%
DOUGLAS	7,191	4,262	2,829	100	1,433 R	59.3%	39.3%	60.1%	39.9%
FARIBAULT	8,506	5,885	2,545	76	3,340 R	69.2%	29.9%	69.8%	30.2%
FILLMORE	9,925	7,719	2,143	63	5,576 R	77.8%	21.6%	78.3%	21.7%
FREEBORN	10,750	7,815	2,859	76	4,956 R	72.7%	26.6%	73.2%	26.8%
GOODHUE	13,372	9,752	3,520	100	6,232 R	72.9%	26.3%	73.5%	26.5%
GRANT	3,786	2,057	1,687	42	370 R	54.3%	44.6%	54.9%	45.1%
HENNEPIN	208,447	125,472	80,851	2,124	44,621 R	60.2%	38.8%	60.8%	39.2%
HOUSTON	5,573	3,615	1,937	21	1,678 R	64.9%	34.8%	65.1%	34.9%
HUBBARD	3,484	2,291	1,120	73	1,171 R	65.8%	32.1%	67.2%	32.8%
ISANTI	4,410	3,137	1,191	82	1,946 R	71.1%	27.0%	72.5%	27.5%
ITASCA	8,656	5,103	3,122	431	1,981 R	59.0%	36.1%	62.0%	38.0%
JACKSON	5,628	3,099	2,503	26	596 R	55.1%	44.5%	55.3%	44.7%
KANABEC	3,482	2,380	1,040	62	1,340 R	68.4%	29.9%	69.6%	30.4%
KANDIYOHI	8,543	5,780	2,481	282	3,299 R	67.7%	29.1%	70.0%	30.0%
KITTSON	3,545	1,957	1,383	205	574 R	55.2%	39.0%	58.6%	41.4%
KOOCHICHING	4,843	2,599	2,110	134	489 R	53.7%	43.6%	55.2%	44.8%
LAC QUI PARLE	5,710	3,406	2,245	59	1,161 R	59.6%	39.3%	60.3%	39.7%
LAKE	2,765	2,014	618	133	1,396 R	72.8%	22.4%	76.5%	23.5%
LAKE OF THE WOODS	1,508	781	671	56	110 R	51.8%	44.5%	53.8%	46.2%
LE SUEUR	8,054	3,401	4,615	38	1,214 D	42.2%	57.3%	42.4%	57.6%
LINCOLN	4,050	1,952	2,064	34	112 D	48.2%	51.0%	48.6%	51.4%
LYON	7,388	4,058	3,274	56	784 R	54.9%	44.3%	55.3%	44.7%
MCLEOD	7,757	4,252	3,445	60	807 R	54.8%	44.4%	55.2%	44.8%
MAHNOMEN	2,027	606	1,378	43	772 D	29.9%	68.0%	30.5%	69.5%
MARSHALL	6,070	3,738	2,200	132	1,538 R	61.6%	36.2%	63.0%	37.0%
MARTIN	7,972	5,110	2,822	40	2,288 R	64.1%	35.4%	64.4%	35.6%
MEEKER	7,002	4,175	2,761	66	1,414 R	59.6%	39.4%	60.2%	39.8%
MILLE LACS	5,552	3,998	1,436	118	2,562 R	72.0%	25.9%	73.6%	26.4%
MORRISON	9,119	3,846	5,222	51	1,376 D	42.2%	57.3%	42.4%	57.6%
MOWER	9,842	6,209	3,587	46	2,622 R	63.1%	36.4%	63.4%	36.6%
MURRAY	4,709	2,602	2,078	29	524 R	55.3%	44.1%	55.6%	44.4%
NICOLLET	6,136	3,628	2,466	42	1,162 R	59.1%	40.2%	59.5%	40.5%
NOBLES	6,563	3,676	2,862	25	814 R	56.0%	43.6%	56.2%	43.8%
NORMAN	4,909	3,308	1,401	200	1,907 R	67.4%	28.5%	70.2%	29.8%
OLMSTED	13,098	8,334	4,720	44	3,614 R	63.6%	36.0%	63.8%	36.2%
OTTER TAIL	17,025	11,624	4,990	411	6,634 R	68.3%	29.3%	70.0%	30.0%
PENNINGTON	3,838	2,506	1,198	134	1,308 R	65.3%	31.2%	67.7%	32.3%
PINE	7,568	4,278	3,185	105	1,093 R	56.5%	42.1%	57.3%	42.7%
PIPESTONE	4,207	2,578	1,591	38	987 R	61.3%	37.8%	61.8%	38.2%
POLK	12,866	7,215	5,357	294	1,858 R	56.1%	41.6%	57.4%	42.6%

PRESIDENT 1932

County	Total Vote	Republican	Democratic	Other	Rep.-Dem. Plurality	Total Vote Rep.	Total Vote Dem.	Major Vote Rep.	Major Vote Dem.
AITKIN	5,743	2,341	2,945	457	604 D	40.8%	51.3%	44.3%	55.7%
ANOKA	7,152	2,718	4,253	181	1,535 D	38.0%	59.5%	39.0%	61.0%
BECKER	8,210	2,299	5,547	364	3,248 D	28.0%	67.5%	29.3%	70.7%
BELTRAMI	7,222	2,318	4,386	518	2,068 D	32.1%	60.7%	34.6%	65.4%
BENTON	5,350	1,329	3,901	120	2,572 D	24.8%	72.9%	25.4%	74.6%
BIG STONE	4,136	868	3,200	68	2,332 D	21.0%	77.4%	21.3%	78.7%
BLUE EARTH	13,691	5,550	7,925	216	2,375 D	40.5%	57.9%	41.2%	58.8%
BROWN	8,955	2,027	6,716	212	4,689 D	22.6%	75.0%	23.2%	76.8%
CARLTON	7,838	3,336	3,586	916	250 D	42.6%	45.8%	48.2%	51.8%
CARVER	6,902	2,508	4,328	66	1,820 D	36.3%	62.7%	36.7%	63.3%
CASS	6,043	2,302	3,494	247	1,192 D	38.1%	57.8%	39.7%	60.3%
CHIPPEWA	5,986	1,940	3,888	158	1,948 D	32.4%	65.0%	33.3%	66.7%
CHISAGO	5,755	2,524	3,047	184	523 D	43.9%	52.9%	45.3%	54.7%
CLAY	8,764	2,556	5,938	270	3,382 D	29.2%	67.8%	30.1%	69.9%
CLEARWATER	3,692	845	2,688	159	1,843 D	22.9%	72.8%	23.9%	76.1%
COOK	966	418	492	56	74 D	43.3%	50.9%	45.9%	54.1%
COTTONWOOD	4,876	1,921	2,877	78	956 D	39.4%	59.0%	40.0%	60.0%
CROW WING	9,578	3,991	5,068	519	1,077 D	41.7%	52.9%	44.1%	55.9%
DAKOTA	13,635	4,439	8,958	238	4,519 D	32.6%	65.7%	33.1%	66.9%
DODGE	4,891	2,129	2,675	87	546 D	43.5%	54.7%	44.3%	55.7%
DOUGLAS	7,656	2,325	5,101	230	2,776 D	30.4%	66.6%	31.3%	68.7%
FARIBAULT	8,892	4,148	4,590	154	442 D	46.6%	51.6%	47.5%	52.5%
FILLMORE	10,325	4,979	5,166	180	187 D	48.2%	50.0%	49.1%	50.9%
FREEBORN	11,052	4,931	5,838	283	907 D	44.6%	52.8%	45.8%	54.2%
GOODHUE	13,310	5,486	7,450	374	1,964 D	41.2%	56.0%	42.4%	57.6%
GRANT	3,935	1,148	2,702	85	1,554 D	29.2%	68.7%	29.8%	70.2%
HENNEPIN	217,566	91,087	119,234	7,245	28,147 D	41.9%	54.8%	43.3%	56.7%
HOUSTON	5,478	2,335	3,052	91	717 D	42.6%	55.7%	43.3%	56.7%
HUBBARD	3,751	1,349	2,230	172	881 D	36.0%	59.5%	37.7%	62.3%
ISANTI	4,877	1,484	3,147	246	1,663 D	30.4%	64.5%	32.0%	68.0%
ITASCA	10,237	3,782	5,616	839	1,834 D	36.9%	54.9%	40.2%	59.8%
JACKSON	5,761	1,524	4,129	108	2,605 D	26.5%	71.7%	27.0%	73.0%
KANABEC	3,605	1,268	2,106	231	838 D	35.2%	58.4%	37.6%	62.4%
KANDIYOHI	8,901	2,674	5,813	414	3,139 D	30.0%	65.3%	31.5%	68.5%
KITTSON	3,416	950	2,332	134	1,382 D	27.8%	68.3%	28.9%	71.1%
KOOCHICHING	4,974	1,427	3,148	399	1,721 D	28.7%	63.3%	31.2%	68.7%
LAC QUI PARLE	6,000	1,911	3,992	97	2,081 D	31.8%	66.5%	32.4%	67.6%
LAKE	3,002	1,290	1,059	653	231 D	43.0%	35.3%	54.9%	45.1%
LAKE OF THE WOODS	1,567	369	972	226	603 D	23.5%	62.0%	27.5%	72.5%
LE SUEUR	8,100	2,121	5,878	101	3,757 D	26.2%	72.6%	26.5%	73.5%
LINCOLN	4,064	974	2,963	127	1,989 D	24.0%	72.9%	24.7%	75.3%
LYON	7,383	2,264	4,989	130	2,725 D	30.7%	67.6%	31.2%	68.8%
MCLEOD	7,608	2,293	5,187	128	2,894 D	30.1%	68.2%	30.7%	69.3%
MAHNOMEN	2,069	264	1,734	71	1,470 D	12.8%	83.8%	13.2%	86.8%
MARSHALL	5,463	1,866	3,259	338	1,393 D	34.2%	59.7%	36.4%	63.6%
MARTIN	7,851	3,004	4,731	116	1,727 D	38.3%	60.3%	38.8%	61.2%
MEEKER	7,147	2,273	4,723	151	2,450 D	31.8%	66.1%	32.5%	67.5%
MILLE LACS	5,836	1,986	3,538	312	1,552 D	34.0%	60.6%	36.0%	64.0%
MORRISON	9,123	2,198	6,712	213	4,514 D	24.1%	73.6%	24.7%	75.3%
MOWER	10,599	4,005	6,421	173	2,416 D	37.8%	60.6%	38.4%	61.6%
MURRAY	4,658	1,314	3,264	80	1,950 D	28.2%	70.1%	28.7%	71.3%
NICOLLET	6,328	2,217	3,960	151	1,743 D	35.0%	62.6%	35.9%	64.1%
NOBLES	6,838	2,417	4,343	78	1,926 D	35.3%	63.5%	35.8%	64.2%
NORMAN	5,234	1,313	3,601	320	2,288 D	25.1%	68.8%	26.7%	73.3%
OLMSTED	12,874	5,254	7,340	280	2,086 D	40.8%	57.0%	41.7%	58.3%
OTTER TAIL	16,964	7,416	8,805	743	1,389 D	43.7%	51.9%	45.7%	54.3%
PENNINGTON	4,310	1,212	2,743	355	1,531 D	28.1%	63.6%	30.6%	69.4%
PINE	7,801	2,304	4,862	635	2,558 D	29.5%	62.3%	32.2%	67.8%
PIPESTONE	4,578	1,509	2,996	73	1,487 D	33.0%	65.4%	33.5%	66.5%
POLK	13,190	3,604	8,751	835	5,147 D	27.3%	66.3%	29.2%	70.8%

MINNESOTA

PRESIDENT 1928

County	Total Vote	Republican	Democratic	Other	Rep.-Dem. Plurality	Total Vote Rep.	Total Vote Dem.	Major Vote Rep.	Major Vote Dem.
POPE	5,114	3,382	1,667	65	1,715 R	65.1%	32.6%	67.0%	33.0%
RAMSEY	110,910	53,054	56,807	1,049	3,753 D	47.8%	51.2%	48.3%	51.7%
RED LAKE	2,256	712	1,507	37	795 D	31.6%	66.8%	32.1%	67.9%
REDWOOD	8,089	5,111	2,899	79	2,212 R	63.2%	35.8%	63.8%	36.2%
RENVILLE	8,932	5,107	3,731	94	1,376 R	57.2%	41.8%	57.8%	42.2%
RICE	11,639	6,576	5,014	49	1,562 R	56.5%	43.1%	56.7%	43.3%
ROCK	4,053	2,433	1,607	13	826 R	60.0%	39.6%	60.2%	39.8%
ROSEAU	4,145	2,618	1,342	185	1,276 R	63.2%	32.4%	66.1%	33.9%
ST LOUIS	72,517	44,331	25,401	2,785	13,930 R	61.1%	35.0%	63.6%	36.4%
SCOTT	6,162	1,732	4,419	11	2,687 D	28.1%	71.7%	28.2%	71.8%
SHERBURNE	3,528	2,437	1,064	27	1,373 R	69.1%	30.2%	69.6%	30.4%
SIBLEY	5,901	3,301	2,553	47	748 R	55.9%	43.3%	56.4%	43.6%
STEARNS	22,615	6,459	16,104	52	9,645 D	28.6%	71.2%	28.6%	71.4%
STEELE	7,595	4,744	2,826	25	1,918 R	62.5%	37.2%	62.7%	37.3%
STEVENS	3,748	2,275	1,457	16	818 R	61.7%	38.9%	61.0%	39.0%
SWIFT	5,613	2,791	2,733	89	58 R	49.7%	48.7%	50.5%	49.5%
TODD	9,500	5,682	3,733	85	1,949 R	59.8%	39.3%	60.4%	39.6%
TRAVERSE	3,130	1,214	1,899	17	685 D	38.8%	50.7%	39.0%	61.0%
WABASHA	7,063	3,944	3,087	32	857 R	55.8%	43.7%	56.1%	43.9%
WADENA	4,044	2,592	1,343	109	1,249 R	64.1%	33.2%	65.9%	34.1%
WASECA	5,710	3,251	2,418	41	833 R	56.9%	42.3%	57.3%	42.7%
WASHINGTON	10,351	6,113	4,158	80	1,955 R	59.1%	40.2%	59.5%	40.5%
WATONWAN	4,744	3,306	1,412	26	1,894 R	69.7%	29.8%	70.1%	29.9%
WILKIN	3,477	1,874	1,578	25	296 R	53.9%	45.4%	54.3%	45.7%
WINONA	14,031	7,459	6,484	88	975 R	53.2%	46.2%	53.5%	46.5%
WRIGHT	10,626	6,011	4,483	132	1,528 R	56.6%	42.2%	57.3%	42.7%
YELLOW MEDICINE	6,235	3,302	2,861	72	441 R	53.0%	45.9%	53.6%	46.4%
TOTAL	970,976	560,977	396,451	13,548	164,526 R	57.8%	40.8%	58.6%	41.4%

PRESIDENT 1932

County	Total Vote	Republican	Democratic	Other	Rep.-Dem. Plurality	Total Vote Rep.	Total Vote Dem.	Major Vote Rep.	Major Vote Dem.
POPE	5,365	1,688	3,571	106	1,883 D	31.5%	66.6%	32.1%	67.9%
RAMSEY	107,980	38,589	66,128	3,263	27,539 D	35.7%	61.2%	36.9%	63.1%
RED LAKE	2,341	351	1,893	97	1,542 D	15.0%	80.9%	15.6%	84.4%
REDWOOD	7,480	2,634	4,727	119	2,093 D	35.2%	63.2%	35.8%	64.2%
RENVILLE	8,761	2,631	5,967	163	3,336 D	30.0%	68.1%	30.6%	69.4%
RICE	11,215	4,743	6,289	183	1,546 D	42.3%	56.1%	43.0%	57.0%
ROCK	4,201	1,452	2,695	54	1,243 D	34.6%	64.2%	35.0%	65.0%
ROSEAU	4,224	1,078	2,805	341	1,727 D	25.5%	66.4%	27.8%	72.2%
ST LOUIS	83,729	34,883	40,181	8,665	5,298 D	41.7%	48.0%	46.5%	53.5%
SCOTT	6,049	1,134	4,878	37	3,744 D	18.7%	80.6%	18.9%	81.1%
SHERBURNE	3,625	1,601	1,938	86	337 D	44.2%	53.5%	45.2%	54.8%
SIBLEY	6,236	1,398	4,756	82	3,358 D	22.4%	76.3%	22.7%	77.3%
STEARNS	23,050	4,499	18,293	258	13,794 D	19.5%	79.4%	19.7%	80.3%
STEELE	7,790	3,365	4,318	107	953 D	43.2%	55.4%	43.8%	56.2%
STEVENS	3,990	1,396	2,552	42	1,156 D	35.0%	64.0%	35.4%	64.6%
SWIFT	5,732	1,308	4,339	135	3,031 D	22.6%	75.0%	23.2%	76.8%
TODD	9,337	3,114	6,023	250	2,909 D	33.2%	64.2%	34.1%	65.9%
TRAVERSE	3,232	608	2,633	41	2,025 D	18.5%	80.2%	18.8%	81.2%
WABASHA	6,978	2,319	4,540	119	2,221 D	33.2%	65.1%	33.8%	66.2%
WADENA	4,030	1,585	2,300	145	715 D	39.3%	57.1%	40.8%	59.2%
WASECA	5,903	2,012	3,805	86	1,793 D	34.1%	64.5%	34.6%	65.4%
WASHINGTON	10,656	3,996	6,413	247	2,417 D	37.5%	60.2%	38.4%	61.6%
WATONWAN	4,843	1,919	2,795	129	876 D	39.6%	57.7%	40.7%	59.3%
WILKIN	3,662	1,126	2,488	48	1,362 D	30.7%	67.9%	31.2%	68.8%
WINONA	13,308	4,751	8,305	252	3,554 D	35.7%	62.4%	36.4%	63.6%
WRIGHT	10,830	3,406	7,205	219	3,799 D	31.4%	66.5%	32.1%	67.9%
YELLOW MEDICINE	6,438	1,739	4,580	119	2,841 D	27.0%	71.1%	27.5%	72.5%
TOTAL	1,002,843	363,959	600,806	38,078	236,847 D	36.3%	59.9%	37.7%	62.3%

MINNESOTA

PRESIDENT 1936

County	Total Vote	Republican	Democratic	Other	Rep.-Dem. Plurality	%TV Rep.	%TV Dem.	%MV Rep.	%MV Dem.
AITKIN	6,611	2,466	3,806	339	1,340 D	37.3	57.6	39.3	60.7
ANOKA	7,909	2,586	4,501	822	1,915 D	32.7	56.9	36.5	63.5
BECKER	9,466	2,683	6,473	310	3,790 D	28.3	68.4	29.3	70.7
BELTRAMI	8,957	2,182	6,507	268	4,325 D	24.4	72.6	25.1	74.9
BENTON	5,813	1,783	3,111	919	1,328 D	30.7	53.5	36.4	63.6
BIG STONE	3,999	1,116	2,648	235	1,532 D	27.9	66.2	29.6	70.4
BLUE EARTH	14,769	5,550	8,255	964	2,705 D	37.6	55.9	40.2	59.8
BROWN	10,267	2,679	6,637	951	3,958 D	26.1	64.6	28.8	71.2
CARLTON	9,478	2,163	7,136	179	4,973 D	22.8	75.3	23.3	76.7
CARVER	7,292	3,095	2,814	1,383	281 R	42.4	38.6	52.4	47.6
CASS	7,334	2,634	4,440	260	1,806 D	35.9	60.5	37.2	62.8
CHIPPEWA	6,559	2,223	4,027	309	1,804 D	33.9	61.4	35.6	64.4
CHISAGO	6,080	2,462	3,360	258	898 D	40.5	55.3	42.3	57.7
CLAY	9,621	2,880	6,282	459	3,402 D	29.9	65.3	31.4	68.6
CLEARWATER	4,258	939	3,208	111	2,269 D	22.1	75.3	22.6	77.4
COOK	1,204	387	793	24	406 D	32.1	65.9	32.8	67.2
COTTONWOOD	6,623	2,509	3,929	185	1,420 D	37.9	59.3	39.0	61.0
CROW WING	10,673	3,611	6,561	501	2,950 D	33.8	61.5	35.5	64.5
DAKOTA	15,398	4,043	8,890	2,465	4,847 D	26.3	57.7	31.3	68.7
DODGE	5,138	2,138	2,812	188	674 D	41.6	54.7	43.2	56.8
DOUGLAS	7,364	2,681	4,186	497	1,505 D	36.4	56.8	39.0	61.0
FARIBAULT	9,847	3,773	5,603	471	1,830 D	38.3	56.9	40.2	59.8
FILLMORE	10,404	5,054	4,764	586	290 R	48.6	45.8	51.5	48.5
FREEBORN	12,305	4,653	7,378	274	2,725 D	37.8	60.0	38.7	61.3
GOODHUE	14,361	5,662	8,257	442	2,575 D	39.6	57.5	40.8	59.2
GRANT	4,075	1,566	2,358	151	792 D	38.4	57.9	39.9	60.1
HENNEPIN	245,480	81,206	144,289	19,985	63,083 D	33.1	58.8	36.0	64.0
HOUSTON	6,100	2,701	3,156	243	455 D	44.3	51.7	46.1	53.9
HUBBARD	4,062	1,618	2,312	132	694 D	39.8	56.9	41.2	58.8
ISANTI	5,123	1,437	3,442	244	2,005 D	28.0	67.2	29.5	70.5
ITASCA	12,819	3,594	8,896	329	5,302 D	28.0	69.4	28.8	71.2
JACKSON	7,195	1,676	5,187	332	3,511 D	23.3	72.1	24.4	75.6
KANABEC	4,088	1,350	2,579	159	1,229 D	33.0	63.1	34.4	65.6
KANDIYOHI	9,524	2,500	6,595	429	4,095 D	26.2	69.2	27.5	72.5
KITTSON	4,269	1,080	3,127	62	2,047 D	25.3	73.2	25.7	74.3
KOOCHICHING	6,513	1,316	5,065	132	3,749 D	20.2	77.8	20.6	79.4
LAC QUI PARLE	5,996	2,066	3,243	687	1,177 D	34.5	54.1	38.9	61.1
LAKE	3,390	617	2,717	56	2,100 D	18.2	80.1	18.5	81.5
LAKE OF THE WOODS	2,052	385	1,566	101	1,181 D	18.8	76.3	19.7	80.3
LE SUEUR	8,865	2,849	5,077	939	2,228 D	32.1	57.3	35.9	64.1
LINCOLN	4,334	1,199	2,662	473	1,463 D	27.7	61.4	31.1	68.9
LYON	8,424	2,551	5,163	710	2,612 D	30.3	61.3	33.1	66.9
MCLEOD	8,058	2,941	4,449	668	1,508 D	36.5	55.2	39.8	60.2
MAHNOMEN	2,634	474	2,025	135	1,551 D	18.0	76.9	19.0	81.0
MARSHALL	6,852	1,904	4,802	146	2,898 D	27.8	70.1	28.4	71.6
MARTIN	9,825	3,090	6,492	243	3,402 D	31.5	66.1	32.2	67.8
MEEKER	7,542	2,479	4,242	821	1,763 D	32.9	56.2	36.9	63.1
MILLE LACS	6,848	2,091	3,767	990	1,676 D	30.5	55.0	35.7	64.3
MORRISON	9,848	2,682	6,112	1,054	3,430 D	27.2	62.1	30.5	69.5
MOWER	13,487	4,743	8,228	516	3,485 D	35.2	61.0	36.6	63.4
MURRAY	5,855	1,601	3,926	328	2,325 D	27.3	67.1	29.0	71.0
NICOLLET	7,003	2,360	4,156	507	1,796 D	33.7	59.3	36.3	63.7
NOBLES	8,072	2,601	4,919	552	2,318 D	32.2	60.9	34.6	65.4
NORMAN	5,502	1,570	3,778	154	2,208 D	28.5	68.7	29.4	70.6
OLMSTED	14,919	5,516	8,958	645	3,442 D	37.0	60.0	38.1	61.9
OTTER TAIL	18,110	8,899	8,642	569	257 R	49.1	47.7	50.7	49.3
PENNINGTON	5,155	1,258	3,736	161	2,478 D	24.4	72.5	25.2	74.8
PINE	8,638	2,452	5,797	389	3,345 D	28.4	67.1	29.7	70.3
PIPESTONE	5,170	1,881	3,026	263	1,145 D	36.4	58.5	38.3	61.7
POLK	15,437	3,751	11,337	349	7,586 D	24.3	73.4	24.9	75.1

PRESIDENT 1940

County	Total Vote	Republican	Democratic	Other	Rep.-Dem. Plurality	%TV Rep.	%TV Dem.	%MV Rep.	%MV Dem.
AITKIN	7,470	3,744	3,610	116	134 R	50.1	48.3	50.9	49.1
ANOKA	9,883	4,302	5,501	80	1,199 D	43.5	55.7	43.5	56.1
BECKER	10,816	4,292	6,432	92	2,140 D	39.7	59.5	40.0	60.0
BELTRAMI	10,713	3,511	7,036	166	3,525 D	32.8	65.7	33.3	66.7
BENTON	6,261	3,491	2,742	28	749 R	55.8	43.8	56.0	44.0
BIG STONE	4,482	1,925	2,517	40	592 D	42.9	56.2	43.3	56.7
BLUE EARTH	15,584	9,642	5,880	62	3,762 R	61.9	37.7	62.1	37.9
BROWN	11,301	7,533	3,678	90	3,855 R	66.7	32.5	67.2	32.8
CARLTON	10,670	3,400	7,159	111	3,759 D	31.9	67.1	32.2	67.8
CARVER	8,303	6,528	1,753	22	4,775 R	78.6	21.1	78.8	21.2
CASS	8,533	4,089	4,392	52	303 D	47.9	51.5	48.2	51.8
CHIPPEWA	7,340	3,307	3,969	64	662 D	45.1	54.1	45.5	54.5
CHISAGO	6,377	3,569	2,746	62	823 R	56.0	43.1	56.5	43.5
CLAY	10,793	4,450	6,295	48	1,845 D	41.2	58.3	41.4	58.6
CLEARWATER	4,678	1,354	3,289	35	1,935 D	28.9	70.3	29.2	70.8
COOK	1,366	673	686	7	13 D	49.3	50.2	49.5	50.5
COTTONWOOD	7,255	4,224	2,991	36	1,237 R	58.3	41.2	58.5	41.5
CROW WING	12,550	5,524	6,876	150	1,352 D	44.0	54.8	44.5	55.5
DAKOTA	17,743	8,327	9,327	77	988 D	46.9	52.6	47.2	52.8
DODGE	5,625	3,257	2,357	11	900 R	57.9	41.9	58.0	42.0
DOUGLAS	9,207	4,652	4,507	48	145 R	50.5	49.0	50.8	49.2
FARIBAULT	10,971	6,816	4,099	56	2,717 R	62.1	37.4	62.4	37.6
FILLMORE	11,704	7,839	3,826	39	4,013 R	67.0	32.7	67.2	32.8
FREEBORN	13,680	6,683	6,942	55	259 D	48.9	50.7	49.0	51.0
GOODHUE	15,656	9,095	6,475	86	2,620 R	58.1	41.4	58.4	41.6
GRANT	4,764	2,443	2,291	30	152 R	51.3	48.1	51.6	48.4
HENNEPIN	270,358	122,960	145,168	2,230	22,208 D	45.5	53.7	45.9	54.1
HOUSTON	6,945	4,826	2,082	37	2,743 R	69.5	30.0	69.9	30.1
HUBBARD	4,711	2,544	2,141	26	403 R	54.0	45.4	54.3	45.7
ISANTI	5,361	2,617	2,654	90	37 D	48.8	49.5	49.6	50.4
ITASCA	15,254	5,196	9,899	159	4,703 D	34.1	64.9	34.4	65.6
JACKSON	7,482	3,387	4,065	30	678 D	45.3	54.3	45.5	54.5
KANABEC	4,545	2,311	2,185	49	126 R	50.8	48.1	51.4	48.6
KANDIYOHI	11,540	4,263	7,187	90	2,924 D	36.9	62.3	37.2	62.8
KITTSON	4,480	1,279	3,167	34	1,888 D	28.5	70.7	28.8	71.2
KOOCHICHING	7,353	2,095	5,219	39	3,124 D	28.5	71.0	28.6	71.4
LAC QUI PARLE	6,923	3,789	3,106	28	683 R	54.7	44.9	55.0	45.0
LAKE	3,733	933	2,750	50	1,817 D	25.0	73.7	25.3	74.7
LAKE OF THE WOODS	2,528	850	1,638	40	788 D	33.6	64.8	34.2	65.8
LE SUEUR	9,313	5,543	3,750	20	1,793 R	59.5	40.3	59.6	40.4
LINCOLN	4,789	2,220	2,536	33	316 D	46.4	53.0	46.7	53.3
LYON	9,575	4,305	5,234	36	929 D	45.0	54.7	45.1	54.9
MCLEOD	9,420	6,474	2,884	62	3,590 R	68.7	30.6	69.2	30.8
MAHNOMEN	3,042	1,069	1,959	14	890 D	35.3	64.4	35.3	64.7
MARSHALL	7,034	2,441	4,549	44	2,108 D	34.7	64.7	34.9	65.1
MARTIN	10,720	6,409	4,290	21	2,119 R	59.8	40.0	59.9	40.1
MEEKER	8,686	5,026	3,615	45	1,411 R	57.9	41.6	58.2	41.8
MILLE LACS	7,151	3,459	3,619	73	160 D	48.4	50.6	48.9	51.1
MORRISON	10,936	5,734	5,144	58	590 R	52.4	47.0	52.7	47.3
MOWER	15,217	7,169	7,988	60	819 D	47.1	52.5	47.3	52.7
MURRAY	6,281	3,044	3,203	34	159 D	48.5	51.0	48.7	51.3
NICOLLET	7,537	4,674	2,832	31	1,842 R	62.0	37.6	62.3	37.7
NOBLES	9,059	5,104	3,919	36	1,185 R	56.3	43.3	56.6	43.4
NORMAN	5,916	2,161	3,716	39	1,555 D	36.5	62.8	36.8	63.2
OLMSTED	17,551	9,096	8,393	62	703 R	51.8	47.8	52.0	48.0
OTTER TAIL	21,629	13,737	7,705	187	6,032 R	63.5	35.6	64.1	35.9
PENNINGTON	5,841	1,857	3,886	98	2,029 D	31.8	66.5	32.3	67.7
PINE	9,526	4,106	5,263	157	1,157 D	43.1	55.2	43.8	56.2
PIPESTONE	5,842	3,423	2,390	29	1,033 R	58.6	40.9	58.9	41.1
POLK	15,985	5,200	10,652	133	5,452 D	32.5	66.6	32.8	67.2

MINNESOTA

PRESIDENT 1936

County	Total Vote	Republican	Democratic	Other	Rep.-Dem. Plurality	Percentage Total Vote Rep.	Dem.	Major Vote Rep.	Dem.
POPE	5,242	1,869	3,200	173	1,331 D	35.7%	61.0%	36.9%	63.1%
RAMSEY	130,728	30,553	86,286	13,889	55,733 D	23.4%	66.0%	26.1%	73.9%
RED LAKE	2,653	487	2,057	109	1,570 D	18.4%	77.5%	19.1%	80.9%
REDWOOD	8,972	3,286	4,965	721	1,679 D	36.6%	55.3%	39.8%	60.2%
RENVILLE	9,453	3,049	5,344	1,060	2,295 D	32.3%	56.5%	36.3%	63.7%
RICE	12,327	4,888	5,928	1,511	1,040 D	39.7%	48.1%	45.2%	54.8%
ROCK	4,838	1,752	2,910	176	1,158 D	36.2%	60.1%	37.6%	62.4%
ROSEAU	5,266	1,326	3,761	179	2,435 D	25.2%	71.4%	26.1%	73.9%
ST LOUIS	93,510	22,332	69,365	1,813	47,033 D	23.9%	74.2%	24.4%	75.6%
SCOTT	6,559	1,528	3,861	1,170	2,333 D	23.3%	58.9%	28.4%	71.6%
SHERBURNE	3,737	1,623	1,881	233	258 D	43.4%	50.3%	46.3%	53.7%
SIBLEY	6,735	2,184	4,140	411	1,956 D	32.4%	61.5%	34.5%	65.5%
STEARNS	22,580	5,262	12,760	4,558	7,498 D	23.3%	56.5%	29.2%	70.8%
STEELE	8,224	3,373	4,481	370	1,108 D	41.0%	54.5%	42.9%	57.1%
STEVENS	3,958	1,431	2,352	175	921 D	36.2%	59.4%	37.8%	62.2%
SWIFT	5,986	1,618	3,749	619	2,131 D	27.0%	62.6%	30.1%	69.9%
TODD	10,002	3,780	5,627	595	1,847 D	37.8%	56.3%	40.2%	59.8%
TRAVERSE	3,144	761	2,297	86	1,536 D	24.2%	73.1%	24.9%	75.1%
WABASHA	7,697	2,663	4,122	912	1,459 D	34.6%	53.6%	39.2%	60.8%
WADENA	4,649	1,898	2,605	146	707 D	40.8%	56.0%	42.1%	57.9%
WASECA	6,348	2,482	3,520	346	1,038 D	39.1%	55.5%	41.4%	58.6%
WASHINGTON	11,710	3,863	6,768	1,079	2,905 D	33.0%	57.8%	36.3%	63.7%
WATONWAN	5,772	1,930	3,668	174	1,738 D	33.4%	63.5%	34.5%	65.5%
WILKIN	3,938	1,278	2,428	232	1,150 D	32.5%	61.7%	34.5%	65.5%
WINONA	15,551	5,353	9,268	930	3,915 D	34.4%	59.6%	36.6%	63.4%
WRIGHT	11,351	4,087	5,363	1,901	1,276 D	36.0%	47.2%	43.2%	56.8%
YELLOW MEDICINE	6,679	2,029	3,921	729	1,892 D	30.4%	58.7%	34.1%	65.9%
TOTAL	1,129,975	350,461	698,811	80,703	348,350 D	31.0%	61.8%	33.4%	66.6%

PRESIDENT 1940

Total Vote	Republican	Democratic	Other	Rep.-Dem. Plurality	Percentage Total Vote Rep.	Dem.	Major Vote Rep.	Dem.
6,090	2,805	3,266	19	461 D	46.1%	53.6%	46.2%	53.8%
138,165	57,093	78,990	2,082	21,897 D	41.3%	57.2%	42.0%	58.0%
2,915	876	2,023	16	1,147 D	30.1%	69.4%	30.2%	69.8%
9,782	6,105	3,637	40	2,468 R	62.4%	37.2%	62.7%	37.3%
10,842	6,196	4,588	58	1,608 R	57.1%	42.3%	62.5%	42.5%
12,875	8,143	4,687	45	3,456 R	63.2%	36.4%	63.5%	36.5%
4,951	2,944	1,983	24	961 R	59.5%	40.1%	59.8%	40.2%
6,123	1,730	4,289	104	2,559 D	28.3%	70.0%	28.7%	71.3%
102,623	32,243	68,620	1,760	36,377 D	31.4%	66.9%	32.0%	68.0%
7,172	4,241	2,910	21	1,331 R	59.1%	40.6%	59.3%	40.7%
4,040	2,450	1,570	20	880 R	60.6%	38.9%	60.9%	39.1%
7,589	5,564	1,986	39	3,578 R	73.3%	26.2%	73.7%	26.3%
25,434	16,027	9,305	102	6,722 R	63.0%	36.6%	63.3%	36.7%
9,199	5,517	3,668	14	1,849 R	60.0%	39.9%	60.1%	39.9%
4,652	2,619	2,018	15	601 R	56.3%	43.4%	56.5%	43.5%
6,768	2,815	3,899	54	1,084 D	41.6%	57.6%	41.9%	58.1%
10,916	6,302	4,553	61	1,749 R	57.7%	41.7%	58.1%	41.9%
3,541	1,434	2,094	13	660 D	40.5%	59.1%	40.6%	59.4%
8,324	5,656	2,655	13	3,001 R	68.1%	31.9%	68.1%	31.9%
5,340	2,898	2,405	37	493 R	54.3%	45.0%	54.6%	45.4%
7,213	4,515	2,673	25	1,842 R	62.6%	37.1%	62.8%	37.2%
13,052	6,710	6,288	54	422 R	51.4%	48.2%	51.6%	48.4%
6,239	3,478	2,783	28	695 R	55.3%	44.3%	55.6%	44.4%
4,249	2,067	2,176	6	109 D	48.6%	51.2%	48.7%	51.3%
16,891	9,599	7,187	105	2,412 R	56.8%	42.5%	57.2%	42.8%
12,377	8,297	3,993	87	4,304 R	67.0%	32.3%	67.5%	32.5%
7,739	3,964	3,786	39	178 R	50.9%	48.6%	51.1%	48.9%
1,251,138	556,274	644,196	10,718	47,922 D	47.7%	51.5%	48.1%	51.9%

MINNESOTA

PRESIDENT 1944

County	Total Vote	Republican	Democratic	Other	Rep.-Dem. Plurality	% Total Vote Rep.	% Total Vote Dem.	% Major Vote Rep.	% Major Vote Dem.
AITKIN	5,509	2,720	2,743	46	23 D	49.4	49.8	49.8	50.2
ANOKA	9,468	3,958	5,431	79	1,473 D	41.8	57.4	42.2	57.8
BECKER	8,750	3,803	4,889	58	1,086 D	43.5	55.9	43.8	56.2
BELTRAMI	8,256	2,705	5,490	61	2,785 D	32.8	66.5	33.0	67.0
BENTON	5,264	2,988	2,258	18	730 R	56.8	42.9	57.0	43.0
BIG STONE	3,752	1,608	2,120	24	512 D	42.9	56.5	43.1	56.9
BLUE EARTH	14,581	9,429	5,098	54	4,331 R	64.7	35.0	64.9	35.1
BROWN	9,949	7,018	2,842	89	4,176 R	70.5	28.6	71.2	28.8
CARLTON	8,856	2,653	6,153	50	3,500 D	30.0	69.5	30.1	69.9
CARVER	7,427	5,823	1,565	39	4,258 R	78.4	21.1	78.8	21.2
CASS	6,547	3,135	3,377	35	242 D	47.9	51.6	48.1	51.9
CHIPPEWA	6,279	2,967	3,264	48	297 D	47.3	52.0	47.6	52.4
CHISAGO	5,434	3,020	2,376	38	644 R	55.6	43.7	56.0	44.0
CLAY	9,674	4,392	5,230	52	838 D	45.4	54.1	45.6	54.4
CLEARWATER	3,817	1,125	2,658	34	1,533 D	29.5	69.6	29.7	70.3
COOK	1,066	513	545	8	32 D	48.1	51.1	48.5	51.5
COTTONWOOD	6,308	3,916	2,354	38	1,562 R	62.1	37.3	62.5	37.5
CROW WING	10,067	4,500	5,504	63	1,004 D	44.7	54.7	45.0	55.0
DAKOTA	16,403	7,731	8,562	110	831 D	47.1	52.2	47.4	52.6
DODGE	4,725	2,902	1,808	15	1,094 R	61.4	38.3	61.6	38.4
DOUGLAS	7,867	4,140	3,681	46	459 R	52.6	46.8	52.9	47.1
FARIBAULT	9,487	5,822	3,640	25	2,182 R	61.4	38.4	61.5	38.5
FILLMORE	9,562	6,339	3,183	40	3,156 R	66.3	33.3	66.6	33.4
FREEBORN	12,246	5,728	6,486	32	758 D	46.8	53.0	46.9	53.1
GOODHUE	13,679	7,820	5,791	68	2,029 R	57.2	42.3	57.5	42.5
GRANT	3,879	1,898	1,969	12	71 D	48.9	50.8	49.1	50.9
HENNEPIN	267,320	116,781	148,792	1,747	32,011 D	43.7	55.7	44.0	56.0
HOUSTON	5,908	4,036	1,847	25	2,189 R	68.3	31.3	68.6	31.4
HUBBARD	3,740	2,114	1,613	13	501 R	56.5	43.1	56.7	43.3
ISANTI	4,487	2,205	2,225	57	20 D	49.1	49.6	49.8	50.2
ITASCA	13,095	4,227	8,787	81	4,560 D	32.3	67.1	32.5	67.5
JACKSON	6,230	2,789	3,417	24	628 D	44.8	54.8	44.9	55.1
KANABEC	3,713	1,913	1,776	24	137 R	51.5	47.8	51.9	48.1
KANDIYOHI	10,353	3,784	6,482	87	2,698 D	36.5	62.6	36.9	63.1
KITTSON	3,757	983	2,752	22	1,769 D	26.2	73.2	26.3	73.7
KOOCHICHING	5,639	1,607	3,981	51	2,374 D	28.5	70.6	28.8	71.2
LAC QUI PARLE	5,900	3,104	2,779	17	325 R	52.6	47.1	52.8	47.2
LAKE	3,239	792	2,401	46	1,609 D	24.5	74.1	24.8	75.2
LAKE OF THE WOODS	1,811	642	1,168	1	526 D	35.4	64.5	35.5	64.5
LE SUEUR	7,967	4,560	3,358	49	1,202 R	57.2	42.1	57.6	42.4
LINCOLN	3,917	1,600	2,302	15	702 D	40.8	58.8	41.0	59.0
LYON	8,295	3,617	4,640	38	1,023 D	43.6	55.9	43.8	56.2
MCLEOD	8,361	5,756	2,557	48	3,199 R	68.8	30.6	69.2	30.8
MAHNOMEN	2,260	748	1,494	18	746 D	33.1	66.1	33.4	66.6
MARSHALL	5,864	2,029	3,808	27	1,779 D	34.6	64.9	34.8	65.2
MARTIN	9,654	5,182	4,443	29	739 R	53.7	46.0	53.8	46.2
MEEKER	7,506	4,302	3,159	45	1,143 R	57.3	42.1	57.6	42.4
MILLE LACS	5,707	2,798	2,872	37	74 D	49.0	50.3	49.3	50.7
MORRISON	9,002	5,035	3,920	47	1,115 R	55.9	43.5	56.2	43.8
MOWER	13,835	6,588	7,199	48	611 D	47.6	52.0	47.8	52.2
MURRAY	5,102	2,585	2,495	22	90 R	50.7	48.9	50.9	49.1
NICOLLET	6,702	4,345	2,321	36	2,024 R	64.8	34.6	65.2	34.8
NOBLES	7,597	4,149	3,413	35	736 R	54.6	44.9	54.9	45.1
NORMAN	4,768	1,884	2,846	38	962 D	39.5	59.7	39.8	60.2
OLMSTED	15,274	8,355	6,873	46	1,482 R	54.7	45.0	54.9	45.1
OTTER TAIL	18,284	12,351	5,823	110	6,528 R	67.6	31.8	68.0	32.0
PENNINGTON	4,905	1,525	3,330	50	1,805 D	31.1	67.9	31.4	68.6
PINE	7,829	3,433	4,332	64	899 D	43.8	55.3	44.2	55.8
PIPESTONE	4,994	2,844	2,129	21	715 R	56.9	42.6	57.2	42.8
POLK	13,310	4,402	8,808	100	4,406 D	33.1	66.2	33.3	66.7

PRESIDENT 1948

County	Total Vote	Republican	Democratic	Other	Rep.-Dem. Plurality	% Total Vote Rep.	% Total Vote Dem.	% Major Vote Rep.	% Major Vote Dem.
AITKIN	6,007	2,466	3,277	264	811 D	41.1	54.6	42.9	57.1
ANOKA	11,929	3,853	7,730	346	3,877 D	32.3	64.8	33.3	66.7
BECKER	9,727	3,495	5,885	347	2,390 D	35.9	60.5	37.3	62.7
BELTRAMI	9,580	3,126	6,020	434	2,894 D	32.6	62.8	34.2	65.8
BENTON	6,015	2,297	3,632	86	1,335 D	38.2	60.4	38.7	61.3
BIG STONE	3,886	1,321	2,466	99	1,145 D	34.0	63.5	34.9	65.1
BLUE EARTH	14,954	7,520	7,272	162	248 R	50.3	48.6	50.8	49.2
BROWN	10,016	5,068	4,804	144	264 R	50.6	48.0	51.3	48.7
CARLTON	10,157	2,742	6,967	448	4,225 D	27.0	68.6	28.2	71.8
CARVER	7,482	4,582	2,816	84	1,766 R	61.2	37.6	61.9	38.1
CASS	7,278	3,179	3,933	166	754 D	43.7	54.0	44.7	55.3
CHIPPEWA	6,646	2,569	3,888	189	1,319 D	38.7	58.5	39.8	60.2
CHISAGO	6,065	2,704	3,184	177	480 D	44.6	52.5	45.9	54.1
CLAY	11,145	4,302	6,624	219	2,322 D	38.6	59.4	39.4	60.6
CLEARWATER	4,212	1,171	2,793	248	1,622 D	27.8	66.3	29.5	70.5
COOK	1,406	674	688	44	14 D	47.9	48.9	49.5	50.5
COTTONWOOD	6,632	3,222	3,333	77	111 D	48.6	50.3	49.2	50.8
CROW WING	11,845	4,702	6,773	370	2,071 D	39.7	57.2	41.0	59.0
DAKOTA	19,623	6,819	12,487	317	5,668 D	34.7	63.6	35.3	64.7
DODGE	4,961	2,381	2,523	57	142 D	48.0	50.9	48.6	51.4
DOUGLAS	8,973	3,744	5,022	207	1,278 D	41.7	56.0	42.7	57.3
FARIBAULT	10,014	4,619	5,261	134	642 D	46.1	52.5	46.8	53.2
FILLMORE	10,128	5,587	4,414	127	1,173 R	55.2	43.6	55.9	44.1
FREEBORN	13,742	5,704	7,825	213	2,121 D	41.5	56.9	42.2	57.8
GOODHUE	14,222	6,704	7,313	205	609 D	47.1	51.4	47.8	52.2
GRANT	4,388	1,789	2,378	221	589 D	40.8	54.2	42.9	57.1
HENNEPIN	282,234	121,169	151,920	9,145	30,751 D	42.9	53.8	44.4	55.6
HOUSTON	6,231	3,540	2,623	68	917 R	56.8	42.1	57.4	42.6
HUBBARD	4,241	2,071	2,044	126	27 R	48.8	48.2	50.3	49.7
ISANTI	4,994	1,918	2,758	318	840 D	38.4	55.2	41.0	59.0
ITASCA	14,716	4,334	9,653	729	5,319 D	29.5	65.6	31.0	69.0
JACKSON	6,969	2,288	4,541	140	2,253 D	32.8	65.2	33.5	66.5
KANABEC	3,970	1,531	2,305	134	774 D	38.6	58.1	39.9	60.1
KANDIYOHI	11,593	3,666	7,204	723	3,538 D	31.6	62.1	33.7	66.3
KITTSON	4,183	1,035	2,970	178	1,935 D	24.7	71.0	25.8	74.2
KOOCHICHING	6,968	1,718	4,968	282	3,250 D	24.7	71.3	25.7	74.3
LAC QUI PARLE	6,100	2,330	3,690	80	1,360 D	38.2	60.5	38.7	61.3
LAKE	3,729	924	2,555	250	1,631 D	24.8	68.5	26.6	73.4
LAKE OF THE WOODS	2,005	583	1,302	120	719 D	29.1	64.9	30.9	69.1
LE SUEUR	8,828	3,858	4,890	80	1,032 D	43.7	55.4	44.1	55.9
LINCOLN	4,090	1,312	2,694	84	1,382 D	32.1	65.9	32.8	67.2
LYON	9,286	3,054	6,144	88	3,090 D	32.9	66.2	33.2	66.8
MCLEOD	8,716	4,623	3,987	106	636 R	53.0	45.7	53.7	46.3
MAHNOMEN	2,775	579	2,125	71	1,546 D	20.9	76.6	21.4	78.6
MARSHALL	6,507	2,090	4,126	291	2,036 D	32.1	63.4	33.6	66.4
MARTIN	10,764	4,662	6,015	87	1,353 D	43.3	55.9	43.7	56.3
MEEKER	8,065	3,620	4,333	112	713 D	44.9	53.7	45.5	54.5
MILLE LACS	6,039	2,502	3,343	194	841 D	41.4	55.4	42.8	57.2
MORRISON	10,092	3,922	6,026	144	2,104 D	38.9	59.7	39.4	60.6
MOWER	15,301	5,672	9,468	161	3,796 D	37.1	61.9	37.5	62.5
MURRAY	5,602	1,951	3,594	57	1,643 D	34.8	64.2	35.2	64.8
NICOLLET	7,325	3,576	3,663	86	87 D	48.8	50.0	49.4	50.6
NOBLES	8,382	3,203	5,090	89	1,887 D	38.2	60.7	38.6	61.4
NORMAN	5,157	1,695	3,245	217	1,550 D	32.9	62.9	34.3	65.7
OLMSTED	17,467	8,131	9,155	181	1,024 D	46.6	52.4	47.0	53.0
OTTER TAIL	18,172	11,131	6,546	495	4,585 R	61.3	36.0	63.0	37.0
PENNINGTON	5,608	1,759	3,402	447	1,643 D	31.4	60.7	34.1	65.9
PINE	8,407	3,069	4,978	360	1,909 D	36.5	59.2	38.1	61.9
PIPESTONE	5,180	2,281	2,804	95	523 D	44.0	54.1	44.9	55.1
POLK	14,580	4,662	9,279	639	4,617 D	32.0	63.6	33.4	66.6

MINNESOTA

PRESIDENT 1944

County	Total Vote	Republican	Democratic	Other	Rep.-Dem. Plurality	Total Vote Rep.	Total Vote Dem.	Major Vote Rep.	Major Vote Dem.
POPE	5,401	2,607	2,781	13	174 D	48.3%	51.5%	48.4%	51.6%
RAMSEY	135,744	53,052	78,759	1,933	25,707 D	39.7%	58.9%	40.2%	59.8%
RED LAKE	2,414	757	1,642	15	885 D	31.4%	68.0%	31.6%	68.4%
REDWOOD	8,343	5,428	2,886	29	2,542 R	65.1%	34.6%	65.3%	34.7%
RENVILLE	8,976	5,160	3,747	69	1,413 R	57.5%	41.7%	57.9%	42.1%
RICE	11,322	6,824	4,470	28	2,354 R	60.3%	39.5%	60.4%	39.6%
ROCK	4,260	2,584	1,649	27	935 R	60.7%	38.7%	61.0%	39.0%
ROSEAU	5,250	1,513	3,697	40	2,184 D	28.8%	70.4%	29.0%	71.0%
ST LOUIS	91,942	27,493	63,369	1,080	35,876 D	29.9%	68.9%	30.3%	69.7%
SCOTT	6,150	3,326	2,786	38	540 R	54.1%	45.3%	54.4%	45.6%
SHERBURNE	3,518	2,046	1,447	25	599 R	53.2%	41.1%	58.6%	41.4%
SIBLEY	6,024	4,311	1,683	30	2,628 R	71.6%	27.9%	71.9%	28.1%
STEARNS	22,029	13,298	8,647	84	4,651 R	51.4%	39.3%	60.6%	39.4%
STEELE	8,082	4,760	3,307	15	1,453 R	53.9%	40.9%	59.0%	41.0%
STEVENS	4,082	2,377	1,693	12	684 R	53.2%	41.5%	58.4%	41.6%
SWIFT	5,876	2,519	3,310	47	791 D	42.9%	56.3%	43.2%	56.8%
TODD	9,493	5,636	3,803	54	1,833 R	59.4%	40.1%	59.7%	40.3%
TRAVERSE	3,031	1,296	1,721	14	425 D	42.8%	56.8%	43.0%	57.0%
WABASHA	5,728	4,213	2,482	33	1,731 R	52.6%	36.9%	62.9%	37.1%
WADENA	4,537	2,653	1,868	16	785 R	58.5%	41.2%	58.7%	41.3%
WASECA	5,375	4,146	2,207	22	1,939 R	65.0%	34.6%	65.3%	34.7%
WASHINGTON	11,679	6,014	5,599	66	415 R	51.5%	47.9%	51.8%	48.2%
WATONWAN	5,493	3,346	2,324	23	822 R	57.3%	42.3%	57.5%	42.5%
WILKIN	3,776	1,945	1,819	12	126 R	51.5%	48.2%	51.7%	48.3%
WINONA	14,506	8,296	6,117	93	2,179 R	57.2%	42.2%	57.6%	42.4%
WRIGHT	10,711	6,961	3,678	72	3,283 R	65.0%	34.3%	65.4%	34.6%
YELLOW MEDICINE	6,585	3,337	3,214	34	123 R	50.7%	48.8%	50.9%	49.1%
TOTAL	1,125,504	527,416	539,864	8,224	62,448 D	46.9%	52.4%	47.2%	52.8%

PRESIDENT 1948

County	Total Vote	Republican	Democratic	Other	Rep.-Dem. Plurality	Total Vote Rep.	Total Vote Dem.	Major Vote Rep.	Major Vote Dem.
POPE	5,462	2,114	3,251	97	1,137 D	38.7%	59.5%	39.4%	60.6%
RAMSEY	140,887	48,142	88,528	4,217	40,386 D	34.2%	62.8%	35.2%	64.8%
RED LAKE	2,468	592	1,771	105	1,179 D	24.0%	71.8%	25.1%	74.9%
REDWOOD	8,445	4,160	4,182	103	22 D	49.3%	49.5%	49.9%	50.1%
RENVILLE	9,679	4,297	5,287	155	930 D	44.4%	54.0%	45.1%	54.9%
RICE	12,321	6,301	5,832	188	469 R	51.1%	47.3%	51.9%	48.1%
ROCK	4,234	2,035	2,134	65	99 D	48.1%	50.4%	48.8%	51.2%
ROSEAU	5,528	1,458	3,674	396	2,216 D	26.4%	66.5%	28.4%	71.6%
ST LOUIS	97,292	28,490	62,553	6,249	34,063 D	29.3%	64.3%	31.3%	68.7%
SCOTT	6,935	2,583	4,278	74	1,695 D	37.2%	61.7%	37.6%	62.4%
SHERBURNE	3,895	1,828	1,958	109	130 D	46.9%	50.3%	48.3%	51.7%
SIBLEY	6,157	3,260	2,818	79	442 R	52.9%	45.8%	53.6%	46.4%
STEARNS	25,706	10,153	15,261	292	5,108 D	39.5%	59.4%	40.0%	60.0%
STEELE	8,816	4,451	4,305	60	146 R	50.5%	48.8%	50.8%	49.2%
STEVENS	4,283	1,928	2,313	42	385 D	45.0%	54.0%	45.5%	54.5%
SWIFT	6,468	2,109	4,082	277	1,973 D	32.6%	63.1%	34.1%	65.9%
TODD	9,535	4,166	5,157	212	991 D	43.7%	54.1%	44.7%	55.3%
TRAVERSE	3,223	1,008	2,151	64	1,143 D	31.3%	66.7%	31.9%	68.1%
WABASHA	7,102	3,297	3,730	75	433 D	46.4%	52.5%	46.9%	53.1%
WADENA	4,917	2,272	2,556	89	284 D	46.2%	52.0%	47.1%	52.9%
WASECA	6,680	3,511	3,120	49	391 R	52.6%	46.7%	52.9%	47.1%
WASHINGTON	13,970	5,686	8,039	245	2,353 D	40.7%	57.5%	41.4%	58.6%
WATONWAN	5,698	2,581	3,039	78	458 D	45.3%	53.3%	45.9%	54.1%
WILKIN	4,060	1,700	2,291	69	591 D	41.9%	56.4%	42.6%	57.4%
WINONA	15,313	6,880	8,281	152	1,401 D	44.9%	54.1%	45.4%	54.6%
WRIGHT	11,297	5,589	5,523	185	66 R	49.5%	48.9%	50.3%	49.7%
YELLOW MEDICINE	7,012	2,693	4,164	155	1,471 D	38.4%	59.4%	39.3%	60.7%
TOTAL	1,212,226	483,617	692,966	35,643	209,349 D	39.9%	57.2%	41.1%	58.9%

MINNESOTA

PRESIDENT 1952

County	Total Vote	Republican	Democratic	Other	Rep.-Dem. Plurality	Total Vote Rep.	Total Vote Dem.	Major Vote Rep.	Major Vote Dem.
AITKIN	6,050	3,384	2,577	89	807 R	55.9%	42.6%	56.8%	43.2%
ANOKA	16,839	7,425	9,344	70	1,919 D	44.1%	55.5%	44.3%	55.7%
BECKER	10,414	5,815	4,539	60	1,276 R	55.8%	43.6%	56.2%	43.8%
BELTRAMI	8,962	4,817	4,092	53	725 R	53.7%	45.7%	54.1%	45.9%
BENTON	6,476	3,856	2,587	33	1,269 R	59.5%	39.9%	59.8%	40.2%
BIG STONE	4,392	2,260	2,107	25	153 R	51.5%	48.0%	51.8%	48.2%
BLUE EARTH	16,870	11,867	4,952	51	6,915 R	70.3%	29.4%	70.6%	29.4%
BROWN	11,308	8,152	3,129	27	5,023 R	72.1%	27.7%	72.3%	27.7%
CARLTON	10,698	4,175	6,432	91	2,257 D	39.0%	60.1%	39.4%	60.6%
CARVER	8,848	6,674	2,159	15	4,515 R	75.4%	24.4%	75.6%	24.4%
CASS	7,486	4,601	2,818	67	1,783 R	61.5%	37.6%	62.0%	38.0%
CHIPPEWA	7,618	4,411	3,171	36	1,240 R	57.9%	41.6%	58.2%	41.8%
CHISAGO	6,460	3,892	2,536	32	1,356 R	60.2%	39.3%	60.5%	39.5%
CLAY	12,234	7,178	5,036	20	2,142 R	58.7%	41.2%	58.8%	41.2%
CLEARWATER	4,116	1,971	2,089	56	118 D	47.9%	50.8%	48.5%	51.5%
COOK	1,454	946	503	5	443 R	65.1%	34.6%	65.3%	34.7%
COTTONWOOD	7,674	5,488	2,130	56	3,358 R	71.5%	27.8%	72.0%	28.0%
CROW WING	12,956	6,992	5,883	81	1,109 R	54.0%	45.4%	54.3%	45.7%
DAKOTA	23,879	11,871	11,890	118	19 D	49.7%	49.8%	50.0%	50.0%
DODGE	5,508	3,893	1,582	33	2,311 R	70.7%	28.7%	71.1%	28.9%
DOUGLAS	9,848	6,037	3,768	43	2,269 R	61.3%	38.3%	61.6%	38.4%
FARIBAULT	10,930	7,763	3,120	47	4,643 R	71.0%	28.5%	71.3%	28.7%
FILLMORE	11,057	8,405	2,612	40	5,793 R	76.0%	23.6%	76.3%	23.7%
FREEBORN	15,021	8,450	6,525	46	1,925 R	56.3%	43.4%	56.4%	43.6%
GOODHUE	15,494	10,422	5,037	35	5,385 R	67.3%	32.5%	67.4%	32.6%
GRANT	4,478	2,665	1,791	22	874 R	59.5%	40.0%	59.8%	40.2%
HENNEPIN	337,141	180,338	155,388	1,415	24,950 R	53.5%	46.1%	53.7%	46.3%
HOUSTON	7,223	5,365	1,830	28	3,535 R	74.3%	25.3%	74.5%	25.4%
HUBBARD	4,493	3,099	1,360	34	1,739 R	69.0%	30.3%	69.5%	30.5%
ISANTI	5,142	2,682	2,393	67	289 R	52.2%	46.5%	52.8%	47.2%
ITASCA	15,782	6,573	9,128	81	2,555 D	41.6%	57.8%	41.9%	58.1%
JACKSON	7,342	4,558	2,771	13	1,787 R	62.1%	37.7%	62.2%	37.8%
KANABEC	3,948	2,205	1,714	29	491 R	55.9%	43.4%	56.3%	43.7%
KANDIYOHI	12,747	6,370	6,264	113	106 R	50.0%	49.1%	50.4%	49.6%
KITTSON	4,264	1,837	2,387	40	550 D	43.1%	56.0%	43.5%	56.5%
KOOCHICHING	6,851	2,742	4,078	31	1,336 D	40.0%	59.5%	40.2%	59.8%
LAC QUI PARLE	6,705	3,924	2,753	28	1,171 R	58.5%	41.1%	58.8%	41.2%
LAKE	4,289	1,451	2,814	24	1,363 D	33.8%	65.6%	34.0%	66.0%
LAKE OF THE WOODS	2,027	898	1,117	12	219 D	44.3%	55.1%	44.6%	55.4%
LE SUEUR	9,140	5,776	3,348	16	2,428 R	63.2%	36.6%	63.3%	36.7%
LINCOLN	4,657	2,746	1,892	19	854 R	59.0%	40.6%	59.2%	40.8%
LYON	10,069	6,015	4,030	24	1,985 R	59.7%	40.0%	59.9%	40.1%
MCLEOD	10,048	7,246	2,781	21	4,465 R	72.1%	27.7%	72.3%	27.7%
MAHNOMEN	2,660	1,220	1,436	4	216 D	45.9%	54.0%	45.9%	54.1%
MARSHALL	6,733	3,516	3,132	85	384 R	52.2%	46.5%	52.9%	47.1%
MARTIN	12,123	9,411	2,673	39	6,738 R	77.6%	22.0%	77.9%	22.1%
MEEKER	8,608	5,750	2,833	25	2,917 R	66.8%	32.9%	67.0%	33.0%
MILLE LACS	6,446	3,766	2,639	41	1,127 R	58.4%	40.9%	58.8%	41.2%
MORRISON	10,639	6,050	4,551	38	1,499 R	56.9%	42.8%	57.1%	42.9%
MOWER	18,551	9,862	8,551	138	1,311 R	53.2%	46.1%	53.6%	46.4%
MURRAY	6,223	4,054	2,145	24	1,909 R	65.1%	34.5%	65.4%	34.6%
NICOLLET	8,398	5,775	2,584	39	3,191 R	68.8%	30.8%	69.1%	30.9%
NOBLES	9,717	6,340	3,351	26	2,989 R	65.2%	34.5%	65.4%	34.6%
NORMAN	5,573	3,069	2,465	39	604 R	55.1%	44.2%	55.5%	44.5%
OLMSTED	21,447	14,566	6,792	89	7,774 R	67.9%	31.7%	68.2%	31.8%
OTTER TAIL	21,921	16,447	5,388	86	11,059 R	75.0%	24.6%	75.3%	24.7%
PENNINGTON	5,615	2,726	2,802	87	76 D	48.5%	49.9%	49.3%	50.7%
PINE	8,038	4,255	3,692	91	563 R	52.9%	45.9%	53.5%	46.5%
PIPESTONE	6,221	4,507	1,701	13	2,806 R	72.4%	27.3%	72.6%	27.4%
POLK	15,683	8,326	7,244	113	1,082 R	53.1%	46.2%	53.5%	46.5%

PRESIDENT 1956

County	Total Vote	Republican	Democratic	Other	Rep.-Dem. Plurality	Total Vote Rep.	Total Vote Dem.	Major Vote Rep.	Major Vote Dem.
AITKIN	5,504	2,762	2,733	9	29 R	50.2%	49.7%	50.3%	49.7%
ANOKA	21,092	9,359	11,697	36	2,338 D	44.4%	55.5%	44.4%	55.6%
BECKER	9,251	4,608	4,619	24	11 D	49.8%	49.9%	49.9%	50.1%
BELTRAMI	7,797	3,974	3,807	16	167 R	51.0%	48.8%	51.1%	48.9%
BENTON	6,216	3,591	2,609	16	982 R	57.8%	42.0%	57.9%	42.1%
BIG STONE	3,925	1,737	2,180	8	443 D	44.3%	55.5%	44.3%	55.7%
BLUE EARTH	16,886	11,398	5,467	21	5,931 R	67.5%	32.4%	67.6%	32.4%
BROWN	11,059	7,965	3,067	27	4,898 R	72.0%	27.7%	72.2%	27.8%
CARLTON	10,677	4,168	6,484	25	2,316 D	39.0%	60.7%	39.1%	60.9%
CARVER	8,589	6,226	2,334	29	3,892 R	72.5%	27.2%	72.7%	27.3%
CASS	6,765	4,007	2,748	10	1,259 R	59.2%	40.6%	59.2%	40.7%
CHIPPEWA	7,060	3,623	3,434	3	189 R	51.3%	48.6%	51.3%	48.7%
CHISAGO	6,153	3,413	2,731	9	682 R	55.5%	44.4%	55.6%	44.4%
CLAY	12,855	6,783	6,057	15	726 R	52.8%	47.1%	52.8%	47.2%
CLEARWATER	3,650	1,464	2,171	15	707 D	40.1%	59.5%	40.3%	59.7%
COOK	1,748	1,078	668	2	410 R	61.7%	38.2%	61.7%	38.3%
COTTONWOOD	6,968	4,619	2,344	5	2,275 R	66.3%	33.6%	66.3%	33.7%
CROW WING	12,243	6,657	5,556	30	1,101 R	54.3%	45.4%	54.5%	45.5%
DAKOTA	25,839	13,112	12,672	55	440 R	50.7%	49.0%	50.9%	49.1%
DODGE	5,025	3,205	1,814	6	1,391 R	63.8%	36.1%	63.9%	36.1%
DOUGLAS	9,320	5,114	4,194	12	920 R	54.9%	45.0%	54.9%	45.1%
FARIBAULT	10,465	6,886	3,554	25	3,332 R	65.8%	34.0%	66.0%	34.0%
FILLMORE	10,440	7,004	3,427	9	3,577 R	67.1%	32.8%	67.1%	32.9%
FREEBORN	14,781	7,632	7,138	11	494 R	51.6%	48.3%	51.7%	48.3%
GOODHUE	14,353	9,365	4,969	19	4,396 R	65.2%	34.6%	65.3%	34.7%
GRANT	4,177	2,064	2,107	6	43 D	49.4%	50.4%	49.5%	50.5%
HENNEPIN	333,112	183,248	149,341	523	33,907 R	55.0%	44.8%	55.1%	44.9%
HOUSTON	6,680	4,538	2,133	9	2,405 R	67.9%	31.9%	68.0%	32.0%
HUBBARD	3,913	2,453	1,454	6	999 R	62.7%	37.2%	62.8%	37.2%
ISANTI	4,959	2,348	2,605	6	257 D	47.3%	52.5%	47.4%	52.6%
ITASCA	15,178	6,408	8,737	33	2,329 D	42.2%	57.6%	42.3%	57.7%
JACKSON	6,784	3,543	3,232	9	311 R	52.2%	47.6%	52.3%	47.7%
KANABEC	3,693	1,950	1,736	7	214 R	52.8%	47.0%	52.9%	47.1%
KANDIYOHI	12,305	5,445	6,834	26	1,389 D	44.3%	55.5%	44.3%	55.7%
KITTSON	3,798	1,569	2,222	7	653 D	41.3%	58.5%	41.4%	58.6%
KOOCHICHING	6,468	2,757	3,695	16	938 D	42.6%	57.1%	42.7%	57.3%
LAC QUI PARLE	6,108	3,276	2,826	6	450 R	53.6%	46.3%	53.7%	46.3%
LAKE	5,143	2,055	3,079	9	1,024 D	40.0%	59.9%	40.0%	60.0%
LAKE OF THE WOODS	1,777	723	1,048	6	325 D	40.7%	59.0%	40.8%	59.2%
LE SUEUR	8,599	5,026	3,556	17	1,470 R	58.4%	41.4%	58.6%	41.4%
LINCOLN	4,390	2,060	2,316	14	256 D	46.9%	52.8%	47.1%	52.9%
LYON	9,386	5,188	4,190	8	998 R	55.3%	44.6%	55.3%	44.7%
MCLEOD	9,828	6,743	3,068	17	3,675 R	68.6%	31.2%	68.7%	31.3%
MAHNOMEN	2,392	875	1,513	4	638 D	36.6%	63.3%	36.7%	63.3%
MARSHALL	6,007	2,519	3,478	10	959 D	41.9%	57.9%	42.0%	58.0%
MARTIN	11,456	8,152	3,289	15	4,863 R	71.2%	28.7%	71.3%	28.7%
MEEKER	8,097	4,738	3,348	11	1,390 R	58.5%	41.3%	58.6%	41.4%
MILLE LACS	5,941	3,315	2,619	7	696 R	55.8%	44.0%	55.9%	44.1%
MORRISON	9,727	5,042	4,653	32	389 R	51.8%	47.8%	52.0%	48.0%
MOWER	18,890	9,570	9,219	101	351 R	50.7%	48.8%	50.9%	49.1%
MURRAY	5,971	3,261	2,695	15	566 R	54.6%	45.1%	54.8%	45.2%
NICOLLET	7,966	5,222	2,636	8	2,586 R	65.5%	33.1%	66.5%	33.5%
NOBLES	9,241	5,196	4,036	9	1,160 R	56.2%	43.6%	56.3%	43.7%
NORMAN	5,081	2,338	2,740	3	402 D	46.0%	53.9%	46.0%	54.0%
OLMSTED	21,012	13,789	7,172	51	6,617 R	65.6%	34.1%	65.8%	34.2%
OTTER TAIL	19,375	12,764	6,571	40	6,193 R	65.8%	33.9%	66.0%	34.0%
PENNINGTON	5,359	2,408	2,947	4	539 D	44.9%	54.9%	45.0%	55.0%
PINE	7,041	3,204	3,829	8	625 D	45.5%	54.4%	45.6%	54.4%
PIPESTONE	5,533	3,362	2,165	6	1,197 R	60.8%	39.1%	60.8%	39.2%
POLK	14,853	6,847	7,980	26	1,133 D	46.1%	53.7%	46.2%	53.8%

MINNESOTA

PRESIDENT 1952

County	Total Vote	Republican	Democratic	Other	Rep.-Dem. Plurality	Total Vote Rep.	Total Vote Dem.	Major Vote Rep.	Major Vote Dem.
POPE	5,988	3,593	2,381	14	1,212 R	60.0%	39.8%	60.1%	39.9%
RAMSEY	171,370	76,093	93,783	1,494	17,690 D	44.4%	54.7%	44.8%	55.2%
RED LAKE	2,491	1,034	1,431	26	397 D	41.5%	57.4%	41.9%	58.1%
REDWOOD	9,810	7,093	2,695	22	4,398 R	72.3%	27.5%	72.5%	27.5%
RENVILLE	10,626	6,742	3,828	56	2,914 R	63.4%	36.0%	63.8%	36.2%
RICE	13,693	9,334	4,330	29	5,004 R	68.2%	31.6%	68.3%	31.7%
ROCK	5,067	3,774	1,286	7	2,488 R	74.5%	25.4%	74.6%	25.4%
ROSEAU	5,727	2,596	3,062	69	466 D	45.3%	53.5%	45.9%	54.1%
ST LOUIS	103,286	38,900	63,032	1,354	24,132 D	37.7%	61.0%	38.2%	61.8%
SCOTT	7,606	4,277	3,315	14	962 R	56.2%	43.6%	56.3%	43.7%
SHERBURNE	4,478	2,839	1,630	9	1,209 R	63.4%	36.4%	63.5%	36.5%
SIBLEY	7,214	5,323	1,871	20	3,452 R	73.8%	25.9%	74.0%	26.0%
STEARNS	28,213	18,267	9,907	39	8,360 R	64.7%	35.1%	64.8%	35.2%
STEELE	9,804	6,956	2,819	29	4,137 R	71.0%	28.8%	71.2%	28.8%
STEVENS	4,879	3,288	1,579	12	1,709 R	67.4%	32.4%	67.6%	32.4%
SWIFT	6,871	3,532	3,291	48	241 R	51.4%	47.9%	51.8%	48.2%
TODD	10,211	6,731	3,439	41	3,292 R	65.9%	33.7%	66.2%	33.8%
TRAVERSE	3,573	1,809	1,756	8	53 R	50.6%	49.1%	50.7%	49.3%
WABASHA	7,843	5,461	2,356	26	3,105 R	69.6%	30.0%	69.9%	30.1%
WADENA	5,343	3,662	1,665	16	1,997 R	68.5%	31.2%	68.7%	31.3%
WASECA	7,113	4,962	2,132	19	2,830 R	59.8%	30.0%	69.9%	30.1%
WASHINGTON	17,240	9,408	7,768	64	1,640 R	54.6%	45.1%	54.8%	45.2%
WATONWAN	6,316	4,549	1,752	15	2,797 R	72.0%	27.7%	72.2%	27.8%
WILKIN	4,556	2,979	1,564	13	1,415 R	65.4%	34.3%	65.6%	34.4%
WINONA	16,621	10,723	5,834	64	4,889 R	64.5%	35.1%	64.8%	35.2%
WRIGHT	12,524	8,089	4,373	62	3,716 R	64.6%	34.9%	64.9%	35.1%
YELLOW MEDICINE	7,486	4,322	3,143	21	1,179 R	57.7%	42.0%	57.9%	42.1%
TOTAL	1,379,483	763,211	608,458	7,814	154,753 R	55.3%	44.1%	55.6%	44.4%

PRESIDENT 1956

County	Total Vote	Republican	Democratic	Other	Rep.-Dem. Plurality	Total Vote Rep.	Total Vote Dem.	Major Vote Rep.	Major Vote Dem.
POPE	5,309	2,725	2,577	7	148 R	51.3%	48.5%	51.4%	48.6%
RAMSEY	169,039	80,701	87,784	554	7,083 D	47.7%	51.9%	47.9%	52.1%
RED LAKE	2,345	782	1,555	8	773 D	33.3%	66.3%	33.5%	66.5%
REDWOOD	9,806	5,956	3,039	11	2,917 R	66.1%	33.7%	66.2%	33.8%
RENVILLE	9,958	5,728	4,213	17	1,515 R	57.5%	42.3%	57.6%	42.4%
RICE	12,984	8,471	4,489	24	3,982 R	65.2%	34.6%	65.4%	34.6%
ROCK	4,862	3,267	1,591	4	1,676 R	67.2%	32.7%	67.2%	32.8%
ROSEAU	4,973	1,901	3,062	10	1,161 D	38.2%	61.6%	38.3%	61.7%
ST LOUIS	102,723	39,902	62,190	631	22,288 D	38.8%	60.5%	39.1%	60.9%
SCOTT	7,598	4,148	3,431	19	717 R	54.6%	45.2%	54.7%	45.3%
SHERBURNE	4,487	2,681	1,796	10	885 R	59.8%	40.0%	59.9%	40.1%
SIBLEY	6,842	4,737	2,099	6	2,638 R	69.2%	30.7%	69.3%	30.7%
STEARNS	27,257	17,364	9,829	64	7,535 R	63.7%	36.1%	63.9%	36.1%
STEELE	9,764	6,435	3,293	36	3,142 R	65.9%	33.7%	66.1%	33.9%
STEVENS	4,430	2,606	1,822	2	784 R	58.8%	41.1%	58.9%	41.1%
SWIFT	6,365	2,637	3,720	8	1,083 D	41.4%	58.4%	41.5%	58.5%
TODD	8,981	5,075	3,882	24	1,193 R	56.5%	43.2%	56.7%	43.3%
TRAVERSE	3,198	1,467	1,724	7	257 D	45.9%	53.9%	46.0%	54.0%
WABASHA	7,068	4,728	2,301	39	2,427 R	66.9%	32.6%	67.3%	32.7%
WADENA	4,767	3,028	1,733	6	1,295 R	63.5%	36.4%	63.6%	36.4%
WASECA	6,889	4,663	2,215	11	2,448 R	67.7%	32.2%	67.8%	32.2%
WASHINGTON	17,056	9,562	7,462	32	2,100 R	56.1%	43.8%	56.2%	43.8%
WATONWAN	5,861	3,963	1,886	12	2,077 R	67.6%	32.2%	67.7%	32.3%
WILKIN	4,218	2,335	1,881	2	454 R	55.4%	44.6%	55.4%	44.6%
WINONA	15,893	9,743	6,048	102	3,695 R	61.3%	38.1%	61.7%	38.3%
WRIGHT	12,213	7,257	4,944	12	2,313 R	59.4%	40.5%	59.5%	40.5%
YELLOW MEDICINE	7,018	3,594	3,416	8	178 R	51.2%	48.7%	51.3%	48.7%
TOTAL	1,340,035	719,302	617,525	3,178	101,777 R	53.7%	46.1%	53.8%	46.2%

MINNESOTA

PRESIDENT 1960

County	Total Vote	Republican	Democratic	Other	Rep.-Dem. Plurality	Total Vote % Rep.	Total Vote % Dem.	Major Vote % Rep.	Major Vote % Dem.
AITKIN	6,113	3,097	2,980	36	117 R	50.7	48.7	51.0	49.0
ANOKA	34,511	14,114	20,324	73	6,210 D	40.9	58.9	41.0	59.0
BECKER	10,389	5,090	5,257	42	167 D	49.0	50.6	49.2	50.8
BELTRAMI	9,157	4,482	4,653	22	171 D	48.9	50.8	49.1	50.9
BENTON	7,515	3,324	4,175	16	851 D	44.2	55.6	44.3	55.7
BIG STONE	4,282	1,834	2,437	11	603 D	42.8	56.9	42.9	57.1
BLUE EARTH	19,413	11,328	8,052	33	3,276 R	58.4	41.5	58.5	41.5
BROWN	12,453	7,084	5,353	16	1,731 R	56.9	43.0	57.0	43.0
CARLTON	12,224	4,613	7,576	35	2,963 D	37.7	62.0	37.8	62.2
CARVER	10,227	6,231	3,982	14	2,249 R	60.9	38.9	61.0	39.0
CASS	7,991	4,399	3,578	14	821 R	55.0	44.8	55.1	44.9
CHIPPEWA	7,574	3,915	3,643	16	272 R	51.7	48.1	51.8	48.2
CHISAGO	6,754	3,822	2,907	25	915 R	56.6	43.0	56.8	43.2
CLAY	15,544	8,278	7,241	25	1,037 R	53.3	46.6	53.3	46.7
CLEARWATER	4,135	1,651	2,466	18	815 D	39.9	59.6	40.1	59.9
COOK	1,641	987	650	4	337 R	60.1	39.6	60.3	39.7
COTTONWOOD	7,872	5,087	2,768	17	2,319 R	64.6	35.2	64.8	35.2
CROW WING	14,614	7,727	6,835	52	892 R	52.8	46.8	53.1	46.9
DAKOTA	35,273	15,032	20,150	91	5,118 D	42.6	57.1	42.7	57.3
DODGE	5,943	3,769	2,170	4	1,599 R	63.4	36.5	63.5	36.5
DOUGLAS	10,506	5,594	4,871	41	723 R	53.2	46.4	53.5	46.5
FARIBAULT	11,287	6,975	4,301	11	2,674 R	61.8	38.1	61.9	38.1
FILLMORE	11,444	7,507	3,926	11	3,581 R	65.6	34.3	65.7	34.3
FREEBORN	17,010	8,970	8,018	22	952 R	52.7	47.1	52.8	47.2
GOODHUE	16,073	10,473	5,562	38	4,911 R	65.2	34.6	65.3	34.7
GRANT	4,576	2,239	2,333	4	94 D	48.9	51.0	49.0	51.0
HENNEPIN	388,181	198,992	188,250	939	10,742 R	51.3	48.5	51.4	48.6
HOUSTON	7,890	4,807	3,080	3	1,727 R	60.9	39.0	61.0	39.0
HUBBARD	4,787	2,749	2,029	9	720 R	57.4	42.4	57.5	42.5
ISANTI	5,694	3,067	2,599	28	468 R	53.9	45.6	54.1	45.9
ITASCA	17,408	6,615	10,761	32	4,146 D	38.0	61.8	38.1	61.9
JACKSON	7,502	3,591	3,898	13	307 D	47.9	52.0	48.0	52.0
KANABEC	4,193	2,278	1,890	25	388 R	54.3	45.1	54.7	45.3
KANDIYOHI	13,567	6,786	6,738	43	48 R	50.0	49.7	50.2	49.8
KITTSON	4,165	1,937	2,218	10	281 D	46.5	53.3	46.6	53.4
KOOCHICHING	7,656	3,055	4,578	23	1,523 D	39.9	59.8	40.0	60.0
LAC QUI PARLE	6,449	3,185	3,253	11	68 D	50.4	50.4	49.5	50.5
LAKE	6,180	2,276	3,888	16	1,612 D	36.8	62.9	36.9	63.1
LAKE OF THE WOODS	1,904	835	1,053	16	218 D	43.8	55.3	44.2	55.8
LE SUEUR	9,670	4,426	5,234	10	808 D	45.8	54.1	45.8	54.2
LINCOLN	4,657	2,147	2,500	10	353 D	46.1	53.7	46.2	53.8
LYON	10,305	4,740	5,550	15	810 D	46.0	53.9	46.1	53.9
MCLEOD	11,511	7,214	4,276	21	2,938 R	62.7	37.1	62.8	37.2
MAHNOMEN	2,749	880	1,864	5	984 D	32.0	67.8	32.1	67.9
MARSHALL	6,777	3,006	3,759	12	753 D	44.4	55.5	44.4	55.6
MARTIN	12,692	8,479	4,194	19	4,285 R	66.8	33.0	66.9	33.1
MEEKER	8,560	4,857	3,678	25	1,179 R	56.7	43.0	56.9	43.1
MILLE LACS	6,830	3,913	2,886	31	1,027 R	57.3	42.3	57.6	42.4
MORRISON	11,764	4,403	7,337	24	2,934 D	37.4	62.4	37.5	62.5
MOWER	21,068	11,040	9,961	67	1,079 R	52.4	47.3	52.6	47.4
MURRAY	6,377	3,357	3,009	11	348 R	52.6	47.2	52.7	47.3
NICOLLET	9,255	5,283	3,961	11	1,322 R	57.1	42.8	57.2	42.8
NOBLES	10,594	5,636	4,947	11	689 R	53.2	46.7	53.3	46.7
NORMAN	5,586	2,642	2,932	12	290 D	47.3	52.5	47.4	52.6
OLMSTED	27,065	16,080	10,918	67	5,162 R	59.4	40.3	59.6	40.4
OTTER TAIL	21,843	13,747	8,054	42	5,693 R	62.9	36.9	63.1	36.9
PENNINGTON	5,759	2,537	3,204	18	667 D	44.1	55.6	44.2	55.8
PINE	7,687	3,450	4,211	26	761 D	44.9	54.8	45.0	55.0
PIPESTONE	6,131	3,677	2,443	11	1,234 R	59.8	39.8	60.1	39.9
POLK	16,909	7,528	9,346	35	1,818 D	44.5	55.3	44.6	55.4

PRESIDENT 1964

County	Total Vote	Republican	Democratic	Other	Rep.-Dem. Plurality	Total Vote % Rep.	Total Vote % Dem.	Major Vote % Rep.	Major Vote % Dem.
AITKIN	5,890	2,000	3,874	16	1,874 D	34.0	65.8	34.0	66.0
ANOKA	45,005	13,201	31,714	90	18,513 D	29.3	70.5	29.4	70.6
BECKER	10,220	3,751	6,453	16	2,702 D	36.7	63.1	36.8	63.2
BELTRAMI	9,166	3,184	5,967	15	2,783 D	34.7	65.1	34.8	65.2
BENTON	7,520	2,818	4,679	23	1,861 D	37.5	62.2	37.6	62.4
BIG STONE	4,172	1,331	2,831	10	1,500 D	31.9	67.9	32.0	68.0
BLUE EARTH	18,797	8,009	10,687	101	2,678 D	42.6	56.9	42.8	57.2
BROWN	11,937	5,851	6,069	17	218 D	49.0	50.8	49.1	50.9
CARLTON	12,359	2,780	9,552	27	6,772 D	22.5	77.3	22.5	77.5
CARVER	10,558	5,424	5,123	11	301 R	51.4	48.5	51.4	48.6
CASS	7,754	3,110	4,635	9	1,525 D	40.1	59.8	40.2	59.8
CHIPPEWA	7,365	2,806	4,550	9	1,744 D	38.1	61.8	38.1	61.9
CHISAGO	6,889	2,525	4,347	17	1,822 D	36.7	63.1	36.7	63.3
CLAY	16,285	6,085	10,161	39	4,076 D	37.4	62.4	37.5	62.5
CLEARWATER	3,739	1,137	2,596	6	1,459 D	30.4	69.4	30.5	69.5
COOK	1,742	764	976	2	212 D	43.9	56.0	43.9	56.1
COTTONWOOD	7,528	3,423	4,090	15	667 D	45.5	54.3	45.5	54.4
CROW WING	14,369	5,131	9,197	21	4,066 D	35.8	64.1	35.8	64.2
DAKOTA	42,328	13,856	28,391	81	14,535 D	32.7	67.1	32.8	67.2
DODGE	5,620	2,474	3,138	8	664 D	44.0	55.8	44.1	55.9
DOUGLAS	10,175	4,122	6,040	13	1,918 D	40.5	59.4	40.6	59.4
FARIBAULT	10,775	4,817	5,946	12	1,129 D	44.7	55.2	44.8	55.2
FILLMORE	10,651	4,824	5,813	14	989 D	45.3	54.6	45.4	54.6
FREEBORN	16,709	6,136	10,554	19	4,418 D	36.7	63.2	36.8	63.2
GOODHUE	15,589	6,539	9,035	15	2,496 D	41.9	58.0	42.0	58.0
GRANT	4,366	1,734	2,631	1	897 D	39.7	60.3	39.7	60.3
HENNEPIN	396,727	154,736	241,020	971	86,284 D	39.0	60.8	39.1	60.9
HOUSTON	7,326	3,433	3,885	8	452 D	46.9	53.0	46.9	53.1
HUBBARD	4,843	2,283	2,553	7	270 D	47.1	52.7	47.2	52.8
ISANTI	6,018	1,982	4,026	10	2,044 D	32.9	66.9	33.0	67.0
ITASCA	16,231	4,137	12,054	40	7,917 D	25.5	74.3	25.6	74.4
JACKSON	7,021	2,441	4,576	4	2,135 D	34.8	65.2	34.8	65.2
KANABEC	4,024	1,348	2,666	10	1,318 D	33.5	66.3	33.6	66.4
KANDIYOHI	13,156	4,011	9,108	37	5,097 D	30.5	69.2	30.6	69.4
KITTSON	3,945	1,153	2,790	2	1,637 D	29.2	70.7	29.2	70.8
KOOCHICHING	7,491	1,602	5,878	11	4,276 D	21.4	78.5	21.4	78.6
LAC QUI PARLE	6,180	2,236	3,934	10	1,698 D	36.2	63.6	36.2	63.8
LAKE	5,925	1,205	4,704	16	3,499 D	20.3	79.4	20.4	79.6
LAKE OF THE WOODS	1,765	489	1,266	10	777 D	27.7	71.7	27.9	72.1
LE SUEUR	9,325	3,191	6,117	17	2,926 D	34.2	65.6	34.3	65.7
LINCOLN	4,428	1,393	3,024	11	1,631 D	31.5	68.3	31.5	68.5
LYON	9,822	3,169	6,649	4	3,484 D	32.2	67.7	32.2	67.8
MCLEOD	11,316	5,545	5,755	16	210 D	49.0	50.8	49.1	50.9
MAHNOMEN	2,619	648	1,967	4	1,319 D	24.7	75.1	24.8	75.2
MARSHALL	6,490	1,893	4,594	3	2,701 D	29.2	70.8	29.2	70.8
MARTIN	12,126	6,529	5,575	22	954 R	53.8	46.0	53.9	46.1
MEEKER	8,378	3,099	5,270	9	2,171 D	37.0	62.9	37.0	63.0
MILLE LACS	6,872	2,474	4,369	29	1,895 D	36.0	63.5	36.2	63.8
MORRISON	11,032	3,515	7,492	25	3,977 D	31.9	67.9	31.9	68.1
MOWER	20,140	6,510	13,573	57	7,063 D	32.3	67.4	32.4	67.6
MURRAY	6,152	2,325	3,822	5	1,497 D	37.8	62.1	37.8	62.2
NICOLLET	8,736	3,605	5,121	10	1,516 D	41.3	58.6	41.3	58.7
NOBLES	9,960	3,517	6,431	12	2,914 D	35.3	64.6	35.4	64.6
NORMAN	5,301	1,662	3,631	8	1,969 D	31.4	68.5	31.4	68.6
OLMSTED	28,950	12,699	16,195	56	3,496 D	43.9	55.9	43.9	56.0
OTTER TAIL	20,565	10,542	9,997	26	545 R	51.3	48.6	51.3	48.7
PENNINGTON	5,534	1,630	3,894	10	2,264 D	29.5	70.4	29.5	70.5
PINE	7,420	2,279	5,123	18	2,844 D	30.7	69.0	30.8	69.2
PIPESTONE	5,851	2,481	3,365	5	884 D	42.4	57.5	42.4	57.6
POLK	16,111	5,039	11,052	20	6,013 D	31.3	68.6	31.3	68.7

PRESIDENT 1964

County	Total Vote	Republican	Democratic	Other	Rep.-Dem. Plurality	Total Vote Rep.	Dem.	Major Vote Rep.	Dem.
POPE	5,764	2,213	3,549	2	1,336 D	38.4%	61.6%	38.4%	61.6%
RAMSEY	191,592	56,898	133,948	746	77,050 D	29.7%	69.9%	29.8%	70.2%
RED LAKE	2,450	573	1,861	16	1,288 D	23.4%	76.0%	23.5%	76.5%
REDWOOD	9,277	4,546	4,722	9	176 D	49.0%	50.9%	49.1%	50.9%
RENVILLE	10,437	4,340	6,072	25	1,732 D	41.6%	58.2%	41.7%	58.3%
RICE	14,843	5,518	9,299	26	3,781 D	37.2%	62.6%	37.2%	62.8%
ROCK	5,287	2,389	2,896	2	507 D	45.2%	54.8%	45.2%	54.8%
ROSEAU	5,293	1,651	3,636	6	1,985 D	31.2%	68.7%	31.2%	68.8%
ST LOUIS	105,183	25,246	79,529	408	54,283 D	24.0%	75.6%	24.1%	75.9%
SCOTT	10,570	3,311	7,248	11	3,937 D	31.3%	68.6%	31.4%	68.6%
SHERBURNE	5,940	2,132	3,787	21	1,655 D	35.9%	63.8%	36.0%	64.0%
SIBLEY	7,436	3,854	3,577	5	277 R	51.8%	48.1%	51.9%	48.1%
STEARNS	32,166	13,009	19,063	94	6,054 D	40.4%	59.3%	40.6%	59.4%
STEELE	10,939	4,882	6,022	35	1,140 D	44.6%	55.1%	44.8%	55.2%
STEVENS	5,137	2,220	2,910	7	690 D	43.2%	56.6%	43.3%	56.7%
SWIFT	6,524	2,132	4,380	12	2,248 D	32.7%	67.1%	32.7%	67.3%
TODD	9,702	4,006	5,673	23	1,667 D	41.3%	58.5%	41.4%	58.6%
TRAVERSE	3,322	1,073	2,247	4	1,174 D	32.3%	67.6%	32.3%	67.7%
WABASHA	7,504	3,133	4,367	4	1,234 D	41.8%	58.2%	41.8%	58.2%
WADENA	5,334	2,418	2,908	8	490 D	45.3%	54.5%	45.4%	54.6%
WASECA	7,217	3,570	3,633	14	63 D	49.5%	50.3%	49.6%	50.4%
WASHINGTON	27,022	8,850	18,108	64	9,258 D	32.8%	67.0%	32.8%	67.2%
WATONWAN	6,445	2,823	3,615	7	792 D	43.8%	56.1%	43.8%	56.2%
WILKIN	4,391	1,636	2,751	4	1,115 D	37.3%	62.7%	37.3%	62.7%
WINONA	17,770	6,345	11,397	28	5,052 D	35.7%	64.1%	35.8%	64.2%
WRIGHT	14,185	5,476	8,687	22	3,211 D	38.6%	61.2%	38.7%	61.3%
YELLOW MEDICINE	7,464	2,751	4,707	6	1,956 D	36.9%	63.1%	36.9%	63.1%
TOTAL	1,554,462	559,624	991,117	3,721	431,493 D	36.0%	63.8%	36.1%	63.9%

PRESIDENT 1960

County	Total Vote	Republican	Democratic	Other	Rep.-Dem. Plurality	Total Vote Rep.	Dem.	Major Vote Rep.	Dem.
POPE	5,958	3,062	2,883	13	179 R	51.4%	48.4%	51.5%	48.5%
RAMSEY	186,527	77,408	108,464	655	31,056 D	41.5%	58.1%	41.6%	58.4%
RED LAKE	2,549	679	1,865	5	1,186 D	26.6%	73.2%	26.7%	73.3%
REDWOOD	9,746	5,893	3,839	14	2,054 R	60.5%	39.4%	60.6%	39.4%
RENVILLE	10,857	5,885	4,958	14	927 R	54.2%	45.7%	54.3%	45.7%
RICE	15,031	8,248	6,752	31	1,496 R	54.9%	44.9%	55.0%	45.0%
ROCK	5,297	3,469	1,823	5	1,646 R	65.5%	34.4%	65.6%	34.4%
ROSEAU	5,482	2,274	3,198	10	924 D	41.5%	58.3%	41.6%	58.4%
ST LOUIS	109,522	39,620	69,270	632	29,650 D	36.2%	63.2%	36.4%	63.6%
SCOTT	9,743	3,671	6,061	11	2,390 D	37.7%	62.2%	37.7%	62.3%
SHERBURNE	5,417	2,837	2,568	12	259 R	52.4%	47.4%	52.5%	47.5%
SIBLEY	7,542	4,987	2,541	14	2,446 R	66.1%	33.7%	66.2%	33.8%
STEARNS	32,581	13,522	19,026	33	5,504 D	41.5%	58.4%	41.5%	58.5%
STEELE	11,301	6,795	4,491	15	2,304 R	60.1%	39.7%	60.2%	39.8%
STEVENS	5,126	2,710	2,405	11	305 R	52.9%	46.9%	53.0%	47.0%
SWIFT	6,928	2,848	4,062	18	1,214 D	41.1%	58.6%	41.2%	58.8%
TODD	10,334	5,255	5,051	28	204 R	50.9%	48.9%	51.0%	49.0%
TRAVERSE	3,590	1,463	2,122	5	659 D	40.8%	59.1%	40.8%	59.2%
WABASHA	8,197	4,566	3,628	3	938 R	55.7%	44.3%	55.7%	44.3%
WADENA	5,329	3,082	2,240	7	842 R	57.8%	42.0%	57.9%	42.1%
WASECA	7,636	4,838	2,793	5	2,045 R	63.4%	36.6%	63.4%	36.6%
WASHINGTON	23,133	11,202	11,870	61	668 D	48.4%	51.3%	48.6%	51.4%
WATONWAN	6,595	4,173	2,412	10	1,751 R	63.3%	36.6%	63.4%	36.6%
WILKIN	4,667	2,340	2,319	8	21 R	50.1%	49.7%	50.2%	49.8%
WINONA	17,780	9,271	8,484	25	787 R	52.1%	47.7%	52.2%	47.8%
WRIGHT	13,658	7,180	6,452	26	728 R	52.6%	47.2%	52.7%	47.3%
YELLOW MEDICINE	7,475	3,800	3,649	26	151 R	50.8%	48.8%	51.0%	49.0%
TOTAL	1,542,887	757,915	779,933	4,039	22,018 D	49.2%	50.6%	49.3%	50.7%

MINNESOTA

OTHER VOTE COMPOSITION:

1920   56,106 Socialist; 11,489 Prohibition; 5,828 Socialist Labor.
1924   339,192 Progressive; 4,427 Communist; 1,855 Socialist Labor.
1928   6,774 Socialist; 4,853 Communist; 1,921 Socialist Labor.
1932   25,476 Socialist; 6,101 Communist; 5,731 Farmer-Labor; 770 Socialist Labor.
1936   74,296 Union; 2,872 Socialist; 2,574 Communist; 961 Socialist Labor.

1940   5,454 Socialist; 2,711 Communist; 2,553 Socialist Labor.
1944   5,048 Socialist; 3,176 Socialist Labor.
1948   27,866 Progressive; 4,646 Socialist; 2,525 Socialist Labor; 606 Socialist
         Workers.
1952   2,666 Progressive; 2,383 Socialist Labor; 2,147 Prohibition; 618 Socialist
         Workers.
1956   2,080 Socialist Labor; 1,098 Socialist Workers.

1960   3,077 Socialist Workers; 962 Socialist Labor.
1964   2,544 Socialist Labor; 1,177 Socialist Workers.

SPECIAL CASES:

1920   Socialist candidates ran second in several counties; Prohibition candidates ran
         second in one county.
1924   Progressive candidates carried a number of counties and ran second in all
         others. Lake of the Woods county organized in 1922.

MISSISSIPPI

PRESIDENT 1920

County	Total Vote	Republican	Democratic	Other	Rep.-Dem. Plurality	TV % Rep.	TV % Dem.	MV % Rep.	MV % Dem.
ADAMS	759	114	642	3	528 D	15.0%	84.6%	15.1%	84.9%
ALCORN	1,731	354	1,336	41	982 D	20.5%	77.2%	20.9%	79.1%
AMITE	673	90	578	5	488 D	13.5%	85.9%	13.5%	86.5%
ATTALA	1,478	270	1,187	21	917 D	18.3%	80.3%	18.5%	81.5%
BENTON	535	124	405	6	281 D	23.2%	75.7%	23.4%	76.6%
BOLIVAR	1,370	326	1,039	5	713 D	23.8%	75.8%	23.9%	76.1%
CALHOUN	1,088	160	887	41	727 D	14.7%	81.5%	15.3%	84.7%
CARROLL	865	184	670	11	436 D	21.3%	77.5%	21.5%	78.5%
CHICKASAW	1,165	194	945	26	751 D	16.7%	81.1%	17.0%	83.0%
CHOCTAW	984	191	779	14	538 D	19.4%	79.2%	19.7%	80.3%
CLAIBORNE	416	14	401	1	387 D	3.4%	96.4%	3.4%	96.6%
CLARKE	880	47	809	24	762 D	5.3%	91.9%	5.5%	94.5%
CLAY	821	48	770	3	722 D	5.8%	93.8%	5.9%	94.1%
COAHOMA	954	61	883	10	822 D	6.4%	92.6%	6.5%	93.5%
COPIAH	1,371	60	1,297	14	1,237 D	4.4%	94.6%	4.4%	95.6%
COVINGTON	936	257	650	29	393 D	27.5%	69.4%	28.3%	71.7%
DE SOTO	845	27	816	2	789 D	3.2%	96.6%	3.2%	96.8%
FORREST	1,357	140	1,151	66	1,011 D	10.3%	84.8%	10.8%	89.2%
FRANKLIN	860	203	654	3	451 D	23.6%	76.0%	23.7%	76.3%
GEORGE	335	56	262	17	206 D	16.7%	78.2%	17.6%	82.4%
GREENE	364	24	337	3	313 D	6.6%	92.6%	6.6%	93.4%
GRENADA	552	12	532	8	520 D	2.2%	96.4%	2.2%	97.8%
HANCOCK	439	130	306	3	176 D	29.6%	69.7%	29.8%	70.2%
HARRISON	1,625	314	1,267	44	953 D	19.3%	78.0%	19.9%	80.1%
HINDS	2,737	151	2,519	67	2,368 D	5.5%	92.0%	5.7%	94.3%
HOLMES	1,001	69	917	15	848 D	6.9%	91.6%	7.0%	93.0%
HUMPHREYS	340	21	317	2	296 D	6.2%	93.2%	6.2%	93.8%
ISSAQUENA	96	13	83		70 D	13.5%	86.5%	13.5%	86.5%
ITAWAMBA	1,224	198	1,023	3	825 D	16.2%	83.6%	16.2%	83.8%
JACKSON	703	121	578	4	457 D	17.2%	82.2%	17.3%	82.7%
JASPER	1,012	98	899	15	801 D	9.7%	88.8%	9.8%	90.2%
JEFFERSON	445	14	430	1	416 D	3.1%	96.6%	3.2%	96.8%
JEFFERSON DAVIS	670	179	486	5	307 D	26.7%	72.5%	26.9%	73.1%
JONES	2,057	419	1,398	240	979 D	20.4%	68.0%	23.1%	76.9%
KEMPER	889	129	734	26	605 D	14.5%	82.6%	14.9%	85.1%
LAFAYETTE	1,209	321	876	12	555 D	26.6%	72.5%	26.8%	73.2%
LAMAR	883	192	672	19	480 D	21.7%	76.1%	22.2%	77.8%
LAUDERDALE	2,893	228	2,539	126	2,311 D	7.9%	87.8%	8.2%	91.8%
LAWRENCE	662	131	529	2	398 D	19.8%	79.9%	19.8%	80.2%
LEAKE	1,227	121	1,081	25	960 D	9.9%	88.1%	10.1%	89.9%
LEE	1,967	302	1,655	10	1,353 D	15.4%	84.1%	15.4%	84.6%
LEFLORE	1,012	39	969	4	930 D	3.9%	95.8%	3.9%	96.1%
LINCOLN	1,208	421	774	13	353 D	34.9%	64.1%	35.2%	64.8%
LOWNDES	991	51	931	9	880 D	5.1%	93.9%	5.2%	94.8%
MADISON	896	57	831	8	774 D	6.4%	92.7%	6.4%	93.6%
MARION	772	143	613	16	470 D	18.5%	79.4%	18.9%	81.1%
MARSHALL	856	30	823	3	793 D	3.5%	96.1%	3.5%	96.5%
MONROE	2,034	139	1,881	14	1,742 D	6.8%	92.5%	6.9%	93.1%
MONTGOMERY	918	57	847	14	790 D	6.2%	92.3%	6.3%	93.7%
NESHOBA	1,326	182	1,089	55	907 D	13.7%	82.1%	14.3%	85.7%
NEWTON	1,399	108	1,209	82	1,101 D	7.7%	86.4%	8.2%	91.8%
NOXUBEE	724	24	699	1	675 D	3.3%	96.5%	3.3%	96.7%
OKTIBBEHA	850	70	779	1	709 D	8.2%	91.6%	8.2%	91.8%
PANOLA	926	80	843	3	763 D	8.6%	91.0%	8.7%	91.3%
PEARL RIVER	519	53	464	2	411 D	10.2%	89.4%	10.3%	89.7%
PERRY	345	69	271	5	202 D	20.0%	78.6%	20.3%	79.7%
PIKE	1,312	153	1,114	45	961 D	11.7%	84.9%	12.1%	87.9%
PONTOTOC	1,447	439	991	17	552 D	30.3%	68.5%	30.7%	69.3%
PRENTISS	1,538	496	993	49	497 D	32.2%	64.5%	33.3%	66.7%
QUITMAN	417	39	377	1	338 D	9.4%	90.4%	9.4%	90.6%

PRESIDENT 1924

County	Total Vote	Republican	Democratic	Other	Rep.-Dem. Plurality	TV % Rep.	TV % Dem.	MV % Rep.	MV % Dem.
ADAMS	1,156	304	836	16	532 D	26.3%	72.3%	26.7%	73.3%
ALCORN	2,053	223	1,828	2	1,605 D	10.9%	89.0%	10.9%	89.1%
AMITE	1,012	86	926		840 D	8.5%	91.5%	8.5%	91.5%
ATTALA	1,766	119	1,600	47	1,481 D	6.7%	90.6%	6.9%	93.1%
BENTON	579	35	541	3	506 D	6.0%	93.4%	6.1%	93.9%
BOLIVAR	1,574	266	1,212	96	946 D	16.9%	77.0%	18.0%	82.0%
CALHOUN	1,397	69	1,129	199	1,060 D	4.9%	80.8%	5.8%	94.2%
CARROLL	965	70	895		825 D	7.3%	92.7%	7.3%	92.7%
CHICKASAW	1,415	86	1,301	29	1,215 D	6.1%	91.9%	6.2%	93.8%
CHOCTAW	1,317	98	1,219		1,121 D	7.4%	92.6%	7.4%	92.6%
CLAIBORNE	619	14	605		591 D	2.3%	97.7%	2.3%	97.7%
CLARKE	1,395	87	1,306	2	1,219 D	6.2%	93.6%	6.2%	93.8%
CLAY	1,218	82	1,136		1,054 D	6.7%	93.3%	6.7%	93.3%
COAHOMA	1,483	121	1,362		1,241 D	8.2%	91.8%	8.2%	91.8%
COPIAH	2,130	43	2,087		2,044 D	2.0%	98.0%	2.0%	98.0%
COVINGTON	963	48	822	93	774 D	5.0%	85.4%	5.5%	94.5%
DE SOTO	1,082	17	1,065		1,048 D	1.6%	98.4%	1.6%	98.4%
FORREST	2,134	156	1,826	152	1,670 D	7.3%	85.6%	7.9%	92.1%
FRANKLIN	627	36	591		555 D	5.7%	94.3%	5.7%	94.3%
GEORGE	570	68	502		434 D	11.9%	88.1%	11.9%	88.1%
GREENE	487	31	456		425 D	6.4%	93.6%	6.4%	93.6%
GRENADA	950	17	933		916 D	1.8%	98.2%	1.8%	98.2%
HANCOCK	709	192	467	50	275 D	27.1%	65.9%	29.1%	70.9%
HARRISON	3,739	523	3,044	172	2,521 D	14.0%	81.4%	14.7%	85.3%
HINDS	4,498	245	4,083	170	3,838 D	5.4%	90.8%	5.7%	94.3%
HOLMES	1,265	92	1,173		1,081 D	7.3%	92.7%	7.3%	92.7%
HUMPHREYS	661	33	628		595 D	5.0%	95.0%	5.0%	95.0%
ISSAQUENA	143	17	126		109 D	11.9%	88.1%	11.9%	88.1%
ITAWAMBA	950	62	888		826 D	6.5%	93.5%	6.5%	93.5%
JACKSON	1,170	158	1,010	2	852 D	13.5%	86.3%	13.5%	86.5%
JASPER	1,319	61	1,257	1	1,196 D	4.6%	95.3%	4.6%	95.4%
JEFFERSON	547	50	497		447 D	9.1%	90.9%	9.1%	90.9%
JEFFERSON DAVIS	820	88	732		644 D	10.7%	89.3%	10.7%	89.3%
JONES	3,155	318	2,373	464	2,055 D	10.1%	75.2%	11.8%	88.2%
KEMPER	967	56	911		855 D	5.8%	94.2%	5.8%	94.2%
LAFAYETTE	1,974	89	1,848	37	1,759 D	4.5%	93.6%	4.6%	95.4%
LAMAR	911	80	795	36	715 D	8.8%	87.3%	9.1%	90.9%
LAUDERDALE	4,113	320	3,204	589	2,884 D	7.8%	77.9%	9.1%	90.9%
LAWRENCE	729	55	674		619 D	7.5%	92.5%	7.5%	92.5%
LEAKE	1,303	48	1,255		1,207 D	3.7%	96.3%	3.7%	96.3%
LEE	2,773	152	2,621		2,469 D	5.5%	94.5%	5.5%	94.5%
LEFLORE	1,279	135	1,144		1,009 D	10.6%	89.4%	10.6%	89.4%
LINCOLN	1,502	154	1,278	70	1,124 D	10.3%	85.1%	10.8%	89.2%
LOWNDES	1,717	62	1,655		1,593 D	3.6%	96.4%	3.6%	96.4%
MADISON	1,707	109	1,598		1,489 D	6.4%	93.6%	6.4%	93.6%
MARION	1,138	99	1,039		940 D	8.7%	91.3%	8.7%	91.3%
MARSHALL	1,142	40	1,102		1,062 D	3.5%	96.5%	3.5%	96.5%
MONROE	2,479	121	2,326	32	2,205 D	4.9%	93.8%	4.9%	95.1%
MONTGOMERY	1,170	60	1,015	95	955 D	5.1%	86.8%	5.6%	94.4%
NESHOBA	1,831	228	1,603		1,375 D	12.5%	87.5%	12.5%	87.5%
NEWTON	1,822	72	1,657	93	1,585 D	4.0%	90.9%	4.2%	95.8%
NOXUBEE	1,010	44	966		922 D	4.4%	95.6%	4.4%	95.6%
OKTIBBEHA	1,442	30	1,370	42	1,340 D	2.1%	95.0%	2.1%	97.9%
PANOLA	1,348	53	1,264	31	1,211 D	3.9%	93.8%	4.0%	96.0%
PEARL RIVER	1,118	164	855	99	691 D	14.7%	76.5%	16.1%	83.9%
PERRY	455	55	383	17	328 D	12.1%	84.2%	12.6%	87.4%
PIKE	2,289	197	1,640	452	1,443 D	8.6%	71.6%	10.7%	89.3%
PONTOTOC	1,292	86	1,206		1,120 D	6.7%	93.3%	6.7%	93.3%
PRENTISS	1,406	179	1,225	2	1,046 D	12.7%	87.1%	12.7%	87.3%
QUITMAN	610	36	574		538 D	5.9%	94.1%	5.9%	94.1%

MISSISSIPPI

PRESIDENT 1920

County	Total Vote	Republican	Democratic	Other	Rep.-Dem. Plurality	Percentage Total Vote Rep.	Dem.	Major Vote Rep.	Dem.
RANKIN	952	43	904	5	861 D	4.5%	95.0%	4.5%	95.5%
SCOTT	1,141	64	1,055	22	991 D	5.6%	92.5%	5.7%	94.3%
SHARKEY	235	7	228		221 D	3.0%	97.0%	3.0%	97.0%
SIMPSON	1,025	109	902	14	793 D	10.6%	88.0%	10.8%	89.2%
SMITH	1,256	265	968	23	703 D	21.1%	77.1%	21.5%	78.5%
STONE	320	16	299	5	283 D	5.0%	93.4%	5.1%	94.9%
SUNFLOWER	1,117	47	1,061	9	1,014 D	4.2%	95.0%	4.2%	95.8%
TALLAHATCHIE	1,174	69	1,092	13	1,023 D	5.9%	93.0%	5.9%	94.1%
TATE	1,004	117	876	11	759 D	11.7%	87.3%	11.8%	88.2%
TIPPAH	1,214	237	955	22	718 D	19.5%	78.7%	19.9%	80.1%
TISHOMINGO	1,249	387	841	21	454 D	31.0%	67.3%	31.5%	68.5%
TUNICA	259	2	256	1	254 D	0.8%	98.8%	0.8%	99.2%
UNION	1,665	429	1,224	12	795 D	25.8%	73.5%	26.0%	74.0%
WALTHALL	600	139	446	15	307 D	23.2%	74.3%	23.8%	76.2%
WARREN	1,258	161	1,082	15	921 D	12.8%	86.0%	13.0%	87.0%
WASHINGTON	837	60	776	1	716 D	7.2%	92.7%	7.2%	92.8%
WAYNE	707	112	547	48	435 D	15.8%	77.4%	17.0%	83.0%
WEBSTER	925	299	580	46	281 D	32.3%	62.7%	34.0%	66.0%
WILKINSON	433	15	416	2	401 D	3.5%	96.1%	3.5%	96.5%
WINSTON	1,080	113	950	17	837 D	10.5%	88.0%	10.6%	89.4%
YALOBUSHA	985	82	893	10	811 D	8.3%	90.7%	8.4%	91.6%
YAZOO	1,007	46	948	13	902 D	4.6%	94.1%	4.6%	95.4%
TOTAL	82,351	11,576	69,136	1,639	57,560 D	14.1%	84.0%	14.3%	85.7%

PRESIDENT 1924

County	Total Vote	Republican	Democratic	Other	Rep.-Dem. Plurality	Percentage Total Vote Rep.	Dem.	Major Vote Rep.	Dem.
RANKIN	1,449	34	1,415		1,381 D	2.3%	97.7%	2.3%	97.7%
SCOTT	1,322	53	1,179	90	1,126 D	4.0%	89.2%	4.3%	95.7%
SHARKEY	393	34	353	6	319 D	8.7%	89.8%	8.8%	91.2%
SIMPSON	1,625	100	1,518	7	1,418 D	6.2%	93.4%	6.2%	93.8%
SMITH	1,161	49	1,081	31	1,032 D	4.2%	93.1%	4.3%	95.7%
STONE	468	56	412		356 D	12.0%	88.0%	12.0%	88.0%
SUNFLOWER	1,770	76	1,694		1,618 D	4.3%	95.7%	4.3%	95.7%
TALLAHATCHIE	1,401	15	1,386		1,371 D	1.1%	98.9%	1.1%	98.9%
TATE	1,014	6	1,002	6	996 D	0.6%	98.8%	0.6%	99.4%
TIPPAH	1,552	96	1,411	45	1,315 D	6.2%	90.9%	6.4%	93.6%
TISHOMINGO	1,460	279	1,181		902 D	19.1%	80.9%	19.1%	80.9%
TUNICA	508	13	495		482 D	2.6%	97.4%	2.6%	97.4%
UNION	1,971	135	1,750	86	1,615 D	6.8%	88.8%	7.2%	92.8%
WALTHALL	724	64	660		596 D	8.8%	91.2%	8.8%	91.2%
WARREN	2,122	328	1,794		1,466 D	15.5%	84.5%	15.5%	84.5%
WASHINGTON	1,422	143	1,277	2	1,134 D	10.1%	89.8%	10.1%	89.9%
WAYNE	961	56	905		849 D	5.8%	94.2%	5.8%	94.2%
WEBSTER	1,130	115	918	97	803 D	10.2%	81.2%	11.1%	88.9%
WILKINSON	395	40	355		315 D	10.1%	89.9%	10.1%	89.9%
WINSTON	1,397	53	1,344		1,291 D	3.8%	96.2%	3.8%	96.2%
YALOBUSHA	1,356	53	1,292	11	1,239 D	3.9%	95.3%	3.9%	96.1%
YAZOO	1,405	57	1,348		1,291 D	4.1%	95.9%	4.1%	95.9%
TOTAL	112,442	8,494	100,474	3,474	91,980 D	7.6%	89.4%	7.8%	92.2%

MISSISSIPPI

PRESIDENT 1928

County	Total Vote	Republican	Democratic	Other	Rep.-Dem. Plurality	Total Vote Rep.	Total Vote Dem.	Major Vote Rep.	Major Vote Dem.
ADAMS	2,177	840	1,337		497 D	38.6%	61.4%	38.6%	61.4%
ALCORN	1,866	335	1,531		1,196 D	18.0%	82.0%	18.0%	82.0%
AMITE	1,514	325	1,189		864 D	21.5%	78.5%	21.5%	78.5%
ATTALA	2,371	113	2,258		2,145 D	4.8%	95.2%	4.8%	95.2%
BENTON	840	47	793		746 D	5.6%	94.4%	5.6%	94.4%
BOLIVAR	2,205	266	1,939		1,673 D	12.1%	87.9%	12.1%	87.9%
CALHOUN	1,560	283	1,277		994 D	18.1%	81.9%	18.1%	81.9%
CARROLL	1,151	49	1,102		1,053 D	4.3%	95.7%	4.3%	95.7%
CHICKASAW	1,666	171	1,495		1,324 D	10.3%	89.7%	10.3%	89.7%
CHOCTAW	1,126	118	1,008		890 D	10.5%	89.5%	10.5%	89.5%
CLAIBORNE	751	43	708		665 D	5.7%	94.3%	5.7%	94.3%
CLARKE	1,694	563	1,131		568 D	33.2%	66.8%	33.2%	66.8%
CLAY	1,584	128	1,456		1,328 D	8.1%	91.9%	8.1%	91.9%
COAHOMA	2,001	223	1,778		1,555 D	11.1%	88.9%	11.1%	88.9%
COPIAH	2,894	161	2,733		2,572 D	5.6%	94.4%	5.6%	94.4%
COVINGTON	1,320	189	1,131		942 D	14.3%	85.7%	14.3%	85.7%
DE SOTO	1,421	64	1,357		1,293 D	4.5%	95.5%	4.5%	95.5%
FORREST	3,240	1,447	1,793		346 D	44.7%	55.3%	44.7%	55.3%
FRANKLIN	1,086	181	905		724 D	16.7%	83.3%	16.7%	83.3%
GEORGE	705	369	336		33 R	52.3%	47.7%	52.3%	47.7%
GREENE	935	342	593		251 D	36.6%	63.4%	36.6%	63.4%
GRENADA	1,195	40	1,155		1,115 D	3.3%	96.7%	3.3%	96.7%
HANCOCK	1,720	436	1,284		848 D	25.3%	74.7%	25.3%	74.7%
HARRISON	5,197	1,485	3,712		2,227 D	28.6%	71.4%	28.6%	71.4%
HINDS	6,683	976	5,707		4,731 D	14.6%	85.4%	14.6%	85.4%
HOLMES	2,138	134	2,004		1,870 D	6.3%	93.7%	6.3%	93.7%
HUMPHREYS	1,021	1	1,020		1,019 D	0.1%	99.9%	0.1%	99.9%
ISSAQUENA	140	6	134		128 D	4.3%	95.7%	4.3%	95.7%
ITAWAMBA	1,185	331	854		523 D	27.9%	72.1%	27.9%	72.1%
JACKSON	1,828	567	1,261		694 D	31.0%	69.0%	31.0%	69.0%
JASPER	1,604	625	979		354 D	39.0%	61.0%	39.0%	61.0%
JEFFERSON	891	61	830		769 D	6.8%	93.2%	6.8%	93.2%
JEFFERSON DAVIS	1,019	163	856		693 D	16.0%	84.0%	16.0%	84.0%
JONES	4,088	1,804	2,284		480 D	44.1%	55.9%	44.1%	55.9%
KEMPER	1,562	141	1,421		1,280 D	9.0%	91.0%	9.0%	91.0%
LAFAYETTE	1,783	131	1,652		1,521 D	7.3%	92.7%	7.3%	92.7%
LAMAR	1,128	410	718		308 D	36.3%	63.7%	36.3%	63.7%
LAUDERDALE	5,356	1,798	3,558		1,760 D	33.6%	66.4%	33.6%	66.4%
LAWRENCE	969	210	759		549 D	21.7%	78.3%	21.7%	78.3%
LEAKE	1,907	212	1,695		1,483 D	11.1%	88.9%	11.1%	88.9%
LEE	3,124	367	2,757		2,390 D	11.7%	88.3%	11.7%	88.3%
LEFLORE	2,324	105	2,219		2,114 D	4.5%	95.5%	4.5%	95.5%
LINCOLN	2,613	422	2,191		1,769 D	16.2%	83.8%	16.2%	83.8%
LOWNDES	2,321	185	2,136		1,951 D	8.0%	92.0%	8.0%	92.0%
MADISON	1,643	124	1,519		1,395 D	7.5%	92.5%	7.5%	92.5%
MARION	1,448	526	922		396 D	36.3%	63.7%	36.3%	63.7%
MARSHALL	1,522	100	1,422		1,322 D	6.6%	93.4%	6.6%	93.4%
MONROE	3,409	376	3,033		2,657 D	11.0%	89.0%	11.0%	89.0%
MONTGOMERY	1,705	98	1,607		1,509 D	5.7%	94.3%	5.7%	94.3%
NESHOBA	2,422	516	1,906		1,390 D	21.3%	78.7%	21.3%	78.7%
NEWTON	2,442	368	2,074		1,706 D	15.1%	84.9%	15.1%	84.9%
NOXUBEE	1,255	102	1,153		1,051 D	8.1%	91.9%	8.1%	91.9%
OKTIBBEHA	1,688	111	1,577		1,466 D	6.6%	93.4%	6.6%	93.4%
PANOLA	1,711	142	1,569		1,427 D	8.3%	91.7%	8.3%	91.7%
PEARL RIVER	1,797	918	879		39 R	51.1%	48.9%	51.1%	48.9%
PERRY	560	277	283		6 D	49.5%	50.5%	49.5%	50.5%
PIKE	3,351	920	2,431		1,511 D	27.5%	72.5%	27.5%	72.5%
PONTOTOC	1,798	261	1,537		1,276 D	14.5%	85.5%	14.5%	85.5%
PRENTISS	1,635	269	1,366		1,097 D	16.5%	83.5%	16.5%	83.5%
QUITMAN	879	86	793		707 D	9.8%	90.2%	9.8%	90.2%

PRESIDENT 1932

County	Total Vote	Republican	Democratic	Other	Rep.-Dem. Plurality	Total Vote Rep.	Total Vote Dem.	Major Vote Rep.	Major Vote Dem.
ADAMS	1,819	384	1,420	15	1,036 D	21.1%	78.1%	21.3%	78.7%
ALCORN	2,544	73	2,461	10	2,388 D	2.9%	96.7%	2.9%	97.1%
AMITE	1,318	73	1,237	8	1,164 D	5.5%	93.9%	5.6%	94.4%
ATTALA	2,419	38	2,370	11	2,332 D	1.6%	98.0%	1.6%	98.4%
BENTON	823	8	814	1	806 D	1.0%	98.9%	1.0%	99.0%
BOLIVAR	2,151	204	1,941	6	1,737 D	9.5%	90.2%	9.5%	90.5%
CALHOUN	1,954	27	1,923	4	1,896 D	1.4%	98.4%	1.4%	98.6%
CARROLL	1,199	9	1,189	1	1,180 D	0.8%	99.2%	0.8%	99.2%
CHICKASAW	1,475	16	1,455	4	1,439 D	1.1%	98.6%	1.1%	98.9%
CHOCTAW	1,134	23	1,110	1	1,087 D	2.0%	97.9%	2.0%	98.0%
CLAIBORNE	730	16	713	1	697 D	2.2%	97.8%	2.2%	97.8%
CLARKE	1,542	53	1,482	7	1,429 D	3.4%	96.1%	3.5%	96.5%
CLAY	1,407	34	1,371	2	1,337 D	2.4%	97.4%	2.4%	97.6%
COAHOMA	1,737	62	1,672	3	1,610 D	3.6%	96.3%	3.6%	96.4%
COPIAH	2,403	28	2,371	4	2,343 D	1.2%	98.7%	1.2%	98.8%
COVINGTON	1,380	22	1,352	6	1,330 D	1.6%	98.0%	1.6%	98.4%
DE SOTO	1,413	13	1,396	4	1,383 D	0.9%	98.8%	0.9%	99.1%
FORREST	2,230	182	2,068	30	1,886 D	8.1%	90.7%	8.1%	91.9%
FRANKLIN	990	25	965		940 D	2.5%	97.5%	2.5%	97.5%
GEORGE	844	19	824	1	805 D	2.3%	97.6%	2.3%	97.7%
GREENE	848	29	818	1	789 D	3.4%	96.5%	3.4%	96.6%
GRENADA	1,112	11	1,101		1,090 D	1.0%	99.0%	1.0%	99.0%
HANCOCK	1,472	109	1,349	14	1,240 D	7.4%	91.6%	7.5%	92.5%
HARRISON	4,619	449	4,124	46	3,675 D	9.7%	89.3%	9.8%	90.2%
HINDS	6,983	403	6,541	39	6,138 D	5.8%	93.7%	5.8%	94.2%
HOLMES	1,852	45	1,799	8	1,754 D	2.4%	97.1%	2.4%	97.6%
HUMPHREYS	785	10	775		765 D	1.3%	98.7%	1.3%	98.7%
ISSAQUENA	160	1	159		158 D	0.6%	99.4%	0.6%	99.4%
ITAWAMBA	1,895	40	1,851	4	1,811 D	2.1%	97.7%	2.1%	97.9%
JACKSON	1,770	126	1,634	10	1,508 D	7.1%	92.3%	7.2%	92.8%
JASPER	1,579	38	1,526	15	1,488 D	2.4%	96.6%	2.4%	97.6%
JEFFERSON	782	24	753	5	729 D	3.1%	96.3%	3.1%	96.9%
JEFFERSON DAVIS	972	30	940	2	910 D	3.1%	96.7%	3.1%	96.9%
JONES	4,172	173	3,816	183	3,643 D	4.1%	91.5%	4.3%	95.7%
KEMPER	1,449	27	1,420	2	1,393 D	1.9%	98.0%	1.9%	98.1%
LAFAYETTE	1,861	26	1,831	4	1,805 D	1.4%	98.4%	1.4%	98.6%
LAMAR	1,069	31	1,033	5	1,002 D	2.9%	95.9%	2.9%	96.2%
LAUDERDALE	5,039	191	4,830	18	4,639 D	3.8%	95.9%	3.8%	96.2%
LAWRENCE	965	31	933	1	902 D	3.2%	96.8%	3.3%	96.8%
LEAKE	1,926	14	1,903	9	1,889 D	0.7%	98.8%	0.7%	99.3%
LEE	3,838	129	3,704	5	3,575 D	3.4%	96.5%	3.4%	96.6%
LEFLORE	1,915	34	1,877	4	1,843 D	1.8%	98.0%	1.8%	98.2%
LINCOLN	2,479	92	2,379	8	2,287 D	3.7%	96.0%	3.8%	96.3%
LOWNDES	2,364	50	2,305	9	2,255 D	2.1%	97.5%	2.1%	97.9%
MADISON	1,533	51	1,474	8	1,423 D	3.3%	96.2%	3.3%	96.7%
MARION	2,531	94	2,429	8	2,335 D	3.7%	96.0%	3.7%	96.3%
MARSHALL	1,322	38	1,281	1	1,243 D	2.9%	97.0%	2.9%	97.1%
MONROE	3,533	82	3,448	3	3,366 D	2.3%	97.6%	2.3%	97.7%
MONTGOMERY	1,384	17	1,366	1	1,349 D	1.2%	98.7%	1.2%	98.8%
NESHOBA	2,300	56	2,236	8	2,180 D	2.4%	97.2%	2.4%	97.6%
NEWTON	2,320	56	2,253	11	2,197 D	2.4%	97.1%	2.4%	97.6%
NOXUBEE	1,096	41	1,052	3	1,011 D	3.8%	96.0%	3.8%	96.2%
OKTIBBEHA	1,600	26	1,574		1,548 D	1.6%	98.4%	1.6%	98.4%
PANOLA	1,341	20	1,318	3	1,298 D	1.5%	98.3%	1.5%	98.5%
PEARL RIVER	1,613	99	1,500	14	1,401 D	6.1%	93.0%	6.2%	93.8%
PERRY	542	15	523	4	508 D	2.8%	96.5%	2.8%	97.2%
PIKE	2,528	118	2,400	10	2,282 D	4.7%	94.9%	4.7%	95.3%
PONTOTOC	2,093	131	1,962		1,831 D	6.3%	93.7%	6.3%	93.7%
PRENTISS	2,052	76	1,976		1,900 D	3.7%	96.3%	3.7%	96.3%
QUITMAN	742	18	720	4	702 D	2.4%	97.0%	2.4%	97.6%

MISSISSIPPI

PRESIDENT 1928

County	Total Vote	Republican	Democratic	Other	Rep.-Dem. Plurality	Percentage Total Vote Rep.	Total Vote Dem.	Major Vote Rep.	Major Vote Dem.
RANKIN	1,505	180	1,325		1,145 D	12.0%	88.0%	12.0%	88.0%
SCOTT	2,214	164	2,050		1,886 D	7.4%	92.6%	7.4%	92.6%
SHARKEY	511	36	475		439 D	7.0%	93.0%	7.0%	93.0%
SIMPSON	2,123	231	1,892		1,661 D	10.9%	89.1%	10.9%	89.1%
SMITH	1,869	419	1,450		1,031 D	22.4%	77.6%	22.4%	77.6%
STONE	694	436	258		178 R	62.8%	37.2%	62.8%	37.2%
SUNFLOWER	2,764	88	2,676		2,588 D	3.2%	96.8%	3.2%	96.8%
TALLAHATCHIE	2,317	33	2,284		2,251 D	1.4%	98.6%	1.4%	98.6%
TATE	1,316	42	1,274		1,232 D	3.2%	96.8%	3.2%	96.8%
TIPPAH	1,755	298	1,457		1,159 D	17.0%	83.0%	17.0%	83.0%
TISHOMINGO	1,550	585	965		380 D	37.7%	62.3%	37.7%	62.3%
TUNICA	680	26	654		628 D	3.8%	96.2%	3.8%	96.2%
UNION	2,182	324	1,858		1,534 D	14.8%	85.2%	14.8%	85.2%
WALTHALL	1,082	218	864		646 D	20.1%	79.9%	20.1%	79.9%
WARREN	3,299	530	2,769		2,239 D	16.1%	83.9%	16.1%	83.9%
WASHINGTON	1,742	246	1,496		1,250 D	14.1%	85.9%	14.1%	85.9%
WAYNE	1,206	289	917		628 D	24.0%	76.0%	24.0%	76.0%
WEBSTER	1,440	338	1,102		764 D	23.5%	76.5%	23.5%	76.5%
WILKINSON	840	73	767		694 D	8.7%	91.3%	8.7%	91.3%
WINSTON	1,717	97	1,620		1,523 D	5.6%	94.4%	5.6%	94.4%
YALOBUSHA	1,453	204	1,249		1,045 D	14.0%	86.0%	14.0%	86.0%
YAZOO	2,141	112	2,029		1,917 D	5.2%	94.8%	5.2%	94.8%
TOTAL	151,568	27,030	124,538		97,508 D	17.8%	82.2%	17.8%	82.2%

PRESIDENT 1932

County	Total Vote	Republican	Democratic	Other	Rep.-Dem. Plurality	Percentage Total Vote Rep.	Total Vote Dem.	Major Vote Rep.	Major Vote Dem.
RANKIN	1,590	52	1,536	2	1,484 D	3.3%	96.6%	3.3%	96.7%
SCOTT	1,554	17	1,537		1,520 D	1.1%	98.9%	1.1%	98.9%
SHARKEY	552		551	1	551 D		99.8%		100.0%
SIMPSON	1,989	47	1,941	1	1,894 D	2.4%	97.6%	2.4%	97.6%
SMITH	1,595	17	1,576	2	1,559 D	1.1%	98.8%	1.1%	98.9%
STONE	458	32	424	2	392 D	7.0%	92.6%	7.0%	93.0%
SUNFLOWER	2,450	34	2,411	5	2,377 D	1.4%	98.4%	1.4%	98.6%
TALLAHATCHIE	2,471	16	2,453	2	2,437 D	0.6%	99.3%	0.6%	99.4%
TATE	996	9	986	1	977 D	0.9%	99.0%	0.9%	99.1%
TIPPAH	2,028	52	1,972	4	1,920 D	2.6%	97.2%	2.6%	97.4%
TISHOMINGO	1,754	112	1,636	6	1,524 D	6.4%	93.3%	6.4%	93.6%
TUNICA	581	8	573		565 D	1.4%	98.6%	1.4%	98.6%
UNION	2,346	74	2,264	8	2,190 D	3.2%	96.5%	3.2%	96.8%
WALTHALL	1,101	30	1,069	2	1,039 D	2.7%	97.1%	2.7%	97.3%
WARREN	2,611	169	2,422	20	2,253 D	6.5%	92.8%	6.5%	93.5%
WASHINGTON	1,795	100	1,691	4	1,591 D	5.6%	94.2%	5.6%	94.4%
WAYNE	1,050	23	1,023	4	1,000 D	2.2%	97.4%	2.2%	97.8%
WEBSTER	1,133	35	1,092	6	1,057 D	3.1%	96.4%	3.1%	96.9%
WILKINSON	834	18	813	3	795 D	2.2%	97.5%	2.2%	97.8%
WINSTON	1,736	12	1,720	4	1,708 D	0.7%	99.1%	0.7%	99.3%
YALOBUSHA	1,583	39	1,536	8	1,497 D	2.5%	97.0%	2.5%	97.5%
YAZOO	2,024	24	1,995	5	1,971 D	1.2%	98.6%	1.2%	98.8%
TOTAL	146,034	5,180	140,168	686	134,988 D	3.5%	96.0%	3.6%	96.4%

MISSISSIPPI

PRESIDENT 1936

County	Total Vote	Republican	Democratic	Other	Rep.-Dem. Plurality	% Total Rep.	% Total Dem.	% Major Rep.	% Major Dem.
ADAMS	1,860	124	1,732	4	1,603 D	6.7%	93.1%	6.7%	93.3%
ALCORN	2,457	53	2,396	8	2,343 D	2.2%	97.5%	2.2%	97.8%
AMITE	1,492	56	1,421	15	1,365 D	3.8%	95.2%	3.8%	96.2%
ATTALA	1,897	36	1,855	6	1,819 D	1.9%	97.8%	1.9%	98.1%
BENTON	1,727	10	1,717		1,707 D	0.6%	99.4%	0.6%	99.4%
BOLIVAR	2,397	101	2,296		2,195 D	4.2%	95.8%	4.2%	95.8%
CALHOUN	1,733	40	1,691	2	1,651 D	2.3%	97.6%	2.3%	97.7%
CARROLL	1,050	19	1,030	1	1,011 D	1.8%	98.1%	1.8%	98.2%
CHICKASAW	1,578	18	1,559	1	1,541 D	1.1%	98.8%	1.1%	98.9%
CHOCTAW	1,386	41	1,342	3	1,301 D	3.0%	96.8%	3.0%	97.0%
CLAIBORNE	806	31	774	1	743 D	3.8%	96.0%	3.9%	96.1%
CLARKE	2,123	31	2,089	3	2,058 D	1.5%	98.4%	1.5%	98.5%
CLAY	1,303	32	1,271		1,239 D	2.5%	97.5%	2.5%	97.5%
COAHOMA	2,108	49	2,059		2,010 D	2.3%	97.7%	2.3%	97.7%
COPIAH	2,443	45	2,397	1	2,352 D	1.8%	98.1%	1.8%	98.2%
COVINGTON	1,644	52	1,589	3	1,537 D	3.2%	96.7%	3.2%	96.8%
DE SOTO	1,356	13	1,343		1,330 D	1.0%	99.0%	1.0%	99.0%
FORREST	3,841	234	3,596	11	3,362 D	6.1%	93.6%	6.1%	93.9%
FRANKLIN	1,134	33	1,098	3	1,065 D	2.9%	96.8%	2.9%	97.1%
GEORGE	918	24	892	2	868 D	2.6%	97.2%	2.6%	97.4%
GREENE	879	46	830	3	784 D	5.2%	94.4%	5.3%	94.7%
GRENADA	1,258	13	1,245		1,232 D	1.0%	99.0%	1.0%	99.0%
HANCOCK	1,464	164	1,284	16	1,120 D	11.2%	87.7%	11.3%	88.7%
HARRISON	4,740	495	4,208	37	3,713 D	10.4%	88.8%	10.5%	89.5%
HINDS	8,976	313	8,647	16	8,334 D	3.5%	96.3%	3.5%	96.5%
HOLMES	1,897	12	1,885		1,873 D	0.6%	99.4%	0.6%	99.4%
HUMPHREYS	1,171	7	1,164		1,157 D	0.6%	99.4%	0.6%	99.4%
ISSAQUENA	214		214		214 D		100.0%		100.0%
ITAWAMBA	1,512	47	1,465		1,418 D	3.1%	96.9%	3.1%	96.9%
JACKSON	1,831	120	1,704	7	1,584 D	6.6%	93.1%	6.6%	93.4%
JASPER	2,027	21	2,004	2	1,983 D	1.0%	98.9%	1.0%	99.0%
JEFFERSON	894	9	884	1	875 D	1.0%	98.9%	1.0%	99.0%
JEFFERSON DAVIS	1,394	67	1,325	2	1,258 D	4.8%	95.1%	4.8%	95.2%
JONES	4,695	185	4,461	49	4,276 D	3.9%	95.0%	3.9%	96.0%
KEMPER	1,485	8	1,477		1,469 D	0.5%	99.5%	0.5%	99.5%
LAFAYETTE	1,683	26	1,652	5	1,626 D	1.5%	98.2%	1.5%	98.5%
LAMAR	1,306	91	1,210	5	1,119 D	7.0%	92.6%	7.0%	93.0%
LAUDERDALE	6,154	67	6,075	12	6,008 D	1.1%	98.7%	1.1%	98.9%
LAWRENCE	1,321	34	1,286	1	1,252 D	2.6%	97.4%	2.6%	97.4%
LEAKE	2,584	8	2,566	10	2,558 D	0.3%	99.3%	0.3%	99.7%
LEE	3,627	42	3,585		3,543 D	1.2%	98.8%	1.2%	98.8%
LEFLORE	2,173	35	2,137	1	2,102 D	1.6%	98.3%	1.6%	98.4%
LINCOLN	2,549	74	2,465	10	2,391 D	2.9%	96.7%	2.9%	97.1%
LOWNDES	2,394	56	2,328	10	2,272 D	2.3%	97.2%	2.3%	97.7%
MADISON	1,871	32	1,838	1	1,806 D	1.7%	98.2%	1.7%	98.3%
MARION	1,970	37	1,932	1	1,895 D	1.9%	98.1%	1.9%	98.1%
MARSHALL	1,134	22	1,111	1	1,089 D	1.9%	98.0%	1.9%	98.0%
MONROE	3,257	55	3,199	3	3,144 D	1.7%	98.2%	1.7%	98.3%
MONTGOMERY	1,388	5	1,383		1,378 D	0.4%	99.6%	0.4%	99.6%
NESHOBA	3,565	67	3,495	3	3,428 D	1.9%	98.0%	1.9%	98.1%
NEWTON	2,666	39	2,624	3	2,585 D	1.5%	98.4%	1.5%	98.5%
NOXUBEE	1,360	27	1,332	1	1,305 D	2.0%	97.9%	2.0%	98.0%
OKTIBBEHA	1,734	19	1,714	1	1,695 D	1.1%	98.8%	1.1%	98.9%
PANOLA	1,484	3	1,481		1,478 D	0.2%	99.8%	0.2%	99.8%
PEARL RIVER	1,240	81	1,156	3	1,075 D	6.5%	93.2%	6.5%	93.5%
PERRY	753	16	737		721 D	2.1%	97.9%	2.1%	97.9%
PIKE	3,261	86	3,170	5	3,084 D	2.6%	97.2%	2.6%	97.4%
PONTOTOC	2,388	93	2,286	9	2,193 D	3.9%	95.7%	3.9%	96.1%
PRENTISS	1,863	50	1,809	4	1,759 D	2.7%	97.1%	2.7%	97.3%
QUITMAN	1,035	9	1,025	1	1,016 D	0.9%	99.0%	0.9%	99.1%

PRESIDENT 1940

County	Total Vote	Republican	Democratic	Other	Rep.-Dem. Plurality	% Total Rep.	% Total Dem.	% Major Rep.	% Major Dem.
ADAMS	2,036	166	1,869	1	1,703 D	8.2%	91.8%	8.2%	91.8%
ALCORN	3,068	133	2,934		2,801 D	4.3%	95.6%	4.3%	95.7%
AMITE	1,499	64	1,435		1,371 D	4.3%	95.7%	4.3%	95.7%
ATTALA	2,120	63	2,049	8	1,986 D	3.0%	96.7%	3.0%	97.0%
BENTON	959	24	935		911 D	2.5%	97.5%	2.5%	97.5%
BOLIVAR	3,209	234	2,974	1	2,740 D	7.3%	92.7%	7.3%	92.7%
CALHOUN	2,032	74	1,958		1,884 D	3.6%	96.4%	3.6%	96.4%
CARROLL	1,446	38	1,408		1,370 D	2.6%	97.4%	2.6%	97.4%
CHICKASAW	1,823	58	1,764	1	1,706 D	3.2%	96.8%	3.2%	96.8%
CHOCTAW	1,278	66	1,212		1,146 D	5.2%	94.8%	5.2%	94.8%
CLAIBORNE	779	32	737	10	705 D	4.1%	94.6%	4.2%	95.8%
CLARKE	1,753	42	1,711		1,669 D	2.4%	97.6%	2.4%	97.6%
CLAY	1,336	103	1,232	1	1,129 D	7.7%	92.2%	7.7%	92.3%
COAHOMA	2,577	137	2,440		2,303 D	5.3%	94.7%	5.3%	94.7%
COPIAH	2,384	49	2,335		2,286 D	2.1%	97.9%	2.1%	97.9%
COVINGTON	1,471	52	1,419		1,367 D	3.5%	96.5%	3.5%	96.5%
DE SOTO	1,535	40	1,491	4	1,451 D	2.6%	97.1%	2.6%	97.4%
FORREST	3,313	228	3,075	10	2,847 D	6.9%	92.8%	6.9%	93.1%
FRANKLIN	1,405	29	1,376		1,347 D	2.1%	97.9%	2.1%	97.9%
GEORGE	983	38	945		907 D	3.9%	96.1%	3.9%	96.1%
GREENE	992	66	926		860 D	6.7%	93.3%	6.7%	93.3%
GRENADA	1,425	62	1,354	9	1,292 D	4.4%	95.0%	4.4%	95.6%
HANCOCK	1,748	197	1,550	1	1,353 D	11.3%	88.7%	11.3%	88.7%
HARRISON	6,214	633	5,577	4	4,944 D	10.2%	89.7%	10.2%	89.8%
HINDS	10,459	538	9,917	4	9,379 D	5.1%	94.8%	5.1%	94.9%
HOLMES	2,078	37	2,041		2,004 D	1.8%	98.2%	1.8%	98.2%
HUMPHREYS	1,081	20	1,061		1,041 D	1.9%	98.1%	1.9%	98.1%
ISSAQUENA	227	9	218		209 D	4.0%	96.0%	4.0%	96.0%
ITAWAMBA	1,758	119	1,627	12	1,508 D	6.8%	92.5%	6.8%	93.2%
JACKSON	2,300	171	2,124	5	1,953 D	7.4%	92.3%	7.5%	92.5%
JASPER	1,748	35	1,713		1,678 D	2.0%	98.0%	2.0%	98.0%
JEFFERSON	808	7	801		794 D	0.9%	99.1%	0.9%	99.1%
JEFFERSON DAVIS	1,330	38	1,289	3	1,251 D	2.9%	96.9%	2.9%	97.1%
JONES	4,759	242	4,517		4,275 D	5.1%	94.9%	5.1%	94.9%
KEMPER	1,464	42	1,422		1,380 D	2.9%	97.1%	2.9%	97.1%
LAFAYETTE	2,255	65	2,188	2	2,123 D	2.9%	97.0%	2.9%	97.1%
LAMAR	1,203	55	1,148		1,093 D	4.6%	95.4%	4.6%	95.4%
LAUDERDALE	6,246	303	5,936	7	5,633 D	4.9%	95.0%	4.9%	95.1%
LAWRENCE	1,255	37	1,218		1,181 D	2.9%	97.1%	2.9%	97.1%
LEAKE	2,823	17	2,802	4	2,785 D	0.6%	99.3%	0.6%	99.4%
LEE	3,935	120	3,814	1	3,694 D	3.1%	96.9%	3.1%	96.9%
LEFLORE	2,515	111	2,404		2,293 D	4.4%	95.6%	4.4%	95.6%
LINCOLN	2,440	97	2,332	11	2,235 D	4.0%	95.6%	4.0%	96.0%
LOWNDES	2,418	147	2,268	3	2,121 D	6.1%	93.8%	6.1%	93.9%
MADISON	2,104	66	2,038		1,972 D	3.1%	96.9%	3.1%	96.9%
MARION	2,128	45	2,083		2,038 D	2.1%	97.9%	2.1%	97.9%
MARSHALL	1,451	48	1,403		1,355 D	3.3%	96.7%	3.3%	96.7%
MONROE	3,360	94	3,263	3	3,169 D	2.8%	97.1%	2.8%	97.2%
MONTGOMERY	1,554	44	1,509	1	1,465 D	2.8%	97.1%	2.8%	97.2%
NESHOBA	2,967	77	2,880	10	2,803 D	2.6%	97.1%	2.6%	97.4%
NEWTON	2,539	41	2,495	3	2,454 D	1.6%	98.3%	1.6%	98.4%
NOXUBEE	1,203	51	1,152		1,101 D	4.2%	95.8%	4.2%	95.8%
OKTIBBEHA	2,044	79	1,951	14	1,872 D	3.9%	95.5%	3.9%	95.8%
PANOLA	2,034	45	1,988		1,943 D	2.2%	97.7%	2.2%	97.8%
PEARL RIVER	2,118	88	2,022	8	1,934 D	4.2%	95.5%	4.2%	95.8%
PERRY	846	18	828		810 D	2.1%	97.9%	2.1%	97.9%
PIKE	3,147	185	2,956	6	2,771 D	5.9%	93.9%	5.9%	94.1%
PONTOTOC	2,244	70	2,171	3	2,101 D	3.1%	96.7%	3.1%	96.9%
PRENTISS	2,235	118	2,117		1,999 D	5.3%	94.7%	5.3%	94.7%
QUITMAN	1,182	29	1,152	1	1,123 D	2.5%	97.5%	2.5%	97.5%

MISSISSIPPI

PRESIDENT 1936

County	Total Vote	Republican	Democratic	Other	Rep.-Dem. Plurality	Total Vote Rep.	Total Vote Dem.	Major Vote Rep.	Major Vote Dem.
RANKIN	1,941	54	1,884	3	1,830 D	2.8%	97.1%	2.8%	97.2%
SCOTT	2,131	33	2,097	1	2,064 D	1.5%	98.4%	1.5%	98.5%
SHARKEY	574	7	567		560 D	1.2%	98.8%	1.2%	98.8%
SIMPSON	2,494	48	2,445	1	2,397 D	1.9%	98.0%	1.9%	98.1%
SMITH	1,694	17	1,676	1	1,659 D	1.0%	98.9%	1.0%	99.0%
STONE	700	23	675	2	652 D	3.3%	96.4%	3.3%	96.7%
SUNFLOWER	2,529	21	2,508		2,487 D	0.8%	99.2%	0.8%	99.2%
TALLAHATCHIE	1,572	4	1,567	1	1,563 D	0.3%	99.7%	0.3%	99.7%
TATE	1,095	7	1,088		1,081 D	0.6%	99.4%	0.6%	99.4%
TIPPAH	1,644	19	1,625		1,606 D	1.2%	98.8%	1.2%	98.8%
TISHOMINGO	1,744	115	1,619	10	1,504 D	6.6%	92.8%	6.6%	93.4%
TUNICA	706	5	701		696 D	0.7%	99.3%	0.7%	99.3%
UNION	2,316	63	2,249	4	2,186 D	2.7%	97.1%	2.7%	97.3%
WALTHALL	1,263	28	1,234	1	1,206 D	2.2%	97.7%	2.2%	97.8%
WARREN	3,361	122	3,233	6	3,111 D	3.6%	96.2%	3.6%	96.4%
WASHINGTON	2,241	94	2,143	4	2,049 D	4.2%	95.6%	4.2%	95.8%
WAYNE	1,412	44	1,367	1	1,323 D	3.1%	96.8%	3.1%	96.9%
WEBSTER	1,507	56	1,439	12	1,383 D	3.7%	95.5%	3.7%	96.3%
WILKINSON	790	21	767	2	746 D	2.7%	97.1%	2.7%	97.3%
WINSTON	2,440	21	2,418	1	2,397 D	0.9%	99.1%	0.9%	99.1%
YALOBUSHA	1,377	25	1,350	2	1,325 D	1.8%	98.0%	1.8%	98.2%
YAZOO	2,161	17	2,141	3	2,124 D	0.8%	99.1%	0.8%	99.2%
TOTAL	162,142	4,467	157,333	342	152,866 D	2.8%	97.0%	2.8%	97.2%

PRESIDENT 1940

County	Total Vote	Republican	Democratic	Other	Rep.-Dem. Plurality	Total Vote Rep.	Total Vote Dem.	Major Vote Rep.	Major Vote Dem.
RANKIN	2,151	35	2,110	6	2,075 D	1.6%	98.1%	1.6%	98.4%
SCOTT	2,407	30	2,377		2,347 D	1.2%	98.8%	1.2%	98.8%
SHARKEY	765	18	747		729 D	2.4%	97.6%	2.4%	97.6%
SIMPSON	2,357	40	2,316	1	2,276 D	1.7%	98.3%	1.7%	98.3%
SMITH	1,854	27	1,826	1	1,799 D	1.5%	98.5%	1.5%	98.5%
STONE	830	28	802		774 D	3.4%	96.6%	3.4%	96.6%
SUNFLOWER	3,142	71	3,071		3,000 D	2.3%	97.7%	2.3%	97.7%
TALLAHATCHIE	2,328	33	2,288	7	2,255 D	1.4%	98.3%	1.4%	98.6%
TATE	1,612	3	1,609		1,606 D	0.2%	99.8%	0.2%	99.8%
TIPPAH	2,311	63	2,248		2,185 D	2.7%	97.3%	2.7%	97.3%
TISHOMINGO	1,630	159	1,463	8	1,304 D	9.8%	89.8%	9.8%	90.2%
TUNICA	808	13	795		782 D	1.6%	98.4%	1.6%	98.4%
UNION	2,726	108	2,609	9	2,501 D	4.0%	95.7%	4.0%	96.0%
WALTHALL	1,247	40	1,206	1	1,166 D	3.2%	96.7%	3.2%	96.8%
WARREN	3,241	192	3,048	1	2,856 D	5.9%	94.0%	5.9%	94.1%
WASHINGTON	2,642	292	2,349	1	2,057 D	11.1%	88.9%	11.1%	88.9%
WAYNE	1,410	22	1,388		1,366 D	1.6%	98.4%	1.6%	98.4%
WEBSTER	1,687	87	1,595	5	1,508 D	5.2%	94.5%	5.2%	94.8%
WILKINSON	988	46	942		896 D	4.7%	95.3%	4.7%	95.3%
WINSTON	2,005	26	1,979		1,953 D	1.3%	98.7%	1.3%	98.7%
YALOBUSHA	1,605	50	1,555		1,505 D	3.1%	96.9%	3.1%	96.9%
YAZOO	2,435	45	2,390		2,345 D	1.8%	98.2%	1.8%	98.2%
TOTAL	175,824	7,364	168,267	193	160,903 D	4.2%	95.7%	4.2%	95.8%

MISSISSIPPI

PRESIDENT 1944

County	Total Vote	Republican	Democratic	Other	Rep.-Dem. Plurality	Total Vote % Rep.	Total Vote % Dem.	Major Vote % Rep.	Major Vote % Dem.
ADAMS	1,920	282	1,638		1,356 D	14.7%	85.3%	14.7%	85.3%
ALCORN	2,875	206	2,669		2,463 D	7.2%	92.8%	7.2%	92.8%
AMITE	1,513	87	1,426		1,339 D	5.8%	94.2%	5.8%	94.2%
ATTALA	2,274	87	2,187		2,100 D	3.8%	96.2%	3.8%	96.2%
BENTON	894	42	852		810 D	4.7%	95.3%	4.7%	95.3%
BOLIVAR	2,822	378	2,444		2,066 D	13.4%	86.6%	13.4%	86.6%
CALHOUN	2,169	97	2,072		1,975 D	4.5%	95.5%	4.5%	95.5%
CARROLL	1,506	68	1,438		1,370 D	4.5%	95.5%	4.5%	95.5%
CHICKASAW	2,115	180	1,935		1,755 D	8.5%	91.5%	8.5%	91.5%
CHOCTAW	1,195	76	1,119		1,043 D	6.4%	93.6%	6.4%	93.6%
CLAIBORNE	755	45	710		665 D	6.0%	94.0%	6.0%	94.0%
CLARKE	1,789	95	1,694		1,599 D	5.3%	94.7%	5.3%	94.7%
CLAY	1,267	109	1,158		1,049 D	8.6%	91.4%	8.6%	91.4%
COAHOMA	2,583	191	2,392		2,201 D	7.4%	92.6%	7.4%	92.6%
COPIAH	2,494	85	2,409		2,324 D	3.4%	96.6%	3.4%	96.6%
COVINGTON	1,730	58	1,672		1,614 D	3.4%	96.6%	3.4%	96.6%
DE SOTO	1,684	123	1,561		1,438 D	7.3%	92.7%	7.3%	92.7%
FORREST	4,085	436	3,649		3,213 D	10.7%	89.3%	10.7%	89.3%
FRANKLIN	1,260	49	1,211		1,162 D	3.9%	96.1%	3.9%	96.1%
GEORGE	1,143	92	1,051		959 D	8.0%	92.0%	8.0%	92.0%
GREENE	1,016	109	907		798 D	10.7%	89.3%	10.7%	89.3%
GRENADA	1,490	117	1,373		1,256 D	7.9%	92.1%	7.9%	92.1%
HANCOCK	1,779	137	1,642		1,505 D	7.7%	92.3%	7.7%	92.3%
HARRISON	6,598	622	5,976		5,354 D	9.4%	90.6%	9.4%	90.6%
HINDS	11,428	962	10,466		9,504 D	8.4%	91.6%	8.4%	91.6%
HOLMES	2,076	122	1,954		1,832 D	5.9%	94.1%	5.9%	94.1%
HUMPHREYS	1,185	35	1,150		1,115 D	3.0%	97.0%	3.0%	97.0%
ISSAQUENA	220	5	215		210 D	2.3%	97.7%	2.3%	97.7%
ITAWAMBA	1,533	183	1,350		1,167 D	11.9%	88.1%	11.9%	88.1%
JACKSON	2,849	213	2,636		2,423 D	7.5%	92.5%	7.5%	92.5%
JASPER	1,714	47	1,667		1,620 D	2.7%	97.3%	2.7%	97.3%
JEFFERSON	791	25	766		741 D	3.2%	96.8%	3.2%	96.8%
JEFFERSON DAVIS	1,460	88	1,372		1,284 D	6.0%	94.0%	6.0%	94.0%
JONES	5,119	337	4,782		4,445 D	6.6%	93.4%	6.6%	93.4%
KEMPER	1,382	37	1,345		1,308 D	2.7%	97.3%	2.7%	97.3%
LAFAYETTE	2,235	87	2,148		2,061 D	3.9%	96.1%	3.9%	96.1%
LAMAR	1,158	93	1,065		972 D	8.0%	92.0%	8.0%	92.0%
LAUDERDALE	6,415	379	6,036		5,657 D	5.9%	94.1%	5.9%	94.1%
LAWRENCE	1,580	45	1,535		1,490 D	2.8%	97.2%	2.8%	97.2%
LEAKE	2,824	24	2,800		2,776 D	0.8%	99.2%	0.8%	99.2%
LEE	3,739	230	3,509		3,279 D	6.2%	93.8%	6.2%	93.8%
LEFLORE	2,599	200	2,399		2,199 D	7.7%	92.3%	7.7%	92.3%
LINCOLN	2,548	103	2,445		2,342 D	4.0%	96.0%	4.0%	96.0%
LOWNDES	2,576	360	2,216		1,856 D	14.0%	86.0%	14.0%	86.0%
MADISON	2,025	104	1,921		1,817 D	5.1%	94.9%	5.1%	94.9%
MARION	2,495	54	2,441		2,387 D	2.2%	97.8%	2.2%	97.8%
MARSHALL	1,504	63	1,441		1,378 D	4.2%	95.8%	4.2%	95.8%
MONROE	3,263	159	3,104		2,945 D	4.9%	95.1%	4.9%	95.1%
MONTGOMERY	1,445	74	1,371		1,297 D	5.1%	94.9%	5.1%	94.9%
NESHOBA	3,156	131	3,025		2,894 D	4.2%	95.8%	4.2%	95.8%
NEWTON	2,572	56	2,516		2,460 D	2.2%	97.8%	2.2%	97.8%
NOXUBEE	1,097	103	994		891 D	9.4%	90.6%	9.4%	90.6%
OKTIBBEHA	2,058	110	1,948		1,838 D	5.3%	94.7%	5.3%	94.7%
PANOLA	2,021	90	1,931		1,841 D	4.5%	95.5%	4.5%	95.5%
PEARL RIVER	2,215	84	2,131		2,047 D	3.8%	96.2%	3.8%	96.2%
PERRY	840	44	796		752 D	5.2%	94.8%	5.2%	94.8%
PIKE	3,220	248	2,972		2,724 D	7.7%	92.3%	7.7%	92.3%
PONTOTOC	1,803	87	1,716		1,629 D	4.8%	95.2%	4.8%	95.2%
PRENTISS	1,827	175	1,652		1,477 D	9.6%	90.4%	9.6%	90.4%
QUITMAN	1,165	59	1,106		1,047 D	5.1%	94.9%	5.1%	94.9%

PRESIDENT 1948

County	Total Vote	Republican	Democratic	Other	Rep.-Dem. Plurality	Total Vote % Rep.	Total Vote % Dem.	Major Vote % Rep.	Major Vote % Dem.
ADAMS	2,200	95	71	2,034	24 R	4.3%	3.2%	57.2%	42.8%
ALCORN	3,091	91	1,013	1,987	922 D	2.9%	32.8%	8.2%	91.8%
AMITE	1,631	17	55	1,559	38 D	1.0%	3.4%	23.6%	76.4%
ATTALA	2,467	32	130	2,305	98 D	1.3%	5.3%	19.8%	80.2%
BENTON	810	11	118	681	107 D	1.4%	14.6%	8.5%	91.5%
BOLIVAR	2,914	115	219	2,580	104 D	3.9%	7.5%	34.4%	65.6%
CALHOUN	1,898	36	786	1,076	750 D	1.9%	41.4%	4.4%	95.6%
CARROLL	1,226	14	74	1,138	60 D	1.1%	6.0%	15.9%	84.1%
CHICKASAW	1,954	12	115	1,827	103 D	0.6%	5.9%	9.4%	90.6%
CHOCTAW	1,286	43	131	1,112	88 D	3.3%	10.2%	24.7%	75.3%
CLAIBORNE	775	14	19	742	5 D	1.8%	2.5%	42.4%	57.6%
CLARKE	1,928	17	144	1,767	127 D	0.9%	7.5%	10.6%	89.4%
CLAY	1,686	22	59	1,605	37 D	1.3%	3.5%	27.2%	72.8%
COAHOMA	2,319	113	246	1,960	133 D	4.9%	10.6%	31.5%	68.5%
COPIAH	2,631	19	89	2,523	70 D	0.7%	3.4%	17.6%	82.4%
COVINGTON	1,687	16	135	1,536	119 D	0.9%	8.0%	10.6%	89.4%
DE SOTO	1,450	14	137	1,299	123 D	1.0%	9.4%	9.3%	90.7%
FORREST	5,880	167	406	5,307	239 D	2.8%	6.9%	29.1%	70.9%
FRANKLIN	1,227	12	55	1,160	43 D	1.0%	4.5%	17.9%	82.1%
GEORGE	1,166	25	108	1,033	83 D	2.1%	9.3%	18.8%	81.2%
GREENE	1,018	14	118	886	104 D	1.4%	11.6%	10.6%	89.4%
GRENADA	1,541	26	109	1,406	83 D	1.7%	7.1%	19.3%	80.7%
HANCOCK	1,775	151	222	1,402	71 D	8.5%	12.5%	40.5%	59.5%
HARRISON	7,458	415	692	6,351	277 D	5.6%	9.3%	37.5%	62.5%
HINDS	15,255	492	1,041	13,722	549 D	3.2%	6.8%	32.1%	67.9%
HOLMES	2,224	24	61	2,139	37 D	1.1%	2.7%	28.2%	71.8%
HUMPHREYS	1,144	11	17	1,116	6 D	1.0%	1.5%	39.3%	60.7%
ISSAQUENA	225	5	11	209	6 D	2.2%	4.9%	31.2%	68.8%
ITAWAMBA	1,735	50	634	1,051	584 D	2.9%	36.5%	7.3%	92.7%
JACKSON	3,713	238	783	2,692	545 D	6.4%	21.1%	23.3%	76.7%
JASPER	1,942	26	121	1,795	95 D	1.3%	6.2%	17.7%	82.3%
JEFFERSON	996	14	15	967	1 D	1.4%	1.5%	48.3%	51.7%
JEFFERSON DAVIS	1,544	51	41	1,452	10 R	3.3%	2.7%	55.4%	44.6%
JONES	6,528	193	599	5,736	406 D	3.0%	9.2%	24.4%	75.6%
KEMPER	1,517	29	98	1,390	69 D	1.9%	6.5%	22.8%	77.2%
LAFAYETTE	1,980	48	744	1,188	696 D	2.4%	37.6%	6.1%	93.9%
LAMAR	1,469	36	91	1,342	55 D	2.5%	6.2%	28.3%	71.7%
LAUDERDALE	6,079	171	578	5,330	407 D	2.8%	9.5%	22.8%	77.2%
LAWRENCE	1,341	13	66	1,262	53 D	1.0%	4.9%	16.5%	83.5%
LEAKE	2,584	12	180	2,392	168 D	0.5%	7.0%	6.2%	93.8%
LEE	3,846	82	636	3,128	554 D	2.1%	16.5%	11.4%	88.6%
LEFLORE	2,973	80	139	2,754	59 D	2.7%	4.7%	36.5%	63.5%
LINCOLN	3,177	40	52	3,085	12 D	1.3%	1.6%	43.5%	56.5%
LOWNDES	2,937	66	116	2,755	50 D	2.2%	3.9%	36.3%	63.7%
MADISON	1,965	51	81	1,833	30 D	2.6%	4.1%	38.6%	61.4%
MARION	2,745	49	205	2,491	156 D	1.8%	7.5%	19.3%	80.7%
MARSHALL	1,397	29	152	1,216	123 D	2.1%	10.9%	16.0%	84.0%
MONROE	2,959	54	624	2,281	570 D	1.8%	21.1%	8.0%	92.0%
MONTGOMERY	1,714	35	105	1,574	70 D	2.0%	6.1%	25.0%	75.0%
NESHOBA	3,130	33	260	2,837	227 D	1.1%	8.3%	11.3%	88.7%
NEWTON	2,650	39	169	2,442	130 D	1.5%	6.4%	18.8%	81.2%
NOXUBEE	1,122	17	74	1,031	57 D	1.5%	6.6%	18.7%	81.3%
OKTIBBEHA	2,004	58	158	1,788	100 D	2.9%	7.9%	26.9%	73.1%
PANOLA	2,170	38	195	1,937	157 D	1.8%	9.0%	16.3%	83.7%
PEARL RIVER	2,121	46	146	1,929	100 D	2.2%	6.9%	24.0%	76.0%
PERRY	877	25	87	765	62 D	2.9%	9.9%	22.3%	77.7%
PIKE	3,940	69	221	3,650	152 D	1.8%	5.6%	23.8%	76.2%
PONTOTOC	1,915	28	348	1,539	320 D	1.5%	18.2%	7.4%	92.6%
PRENTISS	1,665	74	602	989	528 D	4.4%	36.2%	10.9%	89.1%
QUITMAN	1,160	21	91	1,048	70 D	1.8%	7.8%	18.8%	81.2%

MISSISSIPPI

PRESIDENT 1944

County	Total Vote	Republican	Democratic	Other	Rep.-Dem. Plurality	Total Vote Rep.	Total Vote Dem.	Major Vote Rep.	Major Vote Dem.
RANKIN	2,472	98	2,374		2,276 D	4.0%	96.0%	4.0%	96.0%
SCOTT	2,225	60	2,165		2,105 D	2.7%	97.3%	2.7%	97.3%
SHARKEY	722	24	698		674 D	3.3%	96.7%	3.3%	96.7%
SIMPSON	2,548	78	2,470		2,392 D	3.1%	96.9%	3.1%	96.9%
SMITH	2,621	165	2,456		2,291 D	6.3%	93.7%	6.3%	93.7%
STONE	1,032	43	989		946 D	4.2%	95.8%	4.2%	95.8%
SUNFLOWER	2,954	155	2,799		2,644 D	5.2%	94.8%	5.2%	94.8%
TALLAHATCHIE	2,441	40	2,401		2,361 D	1.6%	98.4%	1.6%	98.4%
TATE	1,484	29	1,455		1,426 D	2.0%	98.0%	2.0%	98.0%
TIPPAH	2,665	126	2,539		2,413 D	4.7%	95.3%	4.7%	95.3%
TISHOMINGO	1,708	296	1,412		1,116 D	17.3%	82.7%	17.3%	82.7%
TUNICA	756	35	721		686 D	4.6%	95.4%	4.6%	95.4%
UNION	2,323	183	2,140		1,957 D	7.9%	92.1%	7.9%	92.1%
WALTHALL	1,298	68	1,230		1,162 D	5.2%	94.8%	5.2%	94.8%
WARREN	3,506	304	3,202		2,898 D	8.7%	91.3%	8.7%	91.3%
WASHINGTON	2,466	454	2,012		1,558 D	18.4%	81.6%	18.4%	81.6%
WAYNE	1,415	35	1,380		1,345 D	2.5%	97.5%	2.5%	97.5%
WEBSTER	1,631	127	1,504		1,377 D	7.8%	92.2%	7.8%	92.2%
WILKINSON	943	80	863		783 D	8.5%	91.5%	8.5%	91.5%
WINSTON	1,873	51	1,822		1,771 D	2.7%	97.3%	2.7%	97.3%
YALOBUSHA	1,679	97	1,582		1,485 D	5.8%	94.2%	5.8%	94.2%
YAZOO	2,379	78	2,301		2,223 D	3.3%	96.7%	3.3%	96.7%
TOTAL	180,234	11,613	168,621		157,008 D	6.4%	93.6%	6.4%	93.6%

PRESIDENT 1948

County	Total Vote	Republican	Democratic	Other	Rep.-Dem. Plurality	Total Vote Rep.	Total Vote Dem.	Major Vote Rep.	Major Vote Dem.
RANKIN	2,759	23	57	2,679	34 D	0.8%	2.1%	28.8%	71.2%
SCOTT	2,526	15	170	2,341	155 D	0.6%	6.7%	8.1%	91.9%
SHARKEY	778	10	23	745	13 D	1.3%	3.0%	30.3%	69.7%
SIMPSON	2,572	59	171	2,342	112 D	2.3%	6.6%	25.7%	74.3%
SMITH	2,229	33	295	1,901	262 D	1.5%	13.2%	10.1%	89.9%
STONE	1,123	17	50	1,056	33 D	1.5%	4.5%	25.4%	74.6%
SUNFLOWER	2,673	55	136	2,482	81 D	2.1%	5.1%	28.8%	71.2%
TALLAHATCHIE	2,446	37	287	2,122	250 D	1.5%	11.7%	11.4%	88.6%
TATE	1,412	16	199	1,197	183 D	1.1%	14.1%	7.4%	92.6%
TIPPAH	2,152	66	425	1,661	359 D	3.1%	19.7%	13.4%	86.6%
TISHOMINGO	1,884	98	711	1,075	613 D	5.2%	37.7%	12.1%	87.9%
TUNICA	750	12	23	715	11 D	1.6%	3.1%	34.3%	65.7%
UNION	1,964	63	478	1,423	415 D	3.2%	24.3%	11.6%	88.4%
WALTHALL	1,292	5	85	1,202	80 D	0.4%	6.6%	5.6%	94.4%
WARREN	4,170	245	320	3,605	75 D	5.9%	7.7%	43.4%	56.6%
WASHINGTON	2,979	271	260	2,448	11 R	9.1%	8.7%	51.0%	49.0%
WAYNE	1,376	4	137	1,235	133 D	0.3%	10.0%	2.8%	97.2%
WEBSTER	1,404	47	277	1,080	230 D	3.4%	19.7%	14.5%	85.5%
WILKINSON	874	21	43	810	22 D	2.4%	4.9%	32.8%	67.2%
WINSTON	2,105	33	240	1,832	207 D	1.6%	11.4%	12.1%	87.9%
YALOBUSHA	1,568	49	135	1,384	86 D	3.1%	8.6%	26.6%	73.4%
YAZOO	2,393	26	70	2,297	44 D	1.1%	2.9%	27.1%	72.9%
TOTAL	192,190	5,043	19,384	167,763	14,341 D	2.6%	10.1%	20.6%	79.4%

MISSISSIPPI

PRESIDENT 1952

County	Total Vote	Republican	Democratic	Other	Rep.-Dem. Plurality	TV Rep.	TV Dem.	Major Rep.	Major Dem.
ADAMS	4,069	2,372	1,697		675 R	58.3%	41.7%	58.3%	41.7%
ALCORN	4,430	1,155	3,275		2,120 D	26.1%	73.9%	26.1%	73.9%
AMITE	1,898	777	1,121		344 D	40.9%	59.1%	40.9%	59.1%
ATTALA	3,436	1,178	2,258		1,080 D	34.3%	65.7%	34.3%	65.7%
BENTON	1,179	216	963		747 D	18.3%	81.7%	18.3%	81.7%
BOLIVAR	3,939	2,096	1,843		253 R	53.2%	46.8%	53.2%	46.8%
CALHOUN	2,975	691	2,284		1,593 D	23.2%	76.8%	23.2%	76.8%
CARROLL	1,703	535	1,168		633 D	31.4%	68.6%	31.4%	68.6%
CHICKASAW	2,490	685	1,805		1,120 D	27.5%	72.5%	27.5%	72.5%
CHOCTAW	1,911	524	1,387		863 D	27.4%	72.6%	27.4%	72.6%
CLAIBORNE	1,056	560	496		64 R	53.0%	47.0%	53.0%	47.0%
CLARKE	2,754	754	2,000		1,246 D	27.4%	72.6%	27.4%	72.6%
CLAY	2,307	1,077	1,230		153 D	46.7%	53.3%	46.7%	53.3%
COAHOMA	3,734	1,619	2,115		496 D	43.4%	56.6%	43.4%	56.6%
COPIAH	3,577	1,527	2,050		523 D	42.7%	57.3%	42.7%	57.3%
COVINGTON	2,305	770	1,535		765 D	33.4%	66.6%	33.4%	66.6%
DE SOTO	2,042	754	1,288		534 D	36.9%	63.1%	36.9%	63.1%
FORREST	7,416	4,480	2,936		1,544 R	60.4%	39.6%	60.4%	39.6%
FRANKLIN	1,680	514	1,166		652 D	30.6%	69.4%	30.6%	69.4%
GEORGE	1,954	603	1,351		748 D	30.9%	69.1%	30.9%	69.1%
GREENE	1,753	506	1,247		741 D	28.9%	71.1%	28.9%	71.1%
GRENADA	2,174	1,000	1,174		174 D	46.0%	54.0%	46.0%	54.0%
HANCOCK	2,925	1,347	1,578		231 D	46.1%	53.9%	46.1%	53.9%
HARRISON	13,141	5,960	7,181		1,221 D	45.4%	54.6%	45.4%	54.6%
HINDS	23,453	12,520	10,933		1,587 R	53.4%	46.6%	53.4%	46.6%
HOLMES	2,728	1,305	1,423		118 D	47.8%	52.2%	47.8%	52.2%
HUMPHREYS	1,447	589	858		269 D	40.7%	59.3%	40.7%	59.3%
ISSAQUENA	297	127	170		43 D	42.8%	57.2%	42.8%	57.2%
ITAWAMBA	2,792	556	2,236		1,680 D	19.9%	80.1%	19.9%	80.1%
JACKSON	6,316	2,170	4,146		1,976 D	34.4%	65.6%	34.4%	65.6%
JASPER	2,540	668	1,872		1,204 D	26.3%	73.7%	26.3%	73.7%
JEFFERSON	1,149	610	539		71 R	53.1%	46.9%	53.1%	46.9%
JEFFERSON DAVIS	2,099	473	1,626		1,153 D	22.5%	77.5%	22.5%	77.5%
JONES	9,923	4,039	5,884		1,845 D	40.7%	59.3%	40.7%	59.3%
KEMPER	1,965	372	1,593		1,221 D	18.9%	81.1%	18.9%	81.1%
LAFAYETTE	3,231	868	2,363		1,495 D	26.9%	73.1%	26.9%	73.1%
LAMAR	2,294	1,034	1,260		226 D	45.1%	54.9%	45.1%	54.9%
LAUDERDALE	9,978	4,137	5,841		1,704 D	41.5%	58.5%	41.5%	58.5%
LAWRENCE	1,673	556	1,117		561 D	33.2%	66.8%	33.2%	66.8%
LEAKE	3,270	603	2,667		2,064 D	18.4%	81.6%	18.4%	81.6%
LEE	6,176	2,002	4,174		2,172 D	32.4%	67.6%	32.4%	67.6%
LEFLORE	4,279	2,434	1,845		589 R	56.9%	43.1%	56.9%	43.1%
LINCOLN	4,299	2,028	2,271		243 D	47.2%	52.8%	47.2%	52.8%
LOWNDES	4,288	2,670	1,618		1,052 R	62.3%	37.7%	62.3%	37.7%
MADISON	2,921	1,496	1,425		71 R	51.2%	48.8%	51.2%	48.8%
MARION	4,017	1,420	2,597		1,177 D	35.3%	64.7%	35.3%	64.7%
MARSHALL	2,451	604	1,847		1,243 D	24.6%	75.4%	24.6%	75.4%
MONROE	4,929	1,417	3,512		2,095 D	28.7%	71.3%	28.7%	71.3%
MONTGOMERY	2,196	840	1,356		516 D	38.3%	61.7%	38.3%	61.7%
NESHOBA	4,648	1,081	3,567		2,486 D	23.3%	76.7%	23.3%	76.7%
NEWTON	3,311	851	2,460		1,609 D	25.7%	74.3%	25.7%	74.3%
NOXUBEE	1,645	887	758		129 R	53.9%	46.1%	53.9%	46.1%
OKTIBBEHA	3,101	1,435	1,666		231 D	46.3%	53.7%	46.3%	53.7%
PANOLA	3,079	1,032	2,047		1,015 D	33.5%	66.5%	33.5%	66.5%
PEARL RIVER	3,801	1,741	2,060		319 D	45.8%	54.2%	45.8%	54.2%
PERRY	1,293	511	782		271 D	39.5%	60.5%	39.5%	60.5%
PIKE	5,403	2,908	2,495		413 R	53.8%	46.2%	53.8%	46.2%
PONTOTOC	2,929	648	2,281		1,633 D	22.1%	77.9%	22.1%	77.9%
PRENTISS	3,403	731	2,672		1,941 D	21.5%	78.5%	21.5%	78.5%
QUITMAN	1,650	492	1,158		666 D	29.8%	70.2%	29.8%	70.2%

PRESIDENT 1956

County	Total Vote	Republican	Democratic	Other	Rep.-Dem. Plurality	TV Rep.	TV Dem.	Major Rep.	Major Dem.
ADAMS	4,094	1,664	1,279	1,151	385 R	40.6%	31.2%	56.5%	43.5%
ALCORN	4,072	827	3,143	102	2,316 D	20.3%	77.2%	20.8%	79.2%
AMITE	1,716	255	802	659	547 D	14.9%	46.7%	24.1%	75.9%
ATTALA	2,658	445	1,793	420	1,348 D	16.7%	67.5%	19.9%	80.1%
BENTON	944	108	786	50	678 D	11.4%	83.3%	12.1%	87.9%
BOLIVAR	3,511	754	1,176	1,581	422 D	21.5%	33.5%	39.1%	60.9%
CALHOUN	2,217	301	1,763	153	1,462 D	13.6%	79.5%	14.6%	85.4%
CARROLL	1,551	234	1,080	237	846 D	15.1%	69.6%	17.8%	82.2%
CHICKASAW	2,056	231	1,650	175	1,419 D	11.2%	80.3%	12.3%	87.7%
CHOCTAW	1,404	221	1,117	66	896 D	15.7%	79.6%	16.5%	83.5%
CLAIBORNE	822	191	339	292	148 D	23.2%	41.2%	36.0%	64.0%
CLARKE	2,407	500	1,763	144	1,263 D	20.8%	73.2%	22.1%	77.9%
CLAY	2,247	410	1,225	612	815 D	18.2%	54.5%	25.1%	74.9%
COAHOMA	3,299	1,082	1,677	540	595 D	32.8%	50.8%	39.2%	60.8%
COPIAH	2,304	387	1,270	647	883 D	16.8%	55.1%	23.4%	76.6%
COVINGTON	2,051	386	1,382	283	996 D	18.8%	67.4%	21.8%	78.2%
DE SOTO	1,846	398	1,236	212	838 D	21.6%	67.0%	24.4%	75.6%
FORREST	6,013	2,256	1,928	1,829	328 R	37.5%	32.1%	53.9%	46.1%
FRANKLIN	1,544	177	862	505	685 D	11.5%	55.8%	17.0%	83.0%
GEORGE	1,661	403	1,150	108	747 D	24.3%	69.2%	25.9%	74.1%
GREENE	1,229	351	734	144	383 D	28.6%	59.7%	32.4%	67.6%
GRENADA	2,188	407	949	832	542 D	18.6%	43.4%	30.0%	70.0%
HANCOCK	2,674	1,421	1,179	74	242 R	53.1%	44.1%	54.7%	45.3%
HARRISON	13,001	5,742	6,549	710	807 D	44.2%	50.4%	46.7%	53.3%
HINDS	20,278	7,015	7,104	6,159	89 D	34.6%	35.0%	49.7%	50.3%
HOLMES	2,139	215	872	1,052	657 D	10.1%	40.8%	19.8%	80.2%
HUMPHREYS	1,294	127	576	591	449 D	9.8%	44.5%	18.1%	81.9%
ISSAQUENA	289	42	172	75	130 D	14.5%	59.5%	19.6%	80.4%
ITAWAMBA	2,665	298	2,310	57	2,012 D	11.2%	86.7%	11.4%	88.6%
JACKSON	6,906	2,692	3,882	332	1,190 D	39.0%	56.2%	40.9%	59.1%
JASPER	2,445	287	1,958	200	1,671 D	11.7%	80.1%	12.8%	87.2%
JEFFERSON	962	189	440	333	251 D	19.6%	45.7%	30.0%	70.0%
JEFFERSON DAVIS	1,429	156	1,049	224	893 D	10.9%	73.4%	12.9%	87.1%
JONES	8,263	2,463	5,137	663	2,674 D	29.8%	62.2%	32.4%	67.6%
KEMPER	1,823	173	1,586	64	1,413 D	9.5%	87.0%	9.8%	90.2%
LAFAYETTE	2,701	575	1,968	158	1,393 D	21.3%	72.9%	22.6%	77.4%
LAMAR	1,718	429	805	484	376 D	25.0%	46.9%	34.8%	65.2%
LAUDERDALE	9,127	2,817	5,414	896	2,597 D	30.9%	59.3%	34.2%	65.8%
LAWRENCE	1,519	276	1,025	218	749 D	18.2%	67.5%	21.2%	78.8%
LEAKE	2,999	220	2,475	304	2,255 D	7.3%	82.5%	8.2%	91.8%
LEE	5,157	929	3,883	345	2,954 D	18.0%	75.3%	19.3%	80.7%
LEFLORE	3,588	887	1,769	932	882 D	24.7%	49.3%	33.4%	66.6%
LINCOLN	3,773	848	1,942	983	1,094 D	22.5%	51.5%	30.4%	69.6%
LOWNDES	4,126	1,205	2,308	613	1,103 D	29.2%	55.9%	34.3%	65.7%
MADISON	2,395	377	996	1,022	619 D	15.7%	41.6%	27.5%	72.5%
MARION	3,032	611	1,751	670	1,140 D	20.2%	57.8%	25.9%	74.1%
MARSHALL	1,694	287	1,192	215	905 D	16.9%	70.4%	19.4%	80.6%
MONROE	4,624	705	3,630	289	2,925 D	15.2%	78.5%	16.3%	83.7%
MONTGOMERY	1,779	278	1,134	367	856 D	15.6%	63.7%	19.7%	80.3%
NESHOBA	3,629	502	2,827	300	2,325 D	13.8%	77.9%	15.1%	84.9%
NEWTON	3,126	360	2,359	407	1,999 D	11.5%	75.5%	13.2%	86.8%
NOXUBEE	1,320	257	690	373	433 D	19.5%	52.3%	27.1%	72.9%
OKTIBBEHA	2,640	702	1,552	386	850 D	26.6%	58.8%	31.1%	68.9%
PANOLA	2,631	519	1,741	371	1,222 D	19.7%	66.2%	23.0%	77.0%
PEARL RIVER	2,848	1,129	1,274	445	145 D	39.6%	44.7%	47.0%	53.0%
PERRY	1,100	347	581	172	234 D	31.5%	52.8%	37.4%	62.6%
PIKE	4,106	1,210	1,714	1,182	504 D	29.5%	41.7%	41.4%	58.6%
PONTOTOC	2,812	335	2,320	157	1,985 D	11.9%	82.5%	12.6%	87.4%
PRENTISS	2,399	383	1,942	74	1,559 D	16.0%	81.0%	16.5%	83.5%
QUITMAN	1,499	276	954	269	678 D	18.4%	63.6%	22.4%	77.6%

MISSISSIPPI

PRESIDENT 1952

County	Total Vote	Republican	Democratic	Other	Rep.-Dem. Plurality	Percentage Total Vote Rep.	Dem.	Major Vote Rep.	Dem.
RANKIN	3,622	1,545	2,077		532 D	42.7%	57.3%	42.7%	57.3%
SCOTT	3,331	1,123	2,208		1,085 D	33.7%	66.3%	33.7%	66.3%
SHARKEY	988	600	388		212 R	60.7%	39.3%	60.7%	39.3%
SIMPSON	3,645	878	2,767		1,889 D	24.1%	75.9%	24.1%	75.9%
SMITH	3,026	738	2,288		1,550 D	24.4%	75.6%	24.4%	75.6%
STONE	1,534	569	965		396 D	37.1%	62.9%	37.1%	62.9%
SUNFLOWER	4,056	2,007	2,049		42 D	49.5%	50.5%	49.5%	50.5%
TALLAHATCHIE	3,098	748	2,350		1,602 D	24.1%	75.9%	24.1%	75.9%
TATE	1,962	387	1,575		1,188 D	19.7%	80.3%	19.7%	80.3%
TIPPAH	3,389	511	2,878		2,367 D	15.1%	84.9%	15.1%	84.9%
TISHOMINGO	2,274	679	1,595		916 D	29.9%	70.1%	29.9%	70.1%
TUNICA	913	383	530		147 D	41.9%	58.1%	41.9%	58.1%
UNION	3,666	917	2,749		1,832 D	25.0%	75.0%	25.0%	75.0%
WALTHALL	1,848	491	1,357		866 D	26.6%	73.4%	26.6%	73.4%
WARREN	5,824	3,458	2,366		1,092 R	59.4%	40.6%	59.4%	40.6%
WASHINGTON	5,919	3,301	2,618		683 R	55.8%	44.2%	55.8%	44.2%
WAYNE	2,321	717	1,604		887 D	30.9%	69.1%	30.9%	69.1%
WEBSTER	2,218	453	1,765		1,312 D	20.4%	79.6%	20.4%	79.6%
WILKINSON	1,262	699	563		136 R	55.4%	44.6%	55.4%	44.6%
WINSTON	3,330	771	2,559		1,788 D	23.2%	76.8%	23.2%	76.8%
YALOBUSHA	2,099	753	1,346		593 D	35.9%	64.1%	35.9%	64.1%
YAZOO	3,385	1,683	1,702		19 D	49.7%	50.3%	49.7%	50.3%
TOTAL	285,532	112,966	172,566		59,600 D	39.6%	60.4%	39.6%	60.4%

PRESIDENT 1956

County	Total Vote	Republican	Democratic	Other	Rep.-Dem. Plurality	Percentage Total Vote Rep.	Dem.	Major Vote Rep.	Dem.
RANKIN	3,089	556	1,537	996	981 D	18.0%	49.8%	26.6%	73.4%
SCOTT	3,171	503	2,077	591	1,574 D	15.9%	65.5%	19.5%	80.5%
SHARKEY	832	211	308	313	97 D	25.4%	37.0%	40.7%	59.3%
SIMPSON	3,189	467	2,140	582	1,673 D	14.6%	67.1%	17.9%	82.1%
SMITH	2,543	277	2,055	211	1,778 D	10.9%	80.8%	11.9%	88.1%
STONE	1,168	293	761	114	468 D	25.1%	65.2%	27.8%	72.2%
SUNFLOWER	3,120	520	1,585	1,015	1,065 D	16.7%	50.8%	24.7%	75.3%
TALLAHATCHIE	2,687	341	1,969	377	1,628 D	12.7%	73.3%	14.8%	85.2%
TATE	1,749	171	1,414	164	1,243 D	9.8%	80.8%	10.8%	89.2%
TIPPAH	2,955	287	2,569	99	2,282 D	9.7%	86.9%	10.0%	90.0%
TISHOMINGO	2,170	516	1,577	77	1,061 D	23.8%	72.7%	24.7%	75.3%
TUNICA	836	200	470	166	270 D	23.9%	56.2%	29.9%	70.1%
UNION	3,494	427	2,882	185	2,455 D	12.2%	82.5%	12.9%	87.1%
WALTHALL	1,725	306	1,143	276	837 D	17.7%	66.3%	21.1%	78.9%
WARREN	5,328	2,419	1,857	1,052	562 R	45.4%	34.9%	56.6%	43.4%
WASHINGTON	5,490	1,973	2,722	795	749 D	35.9%	49.6%	42.0%	58.0%
WAYNE	2,129	373	1,493	263	1,120 D	17.5%	70.1%	20.0%	80.0%
WEBSTER	1,745	188	1,412	145	1,224 D	10.8%	80.9%	11.8%	88.2%
WILKINSON	851	240	260	351	20 D	28.2%	30.6%	48.0%	52.0%
WINSTON	2,705	361	2,132	212	1,771 D	13.3%	78.8%	14.5%	85.5%
YALOBUSHA	1,696	414	1,015	267	601 D	24.4%	59.8%	29.0%	71.0%
YAZOO	3,088	370	911	1,807	541 D	12.0%	29.5%	28.9%	71.1%
TOTAL	248,104	60,685	144,453	42,966	83,768 D	24.5%	58.2%	29.6%	70.4%

MISSISSIPPI

PRESIDENT 1960

County	Total Vote	Republican	Democratic	Other	Rep.-Dem. Plurality	Total Vote Rep.	Total Vote Dem.	Major Vote Rep.	Major Vote Dem.
ADAMS	5,205	1,227	1,452	2,526	225 D	23.6%	27.9%	45.8%	54.2%
ALCORN	4,475	820	3,054	601	2,234 D	18.3%	68.2%	21.2%	78.8%
AMITE	2,276	283	338	1,655	55 D	12.4%	14.9%	45.6%	54.4%
ATTALA	3,268	650	1,337	1,281	687 D	19.9%	40.9%	32.7%	67.3%
BENTON	1,091	175	568	348	393 D	16.0%	52.1%	23.6%	76.4%
BOLIVAR	3,769	1,012	1,119	1,638	107 D	26.9%	29.7%	47.5%	52.5%
CALHOUN	2,447	383	765	1,299	382 D	15.7%	31.3%	33.4%	66.6%
CARROLL	1,472	207	425	840	218 D	14.1%	28.9%	32.8%	67.2%
CHICKASAW	2,538	385	791	1,362	406 D	15.2%	31.2%	32.7%	67.3%
CHOCTAW	1,646	245	817	584	572 D	14.9%	49.6%	23.1%	76.9%
CLAIBORNE	1,036	180	205	651	25 D	17.4%	19.8%	46.8%	53.2%
CLARKE	3,308	586	1,244	1,478	658 D	17.7%	37.6%	32.0%	68.0%
CLAY	2,372	451	626	1,295	175 D	19.0%	26.4%	41.9%	58.1%
COAHOMA	3,667	1,096	1,386	1,385	290 D	29.9%	35.8%	44.2%	55.8%
COPIAH	3,614	761	896	1,957	135 D	21.1%	24.8%	45.9%	54.1%
COVINGTON	2,198	371	842	985	471 D	16.9%	38.3%	30.6%	69.4%
DE SOTO	2,082	553	795	734	242 D	26.6%	38.2%	41.0%	59.0%
FORREST	8,632	3,412	2,068	3,152	1,344 R	39.5%	24.0%	62.3%	37.7%
FRANKLIN	1,680	124	441	1,115	317 D	7.4%	26.2%	21.9%	78.1%
GEORGE	2,071	310	844	917	534 D	15.0%	40.8%	26.9%	73.1%
GREENE	1,578	247	550	781	303 D	15.7%	34.9%	31.0%	69.0%
GRENADA	2,343	682	529	1,132	153 R	29.1%	22.6%	56.3%	43.7%
HANCOCK	3,353	719	2,132	502	1,413 D	21.4%	63.6%	25.2%	74.8%
HARRISON	16,759	5,177	8,961	2,621	3,784 D	30.9%	53.5%	36.6%	63.4%
HINDS	28,988	11,083	5,811	12,094	5,272 R	38.2%	20.0%	65.6%	34.4%
HOLMES	2,567	455	628	1,484	173 D	17.7%	24.5%	42.0%	58.0%
HUMPHREYS	1,422	231	459	732	228 D	16.2%	32.3%	33.5%	66.5%
ISSAQUENA	423	64	178	181	114 D	15.1%	42.1%	26.4%	73.6%
ITAWAMBA	2,771	366	1,752	653	1,386 D	13.2%	63.2%	17.3%	82.7%
JACKSON	9,174	2,266	5,000	1,908	2,734 D	24.7%	54.5%	31.2%	68.8%
JASPER	2,435	362	1,147	926	785 D	14.9%	47.1%	24.0%	76.0%
JEFFERSON	1,094	137	229	728	92 D	12.5%	20.9%	37.4%	62.6%
JEFFERSON DAVIS	1,723	225	510	988	285 D	13.1%	29.6%	30.6%	69.4%
JONES	10,528	2,729	4,871	2,928	2,142 D	25.9%	46.3%	35.9%	64.1%
KEMPER	1,711	193	931	587	738 D	11.3%	54.4%	17.2%	82.8%
LAFAYETTE	2,922	705	1,308	909	603 D	24.1%	44.8%	35.0%	65.0%
LAMAR	2,333	636	651	1,046	15 D	27.3%	27.9%	49.4%	50.6%
LAUDERDALE	10,745	2,836	3,755	4,154	919 D	26.4%	34.9%	43.0%	57.0%
LAWRENCE	1,651	259	469	923	210 D	15.7%	28.4%	35.6%	64.4%
LEAKE	3,250	286	953	2,011	667 D	8.8%	29.3%	23.1%	76.9%
LEE	6,641	1,550	3,653	1,438	2,103 D	23.3%	55.0%	29.8%	70.2%
LEFLORE	4,641	1,317	1,212	2,112	105 R	28.4%	26.1%	52.1%	47.9%
LINCOLN	4,885	1,251	1,449	2,185	198 D	25.6%	29.7%	46.3%	53.7%
LOWNDES	4,680	2,010	1,240	1,430	770 R	42.9%	26.5%	61.8%	38.2%
MADISON	2,861	525	753	1,583	228 D	18.4%	26.3%	41.1%	58.9%
MARION	3,045	698	1,082	1,265	384 D	22.9%	35.5%	39.2%	60.8%
MARSHALL	1,785	404	681	700	277 D	22.6%	38.2%	37.2%	52.8%
MONROE	4,860	1,400	1,901	1,559	501 D	28.8%	39.1%	42.4%	57.6%
MONTGOMERY	1,969	585	623	761	38 D	29.7%	31.6%	48.4%	51.6%
NESHOBA	4,136	580	1,840	1,716	1,260 D	14.0%	44.5%	24.0%	76.0%
NEWTON	3,376	508	912	1,956	404 D	15.0%	27.0%	35.8%	64.2%
NOXUBEE	1,489	342	277	870	65 R	23.0%	18.6%	55.3%	44.7%
OKTIBBEHA	3,416	829	915	1,672	86 D	24.3%	26.8%	47.5%	52.5%
PANOLA	2,888	643	841	1,404	198 D	22.3%	29.1%	43.3%	56.7%
PEARL RIVER	3,483	651	1,276	1,556	625 D	18.7%	36.6%	33.8%	66.2%
PERRY	1,344	274	514	556	240 D	20.4%	38.2%	34.8%	65.2%
PIKE	5,357	1,467	1,258	2,632	209 R	27.4%	23.5%	53.8%	46.3%
PONTOTOC	2,704	328	1,584	792	1,256 D	12.1%	58.6%	17.2%	82.8%
PRENTISS	2,985	740	1,777	468	1,037 D	24.8%	59.5%	29.4%	70.6%
QUITMAN	1,556	299	583	674	284 D	19.2%	37.5%	33.9%	66.1%

PRESIDENT 1964

County	Total Vote	Republican	Democratic	Other	Rep.-Dem. Plurality	Total Vote Rep.	Total Vote Dem.	Major Vote Rep.	Major Vote Dem.
ADAMS	6,993	5,900	1,093		4,807 R	84.4%	15.6%	84.4%	15.6%
ALCORN	5,294	3,377	1,917		1,460 R	63.8%	36.2%	63.8%	36.2%
AMITE	2,845	2,742	103		2,639 R	96.4%	3.6%	96.4%	3.6%
ATTALA	4,672	4,409	263		4,146 R	94.4%	5.6%	94.4%	5.6%
BENTON	1,170	934	236		698 R	79.8%	20.2%	79.8%	20.2%
BOLIVAR	5,411	4,680	731		3,949 R	86.5%	13.5%	86.5%	13.5%
CALHOUN	3,518	3,224	294		2,930 R	91.6%	8.4%	91.6%	8.4%
CARROLL	2,141	2,043	98		1,945 R	95.4%	4.6%	95.4%	4.6%
CHICKASAW	3,417	3,138	279		2,859 R	91.8%	8.2%	91.8%	8.2%
CHOCTAW	2,246	2,096	150		1,946 R	93.3%	6.7%	93.3%	6.7%
CLAIBORNE	1,310	1,226	84		1,142 R	93.6%	6.4%	93.6%	6.4%
CLARKE	3,844	3,591	253		3,338 R	93.4%	6.6%	93.4%	6.6%
CLAY	3,074	2,848	226		2,622 R	92.6%	7.4%	92.6%	7.4%
COAHOMA	5,136	4,172	964		3,208 R	81.2%	18.8%	81.2%	18.8%
COPIAH	4,745	4,506	239		4,267 R	95.0%	5.0%	95.0%	5.0%
COVINGTON	3,425	3,033	392		2,641 R	88.6%	11.4%	88.6%	11.4%
DE SOTO	3,389	2,928	461		2,467 R	86.4%	13.6%	86.4%	13.6%
FORREST	10,419	9,291	1,128		8,163 R	89.2%	10.8%	89.2%	10.8%
FRANKLIN	2,302	2,211	91		2,120 R	96.0%	4.0%	96.0%	4.0%
GEORGE	2,797	2,555	242		2,313 R	92.0%	8.0%	92.0%	8.0%
GREENE	2,061	1,845	216		1,629 R	89.5%	10.5%	89.5%	10.5%
GRENADA	3,803	3,648	155		3,493 R	95.9%	4.1%	95.9%	4.1%
HANCOCK	4,051	2,550	1,501		1,049 R	62.9%	37.1%	62.9%	37.1%
HARRISON	21,694	16,301	5,393		10,908 R	75.1%	24.9%	75.1%	24.9%
HINDS	41,889	36,831	5,058		31,773 R	87.9%	12.1%	87.9%	12.1%
HOLMES	3,225	3,115	110		3,005 R	96.6%	3.4%	96.6%	3.4%
HUMPHREYS	1,947	1,863	84		1,779 R	95.7%	4.3%	95.7%	4.3%
ISSAQUENA	490	456	34		422 R	93.1%	6.9%	93.1%	6.9%
ITAWAMBA	3,267	2,140	1,127		1,013 R	65.5%	34.5%	65.5%	34.5%
JACKSON	13,728	11,357	2,371		8,986 R	82.7%	17.3%	82.7%	17.3%
JASPER	3,230	2,994	236		2,758 R	92.7%	7.3%	92.7%	7.3%
JEFFERSON	1,327	1,258	69		1,189 R	94.8%	5.2%	94.8%	5.2%
JEFFERSON DAVIS	2,586	2,351	235		2,116 R	90.9%	9.1%	90.9%	9.1%
JONES	14,104	12,123	1,981		10,142 R	86.0%	14.0%	86.0%	14.0%
KEMPER	2,376	2,185	191		1,994 R	92.0%	8.0%	92.0%	8.0%
LAFAYETTE	3,922	3,202	720		2,482 R	81.6%	18.4%	81.6%	18.4%
LAMAR	3,706	3,372	334		3,038 R	91.0%	9.0%	91.0%	9.0%
LAUDERDALE	14,874	13,291	1,583		11,708 R	89.4%	10.6%	89.4%	10.6%
LAWRENCE	2,609	2,373	236		2,137 R	91.0%	9.0%	91.0%	9.0%
LEAKE	4,513	4,343	170		4,173 R	96.2%	3.8%	96.2%	3.8%
LEE	7,574	5,165	2,409		2,756 R	68.2%	31.8%	68.2%	31.8%
LEFLORE	5,969	5,589	380		5,209 R	93.6%	6.4%	93.6%	6.4%
LINCOLN	7,187	6,750	437		6,313 R	93.9%	6.1%	93.9%	6.1%
LOWNDES	6,668	6,135	533		5,602 R	92.0%	8.0%	92.0%	8.0%
MADISON	3,534	3,283	251		3,032 R	92.9%	7.1%	92.9%	7.1%
MARION	5,974	5,469	505		4,964 R	91.5%	8.5%	91.5%	8.5%
MARSHALL	2,592	2,250	342		1,908 R	86.8%	13.2%	86.8%	13.2%
MONROE	6,612	5,627	985		4,642 R	85.1%	14.9%	85.1%	14.9%
MONTGOMERY	3,181	3,032	149		2,883 R	95.5%	4.5%	95.5%	4.5%
NESHOBA	5,724	5,431	293		5,138 R	94.9%	5.1%	94.9%	5.1%
NEWTON	4,973	4,735	238		4,497 R	95.2%	4.8%	95.2%	4.8%
NOXUBEE	2,050	1,980	70		1,910 R	96.6%	3.4%	96.6%	3.4%
OKTIBBEHA	4,185	3,795	390		3,405 R	90.7%	9.3%	90.7%	9.3%
PANOLA	4,415	4,002	413		3,589 R	90.6%	9.4%	90.6%	9.4%
PEARL RIVER	4,744	4,009	735		3,274 R	84.5%	15.5%	84.5%	15.5%
PERRY	2,054	1,775	279		1,496 R	86.4%	13.6%	86.4%	13.6%
PIKE	6,961	6,418	543		5,875 R	92.2%	7.8%	92.2%	7.8%
PONTOTOC	3,401	2,699	702		1,997 R	79.4%	20.6%	79.4%	20.6%
PRENTISS	3,302	2,289	1,013		1,276 R	69.3%	30.7%	69.3%	30.7%
QUITMAN	2,401	2,065	336		1,729 R	86.0%	14.0%	86.0%	14.0%

MISSISSIPPI

PRESIDENT 1960

County	Total Vote	Republican	Democratic	Other	Rep.-Dem. Plurality	Percentage Total Vote Rep.	Percentage Total Vote Dem.	Percentage Major Vote Rep.	Percentage Major Vote Dem.
RANKIN	4,782	818	850	3,114	32 D	17.1%	17.8%	49.0%	51.0%
SCOTT	3,472	607	1,024	1,841	417 D	17.5%	29.5%	37.2%	62.8%
SHARKEY	1,007	313	263	431	50 R	31.1%	26.1%	54.3%	45.7%
SIMPSON	3,208	606	1,034	1,568	428 D	18.9%	32.2%	37.0%	63.0%
SMITH	2,946	353	1,568	1,025	1,215 D	12.0%	53.2%	18.4%	81.6%
STONE	1,436	275	343	818	68 D	19.2%	23.9%	44.5%	55.5%
SUNFLOWER	3,451	1,177	1,033	1,241	144 R	34.1%	29.9%	53.3%	46.7%
TALLAHATCHIE	2,597	346	830	1,421	484 D	13.3%	32.0%	29.4%	70.6%
TATE	1,772	241	686	845	445 D	13.6%	38.7%	26.0%	74.0%
TIPPAH	2,892	486	1,939	467	1,453 D	16.8%	67.0%	20.0%	80.0%
TISHOMINGO	2,427	536	1,222	669	686 D	22.1%	50.4%	30.5%	69.5%
TUNICA	897	334	323	240	11 R	37.2%	36.0%	50.8%	49.2%
UNION	3,295	605	2,001	689	1,396 D	18.4%	60.7%	23.2%	76.8%
WALTHALL	2,139	310	747	1,082	437 D	14.5%	34.9%	29.3%	70.7%
WARREN	6,587	2,277	2,289	2,021	12 D	34.6%	34.8%	49.9%	50.1%
WASHINGTON	6,655	2,292	3,105	1,258	813 D	34.4%	46.7%	42.5%	57.5%
WAYNE	2,233	490	707	1,036	217 D	21.9%	31.7%	40.9%	59.1%
WEBSTER	2,026	299	553	1,174	254 D	14.8%	27.3%	35.1%	64.9%
WILKINSON	1,222	174	216	832	42 D	14.2%	17.7%	44.6%	55.4%
WINSTON	2,966	405	1,056	1,505	651 D	13.7%	35.6%	27.7%	72.3%
YALOBUSHA	1,903	549	650	704	101 D	28.8%	34.2%	45.8%	54.2%
YAZOO	3,340	778	715	1,847	63 R	23.3%	21.4%	52.1%	47.9%
TOTAL	298,171	73,561	108,362	116,248	34,801 D	24.7%	36.3%	40.4%	59.6%

PRESIDENT 1964

County	Total Vote	Republican	Democratic	Other	Rep.-Dem. Plurality	Percentage Total Vote Rep.	Percentage Total Vote Dem.	Percentage Major Vote Rep.	Percentage Major Vote Dem.
RANKIN	7,873	7,541	332		7,209 R	95.8%	4.2%	95.8%	4.2%
SCOTT	4,967	4,729	238		4,491 R	95.2%	4.8%	95.2%	4.8%
SHARKEY	1,244	1,116	128		988 R	89.7%	10.3%	89.7%	10.3%
SIMPSON	5,220	4,949	271		4,678 R	94.8%	5.2%	94.8%	5.2%
SMITH	4,283	4,045	238		3,807 R	94.4%	5.6%	94.4%	5.6%
STONE	1,955	1,776	179		1,597 R	90.8%	9.2%	90.8%	9.2%
SUNFLOWER	4,378	4,127	251		3,876 R	94.3%	5.7%	94.3%	5.7%
TALLAHATCHIE	3,381	3,126	255		2,871 R	92.5%	7.5%	92.5%	7.5%
TATE	2,673	2,390	283		2,107 R	89.4%	10.6%	89.4%	10.6%
TIPPAH	3,456	2,482	974		1,508 R	71.8%	28.2%	71.8%	28.2%
TISHOMINGO	2,911	1,934	977		957 R	66.4%	33.6%	66.4%	33.6%
TUNICA	1,044	945	99		846 R	90.5%	9.5%	90.5%	9.5%
UNION	4,176	2,939	1,237		1,702 R	70.4%	29.6%	70.4%	29.6%
WALTHALL	3,168	3,014	154		2,860 R	95.1%	4.9%	95.1%	4.9%
WARREN	9,040	7,409	1,631		5,778 R	82.0%	18.0%	82.0%	18.0%
WASHINGTON	7,615	5,611	2,004		3,607 R	73.7%	26.3%	73.7%	26.3%
WAYNE	3,815	3,539	276		3,263 R	92.8%	7.2%	92.8%	7.2%
WEBSTER	3,121	2,884	237		2,647 R	92.4%	7.6%	92.4%	7.6%
WILKINSON	1,576	1,473	103		1,370 R	93.5%	6.5%	93.5%	6.5%
WINSTON	4,159	3,922	237		3,685 R	94.3%	5.7%	94.3%	5.7%
YALOBUSHA	2,644	2,385	259		2,126 R	90.2%	9.8%	90.2%	9.8%
YAZOO	5,005	4,801	204		4,597 R	95.9%	4.1%	95.9%	4.1%
TOTAL	409,146	356,528	52,618		303,910 R	87.1%	12.9%	87.1%	12.9%

MISSISSIPPI

OTHER VOTE COMPOSITION:

1920	Socialist.
1924	Progressive.
1928	
1932	Socialist.
1936	Socialist.
1940	Socialist.
1944	
1948	167,538 States Rights; 225 Progressive.
1952	
1956	Independent.
1960	Unpledged Democratic.
1964	

SPECIAL CASES:

1924 Progressive candidates ran second in several counties.

1928 Republican total includes 26,222 Republican, 544 Ligon elector ticket votes, and 264 Rogers elector ticket votes. The Ligon votes represented the Howard group of Republicans. Some sources identify the Rogers votes as Socialist, though they are included with the Republican total in the report of the Clerk of the House of Representatives and are so listed here.

1932 Republican total includes 3,210 Lily White and 1,970 Black-and-Tan votes. Socialist candidates ran second in two counties, in one of which there were no Republican votes cast.

1936 Republican total includes 2,772 Black-and-Tan and 1,695 Lily White votes. Socialist candidates ran second in one county.

1940 Republican total includes 4,550 Independent Republican and 2,814 Republican votes.

1944 Democratic total includes 158,657 votes for a special elector ticket designated by the Legislature and 9,964 Convention votes. Republican total includes 7,860 Independent Republican and 3,753 Republican votes.

1948 Republican total includes 2,595 Republican and 2,448 Independent Republican votes. States Rights candidates carried the state and all counties.

1952 Republican votes are those cast for a group of electors officially listed as Independent "pledged to vote for the nominees of the National Republican Party".

1956 Republican total includes 56,372 Republican and 4,313 Mississippi Black-and-Tan Grand Old Party votes. Independent electors carried several counties and ran second in others.

1960 Unpledged Democratic electors carried the state, winning many counties and running second in most others. These electors voted in the Electoral College for Senators Harry Flood Byrd and Strom Thurmond.

MISSOURI

PRESIDENT 1920

County	Total Vote	Republican	Democratic	Other	Rep.-Dem. Plurality	% Total Vote Rep.	% Total Vote Dem.	% Major Vote Rep.	% Major Vote Dem.
ADAIR	7,878	4,861	2,534	483	2,327 R	61.7%	32.2%	65.7%	34.3%
ANDREW	6,429	3,913	2,466	50	1,447 R	60.9%	38.4%	61.3%	38.7%
ATCHISON	5,514	3,236	2,227	51	1,009 R	58.7%	40.4%	59.2%	40.8%
AUDRAIN	9,409	3,827	5,514	68	1,687 D	40.7%	58.6%	41.0%	59.0%
BARRY	9,049	5,162	3,729	158	1,433 R	57.0%	41.2%	58.1%	41.9%
BARTON	6,814	3,480	3,040	294	440 R	51.1%	44.6%	53.4%	46.6%
BATES	9,708	5,039	4,433	236	606 R	51.9%	45.7%	53.2%	46.8%
BENTON	4,915	3,367	1,506	42	1,861 R	68.5%	30.6%	69.1%	30.9%
BOLLINGER	4,949	2,869	2,019	61	850 R	58.0%	40.8%	58.7%	41.3%
BOONE	12,890	4,077	8,748	65	4,671 D	31.6%	67.9%	31.8%	68.2%
BUCHANAN	33,714	17,191	16,188	335	1,003 R	51.0%	48.0%	51.5%	48.5%
BUTLER	7,442	4,601	2,662	179	1,939 R	61.8%	35.8%	63.3%	36.7%
CALDWELL	6,688	4,168	2,498	22	1,670 R	62.3%	37.4%	62.5%	37.5%
CALLAWAY	9,339	3,274	6,035	30	2,761 D	35.1%	64.6%	35.2%	64.8%
CAMDEN	3,349	2,276	1,034	39	1,242 R	68.0%	30.9%	68.8%	31.2%
CAPE GIRARDEAU	12,273	7,537	4,584	152	2,953 R	61.4%	37.4%	62.2%	37.8%
CARROLL	9,780	5,609	4,075	96	1,534 R	57.2%	41.7%	57.9%	42.1%
CARTER	2,047	1,057	930	60	127 R	51.6%	45.4%	53.2%	46.8%
CASS	9,185	4,055	5,030	100	975 D	44.1%	54.8%	44.6%	55.4%
CEDAR	5,495	3,488	1,936	71	1,552 R	63.5%	35.2%	64.3%	35.7%
CHARITON	9,084	4,331	4,675	78	344 D	47.7%	51.5%	48.1%	51.9%
CHRISTIAN	4,857	3,795	919	143	2,876 R	78.1%	18.9%	80.5%	19.5%
CLARK	5,761	3,310	2,383	68	927 R	57.5%	41.4%	58.1%	41.9%
CLAY	9,118	2,804	6,283	31	3,479 D	30.8%	68.9%	30.9%	69.1%
CLINTON	6,514	3,165	3,304	45	139 D	48.6%	50.7%	48.9%	51.1%
COLE	10,081	5,878	4,167	36	1,711 R	58.3%	41.3%	58.5%	41.5%
COOPER	8,856	5,151	3,657	48	1,494 R	58.2%	41.3%	58.5%	41.5%
CRAWFORD	4,358	2,634	1,658	66	976 R	60.4%	38.0%	61.4%	38.6%
DADE	5,507	3,520	1,892	95	1,628 R	63.9%	34.4%	65.0%	35.0%
DALLAS	3,811	2,665	1,100	46	1,565 R	69.9%	28.9%	70.8%	29.2%
DAVIESS	8,118	4,458	3,560	100	898 R	54.9%	43.9%	55.6%	44.4%
DE KALB	5,189	3,001	2,121	67	880 R	57.8%	40.9%	58.6%	41.4%
DENT	4,264	2,204	1,970	90	234 R	51.7%	46.2%	52.8%	47.2%
DOUGLAS	4,053	3,207	577	149	2,750 R	82.1%	14.2%	85.2%	14.8%
DUNKLIN	9,963	4,455	5,199	309	744 D	44.7%	52.2%	46.1%	53.9%
FRANKLIN	11,733	8,712	2,814	207	5,898 R	74.3%	24.0%	75.6%	24.4%
GASCONADE	4,978	4,481	454	43	4,027 R	90.0%	9.1%	90.8%	9.2%
GENTRY	6,929	3,442	3,374	113	68 R	49.7%	48.7%	50.5%	49.5%
GREENE	28,126	15,755	11,514	857	4,241 R	56.0%	40.9%	57.8%	42.2%
GRUNDY	7,973	5,123	2,721	129	2,402 R	64.3%	34.1%	65.3%	34.7%
HARRISON	7,740	5,151	2,502	87	2,649 R	66.6%	32.3%	67.3%	32.7%
HENRY	10,813	5,313	5,367	133	54 D	49.1%	49.6%	49.7%	50.3%
HICKORY	2,713	2,131	532	50	1,599 R	78.5%	19.6%	80.0%	20.0%
HOLT	6,556	4,153	2,329	74	1,824 R	63.3%	35.5%	64.1%	35.9%
HOWARD	6,888	2,125	4,735	28	2,610 D	30.9%	68.7%	31.0%	69.0%
HOWELL	6,869	4,344	2,323	202	2,021 R	63.2%	33.8%	65.2%	34.8%
IRON	3,071	1,463	1,554	54	91 D	47.6%	50.6%	48.5%	51.5%
JACKSON	158,214	79,875	76,791	1,548	3,084 R	50.5%	48.5%	51.0%	49.0%
JASPER	29,225	17,074	11,006	1,145	6,068 R	58.4%	37.7%	60.8%	39.2%
JEFFERSON	10,595	5,730	4,684	181	1,046 R	54.1%	44.2%	55.0%	45.0%
JOHNSON	11,252	5,700	5,444	108	256 R	50.7%	48.4%	51.1%	48.9%
KNOX	5,061	2,749	2,250	62	499 R	54.3%	44.5%	55.0%	45.0%
LACLEDE	5,734	3,469	2,183	102	1,286 R	60.3%	37.9%	61.4%	38.6%
LAFAYETTE	13,754	7,471	6,189	94	1,302 R	54.3%	45.0%	54.7%	45.3%
LAWRENCE	9,935	6,093	3,532	310	2,561 R	61.3%	35.5%	63.3%	36.7%
LEWIS	6,405	2,810	3,542	53	732 D	43.9%	55.3%	44.2%	55.8%
LINCOLN	6,909	3,209	3,660	40	451 D	46.4%	53.0%	46.7%	53.3%
LINN	10,878	5,557	5,184	137	373 R	51.1%	47.6%	51.7%	48.3%
LIVINGSTON	8,856	5,093	3,666	97	1,427 R	57.5%	41.4%	58.1%	41.9%
MCDONALD	5,291	2,921	2,242	128	679 R	55.2%	42.4%	56.6%	43.4%

PRESIDENT 1924

County	Total Vote	Republican	Democratic	Other	Rep.-Dem. Plurality	% Total Vote Rep.	% Total Vote Dem.	% Major Vote Rep.	% Major Vote Dem.
ADAIR	8,183	4,383	2,800	1,000	1,583 R	53.6%	34.2%	61.0%	39.0%
ANDREW	6,385	3,535	2,648	202	887 R	55.4%	41.5%	57.2%	42.8%
ATCHISON	5,501	2,710	2,617	174	93 R	49.3%	47.6%	50.9%	49.1%
AUDRAIN	9,142	3,125	5,866	151	2,741 D	34.2%	64.2%	34.8%	65.2%
BARRY	8,481	4,065	3,606	810	459 R	47.9%	42.5%	53.0%	47.0%
BARTON	6,075	2,952	2,682	441	270 R	48.6%	44.1%	52.4%	47.6%
BATES	9,663	4,552	4,722	389	170 D	47.1%	48.9%	49.1%	50.9%
BENTON	4,436	2,693	1,588	155	1,105 R	60.7%	35.8%	62.9%	37.1%
BOLLINGER	4,390	2,204	2,075	111	129 R	50.2%	47.3%	51.5%	48.5%
BOONE	12,373	3,547	8,657	169	5,110 D	28.7%	70.0%	29.1%	70.9%
BUCHANAN	34,926	17,509	14,759	2,658	2,750 R	50.1%	42.3%	54.3%	45.7%
BUTLER	8,019	4,489	2,953	577	1,536 R	56.0%	36.8%	60.3%	39.7%
CALDWELL	6,043	3,545	2,383	115	1,162 R	58.7%	39.4%	59.8%	40.2%
CALLAWAY	8,836	2,799	5,904	133	3,105 D	31.7%	66.8%	32.2%	67.8%
CAMDEN	3,031	1,732	1,196	103	536 R	57.1%	39.5%	59.2%	40.8%
CAPE GIRARDEAU	11,666	6,076	4,967	623	1,109 R	52.1%	42.6%	55.0%	45.0%
CARROLL	9,613	4,907	4,502	204	405 R	51.0%	46.8%	52.2%	47.8%
CARTER	1,903	772	1,051	80	279 D	40.6%	55.2%	42.3%	57.7%
CASS	8,561	3,610	4,709	242	1,099 D	42.2%	55.0%	43.4%	56.6%
CEDAR	5,019	2,802	2,007	210	795 R	55.8%	40.0%	58.3%	41.7%
CHARITON	8,194	3,173	4,795	226	1,622 D	38.7%	58.5%	39.8%	60.2%
CHRISTIAN	4,289	2,692	1,281	316	1,411 R	62.8%	29.9%	67.8%	32.2%
CLARK	5,853	2,948	2,770	135	178 R	50.4%	47.3%	51.6%	48.4%
CLAY	9,459	2,998	6,076	385	3,078 D	31.7%	64.2%	33.0%	67.0%
CLINTON	6,162	2,848	3,177	137	329 D	46.2%	51.6%	47.3%	52.7%
COLE	11,821	6,205	5,033	583	1,172 R	52.5%	42.6%	55.2%	44.8%
COOPER	9,012	4,755	4,070	187	685 R	52.8%	45.2%	53.9%	46.1%
CRAWFORD	4,189	2,336	1,697	156	639 R	55.8%	40.5%	57.9%	42.1%
DADE	4,850	2,651	2,007	192	644 R	54.7%	41.4%	56.9%	43.1%
DALLAS	3,585	2,188	1,304	93	884 R	61.0%	36.4%	62.7%	37.3%
DAVIESS	7,524	3,869	3,520	135	349 R	51.4%	46.8%	52.4%	47.6%
DE KALB	5,192	2,730	2,368	94	362 R	52.6%	45.6%	53.6%	46.4%
DENT	4,153	1,779	2,263	111	484 D	42.8%	54.5%	44.0%	56.0%
DOUGLAS	3,784	2,617	909	258	1,708 R	69.2%	24.0%	74.2%	25.8%
DUNKLIN	8,052	3,436	4,357	259	921 D	42.7%	54.1%	44.1%	55.9%
FRANKLIN	10,543	6,253	3,384	906	2,869 R	59.3%	32.1%	64.9%	35.1%
GASCONADE	4,357	3,306	577	474	2,729 R	75.9%	13.2%	85.1%	14.9%
GENTRY	7,222	3,318	3,555	349	237 D	46.0%	49.2%	48.3%	51.7%
GREENE	29,771	13,618	13,084	3,069	534 R	45.7%	43.9%	51.0%	49.0%
GRUNDY	7,467	3,782	2,367	1,318	1,415 R	50.6%	31.7%	61.5%	38.5%
HARRISON	7,300	4,247	2,792	261	1,455 R	58.2%	38.2%	60.3%	39.7%
HENRY	9,871	4,616	4,706	549	90 D	46.6%	47.7%	49.5%	50.5%
HICKORY	2,680	1,895	722	63	1,173 R	70.7%	26.9%	72.4%	27.6%
HOLT	5,719	3,316	2,255	148	1,061 R	58.0%	39.4%	59.5%	40.5%
HOWARD	6,860	1,873	4,759	228	2,886 D	27.3%	69.4%	28.2%	71.8%
HOWELL	6,493	3,130	2,681	682	449 R	48.2%	41.3%	53.9%	46.1%
IRON	3,071	1,328	1,675	68	347 D	43.2%	54.5%	44.2%	55.8%
JACKSON	175,982	91,141	76,002	8,839	15,139 R	51.8%	43.2%	54.5%	45.5%
JASPER	24,860	13,701	9,176	1,983	4,525 R	55.1%	36.9%	59.9%	40.1%
JEFFERSON	9,963	4,870	4,356	737	514 R	48.9%	43.7%	52.8%	47.2%
JOHNSON	11,006	5,248	5,526	232	278 D	47.7%	50.2%	48.7%	51.3%
KNOX	5,220	2,288	2,722	210	434 D	43.8%	52.1%	45.7%	54.3%
LACLEDE	5,735	2,960	2,500	275	460 R	51.6%	43.6%	54.2%	45.8%
LAFAYETTE	12,923	6,517	5,877	529	640 R	50.4%	45.5%	52.6%	47.4%
LAWRENCE	9,116	4,499	3,768	849	731 R	49.4%	41.3%	54.4%	45.6%
LEWIS	6,120	2,416	3,481	223	1,065 D	39.5%	56.9%	41.0%	59.0%
LINCOLN	6,157	2,563	3,419	175	856 D	41.6%	55.5%	42.8%	57.2%
LINN	11,246	5,155	5,386	705	231 D	45.8%	47.9%	48.9%	51.1%
LIVINGSTON	8,988	4,517	4,316	155	201 R	50.3%	48.0%	51.1%	48.9%
MCDONALD	4,916	2,374	2,301	241	73 R	48.3%	46.8%	50.8%	49.2%

MISSOURI

PRESIDENT 1920

County	Total Vote	Republican	Democratic	Other	Rep.-Dem. Plurality	% Total Vote Rep.	% Total Vote Dem.	% Major Vote Rep.	% Major Vote Dem.
MACON	12,192	6,309	5,626	257	683 R	51.7%	46.1%	52.9%	47.1%
MADISON	3,876	2,023	1,830	23	193 R	52.2%	47.2%	52.5%	47.5%
MARIES	3,150	1,445	1,677	28	232 D	45.9%	53.2%	46.3%	53.7%
MARION	11,545	4,660	6,719	166	2,059 D	40.4%	58.2%	41.0%	59.0%
MERCER	4,274	3,170	1,044	60	2,126 R	74.2%	24.4%	75.2%	24.8%
MILLER	5,474	3,555	1,833	86	1,722 R	64.9%	33.5%	66.0%	34.0%
MISSISSIPPI	4,679	2,193	2,442	44	249 D	46.9%	52.2%	47.3%	52.7%
MONITEAU	5,994	3,535	2,405	54	1,130 R	59.0%	40.1%	59.5%	40.5%
MONROE	7,635	1,406	6,136	93	4,730 D	18.4%	80.4%	18.6%	81.4%
MONTGOMERY	7,088	3,910	3,103	75	807 R	55.2%	43.8%	55.8%	44.2%
MORGAN	4,780	2,911	1,834	35	1,077 R	60.9%	38.4%	61.3%	38.7%
NEW MADRID	7,498	3,745	3,637	116	108 R	49.9%	48.5%	50.7%	49.3%
NEWTON	9,912	5,541	4,078	293	1,463 R	55.9%	41.1%	57.6%	42.4%
NODAWAY	12,493	6,971	5,404	118	1,567 R	55.8%	43.3%	56.3%	43.7%
OREGON	3,333	1,319	1,961	53	642 D	39.6%	58.8%	40.2%	59.8%
OSAGE	4,856	3,699	1,118	39	2,581 R	76.2%	23.0%	76.8%	23.2%
OZARK	3,082	2,457	569	56	1,888 R	79.7%	18.5%	81.2%	18.8%
PEMISCOT	8,453	4,443	3,901	109	542 R	52.6%	46.2%	53.2%	46.8%
PERRY	5,181	3,652	1,504	25	2,148 R	70.5%	29.0%	70.8%	29.2%
PETTIS	15,355	8,595	6,561	199	2,034 R	56.0%	42.7%	56.7%	43.3%
PHELPS	5,152	2,692	2,422	38	270 R	52.3%	47.0%	52.6%	47.4%
PIKE	8,963	3,860	5,034	69	1,174 D	43.1%	56.2%	43.4%	56.6%
PLATTE	6,102	1,724	4,361	17	2,637 D	28.3%	71.5%	28.3%	71.7%
POLK	7,907	4,967	2,847	93	2,120 R	62.8%	36.0%	63.6%	36.4%
PULASKI	3,870	1,853	1,978	39	125 D	47.9%	51.1%	48.4%	51.6%
PUTNAM	5,321	3,880	1,315	126	2,565 R	72.9%	24.7%	74.7%	25.3%
RALLS	4,197	1,362	2,803	32	1,441 D	32.5%	66.8%	32.7%	67.3%
RANDOLPH	11,968	3,768	8,115	85	4,347 D	31.5%	67.8%	31.7%	68.3%
RAY	8,165	3,228	4,865	72	1,637 D	39.5%	59.6%	39.9%	60.1%
REYNOLDS	3,046	1,173	1,837	36	664 D	38.5%	60.3%	39.0%	61.0%
RIPLEY	3,676	1,752	1,735	189	17 R	47.7%	47.2%	50.2%	49.8%
ST CHARLES	9,213	6,645	2,472	96	4,173 R	72.1%	26.8%	72.9%	27.1%
ST CLAIR	5,706	3,249	2,296	161	953 R	56.9%	40.2%	58.6%	41.4%
ST FRANCOIS	11,039	5,504	5,300	235	204 R	49.9%	48.0%	50.9%	49.1%
ST LOUIS	39,342	25,008	12,438	1,896	12,570 R	63.5%	31.6%	66.8%	33.2%
ST LOUIS CITY	282,652	163,047	106,047	13,325	57,233 R	57.8%	37.5%	60.6%	39.4%
STE GENEVIEVE	3,088	1,917	1,149	22	768 R	62.1%	37.2%	62.5%	37.5%
SALINE	12,812	5,613	7,114	85	1,501 D	43.8%	55.5%	44.1%	55.9%
SCHUYLER	3,637	1,806	1,793	38	13 R	49.7%	49.3%	50.2%	49.8%
SCOTLAND	4,724	2,509	2,124	91	385 R	53.1%	45.0%	54.2%	45.8%
SCOTT	8,579	4,204	4,157	218	47 R	49.0%	48.5%	50.3%	49.7%
SHANNON	3,371	1,639	1,661	71	22 D	48.6%	49.3%	49.7%	50.3%
SHELBY	6,334	2,128	3,935	271	1,807 D	34.7%	64.9%	35.1%	64.9%
STODDARD	9,441	4,641	4,448	372	213 R	49.2%	47.1%	51.2%	48.8%
STONE	3,500	2,749	672	79	2,077 R	78.5%	19.2%	80.4%	19.6%
SULLIVAN	8,121	4,576	3,475	70	1,101 R	56.3%	42.8%	56.8%	43.2%
TANEY	2,956	2,001	913	42	1,088 R	67.7%	30.9%	68.7%	31.3%
TEXAS	6,585	3,552	2,965	68	587 R	53.9%	45.0%	54.5%	45.5%
VERNON	10,246	4,645	5,419	182	774 D	45.3%	52.9%	46.2%	53.8%
WARREN	4,133	3,512	545	76	2,967 R	85.0%	13.2%	86.6%	13.4%
WASHINGTON	4,486	2,618	1,837	31	781 R	58.4%	40.9%	58.8%	41.2%
WAYNE	4,552	2,380	2,072	100	308 R	52.3%	45.5%	53.5%	46.5%
WEBSTER	6,509	4,000	2,428	81	1,572 R	61.5%	37.3%	62.2%	37.8%
WORTH	3,450	1,888	1,532	30	356 R	54.7%	44.4%	55.2%	44.8%
WRIGHT	5,748	3,661	2,008	79	1,653 R	63.7%	34.9%	64.6%	35.4%
TOTAL	1,332,140	727,252	574,699	30,189	152,553 R	54.6%	43.1%	55.9%	44.1%

PRESIDENT 1924

County	Total Vote	Republican	Democratic	Other	Rep.-Dem. Plurality	% Total Vote Rep.	% Total Vote Dem.	% Major Vote Rep.	% Major Vote Dem.
MACON	10,950	4,909	5,538	503	629 D	44.8%	50.6%	47.0%	53.0%
MADISON	3,265	1,569	1,665	31	96 D	48.1%	51.0%	48.5%	51.5%
MARIES	3,042	1,004	1,913	125	909 D	33.0%	62.9%	34.4%	65.6%
MARION	12,297	5,408	5,739	1,150	331 D	44.0%	46.7%	48.5%	51.5%
MERCER	4,010	2,508	1,209	293	1,299 R	62.5%	30.1%	67.5%	32.5%
MILLER	5,361	3,011	1,962	388	1,049 R	56.2%	36.6%	60.5%	39.5%
MISSISSIPPI	4,310	1,797	2,360	153	563 D	41.7%	54.8%	43.2%	56.8%
MONITEAU	5,910	3,138	2,601	171	537 R	53.2%	44.1%	54.7%	45.3%
MONROE	6,910	1,141	5,597	172	4,456 D	16.5%	81.0%	16.9%	83.1%
MONTGOMERY	6,648	3,563	2,938	147	625 R	53.6%	44.2%	54.8%	45.2%
MORGAN	4,397	2,489	1,842	66	647 R	56.6%	41.9%	57.5%	42.5%
NEW MADRID	8,312	4,018	4,167	127	149 D	48.3%	50.1%	49.1%	50.9%
NEWTON	9,011	4,592	3,970	449	622 R	51.0%	44.1%	53.6%	46.4%
NODAWAY	12,521	6,242	5,803	476	439 R	49.9%	46.3%	51.8%	48.2%
OREGON	3,487	896	2,231	360	1,335 D	25.7%	64.0%	28.7%	71.3%
OSAGE	4,802	2,496	1,986	320	510 R	52.0%	41.4%	55.7%	44.3%
OZARK	2,546	1,758	688	100	1,070 R	69.0%	27.0%	71.9%	28.1%
PEMISCOT	10,573	4,811	5,616	146	805 D	45.5%	53.1%	46.1%	53.9%
PERRY	4,771	2,656	1,826	289	830 R	55.7%	38.3%	59.3%	40.7%
PETTIS	15,236	7,280	6,568	1,388	712 R	47.8%	43.1%	52.6%	47.4%
PHELPS	5,500	2,085	2,918	497	833 D	37.9%	53.1%	41.7%	58.3%
PIKE	7,999	3,715	4,040	244	325 D	46.4%	50.5%	47.9%	52.1%
PLATTE	5,744	1,999	3,674	71	1,675 D	34.8%	64.0%	35.2%	64.8%
POLK	7,291	4,097	3,033	161	1,064 R	56.2%	41.6%	57.5%	42.5%
PULASKI	3,867	1,578	2,127	162	549 D	40.8%	55.0%	42.6%	57.4%
PUTNAM	5,108	3,340	1,495	273	1,845 R	65.4%	29.3%	69.1%	30.9%
RALLS	4,072	1,365	2,617	90	1,252 D	33.5%	64.3%	34.3%	65.7%
RANDOLPH	11,569	2,991	7,372	1,206	4,381 D	25.9%	63.7%	28.9%	71.1%
RAY	8,041	2,753	4,989	299	2,236 D	34.2%	62.0%	35.6%	64.4%
REYNOLDS	2,724	873	1,822	29	949 D	32.0%	66.9%	32.4%	67.6%
RIPLEY	3,424	1,428	1,863	133	435 D	41.7%	54.4%	43.4%	56.6%
ST CHARLES	7,897	4,668	2,364	865	2,304 R	59.1%	29.9%	66.4%	33.6%
ST CLAIR	5,849	2,907	2,640	302	267 R	49.7%	45.1%	52.4%	47.6%
ST FRANCOIS	11,956	6,117	5,542	297	575 R	51.2%	46.4%	52.5%	47.5%
ST LOUIS	47,834	26,669	16,075	5,090	10,594 R	55.8%	33.6%	62.4%	37.6%
ST LOUIS CITY	264,597	139,433	95,888	29,276	43,545 R	52.7%	36.2%	59.3%	40.7%
STE GENEVIEVE	2,703	1,330	1,257	116	73 R	49.2%	46.5%	51.4%	48.6%
SALINE	12,125	4,990	6,564	571	1,574 D	41.2%	54.1%	43.2%	56.8%
SCHUYLER	3,592	1,522	1,982	88	460 D	42.4%	55.2%	43.4%	56.6%
SCOTLAND	5,092	2,282	2,595	215	313 D	44.8%	51.0%	46.8%	53.2%
SCOTT	8,226	3,335	3,633	1,258	298 D	40.5%	44.2%	47.9%	52.1%
SHANNON	3,415	1,174	2,107	134	933 D	34.4%	61.7%	35.8%	64.2%
SHELBY	5,788	1,737	3,957	94	2,220 D	30.0%	68.4%	30.5%	69.5%
STODDARD	8,680	3,844	4,348	488	504 D	44.3%	50.1%	46.9%	53.1%
STONE	2,860	1,871	626	363	1,245 R	65.4%	21.9%	74.9%	25.1%
SULLIVAN	7,875	3,885	3,703	287	182 R	49.3%	47.0%	51.2%	48.8%
TANEY	2,781	1,710	981	90	729 R	61.5%	35.3%	63.5%	36.5%
TEXAS	6,400	2,787	3,421	192	634 D	43.5%	53.4%	44.9%	55.1%
VERNON	9,239	3,593	4,839	807	1,246 D	38.9%	52.4%	42.6%	57.4%
WARREN	3,508	2,667	644	197	2,023 R	76.0%	18.4%	80.5%	19.5%
WASHINGTON	4,405	2,397	1,955	53	442 R	54.4%	44.4%	55.1%	44.9%
WAYNE	4,439	1,958	2,283	198	325 D	44.1%	51.4%	46.2%	53.8%
WEBSTER	6,197	3,168	2,730	299	438 R	51.1%	44.1%	53.7%	46.3%
WORTH	3,355	1,666	1,650	39	16 R	49.7%	49.2%	50.2%	49.8%
WRIGHT	5,641	3,105	2,303	233	802 R	55.0%	40.8%	57.4%	42.6%
TOTAL	1,310,095	648,488	574,962	86,645	73,526 R	49.5%	43.9%	53.0%	47.0%

MISSOURI

PRESIDENT 1928

County	Total Vote	Republican	Democratic	Other	Rep.-Dem. Plurality	%Total Rep.	%Total Dem.	%Major Rep.	%Major Dem.
ADAIR	8,429	5,538	2,841	50	2,697 R	65.7%	33.7%	66.1%	33.9%
ANDREW	6,373	4,243	2,118	12	2,125 R	66.6%	33.2%	66.7%	33.3%
ATCHISON	5,786	3,239	2,535	12	704 R	56.0%	43.8%	56.1%	43.9%
AUDRAIN	9,222	4,141	5,067	14	926 D	44.9%	54.9%	45.0%	55.0%
BARRY	9,383	5,901	3,431	51	2,470 R	62.9%	36.6%	63.2%	36.8%
BARTON	5,985	3,662	2,275	48	1,387 R	61.2%	38.0%	61.7%	38.3%
BATES	9,781	6,133	3,594	54	2,539 R	62.7%	36.7%	63.1%	36.9%
BENTON	4,716	3,411	1,296	9	2,115 R	72.3%	27.5%	72.5%	27.5%
BOLLINGER	4,846	3,014	1,824	8	1,190 R	62.2%	37.6%	62.3%	37.7%
BOONE	13,319	4,876	8,422	21	3,546 D	36.6%	63.2%	36.7%	63.3%
BUCHANAN	32,624	20,459	12,110	55	8,349 R	62.7%	37.1%	62.8%	37.2%
BUTLER	8,949	5,591	3,320	38	2,271 R	62.5%	37.1%	62.7%	37.3%
CALDWELL	6,331	4,167	2,164		2,003 R	65.8%	34.2%	65.8%	34.2%
CALLAWAY	8,437	3,269	5,153	15	1,884 D	38.7%	61.1%	38.8%	61.2%
CAMDEN	2,695	2,085	606	4	1,479 R	77.4%	22.5%	77.5%	22.5%
CAPE GIRARDEAU	12,829	7,344	5,464	21	1,880 R	57.2%	42.6%	57.3%	42.7%
CARROLL	9,624	5,875	3,735	14	2,140 R	61.0%	38.8%	61.1%	38.9%
CARTER	1,962	989	963	10		50.4%	49.1%	50.7%	49.3%
CASS	8,964	5,299	3,647	18	1,652 R	59.1%	40.7%	59.2%	40.8%
CEDAR	5,080	3,340	1,728	12	1,612 R	65.7%	34.0%	65.9%	34.1%
CHARITON	8,501	3,929	4,559	13	630 D	46.2%	53.6%	46.3%	53.7%
CHRISTIAN	4,721	3,576	1,124	21	2,452 R	75.7%	23.8%	76.1%	23.9%
CLARK	5,447	3,259	2,174	18	1,089 R	59.8%	39.9%	60.0%	40.0%
CLAY	11,185	5,584	5,574	27	10 R	49.9%	49.8%	50.0%	50.0%
CLINTON	6,229	3,736	2,485	8	1,251 R	60.0%	39.9%	60.1%	39.9%
COLE	13,133	6,637	6,481	15	156 R	50.5%	49.3%	50.6%	49.4%
COOPER	9,216	4,794	4,413	9	381 R	52.0%	47.9%	52.1%	47.9%
CRAWFORD	4,428	2,926	1,476	26	1,450 R	66.1%	33.3%	66.5%	33.5%
DADE	4,957	3,497	1,453	7	2,044 R	70.5%	29.3%	70.6%	29.4%
DALLAS	3,783	2,835	931	17	1,904 R	74.9%	24.3%	75.3%	24.7%
DAVIESS	7,057	4,254	2,789	14	1,465 R	60.3%	39.5%	60.4%	39.6%
DE KALB	5,254	3,338	1,898	18	1,440 R	63.5%	36.1%	63.8%	36.2%
DENT	4,266	2,367	1,871	28	496 R	55.5%	43.9%	55.9%	44.1%
DOUGLAS	4,474	3,758	681	35	3,077 R	84.0%	15.2%	84.1%	15.3%
DUNKLIN	8,501	3,602	4,879	20	1,277 D	42.4%	57.4%	42.5%	57.5%
FRANKLIN	13,292	7,831	5,429	32	2,402 R	58.9%	40.8%	59.1%	40.9%
GASCONADE	5,242	4,171	1,058	13	3,113 R	79.5%	20.2%	79.8%	20.2%
GENTRY	6,256	3,506	2,735	15	771 R	56.0%	43.7%	56.2%	43.8%
GREENE	33,151	22,166	10,901	84	11,265 R	66.9%	32.9%	67.0%	33.0%
GRUNDY	7,604	5,226	2,332	46	2,894 R	68.7%	30.7%	68.7%	30.9%
HARRISON	7,153	4,818	2,319	16	2,499 R	67.4%	32.4%	67.5%	32.5%
HENRY	10,603	6,263	4,399	21	1,864 R	59.1%	40.7%	59.2%	40.8%
HICKORY	2,637	2,233	399	5	1,834 R	84.7%	15.1%	84.8%	15.2%
HOLT	5,776	3,845	1,919	12	1,926 R	66.5%	33.2%	66.7%	33.3%
HOWARD	6,720	2,254	4,452	14	2,198 D	33.5%	66.2%	33.6%	66.4%
HOWELL	7,461	4,869	2,543	49	2,326 R	65.3%	34.1%	65.6%	34.3%
IRON	3,255	1,910	1,342	3	568 R	58.7%	41.2%	58.7%	41.3%
JACKSON	223,677	126,589	96,703	385	29,886 R	56.7%	43.2%	56.7%	43.3%
JASPER	29,059	20,587	8,292	180	12,295 R	70.8%	28.5%	71.3%	28.7%
JEFFERSON	11,538	6,285	5,231	22	1,054 R	54.5%	45.3%	54.6%	45.4%
JOHNSON	11,367	7,032	4,316	19	2,716 R	61.9%	38.0%	62.0%	38.0%
KNOX	4,848	2,628	2,213	7	415 R	54.2%	45.6%	54.3%	45.7%
LACLEDE	6,025	3,971	2,031	23	1,940 R	65.9%	33.7%	66.2%	33.8%
LAFAYETTE	13,658	7,687	5,939	32	1,748 R	56.3%	43.5%	56.4%	43.6%
LAWRENCE	10,017	6,328	3,646	43	2,682 R	63.2%	36.4%	63.4%	36.6%
LEWIS	5,646	2,741	2,882	23	141 D	48.5%	51.0%	48.7%	51.3%
LINCOLN	6,088	2,722	3,356	10	634 D	44.7%	55.1%	44.8%	55.2%
LINN	11,411	6,996	4,395	20	2,601 R	61.3%	38.5%	61.3%	38.6%
LIVINGSTON	8,980	5,742	3,221	17	2,521 R	63.9%	35.9%	64.1%	35.9%
MCDONALD	5,686	3,684	1,986	16	1,698 R	64.8%	34.9%	65.0%	35.0%

PRESIDENT 1932

County	Total Vote	Republican	Democratic	Other	Rep.-Dem. Plurality	%Total Rep.	%Total Dem.	%Major Rep.	%Major Dem.
ADAIR	7,760	2,991	4,623	146	1,632 D	38.5%	59.6%	39.3%	60.7%
ANDREW	6,138	2,826	3,280	32	454 D	46.0%	53.4%	46.3%	53.4%
ATCHISON	5,806	2,155	3,617	34	1,462 D	37.1%	62.3%	37.3%	62.7%
AUDRAIN	10,392	3,037	7,301	54	4,264 D	29.2%	70.3%	29.4%	70.6%
BARRY	10,588	4,497	5,957	134	1,460 D	42.5%	56.3%	43.0%	57.0%
BARTON	6,104	2,092	3,897	115	1,805 D	34.3%	63.8%	34.9%	65.1%
BATES	9,694	3,395	6,220	79	2,825 D	35.0%	64.2%	35.3%	64.7%
BENTON	4,672	2,038	2,596	38	558 D	43.6%	55.6%	44.0%	56.0%
BOLLINGER	5,444	2,411	2,994	39	583 D	44.3%	55.0%	44.6%	55.4%
BOONE	14,979	3,241	11,554	184	8,313 D	21.6%	77.1%	21.9%	78.1%
BUCHANAN	40,922	14,602	26,060	260	11,458 D	35.7%	63.7%	35.9%	64.1%
BUTLER	10,303	4,155	6,058	90	1,903 D	40.3%	58.8%	40.7%	59.3%
CALDWELL	5,677	2,688	2,949	40	261 D	47.3%	51.9%	47.7%	52.3%
CALLAWAY	9,172	2,079	7,042	51	4,963 D	22.7%	76.8%	22.8%	77.2%
CAMDEN	3,313	1,497	1,801	15	304 D	45.2%	54.4%	45.4%	54.6%
CAPE GIRARDEAU	14,307	5,796	8,394	117	2,598 D	40.5%	58.7%	40.8%	59.2%
CARROLL	9,003	3,894	5,072	37	1,178 D	43.3%	56.3%	43.4%	56.6%
CARTER	2,309	750	1,522	37	772 D	32.5%	65.9%	33.0%	67.0%
CASS	8,847	3,009	5,772	66	2,763 D	34.0%	65.2%	34.0%	65.5%
CEDAR	5,412	2,515	2,834	63	319 D	46.5%	52.4%	47.0%	53.0%
CHARITON	7,367	1,835	5,498	34	3,663 D	24.9%	74.6%	25.0%	75.0%
CHRISTIAN	5,055	2,395	2,577	83	182 D	47.4%	51.0%	48.2%	51.8%
CLARK	5,324	2,223	3,072	29	849 D	41.8%	57.7%	42.0%	58.0%
CLAY	12,612	3,117	9,398	97	6,281 D	24.7%	74.5%	24.9%	75.1%
CLINTON	5,867	1,805	4,042	20	2,237 D	30.8%	68.9%	30.9%	69.1%
COLE	14,731	5,636	9,068	27	3,432 D	38.3%	61.6%	38.3%	61.7%
COOPER	9,226	3,695	5,493	38	1,798 D	40.0%	59.5%	40.2%	59.8%
CRAWFORD	5,425	2,213	3,166	46	953 D	40.8%	58.4%	41.1%	58.9%
DADE	5,228	2,340	2,833	55	493 D	44.8%	54.2%	45.2%	54.8%
DALLAS	4,136	1,958	2,143	35	185 D	47.3%	51.8%	47.7%	52.3%
DAVIESS	5,906	2,351	3,523	32	1,172 D	39.8%	59.7%	40.0%	60.0%
DE KALB	4,288	1,747	2,519	22	772 D	40.7%	58.7%	41.0%	59.0%
DENT	5,017	1,701	3,293	23	1,592 D	33.9%	65.6%	34.1%	65.9%
DOUGLAS	4,415	2,362	1,922	131	440 R	53.5%	43.5%	55.1%	44.9%
DUNKLIN	11,211	1,977	9,141	93	7,164 D	17.6%	81.5%	17.8%	82.2%
FRANKLIN	13,992	5,369	8,479	144	3,110 D	38.4%	60.6%	38.8%	61.2%
GASCONADE	4,610	2,571	1,998	41	573 R	55.8%	43.3%	56.3%	43.7%
GENTRY	5,563	1,877	3,677	41	1,800 D	33.7%	66.1%	33.8%	66.2%
GREENE	32,794	13,943	18,255	596	4,312 D	42.5%	55.7%	43.3%	56.7%
GRUNDY	7,020	2,953	4,006	61	1,053 D	42.1%	57.1%	42.4%	57.6%
HARRISON	5,883	2,476	3,376	31	900 D	42.1%	57.4%	42.3%	57.7%
HENRY	10,500	3,631	6,809	60	3,178 D	34.6%	64.8%	34.8%	65.2%
HICKORY	2,479	1,586	878	15	708 R	64.0%	35.4%	64.4%	35.6%
HOLT	5,394	2,253	3,117	24	864 D	41.8%	57.8%	42.0%	58.0%
HOWARD	6,737	1,337	5,354	46	4,017 D	19.8%	79.5%	20.0%	80.0%
HOWELL	8,540	3,660	4,775	105	1,115 D	42.9%	55.9%	43.4%	56.6%
IRON	4,172	1,439	2,689	44	1,250 D	34.5%	64.5%	34.9%	65.1%
JACKSON	256,885	83,214	172,456	1,215	89,242 D	32.4%	67.1%	32.5%	67.5%
JASPER	29,604	11,788	17,349	467	5,561 D	39.8%	58.6%	40.5%	59.5%
JEFFERSON	12,844	4,559	8,130	155	3,571 D	35.5%	63.3%	35.9%	64.1%
JOHNSON	10,645	4,088	6,481	76	2,393 D	38.4%	60.9%	38.7%	61.3%
KNOX	4,562	1,465	3,045	52	1,580 D	32.1%	66.7%	32.5%	67.5%
LACLEDE	6,823	2,804	3,960	59	1,156 D	41.1%	58.0%	41.5%	58.5%
LAFAYETTE	13,613	5,670	7,906	37	2,236 D	41.7%	58.1%	41.8%	58.2%
LAWRENCE	10,732	4,146	6,411	175	2,265 D	38.6%	59.7%	39.3%	60.7%
LEWIS	5,143	1,341	3,746	56	2,405 D	26.1%	72.8%	26.4%	73.6%
LINCOLN	6,061	1,604	4,428	29	2,824 D	26.5%	73.1%	26.6%	73.4%
LINN	9,858	3,611	6,177	70	2,566 D	36.6%	62.7%	36.9%	63.1%
LIVINGSTON	8,431	3,659	4,742	30	1,083 D	43.4%	56.2%	43.6%	56.4%
MCDONALD	6,465	2,464	3,943	58	1,479 D	38.1%	61.0%	38.5%	61.5%

MISSOURI

PRESIDENT 1928

County	Total Vote	Republican	Democratic	Other	Rep.-Dem. Plurality	Total Vote Rep.	Total Vote Dem.	Major Vote Rep.	Major Vote Dem.
MACON	10,510	5,618	4,838	54	780 R	53.5%	46.0%	53.7%	46.3%
MADISON	3,491	2,165	1,326		839 R	62.0%	38.0%	62.0%	38.0%
MARIES	3,231	1,415	1,808	8	393 D	43.8%	56.0%	43.9%	56.1%
MARION	13,367	7,664	5,679	24	1,985 R	57.3%	42.5%	57.4%	42.5%
MERCER	3,798	2,869	925	4	1,944 R	75.5%	24.4%	75.6%	24.4%
MILLER	5,376	3,379	1,979	18	1,400 R	62.9%	36.8%	63.1%	36.9%
MISSISSIPPI	4,609	1,999	2,602	8	603 D	43.4%	56.5%	43.4%	56.5%
MONITEAU	5,839	3,496	2,310	33	1,186 R	59.9%	39.6%	60.2%	39.3%
MONROE	6,354	1,378	4,957	19	3,579 D	21.7%	78.0%	21.7%	78.2%
MONTGOMERY	6,203	3,910	2,285	8	1,625 R	63.0%	36.8%	63.1%	36.9%
MORGAN	4,458	3,017	1,432	9	1,585 R	67.7%	32.1%	67.8%	32.2%
NEW MADRID	8,925	4,750	4,153	22	597 R	53.2%	46.5%	53.4%	46.5%
NEWTON	10,408	7,054	3,269	85	3,785 R	67.8%	31.4%	68.3%	31.7%
NODAWAY	12,474	7,160	5,297	17	1,863 R	57.4%	42.5%	57.5%	42.5%
OREGON	3,550	1,662	1,884	4	222 D	46.8%	53.1%	46.9%	53.1%
OSAGE	5,572	2,474	3,092	6	618 D	44.4%	55.6%	44.4%	55.6%
OZARK	3,104	2,616	529	19	2,087 R	82.7%	16.7%	83.2%	16.8%
PEMISCOT	11,515	6,256	5,259		997 R	54.3%	45.7%	54.3%	45.7%
PERRY	5,245	2,648	2,591	6	57 R	50.5%	49.4%	50.5%	49.5%
PETTIS	15,939	10,346	5,554	39	4,792 R	64.9%	34.8%	65.1%	34.9%
PHELPS	5,874	2,967	2,896	11	71 R	50.5%	49.3%	50.6%	49.4%
PIKE	8,347	4,569	3,749	29	820 R	54.7%	44.9%	54.9%	45.1%
PLATTE	5,777	2,423	3,344	10	921 D	41.9%	57.9%	42.0%	58.0%
POLK	7,622	5,307	2,303	12	3,004 R	69.6%	30.2%	69.7%	30.3%
PULASKI	4,171	2,229	1,934	8	295 R	53.4%	46.4%	53.5%	46.5%
PUTNAM	4,755	3,498	1,247	10	2,251 R	73.6%	26.2%	73.7%	26.2%
RALLS	4,071	1,794	2,273	4	479 D	44.1%	55.8%	44.1%	55.8%
RANDOLPH	10,842	4,825	6,008	9	1,183 D	44.5%	55.4%	44.5%	55.5%
RAY	7,866	3,280	4,570	16	1,290 D	41.7%	58.1%	41.8%	58.2%
REYNOLDS	2,835	1,247	1,582	6	335 D	44.0%	55.8%	44.1%	55.9%
RIPLEY	3,631	2,226	1,395	10	831 R	61.3%	38.4%	61.5%	38.5%
ST CHARLES	10,507	5,404	5,081	22	323 R	51.4%	48.4%	51.5%	48.5%
ST CLAIR	5,584	3,846	1,701	37	2,145 R	68.9%	30.5%	69.3%	30.7%
ST FRANCOIS	13,228	9,040	4,171	17	4,869 R	68.3%	31.5%	68.4%	31.6%
ST LOUIS	76,667	42,572	33,802	293	8,770 R	55.5%	44.1%	55.7%	44.3%
ST LOUIS CITY	339,194	161,701	176,428	1,065	14,727 D	47.7%	52.0%	47.8%	52.2%
STE GENEVIEVE	3,652	1,099	2,547	6	1,448 D	30.1%	69.7%	30.1%	69.9%
SALINE	13,044	6,780	6,251	13	529 R	52.0%	47.9%	52.0%	48.0%
SCHUYLER	3,628	1,822	1,797	9	25 R	50.2%	49.5%	50.3%	49.7%
SCOTLAND	4,566	2,350	2,194	22	156 R	51.5%	48.1%	51.7%	48.3%
SCOTT	8,944	3,779	5,159	6	1,380 D	42.3%	57.7%	42.3%	57.7%
SHANNON	3,456	1,542	1,884	30	342 D	44.6%	54.5%	45.0%	55.0%
SHELBY	5,468	2,303	3,158	7	855 D	42.1%	57.8%	42.2%	57.8%
STODDARD	8,951	4,906	4,016	29	890 R	54.8%	44.9%	55.0%	45.0%
STONE	3,543	2,972	559	12	2,413 R	83.9%	15.8%	84.2%	15.8%
SULLIVAN	7,496	4,183	3,292	21	891 R	55.8%	43.9%	56.0%	44.0%
TANEY	3,302	2,319	971	12	1,348 R	70.2%	29.4%	70.5%	29.5%
TEXAS	7,133	4,050	3,676	16	983 R	56.8%	56.9%	38.7%	43.1%
VERNON	9,490	5,783	3,676	31	2,107 R	60.9%	38.7%	61.1%	38.9%
WARREN	3,620	2,610	999	11	1,611 R	72.1%	27.6%	72.3%	27.7%
WASHINGTON	5,120	3,019	2,091	10	928 R	59.0%	40.8%	59.1%	40.9%
WAYNE	4,685	2,662	2,011	12	651 R	56.8%	42.9%	57.0%	43.0%
WEBSTER	6,353	4,002	2,343	8	1,659 R	63.0%	36.9%	63.1%	36.9%
WORTH	3,257	1,839	1,407	11	432 R	56.5%	43.2%	56.7%	43.3%
WRIGHT	6,501	4,504	1,973	24	2,531 R	69.3%	30.3%	69.5%	30.5%
TOTAL	1,500,845	834,080	662,684	4,081	171,396 R	55.6%	44.2%	55.7%	44.3%

PRESIDENT 1932

County	Total Vote	Republican	Democratic	Other	Rep.-Dem. Plurality	Total Vote Rep.	Total Vote Dem.	Major Vote Rep.	Major Vote Dem.
MACON	9,718	3,266	6,370	82	3,104 D	33.6%	65.5%	33.9%	66.1%
MADISON	3,788	1,428	2,347	13	919 D	37.7%	62.0%	37.8%	62.2%
MARIES	3,521	1,745	2,758	18	2,013 D	21.2%	78.3%	21.3%	78.7%
MARION	14,519	4,123	10,293	103	6,170 D	28.4%	70.9%	28.6%	71.4%
MERCER	2,901	1,357	1,520	24	163 D	46.8%	52.4%	47.2%	52.8%
MILLER	6,435	2,615	3,776	44	1,161 D	40.6%	58.7%	40.9%	59.1%
MISSISSIPPI	4,858	1,687	3,136	35	1,449 D	34.7%	64.6%	35.0%	65.0%
MONITEAU	6,114	2,331	3,767	16	1,436 D	38.1%	61.6%	38.2%	61.8%
MONROE	6,968	714	6,210	44	5,496 D	10.2%	89.1%	10.3%	89.7%
MONTGOMERY	6,241	2,607	3,600	34	993 D	41.8%	57.7%	42.0%	58.0%
MORGAN	4,807	2,000	2,768	39	768 D	41.6%	57.6%	41.9%	58.1%
NEW MADRID	11,652	3,768	7,837	47	4,069 D	32.3%	67.3%	32.5%	67.5%
NEWTON	12,209	4,806	7,224	179	2,418 D	39.4%	59.2%	40.0%	60.0%
NODAWAY	10,602	3,584	6,959	59	3,375 D	33.8%	65.6%	34.0%	66.0%
OREGON	4,423	786	3,599	38	2,813 D	17.8%	81.4%	17.9%	82.1%
OSAGE	5,387	1,798	3,567	22	1,769 D	33.4%	66.2%	33.5%	66.5%
OZARK	3,106	1,730	1,358	18	372 R	55.7%	43.7%	56.0%	44.0%
PEMISCOT	12,356	4,415	7,909	32	3,494 D	35.7%	64.0%	35.8%	64.2%
PERRY	5,917	2,396	3,502	19	1,106 D	40.5%	59.2%	40.6%	59.4%
PETTIS	15,545	5,982	9,474	89	3,492 D	38.5%	60.9%	38.7%	61.3%
PHELPS	6,720	1,794	4,858	68	3,064 D	26.7%	72.3%	27.0%	73.0%
PIKE	8,379	2,462	5,783	134	3,321 D	29.4%	69.0%	29.9%	70.1%
PLATTE	6,358	1,160	5,179	19	4,019 D	18.2%	81.5%	18.3%	81.7%
POLK	8,213	3,811	4,355	47	544 D	46.4%	53.0%	46.7%	53.3%
PULASKI	4,766	1,489	3,260	17	1,771 D	31.2%	68.4%	31.4%	68.6%
PUTNAM	4,315	2,180	1,987	148	193 R	50.5%	46.0%	52.3%	47.7%
RALLS	4,307	761	3,526	20	2,765 D	17.6%	81.9%	18.3%	82.2%
RANDOLPH	11,935	2,575	9,294	66	6,719 D	21.6%	77.9%	21.7%	78.3%
RAY	7,846	1,706	6,088	52	4,382 D	21.7%	77.6%	21.9%	78.1%
REYNOLDS	3,252	792	2,439	21	1,647 D	24.4%	75.0%	24.5%	75.5%
RIPLEY	3,934	1,139	2,600	95	1,461 D	29.7%	67.8%	30.5%	69.5%
ST CHARLES	10,737	3,664	6,911	162	3,247 D	34.1%	64.4%	34.6%	65.4%
ST CLAIR	6,022	2,271	3,681	70	1,410 D	37.7%	61.1%	38.2%	61.8%
ST FRANCOIS	13,304	6,017	7,613	174	1,596 D	43.6%	55.2%	44.1%	55.9%
ST LOUIS	98,257	35,872	59,044	3,341	23,172 D	36.5%	60.1%	37.8%	62.2%
ST LOUIS CITY	357,105	123,448	226,338	7,319	102,890 D	34.6%	63.4%	35.3%	64.7%
STE GENEVIEVE	4,215	1,109	3,087	19	1,978 D	26.3%	73.2%	26.4%	73.6%
SALINE	12,245	3,783	8,389	73	4,606 D	30.9%	68.5%	31.1%	68.9%
SCHUYLER	3,372	1,109	2,239	24	1,130 D	32.9%	66.4%	33.1%	66.9%
SCOTLAND	4,205	1,410	2,738	57	1,328 D	33.5%	65.1%	34.0%	66.0%
SCOTT	9,333	2,310	6,948	75	4,638 D	24.8%	74.4%	25.0%	75.0%
SHANNON	3,924	879	2,949	96	2,070 D	22.4%	75.2%	23.0%	77.0%
SHELBY	5,344	1,104	4,215	25	3,111 D	20.7%	78.9%	20.8%	79.2%
STODDARD	10,485	3,234	7,139	112	3,905 D	30.8%	68.1%	31.2%	68.8%
STONE	3,688	1,748	1,911	29	163 D	47.4%	51.8%	47.8%	52.2%
SULLIVAN	7,453	3,373	4,053	27	680 D	45.3%	54.4%	45.4%	54.6%
TANEY	3,687	2,045	1,911	31	134 R	51.3%	47.9%	51.7%	48.3%
TEXAS	7,675	2,621	4,996	58	2,375 D	34.1%	65.1%	34.4%	65.6%
VERNON	9,681	2,856	6,687	138	3,831 D	29.5%	69.1%	29.9%	70.1%
WARREN	3,516	1,974	1,513	29	461 R	56.1%	43.0%	56.6%	43.4%
WASHINGTON	5,559	2,246	3,275	38	1,029 D	40.4%	58.9%	40.7%	59.3%
WAYNE	5,169	1,955	3,172	42	1,217 D	37.8%	61.4%	38.1%	61.9%
WEBSTER	7,357	3,041	4,211	63	1,128 D	41.9%	57.2%	42.3%	57.7%
WORTH	2,821	1,041	1,763	17	722 D	36.9%	62.5%	37.1%	62.9%
WRIGHT	6,948	3,023	3,862	63	839 D	43.5%	55.6%	43.9%	56.1%
TOTAL	1,609,894	564,713	1,025,406	19,775	460,693 D	35.1%	63.7%	35.5%	64.5%

MISSOURI

PRESIDENT 1936

County	Total Vote	Republican	Democratic	Other	Rep.-Dem. Plurality	Total Vote Rep.	Total Vote Dem.	Major Vote Rep.	Major Vote Dem.
ADAIR	10,127	4,685	5,315	127	630 D	46.3%	52.5%	46.8%	53.2%
ANDREW	7,693	3,987	3,702	4	285 R	51.8%	48.1%	51.9%	48.1%
ATCHISON	6,503	3,044	3,452	7	408 D	46.8%	53.1%	46.9%	53.1%
AUDRAIN	9,994	2,508	7,455	31	4,947 D	25.1%	74.6%	25.2%	74.8%
BARRY	11,699	5,906	5,744	49	162 R	50.5%	49.1%	50.7%	49.3%
BARTON	7,249	3,164	4,048	37	884 D	43.6%	55.8%	43.9%	56.1%
BATES	10,777	5,022	5,681	74	659 D	46.6%	52.7%	46.9%	53.1%
BENTON	5,346	3,375	1,950	21	1,425 R	63.1%	36.5%	63.4%	36.6%
BOLLINGER	5,869	2,988	2,816	65	172 R	50.9%	48.0%	51.5%	48.5%
BOONE	14,926	3,624	11,241	61	7,617 D	24.3%	75.3%	24.4%	75.6%
BUCHANAN	44,933	15,912	28,825	196	12,913 D	35.4%	64.2%	35.6%	64.4%
BUTLER	12,631	6,355	6,234	42	121 R	50.3%	49.4%	50.5%	49.5%
CALDWELL	6,813	3,792	3,014	7	778 R	55.7%	44.2%	55.7%	44.3%
CALLAWAY	10,293	3,112	7,160	21	4,048 D	30.2%	69.6%	30.3%	69.7%
CAMDEN	4,195	2,281	1,908	6	373 R	54.4%	45.5%	54.5%	45.5%
CAPE GIRARDEAU	16,330	7,374	8,892	64	1,518 D	45.2%	54.5%	45.3%	54.7%
CARROLL	10,605	5,432	5,141	32	291 R	51.2%	48.5%	51.4%	48.6%
CARTER	2,689	1,073	1,590	26	517 D	39.9%	59.1%	40.3%	59.7%
CASS	9,853	4,070	5,731	52	1,661 D	41.3%	58.2%	41.5%	58.5%
CEDAR	6,012	3,535	2,443	34	1,092 R	58.8%	40.6%	59.1%	40.9%
CHARITON	8,957	3,433	5,490	34	2,057 D	38.3%	61.3%	38.5%	61.5%
CHRISTIAN	6,501	4,022	2,462	17	1,560 R	61.9%	37.9%	62.0%	38.0%
CLARK	5,840	2,812	3,003	25	191 D	48.2%	51.4%	48.4%	51.6%
CLAY	14,084	4,491	9,535	58	5,044 D	31.9%	67.7%	32.0%	68.0%
CLINTON	6,727	2,512	4,166	49	1,654 D	37.3%	61.9%	37.6%	62.4%
COLE	15,106	6,180	8,831	95	2,651 D	40.9%	58.5%	41.2%	58.8%
COOPER	10,197	4,980	5,188	29	208 D	49.0%	50.9%	49.0%	51.0%
CRAWFORD	5,961	3,041	2,879	41	162 R	51.0%	48.3%	51.4%	48.6%
DADE	5,669	3,326	2,312	31	1,014 R	58.7%	40.8%	58.9%	41.0%
DALLAS	4,828	3,066	1,749	13	1,317 R	63.5%	36.2%	63.7%	36.3%
DAVIESS	7,902	3,924	3,953	25	29 D	49.7%	50.0%	49.8%	50.2%
DE KALB	5,570	2,872	2,680	18	192 R	51.6%	48.1%	51.7%	48.3%
DENT	5,514	2,313	3,168	33	855 D	41.9%	57.5%	42.2%	57.8%
DOUGLAS	6,187	4,031	2,118	38	1,913 R	65.2%	34.2%	65.6%	34.4%
DUNKLIN	14,066	3,775	10,233	58	6,458 D	26.8%	72.7%	26.9%	73.1%
FRANKLIN	15,920	7,708	7,565	647	143 R	48.4%	47.5%	50.5%	49.5%
GASCONADE	5,716	4,202	1,492	22	2,710 R	73.5%	26.1%	73.8%	26.2%
GENTRY	7,306	3,115	4,173	18	1,058 D	42.6%	57.1%	42.7%	57.3%
GREENE	38,906	17,298	21,489	119	4,191 D	44.5%	55.2%	44.6%	55.4%
GRUNDY	8,763	4,521	4,187	55	334 R	51.6%	47.8%	51.9%	48.1%
HARRISON	8,852	4,888	3,942	22	946 R	55.2%	44.5%	55.4%	44.6%
HENRY	12,111	4,927	7,145	39	2,218 D	40.7%	59.0%	40.8%	59.2%
HICKORY	3,247	2,329	910	8	1,419 R	71.7%	28.0%	71.9%	28.1%
HOLT	6,499	3,409	3,076	14	333 R	52.5%	47.3%	52.5%	47.4%
HOWARD	7,092	1,745	5,326	21	3,581 D	24.6%	75.1%	24.7%	75.3%
HOWELL	10,064	5,297	4,725	42	572 R	52.6%	46.9%	52.9%	47.1%
IRON	4,029	1,605	2,413	11	808 D	39.8%	59.9%	39.9%	60.1%
JACKSON	295,319	79,119	215,120	1,080	136,001 D	26.8%	72.8%	26.9%	73.1%
JASPER	34,585	14,440	19,822	323	5,382 D	41.8%	57.3%	42.1%	57.9%
JEFFERSON	14,974	5,575	9,158	241	3,583 D	37.2%	61.2%	37.8%	62.2%
JOHNSON	12,113	5,797	6,294	22	497 D	47.9%	52.0%	47.9%	52.1%
KNOX	5,193	2,134	3,030	29	896 D	41.1%	58.3%	41.3%	58.7%
LACLEDE	7,977	4,258	3,691	28	567 R	53.4%	46.3%	53.6%	46.4%
LAFAYETTE	14,861	7,535	7,275	51	260 R	50.7%	49.0%	50.9%	49.1%
LAWRENCE	12,439	6,185	6,184	70	1 R	49.7%	49.7%	50.0%	50.0%
LEWIS	5,903	1,994	3,859	50	1,865 D	33.8%	65.4%	34.1%	65.9%
LINCOLN	6,924	2,258	4,625	41	2,367 D	32.6%	66.8%	32.8%	67.2%
LINN	11,915	5,118	6,744	53	1,626 D	43.0%	56.6%	43.1%	56.9%
LIVINGSTON	9,944	4,678	5,226	40	548 D	47.0%	52.5%	47.2%	52.8%
MCDONALD	6,819	3,312	3,503	4	191 D	48.6%	51.4%	48.6%	51.4%

PRESIDENT 1940

County	Total Vote	Republican	Democratic	Other	Rep.-Dem. Plurality	Total Vote Rep.	Total Vote Dem.	Major Vote Rep.	Major Vote Dem.
ADAIR	10,566	5,688	4,813	65	875 R	53.8%	45.6%	54.2%	45.8%
ANDREW	7,454	4,384	3,059	11	1,325 R	58.8%	41.0%	58.9%	41.1%
ATCHISON	6,358	3,322	3,025	11	297 R	52.2%	47.6%	52.3%	47.7%
AUDRAIN	11,224	3,447	7,768	9	4,321 D	30.7%	69.2%	30.7%	69.3%
BARRY	11,804	6,573	5,207	24	1,366 R	55.7%	44.1%	55.8%	44.2%
BARTON	7,315	3,737	3,539	39	198 R	51.1%	48.4%	51.4%	48.6%
BATES	10,738	5,727	4,978	33	749 R	53.3%	46.4%	53.5%	46.5%
BENTON	5,695	3,912	1,765	18	2,147 R	68.7%	31.0%	68.9%	31.1%
BOLLINGER	5,934	3,415	2,511	8	904 R	57.5%	42.3%	57.6%	42.4%
BOONE	16,543	4,869	11,615	59	6,746 D	29.4%	70.2%	29.5%	70.5%
BUCHANAN	41,995	17,484	24,482	29	6,998 D	41.6%	58.3%	41.7%	58.3%
BUTLER	14,275	8,024	6,213	38	1,811 R	56.2%	43.5%	56.4%	43.6%
CALDWELL	6,713	3,976	2,728	9	1,248 R	59.2%	40.6%	59.3%	40.7%
CALLAWAY	10,757	3,574	7,162	21	3,588 D	33.2%	66.6%	33.3%	66.7%
CAMDEN	4,246	2,692	1,549	5	1,143 R	63.4%	36.5%	63.5%	36.5%
CAPE GIRARDEAU	17,978	9,297	8,642	39	655 R	51.7%	48.1%	51.8%	48.2%
CARROLL	10,457	6,000	4,446	11	1,554 R	57.4%	42.5%	57.5%	42.6%
CARTER	2,697	1,195	1,499	3	304 D	44.3%	55.6%	44.4%	55.6%
CASS	10,479	4,983	5,479	17	496 D	47.5%	52.3%	47.6%	52.4%
CEDAR	6,073	4,068	1,973	32	2,095 R	67.0%	32.5%	67.3%	32.7%
CHARITON	9,497	4,439	5,053	5	614 D	46.7%	53.2%	46.8%	53.2%
CHRISTIAN	6,253	4,509	1,729	15	2,780 R	72.1%	27.7%	72.3%	27.7%
CLARK	5,917	3,171	2,728	18	443 R	53.6%	46.1%	53.8%	46.2%
CLAY	15,861	6,159	9,672	30	3,513 D	38.8%	61.0%	38.9%	61.1%
CLINTON	6,847	3,030	3,800	17	770 D	44.3%	55.5%	44.4%	55.6%
COLE	15,892	7,664	8,219	9	555 D	48.2%	51.7%	48.3%	51.7%
COOPER	10,343	5,720	4,606	17	1,114 R	55.3%	44.5%	55.4%	44.6%
CRAWFORD	6,365	3,615	2,736	14	879 R	56.8%	43.0%	56.9%	43.1%
DADE	5,761	3,910	1,835	16	2,075 R	67.9%	31.9%	68.1%	31.9%
DALLAS	5,435	3,859	1,566	10	2,293 R	71.0%	28.8%	71.1%	28.9%
DAVIESS	7,625	4,289	3,325	11	964 R	56.2%	43.6%	56.3%	43.7%
DE KALB	5,593	3,072	2,505	16	567 R	54.9%	44.8%	55.1%	44.9%
DENT	5,766	2,652	3,101	13	449 D	46.0%	53.8%	46.1%	53.9%
DOUGLAS	6,252	4,870	1,350	32	3,520 R	77.9%	21.6%	78.3%	21.6%
DUNKLIN	16,680	5,516	11,132	32	5,616 D	33.1%	66.7%	33.1%	66.9%
FRANKLIN	17,555	10,283	7,237	35	3,046 R	58.6%	41.2%	58.7%	41.3%
GASCONADE	6,501	5,333	1,163	5	4,170 R	82.0%	17.9%	82.1%	17.9%
GENTRY	7,154	3,446	3,689	19	243 D	48.2%	51.6%	48.3%	51.7%
GREENE	43,695	21,456	22,130	109	674 D	49.1%	50.6%	49.2%	50.8%
GRUNDY	8,404	4,558	3,813	33	745 R	54.2%	45.4%	54.4%	45.6%
HARRISON	8,636	5,304	3,325	7	1,979 R	61.4%	38.5%	61.5%	38.5%
HENRY	12,423	6,332	6,069	22	263 R	51.0%	48.9%	51.1%	48.9%
HICKORY	3,291	2,496	787	8	1,709 R	75.8%	23.9%	76.0%	24.0%
HOLT	6,422	3,739	2,677	6	1,062 R	58.2%	41.7%	58.3%	41.7%
HOWARD	7,123	2,333	4,770	20	2,437 D	32.8%	67.0%	32.8%	67.2%
HOWELL	10,397	6,158	4,218	21	1,940 R	59.2%	40.6%	59.3%	40.7%
IRON	4,565	2,062	2,495	8	433 D	45.2%	54.7%	45.2%	54.8%
JACKSON	239,019	101,568	137,285	366	35,717 D	42.5%	57.4%	42.5%	57.5%
JASPER	37,111	18,755	18,249	107	506 R	50.5%	49.2%	50.7%	49.3%
JEFFERSON	17,115	7,517	9,553	45	2,036 D	43.9%	55.8%	44.0%	56.0%
JOHNSON	11,928	6,468	5,441	19	1,027 R	54.2%	45.6%	54.3%	45.7%
KNOX	4,983	2,370	2,594	19	224 D	47.6%	52.1%	47.6%	52.3%
LACLEDE	8,278	4,941	3,323	14	1,618 R	59.7%	40.1%	59.8%	40.2%
LAFAYETTE	15,744	8,802	6,913	29	1,889 R	55.9%	43.9%	56.0%	44.0%
LAWRENCE	12,641	7,317	5,279	45	2,038 R	57.9%	41.8%	58.1%	41.9%
LEWIS	5,942	2,428	3,484	30	1,056 D	40.9%	58.6%	41.1%	58.9%
LINCOLN	7,480	3,035	4,420	25	1,385 D	40.7%	59.1%	40.7%	59.3%
LINN	11,934	5,664	6,246	24	582 D	47.5%	52.3%	47.6%	52.4%
LIVINGSTON	9,956	5,298	4,633	25	665 R	53.2%	46.5%	53.3%	46.7%
MCDONALD	7,394	4,063	3,312	19	751 R	54.9%	44.8%	55.1%	44.9%

MISSOURI

PRESIDENT 1936

County	Total Vote	Republican	Democratic	Other	Rep.-Dem. Plurality	Total Vote Rep.	Total Vote Dem.	Major Vote Rep.	Major Vote Dem.
MACON	11,262	4,808	6,417	37	1,609 D	42.7%	57.0%	42.8%	57.2%
MADISON	4,342	2,013	2,323	6	310 D	46.4%	53.5%	46.4%	53.6%
MARIES	3,740	1,306	2,414	20	1,108 D	34.9%	64.5%	35.1%	64.9%
MARION	15,747	4,628	11,068	51	6,440 D	29.4%	70.3%	29.5%	70.5%
MERCER	4,605	2,757	1,834	14	923 R	59.9%	39.8%	60.1%	39.9%
MILLER	7,086	3,607	3,436	43	171 R	50.9%	48.5%	51.2%	48.8%
MISSISSIPPI	6,737	2,552	4,160	25	1,608 D	37.9%	61.7%	38.0%	62.0%
MONITEAU	6,466	3,238	3,210	18	28 D	50.1%	49.6%	50.2%	49.8%
MONROE	7,340	939	6,376	25	5,437 D	12.8%	86.9%	12.8%	87.2%
MONTGOMERY	6,937	3,468	3,458	11	10 R	49.9%	49.8%	50.1%	49.9%
MORGAN	5,596	2,993	2,585	18	408 R	53.5%	46.2%	53.7%	46.3%
NEW MADRID	12,872	5,056	7,791	25	2,735 D	39.3%	60.5%	39.4%	60.6%
NEWTON	13,448	6,437	6,929	82	492 D	48.2%	51.8%	48.2%	51.8%
NODAWAY	13,399	5,817	7,499	83	1,682 D	43.4%	56.0%	43.7%	56.3%
OREGON	4,970	1,461	3,504	5	2,043 D	29.4%	70.5%	29.4%	70.6%
OSAGE	5,899	2,836	2,995	68	159 D	48.1%	50.8%	48.6%	51.4%
OZARK	4,354	2,981	1,359	14	1,622 R	68.5%	31.2%	68.7%	31.3%
PEMISCOT	12,324	4,139	8,171	14	4,032 D	33.6%	66.3%	33.6%	66.4%
PERRY	6,606	3,382	3,098	126	284 R	51.2%	46.9%	52.2%	47.8%
PETTIS	16,821	7,435	9,265	121	1,830 D	44.2%	55.1%	44.5%	55.5%
PHELPS	7,381	2,690	4,658	33	1,968 D	36.4%	63.1%	36.6%	63.4%
PIKE	8,827	2,871	5,898	58	3,027 D	32.5%	66.8%	32.7%	67.3%
PLATTE	6,691	1,787	4,884	20	3,097 D	26.7%	73.0%	26.8%	73.2%
POLK	9,048	5,126	3,899	23	1,227 R	56.7%	43.1%	56.8%	43.2%
PULASKI	5,076	2,177	2,886	13	709 D	42.9%	56.9%	43.0%	57.0%
PUTNAM	5,402	3,458	1,902	42	1,556 R	64.0%	35.2%	64.5%	35.5%
RALLS	4,885	1,051	3,822	12	2,771 D	21.5%	78.2%	21.6%	78.4%
RANDOLPH	12,491	2,723	9,733	35	7,010 D	21.8%	77.9%	21.9%	78.1%
RAY	9,124	2,805	6,300	19	3,495 D	30.7%	69.0%	30.8%	69.2%
REYNOLDS	3,396	915	2,476	5	1,561 D	26.9%	72.9%	27.0%	73.0%
RIPLEY	4,397	1,911	2,466	20	555 D	43.5%	56.1%	43.7%	56.3%
ST CHARLES	12,068	5,156	5,903	1,009	747 D	42.7%	48.9%	46.4%	53.4%
ST CLAIR	6,684	3,351	3,302	31	49 R	50.1%	49.4%	50.4%	49.6%
ST FRANCOIS	15,213	7,271	7,876	66	605 D	47.8%	51.8%	48.0%	52.0%
ST LOUIS	112,100	45,541	63,226	3,333	17,685 D	40.6%	56.4%	41.9%	58.1%
ST LOUIS CITY	396,830	127,887	260,063	8,880	132,176 D	32.2%	65.5%	33.0%	67.0%
STE GENEVIEVE	4,182	1,664	2,446	72	782 D	39.8%	58.5%	40.5%	59.5%
SALINE	14,776	6,108	8,622	46	2,514 D	41.3%	58.4%	41.5%	58.5%
SCHUYLER	3,629	1,447	2,173	9	726 D	39.9%	59.9%	40.0%	60.0%
SCOTLAND	4,772	1,940	2,768	64	828 D	40.7%	58.0%	41.2%	58.8%
SCOTT	10,941	3,126	7,763	52	4,637 D	28.6%	71.0%	28.7%	71.3%
SHANNON	4,349	1,225	3,069	55	1,844 D	28.2%	70.6%	28.5%	71.5%
SHELBY	6,102	1,697	4,367	38	2,670 D	27.8%	71.5%	28.0%	72.0%
STODDARD	11,491	4,828	6,608	55	1,780 D	42.0%	57.5%	42.2%	57.8%
STONE	4,745	3,366	1,366	13	2,000 R	70.9%	28.8%	71.1%	28.9%
SULLIVAN	8,025	4,019	3,986	20	33 R	50.1%	49.7%	50.2%	49.8%
TANEY	4,550	2,827	1,710	23	1,117 R	62.0%	37.5%	62.3%	37.7%
TEXAS	8,884	4,132	4,718	34	586 D	46.5%	53.1%	46.7%	53.3%
VERNON	11,478	4,546	6,872	60	2,326 D	39.6%	59.9%	39.6%	60.2%
WARREN	3,941	2,639	1,277	25	1,362 R	67.0%	32.4%	67.4%	32.6%
WASHINGTON	5,902	2,909	2,942	51	33 D	49.3%	49.8%	49.7%	50.3%
WAYNE	5,745	2,494	3,235	16	741 D	43.4%	56.3%	43.5%	56.5%
WEBSTER	8,102	4,469	3,612	21	857 R	55.2%	44.6%	55.3%	44.7%
WORTH	3,556	1,581	1,702	31	363 D	44.4%	47.8%	44.5%	55.5%
WRIGHT	8,174	4,837	3,296	41	1,541 R	59.2%	40.3%	59.5%	40.5%
TOTAL	1,828,635	697,891	1,111,043	19,701	413,152 D	38.2%	60.8%	38.6%	61.4%

PRESIDENT 1940

County	Total Vote	Republican	Democratic	Other	Rep.-Dem. Plurality	Total Vote Rep.	Total Vote Dem.	Major Vote Rep.	Major Vote Dem.
MACON	11,519	5,384	6,120	15	736 D	46.7%	53.1%	46.8%	53.2%
MADISON	4,905	2,495	2,405	5	90 R	50.8%	49.0%	50.9%	49.1%
MARIES	3,836	1,749	2,078	9	329 D	45.6%	54.2%	45.7%	54.3%
MARION	15,660	5,892	9,723	45	3,831 D	37.6%	62.1%	37.7%	62.3%
MERCER	4,161	2,787	1,364	10	1,423 R	67.0%	32.8%	67.1%	32.9%
MILLER	7,107	3,971	3,113	23	858 R	55.9%	43.8%	56.1%	43.9%
MISSISSIPPI	7,462	3,073	4,362	27	1,289 D	41.3%	58.5%	41.3%	58.7%
MONITEAU	6,556	3,627	2,922	7	705 R	55.3%	44.6%	55.4%	44.6%
MONROE	7,231	1,610	6,205	13	4,818 D	16.6%	83.1%	16.6%	83.4%
MONTGOMERY	7,151	3,930	3,205	16	725 D	55.0%	44.8%	55.1%	44.9%
MORGAN	5,556	3,166	2,376	14	790 R	57.0%	42.8%	57.1%	42.9%
NEW MADRID	15,933	6,318	9,591	24	3,273 D	39.7%	60.2%	39.7%	60.3%
NEWTON	14,564	8,064	6,256	44	1,808 R	56.3%	43.5%	56.3%	43.7%
NODAWAY	13,461	6,759	6,696	6	63 R	50.2%	49.7%	50.2%	49.8%
OREGON	5,434	1,826	3,593	15	1,767 D	33.6%	66.1%	33.7%	66.3%
OSAGE	6,086	3,743	2,332	11	1,411 R	61.5%	38.3%	61.6%	38.3%
OZARK	4,405	3,421	965	19	2,456 R	77.7%	21.9%	78.0%	22.0%
PEMISCOT	15,453	6,011	9,391	51	2,380 D	38.9%	60.8%	39.0%	61.0%
PERRY	7,019	4,656	2,354	9	2,302 R	66.3%	33.5%	66.4%	33.6%
PETTIS	17,492	8,905	8,570	17	335 R	50.9%	49.0%	51.0%	49.0%
PHELPS	8,114	3,319	4,780	15	1,461 D	40.9%	58.9%	41.0%	59.0%
PIKE	9,489	3,707	5,742	40	2,035 D	39.1%	60.5%	39.2%	60.8%
PLATTE	7,193	2,545	4,635	13	2,090 D	35.4%	64.4%	35.4%	64.6%
POLK	8,928	5,534	3,380	14	2,154 R	62.0%	37.9%	62.1%	37.9%
PULASKI	5,127	2,367	2,752	8	385 D	46.2%	53.7%	46.2%	53.8%
PUTNAM	5,551	3,828	1,708	25	2,120 R	68.8%	30.7%	69.1%	30.9%
RALLS	4,930	1,412	3,562	6	2,150 D	28.4%	72.5%	28.4%	72.5%[?]
RANDOLPH	12,497	3,319	9,155	23	5,836 D	26.6%	73.3%	26.6%	73.4%
RAY	9,201	3,399	5,786	16	2,387 D	36.9%	62.9%	37.0%	63.0%
REYNOLDS	3,610	1,187	2,406	17	1,219 D	33.0%	66.8%	33.0%	67.0%
RIPLEY	4,725	2,291	2,419	15	128 D	48.5%	51.2%	48.6%	51.4%
ST CHARLES	13,176	5,792	5,334	50	458 R	59.1%	40.5%	59.4%	40.6%
ST CLAIR	6,834	3,950	2,859	25	1,091 R	57.8%	41.8%	58.0%	58.0%[?]
ST FRANCOIS	16,851	8,687	8,132	32	555 R	51.6%	48.3%	51.6%	48.4%
ST LOUIS	119,747	66,909	52,380	458	14,529 R	55.9%	43.7%	56.1%	43.9%
ST LOUIS CITY	402,451	168,165	233,338	948	65,173 D	41.8%	58.0%	41.9%	58.1%
STE GENEVIEVE	4,856	2,750	2,098	8	652 D	56.6%	43.2%	56.7%	43.3%
SALINE	15,352	7,336	7,988	28	652 D	47.8%	52.0%	47.9%	52.1%
SCHUYLER	3,748	1,732	1,998	18	266 D	46.2%	53.3%	46.4%	53.5%
SCOTLAND	4,787	2,329	2,435	23	106 D	48.7%	50.9%	48.9%	51.1%
SCOTT	12,342	4,401	7,899	42	3,498 D	35.7%	64.0%	35.8%	64.2%
SHANNON	4,423	1,589	2,806	28	1,217 D	35.9%	64.7%	36.2%	63.3%
SHELBY	6,221	2,167	4,028	26	1,861 D	34.8%	64.7%	35.0%	65.0%
STODDARD	12,818	6,055	6,725	38	670 D	47.2%	52.5%	47.4%	52.6%
STONE	4,647	3,598	1,041	8	2,557 R	77.4%	22.4%	77.6%	22.4%
SULLIVAN	7,836	4,080	3,743	13	337 R	52.1%	47.8%	52.2%	47.8%
TANEY	4,684	3,167	1,497	20	1,670 R	67.6%	32.0%	67.9%	32.1%
TEXAS	11,735	4,730	6,271	21	233 D	51.3%	53.4%	46.5%	53.5%
VERNON	11,735	5,443	6,271	21	828 D	46.4%	53.4%	46.5%	53.5%
WARREN	4,344	3,403	914	27	2,489 R	78.3%	21.0%	78.8%	21.2%
WASHINGTON	6,706	3,817	2,881	8	936 R	56.9%	42.9%	57.0%	43.0%
WAYNE	5,739	2,735	2,991	13	256 D	47.7%	52.1%	47.8%	52.2%
WEBSTER	8,352	4,818	3,518	16	1,300 R	57.7%	42.1%	57.8%	42.2%
WORTH	3,513	1,807	1,702	4	105 R	51.4%	48.4%	51.5%	48.5%
WRIGHT	7,843	5,096	2,727	20	2,369 R	65.0%	34.8%	65.1%	34.9%
TOTAL	1,833,729	871,009	958,476	4,244	87,467 D	47.5%	52.3%	47.6%	52.4%

MISSOURI

PRESIDENT 1944

County	Total Vote	Republican	Democratic	Other	Rep.-Dem. Plurality	% Total Rep.	% Total Dem.	% Major Rep.	% Major Dem.
ADAIR	8,544	4,909	3,606	26	1,303 R	57.5	42.2	57.7	42.3
ANDREW	5,995	3,734	2,254	7	1,480 R	62.3	37.6	62.4	37.6
ATCHISON	5,021	2,803	2,214	4	589 R	55.8	44.1	55.9	44.1
AUDRAIN	9,939	3,455	6,471	13	3,016 D	34.8	65.1	34.8	65.1
BARRY	9,848	5,796	4,029	23	1,767 R	58.9	40.9	59.0	41.0
BARTON	6,067	3,356	2,688	23	668 R	55.3	44.3	55.5	44.5
BATES	9,236	5,122	4,096	18	1,026 R	55.5	44.3	55.6	44.4
BENTON	4,408	3,294	1,108	6	2,186 R	74.7	25.1	74.8	25.2
BOLLINGER	4,694	2,850	1,841	3	1,009 R	60.7	39.2	60.8	39.2
BOONE	13,929	4,195	9,704	30	5,509 D	30.1	69.6	30.2	69.8
BUCHANAN	35,224	15,113	20,091	20	4,978 D	42.9	57.0	42.9	57.1
BUTLER	10,626	6,375	4,219	32	2,156 R	60.0	39.7	60.2	39.8
CALDWELL	5,393	3,384	2,001	8	1,383 R	62.7	37.1	62.8	37.2
CALLAWAY	8,924	3,143	5,757	24	2,614 D	35.2	64.5	35.3	64.7
CAMDEN	3,175	2,180	990	5	1,190 R	68.7	31.2	68.8	31.2
CAPE GIRARDEAU	15,195	8,339	6,845	11	1,494 R	54.9	45.0	55.1	45.1
CARROLL	8,430	5,127	3,283	20	1,844 R	60.8	38.9	61.0	39.0
CARTER	2,252	1,033	1,207	12	174 D	45.9	53.6	46.1	53.9
CASS	9,041	4,687	4,347	7	340 R	51.8	48.1	51.9	48.1
CEDAR	5,059	3,576	1,478	5	2,098 R	70.7	29.2	70.8	29.2
CHARITON	7,740	3,802	3,930	8	128 D	49.1	50.8	49.2	50.8
CHRISTIAN	5,310	4,167	1,134	9	3,033 R	78.5	21.4	78.6	21.4
CLARK	4,868	2,707	2,155	6	552 R	55.6	44.3	55.7	44.3
CLAY	15,446	6,724	8,682	40	1,958 D	43.5	56.2	43.6	56.4
CLINTON	5,996	2,912	3,079	5	167 D	48.6	51.4	48.6	51.4
COLE	14,507	7,364	7,139	4	225 R	50.8	49.2	50.8	49.2
COOPER	8,677	4,928	3,729	20	1,199 R	56.8	43.0	56.8	43.1
CRAWFORD	5,264	3,077	2,177	10	900 R	58.5	41.4	58.6	41.4
DADE	4,786	3,316	1,462	8	1,854 R	69.3	30.5	69.4	30.6
DALLAS	4,306	3,232	1,064	10	2,168 R	75.1	24.7	75.2	24.8
DAVIESS	6,169	3,597	2,567	5	1,030 R	58.3	41.6	58.4	41.6
DE KALB	4,625	2,658	1,961	6	697 R	57.5	42.4	57.5	42.5
DENT	5,162	2,456	2,699	7	243 D	47.6	52.3	47.6	52.4
DOUGLAS	4,330	3,570	746	14	2,824 R	82.4	17.2	82.7	17.3
DUNKLIN	12,732	4,274	8,431	27	4,157 D	33.6	66.2	33.6	66.4
FRANKLIN	15,326	9,325	5,958	43	3,367 R	60.8	38.9	61.0	39.0
GASCONADE	6,013	5,007	994	12	4,013 R	83.3	16.5	83.4	16.6
GENTRY	6,000	2,970	3,022	8	52 D	49.5	50.4	49.6	50.4
GREENE	38,886	21,531	17,287	68	4,244 R	55.3	44.5	55.5	44.5
GRUNDY	7,167	4,158	2,997	12	1,161 R	58.0	41.8	58.1	41.9
HARRISON	6,964	4,330	2,623	11	1,707 R	62.2	37.7	62.3	37.7
HENRY	10,174	5,564	4,587	23	977 R	54.7	45.1	54.8	45.2
HICKORY	2,734	2,171	560	3	1,611 R	79.4	20.5	79.5	20.5
HOLT	4,946	3,152	1,785	9	1,367 R	63.7	36.1	63.8	36.2
HOWARD	5,918	1,951	3,958	9	2,007 D	33.0	66.9	33.0	67.0
HOWELL	8,185	5,151	3,020	14	2,131 R	62.9	36.9	63.0	37.0
IRON	3,854	1,649	2,205		556 D	42.8	57.2	42.8	57.2
JACKSON	209,632	95,406	113,803	423	18,397 D	45.5	54.3	45.6	54.4
JASPER	30,475	17,301	13,111	63	4,190 R	56.8	43.0	56.9	43.1
JEFFERSON	14,745	6,758	7,953	34	1,195 D	45.8	53.9	45.9	54.1
JOHNSON	10,378	5,949	4,419	10	1,530 R	57.3	42.6	57.4	42.6
KNOX	4,008	2,057	1,943	8	114 R	51.3	48.5	51.4	48.6
LACLEDE	7,687	4,670	3,011	6	1,659 R	60.8	39.2	60.8	39.2
LAFAYETTE	13,561	7,951	5,603	7	2,348 R	58.6	41.3	58.7	41.3
LAWRENCE	10,722	6,836	3,859	27	2,977 R	63.8	36.0	63.9	36.1
LEWIS	4,882	1,988	2,883	11	895 D	40.7	59.1	40.8	59.2
LINCOLN	6,698	2,910	3,773	15	863 D	43.4	56.3	43.5	56.5
LINN	10,193	4,942	5,242	9	300 D	48.5	51.4	48.5	51.5
LIVINGSTON	8,610	4,697	3,887	26	810 R	54.6	45.1	54.7	45.3
MCDONALD	6,056	3,520	2,523	13	997 R	58.1	41.7	58.2	41.8

PRESIDENT 1948

County	Total Vote	Republican	Democratic	Other	Rep.-Dem. Plurality	% Total Rep.	% Total Dem.	% Major Rep.	% Major Dem.
ADAIR	8,201	4,024	4,136	41	112 D	49.1	50.4	49.3	50.7
ANDREW	5,729	3,142	2,576	11	566 R	54.8	45.0	54.9	45.1
ATCHISON	4,693	2,190	2,498	5	308 D	46.7	53.2	46.7	53.3
AUDRAIN	10,250	2,730	7,495	16	4,756 D	26.7	73.1	26.8	73.2
BARRY	9,536	4,812	4,724		88 R	50.5	49.5	50.5	49.5
BARTON	5,592	2,577	3,008	7	431 D	46.1	53.8	46.1	53.9
BATES	8,533	4,156	4,371	6	215 D	48.7	51.2	48.7	51.3
BENTON	4,131	2,768	1,360	3	1,408 R	67.0	32.9	67.1	32.9
BOLLINGER	4,267	2,187	2,075	5	112 R	51.3	48.6	51.3	48.7
BOONE	14,653	4,289	10,200	164	5,911 D	29.3	69.6	29.6	70.4
BUCHANAN	36,034	13,002	22,975	57	9,973 D	36.1	63.8	36.1	63.9
BUTLER	9,630	4,276	5,319	35	1,043 D	44.4	55.2	44.5	55.4
CALDWELL	4,676	2,687	1,985	4	702 R	57.5	42.5	57.5	42.5
CALLAWAY	8,658	2,433	6,215	10	3,782 D	28.1	71.8	28.1	71.9
CAMDEN	3,291	2,020	1,264	7	756 R	61.4	38.4	61.5	38.5
CAPE GIRARDEAU	14,971	7,084	7,872	15	788 D	47.3	52.6	47.4	52.6
CARROLL	7,618	4,212	3,401	5	811 R	55.3	44.6	55.3	44.7
CARTER	2,237	964	1,255	18	291 D	43.1	56.1	43.4	56.6
CASS	9,045	3,614	5,415	16	1,801 D	40.0	59.9	40.0	60.0
CEDAR	5,000	2,928	2,062	10	866 R	58.6	41.2	58.7	41.3
CHARITON	6,791	2,615	4,170	6	1,555 D	38.5	61.4	38.5	61.5
CHRISTIAN	4,735	3,119	1,600	16	1,529 R	66.1	33.8	66.2	33.8
CLARK	4,619	2,264	2,352	3	88 D	49.0	50.9	49.0	51.0
CLAY	18,304	6,408	11,855	41	5,447 D	35.0	64.8	35.1	64.9
CLINTON	5,715	2,227	3,481	7	1,254 D	39.0	60.9	39.0	61.0
COLE	14,825	6,909	7,891	25	982 D	46.6	53.2	46.7	53.3
COOPER	7,968	4,094	3,865	9	229 D	51.4	48.5	51.4	48.6
CRAWFORD	4,949	2,650	2,289	10	361 R	53.5	46.3	53.7	46.3
DADE	4,521	2,783	1,733	5	1,050 R	61.5	38.3	61.6	38.4
DALLAS	4,296	2,695	1,590	11	1,105 R	62.7	37.0	62.9	37.1
DAVIESS	5,693	2,823	2,868	2	45 D	49.6	50.4	49.6	50.4
DE KALB	4,135	2,098	2,033	4	65 R	50.7	49.2	50.8	49.2
DENT	4,990	2,003	2,973	14	970 D	40.1	59.6	40.3	59.7
DOUGLAS	3,914	2,734	1,163	17	1,571 R	69.9	29.7	70.2	29.8
DUNKLIN	13,461	2,466	10,979	16	8,513 D	18.3	81.6	18.3	81.7
FRANKLIN	15,585	7,725	7,822	38	97 D	49.6	50.2	49.7	50.3
GASCONADE	5,485	4,268	1,204	13	3,064 R	77.8	22.0	78.0	22.0
GENTRY	6,044	2,633	3,410	1	777 D	43.6	56.4	43.6	56.4
GREENE	39,664	18,836	20,762	66	1,926 D	47.5	52.3	47.6	52.4
GRUNDY	6,512	3,331	3,177	4	154 R	51.2	48.8	51.2	48.8
HARRISON	6,513	3,646	2,854	13	792 R	56.0	43.8	56.1	43.9
HENRY	10,174	4,619	5,551	4	932 D	45.4	54.6	45.4	54.6
HICKORY	2,462	1,728	733	1	995 R	70.2	29.8	70.2	29.8
HOLT	4,651	2,607	2,040	4	567 R	56.1	43.9	56.1	43.9
HOWARD	5,693	1,538	4,143	12	2,605 D	27.0	72.8	27.1	72.9
HOWELL	8,060	4,427	3,599	34	828 R	54.9	44.7	55.2	44.8
IRON	3,994	1,435	2,552	7	1,117 D	35.9	63.9	36.0	64.0
JACKSON	226,527	86,471	139,186	870	52,715 D	38.2	61.4	38.3	61.7
JASPER	30,078	15,404	14,593	81	811 R	51.2	48.5	51.4	51.4
JEFFERSON	16,435	6,085	10,280	70	4,195 R	37.0	62.5	37.2	62.8
JOHNSON	9,805	4,903	4,888	14	15 R	50.0	49.9	50.1	49.9
KNOX	3,889	1,620	2,268	1	648 D	41.7	58.3	41.7	58.3
LACLEDE	7,015	3,773	3,221	21	552 R	53.8	45.9	53.9	46.1
LAFAYETTE	12,642	6,634	5,988	20	646 R	52.5	47.4	52.6	47.4
LAWRENCE	10,058	5,392	4,649	17	743 R	53.6	46.2	53.7	46.3
LEWIS	4,731	1,564	3,155	12	1,591 D	33.1	66.7	33.1	66.9
LINCOLN	6,336	2,135	4,190	11	2,055 D	33.7	66.1	33.8	66.2
LINN	9,833	4,034	5,788	11	1,754 D	41.0	58.9	41.1	58.9
LIVINGSTON	8,031	3,835	4,182	14	347 D	47.8	52.1	47.8	52.2
MCDONALD	5,915	2,979	2,925	11	54 R	50.4	49.5	50.5	49.5

MISSOURI

PRESIDENT 1944

County	Total Vote	Republican	Democratic	Other	Rep.-Dem. Plurality	Total Vote Rep.	Total Vote Dem.	Major Vote Rep.	Major Vote Dem.
MACON	9,581	4,796	4,772	13	24 R	50.1%	49.8%	50.1%	49.9%
MADISON	4,488	2,277	2,203	8	74 R	50.7%	49.1%	50.8%	49.2%
MARIES	3,366	1,519	1,824	23	305 D	45.1%	54.2%	45.4%	54.6%
MARION	13,149	4,560	8,575	14	4,015 D	34.7%	65.2%	34.7%	65.3%
MERCER	3,288	2,249	1,035	4	1,214 R	68.4%	31.5%	68.5%	31.5%
MILLER	5,850	3,609	2,229	12	1,380 R	61.7%	38.1%	61.8%	38.2%
MISSISSIPPI	6,153	1,944	4,182	27	2,238 D	31.6%	68.0%	31.7%	68.3%
MONITEAU	5,577	3,237	2,327	13	910 R	58.0%	41.7%	58.2%	41.8%
MONROE	6,106	1,098	5,000	8	3,902 D	18.0%	81.9%	18.0%	82.0%
MONTGOMERY	6,276	3,527	2,743	6	784 R	56.2%	43.7%	56.3%	43.7%
MORGAN	4,641	2,896	1,735	10	1,161 R	62.4%	37.4%	62.5%	37.5%
NEW MADRID	11,752	4,108	7,626	18	3,518 D	35.0%	64.9%	35.0%	65.0%
NEWTON	12,154	6,985	5,146	23	1,839 R	57.5%	42.3%	57.6%	42.4%
NODAWAY	11,180	5,766	5,407	7	359 R	51.6%	48.4%	51.6%	48.4%
OREGON	4,314	1,573	2,734	7	1,161 D	36.5%	63.4%	36.5%	63.5%
OSAGE	5,412	3,284	2,121	7	1,163 R	60.7%	39.2%	60.8%	39.2%
OZARK	3,338	2,707	628	3	2,079 R	81.1%	18.8%	81.2%	18.8%
PEMISCOT	11,733	4,333	7,380	20	3,047 D	36.9%	62.9%	37.0%	63.0%
PERRY	6,226	4,207	2,014	5	2,193 R	67.6%	32.3%	67.6%	32.4%
PETTIS	14,894	7,696	7,176	22	520 R	51.7%	48.2%	51.7%	48.3%
PHELPS	7,449	3,180	4,256	13	1,076 D	42.7%	57.1%	42.8%	57.2%
PIKE	8,032	3,351	4,659	22	1,308 D	41.7%	58.0%	41.8%	58.2%
PLATTE	7,093	3,344	3,741	8	397 D	47.1%	52.7%	47.2%	52.8%
POLK	7,585	5,040	2,527	18	2,513 R	66.4%	33.3%	66.6%	33.4%
PULASKI	5,400	2,345	3,048	7	703 D	43.4%	56.4%	43.5%	56.5%
PUTNAM	4,281	3,106	1,168	7	1,938 R	72.6%	27.3%	72.7%	27.3%
RALLS	3,966	1,164	2,799	3	1,635 D	29.3%	70.5%	29.4%	70.6%
RANDOLPH	10,525	2,879	7,629	17	4,750 D	27.4%	72.5%	27.4%	72.6%
RAY	7,627	3,094	4,521	12	1,427 D	40.6%	59.3%	40.6%	59.4%
REYNOLDS	2,833	951	1,877	5	926 D	33.6%	66.3%	33.6%	66.4%
RIPLEY	3,779	1,841	1,923	15	82 D	48.7%	50.9%	48.9%	51.1%
ST CHARLES	11,966	7,050	4,880	36	2,170 R	58.9%	40.8%	59.1%	40.9%
ST CLAIR	5,431	3,306	2,119	6	1,187 R	60.9%	39.0%	60.9%	39.1%
ST FRANCOIS	14,076	7,320	6,745	11	575 R	52.0%	47.9%	52.0%	48.0%
ST LOUIS	122,266	64,131	57,780	355	6,351 R	52.5%	47.3%	52.6%	47.4%
ST LOUIS CITY	339,919	134,411	204,687	821	70,276 D	39.5%	60.2%	39.6%	60.4%
STE GENEVIEVE	4,098	2,214	1,878	6	336 R	54.0%	45.8%	54.1%	45.9%
SALINE	12,753	6,022	6,715	16	693 D	47.2%	52.6%	47.3%	52.7%
SCHUYLER	3,264	1,526	1,729	9	203 D	46.8%	52.9%	46.9%	53.1%
SCOTLAND	4,222	2,058	2,158	6	100 D	48.7%	51.1%	48.8%	51.2%
SCOTT	11,168	3,995	7,132	41	3,137 D	35.8%	63.9%	35.9%	64.1%
SHANNON	3,214	1,113	2,093	8	980 D	34.6%	65.1%	34.7%	65.3%
SHELBY	5,387	1,934	3,435	18	1,501 D	35.9%	63.8%	36.0%	64.0%
STODDARD	11,086	5,079	5,982	25	903 D	45.8%	54.0%	45.9%	54.1%
STONE	3,818	3,080	737	1	2,343 R	80.7%	19.3%	80.7%	19.3%
SULLIVAN	6,147	3,262	2,880	5	382 R	53.1%	46.8%	53.1%	46.9%
TANEY	3,444	2,499	936	9	1,563 R	72.6%	27.1%	72.8%	27.2%
TEXAS	7,938	3,916	4,011	11	95 D	49.3%	50.5%	49.4%	50.6%
VERNON	10,062	5,171	4,885	6	286 R	51.3%	48.5%	51.4%	48.5%
WARREN	3,847	3,017	815	15	2,202 R	78.4%	21.1%	78.7%	21.3%
WASHINGTON	4,974	2,900	2,065	9	835 R	58.3%	41.5%	58.4%	41.5%
WAYNE	4,349	2,171	2,169	9	2 R	49.9%	49.8%	50.0%	50.0%
WEBSTER	7,073	4,281	2,777	15	1,504 R	60.5%	39.3%	60.6%	39.4%
WORTH	2,881	1,444	1,437		7 R	50.1%	49.9%	50.1%	49.9%
WRIGHT	6,537	4,413	2,116	8	2,297 R	67.5%	32.4%	67.6%	32.4%
TOTAL	1,571,697	761,175	807,356	3,166	46,181 D	48.4%	51.4%	48.5%	51.5%

PRESIDENT 1948

County	Total Vote	Republican	Democratic	Other	Rep.-Dem. Plurality	Total Vote Rep.	Total Vote Dem.	Major Vote Rep.	Major Vote Dem.
MACON	9,039	3,833	5,193	13	1,360 D	42.4%	57.5%	42.5%	57.5%
MADISON	4,599	2,086	2,509	4	423 D	45.4%	54.6%	45.4%	54.6%
MARIES	2,846	894	1,948	4	1,054 D	31.4%	68.4%	31.5%	68.5%
MARION	12,944	3,802	9,122	20	5,320 D	29.4%	70.5%	29.4%	70.6%
MERCER	2,605	1,595	1,008	2	587 R	61.2%	38.7%	61.3%	38.7%
MILLER	5,611	3,088	2,514	9	574 R	55.0%	44.8%	55.1%	44.9%
MISSISSIPPI	5,915	1,293	4,592	30	3,299 D	21.9%	77.6%	22.0%	78.0%
MONITEAU	5,385	2,594	2,787	4	193 D	48.2%	51.8%	48.2%	51.8%
MONROE	5,585	809	4,769	7	3,960 D	14.5%	85.4%	14.5%	85.5%
MONTGOMERY	5,693	2,889	2,792	12	97 R	50.7%	49.0%	50.9%	49.1%
MORGAN	4,238	2,365	1,862	11	503 R	55.8%	43.9%	55.9%	44.1%
NEW MADRID	11,018	2,082	8,925	11	6,843 D	18.9%	81.0%	18.9%	81.1%
NEWTON	11,443	5,820	5,598	25	222 R	50.9%	48.9%	51.0%	49.0%
NODAWAY	11,161	4,886	6,253	22	1,367 D	43.8%	56.0%	43.9%	56.1%
OREGON	4,357	1,214	3,133	10	1,919 D	27.9%	71.9%	27.9%	72.1%
OSAGE	5,170	2,488	2,672	10	184 D	48.1%	51.7%	48.2%	51.8%
OZARK	2,832	1,967	859	6	1,108 R	69.5%	30.3%	69.6%	30.4%
PEMISCOT	12,526	2,249	10,269	8	8,020 D	18.0%	82.0%	18.0%	82.0%
PERRY	5,043	2,903	2,133	7	770 R	57.6%	42.3%	57.6%	42.4%
PETTIS	15,069	6,657	8,388	24	1,731 D	44.2%	55.7%	44.2%	55.8%
PHELPS	8,277	3,053	5,202	22	2,149 D	36.9%	62.8%	37.0%	63.0%
PIKE	7,400	2,448	4,934	18	2,486 D	33.1%	66.7%	33.2%	66.8%
PLATTE	6,014	1,644	4,354	16	2,710 D	27.3%	72.4%	27.4%	72.6%
POLK	7,107	4,026	3,079	2	947 R	56.7%	43.3%	56.7%	43.3%
PULASKI	4,513	1,644	2,858	11	1,214 D	36.4%	63.3%	36.5%	63.5%
PUTNAM	3,977	2,499	1,463	15	1,036 R	62.8%	36.8%	63.1%	36.9%
RALLS	3,922	908	3,013	1	2,105 D	23.2%	76.8%	23.2%	76.8%
RANDOLPH	10,178	2,256	7,912	10	5,656 D	22.2%	77.7%	22.2%	77.8%
RAY	6,937	2,102	4,826	9	2,724 D	30.3%	69.6%	30.3%	69.7%
REYNOLDS	2,748	692	2,050	6	1,358 D	25.2%	74.6%	25.2%	74.8%
RIPLEY	3,858	1,533	2,304	21	771 D	39.7%	59.7%	40.0%	60.0%
ST CHARLES	12,064	5,976	6,049	39	73 D	49.5%	50.1%	49.7%	50.3%
ST CLAIR	5,044	2,548	2,489	7	59 R	50.5%	49.3%	50.6%	49.4%
ST FRANCOIS	13,542	6,234	7,276	32	1,042 D	46.0%	53.7%	46.1%	53.9%
ST LOUIS	133,383	69,592	62,684	1,107	6,908 R	52.2%	47.0%	52.6%	47.4%
ST LOUIS CITY	343,770	120,656	220,654	2,460	99,998 D	35.1%	64.2%	35.4%	64.6%
STE GENEVIEVE	3,568	1,567	1,984	17	417 D	43.9%	55.6%	44.1%	55.9%
SALINE	12,029	4,822	7,185	22	2,363 D	40.1%	59.7%	40.2%	59.8%
SCHUYLER	3,277	1,377	1,892	8	515 D	42.0%	57.7%	42.1%	57.9%
SCOTLAND	4,153	1,693	2,451	9	758 D	40.8%	59.0%	40.9%	59.1%
SCOTT	10,803	2,519	8,266	18	5,747 D	23.3%	76.5%	23.4%	76.6%
SHANNON	3,174	805	2,352	17	1,547 D	25.4%	74.1%	25.5%	74.5%
SHELBY	4,760	1,348	3,400	12	2,052 D	28.3%	71.4%	28.4%	71.6%
STODDARD	10,169	3,117	7,029	23	3,912 D	30.7%	69.1%	30.7%	69.3%
STONE	3,121	2,222	892	7	1,330 R	71.2%	28.6%	71.4%	28.6%
SULLIVAN	6,592	3,140	3,443	9	303 D	47.6%	52.2%	47.7%	52.3%
TANEY	3,797	2,361	1,427	9	934 R	62.2%	37.6%	62.3%	37.7%
TEXAS	7,994	3,320	4,664	10	1,344 D	41.5%	58.3%	41.6%	58.4%
VERNON	9,164	3,808	5,342	14	1,534 D	41.6%	58.3%	41.6%	58.4%
WARREN	3,468	2,380	1,071	17	1,309 R	68.6%	30.9%	69.0%	31.0%
WASHINGTON	4,585	2,200	2,370	15	170 D	48.0%	51.7%	48.1%	51.9%
WAYNE	4,634	1,937	2,695	2	758 D	41.8%	58.2%	41.8%	58.2%
WEBSTER	6,890	3,581	3,292	17	289 R	52.0%	47.7%	52.1%	47.9%
WORTH	2,732	1,162	1,563	7	401 D	42.5%	57.2%	42.6%	57.4%
WRIGHT	6,058	3,542	2,505	11	1,037 R	58.5%	41.4%	58.6%	41.4%
TOTAL	1,578,628	655,039	917,315	6,274	262,276 D	41.5%	58.1%	41.7%	58.3%

MISSOURI

PRESIDENT 1952

County	Total Vote	Republican	Democratic	Other	Rep.-Dem. Plurality	Total Vote Rep.	Total Vote Dem.	Major Vote Rep.	Major Vote Dem.
ADAIR	9,120	5,748	3,339	33	2,409 R	63.0%	36.6%	63.3%	36.7%
ANDREW	6,562	4,452	2,104	6	2,348 R	67.8%	32.1%	67.9%	32.1%
ATCHISON	5,297	3,259	2,028	10	1,231 R	61.5%	38.3%	61.6%	38.4%
AUDRAIN	11,554	4,767	6,775	12	2,008 D	41.3%	58.7%	41.3%	58.7%
BARRY	10,788	6,664	4,124		2,540 R	61.8%	38.2%	61.8%	38.2%
BARTON	6,741	4,056	2,661	24	1,395 R	60.2%	39.5%	60.4%	39.6%
BATES	9,999	6,002	3,995		2,007 R	60.0%	40.0%	60.0%	40.0%
BENTON	4,799	3,470	1,303	26	2,167 R	72.3%	27.2%	72.7%	27.3%
BOLLINGER	5,245	3,070	2,182	3	878 R	58.3%	41.6%	58.4%	41.6%
BOONE	17,785	7,545	10,206	34	2,661 D	42.4%	57.4%	42.5%	57.5%
BUCHANAN	41,985	22,087	19,854	44	2,233 R	52.6%	47.3%	52.7%	47.3%
BUTLER	14,285	7,843	6,426	16	1,417 R	54.9%	45.0%	55.0%	45.0%
CALDWELL	5,619	3,755	1,860	4	1,895 R	66.6%	33.1%	66.6%	33.4%
CALLAWAY	9,321	3,818	5,484	19	1,666 D	41.0%	58.8%	41.0%	59.0%
CAMDEN	4,025	2,789	1,226	10	1,563 R	69.3%	30.5%	69.5%	30.5%
CAPE GIRARDEAU	18,684	10,729	7,933	22	2,796 R	57.4%	42.5%	57.5%	42.5%
CARROLL	8,568	5,410	3,146	12	2,264 R	63.1%	36.7%	63.2%	36.8%
CARTER	2,223	1,110	1,123		23 D	49.5%	50.5%	49.5%	50.5%
CASS	11,102	6,000	5,089	13	911 R	54.0%	45.8%	54.1%	45.9%
CEDAR	5,319	3,814	1,483	22	2,331 R	71.7%	27.9%	72.0%	28.0%
CHARITON	7,627	3,883	3,730	14	153 R	50.9%	48.9%	51.0%	49.0%
CHRISTIAN	5,824	4,440	1,374	10	3,066 R	76.2%	23.6%	76.4%	23.6%
CLARK	4,918	2,850	2,045	23	805 R	58.0%	41.6%	58.2%	41.8%
CLAY	25,598	13,043	12,502	53	541 R	51.1%	48.8%	51.1%	48.9%
CLINTON	6,742	3,685	3,048	9	637 R	54.7%	45.2%	54.7%	45.3%
COLE	17,210	9,700	7,507	3	2,193 R	56.4%	43.6%	56.4%	43.6%
COOPER	8,695	5,208	3,475	12	1,733 R	59.9%	40.0%	60.0%	40.0%
CRAWFORD	6,220	3,753	2,453	14	1,300 R	60.3%	39.4%	60.5%	39.5%
DADE	4,747	3,395	1,340	12	2,055 R	71.5%	28.3%	71.7%	28.3%
DALLAS	4,726	3,459	1,258	9	2,201 R	73.2%	26.6%	73.3%	26.7%
DAVIESS	6,282	3,845	2,424	13	1,421 R	61.2%	38.6%	61.3%	38.7%
DE KALB	4,856	3,073	1,773	10	1,300 R	63.3%	36.5%	63.4%	36.6%
DENT	5,497	2,795	2,738		17 R	50.1%	49.8%	50.2%	49.8%
DOUGLAS	4,971	4,051	909	11	3,142 R	81.5%	18.3%	81.7%	18.3%
DUNKLIN	14,924	5,400	9,515	9	4,115 D	36.2%	63.8%	36.2%	63.8%
FRANKLIN	20,004	11,367	8,610	27	2,757 R	56.8%	43.0%	56.9%	43.1%
GASCONADE	6,633	5,339	1,285	9	4,054 R	80.5%	19.4%	80.6%	19.4%
GENTRY	5,937	3,429	2,508		921 R	57.8%	42.2%	57.8%	42.2%
GREENE	48,988	29,673	19,234	81	10,439 R	60.6%	39.3%	60.7%	39.3%
GRUNDY	7,555	4,790	2,747	18	2,043 R	63.4%	36.4%	63.6%	36.4%
HARRISON	7,465	5,191	2,261	13	2,930 R	69.7%	30.3%	69.7%	30.3%
HENRY	11,220	6,628	4,576	16	2,052 R	59.2%	40.8%	59.2%	40.8%
HICKORY	2,686	2,054	622	10	1,432 R	76.5%	23.2%	76.8%	23.2%
HOLT	4,985	3,476	1,487	22	1,989 R	69.7%	29.8%	70.0%	30.0%
HOWARD	5,982	2,330	3,635	27	1,295 D	39.1%	60.8%	39.2%	60.8%
HOWELL	9,983	6,608	3,349	26	3,259 R	66.2%	33.5%	66.4%	33.6%
IRON	4,124	1,831	2,286	7	455 D	44.4%	55.4%	44.5%	55.5%
JACKSON	272,297	133,093	138,792	412	5,699 D	48.9%	51.0%	49.0%	51.0%
JASPER	37,812	23,065	14,665	82	8,400 R	61.0%	38.8%	61.1%	38.9%
JEFFERSON	22,437	9,607	12,808	22	3,201 D	42.8%	57.1%	42.9%	57.1%
JOHNSON	11,307	6,990	4,294	23	2,696 R	61.9%	38.0%	61.9%	38.1%
KNOX	4,224	2,229	1,988	7	241 R	52.8%	47.1%	52.9%	47.1%
LACLEDE	8,155	5,312	2,839	4	2,473 R	65.1%	34.8%	65.2%	34.8%
LAFAYETTE	14,857	8,805	6,020	32	2,785 R	59.3%	40.5%	59.4%	40.6%
LAWRENCE	12,295	8,029	4,232	34	3,797 R	65.3%	34.4%	65.5%	34.5%
LEWIS	5,320	2,416	2,896	8	480 D	45.4%	54.4%	45.5%	54.5%
LINCOLN	7,487	3,458	4,020	9	562 D	46.2%	53.7%	46.2%	53.8%
LINN	10,751	5,551	5,189	11	362 R	51.6%	48.3%	51.7%	48.3%
LIVINGSTON	9,359	5,594	3,757	8	1,837 R	59.8%	40.1%	59.8%	40.2%
MCDONALD	6,657	4,121	2,525	11	1,596 R	61.9%	37.9%	62.0%	38.0%

PRESIDENT 1956

County	Total Vote	Republican	Democratic	Other	Rep.-Dem. Plurality	Total Vote Rep.	Total Vote Dem.	Major Vote Rep.	Major Vote Dem.
ADAIR	8,740	5,322	3,418		1,904 R	60.9%	39.1%	60.9%	39.1%
ANDREW	6,002	3,609	2,393		1,216 R	60.1%	39.9%	60.1%	39.9%
ATCHISON	5,095	2,774	2,321		453 R	54.4%	45.6%	54.4%	45.6%
AUDRAIN	10,615	4,664	5,951		1,287 D	43.9%	56.1%	43.9%	56.1%
BARRY	10,586	6,063	4,523		1,540 R	57.3%	42.7%	57.3%	42.7%
BARTON	6,428	3,547	2,881		666 R	55.2%	44.8%	55.2%	44.8%
BATES	9,767	5,467	4,300		1,167 R	56.0%	44.0%	56.0%	44.0%
BENTON	4,708	3,145	1,563		1,582 R	66.8%	33.2%	66.8%	33.2%
BOLLINGER	5,030	2,845	2,185		660 R	56.6%	43.4%	56.6%	43.4%
BOONE	18,601	8,197	10,404		2,207 D	44.1%	55.9%	44.1%	55.9%
BUCHANAN	38,695	20,311	18,384		1,927 R	52.5%	47.5%	52.5%	47.5%
BUTLER	13,085	7,216	5,869		1,347 R	55.1%	44.9%	55.1%	44.9%
CALDWELL	5,145	3,216	1,929		1,287 R	62.5%	37.5%	62.5%	37.5%
CALLAWAY	8,737	3,572	5,165		1,593 D	40.9%	59.1%	40.9%	59.1%
CAMDEN	4,277	2,817	1,460		1,357 R	65.9%	34.1%	65.9%	34.1%
CAPE GIRARDEAU	18,271	10,638	7,633		3,005 R	58.2%	41.8%	58.2%	41.8%
CARROLL	8,183	4,751	3,432		1,319 R	58.1%	41.9%	58.1%	41.9%
CARTER	2,110	1,033	1,067		34 D	49.2%	50.8%	49.2%	50.8%
CASS	11,164	5,589	5,575		14 R	50.1%	49.9%	50.1%	49.9%
CEDAR	4,996	3,276	1,720		1,556 R	65.6%	34.4%	65.6%	34.4%
CHARITON	7,130	3,459	3,671		212 D	48.5%	51.5%	48.5%	51.5%
CHRISTIAN	5,462	3,732	1,730		2,002 R	68.3%	31.7%	68.3%	31.7%
CLARK	4,816	2,623	2,193		430 R	54.5%	45.5%	54.5%	45.5%
CLAY	27,041	13,436	13,605		169 D	49.7%	50.3%	49.7%	50.3%
CLINTON	6,002	3,026	2,976		50 R	50.4%	49.6%	50.4%	49.6%
COLE	16,711	9,323	7,388		1,935 R	55.8%	44.2%	55.8%	44.2%
COOPER	8,506	4,995	3,511		1,484 R	58.7%	41.3%	58.7%	41.3%
CRAWFORD	6,049	3,594	2,455		1,139 R	59.4%	40.6%	59.4%	40.6%
DADE	4,120	2,641	1,479		1,162 R	64.1%	35.9%	64.1%	35.9%
DALLAS	4,587	2,987	1,600		1,387 R	65.1%	34.9%	65.1%	34.9%
DAVIESS	5,937	3,326	2,611		715 R	56.0%	44.0%	56.0%	44.0%
DE KALB	4,410	2,538	1,872		666 R	57.6%	42.4%	57.6%	42.4%
DENT	5,619	2,658	2,961		303 D	47.3%	52.7%	47.3%	52.7%
DOUGLAS	4,043	2,910	1,133		1,777 R	72.0%	28.0%	72.0%	28.0%
DUNKLIN	13,641	4,943	8,698		3,755 D	36.2%	63.8%	36.2%	63.8%
FRANKLIN	19,996	11,605	8,391		3,214 R	58.0%	42.0%	58.0%	42.0%
GASCONADE	6,433	5,080	1,353		3,727 R	79.0%	21.0%	79.0%	21.0%
GENTRY	5,682	3,020	2,662		358 R	53.2%	46.8%	53.2%	46.8%
GREENE	50,150	29,944	20,206		9,738 R	59.7%	40.3%	59.7%	40.3%
GRUNDY	6,891	4,139	2,752		1,387 R	60.1%	39.9%	60.1%	39.9%
HARRISON	6,659	4,141	2,518		1,623 R	62.2%	37.8%	62.2%	37.8%
HENRY	10,689	5,789	4,900		889 D	54.2%	45.8%	54.2%	45.8%
HICKORY	2,356	1,661	695		966 R	70.5%	29.5%	70.5%	29.5%
HOLT	4,601	2,888	1,713		1,175 R	62.8%	37.2%	62.8%	37.2%
HOWARD	5,719	2,177	3,542		1,365 D	38.1%	61.9%	38.1%	61.9%
HOWELL	8,539	5,473	3,066		2,407 R	64.1%	35.9%	64.1%	35.9%
IRON	3,780	1,810	1,970		160 D	47.9%	52.1%	47.9%	52.1%
JACKSON	255,704	122,182	133,522		11,340 D	47.8%	52.1%	47.8%	52.2%
JASPER	33,818	20,414	13,404		7,010 R	60.4%	39.6%	60.4%	39.6%
JEFFERSON	24,580	10,712	13,868		3,156 D	43.6%	56.4%	43.6%	56.4%
JOHNSON	11,129	6,599	4,530		2,069 R	59.3%	40.7%	59.3%	40.7%
KNOX	3,784	1,934	1,850		84 R	51.1%	48.9%	51.1%	48.9%
LACLEDE	8,366	5,079	3,287		1,792 R	60.7%	39.3%	60.7%	39.3%
LAFAYETTE	14,214	8,133	6,081		2,052 R	57.2%	42.8%	57.2%	42.8%
LAWRENCE	12,161	7,372	4,789		2,583 R	60.6%	39.4%	60.6%	39.4%
LEWIS	5,029	2,301	2,728		427 D	45.8%	54.2%	45.8%	54.2%
LINCOLN	7,104	3,114	3,990		876 D	43.8%	56.2%	43.8%	56.2%
LINN	10,083	5,028	5,055		27 D	49.9%	50.1%	49.9%	50.1%
LIVINGSTON	10,950	5,165	3,785		1,380 R	57.7%	42.3%	57.7%	42.3%
MCDONALD	6,403	3,646	2,757		889 R	56.9%	43.1%	56.9%	43.1%

MISSOURI

PRESIDENT 1952

County	Total Vote	Republican	Democratic	Other	Rep.-Dem. Plurality	Total Vote Rep.	Total Vote Dem.	Major Vote Rep.	Major Vote Dem.
MACON	10,129	5,537	4,577	15	960 R	54.7%	45.2%	54.7%	45.3%
MADISON	5,051	2,676	2,375		301 R	53.0%	47.0%	53.0%	47.0%
MARIES	3,290	1,501	1,783	6	282 D	45.6%	54.2%	45.7%	54.3%
MARION	14,637	6,162	8,457	18	2,295 D	42.1%	57.8%	42.2%	57.8%
MERCER	3,428	2,482	936	10	1,546 R	72.4%	27.3%	72.6%	27.4%
MILLER	6,681	4,237	2,426	18	1,811 R	63.4%	36.3%	63.6%	36.4%
MISSISSIPPI	6,730	2,380	4,331	19	1,951 D	35.4%	64.3%	35.5%	64.5%
MONITEAU	6,081	3,658	2,416	7	1,242 R	60.2%	39.7%	60.2%	39.8%
MONROE	6,259	1,488	4,760	11	3,272 D	23.8%	76.1%	23.8%	76.2%
MONTGOMERY	6,510	3,670	2,835	5	835 R	56.4%	43.5%	56.4%	43.6%
MORGAN	5,147	3,390	1,750	7	1,640 R	65.9%	34.0%	66.0%	34.0%
NEW MADRID	12,329	3,809	8,504	16	4,695 D	30.9%	69.0%	30.9%	69.1%
NEWTON	13,677	8,577	5,070	30	3,507 R	62.7%	37.1%	62.8%	37.2%
NODAWAY	12,441	7,614	4,805	22	2,809 R	61.2%	38.6%	61.3%	38.7%
OREGON	4,744	1,804	2,926	14	1,122 D	38.0%	61.7%	38.1%	61.9%
OSAGE	5,605	3,404	2,191	10	1,213 R	60.7%	39.1%	60.8%	39.2%
OZARK	3,309	2,572	734	3	1,838 R	77.7%	22.2%	77.8%	22.2%
PEMISCOT	13,043	4,118	8,913	12	4,795 D	31.6%	68.3%	31.6%	68.4%
PERRY	6,960	4,633	2,324	3	2,309 R	66.6%	33.4%	66.6%	33.4%
PETTIS	16,636	9,261	7,363	12	1,898 R	55.7%	44.3%	55.7%	44.3%
PHELPS	9,554	4,694	4,846	14	152 D	49.1%	50.7%	49.2%	50.8%
PIKE	8,436	3,836	4,582	18	746 D	45.5%	54.3%	45.5%	54.4%
PLATTE	8,683	3,990	4,684	9	694 D	45.9%	53.9%	46.0%	54.0%
POLK	7,761	5,263	2,474	24	2,789 R	67.8%	31.8%	68.0%	32.0%
PULASKI	5,712	2,678	3,026	8	348 D	46.9%	52.9%	46.9%	53.1%
PUTNAM	4,368	3,202	1,149	17	2,053 R	73.3%	26.3%	73.6%	26.4%
RALLS	4,465	1,437	3,020	8	1,583 D	32.1%	67.6%	32.2%	67.8%
RANDOLPH	11,496	3,968	7,501	27	3,533 D	34.5%	65.2%	34.6%	65.4%
RAY	8,240	3,349	4,869	22	1,520 D	40.6%	59.0%	40.8%	59.2%
REYNOLDS	3,079	949	2,124	6	1,175 D	30.8%	69.0%	30.9%	69.1%
RIPLEY	4,650	2,444	2,194	12	250 R	52.6%	47.2%	52.7%	47.3%
ST CHARLES	14,964	8,451	6,493	20	1,958 R	56.5%	43.4%	56.5%	43.4%
ST CLAIR	5,400	3,465	1,914	21	1,551 R	64.2%	35.4%	64.4%	35.6%
ST FRANCOIS	17,729	9,672	8,040	17	1,632 R	54.6%	45.3%	54.6%	45.4%
ST LOUIS	212,480	116,821	95,457	202	21,364 R	55.0%	44.9%	55.0%	45.0%
ST LOUIS CITY	381,148	144,828	235,893	427	91,065 D	38.0%	61.9%	38.0%	62.0%
STE GENEVIEVE	5,069	2,682	2,385	2	297 R	52.9%	47.0%	52.9%	47.1%
SALINE	13,271	6,926	6,318	27	608 R	52.2%	47.6%	52.3%	47.7%
SCHUYLER	3,323	1,636	1,680	7	44 D	49.2%	50.5%	49.3%	50.7%
SCOTLAND	4,226	2,123	2,093	10	30 R	50.2%	49.5%	50.4%	49.6%
SCOTT	11,814	4,661	7,127	26	2,466 D	39.5%	60.3%	39.5%	60.5%
SHANNON	3,327	1,291	2,028	8	737 D	38.8%	61.0%	38.9%	61.1%
SHELBY	5,424	2,163	3,237	24	1,074 D	39.9%	59.7%	40.1%	59.9%
STODDARD	11,649	5,514	6,110	25	596 D	47.3%	52.5%	47.4%	52.6%
STONE	3,931	3,172	748	11	2,424 R	80.7%	19.0%	80.9%	19.1%
SULLIVAN	6,792	3,746	3,041	5	705 R	55.2%	44.8%	55.2%	44.8%
TANEY	4,148	3,037	1,099	12	1,938 R	73.2%	26.5%	73.4%	26.6%
TEXAS	9,225	4,824	4,372	29	452 R	52.3%	47.4%	52.5%	47.5%
VERNON	10,408	5,924	4,450	34	1,474 R	56.9%	42.8%	57.1%	42.9%
WARREN	4,097	2,977	1,112	8	1,865 R	72.7%	27.1%	72.8%	27.2%
WASHINGTON	6,033	3,338	2,684	11	654 R	55.3%	44.5%	55.4%	44.6%
WAYNE	4,937	2,423	2,500	14	77 D	49.1%	50.6%	49.2%	50.8%
WEBSTER	7,615	4,701	2,894	20	1,807 R	61.7%	38.0%	61.9%	38.1%
WORTH	2,914	1,682	1,227	5	455 R	57.7%	42.1%	57.8%	42.2%
WRIGHT	7,309	5,285	2,006	18	3,279 R	72.3%	27.4%	72.5%	27.5%
TOTAL	1,892,062	959,429	929,830	2,803	29,599 R	50.7%	49.1%	50.8%	49.2%

PRESIDENT 1956

County	Total Vote	Republican	Democratic	Other	Rep.-Dem. Plurality	Total Vote Rep.	Total Vote Dem.	Major Vote Rep.	Major Vote Dem.
MACON	9,031	4,694	4,337		357 R	52.0%	48.0%	52.0%	48.0%
MADISON	5,043	2,763	2,280		483 R	54.8%	45.2%	54.8%	45.2%
MARIES	3,277	1,392	1,885		493 D	42.5%	57.5%	42.5%	57.5%
MARION	12,531	5,657	6,874		1,217 D	45.1%	54.9%	45.1%	54.9%
MERCER	3,144	2,035	1,109		926 R	64.7%	35.3%	64.7%	35.3%
MILLER	6,620	4,085	2,535		1,550 R	61.7%	38.3%	61.7%	38.3%
MISSISSIPPI	5,764	2,111	3,653		1,542 D	36.6%	63.4%	36.6%	63.4%
MONITEAU	5,791	3,239	2,552		687 R	55.9%	44.1%	55.9%	44.1%
MONROE	5,743	1,331	4,412		3,081 D	23.2%	76.8%	23.2%	76.8%
MONTGOMERY	6,287	3,443	2,844		599 R	54.8%	45.2%	54.8%	45.2%
MORGAN	5,294	3,163	2,131		1,032 R	59.7%	40.3%	59.7%	40.3%
NEW MADRID	11,971	3,552	8,419		4,867 D	29.7%	70.3%	29.7%	70.3%
NEWTON	13,321	7,792	5,529		2,263 R	58.5%	41.5%	58.5%	41.5%
NODAWAY	11,752	6,381	5,371		1,010 R	54.3%	45.7%	54.3%	45.7%
OREGON	3,908	1,436	2,472		1,036 D	36.7%	63.3%	36.7%	63.3%
OSAGE	5,522	3,077	2,445		632 R	55.7%	44.3%	55.7%	44.3%
OZARK	3,028	2,141	887		1,254 R	70.7%	29.3%	70.7%	29.3%
PEMISCOT	12,033	3,969	8,064		4,095 D	33.0%	67.0%	33.0%	67.0%
PERRY	6,746	4,400	2,346		2,054 R	65.2%	34.8%	65.2%	34.8%
PETTIS	15,852	8,766	7,086		1,680 R	55.3%	44.7%	55.3%	44.7%
PHELPS	9,534	4,773	4,761		12 R	50.1%	49.9%	50.1%	49.9%
PIKE	7,706	3,474	4,232		758 D	45.1%	54.9%	45.1%	54.9%
PLATTE	8,867	3,596	5,271		1,675 D	40.6%	59.4%	40.6%	59.4%
POLK	7,378	4,410	2,968		1,442 R	59.8%	40.2%	59.8%	40.2%
PULASKI	5,468	2,532	2,936		404 D	46.3%	53.7%	46.3%	53.7%
PUTNAM	3,789	2,674	1,115		1,559 R	70.6%	29.4%	70.6%	29.4%
RALLS	4,005	1,373	2,632		1,259 D	34.3%	65.7%	34.3%	65.7%
RANDOLPH	10,506	3,709	6,797		3,088 D	35.3%	64.7%	35.3%	64.7%
RAY	7,677	3,041	4,636		1,595 D	39.6%	60.4%	39.6%	60.4%
REYNOLDS	2,513	917	1,596		679 D	36.5%	63.5%	36.5%	63.5%
RIPLEY	4,338	2,189	2,149		40 R	50.5%	49.5%	50.5%	49.5%
ST CHARLES	17,080	9,462	7,618		1,844 R	55.4%	44.6%	55.4%	44.6%
ST CLAIR	5,218	3,018	2,200		818 R	57.8%	42.2%	57.8%	42.2%
ST FRANCOIS	17,534	9,968	7,566		2,402 R	56.8%	43.2%	56.8%	43.2%
ST LOUIS	259,992	138,111	121,881		16,230 R	53.1%	46.9%	53.1%	46.9%
ST LOUIS CITY	332,255	130,045	202,210		72,165 D	39.1%	60.9%	39.1%	60.9%
STE GENEVIEVE	4,996	2,633	2,363		270 R	52.7%	47.3%	52.7%	47.3%
SALINE	11,811	5,970	5,841		129 R	50.5%	49.5%	50.5%	49.5%
SCHUYLER	3,148	1,500	1,648		148 D	47.6%	52.4%	47.6%	52.4%
SCOTLAND	3,779	1,735	2,044		309 D	45.9%	54.1%	45.9%	54.1%
SCOTT	11,337	4,654	6,683		2,029 D	41.1%	58.9%	41.1%	58.9%
SHANNON	2,993	1,171	1,822		651 D	39.1%	60.9%	39.1%	60.9%
SHELBY	5,034	1,990	3,044		1,054 D	39.5%	60.5%	39.5%	60.5%
STODDARD	11,201	4,832	6,369		1,537 D	43.1%	56.9%	43.1%	56.9%
STONE	3,988	2,939	1,049		1,890 R	73.7%	26.3%	73.7%	26.3%
SULLIVAN	6,162	3,357	2,805		552 R	54.5%	45.5%	54.5%	45.5%
TANEY	4,695	3,218	1,477		1,741 R	68.5%	31.5%	68.5%	31.5%
TEXAS	8,858	4,352	4,506		154 D	49.1%	50.9%	49.1%	50.9%
VERNON	9,731	5,184	4,547		637 R	53.3%	46.7%	53.3%	46.7%
WARREN	4,063	2,852	1,211		1,641 R	70.2%	29.8%	70.2%	29.8%
WASHINGTON	5,723	3,363	2,360		1,003 R	58.7%	41.3%	58.7%	41.3%
WAYNE	4,964	2,513	2,451		62 R	50.6%	49.4%	50.6%	49.4%
WEBSTER	7,072	3,940	3,132		808 R	55.7%	44.3%	55.7%	44.3%
WORTH	2,692	1,338	1,354		16 D	49.7%	50.3%	49.7%	50.3%
WRIGHT	6,638	4,360	2,278		2,082 R	65.7%	34.3%	65.7%	34.3%
TOTAL	1,832,562	914,289	918,273		3,984 D	49.9%	50.1%	49.9%	50.1%

MISSOURI

PRESIDENT 1960

County	Total Vote	Republican	Democratic	Other	Rep.-Dem. Plurality	Total Vote Rep.	Total Vote Dem.	Major Vote Rep.	Major Vote Dem.
ADAIR	8,629	5,469	3,160		2,309 R	63.4%	36.6%	63.4%	36.6%
ANDREW	5,886	3,716	2,170		1,546 R	63.1%	36.9%	63.1%	36.9%
ATCHISON	4,826	2,659	2,167		492 R	55.1%	44.9%	55.1%	44.9%
AUDRAIN	11,365	4,955	6,410		1,455 D	43.6%	56.4%	43.6%	56.4%
BARRY	10,625	6,706	3,919		2,787 R	63.1%	36.9%	63.1%	36.9%
BARTON	6,120	3,703	2,417		1,286 R	60.5%	39.5%	60.5%	39.5%
BATES	9,335	5,429	3,906		1,523 R	58.2%	41.8%	58.2%	41.8%
BENTON	4,980	3,484	1,496		1,988 R	70.0%	30.0%	70.0%	30.0%
BOLLINGER	4,821	2,886	1,935		951 R	59.9%	40.1%	59.9%	40.1%
BOONE	21,967	10,453	11,514		1,061 D	47.6%	52.4%	47.6%	52.4%
BUCHANAN	40,796	21,448	19,348		2,100 R	52.6%	47.4%	52.6%	47.4%
BUTLER	14,157	8,751	5,406		3,345 R	61.8%	38.2%	61.8%	38.2%
CALDWELL	4,851	3,115	1,736		1,379 R	64.2%	35.8%	64.2%	35.8%
CALLAWAY	9,398	4,054	5,344		1,290 D	43.1%	56.9%	43.1%	56.9%
CAMDEN	5,268	3,509	1,759		1,750 R	66.6%	33.4%	66.6%	33.4%
CAPE GIRARDEAU	19,503	11,331	8,172		3,159 R	58.1%	41.9%	58.1%	41.9%
CARROLL	7,851	4,555	3,296		1,259 R	58.0%	42.0%	58.0%	42.0%
CARTER	1,732	1,049	683		366 R	60.6%	39.4%	60.6%	39.4%
CASS	12,241	6,523	5,718		805 R	53.3%	46.7%	53.3%	46.7%
CEDAR	5,277	3,730	1,547		2,183 R	70.7%	29.3%	70.7%	29.3%
CHARITON	6,652	3,102	3,550		448 D	46.6%	53.4%	46.6%	53.4%
CHRISTIAN	6,249	4,627	1,622		3,005 R	74.0%	26.0%	74.0%	26.0%
CLARK	4,681	2,642	2,039		603 R	56.4%	43.6%	56.4%	43.6%
CLAY	36,273	18,955	17,318		1,637 R	52.3%	47.7%	52.3%	47.7%
CLINTON	6,558	3,391	3,167		224 R	51.7%	48.3%	51.7%	48.3%
COLE	18,295	9,763	8,532		1,231 R	53.4%	46.6%	53.4%	46.6%
COOPER	8,550	4,672	3,858		814 R	54.8%	45.2%	54.8%	45.2%
CRAWFORD	6,452	4,065	2,387		1,678 R	63.0%	37.0%	63.0%	37.0%
DADE	4,204	2,987	1,217		1,770 R	71.1%	28.9%	71.1%	28.9%
DALLAS	5,004	3,522	1,482		2,040 R	70.4%	29.6%	70.4%	29.6%
DAVIESS	5,411	3,191	2,220		971 R	59.0%	41.0%	59.0%	41.0%
DE KALB	4,181	2,484	1,697		787 R	59.4%	40.6%	59.4%	40.6%
DENT	5,805	3,212	2,593		619 R	55.3%	44.7%	55.3%	44.7%
DOUGLAS	4,625	3,611	1,014		2,597 R	78.1%	21.9%	78.1%	21.9%
DUNKLIN	13,276	6,708	6,568		140 R	50.5%	49.5%	50.5%	49.5%
FRANKLIN	21,934	11,610	10,324		1,286 R	52.9%	47.1%	52.9%	47.1%
GASCONADE	6,505	4,854	1,651		3,203 R	74.6%	25.4%	74.6%	25.4%
GENTRY	5,327	2,888	2,439		449 R	54.2%	45.8%	54.2%	45.8%
GREENE	57,400	36,943	20,457		16,486 R	64.4%	35.6%	64.4%	35.6%
GRUNDY	6,837	4,422	2,415		2,007 R	64.7%	35.3%	64.7%	35.3%
HARRISON	6,366	4,166	2,200		1,966 R	65.4%	34.6%	65.4%	34.6%
HENRY	10,613	6,012	4,601		1,411 R	56.6%	43.4%	56.6%	43.4%
HICKORY	2,500	1,885	615		1,270 R	75.4%	24.6%	75.4%	24.6%
HOLT	4,271	2,720	1,551		1,169 R	63.7%	36.3%	63.7%	36.3%
HOWARD	5,377	2,075	3,302		1,227 D	38.6%	61.4%	38.6%	61.4%
HOWELL	9,829	7,095	2,734		4,361 R	72.2%	27.8%	72.2%	27.8%
IRON	3,973	2,122	1,851		271 R	53.4%	46.6%	53.4%	46.6%
JACKSON	266,458	123,589	142,869		19,280 D	46.4%	53.6%	46.4%	53.6%
JASPER	36,766	21,804	14,962		6,842 R	59.3%	40.7%	59.3%	40.7%
JEFFERSON	29,964	12,910	17,054		4,144 D	43.1%	56.9%	43.1%	56.9%
JOHNSON	11,682	6,970	4,712		2,258 R	59.7%	40.3%	59.7%	40.3%
KNOX	3,670	1,874	1,796		78 R	51.1%	48.9%	51.1%	48.9%
LACLEDE	8,961	5,605	3,156		2,449 R	64.8%	35.2%	64.8%	35.2%
LAFAYETTE	13,566	8,011	5,555		2,456 R	59.1%	40.9%	59.1%	40.9%
LAWRENCE	12,889	8,406	4,483		3,923 R	65.2%	34.8%	65.2%	34.8%
LEWIS	5,286	2,560	2,726		166 D	48.4%	51.6%	48.4%	51.6%
LINCOLN	7,264	3,471	3,793		322 D	47.8%	52.2%	47.8%	52.2%
LINN	9,620	5,086	4,534		552 R	52.9%	47.1%	52.9%	47.1%
LIVINGSTON	8,840	5,045	3,795		1,250 R	57.1%	42.9%	57.1%	42.9%
MCDONALD	6,451	3,955	2,496		1,459 R	61.3%	38.7%	61.3%	38.7%

PRESIDENT 1964

County	Total Vote	Republican	Democratic	Other	Rep.-Dem. Plurality	Total Vote Rep.	Total Vote Dem.	Major Vote Rep.	Major Vote Dem.
ADAIR	7,808	3,573	4,235		662 D	45.8%	54.2%	45.8%	54.2%
ANDREW	5,805	2,594	3,211		617 D	44.7%	55.3%	44.7%	55.3%
ATCHISON	4,523	1,653	2,870		1,217 D	36.5%	63.5%	36.5%	63.5%
AUDRAIN	10,703	3,316	7,387		4,071 D	31.0%	69.0%	31.0%	69.0%
BARRY	10,064	4,757	5,307		550 D	47.3%	52.7%	47.3%	52.7%
BARTON	5,505	2,332	3,173		841 D	42.4%	57.6%	42.4%	57.6%
BATES	8,676	3,514	5,162		1,648 D	40.5%	59.5%	40.5%	59.5%
BENTON	4,507	2,477	2,030		447 R	55.0%	45.0%	55.0%	45.0%
BOLLINGER	4,917	2,125	2,792		667 D	43.2%	56.8%	43.2%	56.8%
BOONE	22,453	7,695	14,758		7,063 D	34.3%	65.7%	34.3%	65.7%
BUCHANAN	35,665	11,501	24,164		12,663 D	32.2%	67.8%	32.2%	67.8%
BUTLER	13,326	5,616	7,710		2,094 D	42.1%	57.9%	42.1%	57.9%
CALDWELL	4,600	2,125	2,475		350 D	46.2%	53.8%	46.2%	53.8%
CALLAWAY	8,899	2,983	5,916		2,933 D	33.5%	66.5%	33.5%	66.5%
CAMDEN	5,199	2,607	2,592		85 R	50.8%	49.2%	50.8%	49.2%
CAPE GIRARDEAU	20,207	8,776	11,431		2,655 D	43.4%	56.6%	43.4%	56.6%
CARROLL	7,063	2,994	4,069		1,075 D	42.4%	57.6%	42.4%	57.6%
CARTER	1,993	761	1,232		471 D	38.2%	61.8%	38.2%	61.8%
CASS	10,323	3,665	6,658		2,993 D	35.5%	64.5%	35.5%	64.5%
CEDAR	4,725	2,478	2,247		231 R	52.4%	47.6%	52.4%	47.6%
CHARITON	5,794	1,932	3,862		1,930 D	33.3%	66.7%	33.3%	66.7%
CHRISTIAN	5,878	3,232	2,646		586 R	55.0%	45.0%	55.0%	45.0%
CLARK	3,883	1,660	2,223		563 D	42.8%	57.2%	42.8%	57.2%
CLAY	37,990	13,997	23,993		9,996 D	36.8%	63.2%	36.8%	63.2%
CLINTON	5,398	1,800	3,598		1,798 D	33.3%	66.7%	33.3%	66.7%
COLE	18,195	10,068	8,127		1,941 R	55.3%	44.7%	55.3%	44.7%
COOPER	7,731	3,530	4,201		671 D	45.7%	54.3%	45.7%	54.3%
CRAWFORD	6,104	2,660	3,444		784 D	43.6%	56.4%	43.6%	56.4%
DADE	3,572	1,931	1,641		290 R	54.1%	45.9%	54.1%	45.9%
DALLAS	4,251	2,268	1,983		285 R	53.4%	46.6%	53.4%	46.6%
DAVIESS	4,613	1,874	2,739		865 D	40.6%	59.4%	40.6%	59.4%
DE KALB	4,026	1,679	2,347		668 D	41.7%	58.3%	41.7%	58.3%
DENT	4,648	1,788	2,860		1,072 D	38.5%	61.5%	38.5%	61.5%
DOUGLAS	3,873	2,280	1,593		687 R	58.9%	41.1%	58.9%	41.1%
DUNKLIN	11,932	3,465	8,467		5,002 D	29.0%	71.0%	29.0%	71.0%
FRANKLIN	21,777	8,313	13,464		5,151 D	38.2%	61.8%	38.2%	61.8%
GASCONADE	5,798	3,672	2,126		1,546 R	63.3%	36.7%	63.3%	36.7%
GENTRY	4,875	1,677	3,198		1,521 D	34.4%	65.6%	34.4%	65.6%
GREENE	54,119	23,989	30,130		6,141 D	44.3%	55.7%	44.3%	55.7%
GRUNDY	5,774	2,411	3,363		952 D	41.8%	58.2%	41.8%	58.2%
HARRISON	5,303	2,516	2,787		271 D	47.4%	52.6%	47.4%	52.6%
HENRY	8,844	3,083	5,761		2,678 D	34.9%	65.1%	34.9%	65.1%
HICKORY	2,011	1,157	854		303 R	57.5%	42.5%	57.5%	42.5%
HOLT	3,597	1,726	1,871		145 D	48.0%	52.0%	48.0%	52.0%
HOWARD	4,846	1,339	3,507		2,168 D	27.6%	72.4%	27.6%	72.4%
HOWELL	9,600	4,632	4,968		336 D	48.2%	51.8%	48.2%	51.8%
IRON	3,780	1,050	2,730		1,680 D	27.8%	72.2%	27.8%	72.2%
JACKSON	240,056	78,766	161,290		82,524 D	32.8%	67.2%	32.8%	67.2%
JASPER	33,526	15,481	18,045		2,564 D	46.2%	53.8%	46.2%	53.8%
JEFFERSON	26,803	7,887	18,916		11,029 D	29.4%	70.6%	29.4%	70.6%
JOHNSON	10,760	4,348	6,412		2,064 D	40.4%	59.6%	40.4%	59.6%
KNOX	3,390	1,305	2,085		780 D	38.5%	61.5%	38.5%	61.5%
LACLEDE	8,365	3,848	4,517		669 D	46.0%	54.0%	46.0%	54.0%
LAFAYETTE	12,893	5,493	7,400		1,907 D	42.6%	57.4%	42.6%	57.4%
LAWRENCE	12,430	6,047	6,383		336 D	48.6%	51.4%	48.6%	51.4%
LEWIS	4,520	1,239	3,281		2,042 D	27.4%	72.6%	27.4%	72.6%
LINCOLN	7,264	2,271	4,993		2,722 D	31.3%	68.7%	31.3%	68.7%
LINN	8,618	2,883	5,735		2,852 D	33.5%	66.5%	33.5%	66.5%
LIVINGSTON	8,023	2,703	5,320		2,617 D	33.7%	66.3%	33.7%	66.3%
MCDONALD	6,543	3,055	3,488		433 D	46.7%	53.3%	46.7%	53.3%

MISSOURI

PRESIDENT 1960

County	Total Vote	Republican	Democratic	Other	Rep.-Dem. Plurality	Total Vote Rep.	Total Vote Dem.	Major Vote Rep.	Major Vote Dem.
MACON	9,133	4,925	4,208		717 R	53.9%	46.1%	53.9%	46.1%
MADISON	4,834	2,960	1,874		1,085 R	61.2%	38.8%	61.2%	38.8%
MARIES	3,400	1,684	1,716		32 D	49.5%	50.5%	49.5%	50.5%
MARION	13,189	6,431	6,758		327 D	48.8%	51.2%	48.8%	51.2%
MERCER	3,500	2,354	1,146		1,203 R	67.3%	32.7%	67.3%	32.7%
MILLER	7,066	4,482	2,584		1,893 R	63.4%	36.6%	63.4%	36.6%
MISSISSIPPI	6,484	2,629	3,855		1,225 D	40.5%	59.5%	40.5%	59.5%
MONITEAU	5,724	3,453	2,271		1,182 R	60.3%	39.7%	60.3%	39.7%
MONROE	5,530	1,519	4,011		2,492 D	27.5%	72.5%	27.5%	72.5%
MONTGOMERY	6,258	3,454	2,804		650 R	55.2%	44.8%	55.2%	44.8%
MORGAN	5,218	3,239	1,979		1,260 R	62.1%	37.9%	62.1%	37.9%
NEW MADRID	11,578	4,205	7,373		3,168 D	36.3%	63.7%	36.3%	63.7%
NEWTON	14,688	9,010	5,678		3,332 R	61.3%	38.7%	61.3%	38.7%
NODAWAY	11,311	5,993	5,318		675 R	53.0%	47.0%	53.0%	47.0%
OREGON	3,908	1,974	1,934		40 R	50.5%	49.5%	50.5%	49.5%
OSAGE	5,578	2,678	2,900		222 D	48.0%	52.0%	48.0%	52.0%
OZARK	3,316	2,595	721		1,874 R	78.3%	21.7%	78.3%	21.7%
PEMISCOT	11,776	4,464	7,312		2,848 D	37.9%	62.1%	37.9%	62.1%
PERRY	6,877	3,886	2,991		895 R	56.5%	43.5%	56.5%	43.5%
PETTIS	16,063	9,066	6,997		2,069 R	56.4%	43.6%	56.4%	43.6%
PHELPS	10,239	5,663	4,576		1,087 R	55.3%	44.7%	55.3%	44.7%
PIKE	7,996	3,900	4,096		196 D	48.8%	51.2%	48.8%	51.2%
PLATTE	10,631	4,771	5,860		1,089 D	44.9%	55.1%	44.9%	55.1%
POLK	7,289	4,849	2,440		2,409 R	66.5%	33.5%	66.5%	33.5%
PULASKI	6,381	3,285	3,096		189 R	51.5%	48.5%	51.5%	48.5%
PUTNAM	3,771	2,711	1,060		1,651 R	71.9%	28.1%	71.9%	28.1%
RALLS	3,980	1,485	2,495		1,010 D	37.3%	62.7%	37.3%	62.7%
RANDOLPH	10,614	4,180	6,434		2,254 D	39.4%	60.6%	39.4%	60.6%
RAY	8,107	3,542	4,565		1,023 D	43.7%	56.3%	43.7%	56.3%
REYNOLDS	2,183	1,139	1,044		95 R	52.2%	47.8%	52.2%	47.8%
RIPLEY	4,528	2,811	1,717		1,094 R	62.1%	37.9%	62.1%	37.9%
ST CHARLES	22,778	10,888	11,890		1,002 D	47.8%	52.2%	47.8%	52.2%
ST CLAIR	5,061	2,394	2,667		273 D	47.3%	52.7%	47.3%	52.7%
ST FRANCOIS	17,336	10,131	7,205		2,926 R	58.4%	41.6%	58.4%	41.6%
ST LOUIS	324,500	157,992	166,508		8,516 D	48.7%	51.3%	48.7%	51.3%
ST LOUIS CITY	303,650	101,331	202,319		100,988 D	33.4%	66.6%	33.4%	66.6%
STE GENEVIEVE	5,167	1,956	3,211		1,255 D	37.9%	62.1%	37.9%	62.1%
SALINE	12,054	6,085	5,969		116 R	50.5%	49.5%	50.5%	49.5%
SCHUYLER	3,027	1,666	1,361		305 R	55.0%	45.0%	55.0%	45.0%
SCOTLAND	3,783	1,899	1,884		15 R	50.2%	49.8%	50.2%	49.8%
SCOTT	12,156	5,807	6,349		542 D	47.8%	52.2%	47.8%	52.2%
SHANNON	2,815	1,429	1,386		43 R	50.8%	49.2%	50.8%	49.2%
SHELBY	4,932	2,062	2,870		808 D	41.8%	58.2%	41.8%	58.2%
STODDARD	11,683	6,366	5,317		1,049 R	54.5%	45.5%	54.5%	45.5%
STONE	4,091	3,201	890		2,311 R	78.2%	21.8%	78.2%	21.8%
SULLIVAN	5,706	3,202	2,504		698 R	56.1%	43.9%	56.1%	43.9%
TANEY	5,131	3,692	1,439		2,253 R	72.0%	28.0%	72.0%	28.0%
TEXAS	8,864	5,258	3,606		1,652 R	59.3%	40.7%	59.3%	40.7%
VERNON	9,573	5,387	4,186		1,201 R	56.3%	43.7%	56.3%	43.7%
WARREN	4,353	2,946	1,407		1,539 R	67.7%	32.3%	67.7%	32.3%
WASHINGTON	6,086	3,437	2,649		788 R	56.5%	43.5%	56.5%	43.5%
WAYNE	5,221	3,069	2,152		917 R	58.8%	41.2%	58.8%	41.2%
WEBSTER	7,310	4,603	2,707		1,896 R	63.0%	37.0%	63.0%	37.0%
WORTH	2,678	1,355	1,323		32 R	50.6%	49.4%	50.6%	49.4%
WRIGHT	7,144	5,191	1,953		3,238 R	72.7%	27.3%	72.7%	27.3%
TOTAL	1,934,422	962,221	972,201		9,980 D	49.7%	50.3%	49.7%	50.3%

PRESIDENT 1964

County	Total Vote	Republican	Democratic	Other	Rep.-Dem. Plurality	Total Vote Rep.	Total Vote Dem.	Major Vote Rep.	Major Vote Dem.
MACON	8,226	2,837	5,389		2,552 D	34.5%	65.5%	34.5%	65.5%
MADISON	4,474	1,756	2,718		962 D	39.2%	60.8%	39.2%	60.8%
MARIES	3,246	1,183	2,063		880 D	36.4%	63.6%	36.4%	63.6%
MARION	11,919	3,605	8,314		4,709 D	30.2%	69.8%	30.2%	69.8%
MERCER	2,324	1,040	1,284		244 D	44.8%	55.2%	44.8%	55.2%
MILLER	6,642	3,784	2,858		926 R	57.0%	43.0%	57.0%	43.0%
MISSISSIPPI	5,680	1,665	4,015		2,350 D	29.3%	70.7%	29.3%	70.7%
MONITEAU	5,382	2,758	2,624		134 R	51.2%	48.8%	51.2%	48.8%
MONROE	5,031	928	4,103		3,175 D	18.4%	81.6%	18.4%	81.6%
MONTGOMERY	5,899	2,610	3,289		679 D	44.2%	55.8%	44.2%	55.8%
MORGAN	5,210	2,742	2,468		274 R	52.6%	47.4%	52.6%	47.4%
NEW MADRID	9,998	2,583	7,415		4,832 D	25.8%	74.2%	25.8%	74.2%
NEWTON	14,799	6,660	8,139		1,479 D	45.0%	55.0%	45.0%	55.0%
NODAWAY	10,479	3,789	6,690		2,901 D	36.2%	63.8%	36.2%	63.8%
OREGON	3,900	992	2,908		1,916 D	25.4%	74.6%	25.4%	74.6%
OSAGE	5,320	2,712	2,608		104 R	51.0%	49.0%	51.0%	49.0%
OZARK	2,604	1,540	1,064		476 R	59.1%	40.9%	59.1%	40.9%
PEMISCOT	7,741	2,658	5,083		2,425 D	34.3%	65.7%	34.3%	65.7%
PERRY	6,293	2,837	3,456		619 D	45.1%	54.9%	45.1%	54.9%
PETTIS	14,396	5,409	8,987		3,578 D	37.6%	62.4%	37.6%	62.4%
PHELPS	9,531	3,755	5,776		2,021 D	39.4%	60.6%	39.4%	60.6%
PIKE	7,217	1,944	5,273		3,329 D	26.9%	73.1%	26.9%	73.1%
PLATTE	9,202	3,059	6,143		3,084 D	33.2%	66.8%	33.2%	66.8%
POLK	6,641	3,288	3,353		65 D	49.5%	50.5%	49.5%	50.5%
PULASKI	5,239	1,856	3,383		1,527 D	35.4%	64.6%	35.4%	64.6%
PUTNAM	3,031	1,547	1,484		63 R	51.0%	49.0%	51.0%	49.0%
RALLS	3,583	736	2,847		2,111 D	20.5%	79.5%	20.5%	79.5%
RANDOLPH	9,473	2,485	6,988		4,503 D	26.2%	73.8%	26.2%	73.8%
RAY	6,923	1,734	5,189		3,455 D	25.0%	75.0%	25.0%	75.0%
REYNOLDS	2,365	530	1,835		1,305 D	22.4%	77.6%	22.4%	77.6%
RIPLEY	4,372	1,684	2,688		1,004 D	38.5%	61.5%	38.5%	61.5%
ST CHARLES	23,550	9,020	14,530		5,510 D	38.3%	61.7%	38.3%	61.7%
ST CLAIR	4,554	1,961	2,593		632 D	43.1%	56.9%	43.1%	56.9%
ST FRANCOIS	16,257	5,690	10,567		4,877 D	35.0%	65.0%	35.0%	65.0%
ST LOUIS	348,620	134,962	213,658		78,696 D	38.7%	61.3%	38.7%	61.3%
ST LOUIS CITY	267,562	59,604	207,958		148,354 D	22.3%	77.7%	22.3%	77.7%
STE GENEVIEVE	6,220	2,452	3,768		1,316 D	25.9%	74.1%	25.9%	74.1%
SALINE	10,943	3,635	7,308		3,673 D	33.2%	66.8%	33.2%	66.8%
SCHUYLER	2,521	1,072	1,449		377 D	42.5%	57.5%	42.5%	57.5%
SCOTLAND	3,402	1,215	2,187		972 D	35.7%	64.3%	35.7%	64.3%
SCOTT	10,724	3,212	7,512		4,300 D	30.0%	70.0%	30.0%	70.0%
SHANNON	3,216	904	2,312		1,408 D	28.1%	71.9%	28.1%	71.9%
SHELBY	4,368	1,212	3,156		1,944 D	27.7%	72.3%	27.7%	72.3%
STODDARD	8,958	3,014	5,944		2,930 D	33.6%	66.4%	33.6%	66.4%
STONE	4,212	2,377	1,835		542 R	56.4%	43.6%	56.4%	43.6%
SULLIVAN	4,747	2,052	2,695		643 D	43.2%	56.8%	43.2%	56.8%
TANEY	5,285	2,741	2,544		197 R	51.9%	48.1%	51.9%	48.1%
TEXAS	7,836	2,902	4,934		2,032 D	37.0%	63.0%	37.0%	63.0%
VERNON	9,035	3,077	5,958		2,881 D	34.1%	65.9%	34.1%	65.9%
WARREN	4,226	2,323	1,903		420 R	55.0%	45.0%	55.0%	45.0%
WASHINGTON	6,194	2,286	3,908		1,622 D	36.9%	63.1%	36.9%	63.1%
WAYNE	5,024	2,019	3,005		986 D	40.2%	59.8%	40.2%	59.8%
WEBSTER	7,165	3,341	3,824		483 D	46.6%	53.4%	46.6%	53.4%
WORTH	2,204	831	1,373		542 D	37.7%	62.3%	37.7%	62.3%
WRIGHT	6,758	3,466	3,292		174 R	51.3%	48.7%	51.3%	48.7%
TOTAL	1,817,879	653,535	1,164,344		510,809 D	36.0%	64.0%	36.0%	64.0%

MISSOURI

OTHER VOTE COMPOSITION:

1920   20,342 Socialist; 5,152 Prohibition; 3,108 Farmer-Labor; 1,587 Socialist Labor.

1924   83,996 Progressive; 1,418 Prohibition; 1,066 Socialist Labor; 165 Commonwealth Land.

1928   3,739 Socialist; 342 Socialist Labor.

1932   16,374 Socialist; 2,429 Prohibition; 568 Communist; 404 Socialist Labor.

1936   14,630 Union; 3,454 Socialist; 908 Prohibition; 417 Communist; 292 Socialist Labor.

1940   2,226 Socialist; 1,809 Prohibition; 209 Socialist Labor.

1944   1,751 Socialist; 1,195 Prohibition; 220 Socialist Labor.

1948   3,998 Progressive; 2,222 Socialist; 54 scattered. The scattered vote is not included in the county-by-county figures; it is reported only as a part of the state-wide total.

1952   987 Progressive; 885 Prohibition; 535 Christian Nationalist-America First (MacArthur); 227 Socialist; 169 Socialist Labor.

1956

1960
1964

SPECIAL CASES:

1924   Progressive total includes 56,733 Socialist and 27,263 Liberal votes.

1952   MacArthur total includes 302 Christian Nationalist and 233 America First votes.

MONTANA

PRESIDENT 1920

County	Total Vote	Republican	Democratic	Other	Rep.-Dem. Plurality	TV Rep.	TV Dem.	MV Rep.	MV Dem.
BEAVERHEAD	2,978	2,049	833	96	1,216 R	68.8%	28.0%	71.1%	28.9%
BIG HORN	1,605	1,062	475	68	587 R	66.2%	29.6%	69.1%	30.9%
BLAINE	2,753	1,720	848	185	872 R	62.5%	30.8%	67.0%	33.0%
BROADWATER	1,404	723	622	59	101 R	51.5%	44.3%	53.8%	46.2%
CARBON	4,214	2,700	1,107	407	1,593 R	64.1%	26.3%	70.9%	29.1%
CARTER	1,170	782	342	46	440 R	66.8%	29.2%	69.6%	30.4%
CASCADE	11,572	6,808	3,938	826	2,870 R	58.8%	34.0%	63.4%	36.6%
CHOUTEAU	4,348	2,646	1,436	266	1,210 R	60.9%	33.0%	64.8%	35.2%
CUSTER	3,637	2,347	1,127	163	1,220 R	64.5%	31.0%	67.6%	32.4%
DANIELS	1,349	811	289	249	522 R	60.1%	21.4%	73.7%	26.3%
DAWSON	2,791	1,784	875	132	909 R	63.9%	31.4%	67.1%	32.9%
DEER LODGE	5,219	3,130	1,567	522	1,563 R	60.0%	30.0%	66.6%	33.4%
FALLON	1,491	1,064	381	46	683 R	71.4%	25.6%	73.6%	26.4%
FERGUS	9,727	5,858	3,371	498	2,487 R	60.2%	34.7%	63.5%	36.5%
FLATHEAD	6,581	3,900	2,241	440	1,659 R	59.3%	34.1%	63.5%	36.5%
GALLATIN	5,920	3,238	2,370	312	868 R	54.7%	40.0%	57.7%	42.3%
GARFIELD	1,798	1,226	484	88	742 R	68.2%	26.9%	71.7%	28.3%
GLACIER	1,876	1,297	531	48	766 R	69.1%	28.3%	71.0%	29.0%
GOLDEN VALLEY	1,633	1,185	381	67	804 R	72.5%	23.3%	75.7%	24.3%
GRANITE	1,478	949	439	90	510 R	64.2%	29.7%	68.4%	31.6%
HILL	4,004	2,220	1,388	396	832 R	55.4%	34.7%	61.5%	38.5%
JEFFERSON	1,779	969	688	122	281 R	54.5%	38.7%	58.5%	41.5%
JUDITH BASIN									
LAKE									
LEWIS AND CLARK	6,913	4,348	2,413	152	1,935 R	62.9%	34.9%	64.3%	35.7%
LIBERTY	1,190	757	331	102	426 R	63.6%	27.8%	69.6%	30.4%
LINCOLN	2,063	1,187	683	193	504 R	57.5%	33.7%	63.5%	36.5%
MCCONE	1,898	1,177	537	184	640 R	62.0%	28.3%	68.7%	31.3%
MADISON	2,646	1,672	877	97	795 R	63.2%	33.1%	65.6%	34.4%
MEAGHER	1,077	744	314	19	430 R	69.1%	29.2%	70.3%	29.7%
MINERAL	889	347	362	180	15 D	39.0%	40.7%	48.9%	51.1%
MISSOULA	8,314	4,374	3,292	648	1,082 R	52.6%	39.6%	57.1%	42.9%
MUSSELSHELL	3,225	1,910	951	364	959 R	59.2%	29.5%	66.8%	33.2%
PARK	4,020	2,537	1,155	328	1,382 R	63.1%	28.7%	68.7%	31.3%
PETROLEUM									
PHILLIPS	2,522	1,693	648	181	1,045 R	67.1%	25.7%	72.3%	27.7%
PONDERA	2,647	1,654	893	100	761 R	62.5%	33.7%	64.9%	35.1%
POWDER RIVER	1,340	955	330	55	625 R	71.3%	24.6%	74.3%	25.7%
POWELL	2,352	1,345	787	220	558 R	57.2%	33.5%	63.1%	36.9%
PRAIRIE	1,149	881	242	26	639 R	76.7%	21.1%	78.5%	21.5%
RAVALLI	3,488	2,110	1,224	154	886 R	60.5%	35.1%	63.3%	36.7%
RICHLAND	2,687	1,759	744	184	1,015 R	65.5%	27.7%	70.3%	29.7%
ROOSEVELT	3,282	2,239	873	170	1,366 R	68.2%	26.6%	71.9%	28.1%
ROSEBUD	2,279	1,624	555	100	1,069 R	71.3%	24.4%	74.5%	25.5%
SANDERS	2,010	1,035	741	234	294 R	51.5%	36.9%	58.3%	41.7%
SHERIDAN	2,497	1,335	610	552	725 R	53.5%	24.4%	68.6%	31.4%
SILVER BOW	18,198	10,074	6,394	1,730	3,680 R	55.4%	35.1%	61.2%	38.8%
STILLWATER	2,441	1,721	664	56	1,057 R	70.5%	27.2%	72.2%	27.8%
SWEET GRASS	1,408	1,035	349	24	686 R	73.5%	24.8%	74.8%	25.2%
TETON	2,119	1,319	671	129	648 R	62.2%	31.7%	66.3%	33.7%
TOOLE	1,405	861	405	139	456 R	61.3%	28.8%	68.0%	32.0%
TREASURE	724	517	174	33	343 R	71.4%	24.0%	74.8%	25.2%
VALLEY	3,333	2,096	895	342	1,201 R	62.9%	26.9%	70.1%	29.9%
WHEATLAND	1,817	1,250	520	47	730 R	68.4%	28.6%	70.6%	29.4%
WIBAUX	966	692	223	51	469 R	71.6%	23.1%	75.6%	24.4%
YELLOWSTONE	8,780	5,714	2,782	284	2,932 R	65.1%	31.7%	67.3%	32.7%
TOTAL	179,006	109,430	57,372	12,204	52,058 R	61.1%	32.1%	65.6%	34.4%

PRESIDENT 1924

County	Total Vote	Republican	Democratic	Other	Rep.-Dem. Plurality	TV Rep.	TV Dem.	MV Rep.	MV Dem.
BEAVERHEAD	2,742	1,386	766	590	620 R	50.5%	27.9%	64.4%	35.6%
BIG HORN	1,874	1,082	327	465	755 R	57.7%	17.4%	76.8%	23.2%
BLAINE	1,808	827	337	644	490 R	45.7%	18.6%	71.0%	29.0%
BROADWATER	1,408	531	486	391	45 R	37.7%	34.5%	52.2%	47.8%
CARBON	4,266	1,891	698	1,677	1,193 R	44.3%	16.4%	73.0%	27.0%
CARTER	1,235	669	283	283	386 R	54.2%	22.9%	70.3%	29.7%
CASCADE	11,706	5,081	2,220	4,405	2,861 R	43.4%	19.0%	69.6%	30.4%
CHOUTEAU	2,919	1,347	706	866	641 R	46.1%	24.2%	65.6%	34.4%
CUSTER	3,776	1,554	412	1,712	1,242 R	43.8%	12.9%	80.1%	19.9%
DANIELS	1,435	505	185	745	320 R	35.2%	12.9%	73.2%	26.8%
DAWSON	2,619	1,326	346	947	980 R	50.6%	13.2%	79.3%	20.7%
DEER LODGE	5,467	1,937	1,611	1,919	326 R	35.4%	29.5%	54.6%	45.4%
FALLON	1,314	731	220	363	511 R	55.6%	16.7%	76.9%	23.1%
FERGUS	7,642	2,942	1,580	3,120	1,362 R	38.5%	20.7%	65.1%	34.9%
FLATHEAD	5,871	2,541	788	2,542	1,753 R	43.3%	13.4%	76.3%	23.7%
GALLATIN	5,623	2,494	1,564	1,565	930 R	44.4%	27.8%	61.5%	38.5%
GARFIELD	1,733	876	355	502	521 R	50.5%	20.5%	71.2%	28.8%
GLACIER	1,406	586	511	309	75 R	41.7%	36.3%	53.4%	46.6%
GOLDEN VALLEY	1,114	422	118	574	304 R	37.9%	10.6%	78.1%	21.9%
GRANITE	1,339	582	353	404	229 R	43.5%	26.4%	62.2%	37.8%
HILL	3,628	1,110	602	1,916	508 R	30.6%	16.6%	64.8%	35.2%
JEFFERSON	1,776	648	434	694	214 R	36.5%	24.4%	59.9%	40.1%
JUDITH BASIN	2,148	888	480	780	408 R	41.3%	22.3%	64.9%	35.1%
LAKE	3,157	884	340	1,933	544 R	28.0%	10.8%	72.2%	27.8%
LEWIS AND CLARK	6,875	3,433	1,869	1,573	1,564 R	49.9%	27.2%	64.7%	35.3%
LIBERTY	709	239	141	329	98 R	33.7%	19.9%	62.9%	37.1%
LINCOLN	2,387	976	374	1,037	602 R	40.9%	15.7%	72.3%	27.7%
MCCONE	1,294	494	143	657	351 R	38.2%	11.1%	77.6%	22.4%
MADISON	2,274	1,137	672	465	465 R	45.8%	27.1%	62.9%	37.1%
MEAGHER	1,047	624	257	166	367 R	59.6%	24.5%	70.8%	29.2%
MINERAL	1,032	223	123	686	100 R	21.0%	11.9%	64.5%	35.5%
MISSOULA	8,104	2,386	1,012	4,706	1,374 R	29.4%	12.5%	70.2%	29.8%
MUSSELSHELL	3,267	1,488	247	1,532	1,241 R	45.5%	7.6%	85.8%	14.2%
PARK	4,337	2,199	688	1,450	1,511 R	50.7%	15.9%	76.2%	23.8%
PETROLEUM									
PHILLIPS	2,647	1,236	473	938	763 R	46.7%	17.9%	72.3%	27.7%
PONDERA	2,028	764	414	850	350 R	37.7%	20.4%	64.9%	35.1%
POWDER RIVER	986	480	123	383	357 R	48.7%	12.5%	79.6%	20.4%
POWELL	2,431	982	559	890	423 R	40.4%	23.0%	63.7%	36.3%
PRAIRIE	1,215	683	162	370	521 R	56.2%	13.3%	80.8%	19.2%
RAVALLI	3,469	1,311	562	1,596	749 R	37.8%	16.2%	70.0%	30.0%
RICHLAND	1,854	926	238	690	688 R	49.9%	12.8%	79.6%	20.4%
ROOSEVELT	2,468	965	389	1,114	576 R	39.1%	15.8%	71.3%	28.7%
ROSEBUD	2,270	1,115	259	896	856 R	49.1%	11.4%	81.1%	18.9%
SANDERS	2,052	588	188	1,276	400 R	28.7%	9.2%	75.8%	24.2%
SHERIDAN	2,562	905	176	1,481	729 R	35.3%	6.9%	83.7%	16.3%
SILVER BOW	18,814	6,520	5,393	6,901	1,127 R	34.7%	28.7%	54.7%	45.3%
STILLWATER	2,358	1,412	375	571	1,037 R	59.9%	15.9%	79.0%	21.0%
SWEET GRASS	1,432	853	248	331	605 R	59.6%	17.3%	77.5%	22.5%
TETON	1,920	775	396	749	379 R	40.4%	20.6%	66.2%	33.8%
TOOLE	1,859	697	439	723	258 R	37.5%	23.6%	61.4%	38.6%
TREASURE	522	289	84	149	205 R	55.4%	16.1%	77.5%	22.5%
VALLEY	3,043	1,555	497	991	1,058 R	51.1%	16.3%	75.8%	24.2%
WHEATLAND	1,635	723	221	691	502 R	44.2%	13.5%	76.6%	23.4%
WIBAUX	887	505	189	193	316 R	56.9%	21.3%	72.8%	27.2%
YELLOWSTONE	8,433	4,715	1,172	2,546	3,543 R	55.9%	13.9%	80.1%	19.9%
TOTAL	174,425	74,138	33,805	66,482	40,333 R	42.5%	19.4%	68.7%	31.3%

MONTANA

PRESIDENT 1928

County	Total Vote	Republican	Democratic	Other	Rep.-Dem. Plurality	Total Vote Rep.	Total Vote Dem.	Major Vote Rep.	Major Vote Dem.
BEAVERHEAD	3,064	1,906	1,144	14	762 R	62.2%	37.3%	62.5%	37.5%
BIG HORN	2,297	1,274	1,017	6	257 R	55.5%	44.3%	55.6%	44.4%
BLAINE	2,714	1,537	1,160	17	377 R	56.6%	42.7%	57.0%	43.0%
BROADWATER	1,415	743	663	9	80 R	52.5%	46.9%	52.8%	47.2%
CARBON	4,327	2,514	1,674	139	840 R	58.1%	38.7%	60.0%	40.0%
CARTER	1,192	763	420	9	343 R	64.0%	35.2%	64.5%	35.5%
CASCADE	14,856	8,183	6,540	133	1,643 R	55.1%	44.0%	55.6%	44.4%
CHOUTEAU	3,106	1,837	1,232	37	605 R	59.1%	39.7%	59.9%	40.1%
CUSTER	3,906	2,503	1,386	17	1,117 R	64.1%	35.5%	64.4%	35.6%
DANIELS	1,736	936	780	20	156 R	53.9%	44.9%	54.5%	45.5%
DAWSON	3,286	2,207	1,065	14	1,142 R	67.2%	32.4%	67.5%	32.5%
DEER LODGE	5,901	2,695	3,184	22	489 D	45.7%	54.0%	45.8%	54.2%
FALLON	1,500	1,036	454	10	582 R	69.1%	30.3%	69.5%	30.5%
FERGUS	6,858	4,109	2,657	62	1,442 R	60.1%	39.0%	60.6%	39.4%
FLATHEAD	6,152	4,098	1,972	82	2,126 R	66.6%	32.1%	67.5%	32.5%
GALLATIN	6,318	3,861	2,423	34	1,438 R	61.1%	38.4%	61.4%	38.6%
GARFIELD	1,688	1,176	499	13	677 R	69.7%	29.6%	70.2%	29.8%
GLACIER	1,826	847	976	3	129 D	46.4%	53.5%	46.4%	53.5%
GOLDEN VALLEY	978	625	346	7	279 R	63.9%	35.4%	64.4%	35.6%
GRANITE	1,366	849	509	8	340 R	62.2%	37.3%	62.5%	37.5%
HILL	4,377	2,336	2,022	19	314 R	53.4%	46.2%	53.6%	46.4%
JEFFERSON	1,778	1,013	751	14	262 R	57.0%	42.2%	57.4%	42.6%
JUDITH BASIN	2,364	1,342	978	44	364 R	56.8%	41.4%	57.8%	42.2%
LAKE	3,151	1,876	1,256	25	620 R	59.5%	39.8%	59.9%	40.1%
LEWIS AND CLARK	7,744	4,441	3,278	25	1,163 R	57.3%	42.3%	57.5%	42.5%
LIBERTY	786	446	332	8	114 R	56.7%	42.2%	57.3%	42.7%
LINCOLN	2,327	1,217	1,067	43	150 R	52.3%	45.9%	53.3%	46.7%
MCCONE	1,529	946	554	29	392 R	61.9%	36.2%	63.1%	36.9%
MADISON	2,611	1,785	812	14	973 R	68.4%	31.1%	68.7%	31.3%
MEAGHER	1,051	714	335	2	379 R	67.9%	31.9%	68.1%	31.9%
MINERAL	832	443	370	19	73 R	53.2%	44.5%	54.5%	45.5%
MISSOULA	8,467	5,056	3,291	120	1,765 R	59.7%	38.9%	60.5%	39.4%
MUSSELSHELL	3,181	1,608	1,444	129	164 R	50.6%	45.4%	52.7%	47.3%
PARK	4,496	3,095	1,338	63	1,757 R	68.8%	29.8%	69.8%	30.2%
PETROLEUM	963	586	372	5	214 R	60.8%	38.6%	61.2%	38.8%
PHILLIPS	2,828	1,671	1,135	22	536 R	59.1%	40.1%	59.1%	40.4%
PONDERA	2,283	1,324	944	15	380 R	58.0%	41.3%	58.4%	41.6%
POWDER RIVER	1,199	780	410	9	370 R	65.1%	34.2%	65.5%	34.5%
POWELL	2,622	1,560	1,031	23	529 R	59.5%	39.3%	60.3%	39.7%
PRAIRIE	1,379	968	405	6	563 R	70.2%	29.4%	70.5%	29.5%
RAVALLI	3,724	2,551	1,112	61	1,439 R	68.5%	29.9%	69.6%	30.4%
RICHLAND	2,594	1,648	917	29	731 R	63.5%	35.4%	64.2%	35.8%
ROOSEVELT	2,949	1,630	1,296	23	334 R	55.3%	43.9%	55.7%	44.3%
ROSEBUD	2,558	1,519	1,025	14	494 R	59.4%	40.1%	59.7%	40.3%
SANDERS	2,128	1,142	873	113	269 R	53.7%	41.0%	56.7%	43.3%
SHERIDAN	2,971	1,624	1,190	157	434 R	54.7%	40.1%	57.7%	42.3%
SILVER BOW	21,103	9,456	11,228	419	1,772 D	44.8%	53.2%	45.7%	54.3%
STILLWATER	2,408	1,687	711	10	976 R	70.1%	29.5%	70.4%	29.6%
SWEET GRASS	1,605	1,163	435	7	728 R	72.5%	27.1%	72.8%	27.2%
TETON	2,085	1,263	804	18	459 R	60.6%	38.6%	61.1%	38.9%
TOOLE	2,422	1,325	1,076	21	249 R	54.7%	44.4%	55.2%	44.8%
TREASURE	541	354	186	1	168 R	65.4%	34.4%	65.6%	34.4%
VALLEY	3,649	2,330	1,294	25	1,036 R	63.9%	35.5%	64.3%	35.7%
WHEATLAND	1,754	1,207	542	5	665 R	68.8%	30.9%	69.0%	31.0%
WIBAUX	1,036	583	448	5	135 R	56.3%	43.2%	56.5%	43.5%
YELLOWSTONE	10,141	6,904	3,205	32	3,699 R	68.1%	31.6%	68.3%	31.7%
TOTAL	194,108	113,300	78,578	2,230	34,722 R	58.4%	40.5%	59.0%	41.0%

PRESIDENT 1932

County	Total Vote	Republican	Democratic	Other	Rep.-Dem. Plurality	Total Vote Rep.	Total Vote Dem.	Major Vote Rep.	Major Vote Dem.
BEAVERHEAD	3,291	1,418	1,834	39	416 D	43.1%	55.7%	43.6%	56.4%
BIG HORN	2,628	957	1,637	34	680 D	36.4%	62.3%	36.9%	63.1%
BLAINE	3,160	1,063	1,977	120	914 D	33.6%	62.6%	35.0%	65.0%
BROADWATER	1,519	512	988	19	476 D	33.7%	65.0%	34.1%	65.9%
CARBON	5,076	1,942	2,872	262	930 D	38.3%	56.6%	40.3%	59.7%
CARTER	1,511	565	915	31	350 D	37.4%	60.6%	38.2%	61.8%
CASCADE	16,023	5,800	10,047	976	4,247 D	34.5%	59.7%	36.6%	63.4%
CHOUTEAU	3,477	1,232	2,093	152	861 D	35.4%	60.2%	37.1%	62.9%
CUSTER	4,528	1,675	2,729	124	1,054 D	37.0%	60.3%	38.0%	62.0%
DANIELS	1,886	482	1,172	232	690 D	25.6%	62.1%	29.1%	70.9%
DAWSON	3,457	1,470	1,929	58	459 D	42.5%	55.8%	43.2%	56.8%
DEER LODGE	6,204	2,198	3,893	113	1,695 D	35.4%	62.7%	36.1%	63.9%
FALLON	1,734	690	973	71	283 D	39.8%	56.1%	41.5%	58.5%
FERGUS	7,136	2,400	4,470	266	2,070 D	33.6%	62.6%	34.9%	65.1%
FLATHEAD	7,683	2,978	4,026	679	1,048 D	38.8%	52.4%	42.5%	57.5%
GALLATIN	7,095	2,553	4,359	183	1,806 D	36.0%	61.4%	36.9%	63.0%
GARFIELD	1,785	678	1,044	63	366 D	38.0%	58.5%	39.4%	60.6%
GLACIER	2,439	702	1,717	20	1,015 D	28.8%	70.4%	29.0%	71.0%
GOLDEN VALLEY	912	423	469	20	46 D	46.4%	51.4%	47.4%	52.6%
GRANITE	1,439	536	855	48	319 D	37.2%	59.4%	38.5%	61.5%
HILL	5,054	1,589	3,257	208	1,668 D	31.4%	64.4%	32.8%	67.2%
JEFFERSON	2,111	784	1,246	84	462 D	37.1%	58.9%	38.6%	61.4%
JUDITH BASIN	2,131	720	1,280	131	560 D	33.8%	60.1%	36.0%	64.0%
LAKE	4,082	1,361	2,514	207	1,153 D	33.3%	61.6%	35.1%	64.9%
LEWIS AND CLARK	8,596	3,671	4,714	211	1,043 D	42.7%	54.8%	43.8%	56.2%
LIBERTY	1,010	252	731	27	479 D	25.0%	72.4%	25.6%	74.4%
LINCOLN	2,906	833	1,867	206	1,034 D	28.7%	64.2%	30.9%	69.1%
MCCONE	1,731	456	1,020	255	564 D	26.3%	58.9%	30.9%	69.1%
MADISON	2,976	1,097	1,764	115	667 D	36.9%	59.3%	38.3%	61.7%
MEAGHER	1,101	462	621	18	159 D	42.0%	56.4%	42.7%	57.3%
MINERAL	955	260	578	117	318 D	27.2%	60.5%	31.0%	69.0%
MISSOULA	9,616	3,819	5,242	555	1,423 D	39.7%	54.5%	42.1%	57.9%
MUSSELSHELL	2,640	1,021	1,584	235	563 D	36.0%	55.8%	39.2%	60.8%
PARK	4,609	1,695	2,533	181	638 D	41.1%	55.0%	42.8%	57.2%
PETROLEUM	924	351	544	29	193 D	38.0%	58.9%	39.2%	60.8%
PHILLIPS	3,324	1,127	2,054	143	927 D	33.9%	61.8%	35.4%	64.6%
PONDERA	2,875	930	1,805	140	875 D	32.3%	62.8%	34.0%	66.0%
POWDER RIVER	1,450	515	875	60	360 D	35.5%	60.3%	37.1%	62.9%
POWELL	2,995	1,031	1,869	95	838 D	34.4%	62.4%	35.6%	64.4%
PRAIRIE	1,387	634	732	21	98 D	45.7%	52.8%	46.4%	53.6%
RAVALLI	4,311	1,714	2,292	305	578 D	39.8%	53.2%	42.8%	57.2%
RICHLAND	3,116	1,216	1,768	132	552 D	39.0%	56.7%	40.8%	59.2%
ROOSEVELT	3,500	965	2,263	272	1,298 D	27.6%	64.7%	29.9%	70.1%
ROSEBUD	2,804	1,027	1,646	131	619 D	36.6%	60.6%	38.4%	61.6%
SANDERS	2,601	760	1,577	264	817 D	29.2%	60.6%	32.5%	67.5%
SHERIDAN	3,246	739	1,450	1,057	711 D	22.8%	44.7%	33.8%	66.2%
SILVER BOW	21,834	6,792	13,626	1,416	6,834 D	31.1%	62.4%	33.3%	66.7%
STILLWATER	2,453	1,085	1,281	87	196 D	44.2%	52.2%	45.9%	54.1%
SWEET GRASS	1,594	784	761	49	23 R	49.2%	47.7%	50.7%	49.3%
TETON	2,428	875	1,496	57	621 D	36.0%	61.6%	36.9%	63.1%
TOOLE	2,874	862	1,917	95	1,055 D	30.0%	66.7%	31.0%	69.0%
TREASURE	596	276	310	10	34 D	46.3%	52.0%	47.1%	52.9%
VALLEY	4,092	1,242	2,499	351	1,257 D	30.4%	61.1%	33.2%	66.8%
WHEATLAND	1,836	828	996	12	168 D	45.1%	54.2%	45.4%	54.6%
WIBAUX	1,252	445	798	9	353 D	35.5%	63.7%	35.8%	64.2%
YELLOWSTONE	11,483	5,386	5,777	320	391 D	46.9%	50.3%	48.2%	51.8%
TOTAL	216,479	78,078	127,286	11,115	49,208 D	36.1%	58.8%	38.0%	62.0%

MONTANA

PRESIDENT 1936

County	Total Vote	Republican	Democratic	Other	Rep.-Dem. Plurality	Total Vote Rep.	Total Vote Dem.	Major Vote Rep.	Major Vote Dem.
BEAVERHEAD	3,538	1,304	2,153	81	847 D	36.9%	60.9%	37.7%	62.3%
BIG HORN	3,186	1,087	2,037	62	953 D	34.1%	63.9%	34.8%	65.2%
BLAINE	3,074	851	2,166	57	1,315 D	27.7%	70.5%	28.2%	71.8%
BROADWATER	1,597	502	1,071	24	569 D	31.4%	67.1%	31.9%	68.1%
CARBON	4,876	1,617	3,116	143	1,499 D	33.2%	63.9%	34.2%	65.8%
CARTER	1,414	464	929	21	465 D	32.8%	65.7%	33.3%	66.7%
CASCADE	17,789	4,077	13,325	387	9,248 D	22.9%	74.9%	23.4%	76.6%
CHOUTEAU	3,657	878	2,734	45	1,856 D	24.0%	74.8%	24.3%	75.7%
CUSTER	4,713	1,381	3,196	136	1,815 D	29.3%	67.8%	30.2%	69.8%
DANIELS	2,115	467	1,596	52	1,129 D	22.1%	75.5%	22.6%	77.4%
DAWSON	3,410	1,221	2,169	20	948 D	35.8%	63.6%	36.0%	64.0%
DEER LODGE	6,549	1,640	4,813	96	3,173 D	25.0%	73.5%	25.4%	74.6%
FALLON	1,661	598	1,015	48	417 D	36.0%	61.1%	37.1%	62.9%
FERGUS	6,745	1,821	4,675	249	2,854 D	27.0%	69.3%	28.0%	72.0%
FLATHEAD	8,532	2,460	5,408	664	2,948 D	28.8%	63.4%	31.3%	68.7%
GALLATIN	7,168	2,151	4,697	320	2,546 D	30.0%	65.5%	31.4%	68.6%
GARFIELD	1,577	548	991	38	443 D	34.7%	62.8%	35.6%	64.4%
GLACIER	3,265	781	2,453	31	1,672 D	23.9%	75.1%	24.1%	75.9%
GOLDEN VALLEY	821	331	474	16	143 D	40.3%	57.7%	41.1%	58.9%
GRANITE	1,724	475	1,227	22	752 D	27.6%	71.2%	27.9%	72.1%
HILL	5,520	1,014	4,328	178	3,314 D	18.4%	78.4%	19.0%	81.0%
JEFFERSON	2,063	573	1,409	81	836 D	27.8%	68.3%	28.9%	71.1%
JUDITH BASIN	2,231	645	1,534	52	889 D	28.9%	68.8%	29.6%	70.4%
LAKE	4,422	1,401	2,656	365	1,255 D	31.7%	60.1%	34.5%	65.5%
LEWIS AND CLARK	8,725	2,951	5,614	160	2,663 D	33.8%	64.3%	34.5%	65.5%
LIBERTY	1,065	276	758	31	482 D	25.9%	71.2%	26.7%	73.3%
LINCOLN	3,050	745	2,117	188	1,372 D	24.4%	69.4%	26.0%	74.0%
MCCONE	1,739	332	1,366	41	1,034 D	19.1%	78.6%	19.6%	80.4%
MADISON	2,890	1,006	1,819	65	813 D	34.8%	62.9%	35.6%	64.4%
MEAGHER	1,280	495	767	18	272 D	38.7%	59.9%	39.2%	60.8%
MINERAL	960	215	657	88	442 D	22.4%	68.4%	24.7%	75.3%
MISSOULA	10,803	2,697	7,690	416	4,993 D	25.0%	71.2%	26.0%	74.0%
MUSSELSHELL	3,014	771	2,092	151	1,321 D	25.6%	69.4%	26.9%	73.1%
PARK	4,793	1,583	2,968	242	1,385 D	33.0%	61.9%	34.8%	65.2%
PETROLEUM	806	258	523	25	265 D	32.0%	64.9%	33.0%	67.0%
PHILLIPS	3,494	850	2,555	89	1,705 D	24.3%	73.1%	25.0%	75.0%
PONDERA	2,934	658	2,213	63	1,555 D	22.4%	75.4%	22.8%	77.1%
POWDER RIVER	1,349	545	758	46	213 D	43.4%	56.2%	41.8%	58.2%
POWELL	2,914	799	2,060	55	1,261 D	27.4%	70.7%	28.0%	72.1%
PRAIRIE	1,363	454	877	32	423 D	33.3%	64.3%	34.1%	65.9%
RAVALLI	4,732	1,580	2,859	293	1,279 D	33.4%	60.4%	35.6%	64.4%
RICHLAND	3,663	1,052	2,516	95	1,464 D	28.7%	68.7%	29.5%	70.5%
ROOSEVELT	4,091	1,034	2,923	134	1,889 D	25.3%	71.5%	26.1%	73.9%
ROSEBUD	2,670	866	1,624	180	758 D	32.4%	60.8%	34.8%	65.2%
SANDERS	2,735	718	1,788	229	1,070 D	26.3%	65.4%	28.7%	71.3%
SHERIDAN	3,168	513	2,503	152	1,990 D	16.2%	79.0%	17.0%	83.0%
SILVER BOW	22,623	4,528	17,697	398	13,169 D	20.0%	78.2%	20.4%	79.6%
STILLWATER	2,422	1,034	1,292	96	258 D	42.7%	53.3%	44.5%	55.5%
SWEET GRASS	1,544	664	783	97	119 D	43.0%	50.7%	45.9%	54.1%
TETON	2,550	604	1,917	29	1,313 D	23.7%	75.2%	24.0%	76.0%
TOOLE	2,884	654	2,120	110	1,466 D	22.7%	73.5%	23.6%	76.4%
TREASURE	669	244	398	27	154 D	36.5%	59.5%	38.0%	62.0%
VALLEY	7,057	996	5,862	199	4,866 D	14.1%	83.1%	14.5%	85.5%
WHEATLAND	1,659	602	1,037	20	435 D	36.3%	62.5%	36.7%	63.3%
WIBAUX	1,161	362	790	9	428 D	31.2%	68.0%	31.4%	68.6%
YELLOWSTONE	14,016	5,193	8,575	248	3,382 D	37.1%	61.2%	37.7%	62.3%
TOTAL	230,502	63,598	159,690	7,214	96,092 D	27.6%	69.3%	28.5%	71.5%

PRESIDENT 1940

County	Total Vote	Republican	Democratic	Other	Rep.-Dem. Plurality	Total Vote Rep.	Total Vote Dem.	Major Vote Rep.	Major Vote Dem.
BEAVERHEAD	3,371	1,725	1,632	14	93 R	51.2%	48.4%	51.4%	48.6%
BIG HORN	3,560	1,616	1,926	18	310 D	45.4%	54.1%	45.6%	54.4%
BLAINE	3,327	1,165	2,129	33	964 D	35.0%	64.0%	35.4%	64.6%
BROADWATER	1,613	755	854	4	99 D	46.8%	52.9%	46.9%	53.1%
CARBON	5,161	2,421	2,678	62	257 D	46.9%	51.9%	47.5%	52.5%
CARTER	1,292	556	734	2	178 D	43.0%	56.8%	43.1%	56.9%
CASCADE	20,324	6,443	13,637	244	7,194 D	31.7%	67.1%	31.8%	67.9%
CHOUTEAU	3,475	1,235	2,213	27	978 D	35.5%	63.7%	35.8%	64.2%
CUSTER	4,834	2,007	2,782	45	775 D	41.7%	57.6%	42.0%	58.0%
DANIELS	1,921	807	1,086	28	279 D	42.0%	56.5%	42.6%	57.4%
DAWSON	3,392	1,612	1,765	15	153 D	47.5%	52.0%	47.7%	52.3%
DEER LODGE	7,345	2,397	4,916	32	2,519 D	32.6%	66.9%	32.8%	67.2%
FALLON	1,624	925	686	13	239 R	57.0%	42.2%	57.4%	42.6%
FERGUS	6,619	2,706	3,873	40	1,167 D	40.9%	58.5%	41.1%	58.9%
FLATHEAD	9,771	4,403	5,217	151	814 D	45.1%	53.4%	45.8%	54.2%
GALLATIN	8,198	3,430	4,718	50	1,288 D	41.8%	57.6%	42.1%	57.9%
GARFIELD	1,271	625	644	2	19 D	49.2%	50.7%	49.3%	50.7%
GLACIER	3,760	1,352	2,399	9	1,047 D	36.0%	63.8%	36.0%	64.0%
GOLDEN VALLEY	759	402	351	6	51 R	53.0%	46.3%	53.4%	46.6%
GRANITE	1,710	784	917	9	133 D	45.8%	53.6%	46.1%	53.9%
HILL	5,617	1,842	3,700	75	1,858 D	32.8%	65.9%	33.2%	66.8%
JEFFERSON	2,137	830	1,259	48	429 D	38.8%	58.9%	39.7%	60.3%
JUDITH BASIN	1,913	670	1,215	28	545 D	35.0%	63.5%	35.5%	64.5%
LAKE	5,181	2,718	2,379	84	339 R	52.5%	45.9%	53.3%	46.7%
LEWIS AND CLARK	10,683	4,762	5,814	107	1,052 D	44.6%	54.4%	45.0%	55.0%
LIBERTY	994	434	550	10	116 D	43.7%	55.3%	44.1%	55.9%
LINCOLN	3,448	1,250	2,150	48	900 D	36.3%	62.4%	36.8%	63.2%
MCCONE	1,501	529	928	44	399 D	35.2%	61.8%	36.3%	63.7%
MADISON	3,256	1,557	1,674	25	117 D	47.8%	51.4%	48.2%	51.8%
MEAGHER	1,157	520	621	16	101 D	44.9%	53.7%	45.6%	54.4%
MINERAL	1,068	402	645	21	243 D	37.6%	60.4%	38.4%	61.6%
MISSOULA	13,527	5,640	7,747	150	2,107 D	41.7%	57.2%	42.1%	57.9%
MUSSELSHELL	2,952	1,086	1,807	59	721 D	36.8%	61.2%	37.5%	62.5%
PARK	5,319	2,433	2,833	53	400 D	45.7%	53.3%	46.2%	53.8%
PETROLEUM	631	313	316	2	3 D	49.6%	50.1%	49.8%	50.2%
PHILLIPS	3,366	1,110	2,225	31	1,115 D	33.0%	66.1%	33.3%	66.7%
PONDERA	2,980	1,038	1,899	43	861 D	34.8%	63.7%	35.3%	64.7%
POWDER RIVER	1,212	633	561	18	72 R	52.2%	46.3%	53.0%	47.0%
POWELL	2,902	1,116	1,765	21	649 D	38.5%	60.8%	38.7%	61.3%
PRAIRIE	1,161	597	554	10	43 R	51.4%	47.7%	51.9%	48.1%
RAVALLI	5,313	2,483	2,773	57	290 D	46.7%	52.2%	47.2%	52.8%
RICHLAND	3,645	1,497	2,095	53	598 D	41.1%	57.5%	41.7%	58.3%
ROOSEVELT	3,982	1,503	2,418	61	915 D	37.7%	60.7%	38.3%	61.7%
ROSEBUD	2,677	1,252	1,399	26	147 D	46.8%	52.3%	47.2%	52.8%
SANDERS	2,794	1,088	1,634	72	546 D	38.9%	58.5%	40.0%	60.0%
SHERIDAN	3,052	892	2,108	52	1,216 D	29.2%	69.1%	29.7%	70.3%
SILVER BOW	25,734	7,932	17,467	335	9,535 D	30.8%	67.9%	31.2%	68.8%
STILLWATER	2,475	1,255	1,201	19	54 R	50.7%	48.5%	51.1%	48.9%
SWEET GRASS	1,611	861	741	9	120 R	53.4%	46.0%	53.7%	46.3%
TETON	2,894	1,132	1,735	27	603 D	39.1%	60.0%	39.5%	60.5%
TOOLE	3,182	1,218	1,954	10	736 D	38.3%	61.4%	38.4%	61.6%
TREASURE	610	287	321	2	34 D	47.0%	52.6%	47.2%	52.8%
VALLEY	5,162	1,597	3,493	72	1,896 D	30.9%	67.7%	31.4%	68.6%
WHEATLAND	1,742	786	948	8	162 D	45.1%	54.4%	45.3%	54.7%
WIBAUX	1,043	461	576	6	115 D	44.2%	55.2%	44.5%	55.5%
YELLOWSTONE	17,655	8,479	9,036	140	557 D	48.0%	51.2%	48.4%	51.6%
TOTAL	247,873	99,579	145,698	2,596	46,119 D	40.2%	58.8%	40.6%	59.4%

MONTANA

PRESIDENT 1944

County	Total Vote	Republican	Democratic	Other	Rep.-Dem. Plurality	% Total Vote Rep.	% Total Vote Dem.	% Major Vote Rep.	% Major Vote Dem.
BEAVERHEAD	2,832	1,556	1,263	13	293 R	54.9%	44.6%	55.2%	44.8%
BIG HORN	2,695	1,394	1,289	12	105 R	51.7%	47.8%	52.0%	48.0%
BLAINE	2,479	990	1,469	20	479 D	39.9%	59.3%	40.3%	59.7%
BROADWATER	1,323	760	558	5	202 R	57.4%	42.2%	57.7%	42.3%
CARBON	4,230	2,126	2,073	31	53 R	50.3%	49.0%	50.6%	49.4%
CARTER	1,118	507	610	1	103 D	45.3%	54.6%	45.4%	54.6%
CASCADE	17,437	6,372	10,924	141	4,552 D	36.5%	62.6%	36.8%	63.2%
CHOUTEAU	3,153	1,220	1,906	27	686 D	38.7%	60.5%	39.0%	61.0%
CUSTER	3,897	1,830	2,038	29	208 D	47.0%	52.3%	47.3%	52.7%
DANIELS	1,516	680	824	12	144 D	44.9%	54.4%	45.2%	54.8%
DAWSON	2,927	1,549	1,362	16	187 R	52.9%	46.5%	53.2%	46.8%
DEER LODGE	6,556	2,176	4,347	33	2,171 D	33.2%	66.3%	33.4%	66.6%
FALLON	1,371	870	494	7	376 R	63.5%	36.0%	63.8%	36.2%
FERGUS	5,422	2,229	3,164	29	935 D	41.1%	58.4%	41.3%	58.7%
FLATHEAD	7,786	4,066	3,608	112	458 R	52.2%	46.3%	53.0%	47.0%
GALLATIN	6,632	3,120	3,479	33	359 D	47.0%	52.5%	47.3%	52.7%
GARFIELD	1,053	553	478	22	75 R	52.5%	45.3%	53.6%	46.4%
GLACIER	3,379	1,228	2,142	9	914 D	36.3%	63.4%	36.4%	63.6%
GOLDEN VALLEY	662	395	266	1	129 R	59.7%	40.2%	59.8%	40.2%
GRANITE	1,288	702	574	12	128 R	54.5%	44.6%	55.0%	45.0%
HILL	4,669	1,646	2,986	37	1,340 D	35.3%	64.0%	35.5%	64.5%
JEFFERSON	1,603	797	803	3	6 D	49.7%	50.1%	49.8%	50.2%
JUDITH BASIN	1,747	691	1,049	7	358 D	39.6%	60.0%	39.7%	60.3%
LAKE	4,059	2,265	1,750	44	515 R	55.8%	43.1%	56.4%	43.6%
LEWIS AND CLARK	9,258	4,482	4,737	39	255 D	48.4%	51.2%	48.6%	51.4%
LIBERTY	842	393	440	9	47 D	46.7%	52.3%	47.2%	52.8%
LINCOLN	2,589	1,109	1,445	35	336 D	42.8%	55.8%	43.4%	56.6%
MCCONE	1,320	526	763	31	237 D	39.8%	57.8%	40.8%	59.2%
MADISON	2,313	1,278	1,022	13	256 R	55.3%	44.2%	55.6%	44.4%
MEAGHER	993	509	482	2	27 R	51.3%	48.5%	51.4%	48.6%
MINERAL	792	380	401	11	21 D	48.0%	50.6%	48.7%	51.3%
MISSOULA	11,028	5,371	5,558	99	187 D	48.7%	50.4%	49.1%	50.9%
MUSSELSHELL	2,375	1,004	1,342	29	338 D	42.3%	56.5%	42.8%	57.2%
PARK	4,677	2,396	2,245	36	151 R	51.2%	48.0%	51.6%	48.4%
PETROLEUM	481	253	225	3	28 R	52.6%	46.8%	52.9%	47.1%
PHILLIPS	2,543	1,089	1,435	19	346 D	42.8%	56.4%	43.1%	56.9%
PONDERA	2,361	890	1,448	23	558 D	37.7%	61.3%	38.1%	61.9%
POWDER RIVER	1,137	650	476	11	174 R	57.2%	41.9%	57.7%	42.3%
POWELL	2,645	1,100	1,527	18	427 D	41.6%	57.7%	41.9%	58.1%
PRAIRIE	1,074	598	468	8	130 R	55.7%	43.6%	56.1%	43.9%
RAVALLI	4,311	2,342	1,926	43	416 R	54.3%	44.7%	54.9%	45.1%
RICHLAND	3,161	1,347	1,777	37	430 D	42.6%	56.2%	43.1%	56.9%
ROOSEVELT	3,168	1,281	1,848	39	567 D	40.4%	58.3%	40.9%	59.1%
ROSEBUD	2,301	1,154	1,114	33	40 R	50.2%	48.4%	50.9%	49.1%
SANDERS	2,278	1,070	1,184	24	114 D	47.0%	52.0%	47.5%	52.5%
SHERIDAN	2,548	791	1,713	44	922 D	31.0%	67.2%	31.6%	68.4%
SILVER BOW	21,040	7,610	13,228	202	5,618 D	36.2%	62.9%	36.5%	63.5%
STILLWATER	2,142	1,201	934	7	267 R	56.1%	43.6%	56.3%	43.7%
SWEET GRASS	1,440	897	533	10	364 R	62.3%	37.0%	62.7%	37.3%
TETON	2,601	1,074	1,508	19	434 D	41.3%	58.0%	41.6%	58.4%
TOOLE	2,668	1,113	1,545	10	432 D	41.7%	57.9%	41.9%	58.1%
TREASURE	573	287	282	4	5 R	50.1%	49.2%	50.4%	49.6%
VALLEY	3,582	1,341	2,196	45	855 D	37.4%	61.3%	37.9%	62.1%
WHEATLAND	1,516	767	733	16	34 R	50.6%	48.4%	50.8%	48.9%
WIBAUX	859	432	425	2	7 R	50.3%	49.5%	50.4%	49.6%
YELLOWSTONE	16,925	8,706	8,140	79	566 R	51.4%	48.1%	51.7%	48.3%
TOTAL	207,355	93,163	112,556	1,636	19,393 D	44.9%	54.3%	45.3%	54.7%

PRESIDENT 1948

County	Total Vote	Republican	Democratic	Other	Rep.-Dem. Plurality	% Total Vote Rep.	% Total Vote Dem.	% Major Vote Rep.	% Major Vote Dem.
BEAVERHEAD	3,005	1,583	1,356	66	227 R	52.7%	45.1%	53.9%	46.1%
BIG HORN	2,702	1,334	1,328	40	6 R	49.4%	49.1%	50.1%	49.9%
BLAINE	2,748	997	1,669	82	672 D	36.3%	60.7%	37.4%	62.6%
BROADWATER	1,266	704	536	26	168 R	55.6%	42.3%	56.8%	43.2%
CARBON	4,169	1,901	1,997	271	96 D	45.6%	47.9%	48.8%	51.2%
CARTER	1,084	501	568	15	67 D	46.2%	52.4%	46.9%	53.1%
CASCADE	19,817	6,830	12,082	905	5,252 D	34.5%	61.0%	36.1%	63.9%
CHOUTEAU	3,138	1,181	1,832	125	651 D	37.6%	58.4%	39.2%	60.8%
CUSTER	4,263	1,845	2,359	59	514 D	43.3%	55.3%	43.9%	56.1%
DANIELS	1,523	624	826	73	202 D	41.0%	54.2%	43.0%	57.0%
DAWSON	3,017	1,555	1,397	65	158 R	51.5%	46.3%	52.7%	47.3%
DEER LODGE	6,212	2,036	3,862	314	1,826 D	32.8%	62.2%	34.5%	65.5%
FALLON	1,329	678	623	28	55 R	51.0%	46.9%	52.1%	47.9%
FERGUS	5,652	2,411	3,059	182	648 D	42.7%	54.1%	44.1%	55.9%
FLATHEAD	9,193	4,240	4,546	407	306 D	46.1%	49.5%	48.3%	51.7%
GALLATIN	7,950	4,220	3,548	182	672 R	53.1%	44.6%	54.3%	45.7%
GARFIELD	973	501	451	21	50 R	51.5%	46.4%	52.6%	47.4%
GLACIER	3,508	1,238	2,238	32	1,000 D	35.3%	63.8%	35.6%	64.4%
GOLDEN VALLEY	663	352	295	16	57 R	53.1%	44.5%	54.4%	45.6%
GRANITE	1,268	659	567	42	92 R	52.0%	44.7%	53.8%	46.2%
HILL	5,181	1,645	3,321	215	1,676 D	31.8%	64.1%	33.1%	66.9%
JEFFERSON	1,644	750	836	58	86 D	45.6%	50.8%	47.3%	52.7%
JUDITH BASIN	1,662	609	934	119	325 D	36.6%	56.2%	39.5%	60.5%
LAKE	4,650	2,295	2,177	178	118 R	49.4%	46.8%	51.3%	48.7%
LEWIS AND CLARK	10,176	5,174	4,745	257	429 R	50.8%	46.6%	52.2%	47.8%
LIBERTY	926	354	542	30	188 D	38.2%	58.5%	39.5%	60.5%
LINCOLN	2,893	1,079	1,689	125	610 D	37.3%	58.4%	39.0%	61.0%
MCCONE	1,371	518	702	151	184 D	37.8%	51.2%	42.5%	57.5%
MADISON	2,357	1,300	1,006	51	294 R	55.2%	42.7%	56.4%	43.6%
MEAGHER	1,035	518	497	20	21 R	50.0%	48.0%	51.0%	49.0%
MINERAL	860	338	475	47	137 D	39.3%	55.2%	41.6%	58.4%
MISSOULA	13,873	6,426	7,005	442	579 D	46.3%	50.5%	47.8%	52.2%
MUSSELSHELL	2,496	1,010	1,188	298	178 D	40.5%	47.6%	46.0%	54.0%
PARK	4,845	2,461	2,222	162	239 R	50.8%	45.9%	52.5%	47.5%
PETROLEUM	461	214	235	12	21 D	46.4%	51.0%	47.7%	52.3%
PHILLIPS	2,569	964	1,506	99	542 D	37.5%	58.6%	39.0%	61.0%
PONDERA	2,550	902	1,555	93	653 D	35.4%	61.0%	36.7%	63.3%
POWDER RIVER	1,303	784	480	39	304 R	60.2%	36.8%	62.0%	38.0%
POWELL	2,674	1,163	1,427	84	264 D	43.5%	53.4%	44.9%	55.1%
PRAIRIE	1,042	499	527	16	28 D	47.9%	50.6%	48.6%	51.4%
RAVALLI	4,723	2,354	2,159	210	195 R	49.8%	45.7%	52.2%	47.8%
RICHLAND	3,090	1,332	1,673	85	341 D	43.1%	54.1%	44.3%	55.7%
ROOSEVELT	3,128	1,142	1,820	166	678 D	36.5%	58.2%	38.6%	61.4%
ROSEBUD	2,181	1,106	1,031	44	75 R	50.7%	47.3%	51.8%	48.2%
SANDERS	2,767	1,191	1,425	151	234 D	43.0%	51.5%	45.5%	54.5%
SHERIDAN	2,453	699	1,515	239	816 D	28.5%	61.8%	31.6%	68.4%
SILVER BOW	21,335	7,305	12,715	1,315	5,410 D	34.2%	59.6%	36.5%	63.5%
STILLWATER	2,087	1,137	890	60	247 R	54.5%	42.6%	56.1%	43.9%
SWEET GRASS	1,366	843	499	24	344 R	61.7%	36.5%	62.8%	37.2%
TETON	2,720	1,005	1,632	83	627 D	36.9%	60.0%	38.1%	61.9%
TOOLE	2,888	1,092	1,756	40	664 D	37.8%	60.8%	38.3%	61.7%
TREASURE	560	253	291	16	38 D	45.2%	52.0%	46.5%	53.5%
VALLEY	4,110	1,375	2,535	200	1,160 D	33.5%	61.7%	35.2%	64.8%
WHEATLAND	1,533	780	733	20	47 R	50.9%	47.8%	51.6%	48.4%
WIBAUX	905	421	471	13	50 D	46.5%	52.0%	47.2%	52.8%
YELLOWSTONE	20,384	10,342	9,718	324	624 R	50.7%	47.7%	51.6%	48.4%
TOTAL	224,278	96,770	119,071	8,437	22,301 D	43.1%	53.1%	44.8%	55.2%

MONTANA

PRESIDENT 1952

County	Total Vote	Republican	Democratic	Other	Rep.-Dem. Plurality	Total Vote Rep.	Dem.	Major Vote Rep.	Dem.
BEAVERHEAD	3,128	2,196	920	12	1,276 R	70.2%	29.4%	70.5%	29.5%
BIG HORN	3,285	2,165	1,114	6	1,051 R	65.9%	33.9%	66.0%	34.0%
BLAINE	3,106	1,890	1,207	9	683 R	60.8%	38.9%	61.0%	39.0%
BROADWATER	1,397	962	435	-	527 R	68.9%	31.1%	68.9%	31.1%
CARBON	4,470	2,734	1,713	23	1,021 R	61.2%	38.3%	61.5%	38.5%
CARTER	1,277	921	351	5	570 R	72.1%	27.5%	72.4%	27.6%
CASCADE	23,373	12,176	11,051	146	1,125 R	52.1%	47.3%	52.4%	47.6%
CHOUTEAU	3,535	2,098	1,423	14	675 R	59.3%	40.3%	59.6%	40.4%
CUSTER	5,535	3,461	2,050	24	1,411 R	62.5%	37.0%	62.8%	37.2%
DANIELS	1,748	1,092	649	7	443 R	62.5%	37.1%	62.7%	37.3%
DAWSON	3,658	2,396	1,247	15	1,149 R	65.5%	34.1%	65.8%	34.2%
DEER LODGE	7,217	3,001	4,162	54	1,151 D	41.6%	57.7%	41.9%	58.1%
FALLON	1,494	1,046	440	8	606 R	70.0%	29.5%	70.4%	29.6%
FERGUS	6,691	4,402	2,271	18	2,131 R	65.8%	33.9%	66.0%	34.0%
FLATHEAD	12,476	7,372	4,994	110	2,378 R	59.1%	40.0%	59.6%	40.4%
GALLATIN	9,729	6,998	2,697	34	4,301 R	71.9%	27.7%	72.2%	27.8%
GARFIELD	994	723	269	2	454 R	72.7%	27.1%	72.9%	27.1%
GLACIER	3,769	2,061	1,698	10	363 R	54.7%	45.1%	54.8%	45.2%
GOLDEN VALLEY	669	471	198	-	273 R	70.4%	29.6%	70.4%	29.6%
GRANITE	1,401	923	473	5	450 R	65.9%	33.8%	66.1%	33.9%
HILL	6,266	3,474	2,748	44	726 R	55.4%	43.9%	55.8%	44.2%
JEFFERSON	1,784	1,084	687	13	397 R	60.8%	38.5%	61.2%	38.8%
JUDITH BASIN	1,853	1,074	746	33	328 R	58.0%	40.3%	59.0%	41.0%
LAKE	5,609	3,651	1,893	65	1,758 R	65.1%	33.7%	65.9%	34.1%
LEWIS AND CLARK	12,246	7,663	4,563	20	3,100 R	62.6%	37.3%	62.7%	37.3%
LIBERTY	1,088	671	411	6	250 R	61.7%	37.8%	62.0%	38.0%
LINCOLN	3,821	1,881	1,907	33	26 D	49.2%	49.9%	49.7%	50.3%
MCCONE	1,598	900	674	24	226 R	56.3%	42.2%	57.2%	42.8%
MADISON	2,752	1,993	751	8	1,242 R	72.4%	27.3%	72.6%	27.4%
MEAGHER	1,120	792	326	2	456 R	70.7%	29.1%	70.8%	29.2%
MINERAL	1,054	553	491	10	52 R	52.5%	46.6%	53.0%	47.0%
MISSOULA	17,041	10,053	6,901	87	3,152 R	59.0%	40.5%	59.3%	40.7%
MUSSELSHELL	2,502	1,253	1,240	9	13 R	50.1%	49.6%	50.3%	49.7%
PARK	6,150	4,152	1,969	29	2,183 R	67.5%	32.0%	67.8%	32.2%
PETROLEUM	474	319	155	-	154 R	67.3%	32.7%	67.3%	32.7%
PHILLIPS	3,017	1,771	1,224	22	547 R	58.7%	40.6%	59.1%	40.9%
PONDERA	2,992	1,719	1,246	27	473 R	57.5%	41.6%	58.0%	42.0%
POWDER RIVER	1,222	888	327	7	561 R	72.7%	26.8%	73.1%	26.9%
POWELL	3,082	1,783	1,281	18	502 R	57.9%	41.6%	58.2%	41.8%
PRAIRIE	1,120	771	338	5	433 R	69.2%	30.3%	69.5%	30.5%
RAVALLI	5,329	3,537	1,750	42	1,787 R	66.4%	32.8%	66.9%	33.1%
RICHLAND	3,725	2,506	1,196	23	1,310 R	67.3%	32.1%	67.7%	32.3%
ROOSEVELT	3,483	1,998	1,466	19	532 R	57.4%	42.1%	57.7%	42.3%
ROSEBUD	2,553	1,734	805	14	929 R	67.9%	31.5%	68.3%	31.7%
SANDERS	3,078	1,724	1,311	43	413 R	56.0%	42.5%	56.8%	43.2%
SHERIDAN	2,711	1,339	1,347	25	8 D	49.4%	49.7%	49.8%	50.1%
SILVER BOW	23,458	10,196	13,114	148	2,918 D	43.5%	55.9%	43.7%	56.3%
STILLWATER	2,520	1,689	816	15	873 R	67.0%	32.4%	67.4%	32.6%
SWEET GRASS	1,704	1,315	372	17	943 R	77.2%	21.8%	77.9%	22.1%
TETON	3,378	1,978	1,389	11	589 R	58.6%	41.1%	58.7%	41.3%
TOOLE	3,294	1,853	1,426	15	427 R	56.3%	43.3%	56.5%	43.5%
TREASURE	597	392	205	-	187 R	65.7%	34.3%	65.7%	34.3%
VALLEY	4,621	2,462	2,130	29	332 R	53.3%	46.1%	53.6%	46.4%
WHEATLAND	1,607	1,026	572	9	454 R	63.8%	35.6%	64.2%	35.8%
WIBAUX	885	556	324	5	232 R	62.8%	36.6%	63.2%	36.8%
YELLOWSTONE	26,357	17,556	8,750	51	8,806 R	66.6%	33.2%	66.7%	33.3%
TOTAL	265,037	157,394	106,213	1,430	51,181 R	59.4%	40.1%	59.7%	40.3%

PRESIDENT 1956

County	Total Vote	Republican	Democratic	Other	Rep.-Dem. Plurality	Total Vote Rep.	Dem.	Major Vote Rep.	Dem.
BEAVERHEAD	2,984	1,955	1,029	-	926 R	65.5%	34.5%	65.5%	34.5%
BIG HORN	3,081	1,739	1,342	-	397 R	56.4%	43.6%	56.4%	43.6%
BLAINE	2,898	1,460	1,438	-	22 R	50.4%	49.6%	50.4%	49.6%
BROADWATER	1,318	869	449	-	420 R	65.9%	34.1%	65.9%	34.1%
CARBON	4,165	2,345	1,820	-	525 R	56.3%	43.7%	56.3%	43.7%
CARTER	1,134	698	436	-	262 R	61.6%	38.4%	61.6%	38.4%
CASCADE	23,553	12,455	11,098	-	1,357 R	52.9%	47.1%	52.9%	47.1%
CHOUTEAU	3,515	1,721	1,794	-	73 D	49.0%	51.0%	49.0%	51.0%
CUSTER	5,557	3,240	2,317	-	923 R	58.3%	41.7%	58.3%	41.7%
DANIELS	1,928	982	946	-	36 R	50.9%	49.1%	50.9%	49.1%
DAWSON	4,392	2,463	1,929	-	534 R	56.1%	43.9%	56.1%	43.9%
DEER LODGE	7,343	3,551	3,792	-	241 D	48.4%	51.6%	48.4%	51.6%
FALLON	1,579	967	612	-	355 R	61.2%	38.8%	61.2%	38.8%
FERGUS	6,528	3,771	2,757	-	1,014 R	57.8%	42.2%	57.8%	42.2%
FLATHEAD	14,091	8,088	6,003	-	2,085 R	57.4%	42.6%	57.4%	42.6%
GALLATIN	9,940	6,680	3,260	-	3,420 R	67.2%	32.8%	67.2%	32.8%
GARFIELD	982	558	424	-	134 R	56.8%	43.2%	56.8%	43.2%
GLACIER	3,876	2,054	1,822	-	232 R	53.0%	47.0%	53.0%	47.0%
GOLDEN VALLEY	639	383	256	-	127 R	59.9%	40.1%	59.9%	40.1%
GRANITE	1,429	896	533	-	363 R	62.7%	37.3%	62.7%	37.3%
HILL	6,414	3,415	2,999	-	416 R	53.2%	46.8%	53.2%	46.8%
JEFFERSON	1,709	1,049	660	-	389 R	61.4%	38.6%	61.4%	38.6%
JUDITH BASIN	1,637	789	848	-	59 D	48.2%	51.8%	48.2%	51.8%
LAKE	5,616	3,363	2,253	-	1,110 R	59.9%	40.1%	59.9%	40.1%
LEWIS AND CLARK	12,356	7,959	4,397	-	3,562 R	64.4%	35.6%	64.4%	35.6%
LIBERTY	1,089	601	488	-	113 R	55.2%	44.8%	55.2%	44.8%
LINCOLN	4,607	2,321	2,286	-	35 R	50.4%	49.6%	50.4%	49.6%
MCCONE	1,641	752	889	-	137 D	45.8%	54.2%	45.8%	54.2%
MADISON	2,587	1,662	925	-	737 R	64.2%	35.8%	64.2%	35.8%
MEAGHER	1,067	712	355	-	357 R	66.7%	33.3%	66.7%	33.3%
MINERAL	1,158	606	552	-	54 R	52.3%	47.7%	52.3%	47.7%
MISSOULA	17,387	10,627	6,760	-	3,867 R	61.1%	38.9%	61.1%	38.9%
MUSSELSHELL	2,280	1,165	1,115	-	50 R	51.1%	48.9%	51.1%	48.9%
PARK	5,884	3,733	2,151	-	1,582 R	63.4%	36.6%	63.4%	36.6%
PETROLEUM	463	258	205	-	53 R	55.7%	44.3%	55.7%	44.3%
PHILLIPS	3,032	1,605	1,427	-	178 R	52.9%	47.1%	52.9%	47.1%
PONDERA	3,089	1,651	1,438	-	213 R	53.4%	46.6%	53.4%	46.6%
POWDER RIVER	1,156	700	456	-	244 R	60.6%	39.4%	60.6%	39.4%
POWELL	2,897	1,683	1,214	-	469 R	58.1%	41.9%	58.1%	41.9%
PRAIRIE	1,040	637	403	-	234 R	61.2%	38.8%	61.2%	38.8%
RAVALLI	5,598	3,437	2,161	-	1,276 R	61.4%	38.6%	61.4%	38.6%
RICHLAND	4,250	2,356	1,884	-	482 R	55.7%	44.3%	55.7%	44.3%
ROOSEVELT	4,190	1,985	2,205	-	220 D	47.4%	52.6%	47.4%	52.6%
ROSEBUD	2,406	1,516	890	-	626 R	63.0%	37.0%	63.0%	37.0%
SANDERS	3,168	1,649	1,519	-	130 R	52.1%	47.9%	52.1%	47.9%
SHERIDAN	3,010	1,153	1,857	-	704 D	38.3%	61.7%	38.3%	61.7%
SILVER BOW	23,094	11,619	11,475	-	144 R	50.3%	49.7%	50.3%	49.7%
STILLWATER	2,553	1,540	1,013	-	527 R	60.3%	39.7%	60.3%	39.7%
SWEET GRASS	1,584	1,129	455	-	674 R	71.3%	28.7%	71.3%	28.7%
TETON	3,350	1,728	1,622	-	106 R	51.6%	48.4%	51.6%	48.4%
TOOLE	3,387	1,927	1,460	-	467 R	56.9%	43.1%	56.9%	43.1%
TREASURE	589	337	252	-	85 R	57.2%	42.8%	57.2%	42.8%
VALLEY	4,868	2,357	2,511	-	154 D	48.4%	51.6%	48.4%	51.6%
WHEATLAND	1,510	932	578	-	354 R	61.7%	38.3%	61.7%	38.3%
WIBAUX	821	431	390	-	41 R	52.5%	47.5%	52.5%	47.5%
YELLOWSTONE	28,752	18,664	10,088	-	8,576 R	64.9%	35.1%	64.9%	35.1%
TOTAL	271,171	154,933	116,238	-	38,695 R	57.1%	42.9%	57.1%	42.9%

MONTANA

PRESIDENT 1960

County	Total Vote	Republican	Democratic	Other	Rep.-Dem. Plurality	% Total Vote Rep.	% Total Vote Dem.	% Major Vote Rep.	% Major Vote Dem.
BEAVERHEAD	3,043	1,731	1,307	5	424 R	56.9	43.0	57.0	43.0
BIG HORN	3,224	1,724	1,497	3	227 R	53.5	46.4	53.5	46.5
BLAINE	2,876	1,290	1,569	17	279 D	44.9	54.6	45.1	54.9
BROADWATER	1,311	680	631	–	49 R	51.9	48.1	51.9	48.1
CARBON	3,961	2,050	1,903	8	147 R	51.8	48.0	51.9	48.1
CARTER	1,075	688	383	4	305 R	64.0	35.6	64.2	35.8
CASCADE	26,090	11,928	14,117	45	2,189 D	45.7	54.1	45.8	54.2
CHOUTEAU	3,389	1,672	1,708	9	36 D	49.3	50.4	49.5	50.5
CUSTER	5,351	2,943	2,393	15	550 R	55.0	44.7	55.2	44.8
DANIELS	1,724	763	960	1	197 D	44.3	55.7	44.3	55.7
DAWSON	4,582	2,460	2,108	14	352 R	53.7	46.0	53.9	46.1
DEER LODGE	7,344	2,188	5,149	7	2,961 D	29.8	70.1	29.8	70.2
FALLON	1,516	918	597	1	321 R	60.5	39.4	60.6	39.4
FERGUS	6,306	3,294	2,999	13	295 R	52.2	47.6	52.3	47.7
FLATHEAD	14,267	7,554	6,689	24	865 R	52.9	46.9	53.0	47.0
GALLATIN	10,652	6,870	3,761	21	3,109 R	64.5	35.3	64.6	35.4
GARFIELD	880	515	363	2	152 R	58.5	41.2	58.7	41.3
GLACIER	4,039	1,775	2,260	4	485 D	43.9	56.0	44.0	56.0
GOLDEN VALLEY	639	362	277	–	85 R	56.6	43.3	56.7	43.3
GRANITE	1,323	722	592	9	130 R	54.6	44.7	54.9	45.1
HILL	6,916	3,163	3,741	12	578 D	45.7	54.1	45.8	54.2
JEFFERSON	1,590	817	769	4	48 R	51.4	48.4	51.5	48.5
JUDITH BASIN	1,564	721	842	1	121 D	46.1	53.8	46.1	53.9
LAKE	5,709	3,240	2,462	7	778 R	56.8	43.1	56.8	43.2
LEWIS AND CLARK	13,285	7,260	6,008	17	1,252 R	54.6	45.2	54.7	45.3
LIBERTY	1,100	597	501	2	96 R	54.3	45.5	54.4	45.6
LINCOLN	4,546	1,902	2,623	21	721 D	41.8	57.7	42.0	58.0
MCCONE	1,515	743	764	8	21 D	49.0	50.4	49.3	50.7
MADISON	2,469	1,456	1,010	3	446 R	59.0	40.9	59.0	41.0
MEAGHER	1,048	613	431	4	182 R	58.5	41.1	58.7	41.3
MINERAL	1,240	549	686	5	137 D	44.3	55.3	44.5	55.5
MISSOULA	19,337	10,396	8,876	65	1,520 R	53.8	45.9	53.9	46.1
MUSSELSHELL	2,210	1,107	1,100	3	7 R	50.1	49.8	50.2	49.8
PARK	5,601	3,329	2,249	23	1,080 R	59.4	40.2	59.7	40.3
PETROLEUM	476	255	221	–	34 R	53.6	46.4	53.6	46.4
PHILLIPS	2,925	1,457	1,455	13	2 R	49.8	49.7	50.0	50.0
PONDERA	4,269	2,395	1,863	11	532 R	56.1	43.6	56.1	43.8
POWDER RIVER	1,105	665	438	2	227 R	60.2	39.6	60.3	39.7
POWELL	3,025	1,497	1,522	6	25 D	49.5	50.3	49.6	50.4
PRAIRIE	987	649	338	–	311 R	65.8	34.2	65.8	34.2
RAVALLI	5,528	3,121	2,381	26	740 R	56.5	43.1	56.7	43.3
RICHLAND	4,269	2,395	1,863	11	532 R	56.1	43.6	56.2	43.8
ROOSEVELT	4,132	1,876	2,227	29	351 D	45.4	53.9	45.7	54.3
ROSEBUD	2,399	1,386	1,002	11	384 R	57.8	41.8	58.0	42.0
SANDERS	2,984	1,497	1,469	18	28 R	50.2	49.2	50.5	49.5
SHERIDAN	2,754	1,196	1,549	9	353 D	43.4	56.2	43.6	56.4
SILVER BOW	21,190	7,290	13,754	146	6,464 D	34.4	64.9	34.6	65.4
STILLWATER	2,491	1,455	1,036	–	419 R	58.4	41.6	58.4	41.6
SWEET GRASS	1,617	1,096	521	–	575 R	67.8	32.2	67.8	32.2
TETON	3,276	1,623	1,648	5	25 D	49.5	50.3	49.6	50.4
TOOLE	3,348	1,577	1,767	4	190 D	47.1	52.8	47.2	52.8
TREASURE	570	300	270	–	30 R	52.6	47.4	52.6	47.4
VALLEY	5,346	2,387	2,953	6	566 D	44.7	55.2	44.7	55.3
WHEATLAND	1,518	793	724	1	69 R	52.3	47.7	52.3	47.7
WIBAUX	806	387	419	–	32 D	48.0	52.0	48.0	52.0
YELLOWSTONE	32,006	19,467	12,356	183	7,111 R	60.8	38.6	61.2	38.8
TOTAL	277,579	141,841	134,891	847	6,950 R	51.1	48.6	51.3	48.7

PRESIDENT 1964

County	Total Vote	Republican	Democratic	Other	Rep.-Dem. Plurality	% Total Vote Rep.	% Total Vote Dem.	% Major Vote Rep.	% Major Vote Dem.
BEAVERHEAD	3,231	1,754	1,469	8	285 R	54.3	45.5	54.4	45.6
BIG HORN	3,993	1,481	2,509	3	1,028 D	37.1	62.8	37.1	62.8
BLAINE	2,703	961	1,742	–	781 D	35.6	64.4	35.6	64.4
BROADWATER	1,204	609	595	–	14 R	50.6	49.4	50.6	49.4
CARBON	3,633	1,535	2,098	–	563 D	42.3	57.7	42.3	57.7
CARTER	1,029	576	453	–	123 R	56.0	44.0	56.0	44.0
CASCADE	26,714	8,986	17,609	119	8,623 D	33.8	65.9	33.8	66.2
CHOUTEAU	3,276	1,444	1,827	5	383 D	44.1	55.8	44.1	55.9
CUSTER	5,101	2,302	2,790	9	488 D	45.1	54.7	45.2	54.8
DANIELS	1,730	742	987	1	245 D	42.9	57.1	42.9	57.1
DAWSON	4,637	1,938	2,691	8	753 D	41.8	58.0	41.9	58.1
DEER LODGE	6,259	1,415	4,835	9	3,420 D	22.6	77.2	22.6	77.4
FALLON	1,595	827	765	3	62 R	51.8	47.9	51.9	48.1
FERGUS	6,293	2,980	3,300	13	320 D	47.4	52.4	47.5	52.5
FLATHEAD	14,370	6,325	8,015	30	1,690 D	44.0	55.8	44.1	55.9
GALLATIN	11,248	5,621	5,600	27	21 R	50.0	49.8	50.1	49.9
GARFIELD	896	509	384	3	125 R	56.8	42.9	57.0	43.0
GLACIER	3,697	1,458	2,218	21	760 D	39.4	60.0	39.7	60.3
GOLDEN VALLEY	604	252	352	–	100 D	41.7	58.3	41.7	58.3
GRANITE	1,187	527	658	2	131 D	44.4	55.4	44.5	55.5
HILL	6,604	2,101	4,491	12	2,390 D	31.8	68.0	31.9	68.1
JEFFERSON	1,631	662	967	2	305 D	40.6	59.3	40.6	59.4
JUDITH BASIN	1,502	678	822	2	144 D	45.1	54.7	45.2	54.8
LAKE	5,986	2,828	3,148	10	320 D	47.2	52.6	47.3	52.7
LEWIS AND CLARK	13,687	6,155	7,506	26	1,351 D	45.0	54.8	45.1	54.9
LIBERTY	1,155	533	619	3	86 D	46.1	53.6	46.3	53.7
LINCOLN	4,709	1,554	3,140	15	1,586 D	33.0	66.7	33.1	66.9
MCCONE	1,507	615	891	1	276 D	40.8	59.1	40.8	59.2
MADISON	2,403	1,276	1,125	2	151 R	53.1	46.8	53.1	46.9
MEAGHER	913	506	405	2	101 R	55.4	44.4	55.5	44.5
MINERAL	1,274	368	901	5	533 D	28.9	70.7	29.0	71.0
MISSOULA	21,004	8,065	12,900	39	4,835 D	38.4	61.4	38.5	61.5
MUSSELSHELL	2,012	823	1,189	–	366 D	40.9	59.1	40.9	59.1
PARK	5,053	2,619	2,824	10	205 D	48.0	51.8	48.1	51.9
PETROLEUM	401	190	210	1	20 D	47.4	52.4	47.5	52.5
PHILLIPS	2,857	1,242	1,612	3	370 D	43.5	56.4	43.5	56.5
PONDERA	2,877	1,110	1,759	8	649 D	38.6	61.1	38.7	61.3
POWDER RIVER	1,099	649	449	1	200 R	59.1	40.9	59.1	40.9
POWELL	3,040	1,140	1,896	4	756 D	37.5	62.4	37.5	62.5
PRAIRIE	1,048	555	488	5	67 R	53.0	46.6	53.2	46.8
RAVALLI	5,662	2,350	3,300	12	950 D	41.5	58.3	41.6	58.4
RICHLAND	4,131	1,784	2,320	27	536 D	43.2	56.2	43.5	56.5
ROOSEVELT	4,078	1,612	2,463	4	851 D	39.5	60.4	39.6	60.4
ROSEBUD	2,321	1,105	1,212	4	107 D	47.6	52.2	47.7	52.3
SANDERS	3,013	1,163	1,836	14	673 D	38.6	60.9	38.8	61.2
SHERIDAN	2,754	837	1,905	12	1,068 D	30.4	69.2	30.5	69.5
SILVER BOW	21,239	4,873	15,751	615	10,878 D	22.9	74.2	23.6	76.4
STILLWATER	2,271	1,140	1,130	1	10 R	50.2	49.8	50.2	49.8
SWEET GRASS	1,514	856	653	5	203 R	56.5	43.1	56.7	43.3
TETON	3,199	1,388	1,808	3	420 D	43.4	56.5	43.4	56.6
TOOLE	2,874	1,223	1,649	2	426 D	42.6	57.4	42.6	57.4
TREASURE	536	251	285	–	34 D	46.8	53.2	46.8	53.2
VALLEY	5,125	2,077	3,032	16	955 D	40.5	59.2	40.7	59.3
WHEATLAND	1,373	583	790	–	207 D	42.5	57.5	42.5	57.5
WIBAUX	737	308	427	2	119 D	41.8	57.9	41.9	58.1
YELLOWSTONE	33,239	15,571	17,446	222	1,875 D	46.8	52.5	47.2	52.8
TOTAL	278,628	113,032	164,246	1,350	51,214 D	40.6	58.9	40.8	59.2

MONTANA

OTHER VOTE COMPOSITION:

1920	Farmer-Labor.
1924	66,124 Progressive; 358 Communist.
1928	1,667 Socialist; 563 Communist.
1932	7,891 Socialist; 1,775 Communist; 1,449 Liberty.
1936	5,539 Union; 1,066 Socialist; 385 Communist; 224 Prohibition.
1940	1,443 Socialist; 664 Prohibition; 489 Communist.
1944	1,296 Socialist; 340 Prohibition.
1948	7,313 Progressive; 695 Socialist; 429 Prohibition.
1952	723 Progressive; 548 Prohibition; 159 Socialist.
1956	
1960	456 Prohibition; 391 Socialist Workers.
1964	519 National States Rights; 499 Prohibition; 332 Socialist Workers.

SPECIAL CASES:

1924   Progressive total includes 61,105 La Follette-Wheeler Independent, 4,771 Farmer-Labor, and 248 Socialist votes. This combined vote carried a number of counties and was second in most others. Judith Basin county organized late in 1920; Lake county organized in 1923.

1928   Petroleum county organized in 1925.

NEBRASKA

PRESIDENT 1920

County	Total Vote	Republican	Democratic	Other	Rep.-Dem. Plurality	% Total Rep.	% Total Dem.	% Major Rep.	% Major Dem.
ADAMS	7,008	4,849	1,932	227	2,917 R	69.2%	27.6%	71.5%	28.5%
ANTELOPE	4,685	3,322	1,154	209	2,168 R	70.9%	24.6%	74.2%	25.8%
ARTHUR	293	167	94	32	73 R	57.0%	32.1%	64.0%	36.0%
BANNER	356	258	69	29	189 R	72.5%	19.4%	78.9%	21.1%
BLAINE	514	328	176	10	152 R	63.8%	34.2%	65.1%	34.9%
BOONE	4,711	3,108	1,461	142	1,647 R	66.0%	31.0%	68.0%	32.0%
BOX BUTTE	2,503	1,630	756	117	874 R	65.1%	30.2%	68.3%	31.7%
BOYD	2,116	1,482	527	107	955 R	70.0%	24.9%	73.8%	26.2%
BROWN	2,065	1,417	558	90	859 R	68.6%	27.0%	71.7%	28.3%
BUFFALO	7,557	4,954	2,258	345	2,696 R	65.6%	29.9%	68.7%	31.3%
BURT	4,228	2,969	1,194	65	1,775 R	70.2%	28.2%	71.3%	28.7%
BUTLER	4,486	2,478	1,918	90	560 R	55.2%	42.8%	56.4%	43.6%
CASS	6,127	3,575	2,192	360	1,383 R	58.3%	35.8%	62.0%	38.0%
CEDAR	5,243	3,906	1,279	58	2,627 R	74.5%	24.4%	75.3%	24.7%
CHASE	1,475	976	414	85	562 R	66.2%	28.1%	70.2%	29.8%
CHERRY	2,465	1,636	711	118	925 R	66.4%	28.8%	69.7%	30.3%
CHEYENNE	2,582	1,857	604	121	1,253 R	71.9%	23.4%	75.5%	24.5%
CLAY	5,008	3,392	1,466	150	1,926 R	67.7%	29.3%	69.8%	30.2%
COLFAX	3,005	1,992	957	56	1,035 R	66.3%	31.8%	67.5%	32.5%
CUMING	4,040	3,177	764	99	2,413 R	78.6%	18.9%	80.6%	19.4%
CUSTER	8,387	4,974	2,739	674	2,235 R	59.3%	32.7%	64.5%	35.5%
DAKOTA	2,437	1,525	873	39	652 R	62.6%	35.8%	63.6%	36.4%
DAWES	2,788	1,801	900	87	901 R	64.6%	32.3%	66.7%	33.3%
DAWSON	5,128	3,384	1,444	300	1,940 R	66.0%	28.2%	70.1%	29.9%
DEUEL	1,055	684	321	50	363 R	64.8%	30.4%	68.1%	31.9%
DIXON	3,409	2,435	911	63	1,524 R	71.4%	26.7%	72.8%	27.2%
DODGE	6,864	4,832	1,799	233	3,033 R	70.4%	26.2%	72.9%	27.1%
DOUGLAS	49,375	28,543	18,439	2,393	10,104 R	57.8%	37.3%	60.8%	39.2%
DUNDY	1,572	1,094	375	103	719 R	69.6%	23.9%	74.5%	25.5%
FILLMORE	4,419	2,803	1,549	67	1,254 R	63.4%	35.1%	64.4%	35.6%
FRANKLIN	3,403	2,294	1,030	79	1,264 R	67.4%	30.3%	69.0%	31.0%
FRONTIER	2,570	1,750	673	147	1,077 R	68.1%	26.2%	72.2%	27.8%
FURNAS	4,039	2,445	1,371	223	1,074 R	60.5%	33.9%	64.1%	35.9%
GAGE	8,786	6,059	2,477	250	3,582 R	69.0%	28.2%	71.0%	29.0%
GARDEN	1,395	924	421	50	503 R	66.2%	30.2%	68.7%	31.3%
GARFIELD	950	611	252	87	359 R	64.3%	26.5%	70.8%	29.2%
GOSPER	1,368	794	486	88	308 R	58.0%	35.5%	62.0%	38.0%
GRANT	399	256	141	2	115 R	64.2%	35.3%	64.5%	35.5%
GREELEY	2,618	1,345	1,180	93	165 R	51.4%	45.1%	53.3%	46.7%
HALL	7,123	4,719	1,724	680	2,995 R	66.3%	24.2%	73.2%	26.8%
HAMILTON	4,410	2,950	1,356	104	1,594 R	66.9%	30.7%	68.5%	31.5%
HARLAN	2,947	1,756	974	217	782 R	59.6%	33.1%	64.3%	35.7%
HAYES	771	512	207	52	305 R	66.4%	26.8%	71.2%	28.8%
HITCHCOCK	1,830	1,127	615	88	512 R	61.6%	33.6%	64.7%	35.3%
HOLT	4,898	3,163	1,577	158	1,586 R	64.6%	32.2%	66.7%	33.3%
HOOKER	362	230	117	15	113 R	63.5%	32.3%	66.3%	33.7%
HOWARD	2,971	1,508	1,311	152	197 R	50.8%	44.1%	53.5%	46.5%
JEFFERSON	5,134	3,488	1,408	238	2,080 R	67.9%	27.4%	71.2%	28.8%
JOHNSON	3,389	2,416	909	64	1,507 R	71.3%	26.8%	72.7%	27.3%
KEARNEY	3,043	1,683	1,273	87	410 R	55.3%	41.8%	56.9%	43.1%
KEITH	1,622	1,050	472	100	578 R	64.7%	29.1%	69.0%	31.0%
KEYA PAHA	740	479	218	43	261 R	64.7%	29.5%	68.7%	31.3%
KIMBALL	1,299	910	339	50	571 R	70.1%	26.1%	72.9%	27.1%
KNOX	5,264	3,678	1,470	116	2,208 R	69.9%	27.9%	71.4%	28.6%
LANCASTER	24,990	15,638	8,435	917	7,203 R	62.6%	33.8%	65.0%	35.0%
LINCOLN	5,822	3,342	1,896	584	1,446 R	57.4%	32.6%	63.8%	36.2%
LOGAN	540	312	180	48	132 R	57.8%	33.3%	63.4%	36.6%
LOUP	514	343	117	54	226 R	66.7%	22.8%	74.6%	25.4%
MCPHERSON	327	229	75	23	154 R	70.0%	22.9%	75.3%	24.7%
MADISON	7,056	5,171	1,716	169	3,455 R	73.3%	24.3%	75.1%	24.9%

PRESIDENT 1924

County	Total Vote	Republican	Democratic	Other	Rep.-Dem. Plurality	% Total Rep.	% Total Dem.	% Major Rep.	% Major Dem.
ADAMS	8,516	4,824	2,353	1,339	2,471 R	56.6%	27.6%	67.2%	32.8%
ANTELOPE	4,913	2,998	1,150	765	1,848 R	61.0%	23.4%	72.3%	27.7%
ARTHUR	410	143	101	166	42 R	34.9%	24.6%	58.6%	41.4%
BANNER	492	245	88	159	157 R	49.8%	17.9%	73.6%	26.4%
BLAINE	583	253	132	198	121 R	43.4%	22.6%	65.7%	34.3%
BOONE	5,537	2,013	1,782	1,742	231 R	36.4%	32.2%	53.0%	47.0%
BOX BUTTE	3,545	1,506	814	1,225	692 R	42.5%	23.0%	64.9%	35.1%
BOYD	2,648	991	532	1,125	459 R	37.4%	20.1%	65.1%	34.9%
BROWN	2,452	1,104	714	634	390 R	45.0%	29.1%	60.7%	39.3%
BUFFALO	8,751	4,746	2,337	1,668	2,409 R	54.1%	26.6%	67.0%	33.0%
BURT	5,179	2,813	1,870	496	943 R	54.3%	36.1%	60.1%	39.9%
BUTLER	5,434	2,435	2,444	555	9 D	44.8%	45.0%	49.9%	50.1%
CASS	7,344	3,639	2,352	1,353	1,287 R	49.6%	32.0%	60.7%	39.3%
CEDAR	6,115	2,441	1,747	1,927	694 R	39.9%	28.6%	58.3%	41.7%
CHASE	1,908	919	570	419	349 R	48.2%	29.9%	61.7%	38.3%
CHERRY	3,806	1,663	1,169	974	494 R	43.7%	30.7%	58.7%	41.3%
CHEYENNE	3,321	1,719	555	1,047	1,164 R	51.8%	16.7%	75.6%	24.4%
CLAY	5,481	2,758	1,716	1,007	1,042 R	50.3%	31.3%	61.6%	38.4%
COLFAX	3,716	1,450	1,293	973	157 R	39.0%	34.8%	52.9%	47.1%
CUMING	4,473	1,642	981	1,850	661 R	36.7%	21.9%	62.6%	37.4%
CUSTER	9,595	3,833	2,575	3,187	1,258 R	39.9%	26.8%	59.8%	40.2%
DAKOTA	3,136	1,235	964	937	271 R	39.4%	30.7%	56.2%	43.8%
DAWES	3,818	1,575	595	1,648	980 R	41.3%	15.6%	72.6%	27.4%
DAWSON	5,952	3,016	1,526	1,410	1,490 R	50.7%	25.6%	66.4%	33.6%
DEUEL	1,331	775	316	240	459 R	58.2%	23.7%	71.0%	29.0%
DIXON	4,223	2,153	1,090	980	1,063 R	51.0%	25.8%	66.4%	33.6%
DODGE	8,323	3,798	2,183	2,342	1,615 R	45.6%	26.2%	63.5%	36.5%
DOUGLAS	65,340	29,390	18,672	17,278	10,718 R	45.0%	28.6%	61.2%	38.8%
DUNDY	1,828	1,036	459	333	577 R	56.7%	25.1%	69.3%	30.7%
FILLMORE	5,351	2,758	2,156	437	602 R	51.5%	40.3%	56.1%	43.9%
FRANKLIN	3,745	1,920	1,331	494	589 R	51.3%	35.5%	59.1%	40.9%
FRONTIER	2,864	1,497	599	768	898 R	52.3%	20.9%	71.4%	28.6%
FURNAS	4,728	2,378	1,534	816	844 R	50.3%	32.4%	60.8%	39.2%
GAGE	10,514	5,331	3,330	1,853	2,001 R	50.7%	31.7%	61.6%	38.4%
GARDEN	1,553	725	459	369	266 R	46.7%	29.6%	61.2%	38.8%
GARFIELD	1,280	757	251	272	506 R	59.1%	19.6%	75.1%	24.9%
GOSPER	1,487	540	394	553	146 R	36.3%	26.5%	57.8%	42.2%
GRANT	534	260	191	83	69 R	48.7%	35.8%	57.6%	42.4%
GREELEY	2,919	773	1,220	926	447 D	26.5%	41.8%	38.8%	61.2%
HALL	8,525	4,040	1,863	2,622	2,177 R	47.4%	21.9%	68.4%	31.6%
HAMILTON	5,230	2,935	1,545	750	1,390 R	56.1%	29.5%	65.5%	34.5%
HARLAN	3,689	1,845	1,216	628	629 R	50.0%	33.0%	60.3%	39.7%
HAYES	1,115	475	288	352	187 R	42.6%	25.8%	62.3%	37.7%
HITCHCOCK	2,155	987	633	535	354 R	45.8%	29.4%	60.9%	39.1%
HOLT	5,943	2,207	1,529	2,207	678 R	37.1%	25.7%	59.1%	40.9%
HOOKER	440	176	111	153	65 R	40.0%	25.2%	61.3%	38.7%
HOWARD	3,455	1,091	1,434	930	343 D	31.6%	41.5%	43.2%	56.8%
JEFFERSON	5,719	2,752	1,824	1,143	928 R	48.1%	31.9%	60.1%	39.9%
JOHNSON	3,834	2,075	1,285	474	790 R	54.1%	33.5%	61.8%	38.2%
KEARNEY	3,226	1,453	1,243	530	210 R	45.0%	38.5%	53.9%	46.1%
KEITH	2,141	1,069	602	470	467 R	49.9%	28.1%	64.0%	36.0%
KEYA PAHA	1,215	504	251	460	253 R	41.5%	20.7%	66.8%	33.2%
KIMBALL	1,464	750	253	461	497 R	51.2%	17.3%	74.8%	25.2%
KNOX	6,226	2,405	1,532	2,289	873 R	38.6%	24.6%	61.1%	38.9%
LANCASTER	33,199	18,061	11,563	3,575	6,498 R	54.4%	34.8%	61.0%	39.0%
LINCOLN	6,979	2,857	1,373	2,749	1,484 R	40.9%	19.7%	67.5%	32.5%
LOGAN	683	277	165	241	112 R	40.6%	24.2%	62.7%	37.3%
LOUP	594	285	105	204	180 R	48.0%	17.7%	73.1%	26.9%
MCPHERSON	528	213	96	219	117 R	40.3%	18.2%	68.9%	31.1%
MADISON	8,695	3,537	1,959	3,199	1,578 R	40.7%	22.5%	64.4%	35.6%

NEBRASKA

PRESIDENT 1920

County	Total Vote	Republican	Democratic	Other	Rep.-Dem. Plurality		Total Vote % Rep.	Dem.	Major Vote Rep.	Dem.
MERRICK	3,663	2,385	1,075	203	1,310	R	65.1%	29.3%	68.9%	31.1%
MORRILL	2,085	1,366	667	52	699	R	65.5%	32.0%	67.2%	32.8%
NANCE	2,701	1,877	746	78	1,131	R	69.5%	27.6%	71.6%	28.4%
NEMAHA	4,511	2,888	1,512	111	1,376	R	64.0%	33.5%	65.6%	34.4%
NUCKOLLS	4,116	2,637	1,337	142	1,300	R	64.1%	32.5%	66.4%	33.6%
OTOE	5,722	3,869	1,671	182	2,198	R	67.6%	29.2%	69.8%	30.2%
PAWNEE	3,592	2,510	972	110	1,538	R	69.5%	27.1%	72.1%	27.9%
PERKINS	1,180	722	387	71	335	R	61.2%	32.8%	65.1%	34.9%
PHELPS	3,754	2,324	1,169	261	1,155	R	61.9%	31.1%	66.5%	33.5%
PIERCE	3,299	2,478	743	78	1,735	R	75.1%	22.5%	76.9%	23.1%
PLATTE	5,493	4,058	1,367	68	2,691	R	73.9%	24.9%	74.8%	25.2%
POLK	3,751	2,393	1,236	122	1,157	R	63.8%	33.0%	65.9%	34.1%
RED WILLOW	3,385	1,993	1,133	259	860	R	58.9%	33.5%	63.8%	36.2%
RICHARDSON	7,284	4,496	2,679	109	1,817	R	61.7%	36.8%	62.7%	37.3%
ROCK	885	621	239	25	382	R	70.2%	27.0%	72.2%	27.8%
SALINE	5,449	3,197	2,172	80	1,025	R	58.7%	39.9%	59.5%	40.5%
SARPY	2,780	1,662	1,027	91	635	R	59.8%	36.9%	61.8%	38.2%
SAUNDERS	6,223	3,733	2,296	194	1,437	R	60.0%	36.9%	61.9%	38.1%
SCOTTS BLUFF	4,459	3,189	969	301	2,220	R	71.5%	21.7%	76.7%	23.3%
SEWARD	5,273	3,690	1,497	86	2,193	R	70.0%	28.4%	71.1%	28.9%
SHERIDAN	2,656	1,714	784	158	930	R	64.5%	29.5%	68.6%	31.4%
SHERMAN	2,595	1,582	848	165	734	R	61.0%	32.7%	65.1%	34.9%
SIOUX	965	627	252	86	375	R	65.0%	26.1%	71.3%	28.7%
STANTON	2,005	1,457	501	47	956	R	72.7%	25.0%	74.4%	25.6%
THAYER	4,714	3,456	1,120	138	2,336	R	73.3%	23.8%	75.5%	24.5%
THOMAS	546	305	207	34	98	R	55.9%	37.9%	59.6%	40.4%
THURSTON	2,632	1,667	925	40	742	R	63.3%	35.1%	64.3%	35.7%
VALLEY	2,986	1,935	912	139	1,023	R	64.8%	30.5%	68.0%	32.0%
WASHINGTON	3,788	2,409	1,295	84	1,114	R	63.6%	34.2%	65.0%	35.0%
WAYNE	3,105	2,312	681	112	1,631	R	74.5%	21.9%	77.2%	22.8%
WEBSTER	3,675	2,599	913	163	1,686	R	70.7%	24.8%	74.0%	26.0%
WHEELER	612	352	165	95	187	R	57.5%	27.0%	68.1%	31.9%
YORK	6,378	4,265	1,857	256	2,408	R	66.9%	29.1%	69.7%	30.3%
TOTAL	382,743	247,498	119,608	15,637	127,890	R	64.7%	31.3%	67.4%	32.6%

PRESIDENT 1924

County	Total Vote	Republican	Democratic	Other	Rep.-Dem. Plurality		Total Vote % Rep.	Dem.	Major Vote Rep.	Dem.
MERRICK	4,277	2,324	1,137	816	1,187	R	54.3%	26.6%	67.1%	32.9%
MORRILL	2,519	1,153	734	632	419	R	45.8%	29.1%	61.1%	38.9%
NANCE	3,319	1,574	1,130	615	444	R	47.4%	34.0%	58.2%	41.8%
NEMAHA	4,856	2,378	1,871	607	507	R	49.0%	38.5%	56.0%	44.0%
NUCKOLLS	4,804	2,595	1,596	613	999	R	54.0%	33.2%	61.9%	38.1%
OTOE	6,475	3,245	2,208	1,022	1,037	R	50.1%	34.1%	59.5%	40.5%
PAWNEE	3,844	2,147	1,365	332	782	R	55.9%	35.5%	61.1%	38.9%
PERKINS	1,652	836	493	323	343	R	50.6%	29.8%	62.9%	37.1%
PHELPS	3,944	1,928	993	1,023	935	R	48.9%	25.2%	66.0%	34.0%
PIERCE	3,706	1,570	760	1,376	810	R	42.4%	20.5%	67.4%	32.6%
PLATTE	6,867	2,108	2,173	2,586	65	D	30.7%	31.6%	49.2%	50.8%
POLK	4,167	2,354	1,229	584	1,125	R	56.5%	29.5%	65.7%	34.3%
RED WILLOW	4,329	1,931	1,122	1,276	809	R	44.6%	25.9%	63.2%	36.8%
RICHARDSON	7,517	3,625	3,089	803	536	R	48.2%	41.1%	54.0%	46.0%
ROCK	1,236	585	293	358	292	R	47.3%	23.7%	66.6%	33.4%
SALINE	6,576	2,834	3,123	619	289	D	43.1%	47.5%	47.6%	52.4%
SARPY	3,631	1,411	1,247	973	164	R	38.9%	34.3%	53.1%	46.9%
SAUNDERS	7,749	3,499	2,823	1,427	676	R	45.2%	36.4%	55.3%	44.7%
SCOTTS BLUFF	5,474	3,410	1,132	932	2,278	R	62.3%	20.7%	75.1%	24.9%
SEWARD	5,684	2,797	1,848	1,039	949	R	49.2%	32.5%	60.2%	39.8%
SHERIDAN	3,640	1,509	661	1,470	848	R	41.5%	18.2%	69.5%	30.5%
SHERMAN	2,964	1,182	1,048	734	134	R	39.9%	35.4%	53.0%	47.0%
SIOUX	1,333	480	149	704	331	R	36.0%	11.2%	76.3%	23.7%
STANTON	2,440	962	596	882	366	R	39.4%	24.4%	61.7%	38.3%
THAYER	5,399	2,847	1,719	833	1,128	R	52.7%	31.8%	62.4%	37.6%
THOMAS	581	206	216	159	10	D	35.5%	37.2%	48.8%	51.2%
THURSTON	3,239	1,210	1,191	838	19	R	37.4%	36.8%	50.4%	49.6%
VALLEY	3,659	2,014	802	843	1,212	R	55.0%	21.9%	71.5%	28.5%
WASHINGTON	4,154	1,876	1,231	1,047	645	R	45.2%	29.6%	60.4%	39.6%
WAYNE	3,505	1,840	775	890	1,065	R	52.5%	22.1%	70.4%	29.6%
WEBSTER	4,033	2,194	1,207	632	987	R	54.4%	29.9%	64.5%	35.5%
WHEELER	759	205	145	409	60	R	27.0%	19.1%	58.6%	41.4%
YORK	7,007	4,110	1,778	1,119	2,332	R	58.7%	25.4%	69.8%	30.2%
TOTAL	463,559	218,985	137,299	107,275	81,686	R	47.2%	29.6%	61.5%	38.5%

NEBRASKA

PRESIDENT 1928

County	Total Vote	Republican	Democratic	Other	Rep.-Dem. Plurality	Total Vote Rep.	Total Vote Dem.	Major Vote Rep.	Major Vote Dem.
ADAMS	10,186	7,194	2,926	66	4,268 R	70.6%	28.7%	71.1%	28.9%
ANTELOPE	6,308	4,277	2,016	15	2,261 R	67.8%	32.0%	68.0%	32.0%
ARTHUR	579	402	169	8	233 R	69.4%	29.2%	70.4%	29.6%
BANNER	635	548	81	6	467 R	86.3%	12.8%	87.1%	12.9%
BLAINE	662	484	175	3	309 R	73.1%	26.4%	73.4%	26.6%
BOONE	6,099	3,816	2,260	23	1,556 R	62.6%	37.1%	62.8%	37.2%
BOX BUTTE	4,282	3,028	1,238	16	1,790 R	70.7%	28.9%	71.0%	29.0%
BOYD	2,815	1,653	1,143	19	510 R	58.7%	40.6%	59.1%	40.9%
BROWN	2,575	1,907	636	32	1,271 R	74.1%	24.7%	75.0%	25.0%
BUFFALO	10,329	7,460	2,801	68	4,659 R	72.2%	27.1%	72.7%	27.3%
BURT	5,353	3,551	1,783	19	1,768 R	66.3%	33.3%	66.6%	33.4%
BUTLER	6,418	2,930	3,465	23	535 D	45.7%	54.0%	45.8%	54.2%
CASS	7,777	4,970	2,739	68	2,231 R	63.9%	35.2%	64.5%	35.5%
CEDAR	6,467	3,206	3,241	20	35 D	49.6%	50.1%	49.7%	50.3%
CHASE	2,142	1,540	579	23	961 R	71.9%	27.0%	72.7%	27.3%
CHERRY	4,208	2,905	1,285	18	1,620 R	69.0%	30.5%	69.3%	30.7%
CHEYENNE	4,203	2,618	1,563	22	1,055 R	62.3%	37.2%	62.6%	37.4%
CLAY	5,926	4,115	1,767	54	2,338 R	69.3%	29.8%	69.9%	30.1%
COLFAX	4,194	1,432	2,746	16	1,314 D	34.1%	65.5%	34.3%	65.7%
CUMING	5,043	2,418	2,597	28	179 D	47.9%	51.5%	48.2%	51.8%
CUSTER	10,967	8,379	2,506	82	5,873 R	76.4%	22.9%	77.0%	23.0%
DAKOTA	3,463	1,709	1,754		45 D	49.4%	50.6%	49.4%	50.6%
DAWES	4,468	3,276	1,173	19	2,103 R	73.3%	26.3%	73.6%	26.4%
DAWSON	6,902	5,125	1,718	59	3,407 R	74.3%	24.9%	74.8%	25.1%
DEUEL	1,609	1,197	403	9	794 R	74.4%	25.0%	74.8%	25.2%
DIXON	4,601	2,982	1,607	12	1,375 R	64.8%	34.9%	65.0%	35.0%
DODGE	10,315	6,250	4,030	35	2,220 R	60.6%	39.1%	60.8%	39.2%
DOUGLAS	90,405	47,551	42,267	587	5,284 R	52.6%	46.8%	52.9%	47.1%
DUNDY	2,061	1,575	472	14	1,103 R	76.4%	22.9%	76.9%	23.1%
FILLMORE	5,746	3,479	2,235	32	1,244 R	60.5%	38.9%	60.9%	39.1%
FRANKLIN	3,993	2,533	1,443	17	1,090 R	63.4%	36.1%	63.7%	36.3%
FRONTIER	3,254	2,335	879	40	1,456 R	71.8%	27.0%	72.7%	27.3%
FURNAS	5,139	3,760	1,339	40	2,421 R	73.2%	26.1%	73.7%	26.3%
GAGE	11,998	8,378	3,526	94	4,852 R	69.8%	29.4%	70.4%	29.6%
GARDEN	1,889	1,470	404	15	1,066 R	77.8%	21.4%	78.4%	21.6%
GARFIELD	1,421	1,180	235	6	945 R	83.0%	16.5%	83.4%	16.6%
GOSPER	1,465	975	480	10	495 R	66.6%	32.8%	67.0%	33.0%
GRANT	561	398	160	3	238 R	70.9%	28.5%	71.3%	28.7%
GREELEY	3,564	1,457	2,098	9	641 D	41.0%	58.9%	41.0%	59.0%
HALL	10,306	6,862	3,391	53	3,471 R	66.6%	32.9%	66.9%	33.1%
HAMILTON	5,284	3,634	1,606	44	2,028 R	68.8%	30.4%	69.4%	30.6%
HARLAN	3,861	2,702	1,055	104	1,647 R	70.0%	27.3%	71.9%	28.1%
HAYES	1,393	917	440	36	477 R	65.8%	31.6%	67.6%	32.4%
HITCHCOCK	2,743	2,022	698	23	1,324 R	73.7%	25.4%	74.3%	25.7%
HOLT	6,882	3,746	3,126	10	620 R	54.4%	45.4%	54.5%	45.5%
HOOKER	467	355	110	2	245 R	76.0%	23.6%	76.3%	23.7%
HOWARD	4,157	1,937	2,197	23	260 D	46.6%	52.9%	46.9%	53.1%
JEFFERSON	6,609	4,359	2,193	57	2,166 R	66.0%	33.2%	66.5%	33.5%
JOHNSON	4,134	2,636	1,485	13	1,147 R	63.8%	35.9%	63.9%	36.3%
KEARNEY	3,553	2,426	1,093	34	1,333 R	68.3%	30.8%	68.9%	31.1%
KEITH	2,556	1,715	832	9	883 R	67.1%	32.6%	67.3%	32.7%
KEYA PAHA	1,240	989	232	19	757 R	79.8%	18.7%	81.0%	19.0%
KIMBALL	1,751	1,296	438	17	858 R	74.0%	25.0%	74.7%	25.3%
KNOX	6,614	3,668	2,914	32	754 R	55.5%	44.1%	55.7%	44.3%
LANCASTER	40,605	30,523	9,840	242	20,683 R	75.2%	24.2%	75.6%	24.4%
LINCOLN	8,425	5,946	2,381	98	3,565 R	70.6%	28.3%	71.4%	28.6%
LOGAN	800	595	195	10	400 R	74.4%	24.4%	75.3%	24.7%
LOUP	709	594	106	9	488 R	83.8%	15.0%	84.9%	15.1%
MCPHERSON	497	419	69	9	350 R	84.3%	13.9%	85.9%	14.1%
MADISON	9,684	6,229	3,407	48	2,822 R	64.3%	35.2%	64.6%	35.4%

PRESIDENT 1932

County	Total Vote	Republican	Democratic	Other	Rep.-Dem. Plurality	Total Vote Rep.	Total Vote Dem.	Major Vote Rep.	Major Vote Dem.
ADAMS	9,934	3,915	5,611	408	1,696 D	39.4%	56.5%	41.1%	58.9%
ANTELOPE	6,416	2,270	4,053	93	1,783 D	35.4%	63.2%	35.9%	64.1%
ARTHUR	596	237	338	21	101 D	39.8%	56.7%	41.2%	58.8%
BANNER	651	285	357	9	72 D	43.8%	54.8%	44.4%	55.6%
BLAINE	689	244	431	14	187 D	35.4%	62.6%	36.1%	63.9%
BOONE	6,291	1,862	4,360	69	2,498 D	29.6%	69.3%	29.9%	70.1%
BOX BUTTE	4,525	1,772	2,688	65	916 D	39.2%	59.4%	39.9%	60.3%
BOYD	2,957	808	2,098	51	1,290 D	27.3%	71.0%	27.8%	72.2%
BROWN	2,750	1,174	1,565	11	391 D	42.7%	56.9%	42.9%	57.1%
BUFFALO	9,923	3,773	5,872	278	2,099 D	38.0%	59.2%	39.1%	60.9%
BURT	5,656	1,857	3,734	65	1,877 D	32.8%	66.0%	33.2%	66.8%
BUTLER	6,203	1,712	4,456	35	2,744 D	27.6%	71.8%	27.8%	72.2%
CASS	8,072	2,756	5,155	161	2,399 D	34.1%	63.9%	34.8%	65.2%
CEDAR	6,732	1,696	4,981	55	3,285 D	25.2%	74.0%	25.4%	74.6%
CHASE	2,455	948	1,408	99	460 D	38.6%	57.4%	40.2%	59.8%
CHERRY	4,703	1,754	2,912	37	1,158 D	37.3%	61.9%	37.6%	62.4%
CHEYENNE	4,465	1,285	3,068	112	1,783 D	28.8%	68.7%	29.5%	70.5%
CLAY	6,376	2,320	3,878	178	1,558 D	36.4%	60.8%	37.4%	62.6%
COLFAX	4,779	648	4,076	55	3,428 D	13.6%	85.3%	13.7%	86.3%
CUMING	5,639	1,191	4,391	57	3,200 D	21.1%	77.9%	21.3%	78.7%
CUSTER	11,086	3,953	6,844	289	2,891 D	35.7%	61.7%	36.6%	63.4%
DAKOTA	3,937	863	3,044	30	2,181 D	21.9%	77.3%	22.1%	77.9%
DAWES	4,672	2,095	2,457	120	362 D	44.8%	52.6%	46.0%	54.0%
DAWSON	7,505	2,859	4,513	133	1,654 D	38.1%	60.1%	38.8%	61.2%
DEUEL	1,765	630	1,093	42	463 D	35.7%	61.9%	36.6%	63.4%
DIXON	4,653	1,620	2,953	80	1,333 D	34.8%	63.5%	35.4%	64.6%
DODGE	10,855	3,489	7,247	119	3,758 D	32.1%	66.8%	32.5%	67.5%
DOUGLAS	94,768	33,938	59,347	1,483	25,409 D	35.8%	62.6%	36.4%	63.6%
DUNDY	2,354	974	1,344	36	370 D	41.4%	57.1%	42.0%	58.0%
FILLMORE	5,881	2,178	3,655	48	1,477 D	37.0%	62.1%	37.3%	62.7%
FRANKLIN	4,091	1,404	2,633	54	1,229 D	34.3%	64.4%	34.8%	65.2%
FRONTIER	3,595	1,353	2,188	54	835 D	37.6%	60.9%	38.2%	61.8%
FURNAS	5,477	2,087	3,303	87	1,216 D	38.1%	60.3%	38.7%	61.3%
GAGE	11,585	4,315	7,036	234	2,721 D	37.2%	60.7%	38.0%	62.0%
GARDEN	2,010	768	1,204	38	436 D	38.2%	59.9%	38.9%	61.1%
GARFIELD	1,417	622	775	20	153 D	43.9%	54.7%	44.5%	55.5%
GOSPER	1,758	477	1,263	18	786 D	27.1%	71.8%	27.4%	72.6%
GRANT	671	251	395	25	144 D	37.4%	58.9%	38.9%	61.1%
GREELEY	3,743	817	2,832	94	2,015 D	21.8%	75.7%	22.4%	77.6%
HALL	10,492	3,743	6,266	483	2,523 D	35.7%	59.7%	37.4%	62.6%
HAMILTON	5,051	2,003	2,969	79	966 D	39.7%	58.8%	40.3%	59.7%
HARLAN	3,879	1,272	2,486	121	1,214 D	32.8%	64.1%	33.8%	66.2%
HAYES	1,508	506	962	40	456 D	33.6%	63.8%	34.5%	65.5%
HITCHCOCK	2,983	1,168	1,772	43	604 D	39.2%	59.4%	39.7%	60.3%
HOLT	7,200	2,375	4,761	64	2,386 D	33.0%	66.1%	33.3%	66.7%
HOOKER	511	162	342	7	180 D	31.7%	66.9%	32.1%	67.9%
HOWARD	4,306	734	3,409	163	2,675 D	17.0%	79.2%	17.7%	82.3%
JEFFERSON	7,402	2,453	4,819	130	2,366 D	33.1%	65.1%	33.7%	66.3%
JOHNSON	4,181	1,644	2,505	32	861 D	39.3%	59.9%	39.6%	60.4%
KEARNEY	3,569	1,129	2,367	73	1,238 D	31.6%	66.3%	32.3%	67.7%
KEITH	2,991	946	2,009	36	1,063 D	31.6%	67.2%	32.0%	68.0%
KEYA PAHA	1,336	675	645	16	30 R	50.5%	48.3%	51.1%	48.9%
KIMBALL	2,110	793	1,268	49	475 D	37.6%	60.1%	38.5%	61.5%
KNOX	7,128	1,830	5,229	69	3,399 D	25.7%	73.4%	25.9%	74.1%
LANCASTER	39,723	20,772	18,190	761	2,582 R	52.3%	45.8%	53.3%	46.7%
LINCOLN	9,431	3,082	6,047	302	2,965 D	32.7%	64.1%	33.8%	66.2%
LOGAN	927	346	564	17	218 D	37.3%	60.8%	38.0%	62.0%
LOUP	703	287	389	27	102 D	40.8%	55.3%	42.5%	57.5%
MCPHERSON	669	291	367	11	76 D	43.5%	54.9%	44.2%	55.8%
MADISON	10,954	3,489	7,366	99	3,877 D	31.9%	67.2%	32.1%	67.9%

NEBRASKA

PRESIDENT 1928

County	Total Vote	Republican	Democratic	Other	Rep.-Dem. Plurality	%Total Rep.	%Total Dem.	%Major Rep.	%Major Dem.
MERRICK	4,699	3,269	1,403	27	1,866 R	59.6	29.9	70.0	30.0
MORRILL	3,112	2,318	756	38	1,562 R	74.5	24.3	75.4	24.6
NANCE	3,632	2,299	1,318	15	981 R	53.3	36.3	63.6	36.4
NEMAHA	5,548	3,777	1,767	4	2,010 R	68.1	31.8	68.1	31.9
NUCKOLLS	5,027	3,299	1,684	44	1,615 R	65.6	33.5	66.2	33.8
OTOE	8,077	5,063	2,959	55	2,104 R	62.7	36.6	63.1	36.9
PAWNEE	4,394	2,825	1,547	22	1,278 R	64.3	35.2	64.6	35.4
PERKINS	2,106	1,461	631	14	830 R	69.4	30.0	69.8	30.2
PHELPS	4,251	3,297	927	27	2,370 R	77.6	21.8	78.1	21.9
PIERCE	4,137	2,542	1,586	9	956 R	61.4	38.3	61.6	38.4
PLATTE	8,210	3,435	4,748	27	1,313 D	41.8	57.8	42.0	58.0
POLK	4,609	3,096	1,494	19	1,602 R	67.2	32.4	67.5	32.5
RED WILLOW	5,384	3,559	1,770	55	1,789 R	66.1	32.9	66.8	33.2
RICHARDSON	8,962	5,833	3,072	57	2,761 R	65.1	34.3	65.5	34.5
ROCK	1,341	1,034	305	2	729 R	77.1	22.7	77.2	22.8
SALINE	7,328	3,347	3,955	26	606 D	45.7	54.0	45.8	54.2
SARPY	3,940	2,011	1,900	29	111 R	51.0	48.2	51.4	48.6
SAUNDERS	9,186	5,356	3,793	37	1,563 R	58.3	41.3	58.5	41.5
SCOTTS BLUFF	8,167	6,677	1,403	87	5,274 R	81.8	17.1	82.6	17.4
SEWARD	5,930	3,539	2,367	24	1,172 R	59.7	39.9	59.9	40.1
SHERIDAN	4,315	3,030	1,226	59	1,804 R	70.2	28.4	71.2	28.8
SHERMAN	3,435	1,675	1,733	27	58 D	48.8	50.5	49.1	50.9
SIOUX	1,624	1,178	435	11	743 R	72.5	26.8	73.0	27.0
STANTON	2,514	1,211	1,296	7	85 D	48.2	51.6	48.3	51.7
THAYER	5,748	3,552	2,173	23	1,379 R	61.8	37.8	62.0	38.0
THOMAS	562	406	152	4	254 R	72.2	27.0	72.8	27.2
THURSTON	3,393	1,538	1,837	18	299 D	45.3	54.1	45.6	54.4
VALLEY	3,996	2,768	1,205	23	1,563 R	69.3	30.2	69.7	30.3
WASHINGTON	4,684	2,750	1,912	22	838 R	58.7	40.8	59.0	41.0
WAYNE	3,628	2,354	1,235	39	1,119 R	64.9	34.0	65.6	34.4
WEBSTER	4,286	2,924	1,342	20	1,582 R	68.2	31.3	68.5	31.5
WHEELER	832	534	293	5	241 R	64.2	35.2	64.5	35.4
YORK	7,779	5,769	1,979	31	3,790 R	74.2	25.4	74.5	25.5
TOTAL	547,128	345,745	197,950	3,433	147,795 R	63.2	36.2	63.6	36.4

PRESIDENT 1932

County	Total Vote	Republican	Democratic	Other	Rep.-Dem. Plurality	%Total Rep.	%Total Dem.	%Major Rep.	%Major Dem.
MERRICK	4,696	1,698	2,881	117	1,183 D	36.2	61.4	37.1	62.9
MORRILL	3,476	1,406	2,008	62	602 D	40.4	57.8	41.2	58.8
NANCE	3,661	1,156	2,479	26	1,323 D	31.6	67.7	31.8	68.2
NEMAHA	5,709	2,075	3,593	41	1,518 D	36.3	62.9	36.6	63.4
NUCKOLLS	5,333	1,812	3,420	101	1,608 D	34.0	64.1	34.6	65.4
OTOE	7,959	3,119	4,752	88	1,633 D	39.2	59.7	39.6	60.4
PAWNEE	4,249	1,568	2,641	40	1,073 D	36.9	62.2	37.3	62.7
PERKINS	2,398	674	1,669	55	995 D	28.1	69.6	28.8	71.2
PHELPS	4,372	1,709	2,589	74	880 D	39.1	59.2	39.8	60.2
PIERCE	4,143	1,128	2,980	35	1,852 D	27.2	71.9	27.5	72.5
PLATTE	8,627	1,864	6,691	72	4,827 D	21.6	77.6	21.8	78.2
POLK	4,628	1,636	2,939	53	1,303 D	35.4	63.5	35.8	64.2
RED WILLOW	5,592	1,972	3,479	141	1,507 D	35.3	62.2	36.2	63.8
RICHARDSON	8,249	2,802	5,383	64	2,581 D	34.0	65.3	34.2	65.8
ROCK	1,445	613	810	22	197 D	42.4	56.1	43.1	56.9
SALINE	7,896	1,993	5,831	72	3,838 D	25.2	73.8	25.5	74.5
SARPY	4,329	1,148	3,112	69	1,964 D	26.5	71.9	26.9	73.1
SAUNDERS	9,134	2,772	6,134	228	3,362 D	30.3	67.2	31.1	68.9
SCOTTS BLUFF	9,011	4,108	4,792	111	684 D	45.6	53.2	46.2	53.8
SEWARD	6,571	2,298	4,208	65	1,910 D	35.0	64.0	35.3	64.7
SHERIDAN	4,865	1,820	2,945	100	1,125 D	37.4	60.5	38.2	61.8
SHERMAN	3,692	952	2,670	70	1,718 D	25.8	72.3	26.3	73.7
SIOUX	1,704	667	1,006	31	339 D	39.1	59.0	39.9	60.1
STANTON	2,879	568	2,302	9	1,734 D	19.7	80.0	19.8	80.2
THAYER	5,809	1,878	3,841	90	1,963 D	32.3	66.1	32.8	67.2
THOMAS	721	262	437	22	175 D	36.3	60.6	37.5	62.5
THURSTON	4,056	739	3,273	44	2,534 D	18.2	80.7	18.4	81.6
VALLEY	4,057	1,584	2,400	73	816 D	39.0	59.2	39.8	60.2
WASHINGTON	5,157	1,382	3,709	66	2,327 D	26.8	71.9	27.1	72.9
WAYNE	4,154	1,455	2,608	91	1,153 D	35.0	62.8	35.8	64.2
WEBSTER	4,389	1,627	2,632	130	1,005 D	37.1	60.0	38.2	61.8
WHEELER	906	219	658	29	439 D	24.2	72.6	25.0	75.0
YORK	7,579	3,573	3,920	86	347 D	47.1	51.7	47.7	52.3
TOTAL	570,135	201,177	359,082	9,876	157,905 D	35.3	63.0	35.9	64.1

NEBRASKA

PRESIDENT 1936

County	Total Vote	Republican	Democratic	Other	Rep.-Dem. Plurality	% Total Vote Rep.	% Total Vote Dem.	% Major Vote Rep.	% Major Vote Dem.
ADAMS	10,621	4,094	6,126	401	2,032 D	38.5%	57.7%	40.1%	59.9%
ANTELOPE	6,672	3,304	3,165	203	139 R	49.5%	47.4%	51.1%	48.9%
ARTHUR	550	312	235	3	77 R	56.7%	42.7%	57.0%	43.0%
BANNER	650	277	367	6	90 D	42.6%	56.5%	43.0%	57.0%
BLAINE	716	342	365	9	23 D	47.8%	51.0%	48.4%	51.6%
BOONE	6,025	2,728	3,095	202	367 D	45.3%	51.4%	46.8%	53.2%
BOX BUTTE	4,663	1,711	2,900	52	1,189 D	36.7%	62.2%	37.1%	62.9%
BOYD	2,900	1,290	1,555	55	265 D	44.5%	53.6%	45.3%	54.7%
BROWN	2,638	1,419	1,188	31	231 R	53.8%	45.0%	54.4%	45.6%
BUFFALO	10,972	4,595	6,002	375	1,407 D	41.9%	54.7%	43.4%	56.6%
BURT	5,901	2,710	3,120	71	410 D	45.9%	52.9%	46.5%	53.5%
BUTLER	6,926	2,442	4,360	124	1,918 D	35.3%	63.0%	35.9%	64.1%
CASS	8,645	3,669	4,922	54	1,253 D	42.4%	56.9%	42.7%	57.3%
CEDAR	6,793	2,394	3,781	618	1,387 D	35.2%	55.7%	38.8%	61.2%
CHASE	2,587	1,031	1,493	63	462 D	39.9%	57.7%	40.8%	59.2%
CHERRY	3,939	1,874	2,010	55	136 D	47.6%	51.0%	48.2%	51.8%
CHEYENNE	4,442	1,374	2,950	118	1,576 D	30.9%	66.4%	31.8%	68.2%
CLAY	5,918	2,856	2,932	130	76 D	48.3%	49.5%	49.3%	50.7%
COLFAX	5,075	1,644	3,210	221	1,566 D	32.4%	63.3%	33.9%	66.1%
CUMING	5,840	2,275	3,114	451	839 D	39.0%	53.3%	42.2%	57.8%
CUSTER	11,495	5,250	5,907	338	657 D	45.7%	51.4%	47.1%	52.9%
DAKOTA	4,282	1,264	2,741	277	1,477 D	29.5%	64.0%	31.6%	68.4%
DAWES	5,122	2,083	2,784	255	701 D	40.7%	54.4%	42.8%	57.2%
DAWSON	7,702	3,573	4,021	108	448 D	46.4%	52.2%	47.1%	52.9%
DEUEL	1,808	747	1,020	41	273 D	41.3%	56.4%	42.3%	57.7%
DIXON	4,870	2,108	2,640	122	532 D	43.3%	54.2%	44.4%	55.6%
DODGE	11,339	4,561	6,317	461	1,756 D	40.2%	55.7%	41.9%	58.1%
DOUGLAS	107,076	35,349	70,245	1,482	34,896 D	33.0%	65.6%	33.5%	66.5%
DUNDY	2,408	1,054	1,328	26	274 D	43.8%	55.1%	44.2%	55.8%
FILLMORE	6,062	2,858	3,154	50	296 D	47.1%	52.0%	47.5%	52.5%
FRANKLIN	4,165	1,685	2,350	130	665 D	40.5%	56.4%	41.8%	58.2%
FRONTIER	3,509	1,576	1,883	50	307 D	44.9%	53.7%	45.6%	54.4%
FURNAS	5,424	2,642	2,682	100	40 D	48.7%	49.4%	49.6%	50.4%
GAGE	12,745	5,291	7,227	227	1,936 D	41.5%	56.7%	42.3%	57.7%
GARDEN	2,007	996	986	25	10 R	49.6%	49.1%	50.3%	49.7%
GARFIELD	1,476	744	697	35	47 R	50.4%	47.2%	51.6%	48.4%
GOSPER	1,783	647	1,118	18	471 D	36.3%	62.7%	36.7%	63.3%
GRANT	590	321	267	2	54 R	54.4%	45.3%	54.6%	45.4%
GREELEY	3,525	1,107	1,988	430	881 D	31.4%	56.4%	35.8%	64.2%
HALL	11,810	5,146	6,295	369	1,149 D	43.6%	53.3%	45.0%	55.0%
HAMILTON	5,449	2,748	2,653	48	95 R	50.4%	48.7%	50.9%	49.1%
HARLAN	3,814	1,692	2,084	38	392 D	44.4%	54.6%	44.8%	55.2%
HAYES	1,482	654	818	10	164 D	44.1%	55.2%	44.4%	55.6%
HITCHCOCK	3,045	1,285	1,738	22	453 D	42.2%	57.1%	42.5%	57.5%
HOLT	7,764	3,714	3,902	148	188 D	47.8%	50.3%	48.8%	51.2%
HOOKER	482	288	191	3	97 R	59.8%	39.6%	60.1%	39.9%
HOWARD	4,494	1,223	3,148	123	1,925 D	27.2%	70.0%	28.0%	72.0%
JEFFERSON	7,624	3,048	4,526	50	1,478 D	40.0%	59.4%	40.2%	59.8%
JOHNSON	4,525	2,126	2,359	40	233 D	47.0%	52.1%	47.4%	52.6%
KEARNEY	3,711	1,214	2,445	52	1,231 D	32.7%	65.9%	33.2%	66.8%
KEITH	3,152	1,094	2,000	58	906 D	34.7%	63.5%	35.4%	64.6%
KEYA PAHA	1,393	830	556	7	274 R	59.6%	39.9%	59.9%	40.1%
KIMBALL	2,032	842	1,137	53	295 D	41.4%	56.0%	42.5%	57.5%
KNOX	7,583	2,949	4,449	185	1,500 D	38.9%	58.7%	39.9%	60.1%
LANCASTER	44,106	20,902	22,366	838	1,464 D	47.4%	50.7%	48.3%	51.7%
LINCOLN	10,796	3,857	6,742	197	2,885 D	35.7%	62.4%	36.4%	63.6%
LOGAN	874	410	456	8	46 D	46.9%	52.2%	47.3%	52.7%
LOUP	787	438	335	14	103 R	55.7%	42.6%	56.7%	43.3%
MCPHERSON	584	326	250	8	76 R	55.8%	42.8%	56.6%	43.4%
MADISON	11,340	5,149	6,044	147	895 D	45.4%	53.3%	46.0%	54.0%

PRESIDENT 1940

County	Total Vote	Republican	Democratic	Other	Rep.-Dem. Plurality	% Total Vote Rep.	% Total Vote Dem.	% Major Vote Rep.	% Major Vote Dem.
ADAMS	10,941	6,630	4,311		2,319 R	60.6%	39.4%	60.6%	39.4%
ANTELOPE	6,486	4,331	2,155		2,176 R	66.8%	33.2%	66.8%	33.2%
ARTHUR	542	348	194		154 R	64.2%	35.8%	64.2%	35.8%
BANNER	676	450	226		224 R	66.6%	33.4%	66.6%	33.4%
BLAINE	765	454	311		143 R	59.3%	40.7%	59.3%	40.7%
BOONE	5,348	3,334	2,014		1,320 R	62.3%	37.7%	62.3%	37.7%
BOX BUTTE	5,137	2,942	2,195		747 R	57.3%	42.7%	57.3%	42.7%
BOYD	2,791	1,734	1,057		677 R	62.1%	37.9%	62.1%	37.9%
BROWN	2,758	1,783	975		808 R	64.6%	35.4%	64.6%	35.4%
BUFFALO	10,447	6,387	4,060		2,327 R	61.1%	38.9%	61.1%	38.9%
BURT	6,032	3,443	2,589		854 R	57.1%	42.9%	57.1%	42.9%
BUTLER	6,212	2,966	3,246		280 D	47.7%	52.3%	47.7%	52.3%
CASS	8,331	4,704	3,627		1,077 R	56.5%	43.5%	56.5%	43.5%
CEDAR	7,016	4,397	2,619		1,778 R	62.7%	37.3%	62.7%	37.3%
CHASE	2,461	1,557	904		653 R	63.3%	36.7%	63.3%	36.7%
CHERRY	4,486	2,705	1,781		924 R	60.3%	39.7%	60.3%	39.7%
CHEYENNE	4,337	2,394	1,943		451 R	55.2%	44.8%	55.2%	44.8%
CLAY	5,339	3,576	1,763		1,813 R	67.0%	33.0%	67.0%	33.0%
COLFAX	4,948	2,587	2,361		226 R	52.3%	47.7%	52.3%	47.7%
CUMING	5,978	4,383	1,595		2,788 R	73.3%	26.7%	73.3%	26.7%
CUSTER	10,507	6,269	4,238		2,031 R	59.7%	40.3%	59.7%	40.3%
DAKOTA	4,562	2,140	2,422		282 D	46.9%	53.1%	46.9%	53.1%
DAWES	4,955	3,184	1,771		1,413 R	64.3%	35.7%	64.3%	35.7%
DAWSON	8,248	5,445	2,803		2,642 R	66.0%	34.0%	66.0%	34.0%
DEUEL	1,721	1,156	565		591 R	67.2%	32.8%	67.2%	32.8%
DIXON	4,950	3,038	1,912		1,126 R	61.4%	38.6%	61.4%	38.6%
DODGE	11,423	7,141	4,282		2,859 R	62.5%	37.5%	62.5%	37.5%
DOUGLAS	120,165	53,325	66,840		13,515 D	44.4%	55.6%	44.4%	55.6%
DUNDY	2,244	1,441	803		638 R	64.2%	35.8%	64.2%	35.8%
FILLMORE	5,646	3,677	1,969		1,708 R	65.1%	34.9%	65.1%	34.9%
FRANKLIN	3,732	2,354	1,378		976 R	63.1%	36.9%	63.1%	36.9%
FRONTIER	3,131	2,069	1,062		1,007 R	66.1%	33.9%	66.1%	33.9%
FURNAS	5,113	3,316	1,797		1,519 R	64.9%	35.1%	64.9%	35.1%
GAGE	13,252	8,156	5,096		3,060 R	61.5%	38.5%	61.5%	38.5%
GARDEN	2,087	1,351	736		615 R	64.7%	35.3%	64.7%	35.3%
GARFIELD	1,586	1,053	533		520 R	66.4%	33.6%	66.4%	33.6%
GOSPER	1,629	1,001	628		373 R	61.4%	38.6%	61.4%	38.6%
GRANT	666	423	243		180 R	63.5%	36.5%	63.5%	36.5%
GREELEY	3,032	1,530	1,502		28 R	50.5%	49.5%	50.5%	49.5%
HALL	12,099	7,412	4,687		2,725 R	61.3%	38.7%	61.3%	38.7%
HAMILTON	4,952	3,286	1,666		1,620 R	66.4%	33.6%	66.4%	33.6%
HARLAN	3,535	2,182	1,353		829 R	61.7%	38.3%	61.7%	38.3%
HAYES	1,357	759	598		161 R	55.9%	44.1%	55.9%	44.1%
HITCHCOCK	2,851	1,663	1,188		475 R	58.3%	41.7%	58.3%	41.7%
HOLT	7,856	4,840	3,016		1,824 R	61.6%	38.4%	61.6%	38.4%
HOOKER	550	403	147		256 R	73.3%	26.7%	73.3%	26.7%
HOWARD	3,934	1,696	2,238		542 D	43.1%	56.9%	43.1%	56.9%
JEFFERSON	7,739	4,980	2,759		2,221 R	64.3%	35.7%	64.3%	35.7%
JOHNSON	4,276	2,919	1,357		1,562 R	68.3%	31.7%	68.3%	31.7%
KEARNEY	3,353	1,792	1,561		231 R	53.4%	46.6%	53.4%	46.6%
KEITH	3,781	2,022	1,759		263 R	53.5%	46.5%	53.5%	46.5%
KEYA PAHA	1,506	1,004	502		502 R	66.7%	33.3%	66.7%	33.3%
KIMBALL	1,925	1,190	735		455 R	61.8%	38.2%	61.8%	38.2%
KNOX	7,531	4,352	3,179		1,173 R	57.8%	42.2%	57.8%	42.2%
LANCASTER	46,705	27,384	19,321		8,063 R	58.6%	41.4%	58.6%	41.4%
LINCOLN	10,868	5,908	4,960		948 R	54.4%	45.6%	54.4%	45.6%
LOGAN	823	498	325		173 R	60.5%	39.5%	60.5%	39.5%
LOUP	828	539	289		250 R	65.1%	34.9%	65.1%	34.9%
MCPHERSON	578	414	164		250 R	71.6%	28.4%	71.6%	28.4%
MADISON	11,335	7,353	3,982		3,371 R	64.9%	35.1%	64.9%	35.1%

NEBRASKA

PRESIDENT 1936

County	Total Vote	Republican	Democratic	Other	Rep.-Dem. Plurality	Total Vote Rep.	Total Vote Dem.	Major Vote Rep.	Major Vote Dem.
MERRICK	4,887	2,367	2,401	119	34 D	48.4%	49.1%	49.6%	50.4%
MORRILL	3,404	1,354	1,999	51	645 D	39.8%	58.7%	40.4%	59.6%
NANCE	3,831	1,770	2,012	49	242 D	46.2%	52.5%	46.8%	53.2%
NEMAHA	6,202	2,720	3,459	23	739 D	43.9%	55.8%	44.0%	56.0%
NUCKOLLS	5,171	2,317	2,778	76	461 D	44.8%	53.7%	45.5%	54.5%
OTOE	8,634	4,399	4,173	62	226 R	50.9%	48.3%	51.3%	48.7%
PAWNEE	4,404	2,074	2,297	33	223 D	47.1%	52.2%	47.4%	52.6%
PERKINS	2,460	861	1,584	15	703 D	35.0%	64.4%	35.2%	64.8%
PHELPS	4,490	1,884	2,587	19	703 D	42.0%	57.6%	42.1%	57.9%
PIERCE	4,495	2,016	2,357	122	341 D	44.8%	52.4%	45.1%	53.9%
PLATTE	9,512	2,850	5,249	413	3,399 D	30.0%	65.7%	31.3%	68.7%
POLK	4,823	2,256	2,519	48	263 D	46.8%	52.2%	47.2%	52.8%
RED WILLOW	5,692	2,078	3,445	169	1,367 D	36.5%	60.5%	37.6%	62.4%
RICHARDSON	9,758	3,908	5,813	37	1,905 D	40.0%	59.6%	40.2%	59.8%
ROCK	1,672	944	710	18	234 R	56.5%	42.5%	57.1%	42.9%
SALINE	8,206	2,637	5,480	89	2,843 D	32.1%	65.8%	32.5%	67.5%
SARPY	4,649	1,569	3,030	50	1,461 D	33.7%	65.2%	34.1%	65.9%
SAUNDERS	9,587	3,773	5,514	300	1,741 D	39.4%	57.5%	40.6%	59.4%
SCOTTS BLUFF	9,996	4,051	5,768	177	1,717 D	40.5%	57.7%	41.3%	58.7%
SEWARD	7,039	3,123	3,866	50	743 D	44.4%	54.9%	44.7%	55.3%
SHERIDAN	4,485	1,907	2,428	150	521 D	42.5%	54.1%	44.0%	56.0%
SHERMAN	4,043	1,294	2,701	48	1,407 D	32.0%	66.8%	32.4%	67.6%
SIOUX	1,658	674	956	28	282 D	40.7%	57.7%	41.3%	58.7%
STANTON	3,198	1,169	1,917	112	748 D	36.6%	59.9%	37.9%	62.1%
THAYER	6,125	2,628	3,418	79	790 D	42.9%	55.8%	43.5%	56.5%
THOMAS	753	366	374	13	8 D	48.6%	49.7%	49.5%	50.5%
THURSTON	4,062	1,195	2,676	191	1,481 D	29.4%	65.9%	30.9%	69.1%
VALLEY	4,095	2,033	1,960	102	73 R	49.6%	47.9%	50.9%	49.1%
WASHINGTON	5,734	2,263	3,426	45	1,163 D	39.5%	59.7%	39.8%	60.2%
WAYNE	4,547	2,149	2,322	76	173 D	47.3%	51.1%	48.1%	51.9%
WEBSTER	4,368	1,912	2,408	48	496 D	43.8%	55.1%	44.3%	55.7%
WHEELER	920	358	484	78	126 D	38.9%	52.6%	42.5%	57.5%
YORK	8,415	4,554	3,741	120	813 R	54.1%	44.5%	54.9%	45.1%
TOTAL	608,023	247,731	347,445	12,847	99,714 D	40.7%	57.1%	41.6%	58.4%

PRESIDENT 1940

County	Total Vote	Republican	Democratic	Other	Rep.-Dem. Plurality	Total Vote Rep.	Total Vote Dem.	Major Vote Rep.	Major Vote Dem.
MERRICK	4,352	2,886	1,466		1,420 R	66.3%	33.7%	66.3%	33.7%
MORRILL	3,685	2,214	1,471		743 R	60.1%	39.9%	60.1%	39.9%
NANCE	3,398	1,963	1,435		528 R	57.8%	42.2%	57.8%	42.2%
NEMAHA	6,366	3,817	2,549		1,268 R	60.0%	40.0%	60.0%	40.0%
NUCKOLLS	4,890	3,017	1,873		1,144 R	61.7%	38.3%	61.7%	38.3%
OTOE	8,726	5,799	2,927		2,872 R	66.5%	33.5%	66.5%	33.5%
PAWNEE	4,239	2,643	1,596		1,047 R	62.3%	37.7%	62.3%	37.7%
PERKINS	2,467	1,413	1,054		359 R	57.3%	42.7%	57.3%	42.7%
PHELPS	4,359	2,512	1,847		665 R	57.6%	42.4%	57.6%	42.4%
PIERCE	4,720	3,271	1,449		1,822 R	69.3%	30.7%	69.3%	30.7%
PLATTE	6,791	4,929	3,862		1,067 R	56.1%	43.9%	56.1%	43.9%
POLK	4,288	2,653	1,635		1,018 R	61.9%	38.1%	61.9%	38.1%
RED WILLOW	5,600	3,119	2,481		638 R	55.7%	44.3%	55.7%	44.3%
RICHARDSON	8,938	4,833	4,105		728 R	54.1%	45.9%	54.1%	45.9%
ROCK	1,704	1,104	600		504 R	64.8%	35.2%	64.8%	35.2%
SALINE	7,902	3,673	4,229		556 D	46.5%	53.5%	46.5%	53.5%
SARPY	4,702	2,165	2,537		372 D	46.0%	54.0%	46.0%	54.0%
SAUNDERS	9,079	4,917	4,162		755 R	54.2%	45.8%	54.2%	45.8%
SCOTTS BLUFF	12,444	7,989	4,455		3,534 R	64.2%	35.8%	64.2%	35.8%
SEWARD	6,646	4,117	2,529		1,588 R	61.9%	38.1%	61.9%	38.1%
SHERIDAN	4,727	3,161	1,566		1,595 R	66.9%	33.1%	66.9%	33.1%
SHERMAN	3,382	1,494	1,888		394 D	44.2%	55.8%	44.2%	55.8%
SIOUX	1,690	1,072	618		454 R	63.4%	36.6%	63.4%	36.6%
STANTON	3,155	2,074	1,081		993 R	65.7%	34.3%	65.7%	34.3%
THAYER	5,970	3,893	2,077		1,816 R	65.2%	34.8%	65.2%	34.8%
THOMAS	763	486	277		209 R	63.7%	36.3%	63.7%	36.3%
THURSTON	4,012	1,973	2,039		66 D	49.2%	50.8%	49.2%	50.8%
VALLEY	4,039	2,449	1,590		859 R	60.6%	39.4%	60.6%	39.4%
WASHINGTON	5,558	2,922	2,636		286 R	52.6%	47.4%	52.6%	47.4%
WAYNE	4,604	3,209	1,395		1,814 R	69.7%	30.3%	69.7%	30.3%
WEBSTER	4,175	2,847	1,329		1,518 R	68.2%	31.8%	68.2%	31.8%
WHEELER	922	495	427		68 R	53.7%	46.3%	53.7%	46.3%
YORK	7,522	5,322	2,200		3,122 R	70.8%	29.2%	70.8%	29.2%
TOTAL	615,878	352,201	263,677		88,524 R	57.2%	42.8%	57.2%	42.8%

NEBRASKA

PRESIDENT 1944

County	Total Vote	Republican	Democratic	Other	Rep.-Dem. Plurality	Total Vote Rep.	Total Vote Dem.	Major Vote Rep.	Major Vote Dem.
ADAMS	11,777	7,165	4,612		2,553 R	60.8%	39.2%	60.8%	39.2%
ANTELOPE	5,506	3,888	1,618		2,270 R	70.6%	29.4%	70.6%	29.4%
ARTHUR	421	268	153		115 R	63.7%	36.3%	63.7%	36.3%
BANNER	532	378	154		224 R	71.1%	28.9%	71.1%	28.9%
BLAINE	614	366	248		118 R	59.6%	40.4%	59.6%	40.4%
BOONE	4,530	2,865	1,665		1,200 R	63.2%	36.8%	63.2%	36.8%
BOX BUTTE	4,730	2,994	1,736		1,258 R	63.3%	36.7%	63.3%	36.7%
BOYD	2,351	1,456	895		561 R	61.9%	38.1%	61.9%	38.1%
BROWN	2,294	1,549	745		804 R	67.5%	32.5%	67.5%	32.5%
BUFFALO	9,925	6,073	3,852		2,221 R	61.2%	38.8%	61.2%	38.8%
BURT	5,351	3,189	2,162		1,027 R	59.6%	40.4%	59.6%	40.4%
BUTLER	5,415	2,493	2,922		429 D	46.0%	54.0%	46.0%	54.0%
CASS	7,732	4,588	3,144		1,444 R	59.3%	40.7%	59.3%	40.7%
CEDAR	5,455	3,616	1,839		1,777 R	66.3%	33.7%	66.3%	33.7%
CHASE	2,092	1,444	648		796 R	69.0%	31.0%	69.0%	31.0%
CHERRY	3,685	2,314	1,371		943 R	62.8%	37.2%	62.8%	37.2%
CHEYENNE	4,406	2,654	1,752		902 R	60.2%	39.8%	60.2%	39.8%
CLAY	4,905	3,375	1,530		1,845 R	68.8%	31.2%	68.8%	31.2%
COLFAX	4,492	2,314	2,178		136 R	51.5%	48.5%	51.5%	48.5%
CUMING	5,409	4,008	1,401		2,607 R	74.1%	25.9%	74.1%	25.9%
CUSTER	8,651	5,330	3,321		2,009 R	61.6%	38.4%	61.6%	38.4%
DAKOTA	3,692	1,703	1,989		286 D	46.1%	53.9%	46.1%	53.9%
DAWES	4,194	2,747	1,447		1,300 R	65.5%	34.5%	65.5%	34.5%
DAWSON	7,287	5,017	2,270		2,747 R	68.8%	31.2%	68.8%	31.2%
DEUEL	1,531	1,125	406		719 R	73.5%	26.5%	73.5%	26.5%
DIXON	3,845	2,382	1,463		919 R	62.0%	38.0%	62.0%	38.0%
DODGE	11,081	6,803	4,278		2,525 R	61.4%	38.6%	61.4%	38.6%
DOUGLAS	117,205	53,443	63,762		10,319 D	45.6%	54.4%	45.6%	54.4%
DUNDY	1,933	1,320	613		707 R	68.3%	31.7%	68.3%	31.7%
FILLMORE	5,150	3,362	1,788		1,574 R	65.3%	34.7%	65.3%	34.7%
FRANKLIN	3,054	2,085	969		1,116 R	68.3%	31.7%	68.3%	31.7%
FRONTIER	2,613	1,855	758		1,097 R	71.0%	29.0%	71.0%	29.0%
FURNAS	4,199	2,870	1,329		1,541 R	68.3%	31.7%	68.3%	31.7%
GAGE	11,590	7,352	4,238		3,114 R	63.4%	36.6%	63.4%	36.6%
GARDEN	1,789	1,248	541		707 R	69.8%	30.2%	69.8%	30.2%
GARFIELD	1,304	896	408		488 R	68.7%	31.3%	68.7%	31.3%
GOSPER	1,419	935	484		451 R	65.9%	34.1%	65.9%	34.1%
GRANT	499	327	172		155 R	65.5%	34.5%	65.5%	34.5%
GREELEY	2,507	1,242	1,265		23 D	49.5%	50.5%	49.5%	50.5%
HALL	12,419	7,651	4,768		2,883 R	61.6%	38.4%	61.6%	38.4%
HAMILTON	4,387	3,057	1,330		1,727 R	69.7%	30.3%	69.7%	30.3%
HARLAN	2,997	1,991	1,006		985 R	66.4%	33.6%	66.4%	33.6%
HAYES	1,169	782	387		395 R	66.9%	33.1%	66.9%	33.1%
HITCHCOCK	2,433	1,556	877		679 R	64.0%	36.0%	64.0%	36.0%
HOLT	6,763	4,198	2,565		1,633 R	62.1%	37.9%	62.1%	37.9%
HOOKER	433	330	103		227 R	76.2%	23.8%	76.2%	23.8%
HOWARD	3,598	1,556	2,042		486 D	43.2%	56.8%	43.2%	56.8%
JEFFERSON	6,444	4,257	2,187		2,070 R	66.1%	33.9%	66.1%	33.9%
JOHNSON	3,668	2,649	1,019		1,630 R	72.2%	27.8%	72.2%	27.8%
KEARNEY	3,049	1,782	1,267		515 R	58.4%	41.6%	58.4%	41.6%
KEITH	2,886	1,739	1,147		592 R	60.3%	39.7%	60.3%	39.7%
KEYA PAHA	1,115	781	334		447 R	70.0%	30.0%	70.0%	30.0%
KIMBALL	1,745	1,169	576		593 R	67.0%	33.0%	67.0%	33.0%
KNOX	6,249	3,762	2,487		1,275 R	60.2%	39.8%	60.2%	39.8%
LANCASTER	46,053	26,715	19,338		7,377 R	58.0%	42.0%	58.0%	42.0%
LINCOLN	10,313	5,969	4,344		1,625 R	57.9%	42.1%	57.9%	42.1%
LOGAN	694	450	244		206 R	64.8%	35.2%	64.8%	35.2%
LOUP	670	488	182		306 R	72.8%	27.2%	72.8%	27.2%
MCPHERSON	428	310	118		192 R	72.4%	27.6%	72.4%	27.6%
MADISON	10,265	6,892	3,373		3,519 R	67.1%	32.9%	67.1%	32.9%

PRESIDENT 1948

County	Total Vote	Republican	Democratic	Other	Rep.-Dem. Plurality	Total Vote Rep.	Total Vote Dem.	Major Vote Rep.	Major Vote Dem.
ADAMS	10,212	5,560	4,652		908 R	54.4%	45.6%	54.4%	45.6%
ANTELOPE	4,741	2,868	1,873		995 R	60.5%	39.5%	60.5%	39.5%
ARTHUR	346	199	147		52 R	57.5%	42.5%	57.5%	42.5%
BANNER	538	309	229		80 R	57.4%	42.6%	57.4%	42.6%
BLAINE	500	252	248		4 R	50.4%	49.6%	50.4%	49.6%
BOONE	4,013	2,235	1,778		457 R	55.7%	44.3%	55.7%	44.3%
BOX BUTTE	4,374	2,351	2,023		328 R	53.7%	46.3%	53.7%	46.3%
BOYD	2,095	1,060	1,035		25 R	50.6%	49.4%	50.6%	49.4%
BROWN	1,874	1,174	700		474 R	62.6%	37.4%	62.6%	37.4%
BUFFALO	8,578	4,862	3,716		1,146 R	56.7%	43.3%	56.7%	43.3%
BURT	4,556	2,656	1,900		756 R	58.3%	41.7%	58.3%	41.7%
BUTLER	4,710	2,105	2,605		500 D	44.7%	55.3%	44.7%	55.3%
CASS	6,568	3,527	3,041		486 R	53.7%	46.3%	53.7%	46.3%
CEDAR	5,194	2,616	2,578		38 R	50.4%	49.6%	50.4%	49.6%
CHASE	1,830	1,094	736		358 R	59.8%	40.2%	59.8%	40.2%
CHERRY	3,633	2,141	1,492		649 R	58.9%	41.1%	58.9%	41.1%
CHEYENNE	4,300	2,161	2,139		22 R	50.3%	49.7%	50.3%	49.7%
CLAY	4,100	2,511	1,589		922 R	61.2%	38.8%	61.2%	38.8%
COLFAX	3,825	1,928	1,897		31 R	50.4%	49.6%	50.4%	49.6%
CUMING	4,587	2,930	1,657		1,273 R	63.9%	36.1%	63.9%	36.1%
CUSTER	7,413	4,057	3,356		701 R	54.7%	45.3%	54.7%	45.3%
DAKOTA	3,751	1,379	2,372		993 D	36.8%	63.2%	36.8%	63.2%
DAWES	3,898	2,399	1,499		900 R	61.5%	38.5%	61.5%	38.5%
DAWSON	6,806	4,203	2,603		1,600 R	61.8%	38.2%	61.8%	38.2%
DEUEL	1,455	1,043	412		631 R	71.7%	28.3%	71.7%	28.3%
DIXON	3,621	1,899	1,722		177 R	52.4%	47.6%	52.4%	47.6%
DODGE	10,718	5,848	4,870		978 R	54.6%	45.4%	54.6%	45.4%
DOUGLAS	96,433	47,175	49,258		2,083 D	48.9%	51.1%	48.9%	51.1%
DUNDY	1,581	935	646		289 R	59.1%	40.9%	59.1%	40.9%
FILLMORE	4,573	2,677	1,896		781 R	58.5%	41.5%	58.5%	41.5%
FRANKLIN	2,895	1,555	1,340		215 R	53.7%	46.3%	53.7%	46.3%
FRONTIER	2,154	1,307	846		461 R	60.7%	39.3%	60.7%	39.3%
FURNAS	3,752	2,258	1,494		764 R	60.2%	39.8%	60.2%	39.8%
GAGE	9,435	5,311	4,124		1,187 R	56.3%	43.7%	56.3%	43.7%
GARDEN	1,442	923	519		404 R	64.0%	36.0%	64.0%	36.0%
GARFIELD	1,244	702	542		160 R	56.4%	43.6%	56.4%	43.6%
GOSPER	1,193	621	572		49 R	52.1%	47.9%	52.1%	47.9%
GRANT	412	273	139		134 R	66.3%	33.7%	66.3%	33.7%
GREELEY	2,094	829	1,265		436 D	39.6%	60.4%	39.6%	60.4%
HALL	10,284	5,694	4,590		1,104 R	55.4%	44.6%	55.4%	44.6%
HAMILTON	3,915	2,406	1,509		897 R	61.5%	38.5%	61.5%	38.5%
HARLAN	2,710	1,490	1,220		270 R	55.0%	45.0%	55.0%	45.0%
HAYES	947	529	418		111 R	55.9%	44.1%	55.9%	44.1%
HITCHCOCK	2,131	1,208	923		285 R	56.7%	43.3%	56.7%	43.3%
HOLT	5,769	3,147	2,622		525 R	54.6%	45.4%	54.6%	45.4%
HOOKER	335	249	86		163 R	74.3%	25.7%	74.3%	25.7%
HOWARD	3,026	1,133	1,893		760 D	37.4%	62.6%	37.4%	62.6%
JEFFERSON	5,560	3,352	2,208		1,144 R	60.3%	39.7%	60.3%	39.7%
JOHNSON	3,108	1,817	1,291		526 R	58.5%	41.5%	58.5%	41.5%
KEARNEY	2,840	1,440	1,400		40 R	50.7%	49.3%	50.7%	49.3%
KEITH	2,709	1,600	1,109		491 R	59.1%	40.9%	59.1%	40.9%
KEYA PAHA	935	538	397		141 R	57.5%	42.5%	57.5%	42.5%
KIMBALL	1,696	1,024	672		352 R	60.4%	39.6%	60.4%	39.6%
KNOX	5,375	2,778	2,597		181 R	51.7%	48.3%	51.7%	48.3%
LANCASTER	41,958	23,620	18,338		5,282 R	56.3%	43.7%	56.3%	43.7%
LINCOLN	8,550	4,419	4,131		288 R	51.7%	48.3%	51.7%	48.3%
LOGAN	487	254	233		21 R	52.2%	47.8%	52.2%	47.8%
LOUP	557	294	263		31 R	52.8%	47.2%	52.8%	47.2%
MCPHERSON	307	209	98		111 R	68.1%	31.9%	68.1%	31.9%
MADISON	8,790	5,486	3,304		2,182 R	62.4%	37.6%	62.4%	37.6%

NEBRASKA

PRESIDENT 1944

County	Total Vote	Republican	Democratic	Other	Rep.-Dem. Plurality	Total Vote Rep.	Total Vote Dem.	Major Vote Rep.	Major Vote Dem.
MERRICK	4,081	2,691	1,390		1,301 R	65.9%	34.1%	65.9%	34.1%
MORRILL	3,106	1,998	1,108		890 R	64.3%	35.7%	64.3%	35.7%
NANCE	2,810	1,697	1,113		584 R	60.4%	39.6%	60.4%	39.6%
NEMAHA	5,052	3,267	1,785		1,482 R	64.7%	35.3%	64.7%	35.3%
NUCKOLLS	4,292	2,685	1,607		1,078 R	62.6%	37.4%	62.6%	37.4%
OTOE	7,955	5,291	2,664		2,627 R	66.5%	33.5%	66.5%	33.5%
PAWNEE	3,529	2,254	1,275		979 R	63.9%	36.1%	63.9%	36.1%
PERKINS	2,107	1,301	806		495 R	61.7%	38.3%	61.7%	38.3%
PHELPS	3,911	2,460	1,451		1,009 R	62.9%	37.1%	62.9%	37.1%
PIERCE	4,160	2,956	1,204		1,752 R	71.1%	28.9%	71.1%	28.9%
PLATTE	7,957	4,509	3,448		1,061 R	56.7%	43.3%	56.7%	43.3%
POLK	3,874	2,357	1,517		840 R	60.8%	39.2%	60.8%	39.2%
RED WILLOW	5,239	3,107	2,132		975 R	59.3%	40.7%	59.3%	40.7%
RICHARDSON	7,965	4,482	3,483		999 R	56.3%	43.7%	56.3%	43.7%
ROCK	1,490	984	506		478 R	66.0%	34.0%	66.0%	34.0%
SALINE	7,154	3,255	3,899		644 D	45.5%	54.5%	45.5%	54.5%
SARPY	5,295	2,641	2,654		13 D	49.9%	50.1%	49.9%	50.1%
SAUNDERS	10,814	6,615	4,199		2,416 R	61.2%	38.8%	61.2%	38.8%
SCOTTS BLUFF	10,680	6,947	3,733		3,214 R	65.0%	35.0%	65.0%	35.0%
SEWARD	5,804	3,721	2,083		1,638 R	64.1%	35.9%	64.1%	35.9%
SHERIDAN	3,601	2,570	1,031		1,539 R	71.4%	28.6%	71.4%	28.6%
SHERMAN	2,893	1,309	1,584		275 D	45.2%	54.8%	45.2%	54.8%
SIOUX	1,284	876	408		468 R	68.2%	31.8%	68.2%	31.8%
STANTON	2,556	1,682	874		808 R	65.8%	34.2%	65.8%	34.2%
THAYER	5,198	3,554	1,644		1,910 R	68.4%	31.6%	68.4%	31.6%
THOMAS	552	338	214		124 R	61.2%	38.8%	61.2%	38.8%
THURSTON	3,216	1,584	1,632		48 D	49.3%	50.7%	49.3%	50.7%
VALLEY	3,571	2,096	1,475		621 R	58.7%	41.3%	58.7%	41.3%
WASHINGTON	5,118	2,844	2,274		570 R	55.6%	44.4%	55.6%	44.4%
WAYNE	3,907	2,886	1,021		1,865 R	73.9%	26.1%	73.9%	26.1%
WEBSTER	3,617	2,523	1,094		1,429 R	69.8%	30.2%	69.8%	30.2%
WHEELER	702	392	310		82 R	55.8%	44.2%	55.8%	44.2%
YORK	6,693	4,885	1,808		3,077 R	73.0%	27.0%	73.0%	27.0%
TOTAL	563,126	329,880	233,246		96,634 R	58.6%	41.4%	58.6%	41.4%

PRESIDENT 1948

County	Total Vote	Republican	Democratic	Other	Rep.-Dem. Plurality	Total Vote Rep.	Total Vote Dem.	Major Vote Rep.	Major Vote Dem.
MERRICK	3,341	2,074	1,267		807 R	62.1%	37.9%	62.1%	37.9%
MORRILL	2,798	1,478	1,320		158 R	52.8%	47.2%	52.8%	47.2%
NANCE	2,358	1,339	1,019		320 R	56.8%	43.2%	56.8%	43.2%
NEMAHA	4,100	2,413	1,687		726 R	58.9%	41.1%	58.9%	41.1%
NUCKOLLS	3,863	2,036	1,827		209 R	52.7%	47.3%	52.7%	47.3%
OTOE	6,575	4,060	2,515		1,545 R	61.7%	38.3%	61.7%	38.3%
PAWNEE	2,996	1,725	1,271		454 R	57.6%	42.4%	57.6%	42.4%
PERKINS	1,767	904	863		41 R	51.2%	48.8%	51.2%	48.8%
PHELPS	4,304	2,489	1,815		674 R	57.8%	42.2%	57.8%	42.2%
PIERCE	3,249	1,866	1,383		483 R	57.4%	42.6%	57.4%	42.6%
PLATTE	7,129	3,812	3,317		495 R	53.5%	46.5%	53.5%	46.5%
POLK	3,422	2,026	1,396		630 R	59.2%	40.8%	59.2%	40.8%
RED WILLOW	4,848	2,610	2,238		372 R	53.8%	46.2%	53.8%	46.2%
RICHARDSON	7,297	3,778	3,519		259 R	51.8%	48.2%	51.8%	48.2%
ROCK	1,264	809	455		354 R	64.0%	36.0%	64.0%	36.0%
SALINE	6,239	2,641	3,598		957 D	42.3%	57.7%	42.3%	57.7%
SARPY	5,002	2,367	2,635		268 D	47.3%	52.7%	47.3%	52.7%
SAUNDERS	7,639	3,660	3,979		319 D	47.9%	52.1%	47.9%	52.1%
SCOTTS BLUFF	9,795	5,409	4,386		1,023 R	55.2%	44.8%	55.2%	44.8%
SEWARD	5,190	2,916	2,274		642 R	56.2%	43.8%	56.2%	43.8%
SHERIDAN	3,361	2,180	1,181		999 R	64.9%	35.1%	64.9%	35.1%
SHERMAN	2,611	1,003	1,608		605 D	38.4%	61.6%	38.4%	61.6%
SIOUX	1,177	657	520		137 R	55.8%	44.2%	55.8%	44.2%
STANTON	2,248	1,259	989		270 R	56.0%	44.0%	56.0%	44.0%
THAYER	4,532	2,601	1,931		670 R	57.4%	42.6%	57.4%	42.6%
THOMAS	550	312	238		74 R	56.7%	43.3%	56.7%	43.3%
THURSTON	3,039	1,149	1,890		741 D	37.8%	62.2%	37.8%	62.2%
VALLEY	3,055	1,670	1,385		285 R	54.7%	45.3%	54.7%	45.3%
WASHINGTON	4,306	2,400	1,906		494 R	55.7%	44.3%	55.7%	44.3%
WAYNE	3,481	2,323	1,158		1,165 R	66.7%	33.3%	66.7%	33.3%
WEBSTER	3,329	1,964	1,365		599 R	59.0%	41.0%	59.0%	41.0%
WHEELER	591	264	327		63 D	44.7%	55.3%	44.7%	55.3%
YORK	6,051	3,960	2,091		1,869 R	65.4%	34.6%	65.4%	34.6%
TOTAL	488,940	264,774	224,165		40,609 R	54.2%	45.8%	54.2%	45.8%

NEBRASKA

PRESIDENT 1952

County	Total Vote	Republican	Democratic	Other	Rep.-Dem. Plurality	Total Vote Rep.	Total Vote Dem.	Major Vote Rep.	Major Vote Dem.
ADAMS	12,778	9,033	3,745		5,288 R	70.7%	29.3%	70.7%	29.3%
ANTELOPE	5,445	4,377	1,068		3,309 R	80.4%	19.6%	80.4%	19.6%
ARTHUR	369	307	62		245 R	83.2%	16.8%	83.2%	16.8%
BANNER	623	484	139		345 R	77.7%	22.3%	77.7%	22.3%
BLAINE	595	458	137		321 R	77.0%	23.0%	77.0%	23.0%
BOONE	4,736	3,453	1,283		2,170 R	72.9%	27.1%	72.9%	27.1%
BOX BUTTE	5,665	4,426	1,239		3,187 R	78.1%	21.9%	78.1%	21.9%
BOYD	2,413	1,656	757		899 R	68.6%	31.4%	68.6%	31.4%
BROWN	2,493	1,950	543		1,407 R	78.2%	21.8%	78.2%	21.8%
BUFFALO	10,968	8,467	2,501		5,966 R	77.2%	22.8%	77.2%	22.8%
BURT	5,397	4,154	1,243		2,911 R	77.0%	23.0%	77.0%	23.0%
BUTLER	5,413	3,459	1,954		1,505 R	63.9%	36.1%	63.9%	36.1%
CASS	7,690	5,088	2,602		2,486 R	66.2%	33.8%	66.2%	33.8%
CEDAR	6,170	4,753	1,417		3,336 R	77.0%	23.0%	77.0%	23.0%
CHASE	2,404	1,941	463		1,478 R	80.7%	19.3%	80.7%	19.3%
CHERRY	4,108	3,148	960		2,188 R	76.6%	23.4%	76.6%	23.4%
CHEYENNE	6,423	4,206	2,217		1,989 R	65.5%	34.5%	65.5%	34.5%
CLAY	4,674	3,559	1,115		2,444 R	76.1%	23.9%	76.1%	23.9%
COLFAX	4,790	3,332	1,458		1,874 R	69.6%	30.4%	69.6%	30.4%
CUMING	5,652	4,557	1,095		3,462 R	80.6%	19.4%	80.6%	19.4%
CUSTER	9,256	7,143	2,113		5,030 R	77.2%	22.8%	77.2%	22.8%
DAKOTA	4,606	2,643	1,963		680 R	57.4%	42.6%	57.4%	42.6%
DAWES	4,740	3,583	1,157		2,426 R	75.6%	24.4%	75.6%	24.4%
DAWSON	8,950	7,130	1,820		5,310 R	79.7%	20.3%	79.7%	20.3%
DEUEL	1,613	1,372	241		1,131 R	85.1%	14.9%	85.1%	14.9%
DIXON	4,226	2,977	1,249		1,728 R	70.4%	29.6%	70.4%	29.6%
DODGE	12,938	9,256	3,682		5,574 R	71.5%	28.5%	71.5%	28.5%
DOUGLAS	127,048	71,457	55,591		15,866 R	56.2%	43.8%	56.2%	43.8%
DUNDY	2,067	1,670	397		1,273 R	80.8%	19.2%	80.8%	19.2%
FILLMORE	4,819	3,603	1,216		2,387 R	74.8%	25.2%	74.8%	25.2%
FRANKLIN	3,213	2,438	775		1,663 R	75.9%	24.1%	75.9%	24.1%
FRONTIER	2,569	1,980	589		1,391 R	77.1%	22.9%	77.1%	22.9%
FURNAS	4,482	3,464	1,018		2,446 R	77.3%	22.7%	77.3%	22.7%
GAGE	12,071	8,917	3,154		5,763 R	73.9%	26.1%	73.9%	26.1%
GARDEN	1,798	1,457	341		1,116 R	81.0%	19.0%	81.0%	19.0%
GARFIELD	1,295	1,042	253		789 R	80.5%	19.5%	80.5%	19.5%
GOSPER	1,310	1,017	293		724 R	77.6%	22.4%	77.6%	22.4%
GRANT	557	452	105		347 R	81.1%	18.9%	81.1%	18.9%
GREELEY	2,467	1,543	924		619 R	62.5%	37.5%	62.5%	37.5%
HALL	15,043	10,435	4,608		5,827 R	69.4%	30.6%	69.4%	30.6%
HAMILTON	4,709	3,579	1,130		2,449 R	76.0%	24.0%	76.0%	24.0%
HARLAN	3,030	2,300	730		1,570 R	75.9%	24.1%	75.9%	24.1%
HAYES	1,152	932	220		712 R	80.9%	19.1%	80.9%	19.1%
HITCHCOCK	2,677	2,008	669		1,339 R	75.0%	25.0%	75.0%	25.0%
HOLT	6,814	5,088	1,726		3,362 R	74.7%	25.3%	74.7%	25.3%
HOOKER	483	411	72		339 R	85.1%	14.9%	85.1%	14.9%
HOWARD	3,571	2,115	1,456		659 R	59.2%	40.8%	59.2%	40.8%
JEFFERSON	6,491	4,941	1,550		3,391 R	76.1%	23.9%	76.1%	23.9%
JOHNSON	3,765	2,787	978		1,809 R	74.0%	26.0%	74.0%	26.0%
KEARNEY	3,352	2,422	930		1,492 R	72.3%	27.7%	72.3%	27.7%
KEITH	3,559	2,790	769		2,021 R	78.4%	21.6%	78.4%	21.6%
KEYA PAHA	993	785	208		577 R	79.1%	20.9%	79.1%	20.9%
KIMBALL	2,121	1,646	475		1,171 R	77.6%	22.4%	77.6%	22.4%
KNOX	6,413	4,840	1,573		3,267 R	75.5%	24.5%	75.5%	24.5%
LANCASTER	54,525	36,797	17,728		19,069 R	67.5%	32.5%	67.5%	32.5%
LINCOLN	12,018	8,292	3,726		4,566 R	69.0%	31.0%	69.0%	31.0%
LOGAN	603	447	156		291 R	74.1%	25.9%	74.1%	25.9%
LOUP	616	507	109		398 R	82.3%	17.7%	82.3%	17.7%
MCPHERSON	408	355	53		302 R	87.0%	13.0%	87.0%	13.0%
MADISON	10,883	8,294	2,589		5,705 R	76.2%	23.8%	76.2%	23.8%

PRESIDENT 1956

County	Total Vote	Republican	Democratic	Other	Rep.-Dem. Plurality	Total Vote Rep.	Total Vote Dem.	Major Vote Rep.	Major Vote Dem.
ADAMS	12,231	8,186	4,045		4,141 R	66.9%	33.1%	66.9%	33.1%
ANTELOPE	4,941	3,607	1,334		2,273 R	73.0%	27.0%	73.0%	27.0%
ARTHUR	316	248	68		180 R	78.5%	21.5%	78.5%	21.5%
BANNER	514	329	185		144 R	64.0%	36.0%	64.0%	36.0%
BLAINE	565	416	149		267 R	73.6%	26.4%	73.6%	26.4%
BOONE	4,298	3,021	1,277		1,744 R	70.3%	29.7%	70.3%	29.7%
BOX BUTTE	4,353	2,991	1,362		1,629 R	68.7%	31.3%	68.7%	31.3%
BOYD	2,262	1,414	848		566 R	62.5%	37.5%	62.5%	37.5%
BROWN	2,114	1,566	548		1,018 R	74.1%	25.9%	74.1%	25.9%
BUFFALO	10,442	7,342	3,100		4,242 R	70.3%	29.7%	70.3%	29.7%
BURT	4,978	3,459	1,519		1,940 R	69.5%	30.5%	69.5%	30.5%
BUTLER	5,108	2,864	2,244		620 R	56.1%	43.9%	56.1%	43.9%
CASS	7,537	4,814	2,723		2,091 R	63.9%	36.1%	63.9%	36.1%
CEDAR	5,887	3,809	2,078		1,731 R	64.7%	35.3%	64.7%	35.3%
CHASE	2,114	1,444	670		774 R	68.3%	31.7%	68.3%	31.7%
CHERRY	3,298	2,414	884		1,530 R	73.2%	26.8%	73.2%	26.8%
CHEYENNE	5,991	3,809	2,182		1,627 R	63.6%	36.4%	63.6%	36.4%
CLAY	4,339	3,099	1,240		1,859 R	71.4%	28.6%	71.4%	28.6%
COLFAX	4,369	2,843	1,526		1,317 R	65.1%	34.9%	65.1%	34.9%
CUMING	5,525	4,223	1,302		2,921 R	76.4%	23.6%	76.4%	23.6%
CUSTER	8,223	5,798	2,425		3,373 R	70.5%	29.5%	70.5%	29.5%
DAKOTA	4,740	2,516	2,224		292 R	53.1%	46.9%	53.1%	46.9%
DAWES	3,416	2,523	893		1,630 R	73.9%	26.1%	73.9%	26.1%
DAWSON	8,542	6,503	2,039		4,464 R	76.1%	23.9%	76.1%	23.9%
DEUEL	1,459	1,165	294		871 R	79.8%	20.2%	79.8%	20.2%
DIXON	4,219	2,493	1,726		767 R	59.1%	40.9%	59.1%	40.9%
DODGE	13,298	9,210	4,088		5,122 R	69.3%	30.7%	69.3%	30.7%
DOUGLAS	123,380	73,270	50,110		23,160 R	59.4%	40.6%	59.4%	40.6%
DUNDY	1,691	1,196	495		701 R	70.7%	29.3%	70.7%	29.3%
FILLMORE	4,686	3,137	1,549		1,588 R	66.9%	33.1%	66.9%	33.1%
FRANKLIN	2,843	1,955	888		1,067 R	68.8%	31.2%	68.8%	31.2%
FRONTIER	2,236	1,602	634		968 R	71.6%	28.4%	71.6%	28.4%
FURNAS	4,005	2,894	1,111		1,783 R	72.3%	27.7%	72.3%	27.7%
GAGE	11,109	7,514	3,595		3,919 R	67.6%	32.4%	67.6%	32.4%
GARDEN	1,502	1,167	335		832 R	77.7%	22.3%	77.7%	22.3%
GARFIELD	1,198	936	262		674 R	78.1%	21.9%	78.1%	21.9%
GOSPER	1,139	814	325		489 R	71.5%	28.5%	71.5%	28.5%
GRANT	520	433	87		346 R	83.3%	16.7%	83.3%	16.7%
GREELEY	2,150	1,240	910		330 R	57.7%	42.3%	57.7%	42.3%
HALL	14,351	9,536	4,815		4,721 R	66.4%	33.6%	66.4%	33.6%
HAMILTON	4,292	3,217	1,075		2,142 R	75.0%	25.0%	75.0%	25.0%
HARLAN	2,698	1,850	848		1,002 R	68.6%	31.4%	68.6%	31.4%
HAYES	1,037	726	311		415 R	70.0%	30.0%	70.0%	30.0%
HITCHCOCK	2,311	1,570	741		829 R	67.9%	32.1%	67.9%	32.1%
HOLT	6,111	4,237	1,874		2,363 R	69.3%	30.7%	69.3%	30.7%
HOOKER	432	368	64		304 R	85.2%	14.8%	85.2%	14.8%
HOWARD	3,150	1,701	1,449		252 R	54.0%	46.0%	54.0%	46.0%
JEFFERSON	5,989	4,267	1,722		2,545 R	71.2%	28.8%	71.2%	28.8%
JOHNSON	3,300	2,160	1,140		1,020 R	65.5%	34.5%	65.5%	34.5%
KEARNEY	3,330	2,158	1,172		986 R	64.8%	35.2%	64.8%	35.2%
KEITH	3,554	2,624	930		1,694 R	73.8%	26.2%	73.8%	26.2%
KEYA PAHA	898	635	263		372 R	70.7%	29.3%	70.7%	29.3%
KIMBALL	2,246	1,590	656		934 R	70.8%	29.2%	70.8%	29.2%
KNOX	5,924	3,814	2,110		1,704 R	64.4%	35.6%	64.4%	35.6%
LANCASTER	54,808	35,591	19,217		16,374 R	64.9%	35.1%	64.9%	35.1%
LINCOLN	11,998	7,523	4,475		3,048 R	62.7%	37.3%	62.7%	37.3%
LOGAN	515	367	148		219 R	71.3%	28.7%	71.3%	28.7%
LOUP	580	441	139		302 R	76.0%	24.0%	76.0%	24.0%
MCPHERSON	379	281	98		183 R	74.1%	25.9%	74.1%	25.9%
MADISON	10,917	7,968	2,949		5,019 R	73.0%	27.0%	73.0%	27.0%

NEBRASKA

PRESIDENT 1952

County	Total Vote	Republican	Democratic	Other	Rep.-Dem. Plurality	Total Vote Rep.	Total Vote Dem.	Major Vote Rep.	Major Vote Dem.
MERRICK	4,253	3,288	965		2,323 R	77.3%	22.7%	77.3%	22.7%
MORRILL	3,382	2,485	897		1,588 R	73.5%	26.5%	73.5%	26.5%
NANCE	2,863	2,112	751		1,361 R	73.8%	26.2%	73.8%	26.2%
NEMAHA	5,167	3,735	1,432		2,303 R	72.3%	27.7%	72.3%	27.7%
NUCKOLLS	4,622	3,251	1,371		1,880 R	70.3%	29.7%	70.3%	29.7%
OTOE	8,021	6,082	1,939		4,143 R	75.8%	24.2%	75.8%	24.2%
PAWNEE	3,242	2,432	810		1,622 R	75.0%	25.0%	75.0%	25.0%
PERKINS	2,088	1,637	451		1,186 R	78.4%	21.6%	78.4%	21.6%
PHELPS	4,901	3,822	1,079		2,743 R	78.0%	22.0%	78.0%	22.0%
PIERCE	4,143	3,234	909		2,325 R	78.1%	21.9%	78.1%	21.9%
PLATTE	9,340	6,695	2,645		4,050 R	71.7%	28.3%	71.7%	28.3%
POLK	3,924	3,008	916		2,092 R	76.7%	23.3%	76.7%	23.3%
RED WILLOW	6,064	4,433	1,631		2,802 R	73.1%	26.9%	73.1%	26.9%
RICHARDSON	8,050	5,688	2,362		3,326 R	70.7%	29.3%	70.7%	29.3%
ROCK	1,493	1,226	267		959 R	82.1%	17.9%	82.1%	17.9%
SALINE	7,013	4,221	2,792		1,429 R	60.2%	39.8%	60.2%	39.8%
SARPY	6,178	3,649	2,529		1,120 R	59.1%	40.9%	59.1%	40.9%
SAUNDERS	8,487	5,525	2,962		2,563 R	65.1%	34.9%	65.1%	34.9%
SCOTTS BLUFF	13,263	9,674	3,589		6,085 R	72.9%	27.1%	72.9%	27.1%
SEWARD	5,942	4,257	1,685		2,572 R	71.6%	28.4%	71.6%	28.4%
SHERIDAN	4,353	3,512	841		2,671 R	80.7%	19.3%	80.7%	19.3%
SHERMAN	2,950	1,784	1,166		618 R	60.5%	39.5%	60.5%	39.5%
SIOUX	1,393	1,093	300		793 R	78.5%	21.5%	78.5%	21.5%
STANTON	2,655	1,983	672		1,311 R	74.7%	25.3%	74.7%	25.3%
THAYER	5,258	3,992	1,266		2,726 R	75.9%	24.1%	75.9%	24.1%
THOMAS	610	490	120		370 R	80.3%	19.7%	80.3%	19.7%
THURSTON	3,092	1,918	1,174		744 R	62.0%	38.0%	62.0%	38.0%
VALLEY	3,657	2,630	1,027		1,603 R	71.9%	28.1%	71.9%	28.1%
WASHINGTON	5,455	3,770	1,685		2,085 R	69.1%	30.9%	69.1%	30.9%
WAYNE	4,204	3,338	866		2,472 R	79.4%	20.6%	79.4%	20.6%
WEBSTER	3,644	2,719	925		1,794 R	74.6%	25.4%	74.6%	25.4%
WHEELER	686	455	231		224 R	66.3%	33.7%	66.3%	33.7%
YORK	7,210	5,742	1,468		4,274 R	79.6%	20.4%	79.6%	20.4%
TOTAL	609,660	421,603	188,057		233,546 R	69.2%	30.8%	69.2%	30.8%

PRESIDENT 1956

County	Total Vote	Republican	Democratic	Other	Rep.-Dem. Plurality	Total Vote Rep.	Total Vote Dem.	Major Vote Rep.	Major Vote Dem.
MERRICK	3,983	2,857	1,126		1,731 R	71.7%	28.3%	71.7%	28.3%
MORRILL	2,839	1,810	1,029		781 R	63.8%	36.2%	63.8%	36.2%
NANCE	2,558	1,779	779		1,000 R	69.5%	30.5%	69.5%	30.5%
NEMAHA	4,575	3,141	1,434		1,707 R	68.7%	31.3%	68.7%	31.3%
NUCKOLLS	4,157	2,672	1,485		1,187 R	64.3%	35.7%	64.3%	35.7%
OTOE	7,571	5,275	2,296		2,979 R	69.7%	30.3%	69.7%	30.3%
PAWNEE	2,852	1,830	1,022		808 R	64.2%	35.8%	64.2%	35.8%
PERKINS	1,962	1,296	666		630 R	66.1%	33.9%	66.1%	33.9%
PHELPS	4,815	3,502	1,313		2,189 R	72.7%	27.3%	72.7%	27.3%
PIERCE	3,952	2,800	1,152		1,648 R	70.9%	29.1%	70.9%	29.1%
PLATTE	9,496	6,574	2,922		3,652 R	69.2%	30.8%	69.2%	30.8%
POLK	3,617	2,482	1,135		1,347 R	68.6%	31.4%	68.6%	31.4%
RED WILLOW	5,431	3,806	1,625		2,181 R	70.1%	29.9%	70.1%	29.9%
RICHARDSON	6,994	4,480	2,514		1,966 R	64.1%	35.9%	64.1%	35.9%
ROCK	1,209	928	281		647 R	76.8%	23.2%	76.8%	23.2%
SALINE	6,643	3,248	3,395		147 D	48.9%	51.1%	48.9%	51.1%
SARPY	6,327	3,826	2,501		1,325 R	60.5%	39.5%	60.5%	39.5%
SAUNDERS	8,308	4,973	3,335		1,638 R	59.9%	40.1%	59.9%	40.1%
SCOTTS BLUFF	12,717	8,027	4,690		3,337 R	63.1%	36.9%	63.1%	36.9%
SEWARD	5,598	3,688	1,910		1,778 R	65.9%	34.1%	65.9%	34.1%
SHERIDAN	3,511	2,618	893		1,725 R	74.6%	25.4%	74.6%	25.4%
SHERMAN	2,648	1,429	1,219		210 R	54.0%	46.0%	54.0%	46.0%
SIOUX	759	499	260		239 R	65.7%	34.3%	65.7%	34.3%
STANTON	2,573	1,676	897		779 R	65.1%	34.9%	65.1%	34.9%
THAYER	4,793	3,346	1,447		1,899 R	69.8%	30.2%	69.8%	30.2%
THOMAS	543	422	121		301 R	77.7%	22.3%	77.7%	22.3%
THURSTON	3,128	1,722	1,406		316 R	55.1%	44.9%	55.1%	44.9%
VALLEY	3,278	2,189	1,089		1,100 R	66.8%	33.2%	66.8%	33.2%
WASHINGTON	5,262	3,531	1,731		1,800 R	67.1%	32.9%	67.1%	32.9%
WAYNE	4,183	3,040	1,143		1,897 R	72.7%	27.3%	72.7%	27.3%
WEBSTER	3,254	2,298	956		1,342 R	70.6%	29.4%	70.6%	29.4%
WHEELER	609	391	218		173 R	64.2%	35.8%	64.2%	35.8%
YORK	6,634	5,065	1,569		3,496 R	76.3%	23.7%	76.3%	23.7%
TOTAL	577,137	378,108	199,029		179,079 R	65.5%	34.5%	65.5%	34.5%

NEBRASKA

PRESIDENT 1960

County	Total Vote	Republican	Democratic	Other	Rep.-Dem. Plurality	Total Vote Rep.	Total Vote Dem.	Major Vote Rep.	Major Vote Dem.
ADAMS	12,296	7,932	4,364		3,568 R	64.5%	35.5%	64.5%	35.5%
ANTELOPE	5,087	3,617	1,470		2,147 R	71.1%	28.9%	71.1%	28.9%
ARTHUR	351	283	68		215 R	80.6%	19.4%	80.6%	19.4%
BANNER	635	424	211		213 R	66.8%	33.2%	66.8%	33.2%
BLAINE	533	420	113		307 R	78.8%	21.2%	78.8%	21.2%
BOONE	4,356	2,809	1,547		1,262 R	64.5%	35.5%	64.5%	35.5%
BOX BUTTE	5,043	3,157	1,886		1,271 R	62.6%	37.4%	62.6%	37.4%
BOYD	2,161	1,393	768		625 R	64.5%	35.5%	64.5%	35.5%
BROWN	2,249	1,735	514		1,221 R	77.1%	22.9%	77.1%	22.9%
BUFFALO	11,486	7,595	3,891		3,704 R	66.1%	33.9%	66.1%	33.9%
BURT	4,979	3,613	1,366		2,247 R	72.6%	27.4%	72.6%	27.4%
BUTLER	4,995	2,253	2,742		489 D	45.1%	54.9%	45.1%	54.9%
CASS	7,305	4,506	2,799		1,707 R	61.7%	38.3%	61.7%	38.3%
CEDAR	5,999	3,060	2,939		121 R	51.0%	49.0%	51.0%	49.0%
CHASE	2,139	1,482	657		825 R	69.3%	30.7%	69.3%	30.7%
CHERRY	3,739	2,695	1,044		1,651 R	72.1%	27.9%	72.1%	27.9%
CHEYENNE	6,394	3,814	2,580		1,234 R	59.6%	40.4%	59.6%	40.4%
CLAY	4,336	3,005	1,331		1,674 R	69.3%	30.7%	69.3%	30.7%
COLFAX	4,479	2,504	1,975		529 R	55.9%	44.1%	55.9%	44.1%
CUMING	5,773	3,894	1,879		2,015 R	67.5%	32.5%	67.5%	32.5%
CUSTER	8,066	5,716	2,350		3,366 R	70.9%	29.1%	70.9%	29.1%
DAKOTA	5,304	2,977	2,327		650 R	56.1%	43.9%	56.1%	43.9%
DAWES	4,385	3,106	1,279		1,827 R	70.8%	29.2%	70.8%	29.2%
DAWSON	8,868	6,480	2,388		4,092 R	73.1%	26.9%	73.1%	26.9%
DEUEL	1,674	1,276	398		878 R	76.2%	23.8%	76.2%	23.8%
DIXON	4,097	2,713	1,384		1,329 R	66.2%	33.8%	66.2%	33.8%
DODGE	14,340	9,638	4,702		4,936 R	67.2%	32.8%	67.2%	32.8%
DOUGLAS	136,065	72,005	64,060		7,945 R	52.9%	47.1%	52.9%	47.1%
DUNDY	1,731	1,245	486		759 R	71.9%	28.1%	71.9%	28.1%
FILLMORE	4,652	2,842	1,810		1,032 R	61.1%	38.9%	61.1%	38.9%
FRANKLIN	2,801	1,798	1,003		795 R	64.2%	35.8%	64.2%	35.8%
FRONTIER	2,197	1,615	582		1,033 R	73.5%	26.5%	73.5%	26.5%
FURNAS	3,945	2,854	1,091		1,763 R	72.3%	27.7%	72.3%	27.7%
GAGE	11,615	7,754	3,861		3,893 R	66.8%	33.2%	66.8%	33.2%
GARDEN	1,802	1,376	426		950 R	76.4%	23.6%	76.4%	23.6%
GARFIELD	1,352	1,047	305		742 R	77.4%	22.6%	77.4%	22.6%
GOSPER	1,193	854	339		515 R	71.6%	28.4%	71.6%	28.4%
GRANT	537	410	127		283 R	76.4%	23.6%	76.4%	23.6%
GREELEY	2,223	960	1,263		303 D	43.2%	56.8%	43.2%	56.8%
HALL	15,259	9,763	5,496		4,267 R	64.0%	36.0%	64.0%	36.0%
HAMILTON	4,472	3,249	1,223		2,026 R	72.7%	27.3%	72.7%	27.3%
HARLAN	2,659	1,766	893		873 R	66.4%	33.6%	66.4%	33.6%
HAYES	980	699	281		418 R	71.3%	28.7%	71.3%	28.7%
HITCHCOCK	2,312	1,634	678		956 R	70.7%	29.3%	70.7%	29.3%
HOLT	6,588	4,150	2,438		1,712 R	63.0%	37.0%	63.0%	37.0%
HOOKER	514	443	71		372 R	86.2%	13.8%	86.2%	13.8%
HOWARD	3,194	1,676	1,518		158 R	52.5%	47.5%	52.5%	47.5%
JEFFERSON	5,942	4,047	1,895		2,152 R	68.1%	31.9%	68.1%	31.9%
JOHNSON	3,249	2,098	1,151		947 R	64.6%	35.4%	64.6%	35.4%
KEARNEY	3,328	2,065	1,263		802 R	62.0%	38.0%	62.0%	38.0%
KEITH	3,891	2,680	1,211		1,469 R	68.9%	31.1%	68.9%	31.1%
KEYA PAHA	887	646	241		405 R	72.8%	27.2%	72.8%	27.2%
KIMBALL	3,168	2,152	1,016		1,136 R	67.9%	32.1%	67.9%	32.1%
KNOX	5,969	3,847	2,122		1,725 R	64.4%	35.6%	64.4%	35.6%
LANCASTER	60,289	37,725	22,564		15,161 R	62.6%	37.4%	62.6%	37.4%
LINCOLN	12,497	7,685	4,812		2,873 R	61.5%	38.5%	61.5%	38.5%
LOGAN	554	391	163		228 R	70.6%	29.4%	70.6%	29.4%
LOUP	574	445	129		316 R	77.5%	22.5%	77.5%	22.5%
McPHERSON	370	303	67		236 R	81.9%	18.1%	81.9%	18.1%
MADISON	11,400	8,350	3,050		5,300 R	73.2%	26.8%	73.2%	26.8%

PRESIDENT 1964

County	Total Vote	Republican	Democratic	Other	Rep.-Dem. Plurality	Total Vote Rep.	Total Vote Dem.	Major Vote Rep.	Major Vote Dem.
ADAMS	12,027	5,586	6,441		855 D	46.4%	53.6%	46.4%	53.6%
ANTELOPE	4,570	2,566	2,004		562 R	56.1%	43.9%	56.1%	43.9%
ARTHUR	369	243	126		117 R	65.9%	34.1%	65.9%	34.1%
BANNER	553	357	196		161 R	64.6%	35.4%	64.6%	35.4%
BLAINE	521	326	195		131 R	62.6%	37.4%	62.6%	37.4%
BOONE	3,798	1,893	1,905		12 D	49.8%	50.2%	49.8%	50.2%
BOX BUTTE	4,693	2,725	1,968		757 R	58.1%	41.9%	58.1%	41.9%
BOYD	2,008	1,100	908		192 R	54.8%	45.2%	54.8%	45.2%
BROWN	2,157	1,272	885		387 R	59.0%	41.0%	59.0%	41.0%
BUFFALO	10,861	5,425	5,436		11 D	49.9%	50.1%	49.9%	50.1%
BURT	4,533	2,459	2,074		385 R	54.2%	45.8%	54.2%	45.8%
BUTLER	4,635	1,642	2,993		1,351 D	35.4%	64.6%	35.4%	64.6%
CASS	6,922	2,947	3,975		1,028 D	42.6%	57.4%	42.6%	57.4%
CEDAR	5,403	2,299	3,104		805 D	42.6%	57.4%	42.6%	57.4%
CHASE	1,988	1,081	907		174 R	54.4%	45.6%	54.4%	45.6%
CHERRY	3,672	2,244	1,428		816 R	61.1%	38.9%	61.1%	38.9%
CHEYENNE	5,818	3,129	2,689		440 R	53.8%	46.2%	53.8%	46.2%
CLAY	3,880	1,879	2,001		122 D	48.4%	51.6%	48.4%	51.6%
COLFAX	4,179	1,972	2,207		235 D	47.2%	52.8%	47.2%	52.8%
CUMING	5,129	3,064	2,065		799 R	57.5%	42.5%	57.5%	42.5%
CUSTER	7,391	3,916	3,475		441 R	53.0%	47.0%	53.0%	47.0%
DAKOTA	4,560	1,906	2,654		748 D	41.8%	58.2%	41.8%	58.2%
DAWES	4,087	2,518	1,569		949 R	61.6%	38.4%	61.6%	38.4%
DAWSON	8,367	4,577	3,790		787 R	54.7%	45.3%	54.7%	45.3%
DEUEL	1,505	972	533		439 R	64.6%	35.4%	64.6%	35.4%
DIXON	3,757	1,845	1,912		67 D	49.1%	50.9%	49.1%	50.9%
DODGE	13,543	6,812	6,731		81 R	50.3%	49.7%	50.3%	49.7%
DOUGLAS	139,093	61,613	77,480		15,867 D	44.3%	55.7%	44.3%	55.7%
DUNDY	1,623	911	712		199 R	56.1%	43.9%	56.1%	43.9%
FILLMORE	4,433	1,936	2,497		561 D	43.7%	56.3%	43.7%	56.3%
FRANKLIN	2,650	1,241	1,409		168 D	46.8%	53.2%	46.8%	53.2%
FRONTIER	1,931	1,090	841		249 R	56.4%	43.6%	56.4%	43.6%
FURNAS	3,680	2,011	1,669		342 R	54.6%	45.4%	54.6%	45.4%
GAGE	10,446	4,035	6,411		2,376 D	38.6%	61.4%	38.6%	61.4%
GARDEN	1,665	1,106	559		547 R	66.4%	33.6%	66.4%	33.6%
GARFIELD	1,244	761	483		278 R	61.2%	38.8%	61.2%	38.8%
GOSPER	1,059	547	512		35 R	51.7%	48.3%	51.7%	48.3%
GRANT	503	304	199		105 R	60.4%	39.6%	60.4%	39.6%
GREELEY	2,080	775	1,305		530 D	37.3%	62.7%	37.3%	62.7%
HALL	14,988	6,715	8,273		1,558 D	44.8%	55.2%	44.8%	55.2%
HAMILTON	3,991	2,105	1,886		219 R	52.7%	47.3%	52.7%	47.3%
HARLAN	2,478	1,283	1,195		88 R	51.8%	48.2%	51.8%	48.2%
HAYES	865	503	362		141 R	58.2%	41.8%	58.2%	41.8%
HITCHCOCK	2,095	1,149	946		203 R	54.8%	45.2%	54.8%	45.2%
HOLT	5,933	3,194	2,739		455 R	53.8%	46.2%	53.8%	46.2%
HOOKER	472	335	137		198 R	71.0%	29.0%	71.0%	29.0%
HOWARD	3,044	1,019	2,025		1,006 D	33.5%	66.5%	33.5%	66.5%
JEFFERSON	5,079	2,275	2,804		529 D	44.8%	55.2%	44.8%	55.2%
JOHNSON	2,866	1,312	1,554		242 D	45.8%	54.2%	45.8%	54.2%
KEARNEY	3,119	1,352	1,767		415 D	43.3%	56.7%	43.3%	56.7%
KEITH	3,711	1,927	1,784		143 R	51.9%	48.1%	51.9%	48.1%
KEYA PAHA	826	506	320		186 R	61.3%	38.7%	61.3%	38.7%
KIMBALL	2,815	1,573	1,242		331 R	55.9%	44.1%	55.9%	44.1%
KNOX	5,369	2,752	2,617		135 R	51.3%	48.7%	51.3%	48.7%
LANCASTER	58,390	23,887	34,503		10,616 D	40.9%	59.1%	40.9%	59.1%
LINCOLN	11,257	4,811	6,446		1,635 D	42.7%	57.3%	42.7%	57.3%
LOGAN	563	267	296		29 D	47.4%	52.6%	47.4%	52.6%
LOUP	524	348	176		172 R	66.4%	33.6%	66.4%	33.6%
McPHERSON	323	219	104		115 R	67.8%	32.2%	67.8%	32.2%
MADISON	10,816	6,155	4,661		1,494 R	56.9%	43.1%	56.9%	43.1%

NEBRASKA

PRESIDENT 1960

County	Total Vote	Republican	Democratic	Other	Rep.-Dem. Plurality	Total Vote Rep.	Total Vote Dem.	Major Vote Rep.	Major Vote Dem.
MERRICK	3,978	2,744	1,234		1,510 R	69.0%	31.0%	69.0%	31.0%
MORRILL	3,219	2,020	1,199		821 R	62.8%	37.2%	62.8%	37.2%
NANCE	2,711	1,699	1,012		687 R	62.7%	37.3%	62.7%	37.3%
NEMAHA	4,408	3,031	1,377		1,654 R	68.8%	31.2%	68.8%	31.2%
NUCKOLLS	4,011	2,441	1,570		871 R	60.9%	39.1%	60.9%	39.1%
OTOE	7,600	5,057	2,543		2,514 R	66.5%	33.5%	66.5%	33.5%
PAWNEE	2,737	1,728	1,009		719 R	63.1%	36.9%	63.1%	36.9%
PERKINS	1,998	1,301	697		604 R	65.1%	34.9%	65.1%	34.9%
PHELPS	5,047	3,795	1,252		2,543 R	75.2%	24.8%	75.2%	24.8%
PIERCE	4,070	2,963	1,107		1,856 R	72.8%	27.2%	72.8%	27.2%
PLATTE	10,516	6,129	4,387		1,742 R	58.3%	41.7%	58.3%	41.7%
POLK	3,581	2,397	1,184		1,213 R	66.9%	33.1%	66.9%	33.1%
RED WILLOW	5,812	3,890	1,922		1,968 R	66.9%	33.1%	66.9%	33.1%
RICHARDSON	7,151	4,481	2,670		1,811 R	62.7%	37.3%	62.7%	37.3%
ROCK	1,337	1,084	253		831 R	81.1%	18.9%	81.1%	18.9%
SALINE	6,404	2,881	3,523		642 D	45.0%	55.0%	45.0%	55.0%
SARPY	8,449	4,672	3,777		895 R	55.3%	44.7%	55.3%	44.7%
SAUNDERS	8,258	4,702	3,556		1,146 R	56.9%	43.1%	56.9%	43.1%
SCOTTS BLUFF	14,374	8,728	5,646		3,082 R	60.7%	39.3%	60.7%	39.3%
SEWARD	5,683	3,588	2,095		1,493 R	63.1%	36.9%	63.1%	36.9%
SHERIDAN	4,014	2,870	1,144		1,726 R	71.5%	28.5%	71.5%	28.5%
SHERMAN	2,558	1,131	1,427		296 D	44.2%	55.8%	44.2%	55.8%
SIOUX	1,160	745	415		330 R	64.2%	35.8%	64.2%	35.8%
STANTON	2,537	1,680	857		823 R	66.2%	33.8%	66.2%	33.8%
THAYER	4,752	3,202	1,550		1,652 R	67.4%	32.6%	67.4%	32.6%
THOMAS	561	420	141		279 R	74.9%	25.1%	74.9%	25.1%
THURSTON	3,072	1,757	1,315		442 R	57.2%	42.8%	57.2%	42.8%
VALLEY	3,293	2,045	1,248		797 R	62.1%	37.9%	62.1%	37.9%
WASHINGTON	5,466	3,772	1,694		2,078 R	69.0%	31.0%	69.0%	31.0%
WAYNE	4,299	3,274	1,025		2,249 R	76.2%	23.8%	76.2%	23.8%
WEBSTER	3,129	2,026	1,103		923 R	64.7%	35.3%	64.7%	35.3%
WHEELER	663	424	239		185 R	64.0%	36.0%	64.0%	36.0%
YORK	6,969	5,205	1,764		3,441 R	74.7%	25.3%	74.7%	25.3%
TOTAL	613,095	380,553	232,542		148,011 R	62.1%	37.9%	62.1%	37.9%

PRESIDENT 1964

County	Total Vote	Republican	Democratic	Other	Rep.-Dem. Plurality	Total Vote Rep.	Total Vote Dem.	Major Vote Rep.	Major Vote Dem.
MERRICK	3,539	1,798	1,741		57 R	50.8%	49.2%	50.8%	49.2%
MORRILL	2,877	1,649	1,228		421 R	57.3%	42.7%	57.3%	42.7%
NANCE	2,478	1,155	1,323		168 D	46.6%	53.4%	46.6%	53.4%
NEMAHA	4,020	1,936	2,084		148 D	48.2%	51.8%	48.2%	51.8%
NUCKOLLS	3,727	1,546	2,181		635 D	41.5%	58.5%	41.5%	58.5%
OTOE	6,795	3,626	3,169		457 R	53.4%	46.6%	53.4%	46.6%
PAWNEE	2,277	1,166	1,111		55 R	51.2%	48.8%	51.2%	48.8%
PERKINS	1,789	912	877		35 R	51.0%	49.0%	51.0%	49.0%
PHELPS	4,593	2,440	2,153		287 R	53.1%	46.9%	53.1%	46.9%
PIERCE	3,596	1,965	1,631		334 R	54.6%	45.4%	54.6%	45.4%
PLATTE	9,865	4,705	5,160		455 D	47.7%	52.3%	47.7%	52.3%
POLK	3,337	1,607	1,730		123 D	48.2%	51.8%	48.2%	51.8%
RED WILLOW	5,156	2,740	2,416		324 R	53.1%	46.9%	53.1%	46.9%
RICHARDSON	6,095	2,850	3,245		395 D	46.8%	53.2%	46.8%	53.2%
ROCK	1,211	835	376		459 R	69.0%	31.0%	69.0%	31.0%
SALINE	5,905	1,780	4,125		2,345 D	30.1%	69.9%	30.1%	69.9%
SARPY	9,999	4,418	5,581		1,163 D	44.2%	55.8%	44.2%	55.8%
SAUNDERS	7,517	3,345	4,172		827 D	44.5%	55.5%	44.5%	55.5%
SCOTTS BLUFF	13,333	6,965	6,368		597 R	52.2%	47.8%	52.2%	47.8%
SEWARD	5,568	2,221	3,347		1,126 D	39.9%	60.1%	39.9%	60.1%
SHERIDAN	3,596	2,440	1,156		1,284 R	67.9%	32.1%	67.9%	32.1%
SHERMAN	2,394	762	1,632		870 D	31.8%	68.2%	31.8%	68.2%
SIOUX	1,077	698	379		319 R	64.8%	35.2%	64.8%	35.2%
STANTON	2,313	1,299	1,014		285 R	56.2%	43.8%	56.2%	43.8%
THAYER	4,430	2,132	2,298		166 D	48.1%	51.9%	48.1%	51.9%
THOMAS	531	319	212		107 R	60.1%	39.9%	60.1%	39.9%
THURSTON	2,894	1,194	1,700		506 D	41.3%	58.7%	41.3%	58.7%
VALLEY	3,202	1,657	1,545		112 R	51.7%	48.3%	51.7%	48.3%
WASHINGTON	5,339	2,638	2,701		63 D	49.4%	50.6%	49.4%	50.6%
WAYNE	3,989	2,359	1,630		729 R	59.1%	40.9%	59.1%	40.9%
WEBSTER	2,848	1,191	1,657		466 D	41.8%	58.2%	41.8%	58.2%
WHEELER	565	317	248		69 R	56.1%	43.9%	56.1%	43.9%
YORK	6,242	3,410	2,832		578 R	54.6%	45.4%	54.6%	45.4%
TOTAL	584,154	276,847	307,307		30,460 D	47.4%	52.6%	47.4%	52.6%

NEBRASKA

OTHER VOTE COMPOSITION:

1920	9,600 Socialist; 5,947 Prohibition; 90 scattered.
1924	105,681 Progressive; 1,594 Prohibition.
1928	Socialist.
1932	Socialist.
1936	Union.
1940	
1944	
1948	Scattered.
1952	
1956	
1960	
1964	

SPECIAL CASES:

1924	Progressive candidates carried several counties and ran second in others.

NEVADA

PRESIDENT 1920

County	Total Vote	Republican	Democratic	Other	Rep.-Dem. Plurality	Total Vote Rep.	Total Vote Dem.	Major Vote Rep.	Major Vote Dem.
CHURCHILL	1,616	873	506	237	367 R	54.0%	31.3%	63.3%	36.7%
CLARK	1,320	589	620	111	31 D	44.6%	47.0%	48.7%	51.3%
DOUGLAS	656	503	147	6	356 R	76.7%	22.4%	77.4%	22.6%
ELKO	2,521	1,369	1,029	123	340 R	54.3%	40.8%	57.1%	42.9%
ESMERALDA	940	466	347	127	119 R	49.6%	36.9%	57.3%	42.7%
EUREKA	491	313	157	21	156 R	53.7%	32.0%	66.6%	33.4%
HUMBOLDT	1,284	660	532	92	128 R	51.4%	41.4%	55.4%	44.6%
LANDER	709	416	254	39	162 R	58.7%	35.8%	62.1%	37.9%
LINCOLN	783	373	366	44	7 R	47.6%	46.7%	50.5%	49.5%
LYON	1,408	945	344	119	601 R	67.1%	24.4%	73.3%	26.7%
MINERAL	629	374	209	46	165 R	59.5%	33.2%	64.2%	35.8%
NYE	2,899	1,576	1,007	316	569 R	54.4%	34.7%	61.0%	39.0%
ORMSBY	1,024	592	413	19	179 R	57.8%	40.3%	58.9%	41.1%
PERSHING	996	563	389	44	174 R	56.5%	39.1%	59.1%	40.9%
STOREY	617	324	272	21	52 R	52.5%	44.1%	54.4%	45.6%
WASHOE	6,865	4,189	2,357	319	1,832 R	61.0%	34.3%	64.0%	36.0%
WHITE PINE	2,436	1,354	902	180	452 R	55.6%	37.0%	60.0%	40.0%
TOTAL	27,194	15,479	9,851	1,864	5,628 R	56.9%	36.2%	61.1%	38.9%

PRESIDENT 1924

County	Total Vote	Republican	Democratic	Other	Rep.-Dem. Plurality	Total Vote Rep.	Total Vote Dem.	Major Vote Rep.	Major Vote Dem.
CHURCHILL	1,573	655	310	608	345 R	41.6%	19.7%	67.9%	32.1%
CLARK	1,636	533	288	815	245 R	32.6%	17.6%	64.9%	35.1%
DOUGLAS	581	343	95	143	248 R	59.0%	16.4%	78.3%	21.7%
ELKO	2,868	1,113	604	1,151	509 R	38.8%	21.1%	64.8%	35.2%
ESMERALDA	726	241	150	335	91 R	33.2%	20.7%	61.6%	38.4%
EUREKA	418	209	94	115	115 R	50.0%	22.5%	69.0%	31.0%
HUMBOLDT	1,133	400	248	485	152 R	35.3%	21.9%	61.7%	38.3%
LANDER	545	254	138	153	116 R	46.6%	25.3%	64.8%	35.2%
LINCOLN	738	200	257	281	57 D	27.1%	34.8%	43.8%	56.2%
LYON	1,303	618	231	454	387 R	47.4%	17.7%	72.8%	27.2%
MINERAL	504	191	84	229	107 R	37.9%	16.7%	69.5%	30.5%
NYE	2,227	884	454	889	430 R	39.7%	20.4%	66.1%	33.9%
ORMSBY	932	413	415	104	2 D	44.3%	44.5%	49.9%	50.1%
PERSHING	854	308	164	382	144 R	36.1%	19.2%	65.3%	34.7%
STOREY	761	283	209	269	74 R	37.2%	27.5%	57.5%	42.5%
WASHOE	7,766	3,549	1,669	2,548	1,880 R	45.7%	21.5%	68.0%	32.0%
WHITE PINE	2,356	1,049	499	808	550 R	44.5%	21.2%	67.8%	32.2%
TOTAL	26,921	11,243	5,909	9,769	5,334 R	41.8%	21.9%	65.5%	34.5%

NEVADA

PRESIDENT 1928

County	Total Vote	Republican	Democratic	Other	Rep.-Dem. Plurality	Total Vote Rep.	Total Vote Dem.	Major Vote Rep.	Major Vote Dem.
CHURCHILL	1,877	1,126	751		375 R	60.0%	40.0%	60.0%	40.0%
CLARK	2,268	1,284	984		300 R	56.6%	43.4%	56.6%	43.4%
DOUGLAS	642	456	186		270 R	71.0%	29.0%	71.0%	29.0%
ELKO	3,318	1,876	1,442		434 R	56.5%	43.5%	56.5%	43.5%
ESMERALDA	646	305	341		36 D	47.2%	52.8%	47.2%	52.8%
EUREKA	512	251	261		10 D	49.0%	51.0%	49.0%	51.0%
HUMBOLDT	1,385	783	602		181 R	56.5%	43.5%	56.5%	43.5%
LANDER	770	456	314		142 R	59.2%	40.8%	59.2%	40.8%
LINCOLN	1,095	553	542		11 R	50.5%	49.5%	50.5%	49.5%
LYON	1,631	927	704		223 R	56.8%	43.2%	56.8%	43.2%
MINERAL	601	275	326		51 D	45.3%	54.2%	45.8%	54.2%
NYE	2,081	958	1,123		165 D	46.3%	54.0%	46.0%	54.0%
ORMSBY	1,016	590	426		164 R	58.1%	41.9%	58.1%	41.9%
PERSHING	995	543	452		91 R	54.5%	45.4%	54.6%	45.4%
STOREY	456	185	271		85 D	40.5%	59.4%	40.6%	59.4%
WASHOE	9,719	5,767	3,952		1,815 R	59.3%	40.7%	59.3%	40.7%
WHITE PINE	3,405	1,992	1,413		579 R	58.5%	41.5%	58.5%	41.5%
TOTAL	32,417	18,327	14,090		4,237 R	56.5%	43.5%	56.5%	43.5%

PRESIDENT 1932

County	Total Vote	Republican	Democratic	Other	Rep.-Dem. Plurality	Total Vote Rep.	Total Vote Dem.	Major Vote Rep.	Major Vote Dem.
CHURCHILL	2,192	674	1,518		844 D	30.7%	69.3%	30.7%	69.3%
CLARK	7,184	1,347	5,837		4,490 D	18.8%	81.2%	18.8%	81.2%
DOUGLAS	729	331	398		67 D	45.4%	54.6%	45.4%	54.6%
ELKO	3,887	1,325	2,562		1,237 D	34.1%	65.9%	34.1%	65.9%
ESMERALDA	573	147	426		279 D	25.7%	74.3%	25.7%	74.3%
EUREKA	521	136	385		249 D	26.1%	73.9%	26.1%	73.9%
HUMBOLDT	1,531	405	1,126		721 D	26.5%	73.5%	26.5%	73.5%
LANDER	808	272	536		264 D	33.7%	66.3%	33.7%	66.3%
LINCOLN	1,400	295	1,105		810 D	21.1%	78.9%	21.1%	78.9%
LYON	1,439	456	983		527 D	31.7%	68.3%	31.7%	68.3%
MINERAL	885	238	647		409 D	26.9%	73.1%	26.9%	73.1%
NYE	1,802	506	1,296		790 D	28.1%	71.9%	28.1%	71.9%
ORMSBY	1,065	486	579		93 D	45.6%	54.4%	45.6%	54.4%
PERSHING	1,039	247	792		545 D	23.8%	76.2%	23.8%	76.2%
STOREY	371	124	247		123 D	33.4%	66.6%	33.4%	66.6%
WASHOE	12,474	4,333	8,141		3,808 D	34.7%	65.3%	34.7%	65.3%
WHITE PINE	3,530	1,352	2,178		826 D	38.3%	61.7%	38.3%	61.7%
TOTAL	41,430	12,674	28,756		16,082 D	30.6%	69.4%	30.6%	69.4%

NEVADA

PRESIDENT 1936

County	Total Vote	Republican	Democratic	Other	Rep.-Dem. Plurality	Total Vote Rep.	Total Vote Dem.	Major Vote Rep.	Major Vote Dem.
CHURCHILL	2,049	759	1,290		531 D	37.0%	63.0%	37.0%	63.0%
CLARK	6,269	1,178	5,091		3,913 D	18.8%	81.2%	18.8%	81.2%
DOUGLAS	812	346	466		120 D	42.6%	57.4%	42.6%	57.4%
ELKO	3,953	1,065	2,888		1,823 D	26.9%	73.1%	26.9%	73.1%
ESMERALDA	722	156	566		410 D	21.6%	78.4%	21.6%	78.4%
EUREKA	576	180	396		216 D	31.2%	68.8%	31.2%	68.8%
HUMBOLDT	1,600	390	1,210		820 D	24.4%	75.6%	24.4%	75.6%
LANDER	822	237	585		348 D	28.8%	71.2%	28.8%	71.2%
LINCOLN	1,893	254	1,639		1,385 D	13.4%	86.6%	13.4%	86.6%
LYON	1,690	487	1,203		716 D	28.8%	71.2%	28.8%	71.2%
MINERAL	1,014	236	778		542 D	23.3%	76.7%	23.3%	76.7%
NYE	1,959	464	1,495		1,031 D	23.7%	76.3%	23.7%	76.3%
ORMSBY	1,278	533	745		212 D	41.7%	58.3%	41.7%	58.3%
PERSHING	1,130	269	861		592 D	23.8%	76.2%	23.8%	76.2%
STOREY	531	139	392		253 D	26.2%	73.8%	26.2%	73.8%
WASHOE	13,872	4,358	9,514		5,156 D	31.4%	68.6%	31.4%	68.6%
WHITE PINE	3,678	872	2,806		1,934 D	23.7%	76.3%	23.7%	76.3%
TOTAL	43,848	11,923	31,925		20,002 D	27.2%	72.8%	27.2%	72.8%

PRESIDENT 1940

County	Total Vote	Republican	Democratic	Other	Rep.-Dem. Plurality	Total Vote Rep.	Total Vote Dem.	Major Vote Rep.	Major Vote Dem.
CHURCHILL	2,438	1,171	1,267		96 D	48.0%	52.0%	48.0%	52.0%
CLARK	7,324	2,170	5,154		2,984 D	29.6%	70.4%	29.6%	70.4%
DOUGLAS	922	592	330		262 R	64.2%	35.8%	64.2%	35.8%
ELKO	4,799	1,783	3,016		1,233 D	37.2%	62.8%	37.2%	62.8%
ESMERALDA	931	292	639		347 D	31.4%	68.6%	31.4%	68.6%
EUREKA	637	284	353		69 D	44.6%	55.4%	44.6%	55.4%
HUMBOLDT	2,156	789	1,367		578 D	36.6%	63.4%	36.6%	63.4%
LANDER	868	393	475		82 D	45.3%	54.7%	45.3%	54.7%
LINCOLN	2,062	461	1,601		1,140 D	22.4%	77.6%	22.4%	77.6%
LYON	2,030	963	1,067		104 D	47.4%	52.6%	47.4%	52.6%
MINERAL	1,099	406	693		287 D	36.9%	63.1%	36.9%	63.1%
NYE	1,935	729	1,206		477 D	37.7%	62.3%	37.7%	62.3%
ORMSBY	1,533	748	785		37 D	48.8%	51.2%	48.8%	51.2%
PERSHING	1,290	594	696		102 D	46.0%	54.0%	46.0%	54.0%
STOREY	606	224	382		158 D	37.0%	63.0%	37.0%	63.0%
WASHOE	17,305	8,062	9,243		1,181 D	46.6%	53.4%	46.6%	53.4%
WHITE PINE	5,239	1,568	3,671		2,103 D	29.9%	70.1%	29.9%	70.1%
TOTAL	53,174	21,229	31,945		10,716 D	39.9%	60.1%	39.9%	60.1%

NEVADA

PRESIDENT 1944

County	Total Vote	Republican	Democratic	Other	Rep.-Dem. Plurality	Total Vote Rep.	Total Vote Dem.	Major Vote Rep.	Major Vote Dem.
CHURCHILL	2,176	1,130	1,046		84 R	51.9%	48.1%	51.9%	48.1%
CLARK	11,893	4,543	7,350		2,807 D	38.2%	61.8%	38.2%	61.8%
DOUGLAS	838	556	282		274 R	66.3%	33.7%	66.3%	33.7%
ELKO	3,922	1,642	2,280		638 D	41.9%	58.1%	41.9%	58.1%
ESMERALDA	373	150	223		73 D	40.2%	59.8%	40.2%	59.8%
EUREKA	534	317	217		100 R	59.4%	40.6%	59.4%	40.6%
HUMBOLDT	1,829	835	994		159 D	45.7%	54.3%	45.7%	54.3%
LANDER	808	425	383		42 R	52.6%	47.4%	52.6%	47.4%
LINCOLN	1,819	524	1,295		771 D	28.8%	71.2%	28.8%	71.2%
LYON	1,603	895	708		187 R	55.8%	44.2%	55.8%	44.2%
MINERAL	2,095	751	1,344		593 D	35.8%	64.2%	35.8%	64.2%
NYE	1,666	723	943		220 D	43.4%	56.6%	43.4%	56.6%
ORMSBY	1,506	841	665		176 R	55.8%	44.2%	55.8%	44.2%
PERSHING	1,062	538	524		14 R	50.7%	49.3%	50.7%	49.3%
STOREY	336	163	173		10 D	48.5%	51.5%	48.5%	51.5%
WASHOE	17,408	9,024	8,384		640 R	51.8%	48.2%	51.8%	48.2%
WHITE PINE	4,366	1,554	2,812		1,258 D	35.6%	64.4%	35.6%	64.4%
TOTAL	54,234	24,611	29,623		5,012 D	45.4%	54.6%	45.4%	54.6%

PRESIDENT 1948

County	Total Vote	Republican	Democratic	Other	Rep.-Dem. Plurality	Total Vote Rep.	Total Vote Dem.	Major Vote Rep.	Major Vote Dem.
CHURCHILL	2,372	1,206	1,055	111	151 R	50.8%	44.5%	53.3%	46.7%
CLARK	17,453	6,382	10,787	284	4,405 D	36.6%	61.8%	37.2%	62.8%
DOUGLAS	1,032	719	298	15	421 R	69.7%	28.9%	70.7%	29.3%
ELKO	3,771	1,683	2,026	62	343 D	44.6%	53.7%	45.4%	54.6%
ESMERALDA	365	164	183	18	19 D	44.9%	50.1%	47.3%	52.7%
EUREKA	603	312	278	13	34 R	51.7%	46.1%	52.9%	47.1%
HUMBOLDT	1,831	901	886	44	15 R	49.2%	48.4%	50.4%	49.6%
LANDER	704	397	298	9	99 R	56.4%	42.3%	57.1%	42.9%
LINCOLN	1,553	520	1,004	29	484 D	33.5%	64.6%	34.1%	65.9%
LYON	1,633	967	629	37	338 R	59.2%	38.5%	60.6%	39.4%
MINERAL	1,928	706	1,194	28	488 D	36.6%	61.9%	37.2%	62.8%
NYE	1,390	722	595	73	127 R	51.9%	42.8%	54.8%	45.2%
ORMSBY	1,801	1,095	681	25	414 R	60.8%	37.8%	61.7%	38.3%
PERSHING	1,262	677	541	44	136 R	53.6%	42.9%	55.6%	44.4%
STOREY	388	187	184	17	3 R	48.2%	47.4%	50.4%	49.6%
WASHOE	20,188	11,323	8,365	500	2,958 R	56.1%	41.4%	57.5%	42.5%
WHITE PINE	3,843	1,396	2,287	160	891 D	36.3%	59.5%	37.9%	62.1%
TOTAL	62,117	29,357	31,291	1,469	1,934 D	47.3%	50.4%	48.4%	51.6%

NEVADA

PRESIDENT 1952

County	Total Vote	Republican	Democratic	Other	Rep.-Dem. Plurality	Total Vote Rep.	Total Vote Dem.	Major Vote Rep.	Major Vote Dem.
CHURCHILL	2,851	1,948	903		1,045 R	68.3%	31.7%	68.3%	31.7%
CLARK	25,188	13,333	11,855		1,478 R	52.9%	47.1%	52.9%	47.1%
DOUGLAS	1,125	948	177		771 R	84.3%	15.7%	84.3%	15.7%
ELKO	4,859	3,104	1,755		1,349 R	63.9%	36.1%	63.9%	36.1%
ESMERALDA	313	174	139		35 R	55.6%	44.4%	55.6%	44.4%
EUREKA	536	379	157		222 R	70.7%	29.3%	70.7%	29.3%
HUMBOLDT	2,089	1,398	691		707 R	66.9%	33.1%	66.9%	33.1%
LANDER	738	501	237		264 R	67.9%	32.1%	67.9%	32.1%
LINCOLN	1,844	903	941		38 D	49.0%	51.0%	49.0%	51.0%
LYON	2,029	1,453	576		877 R	71.6%	28.4%	71.6%	28.4%
MINERAL	2,666	1,297	1,369		72 D	48.6%	51.4%	48.6%	51.4%
NYE	1,604	1,037	567		470 R	64.7%	35.3%	64.7%	35.3%
ORMSBY	2,232	1,653	579		1,074 R	74.1%	25.9%	74.1%	25.9%
PERSHING	1,441	919	522		397 R	63.8%	36.2%	63.8%	36.2%
STOREY	355	206	149		57 R	58.0%	42.0%	58.0%	42.0%
WASHOE	27,932	19,044	8,888		10,156 R	68.2%	31.8%	68.2%	31.8%
WHITE PINE	4,388	2,205	2,183		22 R	50.3%	49.7%	50.3%	49.7%
TOTAL	82,190	50,502	31,688		18,814 R	61.4%	38.6%	61.4%	38.6%

PRESIDENT 1956

County	Total Vote	Republican	Democratic	Other	Rep.-Dem. Plurality	Total Vote Rep.	Total Vote Dem.	Major Vote Rep.	Major Vote Dem.
CHURCHILL	3,082	2,013	1,069		944 R	65.3%	34.7%	65.3%	34.7%
CLARK	37,679	18,584	19,095		511 D	49.3%	50.7%	49.3%	50.7%
DOUGLAS	1,319	1,063	256		807 R	80.6%	19.4%	80.6%	19.4%
ELKO	4,717	2,981	1,736		1,245 R	63.2%	36.8%	63.2%	36.8%
ESMERALDA	288	164	124		40 R	56.9%	43.1%	56.9%	43.1%
EUREKA	513	330	183		147 R	64.3%	35.7%	64.3%	35.7%
HUMBOLDT	2,132	1,292	840		452 R	60.6%	39.4%	60.6%	39.4%
LANDER	823	540	283		257 R	65.6%	34.4%	65.6%	34.4%
LINCOLN	1,688	885	803		82 R	52.4%	47.6%	52.4%	47.6%
LYON	2,478	1,697	781		916 R	68.5%	31.5%	68.5%	31.5%
MINERAL	2,848	1,433	1,415		18 R	50.3%	49.7%	50.3%	49.7%
NYE	1,695	946	749		197 R	55.8%	44.2%	55.8%	44.2%
ORMSBY	2,571	1,749	822		927 R	68.0%	32.0%	68.0%	32.0%
PERSHING	1,457	895	562		333 R	61.4%	38.6%	61.4%	38.6%
STOREY	376	226	150		76 R	60.1%	39.9%	60.1%	39.9%
WASHOE	28,390	18,865	9,525		9,340 R	66.4%	33.6%	66.4%	33.6%
WHITE PINE	4,633	2,386	2,247		139 R	51.5%	48.5%	51.5%	48.5%
TOTAL	96,669	56,049	40,640		15,409 R	58.0%	42.0%	58.0%	42.0%

NEVADA

PRESIDENT 1960

County	Total Vote	Republican	Democratic	Other	Rep.-Dem. Plurality	Total Vote Rep.	Total Vote Dem.	Major Vote Rep.	Major Vote Dem.
CHURCHILL	3,074	1,765	1,309		456 R	57.4%	42.6%	57.4%	42.6%
CLARK	42,146	18,197	23,949		5,752 D	43.2%	56.8%	43.2%	56.8%
DOUGLAS	1,751	1,164	587		577 R	66.5%	33.5%	66.5%	33.5%
ELKO	4,922	2,427	2,495		68 D	49.3%	50.7%	49.3%	50.7%
ESMERALDA	371	156	215		59 D	42.0%	58.0%	42.0%	58.0%
EUREKA	462	239	223		16 R	51.7%	48.3%	51.7%	48.3%
HUMBOLDT	2,330	1,157	1,173		16 D	49.7%	50.3%	49.7%	50.3%
LANDER	774	383	391		8 D	49.5%	50.5%	49.5%	50.5%
LINCOLN	1,301	530	771		241 D	40.7%	59.3%	40.7%	59.3%
LYON	2,503	1,494	1,009		485 R	59.7%	40.3%	59.7%	40.3%
MINERAL	2,536	930	1,606		676 D	36.7%	63.3%	36.7%	63.3%
NYE	1,756	763	993		230 D	43.5%	56.5%	43.5%	56.5%
ORMSBY	3,229	1,946	1,283		663 R	60.3%	39.7%	60.3%	39.7%
PERSHING	1,364	648	716		68 D	47.5%	52.5%	47.5%	52.5%
STOREY	370	203	167		36 R	54.9%	45.1%	54.9%	45.1%
WASHOE	34,113	18,833	15,280		3,553 R	55.2%	44.8%	55.2%	44.8%
WHITE PINE	4,265	1,552	2,713		1,161 D	36.4%	63.6%	36.4%	63.6%
TOTAL	107,267	52,387	54,880		2,493 D	48.8%	51.2%	48.8%	51.2%

PRESIDENT 1964

County	Total Vote	Republican	Democratic	Other	Rep.-Dem. Plurality	Total Vote Rep.	Total Vote Dem.	Major Vote Rep.	Major Vote Dem.
CHURCHILL	3,172	1,607	1,565		42 R	50.7%	49.3%	50.7%	49.3%
CLARK	64,681	23,921	40,760		16,839 D	37.0%	63.0%	37.0%	63.0%
DOUGLAS	2,137	1,127	1,010		117 R	52.7%	47.3%	52.7%	47.3%
ELKO	4,641	1,856	2,785		929 D	40.0%	60.0%	40.0%	60.0%
ESMERALDA	318	131	187		56 D	41.2%	58.8%	41.2%	58.8%
EUREKA	528	243	285		42 D	46.0%	54.0%	46.0%	54.0%
HUMBOLDT	2,527	1,106	1,421		315 D	43.8%	56.2%	43.8%	56.2%
LANDER	729	338	391		53 D	46.4%	53.6%	46.4%	53.6%
LINCOLN	1,225	440	785		345 D	35.9%	64.1%	35.9%	64.1%
LYON	2,724	1,397	1,327		70 R	51.3%	48.7%	51.3%	48.7%
MINERAL	2,367	927	1,440		513 D	39.2%	60.8%	39.2%	60.8%
NYE	2,098	822	1,276		454 D	39.2%	60.8%	39.2%	60.8%
ORMSBY	4,126	1,997	2,129		132 D	48.4%	51.6%	48.4%	51.6%
PERSHING	1,224	486	738		252 D	39.7%	60.3%	39.7%	60.3%
STOREY	433	172	261		89 D	39.7%	60.3%	39.7%	60.3%
WASHOE	38,520	16,350	20,170		1,820 D	47.6%	52.4%	47.6%	52.4%
WHITE PINE	3,983	1,174	2,809		1,635 D	29.5%	70.5%	29.5%	70.5%
TOTAL	135,433	56,094	79,339		23,245 D	41.4%	58.6%	41.4%	58.6%

NEVADA

OTHER VOTE COMPOSITION:

1920	Socialist.
1924	Progressive.
1928	
1932	
1936	
1940	
1944	
1948	Progressive.
1952	
1956	
1960	
1964	

SPECIAL CASES:

1924   Progressive candidates carried several counties and ran second in most others.

NEW HAMPSHIRE

PRESIDENT 1920

County	Total Vote	Republican	Democratic	Other	Rep.-Dem. Plurality	Total Vote Rep.	Total Vote Dem.	Major Vote Rep.	Major Vote Dem.
BELKNAP	9,115	5,628	3,464	23	2,164 R	61.7%	38.0%	61.9%	38.1%
CARROLL	6,510	4,214	2,279	17	1,935 R	64.7%	35.0%	64.9%	35.1%
CHESHIRE	10,092	6,644	3,374	74	3,270 R	65.8%	33.4%	66.3%	33.7%
COOS	11,228	6,114	4,985	129	1,129 R	54.5%	44.4%	55.1%	44.9%
GRAFTON	15,794	9,650	6,102	42	3,548 R	61.1%	38.6%	61.3%	38.7%
HILLSBOROUGH	42,322	23,040	18,736	546	4,304 R	54.4%	44.3%	55.2%	44.8%
MERRIMACK	21,872	12,748	8,976	148	3,772 R	58.3%	41.0%	58.7%	41.3%
ROCKINGHAM	20,525	13,811	6,582	132	7,229 R	67.3%	32.1%	67.7%	32.3%
STRAFFORD	14,412	8,700	5,643	69	3,057 R	60.4%	39.2%	60.7%	39.3%
SULLIVAN	7,222	4,647	2,521	54	2,126 R	64.3%	34.9%	64.8%	35.2%
TOTAL	159,092	95,196	62,662	1,234	32,534 R	59.8%	39.4%	60.3%	39.7%

PRESIDENT 1924

County	Total Vote	Republican	Democratic	Other	Rep.-Dem. Plurality	Total Vote Rep.	Total Vote Dem.	Major Vote Rep.	Major Vote Dem.
BELKNAP	9,399	5,996	3,217	186	2,779 R	63.8%	34.2%	65.1%	34.9%
CARROLL	6,685	4,372	2,213	100	2,159 R	65.4%	33.1%	66.4%	33.6%
CHESHIRE	10,156	7,008	2,720	428	4,288 R	69.0%	26.8%	72.0%	28.0%
COOS	11,651	6,137	4,620	894	1,517 R	52.7%	39.7%	57.1%	42.9%
GRAFTON	16,364	10,493	5,360	511	5,133 R	64.1%	32.8%	66.2%	33.8%
HILLSBOROUGH	42,773	22,098	16,002	4,673	6,096 R	51.7%	37.4%	58.0%	42.0%
MERRIMACK	22,692	13,587	8,283	822	5,304 R	59.9%	36.5%	62.1%	37.9%
ROCKINGHAM	21,237	14,530	6,073	634	8,457 R	68.4%	28.6%	70.5%	29.5%
STRAFFORD	16,187	9,167	6,445	575	2,722 R	56.6%	39.8%	58.7%	41.3%
SULLIVAN	7,625	5,187	2,268	170	2,919 R	68.0%	29.7%	69.6%	30.4%
TOTAL	164,769	93,575	57,201	8,993	41,374 R	59.8%	34.7%	63.3%	36.7%

NEW HAMPSHIRE

PRESIDENT 1928

County	Total Vote	Republican	Democratic	Other	Rep.-Dem. Plurality	Total Vote Rep.	Total Vote Dem.	Major Vote Rep.	Major Vote Dem.
BELKNAP	10,462	6,762	3,689	11	3,073 R	64.6%	35.3%	64.7%	35.3%
CARROLL	7,117	5,509	1,592	16	3,917 R	77.4%	22.4%	77.6%	22.4%
CHESHIRE	13,756	8,673	5,025	58	3,648 R	63.0%	36.5%	63.3%	36.7%
COOS	13,931	7,891	6,006	34	1,885 R	56.6%	43.1%	56.8%	43.2%
GRAFTON	18,759	12,566	6,035	158	6,531 R	67.0%	32.2%	67.6%	32.4%
HILLSBOROUGH	54,087	24,465	29,457	165	4,992 D	45.2%	54.5%	45.4%	54.6%
MERRIMACK	25,935	15,724	10,139	72	5,585 R	60.6%	39.1%	60.8%	39.2%
ROCKINGHAM	25,425	17,590	7,782	53	9,808 R	69.2%	30.6%	69.3%	30.7%
STRAFFORD	17,939	10,470	7,441	28	3,029 R	58.4%	41.5%	58.5%	41.5%
SULLIVAN	9,346	5,754	3,549	43	2,205 R	61.6%	38.0%	61.9%	38.1%
TOTAL	196,757	115,404	80,715	638	34,689 R	58.7%	41.0%	58.8%	41.2%

PRESIDENT 1932

County	Total Vote	Republican	Democratic	Other	Rep.-Dem. Plurality	Total Vote Rep.	Total Vote Dem.	Major Vote Rep.	Major Vote Dem.
BELKNAP	10,988	6,048	4,911	29	1,137 R	55.0%	44.7%	55.2%	44.8%
CARROLL	8,161	5,269	2,873	19	2,396 R	64.6%	35.2%	64.7%	35.3%
CHESHIRE	13,692	7,904	5,662	126	2,242 R	57.7%	41.4%	58.3%	41.7%
COOS	15,205	7,189	7,928	88	739 D	47.3%	52.1%	47.6%	52.4%
GRAFTON	19,323	10,810	8,342	171	2,468 R	55.9%	43.2%	56.4%	43.6%
HILLSBOROUGH	56,161	23,308	32,458	395	9,150 D	41.5%	57.8%	41.8%	58.2%
MERRIMACK	26,908	13,986	12,805	117	1,181 R	52.0%	47.6%	52.2%	47.8%
ROCKINGHAM	26,405	14,902	11,363	140	3,539 R	56.4%	43.0%	56.7%	43.3%
STRAFFORD	19,098	9,060	9,970	68	910 D	47.4%	52.2%	47.6%	52.4%
SULLIVAN	9,579	5,153	4,368	58	785 R	53.8%	45.6%	54.1%	45.9%
TOTAL	205,520	103,629	100,680	1,211	2,949 R	50.4%	49.0%	50.7%	49.3%

NEW HAMPSHIRE

PRESIDENT 1936

County	Total Vote	Republican	Democratic	Other	Rep.-Dem. Plurality	Total Vote Rep.	Total Vote Dem.	Major Vote Rep.	Major Vote Dem.
BELKNAP	11,522	6,219	5,150	153	1,069 R	54.0%	44.7%	54.7%	45.3%
CARROLL	8,325	5,521	2,769	35	2,752 R	66.3%	33.3%	66.6%	33.4%
CHESHIRE	14,574	8,052	6,322	200	1,730 R	55.2%	43.4%	56.0%	44.0%
COOS	15,694	6,737	8,737	220	2,000 D	42.9%	55.7%	43.5%	56.5%
GRAFTON	20,016	11,336	8,520	160	2,816 D	56.6%	42.6%	57.1%	42.9%
HILLSBOROUGH	61,180	23,293	34,992	2,895	11,699 D	38.1%	57.2%	40.0%	60.0%
MERRIMACK	28,319	14,456	13,645	218	811 R	51.0%	48.2%	51.4%	48.6%
ROCKINGHAM	28,249	15,466	12,207	576	3,259 R	54.7%	43.2%	55.9%	44.1%
STRAFFORD	19,697	8,215	11,005	477	2,790 D	41.7%	55.9%	42.7%	57.3%
SULLIVAN	10,538	5,347	5,113	78	234 D	50.7%	48.5%	51.1%	48.9%
TOTAL	218,114	104,642	108,460	5,012	3,818 D	48.0%	49.7%	49.1%	50.9%

PRESIDENT 1940

County	Total Vote	Republican	Democratic	Other	Rep.-Dem. Plurality	Total Vote Rep.	Total Vote Dem.	Major Vote Rep.	Major Vote Dem.
BELKNAP	11,768	6,115	5,653		462 R	52.0%	48.0%	52.0%	48.0%
CARROLL	8,526	5,656	2,870		2,786 R	66.3%	33.7%	66.3%	33.7%
CHESHIRE	15,218	8,302	6,916		1,386 R	54.6%	45.4%	54.6%	45.4%
COOS	16,750	6,650	10,100		3,450 D	39.7%	60.3%	39.7%	60.3%
GRAFTON	21,239	11,478	9,761		1,717 D	54.0%	46.0%	54.0%	46.0%
HILLSBOROUGH	68,781	26,201	42,580		16,379 D	38.1%	61.9%	38.1%	61.9%
MERRIMACK	29,615	14,923	14,692		231 R	50.4%	49.6%	50.4%	49.6%
ROCKINGHAM	30,224	16,223	14,001		2,222 R	53.7%	46.3%	53.7%	46.3%
STRAFFORD	21,843	8,996	12,847		3,851 D	41.2%	58.8%	41.2%	58.8%
SULLIVAN	11,455	5,583	5,872		289 D	48.7%	51.3%	48.7%	51.3%
TOTAL	235,419	110,127	125,292		15,165 D	46.8%	53.2%	46.8%	53.2%

NEW HAMPSHIRE

PRESIDENT 1944

County	Total Vote	Republican	Democratic	Other	Rep.-Dem. Plurality	Total Vote Rep.	Total Vote Dem.	Major Vote Rep.	Major Vote Dem.
BELKNAP	11,515	6,188	5,325	2	863 R	53.7%	46.2%	53.7%	46.3%
CARROLL	7,713	5,251	2,461	1	2,790 R	68.1%	31.9%	68.1%	31.9%
CHESHIRE	15,432	8,334	7,098		1,236 R	54.0%	46.0%	54.0%	46.0%
COOS	14,922	6,209	8,709	4	2,500 D	41.6%	58.4%	41.6%	58.4%
GRAFTON	19,697	10,947	8,743	7	2,204 R	55.6%	44.4%	55.6%	44.4%
HILLSBOROUGH	68,236	25,921	42,306	9	16,385 D	38.0%	62.0%	38.0%	62.0%
MERRIMACK	27,983	14,599	13,382	2	1,217 R	52.2%	47.8%	52.2%	47.8%
ROCKINGHAM	30,316	17,144	13,170	2	3,974 R	56.6%	43.4%	56.6%	43.4%
STRAFFORD	21,898	9,388	12,497	13	3,109 D	42.9%	57.1%	42.9%	57.1%
SULLIVAN	11,913	5,935	5,972	6	37 D	49.8%	50.1%	49.8%	50.2%
TOTAL	229,625	109,916	119,663	46	9,747 D	47.9%	52.1%	47.9%	52.1%

PRESIDENT 1948

County	Total Vote	Republican	Democratic	Other	Rep.-Dem. Plurality	Total Vote Rep.	Total Vote Dem.	Major Vote Rep.	Major Vote Dem.
BELKNAP	11,039	7,152	3,822	65	3,330 R	64.8%	34.6%	65.2%	34.8%
CARROLL	8,050	6,127	1,869	54	4,258 R	76.1%	23.2%	76.6%	23.4%
CHESHIRE	15,506	9,043	6,337	126	2,706 R	58.3%	40.9%	58.8%	41.2%
COOS	15,165	7,005	7,930	230	925 D	46.2%	52.3%	46.9%	53.1%
GRAFTON	19,281	12,248	6,841	192	5,407 R	63.5%	35.5%	64.2%	35.8%
HILLSBOROUGH	70,742	28,257	41,789	696	13,532 D	39.9%	59.1%	40.3%	59.7%
MERRIMACK	27,935	16,586	11,171	178	5,415 R	59.4%	40.0%	59.8%	40.2%
ROCKINGHAM	31,128	18,890	11,937	301	6,953 R	60.7%	38.3%	61.3%	38.7%
STRAFFORD	21,776	9,988	11,603	185	1,615 D	45.9%	53.3%	46.3%	53.7%
SULLIVAN	10,818	6,003	4,696	119	1,307 R	55.5%	43.4%	56.1%	43.9%
TOTAL	231,440	121,299	107,995	2,146	13,304 R	52.4%	46.7%	52.9%	47.1%

NEW HAMPSHIRE

PRESIDENT 1952

County	Total Vote	Republican	Democratic	Other	Rep.-Dem. Plurality	Total Vote Rep.	Total Vote Dem.	Major Vote Rep.	Major Vote Dem.
BELKNAP	13,322	9,567	3,755		5,812 R	71.8%	28.2%	71.8%	28.2%
CARROLL	9,076	7,498	1,578		5,920 R	82.6%	17.4%	82.6%	17.4%
CHESHIRE	18,607	11,897	6,710		5,187 R	63.9%	36.1%	63.9%	36.1%
COOS	17,823	9,975	7,848		2,127 R	56.0%	44.0%	56.0%	44.0%
GRAFTON	22,061	15,937	6,124		9,813 R	72.2%	27.8%	72.2%	27.8%
HILLSBOROUGH	83,065	41,263	41,802		539 D	49.7%	50.3%	49.7%	50.3%
MERRIMACK	32,134	21,824	10,310		11,514 R	67.9%	32.1%	67.9%	32.1%
ROCKINGHAM	38,320	26,280	12,040		14,240 R	68.6%	31.4%	68.6%	31.4%
STRAFFORD	25,482	13,729	11,753		1,976 R	53.9%	46.1%	53.9%	46.1%
SULLIVAN	13,060	8,317	4,743		3,574 R	63.7%	36.3%	63.7%	36.3%
TOTAL	272,950	166,287	106,663		59,624 R	60.9%	39.1%	60.9%	39.1%

PRESIDENT 1956

County	Total Vote	Republican	Democratic	Other	Rep.-Dem. Plurality	Total Vote Rep.	Total Vote Dem.	Major Vote Rep.	Major Vote Dem.
BELKNAP	13,038	9,902	3,131	5	6,771 R	75.9%	24.0%	76.0%	24.0%
CARROLL	8,816	7,527	1,281	8	6,246 R	85.4%	14.5%	85.5%	14.5%
CHESHIRE	18,170	12,585	5,574	11	7,011 R	69.3%	30.7%	69.3%	30.7%
COOS	17,338	11,465	5,871	2	5,594 R	66.1%	33.9%	66.1%	33.9%
GRAFTON	21,081	15,609	5,466	6	10,143 R	74.0%	25.9%	74.1%	25.9%
HILLSBOROUGH	81,528	45,248	36,234	46	9,014 R	55.5%	44.4%	55.5%	44.5%
MERRIMACK	30,774	22,060	8,711	3	13,349 R	71.7%	28.3%	71.7%	28.3%
ROCKINGHAM	38,442	28,226	10,198	18	18,028 R	73.4%	26.5%	73.5%	26.5%
STRAFFORD	25,160	15,494	9,659	7	5,835 R	61.6%	38.4%	61.6%	38.4%
SULLIVAN	12,647	8,403	4,239	5	4,164 R	66.4%	33.5%	66.5%	33.5%
TOTAL	266,994	176,519	90,364	111	86,155 R	66.1%	33.8%	66.1%	33.9%

NEW HAMPSHIRE

PRESIDENT 1960

County	Total Vote	Republican	Democratic	Other	Rep.-Dem. Plurality	Total Vote Rep.	Total Vote Dem.	Major Vote Rep.	Major Vote Dem.
BELKNAP	14,786	9,156	5,630		3,526 R	61.9%	38.1%	61.9%	38.1%
CARROLL	9,405	7,487	1,918		5,569 R	79.6%	20.4%	79.6%	20.4%
CHESHIRE	20,262	11,594	8,668		2,926 R	57.2%	42.8%	57.2%	42.8%
COOS	18,252	7,797	10,455		2,658 D	42.7%	57.3%	42.7%	57.3%
GRAFTON	22,275	14,454	7,821		6,633 R	64.9%	35.1%	64.9%	35.1%
HILLSBOROUGH	90,565	38,430	52,135		13,705 D	42.4%	57.6%	42.4%	57.6%
MERRIMACK	33,673	20,395	13,278		7,117 R	60.6%	39.4%	60.6%	39.4%
ROCKINGHAM	45,095	28,032	17,063		10,969 R	62.2%	37.8%	62.2%	37.8%
STRAFFORD	27,874	13,539	14,335		796 D	48.6%	51.4%	48.6%	51.4%
SULLIVAN	13,574	7,105	6,469		636 R	52.3%	47.7%	52.3%	47.7%
TOTAL	295,761	157,989	137,772		20,217 R	53.4%	46.6%	53.4%	46.6%

PRESIDENT 1964

County	Total Vote	Republican	Democratic	Other	Rep.-Dem. Plurality	Total Vote Rep.	Total Vote Dem.	Major Vote Rep.	Major Vote Dem.
BELKNAP	13,932	5,908	8,024		2,116 D	42.4%	57.6%	42.4%	57.6%
CARROLL	9,015	4,957	4,058		899 R	55.0%	45.0%	55.0%	45.0%
CHESHIRE	19,584	5,958	13,626		7,668 D	30.4%	69.6%	30.4%	69.6%
COOS	16,819	4,863	11,956		7,093 D	28.9%	71.1%	28.9%	71.1%
GRAFTON	21,027	8,461	12,566		4,105 D	40.2%	59.8%	40.2%	59.8%
HILLSBOROUGH	89,739	29,503	60,236		30,733 D	32.9%	67.1%	32.9%	67.1%
MERRIMACK	32,382	12,564	19,818		7,254 D	38.8%	61.2%	38.8%	61.2%
ROCKINGHAM	46,754	19,498	27,256		7,758 D	41.7%	58.3%	41.7%	58.3%
STRAFFORD	26,079	9,342	17,737		9,395 D	32.0%	68.0%	32.0%	68.0%
SULLIVAN	12,762	3,975	8,787		4,812 D	31.1%	68.9%	31.1%	68.9%
TOTAL	288,093	104,029	184,064		80,035 D	36.1%	63.9%	36.1%	63.9%

NEW HAMPSHIRE

OTHER VOTE COMPOSITION:

1920   Socialist.
1924   Progressive.
1928   465 Socialist; 173 Communist.
1932   947 Socialist; 264 Communist.
1936   4,819 Union; 193 Communist.

1940
1944   Socialist.
1948   1,970 Progressive; 86 Socialist; 83 Socialist Labor; 7 States Rights.
1952
1956   States Rights.

1960
1964

NEW JERSEY

PRESIDENT 1920

County	Total Vote	Republican	Democratic	Other	Rep.-Dem. Plurality	Total Vote Rep.	Total Vote Dem.	Major Vote Rep.	Major Vote Dem.
ATLANTIC	27,725	21,245	5,753	727	15,492 R	76.6%	20.8%	78.7%	21.3%
BERGEN	62,305	47,512	12,396	2,397	35,116 R	76.3%	19.9%	79.3%	20.7%
BURLINGTON	26,041	17,898	7,532	611	10,366 R	68.7%	28.9%	70.4%	29.6%
CAMDEN	62,087	40,771	17,893	3,423	22,878 R	65.7%	28.8%	69.5%	30.5%
CAPE MAY	8,175	5,785	2,198	192	3,587 R	70.8%	26.9%	72.5%	27.5%
CUMBERLAND	17,427	11,913	4,487	1,027	7,426 R	68.4%	25.7%	72.6%	27.4%
ESSEX	163,848	116,168	40,970	6,710	75,198 R	70.9%	25.0%	73.9%	26.1%
GLOUCESTER	17,557	11,693	4,869	995	6,824 R	66.6%	27.7%	70.6%	29.4%
HUDSON	170,793	101,759	62,637	6,397	39,122 R	59.6%	36.7%	61.9%	38.1%
HUNTERDON	13,686	7,443	6,067	176	1,376 R	54.4%	44.3%	55.1%	44.9%
MERCER	46,683	29,626	15,713	1,344	13,913 R	63.5%	33.7%	65.3%	34.7%
MIDDLESEX	42,088	29,334	11,618	1,136	17,716 R	69.7%	27.6%	71.6%	28.4%
MONMOUTH	42,336	28,818	12,975	543	15,843 R	68.1%	30.6%	69.0%	31.0%
MORRIS	28,931	20,686	7,256	989	13,430 R	71.5%	25.1%	74.0%	26.0%
OCEAN	9,139	6,840	2,138	161	4,702 R	74.8%	23.4%	76.2%	23.8%
PASSAIC	59,225	42,692	11,873	4,660	30,819 R	72.1%	20.0%	78.2%	21.8%
SALEM	11,485	7,638	3,483	364	4,155 R	66.5%	30.3%	68.7%	31.3%
SOMERSET	15,435	10,962	4,192	281	6,770 R	71.0%	27.2%	72.3%	27.7%
SUSSEX	8,892	5,224	3,516	152	1,708 R	58.7%	39.5%	59.8%	40.2%
UNION	54,303	39,409	12,103	2,791	27,306 R	72.6%	22.3%	76.5%	23.5%
WARREN	15,663	8,035	7,218	430	817 R	51.2%	46.0%	52.7%	47.3%
TOTAL	910,251	615,333	258,761	36,157	356,572 R	67.6%	28.4%	70.4%	29.6%

PRESIDENT 1924

County	Total Vote	Republican	Democratic	Other	Rep.-Dem. Plurality	Total Vote Rep.	Total Vote Dem.	Major Vote Rep.	Major Vote Dem.
ATLANTIC	37,939	27,936	6,937	3,066	20,999 R	73.6%	18.3%	80.1%	19.9%
BERGEN	87,598	60,803	16,844	9,951	43,959 R	69.4%	19.2%	78.3%	21.7%
BURLINGTON	30,780	21,617	7,794	1,369	13,823 R	70.2%	25.3%	73.5%	26.5%
CAMDEN	72,622	48,154	17,577	6,891	30,577 R	66.3%	24.2%	73.3%	26.7%
CAPE MAY	11,246	8,139	2,611	496	5,528 R	72.4%	23.2%	75.7%	24.3%
CUMBERLAND	22,084	15,691	4,780	1,613	10,911 R	71.1%	21.6%	76.6%	23.4%
ESSEX	186,673	123,614	41,708	21,351	81,906 R	66.2%	22.3%	74.8%	25.2%
GLOUCESTER	21,328	15,513	4,167	1,648	11,346 R	72.7%	19.5%	78.8%	21.2%
HUDSON	133,952	80,892	91,094	21,966	10,202 D	41.7%	47.0%	47.0%	53.0%
HUNTERDON	14,747	8,940	5,103	704	3,837 R	60.6%	34.6%	63.7%	36.3%
MERCER	51,551	30,689	14,639	6,223	16,050 R	59.5%	28.4%	67.7%	32.3%
MIDDLESEX	55,482	34,556	16,373	4,553	18,183 R	62.3%	29.5%	67.9%	32.1%
MONMOUTH	52,482	34,451	14,931	3,100	19,520 R	65.6%	28.4%	69.8%	30.2%
MORRIS	35,655	24,812	8,042	2,801	16,770 R	69.6%	22.6%	75.5%	24.5%
OCEAN	12,222	8,677	2,594	951	6,083 R	71.0%	21.2%	77.0%	23.0%
PASSAIC	69,599	43,384	11,644	14,571	31,740 R	62.3%	16.7%	78.8%	21.2%
SALEM	11,657	8,027	3,206	424	4,821 R	68.9%	27.5%	71.5%	28.5%
SOMERSET	18,260	12,986	4,143	1,131	8,843 R	71.1%	22.7%	75.8%	24.2%
SUSSEX	10,298	6,319	3,632	347	2,687 R	61.4%	35.3%	63.5%	36.5%
UNION	74,000	50,356	14,738	8,906	35,618 R	68.0%	19.9%	77.4%	22.6%
WARREN	15,844	9,606	5,186	1,052	4,420 R	60.6%	32.7%	64.9%	35.1%
TOTAL	1,088,054	676,277	298,043	113,734	378,234 R	62.2%	27.4%	69.4%	30.6%

NEW JERSEY

PRESIDENT 1928

County	Total Vote	Republican	Democratic	Other	Rep.-Dem. Plurality	Percentage Total Vote Rep.	Dem.	Major Vote Rep.	Dem.
ATLANTIC	56,465	37,238	19,152	75	18,086 R	65.9%	33.9%	66.0%	34.0%
BERGEN	140,067	89,105	50,373	589	38,732 R	63.6%	36.0%	63.9%	36.1%
BURLINGTON	41,294	30,224	10,972	98	19,252 R	73.2%	26.6%	73.4%	26.6%
CAMDEN	108,228	75,517	32,151	560	43,366 R	69.8%	29.7%	70.1%	29.9%
CAPE MAY	15,978	12,207	3,731	40	8,476 R	76.4%	23.4%	76.6%	23.4%
CUMBERLAND	30,699	23,921	6,694	84	17,227 R	77.9%	21.8%	78.1%	21.9%
ESSEX	288,514	168,856	118,268	1,390	50,588 R	58.5%	41.0%	58.8%	41.2%
GLOUCESTER	32,302	25,627	6,594	81	19,033 R	79.3%	20.4%	79.5%	20.5%
HUDSON	254,071	99,972	153,009	1,090	53,037 D	39.3%	60.2%	39.5%	60.5%
HUNTERDON	16,076	11,820	4,225	31	7,595 R	73.5%	26.3%	73.7%	26.3%
MERCER	69,338	41,056	27,908	374	13,148 R	59.2%	40.2%	59.5%	40.5%
MIDDLESEX	73,950	38,714	34,908	328	3,806 R	52.4%	47.2%	52.6%	47.4%
MONMOUTH	71,454	47,046	24,286	122	22,760 R	65.8%	34.0%	66.0%	34.0%
MORRIS	48,559	33,189	15,188	182	18,001 R	68.3%	31.3%	68.6%	31.4%
OCEAN	16,807	12,301	4,452	54	7,849 R	73.2%	26.5%	73.4%	26.6%
PASSAIC	105,834	57,708	47,167	959	10,541 R	54.5%	44.6%	55.0%	45.0%
SALEM	15,360	12,323	3,001	36	9,322 R	80.2%	19.5%	80.4%	19.6%
SOMERSET	24,580	16,386	8,120	74	8,266 R	66.7%	33.0%	66.9%	33.1%
SUSSEX	12,032	8,964	3,043	25	5,921 R	74.5%	25.3%	74.7%	25.3%
UNION	106,092	68,119	37,476	497	30,643 R	64.2%	35.3%	64.5%	35.5%
WARREN	20,495	14,992	5,444	59	9,548 R	73.1%	26.6%	73.4%	26.6%
TOTAL	1,549,381	926,050	616,517	6,814	309,533 R	59.8%	39.8%	60.0%	40.0%

PRESIDENT 1932

County	Total Vote	Republican	Democratic	Other	Rep.-Dem. Plurality	Percentage Total Vote Rep.	Dem.	Major Vote Rep.	Dem.
ATLANTIC	60,261	31,264	28,071	926	3,193 R	51.9%	46.6%	52.7%	47.3%
BERGEN	165,743	86,885	73,921	4,937	12,964 R	52.4%	44.6%	54.0%	46.0%
BURLINGTON	40,629	23,623	15,824	1,182	7,799 R	58.1%	38.9%	59.9%	40.1%
CAMDEN	109,847	55,856	48,825	5,166	7,031 R	50.8%	44.4%	53.4%	46.6%
CAPE MAY	17,482	10,112	7,160	210	2,952 R	57.8%	41.0%	58.5%	41.5%
CUMBERLAND	29,971	16,668	12,371	932	4,297 R	55.6%	41.3%	57.4%	42.6%
ESSEX	290,772	149,630	132,666	8,476	16,964 R	51.5%	45.6%	53.0%	47.0%
GLOUCESTER	33,561	18,782	13,817	962	4,965 R	56.0%	41.2%	57.6%	42.4%
HUDSON	257,019	66,937	184,676	5,406	117,739 D	26.0%	71.9%	26.6%	73.4%
HUNTERDON	16,326	8,476	7,531	319	945 R	51.9%	46.1%	53.0%	47.0%
MERCER	66,879	33,715	30,284	2,880	3,431 R	50.4%	45.3%	52.7%	47.3%
MIDDLESEX	80,781	32,673	45,997	2,111	13,324 D	40.4%	56.9%	41.5%	58.5%
MONMOUTH	76,741	40,467	35,219	1,055	5,248 R	52.7%	45.9%	53.5%	46.5%
MORRIS	53,202	31,481	20,117	1,604	11,364 R	59.2%	37.8%	61.0%	39.0%
OCEAN	18,460	10,513	7,508	439	3,005 R	57.0%	40.7%	58.3%	41.7%
PASSAIC	109,404	49,218	54,576	5,610	5,358 D	45.0%	49.9%	47.4%	52.6%
SALEM	17,425	9,870	7,357	198	2,513 R	56.6%	42.2%	57.3%	42.7%
SOMERSET	28,273	15,317	12,345	611	2,972 R	54.2%	43.7%	55.4%	44.6%
SUSSEX	13,408	7,130	6,136	142	994 R	53.2%	45.8%	53.7%	46.3%
UNION	122,961	67,512	51,357	4,092	16,155 R	54.9%	41.8%	56.8%	43.2%
WARREN	20,355	9,277	10,636	442	1,359 D	45.6%	52.3%	46.6%	53.4%
TOTAL	1,630,063	775,684	806,630	47,749	30,946 D	47.6%	49.5%	49.0%	51.0%

NEW JERSEY

PRESIDENT 1936

County	Total Vote	Republican	Democratic	Other	Rep.-Dem. Plurality	Total Vote Rep.	Total Vote Dem.	Major Vote Rep.	Major Vote Dem.
ATLANTIC	64,688	24,680	39,605	403	14,925 D	38.2%	61.2%	38.4%	61.6%
BERGEN	181,878	89,628	91,107	1,143	1,479 D	49.3%	50.1%	49.6%	50.4%
BURLINGTON	45,159	18,644	26,095	420	7,451 D	41.3%	57.8%	41.7%	58.3%
CAMDEN	123,742	35,874	86,300	1,568	50,426 D	29.0%	69.7%	29.4%	70.6%
CAPE MAY	17,952	8,531	9,363	58	832 D	47.5%	52.2%	47.7%	52.3%
CUMBERLAND	35,292	14,500	20,492	300	5,992 D	41.1%	58.1%	41.4%	58.6%
ESSEX	319,441	140,991	174,857	3,593	33,866 D	44.1%	54.7%	44.6%	55.4%
GLOUCESTER	36,622	15,813	20,516	293	4,703 D	43.2%	56.0%	43.5%	56.5%
HUDSON	300,559	65,110	233,390	2,059	168,280 D	21.7%	77.7%	21.8%	78.2%
HUNTERDON	18,409	8,832	9,526	51	694 D	48.0%	51.7%	48.1%	51.9%
MERCER	77,564	29,283	47,702	579	18,419 D	37.8%	61.5%	38.0%	62.0%
MIDDLESEX	95,340	32,959	61,679	702	28,720 D	34.6%	64.7%	34.8%	65.2%
MONMOUTH	80,767	41,460	38,914	393	2,546 R	51.3%	48.2%	51.6%	48.4%
MORRIS	57,943	32,365	24,978	600	7,387 R	55.9%	43.1%	56.4%	43.6%
OCEAN	21,372	11,293	9,889	190	1,404 R	52.8%	46.3%	53.3%	46.7%
PASSAIC	122,190	49,046	71,384	1,760	22,338 D	40.1%	58.4%	40.7%	59.3%
SALEM	19,402	7,671	11,614	117	3,943 D	39.5%	59.9%	39.8%	60.2%
SOMERSET	31,887	15,806	15,987	94	181 D	49.6%	50.1%	49.7%	50.3%
SUSSEX	14,861	7,945	6,862	54	1,083 R	53.5%	46.2%	53.7%	46.3%
UNION	132,097	59,553	70,813	1,731	11,260 D	45.1%	53.6%	45.7%	54.3%
WARREN	21,957	9,437	12,476	44	3,039 D	43.0%	56.8%	43.1%	56.9%
TOTAL	1,820,437	720,322	1,083,850	16,265	363,528 D	39.6%	59.5%	39.9%	60.1%

PRESIDENT 1940

County	Total Vote	Republican	Democratic	Other	Rep.-Dem. Plurality	Total Vote Rep.	Total Vote Dem.	Major Vote Rep.	Major Vote Dem.
ATLANTIC	66,798	30,551	36,155	92	5,604 D	45.7%	54.1%	45.8%	54.2%
BERGEN	208,823	131,588	76,541	694	55,047 R	63.0%	36.7%	63.2%	36.8%
BURLINGTON	47,878	21,161	26,574	143	5,413 D	44.2%	55.5%	44.3%	55.7%
CAMDEN	128,919	43,480	84,837	602	41,357 D	33.7%	65.8%	33.9%	66.1%
CAPE MAY	17,944	9,429	8,485	30	944 R	52.5%	47.3%	52.6%	47.4%
CUMBERLAND	35,680	16,322	19,251	107	2,929 D	45.7%	54.0%	45.9%	54.1%
ESSEX	344,034	182,124	154,363	7,547	27,761 R	52.9%	44.9%	54.1%	45.9%
GLOUCESTER	38,111	17,674	20,284	153	2,610 D	46.4%	53.2%	46.6%	53.4%
HUDSON	316,508	107,552	208,429	527	100,877 D	34.0%	65.9%	34.0%	66.0%
HUNTERDON	18,203	10,284	7,872	47	2,412 R	56.5%	43.2%	56.6%	43.4%
MERCER	87,533	37,190	50,121	222	12,931 D	42.5%	57.3%	42.6%	57.4%
MIDDLESEX	109,013	41,709	67,140	164	25,431 D	38.3%	61.6%	38.3%	61.7%
MONMOUTH	86,047	49,675	36,298	74	13,377 R	57.7%	42.2%	57.8%	42.2%
MORRIS	64,612	39,720	24,698	194	15,022 R	61.5%	38.2%	61.7%	38.3%
OCEAN	22,182	13,394	8,762	26	4,632 R	60.4%	39.5%	60.5%	39.5%
PASSAIC	135,907	65,523	69,880	504	4,357 D	48.2%	51.4%	48.4%	51.6%
SALEM	20,433	8,132	12,244	57	4,112 D	39.8%	59.9%	39.9%	60.1%
SOMERSET	36,755	20,169	16,490	96	3,679 R	54.9%	44.9%	55.0%	45.0%
SUSSEX	14,984	8,642	6,314	28	2,328 R	57.7%	42.1%	57.8%	42.2%
UNION	152,296	79,962	70,737	1,597	9,225 R	52.5%	46.4%	53.1%	46.9%
WARREN	21,555	10,595	10,929	31	334 D	49.2%	50.7%	49.2%	50.8%
TOTAL	1,972,552	945,475	1,016,808	10,269	71,333 D	47.9%	51.5%	48.2%	51.8%

NEW JERSEY

PRESIDENT 1944

County	Total Vote	Republican	Democratic	Other	Rep.-Dem. Plurality	Total Vote Rep.	Total Vote Dem.	Major Vote Rep.	Major Vote Dem.
ATLANTIC	54,794	25,593	28,972	229	3,379 D	46.7%	52.9%	46.9%	53.1%
BERGEN	219,752	142,836	76,350	566	66,486 R	65.0%	34.7%	65.2%	34.8%
BURLINGTON	41,460	18,765	22,623	72	3,858 D	45.3%	54.6%	45.3%	54.7%
CAMDEN	128,357	42,197	85,691	469	43,494 D	32.9%	66.8%	33.0%	67.0%
CAPE MAY	15,114	8,252	6,835	27	1,417 R	54.6%	45.2%	54.7%	45.3%
CUMBERLAND	30,218	14,477	15,674	67	1,197 D	47.9%	51.9%	48.0%	52.0%
ESSEX	360,742	178,989	174,320	7,433	4,669 R	49.6%	48.3%	50.7%	49.3%
GLOUCESTER	34,555	16,684	17,758	113	1,074 D	48.3%	51.4%	48.4%	51.6%
HUDSON	309,135	117,087	191,354	694	74,267 D	37.9%	61.9%	38.0%	62.0%
HUNTERDON	16,652	9,843	6,774	35	3,069 R	59.1%	40.7%	59.2%	40.8%
MERCER	89,371	36,844	52,383	144	15,539 D	41.2%	58.6%	41.3%	58.7%
MIDDLESEX	107,378	45,232	60,504	1,642	15,272 D	42.1%	56.3%	42.8%	57.2%
MONMOUTH	84,122	49,349	34,720	53	14,629 R	58.7%	41.3%	58.7%	41.3%
MORRIS	61,372	39,732	21,454	186	18,278 R	64.7%	35.0%	64.9%	35.1%
OCEAN	21,032	13,317	7,683	32	5,634 R	63.3%	36.5%	63.4%	36.6%
PASSAIC	137,182	67,856	68,737	589	881 D	49.5%	50.1%	49.7%	50.3%
SALEM	18,310	7,942	10,345	23	2,403 D	43.4%	56.5%	43.4%	56.6%
SOMERSET	34,770	20,266	14,467	37	5,799 R	58.3%	41.6%	58.3%	41.7%
SUSSEX	14,066	8,817	5,237	12	3,580 R	62.7%	37.2%	62.7%	37.3%
UNION	164,625	86,543	75,969	2,113	10,574 R	52.6%	46.1%	53.3%	46.7%
WARREN	20,754	10,714	10,024	16	690 R	51.6%	48.3%	51.7%	48.3%
TOTAL	1,963,761	961,335	987,874	14,552	26,539 D	49.0%	50.3%	49.3%	50.7%

PRESIDENT 1948

County	Total Vote	Republican	Democratic	Other	Rep.-Dem. Plurality	Total Vote Rep.	Total Vote Dem.	Major Vote Rep.	Major Vote Dem.
ATLANTIC	58,071	31,608	25,313	1,150	6,295 R	54.4%	43.6%	55.5%	44.5%
BERGEN	217,131	142,657	69,132	5,342	73,525 R	65.7%	31.8%	67.4%	32.6%
BURLINGTON	42,432	21,183	20,801	448	382 R	49.9%	49.0%	50.5%	49.5%
CAMDEN	121,132	51,977	66,388	2,767	14,411 D	42.9%	54.8%	43.9%	56.1%
CAPE MAY	17,417	11,227	6,031	159	5,196 R	64.5%	34.6%	65.1%	34.9%
CUMBERLAND	32,313	16,556	15,195	562	1,361 R	51.2%	47.0%	52.1%	47.9%
ESSEX	343,567	166,963	155,468	21,136	11,495 R	48.6%	45.3%	51.8%	48.2%
GLOUCESTER	35,765	19,477	15,785	503	3,692 R	54.5%	44.1%	55.2%	44.8%
HUDSON	304,653	111,113	182,979	10,561	71,866 D	36.5%	60.1%	37.8%	62.2%
HUNTERDON	17,509	10,654	6,515	340	4,139 R	60.8%	37.2%	62.1%	37.9%
MERCER	89,436	37,794	49,690	1,952	11,896 D	42.3%	55.6%	43.2%	56.8%
MIDDLESEX	116,210	49,810	61,634	4,766	11,824 D	42.8%	53.0%	44.7%	55.3%
MONMOUTH	85,033	52,908	30,507	1,618	22,401 R	62.2%	35.9%	63.4%	36.6%
MORRIS	62,574	42,558	18,864	1,152	23,694 R	68.0%	30.1%	69.3%	30.7%
OCEAN	23,767	16,740	6,366	661	10,374 R	70.4%	26.8%	72.4%	27.6%
PASSAIC	130,430	59,675	60,147	10,608	472 D	45.8%	46.1%	49.8%	50.2%
SALEM	18,418	8,961	9,278	179	317 D	48.7%	50.4%	49.1%	50.9%
SOMERSET	36,862	22,034	14,104	724	7,930 R	59.8%	38.3%	61.0%	39.0%
SUSSEX	13,939	9,269	4,527	143	4,742 R	66.5%	32.5%	67.2%	32.8%
UNION	162,180	87,402	66,759	8,019	20,643 R	53.9%	41.2%	56.7%	43.3%
WARREN	20,716	10,558	9,972	186	586 R	51.0%	48.1%	51.4%	48.6%
TOTAL	1,949,555	981,124	895,455	72,976	85,669 R	50.3%	45.9%	52.3%	47.7%

NEW JERSEY

PRESIDENT 1952

County	Total Vote	Republican	Democratic	Other	Rep.-Dem. Plurality	Total Vote Rep.	Dem.	Major Vote Rep.	Dem.
ATLANTIC	69,375	40,259	28,953	163	11,306 R	58.0%	41.7%	58.2%	41.8%
BERGEN	307,502	212,842	93,373	1,287	119,469 R	69.2%	30.4%	69.5%	30.5%
BURLINGTON	55,744	30,202	25,482	60	4,720 R	54.2%	45.7%	54.2%	45.8%
CAMDEN	154,541	72,335	81,444	762	9,109 D	46.8%	52.7%	47.0%	53.0%
CAPE MAY	22,209	15,218	6,984	7	8,234 R	68.5%	31.4%	68.5%	31.5%
CUMBERLAND	40,859	21,819	18,929	111	2,890 R	53.4%	46.3%	53.5%	46.5%
ESSEX	407,635	219,863	180,501	7,271	39,362 R	53.9%	44.3%	54.9%	45.1%
GLOUCESTER	45,737	25,103	20,536	98	4,567 R	54.9%	44.9%	55.0%	45.0%
HUDSON	324,280	153,583	161,469	9,228	7,886 D	47.4%	49.8%	48.7%	51.3%
HUNTERDON	21,400	14,439	6,878	83	7,561 R	67.5%	32.1%	67.7%	32.3%
MERCER	108,662	50,423	57,751	488	7,328 D	46.4%	53.1%	46.6%	53.4%
MIDDLESEX	146,224	73,577	70,234	2,413	3,343 R	50.3%	48.0%	51.2%	48.8%
MONMOUTH	110,491	73,228	37,006	257	36,222 R	66.3%	33.5%	66.4%	33.6%
MORRIS	86,629	62,847	23,662	120	39,185 R	72.5%	27.3%	72.6%	27.4%
OCEAN	32,267	23,490	8,660	117	14,830 R	72.8%	26.8%	73.1%	26.9%
PASSAIC	164,190	89,083	70,727	4,380	18,356 R	54.3%	43.1%	55.7%	44.3%
SALEM	23,442	12,026	11,362	54	664 R	51.3%	48.5%	51.4%	48.6%
SOMERSET	49,320	31,239	18,007	74	13,232 R	63.3%	36.5%	63.4%	36.6%
SUSSEX	17,963	13,415	4,534	14	8,881 R	74.7%	25.2%	74.7%	25.3%
UNION	203,245	122,885	78,336	2,024	44,549 R	60.5%	38.5%	61.1%	38.9%
WARREN	26,839	15,737	11,074	28	4,663 R	58.6%	41.3%	58.7%	41.3%
TOTAL	2,413,554	1,373,613	1,015,902	29,039	357,711 R	56.8%	42.0%	57.5%	42.5%

PRESIDENT 1956

County	Total Vote	Republican	Democratic	Other	Rep.-Dem. Plurality	Total Vote Rep.	Dem.	Major Vote Rep.	Dem.
ATLANTIC	68,038	44,698	21,668	1,672	23,030 R	65.7%	31.8%	67.4%	32.6%
BERGEN	338,113	254,334	82,169	1,610	172,165 R	75.2%	24.3%	75.6%	24.4%
BURLINGTON	62,471	38,145	24,258	68	13,887 R	61.1%	38.8%	61.1%	38.9%
CAMDEN	160,953	85,067	75,152	734	9,915 R	52.9%	46.7%	53.1%	46.9%
CAPE MAY	22,815	16,887	5,897	31	10,990 R	74.0%	25.8%	74.1%	25.9%
CUMBERLAND	41,444	24,067	17,309	68	6,758 R	58.1%	41.8%	58.2%	41.8%
ESSEX	388,253	234,682	146,313	7,258	88,369 R	60.4%	37.7%	61.6%	38.4%
GLOUCESTER	50,728	30,646	20,007	75	10,639 R	60.4%	39.4%	60.5%	39.5%
HUDSON	297,585	183,919	107,098	6,568	76,821 R	61.8%	36.0%	63.2%	36.8%
HUNTERDON	22,193	16,150	5,957	86	10,193 R	72.8%	26.8%	73.1%	26.9%
MERCER	109,105	56,029	52,684	392	3,345 R	51.4%	48.3%	51.5%	48.5%
MIDDLESEX	165,286	100,071	64,538	677	35,533 R	60.5%	39.0%	60.8%	39.2%
MONMOUTH	116,751	83,828	32,329	594	51,499 R	71.8%	27.7%	72.2%	27.8%
MORRIS	96,469	76,571	19,503	395	57,068 R	79.4%	20.2%	79.7%	20.3%
OCEAN	37,479	28,033	9,367	79	18,666 R	74.8%	25.0%	75.0%	25.0%
PASSAIC	166,676	101,182	61,859	3,635	39,323 R	60.7%	37.1%	62.1%	37.9%
SALEM	23,423	14,091	9,276	56	4,815 R	60.2%	39.6%	60.3%	39.7%
SOMERSET	52,789	37,930	14,529	330	23,401 R	71.9%	27.5%	72.3%	27.7%
SUSSEX	19,659	15,867	3,756	46	12,111 R	80.7%	19.1%	80.9%	19.1%
UNION	216,414	146,228	67,540	2,646	78,688 R	67.6%	31.2%	68.4%	31.6%
WARREN	27,658	18,517	9,128	13	9,389 R	66.9%	33.0%	67.0%	33.0%
TOTAL	2,484,312	1,605,942	850,337	27,033	756,605 R	64.7%	34.2%	65.4%	34.6%

NEW JERSEY

PRESIDENT 1960

County	Total Vote	Republican	Democratic	Other	Rep.-Dem. Plurality	Total Vote Rep.	Total Vote Dem.	Major Vote Rep.	Major Vote Dem.
ATLANTIC	76,969	39,158	36,129	1,682	3,029 R	50.9%	46.9%	52.0%	48.0%
BERGEN	381,808	224,969	156,165	674	68,804 R	58.9%	40.9%	59.0%	41.0%
BURLINGTON	81,539	42,112	39,321	106	2,791 R	51.6%	48.2%	51.7%	48.3%
CAMDEN	186,515	84,066	102,083	366	18,017 D	45.1%	54.7%	45.2%	54.8%
CAPE MAY	26,222	16,076	10,137	9	5,939 R	61.3%	38.7%	61.3%	38.7%
CUMBERLAND	44,512	21,283	23,199	30	1,916 D	47.8%	52.1%	47.8%	52.2%
ESSEX	393,623	167,848	217,878	7,897	50,030 D	42.6%	55.4%	43.5%	56.5%
GLOUCESTER	62,259	32,474	29,752	33	2,722 R	52.2%	47.8%	52.2%	47.8%
HUDSON	291,292	113,972	174,754	2,566	60,782 D	39.1%	60.0%	39.5%	60.5%
HUNTERDON	24,731	15,842	8,863	26	6,979 R	64.1%	35.8%	64.1%	35.9%
MERCER	121,269	46,924	74,166	179	27,242 D	38.7%	61.2%	38.8%	61.2%
MIDDLESEX	199,556	83,025	116,095	436	33,070 D	41.6%	58.2%	41.7%	58.3%
MONMOUTH	144,060	81,382	62,434	244	18,948 R	56.5%	43.3%	56.6%	43.4%
MORRIS	117,883	75,039	42,698	146	32,341 R	63.7%	36.2%	63.7%	36.3%
OCEAN	51,898	31,430	20,113	355	11,317 R	60.6%	38.8%	61.0%	39.0%
PASSAIC	179,402	80,853	90,950	7,599	10,097 D	45.1%	50.7%	47.1%	52.9%
SALEM	26,607	14,192	12,394	21	1,798 R	53.3%	46.6%	53.4%	46.6%
SOMERSET	64,863	36,200	28,489	174	7,711 R	55.8%	43.9%	56.0%	44.0%
SUSSEX	23,642	16,362	7,269	11	9,093 R	69.2%	30.7%	69.2%	30.8%
UNION	245,008	123,224	119,986	1,798	3,238 R	50.3%	49.0%	50.7%	49.3%
WARREN	29,453	16,893	12,540	20	4,353 R	57.4%	42.6%	57.4%	42.6%
TOTAL	2,773,111	1,363,324	1,385,415	24,372	22,091 D	49.2%	50.0%	49.6%	50.4%

PRESIDENT 1964

County	Total Vote	Republican	Democratic	Other	Rep.-Dem. Plurality	Total Vote Rep.	Total Vote Dem.	Major Vote Rep.	Major Vote Dem.
ATLANTIC	78,019	25,626	50,945	1,448	25,319 D	32.8%	65.3%	33.5%	66.5%
BERGEN	394,358	158,230	235,409	719	77,179 D	40.1%	59.7%	40.2%	59.8%
BURLINGTON	88,945	31,215	57,638	92	26,423 D	35.1%	64.8%	35.1%	64.9%
CAMDEN	185,761	60,844	124,620	297	63,776 D	32.8%	67.1%	32.8%	67.2%
CAPE MAY	26,380	11,390	14,943	47	3,553 D	43.2%	56.6%	43.3%	56.7%
CUMBERLAND	46,215	12,611	33,593	11	20,982 D	27.3%	72.7%	27.3%	72.7%
ESSEX	396,477	116,172	277,042	3,263	160,870 D	29.3%	69.9%	29.5%	70.5%
GLOUCESTER	64,052	23,702	40,305	45	16,603 D	37.0%	62.9%	37.0%	63.0%
HUDSON	272,009	69,515	200,051	2,443	130,536 D	25.6%	73.5%	25.8%	74.2%
HUNTERDON	25,283	10,173	15,091	19	4,918 D	40.2%	59.7%	40.3%	59.7%
MERCER	122,214	35,081	86,985	148	51,904 D	28.7%	71.2%	28.7%	71.3%
MIDDLESEX	215,618	63,370	151,196	1,052	87,826 D	29.4%	70.1%	29.5%	70.5%
MONMOUTH	157,055	61,367	95,320	368	33,993 D	39.1%	60.7%	39.2%	60.8%
MORRIS	128,913	55,024	73,684	205	18,660 D	42.7%	57.2%	42.8%	57.2%
OCEAN	63,714	25,985	36,892	837	10,907 D	40.8%	57.9%	41.3%	58.7%
PASSAIC	179,699	63,114	113,919	2,666	50,805 D	35.1%	63.4%	35.7%	64.3%
SALEM	26,545	8,682	17,846	17	9,164 D	32.7%	67.2%	32.7%	67.3%
SOMERSET	72,270	28,416	43,659	195	15,243 D	39.3%	60.4%	39.4%	60.6%
SUSSEX	26,197	11,836	14,349	12	2,513 D	45.2%	54.8%	45.2%	54.8%
UNION	249,347	82,999	164,989	1,359	81,990 D	33.3%	66.2%	33.5%	66.5%
WARREN	28,592	8,822	19,755	15	10,933 D	30.9%	69.1%	30.9%	69.1%
TOTAL	2,847,663	964,174	1,868,231	15,258	904,057 D	33.9%	65.6%	34.0%	66.0%

NEW JERSEY

OTHER VOTE COMPOSITION:

1920   27,385 Socialist; 4,895 Prohibition; 2,264 Farmer-Labor; 1,010 Socialist Labor; 603 Single Tax.

1924   109,028 Progressive; 1,660 Prohibition; 1,560 Communist; 853 Socialist Labor; 368 American; 265 Commonwealth Land.

1928   4,897 Socialist; 1,257 Communist; 500 Socialist Labor; 160 Prohibition.

1932   42,998 Socialist; 2,915 Communist; 1,062 Socialist Labor; 774 Prohibition.

1936   9,407 Union; 3,931 Socialist; 1,639 Communist; 926 Prohibition; 362 Socialist Labor.

1940   6,508 Communist; 2,433 Socialist; 873 Prohibition; 455 Socialist Labor.

1944   6,939 Socialist Labor; 4,255 Prohibition; 3,358 Socialist.

1948   42,683 Progressive; 10,593 Prohibition; 10,521 Socialist; 5,825 Socialist Workers; 3,354 Socialist Labor.

1952   8,593 Socialist; 5,815 Socialist Labor; 5,589 Progressive; 4,203 Poor Man's Party; 3,850 Socialist Workers; 989 Prohibition.

1956   9,147 Prohibition; 6,736 Socialist Labor; 5,317 States Rights; 4,004 Socialist Workers; 1,829 American Third Party.

1960   11,402 Socialist Workers; 8,708 Conservative (Lee); 4,262 Socialist Labor.

1964   8,183 Socialist Workers; 7,075 Socialist Labor.

SPECIAL CASES:

1920   In this election, and in all elections through 1940, state totals are for the highest elector for each party, but the individual county figures are the average elector vote, as reported by the state canvass. Adding the individual county figures will thus produce slightly smaller totals than those on the state total line.

1924   See note above. Progressive candidates ran second in one county.

1928   See note above.

1932   See note above.

1936   See note above.

1940   See note above. In this election, other party county-by-county figures exceed the state total, since the state canvass reported an average elector vote for several minor parties greater than the vote cast for the highest elector candidates of these parties.

NEW MEXICO

PRESIDENT 1920

County	Total Vote	Republican	Democratic	Other	Rep.-Dem. Plurality	Total Vote Rep.	Total Vote Dem.	Major Vote Rep.	Major Vote Dem.
BERNALILLO	9,833	4,969	4,808	56	161 R	50.5%	48.9%	50.8%	49.2%
CATRON									
CHAVES	3,876	1,765	2,080	31	315 D	45.5%	53.7%	45.9%	54.1%
COLFAX	6,107	3,351	2,709	47	642 R	54.9%	44.4%	55.3%	44.7%
CURRY	3,179	884	2,143	152	1,259 D	27.8%	67.4%	29.2%	70.8%
DE BACA	1,121	412	693	16	281 D	36.8%	61.8%	37.3%	62.7%
DONA ANA	3,964	2,627	1,318	19	1,309 R	66.3%	33.2%	66.6%	33.4%
EDDY	2,624	982	1,611	31	629 D	37.4%	61.4%	37.9%	62.1%
GRANT	4,147	2,230	1,879	38	351 R	53.8%	45.3%	54.3%	45.7%
GUADALUPE	2,840	1,599	1,224	17	375 R	56.3%	43.1%	56.6%	43.4%
HARDING									
HIDALGO	1,003	443	551	9	108 D	44.2%	54.9%	44.6%	55.4%
LEA	1,011	255	733	23	478 D	25.2%	72.5%	25.8%	74.2%
LINCOLN	2,540	1,456	1,047	37	409 R	57.3%	41.2%	58.2%	41.8%
LOS ALAMOS									
LUNA	1,868	834	1,000	34	166 D	44.6%	53.5%	45.5%	54.5%
MCKINLEY	2,541	1,525	989	27	536 R	60.0%	38.9%	60.7%	39.3%
MORA	4,685	2,478	2,179	28	299 R	52.9%	46.5%	53.2%	46.8%
OTERO	2,393	1,229	1,095	69	134 R	51.4%	45.8%	52.9%	47.1%
QUAY	3,098	1,213	1,813	72	600 D	39.2%	58.5%	40.1%	59.9%
RIO ARRIBA	6,042	3,986	2,056		1,930 R	66.0%	34.0%	66.0%	34.0%
ROOSEVELT	1,817	571	1,178	68	607 D	31.4%	64.8%	32.6%	67.4%
SANDOVAL	2,078	1,194	884		310 R	57.5%	42.5%	57.5%	42.5%
SAN JUAN	1,845	985	831	29	154 R	53.4%	45.0%	54.2%	45.8%
SAN MIGUEL	9,525	5,535	3,990		1,545 R	58.1%	41.9%	58.1%	41.9%
SANTA FE	4,787	3,060	1,700	27	1,360 R	63.9%	35.5%	64.3%	35.7%
SIERRA	1,518	862	642	14	220 R	56.8%	42.3%	57.3%	42.7%
SOCORRO	4,987	3,150	1,807	30	1,343 R	63.2%	36.2%	63.5%	36.5%
TAOS	3,884	2,519	1,359	6	1,160 R	64.9%	35.0%	65.0%	35.0%
TORRANCE	2,905	1,751	1,125	29	626 R	60.3%	38.7%	60.9%	39.1%
UNION	5,388	2,930	2,273	185	657 R	54.4%	42.2%	56.3%	43.7%
VALENCIA	3,806	2,839	951	16	1,888 R	74.6%	25.0%	74.9%	25.1%
TOTAL	105,412	57,634	46,668	1,110	10,966 R	54.7%	44.3%	55.3%	44.7%

PRESIDENT 1924

County	Total Vote	Republican	Democratic	Other	Rep.-Dem. Plurality	Total Vote Rep.	Total Vote Dem.	Major Vote Rep.	Major Vote Dem.
BERNALILLO	14,284	7,078	6,023	1,183	1,055 R	49.6%	42.2%	54.0%	46.0%
CATRON	1,055	499	418	138	81 R	47.3%	39.6%	54.4%	45.6%
CHAVES	3,855	1,519	2,168	168	649 D	39.4%	56.2%	41.2%	58.8%
COLFAX	7,307	3,512	3,067	728	445 R	48.1%	42.0%	53.4%	46.6%
CURRY	3,255	669	1,738	848	1,069 D	20.6%	53.4%	27.8%	72.2%
DE BACA	930	270	574	86	304 D	29.0%	61.7%	32.0%	68.0%
DONA ANA	4,819	2,823	1,775	221	1,048 R	58.6%	36.8%	61.4%	38.6%
EDDY	2,320	658	1,524	138	866 D	28.4%	65.7%	30.2%	69.8%
GRANT	4,436	1,756	2,085	595	329 D	39.6%	47.0%	45.7%	54.3%
GUADALUPE	2,564	1,329	1,056	179	273 R	51.8%	41.2%	55.7%	44.3%
HARDING	1,711	721	714	276	7 R	42.1%	41.7%	50.2%	49.8%
HIDALGO	926	261	476	189	215 D	28.2%	51.4%	35.4%	64.6%
LEA	736	138	552	46	414 D	18.8%	75.0%	20.0%	80.0%
LINCOLN	2,216	1,087	837	292	250 R	49.1%	37.8%	56.5%	43.5%
LOS ALAMOS									
LUNA	1,638	709	596	333	113 R	43.3%	36.4%	54.3%	45.7%
MCKINLEY	3,226	1,653	1,150	423	503 R	51.2%	35.6%	59.0%	41.0%
MORA	4,316	2,197	2,087	32	110 R	50.9%	48.4%	51.3%	48.7%
OTERO	2,021	832	886	303	54 D	41.2%	43.8%	48.4%	51.6%
QUAY	3,057	851	1,548	658	697 D	27.8%	50.6%	35.5%	64.5%
RIO ARRIBA	6,591	3,707	2,734	150	973 R	56.2%	41.5%	57.6%	42.4%
ROOSEVELT	2,037	398	1,340	299	942 D	19.5%	65.7%	22.9%	77.1%
SANDOVAL	2,712	1,587	1,096	29	491 R	58.5%	40.4%	59.2%	40.8%
SAN JUAN	1,981	889	819	273	70 R	44.9%	41.3%	52.0%	48.0%
SAN MIGUEL	7,702	3,894	3,543	265	351 R	50.6%	46.0%	52.4%	47.6%
SANTA FE	6,791	4,010	2,602	179	1,408 R	59.0%	38.3%	60.6%	39.4%
SIERRA	1,312	632	546	134	86 R	48.2%	41.6%	53.7%	46.3%
SOCORRO	3,742	2,332	1,251	159	1,081 R	62.3%	33.4%	65.1%	34.9%
TAOS	4,209	2,470	1,655	84	815 R	58.7%	39.3%	59.9%	40.1%
TORRANCE	3,255	1,666	1,269	320	397 R	51.2%	39.0%	56.8%	43.2%
UNION	3,746	1,415	1,735	596	320 D	37.8%	46.3%	44.9%	55.1%
VALENCIA	4,080	3,183	678	219	2,505 R	78.0%	16.6%	82.4%	17.6%
TOTAL	112,830	54,745	48,542	9,543	6,203 R	48.5%	43.0%	53.0%	47.0%

NEW MEXICO

PRESIDENT 1928

County	Total Vote	Republican	Democratic	Other	Rep.-Dem. Plurality	Total Vote Rep.	Total Vote Dem.	Major Vote Rep.	Major Vote Dem.
BERNALILLO	15,311	8,725	6,572	14	2,153 R	57.0%	42.9%	57.0%	43.0%
CATRON	1,195	774	420	1	354 R	64.8%	35.1%	64.8%	35.2%
CHAVES	4,496	3,124	1,364	8	1,760 R	69.5%	30.3%	69.6%	30.4%
COLFAX	6,936	3,904	3,022	10	882 R	56.3%	43.6%	56.4%	43.6%
CURRY	3,504	1,968	1,530	6	438 R	56.2%	43.7%	56.3%	43.7%
DE BACA	991	474	514	3	40 D	47.8%	51.9%	48.0%	52.0%
DONA ANA	5,318	3,141	2,169	8	972 R	59.1%	40.8%	59.2%	40.8%
EDDY	2,833	1,618	1,212	3	406 R	57.1%	42.8%	57.2%	42.8%
GRANT	4,060	2,058	1,994	8	64 R	50.7%	49.1%	50.8%	49.2%
GUADALUPE	2,811	1,718	1,093		625 R	61.1%	38.9%	61.1%	38.9%
HARDING	1,644	916	726	2	190 R	55.7%	44.2%	55.8%	44.2%
HIDALGO	1,071	561	509	1	52 R	52.4%	47.5%	52.4%	47.6%
LEA	1,014	537	474	3	63 R	53.0%	46.7%	53.1%	46.7%
LINCOLN	2,315	1,489	821	5	668 R	64.3%	35.5%	64.5%	35.5%
LUNA	1,514	860	647	7	213 R	56.8%	42.7%	57.1%	42.9%
MCKINLEY	3,335	2,075	1,247	13	828 R	62.2%	37.4%	62.5%	37.5%
MORA	3,797	1,998	1,799		199 R	52.6%	47.4%	52.6%	47.4%
OTERO	2,408	1,250	1,148	10	102 R	51.9%	47.7%	52.1%	47.9%
QUAY	3,215	1,616	1,594	5	22 R	50.3%	49.6%	50.3%	49.7%
RIO ARRIBA	6,557	4,109	2,444	4	1,665 R	62.7%	37.3%	62.7%	37.3%
ROOSEVELT	2,264	1,157	1,098	9	59 R	51.1%	48.5%	51.3%	48.7%
SANDOVAL	2,860	1,700	1,159	1	541 R	59.4%	40.5%	59.5%	40.5%
SAN JUAN	2,164	1,436	724	4	712 R	66.4%	33.5%	66.5%	33.5%
SAN MIGUEL	8,748	5,184	3,560	4	1,624 R	59.3%	40.7%	59.3%	40.7%
SANTA FE	7,685	4,630	3,051	4	1,579 R	60.2%	39.7%	60.3%	39.7%
SIERRA	1,424	766	657	1	109 R	53.8%	46.1%	53.8%	46.2%
SOCORRO	3,507	1,940	1,564	3	376 R	55.3%	44.6%	55.4%	44.6%
TAOS	4,284	2,441	1,842	1	599 R	57.0%	43.0%	57.0%	43.0%
TORRANCE	3,034	1,958	1,070	6	888 R	64.5%	35.3%	64.7%	35.3%
UNION	3,400	2,081	1,306	13	775 R	61.2%	38.4%	61.4%	38.6%
VALENCIA	4,382	3,500	881	1	2,619 R	79.9%	20.1%	79.9%	20.1%
TOTAL	118,077	69,708	48,211	158	21,497 R	59.0%	40.8%	59.1%	40.9%

PRESIDENT 1932

County	Total Vote	Republican	Democratic	Other	Rep.-Dem. Plurality	Total Vote Rep.	Total Vote Dem.	Major Vote Rep.	Major Vote Dem.
BERNALILLO	18,243	7,309	10,722	212	3,413 D	40.1%	58.8%	40.5%	59.5%
CATRON	1,608	610	972	26	362 D	37.9%	60.4%	38.6%	61.4%
CHAVES	6,322	1,830	4,257	235	2,427 D	28.9%	67.3%	30.1%	69.9%
COLFAX	7,547	3,214	4,282	51	1,068 D	42.6%	56.7%	42.9%	57.1%
CURRY	5,079	932	3,738	409	2,806 D	18.4%	73.6%	20.0%	80.0%
DE BACA	1,305	264	1,023	18	759 D	20.2%	78.4%	20.5%	79.5%
DONA ANA	7,595	2,354	5,133	108	2,779 D	31.0%	67.6%	31.4%	68.6%
EDDY	4,459	818	3,565	76	2,747 D	18.3%	80.0%	18.7%	81.3%
GRANT	4,795	1,381	3,344	70	1,963 D	28.8%	69.7%	29.2%	70.8%
GUADALUPE	3,542	1,621	1,909	12	288 D	45.8%	53.9%	45.9%	54.1%
HARDING	2,293	779	1,478	36	699 D	34.0%	64.5%	34.5%	65.5%
HIDALGO	1,460	299	1,131	30	832 D	20.5%	77.5%	20.9%	79.1%
LEA	2,756	271	2,371	114	2,100 D	9.8%	86.0%	10.3%	89.7%
LINCOLN	3,413	1,172	2,225	21	1,053 D	34.3%	65.1%	34.5%	65.5%
LUNA	2,285	641	1,605	40	964 D	28.0%	70.2%	28.5%	71.5%
MCKINLEY	3,489	1,373	2,096	20	723 D	39.4%	60.1%	39.6%	60.4%
MORA	4,407	1,444	2,962	1	1,518 D	32.8%	67.2%	32.8%	67.2%
OTERO	3,127	969	2,091	67	1,122 D	31.0%	66.9%	31.7%	68.3%
QUAY	4,077	852	3,058	167	2,206 D	20.9%	75.0%	21.8%	78.2%
RIO ARRIBA	8,229	2,880	5,337	12	2,457 D	35.0%	64.9%	35.0%	65.0%
ROOSEVELT	3,404	475	2,826	103	2,351 D	14.0%	83.0%	14.4%	85.6%
SANDOVAL	3,378	1,562	1,808	8	246 D	46.2%	53.5%	46.4%	53.6%
SAN JUAN	2,635	925	1,506	204	581 D	35.1%	57.2%	38.1%	61.9%
SAN MIGUEL	10,460	5,364	5,076	20	288 R	51.3%	48.5%	51.4%	48.6%
SANTA FE	9,390	3,625	5,739	26	2,114 D	38.6%	61.1%	38.7%	61.3%
SIERRA	2,210	667	1,515	28	848 D	30.2%	68.6%	30.6%	69.4%
SOCORRO	4,438	1,931	2,495	12	564 D	43.5%	56.2%	43.6%	56.4%
TAOS	5,723	2,416	3,277	30	861 D	42.2%	57.3%	42.4%	57.6%
TORRANCE	4,071	1,803	2,202	66	399 D	44.3%	54.1%	45.0%	55.0%
UNION	4,353	1,173	3,117	63	1,944 D	26.9%	71.6%	27.3%	72.7%
VALENCIA	5,507	3,263	2,229	15	1,034 R	59.3%	40.5%	59.4%	40.6%
TOTAL	151,606	54,217	95,089	2,300	40,872 D	35.8%	62.7%	36.3%	63.7%

NEW MEXICO

PRESIDENT 1936

County	Total Vote	Republican	Democratic	Other	Rep.-Dem. Plurality	Percentage Total Vote Rep.	Dem.	Major Vote Rep.	Dem.
BERNALILLO	22,582	7,107	15,305	170	8,198 D	31.5%	67.8%	31.7%	68.3%
CATRON	2,272	798	1,456	18	658 D	35.1%	64.1%	35.4%	64.6%
CHAVES	7,017	2,505	4,394	118	1,889 D	35.7%	62.6%	36.3%	63.7%
COLFAX	7,451	2,745	4,661	45	1,916 D	36.8%	62.6%	37.1%	62.9%
CURRY	5,797	1,023	4,689	85	3,666 D	17.6%	80.9%	17.9%	82.1%
DE BACA	1,460	444	1,010	6	566 D	30.4%	69.2%	30.5%	69.5%
DONA ANA	8,102	2,494	5,544	64	3,050 D	30.8%	68.4%	31.0%	69.0%
EDDY	5,425	1,027	4,349	49	3,322 D	18.9%	80.2%	19.1%	80.9%
GRANT	4,736	1,469	3,215	52	1,746 D	31.0%	67.9%	31.4%	68.6%
GUADALUPE	3,966	1,775	2,187	4	412 D	44.8%	55.1%	44.8%	55.2%
HARDING	2,169	888	1,276	5	388 D	40.9%	58.8%	41.0%	59.0%
HIDALGO	1,459	326	1,115	18	789 D	22.3%	76.4%	22.6%	77.4%
LEA	4,491	549	3,905	37	3,356 D	12.2%	87.0%	12.3%	87.7%
LINCOLN	3,641	1,579	2,021	41	442 D	43.4%	55.5%	43.9%	56.1%
LOS ALAMOS									
LUNA	2,367	806	1,500	61	694 D	34.1%	63.4%	35.0%	65.0%
MCKINLEY	3,944	1,404	2,526	14	1,122 D	35.6%	64.0%	35.7%	64.3%
MORA	4,725	2,259	2,460	6	201 D	47.8%	52.1%	47.9%	52.1%
OTERO	3,355	1,333	1,989	33	656 D	39.7%	59.3%	40.1%	59.9%
QUAY	4,290	816	3,423	51	2,607 D	19.0%	79.8%	19.2%	80.8%
RIO ARRIBA	8,802	4,093	4,691	18	598 D	46.5%	53.3%	46.6%	53.4%
ROOSEVELT	3,855	677	2,951	227	2,274 D	17.6%	76.5%	18.7%	81.3%
SANDOVAL	3,898	1,800	2,094	4	294 D	46.2%	53.7%	46.2%	53.8%
SAN JUAN	2,944	1,345	1,530	69	185 D	45.7%	52.0%	46.8%	53.2%
SAN MIGUEL	10,906	4,697	6,199	10	1,502 D	43.1%	56.8%	43.1%	56.9%
SANTA FE	11,132	4,960	6,145	27	1,185 D	44.6%	55.2%	44.7%	55.3%
SIERRA	2,562	951	1,587	24	636 D	37.1%	61.9%	37.5%	62.5%
SOCORRO	5,023	2,530	2,477	16	53 R	50.4%	49.3%	50.5%	49.5%
TAOS	5,979	2,918	3,051	10	133 D	48.8%	51.0%	48.9%	51.1%
TORRANCE	4,227	1,843	2,346	38	503 D	43.6%	55.5%	44.0%	56.0%
UNION	4,267	1,625	2,605	37	980 D	38.1%	61.0%	38.4%	61.6%
VALENCIA	6,291	2,941	3,336	14	395 D	46.7%	53.0%	46.9%	53.1%
TOTAL	169,135	61,727	106,037	1,371	44,310 D	36.5%	62.7%	36.8%	63.2%

PRESIDENT 1940

County	Total Vote	Republican	Democratic	Other	Rep.-Dem. Plurality	Percentage Total Vote Rep.	Dem.	Major Vote Rep.	Dem.
BERNALILLO	26,461	11,999	14,428	34	2,429 D	45.3%	54.5%	45.4%	54.6%
CATRON	1,988	949	1,039		90 D	47.7%	52.3%	47.7%	52.3%
CHAVES	7,299	2,981	4,304	14	1,323 D	40.8%	59.0%	40.9%	59.1%
COLFAX	7,690	3,452	4,234	4	782 D	44.9%	55.1%	44.9%	55.1%
CURRY	6,319	1,629	4,670	20	3,041 D	25.8%	73.9%	25.9%	74.1%
DE BACA	1,449	479	970		491 D	33.1%	66.9%	33.1%	66.9%
DONA ANA	8,936	3,720	5,208	8	1,488 D	41.6%	58.3%	41.7%	58.3%
EDDY	6,604	1,625	4,968	11	3,343 D	24.6%	75.2%	24.6%	75.4%
GRANT	5,930	2,015	3,914	1	1,899 D	34.0%	66.0%	34.0%	66.0%
GUADALUPE	3,889	1,807	2,082		275 D	46.5%	53.5%	46.5%	53.5%
HARDING	2,011	998	1,004	9	6 D	49.6%	49.9%	49.9%	50.1%
HIDALGO	1,565	516	1,049		533 D	33.0%	67.0%	33.0%	67.0%
LEA	5,592	1,286	4,295	11	3,009 D	23.0%	76.8%	23.0%	77.0%
LINCOLN	3,570	1,794	1,763	13	31 R	50.3%	49.4%	50.4%	49.6%
LOS ALAMOS									
LUNA	2,460	1,066	1,388	6	322 D	43.3%	56.4%	43.4%	56.6%
MCKINLEY	4,232	1,701	2,525	6	824 D	40.2%	59.7%	40.3%	59.7%
MORA	4,401	2,440	1,960	1	480 R	55.5%	44.5%	55.5%	44.5%
OTERO	3,389	1,596	1,788	5	192 D	47.1%	52.8%	47.2%	52.8%
QUAY	4,650	1,413	3,215	22	1,802 D	30.4%	69.1%	30.5%	69.5%
RIO ARRIBA	9,247	4,289	4,952	6	663 D	46.4%	53.6%	46.4%	53.6%
ROOSEVELT	4,590	1,384	3,190	16	1,806 D	30.2%	69.5%	30.3%	69.7%
SANDOVAL	4,051	1,990	2,060	1	70 D	49.1%	50.9%	49.1%	50.9%
SAN JUAN	3,207	1,757	1,445	5	312 R	54.8%	45.1%	54.9%	45.1%
SAN MIGUEL	10,943	4,882	6,054	7	1,172 D	44.6%	55.3%	44.6%	55.4%
SANTA FE	12,770	6,285	6,482	3	197 D	49.2%	50.8%	49.2%	50.8%
SIERRA	2,910	1,372	1,534	4	162 D	47.1%	52.7%	47.2%	52.8%
SOCORRO	5,197	2,703	2,489	5	214 R	52.0%	47.9%	52.1%	47.9%
TAOS	6,810	3,342	3,463	5	121 D	49.1%	50.9%	49.1%	50.9%
TORRANCE	4,439	2,509	1,921	9	588 R	56.5%	43.3%	56.6%	43.4%
UNION	3,899	1,900	1,987	12	87 D	48.7%	51.0%	48.9%	51.1%
VALENCIA	6,760	3,436	3,318	6	118 R	50.8%	49.1%	50.9%	49.1%
TOTAL	183,258	79,315	103,699	244	24,384 D	43.3%	56.6%	43.3%	56.7%

NEW MEXICO

PRESIDENT 1944

County	Total Vote	Republican	Democratic	Other	Rep.-Dem. Plurality	Total Vote Rep.	Total Vote Dem.	Major Vote Rep.	Major Vote Dem.
BERNALILLO	23,904	11,662	12,229	13	557 D	48.8%	51.2%	48.8%	51.2%
CATRON	1,289	699	589	1	110 R	54.2%	45.7%	54.3%	45.7%
CHAVES	6,516	3,149	3,350	17	201 D	48.3%	51.4%	48.5%	51.5%
COLFAX	5,685	2,661	3,017	7	356 D	46.8%	53.1%	46.9%	53.1%
CURRY	5,609	2,326	3,271	12	945 D	41.5%	58.3%	41.6%	58.4%
DE BACA	1,216	554	660	2	106 D	45.6%	54.3%	45.6%	54.4%
DONA ANA	7,327	3,149	4,172	6	1,023 D	43.0%	56.9%	43.0%	57.0%
EDDY	7,327	2,083	5,228	16	3,145 D	28.4%	71.4%	28.5%	71.5%
GRANT	5,446	1,970	3,472	4	1,502 D	36.2%	63.8%	36.2%	63.8%
GUADALUPE	3,188	1,649	1,539		110 R	51.7%	48.3%	51.7%	48.3%
HARDING	1,467	820	647		173 R	55.9%	44.1%	55.9%	44.1%
HIDALGO	1,174	367	807		440 D	31.3%	68.7%	31.3%	68.7%
LEA	4,168	1,227	2,938	3	1,711 D	29.4%	70.5%	29.5%	70.5%
LINCOLN	2,801	1,455	1,342	4	113 R	51.9%	47.9%	52.0%	48.0%
LOS ALAMOS									
LUNA	2,459	1,074	1,383	2	309 D	43.7%	56.2%	43.7%	56.3%
MCKINLEY	3,760	1,547	2,210	3	663 D	41.1%	58.8%	41.2%	58.8%
MORA	3,209	1,783	1,425	1	358 R	55.6%	44.4%	55.6%	44.4%
OTERO	3,362	1,467	1,892	3	425 D	43.6%	56.3%	43.7%	56.3%
QUAY	3,732	1,449	2,272	11	823 D	38.8%	60.9%	38.9%	61.1%
RIO ARRIBA	7,327	3,532	3,792	3	260 D	48.2%	51.8%	48.2%	51.8%
ROOSEVELT	3,969	1,610	2,359		749 D	40.6%	59.4%	40.6%	59.4%
SANDOVAL	2,795	1,439	1,354	2	85 R	51.5%	48.4%	51.5%	48.5%
SAN JUAN	2,540	1,438	1,093	9	345 R	56.6%	43.0%	56.8%	43.2%
SAN MIGUEL	8,702	4,014	4,684	4	670 D	46.1%	53.8%	46.1%	53.9%
SANTA FE	10,397	5,482	4,915		567 R	52.7%	47.3%	52.7%	47.3%
SIERRA	2,128	1,112	1,008	8	104 R	52.3%	47.4%	52.5%	47.5%
SOCORRO	4,000	2,030	1,967	3	63 R	50.8%	49.2%	50.8%	49.2%
TAOS	5,084	2,557	2,525	2	32 R	50.3%	49.7%	50.3%	49.7%
TORRANCE	3,456	2,014	1,438	4	576 R	58.3%	41.6%	58.3%	41.7%
UNION	2,959	1,604	1,350	5	254 R	54.2%	45.6%	54.3%	45.7%
VALENCIA	5,229	2,765	2,461	3	304 R	52.9%	47.1%	52.9%	47.1%
TOTAL	152,225	70,688	81,389	148	10,701 D	46.4%	53.5%	46.5%	53.5%

PRESIDENT 1948

County	Total Vote	Republican	Democratic	Other	Rep.-Dem. Plurality	Total Vote Rep.	Total Vote Dem.	Major Vote Rep.	Major Vote Dem.
BERNALILLO	35,364	16,668	18,305	391	1,637 D	47.1%	51.8%	47.7%	52.3%
CATRON	1,173	521	648	4	127 D	44.4%	55.2%	44.6%	55.4%
CHAVES	7,725	3,123	4,569	33	1,446 D	40.4%	59.1%	40.6%	59.4%
COLFAX	6,480	2,575	3,871	34	1,296 D	39.7%	59.7%	39.9%	60.1%
CURRY	7,941	2,132	5,759	50	3,627 D	26.8%	72.5%	27.0%	73.0%
DE BACA	1,131	458	670	3	212 D	40.5%	59.2%	40.6%	59.4%
DONA ANA	8,553	3,440	5,116	37	1,676 D	40.0%	59.5%	40.2%	59.8%
EDDY	10,021	2,305	7,593	123	5,288 D	23.0%	75.8%	23.3%	76.7%
GRANT	5,727	1,999	3,592	136	1,593 D	34.9%	62.7%	35.8%	64.2%
GUADALUPE	3,115	1,565	1,550		15 R	50.2%	49.8%	50.2%	49.8%
HARDING	1,307	649	653	5	4 D	49.7%	50.0%	49.8%	50.2%
HIDALGO	1,242	374	859	9	485 D	30.1%	69.2%	30.3%	69.7%
LEA	6,025	1,273	4,708	44	3,435 D	21.1%	78.1%	21.3%	78.7%
LINCOLN	3,005	1,575	1,406	24	169 R	52.4%	46.8%	52.8%	47.2%
LOS ALAMOS									
LUNA	2,584	941	1,629	14	688 D	36.4%	63.0%	36.6%	63.4%
MCKINLEY	5,149	2,109	2,995	45	886 D	41.0%	58.2%	41.3%	58.7%
MORA	3,437	1,893	1,541	3	352 R	55.1%	44.8%	55.1%	44.9%
OTERO	3,753	1,354	2,361	18	1,007 D	36.3%	63.2%	36.4%	63.6%
QUAY	4,493	1,392	3,063	38	1,671 D	31.0%	68.2%	31.2%	68.8%
RIO ARRIBA	9,043	4,273	4,753	17	480 D	47.3%	52.6%	47.3%	52.7%
ROOSEVELT	4,075	956	3,087	32	2,131 D	23.5%	75.8%	23.6%	76.4%
SANDOVAL	3,539	1,675	1,851	13	176 D	47.3%	52.3%	47.5%	52.5%
SAN JUAN	3,965	2,407	1,544	14	863 R	60.7%	38.9%	60.9%	39.1%
SAN MIGUEL	9,629	4,655	4,953	21	298 D	48.3%	51.4%	48.4%	51.6%
SANTA FE	13,731	7,491	6,172	68	1,319 R	54.6%	44.9%	54.8%	45.2%
SIERRA	2,680	1,274	1,389	17	115 D	47.5%	51.8%	47.8%	52.2%
SOCORRO	3,798	2,139	1,650	9	489 R	56.3%	43.4%	56.5%	43.5%
TAOS	5,870	2,852	2,977	41	125 D	48.6%	50.7%	48.9%	51.1%
TORRANCE	3,412	1,709	1,696	7	13 R	50.1%	49.7%	50.2%	49.8%
UNION	2,849	1,246	1,590	13	344 D	43.7%	55.8%	43.9%	56.1%
VALENCIA	6,227	3,280	2,914	33	366 R	52.7%	46.8%	53.0%	47.0%
TOTAL	187,063	80,303	105,464	1,296	25,161 D	42.9%	56.4%	43.2%	56.8%

NEW MEXICO

PRESIDENT 1952

County	Total Vote	Republican	Democratic	Other	Rep.-Dem. Plurality	Total Vote Rep.	Total Vote Dem.	Major Vote Rep.	Major Vote Dem.
BERNALILLO	57,200	33,964	23,164	72	10,800 R	59.4%	40.5%	59.5%	40.5%
CATRON	1,205	741	464		277 R	61.5%	38.5%	61.5%	38.5%
CHAVES	10,979	7,018	3,880	81	3,138 R	63.9%	35.3%	64.4%	35.6%
COLFAX	6,566	3,397	3,184	5	213 R	51.6%	48.3%	51.6%	48.4%
CURRY	8,459	5,023	3,422	14	1,601 R	59.4%	40.5%	59.5%	40.5%
DE BACA	1,376	782	591	3	191 R	56.8%	43.0%	57.0%	43.0%
DONA ANA	10,478	5,902	4,556	20	1,346 R	56.3%	43.5%	56.4%	43.6%
EDDY	13,591	6,041	7,495	55	1,454 D	44.4%	55.1%	44.6%	55.4%
GRANT	7,922	3,421	4,315	186	894 D	43.2%	54.5%	44.2%	55.8%
GUADALUPE	2,922	1,575	1,347		228 R	53.9%	46.1%	53.9%	46.1%
HARDING	1,197	760	436	1	324 R	63.5%	36.4%	63.5%	36.5%
HIDALGO	1,544	781	757	6	24 R	50.6%	49.0%	50.8%	49.2%
LEA	9,971	4,738	5,204	29	466 D	47.5%	52.2%	47.7%	52.3%
LINCOLN	3,106	2,004	1,095	7	909 R	64.5%	35.3%	64.7%	35.3%
LOS ALAMOS	4,515	2,226	2,281	8	55 D	49.3%	50.5%	49.4%	50.6%
LUNA	3,095	1,729	1,332	34	397 R	55.9%	43.0%	56.5%	43.5%
MCKINLEY	6,207	3,091	3,097	19	6 D	49.8%	49.9%	50.0%	50.0%
MORA	3,266	1,849	1,413	4	436 R	56.6%	43.3%	56.7%	43.3%
OTERO	4,620	2,456	2,162	2	294 R	53.2%	46.8%	53.2%	46.8%
QUAY	5,115	2,711	2,375	29	336 R	53.0%	46.4%	53.3%	46.7%
RIO ARRIBA	8,905	4,336	4,564	5	228 D	48.7%	51.3%	48.7%	51.3%
ROOSEVELT	5,330	3,030	2,298	12	732 R	56.7%	43.0%	56.9%	43.1%
SANDOVAL	3,448	1,795	1,647	6	148 R	52.1%	47.8%	52.1%	47.9%
SAN JUAN	5,541	3,864	1,659	18	2,205 R	69.7%	29.9%	70.0%	30.0%
SAN MIGUEL	9,818	5,360	4,451	7	909 R	54.6%	45.3%	54.6%	45.4%
SANTA FE	15,916	9,011	6,786	119	2,225 R	56.6%	42.6%	57.0%	43.0%
SIERRA	3,196	2,033	1,158	5	875 R	63.6%	36.2%	63.7%	36.3%
SOCORRO	4,006	2,224	1,777	5	447 R	55.5%	44.4%	55.6%	44.4%
TAOS	5,646	2,763	2,877	6	114 D	48.9%	51.0%	49.0%	51.0%
TORRANCE	3,177	1,747	1,422	8	325 R	55.0%	44.8%	55.1%	44.9%
UNION	3,136	1,988	1,142	6	846 R	63.4%	36.4%	63.5%	36.5%
VALENCIA	7,125	3,810	3,310	5	500 R	53.5%	46.5%	53.5%	46.5%
TOTAL	238,608	132,170	105,661	777	26,509 R	55.4%	44.3%	55.6%	44.4%

PRESIDENT 1956

County	Total Vote	Republican	Democratic	Other	Rep.-Dem. Plurality	Total Vote Rep.	Total Vote Dem.	Major Vote Rep.	Major Vote Dem.
BERNALILLO	65,143	41,893	22,954	296	18,939 R	64.3%	35.2%	64.6%	35.4%
CATRON	1,188	711	477		234 R	59.8%	40.2%	59.8%	40.2%
CHAVES	11,896	7,538	4,270	88	3,268 R	63.4%	35.9%	63.8%	36.2%
COLFAX	5,409	2,959	2,450		509 R	54.7%	45.3%	54.7%	45.3%
CURRY	8,427	4,826	3,545	56	1,281 R	57.3%	42.1%	57.7%	42.3%
DE BACA	1,313	779	528	6	251 R	59.3%	40.2%	59.6%	40.4%
DONA ANA	11,991	7,025	4,918	48	2,107 R	58.6%	41.0%	58.8%	41.2%
EDDY	14,618	6,691	7,820	107	1,129 D	45.8%	53.5%	46.1%	53.9%
GRANT	7,377	3,224	4,122	31	898 D	43.7%	55.9%	43.9%	56.1%
GUADALUPE	2,723	1,529	1,191	3	338 R	56.2%	43.7%	56.2%	43.8%
HARDING	1,083	671	412		259 R	62.0%	38.0%	62.0%	38.0%
HIDALGO	1,564	790	771	3	19 R	50.5%	49.3%	50.6%	49.4%
LEA	11,879	5,661	6,140	78	479 D	47.7%	51.7%	48.0%	52.0%
LINCOLN	3,020	1,956	1,059	5	897 R	64.8%	35.1%	64.9%	35.1%
LOS ALAMOS	4,629	2,406	2,214	9	192 R	52.0%	47.8%	52.1%	47.9%
LUNA	3,067	1,526	1,506	35	20 R	49.8%	49.1%	50.3%	49.7%
MCKINLEY	7,811	4,450	3,331	30	1,119 R	57.0%	42.6%	57.2%	42.8%
MORA	2,969	1,736	1,233		503 R	58.5%	41.5%	58.5%	41.5%
OTERO	6,483	3,919	2,558	6	1,361 R	60.5%	39.5%	60.5%	39.5%
QUAY	4,318	2,311	1,988	19	323 R	53.5%	46.0%	53.8%	46.2%
RIO ARRIBA	8,860	4,566	4,291	3	275 R	51.5%	48.4%	51.6%	48.4%
ROOSEVELT	4,963	2,708	2,247	8	461 R	54.6%	45.3%	54.7%	45.3%
SANDOVAL	3,554	1,979	1,574	1	405 R	55.7%	44.3%	55.7%	44.3%
SAN JUAN	7,690	5,194	2,425	71	2,769 R	67.5%	31.5%	68.2%	31.8%
SAN MIGUEL	9,100	5,083	4,014	3	1,069 R	55.9%	44.1%	55.9%	44.1%
SANTA FE	16,441	9,359	6,997	85	2,362 R	56.9%	42.6%	57.2%	42.8%
SIERRA	3,006	1,954	1,035	17	919 R	65.0%	34.4%	65.4%	34.6%
SOCORRO	3,841	2,365	1,476		889 R	61.6%	38.4%	61.6%	38.4%
TAOS	5,847	3,100	2,743	4	357 R	53.0%	46.9%	53.1%	46.9%
TORRANCE	2,787	1,567	1,201	19	366 R	56.2%	43.1%	56.6%	43.4%
UNION	2,711	1,649	1,061	1	588 R	60.8%	39.1%	60.8%	39.2%
VALENCIA	8,218	4,663	3,547	8	1,116 R	56.7%	43.2%	56.8%	43.2%
TOTAL	253,926	146,788	106,098	1,040	40,690 R	57.8%	41.8%	58.0%	42.0%

NEW MEXICO

PRESIDENT 1960

County	Total Vote	Republican	Democratic	Other	Rep.-Dem. Plurality	Total Vote Rep.	Total Vote Dem.	Major Vote Rep.	Major Vote Dem.
BERNALILLO	86,061	44,805	40,908	348	3,897 R	52.1%	47.5%	52.3%	47.7%
CATRON	1,245	671	573	1	98 R	53.9%	46.0%	53.9%	46.1%
CHAVES	15,392	9,089	6,212	91	2,877 R	59.1%	40.4%	59.4%	40.6%
COLFAX	5,528	2,316	3,187	25	871 D	41.9%	57.7%	42.1%	57.9%
CURRY	9,639	6,153	3,421	65	2,732 R	63.8%	35.5%	64.3%	35.7%
DE BACA	1,355	734	619	2	115 R	54.2%	45.7%	54.2%	45.8%
DONA ANA	16,755	7,789	8,905	61	1,116 D	46.5%	53.1%	46.7%	53.3%
EDDY	16,780	7,986	8,707	87	721 D	47.6%	51.9%	47.8%	52.2%
GRANT	6,868	2,468	4,378	22	1,910 D	35.9%	63.7%	36.1%	63.9%
GUADALUPE	2,834	1,242	1,589	3	347 D	43.8%	56.1%	43.9%	56.1%
HARDING	1,012	616	396		220 R	60.9%	39.1%	60.9%	39.1%
HIDALGO	1,643	750	889	4	139 D	45.6%	54.1%	45.8%	54.2%
LEA	15,474	7,548	7,806	120	258 D	48.8%	50.4%	49.2%	50.8%
LINCOLN	3,503	2,042	1,459	2	583 R	58.3%	41.7%	58.3%	41.7%
LOS ALAMOS	5,283	2,574	2,692	17	118 D	48.7%	51.0%	48.9%	51.1%
LUNA	3,306	1,583	1,708	15	125 D	47.9%	51.7%	48.1%	51.9%
MCKINLEY	9,893	4,262	5,599	32	1,337 D	43.1%	56.6%	43.2%	56.8%
MORA	2,807	1,349	1,458		109 D	48.1%	51.9%	48.1%	51.9%
OTERO	9,426	4,507	4,916	3	409 D	47.8%	52.2%	47.8%	52.2%
QUAY	4,704	2,652	2,050	2	602 R	56.4%	43.6%	56.4%	43.6%
RIO ARRIBA	9,969	3,716	6,250	3	2,534 D	37.3%	62.7%	37.3%	62.7%
ROOSEVELT	5,804	4,039	1,761	4	2,278 R	69.6%	30.3%	69.6%	30.4%
SANDOVAL	4,119	1,447	2,672		1,225 D	35.1%	64.9%	35.1%	64.9%
SAN JUAN	13,185	7,521	5,370	294	2,151 R	57.0%	40.7%	58.3%	41.7%
SAN MIGUEL	9,514	3,988	5,520	6	1,532 D	41.9%	58.0%	41.9%	58.1%
SANTA FE	17,890	7,411	10,385	94	2,974 D	41.4%	58.0%	41.6%	58.4%
SIERRA	3,117	1,890	1,220	7	670 R	60.6%	39.1%	60.8%	39.2%
SOCORRO	4,128	1,796	2,327	5	531 D	43.5%	56.4%	43.6%	56.4%
TAOS	6,257	2,620	3,631	6	1,011 D	41.9%	58.0%	41.9%	58.1%
TORRANCE	2,884	1,554	1,308	22	246 R	53.9%	45.4%	54.3%	45.7%
UNION	2,756	1,686	1,068	2	618 R	61.2%	38.8%	61.2%	38.8%
VALENCIA	11,976	4,929	7,043	4	2,114 D	41.2%	58.8%	41.2%	58.8%
TOTAL	311,107	153,733	156,027	1,347	2,294 D	49.4%	50.2%	49.6%	50.4%

PRESIDENT 1964

County	Total Vote	Republican	Democratic	Other	Rep.-Dem. Plurality	Total Vote Rep.	Total Vote Dem.	Major Vote Rep.	Major Vote Dem.
BERNALILLO	98,317	42,583	55,036	698	12,453 D	43.3%	56.0%	43.6%	56.4%
CATRON	1,209	584	624	1	40 D	48.3%	51.6%	48.3%	51.7%
CHAVES	17,113	8,419	8,650	44	231 D	49.2%	50.5%	49.3%	50.7%
COLFAX	5,029	1,636	3,367	26	1,731 D	32.5%	67.0%	32.7%	67.3%
CURRY	10,378	5,120	5,228	30	108 D	49.3%	50.4%	49.5%	50.5%
DE BACA	1,240	559	674	7	115 D	45.1%	54.4%	45.3%	54.7%
DONA ANA	18,085	7,280	10,748	57	3,468 D	40.3%	59.4%	40.4%	59.6%
EDDY	18,032	6,747	11,216	69	4,469 D	37.4%	62.2%	37.6%	62.4%
GRANT	7,314	2,042	5,253	19	3,211 D	27.9%	71.8%	28.0%	72.0%
GUADALUPE	2,713	1,058	1,649	6	591 D	39.0%	60.8%	39.1%	60.9%
HARDING	905	473	431	1	42 R	52.3%	47.6%	52.3%	47.7%
HIDALGO	1,635	628	995	12	367 D	38.4%	60.9%	38.7%	61.3%
LEA	15,948	7,033	8,862	53	1,829 D	44.1%	55.6%	44.2%	55.8%
LINCOLN	3,351	1,761	1,565	25	196 R	52.6%	46.7%	52.9%	47.1%
LOS ALAMOS	5,711	1,895	3,767	49	1,872 D	33.2%	66.0%	33.5%	66.5%
LUNA	3,969	1,665	2,286	18	621 D	42.0%	57.6%	42.1%	57.9%
MCKINLEY	10,000	2,965	6,913	122	3,948 D	29.6%	69.1%	30.0%	70.0%
MORA	2,527	1,014	1,509	4	495 D	40.1%	59.7%	40.2%	59.8%
OTERO	9,560	3,498	6,035	27	2,537 D	36.6%	63.1%	36.7%	63.3%
QUAY	4,515	2,161	2,333	21	172 D	47.9%	51.7%	48.1%	51.9%
RIO ARRIBA	9,757	2,906	6,787	64	3,881 D	29.8%	69.6%	30.0%	70.0%
ROOSEVELT	5,635	2,732	2,875	28	143 D	48.5%	51.0%	48.7%	51.3%
SANDOVAL	4,420	1,077	3,332	11	2,255 D	24.4%	75.4%	24.4%	75.6%
SAN JUAN	13,892	6,808	6,901	183	93 D	49.0%	49.7%	49.7%	50.3%
SAN MIGUEL	8,505	2,714	5,767	24	3,053 D	31.9%	67.8%	32.0%	68.0%
SANTA FE	18,524	5,834	12,616	74	6,782 D	31.5%	68.1%	31.6%	68.4%
SIERRA	3,149	1,501	1,633	15	132 D	47.7%	51.9%	47.9%	52.1%
SOCORRO	4,181	1,774	2,397	10	623 D	42.4%	57.3%	42.5%	57.5%
TAOS	6,238	2,006	4,204	28	2,198 D	32.2%	67.4%	32.3%	67.7%
TORRANCE	2,635	1,183	1,446	6	263 D	44.9%	54.9%	45.0%	55.0%
UNION	2,401	1,232	1,159	10	73 R	51.3%	48.3%	51.5%	48.5%
VALENCIA	11,757	3,950	7,757	50	3,807 D	33.6%	66.0%	33.7%	66.3%
TOTAL	328,645	132,838	194,015	1,792	61,177 D	40.4%	59.0%	40.6%	59.4%

NEW MEXICO

OTHER VOTE COMPOSITION:

1920	1,104 Farmer-Labor; 2 Socialist; 4 scattered.
1924	Progressive.
1928	Communist.
1932	1,776 Socialist; 389 Liberty; 135 Communist.
1936	924 Union; 343 Socialist; 61 Prohibition; 43 Communist.

1940	144 Socialist; 100 Prohibition.
1944	Prohibition.
1948	1,037 Progressive; 127 Prohibition; 83 Socialist; 49 Socialist Labor.
1952	297 Prohibition; 225 Progressive; 220 Christian Nationalist (MacArthur); 35 Socialist Labor.
1956	607 Prohibition; 364 States Rights; 69 Socialist Labor.

1960	777 Prohibition; 570 Socialist Labor.
1964	1,217 Socialist Labor; 543 Prohibition; 32 scattered.

SPECIAL CASES:

1924	Progressive candidates ran second in one county. Catron and Harding counties organized in 1921.
1952	Los Alamos county organized in 1949.

NEW YORK

PRESIDENT 1920

County	Total Vote	Republican	Democratic	Other	Rep.-Dem. Plurality	Total Vote Rep.	Total Vote Dem.	Major Vote Rep.	Major Vote Dem.
ALBANY	78,989	48,750	28,376	1,863	20,374 R	61.7%	35.9%	63.2%	36.8%
ALLEGANY	14,697	10,898	2,799	1,000	8,099 R	74.2%	19.0%	79.6%	20.4%
BRONX	187,329	106,050	45,741	35,538	60,309 R	56.6%	24.4%	69.9%	30.1%
BROOME	35,903	24,759	9,251	1,893	15,508 R	65.0%	25.8%	72.8%	27.2%
CATTARAUGUS	24,029	16,083	6,693	1,253	9,390 R	66.9%	27.9%	70.6%	29.4%
CAYUGA	22,510	15,234	6,343	933	8,891 R	67.7%	28.2%	70.6%	29.4%
CHAUTAUQUA	38,587	27,658	6,781	4,188	20,637 R	71.6%	17.6%	80.3%	19.7%
CHEMUNG	26,068	17,864	7,060	1,144	10,804 R	63.5%	27.1%	71.7%	28.3%
CHENANGO	14,224	10,116	3,735	373	6,381 R	71.1%	26.3%	73.0%	27.0%
CLINTON	13,385	9,062	4,110	213	4,952 R	67.7%	30.7%	68.8%	31.2%
COLUMBIA	14,823	9,284	5,203	336	4,081 R	62.6%	35.1%	64.1%	35.9%
CORTLAND	12,516	9,606	2,541	369	7,065 R	76.7%	20.3%	79.1%	20.9%
DELAWARE	16,701	11,719	4,528	454	7,191 R	70.2%	27.1%	72.1%	27.9%
DUTCHESS	32,246	21,552	9,938	1,156	11,614 R	65.6%	30.8%	68.0%	32.0%
ERIE	157,796	99,762	40,436	17,598	59,326 R	63.2%	25.6%	71.2%	28.8%
ESSEX	10,379	8,042	2,218	119	5,824 R	77.5%	21.4%	78.4%	21.6%
FRANKLIN	13,865	9,786	3,825	254	5,961 R	70.6%	27.6%	71.9%	28.1%
FULTON	15,539	10,946	3,192	1,401	7,754 R	70.4%	20.5%	77.4%	22.6%
GENESEE	12,923	9,628	2,570	725	7,058 R	74.5%	19.9%	78.9%	21.1%
GREENE	10,282	6,323	3,498	461	2,825 R	61.5%	34.0%	64.4%	35.6%
HAMILTON	1,406	881	516	9	365 R	62.3%	36.7%	63.1%	36.9%
HERKIMER	21,924	14,310	6,507	1,107	7,803 R	65.3%	29.7%	68.7%	31.3%
JEFFERSON	31,201	22,072	7,925	1,204	14,147 R	70.7%	25.4%	73.6%	26.4%
KINGS	462,248	292,692	119,612	49,944	173,080 R	63.3%	25.9%	71.0%	29.0%
LEWIS	8,692	5,906	2,673	113	3,233 R	67.9%	30.8%	68.8%	31.2%
LIVINGSTON	13,783	9,488	3,571	724	5,917 R	68.8%	25.9%	72.7%	27.3%
MADISON	15,348	11,094	3,797	457	7,297 R	72.3%	24.7%	74.5%	25.5%
MONROE	115,721	73,809	29,523	13,389	44,286 R	63.8%	25.4%	72.1%	27.9%
MONTGOMERY	19,425	12,885	5,941	679	6,944 R	66.1%	30.4%	68.5%	31.5%
NASSAU	43,331	33,099	8,595	1,637	24,504 R	76.4%	19.8%	79.4%	20.6%
NEW YORK	464,420	275,013	135,249	54,158	139,764 R	59.2%	29.1%	67.0%	33.0%
NIAGARA	31,032	21,193	7,416	2,423	13,777 R	68.3%	23.9%	74.1%	25.9%
ONEIDA	54,791	36,311	15,560	2,920	20,751 R	66.3%	28.4%	70.0%	30.0%
ONONDAGA	86,047	57,008	23,308	5,731	33,700 R	66.3%	27.1%	71.0%	29.0%
ONTARIO	20,184	13,361	5,678	1,145	7,683 R	66.2%	28.1%	70.2%	29.8%
ORANGE	37,135	24,558	10,567	2,010	13,991 R	66.1%	28.5%	69.9%	30.1%
ORLEANS	11,410	8,305	2,266	839	6,039 R	72.8%	19.9%	78.6%	21.4%
OSWEGO	28,258	17,844	9,373	1,041	8,471 R	63.1%	33.2%	65.6%	34.4%
OTSEGO	16,897	11,169	5,057	671	6,112 R	66.1%	29.9%	69.0%	31.0%
PUTNAM	4,911	3,447	1,405	59	2,042 R	70.2%	28.6%	71.0%	29.0%
QUEENS	137,324	94,360	35,296	7,668	59,064 R	68.7%	25.7%	72.8%	27.2%
RENSSELAER	51,371	28,810	20,224	2,337	8,586 R	55.1%	39.4%	58.6%	41.4%
RICHMOND	28,258	17,844	9,373	1,041	8,471 R	63.1%	33.2%	65.6%	34.4%
ROCKLAND	16,897	11,169	5,057	671	6,112 R	66.1%	29.9%	69.0%	31.0%
ST LAWRENCE	32,606	24,651	7,213	742	17,438 R	75.6%	22.1%	77.4%	22.6%
SARATOGA	23,858	16,222	6,905	731	9,317 R	68.0%	28.9%	70.1%	29.9%
SCHENECTADY	33,582	19,208	12,741	1,633	6,467 R	57.2%	36.0%	60.7%	39.3%
SCHOHARIE	9,537	5,572	3,697	268	1,875 R	58.4%	38.8%	60.1%	39.9%
SCHUYLER	5,368	3,827	1,231	310	2,596 R	71.3%	22.9%	75.7%	24.3%
SENECA	9,696	6,260	3,023	413	3,237 R	64.1%	32.2%	67.4%	32.6%
STEUBEN	27,868	18,335	7,401	2,132	10,934 R	65.3%	26.6%	71.2%	28.8%
SUFFOLK	36,574	26,737	8,852	985	17,885 R	73.1%	24.2%	75.1%	24.9%
SULLIVAN	12,458	8,029	3,623	806	4,406 R	64.4%	29.1%	68.9%	31.1%
TIOGA	9,511	6,772	2,406	333	4,366 R	71.2%	25.3%	73.8%	26.2%
TOMPKINS	13,573	9,508	3,487	578	6,021 R	70.1%	25.7%	73.2%	26.8%
ULSTER	28,612	19,001	8,759	852	10,242 R	66.1%	30.6%	68.4%	31.6%
WARREN	12,555	9,009	3,227	319	5,782 R	71.4%	25.7%	73.6%	26.4%
WASHINGTON	18,093	13,647	4,124	322	9,523 R	75.4%	22.8%	76.7%	23.2%
WAYNE	18,205	13,333	4,289	583	9,044 R	73.2%	23.6%	75.7%	24.3%
WESTCHESTER	111,335	76,020	28,060	7,255	47,960 R	68.3%	25.2%	73.0%	27.0%

PRESIDENT 1924

County	Total Vote	Republican	Democratic	Other	Rep.-Dem. Plurality	Total Vote Rep.	Total Vote Dem.	Major Vote Rep.	Major Vote Dem.
ALBANY	92,772	48,253	38,671	5,848	9,582 R	52.0%	41.7%	55.5%	44.5%
ALLEGANY	16,196	12,203	2,755	1,238	9,448 R	75.3%	17.0%	81.6%	18.4%
BRONX	216,657	79,583	72,840	64,234	6,743 R	36.7%	33.6%	52.2%	47.8%
BROOME	41,749	28,262	9,289	4,198	18,973 R	67.7%	22.2%	75.3%	24.7%
CATTARAUGUS	27,066	17,307	5,369	4,390	11,938 R	63.9%	19.8%	76.3%	23.7%
CAYUGA	27,100	17,252	7,369	2,479	9,883 R	63.7%	27.2%	70.1%	29.9%
CHAUTAUQUA	41,764	29,757	5,560	6,447	24,197 R	71.3%	13.3%	84.3%	15.7%
CHEMUNG	28,765	18,599	7,162	3,004	11,437 R	64.7%	24.9%	72.2%	27.8%
CHENANGO	15,596	11,323	3,392	881	7,931 R	72.6%	21.7%	76.9%	23.1%
CLINTON	13,698	7,918	5,138	642	2,780 R	57.8%	37.5%	60.6%	39.4%
COLUMBIA	16,914	10,774	5,466	674	5,308 R	63.7%	32.3%	66.3%	33.7%
CORTLAND	13,041	10,032	2,170	839	7,862 R	76.9%	16.6%	82.2%	17.8%
DELAWARE	17,919	13,020	4,158	741	8,862 R	72.7%	23.2%	75.8%	24.2%
DUTCHESS	34,303	26,173	8,864	3,266	17,309 R	64.6%	25.8%	71.4%	28.6%
ERIE	191,480	112,070	40,780	38,630	71,290 R	58.5%	21.3%	73.3%	26.7%
ESSEX	11,565	8,553	2,639	373	5,914 R	74.0%	22.8%	76.4%	23.6%
FRANKLIN	14,515	9,352	4,364	799	4,988 R	64.4%	30.1%	68.2%	31.8%
FULTON	15,358	11,858	3,143	1,357	8,715 R	72.5%	19.2%	79.0%	21.0%
GENESEE	15,542	11,101	3,384	1,057	7,717 R	71.4%	21.8%	76.6%	23.4%
GREENE	12,188	7,503	3,951	734	3,552 R	61.6%	32.4%	65.5%	34.5%
HAMILTON	1,736	1,063	631	42	432 R	61.3%	36.3%	62.8%	37.2%
HERKIMER	23,563	15,625	6,464	1,474	9,161 R	66.3%	27.4%	70.7%	29.3%
JEFFERSON	30,942	21,159	7,665	2,118	13,494 R	68.4%	24.8%	73.4%	26.6%
KINGS	498,667	236,877	158,901	102,903	77,970 R	47.5%	31.9%	59.9%	40.1%
LEWIS	9,057	6,066	2,801	190	3,265 R	67.0%	30.9%	68.4%	31.6%
LIVINGSTON	15,055	10,472	3,676	907	6,796 R	69.6%	24.4%	74.0%	26.0%
MADISON	16,331	11,589	3,430	1,302	8,159 R	71.0%	21.0%	77.2%	22.8%
MONROE	141,428	80,577	28,956	31,595	51,621 R	57.1%	20.5%	73.6%	26.4%
MONTGOMERY	20,352	12,869	5,939	1,554	6,930 R	63.4%	29.2%	68.4%	31.6%
NASSAU	65,031	45,825	14,322	4,884	31,503 R	70.5%	22.0%	76.2%	23.8%
NEW YORK	463,326	190,871	183,249	89,206	7,622 R	41.2%	39.6%	51.0%	49.0%
NIAGARA	38,062	25,874	7,993	4,195	17,881 R	68.0%	21.0%	76.4%	23.6%
ONEIDA	60,734	37,545	18,124	5,065	19,421 R	61.8%	29.8%	67.4%	32.6%
ONONDAGA	100,769	65,395	24,773	10,601	40,622 R	64.9%	24.6%	72.5%	27.5%
ONTARIO	22,523	15,013	5,933	1,577	9,080 R	66.7%	26.3%	71.7%	28.3%
ORANGE	43,083	29,184	9,765	4,134	19,419 R	67.7%	22.7%	74.9%	25.1%
ORLEANS	11,880	8,543	2,320	1,017	6,223 R	71.9%	19.5%	78.6%	21.4%
OSWEGO	28,542	18,576	7,864	2,102	10,712 R	65.1%	27.6%	70.3%	29.7%
OTSEGO	20,670	12,869	5,841	1,256	7,028 R	60.9%	28.3%	69.0%	30.1%
PUTNAM	5,605	3,796	1,472	337	2,324 R	67.7%	26.3%	72.1%	27.9%
QUEENS	188,169	100,793	58,402	28,974	42,391 R	53.6%	31.0%	63.3%	36.7%
RENSSELAER	54,673	30,549	19,783	4,341	10,766 R	55.9%	36.2%	60.7%	39.3%
RICHMOND	37,586	18,007	15,801	3,778	2,206 R	47.9%	42.0%	53.3%	46.7%
ROCKLAND	19,559	11,915	5,640	2,004	6,275 R	60.9%	28.8%	67.9%	32.1%
ST LAWRENCE	31,584	22,583	7,103	1,898	15,480 R	71.5%	22.5%	76.1%	23.9%
SARATOGA	26,856	17,682	7,026	2,148	10,656 R	65.8%	26.2%	71.6%	28.4%
SCHENECTADY	39,639	24,514	9,163	5,962	15,347 R	61.7%	23.1%	72.8%	27.2%
SCHOHARIE	9,879	6,142	3,413	324	2,729 R	62.2%	34.5%	64.3%	35.7%
SCHUYLER	6,074	4,301	1,555	218	2,746 R	70.8%	25.6%	73.4%	26.6%
SENECA	9,974	6,598	2,727	649	3,871 R	66.2%	27.3%	70.8%	29.2%
STEUBEN	32,160	21,481	7,194	3,485	14,287 R	66.8%	22.4%	74.9%	25.1%
SUFFOLK	45,455	31,456	10,024	3,975	21,432 R	69.2%	24.1%	75.8%	24.2%
SULLIVAN	13,604	7,734	4,057	1,813	3,677 R	56.9%	29.1%	65.6%	34.4%
TIOGA	10,810	7,834	2,234	742	5,600 R	72.5%	20.7%	77.8%	22.2%
TOMPKINS	16,123	11,766	3,701	656	8,065 R	73.0%	23.0%	76.1%	23.9%
ULSTER	31,660	20,048	9,361	2,251	10,687 R	63.3%	29.6%	68.2%	31.8%
WARREN	14,168	9,527	3,663	878	5,964 R	67.9%	25.9%	72.4%	27.6%
WASHINGTON	19,264	13,774	4,321	1,169	9,453 R	71.5%	22.4%	76.1%	23.9%
WAYNE	19,485	14,358	3,991	1,136	10,367 R	73.7%	20.5%	78.2%	21.8%
WESTCHESTER	133,035	85,029	30,964	17,042	54,065 R	63.9%	23.3%	73.3%	26.7%

NEW YORK

PRESIDENT 1920

County	Total Vote	Republican	Democratic	Other	Rep.-Dem. Plurality	Percentage Total Vote Rep.	Dem.	Major Vote Rep.	Dem.
WYOMING	12,101	9,134	2,442	525	6,692 R	75.5%	20.2%	78.9%	21.1%
YATES	7,391	5,638	1,571	182	4,067 R	76.3%	21.3%	78.2%	21.8%
TOTAL	2,898,513	1,871,167	781,238	246,108	1,089,929 R	64.6%	27.0%	70.5%	29.5%

PRESIDENT 1924

County	Total Vote	Republican	Democratic	Other	Rep.-Dem. Plurality	Percentage Total Vote Rep.	Dem.	Major Vote Rep.	Dem.
WYOMING	13,705	10,148	2,512	1,045	7,636 R	74.0%	18.3%	80.2%	19.8%
YATES	8,153	6,334	1,568	251	4,766 R	77.7%	19.2%	80.2%	19.8%
TOTAL	3,263,939	1,820,058	950,796	493,085	869,262 R	55.8%	29.1%	65.7%	34.3%

NEW YORK

PRESIDENT 1928

County	Total Vote	Republican	Democratic	Other	Rep.-Dem. Plurality	%TV Rep	%TV Dem	%MV Rep	%MV Dem
ALBANY	113,437	48,762	62,380	2,295	13,618 D	43.0%	55.0%	43.9%	56.1%
ALLEGANY	19,399	15,306	3,491	602	11,815 R	78.9%	18.0%	81.4%	18.6%
BRONX	343,947	98,636	232,766	12,545	134,130 D	28.7%	67.7%	29.8%	70.2%
BROOME	61,092	39,860	19,563	1,669	20,257 R	65.2%	32.0%	67.1%	32.9%
CATTARAUGUS	33,001	22,135	10,229	637	11,906 R	67.1%	31.0%	68.4%	31.6%
CAYUGA	32,525	20,202	11,787	536	8,415 R	62.1%	36.2%	63.2%	36.8%
CHAUTAUQUA	52,584	38,220	13,223	1,141	24,957 R	72.7%	25.1%	74.3%	25.7%
CHEMUNG	37,354	25,029	12,189	136	12,840 R	67.0%	32.6%	67.2%	32.8%
CHENANGO	18,073	13,955	3,986	132	9,969 R	77.2%	22.1%	77.8%	22.2%
CLINTON	18,771	7,824	10,888	59	3,064 D	41.7%	58.0%	41.8%	58.2%
COLUMBIA	20,612	14,000	6,403	209	7,557 R	67.9%	31.1%	68.6%	31.4%
CORTLAND	15,869	11,960	3,662	247	8,298 R	75.4%	23.1%	76.5%	23.4%
DELAWARE	20,645	16,225	4,362	58	11,863 R	78.6%	21.1%	78.8%	21.2%
DUTCHESS	46,801	28,687	16,748	1,366	11,939 R	61.1%	35.1%	63.1%	36.9%
ERIE	281,789	144,726	126,449	10,614	18,277 R	51.4%	44.9%	53.4%	46.6%
ESSEX	15,770	10,462	5,291	17	5,171 R	66.3%	33.6%	66.4%	33.6%
FRANKLIN	19,045	9,495	9,501	49	6 D	49.9%	49.9%	50.0%	50.0%
FULTON	21,139	15,043	5,728	368	9,315 R	71.2%	27.1%	72.4%	27.6%
GENESEE	19,195	13,251	5,181	763	8,070 R	69.0%	27.0%	71.9%	28.1%
GREENE	14,285	9,529	4,440	316	5,089 R	66.7%	31.1%	68.2%	31.8%
HAMILTON	2,351	1,399	952	—	447 R	59.5%	40.5%	59.5%	40.5%
HERKIMER	29,709	18,624	10,654	431	7,970 R	62.7%	35.9%	63.5%	36.4%
JEFFERSON	39,695	26,361	12,908	426	13,453 R	66.4%	32.5%	67.1%	32.9%
KINGS	679,837	245,622	404,393	29,822	158,771 D	36.1%	59.5%	37.8%	62.2%
LEWIS	11,344	7,175	4,161	8	3,014 R	63.2%	36.7%	63.3%	36.7%
LIVINGSTON	18,160	11,632	5,545	983	6,087 R	64.1%	30.5%	67.7%	32.3%
MADISON	19,851	14,333	5,217	301	9,116 R	72.2%	26.3%	73.3%	26.7%
MONROE	179,078	99,803	73,759	5,516	26,044 R	55.7%	41.2%	57.5%	42.5%
MONTGOMERY	25,309	15,257	9,845	207	5,412 R	60.3%	38.9%	60.8%	39.2%
NASSAU	113,140	71,015	40,079	2,046	30,936 R	62.8%	35.4%	63.9%	36.1%
NEW YORK	452,558	186,396	317,227	17,935	130,831 D	35.7%	60.8%	37.0%	63.0%
NIAGARA	52,453	33,229	16,881	2,343	16,348 R	63.4%	32.2%	66.3%	33.7%
ONEIDA	84,786	44,782	38,231	1,773	6,551 R	52.8%	45.1%	53.9%	46.1%
ONONDAGA	133,716	76,278	54,706	2,732	21,572 R	57.0%	40.9%	58.2%	41.8%
ONTARIO	27,225	17,769	8,491	965	9,278 R	65.3%	31.2%	67.7%	32.3%
ORANGE	58,240	37,334	19,047	1,859	18,287 R	64.1%	32.7%	66.2%	33.8%
ORLEANS	14,292	9,828	3,792	672	6,036 R	68.8%	26.5%	72.2%	27.8%
OSWEGO	33,930	21,849	11,639	442	10,210 R	64.4%	34.3%	65.2%	34.8%
OTSEGO	24,606	18,286	6,006	314	12,280 R	74.3%	24.4%	75.3%	24.7%
PUTNAM	6,981	4,534	2,278	169	2,256 R	64.9%	32.6%	66.5%	33.4%
QUEENS	345,556	158,505	184,640	2,411	26,135 D	45.9%	53.4%	46.2%	53.8%
RENSSELAER	66,191	32,370	33,094	727	724 D	48.9%	50.0%	49.4%	50.6%
RICHMOND	54,234	24,995	28,945	294	3,950 D	46.1%	53.4%	46.3%	53.7%
ROCKLAND	26,072	15,732	9,769	571	5,963 R	60.3%	37.5%	61.7%	38.3%
ST LAWRENCE	38,960	25,804	12,567	589	13,237 R	66.2%	32.3%	67.2%	32.8%
SARATOGA	32,187	19,183	12,247	757	6,936 R	59.6%	38.0%	61.0%	39.0%
SCHENECTADY	52,209	29,428	21,277	1,304	8,151 R	56.4%	40.8%	58.0%	42.0%
SCHOHARIE	10,209	6,906	2,926	377	3,980 R	67.6%	28.7%	70.2%	29.8%
SCHUYLER	6,587	4,749	1,731	107	3,018 R	72.1%	26.3%	73.2%	26.8%
SENECA	11,938	7,911	3,873	154	4,038 R	66.3%	32.4%	67.1%	32.9%
STEUBEN	40,466	28,028	10,699	1,739	17,329 R	69.3%	26.4%	72.4%	27.6%
SUFFOLK	63,315	41,199	19,497	2,619	21,702 R	65.1%	30.8%	67.9%	32.1%
SULLIVAN	16,861	10,331	6,207	323	4,124 R	61.3%	36.8%	62.5%	37.5%
TIOGA	12,958	9,963	2,779	216	7,184 R	76.9%	21.4%	78.2%	21.8%
TOMPKINS	19,866	14,471	5,114	281	9,357 R	72.8%	25.7%	73.9%	26.1%
ULSTER	40,695	25,418	14,200	1,077	11,218 R	62.5%	34.9%	64.2%	35.8%
WARREN	18,519	11,697	6,793	29	4,904 R	63.2%	36.7%	63.3%	36.7%
WASHINGTON	23,163	15,497	7,221	445	8,276 R	66.9%	31.2%	68.2%	31.8%
WAYNE	24,155	18,187	5,338	630	12,849 R	75.3%	22.1%	77.3%	22.7%
WESTCHESTER	195,544	109,939	80,926	4,679	29,013 R	56.2%	41.4%	57.6%	42.4%

PRESIDENT 1932

County	Total Vote	Republican	Democratic	Other	Rep.-Dem. Plurality	%TV Rep	%TV Dem	%MV Rep	%MV Dem
ALBANY	120,759	46,244	73,194	1,321	26,950 D	38.3%	60.6%	38.7%	61.3%
ALLEGANY	17,777	12,348	4,961	468	7,387 R	69.5%	27.9%	71.3%	28.7%
BRONX	399,919	76,587	281,330	42,002	204,743 D	19.2%	70.3%	21.4%	78.6%
BROOME	56,494	32,751	22,802	941	9,949 R	58.0%	40.4%	59.0%	41.0%
CATTARAUGUS	30,786	18,071	11,467	1,248	6,604 R	58.7%	37.2%	61.2%	38.8%
CAYUGA	31,043	17,280	12,989	774	4,291 R	55.7%	41.8%	57.1%	42.9%
CHAUTAUQUA	50,275	30,479	16,914	2,882	13,565 R	60.6%	33.6%	64.3%	35.7%
CHEMUNG	34,750	20,152	13,825	773	6,327 R	58.0%	39.8%	59.3%	40.7%
CHENANGO	17,719	11,566	5,953	200	5,613 R	65.3%	33.6%	66.0%	34.0%
CLINTON	19,365	8,263	11,027	75	2,764 D	42.7%	56.9%	42.8%	57.2%
COLUMBIA	20,931	11,667	9,083	181	2,584 R	55.7%	43.4%	56.2%	43.8%
CORTLAND	14,585	9,859	4,425	301	5,434 R	67.6%	30.3%	69.0%	31.0%
DELAWARE	19,980	13,050	6,723	207	6,327 R	65.3%	33.6%	66.0%	34.0%
DUTCHESS	46,871	25,757	20,374	740	5,383 R	55.0%	43.5%	55.8%	44.2%
ERIE	282,930	141,059	131,012	10,859	10,047 R	49.9%	46.3%	51.8%	48.2%
ESSEX	15,786	10,062	5,597	127	4,465 R	63.7%	35.5%	64.3%	35.7%
FRANKLIN	19,857	9,422	10,318	117	896 D	47.4%	52.0%	47.7%	52.3%
FULTON	20,988	14,984	5,678	326	9,306 R	71.4%	27.1%	72.5%	27.5%
GENESEE	18,635	11,881	6,452	302	5,429 R	64.8%	33.6%	65.9%	34.1%
GREENE	14,261	7,334	6,794	133	540 R	51.4%	47.6%	51.9%	48.1%
HAMILTON	2,728	1,603	1,107	18	496 R	58.8%	40.6%	59.2%	40.8%
HERKIMER	26,790	15,158	11,194	438	3,964 R	56.6%	41.8%	57.5%	42.5%
JEFFERSON	36,724	22,760	13,478	486	9,282 R	62.0%	36.7%	62.8%	37.2%
KINGS	769,008	192,536	514,172	62,300	321,636 D	25.0%	66.9%	27.2%	72.8%
LEWIS	10,424	6,258	4,086	80	2,172 R	60.0%	39.2%	60.5%	39.5%
LIVINGSTON	17,888	11,114	6,529	245	4,585 R	62.1%	36.5%	63.0%	37.0%
MADISON	19,272	11,931	6,896	445	5,035 R	61.9%	35.8%	63.4%	36.6%
MONROE	185,960	95,964	83,208	6,788	12,756 R	51.6%	44.7%	53.6%	46.4%
MONTGOMERY	26,076	14,104	11,700	272	2,404 R	54.1%	44.9%	54.7%	45.3%
NASSAU	144,100	78,544	61,752	3,804	16,792 R	54.5%	42.9%	56.0%	44.0%
NEW YORK	565,205	157,014	378,077	30,114	221,063 D	27.8%	66.9%	29.3%	70.7%
NIAGARA	52,891	30,852	20,765	1,274	10,087 R	58.3%	39.3%	59.7%	40.3%
ONEIDA	83,148	41,193	38,413	1,542	2,780 R	50.8%	47.3%	51.7%	48.3%
ONONDAGA	133,250	60,363	62,227	10,660	1,864 D	45.4%	46.7%	49.2%	50.8%
ONTARIO	25,320	15,624	9,273	423	6,351 R	61.7%	36.6%	62.8%	37.2%
ORANGE	54,423	30,687	22,971	765	7,716 R	56.4%	42.2%	57.2%	42.8%
ORLEANS	14,321	9,735	4,303	283	5,432 R	68.0%	30.0%	69.3%	30.7%
OSWEGO	32,201	18,322	13,314	565	5,008 R	56.9%	41.3%	57.9%	42.1%
OTSEGO	23,265	14,904	8,114	247	6,790 R	64.1%	34.9%	64.7%	35.3%
PUTNAM	8,512	4,633	3,730	149	903 R	54.4%	43.8%	55.4%	44.6%
QUEENS	398,141	136,641	244,740	16,760	108,099 D	34.3%	61.5%	35.8%	64.2%
RENSSELAER	64,217	30,606	32,783	828	2,177 D	47.7%	51.1%	48.3%	51.7%
RICHMOND	60,345	21,278	36,857	2,210	15,579 D	35.3%	61.1%	36.6%	63.4%
ROCKLAND	27,982	13,963	13,347	672	616 R	49.9%	47.7%	51.1%	48.9%
ST LAWRENCE	35,680	22,650	12,687	343	9,963 R	63.5%	35.6%	64.1%	35.9%
SARATOGA	31,578	17,990	13,053	535	4,937 R	57.0%	41.3%	58.0%	42.0%
SCHENECTADY	53,371	28,187	22,230	2,954	5,957 R	52.8%	41.7%	55.9%	44.1%
SCHOHARIE	10,318	5,513	4,684	121	829 R	53.4%	45.4%	54.1%	45.9%
SCHUYLER	6,881	4,491	2,255	135	2,236 R	65.3%	32.8%	66.5%	33.4%
SENECA	11,486	6,502	4,764	220	1,738 R	56.6%	41.5%	57.7%	42.3%
STEUBEN	36,959	22,986	13,219	754	9,767 R	62.2%	35.8%	63.5%	36.5%
SUFFOLK	72,528	40,247	30,799	1,482	9,448 R	55.5%	42.5%	56.6%	43.4%
SULLIVAN	18,517	8,294	9,656	567	1,362 D	44.8%	52.1%	46.2%	53.8%
TIOGA	12,328	8,047	4,067	214	3,980 R	65.3%	33.0%	66.4%	33.6%
TOMPKINS	18,916	12,185	6,180	551	6,005 R	64.4%	32.7%	66.3%	33.7%
ULSTER	39,721	21,002	18,092	627	2,910 R	52.9%	45.5%	53.7%	46.3%
WARREN	18,392	11,585	6,661	146	4,924 R	63.0%	36.2%	63.5%	36.5%
WASHINGTON	22,184	14,478	7,512	194	6,966 R	65.3%	33.9%	65.8%	34.2%
WAYNE	22,675	15,031	7,122	522	7,909 R	66.3%	31.4%	67.9%	32.1%
WESTCHESTER	220,788	112,747	101,435	6,606	11,312 R	51.1%	45.9%	52.6%	47.4%

NEW YORK

PRESIDENT 1928

County	Total Vote	Republican	Democratic	Other	Rep.-Dem. Plurality	Percentage Total Vote Rep.	Dem.	Major Vote Rep.	Dem.
WYOMING	15,152	10,830	3,992	330	6,838 R	71.5%	26.3%	73.1%	26.9%
YATES	9,395	7,386	1,950	59	5,436 R	78.6%	20.8%	79.1%	20.9%
TOTAL	4,405,626	2,193,344	2,089,863	122,419	103,481 R	49.8%	47.4%	51.2%	48.8%

PRESIDENT 1932

Total Vote	Republican	Democratic	Other	Rep.-Dem. Plurality	Percentage Total Vote Rep.	Dem.	Major Vote Rep.	Dem.
14,137	9,377	4,490	270	4,887 R	66.3%	31.8%	67.6%	32.4%
8,584	6,048	2,399	137	3,649 R	70.5%	27.9%	71.6%	28.4%
4,688,614	1,937,963	2,534,959	215,692	596,996 D	41.3%	54.1%	43.3%	56.7%

NEW YORK

PRESIDENT 1936

County	Total Vote	Republican	Democratic	Other	Rep.-Dem. Plurality	Total Vote Rep.	Total Vote Dem.	Major Vote Rep.	Major Vote Dem.
ALBANY	127,511	52,962	71,631	2,918	18,669 D	41.5%	56.2%	42.5%	57.5%
ALLEGANY	19,508	13,829	5,288	391	8,541 R	70.9%	27.1%	72.3%	27.7%
BRONX	528,818	93,151	419,625	16,042	326,474 D	17.5%	79.4%	18.2%	81.8%
BROOME	67,603	36,945	29,708	950	7,237 R	54.6%	43.9%	55.4%	44.6%
CATTARAUGUS	32,984	20,484	11,901	599	8,583 R	62.1%	36.1%	63.3%	36.7%
CAYUGA	33,200	20,203	12,158	839	8,045 R	60.9%	36.6%	62.4%	37.6%
CHAUTAUQUA	54,927	30,435	23,283	1,209	7,152 R	55.4%	42.4%	56.7%	43.3%
CHEMUNG	36,195	20,515	15,542	138	4,973 R	56.7%	42.9%	56.9%	43.1%
CHENANGO	18,995	13,772	5,143	80	8,629 R	72.5%	27.1%	72.8%	27.2%
CLINTON	21,538	10,521	10,898	119	377 D	48.8%	50.6%	49.1%	50.9%
COLUMBIA	21,673	13,034	8,375	264	4,659 R	60.1%	38.6%	60.9%	39.1%
CORTLAND	16,637	11,718	4,606	313	7,112 R	70.4%	27.7%	71.8%	28.2%
DELAWARE	21,364	15,164	6,142	58	9,022 R	71.0%	28.7%	71.2%	28.8%
DUTCHESS	54,345	28,868	24,467	1,010	4,401 R	53.1%	45.0%	54.1%	45.9%
ERIE	342,208	152,312	183,555	6,341	31,243 D	44.5%	53.6%	45.3%	54.7%
ESSEX	17,088	11,599	5,447	42	6,152 R	67.9%	31.9%	68.0%	32.0%
FRANKLIN	20,478	11,521	8,799	158	2,722 R	56.3%	43.0%	56.7%	43.3%
FULTON	23,737	14,253	8,977	507	5,276 R	60.0%	37.8%	61.4%	38.6%
GENESEE	20,069	13,292	6,177	600	7,115 R	66.2%	30.8%	68.3%	31.7%
GREENE	16,060	9,060	6,744	256	2,316 R	56.4%	42.0%	57.3%	42.7%
HAMILTON	2,629	1,695	934		761 R	64.5%	35.5%	64.5%	35.5%
HERKIMER	29,129	15,941	12,975	341	2,966 R	54.7%	44.5%	55.4%	44.6%
JEFFERSON	39,466	24,925	13,975	566	10,950 R	63.2%	35.4%	64.1%	35.9%
KINGS	974,301	234,852	738,306	23,143	503,454 D	24.1%	75.8%	24.2%	77.6%
LEWIS	11,426	8,048	3,263	115	4,785 R	70.4%	28.6%	71.2%	28.8%
LIVINGSTON	18,953	12,353	6,088	512	6,265 R	65.2%	32.1%	67.0%	33.0%
MADISON	20,590	14,353	5,867	370	8,486 R	69.7%	28.5%	71.0%	29.0%
MONROE	210,523	93,055	114,286	3,182	21,231 D	44.2%	54.3%	44.9%	55.1%
MONTGOMERY	29,139	14,127	14,698	314	571 D	48.5%	50.4%	49.0%	51.0%
NASSAU	172,779	94,968	74,232	3,579	20,736 R	55.0%	43.0%	56.1%	43.9%
NEW YORK	711,253	174,299	517,134	19,820	342,835 D	24.5%	72.7%	25.2%	74.8%
NIAGARA	61,415	30,114	29,237	2,064	937 R	49.1%	47.6%	50.8%	49.2%
ONEIDA	91,111	46,317	42,939	1,855	2,873 R	50.8%	47.1%	51.6%	48.3%
ONONDAGA	146,270	80,498	62,945	2,827	17,553 R	55.0%	43.0%	56.1%	43.9%
ONTARIO	27,215	17,812	8,787	616	9,025 R	65.4%	32.3%	67.0%	33.0%
ORANGE	63,276	34,428	27,528	1,320	6,900 R	54.4%	43.5%	55.6%	44.4%
ORLEANS	14,994	10,569	4,016	409	6,553 R	70.5%	26.8%	72.5%	27.5%
OSWEGO	34,376	22,803	11,068	505	11,735 R	66.3%	32.2%	67.3%	32.7%
OTSEGO	24,765	16,682	7,807	276	8,875 R	67.4%	31.5%	68.1%	31.9%
PUTNAM	10,633	5,761	4,682	190	1,079 R	54.2%	44.0%	55.2%	44.8%
QUEENS	493,009	162,797	320,053	10,159	157,256 D	33.0%	64.9%	33.7%	66.3%
RENSSELAER	68,621	34,772	31,754	2,095	3,018 R	50.7%	46.3%	52.3%	47.7%
RICHMOND	70,389	22,882	46,229	1,308	23,337 D	32.5%	65.7%	33.1%	66.9%
ROCKLAND	32,090	15,583	15,876	631	293 D	48.6%	49.5%	49.5%	50.5%
ST LAWRENCE	39,556	26,031	12,763	762	13,268 R	65.8%	32.3%	67.1%	32.9%
SARATOGA	34,266	19,153	14,619	494	4,534 R	55.9%	42.7%	56.7%	43.3%
SCHENECTADY	59,407	26,914	31,027	1,466	4,113 D	45.3%	52.2%	46.5%	53.5%
SCHOHARIE	11,434	6,995	4,229	310	2,656 R	60.3%	37.0%	62.0%	38.0%
SCHUYLER	7,435	4,819	2,551	85	2,258 R	64.6%	34.2%	65.4%	34.6%
SENECA	12,454	7,919	4,295	240	3,624 R	63.6%	34.5%	64.8%	35.2%
STEUBEN	40,810	24,987	14,978	845	10,039 R	61.2%	36.7%	62.5%	37.5%
SUFFOLK	84,335	48,970	33,078	2,287	15,892 R	58.1%	39.2%	59.7%	40.3%
SULLIVAN	19,982	9,757	9,908	317	151 D	48.8%	49.6%	49.6%	50.4%
TIOGA	13,640	9,163	4,305	172	4,858 R	67.2%	31.6%	68.0%	32.0%
TOMPKINS	20,746	13,332	7,007	407	6,325 R	64.3%	33.8%	65.5%	34.5%
ULSTER	44,611	24,678	19,118	815	5,560 R	55.3%	42.9%	56.3%	43.7%
WARREN	19,871	12,873	6,807	191	6,066 R	64.8%	34.3%	65.4%	34.6%
WASHINGTON	23,317	15,186	7,713	418	7,473 R	65.1%	33.1%	66.3%	33.7%
WAYNE	25,534	17,901	7,099	534	10,802 R	70.1%	27.8%	71.6%	28.4%
WESTCHESTER	261,569	133,670	123,561	4,338	10,109 R	51.1%	47.2%	52.0%	48.0%

PRESIDENT 1940

County	Total Vote	Republican	Democratic	Other	Rep.-Dem. Plurality	Total Vote Rep.	Total Vote Dem.	Major Vote Rep.	Major Vote Dem.
ALBANY	136,167	58,912	77,052	203	18,140 D	43.3%	56.6%	43.3%	56.7%
ALLEGANY	20,767	15,611	5,077	79	10,534 R	75.2%	24.4%	75.5%	24.5%
BRONX	620,518	198,293	418,931	3,294	220,638 D	32.0%	67.5%	32.1%	67.9%
BROOME	76,284	44,013	32,092	179	11,921 R	57.7%	42.1%	57.8%	42.2%
CATTARAUGUS	35,055	22,987	11,924	144	11,063 R	65.6%	34.0%	65.8%	34.2%
CAYUGA	35,173	21,032	13,985	156	7,047 R	59.8%	39.8%	60.1%	39.9%
CHAUTAUQUA	57,316	35,536	21,524	256	14,012 R	62.0%	37.6%	62.3%	37.7%
CHEMUNG	37,497	22,156	15,203	138	6,953 R	59.1%	40.5%	59.3%	40.7%
CHENANGO	19,452	14,168	5,241	43	8,927 R	72.8%	26.9%	73.0%	27.0%
CLINTON	21,800	10,369	11,378	53	1,009 D	47.6%	52.2%	47.7%	52.3%
COLUMBIA	22,162	13,527	8,591	44	4,936 R	61.0%	38.8%	61.2%	38.8%
CORTLAND	17,411	12,233	5,147	31	7,086 R	70.3%	29.6%	70.4%	29.6%
DELAWARE	21,700	15,684	5,968	48	9,716 R	72.3%	27.5%	72.4%	27.6%
DUTCHESS	58,049	32,329	25,598	122	6,731 R	55.7%	44.1%	55.7%	44.2%
ERIE	374,435	183,664	189,779	992	6,115 D	49.1%	50.7%	49.2%	50.8%
ESSEX	17,451	11,868	5,545	38	6,323 R	68.0%	31.8%	68.2%	31.8%
FRANKLIN	20,958	11,446	9,479	33	1,967 R	54.6%	45.2%	54.7%	45.3%
FULTON	24,015	14,896	9,040	79	5,856 R	62.0%	37.6%	62.2%	37.8%
GENESEE	21,229	14,503	6,664	62	7,839 R	68.3%	31.4%	68.5%	31.5%
GREENE	16,616	10,153	6,425	38	3,728 R	61.1%	38.7%	61.2%	38.8%
HAMILTON	2,873	2,029	840	4	1,189 R	70.6%	29.2%	70.7%	29.3%
HERKIMER	30,657	17,590	13,013	54	4,577 R	57.4%	42.4%	57.5%	42.5%
JEFFERSON	40,262	25,584	14,581	97	11,003 R	63.5%	36.2%	63.7%	36.3%
KINGS	1,141,613	394,554	742,668	4,411	348,114 D	34.6%	65.1%	34.7%	65.3%
LEWIS	11,532	8,049	3,466	17	4,583 R	69.8%	30.1%	69.9%	30.1%
LIVINGSTON	19,084	12,629	6,397	58	6,232 R	66.2%	33.5%	66.4%	33.6%
MADISON	21,662	15,262	6,301	99	8,961 R	70.5%	29.1%	70.8%	51.3%
MONROE	236,064	114,383	120,613	1,068	6,230 D	48.5%	51.1%	48.7%	51.3%
MONTGOMERY	30,659	15,546	15,079	34	467 R	50.7%	49.2%	50.8%	49.2%
NASSAU	217,293	143,672	73,171	450	70,501 R	66.1%	33.7%	66.3%	33.7%
NEW YORK	774,507	292,480	478,153	3,874	185,673 D	37.8%	61.7%	38.0%	62.0%
NIAGARA	70,101	36,729	33,207	165	3,522 R	52.4%	47.4%	52.5%	47.5%
ONEIDA	101,742	52,362	49,109	271	3,253 R	51.5%	48.3%	51.5%	48.4%
ONONDAGA	156,022	91,056	67,481	485	23,575 R	58.4%	43.2%	57.4%	42.6%
ONTARIO	26,162	18,932	9,110	120	9,822 R	67.2%	32.3%	67.5%	32.6%
ORANGE	66,685	38,913	27,632	140	11,281 R	58.4%	41.4%	58.5%	41.5%
ORLEANS	15,519	10,958	4,525	36	6,433 R	70.6%	29.2%	70.8%	29.2%
OSWEGO	36,230	22,688	13,459	83	9,229 R	62.6%	37.1%	62.8%	37.2%
OTSEGO	24,647	16,771	7,798	78	8,973 R	68.0%	31.6%	68.3%	31.7%
PUTNAM	11,997	7,164	4,794	39	2,370 R	59.7%	40.0%	59.9%	40.1%
QUEENS	613,332	323,406	288,024	1,902	35,382 R	52.7%	47.0%	52.9%	47.1%
RENSSELAER	72,132	39,648	32,387	97	7,261 R	55.0%	44.9%	55.0%	45.0%
RICHMOND	77,448	38,911	38,307	230	604 R	50.2%	49.5%	50.4%	49.6%
ROCKLAND	35,064	20,040	14,897	127	5,143 R	57.2%	42.5%	57.4%	42.5%
ST LAWRENCE	39,990	24,339	15,569	82	8,770 R	60.9%	38.9%	61.0%	39.0%
SARATOGA	36,433	21,298	15,037	98	6,261 R	58.6%	41.3%	58.6%	41.4%
SCHENECTADY	66,469	34,101	32,041	327	2,060 R	51.3%	48.2%	51.6%	48.4%
SCHOHARIE	11,414	7,316	4,073	25	3,243 R	64.1%	35.7%	64.2%	35.8%
SCHUYLER	7,171	4,936	2,211	24	2,725 R	68.8%	30.8%	69.1%	30.9%
SENECA	12,598	8,364	4,203	31	4,161 R	66.4%	33.4%	66.6%	33.4%
STEUBEN	42,365	27,587	14,651	127	12,936 R	65.1%	34.6%	65.3%	34.7%
SUFFOLK	97,335	63,722	33,853	270	29,869 R	65.1%	34.6%	65.3%	34.7%
SULLIVAN	21,738	11,877	9,785	76	2,092 R	54.6%	45.0%	54.8%	45.2%
TIOGA	13,758	9,618	4,081	59	5,537 R	69.9%	29.7%	70.2%	29.8%
TOMPKINS	21,552	14,325	7,118	109	7,207 R	66.5%	33.0%	66.8%	33.2%
ULSTER	47,695	27,186	20,403	107	6,783 R	57.0%	42.8%	57.1%	42.9%
WARREN	20,923	13,657	7,226	40	6,431 R	65.3%	34.5%	65.4%	34.5%
WASHINGTON	23,975	15,960	7,977	38	7,983 R	66.6%	33.3%	66.7%	33.3%
WAYNE	22,616	15,196	7,358	62	7,838 R	72.1%	27.3%	72.3%	27.6%
WESTCHESTER	293,691	182,883	110,114	694	72,769 R	62.3%	37.5%	62.4%	37.6%

NEW YORK

PRESIDENT 1936

County	Total Vote	Republican	Democratic	Other	Rep.-Dem. Plurality	Percentage						
						Total Vote		Major Vote				
						Rep.	Dem.	Rep.	Dem.			
WYOMING	14,841	10,253	4,420	168	5,833 R	69.1%	29.8%	69.9%	30.1%			
YATES	9,280	6,897	2,257	126	4,640 R	74.3%	24.3%	75.3%	24.7%			
TOTAL	5,596,398	2,180,670	3,293,222	122,506	1,112,552 D	39.0%	58.8%	39.8%	60.2%			

PRESIDENT 1940

County	Total Vote	Republican	Democratic	Other	Rep.-Dem. Plurality	Percentage				
						Total Vote		Major Vote		
						Rep.	Dem.	Rep.	Dem.	
WYOMING	15,755	11,323	4,393	39	6,930 R	71.9%	27.9%	72.0%	28.0%
YATES	9,275	7,084	2,170	21	4,914 R	76.4%	23.4%	76.6%	23.4%
TOTAL	6,301,596	3,027,478	3,251,918	22,200	224,440 D	48.0%	51.6%	48.2%	51.8%

NEW YORK

PRESIDENT 1944

County	Total Vote	Republican	Democratic	Other	Rep.-Dem. Plurality	Total Vote Rep.	Total Vote Dem.	Major Vote Rep.	Major Vote Dem.
ALBANY	131,960	60,543	71,128	289	10,585 D	45.9%	53.9%	46.0%	54.0%
ALLEGANY	18,279	13,454	4,786	39	8,668 R	73.6	26.2	73.8	26.2
BRONX	665,035	211,158	450,525	3,352	239,367 D	31.8	67.7	31.9	68.1
BROOME	75,206	44,013	31,056	137	12,957 R	58.5	41.3	58.6	41.4
CATTARAUGUS	31,795	19,907	11,787	101	8,120 R	62.6	37.1	62.8	37.2
CAYUGA	32,629	18,680	13,849	100	4,831 R	57.2	42.4	57.4	42.6
CHAUTAUQUA	55,174	32,824	22,086	264	10,738 R	59.5	40.0	59.8	40.2
CHEMUNG	37,357	22,198	15,064	95	7,134 R	59.4	40.3	59.6	40.4
CHENANGO	17,779	12,745	4,997	37	7,748 R	71.7	28.1	71.8	28.2
CLINTON	18,806	8,775	9,996	35	1,221 D	46.7	53.2	46.7	53.3
COLUMBIA	20,078	13,055	6,969	54	6,086 R	65.0	34.7	65.2	34.8
CORTLAND	15,441	10,450	4,967	24	5,483 R	67.7	32.2	67.8	32.2
DELAWARE	20,069	14,916	5,128	25	9,788 R	74.3	25.6	74.4	25.6
DUTCHESS	55,826	32,890	22,778	158	10,112 R	58.9	40.8	59.1	40.9
ERIE	383,235	185,975	195,905	1,355	9,930 D	48.5	51.1	48.7	51.3
ESSEX	14,798	10,128	4,637	33	5,491 R	68.4	31.3	68.6	31.4
FRANKLIN	17,324	9,225	8,060	39	1,165 R	53.2	46.5	53.4	46.6
FULTON	22,070	13,195	8,813	62	4,382 R	59.8	39.9	60.0	40.0
GENESEE	20,324	13,478	6,796	50	6,682 R	66.3	33.4	66.5	33.5
GREENE	15,064	9,807	5,231	26	4,576 R	65.1	34.7	65.2	34.8
HAMILTON	2,673	1,834	830	9	1,004 R	68.6	31.1	68.8	31.2
HERKIMER	28,085	15,656	12,381	48	3,275 R	55.7	44.1	55.8	44.2
JEFFERSON	36,329	21,834	14,449	46	7,385 R	60.1	39.8	60.2	39.8
KINGS	1,158,364	393,926	758,270	6,168	364,344 D	34.0	65.5	34.2	65.8
LEWIS	9,715	6,256	3,441	18	2,815 R	64.4	35.4	64.5	35.5
LIVINGSTON	17,775	11,383	6,351	41	5,032 R	64.0	35.7	64.2	35.8
MADISON	19,514	13,369	6,109	36	7,260 R	68.5	31.3	68.6	31.4
MONROE	232,273	111,725	119,672	876	7,947 D	48.1	51.5	48.3	51.7
MONTGOMERY	29,189	14,726	14,400	63	326 R	50.5	49.3	50.6	49.4
NASSAU	238,801	159,713	78,512	576	81,201 R	66.9	32.9	67.0	33.0
NEW YORK	772,761	258,650	509,263	4,848	250,613 D	33.5	65.9	33.7	66.3
NIAGARA	72,666	37,514	34,850	224	2,764 R	51.6	48.0	51.9	48.1
ONEIDA	97,344	48,749	48,371	224	378 R	50.1	49.7	50.2	49.8
ONONDAGA	154,638	80,507	73,562	569	6,945 R	52.1	47.6	52.3	47.7
ONTARIO	26,364	16,859	9,437	68	7,422 R	63.9	35.8	64.1	35.9
ORANGE	63,262	39,041	24,059	162	14,982 R	61.7	38.0	61.9	38.1
ORLEANS	14,026	9,998	4,006	22	5,992 R	71.3	28.6	71.4	28.6
OSWEGO	32,355	19,733	12,593	29	7,140 R	61.0	38.9	61.0	39.0
OTSEGO	23,313	15,427	7,849	37	7,578 R	66.2	33.7	66.3	33.7
PUTNAM	11,294	7,010	4,251	33	2,759 R	62.1	37.6	62.3	37.7
QUEENS	660,375	365,365	292,940	2,070	72,425 R	55.3	44.4	55.5	44.5
RENSSELAER	68,131	37,819	30,173	139	7,646 R	55.5	44.3	55.7	44.5
RICHMOND	73,915	42,188	31,502	225	10,686 R	57.1	42.6	57.3	42.7
ROCKLAND	32,998	19,471	13,437	90	6,034 R	59.0	40.7	59.2	40.8
ST LAWRENCE	37,219	21,919	15,223	77	6,696 R	58.9	40.9	59.0	41.0
SARATOGA	34,083	20,197	13,788	98	6,409 R	59.3	40.5	59.4	40.6
SCHENECTADY	68,868	35,178	33,397	293	1,781 R	51.6	48.5	51.3	48.7
SCHOHARIE	10,801	6,546	4,219	36	2,327 R	60.6	39.1	60.8	39.2
SCHUYLER	6,279	4,506	1,767	6	2,739 R	71.8	28.1	71.9	28.2
SENECA	11,688	7,424	4,236	28	3,188 R	63.5	36.2	63.7	36.3
STEUBEN	39,072	25,538	13,461	73	12,077 R	65.4	34.5	65.5	34.5
SUFFOLK	97,133	65,650	31,231	252	34,419 R	67.6	32.2	67.8	32.2
SULLIVAN	20,157	11,258	8,836	73	2,422 R	55.8	43.8	56.0	44.0
TIOGA	12,790	8,934	3,831	25	5,103 R	69.9	30.0	70.0	30.0
TOMPKINS	20,053	12,805	7,174	74	5,631 R	63.9	35.8	64.1	35.9
ULSTER	43,763	26,703	16,943	117	9,760 R	61.0	38.7	61.2	38.8
WARREN	18,897	12,144	6,716	37	5,428 R	64.3	35.5	64.4	35.6
WASHINGTON	20,992	13,861	7,100	31	6,761 R	66.0	33.8	66.1	33.9
WAYNE	24,555	17,523	6,999	33	10,524 R	71.4	28.5	71.5	28.5
WESTCHESTER	282,980	174,635	107,591	754	67,044 R	61.7	38.0	61.9	38.1

PRESIDENT 1948

County	Total Vote	Republican	Democratic	Other	Rep.-Dem. Plurality	Total Vote Rep.	Total Vote Dem.	Major Vote Rep.	Major Vote Dem.
ALBANY	140,733	59,965	75,419	5,346	15,454 D	42.6%	53.6%	44.3%	55.7%
ALLEGANY	17,639	12,689	4,711	239	7,978 R	71.9	26.7	72.9	27.1
BRONX	622,355	173,044	337,129	112,182	164,085 D	27.8	54.2	33.9	66.1
BROOME	70,985	43,110	25,654	2,222	17,456 R	60.7	36.1	62.7	37.3
CATTARAUGUS	30,393	16,246	11,289	858	6,957 R	60.0	37.1	61.8	38.2
CAYUGA	33,747	19,017	14,317	413	4,700 R	56.4	42.4	57.0	43.0
CHAUTAUQUA	52,144	29,969	20,683	1,492	9,286 R	57.5	36.2	59.2	40.8
CHEMUNG	36,919	22,754	13,352	813	9,402 R	61.6	36.2	63.0	37.0
CHENANGO	16,982	11,988	4,764	230	7,224 R	70.6	28.1	71.6	28.4
CLINTON	19,755	9,694	9,357	704	337 R	49.1	47.4	50.9	49.1
COLUMBIA	20,880	13,758	6,527	595	7,231 R	65.9	31.3	67.8	32.2
CORTLAND	15,283	10,433	4,614	236	5,819 R	68.3	30.2	69.3	30.7
DELAWARE	19,474	14,226	4,965	283	9,261 R	73.1	25.5	74.1	25.9
DUTCHESS	53,039	34,067	17,439	1,533	16,628 R	64.2	32.9	66.1	33.9
ERIE	383,372	175,118	197,618	10,636	22,500 D	45.7	51.5	47.0	53.0
ESSEX	14,717	10,287	4,088	342	6,199 R	69.6	27.7	71.6	28.4
FRANKLIN	16,302	8,993	6,799	510	2,194 R	55.2	41.7	56.9	43.1
FULTON	21,134	12,787	7,667	680	5,120 R	60.5	36.3	62.5	37.5
GENESEE	20,142	12,650	7,024	468	5,626 R	62.8	34.9	64.3	35.7
GREENE	15,883	10,566	4,955	362	5,611 R	66.5	31.2	68.1	31.9
HAMILTON	2,790	2,000	744	46	1,256 R	71.7	26.7	72.9	27.1
HERKIMER	28,338	14,688	12,577	1,073	2,111 R	51.8	44.4	53.9	46.1
JEFFERSON	33,351	19,661	13,176	514	6,485 R	59.0	39.5	59.9	40.1
KINGS	1,083,801	330,494	579,922	173,385	249,428 D	30.5	53.5	36.3	63.7
LEWIS	9,078	5,692	3,211	175	2,481 R	62.7	35.4	63.9	36.1
LIVINGSTON	18,062	11,310	6,409	343	4,901 R	62.6	35.5	63.8	36.2
MADISON	19,658	13,413	5,937	308	7,476 R	68.2	30.2	69.3	30.7
MONROE	227,790	109,608	110,641	7,541	1,033 D	48.1	48.6	49.8	50.2
MONTGOMERY	29,064	14,212	14,085	767	127 R	48.9	48.5	50.2	49.8
NASSAU	265,238	184,284	70,492	10,462	113,792 R	69.5	26.6	72.3	27.7
NEW YORK	738,237	241,752	380,310	116,175	138,558 D	32.7	51.5	38.9	61.1
NIAGARA	72,219	35,858	34,119	2,242	1,739 R	49.7	47.2	51.2	48.8
ONEIDA	97,613	46,735	48,332	2,526	1,577 D	47.9	49.5	49.2	50.8
ONONDAGA	156,648	84,370	66,295	5,983	18,075 R	53.9	42.3	56.0	44.0
ONTARIO	25,439	16,156	8,852	431	7,304 R	63.5	34.8	64.6	35.4
ORANGE	60,796	38,351	20,638	1,807	17,713 R	63.1	33.9	65.0	35.0
ORLEANS	13,834	9,566	4,009	259	5,557 R	69.1	29.0	70.5	29.5
OSWEGO	32,904	19,095	12,820	989	6,275 R	58.0	39.0	59.8	40.2
OTSEGO	23,197	15,437	7,174	586	8,263 R	66.5	30.9	68.3	31.7
PUTNAM	12,877	8,222	4,012	643	4,210 R	63.9	31.2	67.2	32.8
QUEENS	639,543	323,459	268,742	47,342	54,717 R	50.6	42.0	54.6	45.4
RENSSELAER	71,197	40,375	28,468	2,354	11,907 R	56.7	40.0	58.6	41.4
RICHMOND	73,134	39,539	30,440	3,155	9,097 R	54.1	41.6	56.5	43.5
ROCKLAND	35,681	20,661	13,066	1,954	7,595 R	57.9	36.6	61.3	38.7
ST LAWRENCE	34,925	21,160	13,200	565	7,960 R	60.6	37.8	61.6	38.4
SARATOGA	33,666	20,706	11,457	1,503	9,249 R	61.5	34.0	64.4	35.6
SCHENECTADY	67,391	35,495	28,225	3,671	7,270 R	52.7	41.9	55.7	44.3
SCHOHARIE	11,019	6,751	4,032	236	2,719 R	61.3	36.6	62.6	37.4
SCHUYLER	6,431	4,452	1,868	111	2,584 R	69.2	29.0	70.4	29.6
SENECA	12,516	7,266	4,897	353	2,369 R	58.1	39.1	59.7	40.3
STEUBEN	36,736	22,938	12,895	903	10,043 R	62.4	35.1	64.0	36.0
SUFFOLK	108,265	75,519	29,104	3,642	46,415 R	69.8	26.9	72.2	27.8
SULLIVAN	21,552	11,253	7,654	2,245	3,599 R	53.2	36.2	59.5	40.5
TIOGA	12,362	8,673	3,385	304	5,288 R	70.2	27.4	71.9	28.1
TOMPKINS	20,444	13,719	5,721	1,004	7,998 R	67.1	28.0	70.6	29.4
ULSTER	45,012	28,941	14,441	1,630	14,500 R	64.3	32.1	66.7	33.3
WARREN	18,703	12,884	5,486	333	7,398 R	68.8	29.3	70.1	29.9
WASHINGTON	20,464	13,975	6,017	472	7,958 R	68.3	29.4	69.9	30.1
WAYNE	23,270	16,167	6,749	354	9,418 R	69.5	29.0	70.5	29.5
WESTCHESTER	289,765	177,077	95,681	17,007	81,396 R	61.1	33.0	64.9	35.1

NEW YORK

PRESIDENT 1944

County	Total Vote	Republican	Democratic	Other	Rep.-Dem. Plurality	Percentage Total Vote Rep.	Dem.	Major Vote Rep.	Dem.
WYOMING	14,689	10,219	4,455	15	5,764 R	69.6%	30.3%	69.6%	30.4%
YATES	8,352	6,338	2,005	9	4,333 R	75.9%	24.0%	76.0%	24.0%
TOTAL	6,316,790	2,987,647	3,304,238	24,905	316,591 D	47.3%	52.3%	47.5%	52.5%

PRESIDENT 1948

Total Vote	Republican	Democratic	Other	Rep.-Dem. Plurality	Percentage Total Vote Rep.	Dem.	Major Vote Rep.	Dem.
14,564	9,871	4,508	185	5,363 R	67.8%	31.0%	68.6%	31.4%
8,159	5,997	2,040	122	3,957 R	73.5%	25.0%	74.6%	25.4%
6,177,337	2,841,163	2,780,204	555,970	60,959 R	46.0%	45.0%	50.5%	49.5%

NEW YORK

PRESIDENT 1952

County	Total Vote	Republican	Democratic	Other	Rep.-Dem. Plurality	Total Vote Rep.	Total Vote Dem.	Major Vote Rep.	Major Vote Dem.
ALBANY	152,806	79,871	72,633	302	7,238 R	52.3%	47.5%	52.4%	47.6%
ALLEGANY	20,324	16,365	3,943	16	12,422 R	80.5%	19.4%	80.6%	19.4%
BRONX	648,753	241,898	392,477	14,378	150,579 D	37.3%	60.5%	38.1%	61.9%
BROOME	90,717	64,738	25,833	146	38,905 R	71.4%	28.5%	71.5%	28.5%
CATTARAUGUS	36,195	24,808	11,333	54	13,475 R	68.5%	31.3%	68.6%	31.4%
CAYUGA	36,804	25,037	11,695	72	13,342 R	68.0%	31.8%	68.2%	31.8%
CHAUTAUQUA	65,620	42,043	23,427	150	18,616 R	64.1%	35.7%	64.2%	35.8%
CHEMUNG	44,022	30,188	13,729	105	16,459 R	68.5%	31.1%	68.7%	31.3%
CHENANGO	20,167	16,062	4,089	16	11,973 R	79.6%	20.3%	79.7%	20.3%
CLINTON	22,546	14,535	7,963	48	6,572 R	64.5%	35.3%	64.6%	35.4%
COLUMBIA	23,659	17,539	6,075	45	11,464 R	74.1%	25.7%	74.3%	25.7%
CORTLAND	18,093	13,985	4,079	29	9,905 R	77.3%	22.5%	77.4%	22.6%
DELAWARE	21,879	17,737	4,116	26	13,621 R	81.1%	18.8%	81.2%	18.8%
DUTCHESS	65,198	46,381	18,644	173	27,737 R	71.1%	28.6%	71.3%	28.7%
ERIE	451,249	253,927	196,378	944	57,549 R	56.3%	43.5%	56.4%	43.6%
ESSEX	16,959	12,800	4,130	29	8,670 R	75.5%	24.4%	75.6%	24.4%
FRANKLIN	18,828	12,212	6,591	25	5,621 R	64.9%	35.0%	64.9%	35.1%
FULTON	25,710	18,068	7,570	72	10,498 R	70.5%	29.4%	70.5%	29.5%
GENESEE	23,443	18,606	6,819	18	11,787 R	70.8%	29.1%	71.0%	29.1%
GREENE	17,435	12,907	4,504	24	8,403 R	74.0%	25.8%	74.1%	25.9%
HAMILTON	3,165	2,615	546	4	2,069 R	82.6%	17.3%	82.7%	17.3%
HERKIMER	32,668	20,980	11,599	89	9,381 R	64.2%	35.5%	64.4%	35.6%
JEFFERSON	39,983	27,932	12,026	25	15,906 R	69.8%	30.1%	69.9%	30.1%
KINGS	1,123,249	446,708	656,229	20,312	209,521 D	39.8%	58.4%	40.5%	59.5%
LEWIS	10,576	7,622	2,927	27	4,695 R	72.1%	27.7%	72.3%	27.7%
LIVINGSTON	20,690	14,760	5,901	29	8,859 R	71.3%	28.5%	71.4%	28.6%
MADISON	23,101	17,715	5,353	33	12,362 R	76.7%	23.2%	76.8%	23.2%
MONROE	270,400	159,172	110,723	505	48,449 R	58.9%	40.9%	59.0%	41.0%
MONTGOMERY	32,533	19,554	12,934	45	6,620 R	60.1%	39.8%	60.2%	39.8%
NASSAU	438,090	305,900	130,267	1,923	175,633 R	69.8%	29.7%	70.1%	29.9%
NEW YORK	765,183	300,284	446,727	18,172	146,443 D	39.2%	58.4%	40.2%	59.8%
NIAGARA	91,499	54,843	36,504	152	18,339 R	59.9%	39.9%	60.0%	40.0%
ONEIDA	114,283	69,652	44,438	193	25,214 R	60.9%	38.9%	61.1%	38.9%
ONONDAGA	183,714	119,268	64,022	424	55,246 R	64.9%	34.8%	65.1%	34.9%
ONTARIO	30,448	21,659	8,763	26	12,896 R	71.1%	28.8%	71.2%	28.8%
ORANGE	71,949	51,217	20,585	147	30,632 R	71.2%	28.6%	71.3%	28.7%
ORLEANS	15,590	11,686	3,893	11	7,793 R	75.0%	25.0%	75.0%	25.0%
OSWEGO	36,082	24,309	11,444	29	12,865 R	70.6%	29.3%	70.7%	29.3%
OTSEGO	26,458	20,304	6,115	39	14,189 R	76.7%	23.1%	76.9%	23.1%
PUTNAM	16,118	11,038	5,001	79	6,037 R	68.5%	31.0%	68.8%	31.2%
QUEENS	789,682	450,610	331,217	7,855	119,393 R	57.1%	41.9%	57.6%	42.4%
RENSSELAER	77,337	51,453	25,734	150	25,719 R	66.5%	33.2%	66.6%	33.3%
RICHMOND	84,606	55,991	28,280	335	27,711 R	66.2%	33.4%	66.4%	33.6%
ROCKLAND	42,973	27,657	15,084	232	12,573 R	64.4%	35.1%	64.7%	35.3%
ST LAWRENCE	41,087	28,036	13,000	51	15,036 R	68.2%	31.6%	68.3%	31.7%
SARATOGA	41,186	29,712	11,413	61	18,299 R	72.1%	27.7%	72.2%	27.8%
SCHENECTADY	81,699	54,272	27,157	270	27,115 R	66.4%	33.2%	66.6%	33.4%
SCHOHARIE	12,509	8,972	3,509	28	5,463 R	71.7%	28.0%	71.9%	28.1%
SCHUYLER	7,409	5,604	1,784	21	3,820 R	75.6%	24.0%	75.9%	24.1%
SENECA	14,020	9,669	4,328	23	5,341 R	69.0%	30.9%	69.1%	30.9%
STEUBEN	43,342	32,123	11,154	65	20,969 R	74.1%	25.7%	74.2%	25.8%
SUFFOLK	155,050	115,570	39,120	360	76,450 R	74.5%	25.2%	74.7%	25.3%
SULLIVAN	23,626	14,926	8,421	279	6,505 R	63.2%	35.6%	63.9%	36.1%
TIOGA	15,095	11,799	3,259	37	8,540 R	78.2%	21.6%	78.4%	21.6%
TOMPKINS	25,019	18,673	6,285	61	12,388 R	74.6%	25.1%	74.8%	25.2%
ULSTER	52,085	36,141	15,733	211	20,408 R	69.4%	30.2%	69.7%	30.3%
WARREN	22,131	17,046	5,051	34	11,995 R	77.0%	22.8%	77.1%	22.9%
WASHINGTON	23,789	17,551	6,210	28	11,341 R	73.8%	26.1%	73.9%	26.1%
WAYNE	28,362	21,693	6,621	48	15,072 R	76.5%	23.3%	76.6%	23.4%
WESTCHESTER	352,170	237,105	113,358	1,707	123,747 R	67.3%	32.2%	67.7%	32.3%

PRESIDENT 1956

County	Total Vote	Republican	Democratic	Other	Rep.-Dem. Plurality	Total Vote Rep.	Total Vote Dem.	Major Vote Rep.	Major Vote Dem.
ALBANY	152,193	86,202	65,982	9	20,220 R	56.6%	43.4%	56.6%	43.4%
ALLEGANY	19,736	16,068	3,668		12,400 R	81.4%	18.6%	81.4%	18.6%
BRONX	601,588	257,382	343,823	383	86,441 D	42.8%	57.2%	42.8%	57.2%
BROOME	90,241	67,024	23,217		43,807 R	74.3%	25.7%	74.3%	25.7%
CATTARAUGUS	34,895	25,282	9,613		15,669 R	72.5%	27.5%	72.5%	27.5%
CAYUGA	36,775	26,503	10,268	4	16,235 R	72.1%	27.9%	72.1%	27.9%
CHAUTAUQUA	64,432	44,149	20,269	14	23,880 R	68.5%	31.5%	68.5%	31.5%
CHEMUNG	44,862	33,270	11,592		21,678 R	74.2%	25.8%	74.2%	25.8%
CHENANGO	20,118	16,314	3,804		12,510 R	81.1%	18.9%	81.1%	18.9%
CLINTON	23,130	16,295	6,833	2	9,462 R	70.4%	29.5%	70.5%	29.5%
COLUMBIA	24,003	19,004	4,999		14,005 R	79.2%	20.8%	79.2%	20.8%
CORTLAND	17,697	14,085	3,612		10,473 R	79.6%	20.4%	79.6%	20.4%
DELAWARE	21,199	17,364	3,835		13,529 R	81.9%	18.1%	81.9%	18.1%
DUTCHESS	68,724	53,840	14,876	8	38,964 R	78.3%	21.6%	78.4%	21.6%
ERIE	459,649	292,657	166,930	62	125,727 R	63.7%	36.3%	63.7%	36.3%
ESSEX	16,965	13,930	3,035		10,895 R	82.1%	17.9%	82.1%	17.9%
FRANKLIN	18,229	13,003	5,226		7,777 R	71.3%	28.7%	71.3%	28.7%
FULTON	24,596	18,244	6,352		11,892 R	74.2%	25.8%	74.2%	25.8%
GENESEE	23,600	17,614	5,986		11,628 R	74.6%	25.4%	74.6%	25.4%
GREENE	18,073	14,262	3,811		10,451 R	78.9%	21.1%	78.9%	21.1%
HAMILTON	3,089	2,619	470		2,149 R	84.8%	15.2%	84.8%	15.2%
HERKIMER	31,035	22,246	8,789		13,457 R	71.7%	28.3%	71.7%	28.3%
JEFFERSON	38,389	28,429	9,959	1	18,470 R	74.1%	25.9%	74.1%	25.9%
KINGS	1,018,479	460,456	557,655	368	97,199 D	45.2%	54.8%	45.2%	54.8%
LEWIS	10,300	7,764	2,536		5,228 R	75.4%	24.6%	75.4%	24.6%
LIVINGSTON	20,513	15,523	4,989	1	10,534 R	75.7%	24.3%	75.7%	24.3%
MADISON	23,462	18,555	4,903	23	13,652 R	79.1%	20.9%	79.1%	20.9%
MONROE	274,931	183,517	91,001	111	92,586 R	66.8%	33.2%	66.8%	33.2%
MONTGOMERY	30,685	20,678	9,996	11	10,682 R	67.4%	32.6%	67.4%	32.6%
NASSAU	539,463	372,358	166,646	459	205,712 R	69.0%	30.9%	69.1%	30.9%
NEW YORK	678,317	300,004	377,856	457	77,852 D	44.2%	55.7%	44.3%	55.7%
NIAGARA	92,594	62,433	30,161		32,272 R	67.4%	32.6%	67.4%	32.6%
ONEIDA	114,827	80,178	34,649		45,529 R	69.8%	30.2%	69.8%	30.2%
ONONDAGA	187,772	137,852	49,918		87,934 R	73.4%	26.6%	73.4%	26.6%
ONTARIO	30,041	22,317	7,719	5	14,598 R	74.3%	25.7%	74.3%	25.7%
ORANGE	74,490	57,739	16,722	29	41,017 R	77.5%	22.4%	77.5%	22.4%
ORLEANS	15,359	11,895	3,464		8,431 R	77.4%	22.6%	77.4%	22.6%
OSWEGO	38,086	29,277	8,609		20,468 R	76.9%	23.1%	76.9%	23.1%
OTSEGO	25,123	19,484	5,644		13,840 R	77.5%	22.5%	77.5%	22.5%
PUTNAM	17,505	12,898	4,694	13	8,204 R	73.3%	26.7%	73.3%	26.7%
QUEENS	787,265	471,223	315,898	144	155,325 R	59.9%	40.1%	59.9%	40.1%
RENSSELAER	75,702	55,186	20,516		34,670 R	72.9%	27.1%	72.9%	27.1%
RICHMOND	83,935	64,233	19,644	59	44,589 R	76.5%	23.4%	76.5%	23.4%
ROCKLAND	47,940	34,049	13,881	10	20,168 R	71.0%	29.0%	71.0%	29.0%
ST LAWRENCE	42,789	31,897	10,892		21,005 R	74.5%	25.5%	74.5%	25.5%
SARATOGA	41,866	32,540	9,338	6	23,184 R	77.7%	22.3%	77.7%	22.3%
SCHENECTADY	80,235	56,540	21,673	22	36,867 R	73.0%	27.0%	73.0%	27.0%
SCHOHARIE	12,078	8,851	3,227		5,624 R	73.3%	26.7%	73.3%	26.7%
SCHUYLER	7,408	5,795	1,613		4,182 R	78.2%	21.8%	78.2%	21.8%
SENECA	14,040	10,417	3,623		6,794 R	74.2%	25.8%	74.2%	25.8%
STEUBEN	43,342	33,902	9,440		24,462 R	78.2%	21.8%	78.2%	21.8%
SUFFOLK	216,232	167,805	48,323	104	119,482 R	77.6%	22.3%	77.6%	22.4%
SULLIVAN	24,782	15,845	8,937		6,908 R	63.9%	36.1%	63.9%	36.1%
TIOGA	15,149	11,958	3,188	3	8,770 R	78.9%	21.0%	79.0%	21.0%
TOMPKINS	25,224	19,749	5,475		14,274 R	78.3%	21.7%	78.3%	21.7%
ULSTER	56,360	43,034	13,321	5	29,713 R	76.4%	23.6%	76.4%	23.6%
WARREN	21,749	17,852	3,897		13,955 R	82.1%	17.9%	82.1%	17.9%
WASHINGTON	23,266	18,449	4,817		13,632 R	79.3%	20.7%	79.3%	20.7%
WAYNE	28,850	22,940	5,910		17,030 R	79.5%	20.5%	79.5%	20.5%
WESTCHESTER	377,078	271,906	104,857	315	167,049 R	72.1%	27.8%	72.2%	27.8%

NEW YORK

PRESIDENT 1952

County	Total Vote	Republican	Democratic	Other	Rep.-Dem. Plurality	Total Vote Rep.	Total Vote Dem.	Major Vote Rep.	Major Vote Dem.
WYOMING	16,206	12,154	4,038	14	8,116 R	75.0%	24.9%	75.1%	24.9%
YATES	9,670	7,831	1,820	19	6,011 R	81.0%	18.8%	81.1%	18.9%
TOTAL	7,128,239	3,952,813	3,104,601	70,825	848,212 R	55.5%	43.6%	56.0%	44.0%

PRESIDENT 1956

County	Total Vote	Republican	Democratic	Other	Rep.-Dem. Plurality	Total Vote Rep.	Total Vote Dem.	Major Vote Rep.	Major Vote Dem.
WYOMING	15,896	12,499	3,397		9,102 R	78.6%	21.4%	78.6%	21.4%
YATES	9,516	7,910	1,606		6,304 R	83.1%	16.9%	83.1%	16.9%
TOTAL	7,095,971	4,345,506	2,747,944	2,521	1,597,562 R	61.2%	38.7%	61.3%	38.7%

NEW YORK

PRESIDENT 1960

County	Total Vote	Republican	Democratic	Other	Rep.-Dem. Plurality	% Total Rep.	% Total Dem.	% Major Rep.	% Major Dem.
ALBANY	153,692	61,600	91,973	119	30,373 D	40.1	59.8	40.1	59.9
ALLEGANY	19,695	14,408	5,280	7	9,128 R	73.2	26.8	73.2	26.8
BRONX	574,282	182,393	389,818	2,071	207,425 D	31.8	67.9	31.9	68.1
BROOME	94,991	56,467	38,462	62	18,005 R	59.4	40.5	59.5	40.5
CATTARAUGUS	36,573	21,749	14,797	27	6,952 R	59.5	40.5	59.5	40.5
CAYUGA	37,722	20,437	17,257	28	3,180 R	54.2	45.7	54.2	45.8
CHAUTAUQUA	66,031	37,836	28,143	52	9,693 R	57.3	42.6	57.3	42.7
CHEMUNG	44,396	26,469	17,899	28	8,570 R	59.6	40.3	59.7	40.3
CHENANGO	20,204	14,533	5,659	12	8,874 R	71.9	28.0	72.0	28.0
CLINTON	24,951	11,154	13,782	15	2,628 D	44.7	55.2	44.7	55.3
COLUMBIA	24,664	15,893	8,747	24	7,146 R	64.4	35.5	64.5	35.5
CORTLAND	18,235	12,305	5,921	9	6,384 R	67.5	32.5	67.5	32.5
DELAWARE	22,013	16,336	5,662	15	10,674 R	74.2	25.7	74.3	25.7
DUTCHESS	76,004	46,109	29,842	53	16,267 R	60.7	39.3	60.7	39.3
ERIE	489,564	211,997	277,203	404	65,206 D	43.3	56.6	43.3	56.7
ESSEX	17,901	11,557	6,334	10	5,223 R	64.6	35.4	64.6	35.4
FRANKLIN	15,358	9,385	5,946	27	3,439 R	61.1	38.7	61.2	38.8
FULTON	24,883	14,455	10,409	19	4,046 R	58.1	41.8	58.1	41.9
GENESEE	25,085	14,724	10,343	18	4,381 R	58.7	41.2	58.7	41.3
GREENE	16,320	9,878	6,441	1	3,437 R	60.5	39.5	60.5	39.5
HAMILTON	2,964	2,168	795	1	1,373 R	73.1	26.8	73.2	26.8
HERKIMER	32,768	17,758	14,977	33	2,781 R	54.2	45.7	54.2	45.8
JEFFERSON	40,115	24,290	15,800	25	8,490 R	60.6	39.4	60.6	39.4
KINGS	977,306	327,497	646,582	3,227	319,085 D	33.5	66.2	33.6	66.4
LEWIS	10,697	6,632	4,056	9	2,576 R	62.0	37.9	62.1	37.9
LIVINGSTON	21,454	13,681	7,765	8	5,916 R	63.8	36.2	63.8	36.2
MADISON	24,697	16,245	8,433	19	7,812 R	65.8	34.1	65.8	34.2
MONROE	289,948	148,423	141,378	147	7,045 R	51.2	48.8	51.2	48.8
MONTGOMERY	31,827	14,837	16,976	14	2,139 D	46.6	53.3	46.6	53.4
NASSAU	588,319	324,255	263,303	761	60,952 R	55.1	44.8	55.2	44.8
NEW YORK	635,567	217,271	414,902	3,394	197,631 D	34.2	65.3	34.4	65.6
NIAGARA	101,765	50,001	51,680	84	1,679 D	49.1	50.8	49.2	50.8
ONEIDA	122,981	59,513	63,368	100	3,855 D	48.4	51.5	48.4	51.6
ONONDAGA	198,156	107,170	90,836	150	16,334 R	54.1	45.8	54.1	45.9
ONTARIO	31,931	19,654	12,251	26	7,403 R	61.6	38.4	61.6	38.4
ORANGE	80,182	48,646	31,471	65	17,175 R	60.7	39.2	60.7	39.3
ORLEANS	15,864	10,344	5,515	5	4,829 R	65.2	34.8	65.2	34.8
OSWEGO	39,568	24,013	15,544	11	8,469 R	60.7	39.3	60.7	39.3
OTSEGO	25,347	17,422	7,899	26	9,523 R	68.7	31.2	68.8	31.2
PUTNAM	19,987	11,946	8,013	28	3,933 R	59.8	40.1	59.9	40.1
QUEENS	815,899	367,688	446,348	1,863	78,660 D	45.1	54.7	45.2	54.8
RENSSELAER	76,294	40,124	36,109	61	4,015 R	52.6	47.3	52.6	47.4
RICHMOND	89,123	50,356	38,673	94	11,683 R	56.5	43.4	56.6	43.4
ROCKLAND	60,398	33,107	27,178	113	5,929 R	54.8	45.0	54.9	45.1
ST LAWRENCE	45,302	25,848	19,430	24	6,418 R	57.1	42.9	57.1	42.9
SARATOGA	43,250	25,035	18,179	36	6,856 R	57.9	42.0	57.9	42.1
SCHENECTADY	77,253	40,180	37,003	70	3,177 R	52.0	47.9	52.1	47.9
SCHOHARIE	12,002	7,644	4,342	16	3,302 R	63.7	36.2	63.8	36.2
SCHUYLER	7,527	5,201	2,315	11	2,886 R	69.1	30.8	69.2	30.8
SENECA	14,435	8,741	5,693	1	3,048 R	60.6	39.4	60.6	39.4
STEUBEN	43,549	29,638	13,898	13	15,740 R	68.1	31.9	68.1	31.9
SUFFOLK	280,945	166,644	114,033	268	52,611 R	59.3	40.6	59.4	40.6
SULLIVAN	25,274	13,744	11,486	44	2,258 R	54.4	45.5	54.5	45.5
TIOGA	17,431	12,572	4,855	4	7,717 R	72.1	27.9	72.1	27.9
TOMPKINS	25,733	17,061	8,659	13	8,402 R	66.3	33.6	66.3	33.7
ULSTER	59,502	36,418	23,017	67	13,401 R	61.2	38.7	61.3	38.7
WARREN	21,778	14,433	7,328	17	7,105 R	66.3	33.6	66.3	33.7
WASHINGTON	23,317	15,037	8,274	6	6,763 R	64.5	35.5	64.5	35.5
WAYNE	30,777	21,290	9,476	11	11,814 R	69.2	30.8	69.2	30.8
WESTCHESTER	396,663	224,562	171,410	691	53,152 R	56.6	43.2	56.7	43.3

PRESIDENT 1964

County	Total Vote	Republican	Democratic	Other	Rep.-Dem. Plurality	% Total Rep.	% Total Dem.	% Major Rep.	% Major Dem.
ALBANY	147,152	32,224	114,827	101	82,603 D	21.9	78.0	21.9	78.1
ALLEGANY	18,039	7,688	10,329	22	2,641 D	42.6	57.3	42.7	57.3
BRONX	539,559	135,780	402,960	819	267,180 D	25.2	74.7	25.2	74.8
BROOME	91,139	32,048	59,021	70	26,973 D	35.2	64.8	35.2	64.8
CATTARAUGUS	32,933	10,907	21,994	32	11,087 D	33.1	66.8	33.2	66.8
CAYUGA	35,566	11,453	24,090	23	12,637 D	32.2	67.7	32.2	67.8
CHAUTAUQUA	62,064	19,069	42,924	71	23,855 D	30.7	69.2	30.8	69.2
CHEMUNG	41,082	14,716	26,332	34	11,616 D	35.8	64.1	35.9	64.1
CHENANGO	18,952	7,293	11,653	6	4,360 D	38.5	61.5	38.5	61.5
CLINTON	24,492	6,078	18,398	16	12,320 D	24.8	75.1	24.8	75.2
COLUMBIA	23,558	9,023	14,516	19	5,493 D	38.3	61.6	38.3	61.7
CORTLAND	17,272	6,149	11,110	13	4,961 D	35.6	64.3	35.6	64.4
DELAWARE	20,064	8,359	11,686	19	3,327 D	41.7	58.2	41.7	58.3
DUTCHESS	79,735	29,503	50,179	53	20,676 D	37.0	62.9	37.0	63.0
ERIE	471,576	125,962	344,910	704	218,948 D	26.7	73.1	26.8	73.2
ESSEX	16,585	5,837	10,739	9	4,902 D	35.2	64.8	35.2	64.8
FRANKLIN	23,149	7,278	15,846	25	8,568 D	31.4	68.5	31.5	68.5
FULTON	23,841	8,114	15,713	14	7,599 D	34.0	65.9	34.1	65.9
GENESEE	17,895	7,842	10,034	19	2,192 D	43.8	56.1	43.9	56.1
GREENE	17,329	7,641	9,669	19	2,028 D	44.1	55.8	44.1	55.8
HAMILTON	2,873	1,269	1,603	1	334 D	44.2	55.8	44.2	55.8
HERKIMER	30,317	10,159	20,136	22	9,977 D	33.5	66.4	33.5	66.5
JEFFERSON	35,922	10,718	25,175	29	14,457 D	29.8	70.1	29.9	70.1
KINGS	915,510	229,291	684,839	1,380	455,548 D	25.0	74.8	25.1	74.9
LEWIS	9,779	3,185	6,584	10	3,399 D	32.6	67.3	32.6	67.4
LIVINGSTON	20,619	7,120	13,481	18	6,361 D	34.5	65.4	34.6	65.4
MADISON	23,180	8,858	14,313	9	5,455 D	38.2	61.7	38.2	61.8
MONROE	285,582	80,099	205,226	257	125,127 D	28.0	71.9	28.1	71.9
MONTGOMERY	27,861	8,471	19,370	20	10,899 D	30.4	69.5	30.4	69.6
NASSAU	632,115	248,886	382,590	639	133,704 D	39.4	60.5	39.4	60.6
NEW YORK	625,772	120,125	503,848	1,799	383,723 D	19.3	80.5	19.3	80.7
NIAGARA	95,985	28,663	67,260	62	38,597 D	29.9	70.1	29.9	70.1
ONEIDA	113,210	39,737	73,359	114	33,622 D	35.1	64.8	35.1	64.9
ONONDAGA	192,014	63,205	128,630	179	65,425 D	32.9	67.0	32.9	67.1
ONTARIO	30,788	10,847	19,922	19	9,075 D	35.2	64.7	35.3	64.7
ORANGE	78,932	30,610	48,244	78	17,634 D	38.8	61.1	38.8	61.2
ORLEANS	14,896	5,567	9,304	25	3,737 D	37.4	62.4	37.4	62.6
OSWEGO	37,226	12,415	24,788	23	12,373 D	33.4	66.5	33.4	66.6
OTSEGO	23,859	8,643	15,192	24	6,547 D	36.2	63.7	36.2	63.7
PUTNAM	21,879	9,219	12,636	24	3,417 D	42.1	57.8	42.2	57.8
QUEENS	816,875	274,351	541,418	1,106	267,067 D	33.6	66.3	33.6	66.4
RENSSELAER	72,060	20,814	51,170	76	30,356 D	28.9	71.0	28.9	71.1
RICHMOND	92,946	42,330	50,524	92	8,194 D	45.5	54.4	45.5	54.4
ROCKLAND	72,460	26,187	46,173	100	19,986 D	36.1	63.7	36.2	63.8
ST LAWRENCE	41,307	12,102	29,173	32	17,071 D	29.3	70.6	29.3	70.7
SARATOGA	42,688	13,364	29,264	60	15,900 D	31.3	68.5	31.4	68.6
SCHENECTADY	73,868	21,848	51,892	128	30,044 D	29.5	70.2	29.6	70.4
SCHOHARIE	11,391	4,193	7,187	11	2,994 D	36.8	63.0	36.8	63.1
SCHUYLER	7,256	2,925	4,326	5	1,401 D	40.3	59.6	40.3	59.6
SENECA	13,376	4,473	8,890	13	4,417 D	33.4	66.5	33.5	66.5
STEUBEN	40,645	15,988	24,634	23	8,646 D	39.3	60.6	39.4	60.6
SUFFOLK	325,333	144,350	180,598	385	36,248 D	44.4	55.5	44.4	55.6
SULLIVAN	24,775	8,006	16,728	41	8,722 D	32.3	67.5	32.4	67.6
TIOGA	17,569	7,147	10,411	11	3,264 D	40.7	59.3	40.7	59.3
TOMPKINS	25,203	9,070	16,103	30	7,033 D	36.0	63.9	36.0	64.0
ULSTER	59,326	23,749	35,486	91	11,737 D	40.1	59.8	40.1	59.9
WARREN	20,620	7,834	12,772	14	4,938 D	38.0	61.9	38.0	62.0
WASHINGTON	21,994	8,160	13,826	8	5,666 D	37.1	62.8	37.1	62.9
WAYNE	29,342	10,586	18,729	27	8,143 D	36.1	63.8	36.1	63.9
WESTCHESTER	393,297	149,052	243,723	522	94,671 D	37.9	62.0	37.9	62.1

NEW YORK

PRESIDENT 1960

County	Total Vote	Republican	Democratic	Other	Rep.-Dem. Plurality	Percentage Total Vote Rep.	Dem.	Major Vote Rep.	Dem.
WYOMING	16,307	10,793	5,508	6	5,285 R	66.2%	33.8%	66.2%	33.8%
YATES	9,308	6,892	2,409	7	4,483 R	74.0%	25.9%	74.1%	25.9%
TOTAL	7,291,079	3,446,419	3,830,085	14,575	383,666 D	47.3%	52.5%	47.4%	52.6%

PRESIDENT 1964

Total Vote	Republican	Democratic	Other	Rep.-Dem. Plurality	Percentage Total Vote Rep.	Dem.	Major Vote Rep.	Dem.
14,980	6,099	8,866	15	2,767 D	40.7%	59.2%	40.8%	59.2%
8,663	3,675	4,983	5	1,308 D	42.4%	57.5%	42.4%	57.6%
7,166,275	2,243,559	4,913,102	9,614	2,669,543 D	31.3%	68.6%	31.3%	68.7%

NEW YORK

OTHER VOTE COMPOSITION:

1920	203,201 Socialist; 19,653 Prohibition; 18,413 Farmer-Labor; 4,841 Socialist Labor.
1924	474,913 Progressive; 9,928 Socialist Labor; 8,244 Communist.
1928	107,332 Socialist; 10,876 Communist; 4,211 Socialist Labor.
1932	177,397 Socialist; 27,956 Communist; 10,339 Socialist Labor.
1936	86,897 Socialist; 35,609 Communist.
1940	18,950 Socialist; 3,250 Prohibition.
1944	14,352 Socialist Labor; 10,553 Socialist.
1948	509,559 Progressive; 40,879 Socialist; 2,729 Socialist Labor; 2,675 Socialist Workers; 128 scattered. The scattered vote is not included in the county-by-county figures; it is reported only as a part of the state-wide total.
1952	64,211 Progressive; 2,664 Socialist; 2,212 Socialist Workers; 1,560 Socialist Labor; 178 scattered.
1956	1,027 States Rights; 150 Socialist Labor; 82 Socialist; 1,262 scattered.
1960	14,319 Socialist Workers; 256 scattered.
1964	6,118 Socialist Labor; 3,228 Socialist Workers; 268 scattered.

SPECIAL CASES:

1924	Progressive total includes 268,518 Socialist and 206,395 Progressive votes. This combined vote was second in two counties.
1936	Democratic total includes 3,018,298 Democratic and 274,924 American Labor votes.
1940	Democratic total includes 2,834,500 Democratic and 417,418 American Labor votes.
1944	Democratic total includes 2,478,598 Democratic and 496,405 American Labor and 329,235 Liberal votes.
1948	Democratic total includes 2,557,642 Democratic and 222,562 Liberal votes.
1952	Democratic total includes 2,687,890 Democratic and 416,711 Liberal votes.
1956	Democratic total includes 2,455,457 Democratic and 292,487 Liberal votes.
1960	Democratic total includes 3,423,909 Democratic and 406,176 Liberal votes.
1964	Democratic total includes 4,570,670 Democratic and 342,432 Liberal votes.

NORTH CAROLINA

PRESIDENT 1920

County	Total Vote	Republican	Democratic	Other	Rep.-Dem. Plurality	% Total Vote Rep.	% Total Vote Dem.	% Major Vote Rep.	% Major Vote Dem.
ALAMANCE	9,874	4,619	5,255		636 D	46.8	53.2	46.8	53.2
ALEXANDER	4,688	2,643	2,045		598 R	56.4	43.6	56.4	43.6
ALLEGHANY	2,610	1,201	1,409		208 D	46.0	54.0	46.0	54.0
ANSON	3,608	433	3,175		2,742 D	12.0	88.0	12.0	88.0
ASHE	7,239	3,808	3,431		377 R	52.6	47.4	52.6	47.4
AVERY	2,900	2,503	397		2,106 R	86.3	13.7	86.3	13.7
BEAUFORT	5,788	2,266	3,522		1,256 D	39.1	60.9	39.1	60.9
BERTIE	2,052	212	1,840		1,628 D	10.3	89.7	10.3	89.7
BLADEN	3,003	1,064	1,939		875 D	35.4	64.6	35.4	64.6
BRUNSWICK	2,615	1,362	1,253		109 R	52.1	47.9	52.1	47.9
BUNCOMBE	18,184	8,017	10,167		2,150 D	44.1	55.9	44.1	55.9
BURKE	6,854	3,592	3,262		330 R	52.4	47.6	52.4	47.6
CABARRUS	9,566	5,148	4,418		730 R	53.8	46.2	53.8	46.2
CALDWELL	6,229	3,298	2,931		367 R	52.9	47.1	52.9	47.1
CAMDEN	682	142	540		398 D	20.8	79.2	20.8	79.2
CARTERET	4,385	2,315	2,070		245 R	52.8	47.2	52.8	47.2
CASWELL	1,744	505	1,239		734 D	29.0	71.0	29.0	71.0
CATAWBA	11,339	5,935	5,404		531 R	52.3	47.7	52.3	47.7
CHATHAM	6,092	2,906	3,186		280 D	47.7	52.3	47.7	52.3
CHEROKEE	4,267	2,506	1,761		745 R	58.7	41.3	58.7	41.3
CHOWAN	1,300	209	1,091		882 D	16.1	83.9	16.1	83.9
CLAY	1,666	911	755		156 R	54.7	45.3	54.7	45.3
CLEVELAND	8,134	2,953	5,181		2,228 D	36.3	63.7	36.3	63.7
COLUMBUS	4,894	1,783	3,111		1,328 D	36.4	63.6	36.4	63.6
CRAVEN	4,144	731	3,413		2,682 D	17.6	82.4	17.6	82.4
CUMBERLAND	5,205	1,972	3,233		1,261 D	37.9	62.1	37.9	62.1
CURRITUCK	1,086	86	1,000		914 D	7.9	92.1	7.9	92.1
DARE	1,457	632	825		193 D	43.4	56.6	43.4	56.6
DAVIDSON	10,757	5,960	4,797		1,163 R	55.4	44.6	55.4	44.6
DAVIE	4,215	2,591	1,624		967 R	61.5	38.5	61.5	38.5
DUPLIN	6,095	2,697	3,398		701 D	44.2	55.8	44.2	55.8
DURHAM	8,196	3,550	4,646		1,096 D	43.3	56.7	43.3	56.7
EDGECOMBE	3,367	24	3,343		3,319 D	0.7	99.3	0.7	99.3
FORSYTH	14,915	6,792	8,123		1,331 D	45.5	54.5	45.5	54.5
FRANKLIN	3,331	589	2,742		2,153 D	17.7	82.3	17.7	82.3
GASTON	12,951	5,803	7,148		1,345 D	44.8	55.2	44.8	55.2
GATES	1,123	327	796		469 D	29.1	70.9	29.1	70.9
GRAHAM	1,559	915	644		271 R	58.7	41.3	58.7	41.3
GRANVILLE	3,455	833	2,622		1,789 D	24.1	75.9	24.1	75.9
GREENE	2,088	439	1,649		1,210 D	21.0	79.0	21.0	79.0
GUILFORD	17,535	7,920	9,615		1,695 D	45.2	54.8	45.2	54.8
HALIFAX	3,953	524	3,429		2,905 D	13.3	86.7	13.3	86.7
HARNETT	7,230	3,311	3,919		608 D	45.8	54.2	45.8	54.2
HAYWOOD	7,229	3,000	4,229		1,229 D	41.5	58.5	41.5	58.5
HENDERSON	5,833	3,337	2,496		841 R	57.2	42.8	57.2	42.8
HERTFORD	1,325	221	1,104		883 D	16.7	83.3	16.7	83.3
HOKE	1,432	166	1,266		1,100 D	11.6	88.4	11.6	88.4
HYDE	1,664	530	1,134		604 D	31.9	68.1	31.9	68.1
IREDELL	10,872	4,402	6,470		2,068 D	40.5	59.5	40.5	59.5
JACKSON	4,740	2,355	2,385		30 D	49.7	50.3	49.7	50.3
JOHNSTON	11,618	5,588	6,030		442 D	48.1	51.9	48.1	51.9
JONES	1,349	385	964		579 D	28.5	71.5	28.5	71.5
LEE	3,470	1,143	2,327		1,184 D	32.9	67.1	32.9	67.1
LENOIR	3,713	1,153	2,560		1,407 D	31.1	68.9	31.1	68.9
LINCOLN	6,468	3,137	3,331		194 D	48.5	51.5	48.5	51.5
MCDOWELL	5,370	2,561	2,809		248 D	47.7	52.3	47.7	52.3
MACON	4,227	2,050	2,177		127 D	48.5	51.5	48.5	51.5
MADISON	4,956	3,616	1,340		2,276 R	73.0	27.0	73.0	27.0
MARTIN	3,091	530	2,561		2,031 D	17.1	82.9	17.1	82.9
MECKLENBURG	14,734	3,421	11,313		7,892 D	23.2	76.8	23.2	76.8

PRESIDENT 1924

County	Total Vote	Republican	Democratic	Other	Rep.-Dem. Plurality	% Total Vote Rep.	% Total Vote Dem.	% Major Vote Rep.	% Major Vote Dem.
ALAMANCE	8,169	3,217	4,859	93	1,642 D	39.4	59.5	39.8	60.2
ALEXANDER	4,748	2,437	2,291	20	146 D	51.3	48.3	51.5	48.5
ALLEGHANY	2,883	1,234	1,643	6	409 D	42.8	57.0	42.9	57.1
ANSON	2,622	225	2,372	25	2,147 D	8.6	90.5	8.7	91.3
ASHE	8,288	3,952	4,333	3	381 D	47.7	52.3	47.7	52.3
AVERY	2,560	2,189	357	14	1,832 R	85.5	13.9	86.0	14.0
BEAUFORT	4,643	1,502	3,048	93	1,546 D	32.3	65.6	33.0	67.0
BERTIE	1,949	159	1,785	5	1,626 D	8.2	91.6	8.2	91.8
BLADEN	2,360	786	1,551	23	765 D	33.3	65.7	33.6	66.4
BRUNSWICK	2,455	1,296	1,118	41	178 R	52.8	45.5	53.7	46.3
BUNCOMBE	16,850	6,285	10,098	467	3,813 D	37.3	59.9	38.4	61.6
BURKE	7,327	3,190	4,137		947 D	43.5	56.5	43.5	56.5
CABARRUS	8,148	3,510	4,449	189	939 D	43.1	54.6	44.1	55.9
CALDWELL	5,877	2,503	3,348	26	845 D	42.6	57.0	42.8	57.2
CAMDEN	577	132	436	9	304 D	22.9	75.6	23.2	76.8
CARTERET	4,130	1,854	2,261	15	407 D	44.9	54.7	45.1	54.9
CASWELL	1,546	467	1,075	4	608 D	30.2	69.5	30.3	69.7
CATAWBA	11,919	5,998	5,754	167	244 D	50.3	48.3	51.0	49.0
CHATHAM	6,216	2,755	3,446	15	691 D	44.3	55.4	44.4	55.6
CHEROKEE	4,079	2,314	1,742	23	572 R	56.7	42.7	57.1	42.9
CHOWAN	817	98	714	5	616 D	12.0	87.4	12.1	87.9
CLAY	2,061	1,090	953	18	137 R	52.9	46.2	53.4	46.6
CLEVELAND	5,529	1,743	3,749	37	2,006 D	31.5	67.8	31.7	68.3
COLUMBUS	4,412	1,629	2,757	26	1,128 D	36.9	62.5	37.1	62.9
CRAVEN	3,311	325	2,942	44	2,617 D	9.8	88.9	9.9	90.1
CUMBERLAND	4,332	1,372	2,923	37	1,551 D	31.7	67.5	31.9	68.1
CURRITUCK	735	52	670	13	618 D	7.1	91.2	7.2	92.8
DARE	1,457	629	826	2	197 D	43.2	56.7	43.2	56.8
DAVIDSON	12,790	6,227	6,507	56	280 D	48.7	50.9	48.9	51.1
DAVIE	4,480	2,672	1,795	13	877 R	59.6	40.1	59.8	40.2
DUPLIN	4,503	1,542	2,924	37	1,382 D	34.2	64.9	34.5	65.5
DURHAM	8,151	3,093	4,837	221	1,744 D	37.9	59.3	39.0	61.0
EDGECOMBE	2,554	171	2,274	109	2,103 D	6.7	89.0	7.0	93.0
FORSYTH	13,178	5,315	7,404	459	2,089 D	40.3	56.2	41.8	58.2
FRANKLIN	2,306	302	1,991	13	1,689 D	13.1	86.3	13.2	86.8
GASTON	10,202	3,566	6,554	82	2,988 D	35.0	64.2	35.2	64.8
GATES	895	215	679	1	464 D	24.0	75.9	24.0	76.0
GRAHAM	1,759	907	841	11	66 R	51.6	47.8	51.9	48.1
GRANVILLE	2,695	461	2,220	14	1,759 D	17.1	82.4	17.2	82.8
GREENE	1,308	182	1,119	7	937 D	13.9	85.6	14.0	86.0
GUILFORD	15,943	6,822	8,804	317	1,982 D	42.8	55.2	43.7	56.3
HALIFAX	3,583	268	2,964	83	2,696 D	7.5	90.2	7.7	92.3
HARNETT	6,202	2,895	3,296	11	401 D	46.7	53.1	46.8	53.2
HAYWOOD	7,030	2,440	4,582	8	2,142 D	34.7	65.2	34.7	65.3
HENDERSON	6,603	3,548	3,007	48	541 R	53.7	45.5	54.1	45.9
HERTFORD	1,099	164	932	3	768 D	14.9	84.8	15.0	85.0
HOKE	1,291	141	1,146	4	1,005 D	10.9	88.8	11.0	89.0
HYDE	974	305	653	16	348 D	31.3	67.0	31.8	68.2
IREDELL	10,150	3,565	6,449	136	2,884 D	35.1	63.5	35.6	64.4
JACKSON	5,905	2,788	3,100	17	312 D	47.4	52.5	47.4	52.6
JOHNSTON	9,589	4,910	4,656	23	254 R	51.2	48.6	51.3	48.7
JONES	873	179	692	2	513 D	20.5	79.3	20.6	79.4
LEE	2,554	710	1,834	10	1,124 D	27.8	71.8	27.9	72.1
LENOIR	2,730	514	2,191	25	1,677 D	18.8	80.3	19.0	81.0
LINCOLN	5,609	2,658	2,909	42	251 D	47.4	51.9	47.7	52.3
MCDOWELL	5,638	2,590	3,023	25	433 D	45.9	53.6	46.1	53.9
MACON	4,211	2,015	2,178	18	163 D	47.9	51.7	48.1	51.9
MADISON	4,797	3,252	1,471	74	1,781 R	67.8	30.7	68.9	31.1
MARTIN	2,224	216	1,999	9	1,783 D	9.7	89.9	9.8	90.2
MECKLENBURG	11,452	2,572	8,443	437	5,871 D	22.5	73.7	23.3	76.7

NORTH CAROLINA

PRESIDENT 1920

County	Total Vote	Republican	Democratic	Other	Rep.-Dem. Plurality	Total Vote Rep.	Total Vote Dem.	Major Vote Rep.	Major Vote Dem.
MITCHELL	2,850	2,153	697		1,456 R	75.5%	24.5%	75.5%	24.5%
MONTGOMERY	4,625	2,304	2,321		17 D	49.8%	50.2%	49.8%	50.2%
MOORE	4,958	2,279	2,679		400 D	46.0%	54.0%	46.0%	54.0%
NASH	5,587	1,556	4,031		2,475 D	27.9%	72.1%	27.9%	72.1%
NEW HANOVER	4,814	712	4,102		3,390 D	14.8%	85.2%	14.8%	85.2%
NORTHAMPTON	2,470	165	2,305		2,140 D	6.7%	93.3%	6.7%	93.3%
ONSLOW	2,410	853	1,557		704 D	35.4%	64.6%	35.4%	64.6%
ORANGE	3,730	1,737	1,993		256 D	46.6%	53.4%	46.6%	53.4%
PAMLICO	2,294	1,008	1,286		278 D	43.9%	56.1%	43.9%	56.1%
PASQUOTANK	2,243	507	1,736		1,229 D	22.6%	77.4%	22.6%	77.4%
PENDER	2,279	699	1,580		881 D	30.7%	69.3%	30.7%	69.3%
PERQUIMANS	1,529	487	1,042		555 D	31.9%	68.1%	31.9%	68.1%
PERSON	3,212	1,566	1,646		80 D	48.8%	51.2%	48.8%	51.2%
PITT	5,060	864	4,196		3,332 D	17.1%	82.9%	17.1%	82.9%
POLK	2,687	1,326	1,361		35 D	49.3%	50.7%	49.3%	50.7%
RANDOLPH	11,407	6,297	5,110		1,187 R	55.2%	44.8%	55.2%	44.8%
RICHMOND	4,465	1,124	3,341		2,217 D	25.2%	74.8%	25.2%	74.8%
ROBESON	8,403	2,220	6,183		3,963 D	26.4%	73.6%	26.4%	73.6%
ROCKINGHAM	8,112	3,605	4,507		902 D	44.4%	55.6%	44.4%	55.6%
ROWAN	11,309	4,888	6,421		1,533 D	43.2%	56.8%	43.2%	56.8%
RUTHERFORD	9,116	4,015	5,101		1,086 D	44.0%	56.0%	44.0%	56.0%
SAMPSON	7,779	5,353	2,426		2,927 R	68.8%	31.2%	68.8%	31.2%
SCOTLAND	2,011	306	1,705		1,399 D	15.2%	84.8%	15.2%	84.8%
STANLY	8,155	4,312	3,843		469 R	52.9%	47.1%	52.9%	47.1%
STOKES	4,925	2,926	1,999		927 R	59.4%	40.6%	59.4%	40.6%
SURRY	8,717	5,170	3,547		1,623 R	59.3%	40.7%	59.3%	40.7%
SWAIN	3,673	2,239	1,434		805 R	61.0%	39.0%	61.0%	39.0%
TRANSYLVANIA	3,222	1,680	1,542		138 R	52.1%	47.9%	52.1%	47.9%
TYRRELL	1,250	532	718		186 D	42.6%	57.4%	42.6%	57.4%
UNION	5,572	1,404	4,168		2,764 D	25.2%	74.8%	25.2%	74.8%
VANCE	3,277	816	2,461		1,645 D	24.9%	75.1%	24.9%	75.1%
WAKE	11,673	3,653	8,020		4,367 D	31.3%	68.7%	31.3%	68.7%
WARREN	2,160	295	1,865		1,570 D	13.7%	86.3%	13.7%	86.3%
WASHINGTON	2,087	971	1,116		145 D	46.5%	53.5%	46.5%	53.5%
WATAUGA	4,352	2,631	1,721		910 R	60.5%	39.5%	60.5%	39.5%
WAYNE	7,616	2,822	4,794		1,972 D	37.1%	62.9%	37.1%	62.9%
WILKES	9,294	6,451	2,843		3,608 R	69.4%	30.6%	69.4%	30.6%
WILSON	4,870	1,374	3,496		2,122 D	28.2%	71.8%	28.2%	71.8%
YADKIN	4,651	3,301	1,350		1,951 R	71.0%	29.0%	71.0%	29.0%
YANCEY	4,876	2,596	2,280		316 R	53.2%	46.8%	53.2%	46.8%
TOTAL	538,649	232,819	305,367	463	72,548 D	43.2%	56.7%	43.3%	56.7%

PRESIDENT 1924

County	Total Vote	Republican	Democratic	Other	Rep.-Dem. Plurality	Total Vote Rep.	Total Vote Dem.	Major Vote Rep.	Major Vote Dem.
MITCHELL	2,237	1,540	689	8	851 R	68.8%	30.8%	69.1%	30.9%
MONTGOMERY	4,565	2,077	2,483	5	406 D	45.5%	54.4%	45.5%	54.5%
MOORE	4,783	1,974	2,771	38	797 D	41.3%	57.9%	41.6%	58.4%
NASH	4,083	823	3,129	131	2,306 D	20.2%	76.6%	20.8%	79.2%
NEW HANOVER	6,330	1,190	4,735	405	3,545 D	18.8%	74.8%	20.1%	79.9%
NORTHAMPTON	1,823	144	1,662	17	1,518 D	7.9%	91.2%	8.0%	92.0%
ONSLOW	1,576	423	1,122	31	699 D	26.8%	71.2%	27.4%	72.6%
ORANGE	3,010	1,065	1,879	66	814 D	35.4%	62.4%	36.2%	63.8%
PAMLICO	1,257	459	798		339 D	36.5%	63.5%	36.5%	63.5%
PASQUOTANK	1,553	305	1,236	12	931 D	19.6%	79.6%	19.8%	80.2%
PENDER	1,445	253	1,175	17	922 D	17.5%	81.3%	17.7%	82.3%
PERQUIMANS	853	295	550	8	255 D	34.6%	64.5%	34.9%	65.1%
PERSON	2,604	1,025	1,576	3	551 D	39.4%	60.5%	39.4%	60.6%
PITT	3,765	512	3,197	56	2,685 D	13.6%	84.9%	13.8%	86.2%
POLK	3,071	1,445	1,613	13	168 D	47.1%	52.5%	47.3%	52.7%
RANDOLPH	11,757	6,336	5,397	24	939 R	53.9%	45.9%	54.0%	46.0%
RICHMOND	3,237	599	2,475	163	1,876 D	18.5%	76.5%	19.5%	80.5%
ROBESON	4,392	314	4,064	14	3,750 D	7.1%	92.5%	7.2%	92.8%
ROCKINGHAM	7,122	2,566	4,467	89	1,901 D	36.0%	62.7%	36.5%	63.5%
ROWAN	9,114	3,560	4,816	738	1,256 D	39.1%	52.8%	42.5%	57.5%
RUTHERFORD	9,027	3,897	5,101	29	1,204 D	43.2%	56.5%	43.3%	56.7%
SAMPSON	5,244	3,188	2,021	35	1,167 R	60.8%	38.5%	61.2%	38.8%
SCOTLAND	1,685	205	1,469	11	1,264 D	12.2%	87.2%	12.2%	87.8%
STANLY	7,476	3,594	3,832	50	238 D	48.1%	51.3%	48.4%	51.6%
STOKES	4,835	2,482	2,309	44	173 R	51.3%	47.8%	51.8%	48.2%
SURRY	9,474	4,990	4,448	66	572 R	52.7%	46.6%	53.0%	47.0%
SWAIN	3,971	2,178	1,769	24	409 R	54.8%	44.5%	55.2%	44.8%
TRANSYLVANIA	3,612	1,814	1,776	22	38 R	50.2%	49.0%	50.5%	49.5%
TYRRELL	1,081	442	638	1	196 D	40.9%	59.0%	40.9%	59.1%
UNION	3,425	672	2,721	32	2,049 D	19.6%	79.4%	19.8%	80.2%
VANCE	2,504	470	2,013	21	1,543 D	18.8%	80.4%	18.9%	81.1%
WAKE	11,836	2,975	8,376	485	5,401 D	25.1%	70.8%	26.2%	73.8%
WARREN	1,970	166	1,742	62	1,576 D	8.4%	88.4%	8.7%	91.3%
WASHINGTON	1,723	834	883	6	49 D	48.4%	51.2%	48.6%	51.4%
WATAUGA	5,038	2,665	2,365	8	300 R	52.9%	46.9%	53.0%	47.0%
WAYNE	4,787	1,379	3,366	42	1,987 D	28.8%	70.3%	29.1%	70.9%
WILKES	9,728	6,131	3,586	11	2,545 R	63.0%	36.9%	63.1%	36.9%
WILSON	3,274	574	2,619	81	2,045 D	17.5%	80.0%	18.0%	82.0%
YADKIN	4,281	2,889	1,381	11	1,508 R	67.4%	32.3%	67.7%	32.3%
YANCEY	4,769	2,156	2,592	21	436 D	45.2%	54.4%	45.4%	54.6%
TOTAL	481,608	190,754	284,190	6,664	93,436 D	39.6%	59.0%	40.2%	59.8%

NORTH CAROLINA

PRESIDENT 1928

County	Total Vote	Republican	Democratic	Other	Rep.-Dem. Plurality	Total Vote Rep.	Total Vote Dem.	Major Vote Rep.	Major Vote Dem.
ALAMANCE	11,070	6,810	4,260		2,550 R	61.5%	38.5%	61.5%	38.5%
ALEXANDER	4,327	2,605	1,722		883 R	60.2%	39.8%	60.2%	39.8%
ALLEGHANY	2,782	1,368	1,414		46 D	49.2%	50.8%	49.2%	50.8%
ANSON	3,673	726	2,947		2,221 D	19.8%	80.2%	19.8%	80.2%
ASHE	7,795	4,337	3,458		879 R	55.6%	44.4%	55.6%	44.4%
AVERY	3,663	3,273	390		2,883 R	89.4%	10.6%	89.4%	10.6%
BEAUFORT	6,054	2,521	3,533		1,012 D	41.6%	58.4%	41.6%	58.4%
BERTIE	2,374	374	2,000		1,626 D	15.8%	84.2%	15.8%	84.2%
BLADEN	3,463	1,911	1,552		359 R	55.2%	44.8%	55.2%	44.8%
BRUNSWICK	2,949	1,931	1,018		913 R	65.5%	34.5%	65.5%	34.5%
BUNCOMBE	28,995	16,590	12,405		4,185 R	57.2%	42.8%	57.2%	42.8%
BURKE	7,989	5,108	2,881		2,227 R	63.9%	36.1%	63.9%	36.1%
CABARRUS	11,417	6,548	4,869		1,679 R	57.4%	42.6%	57.4%	42.6%
CALDWELL	6,498	4,207	2,291		1,916 R	64.7%	35.3%	64.7%	35.3%
CAMDEN	869	245	624		379 D	28.2%	71.8%	28.2%	71.8%
CARTERET	5,178	3,133	2,045		1,088 R	60.5%	39.5%	60.5%	39.5%
CASWELL	1,685	749	936		187 D	44.5%	55.5%	44.5%	55.5%
CATAWBA	12,472	7,556	4,916		2,640 R	60.6%	39.4%	60.6%	39.4%
CHATHAM	5,998	3,318	2,680		638 R	55.3%	44.7%	55.3%	44.7%
CHEROKEE	5,150	3,239	1,911		1,328 R	62.9%	37.1%	62.9%	37.1%
CHOWAN	1,288	352	936		584 D	27.3%	72.7%	27.3%	72.7%
CLAY	2,009	1,106	903		203 R	55.1%	44.9%	55.1%	44.9%
CLEVELAND	9,680	4,766	4,914		148 D	49.2%	50.8%	49.2%	50.8%
COLUMBUS	6,387	3,533	2,854		679 R	55.3%	44.7%	55.3%	44.7%
CRAVEN	4,731	2,237	2,494		257 D	47.3%	52.7%	47.3%	52.7%
CUMBERLAND	6,831	3,534	3,297		237 R	51.7%	48.3%	51.7%	48.3%
CURRITUCK	1,419	166	1,253		1,087 D	11.7%	88.3%	11.7%	88.3%
DARE	1,697	814	883		69 D	48.0%	52.0%	48.0%	52.0%
DAVIDSON	14,180	8,960	5,220		3,740 R	63.2%	36.8%	63.2%	36.8%
DAVIE	4,044	2,959	1,085		1,874 R	73.2%	26.8%	73.2%	26.8%
DUPLIN	5,558	2,911	2,647		264 R	52.4%	47.6%	52.4%	47.6%
DURHAM	13,205	8,723	4,482		4,241 R	66.1%	33.9%	66.1%	33.9%
EDGECOMBE	5,161	977	4,184		3,207 D	18.9%	81.1%	18.9%	81.1%
FORSYTH	19,897	13,258	6,639		6,619 R	66.6%	33.4%	66.6%	33.4%
FRANKLIN	3,560	729	2,831		2,102 D	20.5%	79.5%	20.5%	79.5%
GASTON	16,404	9,702	6,702		3,000 R	59.1%	40.9%	59.1%	40.9%
GATES	1,130	558	572		14 D	49.4%	50.6%	49.4%	50.6%
GRAHAM	2,223	1,260	963		297 R	56.7%	43.3%	56.7%	43.3%
GRANVILLE	3,820	858	2,962		2,104 D	22.5%	77.5%	22.5%	77.5%
GREENE	1,723	542	1,181		639 D	31.5%	68.5%	31.5%	68.5%
GUILFORD	26,413	16,541	9,872		6,669 R	62.6%	37.4%	62.6%	37.4%
HALIFAX	5,772	890	4,882		3,992 D	15.4%	84.6%	15.4%	84.6%
HARNETT	8,294	4,740	3,554		1,186 R	57.1%	42.9%	57.1%	42.9%
HAYWOOD	8,645	4,472	4,173		299 R	51.7%	48.3%	51.7%	48.3%
HENDERSON	8,359	5,210	3,149		2,061 R	62.3%	37.7%	62.3%	37.7%
HERTFORD	1,423	393	1,030		637 D	27.6%	72.4%	27.6%	72.4%
HOKE	1,465	311	1,154		843 D	21.2%	78.8%	21.2%	78.8%
HYDE	1,272	682	590		92 R	53.6%	46.4%	53.6%	46.4%
IREDELL	11,548	6,712	4,836		1,876 R	58.1%	41.9%	58.1%	41.9%
JACKSON	6,683	3,512	3,171		341 R	52.6%	47.4%	52.6%	47.4%
JOHNSTON	12,737	7,696	5,041		2,655 R	60.4%	39.6%	60.4%	39.6%
JONES	1,144	658	486		172 R	57.5%	42.5%	57.5%	42.5%
LEE	3,131	1,416	1,715		299 D	45.2%	54.8%	45.2%	54.8%
LENOIR	3,674	1,311	2,363		1,052 D	35.7%	64.3%	35.7%	64.3%
LINCOLN	6,843	3,930	2,913		1,017 R	57.4%	42.6%	57.4%	42.6%
MCDOWELL	6,853	3,423	3,430		7 D	49.9%	50.1%	49.9%	50.1%
MACON	5,094	2,903	2,191		712 R	57.0%	43.0%	57.0%	43.0%
MADISON	5,869	4,776	1,093		3,683 R	81.4%	18.6%	81.4%	18.6%
MARTIN	3,229	411	2,818		2,407 D	12.7%	87.3%	12.7%	87.3%
MECKLENBURG	21,731	12,041	9,690		2,351 R	55.4%	44.6%	55.4%	44.6%

PRESIDENT 1932

County	Total Vote	Republican	Democratic	Other	Rep.-Dem. Plurality	Total Vote Rep.	Total Vote Dem.	Major Vote Rep.	Major Vote Dem.
ALAMANCE	12,882	4,478	8,240	164	3,762 D	34.8%	64.0%	35.2%	64.8%
ALEXANDER	4,933	1,952	2,953	28	1,001 D	39.6%	59.9%	39.8%	60.2%
ALLEGHANY	2,776	810	1,951	15	1,141 D	29.2%	70.3%	29.3%	70.7%
ANSON	4,480	223	4,252	5	4,029 D	5.0%	94.9%	5.0%	95.0%
ASHE	8,660	3,871	4,751	38	880 D	44.7%	54.9%	44.9%	55.1%
AVERY	3,900	2,833	1,045	22	1,788 R	72.6%	26.8%	73.0%	26.9%
BEAUFORT	6,431	839	5,552	40	4,713 D	13.0%	86.3%	13.1%	86.9%
BERTIE	3,224	65	3,154	5	3,089 D	2.0%	97.8%	2.0%	98.0%
BLADEN	3,495	808	2,651	36	1,843 D	23.1%	75.9%	23.4%	76.6%
BRUNSWICK	4,060	1,798	2,245	17	447 D	44.3%	55.3%	44.5%	55.5%
BUNCOMBE	27,353	8,745	18,241	367	9,496 D	32.0%	66.7%	32.4%	67.6%
BURKE	10,736	4,823	5,866	47	1,043 D	44.9%	54.6%	45.1%	54.9%
CABARRUS	11,977	3,444	8,465	68	5,021 D	28.8%	70.7%	28.9%	71.1%
CALDWELL	9,275	3,750	5,479	46	1,729 D	40.4%	59.1%	40.6%	59.4%
CAMDEN	994	78	915	1	837 D	7.8%	92.1%	7.9%	92.1%
CARTERET	5,275	1,765	3,455	55	1,690 D	33.5%	65.5%	33.8%	66.2%
CASWELL	2,033	169	1,858	6	1,689 D	8.3%	91.4%	8.3%	91.7%
CATAWBA	14,340	5,817	8,446	77	2,629 D	40.6%	58.9%	40.8%	59.2%
CHATHAM	6,912	2,590	4,263	59	1,673 D	37.5%	61.7%	37.8%	62.2%
CHEROKEE	6,504	3,131	3,348	25	217 D	48.1%	51.5%	48.3%	51.7%
CHOWAN	1,708	64	1,639	5	1,575 D	3.7%	96.0%	3.8%	96.2%
CLAY	2,614	1,265	1,341	8	76 D	48.4%	51.3%	48.5%	51.5%
CLEVELAND	9,945	1,904	8,016	25	6,112 D	19.1%	80.6%	19.2%	80.8%
COLUMBUS	5,890	739	5,098	53	4,359 D	12.5%	86.6%	12.9%	87.3%
CRAVEN	4,860	466	4,375	19	3,909 D	9.6%	90.0%	9.6%	90.4%
CUMBERLAND	5,983	931	5,012	40	4,081 D	15.6%	83.8%	15.7%	84.3%
CURRITUCK	1,832	69	1,759	4	1,690 D	3.7%	96.0%	3.8%	96.2%
DARE	1,744	497	1,241	6	744 D	28.5%	71.2%	28.6%	71.4%
DAVIDSON	15,500	6,051	9,292	157	3,241 D	39.0%	59.9%	39.4%	60.6%
DAVIE	4,895	2,473	2,381	41	92 R	50.5%	48.6%	50.9%	49.1%
DUPLIN	5,882	1,173	4,674	35	3,501 D	19.9%	79.5%	20.1%	79.9%
DURHAM	10,680	2,770	7,559	351	4,789 D	25.9%	70.8%	26.6%	73.2%
EDGECOMBE	6,141	248	5,872	21	5,624 D	4.1%	95.0%	4.1%	95.9%
FORSYTH	20,100	5,727	14,016	357	8,289 D	28.5%	69.7%	29.4%	70.6%
FRANKLIN	4,504	199	4,294	11	4,095 D	4.4%	95.3%	4.4%	95.6%
GASTON	18,211	5,164	12,890	157	7,726 D	28.4%	70.8%	28.6%	71.4%
GATES	1,288	89	1,198	1	1,109 D	6.9%	93.0%	6.9%	93.1%
GRAHAM	2,558	1,183	1,364	11	181 D	46.2%	53.3%	46.6%	53.4%
GRANVILLE	4,029	212	3,808	9	3,596 D	5.3%	94.5%	5.3%	94.7%
GREENE	2,607	94	2,510	3	2,416 D	3.6%	96.3%	3.6%	96.4%
GUILFORD	29,059	9,263	19,301	495	10,038 D	31.9%	66.4%	32.4%	67.6%
HALIFAX	6,752	306	6,413	33	6,107 D	4.5%	95.0%	4.6%	95.4%
HARNETT	9,012	2,617	6,346	49	3,729 D	29.0%	70.4%	29.2%	70.8%
HAYWOOD	9,906	3,082	6,790	34	3,708 D	31.1%	68.5%	31.2%	68.8%
HENDERSON	9,490	4,172	5,255	63	1,083 D	44.0%	55.4%	44.3%	55.7%
HERTFORD	1,930	88	1,835	7	1,747 D	4.6%	95.1%	4.6%	95.4%
HOKE	1,850	65	1,780	5	1,715 D	3.5%	96.2%	3.5%	96.5%
HYDE	1,201	147	1,050	4	903 D	12.3%	87.4%	12.3%	87.7%
IREDELL	12,005	3,583	8,367	55	4,784 D	29.8%	69.7%	30.2%	70.0%
JACKSON	7,208	2,813	4,360	35	1,547 D	30.0%	60.5%	30.2%	60.8%
JOHNSTON	13,511	3,887	9,574	50	5,687 D	28.8%	70.9%	28.9%	71.1%
JONES	1,585	132	1,449	4	1,317 D	8.3%	91.4%	8.3%	91.7%
LEE	3,752	681	3,058	13	2,377 D	18.2%	81.5%	18.2%	81.8%
LENOIR	5,051	350	4,677	24	4,327 D	7.0%	92.6%	7.0%	93.0%
LINCOLN	7,996	3,563	4,399	34	836 D	44.6%	55.0%	44.8%	55.2%
MCDOWELL	7,323	2,478	4,810	35	2,332 D	33.8%	65.7%	34.0%	66.0%
MACON	5,560	2,307	3,223	30	916 D	41.5%	58.0%	41.7%	58.3%
MADISON	7,370	4,552	2,769	49	1,783 R	61.8%	37.6%	62.2%	37.8%
MARTIN	3,883	94	3,781	8	3,687 D	2.4%	97.4%	2.4%	97.6%
MECKLENBURG	23,321	4,973	18,167	181	13,194 D	21.3%	77.9%	21.5%	78.5%

NORTH CAROLINA

PRESIDENT 1928

County	Total Vote	Republican	Democratic	Other	Rep.-Dem. Plurality	Total Vote Rep.	Total Vote Dem.	Major Vote Rep.	Major Vote Dem.
MITCHELL	4,263	3,436	827		2,609 R	80.6%	19.4%	80.6%	19.4%
MONTGOMERY	4,669	2,653	2,016		637 R	56.8%	43.2%	56.8%	43.2%
MOORE	5,929	3,290	2,639		651 R	55.5%	44.5%	55.5%	44.5%
NASH	6,315	2,066	4,249		2,183 D	32.7%	67.3%	32.7%	67.3%
NEW HANOVER	7,008	4,248	2,760		1,488 R	60.6%	39.4%	60.6%	39.4%
NORTHAMPTON	2,179	456	1,723		1,267 D	20.9%	79.1%	20.9%	79.1%
ONSLOW	2,325	1,253	1,072		181 R	53.9%	46.1%	53.9%	46.1%
ORANGE	4,363	2,564	1,799		765 R	58.8%	41.2%	58.8%	41.2%
PAMLICO	1,977	1,099	878		221 R	55.6%	44.4%	55.6%	44.4%
PASQUOTANK	2,757	814	1,943		1,129 D	29.5%	70.5%	29.5%	70.5%
PENDER	2,298	1,300	998		302 R	56.6%	43.4%	56.6%	43.4%
PERQUIMANS	1,209	600	609		9 D	49.6%	50.4%	49.6%	50.4%
PERSON	2,358	1,123	1,235		112 D	47.6%	52.4%	47.6%	52.4%
PITT	6,041	1,395	4,646		3,251 D	23.1%	76.9%	23.1%	76.9%
POLK	3,489	1,873	1,616		257 R	53.7%	46.3%	53.7%	46.3%
RANDOLPH	11,602	7,414	4,188		3,226 R	63.9%	36.1%	63.9%	36.1%
RICHMOND	5,020	2,045	2,975		930 D	40.7%	59.3%	40.7%	59.3%
ROBESON	7,497	2,767	4,730		1,963 D	36.9%	63.1%	36.9%	63.1%
ROCKINGHAM	8,996	5,585	3,411		2,174 R	62.1%	37.9%	62.1%	37.9%
ROWAN	12,740	7,957	4,783		3,174 R	62.5%	37.5%	62.5%	37.5%
RUTHERFORD	9,908	5,762	4,146		1,616 R	58.2%	41.8%	58.2%	41.8%
SAMPSON	7,864	5,579	2,285		3,294 R	70.9%	29.1%	70.9%	29.1%
SCOTLAND	2,349	588	1,761		1,173 D	25.0%	75.0%	25.0%	75.0%
STANLY	7,597	4,597	3,000		1,597 R	60.5%	39.5%	60.5%	39.5%
STOKES	5,729	3,759	1,970		1,789 R	65.6%	34.4%	65.6%	34.4%
SURRY	10,662	7,015	3,647		3,368 R	65.8%	34.2%	65.8%	34.2%
SWAIN	4,207	2,484	1,723		761 R	59.0%	41.0%	59.0%	41.0%
TRANSYLVANIA	3,887	2,165	1,722		443 R	55.7%	44.3%	55.7%	44.3%
TYRRELL	980	505	475		30 R	51.5%	48.5%	51.5%	48.5%
UNION	5,288	2,448	2,840		392 D	46.3%	53.7%	46.3%	53.7%
VANCE	3,844	1,449	2,395		946 D	37.7%	62.3%	37.7%	62.3%
WAKE	16,061	6,720	9,341		2,621 D	41.8%	58.2%	41.8%	58.2%
WARREN	2,416	379	2,037		1,658 D	15.7%	84.3%	15.7%	84.3%
WASHINGTON	2,081	1,183	898		285 R	56.8%	43.2%	56.8%	43.2%
WATAUGA	5,750	3,159	2,591		568 R	54.9%	45.1%	54.9%	45.1%
WAYNE	8,060	4,340	3,720		620 R	53.8%	46.2%	53.8%	46.2%
WILKES	10,610	7,808	2,802		5,006 R	73.6%	26.4%	73.6%	26.4%
WILSON	5,468	1,933	3,535		1,602 D	35.4%	64.6%	35.4%	64.6%
YADKIN	4,639	3,878	761		3,117 R	83.6%	16.4%	83.6%	16.4%
YANCEY	5,188	2,712	2,476		236 R	52.3%	47.7%	52.3%	47.7%
TOTAL	635,150	348,923	286,227		62,696 R	54.9%	45.1%	54.9%	45.1%

PRESIDENT 1932

County	Total Vote	Republican	Democratic	Other	Rep.-Dem. Plurality	Total Vote Rep.	Total Vote Dem.	Major Vote Rep.	Major Vote Dem.
MITCHELL	5,580	3,798	1,773	9	2,025 R	68.1%	31.8%	68.2%	31.8%
MONTGOMERY	5,098	2,153	2,927	18	774 D	42.2%	57.4%	42.4%	57.6%
MOORE	6,793	2,459	4,287	47	1,828 D	36.2%	63.1%	36.5%	63.5%
NASH	8,053	532	7,472	49	6,940 D	6.6%	92.8%	6.6%	93.4%
NEW HANOVER	7,601	1,430	6,030	141	4,600 D	18.8%	79.3%	19.2%	80.8%
NORTHAMPTON	3,397	147	3,243	7	3,096 D	4.3%	95.5%	4.3%	95.7%
ONSLOW	2,877	253	2,615	9	2,362 D	8.8%	90.9%	8.8%	91.2%
ORANGE	4,203	1,114	2,924	165	1,810 D	26.5%	69.6%	27.6%	72.4%
PAMLICO	2,265	665	1,526	75	861 D	29.3%	67.3%	30.4%	69.6%
PASQUOTANK	3,292	328	2,946	18	2,618 D	10.0%	89.5%	10.0%	90.0%
PENDER	2,274	270	1,993	11	1,723 D	11.9%	87.6%	11.9%	88.1%
PERQUIMANS	1,507	225	1,280	2	1,055 D	14.9%	84.9%	15.0%	85.0%
PERSON	3,049	660	2,372	17	1,712 D	21.6%	77.8%	21.8%	78.2%
PITT	8,000	255	7,724	21	7,469 D	3.2%	96.6%	3.2%	96.8%
POLK	3,843	1,421	2,401	21	980 D	37.0%	62.5%	37.2%	62.8%
RANDOLPH	13,492	6,072	7,345	75	1,273 D	45.0%	54.4%	45.3%	54.7%
RICHMOND	5,591	693	4,862	36	4,169 D	12.4%	87.0%	12.5%	87.5%
ROBESON	8,687	783	7,860	44	7,077 D	9.0%	90.5%	9.1%	90.9%
ROCKINGHAM	10,771	2,896	7,795	80	4,899 D	26.9%	72.4%	27.1%	72.9%
ROWAN	14,426	4,464	9,782	180	5,318 D	30.9%	67.8%	31.3%	68.7%
RUTHERFORD	12,838	4,448	8,336	54	3,888 D	34.6%	64.9%	34.8%	65.2%
SAMPSON	9,152	4,127	4,911	114	784 D	45.1%	53.7%	45.7%	54.3%
SCOTLAND	2,822	208	2,608	6	2,400 D	7.4%	92.4%	7.4%	92.6%
STANLY	9,826	3,992	5,785	49	1,793 D	40.6%	58.9%	40.8%	59.2%
STOKES	6,333	2,577	3,721	35	1,144 D	40.7%	58.8%	40.9%	59.1%
SURRY	12,070	4,511	7,490	69	2,979 D	37.4%	62.1%	37.6%	62.4%
SWAIN	4,324	1,893	2,412	19	519 D	43.8%	55.8%	44.0%	56.0%
TRANSYLVANIA	4,216	1,671	2,523	22	852 D	39.6%	59.8%	39.8%	60.2%
TYRRELL	1,137	258	873	6	615 D	22.7%	76.8%	22.8%	77.2%
UNION	6,870	710	6,103	57	5,393 D	10.3%	88.8%	10.4%	89.6%
VANCE	4,165	318	3,833	14	3,515 D	7.6%	92.0%	7.7%	92.3%
WAKE	17,295	2,170	14,863	246	12,693 D	12.6%	86.0%	12.7%	87.3%
WARREN	2,777	110	2,661	6	2,551 D	4.0%	95.8%	4.0%	96.0%
WASHINGTON	2,312	619	1,681	12	1,062 D	26.8%	72.7%	26.9%	73.1%
WATAUGA	6,606	3,166	3,419	21	253 D	47.9%	51.8%	48.1%	51.9%
WAYNE	8,056	1,631	6,365	60	4,734 D	20.2%	79.0%	20.4%	79.6%
WILKES	12,159	6,522	5,598	39	924 R	53.6%	46.0%	53.8%	46.2%
WILSON	6,721	517	6,153	51	5,636 D	7.7%	91.5%	7.8%	92.2%
YADKIN	6,242	3,482	2,729	31	633 R	54.8%	44.7%	55.1%	44.9%
YANCEY	5,817	2,396	3,412	9	1,016 D	41.2%	58.7%	41.3%	58.7%
TOTAL	711,498	208,344	497,566	5,588	289,222 D	29.3%	69.9%	29.5%	70.5%

NORTH CAROLINA

PRESIDENT 1936

County	Total Vote	Republican	Democratic	Other	Rep.-Dem. Plurality	Total Vote Rep.	Total Vote Dem.	Major Vote Rep.	Major Vote Dem.
ALAMANCE	14,872	3,847	11,025		7,178 D	25.9%	74.1%	25.9%	74.1%
ALEXANDER	5,713	2,451	3,262		811 D	42.9%	57.1%	42.9%	57.1%
ALLEGHANY	3,843	1,498	2,345		847 D	39.0%	61.0%	39.0%	61.0%
ANSON	5,010	381	4,629		4,248 D	7.6%	92.4%	7.6%	92.4%
ASHE	10,109	4,557	5,552		995 D	45.1%	54.9%	45.1%	54.9%
AVERY	3,810	2,971	839		2,132 R	78.0%	22.0%	78.0%	22.0%
BEAUFORT	7,097	964	6,133		5,169 D	13.6%	86.4%	13.6%	86.4%
BERTIE	3,943	115	3,828		3,713 D	2.9%	97.1%	2.9%	97.1%
BLADEN	3,911	551	3,360		2,809 D	14.1%	85.9%	14.1%	85.9%
BRUNSWICK	4,335	1,625	2,710		1,085 D	37.5%	62.5%	37.5%	62.5%
BUNCOMBE	33,116	9,470	23,646		14,176 D	28.6%	71.4%	28.6%	71.4%
BURKE	12,960	5,506	7,454		1,948 D	42.5%	57.5%	42.5%	57.5%
CABARRUS	15,122	2,825	12,297		9,472 D	18.7%	81.3%	18.7%	81.3%
CALDWELL	10,230	3,421	6,809		3,388 D	33.4%	66.6%	33.4%	66.6%
CAMDEN	1,125	117	1,008		891 D	10.4%	89.6%	10.4%	89.6%
CARTERET	5,669	1,889	3,780		1,891 D	33.3%	66.7%	33.3%	66.7%
CASWELL	2,700	207	2,493		2,286 D	7.7%	92.3%	7.7%	92.3%
CATAWBA	17,404	6,387	11,017		4,630 D	36.7%	63.3%	36.7%	63.3%
CHATHAM	6,555	2,182	4,373		2,191 D	33.3%	66.7%	33.3%	66.7%
CHEROKEE	6,687	3,214	3,473		259 D	48.1%	51.9%	48.1%	51.9%
CHOWAN	1,646	96	1,550		1,454 D	5.8%	94.2%	5.8%	94.2%
CLAY	2,865	1,525	1,340		185 R	53.2%	46.8%	53.2%	46.8%
CLEVELAND	13,509	2,116	11,393		9,277 D	15.7%	84.3%	15.7%	84.3%
COLUMBUS	7,573	1,214	6,359		5,145 D	16.0%	84.0%	16.0%	84.0%
CRAVEN	5,996	453	5,543		5,090 D	7.6%	92.4%	7.6%	92.4%
CUMBERLAND	7,529	1,024	6,505		5,481 D	13.6%	86.4%	13.6%	86.4%
CURRITUCK	1,753	128	1,625		1,497 D	7.3%	92.7%	7.3%	92.7%
DARE	1,931	542	1,389		847 D	28.1%	71.9%	28.1%	71.9%
DAVIDSON	18,500	7,656	10,844		3,188 D	41.4%	58.6%	41.4%	58.6%
DAVIE	4,978	2,502	2,476		26 R	50.3%	49.7%	50.3%	49.7%
DUPLIN	7,512	1,546	5,966		4,420 D	20.6%	79.4%	20.6%	79.4%
DURHAM	14,993	2,189	12,804		10,615 D	14.6%	85.4%	14.6%	85.4%
EDGECOMBE	6,950	266	6,684		6,418 D	3.8%	96.2%	3.8%	96.2%
FORSYTH	23,990	5,256	18,734		13,478 D	21.9%	78.1%	21.9%	78.1%
FRANKLIN	5,440	231	5,209		4,978 D	4.2%	95.8%	4.2%	95.8%
GASTON	22,327	4,772	17,555		12,783 D	21.4%	78.6%	21.4%	78.6%
GATES	1,612	128	1,484		1,356 D	7.9%	92.1%	7.9%	92.1%
GRAHAM	2,798	1,325	1,473		148 D	47.4%	52.6%	47.4%	52.6%
GRANVILLE	4,464	185	4,279		4,094 D	4.1%	95.9%	4.1%	95.9%
GREENE	3,213	116	3,097		2,981 D	3.6%	96.4%	3.6%	96.4%
GUILFORD	35,093	9,514	25,579		16,065 D	27.1%	72.9%	27.1%	72.9%
HALIFAX	8,538	308	8,230		7,922 D	3.6%	96.4%	3.6%	96.4%
HARNETT	10,282	2,264	8,018		5,754 D	22.0%	78.0%	22.0%	78.0%
HAYWOOD	10,806	3,331	8,175		4,844 D	29.0%	71.0%	29.0%	71.0%
HENDERSON	10,846	5,099	5,747		648 D	47.0%	53.0%	47.0%	53.0%
HERTFORD	2,411	84	2,327		2,243 D	3.5%	96.5%	3.5%	96.5%
HOKE	2,094	141	1,953		1,812 D	6.7%	93.3%	6.7%	93.3%
HYDE	1,459	302	1,157		855 D	20.7%	79.3%	20.7%	79.3%
IREDELL	15,125	3,817	11,308		7,491 D	25.2%	74.8%	25.2%	74.8%
JACKSON	7,641	3,061	4,580		1,519 D	40.1%	59.9%	40.1%	59.9%
JOHNSTON	15,592	4,339	11,253		6,914 D	27.8%	72.2%	27.8%	72.2%
JONES	1,751	188	1,563		1,375 D	10.7%	89.3%	10.7%	89.3%
LEE	4,393	670	3,723		3,053 D	15.3%	84.7%	15.3%	84.7%
LENOIR	6,205	351	5,854		5,503 D	5.7%	94.3%	5.7%	94.3%
LINCOLN	9,016	3,501	5,515		2,014 D	38.8%	61.2%	38.8%	61.2%
MCDOWELL	8,466	3,114	5,352		2,238 D	36.8%	63.2%	36.8%	63.2%
MACON	5,865	2,554	3,331		757 D	43.5%	56.5%	43.5%	56.5%
MADISON	8,232	5,099	3,133		1,966 R	61.9%	38.1%	61.9%	38.1%
MARTIN	4,588	111	4,477		4,366 D	2.4%	97.6%	2.4%	97.6%
MECKLENBURG	30,878	4,709	26,169		21,460 D	15.3%	84.7%	15.3%	84.7%

PRESIDENT 1940

County	Total Vote	Republican	Democratic	Other	Rep.-Dem. Plurality	Total Vote Rep.	Total Vote Dem.	Major Vote Rep.	Major Vote Dem.
ALAMANCE	14,811	3,382	11,429		8,047 D	22.8%	77.2%	22.8%	77.2%
ALEXANDER	4,956	2,217	2,739		522 D	44.7%	55.3%	44.7%	55.3%
ALLEGHANY	3,169	1,217	1,952		735 D	38.4%	61.6%	38.4%	61.6%
ANSON	4,923	371	4,552		4,181 D	7.5%	92.5%	7.5%	92.5%
ASHE	8,891	4,175	4,716		541 D	47.0%	53.0%	47.0%	53.0%
AVERY	4,138	2,944	1,194		1,750 R	71.1%	28.9%	71.1%	28.9%
BEAUFORT	6,464	936	5,528		4,592 D	14.5%	85.5%	14.5%	85.5%
BERTIE	3,385	98	3,287		3,189 D	2.9%	97.1%	2.9%	97.1%
BLADEN	3,468	543	2,925		2,382 D	15.7%	84.3%	15.7%	84.3%
BRUNSWICK	4,239	1,522	2,717		1,195 D	35.9%	64.1%	35.9%	64.1%
BUNCOMBE	33,601	8,723	24,878		16,155 D	26.0%	74.0%	26.0%	74.0%
BURKE	12,131	4,889	7,242		2,353 D	40.3%	59.7%	40.3%	59.7%
CABARRUS	14,355	2,579	11,776		9,197 D	18.0%	82.0%	18.0%	82.0%
CALDWELL	9,339	3,005	6,334		3,329 D	32.2%	67.8%	32.2%	67.8%
CAMDEN	1,095	134	961		827 D	12.2%	87.8%	12.2%	87.8%
CARTERET	5,685	1,789	3,896		2,107 D	31.5%	68.5%	31.5%	68.5%
CASWELL	2,686	351	2,335		1,984 D	13.1%	86.9%	13.1%	86.9%
CATAWBA	16,889	5,656	11,233		5,577 D	33.5%	66.5%	33.5%	66.5%
CHATHAM	5,854	1,829	4,025		2,196 D	31.2%	68.8%	31.2%	68.8%
CHEROKEE	5,854	2,674	3,180		506 D	45.7%	54.3%	45.7%	54.3%
CHOWAN	1,634	87	1,547		1,460 D	5.3%	94.7%	5.3%	94.7%
CLAY	2,525	1,176	1,349		173 D	46.6%	53.4%	46.6%	53.4%
CLEVELAND	11,316	1,970	9,346		7,376 D	17.4%	82.6%	17.4%	82.6%
COLUMBUS	6,834	934	5,900		4,966 D	13.7%	86.3%	13.7%	86.3%
CRAVEN	5,542	626	4,916		4,290 D	11.3%	88.7%	11.3%	88.7%
CUMBERLAND	7,168	1,118	6,050		4,932 D	15.6%	84.4%	15.6%	84.4%
CURRITUCK	1,634	102	1,532		1,430 D	6.2%	93.8%	6.2%	93.8%
DARE	1,529	315	1,214		899 D	20.6%	79.4%	20.6%	79.4%
DAVIDSON	18,062	6,978	11,084		4,106 D	38.6%	61.4%	38.6%	61.4%
DAVIE	5,428	2,532	2,896		364 D	46.6%	53.4%	46.6%	53.4%
DUPLIN	6,654	1,260	5,394		4,134 D	18.9%	81.1%	18.9%	81.1%
DURHAM	17,301	2,491	14,810		12,319 D	14.4%	85.6%	14.4%	85.6%
EDGECOMBE	7,832	316	7,516		7,200 D	4.0%	96.0%	4.0%	96.0%
FORSYTH	27,789	7,125	20,664		13,539 D	25.6%	74.4%	25.6%	74.4%
FRANKLIN	4,951	227	4,724		4,497 D	4.6%	95.4%	4.6%	95.4%
GASTON	21,556	4,294	17,262		12,968 D	19.9%	80.1%	19.9%	80.1%
GATES	1,496	108	1,388		1,280 D	7.2%	92.8%	7.2%	92.8%
GRAHAM	2,493	1,089	1,404		315 D	43.7%	56.3%	43.7%	56.3%
GRANVILLE	4,137	213	3,924		3,711 D	5.1%	94.9%	5.1%	94.9%
GREENE	3,094	104	2,990		2,886 D	3.4%	96.6%	3.4%	96.6%
GUILFORD	36,335	9,770	26,565		16,795 D	26.9%	73.1%	26.9%	73.1%
HALIFAX	8,343	361	7,982		7,621 D	4.3%	95.7%	4.3%	95.7%
HARNETT	8,882	2,280	6,602		4,322 D	25.7%	74.3%	25.7%	74.3%
HAYWOOD	10,988	2,357	8,631		6,274 D	21.5%	78.5%	21.5%	78.5%
HENDERSON	10,048	3,712	6,336		2,624 D	36.9%	63.1%	36.9%	63.1%
HERTFORD	2,556	92	2,464		2,372 D	3.6%	96.4%	3.6%	96.4%
HOKE	2,021	117	1,904		1,787 D	5.8%	94.2%	5.8%	94.2%
HYDE	1,511	309	1,202		893 D	20.5%	79.5%	20.5%	79.5%
IREDELL	14,148	3,820	10,328		6,508 D	27.0%	73.0%	27.0%	73.0%
JACKSON	6,973	2,410	4,563		2,153 D	34.6%	65.4%	34.6%	65.4%
JOHNSTON	14,168	4,192	9,976		5,784 D	29.6%	70.4%	29.6%	70.4%
JONES	1,604	233	1,371		1,138 D	14.5%	85.5%	14.5%	85.5%
LEE	4,209	527	3,682		3,155 D	12.5%	87.5%	12.5%	87.5%
LENOIR	6,687	440	6,247		5,807 D	6.6%	93.4%	6.6%	93.4%
LINCOLN	8,000	3,099	4,901		1,802 D	38.7%	61.3%	38.7%	61.3%
MCDOWELL	7,506	2,216	5,290		3,074 D	29.5%	70.5%	29.5%	70.5%
MACON	5,253	2,312	2,941		629 D	44.0%	56.0%	44.0%	56.0%
MADISON	7,788	4,617	3,171		1,446 R	59.3%	40.7%	59.3%	40.7%
MARTIN	4,734	106	4,628		4,522 D	2.2%	97.8%	2.2%	97.8%
MECKLENBURG	35,781	7,013	28,768		21,755 D	19.6%	80.4%	19.6%	80.4%

NORTH CAROLINA

PRESIDENT 1936

County	Total Vote	Republican	Democratic	Other	Rep.-Dem. Plurality	Total Vote Rep.	Total Vote Dem.	Major Vote Rep.	Major Vote Dem.
MITCHELL	5,067	3,380	1,687		1,693 R	66.7%	33.3%	66.7%	33.3%
MONTGOMERY	5,990	2,506	3,484		978 D	41.8%	58.2%	41.8%	58.2%
MOORE	6,947	2,481	4,466		1,985 D	35.7%	64.3%	35.7%	64.3%
NASH	9,199	517	8,682		8,165 D	5.6%	94.4%	5.6%	94.4%
NEW HANOVER	8,685	1,306	7,379		6,073 D	15.0%	85.0%	15.0%	85.0%
NORTHAMPTON	3,894	109	3,785		3,676 D	2.8%	97.2%	2.8%	97.2%
ONSLOW	2,993	235	2,758		2,523 D	7.9%	92.1%	7.9%	92.1%
ORANGE	5,335	1,446	3,860	29	2,414 D	27.1%	72.4%	27.3%	72.1%
PAMLICO	2,487	860	1,627		767 D	34.6%	65.4%	34.6%	65.4%
PASQUOTANK	3,555	324	3,226	5	2,902 D	9.1%	90.7%	9.1%	90.9%
PENDER	2,712	333	2,379		2,046 D	12.3%	87.7%	12.3%	87.7%
PERQUIMANS	1,131	161	970		809 D	14.2%	85.8%	14.2%	85.8%
PERSON	3,282	384	2,898		2,514 D	11.7%	88.3%	11.7%	88.3%
PITT	9,864	325	9,539		9,214 D	3.3%	96.7%	3.3%	96.7%
POLK	4,315	1,794	2,521		727 D	41.6%	58.4%	41.6%	58.4%
RANDOLPH	15,017	6,927	8,090		1,163 D	46.1%	53.9%	46.1%	53.9%
RICHMOND	7,316	607	6,709		6,102 D	8.3%	91.7%	8.3%	91.7%
ROBESON	11,012	732	10,280		9,548 D	6.6%	93.4%	6.6%	93.4%
ROCKINGHAM	13,888	2,522	11,366		8,844 D	18.2%	81.8%	18.2%	81.8%
ROWAN	17,114	4,306	12,808		8,502 D	25.2%	74.8%	25.2%	74.8%
RUTHERFORD	14,741	4,830	9,911		5,081 D	32.3%	67.2%	32.8%	67.2%
SAMPSON	10,885	4,948	5,937		989 D	45.5%	54.5%	45.5%	54.5%
SCOTLAND	3,497	314	3,183		2,869 D	9.0%	91.0%	9.0%	91.0%
STANLY	11,028	4,523	6,505		1,982 D	41.0%	59.0%	41.0%	59.0%
STOKES	7,643	3,259	4,384		1,125 D	42.5%	57.4%	42.6%	57.4%
SURRY	13,599	4,766	8,833		4,067 D	35.0%	65.0%	35.0%	65.0%
SWAIN	4,703	2,084	2,619		535 D	44.3%	55.7%	44.3%	55.7%
TRANSYLVANIA	4,846	2,001	2,845		844 D	41.3%	58.7%	41.3%	58.7%
TYRRELL	1,353	304	1,049		745 D	22.5%	77.5%	22.5%	77.5%
UNION	8,081	601	7,480		6,879 D	7.4%	92.6%	7.4%	92.6%
VANCE	4,851	315	4,536		4,221 D	6.5%	93.5%	6.5%	93.5%
WAKE	22,312	2,456	19,850	6	17,394 D	11.0%	89.0%	11.0%	89.0%
WARREN	3,187	140	3,047		2,907 D	4.4%	95.6%	4.4%	95.6%
WASHINGTON	2,410	535	1,875		1,340 D	22.2%	77.8%	22.2%	77.8%
WATAUGA	7,289	3,409	3,880		471 D	46.8%	53.2%	46.8%	53.2%
WAYNE	8,838	1,751	7,087		5,336 D	19.8%	80.2%	19.8%	80.2%
WILKES	14,864	8,358	6,506		1,852 R	56.2%	43.8%	56.2%	43.8%
WILSON	8,071	549	7,522		6,973 D	6.8%	93.2%	6.8%	93.2%
YADKIN	7,409	4,200	3,209		991 R	56.7%	43.3%	56.7%	43.3%
YANCEY	6,294	2,691	3,603		912 D	42.8%	57.2%	42.8%	57.2%
TOTAL	839,475	223,294	616,141	40	392,847 D	26.6%	73.4%	26.6%	73.4%

PRESIDENT 1940

County	Total Vote	Republican	Democratic	Other	Rep.-Dem. Plurality	Total Vote Rep.	Total Vote Dem.	Major Vote Rep.	Major Vote Dem.
MITCHELL	4,740	3,290	1,450		1,840 R	69.4%	30.6%	69.4%	30.6%
MONTGOMERY	4,796	1,789	3,007		1,218 D	37.3%	62.7%	37.3%	62.7%
MOORE	6,917	2,587	4,330		1,743 D	37.4%	62.6%	37.4%	62.6%
NASH	9,069	613	8,456		7,843 D	6.8%	93.2%	6.8%	93.2%
NEW HANOVER	10,235	1,535	8,600		6,965 D	16.0%	84.0%	16.0%	84.0%
NORTHAMPTON	3,931	105	3,826		3,721 D	2.7%	97.3%	2.7%	97.3%
ONSLOW	2,654	271	2,383		2,112 D	10.2%	89.8%	10.2%	89.8%
ORANGE	4,773	1,100	3,673		2,573 D	23.0%	77.0%	23.0%	77.0%
PAMLICO	2,178	730	1,448		718 D	33.5%	66.5%	33.5%	66.5%
PASQUOTANK	3,820	506	3,314		2,808 D	13.2%	86.8%	13.2%	86.8%
PENDER	2,554	305	2,249		1,944 D	11.9%	88.1%	11.9%	88.1%
PERQUIMANS	1,404	228	1,176		948 D	16.2%	83.8%	16.2%	83.8%
PERSON	3,671	432	3,239		2,807 D	11.8%	88.2%	11.8%	88.2%
PITT	10,436	369	10,067		9,698 D	3.5%	96.5%	3.5%	96.5%
POLK	3,982	1,528	2,454		926 D	38.4%	61.6%	38.4%	61.6%
RANDOLPH	15,511	7,056	8,455		1,399 D	45.5%	54.5%	45.5%	54.5%
RICHMOND	7,309	779	6,530		5,751 D	10.7%	89.3%	10.7%	89.3%
ROBESON	10,182	931	9,251		8,320 D	9.1%	90.9%	9.1%	90.9%
ROCKINGHAM	13,713	2,398	11,315		8,917 D	17.5%	82.5%	17.5%	82.5%
ROWAN	17,082	4,059	13,023		8,964 D	23.8%	76.2%	23.8%	76.2%
RUTHERFORD	13,073	4,204	8,869		4,665 D	32.2%	67.8%	32.2%	67.8%
SAMPSON	10,876	5,769	5,107		662 R	53.0%	47.0%	53.0%	47.0%
SCOTLAND	3,231	250	2,981		2,731 D	7.7%	92.3%	7.7%	92.3%
STANLY	10,890	4,569	6,321		1,752 D	42.0%	58.0%	42.0%	58.0%
STOKES	6,986	2,712	4,274		1,562 D	38.8%	61.2%	38.8%	61.2%
SURRY	13,049	4,178	8,871		4,693 D	32.0%	68.0%	32.0%	68.0%
SWAIN	3,847	1,425	2,422		997 D	37.0%	63.0%	37.0%	63.0%
TRANSYLVANIA	5,331	2,019	3,312		1,293 D	37.9%	62.1%	37.9%	62.1%
TYRRELL	1,555	415	1,140		725 D	26.7%	73.3%	26.7%	73.3%
UNION	7,813	634	7,179		6,545 D	8.1%	91.9%	8.1%	91.9%
VANCE	4,632	380	4,252		3,872 D	8.2%	91.8%	8.2%	91.8%
WAKE	20,748	2,665	18,083		15,418 D	12.8%	87.2%	12.8%	87.2%
WARREN	2,923	247	2,676		2,429 D	8.5%	91.5%	8.5%	91.5%
WASHINGTON	2,086	362	1,724		1,362 D	17.4%	82.6%	17.4%	82.6%
WATAUGA	7,354	3,739	3,615		124 R	50.8%	49.2%	50.8%	49.2%
WAYNE	8,871	1,649	7,222		5,573 D	18.6%	81.4%	18.6%	81.4%
WILKES	15,745	8,446	7,299		1,147 R	53.6%	46.4%	53.6%	46.4%
WILSON	8,496	584	7,912		7,328 D	6.9%	93.1%	6.9%	93.1%
YADKIN	7,737	4,077	3,660		417 R	52.7%	47.3%	52.7%	47.3%
YANCEY	6,005	2,516	3,489		973 D	41.9%	58.1%	41.9%	58.1%
TOTAL	822,648	213,633	609,015		395,382 D	26.0%	74.0%	26.0%	74.0%

NORTH CAROLINA

PRESIDENT 1944

County	Total Vote	Republican	Democratic	Other	Rep.-Dem. Plurality	% Total Vote Rep.	% Total Vote Dem.	% Major Vote Rep.	% Major Vote Dem.
ALAMANCE	14,160	4,976	9,184		4,208 D	35.1%	64.9%	35.1%	64.9%
ALEXANDER	5,253	2,971	2,282		689 R	56.6%	43.4%	56.6%	43.4%
ALLEGHANY	3,305	1,495	1,810		315 D	45.2%	54.8%	45.2%	54.8%
ANSON	4,092	510	3,582		3,072 D	12.5%	87.5%	12.5%	87.5%
ASHE	8,887	4,524	4,363		161 R	50.9%	49.1%	50.9%	49.1%
AVERY	4,016	3,178	838		2,340 R	79.1%	20.9%	79.1%	20.9%
BEAUFORT	5,839	1,133	4,706		3,573 D	19.4%	80.6%	19.4%	80.6%
BERTIE	3,266	124	3,142		3,018 D	3.8%	96.2%	3.8%	96.2%
BLADEN	3,273	731	2,542		1,811 D	22.3%	77.7%	22.3%	77.7%
BRUNSWICK	4,343	1,997	2,346		349 D	46.0%	54.0%	46.0%	54.0%
BUNCOMBE	30,276	9,398	20,878		11,480 D	31.0%	69.0%	31.0%	69.0%
BURKE	12,650	5,855	6,795		940 D	46.3%	53.7%	46.3%	53.7%
CABARRUS	13,297	4,233	9,064		4,831 D	31.8%	68.2%	31.8%	68.2%
CALDWELL	9,784	4,365	5,419		1,054 D	44.6%	55.4%	44.6%	55.4%
CAMDEN	915	193	722		529 D	21.1%	78.9%	21.1%	78.9%
CARTERET	5,055	1,566	3,489		1,923 D	31.0%	69.0%	31.0%	69.0%
CASWELL	2,415	492	1,923		1,431 D	20.4%	79.6%	20.4%	79.6%
CATAWBA	17,357	7,211	10,146		2,935 D	41.5%	58.5%	41.5%	58.5%
CHATHAM	6,287	2,431	3,856		1,425 D	38.7%	61.3%	38.7%	61.3%
CHEROKEE	5,207	2,625	2,582		43 R	50.4%	49.6%	50.4%	49.6%
CHOWAN	1,480	166	1,314		1,148 D	11.2%	88.8%	11.2%	88.8%
CLAY	2,508	1,263	1,245		18 R	50.4%	49.6%	50.4%	49.6%
CLEVELAND	10,806	2,636	8,170		5,534 D	24.4%	75.6%	24.4%	75.6%
COLUMBUS	7,269	1,552	5,717		4,165 D	21.4%	78.6%	21.4%	78.6%
CRAVEN	5,698	826	4,872		4,046 D	14.5%	85.5%	14.5%	85.5%
CUMBERLAND	8,629	2,014	6,615		4,601 D	23.3%	76.7%	23.3%	76.7%
CURRITUCK	1,280	231	1,049		818 D	18.0%	82.0%	18.0%	82.0%
DARE	1,225	259	966		707 D	21.1%	78.9%	21.1%	78.9%
DAVIDSON	18,900	9,445	9,455		10 D	50.0%	50.0%	50.0%	50.0%
DAVIE	5,510	3,244	2,266		978 R	58.9%	41.1%	58.9%	41.1%
DUPLIN	6,901	1,437	5,464		4,027 D	20.8%	79.2%	20.8%	79.2%
DURHAM	16,453	3,690	12,763		9,073 D	22.4%	77.6%	22.4%	77.6%
EDGECOMBE	7,210	448	6,762		6,314 D	6.2%	93.8%	6.2%	93.8%
FORSYTH	26,404	10,014	16,390		6,376 D	37.9%	62.1%	37.9%	62.1%
FRANKLIN	4,256	289	3,967		3,678 D	6.8%	93.2%	6.8%	93.2%
GASTON	19,767	6,023	13,744		7,721 D	30.5%	69.5%	30.5%	69.5%
GATES	1,258	153	1,105		952 D	12.2%	87.8%	12.2%	87.8%
GRAHAM	3,245	1,356	1,889		533 D	41.8%	58.2%	41.8%	58.2%
GRANVILLE	3,540	325	3,215		2,890 D	9.2%	90.8%	9.2%	90.8%
GREENE	2,641	113	2,528		2,415 D	4.3%	95.7%	4.3%	95.7%
GUILFORD	36,457	12,962	23,495		10,533 D	35.6%	64.4%	35.6%	64.4%
HALIFAX	7,429	440	6,989		6,549 D	5.9%	94.1%	5.9%	94.1%
HARNETT	9,770	3,191	6,579		3,388 D	32.7%	67.3%	32.7%	67.3%
HAYWOOD	10,674	2,919	7,755		4,836 D	27.3%	72.7%	27.3%	72.7%
HENDERSON	10,292	4,613	5,679		1,066 D	44.8%	55.2%	44.8%	55.2%
HERTFORD	2,121	125	1,996		1,871 D	5.9%	94.1%	5.9%	94.1%
HOKE	1,942	160	1,782		1,622 D	8.2%	91.8%	8.2%	91.8%
HYDE	1,247	323	924		601 D	25.9%	74.1%	25.9%	74.1%
IREDELL	13,222	4,864	8,358		3,494 D	36.8%	63.2%	36.8%	63.2%
JACKSON	6,803	2,694	4,109		1,415 D	39.6%	60.4%	39.6%	60.4%
JOHNSTON	12,705	4,423	8,282		3,859 D	34.8%	65.2%	34.8%	65.2%
JONES	1,432	211	1,221		1,010 D	14.7%	85.3%	14.7%	85.3%
LEE	4,256	808	3,448		2,640 D	19.0%	81.0%	19.0%	81.0%
LENOIR	5,807	554	5,253		4,699 D	9.5%	90.5%	9.5%	90.5%
LINCOLN	7,846	3,678	4,168		490 D	46.9%	53.1%	46.9%	53.1%
MCDOWELL	6,266	2,258	4,008		1,750 D	36.0%	64.0%	36.0%	64.0%
MACON	5,365	2,510	2,855		345 D	46.8%	53.2%	46.8%	53.2%
MADISON	6,679	4,388	2,291		2,097 R	65.7%	34.3%	65.7%	34.3%
MARTIN	4,541	133	4,408		4,275 D	2.9%	97.1%	2.9%	97.1%
MECKLENBURG	35,384	9,434	25,950		16,516 D	26.7%	73.3%	26.7%	73.3%

PRESIDENT 1948

County	Total Vote	Republican	Democratic	Other	Rep.-Dem. Plurality	% Total Vote Rep.	% Total Vote Dem.	% Major Vote Rep.	% Major Vote Dem.
ALAMANCE	15,380	5,124	8,287	1,969	3,163 D	33.3%	53.9%	38.2%	61.8%
ALEXANDER	4,823	2,314	2,057	452	257 R	48.0%	42.6%	52.9%	47.1%
ALLEGHANY	3,241	1,374	1,667	200	293 D	42.4%	51.4%	45.2%	54.8%
ANSON	3,711	447	2,692	572	2,245 D	12.0%	72.5%	14.2%	85.8%
ASHE	9,127	4,266	4,633	228	367 D	46.7%	50.8%	47.9%	52.1%
AVERY	4,008	2,995	933	80	2,062 R	74.7%	23.3%	76.2%	23.8%
BEAUFORT	6,030	1,055	4,675	300	3,620 D	17.5%	77.5%	18.4%	81.6%
BERTIE	3,170	85	3,034	51	2,949 D	2.7%	95.7%	2.7%	97.3%
BLADEN	3,914	500	2,831	583	2,331 D	12.8%	72.3%	15.0%	85.0%
BRUNSWICK	4,683	1,896	2,052	735	156 D	40.5%	43.8%	48.0%	52.0%
BUNCOMBE	30,851	11,460	17,052	2,319	5,612 D	37.1%	55.3%	40.2%	59.8%
BURKE	13,488	6,374	6,226	888	148 R	47.3%	46.2%	50.6%	49.4%
CABARRUS	12,826	4,294	5,059	3,473	765 D	33.5%	39.4%	45.9%	54.1%
CALDWELL	10,785	4,987	5,033	765	46 D	46.2%	46.7%	49.8%	50.2%
CAMDEN	779	127	576	76	449 D	16.3%	73.9%	18.1%	81.9%
CARTERET	5,160	1,520	3,491	149	1,971 D	29.5%	67.7%	30.3%	69.7%
CASWELL	2,399	351	1,651	397	1,300 D	14.6%	68.8%	17.5%	82.5%
CATAWBA	19,937	9,471	8,844	1,622	627 R	47.5%	44.4%	51.7%	48.3%
CHATHAM	5,795	2,008	3,396	391	1,388 D	34.7%	58.6%	37.2%	62.8%
CHEROKEE	5,572	2,615	2,771	186	156 D	46.9%	49.7%	48.6%	51.4%
CHOWAN	1,274	124	1,070	80	946 D	9.7%	84.0%	10.4%	89.6%
CLAY	2,575	1,213	1,307	55	94 D	47.1%	50.8%	48.1%	51.9%
CLEVELAND	9,261	1,905	6,039	1,317	4,134 D	20.6%	65.2%	24.0%	76.0%
COLUMBUS	7,369	1,105	5,511	753	4,406 D	15.0%	74.8%	16.7%	83.3%
CRAVEN	6,278	745	5,039	494	4,294 D	11.9%	80.3%	12.9%	87.1%
CUMBERLAND	9,062	1,741	4,996	2,325	3,255 D	19.2%	55.1%	25.8%	74.2%
CURRITUCK	1,368	130	1,144	94	1,014 D	9.5%	83.6%	10.2%	89.8%
DARE	1,214	373	802	39	429 D	30.7%	66.1%	31.7%	68.3%
DAVIDSON	17,314	8,539	7,991	784	548 R	49.3%	46.2%	51.7%	48.3%
DAVIE	4,959	2,679	1,917	363	762 R	54.0%	38.7%	58.3%	41.7%
DUPLIN	7,220	1,024	5,866	330	4,842 D	14.2%	81.2%	14.9%	85.1%
DURHAM	17,613	4,531	11,530	1,552	6,999 D	25.7%	65.5%	28.2%	71.8%
EDGECOMBE	7,142	478	6,410	254	5,932 D	6.7%	89.8%	6.9%	93.1%
FORSYTH	24,725	10,147	12,201	2,377	2,054 D	41.0%	49.3%	45.4%	54.6%
FRANKLIN	4,957	234	4,538	185	4,304 D	4.7%	91.5%	4.9%	95.1%
GASTON	18,968	6,180	8,966	3,822	2,786 D	32.6%	47.3%	40.8%	59.2%
GATES	1,080	89	939	52	850 D	8.2%	86.9%	8.7%	91.3%
GRAHAM	2,715	1,115	1,527	73	412 D	41.1%	56.2%	42.2%	57.8%
GRANVILLE	4,121	334	3,513	274	3,179 D	8.1%	85.2%	8.7%	91.3%
GREENE	2,786	65	2,687	34	2,622 D	2.3%	96.4%	2.4%	97.6%
GUILFORD	35,349	14,167	17,224	3,958	3,057 D	40.1%	48.7%	45.1%	54.9%
HALIFAX	7,109	505	6,172	432	5,667 D	7.1%	86.8%	7.6%	92.4%
HARNETT	8,916	1,985	6,608	323	4,623 D	22.3%	74.1%	23.1%	76.9%
HAYWOOD	10,266	2,684	7,373	209	4,689 D	26.1%	71.8%	26.7%	73.3%
HENDERSON	9,632	4,971	3,311	1,350	1,660 D	51.6%	34.4%	60.0%	40.0%
HERTFORD	2,438	196	2,165	77	1,969 D	8.0%	88.8%	8.3%	91.7%
HOKE	1,659	142	1,339	178	1,197 D	8.6%	80.7%	9.6%	90.4%
HYDE	1,052	214	800	38	586 D	20.3%	76.0%	21.1%	78.9%
IREDELL	12,136	4,441	5,761	1,934	1,320 D	36.6%	47.5%	43.5%	56.5%
JACKSON	6,725	2,520	4,005	200	1,485 D	37.5%	59.6%	38.6%	61.4%
JOHNSTON	12,997	3,211	9,188	598	5,977 D	24.7%	70.7%	25.9%	74.1%
JONES	1,406	113	1,238	55	1,125 D	8.0%	88.1%	8.4%	91.6%
LEE	4,348	871	3,234	243	2,363 D	20.0%	74.4%	21.2%	78.8%
LENOIR	6,150	515	5,445	190	4,930 D	8.4%	88.5%	8.6%	91.4%
LINCOLN	8,358	3,635	3,570	1,153	65 R	43.5%	42.7%	50.5%	49.5%
MCDOWELL	7,152	2,709	3,805	638	1,096 D	37.9%	53.2%	41.6%	58.4%
MACON	5,309	2,388	2,785	136	397 D	45.0%	52.5%	46.2%	53.8%
MADISON	5,995	3,341	2,558	96	783 R	55.7%	42.7%	56.6%	43.4%
MARTIN	4,853	163	4,636	54	4,473 D	3.4%	95.5%	3.4%	96.6%
MECKLENBURG	33,185	11,518	14,353	7,314	2,835 D	34.7%	43.3%	44.5%	55.5%

NORTH CAROLINA

PRESIDENT 1944

County	Total Vote	Republican	Democratic	Other	Rep.-Dem. Plurality	Total Vote Rep.	Total Vote Dem.	Major Vote Rep.	Major Vote Dem.
MITCHELL	4,216	3,192	1,024		2,168 R	75.7%	24.3%	75.7%	24.3%
MONTGOMERY	4,628	1,963	2,665		702 D	42.4%	57.6%	42.4%	57.6%
MOORE	6,374	2,663	3,711		1,048 D	41.8%	58.2%	41.8%	58.2%
NASH	8,453	876	7,577		6,701 D	10.4%	89.6%	10.4%	89.6%
NEW HANOVER	12,305	2,829	9,476		6,647 D	23.0%	77.0%	23.0%	77.0%
NORTHAMPTON	3,642	172	3,470		3,298 D	4.7%	95.3%	4.7%	95.3%
ONSLOW	3,144	433	2,711		2,278 D	13.8%	86.2%	13.8%	86.2%
ORANGE	4,741	1,467	3,274		1,807 D	30.9%	69.1%	30.9%	69.1%
PAMLICO	2,014	719	1,295		576 D	35.7%	64.3%	35.7%	64.3%
PASQUOTANK	3,400	860	2,540		1,680 D	25.3%	74.7%	25.3%	74.7%
PENDER	2,173	441	1,732		1,291 D	20.3%	79.7%	20.3%	79.7%
PERQUIMANS	1,226	266	960		694 D	21.7%	78.3%	21.7%	78.3%
PERSON	3,114	607	2,507		1,900 D	19.5%	80.5%	19.5%	80.5%
PITT	9,051	495	8,556		8,061 D	5.5%	94.5%	5.5%	94.5%
POLK	4,018	1,678	2,340		662 D	41.8%	58.2%	41.8%	58.2%
RANDOLPH	16,045	8,768	7,277		1,491 R	54.6%	45.4%	54.6%	45.4%
RICHMOND	6,332	938	5,394		4,456 D	14.8%	85.2%	14.8%	85.2%
ROBESON	8,396	1,118	7,278		6,160 D	13.3%	86.7%	13.3%	86.7%
ROCKINGHAM	11,779	3,024	8,755		5,731 D	25.7%	74.3%	25.7%	74.3%
ROWAN	15,583	5,862	9,721		3,859 D	37.6%	62.4%	37.6%	62.4%
RUTHERFORD	12,077	4,698	7,379		2,681 D	38.9%	61.1%	38.9%	61.1%
SAMPSON	10,282	6,062	4,220		1,842 R	59.0%	41.0%	59.0%	41.0%
SCOTLAND	2,675	303	2,372		2,069 D	11.3%	88.7%	11.3%	88.7%
STANLY	11,582	6,083	5,499		584 R	52.5%	47.5%	52.5%	47.5%
STOKES	7,486	3,376	4,110		734 D	45.1%	54.9%	45.1%	54.9%
SURRY	12,795	5,116	7,679		2,563 D	40.0%	60.0%	40.0%	60.0%
SWAIN	3,615	1,505	2,110		605 D	41.6%	58.4%	41.6%	58.4%
TRANSYLVANIA	5,270	2,251	3,019		768 D	42.7%	57.3%	42.7%	57.3%
TYRRELL	892	281	611		330 D	31.5%	68.5%	31.5%	68.5%
UNION	6,843	1,114	5,729		4,615 D	16.3%	83.7%	16.3%	83.7%
VANCE	4,638	528	4,110		3,582 D	11.4%	88.6%	11.4%	88.6%
WAKE	22,046	3,996	18,050		14,054 D	18.1%	81.9%	18.1%	81.9%
WARREN	2,722	242	2,480		2,238 D	8.9%	91.1%	8.9%	91.1%
WASHINGTON	2,279	497	1,782		1,285 D	21.8%	78.2%	21.8%	78.2%
WATAUGA	7,168	3,954	3,214		740 R	55.2%	44.8%	55.2%	44.8%
WAYNE	8,142	1,914	6,228		4,314 D	23.5%	76.5%	23.5%	76.5%
WILKES	14,699	9,121	5,578		3,543 R	62.1%	37.9%	62.1%	37.9%
WILSON	7,249	769	6,480		5,711 D	10.6%	89.4%	10.6%	89.4%
YADKIN	6,862	4,392	2,470		1,922 R	64.0%	36.0%	64.0%	36.0%
YANCEY	5,703	2,402	3,301		899 D	42.1%	57.9%	42.1%	57.9%
TOTAL	790,554	263,155	527,399		264,244 D	33.3%	65.7%	33.3%	66.7%

PRESIDENT 1948

County	Total Vote	Republican	Democratic	Other	Rep.-Dem. Plurality	Total Vote Rep.	Total Vote Dem.	Major Vote Rep.	Major Vote Dem.
MITCHELL	3,809	2,908	818	83	2,090 R	76.3%	21.5%	78.0%	22.0%
MONTGOMERY	4,558	1,975	2,165	418	190 D	43.3%	47.5%	47.7%	52.3%
MOORE	6,750	2,719	3,341	690	622 D	40.3%	49.5%	44.9%	55.1%
NASH	8,576	684	7,590	302	6,906 D	8.0%	88.5%	8.3%	91.7%
NEW HANOVER	11,193	3,162	5,364	2,667	2,202 D	28.2%	47.9%	37.1%	62.9%
NORTHAMPTON	3,896	179	3,591	126	3,412 D	4.6%	92.2%	4.7%	95.3%
ONSLOW	3,799	316	3,318	165	3,002 D	8.3%	87.3%	8.7%	91.3%
ORANGE	5,843	1,813	3,523	507	1,710 D	31.0%	60.3%	34.0%	66.0%
PAMLICO	2,197	685	1,370	142	685 D	31.2%	62.4%	33.3%	66.7%
PASQUOTANK	2,916	701	1,976	239	1,275 D	24.0%	67.8%	26.2%	73.8%
PENDER	2,138	304	1,334	500	1,030 D	14.2%	62.4%	18.6%	81.4%
PERQUIMANS	1,060	135	849	76	714 D	12.7%	80.1%	13.7%	86.3%
PERSON	3,752	480	3,087	185	2,607 D	12.8%	82.3%	13.5%	86.5%
PITT	9,522	602	8,519	401	7,917 D	6.3%	89.5%	6.6%	93.4%
POLK	3,991	1,636	2,078	277	442 D	41.0%	52.1%	44.0%	56.0%
RANDOLPH	15,682	8,372	6,567	743	1,805 R	53.4%	41.9%	56.0%	44.0%
RICHMOND	6,082	866	4,376	840	3,510 D	14.2%	72.0%	16.5%	83.5%
ROBESON	9,133	1,036	7,056	1,041	6,020 D	11.3%	77.3%	12.8%	87.2%
ROCKINGHAM	12,415	2,936	8,553	926	5,617 D	23.6%	68.9%	25.6%	74.4%
ROWAN	15,702	5,722	6,799	3,181	1,077 D	36.4%	43.3%	45.7%	54.3%
RUTHERFORD	11,750	4,342	5,992	1,416	1,650 D	37.0%	51.0%	42.0%	58.0%
SAMPSON	10,548	4,932	4,965	651	33 D	46.8%	47.1%	49.8%	50.2%
SCOTLAND	2,819	359	1,957	503	1,598 D	12.7%	69.4%	15.5%	84.5%
STANLY	11,674	5,902	4,415	1,357	1,487 R	50.6%	37.8%	57.2%	42.8%
STOKES	7,891	3,291	4,431	169	1,140 D	41.0%	56.2%	42.6%	54.3%
SURRY	12,253	4,643	6,956	654	2,313 D	37.9%	56.8%	40.0%	60.0%
SWAIN	3,367	1,389	1,908	70	519 D	41.3%	56.7%	42.1%	57.9%
TRANSYLVANIA	6,163	2,861	2,975	327	114 D	46.4%	48.3%	49.0%	51.0%
TYRRELL	1,113	336	732	45	396 D	30.2%	65.8%	31.5%	68.5%
UNION	5,144	738	3,407	999	2,669 D	14.3%	66.2%	17.8%	82.2%
VANCE	4,627	549	3,679	399	3,130 D	11.9%	79.5%	13.0%	87.0%
WAKE	24,423	4,850	17,939	1,634	13,089 D	19.9%	73.5%	21.3%	78.7%
WARREN	2,771	192	2,376	203	2,184 D	6.9%	85.7%	7.5%	92.5%
WASHINGTON	2,057	333	1,675	49	1,342 D	16.2%	81.4%	16.6%	83.4%
WATAUGA	7,400	3,851	3,379	170	472 R	52.0%	45.7%	53.3%	46.7%
WAYNE	8,348	1,658	6,111	579	4,453 D	19.9%	73.2%	21.3%	78.7%
WILKES	14,400	8,234	5,784	382	2,450 R	57.2%	40.2%	58.7%	41.3%
WILSON	6,966	665	6,008	293	5,343 D	9.5%	86.2%	10.0%	90.0%
YADKIN	5,934	3,631	2,083	220	1,548 R	61.2%	35.1%	63.5%	36.5%
YANCEY	5,832	2,282	3,481	69	1,199 D	39.1%	59.7%	39.6%	64.0%
TOTAL	791,209	258,572	459,070	73,567	200,498 D	32.7%	58.0%	36.0%	64.0%

NORTH CAROLINA

PRESIDENT 1952

County	Total Vote	Republican	Democratic	Other	Rep.-Dem. Plurality	Total Vote Rep.	Total Vote Dem.	Major Vote Rep.	Major Vote Dem.
ALAMANCE	24,790	11,388	13,402		2,014 D	45.9%	54.1%	45.9%	54.1%
ALEXANDER	6,262	3,597	2,665		932 R	57.4%	42.6%	57.4%	42.6%
ALLEGHANY	3,598	1,789	1,809		20 D	49.7%	50.3%	49.7%	50.3%
ANSON	5,986	1,843	4,143		2,300 D	30.8%	69.2%	30.8%	69.2%
ASHE	9,099	4,563	4,536		27 R	50.1%	49.9%	50.1%	49.9%
AVERY	4,689	3,725	964		2,761 R	79.4%	20.6%	79.4%	20.6%
BEAUFORT	7,833	2,404	5,429		3,025 D	30.7%	69.3%	30.7%	69.3%
BERTIE	3,941	384	3,557		3,173 D	9.7%	90.3%	9.7%	90.3%
BLADEN	5,216	1,710	3,506		1,796 D	32.8%	67.2%	32.8%	67.2%
BRUNSWICK	5,909	2,958	2,951		7 R	50.1%	49.9%	50.1%	49.9%
BUNCOMBE	46,869	24,444	22,425		2,019 R	52.2%	47.8%	52.2%	47.8%
BURKE	18,845	11,113	7,732		3,381 R	59.0%	41.0%	59.0%	41.0%
CABARRUS	24,193	15,053	9,140		5,913 R	62.2%	37.8%	62.2%	37.8%
CALDWELL	16,693	9,160	7,533		1,627 R	54.9%	45.1%	54.9%	45.1%
CAMDEN	1,336	340	996		656 D	25.4%	74.6%	25.4%	74.6%
CARTERET	7,247	2,967	4,280		1,313 D	40.9%	59.1%	40.9%	59.1%
CASWELL	3,570	973	2,597		1,624 D	27.3%	72.7%	27.3%	72.7%
CATAWBA	28,368	16,814	11,554		5,260 R	59.3%	40.7%	59.3%	40.7%
CHATHAM	7,909	3,606	4,303		697 D	45.6%	54.4%	45.6%	54.4%
CHEROKEE	6,591	3,228	3,363		135 D	49.0%	51.0%	49.0%	51.0%
CHOWAN	1,985	537	1,448		911 D	27.1%	72.9%	27.1%	72.9%
CLAY	2,882	1,443	1,439		4 R	50.1%	49.9%	50.1%	49.9%
CLEVELAND	17,315	7,606	9,709		2,103 D	43.9%	56.1%	43.9%	56.1%
COLUMBUS	9,942	3,001	6,941		3,940 D	30.2%	69.8%	30.2%	69.8%
CRAVEN	8,914	2,822	6,092		3,270 D	31.7%	68.3%	31.7%	68.3%
CUMBERLAND	16,313	7,474	8,839		1,365 D	45.8%	54.2%	45.8%	54.2%
CURRITUCK	1,885	414	1,471		1,057 D	22.0%	78.0%	22.0%	78.0%
DARE	1,726	767	959		192 D	44.4%	55.6%	44.4%	55.6%
DAVIDSON	25,230	14,299	10,931		3,368 R	56.7%	43.3%	56.7%	43.3%
DAVIE	6,416	4,010	2,406		1,604 R	62.5%	37.5%	62.5%	37.5%
DUPLIN	8,507	2,115	6,392		4,277 D	24.9%	75.1%	24.9%	75.1%
DURHAM	30,198	11,301	18,897		7,596 D	37.4%	62.6%	37.4%	62.6%
EDGECOMBE	10,431	1,927	8,504		6,577 D	18.5%	81.5%	18.5%	81.5%
FORSYTH	50,971	26,436	24,535		1,901 D	51.9%	48.1%	51.9%	48.1%
FRANKLIN	6,116	740	5,376		4,636 D	12.1%	87.9%	12.1%	87.9%
GASTON	36,938	19,157	17,781		1,376 R	51.9%	48.1%	51.9%	48.1%
GATES	1,611	364	1,247		883 D	22.6%	77.4%	22.6%	77.4%
GRAHAM	2,970	1,380	1,590		210 D	46.5%	53.5%	46.5%	53.5%
GRANVILLE	5,749	1,166	4,583		3,417 D	20.3%	79.7%	20.3%	79.7%
GREENE	3,162	186	2,976		2,790 D	5.9%	94.1%	5.9%	94.1%
GUILFORD	62,338	33,310	29,028		4,282 R	53.4%	46.6%	53.4%	46.6%
HALIFAX	11,017	2,210	8,807		6,597 D	20.1%	79.9%	20.1%	79.9%
HARNETT	11,901	4,306	7,595		3,289 D	36.2%	63.8%	36.2%	63.8%
HAYWOOD	14,885	6,124	8,761		2,637 D	41.1%	58.9%	41.1%	58.9%
HENDERSON	12,571	8,768	3,803		4,965 R	69.7%	30.3%	69.7%	30.3%
HERTFORD	3,438	579	2,859		2,280 D	16.8%	83.2%	16.8%	83.2%
HOKE	2,377	616	1,761		1,145 D	25.9%	74.1%	25.9%	74.1%
HYDE	1,325	406	919		513 D	30.6%	69.4%	30.6%	69.4%
IREDELL	20,384	11,804	8,580		3,224 R	57.9%	42.1%	57.9%	42.1%
JACKSON	7,976	3,680	4,296		616 D	46.1%	53.9%	46.1%	53.9%
JOHNSTON	15,426	5,429	9,997		4,568 D	35.2%	64.8%	35.2%	64.8%
JONES	2,004	331	1,673		1,342 D	16.5%	83.5%	16.5%	83.5%
LEE	6,793	2,105	4,688		2,583 D	31.0%	69.0%	31.0%	69.0%
LENOIR	8,946	2,223	6,723		4,500 D	24.8%	75.2%	24.8%	75.2%
LINCOLN	11,617	6,228	5,389		839 R	53.6%	46.4%	53.6%	46.4%
MCDOWELL	9,465	4,710	4,755		45 D	49.8%	50.2%	49.8%	50.2%
MACON	6,723	3,327	3,396		69 D	49.5%	50.5%	49.5%	50.5%
MADISON	8,417	4,751	3,666		1,085 R	56.4%	43.6%	56.4%	43.6%
MARTIN	5,908	415	5,493		5,078 D	7.0%	93.0%	7.0%	93.0%
MECKLENBURG	77,378	44,334	33,044		11,290 R	57.3%	42.7%	57.3%	42.7%

PRESIDENT 1956

County	Total Vote	Republican	Democratic	Other	Rep.-Dem. Plurality	Total Vote Rep.	Total Vote Dem.	Major Vote Rep.	Major Vote Dem.
ALAMANCE	23,152	12,123	11,029		1,094 R	52.4%	47.6%	52.4%	47.6%
ALEXANDER	6,477	3,767	2,710		1,057 R	58.2%	41.8%	58.2%	41.8%
ALLEGHANY	3,369	1,669	1,700		29 D	49.6%	50.4%	49.6%	50.4%
ANSON	5,238	1,640	3,598		1,958 D	31.3%	68.7%	31.3%	68.7%
ASHE	8,570	4,588	3,982		606 R	53.5%	46.5%	53.5%	46.5%
AVERY	4,978	4,009	969		3,040 R	80.5%	19.5%	80.5%	19.5%
BEAUFORT	8,007	2,277	5,730		3,453 D	28.4%	71.6%	28.4%	71.6%
BERTIE	3,842	469	3,373		2,904 D	12.2%	87.8%	12.2%	87.8%
BLADEN	5,620	1,542	4,078		2,536 D	27.4%	72.6%	27.4%	72.6%
BRUNSWICK	6,596	3,299	3,297		2 R	50.0%	50.0%	50.0%	50.0%
BUNCOMBE	41,699	22,655	19,044		3,611 R	54.3%	45.7%	54.3%	45.7%
BURKE	19,822	11,823	7,999		3,824 R	59.6%	40.4%	59.6%	40.4%
CABARRUS	21,635	14,462	7,173		7,289 R	66.8%	33.2%	66.8%	33.2%
CALDWELL	17,694	10,833	6,861		3,972 R	61.2%	38.8%	61.2%	38.8%
CAMDEN	1,156	343	813		470 D	29.7%	70.3%	29.7%	70.3%
CARTERET	7,679	3,804	3,875		71 D	49.5%	50.5%	49.5%	50.5%
CASWELL	3,672	1,204	2,468		1,264 D	32.8%	67.2%	32.8%	67.2%
CATAWBA	30,670	19,266	11,404		7,862 R	62.8%	37.2%	62.8%	37.2%
CHATHAM	7,880	3,729	4,151		422 D	47.3%	52.7%	47.3%	52.7%
CHEROKEE	6,673	3,830	2,843		987 R	57.4%	42.6%	57.4%	42.6%
CHOWAN	2,041	556	1,485		929 D	27.2%	72.8%	27.2%	72.8%
CLAY	2,729	1,442	1,287		155 R	52.8%	47.2%	52.8%	47.2%
CLEVELAND	15,484	7,076	8,408		1,332 D	45.7%	54.3%	45.7%	54.3%
COLUMBUS	10,105	2,300	7,805		5,505 D	22.8%	77.2%	22.8%	77.2%
CRAVEN	9,273	2,956	6,317		3,361 D	31.9%	68.1%	31.9%	68.1%
CUMBERLAND	15,561	6,699	8,862		2,163 D	43.0%	57.0%	43.0%	57.0%
CURRITUCK	1,913	488	1,425		937 D	25.5%	74.5%	25.5%	74.5%
DARE	1,867	839	1,028		189 D	44.9%	55.1%	44.9%	55.1%
DAVIDSON	26,165	16,178	9,987		6,191 R	61.8%	38.2%	61.8%	38.2%
DAVIE	6,709	4,599	2,110		2,489 R	68.5%	31.5%	68.5%	31.5%
DUPLIN	9,041	2,110	6,931		4,821 D	23.3%	76.7%	23.3%	76.7%
DURHAM	27,061	13,226	13,835		609 D	48.9%	51.1%	48.9%	51.1%
EDGECOMBE	9,670	1,840	7,830		5,990 D	19.0%	81.0%	19.0%	81.0%
FORSYTH	45,187	29,368	15,819		13,549 R	65.0%	35.0%	65.0%	35.0%
FRANKLIN	6,090	792	5,298		4,506 D	13.0%	87.0%	13.0%	87.0%
GASTON	33,830	18,159	15,671		2,488 R	53.7%	46.3%	53.7%	46.3%
GATES	1,585	341	1,244		903 D	21.5%	78.5%	21.5%	78.5%
GRAHAM	3,248	1,762	1,486		276 R	54.2%	45.8%	54.2%	45.8%
GRANVILLE	5,476	1,463	4,013		2,550 D	26.7%	73.3%	26.7%	73.3%
GREENE	3,507	222	3,285		3,063 D	6.3%	93.7%	6.3%	93.7%
GUILFORD	54,699	32,751	21,948		10,803 R	59.9%	40.1%	59.9%	40.1%
HALIFAX	10,206	2,346	7,860		5,514 D	23.0%	77.0%	23.0%	77.0%
HARNETT	11,419	3,998	7,421		3,423 D	35.0%	65.0%	35.0%	65.0%
HAYWOOD	14,553	6,955	7,598		643 D	47.8%	52.2%	47.8%	52.2%
HENDERSON	13,246	9,243	4,003		5,240 R	69.8%	30.2%	69.8%	30.2%
HERTFORD	3,437	729	2,708		1,979 D	21.2%	78.8%	21.2%	78.8%
HOKE	2,457	513	1,944		1,431 D	20.9%	79.1%	20.9%	79.1%
HYDE	1,519	491	1,028		537 D	32.3%	67.7%	32.3%	67.7%
IREDELL	18,411	11,125	7,286		3,839 R	60.4%	39.6%	60.4%	39.6%
JACKSON	7,290	3,503	3,787		284 D	48.1%	51.9%	48.1%	51.9%
JOHNSTON	14,745	4,893	9,852		4,959 D	33.2%	66.8%	33.2%	66.8%
JONES	2,367	415	1,952		1,537 D	17.5%	82.5%	17.5%	82.5%
LEE	6,111	1,948	4,163		2,215 D	31.9%	68.1%	31.9%	68.1%
LENOIR	9,411	2,564	6,847		4,283 D	27.2%	72.8%	27.2%	72.8%
LINCOLN	12,475	6,637	5,838		799 R	53.2%	46.8%	53.2%	46.8%
MCDOWELL	9,860	5,468	4,392		1,076 R	55.5%	44.5%	55.5%	44.5%
MACON	6,433	3,408	3,025		383 R	53.0%	47.0%	53.0%	47.0%
MADISON	7,956	4,263	3,693		570 R	53.6%	46.4%	53.6%	46.4%
MARTIN	6,179	449	5,730		5,281 D	7.3%	92.7%	7.3%	92.7%
MECKLENBURG	71,696	44,469	27,227		17,242 R	62.0%	38.0%	62.0%	38.0%

NORTH CAROLINA

PRESIDENT 1952

County	Total Vote	Republican	Democratic	Other	Rep.-Dem. Plurality	Percentage Total Vote Rep.	Total Vote Dem.	Major Vote Rep.	Major Vote Dem.
MITCHELL	5,245	4,009	1,236		2,773 R	76.4%	23.6%	76.4%	23.6%
MONTGOMERY	6,357	3,181	3,176		5 R	50.0%	50.0%	50.0%	50.0%
MOORE	10,508	5,442	5,066		376 R	51.8%	48.2%	51.8%	48.2%
NASH	13,660	2,636	10,424		7,788 D	20.2%	79.8%	20.2%	79.8%
NEW HANOVER	19,660	9,330	10,330		1,000 D	47.5%	52.5%	47.5%	52.5%
NORTHAMPTON	4,917	583	4,334		3,751 D	11.9%	88.1%	11.9%	88.1%
ONSLOW	5,536	1,261	4,275		3,014 D	22.8%	77.2%	22.8%	77.2%
ORANGE	8,969	3,813	5,156		1,343 D	42.5%	57.5%	42.5%	57.5%
PAMLICO	2,331	903	1,428		525 D	38.7%	61.3%	38.7%	61.3%
PASQUOTANK	5,680	2,101	3,579		1,473 D	37.0%	63.0%	37.0%	63.0%
PENDER	3,181	1,152	2,029		877 D	36.2%	63.8%	36.2%	63.8%
PERQUIMANS	1,889	644	1,245		601 D	34.1%	65.9%	34.1%	65.9%
PERSON	5,640	1,374	4,266		2,892 D	24.4%	75.6%	24.4%	75.6%
PITT	13,474	2,203	11,271		9,068 D	16.4%	83.6%	16.4%	83.6%
POLK	5,302	2,561	2,741		180 D	48.3%	51.7%	48.3%	51.7%
RANDOLPH	21,404	12,429	8,975		3,454 R	58.1%	41.9%	58.1%	41.9%
RICHMOND	10,701	3,361	7,340		3,979 D	31.4%	68.6%	31.4%	68.6%
ROBESON	13,438	4,127	9,311		5,184 D	30.7%	69.3%	30.7%	69.3%
ROCKINGHAM	19,308	6,885	12,423		5,538 D	35.7%	64.3%	35.7%	64.3%
ROWAN	28,831	17,535	11,296		6,239 R	60.8%	39.2%	60.8%	39.2%
RUTHERFORD	16,142	8,387	7,755		632 R	52.0%	48.0%	52.0%	48.0%
SAMPSON	13,405	6,449	6,956		507 D	48.1%	51.9%	48.1%	51.9%
SCOTLAND	4,502	1,590	2,912		1,322 D	35.3%	64.7%	35.3%	64.7%
STANLY	17,295	10,093	7,202		2,891 R	58.4%	41.6%	58.4%	41.6%
STOKES	8,296	3,792	4,504		712 D	45.7%	54.3%	45.7%	54.3%
SURRY	15,797	7,591	6,206		615 D	48.1%	51.9%	48.1%	51.9%
SWAIN	3,629	1,680	1,949		269 D	46.3%	53.7%	46.3%	53.7%
TRANSYLVANIA	7,688	4,047	3,641		406 R	52.6%	47.4%	52.6%	47.4%
TYRRELL	1,301	385	916		531 D	29.6%	70.4%	29.6%	70.4%
UNION	11,206	3,790	7,416		3,626 D	33.8%	66.2%	33.8%	66.2%
VANCE	7,418	1,721	5,697		3,976 D	23.2%	76.8%	23.2%	76.8%
WAKE	38,450	15,057	23,393		8,336 D	39.2%	60.8%	39.2%	60.8%
WARREN	3,624	664	2,960		2,296 D	18.3%	81.7%	18.3%	81.7%
WASHINGTON	2,748	774	1,974		1,200 D	28.2%	71.8%	28.2%	71.8%
WATAUGA	8,127	4,527	3,600		927 R	55.7%	44.3%	55.7%	44.3%
WAYNE	11,943	4,662	7,281		2,619 D	39.0%	61.0%	39.0%	61.0%
WILKES	18,589	11,446	7,143		4,303 R	61.6%	38.4%	61.6%	38.4%
WILSON	11,253	2,569	8,684		6,115 D	22.8%	77.2%	22.8%	77.2%
YADKIN	8,326	5,540	2,786		2,754 R	66.5%	33.5%	66.5%	33.5%
YANCEY	6,646	2,953	3,693		740 D	44.4%	55.6%	44.4%	55.6%
TOTAL	1,210,910	558,107	652,803		94,696 D	46.1%	53.9%	46.1%	53.9%

PRESIDENT 1956

County	Total Vote	Republican	Democratic	Other	Rep.-Dem. Plurality	Percentage Total Vote Rep.	Total Vote Dem.	Major Vote Rep.	Major Vote Dem.
MITCHELL	5,338	4,269	1,069		3,200 R	80.0%	20.0%	80.0%	20.0%
MONTGOMERY	6,447	3,359	3,088		271 R	52.1%	47.9%	52.1%	47.9%
MOORE	9,967	5,238	4,729		509 R	52.6%	47.4%	52.6%	47.4%
NASH	12,634	2,665	9,969		7,304 D	21.1%	78.9%	21.1%	78.9%
NEW HANOVER	19,717	9,470	10,247		777 D	48.0%	52.0%	48.0%	52.0%
NORTHAMPTON	4,989	747	4,242		3,495 D	15.0%	85.0%	15.0%	85.0%
ONSLOW	6,318	1,626	4,692		3,066 D	25.7%	74.3%	25.7%	74.3%
ORANGE	9,139	4,396	4,743		347 D	48.1%	51.9%	48.1%	51.9%
PAMLICO	2,330	954	1,376		422 D	40.9%	59.1%	40.9%	59.1%
PASQUOTANK	4,790	1,827	2,963		1,136 D	38.1%	61.9%	38.1%	61.9%
PENDER	3,205	1,009	2,196		1,187 D	31.5%	68.5%	31.5%	68.5%
PERQUIMANS	1,731	709	1,022		313 D	41.0%	59.0%	41.0%	59.0%
PERSON	5,173	1,740	3,433		1,693 D	33.6%	66.4%	33.6%	66.4%
PITT	14,388	2,515	11,873		9,358 D	17.5%	82.5%	17.5%	82.5%
POLK	5,350	2,823	2,527		296 R	52.8%	47.2%	52.8%	47.2%
RANDOLPH	21,578	13,174	8,404		4,770 R	61.1%	38.9%	61.1%	38.9%
RICHMOND	9,499	2,907	6,592		3,685 D	30.6%	69.4%	30.6%	69.4%
ROBESON	13,301	2,785	10,516		7,731 D	20.9%	79.1%	20.9%	79.1%
ROCKINGHAM	17,887	8,991	8,896		95 R	50.3%	49.7%	50.3%	49.7%
ROWAN	27,323	17,562	9,761		7,801 R	64.3%	35.7%	64.3%	35.7%
RUTHERFORD	15,408	8,200	7,208		992 R	53.2%	46.8%	53.2%	46.8%
SAMPSON	13,882	6,685	7,197		512 D	48.2%	51.8%	48.2%	51.8%
SCOTLAND	4,213	1,171	3,042		1,871 D	27.8%	72.2%	27.8%	72.2%
STANLY	17,360	10,667	6,693		3,974 R	61.4%	38.6%	61.4%	38.6%
STOKES	8,289	4,341	3,948		393 R	52.4%	47.6%	52.4%	47.6%
SURRY	16,021	9,001	7,020		1,981 R	56.2%	43.8%	56.2%	43.8%
SWAIN	3,820	2,026	1,794		232 R	53.0%	47.0%	53.0%	47.0%
TRANSYLVANIA	7,336	3,901	3,435		466 R	53.2%	46.8%	53.2%	46.8%
TYRRELL	1,035	420	615		195 D	40.6%	59.4%	40.6%	59.4%
UNION	9,745	3,362	6,383		3,021 D	34.5%	65.5%	34.5%	65.5%
VANCE	6,877	1,955	4,922		2,967 D	28.4%	71.6%	28.4%	71.6%
WAKE	37,621	15,194	22,427		7,233 D	40.4%	59.6%	40.4%	59.6%
WARREN	3,451	718	2,733		2,015 D	20.8%	79.2%	20.8%	79.2%
WASHINGTON	2,980	1,033	1,947		914 D	34.7%	65.3%	34.7%	65.3%
WATAUGA	7,859	4,636	3,223		1,413 R	59.0%	41.0%	59.0%	41.0%
WAYNE	10,976	4,220	6,756		2,536 D	38.4%	61.6%	38.4%	61.6%
WILKES	17,414	11,544	5,870		5,674 R	66.3%	33.7%	66.3%	33.7%
WILSON	11,158	2,830	8,328		5,498 D	25.4%	74.6%	25.4%	74.6%
YADKIN	7,830	5,469	2,361		3,108 R	69.8%	30.2%	69.8%	30.2%
YANCEY	5,772	2,808	2,964		156 D	48.6%	51.4%	48.6%	51.4%
TOTAL	1,165,592	575,062	590,530		15,468 D	49.3%	50.7%	49.3%	50.7%

NORTH CAROLINA

PRESIDENT 1960

County	Total Vote	Republican	Democratic	Other	Rep.-Dem. Plurality	Total Vote Rep.	Total Vote Dem.	Major Vote Rep.	Major Vote Dem.
ALAMANCE	28,417	14,818	13,599		1,219 R	52.1%	47.9%	52.1%	47.9%
ALEXANDER	8,131	4,175	3,956		219 R	51.3%	48.7%	51.3%	48.7%
ALLEGHANY	4,099	1,978	2,121		143 D	48.3%	51.7%	48.3%	51.7%
ANSON	5,717	1,597	4,120		2,523 D	27.9%	72.1%	27.9%	72.1%
ASHE	9,300	4,823	4,477		346 R	51.9%	48.1%	51.9%	48.1%
AVERY	5,223	4,176	1,047		3,129 R	80.0%	20.0%	80.0%	20.0%
BEAUFORT	8,733	2,694	6,039		3,345 D	30.8%	69.2%	30.8%	69.2%
BERTIE	4,259	577	3,682		3,105 D	13.5%	86.5%	13.5%	86.5%
BLADEN	6,207	1,854	4,353		2,499 D	29.9%	70.1%	29.9%	70.1%
BRUNSWICK	7,220	2,915	4,305		1,390 D	40.4%	59.6%	40.4%	59.6%
BUNCOMBE	51,343	28,040	23,303		4,737 R	54.6%	45.4%	54.6%	45.4%
CABARRUS	22,940	12,925	10,015		2,910 R	56.3%	43.7%	56.3%	43.7%
CALDWELL	24,358	15,678	8,680		6,998 R	64.4%	35.6%	64.4%	35.6%
CAMDEN	1,352	338	1,014		676 D	25.0%	75.0%	25.0%	75.0%
CARTERET	9,757	4,493	5,264		771 D	46.0%	54.0%	46.0%	54.0%
CASWELL	4,104	1,272	2,832		1,560 D	31.0%	69.0%	31.0%	69.0%
CATAWBA	32,626	19,135	13,491		5,644 R	58.6%	41.4%	58.6%	41.4%
CHATHAM	8,991	4,308	4,683		375 D	47.9%	52.1%	47.9%	52.1%
CHEROKEE	7,491	4,294	3,197		1,097 R	57.3%	42.7%	57.3%	42.7%
CHOWAN	2,453	533	1,920		1,387 D	21.7%	78.3%	21.7%	78.3%
CLAY	2,921	1,657	1,264		393 R	56.7%	43.3%	56.7%	43.3%
CLEVELAND	18,802	8,257	10,545		2,288 D	43.9%	56.1%	43.9%	56.1%
COLUMBUS	14,110	3,655	10,455		6,800 D	25.9%	74.1%	25.9%	74.1%
CRAVEN	10,838	3,680	7,158		3,478 D	34.0%	66.0%	34.0%	66.0%
CUMBERLAND	19,673	8,072	11,601		3,529 D	41.0%	59.0%	41.0%	59.0%
CURRITUCK	2,115	464	1,651		1,187 D	21.9%	78.1%	21.9%	78.1%
DARE	2,305	1,058	1,247		189 D	45.9%	54.1%	45.9%	54.1%
DAVIDSON	31,915	18,797	13,118		5,679 R	58.9%	41.1%	58.9%	41.1%
DAVIE	7,259	4,788	2,471		2,317 R	66.0%	34.0%	66.0%	34.0%
DUPLIN	10,222	2,953	7,269		4,316 D	28.9%	71.1%	28.9%	71.1%
DURHAM	33,620	14,322	19,298		4,976 D	42.6%	57.4%	42.6%	57.4%
EDGECOMBE	10,325	2,279	8,046		5,767 D	22.1%	77.9%	22.1%	77.9%
FORSYTH	57,409	33,374	24,035		9,339 R	58.1%	41.9%	58.1%	41.9%
FRANKLIN	6,189	1,108	5,081		3,973 D	17.9%	82.1%	17.9%	82.1%
GASTON	41,354	21,250	20,104		1,146 R	51.4%	48.6%	51.4%	48.6%
GATES	1,934	385	1,549		1,164 D	19.9%	80.1%	19.9%	80.1%
GRAHAM	3,056	1,721	1,335		386 R	56.3%	43.7%	56.3%	43.7%
GRANVILLE	6,743	1,798	4,945		3,147 D	26.7%	73.3%	26.7%	73.3%
GREENE	3,543	451	3,092		2,641 D	12.7%	87.3%	12.7%	87.3%
GUILFORD	71,843	41,357	30,486		10,871 R	57.6%	42.4%	57.6%	42.4%
HALIFAX	11,215	2,343	8,872		6,529 D	20.9%	79.1%	20.9%	79.1%
HARNETT	13,193	5,301	7,892		2,591 D	40.2%	59.8%	40.2%	59.8%
HAYWOOD	16,627	8,583	8,044		539 R	51.6%	48.4%	51.6%	48.4%
HENDERSON	15,446	10,835	4,611		6,224 R	70.1%	29.9%	70.1%	29.9%
HERTFORD	3,886	781	3,105		2,324 D	20.1%	79.9%	20.1%	79.9%
HOKE	2,702	596	2,106		1,510 D	22.1%	77.9%	22.1%	77.9%
HYDE	1,628	481	1,147		666 D	29.5%	70.5%	29.5%	70.5%
IREDELL	21,058	12,085	8,973		3,112 R	57.4%	42.6%	57.4%	42.6%
JACKSON	7,917	4,017	3,900		117 R	50.7%	49.3%	50.7%	49.3%
JOHNSTON	16,574	6,660	9,914		3,254 D	40.2%	59.8%	40.2%	59.8%
JONES	2,505	585	1,920		1,335 D	23.4%	76.6%	23.4%	76.6%
LEE	7,236	2,563	4,673		2,110 D	35.4%	64.6%	35.4%	64.6%
LENOIR	11,784	3,658	8,126		4,468 D	31.0%	69.0%	31.0%	69.0%
LINCOLN	13,544	6,816	6,728		88 R	50.3%	49.7%	50.3%	49.7%
MCDOWELL	11,037	6,148	4,889		1,259 R	55.7%	44.3%	55.7%	44.3%
MACON	6,833	3,735	3,098		637 R	54.7%	45.3%	54.7%	45.3%
MADISON	8,968	4,422	4,546		124 D	49.3%	50.7%	49.3%	50.7%
MARTIN	6,563	737	5,826		5,089 D	11.2%	88.8%	11.2%	88.8%
MECKLENBURG	87,612	48,250	39,362		8,888 R	55.1%	44.9%	55.1%	44.9%

PRESIDENT 1964

County	Total Vote	Republican	Democratic	Other	Rep.-Dem. Plurality	Total Vote Rep.	Total Vote Dem.	Major Vote Rep.	Major Vote Dem.
ALAMANCE	30,574	15,177	15,397		220 D	49.6%	50.4%	49.6%	50.4%
ALEXANDER	7,482	3,760	3,722		38 R	50.3%	49.7%	50.3%	49.7%
ALLEGHANY	3,941	1,573	2,368		795 D	39.9%	60.1%	39.9%	60.1%
ANSON	5,865	1,721	4,144		2,423 D	29.3%	70.7%	29.3%	70.7%
ASHE	9,156	4,191	4,965		774 D	45.8%	54.2%	45.8%	54.2%
AVERY	4,179	2,656	1,523		1,133 R	63.6%	36.4%	63.6%	36.4%
BEAUFORT	9,685	3,595	6,090		2,495 D	37.1%	62.9%	37.1%	62.9%
BERTIE	4,263	931	3,332		2,401 D	21.8%	78.2%	21.8%	78.2%
BLADEN	6,685	2,169	4,516		2,347 D	32.4%	67.6%	32.4%	67.6%
BRUNSWICK	7,961	3,721	4,240		519 D	46.7%	53.3%	46.7%	53.3%
BUNCOMBE	50,995	19,372	31,623		12,251 D	38.0%	62.0%	38.0%	62.0%
CABARRUS	22,896	10,081	12,815		2,734 D	44.0%	56.0%	44.0%	56.0%
CALDWELL	25,099	13,178	11,921		1,257 R	52.5%	47.5%	52.5%	47.5%
CAMDEN	1,404	534	870		336 D	38.0%	62.0%	38.0%	62.0%
CARTERET	10,520	4,289	6,231		1,942 D	40.8%	59.2%	40.8%	59.2%
CASWELL	4,306	1,793	2,513		720 D	41.6%	58.4%	41.6%	58.4%
CATAWBA	32,930	17,116	15,814		1,302 R	52.0%	48.0%	52.0%	48.0%
CHATHAM	9,406	4,111	5,295		1,184 D	43.7%	56.3%	43.7%	56.3%
CHEROKEE	6,929	3,106	3,823		717 D	44.8%	55.2%	44.8%	55.2%
CHOWAN	2,483	787	1,696		909 D	31.7%	68.3%	31.7%	68.3%
CLAY	2,743	1,286	1,457		171 D	46.9%	53.1%	46.9%	53.1%
CLEVELAND	18,710	7,874	10,836		2,962 D	42.1%	57.9%	42.1%	57.9%
COLUMBUS	13,475	4,471	9,004		4,533 D	33.2%	66.8%	33.2%	66.8%
CRAVEN	12,113	4,691	7,422		2,731 D	38.7%	61.3%	38.7%	61.3%
CUMBERLAND	22,957	9,093	13,864		4,771 D	39.6%	60.4%	39.6%	60.4%
CURRITUCK	2,196	741	1,455		714 D	33.7%	66.3%	33.7%	66.3%
DARE	2,343	867	1,476		609 D	37.0%	63.0%	37.0%	63.0%
DAVIDSON	31,027	17,292	13,735		3,557 R	55.7%	44.3%	55.7%	44.3%
DAVIE	7,546	4,460	3,086		1,374 R	59.1%	40.9%	59.1%	40.9%
DUPLIN	10,990	3,821	7,169		3,348 D	34.8%	65.2%	34.8%	65.2%
DURHAM	38,138	15,264	22,874		7,610 D	40.0%	60.0%	40.0%	60.0%
EDGECOMBE	11,766	3,932	7,834		3,902 D	33.4%	66.6%	33.4%	66.6%
FORSYTH	61,891	30,276	31,615		1,339 D	48.9%	51.1%	48.9%	51.1%
FRANKLIN	6,651	2,097	4,554		2,457 D	31.5%	68.5%	31.5%	68.5%
GASTON	37,326	17,129	20,197		3,068 D	45.9%	54.1%	45.9%	54.1%
GATES	2,258	556	1,702		1,146 D	24.6%	75.4%	24.6%	75.4%
GRAHAM	3,135	1,398	1,737		339 D	44.6%	55.4%	44.6%	55.4%
GRANVILLE	7,220	2,624	4,596		1,972 D	36.3%	63.7%	36.3%	63.7%
GREENE	3,613	901	2,712		1,811 D	24.9%	75.1%	24.9%	75.1%
GUILFORD	75,604	35,635	39,969		4,334 D	47.1%	52.9%	47.1%	52.9%
HALIFAX	13,709	4,757	8,952		4,195 D	34.7%	65.3%	34.7%	65.3%
HARNETT	13,360	5,883	7,477		1,594 D	44.0%	56.0%	44.0%	56.0%
HAYWOOD	16,239	5,575	10,664		5,089 D	34.3%	65.7%	34.3%	65.7%
HENDERSON	14,846	8,780	6,066		2,714 R	59.1%	40.9%	59.1%	40.9%
HERTFORD	4,947	994	3,953		2,959 D	20.1%	79.9%	20.1%	79.9%
HOKE	3,033	779	2,254		1,475 D	25.7%	74.3%	25.7%	74.3%
HYDE	1,641	514	1,127		613 D	31.3%	68.7%	31.3%	68.7%
IREDELL	24,123	12,892	11,231		1,661 R	53.4%	46.6%	53.4%	46.6%
JACKSON	8,088	3,183	4,905		1,722 D	39.4%	60.6%	39.4%	60.6%
JOHNSTON	17,849	7,523	10,326		2,803 D	42.1%	57.9%	42.1%	57.9%
JONES	2,905	776	2,129		1,353 D	26.7%	73.3%	26.7%	73.3%
LEE	7,483	2,753	4,730		1,977 D	36.8%	63.2%	36.8%	63.2%
LENOIR	13,234	5,617	7,617		2,000 D	42.4%	57.6%	42.4%	57.6%
LINCOLN	13,173	5,869	7,304		1,435 D	44.6%	55.4%	44.6%	55.4%
MCDOWELL	10,488	4,174	6,314		2,140 D	39.8%	60.2%	39.8%	60.2%
MACON	6,674	2,900	3,774		874 D	43.5%	56.5%	43.5%	56.5%
MADISON	7,165	3,336	3,829		493 D	46.6%	53.4%	46.6%	53.4%
MARTIN	6,332	1,511	4,821		3,310 D	23.9%	76.1%	23.9%	76.1%
MECKLENBURG	96,171	46,589	49,582		2,993 D	48.4%	51.6%	48.4%	51.6%

NORTH CAROLINA

PRESIDENT 1960

County	Total Vote	Republican	Democratic	Other	Rep.-Dem. Plurality	Total Vote Rep.	Total Vote Dem.	Major Vote Rep.	Major Vote Dem.
MITCHELL	6,005	4,831	1,174		3,657 R	80.4%	19.6%	80.4%	19.6%
MONTGOMERY	6,946	3,649	3,297		352 R	52.5%	47.5%	52.5%	47.5%
MOORE	11,363	5,815	5,548		267 R	51.2%	48.8%	51.2%	48.8%
NASH	13,982	3,896	10,086		6,190 D	27.9%	72.1%	27.9%	72.1%
NEW HANOVER	22,957	9,775	13,182		3,407 D	42.6%	57.4%	42.6%	57.4%
NORTHAMPTON	5,434	678	4,756		4,078 D	12.5%	87.5%	12.5%	87.5%
ONSLOW	8,376	2,812	5,564		2,752 D	33.6%	66.4%	33.6%	66.4%
ORANGE	12,411	5,231	7,180		1,949 D	42.1%	57.9%	42.1%	57.9%
PAMLICO	2,758	1,061	1,697		636 D	38.5%	61.5%	38.5%	61.5%
PASQUOTANK	6,357	1,827	4,530		2,703 D	28.7%	71.3%	28.7%	71.3%
PENDER	4,018	1,274	2,744		1,470 D	31.7%	68.3%	31.7%	68.3%
PERQUIMANS	2,097	637	1,460		823 D	30.4%	69.6%	30.4%	69.6%
PERSON	6,231	1,926	4,305		2,379 D	30.9%	69.1%	30.9%	69.1%
PITT	15,984	3,458	12,526		9,068 D	21.6%	78.4%	21.6%	78.4%
POLK	5,618	2,856	2,762		94 R	50.8%	49.2%	50.8%	49.2%
RANDOLPH	25,561	15,772	9,789		5,983 R	61.7%	38.3%	61.7%	38.3%
RICHMOND	11,578	3,285	8,293		5,008 D	28.4%	71.6%	28.4%	71.6%
ROBESON	15,203	3,580	11,623		8,043 D	23.5%	76.5%	23.5%	76.5%
ROCKINGHAM	20,663	9,456	11,207		1,751 D	45.8%	54.2%	45.8%	54.2%
ROWAN	30,645	17,726	12,919		4,807 R	57.8%	42.2%	57.8%	42.2%
RUTHERFORD	17,547	8,993	8,554		439 R	51.3%	48.7%	51.3%	48.7%
SAMPSON	14,970	7,338	7,632		294 D	49.0%	51.0%	49.0%	51.0%
SCOTLAND	4,922	1,279	3,643		2,364 D	26.0%	74.0%	26.0%	74.0%
STANLY	19,339	11,080	8,259		2,821 R	57.3%	42.7%	57.3%	42.7%
STOKES	9,359	4,872	4,487		385 R	52.1%	47.9%	52.1%	47.9%
SURRY	18,220	10,035	8,185		1,850 R	55.1%	44.9%	55.1%	44.9%
SWAIN	4,283	2,112	2,171		59 D	49.3%	50.7%	49.3%	50.7%
TRANSYLVANIA	7,609	4,221	3,388		833 R	55.5%	44.5%	55.5%	44.5%
TYRRELL	1,275	349	926		577 D	27.4%	72.6%	27.4%	72.6%
UNION	11,423	4,030	7,393		3,363 D	35.3%	64.7%	35.3%	64.7%
VANCE	7,706	2,012	5,694		3,682 D	26.1%	73.9%	26.1%	73.9%
WAKE	44,486	18,436	26,050		7,614 D	41.4%	58.6%	41.4%	58.6%
WARREN	3,714	717	2,997		2,280 D	19.3%	80.7%	19.3%	80.7%
WASHINGTON	3,442	1,027	2,415		1,388 D	29.8%	70.2%	29.8%	70.2%
WATAUGA	8,460	5,020	3,440		1,580 R	59.3%	40.7%	59.3%	40.7%
WAYNE	13,330	5,474	7,856		2,382 D	41.1%	58.9%	41.1%	58.9%
WILKES	21,002	13,016	7,986		5,030 R	62.0%	38.0%	62.0%	38.0%
WILSON	11,135	3,114	8,021		4,907 D	28.0%	72.0%	28.0%	72.0%
YADKIN	10,053	7,268	2,825		4,443 R	72.3%	27.7%	72.3%	27.7%
YANCEY	6,594	3,284	3,310		26 D	49.8%	50.2%	49.8%	50.2%
TOTAL	1,368,556	655,420	713,136		57,716 D	47.9%	52.1%	47.9%	52.1%

PRESIDENT 1964

County	Total Vote	Republican	Democratic	Other	Rep.-Dem. Plurality	Total Vote Rep.	Total Vote Dem.	Major Vote Rep.	Major Vote Dem.
MITCHELL	4,999	3,263	1,736		1,527 R	65.3%	34.7%	65.3%	34.7%
MONTGOMERY	7,318	3,385	3,933		548 D	46.3%	53.7%	46.3%	53.7%
MOORE	11,546	5,162	6,384		1,222 D	44.7%	55.3%	44.7%	55.3%
NASH	15,559	6,396	9,163		2,767 D	41.1%	58.9%	41.1%	58.9%
NEW HANOVER	24,724	12,140	12,584		444 D	49.1%	50.9%	49.1%	50.9%
NORTHAMPTON	6,233	1,187	5,046		3,859 D	19.0%	81.0%	19.0%	81.0%
ONSLOW	9,726	3,771	5,955		2,184 D	38.8%	61.2%	38.8%	61.2%
ORANGE	14,991	5,785	9,206		3,421 D	38.6%	61.4%	38.6%	61.4%
PAMLICO	2,900	1,036	1,864		828 D	35.7%	64.3%	35.7%	64.3%
PASQUOTANK	6,649	2,380	4,269		1,889 D	35.8%	64.2%	35.8%	64.2%
PENDER	5,166	1,961	3,205		1,244 D	38.0%	62.0%	38.0%	62.0%
PERQUIMANS	2,399	941	1,458		517 D	39.2%	60.8%	39.2%	60.8%
PERSON	6,902	2,162	4,740		2,578 D	31.3%	68.7%	31.3%	68.7%
PITT	16,466	5,149	11,317		6,168 D	31.3%	68.7%	31.3%	68.7%
POLK	5,782	2,765	3,017		252 D	47.8%	52.2%	47.8%	52.2%
RANDOLPH	24,377	13,739	10,638		3,101 R	56.4%	43.6%	56.4%	43.6%
RICHMOND	11,639	3,123	8,516		5,393 D	26.8%	73.2%	26.8%	73.2%
ROBESON	17,387	3,591	13,796		10,205 D	20.7%	79.3%	20.7%	79.3%
ROCKINGHAM	20,495	9,063	11,432		2,369 D	44.2%	55.8%	44.2%	55.8%
ROWAN	29,738	14,804	14,934		130 D	49.8%	50.2%	49.8%	50.2%
RUTHERFORD	16,656	7,115	9,541		2,426 D	42.7%	57.3%	42.7%	57.3%
SAMPSON	15,701	7,634	8,067		433 D	48.6%	51.4%	48.6%	51.4%
SCOTLAND	5,073	1,229	3,844		2,615 D	24.2%	75.8%	24.2%	75.8%
STANLY	16,855	8,924	7,931		993 R	52.9%	47.1%	52.9%	47.1%
STOKES	9,562	4,664	4,898		234 D	48.8%	51.2%	48.8%	51.2%
SURRY	17,780	7,970	9,810		1,840 D	44.8%	55.2%	44.8%	55.2%
SWAIN	3,828	1,534	2,294		760 D	40.1%	59.9%	40.1%	59.9%
TRANSYLVANIA	8,030	3,547	4,483		936 D	44.2%	55.8%	44.2%	55.8%
TYRRELL	1,370	374	996		622 D	27.3%	72.7%	27.3%	72.7%
UNION	11,437	4,229	7,208		2,979 D	37.0%	63.0%	37.0%	63.0%
VANCE	8,638	3,452	5,186		1,734 D	40.0%	60.0%	40.0%	60.0%
WAKE	54,195	22,542	31,653		9,111 D	41.6%	58.4%	41.6%	58.4%
WARREN	4,758	1,909	2,849		940 D	40.1%	59.9%	40.1%	59.9%
WASHINGTON	3,649	1,144	2,505		1,361 D	31.4%	68.6%	31.4%	68.6%
WATAUGA	7,963	3,932	4,031		99 D	49.4%	50.6%	49.4%	50.6%
WAYNE	17,346	7,555	9,791		2,236 D	43.6%	56.4%	43.6%	56.4%
WILKES	20,190	11,014	9,176		1,838 R	54.6%	45.4%	54.6%	45.4%
WILSON	12,240	5,002	7,238		2,236 D	40.9%	59.1%	40.9%	59.1%
YADKIN	9,498	5,860	3,638		2,222 R	61.7%	38.3%	61.7%	38.3%
YANCEY	5,718	2,004	3,714		1,710 D	35.0%	65.0%	35.0%	65.0%
TOTAL	1,424,983	624,844	800,139		175,295 D	43.8%	56.2%	43.8%	56.2%

NORTH CAROLINA

OTHER VOTE COMPOSITION:

1920   446 Socialist; 17 Prohibition. Votes reported as state-wide totals, not by counties.

1924   6,651 Progressive; 13 Prohibition. The county-by-county figures include only the
        Progressive vote; the state-wide total also includes the Prohibition
        vote.

1928

1932   Socialist.

1936   21 Socialist; 11 Communist; 2 Union; 6 scattered.

1940

1944

1948   69,652 States Rights; 3,915 Progressive.

1952

1956

1960

1964

SPECIAL CASES:

1948   States Rights candidates ran second in several counties.

NORTH DAKOTA

PRESIDENT 1920

County	Total Vote	Republican	Democratic	Other	Rep.-Dem. Plurality	Total Vote Rep.	Total Vote Dem.	Major Vote Rep.	Major Vote Dem.
ADAMS	1,768	1,377	347	44	1,030 R	77.9%	19.6%	79.9%	20.1%
BARNES	6,416	5,150	1,101	165	4,049 R	80.3%	17.2%	82.4%	17.6%
BENSON	4,365	3,540	680	145	2,860 R	81.1%	15.6%	83.9%	16.1%
BILLINGS	860	787	61	12	726 R	91.5%	7.1%	92.8%	7.2%
BOTTINEAU	4,808	3,487	970	351	2,517 R	72.5%	20.2%	78.2%	21.8%
BOWMAN	1,708	1,192	321	195	871 R	69.8%	18.8%	78.8%	21.2%
BURKE	2,694	1,911	456	327	1,455 R	70.9%	16.9%	80.7%	19.3%
BURLEIGH	5,564	4,300	943	321	3,357 R	77.3%	16.9%	82.0%	18.0%
CASS	13,938	10,735	2,817	386	7,918 R	77.0%	20.2%	79.2%	20.8%
CAVALIER	4,969	3,936	981	52	2,955 R	79.2%	19.7%	80.0%	20.0%
DICKEY	3,809	2,887	766	156	2,121 R	75.8%	20.1%	79.0%	21.0%
DIVIDE	3,017	2,438	462	117	1,976 R	80.8%	15.3%	84.1%	15.9%
DUNN	2,608	2,102	457	49	1,645 R	80.6%	17.5%	82.1%	17.9%
EDDY	2,218	1,525	577	116	948 R	68.8%	26.0%	72.5%	27.5%
EMMONS	3,160	2,900	238	22	2,662 R	91.8%	7.5%	92.4%	7.6%
FOSTER	2,004	1,583	371	50	1,212 R	79.0%	18.5%	81.0%	19.0%
GOLDEN VALLEY	1,527	1,177	286	64	891 R	77.1%	18.7%	80.5%	19.5%
GRAND FORKS	10,332	7,646	2,527	159	5,119 R	74.0%	24.5%	75.2%	24.8%
GRANT	2,626	2,184	296	146	1,888 R	83.2%	11.3%	88.1%	11.9%
GRIGGS	2,355	1,739	530	86	1,209 R	73.8%	22.5%	76.6%	23.4%
HETTINGER	2,216	1,849	327	40	1,522 R	83.4%	14.8%	85.0%	15.0%
KIDDER	2,299	1,855	336	108	1,519 R	80.7%	14.6%	84.7%	15.3%
LA MOURE	3,855	2,991	645	219	2,346 R	77.6%	16.7%	82.3%	17.7%
LOGAN	1,773	1,590	154	29	1,436 R	89.7%	8.7%	91.2%	8.8%
MCHENRY	4,770	3,534	848	388	2,686 R	74.1%	17.8%	80.6%	19.4%
MCINTOSH	1,889	1,782	79	28	1,703 R	94.3%	4.2%	95.8%	4.2%
MCKENZIE	3,254	2,587	511	156	2,076 R	79.5%	15.7%	83.5%	16.5%
MCLEAN	5,017	3,724	748	545	2,976 R	74.2%	14.9%	83.3%	16.5%
MERCER	2,047	1,786	172	89	1,614 R	87.2%	8.4%	91.2%	8.8%
MORTON	5,347	4,618	632	97	3,986 R	86.4%	11.8%	88.0%	12.0%
MOUNTRAIL	4,070	2,960	687	423	2,273 R	72.7%	16.9%	81.2%	18.8%
NELSON	3,701	3,127	501	73	2,626 R	84.5%	13.5%	86.2%	13.8%
OLIVER	1,287	1,105	111	71	994 R	85.9%	8.6%	90.9%	9.1%
PEMBINA	5,359	3,925	1,405	29	2,520 R	73.2%	26.2%	73.6%	26.4%
PIERCE	2,485	2,102	294	89	1,808 R	84.6%	11.8%	87.7%	12.3%
RAMSEY	5,037	3,996	937	104	3,059 R	79.3%	18.6%	81.0%	19.0%
RANSOM	3,894	3,010	802	82	2,208 R	77.3%	20.6%	79.0%	21.0%
RENVILLE	2,698	1,987	581	130	1,406 R	73.6%	21.5%	77.4%	22.6%
RICHLAND	6,900	5,483	1,339	78	4,144 R	79.5%	19.4%	80.4%	19.6%
ROLETTE	2,850	2,139	535	176	1,604 R	75.1%	18.8%	80.0%	20.0%
SARGENT	3,565	2,787	673	105	2,114 R	78.2%	18.9%	80.5%	19.5%
SHERIDAN	1,928	1,776	134	18	1,642 R	92.1%	7.0%	93.0%	7.0%
SIOUX	961	776	163	22	613 R	80.7%	17.0%	82.6%	17.4%
SLOPE	1,493	1,143	235	115	908 R	76.6%	15.7%	82.9%	17.1%
STARK	4,089	3,526	532	31	2,994 R	86.2%	13.0%	86.9%	13.1%
STEELE	2,609	2,222	337	50	1,885 R	85.2%	12.9%	86.8%	13.2%
STUTSMAN	7,145	5,531	1,394	220	4,137 R	77.4%	19.5%	79.9%	20.1%
TOWNER	2,763	2,192	476	95	1,716 R	79.3%	17.2%	82.2%	17.8%
TRAILL	4,263	3,666	523	74	3,143 R	86.0%	12.3%	87.5%	12.5%
WALSH	6,824	4,581	2,047	196	2,534 R	67.1%	30.0%	69.1%	30.9%
WARD	9,147	6,166	2,291	690	3,875 R	67.4%	25.0%	72.9%	27.1%
WELLS	3,736	3,202	456	78	2,746 R	85.7%	12.2%	87.5%	12.5%
WILLIAMS	5,769	3,768	1,330	671	2,438 R	65.3%	23.1%	73.9%	26.1%
TOTAL	205,786	160,082	37,422	8,282	122,660 R	77.8%	18.2%	81.1%	18.9%

PRESIDENT 1924

County	Total Vote	Republican	Democratic	Other	Rep.-Dem. Plurality	Total Vote Rep.	Total Vote Dem.	Major Vote Rep.	Major Vote Dem.
ADAMS	1,928	776	106	1,046	670 R	40.2%	5.5%	88.0%	12.0%
BARNES	6,228	3,205	346	2,677	2,859 R	51.5%	5.6%	90.3%	9.7%
BENSON	4,156	1,870	246	2,040	1,624 R	45.0%	5.9%	88.4%	11.6%
BILLINGS	871	421	32	418	389 R	48.3%	3.7%	92.9%	7.1%
BOTTINEAU	4,182	1,338	221	2,623	1,117 R	32.0%	5.3%	85.8%	14.2%
BOWMAN	1,718	776	67	875	709 R	45.2%	3.9%	92.1%	7.9%
BURKE	2,514	996	135	1,383	861 R	39.6%	5.4%	88.1%	11.9%
BURLEIGH	5,928	3,152	379	2,397	2,773 R	53.2%	6.4%	89.3%	10.7%
CASS	15,041	9,906	1,352	3,783	8,554 R	65.9%	9.0%	88.0%	12.0%
CAVALIER	4,443	2,428	539	1,476	1,889 R	54.6%	12.1%	81.8%	18.2%
DICKEY	3,930	1,716	352	1,862	1,364 R	43.7%	9.0%	83.0%	17.0%
DIVIDE	2,442	743	91	1,608	652 R	30.4%	3.7%	89.1%	10.9%
DUNN	2,291	980	190	1,121	790 R	42.8%	8.3%	83.8%	16.2%
EDDY	2,240	881	101	1,258	780 R	39.3%	4.5%	89.7%	10.3%
EMMONS	3,021	1,198	123	1,700	1,075 R	39.7%	4.1%	90.7%	9.3%
FOSTER	2,043	922	287	834	635 R	45.1%	14.0%	76.3%	23.7%
GOLDEN VALLEY	1,487	718	140	629	578 R	48.3%	9.4%	83.7%	16.3%
GRAND FORKS	10,651	6,690	943	3,018	5,747 R	62.8%	8.9%	87.6%	12.4%
GRANT	2,887	1,120	125	1,622	995 R	39.1%	4.4%	90.0%	10.0%
GRIGGS	2,214	738	116	1,360	622 R	33.3%	5.2%	86.4%	13.6%
HETTINGER	2,356	936	128	1,292	808 R	39.7%	5.4%	88.0%	12.0%
KIDDER	2,141	844	110	1,187	734 R	39.4%	5.1%	88.5%	11.5%
LA MOURE	3,810	1,647	221	1,942	1,426 R	43.2%	5.8%	88.2%	11.8%
LOGAN	1,816	787	29	1,000	758 R	43.3%	1.6%	96.4%	3.6%
MCHENRY	4,587	1,692	264	2,631	1,428 R	36.9%	5.8%	86.5%	13.5%
MCINTOSH	1,849	637	39	1,173	598 R	34.5%	2.1%	94.2%	5.8%
MCKENZIE	2,918	1,113	137	1,668	976 R	38.1%	4.7%	89.0%	11.0%
MCLEAN	4,583	1,651	194	2,738	1,457 R	36.0%	4.2%	89.5%	10.5%
MERCER	2,086	522	70	1,494	452 R	25.0%	3.4%	88.2%	11.8%
MORTON	5,370	2,377	265	2,728	2,112 R	44.3%	4.9%	90.0%	10.0%
MOUNTRAIL	3,741	1,354	130	2,257	1,224 R	36.2%	3.5%	91.2%	8.8%
NELSON	3,449	1,567	175	1,577	1,522 R	49.2%	5.1%	90.7%	9.3%
OLIVER	1,141	367	31	743	336 R	32.2%	2.7%	92.2%	7.8%
PEMBINA	4,715	2,783	588	1,344	2,195 R	59.0%	12.5%	82.6%	17.4%
PIERCE	2,474	1,160	157	1,157	1,003 R	46.9%	6.3%	88.1%	11.9%
RAMSEY	4,988	3,110	359	1,519	2,751 R	62.3%	7.2%	89.7%	10.3%
RANSOM	4,084	1,862	303	1,919	1,559 R	45.6%	7.4%	86.0%	14.0%
RENVILLE	2,017	649	120	1,248	529 R	32.2%	5.9%	84.4%	15.6%
RICHLAND	6,624	3,235	769	2,620	2,466 R	48.8%	11.6%	80.8%	19.2%
ROLETTE	2,419	869	137	1,413	732 R	35.9%	5.7%	86.4%	13.6%
SARGENT	3,361	1,468	232	1,661	1,236 R	43.7%	6.9%	86.4%	13.6%
SHERIDAN	1,714	594	49	1,071	545 R	34.7%	2.9%	92.4%	7.6%
SIOUX	1,249	777	58	414	719 R	62.2%	4.6%	93.1%	6.9%
SLOPE	1,576	616	47	913	569 R	39.1%	3.0%	92.9%	7.1%
STARK	4,211	2,130	266	1,815	1,864 R	50.6%	6.3%	88.9%	11.1%
STEELE	2,363	1,247	85	1,031	1,152 R	52.8%	3.6%	93.6%	6.4%
STUTSMAN	6,973	3,952	463	2,558	3,489 R	56.7%	6.6%	89.5%	10.5%
TOWNER	2,461	1,173	223	1,065	950 R	47.7%	9.1%	84.0%	16.0%
TRAILL	4,583	2,596	234	1,753	2,362 R	56.6%	5.1%	91.7%	8.3%
WALSH	5,770	2,837	917	2,016	1,920 R	49.2%	15.9%	75.6%	24.4%
WARD	8,681	4,166	721	3,794	3,445 R	48.0%	8.3%	85.2%	14.8%
WELLS	3,703	1,644	138	1,921	1,506 R	44.4%	3.7%	92.3%	7.7%
WILLIAMS	5,073	1,865	308	2,900	1,557 R	36.8%	6.1%	85.8%	14.2%
TOTAL	199,081	94,931	13,858	90,292	81,073 R	47.7%	7.0%	87.3%	12.7%

NORTH DAKOTA

PRESIDENT 1928

County	Total Vote	Republican	Democratic	Other	Rep.-Dem. Plurality	Total Vote Rep.	Total Vote Dem.	Major Vote Rep.	Major Vote Dem.
ADAMS	2,250	1,590	644	16	946 R	70.7%	28.6%	71.2%	28.8%
BARNES	7,083	3,755	3,293	35	462 R	53.0%	46.5%	53.3%	46.7%
BENSON	4,872	2,621	2,194	57	427 R	53.8%	45.0%	54.4%	45.6%
BILLINGS	877	458	412	7	46 R	52.2%	47.0%	52.6%	47.4%
BOTTINEAU	5,383	2,680	2,648	55	32 R	49.8%	49.2%	50.3%	49.7%
BOWMAN	1,875	1,031	821	23	210 R	55.0%	43.8%	55.7%	44.3%
BURKE	3,429	2,002	1,336	91	666 R	58.4%	39.0%	60.0%	40.0%
BURLEIGH	7,115	3,955	3,076	84	879 R	55.6%	43.2%	56.3%	43.7%
CASS	18,858	12,480	6,315	63	6,165 R	66.2%	33.5%	66.4%	33.6%
CAVALIER	5,592	3,068	2,510	14	558 R	54.9%	44.9%	55.0%	45.0%
DICKEY	4,253	2,250	1,977	26	273 R	52.9%	46.5%	53.2%	46.8%
DIVIDE	3,252	1,963	1,250	39	713 R	60.4%	38.4%	61.1%	38.9%
DUNN	2,925	1,360	1,561	4	201 D	46.5%	53.4%	46.6%	53.4%
EDDY	2,322	1,071	1,240	11	169 D	46.1%	53.4%	46.3%	53.7%
EMMONS	3,875	1,792	2,066	17	274 D	46.2%	53.3%	46.4%	53.6%
FOSTER	2,321	1,137	1,178	6	41 D	49.0%	50.8%	49.1%	50.9%
GOLDEN VALLEY	1,499	937	552	10	385 R	62.5%	36.8%	62.9%	37.1%
GRAND FORKS	12,371	8,024	4,300	47	3,724 R	64.9%	34.8%	65.1%	34.9%
GRANT	3,222	1,759	1,434	29	325 R	54.6%	44.5%	55.1%	44.9%
GRIGGS	2,534	1,329	1,182	23	147 R	52.4%	46.6%	52.9%	47.1%
HETTINGER	2,883	1,553	1,323	7	230 R	53.9%	45.9%	54.0%	46.0%
KIDDER	2,403	1,200	1,190	13	10 R	49.9%	49.5%	50.2%	49.8%
LA MOURE	4,082	2,245	1,800	37	445 R	55.0%	44.1%	55.5%	44.5%
LOGAN	2,321	1,013	1,293	15	280 D	43.6%	55.7%	43.9%	56.1%
MCHENRY	5,494	2,914	2,535	45	379 R	53.0%	46.1%	53.5%	46.5%
MCINTOSH	2,670	1,196	1,474		278 D	44.8%	55.2%	44.8%	55.2%
MCKENZIE	3,435	2,100	1,289	46	811 R	61.1%	37.5%	62.0%	38.0%
MCLEAN	5,746	2,730	2,855	161	125 D	47.5%	49.7%	48.9%	51.1%
MERCER	2,593	971	1,619	3	648 D	37.4%	62.4%	37.5%	62.5%
MORTON	6,653	2,881	3,646	126	765 D	43.3%	54.8%	44.1%	55.9%
MOUNTRAIL	4,501	2,354	2,003	144	351 R	52.3%	44.5%	54.0%	46.0%
NELSON	3,928	2,364	1,542	22	822 R	60.2%	39.3%	60.5%	39.5%
OLIVER	1,316	680	631	5	49 R	51.7%	47.9%	51.9%	48.1%
PEMBINA	5,472	3,324	2,141	7	1,183 R	60.7%	39.1%	60.8%	39.2%
PIERCE	3,086	1,469	1,606	11	137 D	47.6%	52.0%	47.8%	52.2%
RAMSEY	5,943	3,246	2,672	25	574 R	54.6%	45.0%	54.8%	45.2%
RANSOM	4,145	2,613	1,505	27	1,108 R	63.0%	36.3%	63.5%	36.5%
RENVILLE	2,674	1,473	1,174	27	299 R	55.1%	43.9%	55.6%	44.4%
RICHLAND	7,889	4,251	3,604	34	647 R	53.9%	45.7%	54.1%	45.9%
ROLETTE	3,539	1,327	2,181	31	854 D	37.5%	61.6%	37.8%	62.2%
SARGENT	3,780	1,772	1,989	19	217 D	46.9%	52.6%	47.1%	52.9%
SHERIDAN	2,194	1,242	944	8	298 R	56.6%	43.0%	56.8%	43.2%
SIOUX	1,698	687	988	23	301 D	40.5%	58.2%	41.0%	59.0%
SLOPE	1,434	873	542	19	331 R	60.9%	37.8%	61.7%	38.3%
STARK	5,161	1,924	3,231	6	1,307 D	37.3%	62.6%	37.3%	62.7%
STEELE	2,745	1,574	1,152	19	422 R	57.3%	42.0%	57.7%	42.3%
STUTSMAN	8,684	4,782	3,873	29	909 R	55.1%	44.6%	55.3%	44.7%
TOWNER	2,928	1,588	1,324	16	264 R	54.2%	45.2%	54.5%	45.5%
TRAILL	5,098	3,638	1,447	13	2,191 R	71.4%	28.4%	71.5%	28.5%
WALSH	7,472	3,657	3,798	17	141 D	48.9%	50.8%	49.1%	50.9%
WARD	10,986	6,561	4,362	63	2,199 R	59.7%	39.7%	60.1%	39.9%
WELLS	4,512	2,364	2,123	25	241 R	52.4%	47.1%	52.7%	47.3%
WILLIAMS	6,272	3,591	2,503	178	1,088 R	57.3%	39.9%	58.9%	41.1%
TOTAL	239,845	131,419	106,648	1,778	24,771 R	54.8%	44.5%	55.2%	44.8%

PRESIDENT 1932

County	Total Vote	Republican	Democratic	Other	Rep.-Dem. Plurality	Total Vote Rep.	Total Vote Dem.	Major Vote Rep.	Major Vote Dem.
ADAMS	2,606	915	1,514	177	599 D	35.1%	58.1%	37.7%	62.3%
BARNES	7,667	2,527	4,833	307	2,306 D	33.0%	63.0%	34.3%	65.7%
BENSON	4,917	1,170	3,650	97	2,480 D	23.8%	74.2%	24.3%	75.7%
BILLINGS	1,079	295	760	24	465 D	27.3%	70.4%	28.0%	72.0%
BOTTINEAU	5,567	1,201	4,178	188	2,977 D	21.6%	75.0%	22.3%	77.7%
BOWMAN	2,176	616	1,292	268	676 D	28.3%	59.4%	32.3%	67.7%
BURKE	3,594	906	2,473	215	1,567 D	25.2%	68.8%	26.8%	73.2%
BURLEIGH	8,439	2,687	5,621	131	2,934 D	31.8%	66.6%	32.3%	67.7%
CASS	20,394	8,937	11,094	363	2,157 D	43.8%	54.4%	44.6%	55.4%
CAVALIER	5,285	1,471	3,770	44	2,299 D	27.8%	71.3%	28.1%	71.9%
DICKEY	4,643	1,424	3,068	151	1,644 D	30.7%	66.1%	31.7%	68.3%
DIVIDE	3,402	817	2,374	211	1,557 D	24.0%	69.8%	25.6%	74.4%
DUNN	3,008	569	2,380	59	1,811 D	18.9%	79.1%	19.3%	80.7%
EDDY	2,527	537	1,888	102	1,351 D	21.3%	74.7%	22.1%	77.9%
EMMONS	4,049	916	3,089	44	2,173 D	22.6%	76.3%	22.9%	77.1%
FOSTER	2,471	609	1,838	24	1,229 D	24.6%	74.4%	24.9%	75.1%
GOLDEN VALLEY	1,695	653	1,023	19	370 D	38.5%	60.4%	39.0%	61.0%
GRAND FORKS	12,900	5,090	7,579	231	2,489 D	39.5%	58.8%	40.2%	59.8%
GRANT	3,654	657	2,912	85	2,255 D	18.0%	79.7%	18.4%	81.6%
GRIGGS	2,431	482	1,838	111	1,356 D	19.8%	75.6%	20.8%	79.2%
HETTINGER	3,358	921	2,336	101	1,415 D	27.4%	69.6%	28.3%	71.7%
KIDDER	2,792	709	2,042	41	1,333 D	25.4%	73.1%	25.8%	74.2%
LA MOURE	4,583	1,134	3,310	139	2,176 D	24.7%	72.2%	25.5%	74.5%
LOGAN	2,767	390	2,350	27	1,960 D	14.1%	84.9%	14.2%	85.8%
MCHENRY	5,566	1,396	3,937	233	2,541 D	25.1%	70.7%	26.2%	73.8%
MCINTOSH	3,543	465	3,078		2,613 D	13.1%	86.9%	13.1%	86.9%
MCKENZIE	3,547	710	2,655	182	1,945 D	20.0%	74.9%	21.1%	78.9%
MCLEAN	5,723	1,369	4,354		2,985 D	23.9%	76.1%	23.9%	76.1%
MERCER	2,993	480	2,491	22	2,011 D	16.0%	83.2%	16.2%	83.8%
MORTON	7,430	1,828	5,548	54	3,720 D	24.6%	74.7%	24.8%	75.2%
MOUNTRAIL	4,448	986	3,284	178	2,298 D	22.2%	73.8%	23.1%	76.9%
NELSON	4,132	956	3,176		2,220 D	23.1%	76.9%	23.1%	76.9%
OLIVER	1,469	302	1,152	15	850 D	20.6%	78.4%	20.8%	79.2%
PEMBINA	5,590	1,911	3,636	43	1,725 D	34.2%	65.0%	34.5%	65.5%
PIERCE	3,333	856	2,439	38	1,583 D	25.7%	73.2%	26.0%	74.0%
RAMSEY	6,329	1,917	4,337	75	2,420 D	30.3%	68.5%	30.7%	69.3%
RANSOM	4,563	1,445	3,025	93	1,580 D	31.7%	66.3%	32.3%	67.7%
RENVILLE	2,731	689	1,969	73	1,280 D	25.2%	72.1%	25.9%	74.1%
RICHLAND	8,183	2,304	5,663	216	3,359 D	28.2%	69.2%	28.9%	71.1%
ROLETTE	3,604	706	2,855	43	2,149 D	19.6%	79.2%	19.8%	80.2%
SARGENT	3,709	785	2,818	106	2,033 D	21.2%	76.0%	21.8%	78.2%
SHERIDAN	2,453	468	1,945	40	1,477 D	19.1%	79.3%	19.4%	80.6%
SIOUX	1,722	350	1,328	44	978 D	20.3%	77.1%	20.9%	79.1%
SLOPE	1,660	461	1,136	63	675 D	27.8%	68.4%	28.9%	71.1%
STARK	6,229	1,443	4,786		3,343 D	23.2%	76.8%	23.2%	76.8%
STEELE	2,685	695	1,925	65	1,230 D	25.9%	71.7%	26.5%	73.5%
STUTSMAN	8,878	2,577	6,182	119	3,605 D	29.0%	69.6%	29.4%	70.6%
TOWNER	2,999	765	2,190	44	1,425 D	25.5%	73.0%	25.9%	74.1%
TRAILL	5,074	1,893	3,112	69	1,219 D	37.3%	61.3%	37.8%	62.2%
WALSH	7,244	1,616	5,342	286	3,726 D	22.3%	73.7%	23.2%	76.8%
WARD	12,626	4,195	8,129	302	3,934 D	33.2%	64.4%	34.0%	66.0%
WELLS	4,939	1,062	3,823	54	2,761 D	21.5%	77.4%	21.7%	78.3%
WILLIAMS	6,884	1,509	4,823	552	3,314 D	21.9%	70.1%	23.8%	76.2%
TOTAL	256,290	71,772	178,350	6,168	106,578 D	28.0%	69.6%	28.7%	71.3%

NORTH DAKOTA

PRESIDENT 1936

County	Total Vote	Republican	Democratic	Other	Rep.-Dem. Plurality	% T.V. Rep.	% T.V. Dem.	% M.V. Rep.	% M.V. Dem.
ADAMS	2,404	746	1,321	337	575 D	31.0%	55.0%	36.1%	63.9%
BARNES	7,746	2,324	4,484	938	2,160 D	30.0%	57.9%	34.1%	65.9%
BENSON	5,363	1,020	3,343	1,000	2,323 D	19.0%	62.3%	23.4%	76.6%
BILLINGS	1,232	329	729	174	430 D	26.7%	59.2%	31.1%	68.9%
BOTTINEAU	5,779	1,224	3,286	1,269	2,062 D	21.2%	56.9%	27.1%	72.9%
BOWMAN	2,010	534	1,118	358	584 D	26.6%	55.6%	32.3%	67.7%
BURKE	3,731	684	1,821	1,226	1,137 D	18.3%	48.8%	27.3%	72.7%
BURLEIGH	9,723	2,447	6,314	962	3,867 D	25.2%	64.9%	27.9%	72.1%
CASS	21,670	7,632	12,400	1,638	4,768 D	35.2%	57.2%	38.1%	61.9%
CAVALIER	5,809	1,657	3,533	619	1,876 D	28.5%	60.8%	31.9%	68.1%
DICKEY	4,458	1,533	2,287	638	754 D	34.4%	51.3%	40.1%	59.9%
DIVIDE	3,536	585	2,212	739	1,627 D	16.5%	62.6%	20.9%	79.1%
DUNN	3,381	732	2,257	392	1,525 D	21.7%	66.8%	24.5%	75.5%
EDDY	2,711	579	1,729	403	1,150 D	21.4%	63.8%	25.1%	74.9%
EMMONS	4,183	1,117	2,424	642	1,307 D	26.7%	57.9%	31.5%	68.5%
FOSTER	2,759	685	1,894	180	1,209 D	24.8%	68.6%	26.6%	73.4%
GOLDEN VALLEY	1,659	581	991	87	410 D	35.0%	59.7%	37.0%	63.0%
GRAND FORKS	14,549	4,312	9,222	1,015	4,910 D	29.6%	63.4%	31.9%	68.1%
GRANT	3,456	1,022	1,858	576	836 D	29.6%	53.8%	35.5%	64.5%
GRIGGS	2,723	666	1,665	392	999 D	24.5%	61.1%	28.6%	71.4%
HETTINGER	3,317	989	1,383	945	394 D	29.8%	41.7%	41.7%	58.3%
KIDDER	2,932	872	1,492	568	620 D	29.7%	50.9%	36.9%	63.1%
LA MOURE	4,871	1,614	2,412	845	798 D	33.1%	49.5%	40.1%	59.9%
LOGAN	2,864	984	1,292	588	308 D	34.4%	45.1%	43.2%	56.8%
MCHENRY	6,169	1,619	3,294	1,256	1,675 D	26.2%	53.4%	33.0%	67.0%
MCINTOSH	3,629	1,469	1,900	260	431 D	40.5%	52.4%	43.6%	56.4%
MCKENZIE	3,888	570	2,885	433	2,315 D	14.7%	74.2%	16.5%	83.5%
MCLEAN	6,862	1,732	4,018	1,112	2,286 D	25.2%	58.6%	30.1%	69.9%
MERCER	3,619	1,142	1,924	553	782 D	31.6%	53.2%	37.2%	62.8%
MORTON	8,090	1,857	5,612	621	3,755 D	23.0%	69.4%	24.9%	75.1%
MOUNTRAIL	4,769	700	2,775	1,294	2,075 D	14.7%	58.2%	20.1%	79.9%
NELSON	4,491	1,002	2,954	535	1,952 D	22.3%	65.8%	25.3%	74.7%
OLIVER	1,573	469	906	198	437 D	29.8%	57.6%	34.1%	65.9%
PEMBINA	6,481	2,040	4,139	302	2,099 D	31.5%	63.9%	33.0%	67.0%
PIERCE	3,764	912	2,168	684	1,256 D	24.2%	57.6%	29.6%	70.4%
RAMSEY	6,993	1,784	4,559	650	2,775 D	25.5%	65.2%	28.1%	71.9%
RANSOM	4,298	1,303	2,385	610	1,082 D	30.3%	55.5%	35.3%	64.7%
RENVILLE	2,861	611	1,766	484	1,155 D	21.4%	61.7%	25.7%	74.3%
RICHLAND	7,596	2,386	3,792	1,418	1,406 D	31.4%	49.9%	38.6%	61.4%
ROLETTE	4,432	857	3,186	389	2,329 D	19.3%	71.9%	21.2%	78.8%
SARGENT	3,577	863	2,306	408	1,443 D	24.1%	64.5%	27.2%	72.8%
SHERIDAN	2,798	834	1,150	814	316 D	29.8%	41.1%	42.0%	58.0%
SIOUX	1,664	585	877	202	292 D	35.2%	52.7%	40.0%	60.0%
SLOPE	1,421	331	896	194	565 D	23.3%	63.1%	27.0%	73.0%
STARK	6,139	1,602	4,012	525	2,410 D	26.1%	65.4%	28.5%	71.5%
STEELE	2,873	724	1,444	705	720 D	25.2%	50.3%	33.4%	66.6%
STUTSMAN	9,369	2,725	5,564	1,080	2,839 D	29.1%	59.4%	32.9%	67.1%
TOWNER	3,214	720	1,744	750	1,024 D	22.4%	54.3%	29.2%	70.8%
TRAILL	5,269	1,807	2,780	682	973 D	34.3%	52.8%	39.4%	60.6%
WALSH	8,185	1,813	5,756	616	3,943 D	22.2%	70.3%	24.0%	76.0%
WARD	14,055	3,142	8,872	2,041	5,730 D	22.4%	63.1%	26.2%	73.8%
WELLS	5,298	1,263	3,114	921	1,851 D	23.8%	58.8%	28.9%	71.1%
WILLIAMS	7,473	1,021	4,903	1,549	3,382 D	13.7%	65.6%	17.2%	82.8%
TOTAL	273,716	72,751	163,148	37,817	90,397 D	26.6%	59.6%	30.8%	69.2%

PRESIDENT 1940

County	Total Vote	Republican	Democratic	Other	Rep.-Dem. Plurality	% T.V. Rep.	% T.V. Dem.	% M.V. Rep.	% M.V. Dem.
ADAMS	2,095	1,231	837	27	394 R	58.8%	40.0%	59.5%	40.5%
BARNES	8,062	4,649	3,384	29	1,265 R	57.7%	42.0%	57.9%	42.1%
BENSON	5,420	2,485	2,898	37	413 D	45.8%	53.5%	46.2%	53.8%
BILLINGS	1,068	663	404	1	259 R	62.1%	37.8%	62.1%	37.9%
BOTTINEAU	5,628	3,129	2,469	30	660 R	55.6%	43.9%	55.9%	44.1%
BOWMAN	1,831	927	882	22	45 R	50.6%	48.2%	51.2%	48.8%
BURKE	3,391	1,951	1,342	98	609 R	57.5%	39.6%	59.2%	40.8%
BURLEIGH	10,266	5,858	4,350	58	1,508 R	57.1%	42.4%	57.4%	42.6%
CASS	24,586	12,567	11,911	108	656 R	51.1%	48.4%	51.3%	48.7%
CAVALIER	5,618	2,845	2,757	16	88 R	50.6%	49.1%	50.8%	49.2%
DICKEY	4,835	2,777	1,721	337	1,056 R	57.4%	35.6%	61.7%	38.3%
DIVIDE	3,242	1,437	1,771	34	334 D	44.3%	54.6%	44.8%	55.2%
DUNN	3,536	2,132	1,392	12	740 R	60.3%	39.4%	60.5%	39.5%
EDDY	2,724	1,319	1,368	37	49 D	48.4%	50.2%	49.1%	50.9%
EMMONS	4,548	3,515	1,004	29	2,511 R	77.3%	22.1%	77.8%	22.2%
FOSTER	2,567	1,109	1,446	12	337 D	43.2%	56.3%	43.4%	56.6%
GOLDEN VALLEY	1,571	873	689	9	184 R	55.6%	43.9%	55.9%	44.1%
GRAND FORKS	15,506	7,043	8,396	67	1,353 D	45.4%	54.1%	45.6%	54.4%
GRANT	3,453	2,815	627	11	2,188 R	81.5%	18.2%	81.8%	18.2%
GRIGGS	2,592	1,117	1,464	11	347 D	43.1%	56.5%	43.3%	56.7%
HETTINGER	3,151	2,468	671	12	1,797 R	78.3%	21.3%	78.6%	21.4%
KIDDER	2,951	1,563	1,377	11	186 R	53.0%	46.7%	53.2%	46.8%
LA MOURE	4,620	2,943	1,637	40	1,306 R	63.7%	35.4%	64.3%	35.7%
LOGAN	3,077	2,572	498	7	2,074 R	83.6%	16.2%	83.8%	16.2%
MCHENRY	6,174	3,894	2,225	55	1,669 R	63.1%	36.0%	63.6%	36.4%
MCINTOSH	3,812	3,494	318	0	3,176 R	91.7%	8.3%	91.7%	8.3%
MCKENZIE	4,046	1,563	2,440	43	877 D	38.6%	60.3%	39.0%	61.0%
MCLEAN	6,972	4,113	2,666	193	1,447 R	59.0%	38.2%	60.7%	39.3%
MERCER	3,914	3,341	567	6	2,774 R	85.4%	14.5%	85.5%	14.5%
MORTON	8,428	5,499	2,889	40	2,610 R	65.2%	34.3%	65.6%	34.4%
MOUNTRAIL	4,435	1,981	2,392	62	411 D	44.7%	53.9%	45.3%	54.7%
NELSON	4,316	1,859	2,435	22	576 D	43.1%	56.4%	43.5%	56.5%
OLIVER	1,623	1,356	266	1	1,090 R	83.5%	16.4%	83.6%	16.4%
PEMBINA	6,655	2,924	3,711	20	787 D	43.9%	55.8%	44.1%	55.9%
PIERCE	3,811	2,349	1,451	11	898 R	61.6%	38.1%	61.8%	38.2%
RAMSEY	7,194	3,629	3,530	35	99 R	50.4%	49.1%	50.7%	49.3%
RANSOM	4,589	2,579	1,986	24	593 R	56.2%	43.3%	56.5%	43.5%
RENVILLE	2,556	1,202	1,298	56	96 D	47.0%	50.8%	48.1%	51.9%
RICHLAND	8,734	5,102	3,584	48	1,518 R	58.4%	41.0%	58.7%	41.3%
ROLETTE	4,392	1,555	2,820	17	1,265 D	35.4%	64.2%	35.5%	64.5%
SARGENT	3,843	1,922	1,894	27	28 R	50.0%	49.3%	50.4%	49.6%
SHERIDAN	2,957	2,405	543	9	1,862 R	81.3%	18.4%	81.6%	18.4%
SIOUX	1,746	578	1,167	1	589 D	33.1%	66.8%	33.1%	66.9%
SLOPE	1,391	801	585	5	216 R	57.6%	42.1%	57.8%	42.2%
STARK	6,457	4,367	2,075	15	2,292 R	67.6%	32.1%	67.8%	32.2%
STEELE	2,784	1,328	1,434	22	106 D	47.7%	51.5%	48.1%	51.9%
STUTSMAN	9,562	5,634	3,897	31	1,737 R	58.9%	40.8%	59.1%	40.9%
TOWNER	3,241	1,630	1,596	15	34 R	50.3%	49.2%	50.5%	49.5%
TRAILL	5,390	2,882	2,476	32	406 R	53.5%	45.9%	53.8%	46.2%
WALSH	8,568	3,051	5,499	18	2,448 D	35.6%	64.2%	35.7%	64.3%
WARD	14,293	6,519	7,669	105	1,150 D	45.6%	53.7%	45.9%	54.1%
WELLS	5,232	3,335	1,878	19	1,457 R	63.7%	35.9%	64.0%	36.0%
WILLIAMS	7,211	2,470	4,579	162	2,109 D	34.3%	63.5%	35.0%	65.0%
TOTAL	280,775	154,590	124,036	2,149	30,554 R	55.1%	44.2%	55.5%	44.5%

NORTH DAKOTA

PRESIDENT 1944

County	Total Vote	Republican	Democratic	Other	Rep.-Dem. Plurality	Total Vote Rep.	Total Vote Dem.	Major Vote Rep.	Major Vote Dem.
ADAMS	1,648	966	668	14	298 R	58.6%	40.5%	59.1%	40.9%
BARNES	6,653	3,696	2,922	35	774 R	55.6%	43.9%	55.8%	44.2%
BENSON	4,010	1,726	2,261	23	535 D	43.0%	56.4%	43.3%	56.7%
BILLINGS	566	354	209	3	145 R	62.5%	36.9%	62.9%	37.1%
BOTTINEAU	4,660	2,663	1,953	44	710 R	57.1%	41.9%	57.7%	42.3%
BOWMAN	1,410	785	609	16	176 R	55.7%	43.2%	56.3%	43.7%
BURKE	2,827	1,540	1,226	61	314 R	54.5%	43.4%	55.7%	44.3%
BURLEIGH	7,700	4,616	3,061	23	1,555 R	59.9%	39.8%	60.1%	39.9%
CASS	21,167	10,661	10,390	116	271 R	50.4%	49.1%	50.6%	49.4%
CAVALIER	4,308	2,011	2,274	23	263 D	46.7%	52.8%	46.9%	53.1%
DICKEY	3,492	2,134	1,339	19	795 R	61.1%	38.3%	61.4%	38.6%
DIVIDE	2,772	1,225	1,513	34	288 D	44.2%	54.6%	44.7%	55.3%
DUNN	2,298	1,374	919	5	455 R	59.8%	40.0%	59.9%	40.1%
EDDY	2,048	974	1,042	32	68 D	47.6%	50.9%	48.3%	51.7%
EMMONS	2,929	2,255	656	18	1,599 R	77.0%	22.4%	77.5%	22.5%
FOSTER	2,007	891	1,102	14	211 D	44.4%	54.9%	44.7%	55.3%
GOLDEN VALLEY	1,158	709	443	6	266 R	61.2%	38.3%	61.5%	38.5%
GRAND FORKS	13,434	5,668	7,707	59	2,039 D	42.2%	57.4%	42.4%	57.6%
GRANT	2,164	1,745	410	9	1,335 R	80.6%	18.9%	81.0%	19.0%
GRIGGS	2,227	990	1,228	9	238 D	44.5%	55.1%	44.6%	55.4%
HETTINGER	2,371	1,812	554	5	1,258 R	76.4%	23.4%	76.6%	23.4%
KIDDER	2,103	1,397	693	13	704 R	66.4%	33.0%	66.8%	33.2%
LA MOURE	3,752	2,298	1,422	32	876 R	61.2%	37.9%	61.8%	38.2%
LOGAN	2,202	1,904	294	4	1,610 R	86.5%	13.4%	86.6%	13.4%
MCHENRY	5,112	3,141	1,934	37	1,207 R	61.4%	37.8%	61.9%	38.1%
MCINTOSH	2,916	2,682	226	8	2,456 R	92.0%	7.8%	92.2%	7.8%
MCKENZIE	2,863	1,241	1,592	30	351 D	43.3%	55.6%	43.8%	56.2%
MCLEAN	5,288	2,822	2,326	140	496 R	53.4%	44.0%	54.8%	45.2%
MERCER	2,956	2,504	445	7	2,059 R	84.7%	15.1%	84.9%	15.1%
MORTON	5,415	3,537	1,850	28	1,687 R	65.3%	34.2%	65.7%	34.3%
MOUNTRAIL	3,693	1,666	1,981	46	315 D	45.1%	53.6%	45.7%	54.3%
NELSON	3,441	1,506	1,925	10	419 D	43.8%	55.9%	43.9%	56.1%
OLIVER	984	756	219	9	537 R	76.8%	22.3%	77.5%	22.5%
PEMBINA	5,361	2,410	2,903	48	493 D	45.0%	54.2%	45.4%	54.6%
PIERCE	3,316	1,992	1,307	17	685 R	60.1%	39.4%	60.4%	39.6%
RAMSEY	5,083	2,505	2,539	39	34 D	49.3%	50.0%	49.7%	50.3%
RANSOM	3,712	2,044	1,639	29	405 R	55.1%	44.2%	55.5%	44.5%
RENVILLE	2,164	1,046	1,095	23	49 D	48.3%	50.6%	48.9%	51.1%
RICHLAND	7,624	4,402	3,192	30	1,210 R	57.7%	41.9%	58.0%	42.0%
ROLETTE	2,832	1,070	1,745	17	675 D	37.8%	61.6%	38.0%	62.0%
SARGENT	2,934	1,488	1,426	20	62 R	50.7%	48.6%	51.1%	48.9%
SHERIDAN	2,308	1,910	386	12	1,524 R	82.8%	16.7%	83.2%	16.8%
SIOUX	1,122	673	445	4	228 R	60.0%	39.7%	60.2%	39.8%
SLOPE	878	434	439	5	5 D	49.4%	50.0%	49.7%	50.3%
STARK	4,398	2,852	1,534	12	1,318 R	64.8%	34.9%	65.0%	35.0%
STEELE	2,374	1,042	1,320	12	278 D	43.9%	55.6%	44.1%	55.9%
STUTSMAN	7,509	4,220	3,243	46	977 R	56.5%	43.2%	56.5%	43.5%
TOWNER	2,286	1,097	1,185	4	88 D	48.0%	51.8%	48.1%	51.9%
TRAILL	4,869	2,370	2,479	20	109 D	48.7%	50.9%	48.9%	51.1%
WALSH	7,252	2,471	4,747	34	2,276 D	34.1%	65.5%	34.2%	65.8%
WARD	11,417	5,514	5,822	81	308 D	48.3%	51.0%	48.6%	51.4%
WELLS	4,106	2,529	1,557	20	972 R	61.6%	37.9%	61.9%	38.1%
WILLIAMS	6,063	2,217	3,748	98	1,531 D	36.6%	61.8%	36.7%	62.8%
TOTAL	220,182	118,535	100,144	1,503	18,391 R	53.8%	45.5%	54.2%	45.8%

PRESIDENT 1948

County	Total Vote	Republican	Democratic	Other	Rep.-Dem. Plurality	Total Vote Rep.	Total Vote Dem.	Major Vote Rep.	Major Vote Dem.
ADAMS	1,780	908	753	119	155 R	51.0%	42.3%	54.7%	45.3%
BARNES	6,594	3,385	2,892	317	493 R	51.3%	43.9%	53.9%	46.1%
BENSON	4,331	1,920	2,216	195	296 D	44.3%	51.2%	46.4%	53.6%
BILLINGS	736	372	311	53	61 R	50.5%	42.3%	54.5%	45.5%
BOTTINEAU	4,231	2,513	1,571	147	942 R	59.4%	37.1%	61.5%	38.5%
BOWMAN	1,451	723	597	131	126 R	49.8%	41.1%	54.8%	45.2%
BURKE	2,379	1,212	972	195	240 R	50.9%	40.9%	55.5%	44.5%
BURLEIGH	8,493	5,049	3,117	327	1,932 R	59.4%	36.7%	61.8%	38.2%
CASS	21,836	11,430	9,937	469	1,493 R	52.3%	45.5%	53.5%	46.5%
CAVALIER	4,158	1,864	2,198	96	334 D	44.8%	52.9%	45.9%	54.1%
DICKEY	3,232	1,774	1,264	194	510 R	54.9%	39.1%	58.4%	41.6%
DIVIDE	2,038	981	887	170	94 R	48.1%	43.5%	52.5%	47.5%
DUNN	2,423	1,244	1,074	105	170 R	51.3%	44.3%	53.7%	46.3%
EDDY	2,032	952	919	161	33 R	46.9%	45.2%	50.9%	49.1%
EMMONS	3,503	2,223	1,187	93	1,036 R	63.5%	33.9%	65.2%	34.8%
FOSTER	2,093	938	1,089	66	151 D	44.8%	52.0%	46.3%	53.7%
GOLDEN VALLEY	1,401	788	585	28	203 R	56.2%	41.8%	57.4%	42.6%
GRAND FORKS	13,789	6,374	6,996	419	866 D	46.2%	50.7%	47.7%	52.3%
GRANT	2,323	1,555	689	79	866 R	66.9%	29.7%	69.3%	30.7%
GRIGGS	2,338	1,036	1,180	122	144 D	44.3%	50.5%	46.8%	53.2%
HETTINGER	2,358	1,517	752	89	765 R	64.3%	31.9%	66.9%	33.1%
KIDDER	2,370	1,510	773	87	737 R	63.7%	32.6%	66.1%	33.9%
LA MOURE	3,708	1,999	1,481	228	518 R	53.9%	39.9%	57.4%	42.6%
LOGAN	2,218	1,585	557	76	1,028 R	71.5%	25.1%	74.0%	26.0%
MCHENRY	4,567	2,578	1,770	219	808 R	56.4%	38.8%	59.3%	40.7%
MCINTOSH	2,776	2,203	513	60	1,690 R	79.4%	18.5%	81.1%	18.9%
MCKENZIE	2,591	1,168	1,227	196	59 D	45.1%	47.4%	48.8%	51.2%
MCLEAN	5,513	2,762	2,283	468	479 R	50.1%	41.4%	54.7%	45.3%
MERCER	2,948	2,219	643	86	1,576 R	75.3%	21.8%	77.5%	22.5%
MORTON	6,394	3,607	2,521	266	1,086 R	56.4%	39.4%	58.9%	41.1%
MOUNTRAIL	3,304	1,395	1,521	388	126 D	42.2%	46.0%	47.8%	52.2%
NELSON	3,538	1,672	1,629	237	43 R	47.3%	46.0%	50.7%	49.3%
OLIVER	1,104	749	304	51	445 R	67.8%	27.5%	71.1%	28.9%
PEMBINA	5,155	2,406	2,666	83	260 D	46.7%	51.7%	47.4%	52.6%
PIERCE	2,953	1,738	1,147	68	591 R	58.9%	38.8%	60.2%	39.8%
RAMSEY	5,555	2,891	2,458	206	433 R	52.0%	44.2%	54.0%	46.0%
RANSOM	3,485	1,772	1,595	118	177 R	50.8%	45.8%	52.6%	47.4%
RENVILLE	1,742	812	838	92	26 D	46.6%	48.1%	49.2%	50.8%
RICHLAND	7,075	3,448	3,413	214	35 R	48.7%	48.2%	50.3%	49.7%
ROLETTE	2,869	1,179	1,565	125	386 D	41.1%	54.5%	43.0%	57.0%
SARGENT	3,033	1,387	1,506	140	119 D	45.7%	49.7%	47.9%	52.1%
SHERIDAN	1,969	1,554	372	43	1,182 R	78.9%	18.9%	80.7%	19.3%
SIOUX	1,166	667	465	34	202 R	57.2%	39.9%	58.9%	41.1%
SLOPE	885	447	388	50	59 R	50.5%	43.8%	53.5%	46.5%
STARK	5,357	3,222	2,017	118	1,205 R	60.1%	37.7%	61.5%	38.5%
STEELE	2,338	1,052	1,163	123	111 D	45.0%	49.7%	47.5%	52.5%
STUTSMAN	7,957	4,208	3,415	334	793 R	52.9%	42.9%	55.2%	44.8%
TOWNER	2,301	1,145	1,100	56	45 R	49.8%	47.8%	51.0%	49.0%
TRAILL	4,477	2,328	1,874	275	454 R	52.0%	41.9%	55.4%	44.6%
WALSH	7,031	2,646	4,170	215	1,524 D	37.6%	59.3%	38.8%	61.2%
WARD	11,337	5,514	5,189	634	325 R	48.6%	45.8%	51.5%	48.5%
WELLS	3,986	2,385	1,492	109	893 R	59.8%	37.4%	61.5%	38.5%
WILLIAMS	5,495	2,133	2,571	791	438 D	38.8%	46.8%	45.3%	54.7%
TOTAL	220,716	115,139	95,812	9,765	19,327 R	52.2%	43.4%	54.6%	45.4%

NORTH DAKOTA

PRESIDENT 1952

County	Total Vote	Republican	Democratic	Other	Rep.-Dem. Plurality	TV Rep. %	TV Dem. %	MV Rep. %	MV Dem. %
ADAMS	2,213	1,561	633	19	928 R	70.5	28.6	71.1	28.9
BARNES	7,703	5,534	2,120	49	3,414 R	71.8	27.5	72.3	27.7
BENSON	4,584	3,192	1,353	39	1,839 R	69.6	29.5	70.2	29.8
BILLINGS	822	674	143	5	531 R	82.0	17.4	82.5	17.5
BOTTINEAU	5,034	3,911	1,094	29	2,817 R	77.7	21.7	78.1	21.9
BOWMAN	1,931	1,375	540	16	835 R	71.2	28.0	71.8	28.2
BURKE	2,841	1,986	811	44	1,175 R	69.9	28.5	71.0	29.0
BURLEIGH	11,975	9,526	2,400	49	7,126 R	79.5	20.0	79.9	20.1
CASS	27,344	18,094	9,193	57	8,901 R	66.2	33.6	66.3	33.7
CAVALIER	5,052	3,519	1,496	37	2,023 R	69.7	29.6	70.2	29.8
DICKEY	4,095	2,917	1,150	28	1,767 R	71.2	28.1	71.7	28.3
DIVIDE	2,824	1,999	807	18	1,192 R	70.8	28.6	71.2	28.8
DUNN	2,924	2,237	664	23	1,573 R	76.5	22.7	77.1	22.9
EDDY	2,288	1,534	728	26	806 R	67.0	31.8	67.8	32.2
EMMONS	3,910	3,369	522	19	2,847 R	86.2	13.4	86.6	13.4
FOSTER	2,428	1,558	862	8	696 R	64.2	35.5	64.4	35.6
GOLDEN VALLEY	1,562	1,186	376	84	810 R	75.9	24.1	75.9	24.1
GRAND FORKS	16,662	10,939	5,639	21	5,300 R	65.7	33.8	66.0	34.0
GRANT	2,889	2,465	403	10	2,062 R	85.3	13.9	85.4	14.1
GRIGGS	2,609	1,727	872	63	855 R	66.2	33.4	66.4	33.6
HETTINGER	2,654	2,330	297	27	2,033 R	87.8	11.2	88.7	11.3
KIDDER	2,679	2,195	468	16	1,727 R	81.9	17.5	82.4	17.6
LA MOURE	4,379	3,202	1,145	32	2,057 R	73.1	26.1	73.7	26.3
LOGAN	2,544	2,165	369	10	1,796 R	85.1	14.5	85.4	14.5
MCHENRY	5,518	4,227	1,228	63	2,999 R	76.6	22.3	77.5	22.5
MCINTOSH	3,348	3,043	276	29	2,767 R	90.9	8.2	91.7	8.3
MCKENZIE	3,152	2,260	846	46	1,414 R	71.7	26.8	72.8	27.2
MCLEAN	7,555	5,184	2,295	76	2,889 R	68.6	30.4	69.3	30.7
MERCER	3,524	2,994	512	18	2,482 R	85.0	14.5	85.4	14.6
MORTON	8,426	6,309	2,079	38	4,230 R	74.9	24.7	75.2	24.8
MOUNTRAIL	3,998	2,516	1,437	45	1,079 R	62.9	35.9	63.6	36.4
NELSON	3,880	2,443	1,418	19	1,025 R	63.0	36.5	63.5	36.5
OLIVER	1,289	1,132	143	14	989 R	87.8	11.1	88.8	11.2
PEMBINA	5,944	4,012	1,891	41	2,121 R	67.5	31.8	68.0	32.0
PIERCE	3,608	2,606	773	29	1,833 R	77.3	21.4	78.4	21.6
RAMSEY	6,489	4,670	1,794	25	2,876 R	72.1	27.6	72.2	27.8
RANSOM	4,347	3,051	1,265	31	1,786 R	70.2	29.1	70.7	29.3
RENVILLE	2,360	1,571	767	22	804 R	66.5	32.5	67.2	32.8
RICHLAND	8,630	6,022	2,541	67	3,481 R	69.3	29.4	70.3	29.7
ROLETTE	3,365	2,188	1,160	17	1,028 R	65.0	34.5	65.4	34.6
SARGENT	3,230	2,124	1,090	16	1,034 R	65.8	33.7	66.1	33.9
SHERIDAN	2,309	2,016	267	26	1,749 R	87.3	11.6	88.3	11.7
SIOUX	1,322	968	336	18	632 R	73.2	25.4	74.2	25.8
SLOPE	983	682	290	11	392 R	69.4	29.5	70.0	30.0
STARK	6,688	5,322	1,332	34	3,990 R	79.6	19.9	80.0	20.0
STEELE	2,434	1,513	911	10	602 R	62.2	37.4	62.4	37.6
STUTSMAN	9,916	6,713	3,156	47	3,557 R	67.7	31.8	68.0	31.9
TOWNER	2,831	1,960	843	28	1,117 R	69.2	29.8	69.9	30.1
TRAILL	5,391	3,884	1,484	23	2,400 R	72.0	27.5	72.4	27.6
WALSH	8,304	4,761	3,494	49	1,267 R	57.3	42.1	57.7	42.3
WARD	15,211	10,130	4,966	115	5,164 R	66.6	32.6	67.1	32.5
WELLS	4,762	3,709	1,016	37	2,693 R	77.9	21.3	78.5	21.5
WILLIAMS	7,367	4,307	2,999	61	1,308 R	58.5	40.7	59.0	41.0
TOTAL	270,127	191,712	76,694	1,721	115,018 R	71.0	28.4	71.4	28.6

PRESIDENT 1956

County	Total Vote	Republican	Democratic	Other	Rep.-Dem. Plurality	TV Rep. %	TV Dem. %	MV Rep. %	MV Dem. %
ADAMS	2,053	1,338	723	2	615 R	64.9	35.0	64.9	35.1
BARNES	7,219	4,475	2,730	14	1,745 R	62.0	37.8	62.1	37.9
BENSON	4,203	2,340	1,851	12	489 R	55.7	44.0	55.8	44.2
BILLINGS	689	437	248	4	189 R	63.4	36.0	63.8	36.2
BOTTINEAU	4,646	2,923	1,718	5	1,205 R	62.9	37.0	63.0	37.0
BOWMAN	1,726	1,007	715	4	292 R	58.3	41.4	58.5	41.5
BURKE	2,359	1,415	936	8	479 R	60.0	39.7	60.2	39.8
BURLEIGH	12,467	9,199	3,231	37	5,968 R	73.8	25.9	74.0	26.0
CASS	26,770	16,932	9,821	17	7,111 R	63.2	36.7	63.3	36.7
CAVALIER	4,295	2,450	1,836	9	614 R	57.0	42.7	57.2	42.8
DICKEY	3,770	2,327	1,435	8	892 R	61.7	38.1	61.9	38.1
DIVIDE	2,493	1,296	1,194	3	102 R	52.0	47.9	52.0	48.0
DUNN	2,612	1,567	1,055	6	512 R	59.6	40.1	59.8	40.2
EDDY	2,212	1,239	973		266 R	56.0	44.0	56.0	44.0
EMMONS	3,617	2,789	825	3	1,964 R	77.1	22.8	77.2	22.8
FOSTER	2,306	1,234	1,062	10	172 R	53.5	46.1	53.7	46.3
GOLDEN VALLEY	1,397	824	567	6	257 R	59.0	40.6	59.2	40.8
GRAND FORKS	16,550	10,289	6,231	30	4,058 R	62.2	37.6	62.3	37.7
GRANT	2,599	1,872	718	9	1,154 R	72.0	27.6	72.3	27.7
GRIGGS	2,387	1,212	1,173	2	39 R	50.8	49.1	50.8	49.2
HETTINGER	2,682	1,882	796	4	1,086 R	70.2	29.7	70.3	29.7
KIDDER	2,237	1,523	708	6	815 R	68.1	31.6	68.3	31.7
LA MOURE	4,134	2,433	1,694	7	739 R	58.9	41.0	59.0	41.0
LOGAN	2,358	1,807	547	4	1,260 R	76.6	23.2	76.8	23.2
MCHENRY	4,860	3,019	1,825	16	1,194 R	62.1	37.6	62.3	37.7
MCINTOSH	3,193	2,689	498	6	2,191 R	84.2	15.6	84.4	15.6
MCKENZIE	3,027	1,609	1,405	13	204 R	53.2	46.4	53.4	46.6
MCLEAN	6,280	3,653	2,609	18	1,044 R	58.2	41.5	58.3	41.7
MERCER	3,227	2,555	666	6	1,889 R	79.2	20.6	79.3	20.7
MORTON	7,890	5,232	2,628	30	2,604 R	66.3	33.3	66.6	33.4
MOUNTRAIL	3,597	1,699	1,891	7	192 D	47.2	52.6	47.3	52.7
NELSON	3,617	1,821	1,794	2	27 D	50.3	49.6	50.4	49.6
OLIVER	1,079	788	279	12	509 R	73.0	25.9	73.9	26.1
PEMBINA	4,977	3,077	1,887	13	1,190 R	61.8	37.9	62.0	38.0
PIERCE	3,342	1,997	1,340	5	657 R	59.8	40.1	59.8	40.2
RAMSEY	5,930	3,821	2,103	6	1,718 R	64.4	35.5	64.5	35.5
RANSOM	4,174	2,361	1,808	5	553 R	56.6	43.3	56.6	43.4
RENVILLE	2,061	1,035	1,025	1	10 R	50.2	49.7	50.2	49.8
RICHLAND	8,154	4,971	3,171	12	1,800 R	60.0	38.8	61.0	38.9
ROLETTE	3,178	1,444	1,728	6	284 D	45.4	54.4	45.5	54.5
SARGENT	3,142	1,662	1,473	7	189 R	52.9	46.9	53.0	47.0
SHERIDAN	2,118	1,646	472		1,174 R	77.7	22.3	77.7	22.3
SIOUX	1,197	718	476	3	242 R	60.0	39.8	60.1	39.9
SLOPE	833	433	397	3	36 R	52.0	47.7	52.2	47.8
STARK	6,040	4,251	1,778	11	2,473 R	70.4	29.4	70.5	29.5
STEELE	2,337	1,188	1,148	1	40 R	50.8	49.1	50.9	49.1
STUTSMAN	9,554	5,718	3,825	11	1,893 R	59.8	40.0	59.9	40.0
TOWNER	2,564	1,391	1,169	4	222 R	54.3	45.6	54.3	45.7
TRAILL	5,062	3,090	1,969	3	1,121 R	61.0	38.9	61.1	38.9
WALSH	7,200	3,946	3,238	16	708 R	54.8	45.0	54.9	45.1
WARD	14,832	9,042	5,762	28	3,280 R	61.0	38.8	61.1	38.9
WELLS	4,355	2,912	1,434	9	1,478 R	66.9	32.9	67.0	33.0
WILLIAMS	8,364	4,188	4,157	19	31 R	50.1	49.7	50.2	49.8
TOTAL	253,991	156,766	96,742	483	60,024 R	61.7	38.1	61.8	38.2

NORTH DAKOTA

PRESIDENT 1960

County	Total Vote	Republican	Democratic	Other	Rep.-Dem. Plurality	TV % Rep.	TV % Dem.	MV % Rep.	MV % Dem.
ADAMS	2,064	1,232	832		400 R	59.7%	40.3%	59.7%	40.3%
BARNES	7,629	4,403	3,223	3	1,180 R	57.7%	42.2%	57.7%	42.3%
BENSON	4,443	2,259	2,181	3	78 R	50.8%	49.1%	50.9%	49.1%
BILLINGS	768	368	400		32 D	47.9%	52.1%	47.9%	52.1%
BOTTINEAU	5,069	3,092	1,974	3	1,118 R	61.0%	38.9%	61.0%	39.0%
BOWMAN	1,888	1,038	847	3	191 R	55.0%	44.9%	55.1%	44.9%
BURKE	2,687	1,609	1,076	2	533 R	59.9%	40.0%	59.9%	40.1%
BURLEIGH	15,278	9,492	5,761	25	3,731 R	62.1%	37.7%	62.2%	37.8%
CASS	29,711	17,498	12,213		5,285 R	58.9%	41.1%	58.9%	41.1%
CAVALIER	4,743	2,430	2,312	1	118 R	51.2%	48.7%	51.2%	48.8%
DICKEY	3,856	2,420	1,433	3	987 R	62.8%	37.2%	62.8%	37.2%
DIVIDE	2,595	1,348	1,243	4	105 R	51.9%	47.9%	52.0%	48.0%
DUNN	2,783	1,462	1,321		141 R	52.5%	47.5%	52.5%	47.5%
EDDY	2,342	1,188	1,152	2	36 R	50.7%	49.2%	50.8%	49.2%
EMMONS	3,845	1,785	2,058	2	273 D	46.4%	53.5%	46.4%	53.6%
FOSTER	2,533	1,351	1,182		169 R	53.3%	46.7%	53.3%	46.7%
GOLDEN VALLEY	1,499	825	672	2	153 R	55.0%	44.8%	55.0%	44.9%
GRAND FORKS	19,343	10,997	8,341	5	2,656 R	56.9%	43.1%	56.9%	43.1%
GRANT	2,751	1,794	955	2	839 R	65.2%	34.7%	65.3%	34.7%
GRIGGS	2,561	1,278	1,279	4	1 D	49.9%	49.9%	50.0%	50.0%
HETTINGER	2,762	1,541	1,219	2	322 R	55.8%	44.1%	55.8%	44.2%
KIDDER	2,443	1,574	868	1	706 R	64.4%	35.5%	64.5%	35.5%
LA MOURE	4,090	2,511	1,575	4	936 R	61.4%	38.5%	61.5%	38.5%
LOGAN	2,499	1,601	898		703 R	64.1%	35.9%	64.1%	35.9%
MCHENRY	4,948	2,715	2,231	2	484 R	54.9%	45.1%	54.9%	45.1%
MCINTOSH	3,322	2,694	628		2,066 R	81.1%	18.9%	81.1%	18.9%
MCKENZIE	3,231	1,715	1,514	2	201 R	53.1%	46.9%	53.1%	46.9%
MCLEAN	6,173	3,398	2,771	4	627 R	55.0%	44.9%	55.1%	44.9%
MERCER	3,239	2,395	844		1,551 R	73.9%	26.1%	73.9%	26.1%
MORTON	8,895	4,028	4,866	1	838 D	45.3%	54.7%	45.3%	54.7%
MOUNTRAIL	4,163	1,894	2,264	5	370 D	45.5%	54.4%	45.6%	54.4%
NELSON	3,719	1,934	1,783	2	151 R	52.0%	47.9%	52.0%	48.0%
OLIVER	1,198	703	494	1	209 R	58.7%	41.2%	58.7%	41.3%
PEMBINA	5,810	3,348	2,460	2	888 R	57.6%	42.3%	57.6%	42.4%
PIERCE	3,313	1,464	1,848	1	384 D	44.2%	55.8%	44.2%	55.8%
RAMSEY	6,413	3,599	2,813	1	786 R	56.1%	43.9%	56.1%	43.9%
RANSOM	4,131	2,324	1,806	1	518 R	56.3%	43.7%	56.3%	43.7%
RENVILLE	2,230	1,012	1,217	1	205 D	45.4%	54.6%	45.4%	54.6%
RICHLAND	6,718	4,711	4,003	4	708 R	54.0%	45.9%	54.1%	45.9%
ROLETTE	3,615	1,277	2,335	3	1,058 D	35.3%	64.6%	35.4%	64.6%
SARGENT	3,248	1,591	1,655	2	64 D	49.0%	51.0%	49.0%	51.0%
SHERIDAN	2,098	1,552	539	7	1,013 R	74.0%	25.7%	74.2%	25.8%
SIOUX	1,259	571	688		117 D	45.4%	54.6%	45.4%	54.6%
SLOPE	906	475	431		44 R	52.4%	47.6%	52.4%	47.6%
STARK	7,421	3,223	4,197	1	974 D	43.4%	56.6%	43.4%	56.6%
STEELE	2,382	1,209	1,173		36 R	50.8%	49.2%	50.8%	49.2%
STUTSMAN	10,399	5,905	4,481	13	1,424 R	56.8%	43.1%	56.9%	43.1%
TOWNER	2,703	1,410	1,292	1	118 R	52.2%	47.8%	52.2%	47.8%
TRAILL	5,303	3,218	2,084	1	1,134 R	60.7%	39.3%	60.7%	39.3%
WALSH	8,047	4,036	4,009	2	27 R	50.2%	49.8%	50.2%	49.8%
WARD	17,653	9,680	7,954	19	1,726 R	54.8%	45.1%	54.9%	45.1%
WELLS	4,535	2,641	1,885	9	756 R	58.2%	41.6%	58.4%	41.6%
WILLIAMS	9,177	4,492	4,683	2	191 D	48.9%	51.0%	49.0%	51.0%
TOTAL	278,431	154,310	123,963	158	30,347 R	55.4%	44.5%	55.5%	44.5%

PRESIDENT 1964

County	Total Vote	Republican	Democratic	Other	Rep.-Dem. Plurality	TV % Rep.	TV % Dem.	MV % Rep.	MV % Dem.
ADAMS	1,888	877	1,010	1	133 D	46.5%	53.5%	46.5%	53.5%
BARNES	7,008	2,987	4,007	14	1,020 D	42.6%	57.2%	42.7%	57.3%
BENSON	4,060	1,489	2,566	5	1,077 D	36.7%	63.2%	36.7%	63.3%
BILLINGS	688	340	348		8 D	49.4%	50.6%	49.4%	50.6%
BOTTINEAU	4,607	2,060	2,546	1	486 D	44.7%	55.3%	44.7%	55.3%
BOWMAN	1,827	756	1,070	1	314 D	41.4%	58.6%	41.4%	58.6%
BURKE	2,434	974	1,454	6	480 D	40.0%	59.7%	40.1%	59.9%
BURLEIGH	15,419	7,239	8,120	60	881 D	46.9%	52.7%	47.1%	52.9%
CASS	28,669	12,972	15,674	23	2,702 D	45.3%	54.7%	45.2%	54.7%
CAVALIER	4,231	1,417	2,810	4	1,393 D	33.5%	66.4%	33.5%	66.5%
DICKEY	3,630	1,808	1,818	4	10 D	49.8%	50.1%	49.9%	50.1%
DIVIDE	2,281	779	1,498	4	719 D	34.2%	65.7%	34.2%	65.8%
DUNN	2,432	1,079	1,351	2	272 D	44.4%	55.6%	44.4%	55.6%
EDDY	2,088	747	1,337	4	590 D	35.8%	64.2%	35.8%	64.2%
EMMONS	3,315	1,759	1,556		203 R	53.1%	46.9%	53.1%	46.9%
FOSTER	2,244	927	1,315	2	388 D	41.3%	58.6%	41.3%	58.6%
GOLDEN VALLEY	1,324	722	602		120 R	54.5%	45.5%	54.5%	45.5%
GRAND FORKS	18,175	7,367	10,740	68	3,373 D	40.5%	59.1%	40.7%	59.3%
GRANT	2,488	1,421	1,063	4	358 R	57.1%	42.7%	57.2%	42.8%
GRIGGS	2,390	885	1,505		620 D	37.0%	63.0%	37.0%	63.0%
HETTINGER	2,465	1,188	1,275	2	87 D	48.2%	51.7%	48.2%	51.8%
KIDDER	2,151	1,104	1,047		57 R	51.3%	48.7%	51.3%	48.7%
LA MOURE	3,755	1,604	2,145	6	541 D	42.7%	57.1%	42.8%	57.2%
LOGAN	2,141	1,187	951	3	236 R	55.4%	44.5%	55.5%	44.5%
MCHENRY	4,379	1,728	2,643	8	915 D	39.5%	60.4%	39.5%	60.5%
MCINTOSH	2,841	1,891	950		941 R	66.6%	33.4%	66.6%	33.4%
MCKENZIE	2,938	1,352	1,584	2	232 D	46.0%	53.9%	46.0%	54.0%
MCLEAN	5,547	2,204	3,339	4	1,135 D	39.7%	60.2%	39.8%	60.2%
MERCER	2,850	1,540	1,310		230 R	54.0%	46.0%	54.0%	46.0%
MORTON	8,138	2,955	5,173	10	2,218 D	36.3%	63.6%	36.4%	63.6%
MOUNTRAIL	3,683	1,131	2,548	4	1,417 D	30.7%	69.2%	30.7%	69.3%
NELSON	3,287	1,101	2,186		1,085 D	33.5%	66.5%	33.5%	66.5%
OLIVER	1,017	469	548		79 D	46.1%	53.9%	46.1%	53.9%
PEMBINA	5,167	1,961	3,198	8	1,237 D	38.0%	61.9%	38.0%	62.0%
PIERCE	3,073	1,178	1,893	2	715 D	38.3%	61.6%	38.4%	61.6%
RAMSEY	5,987	2,409	3,572	6	1,163 D	40.2%	59.7%	40.3%	59.7%
RANSOM	3,717	1,647	2,063	7	416 D	44.3%	55.5%	44.4%	55.6%
RENVILLE	1,997	640	1,356	1	716 D	32.0%	67.9%	32.1%	67.9%
RICHLAND	7,955	3,425	4,525	5	1,100 D	43.1%	56.9%	43.1%	56.9%
ROLETTE	3,458	892	2,566		1,674 D	25.8%	74.2%	25.8%	74.2%
SARGENT	3,033	1,189	1,840	4	651 D	39.2%	60.7%	39.3%	60.7%
SHERIDAN	1,911	1,187	724		463 R	62.1%	37.9%	62.1%	37.9%
SIOUX	1,013	314	695	4	381 D	31.0%	68.9%	31.1%	68.9%
SLOPE	765	329	436		107 D	43.0%	57.0%	43.0%	57.0%
STARK	7,161	2,888	4,270	3	1,382 D	40.3%	59.6%	40.3%	59.7%
STEELE	2,203	796	1,404	3	608 D	36.1%	63.7%	36.2%	63.8%
STUTSMAN	9,474	3,990	5,463	21	1,473 D	42.1%	57.7%	42.2%	57.8%
TOWNER	2,417	788	1,628	1	840 D	32.6%	67.4%	32.6%	67.4%
TRAILL	4,929	2,312	2,614	3	302 D	46.9%	53.0%	46.9%	53.1%
WALSH	7,376	2,454	4,911	11	2,457 D	33.3%	66.6%	33.3%	66.7%
WARD	17,735	6,798	10,871	66	4,073 D	38.3%	61.3%	38.5%	61.5%
WELLS	4,189	1,875	2,314		439 D	44.8%	55.2%	44.8%	55.2%
WILLIAMS	8,439	3,076	5,352	11	2,276 D	36.4%	63.4%	36.5%	63.5%
TOTAL	258,389	108,207	149,784	398	41,577 D	41.9%	58.0%	41.9%	58.1%

NORTH DAKOTA

OTHER VOTE COMPOSITION:

1920	Socialist.
1924	89,922 Progressive; 370 Communist.
1928	936 Socialist; 842 Communist.
1932	3,521 Socialist; 1,817 Liberty; 830 Communist.
1936	36,708 Union; 552 Socialist; 360 Communist; 197 Prohibition.
1940	1,279 Socialist; 545 Alfred Knutson; 325 Prohibition.
1944	954 Socialist; 549 Prohibition.
1948	8,391 Progressive; 1,000 Socialist; 374 States Rights.
1952	1,075 Christian Nationalist (MacArthur); 344 Progressive; 302 Prohibition.
1956	States Rights.
1960	Socialist Workers.
1964	224 Socialist Workers; 174 Prohibition.

SPECIAL CASES:

1924	Progressive candidates carried many counties and ran second in all others.
1936	Union candidates ran second in several counties.
1940	The votes for Alfred Knutson were cast for him as an individual under the designation "Peace--Jobs--Security--Civil Rights"; in some sources these votes are listed as Communist.

OHIO

PRESIDENT 1920

County	Total Vote	Republican	Democratic	Other	Rep.-Dem. Plurality	% Total Vote Rep.	% Total Vote Dem.	% Major Vote Rep.	% Major Vote Dem.
ADAMS	9,199	4,974	4,194	31	780 R	54.1%	45.6%	54.3%	45.7%
ALLEN	26,082	13,978	11,658	446	2,320 R	53.6%	44.7%	54.5%	45.5%
ASHLAND	11,757	5,951	5,705	101	246 R	50.6%	48.5%	51.1%	48.9%
ASHTABULA	20,229	14,099	5,413	717	8,686 R	69.7%	26.8%	72.3%	27.7%
ATHENS	17,900	11,016	6,523	361	4,493 R	61.5%	36.4%	62.8%	37.2%
AUGLAIZE	11,752	6,752	4,792	208	1,960 R	57.5%	40.8%	58.5%	41.5%
BELMONT	29,201	14,761	13,347	1,093	1,414 R	50.5%	45.7%	52.5%	47.5%
BROWN	9,370	4,009	5,317	44	1,308 D	42.8%	56.7%	43.0%	57.0%
BUTLER	33,396	14,998	16,437	1,961	1,439 D	44.9%	49.2%	47.7%	52.3%
CARROLL	6,258	4,392	1,755	111	2,637 R	70.2%	28.0%	71.4%	28.6%
CHAMPAIGN	12,128	7,285	4,775	68	2,510 R	60.1%	39.4%	60.4%	39.6%
CLARK	34,540	19,869	14,097	574	5,772 R	57.5%	40.8%	58.5%	41.5%
CLERMONT	13,210	6,857	6,245	108	612 R	51.9%	47.3%	52.3%	47.7%
CLINTON	10,588	6,947	3,598	43	3,349 R	65.6%	34.0%	65.9%	34.1%
COLUMBIANA	28,023	16,846	9,774	1,403	7,072 R	60.1%	34.9%	63.3%	36.7%
COSHOCTON	12,051	6,154	5,617	280	537 R	51.1%	46.6%	52.3%	47.7%
CRAWFORD	15,829	7,082	8,467	280	1,385 D	44.7%	53.5%	45.5%	54.5%
CUYAHOGA	231,279	148,857	70,518	11,904	78,339 R	64.4%	30.5%	67.9%	32.1%
DARKE	18,162	9,552	8,459	151	1,093 R	52.6%	46.6%	53.0%	47.0%
DEFIANCE	9,890	5,987	3,723	180	2,264 R	60.5%	37.6%	61.7%	38.3%
DELAWARE	13,004	7,700	5,241	63	2,459 R	59.2%	40.3%	59.5%	40.5%
ERIE	14,039	8,755	4,831	453	3,924 R	62.4%	34.4%	64.4%	35.6%
FAIRFIELD	16,298	7,572	8,610	116	1,038 D	46.5%	52.8%	46.8%	53.2%
FAYETTE	9,301	5,446	3,612	43	1,634 R	58.6%	38.8%	60.2%	41.2%
FRANKLIN	110,064	59,691	48,452	1,921	11,239 R	54.2%	44.0%	55.2%	44.8%
FULTON	8,271	6,111	2,049	111	4,062 R	73.9%	24.8%	74.9%	25.1%
GALLIA	7,994	5,388	2,562	44	2,826 R	67.4%	32.0%	67.8%	32.2%
GEAUGA	4,853	3,722	1,081	50	2,641 R	76.7%	22.3%	77.5%	22.5%
GREENE	12,788	8,600	4,016	172	4,584 R	67.3%	31.4%	68.2%	31.8%
GUERNSEY	16,122	8,764	6,888	470	1,876 R	54.4%	42.7%	56.0%	44.0%
HAMILTON	196,966	112,590	77,598	6,778	34,992 R	57.2%	39.4%	59.2%	40.8%
HANCOCK	16,390	9,746	6,386	258	3,360 R	59.5%	39.0%	60.4%	39.6%
HARDIN	14,003	8,071	5,817	115	2,254 R	57.6%	41.5%	58.1%	41.9%
HARRISON	7,584	5,053	2,473	58	2,580 R	66.6%	32.6%	67.1%	32.9%
HENRY	8,681	5,738	2,829	114	2,909 R	66.1%	32.6%	67.0%	33.0%
HIGHLAND	13,267	7,570	5,654	43	1,916 R	57.1%	42.6%	57.2%	42.8%
HOCKING	8,527	4,335	4,082	110	253 R	50.8%	47.9%	51.5%	48.5%
HOLMES	5,325	2,065	3,211	49	1,146 D	38.8%	60.3%	39.1%	60.9%
HURON	13,915	9,348	4,398	169	4,950 R	67.2%	31.6%	68.0%	32.0%
JACKSON	10,929	5,949	4,878	102	1,071 R	54.4%	44.6%	54.9%	45.1%
JEFFERSON	21,816	13,038	8,064	714	4,974 R	59.8%	37.0%	61.8%	38.2%
KNOX	14,610	8,178	6,361	71	1,817 R	56.0%	43.5%	56.2%	43.8%
LAKE	10,323	7,465	2,711	147	4,754 R	72.3%	26.3%	73.4%	26.6%
LAWRENCE	11,782	7,616	3,955	131	3,661 R	65.1%	33.8%	65.8%	34.2%
LICKING	22,981	11,924	10,679	378	1,245 R	51.9%	46.5%	52.8%	47.2%
LOGAN	13,481	8,521	4,904	56	3,617 R	63.2%	36.4%	63.5%	36.5%
LORAIN	27,529	18,125	8,640	764	9,485 R	65.8%	31.4%	67.7%	32.3%
LUCAS	88,769	52,449	30,452	5,868	21,997 R	59.1%	34.3%	63.3%	36.7%
MADISON	9,185	5,397	3,769	19	1,628 R	58.8%	41.0%	58.9%	41.1%
MAHONING	46,570	29,736	14,941	1,893	14,795 R	63.9%	32.1%	66.6%	33.4%
MARION	19,541	11,320	8,065	156	3,255 R	57.9%	41.3%	58.4%	41.6%
MEDINA	10,122	6,846	3,120	156	3,726 R	67.6%	30.8%	68.7%	31.3%
MEIGS	10,324	6,541	3,606	177	2,935 R	63.4%	34.9%	64.5%	35.5%
MERCER	10,140	5,692	4,404	44	1,288 R	56.1%	43.4%	56.4%	43.6%
MIAMI	21,770	13,122	8,076	572	5,046 R	60.3%	37.1%	61.9%	38.1%
MONROE	6,736	2,825	3,861	50	1,036 D	41.9%	57.3%	42.3%	57.7%
MONTGOMERY	89,975	46,493	38,433	5,049	8,060 R	51.7%	42.7%	54.7%	45.3%
MORGAN	6,422	4,127	2,157	138	1,970 R	64.3%	33.6%	65.7%	34.3%
MORROW	7,378	4,484	2,858	36	1,626 R	60.8%	38.7%	61.1%	38.9%
MUSKINGUM	23,671	13,862	9,437	372	4,425 R	58.6%	39.9%	59.5%	40.5%

PRESIDENT 1924

County	Total Vote	Republican	Democratic	Other	Rep.-Dem. Plurality	% Total Vote Rep.	% Total Vote Dem.	% Major Vote Rep.	% Major Vote Dem.
ADAMS	8,226	4,315	3,762	149	553 R	52.5%	45.7%	53.4%	46.6%
ALLEN	25,437	15,711	7,378	2,348	8,333 R	61.8%	29.0%	68.0%	32.0%
ASHLAND	10,966	5,777	4,377	812	1,400 R	52.7%	39.9%	56.9%	43.1%
ASHTABULA	21,937	14,767	2,135	4,435	12,632 R	69.2%	10.0%	87.4%	12.6%
ATHENS	14,943	8,695	2,669	3,579	6,026 R	58.2%	17.9%	76.5%	23.5%
AUGLAIZE	10,618	5,507	3,952	1,159	1,555 R	51.9%	37.2%	58.2%	41.8%
BELMONT	30,035	16,398	8,074	5,583	8,304 R	54.5%	26.9%	67.0%	33.0%
BROWN	8,399	3,616	4,120	663	504 D	43.1%	49.1%	46.7%	53.3%
BUTLER	34,398	19,349	11,612	3,437	7,737 R	56.3%	33.8%	62.5%	37.5%
CARROLL	6,173	4,369	1,430	374	2,939 R	70.8%	23.2%	75.3%	24.7%
CHAMPAIGN	10,245	6,181	3,575	489	2,606 R	60.3%	34.9%	63.4%	36.6%
CLARK	30,615	20,340	8,415	1,860	11,925 R	66.4%	27.5%	70.7%	29.3%
CLERMONT	12,445	6,867	4,544	1,034	2,323 R	55.2%	36.5%	60.2%	39.8%
CLINTON	8,876	5,954	2,496	426	3,458 R	67.1%	28.1%	70.5%	29.5%
COLUMBIANA	29,272	20,483	4,685	4,104	15,798 R	70.0%	16.0%	81.4%	18.6%
COSHOCTON	11,729	5,837	4,415	1,477	1,422 R	49.8%	37.6%	56.9%	43.1%
CRAWFORD	14,440	5,896	4,384	4,160	1,512 R	40.8%	30.4%	57.4%	42.6%
CUYAHOGA	264,066	130,166	24,000	109,897	106,169 R	49.3%	9.1%	84.4%	15.6%
DARKE	17,320	9,166	7,315	839	1,851 R	52.9%	42.2%	55.6%	44.4%
DEFIANCE	9,213	4,841	3,227	1,145	1,614 R	52.5%	35.0%	60.0%	40.0%
DELAWARE	11,142	6,731	3,537	874	3,194 R	60.4%	31.7%	65.6%	34.4%
ERIE	14,151	7,689	2,968	3,494	4,721 R	54.3%	21.0%	72.1%	27.9%
FAIRFIELD	15,393	8,281	5,890	1,222	2,391 R	53.8%	38.3%	58.4%	41.6%
FAYETTE	7,536	4,542	2,696	298	1,846 R	60.2%	35.8%	62.8%	37.2%
FRANKLIN	107,295	61,891	26,505	18,899	35,386 R	57.7%	24.7%	70.0%	30.0%
FULTON	7,118	4,951	1,333	834	3,618 R	69.6%	18.7%	78.8%	21.2%
GALLIA	7,066	4,325	2,284	457	2,041 R	61.2%	32.3%	65.4%	34.6%
GEAUGA	4,662	3,375	635	652	2,740 R	72.4%	13.6%	84.2%	15.8%
GREENE	11,523	8,410	2,471	642	5,939 R	73.0%	21.4%	77.3%	22.7%
GUERNSEY	15,106	8,997	3,604	2,505	5,393 R	59.6%	23.9%	71.4%	28.6%
HAMILTON	191,029	115,950	34,916	40,163	81,034 R	60.7%	18.3%	76.9%	23.1%
HANCOCK	16,074	9,167	5,111	1,796	4,056 R	57.0%	31.8%	64.2%	35.8%
HARDIN	13,254	7,112	5,523	619	1,589 R	53.7%	41.7%	56.3%	43.7%
HARRISON	7,434	4,904	1,999	531	2,905 R	66.0%	26.9%	71.0%	29.0%
HENRY	8,470	3,855	2,922	1,693	933 R	45.5%	34.5%	56.9%	43.1%
HIGHLAND	11,976	6,845	4,583	548	2,262 R	57.2%	38.3%	59.9%	40.1%
HOCKING	8,098	4,086	2,854	1,158	1,232 R	50.5%	35.2%	58.8%	41.2%
HOLMES	4,768	1,824	2,539	405	715 D	38.3%	53.3%	41.8%	58.2%
HURON	13,425	8,340	2,871	2,214	5,469 R	62.1%	21.4%	74.4%	25.6%
JACKSON	9,727	5,977	2,848	902	3,129 R	61.4%	29.3%	67.7%	32.3%
JEFFERSON	21,963	14,929	3,840	3,194	11,089 R	68.0%	17.5%	79.5%	20.5%
KNOX	13,133	7,519	4,721	893	2,798 R	57.3%	35.9%	61.4%	38.6%
LAKE	10,927	7,727	974	2,226	6,753 R	70.7%	8.9%	88.8%	11.2%
LAWRENCE	10,648	6,798	2,729	1,121	4,069 R	63.8%	25.6%	71.4%	28.6%
LICKING	23,788	13,914	7,428	2,446	6,486 R	58.5%	31.2%	65.2%	34.8%
LOGAN	11,774	7,186	3,176	1,412	4,010 R	61.0%	27.0%	69.3%	30.7%
LORAIN	27,774	17,062	3,965	6,747	13,097 R	61.4%	14.3%	81.1%	18.9%
LUCAS	96,902	53,670	11,948	31,284	41,722 R	55.4%	12.3%	81.8%	18.2%
MADISON	7,792	4,829	2,685	278	2,144 R	62.0%	34.5%	64.3%	35.7%
MAHONING	55,264	37,647	9,335	8,282	28,312 R	68.1%	16.9%	80.1%	19.9%
MARION	16,901	9,161	5,234	2,506	3,927 R	54.2%	31.0%	63.6%	36.4%
MEDINA	9,971	6,756	1,884	1,371	4,912 R	67.8%	18.5%	78.6%	21.4%
MEIGS	8,492	4,864	1,944	1,684	2,920 R	57.3%	22.9%	71.4%	28.6%
MERCER	10,434	4,215	5,135	1,084	920 D	40.4%	49.2%	45.1%	54.9%
MIAMI	18,901	11,851	5,296	1,754	6,555 R	62.7%	28.0%	69.1%	30.9%
MONROE	6,589	2,674	3,742	173	1,068 D	40.6%	56.8%	41.7%	58.3%
MONTGOMERY	81,210	50,845	21,860	8,505	28,985 R	62.6%	26.9%	69.9%	30.1%
MORGAN	5,830	3,553	2,072	205	1,481 R	60.9%	35.5%	63.2%	36.8%
MORROW	6,604	3,790	2,379	435	1,411 R	57.4%	36.0%	61.4%	38.6%
MUSKINGUM	23,697	15,571	6,709	1,417	8,862 R	65.7%	28.3%	69.9%	30.1%

OHIO

PRESIDENT 1920

County	Total Vote	Republican	Democratic	Other	Rep.-Dem. Plurality	Total Vote Rep.	Total Vote Dem.	Major Vote Rep.	Major Vote Dem.
NOBLE	7,106	4,197	2,909		1,288 R	59.1%	40.9%	59.1%	40.9%
OTTAWA	7,299	4,336	2,867	96	1,469 R	59.4%	39.3%	60.2%	39.8%
PAULDING	7,366	4,549	2,739	78	1,810 R	61.8%	37.2%	62.4%	37.6%
PERRY	14,018	7,685	5,917	416	1,768 R	54.8%	42.2%	56.5%	43.5%
PICKAWAY	10,939	5,273	5,645	21	372 D	48.2%	51.6%	48.3%	51.7%
PIKE	5,904	3,075	2,799	30	276 R	52.1%	47.4%	52.3%	47.7%
PORTAGE	13,953	8,231	5,405	317	2,826 R	59.0%	38.7%	60.4%	39.6%
PREBLE	11,231	6,258	4,933	40	1,325 R	55.7%	43.9%	55.9%	44.1%
PUTNAM	9,899	5,157	4,673	69	484 R	52.1%	47.2%	52.5%	47.5%
RICHLAND	20,727	10,940	9,349	438	1,591 R	52.8%	45.1%	53.9%	46.1%
ROSS	16,526	9,330	7,063	133	2,267 R	56.5%	42.7%	56.9%	43.1%
SANDUSKY	14,461	8,933	5,295	233	3,638 R	61.8%	36.6%	62.8%	37.2%
SCIOTO	20,135	11,871	7,682	582	4,189 R	59.0%	38.2%	60.7%	39.3%
SENECA	18,500	10,064	8,175	261	1,889 R	54.4%	44.2%	55.2%	44.8%
SHELBY	11,176	5,452	5,642	82	190 D	48.8%	50.5%	49.1%	50.9%
STARK	59,608	37,483	18,437	3,688	19,046 R	62.9%	30.9%	67.0%	33.0%
SUMMIT	73,363	43,721	27,857	1,785	15,864 R	59.6%	38.0%	61.1%	38.9%
TRUMBULL	25,259	17,343	6,815	1,101	10,528 R	68.7%	27.0%	71.8%	28.2%
TUSCARAWAS	22,919	11,908	10,167	844	1,741 R	52.0%	44.4%	53.9%	46.1%
UNION	9,865	6,544	3,286	35	3,258 R	66.3%	33.3%	66.6%	33.4%
VAN WERT	12,493	7,495	4,899	99	2,596 R	60.0%	39.2%	60.5%	39.5%
VINTON	4,734	2,559	2,124	51	435 R	54.1%	44.9%	54.6%	45.4%
WARREN	11,491	7,464	3,956	71	3,508 R	65.0%	34.4%	65.4%	34.6%
WASHINGTON	15,944	9,279	6,286	379	2,993 R	58.2%	39.4%	59.6%	40.4%
WAYNE	16,890	8,932	7,751	207	1,181 R	52.9%	45.9%	53.5%	46.5%
WILLIAMS	11,336	7,000	4,183	153	2,817 R	61.8%	36.9%	62.6%	37.4%
WOOD	17,272	12,042	4,965	265	7,077 R	69.7%	28.7%	70.8%	29.2%
WYANDOT	9,029	4,560	4,443	26	117 R	50.5%	49.2%	50.6%	49.4%
TOTAL	2,021,653	1,182,022	780,037	59,594	401,985 R	58.5%	38.6%	60.2%	39.8%

PRESIDENT 1924

County	Total Vote	Republican	Democratic	Other	Rep.-Dem. Plurality	Total Vote Rep.	Total Vote Dem.	Major Vote Rep.	Major Vote Dem.
NOBLE	7,048	4,284	2,485	279	1,799 R	60.8%	35.3%	63.3%	36.7%
OTTAWA	7,991	4,137	2,571	1,283	1,566 R	51.8%	32.2%	61.7%	38.3%
PAULDING	6,312	3,648	2,242	422	1,406 R	57.8%	35.5%	61.9%	38.1%
PERRY	13,065	7,592	3,702	1,771	3,890 R	58.1%	28.3%	67.2%	32.8%
PICKAWAY	9,009	4,166	4,539	304	373 D	46.2%	50.4%	47.9%	52.1%
PIKE	5,856	2,569	3,185	102	616 D	43.9%	54.4%	44.6%	55.4%
PORTAGE	13,749	8,583	2,994	2,172	5,589 R	62.4%	21.8%	74.1%	25.9%
PREBLE	10,001	5,676	4,033	292	1,643 R	56.8%	40.3%	58.5%	41.5%
PUTNAM	10,465	4,377	4,795	1,293	418 D	41.8%	45.8%	47.7%	52.3%
RICHLAND	21,645	12,013	6,703	2,929	5,310 R	55.5%	31.0%	64.2%	35.8%
ROSS	15,653	8,431	6,028	1,194	2,403 R	53.9%	38.5%	58.3%	41.7%
SANDUSKY	15,408	9,381	4,388	1,639	4,993 R	60.9%	28.5%	68.1%	31.9%
SCIOTO	19,401	12,189	5,532	1,680	6,657 R	62.8%	28.5%	68.8%	31.2%
SENECA	18,091	9,641	6,290	2,160	3,351 R	53.3%	34.8%	60.5%	39.5%
SHELBY	9,816	4,359	4,840	617	481 D	44.4%	49.3%	47.4%	52.6%
STARK	63,562	40,858	12,544	10,160	28,314 R	64.3%	19.7%	76.5%	23.5%
SUMMIT	82,371	53,774	17,533	11,064	36,241 R	65.3%	21.3%	75.4%	24.6%
TRUMBULL	30,049	22,341	4,007	3,701	18,334 R	74.3%	13.3%	84.8%	15.2%
TUSCARAWAS	23,825	13,573	5,566	4,686	8,007 R	57.0%	23.4%	70.9%	29.1%
UNION	8,378	5,256	2,571	551	2,685 R	62.7%	30.7%	67.2%	32.8%
VAN WERT	11,678	6,206	4,318	1,154	1,888 R	53.1%	37.0%	59.0%	41.0%
VINTON	4,326	2,244	1,838	244	406 R	51.9%	42.5%	55.0%	45.0%
WARREN	9,749	6,729	2,406	614	4,323 R	69.0%	24.7%	73.7%	26.3%
WASHINGTON	15,239	8,704	5,727	808	2,977 R	57.1%	37.6%	60.3%	39.7%
WAYNE	16,594	8,928	6,023	1,643	2,905 R	53.8%	36.3%	59.7%	40.3%
WILLIAMS	10,285	5,802	2,795	1,688	3,007 R	56.4%	27.2%	67.5%	32.5%
WOOD	16,325	10,665	3,291	2,369	7,374 R	65.4%	20.2%	76.4%	23.6%
WYANDOT	7,811	3,973	3,271	567	702 R	50.9%	41.9%	54.8%	45.2%
TOTAL	2,016,296	1,176,130	477,887	362,279	698,243 R	58.3%	23.7%	71.1%	28.9%

OHIO

PRESIDENT 1928

County	Total Vote	Republican	Democratic	Other	Rep.-Dem. Plurality	% Total Rep.	% Total Dem.	% Major Rep.	% Major Dem.
ADAMS	8,685	5,665	3,000	20	2,665 R	65.2	34.5	65.4	34.6
ALLEN	30,337	20,693	9,462	182	11,231 R	68.2	31.2	68.6	31.4
ASHLAND	12,097	8,745	3,256	96	5,489 R	72.3	26.9	72.9	27.1
ASHTABULA	25,118	18,870	5,951	297	12,919 R	75.1	23.7	76.0	24.0
ATHENS	15,855	11,101	4,546	208	6,555 R	70.0	28.7	70.9	29.1
AUGLAIZE	12,798	7,794	4,954	50	2,840 R	60.9	38.7	61.1	38.9
BELMONT	34,468	20,969	12,807	692	8,162 R	60.8	37.2	62.1	37.9
BROWN	9,155	5,681	3,422	52	2,259 R	62.1	37.4	62.4	37.6
BUTLER	45,042	29,124	15,663	255	13,461 R	64.7	34.8	65.0	35.0
CARROLL	6,937	5,572	1,321	44	4,251 R	80.3	19.0	80.8	19.2
CHAMPAIGN	11,006	7,651	3,296	59	4,355 R	69.5	29.9	69.9	30.1
CLARK	37,183	26,666	10,316	201	16,350 R	71.7	27.7	72.1	27.9
CLERMONT	13,983	9,732	4,194	57	5,538 R	69.6	30.0	69.9	30.1
CLINTON	9,797	7,150	2,603	44	4,547 R	73.0	26.6	73.3	26.7
COLUMBIANA	34,158	26,405	7,461	292	18,944 R	77.3	21.8	78.0	22.0
COSHOCTON	12,970	9,154	3,745	71	5,409 R	70.6	28.9	71.0	29.0
CRAWFORD	16,793	11,235	5,472	86	5,763 R	66.9	32.6	67.2	32.8
CUYAHOGA	364,108	194,508	166,188	3,412	28,320 R	53.4	45.6	53.9	46.1
DARKE	17,734	11,765	5,822	147	5,943 R	66.3	32.8	66.9	33.1
DEFIANCE	9,776	6,289	3,487		2,802 R	64.3	35.7	64.3	35.7
DELAWARE	11,880	8,049	3,720	111	4,329 R	67.8	31.3	68.4	31.6
ERIE	17,996	10,380	7,570	46	2,810 R	57.7	42.1	57.8	42.2
FAIRFIELD	17,788	12,072	5,619	97	6,453 R	67.9	31.6	68.2	31.8
FAYETTE	8,050	5,251	2,752	47	2,499 R	65.2	34.2	65.6	34.4
FRANKLIN	139,712	92,019	47,084	609	44,935 R	65.9	33.7	66.2	33.8
FULTON	8,253	6,416	1,788	49	4,628 R	77.7	21.7	78.2	21.8
GALLIA	7,509	5,513	1,916	80	3,597 R	73.4	25.5	74.2	25.8
GEAUGA	5,378	4,161	1,180	37	2,981 R	77.4	21.9	77.9	22.1
GREENE	13,528	10,030	3,385	113	6,645 R	74.1	25.0	74.8	25.2
GUERNSEY	15,080	11,174	3,709	197	7,465 R	74.1	24.6	75.1	24.9
HAMILTON	258,692	147,534	110,151	1,007	37,383 R	57.0	42.6	57.3	42.7
HANCOCK	17,410	13,151	4,158	101	8,993 R	75.5	23.9	76.0	24.0
HARDIN	13,517	8,137	5,306	74	2,831 R	60.2	39.3	60.5	39.5
HARRISON	7,676	6,095	1,516	65	4,579 R	79.4	19.7	80.1	19.9
HENRY	9,057	5,370	3,647	40	1,723 R	59.3	40.3	59.6	40.4
HIGHLAND	12,221	8,325	3,836	60	4,489 R	68.1	31.4	68.5	31.5
HOCKING	8,093	5,497	2,502	94	2,995 R	67.9	30.9	68.7	31.3
HOLMES	5,127	3,457	1,631	39	1,826 R	67.4	31.8	67.9	32.1
HURON	15,930	10,702	5,157	71	5,545 R	67.2	32.4	67.5	32.5
JACKSON	9,985	7,129	2,775	81	4,354 R	71.4	27.8	72.0	28.0
JEFFERSON	28,161	19,175	8,711	275	10,464 R	68.1	30.9	68.8	31.2
KNOX	13,724	10,028	3,601	95	6,427 R	73.1	26.2	73.6	26.4
LAKE	15,926	11,823	4,024	79	7,799 R	74.2	25.3	74.6	25.4
LAWRENCE	13,885	10,346	3,470	69	6,876 R	74.5	25.0	74.9	25.1
LICKING	26,517	19,130	7,244	143	11,886 R	72.1	27.3	72.5	27.5
LOGAN	12,531	9,602	2,858	71	6,744 R	76.6	22.8	77.1	22.9
LORAIN	38,205	24,386	13,607	212	10,779 R	63.8	35.6	64.2	35.8
LUCAS	124,081	78,435	44,977	669	33,458 R	63.2	36.2	63.6	36.4
MADISON	8,105	5,522	2,527	56	2,995 R	68.1	31.2	68.6	31.4
MAHONING	75,748	48,341	26,928	479	21,413 R	63.8	35.5	64.2	35.8
MARION	19,060	13,398	5,468	194	7,930 R	70.3	28.7	71.0	29.0
MEDINA	11,950	9,510	2,357	83	7,153 R	79.6	19.7	80.1	19.9
MEIGS	9,314	6,580	2,661	73	3,919 R	70.6	28.6	71.2	28.8
MERCER	11,326	5,129	6,155	42	1,026 D	45.3	54.3	45.5	54.5
MIAMI	22,066	16,063	5,867	136	10,196 R	72.8	26.6	73.2	26.8
MONROE	7,059	4,287	2,729	43	1,558 R	60.7	38.7	61.1	38.9
MONTGOMERY	110,461	71,279	38,517	665	32,762 R	64.5	34.9	64.9	35.1
MORGAN	5,805	4,359	1,397	49	2,962 R	75.1	24.1	75.7	24.3
MORROW	6,699	4,801	1,818	80	2,983 R	71.7	27.1	72.5	27.5
MUSKINGUM	28,798	22,120	6,507	171	15,613 R	76.8	22.6	77.3	22.7

PRESIDENT 1932

County	% Total Rep.	% Total Dem.	% Major Rep.	% Major Dem.	Total Vote	Republican	Democratic	Other	Rep.-Dem. Plurality
ADAMS	44.4	54.1	45.1	54.9	10,931	4,857	5,909	165	1,052 D
ALLEN	46.0	52.2	46.8	53.2	31,930	14,678	16,676	576	1,998 D
ASHLAND	46.5	51.8	47.3	52.7	14,086	6,549	7,302	235	753 D
ASHTABULA	55.3	40.3	57.9	42.1	28,282	15,644	11,386	1,252	4,258 R
ATHENS	51.2	46.1	52.6	47.4	19,343	9,897	8,915	531	982 R
AUGLAIZE	38.1	60.8	38.5	61.5	13,210	5,039	8,036	135	2,997 D
BELMONT	40.7	55.0	42.6	57.4	36,885	15,029	20,291	1,565	5,262 D
BROWN	36.9	61.9	37.3	62.7	10,662	3,930	6,601	131	2,671 D
BUTLER	44.7	51.2	46.6	53.4	44,008	19,673	22,516	1,819	2,843 D
CARROLL	59.7	37.3	61.6	38.4	7,510	4,487	2,802	221	1,685 R
CHAMPAIGN	48.7	50.3	49.2	50.8	12,712	6,191	6,396	125	205 D
CLARK	51.5	46.9	52.4	47.6	36,952	19,028	17,314	610	1,714 D
CLERMONT	46.1	52.0	47.0	53.0	16,667	7,684	8,662	321	978 D
CLINTON	52.4	46.2	53.1	46.9	11,368	5,953	5,252	163	701 R
COLUMBIANA	55.6	40.3	58.0	42.0	35,430	19,707	14,284	1,439	5,423 R
COSHOCTON	41.5	56.3	42.5	57.5	14,555	6,040	8,188	327	2,148 D
CRAWFORD	37.3	60.5	38.2	61.8	17,517	6,538	10,593	386	4,055 D
CUYAHOGA	44.9	50.1	47.2	52.8	370,578	166,337	185,731	18,510	19,394 D
DARKE	42.1	56.5	42.7	57.3	19,689	8,284	11,122	283	2,838 D
DEFIANCE	36.5	61.7	37.2	62.8	10,595	3,871	6,532	192	2,661 D
DELAWARE	51.4	46.6	52.4	47.6	13,300	6,833	6,196	271	637 R
ERIE	40.7	57.1	41.6	58.4	18,843	7,666	10,765	412	3,099 D
FAIRFIELD	43.0	55.7	43.6	56.4	18,704	8,050	10,410	244	2,360 D
FAYETTE	44.7	54.2	45.2	54.8	9,508	4,254	5,157	97	903 D
FRANKLIN	52.2	45.0	53.7	46.3	130,160	67,957	58,539	3,664	9,418 R
FULTON	48.0	50.0	49.0	51.0	9,344	4,487	4,673	184	186 D
GALLIA	56.4	41.9	57.4	42.6	10,002	5,646	4,190	166	1,456 R
GEAUGA	59.4	37.1	61.6	38.4	6,454	3,836	2,396	222	1,440 R
GREENE	54.6	42.6	56.2	43.8	15,481	8,455	6,600	426	1,855 R
GUERNSEY	48.3	49.9	49.2	50.8	18,106	8,750	9,026	330	276 D
HAMILTON	47.7	49.4	49.1	50.9	249,076	118,804	123,109	7,163	4,305 D
HANCOCK	48.6	49.2	49.7	50.3	19,061	9,260	9,370	431	110 D
HARDIN	44.9	54.2	45.3	54.7	16,084	7,215	8,717	152	1,502 D
HARRISON	56.4	41.6	57.5	42.5	8,439	4,759	3,512	168	1,247 R
HENRY	30.1	68.6	30.5	69.5	10,188	3,067	6,987	134	3,920 D
HIGHLAND	49.0	50.1	49.4	50.6	14,137	6,924	7,079	134	155 D
HOCKING	40.8	56.6	41.9	58.1	9,348	3,811	5,287	250	1,476 D
HOLMES	31.6	66.3	32.3	67.7	6,180	1,953	4,096	131	2,143 D
HURON	49.2	49.7	49.7	50.3	17,701	8,702	8,795	204	93 D
JACKSON	55.1	44.0	55.6	44.4	12,590	6,932	5,543	115	1,389 R
JEFFERSON	44.9	50.9	46.9	53.1	31,544	14,179	16,066	1,299	1,887 D
KNOX	53.4	45.3	54.1	45.9	15,486	8,272	7,008	206	1,264 R
LAKE	61.4	35.4	63.4	36.6	19,196	11,792	6,801	603	4,991 R
LAWRENCE	50.8	48.2	51.3	48.7	16,915	8,598	8,157	160	441 R
LICKING	48.0	50.0	49.0	51.0	27,815	13,355	13,904	556	549 D
LOGAN	52.0	46.5	52.8	47.2	14,352	7,469	6,678	205	791 R
LORAIN	51.0	45.8	52.7	47.3	40,971	20,897	18,753	1,321	2,144 R
LUCAS	40.8	55.4	42.4	57.6	117,060	47,796	64,902	4,362	17,106 D
MADISON	49.1	50.1	49.5	50.5	9,426	4,631	4,722	73	91 D
MAHONING	52.3	43.7	54.5	45.5	75,861	39,713	33,139	3,009	6,574 R
MARION	44.1	53.3	45.3	54.7	19,429	8,569	10,354	506	1,785 D
MEDINA	55.1	41.5	57.0	43.0	14,074	7,753	5,841	480	1,912 R
MEIGS	53.0	45.4	53.9	46.1	11,244	5,964	5,105	175	859 R
MERCER	27.8	70.9	28.1	71.9	11,929	3,314	8,462	153	5,148 D
MIAMI	52.0	45.6	53.2	46.8	23,402	12,157	10,677	568	1,480 R
MONROE	34.0	64.6	34.5	65.5	8,146	2,767	5,263	116	2,496 D
MONTGOMERY	46.6	48.5	49.0	51.0	105,717	49,267	51,270	5,180	2,003 D
MORGAN	54.3	42.7	56.0	44.0	7,282	3,957	3,107	218	850 R
MORROW	48.8	49.3	49.8	50.2	7,806	3,811	3,849	146	38 D
MUSKINGUM	54.0	44.2	55.0	45.0	30,285	16,366	13,378	541	2,988 R

OHIO

PRESIDENT 1928

County	Total Vote	Republican	Democratic	Other	Rep.-Dem. Plurality	Total Vote Rep.	Total Vote Dem.	Major Vote Rep.	Major Vote Dem.
NOBLE	6,715	4,462	2,190	63	2,272 R	66.5%	32.6%	67.1%	32.9%
OTTAWA	9,229	5,772	3,435	22	2,337 R	62.5%	37.2%	62.7%	37.3%
PAULDING	6,624	4,093	2,473	58	1,620 R	61.8%	37.3%	62.3%	37.7%
PERRY	13,279	8,551	4,653	75	3,898 R	64.4%	35.0%	64.8%	35.2%
PICKAWAY	9,806	5,871	3,894	41	1,977 R	59.9%	39.7%	60.1%	39.9%
PIKE	5,955	3,246	2,709		537 R	54.5%	45.5%	54.5%	45.5%
PORTAGE	16,948	12,086	4,756	106	7,330 R	71.3%	28.1%	71.8%	28.2%
PREBLE	10,263	6,693	3,513	57	3,180 R	65.2%	34.2%	65.6%	34.4%
PUTNAM	11,254	5,537	5,667	50	130 D	49.2%	50.4%	49.4%	50.6%
RICHLAND	25,909	18,468	7,295	146	11,173 R	71.3%	28.2%	71.7%	28.3%
ROSS	17,308	11,179	6,062	67	5,117 R	64.6%	35.0%	64.8%	35.2%
SANDUSKY	18,119	12,200	5,834	85	6,366 R	67.3%	32.2%	67.6%	32.4%
SCIOTO	28,530	20,997	7,425	108	13,572 R	73.6%	26.0%	73.9%	26.1%
SENECA	21,587	13,369	8,136	82	5,233 R	61.9%	37.7%	62.2%	37.8%
SHELBY	11,460	5,975	5,448	37	527 R	52.1%	47.5%	52.3%	47.7%
STARK	84,075	59,564	23,840	671	35,724 R	70.8%	28.4%	71.4%	28.6%
SUMMIT	110,785	78,504	31,506	775	46,998 R	70.9%	28.4%	71.4%	28.6%
TRUMBULL	39,194	29,710	9,110	374	20,600 R	75.8%	23.2%	76.5%	23.5%
TUSCARAWAS	27,568	20,494	6,805	269	13,689 R	74.3%	24.7%	75.1%	24.9%
UNION	8,331	5,876	2,386	69	3,490 R	70.5%	28.6%	71.1%	28.9%
VAN WERT	12,696	7,540	5,089	67	2,451 R	59.4%	40.1%	59.7%	40.3%
VINTON	4,408	2,810	1,559	39	1,251 R	63.7%	35.4%	64.3%	35.7%
WARREN	11,219	8,708	2,455	56	6,253 R	77.6%	21.9%	78.0%	22.0%
WASHINGTON	17,447	12,767	4,582	98	8,185 R	73.2%	26.3%	73.6%	26.4%
WAYNE	19,024	14,192	4,825	7	9,367 R	74.6%	25.4%	74.6%	25.4%
WILLIAMS	11,332	8,138	3,136	58	5,002 R	71.8%	27.7%	72.2%	27.8%
WOOD	20,126	15,409	4,612	105	10,797 R	76.6%	22.9%	77.0%	23.0%
WYANDOT	8,852	5,790	3,024	38	2,766 R	65.4%	34.2%	65.7%	34.3%
TOTAL	2,508,346	1,627,546	864,210	16,590	763,336 R	64.9%	34.5%	65.3%	34.7%

PRESIDENT 1932

County	Total Vote	Republican	Democratic	Other	Rep.-Dem. Plurality	Total Vote Rep.	Total Vote Dem.	Major Vote Rep.	Major Vote Dem.
NOBLE	8,020	3,950	3,966	104	16 D	49.3%	49.5%	49.9%	50.1%
OTTAWA	10,532	3,600	6,817	115	3,217 D	34.2%	64.7%	34.6%	65.4%
PAULDING	7,485	3,201	4,165	119	964 D	42.8%	55.6%	43.5%	56.5%
PERRY	14,643	7,225	6,714	704	511 R	49.3%	45.9%	51.8%	48.2%
PICKAWAY	10,907	4,395	6,414	98	2,019 D	40.3%	58.8%	40.7%	59.3%
PIKE	7,908	2,743	5,107	58	2,364 D	34.7%	64.6%	34.9%	65.1%
PORTAGE	19,981	9,586	9,662	733	76 D	48.0%	48.4%	49.8%	50.2%
PREBLE	11,625	5,205	6,221	199	1,016 D	44.8%	53.5%	45.6%	54.4%
PUTNAM	11,879	3,646	8,078	155	4,432 D	30.7%	68.0%	31.1%	68.9%
RICHLAND	28,249	12,531	15,225	493	2,694 D	44.4%	53.9%	45.1%	54.9%
ROSS	20,227	9,575	10,542	110	967 D	47.3%	52.1%	47.6%	52.4%
SANDUSKY	19,490	8,915	10,299	276	1,384 D	45.7%	52.8%	46.4%	53.6%
SCIOTO	33,590	17,225	15,817	548	1,408 R	51.3%	47.1%	52.1%	47.9%
SENECA	21,284	9,007	11,894	383	2,887 D	42.3%	55.9%	43.1%	56.9%
SHELBY	12,741	4,281	8,299	161	4,018 D	33.6%	65.1%	34.0%	66.0%
STARK	79,654	40,672	35,757	3,225	4,915 R	51.1%	44.9%	53.2%	46.8%
SUMMIT	105,911	47,691	53,965	4,255	6,274 D	45.0%	51.0%	46.9%	53.1%
TRUMBULL	42,913	23,029	17,871	2,013	5,158 R	53.7%	41.6%	56.3%	43.7%
TUSCARAWAS	29,905	12,369	16,648	888	4,279 D	41.4%	55.7%	42.6%	57.4%
UNION	9,969	4,912	4,943	114	31 D	49.3%	49.6%	49.8%	50.2%
VAN WERT	14,078	5,918	7,977	183	2,059 D	42.0%	56.7%	42.6%	57.4%
VINTON	5,419	2,715	2,655	49	60 R	50.1%	49.0%	50.6%	49.4%
WARREN	13,165	7,421	5,547	197	1,874 R	56.4%	42.1%	57.2%	42.8%
WASHINGTON	19,876	9,352	10,208	316	856 D	47.1%	51.4%	47.8%	52.2%
WAYNE	22,097	10,787	10,870	440	83 D	48.8%	49.2%	49.8%	50.2%
WILLIAMS	12,597	5,459	6,860	278	1,401 D	43.3%	54.5%	44.3%	55.7%
WOOD	22,318	10,566	11,332	420	766 D	47.3%	50.8%	48.3%	51.7%
WYANDOT	9,509	3,939	5,451	119	1,512 D	41.4%	57.3%	41.9%	58.1%
TOTAL	2,609,728	1,227,319	1,301,695	80,714	74,376 D	47.0%	49.9%	48.5%	51.5%

OHIO

PRESIDENT 1936

County	Total Vote	Republican	Democratic	Other	Rep.-Dem. Plurality	TV Rep. %	TV Dem. %	MV Rep. %	MV Dem. %
ADAMS	11,770	5,910	5,832	28	78 R	50.2	49.5	50.3	49.7
ALLEN	33,592	15,079	16,500	2,013	1,421 D	44.9	49.1	47.8	52.2
ASHLAND	15,352	6,154	8,818	380	2,664 D	40.1	57.4	41.1	58.9
ASHTABULA	30,010	14,025	14,468	1,517	443 D	46.7	48.2	49.2	50.8
ATHENS	22,922	9,509	13,205	208	3,696 D	41.5	57.6	41.9	58.1
AUGLAIZE	14,305	5,526	7,835	944	2,309 D	38.6	54.8	41.4	58.6
BELMONT	45,481	14,511	30,545	425	16,034 D	31.9	67.2	32.2	67.8
BROWN	11,088	4,511	6,316	261	1,805 D	40.7	57.0	41.7	58.3
BUTLER	49,832	17,842	29,892	2,098	12,050 D	35.8	60.0	37.4	62.6
CARROLL	8,337	4,440	3,801	96	639 R	53.3	45.6	53.9	46.1
CHAMPAIGN	13,719	6,872	6,485	362	387 R	50.1	47.3	51.4	48.6
CLARK	42,540	15,483	26,138	919	10,655 D	36.4	61.4	37.2	62.8
CLERMONT	17,270	7,608	9,204	458	1,596 D	44.1	53.3	45.3	54.7
CLINTON	12,127	6,265	5,785	77	480 R	51.7	47.7	52.0	48.0
COLUMBIANA	40,198	16,986	22,664	548	5,678 D	42.3	56.4	42.8	57.2
COSHOCTON	15,866	6,449	9,316	101	2,867 D	40.6	58.7	40.9	59.1
CRAWFORD	18,419	6,638	10,955	826	4,317 D	36.0	59.5	37.7	62.3
CUYAHOGA	475,418	128,947	311,117	35,354	182,170 D	27.1	65.4	29.3	70.7
DARKE	20,283	8,375	11,114	794	2,739 D	41.3	54.8	43.0	57.0
DEFIANCE	11,670	5,000	5,608	1,062	608 D	42.8	48.1	47.1	52.9
DELAWARE	14,709	7,364	7,045	300	319 R	50.1	47.9	51.1	48.9
ERIE	18,720	6,869	10,376	1,475	3,507 D	36.7	55.4	39.8	60.2
FAIRFIELD	20,830	8,062	12,322	446	4,260 D	38.7	59.2	39.6	60.4
FAYETTE	10,689	4,841	5,807	41	966 D	45.3	54.3	45.5	54.5
FRANKLIN	158,047	63,830	90,746	3,471	26,916 D	40.4	57.4	41.3	58.7
FULTON	10,224	6,152	3,582	490	2,570 R	60.2	35.0	63.2	36.8
GALLIA	11,275	6,700	4,548	27	2,152 R	59.4	40.3	59.6	40.4
GEAUGA	7,314	3,620	3,400	294	220 R	49.5	46.5	51.6	48.4
GREENE	16,712	7,449	8,946	317	1,497 D	44.6	53.5	45.4	54.6
GUERNSEY	20,070	8,532	11,404	134	2,872 D	42.5	56.8	42.8	57.2
HAMILTON	280,436	108,506	153,117	18,813	44,611 D	38.7	54.6	41.5	58.5
HANCOCK	20,784	9,816	9,929	1,039	113 D	47.2	47.8	49.7	50.3
HARDIN	16,283	7,631	8,441	215	810 D	46.9	51.8	47.5	52.5
HARRISON	10,045	4,779	5,231	35	452 D	47.6	52.1	47.7	52.3
HENRY	10,668	4,108	5,472	1,088	1,364 D	38.5	51.3	42.9	57.1
HIGHLAND	15,451	7,392	8,011	48	619 D	47.8	51.8	48.0	52.0
HOCKING	10,678	3,960	6,580	138	2,620 D	37.1	61.6	37.6	62.4
HOLMES	6,432	2,247	4,097	88	1,850 D	34.9	63.7	35.4	64.6
HURON	18,022	8,318	8,550	1,204	182 D	46.2	47.4	49.5	50.5
JACKSON	13,694	6,853	6,802	39	51 R	50.0	49.7	50.2	49.8
JEFFERSON	40,935	13,044	27,472	419	14,428 D	31.9	67.1	32.2	67.8
KNOX	16,641	7,956	8,315	370	359 D	47.8	50.0	48.9	51.1
LAKE	21,707	9,386	11,213	1,108	1,827 D	43.2	51.7	45.5	54.5
LAWRENCE	20,066	8,498	11,471	97	2,973 D	42.3	57.2	42.6	57.4
LICKING	30,372	11,958	17,785	629	5,827 D	39.4	58.6	40.2	59.8
LOGAN	15,905	8,363	7,353	189	1,010 R	52.6	46.2	53.2	46.8
LORAIN	42,656	15,906	24,393	2,357	8,487 D	37.3	57.2	39.5	60.5
LUCAS	132,979	45,893	74,195	12,891	28,302 D	34.5	55.8	38.2	61.8
MADISON	10,130	4,843	5,184	103	341 D	47.8	51.2	48.3	51.7
MAHONING	90,858	24,825	64,886	1,147	40,061 D	27.3	71.4	27.7	72.3
MARION	21,427	9,070	11,881	476	2,811 D	42.3	55.4	43.3	56.7
MEDINA	15,058	7,283	7,400	375	117 D	48.4	49.1	48.5	50.4
MEIGS	12,549	6,464	6,085		379 R	51.5	48.5	51.5	48.5
MERCER	13,204	3,602	7,217	2,385	3,615 D	27.3	54.7	33.3	66.7
MIAMI	25,286	11,343	12,754	1,189	1,411 D	44.9	50.4	47.1	52.9
MONROE	8,709	3,211	5,368	130	2,157 D	36.9	61.6	37.4	62.6
MONTGOMERY	127,778	44,742	76,430	6,606	31,688 D	35.0	59.8	36.9	63.1
MORGAN	7,801	4,630	3,093	78	1,537 R	59.4	39.6	60.0	40.0
MORROW	8,252	4,086	3,947	219	139 R	49.5	47.8	50.9	49.1
MUSKINGUM	32,573	15,454	16,265	854	811 D	47.4	49.9	48.7	51.3

PRESIDENT 1940

County	Total Vote	Republican	Democratic	Other	Rep.-Dem. Plurality	TV Rep. %	TV Dem. %	MV Rep. %	MV Dem. %
ADAMS	11,187	6,180	5,007		1,173 R	55.2	44.8	55.2	44.8
ALLEN	35,144	20,675	14,469		6,206 R	58.8	41.2	58.8	41.2
ASHLAND	16,459	8,624	7,835		789 R	52.4	47.6	52.4	47.6
ASHTABULA	32,945	18,491	14,454		4,037 R	56.1	43.9	56.1	43.9
ATHENS	22,662	11,213	11,449		236 D	49.5	50.5	49.5	50.5
AUGLAIZE	14,657	8,953	5,704		3,249 R	61.1	38.9	61.1	38.9
BELMONT	46,323	17,705	28,618		10,913 D	38.2	61.8	38.2	61.8
BROWN	11,121	5,477	5,644		167 D	49.2	50.8	49.2	50.8
BUTLER	54,201	23,380	30,821		7,441 D	43.1	56.9	43.1	56.9
CARROLL	8,749	5,160	3,589		1,571 R	59.0	41.0	59.0	41.0
CHAMPAIGN	13,770	7,841	5,929		1,912 R	56.9	43.1	56.9	43.1
CLARK	46,569	20,681	25,888		5,207 D	44.4	55.6	44.4	55.6
CLERMONT	18,309	9,367	8,942		425 R	51.2	48.8	51.2	48.8
CLINTON	11,991	7,027	4,964		2,063 R	58.6	41.4	58.6	41.4
COLUMBIANA	43,570	21,221	22,349		1,128 D	48.7	51.3	48.7	51.3
COSHOCTON	16,512	8,623	7,889		734 R	52.2	47.8	52.2	47.8
CRAWFORD	19,302	10,336	8,966		1,370 R	53.5	46.5	53.5	46.5
CUYAHOGA	556,188	209,070	347,118		138,048 D	37.6	62.4	37.6	62.4
DARKE	20,798	11,147	9,651		1,496 R	53.6	46.4	53.6	46.4
DEFIANCE	12,323	8,010	4,313		3,697 R	65.0	35.0	65.0	35.0
DELAWARE	15,236	9,570	5,666		3,904 R	62.8	37.2	62.8	37.2
ERIE	20,521	11,267	9,254		2,013 R	54.9	45.1	54.9	45.1
FAIRFIELD	22,111	10,813	11,298		485 D	48.9	51.1	48.9	51.1
FAYETTE	11,233	5,984	5,249		735 R	53.3	46.7	53.3	46.7
FRANKLIN	189,134	92,533	96,601		4,068 D	48.9	51.1	48.9	51.1
FULTON	11,183	8,653	2,530		6,123 R	77.4	22.6	77.4	22.6
GALLIA	11,228	7,285	3,943		3,342 R	64.9	35.1	64.9	35.1
GEAUGA	8,689	5,371	3,318		2,053 R	61.8	38.2	61.8	38.2
GREENE	18,154	9,273	8,881		392 R	51.1	48.9	51.1	48.9
GUERNSEY	18,835	10,125	8,710		1,415 R	53.8	46.2	53.8	46.2
HAMILTON	303,640	154,733	148,907		5,826 R	51.0	49.0	51.0	49.0
HANCOCK	21,929	14,174	7,755		6,419 R	64.6	35.4	64.6	35.4
HARDIN	15,739	9,192	6,547		2,645 R	58.4	41.6	58.4	41.6
HARRISON	10,288	5,729	4,559		1,170 R	55.7	44.3	55.7	44.3
HENRY	11,292	7,784	3,508		4,276 R	68.9	31.1	68.9	31.1
HIGHLAND	15,451	8,530	6,921		1,609 R	55.2	44.8	55.2	44.8
HOCKING	11,024	5,336	5,688		352 D	48.4	51.6	48.9	51.1
HOLMES	6,550	3,201	3,349		148 D	48.9	51.1	48.9	51.1
HURON	18,499	11,758	6,741		5,017 R	63.6	36.4	63.6	36.4
JACKSON	13,933	7,551	6,382		1,169 R	54.2	45.8	54.2	45.8
JEFFERSON	46,092	16,578	29,514		12,936 D	36.0	64.0	36.0	64.0
KNOX	17,384	10,303	7,081		3,222 R	59.3	40.7	59.3	40.7
LAKE	25,872	13,464	12,408		1,056 R	52.0	48.0	52.0	48.0
LAWRENCE	20,935	10,274	10,661		387 D	49.1	50.9	49.1	50.9
LICKING	32,667	16,288	16,379		91 D	49.9	50.1	49.9	50.1
LOGAN	16,212	9,861	6,351		3,510 R	60.8	39.2	60.8	39.2
LORAIN	49,253	23,422	25,831		2,409 D	47.6	52.4	47.6	52.4
LUCAS	154,353	76,405	77,948		1,543 D	49.5	50.5	49.5	50.5
MADISON	10,294	5,904	4,390		1,514 R	57.4	42.6	57.4	42.6
MAHONING	113,937	37,496	76,441		38,945 D	32.9	67.1	32.9	67.1
MARION	22,279	11,817	10,462		1,355 R	53.0	47.0	53.0	47.0
MEDINA	16,838	10,116	6,722		3,394 R	60.1	39.9	60.1	39.9
MEIGS	12,222	7,239	4,983		2,256 R	59.2	40.8	59.2	40.8
MERCER	13,019	7,905	5,114		2,791 R	60.7	39.3	60.7	39.3
MIAMI	26,524	14,725	11,799		2,926 R	55.5	44.5	55.5	44.5
MONROE	8,672	4,534	4,138		396 R	52.3	47.7	52.3	47.7
MONTGOMERY	143,950	57,866	86,084		28,218 D	40.2	59.8	40.2	59.8
MORGAN	7,603	4,966	2,637		2,329 R	65.3	34.7	65.3	34.7
MORROW	8,672	5,457	3,215		2,242 R	62.9	37.1	62.9	37.1
MUSKINGUM	35,148	19,395	15,753		3,642 R	55.2	44.8	55.2	44.8

OHIO

PRESIDENT 1936

County	Total Vote	Republican	Democratic	Other	Rep.-Dem. Plurality	Percentage Total Vote Rep.	Dem.	Major Vote Rep.	Dem.
NOBLE	8,319	4,384	3,865	70	519 R	52.7%	46.5%	53.1%	46.9%
OTTAWA	11,139	4,006	6,335	798	2,329 D	36.0%	56.9%	38.7%	51.3%
PAULDING	8,251	3,853	4,179	219	326 D	46.7%	50.6%	48.0%	52.0%
PERRY	15,785	6,826	8,508	451	1,582 D	43.2%	53.9%	44.5%	55.5%
PICKAWAY	12,763	4,920	7,813	30	2,893 D	38.5%	61.2%	38.6%	61.4%
PIKE	8,244	2,953	5,287	4	2,334 D	35.8%	64.1%	35.8%	64.2%
PORTAGE	22,463	8,035	13,798	630	5,763 D	35.8%	61.4%	36.8%	63.2%
PREBLE	12,290	5,593	6,366	331	773 D	45.5%	51.8%	46.8%	53.2%
PUTNAM	12,517	4,151	5,786	2,580	1,635 D	33.2%	46.2%	41.8%	58.2%
RICHLAND	32,758	11,220	20,070	1,468	8,350 D	34.3%	61.3%	35.9%	64.1%
ROSS	22,441	9,817	12,503	121	2,586 D	43.7%	55.7%	44.0%	56.0%
SANDUSKY	20,265	8,692	9,171	2,402	479 D	42.9%	45.3%	48.7%	51.3%
SCIOTO	40,380	17,860	22,243	277	4,383 D	44.2%	55.1%	44.5%	55.5%
SENECA	22,259	9,953	8,982	3,324	971 R	44.7%	40.4%	52.6%	47.4%
SHELBY	13,307	4,482	7,110	1,715	2,628 D	33.7%	53.4%	38.7%	61.3%
STARK	96,612	34,693	57,931	3,988	23,238 D	35.9%	60.0%	37.5%	62.5%
SUMMIT	133,696	38,991	91,836	2,869	52,845 D	29.2%	68.7%	29.8%	70.2%
TRUMBULL	50,329	16,887	32,384	1,058	15,497 D	33.6%	64.3%	34.3%	65.7%
TUSCARAWAS	32,965	10,317	21,991	657	11,574 D	31.3%	66.7%	31.9%	68.1%
UNION	10,950	5,673	5,157	120	516 R	51.8%	47.1%	52.4%	47.6%
VAN WERT	14,733	6,275	7,744	714	1,469 D	42.6%	52.6%	44.8%	55.2%
VINTON	5,974	3,056	2,902	16	154 R	51.2%	48.6%	51.3%	48.7%
WARREN	14,707	7,359	7,209	139	150 R	50.0%	49.0%	50.5%	49.5%
WASHINGTON	21,354	10,826	10,203	325	623 R	50.7%	47.8%	51.5%	48.5%
WAYNE	23,423	10,331	12,666	426	2,335 D	44.1%	54.1%	44.9%	55.1%
WILLIAMS	13,302	7,050	5,628	624	1,422 R	53.0%	42.3%	55.6%	44.4%
WOOD	24,778	11,716	11,255	1,807	461 R	47.3%	45.4%	51.0%	49.0%
WYANDOT	10,286	4,260	5,597	429	1,337 D	41.4%	54.4%	43.2%	56.8%
TOTAL	3,012,660	1,127,855	1,747,140	137,665	619,285 D	37.4%	58.0%	39.2%	60.8%

PRESIDENT 1940

County	Total Vote	Republican	Democratic	Other	Rep.-Dem. Plurality	Percentage Total Vote Rep.	Dem.	Major Vote Rep.	Dem.
NOBLE	7,959	4,922	3,037		1,885 R	61.8%	38.2%	61.8%	38.2%
OTTAWA	12,428	6,872	5,556		1,316 R	55.3%	44.7%	55.3%	44.7%
PAULDING	8,104	4,949	3,155		1,794 R	61.1%	38.9%	61.1%	38.9%
PERRY	15,609	8,656	6,953		1,703 R	55.5%	44.5%	55.5%	44.5%
PICKAWAY	12,869	5,974	6,895		921 D	46.4%	53.6%	46.4%	53.6%
PIKE	8,127	3,165	4,962		1,797 D	38.9%	61.1%	38.9%	61.1%
PORTAGE	24,464	11,777	12,687		910 D	48.1%	51.9%	48.1%	51.9%
PREBLE	12,246	6,511	5,735		776 R	53.2%	46.8%	53.2%	46.8%
PUTNAM	12,601	8,946	3,655		5,291 R	71.0%	29.0%	71.0%	29.0%
RICHLAND	35,802	17,157	18,645		1,488 D	47.9%	52.1%	47.9%	52.1%
ROSS	24,227	11,780	12,447		667 D	48.6%	51.4%	48.6%	51.4%
SANDUSKY	21,170	14,054	7,116		6,938 R	66.4%	33.6%	66.4%	33.6%
SCIOTO	41,388	19,462	21,926		2,464 D	47.0%	53.0%	47.0%	53.0%
SENECA	23,736	16,272	7,464		8,808 R	68.6%	31.4%	68.6%	31.4%
SHELBY	13,235	7,130	6,105		1,025 R	53.9%	46.1%	53.9%	46.1%
STARK	105,880	46,384	59,496		13,112 D	43.8%	56.2%	43.8%	56.2%
SUMMIT	152,960	63,405	89,555		26,150 D	41.5%	58.5%	41.5%	58.5%
TRUMBULL	59,641	25,026	34,615		9,589 D	42.0%	58.0%	42.0%	58.0%
TUSCARAWAS	33,679	14,675	19,004		4,329 D	43.6%	56.4%	43.6%	56.4%
UNION	11,161	7,214	3,947		3,267 R	64.6%	35.4%	64.6%	35.4%
VAN WERT	14,910	8,656	6,254		2,402 R	58.1%	41.9%	58.1%	41.9%
VINTON	5,594	3,190	2,404		786 R	57.0%	43.0%	57.0%	43.0%
WARREN	15,617	8,722	6,895		1,827 R	55.8%	44.2%	55.8%	44.2%
WASHINGTON	22,142	13,558	8,584		4,974 R	61.2%	38.8%	61.2%	38.8%
WAYNE	24,273	13,525	10,748		2,777 R	55.7%	44.3%	55.7%	44.3%
WILLIAMS	13,528	9,463	4,065		5,398 R	70.0%	30.0%	70.0%	30.0%
WOOD	26,709	16,998	9,711		7,287 R	63.6%	36.4%	63.6%	36.4%
WYANDOT	10,478	6,272	4,206		2,066 R	59.9%	40.1%	59.9%	40.1%
TOTAL	3,319,912	1,586,773	1,733,139		146,366 D	47.8%	52.2%	47.8%	52.2%

OHIO

PRESIDENT 1944

County	Total Vote	Republican	Democratic	Other	Rep.-Dem. Plurality	TV Rep.	TV Dem.	MV Rep.	MV Dem.
ADAMS	9,588	5,590	3,998		1,592 R	58.3%	41.7%	58.3%	41.7%
ALLEN	33,588	21,024	12,564		8,460 R	62.6%	37.4%	62.6%	37.4%
ASHLAND	15,124	8,994	6,130		2,864 R	59.5%	40.5%	59.5%	40.5%
ASHTABULA	30,500	17,181	13,319		3,862 R	56.3%	43.7%	56.3%	43.7%
ATHENS	17,764	10,326	7,438		2,888 R	58.1%	41.9%	58.1%	41.9%
AUGLAIZE	13,868	8,980	4,888		4,092 R	64.8%	35.2%	64.8%	35.2%
BELMONT	39,578	15,485	24,093		8,608 D	39.1%	60.9%	39.1%	60.9%
BROWN	9,767	5,024	4,743		281 R	51.4%	48.6%	51.4%	48.6%
BUTLER	49,400	22,702	26,698		3,996 D	46.0%	54.0%	46.0%	54.0%
CARROLL	7,805	4,898	2,907		1,991 R	62.8%	37.2%	62.8%	37.2%
CHAMPAIGN	12,595	7,795	4,800		2,995 R	61.9%	38.1%	61.9%	38.1%
CLARK	44,569	22,207	22,362		155 D	49.8%	50.2%	49.8%	50.2%
CLERMONT	17,062	9,125	7,937		1,188 R	53.5%	46.5%	53.5%	46.5%
CLINTON	10,913	7,200	3,713		3,487 R	66.0%	34.0%	66.0%	34.0%
COLUMBIANA	38,772	19,976	18,796		1,180 R	51.5%	48.5%	51.5%	48.5%
COSHOCTON	14,043	7,917	6,126		1,791 R	56.4%	43.6%	56.4%	43.6%
CRAWFORD	17,543	10,464	7,079		3,385 R	59.6%	40.4%	59.6%	40.4%
CUYAHOGA	548,483	217,824	330,659		112,835 D	39.7%	60.3%	39.7%	60.3%
DARKE	19,171	11,135	8,036		3,099 R	58.1%	41.9%	58.1%	41.9%
DEFIANCE	11,084	7,450	3,634		3,816 R	67.2%	32.8%	67.2%	32.8%
DELAWARE	13,755	9,186	4,569		4,617 R	66.8%	33.2%	66.8%	33.2%
ERIE	18,416	10,663	7,753		2,910 R	57.9%	42.1%	57.9%	42.1%
FAIRFIELD	19,574	11,135	8,439		2,696 R	56.9%	43.1%	56.9%	43.1%
FAYETTE	9,878	5,933	3,945		1,988 R	60.1%	39.9%	60.1%	39.9%
FRANKLIN	188,686	99,292	89,394		9,898 R	52.6%	47.4%	52.6%	47.4%
FULTON	10,405	8,258	2,147		6,111 R	79.4%	20.6%	79.4%	20.6%
GALLIA	9,432	6,464	2,968		3,496 R	68.5%	31.5%	68.5%	31.5%
GEAUGA	8,559	5,295	3,264		2,031 R	61.9%	38.1%	61.9%	38.1%
GREENE	17,617	9,680	7,937		1,743 R	54.9%	45.1%	54.9%	45.1%
GUERNSEY	15,390	8,878	6,512		2,366 R	57.7%	42.3%	57.7%	42.3%
HAMILTON	299,430	154,960	144,470		10,490 R	51.8%	48.2%	51.8%	48.2%
HANCOCK	19,702	13,450	6,252		7,198 R	68.3%	31.7%	68.3%	31.7%
HARDIN	13,636	8,566	5,128		3,438 R	62.6%	37.4%	62.6%	37.4%
HARRISON	8,575	5,194	3,381		1,813 R	60.6%	39.4%	60.6%	39.4%
HENRY	9,846	7,241	2,605		4,636 R	73.5%	26.5%	73.5%	26.5%
HIGHLAND	13,299	7,963	5,336		2,627 R	59.9%	40.1%	59.9%	40.1%
HOCKING	8,301	4,535	3,766		769 R	54.6%	45.4%	54.6%	45.4%
HOLMES	5,656	3,093	2,563		530 R	54.7%	45.3%	54.7%	45.3%
HURON	17,321	11,442	5,879		5,563 R	66.1%	33.9%	66.1%	33.9%
JACKSON	11,452	6,786	4,666		2,120 R	59.3%	40.7%	59.3%	40.7%
JEFFERSON	40,323	15,496	24,827		9,331 D	38.4%	61.6%	38.4%	61.6%
KNOX	15,536	9,963	5,573		4,390 R	64.1%	35.9%	64.1%	35.9%
LAKE	26,410	13,697	12,713		984 R	51.9%	48.1%	51.9%	48.1%
LAWRENCE	17,278	9,312	7,966		1,346 R	53.9%	46.1%	53.9%	46.1%
LICKING	29,634	16,815	12,819		3,996 R	56.7%	43.3%	56.7%	43.3%
LOGAN	14,826	9,882	4,944		4,938 R	66.7%	33.3%	66.7%	33.3%
LORAIN	49,120	23,866	25,254		1,388 D	48.6%	51.4%	48.6%	51.4%
LUCAS	153,356	77,247	76,109		1,138 R	50.4%	49.6%	50.4%	49.6%
MADISON	8,920	5,546	3,374		2,172 R	62.2%	37.8%	62.2%	37.8%
MAHONING	105,286	35,184	70,102		34,918 D	33.4%	66.6%	33.4%	66.6%
MARION	20,700	11,925	8,775		3,150 R	57.6%	42.4%	57.6%	42.4%
MEDINA	16,378	10,375	6,003		4,372 R	63.3%	36.7%	63.3%	36.7%
MEIGS	9,800	6,401	3,399		3,002 R	65.3%	34.7%	65.3%	34.7%
MERCER	12,234	7,712	4,522		3,190 R	63.0%	37.0%	63.0%	37.0%
MIAMI	25,227	14,751	10,476		4,275 R	58.5%	41.5%	58.5%	41.5%
MONROE	7,191	3,617	3,574		43 R	50.3%	49.7%	50.3%	49.7%
MONTGOMERY	145,703	63,336	82,367		19,031 D	43.5%	56.5%	43.5%	56.5%
MORGAN	5,974	4,309	1,665		2,644 R	72.1%	27.9%	72.1%	27.9%
MORROW	7,795	5,439	2,356		3,083 R	69.8%	30.2%	69.8%	30.2%
MUSKINGUM	30,306	17,577	12,729		4,848 R	58.0%	42.0%	58.0%	42.0%

PRESIDENT 1948

County	Total Vote	Republican	Democratic	Other	Rep.-Dem. Plurality	TV Rep.	TV Dem.	MV Rep.	MV Dem.
ADAMS	9,408	5,103	4,293	12	810 R	54.2%	45.6%	54.3%	45.7%
ALLEN	30,668	17,380	13,161	127	4,219 R	56.7%	42.9%	56.9%	43.1%
ASHLAND	14,191	8,027	6,095	69	1,932 R	56.6%	42.9%	56.8%	43.2%
ASHTABULA	28,326	15,389	12,560	377	2,829 R	54.3%	44.3%	55.1%	44.9%
ATHENS	16,354	8,902	7,398	54	1,504 R	54.4%	45.2%	54.6%	45.4%
AUGLAIZE	12,522	6,818	5,670	34	1,148 R	54.4%	45.3%	54.6%	45.4%
BELMONT	37,143	13,283	23,217	643	9,934 D	35.8%	62.5%	36.4%	63.6%
BROWN	9,099	3,931	5,140	28	1,209 D	43.2%	56.5%	43.3%	56.7%
BUTLER	45,991	21,393	24,276	322	2,883 D	46.5%	52.8%	46.8%	53.2%
CARROLL	7,313	4,283	2,996	34	1,287 R	58.6%	41.0%	58.8%	41.2%
CHAMPAIGN	11,100	6,492	4,585	23	1,907 R	58.5%	41.3%	58.6%	41.4%
CLARK	35,917	18,548	17,236	133	1,312 R	51.6%	48.0%	51.8%	48.2%
CLERMONT	16,887	8,592	8,224	71	368 R	50.9%	48.7%	51.1%	48.9%
CLINTON	9,799	6,009	3,758	32	2,251 R	61.3%	38.4%	61.5%	38.5%
COLUMBIANA	34,538	17,724	16,588	226	1,136 R	51.3%	48.0%	51.7%	48.3%
COSHOCTON	13,634	7,096	6,457	81	639 R	52.0%	47.4%	52.4%	47.6%
CRAWFORD	16,503	8,862	7,600	41	1,262 R	53.7%	46.1%	53.8%	46.2%
CUYAHOGA	490,628	214,889	257,958	17,781	43,069 D	43.8%	52.6%	45.4%	54.6%
DARKE	17,813	8,956	8,770	87	186 R	50.3%	49.2%	50.5%	49.5%
DEFIANCE	10,409	5,927	4,454	28	1,473 R	56.9%	42.8%	57.1%	42.9%
DELAWARE	12,506	8,089	4,371	46	3,718 R	64.7%	35.0%	64.9%	35.1%
ERIE	18,302	9,568	8,644	90	924 R	52.3%	47.2%	52.5%	47.5%
FAIRFIELD	18,907	9,471	9,375	61	96 R	50.1%	49.6%	50.3%	49.7%
FAYETTE	8,395	4,865	3,513	17	1,352 R	58.0%	41.8%	58.1%	41.9%
FRANKLIN	184,999	98,707	84,806	1,486	13,901 R	53.4%	45.8%	53.8%	46.2%
FULTON	9,230	6,523	2,672	35	3,851 R	70.7%	28.9%	70.9%	29.1%
GALLIA	9,207	5,743	3,430	34	2,313 R	62.4%	37.3%	62.6%	37.4%
GEAUGA	8,622	5,535	2,960	127	2,575 R	64.2%	34.3%	65.2%	34.8%
GREENE	18,300	9,186	8,970	144	216 R	50.2%	49.0%	50.6%	49.4%
GUERNSEY	14,380	7,651	6,639	90	1,012 R	53.2%	46.2%	53.5%	46.5%
HAMILTON	288,413	151,055	135,290	2,068	15,765 R	52.4%	46.9%	52.7%	47.2%
HANCOCK	18,079	11,427	6,598	54	4,829 R	63.2%	36.5%	63.4%	36.6%
HARDIN	12,967	7,441	5,474	52	1,967 R	57.4%	42.2%	57.6%	42.4%
HARRISON	7,700	4,215	3,422	63	793 R	54.7%	44.4%	55.2%	44.8%
HENRY	8,724	5,024	3,689	11	1,335 R	57.6%	42.3%	57.7%	42.3%
HIGHLAND	12,540	6,849	5,675	16	1,174 R	54.6%	45.3%	54.7%	45.3%
HOCKING	8,212	3,733	4,462	17	729 D	45.5%	54.3%	45.6%	54.4%
HOLMES	4,982	2,496	2,480	6	16 R	50.1%	49.8%	50.2%	49.8%
HURON	15,134	9,004	6,073	57	2,931 R	59.5%	40.1%	59.7%	40.3%
JACKSON	10,874	5,782	5,059	33	723 R	53.2%	46.5%	53.3%	46.7%
JEFFERSON	38,409	14,230	23,725	454	9,495 D	37.0%	61.8%	37.5%	62.5%
KNOX	14,755	8,607	6,120	28	2,487 R	58.3%	41.5%	58.4%	41.6%
LAKE	24,108	12,973	10,844	291	2,129 R	53.8%	45.0%	54.5%	45.5%
LAWRENCE	17,684	8,113	9,495	76	1,382 D	45.9%	53.7%	46.1%	53.9%
LICKING	27,762	15,164	12,511	87	2,653 R	54.6%	45.1%	54.8%	45.2%
LOGAN	13,305	8,118	5,149	38	2,969 R	61.0%	38.7%	61.2%	38.8%
LORAIN	43,638	21,616	21,397	625	219 R	49.5%	49.0%	50.3%	49.7%
LUCAS	142,853	66,798	74,064	1,991	7,266 D	46.8%	51.8%	47.4%	52.6%
MADISON	8,094	4,730	3,356	8	1,374 R	58.4%	41.5%	58.5%	41.5%
MAHONING	101,146	37,365	62,468	1,313	25,103 D	36.9%	61.8%	37.4%	62.6%
MARION	18,606	10,333	8,223	50	2,110 R	55.5%	44.2%	55.7%	44.3%
MEDINA	14,717	9,462	5,133	122	4,329 R	64.3%	34.9%	64.8%	35.2%
MEIGS	9,193	5,564	3,595	34	1,969 R	60.5%	39.1%	60.7%	39.3%
MERCER	11,202	5,266	5,928	8	662 D	47.0%	52.9%	47.0%	53.0%
MIAMI	23,255	13,100	10,066	89	3,034 R	56.3%	43.3%	56.5%	43.5%
MONROE	6,454	2,574	3,873	7	1,299 D	39.9%	60.0%	39.9%	60.1%
MONTGOMERY	138,114	60,048	76,879	1,187	16,831 D	43.5%	55.7%	43.9%	56.1%
MORGAN	5,276	3,480	1,783	13	1,697 R	66.0%	33.8%	66.1%	33.9%
MORROW	6,955	4,327	2,616	12	1,711 R	62.2%	37.6%	62.3%	37.7%
MUSKINGUM	28,895	16,049	12,765	81	3,284 R	55.5%	44.2%	55.7%	44.3%

OHIO

PRESIDENT 1944

County	Total Vote	Republican	Democratic	Other	Rep.-Dem. Plurality	Total Vote Rep.	Total Vote Dem.	Major Vote Rep.	Major Vote Dem.
NOBLE	6,365	4,130	2,235		1,895 R	64.9%	35.1%	64.9%	35.1%
OTTAWA	11,863	6,922	4,941		1,981 R	58.3%	41.7%	58.3%	41.7%
PAULDING	6,870	4,515	2,355		2,160 R	65.7%	34.3%	65.7%	34.3%
PERRY	12,389	7,339	5,050		2,289 R	59.2%	40.8%	59.2%	40.8%
PICKAWAY	11,359	5,997	5,362		635 R	52.8%	47.2%	52.8%	47.2%
PIKE	7,085	3,117	3,968		851 D	44.0%	56.0%	44.0%	56.0%
PORTAGE	24,817	12,284	12,533		249 D	49.5%	50.5%	49.5%	50.5%
PREBLE	11,481	6,609	4,872		1,737 R	57.6%	42.4%	57.6%	42.4%
PUTNAM	11,149	8,004	3,145		4,859 R	71.8%	28.2%	71.8%	28.2%
RICHLAND	33,471	18,065	15,406		2,659 R	54.0%	46.0%	54.0%	46.0%
ROSS	21,352	11,424	9,928		1,496 R	53.5%	46.5%	53.5%	46.5%
SANDUSKY	19,892	13,763	6,129		7,634 R	69.2%	30.8%	69.2%	30.8%
SCIOTO	34,623	17,489	17,134		355 R	50.5%	49.5%	50.5%	49.5%
SENECA	21,361	15,137	6,224		8,913 R	70.9%	29.1%	70.9%	29.1%
SHELBY	12,706	7,084	5,622		1,462 R	55.8%	44.2%	55.8%	44.2%
STARK	108,899	51,506	57,393		5,887 D	47.3%	52.7%	47.3%	52.7%
SUMMIT	155,479	64,696	90,783		26,087 D	41.6%	58.4%	41.6%	58.4%
TRUMBULL	59,462	25,150	34,312		9,162 D	42.3%	57.7%	42.3%	57.7%
TUSCARAWAS	30,541	14,357	16,184		1,827 D	47.0%	53.0%	47.0%	53.0%
UNION	9,815	6,908	2,907		4,001 R	70.4%	29.6%	70.4%	29.6%
VAN WERT	13,575	8,529	5,046		3,483 R	62.8%	37.2%	62.8%	37.2%
VINTON	4,545	2,719	1,826		893 R	59.8%	40.2%	59.8%	40.2%
WARREN	14,363	8,598	5,765		2,833 R	59.9%	40.1%	59.9%	40.1%
WASHINGTON	18,699	11,676	7,023		4,653 R	62.4%	37.6%	62.4%	37.6%
WAYNE	23,122	13,616	9,506		4,110 R	58.9%	41.1%	58.9%	41.1%
WILLIAMS	12,155	8,738	3,417		5,321 R	71.9%	28.1%	71.9%	28.1%
WOOD	24,041	16,016	8,025		7,991 R	66.6%	33.4%	66.6%	33.4%
WYANDOT	9,375	6,144	3,231		2,913 R	65.5%	34.5%	65.5%	34.5%
TOTAL	3,153,056	1,582,293	1,570,763		11,530 R	50.2%	49.8%	50.2%	49.8%

PRESIDENT 1948

County	Total Vote	Republican	Democratic	Other	Rep.-Dem. Plurality	Total Vote Rep.	Total Vote Dem.	Major Vote Rep.	Major Vote Dem.
NOBLE	5,943	3,494	2,425	24	1,069 R	58.8%	40.8%	59.0%	41.0%
OTTAWA	11,783	5,591	6,157	35	566 D	47.4%	52.3%	47.6%	52.4%
PAULDING	6,110	3,579	2,512	19	1,067 R	58.6%	41.1%	58.8%	41.2%
PERRY	10,992	5,692	5,264	36	428 R	51.8%	47.9%	52.0%	48.0%
PICKAWAY	10,262	4,965	5,290	7	325 D	48.4%	51.5%	48.4%	51.6%
PIKE	7,161	2,639	4,516	6	1,877 D	36.9%	63.1%	36.9%	63.1%
PORTAGE	23,876	11,621	11,987	268	366 D	48.7%	50.2%	49.2%	50.8%
PREBLE	10,516	5,837	4,656	23	1,181 R	55.5%	44.3%	55.6%	44.4%
PUTNAM	10,148	5,006	5,114	28	108 D	49.3%	50.4%	49.5%	50.5%
RICHLAND	30,886	15,894	14,712	280	1,182 R	51.5%	47.6%	51.9%	48.1%
ROSS	19,964	10,398	9,524	42	874 R	52.1%	47.7%	52.2%	47.8%
SANDUSKY	18,099	10,847	7,216	36	3,631 R	59.9%	39.9%	60.1%	39.9%
SCIOTO	34,852	16,800	17,923	129	1,123 D	48.2%	51.4%	48.4%	51.6%
SENECA	19,524	11,493	7,954	77	3,539 R	58.9%	40.7%	59.1%	40.9%
SHELBY	12,377	5,406	6,939	32	1,533 D	43.7%	56.1%	43.8%	56.2%
STARK	100,150	51,482	47,533	1,135	3,949 R	51.4%	47.5%	52.0%	48.0%
SUMMIT	140,950	60,174	78,096	2,680	17,922 D	42.7%	55.4%	43.5%	56.5%
TRUMBULL	63,392	25,297	37,097	998	11,800 D	39.9%	58.5%	40.5%	59.5%
TUSCARAWAS	26,817	11,873	14,799	145	2,926 D	44.3%	55.2%	44.5%	55.5%
UNION	8,713	5,688	3,008	17	2,680 R	65.3%	34.5%	65.4%	34.6%
VAN WERT	11,936	6,785	5,127	24	1,658 R	56.8%	43.0%	57.0%	43.0%
VINTON	4,355	2,323	2,016	16	307 R	53.3%	46.3%	53.5%	46.5%
WARREN	13,409	7,584	5,293	32	1,791 R	56.6%	43.2%	56.7%	43.3%
WASHINGTON	17,936	10,349	7,542	45	2,807 R	57.7%	42.0%	57.8%	42.2%
WAYNE	21,090	12,152	8,868	70	3,284 R	57.6%	42.0%	57.8%	42.2%
WILLIAMS	10,470	6,784	3,662	24	3,122 R	64.8%	35.0%	64.9%	35.1%
WOOD	23,041	13,197	9,725	119	3,472 R	57.3%	42.2%	57.6%	42.4%
WYANDOT	8,182	4,849	3,308	25	1,541 R	59.3%	40.4%	59.4%	40.6%
TOTAL	2,936,071	1,445,684	1,452,791	37,596	7,107 D	49.2%	49.5%	49.9%	50.1%

OHIO

PRESIDENT 1952

County	Total Vote	Republican	Democratic	Other	Rep.-Dem. Plurality	Total Vote Rep.	Total Vote Dem.	Major Vote Rep.	Major Vote Dem.
ADAMS	9,585	5,648	3,937		1,711 R	58.9%	41.1%	58.9%	41.1%
ALLEN	40,535	26,396	14,139		12,257 R	65.1%	34.9%	65.1%	34.9%
ASHLAND	17,703	12,459	5,244		7,215 R	70.4%	29.6%	70.4%	29.6%
ASHTABULA	37,861	23,185	14,676		8,509 R	61.2%	38.8%	61.2%	38.8%
ATHENS	17,937	10,829	7,108		3,721 R	60.4%	39.6%	60.4%	39.6%
AUGLAIZE	15,748	10,599	5,149		5,450 R	67.3%	32.7%	67.3%	32.7%
BELMONT	42,452	17,693	24,759		7,066 D	41.7%	58.3%	41.7%	58.3%
BROWN	10,463	5,635	4,828		807 R	53.9%	46.1%	53.9%	46.1%
BUTLER	66,520	35,769	30,751		5,018 R	53.8%	46.2%	53.8%	46.2%
CARROLL	8,841	5,707	3,134		2,573 R	64.6%	35.4%	64.6%	35.4%
CHAMPAIGN	13,443	8,880	4,563		4,317 R	66.1%	33.9%	66.1%	33.9%
CLARK	48,250	27,464	20,786		6,678 R	56.9%	43.1%	56.9%	43.1%
CLERMONT	22,923	13,221	9,702		3,519 R	57.7%	42.3%	57.7%	42.3%
CLINTON	12,076	8,191	3,885		4,306 R	67.8%	32.2%	67.8%	32.2%
COLUMBIANA	45,764	26,707	19,057		7,650 R	58.4%	41.6%	58.4%	41.6%
COSHOCTON	15,631	9,832	5,799		4,033 R	62.9%	37.1%	62.9%	37.1%
CRAWFORD	20,222	13,370	6,852		6,518 R	66.1%	33.9%	66.1%	33.9%
CUYAHOGA	654,427	329,465	324,962		4,503 R	50.3%	49.7%	50.3%	49.7%
DARKE	21,267	13,670	7,597		6,073 R	64.3%	35.7%	64.3%	35.7%
DEFIANCE	12,995	8,834	4,161		4,673 R	68.0%	32.0%	68.0%	32.0%
DELAWARE	14,921	10,682	4,239		6,443 R	71.6%	28.4%	71.6%	28.4%
ERIE	21,794	14,245	7,549		6,696 R	65.4%	34.6%	65.4%	34.6%
FAIRFIELD	24,167	15,027	9,140		5,887 R	62.2%	37.8%	62.2%	37.8%
FAYETTE	10,682	6,800	3,882		2,918 R	63.7%	36.3%	63.7%	36.3%
FRANKLIN	230,514	138,894	91,620		47,274 R	60.3%	39.7%	60.3%	39.7%
FULTON	11,756	9,191	2,565		6,626 R	78.2%	21.8%	78.2%	21.8%
GALLIA	9,916	6,763	3,153		3,610 R	68.2%	31.8%	68.2%	31.8%
GEAUGA	13,182	8,975	4,207		4,768 R	68.1%	31.9%	68.1%	31.9%
GREENE	22,023	12,900	9,123		3,777 R	58.6%	41.4%	58.6%	41.4%
GUERNSEY	16,380	9,749	6,631		3,118 R	59.5%	40.5%	59.5%	40.5%
HAMILTON	348,475	207,690	140,785		66,905 R	59.6%	40.4%	59.6%	40.4%
HANCOCK	20,365	14,999	5,366		9,633 R	73.7%	26.3%	73.7%	26.3%
HARDIN	14,299	9,235	5,064		4,171 R	64.6%	35.4%	64.6%	35.4%
HARRISON	8,920	5,306	3,614		1,692 R	59.5%	40.5%	59.5%	40.5%
HENRY	11,039	8,029	3,010		5,019 R	72.7%	27.3%	72.7%	27.3%
HIGHLAND	13,787	8,568	5,219		3,349 R	62.1%	37.9%	62.1%	37.9%
HOCKING	8,681	4,743	3,938		805 R	54.6%	45.4%	54.6%	45.4%
HOLMES	5,980	3,891	2,089		1,802 R	65.1%	34.9%	65.1%	34.9%
HURON	17,247	12,372	4,875		7,497 R	71.7%	28.3%	71.7%	28.3%
JACKSON	12,206	7,223	4,983		2,240 R	59.2%	40.8%	59.2%	40.8%
JEFFERSON	47,068	19,569	27,499		7,930 D	41.6%	58.4%	41.6%	58.4%
KNOX	18,399	12,705	5,694		7,011 R	69.1%	30.9%	69.1%	30.9%
LAKE	38,829	23,483	15,346		8,137 R	60.5%	39.5%	60.5%	39.5%
LAWRENCE	21,278	11,962	9,316		2,646 R	56.2%	43.8%	56.2%	43.8%
LICKING	32,103	20,385	11,718		8,667 R	63.5%	36.5%	63.5%	36.5%
LOGAN	15,877	11,084	4,793		6,291 R	69.8%	30.2%	69.8%	30.2%
LORAIN	60,019	33,825	26,194		7,631 R	56.4%	43.6%	56.4%	43.6%
LUCAS	188,533	97,490	91,043		6,447 R	51.7%	48.3%	51.7%	48.3%
MADISON	9,456	6,279	3,177		3,102 R	66.4%	33.6%	66.4%	33.6%
MAHONING	120,886	53,164	67,722		14,558 D	44.0%	56.0%	44.0%	56.0%
MARION	23,434	14,583	8,851		5,732 R	62.2%	37.8%	62.2%	37.8%
MEDINA	20,504	14,433	6,071		8,362 R	70.4%	29.6%	70.4%	29.6%
MEIGS	10,036	6,700	3,336		3,364 R	66.8%	33.2%	66.8%	33.2%
MERCER	13,783	9,058	4,725		4,333 R	65.7%	34.3%	65.7%	34.3%
MIAMI	29,987	19,525	10,462		9,063 R	65.1%	34.9%	65.1%	34.9%
MONROE	6,706	3,493	3,213		280 R	52.1%	47.9%	52.1%	47.9%
MONTGOMERY	171,765	91,905	79,860		12,045 R	53.5%	46.5%	53.5%	46.5%
MORGAN	5,981	4,303	1,678		2,625 R	71.9%	28.1%	71.9%	28.1%
MORROW	8,485	6,106	2,379		3,727 R	72.0%	28.0%	72.0%	28.0%
MUSKINGUM	33,734	21,244	12,490		8,754 R	63.0%	37.0%	63.0%	37.0%

PRESIDENT 1956

County	Total Vote	Republican	Democratic	Other	Rep.-Dem. Plurality	Total Vote Rep.	Total Vote Dem.	Major Vote Rep.	Major Vote Dem.
ADAMS	9,531	5,637	3,894		1,743 R	59.1%	40.9%	59.1%	40.9%
ALLEN	40,430	28,388	12,042		16,346 R	70.2%	29.8%	70.2%	29.8%
ASHLAND	17,426	12,792	4,634		8,158 R	73.4%	26.6%	73.4%	26.6%
ASHTABULA	37,360	24,165	13,195		10,970 R	64.7%	35.3%	64.7%	35.3%
ATHENS	16,753	10,794	5,959		4,835 R	64.4%	35.6%	64.4%	35.6%
AUGLAIZE	15,891	11,453	4,438		7,015 R	72.1%	27.9%	72.1%	27.9%
BELMONT	38,221	19,230	18,991		239 R	50.3%	49.7%	50.3%	49.7%
BROWN	10,036	5,690	4,346		1,344 R	56.7%	43.3%	56.7%	43.3%
BUTLER	66,116	41,785	24,331		17,454 R	63.2%	36.8%	63.2%	36.8%
CARROLL	8,506	5,916	2,590		3,326 R	69.6%	30.4%	69.6%	30.4%
CHAMPAIGN	12,618	8,767	3,851		4,916 R	69.5%	30.5%	69.5%	30.5%
CLARK	46,447	28,767	17,680		11,087 R	61.9%	38.1%	61.9%	38.1%
CLERMONT	23,940	14,914	9,026		5,888 R	62.3%	37.7%	62.3%	37.7%
CLINTON	11,301	7,919	3,382		4,537 R	70.1%	29.9%	70.1%	29.9%
COLUMBIANA	43,299	28,783	14,516		14,267 R	66.5%	33.5%	66.5%	33.5%
COSHOCTON	14,338	9,549	4,789		4,760 R	66.6%	33.4%	66.6%	33.4%
CRAWFORD	19,532	13,763	5,769		7,994 R	70.5%	29.5%	70.5%	29.5%
CUYAHOGA	658,032	353,474	304,558		48,916 R	53.7%	46.3%	53.7%	46.3%
DARKE	20,585	13,447	7,138		6,309 R	65.3%	34.7%	65.3%	34.7%
DEFIANCE	12,727	8,786	3,941		4,845 R	69.0%	31.0%	69.0%	31.0%
DELAWARE	14,736	10,739	3,997		6,742 R	72.9%	27.1%	72.9%	27.1%
ERIE	21,047	14,771	6,276		8,495 R	70.2%	29.8%	70.2%	29.8%
FAIRFIELD	23,984	15,647	8,337		7,310 R	65.2%	34.8%	65.2%	34.8%
FAYETTE	10,145	6,696	3,449		3,247 R	66.0%	34.0%	66.0%	34.0%
FRANKLIN	230,396	151,544	78,852		72,692 R	65.8%	34.2%	65.8%	34.2%
FULTON	11,652	9,030	2,622		6,408 R	77.5%	22.5%	77.5%	22.5%
GALLIA	9,917	7,040	2,877		4,163 R	71.0%	29.0%	71.0%	29.0%
GEAUGA	15,789	10,971	4,818		6,153 R	69.5%	30.5%	69.5%	30.5%
GREENE	25,332	15,471	9,861		5,610 R	61.1%	38.9%	61.1%	38.9%
GUERNSEY	15,373	10,224	5,149		5,075 R	66.5%	33.5%	66.5%	33.5%
HAMILTON	335,806	222,009	113,797		108,212 R	66.1%	33.9%	66.1%	33.9%
HANCOCK	21,002	15,713	5,289		10,424 R	74.8%	25.2%	74.8%	25.2%
HARDIN	13,605	9,049	4,556		4,493 R	66.5%	33.5%	66.5%	33.5%
HARRISON	8,275	5,444	2,831		2,613 R	65.8%	34.2%	65.8%	34.2%
HENRY	10,939	8,164	2,775		5,389 R	74.6%	25.4%	74.6%	25.4%
HIGHLAND	13,223	8,397	4,826		3,571 R	63.5%	36.5%	63.5%	36.5%
HOCKING	8,259	4,925	3,334		1,591 R	59.6%	40.4%	59.6%	40.4%
HOLMES	5,750	3,955	1,795		2,160 R	68.8%	31.2%	68.8%	31.2%
HURON	16,626	12,208	4,418		7,790 R	73.4%	26.6%	73.4%	26.6%
JACKSON	12,538	8,106	4,432		3,674 R	64.7%	35.3%	64.7%	35.3%
JEFFERSON	43,865	22,162	21,703		459 R	50.5%	49.5%	50.5%	49.5%
KNOX	17,305	12,347	4,958		7,389 R	71.3%	28.7%	71.3%	28.7%
LAKE	50,735	31,017	19,718		11,299 R	61.1%	38.9%	61.1%	38.9%
LAWRENCE	20,099	12,607	7,492		5,115 R	62.7%	37.3%	62.7%	37.3%
LICKING	32,493	21,912	10,581		11,331 R	67.4%	32.6%	67.4%	32.6%
LOGAN	15,455	11,229	4,226		7,003 R	72.7%	27.3%	72.7%	27.3%
LORAIN	67,114	40,340	26,774		13,566 R	60.1%	39.9%	60.1%	39.9%
LUCAS	189,099	100,501	88,598		11,903 R	53.1%	46.9%	53.1%	46.9%
MADISON	9,358	6,483	2,875		3,608 R	69.3%	30.7%	69.3%	30.7%
MAHONING	123,118	63,992	59,126		4,866 R	52.0%	48.0%	52.0%	48.0%
MARION	22,550	15,125	7,425		7,700 R	67.1%	32.9%	67.1%	32.9%
MEDINA	21,520	15,155	6,365		8,790 R	70.4%	29.6%	70.4%	29.6%
MEIGS	9,376	6,593	2,783		3,810 R	70.3%	29.7%	70.3%	29.7%
MERCER	13,728	9,456	4,272		5,184 R	68.9%	31.1%	68.9%	31.1%
MIAMI	29,364	20,135	9,229		10,906 R	68.6%	31.4%	68.6%	31.4%
MONROE	6,316	3,738	2,578		1,160 R	59.2%	40.8%	59.2%	40.8%
MONTGOMERY	183,548	107,278	76,270		31,008 R	58.4%	41.6%	58.4%	41.6%
MORGAN	5,600	4,134	1,466		2,668 R	73.8%	26.2%	73.8%	26.2%
MORROW	8,224	5,885	2,339		3,546 R	71.6%	28.4%	71.6%	28.4%
MUSKINGUM	32,898	22,788	10,110		12,678 R	69.3%	30.7%	69.3%	30.7%

OHIO

PRESIDENT 1952

County	Total Vote	Republican	Democratic	Other	Rep.-Dem. Plurality	Total Vote Rep.	Total Vote Dem.	Major Vote Rep.	Major Vote Dem.
NOBLE	6,100	4,046	2,054		1,992 R	66.3%	33.7%	66.3%	33.7%
OTTAWA	14,516	8,708	5,808		2,900 R	60.0%	40.0%	60.0%	40.0%
PAULDING	7,223	4,837	2,386		2,451 R	67.0%	33.0%	67.0%	33.0%
PERRY	12,700	7,425	5,275		2,150 R	58.5%	41.5%	58.5%	41.5%
PICKAWAY	11,945	6,836	5,109		1,727 R	57.2%	42.8%	57.2%	42.8%
PIKE	6,875	2,982	3,893		911 D	43.4%	56.6%	43.4%	56.6%
PORTAGE	30,721	17,168	13,553		3,515 R	55.9%	44.1%	55.9%	44.1%
PREBLE	13,241	8,405	4,836		3,569 R	63.5%	36.5%	63.5%	36.5%
PUTNAM	12,197	8,398	3,799		4,599 R	68.9%	31.1%	68.9%	31.1%
RICHLAND	40,609	25,829	14,780		11,049 R	63.6%	36.4%	63.6%	36.4%
ROSS	22,016	13,431	8,585		4,846 R	61.0%	39.0%	61.0%	39.0%
SANDUSKY	20,987	14,939	6,048		8,891 R	71.2%	28.8%	71.2%	28.8%
SCIOTO	38,548	20,403	18,145		2,258 R	52.9%	47.1%	52.9%	47.1%
SENECA	24,810	17,750	7,060		10,690 R	71.5%	28.5%	71.5%	28.5%
SHELBY	14,290	8,957	5,333		3,624 R	62.7%	37.3%	62.7%	37.3%
STARK	129,960	74,929	55,031		19,898 R	57.7%	42.3%	57.7%	42.3%
SUMMIT	188,611	91,168	97,443		6,275 D	48.3%	51.7%	48.3%	51.7%
TRUMBULL	76,855	37,793	39,062		1,269 D	49.2%	50.8%	49.2%	50.8%
TUSCARAWAS	34,952	18,620	16,332		2,288 R	53.3%	46.7%	53.3%	46.7%
UNION	10,604	7,761	2,843		4,918 R	73.2%	26.8%	73.2%	26.8%
VAN WERT	14,463	9,355	5,108		4,247 R	64.7%	35.3%	64.7%	35.3%
VINTON	4,932	2,903	2,029		874 R	58.9%	41.1%	58.9%	41.1%
WARREN	18,583	11,529	7,054		4,475 R	62.0%	38.0%	62.0%	38.0%
WASHINGTON	21,217	13,841	7,376		6,465 R	65.2%	34.8%	65.2%	34.8%
WAYNE	26,488	18,074	8,414		9,660 R	68.2%	31.8%	68.2%	31.8%
WILLIAMS	13,246	9,888	3,358		6,530 R	74.6%	25.4%	74.6%	25.4%
WOOD	26,437	17,269	9,168		8,101 R	65.3%	34.7%	65.3%	34.7%
WYANDOT	9,792	7,015	2,777		4,238 R	71.6%	28.4%	71.6%	28.4%
TOTAL	3,700,758	2,100,391	1,600,367		500,024 R	56.8%	43.2%	56.8%	43.2%

PRESIDENT 1956

County	Total Vote	Republican	Democratic	Other	Rep.-Dem. Plurality	Total Vote Rep.	Total Vote Dem.	Major Vote Rep.	Major Vote Dem.
NOBLE	5,804	3,861	1,943		1,918 R	66.5%	33.5%	66.5%	33.5%
OTTAWA	13,982	8,806	5,176		3,630 R	63.0%	37.0%	63.0%	37.0%
PAULDING	7,055	4,885	2,170		2,715 R	69.2%	30.8%	69.2%	30.8%
PERRY	11,634	7,511	4,123		3,388 R	64.6%	35.4%	64.6%	35.4%
PICKAWAY	11,465	6,956	4,509		2,447 R	60.7%	39.3%	60.7%	39.3%
PIKE	7,310	3,447	3,863		416 D	47.2%	52.8%	47.2%	52.8%
PORTAGE	32,071	18,943	13,128		5,815 R	59.1%	40.9%	59.1%	40.9%
PREBLE	12,673	8,099	4,574		3,525 R	63.9%	36.1%	63.9%	36.1%
PUTNAM	11,946	8,408	3,538		4,870 R	70.4%	29.6%	70.4%	29.6%
RICHLAND	39,676	26,098	13,578		12,520 R	65.8%	34.2%	65.8%	34.2%
ROSS	20,454	13,036	7,418		5,618 R	63.7%	36.3%	63.7%	36.3%
SANDUSKY	20,696	15,009	5,687		9,322 R	72.5%	27.5%	72.5%	27.5%
SCIOTO	37,095	22,110	14,985		7,125 R	59.6%	40.4%	59.6%	40.4%
SENECA	23,988	17,728	6,260		11,468 R	73.9%	26.1%	73.9%	26.1%
SHELBY	13,967	9,452	4,515		4,937 R	67.7%	32.3%	67.7%	32.3%
STARK	133,112	83,667	49,445		34,222 R	62.9%	37.1%	62.9%	37.1%
SUMMIT	196,250	102,872	93,378		9,494 R	52.4%	47.6%	52.4%	47.6%
TRUMBULL	76,849	43,936	32,913		11,023 R	57.2%	42.8%	57.2%	42.8%
TUSCARAWAS	32,784	19,876	12,908		6,968 R	60.6%	39.4%	60.6%	39.4%
UNION	10,228	7,575	2,653		4,922 R	74.1%	25.9%	74.1%	25.9%
VAN WERT	14,042	9,834	4,208		5,626 R	70.0%	30.0%	70.0%	30.0%
VINTON	4,914	2,998	1,916		1,082 R	61.0%	39.0%	61.0%	39.0%
WARREN	20,866	13,673	7,193		6,480 R	65.5%	34.5%	65.5%	34.5%
WASHINGTON	19,995	13,927	6,068		7,859 R	69.7%	30.3%	69.7%	30.3%
WAYNE	26,453	19,469	6,984		12,485 R	73.6%	26.4%	73.6%	26.4%
WILLIAMS	13,009	9,784	3,225		6,559 R	75.2%	24.8%	75.2%	24.8%
WOOD	25,397	16,844	8,553		8,291 R	66.3%	33.7%	66.3%	33.7%
WYANDOT	9,302	6,807	2,495		4,312 R	73.2%	26.8%	73.2%	26.8%
TOTAL	3,702,265	2,262,610	1,439,655		822,955 R	61.1%	38.9%	61.1%	38.9%

OHIO

PRESIDENT 1960

County	Total Vote	Republican	Democratic	Other	Rep.-Dem. Plurality	% Total Vote Rep.	% Total Vote Dem.	% Major Vote Rep.	% Major Vote Dem.
ADAMS	9,896	5,996	3,900		2,096 R	60.6%	39.4%	60.6%	39.4%
ALLEN	42,732	28,007	14,725		13,282 R	65.5%	34.5%	65.5%	34.5%
ASHLAND	18,812	13,112	5,700		7,412 R	69.7%	30.3%	69.7%	30.3%
ASHTABULA	41,561	22,406	19,155		3,251 R	53.9%	46.1%	53.9%	46.1%
ATHENS	18,289	10,747	7,542		3,205 R	58.8%	41.2%	58.8%	41.2%
AUGLAIZE	17,465	11,183	6,282		4,901 R	64.0%	36.0%	64.0%	36.0%
BELMONT	41,951	18,146	23,805		5,659 D	43.3%	56.7%	43.3%	56.7%
BROWN	11,594	6,461	5,133		1,328 R	55.7%	44.3%	55.7%	44.3%
BUTLER	79,296	46,518	32,778		13,740 R	58.7%	41.3%	58.7%	41.3%
CARROLL	9,583	6,095	3,488		2,607 R	63.6%	36.4%	63.6%	36.4%
CHAMPAIGN	13,701	9,141	4,560		4,581 R	66.7%	33.3%	66.7%	33.3%
CLARK	53,044	30,588	22,456		8,132 R	57.7%	42.3%	57.7%	42.3%
CLERMONT	30,525	18,802	11,723		7,079 R	61.6%	38.4%	61.6%	38.4%
CLINTON	12,962	8,464	4,498		3,966 R	65.3%	34.7%	65.3%	34.7%
COLUMBIANA	48,451	28,414	20,037		8,377 R	58.6%	41.4%	58.6%	41.4%
COSHOCTON	15,309	9,913	5,396		4,517 R	64.8%	35.2%	64.8%	35.2%
CRAWFORD	21,639	14,558	6,981		7,577 R	67.6%	32.4%	67.6%	32.4%
CUYAHOGA	717,086	288,056	429,030		140,974 D	40.2%	59.8%	40.2%	59.8%
DARKE	21,763	14,048	7,715		6,333 R	64.5%	35.5%	64.5%	35.5%
DEFIANCE	14,119	8,912	5,207		3,705 R	63.1%	36.9%	63.1%	36.9%
DELAWARE	16,725	11,391	5,334		6,057 R	68.1%	31.9%	68.1%	31.9%
ERIE	26,046	15,092	10,954		4,138 R	57.9%	42.1%	57.9%	42.1%
FAIRFIELD	26,871	17,743	9,128		8,615 R	66.0%	34.0%	66.0%	34.0%
FAYETTE	11,051	7,085	3,966		3,119 R	64.1%	35.9%	64.1%	35.9%
FRANKLIN	271,461	161,178	110,283		50,895 R	59.4%	40.6%	59.4%	40.6%
FULTON	12,969	9,695	3,274		6,421 R	74.8%	25.2%	74.8%	25.2%
GALLIA	11,100	7,602	3,498		4,104 R	68.5%	31.5%	68.5%	31.5%
GEAUGA	21,013	12,491	8,522		3,969 R	59.4%	40.6%	59.4%	40.6%
GREENE	33,797	19,642	14,155		5,487 R	58.1%	41.9%	58.1%	41.9%
GUERNSEY	16,928	10,396	6,532		3,864 R	61.4%	38.6%	61.4%	38.6%
HAMILTON	387,283	211,068	176,215		34,853 R	54.5%	45.5%	54.5%	45.5%
HANCOCK	23,771	17,059	6,712		10,347 R	71.8%	28.2%	71.8%	28.2%
HARDIN	14,038	9,042	4,996		4,046 R	64.4%	35.6%	64.4%	35.6%
HARRISON	8,832	5,191	3,641		1,550 R	58.8%	41.2%	58.8%	41.2%
HENRY	11,666	8,251	3,415		4,836 R	70.7%	29.3%	70.7%	29.3%
HIGHLAND	14,371	8,948	5,423		3,525 R	62.3%	37.7%	62.3%	37.7%
HOCKING	9,319	5,262	4,057		1,205 R	56.5%	43.5%	56.5%	43.5%
HOLMES	6,385	4,432	1,953		2,479 R	69.4%	30.6%	69.4%	30.6%
HURON	19,795	12,261	7,534		4,727 R	61.9%	38.1%	61.9%	38.1%
JACKSON	13,522	7,973	5,549		2,424 R	59.0%	41.0%	59.0%	41.0%
JEFFERSON	48,141	21,186	26,955		5,769 D	44.0%	56.0%	44.0%	56.0%
KNOX	19,276	12,711	6,565		6,146 R	65.9%	34.1%	65.9%	34.1%
LAKE	65,463	32,038	33,425		1,387 D	48.9%	51.1%	48.9%	51.1%
LAWRENCE	21,815	13,159	8,656		4,503 R	60.3%	39.7%	60.3%	39.7%
LICKING	36,988	23,653	13,335		10,318 R	63.9%	36.1%	63.9%	36.1%
LOGAN	16,590	11,311	5,279		6,032 R	68.2%	31.8%	68.2%	31.8%
LORAIN	82,848	39,361	43,487		4,126 D	47.5%	52.5%	47.5%	52.5%
LUCAS	197,504	94,679	102,825		8,146 D	47.9%	52.1%	47.9%	52.1%
MADISON	10,933	7,256	3,677		3,579 R	66.4%	33.6%	66.4%	33.6%
MAHONING	134,070	51,927	82,143		30,216 D	38.7%	61.3%	38.7%	61.3%
MARION	24,808	15,210	9,598		5,612 R	61.3%	38.7%	61.3%	38.7%
MEDINA	25,919	16,123	9,796		6,327 R	62.2%	37.8%	62.2%	37.8%
MEIGS	10,448	6,976	3,472		3,504 R	66.8%	33.2%	66.8%	33.2%
MERCER	15,465	7,735	7,730		5 R	50.0%	50.0%	50.0%	50.0%
MIAMI	33,921	22,151	11,770		10,381 R	65.3%	34.7%	65.3%	34.7%
MONROE	7,250	4,106	3,144		962 R	56.6%	43.4%	56.6%	43.4%
MONTGOMERY	207,927	109,602	98,325		11,277 R	52.7%	47.3%	52.7%	47.3%
MORGAN	6,247	4,424	1,823		2,601 R	70.8%	29.2%	70.8%	29.2%
MORROW	9,093	6,357	2,736		3,621 R	69.9%	30.1%	69.9%	30.1%
MUSKINGUM	34,772	21,518	13,254		8,264 R	61.9%	38.1%	61.9%	38.1%

PRESIDENT 1964

County	Total Vote	Republican	Democratic	Other	Rep.-Dem. Plurality	% Total Vote Rep.	% Total Vote Dem.	% Major Vote Rep.	% Major Vote Dem.
ADAMS	8,707	3,702	5,005		1,303 D	42.5%	57.5%	42.5%	57.5%
ALLEN	38,887	19,897	18,990		907 R	51.2%	48.8%	51.2%	48.8%
ASHLAND	15,801	7,308	8,493		1,185 D	46.3%	53.7%	46.3%	53.7%
ASHTABULA	37,287	13,183	24,104		10,921 D	35.4%	64.6%	35.4%	64.6%
ATHENS	16,844	6,211	10,633		4,422 D	36.9%	63.1%	36.9%	63.1%
AUGLAIZE	16,586	7,954	8,632		678 D	48.0%	52.0%	48.0%	52.0%
BELMONT	37,873	9,693	28,180		18,487 D	25.6%	74.4%	25.6%	74.4%
BROWN	10,887	3,904	6,983		3,079 D	35.9%	64.1%	35.9%	64.1%
BUTLER	73,691	31,413	42,278		10,865 D	42.6%	57.4%	42.6%	57.4%
CARROLL	8,705	3,655	5,050		1,395 D	42.0%	58.0%	42.0%	58.0%
CHAMPAIGN	12,726	5,588	7,138		1,550 D	43.9%	56.1%	43.9%	56.1%
CLARK	53,387	19,112	34,275		15,163 D	35.8%	64.2%	35.8%	64.2%
CLERMONT	29,890	13,367	16,523		3,156 D	44.7%	55.3%	44.7%	55.3%
CLINTON	12,596	6,082	6,514		432 D	48.3%	51.7%	48.3%	51.7%
COLUMBIANA	44,533	15,827	28,706		12,879 D	35.5%	64.5%	35.5%	64.5%
COSHOCTON	14,347	5,965	8,382		2,417 D	41.6%	58.4%	41.6%	58.4%
CRAWFORD	20,938	8,970	11,968		2,998 D	42.8%	57.2%	42.8%	57.2%
CUYAHOGA	689,347	196,436	492,911		296,475 D	28.5%	71.5%	28.5%	71.5%
DARKE	21,014	8,581	12,433		3,852 D	40.8%	59.2%	40.8%	59.2%
DEFIANCE	13,755	5,048	8,707		3,659 D	36.7%	63.3%	36.7%	63.3%
DELAWARE	16,475	8,395	8,080		315 R	51.0%	49.0%	51.0%	49.0%
ERIE	25,949	9,981	15,968		5,987 D	38.5%	61.5%	38.5%	61.5%
FAIRFIELD	27,091	11,480	15,611		4,131 D	42.4%	57.6%	42.4%	57.6%
FAYETTE	10,695	4,567	6,128		1,561 D	42.7%	57.3%	42.7%	57.3%
FRANKLIN	285,872	131,345	154,527		23,182 D	45.9%	54.1%	45.9%	54.1%
FULTON	11,577	5,973	5,604		369 R	51.6%	48.4%	51.6%	48.4%
GALLIA	9,148	4,408	4,740		332 D	48.2%	51.8%	48.2%	51.8%
GEAUGA	21,635	9,423	12,212		2,789 D	43.6%	56.4%	43.6%	56.4%
GREENE	35,847	14,571	21,276		6,705 D	40.6%	59.4%	40.6%	59.4%
GUERNSEY	15,932	6,429	9,503		3,074 D	40.4%	59.6%	40.4%	59.6%
HAMILTON	360,306	161,179	199,127		37,948 D	44.7%	55.3%	44.7%	55.3%
HANCOCK	23,157	11,610	11,547		63 R	50.1%	49.9%	50.1%	49.9%
HARDIN	13,003	5,679	7,324		1,645 D	43.7%	56.3%	43.7%	56.3%
HARRISON	8,087	2,928	5,159		2,231 D	36.2%	63.8%	36.2%	63.8%
HENRY	10,939	5,094	5,845		751 D	46.6%	53.4%	46.6%	53.4%
HIGHLAND	13,266	5,985	7,281		1,296 D	45.1%	54.9%	45.1%	54.9%
HOCKING	8,809	2,858	5,951		3,093 D	32.4%	67.6%	32.4%	67.6%
HOLMES	5,665	2,106	3,559		1,453 D	37.2%	62.8%	37.2%	62.8%
HURON	18,435	7,655	10,780		3,125 D	41.5%	58.5%	41.5%	58.5%
JACKSON	12,005	4,949	7,056		2,107 D	41.2%	58.8%	41.2%	58.8%
JEFFERSON	44,823	11,784	33,039		21,255 D	26.3%	73.7%	26.3%	73.7%
KNOX	18,480	7,258	11,222		3,964 D	39.3%	60.7%	39.3%	60.7%
LAKE	61,834	23,282	38,552		15,270 D	37.7%	62.3%	37.7%	62.3%
LAWRENCE	20,392	7,757	12,635		4,878 D	38.0%	62.0%	38.0%	62.0%
LICKING	38,460	15,096	23,364		8,268 D	39.3%	60.7%	39.3%	60.7%
LOGAN	15,167	6,683	8,484		1,801 D	44.1%	55.9%	44.1%	55.9%
LORAIN	82,438	26,683	55,755		29,072 D	32.4%	67.6%	32.4%	67.6%
LUCAS	185,892	57,782	128,110		70,328 D	31.1%	68.9%	31.1%	68.9%
MADISON	10,209	4,945	5,264		319 D	48.4%	51.6%	48.4%	51.6%
MAHONING	124,709	33,775	90,934		57,159 D	27.1%	72.9%	27.1%	72.9%
MARION	24,450	10,050	14,400		4,350 D	41.1%	58.9%	41.1%	58.9%
MEDINA	24,950	10,221	14,729		4,508 D	41.0%	59.0%	41.0%	59.0%
MEIGS	9,106	3,973	5,133		1,160 D	43.6%	56.4%	43.6%	56.4%
MERCER	14,454	4,373	10,081		5,708 D	30.3%	69.7%	30.3%	69.7%
MIAMI	32,364	12,985	19,379		6,394 D	40.1%	59.9%	40.1%	59.9%
MONROE	6,720	1,944	4,776		2,832 D	28.9%	71.1%	28.9%	71.1%
MONTGOMERY	198,612	71,979	126,633		54,654 D	36.2%	63.8%	36.2%	63.8%
MORGAN	5,334	2,281	3,053		772 D	42.8%	57.2%	42.8%	57.2%
MORROW	8,766	4,194	4,572		378 D	47.8%	52.2%	47.8%	52.2%
MUSKINGUM	32,427	11,635	20,792		9,157 D	35.9%	64.1%	35.9%	64.1%

OHIO

PRESIDENT 1960

County	Total Vote	Republican	Democratic	Other	Rep.-Dem. Plurality	Total Vote Rep.	Total Vote Dem.	Major Vote Rep.	Major Vote Dem.
NOBLE	5,987	3,951	2,036		1,915 R	66.0%	34.0%	66.0%	34.0%
OTTAWA	15,872	9,260	6,612		2,648 R	58.3%	41.7%	58.3%	41.7%
PAULDING	7,786	4,961	2,825		2,136 R	63.7%	36.3%	63.7%	36.3%
PERRY	12,849	7,658	5,191		2,467 R	59.6%	40.4%	59.6%	40.4%
PICKAWAY	12,691	7,821	4,870		2,951 R	61.6%	38.4%	61.6%	38.4%
PIKE	8,023	3,684	4,339		655 D	45.9%	54.1%	45.9%	54.1%
PORTAGE	38,162	19,634	18,528		1,106 R	51.4%	48.6%	51.4%	48.6%
PREBLE	14,269	8,802	5,467		3,335 R	61.7%	38.3%	61.7%	38.3%
PUTNAM	12,873	6,834	6,039		795 R	53.1%	46.9%	53.1%	46.9%
RICHLAND	46,962	27,317	19,645		7,672 R	58.2%	41.8%	58.2%	41.8%
ROSS	23,111	14,075	9,036		5,039 R	60.9%	39.1%	60.9%	39.1%
SANDUSKY	22,737	14,566	8,171		6,395 R	64.1%	35.9%	64.1%	35.9%
SCIOTO	38,418	21,771	16,647		5,124 R	56.7%	43.3%	56.7%	43.3%
SENECA	25,773	15,772	10,001		5,771 R	61.2%	38.8%	61.2%	38.8%
SHELBY	15,632	8,766	6,866		1,900 R	56.1%	43.9%	56.1%	43.9%
STARK	150,086	82,881	67,205		15,676 R	55.2%	44.8%	55.2%	44.8%
SUMMIT	219,918	109,066	110,852		1,786 D	49.6%	50.4%	49.6%	50.4%
TRUMBULL	87,652	40,724	46,928		6,204 D	46.5%	53.5%	46.5%	53.5%
TUSCARAWAS	36,720	20,637	16,083		4,554 R	56.2%	43.8%	56.2%	43.8%
UNION	10,954	7,838	3,116		4,722 R	71.6%	28.4%	71.6%	28.4%
VAN WERT	14,716	9,666	5,050		4,616 R	65.7%	34.3%	65.7%	34.3%
VINTON	5,074	3,043	2,031		1,012 R	60.0%	40.0%	60.0%	40.0%
WARREN	22,450	14,505	7,945		6,560 R	64.6%	35.4%	64.6%	35.4%
WASHINGTON	22,053	14,197	7,856		6,341 R	64.4%	35.6%	64.4%	35.6%
WAYNE	30,784	21,273	9,511		11,762 R	69.1%	30.9%	69.1%	30.9%
WILLIAMS	14,363	10,319	4,044		6,275 R	71.8%	28.2%	71.8%	28.2%
WOOD	29,533	18,952	10,581		8,371 R	64.2%	35.8%	64.2%	35.8%
WYANDOT	10,312	6,786	3,526		3,260 R	65.8%	34.2%	65.8%	34.2%
TOTAL	4,161,859	2,217,611	1,944,248		273,363 R	53.3%	46.7%	53.3%	46.7%

PRESIDENT 1964

County	Total Vote	Republican	Democratic	Other	Rep.-Dem. Plurality	Total Vote Rep.	Total Vote Dem.	Major Vote Rep.	Major Vote Dem.
NOBLE	5,175	2,250	2,925		675 D	43.5%	56.5%	43.5%	56.5%
OTTAWA	15,257	5,639	9,618		3,979 D	37.0%	63.0%	37.0%	63.0%
PAULDING	7,719	3,254	4,465		1,211 D	42.2%	57.8%	42.2%	57.8%
PERRY	11,711	3,895	7,816		3,921 D	33.3%	66.7%	33.3%	66.7%
PICKAWAY	12,627	5,317	7,310		1,993 D	42.1%	57.9%	42.1%	57.9%
PIKE	7,898	2,567	5,331		2,764 D	32.5%	67.5%	32.5%	67.5%
PORTAGE	34,150	10,842	23,308		12,466 D	31.7%	68.3%	31.7%	68.3%
PREBLE	13,413	5,839	7,574		1,735 D	43.5%	56.5%	43.5%	56.5%
PUTNAM	12,235	5,221	7,014		1,793 D	42.7%	57.3%	42.7%	57.3%
RICHLAND	43,632	18,833	24,799		5,966 D	43.2%	56.8%	43.2%	56.8%
ROSS	22,327	9,623	12,704		3,081 D	43.1%	56.9%	43.1%	56.9%
SANDUSKY	21,735	8,254	13,481		5,227 D	38.0%	62.0%	38.0%	62.0%
SCIOTO	35,024	13,465	21,559		8,094 D	38.4%	61.6%	38.4%	61.6%
SENECA	24,054	9,536	14,518		4,982 D	39.6%	60.4%	39.6%	60.4%
SHELBY	15,194	5,190	10,004		4,814 D	34.2%	65.8%	34.2%	65.8%
STARK	142,336	53,632	88,704		35,072 D	37.7%	62.3%	37.7%	62.3%
SUMMIT	210,319	66,000	142,319		74,319 D	32.3%	67.7%	32.3%	67.7%
TRUMBULL	81,401	27,059	54,342		27,283 D	33.2%	66.8%	33.2%	66.8%
TUSCARAWAS	33,585	9,962	23,623		13,661 D	29.7%	70.3%	29.7%	70.3%
UNION	10,489	5,504	4,985		519 R	52.5%	47.5%	52.5%	47.5%
VAN WERT	13,889	6,194	7,695		1,501 D	44.6%	55.4%	44.6%	55.4%
VINTON	4,537	1,919	2,618		699 D	42.3%	57.7%	42.3%	57.7%
WARREN	23,388	10,982	12,406		1,424 D	47.0%	53.0%	47.0%	53.0%
WASHINGTON	20,066	8,873	11,193		2,320 D	44.2%	55.8%	44.2%	55.8%
WAYNE	24,696	9,890	14,806		4,916 D	40.0%	60.0%	40.0%	60.0%
WILLIAMS	13,200	5,653	7,547		1,894 D	42.8%	57.2%	42.8%	57.2%
WOOD	28,446	12,142	16,304		4,162 D	42.7%	57.3%	42.7%	57.3%
WYANDOT	9,412	4,139	5,273		1,134 D	44.0%	56.0%	44.0%	56.0%
TOTAL	3,969,196	1,470,865	2,498,331		1,027,466 D	37.1%	62.9%	37.1%	62.9%

OHIO

OTHER VOTE COMPOSITION:

1920	57,147 Socialist; 2,153 Single Tax; 294 Prohibition.
1924	358,008 Progressive; 3,025 Socialist Labor; 1,246 Commonwealth Land.
1928	8,683 Socialist; 3,556 Prohibition; 2,836 Communist; 1,515 Socialist Labor.
1932	64,094 Socialist; 7,421 Prohibition; 7,231 Communist; 1,968 Socialist Labor.
1936	132,212 Union; 5,251 Communist; 167 Socialist; 28 Socialist Labor; 7 scattered.

The county-by-county figures include only the Union and Communist vote; the state-wide total also includes the Socialist, Socialist Labor, and scattered vote.

1940
1944
1948   Progressive.
1952
1956

1960
1964

SPECIAL CASES:

1924   Progressive candidates ran second in several counties.

OKLAHOMA

PRESIDENT 1920

County	Total Vote	Republican	Democratic	Other	Rep.-Dem. Plurality	%Total Rep.	%Total Dem.	%Major Rep.	%Major Dem.
ADAIR	3,761	2,181	1,559	21	622 R	58.0%	41.5%	58.3%	41.7%
ALFALFA	4,717	3,005	1,350	362	1,655 R	63.7%	28.6%	69.0%	31.0%
ATOKA	4,818	2,081	2,100	637	19 D	43.2%	43.6%	49.8%	50.2%
BEAVER	3,289	1,973	1,076	240	897 R	60.0%	32.7%	64.7%	35.3%
BECKHAM	4,745	1,755	2,347	643	592 D	37.0%	49.5%	42.8%	57.2%
BLAINE	4,520	2,786	1,296	438	1,490 R	61.6%	28.7%	68.3%	31.7%
BRYAN	8,053	3,127	4,502	424	1,375 D	38.8%	55.9%	41.0%	59.0%
CADDO	9,071	4,823	3,594	654	1,229 R	53.2%	39.6%	57.3%	42.7%
CANADIAN	7,444	3,881	3,268	295	613 R	52.1%	43.9%	54.3%	45.7%
CARTER	10,133	3,561	5,997	575	2,436 D	35.1%	59.2%	37.3%	62.7%
CHEROKEE	4,469	2,524	1,859	86	665 R	56.5%	41.6%	57.6%	42.4%
CHOCTAW	4,908	2,094	2,531	283	437 D	42.7%	51.6%	45.3%	54.7%
CIMARRON	1,178	630	465	83	165 R	53.5%	39.5%	57.5%	42.5%
CLEVELAND	4,985	2,283	2,397	305	114 D	45.8%	48.1%	48.8%	51.2%
COAL	3,997	1,744	1,768	485	24 D	43.6%	44.2%	49.7%	50.3%
COMANCHE	6,775	3,332	3,037	406	295 R	49.2%	44.8%	52.3%	47.7%
COTTON	4,252	1,820	2,260	172	440 D	42.8%	53.2%	44.6%	55.4%
CRAIG	6,081	3,094	2,903	84	191 R	50.9%	47.7%	51.6%	48.4%
CREEK	13,974	7,948	5,408	618	2,540 R	56.9%	38.7%	59.5%	40.5%
CUSTER	5,838	3,224	2,271	343	953 R	55.2%	38.9%	58.7%	41.3%
DELAWARE	3,480	2,059	1,282	139	777 R	59.2%	36.8%	61.6%	38.4%
DEWEY	3,358	1,738	995	625	743 R	51.8%	29.6%	63.6%	36.4%
ELLIS	3,012	1,786	845	381	941 R	59.3%	28.1%	67.9%	32.1%
GARFIELD	10,858	6,611	3,671	576	2,940 R	60.9%	33.8%	64.3%	35.7%
GARVIN	7,289	2,922	4,093	274	1,171 D	40.1%	56.2%	41.7%	58.3%
GRADY	8,158	3,403	4,277	478	874 D	41.7%	52.4%	44.3%	55.7%
GRANT	5,299	3,210	1,883	206	1,327 R	60.6%	35.5%	63.0%	37.0%
GREER	3,093	1,013	1,854	226	841 D	32.8%	59.9%	35.3%	64.7%
HARMON	1,881	643	1,123	115	480 D	34.2%	59.7%	36.4%	63.6%
HARPER	2,339	1,404	753	182	651 R	60.0%	32.2%	65.1%	34.9%
HASKELL	5,075	2,673	2,201	201	472 R	52.7%	43.4%	54.8%	45.2%
HUGHES	6,686	3,049	3,487	150	438 D	45.6%	52.2%	46.6%	53.4%
JACKSON	4,456	1,345	2,694	417	1,349 D	30.2%	60.5%	33.3%	66.7%
JEFFERSON	4,403	1,733	2,289	381	556 D	39.4%	52.0%	43.1%	56.9%
JOHNSTON	4,459	1,950	2,117	392	167 D	43.7%	47.5%	47.9%	52.1%
KAY	10,736	5,959	4,546	231	1,413 R	55.5%	42.3%	56.7%	43.3%
KINGFISHER	5,213	3,220	1,744	249	1,476 R	61.8%	33.5%	64.9%	35.1%
KIOWA	5,610	2,649	2,518	443	131 R	47.2%	44.9%	51.3%	48.7%
LATIMER	2,941	1,410	1,200	331	210 R	47.9%	40.8%	54.0%	46.0%
LE FLORE	9,284	4,934	3,764	386	1,170 R	53.1%	40.5%	56.7%	43.3%
LINCOLN	8,881	5,261	2,980	640	2,281 R	59.2%	33.6%	63.8%	36.2%
LOGAN	7,109	4,618	2,209	282	2,409 R	65.0%	31.1%	67.6%	32.4%
LOVE	2,525	711	1,662	152	951 D	28.2%	65.8%	30.0%	70.0%
MCCLAIN	4,298	1,733	2,315	250	582 D	40.3%	53.9%	42.8%	57.2%
MCCURTAIN	4,887	1,966	2,603	318	637 D	40.2%	53.3%	43.0%	57.0%
MCINTOSH	5,259	2,358	2,642	259	284 D	44.8%	50.2%	47.2%	52.8%
MAJOR	3,201	1,921	784	496	1,137 R	60.0%	24.5%	71.0%	29.0%
MARSHALL	3,345	1,487	1,589	269	102 D	44.5%	47.5%	48.3%	51.7%
MAYES	4,597	2,447	1,987	163	460 R	53.2%	43.2%	55.2%	44.8%
MURRAY	3,227	1,362	1,744	121	382 D	42.2%	54.0%	43.9%	56.1%
MUSKOGEE	11,664	5,187	6,378	99	1,191 D	44.5%	54.7%	44.9%	55.1%
NOBLE	4,133	2,467	1,515	151	952 R	59.7%	36.7%	61.9%	38.1%
NOWATA	4,451	2,679	1,697	75	982 R	60.2%	38.1%	61.2%	38.8%
OKFUSKEE	3,652	1,760	1,650	242	110 R	48.2%	45.2%	51.6%	48.4%
OKLAHOMA	34,359	15,350	17,820	1,189	2,470 D	44.7%	51.9%	46.3%	53.7%
OKMULGEE	10,455	5,367	4,495	593	872 R	51.3%	43.0%	54.4%	45.6%
OSAGE	8,622	4,567	3,801	254	766 R	53.0%	44.1%	54.6%	45.4%
OTTAWA	9,616	5,270	3,974	372	1,296 R	54.8%	41.3%	57.0%	43.0%
PAWNEE	5,303	2,976	1,955	372	1,021 R	56.1%	36.9%	60.4%	39.6%
PAYNE	8,370	4,583	3,238	549	1,345 R	54.8%	38.7%	58.6%	41.4%

PRESIDENT 1924

County	Total Vote	Republican	Democratic	Other	Rep.-Dem. Plurality	%Total Rep.	%Total Dem.	%Major Rep.	%Major Dem.
ADAIR	4,488	2,317	1,942	229	375 R	51.6%	43.3%	54.4%	45.6%
ALFALFA	5,181	2,967	1,558	656	1,409 R	57.3%	30.1%	65.6%	34.4%
ATOKA	4,059	1,130	2,204	725	1,074 D	27.8%	54.3%	33.9%	66.1%
BEAVER	3,167	1,565	1,195	407	370 R	49.4%	37.7%	56.7%	43.3%
BECKHAM	4,387	1,357	2,496	534	1,139 D	30.9%	56.9%	35.2%	64.8%
BLAINE	4,647	2,255	1,488	904	767 R	48.5%	32.0%	60.2%	39.8%
BRYAN	7,072	1,780	4,593	699	2,813 D	25.2%	64.9%	27.9%	72.1%
CADDO	9,530	4,388	4,211	931	177 R	46.0%	44.2%	51.0%	49.0%
CANADIAN	7,397	3,070	3,065	1,262	5 R	41.5%	41.4%	50.0%	50.0%
CARTER	10,862	3,164	7,134	564	3,970 D	29.1%	65.7%	30.7%	69.3%
CHEROKEE	5,261	2,622	2,454	185	168 R	49.8%	46.6%	51.7%	48.3%
CHOCTAW	5,278	2,013	2,528	737	515 D	38.1%	47.9%	44.3%	55.7%
CIMARRON	1,422	586	672	164	86 D	41.2%	47.3%	46.6%	53.4%
CLEVELAND	5,008	1,672	2,841	495	1,169 D	33.4%	56.7%	37.0%	63.0%
COAL	3,179	800	1,772	607	972 D	25.2%	55.7%	31.1%	68.9%
COMANCHE	7,448	3,084	3,523	841	439 D	41.4%	47.3%	46.7%	53.3%
COTTON	3,705	1,581	1,825	299	244 D	42.7%	49.3%	46.4%	53.6%
CRAIG	5,786	2,519	3,096	171	577 D	43.5%	53.5%	44.9%	55.1%
CREEK	15,564	6,894	7,819	851	925 D	44.3%	50.2%	46.9%	53.1%
CUSTER	5,629	2,409	2,473	747	64 D	42.8%	43.9%	49.3%	50.7%
DELAWARE	3,555	1,563	1,729	263	166 D	44.0%	48.6%	47.5%	52.5%
DEWEY	3,464	1,539	1,126	799	413 R	44.4%	32.5%	57.7%	42.3%
ELLIS	3,078	1,499	879	700	620 R	48.7%	28.6%	63.0%	37.0%
GARFIELD	13,369	7,524	3,791	2,054	3,733 R	56.3%	28.4%	66.5%	33.5%
GARVIN	6,933	1,863	4,758	312	2,895 D	26.9%	68.6%	28.1%	71.9%
GRADY	8,586	2,640	5,091	855	2,451 D	30.7%	59.3%	34.1%	65.9%
GRANT	5,412	2,800	1,990	622	810 R	51.7%	36.8%	58.5%	41.5%
GREER	2,826	551	1,982	293	1,431 D	19.5%	70.1%	21.8%	78.2%
HARMON	1,456	339	1,049	68	710 D	23.3%	72.0%	24.4%	75.6%
HARPER	2,415	1,226	824	365	402 R	50.8%	34.1%	59.8%	40.2%
HASKELL	4,816	1,935	2,480	401	545 D	40.2%	51.5%	43.8%	56.2%
HUGHES	6,200	1,994	3,996	210	2,002 D	32.2%	64.5%	33.3%	66.7%
JACKSON	3,804	941	2,342	521	1,401 D	24.7%	61.6%	28.7%	71.3%
JEFFERSON	3,763	1,108	2,441	214	1,333 D	29.4%	64.9%	31.2%	68.8%
JOHNSTON	3,621	923	2,122	576	1,199 D	25.5%	58.6%	30.3%	69.7%
KAY	14,448	7,392	6,049	1,007	1,343 R	51.2%	41.9%	55.0%	45.0%
KINGFISHER	5,095	2,834	1,644	617	1,190 R	55.6%	32.3%	63.3%	36.7%
KIOWA	4,854	1,688	2,635	531	947 D	34.8%	54.3%	39.0%	61.0%
LATIMER	2,702	971	1,457	274	486 D	35.9%	53.9%	40.0%	60.0%
LE FLORE	8,247	3,326	4,069	852	743 D	40.3%	49.3%	45.0%	55.0%
LINCOLN	8,242	4,220	3,283	739	937 R	51.2%	39.8%	56.2%	43.8%
LOGAN	7,562	4,445	2,366	751	2,079 R	58.8%	31.3%	65.3%	34.7%
LOVE	2,728	479	1,713	536	1,234 D	17.6%	62.8%	21.9%	78.1%
MCCLAIN	4,011	1,233	2,519	259	1,286 D	30.7%	62.8%	32.9%	67.1%
MCCURTAIN	5,185	1,669	3,279	237	1,610 D	32.2%	63.2%	33.7%	66.3%
MCINTOSH	4,495	1,675	2,723	97	1,048 D	37.3%	60.6%	38.1%	61.9%
MAJOR	3,044	1,781	649	614	1,132 R	58.5%	21.3%	73.3%	26.7%
MARSHALL	3,346	866	1,935	545	1,069 D	25.9%	57.8%	30.9%	69.1%
MAYES	4,888	2,317	2,246	325	71 R	47.4%	45.9%	50.8%	49.2%
MURRAY	3,015	784	2,083	148	1,299 D	26.0%	69.1%	27.3%	72.7%
MUSKOGEE	13,697	6,158	6,895	644	737 D	45.0%	50.3%	47.2%	52.8%
NOBLE	5,240	2,680	1,927	633	753 R	51.1%	36.8%	58.2%	41.8%
NOWATA	4,500	2,296	2,049	155	247 R	51.0%	45.5%	52.8%	47.2%
OKFUSKEE	4,349	1,431	2,654	264	1,223 D	32.9%	61.0%	35.0%	65.0%
OKLAHOMA	43,085	17,504	21,708	3,873	4,204 D	40.6%	50.4%	44.6%	55.4%
OKMULGEE	12,838	6,015	5,927	896	88 R	46.9%	46.2%	50.4%	49.6%
OSAGE	14,202	6,363	7,070	769	707 D	44.8%	49.8%	47.4%	52.6%
OTTAWA	10,377	5,197	4,522	658	675 R	50.1%	43.6%	53.5%	46.5%
PAWNEE	6,021	3,093	2,376	552	717 R	51.4%	39.5%	56.6%	43.4%
PAYNE	9,933	4,817	4,342	774	475 R	48.5%	43.7%	52.6%	47.4%

OKLAHOMA

PRESIDENT 1920

County	Total Vote	Republican	Democratic	Other	Rep.-Dem. Plurality	Total Vote Rep.	Total Vote Dem.	Major Vote Rep.	Major Vote Dem.
PITTSBURG	11,387	5,371	5,361	655	10 R	47.2%	47.1%	50.0%	50.0%
PONTOTOC	6,376	2,370	3,800	206	1,430 D	37.2%	59.6%	38.4%	61.6%
POTTAWATOMIE	11,260	5,355	5,310	595	45 R	47.6%	47.2%	50.2%	49.8%
PUSHMATAHA	3,496	1,864	1,365	267	499 R	53.3%	39.0%	57.7%	42.3%
ROGER MILLS	2,552	1,193	931	428	262 R	46.7%	36.5%	56.2%	43.8%
ROGERS	5,519	2,844	2,459	216	385 R	51.5%	44.6%	53.6%	46.4%
SEMINOLE	5,569	3,382	1,869	318	1,513 R	60.7%	33.6%	64.4%	35.6%
SEQUOYAH	5,813	3,195	2,505	113	690 R	55.0%	43.1%	56.1%	43.9%
STEPHENS	5,197	2,035	2,816	346	781 D	39.2%	54.2%	42.0%	58.0%
TEXAS	3,295	1,762	1,398	135	364 R	53.5%	42.4%	55.8%	44.2%
TILLMAN	4,338	1,539	2,649	150	1,110 D	35.5%	61.1%	36.7%	63.3%
TULSA	24,999	14,357	10,025	617	4,332 R	57.4%	40.1%	58.9%	41.1%
WAGONER	2,965	1,432	1,375	158	57 R	48.3%	46.4%	51.0%	49.0%
WASHINGTON	7,099	4,105	2,805	189	1,300 R	57.8%	39.5%	59.4%	40.6%
WASHITA	4,515	2,070	2,125	320	55 D	45.8%	47.1%	49.3%	50.7%
WOODS	4,687	2,827	1,530	330	1,297 R	60.3%	32.6%	64.9%	35.1%
WOODWARD	4,219	2,492	1,437	290	1,055 R	59.1%	34.1%	63.4%	36.6%
TOTAL	485,678	243,840	216,122	25,716	27,718 R	50.2%	44.5%	53.0%	47.0%

PRESIDENT 1924

County	Total Vote	Republican	Democratic	Other	Rep.-Dem. Plurality	Total Vote Rep.	Total Vote Dem.	Major Vote Rep.	Major Vote Dem.
PITTSBURG	10,765	3,554	6,062	1,149	2,508 D	33.0%	56.3%	37.0%	63.0%
PONTOTOC	6,620	1,859	4,268	493	2,409 D	28.1%	64.5%	30.3%	69.7%
POTTAWATOMIE	10,407	4,040	5,072	1,295	1,032 D	38.8%	48.7%	44.3%	55.7%
PUSHMATAHA	3,006	1,084	1,647	275	563 D	36.1%	54.8%	39.7%	60.3%
ROGER MILLS	2,783	946	1,318	519	372 D	34.0%	47.4%	41.8%	58.2%
ROGERS	5,345	2,207	2,901	237	694 D	41.3%	54.3%	43.2%	56.8%
SEMINOLE	5,808	2,326	3,007	475	681 D	40.0%	51.8%	43.6%	56.4%
SEQUOYAH	6,374	2,875	3,429	70	554 D	45.1%	53.8%	45.6%	54.4%
STEPHENS	7,534	2,377	4,745	412	2,368 D	31.6%	63.0%	33.6%	66.6%
TEXAS	3,962	1,745	1,812	405	67 D	44.0%	45.7%	49.1%	50.9%
TILLMAN	4,163	1,326	2,653	184	1,327 D	31.9%	63.7%	33.3%	66.7%
TULSA	35,179	19,537	14,377	1,265	5,160 R	55.5%	40.9%	57.6%	42.4%
WAGONER	3,903	1,646	1,985	272	339 D	42.2%	50.9%	45.3%	54.7%
WASHINGTON	8,300	4,579	3,487	234	1,092 R	55.2%	42.0%	56.8%	43.2%
WASHITA	4,054	1,357	2,325	372	968 D	33.5%	57.4%	36.9%	63.1%
WOODS	4,988	2,615	1,533	840	1,082 R	52.4%	30.7%	63.0%	37.0%
WOODWARD	4,015	1,831	1,418	766	413 R	45.6%	35.3%	56.4%	43.6%
TOTAL	527,828	225,756	255,798	46,274	30,042 D	42.8%	48.5%	46.9%	53.1%

OKLAHOMA

PRESIDENT 1928

County	Total Vote	Republican	Democratic	Other	Rep.-Dem. Plurality	Total Vote % Rep.	Total Vote % Dem.	Major Vote % Rep.	Major Vote % Dem.
ADAIR	4,831	2,867	1,944	20	923 R	59.3%	40.2%	59.6%	40.4%
ALFALFA	5,417	4,224	1,086	107	3,138 R	78.1%	20.0%	79.5%	20.5%
ATOKA	3,661	1,572	2,056	33	484 D	42.9%	56.2%	43.3%	56.7%
BEAVER	3,524	2,596	887	41	1,709 R	73.7%	25.2%	74.5%	25.5%
BECKHAM	6,110	3,810	2,201	99	1,609 R	62.4%	36.0%	63.4%	36.6%
BLAINE	5,032	3,413	1,543	76	1,870 R	67.8%	30.7%	68.9%	31.1%
BRYAN	6,950	3,014	3,885	51	871 D	43.4%	55.9%	43.7%	56.3%
CADDO	11,378	7,313	3,885	180	3,428 R	64.3%	34.1%	65.3%	34.7%
CANADIAN	7,875	5,011	2,786	78	2,225 R	63.6%	35.4%	64.3%	35.7%
CARTER	11,716	6,538	5,086	92	1,452 R	55.8%	43.4%	56.2%	43.8%
CHEROKEE	5,438	2,963	2,446	29	517 R	54.5%	45.0%	54.8%	45.2%
CHOCTAW	5,152	2,541	2,581	30	40 D	49.3%	50.1%	49.6%	50.4%
CIMARRON	1,725	1,139	566	20	573 R	66.1%	32.8%	66.8%	33.2%
CLEVELAND	6,093	3,738	2,291	64	1,447 R	61.3%	37.6%	62.0%	38.0%
COAL	2,996	1,283	1,681	32	398 D	42.8%	56.1%	43.3%	56.7%
COMANCHE	8,117	5,069	2,956	92	2,113 R	62.4%	36.4%	63.2%	36.8%
COTTON	4,048	2,419	1,605	24	814 R	59.8%	39.6%	60.1%	39.9%
CRAIG	6,444	3,511	2,897	36	614 R	54.5%	45.0%	54.8%	45.2%
CREEK	18,042	12,254	5,693	95	6,561 R	67.9%	31.6%	68.3%	31.7%
CUSTER	6,674	4,576	1,995	103	2,581 R	68.6%	29.9%	69.6%	30.4%
DELAWARE	4,360	2,603	1,706	51	897 R	59.7%	39.1%	60.4%	39.6%
DEWEY	3,804	2,486	1,175	143	1,311 R	65.4%	30.9%	67.9%	32.1%
ELLIS	3,110	1,953	1,122	35	831 R	62.8%	36.1%	63.5%	36.5%
GARFIELD	16,392	12,748	3,503	141	9,245 R	77.8%	21.4%	78.4%	21.6%
GARVIN	7,001	3,321	3,589	91	268 D	47.4%	51.3%	48.1%	51.9%
GRADY	10,109	6,332	3,667	110	2,665 R	62.6%	36.3%	63.3%	36.7%
GRANT	5,883	4,371	1,449	63	2,922 R	74.3%	24.6%	75.1%	24.9%
GREER	3,935	2,262	1,645	28	617 R	57.5%	41.8%	57.9%	42.1%
HARMON	2,517	1,431	1,060	26	371 R	56.9%	42.1%	57.4%	42.6%
HARPER	2,775	1,844	872	59	972 R	66.5%	31.4%	67.9%	32.1%
HASKELL	4,782	2,580	2,172	30	408 R	54.0%	45.4%	54.3%	45.7%
HUGHES	7,135	3,937	3,169	29	768 R	55.2%	44.4%	55.4%	44.6%
JACKSON	5,960	3,440	2,493	27	947 R	57.7%	41.8%	58.0%	42.0%
JEFFERSON	4,185	2,251	1,916	18	335 R	53.8%	45.8%	54.0%	46.0%
JOHNSTON	3,096	1,294	1,766	36	472 D	41.8%	57.0%	42.3%	57.7%
KAY	18,161	13,829	4,196	136	9,633 R	76.1%	23.1%	76.7%	23.3%
KINGFISHER	5,882	4,063	1,780	39	2,283 R	69.1%	30.3%	69.5%	30.5%
KIOWA	6,478	4,116	2,270	92	1,846 R	63.5%	35.0%	64.5%	35.5%
LATIMER	2,989	1,368	1,583	38	215 D	45.8%	53.0%	46.4%	53.6%
LE FLORE	9,847	5,168	4,622	57	546 R	52.5%	46.9%	52.8%	47.2%
LINCOLN	8,649	6,118	2,405	126	3,713 R	70.7%	27.8%	71.8%	28.2%
LOGAN	8,632	6,277	2,251	104	4,026 R	72.7%	26.1%	73.6%	26.4%
LOVE	2,111	843	1,268		425 D	39.9%	60.1%	39.9%	60.1%
MCCLAIN	4,356	2,399	1,913	44	486 R	55.1%	43.9%	55.6%	44.4%
MCCURTAIN	4,813	1,915	2,877	21	962 D	39.8%	59.8%	40.0%	60.0%
MCINTOSH	4,821	2,742	2,044	35	698 R	56.9%	42.4%	57.3%	42.7%
MAJOR	3,672	2,891	674	107	2,217 R	78.7%	18.4%	81.1%	18.9%
MARSHALL	2,501	1,063	1,358	80	295 D	42.5%	54.3%	43.9%	56.1%
MAYES	5,214	3,004	2,161	49	843 R	57.6%	41.4%	58.2%	41.8%
MURRAY	3,165	1,631	1,498	36	133 R	51.5%	47.3%	52.1%	47.9%
MUSKOGEE	16,369	9,972	6,343	54	3,629 R	60.9%	38.8%	61.1%	38.9%
NOBLE	5,448	3,607	1,777	64	1,830 R	66.2%	32.6%	67.0%	33.0%
NOWATA	4,712	2,930	1,763	19	1,167 R	62.2%	37.4%	62.4%	37.6%
OKFUSKEE	6,201	3,612	2,513	76	1,099 R	58.2%	40.5%	59.0%	41.0%
OKLAHOMA	52,953	36,608	16,073	272	20,535 R	69.1%	30.4%	69.5%	30.5%
OKMULGEE	15,056	9,149	5,834	73	3,315 R	60.8%	38.7%	61.1%	38.9%
OSAGE	15,632	10,555	5,010	67	5,545 R	67.5%	32.0%	67.8%	32.2%
OTTAWA	12,720	8,114	4,488	88	3,626 R	63.8%	35.3%	64.4%	35.5%
PAWNEE	6,523	4,489	1,949	85	2,540 R	68.8%	29.9%	69.7%	30.3%
PAYNE	10,893	7,864	2,904	125	4,960 R	72.2%	26.7%	73.0%	27.0%

PRESIDENT 1932

County	Total Vote	Republican	Democratic	Other	Rep.-Dem. Plurality	Total Vote % Rep.	Total Vote % Dem.	Major Vote % Rep.	Major Vote % Dem.
ADAIR	5,753	1,941	3,812		1,871 D	33.7%	66.3%	33.7%	66.3%
ALFALFA	5,679	2,037	3,642		1,605 D	35.9%	64.1%	35.9%	64.1%
ATOKA	4,240	562	3,678		3,116 D	13.3%	86.7%	13.3%	86.7%
BEAVER	3,911	1,358	2,553		1,195 D	34.7%	65.3%	34.7%	65.3%
BECKHAM	6,871	892	5,979		5,087 D	13.0%	87.0%	13.0%	87.0%
BLAINE	6,447	1,728	4,719		2,991 D	26.8%	73.2%	26.8%	73.2%
BRYAN	8,506	825	7,681		6,856 D	9.7%	90.3%	9.7%	90.3%
CADDO	13,973	2,972	11,001		8,029 D	21.3%	78.7%	21.3%	78.7%
CANADIAN	9,316	2,549	6,767		4,218 D	27.4%	72.6%	27.4%	72.6%
CARTER	11,366	1,733	9,633		7,900 D	15.2%	84.8%	15.2%	84.8%
CHEROKEE	6,908	2,275	4,633		2,358 D	32.9%	67.1%	32.9%	67.1%
CHOCTAW	5,948	1,040	4,908		3,868 D	17.5%	82.5%	17.5%	82.5%
CIMARRON	2,466	571	1,895		1,324 D	23.2%	76.8%	23.2%	76.8%
CLEVELAND	7,837	1,868	5,969		4,101 D	23.8%	76.2%	23.8%	76.2%
COAL	3,088	300	2,788		2,488 D	9.7%	90.3%	9.7%	90.3%
COMANCHE	9,632	2,046	7,586		5,540 D	21.2%	78.8%	21.2%	78.8%
COTTON	5,184	758	4,426		3,668 D	14.6%	85.4%	14.6%	85.4%
CRAIG	6,985	2,124	4,861		2,737 D	30.4%	69.6%	30.4%	69.6%
CREEK	19,749	6,786	12,963		6,177 D	34.4%	65.6%	34.4%	65.6%
CUSTER	8,257	1,684	6,573		4,889 D	20.4%	79.6%	20.4%	79.6%
DELAWARE	5,153	1,469	3,684		2,215 D	28.5%	71.5%	28.5%	71.5%
DEWEY	4,906	1,051	3,855		2,804 D	21.4%	78.6%	21.4%	78.6%
ELLIS	3,884	1,089	2,795		1,706 D	28.0%	72.0%	28.0%	72.0%
GARFIELD	17,610	6,837	10,773		3,936 D	38.8%	61.2%	38.8%	61.2%
GARVIN	8,868	1,034	7,834		6,800 D	11.7%	88.3%	11.7%	88.3%
GRADY	11,281	2,034	9,247		7,213 D	18.0%	82.0%	18.0%	82.0%
GRANT	6,334	1,902	4,432		2,530 D	30.0%	70.0%	30.0%	70.0%
GREER	4,658	418	4,240		3,822 D	9.0%	91.0%	9.0%	91.0%
HARMON	3,231	189	3,042		2,853 D	5.8%	94.2%	5.8%	94.2%
HARPER	2,922	783	2,139		1,356 D	26.8%	73.2%	26.8%	73.2%
HASKELL	5,796	1,439	4,357		2,918 D	24.8%	75.2%	24.8%	75.2%
HUGHES	7,599	1,114	6,485		5,371 D	14.7%	85.3%	14.7%	85.3%
JACKSON	6,362	603	5,759		5,156 D	9.5%	90.5%	9.5%	90.5%
JEFFERSON	4,051	485	3,566		3,081 D	12.0%	88.0%	12.0%	88.0%
JOHNSTON	3,606	329	3,277		2,948 D	9.1%	90.9%	9.1%	90.9%
KAY	18,725	5,884	12,841		6,957 D	31.4%	68.6%	31.4%	68.6%
KINGFISHER	6,089	2,103	3,986		1,883 D	34.5%	65.5%	34.5%	65.5%
KIOWA	6,170	966	5,204		4,238 D	15.7%	84.3%	15.7%	84.3%
LATIMER	3,847	728	3,119		2,391 D	18.9%	81.1%	18.9%	81.1%
LE FLORE	11,843	2,363	8,680		6,317 D	21.4%	78.6%	21.4%	78.6%
LINCOLN	11,146	3,505	7,641		4,136 D	31.4%	68.6%	31.4%	68.6%
LOGAN	9,732	3,959	5,773		1,814 D	40.7%	59.3%	40.7%	59.3%
LOVE	2,613	187	2,426		2,239 D	7.2%	92.8%	7.2%	92.8%
MCCLAIN	5,905	818	5,087		4,269 D	13.9%	86.1%	13.9%	86.1%
MCCURTAIN	6,473	587	5,886		5,299 D	9.1%	90.9%	9.1%	90.9%
MCINTOSH	5,610	1,077	4,533		3,456 D	19.2%	80.8%	19.2%	80.8%
MAJOR	3,899	1,374	2,525		1,151 D	35.2%	64.8%	35.2%	64.8%
MARSHALL	3,555	319	3,236		2,917 D	9.0%	91.0%	9.0%	91.0%
MAYES	6,040	1,596	4,444		2,848 D	26.4%	73.6%	26.4%	73.6%
MURRAY	3,618	532	3,086		2,554 D	14.7%	85.3%	14.7%	85.3%
MUSKOGEE	17,972	5,351	12,621		7,270 D	29.8%	70.2%	29.8%	70.2%
NOBLE	6,049	1,635	4,414		2,779 D	27.0%	73.0%	27.0%	73.0%
NOWATA	5,673	1,900	3,773		1,873 D	33.5%	66.5%	33.5%	66.5%
OKFUSKEE	6,541	1,415	5,126		3,711 D	21.6%	78.4%	21.6%	78.4%
OKLAHOMA	62,368	21,238	41,130		19,892 D	34.1%	65.9%	34.1%	65.9%
OKMULGEE	16,049	4,762	11,287		6,525 D	29.7%	70.3%	29.7%	70.3%
OSAGE	15,608	4,775	10,833		6,058 D	30.6%	69.4%	30.6%	69.4%
OTTAWA	11,385	3,210	8,175		4,965 D	28.2%	71.8%	28.2%	71.8%
PAWNEE	7,280	2,280	5,000		2,720 D	31.3%	68.7%	31.3%	68.7%
PAYNE	11,693	3,874	7,819		3,945 D	33.1%	66.9%	33.1%	66.9%

OKLAHOMA

PRESIDENT 1928

County	Total Vote	Republican	Democratic	Other	Rep.-Dem. Plurality	Percentage Total Vote Rep.	Dem.	Major Vote Rep.	Dem.
PITTSBURG	11,942	5,875	5,960	107	85 D	49.2%	49.9%	49.6%	50.4%
PONTOTOC	6,597	3,356	3,203	38	153 R	50.9%	48.6%	51.2%	48.8%
POTTAWATOMIE	12,364	8,478	3,797	89	4,681 R	68.6%	30.7%	69.1%	30.9%
PUSHMATAHA	3,056	1,616	1,384	56	232 R	52.9%	45.3%	53.9%	46.1%
ROGER MILLS	3,067	1,948	986	133	962 R	63.5%	32.1%	66.4%	33.6%
ROGERS	5,665	3,477	2,147	41	1,330 R	61.4%	37.9%	61.8%	38.2%
SEMINOLE	12,495	8,072	4,423		3,649 R	64.6%	35.4%	64.6%	35.4%
SEQUOYAH	5,988	3,296	2,692		604 R	55.0%	45.0%	55.0%	45.0%
STEPHENS	8,279	5,192	2,982	105	2,210 R	62.7%	36.0%	63.5%	36.5%
TEXAS	4,179	2,890	1,240	49	1,650 R	69.2%	29.7%	70.0%	30.0%
TILLMAN	5,497	3,331	2,141	25	1,190 R	60.6%	38.9%	60.9%	39.1%
TULSA	54,998	38,769	16,062	167	22,707 R	70.5%	29.2%	70.7%	29.3%
WAGONER	4,497	2,726	1,745	26	981 R	60.6%	38.8%	61.0%	39.0%
WASHINGTON	9,877	7,258	2,563	56	4,695 R	73.5%	25.9%	73.9%	26.1%
WASHITA	5,645	3,572	2,024	49	1,548 R	63.3%	35.9%	63.8%	36.2%
WOODS	5,600	3,941	1,550	109	2,391 R	70.4%	27.7%	71.8%	28.2%
WOODWARD	4,616	3,188	1,347	81	1,841 R	69.1%	29.2%	70.3%	29.7%
TOTAL	618,427	394,046	219,174	5,207	174,872 R	63.7%	35.4%	64.3%	35.7%

PRESIDENT 1932

Total Vote	Republican	Democratic	Other	Rep.-Dem. Plurality	Percentage Total Vote Rep.	Dem.	Major Vote Rep.	Dem.
12,932	2,396	10,536		8,140 D	18.5%	81.5%	18.5%	81.5%
8,434	1,207	7,227		6,020 D	14.3%	85.7%	14.3%	85.7%
16,076	4,063	12,013		7,950 D	25.3%	74.7%	25.3%	74.7%
3,909	490	3,419		2,929 D	12.5%	87.5%	12.5%	87.5%
4,159	511	3,648		3,137 D	12.3%	87.7%	12.3%	87.7%
7,226	1,879	5,347		3,468 D	26.0%	74.0%	26.0%	74.0%
15,502	3,348	12,154		8,806 D	21.6%	78.4%	21.6%	78.4%
6,537	1,833	4,704		2,871 D	28.0%	72.0%	28.0%	72.0%
8,718	1,012	7,706		6,694 D	11.6%	88.4%	11.6%	88.4%
5,405	1,372	4,033		2,661 D	25.4%	74.6%	25.4%	74.6%
5,483	523	4,960		4,437 D	9.5%	90.5%	9.5%	90.5%
60,871	25,541	35,330		9,789 D	42.0%	58.0%	42.0%	58.0%
5,520	1,505	4,015		2,510 D	27.3%	72.7%	27.3%	72.7%
11,576	4,713	6,863		2,150 D	40.7%	59.3%	40.7%	59.3%
6,936	887	6,049		5,162 D	12.8%	87.2%	12.8%	87.2%
6,287	2,008	4,279		2,271 D	31.9%	68.1%	31.9%	68.1%
5,602	1,614	3,988		2,374 D	28.8%	71.2%	28.8%	71.2%
704,633	188,165	516,468		328,303 D	26.7%	73.3%	26.7%	73.3%

OKLAHOMA

PRESIDENT 1936

County	Total Vote	Republican	Democratic	Other	Rep.-Dem. Plurality	Pct. Total Rep.	Pct. Total Dem.	Pct. Major Rep.	Pct. Major Dem.
ADAIR	5,972	2,699	3,257	16	558 D	45.2%	54.5%	45.3%	54.7%
ALFALFA	6,026	2,573	3,398	55	825 D	42.7%	56.4%	43.1%	56.9%
ATOKA	4,323	1,141	3,173	9	2,032 D	26.4%	73.4%	26.4%	73.6%
BEAVER	3,863	1,340	2,502	21	1,162 D	34.7%	64.8%	34.9%	65.1%
BECKHAM	6,780	1,352	5,372	56	4,020 D	19.9%	79.2%	20.1%	79.9%
BLAINE	7,196	2,877	4,242	77	1,365 D	40.0%	58.9%	40.4%	59.6%
BRYAN	9,488	1,362	8,106	20	6,744 D	14.4%	85.4%	14.4%	85.6%
CADDO	14,669	5,205	9,358	106	4,153 D	35.5%	63.8%	35.7%	64.3%
CANADIAN	9,508	3,325	6,135	48	2,810 D	35.0%	64.5%	35.1%	64.9%
CARTER	11,669	2,247	9,387	35	7,140 D	19.3%	80.4%	19.3%	80.7%
CHEROKEE	6,904	2,917	3,966	21	1,049 D	42.3%	57.4%	42.4%	57.6%
CHOCTAW	5,910	1,269	4,624	17	3,355 D	21.5%	78.2%	21.5%	78.5%
CIMARRON	1,910	555	1,342	13	787 D	29.1%	70.3%	29.3%	70.7%
CLEVELAND	9,022	2,643	6,304	75	3,661 D	29.3%	69.9%	29.5%	70.5%
COAL	3,160	603	2,550	7	1,947 D	19.1%	80.7%	19.1%	80.9%
COMANCHE	10,140	3,039	7,026	75	3,987 D	30.0%	69.3%	30.2%	69.8%
COTTON	5,040	1,181	3,842	17	2,661 D	23.4%	76.2%	23.5%	76.5%
CRAIG	7,354	2,964	4,377	13	1,413 D	40.3%	59.5%	40.4%	59.6%
CREEK	19,903	7,257	12,540	106	5,283 D	36.5%	63.0%	36.7%	63.3%
CUSTER	7,525	2,386	5,093	46	2,707 D	31.7%	67.7%	31.9%	68.1%
DELAWARE	6,045	2,632	3,398	15	766 D	43.5%	56.2%	43.6%	56.4%
DEWEY	4,863	1,846	2,980	37	1,134 D	38.0%	61.3%	38.3%	61.7%
ELLIS	3,847	1,324	2,493	30	1,169 D	34.4%	64.8%	34.7%	65.3%
GARFIELD	18,723	7,457	11,142	124	3,685 D	39.8%	59.5%	40.1%	59.9%
GARVIN	8,034	1,700	6,276	58	4,576 D	21.2%	78.1%	21.3%	78.7%
GRADY	12,099	3,013	9,025	61	6,012 D	24.9%	74.6%	25.0%	75.0%
GRANT	6,294	2,307	3,955	32	1,648 D	36.7%	62.8%	36.8%	63.2%
GREER	4,522	766	3,745	11	2,979 D	16.9%	82.8%	17.0%	83.0%
HARMON	2,912	331	2,570	11	2,239 D	11.4%	88.2%	11.4%	88.6%
HARPER	2,911	1,068	1,836	7	768 D	36.7%	63.1%	36.8%	63.2%
HASKELL	6,144	2,182	3,961	1	1,779 D	35.5%	64.5%	35.5%	64.5%
HUGHES	8,030	2,032	5,990	8	3,958 D	25.3%	74.2%	25.4%	74.7%
JACKSON	6,571	1,095	5,435	41	4,340 D	16.7%	82.7%	16.8%	83.2%
JEFFERSON	4,773	1,032	3,719	22	2,687 D	21.6%	77.9%	21.7%	78.3%
JOHNSTON	3,865	743	3,099	23	2,356 D	19.2%	80.2%	19.3%	80.7%
KAY	18,649	6,671	11,846	132	5,175 D	35.8%	63.5%	36.0%	64.0%
KINGFISHER	6,652	2,539	4,081	32	1,542 D	38.2%	61.3%	38.4%	61.6%
KIOWA	7,161	1,684	5,424	53	3,740 D	23.5%	75.7%	23.7%	76.3%
LATIMER	4,286	1,344	2,923	19	1,579 D	31.4%	68.2%	31.5%	68.5%
LE FLORE	11,969	3,894	8,061	14	4,167 D	32.5%	67.3%	32.6%	67.4%
LINCOLN	11,407	5,452	5,903	52	451 D	47.8%	51.7%	48.0%	52.0%
LOGAN	10,095	4,609	5,425	61	816 D	45.7%	53.7%	45.9%	54.1%
LOVE	2,687	440	2,227	20	1,787 D	16.4%	82.9%	16.5%	83.5%
MCCLAIN	5,300	1,191	4,092	17	2,901 D	22.5%	77.2%	22.5%	77.5%
MCCURTAIN	6,221	1,119	5,089	13	3,970 D	18.0%	81.8%	18.0%	82.0%
MCINTOSH	6,384	2,470	3,898	16	1,428 D	38.7%	61.1%	38.8%	61.2%
MAJOR	4,204	2,230	1,929	45	301 R	53.0%	45.9%	53.6%	46.4%
MARSHALL	3,278	415	2,840	23	2,425 D	12.7%	86.6%	12.7%	87.3%
MAYES	6,334	2,690	3,631	13	941 D	42.5%	57.3%	42.6%	57.4%
MURRAY	4,027	823	3,181	23	2,358 D	20.4%	79.0%	20.6%	79.4%
MUSKOGEE	19,829	6,452	13,344	33	6,892 D	32.5%	67.3%	32.6%	67.4%
NOBLE	6,375	2,461	3,901	13	1,440 D	38.6%	61.2%	38.7%	61.3%
NOWATA	6,084	2,552	3,512	20	960 D	42.0%	57.7%	42.1%	57.9%
OKFUSKEE	7,052	2,162	4,843	47	2,681 D	30.7%	68.7%	30.9%	69.1%
OKLAHOMA	75,631	24,312	50,946	373	26,634 D	32.1%	67.4%	32.3%	67.7%
OKMULGEE	17,093	4,975	12,061	57	7,086 D	29.1%	70.6%	29.2%	70.8%
OSAGE	15,056	4,917	10,090	49	5,173 D	32.7%	67.0%	32.8%	67.2%
OTTAWA	12,412	4,697	7,658	57	2,961 D	37.8%	61.7%	38.0%	62.0%
PAWNEE	7,064	2,961	4,031	72	1,070 D	41.9%	57.1%	42.3%	57.7%
PAYNE	12,921	4,783	8,081	57	3,298 D	37.0%	62.5%	37.2%	62.8%

PRESIDENT 1940

County	Total Vote	Republican	Democratic	Other	Rep.-Dem. Plurality	Pct. Total Rep.	Pct. Total Dem.	Pct. Major Rep.	Pct. Major Dem.
ADAIR	6,484	3,275	3,203	6	72 R	50.5%	49.4%	50.6%	49.4%
ALFALFA	6,455	3,675	2,720	60	955 R	56.9%	42.1%	57.5%	42.5%
ATOKA	5,832	2,218	3,601	13	1,383 D	38.0%	61.7%	38.1%	61.9%
BEAVER	4,282	2,219	2,034	29	185 R	51.8%	47.5%	52.2%	47.8%
BECKHAM	6,783	2,148	4,598	37	2,450 D	31.7%	67.8%	31.8%	68.2%
BLAINE	7,216	4,080	3,095	41	985 R	56.5%	42.9%	56.9%	43.1%
BRYAN	11,310	2,190	9,095	25	6,905 D	19.4%	80.4%	19.4%	80.6%
CADDO	14,645	6,304	8,280	61	1,976 D	43.0%	56.5%	43.2%	56.8%
CANADIAN	10,237	4,699	5,506	32	807 D	45.9%	53.8%	46.0%	54.0%
CARTER	13,746	3,270	10,441	35	7,171 D	23.8%	76.0%	23.8%	76.2%
CHEROKEE	8,098	4,128	3,952	18	176 R	51.0%	48.8%	51.1%	48.9%
CHOCTAW	7,561	2,365	5,177	19	2,812 D	31.3%	68.5%	31.4%	68.6%
CIMARRON	1,853	841	989	23	148 D	45.4%	53.4%	46.0%	54.0%
CLEVELAND	9,650	3,660	5,933	57	2,273 D	37.9%	61.5%	38.2%	61.8%
COAL	3,535	1,148	2,377	10	1,229 D	32.5%	67.2%	32.6%	67.4%
COMANCHE	10,535	3,703	6,796	36	3,093 D	35.1%	64.5%	35.3%	64.7%
COTTON	4,760	1,616	3,121	23	1,505 D	33.9%	65.5%	34.1%	65.6%
CRAIG	7,917	3,582	4,316	19	734 D	45.2%	54.5%	45.4%	54.6%
CREEK	20,495	9,468	10,976	51	1,508 D	46.2%	53.5%	46.3%	53.7%
CUSTER	8,071	3,419	4,612	40	1,193 D	42.4%	57.1%	42.6%	57.4%
DELAWARE	6,739	3,305	3,417	17	112 D	49.0%	50.7%	49.2%	50.8%
DEWEY	5,038	2,613	2,391	34	222 R	51.9%	47.5%	52.2%	47.8%
ELLIS	3,836	2,162	1,657	17	505 R	56.4%	43.2%	56.6%	43.4%
GARFIELD	20,502	10,792	9,544	166	1,248 R	52.6%	46.5%	53.1%	46.9%
GARVIN	9,999	2,958	7,001	40	4,043 D	29.6%	70.0%	29.7%	70.3%
GRADY	12,417	4,299	8,075	43	3,776 D	34.6%	65.0%	34.7%	65.3%
GRANT	6,402	3,394	2,970	38	424 R	53.0%	46.4%	53.3%	46.7%
GREER	4,740	1,195	3,524	21	2,329 D	25.2%	74.3%	25.3%	74.7%
HARMON	3,041	731	2,292	18	1,561 D	24.0%	75.4%	24.2%	75.8%
HARPER	3,073	1,616	1,419	38	197 R	52.6%	46.2%	53.2%	46.8%
HASKELL	6,566	2,661	3,896	9	1,235 D	40.5%	59.3%	40.6%	59.4%
HUGHES	8,863	2,837	6,005	21	3,168 D	34.5%	65.3%	34.5%	65.5%
JACKSON	6,408	1,540	4,832	36	3,292 D	24.0%	75.4%	24.2%	75.8%
JEFFERSON	5,060	1,226	3,814	20	2,588 D	24.2%	75.4%	24.3%	75.7%
JOHNSTON	4,329	1,362	2,955	12	1,593 D	31.5%	68.3%	31.5%	68.5%
KAY	20,884	10,003	10,725	156	722 D	47.9%	51.4%	48.3%	51.7%
KINGFISHER	6,617	3,718	2,865	34	853 R	56.2%	43.3%	56.5%	43.5%
KIOWA	7,252	2,539	4,679	34	2,140 D	35.0%	64.5%	35.2%	64.8%
LATIMER	4,766	1,600	3,138	28	1,538 D	33.6%	65.8%	33.8%	66.2%
LE FLORE	13,087	4,664	8,379	44	3,715 D	35.6%	64.0%	35.8%	64.2%
LINCOLN	11,574	6,269	5,271	34	998 R	54.2%	45.5%	54.3%	45.7%
LOGAN	10,225	5,427	4,752	46	675 R	53.1%	46.5%	53.3%	46.7%
LOVE	3,183	687	2,485	11	1,798 D	21.6%	78.1%	21.6%	78.3%
MCCLAIN	5,641	1,862	3,768	11	1,906 D	33.0%	66.8%	33.1%	66.9%
MCCURTAIN	9,248	2,225	6,994	29	4,769 D	24.1%	75.6%	24.1%	75.9%
MCINTOSH	7,275	3,487	3,771	17	284 D	47.9%	51.8%	48.0%	52.0%
MAJOR	4,891	3,453	1,404	34	2,049 R	70.6%	28.7%	71.1%	28.9%
MARSHALL	3,770	1,032	2,723	15	1,691 D	27.4%	72.2%	27.5%	72.5%
MAYES	7,709	3,631	4,057	21	426 D	47.1%	52.6%	47.2%	52.8%
MURRAY	4,381	1,238	3,126	17	1,888 D	28.3%	71.4%	28.4%	71.6%
MUSKOGEE	22,551	9,585	12,917	49	3,332 D	42.5%	57.3%	42.6%	57.4%
NOBLE	6,674	3,441	3,226	7	215 R	51.6%	48.3%	51.6%	48.4%
NOWATA	7,060	3,406	3,615	39	209 D	48.2%	51.2%	48.5%	51.5%
OKFUSKEE	7,599	3,001	4,574	24	1,573 D	39.5%	60.2%	39.6%	60.4%
OKLAHOMA	89,617	35,639	53,649	329	18,010 D	39.8%	59.9%	39.9%	60.1%
OKMULGEE	17,796	6,696	11,016	84	4,320 D	37.6%	61.9%	37.8%	62.2%
OSAGE	15,481	6,419	9,019	43	2,600 D	41.5%	58.3%	41.6%	58.4%
OTTAWA	13,646	5,738	7,873	35	2,135 D	42.0%	57.7%	42.2%	57.8%
PAWNEE	7,464	3,991	3,435	38	556 R	53.5%	46.0%	53.7%	46.3%
PAYNE	14,539	6,772	7,704	63	932 D	46.6%	53.0%	46.8%	53.2%

OKLAHOMA

PRESIDENT 1936

County	Total Vote	Republican	Democratic	Other	Rep.-Dem. Plurality	Percentage Total Vote Rep.	Dem.	Major Vote Rep.	Dem.
PITTSBURG	13,668	3,651	9,974	43	6,323 D	26.7%	73.0%	26.8%	73.2%
PONTOTOC	10,136	2,015	8,079	42	6,064 D	19.9%	79.7%	20.0%	80.0%
POTTAWATOMIE	16,968	4,703	12,187	78	7,484 D	27.7%	71.8%	27.8%	72.2%
PUSHMATAHA	4,505	1,097	3,389	19	2,292 D	24.4%	75.2%	24.5%	75.5%
ROGER MILLS	4,429	989	3,383	57	2,394 D	22.3%	76.4%	22.6%	77.4%
ROGERS	7,451	3,119	4,290	42	1,171 D	41.9%	57.6%	42.1%	57.9%
SEMINOLE	15,768	4,001	11,695	72	7,694 D	25.4%	74.2%	25.5%	74.5%
SEQUOYAH	6,890	2,609	4,281		1,672 D	37.9%	62.1%	37.9%	62.1%
STEPHENS	8,071	1,636	6,390	45	4,754 D	20.3%	79.2%	20.4%	79.6%
TEXAS	4,471	1,223	3,229	19	2,006 D	27.4%	72.2%	27.5%	72.5%
TILLMAN	6,410	1,126	5,268	16	4,142 D	17.6%	82.2%	17.6%	82.4%
TULSA	70,343	28,759	41,256	328	12,497 D	40.9%	58.6%	41.1%	58.9%
WAGONER	5,117	2,119	2,977	21	858 D	41.4%	58.2%	41.6%	58.4%
WASHINGTON	11,429	5,201	6,202	26	1,001 D	45.5%	54.3%	45.6%	54.4%
WASHITA	7,029	1,792	5,205	32	3,413 D	25.5%	74.1%	25.6%	74.4%
WOODS	6,569	2,346	4,179	44	1,833 D	35.7%	63.6%	36.0%	64.0%
WOODWARD	5,831	2,430	3,361	40	931 D	41.7%	57.6%	42.0%	58.0%
TOTAL	749,740	245,122	501,069	3,549	255,947 D	32.7%	66.8%	32.8%	67.2%

PRESIDENT 1940

County	Total Vote	Republican	Democratic	Other	Rep.-Dem. Plurality	Percentage Total Vote Rep.	Dem.	Major Vote Rep.	Dem.
PITTSBURG	14,676	4,484	10,169	23	5,685 D	30.6%	69.3%	30.6%	69.4%
PONTOTOC	12,794	3,449	9,310	35	5,861 D	27.0%	72.8%	27.0%	73.0%
POTTAWATOMIE	18,912	6,776	12,058	78	5,282 D	35.8%	63.8%	36.0%	64.0%
PUSHMATAHA	5,670	1,709	3,952	9	2,243 D	30.1%	69.7%	30.2%	69.8%
ROGER MILLS	4,106	1,504	2,580	22	1,076 D	36.6%	62.8%	36.8%	63.2%
ROGERS	8,139	4,086	4,028	25	58 R	50.2%	49.5%	50.4%	49.6%
SEMINOLE	18,083	6,880	11,167	36	4,287 D	38.0%	61.8%	38.1%	61.9%
SEQUOYAH	8,281	3,803	4,469	9	666 D	45.9%	54.0%	46.0%	54.0%
STEPHENS	9,172	2,989	6,149	34	3,160 D	32.6%	67.0%	32.7%	67.3%
TEXAS	4,777	1,918	2,831	28	913 D	40.2%	59.3%	40.4%	59.6%
TILLMAN	6,508	1,564	4,920	24	3,356 D	24.0%	75.6%	24.1%	75.9%
TULSA	73,575	40,342	33,098	135	7,244 R	54.8%	45.0%	54.9%	45.1%
WAGONER	7,618	4,647	2,946	25	1,701 R	61.0%	38.7%	61.2%	38.8%
WASHINGTON	13,676	7,347	6,289	40	1,058 R	53.7%	46.0%	53.9%	46.1%
WASHITA	7,245	2,978	4,256	11	1,278 D	41.1%	58.7%	41.2%	58.8%
WOODS	7,007	3,440	3,506	61	66 D	49.1%	50.0%	49.5%	50.5%
WOODWARD	6,243	3,403	2,806	34	597 R	54.5%	44.9%	54.8%	45.2%
TOTAL	826,212	348,872	474,313	3,027	125,441 D	42.2%	57.4%	42.4%	57.6%

OKLAHOMA

PRESIDENT 1944

County	Total Vote	Republican	Democratic	Other	Rep.-Dem. Plurality	Total Vote Rep.	Total Vote Dem.	Major Vote Rep.	Major Vote Dem.
ADAIR	5,564	2,792	2,760	12	32 R	50.2%	49.6%	50.3%	49.7%
ALFALFA	5,182	3,434	1,716	32	1,718 R	66.3%	33.1%	66.7%	33.3%
ATOKA	3,693	1,515	2,172	6	657 D	41.0%	58.8%	41.1%	58.9%
BEAVER	3,295	1,913	1,355	27	558 R	58.1%	41.1%	58.5%	41.5%
BECKHAM	5,557	2,034	3,508	15	1,574 D	36.0%	63.8%	36.1%	63.9%
BLAINE	5,591	3,480	2,097	14	1,383 R	62.2%	37.5%	62.4%	37.6%
BRYAN	8,874	1,677	7,180	17	5,503 D	18.9%	80.9%	18.9%	81.1%
CADDO	12,403	5,529	6,850	24	1,321 D	44.6%	55.2%	44.7%	55.3%
CANADIAN	9,492	4,674	4,800	18	126 D	49.2%	50.6%	49.3%	50.7%
CARTER	11,654	2,446	9,184	24	6,738 D	21.0%	78.8%	21.0%	79.0%
CHEROKEE	6,763	3,336	3,415	12	79 D	49.3%	50.5%	49.4%	50.6%
CHOCTAW	5,775	1,404	4,358	13	2,954 D	24.3%	75.5%	24.4%	75.6%
CIMARRON	1,579	822	746	11	76 R	52.1%	47.2%	52.4%	47.6%
CLEVELAND	8,903	3,642	5,240	21	1,598 D	40.9%	58.9%	41.0%	59.0%
COAL	2,724	760	1,959	5	1,199 D	27.9%	71.9%	28.0%	72.0%
COMANCHE	11,479	4,109	7,342	28	3,233 D	35.8%	64.0%	35.9%	64.1%
COTTON	3,994	1,266	2,711	17	1,445 D	31.7%	67.9%	31.8%	68.2%
CRAIG	6,485	3,111	3,363	11	252 D	48.0%	51.9%	48.1%	51.9%
CREEK	15,932	7,549	8,342	41	793 D	47.4%	52.4%	47.5%	52.5%
CUSTER	7,302	3,349	3,928	25	579 D	45.9%	53.8%	46.0%	54.0%
DELAWARE	5,126	2,660	2,373	93	287 R	51.9%	46.3%	52.0%	47.1%
DEWEY	3,987	2,166	1,808	13	358 R	54.3%	45.3%	54.5%	45.5%
ELLIS	3,051	1,939	1,104	8	835 R	63.6%	36.2%	63.7%	36.3%
GARFIELD	19,155	11,211	7,879	65	3,332 R	58.5%	41.1%	58.7%	41.3%
GARVIN	7,421	2,086	5,328	7	3,242 D	28.1%	71.8%	28.1%	71.9%
GRADY	11,778	4,069	7,689	20	3,620 D	34.5%	65.3%	34.6%	65.4%
GRANT	5,079	3,021	2,045	13	976 R	59.5%	40.3%	59.6%	40.4%
GREER	4,064	1,075	2,984	5	1,909 D	26.5%	73.4%	26.5%	73.5%
HARMON	2,446	503	1,933	10	1,430 D	20.6%	79.0%	20.6%	79.4%
HARPER	2,473	1,394	1,056	23	338 R	56.4%	42.7%	56.9%	43.1%
HASKELL	5,041	2,102	2,924	15	822 D	41.7%	58.0%	41.8%	58.2%
HUGHES	7,506	2,484	5,009	13	2,525 D	33.1%	66.7%	33.2%	66.8%
JACKSON	6,192	1,313	4,866	13	3,553 D	21.2%	78.6%	21.2%	78.8%
JEFFERSON	3,937	974	2,948	15	1,974 D	24.7%	74.9%	24.8%	75.2%
JOHNSTON	3,278	925	2,339	14	1,414 D	28.2%	71.4%	28.3%	71.7%
KAY	18,242	9,498	8,656	88	842 R	52.1%	47.5%	52.3%	47.7%
KINGFISHER	5,609	3,417	2,175	17	1,242 R	60.9%	38.8%	61.1%	58.9%
KIOWA	6,280	2,081	4,175	24	2,094 D	33.1%	66.5%	33.3%	66.7%
LATIMER	3,255	1,296	1,948	11	652 D	39.8%	59.8%	40.0%	60.0%
LE FLORE	9,349	3,667	5,660	22	1,993 D	39.2%	60.5%	39.3%	60.7%
LINCOLN	8,739	4,801	3,910	28	891 R	54.9%	44.7%	55.1%	44.9%
LOGAN	8,417	4,586	3,795	36	791 R	54.5%	45.1%	54.7%	45.3%
LOVE	2,405	446	1,955	4	1,509 D	18.5%	81.3%	18.6%	81.4%
MCCLAIN	4,801	1,492	3,301	8	1,809 D	31.1%	68.8%	31.4%	68.6%
MCCURTAIN	6,751	1,419	5,322	10	3,903 D	21.0%	78.8%	21.1%	78.9%
MCINTOSH	5,771	2,569	3,190	12	621 D	44.5%	55.3%	44.6%	55.4%
MAJOR	4,005	3,019	965	21	2,054 R	75.4%	24.1%	75.8%	24.2%
MARSHALL	3,024	752	2,261	11	1,509 D	24.9%	74.8%	25.0%	75.0%
MAYES	7,671	3,822	3,830	19	8 D	49.8%	49.9%	49.9%	50.1%
MURRAY	3,616	1,005	2,602	9	1,597 D	27.8%	72.0%	27.9%	72.1%
MUSKOGEE	19,990	8,280	11,679	31	3,399 D	41.4%	58.4%	41.5%	58.5%
NOBLE	5,373	3,060	2,300	13	760 R	57.0%	42.8%	57.1%	42.9%
NOWATA	5,326	2,730	2,581	15	149 R	51.3%	48.5%	51.4%	48.6%
OKFUSKEE	5,477	2,177	3,291	9	1,114 D	39.7%	60.1%	39.8%	60.2%
OKLAHOMA	100,392	42,464	57,812	116	15,348 D	42.3%	57.6%	42.3%	57.7%
OKMULGEE	15,192	5,430	9,737	25	4,307 D	35.7%	64.1%	35.8%	64.2%
OSAGE	12,410	5,557	6,846	7	1,289 D	44.8%	55.2%	44.8%	55.2%
OTTAWA	10,945	5,056	5,876	13	820 D	46.2%	53.7%	46.2%	53.8%
PAWNEE	5,786	3,310	2,460	16	850 R	57.2%	42.5%	57.4%	42.5%
PAYNE	11,702	6,048	5,624	30	424 R	51.7%	48.1%	51.8%	48.2%

PRESIDENT 1948

County	Total Vote	Republican	Democratic	Other	Rep.-Dem. Plurality	Total Vote Rep.	Total Vote Dem.	Major Vote Rep.	Major Vote Dem.
ADAIR	5,474	2,407	3,067		660 D	44.0%	56.0%	44.0%	56.0%
ALFALFA	4,603	2,765	1,838		927 R	60.1%	39.9%	60.1%	39.9%
ATOKA	4,137	1,033	3,104		2,071 D	25.0%	75.0%	25.0%	75.0%
BEAVER	3,016	1,420	1,596		176 D	47.1%	52.9%	47.1%	52.9%
BECKHAM	5,854	1,310	4,544		3,234 D	22.4%	77.6%	22.4%	77.6%
BLAINE	5,430	2,835	2,595		240 R	52.2%	47.8%	52.2%	47.8%
BRYAN	9,114	1,366	7,748		6,382 D	15.0%	85.0%	15.0%	85.0%
CADDO	11,903	3,793	8,110		4,317 D	31.9%	68.1%	31.9%	68.1%
CANADIAN	9,297	3,729	5,568		1,839 D	40.1%	59.9%	40.1%	59.9%
CARTER	11,621	2,147	9,474		7,327 D	18.5%	81.5%	18.5%	81.5%
CHEROKEE	7,034	2,785	4,249		1,464 D	39.6%	60.4%	39.6%	60.4%
CHOCTAW	5,786	1,036	4,750		3,714 D	17.9%	82.1%	17.9%	82.1%
CIMARRON	1,544	650	894		244 D	42.1%	57.9%	42.1%	57.9%
CLEVELAND	10,227	3,671	6,556		2,885 D	35.9%	64.1%	35.9%	64.1%
COAL	2,588	464	2,124		1,660 D	17.9%	82.1%	17.9%	82.1%
COMANCHE	10,742	2,787	7,955		5,168 D	25.9%	74.1%	25.9%	74.1%
COTTON	3,351	738	2,613		1,875 D	22.0%	78.0%	22.0%	78.0%
CRAIG	6,989	2,807	4,182		1,375 D	40.2%	59.8%	40.2%	59.8%
CREEK	15,730	6,532	9,198		2,666 D	41.5%	58.5%	41.5%	58.5%
CUSTER	7,186	2,568	4,618		2,050 D	35.7%	64.3%	35.7%	64.3%
DELAWARE	5,500	2,343	3,157		814 D	42.6%	57.4%	42.6%	57.4%
DEWEY	3,543	1,494	2,049		555 D	42.2%	57.8%	42.2%	57.8%
ELLIS	2,942	1,522	1,420		102 R	51.7%	48.3%	51.7%	48.3%
GARFIELD	18,569	10,352	8,217		2,135 R	55.7%	44.3%	55.7%	44.3%
GARVIN	8,460	1,681	6,779		5,098 D	19.9%	80.1%	19.9%	80.1%
GRADY	11,018	2,882	8,136		5,254 D	26.2%	73.8%	26.2%	73.8%
GRANT	4,597	2,471	2,126		345 R	53.8%	46.2%	53.8%	46.2%
GREER	3,757	713	3,044		2,331 D	19.0%	81.0%	19.0%	81.0%
HARMON	2,606	266	2,340		2,074 D	10.2%	89.8%	10.2%	89.8%
HARPER	2,502	1,221	1,281		60 D	48.8%	51.2%	48.8%	51.2%
HASKELL	4,596	1,390	3,206		1,816 D	30.2%	69.8%	30.2%	69.8%
HUGHES	7,168	1,676	5,492		3,816 D	23.4%	76.6%	23.4%	76.6%
JACKSON	6,373	923	5,450		4,527 D	14.5%	85.5%	14.5%	85.5%
JEFFERSON	3,882	556	3,326		2,770 D	14.3%	85.7%	14.3%	85.7%
JOHNSTON	3,520	584	2,936		2,352 D	16.6%	83.4%	16.6%	83.4%
KAY	19,101	8,982	10,119		1,137 D	47.0%	53.0%	47.0%	53.0%
KINGFISHER	5,419	2,931	2,488		443 R	54.1%	45.9%	54.1%	45.9%
KIOWA	5,793	1,530	4,263		2,733 D	26.4%	73.6%	26.4%	73.6%
LATIMER	3,455	919	2,536		1,617 D	26.6%	73.4%	26.6%	73.4%
LE FLORE	9,607	2,821	6,786		3,965 D	29.4%	70.6%	29.4%	70.6%
LINCOLN	8,811	3,898	4,913		1,015 D	44.2%	55.8%	44.2%	55.8%
LOGAN	7,926	3,817	4,109		292 D	48.2%	51.8%	48.2%	51.8%
LOVE	2,440	249	2,191		1,942 D	10.2%	89.8%	10.2%	89.8%
MCCLAIN	4,359	908	3,451		2,543 D	20.8%	79.2%	20.8%	79.2%
MCCURTAIN	7,314	1,091	6,223		5,132 D	14.9%	85.1%	14.9%	85.1%
MCINTOSH	5,116	1,442	3,674		2,232 D	28.2%	71.8%	28.2%	71.8%
MAJOR	3,694	2,467	1,227		1,240 R	66.8%	33.2%	66.8%	33.2%
MARSHALL	2,924	469	2,455		1,986 D	16.0%	84.0%	16.0%	84.0%
MAYES	7,055	2,854	4,201		1,347 D	40.5%	59.5%	40.5%	59.5%
MURRAY	3,852	798	3,054		2,256 D	20.7%	79.3%	20.7%	79.3%
MUSKOGEE	20,452	6,592	13,860		7,268 D	32.2%	67.8%	32.2%	67.8%
NOBLE	5,200	2,430	2,770		340 D	46.7%	53.3%	46.7%	53.3%
NOWATA	4,807	2,119	2,688		569 D	44.1%	55.9%	44.1%	55.9%
OKFUSKEE	4,959	1,624	3,335		1,711 D	32.7%	67.3%	32.7%	67.3%
OKLAHOMA	100,115	40,161	59,954		19,793 D	40.1%	59.9%	40.1%	59.9%
OKMULGEE	14,835	4,368	10,467		6,099 D	29.4%	70.6%	29.4%	70.6%
OSAGE	11,107	3,951	7,156		3,205 D	35.6%	64.4%	35.6%	64.4%
OTTAWA	11,547	4,304	7,243		2,939 D	37.3%	62.7%	37.3%	62.7%
PAWNEE	5,372	2,651	2,721		70 D	49.3%	50.7%	49.3%	50.7%
PAYNE	13,189	5,799	7,390		1,591 D	44.0%	56.0%	44.0%	56.0%

OKLAHOMA

PRESIDENT 1944

County	Total Vote	Republican	Democratic	Other	Rep.-Dem. Plurality	Total Vote Rep.	Total Vote Dem.	Major Vote Rep.	Major Vote Dem.
PITTSBURG	12,626	4,068	8,535	23	4,467 D	32.2%	67.6%	32.3%	67.7%
PONTOTOC	9,533	2,960	6,552	21	3,592 D	31.1%	68.7%	31.1%	68.9%
POTTAWATOMIE	15,659	6,486	9,130	43	2,644 D	41.4%	58.3%	41.5%	58.5%
PUSHMATAHA	4,040	1,181	2,848	11	1,667 D	29.2%	70.5%	29.3%	70.7%
ROGER MILLS	3,176	1,148	2,015	13	867 D	36.1%	63.4%	36.3%	63.7%
ROGERS	6,956	3,739	3,209	8	530 R	53.8%	46.1%	53.8%	46.2%
SEMINOLE	11,692	4,560	7,116	16	2,556 D	39.0%	60.9%	39.1%	60.9%
SEQUOYAH	6,472	2,893	3,571	8	678 D	44.7%	55.2%	44.8%	55.2%
STEPHENS	8,974	2,766	6,189	19	3,423 D	30.8%	69.0%	30.9%	69.1%
TEXAS	3,870	1,731	2,119	20	388 D	44.7%	54.8%	45.0%	55.0%
TILLMAN	5,410	1,496	3,902	12	2,406 D	27.7%	72.1%	27.7%	72.3%
TULSA	76,188	42,663	33,436	89	9,227 R	56.0%	43.9%	56.1%	43.9%
WAGONER	5,848	3,467	2,373	8	1,094 R	59.3%	40.6%	59.4%	40.6%
WASHINGTON	11,641	6,553	5,090	18	1,443 R	56.1%	43.7%	56.2%	43.8%
WASHITA	6,248	2,706	3,524	18	818 D	43.3%	56.4%	43.4%	56.6%
WOODS	5,675	3,226	2,426	23	800 R	56.8%	42.7%	57.1%	42.9%
WOODWARD	5,225	3,055	2,152	18	903 R	58.5%	41.2%	58.7%	41.3%
TOTAL	722,636	319,424	401,549	1,663	82,125 D	44.2%	55.6%	44.3%	55.7%

PRESIDENT 1948

County	Total Vote	Republican	Democratic	Other	Rep.-Dem. Plurality	Total Vote Rep.	Total Vote Dem.	Major Vote Rep.	Major Vote Dem.
PITTSBURG	12,469	2,893	9,576		6,683 D	23.2%	76.8%	23.2%	76.8%
PONTOTOC	10,039	2,289	7,750		5,461 D	22.8%	77.2%	22.8%	77.2%
POTTAWATOMIE	14,980	4,760	10,220		5,460 D	31.8%	68.2%	31.8%	68.2%
PUSHMATAHA	3,766	789	2,977		2,188 D	21.0%	79.0%	21.0%	79.0%
ROGER MILLS	2,685	509	2,176		1,667 D	19.0%	81.0%	19.0%	81.0%
ROGERS	7,046	2,849	4,197		1,348 D	40.4%	59.6%	40.4%	59.6%
SEMINOLE	11,545	3,423	8,122		4,699 D	29.6%	70.4%	29.6%	70.4%
SEQUOYAH	6,526	2,077	4,449		2,372 D	31.8%	68.2%	31.8%	68.2%
STEPHENS	8,611	1,909	6,702		4,793 D	22.2%	77.8%	22.2%	77.8%
TEXAS	4,369	1,676	2,693		1,017 D	38.4%	61.6%	38.4%	61.6%
TILLMAN	5,129	1,058	4,071		3,013 D	20.6%	79.4%	20.6%	79.4%
TULSA	81,440	42,892	38,548		4,344 R	52.7%	47.3%	52.7%	47.3%
WAGONER	6,055	2,666	3,389		723 D	44.0%	56.0%	44.0%	56.0%
WASHINGTON	11,544	6,036	5,508		528 R	52.3%	47.7%	52.3%	47.7%
WASHITA	5,963	1,637	4,326		2,689 D	27.5%	72.5%	27.5%	72.5%
WOODS	5,753	2,871	2,882		11 D	49.9%	50.1%	49.9%	50.1%
WOODWARD	4,571	2,391	2,180		211 R	52.3%	47.7%	52.3%	47.7%
TOTAL	721,599	268,817	452,782		183,965 D	37.3%	62.7%	37.3%	62.7%

OKLAHOMA

PRESIDENT 1952

County	Total Vote	Republican	Democratic	Other	Rep.-Dem. Plurality	Total Vote Rep.	Total Vote Dem.	Major Vote Rep.	Major Vote Dem.
ADAIR	5,762	3,037	2,725		312 R	52.7%	47.3%	52.7%	47.3%
ALFALFA	5,273	4,155	1,118		3,037 R	78.8%	21.2%	78.8%	21.2%
ATOKA	4,658	2,004	2,654		650 D	43.0%	57.0%	43.0%	57.0%
BEAVER	3,358	2,539	819		1,720 R	75.6%	24.4%	75.6%	24.4%
BECKHAM	8,476	4,504	3,972		532 R	53.1%	46.9%	53.1%	46.9%
BLAINE	6,677	4,851	1,826		3,025 R	72.7%	27.3%	72.7%	27.3%
BRYAN	10,079	3,340	6,739		3,399 D	33.1%	65.9%	33.1%	66.9%
CADDO	12,987	6,834	6,153		681 R	52.6%	47.4%	52.6%	47.4%
CANADIAN	11,492	7,289	4,203		3,086 R	63.4%	36.6%	63.4%	36.6%
CARTER	16,250	5,974	10,276		4,302 D	36.8%	63.2%	36.8%	63.2%
CHEROKEE	6,560	3,326	3,234		92 R	50.7%	49.3%	50.7%	49.3%
CHOCTAW	6,511	2,251	4,260		2,009 D	34.6%	65.4%	34.6%	65.4%
CIMARRON	2,143	1,438	705		733 R	67.1%	32.9%	67.1%	32.9%
CLEVELAND	14,339	8,149	6,190		1,959 R	56.8%	43.2%	56.8%	43.2%
COAL	2,861	1,106	1,755		649 D	38.7%	61.3%	38.7%	61.3%
COMANCHE	17,785	8,756	9,029		273 D	49.2%	50.8%	49.2%	50.8%
COTTON	4,014	1,897	2,117		220 D	47.3%	52.7%	47.3%	52.7%
CRAIG	6,965	3,830	3,135		695 R	55.0%	45.0%	55.0%	45.0%
CREEK	18,075	9,257	8,818		439 R	51.2%	48.8%	51.2%	48.8%
CUSTER	8,893	5,667	3,226		2,441 R	63.7%	36.3%	63.7%	36.3%
DELAWARE	6,085	3,399	2,686		713 R	55.9%	44.1%	55.9%	44.1%
DEWEY	3,864	2,583	1,281		1,302 R	66.8%	33.2%	66.8%	33.2%
ELLIS	3,300	2,583	717		1,866 R	78.3%	21.7%	78.3%	21.7%
GARFIELD	24,636	17,589	7,047		10,542 R	71.4%	28.6%	71.4%	28.6%
GARVIN	11,246	4,402	6,844		2,442 D	39.1%	60.9%	39.1%	60.9%
GRADY	14,058	6,348	7,710		1,362 D	45.2%	54.8%	45.2%	54.8%
GRANT	5,517	3,996	1,521		2,475 R	72.4%	27.6%	72.4%	27.6%
GREER	4,468	2,147	2,321		174 D	48.1%	51.9%	48.1%	51.9%
HARMON	2,961	1,057	1,904		847 D	35.7%	64.3%	35.7%	64.3%
HARPER	2,793	2,057	736		1,321 R	73.6%	26.4%	73.6%	26.4%
HASKELL	4,491	1,872	2,619		747 D	41.7%	58.3%	41.7%	58.3%
HUGHES	7,651	3,012	4,639		1,627 D	39.4%	60.6%	39.4%	60.6%
JACKSON	7,548	2,627	4,921		2,294 D	34.8%	65.2%	34.8%	65.2%
JEFFERSON	4,256	1,384	2,872		1,488 D	32.5%	67.5%	32.5%	67.5%
JOHNSTON	3,844	1,349	2,495		1,146 D	35.1%	64.9%	35.1%	64.9%
KAY	24,842	16,460	8,382		8,078 R	66.3%	33.7%	66.3%	33.7%
KINGFISHER	6,332	4,873	1,459		3,414 R	77.0%	23.0%	77.0%	23.0%
KIOWA	7,589	4,100	3,489		611 R	54.0%	46.0%	54.0%	46.0%
LATIMER	3,951	1,668	2,283		615 D	42.2%	57.8%	42.2%	57.8%
LE FLORE	10,980	4,631	6,349		1,718 D	42.2%	57.8%	42.2%	57.8%
LINCOLN	9,849	5,778	4,071		1,707 R	58.7%	41.3%	58.7%	41.3%
LOGAN	9,616	6,172	3,444		2,728 R	64.2%	35.8%	64.2%	35.8%
LOVE	2,778	806	1,972		1,166 D	29.0%	71.0%	29.0%	71.0%
MCCLAIN	5,527	2,326	3,201		875 D	42.1%	57.9%	42.1%	57.9%
MCCURTAIN	8,541	2,748	5,793		3,045 D	32.2%	67.8%	32.2%	67.8%
MCINTOSH	5,302	2,295	3,007		712 D	43.3%	56.7%	43.3%	56.7%
MAJOR	4,340	3,495	845		2,650 R	80.5%	19.5%	80.5%	19.5%
MARSHALL	3,492	1,204	2,288		1,084 D	34.5%	65.5%	34.5%	65.5%
MAYES	8,541	4,704	3,837		867 R	55.1%	44.9%	55.1%	44.9%
MURRAY	4,753	1,885	2,868		983 D	39.7%	60.3%	39.7%	60.3%
MUSKOGEE	24,850	11,810	13,040		1,230 D	47.5%	52.5%	47.5%	52.5%
NOBLE	6,225	4,422	1,803		2,619 R	71.0%	29.0%	71.0%	29.0%
NOWATA	5,883	3,226	2,657		569 R	54.8%	45.2%	54.8%	45.2%
OKFUSKEE	5,244	2,469	2,775		306 D	47.1%	52.9%	47.1%	52.9%
OKLAHOMA	165,691	95,492	70,199		25,293 R	57.6%	42.4%	57.6%	42.4%
OKMULGEE	16,832	6,717	10,115		3,398 D	39.9%	60.1%	39.9%	60.1%
OSAGE	14,445	7,731	6,714		1,017 R	53.5%	46.5%	53.5%	46.5%
OTTAWA	13,903	7,211	6,692		519 R	51.9%	48.1%	51.9%	48.1%
PAWNEE	6,249	3,975	2,274		1,701 R	63.6%	36.4%	63.6%	36.4%
PAYNE	17,095	10,605	6,490		4,115 R	62.0%	38.0%	62.0%	38.0%

PRESIDENT 1956

County	Total Vote	Republican	Democratic	Other	Rep.-Dem. Plurality	Total Vote Rep.	Total Vote Dem.	Major Vote Rep.	Major Vote Dem.
ADAIR	5,570	3,152	2,418		734 R	56.6%	43.4%	56.6%	43.4%
ALFALFA	4,622	3,251	1,371		1,880 R	70.3%	29.7%	70.3%	29.7%
ATOKA	4,155	1,731	2,424		693 D	41.7%	58.3%	41.7%	58.3%
BEAVER	2,992	2,046	946		1,100 R	68.4%	31.6%	68.4%	31.6%
BECKHAM	6,755	3,194	3,561		367 D	47.3%	52.7%	47.3%	52.7%
BLAINE	5,699	3,855	1,844		2,011 R	67.6%	32.4%	67.6%	32.4%
BRYAN	8,668	2,939	5,729		2,790 D	33.9%	66.1%	33.9%	66.1%
CADDO	11,215	5,331	5,884		553 D	47.5%	52.5%	47.5%	52.5%
CANADIAN	9,598	5,702	3,896		1,806 R	59.4%	40.6%	59.4%	40.6%
CARTER	15,315	5,974	9,341		3,367 D	39.0%	61.0%	39.0%	61.0%
CHEROKEE	6,268	3,277	2,991		286 R	52.3%	47.7%	52.3%	47.7%
CHOCTAW	5,675	2,206	3,469		1,263 D	38.9%	61.1%	38.9%	61.1%
CIMARRON	1,865	1,053	812		241 R	56.5%	43.5%	56.5%	43.5%
CLEVELAND	13,753	7,766	5,987		1,779 R	56.5%	43.5%	56.5%	43.5%
COAL	2,516	920	1,596		676 D	36.6%	63.4%	36.6%	63.4%
COMANCHE	16,288	7,532	8,756		1,224 D	46.2%	53.8%	46.2%	53.8%
COTTON	3,287	1,398	1,689		491 D	42.5%	57.5%	42.5%	57.5%
CRAIG	6,649	3,543	3,106		437 R	53.3%	46.7%	53.3%	46.7%
CREEK	15,397	8,295	7,102		1,193 R	53.9%	46.1%	53.9%	46.1%
CUSTER	7,208	4,182	3,026		1,156 R	58.0%	42.0%	58.0%	42.0%
DELAWARE	5,757	3,078	2,679		399 R	53.5%	46.5%	53.5%	46.5%
DEWEY	3,344	1,896	1,448		448 R	56.7%	43.3%	56.7%	43.3%
ELLIS	2,836	1,916	920		996 R	67.6%	32.4%	67.6%	32.4%
GARFIELD	22,117	15,348	6,769		8,579 R	69.4%	30.6%	69.4%	30.6%
GARVIN	10,301	3,850	6,451		2,601 D	37.4%	62.6%	37.4%	62.6%
GRADY	11,964	5,191	6,773		1,582 D	43.4%	56.6%	43.4%	56.6%
GRANT	4,741	2,788	1,953		835 R	58.8%	41.2%	58.8%	41.2%
GREER	3,406	1,499	1,907		408 D	44.0%	56.0%	44.0%	56.0%
HARMON	2,580	837	1,743		906 D	32.4%	67.6%	32.4%	67.6%
HARPER	2,332	1,596	736		860 R	68.4%	31.6%	68.4%	31.6%
HASKELL	4,139	1,758	2,381		623 D	42.5%	57.5%	42.5%	57.5%
HUGHES	7,061	2,783	4,278		1,495 D	39.4%	60.6%	39.4%	60.6%
JACKSON	6,778	2,343	4,435		2,092 D	34.6%	65.4%	34.6%	65.4%
JEFFERSON	3,725	1,186	2,539		1,353 D	31.8%	68.2%	31.8%	68.2%
JOHNSTON	3,389	1,157	2,232		1,075 D	34.1%	65.9%	34.1%	65.9%
KAY	22,908	14,837	8,071		6,766 R	64.8%	35.2%	64.8%	35.2%
KINGFISHER	5,603	3,935	1,668		2,267 R	70.2%	29.8%	70.2%	29.8%
KIOWA	6,084	2,713	3,371		658 D	44.6%	55.4%	44.6%	55.4%
LATIMER	3,381	1,387	1,994		607 D	41.0%	59.0%	41.0%	59.0%
LE FLORE	9,586	4,310	5,276		966 D	45.0%	55.0%	45.0%	55.0%
LINCOLN	8,902	4,993	3,909		1,084 R	56.1%	43.9%	56.1%	43.9%
LOGAN	8,201	5,326	2,875		2,451 R	64.9%	35.1%	64.9%	35.1%
LOVE	2,487	731	1,756		1,025 D	29.4%	70.6%	29.4%	70.6%
MCCLAIN	5,062	2,081	2,981		900 D	41.1%	58.9%	41.1%	58.9%
MCCURTAIN	7,468	2,707	4,761		2,054 D	36.2%	63.8%	36.2%	63.8%
MCINTOSH	4,877	2,149	2,728		579 D	44.1%	55.9%	44.1%	55.9%
MAJOR	3,777	2,826	951		1,875 R	74.8%	25.2%	74.8%	25.2%
MARSHALL	3,251	1,151	2,100		949 D	35.4%	64.6%	35.4%	64.6%
MAYES	8,437	4,677	3,760		917 R	55.4%	44.6%	55.4%	44.6%
MURRAY	4,291	1,809	2,482		673 D	42.2%	57.8%	42.2%	57.8%
MUSKOGEE	21,470	11,057	10,413		644 R	51.5%	48.5%	51.5%	48.5%
NOBLE	5,553	3,536	2,017		1,519 R	63.7%	36.3%	63.7%	36.3%
NOWATA	5,436	3,168	2,268		900 R	58.3%	41.7%	58.3%	41.7%
OKFUSKEE	4,630	2,299	2,331		32 D	49.7%	50.3%	49.7%	50.3%
OKLAHOMA	142,907	85,395	57,512		27,883 R	59.8%	40.2%	59.8%	40.2%
OKMULGEE	14,329	6,703	7,626		923 D	46.8%	53.2%	46.8%	53.2%
OSAGE	13,235	7,296	5,939		1,357 R	55.1%	44.9%	55.1%	44.9%
OTTAWA	12,451	6,730	5,721		1,009 R	54.1%	45.9%	54.1%	45.9%
PAWNEE	5,654	3,390	2,264		1,126 R	60.0%	40.0%	60.0%	40.0%
PAYNE	15,701	9,381	6,320		3,061 R	59.7%	40.3%	59.7%	40.3%

OKLAHOMA

PRESIDENT 1952

County	Total Vote	Republican	Democratic	Other	Rep.-Dem. Plurality	Total Vote Rep.	Total Vote Dem.	Major Vote Rep.	Major Vote Dem.
PITTSBURG	15,455	5,909	9,546		3,637 D	38.2%	61.8%	38.2%	61.8%
PONTOTOC	12,597	5,389	7,208		1,819 D	42.8%	57.2%	42.8%	57.2%
POTTAWATOMIE	19,554	10,099	9,455		644 R	51.6%	48.4%	51.6%	48.4%
PUSHMATAHA	4,218	1,640	2,578		938 D	38.9%	61.1%	38.9%	61.1%
ROGER MILLS	3,146	1,667	1,479		188 R	53.0%	47.0%	53.0%	47.0%
ROGERS	8,703	4,873	3,830		1,043 R	56.0%	44.0%	56.0%	44.0%
SEMINOLE	13,744	6,668	7,076		408 D	48.5%	51.5%	48.5%	51.5%
SEQUOYAH	7,360	3,288	4,072		784 D	44.7%	55.3%	44.7%	55.3%
STEPHENS	14,490	6,461	8,029		1,568 D	44.6%	55.4%	44.6%	55.4%
TEXAS	6,111	4,196	1,915		2,281 R	68.7%	31.3%	68.7%	31.3%
TILLMAN	6,296	2,657	3,639		982 D	42.2%	57.8%	42.2%	57.8%
TULSA	120,590	73,862	46,728		27,134 R	61.3%	38.7%	61.3%	38.7%
WAGONER	6,287	3,321	2,966		355 R	52.8%	47.2%	52.8%	47.2%
WASHINGTON	17,572	11,334	6,238		5,096 R	64.5%	35.5%	64.5%	35.5%
WASHITA	7,091	3,914	3,177		737 R	55.2%	44.8%	55.2%	44.8%
WOODS	6,891	4,892	1,999		2,893 R	71.0%	29.0%	71.0%	29.0%
WOODWARD	6,153	4,463	1,690		2,773 R	72.5%	27.5%	72.5%	27.5%
TOTAL	948,984	518,045	430,939		87,106 R	54.6%	45.4%	54.6%	45.4%

PRESIDENT 1956

County	Total Vote	Republican	Democratic	Other	Rep.-Dem. Plurality	Total Vote Rep.	Total Vote Dem.	Major Vote Rep.	Major Vote Dem.
PITTSBURG	13,621	5,239	8,382		3,143 D	38.5%	61.5%	38.5%	61.5%
PONTOTOC	10,764	4,814	5,950		1,136 D	44.7%	55.3%	44.7%	55.3%
POTTAWATOMIE	17,391	8,496	8,895		399 D	48.9%	51.1%	48.9%	51.1%
PUSHMATAHA	3,772	1,499	2,273		774 D	39.7%	60.3%	39.7%	60.3%
ROGER MILLS	2,439	1,072	1,367		295 D	44.0%	56.0%	44.0%	56.0%
ROGERS	7,672	4,487	3,185		1,302 R	58.5%	41.5%	58.5%	41.5%
SEMINOLE	11,127	5,230	5,897		667 D	47.0%	53.0%	47.0%	53.0%
SEQUOYAH	6,890	3,330	3,560		230 D	48.3%	51.7%	48.3%	51.7%
STEPHENS	13,848	6,324	7,524		1,200 D	45.7%	54.3%	45.7%	54.3%
TEXAS	5,206	3,320	1,886		1,434 R	63.8%	36.2%	63.8%	36.2%
TILLMAN	5,176	1,810	3,366		1,556 D	35.0%	65.0%	35.0%	65.0%
TULSA	127,024	83,219	43,805		39,414 R	65.5%	34.5%	65.5%	34.5%
WAGONER	6,081	3,537	2,544		993 R	58.2%	41.8%	58.2%	41.8%
WASHINGTON	18,017	12,488	5,529		6,959 R	69.3%	30.7%	69.3%	30.7%
WASHITA	5,743	2,552	3,191		639 D	44.4%	55.6%	44.4%	55.6%
WOODS	5,910	3,787	2,123		1,664 R	64.1%	35.9%	64.1%	35.9%
WOODWARD	5,023	3,405	1,618		1,787 R	67.8%	32.2%	67.8%	32.2%
TOTAL	859,350	473,769	385,581		88,188 R	55.1%	44.9%	55.1%	44.9%

OKLAHOMA

PRESIDENT 1960

County	Total Vote	Republican	Democratic	Other	Rep.-Dem. Plurality	%Total Rep.	%Total Dem.	%Major Rep.	%Major Dem.
ADAIR	5,558	3,655	1,903		1,752 R	65.8%	34.2%	65.8%	34.2%
ALFALFA	4,399	3,332	1,067		2,265 R	75.7%	24.3%	75.7%	24.3%
ATOKA	3,651	1,892	1,759		133 R	51.8%	48.2%	51.8%	48.2%
BEAVER	3,329	2,442	887		1,555 R	73.4%	26.6%	73.4%	26.6%
BECKHAM	6,979	4,258	2,721		1,537 R	61.0%	39.0%	61.0%	39.0%
BLAINE	5,371	3,646	1,725		1,921 R	67.9%	32.1%	67.9%	32.1%
BRYAN	8,273	3,845	4,428		583 D	46.5%	53.5%	46.5%	53.5%
CADDO	11,035	5,920	5,115		805 R	53.6%	46.4%	53.6%	46.4%
CANADIAN	9,931	5,697	4,234		1,463 R	57.4%	42.6%	57.4%	42.6%
CARTER	14,729	6,288	8,441		2,153 D	42.7%	57.3%	42.7%	57.3%
CHEROKEE	6,258	3,571	2,687		884 R	57.1%	42.9%	57.1%	42.9%
CHOCTAW	5,472	2,531	2,941		410 D	46.3%	53.7%	46.3%	53.7%
CIMARRON	2,012	1,316	696		620 R	65.4%	34.6%	65.4%	34.6%
CLEVELAND	15,689	9,292	6,397		2,895 R	59.2%	40.8%	59.2%	40.8%
COAL	2,288	1,019	1,269		250 D	44.5%	55.5%	44.5%	55.5%
COMANCHE	20,253	10,691	9,562		1,129 R	52.8%	47.2%	52.8%	47.2%
COTTON	3,253	1,619	1,634		15 D	49.8%	50.2%	49.8%	50.2%
CRAIG	6,562	3,770	2,792		978 R	57.5%	42.5%	57.5%	42.5%
CREEK	14,990	8,785	6,205		2,580 R	58.6%	41.4%	58.6%	41.4%
CUSTER	7,793	5,050	2,743		2,307 R	64.8%	35.2%	64.8%	35.2%
DELAWARE	5,921	3,639	2,282		1,357 R	61.5%	38.5%	61.5%	38.5%
DEWEY	3,197	2,115	1,082		1,033 R	66.2%	33.8%	66.2%	33.8%
ELLIS	2,794	2,085	709		1,376 R	74.6%	25.4%	74.6%	25.4%
GARFIELD	21,442	14,860	6,582		8,278 R	69.3%	30.7%	69.3%	30.7%
GARVIN	9,920	5,125	4,795		330 R	51.7%	48.3%	51.7%	48.3%
GRADY	11,359	5,913	5,446		467 R	52.1%	47.9%	52.1%	47.9%
GREER	4,533	2,810	1,723		1,087 R	62.0%	38.0%	62.0%	38.0%
HARMON	3,856	2,158	1,698		460 R	56.0%	44.0%	56.0%	44.0%
HARPER	2,407	1,142	1,265		123 D	47.4%	52.6%	47.4%	52.6%
HASKELL	3,570	1,858	1,712		146 R	52.0%	48.0%	52.0%	48.0%
HUGHES	6,174	3,117	3,057		60 R	50.5%	49.5%	50.5%	49.5%
JACKSON	7,136	3,375	3,761		386 D	47.3%	52.7%	47.3%	52.7%
JEFFERSON	3,288	1,343	1,945		602 D	40.8%	59.2%	40.8%	59.2%
JOHNSTON	3,263	1,441	1,822		381 D	44.2%	55.8%	44.2%	55.8%
KAY	23,405	15,156	8,249		6,907 R	64.8%	35.2%	64.8%	35.2%
KINGFISHER	5,322	3,501	1,821		1,680 R	65.8%	34.2%	65.8%	34.2%
KIOWA	6,153	3,515	2,638		877 R	57.1%	42.9%	57.1%	42.9%
LATIMER	2,988	1,454	1,534		80 D	48.7%	51.3%	48.7%	51.3%
LE FLORE	10,146	5,302	4,844		458 R	52.3%	47.7%	52.3%	47.7%
LINCOLN	8,783	5,528	3,255		2,273 R	62.9%	37.1%	62.9%	37.1%
LOGAN	7,941	5,121	2,820		2,301 R	64.5%	35.5%	64.5%	35.5%
LOVE	2,375	932	1,443		511 D	39.2%	60.8%	39.2%	60.8%
MCCLAIN	4,912	2,547	2,365		182 R	51.9%	48.1%	51.9%	48.1%
MCCURTAIN	7,764	3,562	4,202		640 D	45.9%	54.1%	45.9%	54.1%
MCINTOSH	4,406	2,221	2,185		36 R	50.4%	49.6%	50.4%	49.6%
MAJOR	3,608	2,892	716		2,176 R	80.2%	19.8%	80.2%	19.8%
MARSHALL	3,118	1,325	1,793		468 D	42.5%	57.5%	42.5%	57.5%
MAYES	8,915	5,194	3,721		1,473 R	58.3%	41.7%	58.3%	41.7%
MURRAY	4,122	1,993	2,129		136 D	48.4%	51.6%	48.4%	51.6%
MUSKOGEE	23,485	12,403	11,082		1,321 R	52.8%	47.2%	52.8%	47.2%
NOBLE	5,108	3,198	1,910		1,288 R	62.6%	37.4%	62.6%	37.4%
NOWATA	5,139	3,014	2,125		889 R	58.6%	41.4%	58.6%	41.4%
OKFUSKEE	4,478	2,510	1,968		542 R	56.1%	43.9%	56.1%	43.9%
OKLAHOMA	167,640	102,992	64,648		38,344 R	61.4%	38.6%	61.4%	38.6%
OKMULGEE	14,369	7,107	7,262		155 D	49.5%	50.5%	49.5%	50.5%
OSAGE	13,309	7,508	5,801		1,707 R	56.4%	43.6%	56.4%	43.6%
OTTAWA	12,225	6,520	5,705		815 R	53.3%	46.7%	53.3%	46.7%
PAWNEE	4,792	3,153	1,639		1,514 R	65.8%	34.2%	65.8%	34.2%
PAYNE	15,637	9,943	5,694		4,249 R	63.6%	36.4%	63.6%	36.4%

PRESIDENT 1964

County	Total Vote	Republican	Democratic	Other	Rep.-Dem. Plurality	%Total Rep.	%Total Dem.	%Major Rep.	%Major Dem.
ADAIR	5,862	2,859	3,003		144 D	48.8%	51.2%	48.8%	51.2%
ALFALFA	4,180	2,450	1,730		720 R	58.6%	41.4%	58.6%	41.4%
ATOKA	3,883	1,424	2,459		1,035 D	36.7%	63.3%	36.7%	63.3%
BEAVER	3,490	1,982	1,508		474 R	56.8%	43.2%	56.8%	43.2%
BECKHAM	6,672	2,557	4,115		1,558 D	38.3%	61.7%	38.3%	61.7%
BLAINE	5,125	2,741	2,384		357 R	53.5%	46.5%	53.5%	46.5%
BRYAN	8,586	2,652	5,934		3,282 D	30.9%	69.1%	30.9%	69.1%
CADDO	11,171	3,724	7,447		3,723 D	33.3%	66.7%	33.3%	66.7%
CANADIAN	10,940	5,193	5,747		554 D	47.5%	52.5%	47.5%	52.5%
CARTER	15,631	4,986	10,645		5,659 D	31.9%	68.1%	31.9%	68.1%
CHEROKEE	7,916	3,467	4,449		982 D	43.8%	56.2%	43.8%	56.2%
CHOCTAW	5,687	1,718	3,969		2,251 D	30.2%	69.8%	30.2%	69.8%
CIMARRON	2,103	1,225	878		347 R	58.3%	41.7%	58.3%	41.7%
CLEVELAND	21,255	9,656	11,599		1,943 D	45.4%	54.6%	45.4%	54.6%
COAL	2,334	721	1,613		892 D	30.9%	69.1%	30.9%	69.1%
COMANCHE	21,521	7,936	13,585		5,649 D	36.9%	63.1%	36.9%	63.1%
COTTON	3,339	1,123	2,216		1,093 D	33.6%	66.4%	33.6%	66.4%
CRAIG	6,379	2,541	3,838		1,297 D	39.8%	60.2%	39.8%	60.2%
CREEK	16,191	6,355	9,836		3,481 D	39.3%	60.7%	39.3%	60.7%
CUSTER	7,826	3,362	4,464		1,102 D	43.0%	57.0%	43.0%	57.0%
DELAWARE	6,445	2,743	3,702		959 D	42.6%	57.4%	42.6%	57.4%
DEWEY	3,055	1,438	1,617		179 D	47.1%	52.9%	47.1%	52.9%
ELLIS	2,572	1,452	1,120		332 R	56.5%	43.5%	56.5%	43.5%
GARFIELD	22,472	12,297	10,175		2,122 R	54.7%	45.3%	54.7%	45.3%
GARVIN	10,483	3,470	7,013		3,543 D	33.1%	66.9%	33.1%	66.9%
GRADY	11,162	3,569	7,593		4,024 D	32.0%	68.0%	32.0%	68.0%
GREER	4,112	1,992	2,120		128 D	48.4%	51.6%	48.4%	51.6%
HARMON	3,918	1,247	2,671		1,424 D	31.8%	68.2%	31.8%	68.2%
HARPER	2,267	602	1,665		1,063 D	26.6%	73.4%	26.6%	73.4%
HASKELL	2,619	1,379	1,240		139 R	52.7%	47.3%	52.7%	47.3%
HUGHES	3,897	1,355	2,542		1,187 D	34.8%	65.2%	34.8%	65.2%
JACKSON	6,169	1,692	4,477		2,785 D	27.4%	72.6%	27.4%	72.6%
JEFFERSON	3,366	811	2,555		1,744 D	24.1%	75.9%	24.1%	75.9%
JOHNSTON	3,435	1,065	2,370		1,305 D	31.0%	69.0%	31.0%	69.0%
KAY	23,329	12,033	11,296		737 R	51.6%	48.4%	51.6%	48.4%
KINGFISHER	5,629	3,117	2,512		605 R	55.4%	44.6%	55.4%	44.6%
KIOWA	5,892	2,206	3,686		1,480 D	37.4%	62.6%	37.4%	62.6%
LATIMER	3,146	849	2,297		1,448 D	27.0%	73.0%	27.0%	73.0%
LE FLORE	11,009	3,904	7,105		3,201 D	35.5%	64.5%	35.5%	64.5%
LINCOLN	8,900	3,854	5,046		1,192 D	43.3%	56.7%	43.3%	56.7%
LOGAN	8,066	3,787	4,279		492 D	47.0%	53.0%	47.0%	53.0%
LOVE	2,526	663	1,863		1,200 D	26.2%	73.8%	26.2%	73.8%
MCCLAIN	5,276	1,638	3,638		2,000 D	31.0%	69.0%	31.0%	69.0%
MCCURTAIN	8,963	2,981	5,982		3,001 D	33.3%	66.7%	33.3%	66.7%
MCINTOSH	4,925	1,428	3,497		2,069 D	29.0%	71.0%	29.0%	71.0%
MAJOR	3,727	2,436	1,291		1,145 R	65.4%	34.6%	65.4%	34.6%
MARSHALL	3,419	1,101	2,318		1,217 D	32.2%	67.8%	32.2%	67.8%
MAYES	9,578	4,157	5,421		1,264 D	43.4%	56.6%	43.4%	56.6%
MURRAY	4,319	1,236	3,083		1,847 D	28.6%	71.4%	28.6%	71.4%
MUSKOGEE	24,838	8,508	16,330		7,822 D	34.3%	65.7%	34.3%	65.7%
NOBLE	4,870	2,157	2,713		556 D	44.3%	55.7%	44.3%	55.7%
NOWATA	4,786	2,142	2,644		502 D	44.8%	55.2%	44.8%	55.2%
OKFUSKEE	4,534	1,629	2,905		1,276 D	35.9%	64.1%	35.9%	64.1%
OKLAHOMA	174,301	83,660	90,641		6,981 D	48.0%	52.0%	48.0%	52.0%
OKMULGEE	14,899	4,704	10,195		5,491 D	31.6%	68.4%	31.6%	68.4%
OSAGE	13,090	5,695	7,395		1,700 D	43.5%	56.5%	43.5%	56.5%
OTTAWA	11,679	4,090	7,589		3,499 D	35.0%	65.0%	35.0%	65.0%
PAWNEE	4,667	2,278	2,389		111 D	48.8%	51.2%	48.8%	51.2%
PAYNE	16,842	7,936	8,906		970 D	47.1%	52.9%	47.1%	52.9%

OKLAHOMA

PRESIDENT 1960

County	Total Vote	Republican	Democratic	Other	Rep.-Dem. Plurality	Percentage Total Vote Rep.	Total Vote Dem.	Major Vote Rep.	Major Vote Dem.
PITTSBURG	13,144	5,834	7,310		1,476 D	44.4%	55.6%	44.4%	55.6%
PONTOTOC	10,517	5,863	4,654		1,209 R	55.7%	44.3%	55.7%	44.3%
POTTAWATOMIE	17,488	9,421	8,067		1,354 R	53.9%	46.1%	53.9%	46.1%
PUSHMATAHA	3,358	1,728	1,630		98 R	51.5%	48.5%	51.5%	48.5%
ROGER MILLS	2,272	1,463	809		654 R	64.4%	35.6%	64.4%	35.6%
ROGERS	8,579	5,412	3,167		2,245 R	63.1%	36.9%	63.1%	36.9%
SEMINOLE	9,761	5,505	4,256		1,249 R	56.4%	43.6%	56.4%	43.6%
SEQUOYAH	6,804	3,862	2,942		920 R	56.8%	43.2%	56.8%	43.2%
STEPHENS	14,983	8,084	6,899		1,185 R	54.0%	46.0%	54.0%	46.0%
TEXAS	5,863	4,314	1,549		2,765 R	73.6%	26.4%	73.6%	26.4%
TILLMAN	5,414	2,678	2,736		58 D	49.5%	50.5%	49.5%	50.5%
TULSA	142,624	89,899	52,725		37,174 R	63.0%	37.0%	63.0%	37.0%
WAGONER	6,277	3,570	2,707		863 R	56.9%	43.1%	56.9%	43.1%
WASHINGTON	19,179	13,700	5,479		8,221 R	71.4%	28.6%	71.4%	28.6%
WASHITA	5,623	3,209	2,414		795 R	57.1%	42.9%	57.1%	42.9%
WOODS	5,966	4,064	1,902		2,162 R	68.1%	31.9%	68.1%	31.9%
WOODWARD	5,672	4,185	1,487		2,698 R	73.8%	26.2%	73.8%	26.2%
TOTAL	903,150	533,039	370,111		162,928 R	59.0%	41.0%	59.0%	41.0%

PRESIDENT 1964

County	Total Vote	Republican	Democratic	Other	Rep.-Dem. Plurality	Percentage Total Vote Rep.	Total Vote Dem.	Major Vote Rep.	Major Vote Dem.
PITTSBURG	13,458	3,555	9,903		6,348 D	26.4%	73.6%	26.4%	73.6%
PONTOTOC	11,615	4,166	7,449		3,283 D	35.9%	64.1%	35.9%	64.1%
POTTAWATOMIE	17,725	6,841	10,884		4,043 D	38.6%	61.4%	38.6%	61.4%
PUSHMATAHA	3,895	1,332	2,563		1,231 D	34.2%	65.8%	34.2%	65.8%
ROGER MILLS	2,271	926	1,345		419 D	40.8%	59.2%	40.8%	59.2%
ROGERS	9,651	4,202	5,449		1,247 D	43.5%	56.5%	43.5%	56.5%
SEMINOLE	10,258	3,676	6,582		2,906 D	35.8%	64.2%	35.8%	64.2%
SEQUOYAH	7,150	2,846	4,304		1,458 D	39.8%	60.2%	39.8%	60.2%
STEPHENS	14,595	5,323	9,272		3,949 D	36.5%	63.5%	36.5%	63.5%
TEXAS	5,839	3,339	2,500		839 R	57.2%	42.8%	57.2%	42.8%
TILLMAN	5,355	2,001	3,354		1,353 D	37.4%	62.6%	37.4%	62.6%
TULSA	138,254	76,770	61,484		15,286 D	55.5%	44.5%	55.5%	44.5%
WAGONER	6,797	2,840	3,957		1,117 D	41.8%	58.2%	41.8%	58.2%
WASHINGTON	20,953	12,382	8,571		3,811 R	59.1%	40.9%	59.1%	40.9%
WASHITA	5,486	2,147	3,339		1,192 D	39.1%	60.9%	39.1%	60.9%
WOODS	5,636	2,886	2,750		136 R	51.2%	48.8%	51.2%	48.8%
WOODWARD	6,028	3,094	2,934		160 R	51.3%	48.7%	51.3%	48.7%
TOTAL	932,499	412,665	519,834		107,169 D	44.3%	55.7%	44.3%	55.7%

OKLAHOMA

OTHER VOTE COMPOSITION:

1920   Socialist.
1924   Progressive.
1928   3,924 Socialist; 1,283 Farmer-Labor.
1932
1936   2,221 Socialist; 1,328 Prohibition.

1940   Prohibition.
1944   Prohibition.
1948
1952
1956

1960
1964

SPECIAL CASES:

1920   Sources vary in their county-by-county figures for this election. Frequently
        data on the Senatorial vote for 1920 have been used in place of the Presi-
        dential vote. In this compilation county figures for each elector have been
        inspected and adjusted to produce the most reasonable construction of each
        county's 1920 vote for President.

1924   Progressive total includes 41,142 Farmer-Labor and 5,132 Socialist votes.
        This combined vote was second in one country.

1960   One Republican elector voted in the Electoral College for Senators Harry
        Flood Byrd and Barry M. Goldwater.

OREGON

PRESIDENT 1920

County	Total Vote	Republican	Democratic	Other	Rep.-Dem. Plurality	Total Vote Rep.	Total Vote Dem.	Major Vote Rep.	Major Vote Dem.
BAKER	5,961	3,495	2,171	295	1,324 R	58.6%	36.4%	61.7%	38.3%
BENTON	5,663	3,752	1,719	192	2,033 R	66.3%	30.4%	68.6%	31.4%
CLACKAMAS	11,639	6,928	3,740	971	3,188 R	59.5%	32.1%	64.9%	35.1%
CLATSOP	5,697	3,498	1,687	512	1,811 R	61.4%	29.6%	67.5%	32.5%
COLUMBIA	3,262	2,007	970	285	1,037 R	61.5%	29.7%	67.4%	32.6%
COOS	6,205	3,272	2,297	636	975 R	52.7%	37.0%	58.8%	41.2%
CROOK	1,473	872	528	73	344 R	59.2%	35.8%	62.3%	37.7%
CURRY	984	599	280	105	319 R	60.9%	28.5%	68.1%	31.9%
DESCHUTES	3,040	1,649	1,072	319	577 R	54.2%	35.3%	60.6%	39.4%
DOUGLAS	7,315	4,402	2,428	485	1,974 R	60.2%	33.2%	64.5%	35.5%
GILLIAM	1,355	821	498	36	323 R	60.6%	36.8%	62.2%	37.8%
GRANT	1,910	1,310	497	103	813 R	68.6%	26.0%	72.5%	27.5%
HARNEY	1,622	1,026	479	117	547 R	63.3%	29.5%	68.2%	31.8%
HOOD RIVER	2,417	1,449	761	207	688 R	60.0%	31.5%	65.6%	34.4%
JACKSON	7,326	4,382	2,503	441	1,879 R	59.8%	34.2%	63.6%	36.4%
JEFFERSON	1,012	623	300	89	323 R	61.6%	29.6%	67.5%	32.5%
JOSEPHINE	2,581	1,606	819	156	787 R	62.2%	31.7%	66.2%	33.8%
KLAMATH	3,907	2,742	901	264	1,841 R	70.2%	23.1%	75.3%	24.7%
LAKE	1,576	1,136	358	82	778 R	72.1%	22.7%	76.0%	24.0%
LANE	12,447	7,714	3,986	747	3,728 R	62.0%	32.0%	65.9%	34.1%
LINCOLN	2,080	1,229	669	182	560 R	59.1%	32.2%	64.8%	35.2%
LINN	8,355	4,693	3,177	485	1,516 R	56.2%	38.0%	59.6%	40.4%
MALHEUR	3,620	2,352	1,075	193	1,277 R	65.0%	29.7%	68.6%	31.4%
MARION	13,298	8,798	3,831	669	4,967 R	66.2%	28.8%	69.7%	30.3%
MORROW	1,725	1,186	451	88	735 R	68.8%	26.1%	72.4%	27.6%
MULTNOMAH	77,174	44,806	27,607	4,761	17,199 R	58.1%	35.8%	61.9%	38.1%
POLK	4,594	2,709	1,653	232	1,056 R	59.0%	36.0%	62.1%	37.9%
SHERMAN	1,362	893	423	46	470 R	65.6%	31.1%	67.9%	32.1%
TILLAMOOK	2,737	1,664	828	245	836 R	60.8%	30.3%	66.8%	33.2%
UMATILLA	8,580	4,979	3,255	346	1,724 R	58.0%	37.9%	60.5%	39.5%
UNION	5,020	2,844	1,899	277	945 R	56.7%	37.8%	60.0%	40.0%
WALLOWA	2,674	1,612	896	166	716 R	60.3%	33.5%	64.3%	35.7%
WASCO	4,334	2,698	1,434	202	1,264 R	62.3%	33.1%	65.3%	34.7%
WASHINGTON	7,641	4,947	2,262	432	2,685 R	64.7%	29.6%	68.6%	31.4%
WHEELER	1,041	797	212	32	585 R	76.6%	20.4%	79.0%	21.0%
YAMHILL	6,895	4,102	2,353	440	1,749 R	59.5%	34.1%	63.5%	36.5%
TOTAL	238,522	143,592	80,019	14,911	63,573 R	60.2%	33.5%	64.2%	35.8%

PRESIDENT 1924

County	Total Vote	Republican	Democratic	Other	Rep.-Dem. Plurality	Total Vote Rep.	Total Vote Dem.	Major Vote Rep.	Major Vote Dem.
BAKER	6,172	2,803	2,004	1,365	799 R	45.4%	32.5%	58.3%	41.7%
BENTON	5,631	3,417	1,579	635	1,838 R	60.7%	28.0%	68.4%	31.6%
CLACKAMAS	13,548	5,864	3,099	4,585	2,765 R	43.3%	22.9%	65.4%	34.6%
CLATSOP	5,881	3,313	1,373	1,195	1,940 R	56.3%	23.3%	70.7%	29.3%
COLUMBIA	4,418	2,483	1,015	920	1,468 R	56.2%	23.0%	71.0%	29.0%
COOS	8,070	3,905	1,757	2,408	2,148 R	48.4%	21.8%	69.0%	31.0%
CROOK	1,429	725	434	270	291 R	50.7%	30.4%	62.6%	37.4%
CURRY	1,214	664	224	326	440 R	54.7%	18.5%	74.8%	25.2%
DESCHUTES	4,378	2,321	1,015	1,042	1,306 R	53.0%	23.2%	69.5%	30.4%
DOUGLAS	7,849	4,219	1,666	1,964	2,553 R	53.8%	21.2%	71.7%	28.3%
GILLIAM	1,470	738	521	211	217 R	50.2%	35.4%	58.6%	41.4%
GRANT	1,979	1,126	459	394	667 R	56.9%	23.2%	71.0%	29.0%
HARNEY	1,581	851	436	294	415 R	53.8%	27.6%	66.1%	33.9%
HOOD RIVER	2,506	1,214	683	609	531 R	48.4%	27.3%	64.0%	36.0%
JACKSON	9,141	4,868	1,840	2,433	3,028 R	53.3%	20.1%	72.6%	27.4%
JEFFERSON	959	374	242	343	132 R	39.0%	25.2%	60.7%	39.3%
JOSEPHINE	3,257	1,756	650	851	1,106 R	53.9%	20.0%	73.0%	27.0%
KLAMATH	5,189	2,775	680	1,734	2,095 R	53.5%	13.1%	80.3%	19.7%
LAKE	1,520	917	304	299	613 R	60.3%	20.0%	75.1%	24.9%
LANE	14,275	8,551	3,255	2,469	5,296 R	59.9%	22.8%	72.4%	27.6%
LINCOLN	2,544	1,328	641	575	687 R	52.2%	25.2%	67.4%	32.6%
LINN	8,355	4,141	2,618	1,596	1,523 R	49.6%	31.3%	61.3%	38.7%
MALHEUR	3,217	1,671	828	718	843 R	51.9%	25.7%	66.9%	33.1%
MARION	16,016	8,351	3,996	3,669	4,355 R	52.1%	25.0%	67.6%	32.4%
MORROW	1,858	991	397	470	594 R	53.3%	21.4%	71.4%	28.6%
MULTNOMAH	97,764	48,866	21,733	27,165	27,133 R	50.0%	22.2%	69.2%	30.8%
POLK	5,223	2,755	1,621	847	1,134 R	52.7%	31.0%	63.0%	37.0%
SHERMAN	1,352	756	367	229	389 R	55.9%	27.1%	67.3%	32.7%
TILLAMOOK	3,719	2,201	795	723	1,406 R	59.2%	21.4%	73.5%	26.5%
UMATILLA	8,620	3,854	3,052	1,714	802 R	44.7%	35.4%	55.8%	44.2%
UNION	5,663	2,428	1,816	1,419	612 R	42.9%	32.1%	57.2%	42.8%
WALLOWA	2,707	1,253	973	481	280 R	46.3%	35.9%	56.3%	43.7%
WASCO	4,681	2,459	1,185	1,087	1,274 R	52.5%	25.3%	67.0%	33.0%
WASHINGTON	9,341	4,203	2,103	2,035	2,100 R	46.0%	23.0%	66.7%	33.3%
WHEELER	1,001	685	213	103	472 R	68.4%	21.3%	76.3%	23.7%
YAMHILL	7,160	3,803	2,015	1,342	1,788 R	53.1%	28.1%	65.4%	34.6%
TOTAL	279,488	142,579	67,589	69,320	74,990 R	51.0%	24.2%	67.8%	32.2%

OREGON

PRESIDENT 1928

County	Total Vote	Republican	Democratic	Other	Rep.-Dem. Plurality	Total Vote Rep.	Total Vote Dem.	Major Vote Rep.	Major Vote Dem.
BAKER	5,679	3,721	1,861	97	1,860 R	65.5%	32.8%	66.7%	33.3%
BENTON	6,095	4,605	1,412	78	3,193 R	75.6%	23.2%	76.5%	23.5%
CLACKAMAS	15,486	9,216	5,918	352	3,298 R	59.5%	38.2%	60.9%	39.1%
CLATSOP	6,454	4,087	2,208	159	1,879 R	63.3%	34.2%	64.9%	35.1%
COLUMBIA	5,396	3,519	1,775	102	1,744 R	65.2%	32.9%	66.5%	33.5%
COOS	8,126	4,929	3,040	157	1,889 R	60.7%	37.4%	61.9%	38.1%
CROOK	1,382	877	487	18	390 R	63.5%	35.2%	64.3%	35.7%
CURRY	1,173	694	453	26	241 R	59.2%	38.6%	60.5%	39.5%
DESCHUTES	4,628	2,815	1,702	111	1,113 R	60.8%	36.8%	62.3%	37.7%
DOUGLAS	7,954	5,609	2,191	154	3,418 R	70.5%	27.5%	71.9%	28.1%
GILLIAM	1,408	880	515	13	365 R	62.5%	36.6%	63.1%	36.9%
GRANT	1,906	1,411	469	26	942 R	74.0%	24.6%	75.1%	24.9%
HARNEY	1,571	952	600	19	352 R	60.6%	38.2%	61.3%	38.7%
HOOD RIVER	2,769	1,806	905	58	901 R	65.2%	32.7%	66.6%	33.4%
JACKSON	10,676	8,053	2,463	160	5,590 R	75.4%	23.1%	76.6%	23.4%
JEFFERSON	811	481	308	22	173 R	59.3%	38.0%	61.0%	39.0%
JOSEPHINE	3,681	2,625	959	97	1,666 R	71.3%	26.1%	73.2%	26.8%
KLAMATH	7,267	4,453	2,721	93	1,732 R	61.3%	37.4%	62.1%	37.9%
LAKE	1,594	1,014	549	31	465 R	63.6%	34.4%	64.9%	35.1%
LANE	18,205	13,647	4,213	345	9,434 R	75.0%	23.1%	76.4%	23.6%
LINCOLN	3,663	2,100	1,464	99	636 R	57.3%	40.0%	58.9%	41.1%
LINN	8,691	5,877	2,645	169	3,232 R	67.6%	30.4%	69.0%	31.0%
MALHEUR	3,213	2,164	1,016	33	1,148 R	67.4%	31.6%	68.1%	31.9%
MARION	18,971	11,754	6,998	219	4,756 R	62.0%	36.9%	62.7%	37.3%
MORROW	1,685	1,093	543	49	550 R	64.9%	32.2%	66.8%	33.2%
MULTNOMAH	122,859	75,731	45,177	1,951	30,554 R	61.6%	36.8%	62.6%	37.4%
POLK	5,034	3,244	1,724	66	1,520 R	64.4%	34.2%	65.3%	34.7%
SHERMAN	1,144	759	375	10	384 R	66.3%	32.8%	66.9%	33.1%
TILLAMOOK	3,850	2,570	1,204	76	1,366 R	66.8%	31.3%	68.1%	31.9%
UMATILLA	7,780	5,277	2,390	113	2,887 R	67.8%	30.7%	68.8%	31.2%
UNION	5,444	3,219	2,154	71	1,065 R	59.1%	39.6%	59.9%	40.1%
WALLOWA	2,332	1,326	935	71	391 R	56.9%	40.1%	58.6%	41.4%
WASCO	4,513	2,746	1,699	68	1,047 R	60.8%	37.6%	61.8%	38.2%
WASHINGTON	9,879	6,162	3,544	173	2,618 R	62.4%	35.9%	63.5%	36.5%
WHEELER	902	677	224	1	453 R	75.1%	24.8%	75.1%	24.9%
YAMHILL	7,721	5,248	2,382	91	2,866 R	68.0%	30.9%	68.8%	31.2%
TOTAL	319,942	205,341	109,223	5,378	96,118 R	64.2%	34.1%	65.3%	34.7%

PRESIDENT 1932

County	Total Vote	Republican	Democratic	Other	Rep.-Dem. Plurality	Total Vote Rep.	Total Vote Dem.	Major Vote Rep.	Major Vote Dem.
BAKER	6,674	2,097	4,420	157	2,323 D	31.4%	66.2%	32.2%	67.8%
BENTON	7,431	4,068	3,121	242	947 R	54.7%	42.0%	56.6%	43.4%
CLACKAMAS	18,608	5,964	11,575	1,069	5,611 D	32.1%	62.2%	34.0%	66.0%
CLATSOP	7,457	2,570	4,473	414	1,903 D	34.5%	60.0%	36.5%	63.5%
COLUMBIA	5,937	1,975	3,643	319	1,668 D	33.3%	61.4%	35.2%	64.8%
COOS	9,296	3,299	5,504	493	2,205 D	35.5%	59.2%	37.5%	62.5%
CROOK	1,656	626	990	40	364 D	37.8%	59.8%	38.7%	61.3%
CURRY	1,428	395	971	62	576 D	27.7%	68.0%	28.9%	71.1%
DESCHUTES	5,055	1,697	2,962	396	1,265 D	33.6%	58.6%	36.4%	63.6%
DOUGLAS	9,054	4,046	4,638	370	592 D	44.7%	51.2%	46.6%	53.4%
GILLIAM	1,343	470	854	19	384 D	35.0%	63.6%	35.5%	64.5%
GRANT	2,325	733	1,496	96	763 D	31.5%	64.3%	32.9%	67.1%
HARNEY	2,067	687	1,276	104	589 D	33.2%	61.7%	35.0%	65.0%
HOOD RIVER	3,256	1,387	1,685	184	298 D	42.6%	51.8%	45.1%	54.9%
JACKSON	13,639	5,459	7,519	661	2,060 D	40.0%	55.1%	42.1%	57.9%
JEFFERSON	766	253	477	36	224 D	33.0%	62.3%	34.7%	65.3%
JOSEPHINE	5,195	1,757	3,060	378	1,303 D	33.8%	58.9%	36.5%	63.5%
KLAMATH	10,755	3,483	6,772	500	3,289 D	32.4%	63.0%	34.0%	66.0%
LAKE	2,084	839	1,199	46	360 D	40.3%	57.5%	41.2%	58.8%
LANE	24,137	10,547	11,073	2,517	526 D	43.7%	45.9%	48.8%	51.2%
LINCOLN	3,994	1,415	2,376	203	961 D	35.4%	59.5%	37.3%	62.7%
LINN	10,031	4,106	5,366	559	1,260 D	40.9%	53.5%	43.3%	56.7%
MALHEUR	3,754	1,589	2,025	140	436 D	42.3%	53.9%	44.0%	56.0%
MARION	22,118	8,633	12,572	913	3,939 D	39.0%	56.8%	40.7%	59.3%
MORROW	1,601	579	929	93	350 D	36.2%	58.0%	38.4%	61.6%
MULTNOMAH	132,743	47,201	78,898	6,644	31,697 D	35.6%	59.4%	37.4%	62.6%
POLK	6,514	2,548	3,705	261	1,157 D	39.1%	56.9%	40.7%	59.3%
SHERMAN	1,112	423	665	24	242 D	38.0%	59.8%	38.9%	61.1%
TILLAMOOK	4,740	1,722	2,726	292	1,004 D	36.3%	57.5%	38.7%	61.3%
UMATILLA	8,877	2,930	5,631	316	2,701 D	33.0%	63.4%	34.2%	65.8%
UNION	6,350	1,705	4,450	195	2,745 D	26.9%	70.1%	27.7%	72.3%
WALLOWA	2,652	772	1,790	90	1,018 D	29.1%	67.5%	30.1%	69.9%
WASCO	4,664	1,740	2,776	148	1,036 D	37.3%	59.5%	38.5%	61.5%
WASHINGTON	11,554	4,201	6,824	529	2,623 D	36.4%	59.1%	38.1%	61.9%
WHEELER	1,165	519	632	14	113 D	44.5%	54.2%	45.1%	54.9%
YAMHILL	8,719	3,584	4,798	337	1,214 D	41.1%	55.0%	42.8%	57.2%
TOTAL	368,751	136,019	213,871	18,861	77,852 D	36.9%	58.0%	38.9%	61.1%

OREGON

PRESIDENT 1936

County	Total Vote	Republican	Democratic	Other	Rep.-Dem. Plurality	Total Vote Rep.	Total Vote Dem.	Major Vote Rep.	Major Vote Dem.
BAKER	7,151	1,768	4,991	392	3,223 D	24.7%	69.8%	26.2%	73.8%
BENTON	7,423	3,390	3,547	486	157 D	45.7%	47.8%	48.9%	51.1%
CLACKAMAS	21,303	5,830	14,203	1,270	8,373 D	27.4%	66.7%	29.1%	70.9%
CLATSOP	8,832	2,261	6,267	304	4,006 D	25.6%	71.0%	26.5%	73.5%
COLUMBIA	7,801	1,815	5,587	399	3,772 D	23.3%	71.6%	24.5%	75.5%
COOS	10,630	2,576	7,167	887	4,591 D	24.2%	67.4%	26.4%	73.6%
CROOK	1,752	589	1,086	77	497 D	33.6%	62.0%	35.2%	64.8%
CURRY	1,680	497	913	270	416 D	29.6%	54.3%	35.2%	64.8%
DESCHUTES	5,884	1,299	4,278	307	2,979 D	22.1%	72.7%	23.3%	76.7%
DOUGLAS	10,110	4,254	4,893	963	639 D	42.1%	48.4%	46.5%	53.5%
GILLIAM	1,411	362	983	66	621 D	25.7%	69.7%	26.9%	73.1%
GRANT	2,489	697	1,436	356	739 D	28.0%	57.7%	32.2%	67.3%
HARNEY	1,940	546	1,262	132	716 D	28.1%	65.1%	30.2%	69.8%
HOOD RIVER	4,195	1,249	2,759	187	1,510 D	29.8%	65.0%	31.2%	68.8%
JACKSON	13,914	4,866	7,520	1,528	2,654 D	35.0%	54.0%	39.3%	60.7%
JEFFERSON	803	253	514	36	261 D	31.5%	64.0%	33.0%	67.0%
JOSEPHINE	5,955	1,992	2,840	1,123	848 D	33.5%	47.7%	41.2%	58.8%
KLAMATH	12,222	3,225	8,562	435	5,337 D	26.4%	70.1%	27.4%	72.6%
LAKE	2,253	725	1,274	254	549 D	32.2%	56.5%	36.3%	63.7%
LANE	24,215	8,309	13,926	1,980	5,617 D	34.3%	57.5%	37.4%	62.6%
LINCOLN	5,042	1,585	3,024	433	1,439 D	31.4%	60.0%	34.4%	65.6%
LINN	11,211	4,110	5,856	1,245	1,746 D	36.7%	52.2%	41.2%	58.8%
MALHEUR	4,410	1,385	2,630	395	1,245 D	31.4%	59.6%	34.5%	65.5%
MARION	26,071	8,595	15,536	1,940	6,941 D	33.0%	59.6%	35.6%	64.4%
MORROW	1,874	518	1,181	175	663 D	27.6%	63.0%	30.5%	69.5%
MULTNOMAH	152,319	41,405	106,561	4,353	65,156 D	27.2%	70.0%	28.0%	72.0%
POLK	6,498	2,246	3,694	558	1,448 D	34.6%	57.8%	37.8%	62.2%
SHERMAN	1,213	337	823	53	486 D	27.8%	67.8%	29.1%	70.9%
TILLAMOOK	4,583	1,380	2,781	422	1,401 D	30.1%	60.7%	33.2%	66.8%
UMATILLA	9,411	2,943	5,753	715	2,810 D	31.3%	61.1%	33.8%	66.2%
UNION	6,712	1,517	4,643	552	3,126 D	22.6%	69.2%	24.6%	75.4%
WALLOWA	3,132	811	2,000	321	1,189 D	25.9%	68.9%	28.9%	71.1%
WASCO	5,184	1,278	3,573	333	2,295 D	24.7%	68.9%	26.3%	73.7%
WASHINGTON	13,612	4,148	8,641	823	4,493 D	30.5%	63.5%	32.4%	67.6%
WHEELER	1,190	502	663	25	161 D	42.2%	55.7%	43.1%	56.9%
YAMHILL	9,596	3,443	5,366	787	1,923 D	35.9%	55.9%	39.1%	60.9%
TOTAL	414,021	122,706	266,733	24,582	144,027 D	29.6%	64.4%	31.5%	68.5%

PRESIDENT 1940

County	Total Vote	Republican	Democratic	Other	Rep.-Dem. Plurality	Total Vote Rep.	Total Vote Dem.	Major Vote Rep.	Major Vote Dem.
BAKER	7,493	3,101	4,353	39	1,252 D	41.4%	58.1%	41.6%	58.4%
BENTON	8,079	5,089	2,942	48	2,147 R	63.0%	36.4%	63.4%	36.6%
CLACKAMAS	25,153	11,416	13,547	190	2,131 D	45.4%	53.9%	45.7%	54.3%
CLATSOP	10,514	3,758	6,686	70	2,928 D	35.7%	63.6%	36.0%	64.0%
COLUMBIA	8,774	2,959	5,758	57	2,799 D	33.7%	65.6%	33.9%	66.1%
COOS	12,988	5,034	7,853	101	2,819 D	38.8%	60.5%	39.1%	60.9%
CROOK	2,398	942	1,439	17	497 D	39.3%	60.0%	39.6%	60.4%
CURRY	1,991	941	1,033	17	92 D	47.3%	51.9%	47.7%	52.3%
DESCHUTES	7,453	2,603	4,775	75	2,172 D	34.9%	64.1%	35.3%	64.7%
DOUGLAS	10,770	5,991	4,707	72	1,284 R	55.6%	43.7%	56.0%	44.0%
GILLIAM	1,307	518	785	4	267 D	39.6%	60.1%	39.8%	60.2%
GRANT	2,695	1,103	1,582	10	479 D	40.9%	58.7%	41.1%	58.9%
HARNEY	2,136	912	1,214	10	302 D	42.7%	56.8%	42.9%	57.1%
HOOD RIVER	4,689	2,305	2,367	17	62 D	49.2%	50.5%	49.3%	50.7%
JACKSON	15,339	8,507	6,754	78	1,753 R	55.5%	44.0%	55.7%	44.3%
JEFFERSON	896	423	467	6	44 D	47.2%	52.1%	47.5%	52.5%
JOSEPHINE	6,932	3,964	2,888	80	1,076 R	57.2%	41.7%	57.9%	42.1%
KLAMATH	15,610	6,169	9,345	96	3,176 D	39.5%	59.9%	39.8%	60.2%
LAKE	2,544	1,121	1,414	9	293 D	44.1%	55.6%	44.2%	55.8%
LANE	31,890	15,349	16,286	255	937 D	48.1%	51.1%	48.5%	51.5%
LINCOLN	6,565	2,962	3,510	93	548 D	45.1%	53.5%	45.8%	54.2%
LINN	12,959	6,523	6,360	76	163 R	50.3%	49.1%	50.6%	49.4%
MALHEUR	5,929	2,929	2,958	42	29 D	49.4%	49.9%	49.8%	50.2%
MARION	31,227	16,940	14,031	256	2,909 R	54.2%	44.9%	54.7%	45.3%
MORROW	1,749	758	979	12	221 D	43.3%	56.0%	43.6%	56.4%
MULTNOMAH	172,313	73,612	97,595	1,106	23,983 D	42.7%	56.6%	43.0%	57.0%
POLK	8,348	4,211	4,077	60	134 R	50.4%	48.8%	50.8%	49.2%
SHERMAN	1,248	575	670	3	95 D	46.1%	53.7%	46.2%	53.8%
TILLAMOOK	5,338	2,516	2,786	36	270 D	47.1%	52.2%	47.5%	52.5%
UMATILLA	10,160	5,193	4,935	32	258 R	51.1%	48.6%	51.3%	48.7%
UNION	7,196	2,642	4,500	54	1,858 D	36.7%	62.5%	37.0%	63.0%
WALLOWA	3,311	1,319	1,974	18	655 D	39.8%	59.6%	40.1%	59.9%
WASCO	5,576	2,553	3,001	22	448 D	45.8%	53.8%	46.0%	54.0%
WASHINGTON	17,103	8,367	8,626	110	259 D	48.9%	50.4%	49.2%	50.8%
WHEELER	1,360	705	652	3	53 R	51.8%	47.9%	52.0%	48.0%
YAMHILL	11,207	5,545	5,566	96	21 D	49.5%	49.7%	49.9%	50.1%
TOTAL	481,240	219,555	258,415	3,270	38,860 D	45.6%	53.7%	45.9%	54.1%

OREGON

PRESIDENT 1944

County	Total Vote	Republican	Democratic	Other	Rep.-Dem. Plurality	% Total Vote Rep.	% Total Vote Dem.	% Major Vote Rep.	% Major Vote Dem.
BAKER	5,641	2,494	3,116	31	522 D	44.2%	55.2%	44.5%	55.5%
BENTON	8,141	5,242	2,830	69	2,412 R	64.4%	34.8%	64.9%	35.1%
CLACKAMAS	26,987	12,492	14,060	435	1,568 D	46.3%	52.1%	47.0%	53.0%
CLATSOP	10,031	3,921	6,038	72	2,117 D	39.1%	60.2%	39.4%	60.6%
COLUMBIA	8,049	2,696	5,213	140	2,517 D	33.5%	64.8%	34.1%	65.9%
COOS	11,225	4,609	6,476	140	1,867 D	41.1%	57.7%	41.6%	58.4%
CROOK	2,105	932	1,145	28	213 D	44.3%	54.4%	44.9%	55.1%
CURRY	1,527	827	678	22	149 R	54.2%	44.4%	55.0%	45.0%
DESCHUTES	6,426	2,547	3,807	72	1,260 D	39.6%	59.2%	40.1%	59.9%
DOUGLAS	10,840	6,134	4,563	143	1,571 R	56.6%	42.1%	57.3%	42.7%
GILLIAM	1,060	492	567	1	75 D	46.4%	53.5%	46.5%	53.5%
GRANT	2,203	1,006	1,072	125	66 D	45.7%	48.7%	48.4%	51.6%
HARNEY	1,794	787	997	10	210 D	43.9%	55.6%	44.1%	55.9%
HOOD RIVER	4,012	2,008	1,960	44	48 R	50.0%	48.9%	50.6%	49.4%
JACKSON	15,426	8,598	6,668	160	1,930 R	55.7%	43.2%	56.3%	43.7%
JEFFERSON	723	419	297	7	122 R	58.0%	41.1%	58.5%	41.5%
JOSEPHINE	7,355	4,010	3,214	131	796 R	54.5%	43.7%	55.5%	44.5%
KLAMATH	12,717	5,969	6,656	92	687 D	45.9%	52.3%	47.3%	52.7%
LAKE	2,169	1,008	1,147	14	139 D	46.5%	52.9%	46.8%	53.2%
LANE	32,397	17,690	14,375	332	3,315 R	54.6%	44.4%	55.2%	44.8%
LINCOLN	5,813	2,801	2,947	65	146 D	48.2%	50.7%	48.7%	51.3%
LINN	13,493	6,877	6,480	136	397 R	51.0%	48.0%	51.5%	48.5%
MALHEUR	5,078	2,797	2,234	47	563 R	55.1%	44.0%	55.6%	44.4%
MARION	28,601	16,176	11,907	518	4,269 R	56.6%	41.6%	57.6%	42.4%
MORROW	1,596	747	836	13	89 D	46.8%	52.4%	47.2%	52.8%
MULTNOMAH	186,218	78,279	105,516	2,423	27,237 D	42.0%	56.7%	42.6%	57.4%
POLK	7,340	3,904	3,318	118	586 R	53.2%	45.2%	54.1%	45.9%
SHERMAN	996	475	518	3	43 D	47.7%	52.0%	47.8%	52.2%
TILLAMOOK	5,186	2,477	2,634	75	157 D	47.8%	50.8%	48.5%	51.5%
UMATILLA	10,391	5,379	4,967	45	412 R	51.8%	47.8%	52.0%	48.0%
UNION	6,424	2,413	3,951	60	1,538 D	37.6%	61.5%	37.9%	62.1%
WALLOWA	2,721	1,152	1,544	25	392 D	42.3%	56.7%	42.7%	57.3%
WASCO	4,786	2,429	2,313	44	116 R	50.8%	48.3%	51.2%	48.8%
WASHINGTON	18,677	9,362	9,110	205	252 R	50.1%	48.8%	50.7%	49.3%
WHEELER	962	544	414	4	130 R	56.5%	43.0%	56.8%	43.2%
YAMHILL	11,037	5,672	5,067	298	605 R	51.4%	45.9%	52.8%	47.2%
TOTAL	480,147	225,365	248,635	6,147	23,270 D	46.9%	51.8%	47.5%	52.5%

PRESIDENT 1948

County	Total Vote	Republican	Democratic	Other	Rep.-Dem. Plurality	% Total Vote Rep.	% Total Vote Dem.	% Major Vote Rep.	% Major Vote Dem.
BAKER	6,040	2,841	3,035	164	194 D	47.0%	50.2%	48.3%	51.7%
BENTON	10,329	6,839	3,135	355	3,704 R	66.2%	30.4%	68.6%	31.4%
CLACKAMAS	30,083	14,431	14,263	1,389	168 R	48.0%	47.4%	50.3%	49.7%
CLATSOP	11,313	5,076	5,574	663	498 D	44.9%	49.3%	47.7%	52.3%
COLUMBIA	8,251	3,049	4,768	434	1,719 D	37.0%	57.8%	39.0%	61.0%
COOS	11,562	5,536	5,453	573	83 R	47.9%	47.2%	50.4%	49.6%
CROOK	2,141	960	1,149	32	189 D	44.8%	53.7%	45.5%	54.5%
CURRY	1,879	1,112	677	90	435 R	59.2%	36.0%	62.2%	37.8%
DESCHUTES	7,163	3,463	3,499	201	36 D	48.3%	48.8%	49.7%	50.3%
DOUGLAS	13,612	7,671	5,500	441	2,171 R	56.4%	40.4%	58.2%	41.8%
GILLIAM	1,184	623	544	17	79 R	52.6%	45.9%	53.4%	46.6%
GRANT	2,293	1,090	1,156	47	66 D	47.5%	50.4%	48.5%	51.5%
HARNEY	1,624	784	802	38	18 D	48.3%	49.4%	49.4%	50.6%
HOOD RIVER	4,042	2,134	1,761	147	373 R	52.8%	43.6%	54.8%	45.2%
JACKSON	19,072	11,226	7,342	504	3,884 R	58.9%	38.5%	60.5%	39.5%
JEFFERSON	1,227	622	559	46	63 R	50.7%	45.6%	52.7%	47.3%
JOSEPHINE	8,588	5,004	3,290	294	1,714 R	58.3%	38.3%	60.3%	39.7%
KLAMATH	14,898	7,072	7,520	306	448 D	47.5%	50.5%	48.5%	51.5%
LAKE	2,254	1,083	1,104	67	21 D	48.0%	49.0%	49.5%	50.5%
LANE	37,709	20,843	15,606	1,260	5,237 R	55.3%	41.4%	57.2%	42.8%
LINCOLN	7,656	3,587	3,720	349	133 D	46.9%	48.6%	49.1%	50.9%
LINN	15,755	7,936	7,260	559	676 R	50.4%	46.1%	52.2%	47.8%
MALHEUR	5,898	3,265	2,499	134	766 R	55.4%	42.4%	56.6%	43.4%
MARION	33,171	18,907	13,183	991	5,814 R	57.3%	39.7%	59.0%	41.0%
MORROW	1,622	751	838	33	87 D	46.3%	51.7%	47.3%	52.7%
MULTNOMAH	169,028	86,519	93,703	8,806	7,184 D	45.8%	49.6%	48.0%	52.0%
POLK	8,012	4,328	3,451	233	877 R	54.0%	43.1%	55.6%	44.4%
SHERMAN	1,000	532	454	14	78 R	53.2%	45.4%	54.0%	46.0%
TILLAMOOK	6,286	2,952	3,128	206	176 D	47.0%	49.8%	48.6%	51.4%
UMATILLA	11,761	5,726	5,891	144	165 D	48.7%	50.1%	49.3%	50.7%
UNION	6,698	2,668	3,808	222	1,140 D	39.8%	56.9%	41.2%	58.8%
WALLOWA	2,675	1,196	1,408	71	212 D	44.7%	52.6%	45.9%	54.1%
WASCO	5,296	2,740	2,438	118	302 R	51.7%	46.0%	52.9%	47.1%
WASHINGTON	21,589	11,455	9,424	710	2,031 R	53.1%	43.7%	54.8%	45.2%
WHEELER	841	414	411	16	3 R	49.2%	48.9%	50.2%	49.8%
YAMHILL	11,528	6,379	4,794	355	1,585 R	55.3%	41.6%	57.1%	42.9%
TOTAL	524,080	260,904	243,147	20,029	17,757 R	49.8%	46.4%	51.8%	48.2%

OREGON

PRESIDENT 1952

County	Total Vote	Republican	Democratic	Other	Rep.-Dem. Plurality	Percentage Total Vote Rep.	Dem.	Major Vote Rep.	Dem.
BAKER	6,838	4,253	2,562	23	1,691 R	62.2%	37.5%	62.4%	37.6%
BENTON	12,262	9,229	2,966	67	6,263 R	75.3%	24.2%	75.7%	24.3%
CLACKAMAS	40,620	24,174	16,219	227	7,955 R	59.5%	39.9%	59.8%	40.2%
CLATSOP	13,511	7,569	5,814	128	1,755 R	56.0%	43.0%	56.6%	43.4%
COLUMBIA	9,834	4,666	5,096	72	430 D	47.4%	51.8%	47.8%	52.2%
COOS	18,389	10,122	8,118	149	2,004 R	55.0%	44.1%	55.5%	44.5%
CROOK	3,681	2,124	1,490	67	634 R	57.7%	40.5%	58.8%	41.2%
CURRY	3,179	2,147	1,005	27	1,142 R	67.5%	31.6%	68.1%	31.9%
DESCHUTES	8,986	5,776	3,174	36	2,602 R	64.3%	35.3%	64.5%	35.5%
DOUGLAS	22,009	14,109	7,837	63	6,272 R	64.1%	35.6%	64.3%	35.7%
GILLIAM	1,329	911	415	3	496 R	68.5%	31.2%	68.7%	31.3%
GRANT	3,148	1,941	1,190	17	751 R	61.7%	37.8%	62.0%	38.0%
HARNEY	2,366	1,378	983	5	395 R	58.2%	41.5%	58.4%	41.6%
HOOD RIVER	5,267	3,310	1,930	27	1,380 R	62.8%	36.6%	63.2%	36.8%
JACKSON	27,060	18,279	8,674	107	9,605 R	67.5%	32.1%	67.8%	32.2%
JEFFERSON	2,217	1,488	723	6	765 R	67.1%	32.6%	67.3%	32.7%
JOSEPHINE	11,655	8,200	3,353	102	4,847 R	70.4%	28.8%	71.0%	29.0%
KLAMATH	17,989	11,517	6,407	65	5,110 R	64.0%	35.6%	64.3%	35.7%
LAKE	2,943	1,727	1,205	11	522 R	58.7%	40.9%	58.9%	41.1%
LANE	55,919	35,693	19,960	266	15,733 R	63.8%	35.7%	64.1%	35.9%
LINCOLN	9,252	5,559	3,632	61	1,927 R	60.1%	39.3%	60.5%	39.5%
LINN	21,959	13,761	8,058	140	5,703 R	62.7%	36.7%	63.1%	36.9%
MALHEUR	7,685	5,414	2,245	26	3,169 R	70.4%	29.2%	70.7%	29.3%
MARION	42,448	29,887	12,337	224	17,550 R	70.4%	29.1%	70.8%	29.2%
MORROW	2,045	1,254	786	5	468 R	61.3%	38.4%	61.5%	38.5%
MULTNOMAH	241,059	132,602	107,118	1,339	25,484 R	55.0%	44.4%	55.3%	44.7%
POLK	9,869	6,850	2,983	36	3,867 R	69.4%	30.2%	69.6%	30.3%
SHERMAN	1,107	747	355	5	392 R	67.5%	32.1%	67.8%	32.2%
TILLAMOOK	8,362	4,931	3,401	30	1,530 R	59.0%	40.7%	59.2%	40.8%
UMATILLA	17,667	10,529	7,098	40	3,431 R	59.6%	40.2%	59.7%	40.3%
UNION	7,663	4,114	3,526	23	588 R	53.7%	46.0%	53.8%	46.2%
WALLOWA	3,183	1,891	1,271	21	620 R	59.4%	39.9%	59.8%	40.2%
WASCO	6,914	4,362	2,517	35	1,845 R	63.1%	36.4%	63.4%	36.6%
WASHINGTON	31,584	20,250	11,191	143	9,059 R	64.1%	35.4%	64.4%	35.6%
WHEELER	1,188	719	468	1	251 R	60.5%	39.4%	60.6%	39.4%
YAMHILL	13,872	9,332	4,472	68	4,860 R	67.3%	32.2%	67.6%	32.4%
TOTAL	695,059	420,815	270,579	3,665	150,236 R	60.5%	38.9%	60.9%	39.1%

PRESIDENT 1956

County	Total Vote	Republican	Democratic	Other	Rep.-Dem. Plurality	Percentage Total Vote Rep.	Dem.	Major Vote Rep.	Dem.
BAKER	7,146	3,706	3,431	9	275 R	51.9%	48.0%	51.9%	48.1%
BENTON	13,230	9,016	4,214		4,802 R	68.1%	31.9%	68.1%	31.9%
CLACKAMAS	45,784	25,314	20,416	54	4,898 R	55.3%	44.6%	55.4%	44.6%
CLATSOP	13,013	6,616	6,372	25	244 R	50.8%	49.0%	50.9%	49.1%
COLUMBIA	9,867	4,275	5,592		1,317 D	43.3%	56.7%	43.3%	56.7%
COOS	20,394	9,201	11,183	10	1,982 D	45.1%	54.8%	45.1%	54.9%
CROOK	3,684	1,879	1,805		74 R	51.0%	49.0%	51.0%	49.0%
CURRY	4,306	2,306	1,996	4	310 R	53.6%	46.4%	53.6%	46.4%
DESCHUTES	9,508	5,399	4,102	7	1,297 R	56.8%	43.1%	56.8%	43.2%
DOUGLAS	25,662	13,837	11,825		2,012 R	53.9%	46.1%	53.9%	46.1%
GILLIAM	1,331	793	538		255 R	59.6%	40.4%	59.6%	40.4%
GRANT	3,085	1,822	1,261	2	561 R	59.1%	40.9%	59.1%	40.9%
HARNEY	2,727	1,512	1,212	3	300 R	55.4%	44.4%	55.5%	44.5%
HOOD RIVER	5,599	3,149	2,445	5	704 R	56.2%	43.7%	56.3%	43.7%
JACKSON	29,948	17,201	12,733	14	4,468 R	57.4%	42.5%	57.5%	42.5%
JEFFERSON	2,476	1,356	1,117	3	239 R	54.8%	45.1%	54.8%	45.2%
JOSEPHINE	12,841	7,967	4,863	11	3,104 R	62.0%	37.9%	62.1%	37.9%
KLAMATH	18,175	9,740	8,434	1	1,306 R	53.6%	46.4%	53.6%	46.4%
LAKE	2,914	1,623	1,289	2	334 R	55.7%	44.2%	55.7%	44.3%
LANE	62,878	35,264	27,534	80	7,730 R	56.1%	43.8%	56.2%	43.8%
LINCOLN	9,979	5,346	4,624	9	722 R	53.6%	46.3%	53.6%	46.4%
LINN	22,622	12,469	10,153		2,316 R	55.1%	44.9%	55.1%	44.9%
MALHEUR	8,140	4,981	3,151	8	1,830 R	61.2%	38.7%	61.3%	38.7%
MARION	45,192	28,990	16,170	32	12,820 R	64.1%	35.8%	64.3%	35.8%
MORROW	1,985	1,092	893		199 R	55.0%	45.0%	55.0%	45.0%
MULTNOMAH	245,769	129,658	115,896	215	13,762 R	52.8%	47.2%	52.8%	47.2%
POLK	10,459	6,404	4,047	8	2,357 R	61.3%	38.7%	61.3%	38.7%
SHERMAN	1,091	671	420		251 R	61.5%	38.5%	61.5%	38.5%
TILLAMOOK	7,999	4,306	3,684	9	622 R	53.8%	46.1%	53.9%	46.1%
UMATILLA	17,339	9,654	7,678	7	1,976 R	55.7%	44.3%	55.7%	44.3%
UNION	8,140	3,749	4,389	2	640 D	46.1%	53.9%	46.1%	53.9%
WALLOWA	3,328	1,604	1,723	1	119 D	48.2%	51.8%	48.2%	51.8%
WASCO	8,497	4,332	4,165		167 R	51.0%	49.0%	51.0%	49.0%
WASHINGTON	36,028	22,001	14,027		7,974 R	61.1%	38.9%	61.1%	39.0%
WHEELER	1,174	605	569		36 R	51.5%	48.5%	51.5%	48.5%
YAMHILL	13,822	8,555	5,253	14	3,302 R	61.9%	38.0%	62.0%	38.0%
TOTAL	736,132	406,393	329,204	535	77,189 R	55.2%	44.7%	55.2%	44.8%

OREGON

PRESIDENT 1960

County	Total Vote	Republican	Democratic	Other	Rep.-Dem. Plurality	Total Vote Rep.	Total Vote Dem.	Major Vote Rep.	Major Vote Dem.
BAKER	7,251	3,514	3,734	3	220 D	48.5%	51.5%	48.5%	51.5%
BENTON	15,125	9,734	5,391		4,343 R	64.4%	35.6%	64.4%	35.6%
CLACKAMAS	52,319	28,531	23,679	109	4,852 R	54.5%	45.3%	54.6%	45.4%
CLATSOP	12,866	6,286	6,530	50	244 D	48.9%	50.8%	49.0%	51.0%
COLUMBIA	9,908	4,356	5,546	6	1,190 D	44.0%	56.0%	44.0%	56.0%
COOS	21,705	8,751	12,893	61	4,142 D	40.3%	59.4%	40.4%	59.6%
CROOK	3,737	1,732	2,005		273 D	46.3%	53.7%	46.3%	53.7%
CURRY	5,153	2,382	2,767	4	385 D	46.2%	53.7%	46.3%	53.7%
DESCHUTES	9,944	5,145	4,776	23	369 R	51.7%	48.0%	51.9%	48.1%
DOUGLAS	25,815	12,493	13,322		829 D	48.4%	51.6%	48.4%	51.6%
GILLIAM	1,318	712	606		106 R	54.0%	46.0%	54.0%	46.0%
GRANT	3,135	1,697	1,438		259 R	54.1%	45.9%	54.1%	45.9%
HARNEY	2,691	1,464	1,220	7	244 R	54.4%	45.3%	54.5%	45.5%
HOOD RIVER	5,555	3,103	2,450	2	653 R	55.9%	44.1%	55.9%	44.1%
JACKSON	32,157	17,554	14,531	72	3,023 R	54.6%	45.2%	54.7%	45.3%
JEFFERSON	2,629	1,413	1,214	2	199 R	53.7%	46.2%	53.8%	46.2%
JOSEPHINE	12,831	7,387	5,419	25	1,968 R	57.6%	42.2%	57.7%	42.3%
KLAMATH	18,023	9,095	8,928		167 R	50.5%	49.5%	50.5%	49.5%
LAKE	2,996	1,555	1,441		114 R	51.9%	48.1%	51.9%	48.1%
LANE	68,862	36,148	32,596	118	3,552 R	52.5%	47.3%	52.6%	47.4%
LINCOLN	10,483	5,231	5,243	9	12 D	49.9%	50.0%	49.9%	50.1%
LINN	23,934	12,889	11,035		1,864 R	53.8%	46.1%	53.9%	46.1%
MALHEUR	8,424	5,043	3,381		1,662 R	59.9%	40.1%	59.9%	40.1%
MARION	49,970	29,124	20,791	55	8,333 R	58.3%	41.6%	58.3%	41.7%
MORROW	2,042	1,003	1,039		36 D	49.1%	50.9%	49.1%	50.9%
MULTNOMAH	251,882	127,271	124,273	338	2,998 R	50.5%	49.3%	50.6%	49.4%
POLK	11,298	6,709	4,578	11	2,131 R	59.4%	40.5%	59.4%	40.6%
SHERMAN	1,165	659	506		153 R	56.6%	43.4%	56.6%	43.4%
TILLAMOOK	8,044	3,935	4,098	11	163 D	48.9%	50.9%	49.0%	51.0%
UMATILLA	17,433	9,374	8,053	6	1,321 R	53.8%	46.2%	53.8%	46.2%
UNION	7,770	3,689	4,081		392 D	47.5%	52.5%	47.5%	52.5%
WALLOWA	3,125	1,440	1,682	3	242 D	46.1%	53.8%	46.1%	53.9%
WASCO	8,784	4,355	4,426	3	71 D	49.6%	50.4%	49.6%	50.4%
WASHINGTON	43,186	25,415	17,736	35	7,679 R	58.9%	41.1%	58.9%	41.1%
WHEELER	1,032	566	466		100 R	54.8%	45.2%	54.8%	45.2%
YAMHILL	13,829	8,295	5,528	6	2,767 R	60.0%	40.0%	60.0%	40.0%
TOTAL	776,421	408,060	367,402	959	40,658 R	52.6%	47.3%	52.6%	47.4%

PRESIDENT 1964

County	Total Vote	Republican	Democratic	Other	Rep.-Dem. Plurality	Total Vote Rep.	Total Vote Dem.	Major Vote Rep.	Major Vote Dem.
BAKER	6,585	2,670	3,903	12	1,233 D	40.5%	59.3%	40.6%	59.4%
BENTON	16,486	7,250	8,971	265	1,721 D	44.0%	54.4%	44.7%	55.3%
CLACKAMAS	57,043	21,299	35,711	33	14,412 D	37.3%	62.6%	37.4%	62.6%
CLATSOP	12,413	4,023	8,371	19	4,348 D	32.4%	67.4%	32.5%	67.5%
COLUMBIA	10,268	2,489	7,728	51	5,239 D	24.2%	75.3%	24.4%	75.6%
COOS	21,149	5,032	16,109	8	11,077 D	23.8%	76.2%	23.8%	76.2%
CROOK	3,586	1,161	2,419	6	1,258 D	32.4%	67.5%	32.4%	67.6%
CURRY	4,686	1,467	3,195	24	1,728 D	31.3%	68.2%	31.5%	68.5%
DESCHUTES	10,095	3,148	6,947		3,799 D	31.2%	68.8%	31.2%	68.8%
DOUGLAS	25,717	9,806	15,909	2	6,103 D	38.1%	61.9%	38.1%	61.9%
GILLIAM	1,220	442	775	3	333 D	36.2%	63.5%	36.3%	63.7%
GRANT	3,032	1,149	1,877	6	728 D	37.9%	61.9%	38.0%	62.0%
HARNEY	2,759	1,172	1,577	10	405 D	42.5%	57.2%	42.6%	57.4%
HOOD RIVER	5,472	1,786	3,564	122	1,778 D	32.6%	65.1%	33.4%	66.6%
JACKSON	34,084	14,598	19,486		4,888 D	42.8%	57.2%	42.8%	57.2%
JEFFERSON	2,938	1,197	1,739	2	542 D	40.7%	59.2%	40.8%	59.2%
JOSEPHINE	13,801	6,918	6,857	26	61 R	50.1%	49.7%	50.2%	49.8%
KLAMATH	17,599	8,530	9,066	3	536 D	48.5%	51.5%	48.5%	51.5%
LAKE	2,723	1,304	1,419		115 D	47.9%	52.1%	47.9%	52.1%
LANE	74,200	24,139	49,785	276	25,646 D	32.5%	67.1%	32.7%	67.3%
LINCOLN	10,323	3,200	7,101	22	3,901 D	31.0%	68.8%	31.1%	68.9%
LINN	23,308	8,382	14,926		6,544 D	36.0%	64.0%	36.0%	64.0%
MALHEUR	7,983	4,177	3,798	8	379 R	52.3%	47.6%	52.4%	47.6%
MARION	51,200	18,897	32,091	221	13,194 D	36.9%	62.7%	37.1%	62.9%
MORROW	2,097	627	1,470		843 D	29.9%	70.1%	29.9%	70.1%
MULTNOMAH	243,739	81,683	161,040	1,016	79,357 D	33.5%	66.1%	33.7%	66.3%
POLK	11,629	4,319	7,292	18	2,973 D	37.1%	62.7%	37.2%	62.8%
SHERMAN	1,353	494	859		365 D	36.5%	63.5%	36.5%	63.5%
TILLAMOOK	7,573	2,318	5,246	9	2,928 D	30.6%	69.3%	30.6%	69.4%
UMATILLA	16,859	6,138	10,689	32	4,551 D	36.4%	63.4%	36.5%	63.5%
UNION	7,489	2,553	4,929	7	2,376 D	34.1%	65.8%	34.1%	65.9%
WALLOWA	2,848	1,055	1,790	3	735 D	37.0%	62.9%	37.1%	62.9%
WASCO	8,597	2,695	5,890	12	3,195 D	31.3%	68.5%	31.4%	68.6%
WASHINGTON	50,181	20,813	29,081	287	8,268 D	41.5%	58.0%	41.7%	58.3%
WHEELER	798	340	458		118 D	42.6%	57.4%	42.6%	57.4%
YAMHILL	14,463	5,508	8,949	6	3,441 D	38.1%	61.9%	38.1%	61.9%
TOTAL	786,305	282,779	501,017	2,509	218,238 D	36.0%	63.7%	36.1%	63.9%

OTHER VOTE COMPOSITION:

1920	9,801 Socialist; 3,595 Prohibition; 1,515 Socialist Labor.
1924	68,403 Progressive; 917 Socialist Labor.
1928	2,720 Socialist; 1,564 Socialist Labor; 1,094 Communist.
1932	15,450 Socialist; 1,730 Socialist Labor; 1,681 Communist.
1936	21,831 Union; 2,143 Socialist; 500 Socialist Labor; 104 Communist; 4 Prohibition.
1940	2,487 Socialist Labor; 398 Socialist; 191 Communist; 154 Prohibition; 40 scattered.
1944	3,785 Socialist; 2,362 Prohibition.
1948	14,978 Progressive; 5,051 Socialist.
1952	Progressive.
1956	Scattered.
1960	Scattered.
1964	Scattered.

SPECIAL CASES:

1924	Progressive candidates ran second in several counties.

PENNSYLVANIA

PRESIDENT 1920

County	Total Vote	Republican	Democratic	Other	Rep.-Dem. Plurality	% Total Rep.	% Total Dem.	% Major Rep.	% Major Dem.
ADAMS	9,349	5,323	3,852	174	1,471 R	56.9%	41.2%	58.0%	42.0%
ALLEGHENY	200,702	138,908	40,278	21,516	98,630 R	69.2%	20.1%	77.5%	22.5%
ARMSTRONG	12,992	8,995	3,262	735	5,733 R	69.2%	25.1%	73.4%	26.6%
BEAVER	18,586	11,691	4,771	2,124	6,920 R	62.9%	25.7%	71.0%	29.0%
BEDFORD	9,405	5,800	2,594	1,011	3,206 R	61.7%	27.6%	69.1%	30.9%
BERKS	46,591	22,221	18,361	6,009	3,860 R	47.7%	39.4%	54.8%	45.2%
BLAIR	26,392	15,035	5,668	5,689	9,367 R	57.0%	21.5%	72.6%	27.4%
BRADFORD	15,900	11,947	2,825	1,128	9,122 R	75.1%	17.8%	80.9%	19.1%
BUCKS	21,681	14,130	6,867	684	7,263 R	65.2%	31.7%	67.3%	32.7%
BUTLER	15,653	10,467	3,829	1,357	6,638 R	66.9%	24.5%	73.2%	26.8%
CAMBRIA	30,712	19,629	6,961	4,122	12,668 R	63.9%	22.7%	73.8%	26.2%
CAMERON	2,004	1,364	497	143	867 R	68.1%	24.8%	73.3%	26.7%
CARBON	13,345	7,900	5,030	415	2,870 R	59.2%	37.7%	61.1%	38.9%
CENTRE	12,372	7,615	4,142	615	3,473 R	61.6%	33.5%	64.8%	35.2%
CHESTER	26,060	18,129	7,004	927	11,125 R	69.6%	26.9%	72.1%	27.9%
CLARION	8,662	4,615	3,487	560	1,128 R	53.3%	40.3%	57.0%	43.0%
CLEARFIELD	18,393	9,615	5,987	2,791	3,628 R	52.3%	32.6%	61.6%	38.4%
CLINTON	7,884	4,303	2,976	605	1,327 R	54.6%	37.7%	59.1%	40.9%
COLUMBIA	13,665	6,238	6,965	462	727 D	45.6%	51.0%	47.2%	52.8%
CRAWFORD	16,098	10,032	4,175	1,891	5,857 R	62.3%	25.9%	70.6%	29.4%
CUMBERLAND	15,674	8,579	6,455	640	2,124 R	54.7%	41.2%	57.1%	42.9%
DAUPHIN	39,923	26,094	11,990	1,839	14,104 R	65.4%	30.0%	68.5%	31.5%
DELAWARE	45,293	34,126	9,602	1,565	24,524 R	75.3%	21.2%	78.0%	22.0%
ELK	7,963	5,267	2,093	603	3,174 R	66.1%	26.3%	71.6%	28.4%
ERIE	30,569	19,465	6,311	4,793	13,154 R	63.7%	20.6%	75.5%	24.5%
FAYETTE	35,611	20,186	13,358	2,067	6,828 R	56.7%	37.5%	60.2%	39.8%
FOREST	1,762	993	389	380	604 R	56.4%	22.1%	71.9%	28.1%
FRANKLIN	13,857	8,376	5,020	461	3,356 R	60.4%	36.2%	62.5%	37.5%
FULTON	2,574	1,292	1,231	51	61 R	50.2%	47.8%	51.2%	48.8%
GREENE	10,028	4,293	5,592	183	1,299 D	42.4%	55.8%	43.2%	56.8%
HUNTINGDON	7,724	5,232	1,784	708	3,448 R	67.7%	23.1%	74.6%	25.4%
INDIANA	11,993	8,616	1,936	1,441	6,680 R	71.8%	16.1%	81.7%	18.3%
JEFFERSON	11,950	7,970	3,060	920	4,910 R	66.7%	25.6%	72.3%	27.7%
JUNIATA	3,628	2,112	1,443	73	669 R	58.2%	39.8%	59.4%	40.6%
LACKAWANNA	67,040	40,593	24,581	1,866	16,012 R	60.6%	36.7%	62.3%	37.7%
LANCASTER	40,542	29,549	9,521	1,472	20,028 R	72.9%	23.5%	75.6%	24.4%
LAWRENCE	14,676	9,448	2,720	2,508	6,728 R	64.4%	18.5%	77.6%	22.4%
LEBANON	12,401	8,778	3,016	607	5,762 R	70.8%	24.3%	74.4%	25.6%
LEHIGH	30,310	18,032	10,863	1,415	7,169 R	59.5%	35.8%	62.4%	37.6%
LUZERNE	75,575	49,419	23,473	2,683	25,946 R	65.4%	31.1%	67.8%	32.2%
LYCOMING	18,635	10,570	5,853	2,212	4,717 R	56.7%	31.4%	64.4%	35.6%
MCKEAN	11,406	7,830	2,505	1,071	5,325 R	68.6%	21.9%	75.8%	24.2%
MERCER	19,199	11,575	4,823	2,801	6,752 R	60.3%	25.1%	70.6%	29.4%
MIFFLIN	7,479	4,780	2,400	299	2,380 R	63.9%	32.1%	66.6%	33.4%
MONROE	6,828	3,278	3,396	154	118 D	48.0%	49.7%	49.1%	50.9%
MONTGOMERY	45,855	31,963	12,239	1,653	19,724 R	69.7%	26.7%	72.3%	27.7%
MONTOUR	4,271	2,296	1,872	103	424 R	53.8%	43.8%	55.1%	44.9%
NORTHAMPTON	24,204	14,227	9,086	891	5,141 R	58.8%	37.5%	61.0%	39.0%
NORTHUMBERLAND	29,581	17,288	9,854	2,439	7,434 R	58.4%	33.3%	63.7%	36.3%
PERRY	6,245	3,787	2,314	144	1,473 R	60.6%	37.1%	62.1%	37.9%
PHILADELPHIA	418,662	307,825	90,151	20,686	217,674 R	73.5%	21.5%	77.3%	22.7%
PIKE	2,272	1,319	880	73	439 R	58.1%	38.7%	60.0%	40.0%
POTTER	5,750	4,036	1,106	608	2,930 R	70.2%	19.2%	78.5%	21.5%
SCHUYLKILL	50,887	30,259	18,746	1,882	11,513 R	59.5%	36.8%	61.7%	38.3%
SNYDER	3,810	2,751	964	95	1,787 R	72.2%	25.3%	74.1%	25.9%
SOMERSET	16,404	12,436	2,912	1,056	9,524 R	75.8%	17.8%	81.0%	19.0%
SULLIVAN	2,814	1,620	1,061	133	559 R	57.6%	37.7%	60.4%	39.6%
SUSQUEHANNA	9,896	6,572	2,905	419	3,667 R	66.4%	29.4%	69.3%	30.7%
TIOGA	11,669	9,718	1,258	693	8,460 R	83.3%	10.8%	88.5%	11.5%
UNION	4,630	3,305	1,155	170	2,150 R	71.4%	24.9%	74.1%	25.9%

PRESIDENT 1924

County	Total Vote	Republican	Democratic	Other	Rep.-Dem. Plurality	% Total Rep.	% Total Dem.	% Major Rep.	% Major Dem.
ADAMS	10,918	5,778	4,840	300	938 R	52.9%	44.3%	54.4%	45.6%
ALLEGHENY	253,013	149,296	21,984	81,733	127,312 R	59.0%	8.7%	87.2%	12.8%
ARMSTRONG	17,439	11,192	2,931	3,316	8,261 R	64.2%	16.8%	79.2%	20.8%
BEAVER	26,141	16,768	3,220	6,153	13,548 R	64.1%	12.3%	83.9%	16.1%
BEDFORD	9,971	6,154	2,315	1,502	3,839 R	61.7%	23.2%	72.7%	27.3%
BERKS	54,893	28,186	17,220	9,487	10,966 R	51.3%	31.4%	62.1%	37.9%
BLAIR	30,808	20,313	4,244	6,251	16,069 R	65.9%	13.8%	82.7%	17.3%
BRADFORD	15,784	11,620	2,307	1,857	9,313 R	73.6%	14.6%	83.4%	16.6%
BUCKS	26,108	17,460	6,582	2,066	10,878 R	66.9%	25.2%	72.6%	27.4%
BUTLER	18,880	13,113	3,462	2,305	9,651 R	69.5%	18.3%	79.1%	20.9%
CAMBRIA	47,764	24,728	13,563	9,473	11,165 R	51.8%	28.4%	64.6%	35.4%
CAMERON	1,770	1,366	260	144	1,106 R	77.2%	14.7%	84.0%	16.0%
CARBON	18,427	10,236	5,150	3,041	5,086 R	55.5%	27.9%	66.5%	33.5%
CENTRE	13,062	7,723	4,443	896	3,280 R	59.1%	34.0%	63.5%	36.5%
CHESTER	29,480	22,333	5,946	1,201	16,387 R	75.8%	20.2%	79.0%	21.0%
CLARION	10,698	5,913	3,642	1,143	2,271 R	55.3%	34.0%	61.9%	38.1%
CLEARFIELD	22,787	13,745	5,027	4,015	8,718 R	60.3%	22.1%	73.2%	26.8%
CLINTON	9,391	5,129	1,939	2,323	3,190 R	54.6%	20.6%	72.6%	27.4%
COLUMBIA	15,469	7,336	7,390	743	54 D	47.4%	47.8%	49.8%	50.2%
CRAWFORD	17,305	10,938	2,969	3,418	7,969 R	63.2%	17.2%	78.6%	21.4%
CUMBERLAND	19,160	10,196	7,643	1,321	2,553 R	53.2%	39.9%	57.2%	42.8%
DAUPHIN	40,916	27,338	9,004	4,074	18,334 R	66.8%	22.0%	75.2%	24.8%
DELAWARE	51,345	41,998	6,368	2,979	35,630 R	81.8%	12.4%	86.8%	13.2%
ELK	9,352	6,926	1,370	1,056	5,556 R	74.1%	14.6%	83.5%	16.5%
ERIE	31,784	19,480	3,502	8,802	15,978 R	61.3%	11.0%	84.8%	15.2%
FAYETTE	35,587	19,064	8,855	7,668	10,209 R	53.6%	24.9%	68.3%	31.7%
FOREST	1,587	1,130	280	177	850 R	71.2%	17.6%	80.1%	19.9%
FRANKLIN	16,645	9,791	5,770	1,084	4,021 R	58.8%	34.7%	62.9%	37.1%
FULTON	2,845	1,412	1,365	68	47 R	49.6%	48.0%	50.8%	49.2%
GREENE	10,976	4,590	5,874	512	1,284 D	41.8%	53.5%	43.9%	56.1%
HUNTINGDON	8,875	6,567	1,488	820	5,079 R	74.0%	16.8%	81.5%	18.5%
INDIANA	18,277	12,848	1,967	3,462	10,881 R	70.3%	10.8%	86.7%	13.3%
JEFFERSON	16,450	10,673	2,664	3,113	8,009 R	64.9%	16.2%	80.0%	20.0%
JUNIATA	3,792	2,177	1,420	195	757 R	57.4%	37.4%	60.5%	39.5%
LACKAWANNA	62,401	37,708	16,859	7,834	20,849 R	60.4%	27.0%	69.1%	30.9%
LANCASTER	58,034	42,787	12,091	3,156	30,696 R	73.7%	20.8%	78.0%	22.0%
LAWRENCE	19,406	12,533	1,880	4,993	10,653 R	64.6%	9.7%	87.0%	13.0%
LEBANON	12,783	9,494	2,464	825	7,030 R	74.3%	19.3%	79.4%	20.6%
LEHIGH	35,284	20,826	10,415	4,043	10,411 R	59.0%	29.5%	66.7%	33.3%
LUZERNE	87,396	46,475	20,472	20,449	26,003 R	53.2%	23.4%	69.4%	30.6%
LYCOMING	23,916	14,039	6,857	3,020	7,182 R	58.7%	28.7%	67.2%	32.8%
MCKEAN	13,149	9,072	2,376	1,701	6,696 R	69.0%	18.1%	79.2%	20.8%
MERCER	22,420	14,639	3,688	4,093	10,951 R	65.3%	16.4%	79.9%	20.1%
MIFFLIN	7,143	4,780	1,999	364	2,781 R	66.9%	28.0%	70.5%	29.5%
MONROE	7,819	3,462	3,901	456	439 D	44.3%	49.9%	47.0%	53.0%
MONTGOMERY	60,154	45,407	11,094	3,653	34,313 R	75.5%	18.4%	80.4%	19.6%
MONTOUR	4,476	2,499	1,799	178	700 R	55.8%	40.2%	58.1%	41.9%
NORTHAMPTON	35,022	20,459	11,459	3,104	9,000 R	58.4%	32.7%	64.1%	35.9%
NORTHUMBERLAND	31,177	17,516	7,571	6,090	9,945 R	56.2%	24.3%	69.8%	30.2%
PERRY	7,276	4,185	2,710	381	1,475 R	57.5%	37.2%	60.7%	39.3%
PHILADELPHIA	447,022	347,457	54,213	45,352	293,244 R	77.7%	12.1%	86.5%	13.5%
PIKE	2,917	1,581	993	343	588 R	54.2%	34.0%	61.4%	38.6%
POTTER	6,241	4,087	1,161	993	2,926 R	65.5%	18.6%	77.9%	22.1%
SCHUYLKILL	53,656	34,578	10,111	8,967	24,467 R	64.4%	18.8%	77.4%	22.6%
SNYDER	4,243	3,055	970	218	2,085 R	72.0%	22.9%	75.9%	24.1%
SOMERSET	17,032	12,389	2,315	2,328	10,074 R	72.7%	13.6%	84.3%	15.7%
SULLIVAN	2,791	1,668	913	210	755 R	59.8%	32.7%	64.6%	35.4%
SUSQUEHANNA	10,784	7,266	2,208	1,310	5,058 R	67.4%	20.5%	76.7%	23.3%
TIOGA	10,406	8,452	1,271	683	7,181 R	81.2%	12.2%	86.9%	13.1%
UNION	5,178	3,707	1,209	262	2,498 R	71.6%	23.3%	75.4%	24.6%

PENNSYLVANIA

PRESIDENT 1920

County	Total Vote	Republican	Democratic	Other	Rep.-Dem. Plurality	Total Vote Rep.	Dem.	Major Vote Rep.	Dem.
VENANGO	11,746	7,718	2,669	1,359	5,049 R	65.7%	22.7%	74.3%	25.7%
WARREN	11,974	7,791	2,180	2,003	5,611 R	65.1%	18.2%	78.1%	21.9%
WASHINGTON	29,625	18,514	8,827	2,284	9,687 R	62.5%	29.8%	67.7%	32.3%
WAYNE	7,060	5,164	1,589	307	3,575 R	73.1%	22.5%	76.5%	23.5%
WESTMORELAND	45,349	27,077	12,845	5,427	14,232 R	59.7%	28.3%	67.8%	32.2%
WYOMING	4,687	3,208	1,247	232	1,961 R	68.4%	26.6%	72.0%	28.0%
YORK	35,679	19,879	14,396	1,404	5,483 R	55.7%	40.3%	58.0%	42.0%
TOTAL	1,851,248	1,218,215	503,202	129,831	715,013 R	65.8%	27.2%	70.8%	29.2%

PRESIDENT 1924

County	Total Vote	Republican	Democratic	Other	Rep.-Dem. Plurality	Total Vote Rep.	Dem.	Major Vote Rep.	Dem.
VENANGO	14,592	10,841	1,886	1,865	8,955 R	74.3%	12.9%	85.2%	14.8%
WARREN	11,986	8,502	2,161	1,323	6,341 R	70.9%	18.0%	79.7%	20.3%
WASHINGTON	36,797	22,315	6,706	7,776	15,609 R	60.6%	18.2%	76.9%	23.1%
WAYNE	7,655	5,578	1,477	600	4,101 R	72.9%	19.3%	79.1%	20.9%
WESTMORELAND	62,514	34,522	10,223	17,769	24,299 R	55.2%	16.4%	77.2%	22.8%
WYOMING	4,721	3,213	1,194	314	2,019 R	68.1%	25.3%	72.9%	27.1%
YORK	41,039	23,044	15,600	2,395	7,444 R	56.2%	38.0%	59.6%	40.4%
TOTAL	2,144,850	1,401,481	409,192	334,177	992,289 R	65.3%	19.1%	77.4%	22.6%

PENNSYLVANIA

PRESIDENT 1928

County	Total Vote	Republican	Democratic	Other	Rep.-Dem. Plurality	Total Vote % Rep.	Total Vote % Dem.	Major Vote % Rep.	Major Vote % Dem.
ADAMS	14,349	9,656	4,635	58	5,021 R	67.3%	32.3%	67.6%	32.4%
ALLEGHENY	379,209	215,626	160,733	2,850	54,893 R	56.9%	42.4%	57.3%	42.7%
ARMSTRONG	22,636	17,625	4,824	187	12,801 R	77.9%	21.3%	78.5%	21.5%
BEAVER	40,217	27,949	11,868	400	16,081 R	69.5%	29.5%	70.2%	29.8%
BEDFORD	11,767	9,602	1,966	199	7,636 R	81.6%	16.7%	83.0%	17.0%
BERKS	73,514	47,073	18,960	7,481	28,113 R	64.0%	25.8%	71.3%	28.7%
BLAIR	46,726	34,356	12,104	266	22,252 R	73.5%	25.9%	73.9%	26.1%
BRADFORD	21,609	17,251	4,281	77	12,970 R	79.8%	19.8%	80.1%	19.9%
BUCKS	37,168	28,421	8,446	301	19,975 R	76.5%	22.7%	77.1%	22.9%
BUTLER	26,327	19,880	6,283	164	13,597 R	75.5%	23.9%	76.0%	24.0%
CAMBRIA	56,945	29,494	27,024	427	2,470 R	51.8%	47.5%	52.2%	47.8%
CAMERON	2,071	1,564	501	6	1,063 R	75.5%	24.2%	75.7%	24.3%
CARBON	23,155	15,047	8,010	98	7,037 R	65.0%	34.6%	65.3%	34.7%
CENTRE	15,557	12,005	3,431	121	8,574 R	77.2%	22.1%	77.8%	22.2%
CHESTER	44,558	36,659	7,689	210	28,970 R	82.3%	17.3%	82.7%	17.3%
CLARION	13,038	9,183	3,746	109	5,437 R	70.4%	28.7%	71.0%	29.0%
CLEARFIELD	24,859	16,719	7,870	270	8,849 R	67.3%	31.7%	68.0%	32.0%
CLINTON	11,029	8,120	2,849	60	5,271 R	73.6%	25.8%	74.0%	26.0%
COLUMBIA	19,781	14,362	5,304	115	9,058 R	72.6%	26.8%	73.0%	27.0%
CRAWFORD	23,989	17,072	6,718	199	10,354 R	71.2%	28.0%	71.8%	28.2%
CUMBERLAND	24,551	19,170	5,189	192	13,981 R	78.1%	21.1%	78.7%	21.3%
DAUPHIN	58,617	49,108	9,115	394	39,993 R	83.8%	15.5%	84.3%	15.7%
DELAWARE	112,941	83,092	29,378	471	53,714 R	73.6%	26.0%	73.9%	26.1%
ELK	13,009	5,234	7,705	70	2,471 D	40.2%	59.2%	40.5%	59.5%
ERIE	50,097	30,542	19,278	277	11,264 R	61.0%	38.5%	61.3%	38.7%
FAYETTE	47,183	27,693	19,063	427	8,630 R	58.7%	40.4%	59.2%	40.8%
FOREST	2,018	1,707	289	22	1,418 R	84.6%	14.3%	85.5%	14.5%
FRANKLIN	19,518	16,345	3,027	146	13,318 R	83.7%	15.5%	84.4%	15.6%
FULTON	3,261	2,179	1,054	28	1,125 R	66.8%	32.3%	67.4%	32.6%
GREENE	12,299	6,910	5,293	96	1,517 R	56.2%	43.0%	56.6%	43.4%
HUNTINGDON	11,502	9,920	1,470	112	8,450 R	86.2%	12.8%	87.1%	12.9%
INDIANA	21,768	16,706	4,810	252	11,896 R	76.7%	22.1%	77.6%	22.4%
JEFFERSON	17,731	13,233	4,325	173	8,908 R	74.6%	24.4%	75.4%	24.6%
JUNIATA	5,361	4,396	919	46	3,477 R	82.0%	17.1%	82.7%	17.3%
LACKAWANNA	99,269	46,510	52,665	94	6,155 D	46.9%	53.1%	46.9%	53.1%
LANCASTER	68,192	55,530	12,146	516	43,384 R	81.4%	17.8%	82.1%	17.9%
LAWRENCE	26,702	20,012	6,417	273	13,595 R	74.9%	24.0%	75.7%	24.3%
LEBANON	20,464	16,841	3,278	345	13,563 R	82.3%	16.0%	83.7%	16.3%
LEHIGH	54,188	40,291	13,463	434	26,828 R	74.4%	24.8%	75.0%	25.0%
LUZERNE	141,411	67,872	73,319	220	5,447 D	48.0%	51.8%	48.1%	51.9%
LYCOMING	36,137	28,720	7,132	285	21,588 R	79.5%	19.7%	80.1%	19.9%
MCKEAN	19,066	14,012	4,964	90	9,048 R	73.5%	26.0%	73.8%	26.2%
MERCER	32,083	22,599	8,204	1,280	14,395 R	70.4%	25.6%	73.4%	26.6%
MIFFLIN	10,270	8,932	1,270	68	7,662 R	87.0%	12.4%	87.6%	12.4%
MONROE	10,762	7,469	3,266	27	4,203 R	69.4%	30.3%	69.6%	30.4%
MONTGOMERY	100,408	76,680	23,026	702	53,654 R	76.4%	22.9%	76.9%	23.1%
MONTOUR	5,150	3,692	1,445	13	2,247 R	71.7%	28.1%	71.9%	28.1%
NORTHAMPTON	52,575	37,403	14,768	404	22,635 R	71.1%	28.1%	71.7%	28.3%
NORTHUMBERLAND	50,490	30,949	19,249	292	11,700 R	61.3%	38.1%	61.7%	38.3%
PERRY	8,330	6,469	1,807	54	4,662 R	77.7%	21.7%	78.2%	21.8%
PHILADELPHIA	700,596	420,320	276,573	3,703	143,747 R	60.0%	39.5%	60.3%	39.7%
PIKE	3,395	2,354	1,024	17	1,330 R	69.3%	30.2%	69.7%	30.3%
POTTER	7,111	5,653	1,416	42	4,237 R	79.5%	19.9%	80.0%	20.0%
SCHUYLKILL	86,768	46,033	40,424	311	5,609 R	53.1%	46.6%	53.2%	46.8%
SNYDER	6,527	5,693	805	29	4,888 R	87.2%	12.3%	87.6%	12.4%
SOMERSET	21,057	16,404	4,489	164	11,915 R	77.9%	21.3%	78.5%	21.5%
SULLIVAN	3,162	2,044	1,101	17	943 R	64.6%	34.8%	65.0%	35.0%
SUSQUEHANNA	13,861	9,445	4,353	63	5,092 R	68.1%	31.4%	68.5%	31.5%
TIOGA	13,498	11,774	1,688	36	10,086 R	87.2%	12.5%	87.5%	12.5%
UNION	6,527	5,708	765	54	4,943 R	87.5%	11.7%	88.2%	11.8%

PRESIDENT 1932

County	Total Vote	Republican	Democratic	Other	Rep.-Dem. Plurality	Total Vote % Rep.	Total Vote % Dem.	Major Vote % Rep.	Major Vote % Dem.
ADAMS	13,494	6,084	7,185	225	1,101 D	45.1%	53.2%	45.9%	54.1%
ALLEGHENY	359,003	152,326	189,839	16,838	37,513 D	42.4%	52.9%	44.5%	55.5%
ARMSTRONG	20,890	10,884	9,230	776	1,654 R	52.1%	44.2%	54.1%	45.9%
BEAVER	41,260	19,751	19,805	1,704	54 D	47.9%	48.0%	49.9%	50.1%
BEDFORD	12,152	6,597	5,075	480	1,522 R	54.3%	41.8%	56.5%	43.5%
BERKS	73,023	27,073	29,763	16,187	2,690 D	37.1%	40.8%	47.6%	52.4%
BLAIR	34,334	19,553	13,709	1,072	5,844 R	56.9%	39.9%	58.8%	41.2%
BRADFORD	18,188	11,521	5,970	697	5,551 R	63.3%	32.8%	65.9%	34.1%
BUCKS	37,807	22,331	14,135	1,341	8,196 R	59.1%	37.4%	61.2%	38.8%
BUTLER	21,075	11,543	8,717	815	2,826 R	54.8%	41.4%	57.0%	43.0%
CAMBRIA	51,145	21,351	28,197	1,597	6,846 D	41.7%	55.1%	43.1%	56.9%
CAMERON	2,236	1,438	748	50	690 R	64.3%	33.5%	65.8%	34.3%
CARBON	20,441	9,918	9,874	649	44 R	48.5%	48.3%	50.1%	49.9%
CENTRE	15,726	8,264	7,053	409	1,211 R	52.5%	44.8%	54.0%	46.0%
CHESTER	42,517	29,425	12,040	1,052	17,385 R	69.2%	28.3%	71.0%	29.0%
CLARION	13,011	5,991	6,651	369	660 D	46.0%	51.1%	47.4%	52.6%
CLEARFIELD	22,597	10,500	11,209	888	709 D	46.5%	49.6%	48.4%	51.6%
CLINTON	11,114	4,851	5,961	302	1,110 D	43.6%	53.6%	44.9%	55.1%
COLUMBIA	19,787	8,791	10,640	356	1,849 D	44.4%	53.8%	45.2%	54.8%
CRAWFORD	21,111	9,382	10,918	811	1,536 D	44.4%	51.7%	46.2%	53.8%
CUMBERLAND	25,751	13,098	12,086	567	1,012 R	50.9%	46.9%	52.0%	48.0%
DAUPHIN	60,152	36,278	22,412	1,462	13,866 R	60.3%	37.3%	61.8%	38.2%
DELAWARE	110,409	75,291	32,413	2,705	42,878 R	68.2%	29.4%	69.9%	30.1%
ELK	12,497	5,797	6,461	239	664 D	46.4%	51.7%	47.3%	52.7%
ERIE	40,442	18,371	19,592	2,479	1,221 D	45.4%	48.4%	48.4%	51.6%
FAYETTE	45,106	15,903	27,662	1,541	11,759 D	35.3%	61.3%	36.5%	63.5%
FOREST	1,721	1,090	569	62	521 R	63.3%	33.1%	65.7%	34.3%
FRANKLIN	20,757	10,992	9,338	427	1,654 R	53.0%	45.0%	54.1%	45.9%
FULTON	2,371	1,410	921	40	489 R	59.5%	38.8%	60.5%	39.5%
GREENE	14,393	4,808	9,322	263	4,514 D	33.4%	64.8%	34.0%	66.0%
HUNTINGDON	11,103	7,371	3,426	306	3,945 R	66.4%	30.9%	68.3%	31.7%
INDIANA	22,235	12,727	8,606	902	4,121 R	57.2%	38.7%	59.7%	40.3%
JEFFERSON	15,713	8,246	6,570	897	1,676 R	52.5%	41.8%	55.7%	44.3%
JUNIATA	5,681	2,752	2,805	124	53 D	48.4%	49.4%	49.5%	50.5%
LACKAWANNA	76,560	34,632	40,793	1,135	6,161 D	45.2%	53.3%	45.9%	54.1%
LANCASTER	61,019	34,502	24,406	2,111	10,096 R	56.5%	40.0%	58.6%	41.4%
LAWRENCE	23,709	13,064	9,390	1,255	3,674 R	55.1%	39.6%	58.2%	41.8%
LEBANON	17,784	10,467	5,924	1,393	4,543 R	58.9%	33.3%	63.9%	36.1%
LEHIGH	45,093	21,169	21,939	1,985	770 D	46.9%	48.7%	49.1%	50.9%
LUZERNE	115,928	52,672	60,975	2,281	8,303 D	45.4%	52.6%	46.3%	53.7%
LYCOMING	29,250	16,212	11,499	1,539	4,713 R	55.4%	39.3%	58.5%	41.5%
MCKEAN	15,335	9,970	4,661	704	5,309 R	65.0%	30.4%	68.1%	31.9%
MERCER	26,258	14,057	10,961	1,240	3,096 R	53.5%	41.7%	56.2%	43.8%
MIFFLIN	9,372	5,525	3,654	193	1,871 R	59.0%	39.0%	60.2%	39.8%
MONROE	11,199	4,659	6,357	183	1,698 D	41.6%	56.8%	42.3%	57.7%
MONTGOMERY	100,961	64,619	32,971	3,371	31,648 R	64.0%	32.7%	66.2%	33.8%
MONTOUR	4,882	2,759	2,079	44	680 R	56.5%	42.6%	57.0%	43.0%
NORTHAMPTON	46,133	20,779	24,009	1,345	3,230 D	45.0%	52.0%	46.4%	53.6%
NORTHUMBERLAND	42,464	17,982	23,114	1,368	5,132 D	42.3%	54.4%	43.8%	56.2%
PERRY	8,259	4,402	3,733	134	669 R	53.2%	45.1%	54.1%	45.9%
PHILADELPHIA	607,014	331,092	260,276	15,646	70,816 R	54.5%	42.9%	56.0%	44.0%
PIKE	3,558	1,649	1,844	65	195 D	46.3%	51.8%	47.2%	52.8%
POTTER	6,573	3,847	2,271	455	1,576 R	58.5%	34.6%	62.9%	37.1%
SCHUYLKILL	69,305	32,492	35,023	1,790	2,531 D	46.9%	50.5%	48.1%	51.9%
SNYDER	5,786	3,423	2,176	167	1,247 R	59.4%	37.7%	61.1%	38.9%
SOMERSET	20,249	11,857	7,919	473	3,938 R	58.6%	39.1%	60.0%	40.0%
SULLIVAN	3,115	1,457	1,602	56	145 D	46.8%	51.4%	47.6%	52.4%
SUSQUEHANNA	12,295	6,884	5,171	240	1,713 R	55.0%	42.1%	57.1%	42.9%
TIOGA	12,778	9,583	3,004	191	6,579 R	75.0%	23.5%	76.1%	23.9%
UNION	5,734	3,534	1,948	252	1,586 R	61.6%	34.0%	64.5%	35.5%

PENNSYLVANIA

PRESIDENT 1928

County	Total Vote	Republican	Democratic	Other	Rep.-Dem. Plurality	Percentage Total Vote Rep.	Dem.	Major Vote Rep.	Dem.
VENANGO	22,089	17,450	4,531	108	12,919 R	79.0%	20.5%	79.4%	20.6%
WARREN	15,056	12,077	2,835	144	9,242 R	80.2%	18.8%	81.0%	19.0%
WASHINGTON	48,893	31,099	17,149	645	13,950 R	63.6%	35.1%	64.5%	35.5%
WAYNE	11,783	8,576	3,148	59	5,428 R	72.8%	26.7%	73.1%	26.9%
WESTMORELAND	83,643	51,760	30,587	1,296	21,173 R	61.9%	36.6%	62.9%	37.1%
WYOMING	6,260	5,321	906	33	4,415 R	85.0%	14.5%	85.5%	14.5%
YORK	57,529	45,791	11,216	522	34,575 R	79.6%	19.5%	80.3%	19.7%
TOTAL	3,150,612	2,055,382	1,067,586	27,644	987,796 R	65.2%	33.9%	65.8%	34.2%

PRESIDENT 1932

County	Total Vote	Republican	Democratic	Other	Rep.-Dem. Plurality	Percentage Total Vote Rep.	Dem.	Major Vote Rep.	Dem.
VENANGO	19,088	12,230	6,174	684	6,056 R	64.1%	32.3%	66.5%	33.5%
WARREN	13,753	7,872	5,254	627	2,618 R	57.2%	38.2%	60.0%	40.0%
WASHINGTON	52,536	21,447	28,934	2,155	7,487 D	40.8%	55.1%	42.6%	57.4%
WAYNE	10,111	6,215	3,666	230	2,549 R	61.5%	36.3%	62.9%	37.1%
WESTMORELAND	80,651	30,426	45,436	4,789	15,010 D	37.7%	56.3%	40.1%	59.9%
WYOMING	6,841	3,968	2,728	145	1,240 R	58.0%	39.9%	59.3%	40.7%
YORK	57,365	25,430	29,313	2,622	3,883 D	44.3%	51.1%	46.5%	53.5%
TOTAL	2,859,021	1,453,540	1,295,948	109,533	157,592 R	50.8%	45.3%	52.9%	47.1%

PENNSYLVANIA

PRESIDENT 1936

County	Total Vote	Republican	Democratic	Other	Rep-Dem Plurality	Total Vote Rep.	Total Vote Dem.	Major Vote Rep.	Major Vote Dem.
ADAMS	17,410	8,313	8,336	761	23 D	47.7%	47.9%	49.9%	50.1%
ALLEGHENY	562,176	176,224	366,593	19,359	190,369 D	31.3%	65.2%	32.5%	67.5%
ARMSTRONG	30,434	14,198	15,955	281	1,757 D	46.7%	52.4%	47.1%	52.9%
BEAVER	58,312	20,223	37,205	884	16,982 D	34.7%	63.8%	35.2%	64.8%
BEDFORD	18,182	9,014	8,937	231	77 R	49.6%	49.2%	50.2%	49.8%
BERKS	88,327	26,699	56,907	4,721	30,208 D	30.2%	64.4%	31.9%	68.1%
BLAIR	52,597	24,711	27,038	848	2,327 D	47.0%	51.4%	47.8%	52.2%
BRADFORD	24,936	16,643	8,078	215	8,565 R	66.7%	32.4%	67.3%	32.7%
BUCKS	48,895	23,860	24,159	876	299 D	48.8%	49.4%	49.7%	50.3%
BUTLER	33,309	16,772	16,008	529	764 R	50.4%	48.1%	51.2%	48.8%
CAMBRIA	72,304	24,378	46,687	1,239	22,309 D	33.7%	64.6%	34.3%	65.7%
CAMERON	3,585	1,801	1,538	46	263 R	53.2%	45.4%	53.9%	46.1%
CARBON	25,811	11,298	14,179	334	2,881 D	43.8%	54.9%	44.3%	55.7%
CENTRE	21,814	9,869	11,734	211	1,865 D	45.2%	53.8%	45.7%	54.3%
CHESTER	56,529	29,340	26,676	613	2,664 R	51.5%	47.1%	52.4%	47.6%
CLARION	17,189	8,477	8,412	300	65 R	49.3%	48.9%	50.2%	49.8%
CLEARFIELD	36,050	14,531	20,799	720	6,268 D	40.3%	57.7%	41.1%	58.9%
CLINTON	14,969	6,479	8,351	139	1,872 D	43.3%	55.8%	43.7%	56.3%
COLUMBIA	24,108	9,674	14,141	293	4,467 D	40.1%	58.7%	40.6%	59.4%
CRAWFORD	28,189	14,463	12,788	938	1,675 R	51.3%	45.4%	53.1%	46.9%
CUMBERLAND	34,021	14,912	18,850	259	3,938 D	43.8%	55.4%	44.2%	55.8%
DAUPHIN	83,500	39,598	43,256	646	3,658 D	47.4%	51.8%	47.8%	52.2%
DELAWARE	143,013	74,899	65,117	2,997	9,782 R	52.4%	45.5%	53.5%	46.5%
ELK	15,631	5,489	9,035	1,107	3,546 D	35.1%	57.8%	37.8%	62.2%
ERIE	65,345	25,607	33,042	6,696	7,435 D	39.2%	50.6%	43.7%	56.3%
FAYETTE	71,144	21,084	48,291	869	26,307 D	30.9%	67.9%	31.3%	68.7%
FOREST	2,953	1,757	1,157	39	600 R	59.5%	39.2%	60.3%	39.7%
FRANKLIN	29,413	13,616	15,632	165	2,016 D	46.3%	53.1%	46.6%	53.4%
FULTON	4,531	2,085	2,431	15	346 D	46.0%	53.7%	46.2%	53.8%
GREENE	18,474	6,359	12,006	109	5,647 D	34.4%	65.0%	34.6%	65.4%
HUNTINGDON	17,392	9,815	7,429	148	2,386 R	56.4%	42.7%	56.9%	43.1%
INDIANA	32,177	16,530	15,353	294	1,177 R	51.4%	47.7%	51.8%	48.2%
JEFFERSON	23,306	11,943	11,080	283	853 R	51.2%	47.5%	51.9%	48.1%
JUNIATA	7,407	3,576	3,782	49	206 D	48.3%	51.1%	48.6%	51.4%
LACKAWANNA	133,801	51,186	80,585	2,030	29,399 D	38.3%	60.2%	38.8%	61.2%
LANCASTER	82,273	42,272	38,454	1,547	3,818 R	51.4%	46.7%	52.4%	47.6%
LAWRENCE	38,090	15,458	21,994	638	6,536 D	40.6%	57.7%	41.3%	58.7%
LEBANON	27,476	13,213	13,800	463	587 D	48.1%	50.2%	48.9%	51.1%
LEHIGH	62,621	25,841	35,325	1,455	9,484 D	41.3%	56.4%	42.2%	57.8%
LUZERNE	188,479	81,672	104,809	1,998	23,137 D	43.3%	55.6%	43.8%	56.2%
LYCOMING	38,280	18,315	19,376	589	1,061 D	47.8%	50.6%	48.6%	51.4%
MCKEAN	22,181	11,837	9,733	611	2,104 R	53.4%	43.9%	54.9%	45.1%
MERCER	40,311	18,493	20,879	939	2,385 D	45.9%	51.8%	47.0%	53.0%
MIFFLIN	16,525	6,867	9,581	77	2,714 D	41.6%	58.0%	41.7%	58.3%
MONROE	14,079	5,778	8,212	89	2,434 D	41.0%	58.3%	41.3%	58.7%
MONTGOMERY	126,506	66,442	57,870	2,194	8,572 R	52.5%	45.7%	53.4%	46.6%
MONTOUR	5,914	2,350	3,534	30	1,184 D	39.7%	59.8%	39.9%	60.1%
NORTHAMPTON	58,926	21,827	36,871	228	15,044 D	37.0%	62.6%	37.2%	62.8%
NORTHUMBERLAND	61,136	24,287	35,849	711	11,562 D	39.7%	58.6%	40.4%	59.6%
PERRY	11,600	5,550	5,780	49	230 D	47.8%	49.8%	49.0%	51.0%
PHILADELPHIA	892,750	329,881	539,757	23,112	209,876 D	37.0%	60.5%	37.9%	62.1%
PIKE	4,741	2,304	2,396	41	92 D	48.6%	50.5%	49.0%	51.0%
POTTER	8,926	5,172	3,553	201	1,619 R	57.9%	39.8%	59.3%	40.7%
SCHUYLKILL	100,921	44,353	55,183	1,385	10,830 D	43.9%	54.7%	44.6%	55.4%
SNYDER	8,598	5,550	2,999	49	2,551 R	64.5%	34.9%	64.9%	35.1%
SOMERSET	33,741	17,375	16,184	182	1,191 R	51.5%	48.0%	51.8%	48.2%
SULLIVAN	3,922	2,121	1,740	61	381 R	54.1%	44.4%	54.9%	45.1%
SUSQUEHANNA	16,534	9,745	6,520	269	3,225 R	58.9%	39.4%	59.9%	40.1%
TIOGA	18,108	12,567	5,442	99	7,125 R	69.4%	30.1%	69.8%	30.2%
UNION	8,602	5,589	2,946	67	2,643 R	65.0%	34.2%	65.5%	34.5%

PRESIDENT 1940

County	Total Vote	Republican	Democratic	Other	Rep-Dem Plurality	Total Vote Rep.	Total Vote Dem.	Major Vote Rep.	Major Vote Dem.
ADAMS	15,983	8,609	7,354	20	1,255 R	53.9%	46.0%	53.9%	46.1%
ALLEGHENY	634,060	263,285	367,926	2,849	104,641 D	41.5%	58.0%	41.7%	58.3%
ARMSTRONG	26,728	14,524	12,144	60	2,380 R	54.3%	45.4%	54.5%	45.5%
BEAVER	58,172	24,324	33,609	239	9,285 D	41.8%	57.8%	42.0%	58.0%
BEDFORD	16,301	8,664	7,388	49	1,476 R	54.4%	45.3%	54.5%	45.5%
BERKS	86,934	32,111	53,301	1,522	21,190 D	36.9%	61.3%	37.6%	62.4%
BLAIR	48,318	26,839	21,573	106	5,066 R	55.1%	44.6%	55.5%	44.7%
BRADFORD	21,480	14,826	6,605	49	8,221 R	69.0%	30.7%	69.2%	30.8%
BUCKS	45,967	25,269	20,586	212	4,683 R	54.8%	44.8%	55.0%	45.0%
BUTLER	33,421	19,450	13,875	96	5,575 R	58.2%	41.5%	58.4%	41.6%
CAMBRIA	73,393	30,336	42,894	193	12,588 D	41.3%	58.4%	41.4%	58.6%
CAMERON	3,251	1,793	1,450	8	343 R	55.2%	44.6%	55.3%	44.7%
CARBON	23,446	10,618	12,777	51	2,159 D	45.3%	54.5%	45.4%	54.6%
CENTRE	20,602	10,665	9,869	68	796 R	51.8%	47.9%	51.9%	48.1%
CHESTER	50,869	28,222	22,473	174	5,749 R	55.5%	44.2%	55.7%	44.3%
CLARION	15,633	9,335	6,564	34	2,471 R	57.8%	42.0%	57.9%	42.1%
CLEARFIELD	33,260	15,407	17,705	148	2,298 D	46.3%	53.2%	46.5%	53.5%
CLINTON	13,732	6,291	7,419	22	1,128 D	45.8%	54.0%	45.9%	54.1%
COLUMBIA	22,062	9,518	12,523	21	3,005 D	43.1%	56.8%	43.2%	56.8%
CRAWFORD	26,203	15,391	10,197	115	5,694 R	60.6%	38.9%	60.9%	39.1%
CUMBERLAND	31,116	15,297	15,758	61	461 D	49.2%	50.6%	49.3%	50.7%
DAUPHIN	80,975	42,394	38,305	276	4,089 R	52.4%	47.3%	52.5%	47.5%
DELAWARE	140,917	80,158	60,225	534	19,933 R	56.9%	42.7%	57.1%	42.9%
ELK	13,900	6,949	6,920	31	29 R	50.0%	49.8%	50.1%	49.8%
ERIE	68,698	36,608	31,735	355	4,873 R	53.3%	46.2%	53.6%	46.4%
FAYETTE	66,114	23,908	41,960	246	18,052 D	36.2%	63.5%	36.3%	63.7%
FOREST	2,736	1,811	919	6	892 R	66.2%	33.6%	66.3%	33.7%
FRANKLIN	25,836	13,084	12,713	39	371 R	50.6%	49.2%	50.7%	49.3%
FULTON	4,095	2,108	1,982	5	126 R	51.5%	48.4%	51.5%	48.5%
GREENE	16,974	6,726	10,242	34	3,488 D	39.6%	60.2%	39.7%	60.3%
HUNTINGDON	14,830	9,141	5,631	58	3,510 R	61.6%	38.0%	61.9%	38.1%
INDIANA	27,687	15,547	12,035	68	3,512 R	56.2%	43.5%	56.4%	43.6%
JEFFERSON	20,687	12,081	8,559	47	3,522 R	58.4%	41.4%	58.5%	41.5%
JUNIATA	7,093	3,510	3,572	11	62 D	49.4%	50.5%	49.5%	50.5%
LACKAWANNA	126,685	54,931	71,343	411	16,412 D	43.4%	56.3%	43.5%	56.5%
LANCASTER	77,394	44,939	32,210	245	12,729 R	58.1%	41.6%	58.2%	41.8%
LAWRENCE	38,342	19,361	18,614	367	747 R	50.5%	48.5%	49.7%	49.7%
LEBANON	26,837	13,449	13,315	73	134 R	50.1%	49.6%	50.3%	49.7%
LEHIGH	62,947	29,584	33,007	356	3,423 D	47.0%	52.4%	47.3%	52.4%
LUZERNE	181,884	79,685	101,577	622	21,892 D	43.8%	55.8%	44.0%	56.0%
LYCOMING	39,877	21,423	18,363	91	3,060 R	53.7%	46.0%	53.8%	46.2%
MCKEAN	21,928	14,822	6,991	115	7,831 R	67.6%	31.9%	68.0%	32.0%
MERCER	38,201	21,058	16,968	175	4,090 R	55.1%	44.6%	55.4%	44.6%
MIFFLIN	13,369	6,352	6,993	24	641 D	47.5%	52.3%	47.6%	52.4%
MONROE	12,687	6,001	6,670	16	669 D	47.3%	52.5%	47.4%	52.6%
MONTGOMERY	123,062	73,250	49,409	403	23,841 R	59.5%	40.1%	59.7%	40.3%
MONTOUR	5,807	2,723	3,080	4	357 D	46.9%	53.0%	46.9%	53.1%
NORTHAMPTON	58,955	25,385	33,304	266	7,919 D	43.1%	56.5%	43.3%	56.7%
NORTHUMBERLAND	49,363	22,914	26,315	134	3,401 D	46.4%	53.3%	46.5%	53.5%
PERRY	10,489	5,877	4,601	11	1,276 R	56.0%	43.9%	56.1%	43.9%
PHILADELPHIA	891,486	354,878	532,149	4,459	177,271 D	39.8%	59.7%	40.0%	60.0%
PIKE	4,426	2,596	1,818	12	778 R	58.7%	41.0%	58.8%	41.2%
POTTER	7,963	5,205	2,731	27	2,474 R	65.4%	34.3%	65.6%	34.4%
SCHUYLKILL	92,475	43,505	48,739	231	5,234 D	47.0%	52.8%	47.2%	52.8%
SNYDER	8,214	5,714	2,478	22	3,244 R	69.7%	30.2%	69.8%	30.2%
SOMERSET	31,506	17,369	14,085	52	3,284 R	55.1%	44.7%	55.2%	44.8%
SULLIVAN	3,692	2,059	1,626	7	433 R	55.8%	44.0%	55.9%	44.1%
SUSQUEHANNA	14,938	9,520	5,383	35	4,137 R	63.7%	36.0%	63.9%	36.1%
TIOGA	16,119	11,645	4,434	40	7,211 R	72.2%	27.5%	72.4%	27.6%
UNION	7,854	5,612	2,220	22	3,392 R	71.5%	28.3%	71.7%	28.3%

PENNSYLVANIA

PRESIDENT 1936

County	Total Vote	Republican	Democratic	Other	Rep.-Dem. Plurality	Percentage Total Vote Rep.	Dem.	Major Vote Rep.	Dem.
VENANGO	27,563	17,676	9,212	675	8,464 R	64.1%	33.4%	65.7%	34.3%
WARREN	18,767	9,440	8,495	832	945 R	50.3%	45.3%	52.6%	47.4%
WASHINGTON	77,168	23,342	52,878	948	29,536 D	30.2%	68.5%	30.6%	69.4%
WAYNE	14,380	9,347	4,864	169	4,483 R	65.0%	33.8%	65.8%	34.2%
WESTMORELAND	111,937	36,079	73,574	2,284	37,495 D	32.2%	65.7%	32.9%	67.1%
WYOMING	8,687	5,321	3,269	97	2,052 R	61.3%	37.6%	61.9%	38.1%
YORK	75,837	29,233	45,142	1,462	15,909 D	38.5%	59.5%	39.3%	60.7%
TOTAL	4,138,105	1,690,300	2,353,788	94,017	663,488 D	40.8%	56.9%	41.8%	58.2%

PRESIDENT 1940

County	Total Vote	Republican	Democratic	Other	Rep.-Dem. Plurality	Percentage Total Vote Rep.	Dem.	Major Vote Rep.	Dem.
VENANGO	24,639	17,728	6,873	38	10,855 R	72.0%	27.9%	72.1%	27.9%
WARREN	16,938	11,016	5,825	97	5,191 R	65.0%	34.4%	65.4%	34.6%
WASHINGTON	80,140	29,026	50,829	285	21,803 D	36.2%	63.4%	36.3%	63.7%
WAYNE	12,693	9,203	3,460	30	5,743 R	72.5%	27.3%	72.7%	27.3%
WESTMORELAND	107,787	42,643	64,567	577	21,924 D	39.6%	59.9%	39.8%	60.2%
WYOMING	7,837	5,273	2,548	16	2,725 R	67.3%	32.5%	67.4%	32.6%
YORK	69,917	30,228	39,543	146	9,315 D	43.2%	56.6%	43.3%	56.7%
TOTAL	4,078,714	1,889,848	2,171,035	17,831	281,187 D	46.3%	53.2%	46.5%	53.5%

PENNSYLVANIA

PRESIDENT 1944

County	Total Vote	Republican	Democratic	Other	Rep.-Dem. Plurality	Total Vote Rep.	Total Vote Dem.	Major Vote Rep.	Major Vote Dem.
ADAMS	14,735	8,787	5,881	67	2,906 R	59.6%	39.9%	59.9%	40.1%
ALLEGHENY	614,301	261,218	350,690	2,393	89,472 D	42.5%	57.1%	42.7%	57.3%
ARMSTRONG	23,984	13,656	10,202	126	3,454 R	56.9%	42.5%	57.2%	42.8%
BEAVER	56,658	23,555	32,743	360	9,188 D	41.6%	57.8%	41.8%	58.2%
BEDFORD	13,946	8,703	5,175	68	3,528 R	62.4%	37.1%	62.7%	37.3%
BERKS	81,410	35,274	43,889	2,247	8,615 D	43.3%	53.9%	44.6%	55.4%
BLAIR	43,106	24,925	18,003	178	6,922 R	57.8%	41.8%	58.1%	41.9%
BRADFORD	19,137	13,472	5,523	142	7,949 R	70.4%	28.9%	70.9%	29.1%
BUCKS	43,727	25,634	17,823	270	7,811 R	58.6%	40.8%	59.0%	41.0%
BUTLER	31,944	19,341	12,377	226	6,964 R	60.5%	38.7%	61.0%	39.0%
CAMBRIA	68,143	28,203	39,676	264	11,473 D	41.4%	58.2%	41.5%	58.5%
CAMERON	2,853	1,729	1,115	9	614 R	60.6%	39.1%	60.8%	39.2%
CARBON	20,970	9,837	11,060	73	1,223 D	46.9%	52.7%	47.1%	52.9%
CENTRE	18,242	10,048	8,064	130	1,984 R	55.1%	44.2%	55.5%	44.5%
CHESTER	45,411	26,655	18,548	208	8,107 R	58.7%	40.8%	59.0%	41.0%
CLARION	13,460	8,098	5,263	99	2,835 R	60.2%	39.1%	60.6%	39.4%
CLEARFIELD	27,836	13,986	13,617	233	369 R	50.2%	48.9%	50.7%	49.3%
CLINTON	11,675	5,915	5,703	57	212 R	50.7%	48.8%	50.9%	49.1%
COLUMBIA	19,053	9,336	9,647	70	311 D	49.0%	50.6%	49.2%	50.8%
CRAWFORD	24,591	15,205	9,216	170	5,989 R	61.8%	37.5%	62.3%	37.7%
CUMBERLAND	29,984	17,782	12,068	134	5,714 R	59.3%	40.2%	59.6%	40.4%
DAUPHIN	75,742	44,725	30,684	333	14,041 R	59.0%	40.5%	59.3%	40.7%
DELAWARE	143,309	78,533	64,021	755	14,512 R	54.8%	44.7%	55.1%	44.9%
ELK	11,809	5,645	6,097	67	452 D	47.8%	51.6%	48.1%	51.9%
ERIE	68,578	35,247	32,912	419	2,335 R	51.4%	48.0%	51.7%	48.3%
FAYETTE	57,489	21,945	35,093	451	13,148 D	38.2%	61.0%	38.5%	61.5%
FOREST	2,038	1,344	673	21	671 R	65.9%	33.0%	66.6%	33.4%
FRANKLIN	22,250	13,380	8,807	63	4,573 R	60.1%	39.6%	60.3%	39.7%
FULTON	3,857	2,084	1,758	15	326 R	54.0%	45.6%	54.2%	45.8%
GREENE	14,192	5,747	8,392	53	2,645 D	40.5%	59.1%	40.6%	59.4%
HUNTINGDON	12,320	8,106	4,131	83	3,975 R	65.8%	33.5%	66.2%	33.8%
INDIANA	23,426	14,388	8,863	175	5,525 R	61.4%	37.8%	61.9%	38.1%
JEFFERSON	17,547	10,970	6,425	152	4,545 R	62.5%	36.6%	63.1%	36.9%
JUNIATA	6,193	3,512	2,666	15	846 R	56.7%	43.0%	56.8%	43.2%
LACKAWANNA	106,578	47,261	59,190	127	11,929 D	44.3%	55.5%	44.4%	55.6%
LANCASTER	72,673	44,888	27,353	432	17,535 R	61.8%	37.6%	62.1%	37.9%
LAWRENCE	36,620	18,886	17,331	403	1,555 R	51.6%	47.3%	52.1%	47.9%
LEBANON	27,153	15,206	11,818	129	3,388 R	56.0%	43.5%	56.3%	43.7%
LEHIGH	61,033	31,584	29,134	315	2,450 R	51.7%	47.7%	52.0%	48.0%
LUZERNE	142,199	67,984	73,674	541	5,690 D	47.8%	51.8%	48.0%	52.0%
LYCOMING	35,741	19,886	15,658	197	4,228 R	55.6%	43.8%	55.9%	44.1%
MCKEAN	18,601	11,988	6,492	121	5,496 R	64.4%	34.9%	64.9%	35.1%
MERCER	36,407	19,606	16,589	212	3,017 R	53.9%	45.6%	54.2%	45.8%
MIFFLIN	11,952	6,205	5,693	54	512 R	51.9%	47.6%	52.2%	47.8%
MONROE	11,729	6,202	5,490	37	712 R	52.9%	46.8%	53.0%	47.0%
MONTGOMERY	126,827	78,260	47,815	752	30,445 R	61.7%	37.7%	62.1%	37.9%
MONTOUR	4,947	2,727	2,212	8	515 R	55.1%	44.7%	55.2%	44.8%
NORTHAMPTON	59,519	26,643	32,584	292	5,941 D	44.8%	54.7%	45.0%	55.0%
NORTHUMBERLAND	42,450	21,995	20,333	122	1,662 R	51.8%	47.9%	52.0%	48.0%
PERRY	9,030	5,722	3,265	43	2,457 R	63.4%	36.2%	63.7%	36.3%
PHILADELPHIA	845,630	346,380	496,367	2,883	149,987 D	41.0%	58.7%	41.1%	58.9%
PIKE	4,101	2,674	1,408	19	1,266 R	65.2%	34.3%	65.5%	34.5%
POTTER	6,404	4,474	1,894	36	2,580 R	69.9%	29.6%	70.3%	29.7%
SCHUYLKILL	76,744	40,671	35,852	221	4,819 R	53.0%	46.7%	53.1%	46.9%
SNYDER	7,514	5,696	1,795	23	3,901 R	75.8%	23.9%	76.0%	24.0%
SOMERSET	26,405	16,039	10,287	79	5,752 R	60.7%	39.0%	60.9%	39.1%
SULLIVAN	3,195	1,858	1,329	8	529 R	58.2%	41.6%	58.3%	41.7%
SUSQUEHANNA	13,080	8,819	4,212	49	4,607 R	67.4%	32.2%	67.7%	32.3%
TIOGA	13,708	10,381	3,248	79	7,133 R	75.7%	23.7%	76.2%	23.8%
UNION	7,330	5,585	1,704	41	3,881 R	76.2%	23.2%	76.6%	23.4%

PRESIDENT 1948

County	Total Vote	Republican	Democratic	Other	Rep.-Dem. Plurality	Total Vote Rep.	Total Vote Dem.	Major Vote Rep.	Major Vote Dem.
ADAMS	13,509	7,988	5,409	112	2,579 R	59.1%	40.0%	59.6%	40.4%
ALLEGHENY	594,506	253,272	326,303	14,931	73,031 D	42.6%	54.9%	43.7%	56.3%
ARMSTRONG	21,912	11,712	9,900	300	1,812 R	53.5%	45.2%	54.2%	45.8%
BEAVER	50,935	22,324	26,629	1,982	4,305 D	43.8%	52.3%	45.6%	54.4%
BEDFORD	9,879	6,028	3,851		2,177 R	61.0%	39.0%	61.0%	39.0%
BERKS	81,726	35,608	43,075	3,043	7,467 D	43.6%	52.7%	45.3%	54.7%
BLAIR	36,886	22,382	14,050	454	8,332 R	60.7%	38.1%	61.4%	38.6%
BRADFORD	16,367	11,783	4,421	163	7,362 R	72.0%	27.0%	72.7%	27.3%
BUCKS	47,084	29,411	16,655	1,018	12,756 R	62.5%	35.4%	63.8%	36.2%
BUTLER	27,724	17,449	9,818	457	7,631 R	62.9%	35.4%	64.0%	36.0%
CAMBRIA	70,422	27,725	41,533	1,164	13,808 D	39.4%	59.0%	40.0%	60.0%
CAMERON	2,465	1,596	858	11	738 R	64.7%	34.8%	65.0%	35.0%
CARBON	19,578	9,744	9,438	396	306 R	49.8%	48.2%	50.8%	49.2%
CENTRE	16,931	10,416	6,515		3,901 R	61.5%	38.5%	61.5%	38.5%
CHESTER	44,478	29,258	14,670	550	14,588 R	65.8%	33.0%	66.6%	33.4%
CLARION	11,850	6,866	4,984		1,882 R	57.9%	42.1%	57.9%	42.1%
CLEARFIELD	23,644	11,810	11,347	487	463 R	49.9%	48.0%	51.0%	49.0%
CLINTON	10,631	5,618	5,013		605 R	52.8%	47.2%	52.8%	47.2%
COLUMBIA	18,784	9,417	9,367		50 R	50.1%	49.9%	50.1%	49.9%
CRAWFORD	23,335	14,161	9,174		4,987 R	60.7%	39.3%	60.7%	39.3%
CUMBERLAND	29,695	18,028	11,421	246	6,607 R	60.7%	38.5%	61.2%	38.8%
DAUPHIN	75,386	46,861	27,729	796	19,132 R	62.2%	36.8%	62.8%	37.2%
DELAWARE	153,315	93,412	57,156	2,747	36,256 R	60.9%	37.3%	62.0%	38.0%
ELK	10,511	5,148	5,363		215 D	49.0%	51.0%	49.0%	51.0%
ERIE	63,245	33,806	28,159	1,280	5,647 R	53.5%	44.5%	54.6%	45.4%
FAYETTE	56,367	20,401	34,971	995	14,570 D	36.2%	62.0%	36.8%	63.2%
FOREST	1,941	1,209	687	45	522 R	62.3%	35.4%	63.8%	36.2%
FRANKLIN	19,664	12,151	7,352	161	4,799 R	61.8%	37.4%	62.3%	37.7%
FULTON	3,475	1,760	1,684	31	76 R	50.6%	48.5%	51.1%	48.9%
GREENE	12,934	4,717	8,015	202	3,298 D	36.5%	62.0%	37.0%	63.0%
HUNTINGDON	10,247	6,943	3,304		3,639 R	67.8%	32.2%	67.8%	32.2%
INDIANA	21,183	12,640	8,543		4,097 R	59.7%	40.3%	59.7%	40.3%
JEFFERSON	15,295	9,395	5,632	268	3,763 R	61.4%	36.8%	62.5%	37.5%
JUNIATA	5,459	3,121	2,299	39	822 R	57.2%	42.1%	57.6%	42.4%
LACKAWANNA	111,749	46,283	64,495	971	18,212 D	41.4%	57.7%	41.8%	58.2%
LANCASTER	68,499	46,306	21,308	885	24,998 R	67.6%	31.1%	68.5%	31.5%
LAWRENCE	32,599	17,186	14,632	781	2,554 R	52.7%	44.9%	54.0%	46.0%
LEBANON	25,241	15,553	9,418	270	6,135 R	61.6%	37.3%	62.3%	37.7%
LEHIGH	60,022	32,202	26,826	994	5,376 R	53.7%	44.7%	54.6%	45.4%
LUZERNE	135,611	71,674	61,869	2,068	9,805 R	52.9%	45.6%	53.7%	46.3%
LYCOMING	33,436	19,118	13,692	626	5,426 R	57.2%	40.9%	58.3%	41.7%
MCKEAN	15,272	10,218	4,785	269	5,433 R	66.9%	31.3%	68.1%	31.9%
MERCER	35,886	18,916	16,108	862	2,808 R	52.7%	44.9%	54.0%	46.0%
MIFFLIN	10,523	5,666	4,762	95	904 R	53.8%	45.3%	54.3%	45.7%
MONROE	12,587	6,674	5,913		761 R	53.0%	47.0%	53.0%	47.0%
MONTGOMERY	128,626	85,576	41,112	1,938	44,464 R	66.5%	32.0%	67.5%	32.5%
MONTOUR	4,670	2,690	1,964	16	726 R	57.6%	42.1%	57.8%	42.2%
NORTHAMPTON	61,504	27,030	33,209	1,265	6,179 D	43.9%	54.0%	44.9%	55.1%
NORTHUMBERLAND	40,485	23,535	16,478	472	7,057 R	58.1%	40.7%	58.8%	41.2%
PERRY	8,040	5,444	2,596		2,848 R	67.7%	32.3%	67.7%	32.3%
PHILADELPHIA	885,297	425,962	432,699	26,636	6,737 D	48.1%	48.9%	49.6%	50.4%
PIKE	4,101	2,893	1,208		1,685 R	70.5%	29.5%	70.5%	29.5%
POTTER	5,401	3,672	1,729		1,943 R	68.0%	32.0%	68.0%	32.0%
SCHUYLKILL	73,492	44,176	28,194	1,122	15,982 R	60.1%	38.4%	61.0%	39.0%
SNYDER	6,671	5,181	1,490		3,691 R	77.7%	22.3%	77.7%	22.3%
SOMERSET	22,978	13,910	8,727	341	5,183 R	60.5%	38.0%	61.4%	38.6%
SULLIVAN	2,862	1,752	1,084	26	668 R	61.2%	37.9%	61.8%	38.2%
SUSQUEHANNA	11,716	7,945	3,621	150	4,324 R	67.8%	30.9%	68.7%	31.3%
TIOGA	13,002	10,016	2,986		7,030 R	77.0%	23.0%	77.0%	23.0%
UNION	6,587	5,058	1,442	87	3,616 R	76.8%	21.9%	77.8%	22.2%

PENNSYLVANIA

PRESIDENT 1944

County	Total Vote	Republican	Democratic	Other	Rep.-Dem. Plurality	Percentage Total Vote Rep.	Dem.	Major Vote Rep.	Dem.
VENANGO	21,646	14,916	6,426	304	8,490 R	68.9%	29.7%	69.9%	30.1%
WARREN	13,853	9,276	4,440	137	4,836 R	67.0%	32.1%	67.6%	32.4%
WASHINGTON	74,030	27,615	46,023	392	18,408 D	37.3%	62.2%	37.5%	62.5%
WAYNE	11,074	8,242	2,793	39	5,449 R	74.4%	25.2%	74.7%	25.3%
WESTMORELAND	104,964	43,202	61,057	705	17,855 D	41.2%	58.2%	41.4%	58.6%
WYOMING	6,582	4,581	1,982	19	2,599 R	69.6%	30.1%	69.8%	30.2%
YORK	71,158	32,617	38,226	315	5,609 D	45.8%	53.7%	46.0%	54.0%
TOTAL	3,794,793	1,835,054	1,940,479	19,260	105,425 D	48.4%	51.1%	48.6%	51.4%

PRESIDENT 1948

County	Total Vote	Republican	Democratic	Other	Rep.-Dem. Plurality	Percentage Total Vote Rep.	Dem.	Major Vote Rep.	Dem.
VENANGO	17,536	11,920	5,144	472	6,776 R	68.0%	29.3%	69.9%	30.1%
WARREN	12,814	8,378	4,103	333	4,275 R	65.4%	32.0%	67.1%	32.9%
WASHINGTON	75,166	26,860	46,327	1,979	19,467 D	35.7%	61.6%	36.7%	63.3%
WAYNE	9,992	7,708	2,284		5,424 R	77.1%	22.9%	77.1%	22.9%
WESTMORELAND	106,814	41,709	61,901	3,204	20,192 D	39.0%	58.0%	40.3%	59.7%
WYOMING	6,127	4,332	1,674	121	2,658 R	70.7%	27.3%	72.1%	27.9%
YORK	68,678	32,494	33,321	2,863	827 D	47.3%	48.5%	49.4%	50.6%
TOTAL	3,735,348	1,902,197	1,752,426	80,725	149,771 R	50.9%	46.9%	52.0%	48.0%

PENNSYLVANIA

PRESIDENT 1952

County	Total Vote	Republican	Democratic	Other	Rep.-Dem. Plurality	Total Vote Rep.	Total Vote Dem.	Major Vote Rep.	Major Vote Dem.
ADAMS	16,737	11,016	5,691	30	5,325 R	65.8%	34.0%	65.9%	34.1%
ALLEGHENY	733,072	359,224	370,945	2,903	11,721 D	49.0%	50.6%	49.2%	50.8%
ARMSTRONG	30,329	16,955	13,221	153	3,734 R	55.9%	43.6%	56.2%	43.8%
BEAVER	70,170	31,700	38,136	334	6,436 D	45.2%	54.3%	45.4%	54.6%
BEDFORD	14,734	9,419	5,255	60	4,164 R	63.9%	35.7%	64.2%	35.8%
BERKS	98,668	51,720	45,874	1,074	5,846 R	52.4%	46.5%	53.0%	47.0%
BLAIR	49,070	32,113	16,851	106	15,262 R	65.4%	34.3%	65.6%	34.4%
BRADFORD	20,908	15,894	4,959	55	10,935 R	76.0%	23.7%	76.2%	23.8%
BUCKS	65,329	40,753	24,301	275	16,452 R	62.4%	37.2%	62.6%	37.4%
BUTLER	40,723	25,243	15,295	185	9,948 R	62.0%	37.6%	62.3%	37.7%
CAMBRIA	90,250	39,294	50,774	182	11,480 D	43.5%	56.3%	43.6%	56.4%
CAMERON	3,341	2,307	1,020	14	1,287 R	69.1%	30.5%	69.3%	30.7%
CARBON	22,988	12,283	10,571	134	1,712 R	53.4%	46.0%	53.7%	46.3%
CENTRE	22,168	14,700	7,391	77	7,309 R	66.3%	33.3%	66.5%	33.5%
CHESTER	61,615	39,961	21,490	164	18,471 R	64.9%	34.9%	65.0%	35.0%
CLARION	14,649	9,340	5,212	97	4,128 R	63.8%	35.6%	64.2%	35.8%
CLEARFIELD	29,519	16,045	13,326	156	2,719 R	54.4%	45.1%	54.6%	45.4%
CLINTON	13,938	8,125	5,758	55	2,367 R	58.3%	41.3%	58.5%	41.5%
COLUMBIA	22,554	13,008	9,467	79	3,541 R	57.7%	42.0%	57.9%	42.1%
CRAWFORD	29,134	19,079	9,874	181	9,205 R	65.5%	33.9%	65.9%	34.1%
CUMBERLAND	39,155	26,302	12,762	91	13,540 R	67.2%	32.6%	67.3%	32.7%
DAUPHIN	89,656	58,385	30,985	286	27,400 R	65.1%	34.6%	65.3%	34.7%
DELAWARE	210,748	129,743	80,316	689	49,427 R	61.6%	38.1%	61.8%	38.2%
ELK	14,195	7,702	6,448	45	1,254 R	54.3%	45.4%	54.4%	45.6%
ERIE	85,846	48,836	36,619	391	12,217 R	56.9%	42.7%	57.1%	42.9%
FAYETTE	71,745	27,348	43,921	476	16,573 D	38.1%	61.2%	38.4%	61.6%
FOREST	2,161	1,511	627	23	884 R	69.9%	29.0%	70.7%	29.3%
FRANKLIN	25,416	16,474	8,868	74	7,606 R	64.8%	34.9%	65.0%	35.0%
FULTON	3,859	2,127	1,718	14	409 R	55.1%	44.5%	55.3%	44.7%
GREENE	17,119	6,964	10,125	30	3,161 D	40.7%	59.1%	40.8%	59.2%
HUNTINGDON	13,962	9,580	4,318	64	5,262 R	68.6%	30.9%	68.9%	31.1%
INDIANA	28,440	16,673	11,620	147	5,053 R	58.6%	40.9%	58.9%	41.1%
JEFFERSON	18,314	11,833	6,365	116	5,468 R	64.6%	34.8%	65.0%	35.0%
JUNIATA	6,589	3,863	2,705	21	1,158 R	58.6%	41.1%	58.8%	41.2%
LACKAWANNA	126,717	61,644	64,926	147	3,282 D	48.6%	51.2%	48.7%	51.3%
LANCASTER	92,721	64,193	28,146	382	36,047 R	69.2%	30.4%	69.5%	30.5%
LAWRENCE	44,738	23,319	21,164	255	2,155 R	52.1%	47.3%	52.4%	47.6%
LEBANON	32,472	20,726	11,611	135	9,115 R	63.8%	35.8%	64.1%	35.9%
LEHIGH	78,479	45,143	33,033	303	12,110 R	57.5%	42.1%	57.7%	42.3%
LUZERNE	162,261	88,967	72,579	715	16,388 R	54.8%	44.7%	55.1%	44.9%
LYCOMING	41,807	25,753	15,870	184	9,883 R	61.6%	38.0%	61.9%	38.1%
MCKEAN	21,776	16,256	5,373	147	10,883 R	74.6%	24.7%	75.2%	24.8%
MERCER	47,537	26,424	20,770	343	5,654 R	55.6%	43.7%	56.0%	44.0%
MIFFLIN	14,556	8,620	5,889	47	2,731 R	59.2%	40.5%	59.4%	40.6%
MONROE	15,304	9,502	5,760	42	3,742 R	62.1%	37.6%	62.3%	37.7%
MONTGOMERY	173,973	115,899	57,701	373	58,198 R	66.6%	33.2%	66.8%	33.2%
MONTOUR	5,996	3,725	2,264	7	1,461 R	62.1%	37.8%	62.2%	37.8%
NORTHAMPTON	75,738	39,131	36,993	614	2,138 R	51.7%	48.8%	51.4%	48.6%
NORTHUMBERLAND	46,769	28,861	17,789	119	11,072 R	61.7%	38.0%	61.9%	38.1%
PERRY	9,792	6,733	3,042	17	3,691 R	68.8%	31.1%	68.9%	31.1%
PHILADELPHIA	958,547	396,874	557,352	4,321	160,478 D	41.4%	58.1%	41.6%	58.4%
PIKE	5,204	3,810	1,383	11	2,427 R	73.2%	26.6%	73.4%	26.6%
POTTER	7,129	5,117	1,974	38	3,143 R	71.8%	27.7%	72.2%	27.8%
SCHUYLKILL	86,610	51,437	34,987	186	16,450 R	59.4%	40.4%	59.5%	40.5%
SNYDER	8,545	6,836	1,686	23	5,150 R	80.0%	19.7%	80.2%	19.8%
SOMERSET	31,820	18,589	13,167	64	5,422 R	58.4%	41.4%	58.5%	41.5%
SULLIVAN	3,253	2,011	1,239	3	772 R	61.8%	38.1%	61.9%	38.1%
SUSQUEHANNA	14,234	10,529	3,653	52	6,876 R	74.0%	25.7%	74.2%	25.8%
TIOGA	14,244	11,203	3,006	35	8,197 R	78.6%	21.1%	78.8%	21.2%
UNION	8,181	6,558	1,610	13	4,948 R	80.2%	19.7%	80.3%	19.7%

PRESIDENT 1956

County	Total Vote	Republican	Democratic	Other	Rep.-Dem. Plurality	Total Vote Rep.	Total Vote Dem.	Major Vote Rep.	Major Vote Dem.
ADAMS	18,531	12,250	6,281		5,969 R	66.1%	33.9%	66.1%	33.9%
ALLEGHENY	702,030	384,939	315,989	1,102	68,950 R	54.8%	45.0%	54.9%	45.1%
ARMSTRONG	32,760	20,055	12,671	34	7,384 R	61.2%	38.7%	61.3%	38.7%
BEAVER	74,715	38,263	36,373	79	1,890 R	51.2%	48.7%	51.3%	48.7%
BEDFORD	17,474	11,423	6,038	13	5,385 R	65.4%	34.6%	65.4%	34.6%
BERKS	99,927	57,258	42,349	320	14,909 R	57.3%	42.4%	57.5%	42.5%
BLAIR	51,191	33,623	17,503	65	16,120 R	65.7%	34.2%	65.8%	34.2%
BRADFORD	20,931	15,399	5,502	30	9,897 R	73.6%	26.3%	73.7%	26.3%
BUCKS	98,583	59,862	38,541	180	21,321 R	60.7%	39.1%	60.8%	39.2%
BUTLER	39,989	26,238	13,672	79	12,566 R	65.6%	34.2%	65.7%	34.3%
CAMBRIA	88,249	46,373	41,753	123	4,620 R	52.5%	47.3%	52.6%	47.4%
CAMERON	3,304	2,462	841	1	1,621 R	74.5%	25.5%	74.5%	25.5%
CARBON	22,961	13,150	9,722	89	3,428 R	57.3%	42.3%	57.5%	42.5%
CENTRE	22,940	15,412	7,483	45	7,929 R	67.2%	32.6%	67.3%	32.7%
CHESTER	67,232	47,225	19,957	50	27,268 R	70.2%	29.7%	70.3%	29.7%
CLARION	15,011	10,048	4,955	8	5,093 R	66.9%	33.0%	67.0%	33.0%
CLEARFIELD	30,460	17,519	12,852	89	4,667 R	57.5%	42.2%	57.7%	42.3%
CLINTON	13,678	8,250	5,411	17	2,839 R	60.3%	39.6%	60.4%	39.6%
COLUMBIA	22,421	13,382	9,024	15	4,358 R	59.7%	40.2%	59.7%	40.3%
CRAWFORD	28,337	18,887	9,346	104	9,541 R	66.7%	33.0%	66.9%	33.1%
CUMBERLAND	43,272	29,468	13,651	153	15,817 R	68.1%	31.5%	68.3%	31.7%
DAUPHIN	90,943	61,342	29,226	375	32,116 R	67.5%	32.1%	67.7%	32.3%
DELAWARE	226,210	143,663	82,024	523	61,639 R	63.5%	36.3%	63.7%	36.3%
ELK	14,468	8,947	5,498	23	3,449 R	61.8%	38.0%	61.9%	38.1%
ERIE	88,555	54,430	33,802	323	20,628 R	61.5%	38.2%	61.7%	38.3%
FAYETTE	66,375	27,857	38,312	206	10,455 D	42.0%	57.7%	42.1%	57.9%
FOREST	2,158	1,535	622	1	913 R	71.1%	28.8%	71.2%	28.8%
FRANKLIN	30,193	19,121	11,060	12	8,061 R	63.3%	36.6%	63.4%	36.6%
FULTON	4,195	2,370	1,819	6	551 R	56.5%	43.4%	56.6%	43.4%
GREENE	17,403	7,562	9,827	14	2,265 D	43.5%	56.5%	43.5%	56.5%
HUNTINGDON	14,333	9,698	4,618	17	5,080 R	67.7%	32.2%	67.7%	32.2%
INDIANA	29,861	18,593	11,268	19	7,325 R	62.3%	37.7%	62.3%	37.7%
JEFFERSON	19,685	13,051	6,627	7	6,424 R	66.3%	33.6%	66.3%	33.7%
JUNIATA	7,644	4,258	2,779	7	1,479 R	60.4%	39.5%	60.5%	39.5%
LACKAWANNA	120,206	64,386	55,741	79	8,645 R	53.6%	46.4%	53.6%	46.4%
LANCASTER	95,801	69,026	26,538	237	42,488 R	72.1%	27.7%	72.2%	27.8%
LAWRENCE	45,025	25,037	19,923	65	5,114 R	55.6%	44.2%	55.7%	44.3%
LEBANON	33,003	22,556	10,406	41	12,150 R	68.3%	31.5%	68.4%	31.6%
LEHIGH	79,882	50,564	29,067	251	21,497 R	63.3%	36.4%	63.5%	36.5%
LUZERNE	158,820	92,458	65,155	1,207	27,303 R	58.2%	41.0%	58.7%	41.3%
LYCOMING	40,540	27,030	13,490	20	13,540 R	66.7%	33.3%	66.7%	33.3%
MCKEAN	19,950	14,725	5,152	73	9,573 R	73.8%	25.8%	74.1%	25.9%
MERCER	48,674	28,785	19,769	120	9,016 R	59.1%	40.6%	59.3%	40.7%
MIFFLIN	13,725	8,638	5,078	9	3,560 R	62.9%	37.0%	63.0%	37.0%
MONROE	15,679	10,081	5,506	92	4,575 R	64.3%	35.1%	64.7%	35.3%
MONTGOMERY	192,583	133,270	59,095	218	74,175 R	69.2%	30.7%	69.3%	30.7%
MONTOUR	6,051	3,976	2,072	3	1,904 R	65.7%	34.2%	65.7%	34.3%
NORTHAMPTON	77,697	43,375	33,749	573	9,626 R	55.8%	43.4%	56.2%	43.8%
NORTHUMBERLAND	45,765	28,583	17,141	41	11,442 R	62.5%	37.4%	62.5%	37.5%
PERRY	11,112	7,511	3,576	25	3,935 R	67.6%	32.2%	67.7%	32.3%
PHILADELPHIA	892,321	383,414	507,289	1,618	123,875 D	43.0%	56.9%	43.0%	57.0%
PIKE	5,383	4,160	1,219	4	2,941 R	77.3%	22.6%	77.3%	22.7%
POTTER	7,460	5,181	2,257	22	2,924 R	69.5%	30.3%	69.7%	30.3%
SCHUYLKILL	83,406	51,670	31,645	91	20,025 R	61.9%	37.9%	62.0%	38.0%
SNYDER	9,064	7,102	1,959	3	5,143 R	78.4%	21.6%	78.4%	21.6%
SOMERSET	33,748	20,568	13,163	17	7,405 R	60.9%	39.0%	61.0%	39.0%
SULLIVAN	3,297	2,007	1,286	4	721 R	60.9%	39.0%	60.9%	39.1%
SUSQUEHANNA	15,055	10,752	4,293	10	6,459 R	71.4%	28.5%	71.5%	28.5%
TIOGA	14,113	10,827	3,280	6	7,547 R	76.7%	23.2%	76.7%	23.3%
UNION	8,478	6,620	1,844	14	4,776 R	78.1%	21.8%	78.2%	21.8%

PENNSYLVANIA

PRESIDENT 1952

County	Total Vote	Republican	Democratic	Other	Rep.-Dem. Plurality	Percentage Total Vote Rep.	Dem.	Major Vote Rep.	Dem.
VENANGO	23,566	17,006	6,356	204	10,650 R	72.2%	27.0%	72.8%	27.2%
WARREN	16,150	11,555	4,442	153	7,113 R	71.5%	27.5%	72.2%	27.8%
WASHINGTON	92,036	36,041	55,725	270	19,684 D	39.2%	60.5%	39.3%	60.7%
WAYNE	12,187	9,623	2,530	34	7,093 R	79.0%	20.8%	79.2%	20.8%
WESTMORELAND	139,494	58,923	80,068	503	21,145 D	42.2%	57.4%	42.4%	57.6%
WYOMING	7,623	5,772	1,815	36	3,957 R	75.7%	23.8%	76.1%	23.9%
YORK	84,351	44,489	39,508	354	4,981 R	52.7%	46.8%	53.0%	47.0%
TOTAL	4,580,969	2,415,789	2,146,269	18,911	269,520 R	52.7%	46.9%	53.0%	47.0%

PRESIDENT 1956

County	Total Vote	Republican	Democratic	Other	Rep.-Dem. Plurality	Percentage Total Vote Rep.	Dem.	Major Vote Rep.	Dem.
VENANGO	22,715	17,107	5,594	14	11,513 R	75.3%	24.6%	75.4%	24.6%
WARREN	16,651	12,145	4,463	43	7,682 R	72.9%	26.8%	73.1%	26.9%
WASHINGTON	87,615	39,465	48,052	98	8,587 D	45.0%	54.8%	45.1%	54.9%
WAYNE	12,768	9,658	3,092	18	6,566 R	75.6%	24.2%	75.7%	24.3%
WESTMORELAND	139,388	66,580	72,616	192	6,036 D	47.8%	52.1%	47.8%	52.2%
WYOMING	8,029	5,906	2,120	3	3,786 R	73.6%	26.4%	73.6%	26.4%
YORK	87,068	48,176	38,743	149	9,433 R	55.3%	44.5%	55.4%	44.6%
TOTAL	4,576,503	2,585,252	1,981,769	9,482	603,483 R	56.5%	43.3%	56.6%	43.4%

PENNSYLVANIA

PRESIDENT 1960

County	Total Vote	Republican	Democratic	Other	Rep-Dem Plurality	Total Vote Rep.	Total Vote Dem.	Major Vote Rep.	Major Vote Dem.
ADAMS	20,854	12,933	7,895	26	5,038 R	62.0%	37.9%	62.1%	37.9%
ALLEGHENY	750,718	320,970	428,455	1,293	107,485 D	42.8%	57.1%	42.8%	57.2%
ARMSTRONG	34,745	19,883	14,799	63	5,084 R	57.2%	42.6%	57.3%	42.7%
BEAVER	84,190	36,796	47,182	212	10,386 D	43.7%	56.0%	43.8%	56.2%
BEDFORD	18,604	12,542	6,030	32	6,512 R	67.4%	32.4%	67.5%	32.5%
BERKS	112,706	61,743	50,572	391	11,171 R	54.8%	44.9%	55.0%	45.0%
BLAIR	54,809	35,297	19,445	67	15,852 R	64.4%	35.5%	64.5%	35.5%
BRADFORD	23,205	16,252	6,920	33	9,332 R	70.0%	29.8%	70.1%	29.9%
BUCKS	125,116	67,501	57,177	438	10,324 R	54.0%	45.7%	54.1%	45.9%
BUTLER	46,305	28,368	17,805	152	10,543 R	61.2%	38.5%	61.4%	38.6%
CAMBRIA	89,622	37,062	52,409	151	15,347 D	41.4%	58.5%	41.4%	58.6%
CAMERON	3,487	2,129	1,353	5	776 R	61.1%	38.8%	61.1%	38.9%
CARBON	25,032	12,586	12,391	55	195 R	50.3%	49.5%	50.4%	49.6%
CENTRE	27,004	18,357	8,601	46	9,756 R	68.0%	31.9%	68.1%	31.9%
CHESTER	83,373	53,059	30,167	147	22,892 R	63.6%	36.2%	63.8%	36.2%
CLARION	15,847	10,307	5,506	34	4,801 R	65.0%	34.7%	65.2%	34.8%
CLEARFIELD	33,195	18,911	14,212	72	4,599 R	57.0%	42.8%	57.1%	42.9%
CLINTON	15,161	9,184	5,965	12	3,219 R	60.6%	39.3%	60.6%	39.4%
COLUMBIA	24,651	15,350	9,322	19	5,988 R	62.1%	37.8%	62.2%	38.0%
CRAWFORD	30,906	18,754	12,050	102	6,704 R	60.7%	39.0%	60.9%	39.1%
CUMBERLAND	51,801	35,636	15,968	197	19,668 R	68.8%	30.8%	69.1%	30.9%
DAUPHIN	96,115	61,726	33,962	427	27,764 R	64.2%	35.3%	64.5%	35.5%
DELAWARE	260,783	135,672	124,629	482	11,043 R	52.0%	47.8%	52.1%	47.9%
ELK	15,567	7,155	8,398	14	1,243 D	46.0%	53.9%	46.0%	54.0%
ERIE	105,543	51,525	53,723	295	2,198 D	48.8%	50.9%	48.8%	51.0%
FAYETTE	68,861	27,120	41,560	181	14,440 D	39.4%	60.4%	39.5%	60.5%
FOREST	2,332	1,497	828	7	569 R	64.4%	35.5%	64.4%	35.6%
FRANKLIN	34,134	22,010	12,088	36	9,922 R	64.5%	35.4%	64.5%	35.5%
FULTON	4,379	2,698	1,672	9	1,026 R	61.6%	38.2%	61.7%	38.3%
GREENE	17,159	7,498	9,645	16	2,147 D	43.7%	56.2%	43.7%	56.3%
HUNTINGDON	15,864	11,116	4,710	38	6,406 R	70.1%	29.7%	70.2%	29.8%
INDIANA	32,013	18,706	13,174	83	5,532 R	58.6%	41.2%	58.7%	41.3%
JEFFERSON	21,694	13,845	7,811	38	6,034 R	63.8%	36.0%	63.9%	36.1%
JUNIATA	7,431	4,885	2,615	11	2,270 R	64.7%	35.2%	64.8%	35.2%
LACKAWANNA	129,783	49,636	80,098	49	30,462 D	38.2%	61.7%	38.3%	61.7%
LANCASTER	111,889	78,390	33,233	266	45,157 R	70.1%	29.7%	70.2%	29.8%
LAWRENCE	48,064	23,646	24,309	109	663 D	49.2%	50.6%	49.3%	50.7%
LEBANON	37,353	25,525	11,761	67	13,764 R	68.3%	31.5%	68.5%	31.5%
LEHIGH	94,167	54,278	39,640	249	14,638 R	57.6%	42.1%	57.8%	42.2%
LUZERNE	174,271	70,711	102,998	562	32,287 D	40.6%	59.1%	40.7%	59.3%
LYCOMING	48,482	30,083	18,351	48	11,732 R	62.0%	37.9%	62.1%	37.9%
MCKEAN	21,532	13,699	7,767	66	5,932 R	63.6%	36.1%	63.8%	36.2%
MERCER	53,480	29,109	24,243	128	4,866 R	54.4%	45.3%	54.5%	45.4%
MIFFLIN	15,203	10,315	4,816	72	5,499 R	67.8%	31.7%	68.2%	31.8%
MONROE	17,726	11,299	6,312	115	4,987 R	63.7%	35.6%	64.2%	35.8%
MONTGOMERY	235,326	142,796	92,212	318	50,584 R	60.7%	39.2%	60.8%	39.2%
MONTOUR	6,791	4,154	2,629	8	1,525 R	61.2%	38.7%	61.2%	38.8%
NORTHAMPTON	82,306	40,683	41,552	71	869 D	49.4%	50.5%	49.5%	50.5%
NORTHUMBERLAND	49,801	27,568	22,233	40	5,335 R	55.3%	44.6%	55.3%	44.6%
PERRY	11,570	8,134	3,413	23	4,721 R	70.3%	29.5%	70.4%	29.6%
PHILADELPHIA	915,277	291,000	622,544	1,733	331,544 D	31.8%	68.0%	31.9%	68.1%
PIKE	5,683	4,000	1,676	7	2,324 R	70.4%	29.5%	70.5%	29.5%
POTTER	7,830	5,099	2,715	16	2,384 R	65.1%	34.7%	65.3%	34.7%
SCHUYLKILL	88,687	44,187	44,430	70	243 D	49.8%	50.1%	49.9%	50.1%
SNYDER	10,117	8,103	1,998	16	6,105 R	80.1%	19.7%	80.2%	19.8%
SOMERSET	35,335	20,554	14,739	42	5,815 R	58.2%	41.7%	58.2%	41.8%
SULLIVAN	3,284	1,808	1,471	5	337 R	55.1%	44.8%	55.1%	44.9%
SUSQUEHANNA	15,970	10,201	5,760	9	4,441 R	63.9%	36.1%	63.9%	36.1%
TIOGA	15,173	11,082	4,076	15	7,006 R	73.0%	26.9%	73.1%	26.9%
UNION	9,472	7,466	1,993	13	5,473 R	78.8%	21.0%	78.9%	21.1%

PRESIDENT 1964

County	Total Vote	Republican	Democratic	Other	Rep-Dem Plurality	Total Vote Rep.	Total Vote Dem.	Major Vote Rep.	Major Vote Dem.
ADAMS	19,860	8,617	11,148	95	2,531 D	43.4%	56.1%	43.6%	56.4%
ALLEGHENY	719,725	244,707	475,207	2,811	230,500 D	33.6%	66.0%	33.7%	66.3%
ARMSTRONG	31,790	10,618	21,098	74	10,480 D	33.4%	66.4%	33.5%	66.5%
BEAVER	83,993	23,174	50,492	327	37,318 D	27.6%	72.0%	27.7%	72.3%
BEDFORD	17,147	7,968	9,165	14	1,197 D	46.5%	53.4%	46.5%	53.5%
BERKS	110,646	36,726	73,444	476	36,718 D	33.2%	66.4%	33.3%	66.7%
BLAIR	50,531	24,301	26,157	73	1,856 D	48.1%	51.8%	48.2%	51.8%
BRADFORD	21,162	10,454	10,714	14	280 D	49.3%	50.6%	49.3%	50.7%
BUCKS	129,176	50,243	78,287	646	28,044 D	38.9%	60.6%	38.9%	60.9%
BUTLER	44,722	17,360	27,267	95	9,907 D	38.8%	61.0%	38.8%	61.1%
CAMBRIA	81,598	26,281	55,183	134	28,902 D	32.2%	67.6%	32.3%	67.6%
CAMERON	3,285	1,376	1,904	5	528 D	41.9%	58.0%	42.0%	58.0%
CARBON	22,641	7,339	15,416	116	8,107 D	32.0%	67.3%	32.2%	67.8%
CENTRE	26,195	9,481	16,556	158	7,075 D	36.2%	63.2%	36.4%	63.6%
CHESTER	88,610	40,280	47,940	390	7,660 D	45.5%	54.1%	45.7%	54.3%
CLARION	15,389	6,143	9,235	11	3,092 D	39.9%	60.0%	39.9%	60.1%
CLEARFIELD	30,652	11,338	19,211	103	7,873 D	37.0%	62.7%	37.1%	62.9%
CLINTON	14,372	4,298	10,038	36	5,740 D	29.9%	69.8%	30.0%	70.0%
COLUMBIA	22,903	8,982	13,885	36	4,903 D	39.2%	60.6%	39.3%	60.6%
CRAWFORD	28,991	10,664	18,212	115	7,548 D	36.8%	62.8%	36.9%	63.1%
CUMBERLAND	50,525	23,685	26,633	207	2,948 D	46.9%	52.7%	47.1%	52.9%
DAUPHIN	89,431	42,718	46,119	594	3,401 D	47.8%	51.6%	48.1%	51.9%
DELAWARE	259,025	111,189	147,189	717	36,000 D	42.9%	56.8%	43.0%	57.0%
ELK	14,828	4,354	10,455	19	6,101 D	29.4%	70.5%	29.4%	70.6%
ERIE	104,886	31,393	72,944	549	41,551 D	29.9%	69.5%	30.1%	69.9%
FAYETTE	61,558	16,127	45,155	276	29,028 D	26.2%	73.4%	26.3%	73.7%
FOREST	2,154	900	1,249	5	349 D	41.8%	58.0%	41.9%	58.1%
FRANKLIN	32,942	13,525	19,332	85	5,807 D	41.1%	58.7%	41.2%	58.8%
FULTON	3,937	1,747	2,180	10	433 D	44.4%	55.4%	44.5%	55.5%
GREENE	15,327	3,896	11,412	19	7,516 D	25.4%	74.5%	25.5%	74.5%
HUNTINGDON	14,039	6,571	7,435	33	864 D	46.8%	53.0%	46.9%	53.1%
INDIANA	29,320	11,706	17,568	46	5,862 D	39.9%	59.9%	40.0%	60.0%
JEFFERSON	19,261	8,373	10,851	37	2,478 D	43.5%	56.3%	43.6%	56.4%
JUNIATA	7,235	3,087	4,138	10	1,051 D	42.7%	57.2%	42.7%	57.3%
LACKAWANNA	119,540	31,272	88,131	137	56,859 D	26.2%	73.7%	26.2%	73.8%
LANCASTER	105,508	52,243	53,041	224	798 D	49.5%	50.3%	49.6%	50.4%
LAWRENCE	45,207	15,998	29,092	117	13,094 D	35.4%	64.4%	35.5%	64.5%
LEBANON	33,845	17,891	15,882	72	2,009 R	52.9%	46.9%	53.0%	47.0%
LEHIGH	93,093	32,245	60,377	471	28,132 D	34.6%	64.9%	34.8%	65.2%
LUZERNE	152,071	43,895	106,397	1,779	62,502 D	28.9%	70.0%	29.2%	70.8%
LYCOMING	44,945	19,011	25,879	55	6,868 D	42.3%	57.6%	42.4%	57.6%
MCKEAN	19,007	7,948	10,950	109	3,002 D	41.8%	57.6%	41.8%	57.9%
MERCER	50,563	18,153	32,199	211	14,046 D	35.9%	63.7%	36.1%	64.1%
MIFFLIN	14,856	6,006	8,811	39	2,805 D	40.4%	59.3%	40.5%	59.5%
MONROE	17,019	6,281	10,422	116	4,141 D	36.9%	62.4%	37.2%	62.8%
MONTGOMERY	239,075	102,714	135,657	704	32,943 D	43.0%	56.7%	43.1%	56.9%
MONTOUR	6,214	2,527	3,683	4	1,156 D	40.7%	59.3%	40.7%	59.3%
NORTHAMPTON	80,485	21,048	58,818	619	37,770 D	26.2%	73.1%	26.4%	73.6%
NORTHUMBERLAND	45,244	17,046	28,082	116	11,036 D	37.7%	62.0%	37.8%	62.2%
PERRY	11,452	5,364	6,054	34	690 D	46.8%	52.9%	47.0%	53.0%
PHILADELPHIA	913,472	239,733	670,645	3,094	430,912 D	26.2%	73.4%	26.3%	73.7%
PIKE	5,426	2,651	2,753	22	102 D	48.8%	50.7%	49.1%	50.9%
POTTER	6,909	3,232	3,652	25	420 D	46.8%	52.9%	46.9%	53.1%
SCHUYLKILL	77,042	26,386	50,560	96	24,174 D	34.2%	65.6%	34.3%	65.7%
SNYDER	9,416	5,195	4,199	22	996 R	55.2%	44.6%	55.3%	44.7%
SOMERSET	32,814	14,817	17,934	63	3,117 D	45.2%	54.7%	45.2%	54.8%
SULLIVAN	3,038	1,344	1,690	4	346 D	44.2%	55.6%	44.3%	55.7%
SUSQUEHANNA	14,417	6,567	7,838	12	1,271 D	45.6%	54.4%	45.6%	54.4%
TIOGA	14,495	7,064	7,415	16	351 D	48.7%	51.2%	48.8%	51.2%
UNION	9,216	4,944	4,262	10	682 R	53.6%	46.2%	53.7%	46.3%

PENNSYLVANIA

PRESIDENT 1960

County	Total Vote	Republican	Democratic	Other	Rep.-Dem. Plurality	Percentage Total Vote Rep.	Dem.	Major Vote Rep.	Dem.
VENANGO	25,280	17,193	8,064	23	9,129 R	68.0%	31.9%	68.1%	31.9%
WARREN	18,195	11,611	6,525	59	5,086 R	63.8%	35.9%	64.0%	36.0%
WASHINGTON	92,197	38,348	53,729	120	15,381 D	41.6%	58.3%	41.6%	58.4%
WAYNE	13,811	9,360	4,425	26	4,935 R	67.8%	32.0%	67.9%	32.1%
WESTMORELAND	154,840	68,825	85,641	374	16,816 D	44.4%	55.3%	44.6%	55.4%
WYOMING	8,921	6,188	2,726	7	3,462 R	69.4%	30.6%	69.4%	30.6%
YORK	95,479	55,922	39,164	393	16,758 R	58.6%	41.0%	58.8%	41.2%
TOTAL	5,006,541	2,439,956	2,556,282	10,303	116,326 D	48.7%	51.1%	48.8%	51.2%

PRESIDENT 1964

County	Total Vote	Republican	Democratic	Other	Rep.-Dem. Plurality	Percentage Total Vote Rep.	Dem.	Major Vote Rep.	Dem.
VENANGO	23,022	9,873	13,065	84	3,192 D	42.9%	56.8%	43.0%	57.0%
WARREN	16,657	5,965	10,598	94	4,633 D	35.8%	63.6%	36.0%	64.0%
WASHINGTON	87,756	24,127	63,482	147	39,355 D	27.5%	72.3%	27.5%	72.5%
WAYNE	12,328	6,512	5,781	35	731 R	52.8%	46.9%	53.0%	47.0%
WESTMORELAND	149,416	41,493	107,131	792	65,638 D	27.8%	71.7%	27.9%	72.1%
WYOMING	8,144	3,864	4,268	12	404 D	47.4%	52.4%	47.5%	52.5%
YORK	92,872	33,677	58,787	408	25,110 D	36.3%	63.3%	36.4%	63.6%
TOTAL	4,822,690	1,673,657	3,130,954	18,079	1,457,297 D	34.7%	64.9%	34.8%	65.2%

PENNSYLVANIA

OTHER VOTE COMPOSITION:

1920   70,021 Socialist; 42,612 Prohibition; 15,642 Farmer-Labor; 803 Single Tax; 753 Socialist Labor.

1924   307,567 Progressive; 13,035 American; 9,779 Prohibition; 2,735 Communist; 634 Socialist Labor; 296 Commonwealth Land; 131 scattered. The scattered vote is not included in the county-by-county figures; it is reported only as a part of the state-wide total.

1928   18,647 Socialist; 4,726 Communist; 3,875 Prohibition; 382 Socialist Labor; 14 scattered.

1932   91,119 Socialist; 11,319 Prohibition; 5,658 Communist; 725 Jobless; 659 Socialist Labor; 53 scattered. The scattered vote is not included in the county-by-county figures; it is reported only as a part of the state-wide total.

1936   67,467 Union; 14,375 Socialist; 6,691 Prohibition; 4,060 Communist; 1,424 Socialist Labor.

1940   10,967 Socialist; 4,519 Communist; 1,518 Socialist Labor; 827 scattered. The scattered vote is not included in the county-by-county figures; it is reported only as a part of the state-wide total.

1944   11,721 Socialist; 5,750 Prohibition; 1,789 Socialist Labor.

1948   55,161 Progressive; 11,325 Socialist; 10,538 Prohibition; 2,133 Socialist Workers; 1,461 Socialist Labor; 107 scattered.

1952   8,951 Prohibition; 4,222 Progressive; 2,698 Socialist; 1,508 Socialist Workers; 1,377 Socialist Labor; 155 scattered.

1956   7,447 Socialist Labor; 2,035 Socialist Workers.

1960   7,185 Socialist Labor; 2,678 Socialist Workers; 440 scattered.

1964   10,456 Socialist Workers; 5,092 Socialist Labor; 2,531 scattered.

SPECIAL CASES:

1924   Progressive total includes 214,126 Labor and 93,441 Socialist votes. This combined vote was second in several counties.

1928   Communist total includes 2,687 Labor and 2,039 Workers votes.

1964   Schuylkill county figures are unofficial.

RHODE ISLAND

PRESIDENT 1920

County	Total Vote	Republican	Democratic	Other	Rep.-Dem. Plurality	Total Vote Rep.	Total Vote Dem.	Major Vote Rep.	Major Vote Dem.
BRISTOL	5,366	3,692	1,569	105	2,123 R	68.8%	29.2%	70.2%	29.8%
KENT	12,110	8,474	3,394	242	5,080 R	70.0%	28.0%	71.4%	28.6%
NEWPORT	12,146	9,319	2,228	599	7,091 R	76.7%	18.3%	80.7%	19.3%
PROVIDENCE	129,791	77,558	45,859	4,374	33,699 R	61.3%	35.3%	63.4%	36.6%
WASHINGTON	8,568	6,420	2,012	136	4,408 R	74.9%	23.5%	76.1%	23.9%
TOTAL	167,981	107,463	55,062	5,456	52,401 R	64.0%	32.8%	66.1%	33.9%

PRESIDENT 1924

County	Total Vote	Republican	Democratic	Other	Rep.-Dem. Plurality	Total Vote Rep.	Total Vote Dem.	Major Vote Rep.	Major Vote Dem.
BRISTOL	6,729	4,076	2,500	153	1,576 R	60.6%	37.2%	62.0%	38.0%
KENT	16,860	11,100	5,429	331	5,671 R	65.8%	32.2%	67.2%	32.8%
NEWPORT	14,289	9,608	3,975	706	5,633 R	67.2%	27.8%	70.7%	29.3%
PROVIDENCE	161,550	92,464	62,336	6,750	30,128 R	57.2%	38.6%	59.7%	40.3%
WASHINGTON	10,687	8,038	2,366	283	5,672 R	75.2%	22.1%	77.3%	22.7%
TOTAL	210,115	125,286	76,606	8,223	48,680 R	59.6%	36.5%	62.1%	37.9%

RHODE ISLAND

PRESIDENT 1928

County	Total Vote	Republican	Democratic	Other	Rep.-Dem. Plurality	Total Vote Rep.	Total Vote Dem.	Major Vote Rep.	Major Vote Dem.
BRISTOL	7,873	3,780	4,080	13	300 D	48.0%	51.8%	48.1%	51.9%
KENT	19,005	11,487	7,460	58	4,027 R	60.4%	39.3%	60.6%	39.4%
NEWPORT	15,359	8,578	6,748	33	1,830 R	55.8%	43.9%	56.0%	44.0%
PROVIDENCE	183,637	85,884	97,185	568	11,301 D	46.8%	52.9%	46.9%	53.1%
WASHINGTON	11,320	7,793	3,500	27	4,293 R	68.8%	30.9%	69.0%	31.0%
TOTAL	237,194	117,522	118,973	699	1,451 D	49.5%	50.2%	49.7%	50.3%

PRESIDENT 1932

County	Total Vote	Republican	Democratic	Other	Rep.-Dem. Plurality	Total Vote Rep.	Total Vote Dem.	Major Vote Rep.	Major Vote Dem.
BRISTOL	8,703	3,833	4,775	95	942 D	44.0%	54.9%	44.5%	55.5%
KENT	21,780	11,096	10,398	286	698 R	50.9%	47.7%	51.6%	48.4%
NEWPORT	16,636	8,633	7,838	165	795 R	51.9%	47.1%	52.4%	47.6%
PROVIDENCE	206,544	84,397	118,546	3,601	34,149 D	40.9%	57.4%	41.6%	58.4%
WASHINGTON	12,507	7,307	5,047	153	2,260 R	58.4%	40.4%	59.1%	40.9%
TOTAL	266,170	115,266	146,604	4,300	31,338 D	43.3%	55.1%	44.0%	56.0%

RHODE ISLAND

PRESIDENT 1936

County	Total Vote	Republican	Democratic	Other	Rep.-Dem. Plurality	Total Vote Rep.	Total Vote Dem.	Major Vote Rep.	Major Vote Dem.
BRISTOL	10,662	4,867	5,327	468	460 D	45.6%	50.0%	47.7%	52.3%
KENT	28,019	13,550	13,238	1,231	312 R	48.4%	47.2%	50.6%	49.4%
NEWPORT	19,361	9,358	9,499	504	141 D	48.3%	49.1%	49.6%	50.4%
PROVIDENCE	238,080	88,492	131,218	18,370	42,726 D	37.2%	55.1%	40.3%	59.7%
WASHINGTON	14,156	8,764	5,056	336	3,708 R	61.9%	35.7%	63.4%	36.6%
TOTAL	310,278	125,031	164,338	20,909	39,307 D	40.3%	53.0%	43.2%	56.8%

PRESIDENT 1940

County	Total Vote	Republican	Democratic	Other	Rep.-Dem. Plurality	Total Vote Rep.	Total Vote Dem.	Major Vote Rep.	Major Vote Dem.
BRISTOL	11,284	5,314	5,967	3	653 D	47.1%	52.9%	47.1%	52.9%
KENT	29,151	14,790	14,333	28	457 R	50.7%	49.2%	50.8%	49.2%
NEWPORT	20,541	9,882	10,645	14	763 D	48.1%	51.8%	48.1%	51.9%
PROVIDENCE	244,925	99,435	145,235	255	45,800 D	40.6%	59.3%	40.6%	59.4%
WASHINGTON	15,251	9,233	6,001	17	3,232 R	60.5%	39.3%	60.6%	39.4%
TOTAL	321,152	138,654	182,181	317	43,527 D	43.2%	56.7%	43.2%	56.8%

RHODE ISLAND

PRESIDENT 1944

County	Total Vote	Republican	Democratic	Other	Rep.-Dem. Plurality	Total Vote Rep.	Total Vote Dem.	Major Vote Rep.	Major Vote Dem.
BRISTOL	11,222	4,919	6,287	16	1,368 D	43.8%	56.0%	43.9%	56.1%
KENT	27,826	13,710	14,059	57	349 D	49.3%	50.5%	49.4%	50.6%
NEWPORT	20,831	9,435	11,375	21	1,940 D	45.3%	54.6%	45.3%	54.7%
PROVIDENCE	224,727	87,190	137,216	321	50,026 D	38.8%	61.1%	38.9%	61.1%
WASHINGTON	14,670	8,233	6,419	18	1,814 R	56.1%	43.8%	56.2%	43.8%
TOTAL	299,276	123,487	175,356	433	51,869 D	41.3%	58.6%	41.3%	58.7%

PRESIDENT 1948

County	Total Vote	Republican	Democratic	Other	Rep.-Dem. Plurality	Total Vote Rep.	Total Vote Dem.	Major Vote Rep.	Major Vote Dem.
BRISTOL	12,982	5,343	7,562	77	2,219 D	41.2%	58.2%	41.4%	58.6%
KENT	31,785	16,299	15,287	199	1,012 R	51.3%	48.1%	51.6%	48.4%
NEWPORT	20,146	10,756	9,254	136	1,502 R	53.4%	45.9%	53.8%	46.2%
PROVIDENCE	245,748	93,867	149,254	2,627	55,387 D	38.2%	60.7%	38.6%	61.4%
WASHINGTON	17,041	9,522	7,379	140	2,143 R	55.9%	43.3%	56.3%	43.7%
TOTAL	327,702	135,787	188,736	3,179	52,949 D	41.4%	57.6%	41.8%	58.2%

RHODE ISLAND

PRESIDENT 1952

County	Total Vote	Republican	Democratic	Other	Rep.-Dem. Plurality	Total Vote Rep.	Total Vote Dem.	Major Vote Rep.	Major Vote Dem.
BRISTOL	16,789	8,468	8,313	8	155 R	50.4%	49.5%	50.5%	49.5%
KENT	45,593	27,745	17,824	24	9,921 R	60.9%	39.1%	60.9%	39.1%
NEWPORT	26,262	15,136	11,116	10	4,020 R	57.6%	42.3%	57.7%	42.3%
PROVIDENCE	304,008	146,197	157,592	219	11,395 D	48.1%	51.8%	48.1%	51.9%
WASHINGTON	21,846	13,389	8,448	9	4,941 R	61.3%	38.7%	61.3%	38.7%
TOTAL	414,498	210,935	203,293	270	7,642 R	50.9%	49.0%	50.9%	49.1%

PRESIDENT 1956

County	Total Vote	Republican	Democratic	Other	Rep.-Dem. Plurality	Total Vote Rep.	Total Vote Dem.	Major Vote Rep.	Major Vote Dem.
BRISTOL	16,818	10,070	6,748		3,322 R	59.9%	40.1%	59.9%	40.1%
KENT	47,846	31,548	16,298		15,250 R	65.9%	34.1%	65.9%	34.1%
NEWPORT	25,496	16,063	9,433		6,630 R	63.0%	37.0%	63.0%	37.0%
PROVIDENCE	275,721	153,860	121,861		31,999 R	55.8%	44.2%	55.8%	44.2%
WASHINGTON	21,728	14,278	7,450		6,828 R	65.7%	34.3%	65.7%	34.3%
TOTAL	387,609	225,819	161,790		64,029 R	58.3%	41.7%	58.3%	41.7%

RHODE ISLAND

PRESIDENT 1960

County	Total Vote	Republican	Democratic	Other	Rep.-Dem. Plurality	Total Vote Rep.	Total Vote Dem.	Major Vote Rep.	Major Vote Dem.
BRISTOL	18,636	7,537	11,099		3,562 D	40.4%	59.6%	40.4%	59.6%
KENT	55,006	24,344	30,662		6,318 D	44.3%	55.7%	44.3%	55.7%
NEWPORT	27,619	11,942	15,677		3,735 D	43.2%	56.8%	43.2%	56.8%
PROVIDENCE	280,043	91,028	189,014	1	97,986 D	32.5%	67.5%	32.5%	67.5%
WASHINGTON	24,231	12,651	11,580		1,071 R	52.2%	47.8%	52.2%	47.8%
TOTAL	405,535	147,502	258,032	1	110,530 D	36.4%	63.6%	36.4%	63.6%

PRESIDENT 1964

County	Total Vote	Republican	Democratic	Other	Rep.-Dem. Plurality	Total Vote Rep.	Total Vote Dem.	Major Vote Rep.	Major Vote Dem.
BRISTOL	18,772	4,466	14,306		9,840 D	23.8%	76.2%	23.8%	76.2%
KENT	56,773	12,297	44,476		32,179 D	21.7%	78.3%	21.7%	78.3%
NEWPORT	27,371	7,286	20,085		12,799 D	26.6%	73.4%	26.6%	73.4%
PROVIDENCE	262,910	43,432	219,465	13	176,033 D	16.5%	83.5%	16.5%	83.5%
WASHINGTON	24,265	7,134	17,131		9,997 D	29.4%	70.6%	29.4%	70.6%
TOTAL	390,091	74,615	315,463	13	240,848 D	19.1%	80.9%	19.1%	80.9%

RHODE ISLAND

OTHER VOTE COMPOSITION:

1920   4,351 Socialist; 510 Prohibition; 495 Socialist Labor; 100 Single Tax.

1924   7,628 Progressive; 289 Communist; 268 Socialist Labor; 38 Commonwealth Land.

1928   416 Socialist Labor; 283 Communist.

1932   3,138 Socialist; 546 Communist; 433 Socialist Labor; 183 Prohibition.

1936   19,569 Union; 929 Socialist Labor; 411 Communist.

1940   243 Communist; 74 Prohibition.

1944   Prohibition.

1948   2,619 Progressive; 429 Socialist; 131 Socialist Labor.

1952   187 Progressive; 83 Socialist Labor.

1956

1960   Scattered.

1964   Scattered.

SOUTH CAROLINA

PRESIDENT 1920

County	Total Vote	Republican	Democratic	Other	Rep.-Dem. Plurality	Total Vote Rep.	Total Vote Dem.	Major Vote Rep.	Major Vote Dem.
ABBEVILLE	881	13	868		855 D	1.5%	98.5%	1.5%	98.5%
AIKEN	1,713	64	1,649		1,585 D	3.7%	96.3%	3.7%	96.3%
ALLENDALE	451	11	440		429 D	2.4%	97.6%	2.4%	97.6%
ANDERSON	2,522	33	2,489		2,456 D	1.3%	98.7%	1.3%	98.7%
BAMBERG	688		688		688 D		100.0%		100.0%
BARNWELL	746	25	721		696 D	3.4%	96.6%	3.4%	96.6%
BEAUFORT	414	149	265		116 D	36.0%	64.0%	36.0%	64.0%
BERKELEY	572	24	548		524 D	4.2%	95.8%	4.2%	95.8%
CALHOUN	672	41	631		590 D	6.1%	93.9%	6.1%	93.9%
CHARLESTON	3,302	373	2,929		2,556 D	11.3%	88.7%	11.3%	88.7%
CHEROKEE	1,819	48	1,771		1,723 D	2.6%	97.4%	2.6%	97.4%
CHESTER	1,259	22	1,237		1,215 D	1.7%	98.3%	1.7%	98.3%
CHESTERFIELD	2,080	14	2,066		2,052 D	0.7%	99.3%	0.7%	99.3%
CLARENDON	902		902		902 D		100.0%		100.0%
COLLETON	1,005	15	990		975 D	1.5%	98.5%	1.5%	98.5%
DARLINGTON	1,280	18	1,262		1,244 D	1.4%	98.6%	1.4%	98.6%
DILLON	1,008	5	1,003		998 D	0.5%	99.5%	0.5%	99.5%
DORCHESTER	932	58	874		816 D	6.2%	93.8%	6.2%	93.8%
EDGEFIELD	976		976		976 D		100.0%		100.0%
FAIRFIELD	752	15	737		722 D	2.0%	98.0%	2.0%	98.0%
FLORENCE	1,842	79	1,763		1,684 D	4.3%	95.7%	4.3%	95.7%
GEORGETOWN	283	38	245		207 D	13.4%	86.6%	13.4%	86.6%
GREENVILLE	4,553	144	4,409		4,265 D	3.2%	96.8%	3.2%	96.8%
GREENWOOD	1,583	15	1,568		1,553 D	0.9%	99.1%	0.9%	99.1%
HAMPTON	623		623		623 D		100.0%		100.0%
HORRY	1,758	49	1,709		1,660 D	2.8%	97.2%	2.8%	97.2%
JASPER	219		219		219 D		100.0%		100.0%
KERSHAW	1,198	42	1,156		1,114 D	3.5%	96.5%	3.5%	96.5%
LANCASTER	1,643	10	1,633		1,623 D	0.6%	99.4%	0.6%	99.4%
LAURENS	2,298	35	2,263		2,228 D	1.5%	98.5%	1.5%	98.5%
LEE	752	18	734		716 D	2.4%	97.6%	2.4%	97.6%
LEXINGTON	1,872	59	1,813		1,754 D	3.2%	96.8%	3.2%	96.8%
MCCORMICK	557	1	556		555 D	0.1%	99.9%	0.1%	99.9%
MARION	809	1	808		807 D	0.1%	99.9%	0.1%	99.9%
MARLBORO	965	5	960		955 D	0.5%	99.5%	0.5%	99.5%
NEWBERRY	2,048	33	2,015		1,982 D	1.6%	98.4%	1.6%	98.4%
OCONEE	1,319	70	1,249		1,179 D	5.3%	94.7%	5.3%	94.7%
ORANGEBURG	2,810	284	2,526		2,242 D	10.1%	89.9%	10.1%	89.9%
PICKENS	1,018	63	955		892 D	6.2%	93.8%	6.2%	93.8%
RICHLAND	2,729	295	2,434		2,139 D	10.8%	89.2%	10.8%	89.2%
SALUDA	1,114	3	1,111		1,108 D	0.3%	99.7%	0.3%	99.7%
SPARTANBURG	4,766	182	4,584		4,402 D	3.8%	96.2%	3.8%	96.2%
SUMTER	1,344	194	1,150		956 D	14.4%	85.6%	14.4%	85.6%
UNION	2,178	16	2,162		2,146 D	0.7%	99.3%	0.7%	99.3%
WILLIAMSBURG	907	12	895		883 D	1.3%	98.7%	1.3%	98.7%
YORK	1,618	35	1,583		1,548 D	2.2%	97.8%	2.2%	97.8%
TOTAL	66,808	2,610	64,170	28	61,560 D	3.9%	96.1%	3.9%	96.1%

PRESIDENT 1924

County	Total Vote	Republican	Democratic	Other	Rep.-Dem. Plurality	Total Vote Rep.	Total Vote Dem.	Major Vote Rep.	Major Vote Dem.
ABBEVILLE	737	19	681	37	662 D	2.6%	92.4%	2.7%	97.3%
AIKEN	1,509	16	1,488	5	1,472 D	1.1%	98.6%	1.1%	98.9%
ALLENDALE	464	14	450		436 D	3.0%	97.0%	3.0%	97.0%
ANDERSON	1,467	9	1,455	3	1,446 D	0.6%	99.2%	0.6%	99.4%
BAMBERG	729	7	708	14	701 D	1.0%	97.1%	1.0%	99.0%
BARNWELL	872	23	847	2	824 D	2.6%	97.1%	2.6%	97.4%
BEAUFORT	438	64	365	9	301 D	14.6%	83.3%	14.9%	85.1%
BERKELEY	527	26	501		475 D	4.9%	95.1%	4.9%	95.1%
CALHOUN	599	5	593	1	588 D	0.8%	99.0%	0.8%	99.2%
CHARLESTON	3,023	361	2,554	108	2,193 D	11.9%	84.5%	12.4%	87.6%
CHEROKEE	1,216	24	1,186	6	1,162 D	2.0%	97.5%	2.0%	98.0%
CHESTER	868	12	850	6	838 D	1.4%	97.9%	1.4%	98.6%
CHESTERFIELD	1,551	11	1,539	1	1,528 D	0.7%	99.2%	0.7%	99.3%
CLARENDON	636	20	615	1	595 D	3.1%	96.7%	3.1%	96.9%
COLLETON	813	11	800	2	789 D	1.4%	98.4%	1.4%	98.6%
DARLINGTON	966	3	956	7	953 D	0.3%	99.0%	0.3%	99.7%
DILLON	601	3	598		595 D	0.5%	99.5%	0.5%	99.5%
DORCHESTER	717	20	697		677 D	2.8%	97.2%	2.8%	97.2%
EDGEFIELD	915		915		915 D		100.0%		100.0%
FAIRFIELD	644	11	631	2	620 D	1.7%	98.0%	1.7%	98.3%
FLORENCE	1,301	32	1,217	52	1,185 D	2.5%	93.5%	2.6%	97.4%
GEORGETOWN	160	24	134	2	110 D	15.0%	83.8%	15.2%	84.8%
GREENVILLE	3,829	59	3,728	42	3,669 D	1.5%	97.4%	1.6%	98.4%
GREENWOOD	1,834	15	1,815	4	1,800 D	0.8%	99.0%	0.8%	99.2%
HAMPTON	737	3	730	4	727 D	0.4%	99.1%	0.4%	99.6%
HORRY	1,350	1	1,346	3	1,345 D	0.1%	99.7%	0.1%	99.9%
JASPER	128		89	39	89 D		69.5%		100.0%
KERSHAW	734	1	733		732 D	0.1%	99.9%	0.1%	100.0%
LANCASTER	1,363	8	1,355		1,347 D	0.6%	99.4%	0.6%	99.4%
LAURENS	2,115	6	2,105	4	2,099 D	0.3%	99.5%	0.3%	99.7%
LEE	1,404	7	1,395	2	1,388 D	0.5%	99.4%	0.5%	99.5%
LEXINGTON	551	15	520	16	505 D	2.7%	94.4%	2.8%	97.2%
MCCORMICK	618	2	616		614 D	0.3%	99.7%	0.3%	99.7%
MARION	716		716		716 D		100.0%		100.0%
MARLBORO									
NEWBERRY	1,817	13	1,802	2	1,789 D	0.7%	99.2%	0.7%	99.3%
OCONEE	1,027	5	989	33	984 D	0.5%	96.3%	0.5%	99.5%
ORANGEBURG	1,807	67	1,727	13	1,660 D	3.7%	95.6%	3.7%	96.3%
PICKENS	1,082	35	1,044	3	1,009 D	3.2%	96.5%	3.2%	96.8%
RICHLAND	2,531	88	2,369	74	2,281 D	3.5%	93.6%	3.6%	96.3%
SALUDA	1,099	3	1,094	2	1,091 D	0.3%	99.5%	0.3%	99.7%
SPARTANBURG									
SUMTER	1,216	18	1,136	62	1,118 D	1.5%	93.4%	1.6%	98.4%
UNION	1,896	27	1,862	7	1,835 D	1.4%	98.2%	1.4%	98.6%
WILLIAMSBURG	676	4	672		668 D	0.6%	99.4%	0.6%	99.4%
YORK	1,472	31	1,385	56	1,354 D	2.1%	94.1%	2.2%	97.8%
TOTAL	50,755	1,123	49,008	624	47,885 D	2.2%	96.6%	2.2%	97.8%

SOUTH CAROLINA

PRESIDENT 1928

County	Total Vote	Republican	Democratic	Other	Rep.-Dem. Plurality	Total Vote % Rep.	Total Vote % Dem.	Major Vote % Rep.	Major Vote % Dem.
ABBEVILLE	1,085	65	1,020		955 D	6.0%	94.0%	6.0%	94.0%
AIKEN	1,553	242	1,308	3	1,066 D	15.6%	84.2%	15.6%	84.4%
ALLENDALE	840	24	816		792 D	2.9%	97.1%	2.9%	97.1%
ANDERSON	1,841	61	1,780		1,719 D	3.3%	96.7%	3.3%	96.7%
BAMBERG	783	4	779		775 D	0.5%	99.5%	0.5%	99.5%
BARNWELL	1,062	34	1,028		994 D	3.2%	96.8%	3.2%	96.8%
BEAUFORT	541	124	414	3	290 D	22.9%	76.5%	23.0%	77.0%
BERKELEY	318	42	276		234 D	13.2%	86.8%	13.2%	86.8%
CALHOUN	584	7	577		570 D	1.2%	98.8%	1.2%	98.8%
CHARLESTON	6,075	1,759	4,298	18	2,539 D	29.0%	70.7%	29.0%	71.0%
CHEROKEE	1,477	89	1,388		1,299 D	6.0%	94.0%	6.0%	94.0%
CHESTER	1,323	36	1,285	2	1,249 D	2.7%	97.1%	2.7%	97.3%
CHESTERFIELD	1,385	23	1,362		1,339 D	1.7%	98.3%	1.7%	98.3%
CLARENDON	772	10	762		752 D	1.3%	98.7%	1.3%	98.7%
COLLETON	1,145	22	1,122	1	1,100 D	1.9%	98.0%	1.9%	98.1%
DARLINGTON	1,183	48	1,135		1,087 D	4.1%	95.9%	4.1%	95.9%
DILLON	579	21	558		537 D	3.6%	96.4%	3.6%	96.4%
DORCHESTER	1,149	44	1,105		1,061 D	3.8%	96.2%	3.8%	96.2%
EDGEFIELD	1,205	4	1,201		1,197 D	0.3%	99.7%	0.3%	99.7%
FAIRFIELD	875	94	781		687 D	10.7%	89.3%	10.7%	89.3%
FLORENCE	1,765	93	1,672		1,579 D	5.3%	94.7%	5.3%	94.7%
GEORGETOWN	660	74	586		512 D	11.2%	88.8%	11.2%	88.8%
GREENVILLE	4,664	546	4,116	2	3,570 D	11.7%	88.2%	11.7%	88.3%
GREENWOOD	2,959	38	2,921		2,883 D	1.3%	98.7%	1.3%	98.7%
HAMPTON	1,117	19	1,098		1,079 D	1.7%	98.3%	1.7%	98.3%
HORRY	1,251	27	1,224		1,197 D	2.2%	97.8%	2.2%	97.8%
JASPER	107	5	102		97 D	4.7%	95.3%	4.7%	95.3%
KERSHAW	1,288	14	1,274		1,260 D	1.1%	98.9%	1.1%	98.9%
LANCASTER	1,444	8	1,436		1,428 D	0.6%	99.4%	0.6%	99.4%
LAURENS	2,037	44	1,989	4	1,945 D	2.2%	97.6%	2.2%	97.8%
LEE	599	6	593		587 D	1.0%	99.0%	1.0%	99.0%
LEXINGTON	1,289	61	1,228		1,167 D	4.7%	95.3%	4.7%	95.3%
MCCORMICK	636	20	615	1	595 D	3.1%	96.7%	3.1%	96.9%
MARION	733	51	682		631 D	7.0%	93.0%	7.0%	93.0%
MARLBORO	756	27	729		702 D	3.6%	96.4%	3.6%	96.4%
NEWBERRY	2,094	12	2,077	5	2,065 D	0.6%	99.2%	0.6%	99.4%
OCONEE	1,335	70	1,263	2	1,193 D	5.2%	94.6%	5.3%	94.7%
ORANGEBURG	1,637	92	1,545		1,453 D	5.6%	94.4%	5.6%	94.4%
PICKENS	1,302	192	1,110		918 D	14.7%	85.3%	14.7%	85.3%
RICHLAND	3,602	444	3,158		2,714 D	12.3%	87.7%	12.3%	87.7%
SALUDA	801	5	796		791 D	0.6%	99.4%	0.6%	99.4%
SPARTANBURG	4,620	760	3,859	1	3,099 D	16.5%	83.5%	16.5%	83.5%
SUMTER	1,376	174	1,202		1,028 D	12.6%	87.4%	12.6%	87.4%
UNION	2,535	174	2,460	1	2,286 D	2.9%	97.1%	2.9%	97.1%
WILLIAMSBURG	847	22	825		803 D	2.6%	97.4%	2.6%	97.4%
YORK	1,376	227	1,145	4	918 D	16.5%	83.2%	16.5%	83.5%
TOTAL	68,605	5,858	62,700	47	56,842 D	8.5%	91.4%	8.5%	91.5%

PRESIDENT 1932

County	Total Vote	Republican	Democratic	Other	Rep.-Dem. Plurality	Total Vote % Rep.	Total Vote % Dem.	Major Vote % Rep.	Major Vote % Dem.
ABBEVILLE	1,194	9	1,184	1	1,175 D	0.8%	99.2%	0.8%	99.2%
AIKEN	3,393	47	3,346		3,299 D	1.4%	98.6%	1.4%	98.6%
ALLENDALE	1,118	10	1,098		1,098 D	0.9%	99.1%	0.9%	99.1%
ANDERSON	4,097	30	4,067		4,037 D	0.7%	99.3%	0.7%	99.3%
BAMBERG	1,613	15	1,598		1,583 D	0.9%	99.1%	0.9%	99.1%
BARNWELL	1,892	15	1,877		1,862 D	0.8%	99.2%	0.8%	99.2%
BEAUFORT	624	63	555	6	492 D	10.1%	88.9%	10.2%	89.8%
BERKELEY	963	22	941		919 D	2.3%	97.7%	2.3%	97.7%
CALHOUN	704	10	694		684 D	1.4%	98.6%	1.4%	98.6%
CHARLESTON	5,833	451	5,351	31	4,900 D	7.7%	91.7%	7.8%	92.2%
CHEROKEE	2,402	37	2,363	2	2,326 D	1.5%	98.4%	1.5%	98.5%
CHESTER	2,043	23	2,020		1,997 D	1.1%	98.9%	1.1%	98.9%
CHESTERFIELD	2,132	23	2,109		2,086 D	1.1%	98.9%	1.1%	98.9%
CLARENDON	987	25	962		937 D	2.5%	97.5%	2.5%	97.5%
COLLETON	1,914	5	1,908	1	1,903 D	0.3%	99.7%	0.3%	99.7%
DARLINGTON	1,441	31	1,409	1	1,378 D	2.2%	97.8%	2.2%	97.8%
DILLON	1,018	20	998		978 D	2.0%	98.0%	2.0%	98.0%
DORCHESTER	1,438	23	1,412	3	1,389 D	1.6%	98.2%	1.6%	98.4%
EDGEFIELD	1,326	10	1,316		1,306 D	0.8%	99.2%	0.8%	99.2%
FAIRFIELD	914	10	901	3	891 D	1.1%	98.6%	1.1%	98.9%
FLORENCE	3,226	29	3,195	2	3,166 D	0.9%	99.0%	0.9%	99.1%
GEORGETOWN	1,717	33	1,684		1,651 D	1.9%	98.1%	1.9%	98.1%
GREENVILLE	8,058	126	7,930	2	7,804 D	1.6%	98.4%	1.6%	98.4%
GREENWOOD	3,255	15	3,240		3,225 D	0.5%	99.5%	0.5%	99.5%
HAMPTON	1,800	18	1,782		1,764 D	1.0%	99.0%	1.0%	99.0%
HORRY	3,253	29	3,224		3,195 D	0.9%	99.1%	0.9%	99.1%
JASPER	410	11	399		388 D	2.7%	97.3%	2.7%	97.3%
KERSHAW	1,059	8	1,051		1,043 D	0.8%	99.2%	0.8%	99.2%
LANCASTER	3,108	5	3,103		3,098 D	0.2%	99.8%	0.2%	99.8%
LAURENS	2,767	13	2,750	4	2,737 D	0.5%	99.4%	0.5%	99.5%
LEE	752	10	742		732 D	1.3%	98.7%	1.3%	98.7%
LEXINGTON	147	5	141	1	136 D	3.4%	95.9%	3.4%	96.6%
MCCORMICK	535	5	530		525 D	0.9%	99.1%	0.9%	99.1%
MARION	960	12	948		936 D	1.2%	98.8%	1.2%	98.8%
MARLBORO	707	22	685		663 D	3.1%	96.9%	3.1%	96.9%
NEWBERRY	3,151	12	3,139		3,127 D	0.4%	99.6%	0.4%	99.6%
OCONEE	1,818	14	1,803	1	1,789 D	0.8%	99.2%	0.8%	99.2%
ORANGEBURG	2,757	111	2,643	3	2,532 D	4.0%	95.9%	4.0%	96.0%
PICKENS	2,742	57	2,685		2,628 D	2.1%	97.9%	2.1%	97.9%
RICHLAND	4,500	119	4,371	10	4,252 D	2.6%	97.1%	2.7%	97.3%
SALUDA	1,314	7	1,307		1,300 D	0.5%	99.5%	0.5%	99.5%
SPARTANBURG	9,444	227	9,216	1	8,989 D	2.4%	97.6%	2.4%	97.6%
SUMTER	1,876	59	1,809	8	1,750 D	3.1%	96.4%	3.2%	96.8%
UNION	3,147	14	3,131	2	3,117 D	0.4%	99.5%	0.4%	99.6%
WILLIAMSBURG	1,253	9	1,244		1,235 D	0.7%	99.3%	0.7%	99.3%
YORK	3,605	129	3,476		3,347 D	3.6%	96.4%	3.6%	96.4%
TOTAL	104,407	1,978	102,347	82	100,369 D	1.9%	98.0%	1.9%	98.1%

SOUTH CAROLINA

PRESIDENT 1936

County	Total Vote	Republican	Democratic	Other	Rep.-Dem. Plurality	Total Vote Rep.	Total Vote Dem.	Major Vote Rep.	Major Vote Dem.
ABBEVILLE	1,288	23	1,265		1,242 D	1.8%	98.2%	1.8%	98.2%
AIKEN	3,333	35	3,298		3,263 D	1.1%	98.9%	1.1%	98.9%
ALLENDALE	1,239	3	1,236		1,233 D	0.2%	99.8%	0.2%	99.8%
ANDERSON	4,051	26	4,025		3,999 D	0.6%	99.4%	0.6%	99.4%
BAMBERG	1,547	5	1,542		1,537 D	0.3%	99.7%	0.3%	99.7%
BARNWELL	2,159	2	2,157		2,155 D	0.1%	99.9%	0.1%	99.9%
BEAUFORT	544	43	501		458 D	7.9%	92.1%	7.9%	92.1%
BERKELEY	698	8	690		682 D	1.1%	98.9%	1.1%	98.9%
CALHOUN	822	1	821		820 D	0.1%	99.9%	0.1%	99.9%
CHARLESTON	8,432	417	8,015		7,598 D	4.9%	95.1%	4.9%	95.1%
CHEROKEE	2,303	23	2,280		2,257 D	1.0%	99.0%	1.0%	99.0%
CHESTER	2,166	11	2,155		2,144 D	0.5%	99.5%	0.5%	99.5%
CHESTERFIELD	3,210	18	3,192		3,174 D	0.6%	99.4%	0.6%	99.4%
CLARENDON	1,277	17	1,260		1,243 D	1.3%	98.7%	1.3%	98.7%
COLLETON	1,471	8	1,463		1,455 D	0.5%	99.5%	0.5%	99.5%
DARLINGTON	2,007	12	1,995		1,983 D	0.6%	99.4%	0.6%	99.4%
DILLON	1,109	5	1,104		1,099 D	0.5%	99.5%	0.5%	99.5%
DORCHESTER	917	28	889		851 D	3.1%	96.9%	3.1%	96.9%
EDGEFIELD	1,305	1	1,304		1,303 D	0.1%	99.9%	0.1%	99.9%
FAIRFIELD	1,018	13	1,005		992 D	1.3%	98.7%	1.3%	98.7%
FLORENCE	4,219	25	4,194		4,169 D	0.6%	99.4%	0.6%	99.4%
GEORGETOWN	1,334	61	1,273		1,212 D	4.6%	95.4%	4.6%	95.4%
GREENVILLE	8,402	92	8,310		8,218 D	1.1%	98.9%	1.1%	98.9%
GREENWOOD	3,083	19	3,064		3,045 D	0.6%	99.4%	0.6%	99.4%
HAMPTON	1,261	8	1,253		1,245 D	0.6%	99.4%	0.6%	99.4%
HORRY	2,927		2,927		2,927 D		100.0%		100.0%
JASPER	456	4	452		448 D	0.9%	99.1%	0.9%	99.1%
KERSHAW	1,420	20	1,400		1,380 D	1.4%	98.6%	1.4%	98.6%
LANCASTER	2,631		2,631		2,631 D		100.0%		100.0%
LAURENS	3,082	13	3,069		3,056 D	0.4%	99.6%	0.4%	99.6%
LEE	1,050	5	1,045		1,040 D	0.5%	99.5%	0.5%	99.5%
LEXINGTON	2,170	32	2,138		2,106 D	1.5%	98.5%	1.5%	98.5%
MCCORMICK	664	8	656		648 D	1.2%	98.8%	1.2%	98.8%
MARION	1,224	5	1,219		1,214 D	0.4%	99.6%	0.4%	99.6%
MARLBORO	995	7	988		981 D	0.7%	99.3%	0.7%	99.3%
NEWBERRY	2,624	9	2,615		2,606 D	0.3%	99.7%	0.3%	99.7%
OCONEE	2,110	53	2,057		2,004 D	2.5%	97.5%	2.5%	97.5%
ORANGEBURG	3,006	59	2,947		2,888 D	2.0%	98.0%	2.0%	98.0%
PICKENS	2,728	50	2,678		2,628 D	1.8%	98.2%	1.8%	98.2%
RICHLAND	6,880	152	6,728		6,576 D	2.2%	97.8%	2.2%	97.8%
SALUDA	1,334	10	1,324		1,314 D	0.7%	99.3%	0.7%	99.3%
SPARTANBURG	10,912	173	10,739		10,566 D	1.6%	98.4%	1.6%	98.4%
SUMTER	2,120	58	2,062		2,004 D	2.7%	97.3%	2.7%	97.3%
UNION	3,467	9	3,458		3,449 D	0.3%	99.7%	0.3%	99.7%
WILLIAMSBURG	1,290	6	1,284		1,278 D	0.5%	99.5%	0.5%	99.5%
YORK	3,152	69	3,083		3,014 D	2.2%	97.8%	2.2%	97.8%
TOTAL	115,437	1,646	113,791		112,145 D	1.4%	98.6%	1.4%	98.6%

PRESIDENT 1940

County	Republican	Democratic	Other	Rep.-Dem. Plurality	Total Vote	Total Vote Rep.	Total Vote Dem.	Major Vote Rep.	Major Vote Dem.
ABBEVILLE	32	1,007		975 D	1,039	3.1%	96.9%	3.1%	96.9%
AIKEN	89	2,772		2,683 D	2,861	3.1%	96.9%	3.1%	96.9%
ALLENDALE	30	905		875 D	935	3.2%	96.8%	3.2%	96.8%
ANDERSON	86	3,763		3,677 D	3,849	2.2%	97.8%	2.2%	97.8%
BAMBERG	13	904		891 D	917	1.4%	98.6%	1.4%	98.6%
BARNWELL	13	1,845		1,832 D	1,858	0.7%	99.3%	0.7%	99.3%
BEAUFORT	91	582		491 D	673	13.5%	86.5%	13.5%	86.5%
BERKELEY	91	490		399 D	581	15.7%	84.3%	15.7%	84.3%
CALHOUN	3	657		654 D	660	0.5%	99.5%	0.5%	99.5%
CHARLESTON	1,372	8,145		6,773 D	9,517	14.4%	85.6%	14.4%	85.6%
CHEROKEE	36	2,069		2,033 D	2,105	1.7%	98.3%	1.7%	98.3%
CHESTER	35	1,930		1,895 D	1,965	1.8%	98.2%	1.8%	98.2%
CHESTERFIELD	20	2,880		2,860 D	2,900	0.7%	99.3%	0.7%	99.3%
CLARENDON	54	1,154		1,100 D	1,208	4.5%	95.5%	4.5%	95.5%
COLLETON	65	1,197		1,132 D	1,262	5.2%	94.8%	5.2%	94.8%
DARLINGTON	60	1,395		1,335 D	1,455	4.1%	95.9%	4.1%	95.9%
DILLON	25	868		843 D	893	2.8%	97.2%	2.8%	97.2%
DORCHESTER	110	993		883 D	1,103	10.0%	90.0%	10.0%	90.0%
EDGEFIELD	9	1,065		1,056 D	1,074	0.8%	99.2%	0.8%	99.2%
FAIRFIELD	20	848		828 D	868	2.3%	97.7%	2.3%	97.7%
FLORENCE	95	2,597		2,502 D	2,692	3.5%	96.5%	3.5%	96.5%
GEORGETOWN	155	1,503		1,348 D	1,658	9.3%	90.7%	9.3%	90.7%
GREENVILLE	514	8,118		7,604 D	8,632	6.0%	94.0%	6.0%	94.0%
GREENWOOD	39	2,914		2,875 D	2,953	1.3%	98.7%	1.3%	98.7%
HAMPTON	24	1,198		1,174 D	1,222	2.0%	98.0%	2.0%	98.0%
HORRY	164	2,111		1,947 D	2,275	7.2%	92.8%	7.2%	92.8%
JASPER	41	418		377 D	459	8.9%	91.1%	8.9%	91.1%
KERSHAW	20	1,174		1,154 D	1,194	1.7%	98.3%	1.7%	98.3%
LANCASTER	14	3,205		3,191 D	3,219	0.4%	99.6%	0.4%	99.6%
LAURENS	40	2,697		2,657 D	2,737	1.5%	98.5%	1.5%	98.5%
LEE	20	825		805 D	845	2.4%	97.6%	2.4%	97.6%
LEXINGTON	17	1,496		1,479 D	1,513	1.1%	98.9%	1.1%	98.9%
MCCORMICK	11	419		408 D	430	2.6%	97.4%	2.6%	97.4%
MARION	18	716		698 D	734	2.5%	97.5%	2.5%	97.5%
MARLBORO	13	526		513 D	539	2.4%	97.6%	2.4%	97.6%
NEWBERRY	35	1,739		1,704 D	1,774	2.0%	98.0%	2.0%	98.0%
OCONEE	143	1,593		1,450 D	1,736	8.2%	91.8%	8.2%	91.8%
ORANGEBURG	56	2,356		2,300 D	2,412	2.3%	97.7%	2.3%	97.7%
PICKENS	76	2,122		2,046 D	2,198	3.5%	96.5%	3.5%	96.5%
RICHLAND	167	4,781		4,614 D	4,948	3.4%	96.6%	3.4%	96.6%
SALUDA	15	1,115		1,100 D	1,130	1.3%	98.7%	1.3%	98.7%
SPARTANBURG	248	9,119		8,871 D	9,367	2.6%	97.4%	2.6%	97.4%
SUMTER	29	3,662		3,633 D	3,691	0.8%	99.2%	0.8%	99.2%
UNION									
WILLIAMSBURG	34	1,089		1,055 D	1,123	3.0%	97.0%	3.0%	97.0%
YORK	118	2,508		2,390 D	2,626	4.5%	95.5%	4.5%	95.5%
TOTAL	4,360	95,470		91,110 D	99,830	4.4%	95.6%	4.4%	95.6%

SOUTH CAROLINA

PRESIDENT 1944

County	Total Vote	Republican	Democratic	Other	Rep.-Dem. Plurality	% Total Vote Rep.	% Total Vote Dem.	% Major Vote Rep.	% Major Vote Dem.
ABBEVILLE	819	19	789	11	770 D	2.3%	96.3%	2.4%	97.6%
AIKEN	2,633	60	2,403	170	2,343 D	2.3%	91.3%	2.4%	97.6%
ALLENDALE	718	8	678	32	670 D	1.1%	94.4%	1.2%	98.8%
ANDERSON	2,978	89	2,687	202	2,598 D	3.0%	90.2%	3.2%	96.8%
BAMBERG	1,041	106	737	198	631 D	10.2%	70.8%	12.6%	87.4%
BARNWELL	1,506	8	1,482	16	1,474 D	0.5%	98.4%	0.5%	99.5%
BEAUFORT	797	108	594	95	486 D	13.6%	74.5%	15.4%	84.6%
BERKELEY	716	32	521	163	489 D	4.5%	72.8%	5.8%	94.2%
CALHOUN	686	1	602	83	601 D	0.1%	87.8%	0.2%	99.8%
CHARLESTON	8,581	1,184	6,260	1,137	5,076 D	13.8%	73.0%	15.9%	84.1%
CHEROKEE	1,721	68	1,620	33	1,552 D	4.0%	94.1%	4.0%	96.0%
CHESTER	1,625	89	1,441	95	1,352 D	5.5%	88.7%	5.8%	94.2%
CHESTERFIELD	3,262	15	3,222	25	3,207 D	0.5%	98.8%	0.5%	99.5%
CLARENDON	1,289	27	1,053	209	1,026 D	2.1%	81.7%	2.5%	97.5%
COLLETON	1,997	45	1,653	299	1,608 D	2.3%	82.8%	2.7%	97.3%
DARLINGTON	1,978	46	1,808	124	1,762 D	2.3%	91.4%	2.5%	97.5%
DILLON	1,004	27	864	113	837 D	2.7%	86.1%	3.0%	97.0%
DORCHESTER	1,676	65	1,181	430	1,116 D	3.9%	70.5%	5.2%	94.8%
EDGEFIELD	709	3	654	52	651 D	0.4%	92.2%	0.5%	99.5%
FAIRFIELD	863	21	798	44	777 D	2.4%	92.5%	2.6%	97.4%
FLORENCE	3,212	128	2,822	262	2,694 D	4.0%	87.9%	4.3%	95.7%
GEORGETOWN	1,408	52	1,197	159	1,145 D	3.7%	85.0%	4.1%	95.8%
GREENVILLE	8,094	711	7,107	276	6,396 D	8.8%	87.8%	9.1%	90.9%
GREENWOOD	2,686	71	2,381	234	2,310 D	2.6%	88.6%	2.9%	97.1%
HAMPTON	850	3	575	272	572 D	0.4%	67.6%	0.5%	99.5%
HORRY	2,728	137	2,403	188	2,266 D	5.0%	88.1%	5.4%	94.6%
JASPER	454	18	230	206	212 D	4.0%	50.7%	7.3%	92.7%
KERSHAW	1,971	21	1,872	78	1,851 D	1.1%	95.0%	1.1%	98.9%
LANCASTER	2,536	13	2,383	140	2,370 D	0.5%	94.0%	0.5%	99.5%
LAURENS	2,060	38	1,924	98	1,886 D	1.8%	93.4%	1.9%	98.1%
LEE	875	50	764	61	714 D	5.7%	87.3%	6.1%	93.9%
LEXINGTON	2,120	20	1,986	114	1,966 D	0.9%	93.7%	1.0%	99.0%
MCCORMICK	354	1	307	46	306 D	0.3%	86.7%	0.3%	99.7%
MARION	924	9	858	57	849 D	1.0%	92.9%	1.0%	99.0%
MARLBORO	979	34	874	71	840 D	3.5%	89.3%	3.7%	96.3%
NEWBERRY	2,343	70	1,940	333	1,870 D	3.0%	82.8%	3.5%	96.5%
OCONEE	1,498	106	1,316	76	1,210 D	7.1%	87.9%	7.5%	92.5%
ORANGEBURG	2,693	87	2,440	166	2,353 D	3.2%	90.6%	3.4%	96.6%
PICKENS	2,468	211	1,662	595	1,451 D	8.5%	67.3%	11.3%	88.7%
RICHLAND	7,077	140	6,590	347	6,450 D	2.0%	93.1%	2.1%	97.9%
SALUDA	1,080	14	924	142	910 D	1.3%	85.6%	1.5%	98.5%
SPARTANBURG	8,738	402	8,092	244	7,690 D	4.6%	92.6%	4.7%	95.3%
SUMTER	2,401	73	2,111	217	2,038 D	3.0%	87.9%	3.3%	96.7%
UNION	3,152	33	3,041	78	3,008 D	1.0%	96.5%	1.1%	98.9%
WILLIAMSBURG	1,291	27	1,118	146	1,091 D	2.1%	86.6%	2.4%	97.6%
YORK	2,791	127	2,637	27	2,510 D	4.6%	94.5%	4.6%	95.4%
TOTAL	103,382	4,617	90,601	8,164	85,984 D	4.5%	87.6%	4.8%	95.2%

PRESIDENT 1948

County	Total Vote	Republican	Democratic	Other	Rep.-Dem. Plurality	% Total Vote Rep.	% Total Vote Dem.	% Major Vote Rep.	% Major Vote Dem.
ABBEVILLE	1,064	23	254	787	231 D	2.2%	23.9%	8.3%	91.7%
AIKEN	5,299	115	572	4,612	457 D	2.2%	10.8%	16.7%	83.3%
ALLENDALE	1,110	14	55	1,041	41 D	1.3%	5.0%	20.3%	79.7%
ANDERSON	4,028	105	2,581	1,342	2,476 D	2.6%	64.1%	3.9%	96.1%
BAMBERG	1,873	34	124	1,715	90 D	1.8%	6.6%	21.5%	78.5%
BARNWELL	2,064	28	115	1,921	87 D	1.4%	5.6%	19.6%	80.4%
BEAUFORT	1,257	150	253	854	103 D	11.9%	20.1%	37.2%	62.8%
BERKELEY	1,919	58	323	1,538	265 D	3.0%	16.8%	15.2%	84.8%
CALHOUN	881	4	36	841	32 D	0.5%	4.1%	10.0%	90.0%
CHARLESTON	13,893	562	2,660	10,671	2,098 D	4.0%	19.1%	17.4%	82.6%
CHEROKEE	1,758	77	605	1,076	528 D	4.4%	34.4%	11.3%	88.7%
CHESTER	2,012	48	436	1,528	388 D	2.4%	21.7%	9.9%	90.1%
CHESTERFIELD	2,498	31	912	1,555	881 D	1.2%	36.5%	3.3%	96.7%
CLARENDON	1,590	16	107	1,467	91 D	1.0%	6.7%	13.0%	87.0%
COLLETON	2,599	39	223	2,337	184 D	1.5%	8.6%	14.9%	85.1%
DARLINGTON	2,760	104	726	1,930	622 D	3.8%	26.3%	12.5%	87.5%
DILLON	1,800	24	808	968	784 D	1.3%	44.9%	2.9%	97.1%
DORCHESTER	2,950	85	143	2,722	58 D	2.9%	4.8%	37.3%	62.7%
EDGEFIELD	1,830	6	27	1,797	21 D	0.3%	1.5%	18.2%	81.8%
FAIRFIELD	1,349	63	211	1,075	148 D	4.7%	15.6%	23.0%	77.0%
FLORENCE	5,110	192	1,189	3,729	997 D	3.8%	23.3%	13.9%	86.1%
GEORGETOWN	2,470	92	432	1,946	340 D	3.7%	17.5%	17.6%	82.4%
GREENVILLE	9,474	789	2,745	5,940	1,956 D	8.3%	29.0%	22.3%	77.7%
GREENWOOD	3,014	63	440	2,511	377 D	2.1%	14.6%	12.5%	87.5%
HAMPTON	1,622	10	81	1,531	71 D	0.6%	5.0%	11.0%	89.0%
HORRY	3,961	113	503	3,345	390 D	2.9%	12.7%	18.3%	81.7%
JASPER	887	31	141	715	110 D	3.5%	15.9%	18.0%	82.0%
KERSHAW	1,966	49	302	1,615	253 D	2.5%	15.4%	14.0%	86.0%
LANCASTER	2,534	30	855	1,649	825 D	1.2%	33.7%	3.4%	96.6%
LAURENS	2,629	69	513	2,047	444 D	2.6%	19.5%	11.9%	88.1%
LEE	1,333	36	142	1,155	106 D	2.7%	10.7%	20.2%	79.8%
LEXINGTON	2,861	58	566	2,237	508 D	2.0%	19.8%	9.3%	90.7%
MCCORMICK	743		30	713	30 D	0.9%	4.0%	0.9%?	100.0%
MARION	1,534	14	301	1,219	287 D	0.9%	19.6%	4.4%	95.6%
MARLBORO	1,479	41	354	1,084	313 D	2.8%	23.9%	10.4%	89.6%
NEWBERRY	3,161	47	349	2,765	302 D	1.5%	11.0%	11.9%	88.1%
OCONEE	1,957	135	666	1,156	531 D	6.9%	34.0%	16.9%	83.1%
ORANGEBURG	3,763	164	435	3,164	271 D	4.4%	11.6%	27.4%	72.6%
PICKENS	1,944	165	435	1,344	270 D	8.5%	22.4%	27.5%	72.5%
RICHLAND	9,193	670	2,419	6,104	1,749 D	7.3%	26.3%	21.7%	78.3%
SALUDA	1,914	15	187	1,712	172 D	0.8%	9.8%	7.4%	92.6%
SPARTANBURG	12,041	627	6,741	4,673	6,114 D	5.2%	56.0%	8.5%	91.5%
SUMTER	3,477	154	605	2,718	451 D	4.4%	17.4%	20.3%	79.7%
UNION	3,419	46	1,283	2,090	1,237 D	1.3%	37.5%	3.5%	96.5%
WILLIAMSBURG	1,989	23	126	1,840	103 D	1.2%	6.3%	15.4%	84.6%
YORK	3,562	167	1,412	1,983	1,245 D	4.7%	39.6%	10.6%	89.4%
TOTAL	142,571	5,386	34,423	102,762	29,037 D	3.8%	24.1%	13.5%	86.5%

SOUTH CAROLINA

PRESIDENT 1952

County	Total Vote	Republican	Democratic	Other	Rep.-Dem. Plurality	% Total Vote Rep.	% Total Vote Dem.	% Major Vote Rep.	% Major Vote Dem.
ABBEVILLE	3,746	970	2,776		1,806 D	25.9%	74.1%	25.9%	74.1%
AIKEN	8,628	4,282	4,346		64 D	49.6%	50.4%	49.6%	50.4%
ALLENDALE	1,191	751	440		311 R	63.1%	36.9%	63.1%	36.9%
ANDERSON	15,002	3,338	11,664		8,326 D	22.3%	77.7%	22.3%	77.7%
BAMBERG	2,157	1,407	750		657 R	65.2%	34.8%	65.2%	34.8%
BARNWELL	2,255	657	1,598		941 D	29.1%	70.9%	29.1%	70.9%
BEAUFORT	2,705	1,599	1,106		493 R	59.1%	40.9%	59.1%	40.9%
BERKELEY	4,190	2,482	1,708		774 R	59.2%	40.8%	59.2%	40.8%
CALHOUN	1,491	1,107	384		723 R	74.2%	25.8%	74.2%	25.8%
CHARLESTON	30,046	20,087	9,959		10,128 R	66.9%	33.1%	66.9%	33.1%
CHEROKEE	7,074	1,529	5,545		4,016 D	21.6%	78.4%	21.6%	78.4%
CHESTER	5,620	2,777	2,843		66 D	49.4%	50.6%	49.4%	50.6%
CHESTERFIELD	6,444	1,776	4,568		2,892 D	27.6%	72.4%	27.6%	72.4%
CLARENDON	3,026	2,073	953		1,120 R	68.5%	31.5%	68.5%	31.5%
COLLETON	4,665	2,760	1,905		855 R	59.2%	40.8%	59.2%	40.8%
DARLINGTON	9,181	3,463	5,718		2,255 D	37.7%	62.3%	37.7%	62.3%
DILLON	3,051	1,473	1,578		105 D	48.3%	51.7%	48.3%	51.7%
DORCHESTER	3,171	2,319	852		1,467 R	73.1%	26.9%	73.1%	26.9%
EDGEFIELD	2,418	1,665	753		912 R	68.9%	31.1%	68.9%	31.1%
FAIRFIELD	3,197	1,607	1,590		17 R	50.3%	49.7%	50.3%	49.7%
FLORENCE	10,576	5,236	5,340		104 D	49.5%	50.5%	49.5%	50.5%
GEORGETOWN	3,710	2,340	1,370		970 R	63.1%	36.9%	63.1%	36.9%
GREENVILLE	32,606	17,743	14,863		2,880 R	54.4%	45.6%	54.4%	45.6%
GREENWOOD	7,207	3,392	3,815		423 D	47.1%	52.9%	47.1%	52.9%
HAMPTON	2,620	1,833	787		846 R	67.5%	32.5%	67.5%	32.5%
HORRY	8,205	3,716	4,489		773 D	45.3%	54.7%	45.3%	54.7%
JASPER	1,436	800	636		164 R	55.7%	44.3%	55.7%	44.3%
KERSHAW	4,987	2,935	2,052		883 R	58.9%	41.1%	58.9%	41.1%
LANCASTER	8,069	3,080	4,989		1,909 D	38.2%	61.8%	38.2%	61.8%
LAURENS	7,897	3,400	3,697		297 D	47.9%	52.1%	47.9%	52.1%
LEE	2,596	1,669	927		742 R	64.3%	35.7%	64.3%	35.7%
LEXINGTON	7,531	4,018	3,513		505 R	53.4%	46.6%	53.4%	46.6%
MCCORMICK	1,202	577	624	1	47 D	48.0%	51.9%	48.0%	52.0%
MARION	3,923	2,313	1,610		703 R	59.0%	41.0%	59.0%	41.0%
MARLBORO	3,240	1,541	1,699		158 D	47.6%	52.4%	47.6%	52.4%
NEWBERRY	7,544	4,126	3,418		708 R	54.7%	45.3%	54.7%	45.3%
OCONEE	4,854	1,624	3,230		1,606 D	33.5%	66.5%	33.5%	66.5%
ORANGEBURG	7,524	4,695	2,829		1,866 R	62.4%	37.6%	62.4%	37.6%
PICKENS	5,961	3,096	2,865		231 R	51.9%	48.1%	51.9%	48.1%
RICHLAND	24,815	15,925	8,890		7,035 R	64.2%	35.8%	64.2%	35.8%
SALUDA	2,988	1,396	1,592		196 D	46.7%	53.3%	46.7%	53.3%
SPARTANBURG	31,911	10,028	21,883		11,855 D	31.4%	68.6%	31.4%	68.6%
SUMTER	6,740	4,726	2,014		2,712 R	70.1%	29.9%	70.1%	29.9%
UNION	8,015	2,094	5,921		3,827 D	26.1%	73.9%	26.1%	73.9%
WILLIAMSBURG	3,896	2,576	1,320		1,256 R	66.1%	33.9%	66.1%	33.9%
YORK	12,776	5,281	7,495		2,214 D	41.3%	58.7%	41.3%	58.7%
TOTAL	341,087	168,082	173,004	1	4,922 D	49.3%	50.7%	49.3%	50.7%

PRESIDENT 1956

County	Total Vote	Republican	Democratic	Other	Rep.-Dem. Plurality	% Total Vote Rep.	% Total Vote Dem.	% Major Vote Rep.	% Major Vote Dem.
ABBEVILLE	3,581	339	2,985	257	2,646 D	9.5%	83.4%	10.2%	89.8%
AIKEN	12,296	6,195	4,280	1,821	1,915 R	50.4%	34.8%	59.1%	40.9%
ALLENDALE	1,317	262	380	675	118 D	19.9%	28.9%	40.8%	59.2%
ANDERSON	14,771	2,186	11,344	1,241	9,158 D	14.8%	76.8%	16.2%	83.8%
BAMBERG	1,874	326	430	1,118	104 D	17.4%	22.9%	43.1%	56.9%
BARNWELL	3,009	520	1,914	575	1,394 D	17.3%	63.6%	21.4%	78.6%
BEAUFORT	2,777	1,051	710	1,016	341 R	37.8%	25.6%	59.7%	40.3%
BERKELEY	3,736	1,055	902	1,779	153 R	28.2%	24.1%	53.9%	46.1%
CALHOUN	1,180	795	341	44	454 R	67.4%	28.9%	70.0%	30.0%
CHARLESTON	25,073	7,487	4,028	13,558	3,459 R	29.9%	16.1%	65.0%	35.0%
CHEROKEE	4,902	907	3,687	308	2,780 D	18.5%	75.2%	19.7%	80.3%
CHESTER	4,699	1,007	2,951	741	1,944 D	21.4%	62.8%	25.4%	74.6%
CHESTERFIELD	4,988	795	3,559	634	2,764 D	15.9%	71.4%	18.3%	81.7%
CLARENDON	2,672	224	661	1,787	437 D	8.4%	24.7%	25.3%	74.7%
COLLETON	4,046	635	1,463	1,948	828 D	15.7%	36.1%	30.3%	69.7%
DARLINGTON	7,108	1,597	2,908	2,603	1,311 D	22.5%	40.9%	35.4%	64.6%
DILLON	2,984	313	1,879	792	1,566 D	10.5%	63.0%	14.3%	85.7%
DORCHESTER	3,217	504	862	1,851	358 D	15.7%	26.8%	36.9%	63.1%
EDGEFIELD	2,042	516	525	1,001	9 D	25.3%	25.7%	49.6%	50.4%
FAIRFIELD	2,648	519	961	1,168	442 D	19.6%	36.3%	35.1%	64.9%
FLORENCE	9,765	1,855	3,463	4,447	1,608 D	19.0%	35.5%	34.9%	65.1%
GEORGETOWN	4,361	1,057	1,020	2,284	37 R	24.2%	23.4%	50.9%	49.1%
GREENVILLE	27,193	10,752	11,819	4,622	1,067 D	39.5%	43.5%	47.6%	52.4%
GREENWOOD	6,753	1,120	4,386	1,247	3,266 D	16.6%	64.9%	20.3%	79.7%
HAMPTON	2,056	359	564	1,133	205 D	17.5%	27.4%	38.9%	61.1%
HORRY	8,171	1,092	4,835	2,244	3,743 D	13.4%	59.2%	18.4%	81.6%
JASPER	1,271	403	210	658	193 R	31.7%	16.5%	65.7%	34.3%
KERSHAW	5,868	1,558	1,875	2,435	317 D	26.5%	31.9%	45.4%	54.6%
LANCASTER	6,637	1,610	4,398	629	2,788 D	24.3%	66.3%	26.8%	73.2%
LAURENS	6,648	1,377	3,726	1,545	2,349 D	20.7%	56.0%	27.0%	73.0%
LEE	2,465	250	943	1,272	693 D	10.1%	38.3%	21.0%	79.0%
LEXINGTON	5,737	2,188	2,094	1,455	94 R	38.1%	36.5%	51.1%	48.9%
MCCORMICK	869	102	485	282	383 D	11.7%	55.8%	17.4%	82.6%
MARION	3,160	417	1,390	1,353	973 D	13.2%	44.0%	23.1%	76.9%
MARLBORO	2,798	507	1,769	522	1,262 D	18.1%	63.2%	22.3%	77.7%
NEWBERRY	5,130	1,061	2,671	1,398	1,610 D	20.7%	52.1%	28.4%	71.6%
OCONEE	4,797	911	3,510	376	2,599 D	19.0%	73.2%	20.6%	79.4%
ORANGEBURG	6,921	1,467	2,511	2,943	1,044 D	21.2%	36.3%	36.9%	63.1%
PICKENS	4,278	1,747	1,847	684	100 D	40.8%	43.2%	48.6%	51.4%
RICHLAND	22,384	6,714	6,154	9,516	560 R	30.0%	27.5%	52.2%	47.8%
SALUDA	2,286	341	1,080	865	739 D	14.9%	47.2%	24.0%	76.0%
SPARTANBURG	25,683	6,822	16,637	2,124	9,815 D	26.6%	64.8%	29.1%	70.9%
SUMTER	6,034	1,356	937	3,741	419 R	22.5%	15.5%	59.1%	40.9%
UNION	5,688	1,252	3,760	676	2,508 D	22.0%	66.1%	25.0%	75.0%
WILLIAMSBURG	3,752	330	683	2,739	353 D	8.8%	18.2%	32.6%	67.4%
YORK	11,535	3,508	6,835	1,192	3,327 D	30.4%	59.3%	33.9%	66.1%
TOTAL	300,583	75,700	136,372	88,511	60,672 D	25.2%	45.4%	35.7%	64.3%

SOUTH CAROLINA

PRESIDENT 1960

County	Total Vote	Republican	Democratic	Other	Rep.-Dem. Plurality	Total Vote % Rep.	Total Vote % Dem.	Major Vote % Rep.	Major Vote % Dem.
ABBEVILLE	3,909	845	3,064		2,219 D	21.6%	78.4%	21.6%	78.4%
AIKEN	17,389	10,715	6,674		4,041 R	61.6%	38.4%	61.6%	38.4%
ALLENDALE	1,471	888	583		305 R	60.4%	39.6%	60.4%	39.6%
ANDERSON	17,746	3,845	13,901		10,056 D	21.7%	78.3%	21.7%	78.3%
BAMBERG	2,560	1,652	908		744 R	64.5%	35.5%	64.5%	35.5%
BARNWELL	3,173	1,842	1,331		511 R	58.1%	41.9%	58.1%	41.9%
BEAUFORT	3,821	2,021	1,800		221 R	52.9%	47.1%	52.9%	47.1%
BERKELEY	4,964	2,422	2,542		120 D	48.8%	51.2%	48.8%	51.2%
CALHOUN	3,388	852	2,536		316 D...	38.6%	61.4%	38.6%	61.4%
CHARLESTON	33,233	21,223	12,010		9,213 R	63.9%	36.1%	63.9%	36.1%
CHEROKEE	6,956	1,565	5,391		3,826 D	22.5%	77.5%	22.5%	77.5%
CHESTER	5,922	1,660	4,262		2,602 D	28.0%	72.0%	28.0%	72.0%
CHESTERFIELD	5,822	1,372	4,450		3,078 D	23.6%	76.4%	23.6%	76.4%
CLARENDON	2,579	1,445	1,134		311 R	56.0%	44.0%	56.0%	44.0%
COLLETON	4,483	2,521	1,962		559 R	56.2%	43.8%	56.2%	43.8%
DARLINGTON	8,162	3,494	4,668		1,174 D	42.8%	57.2%	42.8%	57.2%
DILLON	4,091	1,439	2,652		1,213 D	35.2%	64.8%	35.2%	64.8%
DORCHESTER	5,882	3,525	2,357		1,168 R	59.9%	40.1%	59.9%	40.1%
EDGEFIELD	2,294	1,448	846		602 R	63.1%	36.9%	63.1%	36.9%
FAIRFIELD	3,182	1,549	1,633		84 D	48.7%	51.3%	48.7%	51.3%
FLORENCE	11,906	5,815	6,090		275 D	48.8%	51.2%	48.8%	51.2%
GEORGETOWN	5,418	2,607	2,811	1	204 D	48.1%	51.9%	48.1%	51.9%
GREENVILLE	36,633	22,657	13,976		8,681 R	61.8%	38.2%	61.8%	38.2%
GREENWOOD	8,251	2,968	5,283		2,315 D	36.0%	64.0%	36.0%	64.0%
HAMPTON	2,112	1,322	790		532 R	62.6%	37.4%	62.6%	37.4%
HORRY	9,774	3,768	6,006		2,238 D	38.6%	61.4%	38.6%	61.4%
JASPER	1,500	779	721		58 R	51.9%	48.1%	51.9%	48.1%
KERSHAW	6,643	3,465	3,178		287 R	52.2%	47.8%	52.2%	47.8%
LANCASTER	8,470	2,909	5,561		2,652 D	34.3%	65.7%	34.3%	65.7%
LAURENS	7,846	3,299	4,547		1,248 D	42.0%	58.0%	42.0%	58.0%
LEE	2,784	1,297	1,487		190 D	46.6%	53.4%	46.6%	53.4%
LEXINGTON	10,670	6,511	4,159		2,352 R	61.0%	39.0%	61.0%	39.0%
MCCORMICK	1,027	347	680		333 D	33.8%	66.2%	33.8%	66.2%
MARION	4,043	1,646	2,397		751 D	40.7%	59.3%	40.7%	59.3%
MARLBORO	3,877	1,291	2,586		1,295 D	33.3%	66.7%	33.3%	66.7%
NEWBERRY	5,984	2,841	3,143		302 D	47.5%	52.5%	47.5%	52.5%
OCONEE	6,214	1,886	4,328		2,442 D	30.4%	69.6%	30.4%	69.6%
ORANGEBURG	9,123	5,233	3,890		1,343 R	57.4%	42.6%	57.4%	42.6%
PICKENS	6,747	4,201	2,546		1,655 R	62.3%	37.7%	62.3%	37.7%
RICHLAND	32,430	20,736	11,694		9,042 R	63.9%	36.1%	63.9%	36.1%
SALUDA	2,621	1,268	1,353		85 D	48.4%	51.6%	48.4%	51.6%
SPARTANBURG	31,074	10,940	20,134		9,194 D	35.2%	64.8%	35.2%	64.8%
SUMTER	7,249	4,633	2,616		2,017 R	63.9%	36.1%	63.9%	36.1%
UNION	7,209	1,980	5,229		3,249 D	27.5%	72.5%	27.5%	72.5%
WILLIAMSBURG	3,837	2,324	1,513		811 R	60.6%	39.4%	60.6%	39.4%
YORK	14,219	5,512	8,707		3,195 D	38.8%	61.2%	38.8%	61.2%
TOTAL	386,688	188,558	198,129	1	9,571 D	48.8%	51.2%	48.8%	51.2%

PRESIDENT 1964

County	Total Vote	Republican	Democratic	Other	Rep.-Dem. Plurality	Total Vote % Rep.	Total Vote % Dem.	Major Vote % Rep.	Major Vote % Dem.
ABBEVILLE	4,137	1,448	2,689		1,241 D	35.0%	65.0%	35.0%	65.0%
AIKEN	25,089	17,467	7,622		9,845 R	69.6%	30.4%	69.6%	30.4%
ALLENDALE	2,512	1,740	772		968 R	69.3%	30.7%	69.3%	30.7%
ANDERSON	20,068	8,398	11,670		3,272 D	41.8%	58.2%	41.8%	58.2%
BAMBERG	3,785	2,366	1,419		947 R	62.5%	37.5%	62.5%	37.5%
BARNWELL	5,052	3,670	1,382		2,288 R	72.6%	27.4%	72.6%	27.4%
BEAUFORT	6,179	3,432	2,747		685 R	55.5%	44.5%	55.5%	44.5%
BERKELEY	9,637	6,100	3,537		2,563 R	63.3%	36.7%	63.3%	36.7%
CALHOUN	2,203	1,591	612		979 R	72.2%	27.8%	72.2%	27.8%
CHARLESTON	47,073	32,509	14,564		17,945 R	69.1%	30.9%	69.1%	30.9%
CHEROKEE	7,885	3,627	4,258		631 D	46.0%	54.0%	46.0%	54.0%
CHESTER	6,797	2,915	3,882		967 D	42.9%	57.1%	42.9%	57.1%
CHESTERFIELD	7,083	2,449	4,634		2,185 D	34.6%	65.4%	34.6%	65.4%
CLARENDON	3,793	2,960	833		2,127 R	78.0%	22.0%	78.0%	22.0%
COLLETON	6,688	4,637	2,051		2,586 R	69.3%	30.7%	69.3%	30.7%
DARLINGTON	11,727	6,717	5,010		1,707 R	57.3%	42.7%	57.3%	42.7%
DILLON	5,515	2,742	2,773		31 D	49.7%	50.3%	49.7%	50.3%
DORCHESTER	6,713	5,109	1,604		3,505 R	76.1%	23.9%	76.1%	23.9%
EDGEFIELD	3,313	2,489	824		1,665 R	75.1%	24.9%	75.1%	24.9%
FAIRFIELD	4,625	1,997	2,628		631 D	43.2%	56.8%	43.2%	56.8%
FLORENCE	17,503	10,346	7,157		3,189 R	59.1%	40.9%	59.1%	40.9%
GEORGETOWN	8,128	4,705	3,423		1,282 R	57.9%	42.1%	57.9%	42.1%
GREENVILLE	46,656	29,358	17,298		12,060 R	62.9%	37.1%	62.9%	37.1%
GREENWOOD	11,132	5,653	5,479		174 R	50.8%	49.2%	50.8%	49.2%
HAMPTON	3,698	2,259	1,439		820 R	61.1%	38.9%	61.1%	38.9%
HORRY	13,737	8,293	5,444		2,849 R	60.4%	39.6%	60.4%	39.6%
JASPER	2,595	1,593	1,002		591 R	61.4%	38.6%	61.4%	38.6%
KERSHAW	8,785	5,617	3,168		2,449 R	63.9%	36.1%	63.9%	36.1%
LANCASTER	9,712	4,742	4,970		228 D	48.8%	51.2%	48.8%	51.2%
LAURENS	9,446	5,081	4,365		716 R	53.8%	46.2%	53.8%	46.2%
LEE	3,645	2,489	1,156		1,333 R	68.3%	31.7%	68.3%	31.7%
LEXINGTON	16,848	12,041	4,807		7,234 R	71.5%	28.5%	71.5%	28.5%
MCCORMICK	1,437	939	498		441 R	65.3%	34.7%	65.3%	34.7%
MARION	5,243	3,197	2,046		1,151 R	61.0%	39.0%	61.0%	39.0%
MARLBORO	4,286	1,864	2,422		558 D	43.5%	56.5%	43.5%	56.5%
NEWBERRY	8,794	5,571	3,222	1	2,349 R	63.4%	36.6%	63.4%	36.6%
OCONEE	8,272	2,712	5,560		2,848 D	32.8%	67.2%	32.8%	67.2%
ORANGEBURG	16,063	10,456	5,607		4,849 R	65.1%	34.9%	65.1%	34.9%
PICKENS	9,391	5,882	3,506	3	2,376 R	62.6%	37.3%	62.7%	37.3%
RICHLAND	45,245	27,306	17,939		9,367 R	60.4%	39.6%	60.4%	39.6%
SALUDA	3,933	2,524	1,409		1,115 R	64.2%	35.8%	64.2%	35.8%
SPARTANBURG	38,445	18,411	20,034		1,623 D	47.9%	52.1%	47.9%	52.1%
SUMTER	11,504	7,729	3,775		3,954 R	67.2%	32.8%	67.2%	32.8%
UNION	7,707	3,815	3,892		77 D	49.5%	50.5%	49.5%	50.5%
WILLIAMSBURG	7,058	4,810	2,248		2,562 R	68.1%	31.9%	68.1%	31.9%
YORK	15,642	7,292	8,346	4	1,054 D	46.6%	53.4%	46.6%	53.4%
TOTAL	524,779	309,048	215,723	8	93,325 R	58.9%	41.1%	58.9%	41.1%

SOUTH CAROLINA

OTHER VOTE COMPOSITION:

1920   Socialist; reported as a state-wide total, not by counties.
1924   623 Progressive; 1 scattered.
1928   Socialist.
1932   Socialist.
1936

1940
1944   7,799 Southern Democratic; 365 Prohibition.
1948   102,607 States Rights; 154 Progressive; 1 Socialist.
1952   Prohibition.
1956   88,509 Independent; 2 States Rights.

1960   Scattered.
1964   Scattered.

SPECIAL CASES:

1920   Republican total includes 2,244 Republican and 366 Insurgent Republican votes.
1924   Progressive candidates ran second in several counties. No returns can-
           vassed for Lee and Spartanburg counties.
1928   Republican total includes 3,188 Republican and 2,670 anti-Smith votes.
1936   Republican total includes 953 Tolbert and 693 Hambright elector ticket votes.
1940   Republican total includes 2,496 Jeffersonian Democratic, 1,727 Republican, and
           137 Tolbert elector ticket votes. No returns canvassed for Sumter County.

1944   Republican total includes 4,554 Republican and 63 Tolbert elector ticket votes.
           Southern Democratic electors ran second in many counties.
1948   States Rights candidates carried the state and all but two counties.
1952   Republican total includes 158,289 Independent and 9,793 Republican votes.
1956   Independent electors carried many counties and ran second in others.

SOUTH DAKOTA

PRESIDENT 1920

County	Total Vote	Republican	Democratic	Other	Rep.-Dem. Plurality	% Total Rep.	% Total Dem.	% Major Rep.	% Major Dem.
ARMSTRONG									
AURORA	2,041	1,004	445	592	559 R	49.2	21.8	69.3	30.7
BEADLE	5,644	2,852	925	1,267	1,927 R	56.5	18.3	75.5	24.5
BENNETT	452	220	199	33	21 R	48.7	44.0	52.5	47.5
BON HOMME	3,517	1,872	960	685	912 R	53.2	27.3	66.1	33.9
BROOKINGS	3,996	2,743	564	689	2,179 R	68.6	14.1	82.9	17.1
BROWN	9,881	5,581	1,364	2,926	4,217 R	56.5	13.8	80.4	19.6
BRULE	2,030	1,036	671	323	365 R	51.0	33.1	60.7	39.3
BUFFALO	335	200	101	34	99 R	59.7	30.1	66.4	33.6
BUTTE	3,159	1,722	672	765	1,050 R	54.5	21.3	71.9	28.1
CAMPBELL	1,583	1,128	67	388	1,061 R	71.3	4.2	94.4	5.6
CHARLES MIX	4,028	2,021	1,305	702	716 R	50.2	32.4	60.8	39.2
CLARK	2,910	1,753	437	720	1,316 R	60.2	15.0	80.0	20.0
CLAY	3,046	1,885	907	254	978 R	61.9	29.8	67.5	32.5
CODINGTON	4,522	2,706	867	949	1,839 R	59.8	19.2	75.7	24.3
CORSON	2,378	1,448	484	446	964 R	60.9	20.4	74.9	25.1
CUSTER	1,289	784	383	122	401 R	60.8	29.7	67.2	32.8
DAVISON	4,810	2,605	1,105	1,100	1,500 R	54.2	23.0	70.2	29.8
DAY	4,579	2,739	436	1,404	2,303 R	59.8	9.5	86.3	13.7
DEUEL	2,243	1,569	159	515	1,410 R	70.0	7.1	90.8	9.2
DEWEY	1,390	880	335	175	545 R	63.3	24.1	72.4	27.6
DOUGLAS	1,964	1,247	386	331	861 R	63.5	19.7	76.4	23.6
EDMUNDS	2,462	1,486	283	693	1,203 R	60.4	11.5	84.0	16.0
FALL RIVER	2,026	1,236	680	110	556 R	61.0	33.6	64.5	35.5
FAULK	2,047	1,341	346	360	995 R	65.5	16.9	79.5	20.5
GRANT	3,022	1,813	350	859	1,463 R	60.0	11.6	83.8	16.2
GREGORY	3,182	1,833	744	605	1,089 R	57.6	23.4	71.1	28.9
HAAKON	1,486	713	393	330	320 R	49.7	27.4	64.5	35.5
HAMLIN	2,076	1,322	337	417	985 R	63.7	16.2	79.7	20.3
HAND	2,474	1,511	655	308	856 R	61.1	26.5	69.8	30.2
HANSON	1,930	1,001	418	511	583 R	51.9	21.7	70.5	29.5
HARDING	1,109	648	213	248	435 R	58.4	19.2	75.3	24.7
HUGHES	1,622	1,313	433	176	880 R	58.3	22.5	75.2	24.8
HUTCHINSON	3,662	1,873	243	1,546	1,630 R	51.1	6.6	88.5	11.5
HYDE	1,036	710	233	93	477 R	68.5	22.5	75.3	24.7
JACKSON	843	595	206	42	389 R	70.6	24.4	74.3	25.7
JERAULD	1,820	1,038	357	425	681 R	57.0	19.6	74.4	25.6
JONES	977	609	255	113	354 R	62.3	14.7	70.5	29.5
KINGSBURY	3,271	2,344	481	446	1,863 R	71.7	14.7	83.0	17.0
LAKE	3,334	2,333	398	603	1,935 R	70.0	11.9	85.4	14.6
LAWRENCE	4,359	2,986	1,201	172	1,785 R	68.5	27.6	71.3	28.7
LINCOLN	3,794	2,790	441	563	2,349 R	73.5	11.6	86.4	13.6
LYMAN	1,761	1,050	463	248	587 R	59.6	26.3	69.4	30.6
MCCOOK	3,080	1,864	565	651	1,299 R	60.5	18.3	76.7	23.3
MCPHERSON	2,016	1,470	112	434	1,358 R	72.9	5.6	92.9	7.1
MARSHALL	2,782	1,557	266	959	1,291 R	56.0	9.6	85.4	14.6
MEADE	3,245	1,894	894	457	1,000 R	58.4	27.6	67.9	32.1
MELLETTE	839	533	261	45	272 R	63.5	31.1	67.1	32.9
MINER	2,556	1,450	651	455	799 R	56.7	25.5	69.0	31.0
MINNEHAHA	13,127	8,290	2,534	2,303	5,756 R	63.2	19.3	76.6	23.4
MOODY	2,623	1,667	371	585	1,296 R	63.6	14.1	81.8	18.2
PENNINGTON	3,998	2,568	1,205	225	1,363 R	64.2	30.1	68.1	31.9
PERKINS	2,195	1,326	417	452	909 R	60.4	19.0	76.1	23.9
POTTER	1,484	1,073	255	156	818 R	72.3	17.2	80.8	19.2
ROBERTS	4,695	2,335	447	1,913	1,888 R	49.7	9.5	83.9	16.1
SANBORN	2,255	1,125	517	613	608 R	49.9	22.9	68.5	31.5
SHANNON									
SPINK	4,491	2,923	785	783	2,138 R	65.1	17.5	78.8	21.2
STANLEY	1,053	598	394	61	204 R	56.8	37.4	60.3	39.7
SULLY	861	542	147	172	395 R	63.0	17.1	78.7	21.3

PRESIDENT 1924

County	Total Vote	Republican	Democratic	Other	Rep.-Dem. Plurality	% Total Rep.	% Total Dem.	% Major Rep.	% Major Dem.
ARMSTRONG									
AURORA	2,663	967	665	1,031	302 R	36.3	25.0	59.3	40.7
BEADLE	6,494	3,466	851	2,177	2,615 R	53.4	13.1	80.3	19.7
BENNETT	778	444	102	232	342 R	57.1	13.1	81.3	18.7
BON HOMME	3,398	1,420	860	1,118	560 R	41.8	25.3	62.3	37.7
BROOKINGS	4,516	2,740	361	1,415	2,379 R	60.7	8.0	88.4	11.6
BROWN	9,705	4,708	1,010	3,987	3,698 R	48.5	10.4	82.3	17.7
BRULE	2,856	1,060	650	1,146	410 R	37.1	22.8	62.0	38.0
BUFFALO	744	309	225	210	84 R	41.5	30.2	57.9	42.1
BUTTE	2,157	1,199	277	681	922 R	55.6	12.8	81.2	18.8
CAMPBELL	1,175	641	46	488	595 R	54.6	3.9	93.3	6.7
CHARLES MIX	5,382	1,680	1,306	2,396	374 R	31.2	24.3	56.3	43.7
CLARK	2,962	1,684	325	953	1,359 R	56.9	11.0	83.8	16.2
CLAY	3,345	1,415	492	1,438	923 R	42.3	14.7	74.2	25.8
CODINGTON	4,500	1,862	627	2,011	1,235 R	41.4	13.9	74.8	25.2
CORSON	2,414	1,364	140	910	1,224 R	56.5	5.8	90.7	9.3
CUSTER	1,561	833	236	492	597 R	53.4	15.1	77.9	22.1
DAVISON	5,417	2,801	578	2,038	2,223 R	51.7	10.7	82.9	17.1
DAY	3,975	2,194	308	1,473	1,886 R	55.2	7.7	87.7	12.3
DEUEL	2,258	1,362	168	728	1,194 R	60.3	7.4	89.0	11.0
DEWEY	1,802	956	222	624	734 R	53.1	12.3	81.2	18.8
DOUGLAS	2,241	1,125	317	799	808 R	50.2	14.1	78.0	22.0
EDMUNDS	2,460	1,043	277	1,140	766 R	42.4	11.3	79.0	21.0
FALL RIVER	2,670	1,392	342	936	1,050 R	52.4	12.8	80.3	19.7
FAULK	1,983	1,112	277	594	835 R	56.1	14.0	80.1	19.9
GRANT	2,920	1,227	202	1,491	1,025 R	42.0	6.9	85.9	14.1
GREGORY	3,683	1,643	818	1,222	825 R	44.6	22.2	66.8	33.2
HAAKON	1,598	797	319	482	478 R	49.9	20.0	71.4	28.6
HAMLIN	2,184	1,144	207	833	937 R	52.4	9.5	84.7	15.3
HAND	3,198	1,727	690	781	1,037 R	54.0	21.6	71.5	28.5
HANSON	2,004	811	299	894	512 R	40.5	14.9	73.1	26.9
HARDING	1,131	702	107	322	595 R	62.1	9.5	86.8	13.2
HUGHES	2,368	1,260	325	783	935 R	53.2	13.7	79.5	20.5
HUTCHINSON	3,623	893	180	2,550	713 R	24.6	5.0	83.2	16.8
HYDE	1,324	669	257	398	412 R	50.5	19.4	72.2	27.8
JACKSON	1,024	583	194	247	389 R	56.9	18.9	75.0	25.0
JERAULD	1,993	1,054	228	711	826 R	52.9	11.4	82.2	17.8
JONES	1,320	732	141	447	591 R	55.5	10.7	83.8	16.2
KINGSBURY	3,415	2,242	333	840	1,909 R	65.5	9.8	87.1	12.9
LAKE	4,163	1,888	297	1,978	1,591 R	45.4	7.1	86.4	13.6
LAWRENCE	4,580	3,255	649	676	2,606 R	71.1	14.2	83.4	16.6
LINCOLN	4,166	1,825	265	2,076	1,560 R	43.8	6.4	87.3	26.7
LYMAN	2,395	1,061	387	947	674 R	44.3	16.2	73.3	26.7
MCCOOK	3,090	1,368	457	1,265	911 R	44.3	14.8	75.0	25.0
MCPHERSON	2,889	833	94	1,962	739 R	28.8	3.3	89.9	10.1
MARSHALL	2,466	1,271	190	1,005	1,081 R	51.5	7.7	87.0	13.0
MEADE	3,493	2,006	786	701	1,220 R	57.4	22.5	71.8	28.2
MELLETTE	1,608	642	604	362	38 R	39.6	37.6	51.5	48.5
MINER	2,791	995	308	1,488	687 R	35.7	11.0	76.4	23.6
MINNEHAHA	15,773	8,822	1,524	5,427	7,298 R	55.9	9.7	85.3	14.7
MOODY	2,833	1,181	234	1,418	947 R	41.7	8.3	83.5	16.5
PENNINGTON	5,035	3,201	854	980	2,347 R	63.6	17.0	78.9	21.1
PERKINS	2,400	1,421	277	702	1,144 R	59.2	11.5	83.7	16.3
POTTER	1,797	1,075	283	439	792 R	59.8	15.7	79.2	20.8
ROBERTS	4,255	1,744	215	2,296	1,529 R	41.0	5.1	89.0	11.0
SANBORN	2,501	1,184	327	990	857 R	47.3	13.1	78.4	21.6
SHANNON	1,116	992	76	48	916 R	88.9	6.8	92.9	7.1
SPINK	4,520	2,613	595	1,312	2,018 R	57.8	13.2	81.5	18.5
STANLEY	1,212	531	249	432	282 R	43.8	20.5	68.1	31.9
SULLY	940	555	138	247	417 R	59.0	14.7	80.1	19.9

SOUTH DAKOTA

PRESIDENT 1920

County	Total Vote	Republican	Democratic	Other	Rep.-Dem. Plurality	Percentage Total Vote Rep.	Dem.	Major Vote Rep.	Dem.
TODD									
TRIPP	3,066	1,819	968	279	851 R	59.3%	31.6%	65.3%	34.7%
TURNER	3,999	2,703	604	692	2,099 R	67.6%	15.1%	81.7%	18.3%
UNION	2,935	1,942	841	152	1,101 R	66.2%	28.7%	69.8%	30.2%
WALWORTH	2,298	1,411	478	409	933 R	61.4%	20.8%	74.7%	25.3%
WASHABAUGH									
WASHINGTON									
YANKTON	4,134	2,555	1,147	432	1,408 R	61.8%	27.7%	69.0%	31.0%
ZIEBACH	775	507	177	91	330 R	65.4%	22.8%	74.1%	25.9%
TOTAL	182,237	110,692	35,938	35,607	74,754 R	60.7%	19.7%	75.5%	24.5%

PRESIDENT 1924

County	Total Vote	Republican	Democratic	Other	Rep.-Dem. Plurality	Percentage Total Vote Rep.	Dem.	Major Vote Rep.	Dem.
TODD	1,249	837	237	175	600 R	67.0%	19.0%	77.9%	22.1%
TRIPP	3,680	1,647	932	1,301	715 R	42.4%	24.0%	63.9%	36.1%
TURNER	3,719	1,708	285	1,726	1,423 R	45.9%	7.7%	85.7%	14.3%
UNION	3,697	1,665	877	1,155	788 R	45.0%	23.7%	65.5%	34.5%
WALWORTH	2,340	1,033	114	1,193	919 R	44.1%	4.9%	90.1%	9.9%
WASHABAUGH	425	246	121	58	125 R	57.9%	28.5%	67.0%	33.0%
WASHINGTON	316	277	31	8	246 R	87.7%	9.8%	89.9%	10.1%
YANKTON	3,781	1,504	693	1,584	811 R	39.8%	18.3%	68.5%	31.5%
ZIEBACH	1,198	659	153	386	506 R	55.0%	12.8%	81.2%	18.8%
TOTAL	203,868	101,299	27,214	75,355	74,085 R	49.7%	13.3%	78.8%	21.2%

SOUTH DAKOTA

PRESIDENT 1928

County	Total Vote	Republican	Democratic	Other	Rep.-Dem. Plurality	%Total Rep.	%Total Dem.	%Major Rep.	%Major Dem.
ARMSTRONG	7		7		7 D		100.0%		100.0%
AURORA	3,001	1,552	1,426	23	126 R	51.7%	47.5%	52.1%	47.9%
BEADLE	8,293	5,094	3,168	31	1,926 R	61.4%	38.2%	61.7%	38.3%
BENNETT	1,317	766	544	7	222 R	58.5%	41.3%	58.5%	41.5%
BON HOMME	4,441	2,262	2,166	13	96 R	50.9%	48.8%	51.1%	48.9%
BROOKINGS	6,547	4,586	1,915	46	2,671 R	70.0%	29.3%	70.5%	29.5%
BROWN	12,522	7,266	5,065	191	2,201 R	58.0%	40.4%	58.9%	41.1%
BRULE	3,080	1,431	1,599	50	168 R	46.5%	51.9%	47.2%	52.8%
BUFFALO	794	405	387	2	18 R	51.0%	48.7%	51.1%	48.9%
BUTTE	2,866	1,988	840	38	1,148 R	69.4%	29.3%	70.3%	29.7%
CAMPBELL	1,947	1,346	588	13	758 R	69.1%	30.2%	69.6%	30.4%
CHARLES MIX	6,140	3,087	3,039	14	48 R	50.3%	49.5%	50.4%	49.6%
CLARK	4,071	2,665	1,370	36	1,295 R	65.5%	33.7%	66.0%	34.0%
CLAY	4,057	2,573	1,474	10	1,099 R	63.4%	36.3%	63.6%	36.4%
CODINGTON	7,087	3,762	3,299	26	463 R	53.1%	46.6%	53.3%	46.7%
CORSON	3,245	1,847	1,374	24	473 R	56.9%	42.3%	57.3%	42.7%
CUSTER	2,190	1,464	715	11	749 R	66.8%	32.6%	67.2%	32.8%
DAVISON	6,571	3,821	2,729	21	1,092 R	58.1%	41.5%	58.3%	41.7%
DAY	5,865	3,180	2,642	43	538 R	54.2%	45.0%	54.6%	45.4%
DEUEL	2,902	1,869	999	34	870 R	64.4%	34.4%	65.2%	34.8%
DEWEY	2,293	1,293	996	4	297 R	56.4%	43.4%	56.5%	43.5%
DOUGLAS	2,838	1,949	879	10	1,070 R	68.7%	31.0%	68.9%	31.1%
EDMUNDS	3,355	1,743	1,597	15	146 R	52.0%	47.6%	52.2%	47.8%
FALL RIVER	3,489	2,216	1,258	15	958 R	63.5%	36.1%	63.8%	36.2%
FAULK	3,053	1,907	1,135	11	772 R	62.5%	37.2%	62.7%	37.3%
GRANT	4,216	2,508	1,656	52	852 R	59.5%	39.3%	60.2%	39.8%
GREGORY	4,287	2,274	2,001	12	273 R	53.0%	46.7%	53.2%	46.8%
HAAKON	1,951	1,255	663	33	592 R	64.3%	34.0%	65.4%	34.6%
HAMLIN	3,100	1,959	1,088	53	871 R	63.2%	35.1%	64.3%	35.7%
HAND	3,841	2,430	1,397	14	1,033 R	63.3%	36.4%	63.5%	36.5%
HANSON	2,711	1,576	1,129	6	447 R	58.1%	41.6%	58.3%	41.7%
HARDING	1,418	1,032	368	18	664 R	72.8%	26.0%	73.7%	26.3%
HUGHES	3,106	1,912	1,171	23	741 R	61.6%	37.7%	62.0%	38.0%
HUTCHINSON	4,077	2,145	1,898	34	247 R	52.6%	46.5%	53.1%	46.9%
HYDE	1,580	961	608	11	353 R	60.8%	38.5%	61.2%	38.8%
JACKSON	1,124	704	417	3	287 R	62.6%	37.1%	62.8%	37.2%
JERAULD	2,420	1,517	875	28	642 R	62.7%	36.2%	63.4%	36.6%
JONES	1,290	857	422	11	435 R	66.4%	32.7%	67.0%	33.0%
KINGSBURY	4,868	3,499	1,352	17	2,147 R	71.9%	27.7%	72.1%	27.9%
LAKE	4,807	3,048	1,744	15	1,304 R	63.4%	36.3%	63.6%	36.4%
LAWRENCE	5,947	4,141	1,785	21	2,356 R	69.6%	30.0%	69.9%	30.1%
LINCOLN	4,850	3,463	1,364	23	2,099 R	71.4%	28.1%	71.7%	28.3%
LYMAN	2,718	1,488	1,222	8	266 R	54.7%	45.0%	54.9%	45.1%
McCOOK	4,005	2,234	1,758	13	476 R	55.8%	43.9%	56.0%	44.0%
McPHERSON	2,711	1,234	1,468	9	234 D	45.5%	54.1%	45.7%	54.3%
MARSHALL	3,252	1,858	1,315	79	543 R	57.1%	40.4%	58.6%	41.4%
MEADE	4,308	2,843	1,441	22	1,404 R	66.0%	33.4%	66.4%	33.6%
MELLETTE	1,881	943	927	11	16 R	50.1%	49.3%	50.4%	49.6%
MINER	3,352	1,990	1,341	21	649 R	59.4%	40.0%	59.7%	40.3%
MINNEHAHA	20,608	13,741	6,805	62	6,936 R	66.7%	33.0%	66.9%	33.1%
MOODY	3,535	2,108	1,416	11	692 R	59.6%	40.1%	59.8%	40.2%
PENNINGTON	6,936	4,645	2,266	25	2,379 R	67.0%	32.7%	67.2%	32.8%
PERKINS	3,299	2,262	1,010	27	1,252 R	68.6%	30.6%	69.1%	30.9%
POTTER	2,350	1,240	1,100	10	140 R	52.8%	46.8%	53.0%	47.0%
ROBERTS	5,625	2,966	2,619	40	347 R	52.7%	46.6%	53.1%	46.9%
SANBORN	2,914	1,576	1,321	17	255 R	54.1%	45.3%	54.4%	45.6%
SHANNON	1,075	469	601	5	132 D	43.6%	55.9%	43.8%	56.2%
SPINK	6,352	3,868	2,451	33	1,417 R	60.9%	38.6%	61.2%	38.8%
STANLEY	1,184	739	437	8	302 R	62.4%	36.9%	62.8%	37.2%
SULLY	1,417	999	415	3	584 R	70.5%	29.3%	70.7%	29.3%

PRESIDENT 1932

County	Total Vote	Republican	Democratic	Other	Rep.-Dem. Plurality	%Total Rep.	%Total Dem.	%Major Rep.	%Major Dem.
ARMSTRONG	17		17		17 D		100.0%		100.0%
AURORA	3,219	860	2,304	55	1,444 D	26.7%	71.6%	27.2%	72.8%
BEADLE	9,346	2,995	6,246	105	3,251 D	32.0%	66.8%	32.4%	67.6%
BENNETT	1,908	453	1,410	45	957 D	23.7%	73.9%	24.3%	75.7%
BON HOMME	4,886	1,354	3,504	28	2,150 D	27.7%	71.7%	27.9%	72.1%
BROOKINGS	6,599	3,231	3,247	121	16 D	49.0%	49.2%	49.9%	50.1%
BROWN	13,601	4,639	8,669	293	4,030 D	34.1%	63.7%	34.9%	65.1%
BRULE	3,315	797	2,465	53	1,668 D	24.0%	74.4%	24.4%	75.6%
BUFFALO	911	270	634	7	364 D	29.6%	69.6%	29.9%	70.1%
BUTTE	3,337	1,594	1,684	59	90 D	47.8%	50.5%	48.6%	51.4%
CAMPBELL	1,904	770	1,116	18	346 D	40.4%	58.6%	40.8%	59.2%
CHARLES MIX	6,846	1,397	5,399	50	4,002 D	20.4%	78.9%	20.6%	79.4%
CLARK	4,300	1,572	2,649	79	1,077 D	36.6%	61.6%	37.2%	62.8%
CLAY	4,624	1,514	3,040	70	1,526 D	32.7%	65.7%	33.2%	66.8%
CODINGTON	7,396	2,538	4,806	52	2,268 D	34.3%	65.0%	34.6%	65.4%
CORSON	3,484	946	2,403	135	1,457 D	27.2%	69.0%	28.2%	71.8%
CUSTER	2,568	977	1,548	43	571 D	38.0%	60.3%	38.7%	61.3%
DAVISON	7,480	2,147	5,233	100	3,086 D	28.7%	70.0%	29.1%	70.9%
DAY	6,191	1,983	3,910	298	1,927 D	32.0%	63.2%	33.7%	66.3%
DEUEL	2,812	1,131	1,658	23	527 D	40.2%	59.0%	40.6%	59.4%
DEWEY	2,327	710	1,591	26	881 D	30.5%	68.4%	30.9%	69.1%
DOUGLAS	3,066	1,045	2,005	16	960 D	34.1%	65.4%	34.3%	65.6%
EDMUNDS	3,836	1,183	2,588	65	1,405 D	30.8%	67.5%	31.4%	68.6%
FALL RIVER	4,029	1,351	2,603	75	1,252 D	33.5%	64.6%	34.2%	65.8%
FAULK	2,930	1,141	1,743	46	602 D	38.9%	59.5%	39.6%	60.4%
GRANT	4,472	1,515	2,887	70	1,372 D	33.9%	64.6%	34.4%	65.6%
GREGORY	4,287	1,169	3,245	25	2,109 D	26.1%	73.3%	26.3%	73.7%
HAAKON	2,234	797	1,797	192	448 D	35.7%	55.7%	39.0%	61.0%
HAMLIN	3,230	1,267	1,920	43	653 D	39.2%	59.4%	39.8%	60.2%
HAND	4,105	1,394	2,658	53	1,264 D	34.0%	64.8%	34.4%	65.6%
HANSON	2,650	845	1,783	22	938 D	31.9%	67.3%	32.2%	67.8%
HARDING	1,444	625	715	104	90 D	43.3%	49.5%	46.6%	53.4%
HUGHES	3,270	1,374	1,852	44	478 D	42.0%	56.6%	42.6%	57.4%
HUTCHINSON	5,192	1,504	3,630	58	2,126 D	29.0%	69.9%	29.3%	70.7%
HYDE	1,596	678	895	23	217 D	42.5%	56.1%	43.1%	56.9%
JACKSON	1,344	499	812	33	313 D	37.1%	60.4%	38.1%	61.9%
JERAULD	2,673	836	1,773	64	937 D	31.3%	66.3%	32.0%	68.0%
JONES	1,455	472	929	54	457 D	32.4%	63.8%	33.7%	66.3%
KINGSBURY	5,033	2,135	2,808	90	673 D	42.4%	55.8%	43.2%	56.8%
LAKE	5,407	2,222	3,090	95	868 D	41.1%	57.1%	41.8%	58.2%
LAWRENCE	6,868	3,708	3,106	54	602 R	54.0%	45.2%	54.4%	45.6%
LINCOLN	5,560	2,160	3,300	100	1,140 D	38.8%	59.3%	39.5%	60.4%
LYMAN	2,730	811	1,879	40	1,068 D	29.7%	68.8%	30.1%	69.9%
McCOOK	4,422	1,436	2,884	102	1,448 D	32.5%	65.2%	33.2%	66.8%
McPHERSON	3,302	606	2,650	46	2,044 D	18.4%	80.3%	18.6%	81.4%
MARSHALL	3,446	935	2,137	374	1,202 D	27.1%	62.0%	30.4%	69.6%
MEADE	4,608	1,735	2,687	186	952 D	37.7%	58.3%	39.2%	60.8%
MELLETTE	2,255	657	1,583	15	926 D	29.1%	70.2%	29.3%	70.7%
MINER	3,416	976	2,332	108	1,356 D	28.6%	68.3%	29.5%	70.5%
MINNEHAHA	23,273	10,288	12,646	339	2,358 D	44.2%	54.3%	44.9%	55.1%
MOODY	3,906	1,289	2,547	70	1,258 D	33.0%	65.2%	33.6%	66.4%
PENNINGTON	8,875	3,638	5,178	59	1,540 D	41.0%	58.3%	41.3%	58.7%
PERKINS	3,438	1,406	1,852	180	446 D	40.9%	53.9%	43.2%	56.8%
POTTER	2,350	660	1,668	22	1,008 D	28.1%	71.0%	28.4%	71.6%
ROBERTS	6,368	1,381	4,440	547	3,059 D	21.7%	69.7%	23.7%	76.3%
SANBORN	3,281	860	2,398	23	1,538 D	26.2%	73.1%	26.4%	73.6%
SHANNON	1,262	463	798	1	335 D	36.7%	63.2%	36.7%	63.3%
SPINK	6,635	2,433	4,046	156	1,613 D	36.7%	61.0%	37.6%	62.4%
STANLEY	1,336	553	757	26	204 D	41.4%	56.7%	42.2%	57.8%
SULLY	1,569	559	961	49	402 D	35.6%	61.2%	36.8%	63.2%

SOUTH DAKOTA

PRESIDENT 1928

County	Total Vote	Republican	Democratic	Other	Rep.-Dem. Plurality	Percentage Total Vote Rep.	Dem.	Major Vote Rep.	Dem.
TODD	1,629	789	831	9	42 D	48.4%	51.0%	48.7%	51.3%
TRIPP	4,519	2,396	2,099	24	297 R	53.0%	46.4%	53.3%	46.7%
TURNER	4,759	3,362	1,380	17	1,982 R	70.6%	29.0%	70.9%	29.1%
UNION	4,540	2,415	2,106	19	309 R	53.2%	46.4%	53.4%	46.6%
WALWORTH	3,092	1,854	1,216	22	638 R	60.0%	39.3%	60.4%	39.6%
WASHABAUGH	580	294	282	4	12 R	50.7%	48.6%	51.0%	49.0%
WASHINGTON	433	205	228		23 D	47.3%	52.7%	47.3%	52.7%
YANKTON	5,839	2,971	2,841	27	130 R	50.9%	48.7%	51.1%	48.9%
ZIEBACH	1,380	759	615	6	144 R	55.0%	44.6%	55.2%	44.8%
TOTAL	261,857	157,603	102,660	1,594	54,943 R	60.2%	39.2%	60.6%	39.4%

PRESIDENT 1932

County	Total Vote	Republican	Democratic	Other	Rep.-Dem. Plurality	Percentage Total Vote Rep.	Dem.	Major Vote Rep.	Dem.
TODD	2,034	533	1,485	16	952 D	26.2%	73.0%	26.4%	73.6%
TRIPP	4,846	1,147	3,647	52	2,500 D	23.7%	75.3%	23.9%	76.1%
TURNER	5,405	2,172	3,170	63	998 D	40.2%	58.6%	40.7%	59.3%
UNION	4,957	1,381	3,530	46	2,149 D	27.9%	71.2%	28.1%	71.9%
WALWORTH	3,320	1,049	2,221	50	1,172 D	31.6%	66.9%	32.1%	67.9%
WASHABAUGH	761	134	612	15	478 D	17.6%	80.4%	18.0%	82.0%
WASHINGTON	503	157	342	4	185 D	31.2%	68.0%	31.5%	68.5%
YANKTON	6,730	1,693	4,930	107	3,237 D	25.2%	73.3%	25.6%	74.4%
ZIEBACH	1,473	462	982	29	520 D	31.4%	66.7%	32.0%	68.0%
TOTAL	288,438	99,212	183,515	5,711	84,303 D	34.4%	63.6%	35.1%	64.9%

SOUTH DAKOTA

PRESIDENT 1936

County	Total Vote	Republican	Democratic	Other	Rep.-Dem. Plurality	Total Vote Rep.	Total Vote Dem.	Major Vote Rep.	Major Vote Dem.
ARMSTRONG									
AURORA	2,963	1,082	1,801	80	719 D	36.5%	60.8%	37.5%	62.5%
BEADLE	9,011	2,965	5,843	203	2,878 D	32.9%	64.8%	33.7%	66.3%
BENNETT	1,349	530	807	12	277 D	39.3%	59.8%	39.6%	60.4%
BON HOMME	5,299	2,236	2,959	104	723 D	42.2%	55.8%	43.0%	57.0%
BROOKINGS	7,302	3,899	3,161	242	738 R	53.4%	43.3%	55.2%	44.8%
BROWN	13,993	4,505	9,177	311	4,672 D	32.2%	65.6%	32.9%	67.1%
BRULE	3,317	982	2,274	61	1,292 D	29.6%	68.6%	30.2%	69.8%
BUFFALO	795	368	410	17	42 D	46.3%	51.6%	47.3%	52.7%
BUTTE	3,145	1,525	1,519	101	6 R	48.5%	48.3%	50.1%	49.9%
CAMPBELL	2,027	1,236	736	55	500 R	61.0%	36.3%	62.7%	37.3%
CHARLES MIX	6,912	2,209	4,628	75	2,419 D	32.0%	67.0%	32.3%	67.7%
CLARK	4,087	1,883	2,036	168	153 D	46.1%	49.8%	48.0%	52.0%
CLAY	5,035	1,692	3,070	273	1,378 D	33.6%	61.0%	35.5%	64.5%
CODINGTON	7,620	3,005	4,256	359	1,251 D	39.4%	55.9%	41.4%	58.6%
CORSON	3,295	1,408	1,781	106	373 D	42.7%	54.1%	44.2%	55.8%
CUSTER	2,912	1,365	1,519	28	154 D	46.9%	52.2%	47.3%	52.7%
DAVISON	7,805	2,510	4,983	312	2,473 D	32.2%	63.8%	33.5%	66.5%
DAY	5,729	2,113	3,335	281	1,222 D	36.9%	58.2%	38.8%	61.2%
DEUEL	3,153	1,595	1,440	118	155 R	50.6%	45.7%	52.6%	47.4%
DEWEY	2,287	1,012	1,216	59	204 D	44.3%	53.2%	45.4%	54.6%
DOUGLAS	3,169	1,418	1,680	71	262 D	44.7%	53.0%	45.8%	54.2%
EDMUNDS	3,888	1,818	2,030	40	212 D	46.8%	52.2%	47.2%	52.8%
FALL RIVER	3,982	1,876	1,927	179	51 D	47.1%	48.4%	49.3%	50.7%
FAULK	2,555	1,111	1,404	40	293 D	43.5%	55.0%	44.2%	55.8%
GRANT	4,059	1,847	2,101	111	254 D	45.5%	51.8%	46.8%	53.2%
GREGORY	4,545	1,868	2,603	74	735 D	41.1%	57.3%	41.8%	58.2%
HAAKON	1,956	933	948	75	15 D	47.7%	48.5%	49.6%	50.4%
HAMLIN	3,554	1,857	1,622	75	235 R	52.3%	45.6%	53.4%	46.6%
HAND	3,237	1,289	1,721	227	432 D	39.8%	53.2%	42.8%	57.2%
HANSON	2,708	1,090	1,530	88	440 D	40.3%	56.5%	41.6%	58.4%
HARDING	1,382	524	819	39	295 D	37.9%	59.3%	39.0%	61.0%
HUGHES	3,312	1,547	1,662	103	115 D	46.7%	50.2%	48.2%	51.8%
HUTCHINSON	5,801	2,804	2,500	497	304 R	48.3%	43.1%	52.9%	47.1%
HYDE	1,514	795	683	36	112 D	52.5%	45.1%	53.8%	46.2%
JACKSON	1,104	481	593	30	112 D	43.6%	53.7%	44.8%	55.2%
JERAULD	2,504	1,075	1,343	86	268 D	42.9%	53.6%	44.5%	55.5%
JONES	1,264	608	620	36	12 D	48.1%	49.1%	49.5%	50.5%
KINGSBURY	5,076	2,813	2,037	226	776 R	55.4%	40.1%	58.0%	42.0%
LAKE	6,009	3,182	2,520	307	662 R	53.0%	41.9%	55.8%	44.2%
LAWRENCE	8,852	4,974	3,809	69	1,165 R	56.2%	43.0%	56.6%	43.4%
LINCOLN	6,026	2,918	2,541	567	377 R	48.4%	42.2%	53.5%	46.5%
LYMAN	2,440	1,090	1,321	29	231 D	44.7%	54.1%	45.2%	54.8%
McCOOK	4,851	2,117	2,536	198	419 D	43.6%	52.3%	45.5%	54.5%
McPHERSON	3,505	1,921	1,556	28	365 R	54.8%	44.4%	55.2%	44.8%
MARSHALL	3,387	1,105	2,220	62	1,115 D	32.6%	65.5%	33.2%	66.8%
MEADE	4,616	2,064	2,304	248	240 D	44.7%	49.9%	47.3%	52.7%
MELLETTE	1,527	711	808	8	97 D	46.6%	52.9%	46.8%	53.2%
MINER	3,552	1,377	2,051	124	674 D	38.8%	57.7%	40.2%	59.8%
MINNEHAHA	26,508	12,418	13,174	916	756 D	46.8%	49.7%	48.5%	51.5%
MOODY	4,560	1,992	2,366	202	374 D	43.7%	51.9%	45.7%	54.3%
PENNINGTON	10,428	4,442	5,557	429	1,115 D	42.6%	53.3%	44.4%	55.6%
PERKINS	3,425	1,408	1,940	77	532 D	41.1%	56.6%	42.1%	57.9%
POTTER	2,306	914	1,338	54	424 D	39.6%	58.0%	40.6%	59.4%
ROBERTS	5,951	1,934	3,820	197	1,886 D	32.5%	64.2%	33.6%	66.4%
SANBORN	3,204	1,174	1,919	111	745 D	36.6%	59.9%	38.0%	62.0%
SHANNON	1,336	667	634	35	33 R	49.9%	47.5%	51.3%	48.7%
SPINK	5,871	2,078	3,569	224	1,491 D	35.4%	60.8%	36.8%	63.2%
STANLEY	1,176	495	629	52	134 D	42.1%	53.5%	44.0%	56.0%
SULLY	1,138	667	437	34	230 R	58.6%	38.4%	60.4%	39.6%

PRESIDENT 1940

County	Total Vote	Republican	Democratic	Other	Rep.-Dem. Plurality	Total Vote Rep.	Total Vote Dem.	Major Vote Rep.	Major Vote Dem.
ARMSTRONG									
AURORA	2,793	1,408	1,385		23 R	50.4%	49.6%	50.4%	49.6%
BEADLE	9,609	4,356	5,253		897 D	45.3%	54.7%	45.3%	54.7%
BENNETT	1,775	915	860		55 R	51.5%	48.5%	51.5%	48.5%
BON HOMME	5,509	3,046	2,463		583 R	55.3%	44.7%	55.3%	44.7%
BROOKINGS	7,687	5,016	2,671		2,345 R	65.3%	34.7%	65.3%	34.7%
BROWN	14,646	6,598	8,048		1,450 D	45.0%	55.0%	45.0%	55.0%
BRULE	3,187	1,352	1,835		483 D	42.4%	57.6%	42.4%	57.6%
BUFFALO	886	491	395		96 R	55.4%	44.6%	55.4%	44.6%
BUTTE	3,548	2,164	1,384		780 R	61.0%	39.0%	61.0%	39.0%
CAMPBELL	2,149	1,733	416		1,317 R	80.6%	19.4%	80.6%	19.4%
CHARLES MIX	6,296	2,993	3,303		310 D	47.5%	52.5%	47.5%	52.5%
CLARK	4,246	2,622	1,624		998 R	61.8%	38.2%	61.8%	38.2%
CLAY	4,729	2,463	2,266		197 R	52.1%	47.9%	52.1%	47.9%
CODINGTON	8,025	4,320	3,705		615 R	53.8%	46.2%	53.8%	46.2%
CORSON	3,037	1,709	1,328		381 R	56.3%	43.7%	56.3%	43.7%
CUSTER	2,947	1,796	1,151		645 R	60.9%	39.1%	60.9%	39.1%
DAVISON	7,889	3,659	4,230		571 D	46.4%	53.6%	46.4%	53.6%
DAY	6,574	3,277	3,297		20 D	49.8%	50.2%	49.8%	50.2%
DEUEL	3,470	2,304	1,166		1,138 R	66.4%	33.6%	66.4%	33.6%
DEWEY	2,477	1,396	1,081		315 R	56.4%	43.6%	56.4%	43.6%
DOUGLAS	3,017	1,977	1,040		937 R	65.5%	34.5%	65.5%	34.5%
EDMUNDS	3,784	2,341	1,443		898 R	61.9%	38.1%	61.9%	38.1%
FALL RIVER	3,825	2,420	1,405		1,015 R	63.3%	36.7%	63.3%	36.7%
FAULK	2,630	1,431	1,199		232 R	54.4%	45.6%	54.4%	45.6%
GRANT	5,020	2,981	2,039		942 R	59.4%	40.6%	59.4%	40.6%
GREGORY	4,513	2,478	2,035		443 R	54.9%	45.1%	54.9%	45.1%
HAAKON	1,836	1,129	707		422 R	61.5%	38.5%	61.5%	38.5%
HAMLIN	3,561	2,279	1,282		997 R	64.0%	36.0%	64.0%	36.0%
HAND	3,610	2,002	1,608		394 R	55.5%	44.5%	55.5%	44.5%
HANSON	2,624	1,408	1,216		192 R	53.7%	46.3%	53.7%	46.3%
HARDING	1,425	755	670		85 R	53.0%	47.0%	53.0%	47.0%
HUGHES	3,344	1,982	1,362		620 R	59.3%	40.7%	59.3%	40.7%
HUTCHINSON	6,154	5,051	1,103		3,948 R	82.1%	17.9%	82.1%	17.9%
HYDE	1,688	1,018	670		348 R	60.3%	39.7%	60.3%	39.7%
JACKSON	1,055	620	435		185 R	58.8%	41.2%	58.8%	41.2%
JERAULD	2,495	1,576	919		657 R	63.2%	36.8%	63.2%	36.8%
JONES	1,340	832	508		324 R	62.1%	37.9%	62.1%	37.9%
KINGSBURY	5,054	3,551	1,503		2,048 R	70.3%	29.7%	70.3%	29.7%
LAKE	6,068	4,179	1,889		2,290 R	68.9%	31.1%	68.9%	31.1%
LAWRENCE	8,803	5,288	3,515		1,773 R	60.1%	39.9%	60.1%	39.9%
LINCOLN	6,129	4,081	2,048		2,033 R	66.6%	33.4%	66.6%	33.4%
LYMAN	2,514	1,409	1,105		304 R	56.0%	44.0%	56.0%	44.0%
McCOOK	5,006	3,310	1,696		1,614 R	66.1%	33.9%	66.1%	33.9%
McPHERSON	3,665	2,839	826		2,013 R	77.5%	22.5%	77.5%	22.5%
MARSHALL	3,961	1,989	1,972		17 R	50.2%	49.8%	50.2%	49.8%
MEADE	4,491	2,560	1,931		629 R	57.0%	43.0%	57.0%	43.0%
MELLETTE	1,895	990	905		85 R	52.2%	47.8%	52.2%	47.8%
MINER	3,460	2,095	1,365		730 R	60.5%	39.5%	60.5%	39.5%
MINNEHAHA	28,923	16,664	12,259		4,405 R	57.6%	42.4%	57.6%	42.4%
MOODY	4,569	2,749	1,820		929 R	60.2%	39.8%	60.2%	39.8%
PENNINGTON	11,481	6,603	4,878		1,725 R	57.5%	42.5%	57.5%	42.5%
PERKINS	3,098	1,777	1,321		456 R	57.4%	42.6%	57.4%	42.6%
POTTER	2,332	1,278	1,054		224 R	54.8%	45.2%	54.8%	45.2%
ROBERTS	7,254	3,504	3,750		246 D	48.3%	51.7%	48.3%	51.7%
SANBORN	3,130	1,732	1,398		334 R	55.3%	44.7%	55.3%	44.7%
SHANNON	1,885	1,094	791		303 R	58.0%	42.0%	58.0%	42.0%
SPINK	6,109	2,975	3,134		159 D	48.7%	51.3%	48.7%	51.3%
STANLEY	1,220	679	541		138 R	55.7%	44.3%	55.7%	44.3%
SULLY	1,298	840	458		382 R	64.7%	35.3%	64.7%	35.3%

SOUTH DAKOTA

PRESIDENT 1936

County	Total Vote	Republican	Democratic	Other	Rep.-Dem. Plurality		Total Vote Rep.	Percentage Total Vote Dem.	Major Vote Rep.	Major Vote Dem.
TODD	1,966	624	1,318	24	694	D	31.7%	67.0%	32.1%	67.9%
TRIPP	4,485	1,693	2,728	84	1,015	D	37.7%	60.4%	38.5%	61.5%
TURNER	6,526	3,214	2,923	389	291	R	49.2%	44.8%	52.4%	47.6%
UNION	5,785	1,845	3,520	420	1,675	D	31.9%	60.8%	34.4%	65.6%
WALWORTH	3,666	1,420	2,212	34	792	D	38.7%	60.3%	39.1%	60.9%
WASHABAUGH	561	238	313	10	75	D	42.4%	55.8%	43.2%	56.8%
WASHINGTON	392	158	234		76	D	40.3%	59.7%	40.3%	59.7%
YANKTON	7,438	2,702	4,349	387	1,647	D	36.3%	58.5%	38.3%	61.7%
ZIEBACH	1,319	561	737	21	176	D	42.5%	55.9%	43.2%	56.8%
TOTAL	296,452	125,977	160,137	10,338	34,160	D	42.5%	54.0%	44.0%	56.0%

PRESIDENT 1940

	Total Vote	Republican	Democratic	Other	Rep.-Dem. Plurality		Total Vote Rep.	Percentage Total Vote Dem.	Major Vote Rep.	Major Vote Dem.
	2,483	1,245	1,238		7	R	50.1%	49.9%	50.1%	49.9%
	4,581	2,492	2,089		403	R	54.4%	45.6%	54.4%	45.6%
	6,418	4,644	1,774		2,870	R	72.4%	27.6%	72.4%	27.6%
	5,724	3,115	2,608		508	R	54.4%	45.6%	54.4%	45.6%
	3,486	1,921	1,565		356	R	55.1%	44.9%	55.1%	44.9%
	732	358	374		16	D	48.9%	51.1%	48.9%	51.1%
	637	335	302		33	R	52.6%	47.4%	52.6%	47.4%
	7,243	4,179	3,064		1,115	R	57.7%	42.3%	57.7%	42.3%
	1,378	691	687		4	R	50.1%	49.9%	50.1%	49.9%
	308,427	177,065	131,362		45,703	R	57.4%	42.6%	57.4%	42.6%

SOUTH DAKOTA

PRESIDENT 1944

County	Total Vote	Republican	Democratic	Other	Rep.-Dem. Plurality	Total Vote Rep.	Total Vote Dem.	Major Vote Rep.	Major Vote Dem.
ARMSTRONG	4		4		4 D		100.0%		100.0%
AURORA	2,174	1,163	1,011		152 R	53.5%	46.5%	53.5%	46.5%
BEADLE	7,452	3,610	3,842		232 D	48.4%	51.6%	48.4%	51.6%
BENNETT	1,060	494	566		72 D	46.6%	53.4%	46.6%	53.4%
BON HOMME	4,534	2,553	1,981		572 R	56.3%	43.7%	56.3%	43.7%
BROOKINGS	6,209	4,136	2,073		2,063 R	66.6%	33.4%	66.6%	33.4%
BROWN	11,963	5,611	6,352		741 D	46.9%	53.1%	46.9%	53.1%
BRULE	2,414	1,002	1,412		410 D	41.5%	58.5%	41.5%	58.5%
BUFFALO	574	324	250		74 R	56.4%	43.6%	56.4%	43.6%
BUTTE	2,752	1,824	928		896 R	66.3%	33.7%	66.3%	33.7%
CAMPBELL	1,255	1,047	208		839 R	83.4%	16.6%	83.4%	16.6%
CHARLES MIX	4,872	2,171	2,701		530 D	44.6%	55.4%	44.6%	55.4%
CLARK	3,145	1,936	1,209		727 R	61.6%	38.4%	61.6%	38.4%
CLAY	3,766	1,970	1,796		174 R	52.3%	47.7%	52.3%	47.7%
CODINGTON	6,468	3,348	3,120		228 R	51.8%	48.2%	51.8%	48.2%
CORSON	1,794	1,008	786		222 R	56.2%	43.8%	56.2%	43.8%
CUSTER	2,000	1,288	712		576 R	64.4%	35.6%	64.4%	35.6%
DAVISON	6,151	2,929	3,222		293 D	47.6%	52.4%	47.6%	52.4%
DAY	5,080	2,593	2,487		106 R	51.0%	49.0%	51.0%	49.0%
DEUEL	3,090	1,910	1,180		730 R	61.8%	38.2%	61.8%	38.2%
DEWEY	1,424	913	511		402 R	64.1%	35.9%	64.1%	35.9%
DOUGLAS	2,202	1,483	719		764 R	67.3%	32.7%	67.3%	32.7%
EDMUNDS	2,723	1,762	961		801 R	64.7%	35.3%	64.7%	35.3%
FALL RIVER	3,060	1,938	1,122		816 R	63.3%	36.7%	63.3%	36.7%
FAULK	1,986	1,090	896		194 R	54.9%	45.1%	54.9%	45.1%
GRANT	3,753	2,278	1,475		803 R	60.7%	39.3%	60.7%	39.3%
GREGORY	3,680	2,067	1,613		454 R	56.2%	43.8%	56.2%	43.8%
HAAKON	1,019	638	381		257 R	62.6%	37.4%	62.6%	37.4%
HAMLIN	2,831	1,811	1,020		791 R	64.0%	36.0%	64.0%	36.0%
HAND	2,704	1,558	1,146		412 R	57.6%	42.4%	57.6%	42.4%
HANSON	1,934	1,070	864		206 R	55.3%	44.7%	55.3%	44.7%
HARDING	1,045	552	493		59 R	52.8%	47.2%	52.8%	47.2%
HUGHES	2,614	1,676	938		738 R	64.1%	35.9%	64.1%	35.9%
HUTCHINSON	4,498	3,799	699		3,100 R	84.5%	15.5%	84.5%	15.5%
HYDE	1,296	842	454		388 R	65.0%	35.0%	65.0%	35.0%
JACKSON	553	340	213		127 R	61.5%	38.5%	61.5%	38.5%
JERAULD	1,948	1,217	731		486 R	62.5%	37.5%	62.5%	37.5%
JONES	729	465	264		201 R	63.8%	36.2%	63.8%	36.2%
KINGSBURY	3,697	2,541	1,156		1,385 R	68.7%	31.3%	68.7%	31.3%
LAKE	4,499	2,956	1,543		1,413 R	65.7%	34.3%	65.7%	34.3%
LAWRENCE	5,394	3,528	1,866		1,662 R	65.4%	34.6%	65.4%	34.6%
LINCOLN	4,923	3,298	1,625		1,673 R	67.0%	33.0%	67.0%	33.0%
LYMAN	1,497	867	630		237 R	57.9%	42.1%	57.9%	42.1%
MCCOOK	3,679	2,516	1,163		1,353 R	68.4%	31.6%	68.4%	31.6%
MCPHERSON	2,700	2,290	410		1,880 R	84.8%	15.2%	84.8%	15.2%
MARSHALL	2,874	1,511	1,363		148 R	52.6%	47.4%	52.6%	47.4%
MEADE	3,076	1,912	1,164		748 R	62.2%	37.8%	62.2%	37.8%
MELLETTE	954	544	410		134 R	57.0%	43.0%	57.0%	43.0%
MINER	2,634	1,544	1,090		454 R	58.6%	41.4%	58.6%	41.4%
MINNEHAHA	24,136	13,920	10,216		3,704 R	57.7%	42.3%	57.7%	42.3%
MOODY	3,500	2,080	1,420		660 R	59.4%	40.6%	59.4%	40.6%
PENNINGTON	8,763	5,246	3,517		1,729 R	59.9%	40.1%	59.9%	40.1%
PERKINS	2,320	1,325	995		330 R	57.1%	42.9%	57.1%	42.9%
POTTER	1,718	1,001	717		284 R	58.3%	41.7%	58.3%	41.7%
ROBERTS	5,745	2,721	3,024		303 D	47.4%	52.6%	47.4%	52.6%
SANBORN	2,210	1,212	998		214 R	54.8%	45.2%	54.8%	45.2%
SHANNON	1,042	562	480		82 R	53.9%	46.1%	53.9%	46.1%
SPINK	4,650	2,365	2,285		80 R	50.9%	49.1%	50.9%	49.1%
STANLEY	618	384	234		150 R	62.1%	37.9%	62.1%	37.9%
SULLY	912	612	300		312 R	67.1%	32.9%	67.1%	32.9%

PRESIDENT 1948

County	Total Vote	Republican	Democratic	Other	Rep.-Dem. Plurality	Total Vote Rep.	Total Vote Dem.	Major Vote Rep.	Major Vote Dem.
ARMSTRONG	7	1	6		5 D	14.3%	85.7%	14.3%	85.7%
AURORA	2,347	1,056	1,275	16	219 D	45.0%	54.3%	45.3%	54.7%
BEADLE	8,111	3,662	4,372	77	710 D	45.1%	53.9%	45.6%	54.4%
BENNETT	1,252	477	758	17	281 D	38.1%	60.5%	38.6%	61.4%
BON HOMME	4,408	2,283	2,077	48	206 R	51.8%	47.1%	52.4%	47.6%
BROOKINGS	6,926	3,975	2,907	44	1,068 R	57.4%	42.0%	57.8%	42.2%
BROWN	12,972	5,632	7,148	192	1,516 D	43.4%	55.1%	44.1%	55.9%
BRULE	2,744	1,056	1,646	42	590 D	38.5%	60.0%	39.1%	60.9%
BUFFALO	652	313	334	5	21 D	48.0%	51.2%	48.4%	51.6%
BUTTE	2,842	1,726	1,065	51	661 R	60.7%	37.5%	61.8%	38.2%
CAMPBELL	1,945	1,518	410	17	1,108 R	78.0%	21.1%	78.7%	21.3%
CHARLES MIX	4,935	1,800	3,086	49	1,286 D	36.5%	62.5%	36.8%	63.2%
CLARK	3,212	1,625	1,559	28	66 R	50.6%	48.5%	51.0%	49.0%
CLAY	4,361	2,228	2,080	53	148 R	51.1%	47.7%	51.7%	48.3%
CODINGTON	7,441	3,349	4,042	50	693 D	45.0%	54.3%	45.3%	54.7%
CORSON	2,325	1,154	1,154	17	300 R	49.6%	49.6%	50.0%	50.0%
CUSTER	2,148	1,217	917	14	300 R	56.7%	42.7%	57.0%	43.0%
DAVISON	7,681	2,996	4,064	68	1,068 D	42.0%	55.4%	42.4%	57.6%
DAY	5,681	2,438	3,146	97	708 D	42.9%	55.4%	43.7%	56.3%
DEUEL	2,719	1,357	1,324	38	33 R	49.9%	48.7%	50.6%	49.4%
DEWEY	1,606	864	727	15	137 R	53.8%	45.3%	54.3%	45.7%
DOUGLAS	2,042	1,301	736	5	565 R	63.7%	36.0%	63.9%	36.1%
EDMUNDS	2,765	1,493	1,253	19	240 R	54.0%	45.3%	54.4%	45.6%
FALL RIVER	3,411	2,037	1,348	26	689 R	59.7%	39.5%	60.2%	39.8%
FAULK	2,047	1,054	971	22	83 R	51.5%	47.4%	52.0%	48.0%
GRANT	4,060	1,972	2,052	36	80 D	48.6%	50.5%	49.0%	51.0%
GREGORY	3,562	1,723	1,793	46	70 D	48.4%	50.3%	49.0%	51.0%
HAAKON	1,300	753	519	28	234 R	57.9%	39.9%	59.2%	40.8%
HAMLIN	2,979	1,608	1,326	45	282 R	54.0%	44.5%	54.8%	45.2%
HAND	2,778	1,402	1,367	9	35 R	50.5%	49.2%	50.6%	49.4%
HANSON	1,828	860	953	15	93 D	47.0%	52.1%	47.4%	52.6%
HARDING	1,040	529	479	32	50 R	50.9%	46.1%	52.5%	47.5%
HUGHES	2,831	1,739	1,080	12	659 R	61.4%	38.1%	61.7%	38.3%
HUTCHINSON	4,151	2,906	1,209	36	1,697 R	70.0%	29.1%	70.6%	29.4%
HYDE	1,379	817	553	9	264 R	59.2%	40.1%	59.6%	40.4%
JACKSON	766	432	321	13	111 R	56.4%	41.9%	57.4%	42.6%
JERAULD	1,987	1,085	876	26	209 R	54.6%	44.1%	55.3%	44.7%
JONES	948	522	414	12	108 R	55.1%	43.7%	55.8%	44.2%
KINGSBURY	3,728	2,332	1,338	58	994 R	62.6%	35.9%	63.5%	36.5%
LAKE	4,982	2,837	2,093	52	744 R	56.9%	42.0%	57.5%	42.5%
LAWRENCE	6,045	3,778	2,209	58	1,569 R	62.5%	36.5%	63.1%	36.9%
LINCOLN	4,656	2,771	1,826	59	945 R	59.5%	39.2%	60.3%	39.7%
LYMAN	1,912	993	904	15	89 R	51.9%	47.3%	52.3%	47.7%
MCCOOK	3,471	2,064	1,387	20	677 R	59.5%	40.0%	59.8%	40.2%
MCPHERSON	2,668	2,034	611	23	1,423 R	76.2%	22.9%	76.9%	23.1%
MARSHALL	3,198	1,419	1,710	69	291 D	44.4%	53.5%	45.3%	54.7%
MEADE	3,769	2,053	1,681	35	372 R	54.5%	44.6%	55.0%	45.0%
MELLETTE	977	482	482	13	185 D	49.3%	49.3%	50.0%	50.0%
MINER	2,587	1,188	1,373	26	185 D	45.9%	53.1%	46.4%	53.6%
MINNEHAHA	26,125	14,047	11,770	308	2,277 R	53.8%	45.1%	54.4%	45.6%
MOODY	3,369	1,691	1,630	48	61 R	50.2%	48.4%	50.9%	49.1%
PENNINGTON	11,413	6,392	4,929	92	1,463 R	56.0%	43.2%	56.5%	43.5%
PERKINS	2,587	1,424	1,096	67	328 R	55.0%	42.4%	56.5%	43.5%
POTTER	2,101	1,044	1,039	18	5 R	49.7%	49.5%	50.1%	49.9%
ROBERTS	5,652	2,211	3,277	164	1,066 D	39.1%	58.0%	40.3%	59.7%
SANBORN	2,061	990	1,046	25	56 D	48.0%	50.8%	48.6%	51.4%
SHANNON	1,454	641	803	10	162 D	44.1%	55.2%	44.4%	55.6%
SPINK	5,067	2,310	2,702	55	392 D	45.6%	53.3%	46.1%	53.9%
STANLEY	887	522	359	6	163 R	58.9%	40.5%	59.3%	40.7%
SULLY	992	579	405	8	174 R	58.4%	40.8%	58.8%	41.2%

SOUTH DAKOTA

PRESIDENT 1944

County	Total Vote	Republican	Democratic	Other	Rep.-Dem. Plurality	Total Vote Rep.	Total Vote Dem.	Major Vote Rep.	Major Vote Dem.
TODD	1,420	737	683		54 R	51.9%	48.1%	51.9%	48.1%
TRIPP	3,551	1,911	1,640		271 R	53.8%	46.2%	53.8%	46.2%
TURNER	4,853	3,549	1,304		2,245 R	73.1%	26.9%	73.1%	26.9%
UNION	4,558	2,501	2,057		444 R	54.9%	45.1%	54.9%	45.1%
WALWORTH	2,755	1,533	1,222		311 R	55.6%	44.4%	55.6%	44.4%
WASHABAUGH	285	139	146		7 D	48.8%	51.2%	48.8%	51.2%
WASHINGTON									
YANKTON	5,672	3,313	2,359		954 R	58.4%	41.6%	58.4%	41.6%
ZIEBACH	685	331	354		23 D	48.3%	51.7%	48.3%	51.7%
TOTAL	232,076	135,365	96,711		38,654 R	58.3%	41.7%	58.3%	41.7%

PRESIDENT 1948

County	Total Vote	Republican	Democratic	Other	Rep.-Dem. Plurality	Total Vote Rep.	Total Vote Dem.	Major Vote Rep.	Major Vote Dem.
TODD	1,438	625	796	17	171 D	43.5%	55.4%	44.0%	56.0%
TRIPP	3,818	1,845	1,918	55	73 D	48.3%	50.2%	49.0%	51.0%
TURNER	4,600	3,048	1,514	38	1,534 R	66.3%	32.9%	66.8%	33.2%
UNION	4,465	2,205	2,237	23	32 D	49.4%	50.1%	49.6%	50.4%
WALWORTH	3,155	1,607	1,513	35	94 R	50.9%	48.0%	51.5%	48.5%
WASHABAUGH	419	192	223	4	31 D	45.8%	53.2%	46.3%	53.7%
YANKTON	5,893	2,904	2,932	57	28 D	49.3%	49.8%	49.8%	50.2%
ZIEBACH	980	463	503	14	40 D	47.2%	51.3%	47.9%	52.1%
TOTAL	250,105	129,651	117,653	2,801	11,998 R	51.8%	47.0%	52.4%	47.6%

SOUTH DAKOTA

PRESIDENT 1952

County	Total Vote	Republican	Democratic	Other	Rep.-Dem. Plurality	% Total Vote Rep.	% Total Vote Dem.	% Major Vote Rep.	% Major Vote Dem.
ARMSTRONG	11	6	5		1 R	54.5%	45.5%	54.5%	45.5%
AURORA	2,455	1,458	997		461 R	59.4%	40.6%	59.4%	40.6%
BEAD-E	9,930	6,487	3,443		3,044 R	65.3%	34.7%	65.3%	34.7%
BENNETT	1,389	873	516		357 R	62.9%	37.1%	62.9%	37.1%
BON HOMME	4,815	3,157	1,658		1,499 R	65.6%	34.4%	65.6%	34.4%
BROOKINGS	7,849	5,988	1,861		4,127 R	76.3%	23.7%	76.3%	23.7%
BROWN	15,721	9,581	6,140		3,441 R	60.9%	39.1%	60.9%	39.1%
BRULE	2,970	1,578	1,392		186 R	53.1%	46.9%	53.1%	46.9%
BUFFALO	672	413	259		154 R	61.5%	38.5%	61.5%	38.5%
BUTTE	3,526	2,689	837		1,852 R	76.3%	23.7%	76.3%	23.7%
CAMPBELL	1,704	1,536	168		1,368 R	90.1%	9.9%	90.1%	9.9%
CHARLES MIX	6,106	3,316	2,790		526 R	54.3%	45.7%	54.3%	45.7%
CLARK	3,768	2,692	1,076		1,616 R	71.4%	28.6%	71.4%	28.6%
CLAY	4,714	3,302	1,412		1,890 R	70.0%	30.0%	70.0%	30.0%
CODINGTON	8,724	5,750	2,974		2,776 R	65.9%	34.1%	65.9%	34.1%
CORSON	2,546	1,757	789		968 R	69.0%	31.0%	69.0%	31.0%
CUSTER	2,377	1,725	652		1,073 R	72.6%	27.4%	72.6%	27.4%
DAVISON	8,001	4,774	3,227		1,547 R	59.7%	40.3%	59.7%	40.3%
DAY	5,999	3,648	2,351		1,297 R	60.8%	39.2%	60.8%	39.2%
DEUEL	3,158	2,279	879		1,400 R	72.2%	27.8%	72.2%	27.8%
DEWEY	1,961	1,301	660		641 R	66.3%	33.7%	66.3%	33.7%
DOUGLAS	2,631	2,103	528		1,575 R	79.9%	20.1%	79.9%	20.1%
EDMUNDS	3,191	2,178	1,013		1,165 R	68.3%	31.7%	68.3%	31.7%
FALL RIVER	3,871	2,863	1,008		1,855 R	74.0%	26.0%	74.0%	26.0%
FAULK	2,357	1,619	738		881 R	68.7%	31.3%	68.7%	31.3%
GRANT	4,734	3,234	1,500		1,734 R	68.3%	31.7%	68.3%	31.7%
GREGORY	3,835	2,463	1,372		1,091 R	64.2%	35.8%	64.2%	35.8%
HAAKON	1,572	1,176	396		780 R	74.8%	25.2%	74.8%	25.2%
HAMLIN	3,345	2,391	954		1,437 R	71.5%	28.5%	71.5%	28.5%
HAND	3,199	2,262	937		1,325 R	70.7%	29.3%	70.7%	29.3%
HANSON	2,093	1,320	773		547 R	63.1%	36.9%	63.1%	36.9%
HARDING	1,103	809	294		515 R	73.3%	26.7%	73.3%	26.7%
HUGHES	3,865	2,932	933		1,999 R	75.9%	24.1%	75.9%	24.1%
HUTCHINSON	5,197	4,322	875		3,447 R	83.2%	16.8%	83.2%	16.8%
HYDE	1,444	1,051	393		658 R	72.8%	27.2%	72.8%	27.2%
JACKSON	861	607	254		353 R	70.5%	29.5%	70.5%	29.5%
JERAULD	2,197	1,520	677		843 R	69.2%	30.8%	69.2%	30.8%
JONES	1,062	739	323		416 R	69.6%	30.4%	69.6%	30.4%
KINGSBURY	4,732	3,703	1,029		2,674 R	78.3%	21.7%	78.3%	21.7%
LAKE	5,486	4,020	1,466		2,554 R	73.3%	26.7%	73.3%	26.7%
LAWRENCE	7,260	5,559	1,701		3,858 R	76.6%	23.4%	76.6%	23.4%
LINCOLN	5,599	4,387	1,212		3,175 R	78.4%	21.6%	78.4%	21.6%
LYMAN	2,227	1,561	666		895 R	70.1%	29.9%	70.1%	29.9%
MCCOOK	4,118	2,991	1,127		1,864 R	72.6%	27.4%	72.6%	27.4%
MCPHERSON	3,351	2,915	436		2,479 R	87.0%	13.0%	87.0%	13.0%
MARSHALL	3,383	2,248	1,135		1,113 R	66.4%	33.6%	66.4%	33.6%
MEADE	4,443	3,109	1,334		1,775 R	70.0%	30.0%	70.0%	30.0%
MELLETTE	1,134	787	347		440 R	69.4%	30.6%	69.4%	30.6%
MINER	2,993	1,964	1,029		935 R	65.6%	34.4%	65.6%	34.4%
MINNEHAHA	32,949	23,559	9,390		14,169 R	71.5%	28.5%	71.5%	28.5%
MOODY	3,817	2,728	1,089		1,639 R	71.5%	28.5%	71.5%	28.5%
PENNINGTON	15,499	11,029	4,470		6,559 R	71.2%	28.8%	71.2%	28.8%
PERKINS	3,009	2,160	849		1,311 R	71.8%	28.2%	71.8%	28.2%
POTTER	2,204	1,625	579		1,046 R	73.7%	26.3%	73.7%	26.3%
ROBERTS	6,090	3,566	2,524		1,042 R	58.6%	41.4%	58.6%	41.4%
SANBORN	2,666	1,761	905		856 R	66.1%	33.9%	66.1%	33.9%
SHANNON	1,731	957	774		183 R	55.3%	44.7%	55.3%	44.7%
SPINK	5,676	3,693	1,983		1,710 R	65.1%	34.9%	65.1%	34.9%
STANLEY	984	695	289		406 R	70.6%	29.4%	70.6%	29.4%
SULLY	1,212	860	352		508 R	71.0%	29.0%	71.0%	29.0%

PRESIDENT 1956

County	Total Vote	Republican	Democratic	Other	Rep.-Dem. Plurality	% Total Vote Rep.	% Total Vote Dem.	% Major Vote Rep.	% Major Vote Dem.
ARMSTRONG									
AURORA	2,429	1,055	1,374		319 D	43.4%	56.6%	43.4%	56.6%
BEAD-E	9,830	5,216	4,614		602 R	53.1%	46.9%	53.1%	46.9%
BENNETT	1,431	746	685		61 R	52.1%	47.9%	52.1%	47.9%
BON HOMME	4,840	2,696	2,144		552 R	55.7%	44.3%	55.7%	44.3%
BROOKINGS	7,913	5,293	2,620		2,673 R	66.9%	33.1%	66.9%	33.1%
BROWN	15,377	8,193	7,184		1,009 R	53.3%	46.7%	53.3%	46.7%
BRULE	3,211	1,317	1,894		577 D	41.0%	59.0%	41.0%	59.0%
BUFFALO	632	314	318		4 D	49.7%	50.3%	49.7%	50.3%
BUTTE	3,259	2,231	1,028		1,203 R	68.5%	31.5%	68.5%	31.5%
CAMPBELL	1,557	1,268	289		979 R	81.4%	18.6%	81.4%	18.6%
CHARLES MIX	5,319	2,202	3,117		915 D	41.4%	58.6%	41.4%	58.6%
CLARK	3,694	2,173	1,521		652 R	58.8%	41.2%	58.8%	41.2%
CLAY	4,560	2,632	1,928		704 R	57.7%	42.3%	57.7%	42.3%
CODINGTON	8,922	5,150	3,772		1,378 R	57.7%	42.3%	57.7%	42.3%
CORSON	2,506	1,394	1,112		282 R	55.6%	44.4%	55.6%	44.4%
CUSTER	2,367	1,514	853		661 R	64.0%	36.0%	64.0%	36.0%
DAVISON	7,865	4,056	3,809		247 R	51.6%	48.4%	51.6%	48.4%
DAY	5,623	2,652	2,971		319 D	47.2%	52.8%	47.2%	52.8%
DEUEL	3,061	1,698	1,363		335 R	55.5%	44.5%	55.5%	44.5%
DEWEY	2,109	1,197	912		285 R	56.8%	43.2%	56.8%	43.2%
DOUGLAS	2,526	1,713	813		900 R	67.8%	32.2%	67.8%	32.2%
EDMUNDS	3,265	1,685	1,580		105 R	51.6%	48.4%	51.6%	48.4%
FALL RIVER	3,527	2,377	1,150		1,227 R	67.4%	32.6%	67.4%	32.6%
FAULK	2,415	1,260	1,155		105 R	52.2%	47.8%	52.2%	47.8%
GRANT	4,691	2,621	2,070		551 R	55.9%	44.1%	55.9%	44.1%
GREGORY	3,740	1,945	1,795		150 R	52.0%	48.0%	52.0%	48.0%
HAAKON	1,530	936	594		342 R	61.2%	38.8%	61.2%	38.8%
HAMLIN	3,377	2,083	1,294		789 R	61.7%	38.3%	61.7%	38.3%
HAND	3,257	1,804	1,453		351 R	55.4%	44.6%	55.4%	44.6%
HANSON	2,237	1,050	1,187		137 D	46.9%	53.1%	46.9%	53.1%
HARDING	1,026	650	376		274 R	63.4%	36.6%	63.4%	36.6%
HUGHES	4,610	2,923	1,687		1,236 R	63.4%	36.6%	63.4%	36.6%
HUTCHINSON	5,290	3,870	1,420		2,450 R	73.2%	26.8%	73.2%	26.8%
HYDE	1,352	755	597		158 R	55.8%	44.2%	55.8%	44.2%
JACKSON	898	490	408		82 R	54.6%	45.4%	54.6%	45.4%
JERAULD	2,180	1,175	1,005		170 R	53.9%	46.1%	53.9%	46.1%
JONES	1,072	601	471		130 R	56.1%	43.9%	56.1%	43.9%
KINGSBURY	4,518	2,933	1,585		1,348 R	64.9%	35.1%	64.9%	35.1%
LAKE	5,462	3,404	2,058		1,346 R	62.3%	37.7%	62.3%	37.7%
LAWRENCE	6,525	4,654	1,871		2,783 R	71.3%	28.7%	71.3%	28.7%
LINCOLN	5,670	3,529	2,141		1,388 R	62.2%	37.8%	62.2%	37.8%
LYMAN	2,024	1,151	873		278 R	56.9%	43.1%	56.9%	43.1%
MCCOOK	4,140	2,382	1,758		624 R	57.5%	42.5%	57.5%	42.5%
MCPHERSON	2,858	2,225	633		1,592 R	77.9%	22.1%	77.9%	22.1%
MARSHALL	3,274	1,639	1,635		4 R	50.1%	49.9%	50.1%	49.9%
MEADE	4,125	2,467	1,658		809 R	59.8%	40.2%	59.8%	40.2%
MELLETTE	1,163	643	520		123 R	55.3%	44.7%	55.3%	44.7%
MINER	2,973	1,456	1,517		61 D	49.0%	51.0%	49.0%	51.0%
MINNEHAHA	35,378	22,285	13,093		9,192 R	63.0%	37.0%	63.0%	37.0%
MOODY	3,973	2,133	1,840		293 R	53.7%	46.3%	53.7%	46.3%
PENNINGTON	16,287	10,955	5,332		5,623 R	67.3%	32.7%	67.3%	32.7%
PERKINS	2,934	1,743	1,191		552 R	59.4%	40.6%	59.4%	40.6%
POTTER	2,288	1,445	843		602 R	63.2%	36.8%	63.2%	36.8%
ROBERTS	6,100	2,854	3,246		392 D	46.8%	53.2%	46.8%	53.2%
SANBORN	2,629	1,327	1,302		25 R	50.5%	49.5%	50.5%	49.5%
SHANNON	1,731	782	949		167 D	45.2%	54.8%	45.2%	54.8%
SPINK	5,556	2,683	2,873		190 D	48.3%	51.7%	48.3%	51.7%
STANLEY	1,154	587	567		20 R	50.9%	49.1%	50.9%	49.1%
SULLY	1,220	726	494		232 R	59.5%	40.5%	59.5%	40.5%

SOUTH DAKOTA

PRESIDENT 1952

County	Total Vote	Republican	Democratic	Other	Rep.-Dem. Plurality	Percentage Total Vote Rep.	Dem.	Major Vote Rep.	Dem.
TODD	1,636	1,025	611		414 R	62.7%	37.3%	62.7%	37.3%
TRIPP	4,235	2,790	1,445		1,345 R	65.9%	34.1%	65.9%	34.1%
TURNER	5,588	4,604	984		3,620 R	82.4%	17.6%	82.4%	17.6%
UNION	5,038	3,393	1,645		1,748 R	67.3%	32.7%	67.3%	32.7%
WALWORTH	3,631	2,369	1,262		1,107 R	65.2%	34.8%	65.2%	34.8%
WASHABAUGH	466	319	147		172 R	63.5%	31.5%	68.5%	31.5%
WASHINGTON									
YANKTON	7,022	4,802	2,220		2,582 R	68.4%	31.6%	68.4%	31.6%
ZIEBACH	1,151	779	372		407 R	67.7%	32.3%	67.7%	32.3%
TOTAL	294,283	203,857	90,426		113,431 R	69.3%	30.7%	69.3%	30.7%

PRESIDENT 1956

County	Total Vote	Republican	Democratic	Other	Rep.-Dem. Plurality	Percentage Total Vote Rep.	Dem.	Major Vote Rep.	Dem.
TODD	1,581	748	833		85 D	47.3%	52.7%	47.3%	52.7%
TRIPP	3,899	2,064	1,835		229 R	52.9%	47.1%	52.9%	47.1%
TURNER	5,778	4,096	1,682		2,414 R	70.9%	29.1%	70.9%	29.1%
UNION	4,979	2,636	2,343		293 R	52.9%	47.1%	52.9%	47.1%
WALWORTH	3,541	2,132	1,409		723 R	60.2%	39.8%	60.2%	39.8%
WASHABAUGH	450	265	185		80 R	58.9%	41.1%	58.9%	41.1%
YANKTON	7,050	4,063	2,987		1,076 R	57.6%	42.4%	57.6%	42.4%
ZIEBACH	1,099	627	472		155 R	57.1%	42.9%	57.1%	42.9%
TOTAL	293,857	171,569	122,288		49,281 R	58.4%	41.6%	58.4%	41.6%

SOUTH DAKOTA

PRESIDENT 1960

County	Total Vote	Republican	Democratic	Other	Rep.-Dem. Plurality	Tot.% Rep.	Tot.% Dem.	Maj.% Rep.	Maj.% Dem.
ARMSTRONG									
AURORA	2,537	1,267	1,270		3 D	49.9%	50.1%	49.9%	50.1%
BEADLE	9,990	5,911	4,079		1,832 R	59.2%	40.8%	59.2%	40.8%
BENNETT	1,386	779	607		172 R	56.2%	43.8%	56.2%	43.8%
BON HOMME	4,782	2,730	2,052		678 R	57.1%	42.9%	57.1%	42.9%
BROOKINGS	8,684	5,710	2,974		2,736 R	65.8%	34.2%	65.8%	34.2%
BROWN	15,930	8,037	7,893		144 R	50.5%	49.5%	50.5%	49.5%
BRULE	3,003	1,403	1,600		197 D	46.7%	53.3%	46.7%	53.3%
BUFFALO	628	294	334		40 D	46.8%	53.2%	46.8%	53.2%
BUTTE	3,814	2,496	1,318		1,178 R	65.4%	34.6%	65.4%	34.6%
CAMPBELL	1,692	1,330	362		968 R	78.6%	21.4%	78.6%	21.4%
CHARLES MIX	5,200	2,446	2,754		308 D	47.0%	53.0%	47.0%	53.0%
CLARK	3,610	2,204	1,406		798 R	61.1%	38.9%	61.1%	38.9%
CLAY	4,650	2,772	1,878		894 R	59.6%	40.4%	59.6%	40.4%
CODINGTON	9,613	5,309	4,304		1,005 R	55.2%	44.8%	55.2%	44.8%
CORSON	2,383	1,290	1,093		197 R	54.1%	45.9%	54.1%	45.9%
CUSTER	2,411	1,533	878		655 R	63.6%	36.4%	63.6%	36.4%
DAVISON	8,213	4,105	4,108		3 D	50.0%	50.0%	50.0%	50.0%
DAY	5,461	2,626	2,835		209 D	48.1%	51.9%	48.1%	51.9%
DEUEL	3,080	1,907	1,173		734 R	61.9%	38.1%	61.9%	38.1%
DEWEY	2,212	1,168	1,044		124 R	52.8%	47.2%	52.8%	47.2%
DOUGLAS	2,543	2,002	541		1,461 R	78.7%	21.3%	78.7%	21.3%
EDMUNDS	3,337	1,728	1,609		119 R	51.8%	48.2%	51.8%	48.2%
FALL RIVER	3,918	2,492	1,426		1,066 R	63.6%	36.4%	63.6%	36.4%
FAULK	2,283	1,240	1,043		197 R	54.3%	45.7%	54.3%	45.7%
GRANT	4,725	2,611	2,114		497 R	55.3%	44.7%	55.3%	44.7%
GREGORY	3,841	2,063	1,778		285 R	53.7%	46.3%	53.7%	46.3%
HAAKON	1,575	980	595		385 R	62.2%	37.8%	62.2%	37.8%
HAMLIN	3,369	2,139	1,230		909 R	63.5%	36.5%	63.5%	36.5%
HAND	3,269	1,872	1,397		475 R	57.3%	42.7%	57.3%	42.7%
HANSON	2,240	1,087	1,153		66 D	48.5%	51.5%	48.5%	51.5%
HARDING	1,058	676	382		294 R	63.9%	36.1%	63.9%	36.1%
HUGHES	5,356	3,320	2,036		1,284 R	62.0%	38.0%	62.0%	38.0%
HUTCHINSON	5,505	3,948	1,557		2,391 R	71.7%	28.3%	71.7%	28.3%
HYDE	1,433	773	660		113 R	53.9%	46.1%	53.9%	46.1%
JACKSON	947	581	366		215 R	61.4%	38.6%	61.4%	38.6%
JERAULD	2,028	1,165	863		302 R	57.4%	42.6%	57.4%	42.6%
JONES	1,067	644	423		221 R	60.4%	39.6%	60.4%	39.6%
KINGSBURY	4,564	2,887	1,677		1,210 R	63.3%	36.7%	63.3%	36.7%
LAKE	5,744	3,520	2,224		1,296 R	61.3%	38.7%	61.3%	38.7%
LAWRENCE	7,695	5,083	2,612		2,471 R	66.1%	33.9%	66.1%	33.9%
LINCOLN	5,538	3,553	1,985		1,568 R	64.2%	35.8%	64.2%	35.8%
LYMAN	2,018	1,166	852		314 R	57.8%	42.2%	57.8%	42.2%
McCOOK	4,172	2,375	1,797		578 R	56.9%	43.1%	56.9%	43.1%
McPHERSON	2,970	2,354	616		1,738 R	79.3%	20.7%	79.3%	20.7%
MARSHALL	3,378	1,704	1,674		30 R	50.4%	49.6%	50.4%	49.6%
MEADE	4,567	2,644	1,923		721 R	57.9%	42.1%	57.9%	42.1%
MELLETTE	1,284	774	510		264 R	60.3%	39.7%	60.3%	39.7%
MINER	2,693	1,377	1,316		61 R	51.1%	48.9%	51.1%	48.9%
MINNEHAHA	38,390	23,238	15,152		8,086 R	60.5%	39.5%	60.5%	39.5%
MOODY	4,037	2,119	1,918		201 R	52.5%	47.5%	52.5%	47.5%
PENNINGTON	18,842	11,364	7,478		3,886 R	60.3%	39.7%	60.3%	39.7%
PERKINS	2,931	1,767	1,164		603 R	60.3%	39.7%	60.3%	39.7%
POTTER	2,330	1,326	1,004		322 R	56.9%	43.1%	56.9%	43.1%
ROBERTS	5,946	2,857	3,089		232 D	48.0%	52.0%	48.0%	52.0%
SANBORN	2,503	1,254	1,249		5 R	50.1%	49.9%	50.1%	49.9%
SHANNON	1,790	655	1,135		480 D	36.6%	63.4%	36.6%	63.4%
SPINK	5,301	2,738	2,563		175 R	51.7%	48.3%	51.7%	48.3%
STANLEY	1,408	678	730		52 D	48.2%	51.8%	48.2%	51.8%
SULLY	1,347	864	483		381 R	64.1%	35.9%	64.1%	35.9%

PRESIDENT 1964

County	Total Vote	Republican	Democratic	Other	Rep.-Dem. Plurality	Tot.% Rep.	Tot.% Dem.	Maj.% Rep.	Maj.% Dem.
ARMSTRONG									
AURORA	2,426	871	1,555		684 D	35.9%	64.1%	35.9%	64.1%
BEADLE	10,019	4,051	5,968		1,917 D	40.4%	59.6%	40.4%	59.6%
BENNETT	1,399	624	775		151 D	44.6%	55.4%	44.6%	55.4%
BON HOMME	4,278	1,784	2,494		710 D	41.7%	58.3%	41.7%	58.3%
BROOKINGS	7,883	3,692	4,191		499 D	46.8%	53.2%	46.8%	53.2%
BROWN	14,631	5,524	9,107		3,583 D	37.8%	62.2%	37.8%	62.2%
BRULE	3,173	968	2,205		1,237 D	30.5%	69.5%	30.5%	69.5%
BUFFALO	779	278	501		223 D	35.7%	64.3%	35.7%	64.3%
BUTTE	3,740	1,877	1,863		14 R	50.2%	49.8%	50.2%	49.8%
CAMPBELL	1,573	1,162	411		751 R	73.9%	26.1%	73.9%	26.1%
CHARLES MIX	5,113	1,625	3,488		1,863 D	31.8%	68.2%	31.8%	68.2%
CLARK	3,282	1,511	1,771		260 D	46.0%	54.0%	46.0%	54.0%
CLAY	4,401	1,802	2,599		797 D	40.9%	59.1%	40.9%	59.1%
CODINGTON	8,946	3,593	5,353		1,760 D	40.2%	59.8%	40.2%	59.8%
CORSON	2,362	1,034	1,328		294 D	43.8%	56.2%	43.8%	56.2%
CUSTER	2,318	1,142	1,176		34 D	49.3%	50.7%	49.3%	50.7%
DAVISON	7,650	2,789	4,861		2,072 D	36.5%	63.5%	36.5%	63.5%
DAY	5,149	1,914	3,235		1,321 D	37.2%	62.8%	37.2%	62.8%
DEUEL	2,841	1,317	1,524		207 D	46.4%	53.6%	46.4%	53.6%
DEWEY	2,240	981	1,259		278 D	43.8%	56.2%	43.8%	56.2%
DOUGLAS	2,338	1,189	1,149		40 R	50.9%	49.1%	50.9%	49.1%
EDMUNDS	3,150	1,442	1,708		266 D	45.8%	54.2%	45.8%	54.2%
FALL RIVER	3,732	2,026	1,706		320 R	54.3%	45.7%	54.3%	45.7%
FAULK	2,199	974	1,225		251 D	44.3%	55.7%	44.3%	55.7%
GRANT	4,437	1,854	2,583		729 D	41.8%	58.2%	41.8%	58.2%
GREGORY	3,639	1,644	1,995		351 D	45.2%	54.8%	45.2%	54.8%
HAAKON	1,457	795	662		133 R	54.6%	45.4%	54.6%	45.4%
HAMLIN	3,086	1,525	1,661		136 D	49.4%	50.6%	49.4%	50.6%
HAND	3,029	1,466	1,563		97 D	48.4%	51.6%	48.4%	51.6%
HANSON	2,034	802	1,232		430 D	39.4%	60.6%	39.4%	60.6%
HARDING	976	489	487		2 R	50.1%	49.9%	50.1%	49.9%
HUGHES	5,338	2,732	2,606		126 R	51.2%	48.8%	51.2%	48.8%
HUTCHINSON	5,073	2,884	2,189		695 R	56.8%	43.2%	56.8%	43.2%
HYDE	1,402	666	736		70 D	47.5%	52.5%	47.5%	52.5%
JACKSON	928	448	480		32 D	48.3%	51.7%	48.3%	51.7%
JERAULD	1,856	857	999		142 D	46.2%	53.8%	46.2%	53.8%
JONES	963	415	548		133 D	43.1%	56.9%	43.1%	56.9%
KINGSBURY	4,131	2,126	2,005		121 R	51.5%	48.5%	51.5%	48.5%
LAKE	5,405	2,417	2,988		571 D	44.7%	55.3%	44.7%	55.3%
LAWRENCE	7,211	3,743	3,468		275 R	51.9%	48.1%	51.9%	48.1%
LINCOLN	5,576	2,740	2,836		96 D	49.1%	50.9%	49.1%	50.9%
LYMAN	1,919	862	1,057		195 D	44.9%	55.1%	44.9%	55.1%
McCOOK	3,937	1,756	2,181		425 D	44.6%	55.4%	44.6%	55.4%
McPHERSON	2,614	1,891	723		1,168 R	72.3%	27.7%	72.3%	27.7%
MARSHALL	3,246	1,183	2,063		880 D	36.4%	63.6%	36.4%	63.6%
MEADE	4,463	2,140	2,323		183 D	47.9%	52.1%	47.9%	52.1%
MELLETTE	1,183	525	658		133 D	44.4%	55.6%	44.4%	55.6%
MINER	2,624	945	1,679		734 D	36.0%	64.0%	36.0%	64.0%
MINNEHAHA	37,695	16,766	20,929		4,163 D	44.5%	55.5%	44.5%	55.5%
MOODY	3,762	1,461	2,301		840 D	38.8%	61.2%	38.8%	61.2%
PENNINGTON	18,807	8,926	9,881		955 D	47.5%	52.5%	47.5%	52.5%
PERKINS	2,664	1,409	1,255		154 R	52.9%	47.1%	52.9%	47.1%
POTTER	2,214	954	1,260		306 D	43.1%	56.9%	43.1%	56.9%
ROBERTS	5,498	1,931	3,567		1,636 D	35.1%	64.9%	35.1%	64.9%
SANBORN	2,313	912	1,401		489 D	39.4%	60.6%	39.4%	60.6%
SHANNON	2,305	557	1,748		1,191 D	24.2%	75.8%	24.2%	75.8%
SPINK	5,073	1,953	3,120		1,167 D	38.5%	61.5%	38.5%	61.5%
STANLEY	1,299	549	750		201 D	42.3%	57.7%	42.3%	57.7%
SULLY	1,263	667	596		71 R	52.8%	47.2%	52.8%	47.2%

SOUTH DAKOTA

PRESIDENT 1960

County	Total Vote	Republican	Democratic	Other	Rep.-Dem. Plurality	Total Vote Rep.	Dem.	Major Vote Rep.	Dem.
TODD	1,813	909	904		5 R	50.1%	49.9%	50.1%	49.9%
TRIPP	4,214	2,466	1,748		718 R	58.5%	41.5%	58.5%	41.5%
TURNER	5,667	4,120	1,547		2,573 R	72.7%	27.3%	72.7%	27.3%
UNION	5,019	2,688	2,331		357 R	53.6%	46.4%	53.6%	46.4%
WALWORTH	3,874	2,406	1,468		938 R	62.1%	37.9%	62.1%	37.9%
WASHABAUGH	473	260	213		47 R	55.0%	45.0%	55.0%	45.0%
WASHINGTON									
YANKTON	7,126	4,065	3,061		1,004 R	57.0%	43.0%	57.0%	43.0%
ZIEBACH	1,080	568	512		56 R	52.6%	47.4%	52.6%	47.4%
TOTAL	306,487	178,417	128,070		50,347 R	58.2%	41.8%	58.2%	41.8%

PRESIDENT 1964

County	Total Vote	Republican	Democratic	Other	Rep.-Dem. Plurality	Total Vote Rep.	Dem.	Major Vote Rep.	Dem.
TODD	1,997	723	1,274		551 D	36.2%	63.8%	36.2%	63.8%
TRIPP	4,178	1,937	2,241		304 D	46.4%	53.6%	46.4%	53.6%
TURNER	5,030	2,846	2,184		662 R	56.6%	43.4%	56.6%	43.4%
UNION	4,555	1,727	2,828		1,101 D	37.9%	62.1%	37.9%	62.1%
WALWORTH	3,801	1,849	1,952		103 D	48.6%	51.4%	48.6%	51.4%
WASHABAUGH	559	211	348		137 D	37.7%	62.3%	37.7%	62.3%
WASHINGTON									
YANKTON	6,955	3,208	3,747		539 D	46.1%	53.9%	46.1%	53.9%
ZIEBACH	1,001	447	554		107 D	44.7%	55.3%	44.7%	55.3%
TOTAL	293,118	130,108	163,010		32,902 D	44.4%	55.6%	44.4%	55.6%

SOUTH DAKOTA

OTHER VOTE COMPOSITION:

1920	34,707 Farmer-Labor; 900 Prohibition.
1924	Progressive.
1928	927 Farmer-Labor; 443 Socialist; 224 Communist.
1932	3,333 Liberty; 1,551 Socialist; 463 Prohibition; 364 Communist.
1936	Union.
1940	
1944	
1948	Progressive.
1952	
1956	
1960	
1964	

SPECIAL CASES:

In several instances individual counties have not been separately returned in the official state canvass; such voting as took place in these areas was reported with neighboring counties.

1920	Farmer-Labor candidates ran second in a number of counties.
1924	Progressive candidates carried a number of counties and ran second in many others.
1944	Washington county merged with Shannon county in 1943.
1956	Armstrong county merged with Dewey county in 1954.

TENNESSEE

PRESIDENT 1920

County	Total Vote	Republican	Democratic	Other	Rep.-Dem. Plurality	% Total Rep.	% Total Dem.	% Major Rep.	% Major Dem.
ANDERSON	3,894	3,127	748	19	2,379 R	80.3	19.2	80.7	19.3
BEDFORD	4,238	2,056	2,182		126 D	48.5	51.5	48.5	51.5
BENTON	3,438	1,514	1,914	10	400 D	44.0	55.7	44.2	55.8
BLEDSOE	1,680	1,198	482		716 R	71.3	28.7	71.3	28.7
BLOUNT	7,094	5,540	1,550	4	3,990 R	78.1	21.8	78.1	21.9
BRADLEY	3,349	2,255	1,058	36	1,197 R	67.3	31.6	68.1	31.9
CAMPBELL	4,018	3,368	650		2,718 R	83.8	16.2	83.8	16.2
CANNON	1,457	687	770		83 D	47.2	52.8	47.2	52.8
CARROLL	7,956	4,741	3,215		1,526 R	59.6	40.4	59.6	40.4
CARTER	6,733	6,059	674		5,385 R	90.0	10.0	90.0	10.0
CHEATHAM	1,791	569	1,219	3	650 D	31.8	68.1	31.8	68.2
CHESTER	2,229	1,088	1,105	36	17 D	48.8	49.6	49.6	50.4
CLAIBORNE	3,848	2,612	1,236		1,376 R	67.9	32.1	67.9	32.1
CLAY	1,827	1,044	772	11	272 R	57.1	42.3	57.5	42.5
COCKE	4,255	3,294	929	32	2,365 R	77.4	21.8	78.0	22.0
COFFEE	2,925	882	2,043		1,161 D	30.2	69.8	30.2	69.8
CROCKETT	4,578	2,326	2,252		74 R	50.8	49.2	50.8	49.2
CUMBERLAND	2,042	1,485	557		928 R	72.7	27.3	72.7	27.3
DAVIDSON	20,346	6,811	13,354	181	6,543 D	33.5	65.6	33.8	66.2
DECATUR	2,780	1,608	1,149	23	459 R	57.8	41.3	58.3	41.7
DE KALB	4,555	2,572	1,983		589 R	56.5	43.5	56.5	43.5
DICKSON	3,617	1,472	2,145		673 D	40.7	59.3	40.7	59.3
DYER	4,417	1,166	3,181	70	2,015 D	26.4	72.0	26.8	73.2
FAYETTE	2,640	346	2,294		1,948 D	13.1	86.9	13.1	86.9
FENTRESS	2,523	1,808	694	21	1,114 R	71.7	27.5	72.3	27.7
FRANKLIN	5,064	1,558	3,504	2	1,946 D	30.8	69.2	30.8	69.2
GIBSON	9,359	3,398	5,942	19	2,544 D	36.3	63.5	36.4	63.6
GILES	5,359	2,224	3,129	6	905 D	41.5	58.4	41.5	58.5
GRAINGER	3,054	2,158	895	1	1,263 R	70.7	29.3	70.7	29.3
GREENE	8,606	5,677	2,924	5	2,753 R	66.0	34.0	66.0	34.0
GRUNDY	1,355	447	745	163	298 D	33.0	55.0	37.5	62.5
HAMBLEN	2,928	1,571	1,301	56	270 R	53.7	44.4	54.7	45.3
HAMILTON	21,037	10,793	9,910	334	883 R	51.3	47.1	52.1	47.9
HANCOCK	2,124	1,740	384		1,356 R	81.9	18.1	81.9	18.1
HARDEMAN	3,190	895	2,272	23	1,377 D	28.1	71.2	28.3	71.7
HARDIN	4,487	3,077	1,398	12	1,679 R	68.6	31.2	68.8	31.2
HAWKINS	4,070	2,650	1,381	39	1,269 R	65.1	33.9	65.7	34.3
HAYWOOD	2,176	101	2,068	7	1,967 D	4.6	95.0	4.7	95.3
HENDERSON	4,346	3,112	1,217	17	1,895 R	71.6	28.0	71.9	28.1
HENRY	6,633	1,957	4,613	63	2,656 D	29.5	69.5	29.8	70.2
HICKMAN	2,847	1,470	1,362	15	108 R	51.6	47.8	51.9	48.1
HOUSTON	1,193	385	790	18	405 D	32.3	66.2	32.8	67.2
HUMPHREYS	2,231	674	1,534	23	860 D	30.2	68.8	30.5	69.5
JACKSON	2,284	1,187	1,097		90 R	52.0	48.0	52.0	48.0
JEFFERSON	4,392	3,583	741	68	2,842 R	81.6	16.9	82.9	17.1
JOHNSON	3,918	3,627	291		3,336 R	92.6	7.4	92.6	7.4
KNOX	18,931	12,005	6,801	125	5,204 R	63.4	35.9	63.8	36.2
LAKE	1,552	352	1,192	8	840 D	22.7	76.8	22.8	77.2
LAUDERDALE	3,503	1,190	2,313		1,123 D	34.0	66.0	34.0	66.0
LAWRENCE	6,453	3,843	2,610		1,233 R	59.6	40.4	59.6	40.4
LEWIS	853	446	403	4	43 R	52.3	47.2	52.5	47.5
LINCOLN	3,560	1,091	2,463	6	1,372 D	30.6	69.2	30.7	69.3
LOUDON	2,575	1,872	686	17	1,186 R	72.7	26.6	73.1	26.9
MCMINN	4,471	2,800	1,636	35	1,164 R	62.6	36.6	63.1	36.9
MCNAIRY	5,075	3,212	1,863		1,349 R	63.3	36.7	63.3	36.7
MACON	4,276	3,208	1,066	2	2,142 R	75.0	24.9	75.1	24.9
MADISON	7,945	2,665	5,280		2,615 D	33.5	66.5	33.5	66.5
MARION	4,580	2,662	1,874	44	788 R	58.1	40.9	58.7	41.3
MARSHALL	2,596	753	1,828	15	1,075 D	29.0	70.4	29.3	70.7
MAURY	4,113	1,379	2,693	41	1,314 D	33.5	65.5	33.9	66.1

PRESIDENT 1924

County	Total Vote	Republican	Democratic	Other	Rep.-Dem. Plurality	% Total Rep.	% Total Dem.	% Major Rep.	% Major Dem.
ANDERSON	2,152	1,487	550	115	937 R	69.1	25.6	73.0	27.0
BEDFORD	2,784	925	1,799	60	874 D	33.2	64.6	34.0	66.0
BENTON	1,856	708	1,109	39	401 D	38.1	59.8	39.0	61.0
BLEDSOE	1,179	686	483	10	203 R	58.2	41.0	58.7	41.3
BLOUNT	3,813	2,754	999	60	1,755 R	72.2	26.2	73.4	26.6
BRADLEY	2,829	1,780	1,011	38	769 R	62.9	35.7	63.8	36.2
CAMPBELL	3,551	2,620	648	283	1,972 R	73.8	18.2	80.2	19.8
CANNON	878	285	581	12	296 D	32.5	66.2	32.9	67.1
CARROLL	4,208	2,178	1,925	105	253 R	51.8	45.7	53.1	46.9
CARTER	4,250	3,665	557	28	3,108 R	86.2	13.1	86.8	13.1
CHEATHAM	1,069	181	868	20	687 D	16.9	81.2	17.3	82.7
CHESTER	1,267	485	768	14	283 D	38.3	60.6	38.7	61.3
CLAIBORNE	2,960	1,775	1,091	94	684 R	60.0	36.9	61.9	38.1
CLAY	1,567	863	673	31	190 R	55.1	42.9	56.2	43.8
COCKE	3,518	2,564	936	18	1,628 R	72.9	26.6	73.3	26.7
COFFEE	2,236	485	1,692	59	1,207 D	21.7	75.7	22.3	77.7
CROCKETT	1,775	587	1,168	20	581 D	33.1	65.8	33.4	66.6
CUMBERLAND	1,517	886	540	91	346 R	58.4	35.6	62.1	37.9
DAVIDSON	17,270	4,511	11,386	1,373	6,875 D	26.1	65.9	28.4	71.6
DECATUR	1,696	799	877	20	78 D	47.1	51.7	47.7	52.3
DE KALB	3,257	1,406	1,829	22	423 D	43.2	56.2	43.5	56.5
DICKSON	2,270	516	1,648	106	1,132 D	22.7	72.6	23.8	76.2
DYER	2,835	477	2,348	10	1,871 D	16.8	82.8	16.9	83.1
FAYETTE	1,273	65	1,181	27	1,116 D	5.1	92.8	5.2	94.8
FENTRESS	1,706	1,197	420	89	777 R	70.2	24.6	74.0	26.0
FRANKLIN	2,840	707	2,075	58	1,368 D	24.9	73.1	25.4	74.6
GIBSON	4,372	1,046	3,277	49	2,231 D	23.9	75.0	24.2	75.8
GILES	3,261	677	2,509	75	1,832 D	20.8	76.9	21.2	78.8
GRAINGER	2,148	1,463	664	21	799 R	68.1	30.9	68.8	31.2
GREENE	5,932	3,295	2,605	32	690 R	55.5	43.9	55.8	44.2
GRUNDY	764	173	394	197	221 D	22.6	51.6	30.5	69.5
HAMBLEN	2,715	1,342	1,316	26	26 R	49.4	48.5	50.5	49.5
HAMILTON	16,780	8,421	7,511	848	910 R	50.2	44.8	52.9	47.1
HANCOCK	1,395	1,028	305	62	723 R	73.7	21.9	77.1	22.9
HARDEMAN	1,904	253	1,595	56	1,342 D	13.3	83.8	13.7	86.3
HARDIN	1,805	1,175	625	5	550 R	65.1	34.6	65.3	34.7
HAWKINS	4,389	2,632	1,705	52	927 R	60.0	38.8	60.7	39.3
HAYWOOD	1,947	60	1,872	15	1,812 D	3.1	96.1	3.1	96.9
HENDERSON	2,677	1,616	1,009	52	607 R	60.4	37.7	61.6	38.4
HENRY	3,193	562	2,478	153	1,916 D	17.6	77.6	18.5	81.5
HICKMAN	1,258	315	922	21	607 D	25.0	73.3	25.5	74.5
HOUSTON	565	95	449	21	354 D	16.8	79.5	17.5	82.5
HUMPHREYS	1,322	216	1,089	17	873 D	16.3	82.4	16.6	83.4
JACKSON	1,123	363	726	34	363 D	32.3	64.6	33.3	66.7
JEFFERSON	3,451	2,701	716	34	1,985 R	78.3	20.7	79.0	21.0
JOHNSON	3,064	2,798	255	11	2,543 R	91.3	8.3	91.6	8.4
KNOX	19,003	10,713	6,952	1,338	3,761 R	56.4	36.6	60.6	39.4
LAKE	912	87	817	8	730 D	9.5	89.6	9.6	90.4
LAUDERDALE	1,868	242	1,596	30	1,354 D	13.0	85.4	13.2	86.8
LAWRENCE	4,689	2,379	2,237	73	142 R	50.7	47.7	51.5	48.5
LEWIS	525	191	307	27	116 D	36.4	58.5	38.4	61.6
LINCOLN	2,753	357	2,360	36	2,003 D	13.0	85.7	13.1	86.9
LOUDON	2,306	1,537	706	63	831 R	66.7	30.6	68.5	31.5
MCMINN	4,502	2,652	1,615	235	1,037 R	58.9	35.9	62.2	37.8
MCNAIRY	2,776	1,625	1,125	26	500 R	58.5	40.5	59.1	40.9
MACON	2,537	1,808	709	20	1,099 R	71.3	27.9	71.8	28.2
MADISON	4,931	1,110	3,422	399	2,312 D	22.5	69.4	24.5	75.5
MARION	2,241	1,076	1,055	110	21 R	48.0	47.1	50.5	49.5
MARSHALL	2,085	349	1,696	40	1,347 D	16.7	81.3	17.1	82.9
MAURY	3,944	844	3,000	100	2,156 D	21.4	76.1	22.0	78.0

TENNESSEE

PRESIDENT 1920

County	Total Vote	Republican	Democratic	Other	Rep.-Dem. Plurality	Total Vote Rep.	Total Vote Dem.	Major Vote Rep.	Major Vote Dem.
MEIGS	1,627	915	712		203 R	56.2%	43.8%	56.2%	43.8%
MONROE	4,420	2,575	1,845		730 R	58.3%	41.7%	58.3%	41.7%
MONTGOMERY	4,384	1,780	2,564	40	784 D	40.6%	58.5%	41.0%	59.0%
MOORE	587		497		407 D	15.3%	84.7%	15.3%	84.7%
MORGAN	3,072	2,248	816	8	1,432 R	73.2%	26.6%	73.4%	26.6%
OBION	5,874	1,307	4,547	20	3,240 D	22.3%	77.4%	22.3%	77.7%
OVERTON	3,735	1,939	1,779	17	160 R	51.9%	47.6%	52.4%	47.6%
PERRY	1,439	747	692		55 R	51.9%	48.1%	51.9%	48.1%
PICKETT	1,503	896	607		289 R	59.6%	40.4%	59.6%	40.4%
POLK	1,811	1,018	775	18	243 R	56.2%	42.8%	56.8%	43.2%
PUTNAM	5,728	2,732	2,996		264 D	47.7%	52.3%	47.7%	52.3%
RHEA	2,413	1,341	1,051	21	290 R	55.6%	43.6%	56.1%	43.9%
ROANE	2,812	1,974	838		1,136 R	70.2%	29.8%	70.2%	29.8%
ROBERTSON	4,248	1,191	3,046	11	1,855 D	28.0%	71.7%	28.1%	71.9%
RUTHERFORD	5,287	1,881	3,406		1,525 D	35.6%	64.4%	35.6%	64.4%
SCOTT	2,802	2,537	221	44	2,316 R	90.5%	7.9%	92.0%	8.0%
SEQUATCHIE	1,057	509	545	3	36 D	48.2%	51.6%	48.3%	51.7%
SEVIER	6,417	6,006	404	7	5,602 R	93.6%	6.3%	93.7%	6.3%
SHELBY	24,843	8,597	15,986	260	7,389 D	34.6%	64.3%	35.0%	65.0%
SMITH	5,131	1,981	3,150		1,169 D	38.6%	61.4%	38.6%	61.4%
STEWART	3,244	849	2,366	29	1,517 D	26.2%	72.9%	26.4%	73.6%
SULLIVAN	7,920	3,593	4,327		734 D	45.4%	54.6%	45.4%	54.6%
SUMNER	4,963	1,268	3,674	21	2,406 D	25.5%	74.0%	25.7%	74.3%
TIPTON	3,776	906	2,816	54	1,910 D	24.0%	74.6%	24.3%	75.7%
TROUSDALE	1,530	574	955	1	381 D	37.5%	62.4%	37.5%	62.5%
UNICOI	3,135	2,584	547	4	2,037 R	82.4%	17.4%	82.5%	17.5%
UNION	3,032	2,607	423	2	2,184 R	86.0%	14.0%	86.0%	14.0%
VAN BUREN	582	223	351	8	128 D	38.3%	60.3%	38.8%	61.1%
WARREN	3,012	1,010	1,986	16	976 D	33.5%	65.9%	33.7%	66.3%
WASHINGTON	7,122	4,858	2,260	4	2,598 R	68.2%	31.7%	68.2%	31.8%
WAYNE	3,284	2,617	654	13	1,963 R	79.7%	19.9%	80.0%	20.0%
WEAKLEY	7,166	2,741	4,395	30	1,654 D	38.3%	61.3%	38.4%	61.6%
WHITE	3,657	1,456	2,201		745 D	39.8%	60.2%	39.8%	60.2%
WILLIAMSON	2,950	946	2,004		1,058 D	32.1%	67.9%	32.1%	67.9%
WILSON	4,296	1,532	2,760	4	1,228 D	35.7%	64.2%	35.7%	64.3%
TOTAL	428,036	219,229	206,558	2,249	12,671 R	51.2%	48.3%	51.5%	48.5%

PRESIDENT 1924

County	Total Vote	Republican	Democratic	Other	Rep.-Dem. Plurality	Total Vote Rep.	Total Vote Dem.	Major Vote Rep.	Major Vote Dem.
MEIGS	1,243	656	572	15	84 R	52.8%	46.0%	53.4%	46.6%
MONROE	4,743	2,487	2,238	18	249 R	52.4%	47.2%	52.6%	47.4%
MONTGOMERY	2,967	943	1,967	57	1,024 D	31.8%	66.3%	32.4%	67.6%
MOORE	537	41	492	4	451 D	7.6%	91.6%	7.7%	92.3%
MORGAN	1,769	1,105	416	248	689 R	62.5%	23.5%	72.6%	27.4%
OBION	3,778	484	3,233	61	2,749 D	12.8%	85.6%	13.0%	87.0%
OVERTON	2,489	904	1,536	49	632 D	36.3%	61.7%	37.0%	63.0%
PERRY	772	268	498	6	230 D	34.7%	64.5%	35.0%	65.0%
PICKETT	1,331	672	649	10	23 R	50.5%	48.8%	50.9%	49.1%
POLK	2,456	1,246	1,160	50	86 R	50.7%	47.2%	51.8%	48.2%
PUTNAM	4,018	1,489	2,474	55	985 D	37.1%	61.6%	37.6%	62.4%
RHEA	2,412	1,165	1,176	71	11 D	48.3%	48.8%	49.8%	50.2%
ROANE	2,638	1,680	812	146	868 R	63.7%	30.8%	67.4%	32.6%
ROBERTSON	1,946	229	1,668	49	1,439 D	11.8%	85.7%	12.1%	87.9%
RUTHERFORD	2,849	680	2,137	32	1,457 D	23.9%	75.0%	24.1%	75.9%
SCOTT	2,073	1,611	274	188	1,337 R	77.7%	13.2%	85.5%	14.5%
SEQUATCHIE	626	247	374	5	127 D	39.5%	59.7%	39.8%	60.2%
SEVIER	4,016	3,534	462	20	3,072 R	88.0%	11.5%	88.4%	11.6%
SHELBY	23,066	7,369	13,695	2,002	6,326 D	31.9%	59.4%	35.0%	65.0%
SMITH	2,449	695	1,723	31	1,028 D	28.4%	70.4%	28.7%	71.3%
STEWART	1,658	264	1,369	25	1,105 D	15.9%	82.6%	16.2%	83.8%
SULLIVAN	5,652	2,247	3,338	67	1,091 D	39.8%	59.1%	40.2%	59.8%
SUMNER	3,149	432	2,655	62	2,223 D	13.7%	84.3%	14.0%	86.0%
TIPTON	2,177	217	1,914	46	1,697 D	10.0%	87.9%	10.2%	89.8%
TROUSDALE	837	139	694	4	555 D	16.6%	82.9%	16.7%	83.3%
UNICOI	1,901	1,379	384	138	995 R	72.5%	20.2%	78.2%	21.8%
UNION	1,965	1,540	368	57	1,172 R	78.4%	18.7%	80.7%	19.3%
VAN BUREN	483	123	357	3	234 D	25.5%	73.9%	25.6%	74.4%
WARREN	1,874	490	1,356	28	866 D	26.1%	72.4%	26.5%	73.5%
WASHINGTON	5,179	3,258	1,842	79	1,416 R	62.9%	35.6%	63.9%	36.1%
WAYNE	1,859	1,395	452	12	943 R	75.0%	24.3%	75.5%	24.5%
WEAKLEY	4,327	1,153	3,150	24	1,997 D	26.6%	72.8%	26.8%	73.2%
WHITE	1,679	453	1,175	51	722 D	27.0%	70.0%	27.8%	72.2%
WILLIAMSON	1,917	243	1,626	48	1,383 D	12.7%	84.8%	13.0%	86.0%
WILSON	2,655	580	2,043	32	1,463 D	21.8%	76.9%	22.1%	77.9%
TOTAL	301,030	130,831	159,339	10,860	28,508 D	43.5%	52.9%	45.1%	54.9%

TENNESSEE

PRESIDENT 1928

County	Total Vote	Republican	Democratic	Other	Rep.-Dem. Plurality	Total Vote Rep.	Total Vote Dem.	Major Vote Rep.	Major Vote Dem.
ANDERSON	2,843	2,306	537		1,769 R	81.1%	18.9%	81.1%	18.9%
BEDFORD	2,937	1,405	1,532		127 D	47.8%	52.2%	47.8%	52.2%
BENTON	2,203	949	1,241	13	292 D	43.1%	56.3%	43.3%	56.7%
BLEDSOE	1,499	899	600		299 R	60.0%	40.0%	60.0%	40.0%
BLOUNT	4,855	4,135	715	5	3,420 R	85.2%	14.7%	85.3%	14.7%
BRADLEY	3,770	2,854	913	3	1,941 R	75.7%	24.2%	75.8%	24.2%
CAMPBELL	3,597	3,007	585	5	2,422 R	83.6%	16.3%	83.7%	16.3%
CANNON	1,210	588	622		34 D	48.6%	51.4%	48.6%	51.4%
CARROLL	4,751	2,987	1,743	21	1,244 R	62.9%	36.7%	63.2%	36.8%
CARTER	5,460	4,934	512	14	4,422 R	90.4%	9.4%	90.6%	9.4%
CHEATHAM	1,403	488	913	2	425 D	34.6%	65.1%	34.8%	65.2%
CHESTER	1,323	588	735		147 D	44.4%	55.6%	44.4%	55.6%
CLAIBORNE	3,790	2,565	1,225		1,340 R	67.7%	32.3%	67.7%	32.3%
CLAY	1,134	556	576	2	20 D	49.0%	50.8%	49.1%	50.9%
COCKE	3,634	2,909	722	3	2,187 R	80.0%	19.9%	80.1%	19.9%
COFFEE	2,311	1,126	1,175	10	49 D	48.7%	50.8%	48.9%	51.1%
CROCKETT	1,459	710	749		39 D	48.7%	51.3%	48.7%	51.3%
CUMBERLAND	1,695	1,188	507		681 R	70.1%	29.9%	70.1%	29.9%
DAVIDSON	28,839	15,359	13,453	27	1,906 R	53.3%	46.6%	53.3%	46.7%
DECATUR	1,560	748	812		64 D	47.9%	52.1%	47.9%	52.1%
DE KALB	3,951	2,261	1,690		571 R	57.2%	42.8%	57.2%	42.8%
DICKSON	2,319	891	1,428		537 D	38.4%	61.6%	38.4%	61.6%
DYER	3,503	842	2,661		1,819 D	24.0%	76.0%	24.0%	76.0%
FAYETTE	1,222	122	1,100		978 D	10.0%	90.0%	10.0%	90.0%
FENTRESS	1,792	1,399	375	18	1,024 R	78.1%	20.9%	78.9%	21.1%
FRANKLIN	2,632	928	1,698	6	770 D	35.3%	64.5%	35.3%	64.7%
GIBSON	4,291	1,372	2,911	8	1,539 D	32.0%	67.9%	32.0%	68.0%
GILES	3,693	1,032	2,661		1,629 D	27.9%	72.1%	27.9%	72.1%
GRAINGER	1,942	1,464	466	12	998 R	75.4%	24.0%	75.9%	24.1%
GREENE	5,896	3,599	2,297		1,302 R	61.0%	39.0%	61.0%	39.0%
GRUNDY	992	380	608	4	228 D	38.3%	61.3%	38.5%	61.5%
HAMBLEN	3,172	1,902	1,270		632 R	60.0%	40.0%	60.0%	40.0%
HAMILTON	20,537	13,244	7,190	103	6,054 R	64.5%	35.0%	64.8%	35.2%
HANCOCK	1,255	1,039	216		823 R	82.8%	17.2%	82.8%	17.2%
HARDEMAN	1,960	491	1,459	10	968 D	25.1%	74.4%	25.2%	74.8%
HARDIN	2,301	1,585	709	7	875 R	68.9%	30.8%	69.1%	30.9%
HAWKINS	4,165	2,969	1,190	6	1,779 R	71.3%	28.6%	71.4%	28.6%
HAYWOOD	2,202	178	2,024		1,846 D	8.1%	91.9%	8.1%	91.9%
HENDERSON	2,752	2,005	714	33	1,291 R	72.9%	25.9%	73.7%	26.3%
HENRY	3,713	1,041	2,667	5	1,626 D	28.0%	71.8%	28.1%	71.9%
HICKMAN	1,550	511	1,039		528 D	33.0%	67.0%	33.0%	67.0%
HOUSTON	632	374	258		116 R	59.2%	40.8%	59.2%	40.8%
HUMPHREYS	1,218	441	771	6	330 D	36.2%	63.3%	36.4%	63.6%
JACKSON	1,464	617	832	15	215 D	42.1%	56.8%	42.6%	57.4%
JEFFERSON	3,019	2,582	437		2,145 R	85.5%	14.5%	85.5%	14.5%
JOHNSON	3,261	3,057	196	8	2,861 R	93.7%	6.0%	94.0%	6.0%
KNOX	20,438	14,627	5,767	44	8,860 R	71.6%	28.2%	71.7%	28.3%
LAKE	1,126	166	960		794 D	14.7%	85.3%	14.7%	85.3%
LAUDERDALE	3,228	430	2,798		2,368 D	13.3%	86.7%	13.3%	86.7%
LAWRENCE	6,373	3,581	2,780	12	801 R	56.2%	43.6%	56.3%	43.7%
LEWIS	683	269	414		145 D	39.4%	60.6%	39.4%	60.6%
LINCOLN	3,127	743	2,377	7	1,634 D	23.8%	76.0%	23.8%	76.2%
LOUDON	2,719	2,128	590	1	1,538 R	78.3%	21.7%	78.3%	21.7%
MCMINN	6,481	4,440	2,025	16	2,415 R	68.5%	31.2%	68.7%	31.3%
MCNAIRY	3,535	2,326	1,209		1,117 R	65.8%	34.2%	65.8%	34.2%
MACON	2,356	1,937	419		1,518 R	82.2%	17.8%	82.2%	17.8%
MADISON	5,471	1,894	3,577		1,683 D	34.6%	65.4%	34.6%	65.4%
MARION	2,820	1,659	1,161		498 R	58.8%	41.2%	58.8%	41.2%
MARSHALL	2,319	735	1,584		849 D	31.7%	68.3%	31.7%	68.3%
MAURY	5,014	1,362	3,652		2,290 D	27.2%	72.8%	27.2%	72.8%

PRESIDENT 1932

County	Total Vote	Republican	Democratic	Other	Rep.-Dem. Plurality	Total Vote Rep.	Total Vote Dem.	Major Vote Rep.	Major Vote Dem.
ANDERSON	2,697	1,605	1,081	11	524 R	59.5%	40.1%	59.8%	40.2%
BEDFORD	2,898	630	2,264	4	1,634 D	21.7%	78.1%	21.8%	78.2%
BENTON	2,021	455	1,540	26	1,085 D	22.5%	76.2%	22.8%	77.2%
BLEDSOE	1,994	960	1,034		74 D	48.1%	51.9%	48.1%	51.9%
BLOUNT	4,867	3,275	1,515	77	1,760 R	67.3%	31.1%	68.4%	31.6%
BRADLEY	2,902	1,570	1,295	37	275 R	54.1%	44.6%	54.8%	45.2%
CAMPBELL	4,609	2,735	1,834	40	901 R	59.3%	39.8%	59.9%	40.1%
CANNON	1,575	360	1,207	8	847 D	22.9%	76.6%	23.0%	77.0%
CARROLL	5,156	2,505	2,603	48	98 D	48.6%	50.5%	49.0%	51.0%
CARTER	6,629	5,055	1,574		3,481 R	76.3%	23.7%	76.3%	23.7%
CHEATHAM	1,562	180	1,370	12	1,190 D	11.5%	87.7%	11.6%	88.4%
CHESTER	1,357	356	985	16	629 D	26.2%	72.6%	26.5%	73.5%
CLAIBORNE	5,265	1,725	3,518	22	1,793 D	32.8%	66.8%	32.9%	67.1%
CLAY	1,196	361	819	16	458 D	30.2%	68.5%	30.6%	69.4%
COCKE	3,915	2,324	1,557	34	767 R	59.4%	39.8%	59.9%	40.1%
COFFEE	2,400	430	1,950	20	1,520 D	17.9%	81.2%	18.1%	81.9%
CROCKETT	2,467	513	1,934	11	1,421 D	20.8%	78.4%	21.0%	79.0%
CUMBERLAND	1,964	957	996	11	39 D	48.7%	50.7%	49.0%	51.0%
DAVIDSON	28,666	7,004	21,233	429	14,229 D	24.4%	74.1%	24.8%	75.2%
DECATUR	1,643	601	1,020	22	419 D	36.6%	62.1%	37.1%	62.9%
DE KALB	3,853	1,530	2,323		793 D	39.7%	60.3%	39.7%	60.3%
DICKSON	2,380	369	2,007	4	1,638 D	15.5%	84.3%	15.5%	84.9%
DYER	4,222	389	3,805	28	3,416 D	9.2%	90.1%	9.3%	90.7%
FAYETTE	1,346	42	1,287	17	1,245 D	3.1%	95.6%	3.2%	96.8%
FENTRESS	2,456	1,383	961	112	422 R	56.3%	39.1%	59.0%	41.0%
FRANKLIN	3,417	360	3,029	28	2,669 D	10.5%	88.6%	10.6%	89.4%
GIBSON	4,705	704	3,972	29	3,268 D	15.0%	84.4%	15.1%	84.9%
GILES	3,417	619	2,773	25	2,154 D	18.1%	81.2%	18.2%	81.8%
GRAINGER	2,353	1,325	995	33	330 R	56.3%	42.3%	57.1%	42.9%
GREENE	7,532	3,223	4,264	45	1,041 D	42.8%	56.6%	43.0%	57.0%
GRUNDY	1,191	198	978	15	780 D	16.6%	82.1%	16.8%	83.2%
HAMBLEN	3,522	1,458	2,032	32	574 D	41.4%	57.7%	41.8%	58.2%
HAMILTON	18,937	7,090	11,469	378	4,379 D	37.4%	60.6%	38.2%	61.8%
HANCOCK	1,680	1,089	551	40	538 R	64.8%	32.8%	66.4%	33.6%
HARDEMAN	2,680	281	2,377	22	2,096 D	10.5%	88.7%	10.6%	89.4%
HARDIN	1,851	1,036	806	9	230 R	56.0%	43.5%	56.2%	43.8%
HAWKINS	5,302	2,890	2,391	21	499 R	54.5%	45.1%	54.7%	45.3%
HAYWOOD	1,882	77	1,788	17	1,711 D	4.1%	95.0%	4.1%	95.9%
HENDERSON	2,229	1,158	1,058	13	100 R	52.0%	47.2%	52.5%	47.5%
HENRY	3,255	340	2,867	48	2,527 D	10.4%	88.1%	10.6%	89.4%
HICKMAN	2,205	385	1,812	8	1,427 D	17.5%	82.2%	17.5%	82.5%
HOUSTON	867	112	750	5	638 D	12.9%	86.5%	13.0%	87.0%
HUMPHREYS	1,703	231	1,455	17	1,224 D	13.6%	85.4%	13.7%	86.3%
JACKSON	1,986	256	1,726	4	1,470 D	12.9%	86.9%	12.9%	87.1%
JEFFERSON	3,317	2,275	975	67	1,300 R	68.6%	29.4%	70.0%	30.0%
JOHNSON	2,840	2,400	425	15	1,975 R	84.5%	15.0%	85.0%	15.0%
KNOX	20,927	9,774	10,755	398	981 D	46.7%	51.4%	47.6%	52.4%
LAKE	1,902	78	1,824		1,746 D	4.1%	95.9%	4.1%	95.9%
LAUDERDALE	2,350	174	2,137	39	1,963 D	7.4%	90.9%	7.5%	92.5%
LAWRENCE	4,948	1,684	3,240	24	1,556 D	34.0%	65.5%	34.2%	65.8%
LEWIS	936	137	799		662 D	14.6%	85.4%	14.6%	85.4%
LINCOLN	3,429	288	3,095	46	2,807 D	8.4%	90.3%	8.5%	91.5%
LOUDON	3,503	1,817	1,629	57	188 R	51.9%	46.5%	52.7%	47.3%
MCMINN	5,495	2,790	2,630	75	160 R	50.8%	47.9%	51.5%	48.5%
MCNAIRY	3,323	1,350	1,961	12	611 D	40.6%	59.0%	40.8%	59.2%
MACON	2,018	1,123	885	10	238 R	55.6%	43.9%	55.9%	44.1%
MADISON	6,029	1,104	4,813	92	3,689 D	18.3%	79.8%	18.6%	81.4%
MARION	3,470	1,322	2,128	20	806 D	38.0%	61.1%	38.3%	61.7%
MARSHALL	2,470	283	2,167	20	1,884 D	11.5%	87.7%	11.6%	88.4%
MAURY	3,952	535	3,392	25	2,857 D	13.5%	85.8%	13.6%	86.4%

TENNESSEE

PRESIDENT 1928

County	Total Vote	Republican	Democratic	Other	Rep.-Dem. Plurality	Percentage Total Vote Rep.	Dem.	Major Vote Rep.	Dem.
MEIGS	1,311	722	589		133 R	55.1%	44.9%	55.1%	44.9%
MONROE	5,343	3,312	2,031		1,281 R	62.0%	38.0%	62.0%	38.0%
MONTGOMERY	3,616	1,748	1,868		120 D	48.3%	51.7%	48.3%	51.7%
MOORE	571	133	431	7	298 D	23.3%	75.5%	23.6%	76.4%
MORGAN	1,933	1,487	446		1,041 R	76.9%	23.1%	76.9%	23.1%
OBION	3,281	789	2,492		1,703 D	24.0%	76.0%	24.0%	76.0%
OVERTON	2,307	1,195	1,105	7	90 R	51.8%	47.9%	52.0%	48.0%
PERRY	982	360	622		262 D	36.7%	63.3%	36.7%	63.3%
PICKETT	1,135	745	383	7	362 R	65.6%	33.7%	66.0%	34.0%
POLK	2,784	1,760	1,012	12	748 R	63.2%	36.4%	63.5%	36.5%
PUTNAM	3,757	1,612	2,145		533 D	42.9%	57.1%	42.9%	57.1%
RHEA	2,434	1,588	846		742 R	65.2%	34.8%	65.2%	34.8%
ROANE	3,754	2,971	761	22	2,210 R	79.1%	20.3%	79.6%	20.4%
ROBERTSON	2,402	848	1,543	11	695 D	35.3%	64.2%	35.5%	64.5%
RUTHERFORD	3,544	1,429	2,115		686 D	40.3%	59.7%	40.3%	59.7%
SCOTT	2,948	2,700	244	4	2,456 R	91.6%	8.3%	91.7%	8.3%
SEQUATCHIE	681	298	383		85 D	43.8%	56.2%	43.8%	56.2%
SEVIER	4,185	3,874	308	3	3,566 R	92.6%	7.4%	92.6%	7.4%
SHELBY	30,101	11,969	18,040	92	6,071 D	39.8%	59.9%	39.9%	60.1%
SMITH	2,606	1,150	1,446	10	296 D	44.1%	55.5%	44.3%	55.7%
STEWART	1,660	403	1,257		854 D	24.3%	75.7%	24.3%	75.7%
SULLIVAN	7,367	4,151	3,216		935 R	56.3%	43.7%	56.3%	43.7%
SUMNER	3,589	1,045	2,541	3	1,496 D	29.1%	70.8%	29.1%	70.9%
TIPTON	2,329	425	1,889	15	1,464 D	18.2%	81.1%	18.4%	81.6%
TROUSDALE	787	179	607	1	428 D	22.7%	77.1%	22.8%	77.2%
UNICOI	2,427	2,044	376	7	1,668 R	84.2%	15.5%	84.5%	15.5%
UNION	2,192	1,826	360	6	1,466 R	83.3%	16.4%	83.5%	16.5%
VAN BUREN	517	257	260		3 D	49.7%	50.3%	49.7%	50.3%
WARREN	2,045	923	1,112	10	189 D	45.1%	54.4%	45.4%	54.6%
WASHINGTON	6,434	4,889	1,545		3,344 R	76.0%	24.0%	76.0%	24.0%
WAYNE	2,149	1,756	382	11	1,374 R	81.7%	17.8%	82.1%	17.9%
WEAKLEY	3,853	1,358	2,495		1,137 D	35.2%	64.8%	35.2%	64.8%
WHITE	1,798	776	1,022		246 D	43.2%	56.8%	43.2%	56.8%
WILLIAMSON	2,295	693	1,595	7	902 D	30.2%	69.5%	30.3%	69.7%
WILSON	2,678	1,049	1,629		580 D	39.2%	60.8%	39.2%	60.8%
TOTAL	353,192	195,388	157,143	661	38,245 R	55.3%	44.5%	55.4%	44.6%

PRESIDENT 1932

County	Total Vote	Republican	Democratic	Other	Rep.-Dem. Plurality	Percentage Total Vote Rep.	Dem.	Major Vote Rep.	Dem.
MEIGS	1,408	564	840	4	276 D	40.1%	59.7%	40.2%	59.8%
MONROE	4,478	1,504	2,954	20	1,450 D	33.6%	66.0%	33.7%	66.3%
MONTGOMERY	3,546	799	2,747		1,948 D	22.5%	77.5%	22.5%	77.5%
MOORE	996	65	923	8	858 D	6.5%	92.7%	6.6%	93.4%
MORGAN	2,185	1,184	983	18	201 R	54.2%	45.0%	54.6%	45.4%
OBION	3,569	334	3,183	52	2,849 D	9.4%	89.2%	9.5%	90.5%
OVERTON	2,905	661	2,231	13	1,570 D	22.8%	76.8%	22.9%	77.1%
PERRY	893	182	705	6	523 D	20.4%	78.9%	20.5%	79.5%
PICKETT	1,416	681	712	23	31 D	48.1%	50.3%	48.9%	51.1%
POLK	4,182	1,642	2,540		898 D	39.3%	60.7%	39.3%	60.7%
PUTNAM	4,214	1,281	2,911	22	1,630 D	30.4%	69.1%	30.6%	69.4%
RHEA	3,046	1,448	1,560	38	112 D	47.5%	51.2%	48.1%	51.9%
ROANE	3,709	2,036	1,625	48	411 R	54.9%	43.8%	55.6%	44.4%
ROBERTSON	3,034	252	2,752	30	2,500 D	8.3%	90.7%	8.4%	91.6%
RUTHERFORD	4,550	606	3,924	20	3,318 D	13.3%	86.2%	13.4%	86.6%
SCOTT	2,940	1,890	1,025	25	865 R	64.3%	34.9%	64.8%	35.2%
SEQUATCHIE	1,076	289	777	10	488 D	26.9%	72.2%	27.1%	72.9%
SEVIER	3,993	3,075	887	31	2,188 R	77.0%	22.2%	77.6%	22.4%
SHELBY	45,209	6,332	38,320	557	31,988 D	14.0%	84.8%	14.2%	85.8%
SMITH	2,668	595	2,057	16	1,462 D	22.3%	77.1%	22.4%	77.6%
STEWART	1,744	184	1,548	12	1,364 D	10.6%	88.8%	10.6%	89.4%
SULLIVAN	8,442	2,999	5,322	121	2,323 D	35.5%	63.0%	36.0%	64.0%
SUMNER	4,303	382	3,893	28	3,511 D	8.9%	90.5%	8.9%	91.1%
TIPTON	3,069	154	2,892	23	2,738 D	5.0%	94.2%	5.1%	94.9%
TROUSDALE	900	64	835	1	771 D	7.1%	92.8%	7.1%	92.9%
UNICOI	2,566	1,716	850		866 R	66.9%	33.1%	66.9%	33.1%
UNION	1,983	1,169	802	12	367 R	59.0%	40.4%	59.3%	40.7%
VAN BUREN	833	196	613	24	417 D	23.5%	73.6%	24.2%	75.8%
WARREN	2,765	410	2,325	30	1,915 D	14.8%	84.1%	15.0%	85.0%
WASHINGTON	7,138	3,691	3,345	102	346 R	51.7%	46.9%	52.5%	47.5%
WAYNE	1,639	1,082	543	14	539 R	66.0%	33.1%	66.6%	33.4%
WEAKLEY	4,577	783	3,777	17	2,994 D	17.1%	82.5%	17.2%	82.8%
WHITE	2,341	390	1,938	13	1,548 D	16.7%	82.8%	16.8%	83.2%
WILLIAMSON	3,087	261	2,516	49	2,516 D	8.5%	90.0%	8.6%	91.4%
WILSON	3,298	567	2,713	18	2,146 D	17.2%	82.3%	17.3%	82.7%
TOTAL	390,273	126,752	259,473	4,048	132,721 D	32.5%	66.5%	32.8%	67.2%

TENNESSEE

PRESIDENT 1936

County	Total Vote	Republican	Democratic	Other	Rep.-Dem. Plurality	%Total Rep.	%Total Dem.	%Major Rep.	%Major Dem.
ANDERSON	4,213	1,805	2,348	60	543 D	42.8%	55.7%	43.5%	56.5%
BEDFORD	2,961	514	2,428	19	1,914 D	17.4%	82.0%	17.5%	82.5%
BENTON	2,429	661	1,762	6	1,101 D	27.2%	72.5%	27.3%	72.7%
BLEDSOE	2,419	1,178	1,218	23	40 D	48.7%	50.4%	49.2%	50.8%
BLOUNT	7,199	4,119	3,056	24	1,063 R	57.2%	42.5%	57.4%	42.6%
BRADLEY	5,376	2,561	2,806	9	245 D	47.5%	52.2%	47.7%	52.3%
CAMPBELL	5,522	2,814	2,703	5	111 R	51.0%	48.9%	51.0%	49.0%
CANNON	1,670	498	1,166	6	668 D	29.8%	69.8%	29.9%	70.1%
CARROLL	5,323	2,282	2,989	52	707 D	42.9%	56.2%	43.3%	55.7%
CARTER	6,722	4,858	1,837	27	3,021 R	72.3%	27.3%	72.6%	27.4%
CHEATHAM	1,543	183	1,352	8	1,169 D	11.9%	87.6%	11.9%	88.1%
CHESTER	1,744	565	1,172	7	607 D	32.4%	67.2%	32.5%	67.5%
CLAIBORNE	5,450	2,400	3,036	14	635 D	44.0%	55.7%	44.2%	55.8%
CLAY	1,059	378	661	20	283 D	35.7%	62.4%	36.4%	63.6%
COCKE	4,954	3,731	1,217	6	2,514 R	75.3%	24.6%	75.4%	24.6%
COFFEE	2,570	408	2,148	14	1,740 D	15.9%	83.6%	16.0%	84.0%
CROCKETT	2,450	525	1,921	4	1,396 D	21.4%	78.4%	21.5%	78.5%
CUMBERLAND	2,849	1,409	1,426	14	17 D	49.5%	50.1%	49.7%	50.3%
DAVIDSON	30,158	4,467	25,530	161	21,063 D	14.8%	84.7%	14.9%	85.1%
DECATUR	2,421	919	1,502		583 D	38.0%	62.0%	38.0%	62.0%
DE KALB	5,105	2,140	2,947	18	807 D	41.9%	57.7%	42.1%	57.9%
DICKSON	2,437	402	2,022	13	1,620 D	16.5%	83.0%	16.6%	83.4%
DYER	3,999	557	3,355	87	2,798 D	13.9%	83.9%	14.2%	85.8%
FAYETTE	1,793	29	1,764		1,735 D	1.6%	98.4%	1.6%	98.4%
FENTRESS	2,111	1,299	743	69	556 R	61.5%	35.2%	63.6%	36.4%
FRANKLIN	4,066	519	3,534	13	3,015 D	12.8%	86.9%	12.8%	87.2%
GIBSON	5,730	958	4,744	28	3,786 D	16.7%	82.8%	16.8%	83.2%
GILES	4,378	600	3,760	18	3,160 D	13.7%	85.9%	13.8%	86.2%
GRAINGER	2,916	1,754	1,153	9	601 R	60.2%	39.5%	60.3%	39.7%
GREENE	9,057	4,313	4,708	36	395 D	47.6%	52.0%	47.8%	52.2%
GRUNDY	1,730	238	1,488	4	1,250 D	13.8%	86.0%	13.8%	86.2%
HAMBLEN	4,699	2,261	2,438		177 D	48.1%	51.9%	48.1%	51.9%
HAMILTON	23,589	6,917	16,568	104	9,651 D	29.3%	70.2%	29.5%	70.5%
HANCOCK	2,633	1,673	960		713 R	63.5%	36.5%	63.5%	36.5%
HARDEMAN	2,029	157	1,869	3	1,712 D	7.7%	92.1%	7.7%	92.3%
HARDIN	2,895	1,348	1,538	9	190 D	46.6%	53.1%	46.7%	53.3%
HAWKINS	5,589	3,300	2,278	11	1,022 R	59.0%	40.8%	59.2%	40.8%
HAYWOOD	1,756	29	1,725	2	1,696 D	1.7%	98.3%	1.7%	98.3%
HENDERSON	2,753	1,380	1,307	66	73 D	50.1%	47.5%	51.4%	48.6%
HENRY	3,718	470	3,223	25	2,753 D	12.6%	86.7%	12.7%	87.3%
HICKMAN	2,165	353	1,804	8	1,451 D	16.3%	83.3%	16.4%	83.6%
HOUSTON	1,006	193	813		620 D	19.2%	80.8%	19.2%	80.8%
HUMPHREYS	1,579	297	1,279	3	982 D	18.8%	81.0%	18.8%	81.2%
JACKSON	2,128	422	1,702	4	1,280 D	19.8%	80.0%	19.9%	80.1%
JEFFERSON	3,448	2,356	1,079	13	1,277 R	68.3%	31.3%	68.6%	31.4%
JOHNSON	3,415	2,882	533		2,349 R	84.4%	15.6%	84.4%	15.6%
KNOX	32,120	12,183	19,837	100	7,654 D	37.9%	61.8%	38.0%	62.0%
LAKE	3,720	113	3,604	3	3,491 D	3.0%	96.9%	3.0%	97.0%
LAUDERDALE	3,755	203	3,540	12	3,337 D	5.4%	94.3%	5.4%	94.6%
LAWRENCE	8,164	3,342	4,773	49	1,431 D	40.9%	58.5%	41.2%	58.8%
LEWIS	1,399	331	1,068		737 D	23.7%	76.3%	23.7%	76.3%
LINCOLN	3,888	430	3,451	7	3,021 D	11.1%	88.8%	11.1%	88.9%
LOUDON	4,507	2,343	2,146	18	197 R	52.0%	47.6%	52.2%	47.8%
MCMINN	8,432	4,310	4,077	45	233 R	51.1%	48.4%	51.4%	48.6%
MCNAIRY	3,403	1,613	1,742	48	129 D	47.4%	51.2%	48.1%	51.9%
MACON	2,290	1,402	876	12	526 R	61.2%	38.3%	61.5%	38.5%
MADISON	7,350	1,223	6,095	32	4,872 D	16.6%	82.9%	16.7%	83.3%
MARION	4,434	1,770	2,664		894 D	39.9%	60.1%	39.9%	60.1%
MARSHALL	2,739	300	2,431	8	2,131 D	11.0%	88.8%	11.0%	89.0%
MAURY	4,325	497	3,809	19	3,312 D	11.5%	88.1%	11.5%	88.5%

PRESIDENT 1940

County	Total Vote	Republican	Democratic	Other	Rep.-Dem. Plurality	%Total Rep.	%Total Dem.	%Major Rep.	%Major Dem.
ANDERSON	4,091	1,852	2,218	21	366 D	45.3%	54.2%	45.5%	54.5%
BEDFORD	3,074	555	2,499	20	1,944 D	18.1%	81.3%	18.2%	81.8%
BENTON	2,877	858	1,996	23	1,138 D	29.8%	69.4%	30.1%	69.9%
BLEDSOE	2,844	1,317	1,527		210 D	46.3%	53.7%	46.3%	53.7%
BLOUNT	7,720	4,312	3,363	45	949 R	55.9%	43.6%	56.2%	43.8%
BRADLEY	4,615	2,617	1,976	22	641 R	56.7%	42.8%	57.0%	43.0%
CAMPBELL	5,512	2,799	2,688	25	111 R	50.8%	48.8%	51.0%	49.0%
CANNON	2,358	638	1,699	21	1,061 D	27.1%	72.1%	27.3%	72.7%
CARROLL	5,642	2,782	2,830	30	48 D	49.3%	50.2%	49.6%	50.4%
CARTER	6,480	4,238	2,171	71	2,067 R	65.4%	33.5%	66.1%	33.9%
CHEATHAM	2,266	331	1,932	3	1,601 D	14.6%	85.3%	14.6%	85.4%
CHESTER	2,552	1,015	1,537		522 D	39.8%	60.2%	39.8%	60.2%
CLAIBORNE	5,764	2,879	2,792	93	87 R	49.9%	48.4%	50.8%	49.2%
CLAY	1,825	537	1,288		751 D	29.4%	70.6%	29.4%	70.6%
COCKE	4,673	3,521	1,098	54	2,423 R	75.3%	23.5%	76.2%	23.8%
COFFEE	2,712	424	2,277	11	1,853 D	15.6%	84.0%	15.7%	84.3%
CROCKETT	2,790	733	2,048	9	1,315 D	26.3%	73.4%	26.4%	73.6%
CUMBERLAND	2,965	1,492	1,443	30	49 D	50.3%	48.7%	50.8%	49.2%
DAVIDSON	36,352	8,763	27,589		18,826 D	24.1%	75.9%	24.1%	75.9%
DECATUR	3,117	1,275	1,832	10	557 D	40.9%	58.8%	41.0%	59.0%
DE KALB	4,871	2,041	2,830	8	789 D	41.9%	58.1%	41.9%	58.1%
DICKSON	3,319	527	2,784	8	2,257 D	15.9%	83.9%	15.9%	84.1%
DYER	4,380	961	3,374	45	2,413 D	21.9%	77.0%	22.2%	77.8%
FAYETTE	1,906	78	1,826	2	1,748 D	4.1%	95.8%	4.1%	95.9%
FENTRESS	2,317	1,365	919	33	446 R	58.9%	39.7%	59.8%	40.2%
FRANKLIN	4,893	569	4,312	12	3,743 D	11.6%	88.1%	11.7%	88.3%
GIBSON	6,356	1,233	5,103	20	3,870 D	19.4%	80.3%	19.5%	80.5%
GILES	4,501	692	3,796	13	3,104 D	15.4%	84.3%	15.4%	84.6%
GRAINGER	2,557	1,688	846	23	842 R	66.0%	32.9%	66.7%	33.3%
GREENE	9,135	4,587	4,406	142	181 R	50.2%	48.2%	51.0%	49.0%
GRUNDY	2,056	298	1,749	9	1,451 D	14.5%	85.1%	14.6%	85.4%
HAMBLEN	3,877	1,794	2,055	28	261 D	46.3%	53.0%	46.6%	53.4%
HAMILTON	26,922	9,771	17,083	68	7,312 D	36.3%	63.5%	36.4%	63.6%
HANCOCK	2,701	1,673	1,014	14	659 R	61.9%	37.5%	62.3%	37.7%
HARDEMAN	2,875	319	2,549	7	2,230 D	11.1%	88.7%	11.1%	88.9%
HARDIN	4,247	2,264	1,957	26	307 R	53.3%	46.1%	53.6%	46.4%
HAWKINS	5,458	3,314	2,108	36	1,206 R	60.7%	38.6%	61.1%	38.9%
HAYWOOD	3,598	128	3,466	4	3,338 D	3.6%	96.3%	3.6%	96.4%
HENDERSON	2,660	605	2,046	9	1,441 D	22.7%	76.9%	22.8%	77.2%
HENRY	3,886	563	3,307	16	2,744 D	14.5%	85.1%	14.5%	85.5%
HICKMAN	3,434	644	2,776	14	2,132 D	18.8%	80.8%	18.8%	81.2%
HOUSTON	1,331	229	1,093	9	864 D	17.2%	82.1%	17.3%	82.7%
HUMPHREYS	2,097	377	1,717	3	1,340 D	18.0%	81.9%	18.0%	82.0%
JACKSON	2,660	605	2,046	9	1,441 D	22.7%	76.9%	22.8%	77.2%
JEFFERSON	3,004	1,921	1,062	21	859 R	63.9%	35.4%	64.4%	35.6%
JOHNSON	2,971	2,502	469		2,033 R	84.2%	15.8%	84.2%	15.8%
KNOX	34,304	13,877	20,226	201	6,349 D	40.5%	59.0%	40.7%	59.3%
LAKE	3,187	213	2,962	12	2,749 D	6.7%	92.9%	6.7%	93.3%
LAUDERDALE	6,603	317	6,279	7	5,962 D	4.8%	95.1%	4.8%	95.2%
LAWRENCE	5,836	1,877	3,936	23	2,059 D	32.2%	67.4%	32.3%	67.7%
LEWIS	1,716	368	1,343	5	975 D	21.4%	78.3%	21.5%	78.5%
LINCOLN	4,315	521	3,781	13	3,260 D	12.1%	87.6%	12.1%	87.9%
LOUDON	4,317	2,226	2,068	23	158 R	51.6%	47.9%	51.8%	48.2%
MCMINN	9,121	3,901	5,192	28	1,291 D	42.8%	56.9%	42.9%	57.1%
MCNAIRY	5,034	2,550	2,484		66 R	50.7%	49.3%	50.7%	49.3%
MACON	2,445	1,730	711	4	1,019 R	70.8%	29.1%	70.9%	29.1%
MADISON	7,448	1,271	6,154	23	4,883 D	17.1%	82.6%	17.1%	82.9%
MARION	5,435	2,158	3,242	35	1,084 D	39.7%	59.7%	40.0%	60.0%
MARSHALL	3,523	389	3,132	2	2,743 D	11.0%	88.9%	11.0%	89.0%
MAURY	5,186	634	4,529	23	3,895 D	12.2%	87.3%	12.3%	87.7%

TENNESSEE

PRESIDENT 1936

County	Total Vote	Republican	Democratic	Other	Rep.-Dem. Plurality	Total Vote Rep.	Total Vote Dem.	Major Vote Rep.	Major Vote Dem.
MEIGS	1,747	740	994	13	254 D	42.4%	56.9%	42.7%	57.3%
MONROE	7,599	3,493	4,106		613 D	46.0%	54.0%	46.0%	54.0%
MONTGOMERY	4,180	838	3,314	28	2,476 D	20.0%	79.3%	20.2%	79.8%
MOORE	825	101	719	5	618 D	12.2%	87.2%	12.3%	87.7%
MORGAN	2,525	1,225	1,291	9	66 D	48.5%	51.1%	48.7%	51.3%
OBION	4,145	417	3,728		3,311 D	10.1%	89.9%	10.1%	89.9%
OVERTON	2,556	942	1,608	6	666 D	36.9%	62.9%	36.9%	63.1%
PERRY	1,111	210	896	5	686 D	18.9%	80.6%	19.0%	81.0%
PICKETT	1,120	651	454	15	197 R	58.1%	40.5%	58.9%	41.1%
POLK	4,062	1,755	2,283	24	528 D	43.2%	56.2%	43.5%	56.5%
PUTNAM	3,832	1,207	2,619	6	1,412 D	31.5%	68.3%	31.5%	68.5%
RHEA	4,201	1,964	2,199	38	235 D	46.8%	52.3%	47.2%	52.8%
ROANE	5,235	2,757	2,467	11	290 R	52.7%	47.1%	52.8%	47.2%
ROBERTSON	3,056	388	2,629	39	2,241 D	12.7%	86.0%	12.9%	87.1%
RUTHERFORD	4,710	580	4,101	29	3,521 D	12.3%	87.1%	12.4%	87.6%
SCOTT	2,847	2,012	827	8	1,185 R	70.7%	29.0%	70.9%	29.1%
SEQUATCHIE	1,198	353	840	5	487 D	29.5%	70.1%	29.6%	70.4%
SEVIER	5,308	4,126	1,144	38	2,982 R	77.7%	21.6%	78.3%	21.7%
SHELBY	63,698	2,113	61,504	81	59,391 D	3.3%	96.6%	3.3%	96.7%
SMITH	2,726	626	2,092	8	1,466 D	23.0%	76.7%	23.0%	77.0%
STEWART	2,028	303	1,718	7	1,415 D	14.9%	84.7%	15.0%	85.0%
SULLIVAN	9,795	3,492	6,269	34	2,777 D	35.7%	64.0%	35.8%	64.2%
SUMNER	3,666	517	3,146	3	2,629 D	14.1%	85.8%	14.1%	85.9%
TIPTON	4,799	116	4,683		4,567 D	2.4%	97.6%	2.4%	97.6%
TROUSDALE	839	72	765	2	693 D	8.6%	91.2%	8.6%	91.4%
UNICOI	2,756	1,850	879	27	971 R	67.1%	31.9%	67.8%	32.2%
UNION	2,759	1,785	963	11	822 R	64.7%	34.9%	65.0%	35.0%
VAN BUREN	941	251	690		439 D	26.7%	73.3%	26.7%	73.3%
WARREN	2,870	553	2,304	13	1,751 D	19.3%	80.3%	19.4%	80.6%
WASHINGTON	9,294	4,788	4,448	58	340 R	51.5%	47.9%	51.8%	48.2%
WAYNE	2,041	1,304	733	4	571 R	63.9%	35.9%	64.0%	36.0%
WEAKLEY	4,212	928	3,254	30	2,326 D	22.0%	77.3%	22.2%	77.8%
WHITE	1,414	591	814	9	223 D	41.8%	57.6%	42.1%	57.9%
WILLIAMSON	3,059	286	2,769	4	2,483 D	9.3%	90.5%	9.4%	90.6%
WILSON	3,650	539	3,108	3	2,569 D	14.8%	85.2%	14.8%	85.2%
TOTAL	477,086	147,055	328,083	1,948	181,028 D	30.8%	68.8%	30.9%	69.1%

PRESIDENT 1940

County	Total Vote	Republican	Democratic	Other	Rep.-Dem. Plurality	Total Vote Rep.	Total Vote Dem.	Major Vote Rep.	Major Vote Dem.
MEIGS	1,462	573	889		316 D	39.2%	60.8%	39.2%	60.8%
MONROE	7,416	3,253	4,121	42	868 D	43.9%	55.6%	44.1%	55.9%
MONTGOMERY	3,990	819	3,158	13	2,339 D	20.5%	79.1%	20.6%	79.4%
MOORE	982	106	869	7	763 D	10.8%	88.5%	10.9%	89.1%
MORGAN	3,231	1,448	1,783		335 D	44.8%	55.2%	44.8%	55.2%
OBION	4,914	536	4,360	18	3,824 D	10.9%	88.7%	10.9%	89.1%
OVERTON	2,733	988	1,718	27	730 D	36.2%	62.9%	36.5%	63.5%
PERRY	1,403	332	1,068	3	736 D	23.7%	76.1%	23.7%	76.3%
PICKETT	1,492	830	652	10	178 R	55.6%	43.7%	56.0%	44.0%
POLK	4,173	562	3,611		3,049 D	13.5%	86.5%	13.5%	86.5%
PUTNAM	4,544	1,576	2,963	5	1,387 D	34.7%	65.2%	34.7%	65.3%
RHEA	4,336	1,956	2,364	16	408 D	45.1%	54.5%	45.3%	54.7%
ROANE	4,650	2,245	2,384	21	139 D	48.3%	51.3%	48.5%	51.5%
ROBERTSON	3,767	490	3,258	19	2,768 D	13.0%	86.5%	13.1%	86.9%
RUTHERFORD	5,009	782	4,207	20	3,425 D	15.6%	84.0%	15.7%	84.3%
SCOTT	3,649	2,187	1,448	14	739 R	59.9%	39.7%	60.2%	39.8%
SEQUATCHIE	1,408	401	1,003	4	602 D	28.5%	71.2%	28.6%	71.4%
SEVIER	5,750	4,569	1,181		3,388 R	79.5%	20.5%	79.5%	20.5%
SHELBY	65,074	7,312	57,664	98	50,352 D	11.2%	88.6%	11.3%	88.7%
SMITH	2,906	648	2,244	14	1,596 D	22.3%	77.2%	22.4%	77.6%
STEWART	3,088	374	2,699	15	2,325 D	12.1%	87.4%	12.2%	87.8%
SULLIVAN	11,421	4,153	7,234	34	3,081 D	36.4%	63.3%	36.5%	63.5%
SUMNER	4,447	834	3,591	22	2,757 D	18.8%	80.8%	18.8%	81.2%
TIPTON	6,113	288	5,815	10	5,527 D	4.7%	95.1%	4.7%	95.3%
TROUSDALE	1,025	94	929	2	835 D	9.2%	90.6%	9.2%	90.8%
UNICOI	2,881	1,863	985	33	878 R	64.7%	34.2%	64.7%	34.6%
UNION	1,824	1,143	673	8	470 R	62.7%	36.9%	62.9%	37.1%
VAN BUREN	1,053	318	732	3	414 D	30.2%	69.5%	30.3%	69.7%
WARREN	2,887	546	2,323	18	1,777 D	18.9%	80.5%	19.0%	81.0%
WASHINGTON	8,327	4,719	3,565	43	1,154 R	56.7%	42.8%	57.0%	43.0%
WAYNE	3,592	2,486	1,100	6	1,386 R	69.2%	30.6%	69.3%	30.7%
WEAKLEY	4,648	1,139	3,474	35	2,335 D	24.5%	74.7%	24.7%	75.3%
WHITE	2,928	657	2,256	15	1,599 D	22.4%	77.0%	22.6%	77.4%
WILLIAMSON	3,746	505	3,215	26	2,710 D	13.5%	85.8%	13.6%	86.4%
WILSON	3,681	655	3,020	6	2,365 D	17.8%	82.0%	17.8%	82.2%
TOTAL	522,823	169,153	351,601	2,069	182,448 D	32.4%	67.3%	32.5%	67.5%

TENNESSEE

PRESIDENT 1944

County	Total Vote	Republican	Democratic	Other	Rep.-Dem. Plurality	%Total Rep.	%Total Dem.	%Major Rep.	%Major Dem.
ANDERSON	6,920	3,424	3,476	20	52 D	49.5	50.2	49.6	50.4
BEDFORD	3,407	733	2,651	23	1,918 D	21.5	77.8	21.7	78.3
BENTON	3,124	1,195	1,901	28	706 D	38.2	60.9	38.6	61.4
BLEDSOE	1,982	1,187	795	—	392 R	59.9	40.1	59.9	40.1
BLOUNT	9,067	6,193	2,836	38	3,357 R	68.3	31.3	68.6	31.4
BRADLEY	3,951	2,616	1,312	23	1,304 R	66.2	33.2	66.6	33.4
CAMPBELL	5,270	3,244	2,008	18	1,236 R	61.6	38.1	61.8	38.2
CANNON	1,630	627	1,002	1	375 D	38.5	61.5	38.5	61.5
CARROLL	5,088	2,996	2,077	15	919 R	58.9	40.8	59.1	40.9
CARTER	6,556	4,873	1,662	21	3,211 R	74.3	25.4	74.6	25.4
CHEATHAM	1,616	216	1,398	2	1,182 D	13.4	86.5	13.4	86.6
CHESTER	2,091	931	1,156	4	225 D	44.5	55.3	44.6	55.4
CLAIBORNE	4,098	2,426	1,649	23	777 R	59.2	40.2	59.5	40.5
CLAY	1,404	650	754	—	104 D	46.3	53.7	46.3	53.7
COCKE	4,558	3,554	989	5	2,565 R	78.0	21.7	78.2	21.8
COFFEE	3,274	568	2,703	3	2,135 D	17.3	82.6	17.4	82.6
CROCKETT	2,212	782	1,421	9	639 D	35.4	64.2	35.5	64.5
CUMBERLAND	2,980	1,786	1,174	20	612 R	59.9	39.4	60.3	39.7
DAVIDSON	36,760	10,174	26,493	93	16,319 D	27.7	72.1	27.7	72.3
DECATUR	2,763	1,235	1,515	13	280 D	44.7	54.8	44.9	55.1
DE KALB	4,502	2,161	2,341	—	180 D	48.0	52.0	48.0	52.0
DICKSON	2,950	600	2,339	11	1,739 D	20.3	79.3	20.4	79.6
DYER	4,576	1,190	3,368	18	2,178 D	26.0	73.6	26.1	73.9
FAYETTE	1,591	172	1,417	2	1,245 D	10.8	89.1	10.8	89.2
FENTRESS	2,376	1,696	657	23	1,039 R	71.4	27.7	72.1	27.9
FRANKLIN	4,573	600	3,958	15	3,358 D	13.2	86.6	13.2	86.8
GIBSON	6,212	1,568	4,632	12	3,064 D	25.3	74.6	25.3	74.7
GILES	5,000	751	4,249	—	3,498 D	15.0	85.0	15.0	85.0
GRAINGER	2,550	1,938	605	7	1,333 R	76.2	23.7	76.2	23.8
GREENE	7,665	4,922	2,726	17	2,196 R	64.2	35.6	64.4	35.6
GRUNDY	1,887	406	1,462	19	1,056 D	21.5	77.5	21.7	78.3
HAMBLEN	3,724	2,001	1,723	—	278 R	53.7	46.3	53.7	46.3
HAMILTON	28,173	10,379	17,527	267	7,148 D	36.8	62.2	37.2	62.8
HANCOCK	2,364	1,929	431	4	1,498 R	81.6	18.2	81.7	18.3
HARDEMAN	2,400	444	1,949	7	1,505 D	18.5	81.2	18.5	81.5
HARDIN	3,500	2,124	1,358	18	766 R	60.7	38.8	61.0	39.0
HAWKINS	5,458	3,692	1,756	10	1,936 R	67.6	32.2	67.7	32.3
HAYWOOD	2,734	208	2,525	1	2,317 D	7.6	92.4	7.6	92.4
HENDERSON	3,579	2,570	1,009	—	1,561 R	71.8	28.2	71.8	28.2
HENRY	3,831	702	3,111	18	2,409 D	18.3	81.2	18.4	81.6
HICKMAN	2,846	618	2,223	5	1,605 D	21.7	78.1	21.7	78.3
HOUSTON	1,701	248	1,453	—	1,205 D	14.6	85.4	14.6	85.4
HUMPHREYS	2,114	367	1,735	12	1,368 D	17.4	82.1	17.5	82.5
JACKSON	3,159	695	2,453	11	1,758 D	22.0	77.6	22.1	77.9
JEFFERSON	4,143	3,159	966	18	2,193 R	76.2	23.3	76.6	23.4
JOHNSON	3,158	2,699	450	9	2,249 R	85.5	14.2	85.7	14.3
KNOX	39,452	20,742	18,482	228	2,260 R	52.6	46.8	52.9	47.1
LAKE	1,590	150	1,440	—	1,290 D	9.4	90.6	9.4	90.6
LAUDERDALE	4,117	381	3,732	4	3,351 D	9.3	90.6	9.3	90.7
LAWRENCE	9,021	4,359	4,662	—	303 D	48.3	51.7	48.3	51.7
LEWIS	1,207	252	955	—	703 D	20.9	79.1	20.9	79.1
LINCOLN	4,316	573	3,735	8	3,162 D	13.3	86.5	13.3	86.7
LOUDON	4,787	3,147	1,632	8	1,515 R	65.7	34.1	65.9	34.1
MCMINN	7,526	3,091	4,435	—	1,344 D	41.1	58.9	41.1	58.9
MCNAIRY	4,409	2,697	1,712	—	985 R	61.2	38.8	61.2	38.8
MACON	3,045	2,322	701	22	1,621 R	76.3	23.0	76.8	23.2
MADISON	7,517	1,793	5,706	18	3,913 D	23.9	75.9	23.9	76.1
MARION	4,533	1,761	2,666	106	905 D	38.9	58.8	39.8	60.2
MARSHALL	4,315	500	3,812	3	3,312 D	11.6	88.3	11.6	88.4
MAURY	5,579	747	4,814	18	4,067 D	13.4	86.3	13.4	86.6

PRESIDENT 1948

County	Total Vote	Republican	Democratic	Other	Rep.-Dem. Plurality	%Total Rep.	%Total Dem.	%Major Rep.	%Major Dem.
ANDERSON	11,837	5,372	5,915	550	543 D	45.4	50.0	47.6	52.4
BEDFORD	4,301	771	2,393	1,137	1,622 D	17.9	55.6	24.4	75.6
BENTON	2,788	908	1,757	123	849 D	32.6	63.0	34.1	65.9
BLEDSOE	2,248	1,103	1,092	53	11 R	49.1	48.6	50.3	49.7
BLOUNT	9,543	6,152	3,141	250	3,011 R	64.5	32.9	66.2	33.8
BRADLEY	5,152	2,942	2,036	174	906 R	57.1	39.5	59.1	40.9
CAMPBELL	5,320	2,922	2,267	131	655 R	54.9	42.6	56.3	43.7
CANNON	2,127	558	1,408	161	850 D	26.2	66.2	28.4	71.6
CARROLL	6,173	2,651	2,818	704	167 D	42.9	45.7	48.5	51.5
CARTER	6,968	4,943	1,809	216	3,134 R	70.9	26.0	73.2	26.8
CHEATHAM	3,083	193	2,731	159	2,538 D	6.3	88.6	6.6	93.4
CHESTER	1,940	766	980	194	214 D	39.5	50.5	43.9	56.1
CLAIBORNE	4,686	2,507	2,068	111	439 R	53.5	44.1	54.8	45.2
CLAY	1,901	703	1,146	52	443 D	37.0	60.3	38.0	62.0
COCKE	4,614	3,576	939	99	2,637 R	77.5	20.4	79.2	20.8
COFFEE	3,601	599	2,041	961	1,442 D	16.6	56.7	22.7	77.3
CROCKETT	2,640	601	1,415	624	814 D	22.8	53.6	29.8	70.2
CUMBERLAND	3,721	1,988	1,607	126	381 R	53.4	43.2	55.3	44.7
DAVIDSON	37,663	8,410	20,877	8,356	12,467 D	22.3	55.5	28.7	71.3
DECATUR	3,020	1,291	1,565	164	274 D	42.7	51.8	45.2	54.8
DE KALB	4,412	1,751	2,412	249	661 D	39.7	54.7	42.1	57.9
DICKSON	3,145	485	2,337	323	1,852 D	15.4	74.3	17.2	82.8
DYER	5,364	989	3,503	872	2,514 D	18.4	65.3	22.0	78.0
FAYETTE	1,785	226	1,493	66	1,267 D	12.7	83.7	13.2	86.8
FENTRESS	2,634	1,587	962	85	625 R	60.3	36.5	62.3	37.7
FRANKLIN	4,461	589	2,948	924	2,359 D	13.2	66.1	16.7	83.3
GIBSON	5,971	1,137	3,917	917	2,780 D	19.0	65.6	22.5	77.5
GILES	4,872	717	3,676	479	2,959 D	14.7	75.5	16.3	83.7
GRAINGER	2,542	1,824	644	74	1,180 R	71.8	25.3	73.9	26.1
GREENE	7,875	4,375	3,282	218	1,093 R	55.6	41.7	57.1	42.9
GRUNDY	2,575	431	2,009	135	1,578 D	16.7	78.0	17.7	82.3
HAMBLEN	3,933	2,116	1,552	265	564 R	53.8	39.5	57.7	42.3
HAMILTON	30,189	10,434	16,968	2,787	6,534 D	34.7	56.2	38.1	61.9
HANCOCK	2,065	1,598	416	51	1,182 R	77.4	20.1	79.3	20.7
HARDEMAN	3,300	317	1,609	1,374	1,292 D	9.6	48.8	16.5	83.5
HARDIN	3,277	1,779	1,270	228	509 R	54.3	38.8	58.3	41.7
HAWKINS	5,619	3,637	1,818	163	1,819 R	64.7	32.4	66.7	33.3
HAYWOOD	2,129	148	1,050	931	902 D	7.0	49.3	12.4	87.6
HENDERSON	3,643	2,278	1,155	210	1,123 R	62.5	31.7	66.4	33.6
HENRY	4,276	604	3,292	380	2,688 D	14.1	77.0	15.5	84.5
HICKMAN	2,878	478	2,140	260	1,662 D	16.6	74.4	18.3	81.7
HOUSTON	1,455	202	1,159	94	957 D	13.9	79.7	14.8	85.2
HUMPHREYS	2,240	355	1,327	558	972 D	15.8	59.2	21.1	78.9
JACKSON	2,187	536	1,502	149	966 D	24.5	68.7	26.3	73.7
JEFFERSON	4,019	2,979	900	140	2,079 R	74.1	22.4	76.8	23.2
JOHNSON	2,908	2,413	433	62	1,980 R	83.0	14.9	84.8	15.2
KNOX	39,196	21,074	15,946	2,176	5,128 R	53.8	40.7	56.9	43.1
LAKE	1,502	179	833	490	654 D	11.9	55.5	17.7	82.3
LAUDERDALE	3,879	298	2,556	1,025	2,258 D	7.7	65.9	10.4	89.6
LAWRENCE	9,084	3,837	4,854	393	1,017 D	42.2	53.4	44.1	55.9
LEWIS	1,636	381	1,148	107	767 D	23.3	70.2	24.9	75.1
LINCOLN	4,088	361	2,969	758	2,608 D	8.8	72.6	10.8	89.2
LOUDON	4,515	2,605	1,673	237	932 R	57.7	37.1	60.9	39.1
MCMINN	7,662	4,432	3,016	214	1,416 R	57.8	39.3	59.5	40.5
MCNAIRY	4,969	2,390	2,267	312	123 R	48.1	45.6	51.3	48.7
MACON	2,510	1,708	738	64	970 R	68.0	29.4	69.8	30.2
MADISON	8,997	1,681	4,722	2,594	3,041 D	18.7	52.5	20.3	73.7
MARION	4,467	1,738	2,554	175	816 D	38.9	57.2	40.5	59.5
MARSHALL	4,295	517	3,059	719	2,542 D	12.0	71.2	14.5	85.5
MAURY	5,635	895	2,906	1,834	2,011 D	15.9	51.6	23.5	76.5

TENNESSEE

PRESIDENT 1944

County	Total Vote	Republican	Democratic	Other	Rep.-Dem. Plurality	Total Vote Rep.	Total Vote Dem.	Major Vote Rep.	Major Vote Dem.
MEIGS	1,259	532	727		195 D	42.3%	57.7%	42.3%	57.7%
MONROE	6,819	3,424	3,385	10	39 R	50.2%	49.6%	50.3%	49.7%
MONTGOMERY	3,686	702	2,971	13	2,269 D	19.0%	80.6%	19.1%	80.9%
MOORE	885	143	742		599 D	16.2%	83.8%	16.2%	83.8%
MORGAN	2,600	1,399	1,201		198 R	53.8%	46.2%	53.8%	46.2%
OBION	4,298	615	3,570	13	3,055 D	14.3%	85.4%	14.3%	85.6%
OVERTON	2,389	935	1,449	5	514 D	39.1%	60.7%	39.2%	60.8%
PERRY	1,158	387	771		384 D	33.4%	66.6%	33.4%	66.6%
PICKETT	1,198	761	416	21	345 R	63.5%	34.7%	64.7%	35.3%
POLK	5,226	378	4,842	6	4,464 D	7.2%	92.7%	7.2%	92.8%
PUTNAM	4,558	1,770	2,788		1,018 D	38.8%	61.2%	38.8%	61.2%
RHEA	3,461	1,880	1,581		299 R	54.3%	45.7%	54.3%	45.7%
ROANE	4,699	2,711	1,971	17	740 R	57.7%	41.9%	57.9%	42.1%
ROBERTSON	3,708	622	3,074	12	2,452 D	16.8%	82.9%	16.8%	83.2%
RUTHERFORD	5,638	879	4,730	29	3,851 D	15.6%	83.9%	15.7%	84.3%
SCOTT	2,832	1,971	850	11	1,121 R	69.6%	30.0%	69.9%	30.1%
SEQUATCHIE	1,268	417	851		434 D	32.9%	67.1%	32.9%	67.1%
SEVIER	5,651	4,930	711	10	4,219 R	87.2%	12.6%	87.4%	12.6%
SHELBY	59,544	10,839	48,625	80	37,786 D	18.2%	81.7%	18.2%	81.8%
SMITH	3,006	887	2,107	12	1,220 D	29.5%	70.1%	29.6%	70.4%
STEWART	2,251	335	1,916		1,581 D	14.9%	85.1%	14.9%	85.1%
SULLIVAN	11,544	5,223	6,290	31	1,067 D	45.2%	54.5%	45.4%	54.6%
SUMNER	5,076	990	4,076	10	3,086 D	19.5%	80.3%	19.5%	80.5%
TIPTON	4,360	310	4,046	4	3,736 D	7.1%	92.8%	7.1%	92.9%
TROUSDALE	1,304	131	1,170	3	1,039 D	10.0%	89.7%	10.1%	89.9%
UNICOI	2,771	1,992	779		1,213 R	71.9%	28.1%	71.9%	28.1%
UNION	2,398	1,768	627	3	1,141 R	73.8%	26.1%	73.8%	26.2%
VAN BUREN	820	291	526	3	235 D	35.5%	64.1%	35.6%	64.4%
WARREN	3,429	848	2,550	21	1,712 D	24.7%	74.3%	24.7%	75.1%
WASHINGTON	10,602	6,485	4,060	57	2,425 R	61.2%	38.3%	61.5%	38.5%
WAYNE	2,820	2,185	630	5	1,555 R	77.5%	22.3%	77.6%	22.4%
WEAKLEY	5,039	1,595	3,434	10	1,839 D	31.7%	68.1%	31.7%	68.3%
WHITE	2,011	668	1,339	4	671 D	33.2%	66.6%	33.3%	66.7%
WILLIAMSON	3,268	602	2,656	10	2,054 D	18.4%	81.3%	18.5%	81.5%
WILSON	4,090	942	3,148		2,206 D	23.0%	77.0%	23.0%	77.0%
TCTAL	510,692	200,311	308,707	1,674	108,396 D	39.2%	60.4%	39.4%	60.6%

PRESIDENT 1948

County	Total Vote	Republican	Democratic	Other	Rep.-Dem. Plurality	Total Vote Rep.	Total Vote Dem.	Major Vote Rep.	Major Vote Dem.
MEIGS	1,590	748	788	54	40 D	47.0%	49.6%	48.7%	51.3%
MONROE	7,546	3,905	3,553	88	352 R	51.7%	47.1%	52.4%	47.6%
MONTGOMERY	4,505	646	3,310	549	2,664 D	14.3%	73.5%	16.3%	83.7%
MOORE	831	102	523	206	421 D	12.3%	62.9%	16.3%	83.7%
MORGAN	3,085	1,570	1,500	15	70 R	50.9%	48.6%	51.1%	48.9%
OBION	4,617	642	3,490	485	2,848 D	13.9%	75.6%	15.5%	84.5%
OVERTON	2,905	917	1,835	153	918 D	31.6%	63.2%	33.3%	66.7%
PERRY	1,748	459	1,196	93	737 D	26.3%	68.4%	27.7%	72.3%
PICKETT	1,437	849	566	22	283 R	59.1%	39.4%	60.0%	40.0%
POLK	2,990	1,529	1,412	49	117 R	51.1%	47.2%	52.0%	48.0%
PUTNAM	5,564	1,879	3,134	551	1,255 D	33.8%	56.3%	37.5%	62.5%
RHEA	4,151	2,077	1,897	177	180 R	50.0%	45.7%	52.3%	47.7%
ROANE	5,781	3,236	2,306	239	930 R	56.0%	39.9%	58.4%	41.6%
ROBERTSON	3,946	376	3,044	526	2,668 D	9.5%	77.1%	11.0%	89.0%
RUTHERFORD	6,078	854	4,151	1,073	3,297 D	14.1%	68.3%	17.1%	82.9%
SCOTT	3,024	2,016	972	36	1,044 R	66.7%	32.1%	67.5%	32.5%
SEQUATCHIE	1,373	420	907	46	487 D	30.6%	66.1%	31.7%	68.3%
SEVIER	6,003	5,049	840	114	4,209 R	84.1%	14.0%	85.7%	14.3%
SHELBY	65,176	14,566	23,854	26,756	9,288 D	22.3%	36.6%	37.9%	62.1%
SMITH	2,828	773	1,764	291	991 D	27.3%	62.4%	30.5%	69.5%
STEWART	2,411	331	1,962	118	1,631 D	13.7%	81.4%	14.4%	85.6%
SULLIVAN	15,120	6,984	7,626	510	642 D	46.2%	50.4%	47.8%	52.2%
SUMNER	5,006	793	3,688	525	2,895 D	15.8%	73.7%	17.7%	82.3%
TIPTON	4,681	209	3,066	1,406	2,857 D	4.5%	65.5%	6.4%	93.6%
TROUSDALE	1,229	104	1,014	111	910 D	8.5%	82.5%	9.3%	90.7%
UNICOI	2,861	1,927	844	90	1,083 R	67.4%	29.5%	69.5%	30.5%
UNION	2,156	1,603	513	40	1,090 R	74.4%	23.8%	75.8%	24.2%
VAN BUREN	978	298	636	44	338 D	30.5%	65.0%	31.9%	68.1%
WARREN	4,464	807	2,969	688	2,162 D	18.1%	66.5%	21.4%	78.6%
WASHINGTON	11,559	7,056	4,023	480	3,033 R	61.0%	34.8%	63.7%	36.3%
WAYNE	2,862	1,957	820	85	1,137 R	68.4%	28.7%	70.5%	29.5%
WEAKLEY	4,841	1,310	3,099	432	1,789 D	27.1%	64.0%	29.7%	70.3%
WHITE	2,682	635	1,719	328	1,084 D	23.7%	64.1%	27.0%	73.0%
WILLIAMSON	3,861	554	1,738	1,011	1,184 D	14.4%	59.4%	19.5%	80.5%
WILSON	4,699	854	3,133	712	2,279 D	18.2%	66.7%	21.4%	78.6%
TCTAL	550,283	202,914	270,402	76,967	67,488 D	36.9%	49.1%	42.9%	57.1%

TENNESSEE

PRESIDENT 1952

County	Total Vote	Republican	Democratic	Other	Rep.-Dem. Plurality	TV Rep.	TV Dem.	MV Rep.	MV Dem.
ANDERSON	19,466	10,489	8,939	38	1,550 R	53.9%	45.9%	54.0%	46.0%
BEDFORD	6,973	2,611	4,362		1,751 D	37.4%	62.6%	37.4%	62.6%
BENTON	3,772	1,304	2,452	16	1,148 D	34.6%	65.0%	34.7%	65.3%
BLEDSOE	2,417	1,229	1,158	30	71 R	50.8%	47.9%	51.5%	48.5%
BLOUNT	16,913	11,708	5,163	42	6,545 R	69.2%	30.5%	69.4%	30.6%
BRADLEY	7,269	4,606	2,646	17	1,960 R	63.4%	36.4%	63.5%	36.5%
CAMPBELL	6,943	4,557	2,346	40	2,211 R	65.6%	33.8%	66.0%	34.0%
CANNON	2,449	930	1,491	28	561 D	38.0%	60.9%	38.4%	61.6%
CARROLL	6,626	3,741	2,841	44	900 R	56.5%	42.9%	56.8%	43.2%
CARTER	11,844	9,019	2,707	118	6,312 R	76.1%	22.9%	76.9%	23.1%
CHEATHAM	2,776	536	2,222	18	1,686 D	19.3%	80.0%	19.4%	80.6%
CHESTER	3,158	1,674	1,484		190 R	53.0%	47.0%	53.0%	47.0%
CLAIBORNE	5,403	3,221	2,182		1,039 R	59.6%	40.4%	59.6%	40.4%
CLAY	1,821	842	968	11	126 D	46.2%	53.2%	46.5%	53.5%
COCKE	6,935	5,688	1,247		4,441 R	82.0%	18.0%	82.0%	18.0%
COFFEE	5,665	2,110	3,537	18	1,427 D	37.2%	62.4%	37.4%	62.6%
CROCKETT	3,509	1,343	2,155	11	812 D	38.5%	61.4%	38.6%	61.4%
CUMBERLAND	5,341	3,282	2,059		1,223 R	61.4%	38.6%	61.4%	38.6%
DAVIDSON	87,630	35,916	51,562	152	15,646 D	41.0%	58.9%	41.1%	58.9%
DECATUR	3,100	1,406	1,681	13	275 D	45.4%	54.2%	45.5%	54.5%
DE KALB	3,763	1,814	1,949		135 D	48.2%	51.8%	48.2%	51.8%
DICKSON	5,611	1,415	4,196		2,781 D	25.2%	74.8%	25.2%	74.8%
DYER	7,823	3,231	4,531	61	1,300 D	41.3%	57.9%	41.6%	58.4%
FAYETTE	2,202	1,029	1,173		144 D	46.7%	53.3%	46.7%	53.3%
FENTRESS	3,077	2,143	934		1,209 R	69.6%	30.4%	69.6%	30.4%
FRANKLIN	6,834	2,015	4,786	33	2,771 D	29.5%	70.0%	29.6%	70.4%
GIBSON	10,491	3,766	6,687	38	2,921 D	35.9%	63.7%	36.0%	64.0%
GILES	6,347	1,649	4,640	58	2,991 D	26.0%	73.1%	26.4%	73.6%
GRAINGER	3,972	3,030	937	5	2,093 R	76.3%	23.6%	76.4%	23.6%
GREENE	10,563	6,864	3,656	43	3,208 R	65.0%	34.6%	65.2%	34.8%
GRUNDY	3,302	709	2,583	10	1,874 D	21.5%	78.2%	21.5%	78.5%
HAMBLEN	7,488	5,031	2,395	62	2,636 R	67.2%	32.0%	67.7%	32.3%
HAMILTON	53,830	29,681	23,832	317	5,849 R	55.1%	44.3%	55.5%	44.5%
HANCOCK	2,302	1,830	458	14	1,372 R	79.5%	19.9%	80.0%	20.0%
HARDEMAN	4,029	1,256	2,747	26	1,491 D	31.2%	68.2%	31.4%	68.6%
HARDIN	4,148	2,459	1,677	12	782 R	59.3%	40.4%	59.5%	40.5%
HAWKINS	7,765	5,295	2,404	66	2,891 R	68.2%	31.0%	68.5%	31.5%
HAYWOOD	3,381	940	2,432	9	1,492 D	27.8%	71.9%	27.9%	72.1%
HENDERSON	4,918	3,317	1,601		1,716 R	67.4%	32.6%	67.4%	32.6%
HENRY	8,132	2,421	5,677	34	3,256 D	29.8%	69.8%	29.9%	70.1%
HICKMAN	3,679	1,044	2,625	10	1,581 D	28.4%	71.4%	28.5%	71.5%
HOUSTON	1,694	465	1,229		764 D	27.4%	72.6%	27.4%	72.6%
HUMPHREYS	3,569	898	2,670	1	1,772 D	25.2%	74.8%	25.2%	74.8%
JACKSON	2,827	1,138	1,686	3	548 D	40.3%	59.6%	40.3%	59.7%
JEFFERSON	5,860	4,622	1,228	10	3,394 R	78.9%	21.0%	79.0%	21.0%
JOHNSON	4,096	3,590	506		3,084 R	87.6%	12.4%	87.6%	12.4%
KNOX	71,178	44,358	26,681	139	17,677 R	62.3%	37.5%	62.4%	37.6%
LAKE	1,975	487	1,475	13	988 D	24.7%	74.7%	24.8%	75.2%
LAUDERDALE	5,730	1,390	4,340		2,950 D	24.3%	75.7%	24.3%	75.7%
LAWRENCE	8,931	4,561	4,299	71	262 R	51.1%	48.1%	51.5%	48.5%
LEWIS	1,859	540	1,308	11	768 D	29.0%	70.4%	29.2%	70.8%
LINCOLN	6,177	1,654	4,510	13	2,856 D	26.8%	73.0%	26.8%	73.2%
LOUDON	6,481	4,311	2,138	32	2,173 R	66.5%	33.0%	66.8%	33.2%
MC MINN	9,261	5,778	3,440	43	2,338 R	62.4%	37.1%	62.7%	37.3%
MC NAIRY	6,124	3,426	2,698		728 R	55.9%	44.1%	55.9%	44.1%
MACON	3,760	2,602	1,158		1,444 R	69.2%	30.8%	69.2%	30.8%
MADISON	15,919	7,243	8,623	53	1,380 D	45.5%	54.2%	45.7%	54.3%
MARION	5,190	2,227	2,938	25	711 D	42.9%	56.6%	43.1%	56.9%
MARSHALL	5,362	1,525	3,837		2,312 D	28.4%	71.6%	28.4%	71.6%
MAURY	10,959	3,582	7,377		3,795 D	32.7%	67.3%	32.7%	67.3%

PRESIDENT 1956

County	Total Vote	Republican	Democratic	Other	Rep.-Dem. Plurality	TV Rep.	TV Dem.	MV Rep.	MV Dem.
ANDERSON	21,121	11,071	9,368	682	1,703 R	52.4%	44.4%	54.2%	45.8%
BEDFORD	6,825	2,258	4,517	50	2,259 D	33.1%	66.2%	33.3%	66.7%
BENTON	3,531	1,279	2,231	21	952 D	36.2%	63.2%	36.4%	63.6%
BLEDSOE	2,526	1,429	1,079	18	350 R	56.6%	42.7%	57.0%	43.0%
BLOUNT	17,867	12,667	5,076	124	7,591 R	70.9%	28.4%	71.4%	28.6%
BRADLEY	9,611	6,247	3,225	139	3,022 R	65.0%	33.6%	66.0%	34.0%
CAMPBELL	7,819	5,065	2,628	126	2,437 R	64.8%	33.6%	65.8%	34.2%
CANNON	2,475	919	1,547	9	628 D	37.1%	62.5%	37.3%	62.7%
CARROLL	7,590	4,235	3,232	123	1,003 R	55.8%	42.6%	56.7%	43.3%
CARTER	14,236	11,218	2,933	85	8,285 R	78.8%	20.6%	79.3%	20.7%
CHEATHAM	2,811	498	2,297	16	1,799 D	17.7%	81.7%	17.8%	82.2%
CHESTER	2,989	1,460	1,495	34	35 D	48.8%	50.0%	49.4%	50.6%
CLAIBORNE	5,428	3,377	1,973	78	1,404 R	62.2%	36.3%	63.1%	36.9%
CLAY	1,867	902	948	17	46 D	48.3%	50.8%	48.8%	51.2%
COCKE	6,715	5,526	1,121	68	4,405 R	82.3%	16.7%	83.1%	16.9%
COFFEE	7,369	2,389	4,930	50	2,541 D	32.4%	66.9%	32.6%	67.4%
CROCKETT	3,107	1,026	1,964	117	938 D	33.0%	63.3%	34.3%	65.1%
CUMBERLAND	5,161	3,200	1,925	36	1,275 R	62.0%	37.3%	62.4%	37.6%
DAVIDSON	94,874	37,207	56,622	975	19,745 D	39.2%	59.9%	39.5%	60.5%
DECATUR	3,101	1,512	1,554	35	42 D	48.8%	50.1%	49.3%	50.7%
DE KALB	3,693	1,690	1,982	21	292 D	45.8%	53.7%	46.0%	54.0%
DICKSON	5,114	1,247	3,799	68	2,552 D	24.4%	74.3%	24.7%	75.3%
DYER	7,407	2,682	4,524	201	1,842 D	36.2%	61.1%	37.2%	62.8%
FAYETTE	1,968	687	639	971	48 R	34.9%	32.5%	51.7%	48.3%
FENTRESS	3,212	2,233	934	45	1,299 R	69.5%	29.1%	70.5%	29.5%
FRANKLIN	6,595	1,727	4,791	77	3,064 D	26.2%	72.6%	26.5%	73.5%
GIBSON	11,713	3,481	7,884	348	4,403 D	29.7%	67.3%	30.6%	69.4%
GILES	6,186	1,401	4,750	35	3,349 D	22.6%	76.8%	22.8%	77.2%
GRAINGER	3,449	2,497	913	39	1,584 R	72.4%	26.5%	73.2%	26.8%
GREENE	11,402	7,396	3,949	57	3,447 R	64.9%	34.6%	65.2%	34.8%
GRUNDY	3,024	918	2,076	30	1,158 D	30.4%	68.7%	30.7%	69.3%
HAMBLEN	8,275	5,608	2,592	75	3,016 R	67.8%	31.3%	68.4%	31.5%
HAMILTON	64,830	34,429	28,287	2,114	6,142 R	53.1%	43.6%	54.9%	45.1%
HANCOCK	2,328	1,939	350	39	1,589 R	83.3%	15.0%	84.7%	15.3%
HARDEMAN	3,353	818	1,754	781	936 D	24.4%	52.3%	31.8%	68.2%
HARDIN	4,680	2,898	1,734	48	1,164 R	61.9%	37.1%	62.6%	37.4%
HAWKINS	10,184	6,988	3,180	68	3,736 R	68.0%	31.3%	68.5%	31.5%
HAYWOOD	3,028	516	2,217	295	1,701 D	17.0%	73.2%	18.9%	81.1%
HENDERSON	4,923	3,294	1,613	16	1,681 R	66.9%	32.8%	67.1%	32.9%
HENRY	8,068	2,337	5,625	106	3,288 D	29.0%	69.7%	29.4%	70.6%
HICKMAN	3,496	1,040	2,439	17	1,399 D	29.7%	69.8%	29.9%	70.1%
HOUSTON	1,385	340	1,033	12	693 D	24.5%	74.6%	24.8%	75.2%
HUMPHREYS	3,566	713	2,841	12	2,128 D	20.0%	79.9%	20.0%	79.9%
JACKSON	2,859	881	1,743	35	862 D	33.1%	65.6%	33.6%	66.4%
JEFFERSON	6,273	4,870	1,338	65	3,532 R	77.6%	21.3%	78.4%	21.6%
JOHNSON	4,220	3,690	503	27	3,187 R	87.4%	11.9%	88.0%	12.0%
KNOX	76,831	46,167	29,768	896	16,399 R	60.1%	38.7%	60.8%	39.2%
LAKE	2,246	512	1,673	61	1,161 D	22.8%	74.5%	23.4%	76.6%
LAUDERDALE	5,540	1,049	4,383	108	3,334 D	18.9%	79.1%	19.3%	80.7%
LAWRENCE	8,880	4,588	4,227	65	361 R	51.7%	47.6%	52.0%	48.0%
LEWIS	1,854	522	1,321	11	799 D	28.2%	71.3%	28.3%	71.7%
LINCOLN	5,692	1,207	4,434	51	3,227 D	21.2%	77.9%	21.4%	78.6%
LOUDON	7,524	4,583	2,844	97	1,739 R	60.9%	37.8%	61.7%	38.3%
MC MINN	10,153	6,075	3,950	128	2,125 R	59.8%	38.9%	60.6%	39.4%
MC NAIRY	5,838	3,349	2,403	86	946 R	57.4%	41.2%	58.2%	41.8%
MACON	3,296	2,207	1,069	20	1,138 R	67.0%	32.4%	67.4%	32.6%
MADISON	16,037	6,642	8,540	855	1,898 D	41.4%	53.3%	43.7%	56.3%
MARION	5,798	2,925	2,781	92	144 R	50.4%	48.0%	51.3%	48.7%
MARSHALL	5,745	1,527	4,100	118	2,573 D	26.6%	71.4%	27.1%	72.9%
MAURY	9,706	2,853	6,662	191	3,809 D	29.4%	68.6%	30.0%	70.0%

TENNESSEE

PRESIDENT 1952

County	Total Vote	Republican	Democratic	Other	Rep.-Dem. Plurality	Total Vote % Rep.	Total Vote % Dem.	Major Vote % Rep.	Major Vote % Dem.
MEIGS	1,625	850	754	21	96 R	52.3%	46.4%	53.0%	47.0%
MONROE	8,313	4,581	3,693	39	888 R	55.1%	44.4%	55.4%	44.6%
MONTGOMERY	8,395	2,573	5,759	63	3,186 D	30.6%	68.6%	30.9%	69.1%
MOORE	1,180	354	826		472 D	30.0%	70.0%	30.0%	70.0%
MORGAN	4,057	2,565	1,492		1,073 R	63.2%	36.8%	63.2%	36.8%
OBION	7,345	2,682	4,623	40	1,941 D	36.5%	62.9%	36.7%	63.3%
OVERTON	3,681	1,453	2,209	19	756 D	39.5%	60.0%	39.7%	60.3%
PERRY	1,954	762	1,192		430 D	39.0%	61.0%	39.0%	61.0%
PICKETT	1,550	1,003	547		456 R	64.7%	35.3%	64.7%	35.3%
POLK	4,104	2,283	1,821		462 R	55.6%	44.4%	55.6%	44.4%
PUTNAM	7,279	3,183	4,096		913 D	43.7%	56.3%	43.7%	56.3%
RHEA	4,627	2,520	2,090	17	430 R	54.5%	45.2%	54.7%	45.3%
ROANE	9,285	5,583	3,702		1,881 R	60.1%	39.9%	60.1%	39.9%
ROBERTSON	6,897	1,834	5,063		3,229 D	26.6%	73.4%	26.6%	73.4%
RUTHERFORD	10,061	3,196	6,793	72	3,597 D	31.8%	67.5%	32.0%	68.0%
SCOTT	4,435	3,274	1,161		2,113 R	73.8%	26.2%	73.8%	26.2%
SEQUATCHIE	1,424	535	882	7	347 D	37.6%	61.9%	37.8%	62.2%
SEVIER	8,310	7,244	1,066		6,178 R	87.2%	12.8%	87.2%	12.8%
SHELBY	137,099	65,170	71,779	150	6,609 D	47.5%	52.4%	47.6%	52.4%
SMITH	4,058	1,412	2,622	24	1,210 D	34.8%	64.6%	35.0%	65.0%
STEWART	2,812	641	2,170	1	1,529 D	22.8%	77.2%	22.8%	77.2%
SULLIVAN	27,563	15,596	11,849	118	3,747 R	56.6%	43.0%	56.8%	43.2%
SUMNER	7,958	2,233	5,674	51	3,441 D	28.1%	71.3%	28.2%	71.8%
TIPTON	6,716	1,312	5,351	53	4,039 D	19.5%	79.7%	19.7%	80.3%
TROUSDALE	1,497	261	1,236		975 D	17.4%	82.6%	17.4%	82.6%
UNICOI	4,616	3,453	1,163		2,290 R	74.8%	25.2%	74.8%	25.2%
UNION	2,754	2,087	667		1,420 R	75.8%	24.2%	75.8%	24.2%
VAN BUREN	1,088	393	674	21	281 D	36.1%	61.9%	36.8%	63.2%
WARREN	5,513	1,912	3,568	33	1,656 D	34.7%	64.7%	34.9%	65.1%
WASHINGTON	17,347	12,023	5,245	79	6,778 R	69.3%	30.2%	69.6%	30.4%
WAYNE	3,451	2,439	1,008	4	1,431 R	70.7%	29.2%	70.8%	29.2%
WEAKLEY	7,275	3,043	4,198	34	1,155 D	41.8%	57.7%	42.0%	58.0%
WHITE	3,714	1,374	2,319	21	945 D	37.0%	62.4%	37.2%	62.8%
WILLIAMSON	6,432	2,326	4,085	21	1,759 D	36.2%	63.5%	36.3%	63.7%
WILSON	7,519	2,449	5,070		2,621 D	32.6%	67.4%	32.6%	67.4%
TOTAL	892,553	446,147	443,710	2,696	2,437 R	50.0%	49.7%	50.1%	49.9%

PRESIDENT 1956

County	Total Vote	Republican	Democratic	Other	Rep.-Dem. Plurality	Total Vote % Rep.	Total Vote % Dem.	Major Vote % Rep.	Major Vote % Dem.
MEIGS	1,631	847	759	25	88 R	51.9%	46.5%	52.7%	47.3%
MONROE	8,576	4,998	3,511	67	1,487 R	58.3%	40.9%	58.7%	41.3%
MONTGOMERY	10,934	2,778	8,034	122	5,256 D	25.4%	73.5%	25.7%	74.3%
MOORE	1,167	270	893	4	623 D	23.1%	76.5%	23.2%	76.8%
MORGAN	3,823	2,402	1,379	42	1,023 R	62.8%	36.1%	63.5%	36.5%
OBION	7,637	2,349	5,185	103	2,836 D	30.8%	67.9%	31.2%	68.8%
OVERTON	3,923	1,508	2,385	30	877 D	38.4%	60.8%	38.7%	61.3%
PERRY	1,760	694	1,052	14	358 D	39.4%	59.8%	39.7%	60.3%
PICKETT	1,556	985	560	11	425 R	63.3%	36.0%	63.8%	36.2%
POLK	3,669	2,136	1,533		603 R	58.2%	41.8%	58.2%	41.8%
PUTNAM	8,004	3,492	4,481	31	989 D	43.6%	56.0%	43.8%	56.2%
RHEA	4,517	2,516	1,930	71	586 D	55.7%	42.7%	55.6%	43.4%
ROANE	10,818	6,147	4,531	140	1,616 R	56.8%	41.9%	57.6%	42.4%
ROBERTSON	6,526	1,517	4,961	48	3,444 D	23.2%	76.0%	23.4%	76.6%
RUTHERFORD	9,306	2,713	6,494	99	3,781 D	29.2%	69.8%	29.5%	70.5%
SCOTT	4,149	3,282	842	25	2,440 R	79.1%	20.3%	79.6%	20.4%
SEQUATCHIE	1,556	683	859	14	176 D	43.9%	55.2%	44.3%	55.7%
SEVIER	8,038	6,950	1,043	45	5,007 R	86.5%	13.0%	87.0%	13.0%
SHELBY	135,025	65,690	62,051	7,284	3,639 R	48.7%	46.0%	51.4%	48.6%
SMITH	4,229	1,267	2,949	13	1,682 D	30.0%	69.7%	30.1%	69.9%
STEWART	2,696	560	2,120	16	1,560 D	20.8%	78.6%	20.9%	79.1%
SULLIVAN	33,506	18,903	14,106	497	4,797 R	56.4%	42.1%	57.3%	42.7%
SUMNER	9,527	2,123	7,368	36	5,245 D	22.3%	77.3%	22.4%	77.6%
TIPTON	6,045	983	4,828	234	3,845 D	16.3%	79.9%	16.9%	83.1%
TROUSDALE	1,247	209	1,032	6	823 D	16.8%	82.8%	16.8%	83.2%
UNICOI	5,119	3,978	1,111	30	2,867 R	77.7%	21.7%	78.2%	21.8%
UNION	2,703	2,154	535	14	1,619 R	79.7%	19.8%	80.1%	19.9%
VAN BUREN	991	381	602	8	221 D	38.4%	60.7%	38.8%	61.2%
WARREN	5,998	1,954	4,014	30	2,060 D	32.6%	66.9%	32.7%	67.3%
WASHINGTON	18,912	13,471	5,314	127	8,157 R	71.2%	28.1%	71.7%	28.3%
WAYNE	3,618	2,557	1,045	16	1,512 R	70.7%	28.9%	71.0%	29.0%
WEAKLEY	7,510	2,720	4,717	73	1,997 D	36.2%	62.8%	36.6%	63.4%
WHITE	3,759	1,346	2,378	35	1,032 D	35.8%	63.3%	36.1%	63.9%
WILLIAMSON	6,211	1,979	4,174	58	2,195 D	31.9%	67.2%	32.2%	67.8%
WILSON	7,544	2,266	5,221	57	2,955 D	30.0%	69.2%	30.3%	69.7%
TOTAL	939,404	462,288	456,507	20,609	5,781 R	49.2%	48.6%	50.3%	49.7%

TENNESSEE

PRESIDENT 1960

County	Total Vote	Republican	Democratic	Other	Rep.-Dem. Plurality	%Total Rep.	%Total Dem.	%Major Rep.	%Major Dem.
ANDERSON	21,221	11,153	9,878	190	1,275 R	52.6%	46.5%	53.0%	47.0%
BEDFORD	7,152	2,633	4,457	62	1,824 D	36.8%	62.3%	37.1%	62.9%
BENTON	3,923	1,773	2,030	120	257 D	45.2%	51.7%	46.6%	53.4%
BLEDSOE	2,452	1,439	981	32	458 R	58.7%	40.0%	59.5%	40.5%
BLOUNT	19,872	13,552	6,213	107	7,339 R	68.2%	31.3%	68.6%	31.4%
BRADLEY	11,285	7,865	3,307	113	4,558 R	69.7%	29.3%	70.4%	29.6%
CAMPBELL	8,297	5,079	3,134	84	1,945 R	61.2%	37.8%	61.8%	38.2%
CANNON	2,487	1,195	1,275	17	80 D	48.0%	51.3%	48.4%	51.6%
CARROLL	7,609	4,517	2,961	131	1,556 R	59.4%	38.9%	60.4%	39.6%
CARTER	15,798	12,214	3,412	172	8,802 R	77.3%	21.6%	78.2%	21.8%
CHEATHAM	2,607	683	1,883	41	1,200 D	26.2%	72.2%	26.6%	73.4%
CHESTER	3,060	1,807	1,192	61	615 R	59.1%	39.0%	60.3%	39.7%
CLAIBORNE	6,056	3,888	2,142	26	1,746 R	64.2%	35.4%	64.5%	35.5%
CLAY	2,106	1,098	976	32	122 R	52.1%	46.3%	52.9%	47.1%
COCKE	8,095	6,581	1,442	72	5,139 R	81.3%	17.8%	82.0%	18.0%
COFFEE	7,686	3,058	4,555	73	1,497 D	39.8%	59.3%	40.2%	59.8%
CROCKETT	3,013	1,467	1,438	108	29 R	48.7%	47.7%	50.5%	49.5%
CUMBERLAND	5,804	3,523	2,189	92	1,334 R	60.7%	37.7%	61.7%	38.3%
DAVIDSON	112,597	52,077	59,649	871	7,572 D	46.3%	53.0%	46.6%	53.4%
DECATUR	3,075	1,684	1,321	70	363 R	54.8%	43.0%	56.0%	44.0%
DE KALB	3,026	1,440	1,547	39	107 D	47.6%	51.1%	48.2%	51.8%
DICKSON	5,894	1,928	3,930	36	2,002 D	32.7%	66.7%	32.9%	67.1%
DYER	8,203	4,097	3,868	238	229 R	49.9%	47.2%	51.4%	48.6%
FAYETTE	2,799	1,370	892	537	478 R	48.9%	31.9%	60.6%	39.4%
FENTRESS	3,792	2,726	1,014	52	1,712 R	71.9%	26.7%	72.9%	27.1%
FRANKLIN	7,139	2,041	5,041	57	3,000 D	28.6%	70.6%	28.8%	71.2%
GIBSON	11,329	5,173	5,796	360	623 D	45.7%	51.2%	47.2%	52.8%
GILES	6,513	1,598	4,879	36	3,281 D	24.5%	74.9%	24.7%	75.3%
GRAINGER	3,977	3,017	939	21	2,078 R	75.9%	23.6%	76.3%	23.7%
GREENE	13,276	8,835	4,406	35	4,429 R	66.5%	33.2%	66.7%	33.3%
GRUNDY	2,960	786	2,143	31	1,357 D	26.6%	72.4%	26.8%	73.2%
HAMBLEN	10,245	7,093	3,122	30	3,971 R	69.2%	30.5%	69.4%	30.6%
HAMILTON	71,277	39,703	30,482	1,092	9,221 R	55.7%	42.8%	56.6%	43.4%
HANCOCK	2,552	2,107	438	7	1,669 R	82.6%	17.2%	82.8%	17.2%
HARDEMAN	3,604	1,601	1,711	292	110 D	44.4%	47.5%	48.3%	51.7%
HARDIN	5,098	3,323	1,690	85	1,633 R	65.2%	33.2%	66.3%	33.7%
HAWKINS	9,672	7,010	2,586	76	4,424 R	72.5%	26.7%	73.1%	26.9%
HAYWOOD	3,334	1,188	1,867	279	679 D	35.6%	56.0%	38.9%	61.1%
HENDERSON	5,128	3,597	1,490	41	2,107 R	70.1%	29.1%	70.7%	29.3%
HENRY	8,213	3,033	5,049	131	2,016 D	36.9%	61.5%	37.5%	62.5%
HICKMAN	3,687	1,224	2,401	62	1,177 D	33.2%	65.1%	33.8%	66.2%
HOUSTON	1,533	366	1,150	17	784 D	23.9%	75.0%	24.1%	75.9%
HUMPHREYS	3,766	1,126	2,592	48	1,466 D	29.9%	68.8%	30.3%	69.7%
JACKSON	2,636	1,049	1,539	48	490 D	39.8%	58.4%	40.5%	59.5%
JEFFERSON	7,794	6,141	1,620	33	4,521 R	78.8%	20.8%	79.1%	20.9%
JOHNSON	4,443	3,854	571	18	3,283 R	86.7%	12.9%	87.1%	12.9%
KNOX	83,300	50,811	31,990	499	18,821 R	61.0%	38.4%	61.4%	38.6%
LAKE	2,151	732	1,346	73	614 D	34.0%	62.6%	35.2%	64.8%
LAUDERDALE	4,832	1,322	3,462	48	2,140 D	27.4%	71.6%	27.6%	72.4%
LAWRENCE	10,639	5,709	4,862	68	847 R	53.7%	45.7%	54.0%	46.0%
LEWIS	2,312	580	1,723	9	1,143 D	25.1%	74.5%	25.2%	74.8%
LINCOLN	6,346	1,428	4,862	56	3,434 D	22.5%	76.6%	22.7%	77.3%
LOUDON	8,181	5,356	2,722	103	2,634 R	65.5%	33.3%	66.3%	33.7%
MCMINN	10,766	6,585	4,111	70	2,474 R	61.2%	38.2%	61.6%	38.4%
MCNAIRY	5,604	3,310	2,173	121	1,137 R	59.1%	38.8%	60.4%	39.6%
MACON	3,782	2,829	915	38	1,914 R	74.8%	24.2%	75.6%	24.4%
MADISON	17,693	8,863	8,083	747	780 R	50.1%	45.7%	52.3%	47.7%
MARION	5,865	2,657	3,124	84	467 D	45.3%	53.3%	46.0%	54.0%
MARSHALL	5,387	1,717	3,625	45	1,908 D	31.9%	67.3%	32.1%	67.9%
MAURY	10,879	4,133	6,615	131	2,482 D	38.0%	60.8%	38.5%	61.5%

PRESIDENT 1964

County	Total Vote	Republican	Democratic	Other	Rep.-Dem. Plurality	%Total Rep.	%Total Dem.	%Major Rep.	%Major Dem.
ANDERSON	21,006	8,860	12,146	2	3,286 D	42.2%	57.8%	42.2%	57.8%
BEDFORD	7,882	2,272	5,610		3,338 D	28.8%	71.2%	28.8%	71.2%
BENTON	3,974	1,363	2,611		1,248 D	34.3%	65.7%	34.3%	65.7%
BLEDSOE	2,843	1,431	1,412		19 R	50.3%	49.7%	50.3%	49.7%
BLOUNT	20,343	11,876	8,459	8	3,417 R	58.4%	41.6%	58.4%	41.6%
BRADLEY	12,410	6,717	5,693		1,024 R	54.1%	45.9%	54.1%	45.9%
CAMPBELL	8,644	4,232	4,412		180 D	49.0%	51.0%	49.0%	51.0%
CANNON	2,936	746	2,190		1,444 D	25.4%	74.6%	25.4%	74.6%
CARROLL	7,790	3,734	4,056		322 D	47.9%	52.1%	47.9%	52.1%
CARTER	13,798	8,472	5,326		3,146 R	61.4%	38.6%	61.4%	38.6%
CHEATHAM	3,554	803	2,750	1	1,947 D	22.6%	77.4%	22.6%	77.4%
CHESTER	3,530	1,767	1,763		4 R	50.1%	49.9%	50.1%	49.9%
CLAIBORNE	5,433	2,852	2,581		271 R	52.5%	47.5%	52.5%	47.5%
CLAY	1,818	622	1,196		574 D	34.2%	65.8%	34.2%	65.8%
COCKE	7,193	5,084	2,109		2,975 R	70.7%	29.3%	70.7%	29.3%
COFFEE	9,849	3,012	6,837		3,825 D	30.6%	69.4%	30.6%	69.4%
CROCKETT	3,690	1,873	1,817		56 R	50.8%	49.2%	50.8%	49.2%
CUMBERLAND	6,048	2,975	3,073		98 D	49.2%	50.8%	49.2%	50.8%
DAVIDSON	124,722	45,335	79,387		34,052 D	36.3%	63.7%	36.3%	63.7%
DECATUR	3,242	1,429	1,813		384 D	44.1%	55.9%	44.1%	55.9%
DE KALB	3,693	1,402	2,291		889 D	38.0%	62.0%	38.0%	62.0%
DICKSON	6,005	1,281	4,724		3,443 D	21.3%	78.7%	21.3%	78.7%
DYER	9,236	4,517	4,717	2	200 D	48.9%	51.1%	48.9%	51.1%
FAYETTE	5,558	2,922	2,636		286 R	52.6%	47.4%	52.6%	47.4%
FENTRESS	3,519	1,969	1,550		419 R	56.0%	44.0%	56.0%	44.0%
FRANKLIN	8,291	2,262	6,029		3,767 D	27.3%	72.7%	27.3%	72.7%
GIBSON	12,733	4,614	8,119		3,505 D	36.2%	63.8%	36.2%	63.8%
GILES	6,318	1,378	4,940		3,562 D	21.8%	78.2%	21.8%	78.2%
GRAINGER	3,943	2,634	1,309		1,325 R	66.8%	33.2%	66.8%	33.2%
GREENE	12,829	6,913	5,916		997 R	53.9%	46.1%	53.9%	46.1%
GRUNDY	3,461	686	2,775		2,089 D	19.8%	80.2%	19.8%	80.2%
HAMBLEN	9,803	5,196	4,607		589 R	53.0%	47.0%	53.0%	47.0%
HAMILTON	78,746	40,200	38,546		1,654 R	51.0%	48.9%	51.1%	48.9%
HANCOCK	2,204	1,517	687		830 R	68.8%	31.2%	68.8%	31.2%
HARDEMAN	5,125	2,450	2,675		225 D	47.8%	52.2%	47.8%	52.2%
HARDIN	5,645	3,025	2,620		405 R	53.6%	46.4%	53.6%	46.4%
HAWKINS	9,903	5,712	4,191		1,521 R	57.7%	42.3%	57.7%	42.3%
HAYWOOD	4,697	2,407	2,290		117 R	51.2%	48.8%	51.2%	48.8%
HENDERSON	5,068	3,133	1,955		1,178 R	61.6%	38.4%	61.6%	38.4%
HENRY	8,135	2,261	5,874		3,613 D	27.8%	72.2%	27.8%	72.2%
HICKMAN	3,895	1,019	2,877		1,858 D	26.2%	73.8%	26.2%	73.8%
HOUSTON	1,859	287	1,572		1,285 D	15.4%	84.6%	15.4%	84.6%
HUMPHREYS	4,146	916	3,230		2,314 D	22.1%	77.9%	22.1%	77.9%
JACKSON	2,842	551	2,291		1,740 D	19.4%	80.6%	19.4%	80.6%
JEFFERSON	7,523	4,923	2,600		2,323 R	65.4%	34.6%	65.4%	34.6%
JOHNSON	3,816	2,889	927		1,962 R	75.7%	24.3%	75.7%	24.3%
KNOX	85,260	42,797	42,463		334 R	50.2%	49.8%	50.2%	49.8%
LAKE	2,404	736	1,667	1	931 D	30.6%	69.4%	30.6%	69.4%
LAUDERDALE	5,727	1,880	3,847		1,967 D	32.8%	67.2%	32.8%	67.2%
LAWRENCE	10,039	4,590	5,449		859 D	45.7%	54.3%	45.7%	54.3%
LEWIS	2,449	388	2,061		1,673 D	15.8%	84.2%	15.8%	84.2%
LINCOLN	6,590	1,728	4,861	1	3,133 D	26.2%	73.8%	26.2%	73.8%
LOUDON	7,524	4,148	3,365	11	783 R	55.1%	44.8%	55.2%	44.8%
MCMINN	10,831	5,624	5,207		417 R	51.9%	48.1%	51.9%	48.1%
MCNAIRY	6,103	3,109	2,994		115 R	50.9%	49.1%	50.9%	49.1%
MACON	3,292	1,846	1,446		400 R	56.1%	43.9%	56.1%	43.9%
MADISON	21,505	10,932	10,573		359 R	50.8%	49.2%	50.8%	49.2%
MARION	6,503	2,728	3,775		1,047 D	41.9%	58.1%	41.9%	58.1%
MARSHALL	5,329	1,340	3,989		2,649 D	25.1%	74.9%	25.1%	74.9%
MAURY	12,322	4,605	7,716	1	3,111 D	37.4%	62.6%	37.4%	62.6%

TENNESSEE

PRESIDENT 1960

County	Total Vote	Republican	Democratic	Other	Rep.-Dem. Plurality	Total Vote Rep.	Total Vote Dem.	Major Vote Rep.	Major Vote Dem.
MEIGS	1,605	901	691	13	210 R	56.1%	43.1%	56.6%	43.4%
MONROE	8,452	4,991	3,375	86	1,616 R	59.1%	39.9%	59.7%	40.3%
MONTGOMERY	10,270	2,550	7,635	85	5,085 D	24.8%	74.3%	25.0%	75.0%
MOORE	1,187	313	863	11	550 D	26.4%	72.7%	26.6%	73.4%
MORGAN	3,855	2,241	1,576	38	665 R	58.1%	40.9%	58.7%	41.3%
OBION	8,196	3,800	4,244	152	444 D	46.4%	51.8%	47.2%	52.8%
OVERTON	4,252	1,831	2,389	32	558 D	43.1%	56.2%	43.4%	56.6%
PERRY	1,737	645	1,076	16	431 D	37.1%	61.9%	37.5%	62.5%
PICKETT	1,721	1,154	567		587 R	67.1%	32.9%	67.1%	32.9%
POLK	3,751	2,187	1,532	32	655 R	58.3%	40.8%	58.8%	41.2%
PUTNAM	8,715	4,240	4,443	32	203 D	48.7%	51.0%	48.8%	51.2%
RHEA	4,552	2,721	1,761	70	960 R	59.8%	38.7%	60.7%	39.3%
ROANE	11,626	6,540	4,953	133	1,587 R	56.3%	42.6%	56.9%	43.1%
ROBERTSON	5,891	1,776	4,053	62	2,277 D	30.1%	68.8%	30.5%	69.5%
RUTHERFORD	11,052	4,526	6,410	116	1,884 D	41.0%	58.0%	41.4%	58.6%
SCOTT	4,411	3,301	1,098	12	2,203 R	74.8%	24.9%	75.0%	25.0%
SEQUATCHIE	1,655	703	930	22	227 D	42.5%	56.2%	43.0%	57.0%
SEVIER	9,192	7,818	1,341	33	6,477 R	85.1%	14.6%	85.4%	14.6%
SHELBY	176,607	87,191	86,270	3,146	921 R	49.4%	48.8%	50.3%	49.7%
SMITH	4,060	1,601	2,411	48	810 D	39.4%	59.4%	39.9%	60.1%
STEWART	2,386	539	1,810	37	1,271 D	22.6%	75.9%	22.9%	77.1%
SULLIVAN	37,598	22,354	14,731	513	7,623 R	59.5%	39.2%	60.3%	39.7%
SUMNER	10,261	3,491	6,687	83	3,196 D	34.0%	65.2%	34.3%	65.7%
*TIPTON	5,917	1,829	3,853	235	2,024 D	30.9%	65.1%	32.2%	67.8%
*TROUSDALE	1,356	308	1,036	12	728 D	22.7%	76.4%	22.9%	77.1%
UNICOI	5,336	4,004	1,322	10	2,682 R	75.0%	24.8%	75.2%	24.8%
UNION	2,753	2,082	652	19	1,430 R	75.6%	23.7%	76.2%	23.8%
VAN BUREN	995	401	577	17	176 D	40.3%	58.0%	41.0%	59.0%
WARREN	5,841	2,682	3,119	40	437 D	45.9%	53.4%	46.2%	53.8%
WASHINGTON	21,236	14,851	6,283	102	8,568 R	69.9%	29.6%	70.3%	29.7%
WAYNE	3,872	2,912	931	29	1,981 R	75.2%	24.0%	75.8%	24.2%
WEAKLEY	8,109	3,543	4,488	78	945 D	43.7%	55.3%	44.1%	55.9%
WHITE	3,998	1,725	2,207	66	482 D	43.1%	55.2%	43.9%	56.1%
WILLIAMSON	7,228	2,999	4,471	58	1,772 D	37.3%	61.9%	37.6%	62.1%
WILSON	8,297	3,383	4,857	57	1,474 D	40.8%	58.5%	41.1%	58.9%
TOTAL	1,051,792	556,577	481,453	13,762	75,124 R	52.9%	45.8%	53.6%	46.4%

PRESIDENT 1964

County	Total Vote	Republican	Democratic	Other	Rep.-Dem. Plurality	Total Vote Rep.	Total Vote Dem.	Major Vote Rep.	Major Vote Dem.
MEIGS	1,740	824	916		92 D	47.4%	52.6%	47.4%	52.6%
MONROE	8,449	4,349	4,100		249 R	51.5%	48.5%	51.5%	48.5%
MONTGOMERY	12,992	2,814	10,178		7,364 D	21.7%	78.3%	21.7%	78.3%
MOORE	1,298	264	1,034		770 D	20.3%	79.7%	20.3%	79.7%
MORGAN	3,799	1,842	1,957		115 D	48.5%	51.5%	48.5%	51.5%
OBION	8,474	2,802	5,672		2,870 D	33.1%	66.9%	33.1%	66.9%
OVERTON	4,413	1,155	3,258		2,103 D	26.2%	73.8%	26.2%	73.8%
PERRY	1,954	514	1,440		926 D	26.3%	73.7%	26.3%	73.7%
PICKETT	1,663	935	728		207 R	56.2%	43.8%	56.2%	43.8%
POLK	3,798	1,685	2,113		428 D	44.4%	55.6%	44.4%	55.6%
PUTNAM	9,304	2,993	6,309	2	3,316 D	32.2%	67.8%	32.2%	67.8%
RHEA	5,367	2,730	2,637		93 R	50.9%	49.1%	50.9%	49.1%
ROANE	11,843	5,735	6,108		373 D	48.4%	51.6%	48.4%	51.6%
ROBERTSON	7,581	1,797	5,784		3,987 D	23.7%	76.3%	23.7%	76.3%
RUTHERFORD	13,668	4,088	9,580		5,492 D	29.9%	70.1%	29.9%	70.1%
SCOTT	4,413	2,406	2,007		399 R	54.5%	45.5%	54.5%	45.5%
SEQUATCHIE	1,966	804	1,162		358 D	40.9%	59.1%	40.9%	59.1%
SEVIER	9,816	6,821	2,995		3,826 R	69.5%	30.5%	69.5%	30.5%
SHELBY	212,026	100,527	111,496	3	10,969 D	47.4%	52.6%	47.4%	52.6%
SMITH	4,018	1,084	2,934		1,850 D	27.0%	73.0%	27.0%	73.0%
STEWART	2,885	441	2,444		2,003 D	15.3%	84.7%	15.3%	84.7%
SULLIVAN	37,199	17,703	19,496		1,793 D	47.6%	52.4%	47.6%	52.4%
SUMNER	12,539	3,437	9,102		5,665 D	27.4%	72.6%	27.4%	72.6%
*TIPTON	6,894	3,073	3,821		748 D	44.6%	55.4%	44.6%	55.4%
*TROUSDALE	1,475	205	1,270		1,065 D	13.9%	86.1%	13.9%	86.1%
UNICOI	4,731	2,731	2,000		731 R	57.7%	42.3%	57.7%	42.3%
UNION	2,861	1,770	1,091		679 R	61.9%	38.1%	61.9%	38.1%
VAN BUREN	1,158	293	865		572 D	25.3%	74.7%	25.3%	74.7%
WARREN	6,782	1,754	5,027	1	3,273 D	25.9%	74.1%	25.9%	74.1%
WASHINGTON	20,865	10,612	10,253		359 R	50.9%	49.1%	50.9%	49.1%
WAYNE	3,688	2,510	1,178		1,332 R	68.1%	31.9%	68.1%	31.9%
WEAKLEY	7,845	2,684	5,161		2,477 D	34.2%	65.8%	34.2%	65.8%
WHITE	4,186	1,199	2,987		1,788 D	28.6%	71.4%	28.6%	71.4%
WILLIAMSON	7,783	2,707	5,075	1	2,368 D	34.8%	65.2%	34.8%	65.2%
WILSON	8,974	2,707	6,267		3,560 D	30.2%	69.8%	30.2%	69.8%
TOTAL	1,144,046	508,965	635,047	34	126,082 D	44.5%	55.5%	44.5%	55.5%

TENNESSEE

OTHER VOTE COMPOSITION:

1920   Socialist.
1924   10,666 Progressive; 100 American; 94 Prohibition.
1928   567 Socialist; 94 Communist.
1932   1,998 Prohibition; 1,796 Socialist; 254 Communist.
1936   692 Socialist; 634 Prohibition; 326 Communist; 296 Union.

1940   1,606 Prohibition; 463 Socialist.
1944   882 Prohibition; 792 Socialist.
1948   73,815 States Rights; 1,864 Progressive; 1,288 Socialist.
1952   1,432 Prohibition; 885 Progressive; 379 Christian Nationalist (MacArthur).
1956   19,820 States Rights; 789 Prohibition.

1960   11,304 National States Rights; 2,458 Prohibition.
1964   Scattered.

SPECIAL CASES:

1924   Progressive candidates ran second in one county.
1948   States Rights candidates carried several counties and ran second in others. One Democratic elector voted in the Electoral College for the States Rights nominees.
1956   States Rights candidates carried one county.

TEXAS

PRESIDENT 1920

County	Total Vote	Republican	Democratic	Other	Rep.-Dem. Plurality	% Total Vote Rep.	% Total Vote Dem.	% Major Vote Rep.	% Major Vote Dem.
ANDERSON	3,926	323	2,355	1,248	2,032 D	8.2%	60.0%	12.1%	87.9%
ANDREWS	83	9	74		65 D	10.8%	89.2%	10.8%	89.2%
ANGELINA	2,672	205	1,661	806	1,456 D	7.7%	62.2%	11.0%	89.0%
ARANSAS	202	49	146	7	97 D	24.3%	72.3%	25.1%	74.9%
ARCHER	641	169	449	23	280 D	26.4%	70.0%	27.3%	72.7%
ARMSTRONG	506	87	405	14	318 D	17.2%	80.0%	17.7%	82.3%
ATASCOSA	766	185	531	50	346 D	24.2%	69.3%	25.8%	74.2%
AUSTIN	2,892	568	538	1,786	30 R	19.6%	18.6%	51.4%	48.6%
BAILEY									
BANDERA	611	249	311	51	62 D	40.8%	50.9%	44.5%	55.5%
BASTROP	2,166	484	1,088	594	604 D	22.3%	50.2%	30.8%	69.2%
BAYLOR	859	139	632	88	493 D	16.2%	73.6%	18.0%	82.0%
BEE	923	283	545	95	262 D	30.7%	59.0%	34.2%	65.8%
BELL	6,081	483	3,595	2,003	3,112 D	7.9%	59.1%	11.8%	88.2%
BEXAR	17,047	8,898	6,926	1,223	1,972 R	52.2%	40.6%	56.2%	43.8%
BLANCO	1,708	378	426	904	48 D	22.1%	24.9%	47.0%	53.0%
BORDEN	105	4	89	12	85 D	3.8%	84.8%	4.3%	95.7%
BOSQUE	2,544	567	1,556	421	989 D	22.3%	61.2%	26.7%	73.3%
BOWIE	3,851	1,032	2,396	423	1,364 D	26.8%	62.2%	30.1%	69.9%
BRAZORIA	2,605	1,235	1,184	186	51 R	47.4%	45.5%	51.1%	48.9%
BRAZOS	2,172	277	1,281	614	1,004 D	12.8%	59.0%	17.8%	82.2%
BREWSTER	347	125	210	12	85 D	36.0%	60.5%	37.3%	62.7%
BRISCOE	332	39	262	31	223 D	11.7%	78.3%	13.0%	87.0%
BROOKS	164	37	127		90 D	22.6%	77.4%	22.6%	77.4%
BROWN	2,436	397	1,708	331	1,311 D	16.3%	70.1%	18.9%	81.1%
BURLESON	1,988	142	981	865	839 D	7.1%	49.3%	12.6%	87.4%
BURNET	1,270	241	795	234	554 D	19.0%	62.6%	23.3%	76.7%
CALDWELL	2,067	269	1,240	558	971 D	13.0%	60.0%	17.8%	82.2%
CALHOUN	561	95	363	103	268 D	16.9%	64.7%	20.7%	79.3%
CALLAHAN	1,204	213	814	187	601 D	17.7%	66.8%	20.9%	79.1%
CAMERON	1,846	909	920	17	11 D	49.2%	49.8%	49.7%	50.3%
CAMP	1,321	156	661	504	505 D	11.8%	50.0%	19.1%	80.9%
CARSON	647	208	428	11	220 D	32.1%	66.2%	32.7%	67.3%
CASS	3,397	1,446	1,563	388	117 D	42.6%	46.0%	48.1%	51.9%
CASTRO	275	111	158	6	47 D	40.4%	57.5%	41.3%	58.7%
CHAMBERS	563	278	240	45	38 R	49.4%	42.6%	53.7%	46.3%
CHEROKEE	3,572	478	2,233	861	1,755 D	13.4%	62.5%	17.6%	82.4%
CHILDRESS	1,441	163	1,206	72	1,043 D	11.3%	83.7%	11.9%	88.1%
CLAY	1,821	446	1,324	51	878 D	24.5%	72.7%	25.2%	74.8%
COCHRAN									
COKE	564	58	444	62	386 D	10.3%	78.7%	11.6%	88.4%
COLEMAN	2,214	355	1,445	414	1,090 D	16.0%	65.3%	19.7%	80.3%
COLLIN	5,778	1,337	4,046	395	2,707 D	23.1%	70.0%	24.9%	75.1%
COLLINGSWORTH	1,007	308	640	60	333 D	30.6%	63.6%	32.4%	67.6%
COLORADO	2,475	477	765	1,233	288 D	19.3%	30.9%	38.4%	61.6%
COMAL	1,820	765	181	874	584 R	42.0%	9.9%	80.9%	19.1%
COMANCHE	2,860	930	1,633	297	703 D	32.5%	57.1%	36.3%	63.7%
CONCHO	675	151	405	119	254 D	22.4%	60.0%	27.2%	72.8%
COOKE	3,388	1,003	2,170	215	1,167 D	29.6%	64.0%	31.6%	68.4%
CORYELL	2,722	444	1,542	736	1,098 D	16.3%	56.6%	22.4%	77.6%
COTTLE	664	121	472	71	351 D	18.2%	71.1%	20.4%	79.6%
CRANE									
CROCKETT	171	80	89	2	9 D	46.8%	52.0%	47.3%	52.7%
CROSBY	782	146	572	64	426 D	18.7%	73.1%	20.3%	79.7%
CULBERSON	47	6	40	1	34 D	12.8%	85.1%	13.0%	87.0%
DALLAM	736	195	478	63	283 D	26.5%	64.9%	29.0%	71.0%
DALLAS	21,349	4,986	14,390	1,973	9,404 D	23.4%	67.4%	25.7%	74.3%
DAWSON	419	75	296	48	221 D	17.9%	70.6%	20.2%	79.8%
DEAF SMITH	666	205	459	2	254 D	30.8%	68.9%	30.9%	69.1%
DELTA	1,499	316	1,081	102	765 D	21.1%	72.1%	22.6%	77.4%

PRESIDENT 1924

County	Total Vote	Republican	Democratic	Other	Rep.-Dem. Plurality	% Total Vote Rep.	% Total Vote Dem.	% Major Vote Rep.	% Major Vote Dem.
ANDERSON	1,191	562	374	255	188 R	47.2%	31.4%	60.0%	40.0%
ANDREWS	71	7	60	4	53 D	9.9%	84.5%	10.4%	89.6%
ANGELINA	4,419	333	3,914	172	3,581 D	7.5%	88.6%	7.8%	92.2%
ARANSAS	278	75	195	8	120 D	27.0%	70.1%	27.8%	72.2%
ARCHER	1,117	146	883	88	737 D	13.1%	79.1%	14.2%	85.8%
ARMSTRONG	556	106	426	24	320 D	19.1%	76.6%	19.9%	80.1%
ATASCOSA	1,389	303	869	217	566 D	21.8%	62.6%	25.9%	74.1%
AUSTIN	3,627	457	2,601	569	2,144 D	12.6%	71.7%	14.9%	85.1%
BAILEY	250	63	166	21	103 D	25.2%	66.4%	27.5%	72.5%
BANDERA	924	442	425	57	17 R	47.8%	46.0%	51.0%	49.0%
BASTROP	3,452	494	2,711	247	2,217 D	14.3%	78.5%	15.4%	84.6%
BAYLOR	1,163	135	1,012	16	877 D	11.6%	87.0%	11.8%	88.2%
BEE	2,077	944	987	146	43 D	45.5%	47.5%	48.9%	51.1%
BELL	9,457	1,632	7,273	552	5,641 D	17.3%	76.9%	18.3%	81.7%
BEXAR	24,699	9,898	10,838	3,963	940 D	40.1%	43.9%	47.7%	52.3%
BLANCO	1,078	317	586	175	269 D	29.4%	54.4%	35.1%	64.9%
BORDEN	96	10	86		76 D	10.4%	89.6%	10.4%	89.6%
BOSQUE	3,017	403	2,534	80	2,131 D	13.4%	84.0%	13.7%	86.3%
BOWIE	4,464	740	3,455	269	2,715 D	16.6%	77.4%	17.6%	82.4%
BRAZORIA	2,994	1,114	1,761	119	647 D	37.2%	58.8%	38.7%	61.3%
BRAZOS	2,444	255	2,128	61	1,873 D	10.4%	87.1%	10.7%	89.3%
BREWSTER	500	113	366	21	253 D	22.6%	73.2%	23.6%	76.4%
BRISCOE	476	53	397	26	344 D	11.1%	83.4%	11.8%	88.2%
BROOKS	268	59	205	4	146 D	22.0%	76.5%	22.3%	77.7%
BROWN	3,963	396	3,467	100	3,071 D	10.0%	87.5%	10.3%	89.7%
BURLESON	2,744	224	2,496	24	2,272 D	8.2%	91.0%	8.2%	91.8%
BURNET	2,060	277	1,725	58	1,448 D	13.4%	83.7%	13.8%	86.2%
CALDWELL	2,797	399	2,194	204	1,795 D	14.3%	78.4%	15.4%	84.6%
CALHOUN	902	181	686	35	505 D	20.1%	76.1%	20.9%	79.1%
CALLAHAN	1,946	244	1,614	88	1,370 D	12.5%	82.9%	13.1%	86.9%
CAMERON	3,667	1,266	2,225	176	959 D	34.5%	60.7%	36.3%	63.7%
CAMP	1,416	187	1,186	43	999 D	13.2%	83.8%	13.6%	86.4%
CARSON	952	306	611	35	305 D	32.1%	64.2%	33.4%	66.6%
CASS	3,211	997	2,125	89	1,128 D	31.0%	66.2%	31.9%	68.1%
CASTRO	369	68	219	82	151 D	18.4%	59.3%	23.7%	76.3%
CHAMBERS	565	239	315	11	76 D	42.3%	55.8%	43.1%	56.9%
CHEROKEE	5,099	666	4,343	90	3,677 D	13.1%	85.2%	13.3%	86.7%
CHILDRESS	1,366	178	1,117	71	939 D	13.0%	81.8%	13.7%	86.3%
CLAY	1,833	318	1,402	113	1,084 D	17.3%	76.5%	18.5%	81.5%
COCHRAN	72	9	59	4	50 D	12.5%	81.9%	13.2%	86.8%
COKE	766	80	673	13	593 D	10.4%	87.9%	10.6%	89.4%
COLEMAN	3,341	502	2,763	76	2,261 D	15.0%	82.7%	15.3%	84.6%
COLLIN	9,365	1,981	7,215	169	5,234 D	21.2%	77.0%	21.5%	78.5%
COLLINGSWORTH	988	234	731	23	497 D	23.7%	74.0%	24.2%	75.8%
COLORADO	3,162	681	2,105	376	1,424 D	21.5%	66.6%	24.4%	75.6%
COMAL	2,465	312	330	1,823	18 D	12.7%	13.4%	48.6%	51.4%
COMANCHE	846	456	276	114	180 R	53.9%	32.6%	62.3%	37.7%
CONCHO	781	90	668	23	578 D	11.5%	85.5%	11.9%	88.1%
COOKE	4,086	525	3,170	391	2,645 D	12.8%	77.6%	14.2%	85.8%
CORYELL	3,389	429	2,890	70	2,461 D	12.7%	85.3%	12.9%	87.1%
COTTLE	658	59	580	19	521 D	9.0%	88.1%	9.2%	90.8%
CRANE									
CROCKETT	182	112	69	1	43 R	61.5%	37.9%	61.9%	38.1%
CROSBY	1,554	278	1,242	34	964 D	17.9%	79.9%	18.3%	81.7%
CULBERSON	117	15	93	9	78 D	12.8%	79.5%	13.9%	86.1%
DALLAM	1,045	254	506	285	252 D	24.3%	48.4%	33.4%	66.6%
DALLAS	39,837	8,618	30,207	1,012	21,589 D	21.6%	75.8%	22.2%	77.8%
DAWSON	1,299	185	1,079	35	894 D	14.2%	83.1%	14.6%	85.4%
DEAF SMITH	763	192	538	33	346 D	25.2%	70.5%	26.3%	73.7%
DELTA	2,716	479	2,186	51	1,707 D	17.6%	80.5%	18.0%	82.0%

TEXAS

PRESIDENT 1920

County	Total Vote	Republican	Democratic	Other	Rep.-Dem. Plurality	% Total Vote Rep.	% Total Vote Dem.	% Major Vote Rep.	% Major Vote Dem.
DENTON	2,600	900	1,257	443	357 D	34.6	48.3	41.7	58.3
DE WITT	3,309	1,277	971	1,061	306 R	38.6	29.3	56.8	43.2
DICKENS	579	109	433	37	324 D	18.8	74.8	20.1	79.9
DIMMIT	343	108	231	4	123 D	31.5	67.3	31.9	68.1
DONLEY	1,001	206	766	29	560 D	20.6	76.5	21.2	78.8
DUVAL	480	86	387	7	301 D	17.9	80.6	18.2	81.8
EASTLAND	4,069	941	2,942	186	2,001 D	23.1	72.3	24.2	75.8
ECTOR	125	23	100	2	77 D	18.4	80.0	18.7	81.3
EDWARDS	529	297	201	31	96 R	56.1	38.0	59.6	40.4
ELLIS	5,857	819	4,081	957	3,262 D	14.0	59.7	16.7	83.3
EL PASO	8,286	4,070	4,143	73	73 D	49.1	50.0	49.6	50.4
ERATH	2,743	358	1,914	471	1,556 D	13.1	59.8	15.8	84.2
FALLS	3,883	585	1,878	1,420	1,293 D	15.1	48.4	23.6	76.4
FANNIN	5,182	1,103	3,461	618	2,358 D	21.3	66.8	24.2	75.8
FAYETTE	4,525	1,099	932	2,494	167 R	24.3	20.6	54.1	45.9
FISHER	994	152	743	99	591 D	15.3	74.7	17.0	83.0
FLOYD	1,066	167	841	58	674 D	15.7	78.9	16.6	83.4
FOARD	1,017	101	491	425	390 D	9.9	48.3	17.1	82.9
FORT BEND	2,484	748	1,299	437	551 D	30.1	52.3	36.5	63.5
FRANKLIN	811	251	529	31	278 D	30.9	65.2	32.2	67.8
FREESTONE	2,752	378	1,463	911	1,085 D	13.7	53.2	20.5	79.5
FRIO	532	102	421	9	319 D	19.2	79.1	19.5	80.5
GAINES	143	9	134		125 D	6.3	93.7	6.3	93.7
GALVESTON	5,372	1,628	2,933	811	1,305 D	30.3	54.6	35.7	64.3
GARZA	473	28	392	53	364 D	5.9	82.9	6.7	93.3
GILLESPIE	2,104	1,270	137	697	1,133 R	60.4	6.5	90.3	9.7
GLASSCOCK	117	25	91	1	66 D	21.4	77.3	21.6	78.4
GOLIAD	2,163	1,513	448	202	1,065 R	69.9	20.7	77.2	22.8
GONZALES	2,484	748	1,299	437	551 D	30.1	52.3	36.5	63.5
GRAY	811	251	529	31	278 D	30.9	65.2	32.2	67.8
GRAYSON	7,945	2,125	5,241	579	3,116 D	26.7	66.0	28.8	71.2
GREGG	1,522	257	1,050	215	793 D	16.9	69.0	19.7	80.3
GRIMES	1,449	214	1,027	208	813 D	14.8	70.9	17.2	82.8
GUADALUPE	3,245	1,839	561	846	1,279 R	56.7	17.3	76.7	23.3
HALE	1,679	352	1,279	48	927 D	21.0	76.2	21.6	78.4
HALL	1,204	194	922	88	728 D	16.1	76.6	17.4	82.6
HAMILTON	1,672	422	1,075	175	653 D	25.2	64.3	28.2	71.8
HANSFORD	184	54	124	6	70 D	29.3	67.4	30.3	69.7
HARDEMAN	1,325	253	967	105	714 D	19.1	73.0	20.7	79.3
HARDIN	1,376	202	999	175	797 D	14.7	72.6	16.8	83.2
HARRIS	28,837	7,735	14,808	6,294	7,073 D	26.8	51.4	34.3	65.7
HARRISON	3,181	377	2,134	670	1,757 D	11.9	67.1	15.0	85.0
HARTLEY	234	81	144	9	63 D	34.6	61.5	36.0	64.0
HASKELL	1,637	254	1,127	256	873 D	15.5	68.8	18.4	81.6
HAYS	1,656	242	1,075	339	833 D	14.6	64.9	18.4	81.6
HEMPHILL	678	253	417	8	164 D	37.3	61.5	37.8	62.2
HENDERSON	2,889	538	1,684	667	1,146 D	18.6	58.3	24.2	75.8
HIDALGO	3,559	1,108	2,409	42	1,301 D	31.1	67.7	31.5	68.5
HILL	5,155	1,022	3,254	879	2,232 D	19.8	63.1	23.9	76.1
HOCKLEY									
HOOD	1,020	175	697	148	522 D	17.2	68.3	20.1	79.9
HOPKINS	3,694	837	2,548	309	1,711 D	22.7	69.0	24.7	75.3
HOUSTON	2,981	385	1,475	1,121	1,090 D	12.9	49.5	20.7	79.3
HOWARD	907	107	703	97	596 D	11.8	77.5	13.2	86.8
HUDSPETH	135	37	97	1	60 D	27.4	71.9	27.6	72.4
HUNT	5,788	880	4,397	511	3,517 D	15.2	76.0	16.7	83.3
HUTCHINSON	247	106	135	6	29 D	42.9	54.7	44.0	56.0
IRION	224	45	148	31	103 D	20.1	66.1	23.3	76.7
JACK	881	253	566	62	313 D	28.7	64.2	30.9	69.1
JACKSON	1,055	355	562	138	207 D	33.6	53.3	38.7	61.3

PRESIDENT 1924

County	Total Vote	Republican	Democratic	Other	Rep.-Dem. Plurality	% Total Vote Rep.	% Total Vote Dem.	% Major Vote Rep.	% Major Vote Dem.
DENTON	5,805	712	4,708	385	3,996 D	12.3	81.1	13.1	86.9
DE WITT	3,791	868	2,131	792	1,263 D	22.9	56.2	28.9	71.1
DICKENS	1,020	161	849	10	688 D	15.8	83.2	15.9	84.1
DIMMIT	493	180	289	24	109 D	36.5	58.6	38.4	61.6
DONLEY	1,234	273	893	68	620 D	22.1	72.4	23.4	76.6
DUVAL	1,057	89	947	21	858 D	8.4	89.6	8.6	91.4
EASTLAND	5,682	972	4,548	162	3,576 D	17.1	80.0	17.6	82.4
ECTOR	155	12	138	5	126 D	7.7	89.0	8.0	92.0
EDWARDS	564	346	204	14	142 R	61.3	36.2	62.9	37.1
ELLIS	9,040	1,220	7,678	142	6,458 D	13.5	84.9	13.7	86.3
EL PASO	3,954	406	3,396	152	2,990 D	10.3	85.9	10.7	89.3
ERATH	3,456	448	2,817	191	2,369 D	13.0	81.5	13.7	86.3
FALLS	6,462	653	5,596	213	4,943 D	10.1	86.6	10.4	89.6
FANNIN	6,455	1,450	3,851	1,154	2,401 D	22.5	59.7	27.4	72.6
FISHER	2,013	302	1,653	58	1,351 D	15.0	82.1	15.4	84.6
FLOYD	1,392	166	1,197	29	1,031 D	11.9	86.0	12.2	87.8
FOARD	715	95	585	35	490 D	13.3	81.8	14.0	86.0
FORT BEND	2,250	356	1,690	204	1,334 D	15.8	75.1	17.4	82.6
FRANKLIN	1,336	118	1,157	61	1,039 D	8.8	86.6	9.3	90.7
FREESTONE	3,172	608	2,484	80	1,876 D	19.2	78.3	19.7	80.3
FRIO	808	158	637	13	479 D	19.6	78.8	19.9	80.1
GAINES	441	37	342	62	305 D	8.4	77.6	9.8	90.2
GALVESTON	7,619	1,912	5,068	639	3,156 D	25.1	66.5	27.4	72.6
GARZA	944	331	588	25	257 D	35.1	62.3	36.0	64.0
GILLESPIE	2,702	768	352	1,582	416 R	28.4	13.0	68.6	31.4
GLASSCOCK	109	14	89	6	75 D	12.8	81.7	13.6	86.4
GOLIAD	1,333	438	733	162	295 D	32.9	55.0	37.4	62.6
GONZALES	3,290	463	2,499	328	2,036 D	14.1	76.0	15.6	84.4
GRAY	1,189	581	608		27 D	48.9	51.1	48.9	51.1
GRAYSON	10,335	1,973	7,413	949	5,440 D	19.1	71.7	21.0	79.0
GREGG	1,671	177	1,286	208	1,109 D	10.5	77.0	12.1	87.9
GRIMES	2,345	177	2,136	32	1,959 D	7.5	91.1	7.6	92.4
GUADALUPE	4,089	1,657	831	1,601	826 R	40.5	20.3	66.6	33.4
HALE	2,041	507	1,446	88	939 D	24.8	70.8	26.0	74.0
HALL	1,353	229	1,060	64	831 D	16.9	78.3	17.8	82.2
HAMILTON	2,327	202	2,035	90	1,833 D	8.7	87.5	9.0	91.0
HANSFORD	363	76	263	24	187 D	20.9	72.5	22.4	77.6
HARDEMAN	1,408	256	1,099	53	843 D	18.2	78.1	18.9	81.1
HARDIN	2,278	645	1,516	117	871 D	28.3	66.5	29.8	70.2
HARRIS	32,479	8,953	20,648	2,878	11,695 D	27.6	63.6	30.2	69.8
HARRISON	3,262	463	2,573	226	2,110 D	14.2	78.9	15.3	84.7
HARTLEY	243	61	156	26	95 D	25.1	64.2	28.1	71.9
HASKELL	2,606	428	2,050	128	1,622 D	16.4	78.7	17.3	82.7
HAYS	2,089	394	1,616	79	1,222 D	18.9	77.4	19.6	80.4
HEMPHILL	643	167	405	71	238 D	26.0	63.0	29.2	70.8
HENDERSON	4,304	405	3,819	80	3,414 D	9.4	88.7	9.6	90.4
HIDALGO	4,872	996	3,662	214	2,666 D	20.4	75.2	21.4	78.6
HILL	6,688	807	5,778	103	4,971 D	12.1	86.6	12.3	87.7
HOCKLEY	94	20	69	5	49 D	21.3	73.4	22.5	77.5
HOOD	1,256	122	1,074	60	952 D	9.7	85.5	10.2	89.8
HOPKINS	4,834	557	4,156	121	3,599 D	11.5	86.0	11.8	88.2
HOUSTON	3,784	457	3,289	38	2,832 D	12.1	86.9	12.2	87.8
HOWARD	1,447	186	1,100	161	914 D	12.9	76.0	14.5	85.5
HUDSPETH	142	34	84	24	50 D	23.9	59.2	28.8	71.2
HUNT	7,810	836	6,828	146	5,992 D	10.7	87.4	10.9	89.1
HUTCHINSON	234	69	159	6	90 D	29.5	67.9	30.3	69.7
IRION	288	73	205	10	132 D	25.3	71.2	26.3	73.7
JACK	1,470	290	1,154	26	864 D	19.7	78.5	20.1	79.9
JACKSON	1,169	354	758	57	404 D	30.3	64.8	31.8	68.2

TEXAS

PRESIDENT 1920

County	Total Vote	Republican	Democratic	Other	Rep.-Dem. Plurality	TV % Rep.	TV % Dem.	MV % Rep.	MV % Dem.
JASPER	1,095	62	793	240	731 D	5.7%	72.4%	7.3%	92.7%
JEFF DAVIS	132	41	91		50 D	31.1%	68.9%	31.1%	68.9%
JEFFERSON	6,450	1,110	4,246	1,094	3,136 D	17.2%	65.8%	20.7%	79.3%
JIM HOGG	93	23	70		47 D	24.7%	75.3%	24.7%	75.3%
JIM WELLS	524	169	304	51	135 D	32.3%	58.0%	35.7%	64.3%
JOHNSON	4,224	661	3,041	522	2,380 D	15.6%	72.0%	17.9%	82.1%
JONES	2,282	270	1,792	220	1,522 D	11.8%	78.5%	13.1%	86.9%
KARNES	1,548	484	642	422	158 D	31.3%	41.5%	43.0%	57.0%
KAUFMAN	4,462	573	3,070	819	2,497 D	12.8%	68.8%	15.7%	84.3%
KENDALL	1,159	846	142	171	704 R	73.0%	12.3%	85.6%	14.4%
KENEDY									
KENT	283	45	214	24	169 D	15.9%	75.6%	17.4%	82.6%
KERR	1,149	464	612	73	148 D	40.4%	53.3%	43.1%	56.9%
KIMBLE	491	150	299	42	149 D	30.5%	60.9%	33.4%	66.6%
KING	160		157	3	157 D		98.1%		100.0%
KINNEY	247	137	98	12	39 R	55.5%	39.7%	58.3%	41.7%
KLEBERG	673	172	455	46	283 D	25.6%	67.6%	27.4%	72.6%
KNOX	1,030	159	773	98	614 D	15.4%	75.0%	17.1%	82.9%
LAMAR	5,006	639	3,765	602	3,126 D	12.8%	75.2%	14.5%	85.5%
LAMB	419	136	264	19	128 D	32.5%	63.0%	34.0%	66.0%
LAMPASAS	1,348	227	778	343	551 D	16.8%	57.7%	22.6%	77.4%
LA SALLE	314	53	252	9	199 D	16.9%	80.3%	17.4%	82.6%
LAVACA	3,194	100	1,249	1,845	1,149 D	3.1%	39.1%	7.4%	92.6%
LEE	2,219	325	712	1,182	387 D	14.6%	32.1%	31.3%	68.7%
LEON	2,079	220	1,124	735	904 D	10.6%	54.1%	16.4%	83.6%
LIBERTY	3,390	408	2,165	817	1,757 D	12.0%	63.9%	15.9%	84.1%
LIMESTONE	821	425	350	46	75 R	51.8%	42.6%	54.8%	45.2%
LIPSCOMB	496	161	234	101	73 D	32.5%	47.2%	40.8%	59.2%
LIVE OAK									
LLANO	1,092	184	665	243	481 D	16.8%	60.9%	21.7%	78.3%
LOVING									
LUBBOCK	1,452	204	1,180	68	976 D	14.0%	81.3%	14.7%	85.3%
LYNN	682	76	538	68	462 D	11.1%	78.9%	12.4%	87.6%
MCCULLOCH	1,130	210	736	184	526 D	18.9%	65.1%	22.0%	78.0%
MCLENNAN	7,809	1,655	4,975	1,179	3,320 D	21.2%	63.7%	25.0%	75.0%
MCMULLEN	106	33	72	1	39 D	31.1%	67.9%	31.4%	68.6%
MADISON	1,126	63	650	413	587 D	5.6%	57.7%	8.8%	91.2%
MARION	1,130	392	430	308	38 D	34.7%	38.1%	47.7%	52.3%
MARTIN	175	33	136	6	103 D	18.9%	77.7%	19.5%	80.5%
MASON	673	269	304	100	35 D	40.0%	45.2%	46.9%	53.1%
MATAGORDA	2,094	918	992	184	74 D	43.8%	47.4%	48.1%	51.9%
MAVERICK	475	296	173	6	123 R	62.3%	36.4%	63.1%	36.9%
MEDINA	1,689	772	519	398	253 R	45.7%	30.7%	59.8%	40.2%
MENARD	426	203	157	26	46 D	47.7%	36.9%	55.2%	44.8%
MIDLAND	341	68	271	2	203 D	19.9%	79.5%	20.1%	79.9%
MILAM	4,828	371	2,558	1,859	2,227 D	7.7%	53.0%	12.5%	87.5%
MILLS	1,181	247	669	265	422 D	20.9%	56.6%	27.0%	73.0%
MITCHELL	850	89	694	67	605 D	10.5%	81.6%	11.4%	88.6%
MONTAGUE	1,395	474	714	207	240 D	34.0%	51.2%	39.9%	60.1%
MONTGOMERY	1,450	203	935	312	732 D	14.0%	64.5%	17.8%	82.2%
MOORE	115	13	101	1	88 D	11.3%	87.8%	11.4%	88.6%
MORRIS	908	164	669	75	505 D	18.1%	73.7%	19.7%	80.3%
MOTLEY	391	40	345	6	305 D	10.2%	88.2%	10.4%	89.6%
NACOGDOCHES	2,727	238	1,794	695	1,556 D	8.7%	65.8%	11.7%	88.3%
NAVARRO	5,172	821	3,328	1,023	2,507 D	15.9%	64.3%	19.8%	80.2%
NEWTON	668	58	420	190	362 D	8.7%	62.9%	12.1%	87.9%
NOLAN	1,154	175	923	56	748 D	15.2%	80.0%	15.9%	84.1%
NUECES	1,778	385	1,245	147	861 D	21.7%	70.1%	23.6%	76.4%
OCHILTREE	416	135	281		146 D	32.5%	67.5%	32.5%	67.5%
OLDHAM	192	52	139	1	87 D	27.1%	72.4%	27.2%	72.8%

PRESIDENT 1924

County	Total Vote	Republican	Democratic	Other	Rep.-Dem. Plurality	TV % Rep.	TV % Dem.	MV % Rep.	MV % Dem.
JASPER	1,719	176	1,526	17	1,350 D	10.2%	88.8%	10.3%	89.7%
JEFF DAVIS	184	49	117	18	68 D	26.6%	63.6%	29.5%	70.5%
JEFFERSON	10,756	4,348	5,925	483	1,577 D	40.4%	55.1%	42.3%	57.7%
JIM HOGG	158	19	139		120 D	12.0%	88.0%	12.0%	88.0%
JIM WELLS	992	213	654	125	441 D	21.5%	65.9%	24.6%	75.4%
JOHNSON	5,761	851	4,600	310	3,749 D	14.8%	79.8%	15.6%	84.4%
JONES	3,677	566	3,010	101	2,444 D	15.4%	81.9%	15.8%	84.2%
KARNES	2,496	531	1,727	238	1,196 D	21.3%	69.2%	23.5%	76.5%
KAUFMAN	6,531	884	5,573	74	4,689 D	13.5%	85.3%	13.7%	86.3%
KENDALL	1,232	689	136	407	553 R	55.9%	11.0%	83.5%	16.5%
KENEDY	75	7	67	1	60 D	9.3%	89.3%	9.5%	90.5%
KENT	474	80	386	8	306 D	16.9%	81.4%	17.2%	82.8%
KERR	1,809	892	735	182	157 R	49.3%	40.6%	54.8%	45.2%
KIMBLE	707	223	465	19	242 D	31.5%	65.8%	32.4%	67.6%
KING	87	4	83		79 D	4.6%	95.4%	4.6%	95.4%
KINNEY	315	158	144	13	14 R	50.2%	45.7%	52.3%	47.7%
KLEBERG	1,155	226	721	208	495 D	19.6%	62.4%	23.9%	76.1%
KNOX	1,935	455	1,399	81	944 D	23.5%	72.3%	24.5%	75.5%
LAMAR	5,979	596	5,224	159	4,628 D	10.0%	87.4%	10.2%	89.8%
LAMB	507	121	356	30	235 D	23.9%	70.2%	25.4%	74.6%
LAMPASAS	1,846	228	1,596	22	1,368 D	12.4%	86.5%	12.5%	87.5%
LA SALLE	541	73	458	10	385 D	13.5%	84.7%	13.7%	86.3%
LAVACA	5,271	746	3,290	1,235	2,544 D	14.2%	62.4%	18.5%	81.5%
LEE	2,284	271	1,561	452	1,290 D	11.9%	68.3%	14.8%	85.2%
LEON	2,394	311	2,004	79	1,693 D	13.0%	83.7%	13.4%	86.6%
LIBERTY	2,189	639	1,506	44	867 D	29.2%	68.8%	29.8%	70.2%
LIMESTONE	5,434	523	4,868	43	4,345 D	9.6%	89.6%	9.7%	90.3%
LIPSCOMB	949	405	430	114	25 R	42.7%	45.3%	48.5%	51.5%
LIVE OAK	1,012	323	596	93	273 D	31.9%	58.9%	35.1%	64.9%
LLANO	1,077	88	928	61	840 D	8.2%	86.2%	8.7%	91.3%
LOVING	14	2	12		10 D	14.3%	85.7%	14.3%	85.7%
LUBBOCK	2,343	411	1,740	192	1,329 D	17.5%	74.3%	19.1%	80.9%
LYNN	1,501	313	1,131	57	818 D	20.9%	75.3%	21.7%	78.3%
MCCULLOCH	1,844	495	1,327	22	832 D	26.8%	72.0%	27.2%	72.8%
MCLENNAN	10,721	2,384	7,882	455	5,498 D	22.2%	73.5%	23.2%	76.8%
MCMULLEN	223	111	109	3	2 R	49.8%	48.9%	50.5%	49.5%
MADISON	1,743	146	1,592	5	1,446 D	8.4%	91.3%	8.4%	91.6%
MARION	1,051	347	620	84	273 D	33.0%	59.0%	35.9%	64.1%
MARTIN	426	92	327	7	235 D	21.6%	76.8%	22.0%	78.0%
MASON	718	171	384	163	213 D	23.8%	53.5%	30.8%	69.2%
MATAGORDA	2,374	893	1,353	128	460 D	37.6%	57.0%	39.8%	60.2%
MAVERICK	491	261	199	31	62 R	53.2%	40.5%	56.7%	43.3%
MEDINA	2,279	816	986	477	170 D	35.8%	43.3%	45.3%	54.7%
MENARD	578	247	304	27	57 D	42.7%	52.6%	44.8%	55.2%
MIDLAND	447	44	399	4	355 D	9.8%	89.3%	9.9%	90.1%
MILAM	6,334	930	5,087	317	4,157 D	14.7%	80.3%	15.5%	84.5%
MILLS	1,515	175	1,289	51	1,114 D	11.6%	85.1%	12.0%	88.0%
MITCHELL	1,446	169	1,242	35	1,073 D	11.7%	85.9%	12.0%	88.0%
MONTAGUE	3,269	586	2,236	447	1,650 D	17.9%	68.4%	20.8%	79.2%
MONTGOMERY	1,689	166	1,500	23	1,334 D	9.8%	88.8%	10.0%	90.0%
MOORE	92	9	82	1	73 D	9.8%	89.1%	9.9%	90.1%
MORRIS									
MOTLEY	525	62	453	10	391 D	11.8%	86.3%	12.0%	88.0%
NACOGDOCHES	3,669	204	3,418	47	3,214 D	5.6%	93.2%	5.6%	94.4%
NAVARRO	7,482	996	6,409	77	5,413 D	13.3%	85.7%	13.5%	86.5%
NEWTON	948	145	782	21	637 D	15.3%	82.5%	15.6%	84.4%
NOLAN	1,840	337	1,421	82	1,084 D	18.3%	77.2%	19.2%	80.8%
NUECES									
OCHILTREE	562	155	352	55	197 D	27.6%	62.6%	30.6%	69.4%
OLDHAM	272	71	187	14	116 D	26.1%	68.8%	27.5%	72.5%

TEXAS

PRESIDENT 1920

County	Total Vote	Republican	Democratic	Other	Rep.-Dem. Plurality		% Total Vote Rep.	% Total Vote Dem.	% Major Vote Rep.	% Major Vote Dem.
ORANGE	1,295	121	1,055	119	934	D	9.3%	81.5%	10.3%	89.7%
PALO PINTO	2,172	342	1,645	185	1,303	D	15.7%	75.7%	17.2%	82.8%
PANOLA	1,659	268	1,086	305	818	D	16.2%	65.5%	19.8%	80.2%
PARKER	2,369	488	1,765	116	1,277	D	20.6%	74.5%	21.7%	78.3%
PARMER	341	140	189	12	49	D	41.1%	55.4%	42.6%	57.4%
PECOS	814	394	386	34	8	R	43.4%	47.4%	50.5%	49.5%
POLK	1,285	255	810	220	555	D	19.8%	73.3%	23.9%	76.1%
POTTER	1,771	358	1,374	39	1,016	D	20.2%	77.5%	20.7%	79.3%
PRESIDIO	366	122	238	6	116	D	33.3%	65.0%	33.9%	66.1%
RAINS	769	189	462	118	273	D	24.6%	60.1%	29.0%	71.0%
RANDALL	551	183	360	8	177	D	33.2%	65.3%	33.7%	66.3%
REAGAN	49		49		49	D		100.0%		100.0%
REAL	310	111	177	22	66	D	35.8%	57.1%	38.5%	61.5%
RED RIVER	3,538	799	2,263	476	1,464	D	22.6%	64.0%	26.1%	73.9%
REEVES	550	91	457	2	366	D	16.5%	83.1%	16.6%	83.4%
REFUGIO	645	360	227	58	133	R	55.8%	35.2%	61.3%	38.7%
ROBERTS	239	60	173	6	113	D	25.1%	72.4%	25.8%	74.2%
ROBERTSON	2,515	225	1,634	656	1,409	D	8.9%	65.0%	12.1%	87.9%
ROCKWALL	994	104	873	17	769	D	10.5%	87.8%	10.6%	89.4%
RUNNELS	1,855	332	1,197	326	865	D	17.9%	64.5%	21.7%	78.3%
RUSK	2,843	745	1,535	563	790	D	26.2%	54.0%	32.7%	67.3%
SABINE	985	61	658	266	597	D	6.2%	66.8%	8.7%	91.3%
SAN AUGUSTINE	1,544	121	658	765	537	D	7.8%	42.6%	15.5%	84.5%
SAN JACINTO	691	127	320	244	193	D	18.4%	46.3%	28.4%	71.6%
SAN PATRICIO	955	308	320	327	12	D	32.2%	33.5%	49.0%	51.0%
SAN SABA	1,476	180	874	422	694	D	12.2%	59.2%	17.1%	82.9%
SCHLEICHER	304	81	211	12	130	D	26.6%	69.4%	27.7%	72.3%
SCURRY	1,006	151	801	54	650	D	15.0%	79.6%	15.9%	84.1%
SHACKELFORD	527	116	342	69	226	D	22.0%	64.9%	25.3%	74.7%
SHELBY	2,336	150	1,700	486	1,550	D	6.4%	72.8%	8.1%	91.9%
SHERMAN	247	77	170		93	D	31.2%	68.8%	31.4%	68.7%
SMITH	4,673	707	2,965	1,001	2,258	D	15.1%	63.4%	19.3%	80.7%
SOMERVELL	374	92	198	84	106	D	24.6%	52.9%	31.7%	68.3%
STARR	510	92	418		326	D	18.0%	82.0%	18.0%	82.0%
STEPHENS	845	141	643	61	502	D	16.7%	76.1%	18.0%	82.0%
STERLING	186	17	152	17	135	D	9.1%	81.7%	10.1%	89.9%
STONEWALL	547	134	356	57	222	D	24.5%	65.1%	27.3%	72.7%
SUTTON	305	104	190	11	86	D	34.1%	62.3%	35.4%	64.6%
SWISHER	601	148	443	10	295	D	24.6%	73.7%	25.0%	75.0%
TARRANT	17,108	3,486	12,431	1,191	8,945	D	20.4%	72.7%	21.9%	78.1%
TAYLOR	2,438	300	1,932	206	1,632	D	12.3%	79.2%	13.4%	86.5%
TERRELL	268	95	155	18	60	D	35.4%	57.8%	38.0%	62.0%
TERRY	355	39	270	46	231	D	11.0%	76.1%	12.6%	87.4%
THROCKMORTON	498	72	399	27	327	D	14.5%	80.1%	15.3%	84.7%
TITUS	1,795	508	1,094	193	586	D	28.3%	60.9%	31.7%	68.3%
TOM GREEN	1,650	256	1,264	130	1,008	D	15.5%	76.6%	16.8%	83.2%
TRAVIS	5,905	1,204	3,541	1,160	2,337	D	20.4%	63.0%	25.4%	74.6%
TRINITY	1,128	125	643	360	518	D	11.1%	57.0%	16.3%	83.7%
TYLER	1,393	115	1,066	212	951	D	8.3%	76.5%	9.7%	90.3%
UPSHUR	2,330	616	1,222	492	606	D	26.4%	52.4%	33.5%	66.5%
UPTON	71	25	46		21	D	35.2%	64.8%	35.2%	64.8%
UVALDE	1,022	237	743	41	506	D	23.2%	72.8%	24.2%	75.8%
VAL VERDE	718	296	418	4	122	D	41.2%	58.2%	41.5%	58.5%
VAN ZANDT	3,206	728	1,958	520	1,230	D	22.7%	61.1%	27.1%	72.9%
VICTORIA	1,879	782	666	411	116	R	41.6%	35.4%	53.3%	46.7%
WALKER	1,723	404	768	531	364	D	23.4%	44.5%	34.5%	65.5%
WALLER	1,250	167	674	409	507	D	13.4%	53.9%	19.9%	80.1%
WARD	265	79	181	5	102	D	29.8%	68.3%	30.4%	69.6%
WASHINGTON	3,222	684	796	1,740	112	D	21.2%	24.7%	46.2%	53.8%
WEBB	1,117	468	633	16	165	D	41.9%	56.7%	42.5%	57.5%

PRESIDENT 1924

County	Total Vote	Republican	Democratic	Other	Rep.-Dem. Plurality		% Total Vote Rep.	% Total Vote Dem.	% Major Vote Rep.	% Major Vote Dem.
ORANGE	1,933	509	1,385	39	876	D	26.3%	71.7%	26.9%	73.1%
PALO PINTO	2,631	473	1,925	232	1,453	D	18.0%	73.2%	19.7%	80.3%
PANOLA	2,233	119	2,083	26	1,969	D	5.3%	93.5%	5.4%	94.6%
PARKER	2,979	436	2,391	150	1,953	D	14.7%	80.3%	15.5%	84.5%
PARMER	341	91	214	36	123	D	26.7%	62.8%	29.8%	70.2%
PECOS	662	192	440	30	248	D	29.0%	66.5%	30.4%	69.6%
POLK	2,142	272	1,839	31	1,567	D	12.7%	85.9%	12.9%	87.1%
POTTER	3,811	831	2,394	586	1,563	D	21.8%	62.8%	25.8%	74.2%
PRESIDIO	348	68	267	13	199	D	19.5%	76.7%	20.3%	79.7%
RAINS	1,098	151	899	48	748	D	13.8%	81.9%	14.4%	85.6%
RANDALL	845	154	627	64	473	D	18.2%	74.2%	19.7%	80.3%
REAGAN	144	31	111	2	80	D	21.5%	77.1%	21.8%	78.2%
REAL	498	300	168	30	112	R	60.2%	37.8%	61.5%	38.5%
RED RIVER	3,543	311	3,163	49	2,872	D	8.8%	89.8%	8.9%	91.1%
REEVES	512	96	367	49	291	D	18.8%	75.6%	19.9%	80.1%
REFUGIO	934	256	585	93	329	D	27.4%	62.6%	30.4%	69.9%
ROBERTS	347	104	241	2	137	D	30.0%	69.5%	30.1%	69.9%
ROBERTSON	2,261	226	1,971	64	1,745	D	10.0%	87.2%	10.3%	89.7%
ROCKWALL	1,471	93	1,371	7	1,278	D	6.3%	93.2%	6.4%	93.6%
RUNNELS	3,162	458	2,564	140	2,106	D	14.5%	81.1%	15.2%	84.8%
RUSK	3,815	651	3,097	67	2,446	D	17.1%	81.2%	17.4%	82.6%
SABINE	1,218	61	1,150	7	1,089	D	5.0%	94.4%	5.0%	95.0%
SAN AUGUSTINE	1,553	78	1,475		1,397	D	5.0%	95.0%	5.0%	95.0%
SAN JACINTO	700	104	585	11	481	D	14.9%	83.5%	15.1%	84.9%
SAN PATRICIO	2,163	987	1,097	79	110	D	45.6%	50.7%	47.4%	52.6%
SAN SABA	2,017	187	1,814	16	1,627	D	9.3%	89.9%	9.3%	90.7%
SCHLEICHER	365	118	246	1	128	D	32.3%	67.4%	32.4%	67.6%
SCURRY	1,610	269	1,292	49	1,023	D	16.7%	80.2%	17.2%	82.8%
SHACKELFORD	1,456	727	729		2	D	49.9%	50.1%	49.9%	50.1%
SHELBY	3,698	150	3,408	140	3,258	D	4.3%	92.2%	4.5%	95.5%
SHERMAN	300	87	188	25	101	D	29.0%	62.7%	31.6%	68.4%
SMITH	5,723	1,079	4,473	171	3,394	D	18.9%	78.2%	19.4%	80.6%
SOMERVELL	779	23	756		733	D	3.0%	97.0%	3.0%	97.0%
STARR	2,661	372	2,184	105	1,812	D	14.0%	82.1%	14.6%	85.4%
STEPHENS										
STERLING	269	25	243	1	218	D	9.3%	90.3%	9.3%	90.7%
STONEWALL	1,067	171	778	118	607	D	16.0%	72.9%	18.0%	82.0%
SUTTON	269	124	143	2	19	D	46.1%	53.3%	46.4%	53.6%
SWISHER	819	212	573	34	361	D	25.9%	70.0%	27.0%	73.0%
TARRANT	22,151	5,859	13,673	2,619	7,814	D	26.5%	61.7%	30.0%	70.0%
TAYLOR	3,660	441	3,157	62	2,716	D	12.0%	86.3%	12.3%	87.7%
TERRELL	316	122	109	85	13	R	38.5%	34.4%	52.8%	47.2%
TERRY	1,000	160	823	18	663	D	16.0%	82.2%	16.3%	83.7%
THROCKMORTON	719	174	539	6	365	D	24.2%	75.0%	24.4%	75.6%
TITUS	1,589		1,589		1,589	D		100.0%		100.0%
TOM GREEN	2,794	554	2,116	124	1,562	D	19.8%	75.7%	20.7%	79.3%
TRAVIS	9,827	1,909	7,573	345	5,664	D	19.4%	77.1%	20.1%	79.9%
TRINITY	1,692	146	1,504	42	1,358	D	8.6%	88.9%	8.8%	91.2%
TYLER	1,044	90	929	25	839	D	8.6%	89.0%	8.8%	91.2%
UPSHUR	2,911	258	2,611	42	2,353	D	8.8%	89.7%	9.0%	91.0%
UPTON	40	4	35	1	31	D	10.0%	87.5%	10.3%	89.7%
UVALDE	1,715	351	1,312	52	961	D	20.5%	76.5%	21.1%	78.9%
VAL VERDE	998	457	434	107	23	R	45.8%	43.5%	51.3%	48.7%
VAN ZANDT	3,957		3,957		3,957	D		100.0%		100.0%
VICTORIA	2,418	459	1,653	306	1,194	D	19.0%	68.4%	21.7%	78.3%
WALKER	1,996	201	1,792	3	1,591	D	10.1%	89.8%	10.1%	89.9%
WALLER	1,461	203	1,239	19	1,036	D	13.9%	84.8%	14.1%	85.9%
WARD	274	42	206	26	164	D	15.3%	75.2%	16.9%	83.1%
WASHINGTON	4,137	496	3,568	73	3,072	D	12.0%	86.2%	12.2%	87.8%
WEBB	1,794	429	1,313	52	884	D	23.9%	73.2%	24.6%	75.4%

TEXAS

PRESIDENT 1920

County	Total Vote	Republican	Democratic	Other	Rep.-Dem. Plurality	Total Vote Rep.	Total Vote Dem.	Major Vote Rep.	Major Vote Dem.
WHARTON	2,363	852	835	675	16 R	36.1%	35.4%	50.5%	49.5%
WHEELER	752	198	515	38	318 D	26.3%	68.6%	27.7%	72.3%
WICHITA	5,410	1,487	3,812	111	2,325 D	27.5%	70.5%	28.1%	71.9%
WILBARGER	1,542	335	1,118	89	783 D	21.7%	72.5%	23.1%	76.9%
WILLACY	62	9	53		44 D	14.5%	85.5%	14.5%	85.5%
WILLIAMSON	5,051	819	2,677	1,555	1,858 D	16.2%	53.0%	23.4%	76.6%
WILSON	1,779	820	753	206	67 R	46.1%	42.3%	52.1%	47.9%
WINKLER	19	2	17		15 D	10.5%	89.5%	10.5%	89.5%
WISE	2,725	579	2,031	115	1,452 D	21.2%	74.5%	22.2%	77.8%
WOOD	3,160	798	1,643	719	845 D	25.3%	52.0%	32.7%	67.3%
YOAKUM	81		79	2	79 D		97.5%		100.0%
YOUNG	1,470	209	1,214	47	1,005 D	14.2%	82.6%	14.7%	85.3%
ZAPATA	162	98	50	14	48 R	60.5%	30.9%	66.2%	33.8%
ZAVALA	381	101	264	16	163 D	26.5%	69.3%	27.7%	72.3%
TOTAL	486,109	114,658	287,920	83,531	173,262 D	23.6%	59.2%	28.5%	71.5%

PRESIDENT 1924

County	Total Vote	Republican	Democratic	Other	Rep.-Dem. Plurality	Total Vote Rep.	Total Vote Dem.	Major Vote Rep.	Major Vote Dem.
WHARTON	2,989	858	2,020	111	1,162 D	28.7%	67.6%	29.8%	70.2%
WHEELER	1,151	197	908	46	711 D	17.1%	78.9%	17.8%	82.2%
WICHITA	8,481	2,189	5,831	461	3,642 D	25.8%	68.8%	27.3%	72.7%
WILBARGER	1,578	269	1,222	87	953 D	17.0%	77.4%	18.0%	82.0%
WILLACY	434	110	307	17	197 D	25.3%	70.7%	26.4%	73.6%
WILLIAMSON	7,578	934	6,324	320	5,390 D	12.3%	83.5%	12.9%	87.1%
WILSON	2,454	495	1,633	326	1,138 D	20.2%	66.5%	23.3%	76.7%
WINKLER	16	1	15		14 D	6.2%	93.8%	6.2%	93.8%
WISE	3,641	532	2,958	151	2,426 D	14.6%	81.2%	15.2%	84.8%
WOOD	3,280	342	2,806	132	2,464 D	10.4%	85.5%	10.9%	89.1%
YOAKUM	112	9	95	8	86 D	8.0%	84.8%	8.7%	91.3%
YOUNG	2,373	322	2,000	51	1,678 D	13.6%	84.3%	13.9%	86.1%
ZAPATA	498	197	300	1	103 D	39.6%	60.2%	39.6%	60.4%
ZAVALA	453	95	326	32	231 D	21.0%	72.0%	22.6%	77.4%
TOTAL	657,054	130,794	483,381	42,879	352,587 D	19.9%	73.6%	21.3%	78.7%

TEXAS

PRESIDENT 1928

County	Total Vote	Republican	Democratic	Other	Rep.-Dem. Plurality	Total Vote Rep.	Total Vote Dem.	Major Vote Rep.	Major Vote Dem.
ANDERSON	3,561	1,814	1,747		67 R	50.9%	49.1%	50.9%	49.1%
ANDREWS	91	66	25		41 R	72.5%	27.5%	72.5%	27.5%
ANGELINA	3,514	1,209	2,305		1,096 D	34.4%	65.6%	34.4%	65.6%
ARANSAS	313	161	152		9 R	51.4%	48.6%	51.4%	48.6%
ARCHER	1,664	799	865		66 D	48.0%	52.0%	48.0%	52.0%
ARMSTRONG	690	316	373	1	57 D	45.8%	54.1%	45.9%	54.1%
ATASCOSA	1,570	888	682		206 R	56.6%	43.4%	56.6%	43.4%
AUSTIN	2,597	466	2,129	2	1,663 D	17.9%	82.0%	18.0%	82.0%
BAILEY	552	410	142		268 R	74.3%	25.7%	74.3%	25.7%
BANDERA	1,256	936	317	3	619 R	74.5%	25.2%	74.7%	25.3%
BASTROP	2,384	850	1,534		684 D	35.7%	64.3%	35.7%	64.3%
BAYLOR	1,275	491	784		293 D	38.5%	61.5%	38.5%	61.5%
BEE	2,236	1,189	1,043	4	146 R	53.2%	46.7%	53.3%	46.7%
BELL	6,452	3,366	3,079	7	287 R	52.2%	47.7%	52.2%	47.8%
BEXAR	33,160	16,477	16,626	57	149 D	49.7%	50.1%	49.8%	50.2%
BLANCO	1,155	615	539	1	76 R	53.2%	46.7%	53.3%	46.7%
BORDEN	171	98	73		25 R	57.3%	42.7%	57.3%	42.7%
BOSQUE	2,765	1,526	1,235	4	291 R	55.2%	44.7%	55.3%	44.7%
BOWIE	5,227	2,225	3,002		777 D	42.6%	57.4%	42.6%	57.4%
BRAZORIA	2,674	1,588	1,086		502 R	59.4%	40.6%	59.4%	40.6%
BRAZOS	2,221	738	1,480	3	742 D	33.2%	66.6%	33.3%	66.7%
BREWSTER	684	406	273	5	133 D	59.4%	39.9%	59.8%	40.2%
BRISCOE	641	301	336	4	35 D	47.0%	52.4%	47.3%	52.7%
BROOKS	492	160	332		172 D	32.5%	67.5%	32.5%	67.5%
BROWN	4,029	2,033	1,992	4	41 R	50.5%	49.4%	50.5%	49.5%
BURLESON	1,897	339	1,558		1,219 D	17.9%	82.1%	17.9%	82.1%
BURNET	1,404	936	467	1	469 R	66.7%	33.3%	66.7%	33.3%
CALDWELL	2,400	1,189	1,211		22 D	49.5%	50.5%	49.5%	50.5%
CALHOUN	711	333	375	3	42 D	46.8%	52.7%	47.0%	53.0%
CALLAHAN	1,919	979	940		39 R	51.0%	49.0%	51.0%	49.0%
CAMERON	6,757	3,544	3,202	11	342 R	52.4%	47.4%	52.5%	47.5%
CAMP	1,134	494	640		146 D	43.6%	56.4%	43.6%	56.4%
CARSON	1,484	891	592	1	299 R	60.0%	39.9%	60.1%	39.9%
CASS	3,021	1,323	1,698		375 D	43.8%	56.2%	43.8%	56.2%
CASTRO	703	319	384		65 D	45.4%	54.6%	45.4%	54.6%
CHAMBERS	498	256	242		14 R	51.4%	48.6%	51.4%	48.6%
CHEROKEE	3,871	1,933	1,938		5 D	49.9%	50.1%	49.9%	50.1%
CHILDRESS	2,164	1,438	726		712 R	66.5%	33.5%	66.5%	33.5%
CLAY	2,487	1,327	1,160		167 R	53.4%	46.6%	53.4%	46.6%
COCHRAN	306	197	109		88 R	64.4%	35.6%	64.4%	35.6%
COKE	656	450	206		244 R	68.6%	31.4%	68.6%	31.4%
COLEMAN	3,104	1,645	1,459		186 R	53.0%	47.0%	53.0%	47.0%
COLLIN	6,876	3,476	3,377	23	99 R	50.5%	49.1%	50.7%	49.3%
COLLINGSWORTH	1,787	1,179	608		571 R	66.0%	34.0%	66.0%	34.0%
COLORADO	2,682	891	1,787	4	896 D	33.2%	66.7%	33.3%	66.7%
COMAL	2,403	508	1,893	2	1,385 D	21.1%	78.8%	21.2%	78.8%
COMANCHE	2,794	1,483	1,311		172 R	53.1%	46.9%	53.1%	46.9%
CONCHO	875	446	426	3	20 R	51.0%	48.7%	51.1%	48.9%
COOKE	4,190	2,262	1,924	4	338 R	54.0%	45.9%	54.0%	46.0%
CORYELL	2,430	1,123	1,306	1	183 D	46.2%	53.7%	46.2%	53.8%
COTTLE	924	473	451		22 R	51.2%	48.8%	51.2%	48.8%
CRANE	286	127	159		32 D	44.4%	55.6%	44.4%	55.6%
CROCKETT	355	291	64		227 R	82.0%	18.0%	82.0%	18.0%
CROSBY	1,732	1,004	728		276 R	58.0%	42.0%	58.0%	42.0%
CULBERSON	157	72	85		13 D	45.9%	54.1%	45.9%	54.1%
DALLAM	1,166	618	539	9	79 R	53.0%	46.2%	53.4%	46.6%
DALLAS	44,787	27,272	17,437	78	9,835 R	60.9%	38.9%	61.0%	39.0%
DAWSON	1,875	1,448	427		1,021 R	77.2%	22.8%	77.2%	22.8%
DEAF SMITH	981	570	411		159 R	58.1%	41.9%	58.1%	41.9%
DELTA	1,713	753	958	2	205 D	44.0%	55.9%	44.0%	56.0%

PRESIDENT 1932

County	Total Vote	Republican	Democratic	Other	Rep.-Dem. Plurality	Total Vote Rep.	Total Vote Dem.	Major Vote Rep.	Major Vote Dem.
ANDERSON	4,627	259	4,354	14	4,095 D	5.6%	94.1%	5.6%	94.4%
ANDREWS	193	6	186	1	180 D	3.1%	96.4%	3.1%	96.9%
ANGELINA	5,253	287	4,962	4	4,675 D	5.5%	94.5%	5.5%	94.5%
ARANSAS	308	39	268	1	229 D	12.7%	87.0%	12.7%	87.3%
ARCHER	1,654	97	1,555	2	1,458 D	5.9%	94.0%	5.9%	94.1%
ARMSTRONG	877	63	813	1	750 D	7.2%	92.7%	7.2%	92.8%
ATASCOSA	2,307	192	2,101	14	1,909 D	8.3%	91.1%	8.4%	91.6%
AUSTIN	2,955	142	2,806	7	2,664 D	4.8%	95.0%	4.8%	95.2%
BAILEY	958	104	851	3	747 D	10.9%	88.8%	10.9%	89.1%
BANDERA	1,249	359	883	7	524 D	28.7%	70.7%	28.9%	71.1%
BASTROP	3,259	180	3,077	2	2,897 D	5.5%	94.4%	5.5%	94.5%
BAYLOR	1,493	55	1,437	1	1,382 D	3.7%	96.2%	3.7%	96.3%
BEE	2,724	534	2,180	10	1,646 D	19.6%	80.0%	19.7%	80.3%
BELL	8,354	724	7,607	23	6,883 D	8.7%	91.0%	8.7%	91.3%
BEXAR	45,594	7,466	37,765	363	30,299 D	16.4%	82.8%	16.5%	83.5%
BLANCO	1,367	127	1,233	7	1,106 D	9.3%	90.2%	9.3%	90.7%
BORDEN	249	7	242		235 D	2.8%	97.2%	2.8%	97.2%
BOSQUE	3,489	272	3,214	3	2,942 D	7.8%	92.1%	7.8%	92.2%
BOWIE	5,829	541	5,269	19	4,728 D	9.3%	90.4%	9.3%	90.7%
BRAZORIA	3,576	617	2,948	11	2,331 D	17.3%	82.4%	17.3%	82.7%
BRAZOS	2,801	195	2,588	18	2,393 D	7.0%	92.4%	7.0%	93.0%
BREWSTER	1,010	130	875	5	745 D	12.9%	86.6%	12.9%	87.1%
BRISCOE	1,023	42	977	4	935 D	4.1%	95.5%	4.1%	95.9%
BROOKS	697	86	608	3	522 D	12.3%	87.2%	12.4%	87.6%
BROWN	4,375	330	4,024	21	3,694 D	7.5%	92.0%	7.6%	92.4%
BURLESON	2,545	119	2,423	3	2,304 D	4.7%	95.2%	4.7%	95.3%
BURNET	2,050	144	1,904	2	1,760 D	7.0%	92.9%	7.0%	93.0%
CALDWELL	3,610	291	3,337	2	3,026 D	8.1%	91.9%	8.0%	91.9%
CALHOUN	944	100	834	10	734 D	10.6%	88.3%	10.7%	89.3%
CALLAHAN	2,285	152	2,133		1,981 D	6.7%	93.3%	6.7%	93.3%
CAMERON	8,985	1,785	7,146	54	5,361 D	19.9%	79.5%	20.0%	80.0%
CAMP	1,491	73	1,416	2	1,343 D	4.9%	95.0%	4.9%	95.1%
CARSON	1,603	224	1,379		1,179 D	13.9%	86.0%	13.9%	86.0%
CASS	3,359	224	3,135		2,911 D	6.7%	93.3%	6.7%	93.3%
CASTRO	1,023	66	949	8	883 D	6.5%	92.8%	6.5%	93.5%
CHAMBERS	939	91	843	5	752 D	9.7%	89.8%	9.7%	90.3%
CHEROKEE	4,368	233	4,125	10	3,892 D	5.3%	94.4%	5.3%	94.7%
CHILDRESS	2,238	153	2,072	13	1,919 D	6.8%	92.6%	6.9%	93.1%
CLAY	2,523	151	2,365	7	2,214 D	6.0%	93.7%	6.0%	94.0%
COCHRAN	388	31	345	12	314 D	8.0%	88.9%	8.2%	91.8%
COKE	1,047	57	983	7	926 D	5.4%	93.9%	5.5%	94.5%
COLEMAN	3,128	235	2,881	12	2,646 D	7.5%	92.1%	7.5%	92.5%
COLLIN	6,698	589	6,059	50	5,470 D	8.8%	90.5%	8.9%	91.1%
COLLINGSWORTH	1,879	115	1,753	11	1,638 D	6.1%	93.3%	6.2%	93.8%
COLORADO	3,069	331	2,715	23	2,384 D	10.8%	88.5%	10.9%	89.1%
COMAL	2,402	176	2,211	15	2,035 D	7.3%	92.0%	7.4%	92.6%
COMANCHE	3,335	192	3,134	13	2,942 D	5.8%	93.9%	5.8%	94.2%
CONCHO	1,174	44	1,126	4	1,082 D	3.7%	95.9%	3.7%	96.2%
COOKE	4,265	470	3,775	20	3,305 D	11.0%	88.5%	11.1%	88.9%
CORYELL	3,541	191	3,347	3	3,156 D	5.4%	94.5%	5.4%	94.6%
COTTLE	1,234	38	1,196		1,158 D	3.1%	96.9%	3.1%	96.9%
CRANE	454	37	416	1	379 D	8.1%	91.6%	8.1%	91.8%
CROCKETT	497	168	329		161 D	33.8%	66.2%	33.8%	66.2%
CROSBY	1,698	108	1,590		1,482 D	6.4%	93.6%	6.4%	93.6%
CULBERSON	304	18	285	1	267 D	5.9%	93.8%	5.9%	94.1%
DALLAM	2,300	341	1,935	24	1,594 D	14.8%	84.1%	15.0%	85.0%
DALLAS	46,653	8,919	37,363	371	28,444 D	19.1%	80.1%	19.3%	80.7%
DAWSON	1,813	153	1,659	1	1,506 D	8.4%	91.5%	8.4%	91.6%
DEAF SMITH	1,505	198	1,307		1,109 D	13.2%	86.8%	13.2%	86.8%
DELTA	2,101	87	2,013	1	1,926 D	4.1%	95.8%	4.1%	95.9%

TEXAS

PRESIDENT 1928

County	Total Vote	Republican	Democratic	Other	Rep.-Dem. Plurality	Total Vote Rep.	Total Vote Dem.	Major Vote Rep.	Major Vote Dem.
DENTON	4,986	2,587	2,384	15	203 R	51.9%	47.8%	52.0%	48.0%
DE WITT	2,741	1,142	1,594	5	452 D	41.7%	58.2%	41.7%	58.3%
DICKENS	1,156	741	415		326 R	64.1%	35.9%	64.1%	35.9%
DIMMIT	884	626	253	2	368 R	70.8%	29.2%	70.8%	29.2%
DONLEY	1,585	1,092	491		601 R	68.9%	31.0%	69.0%	31.0%
DUVAL	1,679	434	1,245		811 D	25.8%	74.2%	25.8%	74.2%
EASTLAND	5,734	3,233	2,501		732 R	56.4%	43.6%	56.4%	43.6%
ECTOR	319	168	151		17 R	52.7%	47.3%	52.7%	47.3%
EDWARDS	609	546	59	4	487 R	89.7%	9.8%	90.2%	9.8%
ELLIS	7,981	3,569	4,399	13	830 D	44.7%	55.1%	44.8%	55.2%
EL PASO	12,164	6,050	6,114		64 D	49.7%	50.3%	49.7%	50.3%
ERATH	3,377	1,923	1,372	82	551 R	56.9%	40.6%	58.4%	41.6%
FALLS	3,368	877	2,484	7	1,607 D	26.0%	73.8%	26.1%	73.9%
FANNIN	4,651	2,122	2,525	4	403 D	45.6%	54.3%	45.7%	54.3%
FAYETTE	4,341	689	3,647	5	2,958 D	15.9%	84.0%	15.9%	84.1%
FISHER	2,096	1,259	837		422 R	60.1%	39.9%	60.1%	39.9%
FLOYD	1,842	1,176	666		510 R	63.8%	36.2%	63.8%	36.2%
FOARD	905	430	466	9	36 D	47.5%	51.5%	48.0%	52.0%
FORT BEND	2,357	631	1,724	2	1,093 D	26.8%	73.1%	26.8%	73.2%
FRANKLIN	1,099	386	713		327 D	35.1%	64.9%	35.1%	64.9%
FREESTONE	2,499	1,178	1,318	3	140 D	47.1%	52.7%	47.2%	52.8%
FRIO	932	673	258	1	415 R	72.2%	27.7%	72.3%	27.7%
GAINES	452	312	140		172 R	69.0%	31.0%	69.0%	31.0%
GALVESTON	10,372	4,401	5,951	20	1,550 D	42.4%	57.4%	42.5%	57.5%
GARZA	1,079	794	285		509 R	73.6%	26.4%	73.6%	26.4%
GILLESPIE	2,625	1,447	1,174	4	273 R	55.1%	44.7%	55.2%	44.8%
GLASSCOCK	158	124	34		90 R	78.5%	21.5%	78.5%	21.5%
GOLIAD	1,024	554	468	2	86 R	54.1%	45.7%	54.2%	45.8%
GONZALES	2,431	1,112	1,319		207 D	45.7%	54.3%	45.7%	54.3%
GRAY	2,863	1,871	986	6	885 R	65.4%	34.5%	65.5%	34.5%
GRAYSON	10,892	6,277	4,600	15	1,677 R	57.6%	42.2%	57.7%	42.3%
GREGG	1,644	646	996	2	350 D	39.3%	60.6%	39.3%	60.7%
GRIMES	1,876	701	1,175		474 D	37.4%	62.6%	37.4%	62.6%
GUADALUPE	3,318	1,442	1,872	4	430 D	43.5%	56.4%	43.5%	56.5%
HALE	3,248	2,143	1,098	7	1,045 R	66.0%	33.8%	66.1%	33.9%
HALL	1,902	1,409	493		916 R	74.1%	25.9%	74.1%	25.9%
HAMILTON	1,916	927	989		62 D	48.4%	51.6%	48.4%	51.6%
HANSFORD	737	417	319	1	98 R	56.6%	43.3%	56.7%	43.3%
HARDEMAN	2,243	1,333	910		423 R	59.4%	40.6%	59.4%	40.6%
HARDIN	1,983	951	1,032		81 D	48.0%	52.0%	48.0%	52.0%
HARRIS	48,810	27,188	21,536	86	5,652 R	55.7%	44.1%	55.8%	44.2%
HARRISON	3,804	1,776	2,023	5	247 D	46.7%	53.1%	46.7%	53.3%
HARTLEY	342	179	163		16 R	52.3%	47.5%	52.3%	47.7%
HASKELL	2,974	1,430	1,532	12	102 D	48.1%	51.5%	48.3%	51.7%
HAYS	1,708	1,088	620		468 R	63.7%	36.3%	63.7%	36.3%
HEMPHILL	806	489	317		172 R	60.7%	39.3%	60.7%	39.3%
HENDERSON	2,854	1,128	1,726		598 D	39.5%	60.5%	39.5%	60.5%
HIDALGO	8,335	4,285	4,034	16	251 R	51.4%	48.4%	51.5%	48.5%
HILL	4,859	2,446	2,413		33 R	50.3%	49.7%	50.3%	49.7%
HOCKLEY	1,009	765	235	9	530 R	75.8%	23.3%	76.5%	23.5%
HOOD	1,121	640	479	2	161 R	57.1%	42.7%	57.2%	42.8%
HOPKINS	3,617	1,767	1,845	5	78 D	48.9%	51.0%	48.9%	51.1%
HOUSTON	2,099	763	1,336		573 D	36.4%	63.6%	36.4%	63.6%
HOWARD	1,774	812	959	3	147 D	45.8%	54.0%	45.9%	54.1%
HUDSPETH	240	123	117		6 R	51.2%	48.8%	51.2%	48.8%
HUNT	6,519	3,009	3,510		501 D	46.2%	53.8%	46.2%	53.8%
HUTCHINSON	1,845	1,115	730		385 R	60.4%	39.6%	60.4%	39.6%
IRION	378	259	119		140 R	68.5%	31.5%	68.5%	31.5%
JACK	1,521	1,068	450	3	618 R	70.2%	29.6%	70.4%	29.6%
JACKSON	1,046	572	473	1	99 R	54.7%	45.2%	54.7%	45.3%

PRESIDENT 1932

County	Total Vote	Republican	Democratic	Other	Rep.-Dem. Plurality	Total Vote Rep.	Total Vote Dem.	Major Vote Rep.	Major Vote Dem.
DENTON	5,677	520	5,115	42	4,595 D	9.2%	90.1%	9.2%	90.8%
DE WITT	3,521	309	3,206	6	2,897 D	8.8%	91.1%	8.8%	91.2%
DICKENS	1,562	63	1,491	8	1,428 D	4.0%	95.5%	4.1%	95.9%
DIMMIT	1,090	241	843	6	602 D	22.1%	77.3%	22.2%	77.8%
DONLEY	1,773	141	1,626	6	1,485 D	8.0%	91.7%	8.0%	92.0%
DUVAL	1,596	30	1,566		1,536 D	1.9%	98.1%	1.9%	98.1%
EASTLAND	5,556	598	4,958		4,360 D	10.8%	89.2%	10.8%	89.2%
ECTOR	595	37	530	28	493 D	6.2%	89.1%	6.5%	93.5%
EDWARDS	804	224	575	5	351 D	27.9%	71.5%	28.0%	72.0%
ELLIS	7,604	527	7,033	44	6,506 D	6.9%	92.5%	7.0%	93.0%
EL PASO	14,392	2,841	11,336	215	8,495 D	19.7%	78.8%	20.0%	80.0%
ERATH	3,629	284	3,319	26	3,035 D	7.8%	91.5%	7.9%	92.1%
FALLS	4,084	181	3,896	7	3,715 D	4.4%	95.4%	4.4%	95.6%
FANNIN	5,815	460	5,338	17	4,878 D	7.9%	91.8%	7.9%	92.1%
FAYETTE	5,233	245	4,985	3	4,740 D	4.7%	95.3%	4.7%	95.3%
FISHER	1,506	105	1,395	6	1,290 D	7.0%	92.6%	7.0%	93.0%
FLOYD	2,126	145	1,976	5	1,831 D	6.8%	92.9%	6.8%	93.2%
FOARD	948	53	882	13	829 D	5.6%	93.0%	5.7%	94.3%
FORT BEND	3,265	148	3,109	8	2,961 D	4.5%	95.2%	4.5%	95.5%
FRANKLIN	1,362	56	1,305	1	1,249 D	4.1%	95.8%	4.1%	95.9%
FREESTONE	2,656	170	2,481	5	2,311 D	6.4%	93.4%	6.4%	93.6%
FRIO	1,140	142	998		856 D	12.5%	87.5%	12.5%	87.5%
GAINES	562	44	510	8	466 D	7.8%	90.7%	7.9%	92.1%
GALVESTON	12,582	2,011	10,491	80	8,480 D	16.0%	83.4%	16.1%	83.9%
GARZA	904	87	812	5	725 D	9.6%	89.8%	9.7%	90.3%
GILLESPIE	3,317	662	2,642	13	1,980 D	20.0%	79.7%	20.0%	80.0%
GLASSCOCK	254	42	212		170 D	16.5%	83.5%	16.5%	83.5%
GOLIAD	1,718	170	1,542	6	1,372 D	9.9%	89.8%	9.9%	90.1%
GONZALES	3,728	337	3,384	7	3,047 D	9.0%	90.8%	9.1%	90.9%
GRAY	3,975	505	3,446	24	2,941 D	12.7%	86.7%	12.8%	87.2%
GRAYSON	10,992	1,317	9,631	44	8,314 D	12.0%	87.6%	12.0%	88.0%
GREGG	5,565	341	5,204	20	4,863 D	6.1%	93.5%	6.1%	93.9%
GRIMES	2,223	153	2,065	5	1,912 D	6.9%	92.9%	6.9%	93.1%
GUADALUPE	4,451	691	3,751	9	3,060 D	15.5%	84.3%	15.6%	84.4%
HALE	3,437	369	3,029	39	2,660 D	10.7%	88.1%	10.9%	89.1%
HALL	2,218	91	2,114	13	2,023 D	4.1%	95.3%	4.1%	95.9%
HAMILTON	2,642	164	2,474	4	2,310 D	6.2%	93.6%	6.2%	93.8%
HANSFORD	901	67	803	31	736 D	7.4%	89.1%	7.7%	92.3%
HARDEMAN	2,135	145	1,985	5	1,840 D	6.8%	93.0%	6.8%	93.2%
HARDIN	2,944	161	2,783		2,622 D	5.5%	94.5%	5.5%	94.5%
HARRIS	55,970	8,604	46,886	480	38,282 D	15.4%	83.8%	15.5%	84.5%
HARRISON	4,604	528	4,057	19	3,529 D	11.5%	88.1%	11.5%	88.5%
HARTLEY	660	74	586		512 D	11.2%	88.8%	11.2%	88.8%
HASKELL	2,500	154	2,330	16	2,176 D	6.2%	93.6%	6.4%	93.6%
HAYS	2,050	220	1,822	8	1,602 D	10.7%	88.9%	10.8%	89.2%
HEMPHILL	1,052	133	918	1	785 D	12.6%	87.3%	12.7%	87.3%
HENDERSON	3,760	219	3,522	19	3,303 D	5.8%	93.7%	5.9%	94.1%
HIDALGO	12,784	2,969	9,695	120	6,726 D	23.2%	75.8%	23.4%	76.6%
HILL	5,662	360	5,297	5	4,937 D	6.4%	93.6%	6.4%	93.6%
HOCKLEY	1,623	76	1,513	34	1,437 D	4.7%	93.2%	4.8%	95.2%
HOOD	1,230	106	1,119	5	1,013 D	8.6%	91.0%	8.7%	91.3%
HOPKINS	5,159	261	4,891	7	4,630 D	5.1%	94.8%	5.1%	94.9%
HOUSTON	3,255	165	3,087	3	2,922 D	5.1%	94.8%	5.1%	94.9%
HOWARD	2,895	149	2,733	13	2,584 D	5.2%	94.4%	5.2%	94.8%
HUDSPETH	373	31	341	1	310 D	8.3%	91.4%	8.3%	91.7%
HUNT	7,340	465	6,856	19	6,391 D	6.3%	93.4%	6.4%	93.6%
HUTCHINSON	2,508	505	1,976	27	1,471 D	20.1%	78.8%	20.4%	79.6%
IRION	456	47	398	11	351 D	10.3%	87.3%	10.6%	89.4%
JACK	1,634	189	1,429	16	1,240 D	11.6%	87.3%	11.7%	88.3%
JACKSON	1,214	182	1,030	2	848 D	15.0%	84.8%	15.0%	85.0%

TEXAS

PRESIDENT 1928

County	Total Vote	Republican	Democratic	Other	Rep.-Dem. Plurality	% Total Vote Rep.	% Total Vote Dem.	% Major Vote Rep.	% Major Vote Dem.
JASPER	1,511	611	898	2	287 D	40.4%	59.4%	40.5%	59.5%
JEFF DAVIS	270	157	112	1	45 R	58.1%	41.5%	58.4%	41.6%
JEFFERSON	16,231	9,209	7,006	16	2,203 R	56.7%	43.2%	56.8%	43.2%
JIM HOGG	372	109	263	-	154 D	29.3%	70.7%	29.3%	70.7%
JIM WELLS	1,173	423	747	3	324 D	36.1%	63.7%	36.2%	63.8%
JOHNSON	5,166	3,181	1,981	4	1,200 R	61.6%	38.3%	61.6%	38.4%
JONES	3,566	1,995	1,563	8	432 R	55.9%	43.8%	56.1%	43.9%
KARNES	1,907	855	1,052	-	197 D	44.8%	55.2%	44.8%	55.2%
KAUFMAN	4,375	1,718	2,657	-	939 D	39.3%	60.7%	39.3%	60.7%
KENDALL	1,042	663	377	2	286 R	63.6%	36.2%	63.8%	36.2%
KENEDY	130	12	118	-	106 D	9.2%	90.8%	9.2%	90.8%
KENT	526	363	163	-	200 R	69.0%	31.0%	69.0%	31.0%
KERR	2,147	1,575	570	2	1,005 R	73.4%	26.5%	73.4%	26.6%
KIMBLE	821	660	157	4	503 R	80.4%	19.1%	80.8%	19.2%
KING	130	85	45	-	40 R	65.4%	34.6%	65.4%	34.6%
KINNEY	382	182	200	-	18 D	47.6%	52.4%	47.6%	52.4%
KLEBERG	1,446	751	695	-	56 R	51.9%	48.1%	51.9%	48.1%
KNOX	1,781	992	784	5	208 R	55.7%	44.0%	55.9%	44.1%
LAMAR	5,058	2,887	2,163	8	724 R	57.1%	42.8%	57.2%	42.8%
LAMB	1,706	1,266	440	-	826 R	74.2%	25.8%	74.2%	25.8%
LAMPASAS	1,475	899	567	10	332 R	60.9%	38.4%	61.3%	38.7%
LA SALLE	806	327	479	-	152 D	40.6%	59.4%	40.5%	59.5%
LAVACA	3,753	911	2,842	-	1,931 D	24.3%	75.7%	24.3%	75.7%
LEE	1,625	449	1,176	-	727 D	27.6%	72.4%	27.6%	72.4%
LEON	1,407	543	862	2	319 D	38.6%	61.3%	38.6%	61.4%
LIBERTY	1,995	1,070	918	7	152 R	53.6%	46.0%	53.8%	46.2%
LIMESTONE	4,250	1,642	2,608	-	966 D	38.6%	61.4%	38.6%	61.4%
LIPSCOMB	1,119	776	331	12	445 R	69.3%	29.6%	70.1%	29.9%
LIVE OAK	867	484	383	-	101 R	55.8%	44.2%	55.8%	44.2%
LLANO	953	439	514	-	75 D	46.1%	53.9%	46.1%	53.9%
LOVING	16	6	10	-	4 D	37.5%	62.5%	37.5%	62.5%
LUBBOCK	5,065	3,079	1,979	7	1,100 R	60.8%	39.1%	60.9%	39.1%
LYNN	2,029	1,268	754	7	514 R	62.5%	37.2%	62.7%	37.3%
MCCULLOCH	2,035	1,294	741	-	553 R	63.6%	36.4%	63.6%	36.4%
MCLENNAN	11,087	5,744	5,330	13	414 R	51.8%	48.1%	51.9%	48.1%
MCMULLEN	192	96	94	2	2 R	50.0%	49.0%	50.5%	49.5%
MADISON	816	364	452	-	88 D	44.6%	55.4%	44.6%	55.4%
MARION	1,083	443	640	-	197 D	40.9%	59.1%	40.9%	59.1%
MARTIN	543	330	213	-	117 R	60.8%	39.2%	60.8%	39.2%
MASON	1,053	807	244	2	563 R	76.8%	23.2%	76.8%	23.2%
MATAGORDA	2,029	1,194	829	6	365 R	58.8%	40.9%	59.0%	41.0%
MAVERICK	491	311	180	-	131 R	63.3%	36.7%	63.3%	36.7%
MEDINA	2,648	1,243	1,400	5	157 D	46.9%	52.9%	47.0%	53.0%
MENARD	823	589	234	-	355 R	71.6%	28.4%	71.6%	28.4%
MIDLAND	700	347	350	3	3 D	49.6%	50.0%	49.8%	50.2%
MILAM	4,116	1,270	2,842	4	1,572 D	30.9%	69.0%	30.9%	69.1%
MILLS	1,216	774	442	-	332 R	63.7%	36.3%	63.7%	36.3%
MITCHELL	1,845	1,099	746	-	353 R	59.5%	40.4%	59.6%	40.4%
MONTAGUE	2,971	1,519	1,452	-	67 R	51.1%	48.9%	51.1%	48.9%
MONTGOMERY	1,519	613	905	1	252 D	40.4%	59.6%	40.4%	59.6%
MOORE	211	87	124	-	37 D	41.2%	58.8%	41.2%	58.8%
MORRIS	1,067	287	780	-	493 D	26.9%	73.1%	26.9%	73.1%
MOTLEY	799	450	349	-	101 R	56.3%	43.7%	56.3%	43.7%
NACOGDOCHES	2,703	822	1,879	2	1,057 D	30.4%	69.5%	30.4%	69.6%
NAVARRO	6,989	3,341	3,648	-	307 D	47.8%	52.2%	47.8%	52.2%
NEWTON	962	397	564	1	157 D	41.3%	58.6%	41.3%	58.7%
NOLAN	2,510	1,475	1,035	-	440 R	58.8%	41.2%	58.8%	41.2%
NUECES	5,469	2,481	2,985	3	504 D	45.4%	54.6%	45.4%	54.6%
OCHILTREE	826	556	270	-	286 R	67.3%	32.7%	67.3%	32.7%
OLDHAM	329	172	157	-	15 R	52.3%	47.7%	52.3%	47.7%

PRESIDENT 1932

County	Total Vote	Republican	Democratic	Other	Rep.-Dem. Plurality	% Total Vote Rep.	% Total Vote Dem.	% Major Vote Rep.	% Major Vote Dem.
JASPER	2,084	93	1,990	1	1,897 D	4.5%	95.5%	4.5%	95.5%
JEFF DAVIS	302	46	252	4	206 D	15.2%	83.4%	15.4%	84.6%
JEFFERSON	20,865	3,534	17,129	152	13,545 D	17.2%	82.1%	17.3%	82.7%
JIM HOGG	479	51	428	-	377 D	10.6%	89.4%	10.6%	89.4%
JIM WELLS	1,621	162	1,449	10	1,287 D	10.0%	89.4%	10.1%	89.9%
JOHNSON	5,405	530	4,858	17	4,328 D	9.8%	89.9%	9.8%	90.2%
JONES	2,940	224	2,710	6	2,486 D	7.0%	92.8%	7.1%	92.9%
KARNES	2,650	186	2,458	6	2,272 D	7.0%	92.8%	7.0%	93.0%
KAUFMAN	4,389	268	4,116	5	3,848 D	6.1%	93.8%	6.1%	93.9%
KENDALL	1,609	416	1,185	8	769 D	25.9%	73.6%	26.0%	74.0%
KENEDY	129	5	123	1	118 D	3.9%	95.3%	3.9%	96.1%
KENT	587	23	561	3	538 D	3.9%	95.6%	3.9%	96.1%
KERR	2,804	623	2,165	16	1,542 D	22.2%	77.2%	22.3%	77.7%
KIMBLE	1,014	121	890	3	769 D	11.9%	87.8%	12.0%	88.0%
KING	228	4	224	-	220 D	1.8%	98.2%	1.8%	98.2%
KINNEY	768	89	678	1	589 D	11.6%	88.3%	11.6%	88.4%
KLEBERG	1,950	198	1,727	25	1,529 D	10.2%	88.6%	10.3%	89.7%
KNOX	1,706	102	1,600	4	1,498 D	6.0%	93.8%	6.0%	94.0%
LAMAR	6,307	375	5,911	21	5,536 D	5.9%	93.7%	6.0%	94.0%
LAMB	3,288	272	2,978	39	2,707 D	8.2%	90.6%	8.3%	91.7%
LAMPASAS	1,944	120	1,824	-	1,704 D	6.2%	93.8%	6.2%	93.8%
LA SALLE	905	92	810	3	718 D	10.2%	89.5%	10.2%	89.8%
LAVACA	4,613	224	4,378	11	4,154 D	4.9%	94.9%	4.9%	95.1%
LEE	1,941	110	1,831	-	1,721 D	5.7%	94.3%	5.7%	94.3%
LEON	2,076	108	1,958	10	1,850 D	5.2%	94.3%	5.2%	94.8%
LIBERTY	2,796	247	2,527	22	2,280 D	8.8%	90.4%	8.9%	91.1%
LIMESTONE	4,635	215	4,416	4	4,201 D	4.6%	95.3%	4.6%	95.4%
LIPSCOMB	1,221	349	865	7	516 D	27.5%	68.1%	28.7%	71.3%
LIVE OAK	1,192	114	1,070	8	956 D	9.6%	89.8%	9.6%	90.4%
LLANO	1,337	108	1,229	-	1,121 D	8.1%	91.9%	8.1%	91.9%
LOVING	215	27	187	1	160 D	12.6%	87.0%	12.6%	87.4%
LUBBOCK	5,953	590	5,330	33	4,740 D	9.9%	89.5%	10.0%	90.0%
LYNN	2,048	110	1,930	8	1,820 D	5.4%	94.2%	5.4%	94.6%
MCCULLOCH	2,277	265	2,006	6	1,741 D	11.6%	88.1%	11.7%	88.3%
MCLENNAN	13,185	1,108	11,972	105	10,864 D	8.4%	90.8%	8.5%	91.5%
MCMULLEN	270	12	246	12	234 D	4.4%	95.6%	4.4%	95.6%
MADISON	1,364	20	1,344	-	1,324 D	1.5%	98.5%	1.5%	98.5%
MARION	901	34	861	6	827 D	3.8%	95.6%	3.8%	96.2%
MARTIN	744	44	694	6	650 D	5.9%	93.3%	5.9%	94.1%
MASON	1,141	309	828	4	519 D	27.1%	72.6%	27.2%	72.8%
MATAGORDA	2,461	408	2,039	14	1,631 D	16.6%	82.9%	16.7%	83.3%
MAVERICK	1,056	199	847	10	648 D	18.8%	80.2%	19.0%	81.0%
MEDINA	3,036	515	2,516	5	2,001 D	17.0%	82.9%	17.0%	83.0%
MENARD	1,053	150	901	2	751 D	14.2%	85.6%	14.3%	85.7%
MIDLAND	1,402	136	1,245	21	1,109 D	9.7%	88.8%	9.8%	90.2%
MILAM	4,963	264	4,676	23	4,412 D	5.3%	94.2%	5.3%	94.7%
MILLS	1,567	133	1,434	-	1,301 D	8.5%	91.5%	8.5%	91.5%
MITCHELL	1,640	148	1,490	2	1,342 D	9.0%	90.9%	9.0%	91.0%
MONTAGUE	3,381	262	3,090	29	2,828 D	7.7%	91.4%	7.8%	92.2%
MONTGOMERY	2,099	126	1,971	2	1,845 D	6.0%	93.9%	6.0%	94.0%
MOORE	607	56	549	2	493 D	9.2%	90.4%	9.3%	90.7%
MORRIS	1,291	38	1,253	-	1,215 D	2.9%	97.1%	2.9%	97.1%
MOTLEY	936	34	900	2	866 D	3.6%	96.2%	3.6%	96.4%
NACOGDOCHES	3,726	117	3,603	6	3,486 D	3.1%	96.7%	3.1%	96.4%
NAVARRO	6,915	512	6,392	11	5,880 D	7.4%	92.4%	7.4%	92.6%
NEWTON	1,635	46	1,586	3	1,540 D	2.8%	97.0%	2.8%	97.2%
NOLAN	2,675	219	2,453	3	2,234 D	8.2%	91.7%	8.2%	91.8%
NUECES	7,662	967	6,659	36	5,692 D	12.6%	86.9%	12.7%	87.3%
OCHILTREE	1,291	183	1,097	11	914 D	14.2%	85.0%	14.3%	85.7%
OLDHAM	493	61	432	-	371 D	12.4%	87.6%	12.4%	87.6%

TEXAS

PRESIDENT 1928

County	Total Vote	Republican	Democratic	Other	Rep.-Dem. Plurality	% Total Rep.	% Total Dem.	% Major Rep.	% Major Dem.
ORANGE	2,166	919	1,247		328 D	42.4%	57.6%	42.4%	57.6%
PALO PINTO	3,162	2,001	1,161		840 R	63.3%	36.7%	63.3%	36.7%
PANOLA	1,735	420	1,312	3	892 D	24.2%	75.8%	24.2%	75.8%
PARKER	3,288	2,178	1,110		1,068 R	66.2%	33.8%	66.2%	33.8%
PARMER	943	620	315	8	305 R	65.7%	33.4%	66.3%	33.7%
PECOS	1,092	524	562	6	38 D	48.0%	51.5%	48.3%	51.7%
POLK	1,506	508	994	4	486 D	33.7%	66.0%	33.8%	66.2%
POTTER	6,264	3,627	2,637		990 R	57.9%	42.1%	57.9%	42.1%
PRESIDIO	569	254	315		61 D	44.6%	55.4%	44.6%	55.4%
RAINS	751	202	544	5	342 D	26.9%	72.4%	27.1%	72.9%
RANDALL	1,392	733	659		74 R	52.7%	47.3%	52.7%	47.3%
REAGAN	616	387	229		158 R	62.8%	37.2%	62.8%	37.2%
REAL	577	479	98		381 R	83.0%	17.0%	83.0%	17.0%
RED RIVER	2,838	1,172	1,666		494 D	41.3%	58.7%	41.3%	58.7%
REEVES	738	344	394		50 D	46.6%	53.4%	46.6%	53.4%
REFUGIO	1,054	383	671		288 D	36.3%	63.7%	36.3%	63.7%
ROBERTS	347	243	104		139 R	70.0%	30.0%	70.0%	30.0%
ROBERTSON	2,239	751	1,487	1	736 D	33.5%	66.4%	33.6%	66.4%
ROCKWALL	1,139	289	850		561 D	25.4%	74.6%	25.4%	74.6%
RUNNELS	3,148	1,645	1,494	9	151 R	52.3%	47.5%	52.4%	47.6%
RUSK	2,765	1,033	1,732		699 D	37.4%	62.6%	37.4%	62.6%
SABINE	1,226	419	807		388 D	34.2%	65.8%	34.2%	65.8%
SAN AUGUSTINE	1,288	467	821		354 D	36.3%	63.7%	36.3%	63.7%
SAN JACINTO	800	296	503	1	207 D	37.0%	63.0%	37.0%	63.0%
SAN PATRICIO	1,967	1,388	579		809 R	70.6%	29.4%	70.6%	29.4%
SAN SABA	1,434	682	752		70 D	47.6%	52.4%	47.6%	52.4%
SCHLEICHER	364	227	137		90 R	62.4%	37.6%	62.4%	37.6%
SCURRY	2,061	1,597	462	2	1,135 R	77.5%	22.4%	77.6%	22.4%
SHACKELFORD	1,092	558	533	1	25 R	51.1%	48.9%	51.1%	48.9%
SHELBY	2,648	676	1,961	11	1,285 D	25.5%	74.1%	25.5%	74.4%
SHERMAN	385	248	137		111 R	64.4%	35.6%	64.4%	35.6%
SMITH	5,836	3,493	2,343		1,150 R	59.9%	40.1%	59.9%	40.1%
SOMERVELL	377	241	136		105 R	63.9%	36.1%	63.9%	36.1%
STARR	815	79	736		657 D	9.7%	90.3%	9.7%	90.3%
STEPHENS	2,952	1,789	1,163		626 R	60.6%	39.4%	60.6%	39.4%
STERLING	289	122	167		45 D	42.2%	57.8%	42.2%	57.8%
STONEWALL	942	442	500		58 D	46.9%	53.1%	46.9%	53.1%
SUTTON	382	290	92		198 R	75.9%	24.1%	75.9%	24.1%
SWISHER	1,261	887	374		513 R	70.3%	29.7%	70.3%	29.7%
TARRANT	29,689	20,481	9,200	8	11,273 R	69.0%	31.0%	69.0%	31.0%
TAYLOR	5,950	4,050	1,891	9	2,159 R	68.1%	31.8%	68.2%	31.8%
TERRELL	451	364	85	2	279 R	81.1%	18.8%	81.1%	18.9%
TERRY	1,029	622	407		215 R	60.4%	39.6%	60.4%	39.6%
THROCKMORTON	1,007	703	304		399 R	69.8%	30.2%	69.8%	30.2%
TITUS	1,618	469	1,149		680 D	29.0%	71.0%	29.0%	71.0%
TOM GREEN	4,148	2,618	1,528	2	1,090 R	63.1%	36.8%	63.1%	36.9%
TRAVIS	9,351	4,847	4,487	17	360 R	51.9%	48.0%	51.9%	48.1%
TRINITY	1,142	456	686		230 D	39.9%	60.1%	39.9%	60.1%
TYLER	965	298	666	1	368 D	30.9%	69.0%	30.9%	69.1%
UPSHUR	2,210	649	1,553	8	904 D	29.5%	70.3%	29.5%	70.5%
UPTON	459	270	189		81 R	58.8%	41.2%	58.8%	41.2%
UVALDE	1,971	1,224	747		477 R	62.1%	37.9%	62.1%	37.9%
VAL VERDE	1,474	854	620		234 R	57.9%	42.1%	57.9%	42.1%
VAN ZANDT	3,312	1,502	1,789	21	287 D	45.4%	54.4%	45.4%	54.4%
VICTORIA	2,373	663	1,710		1,047 D	27.9%	72.1%	27.9%	72.1%
WALKER	1,235	488	747		259 D	39.5%	60.5%	39.5%	60.5%
WALLER	881	376	504	1	128 D	42.7%	57.2%	42.7%	57.2%
WARD	472	216	256		40 D	45.8%	54.2%	45.8%	54.2%
WASHINGTON	2,766	275	2,491		2,216 D	32.2%	67.7%	32.2%	67.8%
WEBB	2,385	767	1,615	3	848 D	32.2%	67.7%	32.2%	67.8%

PRESIDENT 1932

County	Total Vote	Republican	Democratic	Other	Rep.-Dem. Plurality	% Total Rep.	% Total Dem.	% Major Rep.	% Major Dem.
ORANGE	3,078	244	2,830	4	2,586 D	7.9%	91.9%	7.9%	92.1%
PALO PINTO	3,128	392	2,722	14	2,330 D	12.5%	87.0%	12.6%	87.4%
PANOLA	2,709	50	2,630	29	2,580 D	1.8%	97.1%	1.9%	98.1%
PARKER	3,482	372	3,074	36	2,702 D	10.7%	88.3%	10.8%	89.2%
PARMER	1,319	148	1,154	17	1,006 D	11.2%	87.5%	11.4%	88.6%
PECOS	1,448	180	1,261	7	1,081 D	12.4%	87.1%	12.5%	87.5%
POLK	2,229	110	2,117	2	2,007 D	4.9%	95.0%	4.9%	95.1%
POTTER	7,643	1,233	6,366	44	5,133 D	16.1%	83.3%	16.2%	83.8%
PRESIDIO	977	112	863	2	751 D	11.5%	88.3%	11.5%	88.5%
RAINS	985	41	937	7	896 D	4.2%	95.1%	4.2%	95.8%
RANDALL	1,638	231	1,394	13	1,163 D	14.1%	85.1%	14.2%	85.8%
REAGAN	808	124	681	3	557 D	15.3%	84.3%	15.4%	84.6%
REAL	424	89	335		246 D	21.0%	79.0%	21.0%	79.0%
RED RIVER	3,333	145	3,181	7	3,036 D	4.4%	95.4%	4.4%	95.6%
REEVES	1,211	122	1,085	4	963 D	10.1%	89.4%	10.1%	89.9%
REFUGIO	1,394	172	1,201	21	1,029 D	12.3%	86.2%	12.5%	87.5%
ROBERTS	491	36	451	4	415 D	7.3%	91.9%	7.4%	92.6%
ROBERTSON	2,544	148	2,396		2,248 D	5.8%	94.1%	5.8%	94.2%
ROCKWALL	1,299	62	1,237		1,175 D	4.8%	95.2%	4.8%	95.2%
RUNNELS	3,220	235	2,975	10	2,740 D	7.3%	92.4%	7.3%	92.7%
RUSK	5,566	483	5,074	9	4,591 D	8.7%	91.2%	8.7%	91.3%
SABINE	1,849	57	1,789	3	1,732 D	3.1%	96.9%	3.1%	96.9%
SAN AUGUSTINE	1,821	19	1,802		1,783 D	1.0%	99.0%	1.0%	99.0%
SAN JACINTO	848	16	828	4	812 D	1.9%	97.6%	1.9%	98.1%
SAN PATRICIO	2,566	407	2,142	17	1,735 D	15.9%	83.5%	16.0%	84.0%
SAN SABA	2,028	122	1,904	2	1,782 D	6.0%	93.9%	6.0%	94.0%
SCHLEICHER	592	76	516		440 D	12.8%	87.2%	12.8%	87.2%
SCURRY	1,711	105	1,604	2	1,499 D	6.1%	93.7%	6.1%	93.9%
SHACKELFORD	1,438	117	1,316	5	1,199 D	8.1%	91.5%	8.2%	91.8%
SHELBY	3,734	120	3,594	20	3,474 D	3.2%	96.3%	3.2%	96.8%
SHERMAN	609	91	515	3	424 D	14.9%	84.6%	15.0%	85.0%
SMITH	8,201	750	7,424	27	6,674 D	9.1%	90.5%	9.2%	90.8%
SOMERVELL	624	43	561	20	518 D	6.9%	89.9%	7.1%	92.9%
STARR	786	32	754		722 D	4.1%	95.9%	4.1%	95.9%
STEPHENS	2,969	256	2,684	29	2,428 D	8.6%	90.4%	8.7%	91.3%
STERLING	367	13	354		341 D	3.5%	96.5%	3.5%	96.5%
STONEWALL	1,026	50	976		926 D	4.9%	95.1%	4.9%	95.1%
SUTTON	485	113	372		259 D	23.3%	76.7%	23.3%	76.7%
SWISHER	1,631	166	1,448	17	1,282 D	10.2%	88.8%	10.3%	89.7%
TARRANT	33,513	5,251	27,836	426	22,585 D	15.7%	83.1%	15.9%	84.1%
TAYLOR	5,885	639	5,235	11	4,596 D	10.9%	89.0%	10.9%	89.1%
TERRELL	613	133	479	1	346 D	21.7%	78.1%	21.7%	78.3%
TERRY	1,543	87	1,448	8	1,361 D	5.6%	93.8%	5.7%	94.3%
THROCKMORTON	1,029	95	932	2	837 D	9.2%	90.6%	9.3%	90.7%
TITUS	2,602	75	2,523	4	2,448 D	2.9%	97.0%	2.9%	97.1%
TOM GREEN	5,714	739	4,957	18	4,218 D	12.9%	86.8%	13.0%	87.0%
TRAVIS	13,376	1,532	11,718	126	10,186 D	11.5%	87.6%	11.6%	88.4%
TRINITY	1,582	65	1,514	3	1,449 D	4.1%	95.7%	4.1%	95.9%
TYLER	1,495	44	1,450	1	1,406 D	2.9%	97.0%	2.9%	97.1%
UPSHUR	3,040	129	2,900	11	2,771 D	4.2%	95.4%	4.3%	95.7%
UPTON	1,110	92	1,012	6	920 D	8.3%	91.2%	8.3%	91.7%
UVALDE	2,186	422	1,759	5	1,337 D	19.3%	80.5%	19.3%	80.7%
VAL VERDE	1,835	421	1,412	2	991 D	22.9%	76.9%	23.0%	77.0%
VAN ZANDT	4,428	190	4,203	35	4,013 D	4.3%	94.9%	4.3%	95.7%
VICTORIA	2,972	190	2,777	5	2,587 D	6.4%	93.4%	6.4%	93.6%
WALKER	1,903	83	1,811	9	1,728 D	4.4%	95.2%	4.4%	95.6%
WALLER	1,283	89	1,192	2	1,103 D	6.9%	92.9%	6.9%	93.1%
WARD	755	70	678	7	608 D	9.3%	89.8%	9.4%	90.6%
WASHINGTON	3,545	99	3,443	3	3,344 D	2.8%	97.1%	2.8%	97.2%
WEBB	4,969	657	4,299	13	3,642 D	13.2%	86.5%	13.3%	86.7%

TEXAS

PRESIDENT 1928

County	Total Vote	Republican	Democratic	Other	Rep.-Dem. Plurality	Percentage Total Vote Rep.	Dem.	Major Vote Rep.	Dem.
WHARTON	2,696	1,151	1,545		394 D	42.7%	57.3%	42.7%	57.3%
WHEELER	1,794	1,038	750	6	288 R	57.9%	41.8%	58.1%	41.5%
WICHITA	12,079	7,226	4,853		2,373 R	59.8%	40.2%	59.8%	40.2%
WILBARGER	3,040	1,590	1,447	3	143 R	52.3%	47.6%	52.4%	47.6%
WILLACY	785	389	396		7 D	49.6%	50.4%	49.6%	50.4%
WILLIAMSON	5,531	1,833	3,689	9	1,856 D	33.1%	66.7%	33.2%	66.8%
WILSON	2,121	622	1,499		877 D	29.3%	70.7%	29.3%	70.7%
WINKLER	472	162	310		148 D	34.3%	65.7%	34.3%	65.7%
WISE	3,234	2,141	1,093		1,048 R	66.2%	33.8%	66.2%	33.8%
WOOD	2,806	1,161	1,645		484 D	41.4%	58.6%	41.4%	58.6%
YOAKUM	152	86	66		20 R	56.6%	43.4%	56.6%	43.4%
YOUNG	3,101	1,826	1,275		551 R	53.9%	41.1%	58.9%	41.1%
ZAPATA	315	19	296		277 D	5.0%	94.0%	6.0%	94.0%
ZAVALA	800	571	229		342 R	71.4%	28.6%	71.4%	28.6%
TOTAL	717,733	372,324	344,542	867	27,782 R	51.9%	48.0%	51.9%	48.1%

PRESIDENT 1932

County	Total Vote	Republican	Democratic	Other	Rep.-Dem. Plurality	Percentage Total Vote Rep.	Dem.	Major Vote Rep.	Dem.
WHARTON	3,792	405	3,357	30	2,952 D	10.7%	88.5%	10.8%	89.2%
WHEELER	2,445	165	2,263	17	2,098 D	6.7%	92.6%	6.8%	93.2%
WICHITA	10,413	1,479	8,889	45	7,410 D	14.2%	85.4%	14.3%	85.7%
WILBARGER	3,609	199	3,397	13	3,198 D	5.5%	94.1%	5.5%	94.5%
WILLACY	1,302	259	1,042	1	783 D	19.9%	80.0%	19.9%	80.1%
WILLIAMSON	7,214	418	6,783	13	6,365 D	5.8%	94.0%	5.8%	94.2%
WILSON	2,612	174	2,435	3	2,261 D	6.7%	93.2%	6.7%	93.3%
WINKLER	728	78	642	8	564 D	10.7%	88.2%	10.8%	89.2%
WISE	2,980	286	2,681	13	2,395 D	9.6%	90.0%	9.6%	90.4%
WOOD	3,516	189	3,308	19	3,119 D	5.4%	94.1%	5.4%	94.6%
YOAKUM	257	11	245	1	234 D	4.3%	95.3%	4.3%	95.7%
YOUNG	3,482	320	3,156	6	2,836 D	9.2%	90.6%	9.2%	90.8%
ZAPATA	295	24	271		247 D	8.1%	91.9%	8.1%	91.9%
ZAVALA	953	166	783	4	617 D	17.4%	82.2%	17.5%	82.5%
TOTAL	874,382	98,218	771,109	5,055	672,891 D	11.2%	88.2%	11.3%	88.7%

TEXAS

PRESIDENT 1936

County	Total Vote	Republican	Democratic	Other	Rep.-Dem. Plurality	Rep. %	Dem. %	Maj. Rep. %	Maj. Dem. %
ANDERSON	4,040	289	3,749	2	3,460 D	7.2%	92.8%	7.2%	92.8%
ANDREWS	306	18	287	1	269 D	5.9%	93.8%	5.9%	94.1%
ANGELINA	4,290	342	3,943	5	3,601 D	8.0%	91.9%	8.0%	92.0%
ARANSAS	277	60	206	11	146 D	21.7%	74.4%	22.6%	77.4%
ARCHER	1,822	146	1,672	4	1,526 D	8.0%	91.8%	8.0%	92.0%
ARMSTRONG	933	33	897	3	864 D	3.5%	96.1%	3.5%	96.5%
ATASCOSA	2,350	285	2,041	24	1,756 D	12.1%	86.9%	12.3%	87.7%
AUSTIN	1,929	290	1,635	4	1,345 D	15.0%	84.8%	15.1%	84.9%
BAILEY	993	191	788	14	597 D	19.2%	79.4%	19.5%	80.5%
BANDERA	1,171	431	720	20	289 D	36.8%	61.5%	37.4%	62.6%
BASTROP	2,602	198	2,395	9	2,197 D	7.6%	92.0%	7.6%	92.4%
BAYLOR	1,642	100	1,541	1	1,441 D	6.1%	93.8%	6.1%	93.9%
BEE	2,082	603	1,452	17	859 D	29.0%	70.2%	29.2%	70.8%
BELL	6,621	475	6,119	27	5,644 D	7.2%	92.4%	7.2%	92.8%
BEXAR	48,982	12,951	35,731	250	22,830 D	26.4%	73.0%	26.6%	73.4%
BLANCO	1,372	313	1,056	3	743 D	22.8%	77.0%	22.9%	77.1%
BORDEN	248	26	220	2	194 D	10.5%	88.7%	10.6%	89.4%
BOSQUE	2,638	350	2,283	5	1,933 D	13.3%	86.5%	13.3%	86.7%
BOWIE	5,521	472	5,030	19	4,558 D	8.5%	91.1%	8.6%	91.4%
BRAZORIA	2,785	462	2,284	39	1,822 D	16.6%	82.0%	16.8%	83.2%
BRAZOS	2,659	45	2,610	4	2,565 D	1.7%	98.2%	1.7%	98.3%
BREWSTER	981	151	828	2	677 D	15.4%	84.4%	15.4%	84.6%
BRISCOE	913	64	849		785 D	7.0%	93.0%	7.0%	93.0%
BROOKS	483	117	355	1	248 D	24.2%	75.6%	24.3%	75.7%
BROWN	4,458	448	3,971	39	3,523 D	10.0%	89.1%	10.1%	89.9%
BURLESON	1,601	135	1,465		1,331 D	8.4%	91.6%	8.4%	91.6%
BURNET	1,696	111	1,583	2	1,472 D	6.5%	93.3%	6.6%	93.4%
CALDWELL	3,291	247	3,019	25	2,772 D	7.5%	91.7%	7.6%	92.4%
CALHOUN	781	92	685	4	593 D	11.8%	87.7%	11.8%	88.2%
CALLAHAN	1,991	245	1,739	7	1,494 D	12.3%	87.3%	12.3%	87.7%
CAMERON	8,206	2,160	5,887	159	3,727 D	26.3%	71.7%	26.8%	73.2%
CAMP	1,017	78	939		861 D	7.7%	92.3%	7.7%	92.3%
CARSON	1,728	147	1,568	13	1,421 D	8.5%	90.7%	8.6%	91.4%
CASS	2,630	169	2,461		2,292 D	6.4%	93.6%	6.4%	93.6%
CASTRO	1,025	65	950	10	885 D	6.3%	92.7%	6.4%	93.6%
CHAMBERS	1,121	134	984	3	850 D	12.0%	87.8%	12.0%	88.0%
CHEROKEE	4,218	302	3,908	8	3,606 D	7.2%	92.7%	7.2%	92.8%
CHILDRESS	2,307	209	2,076	22	1,867 D	9.1%	90.0%	9.1%	90.9%
CLAY	2,380	196	2,168	16	1,972 D	8.2%	91.1%	8.3%	91.7%
COCHRAN	749	58	683	8	625 D	7.7%	91.2%	7.8%	92.2%
COKE	966	68	888	10	820 D	7.0%	91.9%	7.1%	92.9%
COLEMAN	3,177	269	2,900	8	2,631 D	8.5%	91.3%	8.5%	91.5%
COLLIN	6,210	531	5,669	10	5,138 D	8.5%	91.3%	8.6%	91.4%
COLLINGSWORTH	2,172	158	2,012	2	1,854 D	7.3%	92.6%	7.3%	92.7%
COLORADO	1,815	372	1,435	8	1,063 D	20.5%	79.1%	20.6%	79.4%
COMAL	2,171	554	1,611	6	1,057 D	25.5%	74.2%	25.6%	74.4%
COMANCHE	3,005	355	2,587	63	2,232 D	11.8%	86.1%	12.1%	87.9%
CONCHO	1,165	76	1,089		1,013 D	6.5%	93.5%	6.5%	93.5%
COOKE	4,392	686	3,686	20	3,000 D	15.6%	83.9%	15.7%	84.3%
CORYELL	2,223	150	2,064	9	1,914 D	6.7%	92.8%	6.8%	93.2%
COTTLE	1,359	86	1,265	8	1,179 D	6.3%	93.1%	6.4%	93.6%
CRANE	647	25	622		597 D	3.9%	96.1%	3.9%	96.1%
CROCKETT	308	75	231	2	156 D	24.4%	75.0%	24.5%	75.5%
CROSBY	1,867	153	1,711	3	1,558 D	8.2%	91.2%	8.2%	91.8%
CULBERSON	262	23	239		216 D	8.8%	91.2%	8.8%	91.2%
DALLAM	1,727	220	1,436	71	1,216 D	12.7%	83.1%	13.3%	86.7%
DALLAS	49,657	7,204	42,153	300	34,949 D	14.5%	84.9%	14.6%	85.4%
DAWSON	1,992	156	1,829	7	1,673 D	7.8%	91.8%	7.9%	92.1%
DEAF SMITH	1,387	142	1,236	9	1,094 D	10.2%	89.1%	10.3%	89.7%
DELTA	1,549	82	1,466	1	1,384 D	5.3%	94.6%	5.3%	94.7%

PRESIDENT 1940

County	Total Vote	Republican	Democratic	Other	Rep.-Dem. Plurality	Rep. %	Dem. %	Maj. Rep. %	Maj. Dem. %
ANDERSON	5,976	688	5,281	7	4,593 D	11.5%	88.4%	11.5%	88.5%
ANDREWS	466	26	440		414 D	5.6%	94.4%	5.6%	94.4%
ANGELINA	6,572	572	5,993	7	5,421 D	8.7%	91.2%	8.7%	91.3%
ARANSAS	677	141	536		395 D	20.8%	79.2%	20.8%	79.2%
ARCHER	2,181	276	1,904	1	1,628 D	12.7%	87.3%	12.7%	87.3%
ARMSTRONG	974	82	891	1	809 D	8.4%	91.5%	8.4%	91.6%
ATASCOSA	2,344	418	1,922	4	1,504 D	17.8%	82.0%	17.9%	82.1%
AUSTIN	2,807	1,400	1,404	3	4 D	49.5%	50.0%	49.9%	50.1%
BAILEY	1,397	330	1,066	1	736 D	23.6%	76.3%	23.6%	76.4%
BANDERA	1,317	432	881	4	449 D	32.8%	66.9%	32.9%	67.1%
BASTROP	2,996	502	2,492	2	1,990 D	16.8%	83.2%	16.8%	83.2%
BAYLOR	1,807	139	1,667	1	1,528 D	7.7%	92.3%	7.7%	92.3%
BEE	2,707	948	1,759		811 D	35.0%	65.0%	35.0%	65.0%
BELL	8,468	1,050	7,418		6,368 D	12.4%	87.6%	12.4%	87.6%
BEXAR	56,696	18,270	38,214	212	19,944 D	32.2%	67.4%	32.3%	67.7%
BLANCO	1,567	520	1,042	5	522 D	33.2%	66.5%	33.3%	66.7%
BORDEN	419	44	375		331 D	10.5%	89.5%	10.5%	89.5%
BOSQUE	3,680	595	3,083	2	2,488 D	16.2%	83.8%	16.2%	83.8%
BOWIE	8,049	1,107	6,937	5	5,830 D	13.8%	86.2%	13.8%	86.2%
BRAZORIA	4,585	799	3,781	5	2,982 D	17.4%	82.5%	17.4%	82.6%
BRAZOS	4,777	617	4,151	9	3,534 D	12.9%	86.9%	12.9%	87.1%
BREWSTER	1,248	245	1,001	2	756 D	19.6%	80.2%	19.7%	80.3%
BRISCOE	1,066	154	910	2	756 D	14.4%	85.4%	14.5%	85.5%
BROOKS	875	201	670	4	469 D	23.0%	76.6%	23.1%	76.9%
BROWN	5,195	663	4,523	9	3,860 D	12.8%	87.1%	12.8%	87.2%
BURLESON	2,321	319	1,999	3	1,680 D	13.8%	86.1%	13.8%	86.2%
BURNET	2,412	233	2,177	2	1,944 D	9.7%	90.3%	9.7%	90.3%
CALDWELL	4,159	659	3,499	1	2,840 D	15.8%	84.1%	15.8%	84.2%
CALHOUN	1,088	152	935		783 D	14.0%	85.9%	14.0%	86.0%
CALLAHAN	2,623	309	2,310	4	2,001 D	11.8%	88.1%	11.8%	88.2%
CAMERON	9,433	3,370	6,035	28	2,665 D	35.7%	64.0%	35.8%	64.2%
CAMP	1,545	200	1,343	2	1,143 D	13.0%	86.9%	13.0%	87.0%
CARSON	2,000	362	1,636	2	1,274 D	18.1%	81.8%	18.1%	81.9%
CASS	3,580	454	3,126		2,672 D	12.7%	87.3%	12.7%	87.3%
CASTRO	1,226	224	1,000	2	776 D	18.3%	81.6%	18.3%	81.7%
CHAMBERS	1,500	219	1,279	2	1,060 D	14.6%	85.3%	14.6%	85.4%
CHEROKEE	6,104	801	5,293	10	4,492 D	13.1%	86.7%	13.1%	86.9%
CHILDRESS	3,067	335	2,729	3	2,394 D	10.9%	89.0%	10.9%	89.1%
CLAY	2,790	427	2,357	6	1,930 D	15.3%	84.5%	15.3%	84.7%
COCHRAN	891	122	765	4	643 D	13.7%	85.9%	13.7%	86.2%
COKE	1,066	94	967	5	873 D	8.8%	90.7%	8.9%	91.1%
COLEMAN	3,723	454	3,257	12	2,803 D	12.2%	87.5%	12.2%	87.8%
COLLIN	8,412	1,028	7,373	11	6,345 D	12.2%	87.6%	12.2%	87.8%
COLLINGSWORTH	2,346	307	2,034	5	1,727 D	13.1%	86.7%	13.1%	86.9%
COLORADO	2,844	1,166	1,674	4	508 D	41.0%	58.9%	41.1%	58.9%
COMAL	2,706	1,852	851	3	1,001 R	68.4%	31.4%	68.5%	31.5%
COMANCHE	3,837	610	3,226	1	2,616 D	15.9%	84.1%	15.9%	84.1%
CONCHO	1,500	189	1,310	1	1,121 D	12.6%	87.3%	12.6%	87.4%
COOKE	5,853	1,358	4,483	12	3,125 D	23.2%	76.6%	23.2%	76.8%
CORYELL	3,705	549	3,155	1	2,606 D	14.8%	85.2%	14.8%	85.2%
COTTLE	1,743	237	1,506		1,269 D	13.6%	86.4%	13.6%	86.4%
CRANE	884	68	815	1	747 D	7.7%	92.2%	7.7%	92.3%
CROCKETT	552	132	420		288 D	23.9%	76.1%	23.9%	76.1%
CROSBY	2,002	276	1,720	6	1,444 D	13.8%	85.9%	13.8%	86.2%
CULBERSON	349	45	303	1	258 D	12.9%	86.8%	12.9%	87.1%
DALLAM	1,974	427	1,539	8	1,112 D	21.6%	78.0%	21.7%	78.3%
DALLAS	66,136	16,574	49,431	131	32,857 D	25.1%	74.7%	25.1%	74.9%
DAWSON	3,174	361	2,808	5	2,447 D	11.4%	88.5%	11.4%	88.6%
DEAF SMITH	1,647	423	1,219	5	796 D	25.7%	74.0%	25.8%	74.2%
DELTA	2,404	190	2,214		2,024 D	7.9%	92.1%	7.9%	92.1%

TEXAS

PRESIDENT 1936 / PRESIDENT 1940

County	1936 Total Vote	1936 Republican	1936 Democratic	1936 Other	1936 Rep.-Dem. Plurality	1936 % Total Rep.	1936 % Total Dem.	1936 % Major Rep.	1936 % Major Dem.	1940 Total Vote	1940 Republican	1940 Democratic	1940 Other	1940 Rep.-Dem. Plurality	1940 % Total Rep.	1940 % Total Dem.	1940 % Major Rep.	1940 % Major Dem.
DENTON	5,523	476	5,021	26	4,545 D	8.6%	90.9%	8.7%	91.3%	7,292	899	6,386	7	5,487 D	12.3%	87.6%	12.3%	87.7%
DE WITT	2,612	616	1,977	9	1,361 D	23.7%	76.0%	23.8%	76.2%	3,791	1,735	2,056		321 D	45.8%	54.2%	45.8%	54.2%
DICKENS	1,551	115	1,445	1	1,330 D	7.4%	92.6%	7.4%	92.6%	1,979	246	1,728	5	1,482 D	12.4%	87.3%	12.5%	87.5%
DIMMIT	1,021	296	704	21	408 D	29.0%	69.0%	29.6%	70.4%	1,079	340	736	3	396 D	31.5%	68.2%	31.6%	68.4%
DONLEY	1,654	133	1,513	18	1,380 D	8.0%	90.9%	8.1%	91.9%	1,843	213	1,619	11	1,406 D	11.6%	87.8%	11.6%	88.4%
DUVAL	3,058	163	2,901	4	2,738 D	5.3%	94.6%	5.3%	94.7%	3,384	151	3,232	1	3,081 D	4.5%	95.5%	4.5%	95.5%
EASTLAND	5,418	724	4,659	35	3,935 D	13.4%	86.0%	13.4%	86.6%	6,887	1,063	5,818	6	4,755 D	15.4%	84.5%	15.4%	84.6%
ECTOR	908	81	816	11	735 D	8.9%	89.9%	9.0%	91.0%	3,239	451	2,783	5	2,332 D	13.9%	85.9%	13.9%	86.1%
EDWARDS	514	157	354	3	197 D	30.5%	68.9%	30.7%	69.3%	740	175	565		390 D	23.6%	76.4%	23.6%	76.4%
ELLIS	5,975	319	5,644	12	5,325 D	5.3%	94.5%	5.3%	94.7%	8,578	692	7,881	5	7,189 D	8.1%	91.9%	8.1%	91.9%
EL PASO	13,809	1,773	11,920	116	10,147 D	12.8%	86.3%	12.9%	87.1%	16,165	3,764	12,374	27	8,610 D	23.3%	76.5%	23.3%	76.7%
ERATH	2,995	290	2,694	11	2,404 D	9.7%	89.9%	9.7%	90.3%	4,123	646	3,459	18	2,813 D	15.7%	83.9%	15.7%	84.3%
FALLS	3,556	140	3,411	5	3,271 D	3.9%	95.9%	3.9%	96.1%	4,908	958	3,949	1	2,991 D	19.5%	80.5%	19.5%	80.5%
FANNIN	5,617	368	5,242	7	4,874 D	6.6%	93.3%	6.6%	93.4%	8,276	792	7,478	6	6,686 D	9.6%	90.4%	9.6%	90.4%
FAYETTE	3,420	595	2,820	5	2,225 D	17.4%	82.5%	17.4%	82.6%	5,052	2,441	2,606	5	165 D	48.3%	51.6%	48.4%	51.6%
FISHER	2,229	155	2,068	6	1,913 D	7.0%	92.8%	7.0%	93.0%	2,467	199	2,260	8	2,061 D	8.1%	91.6%	8.1%	91.9%
FLOYD	2,095	217	1,863	15	1,646 D	10.4%	89.3%	10.4%	89.6%	2,371	484	1,880	7	1,396 D	20.4%	79.3%	20.5%	79.5%
FOARD	1,005	74	928	3	854 D	7.4%	92.3%	7.4%	92.6%	1,139	142	997		855 D	12.5%	87.5%	12.5%	87.5%
FORT BEND	2,775	176	2,588	11	2,412 D	6.3%	93.3%	6.4%	93.6%	3,849	748	3,101	2	2,353 D	19.4%	80.6%	19.4%	80.6%
FRANKLIN	1,017	90	925	2	835 D	8.8%	91.0%	8.9%	91.1%	1,806	183	1,621		1,438 D	10.1%	89.8%	10.1%	89.9%
FREESTONE	2,069	134	1,929	6	1,795 D	6.5%	93.2%	6.5%	93.5%	4,000	481	3,514	5	3,033 D	12.0%	87.8%	12.0%	88.0%
FRIO	1,219	193	1,019	7	826 D	15.8%	83.6%	15.9%	84.1%	1,252	236	1,012	4	776 D	18.8%	80.8%	18.9%	81.1%
GAINES	726	42	680	4	638 D	5.8%	93.7%	5.8%	94.2%	1,709	197	1,509	3	1,312 D	11.5%	88.3%	11.5%	88.5%
GALVESTON	11,106	1,666	9,370	70	7,704 D	15.0%	84.4%	15.1%	84.9%	13,632	2,443	11,161	28	8,718 D	17.9%	81.9%	18.0%	82.0%
GARZA	942	132	807	3	675 D	14.0%	85.7%	14.1%	85.9%	1,276	198	1,073	7	875 D	15.5%	84.1%	15.6%	84.4%
GILLESPIE	2,514	1,421	1,016	77	405 R	56.5%	40.4%	58.3%	41.7%	3,704	3,213	487	4	2,726 R	86.7%	13.1%	86.8%	13.2%
GLASSCOCK	283	29	252	2	223 D	10.2%	89.0%	10.3%	89.7%	311	41	268	2	227 D	13.2%	86.2%	13.3%	86.7%
GOLIAD	1,511	323	1,184	4	861 D	21.4%	78.4%	21.4%	78.6%	1,453	580	868	5	288 D	39.9%	59.7%	40.1%	59.9%
GONZALES	3,033	352	2,674	7	2,322 D	11.6%	88.2%	11.6%	88.4%	3,732	722	3,008	2	2,286 D	19.3%	80.6%	19.4%	80.6%
GRAY	4,839	464	4,347	28	3,883 D	9.6%	89.8%	9.6%	90.4%	5,540	1,217	4,315	8	3,098 D	22.0%	77.9%	22.0%	78.0%
GRAYSON	11,597	947	10,627	23	9,680 D	8.2%	91.6%	8.2%	91.8%	13,884	1,340	12,530	14	11,190 D	9.7%	90.2%	9.7%	90.3%
GREGG	7,121	621	6,489	11	5,868 D	8.7%	91.1%	8.7%	91.3%	10,990	1,584	9,391	15	7,807 D	14.4%	85.4%	14.4%	85.9%
GRIMES	1,989	136	1,851	2	1,715 D	6.8%	93.1%	6.8%	93.2%	3,199	298	2,899	2	2,601 D	9.3%	90.6%	9.3%	90.9%
GUADALUPE	4,237	1,266	2,962	9	1,696 D	29.9%	69.9%	29.9%	70.1%	4,661	2,473	2,182	6	291 R	53.1%	46.8%	53.1%	46.9%
HALE	3,582	451	3,109	22	2,658 D	12.6%	86.8%	12.7%	87.3%	4,323	906	3,405	12	2,499 D	21.0%	78.8%	21.0%	79.0%
HALL	2,346	126	2,195	25	2,069 D	5.4%	93.6%	5.4%	94.6%	2,445	219	2,221	5	2,002 D	9.0%	90.8%	9.0%	91.0%
HAMILTON	2,132	202	1,929	1	1,727 D	9.5%	90.5%	9.5%	90.5%	2,922	655	2,263	4	1,608 D	22.4%	77.4%	22.4%	77.6%
HANSFORD	921	74	826	21	752 D	8.0%	89.7%	8.2%	91.8%	880	150	725	5	575 D	17.0%	82.4%	17.1%	82.9%
HARDEMAN	2,208	207	1,991	10	1,784 D	9.3%	90.2%	9.4%	90.6%	2,815	362	2,453		2,091 D	12.9%	87.1%	12.9%	87.1%
HARDIN	2,470	119	2,351		2,232 D	4.8%	95.2%	4.8%	95.2%	3,232	226	2,997	2	2,771 D	7.0%	92.9%	7.0%	93.0%
HARRIS	67,533	8,083	59,205	245	51,122 D	12.0%	87.7%	12.0%	88.0%	94,453	20,797	73,520	136	52,723 D	22.0%	77.8%	22.1%	77.9%
HARRISON	3,708	302	3,400	6	3,098 D	8.1%	91.7%	8.2%	91.8%	5,196	681	4,515		3,834 D	13.1%	86.9%	13.1%	86.9%
HARTLEY	600	40	560		520 D	6.7%	93.3%	6.7%	93.3%	655	110	545		435 D	16.8%	83.2%	16.8%	83.2%
HASKELL	2,872	156	2,713	3	2,557 D	5.4%	94.5%	5.4%	94.6%	3,350	405	2,941	4	2,536 D	12.1%	87.8%	12.1%	87.9%
HAYS	2,259	286	1,964	9	1,578 D	12.7%	86.9%	12.7%	87.3%	2,828	453	2,371	4	1,918 D	16.0%	83.8%	16.0%	84.0%
HEMPHILL	1,134	121	1,008	5	887 D	10.7%	88.9%	10.7%	89.3%	1,038	170	868		698 D	16.4%	83.6%	16.4%	83.6%
HENDERSON	3,525	260	3,259	6	2,999 D	7.4%	92.5%	7.4%	92.6%	4,914	803	4,111		3,308 D	16.3%	83.7%	16.3%	83.7%
HIDALGO	10,053	2,962	6,782	309	3,820 D	29.5%	67.5%	30.4%	69.6%	12,285	4,787	7,471	27	2,684 D	39.0%	60.8%	39.1%	60.9%
HILL	4,980	265	4,710	5	4,445 D	5.3%	94.5%	5.3%	94.7%	6,629	627	6,002		5,375 D	9.5%	90.5%	9.5%	90.5%
HOCKLEY	1,833	90	1,731	12	1,641 D	4.9%	94.4%	4.9%	95.1%	2,649	261	2,382	6	2,121 D	9.9%	89.9%	9.9%	90.1%
HOOD	1,094	102	988	4	886 D	9.3%	90.3%	9.4%	90.6%	1,485	166	1,318	1	1,152 D	11.2%	88.8%	11.2%	88.8%
HOPKINS	3,018	261	2,753	4	2,492 D	8.6%	91.2%	8.7%	91.3%	5,511	551	4,955	5	4,404 D	10.0%	89.9%	10.0%	90.0%
HOUSTON	2,559	99	2,458	2	2,359 D	3.9%	96.1%	3.9%	96.1%	4,056	474	3,579	3	3,105 D	11.7%	88.2%	11.7%	88.3%
HOWARD	3,332	230	3,094	8	2,864 D	6.9%	92.8%	6.9%	93.1%	4,703	367	4,329	7	3,962 D	7.8%	92.0%	7.8%	92.2%
HUDSPETH	388	24	363	1	339 D	6.2%	93.6%	6.2%	93.8%	481	54	426	1	372 D	11.2%	88.6%	11.2%	88.8%
HUNT	6,147	335	5,801	11	5,466 D	5.4%	94.4%	5.5%	94.5%	9,044	877	8,156	11	7,279 D	9.7%	90.2%	9.7%	90.3%
HUTCHINSON	2,873	390	2,478	5	2,088 D	13.6%	86.3%	13.6%	86.4%	4,129	1,101	3,019	9	1,918 D	26.7%	73.1%	26.7%	73.3%
IRION	530	49	476	5	427 D	9.3%	89.8%	9.3%	90.6%	637	74	560	3	486 D	11.6%	87.9%	11.6%	88.3%
JACK	1,306	183	1,113	10	930 D	14.0%	85.2%	14.1%	85.9%	2,352	305	2,046	1	1,741 D	13.0%	87.0%	13.0%	87.0%
JACKSON	1,128	171	952	5	781 D	15.2%	84.4%	15.2%	84.8%	1,804	296	1,506	2	1,210 D	16.4%	83.5%	16.4%	83.6%

TEXAS

PRESIDENT 1936

County	Total Vote	Republican	Democratic	Other	Rep.-Dem. Plurality	TV Rep.	TV Dem.	MV Rep.	MV Dem.
JASPER	1,612	109	1,500	3	1,391 D	6.8%	93.1%	6.8%	93.2%
JEFF DAVIS	325	33	291	1	258 D	10.2%	89.5%	10.2%	89.8%
JEFFERSON	20,808	2,544	18,187	77	15,643 D	12.2%	87.4%	12.2%	87.7%
JIM HOGG	760	48	712		664 D	6.3%	93.7%	6.3%	93.7%
JIM WELLS	2,038	338	1,691	9	1,353 D	16.6%	83.0%	16.6%	83.3%
JOHNSON	4,647	337	4,281	29	3,944 D	7.3%	92.1%	7.3%	92.7%
JONES	3,703	305	3,396	2	3,091 D	8.2%	91.7%	8.2%	91.8%
KARNES	2,447	371	2,067	9	1,696 D	15.2%	84.5%	15.2%	84.8%
KAUFMAN	4,175	229	3,943	3	3,714 D	5.5%	94.4%	5.5%	94.5%
KENDALL	1,104	693	405	6	288 R	62.8%	36.7%	63.1%	36.9%
KENEDY	126	30	96		66 D	23.8%	76.2%	23.8%	76.2%
KENT	564	31	533		502 D	5.5%	94.5%	5.5%	94.5%
KERR	2,589	994	1,586	9	592 D	38.4%	61.3%	38.5%	61.5%
KIMBLE	833	151	681	1	530 D	18.1%	81.8%	18.1%	81.9%
KING	224	13	211		198 D	5.8%	94.2%	5.8%	94.2%
KINNEY	532	175	357		182 D	32.9%	67.1%	32.9%	67.1%
KLEBERG	1,708	156	1,488	64	1,332 D	9.1%	87.1%	9.5%	90.5%
KNOX	2,000	171	1,823	6	1,652 D	8.6%	91.2%	8.6%	91.4%
LAMAR	5,939	308	5,621	10	5,313 D	5.2%	94.6%	5.2%	94.8%
LAMB	2,630	300	2,320	10	2,020 D	11.4%	88.2%	11.5%	88.5%
LAMPASAS	1,599	134	1,462	3	1,328 D	8.4%	91.4%	8.4%	91.6%
LA SALLE	778	74	704		630 D	9.5%	90.5%	9.5%	90.5%
LAVACA	2,620	403	2,204	13	1,801 D	15.4%	84.1%	15.5%	84.5%
LEE	1,427	271	1,155	1	884 D	19.0%	80.9%	19.0%	81.0%
LEON	1,846	97	1,748	1	1,651 D	5.3%	94.7%	5.3%	94.7%
LIBERTY	3,068	244	2,813	11	2,569 D	8.0%	91.7%	8.0%	92.0%
LIMESTONE	4,058	196	3,857	5	3,661 D	4.8%	95.0%	4.8%	95.2%
LIPSCOMB	1,253	273	973	7	700 D	21.8%	77.7%	21.9%	78.1%
LIVE OAK	1,145	231	874	40	643 D	20.2%	76.3%	20.9%	79.1%
LLANO	1,409	107	1,302	1	1,195 D	7.6%	92.4%	7.6%	92.4%
LOVING	163	21	118	24	97 D	12.9%	72.4%	15.1%	84.9%
LUBBOCK	7,053	622	6,425	16	5,803 D	8.8%	91.0%	8.8%	91.2%
LYNN	2,158	169	1,983	16	1,814 D	7.8%	91.9%	7.9%	92.1%
MCCULLOCH	2,351	323	1,772	16	1,449 D	15.3%	83.9%	15.4%	84.6%
MC LENNAN	13,799	1,116	12,489	154	11,373 D	8.1%	90.5%	8.2%	91.8%
MCMULLEN	302	37	265		228 D	12.3%	87.7%	12.3%	87.7%
MADISON	1,172	45	1,127		1,082 D	3.8%	96.2%	3.8%	96.2%
MARION	1,048	129	919		790 D	12.3%	87.7%	12.3%	87.7%
MARTIN	854	70	775	9	705 D	8.2%	90.7%	8.3%	91.7%
MASON	1,147	359	787	1	428 D	31.3%	68.6%	31.3%	68.7%
MATAGORDA	2,164	459	1,700	5	1,241 D	21.2%	78.6%	21.3%	78.7%
MAVERICK	1,096	166	890	40	724 D	15.1%	81.2%	15.7%	84.3%
MEDINA	3,031	969	2,050	12	1,081 D	32.0%	67.6%	32.1%	67.9%
MENARD	853	115	734	4	619 D	13.5%	86.0%	13.5%	86.5%
MIDLAND	1,428	190	1,229	9	1,039 D	13.3%	86.1%	13.4%	86.6%
MILAM	4,383	288	4,077	18	3,789 D	6.6%	93.0%	6.6%	93.4%
MILLS	1,170	165	1,005		840 D	14.1%	85.9%	14.1%	85.9%
MITCHELL	2,231	192	2,035	4	1,843 D	8.6%	91.2%	8.6%	91.4%
MONTAGUE	3,128	324	2,789	15	2,465 D	10.4%	89.2%	10.4%	89.6%
MONTGOMERY	2,638	186	2,443	9	2,257 D	7.1%	92.6%	7.1%	92.9%
MOORE	631	47	583	1	536 D	7.4%	92.4%	7.5%	92.5%
MORRIS	1,272	52	1,220		1,168 D	4.1%	95.9%	4.1%	95.9%
MOTLEY	933	64	867	2	803 D	6.9%	92.9%	6.9%	93.1%
NACOGDOCHES	4,289	209	4,075	5	3,866 D	4.9%	95.0%	4.9%	95.1%
NAVARRO	6,120	293	5,815	12	5,522 D	4.8%	95.0%	4.8%	95.2%
NEWTON	1,206	93	1,111	2	1,018 D	7.7%	92.1%	7.7%	92.3%
NOLAN	3,196	268	2,913	15	2,645 D	8.4%	91.1%	8.4%	91.6%
NUECES	7,940	1,234	6,597	109	5,363 D	15.5%	83.1%	15.8%	84.2%
OCHILTREE	1,262	109	1,111	42	1,002 D	8.6%	88.0%	8.6%	91.1%
OLDHAM	462	20	437	5	417 D	4.3%	94.6%	4.4%	95.6%

PRESIDENT 1940

County	Total Vote	Republican	Democratic	Other	Rep.-Dem. Plurality	TV Rep.	TV Dem.	MV Rep.	MV Dem.
JASPER	2,456	220	2,236		2,016 D	9.0%	91.0%	9.0%	91.0%
JEFF DAVIS	424	50	374		324 D	11.8%	88.2%	11.8%	88.2%
JEFFERSON	24,591	4,860	19,694	37	14,834 D	19.8%	80.1%	19.8%	80.2%
JIM HOGG	910	100	810		710 D	11.0%	89.0%	11.0%	89.0%
JIM WELLS	3,026	914	2,105	7	1,191 D	30.2%	69.6%	30.3%	69.7%
JOHNSON	6,183	649	5,532	2	4,883 D	10.5%	89.5%	10.5%	89.5%
JONES	4,094	401	3,688	5	3,287 D	9.8%	90.1%	9.8%	90.2%
KARNES	2,642	631	2,010	1	1,379 D	23.9%	76.1%	23.9%	76.1%
KAUFMAN	5,751	516	5,232	3	4,716 D	9.0%	91.0%	9.0%	91.0%
KENDALL	1,744	1,321	421	2	900 R	75.7%	24.1%	75.8%	24.2%
KENEDY	106	68	38		30 R	64.2%	35.8%	64.2%	35.8%
KENT	792	79	712	1	633 D	10.0%	89.9%	10.0%	90.0%
KERR	2,756	1,112	1,634	10	522 D	40.3%	59.3%	40.5%	59.5%
KIMBLE	1,336	219	1,117		898 D	16.4%	83.6%	16.4%	83.6%
KING	289	23	266		243 D	8.0%	92.0%	8.0%	92.0%
KINNEY	577	156	418	3	262 D	27.0%	72.4%	27.2%	72.8%
KLEBERG	2,064	429	1,631	4	1,202 D	20.8%	79.0%	20.8%	79.2%
KNOX	1,952	253	1,699		1,446 D	13.0%	87.0%	13.0%	87.0%
LAMAR	8,805	761	8,038	6	7,277 D	8.6%	91.3%	8.6%	91.4%
LAMB	3,783	513	3,259	11	2,746 D	13.6%	86.1%	13.6%	86.4%
LAMPASAS	2,251	244	2,006	1	1,762 D	10.8%	89.1%	10.8%	89.2%
LA SALLE	818	112	706		594 D	13.7%	86.3%	13.7%	86.3%
LAVACA	3,836	1,412	2,419	5	1,007 D	36.8%	63.1%	36.9%	63.1%
LEE	2,106	1,150	954	2	196 R	54.6%	45.3%	54.7%	45.3%
LEON	2,601	252	2,349		2,097 D	9.7%	90.3%	9.7%	90.3%
LIBERTY	3,966	497	3,458	11	2,961 D	12.5%	87.2%	12.6%	87.4%
LIMESTONE	5,345	559	4,784	2	4,225 D	10.5%	89.5%	10.5%	89.5%
LIPSCOMB	1,231	445	774	12	329 D	36.1%	62.9%	36.5%	63.5%
LIVE OAK	1,390	499	888	3	389 D	35.9%	63.9%	36.0%	64.0%
LLANO	1,727	238	1,484	5	1,246 D	13.8%	85.9%	13.8%	86.2%
LOVING	119	21	98		77 D	17.6%	82.4%	17.6%	82.4%
LUBBOCK	9,411	1,283	8,113	15	6,830 D	13.6%	86.2%	13.6%	86.3%
LYNN	2,878	255	2,618	5	2,363 D	8.9%	91.0%	8.9%	91.1%
MCCULLOCH	2,816	443	2,373		1,930 D	15.7%	84.3%	15.7%	84.3%
MC LENNAN	18,165	2,178	15,952	35	13,774 D	12.0%	87.8%	12.0%	88.0%
MCMULLEN	413	77	336		259 D	18.6%	81.4%	18.6%	81.4%
MADISON	1,561	127	1,434		1,307 D	8.1%	91.9%	8.1%	91.9%
MARION	1,420	167	1,253		1,086 D	11.8%	88.2%	11.8%	88.2%
MARTIN	1,181	136	1,044	1	908 D	11.5%	88.4%	11.5%	88.5%
MASON	1,702	634	1,065	3	431 D	37.3%	62.6%	37.3%	62.7%
MATAGORDA	2,813	651	2,156	6	1,505 D	23.1%	76.6%	23.2%	76.8%
MAVERICK	1,045	166	875	4	709 D	15.9%	83.7%	15.9%	84.1%
MEDINA	3,229	1,480	1,749		269 D	45.8%	54.2%	45.8%	54.2%
MENARD	1,400	246	1,153	1	907 D	17.6%	82.4%	17.6%	82.4%
MIDLAND	2,570	646	1,921	3	1,275 D	25.1%	74.7%	25.2%	74.8%
MILAM	5,209	1,110	4,083	16	2,973 D	21.3%	78.4%	21.4%	78.6%
MILLS	1,946	287	1,658	1	1,371 D	14.7%	85.2%	14.8%	85.2%
MITCHELL	2,657	251	2,401	5	2,150 D	9.4%	90.4%	9.4%	90.5%
MONTAGUE	3,888	530	3,352	6	2,822 D	13.6%	86.2%	13.7%	86.3%
MONTGOMERY	3,755	408	3,347		2,939 D	10.9%	89.1%	10.9%	89.1%
MOORE	1,189	224	959	6	735 D	18.9%	80.7%	18.9%	81.1%
MORRIS	1,834	82	1,752		1,670 D	4.5%	95.5%	4.5%	95.5%
MOTLEY	1,007	100	907		807 D	9.9%	90.1%	9.9%	90.1%
NACOGDOCHES	5,432	440	4,988	4	4,548 D	8.1%	91.8%	8.1%	91.9%
NAVARRO	8,415	721	7,683	11	6,962 D	8.6%	91.3%	8.6%	91.4%
NEWTON	2,116	174	1,940	2	1,766 D	8.2%	91.7%	8.2%	91.8%
NOLAN	3,794	471	3,314	9	2,843 D	12.4%	87.3%	12.4%	87.6%
NUECES	12,842	3,065	9,740	37	6,675 D	23.9%	75.8%	23.9%	76.1%
OCHILTREE	1,507	294	1,213		919 D	19.5%	80.5%	19.5%	80.5%
OLDHAM	499	82	416	1	334 D	16.4%	83.4%	16.5%	83.5%

TEXAS

PRESIDENT 1936

County	Total Vote	Republican	Democratic	Other	Rep-Dem Plurality	Total Vote Rep.	Total Vote Dem.	Major Vote Rep.	Major Vote Dem.
ORANGE	2,479	190	2,281	8	2,091 D	7.7%	92.0%	7.7%	92.3%
PALO PINTO	3,123	371	2,735	14	2,367 D	11.9%	87.7%	11.9%	88.1%
PANOLA	2,543	95	2,425	23	2,347 D	3.7%	95.4%	3.8%	96.2%
PARKER	2,896	375	2,493	28	2,118 D	12.9%	86.1%	13.1%	86.9%
PARMER	1,078	135	936	7	801 D	12.5%	86.8%	12.6%	87.4%
PECOS	1,490	167	1,330	1	1,163 D	11.1%	83.0%	11.2%	88.8%
POLK	1,760	141	1,618	1	1,477 D	8.0%	91.9%	8.0%	92.0%
POTTER	7,643	1,018	6,496	129	5,478 D	13.3%	85.0%	13.5%	86.2%
PRESIDIO	1,049	106	938	5	832 D	10.1%	89.4%	10.2%	89.8%
RAINS	741	63	676	2	613 D	8.5%	91.2%	8.5%	91.3%
RANDALL	1,804	142	1,656	6	1,514 D	7.9%	91.8%	7.9%	92.1%
REAGAN	543	66	477	—	411 D	12.2%	87.8%	12.2%	87.8%
REAL	265	55	210	—	155 D	20.8%	79.2%	20.8%	79.2%
RED RIVER	2,887	199	2,665	3	2,466 D	6.9%	93.1%	6.9%	93.1%
REEVES	1,230	100	1,127	3	1,027 D	8.1%	91.6%	8.1%	91.9%
REFUGIO	1,305	242	1,058	5	816 D	18.5%	81.1%	18.6%	81.4%
ROBERTS	453	27	426	—	399 D	6.0%	94.0%	6.0%	94.0%
ROBERTSON	2,721	86	2,633	2	2,547 D	3.2%	96.8%	3.2%	96.8%
ROCKWALL	1,195	26	1,168	1	1,142 D	2.2%	97.7%	2.2%	97.8%
RUNNELS	3,317	313	2,985	19	2,672 D	9.4%	90.0%	9.5%	90.5%
RUSK	6,548	433	6,117	8	5,684 D	6.6%	93.3%	6.6%	93.4%
SABINE	1,376	108	1,216	2	1,108 D	8.1%	91.7%	8.2%	91.8%
SAN AUGUSTINE	1,118	84	1,034	—	950 D	5.7%	94.4%	5.7%	94.3%
SAN JACINTO	631	67	564	—	497 D	10.6%	89.4%	10.6%	89.4%
SAN PATRICIO	2,725	482	2,213	30	1,731 D	17.7%	81.2%	17.9%	82.1%
SAN SABA	1,654	147	1,505	2	1,358 D	8.9%	91.0%	8.9%	91.1%
SCHLEICHER	548	78	470	—	392 D	14.2%	85.6%	14.2%	85.7%
SCURRY	1,912	162	1,746	4	1,584 D	8.5%	91.3%	8.5%	91.5%
SHACKELFORD	1,305	152	1,153	—	1,001 D	11.6%	88.4%	11.6%	88.4%
SHELBY	3,312	136	3,167	9	3,031 D	4.1%	95.6%	4.1%	95.9%
SHERMAN	602	34	568	—	534 D	5.6%	94.3%	5.6%	94.4%
SMITH	7,788	660	7,116	12	6,456 D	8.5%	91.3%	8.5%	91.5%
SOMERVELL	378	57	317	4	260 D	15.1%	83.9%	15.2%	84.8%
STARR	2,618	320	2,289	9	1,969 D	12.2%	87.4%	12.3%	87.7%
STEPHENS	3,080	681	2,380	19	1,699 D	22.1%	77.3%	22.2%	77.6%
STERLING	398	14	384	—	370 D	3.5%	96.5%	3.5%	96.5%
STONEWALL	1,051	59	991	1	942 D	5.6%	94.3%	5.6%	94.4%
SUTTON	452	64	388	—	334 D	13.9%	86.1%	13.9%	86.1%
SWISHER	1,597	140	1,453	4	1,313 D	8.8%	91.0%	8.8%	91.2%
TARRANT	33,762	3,761	29,791	190	26,010 D	11.2%	88.2%	11.2%	88.7%
TAYLOR	6,898	678	6,169	51	5,491 D	9.8%	89.4%	9.9%	91.1%
TERRELL	408	84	324	—	240 D	20.6%	79.4%	20.6%	79.4%
TERRY	1,719	87	1,619	13	1,532 D	5.1%	94.2%	5.1%	94.9%
THROCKMORTON	1,083	132	949	3	817 D	12.2%	87.6%	12.2%	87.8%
TITUS	1,952	77	1,872	3	1,795 D	3.9%	95.9%	4.0%	95.0%
TOM GREEN	5,499	627	4,803	69	4,175 D	11.4%	87.3%	11.5%	88.5%
TRAVIS	13,425	1,314	12,092	179	10,933 D	10.3%	90.1%	9.8%	90.1%
TRINITY	1,348	151	1,196	—	1,045 D	11.2%	88.7%	11.2%	88.8%
TYLER	1,192	116	1,076	—	960 D	9.7%	90.3%	9.7%	90.3%
UPSHUR	2,567	321	2,243	3	1,922 D	12.5%	87.4%	12.5%	87.5%
UPTON	813	81	728	4	647 D	10.0%	89.5%	10.0%	90.0%
UVALDE	2,098	354	1,743	1	1,389 D	16.9%	83.1%	16.9%	83.1%
VAL VERDE	1,771	504	1,262	5	758 D	28.5%	71.3%	28.5%	71.5%
VAN ZANDT	3,531	245	3,257	29	3,012 D	6.9%	92.2%	7.0%	93.0%
VICTORIA	2,435	352	2,081	2	1,729 D	14.3%	85.5%	14.5%	85.5%
WALKER	1,786	69	1,715	2	1,646 D	3.9%	96.0%	3.9%	96.1%
WALLER	1,002	111	889	2	778 D	11.1%	88.7%	11.1%	88.9%
WARD	1,213	98	1,113	2	1,015 D	8.1%	91.7%	8.1%	91.9%
WASHINGTON	2,173	176	1,993	4	1,817 D	8.1%	91.6%	8.1%	91.9%
WEBB	4,290	696	3,594	—	2,898 D	16.2%	83.8%	16.2%	83.8%

PRESIDENT 1940

County	Total Vote	Republican	Democratic	Other	Rep-Dem Plurality	Total Vote Rep.	Total Vote Dem.	Major Vote Rep.	Major Vote Dem.
ORANGE	3,576	358	3,011	7	2,653 D	10.6%	89.2%	10.6%	89.4%
PALO PINTO	3,090	510	2,571	9	2,061 D	16.5%	83.2%	16.6%	83.4%
PANOLA	3,052	179	2,871	2	2,692 D	5.9%	94.1%	5.9%	94.1%
PARKER	4,253	558	3,587	8	3,129 D	13.1%	84.7%	13.1%	86.9%
PARMER	1,435	370	1,062	3	692 D	25.8%	74.0%	25.8%	74.2%
PECOS	1,925	332	1,583	10	1,251 D	17.2%	82.2%	17.3%	82.7%
POLK	2,922	280	2,642	—	2,362 D	9.6%	90.4%	9.6%	90.4%
POTTER	9,914	2,285	7,203	26	4,918 D	23.0%	72.7%	24.0%	75.9%
PRESIDIO	1,084	263	917	4	754 D	15.0%	84.6%	15.1%	84.9%
RAINS	1,333	251	1,080	2	829 D	18.8%	81.0%	18.9%	81.1%
RANDALL	2,162	382	1,779	1	1,397 D	17.7%	82.3%	17.7%	82.3%
REAGAN	609	88	520	1	432 D	14.4%	85.5%	14.5%	85.5%
REAL	579	126	453	—	327 D	21.8%	78.2%	21.8%	78.2%
RED RIVER	4,458	555	3,899	4	3,344 D	12.5%	87.5%	12.5%	87.5%
REEVES	1,554	247	1,305	2	1,058 D	15.9%	84.0%	15.9%	84.1%
REFUGIO	1,952	456	1,487	7	1,029 D	23.5%	76.2%	23.5%	76.5%
ROBERTS	466	55	408	3	353 D	11.8%	87.6%	11.9%	88.1%
ROBERTSON	3,366	175	3,191	—	3,016 D	5.2%	94.8%	5.2%	94.8%
ROCKWALL	1,605	95	1,510	—	1,415 D	5.9%	94.1%	5.9%	94.1%
RUNNELS	3,903	835	3,068	—	2,233 D	21.3%	78.6%	21.3%	78.7%
RUSK	8,613	704	7,901	8	7,197 D	8.2%	91.7%	8.2%	91.8%
SABINE	1,785	157	1,626	2	1,469 D	8.8%	91.1%	8.8%	91.2%
SAN AUGUSTINE	1,444	119	1,325	—	1,206 D	8.2%	91.8%	8.2%	91.8%
SAN JACINTO	884	119	764	1	645 D	13.5%	86.4%	13.5%	86.5%
SAN PATRICIO	3,953	980	2,963	20	1,983 D	24.9%	74.8%	24.9%	75.1%
SAN SABA	2,528	221	2,304	3	2,083 D	8.8%	91.1%	8.7%	91.2%
SCHLEICHER	718	117	601	—	484 D	16.3%	83.7%	16.3%	83.7%
SCURRY	2,583	280	2,303	—	2,023 D	10.8%	89.2%	10.8%	89.2%
SHACKELFORD	1,521	229	1,292	—	1,063 D	13.1%	86.6%	13.1%	86.9%
SHELBY	5,070	349	4,720	1	4,371 D	6.9%	93.1%	6.9%	93.1%
SHERMAN	613	82	528	3	446 D	13.4%	86.1%	13.4%	86.6%
SMITH	10,975	1,557	9,410	8	7,853 D	14.2%	85.1%	14.2%	85.8%
SOMERVELL	670	138	532	—	394 D	20.6%	79.4%	20.6%	79.4%
STARR	1,268	68	1,200	—	1,132 D	5.4%	94.6%	5.4%	94.6%
STEPHENS	3,223	471	2,750	2	2,279 D	14.6%	85.3%	14.0%	85.4%
STERLING	441	16	425	—	409 D	3.6%	96.4%	3.6%	96.4%
STONEWALL	1,328	156	1,172	—	1,016 D	11.7%	88.3%	11.7%	88.3%
SUTTON	657	84	571	2	487 D	12.8%	86.9%	12.8%	87.2%
SWISHER	1,733	298	1,432	3	1,134 D	17.2%	82.6%	17.2%	82.8%
TARRANT	43,589	7,474	36,062	53	28,588 D	17.1%	82.7%	17.2%	82.8%
TAYLOR	8,850	953	7,852	45	6,899 D	11.1%	88.7%	11.1%	88.9%
TERRELL	550	133	417	—	284 D	24.2%	75.8%	24.2%	75.8%
TERRY	2,261	145	2,116	—	1,971 D	6.4%	93.6%	6.4%	93.6%
THROCKMORTON	1,133	138	995	—	857 D	12.2%	87.8%	12.2%	87.8%
TITUS	3,941	255	3,686	—	3,431 D	6.5%	93.5%	6.5%	93.5%
TOM GREEN	7,497	1,049	6,433	15	5,384 D	14.0%	85.8%	14.0%	86.0%
TRAVIS	20,503	3,128	17,300	75	14,172 D	15.3%	84.4%	15.3%	84.7%
TRINITY	2,069	274	1,791	4	1,517 D	13.2%	86.6%	13.3%	86.7%
TYLER	1,550	226	1,326	2	1,098 D	14.7%	85.3%	14.7%	85.4%
UPSHUR	3,998	518	3,480	—	2,962 D	13.0%	87.0%	13.0%	87.0%
UPTON	1,432	370	1,062	—	692 D	25.8%	74.2%	25.8%	74.2%
UVALDE	2,437	556	1,871	6	1,315 D	22.9%	76.9%	22.9%	77.1%
VAL VERDE	2,247	616	1,628	3	1,012 D	27.4%	72.5%	27.5%	72.5%
VAN ZANDT	5,715	721	4,975	19	4,254 D	12.6%	87.1%	12.7%	87.3%
VICTORIA	3,451	956	2,493	2	1,537 D	27.7%	72.2%	27.7%	72.3%
WALKER	2,376	218	2,158	—	1,940 D	9.2%	90.8%	9.2%	90.8%
WALLER	1,366	300	1,065	1	765 D	22.0%	78.0%	22.0%	78.0%
WARD	2,227	281	1,931	15	1,650 D	12.7%	86.3%	12.7%	87.3%
WASHINGTON	3,317	1,868	1,449	—	419 R	56.3%	43.7%	56.3%	43.7%
WEBB	4,926	775	4,147	4	3,372 D	15.7%	84.2%	15.7%	84.3%

TEXAS

PRESIDENT 1936

County	Total Vote	Republican	Democratic	Other	Rep.-Dem. Plurality	Total Vote Rep.	Total Vote Dem.	Major Vote Rep.	Major Vote Dem.
WHARTON	3,355	307	3,034	14	2,727 D	9.2%	90.4%	9.2%	90.8%
WHEELER	2,704	277	2,415	12	2,138 D	10.2%	89.3%	10.3%	89.7%
WICHITA	10,788	1,327	9,428	33	8,101 D	12.3%	87.4%	12.3%	87.7%
WILBARGER	3,613	316	3,279	18	2,963 D	8.7%	90.8%	8.8%	91.2%
WILLACY	1,399	376	1,002	21	626 D	26.9%	71.6%	27.3%	72.7%
WILLIAMSON	5,383	375	4,995	13	4,620 D	7.0%	92.8%	7.0%	93.0%
WILSON	2,864	286	2,573	5	2,287 D	10.0%	89.8%	10.0%	90.0%
WINKLER	975	63	903	9	840 D	6.5%	92.6%	6.5%	93.5%
WISE	3,090	348	2,737	5	2,389 D	11.3%	88.6%	11.3%	88.7%
WOOD	2,950	192	2,751	7	2,559 D	6.5%	93.3%	6.5%	93.5%
YOAKUM	245	13	227	5	214 D	5.3%	92.7%	5.4%	94.6%
YOUNG	3,381	304	3,065	12	2,761 D	9.0%	90.7%	9.0%	91.0%
ZAPATA	316	34	282		248 D	10.8%	89.2%	10.8%	89.2%
ZAVALA	1,002	209	788	5	579 D	20.9%	78.6%	21.0%	79.0%
TOTAL	849,701	104,661	739,952	5,088	635,291 D	12.3%	87.1%	12.4%	87.6%

PRESIDENT 1940

County	Total Vote	Republican	Democratic	Other	Rep.-Dem. Plurality	Total Vote Rep.	Total Vote Dem.	Major Vote Rep.	Major Vote Dem.
WHARTON	4,740	760	3,976	4	3,216 D	16.0%	83.9%	16.0%	84.0%
WHEELER	3,124	517	2,600	7	2,083 D	16.5%	83.2%	16.6%	83.4%
WICHITA	13,887	2,206	11,672	9	9,466 D	15.9%	84.0%	15.9%	84.1%
WILBARGER	3,952	697	3,249	6	2,552 D	17.6%	82.2%	17.7%	82.3%
WILLACY	1,920	740	1,173	7	433 D	38.5%	61.1%	38.7%	61.3%
WILLIAMSON	7,671	1,714	5,944	13	4,230 D	22.3%	77.5%	22.4%	77.6%
WILSON	3,359	605	2,750	4	2,145 D	18.0%	81.9%	18.0%	82.0%
WINKLER	1,512	172	1,340		1,168 D	11.4%	88.6%	11.4%	88.6%
WISE	4,251	498	3,751	2	3,253 D	11.7%	88.2%	11.7%	88.3%
WOOD	4,249	585	3,659	5	3,074 D	13.8%	86.1%	13.8%	86.2%
YOAKUM	1,019	134	885		751 D	13.2%	86.8%	13.2%	86.8%
YOUNG	4,195	478	3,712	5	3,234 D	11.4%	88.5%	11.4%	88.6%
ZAPATA	1,279	495	784		289 D	38.7%	61.3%	38.7%	61.3%
ZAVALA	998	259	739		480 D	26.0%	74.0%	26.0%	74.0%
TOTAL	1,124,437	212,692	909,974	1,771	697,282 D	18.9%	80.9%	18.9%	81.1%

TEXAS

PRESIDENT 1944

County	Total Vote	Republican	Democratic	Other	Rep.-Dem. Plurality	% Total Rep.	% Total Dem.	% Major Rep.	% Major Dem.
ANDERSON	5,474	467	4,342	665	3,875 D	8.5%	79.3%	9.7%	90.3%
ANDREWS	404	48	329	27	281 D	11.9%	81.4%	12.7%	87.3%
ANGELINA	5,898	1,001	4,387	510	3,386 D	17.0%	74.4%	18.6%	81.4%
ARANSAS	621	150	456	15	306 D	24.2%	73.4%	24.8%	75.2%
ARCHER	2,097	194	1,674	229	1,480 D	9.3%	79.8%	10.4%	89.6%
ARMSTRONG	800	132	623	45	491 D	16.5%	77.9%	17.5%	82.5%
ATASCOSA	2,646	685	1,757	204	1,072 D	25.9%	66.4%	28.1%	71.9%
AUSTIN	3,186	619	1,316	1,251	697 D	19.4%	41.3%	32.0%	68.0%
BAILEY	1,458	358	943	157	585 D	24.6%	64.7%	27.5%	72.5%
BANDERA	1,256	634	532	90	102 R	50.4%	42.3%	54.4%	45.6%
BASTROP	3,289	385	2,604	300	2,219 D	11.7%	79.2%	12.9%	87.1%
BAYLOR	1,789	102	1,568	119	1,466 D	5.7%	87.6%	6.1%	93.9%
BEE	2,411	848	1,306	257	458 D	35.2%	54.2%	39.4%	60.6%
BELL	8,955	763	6,960	1,232	6,197 D	8.5%	77.7%	9.9%	90.1%
BEXAR	60,427	23,588	35,024	1,815	11,436 D	39.0%	58.0%	40.2%	59.8%
BLANCO	1,512	533	846	133	313 D	35.3%	56.0%	38.7%	61.3%
BORDEN	303	34	237	32	203 D	11.2%	78.2%	12.5%	87.5%
BOSQUE	3,335	504	2,502	329	1,998 D	15.1%	75.0%	16.8%	83.2%
BOWIE	8,902	790	7,045	1,067	6,255 D	8.9%	79.1%	10.1%	89.9%
BRAZORIA	7,691	850	5,543	1,298	4,693 D	11.1%	72.1%	13.3%	86.7%
BRAZOS	4,375	464	3,358	553	2,894 D	10.6%	76.8%	12.1%	87.9%
BREWSTER	1,186	237	864	85	627 D	20.0%	72.8%	21.5%	78.5%
BRISCOE	828	80	615	133	535 D	9.7%	74.3%	11.5%	88.5%
BROOKS	635	142	403	90	261 D	22.4%	63.5%	26.1%	73.9%
BROWN	3,544	430	2,426	688	1,996 D	12.1%	68.5%	15.1%	84.9%
BURLESON	2,407	158	1,992	257	1,834 D	6.6%	82.8%	7.3%	92.7%
BURNET	2,112	228	1,697	187	1,469 D	10.8%	80.4%	11.8%	88.2%
CALDWELL	3,888	704	2,916	268	2,212 D	18.1%	75.0%	19.4%	80.6%
CALHOUN	1,073	158	732	183	574 D	14.7%	68.2%	17.8%	82.2%
CALLAHAN	2,463	224	1,962	277	1,738 D	9.1%	79.7%	10.2%	89.8%
CAMERON	11,846	5,309	5,998	539	689 D	44.8%	50.6%	47.0%	53.0%
CAMP	1,368	180	977	211	797 D	13.2%	71.4%	15.6%	84.4%
CARSON	1,763	446	1,216	101	770 D	25.3%	69.0%	26.8%	73.2%
CASS	3,742	541	2,866	335	2,325 D	14.5%	76.6%	15.9%	84.1%
CASTRO	1,203	222	838	143	615 D	18.5%	69.7%	20.9%	79.1%
CHAMBERS	1,329	179	1,038	112	859 D	13.5%	78.1%	14.7%	85.3%
CHEROKEE	5,146	598	3,918	630	3,320 D	11.6%	76.1%	13.2%	86.8%
CHILDRESS	2,797	299	2,295	203	1,996 D	10.7%	82.1%	11.5%	88.5%
CLAY	2,980	311	2,307	362	1,996 D	10.4%	77.4%	11.9%	88.1%
COCHRAN	1,030	123	716	191	593 D	11.9%	69.5%	14.7%	85.3%
COKE	959	65	824	70	759 D	6.8%	85.9%	7.3%	92.7%
COLEMAN	3,704	498	2,887	319	2,389 D	13.4%	77.9%	14.7%	85.3%
COLLIN	8,344	974	6,574	796	5,600 D	11.7%	78.8%	12.9%	87.1%
COLLINGSWORTH	2,152	261	1,725	166	1,464 D	12.1%	80.2%	13.1%	86.9%
COLORADO	3,098	638	1,517	943	879 D	20.6%	49.0%	29.6%	70.4%
COMAL	2,989	2,021	787	181	1,234 R	67.6%	26.3%	72.0%	28.0%
COMANCHE	3,787	356	2,941	490	2,585 D	9.4%	77.7%	10.8%	89.2%
CONCHO	1,364	151	1,090	123	939 D	11.1%	79.9%	12.2%	87.8%
COOKE	4,938	919	3,270	749	2,351 D	18.6%	66.2%	21.9%	78.1%
CORYELL	3,159	413	2,518	228	2,105 D	13.1%	79.7%	14.1%	85.9%
COTTLE	2,776	130	2,551	95	2,421 D	4.7%	91.9%	4.8%	95.2%
CRANE	639	58	552	29	494 D	9.1%	86.4%	9.5%	90.5%
CROCKETT	492	112	323	57	211 D	22.8%	65.7%	25.7%	74.3%
CROSBY	2,127	201	1,691	235	1,490 D	9.4%	79.5%	10.6%	89.4%
CULBERSON	251	17	200	34	183 D	6.8%	79.7%	7.8%	92.2%
DALLAM	1,610	323	1,118	169	795 D	20.1%	69.4%	22.4%	77.6%
DALLAS	94,036	21,099	60,909	12,028	39,810 D	22.4%	64.8%	25.7%	74.3%
DAWSON	2,872	472	2,149	251	1,677 D	16.4%	74.8%	18.0%	82.0%
DEAF SMITH	1,805	508	1,117	180	609 D	28.1%	61.9%	31.3%	68.7%
DELTA	1,987	133	1,706	148	1,573 D	6.7%	85.9%	7.2%	92.8%

PRESIDENT 1948

County	Total Vote	Republican	Democratic	Other	Rep.-Dem. Plurality	% Total Rep.	% Total Dem.	% Major Rep.	% Major Dem.
ANDERSON	5,198	1,199	3,242	757	2,043 D	23.1%	62.4%	27.0%	73.0%
ANDREWS	957	101	816	40	715 D	10.6%	85.3%	11.0%	89.0%
ANGELINA	6,339	1,000	4,377	962	3,377 D	15.8%	69.0%	18.6%	81.4%
ARANSAS	685	235	418	32	183 D	34.3%	61.0%	36.0%	64.0%
ARCHER	1,855	191	1,599	65	1,408 D	10.3%	86.2%	10.7%	89.3%
ARMSTRONG	816	97	686	33	589 D	11.9%	84.1%	12.4%	87.6%
ATASCOSA	2,732	704	1,895	133	1,191 D	25.8%	69.4%	27.1%	72.9%
AUSTIN	2,865	1,260	1,252	353	8 R	44.0%	43.7%	50.2%	49.8%
BAILEY	1,452	234	1,115	103	881 D	16.1%	76.8%	17.3%	82.7%
BANDERA	1,132	570	445	117	125 R	50.4%	39.3%	56.2%	43.8%
BASTROP	3,237	443	2,518	276	2,075 D	13.7%	77.8%	15.0%	85.0%
BAYLOR	1,676	101	1,522	53	1,421 D	6.0%	90.8%	6.2%	93.8%
BEE	2,374	801	1,441	132	640 D	33.7%	60.7%	35.7%	64.3%
BELL	9,113	1,069	7,548	496	6,479 D	11.7%	82.8%	12.4%	87.6%
BEXAR	66,279	26,202	35,970	4,107	9,768 D	39.5%	54.3%	42.1%	57.9%
BLANCO	1,569	497	1,003	69	506 D	31.7%	63.9%	33.1%	66.9%
BORDEN	233	18	203	12	185 D	7.7%	87.1%	8.1%	91.9%
BOSQUE	2,956	501	2,303	152	1,802 D	16.9%	77.9%	17.9%	82.1%
BOWIE	10,343	1,161	7,028	2,154	5,867 D	11.2%	67.9%	14.2%	85.8%
BRAZORIA	8,363	2,133	4,783	1,447	2,650 D	25.5%	57.2%	30.8%	69.2%
BRAZOS	5,530	1,533	3,459	538	1,926 D	27.7%	62.5%	30.7%	69.3%
BREWSTER	1,341	312	940	89	628 D	23.3%	70.1%	24.9%	75.1%
BRISCOE	807	83	692	32	609 D	10.3%	85.7%	10.7%	89.3%
BROOKS	1,282	217	1,029	36	812 D	16.9%	80.3%	17.4%	82.6%
BROWN	6,481	1,071	5,059	351	3,988 D	16.5%	78.1%	17.5%	82.5%
BURLESON	2,434	240	2,051	143	1,811 D	9.9%	84.3%	10.5%	89.5%
BURNET	2,324	287	1,955	82	1,668 D	12.3%	84.1%	12.8%	87.2%
CALDWELL	3,616	623	2,792	201	2,169 D	17.2%	77.2%	18.2%	81.8%
CALHOUN	1,030	346	589	95	243 D	33.6%	57.2%	37.0%	63.0%
CALLAHAN	2,211	258	1,844	109	1,586 D	11.7%	83.4%	12.3%	87.7%
CAMERON	11,859	4,689	6,778	392	2,089 D	39.5%	57.2%	40.9%	59.1%
CAMP	1,488	180	923	385	743 D	12.1%	62.0%	16.3%	83.7%
CARSON	1,754	413	1,301	40	888 D	23.5%	74.2%	24.1%	75.9%
CASS	3,899	457	2,540	902	2,083 D	11.7%	65.1%	15.2%	84.8%
CASTRO	1,374	169	1,158	27	989 D	12.3%	84.3%	12.7%	87.3%
CHAMBERS	1,392	302	787	303	485 D	21.7%	56.5%	27.7%	72.3%
CHEROKEE	4,801	1,154	3,079	568	1,925 D	24.0%	64.1%	27.3%	72.7%
CHILDRESS	2,801	273	2,415	113	2,142 D	9.7%	86.2%	10.2%	89.8%
CLAY	2,583	332	2,131	120	1,799 D	12.9%	82.5%	13.5%	86.5%
COCHRAN	1,186	119	852	215	733 D	10.0%	71.8%	12.3%	87.7%
COKE	1,008	65	909	34	844 D	6.4%	90.2%	6.7%	93.3%
COLEMAN	3,429	545	2,695	189	2,150 D	15.9%	78.6%	16.8%	83.2%
COLLIN	7,253	1,155	5,516	582	4,361 D	15.9%	76.1%	17.3%	82.7%
COLLINGSWORTH	2,089	198	1,779	112	1,581 D	9.5%	85.2%	10.0%	90.0%
COLORADO	3,155	900	1,316	939	416 D	28.5%	41.7%	40.6%	59.4%
COMAL	3,074	1,752	1,212	110	540 R	57.0%	39.4%	59.1%	40.9%
COMANCHE	3,505	408	2,915	182	2,507 D	11.6%	83.2%	12.3%	87.7%
CONCHO	1,346	174	1,156	16	982 D	12.9%	85.9%	13.1%	86.9%
COOKE	5,026	1,194	3,241	591	2,047 D	23.8%	64.5%	26.9%	73.1%
CORYELL	2,761	310	2,350	101	2,040 D	11.2%	85.1%	11.7%	88.3%
COTTLE	1,453	102	1,318	33	1,216 D	7.0%	90.7%	7.2%	92.8%
CRANE	921	70	812	39	742 D	7.6%	88.2%	7.9%	92.1%
CROCKETT	545	127	400	18	273 D	23.3%	73.4%	24.1%	75.9%
CROSBY	2,069	168	1,731	170	1,563 D	8.1%	83.7%	8.8%	91.2%
CULBERSON	306	38	244	24	206 D	12.4%	79.7%	13.5%	86.5%
DALLAM	1,943	399	1,504	40	1,105 D	20.5%	77.4%	21.0%	79.0%
DALLAS	94,344	35,664	47,464	11,216	11,800 D	37.8%	50.3%	42.9%	57.1%
DAWSON	3,141	393	2,605	143	2,212 D	12.5%	82.9%	13.1%	86.9%
DEAF SMITH	2,089	535	1,496	58	961 D	25.6%	71.6%	26.3%	73.7%
DELTA	1,900	146	1,594	160	1,448 D	7.7%	83.9%	8.4%	91.6%

TEXAS

PRESIDENT 1944 / PRESIDENT 1948

County	1944 Total Vote	Republican	Democratic	Other	Rep.-Dem. Plurality	%TV Rep	%TV Dem	%MV Rep	%MV Dem	1948 Total Vote	Republican	Democratic	Other	Rep.-Dem. Plurality	%TV Rep	%TV Dem	%MV Rep	%MV Dem
DENTON	7,110	771	5,584	755	4,813 D	10.8%	78.5%	12.1%	87.9%	6,953	1,531	4,549	873	3,018 D	22.0%	65.4%	25.2%	74.8%
DE WITT	4,187	1,879	1,884	424	5 D	44.9%	45.0%	49.9%	50.1%	3,647	1,612	1,808	227	196 D	44.2%	49.6%	47.1%	52.9%
DICKENS	1,879	141	1,517	121	1,476 D	7.5%	86.1%	8.0%	92.0%	1,700	115	1,492	93	1,377 D	6.8%	87.8%	7.2%	92.8%
DIMMIT	977	328	554	95	226 D	33.6%	56.7%	37.2%	62.8%	1,318	384	863	71	479 D	29.1%	65.5%	30.8%	69.2%
DONLEY	1,562	280	1,170	112	890 D	17.9%	74.9%	19.3%	80.7%	1,692	241	1,372	79	1,131 D	14.2%	81.1%	14.9%	85.1%
DUVAL	3,518	136	3,353	29	3,217 D	3.9%	95.3%	3.9%	96.1%	3,679	117	3,551	11	3,434 D	3.2%	96.5%	3.2%	96.8%
EASTLAND	6,072	643	4,607	822	3,964 D	10.6%	75.9%	12.2%	87.8%	6,665	1,177	5,121	367	3,944 D	17.7%	76.8%	18.7%	81.3%
ECTOR	3,091	432	2,265	394	1,833 D	14.0%	73.3%	16.0%	84.0%	5,694	1,145	4,305	244	3,160 D	20.1%	75.6%	21.0%	79.0%
EDWARDS	586	187	348	51	161 D	31.9%	59.4%	35.0%	65.0%	539	185	329	25	144 D	34.3%	61.0%	36.0%	64.0%
ELLIS	8,304	666	7,065	573	6,399 D	8.0%	85.1%	8.6%	91.4%	7,665	1,055	5,792	818	4,737 D	13.8%	75.6%	15.4%	84.6%
EL PASO	15,718	2,072	11,426	2,220	9,354 D	13.2%	72.7%	15.4%	84.6%	21,448	5,544	15,341	563	9,797 D	25.8%	71.5%	26.5%	73.5%
ERATH	4,171	411	3,330	430	2,919 D	9.9%	79.8%	11.0%	89.0%	4,002	598	3,172	232	2,574 D	14.9%	79.3%	15.5%	84.1%
FALLS	4,219	377	3,191	651	2,814 D	8.9%	75.6%	10.6%	89.4%	4,218	546	3,385	287	2,839 D	12.9%	80.3%	13.9%	86.1%
FANNIN	7,163	677	5,984	502	5,307 D	9.5%	83.5%	10.2%	89.8%	7,065	553	6,132	380	5,579 D	7.8%	86.8%	8.3%	91.7%
FAYETTE	6,030	1,611	3,156	1,263	1,545 D	26.7%	52.3%	33.8%	66.2%	5,298	1,737	3,106	455	1,369 D	32.8%	58.6%	35.9%	64.1%
FISHER	2,332	154	2,041	137	1,886 D	6.6%	87.5%	7.0%	93.0%	2,285	149	2,063	73	1,914 D	6.5%	90.3%	6.7%	93.3%
FLOYD	2,448	370	1,756	322	1,386 D	15.1%	71.7%	17.4%	82.6%	2,653	344	2,174	135	1,830 D	13.0%	81.9%	13.7%	86.3%
FOARD	1,080	84	925	71	841 D	7.8%	85.6%	8.3%	91.7%	876	90	751	35	661 D	10.3%	85.7%	10.7%	89.3%
FORT BEND	3,980	442	2,781	757	2,339 D	11.1%	69.9%	13.7%	86.3%	3,613	1,016	2,058	539	1,042 D	28.1%	57.0%	33.1%	66.9%
FRANKLIN	1,601	147	1,336	118	1,189 D	9.2%	83.4%	9.9%	90.1%	1,527	146	1,236	145	1,090 D	9.6%	80.9%	10.6%	89.4%
FREESTONE	3,022	277	2,427	318	2,150 D	9.2%	80.3%	10.2%	89.8%	3,230	460	2,265	505	1,805 D	14.2%	70.1%	16.9%	83.1%
FRIO	1,369	293	951	125	658 D	21.4%	69.5%	23.6%	76.4%	1,341	345	898	98	553 D	25.7%	67.0%	27.8%	72.2%
GAINES	1,471	173	1,173	125	1,000 D	11.8%	79.7%	12.9%	87.1%	1,794	207	1,465	122	1,258 D	11.5%	81.7%	12.4%	87.6%
GALVESTON	15,074	1,542	11,748	1,784	10,206 D	10.2%	77.9%	11.6%	88.4%	18,792	4,857	12,491	1,444	7,634 D	25.8%	66.5%	28.0%	72.0%
GARZA	1,159	144	842	173	698 D	12.4%	72.6%	14.6%	85.4%	1,110	176	861	73	685 D	15.9%	77.6%	17.0%	83.0%
GILLESPIE	3,573	2,950	333	290	2,617 R	82.6%	9.3%	89.9%	10.1%	3,413	2,741	593	79	2,148 R	80.3%	17.4%	82.2%	17.8%
GLASSCOCK	269	34	185	50	151 D	12.6%	68.8%	15.5%	84.5%	278	69	188	21	119 D	24.8%	67.6%	26.8%	73.2%
GOLIAD	1,348	609	641	98	32 D	45.2%	47.6%	48.7%	51.3%	1,035	450	454	131	4 D	43.5%	43.9%	49.8%	50.2%
GONZALES	3,987	841	2,804	342	1,963 D	21.1%	70.3%	23.1%	76.9%	3,599	666	2,612	321	1,946 D	18.5%	72.6%	20.3%	79.7%
GRAY	4,989	1,739	3,067	183	1,328 D	34.9%	61.5%	36.2%	63.8%	5,696	1,594	3,699	403	2,105 D	28.0%	64.9%	30.1%	69.9%
GRAYSON	14,070	1,372	11,636	1,062	10,264 D	9.8%	82.7%	10.5%	89.5%	14,148	2,174	10,991	983	8,817 D	15.4%	77.7%	16.5%	83.5%
GREGG	9,077	1,412	6,401	1,264	4,989 D	15.6%	70.5%	18.1%	81.9%	10,565	2,477	5,104	2,984	2,627 D	23.4%	48.3%	32.7%	67.3%
GRIMES	1,970	137	1,559	274	1,422 D	7.0%	79.1%	8.1%	91.9%	1,720	336	901	483	565 D	19.5%	52.4%	27.2%	72.8%
GUADALUPE	4,343	2,556	1,583	204	973 R	58.9%	36.4%	61.8%	38.2%	4,908	2,502	2,119	287	383 R	51.0%	43.2%	54.1%	45.9%
HALE	4,379	712	3,066	601	2,354 D	16.3%	70.0%	18.8%	81.2%	5,310	1,013	3,995	302	2,982 D	19.1%	75.2%	20.2%	79.8%
HALL	2,108	164	1,812	132	1,648 D	7.8%	86.0%	8.3%	91.7%	2,376	174	2,122	80	1,948 D	7.3%	89.3%	7.6%	92.4%
HAMILTON	2,499	344	1,790	365	1,446 D	13.8%	71.6%	16.1%	83.9%	2,339	478	1,725	136	1,247 D	20.4%	73.7%	21.7%	78.3%
HANSFORD	842	203	590	49	387 D	24.1%	70.1%	25.6%	74.4%	1,128	206	895	27	689 D	18.3%	79.3%	18.7%	81.3%
HARDEMAN	2,173	223	1,756	194	1,533 D	10.3%	80.8%	11.3%	88.7%	1,976	226	1,654	96	1,428 D	11.4%	83.7%	12.1%	88.0%
HARTIN	3,126	243	2,632	251	2,389 D	7.8%	84.2%	8.5%	91.5%	3,043	196	2,233	614	2,037 D	6.4%	73.4%	8.1%	91.9%
HARRIS	104,119	11,843	71,077	21,199	59,234 D	11.4%	68.3%	14.3%	85.7%	122,617	43,117	58,488	21,012	15,371 D	35.2%	47.7%	42.4%	57.6%
HARRISON	5,009	619	3,588	802	2,969 D	12.4%	71.6%	14.7%	85.3%	5,588	946	2,504	2,138	1,558 D	16.9%	44.8%	27.4%	72.6%
HARTLEY	520	26	484	10	458 D	5.0%	93.1%	5.1%	94.9%	567	83	477	7	394 D	14.6%	84.1%	14.8%	85.2%
HASKELL	3,083	261	2,573	249	2,312 D	8.5%	83.5%	9.2%	90.8%	2,999	181	2,735	83	2,554 D	6.0%	91.2%	6.2%	93.8%
HAYS	2,428	495	1,690	243	1,195 D	20.4%	69.6%	22.7%	77.3%	2,987	555	2,239	193	1,684 D	18.6%	75.0%	19.9%	80.1%
HEMPHILL	1,143	274	792	77	518 D	24.0%	69.3%	25.7%	74.3%	1,178	201	930	47	729 D	17.1%	78.9%	17.8%	82.2%
HENDERSON	4,220	427	3,219	574	2,792 D	10.1%	76.3%	11.7%	88.3%	4,413	540	3,669	204	3,129 D	12.2%	83.1%	12.8%	87.2%
HIDALGO	12,034	4,080	7,250	904	3,170 D	33.9%	60.2%	36.0%	64.0%	16,018	6,220	9,526	272	3,306 D	38.8%	59.5%	39.5%	60.5%
HILL	5,984	516	4,876	592	4,360 D	8.6%	81.5%	9.6%	90.4%	5,395	657	4,362	376	3,705 D	12.2%	80.9%	13.2%	86.8%
HOCKLEY	3,367	319	2,641	407	2,322 D	9.5%	78.4%	10.8%	89.2%	3,631	346	3,071	214	2,725 D	9.5%	84.6%	10.1%	89.9%
HOOD	1,472	146	1,203	123	1,057 D	9.9%	81.7%	10.8%	89.2%	1,504	169	1,273	62	1,104 D	11.2%	84.6%	11.7%	88.3%
HOPKINS	4,876	533	3,981	362	3,448 D	10.9%	81.6%	11.8%	88.2%	4,667	479	3,885	303	3,406 D	10.3%	83.2%	11.0%	89.0%
HOUSTON	3,146	233	2,329	584	2,096 D	7.4%	74.0%	9.1%	90.9%	3,104	532	2,014	558	1,482 D	17.1%	64.9%	20.9%	79.1%
HOWARD	4,334	334	3,586	412	3,252 D	7.7%	82.8%	8.5%	91.5%	5,052	561	4,179	312	3,618 D	11.1%	82.7%	11.8%	88.2%
HUDSPETH	396	35	333	28	298 D	8.8%	84.1%	9.5%	90.5%	498	49	437	12	388 D	9.8%	87.8%	10.1%	89.9%
HUNT	8,037	714	6,200	1,123	5,486 D	8.9%	77.1%	10.3%	89.7%	7,067	1,195	5,082	790	3,887 D	16.9%	71.9%	19.0%	81.0%
HUTCHINSON	3,826	864	2,760	202	1,896 D	22.6%	72.1%	23.8%	76.2%	6,009	1,382	4,527	100	3,145 D	23.0%	75.3%	23.4%	76.6%
IRION	453	54	363	36	309 D	11.9%	80.1%	12.9%	87.1%	440	63	366	11	303 D	14.3%	83.2%	14.7%	85.3%
JACK	1,964	217	1,484	263	1,267 D	11.0%	75.6%	12.8%	87.2%	1,817	265	1,426	126	1,161 D	14.6%	78.5%	15.7%	84.3%
JACKSON	2,296	344	1,708	244	1,364 D	15.0%	74.4%	16.8%	83.2%	1,972	488	1,343	141	855 D	24.7%	68.1%	26.7%	73.3%

TEXAS

PRESIDENT 1944

County	Total Vote	Republican	Democratic	Other	Rep.-Dem. Plurality	% Total Vote Rep.	% Total Vote Dem.	% Major Vote Rep.	% Major Vote Dem.
JASPER	2,427	341	1,850	236	1,509 D	14.1%	76.2%	15.6%	84.4%
JEFF DAVIS	457	51	331	35	280 D	12.2%	79.4%	13.4%	86.6%
JEFFERSON	29,080	4,525	22,066	2,489	17,541 D	15.6%	75.9%	17.0%	83.0%
JIM HOGG	713	77	620	16	543 D	10.8%	87.0%	11.0%	89.0%
JIM WELLS	3,191	1,113	1,908	170	795 D	34.9%	59.8%	36.8%	63.2%
JOHNSON	5,896	546	4,757	593	4,211 D	9.3%	80.7%	10.3%	89.7%
JONES	4,117	361	3,417	339	3,056 D	8.8%	83.0%	9.6%	90.4%
KARNES	2,856	692	1,920	244	1,228 D	24.2%	67.2%	26.5%	73.5%
KAUFMAN	5,136	430	4,251	455	3,821 D	8.4%	82.8%	9.2%	90.8%
KENDALL	1,762	1,337	309	116	1,028 R	75.9%	17.5%	81.2%	18.8%
KENEDY	82	60	16	6	44 R	73.2%	19.5%	78.9%	21.1%
KENT	658	31	572	55	541 D	4.7%	86.9%	5.1%	94.9%
KERR	2,943	1,358	1,377	208	19 D	46.1%	46.8%	49.7%	50.3%
KIMBLE	1,247	225	880	142	655 D	18.0%	70.6%	20.4%	79.6%
KING	256	13	228	15	215 D	5.1%	89.1%	5.4%	94.6%
KINNEY	602	200	401	1	201 D	33.2%	66.6%	33.3%	66.7%
KLEBERG	1,957	421	1,473	63	1,052 D	21.5%	75.3%	22.2%	77.8%
KNOX	2,142	156	1,785	201	1,629 D	7.3%	83.3%	8.0%	92.0%
LAMAR	7,747	725	6,283	739	5,558 D	9.4%	81.1%	10.3%	89.7%
LAMB	3,444	616	2,407	421	1,791 D	17.9%	69.9%	20.4%	79.6%
LAMPASAS	2,066	212	1,693	161	1,481 D	10.3%	81.9%	11.1%	88.9%
LA SALLE	860	127	692	41	565 D	14.8%	80.5%	15.5%	84.5%
LAVACA	4,955	960	3,406	589	2,446 D	19.4%	68.7%	22.0%	78.0%
LEE	2,196	771	953	472	182 D	35.1%	43.4%	44.7%	55.3%
LEON	1,898	140	1,569	189	1,429 D	7.4%	82.7%	8.2%	91.8%
LIBERTY	3,455	336	2,561	558	2,225 D	9.7%	74.1%	11.6%	88.4%
LIMESTONE	5,058	239	4,299	520	4,060 D	4.7%	85.0%	5.3%	94.7%
LIPSCOMB	1,032	396	551	85	155 D	38.4%	53.4%	41.8%	58.2%
LIVE OAK	1,405	548	642	215	94 D	39.0%	45.7%	46.1%	53.9%
LLANO	1,538	198	1,199	141	1,001 D	12.9%	78.0%	14.2%	85.8%
LOVING	84	18	60	6	42 D	21.4%	71.4%	23.1%	76.9%
LUBBOCK	10,856	1,169	7,654	2,033	6,485 D	10.8%	70.5%	13.2%	86.8%
LYNN	2,493	263	1,968	262	1,705 D	10.5%	78.9%	11.8%	88.2%
McCULLOCH	2,804	463	2,088	253	1,625 D	16.5%	74.5%	18.1%	81.9%
McLENNAN	18,531	1,668	15,236	1,627	13,568 D	9.0%	82.2%	9.8%	90.2%
McMULLEN	375	106	223	46	117 D	28.3%	59.5%	32.2%	67.8%
MADISON	1,307	65	1,115	127	1,050 D	5.0%	85.3%	5.5%	94.5%
MARION	1,381	219	1,057	105	838 D	15.9%	76.5%	17.2%	82.8%
MARTIN	986	131	758	97	627 D	13.3%	76.9%	14.7%	85.3%
MASON	1,496	420	822	254	402 D	28.1%	54.9%	33.8%	66.2%
MATAGORDA	3,067	412	1,854	801	1,442 D	13.4%	60.4%	18.2%	81.8%
MAVERICK	1,306	302	787	217	485 D	23.1%	60.3%	27.7%	72.3%
MEDINA	3,389	1,607	1,469	313	138 R	47.4%	43.3%	52.2%	47.8%
MENARD	1,122	96	776	250	680 D	8.5%	69.2%	11.0%	89.0%
MIDLAND	2,929	302	1,688	939	1,386 D	10.3%	57.6%	15.2%	84.8%
MILAM	4,974	623	3,537	814	2,914 D	12.5%	71.1%	15.0%	85.0%
MILLS	1,817	172	1,428	217	1,256 D	9.5%	78.6%	10.8%	89.2%
MITCHELL	2,573	218	2,215	140	1,997 D	8.5%	86.1%	9.0%	91.0%
MONTAGUE	3,710	429	2,900	381	2,471 D	11.6%	78.2%	12.9%	87.1%
MONTGOMERY	3,620	219	2,902	499	2,683 D	6.0%	80.2%	7.0%	93.0%
MOORE	1,394	313	999	82	686 D	22.5%	71.7%	23.9%	76.1%
MORRIS	1,476	122	1,269	85	1,147 D	8.3%	86.0%	8.8%	91.2%
MOTLEY	935	107	744	84	637 D	11.4%	79.6%	12.6%	87.4%
NACOGDOCHES	4,182	319	3,226	637	2,907 D	7.6%	77.1%	9.0%	91.0%
NAVARRO	7,401	449	6,298	654	5,849 D	6.1%	85.1%	6.7%	93.3%
NEWTON	1,224	187	910	127	723 D	15.3%	74.3%	17.0%	83.0%
NOLAN	3,747	322	3,071	354	2,749 D	8.6%	82.0%	9.5%	90.5%
NUECES	15,773	3,819	11,091	863	7,272 D	24.2%	70.3%	25.6%	74.4%
OCHILTREE	1,309	307	863	139	556 D	23.5%	65.9%	26.2%	73.8%
OLDHAM	409	93	277	39	184 D	22.7%	67.7%	25.1%	74.9%

PRESIDENT 1948

County	Total Vote	Republican	Democratic	Other	Rep.-Dem. Plurality	% Total Vote Rep.	% Total Vote Dem.	% Major Vote Rep.	% Major Vote Dem.
JASPER	2,527	264	1,777	466	1,493 D	11.2%	70.3%	13.8%	86.2%
JEFF DAVIS	402	75	309	18	234 D	18.7%	76.9%	19.5%	80.5%
JEFFERSON	33,514	5,775	22,475	5,290	16,726 D	17.2%	67.1%	20.4%	79.6%
JIM HOGG	829	73	725	31	652 D	8.8%	87.5%	9.1%	90.9%
JIM WELLS	5,299	1,402	3,781	116	2,379 D	26.5%	71.4%	27.0%	73.0%
JOHNSON	5,202	707	4,042	453	3,335 D	13.6%	77.7%	14.9%	85.1%
JONES	4,177	432	3,599	146	3,167 D	10.3%	86.2%	10.7%	89.3%
KARNES	2,971	592	2,198	181	1,606 D	19.9%	74.0%	21.2%	78.8%
KAUFMAN	4,890	764	3,479	647	2,715 D	15.7%	71.1%	18.0%	82.0%
KENDALL	1,789	1,237	511	71	696 R	67.5%	28.6%	70.3%	29.7%
KENEDY	81	31	45	5	14 D	38.3%	55.6%	40.8%	59.2%
KENT	534	33	479	22	446 D	6.2%	89.7%	6.4%	93.6%
KERR	3,204	1,520	1,505	179	15 R	47.4%	47.0%	50.2%	49.8%
KIMBLE	1,250	303	851	96	548 D	24.2%	68.1%	26.3%	73.7%
KING	241	6	231	4	225 D	2.5%	95.9%	2.5%	97.5%
KINNEY	575	175	370	30	195 D	30.4%	64.3%	32.1%	67.9%
KLEBERG	2,873	697	2,083	93	1,386 D	24.3%	72.5%	25.1%	74.9%
KNOX	2,008	157	1,792	59	1,635 D	7.8%	89.2%	8.1%	91.9%
LAMAR	8,365	1,018	6,306	1,041	5,288 D	12.2%	75.4%	13.9%	86.1%
LAMB	3,947	475	3,286	186	2,811 D	12.0%	83.3%	12.6%	87.4%
LAMPASAS	1,807	276	1,459	72	1,183 D	15.3%	80.7%	15.9%	84.1%
LA SALLE	913	135	719	59	584 D	14.8%	78.8%	15.8%	84.2%
LAVACA	4,511	1,165	3,046	300	1,881 D	25.8%	67.5%	27.7%	72.3%
LEE	2,122	465	1,540	117	1,075 D	21.9%	72.6%	23.2%	76.8%
LEON	1,690	184	1,231	275	1,047 D	10.9%	72.8%	13.0%	87.0%
LIBERTY	3,917	735	2,199	983	1,464 D	18.8%	56.1%	25.1%	74.9%
LIMESTONE	4,532	688	3,289	555	2,601 D	15.2%	72.6%	17.3%	82.7%
LIPSCOMB	1,049	354	668	27	314 D	33.7%	63.7%	34.6%	65.4%
LIVE OAK	1,567	479	945	143	466 D	30.6%	60.3%	33.6%	66.4%
LLANO	1,680	253	1,384	43	1,131 D	15.1%	82.4%	15.5%	84.5%
LOVING	95	29	62	4	33 D	30.5%	65.3%	31.9%	68.1%
LUBBOCK	15,207	2,837	11,114	1,256	8,277 D	18.7%	73.1%	20.3%	79.7%
LYNN	2,529	224	2,179	126	1,955 D	8.9%	86.2%	9.3%	90.7%
McCULLOCH	2,664	393	2,106	165	1,773 D	14.9%	79.5%	15.3%	83.9%
McLENNAN	20,457	3,388	16,034	1,035	12,646 D	16.6%	78.4%	17.4%	82.6%
McMULLEN	302	61	222	19	161 D	20.2%	73.5%	21.6%	78.4%
MADISON	1,134	134	801	199	667 D	11.8%	70.6%	14.3%	85.7%
MARION	1,082	200	703	179	503 D	18.5%	65.0%	22.1%	77.9%
MARTIN	1,077	77	945	55	868 D	7.1%	87.7%	7.5%	92.5%
MASON	1,356	498	836	22	338 D	36.7%	61.7%	37.3%	62.7%
MATAGORDA	3,299	1,016	1,628	655	612 D	30.8%	49.3%	38.5%	61.5%
MAVERICK	994	270	695	29	425 D	27.2%	69.9%	28.0%	72.0%
MEDINA	3,520	1,492	1,875	153	383 D	42.4%	53.3%	44.3%	55.7%
MENARD	996	283	663	50	380 D	28.4%	66.6%	29.9%	70.1%
MIDLAND	3,818	1,410	2,032	376	622 D	36.9%	53.2%	41.0%	59.0%
MILAM	4,292	646	3,261	385	2,615 D	15.1%	76.0%	16.5%	83.5%
MILLS	1,418	205	1,135	78	930 D	14.5%	80.0%	15.3%	84.7%
MITCHELL	2,484	230	2,181	73	1,951 D	9.3%	87.8%	9.5%	90.5%
MONTAGUE	3,557	475	2,872	210	2,397 D	13.3%	80.7%	14.2%	85.8%
MONTGOMERY	3,338	544	1,795	999	1,251 D	16.3%	53.8%	23.3%	76.7%
MOORE	2,101	323	1,748	30	1,425 D	15.4%	83.2%	15.6%	84.4%
MORRIS	1,556	143	1,164	249	1,021 D	9.2%	74.8%	10.9%	89.1%
MOTLEY	901	75	774	52	699 D	8.3%	85.9%	8.8%	91.2%
NACOGDOCHES	4,534	833	3,195	506	2,362 D	18.4%	70.5%	20.7%	79.3%
NAVARRO	6,494	1,188	4,679	627	3,491 D	18.3%	72.1%	20.2%	79.8%
NEWTON	1,399	110	957	332	847 D	7.9%	68.4%	10.3%	89.7%
NOLAN	4,066	552	3,408	106	2,856 D	13.6%	83.8%	13.9%	86.1%
NUECES	21,783	5,577	15,240	966	9,663 D	25.6%	70.0%	26.8%	73.2%
OCHILTREE	1,403	344	1,025	34	681 D	24.5%	73.1%	25.1%	74.9%
OLDHAM	458	100	339	19	239 D	21.8%	74.0%	22.8%	77.2%

TEXAS

PRESIDENT 1944

County	Total Vote	Republican	Democratic	Other	Rep.-Dem. Plurality	Total Vote Rep. %	Total Vote Dem. %	Major Vote Rep. %	Major Vote Dem. %
ORANGE	5,840	910	4,500	430	3,590 D	15.6	77.1	16.8	83.2
PALO PINTO	4,126	416	3,291	419	2,875 D	10.1	79.8	11.2	88.8
PANOLA	2,502	221	2,106	175	1,885 D	6.8	84.2	9.5	90.5
PARKER	4,555	559	3,503	493	2,944 D	12.3	76.9	13.8	86.2
PARMER	1,384	415	810	159	395 D	30.0	58.5	33.9	66.1
PECOS	1,653	305	1,226	122	921 D	18.5	74.2	19.9	80.1
POLK	2,254	154	1,817	283	1,663 D	6.8	80.6	7.8	92.2
POTTER	10,084	2,759	6,519	806	3,760 D	27.4	64.6	29.7	70.3
PRESIDIO	1,024	211	648	165	437 D	20.6	63.3	24.6	75.4
RAINS	916	137	628	151	491 D	15.0	68.5	17.9	82.1
RANDALL	2,115	409	1,439	267	1,030 D	19.3	68.0	22.1	77.9
REAGAN	520	53	426	41	373 D	10.2	81.9	11.1	88.9
REAL	549	163	326	60	163 D	29.7	59.4	33.3	66.7
RED RIVER	3,823	466	2,991	366	2,525 D	12.2	78.2	13.5	86.5
REEVES	1,510	201	1,157	152	956 D	13.3	76.6	14.8	85.2
REFUGIO	1,468	376	991	101	615 D	25.6	67.5	27.5	72.5
ROBERTS	418	89	289	40	200 D	21.3	69.1	23.5	76.5
ROBERTSON	3,042	126	2,681	235	2,555 D	4.1	88.1	4.5	95.5
ROCKWALL	1,358	98	1,153	107	1,055 D	7.2	84.9	7.8	92.2
RUNNELS	3,787	685	2,657	445	1,972 D	18.1	70.2	20.5	79.5
RUSK	6,844	637	5,232	975	4,595 D	9.3	76.4	10.9	89.1
SABINE	1,449	203	1,169	77	966 D	14.0	80.7	14.8	85.2
SAN AUGUSTINE	1,278	102	1,176		1,074 D	8.0	92.0	8.0	92.0
SAN JACINTO	720	53	522	145	469 D	7.4	72.5	7.8	92.2
SAN PATRICIO	3,841	878	2,712	251	1,834 D	22.9	70.6	24.5	75.5
SAN SABA	2,393	177	2,109	107	1,932 D	7.4	88.1	7.7	92.3
SCHLEICHER	695	84	520	91	436 D	12.1	74.8	13.9	86.1
SCURRY	2,176	285	1,761	130	1,476 D	13.1	80.9	13.9	86.1
SHACKELFORD	1,339	135	1,007	197	872 D	10.1	75.2	11.8	88.2
SHELBY	3,564	428	2,927	209	2,499 D	12.0	82.1	12.8	87.2
SHERMAN	584	97	454	33	357 D	16.6	77.7	17.6	82.4
SMITH	9,538	936	6,671	1,931	5,735 D	9.8	69.9	12.3	87.7
SOMERVELL	621	87	406	128	319 D	14.0	65.4	17.6	82.4
STARR	1,395	68	1,312	15	1,244 D	4.9	94.1	4.9	95.1
STEPHENS	2,804	217	2,104	483	1,887 D	7.7	75.0	9.3	90.7
STERLING	358	18	330	10	312 D	5.0	92.2	5.2	94.8
STONEWALL	1,080	89	902	89	813 D	8.2	83.5	9.0	91.0
SUTTON	636	118	449	69	331 D	18.6	70.6	20.8	79.2
SWISHER	1,819	331	1,275	213	944 D	18.2	70.1	20.6	79.4
TARRANT	51,065	4,113	36,791	10,161	32,678 D	8.1	72.0	10.1	89.9
TAYLOR	9,742	602	7,975	1,165	7,373 D	6.2	81.9	7.0	93.0
TERRELL	504	156	329	19	173 D	31.0	65.3	32.2	67.8
TERRY	2,780	273	2,304	203	2,031 D	9.8	82.9	10.6	89.4
THROCKMORTON	1,184	76	970	138	894 D	6.4	81.9	7.3	92.7
TITUS	3,117	265	2,612	230	2,347 D	8.5	84.1	9.2	90.8
TOM GREEN	8,306	1,125	6,272	909	5,147 D	13.5	75.5	15.2	84.8
TRAVIS	19,230	2,324	14,384	2,522	12,060 D	12.1	74.8	13.9	86.1
TRINITY	1,548	127	1,132	289	1,005 D	8.2	73.1	10.1	89.9
TYLER	1,421	219	1,037	165	818 D	15.4	73.0	17.4	82.6
UPSHUR	3,369	446	2,359	554	1,923 D	13.2	70.3	15.8	84.2
UPTON	915	105	742	68	637 D	11.5	81.1	12.4	87.6
UVALDE	2,356	856	1,322	178	466 D	36.3	56.1	39.3	60.7
VAL VERDE	1,985	676	1,210	99	534 D	34.1	61.0	35.8	64.2
VAN ZANDT	4,205	503	3,139	563	2,636 D	12.0	74.6	13.8	86.2
VICTORIA	3,684	936	2,331	417	1,395 D	25.4	63.3	28.7	71.3
WALKER	2,037	145	1,638	254	1,493 D	7.1	80.4	8.1	91.9
WALLER	1,436	190	1,007	239	817 D	13.2	70.1	15.9	84.1
WARD	1,819	268	1,448	103	1,180 D	14.7	79.6	15.6	84.4
WASHINGTON	4,025	534	1,387	2,104	853 D	13.3	34.5	27.8	72.2
WEBB	5,571	776	4,742	53	3,966 D	13.9	85.1	14.1	85.9

PRESIDENT 1948

County	Total Vote	Republican	Democratic	Other	Rep.-Dem. Plurality	Total Vote Rep. %	Total Vote Dem. %	Major Vote Rep. %	Major Vote Dem. %
ORANGE	6,813	987	4,957	869	3,970 D	14.5	72.8	16.6	83.4
PALO PINTO	5,045	977	3,736	332	2,759 D	19.4	74.1	20.7	79.3
PANOLA	2,818	256	1,751	811	1,495 D	9.1	62.1	12.8	87.2
PARKER	4,080	806	3,061	213	2,255 D	19.8	75.0	20.8	79.2
PARMER	1,421	280	1,091	50	811 D	19.7	76.8	20.4	79.6
PECOS	1,801	317	1,430	54	1,113 D	17.6	79.4	18.1	81.9
POLK	2,270	317	1,422	531	1,105 D	14.0	62.6	18.2	81.8
POTTER	14,222	4,110	9,622	490	5,512 D	28.9	67.7	29.9	70.1
PRESIDIO	1,153	212	907	34	695 D	18.4	78.7	18.9	81.1
RAINS	944	111	739	94	628 D	11.8	78.3	13.1	86.9
RANDALL	2,772	722	1,936	114	1,214 D	26.0	69.8	27.2	72.8
REAGAN	579	112	444	23	332 D	19.3	76.7	20.1	79.9
REAL	616	156	446	14	290 D	25.3	72.4	25.9	74.1
RED RIVER	3,957	323	2,987	647	2,664 D	8.2	75.5	9.8	90.2
REEVES	1,789	309	1,383	97	1,074 D	17.3	77.3	18.3	81.7
REFUGIO	2,199	489	1,637	73	1,148 D	22.2	74.4	23.0	77.0
ROBERTS	418	76	317	25	241 D	18.2	75.3	19.3	80.7
ROBERTSON	2,897	246	2,147	504	1,901 D	8.5	74.1	10.3	89.7
ROCKWALL	1,252	117	947	188	830 D	9.3	75.6	11.0	89.0
RUNNELS	3,615	526	2,954	135	2,428 D	14.6	81.7	15.1	84.9
RUSK	7,375	1,294	4,322	1,759	3,028 D	17.5	58.6	23.0	77.0
SABINE	1,432	104	1,078	250	974 D	7.3	75.3	8.8	91.2
SAN AUGUSTINE	1,265	137	858	270	721 D	10.8	67.8	13.8	86.2
SAN JACINTO	774	106	509	159	403 D	13.7	65.8	17.2	82.8
SAN PATRICIO	3,823	963	2,649	211	1,686 D	25.2	69.3	26.7	73.3
SAN SABA	2,303	184	2,050	69	1,866 D	8.0	89.0	8.2	91.8
SCHLEICHER	645	107	495	43	388 D	16.6	76.7	17.8	82.2
SCURRY	2,308	201	2,040	67	1,839 D	8.7	88.4	9.0	91.0
SHACKELFORD	1,146	211	892	43	681 D	18.4	77.8	19.1	80.9
SHELBY	4,036	307	3,051	678	2,744 D	7.6	75.6	9.1	90.9
SHERMAN	592	98	479	15	381 D	16.6	80.9	17.0	83.0
SMITH	11,309	3,181	6,473	1,655	3,292 D	28.1	57.2	33.0	67.0
SOMERVELL	583	91	446	46	355 D	15.6	76.5	16.9	83.1
STARR	2,188	179	1,996	13	1,817 D	8.2	91.2	8.2	91.8
STEPHENS	2,890	572	2,132	186	1,560 D	19.8	73.8	21.2	78.8
STERLING	268	17	244	7	227 D	6.3	91.0	6.5	93.5
STONEWALL	1,064	65	968	31	903 D	6.1	91.0	6.3	93.7
SUTTON	622	131	433	58	302 D	21.1	69.6	23.2	76.8
SWISHER	2,042	307	1,670	65	1,363 D	15.0	81.8	15.5	84.5
TARRANT	60,739	17,157	36,325	7,257	19,168 D	28.2	59.8	32.1	67.9
TAYLOR	10,373	1,658	8,184	531	6,526 D	16.0	78.9	16.8	83.2
TERRELL	265	78	171	16	93 D	29.4	64.5	31.3	68.7
TERRY	2,685	236	2,283	166	2,047 D	8.8	85.0	9.4	90.6
THROCKMORTON	1,120	63	1,026	31	963 D	5.6	91.6	5.8	94.2
TITUS	3,055	379	2,339	337	1,960 D	12.4	76.6	13.9	86.1
TOM GREEN	9,116	1,822	6,777	517	4,955 D	20.0	74.3	21.2	78.8
TRAVIS	27,207	5,994	19,598	1,615	13,604 D	22.0	72.0	23.4	76.6
TRINITY	1,315	150	905	260	755 D	11.4	68.8	14.2	85.8
TYLER	1,551	177	895	479	718 D	11.4	57.7	16.5	83.5
UPSHUR	3,165	555	2,118	492	1,563 D	17.5	66.9	20.8	79.2
UPTON	1,024	155	811	58	656 D	15.1	79.2	16.0	84.0
UVALDE	2,545	866	1,550	129	684 D	34.0	60.7	35.8	64.2
VAL VERDE	1,978	672	1,242	164	570 D	34.0	62.8	35.1	64.9
VAN ZANDT	4,350	578	3,264	508	2,686 D	13.3	75.0	15.0	85.0
VICTORIA	4,042	1,262	2,435	345	1,173 D	31.2	60.2	34.1	65.9
WALKER	2,564	570	1,439	555	869 D	22.2	56.1	28.4	71.6
WALLER	1,634	448	812	374	364 D	27.4	49.7	35.6	64.4
WARD	2,658	414	2,119	125	1,705 D	15.6	79.7	16.3	83.7
WASHINGTON	3,742	1,904	1,647	191	257 R	50.9	44.0	53.6	46.4
WEBB	5,695	1,004	4,595	96	3,591 D	17.6	80.7	17.9	82.1

TEXAS

PRESIDENT 1944

County	Total Vote	Republican	Democratic	Other	Rep.-Dem. Plurality	Percentage Total Vote Rep.	Dem.	Major Vote Rep.	Dem.
WHARTON	5,042	529	3,754	759	3,225 D	10.5%	74.5%	12.4%	87.6%
WHEELER	2,615	511	1,859	235	1,356 D	19.5%	71.5%	21.5%	78.5%
WICHITA	14,616	1,597	11,392	1,627	9,795 D	10.9%	77.9%	12.3%	87.7%
WILBARGER	4,419	517	3,382	520	2,865 D	11.7%	76.5%	13.3%	86.7%
WILLACY	1,737	754	846	137	92 D	43.4%	48.7%	47.1%	52.9%
WILLIAMSON	7,431	1,239	5,284	908	4,045 D	16.7%	71.1%	19.0%	81.0%
WILSON	3,533	676	2,666	191	1,990 D	19.1%	75.5%	20.2%	79.8%
WINKLER	1,193	120	1,004	69	884 D	10.1%	84.2%	10.7%	89.3%
WISE	3,979	444	3,114	421	2,670 D	11.2%	78.3%	12.5%	87.5%
WOOD	4,061	485	3,045	511	2,560 D	12.0%	75.4%	13.7%	86.3%
YOAKUM	839	106	646	87	540 D	12.6%	77.0%	14.1%	85.9%
YOUNG	4,114	327	3,183	604	2,855 D	7.9%	77.4%	9.3%	90.7%
ZAPATA	547	43	501	3	458 D	7.9%	91.6%	7.9%	92.1%
ZAVALA	1,129	342	696	91	354 D	30.3%	61.6%	32.9%	67.1%
TOTAL	1,150,334	191,423	821,605	137,306	630,182 D	16.6%	71.4%	18.9%	81.1%

PRESIDENT 1948

County	Total Vote	Republican	Democratic	Other	Rep.-Dem. Plurality	Percentage Total Vote Rep.	Dem.	Major Vote Rep.	Dem.
WHARTON	4,685	1,354	2,811	520	1,457 D	28.9%	60.0%	32.5%	67.5%
WHEELER	2,460	370	2,010	80	1,640 D	15.0%	81.7%	15.5%	84.5%
WICHITA	15,866	2,887	12,235	744	9,348 D	18.2%	77.1%	19.1%	80.9%
WILBARGER	3,800	529	2,963	308	2,434 D	13.9%	78.0%	15.1%	84.9%
WILLACY	1,924	676	1,139	109	463 D	35.1%	59.2%	37.2%	62.8%
WILLIAMSON	7,026	1,094	5,638	294	4,544 D	15.6%	80.2%	16.3%	83.7%
WILSON	3,020	593	2,313	114	1,720 D	19.6%	76.6%	20.4%	79.6%
WINKLER	1,983	296	1,588	99	1,292 D	14.9%	80.1%	15.7%	84.3%
WISE	3,778	448	3,064	266	2,616 D	11.9%	81.1%	12.8%	87.2%
WOOD	3,885	629	2,590	666	1,961 D	16.2%	66.7%	19.5%	80.5%
YOAKUM	1,020	119	861	40	742 D	11.7%	84.4%	12.1%	87.9%
YOUNG	3,898	516	3,175	207	2,659 D	13.2%	81.5%	14.0%	86.0%
ZAPATA	1,047	414	632	1	218 D	39.5%	60.4%	39.6%	60.4%
ZAVALA	986	306	618	62	312 D	31.0%	62.7%	33.1%	66.9%
TOTAL	1,249,577	303,467	824,235	121,875	520,768 D	24.3%	66.0%	26.9%	73.1%

TEXAS

PRESIDENT 1952

County	Total Vote	Republican	Democratic	Other	Rep.-Dem. Plurality	%TV Rep.	%TV Dem.	%MV Rep.	%MV Dem.
ANDERSON	8,109	4,637	3,462	10	1,175 R	57.2%	42.7%	57.3%	42.7%
ANDREWS	1,729	805	920	4	115 D	46.6%	53.2%	46.7%	53.3%
ANGELINA	10,942	4,705	6,224	13	1,519 D	43.0%	56.9%	43.1%	56.9%
ARANSAS	1,325	818	503	4	315 R	61.7%	38.0%	61.9%	38.1%
ARCHER	2,212	937	1,272	3	335 D	42.4%	57.5%	42.4%	57.6%
ARMSTRONG	996	562	425	9	137 R	56.4%	42.7%	56.9%	43.1%
ATASCOSA	4,281	2,147	2,124	10	23 R	50.2%	49.6%	50.3%	49.7%
AUSTIN	4,413	2,964	1,445	4	1,519 R	67.2%	32.7%	67.2%	32.8%
BAILEY	2,162	1,118	1,039	5	79 R	51.7%	48.0%	51.8%	48.1%
BANDERA	1,710	1,350	358	2	992 R	78.9%	20.9%	79.0%	21.0%
BASTROP	4,694	1,540	3,148	6	1,608 D	32.8%	67.1%	32.8%	67.2%
BAYLOR	2,024	879	1,142	3	263 D	43.4%	56.4%	43.5%	56.5%
BEE	4,126	2,536	1,583	7	953 R	61.5%	38.4%	61.6%	38.4%
BELL	14,358	4,862	9,484	12	4,622 D	33.9%	66.1%	33.9%	66.1%
BEXAR	116,136	65,391	50,260	485	15,131 R	56.3%	43.3%	56.5%	43.5%
BLANCO	1,618	919	697	2	222 R	56.8%	43.1%	56.9%	43.1%
BORDEN	392	182	210		28 D	46.4%	53.6%	46.4%	53.6%
BOSQUE	3,929	1,982	1,940	7	42 R	50.4%	49.4%	50.5%	49.5%
BOWIE	16,954	6,501	10,437	16	3,936 D	38.3%	61.6%	38.4%	61.6%
BRAZORIA	16,761	8,360	8,386	15	26 D	49.9%	50.0%	49.9%	50.1%
BRAZOS	8,896	4,681	4,213	2	468 R	52.6%	47.4%	52.6%	47.4%
BREWSTER	1,705	1,096	609		487 R	64.3%	35.7%	64.3%	35.7%
BRISCOE	1,203	692	508	3	184 R	57.5%	42.2%	57.7%	42.3%
BROOKS	2,387	809	1,577	1	768 D	33.9%	66.1%	33.9%	66.1%
BROWN	8,424	4,635	3,778	11	857 R	55.0%	44.8%	55.1%	44.9%
BURLESON	3,410	1,052	2,347	11	1,295 D	30.9%	68.8%	31.0%	69.0%
BURNET	2,703	1,270	1,431	2	161 D	47.0%	52.9%	47.0%	53.0%
CALDWELL	4,941	2,052	2,687	3	835 D	41.5%	58.4%	41.5%	58.5%
CALHOUN	2,222	1,406	813	3	593 R	63.3%	36.6%	63.4%	36.6%
CALLAHAN	2,938	1,431	1,502	5	71 D	48.7%	51.1%	48.8%	51.2%
CAMERON	21,602	14,018	7,559	25	6,459 R	64.9%	35.0%	65.0%	35.0%
CAMP	2,487	951	1,535	1	584 D	38.2%	61.7%	38.3%	61.7%
CARSON	2,552	1,471	1,071	10	400 R	57.6%	41.9%	57.9%	42.1%
CASS	5,665	2,502	3,160	3	658 D	44.2%	55.8%	44.2%	55.8%
CASTRO	1,996	1,169	825	2	344 R	58.6%	41.3%	58.6%	41.4%
CHAMBERS	2,617	1,497	1,116	4	381 R	57.2%	42.6%	57.3%	42.7%
CHEROKEE	7,707	3,825	3,858	14	43 D	49.6%	50.0%	49.7%	50.3%
CHILDRESS	3,771	1,890	1,879	2	11 R	50.1%	49.8%	50.1%	49.9%
CLAY	3,316	1,272	2,044		772 D	38.4%	61.6%	38.4%	61.6%
COCHRAN	1,893	780	936	7	156 D	46.1%	53.5%	46.3%	53.7%
COKE	1,317	576	736	5	160 D	43.7%	55.9%	43.9%	56.1%
COLEMAN	4,387	2,555	1,824	8	731 R	58.2%	41.6%	58.3%	41.7%
COLLIN	9,950	4,037	5,906	7	1,869 D	40.6%	59.4%	40.6%	59.4%
COLLINGSWORTH	2,657	1,334	1,321	2	13 R	50.2%	49.7%	50.3%	49.8%
COLORADO	5,290	3,237	2,043	10	1,194 R	61.2%	38.6%	61.3%	38.7%
COMAL	4,606	3,350	1,252	4	2,098 R	72.7%	27.2%	72.8%	27.2%
COMANCHE	4,596	2,411	2,181	4	230 R	52.5%	47.5%	52.5%	47.5%
CONCHO	1,516	808	708		100 R	53.3%	46.7%	53.3%	46.7%
COOKE	7,050	4,385	2,657	8	1,728 R	62.2%	37.7%	62.3%	37.7%
CORYELL	4,092	1,658	2,432	2	774 D	40.5%	59.4%	40.5%	59.5%
COTTLE	1,862	494	1,368		874 D	26.5%	73.5%	26.5%	73.5%
CRANE	1,488	621	857	10	236 D	41.7%	57.6%	41.9%	58.0%
CROCKETT	960	654	306		348 R	68.1%	31.9%	68.1%	31.9%
CROSBY	2,603	1,053	1,550		497 D	40.5%	59.5%	40.5%	59.5%
CULBERSON	583	331	252		79 R	56.8%	43.2%	56.8%	43.2%
DALLAM	2,673	1,464	1,197	12	267 R	54.7%	44.8%	55.0%	45.0%
DALLAS	188,462	118,218	69,394	850	48,824 R	62.7%	36.8%	63.0%	37.0%
DAWSON	4,481	2,388	2,093		295 R	53.3%	46.7%	53.3%	46.7%
DEAF SMITH	3,483	2,468	1,005	9	1,462 R	70.9%	28.9%	71.0%	29.0%
DELTA	2,295	707	1,585	3	878 D	30.8%	69.1%	30.8%	69.2%

PRESIDENT 1956

County	Total Vote	Republican	Democratic	Other	Rep.-Dem. Plurality	%TV Rep.	%TV Dem.	%MV Rep.	%MV Dem.
ANDERSON	6,914	4,181	2,710	23	1,471 R	60.5%	39.2%	60.7%	39.3%
ANDREWS	2,113	1,131	968	14	163 R	53.5%	45.8%	53.9%	46.1%
ANGELINA	10,096	5,274	4,781	41	493 R	52.2%	47.4%	52.5%	47.5%
ARANSAS	1,189	757	425	7	332 R	63.7%	35.7%	64.0%	36.0%
ARCHER	1,899	825	1,067	7	242 D	43.4%	56.2%	43.6%	56.4%
ARMSTRONG	798	372	422	4	50 D	46.6%	52.9%	46.9%	53.1%
ATASCOSA	3,307	1,804	1,492	11	312 R	54.6%	45.1%	54.7%	45.3%
AUSTIN	3,726	2,501	1,215	10	1,286 R	67.1%	32.6%	67.3%	32.7%
BAILEY	2,151	871	1,274	6	403 D	40.5%	59.2%	40.6%	59.4%
BANDERA	1,424	1,083	336	5	747 R	76.1%	23.6%	76.3%	23.7%
BASTROP	4,045	1,531	2,504	10	973 D	37.8%	61.9%	37.9%	62.1%
BAYLOR	1,766	715	1,047	4	332 D	40.5%	59.3%	40.6%	59.4%
BEE	4,345	2,401	1,929	15	472 R	55.3%	44.4%	55.5%	44.5%
BELL	13,932	4,285	9,603	44	5,318 D	30.8%	68.9%	30.9%	69.1%
BEXAR	113,331	65,901	46,790	640	19,111 R	58.1%	41.3%	58.5%	41.5%
BLANCO	1,418	796	615	7	181 R	56.4%	43.4%	56.4%	43.6%
BORDEN	368	127	240	1	113 D	34.5%	65.2%	34.6%	65.4%
BOSQUE	3,331	1,654	1,670	7	16 D	49.7%	50.1%	49.8%	50.2%
BOWIE	14,602	6,823	7,675	104	852 D	46.7%	52.5%	47.1%	52.9%
BRAZORIA	16,881	9,536	7,137	208	2,399 R	56.5%	42.3%	57.2%	42.8%
BRAZOS	8,436	4,942	3,463	31	1,479 R	58.6%	41.1%	58.8%	41.2%
BREWSTER	1,324	837	479	8	358 R	63.2%	36.2%	63.6%	36.4%
BRISCOE	1,008	357	648	3	291 D	35.4%	64.3%	35.5%	64.5%
BROOKS	1,920	802	1,108	10	306 D	41.8%	57.7%	42.0%	58.0%
BROWN	6,880	3,664	3,195	21	469 R	53.2%	46.4%	53.4%	46.6%
BURLESON	2,915	1,173	1,726	16	553 D	40.2%	59.2%	40.5%	59.5%
BURNET	2,590	1,163	1,422	5	259 D	44.9%	54.9%	45.0%	55.0%
CALDWELL	4,265	1,747	2,513	5	766 D	41.0%	58.9%	41.0%	59.0%
CALHOUN	2,992	1,912	1,067	13	845 R	63.9%	35.7%	64.2%	35.8%
CALLAHAN	2,353	1,140	1,199	14	59 D	48.4%	51.0%	48.7%	51.3%
CAMERON	21,022	11,952	8,829	241	3,123 R	56.9%	42.0%	57.5%	42.5%
CAMP	2,029	958	1,053	18	95 D	47.2%	51.9%	47.6%	52.4%
CARSON	2,044	1,061	976	7	85 R	51.9%	47.7%	52.1%	47.9%
CASS	5,409	2,970	2,395	44	575 R	54.9%	44.2%	55.4%	44.6%
CASTRO	2,006	697	1,305	4	608 D	34.7%	65.1%	34.8%	65.2%
CHAMBERS	2,393	1,520	860	13	660 R	63.5%	35.9%	63.9%	36.1%
CHEROKEE	6,961	4,022	2,912	27	1,110 R	57.8%	41.8%	58.0%	42.0%
CHILDRESS	2,780	1,268	1,503	9	235 D	45.6%	54.1%	45.8%	54.2%
CLAY	2,808	990	1,813	5	823 D	35.3%	64.6%	35.3%	64.7%
COCHRAN	1,523	599	923	1	324 D	39.3%	60.6%	39.4%	60.6%
COKE	1,245	549	690	6	141 D	44.1%	55.4%	44.3%	55.7%
COLEMAN	3,841	2,247	1,577	17	670 R	58.5%	41.1%	58.8%	41.2%
COLLIN	9,137	3,823	5,280	34	1,457 D	41.8%	57.8%	42.0%	58.0%
COLLINGSWORTH	2,055	815	1,229	11	414 D	39.7%	59.8%	39.9%	60.1%
COLORADO	4,367	2,691	1,648	28	1,043 R	61.6%	37.7%	62.0%	38.0%
COMAL	4,557	3,397	1,140	20	2,257 R	74.5%	25.0%	74.9%	25.1%
COMANCHE	3,878	1,900	1,962	16	62 D	49.0%	50.6%	49.2%	50.8%
CONCHO	1,142	574	567	1	7 R	50.3%	49.6%	50.3%	49.7%
COOKE	6,473	4,164	2,272	37	1,892 R	64.3%	35.1%	64.7%	35.3%
CORYELL	3,883	1,509	2,372	2	863 D	38.9%	61.1%	38.9%	61.1%
COTTLE	1,469	329	1,138	2	809 D	22.4%	77.5%	22.4%	77.6%
CRANE	1,348	626	707	15	81 D	46.4%	52.4%	47.0%	53.0%
CROCKETT	1,009	702	305	2	397 R	69.6%	30.2%	69.7%	30.3%
CROSBY	2,514	704	1,804	6	1,100 D	28.0%	71.8%	28.1%	71.9%
CULBERSON	596	324	269	3	55 R	54.4%	45.1%	54.6%	45.4%
DALLAM	2,103	1,018	1,074	11	56 D	48.4%	51.1%	48.7%	51.3%
DALLAS	192,695	125,361	65,472	1,862	59,889 R	65.1%	34.0%	65.7%	34.3%
DAWSON	3,670	1,615	2,049	6	434 D	44.0%	55.8%	44.1%	55.9%
DEAF SMITH	3,055	1,685	1,361	9	324 R	55.2%	44.5%	55.3%	44.7%
DELTA	1,877	605	1,262	10	657 D	32.2%	67.2%	32.4%	67.6%

TEXAS

PRESIDENT 1952

County	Total Vote	Republican	Democratic	Other	Rep.-Dem. Plurality	Total Vote % Rep.	Total Vote % Dem.	Major Vote % Rep.	Major Vote % Dem.
DENTON	11,137	5,840	5,289	8	551 R	52.4%	47.5%	52.5%	47.5%
DE WITT	6,018	4,075	1,934	9	2,141 R	67.7%	32.1%	67.8%	32.2%
DICKENS	2,035	782	1,249	4	467 D	38.4%	61.4%	38.5%	61.5%
DIMMIT	1,460	954	503	3	451 R	65.3%	34.5%	65.5%	34.5%
DONLEY	2,056	1,150	900	6	250 R	55.9%	43.8%	56.1%	43.9%
DUVAL	3,989	672	3,316	1	2,644 D	16.8%	83.1%	16.9%	83.1%
EASTLAND	7,906	4,518	3,370	18	1,148 R	57.1%	42.6%	57.3%	42.7%
ECTOR	13,537	8,259	5,270	8	2,989 R	61.0%	38.9%	61.0%	39.0%
EDWARDS	796	586	210	2	376 R	73.6%	25.3%	73.6%	26.4%
ELLIS	10,482	4,183	6,275	24	2,092 D	39.9%	59.9%	40.0%	60.0%
EL PASO	34,647	20,005	14,595	47	5,410 R	57.7%	42.1%	57.8%	42.2%
ERATH	5,915	3,249	2,664	2	585 R	54.9%	45.0%	54.9%	45.1%
FALLS	5,257	1,962	3,287	8	1,325 D	37.3%	62.5%	37.4%	62.6%
FANNIN	7,465	2,099	5,363	3	3,264 D	28.1%	71.8%	28.1%	71.9%
FAYETTE	6,800	4,240	2,557	3	1,683 R	62.4%	37.6%	62.4%	37.6%
FISHER	2,359	952	1,405	2	453 D	40.4%	59.6%	40.4%	59.6%
FLOYD	3,534	2,066	1,463	5	603 R	58.5%	41.4%	58.5%	41.5%
FOARD	1,256	418	830	8	412 D	33.3%	66.1%	33.5%	66.5%
FORT BEND	7,226	3,974	3,241	11	733 R	55.0%	44.9%	55.1%	44.9%
FRANKLIN	1,923	564	1,358	1	794 D	29.3%	70.6%	29.3%	70.7%
FREESTONE	4,611	1,707	2,902	2	1,195 D	37.0%	62.9%	37.0%	63.0%
FRIO	2,001	1,011	983	7	28 R	50.5%	49.1%	50.7%	49.3%
GAINES	2,905	1,350	1,540	15	190 D	46.5%	53.0%	46.7%	53.3%
GALVESTON	34,920	15,715	19,058	147	3,343 D	45.0%	54.6%	45.2%	54.8%
GARZA	1,541	742	797	2	55 D	48.2%	51.7%	48.2%	51.8%
GILLESPIE	3,995	3,687	300	8	3,387 R	92.3%	7.5%	92.5%	7.5%
GLASSCOCK	432	235	197		38 R	54.4%	45.6%	54.4%	45.6%
GOLIAD	1,518	1,065	452	1	613 R	70.2%	29.8%	70.2%	29.8%
GONZALES	4,815	2,249	2,563	3	314 D	46.7%	53.2%	46.7%	53.3%
GRAY	8,857	5,467	3,367	23	2,100 R	61.7%	38.0%	61.9%	38.1%
GRAYSON	18,194	7,736	10,435	23	2,699 D	42.6%	57.4%	42.6%	57.4%
GREGG	18,794	10,583	7,969	242	2,614 R	56.3%	42.4%	57.0%	43.0%
GRIMES	2,920	1,557	1,362	1	195 R	53.3%	46.6%	53.3%	46.7%
GUADALUPE	6,740	4,396	2,330	14	2,066 R	65.2%	34.6%	65.4%	34.6%
HALE	8,226	4,858	3,351	17	1,507 R	59.1%	40.7%	59.2%	40.8%
HALL	2,999	1,253	1,744	2	491 D	41.8%	58.2%	41.8%	58.2%
HAMILTON	3,448	2,130	1,313	5	817 R	61.8%	38.1%	61.9%	38.1%
HANSFORD	1,692	1,234	456	2	778 R	72.9%	27.0%	73.0%	27.0%
HARDEMAN	2,821	1,571	1,242	8	329 R	55.7%	44.0%	55.8%	44.2%
HARDIN	5,082	1,653	3,423	6	1,770 D	32.5%	67.4%	32.6%	67.4%
HARRIS	254,497	146,665	107,604	228	39,061 R	57.6%	42.3%	57.7%	42.3%
HARRISON	9,229	4,708	4,516	5	192 R	51.0%	48.9%	51.0%	49.0%
HARTLEY	674	468	402	4	66 R	53.5%	46.0%	53.8%	46.2%
HASKELL	3,777	1,290	2,481	6	1,191 D	34.2%	65.7%	34.2%	65.8%
HAYS	4,208	2,135	2,070	3	65 R	50.7%	49.2%	50.8%	49.2%
HEMPHILL	1,482	892	590		302 R	60.2%	39.8%	60.2%	39.8%
HENDERSON	6,974	2,534	4,439	1	1,905 D	36.3%	63.7%	36.3%	63.7%
HIDALGO	24,602	15,303	9,251	48	6,052 R	62.3%	37.6%	62.3%	37.7%
HILL	7,747	3,242	4,504	1	1,262 D	41.9%	58.1%	41.8%	58.1%
HOCKLEY	5,620	2,651	2,962	7	311 D	47.2%	52.7%	47.2%	52.8%
HOOD	2,136	780	1,356		576 D	36.5%	63.5%	36.5%	63.5%
HOPKINS	6,218	2,460	3,750	8	1,290 D	39.6%	60.3%	39.6%	60.4%
HOUSTON	5,126	2,222	2,900	4	678 D	43.3%	56.6%	43.3%	56.6%
HOWARD	8,202	3,412	4,779	11	1,367 D	41.6%	58.3%	41.7%	58.3%
HUDSPETH	622	355	262	5	93 R	57.1%	42.1%	57.5%	42.5%
HUNT	10,581	5,614	4,953	14	661 R	53.1%	46.8%	53.1%	46.9%
HUTCHINSON	10,465	5,369	5,083	13	286 R	51.3%	48.6%	51.4%	48.6%
IRION	550	268	282		14 D	48.7%	51.3%	48.7%	51.3%
JACK	2,539	1,406	1,130	3	276 R	55.4%	44.5%	55.4%	44.6%
JACKSON	3,698	2,113	1,584	1	529 R	57.1%	42.8%	57.2%	42.8%

PRESIDENT 1956

County	Total Vote	Republican	Democratic	Other	Rep.-Dem. Plurality	Total Vote % Rep.	Total Vote % Dem.	Major Vote % Rep.	Major Vote % Dem.
DENTON	10,346	5,350	4,972	24	378 R	51.7%	48.1%	51.8%	48.2%
DE WITT	4,849	3,401	1,435	13	1,966 R	70.1%	29.6%	70.3%	29.7%
DICKENS	1,808	565	1,243		678 D	31.2%	68.8%	31.2%	68.8%
DIMMIT	1,139	705	427	7	278 R	61.9%	37.5%	62.3%	37.7%
DONLEY	1,731	826	903	2	77 D	47.7%	52.2%	47.8%	52.2%
DUVAL	4,575	1,459	3,110	6	1,651 D	31.9%	68.0%	31.9%	68.1%
EASTLAND	6,103	3,580	2,512	11	1,068 R	58.6%	41.1%	58.8%	41.2%
ECTOR	14,103	8,805	5,109	189	3,696 R	62.4%	36.2%	63.3%	36.7%
EDWARDS	669	533	133	3	400 R	79.7%	19.9%	80.0%	20.0%
ELLIS	8,820	3,585	5,211	24	1,626 D	40.6%	59.1%	40.8%	59.2%
EL PASO	33,882	18,532	15,157	193	3,375 R	54.7%	44.7%	55.0%	45.0%
ERATH	5,171	2,775	2,377	19	398 R	53.7%	46.0%	53.9%	46.1%
FALLS	4,507	1,819	2,674	14	855 D	40.4%	59.3%	40.5%	59.5%
FANNIN	6,420	1,910	4,504	6	2,594 D	29.8%	70.2%	29.8%	70.2%
FAYETTE	5,904	3,574	2,282	48	1,292 R	60.5%	38.7%	61.0%	39.0%
FISHER	2,343	673	1,664	6	991 D	28.8%	71.0%	28.8%	71.2%
FLOYD	3,221	1,445	1,767	9	322 D	44.9%	54.9%	45.0%	55.0%
FOARD	932	243	687	2	444 D	26.1%	73.7%	26.1%	73.9%
FORT BEND	6,316	3,779	2,464	73	1,315 R	59.8%	39.0%	60.5%	39.5%
FRANKLIN	1,641	556	1,082	3	526 D	33.9%	65.9%	33.9%	66.1%
FREESTONE	3,455	1,627	1,813	15	186 D	47.1%	52.5%	47.3%	52.7%
FRIO	1,721	825	886	10	61 D	47.9%	51.5%	48.2%	51.8%
GAINES	2,779	1,244	1,527	8	283 D	44.8%	54.9%	44.9%	55.1%
GALVESTON	33,536	17,567	15,603	336	1,964 R	52.4%	46.6%	53.0%	47.0%
GARZA	1,415	628	786	1	158 D	44.4%	55.5%	44.4%	55.6%
GILLESPIE	3,315	3,070	240	5	2,830 R	92.6%	7.2%	92.7%	7.3%
GLASSCOCK	398	224	174		50 R	56.3%	43.7%	56.3%	43.7%
GOLIAD	1,247	902	338	7	564 R	72.3%	27.1%	72.3%	27.7%
GONZALES	4,037	1,767	2,260	10	493 D	43.8%	56.0%	43.9%	56.1%
GRAY	8,153	5,047	3,034	72	2,013 R	61.9%	37.2%	62.5%	37.5%
GRAYSON	16,330	7,402	8,876	52	1,474 D	45.3%	54.4%	45.5%	54.5%
GREGG	14,559	9,440	4,881	198	4,559 R	65.0%	33.6%	65.3%	34.1%
GRIMES	2,374	1,281	1,079	14	202 R	54.0%	45.5%	54.3%	45.7%
GUADALUPE	6,425	4,296	2,099	30	2,197 R	66.9%	32.7%	67.2%	32.8%
HALE	7,663	3,804	3,848	11	44 D	49.6%	50.2%	49.7%	50.3%
HALL	2,179	687	1,487	5	800 D	31.5%	68.2%	31.6%	68.4%
HAMILTON	2,843	1,709	1,124	10	585 R	60.1%	39.5%	60.3%	39.7%
HANSFORD	1,465	919	545	1	374 R	62.7%	37.2%	62.8%	37.2%
HARDEMAN	2,409	1,119	1,281	9	162 D	46.5%	53.2%	46.6%	53.4%
HARDIN	4,582	2,130	2,371	81	241 D	46.5%	51.7%	47.3%	52.7%
HARRIS	254,549	155,555	93,961	5,033	61,594 R	61.1%	36.9%	62.3%	37.7%
HARRISON	7,795	5,048	2,668	79	2,380 R	64.8%	34.2%	65.4%	34.6%
HARTLEY	810	356	451	3	95 D	44.0%	55.3%	44.1%	55.9%
HASKELL	3,341	993	2,340	8	1,347 D	29.7%	70.0%	29.8%	70.2%
HAYS	3,904	1,873	2,017	14	144 D	48.0%	51.7%	48.1%	51.9%
HEMPHILL	1,022	620	401	1	219 R	60.7%	39.2%	60.7%	39.3%
HENDERSON	5,559	2,479	3,065	15	586 D	44.5%	55.1%	44.7%	55.3%
HIDALGO	23,327	9,804	13,270	253	3,466 D	42.0%	56.9%	42.5%	57.5%
HILL	6,707	2,487	4,199	21	1,712 D	37.1%	62.6%	37.5%	62.9%
HOCKLEY	5,186	2,001	3,175	10	1,174 D	38.6%	61.2%	38.7%	61.3%
HOOD	1,852	751	1,095	6	344 D	40.6%	59.1%	40.7%	59.3%
HOPKINS	5,347	2,206	3,118	23	912 D	41.3%	58.3%	41.4%	58.6%
HOUSTON	3,958	1,941	1,998	19	57 D	49.0%	50.5%	49.3%	50.7%
HOWARD	7,571	3,051	4,506	14	1,455 D	40.3%	59.5%	40.4%	59.6%
HUDSPETH	692	316	368	8	52 D	45.7%	53.2%	46.2%	53.8%
HUNT	8,592	4,508	4,051	33	457 R	52.5%	47.1%	52.7%	47.3%
HUTCHINSON	9,436	5,110	4,184	142	926 R	54.2%	44.8%	55.0%	45.0%
IRION	432	252	178	2	74 R	58.3%	41.2%	58.6%	41.4%
JACK	2,347	1,327	997	23	330 R	56.5%	42.5%	57.1%	42.9%
JACKSON	3,852	2,259	1,571	22	688 R	58.6%	40.8%	59.0%	41.0%

TEXAS

PRESIDENT 1952

County	Total Vote	Republican	Democratic	Other	Rep.-Dem. Plurality	% Total Vote Rep.	% Total Vote Dem.	% Major Vote Rep.	% Major Vote Dem.
JASPER	4,543	1,946	2,595	2	649 D	42.8%	57.1%	42.9%	57.1%
JEFF DAVIS	489	306	183		123 R	62.6%	37.4%	62.6%	37.4%
JEFFERSON	54,795	25,363	29,384	48	4,021 D	46.3%	53.6%	46.3%	53.7%
JIM HOGG	1,362	309	1,053		744 D	22.7%	77.3%	22.7%	77.3%
JIM WELLS	7,339	3,592	3,745	2	153 D	48.9%	51.0%	49.0%	51.0%
JOHNSON	8,485	3,985	4,496	4	511 D	47.0%	53.0%	47.0%	53.0%
JONES	5,633	2,941	2,680	12	261 R	52.2%	47.6%	52.3%	47.7%
KARNES	4,260	2,374	1,884	2	490 R	55.7%	44.2%	55.7%	44.3%
KAUFMAN	6,729	2,964	3,762	3	798 D	44.0%	55.9%	44.1%	55.9%
KENDALL	2,164	1,786	370	8	1,416 R	82.5%	17.1%	82.6%	17.4%
KENEDY	122	108	14		94 R	88.5%	11.5%	88.5%	11.5%
KENT	786	259	526	1	267 D	33.0%	66.9%	33.0%	67.0%
KERR	5,009	3,663	1,337	9	2,326 R	73.2%	26.6%	73.3%	26.6%
KIMBLE	1,605	1,077	525	3	552 R	67.1%	32.7%	67.2%	32.8%
KING	255	66	189		123 D	25.9%	74.1%	25.9%	74.1%
KINNEY	690	384	306		78 R	55.7%	44.3%	55.7%	44.3%
KLEBERG	5,231	2,037	3,193	1	1,156 D	38.9%	61.0%	38.9%	61.1%
KNOX	2,590	1,033	1,556	1	523 D	39.9%	60.1%	39.9%	60.1%
LAMAR	9,453	3,929	5,524		1,595 D	41.6%	58.4%	41.6%	58.4%
LAMB	5,672	2,913	2,748	11	165 R	51.4%	48.4%	51.5%	48.5%
LA SALLE	2,677	1,478	1,199		279 R	55.2%	44.8%	55.2%	44.8%
LAVACA	1,382	565	816	1	251 D	40.9%	59.0%	40.9%	59.1%
LEE	6,361	3,599	2,750	12	849 R	56.6%	43.3%	56.7%	43.3%
LEON	2,707	1,316	1,389	2	73 D	48.7%	51.3%	48.7%	51.3%
LIBERTY	7,746	4,106	3,632	8	474 R	53.0%	46.9%	53.1%	46.9%
LIMESTONE	6,627	2,485	4,132	10	1,647 D	37.5%	62.4%	37.6%	62.4%
LIPSCOMB	1,379	1,174	204	1	970 R	85.1%	14.8%	85.2%	14.8%
LIVE OAK	2,026	1,443	573	10	870 R	71.2%	28.3%	71.6%	28.4%
LLANO	1,944	840	1,102	2	262 D	43.2%	56.7%	43.3%	56.7%
LOVING	95	71	24		47 R	74.7%	25.3%	74.7%	25.3%
LUBBOCK	27,845	16,137	11,650	58	4,487 R	58.0%	41.8%	58.1%	41.9%
LYNN	3,121	1,351	1,762	8	411 D	43.3%	56.5%	43.4%	56.6%
MCCULLOCH	3,460	1,788	1,663	9	125 R	51.7%	48.1%	51.8%	48.2%
MCLENNAN	32,278	14,974	17,251	53	2,277 D	46.4%	53.4%	46.5%	53.5%
MCMULLEN	447	290	156	1	134 R	64.9%	34.9%	65.0%	35.0%
MADISON	1,844	692	1,152		460 D	37.5%	62.5%	37.5%	62.5%
MARION	1,849	877	970	2	93 D	47.4%	52.5%	47.5%	52.5%
MARTIN	1,516	562	952	2	390 D	37.1%	62.9%	37.4%	62.6%
MASON	1,678	1,069	606	3	463 R	63.7%	36.1%	63.8%	36.2%
MATAGORDA	6,224	4,122	2,101	1	2,021 R	66.2%	33.8%	66.2%	33.8%
MAVERICK	1,802	839	962	1	123 D	46.6%	53.4%	46.6%	53.4%
MEDINA	5,044	3,204	1,840		1,364 R	63.5%	36.5%	63.5%	36.5%
MENARD	1,242	843	399		444 R	67.9%	32.1%	67.9%	32.1%
MIDLAND	11,200	7,956	3,244		4,712 R	71.0%	29.0%	71.0%	29.0%
MILAM	5,778	2,539	3,227	12	688 D	43.9%	55.8%	44.0%	56.0%
MILLS	1,966	1,089	875	2	214 R	55.4%	44.5%	55.4%	44.6%
MITCHELL	3,460	1,417	2,031	12	614 D	41.0%	58.7%	41.1%	58.9%
MONTAGUE	5,383	2,367	3,012	4	645 D	44.0%	56.0%	44.0%	56.0%
MONTGOMERY	6,410	2,969	3,432	9	463 D	46.3%	53.5%	46.4%	53.6%
MOORE	4,035	1,909	2,114	12	205 D	47.3%	52.4%	47.5%	52.5%
MORRIS	2,613	890	1,722	1	832 D	34.1%	65.9%	34.1%	65.9%
MOTLEY	1,190	675	513	2	162 R	56.7%	43.1%	56.8%	43.2%
NACOGDOCHES	6,447	2,891	3,556		665 D	44.8%	55.2%	44.8%	55.2%
NAVARRO	12,345	3,592	8,745	8	5,153 D	29.1%	70.8%	29.1%	70.9%
NEWTON	2,548	917	1,630	1	713 D	36.0%	64.0%	36.0%	64.0%
NOLAN	6,043	2,907	3,123	13	216 D	48.1%	51.7%	48.2%	51.8%
NUECES	39,359	19,124	20,156	79	1,032 D	48.6%	51.2%	48.7%	51.3%
OCHILTREE	2,183	1,755	426	2	1,329 R	80.4%	19.5%	80.5%	19.5%
OLDHAM	624	341	280	3	61 R	54.6%	44.9%	54.9%	45.1%

PRESIDENT 1956

County	Total Vote	Republican	Democratic	Other	Rep.-Dem. Plurality	% Total Vote Rep.	% Total Vote Dem.	% Major Vote Rep.	% Major Vote Dem.
JASPER	4,308	2,430	1,856	22	574 R	56.4%	43.1%	56.7%	43.3%
JEFF DAVIS	407	239	165	3	74 R	58.7%	40.5%	59.2%	40.8%
JEFFERSON	55,429	30,102	25,057	270	5,045 R	54.3%	45.2%	54.6%	45.4%
JIM HOGG	906	282	617	7	335 D	31.1%	68.1%	31.4%	68.6%
JIM WELLS	6,122	3,348	2,752	22	596 R	54.7%	44.9%	54.9%	45.1%
JOHNSON	7,340	3,750	3,560	30	190 R	51.1%	48.5%	51.3%	48.7%
JONES	4,677	2,073	2,594	10	521 D	44.3%	55.5%	44.4%	55.6%
KARNES	3,417	1,764	1,636	17	128 R	51.6%	47.9%	51.9%	48.1%
KAUFMAN	5,750	2,816	2,901	32	85 D	49.0%	50.5%	49.2%	50.8%
KENDALL	1,873	1,519	341	13	1,178 R	81.1%	18.2%	81.7%	18.3%
KENEDY	135	125	10		115 R	92.6%	7.4%	92.6%	7.4%
KENT	755	234	519	2	285 D	31.0%	68.7%	31.1%	68.9%
KERR	4,594	3,555	1,025	14	2,530 R	77.4%	22.3%	77.6%	22.4%
KIMBLE	1,307	821	484	2	337 R	62.8%	37.0%	62.9%	37.1%
KING	224	46	177	1	131 D	20.5%	79.0%	20.6%	79.4%
KINNEY	660	368	289	3	79 R	55.8%	43.8%	56.0%	44.0%
KLEBERG	4,572	2,121	2,436	15	315 D	46.4%	53.3%	46.5%	53.5%
KNOX	2,100	835	1,262	3	427 D	39.8%	60.1%	39.8%	60.2%
LAMAR	8,381	4,154	4,202	25	48 D	49.6%	50.1%	49.7%	50.3%
LAMB	5,177	1,840	3,325	12	1,485 D	35.5%	64.2%	35.6%	64.4%
LA SALLE	2,447	1,308	1,134	5	174 R	53.5%	46.3%	53.6%	46.4%
LAVACA	1,024	449	574	1	125 D	43.8%	56.1%	43.9%	56.1%
LEE	4,941	2,509	2,412	20	97 R	50.8%	48.9%	51.0%	49.0%
LEON	2,274	1,200	1,061	13	139 R	52.8%	46.7%	53.1%	46.9%
LIBERTY	6,503	4,129	2,318	56	1,811 R	63.5%	35.6%	64.0%	36.0%
LIMESTONE	5,171	2,097	3,067	7	970 D	40.6%	59.3%	40.6%	59.4%
LIPSCOMB	1,154	806	345	3	461 R	69.8%	29.9%	70.0%	30.0%
LIVE OAK	1,639	1,077	556	41	521 R	65.7%	33.9%	67.4%	32.6%
LLANO	1,709	672	1,034	3	362 D	39.3%	60.5%	39.4%	60.6%
LOVING	91	55	36		19 R	60.4%	39.6%	60.4%	39.6%
LUBBOCK	26,576	13,970	12,540	66	1,430 R	52.6%	47.2%	52.7%	47.3%
LYNN	2,667	861	1,800	6	939 D	32.3%	67.5%	32.4%	67.6%
MCCULLOCH	2,455	1,292	1,158	5	134 R	52.6%	47.2%	52.7%	47.3%
MCLENNAN	31,853	15,561	16,181	111	620 D	48.9%	50.8%	49.0%	51.0%
MCMULLEN	413	226	185	2	41 R	54.7%	44.8%	55.0%	45.0%
MADISON	1,458	733	713	12	20 R	50.9%	48.9%	50.7%	49.3%
MARION	1,848	1,126	709	13	417 R	60.9%	38.4%	61.4%	38.6%
MARTIN	1,227	318	903	6	585 D	25.9%	73.6%	26.0%	74.0%
MASON	1,390	885	504	1	381 R	63.7%	36.3%	63.7%	36.3%
MATAGORDA	5,909	3,927	1,904	78	2,023 R	66.5%	32.2%	67.3%	32.7%
MAVERICK	1,560	721	820	19	99 D	46.2%	52.6%	46.8%	53.2%
MEDINA	4,201	2,668	1,516	17	1,152 R	63.8%	36.1%	63.8%	36.2%
MENARD	932	614	318		296 R	65.9%	34.1%	65.9%	34.1%
MIDLAND	11,841	8,287	3,468	86	4,819 R	70.0%	29.3%	70.5%	29.5%
MILAM	5,466	2,486	2,969	11	483 D	45.5%	54.3%	45.6%	54.4%
MILLS	1,648	912	735	1	177 R	55.4%	44.6%	55.6%	44.4%
MITCHELL	2,982	1,091	1,891		800 D	36.6%	63.4%	36.6%	63.4%
MONTAGUE	4,372	2,003	2,358	11	355 D	45.8%	53.9%	45.9%	54.1%
MONTGOMERY	5,974	3,360	2,572	42	788 R	56.2%	43.1%	56.6%	43.4%
MOORE	4,049	1,820	2,219	10	399 D	44.9%	54.8%	45.1%	54.9%
MORRIS	3,075	1,463	1,592	20	129 D	47.6%	51.8%	47.9%	52.1%
MOTLEY	926	411	511	4	100 D	44.4%	55.2%	44.6%	55.4%
NACOGDOCHES	6,165	3,285	2,855	25	430 R	53.3%	46.3%	53.5%	46.5%
NAVARRO	7,931	3,193	4,723	15	1,530 D	40.3%	59.6%	40.3%	59.7%
NEWTON	2,076	1,030	1,037	9	7 D	49.6%	50.0%	49.8%	50.2%
NOLAN	4,780	2,232	2,535	13	303 D	46.7%	53.0%	46.8%	53.2%
NUECES	40,059	19,985	19,912	162	73 R	49.7%	49.4%	50.1%	49.9%
OCHILTREE	1,740	1,209	512	19	697 R	69.5%	29.4%	70.2%	29.8%
OLDHAM	578	284	294		10 D	49.1%	50.9%	49.1%	50.9%

TEXAS

PRESIDENT 1952

County	Total Vote	Republican	Democratic	Other	Rep.-Dem. Plurality	Total % Rep.	Total % Dem.	Major % Rep.	Major % Dem.
ORANGE	10,913	4,491	6,403	19	1,912 D	41.2%	58.7%	41.2%	58.8%
PALO PINTO	5,917	3,029	2,876	12	153 R	51.2%	48.6%	51.3%	48.7%
PANOLA	4,982	2,080	2,897	5	817 D	41.8%	58.1%	41.8%	58.2%
PARKER	6,976	3,523	3,434	19	89 R	50.5%	49.2%	50.6%	49.4%
PARMER	2,166	1,503	663	—	840 R	69.4%	30.6%	69.4%	30.6%
PECOS	2,650	1,573	1,076	1	497 R	59.4%	40.6%	59.4%	40.6%
POLK	3,694	1,454	2,238	2	784 D	39.4%	60.6%	39.4%	60.6%
POTTER	24,232	14,931	9,259	42	5,672 R	61.6%	38.2%	61.7%	38.3%
PRESIDIO	1,391	770	621	—	149 R	55.4%	44.6%	55.4%	44.6%
RAINS	1,088	500	588	—	88 D	46.0%	54.0%	46.0%	54.0%
RANDALL	6,214	4,305	1,905	4	2,400 R	69.3%	30.7%	69.3%	30.7%
REAGAN	994	533	460	1	73 R	53.5%	46.3%	53.7%	46.3%
REAL	753	450	303	—	147 R	59.8%	40.2%	59.8%	40.2%
RED RIVER	5,450	1,964	3,484	2	1,520 D	36.0%	63.9%	36.0%	64.0%
REEVES	3,118	1,727	1,385	6	342 R	55.4%	44.4%	55.5%	44.5%
REFUGIO	2,832	1,427	1,401	4	26 R	50.4%	49.5%	50.5%	49.5%
ROBERTS	470	379	91	—	288 R	80.6%	19.4%	80.5%	19.4%
ROBERTSON	4,007	1,378	2,526	3	1,248 D	34.4%	65.5%	34.5%	65.5%
ROCKWALL	1,785	602	1,175	8	573 D	33.7%	65.3%	33.9%	65.1%
RUNNELS	4,480	2,622	1,853	5	769 R	58.5%	41.4%	58.6%	41.4%
RUSK	11,340	5,634	5,694	12	50 D	49.7%	50.2%	49.7%	50.3%
SABINE	2,302	729	1,573	—	844 D	31.7%	68.3%	31.7%	68.3%
SAN AUGUSTINE	2,089	730	1,359	—	629 D	34.9%	65.1%	35.0%	65.0%
SAN JACINTO	1,541	494	1,043	4	549 D	32.0%	67.7%	32.1%	67.9%
SAN PATRICIO	6,540	3,220	3,315	5	95 D	49.2%	50.7%	49.3%	50.7%
SAN SABA	2,653	900	1,752	1	852 D	33.9%	66.0%	33.9%	66.1%
SCHLEICHER	1,049	628	421	—	207 R	59.9%	40.1%	59.9%	40.1%
SCURRY	5,100	2,620	2,480	—	140 R	51.4%	48.6%	51.4%	48.6%
SHACKELFORD	1,837	1,057	776	4	281 R	57.5%	42.4%	57.7%	42.3%
SHELBY	6,047	1,792	4,249	6	2,457 D	29.6%	70.3%	29.7%	70.3%
SHERMAN	988	669	317	2	352 R	67.7%	32.1%	67.8%	32.2%
SMITH	19,410	10,947	8,450	13	2,497 R	56.4%	43.5%	56.5%	43.5%
SOMERVELL	953	494	450	9	44 R	51.8%	47.2%	52.3%	47.7%
STARR	3,675	620	3,055	—	2,435 D	16.9%	83.1%	16.9%	83.1%
STEPHENS	3,747	2,272	1,471	4	801 R	60.5%	39.3%	60.7%	39.3%
STERLING	435	277	158	—	119 R	63.7%	36.3%	63.7%	36.3%
STONEWALL	1,157	319	836	2	517 D	27.6%	72.4%	27.6%	72.4%
SUTTON	932	581	351	—	230 R	62.3%	37.7%	62.3%	37.7%
SWISHER	2,922	1,843	1,074	5	769 R	63.1%	36.8%	63.2%	36.8%
TARRANT	109,842	63,680	45,968	194	17,712 R	58.0%	41.8%	58.1%	41.9%
TAYLOR	18,251	10,260	7,936	55	2,324 R	56.2%	43.5%	56.4%	43.6%
TERRELL	722	426	295	1	131 R	59.0%	40.9%	59.0%	40.9%
TERRY	3,931	1,823	2,105	3	282 D	45.4%	53.6%	45.4%	53.6%
THROCKMORTON	1,314	586	728	—	142 D	44.6%	55.4%	44.6%	55.4%
TITUS	5,031	1,887	3,142	2	1,255 D	37.5%	62.5%	37.5%	62.5%
TOM GREEN	15,519	9,698	5,797	24	3,901 R	62.5%	37.4%	62.6%	37.4%
TRAVIS	40,051	20,850	19,155	46	1,695 R	52.1%	47.8%	52.1%	47.8%
TRINITY	2,683	958	1,725	—	767 D	35.7%	64.3%	35.7%	64.3%
TYLER	2,770	1,466	1,304	—	162 R	52.9%	47.1%	52.9%	47.1%
UPSHUR	5,437	2,391	3,040	6	649 D	44.0%	55.9%	44.0%	56.0%
UPTON	1,793	940	850	3	90 R	52.4%	47.4%	52.5%	47.5%
UVALDE	4,044	2,805	1,230	9	1,575 R	69.4%	30.4%	69.5%	30.5%
VAL VERDE	3,373	1,725	1,647	1	78 R	51.1%	48.8%	51.2%	48.8%
VAN ZANDT	6,203	2,279	3,911	13	1,632 D	36.7%	63.1%	36.8%	63.2%
VICTORIA	7,438	4,306	3,128	4	1,178 R	57.9%	42.1%	57.9%	42.1%
WALKER	3,976	1,897	2,078	1	181 D	47.7%	52.3%	47.7%	52.3%
WALLER	2,753	1,487	1,264	2	223 R	54.0%	45.9%	54.1%	45.9%
WARD	3,836	1,994	1,840	2	154 R	52.0%	48.0%	52.0%	48.0%
WASHINGTON	4,876	3,519	1,354	3	2,165 R	72.2%	27.8%	72.2%	27.8%
WEBB	8,996	2,784	6,208	4	3,424 D	30.9%	69.0%	31.0%	69.0%

PRESIDENT 1956

County	Total Vote	Republican	Democratic	Other	Rep.-Dem. Plurality	Total % Rep.	Total % Dem.	Major % Rep.	Major % Dem.
ORANGE	11,462	5,501	5,910	51	409 D	48.0%	51.6%	48.2%	51.8%
PALO PINTO	5,199	2,818	2,369	12	449 R	54.2%	45.6%	54.3%	45.7%
PANOLA	4,836	2,538	2,225	73	313 R	52.5%	46.0%	53.3%	46.7%
PARKER	6,588	3,390	3,165	33	225 R	51.5%	48.0%	51.7%	48.3%
PARMER	2,404	1,028	1,362	14	334 D	42.8%	56.7%	43.0%	57.0%
PECOS	2,367	1,425	931	11	494 R	60.2%	39.3%	60.5%	39.5%
POLK	3,144	1,663	1,465	16	198 R	52.9%	46.6%	53.2%	46.8%
POTTER	20,712	11,943	8,720	49	3,223 R	57.6%	42.1%	57.8%	42.2%
PRESIDIO	1,019	494	517	8	23 D	48.5%	50.7%	48.9%	51.1%
RAINS	952	427	524	1	97 D	44.9%	55.0%	44.9%	55.1%
RANDALL	7,400	4,609	2,774	17	1,835 R	62.3%	37.5%	62.4%	37.6%
REAGAN	1,054	669	384	1	285 R	63.5%	36.4%	63.5%	36.5%
REAL	541	350	191	—	159 R	64.7%	35.3%	64.7%	35.3%
RED RIVER	4,534	1,956	2,567	11	611 D	43.1%	56.6%	43.3%	56.8%
REEVES	2,856	1,492	1,356	8	136 R	52.2%	47.5%	52.4%	47.6%
REFUGIO	2,552	1,355	1,188	9	167 R	53.1%	46.6%	53.3%	46.7%
ROBERTS	399	279	118	2	161 R	69.9%	29.6%	70.3%	29.7%
ROBERTSON	3,508	1,285	2,212	11	927 D	36.6%	63.1%	36.7%	63.3%
ROCKWALL	1,583	657	920	6	263 D	41.5%	58.1%	41.7%	58.3%
RUNNELS	3,863	2,416	1,442	5	974 R	62.5%	37.3%	62.6%	37.4%
RUSK	8,573	5,140	3,381	52	1,759 R	60.0%	39.4%	60.3%	39.7%
SABINE	1,715	801	913	1	112 D	46.7%	53.2%	46.7%	53.3%
SAN AUGUSTINE	1,997	900	1,086	11	186 D	45.1%	54.4%	45.3%	54.7%
SAN JACINTO	1,329	565	755	9	190 D	42.5%	56.8%	42.8%	57.2%
SAN PATRICIO	7,052	3,302	3,728	22	426 D	46.8%	52.9%	47.0%	53.0%
SAN SABA	2,222	797	1,419	6	622 D	35.9%	63.9%	36.0%	64.0%
SCHLEICHER	811	471	336	4	135 R	58.1%	41.4%	58.4%	41.6%
SCURRY	4,949	2,250	2,691	8	441 D	45.5%	54.4%	45.5%	54.5%
SHACKELFORD	1,404	849	555	—	294 R	60.5%	39.4%	60.5%	39.5%
SHELBY	5,440	1,988	3,403	49	1,415 D	36.5%	62.6%	36.9%	63.1%
SHERMAN	869	481	383	5	98 R	55.4%	44.1%	55.7%	44.3%
SMITH	18,792	12,255	6,468	69	5,787 R	65.2%	34.4%	65.5%	34.5%
SOMERVELL	781	467	309	5	158 R	59.8%	39.6%	59.8%	39.8%
STARR	3,274	547	2,727	—	2,180 D	16.7%	83.3%	16.7%	83.3%
STEPHENS	2,971	1,832	1,126	13	706 R	61.7%	37.9%	61.9%	38.1%
STERLING	373	223	150	—	73 R	59.8%	40.2%	59.8%	40.2%
STONEWALL	1,138	306	829	3	523 D	26.9%	72.8%	27.0%	73.0%
SUTTON	838	546	290	2	256 R	65.2%	34.6%	65.3%	34.7%
SWISHER	2,684	876	1,802	6	926 D	32.6%	67.1%	32.7%	67.3%
TARRANT	111,197	66,329	43,922	946	22,407 R	59.6%	39.5%	60.2%	39.8%
TAYLOR	16,699	9,488	7,177	34	2,311 R	56.8%	43.0%	56.9%	43.1%
TERRELL	569	350	217	2	133 R	61.5%	38.1%	61.7%	38.3%
TERRY	3,526	1,473	2,050	3	577 D	41.8%	58.1%	41.8%	58.2%
THROCKMORTON	1,127	466	656	5	190 D	41.3%	58.2%	41.5%	58.5%
TITUS	4,305	1,971	2,301	33	330 D	45.8%	53.4%	46.1%	53.9%
TOM GREEN	14,033	9,070	4,923	40	4,147 R	64.6%	35.1%	64.8%	35.2%
TRAVIS	43,631	23,551	19,982	98	3,569 R	54.0%	45.8%	54.1%	45.9%
TRINITY	1,967	865	1,091	11	226 D	44.0%	55.5%	44.2%	55.8%
TYLER	2,541	1,734	797	10	937 R	68.2%	31.4%	68.5%	31.5%
UPSHUR	4,764	2,737	1,995	32	742 R	57.5%	41.9%	57.8%	42.2%
UPTON	1,840	999	834	7	165 R	54.3%	45.3%	54.5%	45.5%
UVALDE	3,463	2,449	994	20	1,455 R	70.7%	28.7%	71.1%	28.9%
VAL VERDE	3,267	1,660	1,598	9	62 R	50.8%	48.9%	51.0%	49.0%
VAN ZANDT	5,070	2,142	2,919	9	777 D	42.2%	57.6%	42.3%	57.7%
VICTORIA	8,904	5,596	3,280	28	2,316 R	62.8%	36.8%	63.0%	37.0%
WALKER	3,326	1,991	1,287	48	704 R	59.9%	38.7%	60.7%	39.3%
WALLER	2,397	1,426	929	42	497 R	59.5%	38.8%	60.6%	39.4%
WARD	3,432	1,772	1,638	22	134 R	51.6%	47.7%	52.0%	48.0%
WASHINGTON	3,923	2,975	933	15	2,042 R	75.8%	23.8%	76.1%	23.9%
WEBB	8,587	2,744	5,827	16	3,083 D	32.0%	67.9%	32.0%	68.0%

TEXAS

PRESIDENT 1952

County	Total Vote	Republican	Democratic	Other	Rep.-Dem. Plurality	Percentage Total Vote Rep.	Dem.	Major Vote Rep.	Dem.
WHARTON	9,259	5,232	4,022	5	1,210 R	56.5%	43.4%	56.5%	43.5%
WHEELER	3,202	1,645	1,551	6	94 R	51.4%	48.4%	51.5%	48.5%
WICHITA	25,731	12,197	13,505	29	1,308 D	47.4%	52.5%	47.5%	52.5%
WILBARGER	5,666	3,019	2,646	1	373 R	53.3%	46.7%	53.3%	46.7%
WILLACY	3,574	2,244	1,324	6	920 R	62.8%	37.0%	62.9%	37.1%
WILLIAMSON	8,663	3,646	5,010	7	1,364 D	42.1%	57.8%	42.1%	57.9%
WILSON	4,015	1,823	2,187	5	364 D	45.4%	54.5%	45.5%	54.5%
WINKLER	3,064	1,550	1,508	6	42 R	50.6%	49.2%	50.7%	49.3%
WISE	5,434	2,309	3,121	4	812 D	42.5%	57.4%	42.5%	57.5%
WOOD	5,780	2,748	3,026	6	278 D	47.5%	52.4%	47.6%	52.4%
YOAKUM	1,733	858	873	2	15 D	49.5%	50.4%	49.6%	50.4%
YOUNG	5,192	2,649	2,536	7	113 R	51.0%	48.8%	51.1%	48.9%
ZAPATA	1,143	526	616	1	90 D	46.0%	53.9%	46.1%	53.9%
ZAVALA	1,723	1,043	677	3	366 R	60.5%	39.3%	60.6%	39.4%
TOTAL	2,075,946	1,102,878	969,228	3,840	133,650 R	53.1%	46.7%	53.2%	46.8%

PRESIDENT 1956

County	Total Vote	Republican	Democratic	Other	Rep.-Dem. Plurality	Percentage Total Vote Rep.	Dem.	Major Vote Rep.	Dem.
WHARTON	8,203	4,714	3,439	50	1,275 R	57.5%	41.9%	57.8%	42.2%
WHEELER	2,443	1,178	1,252	13	74 D	48.2%	51.2%	48.5%	51.5%
WICHITA	24,948	12,181	12,726	41	545 D	48.8%	51.0%	48.9%	51.1%
WILBARGER	4,587	2,230	2,347	10	117 D	48.6%	51.2%	48.7%	51.3%
WILLACY	2,948	1,656	1,261	31	395 R	56.2%	42.8%	56.8%	43.2%
WILLIAMSON	7,367	2,947	4,402	18	1,455 D	40.0%	59.8%	40.1%	59.9%
WILSON	3,678	1,519	2,149	10	630 D	41.3%	58.4%	41.4%	58.6%
WINKLER	2,777	1,471	1,287	19	184 R	53.0%	46.3%	53.3%	46.7%
WISE	4,524	2,058	2,443	23	385 D	45.5%	54.0%	45.7%	54.3%
WOOD	4,722	2,508	2,199	15	309 R	53.1%	46.6%	53.3%	46.7%
YOAKUM	1,915	923	989	3	66 D	48.2%	51.6%	48.3%	51.7%
YOUNG	4,130	2,083	2,028	19	55 R	50.4%	49.1%	50.7%	49.3%
ZAPATA	1,524	637	886	1	249 D	41.8%	58.1%	41.8%	58.2%
ZAVALA	1,427	896	528	3	368 R	62.8%	37.0%	62.9%	37.1%
TOTAL	1,955,168	1,080,619	859,958	14,591	220,661 R	55.3%	44.0%	55.7%	44.3%

TEXAS

PRESIDENT 1960

County	Total Vote	Republican	Democratic	Other	Rep.-Dem. Plurality	%Total Rep.	%Total Dem.	%Major Rep.	%Major Dem.
ANDERSON	6,982	3,642	3,296	44	346 R	52.2%	47.2%	52.5%	47.5%
ANDREWS	3,409	1,550	1,821	38	271 D	45.5%	53.4%	46.0%	54.0%
ANGELINA	12,510	5,169	7,046	295	1,877 D	41.3%	56.3%	42.3%	57.7%
ARANSAS	1,748	792	948	8	156 D	45.3%	54.2%	45.5%	54.5%
ARCHER	2,023	680	1,341	2	661 D	33.6%	66.3%	33.6%	66.4%
ARMSTRONG	860	488	365	7	123 R	56.7%	42.4%	57.2%	42.8%
ATASCOSA	4,361	1,812	2,544	5	732 D	41.6%	58.3%	41.6%	58.4%
AUSTIN	3,738	1,978	1,725	35	253 R	52.9%	46.1%	53.4%	46.6%
BAILEY	2,271	1,180	1,064	27	115 R	52.0%	46.9%	52.6%	47.4%
BANDERA	1,464	942	539	23	403 R	63.5%	36.3%	63.6%	36.4%
BASTROP	4,080	1,208	2,866	6	1,658 D	29.6%	70.2%	29.7%	70.3%
BAYLOR	1,913	713	1,199	1	486 D	37.3%	62.7%	37.3%	62.7%
BEE	4,787	2,220	2,557	10	337 D	46.4%	53.5%	46.5%	53.5%
BELL	15,288	4,606	10,651	31	6,045 D	30.1%	69.7%	30.2%	69.8%
BEXAR	140,245	63,934	75,373	938	11,439 D	45.6%	53.7%	45.9%	54.1%
BLANCO	1,394	557	830	7	273 D	40.0%	59.5%	40.2%	59.8%
BORDEN	411	166	230	15	64 D	43.4%	56.0%	41.9%	58.1%
BOSQUE	3,525	1,653	1,852	20	199 D	45.9%	52.5%	47.2%	52.8%
BOWIE	15,193	5,927	9,198	68	3,271 D	39.0%	60.5%	39.2%	60.8%
BRAZORIA	21,705	10,880	10,561	264	319 R	50.1%	48.7%	50.7%	49.3%
BRAZOS	10,477	4,553	5,907	17	1,354 D	43.5%	56.4%	43.5%	55.5%
BREWSTER	1,457	736	716	5	20 R	50.5%	49.1%	50.7%	49.3%
BRISCOE	1,112	533	570	9	37 D	47.9%	51.3%	48.3%	51.7%
BROOKS	2,511	567	1,934	10	1,367 D	22.6%	77.0%	22.7%	77.3%
BROWN	7,278	3,512	3,720	46	208 D	48.3%	51.1%	48.6%	51.4%
BURLESON	3,143	672	2,466	5	1,794 D	21.4%	78.5%	21.4%	78.6%
BURNET	2,976	1,189	1,770	17	581 D	40.0%	59.5%	40.2%	59.8%
CALDWELL	4,222	1,482	2,729	11	1,247 D	35.1%	64.6%	35.2%	64.8%
CALHOUN	3,594	1,599	1,961	34	352 D	44.5%	54.6%	44.9%	55.1%
CALLAHAN	2,838	1,261	1,559	18	298 D	44.4%	54.9%	44.6%	55.3%
CAMERON	22,640	10,190	12,416	34	2,226 D	45.0%	54.8%	45.1%	54.9%
CAMP	2,200	873	1,307	20	434 D	39.7%	59.4%	40.0%	60.0%
CARSON	2,407	1,387	1,009	11	378 R	57.6%	41.9%	57.9%	42.1%
CASS	5,290	2,322	2,934	34	612 D	43.9%	55.5%	44.2%	55.8%
CASTRO	2,382	810	1,544	28	734 D	34.0%	64.8%	34.4%	65.6%
CHAMBERS	2,316	1,260	1,524	32	264 D	44.7%	54.1%	45.3%	54.7%
CHEROKEE	7,382	3,233	4,544	105	1,311 D	41.0%	57.7%	41.6%	58.4%
CHILDRESS	2,767	1,571	1,189	7	382 R	56.8%	43.0%	56.9%	43.1%
CLAY	2,718	1,019	1,692	7	673 D	37.5%	62.3%	37.6%	62.4%
COCHRAN	1,674	646	1,028		382 D	38.6%	61.4%	38.6%	61.4%
COKE	1,388	575	799	14	224 D	41.4%	57.6%	41.8%	58.2%
COLEMAN	3,977	1,828	2,134	15	306 D	46.0%	53.6%	46.1%	53.9%
COLLIN	9,158	3,865	5,229	64	1,364 D	42.2%	57.1%	42.5%	57.5%
COLLINGSWORTH	1,782	1,084	691	7	393 R	60.3%	38.9%	61.0%	38.9%
COLORADO	4,247	1,909	2,299	39	390 D	44.9%	54.4%	45.4%	54.6%
COMAL	4,941	3,082	1,845	14	1,237 R	62.4%	37.3%	62.6%	37.4%
COMANCHE	3,830	1,828	1,979	23	151 D	47.7%	51.7%	48.0%	52.0%
CONCHO	1,242	522	718	2	196 D	42.0%	57.8%	42.1%	57.9%
COOKE	7,176	3,983	3,168	25	815 R	55.5%	44.1%	55.7%	44.3%
CORYELL	4,192	1,477	2,700	15	1,223 D	35.2%	64.4%	35.4%	64.6%
COTTLE	1,361	370	986	5	616 D	27.2%	72.4%	27.3%	72.7%
CRANE	1,568	678	848	42	170 D	43.2%	54.1%	44.4%	55.6%
CROCKETT	1,156	635	517	4	118 R	54.9%	44.7%	55.1%	44.9%
CROSBY	2,683	889	1,783	11	894 D	33.1%	66.5%	33.3%	66.7%
CULBERSON	650	300	343	7	43 D	46.2%	52.8%	46.7%	53.3%
DALLAM	1,808	961	835	12	126 R	53.2%	46.2%	53.5%	46.5%
DALLAS	240,299	149,369	88,876	2,054	60,493 R	62.2%	37.0%	62.7%	37.3%
DAWSON	4,246	2,161	2,063	22	98 R	50.9%	48.6%	51.2%	48.8%
DEAF SMITH	3,349	2,024	1,299	26	725 R	60.4%	38.8%	60.9%	39.1%
DELTA	1,832	460	1,360	12	900 D	25.1%	74.2%	25.3%	74.7%

PRESIDENT 1964

County	Total Vote	Republican	Democratic	Other	Rep.-Dem. Plurality	%Total Rep.	%Total Dem.	%Major Rep.	%Major Dem.
ANDERSON	8,181	3,362	4,809	10	1,447 D	41.1%	58.8%	41.1%	58.9%
ANDREWS	3,585	1,442	2,133	10	691 D	40.2%	59.5%	40.3%	59.7%
ANGELINA	13,484	5,262	8,194	28	2,932 D	39.0%	60.8%	39.1%	60.9%
ARANSAS	2,101	602	1,492	7	890 D	28.7%	71.0%	28.7%	71.3%
ARCHER	2,207	441	1,766		1,325 D	20.0%	80.0%	20.0%	80.0%
ARMSTRONG	909	365	544		179 D	40.2%	59.8%	40.2%	59.8%
ATASCOSA	4,516	1,283	3,224	9	1,941 D	28.4%	71.4%	28.4%	71.5%
AUSTIN	3,915	1,545	2,365	5	820 D	39.5%	60.4%	39.5%	60.5%
BAILEY	2,562	1,056	1,503	3	447 D	41.2%	58.7%	41.3%	58.7%
BANDERA	1,639	762	876	1	114 D	46.5%	53.4%	46.5%	53.5%
BASTROP	5,049	1,130	3,912	7	2,782 D	22.4%	77.5%	22.4%	77.6%
BAYLOR	1,794	389	1,403	2	1,014 D	21.7%	78.2%	21.7%	78.3%
BEE	4,832	1,509	3,314	9	1,805 D	31.2%	68.6%	31.3%	68.7%
BELL	17,512	2,938	14,557	17	11,619 D	16.8%	83.1%	16.8%	83.2%
BEXAR	162,520	53,469	108,658	393	55,189 D	32.9%	66.9%	33.0%	67.0%
BLANCO	1,488	290	1,197	1	907 D	19.5%	80.4%	19.5%	80.5%
BORDEN	419	152	266	1	114 D	36.3%	63.4%	36.4%	63.6%
BOSQUE	3,721	1,024	2,690	7	1,666 D	27.5%	72.3%	27.6%	72.4%
BOWIE	17,410	7,018	10,368	24	3,350 D	40.3%	59.6%	40.4%	59.6%
BRAZORIA	24,497	8,477	15,917	103	7,440 D	34.6%	65.0%	34.8%	65.2%
BRAZOS	12,019	4,003	7,998	18	3,995 D	33.3%	66.5%	33.4%	66.6%
BREWSTER	1,887	635	1,251	1	616 D	33.7%	66.3%	33.7%	66.3%
BRISCOE	1,317	348	966	3	618 D	26.4%	73.3%	26.5%	73.5%
BROOKS	2,703	402	2,299	2	1,897 D	14.9%	85.1%	14.9%	85.1%
BROWN	7,293	2,070	5,214	9	3,144 D	28.4%	71.5%	28.4%	71.6%
BURLESON	3,147	617	2,527	3	1,910 D	19.6%	80.3%	19.6%	80.4%
BURNET	3,410	821	2,585	4	1,764 D	24.1%	75.8%	24.1%	75.9%
CALDWELL	4,629	1,046	3,580	3	2,534 D	22.6%	77.3%	22.6%	77.4%
CALHOUN	4,434	1,031	3,398	5	2,367 D	23.3%	76.6%	23.3%	76.7%
CALLAHAN	3,037	849	2,178	10	1,329 D	28.0%	71.7%	28.0%	72.0%
CAMERON	25,659	9,531	16,056	72	6,525 D	37.1%	62.5%	37.2%	62.8%
CAMP	2,577	729	1,841	7	1,112 D	28.3%	71.4%	28.4%	71.6%
CARSON	2,621	1,044	1,574	3	530 D	39.8%	60.0%	39.9%	60.1%
CASS	6,292	2,681	3,603	8	922 D	42.6%	57.3%	42.7%	57.3%
CASTRO	2,494	626	1,865	3	1,239 D	25.1%	74.8%	25.1%	74.9%
CHAMBERS	2,956	1,023	1,921	12	898 D	34.6%	65.0%	34.7%	65.3%
CHEROKEE	8,537	3,043	5,485	9	2,442 D	35.6%	64.2%	35.7%	64.3%
CHILDRESS	2,931	952	1,977	2	1,025 D	32.5%	67.4%	32.5%	67.5%
CLAY	3,020	559	2,357	4	1,798 D	21.8%	78.0%	21.8%	78.1%
COCHRAN	1,761	497	1,260	4	763 D	28.2%	71.6%	28.3%	71.7%
COKE	1,269	366	900	3	534 D	28.8%	70.9%	28.9%	71.1%
COLEMAN	4,105	1,434	2,670	1	1,236 D	34.9%	65.0%	34.9%	65.1%
COLLIN	11,193	3,341	7,833	19	4,492 D	29.8%	70.0%	29.9%	70.1%
COLLINGSWORTH	1,872	724	1,145	3	421 D	38.7%	61.2%	38.7%	61.3%
COLORADO	5,574	1,918	3,650	6	1,732 D	34.4%	65.5%	34.6%	65.6%
COMAL	5,875	2,223	3,644	8	1,421 D	37.8%	62.0%	37.9%	62.1%
COMANCHE	3,819	962	2,851	6	1,889 D	25.2%	74.6%	25.2%	74.8%
CONCHO	1,256	307	948	1	641 D	24.4%	75.5%	24.4%	75.5%
COOKE	7,211	3,117	4,083	11	966 D	43.2%	56.6%	43.3%	56.7%
CORYELL	4,564	877	3,679	8	2,802 D	19.2%	80.6%	19.2%	80.8%
COTTLE	1,353	230	1,122	1	892 D	17.0%	82.9%	17.0%	83.0%
CRANE	1,559	637	919	3	282 D	40.9%	58.9%	40.9%	59.1%
CROCKETT	1,211	409	799	3	390 D	33.8%	66.0%	33.9%	66.1%
CROSBY	2,892	611	2,278	3	1,667 D	21.1%	78.8%	21.1%	78.9%
CULBERSON	787	314	473		159 D	39.9%	60.1%	39.9%	60.1%
DALLAM	1,759	700	1,058	1	358 D	39.8%	60.1%	39.8%	60.2%
DALLAS	304,158	137,065	166,472	621	29,407 D	45.1%	54.7%	45.2%	54.8%
DAWSON	4,868	1,691	3,171	6	1,480 D	34.7%	65.1%	34.8%	65.2%
DEAF SMITH	3,897	1,793	2,094	10	301 D	46.0%	53.7%	46.1%	53.9%
DELTA	1,960	339	1,619	2	1,280 D	17.3%	82.6%	17.3%	82.7%

TEXAS

PRESIDENT 1960

County	Total Vote	Republican	Democratic	Other	Rep.-Dem. Plurality	Total Vote %Rep.	Total Vote %Dem.	Major Vote %Rep.	Major Vote %Dem.
DENTON	11,119	5,724	5,366	29	358 R	51.5%	48.3%	51.6%	48.4%
DE WITT	5,029	2,763	2,253	13	510 R	54.9%	44.8%	55.1%	44.9%
DICKENS	1,607	521	1,075	11	554 D	32.4%	66.9%	32.6%	67.4%
DIMMIT	1,537	648	886	3	238 D	42.2%	57.6%	42.2%	57.8%
DONLEY	1,720	951	764	5	187 R	55.3%	44.4%	55.5%	44.5%
DUVAL	4,614	809	3,803	2	2,994 D	17.5%	82.4%	17.5%	82.5%
EASTLAND	6,449	3,359	3,058	32	301 R	52.1%	47.4%	52.3%	47.7%
ECTOR	20,672	11,145	8,996	531	2,149 R	53.9%	43.5%	55.3%	44.7%
EDWARDS	639	463	168	8	295 R	72.5%	26.3%	73.4%	26.6%
ELLIS	9,543	3,666	5,841	36	2,175 D	38.4%	61.2%	38.6%	61.4%
EL PASO	47,677	21,551	26,027	99	4,476 D	45.2%	54.6%	45.3%	54.7%
ERATH	5,216	2,696	2,490	30	206 R	51.7%	47.7%	52.0%	48.0%
FALLS	4,965	1,559	3,399	7	1,840 D	31.4%	68.5%	31.4%	68.6%
FANNIN	6,138	1,844	4,282	12	2,438 D	30.0%	69.8%	30.1%	69.9%
FAYETTE	5,699	2,213	3,462	24	1,249 D	38.8%	60.7%	39.0%	61.0%
FISHER	2,655	679	1,966	10	1,287 D	25.6%	74.0%	25.7%	74.3%
FLOYD	3,042	1,580	1,437	25	143 R	51.9%	47.2%	52.4%	47.6%
FOARD	995	270	723	2	453 D	27.1%	72.6%	27.2%	72.8%
FORT BEND	7,711	3,301	4,339	71	1,038 D	42.8%	56.3%	43.2%	56.8%
FRANKLIN	1,774	620	1,148	6	528 D	34.9%	64.7%	35.1%	64.9%
FREESTONE	3,650	1,629	1,997	24	368 D	44.6%	54.7%	44.9%	55.1%
FRIO	1,790	713	1,068	9	355 D	39.8%	59.7%	40.0%	60.0%
GAINES	3,041	1,520	1,498	23	22 R	50.0%	49.3%	50.4%	49.6%
GALVESTON	40,828	16,373	23,940	515	7,567 D	40.1%	58.6%	40.6%	59.4%
GARZA	1,576	737	829	10	92 D	46.8%	52.6%	47.1%	52.9%
GILLESPIE	3,507	2,687	816	4	1,871 R	76.6%	23.3%	76.7%	23.3%
GLASSCOCK	366	152	207	7	55 D	41.5%	56.6%	42.3%	57.7%
GOLIAD	1,455	741	711	3	30 R	50.9%	48.9%	51.0%	49.0%
GONZALES	4,291	1,554	2,730	7	1,176 D	36.2%	63.6%	36.3%	63.7%
GRAY	9,013	6,197	2,802	14	3,395 R	68.8%	31.1%	68.9%	31.1%
GRAYSON	17,231	7,312	9,866	53	2,554 D	42.4%	57.3%	42.6%	57.4%
GREGG	18,737	10,679	7,765	293	2,914 R	57.0%	41.4%	57.9%	42.1%
GRIMES	2,778	1,053	1,711	12	660 D	37.9%	61.6%	38.1%	61.9%
GUADALUPE	6,787	3,657	3,116	14	541 R	53.9%	45.9%	54.0%	46.0%
HALE	8,532	4,784	3,695	53	1,089 R	56.1%	43.3%	56.4%	43.6%
HALL	2,133	939	1,192	2	253 D	44.0%	55.9%	44.1%	55.9%
HAMILTON	2,737	1,592	1,136	9	456 R	58.2%	41.5%	58.4%	41.6%
HANSFORD	1,839	1,322	512	5	810 R	71.9%	27.8%	72.1%	27.9%
HARDEMAN	2,655	1,472	1,182	1	290 R	55.4%	44.5%	55.5%	44.5%
HARDIN	6,451	2,115	4,315	21	2,200 D	32.8%	66.9%	32.9%	67.1%
HARRIS	325,399	168,170	148,275	8,954	19,895 R	51.7%	45.6%	53.1%	46.9%
HARRISON	9,945	4,613	5,108	224	495 D	46.4%	51.4%	47.5%	52.5%
HARTLEY	815	413	397	5	16 R	50.7%	48.7%	51.0%	49.0%
HASKELL	3,650	866	2,776	8	1,910 D	23.7%	76.0%	23.8%	76.2%
HAYS	4,529	1,606	2,916	7	1,310 D	35.5%	64.4%	35.5%	64.5%
HEMPHILL	1,181	847	333	1	514 R	71.7%	28.2%	71.8%	28.2%
HENDERSON	5,970	2,521	3,411	38	890 D	42.2%	57.1%	42.5%	57.5%
HIDALGO	32,406	13,628	18,663	115	5,035 D	42.1%	57.6%	42.2%	57.8%
HILL	6,593	2,226	4,340	27	2,114 D	33.8%	65.8%	33.9%	66.1%
HOCKLEY	5,358	2,159	3,169	30	1,010 D	40.3%	59.1%	40.5%	59.5%
HOOD	2,187	943	1,238	6	295 D	43.1%	56.6%	43.3%	56.7%
HOPKINS	5,357	2,117	3,228	12	1,111 D	39.5%	60.3%	39.6%	60.4%
HOUSTON	4,383	1,591	2,703	89	1,112 D	36.3%	61.7%	37.1%	62.9%
HOWARD	8,335	3,403	4,844	88	1,441 D	40.8%	58.1%	41.3%	58.7%
HUDSPETH	685	267	409	9	142 D	39.0%	59.7%	39.5%	60.5%
HUNT	8,242	4,084	4,116	42	32 D	49.6%	49.9%	49.8%	50.2%
HUTCHINSON	9,747	6,432	3,295	20	3,137 R	66.0%	33.8%	66.1%	33.9%
IRION	487	238	246	3	8 D	48.9%	50.5%	49.2%	50.8%
JACK	2,432	1,342	1,079	11	263 R	55.2%	44.4%	55.4%	44.6%
JACKSON	3,972	1,670	2,268	34	598 D	42.0%	57.1%	42.4%	57.6%

PRESIDENT 1964

County	Total Vote	Republican	Democratic	Other	Rep.-Dem. Plurality	Total Vote %Rep.	Total Vote %Dem.	Major Vote %Rep.	Major Vote %Dem.
DENTON	13,494	4,335	9,137	22	4,802 D	32.1%	67.7%	32.2%	67.8%
DE WITT	5,573	2,283	3,286	4	1,003 D	41.0%	59.0%	41.0%	59.0%
DICKENS	1,667	339	1,324	4	985 D	20.3%	79.4%	20.4%	79.6%
DIMMIT	1,688	501	1,184	3	683 D	29.7%	70.1%	29.7%	70.3%
DONLEY	1,776	708	1,068	—	360 D	39.9%	60.1%	39.9%	60.1%
DUVAL	4,789	353	4,432	4	4,079 D	7.4%	92.5%	7.4%	92.6%
EASTLAND	6,752	2,049	4,692	11	2,643 D	30.4%	69.5%	30.4%	69.6%
ECTOR	22,386	11,497	10,826	63	671 R	51.4%	48.4%	51.5%	48.5%
EDWARDS	712	371	337	4	34 R	52.1%	47.3%	52.4%	47.6%
ELLIS	10,062	2,779	7,278	5	4,499 D	27.6%	72.3%	27.6%	72.4%
EL PASO	55,927	20,687	35,050	190	14,363 D	37.0%	62.7%	37.1%	62.9%
ERATH	5,498	1,642	3,851	5	2,209 D	29.9%	70.0%	29.9%	70.1%
FALLS	5,151	1,216	3,933	2	2,717 D	23.6%	76.4%	23.6%	76.4%
FANNIN	7,200	1,219	5,976	5	4,757 D	16.9%	83.0%	16.9%	83.1%
FAYETTE	5,677	2,036	3,630	11	1,594 D	35.9%	63.9%	35.9%	64.1%
FISHER	2,567	454	2,108	5	1,654 D	17.7%	82.1%	17.7%	82.3%
FLOYD	3,621	1,229	2,383	9	1,154 D	33.9%	65.8%	34.0%	66.0%
FOARD	980	146	833	1	687 D	14.9%	85.0%	14.9%	85.1%
FORT BEND	9,699	3,493	6,186	20	2,693 D	36.0%	63.8%	36.1%	63.9%
FRANKLIN	1,944	424	1,520	—	1,096 D	21.8%	78.2%	21.8%	78.2%
FREESTONE	3,892	1,074	2,816	2	1,742 D	27.6%	72.4%	27.6%	72.4%
FRIO	2,117	607	1,507	3	900 D	28.7%	71.2%	28.7%	71.3%
GAINES	3,201	1,153	2,045	3	892 D	36.0%	63.9%	36.1%	63.9%
GALVESTON	43,173	12,365	30,672	136	18,307 D	28.6%	71.0%	28.7%	71.3%
GARZA	1,827	567	1,254	6	687 D	31.0%	68.6%	31.1%	68.9%
GILLESPIE	3,960	1,695	2,264	1	569 D	42.8%	57.2%	42.8%	57.2%
GLASSCOCK	363	183	179	1	4 R	50.4%	49.3%	50.6%	49.4%
GOLIAD	1,541	549	990	2	441 D	35.6%	64.2%	35.7%	64.3%
GONZALES	4,545	1,190	3,348	7	2,158 D	26.2%	73.7%	26.2%	73.8%
GRAY	8,650	5,011	3,633	6	1,378 R	57.9%	42.0%	58.0%	42.0%
GRAYSON	19,728	5,500	14,207	21	8,707 D	27.9%	72.0%	27.9%	72.0%
GREGG	20,584	11,761	8,741	82	3,020 R	57.1%	42.5%	57.4%	42.6%
GRIMES	3,247	1,014	2,229	4	1,215 D	31.2%	68.6%	31.3%	68.7%
GUADALUPE	7,308	2,731	4,568	9	1,837 D	37.4%	62.5%	37.4%	62.6%
HALE	9,594	3,666	5,910	18	2,244 D	38.2%	61.6%	38.3%	61.7%
HALL	2,453	667	1,785	1	1,118 D	27.2%	72.8%	27.2%	72.8%
HAMILTON	3,056	1,006	2,048	2	1,042 D	32.9%	67.0%	32.9%	67.1%
HANSFORD	2,056	1,193	860	3	333 R	58.0%	41.8%	58.1%	41.9%
HARDEMAN	2,532	697	1,835	—	1,138 D	27.5%	72.5%	27.5%	72.5%
HARDIN	7,146	1,987	5,143	16	3,156 D	27.8%	72.0%	27.9%	72.1%
HARRIS	382,985	154,401	227,819	765	73,418 D	40.3%	59.5%	40.4%	59.6%
HARRISON	11,930	5,568	6,351	11	783 D	46.7%	53.2%	46.7%	53.3%
HARTLEY	1,003	437	565	1	128 D	43.6%	56.3%	43.6%	56.4%
HASKELL	3,421	512	2,903	6	2,391 D	15.0%	84.9%	15.0%	85.0%
HAYS	5,064	1,279	3,780	5	2,501 D	25.3%	74.6%	25.3%	74.7%
HEMPHILL	1,213	563	649	1	86 D	46.4%	53.5%	46.5%	53.5%
HENDERSON	6,714	1,988	4,697	29	2,709 D	29.6%	70.0%	29.7%	70.3%
HIDALGO	33,756	11,563	22,110	83	10,547 D	34.3%	65.5%	34.3%	65.5%
HILL	6,696	1,557	5,130	9	3,573 D	23.3%	76.6%	23.3%	76.7%
HOCKLEY	5,733	1,674	4,049	10	2,375 D	29.2%	70.6%	29.3%	70.7%
HOOD	2,087	423	1,661	3	1,238 D	20.3%	79.6%	20.3%	79.7%
HOPKINS	5,651	1,518	4,133	—	2,615 D	26.9%	73.1%	26.9%	73.1%
HOUSTON	5,366	1,675	3,681	10	2,006 D	31.2%	68.6%	31.3%	68.7%
HOWARD	9,367	3,272	6,083	12	2,811 D	34.9%	64.9%	35.0%	65.0%
HUDSPETH	665	224	438	3	214 D	33.7%	65.9%	33.8%	66.2%
HUNT	9,879	3,302	6,567	10	3,265 D	33.4%	66.5%	33.5%	66.5%
HUTCHINSON	10,000	5,358	4,625	17	733 R	53.6%	46.2%	53.7%	46.3%
IRION	550	199	351	—	152 D	36.2%	63.8%	36.2%	63.8%
JACK	2,444	847	1,594	3	747 D	34.7%	65.2%	34.7%	65.3%
JACKSON	3,952	1,168	2,775	9	1,607 D	29.6%	70.2%	29.6%	70.4%

TEXAS

PRESIDENT 1960

County	Total Vote	Republican	Democratic	Other	Rep.-Dem. Plurality	Total Vote Rep.	Total Vote Dem.	Major Vote Rep.	Major Vote Dem.
JASPER	5,123	2,102	3,004	17	902 D	41.0%	58.6%	41.2%	58.8%
JEFF DAVIS	381	182	195	4	13 D	47.6%	51.2%	48.3%	51.7%
JEFFERSON	70,331	29,395	40,533	403	11,138 D	41.8%	57.6%	42.0%	58.0%
JIM HOGG	1,479	224	1,255	—	1,031 D	15.1%	84.9%	15.1%	84.9%
JIM WELLS	8,112	2,773	5,330	9	2,557 D	34.2%	65.7%	34.2%	65.8%
JOHNSON	8,431	4,510	3,844	77	666 R	53.5%	45.6%	54.0%	46.0%
JONES	4,986	2,196	2,772	18	576 D	44.0%	55.6%	44.2%	55.8%
KARNES	4,085	1,526	2,556	3	1,030 D	37.4%	62.6%	37.4%	62.6%
KAUFMAN	5,768	2,717	3,008	43	291 D	47.1%	52.6%	47.5%	52.5%
KENDALL	2,100	1,544	549	7	995 R	73.5%	26.1%	73.8%	26.2%
KENEDY	152	74	78	—	4 D	48.7%	51.3%	48.7%	51.3%
KENT	698	205	491	2	286 D	29.4%	70.3%	29.5%	70.5%
KERR	4,596	3,252	1,323	21	1,929 R	70.8%	28.8%	71.1%	28.9%
KIMBLE	1,253	699	550	4	149 R	55.8%	43.9%	56.0%	44.0%
KING	173	39	133	1	94 D	22.5%	76.9%	22.7%	77.3%
KINNEY	569	211	358	—	147 D	37.1%	62.9%	37.1%	62.9%
KLEBERG	5,866	2,092	3,773	1	1,681 D	35.7%	64.3%	35.7%	64.3%
KNOX	2,098	729	1,365	4	636 D	34.7%	65.1%	34.8%	65.2%
LAMAR	9,076	3,964	5,084	28	1,120 D	43.7%	56.0%	43.8%	56.2%
LAMB	6,007	2,764	3,089	154	325 D	46.0%	51.4%	47.2%	52.8%
LAMPASAS	2,609	1,222	1,372	15	150 D	46.8%	52.6%	47.1%	52.9%
LA SALLE	1,046	326	718	2	392 D	31.2%	68.6%	31.3%	68.7%
LAVACA	5,522	1,507	4,002	13	2,495 D	27.3%	72.5%	27.4%	72.6%
LEE	2,451	1,048	1,369	34	321 D	42.8%	55.8%	43.4%	56.6%
LEON	2,684	868	1,803	13	935 D	32.3%	67.2%	32.5%	67.5%
LIBERTY	7,345	3,361	3,902	82	541 D	45.8%	53.1%	46.3%	53.7%
LIMESTONE	5,511	2,023	3,472	16	1,449 D	36.7%	63.0%	36.8%	63.2%
LIPSCOMB	1,209	939	267	3	672 R	77.7%	22.1%	77.9%	22.1%
LIVE OAK	1,820	1,048	770	2	278 R	57.6%	42.3%	57.6%	42.4%
LLANO	1,840	704	1,131	5	427 D	38.3%	61.5%	38.4%	61.6%
LOVING	95	42	46	7	4 D	44.2%	48.4%	47.7%	52.3%
LUBBOCK	35,607	20,065	15,340	202	4,725 R	56.4%	43.1%	56.7%	43.3%
LYNN	2,843	953	1,872	18	919 D	33.5%	65.8%	33.7%	66.3%
MCCULLOCH	2,748	1,165	1,579	4	414 D	42.4%	57.5%	42.5%	57.5%
MCLENNAN	35,156	14,926	20,100	130	5,174 D	42.5%	57.2%	42.6%	57.4%
MCMULLEN	481	241	240	—	1 R	50.1%	49.9%	50.1%	49.9%
MADISON	1,552	607	909	36	302 D	39.1%	58.6%	40.0%	60.0%
MARION	1,691	742	904	45	162 D	43.9%	53.5%	45.1%	54.9%
MARTIN	1,203	350	831	22	481 D	29.1%	69.1%	29.6%	70.4%
MASON	1,417	833	575	9	258 R	58.6%	40.6%	59.2%	40.8%
MATAGORDA	5,998	2,975	2,971	52	4 R	49.6%	49.5%	50.0%	50.0%
MAVERICK	2,139	639	1,498	2	859 D	29.9%	70.0%	29.9%	70.1%
MEDINA	4,368	2,028	2,335	5	307 D	46.4%	53.4%	46.5%	53.5%
MENARD	1,099	608	491	—	117 R	55.3%	44.7%	55.3%	44.7%
MIDLAND	17,645	11,363	5,842	440	5,521 R	64.3%	33.1%	66.0%	34.0%
MILAM	5,556	1,898	3,640	18	1,742 D	34.2%	65.5%	34.3%	65.7%
MILLS	1,887	1,012	869	6	143 R	53.6%	46.1%	53.8%	46.2%
MITCHELL	3,350	1,208	2,131	11	923 D	36.1%	63.6%	36.2%	63.8%
MONTAGUE	4,465	2,101	2,346	18	245 D	47.1%	52.5%	47.2%	52.8%
MONTGOMERY	6,937	3,309	3,510	118	201 D	47.7%	50.6%	48.5%	51.5%
MOORE	4,025	2,463	1,547	15	916 R	61.2%	38.4%	61.4%	38.6%
MORRIS	3,544	1,569	1,952	23	383 D	44.3%	55.1%	44.6%	55.4%
MOTLEY	932	480	439	13	41 R	51.5%	47.1%	52.2%	47.8%
NACOGDOCHES	6,732	3,042	3,522	168	480 D	45.2%	52.3%	46.3%	53.7%
NAVARRO	8,901	3,361	5,540	—	2,179 D	37.8%	62.2%	37.8%	62.2%
NEWTON	2,590	756	1,815	19	1,059 D	29.2%	70.1%	29.4%	70.6%
NOLAN	5,675	2,421	3,247	7	826 D	42.7%	57.2%	42.7%	57.3%
NUECES	48,368	18,907	29,361	100	10,454 D	39.1%	60.7%	39.2%	60.8%
OCHILTREE	2,394	1,870	521	3	1,349 R	78.1%	21.8%	78.2%	21.8%
OLDHAM	643	313	326	4	13 D	48.7%	50.7%	49.0%	51.0%

PRESIDENT 1964

County	Total Vote	Republican	Democratic	Other	Rep.-Dem. Plurality	Total Vote Rep.	Total Vote Dem.	Major Vote Rep.	Major Vote Dem.
JASPER	5,537	1,919	3,600	18	1,681 D	34.7%	65.0%	34.8%	65.2%
JEFF DAVIS	479	174	304	1	130 D	36.3%	63.5%	36.4%	63.6%
JEFFERSON	73,594	28,771	44,584	239	15,813 D	39.1%	60.6%	39.2%	60.8%
JIM HOGG	1,530	152	1,375	3	1,223 D	9.9%	89.9%	10.0%	90.0%
JIM WELLS	8,837	1,988	6,849	—	4,861 D	22.5%	77.5%	22.5%	77.5%
JOHNSON	9,642	3,251	6,381	10	3,130 D	33.7%	66.2%	33.8%	66.2%
JONES	4,920	1,295	3,622	3	2,327 D	26.3%	73.6%	26.3%	73.7%
KARNES	4,177	993	3,178	6	2,185 D	23.8%	76.1%	23.8%	76.2%
KAUFMAN	6,694	1,922	4,766	6	2,844 D	28.7%	71.2%	28.7%	71.3%
KENDALL	2,173	1,200	970	3	230 R	55.2%	44.6%	55.3%	44.7%
KENEDY	146	30	115	1	85 D	20.5%	78.8%	20.7%	79.3%
KENT	678	115	563	—	448 D	17.0%	83.0%	17.0%	83.0%
KERR	5,608	2,706	2,894	8	188 D	48.3%	51.6%	48.3%	51.7%
KIMBLE	1,383	520	862	1	342 D	37.6%	62.3%	37.6%	62.4%
KING	214	34	180	—	146 D	15.9%	84.1%	15.9%	84.1%
KINNEY	594	155	439	—	284 D	26.1%	73.9%	26.1%	73.9%
KLEBERG	6,230	1,652	4,568	10	2,916 D	26.5%	73.3%	26.6%	73.4%
KNOX	2,216	439	1,773	4	1,334 D	19.8%	80.0%	19.8%	80.2%
LAMAR	8,905	2,594	6,303	8	3,709 D	29.1%	70.7%	29.2%	70.8%
LAMB	6,349	2,022	4,318	9	2,296 D	31.8%	68.0%	31.9%	68.1%
LAMPASAS	2,970	744	2,224	2	1,480 D	25.1%	74.9%	25.1%	74.9%
LA SALLE	1,212	223	988	1	765 D	18.4%	81.5%	18.4%	81.6%
LAVACA	5,517	1,480	4,031	6	2,551 D	26.8%	73.1%	26.9%	73.1%
LEE	2,809	923	1,884	2	961 D	32.9%	67.1%	32.9%	67.1%
LEON	3,022	642	2,373	7	1,731 D	21.2%	78.5%	21.3%	78.7%
LIBERTY	8,257	2,884	5,357	16	2,473 D	34.9%	64.9%	35.0%	65.0%
LIMESTONE	5,363	1,763	3,589	11	1,826 D	32.9%	66.9%	33.0%	67.0%
LIPSCOMB	1,352	763	589	—	174 R	56.4%	43.5%	56.4%	43.6%
LIVE OAK	2,226	795	1,423	8	628 D	35.7%	63.9%	35.8%	64.2%
LLANO	2,384	655	1,727	2	1,072 D	27.5%	72.4%	27.5%	72.5%
LOVING	79	32	46	1	14 D	40.5%	58.2%	41.0%	59.0%
LUBBOCK	39,463	17,372	22,057	34	4,685 D	44.0%	55.9%	44.1%	55.9%
LYNN	3,030	745	2,281	4	1,536 D	24.6%	75.3%	24.6%	75.4%
MCCULLOCH	2,761	655	2,100	6	1,445 D	23.7%	76.1%	23.8%	76.2%
MCLENNAN	39,346	10,892	28,429	25	17,537 D	27.7%	72.3%	27.7%	72.3%
MCMULLEN	443	175	267	1	92 D	39.5%	60.3%	39.6%	60.4%
MADISON	1,945	644	1,298	3	654 D	33.1%	66.7%	33.1%	66.6%
MARION	2,303	927	1,372	4	445 D	40.3%	59.6%	40.3%	59.7%
MARTIN	1,297	402	892	3	490 D	31.0%	68.8%	31.0%	68.8%
MASON	1,535	590	941	4	351 D	38.4%	61.3%	38.5%	61.5%
MATAGORDA	6,555	2,407	4,143	5	1,736 D	36.7%	63.2%	36.7%	63.3%
MAVERICK	2,661	545	2,113	3	1,568 D	20.5%	79.4%	20.5%	79.5%
MEDINA	4,992	1,583	3,408	1	1,825 D	31.7%	68.2%	31.7%	68.3%
MENARD	985	397	588	—	191 D	40.3%	59.7%	40.3%	59.7%
MIDLAND	20,605	11,906	8,646	53	3,260 R	57.8%	42.0%	57.9%	42.1%
MILAM	5,709	1,334	4,368	7	3,034 D	23.4%	76.5%	23.4%	76.6%
MILLS	1,723	495	1,228	—	733 D	28.7%	71.3%	28.7%	71.3%
MITCHELL	3,159	737	2,420	2	1,683 D	23.3%	76.6%	23.3%	76.7%
MONTAGUE	4,856	1,106	3,746	4	2,640 D	22.8%	77.1%	22.8%	77.2%
MONTGOMERY	8,196	3,167	4,989	40	1,822 D	38.6%	60.9%	38.8%	61.2%
MOORE	4,159	1,762	2,393	4	631 D	42.4%	57.5%	42.4%	57.6%
MORRIS	3,594	1,218	2,366	10	1,148 D	33.9%	65.8%	34.0%	66.0%
MOTLEY	1,004	324	678	2	354 D	32.3%	67.5%	32.3%	67.7%
NACOGDOCHES	7,519	2,976	4,524	19	1,548 D	39.6%	60.2%	39.7%	60.3%
NAVARRO	8,953	2,139	6,811	3	4,672 D	23.9%	76.1%	23.9%	76.1%
NEWTON	2,955	738	2,211	6	1,473 D	25.0%	74.8%	25.0%	75.0%
NOLAN	5,162	1,610	3,540	12	1,930 D	31.2%	68.5%	31.3%	68.7%
NUECES	54,558	14,048	40,426	84	26,378 D	25.7%	74.1%	25.7%	74.2%
OCHILTREE	2,737	1,814	920	3	894 R	66.3%	33.6%	66.3%	33.7%
OLDHAM	670	269	397	4	128 D	40.1%	59.3%	40.4%	59.6%

TEXAS

PRESIDENT 1960

County	Total Vote	Republican	Democratic	Other	Rep.-Dem. Plurality	TV Rep.	TV Dem.	MV Rep.	MV Dem.
ORANGE	14,637	5,483	9,178	76	3,595 D	37.5%	62.0%	37.7%	62.3%
PALO PINTO	5,742	2,595	3,322	25	327 D	46.9%	52.6%	47.1%	52.9%
PANOLA	4,518	2,264	2,187	67	77 R	50.1%	48.4%	50.9%	49.1%
PARKER	7,148	3,467	3,329	52	162 D	48.5%	48.9%	48.9%	51.1%
PARMER	2,786	1,674	1,190	22	584 R	60.1%	39.1%	60.6%	39.4%
PECOS	3,167	1,412	1,724	31	312 D	44.0%	54.4%	45.0%	55.0%
POLK	3,360	1,268	2,037	55	769 D	37.7%	60.6%	38.4%	61.6%
POTTER	23,229	14,202	8,989	38	5,213 R	61.1%	38.7%	61.2%	38.8%
PRESIDIO	1,248	376	866	6	490 D	30.1%	69.4%	30.3%	69.7%
RAINS	1,081	401	680		279 D	37.1%	62.9%	37.1%	62.9%
RANDALL	10,269	6,958	3,282	29	3,676 R	67.8%	32.0%	67.9%	32.1%
REAGAN	1,131	489	621	21	132 D	43.2%	54.9%	44.1%	55.9%
REAL	653	377	273	3	104 R	57.7%	41.8%	58.0%	42.0%
RED RIVER	4,389	1,527	2,850	12	1,323 D	34.8%	64.9%	34.9%	65.1%
REEVES	3,822	1,549	2,235	38	686 D	40.5%	58.5%	40.9%	59.1%
REFUGIO	2,842	1,062	1,777	3	715 D	37.4%	62.5%	37.4%	62.6%
ROBERTS	445	339	104	2	235 R	76.2%	23.4%	76.5%	23.5%
ROBERTSON	3,616	935	2,669	12	1,734 D	25.9%	73.8%	25.9%	74.1%
ROCKWALL	1,583	652	917	14	265 D	41.2%	57.9%	41.6%	58.4%
RUNNELS	4,075	2,128	1,938	9	190 R	52.2%	47.6%	52.3%	47.7%
RUSK	10,840	6,001	4,390	449	1,611 D	55.4%	40.5%	57.8%	42.2%
SABINE	1,843	619	1,208	16	589 D	33.6%	65.5%	33.9%	66.1%
SAN AUGUSTINE	1,961	638	1,269	54	631 D	32.5%	64.7%	33.5%	66.5%
SAN JACINTO	1,570	448	1,115	7	667 D	28.5%	71.0%	28.7%	71.3%
SAN PATRICIO	8,391	3,129	5,246	16	2,117 D	37.3%	62.5%	37.4%	62.6%
SAN SABA	2,108	849	1,251	8	402 D	40.3%	59.3%	40.4%	59.6%
SCHLEICHER	809	455	351	3	104 R	56.2%	43.4%	56.5%	43.5%
SCURRY	5,290	2,235	3,020	35	785 D	42.2%	57.1%	42.5%	57.5%
SHACKELFORD	1,397	684	713		29 D	49.0%	51.0%	49.0%	51.0%
SHELBY	4,993	1,679	3,256	48	1,587 D	33.6%	65.4%	34.0%	66.0%
SHERMAN	993	686	335	2	351 R	69.1%	30.7%	69.2%	30.8%
SMITH	20,821	12,042	8,424	285	3,548 R	57.8%	40.8%	58.6%	41.4%
SOMERVELL	800	441	345	14	96 R	55.1%	43.1%	56.1%	43.9%
STARR	4,333	280	4,051	2	3,771 D	6.5%	93.5%	6.5%	93.5%
STEPHENS	3,029	1,664	1,357	8	307 R	54.9%	44.8%	55.1%	44.9%
STERLING	375	182	193		11 D	48.5%	51.5%	48.5%	51.5%
STONEWALL	1,173	306	864	3	558 D	26.1%	73.7%	26.2%	73.8%
SUTTON	911	437	474		37 D	48.0%	52.0%	48.0%	52.0%
SWISHER	3,103	1,310	1,777	16	467 D	42.2%	57.3%	42.4%	57.6%
TARRANT	132,986	72,813	59,385	788	13,428 R	54.8%	44.7%	55.1%	44.9%
TAYLOR	21,650	12,258	9,347	45	2,911 R	56.6%	43.2%	56.7%	43.3%
TERRELL	646	291	352	3	61 D	45.0%	54.5%	45.3%	54.7%
TERRY	4,162	1,908	2,237	17	329 D	45.8%	53.7%	46.0%	54.0%
THROCKMORTON	1,134	442	689		247 D	39.0%	60.5%	39.1%	60.9%
TITUS	4,946	2,216	2,701	29	485 D	44.8%	54.6%	45.1%	54.9%
TOM GREEN	15,246	8,176	7,031	39	1,145 R	53.6%	46.1%	53.8%	46.2%
TRAVIS	49,264	22,107	27,022	135	4,915 D	44.9%	54.9%	45.0%	55.0%
TRINITY	2,264	707	1,521	36	814 D	31.2%	67.2%	31.7%	68.3%
TYLER	2,656	1,401	1,242	13	159 R	52.7%	46.8%	53.0%	47.0%
UPSHUR	5,554	2,262	3,248	44	986 D	40.7%	58.5%	41.1%	58.9%
UPTON	1,760	798	930	32	132 D	45.3%	52.8%	46.2%	53.8%
UVALDE	3,552	2,214	1,324	14	890 R	62.3%	37.3%	62.6%	37.4%
VAL VERDE	3,603	1,551	2,049	3	498 D	43.0%	56.9%	43.1%	56.9%
VAN ZANDT	4,967	2,120	2,825	22	705 D	42.7%	56.9%	42.9%	57.1%
VICTORIA	10,397	4,591	5,779	27	1,188 D	44.2%	55.6%	44.3%	55.7%
WALKER	3,604	1,750	1,832	22	82 D	48.6%	50.8%	48.9%	51.1%
WALLER	2,267	1,115	1,101	51	14 R	49.2%	48.6%	50.3%	49.7%
WARD	3,852	1,763	2,013	71	255 D	45.8%	52.4%	46.6%	53.4%
WASHINGTON	4,489	2,613	1,864	12	749 R	58.2%	41.5%	58.4%	41.6%
WEBB	11,865	1,802	10,059	4	8,257 D	15.2%	84.8%	15.2%	84.8%

PRESIDENT 1964

County	Total Vote	Republican	Democratic	Other	Rep.-Dem. Plurality	TV Rep.	TV Dem.	MV Rep.	MV Dem.
ORANGE	15,645	6,216	9,390	39	3,174 D	39.7%	60.0%	39.8%	60.2%
PALO PINTO	5,541	1,748	3,791	2	2,043 D	31.5%	68.4%	31.6%	68.4%
PANOLA	5,437	2,818	2,608	11	210 R	51.8%	48.0%	51.9%	48.1%
PARKER	7,458	2,175	5,270	13	3,095 D	29.2%	70.7%	29.2%	70.8%
PARMER	2,779	1,216	1,556	7	340 D	43.8%	56.0%	43.9%	56.1%
PECOS	3,473	1,393	2,068	12	675 D	40.1%	59.5%	40.2%	59.8%
POLK	3,700	1,199	2,492	9	1,293 D	32.4%	67.5%	32.5%	67.5%
POTTER	24,419	11,505	12,850	64	1,345 D	47.1%	52.6%	47.2%	52.8%
PRESIDIO	1,588	431	1,156	1	725 D	27.1%	72.8%	27.2%	72.8%
RAINS	1,168	272	893	3	621 D	23.3%	76.5%	23.3%	76.7%
RANDALL	13,881	7,843	6,016	22	1,827 R	56.5%	43.3%	56.6%	43.4%
REAGAN	1,022	406	614	2	208 D	39.7%	60.1%	39.8%	60.2%
REAL	743	255	487	1	232 D	34.3%	65.5%	34.4%	65.6%
RED RIVER	4,654	1,257	3,391	6	2,134 D	27.0%	72.9%	27.0%	73.0%
REEVES	3,595	1,251	2,340	4	1,089 D	34.8%	65.1%	34.8%	65.2%
REFUGIO	3,091	772	2,319		1,547 D	25.0%	75.0%	25.0%	75.0%
ROBERTS	495	297	198		99 D	60.0%	40.0%	60.0%	40.0%
ROBERTSON	4,247	895	3,350	2	2,455 D	21.1%	78.9%	21.1%	78.9%
ROCKWALL	1,755	445	1,305	5	860 D	25.4%	74.4%	25.4%	74.6%
RUNNELS	4,132	1,480	2,645	7	1,165 D	35.8%	64.0%	35.9%	64.1%
RUSK	12,033	5,488	6,528	17	1,040 D	45.6%	54.3%	45.7%	54.3%
SABINE	2,230	428	1,801	1	1,373 D	19.2%	80.8%	19.2%	80.8%
SAN AUGUSTINE	1,940	760	1,173	7	413 D	39.2%	60.5%	39.3%	60.7%
SAN JACINTO	2,026	343	1,680	3	1,337 D	16.9%	82.9%	17.0%	83.0%
SAN PATRICIO	9,384	2,188	7,176	20	4,988 D	23.3%	76.5%	23.4%	76.6%
SAN SABA	2,277	418	1,859		1,441 D	18.4%	81.6%	18.4%	81.6%
SCHLEICHER	903	388	514	1	126 D	43.0%	56.9%	43.0%	56.9%
SCURRY	5,137	1,741	3,381	15	1,640 D	33.9%	65.8%	34.0%	66.0%
SHACKELFORD	1,424	487	934		447 D	34.2%	65.5%	34.3%	65.7%
SHELBY	5,711	2,220	3,487	4	1,267 D	38.9%	61.1%	38.9%	61.1%
SHERMAN	1,092	629	462	1	167 R	57.6%	42.3%	57.7%	42.3%
SMITH	25,472	12,960	12,026	486	934 R	50.9%	49.0%	51.0%	49.0%
SOMERVELL	854	210	641	3	431 D	24.7%	75.1%	24.7%	75.3%
STARR	4,742	678	4,056	8	3,378 D	14.3%	85.5%	14.3%	85.7%
STEPHENS	2,874	1,119	1,753	2	634 D	39.0%	61.0%	39.0%	61.0%
STERLING	384	140	243	1	103 D	36.5%	63.4%	36.6%	63.4%
STONEWALL	1,199	219	978	2	759 D	18.3%	81.6%	18.3%	81.7%
SUTTON	1,051	357	694		337 D	34.0%	66.0%	34.0%	66.0%
SWISHER	3,230	815	2,410	5	1,595 D	25.2%	74.6%	25.3%	74.7%
TARRANT	154,158	56,593	97,092	473	40,499 D	36.7%	63.0%	36.8%	63.2%
TAYLOR	22,620	9,220	13,366	34	4,146 D	40.8%	59.1%	40.8%	59.2%
TERRELL	658	294	364		70 D	44.7%	55.3%	44.7%	55.3%
TERRY	4,632	1,592	3,034	6	1,442 D	34.4%	65.5%	34.4%	65.6%
THROCKMORTON	1,130	247	883		636 D	21.9%	78.1%	21.9%	78.1%
TITUS	5,219	1,687	3,528	4	1,841 D	32.3%	67.6%	32.3%	67.7%
TOM GREEN	16,443	6,664	9,767	12	3,103 D	40.5%	59.4%	40.6%	59.4%
TRAVIS	63,958	19,838	44,058	62	24,220 D	31.0%	68.9%	31.0%	69.0%
TRINITY	2,428	763	1,654	11	891 D	31.6%	68.1%	31.6%	68.4%
TYLER	3,037	1,216	1,818	13	602 D	40.0%	59.9%	40.1%	59.9%
UPSHUR	6,262	2,222	4,027	13	1,805 D	35.5%	64.3%	35.5%	64.4%
UPTON	1,604	636	958	10	322 D	39.7%	60.1%	39.9%	60.1%
UVALDE	4,326	1,963	2,358	5	395 D	45.4%	54.5%	45.5%	54.6%
VAL VERDE	4,902	1,346	3,555	1	2,209 D	27.5%	72.5%	27.5%	72.5%
VAN ZANDT	5,676	1,614	4,047	15	2,433 D	28.4%	71.3%	28.5%	71.5%
VICTORIA	12,367	4,201	8,141	25	3,940 D	34.0%	65.8%	34.0%	66.0%
WALKER	4,436	1,557	2,877	2	1,320 D	35.1%	64.9%	35.1%	64.9%
WALLER	3,149	980	2,167	2	1,187 D	31.1%	68.8%	31.1%	68.9%
WARD	3,954	1,730	2,221	3	491 D	43.8%	56.2%	43.8%	56.2%
WASHINGTON	4,962	2,019	2,938	5	919 D	40.7%	59.3%	40.7%	59.3%
WEBB	11,182	1,094	10,073	15	8,979 D	9.8%	90.1%	9.8%	90.2%

TEXAS

PRESIDENT 1960

County	Total Vote	Republican	Democratic	Other	Rep.-Dem. Plurality	Percentage Total Vote Rep.	Dem.	Major Vote Rep.	Dem.
WHARTON	8,458	3,387	5,004	67	1,617 D	40.0%	59.2%	40.4%	59.6%
WHEELER	2,444	1,428	1,011	5	417 R	58.4%	41.4%	58.5%	41.5%
WICHITA	27,213	12,587	14,587	39	2,000 D	46.3%	53.6%	46.3%	53.7%
WILBARGER	5,129	2,796	2,319	14	477 R	54.5%	45.2%	54.7%	45.3%
WILLACY	3,487	1,367	2,109	11	742 D	39.2%	60.5%	39.3%	60.7%
WILLIAMSON	7,870	2,429	5,410	31	2,981 D	30.9%	68.7%	31.0%	69.0%
WILSON	4,157	1,248	2,905	4	1,657 D	30.0%	69.9%	30.1%	69.9%
WINKLER	3,253	1,562	1,642	49	80 D	48.0%	50.5%	48.8%	51.2%
WISE	5,051	2,562	2,470	19	92 R	50.7%	48.9%	50.9%	49.1%
WOOD	5,112	2,400	2,633	79	233 D	46.9%	51.5%	47.7%	52.3%
YOAKUM	2,215	1,207	994	14	213 R	54.5%	44.9%	54.8%	45.2%
YOUNG	4,509	2,067	2,419	23	352 D	45.3%	53.6%	46.1%	53.9%
ZAPATA	935	260	675		415 D	27.8%	72.2%	27.8%	72.2%
ZAVALA	1,475	761	706	8	55 R	51.5%	47.9%	51.9%	48.1%
TOTAL	2,311,084	1,121,310	1,167,567	22,207	46,257 D	48.5%	50.5%	49.0%	51.3%

PRESIDENT 1964

County	Total Vote	Republican	Democratic	Other	Rep.-Dem. Plurality	Percentage Total Vote Rep.	Dem.	Major Vote Rep.	Dem.
WHARTON	9,020	2,775	6,234	11	3,459 D	30.8%	69.1%	30.8%	69.2%
WHEELER	2,580	1,138	1,440	2	302 D	44.1%	55.8%	44.1%	55.9%
WICHITA	27,730	8,585	19,131	14	10,546 D	31.0%	69.0%	31.0%	69.0%
WILBARGER	4,742	1,539	3,200	3	1,661 D	32.5%	67.5%	32.5%	67.5%
WILLACY	3,388	1,230	2,152	6	922 D	36.3%	63.5%	36.4%	63.6%
WILLIAMSON	9,202	1,766	7,430	6	5,664 D	19.2%	80.7%	19.2%	80.8%
WILSON	4,195	718	3,472	5	2,754 D	17.1%	82.8%	17.1%	82.9%
WINKLER	3,679	1,617	2,059	3	442 D	44.0%	56.0%	44.0%	56.0%
WISE	5,241	1,336	3,852	3	2,466 D	26.4%	73.5%	26.5%	73.5%
WOOD	5,606	2,068	3,528	10	1,460 D	36.9%	62.9%	37.0%	63.0%
YOAKUM	2,280	859	1,415	6	556 D	37.7%	62.1%	37.8%	62.2%
YOUNG	4,996	1,600	3,395	1	1,795 D	32.0%	68.0%	32.0%	68.0%
ZAPATA	1,147	135	1,009	3	874 D	11.8%	88.0%	11.8%	88.2%
ZAVALA	2,385	598	1,784	3	1,186 D	25.1%	74.8%	25.1%	74.9%
TOTAL	2,626,811	958,566	1,663,185	5,060	704,619 D	36.5%	63.3%	36.6%	63.4%

TEXAS

OTHER VOTE COMPOSITION

1920   48,098 American; 27,309 Black-and-Tan Republican; 8,124 Socialist.
1924   Progressive.
1928   658 Socialist; 209 Communist.
1932   4,414 Socialist; 243 Liberty; 207 Communist; 157 Jacksonian; 34 scattered.
The Jacksonian and scattered vote are not included in the county-by-county figures; they are reported only as a part of the state-wide total.
1936   3,187 Union; 1,122 Socialist; 522 Prohibition; 257 Communist. The Prohibition vote is not included in the county-by-county figures; it is included only as a part of the state-wide total.

1940   928 Prohibition; 628 Socialist; 215 Communist.
1944   135,444 Texas Regulars; 1,018 Prohibition; 594 Socialist; 250 America First.
1948   113,920 States Rights; 3,918 Progressive; 3,115 Prohibition; 922 Socialist.
1952   1,983 Prohibition; 1,563 Christian Nationalist-Constitution (MacArthur); 294 Progressive.
1956   States Rights.

1960   18,162 Constitution (Sullivan); 3,870 Prohibition; 175 scattered.
1964   Constitution.

SPECIAL CASES:

State canvass reports for the earlier elections omit all or part of the vote in certain counties. In most of these cases unofficial figures have been used to complete the state records, notably in 1940 (from Edgar Eugene Robinson's studies), and in 1948 (from the files of the American Institute of Public Opinion).

1920   American candidates carried several counties and ran second in others; Black-and-Tan Republican electors ran second in several counties; Socialist candidates ran second in one county in which no Republican votes were cast. In several counties the canvassing report is unclear; in these counties, the interpretations developed in Edgar Eugene Robinson's studies have been used.
1924   Progressive candidates carried several counties and ran second in others. Most of Willacy county renamed Kenedy and a new Willacy county organized in 1921; Hockley county organized in 1921; Cochran county organized in 1924.
1928   Crane county organized in 1927.
1932   Loving county organized in 1931, though it had reported as an electoral unit in earlier elections.
1944   Texas Regulars electors carried one county and ran second in others.

1948   States Rights candidates ran second in a number of counties.
1952   MacArthur total includes 833 Christian Nationalist and 730 Constitution votes.

UTAH

PRESIDENT 1920

County	Total Vote	Republican	Democratic	Other	Rep.-Dem. Plurality	Percentage Total Vote Rep.	Dem.	Percentage Major Vote Rep.	Dem.
BEAVER	1,837	1,056	741	40	315 R	57.5%	40.3%	58.8%	41.2%
BOX ELDER	5,812	3,421	2,330	61	1,091 R	58.9%	40.1%	59.5%	40.5%
CACHE	9,397	5,063	4,239	95	824 R	53.9%	45.1%	54.4%	45.6%
CARBON	3,560	1,675	1,559	326	116 R	47.1%	43.8%	51.8%	48.2%
DAGGETT	128	94	32	2	62 R	73.4%	25.0%	74.6%	25.4%
DAVIS	4,122	2,463	1,632	27	831 R	59.8%	39.6%	60.1%	39.9%
DUCHESNE	2,466	1,523	822	121	701 R	61.8%	33.3%	64.9%	35.1%
EMERY	2,398	1,285	1,029	84	256 R	53.6%	42.9%	55.5%	44.5%
GARFIELD	1,431	1,023	393	15	630 R	71.5%	27.5%	72.2%	27.3%
GRAND	598	306	278	14	28 R	51.2%	46.5%	52.4%	47.5%
IRON	2,010	1,399	561	50	838 R	69.6%	27.9%	71.4%	28.6%
JUAB	3,185	1,692	1,308	185	384 R	53.1%	41.1%	56.4%	43.6%
KANE	690	501	186	3	315 R	72.6%	27.0%	72.9%	27.1%
MILLARD	3,515	2,199	1,167	149	1,032 R	62.6%	33.2%	65.3%	34.7%
MORGAN	945	544	397	4	147 R	57.6%	42.0%	57.8%	42.2%
PIUTE	843	538	283	22	255 R	63.8%	33.6%	65.5%	34.5%
RICH	671	449	222		227 R	66.9%	33.1%	66.9%	33.1%
SALT LAKE	50,873	27,841	19,249	3,783	8,592 R	54.7%	37.8%	59.1%	40.9%
SAN JUAN	807	523	260	24	263 R	64.8%	32.2%	66.8%	33.2%
SANPETE	6,219	3,741	2,406	72	1,335 R	60.2%	38.7%	60.9%	39.1%
SEVIER	3,988	2,506	1,425	57	1,081 R	62.8%	35.7%	63.7%	36.3%
SUMMIT	2,514	1,503	874	137	629 R	59.8%	34.8%	63.2%	36.8%
TOOELE	2,470	1,387	916	167	471 R	56.2%	37.1%	60.2%	39.8%
UINTAH	2,239	1,354	817	68	537 R	60.5%	36.5%	62.4%	37.6%
UTAH	14,532	7,752	6,377	403	1,375 R	53.3%	43.9%	54.9%	45.1%
WASATCH	1,738	1,061	665	12	396 R	61.0%	38.3%	61.5%	38.5%
WASHINGTON	2,156	1,138	1,008	10	130 R	52.8%	46.8%	53.0%	47.0%
WAYNE	639	396	224	19	172 R	62.0%	35.1%	63.9%	36.1%
WEBER	14,045	7,122	5,239	1,684	1,883 R	50.7%	37.3%	57.6%	42.4%
TOTAL	145,828	81,555	56,639	7,634	24,916 R	55.9%	38.8%	59.0%	41.0%

PRESIDENT 1924

County	Total Vote	Republican	Democratic	Other	Rep.-Dem. Plurality	Percentage Total Vote Rep.	Dem.	Percentage Major Vote Rep.	Dem.
BEAVER	1,854	989	578	287	411 R	53.3%	31.2%	63.1%	36.9%
BOX ELDER	5,493	3,086	1,841	566	1,245 R	56.2%	33.5%	62.6%	37.4%
CACHE	9,562	4,973	3,915	674	1,058 R	52.0%	40.9%	56.0%	44.0%
CARBON	4,996	1,878	1,528	1,590	350 R	37.6%	30.6%	55.1%	44.9%
DAGGETT	131	97	26	8	71 R	74.0%	19.8%	78.9%	21.1%
DAVIS	4,080	2,265	1,507	308	758 R	55.5%	36.9%	60.0%	40.0%
DUCHESNE	2,217	1,277	731	209	546 R	57.6%	33.0%	63.6%	36.4%
EMERY	2,278	979	916	383	63 R	43.0%	40.2%	51.7%	48.3%
GARFIELD	1,183	823	308	52	515 R	69.6%	26.0%	72.8%	27.2%
GRAND	580	278	243	59	35 R	47.9%	41.9%	53.4%	46.6%
IRON	2,150	1,429	485	236	944 R	66.5%	22.6%	74.7%	25.3%
JUAB	3,041	1,325	1,241	475	84 R	43.6%	40.8%	51.6%	48.4%
KANE	642	515	117	10	398 R	80.2%	18.2%	81.5%	18.5%
MILLARD	3,439	1,917	1,025	497	892 R	55.7%	29.8%	65.2%	34.8%
MORGAN	891	482	360	49	122 R	54.1%	40.4%	57.2%	42.8%
PIUTE	648	396	208	42	190 R	61.4%	32.1%	65.7%	34.3%
RICH	645	403	211	31	192 R	62.5%	32.7%	65.6%	34.4%
SALT LAKE	58,602	27,215	14,853	16,534	12,362 R	46.4%	25.3%	64.7%	35.3%
SAN JUAN	668	380	232	56	148 R	56.9%	34.7%	62.1%	37.9%
SANPETE	5,983	3,374	2,228	381	1,146 R	56.4%	37.2%	60.2%	39.8%
SEVIER	3,740	2,111	1,201	428	910 R	56.4%	32.1%	63.7%	36.3%
SUMMIT	2,794	1,597	825	372	772 R	57.2%	29.5%	65.9%	34.1%
TOOELE	2,468	1,295	674	499	621 R	52.5%	27.3%	65.8%	34.2%
UINTAH	2,128	1,296	716	116	580 R	60.9%	33.6%	64.4%	35.6%
UTAH	15,010	6,946	5,226	2,838	1,720 R	46.3%	34.8%	57.1%	42.9%
WASATCH	2,139	1,105	727	277	378 R	52.4%	34.5%	60.3%	39.7%
WASHINGTON	2,149	1,181	868	100	313 R	55.0%	40.4%	57.6%	42.4%
WAYNE	578	331	241	6	90 R	57.3%	41.7%	57.9%	42.1%
WEBER	16,931	7,362	3,970	5,579	3,412 R	43.6%	23.4%	65.0%	35.0%
TOTAL	156,990	77,327	47,001	32,662	30,326 R	49.3%	29.9%	62.2%	37.8%

UTAH

PRESIDENT 1928

County	Total Vote	Republican	Democratic	Other	Rep.-Dem. Plurality	% Total Vote Rep.	% Total Vote Dem.	% Major Vote Rep.	% Major Vote Dem.
BEAVER	2,090	1,149	936	5	213 R	55.0%	44.8%	55.1%	44.9%
BOX ELDER	5,825	3,317	2,488	20	829 R	56.9%	42.7%	57.1%	42.9%
CACHE	10,071	5,297	4,748	26	549 R	52.6%	47.1%	52.7%	47.3%
CARBON	5,188	2,184	2,954	50	770 D	42.1%	56.9%	42.5%	57.5%
DAGGETT	138	107	31		76 R	77.5%	22.5%	77.5%	22.5%
DAVIS	4,818	2,508	2,296	14	212 R	52.1%	47.7%	52.2%	47.8%
DUCHESNE	2,497	1,585	899	13	686 R	63.5%	36.0%	63.8%	36.2%
EMERY	2,308	1,317	965	26	352 R	57.1%	41.8%	57.7%	42.3%
GARFIELD	1,354	1,024	325	5	699 R	75.6%	24.0%	75.9%	24.1%
GRAND	660	347	310	3	37 R	52.6%	47.0%	52.8%	47.2%
IRON	2,528	1,823	682	23	1,141 R	72.1%	27.0%	72.8%	27.2%
JUAB	3,279	1,557	1,714	8	157 D	47.5%	52.3%	47.6%	52.4%
KANE	708	566	141	1	425 R	79.9%	19.9%	80.1%	19.9%
MILLARD	3,720	2,263	1,440	17	823 R	60.8%	38.7%	61.1%	38.9%
MORGAN	968	513	454	1	59 R	53.0%	46.9%	53.1%	46.9%
PIUTE	676	434	237	5	197 R	64.2%	35.1%	64.7%	35.3%
RICH	694	470	224		246 R	67.7%	32.3%	67.7%	32.3%
SALT LAKE	68,940	34,393	34,127	420	266 R	49.9%	49.5%	50.2%	49.8%
SAN JUAN	685	449	231	5	218 R	65.5%	33.7%	66.0%	34.0%
SANPETE	6,195	3,694	2,482	19	1,212 R	59.6%	40.1%	59.8%	40.2%
SEVIER	3,840	2,424	1,399	17	1,025 R	63.1%	36.4%	63.4%	36.6%
SUMMIT	3,032	1,748	1,260	24	488 R	57.7%	41.6%	58.1%	41.9%
TOOELE	3,148	1,707	1,421	20	286 R	54.2%	45.1%	54.6%	45.4%
UINTAH	2,483	1,589	860	14	709 R	64.0%	35.1%	64.6%	35.6%
UTAH	16,807	8,771	7,955	81	816 R	52.2%	47.3%	52.4%	47.6%
WASATCH	2,317	1,340	973	4	367 R	57.8%	42.0%	57.9%	42.1%
WASHINGTON	2,547	1,686	857	4	829 R	66.2%	33.6%	66.3%	33.7%
WAYNE	619	422	195	2	227 R	68.2%	31.5%	68.4%	31.6%
WEBER	18,468	9,934	8,361	173	1,573 R	53.8%	45.3%	54.3%	45.7%
TOTAL	176,603	94,618	80,965	1,000	13,633 R	53.6%	45.9%	53.9%	46.1%

PRESIDENT 1932

County	Total Vote	Republican	Democratic	Other	Rep.-Dem. Plurality	% Total Vote Rep.	% Total Vote Dem.	% Major Vote Rep.	% Major Vote Dem.
BEAVER	2,201	969	1,218	14	249 D	44.0%	55.3%	44.3%	55.7%
BOX ELDER	6,827	3,048	3,695	84	647 D	44.6%	54.1%	45.2%	54.8%
CACHE	11,444	4,829	6,522	93	1,693 D	42.2%	57.0%	42.5%	57.5%
CARBON	6,120	1,655	4,239	226	2,584 D	27.0%	69.3%	28.1%	71.9%
DAGGETT	170	90	79	1	11 R	52.9%	46.5%	53.3%	46.7%
DAVIS	5,618	2,562	3,006	50	444 D	45.6%	53.5%	46.0%	54.0%
DUCHESNE	3,072	1,333	1,590	149	257 D	43.4%	51.8%	45.6%	54.4%
EMERY	2,848	1,112	1,613	123	501 D	39.0%	56.6%	40.8%	59.2%
GARFIELD	1,644	1,125	493	26	632 R	68.4%	30.0%	69.5%	30.5%
GRAND	805	278	506	21	228 D	34.5%	62.9%	35.5%	64.5%
IRON	3,163	1,599	1,358	206	241 R	50.6%	42.9%	54.1%	45.9%
JUAB	3,245	1,220	1,969	56	749 D	37.6%	60.7%	38.3%	61.7%
KANE	860	618	229	13	389 R	71.9%	26.6%	73.0%	27.0%
MILLARD	3,855	1,916	1,881	58	35 R	49.7%	48.8%	50.5%	49.5%
MORGAN	1,175	568	602	5	34 D	48.3%	51.2%	48.5%	51.5%
PIUTE	854	433	403	18	30 R	50.7%	47.2%	51.8%	48.2%
RICH	867	398	469		71 D	45.9%	54.1%	45.9%	54.1%
SALT LAKE	82,292	32,224	48,012	2,056	15,788 D	39.2%	58.3%	40.2%	59.8%
SAN JUAN	940	460	459	21	1 R	48.9%	48.8%	50.1%	49.9%
SANPETE	6,833	3,147	3,600	86	453 D	46.1%	52.7%	46.6%	53.4%
SEVIER	4,593	2,225	2,303	65	78 D	48.4%	50.1%	49.1%	50.9%
SUMMIT	3,536	1,434	2,028	74	594 D	40.6%	57.4%	41.4%	58.6%
TOOELE	3,323	1,407	1,865	51	458 D	42.3%	56.1%	43.0%	57.0%
UINTAH	3,190	1,355	1,778	57	423 D	42.5%	55.7%	43.2%	56.8%
UTAH	20,536	7,953	12,136	443	4,187 D	38.7%	59.1%	39.6%	60.4%
WASATCH	2,163	1,042	1,103	18	61 D	48.2%	51.0%	48.6%	51.4%
WASHINGTON	3,047	1,378	1,648	21	270 D	45.2%	54.1%	45.5%	54.5%
WAYNE	808	398	401	9	3 D	49.3%	49.6%	49.8%	50.2%
WEBER	20,549	8,019	11,541	989	3,522 D	39.0%	56.2%	41.0%	59.0%
TOTAL	206,578	84,795	116,750	5,033	31,955 D	41.0%	56.5%	42.1%	57.9%

UTAH

PRESIDENT 1936

County	Total Vote	Republican	Democratic	Other	Rep.-Dem. Plurality	Percentage Total Vote Rep.	Dem.	Major Vote Rep.	Dem.
BEAVER	2,261	913	1,337	11	424 D	40.4%	59.1%	40.6%	59.4%
BOX ELDER	7,231	2,180	5,001	50	2,821 D	30.1%	69.2%	30.4%	69.6%
CACHE	11,957	3,258	8,606	93	5,348 D	27.2%	72.0%	27.5%	72.5%
CARBON	6,510	1,348	5,040	122	3,692 D	20.7%	77.4%	21.1%	78.9%
DAGGETT	208	78	128	2	50 D	37.5%	61.5%	37.9%	62.1%
DAVIS	5,782	1,841	3,920	21	2,079 D	31.8%	67.8%	32.0%	68.0%
DUCHESNE	3,085	1,070	1,970	45	900 D	34.7%	63.9%	35.2%	64.8%
EMERY	2,869	938	1,909	22	971 D	32.7%	66.5%	32.9%	67.1%
GARFIELD	1,772	842	928	2	86 D	47.5%	52.4%	47.6%	52.4%
GRAND	809	272	521	16	249 D	33.6%	64.4%	34.3%	65.7%
IRON	3,289	1,396	1,844	49	448 D	42.4%	56.1%	43.1%	56.9%
JUAB	3,377	1,027	2,319	31	1,292 D	30.4%	68.7%	30.7%	69.3%
KANE	918	519	395	4	124 R	56.5%	43.0%	56.8%	43.2%
MILLARD	3,833	1,466	2,313	54	847 D	38.2%	60.3%	38.8%	61.2%
MORGAN	1,228	483	739	6	256 D	39.3%	60.2%	39.5%	60.5%
PIUTE	951	339	611	1	272 D	35.6%	64.2%	35.7%	64.3%
RICH	880	388	488	4	100 D	44.1%	55.5%	44.3%	55.7%
SALT LAKE	86,929	23,819	62,386	724	38,567 D	27.4%	71.8%	27.6%	72.4%
SAN JUAN	961	432	520	9	88 D	45.0%	54.1%	45.4%	54.6%
SANPETE	6,748	2,738	3,959	51	1,221 D	40.6%	58.7%	40.9%	59.1%
SEVIER	4,767	1,899	2,816	52	917 D	39.8%	59.1%	40.3%	59.7%
SUMMIT	3,784	1,422	2,344	18	922 D	37.5%	61.9%	37.8%	62.2%
TOOELE	3,399	1,029	2,361	9	1,332 D	30.3%	69.5%	30.3%	69.6%
UINTAH	3,258	1,193	1,986	79	793 D	36.6%	61.0%	37.5%	62.5%
UTAH	20,695	6,173	14,387	135	8,214 D	29.8%	69.5%	30.0%	70.3%
WASATCH	2,334	1,029	1,299	6	270 D	44.1%	55.7%	44.2%	55.3%
WASHINGTON	3,164	1,145	2,005	14	860 D	36.2%	63.4%	36.3%	63.7%
WAYNE	854	329	522	3	193 D	38.5%	61.1%	38.7%	61.3%
WEBER	22,826	4,989	17,594	243	12,605 D	21.9%	77.1%	22.1%	77.9%
TOTAL	216,679	64,555	150,248	1,876	85,693 D	29.8%	69.3%	30.1%	69.9%

PRESIDENT 1940

County	Total Vote	Republican	Democratic	Other	Rep.-Dem. Plurality	Percentage Total Vote Rep.	Dem.	Major Vote Rep.	Dem.
BEAVER	2,405	1,101	1,303	1	202 D	45.8%	54.2%	45.8%	54.2%
BOX ELDER	7,986	3,248	4,736	2	1,488 D	40.7%	59.3%	40.7%	59.3%
CACHE	13,058	5,184	7,867	7	2,683 D	39.7%	60.2%	39.7%	60.3%
CARBON	7,456	2,242	5,180	34	2,938 D	30.1%	69.5%	30.2%	69.8%
DAGGETT	256	95	160		64 D	37.5%	62.5%	37.5%	62.5%
DAVIS	6,707	2,835	3,865	6	1,029 D	42.3%	57.6%	42.3%	57.7%
DUCHESNE	3,308	1,322	1,982	4	660 D	40.0%	59.9%	40.0%	60.0%
EMERY	2,919	1,006	1,901	12	895 D	34.5%	65.1%	34.6%	65.4%
GARFIELD	1,844	1,030	814		216 R	55.9%	44.1%	55.9%	44.1%
GRAND	881	432	446	3	14 D	49.0%	50.6%	49.2%	50.8%
IRON	3,998	2,060	1,915	23	145 R	51.5%	47.9%	51.8%	48.2%
JUAB	3,553	1,412	2,136	5	724 D	39.7%	60.1%	39.8%	60.2%
KANE	1,014	675	339		336 R	66.6%	33.4%	66.6%	33.4%
MILLARD	4,255	1,943	2,312	10	359 D	45.7%	54.1%	45.8%	54.2%
MORGAN	1,274	575	699		124 D	45.1%	54.9%	45.1%	54.9%
PIUTE	910	442	466	2	24 D	48.6%	51.2%	48.7%	51.3%
RICH	922	447	475		28 D	48.5%	51.5%	48.5%	51.5%
SALT LAKE	102,926	35,427	67,318	181	31,891 D	34.4%	65.4%	34.5%	65.5%
SAN JUAN	1,047	528	515	4	13 R	50.4%	49.2%	50.6%	49.4%
SANPETE	7,250	3,722	3,524	4	198 R	51.3%	48.6%	51.4%	48.6%
SEVIER	5,228	2,703	2,521	4	182 R	51.7%	48.2%	51.7%	48.3%
SUMMIT	3,948	1,730	2,215	3	485 D	43.8%	56.1%	43.9%	56.1%
TOOELE	4,108	1,476	2,625	7	1,149 D	35.9%	63.9%	36.0%	64.0%
UINTAH	3,399	1,624	1,773	2	149 D	47.8%	52.2%	47.8%	52.2%
UTAH	23,956	8,740	15,168	48	6,428 D	36.5%	63.3%	36.6%	63.4%
WASATCH	2,702	1,199	1,502	1	303 D	44.4%	55.6%	44.4%	55.6%
WASHINGTON	3,621	1,625	1,993	3	368 D	44.9%	55.0%	44.9%	55.1%
WAYNE	881	380	500	1	120 D	43.1%	56.8%	43.2%	56.8%
WEBER	26,007	7,946	18,037	24	10,091 D	30.6%	69.4%	30.6%	69.4%
TOTAL	247,819	93,151	154,277	391	61,126 D	37.6%	62.3%	37.6%	62.4%

UTAH

PRESIDENT 1944

County	Total Vote	Republican	Democratic	Other	Rep.-Dem. Plurality	Percentage Total Vote Rep.	Dem.	Major Vote Rep.	Dem.
BEAVER	2,088	958	1,128	2	170 D	45.9%	54.0%	45.9%	54.1%
BOX ELDER	7,201	3,058	4,138	5	1,080 D	42.5%	57.5%	42.5%	57.5%
CACHE	11,948	4,938	6,998	12	2,060 D	41.3%	58.6%	41.4%	58.6%
CARBON	7,696	2,318	5,354	14	3,046 D	30.1%	69.7%	30.2%	69.8%
DAGGETT	173	75	98		23 D	43.4%	56.6%	43.4%	56.6%
DAVIS	8,851	3,663	5,179	9	1,516 D	41.4%	58.5%	41.4%	58.6%
DUCHESNE	2,769	1,140	1,629		489 D	41.2%	58.8%	41.2%	58.8%
EMERY	2,402	974	1,427	1	453 D	40.5%	59.4%	40.6%	59.4%
GARFIELD	1,402	842	559	1	283 R	60.1%	39.9%	60.1%	39.9%
GRAND	813	428	380	5	48 R	52.6%	46.7%	53.0%	47.0%
IRON	3,621	1,930	1,677	14	253 R	53.3%	46.3%	53.5%	46.5%
JUAB	2,680	1,192	1,483	5	291 D	44.5%	55.3%	44.6%	55.4%
KANE	906	662	244		418 R	73.1%	26.9%	73.1%	26.9%
MILLARD	3,803	1,889	1,909	5	20 D	49.7%	50.2%	49.7%	50.3%
MORGAN	1,206	535	671		136 D	44.4%	55.6%	44.4%	55.6%
PIUTE	727	381	346		35 R	52.4%	47.6%	52.4%	47.6%
RICH	789	394	395		1 D	49.9%	50.1%	49.9%	50.1%
SALT LAKE	105,598	39,327	66,114	157	26,787 D	37.2%	62.6%	37.3%	62.7%
SAN JUAN	881	513	367	1	146 R	58.2%	41.7%	58.3%	41.7%
SANPETE	6,267	3,196	3,071		125 R	51.0%	49.0%	51.0%	49.0%
SEVIER	4,445	2,345	2,095	5	250 R	52.8%	47.1%	52.8%	47.2%
SUMMIT	3,242	1,479	1,76-	2	282 D	45.6%	54.3%	45.6%	54.4%
TOOELE	4,559	1,753	2,802	4	1,049 D	38.5%	61.5%	38.5%	61.5%
UINTAH	3,000	1,479	1,519	2	40 D	49.3%	50.6%	49.3%	50.7%
UTAH	25,713	9,946	15,722	45	5,776 D	38.7%	61.1%	38.7%	61.3%
WASATCH	2,309	1,058	1,249	2	191 D	45.8%	54.1%	45.9%	54.1%
WASHINGTON	3,270	1,575	1,694	1	119 D	48.2%	51.8%	48.2%	51.8%
WAYNE	755	325	430		105 D	43.0%	57.0%	43.0%	57.0%
WEBER	29,205	9,518	19,639	48	10,121 D	32.6%	67.2%	32.6%	67.4%
TOTAL	248,319	97,891	150,088	340	52,197 D	39.4%	60.4%	39.5%	60.5%

PRESIDENT 1948

County	Total Vote	Republican	Democratic	Other	Rep.-Dem. Plurality	Percentage Total Vote Rep.	Dem.	Major Vote Rep.	Dem.
BEAVER	2,264	1,057	1,190	17	133 D	46.7%	52.6%	47.0%	53.0%
BOX ELDER	7,475	3,790	3,667	18	123 R	50.7%	49.1%	50.8%	49.2%
CACHE	12,946	6,514	6,383	49	131 R	50.3%	49.3%	50.5%	49.5%
CARBON	9,360	2,704	6,397	259	3,693 D	28.9%	68.3%	29.7%	70.3%
DAGGETT	165	69	95	1	26 D	41.8%	57.6%	42.1%	57.9%
DAVIS	10,936	4,718	6,147	71	1,429 D	43.1%	56.2%	43.4%	56.6%
DUCHESNE	2,870	1,266	1,588	16	322 D	44.1%	55.3%	44.4%	55.6%
EMERY	2,673	1,147	1,511	15	364 D	42.9%	56.5%	43.2%	56.8%
GARFIELD	1,567	924	642	1	282 R	59.0%	41.0%	59.0%	41.0%
GRAND	827	418	400	9	18 R	50.5%	48.4%	51.1%	48.9%
IRON	3,911	2,289	1,596	26	693 R	58.5%	40.8%	58.9%	41.1%
JUAB	2,912	1,396	1,501	15	105 D	47.9%	51.5%	48.2%	51.8%
KANE	989	769	220		549 R	77.8%	22.2%	77.8%	22.2%
MILLARD	4,029	2,184	1,817	28	367 R	54.2%	45.1%	54.6%	45.4%
MORGAN	1,265	587	670	8	83 D	46.4%	53.0%	46.7%	53.3%
PIUTE	763	440	315	8	125 R	57.7%	41.3%	58.3%	41.7%
RICH	766	399	366	1	33 R	52.1%	47.8%	52.2%	47.8%
SALT LAKE	116,917	52,479	62,957	1,481	10,478 D	44.9%	53.8%	45.5%	54.5%
SAN JUAN	983	558	418	7	140 R	56.8%	42.5%	57.2%	42.8%
SANPETE	6,413	3,336	3,041	36	295 R	52.0%	47.4%	52.3%	47.7%
SEVIER	4,750	2,791	1,943	16	848 R	58.8%	40.9%	59.0%	41.0%
SUMMIT	3,206	1,617	1,556	33	61 R	50.4%	48.5%	51.0%	49.0%
TOOELE	4,884	2,036	2,798	50	762 D	41.7%	57.3%	42.1%	57.9%
UINTAH	3,153	1,513	1,622	18	109 D	48.0%	51.4%	48.3%	51.7%
UTAH	29,886	13,395	16,191	300	2,796 D	44.8%	54.2%	45.3%	54.7%
WASATCH	2,389	1,165	1,219	5	54 D	48.8%	51.0%	49.0%	51.1%
WASHINGTON	3,617	2,029	1,580	8	449 R	56.1%	43.7%	56.2%	43.8%
WAYNE	831	367	460	4	93 D	44.2%	55.4%	44.4%	55.6%
WEBER	33,559	12,445	20,861	253	8,416 D	37.1%	62.2%	37.4%	62.6%
TOTAL	276,306	124,402	149,151	2,753	24,749 D	45.0%	54.0%	45.5%	54.5%

UTAH

PRESIDENT 1952

County	Total Vote	Republican	Democratic	Other	Rep.-Dem. Plurality	Total Vote Rep.	Total Vote Dem.	Major Vote Rep.	Major Vote Dem.
BEAVER	2,315	1,277	1,038		239 R	55.2%	44.8%	55.2%	44.8%
BOX ELDER	8,834	5,850	2,984		2,866 R	66.2%	33.8%	66.2%	33.8%
CACHE	14,409	10,167	4,242		5,925 R	70.6%	29.4%	70.6%	29.4%
CARBON	9,560	3,770	5,790		2,020 D	39.4%	60.6%	39.4%	60.6%
DAGGETT	176	90	86		4 R	51.1%	48.9%	51.1%	48.9%
DAVIS	15,027	9,067	5,960		3,107 R	60.3%	39.7%	60.3%	39.7%
DUCHESNE	3,211	1,969	1,242		727 R	61.3%	38.7%	61.3%	38.7%
EMERY	2,733	1,552	1,181		371 R	56.8%	43.2%	56.8%	43.2%
GARFIELD	1,542	1,065	477		588 R	69.1%	30.9%	69.1%	30.9%
GRAND	934	675	259		416 R	72.3%	27.7%	72.3%	27.7%
IRON	4,771	3,175	1,596		1,579 R	66.5%	33.5%	66.5%	33.5%
JUAB	2,914	1,711	1,203		508 R	58.7%	41.3%	58.7%	41.3%
KANE	1,107	943	154		789 R	85.2%	14.8%	85.2%	14.8%
MILLARD	4,293	2,994	1,299		1,695 R	69.7%	30.3%	69.7%	30.3%
MORGAN	1,329	862	457		395 R	64.9%	35.1%	64.9%	35.1%
PIUTE	738	531	207		324 R	72.0%	28.0%	72.0%	28.0%
RICH	820	569	251		318 R	69.4%	30.6%	69.4%	30.6%
SALT LAKE	143,646	84,176	59,470		24,706 R	58.6%	41.4%	58.6%	41.4%
SAN JUAN	1,297	876	421		455 R	67.5%	32.5%	67.5%	32.5%
SANPETE	6,367	4,146	2,221		1,925 R	65.1%	34.9%	65.1%	34.9%
SEVIER	5,441	3,996	1,445		2,551 R	73.4%	26.6%	73.4%	26.6%
SUMMIT	3,218	1,955	1,263		692 R	60.8%	39.2%	60.8%	39.2%
TOOELE	6,730	3,209	3,521		312 D	47.7%	52.3%	47.7%	52.3%
UINTAH	3,942	2,806	1,136		1,670 R	71.2%	28.8%	71.2%	28.8%
UTAH	36,240	20,913	15,327		5,586 R	57.7%	42.3%	57.7%	42.3%
WASATCH	2,645	1,677	968		709 R	63.4%	36.6%	63.4%	36.6%
WASHINGTON	4,017	2,941	1,076		1,865 R	73.2%	26.8%	73.2%	26.8%
WAYNE	811	536	275		261 R	66.1%	33.9%	66.1%	33.9%
WEBER	40,487	20,692	19,795		897 R	51.1%	48.9%	51.1%	48.9%
TOTAL	329,554	194,190	135,364		58,826 R	58.9%	41.1%	58.9%	41.1%

PRESIDENT 1956

County	Total Vote	Republican	Democratic	Other	Rep.-Dem. Plurality	Total Vote Rep.	Total Vote Dem.	Major Vote Rep.	Major Vote Dem.
BEAVER	2,220	1,190	1,030		160 R	53.6%	46.4%	53.6%	46.4%
BOX ELDER	8,493	5,804	2,689		3,115 R	68.3%	31.7%	68.3%	31.7%
CACHE	14,020	10,349	3,671		6,678 R	73.8%	26.2%	73.8%	26.2%
CARBON	8,967	4,507	4,460		47 R	50.3%	49.7%	50.3%	49.7%
DAGGETT	192	102	90		12 R	53.1%	46.9%	53.1%	46.9%
DAVIS	18,172	12,122	6,050		6,072 R	66.7%	33.3%	66.7%	33.3%
DUCHESNE	2,730	1,856	874		982 R	68.0%	32.0%	68.0%	32.0%
EMERY	2,622	1,679	943		736 R	64.0%	36.0%	64.0%	36.0%
GARFIELD	1,468	1,115	353		762 R	76.0%	24.0%	76.0%	24.0%
GRAND	1,372	1,044	328		716 R	76.1%	23.9%	76.1%	23.9%
IRON	4,632	3,321	1,311		2,010 R	71.7%	28.3%	71.7%	28.3%
JUAB	2,537	1,512	1,025		487 R	59.6%	40.4%	59.6%	40.4%
KANE	1,041	939	102		837 R	90.2%	9.8%	90.2%	9.8%
MILLARD	3,860	2,667	1,193		1,474 R	69.1%	30.9%	69.1%	30.9%
MORGAN	1,343	905	438		467 R	67.4%	32.6%	67.4%	32.6%
PIUTE	728	548	180		368 R	75.3%	24.7%	75.3%	24.7%
RICH	814	561	253		308 R	68.9%	31.1%	68.9%	31.1%
SALT LAKE	148,217	95,179	53,038		42,141 R	64.2%	35.8%	64.2%	35.8%
SAN JUAN	1,544	1,119	425		694 R	72.5%	27.5%	72.5%	27.5%
SANPETE	5,661	3,883	1,778		2,105 R	68.6%	31.4%	68.6%	31.4%
SEVIER	4,878	3,646	1,232		2,414 R	74.7%	25.3%	74.7%	25.3%
SUMMIT	2,911	2,031	880		1,151 R	69.8%	30.2%	69.8%	30.2%
TOOELE	6,073	3,350	2,683		707 R	55.8%	44.2%	55.8%	44.2%
UINTAH	3,650	2,840	820		2,020 R	77.6%	22.4%	77.6%	22.4%
UTAH	38,118	25,371	12,747		12,624 R	66.6%	33.4%	66.6%	33.4%
WASATCH	2,602	1,738	864		874 R	66.8%	33.2%	66.8%	33.2%
WASHINGTON	4,049	3,172	877		2,295 R	78.3%	21.7%	78.3%	21.7%
WAYNE	782	499	283		216 R	63.8%	36.2%	63.8%	36.2%
WEBER	40,299	22,542	17,747		4,795 R	56.0%	44.0%	56.0%	44.0%
TOTAL	333,995	215,631	118,364		97,267 R	64.6%	35.4%	64.6%	35.4%

UTAH

PRESIDENT 1960

County	Total Vote	Republican	Democratic	Other	Rep.-Dem. Plurality	Total Vote Rep.	Total Vote Dem.	Major Vote Rep.	Major Vote Dem.
BEAVER	2,127	971	1,156		185 D	45.7%	54.3%	45.7%	54.3%
BOX ELDER	10,428	6,594	3,831	3	2,763 R	63.2%	36.7%	63.3%	36.7%
CACHE	15,198	10,281	4,917		5,364 R	67.6%	32.4%	67.6%	32.4%
CARBON	9,006	2,953	6,039	14	3,086 D	32.8%	67.1%	32.8%	67.2%
DAGGETT	436	196	239	1	43 D	45.0%	54.8%	45.1%	54.9%
DAVIS	24,034	13,782	10,244	8	3,538 R	57.3%	42.6%	57.4%	42.6%
DUCHESNE	2,713	1,546	1,166	1	380 R	57.0%	43.0%	57.0%	43.0%
EMERY	2,521	1,283	1,238		45 R	50.9%	49.1%	50.9%	49.1%
GARFIELD	1,554	1,083	471		612 R	69.7%	30.3%	69.7%	30.3%
GRAND	1,935	1,130	805		325 R	58.4%	41.6%	58.4%	41.6%
IRON	4,818	3,079	1,738	1	1,341 R	63.9%	36.1%	63.9%	36.1%
JUAB	2,360	1,202	1,158		44 R	50.9%	49.1%	50.9%	49.1%
KANE	1,089	876	213		663 R	80.4%	19.6%	80.4%	19.6%
MILLARD	3,676	2,248	1,425	3	823 R	61.2%	38.8%	61.2%	38.8%
MORGAN	1,398	775	622	1	153 R	55.4%	44.5%	55.5%	44.5%
PIUTE	700	453	247		206 R	64.7%	35.3%	64.7%	35.3%
RICH	802	511	291		220 R	63.7%	36.3%	63.7%	36.3%
SALT LAKE	166,713	90,845	75,868		14,977 R	54.5%	45.5%	54.5%	45.5%
SAN JUAN	2,245	1,408	837		571 R	62.7%	37.3%	62.7%	37.3%
SANPETE	5,505	3,322	2,180	3	1,142 R	60.3%	39.6%	60.4%	39.6%
SEVIER	4,857	3,166	1,690	1	1,476 R	65.2%	34.8%	65.2%	34.8%
SUMMIT	2,824	1,607	1,217		390 R	56.9%	43.1%	56.9%	43.1%
TOOELE	6,688	3,016	3,665	7	649 D	45.1%	54.8%	45.1%	54.9%
UINTAH	4,262	2,882	1,380		1,502 R	67.6%	32.4%	67.6%	32.4%
UTAH	42,708	23,057	19,626	25	3,431 R	54.0%	46.0%	54.0%	46.0%
WASATCH	2,547	1,480	1,066	1	414 R	58.1%	41.9%	58.1%	41.9%
WASHINGTON	4,174	2,876	1,298		1,578 R	68.9%	31.1%	68.9%	31.1%
WAYNE	828	446	382		64 R	53.9%	46.1%	53.9%	46.1%
WEBER	46,563	22,293	24,239	31	1,946 D	47.9%	52.1%	47.9%	52.1%
TOTAL	374,709	205,361	169,248	100	36,113 R	54.8%	45.2%	54.8%	45.2%

PRESIDENT 1964

County	Total Vote	Republican	Democratic	Other	Rep.-Dem. Plurality	Total Vote Rep.	Total Vote Dem.	Major Vote Rep.	Major Vote Dem.
BEAVER	1,981	792	1,189		397 D	40.0%	60.0%	40.0%	60.0%
BOX ELDER	11,964	6,851	5,113		1,738 R	57.3%	42.7%	57.3%	42.7%
CACHE	15,953	9,326	6,627		2,699 R	58.5%	41.5%	58.5%	41.5%
CARBON	7,802	2,130	5,672		3,542 D	27.3%	72.7%	27.3%	72.7%
DAGGETT	282	112	170		58 D	39.7%	60.3%	39.7%	60.3%
DAVIS	28,654	14,477	14,177		300 R	50.5%	49.5%	50.5%	49.5%
DUCHESNE	2,571	1,251	1,320		69 D	48.7%	51.3%	48.7%	51.3%
EMERY	2,537	1,103	1,434		331 D	43.5%	56.5%	43.5%	56.5%
GARFIELD	1,479	821	658		163 R	55.5%	44.5%	55.5%	44.5%
GRAND	2,275	1,130	1,145		15 D	49.7%	50.3%	49.7%	50.3%
IRON	4,575	2,522	2,053		469 R	55.1%	44.9%	55.1%	44.9%
JUAB	2,245	926	1,319		393 D	41.2%	58.8%	41.2%	58.8%
KANE	1,124	784	340		444 R	69.8%	30.2%	69.8%	30.2%
MILLARD	3,435	1,973	1,462		511 R	57.4%	42.6%	57.4%	42.6%
MORGAN	1,407	572	835		263 D	40.7%	59.3%	40.7%	59.3%
PIUTE	634	361	273		88 R	56.9%	43.1%	56.9%	43.1%
RICH	761	435	326		109 R	57.2%	42.8%	57.2%	42.8%
SALT LAKE	182,044	78,118	103,926		25,808 D	42.9%	57.1%	42.9%	57.1%
SAN JUAN	2,364	1,371	993		378 R	58.0%	42.0%	58.0%	42.0%
SANPETE	5,167	2,620	2,547		73 R	50.7%	49.3%	50.7%	49.3%
SEVIER	4,565	2,617	1,948		669 R	57.3%	42.7%	57.3%	42.7%
SUMMIT	2,832	1,335	1,497		162 D	47.1%	52.9%	47.1%	52.9%
TOOELE	7,750	2,511	5,239		2,728 D	32.4%	67.6%	32.4%	67.6%
UINTAH	4,579	2,437	2,142		295 R	53.2%	46.8%	53.2%	46.8%
UTAH	44,848	20,912	23,936		3,024 D	46.6%	53.4%	46.6%	53.4%
WASATCH	2,578	1,158	1,420		262 D	44.9%	55.1%	44.9%	55.1%
WASHINGTON	4,323	2,534	1,789		745 R	58.6%	41.4%	58.6%	41.4%
WAYNE	812	400	412		12 D	49.3%	50.7%	49.3%	50.7%
WEBER	49,872	20,206	29,666		9,460 D	40.5%	59.5%	40.5%	59.5%
TOTAL	401,413	181,785	219,628		37,843 D	45.3%	54.7%	45.3%	54.7%

UTAH

OTHER VOTE COMPOSITION:

1920	4,475 Farmer-Labor; 3,159 Socialist.
1924	Progressive.
1928	954 Socialist; 46 Communist.
1932	4,087 Socialist; 946 Communist.
1936	1,121 Union; 432 Socialist; 280 Communist; 43 Prohibition.
1940	200 Socialist; 191 Communist.
1944	Socialist.
1948	2,679 Progressive; 74 Socialist Workers.
1952	
1956	
1960	Socialist Workers.
1964	

SPECIAL CASES:

1924	Progressive candidates ran second in several counties.

VERMONT

PRESIDENT 1920

County	Total Vote	Republican	Democratic	Other	Rep.-Dem. Plurality	Total Vote Rep.	Total Vote Dem.	Major Vote Rep.	Major Vote Dem.
ADDISON	5,077	4,515	503	59	4,012 R	88.9%	9.9%	90.0%	10.0%
BENNINGTON	5,841	4,172	1,615	54	2,557 R	71.4%	27.6%	72.1%	27.9%
CALEDONIA	7,300	5,537	1,694	69	3,843 R	75.8%	23.2%	76.6%	23.4%
CHITTENDEN	10,865	7,215	3,564	86	3,651 R	66.4%	32.8%	66.9%	33.1%
ESSEX	1,804	1,243	552	9	691 R	68.9%	30.6%	69.2%	30.8%
FRANKLIN	7,298	4,869	2,342	87	2,527 R	66.7%	32.1%	67.5%	32.5%
GRAND ISLE	1,296	928	354	14	574 R	71.6%	27.3%	72.4%	27.6%
LAMOILLE	2,816	2,311	458	47	1,853 R	82.1%	16.3%	83.5%	16.5%
ORANGE	4,704	3,713	938	53	2,775 R	78.9%	19.9%	79.8%	20.2%
ORLEANS	5,177	4,400	738	39	3,662 R	85.0%	14.3%	85.6%	14.4%
RUTLAND	12,229	8,940	3,192	97	5,748 R	73.1%	26.1%	73.7%	26.3%
WASHINGTON	8,471	6,418	1,953	100	4,465 R	75.8%	23.1%	76.7%	23.3%
WINDHAM	6,908	5,551	1,302	55	4,249 R	80.4%	18.8%	81.0%	19.0%
WINDSOR	10,175	8,400	1,714	61	6,686 R	82.6%	16.8%	83.1%	16.9%
TOTAL	89,961	68,212	20,919	830	47,293 R	75.8%	23.3%	76.5%	23.5%

PRESIDENT 1924

County	Total Vote	Republican	Democratic	Other	Rep.-Dem. Plurality	Total Vote Rep.	Total Vote Dem.	Major Vote Rep.	Major Vote Dem.
ADDISON	5,619	4,927	557	135	4,370 R	87.7%	9.9%	89.8%	10.2%
BENNINGTON	7,325	5,341	1,466	518	3,875 R	72.9%	20.0%	78.5%	21.5%
CALEDONIA	7,422	6,205	929	288	5,276 R	83.6%	12.5%	87.0%	13.0%
CHITTENDEN	11,286	8,008	2,658	620	5,350 R	71.0%	23.6%	75.1%	24.9%
ESSEX	2,187	1,391	576	220	815 R	63.6%	26.3%	70.7%	29.3%
FRANKLIN	6,847	4,594	1,649	604	2,945 R	67.1%	24.1%	73.6%	26.4%
GRAND ISLE	1,320	861	343	116	518 R	65.2%	26.0%	71.5%	28.5%
LAMOILLE	2,876	2,480	305	91	2,175 R	86.2%	10.6%	89.0%	11.0%
ORANGE	5,621	4,657	724	240	3,933 R	82.9%	12.9%	86.5%	13.5%
ORLEANS	5,877	5,006	619	252	4,387 R	85.2%	10.5%	89.0%	11.0%
RUTLAND	14,320	10,642	2,477	1,201	8,165 R	74.3%	17.3%	81.1%	18.9%
WASHINGTON	11,474	8,525	1,715	1,234	6,810 R	74.3%	14.9%	83.3%	16.7%
WINDHAM	9,183	7,638	1,091	454	6,547 R	83.2%	11.9%	87.5%	12.5%
WINDSOR	11,560	10,223	1,015	322	9,208 R	88.4%	8.8%	91.0%	9.0%
TOTAL	102,917	80,498	16,124	6,295	64,374 R	78.2%	15.7%	83.3%	16.7%

VERMONT

PRESIDENT 1928

County	Total Vote	Republican	Democratic	Other	Rep.-Dem. Plurality	Total Vote Rep.	Total Vote Dem.	Major Vote Rep.	Major Vote Dem.
ADDISON	7,278	5,247	2,003	28	3,244 R	72.1%	27.5%	72.4%	27.6%
BENNINGTON	9,630	6,114	3,498	18	2,616 R	63.5%	36.3%	63.6%	36.4%
CALEDONIA	8,474	6,616	1,832	26	4,784 R	78.1%	21.6%	78.3%	21.7%
CHITTENDEN	17,235	8,156	9,052	27	896 D	47.3%	52.5%	47.4%	52.6%
ESSEX	2,514	1,703	805	6	898 R	67.7%	32.0%	67.9%	32.1%
FRANKLIN	11,548	6,031	5,477	40	554 R	52.2%	47.4%	52.4%	47.6%
GRAND ISLE	1,642	830	801	11	29 R	50.5%	48.8%	50.9%	49.1%
LAMOILLE	3,854	3,262	576	16	2,686 R	84.6%	14.9%	85.0%	15.0%
ORANGE	6,167	5,223	914	30	4,309 R	84.7%	14.8%	85.1%	14.9%
ORLEANS	6,895	5,561	1,320	14	4,241 R	80.7%	19.1%	80.8%	19.2%
RUTLAND	21,262	12,621	8,609	32	4,012 R	59.4%	40.5%	59.4%	40.6%
WASHINGTON	14,353	9,891	4,408	54	5,483 R	68.9%	30.7%	69.2%	30.8%
WINDHAM	10,824	8,410	2,398	16	6,012 R	77.7%	22.2%	77.8%	22.4%
WINDSOR	13,515	10,739	2,747	29	7,992 R	79.5%	20.3%	79.6%	20.4%
TOTAL	135,191	90,404	44,440	347	45,964 R	66.9%	32.9%	67.0%	33.0%

PRESIDENT 1932

County	Total Vote	Republican	Democratic	Other	Rep.-Dem. Plurality	Total Vote Rep.	Total Vote Dem.	Major Vote Rep.	Major Vote Dem.
ADDISON	8,428	5,295	3,031	102	2,264 R	62.8%	36.0%	63.6%	36.4%
BENNINGTON	9,416	5,250	3,964	202	1,286 R	55.8%	42.1%	57.0%	43.0%
CALEDONIA	9,741	6,066	3,621	54	2,445 R	62.3%	37.2%	62.6%	37.4%
CHITTENDEN	16,435	7,208	9,104	123	1,896 D	43.9%	55.4%	44.2%	55.8%
ESSEX	2,980	1,567	1,397	16	170 R	52.6%	46.9%	52.9%	47.1%
FRANKLIN	11,286	4,999	6,179	108	1,180 D	44.3%	54.7%	44.7%	55.3%
GRAND ISLE	1,477	649	811	17	162 D	43.9%	54.9%	44.5%	55.5%
LAMOILLE	3,729	2,599	1,096	34	1,503 R	69.7%	29.4%	70.3%	29.7%
ORANGE	6,212	4,305	1,830	77	2,475 R	69.3%	29.5%	70.2%	29.8%
ORLEANS	7,729	5,132	2,530	67	2,602 R	66.4%	32.7%	67.0%	33.0%
RUTLAND	19,951	10,821	8,924	206	1,897 R	54.2%	44.7%	54.8%	45.2%
WASHINGTON	14,540	8,393	5,777	370	2,616 R	57.7%	39.7%	59.2%	40.8%
WINDHAM	11,129	7,347	3,659	123	3,688 R	66.0%	32.9%	66.8%	33.2%
WINDSOR	13,927	9,353	4,343	231	5,010 R	67.2%	31.2%	68.3%	31.7%
TOTAL	136,980	78,984	56,266	1,730	22,718 R	57.7%	41.1%	58.4%	41.6%

VERMONT

PRESIDENT 1936

County	Total Vote	Republican	Democratic	Other	Rep.-Dem. Plurality	Total Vote Rep.	Dem.	Major Vote Rep.	Dem.
ADDISON	7,831	5,161	2,646	24	2,515 R	65.9%	33.8%	66.1%	33.9%
BENNINGTON	9,834	5,515	4,166	153	1,349 R	56.1%	42.4%	57.0%	43.0%
CALEDONIA	9,423	6,054	3,342	27	2,712 R	64.2%	35.5%	64.4%	35.6%
CHITTENDEN	18,775	7,757	10,962	56	3,205 D	41.3%	58.4%	41.4%	58.6%
ESSEX	2,680	1,474	1,203	3	271 R	55.0%	44.9%	55.1%	44.9%
FRANKLIN	12,360	5,507	6,817	36	1,310 D	44.6%	55.2%	44.7%	55.3%
GRAND ISLE	1,568	712	852	4	140 D	45.4%	54.3%	45.5%	54.5%
LAMOILLE	4,137	2,846	1,279	12	1,567 R	68.8%	30.9%	69.0%	31.0%
ORANGE	6,763	4,956	1,796	11	3,160 R	73.3%	26.6%	73.4%	26.6%
ORLEANS	7,720	5,038	2,662	20	2,376 R	65.3%	34.5%	65.4%	34.6%
RUTLAND	20,391	10,794	9,543	54	1,251 R	52.9%	46.8%	53.1%	46.9%
WASHINGTON	16,490	8,351	8,073	66	278 R	50.6%	49.0%	50.8%	49.2%
WINDHAM	11,095	7,369	3,699	27	3,670 R	66.4%	33.3%	66.6%	33.4%
WINDSOR	14,622	9,489	5,084	49	4,405 R	64.9%	34.8%	65.1%	34.9%
TOTAL	143,689	81,023	62,124	542	18,899 R	56.4%	43.2%	56.6%	43.4%

PRESIDENT 1940

County	Total Vote	Republican	Democratic	Other	Rep.-Dem. Plurality	Total Vote Rep.	Dem.	Major Vote Rep.	Dem.
ADDISON	7,118	4,500	2,593	25	1,907 R	63.2%	36.4%	63.4%	36.6%
BENNINGTON	10,180	5,845	4,308	27	1,537 R	57.4%	42.3%	57.6%	42.4%
CALEDONIA	9,260	5,793	3,444	23	2,349 R	62.6%	37.2%	62.7%	37.3%
CHITTENDEN	19,061	7,926	11,069	66	3,143 D	41.6%	58.1%	41.7%	58.3%
ESSEX	2,907	1,365	1,531	11	166 D	47.0%	52.7%	47.1%	52.9%
FRANKLIN	12,760	5,258	7,439	63	2,181 D	41.2%	58.3%	41.4%	58.6%
GRAND ISLE	1,719	716	998	5	282 D	41.7%	58.1%	41.8%	58.2%
LAMOILLE	4,034	2,566	1,463	5	1,103 R	63.6%	36.3%	63.7%	36.3%
ORANGE	6,579	4,527	2,029	23	2,498 R	68.8%	30.8%	69.1%	30.9%
ORLEANS	7,789	4,480	3,294	15	1,186 R	57.5%	42.3%	57.6%	42.4%
RUTLAND	19,681	10,829	8,798	54	2,031 R	55.0%	44.7%	55.2%	44.8%
WASHINGTON	16,203	8,426	7,727	50	699 R	52.0%	47.7%	52.2%	47.8%
WINDHAM	11,159	7,031	4,101	27	2,930 R	63.0%	36.8%	63.2%	36.8%
WINDSOR	14,612	9,109	5,475	28	3,634 R	62.3%	37.5%	62.5%	37.5%
TOTAL	143,062	78,371	64,269	422	14,102 R	54.8%	44.9%	54.9%	45.1%

VERMONT

PRESIDENT 1944

County	Total Vote	Republican	Democratic	Other	Rep.-Dem. Plurality	Total Vote Rep.	Dem.	Major Vote Rep.	Dem.
ADDISON	6,184	4,097	2,079	8	2,018 R	66.3%	33.6%	66.3%	33.7%
BENNINGTON	8,961	5,252	3,709		1,543 R	58.6%	41.4%	58.6%	41.4%
CALEDONIA	7,890	5,086	2,804		2,282 R	64.5%	35.5%	64.5%	35.5%
CHITTENDEN	18,301	7,513	10,788		3,275 D	41.1%	58.9%	41.1%	58.9%
ESSEX	2,190	1,064	1,126		52 D	48.6%	51.4%	48.6%	51.4%
FRANKLIN	10,411	4,374	6,036	1	1,662 D	42.0%	58.0%	42.0%	58.0%
GRAND ISLE	1,468	667	801		134 D	45.4%	54.6%	45.4%	54.6%
LAMOILLE	3,243	2,212	1,031		1,181 R	68.2%	31.8%	68.2%	31.8%
ORANGE	5,581	4,117	1,464		2,653 R	73.8%	26.2%	73.8%	26.2%
ORLEANS	6,458	3,801	2,657		1,144 R	58.9%	41.1%	58.9%	41.1%
RUTLAND	16,655	9,544	7,111		2,433 R	57.3%	42.7%	57.3%	42.7%
WASHINGTON	12,911	7,162	5,749		1,413 R	55.5%	44.5%	55.5%	44.5%
WINDHAM	10,089	6,708	3,376	5	3,332 R	66.5%	33.5%	66.5%	33.5%
WINDSOR	15,019	9,930	5,089		4,841 R	66.1%	33.9%	66.1%	33.9%
TOTAL	125,361	71,527	53,820	14	17,707 R	57.1%	42.9%	57.1%	42.9%

PRESIDENT 1948

County	Total Vote	Republican	Democratic	Other	Rep.-Dem. Plurality	Total Vote Rep.	Dem.	Major Vote Rep.	Dem.
ADDISON	5,869	4,148	1,615	106	2,533 R	70.7%	27.5%	72.0%	28.0%
BENNINGTON	9,374	5,840	3,340	194	2,500 R	62.3%	35.6%	63.6%	36.4%
CALEDONIA	8,542	5,873	2,585	84	3,288 R	68.8%	30.3%	69.4%	30.6%
CHITTENDEN	17,739	8,509	8,903	327	394 D	48.0%	50.2%	48.9%	51.1%
ESSEX	1,946	1,055	881	10	174 R	54.2%	45.3%	54.5%	45.5%
FRANKLIN	10,444	4,897	5,455	92	558 D	46.9%	52.2%	47.3%	52.7%
GRAND ISLE	1,563	724	822	17	98 D	46.3%	52.6%	46.8%	53.2%
LAMOILLE	3,181	2,344	816	21	1,528 R	73.7%	25.7%	74.2%	25.8%
ORANGE	5,276	4,061	1,139	76	2,922 R	77.0%	21.6%	78.1%	21.9%
ORLEANS	6,004	3,775	2,204	25	1,571 R	62.9%	36.7%	63.1%	36.9%
RUTLAND	16,853	10,206	6,452	195	3,754 R	60.6%	38.3%	61.3%	38.7%
WASHINGTON	12,883	7,720	4,839	324	2,881 R	59.9%	37.6%	61.5%	38.5%
WINDHAM	10,140	7,148	2,770	222	4,378 R	70.5%	27.3%	72.1%	27.9%
WINDSOR	13,568	9,626	3,736	206	5,890 R	70.9%	27.5%	72.0%	28.0%
TOTAL	123,382	75,926	45,557	1,899	30,369 R	61.5%	36.9%	62.5%	37.5%

VERMONT

PRESIDENT 1952

County	Total Vote	Republican	Democratic	Other	Rep.-Dem. Plurality	Total Vote Rep.	Total Vote Dem.	Major Vote Rep.	Major Vote Dem.
ADDISON	7,748	6,057	1,667	24	4,390 R	78.2%	21.5%	78.4%	21.6%
BENNINGTON	11,437	8,385	3,018	34	5,367 R	73.3%	26.4%	73.5%	26.5%
CALEDONIA	9,423	7,595	1,807	21	5,788 R	80.6%	19.2%	80.8%	19.2%
CHITTENDEN	23,385	13,533	9,746	106	3,787 R	57.9%	41.7%	58.1%	41.9%
ESSEX	2,306	1,592	705	9	887 R	69.0%	30.6%	69.3%	30.7%
FRANKLIN	12,018	6,949	5,018	51	1,931 R	57.8%	41.8%	58.1%	41.9%
GRAND ISLE	1,650	976	665	9	311 R	59.2%	40.3%	59.5%	40.5%
LAMOILLE	4,160	3,516	633	11	2,883 R	84.5%	15.2%	84.7%	15.3%
ORANGE	6,719	5,610	1,082	27	4,528 R	83.5%	16.1%	83.8%	16.2%
ORLEANS	7,858	5,830	2,303	25	3,827 R	74.2%	25.5%	74.4%	25.6%
RUTLAND	19,986	13,980	5,970	36	8,010 R	69.9%	29.9%	70.1%	29.9%
WASHINGTON	16,503	11,979	4,460	64	7,519 R	72.6%	27.0%	72.9%	27.1%
WINDHAM	12,595	9,774	2,790	31	6,984 R	77.6%	22.2%	77.8%	22.2%
WINDSOR	17,769	13,941	3,791	37	10,150 R	78.5%	21.3%	78.6%	21.4%
TOTAL	153,557	109,717	43,355	485	66,362 R	71.5%	28.2%	71.7%	28.3%

PRESIDENT 1956

County	Total Vote	Republican	Democratic	Other	Rep.-Dem. Plurality	Total Vote Rep.	Total Vote Dem.	Major Vote Rep.	Major Vote Dem.
ADDISON	7,658	5,990	1,668		4,322 R	78.2%	21.8%	78.2%	21.8%
BENNINGTON	11,157	8,434	2,719	4	5,715 R	75.6%	24.4%	75.6%	24.4%
CALEDONIA	9,304	7,560	1,744		5,816 R	81.3%	18.7%	81.3%	18.7%
CHITTENDEN	24,582	14,108	10,474		3,634 R	57.4%	42.6%	57.4%	42.6%
ESSEX	2,434	1,714	719	1	995 R	70.4%	29.5%	70.4%	29.6%
FRANKLIN	11,965	7,125	4,840		2,285 R	59.5%	40.5%	59.5%	40.5%
GRAND ISLE	1,582	978	604		374 R	61.8%	38.2%	61.8%	38.2%
LAMOILLE	4,142	3,464	678		2,786 R	83.6%	16.4%	83.6%	16.4%
ORANGE	6,690	5,616	1,072		4,544 R	83.9%	16.0%	84.0%	16.0%
ORLEANS	7,396	5,344	2,052	2	3,292 R	72.3%	27.7%	72.3%	27.7%
RUTLAND	19,735	14,570	5,165		9,405 R	73.8%	26.2%	73.8%	26.2%
WASHINGTON	15,876	11,351	4,520	5	6,831 R	71.5%	28.5%	71.5%	28.5%
WINDHAM	12,475	9,979	2,474	22	7,505 R	80.0%	19.8%	80.1%	19.9%
WINDSOR	17,982	14,157	3,820	5	10,337 R	78.7%	21.2%	78.8%	21.2%
TOTAL	152,978	110,390	42,549	39	67,841 R	72.2%	27.8%	72.2%	27.8%

VERMONT

PRESIDENT 1960

County	Total Vote	Republican	Democratic	Other	Rep.-Dem. Plurality	Total Vote Rep.	Total Vote Dem.	Major Vote Rep.	Major Vote Dem.
ADDISON	8,489	5,520	2,969		2,551 R	65.0%	35.0%	65.0%	35.0%
BENNINGTON	11,602	7,099	4,502		2,597 R	61.2%	38.8%	61.2%	38.8%
CALEDONIA	9,597	6,688	2,909		3,779 R	69.7%	30.3%	69.7%	30.3%
CHITTENDEN	30,031	13,072	16,959	1	3,887 D	43.5%	56.5%	43.5%	56.5%
ESSEX	2,502	1,439	1,063		376 R	57.5%	42.5%	57.5%	42.5%
FRANKLIN	12,472	5,444	7,028		1,584 D	43.6%	56.4%	43.6%	56.4%
GRAND ISLE	1,617	798	819		21 D	49.4%	50.6%	49.4%	50.6%
LAMOILLE	4,304	3,272	1,032		2,240 R	76.0%	24.0%	76.0%	24.0%
ORANGE	6,944	5,363	1,581		3,782 R	77.2%	22.8%	77.2%	22.8%
ORLEANS	8,381	5,027	3,354		1,673 R	60.0%	40.0%	60.0%	40.0%
RUTLAND	21,412	12,166	9,246		2,920 R	56.8%	43.2%	56.8%	43.2%
WASHINGTON	17,578	10,458	7,116	4	3,342 R	59.5%	40.5%	59.5%	40.5%
WINDHAM	13,486	9,128	4,358		4,770 R	67.7%	32.3%	67.7%	32.3%
WINDSOR	18,909	12,657	6,250	2	6,407 R	66.9%	33.1%	66.9%	33.1%
TOTAL	167,324	98,131	69,186	7	28,945 R	58.6%	41.3%	58.6%	41.4%

PRESIDENT 1964

County	Total Vote	Republican	Democratic	Other	Rep.-Dem. Plurality	Total Vote Rep.	Total Vote Dem.	Major Vote Rep.	Major Vote Dem.
ADDISON	8,258	3,500	4,758		1,258 D	42.4%	57.6%	42.4%	57.6%
BENNINGTON	11,254	3,895	7,359		3,464 D	34.6%	65.4%	34.6%	65.4%
CALEDONIA	8,990	3,258	5,732		2,474 D	36.2%	63.8%	36.2%	63.8%
CHITTENDEN	30,867	9,050	21,817		12,767 D	29.3%	70.7%	29.3%	70.7%
ESSEX	2,423	750	1,673		923 D	31.0%	69.0%	31.0%	69.0%
FRANKLIN	12,086	3,261	8,823	2	5,562 D	27.0%	73.0%	27.0%	73.0%
GRAND ISLE	1,503	506	996	1	490 D	33.7%	66.3%	33.7%	66.3%
LAMOILLE	4,412	2,036	2,376		340 D	46.1%	53.9%	46.1%	53.9%
ORANGE	6,642	2,723	3,918	1	1,195 D	41.0%	59.0%	41.0%	59.0%
ORLEANS	7,907	3,009	4,898		1,889 D	38.1%	61.9%	38.1%	61.9%
RUTLAND	20,406	7,165	13,241		6,076 D	35.1%	64.9%	35.1%	64.9%
WASHINGTON	17,763	5,750	12,002	11	6,252 D	32.4%	67.6%	32.4%	67.6%
WINDHAM	12,555	4,180	8,371	4	4,191 D	33.3%	66.7%	33.3%	66.7%
WINDSOR	18,023	5,859	12,163	1	6,304 D	32.5%	67.5%	32.5%	67.5%
TOTAL	163,089	54,942	108,127	20	53,185 D	33.7%	66.3%	33.7%	66.3%

VERMONT

OTHER VOTE COMPOSITION:

1920	774 Prohibition; 56 scattered.
1924	5,964 Progressive; 326 Prohibition; 5 scattered.
1928	338 Prohibition; 9 scattered.
1932	1,533 Socialist; 195 Communist; 2 scattered.
1936	405 Communist; 137 scattered.
1940	411 Communist; 11 scattered.
1944	Scattered.
1948	1,279 Progressive; 585 Socialist; 35 scattered.
1952	282 Progressive; 185 Socialist; 18 scattered.
1956	Scattered.
1960	Scattered.
1964	Scattered.

VIRGINIA

PRESIDENT 1920

County	Total Vote	Republican	Democratic	Other	Rep.-Dem. Plurality	Rep. % (Total)	Dem. % (Total)	Rep. % (Major)	Dem. % (Major)
ACCOMACK	2,480	409	2,026	45	1,617 D	16.5%	81.7%	16.8%	83.2%
ALBEMARLE	2,128	541	1,587		1,046 D	25.4%	74.6%	25.4%	74.6%
ALLEGHANY	1,417	736	663	18	73 R	51.9%	46.8%	52.6%	47.4%
AMELIA	574	179	389	6	210 D	31.2%	67.8%	31.5%	68.5%
AMHERST	1,270	168	1,094	8	926 D	13.2%	86.1%	13.3%	86.7%
APPOMATTOX	1,032	190	837	5	647 D	18.4%	81.1%	18.5%	81.5%
ARLINGTON	1,870	997	835	38	162 R	53.3%	44.7%	54.4%	45.6%
AUGUSTA	3,879	1,707	2,106	66	399 D	44.0%	54.3%	44.8%	55.2%
BATH	710	362	343	5	19 R	51.0%	48.3%	51.3%	48.7%
BEDFORD	2,381	583	1,774	24	1,191 D	24.5%	74.5%	24.7%	75.3%
BLAND	881	478	403		75 R	54.3%	45.7%	54.3%	45.7%
BOTETOURT	2,574	1,240	1,331	3	91 D	48.2%	51.7%	48.2%	51.8%
BRUNSWICK	995	125	866	4	741 D	12.6%	87.0%	12.6%	87.4%
BUCHANAN	1,755	1,078	675	2	403 R	61.4%	38.5%	61.5%	38.5%
BUCKINGHAM	1,062	311	749	2	438 D	29.3%	70.5%	29.3%	70.7%
CAMPBELL	1,738	375	1,341	22	966 D	21.6%	77.2%	21.9%	78.1%
CAROLINE	984	308	665	11	357 D	31.3%	67.6%	31.7%	68.3%
CARROLL	3,791	2,520	1,265	6	1,255 R	66.5%	33.4%	66.6%	33.4%
CHARLES CITY COUNTY	202	82	119	1	37 D	40.6%	58.9%	40.8%	59.2%
CHARLOTTE	1,634	364	1,266	4	902 D	22.3%	77.5%	22.3%	77.7%
CHESTERFIELD	1,279	302	964	13	662 D	23.6%	75.4%	23.9%	76.1%
CLARKE	976	154	774	48	620 D	15.8%	79.3%	16.6%	83.4%
CRAIG	699	315	381	3	66 D	45.1%	54.5%	45.3%	54.7%
CULPEPER	1,306	330	973	3	643 D	25.3%	74.5%	25.3%	74.7%
CUMBERLAND	531	114	413	4	299 D	21.5%	77.8%	21.6%	78.4%
DICKENSON	1,990	1,067	903	20	164 R	53.6%	45.4%	54.2%	45.8%
DINWIDDIE	824	186	636	2	450 D	22.6%	77.2%	22.6%	77.4%
ELIZABETH CITY COUNTY	1,148	439	675	34	236 D	38.2%	58.8%	39.4%	60.6%
ESSEX	420	101	319		218 D	24.0%	76.0%	24.0%	76.0%
FAIRFAX COUNTY	2,617	987	1,598	32	611 D	37.7%	61.1%	38.2%	61.8%
FAUQUIER	1,941	568	1,365	8	797 D	29.3%	70.3%	29.4%	70.6%
FLOYD	1,865	1,355	497	13	858 R	72.7%	26.6%	73.2%	26.8%
FLUVANNA	717	146	562	9	416 D	20.4%	78.4%	20.6%	79.4%
FRANKLIN COUNTY	3,151	1,381	1,765	5	384 D	43.8%	56.0%	43.9%	56.1%
FREDERICK	2,236	875	1,337	24	462 D	39.1%	59.8%	39.6%	60.4%
GILES	1,987	877	1,104	6	227 D	44.1%	55.6%	44.3%	55.7%
GLOUCESTER	969	283	677	9	394 D	29.2%	69.9%	29.5%	70.5%
GOOCHLAND	602	212	384	6	172 D	35.2%	63.8%	35.6%	64.4%
GRAYSON	3,934	2,153	1,781		372 R	54.7%	45.3%	54.7%	45.3%
GREENE	724	414	306	4	108 R	57.2%	42.3%	57.5%	42.5%
GREENSVILLE	538	111	424	3	313 D	20.6%	78.8%	20.7%	79.3%
HALIFAX	2,697	586	2,103	8	1,517 D	21.7%	78.0%	21.8%	78.2%
HANOVER	1,133	224	903	6	679 D	19.8%	79.7%	19.9%	80.1%
HENRICO	1,453	338	1,078	37	740 D	23.3%	74.2%	23.9%	76.1%
HENRY	1,585	698	871	16	173 D	44.0%	54.9%	44.5%	55.5%
HIGHLAND	857	474	379	4	95 R	55.3%	44.2%	55.6%	44.4%
ISLE OF WIGHT	1,005	245	759	1	514 D	24.4%	75.5%	24.4%	75.6%
JAMES CITY COUNTY	271	61	207	3	146 D	22.5%	76.4%	22.8%	77.2%
KING AND QUEEN	528	181	347		166 D	34.3%	65.7%	34.3%	65.7%
KING GEORGE	503	253	249	1	4 R	50.3%	49.5%	50.4%	49.6%
KING WILLIAM	535	176	353	6	177 D	32.9%	66.0%	33.3%	66.7%
LANCASTER	546	138	404	4	266 D	25.3%	74.0%	25.5%	74.5%
LEE	3,761	2,162	1,592	7	570 R	57.5%	42.3%	57.6%	42.4%
LOUDOUN	2,506	757	1,720	29	963 D	30.2%	68.6%	30.6%	69.4%
LOUISA	1,003	312	684	7	372 D	31.1%	68.2%	31.3%	68.7%
LUNENBURG	1,036	208	818	10	610 D	20.1%	79.0%	20.3%	79.7%
MADISON	941	431	499	11	68 D	45.8%	53.0%	46.3%	53.7%
MATHEWS	856	216	624	16	408 D	25.2%	72.9%	25.7%	74.3%
MECKLENBURG	1,890	264	1,619	7	1,355 D	14.0%	85.7%	14.0%	86.0%
MIDDLESEX	609	170	438	1	268 D	27.9%	71.9%	28.0%	72.0%

PRESIDENT 1924

County	Total Vote	Republican	Democratic	Other	Rep.-Dem. Plurality	Rep. % (Total)	Dem. % (Total)	Rep. % (Major)	Dem. % (Major)
ACCOMACK	2,429	307	2,087	35	1,780 D	12.6%	85.9%	12.8%	87.2%
ALBEMARLE	1,802	366	1,383	53	1,017 D	20.3%	76.7%	20.9%	79.1%
ALLEGHANY	1,631	856	589	186	267 R	52.5%	36.1%	59.2%	40.8%
AMELIA	540	153	372	15	219 D	28.3%	68.9%	29.1%	70.9%
AMHERST	1,327	129	1,092	106	963 D	9.7%	82.3%	10.6%	89.4%
APPOMATTOX	1,073	101	952	20	851 D	9.4%	88.7%	9.6%	90.4%
ARLINGTON	2,921	1,307	1,209	405	98 R	44.7%	41.4%	51.9%	48.1%
AUGUSTA	3,265	1,265	1,920	80	655 D	38.7%	58.8%	39.7%	60.3%
BATH	835	407	404	24	3 R	48.7%	48.4%	50.2%	49.8%
BEDFORD	2,274	432	1,811	31	1,379 D	19.0%	79.6%	19.3%	80.7%
BLAND	1,219	609	604	6	5 R	50.0%	49.5%	50.2%	49.8%
BOTETOURT	2,754	1,264	1,427	63	163 D	45.9%	51.8%	47.0%	53.0%
BRUNSWICK	982	65	887	30	822 D	6.6%	90.3%	6.8%	93.2%
BUCHANAN	1,966	1,080	870	16	210 R	54.9%	44.3%	55.4%	44.6%
BUCKINGHAM	851	213	623	15	410 D	25.0%	73.2%	25.5%	74.5%
CAMPBELL	1,983	372	1,468	143	1,096 D	18.8%	74.0%	20.2%	79.8%
CAROLINE	1,083	223	840	20	617 D	20.6%	77.6%	21.0%	79.0%
CARROLL	3,016	1,743	1,257	16	486 R	57.8%	41.7%	58.1%	41.9%
CHARLES CITY COUNTY	232	82	141	9	59 D	35.3%	60.8%	36.8%	63.2%
CHARLOTTE	1,244	154	1,006	84	852 D	12.4%	80.9%	13.3%	86.7%
CHESTERFIELD	1,324	282	967	75	685 D	21.3%	73.0%	22.6%	77.4%
CLARKE	779	76	687	16	611 D	9.8%	88.2%	10.0%	90.0%
CRAIG	833	300	512	21	212 D	36.0%	61.5%	36.9%	63.1%
CULPEPER	1,108	190	876	42	686 D	17.1%	79.1%	17.8%	82.2%
CUMBERLAND	487	61	398	28	337 D	12.5%	81.7%	13.3%	86.7%
DICKENSON	3,047	1,294	1,618	135	324 D	42.5%	53.1%	44.4%	55.6%
DINWIDDIE	830	122	685	23	563 D	14.7%	82.5%	15.1%	84.9%
ELIZABETH CITY COUNTY	1,104	312	698	94	386 D	28.3%	63.2%	30.9%	69.1%
ESSEX	384	60	315	9	255 D	15.6%	82.0%	16.0%	84.0%
FAIRFAX COUNTY	2,550	765	1,586	199	821 D	30.0%	62.2%	32.5%	67.5%
FAUQUIER	1,713	345	1,277	91	932 D	20.1%	74.5%	21.3%	78.7%
FLOYD	1,513	984	515	14	469 R	65.0%	34.0%	65.6%	34.4%
FLUVANNA	617	136	452	29	316 D	22.0%	73.3%	23.1%	76.9%
FRANKLIN COUNTY	2,993	1,077	1,902	14	825 D	36.0%	63.5%	36.2%	63.8%
FREDERICK	1,827	484	1,314	29	830 D	26.5%	71.9%	26.9%	73.1%
GILES	2,230	852	1,319	59	467 D	38.2%	59.1%	39.2%	60.8%
GLOUCESTER	730	109	616	5	507 D	14.9%	84.4%	15.0%	85.0%
GOOCHLAND	598	164	394	40	230 D	27.4%	65.9%	29.4%	70.6%
GRAYSON	3,076	1,442	1,611	23	169 D	46.9%	52.4%	47.2%	52.8%
GREENE	535	240	285	10	45 D	44.9%	53.3%	45.7%	54.3%
GREENSVILLE	573	132	417	24	285 D	23.0%	72.8%	24.0%	76.0%
HALIFAX	2,665	374	2,245	46	1,871 D	14.0%	84.2%	14.3%	85.7%
HANOVER	905	135	732	38	597 D	14.9%	80.9%	15.6%	84.4%
HENRICO	1,605	416	1,052	137	636 D	25.9%	65.5%	28.3%	71.7%
HENRY	1,697	565	1,097	35	532 D	33.3%	64.6%	34.0%	66.0%
HIGHLAND	972	454	508	10	54 D	46.7%	52.3%	47.2%	52.8%
ISLE OF WIGHT	827	190	631	6	441 D	23.0%	76.3%	23.1%	76.9%
JAMES CITY COUNTY	240	54	173	13	119 D	22.5%	72.1%	23.8%	76.2%
KING AND QUEEN	452	134	314	4	180 D	29.6%	69.5%	29.9%	70.1%
KING GEORGE	503	206	280	17	74 D	41.0%	55.7%	42.4%	57.6%
KING WILLIAM	533	148	372	13	224 D	27.8%	69.8%	28.5%	71.5%
LANCASTER	668	90	564	14	474 D	13.5%	84.4%	13.8%	86.2%
LEE	4,946	2,456	2,376	114	80 R	49.7%	48.0%	50.8%	49.2%
LOUDOUN	2,031	152	1,794	85	1,642 D	7.5%	88.3%	7.8%	92.2%
LOUISA	1,046	282	707	57	425 D	27.0%	67.6%	28.5%	71.5%
LUNENBURG	1,036	130	686	220	556 D	12.5%	66.2%	15.9%	84.1%
MADISON	971	347	589	35	242 D	35.7%	60.7%	37.1%	62.9%
MATHEWS	883	195	678	10	483 D	22.1%	76.8%	22.3%	77.7%
MECKLENBURG	1,956	286	1,649	21	1,363 D	14.6%	84.3%	14.8%	85.2%
MIDDLESEX	523	78	438	7	360 D	14.9%	83.7%	15.1%	84.9%

VIRGINIA

PRESIDENT 1920

County	Total Vote	Republican	Democratic	Other	Rep.-Dem. Plurality	Percentage Total Vote Rep.	Total Vote Dem.	Major Vote Rep.	Major Vote Dem.
MONTGOMERY	2,157	1,160	969	28	191 R	53.8%	44.9%	54.5%	45.5%
NANSEMOND	933	243	690		447 D	26.0%	74.0%	26.0%	74.0%
NELSON	1,367	392	973	2	581 D	28.7%	71.2%	28.7%	71.3%
NEW KENT	299	109	190		81 D	36.5%	63.5%	36.5%	63.5%
NORFOLK COUNTY	2,672	813	1,824	35	1,011 D	30.4%	68.3%	30.8%	69.2%
NORTHAMPTON	1,178	217	954	7	737 D	18.4%	81.0%	18.5%	81.5%
NORTHUMBERLAND	763	221	536	6	315 D	29.0%	70.2%	29.2%	73.8%
NOTTOWAY	975	154	821		667 D	15.8%	84.2%	15.8%	84.2%
ORANGE	977	258	718	1	460 D	26.4%	73.5%	26.4%	73.6%
PAGE	1,582	1,126	846	10	280 R	56.6%	42.7%	57.1%	42.9%
PATRICK	2,387	1,230	1,154	3	76 R	51.5%	48.3%	51.6%	48.4%
PITTSYLVANIA	3,896	1,162	2,715	19	1,553 D	29.8%	69.8%	30.0%	70.0%
POWHATAN	406	140	263	3	123 D	34.7%	64.8%	34.7%	65.3%
PRINCE EDWARD	965	189	774	2	585 D	19.5%	80.2%	19.6%	80.4%
PRINCE GEORGE	506	127	375	4	248 D	25.1%	74.1%	25.3%	74.7%
PRINCE WILLIAM	1,182	393	786	3	393 D	33.2%	66.5%	33.3%	66.7%
PRINCESS ANNE	717	105	610	2	505 D	14.6%	85.1%	14.7%	85.3%
PULASKI	3,531	1,710	1,814	7	104 D	48.4%	51.4%	48.5%	51.5%
RAPPAHANNOCK	630	210	418	2	208 D	33.3%	66.3%	33.4%	66.6%
RICHMOND COUNTY	527	206	321		115 D	39.1%	60.9%	39.1%	60.9%
ROANOKE COUNTY	2,282	955	1,286	41	331 D	41.8%	56.4%	42.6%	57.4%
ROCKBRIDGE	2,432	1,054	1,365	13	311 D	43.3%	56.1%	43.3%	56.4%
ROCKINGHAM	4,588	2,464	2,068	56	396 R	53.7%	45.1%	54.4%	45.6%
RUSSELL	3,481	1,772	1,704	5	68 R	50.9%	49.0%	51.0%	49.0%
SCOTT	4,127	2,449	1,671	7	778 R	59.3%	40.5%	59.4%	40.6%
SHENANDOAH	4,787	2,683	2,077	27	606 R	56.0%	43.4%	56.4%	43.6%
SMYTH	3,414	1,883	1,516	15	367 R	55.2%	44.4%	55.4%	44.6%
SOUTHAMPTON	1,582	250	1,314	18	1,064 D	15.8%	83.1%	16.0%	84.0%
SPOTSYLVANIA	834	380	440	14	60 D	45.6%	52.8%	46.0%	53.7%
STAFFORD	1,060	599	459	2	140 R	56.5%	43.3%	56.6%	43.4%
SURRY	492	92	397	3	305 D	18.7%	80.7%	18.8%	81.2%
SUSSEX	717	166	548	3	382 D	23.2%	76.4%	23.2%	76.8%
TAZEWELL	4,187	2,408	1,770	9	638 R	57.5%	42.3%	57.6%	42.4%
WARREN	1,034	293	720	21	427 D	28.3%	69.6%	28.9%	71.1%
WARWICK COUNTY	267	109	152	6	43 D	41.8%	56.9%	41.8%	58.2%
WASHINGTON	4,935	2,672	2,251	12	421 R	54.1%	45.6%	54.3%	45.7%
WESTMORELAND	530	133	396	1	263 D	25.1%	74.7%	25.1%	74.9%
WISE	5,853	3,236	2,587	30	649 R	55.3%	44.2%	55.6%	44.4%
WYTHE	3,582	2,104	1,465	13	639 R	58.7%	40.9%	59.0%	41.0%
YORK	377	92	281	4	189 D	24.4%	74.5%	24.7%	75.3%

PRESIDENT 1924

County	Total Vote	Republican	Democratic	Other	Rep.-Dem. Plurality	Percentage Total Vote Rep.	Total Vote Dem.	Major Vote Rep.	Major Vote Dem.
MONTGOMERY	2,169	964	1,142	63	178 D	44.4%	52.7%	45.8%	54.2%
NANSEMOND	652	99	539	14	440 D	15.2%	82.7%	15.5%	84.5%
NELSON	1,431	350	1,042	39	692 D	24.5%	72.8%	25.1%	74.9%
NEW KENT	279	66	178	15	92 D	30.8%	63.8%	32.6%	67.4%
NORFOLK COUNTY	1,369	289	1,000	80	711 D	21.1%	73.0%	22.4%	77.6%
NORTHAMPTON	1,159	180	941	38	761 D	15.5%	81.2%	16.1%	83.9%
NORTHUMBERLAND	729	130	589	10	459 D	17.8%	80.8%	18.1%	81.9%
NOTTOWAY	1,161	181	840	140	659 D	15.6%	72.4%	17.7%	82.3%
ORANGE	1,068	181	834	53	653 D	16.9%	78.1%	17.8%	82.2%
PAGE	2,057	885	1,015	157	130 D	43.0%	49.3%	46.6%	53.4%
PATRICK	1,932	783	1,138	11	355 D	40.5%	58.9%	40.8%	59.2%
PITTSYLVANIA	3,556	880	2,563	113	1,683 D	24.7%	72.1%	25.6%	74.4%
POWHATAN	368	110	247	11	137 D	29.9%	67.1%	30.8%	69.2%
PRINCE EDWARD	863	140	714	9	574 D	16.2%	82.7%	16.4%	83.6%
PRINCE GEORGE	381	90	279	12	189 D	23.6%	73.2%	24.4%	75.6%
PRINCE WILLIAM	1,170	269	847	54	578 D	23.0%	72.4%	24.1%	75.9%
PRINCESS ANNE	858	137	690	31	553 D	16.0%	80.4%	16.6%	83.4%
PULASKI	3,282	1,422	1,767	93	345 D	43.3%	53.8%	44.6%	55.4%
RAPPAHANNOCK	505	89	395	21	306 D	17.6%	78.2%	18.4%	81.6%
RICHMOND COUNTY	471	125	340	6	215 D	26.5%	72.2%	26.9%	73.1%
ROANOKE COUNTY	1,890	695	1,078	117	383 D	36.8%	57.0%	39.2%	60.8%
ROCKBRIDGE	2,132	680	1,394	58	714 D	31.9%	65.4%	32.8%	67.2%
ROCKINGHAM	4,133	1,982	2,041	110	59 D	48.0%	49.4%	49.3%	50.7%
RUSSELL	4,478	1,848	2,554	76	706 D	41.3%	57.0%	42.0%	58.0%
SCOTT	4,912	2,666	2,177	69	489 R	54.3%	44.3%	55.0%	45.0%
SHENANDOAH	4,537	2,214	2,186	137	28 R	48.8%	48.2%	50.3%	49.7%
SMYTH	4,172	2,232	1,907	133	325 R	53.5%	45.7%	53.9%	46.1%
SOUTHAMPTON	1,404	203	1,119	82	916 D	14.5%	79.7%	15.4%	84.6%
SPOTSYLVANIA	736	255	448	33	193 D	34.6%	60.9%	36.3%	63.7%
STAFFORD	929	433	450	46	17 D	46.6%	48.4%	49.0%	51.0%
SURRY	502	72	388	42	316 D	14.3%	77.3%	15.7%	84.3%
SUSSEX	747	132	607	8	475 D	17.7%	81.3%	17.7%	82.1%
TAZEWELL	5,477	2,631	2,568	278	63 R	48.0%	46.9%	50.6%	49.4%
WARREN	888	150	699	39	549 D	16.9%	78.7%	17.6%	82.3%
WARWICK COUNTY	323	58	248	17	190 D	18.0%	76.8%	19.0%	81.0%
WASHINGTON	6,021	2,848	3,083	90	235 D	47.3%	51.2%	48.0%	52.0%
WESTMORELAND	655	157	484	14	327 D	24.0%	73.9%	24.5%	75.5%
WISE	8,224	3,322	4,157	745	835 D	40.4%	50.5%	44.4%	55.6%
WYTHE	3,966	1,996	1,899	51	97 R	50.6%	48.1%	51.2%	48.8%
YORK	395	75	305	15	230 D	19.0%	77.2%	19.7%	80.3%

VIRGINIA

PRESIDENT 1920

City	Total Vote	Republican	Democratic	Other	Rep.-Dem. Plurality	Total Vote Rep.	Total Vote Dem.	Major Vote Rep.	Major Vote Dem.
ALEXANDRIA	2,379	921	1,417	41	496 D	38.7%	59.6%	39.4%	60.6%
BRISTOL	1,134	344	784	6	440 D	30.3%	69.1%	30.5%	69.5%
BUENA VISTA	417	154	262	1	108 D	36.9%	62.8%	37.0%	63.0%
CHARLOTTESVILLE	1,407	351	1,041	15	690 D	24.9%	74.0%	25.2%	74.8%
CHESAPEAKE									
CLIFTON FORGE	1,033	274	727	32	453 D	26.5%	70.4%	27.4%	72.6%
COLONIAL HEIGHTS									
COVINGTON									
DANVILLE	2,476	551	1,888	37	1,337 D	22.3%	76.3%	22.6%	77.4%
FAIRFAX CITY									
FALLS CHURCH									
FRANKLIN CITY									
FREDERICKSBURG	893	299	581	13	282 D	33.5%	65.1%	34.0%	66.0%
GALAX									
HAMPTON	767	152	601	14	449 D	19.8%	78.4%	20.2%	79.8%
HARRISONBURG	1,307	704	594	9	110 R	53.9%	45.4%	54.2%	45.8%
HOPEWELL	139	41	97	1	56 D	29.5%	69.8%	29.7%	70.3%
LYNCHBURG	2,731	609	2,096	26	1,487 D	22.3%	76.7%	22.5%	77.5%
MARTINSVILLE									
NEWPORT NEWS	3,203	1,450	1,703	50	253 D	45.3%	53.2%	46.0%	54.0%
NORFOLK CITY	8,417	2,386	5,953	78	3,567 D	28.3%	70.7%	28.6%	71.4%
NORTON									
PETERSBURG	2,566	485	2,072	9	1,587 D	18.9%	80.7%	19.0%	81.0%
PORTSMOUTH	4,348	1,061	3,228	59	2,167 D	24.4%	74.2%	24.7%	75.3%
RADFORD	660	245	402	13	157 D	37.1%	60.9%	37.9%	62.1%
RICHMOND CITY	19,595	4,515	14,878	202	10,363 D	23.0%	75.9%	23.3%	76.7%
ROANOKE CITY	7,144	2,329	4,715	100	2,386 D	32.6%	66.0%	33.1%	66.9%
SOUTH BOSTON									
SOUTH NORFOLK									
STAUNTON	1,645	705	931	9	226 D	42.9%	56.6%	43.1%	56.9%
SUFFOLK	1,074	302	761	11	459 D	28.1%	70.9%	28.4%	71.6%
VIRGINIA BEACH									
WARWICK CITY									
WAYNESBORO									
WILLIAMSBURG	228	62	166		104 D	27.2%	72.8%	27.2%	72.8%
WINCHESTER	1,300	540	736	24	196 D	41.5%	56.6%	42.3%	57.7%
TOTAL	231,000	87,456	141,570	1,874	54,214 D	37.9%	61.3%	38.2%	61.8%

PRESIDENT 1924

City	Total Vote	Republican	Democratic	Other	Rep.-Dem. Plurality	Total Vote Rep.	Total Vote Dem.	Major Vote Rep.	Major Vote Dem.
ALEXANDRIA	1,960	556	1,136	268	580 D	28.4%	58.0%	32.9%	67.1%
BRISTOL	1,506	440	1,036	30	596 D	29.2%	68.8%	29.8%	70.2%
BUENA VISTA	392	149	235	8	86 D	38.0%	59.9%	38.8%	61.2%
CHARLOTTESVILLE	1,160	218	831	111	613 D	18.8%	71.6%	20.8%	79.2%
CHESAPEAKE									
CLIFTON FORGE	953	225	447	281	222 D	23.6%	46.9%	33.5%	66.5%
COLONIAL HEIGHTS									
COVINGTON									
DANVILLE	2,241	473	1,577	191	1,104 D	21.1%	70.4%	23.1%	76.9%
FAIRFAX CITY									
FALLS CHURCH									
FRANKLIN CITY									
FREDERICKSBURG	809	223	558	28	335 D	27.6%	69.0%	28.6%	71.4%
GALAX									
HAMPTON	615	129	471	15	342 D	21.0%	76.6%	21.5%	78.5%
HARRISONBURG	1,270	631	624	15	7 R	49.7%	49.1%	50.3%	49.7%
HOPEWELL	491	206	277	8	71 D	42.0%	56.4%	42.7%	57.3%
LYNCHBURG	2,816	602	2,086	128	1,484 D	21.4%	74.1%	22.4%	77.6%
MARTINSVILLE									
NEWPORT NEWS	2,783	917	1,574	292	657 D	33.0%	56.6%	36.8%	63.2%
NORFOLK CITY	7,924	2,447	5,061	416	2,614 D	30.9%	63.9%	32.6%	67.4%
NORTON									
PETERSBURG	1,595	228	1,331	36	1,103 D	14.3%	83.4%	14.6%	85.4%
PORTSMOUTH	3,433	624	2,206	603	1,582 D	18.2%	64.3%	22.0%	78.0%
RADFORD	807	314	394	99	80 D	38.9%	48.8%	44.4%	55.6%
RICHMOND CITY	13,421	2,600	9,904	917	7,304 D	19.4%	73.8%	20.8%	79.2%
ROANOKE CITY	6,435	1,747	3,930	758	2,183 D	27.1%	61.1%	30.8%	69.2%
SOUTH BOSTON									
SOUTH NORFOLK	439	134	281	24	147 D	30.5%	64.0%	32.3%	67.7%
STAUNTON	1,609	549	1,022	38	473 D	34.1%	63.5%	34.9%	65.1%
SUFFOLK	760	179	557	24	378 D	23.6%	73.3%	24.3%	75.7%
VIRGINIA BEACH									
WARWICK CITY									
WAYNESBORO									
WILLIAMSBURG	228	31	196	1	165 D	13.6%	86.0%	13.7%	86.3%
WINCHESTER	1,258	420	820	18	400 D	33.4%	65.2%	33.9%	66.1%
TOTAL	223,603	73,328	139,717	10,558	66,389 D	32.8%	62.5%	34.4%	65.6%

VIRGINIA

PRESIDENT 1928

County	Total Vote	Republican	Democratic	Other	Rep.-Dem. Plurality	% Total Rep.	% Total Dem.	% Major Rep.	% Major Dem.
ACCOMACK	3,195	1,367	1,826	2	459 D	42.8%	57.2%	42.8%	57.2%
ALBEMARLE	2,419	846	1,571	2	725 D	35.0%	64.9%	35.0%	65.0%
ALLEGHANY	2,264	1,642	622		1,020 R	72.5%	27.5%	72.5%	27.5%
AMELIA	776	277	498	1	221 D	35.7%	64.2%	35.7%	64.3%
AMHERST	1,900	447	1,442	11	995 D	23.5%	75.9%	23.7%	76.3%
APPOMATTOX	1,334	446	885	3	439 D	33.4%	66.3%	33.5%	66.5%
ARLINGTON	5,744	4,274	1,444	26	2,830 R	74.4%	25.1%	74.7%	25.3%
AUGUSTA	4,198	2,679	1,507	12	1,172 R	63.8%	35.9%	64.0%	36.0%
BATH	1,144	731	409	4	322 R	63.9%	35.8%	64.1%	35.9%
BEDFORD	2,562	1,118	1,436	8	318 D	43.6%	56.0%	43.8%	56.2%
BLAND	1,402	826	575	1	251 R	58.9%	41.0%	59.0%	41.0%
BOTETOURT	2,778	1,575	1,200	3	375 R	56.7%	43.2%	56.8%	43.2%
BRUNSWICK	1,168	245	922		677 D	21.0%	78.9%	21.0%	79.0%
BUCHANAN	2,707	1,333	1,365	9	32 D	49.2%	50.4%	49.4%	50.6%
BUCKINGHAM	1,178	579	599		20 D	49.2%	50.8%	49.2%	50.8%
CAMPBELL	1,776	801	967	8	166 D	45.1%	54.4%	45.3%	54.7%
CAROLINE	1,280	638	639	3	1 D	49.8%	49.9%	50.0%	50.0%
CARROLL	3,589	2,459	1,117	13	1,342 R	68.5%	31.1%	68.8%	31.2%
CHARLES CITY COUNTY	312	207	105		102 R	66.3%	33.7%	66.5%	33.5%
CHARLOTTE	1,516	403	1,112	1	709 D	26.6%	73.4%	26.6%	73.4%
CHESTERFIELD	2,414	1,325	1,082	7	243 R	54.9%	44.8%	55.0%	45.0%
CLARKE	989	248	740	1	492 D	25.1%	74.8%	25.1%	74.9%
CRAIG	942	451	489	2	38 D	47.6%	51.9%	48.0%	52.0%
CULPEPER	1,590	753	836	1	83 D	47.3%	52.6%	47.5%	52.5%
CUMBERLAND	659	213	442	4	229 D	32.3%	67.1%	32.5%	67.5%
DICKENSON	3,754	1,868	1,879	7	11 D	49.3%	50.1%	49.9%	50.1%
DINWIDDIE	1,280	332	945	3	613 D	25.9%	73.8%	26.0%	74.0%
ELIZABETH CITY COUNTY	1,942	1,122	807	13	315 R	57.8%	41.6%	58.2%	41.8%
ESSEX	516	195	321		126 D	37.8%	62.2%	37.8%	62.2%
FAIRFAX COUNTY	3,743	2,507	1,229	7	1,278 R	67.0%	32.8%	67.1%	32.9%
FAUQUIER	2,506	972	1,531	3	559 D	38.8%	61.1%	38.8%	61.2%
FLOYD	1,915	1,481	433	1	1,048 R	77.3%	22.6%	77.4%	22.6%
FLUVANNA	778	327	447	4	120 D	42.0%	57.5%	42.5%	57.8%
FRANKLIN COUNTY	3,394	1,529	1,861	4	332 D	45.1%	54.8%	45.1%	54.9%
FREDERICK	2,151	1,006	1,140	5	134 D	46.8%	53.0%	46.9%	53.1%
GILES	2,614	1,313	1,293	8	20 R	50.2%	49.5%	50.4%	49.6%
GLOUCESTER	1,201	614	587		27 R	51.1%	48.9%	51.1%	48.9%
GOOCHLAND	754	318	431	5	113 D	42.2%	57.2%	42.5%	57.5%
GRAYSON	4,454	2,728	1,713	13	1,015 R	61.2%	38.5%	61.4%	38.6%
GREENE	683	423	259	1	164 R	61.9%	37.9%	62.0%	38.0%
GREENSVILLE	839	318	519	2	201 D	37.9%	61.9%	38.0%	62.0%
HALIFAX	3,845	1,091	2,742	12	1,651 D	28.4%	71.3%	28.4%	71.5%
HANOVER	1,423	592	831		239 D	41.6%	58.4%	41.6%	58.4%
HENRICO	3,261	1,887	1,349	25	538 R	57.9%	41.4%	58.3%	41.7%
HENRY	2,409	1,139	1,267	3	128 D	47.3%	52.6%	47.3%	52.7%
HIGHLAND	999	623	371	5	252 R	62.4%	37.1%	62.7%	37.3%
ISLE OF WIGHT	1,086	555	531		24 R	51.1%	48.9%	51.1%	48.9%
JAMES CITY COUNTY	407	204	201	2	3 R	50.1%	49.4%	50.4%	49.6%
KING AND QUEEN	603	319	280	4	39 R	52.9%	46.4%	53.3%	46.7%
KING GEORGE	724	413	309	2	104 R	57.0%	42.7%	57.2%	42.8%
KING WILLIAM	764	329	431	4	102 D	43.1%	56.4%	43.3%	56.7%
LANCASTER	835	520	315		205 R	62.3%	37.7%	62.3%	37.7%
LEE	5,731	3,337	2,383	11	954 R	58.2%	41.6%	58.3%	41.7%
LOUDON	3,244	1,915	1,752	1	593 R	40.8%	59.0%	59.1%	40.9%
LOUISA	1,507	772	734	1	33 R	51.2%	48.7%	51.3%	48.7%
LUNENBURG	1,513	314	1,199		885 D	20.3%	79.2%	20.8%	79.2%
MADISON	1,355	772	580	3	192 R	57.0%	42.8%	57.1%	42.9%
MATHEWS	1,287	855	431	1	424 R	66.4%	33.5%	66.5%	33.5%
MECKLENBURG	2,537	784	1,752	1	968 D	30.9%	69.1%	30.9%	69.1%
MIDDLESEX	717	318	397	2	79 D	44.4%	55.4%	44.5%	55.5%

PRESIDENT 1932

County	Total Vote	Republican	Democratic	Other	Rep.-Dem. Plurality	% Total Rep.	% Total Dem.	% Major Rep.	% Major Dem.
ACCOMACK	3,007	527	2,458	22	1,931 D	17.5%	81.7%	17.7%	82.3%
ALBEMARLE	2,491	508	1,949	34	1,441 D	20.4%	78.2%	20.7%	79.3%
ALLEGHANY	2,417	1,095	1,293	29	198 D	45.3%	53.5%	45.9%	54.1%
AMELIA	854	142	701	11	559 D	16.6%	82.1%	16.8%	83.2%
AMHERST	1,980	195	1,764	21	1,569 D	9.8%	89.1%	10.0%	90.0%
APPOMATTOX	1,337	204	1,123	10	919 D	15.3%	84.0%	15.4%	84.6%
ARLINGTON	6,234	2,806	3,285	143	479 D	45.0%	52.7%	46.1%	53.9%
AUGUSTA	4,237	1,541	2,606	90	1,065 D	36.4%	61.5%	37.2%	62.8%
BATH	952	384	594	14	210 D	39.3%	59.9%	39.3%	60.7%
BEDFORD	2,831	469	2,321	41	1,852 D	16.6%	82.0%	16.8%	83.2%
BLAND	1,356	556	783	17	227 D	41.0%	57.7%	41.5%	58.5%
BOTETOURT	3,058	1,209	1,808	41	599 D	39.5%	59.1%	40.1%	59.9%
BRUNSWICK	1,424	52	1,361	11	1,309 D	3.7%	95.6%	3.7%	96.3%
BUCHANAN	2,103	727	1,372	4	645 D	34.6%	65.2%	34.6%	65.4%
BUCKINGHAM	1,090	204	870	16	666 D	18.7%	79.8%	19.0%	81.0%
CAMPBELL	2,021	301	1,692	28	1,391 D	14.9%	83.7%	15.1%	84.9%
CAROLINE	1,364	270	1,076	18	806 D	19.8%	78.9%	20.1%	79.9%
CARROLL	3,226	1,461	1,537	28	76 D	45.3%	50.8%	48.7%	51.3%
CHARLES CITY COUNTY	335	85	245	5	160 D	25.4%	73.1%	25.8%	74.2%
CHARLOTTE	1,477	169	1,300	8	1,131 D	11.4%	88.0%	11.5%	88.5%
CHESTERFIELD	2,698	726	1,886	86	1,160 D	26.9%	69.9%	27.8%	72.2%
CLARKE	973	124	841	8	717 D	12.8%	86.4%	12.8%	87.2%
CRAIG	966	302	649	15	347 D	31.3%	67.2%	31.8%	68.2%
CULPEPER	1,782	417	1,349	16	932 D	23.4%	75.7%	23.6%	76.4%
CUMBERLAND	608	84	511	13	427 D	13.8%	84.0%	14.1%	85.9%
DICKENSON	3,878	1,228	2,635	15	1,407 D	31.7%	67.9%	31.8%	68.2%
DINWIDDIE	1,359	104	1,026	15	924 D	9.1%	90.2%	9.2%	90.8%
ELIZABETH CITY COUNTY	1,959	700	1,226	33	526 D	35.7%	62.6%	36.3%	63.7%
ESSEX	524	101	420	3	319 D	19.3%	80.2%	19.4%	80.6%
FAIRFAX COUNTY	4,154	1,368	2,714	72	1,346 D	32.9%	65.3%	33.5%	66.5%
FAUQUIER	2,396	379	1,999	18	1,620 D	15.8%	83.4%	15.9%	84.1%
FLOYD	1,752	1,051	699	2	352 R	60.0%	39.9%	60.1%	39.9%
FLUVANNA	768	176	579	13	403 D	22.9%	75.4%	23.3%	76.7%
FRANKLIN COUNTY	3,077	812	2,245	20	1,433 D	26.4%	73.0%	26.6%	73.4%
FREDERICK	2,016	456	1,536	24	1,080 D	22.6%	76.2%	22.9%	77.1%
GILES	2,802	1,016	1,754	32	738 D	36.3%	62.6%	36.7%	63.3%
GLOUCESTER	1,211	280	916	15	636 D	23.1%	75.6%	23.4%	76.6%
GOOCHLAND	810	166	629	15	463 D	20.5%	77.7%	20.9%	79.1%
GRAYSON	3,958	1,624	2,306	28	682 D	41.0%	58.3%	41.3%	58.7%
GREENE	652	258	394		136 D	39.6%	60.4%	39.6%	60.4%
GREENSVILLE	811	112	692	7	580 D	13.8%	85.3%	13.9%	86.1%
HALIFAX	3,901	238	3,583	43	3,308 D	7.0%	91.8%	7.1%	92.9%
HANOVER	1,332	238	1,073	21	835 D	17.9%	80.6%	18.2%	81.8%
HENRICO	3,875	1,291	2,458	126	1,167 D	33.3%	63.4%	34.4%	65.6%
HENRY	1,503	342	1,146	15	804 D	22.8%	76.2%	23.0%	77.0%
HIGHLAND	838	355	464	19	109 D	42.4%	55.4%	43.3%	56.7%
ISLE OF WIGHT	1,275	284	982	9	698 D	22.3%	77.0%	22.4%	77.6%
JAMES CITY COUNTY	425	116	302	7	186 D	27.3%	71.1%	27.7%	72.2%
KING AND QUEEN	535	154	368	13	214 D	28.8%	68.8%	29.5%	70.5%
KING GEORGE	632	203	475	4	272 D	29.8%	69.6%	29.9%	70.1%
KING WILLIAM	804	177	612	15	435 D	22.0%	76.1%	22.4%	77.6%
LANCASTER	927	272	639	16	367 D	29.3%	68.9%	29.8%	70.1%
LEE	4,071	1,985	2,892	38	907 D	40.4%	58.8%	40.7%	59.3%
LOUDON	3,071	600	2,440	31	1,840 D	19.5%	79.5%	19.7%	80.3%
LOUISA	1,281	366	879	36	513 D	28.6%	68.6%	29.4%	70.6%
LUNENBURG	1,247	92	1,141	14	1,049 D	7.4%	91.5%	7.5%	92.5%
MADISON	1,380	522	849	9	327 D	37.8%	61.5%	38.1%	61.9%
MATHEWS	1,154	488	652	14	164 D	42.3%	56.5%	42.8%	57.2%
MECKLENBURG	2,478	275	2,188	15	1,913 D	11.1%	88.3%	11.2%	88.8%
MIDDLESEX	742	127	595	20	468 D	17.1%	80.2%	17.6%	82.4%

VIRGINIA

PRESIDENT 1928

County	Total Vote	Republican	Democratic	Other	Rep.-Dem. Plurality	Total Vote Rep.	Total Vote Dem.	Major Vote Rep.	Major Vote Dem.
MONTGOMERY	2,835	1,861	967	7	894 R	65.6%	34.1%	65.8%	34.2%
NANSEMOND	1,387	649	737	1	88 D	46.8%	53.1%	46.8%	53.2%
NELSON	1,835	618	1,216	1	598 D	33.7%	66.3%	33.7%	66.3%
NEW KENT	397	217	178	2	39 R	54.7%	44.8%	54.9%	45.1%
NORFOLK COUNTY	3,349	1,922	1,418	9	504 R	57.4%	42.3%	57.5%	42.5%
NORTHAMPTON	1,623	688	935		247 D	42.4%	57.6%	42.4%	57.6%
NORTHUMBERLAND	1,032	744	286	2	458 R	72.1%	27.7%	72.2%	27.8%
NOTTOWAY	1,654	667	986	1	319 D	40.3%	59.6%	40.4%	59.6%
ORANGE	1,578	732	846		114 D	46.4%	53.6%	46.4%	53.6%
PAGE	2,605	1,580	1,025		555 R	60.7%	39.3%	60.7%	39.3%
PATRICK	2,080	1,191	883	6	308 R	57.3%	42.5%	57.4%	42.6%
PITTSYLVANIA	4,293	2,598	1,688	7	910 R	60.5%	39.3%	60.6%	39.4%
POWHATAN	476	189	287		98 D	39.7%	60.3%	39.7%	60.3%
PRINCE EDWARD	1,198	494	699	5	205 D	41.2%	58.3%	41.4%	58.6%
PRINCE GEORGE	665	235	428	2	193 D	35.3%	64.4%	35.4%	64.6%
PRINCE WILLIAM	1,643	817	826		9 D	49.7%	50.3%	49.7%	50.3%
PRINCESS ANNE	1,883	1,040	841	2	199 R	55.2%	44.7%	55.3%	44.7%
PULASKI	3,819	1,998	1,821		177 R	52.3%	47.7%	52.3%	47.7%
RAPPAHANNOCK	842	329	513		184 D	39.1%	60.9%	39.1%	60.9%
RICHMOND COUNTY	759	467	292		175 R	61.5%	38.5%	61.5%	38.5%
ROANOKE COUNTY	3,961	2,675	1,284	2	1,391 R	67.5%	32.4%	67.6%	32.4%
ROCKBRIDGE	2,524	1,206	1,311	7	105 D	47.8%	51.9%	47.9%	52.1%
ROCKINGHAM	5,231	3,822	1,402	7	2,420 R	73.1%	26.8%	73.2%	26.8%
RUSSELL	4,520	2,006	2,511	3	505 D	44.4%	55.6%	44.4%	55.6%
SCOTT	5,275	2,916	2,355	4	561 R	55.3%	44.6%	55.3%	44.7%
SHENANDOAH	5,029	3,420	1,589	20	1,831 R	68.0%	31.6%	68.3%	31.7%
SMYTH	4,700	2,751	1,937	12	814 R	58.5%	41.2%	58.7%	41.3%
SOUTHAMPTON	1,493	648	844	1	196 D	43.4%	56.5%	43.4%	56.6%
SPOTSYLVANIA	1,094	654	439	1	215 R	59.8%	40.1%	59.8%	40.2%
STAFFORD	1,240	797	441	2	356 R	64.3%	35.6%	64.4%	35.6%
SURRY	700	157	541	2	384 D	22.4%	77.3%	22.5%	77.5%
SUSSEX	932	385	547		162 D	41.3%	58.7%	41.5%	58.5%
TAZEWELL	5,065	3,072	1,879	14	1,093 R	60.7%	39.1%	60.8%	39.2%
WARREN	1,276	564	710	2	146 D	44.2%	55.6%	44.3%	55.7%
WARWICK COUNTY	765	465	298	2	167 R	60.8%	39.0%	60.9%	39.1%
WASHINGTON	6,132	3,449	2,656	17	783 R	56.2%	43.5%	56.4%	43.6%
WESTMORELAND	947	554	393		161 R	58.5%	41.5%	58.5%	41.5%
WISE	9,075	4,504	4,559	12	55 D	49.6%	50.2%	49.7%	50.3%
WYTHE	4,060	2,560	1,556	4	1,024 R	62.6%	37.3%	62.6%	37.4%
YORK	837	642	194	1	448 R	76.7%	23.2%	76.8%	23.2%

PRESIDENT 1932

County	Total Vote	Republican	Democratic	Other	Rep.-Dem. Plurality	Total Vote Rep.	Total Vote Dem.	Major Vote Rep.	Major Vote Dem.
MONTGOMERY	3,405	1,522	1,805	78	283 D	44.7%	53.0%	45.7%	54.3%
NANSEMOND	1,466	196	1,264	6	1,068 D	13.4%	86.2%	13.4%	86.6%
NELSON	1,702	238	1,457	7	1,219 D	14.0%	85.6%	14.0%	86.0%
NEW KENT	406	115	286	5	171 D	28.3%	70.4%	28.7%	71.3%
NORFOLK COUNTY	4,059	1,072	2,926	61	1,854 D	26.4%	72.1%	26.8%	73.2%
NORTHAMPTON	1,577	298	1,264	15	966 D	18.9%	80.2%	19.1%	80.9%
NORTHUMBERLAND	884	245	630	9	385 D	27.7%	71.3%	28.0%	72.0%
NOTTOWAY	1,671	277	1,348	46	1,071 D	16.6%	80.7%	17.0%	83.0%
ORANGE	1,567	309	1,253	5	944 D	19.7%	80.0%	19.8%	80.2%
PAGE	3,158	1,261	1,851	46	590 D	39.9%	58.6%	40.5%	59.5%
PATRICK	1,853	486	1,342	25	856 D	26.2%	72.4%	26.6%	73.4%
PITTSYLVANIA	3,840	656	3,124	60	2,468 D	17.1%	81.4%	17.4%	82.6%
POWHATAN	555	108	433	14	325 D	19.5%	78.0%	20.0%	80.0%
PRINCE EDWARD	1,197	196	970	31	774 D	16.4%	81.0%	16.8%	83.2%
PRINCE GEORGE	719	115	597	7	482 D	16.0%	83.0%	16.2%	83.8%
PRINCE WILLIAM	1,907	386	1,499	22	1,113 D	20.2%	78.6%	20.5%	79.5%
PRINCESS ANNE	1,902	432	1,451	19	1,019 D	22.7%	76.3%	22.9%	77.1%
PULASKI	3,454	1,109	2,314	31	1,205 D	32.1%	67.0%	32.4%	67.6%
RAPPAHANNOCK	720	124	590	6	466 D	17.2%	81.9%	17.4%	82.6%
RICHMOND COUNTY	659	192	461	6	269 D	29.1%	70.0%	29.4%	70.6%
ROANOKE COUNTY	4,268	1,704	2,509	55	805 D	39.9%	58.8%	40.4%	59.6%
ROCKBRIDGE	2,619	811	1,764	44	953 D	31.0%	67.4%	31.5%	68.5%
ROCKINGHAM	5,107	2,194	2,750	163	556 D	43.0%	53.8%	44.4%	55.6%
RUSSELL	4,671	1,386	3,274	11	1,888 D	29.7%	70.1%	29.7%	70.3%
SCOTT	3,841	1,673	2,137	31	464 D	43.6%	55.6%	43.9%	56.1%
SHENANDOAH	5,217	2,514	2,635	68	121 D	48.2%	50.5%	48.8%	51.2%
SMYTH	4,196	1,843	2,287	66	444 D	43.9%	54.5%	44.6%	55.4%
SOUTHAMPTON	1,557	182	1,357	18	1,175 D	11.7%	87.2%	11.8%	88.2%
SPOTSYLVANIA	1,147	346	784	17	438 D	30.2%	68.4%	30.6%	69.4%
STAFFORD	1,191	454	731	6	277 D	38.1%	61.4%	38.3%	61.7%
SURRY	736	73	653	10	580 D	9.9%	88.7%	10.1%	89.9%
SUSSEX	825	122	688	15	566 D	14.8%	83.4%	15.1%	84.9%
TAZEWELL	4,762	2,005	2,713	44	708 D	42.1%	57.0%	42.5%	57.5%
WARREN	1,472	367	1,096	9	729 D	24.9%	74.5%	25.1%	74.9%
WARWICK COUNTY	900	242	645	13	403 D	26.9%	71.7%	27.3%	72.7%
WASHINGTON	4,627	1,774	2,784	69	1,010 D	38.3%	60.2%	38.9%	61.1%
WESTMORELAND	857	212	641	4	429 D	24.7%	74.8%	24.9%	75.1%
WISE	7,744	2,405	5,276	63	2,871 D	31.1%	68.1%	31.3%	68.7%
WYTHE	3,484	1,589	1,866	29	277 D	45.6%	53.6%	46.0%	54.0%
YORK	804	309	457	38	148 D	38.4%	56.8%	40.3%	59.7%

VIRGINIA

PRESIDENT 1928

City	Total Vote	Republican	Democratic	Other	Rep.-Dem. Plurality	Percentage Total Vote Rep.	Percentage Total Vote Dem.	Major Vote Rep.	Major Vote Dem.
ALEXANDRIA	2,926	1,617	1,307	2	310 R	55.3%	44.7%	55.3%	44.7%
BRISTOL	1,556	630	922	4	292 D	40.5%	59.3%	40.6%	59.4%
BUENA VISTA	440	267	172	1	95 R	60.7%	39.1%	60.8%	39.2%
CHARLOTTESVILLE	1,703	708	992	3	284 D	41.6%	58.3%	41.6%	58.4%
CHESAPEAKE									
CLIFTON FORGE	1,372	781	591		190 R	56.9%	43.1%	56.9%	43.1%
COLONIAL HEIGHTS									
COVINGTON	3,561	2,360	1,196	5	1,164 R	66.3%	33.6%	66.4%	33.6%
DANVILLE									
FAIRFAX CITY									
FALLS CHURCH									
FRANKLIN CITY									
FREDERICKSBURG	1,293	697	594	2	103 R	53.9%	45.9%	54.0%	46.0%
GALAX	1,160	544	615	1	71 D	46.9%	53.0%	46.9%	53.1%
HAMPTON									
HARRISONBURG	1,655	1,037	616	2	421 R	62.7%	37.2%	62.7%	37.3%
HOPEWELL	988	505	482	1	23 R	51.1%	48.8%	51.2%	48.8%
LYNCHBURG	4,717	2,730	1,987		743 R	57.9%	42.1%	57.9%	42.1%
MARTINSVILLE									
NEWPORT NEWS	5,083	3,118	1,951	14	1,167 R	61.3%	38.4%	61.5%	38.5%
NORFOLK CITY	14,309	8,392	5,888	29	2,504 R	58.6%	41.1%	58.8%	41.2%
NORTON	2,290	909	1,379	2	470 D	39.7%	60.2%	39.7%	60.3%
PETERSBURG	6,090	3,474	2,587	29	887 R	57.0%	42.5%	57.3%	42.7%
PORTSMOUTH	899	524	373	2	151 R	58.3%	41.5%	58.4%	41.6%
RADFORD									
RICHMOND CITY	21,029	10,767	10,213	49	554 R	51.2%	48.5%	51.3%	48.7%
ROANOKE CITY	10,501	6,471	4,018	12	2,453 R	61.6%	38.3%	61.7%	38.3%
SOUTH BOSTON	1,023	865	158		707 R	84.6%	15.4%	84.6%	15.4%
SOUTH NORFOLK	1,765	1,026	733	6	293 R	58.1%	41.5%	58.3%	41.7%
STAUNTON									
SUFFOLK	1,212	573	637	2	64 D	47.3%	52.6%	47.4%	52.6%
VIRGINIA BEACH									
WARWICK CITY									
WAYNESBORO	408	98	310		212 D	24.0%	76.0%	24.0%	76.0%
WILLIAMSBURG									
WINCHESTER	1,968	1,168	794	6	374 R	59.3%	40.3%	59.5%	40.5%
TOTAL	305,364	164,609	140,146	609	24,463 R	53.9%	45.9%	54.0%	46.0%

PRESIDENT 1932

City	Total Vote	Republican	Democratic	Other	Rep.-Dem. Plurality	Percentage Total Vote Rep.	Percentage Total Vote Dem.	Major Vote Rep.	Major Vote Dem.
ALEXANDRIA	4,184	1,199	2,941	44	1,742 D	28.7%	70.3%	29.0%	71.0%
BRISTOL	1,583	307	1,252	24	945 D	19.4%	79.1%	19.7%	80.3%
BUENA VISTA	438	154	258	26	104 D	35.2%	58.9%	37.4%	62.6%
CHARLOTTESVILLE	1,704	409	1,287	8	878 D	24.0%	75.5%	24.1%	75.9%
CHESAPEAKE									
CLIFTON FORGE	1,271	328	917	26	589 D	25.8%	72.1%	26.3%	73.7%
COLONIAL HEIGHTS									
COVINGTON	3,084	740	2,264	80	1,524 D	24.0%	73.4%	24.6%	75.4%
DANVILLE									
FAIRFAX CITY									
FALLS CHURCH									
FRANKLIN CITY									
FREDERICKSBURG	1,191	366	812	13	446 D	30.7%	68.2%	31.1%	68.9%
GALAX	1,084	294	772	18	478 D	27.1%	71.2%	27.6%	72.4%
HAMPTON									
HARRISONBURG	1,652	665	995	32	330 D	39.3%	58.8%	40.1%	59.9%
HOPEWELL	1,320	342	957	21	615 D	25.9%	72.5%	26.3%	73.7%
LYNCHBURG	4,936	1,200	3,656	80	2,456 D	24.3%	74.1%	24.7%	75.3%
MARTINSVILLE	958	212	739	7	527 D	22.1%	77.1%	22.3%	77.7%
NEWPORT NEWS	4,304	1,515	2,703	86	1,188 D	35.2%	62.8%	35.9%	64.1%
NORFOLK CITY	13,467	4,403	8,814	250	4,411 D	32.7%	65.4%	33.3%	66.7%
NORTON	2,440	490	1,920	30	1,430 D	20.1%	78.7%	20.3%	79.7%
PETERSBURG	5,294	1,840	3,344	110	1,504 D	34.8%	63.2%	35.5%	64.5%
PORTSMOUTH	909	341	542	26	201 D	37.5%	59.6%	38.6%	61.4%
RADFORD									
RICHMOND CITY	20,681	5,602	14,631	448	9,029 D	27.1%	70.7%	27.7%	72.3%
ROANOKE CITY	9,540	3,195	6,215	130	3,020 D	33.5%	65.1%	34.0%	66.0%
SOUTH BOSTON	945	329	597	19	268 D	34.8%	63.2%	35.5%	64.5%
SOUTH NORFOLK	1,555	551	988	16	437 D	35.4%	63.5%	35.8%	64.2%
STAUNTON									
SUFFOLK	1,287	265	1,013	9	748 D	20.6%	78.7%	20.7%	79.3%
VIRGINIA BEACH									
WARWICK CITY									
WAYNESBORO	505	99	387	19	288 D	19.6%	76.6%	20.4%	79.6%
WILLIAMSBURG									
WINCHESTER	1,910	698	1,179	33	481 D	36.5%	61.7%	37.2%	62.8%
TOTAL	297,942	89,637	203,979	4,326	114,342 D	30.1%	68.5%	30.5%	69.5%

VIRGINIA

PRESIDENT 1936

County	Total Vote	Republican	Democratic	Other	Rep.-Dem. Plurality	Total Vote Rep.	Total Vote Dem.	Major Vote Rep.	Major Vote Dem.
ACCOMACK	2,259	670	1,583	6	913 D	29.7%	70.1%	29.7%	70.3%
ALBEMARLE	2,467	635	1,825	7	1,190 D	25.7%	74.0%	25.8%	74.2%
ALLEGHANY	3,345	1,319	2,013	13	694 D	39.4%	60.2%	39.6%	60.4%
AMELIA	997	239	753	5	514 D	24.0%	75.5%	24.1%	75.9%
AMHERST	1,976	236	1,734	6	1,498 D	11.9%	87.8%	12.0%	88.0%
APPOMATTOX	1,587	204	1,375	8	1,171 D	12.9%	86.6%	12.9%	87.1%
ARLINGTON	7,835	2,825	4,971	39	2,146 D	36.1%	63.4%	36.2%	63.8%
AUGUSTA	4,571	1,668	2,872	31	1,204 D	36.5%	62.8%	36.7%	63.3%
BATH	1,130	514	614	2	100 D	45.5%	54.3%	45.6%	54.4%
BEDFORD	2,906	619	2,276	11	1,657 D	21.3%	78.3%	21.4%	78.6%
BLAND	1,425	642	778	5	136 D	45.1%	54.6%	45.2%	54.8%
BOTETOURT	2,901	1,343	1,544	14	201 D	46.3%	53.2%	46.5%	53.5%
BRUNSWICK	1,365	60	1,303	2	1,243 D	4.4%	95.5%	4.4%	95.6%
BUCHANAN	2,699	808	1,886	5	1,078 D	29.9%	69.9%	30.0%	70.0%
BUCKINGHAM	1,220	273	945	2	672 D	22.4%	77.5%	22.4%	77.6%
CAMPBELL	2,363	370	1,987	6	1,617 D	15.7%	84.1%	15.7%	84.3%
CAROLINE	1,367	258	1,104	5	846 D	18.9%	80.8%	18.9%	81.1%
CARROLL	5,368	3,245	2,122	1	1,123 R	60.5%	39.5%	60.5%	39.5%
CHARLES CITY COUNTY	312	79	233		154 D	25.3%	74.7%	25.3%	74.7%
CHARLOTTE	1,922	190	1,727	5	1,537 D	9.9%	89.9%	9.9%	90.1%
CHESTERFIELD	3,173	621	2,522	30	1,901 D	19.6%	79.5%	19.8%	80.2%
CLARKE	1,141	198	940	3	742 D	17.4%	82.4%	17.4%	82.6%
CRAIG	1,049	395	653	1	258 D	37.7%	62.1%	37.7%	62.3%
CULPEPER	1,824	551	1,266	7	715 D	30.2%	69.4%	30.3%	69.7%
CUMBERLAND	616	136	476	4	340 D	22.1%	77.3%	22.2%	77.8%
DICKENSON	3,830	1,146	2,683	1	1,537 D	29.9%	70.1%	29.9%	70.1%
DINWIDDIE	1,475	127	1,343	5	1,216 D	8.6%	91.5%	8.6%	91.4%
ELIZABETH CITY COUNTY	2,540	597	1,925	18	1,328 D	23.5%	76.3%	23.7%	76.3%
ESSEX	645	116	527	2	411 D	18.0%	81.7%	18.0%	82.0%
FAIRFAX COUNTY	4,527	1,584	2,913	30	1,329 D	35.0%	64.3%	35.2%	64.8%
FAUQUIER	2,672	629	2,037	6	1,408 D	23.5%	76.2%	23.6%	76.4%
FLOYD	2,273	1,566	699	8	867 R	68.9%	30.8%	69.1%	30.9%
FLUVANNA	808	217	586	5	369 D	26.9%	72.5%	27.0%	73.0%
FRANKLIN COUNTY	3,272	975	2,285	12	1,310 D	29.8%	69.8%	29.9%	70.1%
FREDERICK	2,058	665	1,386	7	721 D	32.3%	67.3%	32.4%	67.6%
GILES	2,596	1,047	1,547	2	500 D	40.3%	59.6%	40.4%	59.6%
GLOUCESTER	1,297	281	1,012	4	731 D	21.7%	78.3%	21.7%	78.3%
GOOCHLAND	870	228	638	4	410 D	26.2%	73.3%	26.3%	73.7%
GRAYSON	6,352	3,343	3,005	4	338 R	52.6%	47.3%	52.7%	47.3%
GREENE	663	321	341	1	20 D	48.4%	51.4%	48.5%	51.5%
GREENSVILLE	884		884		884 D		100.0%		100.0%
HALIFAX	4,642	302	4,331	9	4,029 D	6.5%	93.3%	6.5%	93.5%
HANOVER	1,736	327	1,397	12	1,070 D	18.8%	80.5%	19.0%	81.0%
HENRICO	4,919	1,285	3,618	16	2,333 D	26.1%	73.7%	26.3%	73.7%
HENRY	2,252	458	1,790	4	1,332 D	20.3%	79.5%	20.4%	79.6%
HIGHLAND	1,040	522	515	3	7 R	50.2%	49.5%	50.3%	49.7%
ISLE OF WIGHT	1,235	207	1,025	3	818 D	16.8%	83.0%	16.8%	83.2%
JAMES CITY COUNTY	372	70	302		232 D	18.8%	81.2%	18.8%	81.2%
KING AND QUEEN	497	124	372	1	248 D	24.9%	74.8%	25.0%	75.0%
KING GEORGE	766	295	469	2	174 D	38.5%	61.2%	38.6%	61.4%
KING WILLIAM	910	211	696	3	485 D	23.2%	76.5%	23.3%	76.7%
LANCASTER	1,014	322	689	3	367 D	31.8%	67.9%	31.8%	68.2%
LEE	6,199	2,066	4,120	13	2,054 D	33.3%	66.5%	33.4%	66.6%
LOUDOUN	3,162	867	2,287	8	1,420 D	27.4%	72.3%	27.5%	72.5%
LOUISA	1,598	486	1,100	12	614 D	30.4%	68.8%	30.6%	69.4%
LUNENBURG	1,370	77	1,291	2	1,214 D	5.6%	94.2%	5.6%	94.4%
MADISON	1,467	662	804	1	142 D	45.1%	54.8%	45.2%	54.8%
MATHEWS	1,079	452	622	5	170 D	41.9%	57.6%	42.1%	57.9%
MECKLENBURG	2,934	202	2,730	2	2,528 D	6.9%	93.0%	6.9%	93.1%
MIDDLESEX	781	123	653	5	530 D	15.7%	83.3%	15.9%	84.1%

PRESIDENT 1940

County	Total Vote	Republican	Democratic	Other	Rep.-Dem. Plurality	Total Vote Rep.	Total Vote Dem.	Major Vote Rep.	Major Vote Dem.
ACCOMACK	2,366	882	1,476	8	594 D	37.3%	62.4%	37.4%	62.6%
ALBEMARLE	2,458	804	1,648	6	844 D	32.7%	67.0%	32.8%	67.0%
ALLEGHANY	3,329	1,164	2,153	12	989 D	35.0%	64.7%	35.1%	64.9%
AMELIA	831	267	562	2	295 D	32.1%	67.6%	32.4%	67.6%
AMHERST	2,347	292	2,048	7	1,756 D	12.4%	87.3%	12.5%	87.5%
APPOMATTOX	1,363	215	1,144	4	929 D	15.8%	83.9%	15.8%	84.2%
ARLINGTON	9,862	4,365	5,440	57	1,075 D	44.3%	55.2%	44.5%	55.5%
AUGUSTA	4,564	1,768	2,774	22	1,006 D	38.7%	60.8%	38.9%	61.1%
BATH	1,163	527	630	6	103 D	45.3%	54.2%	45.5%	54.5%
BEDFORD	3,340	791	2,535	14	1,744 D	23.7%	75.9%	23.8%	76.2%
BLAND	1,449	693	753	3	60 D	47.8%	52.0%	47.9%	52.1%
BOTETOURT	2,422	1,085	1,329	8	244 D	44.8%	54.9%	44.9%	55.1%
BRUNSWICK	1,456	164	1,288	4	1,124 D	11.3%	88.5%	11.3%	88.7%
BUCHANAN	3,848	1,291	2,554	3	1,263 D	33.5%	66.4%	33.6%	66.4%
BUCKINGHAM	1,123	289	829	5	540 D	25.8%	73.8%	25.8%	74.2%
CAMPBELL	2,819	456	2,358	5	1,902 D	16.2%	83.6%	16.2%	83.8%
CAROLINE	1,447	305	1,136	6	831 D	21.1%	78.5%	21.2%	78.8%
CARROLL	3,386	1,835	1,546	5	289 R	54.2%	45.7%	54.3%	45.7%
CHARLES CITY COUNTY	330	92	238		146 D	27.9%	72.1%	27.9%	72.1%
CHARLOTTE	1,721	251	1,467	3	1,216 D	14.6%	85.2%	14.6%	85.4%
CHESTERFIELD	4,261	879	3,354	28	2,475 D	20.6%	78.7%	20.8%	79.2%
CLARKE	1,380	333	1,043	4	710 D	24.1%	75.6%	24.2%	75.8%
CRAIG	957	299	656	2	357 D	31.2%	68.5%	31.3%	68.7%
CULPEPER	1,794	579	1,208	7	629 D	32.3%	67.3%	32.4%	67.6%
CUMBERLAND	559	157	396	6	239 D	28.1%	70.8%	28.4%	71.6%
DICKENSON	4,343	1,785	2,551	7	766 D	41.1%	58.7%	41.2%	58.8%
DINWIDDIE	1,400	264	1,129	7	865 D	18.9%	80.6%	19.0%	81.0%
ELIZABETH CITY COUNTY	3,000	652	2,337	11	1,685 D	21.7%	77.9%	21.8%	78.2%
ESSEX	693	145	547	1	402 D	20.9%	78.9%	21.0%	79.0%
FAIRFAX COUNTY	5,660	2,371	3,263	26	892 D	41.9%	57.7%	42.1%	57.9%
FAUQUIER	2,637	756	1,874	7	1,118 D	28.7%	71.1%	28.7%	71.3%
FLOYD	2,214	1,482	729	3	753 R	66.9%	32.9%	67.0%	33.0%
FLUVANNA	821	241	579	1	338 D	29.4%	70.5%	29.4%	70.6%
FRANKLIN COUNTY	2,968	925	2,037	6	1,112 D	31.2%	68.6%	31.2%	68.8%
FREDERICK	2,406	773	1,631	2	858 D	32.1%	67.8%	32.2%	67.8%
GILES	2,744	1,024	1,716	4	692 D	37.3%	62.5%	37.4%	62.6%
GLOUCESTER	1,180	241	937	2	696 D	20.4%	79.4%	20.5%	79.5%
GOOCHLAND	1,004	180	820	4	640 D	17.9%	81.7%	18.0%	82.0%
GRAYSON	5,526	2,806	2,703	17	103 R	50.8%	48.9%	50.9%	49.1%
GREENE	645	282	363		81 D	43.7%	56.3%	43.7%	56.3%
GREENSVILLE	999	152	843	4	691 D	15.2%	84.4%	15.3%	84.7%
HALIFAX	3,826	373	3,441	12	3,068 D	9.7%	89.9%	9.8%	90.2%
HANOVER	1,719	364	1,347	8	983 D	21.2%	78.4%	21.3%	78.7%
HENRICO	6,027	2,005	3,993	29	1,988 D	33.3%	66.3%	33.4%	66.6%
HENRY	2,280	474	1,795	11	1,321 D	20.8%	78.7%	20.9%	79.1%
HIGHLAND	1,182	628	549	5	79 R	53.1%	46.4%	53.4%	46.6%
ISLE OF WIGHT	1,346	208	1,138		930 D	15.5%	84.5%	15.5%	84.5%
JAMES CITY COUNTY	454	146	306	2	160 D	32.2%	67.4%	32.4%	67.6%
KING AND QUEEN	490	124	365	1	241 D	25.3%	74.5%	25.4%	74.6%
KING GEORGE	683	167	515	1	348 D	24.5%	75.4%	24.5%	75.5%
KING WILLIAM	932	235	697		462 D	25.2%	74.8%	25.2%	74.8%
LANCASTER	1,036	317	711	8	394 D	30.6%	68.6%	30.8%	69.2%
LEE	6,809	2,623	4,180	6	1,557 D	38.5%	61.4%	38.6%	61.4%
LOUDOUN	3,231	1,061	2,156	14	1,095 D	32.8%	66.7%	33.0%	67.0%
LOUISA	1,482	573	896	13	323 D	38.7%	60.5%	39.0%	61.0%
LUNENBURG	1,359	144	1,213	2	1,069 D	10.6%	89.3%	10.6%	89.4%
MADISON	1,342	646	692	4	46 D	48.1%	51.5%	48.3%	51.7%
MATHEWS	947	349	592	6	243 D	36.9%	62.5%	37.1%	62.9%
MECKLENBURG	2,713	308	2,402	3	2,094 D	11.4%	88.5%	11.4%	88.6%
MIDDLESEX	713	125	586	2	461 D	17.5%	82.2%	17.6%	82.4%

VIRGINIA

PRESIDENT 1936

County	Total Vote	Republican	Democratic	Other	Rep.-Dem. Plurality	Total Vote % Rep.	Total Vote % Dem.	Major Vote % Rep.	Major Vote % Dem.
MONTGOMERY	3,713	1,852	1,832	29	20 R	49.9%	49.3%	50.3%	49.7%
NANSEMOND	1,654	175	1,478	1	1,303 D	10.6%	89.4%	10.6%	89.4%
NELSON	1,577	370	1,204	3	834 D	23.5%	76.3%	23.5%	76.5%
NEW KENT	427	120	307		187 D	28.1%	71.9%	28.1%	71.9%
NORFOLK COUNTY	4,406	652	3,734	20	3,082 D	14.8%	84.7%	14.9%	85.1%
NORTHAMPTON	1,255	277	975	3	698 D	22.1%	77.7%	22.1%	77.9%
NORTHUMBERLAND	878	260	618		358 D	29.6%	70.4%	29.6%	70.4%
NOTTOWAY	1,568	260	1,297	11	1,037 D	16.6%	82.7%	16.7%	83.3%
ORANGE	1,636	402	1,227	7	825 D	24.6%	75.0%	24.7%	75.3%
PAGE	3,447	1,551	1,888	8	337 D	45.0%	54.8%	45.1%	54.9%
PATRICK	2,320	726	1,588	6	862 D	31.3%	68.4%	31.4%	68.6%
PITTSYLVANIA	4,255	556	3,694	5	3,138 D	13.1%	86.8%	13.1%	86.9%
POWHATAN	596	158	438		280 D	26.5%	73.5%	26.5%	73.5%
PRINCE EDWARD	1,410	253	1,153	4	900 D	17.9%	81.8%	18.0%	82.0%
PRINCE GEORGE	844	128	713	3	585 D	15.2%	84.5%	15.2%	84.8%
PRINCE WILLIAM	1,982	457	1,512	13	1,055 D	23.1%	76.3%	23.2%	76.8%
PRINCESS ANNE	2,368	436	1,925	7	1,489 D	18.4%	81.3%	18.5%	81.5%
PULASKI	3,521	1,180	2,337	4	1,157 D	33.5%	66.4%	33.6%	66.4%
RAPPAHANNOCK	923	241	686	1	445 D	26.0%	73.9%	26.0%	74.0%
RICHMOND COUNTY	668	217	451		234 D	32.5%	67.5%	32.5%	67.5%
ROANOKE COUNTY	5,558	2,105	3,422	31	1,317 D	37.9%	61.6%	38.1%	61.9%
ROCKBRIDGE	2,516	868	1,635	13	767 D	34.5%	65.0%	34.7%	65.3%
ROCKINGHAM	5,754	2,834	2,916	4	82 D	49.2%	50.7%	49.3%	50.7%
RUSSELL	4,760	1,599	3,143	18	1,544 D	33.6%	66.0%	33.7%	66.3%
SCOTT	4,168	2,046	2,122		76 D	49.1%	50.9%	49.1%	50.9%
SHENANDOAH	6,028	3,152	2,861	15	291 R	52.3%	47.5%	52.4%	47.6%
SMYTH	4,421	2,067	2,337	17	270 D	46.8%	52.9%	46.9%	53.1%
SOUTHAMPTON	1,826	148	1,673	5	1,525 D	8.1%	91.6%	8.1%	91.9%
SPOTSYLVANIA	1,294	453	836	5	383 D	35.0%	64.6%	35.1%	64.9%
STAFFORD	1,250	596	651	3	55 D	47.7%	52.1%	47.8%	52.2%
SURRY	804	87	715	2	628 D	10.8%	88.9%	10.8%	89.2%
SUSSEX	1,006	126	880		754 D	12.5%	87.5%	12.5%	87.5%
TAZEWELL	4,995	1,981	2,992	22	1,011 D	39.7%	59.9%	39.8%	60.2%
WARREN	1,604	426	1,174	4	748 D	26.6%	73.2%	26.6%	73.4%
WARWICK COUNTY	1,075	200	870	5	670 D	18.6%	80.9%	18.7%	81.3%
WASHINGTON	4,654	2,047	2,595	12	548 D	44.0%	55.8%	44.1%	55.9%
WESTMORELAND	1,167	296	871		575 D	25.4%	74.6%	25.4%	74.6%
WISE	7,470	2,057	5,399	14	3,342 D	27.5%	72.3%	27.6%	72.4%
WYTHE	4,878	2,781	2,089	8	692 R	57.0%	42.8%	57.1%	42.9%
YORK	988	228	729	31	501 D	23.1%	73.8%	23.8%	76.2%

PRESIDENT 1940

County	Total Vote	Republican	Democratic	Other	Rep.-Dem. Plurality	Total Vote % Rep.	Total Vote % Dem.	Major Vote % Rep.	Major Vote % Dem.
MONTGOMERY	4,075	1,890	2,168	17	278 D	46.4%	53.2%	46.6%	53.4%
NANSEMOND	1,538	129	1,408	1	1,279 D	8.4%	91.5%	8.4%	91.6%
NELSON	1,626	330	1,291	5	961 D	20.3%	79.4%	20.4%	79.6%
NEW KENT	419	133	286		153 D	31.7%	68.3%	31.7%	68.3%
NORFOLK COUNTY	4,475	639	3,821	15	3,182 D	14.3%	85.4%	14.3%	85.7%
NORTHAMPTON	1,228	359	866	3	507 D	29.2%	70.5%	29.3%	70.7%
NORTHUMBERLAND	1,102	386	712	4	326 D	35.0%	64.6%	35.2%	64.8%
NOTTOWAY	1,674	373	1,290	11	917 D	22.3%	77.1%	22.4%	77.6%
ORANGE	1,759	464	1,283	12	819 D	26.4%	72.9%	26.6%	73.4%
PAGE	3,237	1,630	1,596	11	34 R	50.4%	49.3%	50.5%	49.5%
PATRICK	1,999	514	1,479	6	965 D	25.7%	74.0%	25.8%	74.2%
PITTSYLVANIA	4,455	728	3,710	17	2,982 D	16.3%	83.3%	16.4%	83.6%
POWHATAN	669	157	510	2	353 D	23.5%	76.2%	23.5%	76.5%
PRINCE EDWARD	1,435	313	1,110	12	797 D	21.8%	77.4%	22.0%	78.0%
PRINCE GEORGE	925	156	766	3	610 D	16.9%	82.8%	16.9%	83.1%
PRINCE WILLIAM	1,940	500	1,435	5	935 D	25.8%	74.0%	25.8%	74.2%
PRINCESS ANNE	2,137	445	1,689	3	1,244 D	20.8%	79.0%	20.9%	79.1%
PULASKI	3,255	1,023	2,226	6	1,203 D	31.4%	68.4%	31.5%	68.5%
RAPPAHANNOCK	816	225	588	3	363 D	27.6%	72.1%	27.7%	72.3%
RICHMOND COUNTY	741	257	475	9	218 D	34.7%	64.1%	35.1%	64.9%
ROANOKE COUNTY	5,888	2,302	3,539	47	1,237 D	39.1%	60.1%	39.4%	60.6%
ROCKBRIDGE	2,535	902	1,618	15	716 D	35.6%	63.8%	35.8%	64.2%
ROCKINGHAM	5,544	2,922	2,569	53	353 R	52.7%	46.3%	53.2%	46.8%
RUSSELL	5,200	2,080	3,109	11	1,029 D	40.0%	59.8%	40.1%	59.9%
SCOTT	5,464	2,982	2,474	8	508 R	54.6%	45.3%	54.7%	45.3%
SHENANDOAH	5,991	3,527	2,450	14	1,077 R	58.9%	40.9%	59.0%	41.0%
SMYTH	4,570	2,134	2,420	16	286 D	46.7%	53.0%	46.9%	53.1%
SOUTHAMPTON	1,733	213	1,508	12	1,295 D	12.3%	87.0%	12.4%	87.6%
SPOTSYLVANIA	1,154	365	785	4	420 D	31.6%	68.0%	31.7%	68.3%
STAFFORD	1,269	463	803	3	340 D	36.5%	63.3%	36.6%	63.4%
SURRY	778	120	658		538 D	15.4%	84.6%	15.4%	84.6%
SUSSEX	903	154	737	12	583 D	17.0%	81.6%	17.3%	82.7%
TAZEWELL	5,472	2,356	3,108	8	752 D	43.1%	56.8%	43.1%	56.9%
WARREN	1,833	491	1,338	4	847 D	26.8%	73.0%	26.8%	73.2%
WARWICK COUNTY	1,373	305	1,065	3	760 D	22.2%	77.6%	22.3%	77.7%
WASHINGTON	5,976	2,697	3,245	34	548 D	45.1%	54.3%	45.4%	54.6%
WESTMORELAND	1,203	357	845	1	488 D	29.7%	70.2%	29.7%	70.3%
WISE	5,998	1,448	4,538	12	3,090 D	24.1%	75.7%	24.2%	75.8%
WYTHE	3,215	1,507	1,695	13	188 D	46.9%	52.7%	47.1%	52.9%
YORK	980	177	787	16	610 D	18.1%	80.3%	18.4%	81.6%

VIRGINIA

PRESIDENT 1936 / PRESIDENT 1940

City	1936 Total Vote	Republican	Democratic	Other	Rep.-Dem. Plurality	%TV Rep.	%TV Dem.	%MV Rep.	%MV Dem.	1940 Total Vote	Republican	Democratic	Other	Rep.-Dem. Plurality	%TV Rep.	%TV Dem.	%MV Rep.	%MV Dem.
ALEXANDRIA	4,650	1,225	3,381	44	2,156 D	26.3%	72.7%	26.6%	73.4%	5,831	1,802	4,004	25	2,202 D	30.9%	68.7%	31.0%	69.0%
BRISTOL	1,682	311	1,364	7	1,053 D	18.5%	81.1%	18.6%	81.4%	1,904	423	1,465	16	1,042 D	22.2%	76.9%	22.4%	77.6%
BUENA VISTA	540	177	363		186 D	32.8%	67.2%	32.8%	67.2%	395	113	280	2	167 D	28.6%	70.9%	28.8%	71.2%
CHARLOTTESVILLE	1,742	335	1,393	14	1,058 D	19.2%	80.0%	19.4%	80.6%	2,515	743	1,759	13	1,016 D	29.5%	69.9%	29.7%	70.3%
CHESAPEAKE																		
CLIFTON FORGE	1,550	343	1,199	8	856 D	22.1%	77.4%	22.2%	77.8%	1,543	353	1,179	11	826 D	22.9%	76.4%	23.0%	77.0%
COLONIAL HEIGHTS																		
COVINGTON																		
DANVILLE	3,845	549	3,266	30	2,717 D	14.3%	84.9%	14.4%	85.6%	4,141	787	3,324	30	2,537 D	19.0%	80.3%	19.1%	80.9%
FAIRFAX CITY																		
FALLS CHURCH																		
FRANKLIN CITY																		
FREDERICKSBURG	1,357	411	944	2	533 D	30.3%	69.6%	30.3%	69.7%	1,565	522	1,037	6	515 D	33.4%	66.3%	33.5%	66.5%
GALAX																		
HAMPTON	1,162	190	971	1	781 D	16.4%	83.6%	16.4%	83.6%	1,194	215	975	4	760 D	18.0%	81.7%	18.1%	81.9%
HARRISONBURG	2,297	894	1,390	13	496 D	38.9%	60.5%	39.1%	60.9%	2,481	1,000	1,462	19	462 D	40.3%	58.9%	40.6%	59.4%
HOPEWELL	1,651	332	1,309	10	977 D	20.1%	79.3%	20.2%	79.8%	1,290	308	981	1	673 D	23.9%	76.0%	23.9%	76.0%
LYNCHBURG	5,092	1,373	3,697	22	2,324 D	27.0%	72.6%	27.1%	72.9%	6,631	1,966	4,656	9	2,690 D	29.6%	70.2%	29.7%	70.3%
MARTINSVILLE	1,208	255	949	4	694 D	21.1%	78.6%	21.2%	78.8%	1,254	269	980	5	711 D	21.5%	78.1%	21.5%	78.5%
NEWPORT NEWS	4,962	919	4,021	22	3,102 D	18.5%	81.0%	18.6%	81.4%	4,799	863	3,907	29	3,044 D	18.0%	81.4%	18.1%	81.9%
NORFOLK CITY	13,849	3,229	10,561	59	7,332 D	23.3%	76.3%	23.4%	76.6%	14,304	3,485	10,783	36	7,298 D	24.4%	75.4%	24.4%	75.6%
NORTON																		
PETERSBURG	2,651	444	2,192	15	1,748 D	16.7%	82.7%	16.8%	83.2%	2,815	604	2,193	18	1,589 D	21.5%	77.9%	21.6%	78.4%
PORTSMOUTH	6,509	861	5,617	31	4,756 D	13.2%	86.3%	13.3%	86.7%	5,753	675	5,053	25	4,378 D	11.7%	87.8%	11.8%	88.2%
RADFORD	1,078	421	650	7	229 D	39.1%	60.3%	39.3%	60.7%	1,216	417	793	6	376 D	34.3%	65.2%	34.5%	65.5%
RICHMOND CITY	23,348	4,478	18,784	86	14,306 D	19.2%	80.5%	19.3%	80.7%	25,439	6,031	19,332	76	13,301 D	23.7%	76.0%	23.8%	76.2%
ROANOKE CITY	10,504	3,363	7,087	54	3,724 D	32.0%	67.5%	32.2%	67.8%	10,542	3,553	6,942	47	3,389 D	33.7%	65.9%	33.9%	66.1%
SOUTH BOSTON	1,002	172	823	7	651 D	17.2%	82.1%	17.3%	82.7%	1,076	156	920		764 D	14.5%	85.5%	14.5%	85.5%
SOUTH NORFOLK	1,668	568	1,091	9	523 D	34.1%	65.4%	34.2%	65.8%	1,744	687	1,042	15	355 D	39.4%	59.7%	39.7%	60.3%
STAUNTON																		
SUFFOLK	1,641	281	1,360		1,079 D	17.1%	82.9%	17.1%	82.9%	1,598	383	1,215		832 D	24.0%	76.0%	24.0%	76.0%
VIRGINIA BEACH																		
WARWICK CITY																		
WAYNESBORO	489	96	389	4	293 D	19.6%	79.6%	19.8%	80.2%	541	168	367	6	199 D	31.1%	67.8%	31.4%	68.6%
WILLIAMSBURG																		
WINCHESTER	1,851	743	1,096	12	353 D	40.1%	59.2%	40.4%	59.6%	2,067	945	1,114	8	169 D	45.7%	53.9%	45.9%	54.1%
TOTAL	334,590	98,336	234,980	1,274	136,644 D	29.4%	70.2%	29.5%	70.5%	346,608	109,363	235,961	1,284	126,598 D	31.6%	68.1%	31.7%	68.3%

VIRGINIA

PRESIDENT 1944

County	Total Vote	Republican	Democratic	Other	Rep.-Dem. Plurality	Total Vote Rep. %	Total Vote Dem. %	Major Vote Rep. %	Major Vote Dem. %
ACCOMACK	2,795	1,045	1,747	3	702 D	37.4%	62.5%	37.4%	62.5%
ALBEMARLE	2,701	964	1,725	12	761 D	35.7%	63.9%	35.8%	64.2%
ALLEGHANY	3,300	1,308	1,985	7	677 D	39.6%	60.2%	39.7%	60.3%
AMELIA	851	295	553	3	258 D	34.7%	65.0%	34.8%	65.2%
AMHERST	3,039	442	2,585	12	2,143 D	14.5%	85.1%	14.6%	85.4%
APPOMATTOX	1,385	270	1,109	6	839 D	19.5%	80.1%	19.6%	80.4%
ARLINGTON	15,499	8,317	7,122	60	1,195 R	53.7%	46.0%	53.9%	46.1%
AUGUSTA	5,247	2,319	2,913	15	594 D	44.2%	55.5%	44.3%	55.7%
BATH	1,089	504	581	4	77 D	46.3%	53.4%	46.5%	53.5%
BEDFORD	3,608	1,068	2,534	6	1,466 D	29.6%	70.2%	29.7%	70.3%
BLAND	1,506	744	762		18 D	49.4%	50.6%	49.4%	50.6%
BOTETOURT	2,562	1,272	1,275	15	3 D	49.6%	49.8%	49.9%	50.1%
BRUNSWICK	1,447	208	1,239		1,031 D	14.4%	85.6%	14.4%	85.6%
BUCHANAN	4,805	1,971	2,826	8	855 D	41.0%	58.8%	41.1%	58.9%
BUCKINGHAM	1,012	286	723	3	437 D	28.3%	71.4%	28.3%	71.7%
CAMPBELL	2,633	634	1,995	4	1,361 D	24.1%	75.8%	24.1%	75.9%
CAROLINE	1,391	383	1,004	4	621 D	27.5%	72.2%	27.6%	72.4%
CARROLL	3,729	2,352	1,375	2	977 R	63.1%	36.9%	63.1%	36.9%
CHARLES CITY COUNTY	465	139	326		187 D	29.9%	70.1%	29.9%	70.1%
CHARLOTTE	1,830	356	1,473	1	1,117 D	19.5%	80.5%	19.5%	80.5%
CHESTERFIELD	3,772	901	2,860	11	1,959 D	23.9%	75.8%	24.0%	76.0%
CLARKE	1,235	415	816	4	401 D	33.6%	66.0%	33.8%	66.3%
CRAIG	892	327	564	1	237 D	36.7%	63.2%	36.7%	63.3%
CULPEPER	1,773	750	1,022	1	272 D	42.3%	57.6%	42.3%	57.7%
CUMBERLAND	685	218	463	4	245 D	31.8%	67.6%	32.0%	68.0%
DICKENSON	4,554	1,762	2,786	6	1,024 D	38.7%	61.2%	38.7%	61.3%
DINWIDDIE	1,377	279	1,096	2	817 D	20.3%	79.6%	20.3%	79.7%
ELIZABETH CITY COUNTY	3,704	1,128	2,563	13	1,435 D	30.5%	69.4%	30.6%	69.4%
ESSEX	689	179	508	2	329 D	26.0%	73.7%	26.1%	73.9%
FAIRFAX COUNTY	7,662	4,046	3,582	34	464 R	52.8%	46.8%	53.0%	47.0%
FAUQUIER	3,204	1,089	2,110	5	1,021 D	34.0%	65.9%	34.0%	66.0%
FLOYD	2,052	1,424	630	8	794 R	69.1%	30.6%	69.3%	30.7%
FLUVANNA	870	291	577		286 D	33.5%	66.3%	33.5%	66.5%
FRANKLIN COUNTY	3,224	1,206	2,002	16	796 D	37.4%	62.1%	37.6%	62.4%
FREDERICK	2,156	938	1,213	5	275 D	43.5%	56.3%	43.6%	56.4%
GILES	2,910	1,203	1,703	4	500 D	41.3%	58.5%	41.4%	58.6%
GLOUCESTER	1,349	410	934	5	524 D	30.4%	69.2%	30.5%	69.5%
GOOCHLAND	925	230	691	4	461 D	24.5%	74.7%	25.0%	75.0%
GRAYSON	5,914	3,298	2,607	9	691 R	55.8%	44.1%	55.9%	44.1%
GREENE	676	393	282	1	111 R	58.1%	41.7%	58.2%	41.8%
GREENSVILLE	1,237	279	954	4	675 D	22.6%	77.1%	22.6%	77.4%
HALIFAX	3,870	512	3,351	7	2,839 D	13.2%	86.6%	13.3%	86.7%
HANOVER	2,051	575	1,471	5	896 D	28.1%	71.7%	28.1%	71.9%
HENRICO	4,331	1,263	3,056	12	1,793 D	29.2%	70.6%	29.2%	70.8%
HENRY	2,270	727	1,538	5	811 D	32.1%	67.8%	32.1%	67.9%
HIGHLAND	1,176	641	535		106 R	54.5%	45.5%	54.5%	45.5%
ISLE OF WIGHT	1,608	430	1,178		748 D	26.7%	73.3%	26.7%	73.3%
JAMES CITY COUNTY	478	161	317		156 D	33.7%	66.3%	33.7%	66.3%
KING AND QUEEN	529	166	363		197 D	31.4%	68.6%	31.4%	68.6%
KING GEORGE	690	340	348	2	8 D	49.3%	50.4%	49.4%	50.6%
KING WILLIAM	998	280	718		438 D	28.1%	71.9%	28.1%	71.9%
LANCASTER	1,061	390	666	5	276 D	36.8%	62.8%	36.9%	63.1%
LEE	8,399	3,921	4,470	8	549 D	46.7%	53.2%	46.7%	53.3%
LOUDOUN	3,294	1,485	1,802	7	317 D	45.1%	54.7%	45.2%	54.8%
LOUISA	1,572	634	930	8	296 D	40.3%	59.2%	40.5%	59.5%
LUNENBURG	1,393	184	1,205	4	1,021 D	13.2%	86.5%	13.2%	86.8%
MADISON	1,428	811	616	1	195 R	56.8%	43.1%	56.8%	43.2%
MATHEWS	1,107	491	615	1	124 D	44.4%	55.6%	44.4%	55.6%
MECKLENBURG	2,991	430	2,561		2,131 D	14.4%	85.6%	14.4%	85.6%
MIDDLESEX	816	186	627	3	441 D	22.8%	76.8%	22.9%	77.1%

PRESIDENT 1948

County	Total Vote	Republican	Democratic	Other	Rep.-Dem. Plurality	Total Vote Rep. %	Total Vote Dem. %	Major Vote Rep. %	Major Vote Dem. %
ACCOMACK	3,104	1,088	1,669	347	581 D	35.1%	53.8%	39.5%	60.5%
ALBEMARLE	2,443	984	1,178	281	194 D	40.3%	48.2%	45.5%	54.5%
ALLEGHANY	3,850	1,425	2,253	172	828 D	37.0%	58.5%	38.7%	61.3%
AMELIA	1,058	372	443	243	71 D	35.2%	41.9%	45.6%	54.4%
AMHERST	2,466	460	1,481	525	1,021 D	18.7%	60.1%	23.7%	76.3%
APPOMATTOX	1,666	238	1,182	246	944 D	14.3%	70.9%	16.8%	83.2%
ARLINGTON	20,111	10,774	7,798	1,539	2,976 R	53.6%	38.8%	58.0%	42.0%
AUGUSTA	3,454	1,690	1,355	409	335 R	48.9%	39.2%	55.5%	44.5%
BATH	938	488	375	75	113 R	52.0%	40.0%	56.5%	43.5%
BEDFORD	3,609	1,084	1,556	969	472 D	30.0%	43.1%	41.1%	58.9%
BLAND	1,628	822	738	68	84 R	50.5%	45.3%	52.7%	47.3%
BOTETOURT	2,631	1,363	1,026	242	337 R	51.8%	39.0%	57.1%	42.9%
BRUNSWICK	2,202	229	1,067	906	838 D	10.4%	48.5%	17.7%	82.3%
BUCHANAN	5,325	2,085	3,174	66	1,089 D	39.2%	59.6%	39.6%	60.4%
BUCKINGHAM	1,267	354	728	185	374 D	27.9%	57.5%	32.7%	67.3%
CAMPBELL	2,876	668	1,554	654	886 D	23.2%	54.0%	30.1%	69.9%
CAROLINE	1,312	397	731	184	334 D	30.3%	55.7%	35.2%	64.8%
CARROLL	3,724	2,456	1,196	72	1,260 R	65.7%	32.0%	67.3%	32.7%
CHARLES CITY COUNTY	497	167	258	72	91 D	33.6%	51.9%	39.3%	60.7%
CHARLOTTE	1,667	285	964	418	679 D	17.1%	57.8%	22.8%	77.2%
CHESTERFIELD	4,730	1,428	2,600	702	1,172 D	30.2%	55.0%	35.5%	64.5%
CLARKE	1,158	384	482	292	98 D	33.2%	41.6%	44.3%	55.7%
CRAIG	796	317	456	23	139 D	39.8%	57.3%	41.0%	59.0%
CULPEPER	1,699	682	804	213	122 D	40.1%	47.3%	45.9%	54.1%
CUMBERLAND	813	219	424	170	205 D	26.9%	52.2%	34.1%	65.9%
DICKENSON	5,172	2,197	2,945	30	748 D	42.5%	56.9%	42.7%	57.3%
DINWIDDIE	1,500	264	961	275	697 D	17.6%	64.1%	21.4%	78.6%
ELIZABETH CITY COUNTY	4,788	1,617	2,744	427	1,127 D	33.8%	57.3%	37.1%	62.9%
ESSEX	651	221	329	101	108 D	33.9%	50.5%	40.2%	59.8%
FAIRFAX COUNTY	9,489	4,930	3,719	840	1,211 R	52.5%	39.2%	57.0%	43.0%
FAUQUIER	2,667	1,102	1,291	274	189 D	41.3%	48.4%	46.1%	53.9%
FLOYD	1,745	1,266	434	45	832 R	72.6%	24.9%	74.5%	25.5%
FLUVANNA	852	319	447	86	128 D	37.4%	52.5%	41.6%	58.4%
FRANKLIN COUNTY	2,813	1,100	1,343	370	243 D	39.1%	47.7%	45.0%	55.0%
FREDERICK	2,404	921	1,244	239	323 D	38.3%	51.7%	42.5%	57.5%
GILES	3,115	1,448	1,529	138	81 D	46.5%	49.1%	48.6%	51.4%
GLOUCESTER	1,274	434	719	121	285 D	34.1%	56.4%	37.6%	62.4%
GOOCHLAND	1,140	292	683	165	391 D	25.6%	59.9%	29.9%	70.1%
GRAYSON	6,568	3,669	2,741	158	928 R	55.8%	41.7%	57.2%	42.8%
GREENE	714	420	261	33	159 R	58.8%	36.6%	61.7%	38.3%
GREENSVILLE	1,427	301	710	416	409 D	21.1%	49.8%	29.8%	70.2%
HALIFAX	3,870	521	1,323	2,026	802 D	13.5%	34.2%	28.3%	71.7%
HANOVER	2,202	838	1,048	316	210 D	38.1%	47.6%	44.4%	55.6%
HENRICO	4,970	2,092	2,321	557	229 D	42.1%	46.7%	47.4%	52.6%
HENRY	2,537	730	1,318	489	588 D	28.8%	52.0%	35.6%	64.4%
HIGHLAND	1,090	579	423	88	156 R	53.1%	38.8%	57.8%	42.2%
ISLE OF WIGHT	1,591	442	1,064	85	622 D	27.8%	66.9%	29.3%	70.7%
JAMES CITY COUNTY	439	171	198	70	27 D	39.0%	45.1%	46.3%	53.7%
KING AND QUEEN	547	171	293	83	122 D	31.3%	53.6%	36.9%	63.1%
KING GEORGE	720	316	248	156	68 R	43.9%	34.4%	56.0%	44.0%
KING WILLIAM	971	348	476	147	128 D	35.8%	49.0%	42.2%	57.8%
LANCASTER	1,174	459	560	155	101 D	39.1%	47.7%	45.0%	55.0%
LEE	8,466	4,297	4,069	100	228 R	50.8%	48.1%	51.4%	48.6%
LOUDOUN	3,245	1,430	1,545	270	115 D	44.1%	47.6%	48.1%	51.9%
LOUISA	1,691	701	782	208	81 D	41.5%	46.2%	47.3%	52.7%
LUNENBURG	1,718	251	1,126	341	875 D	14.6%	65.5%	18.2%	81.8%
MADISON	1,188	662	428	98	234 R	55.7%	36.0%	60.7%	39.3%
MATHEWS	1,031	490	458	83	32 R	47.5%	44.4%	51.7%	48.3%
MECKLENBURG	3,053	513	2,117	423	1,604 D	16.8%	69.3%	19.5%	80.5%
MIDDLESEX	879	271	457	151	186 D	30.8%	52.0%	37.2%	62.8%

VIRGINIA

PRESIDENT 1944

County	Total Vote	Republican	Democratic	Other	Rep.-Dem. Plurality	Total Vote Rep.	Total Vote Dem.	Major Vote Rep.	Major Vote Dem.
MONTGOMERY	3,607	1,936	1,652	19	284 R	53.7%	45.8%	54.0%	46.0%
NANSEMOND	1,749	351	1,398		1,047 D	20.1%	79.9%	20.1%	79.9%
NELSON	1,819	427	1,390	2	963 D	23.5%	76.4%	23.5%	76.5%
NEW KENT	487	158	329		171 D	32.4%	67.6%	32.4%	67.6%
NORFOLK COUNTY	7,011	1,527	5,467	17	3,940 D	21.8%	78.0%	21.8%	78.2%
NORTHAMPTON	1,493	381	1,108	4	727 D	25.5%	74.2%	25.6%	74.4%
NORTHUMBERLAND	1,221	525	695	1	170 D	43.0%	56.9%	43.0%	57.0%
NOTTOWAY	1,930	472	1,453	5	981 D	24.5%	75.3%	24.5%	75.5%
ORANGE	1,896	694	1,199	3	505 D	36.6%	63.2%	36.7%	63.3%
PAGE	4,234	2,574	1,653	7	921 R	60.8%	39.0%	60.9%	39.1%
PATRICK	2,096	706	1,383	7	677 D	33.7%	66.0%	33.8%	66.2%
PITTSYLVANIA	4,724	1,224	3,492	8	2,268 D	25.9%	73.9%	26.0%	74.0%
POWHATAN	694	230	461	3	231 D	33.1%	66.4%	33.3%	66.7%
PRINCE EDWARD	1,492	425	1,063	4	638 D	28.5%	71.2%	28.6%	71.4%
PRINCE GEORGE	1,098	301	796	1	495 D	27.4%	72.5%	27.4%	72.6%
PRINCE WILLIAM	2,108	763	1,340	5	577 D	36.2%	63.6%	36.3%	63.7%
PRINCESS ANNE	2,953	993	1,959	1	966 D	33.6%	66.3%	33.6%	66.4%
PULASKI	3,458	1,302	2,155	1	853 D	37.7%	62.3%	37.7%	62.3%
RAPPAHANNOCK	797	297	497	3	200 D	37.3%	62.4%	37.4%	62.6%
RICHMOND COUNTY	701	336	364	1	28 D	47.9%	51.9%	48.0%	52.0%
ROANOKE COUNTY	6,536	3,146	3,380	10	234 D	48.1%	51.7%	48.2%	51.8%
ROCKBRIDGE	2,608	961	1,638	9	677 D	36.8%	62.8%	37.0%	63.0%
ROCKINGHAM	5,839	3,714	2,134	21	1,580 R	63.6%	36.0%	63.8%	36.2%
RUSSELL	5,350	2,385	2,945	20	560 D	44.6%	55.0%	44.7%	55.3%
SCOTT	5,983	3,089	2,888	6	201 R	51.6%	48.3%	51.7%	48.3%
SHENANDOAH	5,485	3,517	1,962	6	1,555 R	64.1%	35.8%	64.2%	35.8%
SMYTH	4,999	2,726	2,266	7	460 R	54.5%	45.3%	54.6%	45.4%
SOUTHAMPTON	1,895	284	1,599	12	1,315 D	15.0%	84.4%	15.1%	84.9%
SPOTSYLVANIA	1,251	504	744	3	240 D	40.3%	59.5%	40.4%	59.6%
STAFFORD	1,418	714	698	6	16 R	50.4%	49.2%	50.6%	49.4%
SURRY	726	123	602	1	479 D	16.9%	82.9%	17.0%	83.0%
SUSSEX	980	201	773	6	572 D	20.5%	78.9%	20.6%	79.4%
TAZEWELL	5,128	2,271	2,832	25	561 D	44.3%	55.2%	44.5%	55.5%
WARREN	1,798	761	1,034	3	273 D	42.3%	57.5%	42.4%	57.6%
WARWICK COUNTY	2,661	807	1,849	5	1,042 D	30.3%	69.5%	30.4%	69.6%
WASHINGTON	5,664	2,792	2,849	23	57 D	49.3%	50.3%	49.5%	50.5%
WESTMORELAND	1,344	532	808	4	276 D	39.6%	60.1%	39.7%	60.3%
WISE	6,420	1,817	4,588	15	2,771 D	28.3%	71.5%	28.4%	71.6%
WYTHE	3,287	1,822	1,465		357 R	55.4%	44.5%	55.5%	44.5%
YORK	1,096	318	760	18	442 D	29.0%	69.3%	29.5%	70.5%

PRESIDENT 1948

County	Total Vote	Republican	Democratic	Other	Rep.-Dem. Plurality	Total Vote Rep.	Total Vote Dem.	Major Vote Rep.	Major Vote Dem.
MONTGOMERY	3,473	2,070	1,126	277	944 R	59.6%	32.4%	64.8%	35.2%
NANSEMOND	2,773	413	2,115	245	1,702 D	14.9%	76.3%	16.3%	83.7%
NELSON	1,741	371	1,204	166	833 D	21.3%	69.2%	23.6%	76.4%
NEW KENT	514	140	277	97	137 D	27.2%	53.9%	33.6%	66.4%
NORFOLK COUNTY	7,089	1,830	4,696	563	2,866 D	25.8%	66.2%	28.0%	72.0%
NORTHAMPTON	1,758	525	997	236	472 D	29.9%	56.7%	34.5%	65.5%
NORTHUMBERLAND	1,146	535	429	182	106 R	46.7%	37.4%	55.5%	44.5%
NOTTOWAY	1,963	486	1,004	473	518 D	24.8%	51.1%	32.6%	67.4%
ORANGE	1,852	726	856	270	130 D	39.2%	46.2%	45.9%	54.1%
PAGE	4,055	2,236	1,611	208	625 R	55.1%	39.7%	58.1%	41.9%
PATRICK	1,840	648	760	432	112 D	35.2%	41.3%	46.0%	54.0%
PITTSYLVANIA	5,666	1,164	3,149	1,353	1,985 D	20.5%	55.6%	27.0%	73.0%
POWHATAN	663	238	338	87	100 D	35.9%	51.0%	41.3%	58.7%
PRINCE EDWARD	1,718	459	740	519	281 D	26.7%	43.1%	38.3%	61.7%
PRINCE GEORGE	1,210	317	745	148	428 D	26.2%	61.6%	29.8%	70.2%
PRINCE WILLIAM	2,083	760	1,162	161	402 D	36.5%	55.8%	39.5%	60.5%
PRINCESS ANNE	3,715	1,329	2,008	378	679 D	35.8%	54.1%	39.8%	60.2%
PULASKI	3,452	1,691	1,412	349	279 R	49.0%	40.9%	54.5%	45.5%
RAPPAHANNOCK	1,034	311	617	106	306 D	30.1%	59.7%	33.5%	66.5%
RICHMOND COUNTY	615	296	240	79	56 R	48.1%	39.0%	55.2%	44.8%
ROANOKE COUNTY	7,455	3,988	2,876	591	1,112 R	53.5%	38.6%	58.1%	41.9%
ROCKBRIDGE	2,284	1,062	994	228	68 R	46.5%	43.5%	51.7%	48.3%
ROCKINGHAM	5,182	3,219	1,680	283	1,539 R	62.1%	32.4%	65.7%	34.3%
RUSSELL	5,243	2,447	2,689	107	242 D	46.7%	51.3%	47.6%	52.4%
SCOTT	6,272	3,520	2,676	76	844 R	56.1%	42.7%	56.8%	43.2%
SHENANDOAH	5,180	3,349	1,603	228	1,746 R	64.7%	30.9%	67.6%	32.4%
SMYTH	4,822	2,897	1,750	175	1,147 R	60.1%	36.3%	62.3%	37.7%
SOUTHAMPTON	2,100	339	1,462	299	1,123 D	16.1%	69.6%	18.8%	81.2%
SPOTSYLVANIA	1,510	517	818	175	301 D	34.2%	54.2%	38.7%	61.3%
STAFFORD	1,579	732	708	139	24 R	46.4%	44.8%	50.8%	49.2%
SURRY	774	134	460	180	326 D	17.3%	59.4%	22.6%	77.4%
SUSSEX	1,220	244	614	362	370 D	20.0%	50.3%	28.4%	71.6%
TAZEWELL	4,706	2,278	2,258	170	20 R	48.4%	48.0%	50.2%	49.8%
WARREN	2,483	1,016	1,291	176	275 D	40.9%	52.0%	44.0%	56.0%
WARWICK COUNTY	3,165	1,014	1,822	329	808 D	32.0%	57.6%	35.8%	64.2%
WASHINGTON	5,693	2,972	2,510	211	462 R	52.2%	44.1%	54.2%	45.8%
WESTMORELAND	1,276	568	503	205	65 R	44.5%	39.4%	53.0%	47.0%
WISE	7,845	2,836	4,862	147	2,026 D	36.2%	62.0%	36.8%	63.2%
WYTHE	3,336	2,077	976	283	1,101 R	62.3%	29.3%	68.0%	32.0%
YORK	1,376	418	826	132	408 D	30.4%	60.0%	33.6%	66.4%

VIRGINIA

PRESIDENT 1944

City	Total Vote	Republican	Democratic	Other	Rep.-Dem. Plurality	Percentage — Total Vote Rep.	Total Vote Dem.	Major Vote Rep.	Major Vote Dem.
ALEXANDRIA	7,823	3,405	4,391	27	986 D	43.5%	56.1%	43.7%	56.3%
BRISTOL	2,198	628	1,561	9	933 D	28.6%	71.0%	28.7%	71.3%
BUENA VISTA	582	179	402	1	223 D	30.8%	69.1%	30.8%	69.2%
CHARLOTTESVILLE	3,255	1,055	2,188	12	1,133 D	32.4%	67.2%	32.5%	67.5%
CHESAPEAKE									
CLIFTON FORGE	1,502	415	1,082	5	667 D	27.6%	72.3%	27.7%	72.3%
COLONIAL HEIGHTS									
COVINGTON									
DANVILLE	4,366	1,231	3,121	14	1,890 D	28.2%	71.5%	28.3%	71.7%
FAIRFAX CITY									
FALLS CHURCH									
FRANKLIN CITY	1,793	698	1,092	3	394 D	38.9%	60.9%	39.0%	61.0%
FREDERICKSBURG									
GALAX	1,287	297	987	3	690 D	23.1%	76.7%	23.1%	76.9%
HAMPTON									
HARRISONBURG	2,602	1,302	1,292	8	10 R	50.0%	49.7%	50.2%	49.8%
HOPEWELL	1,657	368	1,284	5	916 D	22.2%	77.5%	22.3%	77.7%
LYNCHBURG	6,713	2,396	4,302	15	1,906 D	35.7%	64.1%	35.8%	64.2%
MARTINSVILLE	1,553	458	1,093	2	635 D	29.5%	70.4%	29.5%	70.5%
NEWPORT NEWS	5,309	1,237	4,051	21	2,814 D	23.3%	76.3%	23.4%	76.5%
NORFOLK CITY	16,996	4,958	12,010	28	7,052 D	29.2%	71.7%	29.2%	70.8%
NORTON	2,981	719	2,256	6	1,537 D	24.1%	75.7%	24.2%	75.8%
PETERSBURG	6,877	1,129	5,735	13	4,606 D	16.4%	83.4%	16.4%	83.6%
PORTSMOUTH									
RADFORD	1,423	597	824	2	227 D	42.0%	57.9%	42.0%	58.0%
RICHMOND CITY	31,387	8,737	22,584	66	13,847 D	27.8%	72.0%	27.9%	72.1%
ROANOKE CITY	12,451	5,095	7,322	34	2,227 D	40.9%	58.8%	41.0%	59.0%
SOUTH BOSTON	1,168	241	924	3	683 D	20.6%	79.1%	20.7%	79.3%
SOUTH NORFOLK	2,012	847	1,159	6	312 D	42.1%	57.6%	42.2%	57.8%
STAUNTON	1,914	569	1,342	3	773 D	29.7%	70.1%	29.8%	70.2%
SUFFOLK									
VIRGINIA BEACH									
WARWICK CITY	671	211	454	6	243 D	31.4%	67.7%	31.7%	68.3%
WAYNESBORO									
WILLIAMSBURG									
WINCHESTER	2,102	1,095	1,000	7	95 R	52.1%	47.6%	52.3%	47.7%
TOTAL	388,485	145,243	242,276	966	97,033 D	37.4%	62.4%	37.5%	62.5%

PRESIDENT 1948

City	Total Vote	Republican	Democratic	Other	Rep.-Dem. Plurality	Percentage — Total Vote Rep.	Total Vote Dem.	Major Vote Rep.	Major Vote Dem.
ALEXANDRIA	8,707	3,903	3,917	887	14 D	44.8%	45.0%	49.9%	50.1%
BRISTOL	2,462	879	1,451	132	572 D	35.7%	58.9%	37.7%	62.3%
BUENA VISTA	563	234	297	32	63 D	41.6%	52.8%	44.1%	55.9%
CHARLOTTESVILLE	3,367	1,419	1,527	421	108 D	42.1%	45.4%	48.2%	51.8%
CHESAPEAKE									
CLIFTON FORGE	1,405	451	818	136	367 D	32.1%	58.2%	35.5%	64.5%
COLONIAL HEIGHTS									
COVINGTON									
DANVILLE	5,448	1,579	2,334	1,535	755 D	29.0%	42.8%	40.4%	59.6%
FAIRFAX CITY									
FALLS CHURCH									
FRANKLIN CITY	1,931	810	816	305	6 D	41.9%	42.3%	49.8%	50.2%
FREDERICKSBURG									
GALAX	1,235	371	727	137	356 D	30.0%	58.9%	33.8%	66.2%
HAMPTON									
HARRISONBURG	2,352	1,377	751	224	626 R	58.5%	31.9%	64.7%	35.3%
HOPEWELL	1,981	570	1,242	169	672 D	28.8%	62.7%	31.5%	68.5%
LYNCHBURG	6,747	2,373	2,480	1,894	107 D	35.2%	36.8%	48.9%	51.1%
MARTINSVILLE	2,061	642	814	605	172 D	31.1%	39.5%	44.1%	55.9%
NEWPORT NEWS	5,235	1,453	3,420	366	1,967 D	27.7%	65.3%	29.8%	70.2%
NORFOLK CITY	18,460	7,556	9,370	1,534	1,814 D	40.9%	50.8%	44.6%	55.4%
NORTON	3,831	1,189	2,019	623	830 D	31.0%	52.7%	37.1%	62.9%
PETERSBURG	7,381	2,056	4,612	713	2,556 D	27.9%	62.5%	30.8%	69.2%
PORTSMOUTH									
RADFORD	1,765	850	826	89	24 R	48.2%	46.8%	50.7%	49.3%
RICHMOND CITY	35,301	14,549	16,466	4,286	1,917 D	41.2%	46.6%	46.9%	53.1%
ROANOKE CITY	13,200	6,542	5,343	1,315	1,199 R	49.6%	40.5%	55.0%	45.0%
SOUTH BOSTON	1,263	347	857	79	510 D	27.0%	66.8%	28.8%	71.2%
SOUTH NORFOLK	2,673	1,323	914	436	409 R	49.5%	34.2%	59.1%	40.9%
STAUNTON	2,070	741	1,030	299	289 D	35.8%	49.8%	41.8%	58.2%
SUFFOLK									
VIRGINIA BEACH									
WARWICK CITY	1,794	833	839	122	6 D	46.4%	46.8%	49.8%	50.2%
WAYNESBORO	849	334	312	203	22 R	39.3%	36.7%	51.7%	48.3%
WILLIAMSBURG									
WINCHESTER	2,546	1,272	894	380	378 D	50.0%	35.1%	58.7%	41.3%
TOTAL	419,256	172,070	203,786	46,400	28,716 D	41.0%	47.9%	46.1%	53.9%

VIRGINIA

PRESIDENT 1952

County	Total Vote	Republican	Democratic	Other	Rep.-Dem. Plurality	%Tot Rep	%Tot Dem	%Maj Rep	%Maj Dem
ACCOMACK	4,864	2,626	2,220	18	406 R	54.0%	45.6%	54.2%	45.8%
ALBEMARLE	4,183	2,523	1,642	18	881 R	60.3%	39.3%	60.6%	39.4%
ALLEGHANY	4,849	2,564	2,274	11	290 R	52.9%	46.9%	53.0%	47.0%
AMELIA	1,551	832	703	16	129 R	53.6%	45.3%	54.2%	45.8%
AMHERST	3,500	1,407	2,078	15	671 D	40.2%	59.4%	40.4%	59.6%
APPOMATTOX	1,891	929	957	5	28 D	49.1%	50.6%	49.3%	50.7%
ARLINGTON	36,380	22,158	14,132	190	8,126 R	60.9%	38.8%	61.1%	38.9%
AUGUSTA	4,879	3,414	1,453	12	1,961 R	70.0%	29.8%	70.1%	29.9%
BATH	1,221	765	451	5	314 R	62.7%	36.9%	62.9%	37.1%
BEDFORD	5,353	2,916	2,426	11	490 R	54.5%	45.3%	54.6%	45.4%
BLAND	1,748	1,000	743	5	257 R	57.2%	42.5%	57.4%	42.6%
BOTETOURT	3,286	2,021	1,264	1	757 R	61.5%	38.5%	61.5%	38.5%
BRUNSWICK	2,747	1,098	1,635	14	537 D	40.0%	59.5%	40.2%	59.8%
BUCHANAN	6,029	2,330	3,613	86	1,283 D	38.6%	59.9%	39.2%	60.8%
BUCKINGHAM	1,741	811	919	11	108 D	46.6%	52.8%	46.9%	53.1%
CAMPBELL	5,178	2,447	2,713	18	266 D	47.3%	52.4%	47.4%	52.6%
CAROLINE	1,825	858	954	13	96 D	47.0%	52.3%	47.4%	52.6%
CARROLL	5,495	3,774	1,711	10	2,063 R	68.7%	31.1%	68.8%	31.2%
CHARLES CITY COUNTY	850	342	492	16	150 D	40.2%	57.9%	41.0%	59.0%
CHARLOTTE	2,596	949	1,630	17	681 D	36.6%	62.8%	36.8%	63.2%
CHESTERFIELD	8,046	4,482	3,546	18	936 R	55.7%	44.1%	55.8%	44.2%
CLARKE	1,530	809	716	5	93 R	52.9%	46.8%	53.0%	47.0%
CRAIG	915	425	490	—	65 D	46.4%	53.6%	46.4%	53.6%
CULPEPER	2,498	1,507	987	4	520 R	60.3%	39.5%	60.4%	39.6%
CUMBERLAND	1,277	695	574	8	121 R	54.4%	44.9%	54.8%	45.2%
DICKENSON	6,144	2,913	3,210	21	297 D	47.4%	52.2%	47.6%	52.4%
DINWIDDIE	2,472	983	1,462	27	479 D	39.8%	59.1%	40.2%	59.8%
ELIZABETH CITY COUNTY									
ESSEX	1,163	610	545	8	65 R	52.5%	46.9%	52.8%	47.2%
FAIRFAX COUNTY	21,379	13,020	8,329	30	4,691 R	60.9%	39.0%	61.0%	39.0%
FAUQUIER	3,675	2,068	1,597	10	471 R	56.3%	43.5%	56.4%	43.6%
FLOYD	2,268	1,626	619	23	1,007 R	71.7%	27.3%	72.4%	27.6%
FLUVANNA	1,254	724	519	11	205 R	57.7%	41.4%	58.2%	41.8%
FRANKLIN COUNTY	4,026	1,976	2,012	38	36 D	49.1%	50.0%	49.5%	50.5%
FREDERICK	3,134	1,803	1,326	5	477 R	57.5%	42.3%	57.6%	42.4%
GILES	3,655	1,935	1,717	3	218 R	52.9%	47.0%	53.0%	47.0%
GLOUCESTER	2,046	1,073	961	12	112 R	52.4%	47.0%	52.8%	47.2%
GOOCHLAND	1,548	714	820	14	106 D	46.1%	53.0%	46.5%	53.5%
GRAYSON	7,201	4,449	2,734	18	1,715 R	61.8%	38.0%	61.9%	38.1%
GREENE	792	537	250	5	287 R	67.8%	31.6%	68.2%	31.8%
GREENSVILLE	2,273	988	1,259	26	271 D	43.5%	55.4%	44.0%	56.0%
HALIFAX	5,587	2,274	3,296	17	1,022 D	40.7%	59.0%	40.8%	59.2%
HANOVER	3,777	2,257	1,518	2	739 R	59.8%	40.2%	59.8%	40.2%
HENRICO	16,035	10,682	5,339	14	5,343 R	66.6%	33.3%	66.7%	33.3%
HENRY	4,220	1,871	2,323	26	452 D	44.3%	55.0%	44.6%	55.4%
HIGHLAND	1,118	696	419	3	277 R	62.3%	37.5%	62.4%	37.6%
ISLE OF WIGHT	2,237	996	1,227	14	231 D	44.5%	54.9%	44.8%	55.2%
JAMES CITY COUNTY	875	527	346	2	181 R	60.2%	39.5%	60.4%	39.6%
KING AND QUEEN	810	415	387	8	28 R	51.2%	47.8%	51.7%	48.3%
KING GEORGE	1,090	577	503	10	74 R	52.9%	46.1%	53.4%	46.6%
KING WILLIAM	1,272	730	533	9	197 R	57.4%	41.9%	57.8%	42.2%
LANCASTER	1,997	1,228	753	16	475 R	61.5%	37.7%	62.0%	38.0%
LEE	8,891	4,622	4,242	27	380 R	52.0%	47.7%	52.1%	47.9%
LOUDOUN	4,630	2,540	2,075	15	465 R	54.9%	44.8%	55.0%	45.0%
LOUISA	2,172	1,135	1,025	12	110 R	52.3%	47.2%	52.5%	47.5%
LUNENBURG	2,373	837	1,528	8	691 D	35.3%	64.4%	35.4%	64.6%
MADISON	1,558	1,012	540	6	472 R	65.0%	34.7%	65.2%	34.8%
MATHEWS	1,489	951	533	5	418 R	63.9%	35.8%	64.1%	35.9%
MECKLENBURG	4,454	1,891	2,525	38	634 D	42.5%	56.7%	42.8%	57.2%
MIDDLESEX	1,221	705	507	9	198 R	57.7%	41.5%	58.2%	41.8%

PRESIDENT 1956

County	Total Vote	Republican	Democratic	Other	Rep.-Dem. Plurality	%Tot Rep	%Tot Dem	%Maj Rep	%Maj Dem
ACCOMACK	5,204	2,823	2,213	168	610 R	54.2%	42.5%	56.1%	43.9%
ALBEMARLE	4,386	2,508	1,412	466	1,096 R	57.2%	32.2%	64.0%	36.0%
ALLEGHANY	2,054	1,135	822	97	313 R	55.3%	40.0%	58.0%	42.0%
AMELIA	1,729	745	403	580	342 R	43.1%	23.3%	64.9%	35.1%
AMHERST	3,590	1,529	1,933	128	404 D	42.6%	53.8%	44.2%	55.8%
APPOMATTOX	2,086	853	1,079	154	226 D	40.9%	51.7%	44.2%	55.8%
ARLINGTON	39,725	21,868	16,674	1,183	5,194 R	55.0%	42.0%	56.7%	43.3%
AUGUSTA	5,092	3,466	1,484	142	1,982 R	68.1%	29.1%	70.0%	30.0%
BATH	1,264	739	479	46	260 R	58.5%	37.9%	60.7%	39.3%
BEDFORD	6,046	3,148	2,649	249	499 R	52.1%	43.8%	54.3%	45.7%
BLAND	1,947	1,113	813	21	300 R	57.2%	41.8%	57.8%	42.2%
BOTETOURT	3,758	2,280	1,377	101	903 R	60.7%	36.6%	62.3%	37.7%
BRUNSWICK	3,160	799	1,357	1,004	558 D	25.3%	42.9%	37.1%	62.9%
BUCHANAN	6,831	3,191	3,616	24	425 D	46.7%	52.9%	46.9%	53.1%
BUCKINGHAM	1,721	751	648	322	103 R	43.6%	37.7%	53.7%	46.3%
CAMPBELL	5,916	2,827	2,674	415	153 R	47.8%	45.2%	51.4%	48.6%
CAROLINE	1,969	907	853	209	54 R	46.1%	43.3%	51.5%	48.5%
CARROLL	5,828	4,060	1,739	29	2,321 R	69.7%	29.8%	70.0%	30.0%
CHARLES CITY COUNTY	917	661	174	82	487 R	72.1%	19.0%	79.2%	20.8%
CHARLOTTE	2,839	791	1,431	617	640 D	27.9%	50.4%	35.6%	64.4%
CHESTERFIELD	10,894	5,787	3,306	1,801	2,481 R	53.1%	30.3%	63.6%	36.4%
CLARKE	1,605	785	725	95	60 R	48.9%	45.2%	52.0%	48.0%
CRAIG	993	485	501	7	16 D	48.8%	50.5%	49.2%	50.8%
CULPEPER	2,661	1,502	966	193	536 R	56.4%	36.3%	60.9%	39.1%
CUMBERLAND	1,319	566	331	422	235 R	42.9%	25.1%	63.1%	36.9%
DICKENSON	7,153	3,444	3,695	14	251 D	48.1%	51.7%	48.2%	51.8%
DINWIDDIE	2,628	807	1,282	539	475 D	30.7%	48.8%	38.6%	61.4%
ELIZABETH CITY COUNTY									
ESSEX	1,076	597	328	151	269 R	55.5%	30.5%	64.5%	35.5%
FAIRFAX COUNTY	37,267	20,761	15,633	873	5,128 R	55.7%	41.9%	57.0%	43.0%
FAUQUIER	3,802	2,112	1,567	123	545 R	55.5%	41.2%	57.4%	42.6%
FLOYD	2,796	1,970	799	27	1,171 R	70.5%	28.6%	71.1%	28.9%
FLUVANNA	1,363	734	417	212	317 R	53.9%	30.6%	63.8%	36.2%
FRANKLIN COUNTY	4,354	2,125	2,142	87	17 D	48.8%	49.2%	49.8%	50.2%
FREDERICK	3,360	1,882	1,405	73	477 R	56.0%	41.8%	57.3%	42.7%
GILES	4,379	2,270	2,016	93	254 R	51.8%	46.0%	53.0%	47.0%
GLOUCESTER	2,276	1,319	723	234	596 R	58.0%	31.8%	64.6%	35.4%
GOOCHLAND	1,493	748	508	237	240 R	50.1%	34.0%	59.6%	40.4%
GRAYSON	6,496	4,039	2,426	31	1,613 R	62.2%	37.3%	62.5%	37.5%
GREENE	849	539	246	64	293 R	63.5%	29.0%	68.7%	31.3%
GREENSVILLE	2,490	724	994	772	270 D	29.1%	39.9%	42.1%	57.9%
HALIFAX	5,799	1,782	2,470	1,547	688 D	30.7%	42.6%	41.9%	58.1%
HANOVER	4,202	2,272	1,109	821	1,163 R	54.1%	26.4%	67.2%	32.8%
HENRICO	21,101	12,702	5,032	3,367	7,670 R	60.2%	23.8%	71.6%	28.4%
HENRY	5,102	2,436	2,582	84	146 D	47.7%	50.6%	48.5%	51.5%
HIGHLAND	1,091	633	432	26	201 R	58.0%	39.6%	59.5%	40.5%
ISLE OF WIGHT	2,757	1,298	1,324	135	26 D	47.1%	48.0%	49.5%	50.5%
JAMES CITY COUNTY	1,164	728	312	124	416 R	62.5%	26.8%	70.0%	30.0%
KING AND QUEEN	906	495	289	122	206 R	54.6%	31.9%	63.1%	36.9%
KING GEORGE	1,267	655	563	49	92 R	51.7%	44.4%	53.8%	46.2%
KING WILLIAM	1,427	887	357	183	530 R	62.2%	25.0%	71.3%	28.7%
LANCASTER	1,953	1,380	373	200	1,007 R	70.7%	19.1%	78.7%	21.3%
LEE	8,304	4,548	3,714	42	834 R	54.8%	44.7%	55.0%	45.0%
LOUDOUN	4,650	2,479	1,960	211	519 R	53.4%	42.1%	55.9%	44.1%
LOUISA	2,429	1,152	795	482	357 R	47.4%	32.7%	59.2%	40.8%
LUNENBURG	2,339	580	1,111	648	531 D	24.8%	47.5%	34.3%	65.7%
MADISON	1,495	850	533	112	317 R	56.9%	35.7%	61.5%	38.5%
MATHEWS	1,556	1,018	406	132	612 R	65.4%	26.1%	71.5%	28.5%
MECKLENBURG	4,434	1,498	2,004	932	506 D	33.8%	45.2%	42.8%	57.2%
MIDDLESEX	1,243	721	338	184	383 R	58.0%	27.2%	68.1%	31.9%

VIRGINIA

PRESIDENT 1952

County	Total Vote	Republican	Democratic	Other	Rep.-Dem. Plurality	Percentage Total Vote Rep.	Dem.	Major Vote Rep.	Dem.
MONTGOMERY	5,491	3,881	1,600	10	2,281 R	70.7%	29.1%	70.8%	29.2%
NANSEMOND	3,553	1,168	2,360	25	1,192 D	32.9%	66.4%	33.1%	66.9%
NELSON	1,970	740	1,222	8	482 D	37.6%	62.0%	37.7%	62.3%
NEW KENT	862	455	400	7	55 R	52.8%	46.4%	53.2%	46.8%
NORFOLK COUNTY	12,392	5,614	6,766	12	1,152 D	45.3%	54.6%	45.3%	54.7%
NORTHAMPTON	2,608	1,307	1,289	12	18 R	50.1%	49.4%	50.3%	49.7%
NORTHUMBERLAND	1,806	1,230	573	3	657 R	68.1%	31.7%	68.2%	31.8%
NOTTOWAY	2,850	1,454	1,381	15	73 R	51.0%	48.5%	51.3%	48.7%
ORANGE	2,453	1,525	916	12	609 R	62.2%	37.3%	62.5%	37.5%
PAGE	4,101	2,649	1,441	11	1,208 R	64.6%	35.1%	64.8%	35.2%
PATRICK	2,872	1,314	1,554	4	240 D	45.3%	54.1%	45.8%	54.2%
PITTSYLVANIA	6,900	2,893	3,976	31	1,083 D	41.9%	57.6%	42.1%	57.9%
POWHATAN	1,063	558	498	5	60 R	52.5%	46.8%	52.8%	47.2%
PRINCE EDWARD	2,290	1,359	926	5	433 R	59.3%	40.4%	59.5%	40.5%
PRINCE GEORGE	1,166	541	612	13	71 D	45.4%	52.5%	46.9%	53.1%
PRINCE WILLIAM	3,295	1,619	1,653	23	34 D	49.1%	50.2%	49.5%	50.5%
PRINCESS ANNE	6,230	3,180	3,037	13	143 R	51.0%	48.7%	51.2%	48.8%
PULASKI	4,538	2,815	1,715	8	1,100 R	62.0%	37.8%	62.1%	37.9%
RAPPAHANNOCK	1,139	619	518	2	101 R	54.3%	45.5%	54.4%	45.6%
RICHMOND COUNTY	1,055	727	326	2	401 R	68.9%	30.9%	69.0%	31.0%
ROANOKE COUNTY	8,726	6,017	2,689	20	3,328 R	69.0%	30.8%	69.1%	30.9%
ROCKBRIDGE	3,138	2,068	1,059	11	1,009 R	65.9%	33.7%	66.1%	33.9%
ROCKINGHAM	5,950	4,350	1,591	9	2,759 R	73.1%	26.7%	73.2%	26.8%
RUSSELL	6,206	2,937	3,253	16	316 D	47.3%	52.4%	47.4%	52.6%
SCOTT	7,693	4,703	2,990		1,713 R	61.1%	38.9%	61.1%	38.9%
SHENANDOAH	6,024	4,284	1,734	6	2,550 R	71.1%	28.8%	71.2%	28.8%
SMYTH	5,685	3,694	1,972	19	1,722 R	65.0%	34.7%	65.2%	34.8%
SOUTHAMPTON	3,177	1,166	2,000	11	834 D	36.7%	63.0%	36.8%	63.2%
SPOTSYLVANIA	2,397	1,174	1,194	29	20 D	49.0%	49.8%	49.6%	50.4%
STAFFORD	2,504	1,411	1,077	16	334 R	56.3%	43.0%	56.7%	43.3%
SURRY	1,006	414	572	20	158 D	41.2%	56.9%	42.0%	58.0%
SUSSEX	1,851	888	956	7	68 D	48.0%	51.6%	48.2%	51.8%
TAZEWELL	5,789	3,232	2,527	30	705 R	55.8%	43.6%	56.1%	43.9%
WARREN	3,261	1,888	1,362	11	526 R	57.9%	41.8%	58.1%	41.9%
WARWICK COUNTY									
WASHINGTON	6,599	3,810	2,778	11	1,032 R	57.7%	42.1%	57.8%	42.2%
WESTMORELAND	1,877	1,117	754	6	363 R	59.5%	40.2%	59.7%	40.3%
WISE	8,660	3,911	4,729	20	818 D	45.2%	54.6%	45.3%	54.7%
WYTHE	5,246	3,580	1,654	12	1,926 R	68.2%	31.5%	68.4%	31.6%
YORK	2,642	1,335	1,287	20	48 R	50.5%	48.7%	50.9%	49.1%

PRESIDENT 1956

County	Total Vote	Republican	Democratic	Other	Rep.-Dem. Plurality	Percentage Total Vote Rep.	Dem.	Major Vote Rep.	Dem.
MONTGOMERY	6,559	4,598	1,848	113	2,750 R	70.1%	28.2%	71.3%	28.7%
NANSEMOND	4,360	1,753	2,492	115	739 D	40.2%	57.2%	41.3%	58.7%
NELSON	2,054	764	1,215	75	451 D	37.2%	59.2%	38.6%	61.4%
NEW KENT	880	510	178	192	332 R	58.0%	20.2%	74.1%	25.9%
NORFOLK COUNTY	10,920	4,558	6,026	336	1,468 D	41.7%	55.2%	43.1%	56.9%
NORTHAMPTON	2,477	1,264	1,132	81	132 R	51.0%	45.7%	52.8%	47.2%
NORTHUMBERLAND	1,900	1,191	428	281	763 R	62.7%	22.5%	73.6%	26.4%
NOTTOWAY	3,329	1,124	1,242	963	118 D	33.8%	37.3%	47.5%	52.5%
ORANGE	2,510	1,344	794	372	550 R	53.5%	31.6%	62.9%	37.1%
PAGE	3,781	2,372	1,358	51	1,014 R	62.7%	35.9%	63.6%	36.4%
PATRICK	3,062	1,345	1,677	40	332 D	43.9%	54.8%	44.5%	55.5%
PITTSYLVANIA	7,794	2,870	4,136	788	1,266 D	36.8%	53.1%	41.0%	59.0%
POWHATAN	1,348	729	297	322	432 R	54.1%	22.0%	71.1%	28.9%
PRINCE EDWARD	2,965	932	437	1,596	495 R	31.4%	14.7%	68.1%	31.9%
PRINCE GEORGE	1,490	689	642	159	47 R	46.2%	43.1%	51.8%	48.2%
PRINCE WILLIAM	3,970	2,023	1,851	96	172 R	51.0%	46.6%	52.2%	47.8%
PRINCESS ANNE	9,253	4,675	4,342	236	333 R	50.5%	46.9%	51.8%	48.2%
PULASKI	5,578	3,517	1,994	67	1,523 R	63.1%	35.7%	63.8%	36.2%
RAPPAHANNOCK	1,075	514	523	38	9 D	47.8%	48.7%	49.6%	50.4%
RICHMOND COUNTY	1,121	761	274	86	487 R	67.9%	24.4%	73.5%	26.5%
ROANOKE COUNTY	10,753	7,509	2,899	345	4,610 R	69.8%	27.0%	72.1%	27.9%
ROCKBRIDGE	3,418	2,273	1,039	106	1,234 R	66.5%	30.4%	68.6%	31.4%
ROCKINGHAM	6,027	4,324	1,605	98	2,719 R	71.7%	26.6%	72.9%	27.1%
RUSSELL	7,224	3,550	3,641	33	91 D	49.1%	50.4%	49.4%	50.6%
SCOTT	8,754	5,116	3,595	43	1,521 R	58.4%	41.1%	58.7%	41.3%
SHENANDOAH	6,019	4,164	1,769	86	2,395 R	69.2%	29.4%	70.2%	29.8%
SMYTH	7,204	4,771	2,374	59	2,397 R	66.2%	33.0%	66.8%	33.2%
SOUTHAMPTON	3,655	1,290	2,039	326	749 D	35.3%	55.8%	38.8%	61.2%
SPOTSYLVANIA	2,395	1,244	993	158	251 R	51.9%	41.5%	55.6%	44.4%
STAFFORD	2,652	1,553	978	111	585 R	58.9%	36.9%	61.5%	38.5%
SURRY	1,307	425	616	266	191 D	32.5%	47.1%	40.8%	59.2%
SUSSEX	1,997	785	851	361	66 D	39.3%	42.6%	48.0%	52.0%
TAZEWELL	7,535	3,960	3,495	80	465 R	52.6%	46.4%	53.1%	46.9%
WARREN	3,405	2,003	1,322	80	681 R	58.8%	38.8%	60.2%	39.8%
WARWICK COUNTY									
WASHINGTON	8,250	4,651	3,547	52	1,104 R	56.4%	43.0%	56.7%	43.3%
WESTMORELAND	1,897	1,033	695	169	338 R	54.5%	36.6%	59.8%	40.2%
WISE	10,495	4,371	5,766	57	696 D	46.4%	54.7%	46.4%	53.3%
WYTHE	5,307	3,484	1,766	57	1,718 R	65.6%	33.3%	66.4%	33.6%
YORK	2,927	1,759	1,064	104	695 R	60.1%	36.4%	62.3%	37.7%

VIRGINIA

PRESIDENT 1952

City	Total Vote	Republican	Democratic	Other	Rep.-Dem. Plurality	Total Vote % Rep.	Total Vote % Dem.	Major Vote % Rep.	Major Vote % Dem.
ALEXANDRIA	15,072	8,579	6,471	22	2,108 R	56.9%	42.9%	57.0%	43.0%
BRISTOL	3,009	1,574	1,432	3	142 R	52.3%	47.6%	52.4%	47.6%
BUENA VISTA	906	513	392	1	121 R	56.6%	43.3%	56.7%	43.3%
CHARLOTTESVILLE	5,474	3,292	2,174	8	1,118 R	60.1%	39.7%	60.2%	39.8%
CHESAPEAKE									
CLIFTON FORGE	1,751	936	811	4	125 R	53.5%	46.3%	53.6%	46.4%
COLONIAL HEIGHTS	1,732	896	835	1	61 R	51.7%	48.2%	51.8%	48.2%
COVINGTON									
DANVILLE	8,146	4,765	3,323	58	1,442 R	58.5%	40.8%	58.9%	41.1%
FAIRFAX CITY									
FALLS CHURCH	2,317	1,366	930	1	456 R	59.8%	40.1%	59.8%	40.2%
FRANKLIN CITY									
FREDERICKSBURG	2,510	1,536	970	4	566 R	61.2%	38.6%	61.3%	38.7%
GALAX									
HAMPTON	10,481	5,505	4,946	30	559 R	52.5%	47.2%	52.7%	47.3%
HARRISONBURG	2,876	2,238	635	3	1,603 R	77.8%	22.1%	77.9%	22.1%
HOPEWELL	3,308	1,640	1,657	11	17 D	49.6%	50.1%	49.7%	50.1%
LYNCHBURG	10,949	7,090	3,848	11	3,242 R	64.8%	35.1%	64.8%	35.1%
MARTINSVILLE	3,174	1,772	1,391	11	381 R	55.8%	43.8%	56.0%	44.0%
NEWPORT NEWS	6,843	2,769	4,051	23	1,282 D	40.5%	59.2%	40.6%	59.4%
NORFOLK CITY	26,074	14,166	11,862	46	2,304 R	54.3%	45.5%	54.4%	45.6%
NORTON									
PETERSBURG	5,179	2,822	2,342	15	480 R	54.5%	45.2%	54.6%	45.4%
PORTSMOUTH	9,855	3,621	6,138	46	2,567 D	36.7%	62.8%	36.9%	63.1%
RADFORD	2,658	1,523	1,108	7	415 R	57.7%	42.0%	57.9%	42.1%
RICHMOND CITY	48,610	29,300	19,235	75	10,065 R	60.3%	39.6%	60.4%	39.6%
ROANOKE CITY	23,747	15,673	8,042	32	7,631 R	66.0%	33.9%	66.1%	33.9%
SOUTH BOSTON	2,897	1,098	1,782	17	684 D	37.9%	61.5%	38.1%	61.9%
SOUTH NORFOLK	3,528	2,578	945	5	1,633 R	73.1%	26.8%	73.2%	26.8%
STAUNTON									
SUFFOLK	2,837	1,622	1,209	6	413 R	57.2%	42.6%	57.3%	42.7%
VIRGINIA BEACH	2,191	1,310	881		429 R	59.8%	40.2%	59.8%	40.2%
WARWICK CITY	6,124	3,307	2,806	11	501 R	54.0%	45.8%	54.1%	45.9%
WAYNESBORO	2,413	1,680	730	3	950 R	69.6%	30.3%	69.7%	30.3%
WILLIAMSBURG	1,283	797	483	3	314 R	62.1%	37.6%	62.3%	37.7%
WINCHESTER	3,432	2,375	1,055	2	1,320 R	69.2%	30.7%	69.2%	30.8%
TOTAL	619,689	349,037	268,677	1,975	80,360 R	56.3%	43.4%	56.5%	43.5%

PRESIDENT 1956

City	Total Vote	Republican	Democratic	Other	Rep.-Dem. Plurality	Total Vote % Rep.	Total Vote % Dem.	Major Vote % Rep.	Major Vote % Dem.
ALEXANDRIA	16,449	8,633	7,451	365	1,182 R	52.5%	45.3%	53.7%	46.3%
BRISTOL	3,457	1,794	1,645	18	149 R	51.9%	47.6%	52.2%	47.8%
BUENA VISTA	897	545	326	26	219 R	60.8%	36.3%	62.6%	37.4%
CHARLOTTESVILLE	6,023	3,746	1,783	494	1,963 R	62.2%	29.6%	67.8%	32.2%
CHESAPEAKE									
CLIFTON FORGE	1,830	1,125	633	72	492 R	61.5%	34.6%	64.0%	36.0%
COLONIAL HEIGHTS	2,172	1,037	956	179	81 R	47.7%	44.0%	52.0%	48.0%
COVINGTON	2,909	1,639	1,189	81	450 R	56.3%	40.9%	58.0%	42.0%
DANVILLE	7,726	4,561	2,409	756	2,152 R	59.0%	31.2%	65.4%	34.6%
FAIRFAX CITY									
FALLS CHURCH	2,752	1,462	1,233	57	229 R	53.1%	44.8%	54.2%	45.8%
FRANKLIN CITY									
FREDERICKSBURG	2,775	1,672	934	169	738 R	60.3%	33.7%	64.2%	35.8%
GALAX	1,114	761	346	7	415 R	68.3%	31.1%	68.7%	31.3%
HAMPTON	12,983	7,432	5,108	443	2,324 R	57.2%	39.3%	59.3%	40.7%
HARRISONBURG	2,893	2,265	571	57	1,694 R	78.3%	19.7%	79.9%	20.1%
HOPEWELL	3,539	1,908	1,388	243	520 R	53.9%	39.2%	57.9%	42.1%
LYNCHBURG	10,502	6,806	3,362	334	3,444 R	64.8%	32.0%	66.9%	33.1%
MARTINSVILLE	3,561	2,125	1,368	68	757 R	59.7%	38.4%	60.8%	39.2%
NEWPORT NEWS	7,095	3,779	3,069	247	710 R	53.3%	43.3%	55.2%	44.8%
NORFOLK CITY	34,525	18,650	14,571	1,304	4,079 R	54.0%	42.2%	56.1%	43.9%
NORTON	1,241	684	552	5	132 R	55.1%	44.5%	55.3%	44.7%
PETERSBURG	5,449	3,166	1,882	401	1,284 R	58.1%	34.5%	62.7%	37.3%
PORTSMOUTH	11,436	5,390	5,683	363	293 D	47.1%	49.7%	48.7%	51.3%
RADFORD	3,058	1,910	1,118	30	792 R	62.5%	36.6%	63.1%	36.9%
RICHMOND CITY	44,291	27,367	10,758	6,166	16,609 R	61.8%	24.3%	71.8%	28.2%
ROANOKE CITY	24,082	16,708	6,751	623	9,957 R	69.4%	28.0%	71.2%	28.8%
SOUTH BOSTON	3,609	1,521	1,871	217	350 D	42.1%	51.8%	44.8%	55.2%
SOUTH NORFOLK	3,881	2,908	843	130	2,065 R	74.9%	21.7%	77.5%	22.5%
STAUNTON									
SUFFOLK	2,812	1,617	1,103	92	514 R	57.5%	39.2%	59.4%	40.6%
VIRGINIA BEACH	2,543	1,355	1,111	77	244 R	53.3%	43.7%	54.9%	45.1%
WARWICK CITY	8,640	4,872	3,406	362	1,466 R	56.4%	39.4%	58.9%	41.1%
WAYNESBORO	2,886	2,049	748	89	1,301 R	71.0%	25.9%	73.3%	26.7%
WILLIAMSBURG	1,238	775	362	101	413 R	62.6%	29.2%	68.2%	31.8%
WINCHESTER	3,419	2,375	945	99	1,430 R	69.5%	27.6%	71.5%	28.5%
TOTAL	697,978	386,459	267,760	43,759	118,699 R	55.4%	38.4%	59.1%	40.9%

VIRGINIA

PRESIDENT 1960

County	Total Vote	Republican	Democratic	Other	Rep.-Dem. Plurality	%Tot. Rep.	%Tot. Dem.	%Maj. Rep.	%Maj. Dem.
ACCOMACK	5,581	2,676	2,884	21	208 D	47.9	51.7	48.1	51.9
ALBEMARLE	5,272	3,135	2,102	35	1,033 R	59.5	39.9	59.9	40.1
ALLEGHANY	2,488	1,214	1,265	9	51 D	48.8	50.8	49.0	51.0
AMELIA	1,524	784	708	32	76 R	51.4	46.5	52.5	47.5
AMHERST	3,747	1,455	2,280	12	825 D	38.8	60.8	39.0	61.0
APPOMATTOX	2,208	951	1,240	17	289 D	43.1	56.2	43.4	56.6
ARLINGTON	45,977	23,632	22,095	250	1,537 R	51.4	48.1	51.7	48.3
AUGUSTA	5,989	4,034	1,914	41	2,120 R	67.4	32.0	67.8	32.2
BATH	1,277	646	629	2	17 R	50.6	49.3	50.7	49.3
BEDFORD	6,081	2,911	3,150	20	239 D	47.9	51.8	48.0	52.0
BLAND	1,671	848	822	1	26 R	50.7	49.2	50.8	49.2
BOTETOURT	3,802	2,159	1,621	22	538 R	56.8	42.6	57.1	42.9
BRUNSWICK	2,932	926	1,942	64	1,016 D	31.6	66.2	32.3	67.7
BUCHANAN	6,099	2,370	3,706	23	1,336 D	38.9	60.8	39.0	61.0
BUCKINGHAM	1,724	765	947	12	182 D	44.4	54.9	44.7	55.3
CAMPBELL	5,970	2,903	3,030	37	127 D	48.6	50.8	48.9	51.1
CAROLINE	2,367	864	1,483	20	619 D	36.5	62.7	36.8	63.2
CARROLL	5,589	3,705	1,873	11	1,832 R	66.3	33.5	66.4	33.6
CHARLES CITY COUNTY	964	337	623	4	286 D	35.0	64.6	35.1	64.9
CHARLOTTE	2,635	867	1,735	33	868 D	32.9	65.8	33.3	66.7
CHESTERFIELD	15,859	9,787	5,982	90	3,805 R	61.7	37.7	62.1	37.9
CLARKE	1,736	804	923	9	119 D	46.3	53.2	46.6	53.4
CRAIG	967	433	534		101 D	44.8	55.2	44.8	55.2
CULPEPER	2,971	1,630	1,332	9	298 R	54.9	44.8	55.0	45.0
CUMBERLAND	1,262	691	559	12	132 R	54.8	44.3	55.3	44.7
DICKENSON	4,960	2,203	2,756	1	553 D	44.4	55.6	44.4	55.6
DINWIDDIE	2,686	935	1,714	37	779 D	34.8	63.8	35.3	64.7
ELIZABETH CITY COUNTY									
ESSEX	1,117	606	509	2	97 R	54.3	45.6	54.3	45.7
FAIRFAX COUNTY	54,229	28,006	26,064	149	1,942 R	51.6	48.1	51.8	48.2
FAUQUIER	4,094	2,123	1,958	13	165 R	51.9	47.8	52.0	48.0
FLOYD	2,759	1,933	817	9	1,116 R	70.1	29.6	70.3	29.7
FLUVANNA	1,390	763	614	13	149 R	54.9	44.2	55.4	44.6
FRANKLIN COUNTY	5,016	2,080	2,924	12	844 D	41.5	58.3	41.6	58.4
FREDERICK	3,835	2,061	1,757	17	304 R	53.7	45.8	54.0	46.0
GILES	4,327	2,030	2,214	83	184 D	46.9	51.2	47.8	52.2
GLOUCESTER	2,620	1,310	1,297	13	13 R	50.0	49.5	50.2	49.8
GOOCHLAND	1,749	851	862	36	11 D	48.7	49.3	49.7	50.3
GRAYSON	6,638	3,893	2,738	7	1,155 R	58.7	41.2	58.7	41.3
GREENE	892	573	314	5	259 R	64.2	35.2	64.6	35.4
GREENSVILLE	2,766	1,057	1,676	33	619 D	38.2	60.6	38.7	61.3
HALIFAX	4,508	1,784	2,676	48	892 D	39.6	59.4	40.0	60.0
HANOVER	5,085	3,020	2,023	42	997 R	59.4	39.8	59.9	40.1
HENRICO	29,235	19,446	9,626	163	9,820 R	66.5	32.9	66.9	33.1
HENRY	5,643	2,323	3,306	14	983 D	41.2	58.6	41.3	58.7
HIGHLAND	932	527	401	4	126 R	56.5	43.0	56.8	43.2
ISLE OF WIGHT	3,177	1,141	2,020	16	879 D	35.9	63.6	36.1	63.9
JAMES CITY COUNTY	1,729	873	845	11	28 R	50.5	48.9	50.8	49.2
KING AND QUEEN	983	432	536	15	104 D	43.9	54.5	44.6	55.4
KING GEORGE	1,410	685	717	8	32 D	48.6	50.9	48.9	51.1
KING WILLIAM	1,549	793	745	11	48 R	51.2	48.1	51.6	48.4
LANCASTER	2,250	1,340	895	15	445 R	59.6	39.8	60.0	40.0
LEE	7,285	3,363	3,867	55	504 D	46.2	53.1	46.5	53.5
LOUDOUN	4,954	2,526	2,399	29	127 R	51.0	48.4	51.3	48.7
LOUISA	2,458	1,170	1,244	44	74 D	47.6	50.6	48.5	51.5
LUNENBURG	2,379	838	1,451	90	613 D	35.2	61.0	36.6	63.4
MADISON	1,653	998	636	19	362 R	60.4	38.5	61.1	38.9
MATHEWS	1,754	1,069	682	3	387 R	60.9	38.9	61.1	38.9
MECKLENBURG	4,534	1,936	2,533	65	597 D	42.7	55.9	43.3	56.7
MIDDLESEX	1,402	823	574	5	249 R	58.7	40.9	58.9	41.1

PRESIDENT 1964

County	Total Vote	Republican	Democratic	Other	Rep.-Dem. Plurality	%Tot. Rep.	%Tot. Dem.	%Maj. Rep.	%Maj. Dem.
ACCOMACK	6,683	3,145	3,528	10	383 D	47.1	52.8	47.1	52.9
ALBEMARLE	6,315	3,251	3,062	2	189 R	51.5	48.5	51.5	48.5
ALLEGHANY	2,685	1,104	1,580	1	476 D	41.1	58.8	41.1	58.9
AMELIA	2,239	1,348	884	7	464 R	60.2	39.5	60.4	39.6
AMHERST	5,410	2,675	2,730	5	55 D	49.4	50.5	49.5	50.5
APPOMATTOX	3,791	2,444	1,339	8	1,105 R	64.5	35.3	64.6	35.4
ARLINGTON	54,363	20,485	33,567	311	13,082 D	37.7	61.7	37.9	62.1
AUGUSTA	8,372	4,327	4,039	6	288 R	51.7	48.2	51.7	48.3
BATH	1,286	516	770		254 D	40.1	59.9	40.1	59.9
BEDFORD	7,914	3,806	4,076	32	270 D	48.1	51.5	48.3	51.7
BLAND	1,570	717	851	2	134 D	45.7	54.2	45.7	54.3
BOTETOURT	4,476	2,098	2,377	1	279 D	46.9	53.1	46.9	53.1
BRUNSWICK	4,446	1,883	2,560	3	677 D	42.4	57.6	42.4	57.6
BUCHANAN	7,124	2,349	4,756	19	2,407 D	33.0	66.8	33.1	66.9
BUCKINGHAM	2,733	1,547	1,182	4	365 R	56.6	43.2	56.7	43.3
CAMPBELL	9,145	5,713	3,401	31	2,312 R	62.5	37.2	62.7	37.3
CAROLINE	3,243	1,166	2,064	13	898 D	36.0	63.6	36.1	63.9
CARROLL	6,146	3,617	2,517	12	1,100 R	58.9	41.0	59.0	41.0
CHARLES CITY COUNTY	1,358	323	1,023	12	700 D	23.8	75.3	24.0	76.0
CHARLOTTE	3,178	1,974	1,191	13	783 R	62.1	37.5	62.4	37.6
CHESTERFIELD	25,871	17,486	8,376	9	9,110 R	67.6	32.4	67.6	32.4
CLARKE	2,206	1,068	1,136	2	68 D	48.4	51.5	48.5	51.5
CRAIG	1,244	477	767		290 D	38.3	61.7	38.3	61.7
CULPEPER	3,665	1,775	1,886	4	111 D	48.4	51.5	48.5	51.5
CUMBERLAND	1,977	1,099	871	7	228 R	55.6	44.1	55.8	44.2
DICKENSON	5,639	2,143	3,485	11	1,342 D	38.0	61.8	38.1	61.9
DINWIDDIE	4,285	2,096	2,182	7	86 D	48.9	50.9	49.0	51.0
ELIZABETH CITY COUNTY									
ESSEX	1,550	789	760	1	29 R	50.9	49.0	50.9	49.1
FAIRFAX COUNTY	79,517	30,755	48,680	82	17,925 D	38.7	61.2	38.7	61.3
FAUQUIER	6,613	3,101	3,506	6	405 D	46.9	53.0	46.9	53.1
FLOYD	2,985	1,836	1,144	5	692 R	61.5	38.3	61.6	38.4
FLUVANNA	1,834	823	1,008	3	185 D	44.9	55.0	44.9	55.1
FRANKLIN COUNTY	5,757	2,299	3,447	11	1,148 D	39.9	59.9	40.0	60.0
FREDERICK	5,374	2,535	2,830	9	295 D	47.2	52.6	47.3	52.7
GILES	5,167	1,952	3,133	82	1,181 D	37.8	60.6	38.4	61.6
GLOUCESTER	3,583	1,631	1,949	3	318 D	45.5	54.4	45.6	54.4
GOOCHLAND	2,697	1,241	1,452	4	211 D	46.0	53.8	46.1	53.9
GRAYSON	6,352	3,105	3,238	9	133 D	48.9	51.0	49.0	51.0
GREENE	1,104	641	460	3	181 R	58.1	41.7	58.2	41.8
GREENSVILLE	4,519	2,245	2,262	12	17 D	49.7	50.1	49.8	50.2
HALIFAX	6,144	3,928	2,198	18	1,730 R	63.9	35.8	64.1	35.9
HANOVER	7,751	4,879	2,864	8	2,015 R	62.9	36.9	63.0	37.0
HENRICO	42,082	29,286	12,779	17	16,507 R	69.6	30.4	69.6	30.4
HENRY	8,184	2,844	5,295	45	2,451 D	34.8	64.7	34.9	65.1
HIGHLAND	989	511	476	2	35 R	51.7	48.1	51.8	48.2
ISLE OF WIGHT	4,399	1,737	2,656	6	919 D	39.5	60.4	39.5	60.5
JAMES CITY COUNTY	2,839	1,092	1,744	3	652 D	38.5	61.4	38.5	61.5
KING AND QUEEN	1,489	699	786	4	87 D	46.9	52.8	47.1	52.9
KING GEORGE	1,729	644	1,085		441 D	37.2	62.8	37.2	62.8
KING WILLIAM	1,975	1,065	904	6	161 R	53.9	45.8	54.1	45.9
LANCASTER	2,911	1,663	1,245	3	418 R	57.1	42.8	57.2	42.8
LEE	8,626	3,463	5,151	12	1,688 D	40.1	59.7	40.2	59.8
LOUDOUN	6,877	2,594	4,278	5	1,684 D	37.7	62.2	37.7	62.3
LOUISA	3,103	1,369	1,731	3	362 D	44.1	55.8	44.2	55.8
LUNENBURG	2,977	1,847	1,128	2	719 R	62.0	37.9	62.1	37.9
MADISON	1,923	1,060	862	1	198 R	55.1	44.8	55.2	44.8
MATHEWS	2,286	1,149	1,137		12 R	50.3	49.7	50.3	49.7
MECKLENBURG	8,227	4,976	3,238	13	1,738 R	60.5	39.4	60.6	39.4
MIDDLESEX	1,995	1,019	973	3	46 R	51.1	48.8	51.2	48.8

VIRGINIA

PRESIDENT 1960

County	Total Vote	Republican	Democratic	Other	Rep.-Dem. Plurality	Total Vote Rep.	Total Vote Dem.	Major Vote Rep.	Major Vote Dem.
MONTGOMERY	6,445	4,270	2,157	18	2,113 R	66.3%	33.5%	66.4%	33.6%
NANSEMOND	5,323	1,346	3,944	33	2,598 D	25.3%	74.1%	25.4%	74.6%
NELSON	2,268	775	1,480	13	705 D	34.2%	65.3%	34.4%	65.6%
NEW KENT	1,018	526	481	11	45 R	51.7%	47.2%	52.2%	47.8%
NORFOLK COUNTY	8,936	3,769	5,101	66	1,332 D	42.2%	57.1%	42.5%	57.5%
NORTHAMPTON	2,392	995	1,387	10	392 D	41.6%	58.0%	41.8%	58.2%
NORTHUMBERLAND	2,211	1,340	858	13	482 R	60.6%	38.8%	61.0%	39.0%
NOTTOWAY	3,286	1,319	1,882	85	563 D	40.1%	57.3%	41.2%	58.8%
ORANGE	2,603	1,413	1,108	82	305 R	54.3%	42.6%	56.0%	44.0%
PAGE	4,331	2,708	1,508	15	1,100 R	62.5%	37.1%	62.7%	37.3%
PATRICK	3,028	1,362	1,655	11	293 D	45.0%	54.7%	45.1%	54.9%
PITTSYLVANIA	7,954	3,788	4,089	77	301 D	47.6%	51.4%	48.1%	51.9%
POWHATAN	1,328	779	528	21	251 R	58.7%	39.8%	59.6%	40.4%
PRINCE EDWARD	3,214	1,721	1,459	34	262 R	53.5%	45.4%	54.1%	45.9%
PRINCE GEORGE	1,725	727	983	15	256 D	42.1%	57.0%	42.5%	57.5%
PRINCE WILLIAM	5,639	2,624	2,987	28	363 D	46.5%	53.0%	46.8%	53.2%
PRINCESS ANNE	10,843	4,844	5,954	45	1,110 D	44.7%	54.9%	44.9%	55.1%
PULASKI	5,207	3,059	2,134	44	955 R	58.7%	40.4%	59.2%	40.8%
RAPPAHANNOCK	975	426	544	5	118 D	43.7%	55.8%	43.9%	56.1%
RICHMOND COUNTY	1,233	801	425	7	376 R	65.0%	34.5%	65.3%	34.7%
ROANOKE COUNTY	13,532	9,109	4,384	39	4,725 R	67.3%	32.4%	67.5%	32.5%
ROCKBRIDGE	3,585	2,170	1,405	10	765 R	60.5%	39.2%	60.7%	39.3%
ROCKINGHAM	6,872	4,829	2,026	17	2,803 R	70.3%	29.5%	70.4%	29.6%
RUSSELL	6,554	3,044	3,496	14	452 D	46.4%	53.3%	46.5%	53.4%
SCOTT	8,744	4,936	3,789	19	1,147 R	56.5%	43.3%	56.6%	43.4%
SHENANDOAH	6,199	4,144	2,053	2	2,091 R	66.8%	33.1%	66.9%	33.1%
SMYTH	7,138	4,256	2,864	18	1,392 R	59.6%	40.1%	59.8%	40.2%
SOUTHAMPTON	4,125	1,263	2,804	58	1,541 D	30.6%	68.0%	31.1%	68.9%
SPOTSYLVANIA	2,799	1,288	1,482	29	194 D	46.0%	52.9%	46.5%	53.5%
STAFFORD	2,965	1,447	1,494	24	47 D	48.8%	50.4%	49.2%	50.8%
SURRY	1,443	397	1,003	43	606 D	27.5%	69.5%	28.4%	71.6%
SUSSEX	1,993	713	1,253	27	540 D	35.8%	62.9%	36.3%	63.7%
TAZEWELL	7,574	3,139	4,416	19	1,277 D	41.4%	58.3%	41.5%	58.5%
WARREN	3,720	1,842	1,850	28	8 D	49.5%	49.7%	49.9%	50.1%
WARWICK COUNTY									
WASHINGTON	8,347	4,473	3,833	41	640 R	53.6%	45.9%	53.9%	46.1%
WESTMORELAND	2,219	1,176	1,034	9	142 R	53.0%	46.6%	53.2%	46.8%
WISE	9,716	3,876	5,822	18	1,946 D	39.9%	59.9%	40.0%	60.0%
WYTHE	4,993	2,871	2,075	47	796 R	57.5%	41.6%	58.0%	42.0%
YORK	3,795	2,085	1,691	19	394 R	54.9%	44.6%	55.2%	44.8%

PRESIDENT 1964

County	Total Vote	Republican	Democratic	Other	Rep.-Dem. Plurality	Total Vote Rep.	Total Vote Dem.	Major Vote Rep.	Major Vote Dem.
MONTGOMERY	8,489	4,604	3,872	13	732 R	54.2%	45.6%	54.3%	45.7%
NANSEMOND	7,415	2,590	4,804	21	2,214 D	34.9%	64.8%	35.0%	65.0%
NELSON	2,534	893	1,635	6	742 D	35.2%	64.5%	35.3%	64.7%
NEW KENT	1,365	677	684	4	7 D	49.6%	50.1%	49.7%	50.3%
NORFOLK COUNTY									
NORTHAMPTON	3,103	1,586	1,516	1	70 R	51.1%	48.9%	51.1%	48.9%
NORTHUMBERLAND	2,418	1,423	988	7	435 R	58.9%	40.9%	59.0%	41.0%
NOTTOWAY	4,499	2,353	2,138	8	215 R	52.3%	47.5%	52.4%	47.6%
ORANGE	3,107	1,595	1,508	4	87 R	51.3%	48.5%	51.4%	48.6%
PAGE	5,419	2,804	2,606	9	198 R	51.7%	48.1%	51.8%	48.2%
PATRICK	3,776	1,468	2,306	2	838 D	38.9%	61.1%	38.9%	61.1%
PITTSYLVANIA	12,373	7,120	5,228	25	1,892 R	57.5%	42.3%	57.7%	42.3%
POWHATAN	2,152	1,182	969	1	213 R	54.9%	45.0%	55.0%	45.0%
PRINCE EDWARD	4,064	2,545	1,512	7	1,033 R	62.6%	37.2%	62.7%	37.3%
PRINCE GEORGE	3,295	1,790	1,502	3	288 R	54.3%	45.6%	54.4%	45.6%
PRINCE WILLIAM	8,963	3,343	5,611	9	2,268 D	37.3%	62.6%	37.3%	62.7%
PRINCESS ANNE									
PULASKI	6,726	3,101	3,620	5	519 D	46.1%	53.8%	46.1%	53.9%
RAPPAHANNOCK	1,127	449	675	3	226 D	39.8%	59.9%	39.9%	60.1%
RICHMOND COUNTY	1,540	901	636	3	265 R	58.5%	41.3%	58.6%	41.4%
ROANOKE COUNTY	19,536	10,714	8,808	14	1,906 R	54.8%	45.1%	54.9%	45.1%
ROCKBRIDGE	4,806	2,200	2,599	7	399 D	45.8%	54.1%	45.8%	54.2%
ROCKINGHAM	8,363	4,155	4,205	3	50 D	49.7%	50.3%	49.7%	50.3%
RUSSELL	7,367	3,012	4,330	25	1,318 D	40.9%	58.8%	41.0%	59.0%
SCOTT	9,269	4,533	4,720	16	187 D	48.9%	50.9%	49.0%	51.0%
SHENANDOAH	7,168	3,981	3,184	3	797 R	55.5%	44.4%	55.6%	44.4%
SMYTH	7,952	3,830	4,113	9	283 D	48.2%	51.7%	48.2%	51.8%
SOUTHAMPTON	4,090	1,520	2,566	4	1,046 D	37.2%	62.7%	37.2%	62.8%
SPOTSYLVANIA	3,367	1,261	2,097	9	836 D	37.5%	62.3%	37.6%	62.4%
STAFFORD	4,364	1,888	2,469	7	581 D	43.3%	56.6%	43.3%	56.7%
SURRY	2,140	1,004	1,131	5	127 D	46.9%	52.9%	47.0%	53.0%
SUSSEX	2,775	1,537	1,234	4	303 R	55.4%	44.5%	55.5%	44.5%
TAZEWELL	9,417	3,231	6,081	105	2,850 D	34.3%	64.6%	34.7%	65.3%
WARREN	4,390	1,886	2,494	10	608 D	43.0%	56.8%	43.1%	56.9%
WARWICK COUNTY									
WASHINGTON	9,226	4,146	5,070	10	924 D	44.9%	55.0%	45.0%	55.0%
WESTMORELAND	2,499	1,181	1,312	6	131 D	47.3%	52.5%	47.4%	52.6%
WISE	10,539	3,309	7,220	10	3,911 D	31.4%	68.5%	31.5%	68.6%
WYTHE	5,863	2,958	2,879	26	79 R	50.5%	49.1%	50.7%	49.3%
YORK	6,389	2,992	3,385	12	393 D	46.8%	53.0%	46.9%	53.1%

VIRGINIA

PRESIDENT 1960

City	Total Vote	Republican	Democratic	Other	Rep.-Dem. Plurality	Total Vote Rep.	Total Vote Dem.	Major Vote Rep.	Major Vote Dem.
ALEXANDRIA	18,551	8,826	9,662	63	836 D	47.6%	52.1%	47.7%	52.3%
BRISTOL	3,299	1,728	1,561	10	167 R	52.4%	47.3%	52.5%	47.5%
BUENA VISTA	918	487	427	4	60 R	53.1%	46.5%	53.3%	46.7%
CHARLOTTESVILLE	6,628	3,651	2,894	83	757 R	55.1%	43.7%	55.8%	44.2%
CHESAPEAKE									
CLIFTON FORGE	1,663	885	771	7	114 R	53.2%	46.4%	53.4%	46.6%
COLONIAL HEIGHTS	2,581	1,372	1,193	11	174 R	53.2%	46.2%	53.4%	46.6%
COVINGTON	3,001	1,436	1,558	7	122 D	47.9%	51.9%	48.0%	52.1%
DANVILLE	7,794	4,966	2,611	217	2,355 R	63.7%	33.5%	65.5%	34.5%
FAIRFAX CITY									
FALLS CHURCH	3,165	1,525	1,629	11	104 D	48.2%	51.5%	48.4%	51.6%
FRANKLIN CITY									
FREDERICKSBURG	2,915	1,566	1,326	23	240 R	53.7%	45.5%	54.1%	45.9%
GALAX	1,377	867	508	2	359 R	63.0%	36.9%	63.1%	36.9%
HAMPTON	14,808	7,623	7,133	52	490 R	51.5%	48.2%	51.7%	48.3%
HARRISONBURG	3,015	2,172	836	7	1,336 R	72.0%	27.7%	72.2%	27.8%
HOPEWELL	3,999	2,169	1,805	25	364 R	54.2%	45.1%	54.6%	45.4%
LYNCHBURG	12,256	7,271	4,961	24	2,310 R	59.3%	40.5%	59.4%	40.6%
MARTINSVILLE	3,517	1,729	1,699	89	30 R	49.2%	48.3%	50.4%	49.6%
NEWPORT NEWS	18,855	10,098	8,678	79	1,420 R	53.6%	46.0%	53.8%	46.2%
NORFOLK CITY	39,473	17,174	22,037	262	4,863 D	43.5%	55.8%	43.8%	56.2%
NORTON	1,076	549	526	1	23 R	51.0%	48.9%	51.1%	48.9%
PETERSBURG	5,803	2,820	2,950	33	130 D	48.6%	50.8%	48.9%	51.1%
PORTSMOUTH	16,960	6,900	9,902	178	3,002 D	40.6%	58.3%	41.1%	58.9%
RADFORD	2,912	1,663	1,240	9	423 R	57.1%	42.6%	57.3%	42.7%
RICHMOND CITY	45,285	27,307	17,642	256	9,665 R	60.4%	39.0%	60.8%	39.2%
ROANOKE CITY	24,453	15,229	9,175	49	6,054 R	62.3%	37.5%	62.4%	37.6%
SOUTH BOSTON	1,237	807	477	3	330 R	62.7%	37.1%	62.9%	37.1%
SOUTH NORFOLK	3,521	1,341	2,155	25	814 D	38.1%	61.2%	38.4%	61.6%
STAUNTON	4,032	2,789	1,233	10	1,556 R	69.2%	30.6%	69.3%	30.7%
SUFFOLK	2,834	1,406	1,419	9	13 D	49.6%	50.1%	49.8%	50.2%
VIRGINIA BEACH	2,321	986	1,301	34	315 D	42.5%	56.1%	43.1%	56.9%
WARWICK CITY									
WAYNESBORO	3,513	2,444	1,047	22	1,397 R	69.6%	29.3%	70.0%	30.0%
WILLIAMSBURG	1,220	721	486	13	235 R	59.1%	39.8%	59.7%	40.3%
WINCHESTER	3,545	2,326	1,203	16	1,123 R	65.6%	33.9%	65.9%	34.1%
TOTAL	771,449	404,521	362,327	4,601	42,194 R	52.4%	47.0%	52.8%	47.2%

PRESIDENT 1964

City	Total Vote	Republican	Democratic	Other	Rep.-Dem. Plurality	Total Vote Rep.	Total Vote Dem.	Major Vote Rep.	Major Vote Dem.
ALEXANDRIA	25,683	8,825	16,828	30	8,003 D	34.4%	65.5%	34.4%	65.6%
BRISTOL	3,723	1,289	2,429	5	1,140 D	34.6%	65.2%	34.7%	65.3%
BUENA VISTA	1,153	459	691	3	232 D	39.8%	59.9%	39.9%	60.1%
CHARLOTTESVILLE	9,734	4,415	5,205	84	790 D	45.4%	53.5%	45.9%	54.1%
CHESAPEAKE	18,621	9,038	9,532	51	494 D	48.5%	51.2%	48.7%	51.3%
CLIFTON FORGE	2,102	850	1,252		402 D	40.4%	59.6%	40.4%	59.6%
COLONIAL HEIGHTS	3,620	2,420	1,198	2	1,222 R	66.9%	33.1%	66.9%	33.1%
COVINGTON	3,206	1,149	2,055	2	906 D	35.8%	64.1%	35.8%	64.1%
DANVILLE	12,724	7,900	4,539	285	3,361 R	62.1%	35.7%	63.5%	36.5%
FAIRFAX CITY	4,766	1,924	2,835	7	911 D	40.4%	59.5%	40.4%	59.6%
FALLS CHURCH	3,707	1,329	2,371	7	1,042 D	35.9%	64.0%	35.9%	64.1%
FRANKLIN CITY	2,041	783	1,257	1	474 D	38.4%	61.6%	38.4%	61.6%
FREDERICKSBURG	3,928	1,511	2,440		899 D	38.5%	61.4%	38.5%	61.5%
GALAX	1,416	697	717	2	20 D	49.2%	50.6%	49.3%	50.7%
HAMPTON	22,288	8,731	13,542	15	4,811 D	39.2%	60.8%	39.2%	60.8%
HARRISONBURG	3,590	1,820	1,765	5	55 R	50.7%	49.2%	50.8%	49.2%
HOPEWELL	5,691	3,183	2,498	10	685 R	55.9%	43.9%	56.0%	44.0%
LYNCHBURG	16,834	10,044	6,758	32	3,286 R	59.7%	40.1%	59.8%	40.2%
MARTINSVILLE	4,824	1,805	2,943	76	1,138 D	37.4%	61.0%	38.0%	62.0%
NEWPORT NEWS	25,894	10,584	15,296	14	4,712 D	40.9%	59.1%	40.9%	59.1%
NORFOLK CITY	51,546	16,429	32,388	729	13,959 D	35.8%	62.8%	36.3%	63.7%
NORTON	1,196	372	824		452 D	31.1%	68.9%	31.1%	68.9%
PETERSBURG	7,775	3,253	4,521	1	1,268 D	41.8%	58.1%	41.8%	58.2%
PORTSMOUTH	24,544	8,420	16,073	51	7,653 D	34.3%	65.5%	34.4%	65.6%
RADFORD	3,358	1,505	1,850	3	345 D	44.8%	55.1%	44.9%	55.1%
RICHMOND CITY	62,890	27,196	35,662	32	8,466 D	43.2%	56.7%	43.3%	56.7%
ROANOKE CITY	28,496	13,164	15,314	18	2,150 D	46.2%	53.7%	46.2%	53.8%
SOUTH BOSTON	1,843	1,206	636	1	570 R	65.4%	34.5%	65.5%	34.5%
SOUTH NORFOLK									
STAUNTON	5,680	2,969	2,705	6	264 R	52.3%	47.6%	52.3%	47.7%
SUFFOLK	3,044	1,453	1,579	2	116 D	48.1%	51.9%	48.1%	51.9%
VIRGINIA BEACH	23,442	10,529	12,892	21	2,363 D	44.9%	55.0%	45.0%	55.0%
WARWICK CITY									
WAYNESBORO	4,531	2,107	2,369	55	262 D	46.5%	52.3%	47.1%	52.9%
WILLIAMSBURG	2,093	906	1,171	16	265 D	43.3%	55.9%	43.6%	56.4%
WINCHESTER	4,437	2,180	2,254	3	74 D	49.1%	50.8%	49.2%	50.8%
TOTAL	1,042,267	481,334	558,038	2,895	76,704 D	46.2%	53.5%	46.3%	53.7%

VIRGINIA

OTHER VOTE COMPOSITION:

1920	826 Prohibition; 808 Socialist; 240 Farmer-Labor.
1924	10,369 Progressive; 189 Socialist Labor.
1928	249 Socialist; 181 Socialist Labor; 179 Communist.
1932	2,382 Socialist; 1,843 Prohibition; 86 Communist; 15 Jobless.
1936	594 Prohibition; 313 Socialist; 233 Union; 98 Communist; 36 Socialist Labor.
1940	882 Prohibition; 282 Socialist; 72 Communist; 48 Socialist Labor.
1944	459 Prohibition; 417 Socialist; 90 Socialist Labor.
1948	43,393 States Rights; 2,047 Progressive; 726 Socialist; 234 Socialist Labor.
1952	1,160 Socialist Labor; 504 Socialist; 311 Progressive.
1956	42,964 States Rights; 444 Socialist; 351 Socialist Labor.
1960	4,204 Conservative (Coiner); 397 Socialist Labor.
1964	Socialist Labor.

SPECIAL CASES:

The existence in Virginia of a number of "independent city" jurisdictions, not under control of any county, leads to some complexity in election reporting. The actual number of these jurisdictions may change from election to election, sometimes substantially, and the process of territorial annexation and of consolidation is continuous. In this volume returns are for each of the state's subordinate reporting units as of the time of the election concerned.

1924	Progressive candidates ran second in one city and in one county.
1948	States Rights candidates carried one county and ran second in others.
1956	States Rights candidates carried one county and ran second in others.

WASHINGTON

PRESIDENT 1920

County	Total Vote	Republican	Democratic	Other	Rep.-Dem. Plurality	Total Vote Rep.	Total Vote Dem.	Major Vote Rep.	Major Vote Dem.
ADAMS	2,271	1,525	515	231	1,010 R	67.2%	22.7%	74.8%	25.2%
ASOTIN	1,866	1,210	497	159	713 R	64.8%	26.6%	70.9%	29.1%
BENTON	3,847	2,001	975	871	1,026 R	52.0%	25.3%	67.2%	32.8%
CHELAN	6,635	3,885	1,540	1,210	2,345 R	58.6%	23.2%	71.6%	28.4%
CLALLAM	3,302	1,775	489	1,038	1,286 R	53.8%	14.8%	78.4%	21.6%
CLARK	9,295	4,852	2,941	1,502	1,911 R	52.2%	31.6%	62.3%	37.7%
COLUMBIA	2,144	1,376	662	106	714 R	64.2%	30.9%	67.5%	32.5%
COWLITZ	3,687	2,267	801	619	1,466 R	61.5%	21.7%	73.9%	26.1%
DOUGLAS	2,743	1,587	918	238	669 R	57.9%	33.5%	63.4%	36.6%
FERRY	1,359	592	505	262	87 R	43.6%	37.2%	54.0%	46.0%
FRANKLIN	1,887	839	571	477	268 R	44.5%	30.3%	59.5%	40.5%
GARFIELD	1,316	869	370	77	499 R	66.0%	28.1%	70.1%	29.9%
GRANT	2,366	1,378	684	304	694 R	58.2%	28.9%	66.8%	33.2%
GRAYS HARBOR	11,822	5,920	3,378	2,524	2,542 R	50.9%	29.1%	63.7%	36.3%
ISLAND	1,725	883	285	557	598 R	51.2%	16.5%	75.6%	24.4%
JEFFERSON	1,832	1,128	322	382	806 R	61.6%	17.6%	77.8%	22.2%
KING	107,124	58,584	17,369	31,171	41,215 F	54.7%	16.2%	77.1%	22.9%
KITSAP	10,098	4,989	1,350	3,759	3,639 R	49.4%	13.4%	78.7%	21.3%
KITTITAS	5,202	2,837	1,119	1,246	1,718 R	54.5%	21.5%	71.7%	28.3%
KLICKITAT	2,777	1,649	745	383	904 R	59.4%	26.8%	68.9%	31.1%
LEWIS	11,285	6,160	2,212	2,913	3,948 R	54.6%	19.6%	73.5%	26.4%
LINCOLN	4,671	3,038	1,395	238	1,643 R	65.0%	29.9%	68.5%	31.5%
MASON	1,779	997	383	399	614 R	56.0%	21.5%	72.2%	27.8%
OKANOGAN	5,064	2,784	1,260	1,020	1,524 R	55.0%	24.9%	68.8%	31.2%
PACIFIC	3,975	2,607	874	495	1,733 R	65.6%	22.0%	74.9%	25.1%
PEND OREILLE	1,987	1,079	651	257	428 R	54.3%	32.8%	62.4%	37.6%
PIERCE	42,491	22,048	8,259	12,184	13,789 R	51.9%	19.4%	72.7%	27.3%
SAN JUAN	1,250	833	196	221	637 R	66.6%	15.7%	81.0%	19.0%
SKAGIT	10,356	5,320	1,840	3,146	3,480 R	51.6%	17.9%	74.3%	25.7%
SKAMANIA	776	409	247	120	162 R	52.7%	31.8%	62.3%	37.7%
SNOHOMISH	20,567	10,793	3,056	6,718	7,737 R	52.5%	14.9%	77.9%	22.1%
SPOKANE	43,331	26,212	13,412	12,807	12,807 R	60.5%	31.0%	66.2%	33.8%
STEVENS	5,894	3,282	1,452	1,160	1,830 R	55.7%	24.6%	69.3%	30.7%
THURSTON	7,388	3,899	1,367	2,122	2,532 R	52.8%	18.5%	74.0%	26.0%
WAHKIAKUM	857	494	164	199	330 R	57.6%	19.1%	75.1%	24.9%
WALLA WALLA	8,612	5,957	2,338	517	3,619 R	67.6%	26.5%	71.8%	28.2%
WHATCOM	15,920	9,157	2,288	4,475	6,869 R	57.5%	14.4%	80.0%	20.0%
WHITMAN	9,809	6,344	2,806	659	3,538 R	64.7%	28.6%	69.3%	30.7%
YAKIMA	19,484	11,571	4,062	3,851	7,509 R	59.4%	20.8%	74.0%	26.0%
TOTAL	398,715	223,137	84,298	91,280	138,839 R	56.0%	21.1%	72.6%	27.4%

PRESIDENT 1924

County	Total Vote	Republican	Democratic	Other	Rep.-Dem. Plurality	Total Vote Rep.	Total Vote Dem.	Major Vote Rep.	Major Vote Dem.
ADAMS	2,026	763	228	1,038	532 R	37.5%	11.3%	76.9%	23.1%
ASOTIN	2,352	1,094	508	750	586 R	46.5%	21.6%	68.3%	31.7%
BENTON	3,997	1,812	437	1,748	1,375 R	45.3%	10.9%	80.6%	19.4%
CHELAN	8,177	4,543	995	2,639	3,548 R	55.6%	12.2%	82.0%	18.0%
CLALLAM	4,089	2,129	283	1,677	1,846 R	52.1%	6.9%	88.3%	11.7%
CLARK	10,954	5,215	2,004	3,735	3,211 R	47.6%	18.3%	72.2%	27.8%
COLUMBIA	2,153	1,122	522	509	600 R	52.1%	24.2%	68.2%	31.8%
COWLITZ	5,882	3,274	927	1,681	2,347 R	55.7%	15.7%	77.9%	22.1%
DOUGLAS	2,536	1,070	398	1,068	672 R	42.2%	15.7%	72.9%	27.1%
FERRY	1,470	507	349	614	158 R	34.5%	23.7%	59.2%	40.8%
FRANKLIN	2,276	709	237	1,330	472 R	31.2%	10.4%	74.9%	25.1%
GARFIELD	1,341	875	324	142	551 R	65.2%	24.2%	73.0%	27.0%
GRANT	1,989	813	332	844	481 R	40.9%	16.7%	71.0%	29.0%
GRAYS HARBOR	13,751	8,273	1,239	4,239	7,034 R	60.2%	9.0%	87.0%	13.0%
ISLAND	1,799	832	114	853	718 R	46.2%	6.3%	87.9%	12.1%
JEFFERSON	1,763	913	143	707	770 R	51.8%	8.1%	86.5%	13.5%
KING	112,940	60,438	7,404	45,098	53,034 R	53.5%	6.6%	89.0%	10.9%
KITSAP	8,750	3,954	490	4,306	3,464 R	45.2%	5.6%	89.0%	11.0%
KITTITAS	4,998	2,360	455	2,183	1,905 R	47.2%	9.1%	83.8%	16.2%
KLICKITAT	2,811	1,482	518	811	964 R	52.7%	18.4%	74.1%	25.9%
LEWIS	12,007	6,973	1,544	3,490	5,429 R	58.1%	12.9%	81.9%	18.1%
LINCOLN	4,424	2,042	743	1,639	1,299 R	46.2%	16.8%	73.3%	26.7%
MASON	1,840	902	179	759	723 R	49.0%	9.7%	83.4%	16.6%
OKANOGAN	5,021	2,531	721	1,769	1,810 R	50.4%	14.4%	77.8%	22.2%
PACIFIC	4,138	2,672	501	965	2,171 R	64.6%	12.1%	84.2%	15.8%
PEND OREILLE	2,008	1,025	231	752	794 R	51.0%	11.5%	81.6%	18.4%
PIERCE	44,818	21,376	4,232	19,210	17,144 R	47.7%	9.4%	83.5%	16.5%
SAN JUAN	1,116	744	86	286	658 R	66.7%	7.7%	89.6%	10.4%
SKAGIT	10,576	5,071	699	4,806	4,372 R	47.9%	6.6%	87.9%	12.1%
SKAMANIA	1,022	533	207	282	326 R	52.2%	20.3%	72.0%	28.0%
SNOHOMISH	21,473	10,484	1,548	9,441	8,936 R	48.8%	7.2%	87.1%	12.9%
SPOKANE	47,473	23,403	6,036	18,034	17,367 R	49.3%	12.7%	79.5%	20.5%
STEVENS	5,944	2,909	685	2,350	2,224 R	48.9%	11.5%	80.9%	19.1%
THURSTON	8,871	5,125	943	2,803	4,182 R	57.8%	10.6%	84.5%	15.5%
WAHKIAKUM	820	496	89	235	407 R	60.5%	10.9%	84.8%	15.2%
WALLA WALLA	9,290	5,465	1,662	2,163	3,803 R	58.8%	17.9%	76.7%	23.3%
WHATCOM	16,110	9,214	927	5,969	8,287 R	57.2%	5.8%	90.9%	9.1%
WHITMAN	9,516	4,960	1,745	2,811	3,215 R	52.1%	18.3%	74.0%	26.0%
YAKIMA	19,028	12,124	2,157	4,747	9,967 R	63.7%	11.3%	84.9%	15.1%
TOTAL	421,549	220,224	42,842	158,483	177,382 R	52.2%	10.2%	83.7%	16.3%

WASHINGTON

PRESIDENT 1928

County	Total Vote	Republican	Democratic	Other	Rep.-Dem. Plurality	Total Vote Rep.	Total Vote Dem.	Major Vote Rep.	Major Vote Dem.
ADAMS	2,299	1,473	807	19	666 R	64.1%	35.1%	64.6%	35.4%
ASOTIN	2,612	1,812	776	24	1,036 R	69.4%	29.7%	70.0%	30.0%
BENTON	3,789	2,650	1,080	59	1,570 R	69.9%	28.5%	71.0%	29.0%
CHELAN	9,954	7,672	2,239	43	5,433 R	77.1%	22.5%	77.4%	22.6%
CLALLAM	5,065	3,319	1,705	41	1,614 R	65.5%	33.7%	66.1%	33.9%
CLARK	12,442	7,786	4,467	189	3,319 R	62.6%	35.9%	63.5%	36.5%
COLUMBIA	2,041	1,328	689	24	639 R	65.1%	33.8%	65.8%	34.2%
COWLITZ	8,554	5,882	2,581	91	3,301 R	68.8%	30.2%	69.5%	30.5%
DOUGLAS	2,653	1,760	862	31	898 R	66.3%	32.5%	67.1%	32.9%
FERRY	1,399	640	732	27	92 D	45.7%	52.3%	46.6%	53.4%
FRANKLIN	2,161	1,339	799	23	540 R	62.0%	37.0%	62.6%	37.4%
GARFIELD	1,422	1,004	412	6	592 R	70.6%	29.0%	70.9%	29.1%
GRANT	2,067	1,407	541	19	866 R	68.1%	31.0%	68.7%	31.3%
GRAYS HARBOR	16,286	10,798	5,258	230	5,540 R	66.3%	32.3%	67.3%	32.7%
ISLAND	2,087	1,487	556	44	931 R	71.3%	26.6%	72.8%	27.2%
JEFFERSON	2,306	1,472	810	24	662 R	63.8%	35.1%	64.5%	35.5%
KING	146,678	96,263	46,604	3,811	49,659 R	65.6%	31.8%	67.4%	32.6%
KITSAP	10,392	6,544	3,668	180	2,876 R	63.0%	35.3%	64.1%	35.9%
KITTITAS	5,392	3,207	2,136	49	1,071 R	59.5%	39.6%	60.0%	40.0%
KLICKITAT	2,959	1,936	975	48	961 R	65.4%	33.0%	66.5%	33.5%
LEWIS	13,010	9,253	3,591	166	5,662 R	71.1%	27.6%	72.0%	28.0%
LINCOLN	4,559	2,718	1,807	34	911 R	59.6%	39.6%	60.1%	39.9%
MASON	2,772	1,745	992	35	753 R	63.0%	35.8%	63.8%	36.2%
OKANOGAN	5,003	3,245	1,722	36	1,523 R	64.9%	34.4%	65.3%	34.7%
PACIFIC	4,817	3,247	1,523	47	1,724 R	67.4%	31.6%	68.1%	31.9%
PEND OREILLE	2,024	1,206	793	25	413 R	59.6%	39.2%	60.3%	39.7%
PIERCE	54,146	35,748	17,402	996	18,346 R	66.0%	32.1%	67.3%	32.7%
SAN JUAN	1,220	814	400	6	414 R	66.7%	32.8%	67.1%	32.9%
SKAGIT	11,329	8,336	2,843	145	5,488 R	73.6%	25.1%	74.5%	25.5%
SKAMANIA	1,127	631	473	23	158 R	56.0%	42.0%	57.2%	42.8%
SNOHOMISH	24,507	16,516	7,419	572	9,097 R	67.4%	30.3%	69.0%	31.0%
SPOKANE	54,758	35,858	18,527	373	17,331 R	65.5%	33.8%	65.9%	34.1%
STEVENS	6,048	3,813	2,147	88	1,666 R	63.0%	35.5%	64.0%	36.0%
THURSTON	10,351	7,203	3,013	135	4,190 R	69.6%	29.1%	70.5%	29.5%
WAHKIAKUM	975	578	382	15	196 R	59.3%	39.2%	60.2%	39.8%
WALLA WALLA	9,666	6,774	2,859	33	3,915 R	70.1%	29.6%	70.3%	29.7%
WHATCOM	19,021	14,621	4,100	300	10,521 R	76.9%	21.6%	78.1%	21.9%
WHITMAN	10,101	7,065	2,969	67	4,096 R	69.9%	29.4%	70.4%	29.6%
YAKIMA	22,848	16,694	6,008	146	10,686 R	73.1%	26.3%	73.5%	26.5%
TOTAL	500,840	335,844	156,772	8,224	179,072 R	67.1%	31.3%	68.2%	31.8%

PRESIDENT 1932

County	Total Vote	Republican	Democratic	Other	Rep.-Dem. Plurality	Total Vote Rep.	Total Vote Dem.	Major Vote Rep.	Major Vote Dem.
ADAMS	2,430	867	1,504	59	637 D	35.7%	61.9%	36.6%	63.4%
ASOTIN	3,052	960	1,994	98	1,034 D	31.5%	65.3%	32.5%	67.5%
BENTON	4,597	1,694	2,633	270	939 D	36.9%	57.3%	39.1%	60.9%
CHELAN	13,859	5,584	7,316	959	1,732 D	40.3%	52.8%	43.3%	56.7%
CLALLAM	7,537	1,870	3,954	1,713	2,084 D	24.8%	52.5%	32.1%	67.9%
CLARK	15,160	4,901	9,104	1,155	4,203 D	32.3%	60.1%	35.0%	65.0%
COLUMBIA	2,298	714	1,491	93	777 D	31.1%	64.9%	32.4%	67.6%
COWLITZ	11,113	3,767	5,443	1,903	1,676 D	33.9%	49.0%	40.9%	59.1%
DOUGLAS	3,362	1,179	1,941	242	762 D	35.1%	57.7%	37.8%	62.2%
FERRY	1,445	322	1,035	88	713 D	22.3%	71.6%	23.7%	76.3%
FRANKLIN	2,473	838	1,540	95	702 D	33.9%	62.3%	35.2%	64.8%
GARFIELD	1,506	669	818	19	149 D	44.4%	54.3%	45.0%	55.0%
GRANT	2,410	840	1,376	194	536 D	34.9%	57.1%	37.9%	62.1%
GRAYS HARBOR	18,436	5,141	10,310	2,985	5,169 D	27.9%	55.9%	33.3%	66.7%
ISLAND	2,662	803	1,517	342	714 D	30.2%	57.0%	34.6%	65.4%
JEFFERSON	3,267	952	1,994	321	1,042 D	29.1%	61.0%	32.3%	67.7%
KING	184,031	63,346	108,738	11,947	45,392 D	34.4%	59.1%	36.8%	63.2%
KITSAP	14,173	3,465	10,002	706	6,537 D	24.4%	70.6%	25.7%	74.3%
KITTITAS	6,684	1,963	4,266	455	2,303 D	29.4%	63.8%	31.5%	68.5%
KLICKITAT	3,643	1,335	2,155	153	820 D	36.6%	59.2%	38.3%	61.1%
LEWIS	15,594	4,647	8,454	2,493	3,807 D	29.8%	54.2%	35.5%	64.5%
LINCOLN	4,595	1,748	2,725	122	977 D	38.0%	59.3%	39.1%	60.9%
MASON	3,902	995	2,181	726	1,186 D	25.5%	55.9%	31.3%	68.7%
OKANOGAN	6,947	2,277	3,969	701	1,692 D	32.8%	57.1%	36.5%	63.5%
PACIFIC	5,588	1,737	3,099	752	1,362 D	31.1%	55.5%	35.9%	64.1%
PEND OREILLE	2,761	855	1,772	134	917 D	31.0%	64.2%	32.5%	67.5%
PIERCE	65,327	19,006	38,451	7,870	19,445 D	29.1%	58.9%	33.1%	66.9%
SAN JUAN	1,501	607	786	108	179 D	40.4%	52.4%	43.6%	56.4%
SKAGIT	13,888	4,246	8,395	1,247	4,149 D	30.6%	60.4%	33.6%	66.4%
SKAMANIA	1,462	444	934	84	490 D	30.4%	63.9%	32.2%	67.8%
SNOHOMISH	30,963	9,310	18,352	3,301	9,042 D	30.1%	59.3%	33.7%	66.3%
SPOKANE	65,125	24,848	36,953	3,324	12,105 D	38.2%	56.7%	40.2%	59.8%
STEVENS	6,994	2,247	4,262	485	2,015 D	32.1%	60.9%	34.5%	65.5%
THURSTON	13,764	4,241	6,308	3,173	2,067 D	30.9%	46.0%	40.2%	59.8%
WAHKIAKUM	1,364	442	730	192	288 D	32.4%	53.5%	37.7%	62.3%
WALLA WALLA	10,575	4,653	5,578	344	925 D	44.0%	52.7%	45.5%	54.5%
WHATCOM	22,511	9,254	11,355	1,902	2,101 D	41.1%	50.4%	44.9%	55.1%
WHITMAN	11,011	4,727	5,945	339	1,218 D	42.9%	54.0%	44.3%	55.7%
YAKIMA	26,846	11,151	13,880	1,815	2,729 D	41.5%	51.7%	44.5%	55.5%
TOTAL	614,814	208,645	353,260	52,909	144,615 D	33.9%	57.5%	37.1%	62.9%

WASHINGTON

PRESIDENT 1936

County	Total Vote	Republican	Democratic	Other	Rep.-Dem. Plurality	Total Vote Rep.	Total Vote Dem.	Major Vote Rep.	Major Vote Dem.
ADAMS	2,661	657	1,944	60	1,287 D	24.7%	73.1%	25.3%	74.7%
ASOTIN	3,443	916	2,261	266	1,345 D	26.6%	65.7%	28.8%	71.2%
BENTON	4,527	1,610	2,402	515	792 D	35.6%	53.1%	40.1%	59.9%
CHELAN	13,486	4,975	8,030	481	3,055 D	36.9%	59.5%	38.3%	61.7%
CLALLAM	8,418	2,404	5,586	428	3,182 D	28.6%	66.4%	30.1%	69.9%
CLARK	18,554	4,868	12,714	972	7,846 D	26.2%	68.5%	27.7%	72.3%
COLUMBIA	2,412	807	1,391	214	584 D	33.5%	57.7%	36.7%	63.3%
COWLITZ	14,292	3,617	10,147	528	6,530 D	25.3%	71.0%	26.3%	73.7%
DOUGLAS	3,445	1,025	2,290	130	1,265 D	29.8%	66.5%	30.9%	69.1%
FERRY	1,516	320	1,130	66	810 D	21.1%	74.5%	22.1%	77.9%
FRANKLIN	2,594	622	1,784	188	1,162 D	24.0%	58.8%	25.9%	74.1%
GARFIELD	1,679	652	983	44	331 D	38.8%	58.5%	39.9%	60.1%
GRANT	5,328	694	4,560	74	3,866 D	13.0%	85.6%	13.2%	86.8%
GRAYS HARBOR	21,622	5,053	15,851	718	10,798 D	23.4%	73.3%	24.2%	75.8%
ISLAND	2,813	921	1,687	205	766 D	32.7%	60.0%	35.3%	64.7%
JEFFERSON	3,425	1,063	2,279	83	1,216 D	31.0%	66.5%	31.8%	68.2%
KING	210,045	66,544	138,597	4,904	72,053 D	31.7%	66.0%	32.4%	67.6%
KITSAP	16,347	3,440	12,414	493	8,974 D	21.0%	75.9%	21.7%	78.3%
KITTITAS	7,218	1,941	5,044	233	3,103 D	26.9%	69.9%	27.8%	72.2%
KLICKITAT	3,898	1,190	2,545	163	1,355 D	30.5%	65.3%	31.9%	68.1%
LEWIS	16,705	5,885	9,619	1,201	3,734 D	35.2%	57.6%	38.0%	62.0%
LINCOLN	5,069	1,325	3,627	117	2,302 D	26.1%	71.6%	26.8%	73.2%
MASON	4,398	1,015	3,087	296	2,072 D	23.1%	70.2%	24.7%	75.3%
OKANOGAN	8,667	2,367	5,622	678	3,255 D	27.3%	64.9%	29.6%	70.4%
PACIFIC	6,447	1,732	4,395	320	2,663 D	26.9%	68.2%	28.3%	71.7%
PEND OREILLE	2,875	813	1,903	159	1,090 D	28.3%	66.2%	29.9%	70.1%
PIERCE	69,891	18,331	48,938	2,572	30,607 D	26.2%	70.1%	27.2%	72.6%
SAN JUAN	1,595	690	775	130	85 D	43.3%	48.6%	47.1%	52.9%
SKAGIT	15,615	5,222	9,639	754	4,417 D	33.4%	61.7%	35.1%	64.9%
SKAMANIA	2,310	406	1,863	41	1,457 D	17.6%	80.6%	17.9%	82.1%
SNOHOMISH	35,559	8,882	25,081	1,606	16,199 D	25.0%	70.5%	26.2%	73.8%
SPOKANE	70,125	19,951	48,117	2,057	28,166 D	28.5%	68.6%	29.3%	70.7%
STEVENS	6,935	1,981	4,536	418	2,555 D	28.6%	65.4%	30.4%	69.6%
THURSTON	15,775	4,425	10,647	703	6,222 D	28.1%	67.5%	29.4%	70.6%
WAHKIAKUM	1,583	419	1,098	66	679 D	26.5%	69.4%	27.6%	72.4%
WALLA WALLA	11,670	4,584	6,562	524	1,978 D	39.3%	56.2%	41.1%	58.9%
WHATCOM	25,756	9,035	15,428	1,293	6,393 D	35.1%	59.9%	36.9%	63.1%
WHITMAN	11,973	3,955	7,753	265	3,798 D	33.1%	64.8%	33.8%	66.2%
YAKIMA	31,657	12,555	17,200	1,902	4,645 D	39.7%	54.3%	42.2%	57.8%
TOTAL	692,338	206,892	459,579	25,867	252,637 D	29.9%	66.4%	31.0%	69.0%

PRESIDENT 1940

County	Total Vote	Republican	Democratic	Other	Rep.-Dem. Plurality	Total Vote Rep.	Total Vote Dem.	Major Vote Rep.	Major Vote Dem.
ADAMS	2,918	1,508	1,397	13	111 R	51.7%	47.9%	51.9%	48.1%
ASOTIN	3,611	1,483	2,107	21	624 D	41.1%	58.3%	41.3%	58.7%
BENTON	5,139	2,670	2,414	55	256 R	52.0%	47.0%	52.5%	47.5%
CHELAN	15,273	8,019	7,181	73	838 R	52.5%	47.0%	52.8%	47.2%
CLALLAM	9,631	3,555	5,966	110	2,411 D	36.9%	61.9%	37.3%	62.7%
CLARK	21,925	8,776	12,931	218	4,155 D	40.0%	59.0%	40.4%	59.6%
COLUMBIA	2,685	1,461	1,218	6	243 R	54.4%	45.4%	54.5%	45.5%
COWLITZ	17,714	6,073	11,420	216	5,342 D	34.3%	64.5%	34.7%	65.3%
DOUGLAS	3,971	1,959	1,972	40	13 D	49.3%	49.7%	49.8%	50.2%
FERRY	1,849	590	1,247	12	657 D	31.9%	67.4%	32.1%	67.9%
FRANKLIN	2,983	1,064	1,868	31	784 D	36.3%	62.6%	36.7%	63.3%
GARFIELD	1,727	1,003	714	10	289 R	58.1%	41.3%	58.4%	41.6%
GRANT	5,601	1,487	4,097	17	2,610 D	26.5%	73.1%	26.6%	73.4%
GRAYS HARBOR	23,487	8,359	14,861	257	6,492 D	35.6%	63.3%	36.0%	64.0%
ISLAND	3,057	1,371	1,626	60	255 D	44.8%	53.2%	45.7%	54.3%
JEFFERSON	3,655	1,540	2,083	32	543 D	42.1%	57.0%	42.5%	57.5%
KING	241,803	95,504	143,134	3,165	47,630 D	39.5%	59.2%	40.0%	60.0%
KITSAP	19,596	5,525	13,851	210	8,336 D	28.2%	70.7%	28.5%	71.5%
KITTITAS	8,660	3,401	5,203	56	1,802 D	39.3%	60.1%	39.5%	60.5%
KLICKITAT	4,794	2,139	2,627	28	488 D	44.6%	54.8%	44.9%	55.1%
LEWIS	18,726	9,228	9,280	218	52 D	49.3%	49.6%	49.9%	50.1%
LINCOLN	5,552	2,627	2,896	29	269 D	47.3%	52.2%	47.6%	52.4%
MASON	5,346	1,775	3,465	106	1,690 D	33.2%	64.8%	33.9%	66.1%
OKANOGAN	9,655	4,244	5,362	49	1,118 D	44.0%	55.5%	44.2%	55.8%
PACIFIC	7,145	2,704	4,393	48	1,689 D	37.8%	61.5%	38.1%	61.9%
PEND OREILLE	3,097	1,266	1,812	17	544 D	40.9%	58.5%	41.2%	58.8%
PIERCE	80,311	27,188	51,670	1,453	24,482 D	33.9%	64.3%	34.5%	65.5%
SAN JUAN	1,675	808	860	7	52 D	48.2%	51.3%	48.4%	51.6%
SKAGIT	17,970	7,985	9,796	189	1,811 D	44.4%	54.5%	44.9%	55.1%
SKAMANIA	2,079	765	1,292	22	527 D	36.8%	62.1%	37.2%	62.8%
SNOHOMISH	40,535	13,638	26,185	762	12,547 D	33.6%	64.5%	34.2%	65.8%
SPOKANE	78,793	33,238	44,904	713	11,624 D	42.2%	56.9%	42.6%	57.4%
STEVENS	8,208	3,238	4,904	66	1,666 D	39.4%	59.7%	39.8%	60.2%
THURSTON	18,573	7,275	11,092	206	3,817 D	39.2%	59.7%	39.8%	60.4%
WAHKIAKUM	1,625	642	1,164	19	522 D	35.2%	63.8%	35.5%	64.5%
WALLA WALLA	13,821	7,883	5,875	63	2,008 R	57.0%	42.5%	57.3%	42.7%
WHATCOM	28,334	13,351	14,877	606	1,526 D	46.3%	51.6%	47.3%	52.7%
WHITMAN	12,799	6,356	6,351	92	5 R	49.7%	49.3%	50.0%	50.0%
YAKIMA	38,760	20,398	18,092	270	2,306 R	52.6%	46.7%	53.0%	47.0%
TOTAL	793,833	322,123	462,145	9,565	140,022 D	40.6%	58.2%	41.1%	58.9%

WASHINGTON

PRESIDENT 1944

County	Total Vote	Republican	Democratic	Other	Rep.-Dem. Plurality	Percentage Total Vote Rep.	Total Vote Dem.	Major Vote Rep.	Major Vote Dem.
ADAMS	2,740	1,666	1,062	12	604 R	60.8%	38.8%	61.1%	38.9%
ASOTIN	3,270	1,367	1,888	15	521 D	41.8%	57.7%	42.0%	58.0%
BENTON	8,172	3,905	4,283	34	328 D	47.8%	51.8%	48.0%	52.0%
CHELAN	13,713	7,081	6,557	75	524 R	51.6%	47.8%	51.9%	48.1%
CLALLAM	9,051	3,551	5,441	59	1,890 D	39.2%	60.1%	39.5%	60.5%
CLARK	31,549	12,312	18,861	376	6,549 D	39.0%	59.8%	39.5%	60.5%
COLUMBIA	2,270	1,211	1,039	20	172 R	53.3%	45.8%	53.8%	46.2%
COWLITZ	16,799	6,157	10,485	157	4,328 D	36.7%	62.4%	37.0%	63.0%
DOUGLAS	3,665	1,809	1,832	24	23 D	49.4%	50.0%	49.7%	50.3%
FERRY	1,315	518	792	5	274 D	39.4%	60.2%	39.5%	60.5%
FRANKLIN	3,371	1,381	1,974	16	593 D	41.0%	58.6%	41.2%	58.8%
GARFIELD	1,612	925	577	10	248 R	57.4%	42.0%	57.7%	42.3%
GRANT	3,902	1,530	2,354	18	824 D	39.2%	60.3%	39.4%	60.6%
GRAYS HARBOR	21,767	7,834	13,803	130	5,969 D	36.0%	63.4%	36.2%	63.8%
IS-AND	3,187	1,487	1,662	38	175 D	46.7%	52.1%	47.2%	52.8%
JEFFERSON	3,262	1,415	1,829	18	414 D	43.4%	56.1%	43.6%	56.4%
KING	286,604	118,719	165,308	2,577	46,589 D	41.4%	57.7%	41.8%	58.2%
KITSAP	35,491	11,224	24,016	251	12,792 D	31.6%	67.7%	31.9%	68.1%
KITTITAS	7,686	3,423	4,227	36	804 D	44.5%	55.0%	44.7%	55.3%
KLICKITAT	4,127	1,980	2,089	58	109 D	48.0%	50.6%	48.7%	51.3%
LEWIS	16,726	8,896	7,706	124	1,190 R	53.2%	46.1%	53.6%	46.4%
LINCOLN	5,066	2,723	2,328	15	395 R	53.8%	46.0%	53.9%	46.1%
MASON	5,397	1,976	3,379	42	1,403 D	36.6%	62.6%	36.9%	63.1%
OKANOGAN	8,764	4,084	4,642	38	558 D	46.6%	53.0%	46.8%	53.2%
PACIFIC	6,176	2,419	3,745	12	1,326 D	39.2%	60.6%	39.2%	60.8%
PEND OREILLE	2,452	1,052	1,385	15	333 D	42.9%	56.5%	43.2%	56.8%
PIERCE	86,370	31,626	53,269	1,475	21,643 D	36.6%	61.7%	37.3%	62.7%
SAN JUAN	1,354	703	644	7	59 R	51.9%	47.6%	52.2%	47.8%
SKAGIT	17,332	7,805	9,409	118	1,604 D	45.0%	54.3%	45.3%	54.7%
SKAMANIA	1,647	668	968	11	300 D	40.6%	58.8%	40.8%	59.2%
SNOHOMISH	43,130	15,182	27,345	603	12,163 D	35.2%	63.4%	35.7%	64.3%
SPOKANE	82,306	36,359	45,491	456	9,132 D	44.1%	55.1%	44.4%	55.6%
STEVENS	7,165	3,151	3,951	63	800 D	44.0%	55.1%	44.4%	55.6%
THURSTON	17,766	7,900	9,708	158	1,808 D	44.5%	54.6%	44.9%	55.1%
WAHKIAKUM	1,545	532	1,003	10	471 D	34.4%	64.9%	34.7%	65.3%
WALLA WALLA	13,235	7,364	5,793	78	1,571 R	55.6%	43.8%	56.0%	44.0%
WHATCOM	28,098	12,890	14,787	421	1,897 D	45.9%	52.6%	46.6%	53.4%
WHITMAN	11,490	6,000	5,449	41	551 R	52.2%	47.4%	52.4%	47.6%
YAKIMA	36,756	20,864	15,643	249	5,221 R	56.8%	42.6%	57.2%	42.8%
TOTAL	856,328	361,689	486,774	7,865	125,085 D	42.2%	56.8%	42.6%	57.4%

PRESIDENT 1948

County	Total Vote	Republican	Democratic	Other	Rep.-Dem. Plurality	Percentage Total Vote Rep.	Total Vote Dem.	Major Vote Rep.	Major Vote Dem.
ADAMS	2,683	1,394	1,267	22	127 R	52.0%	47.2%	52.4%	47.6%
ASOTIN	3,583	1,384	2,054	145	670 D	38.6%	57.3%	40.3%	59.7%
BENTON	14,467	5,852	8,458	157	2,606 D	40.5%	58.5%	40.9%	59.1%
CHELAN	15,351	7,392	7,702	257	310 D	48.2%	50.2%	49.0%	51.0%
CLALLAM	10,097	4,178	5,412	507	1,234 D	41.4%	53.6%	43.6%	56.4%
CLARK	30,132	11,546	17,154	1,432	5,608 D	38.3%	56.9%	40.2%	59.8%
COLUMBIA	2,112	1,062	1,015	35	47 R	50.3%	48.1%	51.1%	48.9%
COWLITZ	18,902	7,098	11,075	729	3,977 D	37.6%	58.6%	39.1%	60.9%
DOUGLAS	4,033	1,703	2,251	79	548 D	42.2%	55.8%	43.1%	56.9%
FERRY	1,340	473	824	43	351 D	35.3%	61.5%	36.5%	63.5%
FRANKLIN	4,130	1,541	2,525	64	984 D	37.3%	61.1%	37.9%	62.1%
GARFIELD	1,531	749	747	35	2 R	48.9%	48.8%	50.1%	49.9%
GRANT	6,277	2,081	4,067	129	1,986 D	33.2%	64.8%	33.8%	66.2%
GRAYS HARBOR	23,215	8,357	13,660	1,198	5,303 D	36.0%	58.8%	38.0%	62.0%
IS-AND	3,680	1,805	1,694	181	111 R	49.0%	46.0%	51.6%	48.4%
JEFFERSON	3,676	1,610	1,911	155	301 D	43.8%	52.0%	45.7%	54.3%
KING	291,635	131,039	143,295	17,301	12,256 D	44.9%	49.1%	47.8%	52.2%
KITSAP	30,678	9,869	19,538	1,271	9,669 D	32.2%	63.7%	33.6%	66.4%
KITTITAS	8,348	3,446	4,588	314	1,142 D	41.3%	55.0%	42.9%	57.1%
KLICKITAT	4,252	1,951	2,206	95	255 D	45.9%	51.9%	46.9%	53.1%
LEWIS	17,953	9,047	8,394	512	653 R	50.4%	46.8%	51.9%	48.1%
LINCOLN	4,924	2,348	2,518	58	170 D	47.7%	51.1%	48.3%	51.7%
MASON	6,501	2,524	3,613	364	1,089 D	38.8%	55.6%	41.1%	58.9%
OKANOGAN	9,935	4,083	5,644	208	1,561 D	41.1%	56.8%	42.0%	58.0%
PACIFIC	7,052	2,749	3,902	401	1,153 D	39.0%	55.3%	41.3%	58.7%
PEND OREILLE	2,567	1,009	1,465	93	456 D	39.3%	57.1%	40.8%	59.2%
PIERCE	90,786	34,396	50,674	5,716	16,278 D	37.9%	55.8%	40.4%	59.6%
SAN JUAN	1,575	881	636	58	245 R	55.9%	40.4%	58.1%	41.9%
SKAGIT	18,192	8,176	9,080	936	904 D	44.9%	49.9%	47.4%	52.6%
SKAMANIA	1,842	707	1,067	68	360 D	38.4%	57.9%	39.9%	60.1%
SNOHOMISH	46,260	17,018	25,924	3,318	8,906 D	36.8%	56.0%	39.6%	60.4%
SPOKANE	88,988	37,086	49,649	2,253	12,563 D	41.7%	55.8%	42.8%	57.2%
STEVENS	7,434	2,977	4,205	252	1,228 D	40.0%	56.6%	41.5%	58.5%
THURSTON	20,804	9,511	10,461	832	950 D	45.7%	50.3%	47.6%	52.4%
WAHKIAKUM	1,597	622	877	98	255 D	38.9%	54.9%	41.5%	58.5%
WALLA WALLA	15,378	7,993	7,102	283	891 R	52.0%	46.2%	53.0%	47.0%
WHATCOM	28,451	12,850	13,736	1,865	886 D	45.2%	48.3%	48.3%	51.7%
WHITMAN	12,740	6,411	6,015	314	396 R	50.3%	47.2%	51.6%	48.4%
YAKIMA	41,957	21,396	19,760	801	1,636 R	51.0%	47.1%	52.0%	48.0%
TOTAL	905,058	386,314	476,165	42,579	89,851 D	42.7%	52.6%	44.8%	55.2%

WASHINGTON

PRESIDENT 1952

County	Total Vote	Republican	Democratic	Other	Rep.-Dem. Plurality	Total Vote Rep.	Total Vote Dem.	Major Vote Rep.	Major Vote Dem.
ADAMS	3,290	2,181	1,104	5	1,077 R	66.3%	33.6%	66.4%	33.6%
ASOTIN	4,894	2,722	2,160	12	562 R	55.6%	44.1%	55.8%	44.2%
BENTON	23,364	13,412	9,889	63	3,523 R	57.4%	42.3%	57.6%	42.4%
CHELAN	18,084	11,164	6,867	53	4,297 R	61.7%	38.3%	61.9%	38.1%
CLALLAM	11,938	6,442	5,390	106	1,052 R	54.0%	45.1%	54.4%	45.6%
CLARK	37,328	18,973	18,153	202	820 R	50.8%	48.6%	51.1%	48.9%
COLUMBIA	2,283	1,511	765	7	746 R	66.2%	33.5%	66.4%	33.6%
COWLITZ	23,746	12,366	11,242	138	1,124 R	52.1%	47.3%	52.4%	47.6%
DOUGLAS	5,329	2,954	2,361	14	593 R	55.4%	44.3%	55.6%	44.4%
FERRY	1,450	687	754	9	67 D	47.4%	52.0%	47.7%	52.3%
FRANKLIN	6,107	3,291	2,798	18	493 R	53.9%	45.8%	54.0%	46.0%
GARFIELD	1,733	1,157	559	17	598 R	66.8%	32.3%	67.4%	32.6%
GRANT	8,915	4,512	4,381	22	131 R	50.6%	49.1%	50.7%	49.3%
GRAYS HARBOR	24,683	12,168	12,317	198	149 D	49.3%	49.9%	49.7%	50.3%
ISLAND	4,703	2,901	1,772	30	1,129 R	61.7%	37.7%	62.1%	37.9%
JEFFERSON	4,305	2,355	1,933	17	422 R	54.7%	44.9%	54.9%	45.1%
KING	371,771	200,507	165,583	5,681	34,924 R	53.9%	44.5%	54.8%	45.2%
KITSAP	37,596	16,876	20,531	189	3,655 D	44.9%	54.6%	45.1%	54.9%
KITTITAS	9,174	5,201	3,937	36	1,264 R	56.7%	42.9%	56.9%	43.1%
KLICKITAT	5,011	2,845	2,140	26	705 R	56.8%	42.7%	57.1%	42.9%
LEWIS	19,571	12,287	7,115	169	5,172 R	62.8%	36.4%	63.3%	36.7%
LINCOLN	5,405	3,422	1,974	9	1,448 R	63.3%	36.5%	63.4%	36.6%
MASON	7,700	3,827	3,830	43	3 D	49.7%	49.7%	50.0%	50.0%
OKANOGAN	10,950	6,085	4,817	48	1,268 R	55.6%	44.0%	55.8%	44.2%
PACIFIC	7,663	3,846	3,778	39	68 R	50.2%	49.3%	50.4%	49.6%
PEND OREILLE	2,952	1,566	1,380	16	186 R	52.9%	46.6%	53.2%	46.8%
PIERCE	113,811	56,515	56,132	1,164	383 R	49.7%	49.3%	50.2%	49.8%
SAN JUAN	1,766	1,133	619	14	514 R	64.2%	35.1%	64.7%	35.3%
SKAGIT	19,952	11,446	8,321	185	3,125 R	57.4%	41.7%	57.9%	42.1%
SKAMANIA	2,050	1,072	978		94 R	52.3%	47.7%	52.3%	47.7%
SNOHOMISH	55,801	26,749	28,518	534	1,769 D	47.9%	51.1%	48.4%	51.6%
SPOKANE	103,236	56,958	45,827	451	11,131 R	55.2%	44.4%	55.6%	44.6%
STEVENS	7,385	4,458	3,355	72	1,103 R	56.5%	42.5%	57.1%	42.9%
THURSTON	23,880	13,904	9,764	172	4,140 R	58.3%	41.0%	58.7%	41.3%
WAHKIAKUM	1,760	815	928	17	113 D	46.3%	52.7%	46.8%	53.2%
WALLA WALLA	17,817	11,987	5,738	92	6,249 R	67.3%	32.2%	67.6%	32.4%
WHATCOM	30,828	17,590	12,877	361	4,713 R	57.1%	41.8%	57.7%	42.3%
WHITMAN	13,560	8,905	4,611	44	4,294 R	65.7%	34.0%	65.9%	34.1%
YAKIMA	50,447	32,317	17,647	483	14,670 R	64.1%	35.0%	64.7%	35.3%
TOTAL	1,102,708	599,107	492,845	10,756	106,262 R	54.3%	44.7%	54.9%	45.1%

PRESIDENT 1956

County	Total Vote	Republican	Democratic	Other	Rep.-Dem. Plurality	Total Vote Rep.	Total Vote Dem.	Major Vote Rep.	Major Vote Dem.
ADAMS	3,944	2,267	1,673	4	594 R	57.5%	42.4%	57.5%	42.5%
ASOTIN	5,200	2,608	2,586	6	22 R	50.2%	49.7%	50.2%	49.8%
BENTON	25,571	13,807	11,760		2,047 R	54.0%	46.0%	54.0%	46.0%
CHELAN	18,122	10,405	7,600	117	2,805 R	57.4%	41.9%	57.8%	42.2%
CLALLAM	12,500	6,852	5,632	16	1,220 R	54.8%	45.1%	54.9%	45.1%
CLARK	39,046	19,330	19,665	51	335 D	49.5%	50.4%	49.6%	50.4%
COLUMBIA	2,162	1,423	739		684 R	65.8%	34.2%	65.8%	34.2%
COWLITZ	24,410	11,912	12,448	50	536 D	48.8%	51.0%	48.9%	51.1%
DOUGLAS	5,645	2,602	3,034	9	432 D	46.1%	53.7%	46.2%	53.8%
FERRY	1,493	662	830	1	168 D	44.3%	55.6%	44.4%	55.6%
FRANKLIN	8,090	3,763	4,322	5	559 D	46.5%	53.4%	46.5%	53.5%
GARFIELD	1,606	956	639	1	317 R	60.1%	39.8%	60.2%	39.8%
GRANT	13,549	6,603	6,938	8	335 D	48.7%	51.2%	48.8%	51.2%
GRAYS HARBOR	24,514	11,599	12,858	57	1,259 D	47.3%	52.5%	47.4%	52.6%
ISLAND	5,222	3,196	2,009	17	1,187 R	61.2%	38.5%	61.4%	38.6%
JEFFERSON	4,057	2,300	1,750	7	550 R	56.7%	43.1%	56.8%	43.2%
KING	386,223	213,504	167,443	5,276	46,061 R	55.3%	43.4%	56.0%	44.0%
KITSAP	37,685	17,986	19,641	58	1,655 D	47.7%	52.1%	47.8%	52.2%
KITTITAS	8,830	5,097	3,726	7	1,371 R	57.7%	42.2%	57.8%	42.2%
KLICKITAT	5,379	2,794	2,577	8	217 R	51.9%	47.9%	52.0%	48.0%
LEWIS	19,668	11,949	7,714	25	4,235 R	60.7%	39.2%	60.8%	39.2%
LINCOLN	5,390	3,114	2,273	3	841 R	57.8%	42.2%	57.8%	42.2%
MASON	7,886	4,026	3,840	20	186 R	51.1%	48.7%	51.2%	48.8%
OKANOGAN	10,754	5,448	5,298	8	150 R	50.7%	49.3%	50.7%	49.3%
PACIFIC	7,635	3,799	3,824	12	25 D	49.8%	50.1%	49.8%	50.2%
PEND OREILLE	3,031	1,488	1,540	3	52 D	49.1%	50.8%	49.1%	50.8%
PIERCE	115,544	57,078	57,728	738	650 D	49.4%	50.0%	49.7%	50.3%
SAN JUAN	1,693	1,105	584	4	521 R	65.3%	34.5%	65.4%	34.6%
SKAGIT	21,440	12,149	9,243	48	2,906 R	56.6%	43.1%	56.8%	43.2%
SKAMANIA	2,209	1,014	1,193	2	179 D	45.9%	54.0%	45.9%	54.1%
SNOHOMISH	62,327	30,052	31,950	325	1,898 D	48.2%	51.3%	48.5%	51.5%
SPOKANE	109,287	60,335	48,833	119	11,502 R	55.2%	44.7%	55.3%	44.7%
STEVENS	8,322	4,499	3,808	15	691 R	54.1%	45.8%	54.2%	45.8%
THURSTON	24,009	14,093	9,697	19	4,196 R	58.7%	41.2%	58.7%	41.3%
WAHKIAKUM	1,767	808	953	6	145 D	45.7%	53.9%	45.9%	54.1%
WALLA WALLA	17,910	11,827	6,076	7	5,751 R	66.0%	33.9%	66.1%	33.9%
WHATCOM	32,191	17,414	14,533	244	2,881 R	54.1%	45.1%	54.5%	45.5%
WHITMAN	13,434	8,572	4,854	8	3,718 R	63.8%	36.1%	63.6%	36.2%
YAKIMA	53,124	33,984	20,991	149	10,993 R	60.2%	39.5%	60.4%	39.6%
TOTAL	1,150,889	620,430	523,002	7,457	97,428 R	53.9%	45.4%	54.3%	45.7%

WASHINGTON

PRESIDENT 1960

County	Total Vote	Republican	Democratic	Other	Rep.-Dem. Plurality		Total Vote Rep.	Total Vote Dem.	Major Vote Rep.	Major Vote Dem.
ADAMS	4,216	2,479	1,732	5	747	R	58.8%	41.1%	58.9%	41.1%
ASOTIN	5,739	2,640	3,093	6	453	D	46.0%	53.9%	46.0%	54.0%
BENTON	26,344	13,797	12,518	29	1,279	R	52.4%	47.5%	52.4%	47.6%
CHELAN	18,214	9,854	8,177	183	1,677	R	54.1%	44.9%	54.7%	45.3%
CLALLAM	13,080	6,227	6,801	52	574	D	47.6%	52.0%	47.8%	52.2%
CLARK	40,868	20,080	20,771	17	691	D	49.1%	50.8%	49.2%	50.8%
COLUMBIA	2,094	1,301	793		508	R	62.1%	37.9%	62.1%	37.9%
COWLITZ	24,310	12,103	12,054	153	49	R	49.8%	49.6%	50.1%	49.9%
DOUGLAS	6,346	3,241	3,087	18	154	R	51.1%	48.6%	51.2%	48.8%
FERRY	1,546	623	921	2	298	D	40.3%	59.6%	40.3%	59.7%
FRANKLIN	9,409	4,201	5,156	52	955	D	44.6%	54.8%	44.9%	55.1%
GARFIELD	1,607	914	690	3	224	R	56.9%	42.9%	57.0%	43.0%
GRANT	15,005	7,568	7,400	37	168	R	50.4%	49.3%	50.6%	49.4%
GRAYS HARBOR	24,006	10,067	13,773	166	3,706	D	41.9%	57.4%	42.2%	57.8%
ISLAND	6,094	3,596	2,470	28	1,126	R	59.0%	40.5%	59.3%	40.7%
JEFFERSON	4,307	2,103	2,197	7	94	D	48.8%	51.0%	48.9%	51.1%
KING	440,810	224,150	208,756	7,904	15,394	R	50.8%	47.4%	51.8%	48.2%
KITSAP	37,302	17,459	19,662	181	2,203	D	46.8%	52.7%	47.0%	53.0%
KITTITAS	8,953	4,640	4,303	10	337	R	51.8%	48.1%	51.9%	48.1%
KLICKITAT	5,595	2,836	2,744	15	92	R	50.7%	49.0%	50.8%	49.2%
LEWIS	19,480	11,012	8,411	57	2,601	R	56.5%	43.2%	56.7%	43.3%
LINCOLN	5,464	3,211	2,248	5	963	R	58.8%	41.1%	58.8%	41.2%
MASON	7,902	3,703	4,183	16	480	D	46.9%	52.9%	47.0%	53.0%
OKANOGAN	10,698	5,169	5,507	22	338	D	48.3%	51.5%	48.4%	51.6%
PACIFIC	7,090	3,224	3,837	29	613	D	45.5%	54.1%	45.7%	54.3%
PEND OREILLE	2,953	1,305	1,641	7	336	D	44.2%	55.6%	44.3%	55.7%
PIERCE	125,475	57,188	64,292	1,995	7,104	D	46.3%	52.1%	47.1%	52.9%
SAN JUAN	1,740	1,112	624	4	488	R	63.9%	35.9%	64.1%	35.9%
SKAGIT	23,220	12,168	11,083	49	1,165	R	52.4%	47.4%	52.5%	47.5%
SKAMANIA	2,306	1,032	1,269	5	237	D	44.8%	55.0%	44.9%	55.1%
SNOHOMISH	73,163	33,731	38,793	639	5,062	D	46.1%	53.0%	46.5%	53.5%
SPOKANE	115,369	59,557	55,553	259	4,004	R	51.6%	48.2%	51.7%	48.3%
STEVENS	7,955	4,076	3,861	18	215	R	51.2%	48.5%	51.4%	48.6%
THURSTON	25,606	13,921	11,620	65	2,301	R	54.4%	45.4%	54.5%	45.5%
WAHKIAKUM	1,722	796	923	3	127	D	46.2%	53.6%	46.3%	53.7%
WALLA WALLA	18,519	11,786	6,721	12	5,065	R	63.6%	36.3%	63.7%	36.3%
WHATCOM	31,526	16,651	14,298	577	2,353	R	52.8%	45.4%	53.8%	46.2%
WHITMAN	13,544	8,069	5,458	17	2,611	R	59.6%	40.3%	59.7%	40.3%
YAKIMA	53,995	31,683	21,958	354	9,725	R	58.7%	40.7%	59.1%	40.9%
TOTAL	1,241,572	629,273	599,298	13,001	29,975	R	50.7%	48.3%	51.2%	48.8%

PRESIDENT 1964

County	Total Vote	Republican	Democratic	Other	Rep.-Dem. Plurality		Total Vote Rep.	Total Vote Dem.	Major Vote Rep.	Major Vote Dem.
ADAMS	4,273	2,241	2,027	5	214	R	52.4%	47.4%	52.5%	47.5%
ASOTIN	5,436	1,777	3,657	2	1,880	D	32.7%	67.3%	32.7%	67.3%
BENTON	28,372	11,708	16,650	14	4,942	D	41.3%	58.7%	41.3%	58.7%
CHELAN	17,822	7,406	10,295	121	2,889	D	41.6%	57.8%	41.8%	58.2%
CLALLAM	13,455	4,175	9,265	15	5,090	D	31.0%	68.9%	31.1%	68.9%
CLARK	41,790	12,300	29,341	149	17,041	D	29.4%	70.2%	29.5%	70.5%
COLUMBIA	2,187	1,048	1,138	1	90	D	47.9%	52.0%	47.9%	52.1%
COWLITZ	24,501	6,708	17,605	188	10,897	D	27.4%	71.9%	27.6%	72.4%
DOUGLAS	6,376	2,643	3,728	5	1,085	D	41.5%	58.5%	41.5%	58.5%
FERRY	1,459	526	931	2	405	D	36.1%	63.8%	36.1%	63.9%
FRANKLIN	10,058	3,615	6,375	68	2,760	D	35.9%	63.4%	36.2%	63.8%
GARFIELD	1,532	751	781		30	D	49.0%	51.0%	49.0%	51.0%
GRANT	14,427	6,065	8,352	10	2,287	D	42.0%	57.9%	42.0%	57.9%
GRAYS HARBOR	23,027	5,744	17,145	138	11,401	D	24.9%	74.5%	25.1%	74.9%
ISLAND	6,999	3,044	3,946	9	902	D	43.5%	56.4%	43.5%	56.5%
JEFFERSON	4,456	1,432	3,012	12	1,580	D	32.1%	67.6%	32.2%	67.8%
KING	450,640	177,598	268,216	4,826	90,618	D	39.4%	59.5%	39.8%	60.2%
KITSAP	37,714	10,702	26,904	108	16,202	D	28.4%	71.3%	28.5%	71.5%
KITTITAS	8,592	3,280	5,383	9	2,183	D	37.2%	62.7%	37.5%	62.5%
KLICKITAT	5,674	1,850	3,819	5	1,969	D	32.6%	67.3%	32.6%	67.3%
LEWIS	19,022	6,933	12,070	19	5,137	D	36.4%	63.5%	36.5%	63.5%
LINCOLN	5,213	2,911	2,299	3	612	R	55.8%	44.1%	55.9%	44.1%
MASON	8,071	2,549	5,514	8	2,965	D	31.6%	68.3%	31.6%	68.4%
OKANOGAN	10,495	3,931	6,554	10	2,623	D	37.5%	62.4%	37.5%	62.5%
PACIFIC	6,860	1,789	5,056	15	3,267	D	26.1%	73.7%	26.1%	73.9%
PEND OREILLE	2,965	985	1,978		993	D	33.2%	66.7%	33.2%	66.8%
PIERCE	125,973	40,164	84,566	1,243	44,402	D	31.9%	67.1%	32.2%	67.8%
SAN JUAN	1,750	839	906	5	67	D	47.9%	51.8%	48.1%	51.9%
SKAGIT	22,328	8,138	14,162	28	6,024	D	36.4%	63.3%	36.5%	63.5%
SKAMANIA	2,414	653	1,758	3	1,105	D	27.1%	72.8%	27.1%	72.9%
SNOHOMISH	81,405	25,902	55,013	490	29,111	D	31.8%	67.6%	32.0%	68.0%
SPOKANE	111,581	49,387	62,092	102	12,705	D	44.3%	55.5%	44.3%	55.7%
STEVENS	7,578	3,302	4,266	10	964	D	43.6%	56.3%	43.6%	56.4%
THURSTON	27,021	9,351	17,578	92	8,227	D	34.6%	65.1%	34.7%	65.3%
WAHKIAKUM	1,624	446	1,175		729	D	27.5%	72.4%	27.5%	72.5%
WALLA WALLA	17,594	8,102	9,481	11	1,379	D	46.0%	53.9%	46.1%	53.9%
WHATCOM	31,422	10,900	20,297	225	9,397	D	34.7%	64.6%	34.9%	65.1%
WHITMAN	13,538	6,765	6,760	13	5	R	50.0%	49.3%	50.0%	50.0%
YAKIMA	52,730	22,786	29,604	340	6,818	D	43.2%	56.1%	43.5%	56.5%
TOTAL	1,258,374	470,366	779,699	8,309	309,333	D	37.4%	62.0%	37.6%	62.4%

WASHINGTON

OTHER VOTE COMPOSITION:

1920   77,246 Farmer-Labor; 8,913 Socialist; 3,800 Prohibition; 1,321 Socialist Labor.

1924   150,727 Progressive; 5,991 American; 1,004 Socialist Labor; 761 Communist.

1928   4,068 Socialist Labor; 2,615 Socialist; 1,541 Communist.

1932   30,308 Liberty; 17,080 Socialist; 2,972 Communist; 1,540 Prohibition; 1,009 Socialist Labor.

1936   17,463 Union; 3,496 Socialist; 1,907 Communist; 1,598 Christian; 1,041 Prohibition; 362 Socialist Labor.

1940   4,586 Socialist; 2,626 Communist; 1,686 Prohibition; 667 Socialist Labor.

1944   3,824 Socialist; 2,396 Prohibition; 1,645 Socialist Labor.

1948   31,692 Progressive; 6,117 Prohibition; 3,534 Socialist; 1,133 Socialist Labor; 103 Socialist Workers.

1952   7,290 Christian Nationalist (MacArthur); 2,460 Progressive; 633 Socialist Labor; 254 Socialist; 119 Socialist Workers.

1956   Socialist Labor.

1960   10,895 Socialist Labor; 1,401 Constitution (Curtis); 705 Socialist Workers.

1964   7,772 Socialist Labor; 537 Socialist Workers.

SPECIAL CASES:

1920   Farmer-Labor candidates ran second in several counties.

1924   Progressive candidates carried several counties and ran second in most others.

WEST VIRGINIA

PRESIDENT 1920

County	Total Vote	Republican	Democratic	Other	Rep.-Dem. Plurality	Total Vote Rep. %	Total Vote Dem. %	Major Vote Rep. %	Major Vote Dem. %
BARBOUR	6,651	3,763	2,777	111	986 R	56.6%	41.8%	57.5%	42.5%
BERKELEY	9,748	5,259	4,399	90	860 R	53.9%	45.1%	54.5%	45.5%
BOONE	5,315	2,674	2,529	112	145 R	50.3%	47.6%	51.4%	48.6%
BRAXTON	8,563	4,274	4,269	20	5 R	49.9%	49.9%	50.0%	50.0%
BROOKE	5,335	3,060	2,129	146	931 R	57.4%	39.9%	59.0%	41.0%
CABELL	26,283	13,170	12,845	268	325 R	50.1%	48.9%	50.6%	49.4%
CALHOUN	3,447	1,671	1,773	3	102 D	48.5%	51.4%	48.5%	51.5%
CLAY	3,514	1,981	1,533	—	448 R	56.4%	43.6%	56.4%	43.6%
DODDRIDGE	4,297	3,135	1,137	25	1,998 R	73.0%	26.5%	73.4%	26.6%
FAYETTE	19,934	10,561	9,003	370	1,558 R	53.0%	45.2%	54.0%	46.0%
GILMER	3,510	1,635	1,854	21	219 D	46.6%	52.8%	46.9%	53.1%
GRANT	2,942	2,417	492	33	1,925 R	82.2%	16.7%	83.1%	16.9%
GREENBRIER	9,899	4,850	4,994	55	144 D	49.0%	50.4%	49.3%	50.7%
HAMPSHIRE	3,467	1,214	2,221	32	1,007 D	35.0%	64.1%	35.3%	64.5%
HANCOCK	4,364	2,768	1,435	161	1,333 R	63.0%	32.9%	65.3%	34.1%
HARDY	3,375	1,354	2,014	7	660 D	40.1%	59.7%	40.2%	59.8%
HARRISON	24,759	13,784	10,206	769	3,578 R	55.7%	41.2%	57.5%	42.5%
JACKSON	7,181	4,330	2,631	20	1,699 R	60.3%	39.4%	60.5%	39.5%
JEFFERSON	6,147	2,168	3,944	35	1,776 D	35.3%	64.2%	35.5%	64.5%
KANAWHA	43,769	23,781	19,284	704	4,497 R	54.3%	44.1%	55.2%	44.8%
LEWIS	8,082	4,618	3,310	154	1,308 R	57.1%	41.0%	58.2%	41.8%
LINCOLN	6,008	3,339	2,649	20	690 R	55.6%	44.1%	55.8%	44.2%
LOGAN	9,936	4,304	5,588	44	1,284 D	43.3%	56.2%	43.5%	56.5%
MCDOWELL	17,282	12,198	5,068	16	7,130 R	70.6%	29.3%	70.6%	29.4%
MARION	20,811	11,494	8,734	583	2,760 R	55.2%	42.0%	56.8%	43.2%
MARSHALL	12,380	7,208	4,814	358	2,394 R	58.2%	38.9%	60.0%	40.0%
MASON	8,203	4,912	3,177	114	1,735 R	59.9%	38.7%	60.7%	39.3%
MERCER	16,650	8,913	7,981	156	632 R	51.7%	47.9%	51.9%	48.1%
MINERAL	6,297	3,646	2,516	135	1,130 R	57.9%	40.0%	59.2%	40.8%
MINGO	8,906	3,972	4,934	—	962 D	44.6%	55.4%	44.6%	55.4%
MONONGALIA	10,584	6,773	3,442	369	3,331 R	64.0%	32.5%	66.3%	33.7%
MONROE	5,532	3,001	2,519	12	482 R	54.2%	45.5%	54.4%	45.6%
MORGAN	2,542	1,817	712	13	1,105 R	71.5%	28.0%	71.8%	28.2%
NICHOLAS	7,305	3,691	3,554	50	127 R	50.5%	48.8%	50.9%	49.1%
OHIO	26,842	15,735	10,278	829	5,457 R	58.6%	38.3%	60.5%	39.5%
PENDLETON	3,399	1,581	1,814	4	233 D	46.5%	53.4%	46.6%	53.4%
PLEASANTS	3,123	1,657	1,440	26	217 R	53.1%	46.1%	53.5%	46.5%
POCAHONTAS	5,421	2,836	2,540	45	296 R	52.3%	46.9%	52.8%	47.2%
PRESTON	9,004	6,729	2,150	125	4,579 R	74.7%	23.9%	75.8%	24.2%
PUTNAM	5,915	3,223	2,578	114	645 R	54.5%	43.6%	55.6%	44.4%
RALEIGH	13,646	7,668	5,915	62	1,752 R	56.2%	43.4%	56.4%	43.6%
RANDOLPH	9,018	4,158	4,676	184	518 D	46.1%	51.9%	47.1%	52.9%
RITCHIE	6,495	4,377	2,050	68	2,327 R	67.4%	31.6%	68.1%	31.9%
ROANE	7,324	4,232	3,082	10	1,150 R	57.8%	42.1%	57.9%	42.1%
SUMMERS	7,187	3,611	3,552	24	59 R	50.2%	49.4%	50.4%	49.6%
TAYLOR	6,080	3,649	2,311	120	1,338 R	60.0%	38.0%	61.2%	38.8%
TUCKER	4,688	2,498	1,966	224	532 R	53.3%	41.9%	56.0%	44.0%
TYLER	5,509	3,654	1,762	93	1,892 R	66.3%	32.0%	67.5%	32.5%
UPSHUR	6,396	4,936	1,418	42	3,518 R	77.2%	22.3%	77.7%	22.3%
WAYNE	8,244	3,754	4,490	—	736 D	45.5%	54.5%	45.5%	54.5%
WEBSTER	3,509	1,562	1,942	5	380 D	44.5%	55.3%	44.6%	55.4%
WETZEL	7,804	3,619	4,103	82	484 D	46.4%	52.6%	46.9%	53.1%
WIRT	3,061	1,680	1,376	5	304 R	54.9%	45.0%	54.9%	45.0%
WOOD	19,478	10,463	8,839	176	1,624 R	53.7%	45.4%	54.2%	45.8%
WYOMING	4,775	2,950	1,825	—	1,125 R	61.8%	38.2%	61.8%	38.2%
TOTAL	**509,936**	**282,007**	**220,785**	**7,144**	**61,222 R**	**55.3%**	**43.3%**	**56.1%**	**43.9%**

PRESIDENT 1924

County	Total Vote	Republican	Democratic	Other	Rep.-Dem. Plurality	Total Vote Rep. %	Total Vote Dem. %	Major Vote Rep. %	Major Vote Dem. %
BARBOUR	7,371	3,347	3,188	836	159 R	45.4%	43.3%	51.2%	48.8%
BERKELEY	10,205	5,427	4,366	412	1,061 R	53.2%	42.8%	55.4%	44.6%
BOONE	7,284	3,010	3,326	948	316 D	41.3%	45.7%	47.5%	52.5%
BRAXTON	9,490	4,192	5,168	130	976 D	44.2%	54.5%	44.8%	55.2%
BROOKE	6,501	3,858	2,037	606	1,821 R	59.3%	31.3%	65.4%	34.6%
CABELL	32,969	15,581	16,211	1,177	630 D	47.3%	49.2%	49.0%	51.0%
CALHOUN	3,633	1,399	2,231	3	832 D	38.5%	61.4%	38.5%	61.5%
CLAY	3,920	1,843	2,037	40	194 D	47.0%	52.0%	47.5%	52.5%
DODDRIDGE	4,419	2,777	1,594	48	1,183 R	62.8%	36.1%	63.5%	36.5%
FAYETTE	22,558	10,555	9,563	2,440	992 R	46.8%	42.4%	52.5%	47.5%
GILMER	4,350	1,570	2,750	30	1,180 D	36.1%	63.2%	36.3%	63.7%
GRANT	3,105	2,344	658	103	1,686 R	75.5%	21.2%	78.1%	21.9%
GREENBRIER	11,288	4,768	6,048	472	1,280 D	42.2%	53.6%	44.1%	55.9%
HAMPSHIRE	4,204	1,172	2,993	39	1,821 D	27.9%	71.2%	28.1%	71.9%
HANCOCK	5,321	3,775	1,187	359	2,588 R	70.9%	22.3%	76.1%	23.9%
HARDY	3,750	1,272	2,442	36	1,170 D	33.9%	65.1%	34.2%	65.8%
HARRISON	30,710	15,165	13,470	2,075	1,695 R	49.4%	43.9%	53.0%	47.0%
JACKSON	6,734	3,739	2,936	59	803 R	55.5%	43.6%	56.0%	44.0%
JEFFERSON	6,433	1,870	4,368	195	2,498 D	29.1%	67.9%	30.0%	70.0%
KANAWHA	52,951	26,018	22,726	4,207	3,292 R	49.1%	42.9%	53.4%	46.6%
LEWIS	9,470	4,839	4,410	221	429 R	51.1%	46.6%	52.3%	47.7%
LINCOLN	6,690	3,164	3,355	171	191 D	47.3%	50.1%	48.5%	51.5%
LOGAN	15,051	7,062	7,377	612	315 D	46.9%	49.0%	48.9%	51.1%
MCDOWELL	19,732	12,422	5,561	1,749	6,861 R	63.0%	28.2%	69.1%	30.9%
MARION	24,066	12,167	9,386	2,513	2,781 R	50.6%	39.0%	56.5%	43.5%
MARSHALL	13,342	7,413	4,710	1,219	2,703 R	55.6%	35.3%	61.1%	38.9%
MASON	8,090	4,225	3,308	557	917 R	52.2%	40.9%	56.1%	43.9%
MERCER	21,370	9,159	10,058	2,153	899 D	42.9%	47.1%	47.7%	52.3%
MINERAL	7,157	3,551	2,860	746	691 R	49.6%	40.0%	55.4%	44.6%
MINGO	11,070	4,656	5,313	1,101	657 D	42.1%	48.0%	46.7%	53.3%
MONONGALIA	14,110	6,994	4,977	2,139	2,017 R	49.6%	35.3%	58.4%	41.6%
MONROE	5,430	2,713	2,686	31	27 R	50.0%	49.5%	50.3%	49.7%
MORGAN	2,984	1,883	919	182	964 R	63.1%	30.8%	67.2%	32.8%
NICHOLAS	7,434	3,347	3,956	131	609 D	45.0%	53.2%	45.8%	54.2%
OHIO	26,626	14,402	8,753	3,471	5,649 R	54.1%	32.9%	62.2%	37.8%
PENDLETON	3,508	1,462	2,037	9	575 D	41.7%	58.1%	41.8%	58.2%
PLEASANTS	3,323	1,619	1,675	29	56 D	48.7%	50.4%	49.1%	50.9%
POCAHONTAS	5,661	2,782	2,777	102	5 R	49.1%	49.0%	50.0%	50.0%
PRESTON	9,375	6,396	2,445	534	3,951 R	68.2%	26.1%	72.3%	27.7%
PUTNAM	6,123	2,862	2,946	315	84 D	46.7%	48.1%	49.3%	50.7%
RALEIGH	17,486	8,643	7,776	1,067	867 R	49.4%	44.5%	52.6%	47.4%
RANDOLPH	10,263	4,152	5,314	797	1,162 D	40.5%	51.7%	43.9%	56.1%
RITCHIE	6,987	4,507	2,403	77	2,104 R	64.5%	34.4%	65.2%	34.8%
ROANE	7,601	4,097	3,504	—	593 R	53.9%	46.1%	53.9%	46.1%
SUMMERS	7,524	3,124	3,998	402	874 D	41.5%	53.1%	43.9%	56.1%
TAYLOR	6,890	3,683	2,499	708	1,184 R	53.5%	36.3%	59.6%	40.4%
TUCKER	4,992	2,277	2,127	588	150 R	45.6%	42.6%	51.7%	48.3%
TYLER	5,672	3,425	2,137	110	1,288 R	60.4%	37.7%	61.6%	38.4%
UPSHUR	7,019	4,930	1,952	137	2,978 R	70.2%	27.8%	71.6%	28.4%
WAYNE	10,247	3,999	5,870	378	1,871 D	39.0%	57.3%	40.5%	59.5%
WEBSTER	4,180	1,617	2,523	40	906 D	38.7%	60.4%	39.1%	60.9%
WETZEL	8,732	3,458	4,998	276	1,540 D	39.6%	57.2%	40.9%	59.1%
WIRT	3,104	1,491	1,587	26	96 D	48.0%	51.1%	48.4%	51.6%
WOOD	20,055	10,086	9,378	591	708 R	50.3%	46.8%	51.8%	48.2%
WYOMING	6,083	3,327	2,358	398	969 R	54.7%	38.8%	58.5%	41.5%
TOTAL	**583,662**	**288,635**	**257,232**	**37,795**	**31,403 R**	**49.5%**	**44.1%**	**52.9%**	**47.1%**

WEST VIRGINIA

PRESIDENT 1928

County	Total Vote	Republican	Democratic	Other	Rep.-Dem. Plurality	% Total Vote Rep.	% Total Vote Dem.	% Major Vote Rep.	% Major Vote Dem.
BARBOUR	7,514	4,023	3,491		532 R	53.5%	46.5%	53.5%	46.5%
BERKELEY	12,059	8,477	3,540	42	4,937 R	70.3%	29.4%	70.5%	29.5%
BOONE	8,835	4,000	4,805	30	805 D	45.3%	54.4%	45.4%	54.6%
BRAXTON	8,651	4,028	4,582	41	554 D	46.6%	53.05%	46.8%	53.2%
BROOKE	7,744	5,277	2,419	48	2,858 R	68.1%	31.2%	68.6%	31.4%
CABELL	36,583	21,091	15,340	152	5,751 R	57.7%	41.9%	57.9%	42.1%
CALHOUN	3,942	1,745	2,179	18	434 D	44.3%	55.3%	44.5%	55.5%
CLAY	4,494	2,551	1,929	14	622 R	56.8%	42.9%	56.9%	43.1%
DODDRIDGE	4,121	2,919	1,202		1,717 R	70.8%	29.2%	70.8%	29.2%
FAYETTE	25,416	12,961	12,351	104	610 R	51.0%	48.6%	51.2%	48.8%
GILMER	4,044	1,705	2,313	26	608 D	42.2%	57.2%	42.4%	57.6%
GRANT	3,197	2,648	542	7	2,106 R	82.8%	17.0%	83.0%	17.0%
GREENBRIER	12,624	6,423	6,141	60	282 R	50.9%	48.6%	51.1%	48.9%
HAMPSHIRE	3,926	1,779	2,132	15	353 D	45.3%	54.3%	45.5%	54.5%
HANCOCK	7,374	5,461	1,884	29	3,577 R	74.1%	25.5%	74.3%	25.7%
HARDY	3,582	1,611	1,965	6	354 D	45.0%	54.9%	45.1%	54.9%
HARRISON	30,331	17,502	12,483	346	5,019 R	57.7%	41.2%	58.4%	41.6%
JACKSON	6,502	4,050	2,452		1,658 R	62.3%	37.1%	62.9%	37.1%
JEFFERSON	6,384	3,050	3,312	22	262 D	47.8%	51.9%	47.9%	52.1%
KANAWHA	61,535	35,788	25,563	184	10,225 R	58.2%	41.5%	58.5%	41.7%
LEWIS	9,221	5,290	3,825	106	1,465 R	57.4%	41.5%	58.0%	42.0%
LINCOLN	7,239	3,823	3,416		407 R	52.3%	47.2%	52.8%	47.2%
LOGAN	21,389	11,404	9,944	41	1,460 R	53.3%	46.5%	53.4%	46.6%
MCDOWELL	23,135	14,810	8,294	31	6,516 R	64.0%	35.9%	64.1%	35.9%
MARION	26,663	16,088	10,133	442	5,955 R	60.3%	38.0%	61.4%	38.6%
MARSHALL	14,112	9,204	4,785	123	4,419 R	65.2%	33.9%	65.8%	34.2%
MASON	7,992	5,125	2,814	53	2,311 R	64.1%	35.2%	64.6%	35.4%
MERCER	23,210	12,887	10,273	50	2,614 R	55.5%	44.3%	55.6%	44.4%
MINERAL	8,212	5,880	2,310	22	3,570 R	71.4%	28.1%	71.6%	28.3%
MINGO	13,732	6,904	6,801	27	103 R	50.3%	49.5%	50.4%	49.6%
MONONGALIA	17,734	11,364	6,182	188	5,182 R	64.1%	34.9%	64.8%	35.2%
MONROE	5,388	3,025	2,346	17	679 R	56.1%	43.5%	56.5%	43.5%
MORGAN	3,308	2,539	758	11	1,781 R	76.8%	22.9%	77.0%	23.0%
NICHOLAS	7,481	3,917	3,495	69	422 R	52.4%	46.7%	52.8%	47.2%
OHIO	33,415	20,064	13,132	219	6,932 R	60.0%	39.3%	60.4%	39.6%
PENDLETON	3,631	1,710	1,921		211 D	47.1%	52.9%	47.1%	52.9%
PLEASANTS	3,032	1,821	1,210	1	611 R	60.1%	39.9%	60.1%	39.9%
POCAHONTAS	5,454	3,141	2,487	26	654 R	55.6%	44.0%	55.9%	44.1%
PRESTON	10,216	7,783	2,355	78	5,428 R	76.25%	23.1%	76.8%	23.2%
PUTNAM	5,793	3,346	2,406	41	940 R	57.8%	41.5%	58.2%	41.8%
RALEIGH	21,947	11,581	10,366		1,215 R	52.8%	47.2%	52.8%	47.2%
RANDOLPH	9,597	4,436	5,085	76	649 D	46.2%	53.0%	46.6%	53.4%
RITCHIE	5,959	4,195	1,711	53	2,484 R	70.4%	28.7%	71.0%	29.0%
ROANE	7,511	4,472	3,007	32	1,465 R	59.5%	40.0%	59.8%	40.2%
SUMMERS	7,832	4,063	3,752	17	311 R	51.5%	47.9%	52.0%	48.0%
TAYLOR	7,705	5,101	2,548	56	2,553 R	66.2%	33.3%	66.7%	33.3%
TUCKER	4,872	2,525	2,263	84	262 R	51.8%	46.4%	52.7%	47.3%
TYLER	5,533	3,881	1,591	61	2,290 R	70.1%	28.8%	70.9%	29.1%
UPSHUR	7,017	5,277	1,683	57	3,594 R	75.2%	24.0%	75.8%	24.2%
WAYNE	10,849	5,630	5,177	42	453 R	51.9%	47.7%	52.1%	47.9%
WEBSTER	4,252	1,936	2,306	10	370 D	45.5%	54.2%	45.6%	54.4%
WETZEL	8,539	4,428	4,052	59	376 R	51.9%	47.5%	52.2%	47.8%
WIRT	2,869	1,561	1,272	36	289 R	54.4%	44.3%	55.1%	44.9%
WOOD	21,721	15,184	6,412	125	8,772 R	69.9%	29.5%	70.3%	29.7%
WYOMING	7,034	3,987	3,047		940 R	56.7%	43.3%	56.7%	43.3%
TOTAL	642,752	375,551	263,784	3,417	111,767 R	58.4%	41.0%	58.7%	41.3%

PRESIDENT 1932

County	Total Vote	Republican	Democratic	Other	Rep.-Dem. Plurality	% Total Vote Rep.	% Total Vote Dem.	% Major Vote Rep.	% Major Vote Dem.
BARBOUR	8,022	3,652	4,228	142	576 D	45.5%	52.7%	46.3%	53.7%
BERKELEY	13,527	6,370	7,009	148	639 D	47.1%	51.8%	47.6%	52.4%
BOONE	9,593	3,555	5,973	65	2,418 D	37.1%	62.3%	37.3%	62.7%
BRAXTON	9,661	3,563	6,043	58	2,483 D	36.8%	62.6%	37.1%	62.9%
BROOKE	9,206	4,010	4,919	277	909 D	43.6%	53.4%	44.9%	55.1%
CABELL	41,950	17,999	23,498	453	5,499 D	42.9%	56.0%	43.4%	56.6%
CALHOUN	4,724	1,564	3,139	21	1,575 D	33.1%	66.4%	33.3%	66.7%
CLAY	5,499	2,443	3,038	18	595 D	44.4%	55.2%	44.6%	55.4%
DODDRIDGE	4,723	2,780	1,943		837 R	58.9%	41.1%	58.9%	41.1%
FAYETTE	29,509	12,170	17,127	212	4,957 D	41.2%	58.0%	41.5%	58.5%
GILMER	5,078	1,530	3,511	37	1,981 D	30.1%	69.1%	30.4%	69.6%
GRANT	3,433	2,477	920	36	1,557 R	72.2%	26.8%	72.9%	27.1%
GREENBRIER	14,684	5,111	9,467	106	4,356 D	34.8%	64.5%	35.1%	64.9%
HAMPSHIRE	4,988	1,258	3,681	49	2,423 D	25.2%	73.8%	25.5%	74.5%
HANCOCK	9,220	4,328	4,603	289	275 D	46.9%	49.9%	48.5%	51.5%
HARDY	4,116	1,267	2,824	25	1,557 D	30.8%	68.6%	31.0%	69.0%
HARRISON	33,354	14,641	18,081	632	3,440 D	43.9%	54.2%	44.7%	55.3%
JACKSON	8,215	4,084	4,131		47 D	49.7%	50.3%	49.7%	50.3%
JEFFERSON	7,119	1,734	5,350	35	3,616 D	24.4%	75.2%	24.5%	75.5%
KANAWHA	74,821	35,455	38,617	749	3,162 D	47.4%	51.6%	47.9%	52.1%
LEWIS	10,381	4,704	5,546	131	842 D	45.3%	53.4%	45.9%	54.1%
LINCOLN	8,757	3,881	4,876		995 D	44.3%	55.7%	44.3%	55.7%
LOGAN	23,283	10,683	12,529	71	1,846 D	45.9%	53.8%	46.0%	54.0%
MCDOWELL	28,514	16,069	12,365	80	3,704 R	56.4%	43.4%	56.5%	43.5%
MARION	29,464	12,638	15,975	851	3,337 D	42.9%	54.2%	44.2%	55.8%
MARSHALL	15,647	7,416	7,994	237	578 D	47.4%	51.1%	48.1%	51.9%
MASON	9,758	5,027	4,655	76	372 R	51.5%	47.7%	51.9%	48.1%
MERCER	27,093	11,088	15,900	105	4,812 D	40.9%	58.7%	41.1%	58.9%
MINERAL	8,669	4,519	4,098	52	421 R	52.1%	47.3%	52.4%	47.6%
MINGO	16,501	7,801	8,657	43	856 D	47.3%	52.5%	47.4%	52.6%
MONONGALIA	19,221	8,417	10,319	485	1,902 D	43.8%	53.7%	44.9%	55.1%
MONROE	6,247	2,978	3,267	2	289 D	47.7%	52.3%	47.7%	52.3%
MORGAN	3,483	2,082	1,358	43	724 R	59.8%	39.0%	60.5%	39.5%
NICHOLAS	9,097	3,684	5,327	86	1,643 D	40.5%	58.6%	40.9%	59.1%
OHIO	35,020	15,836	18,652	532	2,816 D	45.2%	53.3%	45.9%	54.1%
PENDLETON	4,047	1,502	2,530	15	1,028 D	37.1%	62.5%	37.3%	62.7%
PLEASANTS	3,525	1,580	1,921	24	341 D	44.8%	54.5%	45.1%	54.9%
POCAHONTAS	6,195	2,623	3,531	41	908 D	42.3%	57.0%	42.5%	57.5%
PRESTON	11,346	6,359	4,872	115	1,487 R	56.0%	42.9%	56.6%	43.4%
PUTNAM	7,590	3,411	4,098	81	687 D	44.9%	54.0%	45.4%	54.6%
RALEIGH	27,078	11,441	15,456	181	4,015 D	42.3%	57.1%	42.5%	57.5%
RANDOLPH	10,923	3,418	7,397	108	3,979 D	31.3%	67.7%	31.6%	68.4%
RITCHIE	7,317	4,055	3,179	83	876 R	55.4%	43.4%	56.1%	43.9%
ROANE	9,455	4,361	5,094		733 D	46.1%	53.9%	46.1%	53.9%
SUMMERS	9,010	3,220	5,724	66	2,504 D	35.7%	63.5%	36.0%	64.0%
TAYLOR	8,285	3,856	4,293	136	437 D	46.5%	51.8%	47.3%	52.7%
TUCKER	5,550	2,204	3,244	102	1,040 D	39.7%	58.5%	40.5%	59.5%
TYLER	6,390	3,734	2,582	74	1,152 R	58.4%	40.4%	59.1%	40.9%
UPSHUR	8,292	5,077	3,147	68	1,930 R	61.2%	38.0%	61.7%	38.3%
WAYNE	13,420	4,682	8,648	90	3,966 D	34.9%	64.4%	35.1%	64.9%
WEBSTER	5,475	1,781	3,664	30	1,883 D	32.5%	66.9%	32.7%	67.3%
WETZEL	9,547	3,351	6,118	78	2,767 D	35.1%	64.1%	35.4%	64.6%
WIRT	3,476	1,486	1,944	46	458 D	42.7%	55.9%	43.3%	56.7%
WOOD	25,673	12,144	13,294	235	1,150 D	47.3%	51.8%	47.7%	52.3%
WYOMING	8,403	4,007	4,396		389 D	47.7%	52.3%	47.7%	52.3%
TOTAL	743,774	330,731	405,124	7,919	74,393 D	44.5%	54.5%	44.9%	55.1%

WEST VIRGINIA

PRESIDENT 1936 (left) — **PRESIDENT 1940** (right)

County	1936 Total Vote	1936 Republican	1936 Democratic	1936 Other	1936 Rep.-Dem. Plurality	1936 % Total Vote Rep.	1936 % Total Vote Dem.	1936 % Major Vote Rep.	1936 % Major Vote Dem.	1940 Total Vote	1940 Republican	1940 Democratic	1940 Other	1940 Rep.-Dem. Plurality	1940 % Total Vote Rep.	1940 % Total Vote Dem.	1940 % Major Vote Rep.	1940 % Major Vote Dem.
BARBOUR	9,198	3,875	5,284	39	1,409 D	42.1%	57.4%	42.3%	57.7%	9,601	4,576	5,025		449 D	47.7%	52.3%	47.7%	52.3%
BERKELEY	14,960	6,585	8,336	39	1,751 D	44.0%	55.7%	44.3%	55.7%	15,220	6,562	8,658		2,096 D	43.1%	56.9%	43.1%	56.9%
BOONE	11,174	3,477	7,697	16	4,220 D	31.1%	68.9%	31.1%	68.9%	12,032	4,128	7,904		3,776 D	34.3%	65.7%	34.3%	65.7%
BRAXTON	9,392	3,709	5,667	16	1,958 D	39.5%	60.3%	39.6%	60.4%	9,765	4,056	5,709		1,653 D	41.5%	58.5%	41.5%	58.5%
BROOKE	9,495	3,485	5,955	55	2,470 D	36.7%	62.7%	36.9%	63.1%	10,420	4,004	6,416		2,412 D	38.4%	61.6%	38.4%	61.6%
CABELL	46,409	19,003	27,319	87	8,316 D	40.9%	58.9%	41.0%	59.0%	49,152	21,027	28,125		7,098 D	42.8%	57.2%	42.8%	57.2%
CALHOUN	5,115	1,733	3,369	13	1,636 D	33.9%	65.9%	34.0%	66.0%	4,763	1,891	2,872		981 D	39.7%	60.3%	39.7%	60.3%
CLAY	5,905	2,513	3,387	5	874 D	42.6%	57.4%	42.6%	57.4%	6,366	2,881	3,485		604 D	45.3%	54.7%	45.3%	54.7%
DODDRIDGE	4,744	3,023	1,716	5	1,307 R	63.7%	36.2%	63.8%	36.2%	4,788	3,293	1,495		1,798 R	68.8%	31.2%	68.8%	31.2%
FAYETTE	32,886	8,942	23,864	80	14,922 D	27.2%	72.6%	27.3%	72.7%	32,563	10,307	22,256		11,949 D	31.7%	68.3%	31.7%	68.3%
GILMER	5,291	1,858	3,433		1,575 D	35.1%	64.9%	35.1%	64.9%	5,343	2,067	3,276		1,209 D	38.7%	61.3%	38.7%	61.3%
GRANT	3,923	2,923	995	5	1,928 R	74.5%	25.4%	74.6%	25.4%	4,052	3,195	857		2,338 R	78.8%	21.2%	78.8%	21.2%
GREENBRIER	16,672	5,881	10,738	53	4,857 D	35.3%	64.4%	35.4%	64.6%	16,615	6,451	10,164		3,713 D	38.8%	61.2%	38.8%	61.2%
HAMPSHIRE	5,325	1,512	3,792	21	2,280 D	28.4%	71.2%	28.5%	71.5%	5,028	1,751	3,277		1,526 D	34.8%	65.2%	34.8%	65.2%
HANCOCK	11,771	3,957	7,756	58	3,799 D	33.6%	65.9%	33.8%	66.2%	13,512	4,997	8,515		3,518 D	37.0%	63.0%	37.0%	63.0%
HARDY	4,542	1,581	2,956	5	1,375 D	34.8%	65.1%	34.8%	65.2%	4,364	1,674	2,690		1,016 D	38.4%	61.6%	38.4%	61.6%
HARRISON	38,678	14,180	24,361	137	10,181 D	36.7%	63.0%	36.8%	63.2%	39,657	17,087	22,570		5,483 D	43.1%	56.9%	43.1%	56.9%
JACKSON	8,172	4,711	3,453	8	1,258 R	57.6%	42.3%	57.7%	42.3%	8,403	5,104	3,299		1,805 R	60.7%	39.3%	60.7%	39.3%
JEFFERSON	7,501	2,040	5,443	18	3,403 D	27.2%	72.6%	27.3%	72.7%	7,629	2,332	5,297		2,965 D	30.6%	69.4%	30.6%	69.4%
KANAWHA	86,301	35,387	50,801	113	15,414 D	41.0%	58.9%	41.1%	58.9%	98,045	40,113	57,932		17,819 D	40.9%	59.1%	40.9%	59.1%
LEWIS	11,084	5,499	5,531	54	32 D	49.6%	49.9%	49.9%	50.1%	10,501	5,935	4,566		1,369 R	56.5%	43.5%	56.5%	43.5%
LINCOLN	9,752	4,382	5,370		988 D	44.9%	55.1%	44.9%	55.1%	10,046	4,818	5,228		410 D	48.0%	52.0%	48.0%	52.0%
LOGAN	25,542	7,069	18,424	49	11,355 D	27.7%	72.1%	27.9%	72.3%	26,870	9,860	17,010		7,150 D	36.7%	63.3%	36.7%	63.3%
McDOWELL	35,481	9,975	25,471	35	15,496 D	28.1%	71.8%	28.1%	71.9%	38,355	13,906	24,449		10,543 D	36.3%	63.7%	36.3%	63.7%
MARION	32,443	11,403	20,859	181	9,456 D	35.1%	64.3%	35.3%	64.7%	34,384	13,349	21,035		7,686 D	38.8%	61.2%	38.8%	61.2%
MARSHALL	17,241	7,967	9,198	76	1,231 D	46.2%	53.3%	46.4%	53.6%	18,284	9,324	8,900		424 R	51.2%	48.8%	51.2%	48.8%
MASON	10,762	5,894	4,852	36	1,042 R	54.7%	45.0%	54.8%	45.2%	10,760	6,239	4,521		1,718 R	58.0%	42.0%	58.0%	42.0%
MERCER	29,183	10,762	18,391	30	7,629 D	36.9%	63.0%	36.9%	63.1%	29,558	11,395	18,163		6,768 D	38.6%	61.4%	38.6%	61.4%
MINERAL	9,859	4,486	5,333	40	847 D	45.5%	54.1%	45.6%	54.3%	10,328	5,133	5,195		62 D	49.7%	50.3%	49.7%	50.3%
MINGO	17,064	5,771	11,278	15	5,507 D	33.8%	66.1%	33.8%	66.2%	17,395	5,776	11,619		5,843 D	33.2%	66.8%	33.2%	66.8%
MONONGALIA	22,582	8,811	13,477	94	4,866 D	39.0%	60.6%	39.2%	60.8%	23,307	10,367	12,940		2,573 D	44.5%	55.5%	44.5%	55.5%
MONROE	6,695	3,268	3,413	14	145 D	48.8%	51.0%	48.9%	51.1%	6,686	3,403	3,283		120 R	50.9%	49.1%	50.9%	49.1%
MORGAN	4,184	2,555	1,620	9	935 R	61.1%	38.7%	61.2%	38.8%	3,849	2,563	1,286		1,277 R	66.6%	33.4%	66.6%	33.4%
NICHOLAS	9,906	3,964	5,872	70	1,908 D	40.0%	59.3%	40.1%	59.9%	9,611	4,299	5,312		1,013 D	44.7%	55.3%	44.7%	55.3%
OHIO	36,758	13,743	22,899	116	9,156 D	37.4%	62.3%	37.5%	62.5%	39,786	18,073	21,713		3,640 D	45.4%	54.6%	45.4%	54.6%
PENDLETON	4,450	1,800	2,637	13	837 D	40.4%	59.3%	40.6%	59.4%	4,687	1,977	2,710		733 D	42.2%	57.8%	42.2%	57.8%
PLEASANTS	3,735	1,820	1,907	8	87 D	48.7%	51.1%	48.8%	51.2%	3,675	1,896	1,779		117 R	51.6%	48.4%	51.6%	48.4%
POCAHONTAS	6,978	2,850	4,118	10	1,268 D	40.8%	59.0%	40.8%	59.1%	6,490	2,886	3,604		718 D	44.5%	55.5%	44.5%	55.5%
PRESTON	12,997	7,553	5,410	34	2,143 R	58.1%	41.6%	58.3%	41.7%	12,943	8,213	4,730		3,483 R	63.5%	36.5%	63.5%	36.5%
PUTNAM	8,720	3,938	4,756	26	818 D	45.2%	54.5%	45.3%	54.7%	9,156	4,268	4,888		620 D	46.6%	53.4%	46.6%	53.4%
RALEIGH	31,885	9,001	22,840	44	13,839 D	28.2%	71.6%	28.3%	71.7%	34,857	11,752	23,105		11,353 D	33.7%	66.3%	33.7%	66.3%
RANDOLPH	11,842	3,711	8,189	22	4,398 D	31.3%	68.5%	31.4%	68.6%	12,661	4,196	8,465		4,269 D	33.1%	66.9%	33.1%	66.9%
RITCHIE	7,486	4,639	2,825	22	1,814 R	62.0%	37.7%	62.0%	37.8%	7,421	4,982	2,439		2,543 R	67.1%	32.9%	67.1%	32.9%
ROANE	10,341	5,282	5,047	12	235 R	51.1%	48.8%	51.2%	48.8%	10,475	5,317	5,158		159 R	50.8%	49.2%	50.8%	49.2%
SUMMERS	9,311	3,521	5,779	11	2,258 D	37.8%	62.1%	37.9%	62.1%	9,085	3,644	5,441		1,797 D	40.1%	59.9%	40.1%	59.9%
TAYLOR	9,898	4,061	5,795	42	1,734 D	41.0%	58.5%	41.2%	58.8%	9,809	4,841	4,968		127 D	49.4%	50.6%	49.4%	50.6%
TUCKER	6,169	2,335	3,801	33	1,466 D	37.9%	61.6%	38.1%	61.9%	5,986	2,654	3,332		678 D	44.3%	55.7%	44.3%	55.7%
TYLER	6,559	4,031	2,509	21	1,522 R	61.5%	38.3%	61.6%	38.4%	6,380	4,354	2,026		2,328 R	68.2%	31.8%	68.2%	31.8%
UPSHUR	8,934	5,745	3,163	26	2,582 R	64.3%	35.4%	64.5%	35.5%	8,948	6,086	2,862		3,224 R	68.0%	32.0%	68.0%	32.0%
WAYNE	14,588	5,603	8,954	31	3,351 D	38.4%	61.4%	38.5%	61.5%	15,327	5,701	9,626		3,925 D	37.2%	62.8%	37.2%	62.8%
WEBSTER	6,618	1,987	4,613	18	2,626 D	30.0%	69.7%	30.1%	69.9%	6,646	2,067	4,579		2,512 D	31.1%	68.9%	31.1%	68.9%
WETZEL	10,262	3,770	6,463	29	2,693 D	36.7%	63.0%	36.8%	63.2%	10,033	4,443	5,590		1,147 D	44.3%	55.7%	44.3%	55.7%
WIRT	3,413	1,612	1,783	18	171 D	47.2%	52.2%	47.5%	52.5%	3,372	1,818	1,554		264 R	53.9%	46.1%	53.9%	46.1%
WOOD	29,414	12,574	16,829	11	4,255 D	42.7%	57.2%	42.8%	57.2%	30,967	15,005	15,962		957 D	48.5%	51.5%	48.5%	51.5%
WYOMING	10,335	3,601	6,734		3,133 D	34.8%	65.2%	34.8%	65.2%	12,180	4,378	7,802		3,424 D	35.9%	64.1%	35.9%	64.1%
TOTAL	829,945	325,358	502,582	2,005	177,224 D	39.2%	60.6%	39.3%	60.7%	868,076	372,414	495,662		123,248 D	42.9%	57.1%	42.9%	57.1%

WEST VIRGINIA

PRESIDENT 1944

County	Total Vote	Republican	Democratic	Other	Rep.-Dem. Plurality	Total Vote Rep.	Total Vote Dem.	Major Vote Rep.	Major Vote Dem.
BARBOUR	7,711	3,993	3,718		275 R	51.8%	48.2%	51.8%	48.2%
BERKELEY	11,970	6,151	5,819		332 R	51.4%	48.6%	51.4%	48.6%
BOONE	9,815	3,449	6,366		2,917 D	35.1%	64.9%	35.1%	64.9%
BRAXTON	7,336	3,023	4,313		1,290 D	41.2%	58.8%	41.2%	58.8%
BROOKE	9,314	3,588	5,726		2,138 D	38.5%	61.5%	38.5%	61.5%
CABELL	42,881	19,861	23,020		3,159 D	46.3%	53.7%	46.3%	53.7%
CALHOUN	3,941	1,687	2,254		567 D	42.8%	57.2%	42.8%	57.2%
CLAY	4,509	2,114	2,395		281 D	46.9%	53.1%	46.9%	53.1%
DODDRIDGE	3,611	2,611	1,000		1,611 R	72.3%	27.7%	72.3%	27.7%
FAYETTE	25,461	7,932	17,529		9,597 D	31.2%	68.8%	31.2%	68.8%
GILMER	4,160	1,651	2,509		858 D	39.7%	60.3%	39.7%	60.3%
GRANT	3,566	2,996	570		2,426 R	84.0%	16.0%	84.0%	16.0%
GREENBRIER	12,021	4,790	7,231		2,441 D	39.8%	60.2%	39.8%	60.2%
HAMPSHIRE	4,123	1,638	2,485		847 D	39.7%	60.3%	39.7%	60.3%
HANCOCK	11,619	4,285	7,334		3,049 D	36.9%	63.1%	36.9%	63.1%
HARDY	3,600	1,489	2,111		622 D	41.4%	58.6%	41.4%	58.6%
HARRISON	32,436	14,408	18,028		3,620 D	44.4%	55.6%	44.4%	55.6%
JACKSON	6,887	4,486	2,401		2,085 R	65.1%	34.9%	65.1%	34.9%
JEFFERSON	5,870	2,103	3,767		1,664 D	35.8%	64.2%	35.8%	64.2%
KANAWHA	83,888	36,488	47,400		10,912 D	43.5%	56.5%	43.5%	56.5%
LEWIS	8,334	4,984	3,350		1,634 R	59.8%	40.2%	59.8%	40.2%
LINCOLN	7,829	4,175	3,654		521 R	53.3%	46.7%	53.3%	46.7%
LOGAN	22,692	8,000	14,692		6,692 D	35.3%	64.7%	35.3%	64.7%
MCDOWELL	30,323	11,023	19,300		8,277 D	36.4%	63.6%	36.4%	63.6%
MARION	29,224	11,584	17,640		6,056 D	39.6%	60.4%	39.6%	60.4%
MARSHALL	14,974	7,800	7,174		626 R	52.1%	47.9%	52.1%	47.9%
MASON	9,271	5,609	3,662		1,947 R	60.5%	39.5%	60.5%	39.5%
MERCER	24,895	10,034	14,861		4,827 D	40.3%	59.7%	40.3%	59.7%
MINERAL	8,624	4,635	3,989		646 R	53.7%	46.3%	53.7%	46.3%
MINGO	14,261	4,711	9,550		4,839 D	33.0%	67.0%	33.0%	67.0%
MONONGALIA	20,076	9,647	10,429		782 D	48.1%	51.9%	48.1%	51.9%
MONROE	5,745	3,130	2,615		515 R	54.5%	45.5%	54.5%	45.5%
MORGAN	3,198	2,303	895		1,408 R	72.0%	28.0%	72.0%	28.0%
NICHOLAS	7,564	3,259	4,305		1,046 D	43.1%	56.9%	43.1%	56.9%
OHIO	33,610	16,165	17,445		1,280 D	48.1%	51.9%	48.1%	51.9%
PENDLETON	4,015	1,838	2,177		339 D	45.8%	54.2%	45.8%	54.2%
PLEASANTS	3,129	1,622	1,507		115 R	51.8%	48.2%	51.8%	48.2%
POCAHONTAS	5,237	2,340	2,897		557 D	44.7%	55.3%	44.7%	55.3%
PRESTON	9,782	6,785	2,997		3,788 R	69.4%	30.6%	69.4%	30.6%
PUTNAM	7,943	4,025	3,918		107 R	50.7%	49.3%	50.7%	49.3%
RALEIGH	28,311	10,323	17,988		7,665 D	36.5%	63.5%	36.5%	63.5%
RANDOLPH	9,980	3,681	6,299		2,618 D	36.9%	63.1%	36.9%	63.1%
RITCHIE	5,613	3,963	1,650		2,313 R	70.6%	29.4%	70.6%	29.4%
ROANE	8,437	4,650	3,787		863 R	55.1%	44.9%	55.1%	44.9%
SUMMERS	7,366	2,967	4,399		1,432 D	40.3%	59.7%	40.3%	59.7%
TAYLOR	7,543	3,890	3,653		237 R	51.6%	48.4%	51.6%	48.4%
TUCKER	4,893	2,220	2,673		453 D	45.4%	54.6%	45.4%	54.6%
TYLER	4,857	3,429	1,428		2,001 R	70.6%	29.4%	70.6%	29.4%
UPSHUR	7,358	5,332	2,026		3,306 R	72.5%	27.5%	72.5%	27.5%
WAYNE	11,143	4,516	6,627		2,111 D	40.5%	59.5%	40.5%	59.5%
WEBSTER	4,880	1,595	3,285		1,690 D	32.7%	67.3%	32.7%	67.3%
WETZEL	7,939	3,604	4,335		731 D	45.4%	54.6%	45.4%	54.6%
WIRT	2,588	1,418	1,170		248 R	54.8%	45.2%	54.8%	45.2%
WOOD	28,242	14,566	13,676		890 R	51.6%	48.4%	51.6%	48.4%
WYOMING	11,001	4,253	6,748		2,495 D	38.7%	61.3%	38.7%	61.3%
TOTAL	715,596	322,819	392,777		69,958 D	45.1%	54.9%	45.1%	54.9%

PRESIDENT 1948

County	Total Vote	Republican	Democratic	Other	Rep.-Dem. Plurality	Total Vote Rep.	Total Vote Dem.	Major Vote Rep.	Major Vote Dem.
BARBOUR	8,100	3,834	4,238	28	404 D	47.3%	52.3%	47.5%	52.5%
BERKELEY	12,873	6,042	6,797	34	755 D	46.9%	52.8%	47.1%	52.9%
BOONE	9,697	2,909	6,769	19	3,860 D	30.0%	69.8%	30.1%	69.9%
BRAXTON	7,158	2,664	4,287	7	1,423 D	40.0%	59.9%	40.1%	59.9%
BROOKE	10,512	3,718	6,630	114	2,962 D	35.4%	63.5%	35.8%	64.2%
CABELL	42,410	18,599	23,680	131	5,081 D	43.9%	55.8%	44.0%	56.0%
CALHOUN	3,681	1,549	2,126	6	577 D	42.1%	57.8%	42.1%	57.9%
CLAY	5,352	2,356	2,978	8	612 D	44.2%	55.6%	44.3%	55.7%
DODDRIDGE	3,599	2,433	1,166		1,267 R	67.6%	32.4%	67.6%	32.4%
FAYETTE	29,278	7,451	21,707	120	14,256 D	25.4%	74.1%	25.6%	74.4%
GILMER	3,776	1,421	2,355		934 D	37.6%	62.4%	37.6%	62.4%
GRANT	3,484	2,616	564	4	2,152 R	80.3%	19.1%	80.9%	19.1%
GREENBRIER	12,562	4,935	7,598	29	2,663 D	39.3%	60.5%	39.4%	60.6%
HAMPSHIRE	3,818	1,351	2,357	110	1,006 D	35.3%	61.8%	36.4%	63.6%
HANCOCK	12,973	4,561	8,242	170	3,681 D	35.2%	63.5%	35.6%	64.4%
HARDY	3,878	1,433	2,435	10	1,002 D	37.0%	62.8%	37.0%	63.0%
HARRISON	35,757	14,534	21,109	114	6,575 D	40.6%	59.0%	40.8%	59.2%
JACKSON	6,923	4,277	2,639	7	1,638 R	61.8%	38.1%	61.8%	38.2%
JEFFERSON	6,009	2,199	3,797	13	1,598 D	36.6%	63.2%	36.7%	63.3%
KANAWHA	94,695	41,144	53,213	338	12,069 D	43.4%	56.2%	43.6%	56.4%
LEWIS	8,341	4,829	3,477	35	1,352 R	57.9%	41.7%	58.1%	41.9%
LINCOLN	8,514	4,065	4,433	16	368 D	47.7%	52.1%	47.8%	52.2%
LOGAN	23,559	7,362	16,121	76	8,759 D	31.2%	68.4%	31.4%	68.6%
MCDOWELL	31,472	9,687	21,545	240	11,858 D	30.8%	68.4%	31.0%	69.0%
MARION	31,357	11,201	19,866	290	8,665 D	35.7%	63.4%	36.1%	63.9%
MARSHALL	15,122	6,986	7,989	147	1,003 D	46.2%	52.8%	46.7%	53.3%
MASON	9,491	5,453	4,038		1,415 R	57.5%	42.5%	57.5%	42.5%
MERCER	25,348	10,065	15,201	82	5,136 D	39.7%	60.0%	39.8%	60.2%
MINERAL	8,996	4,382	4,586	28	204 D	48.7%	51.0%	48.9%	51.1%
MINGO	15,292	4,896	10,362	34	5,466 D	32.0%	67.8%	32.1%	67.9%
MONONGALIA	21,683	9,329	12,138	216	2,809 D	43.0%	56.0%	43.5%	56.5%
MONROE	5,588	2,956	2,632		324 R	52.9%	47.1%	52.9%	47.1%
MORGAN	3,267	2,159	1,104	4	1,055 R	66.1%	33.8%	66.2%	33.8%
NICHOLAS	8,432	3,391	5,018	23	1,627 D	40.2%	59.5%	40.3%	59.7%
OHIO	33,147	15,757	16,995	395	1,238 D	47.5%	51.3%	48.1%	51.9%
PENDLETON	3,543	1,592	1,944	7	352 D	44.9%	54.9%	45.0%	55.0%
PLEASANTS	3,099	1,548	1,536	15	12 R	50.0%	49.6%	50.2%	49.8%
POCAHONTAS	5,132	2,373	2,754		381 D	46.2%	53.7%	46.3%	53.7%
PRESTON	9,596	6,020	3,527	49	2,493 R	62.7%	36.8%	63.1%	36.9%
PUTNAM	8,164	3,722	4,426	16	704 D	45.6%	54.2%	45.7%	54.3%
RALEIGH	30,259	10,414	19,697	148	9,283 D	34.4%	65.1%	34.6%	65.4%
RANDOLPH	10,412	3,802	6,586	24	2,784 D	36.5%	63.3%	36.6%	63.4%
RITCHIE	5,345	3,619	1,712	14	1,907 R	67.7%	32.0%	67.9%	32.1%
ROANE	7,908	4,213	3,684	11	529 R	53.3%	46.6%	53.3%	46.7%
SUMMERS	7,412	2,782	4,630		1,848 D	37.5%	62.5%	37.5%	62.5%
TAYLOR	7,871	3,948	3,888	35	60 R	50.2%	49.4%	50.4%	49.6%
TUCKER	4,693	2,102	2,557	34	455 D	44.8%	54.5%	45.1%	54.9%
TYLER	4,753	3,160	1,579	14	1,581 R	66.5%	33.2%	66.7%	33.3%
UPSHUR	7,419	5,068	2,323	28	2,745 R	68.3%	31.3%	68.6%	31.4%
WAYNE	12,031	4,394	7,618	19	3,224 D	36.5%	63.3%	36.6%	63.4%
WEBSTER	5,267	1,527	3,726	14	2,199 D	29.0%	70.7%	29.1%	70.9%
WETZEL	7,829	3,326	4,477	26	1,151 D	42.5%	57.2%	42.6%	57.4%
WIRT	2,532	1,291	1,233	8	58 R	51.0%	48.7%	51.1%	48.9%
WOOD	28,493	14,198	14,224	71	26 D	49.8%	49.9%	50.0%	50.0%
WYOMING	10,948	4,198	6,725	25	2,527 D	38.3%	61.4%	38.4%	61.6%
TOTAL	748,750	316,251	429,188	3,311	112,937 D	42.2%	57.3%	42.4%	57.6%

WEST VIRGINIA

PRESIDENT 1952

County	Total Vote	Republican	Democratic	Other	Rep.-Dem. Plurality	Total Vote Rep.	Total Vote Dem.	Major Vote Rep.	Major Vote Dem.
BARBOUR	8,993	4,504	4,489		15 R	50.1%	49.9%	50.1%	49.9%
BERKELEY	15,260	8,149	7,111		1,038 R	53.4%	46.6%	53.4%	46.6%
BOONE	12,309	4,100	8,209		4,109 D	33.3%	66.7%	33.3%	66.7%
BRAXTON	7,641	3,382	4,259		877 D	44.3%	55.7%	44.3%	55.7%
BROOKE	12,664	5,073	7,591		2,518 D	40.1%	59.9%	40.1%	59.9%
CABELL	49,640	27,461	22,179		5,282 R	55.3%	44.7%	55.3%	44.7%
CALHOUN	4,239	2,101	2,138		37 D	49.6%	50.4%	49.6%	50.4%
CLAY	5,348	2,534	2,814		280 D	47.4%	52.6%	47.4%	52.6%
DODDRIDGE	3,781	2,741	1,040		1,701 R	72.5%	27.5%	72.5%	27.5%
FAYETTE	31,497	9,190	22,307		13,117 D	29.2%	70.8%	29.2%	70.8%
GILMER	4,104	1,813	2,291		478 D	44.2%	55.8%	44.2%	55.8%
GRANT	3,956	3,282	674		2,608 R	83.0%	17.0%	83.0%	17.0%
GREENBRIER	15,460	7,374	8,086		712 D	47.7%	52.3%	47.7%	52.3%
HAMPSHIRE	4,564	2,173	2,391		218 D	47.6%	52.4%	47.6%	52.4%
HANCOCK	16,292	6,520	9,772		3,252 D	40.0%	60.0%	40.0%	60.0%
HARDY	4,448	2,037	2,411		374 D	45.8%	54.2%	45.8%	54.2%
HARRISON	41,720	21,193	20,527		666 R	50.8%	49.2%	50.8%	49.2%
JACKSON	7,442	4,845	2,597		2,248 R	65.1%	34.9%	65.1%	34.9%
JEFFERSON	7,170	3,134	4,036		902 D	43.7%	56.3%	43.7%	56.3%
KANAWHA	111,401	56,861	54,540		2,321 R	51.0%	49.0%	51.0%	49.0%
LEWIS	9,534	6,254	3,280		2,974 R	65.6%	34.4%	65.6%	34.4%
LINCOLN	9,883	4,784	5,099		315 D	48.4%	51.6%	48.4%	51.6%
LOGAN	28,450	9,148	19,302		10,154 D	32.2%	67.8%	32.2%	67.8%
MCDOWELL	35,320	10,663	24,657		13,994 D	30.2%	69.8%	30.2%	69.8%
MARION	34,869	14,979	19,890		4,911 D	43.0%	57.0%	43.0%	57.0%
MARSHALL	17,960	9,271	8,689		582 R	51.6%	48.4%	51.6%	48.4%
MASON	9,926	6,102	3,824		2,278 R	61.5%	38.5%	61.5%	38.5%
MERCER	30,961	14,267	16,674		2,407 D	46.1%	53.9%	46.1%	53.9%
MINERAL	10,143	5,598	4,545		1,053 R	55.2%	44.8%	55.2%	44.8%
MINGO	19,708	6,852	12,856		6,004 D	34.8%	65.2%	34.8%	65.2%
MONONGALIA	26,263	13,111	13,152		41 D	49.9%	50.1%	49.9%	50.1%
MONROE	6,303	3,447	2,856		591 R	54.7%	45.3%	54.7%	45.3%
MORGAN	3,813	2,699	1,114		1,585 R	70.8%	29.2%	70.8%	29.2%
NICHOLAS	10,001	4,386	5,615		1,229 D	43.9%	56.1%	43.9%	56.1%
OHIO	37,121	20,575	16,545		4,029 R	55.4%	44.6%	55.4%	44.6%
PENDLETON	3,850	1,859	1,991		132 D	48.3%	51.7%	48.3%	51.7%
PLEASANTS	3,532	1,900	1,632		268 R	53.8%	46.2%	53.8%	46.2%
POCAHONTAS	5,584	2,841	2,743		98 R	50.9%	49.1%	50.9%	49.1%
PRESTON	12,337	8,059	4,278		3,781 R	65.3%	34.7%	65.3%	34.7%
PUTNAM	9,746	4,944	4,802		142 R	50.7%	49.3%	50.7%	49.3%
RALEIGH	36,709	14,005	22,704		8,699 D	38.2%	61.8%	38.2%	61.8%
RANDOLPH	12,428	5,452	6,976		1,524 D	43.9%	56.1%	43.9%	56.1%
RITCHIE	5,903	4,238	1,665		2,573 R	71.8%	28.2%	71.8%	28.2%
ROANE	8,525	4,922	3,603		1,319 R	57.7%	42.3%	57.7%	42.3%
SUMMERS	7,959	3,496	4,463		967 D	43.9%	56.1%	43.9%	56.1%
TAYLOR	8,463	4,711	3,752		959 R	55.7%	44.3%	55.7%	44.3%
TUCKER	4,812	2,235	2,577		342 D	46.4%	53.6%	46.4%	53.6%
TYLER	5,011	3,488	1,523		1,965 R	69.6%	30.4%	69.6%	30.4%
UPSHUR	8,172	5,938	2,234		3,704 R	72.7%	27.3%	72.7%	27.3%
WAYNE	15,738	7,059	8,679		1,620 D	44.9%	55.1%	44.9%	55.1%
WEBSTER	5,996	2,229	3,767		1,538 D	37.2%	62.8%	37.2%	62.8%
WETZEL	8,851	4,476	4,375		101 R	50.6%	49.4%	50.6%	49.4%
WIRT	2,524	1,474	1,050		424 R	58.4%	41.6%	58.4%	41.6%
WOOD	34,071	19,917	14,154		5,763 R	58.5%	41.5%	58.5%	41.5%
WYOMING	15,153	6,124	9,029		2,905 D	40.4%	59.6%	40.4%	59.6%
TOTAL	873,548	419,970	453,578		33,608 D	48.1%	51.9%	48.1%	51.9%

PRESIDENT 1956

County	Total Vote	Republican	Democratic	Other	Rep.-Dem. Plurality	Total Vote Rep.	Total Vote Dem.	Major Vote Rep.	Major Vote Dem.
BARBOUR	8,167	4,460	3,707		753 R	54.6%	45.4%	54.6%	45.4%
BERKELEY	14,720	9,071	5,649		3,422 R	61.6%	38.4%	61.6%	38.4%
BOONE	12,322	5,196	7,126		1,930 D	42.2%	57.8%	42.2%	57.8%
BRAXTON	7,354	3,441	3,913		472 D	46.8%	53.2%	46.8%	53.2%
BROOKE	13,016	5,944	7,072		1,128 D	45.7%	54.3%	45.7%	54.3%
CABELL	47,290	28,882	18,408		10,474 R	61.1%	38.9%	61.1%	38.9%
CALHOUN	4,022	2,094	1,928		166 R	52.1%	47.9%	52.1%	47.9%
CLAY	5,448	2,820	2,628		192 R	51.8%	48.2%	51.8%	48.2%
DODDRIDGE	3,529	2,594	935		1,659 R	73.5%	26.5%	73.5%	26.5%
FAYETTE	26,504	10,218	16,286		6,068 D	38.6%	61.4%	38.6%	61.4%
GILMER	3,790	1,774	2,016		242 D	46.8%	53.2%	46.8%	53.2%
GRANT	4,042	3,408	634		2,774 R	84.3%	15.7%	84.3%	15.7%
GREENBRIER	14,501	7,684	6,817		867 R	53.0%	47.0%	53.0%	47.0%
HAMPSHIRE	5,032	2,676	2,356		320 R	53.2%	46.8%	53.2%	46.8%
HANCOCK	18,274	8,750	9,524		774 D	47.9%	52.1%	47.9%	52.1%
HARDY	4,461	2,202	2,259		57 D	49.4%	50.6%	49.4%	50.6%
HARRISON	39,461	21,860	17,541		4,319 R	55.5%	44.5%	55.5%	44.5%
JACKSON	7,580	4,984	2,596		2,388 R	65.8%	34.2%	65.8%	34.2%
JEFFERSON	6,733	3,380	3,353		27 R	50.2%	49.8%	50.2%	49.8%
KANAWHA	108,886	58,597	50,289		8,308 R	53.8%	46.2%	53.8%	46.2%
LEWIS	9,397	6,203	3,194		3,009 R	66.0%	34.0%	66.0%	34.0%
LINCOLN	9,926	4,954	4,972		18 D	49.9%	50.1%	49.9%	50.1%
LOGAN	25,382	10,588	14,794		4,206 D	41.7%	58.3%	41.7%	58.3%
MCDOWELL	28,003	11,138	16,865		5,727 D	39.8%	60.2%	39.8%	60.2%
MARION	32,304	16,112	16,192		80 D	49.9%	50.1%	49.9%	50.1%
MARSHALL	17,686	10,223	7,463		2,760 R	57.8%	42.2%	57.8%	42.2%
MASON	10,075	6,306	3,769		2,537 R	62.6%	37.4%	62.6%	37.4%
MERCER	27,884	14,648	13,236		1,412 R	52.5%	47.5%	52.5%	47.5%
MINERAL	10,000	6,412	3,588		2,824 R	64.1%	35.9%	64.1%	35.9%
MINGO	17,930	7,916	10,014		2,098 D	44.1%	55.9%	44.1%	55.9%
MONONGALIA	25,062	14,046	11,016		3,030 R	56.0%	44.0%	56.0%	44.0%
MONROE	6,301	3,529	2,772		757 R	56.0%	44.0%	56.0%	44.0%
MORGAN	4,050	2,946	1,104		1,842 R	72.7%	27.3%	72.7%	27.3%
NICHOLAS	10,143	5,263	4,880		383 R	51.9%	48.1%	51.9%	48.1%
OHIO	35,356	22,165	13,191		8,974 R	62.7%	37.3%	62.7%	37.3%
PENDLETON	3,958	1,959	1,999		40 D	49.5%	50.5%	49.5%	50.5%
PLEASANTS	3,725	2,144	1,581		563 R	57.6%	42.4%	57.6%	42.4%
POCAHONTAS	5,470	2,937	2,533		404 R	53.7%	46.3%	53.7%	46.3%
PRESTON	11,318	7,953	3,365		4,588 R	70.3%	29.7%	70.3%	29.7%
PUTNAM	10,314	5,560	4,754		806 R	53.9%	46.1%	53.9%	46.1%
RALEIGH	32,582	16,318	16,264		54 R	50.1%	49.9%	50.1%	49.9%
RANDOLPH	11,145	5,448	5,697		249 D	48.9%	51.1%	48.9%	51.1%
RITCHIE	5,611	4,140	1,471		2,669 R	73.8%	26.2%	73.8%	26.2%
ROANE	7,854	4,701	3,153		1,548 R	59.9%	40.1%	59.9%	40.1%
SUMMERS	7,577	3,712	3,865		153 D	49.0%	51.0%	49.0%	51.0%
TAYLOR	7,822	4,743	3,079		1,664 R	60.6%	39.4%	60.6%	39.4%
TUCKER	4,455	2,326	2,129		197 R	52.2%	47.8%	52.2%	47.8%
TYLER	4,989	3,671	1,318		2,353 R	73.6%	26.4%	73.6%	26.4%
UPSHUR	7,788	5,707	2,081		3,626 R	73.3%	26.7%	73.3%	26.7%
WAYNE	16,084	8,429	7,655		774 R	52.4%	47.6%	52.4%	47.6%
WEBSTER	5,529	2,457	3,072		615 D	44.4%	55.6%	44.4%	55.6%
WETZEL	8,833	5,024	3,809		1,215 R	56.9%	43.1%	56.9%	43.1%
WIRT	2,628	1,444	1,184		260 R	54.9%	45.1%	54.9%	45.1%
WOOD	34,416	21,096	13,320		7,776 R	61.3%	38.7%	61.3%	38.7%
WYOMING	14,162	7,044	7,118		74 D	49.7%	50.3%	49.7%	50.3%
TOTAL	830,831	449,297	381,534		67,763 R	54.1%	45.9%	54.1%	45.9%

WEST VIRGINIA

PRESIDENT 1960

County	Total Vote	Republican	Democratic	Other	Rep-Dem Plurality	%Total Rep	%Total Dem	%Major Rep	%Major Dem
BARBOUR	7,824	4,006	3,818		188 R	51.2%	48.8%	51.2%	48.8%
BERKELEY	15,441	8,369	7,072		1,297 R	54.2%	45.8%	54.2%	45.8%
BOONE	12,162	4,104	8,158		3,954 D	33.7%	66.3%	33.7%	66.3%
BRAXTON	7,162	2,977	4,185		1,208 D	41.5%	58.4%	41.6%	58.4%
BROOKE	13,592	5,754	7,838		2,084 D	42.3%	57.7%	42.3%	57.7%
CABELL	47,899	26,988	20,911		6,077 R	56.3%	43.7%	56.3%	43.7%
CALHOUN	3,921	1,946	1,975		29 D	49.6%	50.4%	49.6%	50.4%
CLAY	5,265	2,406	2,859		453 D	45.7%	54.3%	45.7%	54.3%
DODDRIDGE	3,455	2,402	1,053		1,349 R	69.5%	30.5%	69.5%	30.5%
FAYETTE	25,646	7,537	18,139		10,602 D	29.4%	70.6%	29.4%	70.6%
GILMER	3,521	1,446	2,075		629 D	41.1%	58.9%	41.1%	58.9%
GRANT	4,241	3,333	908		2,425 R	78.6%	21.4%	78.6%	21.4%
GREENBRIER	14,976	6,633	8,343		1,710 D	44.3%	55.7%	44.3%	55.7%
HAMPSHIRE	5,390	2,541	2,849		308 D	47.1%	52.9%	47.1%	52.9%
HANCOCK	19,207	8,031	11,176		3,145 D	41.8%	58.2%	41.8%	58.2%
HARDY	4,507	2,042	2,465		423 D	45.3%	54.7%	45.3%	54.7%
HARRISON	39,105	18,378	20,727		2,349 D	47.0%	53.0%	47.0%	53.0%
JACKSON	9,550	5,535	3,615		1,920 R	60.5%	39.5%	60.5%	39.5%
JEFFERSON	7,239	2,887	4,352		1,465 D	39.9%	60.1%	39.9%	60.1%
KANAWHA	111,614	57,130	54,484		2,646 R	51.2%	48.8%	51.2%	48.8%
LEWIS	8,806	5,157	3,649		1,508 R	58.6%	41.4%	58.6%	41.4%
LINCOLN	9,602	4,579	5,023		444 D	47.7%	52.3%	47.7%	52.3%
LOGAN	24,196	7,836	16,360		8,524 D	32.4%	67.6%	32.4%	67.6%
MCDOWELL	26,056	6,555	19,501		12,946 D	25.2%	74.8%	25.2%	74.8%
MARION	32,041	14,138	17,903		3,765 D	44.1%	55.9%	44.1%	55.9%
MARSHALL	18,344	9,147	9,197		50 D	49.9%	50.1%	49.9%	50.1%
MASON	10,946	6,424	4,522		1,902 R	58.7%	41.3%	58.7%	41.3%
MERCER	29,008	11,779	17,289		5,510 D	40.4%	59.6%	40.4%	59.6%
MINERAL	10,463	6,299	4,164		2,135 R	60.2%	39.8%	60.2%	39.8%
MINGO	16,162	4,903	11,259		6,356 D	30.3%	69.7%	30.3%	69.7%
MONONGALIA	24,626	11,523	13,103		1,580 D	46.8%	53.2%	46.8%	53.2%
MONROE	6,049	3,139	2,910		229 R	51.9%	48.1%	51.9%	48.1%
MORGAN	4,121	2,752	1,369		1,383 R	66.8%	33.2%	66.8%	33.2%
NICHOLAS	10,071	4,297	5,774		1,477 D	42.7%	57.3%	42.7%	57.3%
OHIO	35,790	17,367	18,423		1,056 D	48.5%	51.5%	48.5%	51.5%
PENDLETON	3,987	1,930	2,057		127 D	48.4%	51.6%	48.4%	51.6%
PLEASANTS	3,724	1,982	1,742		240 R	53.2%	46.8%	53.2%	46.8%
POCAHONTAS	5,291	2,469	2,822		353 D	46.7%	53.3%	46.7%	53.3%
PRESTON	11,129	6,908	4,221		2,687 R	62.1%	37.9%	62.1%	37.9%
PUTNAM	10,670	5,702	4,968		734 R	53.4%	46.6%	53.4%	46.6%
RALEIGH	32,536	12,088	20,448		8,360 D	37.2%	62.8%	37.2%	62.8%
RANDOLPH	12,207	5,018	6,989		1,971 D	41.8%	58.2%	41.8%	58.2%
RITCHIE	5,563	3,972	1,591		2,381 R	71.4%	28.6%	71.4%	28.6%
ROANE	7,723	4,443	3,280		1,163 R	57.5%	42.5%	57.5%	42.5%
SUMMERS	7,759	3,137	4,622		1,485 D	40.4%	59.6%	40.4%	59.6%
TAYLOR	7,481	3,992	3,489		503 R	53.4%	46.6%	53.4%	46.6%
TUCKER	3,977	1,887	2,090		203 D	47.4%	52.6%	47.4%	52.6%
TYLER	5,095	3,537	1,558		1,979 R	69.4%	30.6%	69.4%	30.6%
UPSHUR	7,713	5,123	2,590		2,533 R	66.4%	33.6%	66.4%	33.6%
WAYNE	17,268	8,128	9,140		1,012 D	47.1%	52.9%	47.1%	52.9%
WEBSTER	5,168	1,689	3,479		1,790 D	32.7%	67.3%	32.7%	67.3%
WETZEL	9,487	5,149	4,338		811 D	54.3%	45.7%	54.3%	45.7%
WIRT	2,392	1,347	1,045		302 R	56.3%	43.7%	56.3%	43.7%
WOOD	37,527	22,131	15,396		6,735 R	59.0%	41.0%	59.0%	41.0%
WYOMING	13,686	5,083	8,603		3,520 D	37.1%	62.9%	37.1%	62.9%
TOTAL	837,781	395,995	441,786		45,791 D	47.3%	52.7%	47.3%	52.7%

PRESIDENT 1964

County	Total Vote	Republican	Democratic	Other	Rep-Dem Plurality	%Total Rep	%Total Dem	%Major Rep	%Major Dem
BARBOUR	7,291	2,533	4,758		2,225 D	34.7%	65.3%	34.7%	65.3%
BERKELEY	14,085	5,457	8,628		3,171 D	38.7%	61.3%	38.7%	61.3%
BOONE	11,076	2,467	8,609		6,142 D	22.3%	77.7%	22.3%	77.7%
BRAXTON	6,654	1,867	4,787		2,920 D	28.1%	71.9%	28.1%	71.9%
BROOKE	13,198	3,364	9,634		6,470 D	25.5%	74.5%	25.5%	74.5%
CABELL	45,394	16,957	28,437		11,480 D	37.4%	62.6%	37.4%	62.6%
CALHOUN	3,801	1,275	2,526		1,351 D	32.7%	67.3%	32.7%	67.3%
CLAY	4,548	1,366	3,182		1,816 D	30.0%	70.0%	30.0%	70.0%
DODDRIDGE	3,168	1,581	1,587		16 D	49.9%	50.1%	49.9%	50.1%
FAYETTE	24,041	4,051	19,990		15,939 D	16.9%	83.1%	16.9%	83.1%
GILMER	3,948	1,116	2,832		1,716 D	28.3%	71.7%	28.3%	71.7%
GRANT	3,958	2,464	1,494		970 R	62.3%	37.7%	62.3%	37.7%
GREENBRIER	14,661	4,549	10,112		5,563 D	31.0%	69.0%	31.0%	69.0%
HAMPSHIRE	4,854	1,473	3,381		1,908 D	30.3%	69.7%	30.3%	69.7%
HANCOCK	19,010	5,009	14,001		8,992 D	26.3%	73.7%	26.3%	73.7%
HARDY	4,304	1,308	2,996		1,688 D	30.4%	69.6%	30.4%	69.6%
HARRISON	35,669	9,936	25,683		15,697 D	28.0%	72.0%	28.0%	72.0%
JACKSON	9,381	4,359	5,022		663 D	46.5%	53.5%	46.5%	53.5%
JEFFERSON	6,793	1,901	4,892		2,991 D	28.0%	72.0%	28.0%	72.0%
KANAWHA	108,894	38,383	70,511		32,128 D	35.2%	64.8%	35.2%	64.8%
LEWIS	8,227	2,979	5,248		2,269 D	36.2%	63.8%	36.2%	63.8%
LINCOLN	9,288	3,436	5,852		2,416 D	37.0%	63.0%	37.0%	63.0%
LOGAN	20,775	3,776	16,999		13,223 D	18.2%	81.8%	18.2%	81.8%
MCDOWELL	21,730	3,584	18,046		14,462 D	17.0%	83.0%	17.0%	83.0%
MARION	29,754	7,707	22,047		14,340 D	25.9%	74.1%	25.9%	74.1%
MARSHALL	17,932	6,175	11,757		5,582 D	34.4%	65.6%	34.4%	65.6%
MASON	10,978	4,467	6,511		2,044 D	40.7%	59.3%	40.7%	59.3%
MERCER	27,203	8,905	18,298		9,393 D	32.7%	67.3%	32.7%	67.3%
MINERAL	10,145	3,801	6,344		2,543 D	37.5%	62.5%	37.5%	62.5%
MINGO	15,420	3,154	12,266		9,112 D	20.5%	79.5%	20.5%	79.5%
MONONGALIA	23,831	6,473	17,358		10,885 D	27.2%	72.8%	27.2%	72.8%
MONROE	5,752	2,385	3,367		982 D	41.5%	58.5%	41.5%	58.5%
MORGAN	3,686	1,866	1,820		46 R	50.6%	49.4%	50.6%	49.4%
NICHOLAS	9,506	2,628	6,878		4,250 D	27.6%	72.4%	27.6%	72.4%
OHIO	33,184	12,006	21,178		9,172 D	36.2%	63.8%	36.2%	63.8%
PENDLETON	3,794	1,296	2,498		1,202 D	34.2%	65.8%	34.2%	65.8%
PLEASANTS	3,626	1,339	2,287		948 D	36.9%	63.1%	36.9%	63.1%
POCAHONTAS	5,033	1,716	3,317		1,601 D	34.1%	65.9%	34.1%	65.9%
PRESTON	10,279	4,015	6,264		2,249 D	39.1%	60.9%	39.1%	60.9%
PUTNAM	11,075	4,165	6,910		2,745 D	37.6%	62.4%	37.6%	62.4%
RALEIGH	30,558	6,952	23,606		16,654 D	22.8%	77.2%	22.8%	77.2%
RANDOLPH	10,996	2,984	8,012		5,028 D	27.1%	72.9%	27.1%	72.9%
RITCHIE	4,961	2,717	2,244		473 R	54.8%	45.2%	54.8%	45.2%
ROANE	7,271	3,451	3,820		369 D	47.5%	52.5%	47.5%	52.5%
SUMMERS	6,999	1,962	5,037		3,075 D	28.0%	72.0%	28.0%	72.0%
TAYLOR	6,734	2,292	4,442		2,150 D	34.0%	66.0%	34.0%	66.0%
TUCKER	3,978	1,314	2,664		1,350 D	33.0%	67.0%	33.0%	67.0%
TYLER	4,797	2,522	2,275		247 R	52.6%	47.4%	52.6%	47.4%
UPSHUR	7,380	3,606	3,774		168 D	48.9%	51.1%	48.9%	51.1%
WAYNE	16,918	5,340	11,578		6,238 D	31.6%	68.4%	31.6%	68.4%
WEBSTER	4,691	936	3,755		2,819 D	20.0%	80.0%	20.0%	80.0%
WETZEL	9,454	3,215	6,239		3,024 D	34.0%	66.0%	34.0%	66.0%
WIRT	2,185	899	1,286		387 D	41.1%	58.9%	41.1%	58.9%
WOOD	36,507	14,947	21,560		6,613 D	40.9%	59.1%	40.9%	59.1%
WYOMING	12,565	3,377	9,188		5,811 D	26.9%	73.1%	26.9%	73.1%
TOTAL	792,040	253,953	538,087		284,134 D	32.1%	67.9%	32.1%	67.9%

WEST VIRGINIA

OTHER VOTE COMPOSITION:

1920	5,618 Socialist; 1,526 Prohibition.
1924	36,723 Progressive; 1,072 American.
1928	1,703 Prohibition; 1,313 Socialist; 401 Communist.
1932	5,133 Socialist; 2,342 Prohibition; 444 Communist.
1936	1,173 Prohibition; 832 Socialist.
1940	
1944	
1948	Progressive.
1952	
1956	
1960	
1964	

SPECIAL CASES:

1924   Progressive total includes 21,820 Farmer-Labor and 14,903 Socialist votes.

WISCONSIN

PRESIDENT 1920

County	Total Vote	Republican	Democratic	Other	Rep.-Dem. Plurality	% Total Vote Rep.	% Total Vote Dem.	% Major Vote Rep.	% Major Vote Dem.
ADAMS	2,007	1,528	392	87	1,136 R	76.1%	19.5%	79.6%	20.4%
ASHLAND	5,646	4,005	1,081	560	2,924 R	70.9%	19.1%	78.7%	21.3%
BARRON	8,176	6,887	742	547	6,145 R	84.2%	9.1%	90.3%	9.7%
BAYFIELD	3,458	2,536	589	333	1,947 R	73.3%	17.0%	81.2%	18.8%
BROWN	14,345	8,845	3,877	1,623	4,968 R	61.7%	27.0%	69.5%	30.5%
BUFFALO	3,609	3,082	299	228	2,783 R	85.4%	8.3%	91.2%	8.8%
BURNETT	2,545	2,025	187	333	1,838 R	79.6%	7.3%	91.5%	8.5%
CALUMET	4,766	3,730	586	450	3,144 R	78.3%	12.3%	86.4%	13.6%
CHIPPEWA	8,175	6,750	1,103	322	5,647 R	82.6%	13.5%	86.0%	14.0%
CLARK	7,833	6,246	745	842	5,501 R	79.7%	9.5%	89.3%	10.7%
COLUMBIA	8,882	7,394	1,201	287	6,193 R	83.2%	13.5%	86.0%	14.0%
CRAWFORD	4,845	3,600	1,112	134	2,488 R	74.3%	22.9%	76.4%	23.6%
DANE	29,488	22,842	4,879	1,767	17,963 R	77.5%	16.5%	82.4%	17.6%
DODGE	14,658	11,354	2,293	1,011	9,061 R	77.5%	15.6%	83.2%	16.8%
DOOR	4,321	3,817	385	119	3,432 R	88.3%	8.9%	90.8%	9.2%
DOUGLAS	10,736	7,250	2,111	1,375	5,139 R	67.5%	19.7%	77.4%	22.6%
DUNN	6,370	5,596	491	283	5,105 R	87.8%	7.7%	91.9%	8.1%
EAU CLAIRE	9,625	7,856	1,193	576	6,663 R	81.6%	12.4%	86.8%	13.2%
FLORENCE	1,050	912	98	40	814 R	86.9%	9.3%	90.3%	9.7%
FOND DU LAC	16,819	12,543	3,409	867	9,134 R	74.6%	20.3%	78.6%	21.4%
FOREST	1,902	1,429	379	94	1,050 R	75.1%	19.9%	79.0%	21.0%
GRANT	11,911	9,638	1,971	302	7,657 R	80.9%	16.5%	83.0%	17.0%
GREEN	6,455	5,466	633	356	4,833 R	84.7%	9.8%	89.6%	10.4%
GREEN LAKE	4,580	3,457	890	233	2,567 R	75.5%	19.4%	79.5%	20.5%
IOWA	6,667	5,428	942	297	4,486 R	81.4%	14.1%	85.2%	14.8%
IRON	2,206	1,714	268	224	1,446 R	77.7%	12.1%	86.5%	13.5%
JACKSON	4,250	3,652	410	188	3,242 R	85.9%	9.6%	89.9%	10.1%
JEFFERSON	11,029	8,865	1,844	320	7,021 R	80.4%	16.7%	82.8%	17.2%
JUNEAU	5,399	4,385	774	240	3,611 R	81.2%	14.3%	85.0%	15.0%
KENOSHA	12,584	9,791	1,724	1,069	8,067 R	77.8%	13.7%	85.0%	15.0%
KEWAUNEE	3,326	2,622	598	106	2,024 R	78.8%	18.0%	81.4%	18.6%
LA CROSSE	13,611	10,067	2,588	956	7,479 R	74.0%	19.0%	79.5%	20.5%
LAFAYETTE	6,429	4,893	1,357	179	3,536 R	76.1%	21.1%	78.3%	21.7%
LANGLADE	5,913	4,059	1,619	235	2,440 R	68.6%	27.4%	71.5%	28.5%
LINCOLN	5,149	3,713	838	598	2,875 R	72.1%	16.3%	81.6%	18.4%
MANITOWOC	11,579	6,378	2,018	3,183	4,360 R	55.1%	17.4%	76.0%	24.0%
MARATHON	17,329	11,356	2,133	3,840	9,223 R	65.5%	12.3%	84.2%	15.8%
MARINETTE	8,124	6,138	1,314	672	4,824 R	75.6%	16.2%	82.4%	17.6%
MARQUETTE	3,196	2,436	687	73	1,749 R	76.2%	21.5%	78.0%	22.0%
MENOMINEE									
MILWAUKEE	142,311	73,410	25,464	43,437	47,946 R	51.6%	17.9%	74.2%	25.8%
MONROE	8,146	6,784	978	384	5,806 R	83.3%	12.0%	87.4%	12.6%
OCONTO	6,058	4,735	1,030	293	3,705 R	78.2%	17.0%	82.1%	17.9%
ONEIDA	3,733	2,424	833	476	1,591 R	64.9%	22.3%	74.4%	25.6%
OUTAGAMIE	14,915	11,140	3,121	654	8,019 R	74.7%	20.9%	78.1%	21.9%
OZAUKEE	4,660	3,523	835	302	2,688 R	75.6%	17.9%	80.8%	19.2%
PEPIN	2,140	1,817	265	58	1,552 R	84.9%	12.4%	87.3%	12.7%
PIERCE	5,375	4,441	644	290	3,797 R	82.6%	12.0%	87.3%	12.7%
POLK	5,960	4,796	752	412	4,044 R	80.5%	12.6%	86.4%	13.6%
PORTAGE	8,452	5,527	2,656	269	2,871 R	65.4%	31.4%	67.5%	32.5%
PRICE	4,028	2,990	551	487	2,439 R	74.2%	13.7%	84.4%	15.6%
RACINE	20,021	14,406	3,650	1,965	10,756 R	72.0%	18.2%	79.8%	20.2%
RICHLAND	5,040	3,862	917	261	2,945 R	76.6%	18.2%	80.8%	19.2%
ROCK	19,337	16,152	2,447	738	13,705 R	83.5%	12.7%	86.8%	13.2%
RUSK	3,362	2,609	441	312	2,168 R	77.6%	13.1%	85.5%	14.5%
ST CROIX	7,637	5,601	1,638	398	3,963 R	73.3%	21.4%	77.4%	22.6%
SAUK	9,522	8,074	946	502	7,128 R	84.8%	9.9%	89.5%	10.5%
SAWYER	2,104	1,668	302	134	1,366 R	79.3%	14.4%	84.7%	15.3%
SHAWANO	7,925	5,836	525	1,564	5,311 R	73.6%	6.6%	91.7%	8.3%
SHEBOYGAN	17,396	11,994	1,895	3,507	10,099 R	69.0%	10.9%	86.4%	13.6%

PRESIDENT 1924

County	Total Vote	Republican	Democratic	Other	Rep.-Dem. Plurality	% Total Vote Rep.	% Total Vote Dem.	% Major Vote Rep.	% Major Vote Dem.
ADAMS	2,687	779	173	1,735	606 R	29.0%	6.4%	81.8%	18.2%
ASHLAND	7,004	2,272	449	4,283	1,823 R	32.4%	6.4%	83.5%	16.5%
BARRON	9,180	2,703	377	6,100	2,326 R	29.4%	4.1%	87.8%	12.2%
BAYFIELD	4,600	1,675	205	2,720	1,470 R	36.4%	4.5%	89.1%	10.9%
BROWN	20,080	7,611	2,328	10,141	5,283 R	37.9%	11.6%	76.6%	23.4%
BUFFALO	4,006	1,324	176	2,506	1,148 R	33.1%	4.4%	88.3%	11.7%
BURNETT	3,158	958	76	2,124	882 R	30.3%	2.4%	92.6%	7.4%
CALUMET	5,046	938	569	3,539	369 R	18.6%	11.3%	62.2%	37.8%
CHIPPEWA	12,308	5,135	560	6,613	4,575 R	41.7%	4.5%	90.2%	9.8%
CLARK	10,010	3,130	552	6,328	2,578 R	31.5%	5.5%	85.0%	15.0%
COLUMBIA	11,690	4,724	907	6,059	3,817 R	40.4%	7.8%	83.9%	16.1%
CRAWFORD	5,658	1,687	936	3,035	751 R	29.8%	16.5%	64.3%	35.7%
DANE	39,208	12,280	2,081	24,847	10,199 R	31.3%	5.3%	85.5%	14.5%
DODGE	16,971	5,167	2,019	9,785	3,148 R	30.4%	11.9%	71.9%	28.1%
DOOR	4,904	1,891	235	2,778	1,656 R	38.6%	4.8%	88.9%	11.1%
DOUGLAS	15,039	5,887	638	8,514	5,249 R	39.1%	4.2%	90.2%	9.8%
DUNN	7,916	3,177	284	4,455	2,893 R	40.1%	3.6%	91.8%	8.2%
EAU CLAIRE	11,083	5,149	629	5,305	4,520 R	46.5%	5.7%	89.1%	10.9%
FLORENCE	1,183	594	49	540	545 R	50.2%	4.1%	92.4%	7.6%
FOND DU LAC	20,460	8,516	2,222	9,722	6,294 R	41.6%	10.9%	79.3%	20.7%
FOREST	2,710	1,104	299	1,307	805 R	40.7%	11.0%	78.7%	21.3%
GRANT	14,149	5,714	1,518	6,917	4,196 R	40.3%	10.7%	79.0%	21.0%
GREEN	8,331	2,922	423	4,986	2,499 R	35.1%	5.1%	87.4%	12.6%
GREEN LAKE	5,309	1,988	1,090	2,231	898 R	37.5%	20.5%	64.6%	35.4%
IOWA	8,213	3,291	689	4,233	2,602 R	40.1%	8.4%	82.7%	17.3%
IRON	2,634	1,058	84	1,492	974 R	40.2%	3.2%	92.6%	7.4%
JACKSON	5,155	1,662	255	3,238	1,407 R	32.2%	4.9%	86.7%	13.3%
JEFFERSON	13,611	4,250	1,374	7,987	2,876 R	31.2%	10.1%	75.6%	24.4%
JUNEAU	6,164	1,917	403	3,844	1,514 R	31.1%	6.5%	82.6%	17.4%
KENOSHA	18,649	10,341	1,517	6,791	8,824 R	55.5%	8.1%	87.2%	12.8%
KEWAUNEE	4,260	1,018	395	2,847	623 R	23.9%	9.3%	72.0%	28.0%
LA CROSSE	17,647	5,733	1,252	10,662	4,481 R	32.5%	7.1%	82.1%	17.9%
LAFAYETTE	7,699	2,671	1,265	3,763	1,406 R	34.7%	16.4%	67.9%	32.1%
LANGLADE	7,149	2,572	926	3,651	1,646 R	36.0%	13.0%	73.5%	26.5%
LINCOLN	6,913	1,857	503	4,558	1,354 R	26.8%	7.3%	78.7%	21.3%
MANITOWOC	16,345	4,828	1,599	9,918	3,229 R	29.5%	9.8%	75.1%	24.9%
MARATHON	19,088	5,577	1,109	12,402	4,468 R	29.2%	5.8%	83.4%	16.6%
MARINETTE	8,981	4,911	571	3,499	4,340 R	54.7%	6.4%	89.6%	10.4%
MARQUETTE	3,556	1,119	587	1,860	522 R	31.2%	16.5%	65.4%	34.6%
MENOMINEE									
MILWAUKEE	148,029	50,730	14,510	82,789	36,220 R	34.3%	9.8%	77.8%	22.2%
MONROE	9,965	2,661	428	6,876	2,233 R	26.7%	4.3%	86.1%	13.9%
OCONTO	7,735	2,562	602	4,571	1,960 R	33.1%	7.8%	81.0%	19.0%
ONEIDA	5,350	1,769	324	3,257	1,445 R	33.1%	6.1%	84.5%	15.5%
OUTAGAMIE	18,160	6,426	1,255	10,479	5,171 R	35.4%	6.9%	83.7%	16.3%
OZAUKEE	4,900	1,015	592	3,293	423 R	20.7%	12.1%	63.2%	36.8%
PEPIN	2,194	1,226	206	762	1,020 R	55.9%	9.4%	85.6%	14.4%
PIERCE	6,805	2,788	298	3,719	2,490 R	41.0%	4.4%	90.3%	9.7%
POLK	7,434	2,793	317	4,324	2,476 R	37.6%	4.3%	89.8%	10.2%
PORTAGE	10,280	2,854	2,010	5,416	844 R	27.8%	19.6%	58.7%	41.3%
PRICE	5,346	1,754	323	3,269	1,431 R	32.8%	6.0%	84.4%	15.6%
RACINE	25,969	13,040	1,463	11,466	11,577 R	50.2%	5.6%	89.9%	10.1%
RICHLAND	6,338	2,669	898	2,771	1,771 R	42.1%	14.2%	74.8%	25.2%
ROCK	24,320	14,815	1,453	8,052	13,362 R	60.9%	6.0%	91.1%	8.9%
RUSK	4,940	1,932	272	2,736	1,660 R	39.1%	5.5%	87.7%	12.3%
ST CROIX	9,073	3,600	718	4,755	2,882 R	39.7%	7.9%	83.4%	16.6%
SAUK	11,052	3,935	555	6,562	3,380 R	35.6%	5.0%	87.6%	12.4%
SAWYER	2,638	990	135	1,513	855 R	37.5%	5.1%	88.0%	12.0%
SHAWANO	8,965	2,063	471	6,431	1,592 R	23.0%	5.3%	81.4%	18.6%
SHEBOYGAN	20,181	6,974	1,350	11,857	5,624 R	34.6%	6.7%	83.8%	16.2%

WISCONSIN

PRESIDENT 1920

County	Total Vote	Republican	Democratic	Other	Rep.-Dem. Plurality	Percentage Total Vote Rep.	Dem.	Major Vote Rep.	Dem.
TAYLOR	3,724	2,707	282	735	2,425 R	72.7%	7.6%	90.6%	9.4%
TREMPEALEAU	5,636	4,748	718	170	4,030 R	84.2%	12.7%	86.9%	13.1%
VERNON	6,621	5,694	629	298	5,065 R	86.0%	9.5%	90.1%	9.9%
VILAS	1,367	903	255	209	648 R	66.1%	18.7%	78.0%	22.0%
WALWORTH	10,458	8,437	1,631	390	6,806 R	80.7%	15.6%	83.8%	16.2%
WASHBURN	2,585	2,023	352	210	1,671 R	78.3%	13.6%	85.2%	14.8%
WASHINGTON	7,748	5,949	1,328	471	4,621 R	76.8%	17.1%	81.8%	18.2%
WAUKESHA	12,097	8,665	2,759	673	5,906 R	71.6%	22.8%	75.8%	24.2%
WAUPACA	9,997	8,302	888	807	7,414 R	83.0%	8.9%	90.3%	9.7%
WAUSHARA	4,903	4,176	482	245	3,694 R	85.2%	9.8%	89.7%	10.3%
WINNEBAGO	17,308	12,035	3,397	1,876	8,638 R	69.5%	19.6%	78.0%	22.0%
WOOD	9,721	6,863	1,051	1,807	5,812 R	70.6%	10.8%	86.7%	13.3%
TOTAL	701,281	498,576	113,422	89,283	385,154 R	71.1%	16.2%	81.5%	18.5%

PRESIDENT 1924

County	Total Vote	Republican	Democratic	Other	Rep.-Dem. Plurality	Percentage Total Vote Rep.	Dem.	Major Vote Rep.	Dem.
TAYLOR	4,710	1,389	185	3,136	1,204 R	29.5%	3.9%	88.2%	11.8%
TREMPEALEAU	6,664	2,083	373	4,208	1,710 R	31.3%	5.6%	84.8%	15.2%
VERNON	8,779	2,670	406	5,703	2,264 R	30.4%	4.6%	86.8%	13.2%
VILAS	2,073	873	119	1,081	754 R	42.1%	5.7%	88.0%	12.0%
WALWORTH	13,080	7,484	1,162	4,434	6,322 R	57.2%	8.9%	86.6%	13.4%
WASHBURN	3,655	1,422	158	2,075	1,264 R	38.9%	4.3%	90.0%	10.0%
WASHINGTON	8,131	1,987	980	5,164	1,007 R	24.4%	12.1%	67.0%	33.0%
WAUKESHA	15,459	7,026	1,965	6,468	5,061 R	45.4%	12.7%	78.1%	21.9%
WAUPACA	10,781	3,654	665	6,462	2,989 R	33.9%	6.2%	84.6%	15.4%
WAUSHARA	4,522	1,602	249	2,671	1,353 R	35.4%	5.5%	86.5%	13.5%
WINNEBAGO	23,078	11,239	1,801	10,038	9,438 R	48.7%	7.8%	86.2%	13.8%
WOOD	11,442	3,469	548	7,425	2,921 R	30.3%	4.8%	86.4%	13.6%
TOTAL	840,827	311,614	68,115	461,098	243,499 R	37.1%	8.1%	82.1%	17.9%

WISCONSIN

PRESIDENT 1928

County	Total Vote	Republican	Democratic	Other	Rep.-Dem. Plurality	% Total Vote Rep.	% Total Vote Dem.	% Major Vote Rep.	% Major Vote Dem.
ADAMS	2,580	1,624	914	42	710 R	62.9%	35.4%	64.0%	36.0%
ASHLAND	7,372	3,639	3,570	163	69 R	49.4%	48.4%	50.5%	49.5%
BARRON	11,746	8,455	3,185	106	5,270 R	72.0%	27.1%	72.6%	27.4%
BAYFIELD	5,171	3,279	1,709	183	1,570 R	63.4%	33.0%	65.7%	34.3%
BROWN	26,004	9,371	16,465	168	7,094 D	36.0%	63.3%	36.3%	63.7%
BUFFALO	4,892	3,027	1,836	29	1,191 R	61.9%	37.5%	62.2%	37.8%
BURNETT	3,670	2,742	880	48	1,862 R	74.7%	24.0%	75.7%	24.3%
CALUMET	6,323	2,405	3,871	47	1,466 D	38.0%	61.2%	38.3%	61.7%
CHIPPEWA	13,561	7,514	5,985	62	1,529 R	55.4%	44.1%	55.7%	44.3%
CLARK	11,121	6,948	3,938	235	3,010 R	62.5%	35.4%	63.8%	36.2%
COLUMBIA	12,545	7,615	4,819	111	2,796 R	60.7%	38.4%	61.2%	38.8%
CRAWFORD	6,745	3,452	3,238	55	214 R	51.2%	48.0%	51.6%	48.4%
DANE	43,170	23,680	19,126	364	4,554 R	54.9%	44.3%	55.3%	44.7%
DODGE	19,434	9,660	9,536	238	124 R	49.7%	49.1%	50.3%	49.7%
DOOR	6,134	3,636	2,456	42	1,180 R	59.3%	40.0%	59.7%	40.3%
DOUGLAS	18,432	11,280	6,762	390	4,518 R	61.2%	36.7%	62.5%	37.5%
DUNN	9,274	7,096	2,045	133	5,051 R	76.5%	22.0%	77.6%	22.4%
EAU CLAIRE	14,555	10,079	4,385	91	5,694 R	69.2%	30.1%	69.7%	30.3%
FLORENCE	1,545	993	540	12	453 R	64.3%	35.0%	64.8%	35.2%
FOND DU LAC	24,517	12,593	11,719	205	874 R	51.4%	47.8%	51.8%	48.2%
FOREST	3,631	1,918	1,677	36	241 R	52.8%	46.2%	53.4%	46.6%
GRANT	16,794	10,052	6,630	112	3,422 R	59.9%	39.5%	60.3%	39.7%
GREEN	8,027	5,152	2,812	63	2,340 R	64.2%	35.0%	64.7%	35.3%
GREEN LAKE	5,716	3,038	2,622	56	416 R	53.1%	45.9%	53.7%	46.3%
IOWA	8,669	5,484	3,129	56	2,355 R	63.3%	36.1%	63.7%	36.3%
IRON	3,132	1,274	1,724	134	450 D	40.7%	55.0%	42.5%	57.5%
JACKSON	5,791	4,353	1,364	74	2,989 R	75.2%	23.6%	76.1%	23.9%
JEFFERSON	15,033	8,451	6,466	116	1,985 R	56.2%	43.0%	56.7%	43.3%
JUNEAU	6,541	3,777	2,708	56	1,069 R	57.7%	41.4%	58.2%	41.8%
KENOSHA	22,363	11,330	10,638	395	692 R	50.7%	47.6%	51.6%	48.4%
KEWAUNEE	5,569	1,556	3,988	25	2,432 D	27.9%	71.6%	28.1%	71.9%
LA CROSSE	20,295	11,321	8,877	97	2,444 R	55.8%	43.7%	56.1%	43.9%
LAFAYETTE	8,771	5,134	3,585	52	1,549 R	58.5%	40.9%	58.9%	41.1%
LANGLADE	7,879	3,715	4,078	86	363 D	47.2%	51.8%	47.7%	52.3%
LINCOLN	7,180	4,025	3,091	64	934 R	56.1%	43.1%	56.6%	43.4%
MANITOWOC	18,032	7,519	10,292	221	2,773 D	41.7%	57.1%	42.2%	57.8%
MARATHON	21,091	10,127	10,675	289	548 D	48.0%	50.6%	48.7%	51.3%
MARINETTE	11,424	6,516	4,781	127	1,735 R	57.0%	41.9%	57.7%	42.3%
MARQUETTE	3,903	2,554	1,313	36	1,241 R	65.4%	33.6%	66.0%	34.0%
MENOMINEE									
MILWAUKEE	206,237	82,025	110,668	13,544	28,643 D	39.8%	53.7%	42.6%	57.4%
MONROE	9,759	5,936	3,709	114	2,227 R	60.8%	38.0%	61.5%	38.5%
OCONTO	8,979	4,661	4,253	65	408 R	51.9%	47.4%	52.3%	47.7%
ONEIDA	5,707	3,100	2,504	103	596 R	54.3%	43.9%	55.3%	44.7%
OUTAGAMIE	24,964	12,378	12,474	112	96 D	49.6%	50.0%	49.8%	50.2%
OZAUKEE	6,292	2,338	3,864	90	1,526 D	37.2%	61.4%	37.7%	62.3%
PEPIN	3,140	1,839	1,276	25	563 R	58.6%	40.6%	59.0%	41.0%
PIERCE	6,641	3,537	3,017	87	520 R	53.3%	45.4%	54.0%	46.0%
POLK	9,190	6,905	2,177	108	4,728 R	75.1%	23.7%	76.0%	24.0%
PORTAGE	11,995	5,161	6,764	70	1,603 D	43.0%	56.4%	43.3%	56.7%
PRICE	5,542	3,210	2,223	109	987 R	57.9%	40.1%	59.1%	40.9%
RACINE	30,806	17,423	13,021	362	4,402 R	56.6%	42.3%	57.2%	42.8%
RICHLAND	8,022	5,685	2,262	75	3,423 R	70.9%	28.2%	71.5%	28.5%
ROCK	30,344	21,457	8,726	161	12,731 R	70.7%	28.8%	71.1%	28.9%
RUSK	5,539	3,524	1,925	90	1,599 R	63.6%	34.8%	64.7%	35.3%
ST CROIX	11,026	6,855	4,083	88	2,772 R	62.2%	37.0%	62.7%	37.3%
SAUK	12,729	7,496	5,151	82	2,345 R	58.9%	40.5%	59.3%	40.7%
SAWYER	3,063	1,882	1,129	52	753 R	61.4%	36.9%	62.5%	37.5%
SHAWANO	9,065	5,198	3,779	88	1,419 R	57.3%	41.7%	57.9%	42.1%
SHEBOYGAN	24,701	12,640	11,439	622	1,201 R	51.2%	46.3%	52.5%	47.5%

PRESIDENT 1932

County	Total Vote	Republican	Democratic	Other	Rep.-Dem. Plurality	% Total Vote Rep.	% Total Vote Dem.	% Major Vote Rep.	% Major Vote Dem.
ADAMS	2,949	777	2,120	52	1,343 D	26.3%	71.9%	26.8%	73.2%
ASHLAND	8,328	2,646	5,405	277	2,759 D	31.8%	64.9%	32.9%	67.1%
BARRON	11,701	3,852	7,413	436	3,561 D	32.9%	63.4%	34.2%	65.8%
BAYFIELD	5,335	2,035	2,981	319	946 D	38.1%	55.9%	40.6%	59.4%
BROWN	27,634	7,150	19,990	494	12,840 D	25.9%	72.3%	26.3%	73.7%
BUFFALO	5,028	1,711	3,252	65	1,541 D	34.0%	64.7%	34.5%	65.5%
BURNETT	3,833	1,281	2,437	115	1,156 D	33.4%	63.6%	34.5%	65.5%
CALUMET	6,785	1,213	5,485	87	4,272 D	17.9%	80.8%	18.1%	81.9%
CHIPPEWA	13,421	4,792	8,445	184	3,653 D	35.7%	62.9%	36.2%	63.8%
CLARK	11,999	3,132	8,372	495	5,240 D	26.1%	69.8%	27.2%	72.8%
COLUMBIA	13,641	4,970	8,455	216	3,485 D	36.4%	62.0%	37.0%	63.0%
CRAWFORD	6,768	1,943	4,754	71	2,811 D	28.7%	70.2%	29.0%	71.0%
DANE	47,823	19,083	26,841	1,899	7,758 D	39.9%	56.1%	41.6%	58.4%
DODGE	21,148	4,936	15,874	338	10,938 D	23.3%	75.1%	23.7%	76.3%
DOOR	6,734	2,486	4,149	97	1,663 D	36.9%	61.6%	37.5%	62.5%
DOUGLAS	18,949	7,888	9,715	1,346	1,827 D	41.6%	51.3%	44.8%	55.2%
DUNN	9,108	3,893	4,936	274	1,043 D	42.8%	54.2%	44.1%	55.9%
EAU CLAIRE	15,350	7,487	7,565	298	78 D	48.8%	49.3%	49.7%	50.3%
FLORENCE	1,744	714	965	65	251 D	40.9%	55.3%	42.5%	57.5%
FOND DU LAC	25,004	8,436	16,143	425	7,707 D	33.7%	64.6%	34.3%	65.7%
FOREST	3,413	768	2,595	50	1,827 D	22.5%	76.0%	22.8%	77.2%
GRANT	15,919	5,986	9,701	232	3,715 D	37.6%	60.9%	38.2%	61.8%
GREEN	8,758	3,190	5,406	162	2,216 D	36.4%	61.7%	37.1%	62.9%
GREEN LAKE	6,683	2,179	4,446	58	2,267 D	32.6%	66.5%	32.9%	67.1%
IOWA	7,856	3,113	4,621	122	1,508 D	39.6%	58.8%	40.3%	59.7%
IRON	3,523	891	2,338	294	1,447 D	25.3%	66.4%	27.6%	72.4%
JACKSON	5,919	1,983	3,813	123	1,830 D	33.5%	64.4%	34.2%	65.8%
JEFFERSON	16,448	5,062	11,230	156	6,168 D	30.8%	68.3%	31.1%	68.9%
JUNEAU	6,870	2,018	4,723	129	2,705 D	29.4%	68.7%	29.9%	70.1%
KENOSHA	23,903	7,307	14,373	2,223	7,066 D	30.6%	60.1%	33.7%	66.3%
KEWAUNEE	6,122	879	5,200	43	4,321 D	14.4%	84.9%	14.5%	85.5%
LA CROSSE	20,811	7,686	12,919	206	5,233 D	36.9%	62.1%	37.3%	62.7%
LAFAYETTE	8,213	3,246	4,886	81	1,640 D	39.5%	59.5%	39.9%	60.1%
LANGLADE	8,849	2,340	6,332	177	3,992 D	26.4%	71.6%	27.0%	73.0%
LINCOLN	8,272	2,958	5,093	221	2,135 D	35.8%	61.6%	36.7%	63.3%
MANITOWOC	20,805	4,573	15,696	536	11,123 D	22.0%	75.4%	22.6%	77.4%
MARATHON	24,601	6,210	17,744	647	11,534 D	25.2%	72.1%	25.9%	74.1%
MARINETTE	12,185	5,249	6,508	428	1,259 D	43.1%	53.4%	44.6%	55.4%
MARQUETTE	3,922	1,365	2,504	53	1,139 D	34.8%	63.8%	35.3%	64.7%
MENOMINEE									
MILWAUKEE	259,388	54,693	170,202	34,493	115,509 D	21.1%	65.6%	24.3%	75.7%
MONROE	9,954	3,022	6,757	175	3,735 D	30.4%	67.9%	30.9%	69.1%
OCONTO	9,465	2,915	6,440	110	3,525 D	30.8%	68.0%	31.2%	68.8%
ONEIDA	6,913	1,992	4,542	379	2,550 D	28.8%	65.7%	30.5%	69.5%
OUTAGAMIE	25,118	8,517	16,186	415	7,669 D	33.9%	64.4%	34.5%	65.5%
OZAUKEE	7,150	1,182	5,770	198	4,588 D	16.5%	80.6%	17.0%	83.0%
PEPIN	3,125	1,152	1,931	42	779 D	36.9%	61.8%	37.4%	62.6%
PIERCE	7,980	3,537	4,115	328	578 D	44.3%	51.6%	46.2%	53.8%
POLK	9,232	3,425	5,421	386	1,996 D	37.1%	58.7%	38.7%	61.3%
PORTAGE	12,820	3,434	9,195	191	5,761 D	26.8%	71.7%	27.2%	72.8%
PRICE	6,459	2,023	4,114	322	2,091 D	31.3%	63.7%	33.0%	67.0%
RACINE	33,097	10,754	19,960	2,383	9,206 D	32.5%	60.3%	35.0%	65.0%
RICHLAND	7,435	3,256	4,027	152	771 D	43.8%	54.2%	44.7%	55.3%
ROCK	30,008	16,825	12,612	571	4,213 R	56.1%	42.0%	57.2%	42.8%
RUSK	5,410	1,942	3,194	274	1,252 D	35.9%	59.0%	37.8%	62.2%
ST CROIX	10,698	4,059	6,374	265	2,315 D	37.9%	59.6%	38.9%	61.1%
SAUK	12,867	5,063	7,638	166	2,575 D	39.3%	59.4%	39.9%	60.1%
SAWYER	3,700	1,179	2,381	140	1,202 D	31.9%	64.4%	33.1%	66.9%
SHAWANO	10,367	2,450	7,593	324	5,143 D	23.6%	73.2%	24.4%	75.6%
SHEBOYGAN	26,651	7,454	18,029	1,178	10,575 D	28.0%	67.6%	29.3%	70.7%

WISCONSIN

PRESIDENT 1928

County	Total Vote	Republican	Democratic	Other	Rep.-Dem. Plurality	Total Vote Rep.	Total Vote Dem.	Major Vote Rep.	Major Vote Dem.
TAYLOR	4,849	2,648	2,095	106	553 R	54.6%	43.2%	55.8%	44.2%
TREMPEALEAU	8,613	5,596	2,963	54	2,633 R	65.0%	34.4%	65.4%	34.6%
VERNON	9,254	6,596	2,559	99	4,037 R	71.3%	27.7%	72.0%	28.0%
VILAS	2,753	1,609	1,083	61	526 R	58.4%	39.3%	59.8%	40.2%
WALWORTH	14,196	9,846	4,253	97	5,593 R	69.4%	30.0%	69.8%	30.2%
WASHBURN	4,138	2,898	1,192	48	1,706 R	70.0%	28.8%	70.9%	29.1%
WASHINGTON	10,122	4,163	5,827	132	1,664 D	41.1%	57.6%	41.7%	58.3%
WAUKESHA	20,311	12,218	7,846	247	4,372 R	60.2%	38.6%	60.9%	39.1%
WAUPACA	12,345	8,928	3,307	110	5,621 R	72.3%	26.8%	73.0%	27.0%
WAUSHARA	5,394	4,068	1,260	66	2,808 R	75.4%	23.4%	76.4%	23.6%
WINNEBAGO	26,501	16,191	9,995	315	6,196 R	61.1%	37.7%	61.8%	38.2%
WOOD	12,988	6,655	6,167	166	488 R	51.2%	47.5%	51.9%	48.1%
TOTAL	1,016,831	544,205	450,259	22,367	93,946 R	53.5%	44.3%	54.7%	45.3%

PRESIDENT 1932

County	Total Vote	Republican	Democratic	Other	Rep.-Dem. Plurality	Total Vote Rep.	Total Vote Dem.	Major Vote Rep.	Major Vote Dem.
TAYLOR	5,947	1,107	4,219	621	3,112 D	18.6%	70.9%	20.8%	79.2%
TREMPEALEAU	8,759	2,874	5,786	99	2,912 D	32.8%	66.1%	33.2%	66.8%
VERNON	9,057	2,979	5,939	139	2,960 D	32.9%	65.6%	33.4%	66.6%
VILAS	3,319	1,138	2,036	145	898 D	34.3%	61.3%	35.9%	64.1%
WALWORTH	14,852	7,858	6,790	204	1,068 R	52.9%	45.7%	53.6%	46.4%
WASHBURN	4,328	1,501	2,619	208	1,118 D	34.7%	60.5%	36.4%	63.6%
WASHINGTON	10,985	2,209	8,570	206	6,361 D	20.1%	78.0%	20.5%	79.5%
WAUKESHA	22,609	8,538	13,487	584	4,949 D	37.8%	59.7%	38.8%	61.2%
WAUPACA	13,536	5,082	8,179	275	3,097 D	37.5%	60.4%	38.3%	61.7%
WAUSHARA	5,738	2,541	3,073	124	532 D	44.3%	53.6%	45.3%	54.7%
WINNEBAGO	27,852	11,505	15,591	756	4,086 D	41.3%	56.0%	42.5%	57.5%
WOOD	13,621	4,100	9,215	306	5,115 D	30.1%	67.7%	30.8%	69.2%
TOTAL	1,114,814	347,741	707,410	59,663	359,669 D	31.2%	63.5%	33.0%	67.0%

WISCONSIN

PRESIDENT 1936

County	Total Vote	Republican	Democratic	Other	Rep.-Dem. Plurality		Pct. Total Rep.	Pct. Total Dem.	Pct. Major Rep.	Pct. Major Dem.
ADAMS	3,579	1,191	2,289	99	1,098	D	33.3%	64.0%	34.2%	65.8%
ASHLAND	8,681	2,439	5,904	338	3,465	D	28.1%	68.0%	29.2%	70.8%
BARRON	13,355	5,067	7,419	869	2,352	D	37.9%	55.6%	40.6%	59.4%
BAYFIELD	6,663	2,071	4,366	226	2,295	D	31.1%	65.5%	32.2%	67.8%
BROWN	31,077	8,433	21,417	1,227	12,984	D	27.1%	68.9%	28.3%	71.7%
BUFFALO	6,194	2,481	3,434	279	953	D	40.1%	55.4%	41.9%	58.1%
BURNETT	4,460	1,422	2,801	237	1,379	D	31.9%	62.8%	33.7%	66.3%
CALUMET	7,113	1,972	4,694	447	2,722	D	27.7%	66.0%	29.6%	70.4%
CHIPPEWA	14,796	5,760	7,854	1,182	2,094	D	38.9%	53.1%	42.3%	57.7%
CLARK	13,132	5,196	6,931	1,005	1,735	D	39.6%	52.8%	42.8%	57.2%
COLUMBIA	15,054	5,607	8,935	511	3,329	D	37.2%	59.4%	38.6%	61.4%
CRAWFORD	7,956	2,857	4,377	722	1,520	D	35.9%	55.0%	39.5%	60.5%
DANE	52,908	15,233	35,856	1,819	20,623	D	28.8%	67.8%	29.8%	70.2%
DODGE	22,599	6,829	14,782	988	7,953	D	30.2%	65.4%	31.6%	68.4%
DOOR	7,664	3,146	3,952	566	806	D	41.0%	51.6%	44.3%	55.7%
DOUGLAS	22,163	5,079	16,684	400	11,605	D	22.9%	75.2%	23.3%	76.7%
DUNN	10,975	4,570	5,619	786	1,049	D	41.6%	51.2%	44.9%	55.1%
EAU CLAIRE	17,260	6,802	10,065	393	3,263	D	39.4%	58.3%	40.3%	59.7%
FLORENCE	1,932	800	1,037	95	237	D	41.4%	53.7%	43.5%	56.5%
FOND DU LAC	25,931	9,179	14,821	1,931	5,642	D	35.4%	57.2%	38.2%	61.8%
FOREST	4,535	1,334	3,092	109	1,758	D	29.4%	68.2%	30.1%	69.9%
GRANT	17,503	7,196	9,170	1,137	1,974	D	41.1%	52.4%	44.0%	56.0%
GREEN	9,859	3,700	5,941	218	2,241	D	37.5%	60.3%	38.4%	61.6%
GREEN LAKE	6,877	2,926	3,840	111	914	D	42.5%	55.8%	43.2%	56.8%
IOWA	9,094	3,623	4,988	483	1,365	D	39.8%	54.8%	42.1%	57.9%
IRON	4,341	902	3,319	120	2,417	D	20.8%	76.5%	21.4%	78.6%
JACKSON	6,979	2,235	4,537	207	2,302	D	32.0%	65.0%	33.0%	67.0%
JEFFERSON	17,324	5,599	11,144	581	5,545	D	32.3%	64.3%	33.4%	66.6%
JUNEAU	8,152	3,084	4,544	524	1,460	D	37.8%	55.7%	40.4%	59.6%
KENOSHA	27,245	7,268	18,165	1,812	10,897	D	26.7%	66.7%	28.6%	71.4%
KEWAUNEE	6,717	1,527	4,971	219	3,444	D	22.7%	74.0%	23.5%	76.5%
LA CROSSE	22,840	7,558	14,455	827	6,897	D	33.1%	63.3%	34.3%	65.7%
LAFAYETTE	9,247	3,801	4,976	470	1,175	D	41.1%	53.8%	43.3%	56.7%
LANGLADE	8,684	2,635	5,837	212	3,202	D	30.3%	67.2%	31.1%	68.9%
LINCOLN	9,222	3,120	5,520	582	2,400	D	33.8%	59.9%	36.1%	63.9%
MANITOWOC	24,026	5,094	15,539	3,393	10,445	D	21.2%	64.7%	24.7%	75.3%
MARATHON	27,076	7,328	17,898	1,850	10,570	D	27.1%	66.1%	29.0%	71.0%
MARINETTE	14,272	4,938	8,884	450	3,946	D	34.6%	62.2%	35.7%	64.3%
MARQUETTE	3,917	1,957	1,812	148	145	R	50.0%	46.3%	51.9%	48.1%
MILWAUKEE	296,958	54,811	221,512	20,635	166,701	D	18.5%	74.6%	19.8%	80.2%
MONROE	12,008	4,695	6,491	822	1,796	D	39.1%	54.1%	42.0%	58.0%
OCONTO	11,034	3,774	6,729	531	2,955	D	34.2%	61.0%	35.9%	64.1%
ONEIDA	8,056	2,294	5,208	554	2,914	D	28.5%	64.6%	30.6%	69.4%
OUTAGAMIE	27,364	9,485	16,163	1,716	6,678	D	34.7%	59.1%	37.0%	63.0%
OZAUKEE	7,918	1,785	5,594	539	3,809	D	22.5%	70.6%	24.2%	75.8%
PEPIN	3,446	1,466	1,785	195	319	D	42.5%	51.8%	45.1%	54.9%
PIERCE	9,216	3,935	4,061	1,220	126	D	42.7%	44.1%	49.2%	50.8%
POLK	10,499	3,596	5,618	1,285	2,022	D	34.3%	53.5%	39.0%	61.0%
PORTAGE	14,844	3,969	10,576	299	6,607	D	26.7%	71.2%	27.3%	72.7%
PRICE	7,652	2,215	5,098	339	2,883	D	28.9%	66.6%	30.3%	69.7%
RACINE	37,771	10,850	24,474	2,447	13,624	D	28.7%	64.8%	30.7%	69.3%
RICHLAND	8,686	4,245	4,080	361	165	R	48.9%	47.0%	51.0%	49.0%
ROCK	33,729	14,693	17,991	1,045	3,298	D	43.6%	53.3%	45.0%	55.0%
RUSK	6,780	2,453	3,877	450	1,424	D	36.2%	57.2%	38.8%	61.2%
ST.CROIX	11,218	4,316	4,679	2,223	363	D	38.5%	41.7%	48.0%	52.0%
SAUK	14,812	5,626	8,355	831	2,729	D	38.0%	56.4%	40.2%	59.8%
SAWYER	4,733	1,726	2,834	173	1,108	D	36.5%	59.9%	37.9%	62.1%
SHAWANO	12,925	3,679	8,865	381	5,186	D	28.5%	68.6%	29.3%	70.7%
SHEBOYGAN	28,063	8,865	17,415	1,783	8,550	D	31.6%	62.1%	33.7%	66.3%

PRESIDENT 1940

County	Total Vote	Republican	Democratic	Other	Rep.-Dem. Plurality		Pct. Total Rep.	Pct. Total Dem.	Pct. Major Rep.	Pct. Major Dem.
ADAMS	3,730	1,818	1,883	29	65	D	48.7%	50.5%	49.1%	50.9%
ASHLAND	9,309	3,592	5,586	131	1,994	D	38.6%	60.0%	39.1%	60.9%
BARRON	14,227	7,806	6,183	238	1,623	R	54.9%	43.5%	55.8%	44.2%
BAYFIELD	7,342	2,829	4,387	126	1,558	D	38.5%	59.8%	39.2%	60.8%
BROWN	36,040	16,379	19,526	135	3,147	D	45.4%	54.2%	45.6%	54.4%
BUFFALO	6,675	4,056	2,516	103	1,540	R	60.8%	37.7%	61.7%	38.3%
BURNETT	5,105	2,510	2,513	82	3	D	49.2%	50.0%	50.0%	50.0%
CALUMET	7,725	5,327	2,324	74	3,003	R	69.0%	30.1%	69.6%	30.4%
CHIPPEWA	16,171	8,781	7,250	140	1,531	R	54.3%	44.8%	54.8%	45.2%
CLARK	14,420	9,501	4,683	236	4,818	R	65.9%	32.5%	67.0%	33.0%
COLUMBIA	15,387	8,260	7,021	106	1,239	R	53.7%	45.6%	54.1%	45.9%
CRAWFORD	8,293	4,667	3,595	31	1,072	R	56.3%	43.3%	56.5%	43.5%
DANE	62,787	21,845	40,531	611	18,686	D	34.8%	64.3%	35.0%	65.0%
DODGE	23,859	14,651	8,948	260	5,703	R	61.4%	37.5%	62.1%	37.9%
DOOR	8,260	5,461	2,750	49	2,711	R	66.1%	33.3%	66.5%	33.5%
DOUGLAS	23,515	7,695	15,548	272	7,853	D	32.7%	66.1%	33.1%	66.9%
DUNN	11,639	6,968	4,545	126	2,423	R	59.9%	39.0%	60.5%	39.5%
EAU CLAIRE	19,832	9,595	10,129	108	534	D	48.4%	51.1%	48.6%	51.4%
FLORENCE	2,011	1,008	980	23	28	R	50.1%	48.7%	50.7%	49.3%
FOND DU LAC	27,342	16,804	10,323	215	6,481	R	61.5%	37.8%	61.9%	38.1%
FOREST	4,639	1,672	2,951	16	1,279	D	36.0%	63.6%	36.2%	63.8%
GRANT	18,799	11,143	7,458	158	3,685	R	59.3%	39.7%	59.9%	40.1%
GREEN	10,364	5,711	4,565	88	1,146	R	55.1%	44.0%	55.6%	44.4%
GREEN LAKE	7,314	4,919	2,357	38	2,562	R	67.3%	32.2%	67.6%	32.4%
IOWA	9,140	4,978	4,025	137	953	R	54.5%	44.0%	55.3%	44.7%
IRON	5,269	1,672	3,525	72	1,853	D	31.7%	66.9%	32.2%	67.8%
JACKSON	7,780	3,741	3,975	64	234	D	48.1%	51.1%	48.5%	51.5%
JEFFERSON	18,190	10,178	7,842	149	2,336	R	56.0%	43.1%	56.5%	43.5%
JUNEAU	8,706	5,268	3,354	84	1,914	R	60.5%	38.5%	61.1%	38.9%
KENOSHA	29,777	12,182	17,174	421	4,992	D	40.9%	57.7%	41.5%	58.5%
KEWAUNEE	7,272	3,862	3,389	21	473	R	53.1%	46.6%	53.3%	46.7%
LA CROSSE	26,924	13,711	13,079	134	632	R	50.9%	48.6%	51.2%	48.8%
LAFAYETTE	9,419	5,059	4,315	45	744	R	53.7%	45.8%	54.0%	46.0%
LANGLADE	9,814	4,523	5,190	101	667	D	46.1%	52.9%	46.5%	53.5%
LINCOLN	9,984	5,812	3,951	221	1,861	R	58.2%	39.6%	59.5%	40.5%
MANITOWOC	26,126	12,616	13,142	368	526	D	48.3%	50.3%	49.0%	51.0%
MARATHON	26,469	12,224	13,764	481	1,540	D	46.2%	52.0%	47.0%	53.0%
MARINETTE	15,483	7,688	7,703	92	15	D	49.7%	49.8%	50.0%	50.0%
MARQUETTE	4,312	3,086	1,195	31	1,891	R	71.6%	27.7%	72.1%	27.9%
MILWAUKEE	351,197	131,120	209,861	10,216	78,741	D	37.3%	59.8%	38.5%	61.5%
MONROE	12,863	8,042	4,673	148	3,369	R	62.5%	36.3%	63.2%	36.8%
OCONTO	11,577	6,238	5,273	66	965	R	53.9%	45.5%	54.2%	45.8%
ONEIDA	9,146	3,694	5,375	77	1,681	D	40.4%	58.8%	40.7%	59.3%
OUTAGAMIE	30,067	17,733	12,168	166	5,565	R	59.0%	40.5%	59.3%	40.7%
OZAUKEE	8,723	4,913	3,662	148	1,251	R	56.3%	42.0%	57.3%	42.7%
PEPIN	3,522	2,272	1,194	56	1,078	R	64.5%	33.9%	65.6%	34.4%
PIERCE	9,999	6,624	3,259	116	3,365	R	66.2%	32.6%	67.0%	33.0%
POLK	11,248	6,031	4,979	238	1,052	R	53.6%	44.3%	54.8%	45.2%
PORTAGE	15,912	5,670	10,148	94	4,478	D	35.6%	63.8%	35.8%	64.2%
PRICE	8,093	3,879	4,042	172	163	D	47.9%	49.9%	49.0%	51.0%
RACINE	42,978	18,753	23,532	693	4,779	D	43.6%	54.8%	44.3%	55.7%
RICHLAND	9,139	5,527	3,524	88	2,003	R	60.5%	38.6%	61.1%	38.9%
ROCK	37,398	20,141	17,543	214	2,598	R	53.1%	46.9%	53.4%	46.6%
RUSK	7,160	3,484	3,578	98	94	D	48.7%	50.0%	49.3%	50.7%
ST.CROIX	11,876	6,857	4,898	121	1,959	R	57.7%	41.2%	58.3%	41.7%
SAUK	15,707	9,363	6,106	238	3,257	R	59.6%	38.9%	60.5%	39.5%
SAWYER	5,253	2,745	2,459	49	286	R	52.3%	46.8%	52.8%	47.2%
SHAWANO	11,774	6,377	5,241	156	1,136	R	54.2%	44.5%	54.9%	45.1%
SHEBOYGAN	31,747	15,305	15,800	642	495	D	48.2%	49.8%	49.2%	50.8%

WISCONSIN

PRESIDENT 1936

County	Total Vote	Republican	Democratic	Other	Rep.-Dem. Plurality	Total Vote Rep.	Total Vote Dem.	Major Vote Rep.	Major Vote Dem.
TAYLOR	6,989	1,758	4,721	510	2,963 D	25.2%	67.5%	27.1%	72.9%
TREMPEALEAU	9,832	3,339	5,929	564	2,590 D	34.0%	60.3%	36.0%	64.0%
VERNON	11,357	4,811	6,044	502	1,233 D	42.4%	53.2%	44.3%	55.7%
VILAS	4,145	1,298	2,559	288	1,261 D	31.3%	61.7%	33.7%	66.3%
WALWORTH	16,066	8,462	7,093	511	1,369 R	52.7%	44.1%	54.4%	45.6%
WASHBURN	5,215	1,650	3,220	345	1,570 D	31.6%	61.7%	33.9%	66.1%
WASHINGTON	12,092	3,589	7,129	1,374	3,540 D	29.7%	59.0%	33.5%	66.5%
WAUKESHA	25,194	8,921	14,982	1,291	6,061 D	35.4%	59.5%	37.3%	62.7%
WAUPACA	14,561	6,680	6,920	961	240 D	45.9%	47.5%	49.1%	50.9%
WAUSHARA	6,421	3,302	2,636	483	666 R	51.4%	41.1%	55.6%	44.4%
WINNEBAGO	31,621	11,679	18,522	1,420	6,843 D	36.9%	58.6%	38.7%	61.3%
WOOD	15,953	4,902	9,982	1,069	5,080 D	30.7%	62.6%	32.9%	67.1%
TOTAL	1,258,560	380,828	802,984	74,748	422,156 D	30.3%	63.8%	32.2%	67.8%

PRESIDENT 1940

County	Total Vote	Republican	Democratic	Other	Rep.-Dem. Plurality	Total Vote Rep.	Total Vote Dem.	Major Vote Rep.	Major Vote Dem.
TAYLOR	7,678	3,668	3,771	239	103 D	47.8%	49.1%	49.3%	50.7%
TREMPEALEAU	10,579	5,319	5,175	85	144 R	50.3%	48.9%	50.7%	49.3%
VERNON	12,492	6,614	5,776	102	838 R	52.9%	46.2%	53.4%	46.6%
VILAS	4,798	2,251	2,470	77	219 D	46.9%	51.5%	47.7%	52.3%
WALWORTH	17,154	11,594	5,449	111	6,145 R	67.6%	31.8%	68.0%	32.0%
WASHBURN	5,762	2,805	2,901	56	96 D	48.7%	50.3%	49.2%	50.8%
WASHINGTON	13,380	8,501	4,683	196	3,818 R	63.5%	35.0%	64.5%	35.5%
WAUKESHA	29,943	16,726	12,859	358	3,867 R	55.9%	42.9%	56.5%	43.5%
WAUPACA	15,866	11,099	4,616	151	6,483 R	70.0%	29.1%	70.6%	29.4%
WAUSHARA	6,685	4,872	1,747	66	3,125 R	72.9%	26.1%	73.6%	26.4%
WINNEBAGO	34,535	18,697	15,570	268	3,127 R	54.1%	45.1%	54.6%	45.4%
WOOD	18,402	9,654	8,574	174	1,080 R	52.5%	46.6%	53.0%	47.0%
TOTAL	1,405,522	679,206	704,821	21,495	25,615 D	48.3%	50.1%	49.1%	50.9%

WISCONSIN

PRESIDENT 1944

County	Total Vote	Republican	Democratic	Other	Rep.-Dem. Plurality	Total Vote Rep.	Total Vote Dem.	Major Vote Rep.	Major Vote Dem.
ADAMS	3,072	1,579	1,478	15	101 R	51.4%	48.1%	51.7%	48.3%
ASHLAND	7,839	3,183	4,609	47	1,426 D	40.6%	58.8%	40.8%	59.2%
BARRON	12,823	7,137	5,585	101	1,552 R	55.7%	43.6%	56.1%	43.9%
BAYFIELD	5,890	2,475	3,352	53	887 D	42.0%	57.1%	42.4%	57.6%
BROWN	35,426	17,762	17,576	88	186 R	50.1%	49.6%	50.3%	49.7%
BUFFALO	5,406	3,416	1,948	42	1,468 R	63.2%	36.0%	63.7%	36.3%
BURNETT	4,019	2,119	1,868	32	251 R	52.7%	46.5%	53.1%	46.9%
CALUMET	7,626	5,611	1,966	49	3,645 R	73.6%	25.8%	74.1%	25.9%
CHIPPEWA	14,351	7,691	6,567	93	1,124 R	53.6%	45.8%	53.9%	46.1%
CLARK	12,657	7,948	4,612	97	3,336 R	62.3%	36.4%	63.3%	36.7%
COLUMBIA	13,924	7,867	5,997	60	1,870 R	56.5%	43.1%	56.7%	43.3%
CRAWFORD	7,256	4,199	3,130	22	1,069 R	57.1%	42.4%	57.3%	42.7%
DANE	60,651	23,021	37,076	554	14,055 D	38.0%	61.1%	38.3%	61.7%
DODGE	21,883	14,102	7,667	114	6,435 R	64.4%	35.0%	64.8%	35.2%
DOOR	8,305	5,668	2,599	38	3,069 R	68.2%	31.3%	68.6%	31.4%
DOUGLAS	20,263	7,132	12,985	146	5,853 D	35.2%	64.1%	35.5%	64.5%
DUNN	9,905	5,980	3,853	72	2,127 R	60.4%	38.9%	60.8%	39.2%
EAU CLAIRE	18,520	9,470	8,962	88	508 R	51.1%	48.4%	51.4%	48.6%
FLORENCE	1,678	765	897	16	132 D	45.6%	53.5%	46.0%	54.0%
FOND DU LAC	26,306	16,785	9,378	143	7,407 R	63.8%	35.6%	64.2%	35.8%
FOREST	3,840	1,391	2,436	13	1,045 D	36.2%	63.4%	36.3%	63.7%
GRANT	16,345	10,226	6,091	28	4,135 R	62.6%	37.3%	62.7%	37.3%
GREEN	9,699	5,556	4,101	42	1,455 R	57.3%	42.3%	57.5%	42.5%
GREEN LAKE	6,784	4,571	2,190	23	2,381 R	67.4%	32.3%	67.6%	32.4%
IOWA	8,228	4,608	3,585	35	1,023 R	56.0%	43.6%	56.2%	43.8%
IRON	4,268	1,345	2,894	29	1,549 D	31.5%	67.8%	31.7%	68.3%
JACKSON	6,256	3,182	3,040	34	142 R	50.9%	48.6%	51.1%	48.9%
JEFFERSON	17,317	10,245	6,988	84	3,257 R	59.2%	40.4%	59.4%	40.6%
JUNEAU	7,637	4,733	2,857	47	1,876 R	62.0%	37.4%	62.4%	37.6%
KENOSHA	31,121	12,436	18,325	360	5,889 D	40.0%	58.9%	40.4%	59.6%
KEWAUNEE	6,780	4,153	2,611	16	1,542 R	61.3%	38.5%	61.4%	38.6%
LA CROSSE	25,103	12,784	12,247	72	537 R	50.9%	48.8%	51.1%	48.9%
LAFAYETTE	8,147	4,441	3,696	30	745 R	54.3%	45.4%	54.5%	45.5%
LANGLADE	8,369	4,036	4,310	23	274 D	48.2%	51.5%	48.4%	51.6%
LINCOLN	8,598	5,564	2,938	96	2,626 R	64.7%	34.2%	65.4%	34.6%
MANITOWOC	26,247	14,047	11,949	251	2,098 R	53.5%	45.5%	54.0%	46.0%
MARATHON	29,477	15,782	13,192	503	2,590 R	53.5%	44.8%	54.5%	45.5%
MARINETTE	13,712	7,159	6,483	70	676 R	52.2%	47.3%	52.5%	47.5%
MARQUETTE	3,883	2,853	1,016	14	1,837 R	73.5%	26.2%	73.7%	26.3%
MENOMINEE									
MILWAUKEE	354,830	142,448	205,282	7,100	62,834 D	40.1%	57.9%	41.0%	59.0%
MONROE	11,354	7,277	4,013	64	3,264 R	64.1%	35.3%	64.5%	35.5%
OCONTO	10,322	5,923	4,348	51	1,575 R	57.4%	42.1%	57.7%	42.3%
ONEIDA	7,383	3,253	4,076	54	823 D	44.1%	55.2%	44.4%	55.6%
OUTAGAMIE	28,389	18,294	9,955	140	8,339 R	64.4%	35.1%	64.8%	35.2%
OZAUKEE	9,323	5,655	3,579	89	2,076 R	60.7%	38.4%	61.2%	38.8%
PEPIN	2,959	1,902	1,029	28	873 R	64.3%	34.8%	64.9%	35.1%
PIERCE	8,233	5,137	3,033	63	2,104 R	62.4%	36.8%	62.9%	37.1%
POLK	8,265	4,489	3,649	127	840 R	53.5%	46.0%	54.3%	45.7%
PORTAGE	14,125	5,405	8,678	42	3,273 D	38.3%	61.4%	38.4%	61.6%
PRICE	6,819	3,258	3,515	46	257 D	47.8%	51.5%	48.1%	51.9%
RACINE	44,325	18,220	25,697	408	7,477 D	41.1%	58.0%	41.5%	58.5%
RICHLAND	8,226	5,088	3,109	29	1,979 R	61.9%	37.8%	62.1%	37.9%
ROCK	35,376	18,477	16,766	133	1,711 R	52.2%	47.4%	52.4%	47.6%
RUSK	6,388	3,092	3,238	58	146 D	48.4%	50.7%	48.8%	51.2%
ST CROIX	10,678	5,660	4,930	88	730 R	53.0%	46.2%	53.4%	46.6%
SAUK	15,546	9,751	5,690	105	4,061 R	62.7%	36.6%	63.2%	36.3%
SAWYER	4,400	2,421	1,947	32	474 R	55.0%	44.2%	55.4%	44.5%
SHAWANO	12,811	8,732	4,015	64	4,717 R	68.2%	31.3%	68.5%	31.5%
SHEBOYGAN	30,938	15,291	15,062	585	229 R	49.4%	48.7%	50.4%	49.6%

PRESIDENT 1948

County	Total Vote	Republican	Democratic	Other	Rep.-Dem. Plurality	Total Vote Rep.	Total Vote Dem.	Major Vote Rep.	Major Vote Dem.
ADAMS	2,761	1,259	1,419	83	160 D	45.6%	51.4%	47.0%	53.0%
ASHLAND	7,509	3,135	4,110	264	975 D	41.7%	54.7%	43.3%	56.7%
BARRON	12,016	5,516	6,148	352	632 D	45.9%	51.2%	47.3%	52.7%
BAYFIELD	5,835	2,338	3,081	416	743 D	40.1%	52.8%	43.1%	56.9%
BROWN	36,558	17,729	18,449	380	720 D	48.5%	50.5%	49.0%	51.0%
BUFFALO	4,993	2,350	2,563	80	213 D	47.1%	51.3%	47.8%	52.2%
BURNETT	3,899	1,590	2,177	132	587 D	40.8%	55.8%	42.2%	57.8%
CALUMET	6,909	4,185	2,662	62	1,523 R	60.6%	38.5%	61.1%	38.9%
CHIPPEWA	14,102	6,146	7,702	254	1,556 D	43.6%	54.6%	44.4%	55.6%
CLARK	11,175	5,885	4,840	450	1,045 R	52.7%	43.3%	54.9%	45.1%
COLUMBIA	12,169	6,406	5,615	148	791 R	52.6%	46.1%	53.3%	46.7%
CRAWFORD	7,185	3,465	3,639	81	174 D	48.2%	50.6%	48.8%	51.2%
DANE	60,664	22,934	35,486	2,244	12,552 D	37.8%	58.5%	39.3%	60.7%
DODGE	19,286	10,831	8,212	243	2,619 R	56.2%	42.6%	56.9%	43.1%
DOOR	7,459	4,911	2,440	108	2,471 R	65.8%	32.7%	66.8%	33.2%
DOUGLAS	19,248	6,252	12,278	718	6,026 D	32.5%	63.8%	33.7%	66.3%
DUNN	9,382	4,319	4,894	169	575 D	46.0%	52.2%	46.9%	53.1%
EAU CLAIRE	18,042	7,825	9,971	246	2,146 D	43.4%	55.3%	44.0%	56.0%
FLORENCE	1,758	756	885	117	129 D	43.0%	50.3%	46.1%	53.9%
FOND DU LAC	23,083	13,760	8,904	419	4,856 R	59.6%	38.6%	60.7%	39.3%
FOREST	3,563	1,251	2,208	104	957 D	35.1%	62.0%	36.2%	63.8%
GRANT	15,089	8,299	6,575	215	1,724 R	55.0%	43.6%	55.8%	44.2%
GREEN	8,398	4,403	3,881	114	522 R	52.4%	46.2%	53.2%	46.8%
GREEN LAKE	5,729	3,939	1,722	68	2,217 R	68.8%	30.1%	69.6%	30.4%
IOWA	7,794	3,745	3,917	132	172 D	48.0%	50.3%	48.9%	51.1%
IRON	4,209	1,281	2,665	263	1,384 D	30.4%	63.3%	32.5%	67.5%
JACKSON	5,563	2,553	2,921	89	368 D	45.9%	52.5%	46.6%	53.4%
JEFFERSON	15,728	8,244	7,256	228	988 R	52.4%	46.1%	53.2%	46.8%
JUNEAU	6,809	3,793	2,889	127	904 R	55.7%	42.4%	56.8%	43.2%
KENOSHA	32,109	12,780	17,987	1,342	5,207 D	39.8%	56.0%	41.5%	58.5%
KEWAUNEE	6,476	3,646	2,746	86	900 R	56.3%	42.4%	57.0%	43.0%
LA CROSSE	23,260	10,525	12,345	390	1,820 D	45.2%	53.0%	46.0%	54.0%
LAFAYETTE	7,104	3,288	3,740	76	452 D	46.3%	52.6%	46.8%	53.2%
LANGLADE	8,081	3,441	4,346	294	905 D	42.6%	53.8%	44.2%	55.8%
LINCOLN	7,894	4,339	3,368	187	971 R	55.0%	42.7%	56.3%	43.7%
MANITOWOC	24,863	10,947	13,401	515	2,454 D	44.0%	53.9%	45.0%	55.0%
MARATHON	26,079	11,494	13,898	687	2,404 D	40.9%	56.6%	42.0%	58.0%
MARINETTE	12,565	5,869	6,468	228	599 D	46.7%	51.5%	47.6%	52.4%
MARQUETTE	3,166	2,033	1,095	38	938 R	64.2%	34.6%	65.0%	35.0%
MENOMINEE									
MILWAUKEE	342,910	138,672	187,637	16,601	48,965 D	40.4%	54.7%	42.5%	57.5%
MONROE	10,490	5,347	4,970	173	377 R	51.0%	47.4%	51.8%	48.2%
OCONTO	9,247	4,865	4,269	113	596 R	52.6%	46.2%	53.2%	46.8%
ONEIDA	8,015	3,709	4,061	245	352 D	46.5%	50.2%	47.7%	52.3%
OUTAGAMIE	27,672	16,161	11,253	278	4,928 R	58.4%	40.6%	59.0%	41.0%
OZAUKEE	9,208	4,866	4,159	183	707 R	52.8%	45.2%	53.9%	46.1%
PEPIN	2,764	1,333	1,381	50	48 D	48.2%	49.9%	49.1%	50.9%
PIERCE	8,306	3,753	4,395	158	642 D	45.2%	52.9%	46.1%	53.9%
POLK	9,572	3,974	5,330	268	1,356 D	41.5%	55.7%	42.7%	57.3%
PORTAGE	13,791	5,424	8,154	213	2,730 D	39.3%	59.1%	39.9%	60.1%
PRICE	5,785	2,952	3,373	460	421 D	43.5%	49.7%	46.7%	53.3%
RACINE	43,797	19,029	23,266	1,502	4,237 D	43.4%	53.1%	45.0%	55.0%
RICHLAND	6,906	3,636	2,990	80	846 R	55.5%	43.3%	56.2%	43.8%
ROCK	33,692	17,068	16,150	474	918 R	50.7%	47.9%	51.4%	48.6%
RUSK	6,239	2,623	3,441	175	818 D	42.0%	55.1%	43.3%	56.7%
ST CROIX	10,701	4,326	6,173	202	1,847 D	40.4%	57.7%	41.2%	58.8%
SAUK	13,307	7,140	5,831	336	1,309 R	53.7%	43.8%	55.0%	45.0%
SAWYER	4,559	2,257	2,177	125	80 R	49.5%	47.7%	50.9%	49.1%
SHAWANO	10,659	6,286	4,192	181	2,094 R	59.0%	39.3%	60.0%	40.0%
SHEBOYGAN	28,942	12,459	15,339	1,144	2,880 D	43.0%	53.0%	44.8%	55.2%

WISCONSIN

PRESIDENT 1944

County	Total Vote	Republican	Democratic	Other	Rep.-Dem. Plurality	Percentage Total Vote Rep.	Dem.	Major Vote Rep.	Dem.
TAYLOR	6,621	3,194	3,215	212	21 D	48.2%	48.6%	49.8%	50.2%
TREMPEALEAU	9,242	4,719	4,496	27	223 R	51.1%	48.6%	51.2%	48.8%
VERNON	11,121	5,676	5,409	36	267 R	51.0%	48.6%	51.2%	48.8%
VILAS	4,132	2,021	2,079	32	58 D	48.9%	50.3%	49.3%	50.7%
WALWORTH	16,683	10,901	5,696	86	5,205 R	65.3%	34.1%	65.7%	34.3%
WASHBURN	4,533	2,441	2,059	33	382 R	53.8%	45.4%	54.2%	45.8%
WASHINGTON	12,847	8,921	3,840	86	5,081 R	69.4%	29.9%	69.9%	30.1%
WAUKESHA	31,326	17,995	13,038	293	4,957 R	57.4%	41.6%	58.0%	42.0%
WAUPACA	15,442	11,495	3,879	68	7,616 R	74.4%	25.1%	74.8%	25.2%
WAUSHARA	6,189	4,675	1,485	29	3,190 R	75.5%	24.0%	75.9%	24.1%
WINNEBAGO	32,420	19,310	12,841	269	6,469 R	59.6%	39.6%	60.1%	39.9%
WOOD	16,520	9,569	6,861	90	2,708 R	57.9%	41.5%	58.2%	41.8%
TOTAL	1,339,152	674,532	650,413	14,207	24,119 R	50.4%	48.6%	50.9%	49.1%

PRESIDENT 1948

County	Total Vote	Republican	Democratic	Other	Rep.-Dem. Plurality	Percentage Total Vote Rep.	Dem.	Major Vote Rep.	Dem.
TAYLOR	6,124	2,579	3,184	361	605 D	42.1%	52.0%	44.8%	55.2%
TREMPEALEAU	8,463	3,650	4,711	102	1,061 D	43.1%	55.7%	43.7%	56.3%
VERNON	9,470	4,139	5,226	105	1,087 D	43.7%	55.2%	44.2%	55.8%
VILAS	4,571	2,665	1,688	218	977 R	58.3%	36.9%	61.2%	38.8%
WALWORTH	16,151	10,509	5,377	265	5,132 R	65.1%	33.3%	66.2%	33.8%
WASHBURN	4,925	2,059	2,708	158	649 D	41.8%	55.0%	43.2%	56.8%
WASHINGTON	11,565	6,876	4,495	194	2,381 R	59.5%	38.9%	60.5%	39.5%
WAUKESHA	31,950	17,324	13,952	674	3,372 R	54.2%	43.7%	55.4%	44.6%
WAUPACA	12,982	8,764	4,020	198	4,744 R	67.5%	31.0%	68.6%	31.4%
WAUSHARA	5,164	3,594	1,430	140	2,164 R	69.6%	27.7%	71.5%	28.5%
WINNEBAGO	31,110	17,165	13,116	829	4,049 R	55.2%	42.2%	56.7%	43.3%
WOOD	16,247	8,073	7,999	175	74 R	49.7%	49.2%	50.2%	49.8%
TOTAL	1,276,800	590,959	647,310	38,531	56,351 D	46.3%	50.7%	47.7%	52.3%

WISCONSIN

PRESIDENT 1952

County	Total Vote	Republican	Democratic	Other	Rep.-Dem. Plurality	Total Vote Rep.	Total Vote Dem.	Major Vote Rep.	Major Vote Dem.
ADAMS	3,457	2,259	1,180	18	1,079 R	65.3%	34.1%	65.7%	34.3%
ASHLAND	8,320	4,451	3,828	41	623 R	53.5%	46.0%	53.8%	46.2%
BARRON	14,981	10,013	4,902	66	5,111 R	66.3%	32.7%	67.1%	32.9%
BAYFIELD	6,107	3,419	2,616	72	803 R	56.0%	42.8%	56.7%	43.3%
BROWN	44,836	30,400	14,342	94	16,058 R	67.8%	32.0%	67.9%	32.1%
BUFFALO	6,232	4,233	1,988	11	2,245 R	67.9%	31.9%	68.0%	32.0%
BURNETT	4,440	2,683	1,741	16	942 R	60.4%	39.2%	60.6%	39.4%
CALUMET	8,615	6,640	1,970	5	4,670 R	77.1%	22.9%	77.1%	22.9%
CHIPPEWA	17,854	11,429	6,380	45	5,049 R	64.0%	35.7%	64.2%	35.8%
CLARK	13,116	9,406	3,652	58	5,754 R	71.7%	27.8%	72.0%	28.0%
COLUMBIA	16,425	11,133	5,272	20	5,861 R	67.8%	32.1%	67.9%	32.1%
CRAWFORD	7,588	5,323	2,256	9	3,067 R	70.1%	29.7%	70.2%	29.8%
DANE	76,927	38,724	37,987	216	737 R	50.3%	49.4%	50.5%	49.5%
DODGE	26,336	19,298	7,001	37	12,297 R	73.3%	26.6%	73.4%	26.6%
DOOR	9,430	7,621	1,790	19	5,831 R	80.8%	19.0%	81.0%	19.0%
DOUGLAS	21,313	9,677	11,538	98	1,861 D	45.4%	54.1%	45.6%	54.4%
DUNN	11,094	7,475	3,593	26	3,882 R	67.5%	32.4%	67.6%	32.5%
EAU CLAIRE	23,658	14,069	9,554	35	4,515 R	59.5%	40.4%	59.6%	40.4%
FLORENCE	1,963	1,147	809	7	338 R	58.4%	41.2%	58.6%	41.4%
FOND DU LAC	30,625	22,794	7,724	107	15,070 R	74.4%	25.2%	74.7%	25.3%
FOREST	3,793	1,990	1,791	12	199 R	52.5%	47.2%	52.6%	47.4%
GRANT	18,556	14,327	4,197	32	10,130 R	77.2%	22.6%	77.3%	22.7%
GREEN	11,281	7,949	3,326	6	4,623 R	70.5%	29.5%	70.5%	29.5%
GREEN LAKE	7,717	6,117	1,590	10	4,527 R	79.3%	20.6%	79.4%	20.6%
IOWA	8,952	6,211	2,722	19	3,489 R	69.4%	30.4%	69.5%	30.5%
IRON	4,416	1,733	2,662	21	929 D	39.2%	60.3%	39.4%	60.6%
JACKSON	7,071	4,235	2,819	17	1,416 R	59.9%	39.9%	60.0%	40.0%
JEFFERSON	20,743	13,884	6,827	32	7,057 R	66.9%	32.9%	67.0%	33.0%
JUNEAU	8,164	5,978	2,163	23	3,815 R	73.2%	26.6%	73.4%	26.6%
KENOSHA	38,827	18,917	19,768	142	851 D	48.7%	50.9%	48.9%	51.1%
KEWAUNEE	8,482	6,482	1,972	28	4,510 R	76.4%	23.2%	76.7%	23.3%
LA CROSSE	31,132	19,271	11,808	53	7,463 R	61.9%	37.9%	62.0%	38.0%
LAFAYETTE	8,653	5,731	2,905	17	2,826 R	66.2%	33.6%	66.4%	33.6%
LANGLADE	9,269	5,841	3,371	57	2,470 R	63.0%	36.4%	63.4%	36.6%
LINCOLN	10,007	6,877	3,092	38	3,785 R	68.7%	30.9%	69.0%	31.0%
MANITOWOC	30,901	18,950	11,879	72	7,071 R	61.3%	38.4%	61.5%	38.5%
MARATHON	35,373	20,702	14,541	130	6,161 R	58.5%	41.1%	58.7%	41.3%
MARINETTE	15,087	9,313	5,727	47	3,586 R	61.7%	38.0%	61.9%	38.1%
MARQUETTE	4,218	3,379	835	4	2,544 R	80.1%	19.8%	80.2%	19.8%
MENOMINEE									
MILWAUKEE	426,006	219,477	204,474	2,055	15,003 R	51.5%	48.0%	51.8%	48.2%
MONROE	12,495	8,744	3,717	34	5,027 R	70.0%	29.7%	70.2%	29.8%
OCONTO	11,220	7,807	3,382	31	4,425 R	69.6%	30.1%	69.8%	30.2%
ONEIDA	10,062	6,224	3,808	30	2,416 R	61.9%	37.8%	62.0%	38.0%
OUTAGAMIE	36,020	26,603	9,373	44	17,230 R	73.9%	26.0%	73.9%	26.1%
OZAUKEE	12,939	8,665	4,241	33	4,424 R	67.0%	32.8%	67.1%	32.9%
PEPIN	3,255	2,348	896	11	1,452 R	72.1%	27.5%	72.4%	27.6%
PIERCE	10,021	6,763	3,241	17	3,522 R	67.5%	32.3%	67.6%	32.4%
POLK	11,282	6,966	4,274	42	2,692 R	61.7%	37.9%	62.0%	38.0%
PORTAGE	16,087	8,499	7,537	51	962 R	52.8%	46.9%	53.0%	47.0%
PRICE	7,491	4,376	3,048	67	1,328 R	58.4%	40.7%	58.9%	41.1%
RACINE	56,049	30,628	25,241	180	5,387 R	54.6%	45.0%	54.8%	45.2%
RICHLAND	8,875	6,605	2,260	10	4,345 R	74.5%	25.5%	74.5%	25.5%
ROCK	43,065	27,837	15,183	45	12,654 R	64.6%	35.3%	64.7%	35.3%
RUSK	6,964	4,134	2,777	53	1,357 R	59.4%	39.9%	59.8%	40.2%
ST CROIX	12,726	7,607	5,094	25	2,513 R	59.8%	40.1%	59.9%	40.1%
SAUK	17,666	12,347	5,267	52	7,080 R	69.9%	29.8%	70.1%	29.9%
SAWYER	4,694	3,146	1,527	21	1,619 R	67.0%	32.5%	67.3%	32.7%
SHAWANO	14,501	11,131	3,334	36	7,797 R	76.0%	23.0%	77.0%	23.3%
SHEBOYGAN	37,432	22,084	15,136	212	6,948 R	59.0%	40.4%	59.3%	40.7%

PRESIDENT 1956

County	Total Vote	Republican	Democratic	Other	Rep.-Dem. Plurality	Total Vote Rep.	Total Vote Dem.	Major Vote Rep.	Major Vote Dem.
ADAMS	3,117	1,854	1,244	19	610 R	59.5%	39.9%	59.8%	40.2%
ASHLAND	7,819	4,121	3,677	21	444 R	52.7%	47.0%	52.8%	47.2%
BARRON	14,126	8,634	5,419	73	3,215 R	61.1%	38.4%	61.4%	38.6%
BAYFIELD	5,806	3,096	2,691	19	405 R	53.3%	46.3%	53.5%	46.5%
BROWN	46,808	32,878	13,642	288	19,236 R	70.2%	29.1%	70.7%	29.3%
BUFFALO	5,661	3,387	2,266	8	1,121 R	59.8%	40.0%	59.9%	40.1%
BURNETT	4,198	2,198	1,986	14	212 R	52.4%	47.3%	52.5%	47.5%
CALUMET	8,308	6,166	2,099	43	4,067 R	74.2%	25.3%	74.6%	25.4%
CHIPPEWA	16,461	9,781	6,617	63	3,164 R	59.4%	40.2%	59.6%	40.4%
CLARK	12,754	7,941	4,765	48	3,176 R	62.3%	37.4%	62.5%	37.5%
COLUMBIA	15,330	10,120	5,158	52	4,962 R	66.0%	33.6%	66.2%	33.8%
CRAWFORD	6,681	4,123	2,522	36	1,601 R	61.7%	37.7%	62.0%	38.0%
DANE	76,213	38,955	36,891	367	2,064 R	51.1%	48.4%	51.4%	48.6%
DODGE	24,366	17,569	6,704	93	10,865 R	72.1%	27.5%	72.4%	27.6%
DOOR	8,622	6,722	1,859	41	4,863 R	78.0%	21.6%	78.3%	21.7%
DOUGLAS	20,502	9,183	11,276	43	2,093 D	44.8%	55.0%	44.9%	55.1%
DUNN	10,604	6,401	4,189	14	2,212 R	60.4%	39.5%	60.4%	39.6%
EAU CLAIRE	22,439	13,122	9,276	41	3,846 R	58.5%	41.3%	58.6%	41.3%
FLORENCE	1,731	1,003	723	5	280 R	57.9%	41.8%	58.1%	41.9%
FOND DU LAC	29,666	21,496	7,940	230	13,556 R	72.5%	26.8%	73.0%	27.0%
FOREST	3,575	2,039	1,527	9	512 R	57.0%	42.7%	57.2%	42.8%
GRANT	16,958	11,648	5,208	102	6,440 R	68.7%	30.7%	69.1%	30.9%
GREEN	10,779	7,114	3,614	51	3,500 R	66.0%	33.5%	66.3%	33.7%
GREEN LAKE	7,113	5,441	1,643	29	3,798 R	76.5%	23.1%	76.8%	23.2%
IOWA	8,417	5,201	3,176	40	2,025 R	61.8%	37.7%	62.1%	37.9%
IRON	4,176	1,930	2,226	20	296 D	46.4%	53.3%	46.4%	53.6%
JACKSON	6,378	3,614	2,755	9	859 R	56.7%	43.2%	56.7%	43.4%
JEFFERSON	19,931	13,357	6,452	122	6,905 R	67.0%	32.4%	67.4%	32.6%
JUNEAU	7,598	5,135	2,428	35	2,707 R	67.6%	32.0%	67.9%	32.1%
KENOSHA	38,796	21,367	17,094	335	4,273 R	55.1%	44.1%	55.6%	44.4%
KEWAUNEE	7,509	5,106	2,364	39	2,742 R	68.0%	31.5%	68.4%	31.6%
LA CROSSE	29,622	18,264	11,258	100	7,006 R	61.7%	38.0%	61.9%	38.1%
LAFAYETTE	7,978	4,733	3,212	33	1,521 R	59.3%	40.3%	59.6%	40.4%
LANGLADE	7,841	5,004	2,804	33	2,200 R	64.1%	35.5%	64.1%	35.9%
LINCOLN	9,343	6,329	2,880	134	3,449 R	67.7%	30.8%	68.7%	31.3%
MANITOWOC	29,199	18,078	10,800	321	7,278 R	61.9%	37.0%	62.6%	37.4%
MARATHON	38,051	22,586	15,301	164	7,285 R	59.4%	40.2%	59.6%	40.4%
MARINETTE	14,060	8,874	5,113	73	3,761 R	63.4%	36.4%	63.6%	36.4%
MARQUETTE									
MENOMINEE	3,785	2,796	975	14	1,821 R	73.9%	25.8%	74.1%	25.9%
MILWAUKEE	407,318	227,253	177,286	2,779	49,967 R	56.2%	43.5%	56.2%	43.8%
MONROE	11,811	7,460	4,311	40	3,149 R	63.2%	36.5%	63.4%	36.6%
OCONTO	10,525	6,836	3,632	57	3,204 R	65.0%	34.5%	65.3%	34.7%
ONEIDA	9,648	6,261	3,328	59	2,933 R	65.0%	34.5%	65.3%	34.7%
OUTAGAMIE	34,077	26,090	7,725	262	18,365 R	76.6%	22.7%	77.2%	22.8%
OZAUKEE	14,086	9,808	4,139	139	5,669 R	69.6%	29.4%	70.3%	29.7%
PEPIN	3,015	1,975	1,040		935 R	65.5%	34.5%	65.5%	34.5%
PIERCE	9,458	5,782	3,644	32	2,138 R	61.1%	38.5%	61.3%	38.7%
POLK	10,906	5,894	4,985	27	909 R	54.1%	45.7%	54.3%	45.7%
PORTAGE	15,386	8,320	7,010	56	1,310 R	54.1%	45.6%	54.3%	45.7%
PRICE	6,848	4,028	2,778	42	1,250 R	58.8%	40.6%	59.2%	40.8%
RACINE	54,919	31,968	22,646	305	9,322 R	58.2%	41.2%	58.5%	41.5%
RICHLAND	7,874	5,062	2,783	29	2,279 R	64.3%	35.3%	64.5%	35.5%
ROCK	42,987	28,980	13,834	173	15,146 R	67.4%	32.2%	67.7%	32.3%
RUSK	6,395	3,433	2,929	33	504 R	53.7%	45.8%	54.0%	46.0%
ST CROIX	12,484	6,956	5,499	29	1,457 R	55.7%	44.0%	55.8%	44.2%
SAUK	16,016	10,644	5,292	80	5,352 R	66.5%	33.0%	66.8%	33.2%
SAWYER	4,374	2,823	1,520	31	1,303 R	64.5%	34.8%	65.0%	35.0%
SHAWANO	13,122	9,388	3,675	59	5,713 R	71.5%	28.0%	71.9%	28.1%
SHEBOYGAN	36,852	22,077	14,540	235	7,537 R	59.9%	39.5%	60.3%	39.7%

WISCONSIN

PRESIDENT 1952

County	Total Vote	Republican	Democratic	Other	Rep.-Dem. Plurality	Total Vote Rep.	Total Vote Dem.	Major Vote Rep.	Major Vote Dem.
TAYLOR	7,710	4,892	2,768	50	2,124 R	63.5%	35.9%	63.9%	36.1%
TREMPEALEAU	10,548	6,501	4,021	26	2,480 R	61.6%	38.1%	61.8%	38.2%
VERNON	11,663	7,619	4,032	12	3,587 R	65.3%	34.6%	65.4%	34.6%
VILAS	5,204	3,687	1,497	20	2,190 R	70.8%	28.8%	71.1%	28.9%
WALWORTH	22,372	16,906	5,417	49	11,489 R	75.6%	24.2%	75.7%	24.3%
WASHBURN	5,237	3,184	2,039	14	1,145 R	60.8%	38.9%	61.0%	39.0%
WASHINGTON	17,100	12,626	4,440	34	8,186 R	73.8%	26.0%	74.0%	26.0%
WAUKESHA	46,111	30,238	15,756	117	14,482 R	65.6%	34.2%	65.7%	34.3%
WAUPACA	16,826	13,693	3,105	28	10,588 R	81.4%	18.5%	81.5%	18.5%
WAUSHARA	6,713	5,447	1,242	24	4,205 R	81.1%	18.5%	81.4%	18.6%
WINNEBAGO	41,328	28,172	13,016	140	15,156 R	68.2%	31.5%	68.4%	31.6%
WOOD	21,749	14,707	6,914	128	7,793 R	67.6%	31.8%	68.0%	32.0%
TOTAL	1,607,370	979,744	622,175	5,451	357,569 R	61.0%	38.7%	61.2%	38.8%

PRESIDENT 1956

County	Total Vote	Republican	Democratic	Other	Rep.-Dem. Plurality	Total Vote Rep.	Total Vote Dem.	Major Vote Rep.	Major Vote Dem.
TAYLOR	6,654	3,843	2,759	52	1,084 R	57.8%	41.5%	58.2%	41.8%
TREMPEALEAU	10,094	5,476	4,602	16	874 R	54.3%	45.6%	54.3%	45.7%
VERNON	11,140	6,200	4,923	17	1,277 R	55.7%	44.2%	55.7%	44.3%
VILAS	4,972	3,683	1,267	22	2,416 R	74.1%	25.5%	74.4%	25.6%
WALWORTH	21,790	16,696	4,922	172	11,774 R	76.6%	22.6%	77.2%	22.8%
WASHBURN	4,752	2,798	1,935	19	863 R	58.9%	40.7%	59.1%	40.9%
WASHINGTON	16,683	12,167	4,447	69	7,720 R	72.9%	26.7%	73.2%	26.8%
WAUKESHA	51,084	35,212	15,496	376	19,716 R	68.9%	30.3%	69.4%	30.6%
WAUPACA	15,003	11,798	3,133	72	8,665 R	78.6%	20.9%	79.0%	21.0%
WAUSHARA	6,127	4,717	1,387	23	3,330 R	77.0%	22.6%	77.3%	22.7%
WINNEBAGO	40,254	28,759	11,115	380	17,644 R	71.4%	27.6%	72.1%	27.9%
WOOD	21,583	15,091	6,412	80	8,679 R	69.9%	29.7%	70.2%	29.8%
TOTAL	1,550,558	954,844	586,768	8,946	368,076 R	61.6%	37.8%	61.9%	38.1%

WISCONSIN

PRESIDENT 1960

County	Total Vote	Republican	Democratic	Other	Rep-Dem Plurality	Total Vote Rep.	Total Vote Dem.	Major Vote Rep.	Major Vote Dem.
ADAMS	3,674	2,109	1,551	14	558 R	57.4%	42.2%	57.6%	42.4%
ASHLAND	8,127	3,470	4,644	13	1,174 D	42.7%	57.1%	42.8%	57.2%
BARRON	15,145	8,640	6,464	41	2,176 R	57.0%	42.7%	57.2%	42.8%
BAYFIELD	6,060	2,841	3,196	23	355 D	46.9%	52.7%	47.1%	52.9%
BROWN	52,952	26,329	26,577	46	248 D	49.1%	50.2%	49.8%	50.2%
BUFFALO	6,256	3,464	2,790	2	674 R	55.4%	44.6%	55.4%	44.6%
BURNETT	4,596	2,483	2,095	18	388 R	54.3%	45.6%	54.2%	45.8%
CALUMET	9,486	5,166	4,312	8	854 R	54.5%	45.5%	54.5%	45.5%
CHIPPEWA	18,511	8,690	9,793	28	1,103 D	46.9%	52.9%	47.0%	53.0%
CLARK	13,343	7,368	5,934	41	1,434 R	55.2%	44.5%	55.4%	44.6%
COLUMBIA	16,873	10,282	6,576	15	3,706 R	60.9%	39.0%	61.0%	39.0%
CRAWFORD	7,071	3,719	3,342	10	377 R	52.6%	47.3%	52.7%	47.3%
DANE	90,502	43,245	47,045	212	3,830 D	47.8%	52.0%	47.9%	52.1%
DODGE	27,295	17,152	10,113	30	7,039 R	62.8%	37.1%	62.9%	37.1%
DOOR	9,414	5,790	3,610	14	2,180 R	61.5%	38.3%	61.6%	38.4%
DOUGLAS	21,270	8,307	12,910	53	4,603 D	39.1%	60.7%	39.2%	60.8%
DUNN	11,239	6,723	4,487	29	2,236 R	59.8%	39.9%	60.0%	40.0%
EAU CLAIRE	25,704	14,427	11,240	37	3,187 R	56.1%	43.7%	56.2%	43.8%
FLORENCE	1,791	928	858	5	70 R	51.8%	47.9%	52.0%	48.0%
FOND DU LAC	32,688	19,498	13,132	58	6,366 R	59.6%	40.2%	59.8%	40.2%
FOREST	3,514	1,653	1,851	10	198 D	47.0%	52.7%	47.2%	52.8%
GRANT	19,258	11,564	7,678	16	3,886 R	60.0%	39.9%	60.1%	39.9%
GREEN	11,711	7,939	3,766	6	4,173 R	67.8%	32.2%	67.8%	32.2%
GREEN LAKE	7,893	5,110	2,776	7	2,334 R	64.7%	35.2%	64.8%	35.2%
IOWA	8,694	5,143	3,547	4	1,596 R	59.2%	40.8%	59.2%	40.8%
IRON	4,170	1,290	2,873	7	1,583 D	30.9%	68.9%	31.0%	69.0%
JACKSON	6,813	3,950	2,849	14	1,101 R	58.0%	41.8%	58.1%	41.9%
JEFFERSON	22,929	14,133	8,757	39	5,376 R	61.6%	38.2%	61.7%	38.3%
JUNEAU	8,246	4,997	3,238	11	1,759 R	60.6%	39.2%	60.7%	39.3%
KENOSHA	43,011	19,969	22,956	86	2,987 D	46.4%	53.4%	46.5%	53.5%
KEWAUNEE	8,213	3,950	4,256	7	306 D	48.1%	51.8%	48.1%	51.9%
LA CROSSE	32,665	18,319	14,310	36	4,009 R	56.1%	43.8%	56.1%	43.9%
LAFAYETTE	8,330	4,715	3,607	8	1,108 R	56.6%	43.3%	56.7%	43.3%
LANGLADE	8,655	4,614	4,025	16	589 R	53.3%	46.5%	53.4%	46.6%
LINCOLN	10,089	6,147	3,909	33	2,238 R	60.9%	38.7%	61.1%	38.9%
MANITOWOC	32,080	14,622	17,423	35	2,801 D	45.6%	54.3%	45.6%	54.4%
MARATHON	40,025	21,880	18,145		3,735 R	54.6%	45.3%	54.7%	45.3%
MARINETTE	15,630	8,205	7,408	17	797 R	52.5%	47.4%	52.6%	47.4%
MARQUETTE	4,203	2,947	1,249	7	1,698 R	70.1%	29.7%	70.2%	29.8%
MENOMINEE									
MILWAUKEE	445,807	187,067	257,707	1,033	70,640 D	42.0%	57.8%	42.1%	57.9%
MONROE	12,587	7,410	5,161	16	2,249 R	58.9%	41.0%	58.9%	41.1%
OCONTO	11,283	6,223	5,045	15	1,178 R	55.2%	44.7%	55.2%	44.8%
ONEIDA	10,666	5,676	4,974	16	702 R	53.2%	46.6%	53.3%	46.7%
OUTAGAMIE	41,522	24,146	17,287	89	6,859 R	58.2%	41.6%	58.3%	41.7%
OZAUKEE	17,657	10,401	7,228	28	3,173 R	58.9%	40.9%	59.0%	41.0%
PEPIN	3,380	1,612	1,763	5	151 D	47.7%	52.2%	47.8%	52.2%
PIERCE	9,958	5,632	4,317	9	1,315 R	56.5%	43.4%	56.6%	43.4%
POLK	11,565	6,387	5,148	30	1,239 R	55.2%	44.5%	55.4%	44.6%
PORTAGE	16,972	6,436	10,516	20	4,080 D	37.9%	62.0%	38.0%	62.0%
PRICE	6,957	3,555	3,382	20	173 R	51.1%	48.6%	51.2%	48.8%
RACINE	60,294	29,562	30,596	136	1,034 D	49.0%	50.7%	49.1%	50.9%
RICHLAND	8,229	5,253	2,965	11	2,288 R	63.8%	36.0%	63.9%	36.1%
ROCK	48,945	29,675	19,194	76	10,481 R	60.6%	39.2%	60.7%	39.3%
RUSK	6,803	3,094	3,692	17	598 D	45.5%	54.3%	45.6%	54.4%
ST CROIX	13,478	7,113	6,341	24	772 R	52.8%	47.0%	52.9%	47.1%
SAUK	16,867	10,403	6,441	23	3,962 R	61.7%	38.2%	61.8%	38.2%
SAWYER	4,408	2,385	2,011	12	374 R	54.1%	45.6%	54.2%	45.8%
SHAWANO	14,489	9,734	4,734	21	5,000 R	67.1%	32.6%	67.3%	32.7%
SHEBOYGAN	40,221	21,676	18,425	120	3,251 R	53.9%	45.8%	54.1%	45.9%

PRESIDENT 1964

County	Total Vote	Republican	Democratic	Other	Rep-Dem Plurality	Total Vote Rep.	Total Vote Dem.	Major Vote Rep.	Major Vote Dem.
ADAMS	3,489	1,219	2,262	8	1,043 D	34.9%	64.8%	35.0%	65.0%
ASHLAND	7,591	2,198	5,383	10	3,185 D	29.0%	70.9%	29.0%	71.0%
BARRON	14,056	5,701	8,332	23	2,631 D	40.6%	59.3%	40.6%	59.4%
BAYFIELD	5,777	1,886	3,875	16	1,989 D	32.6%	67.1%	32.7%	67.3%
BROWN	52,064	21,134	30,851	79	9,717 D	40.6%	59.3%	40.7%	59.3%
BUFFALO	5,759	2,091	3,663	5	1,572 D	36.3%	63.6%	36.3%	63.7%
BURNETT	4,463	1,536	2,921	6	1,385 D	34.4%	65.4%	34.5%	65.5%
CALUMET	9,274	3,905	5,356	13	1,451 D	42.2%	57.7%	42.2%	57.8%
CHIPPEWA	17,214	6,277	10,911	26	4,634 D	36.5%	63.4%	36.5%	63.5%
CLARK	12,704	4,897	7,781	26	2,884 D	38.5%	61.2%	38.6%	61.4%
COLUMBIA	16,370	6,253	10,093	24	3,840 D	38.2%	61.7%	38.3%	61.7%
CRAWFORD	6,663	2,726	3,930	7	1,204 D	41.0%	59.0%	41.0%	59.0%
DANE	95,426	27,124	68,118	184	40,994 D	28.4%	71.4%	28.5%	71.5%
DODGE	26,308	10,772	15,497	39	4,725 D	40.9%	58.9%	41.0%	59.0%
DOOR	8,714	4,289	4,416	9	127 D	49.2%	50.7%	49.3%	50.7%
DOUGLAS	19,839	4,579	15,237	23	10,658 D	23.1%	76.8%	23.1%	76.9%
DUNN	10,458	3,964	6,475	19	2,511 D	37.9%	61.9%	38.0%	61.9%
EAU CLAIRE	24,521	8,700	15,775	46	7,075 D	35.5%	64.3%	35.5%	64.5%
FLORENCE	1,627	596	1,029	2	433 D	36.7%	63.2%	36.7%	63.3%
FOND DU LAC	30,778	12,708	18,040	30	5,332 D	41.3%	58.6%	41.3%	58.6%
FOREST	3,552	1,069	2,479	4	1,410 D	30.1%	69.8%	30.1%	69.8%
GRANT	17,211	7,872	9,309	30	1,437 D	45.8%	54.1%	45.8%	54.2%
GREEN	10,929	5,364	5,548	17	184 D	49.2%	50.8%	49.2%	50.8%
GREEN LAKE	7,768	3,871	3,893	4	22 D	49.8%	50.1%	49.9%	50.1%
IOWA	7,907	3,275	4,620	12	1,345 D	41.4%	58.4%	41.5%	58.5%
IRON	3,480	963	2,514	3	1,551 D	27.7%	72.2%	27.7%	72.3%
JACKSON	6,357	2,552	3,818	7	1,266 D	40.1%	60.0%	40.1%	59.9%
JEFFERSON	22,084	8,741	13,295	48	4,554 D	39.6%	60.2%	39.7%	60.3%
JUNEAU	7,567	2,976	4,583	8	1,607 D	39.3%	60.6%	39.4%	60.6%
KENOSHA	45,356	14,764	30,522	70	15,758 D	32.6%	67.3%	32.6%	67.4%
KEWAUNEE	7,780	2,980	4,792	8	1,812 D	38.3%	61.6%	38.3%	61.7%
LA CROSSE	29,803	13,135	16,625	43	3,490 D	44.1%	55.8%	44.1%	55.9%
LAFAYETTE	7,671	3,194	4,471	6	1,277 D	41.6%	58.3%	41.7%	58.3%
LANGLADE	8,081	2,994	5,077	10	2,083 D	37.1%	62.8%	37.1%	62.9%
LINCOLN	9,796	3,894	5,883	19	1,989 D	39.8%	60.1%	39.8%	60.2%
MANITOWOC	31,815	9,849	21,927	39	12,078 D	31.0%	68.9%	31.0%	69.0%
MARATHON	37,426	12,766	24,603	57	11,837 D	34.1%	65.7%	34.2%	65.8%
MARINETTE	15,013	5,332	9,657	24	4,325 D	35.5%	64.3%	35.6%	64.3%
MARQUETTE	3,816	1,881	1,927	8	46 D	49.3%	50.5%	49.4%	50.6%
MENOMINEE	726	78	647	1	569 D	10.7%	89.1%	10.8%	89.2%
MILWAUKEE	439,459	149,962	288,577	920	138,615 D	34.1%	65.2%	34.2%	65.8%
MONROE	11,524	5,126	6,385	13	1,259 D	44.5%	55.4%	44.5%	55.5%
OCONTO	10,795	4,420	6,360	15	1,940 D	41.0%	58.9%	41.0%	59.0%
ONEIDA	10,355	3,909	6,431	15	2,522 D	37.7%	62.1%	37.8%	62.2%
OUTAGAMIE	40,198	18,595	21,556	47	2,961 D	46.3%	53.6%	46.3%	53.7%
OZAUKEE	18,123	8,581	9,517	25	936 D	47.4%	52.5%	47.4%	52.6%
PEPIN	3,229	1,069	2,154	6	1,085 D	33.1%	66.7%	33.2%	66.8%
PIERCE	9,666	3,291	6,351	24	3,060 D	34.1%	65.7%	34.1%	65.9%
POLK	11,003	3,754	7,215	34	3,461 D	34.1%	65.5%	34.2%	65.8%
PORTAGE	16,498	4,579	11,887	32	7,308 D	27.8%	72.1%	27.8%	72.2%
PRICE	6,705	2,406	4,289	10	1,883 D	35.9%	64.0%	35.9%	64.1%
RACINE	59,306	21,434	37,785	87	16,351 D	36.1%	63.7%	36.2%	63.8%
RICHLAND	7,548	3,224	4,315	9	1,091 D	42.7%	57.2%	42.8%	57.2%
ROCK	46,684	20,372	26,257	55	5,885 D	41.8%	58.0%	41.9%	58.1%
RUSK	6,405	2,214	4,176	15	1,962 D	34.5%	65.2%	34.6%	65.4%
ST CROIX	13,458	4,565	8,864	29	4,299 D	33.9%	65.9%	34.0%	66.0%
SAUK	15,656	6,345	9,288	23	2,943 D	40.5%	59.3%	40.6%	59.4%
SAWYER	4,613	2,012	2,591	10	579 D	43.6%	56.2%	43.7%	56.3%
SHAWANO	13,105	6,519	6,560	26	41 D	49.7%	50.2%	49.8%	50.2%
SHEBOYGAN	39,445	12,968	26,410	67	13,442 D	32.9%	67.0%	32.9%	67.1%

WISCONSIN

PRESIDENT 1960

County	Total Vote	Republican	Democratic	Other	Rep.-Dem. Plurality	Total Vote Rep.	Total Vote Dem.	Major Vote Rep.	Major Vote Dem.
TAYLOR	7,237	3,447	3,768	22	321 D	47.6%	52.1%	47.8%	52.2%
TREMPEALEAU	10,781	5,539	5,223	19	316 R	51.4%	48.4%	51.5%	48.5%
VERNON	11,760	6,909	4,836	15	2,073 R	58.8%	41.1%	58.8%	41.2%
VILAS	5,460	3,508	1,942	10	1,566 R	64.2%	35.6%	64.4%	35.6%
WALWORTH	24,401	16,395	7,986	20	8,409 R	67.2%	32.7%	67.2%	32.8%
WASHBURN	5,261	2,848	2,398	15	450 R	54.1%	45.6%	54.3%	45.7%
WASHINGTON	19,991	11,452	8,523	16	2,929 R	57.3%	42.6%	57.3%	42.7%
WAUKESHA	68,419	39,380	28,963	76	10,417 R	57.6%	42.3%	57.6%	42.4%
WAUPACA	16,867	12,247	4,606	14	7,641 R	72.6%	27.3%	72.7%	27.3%
WAUSHARA	6,799	4,906	1,888	5	3,018 R	72.2%	27.8%	72.2%	27.8%
WINNEBAGO	46,334	28,598	17,656	80	10,942 R	61.7%	38.1%	61.8%	38.2%
WOOD	24,930	14,414	10,483	33	3,931 R	57.8%	42.0%	57.9%	42.1%
TOTAL	1,729,082	895,175	830,805	3,102	64,370 R	51.8%	48.0%	51.9%	48.1%

PRESIDENT 1964

County	Total Vote	Republican	Democratic	Other	Rep.-Dem. Plurality	Total Vote Rep.	Total Vote Dem.	Major Vote Rep.	Major Vote Dem.
TAYLOR	6,898	2,261	4,624	13	2,363 D	32.8%	67.0%	32.8%	57.2%
TREMPEALEAU	9,589	3,264	6,320	5	3,056 D	34.0%	65.9%	34.1%	65.9%
VERNON	10,898	4,640	6,242	16	1,602 D	42.6%	57.3%	42.6%	57.4%
VILAS	5,679	2,827	2,841	11	14 D	49.8%	50.0%	49.9%	50.1%
WALWORTH	24,009	12,225	11,746	38	479 R	50.9%	48.9%	51.0%	49.0%
WASHBURN	5,062	1,865	3,181	16	1,316 D	36.8%	62.8%	37.0%	63.0%
WASHINGTON	20,791	9,191	11,563	37	2,372 D	44.2%	55.6%	44.3%	55.7%
WAUKESHA	75,429	35,502	39,796	131	4,294 D	47.1%	52.8%	47.1%	52.9%
WAUPACA	15,389	8,381	6,990	18	1,391 R	54.5%	45.4%	54.5%	45.5%
WAUSHARA	6,441	3,437	3,004		433 R	53.4%	46.6%	53.4%	46.6%
WINNEBAGO	44,835	21,084	23,636	115	2,552 D	47.0%	52.7%	47.1%	52.9%
WOOD	23,787	8,388	15,378	21	6,990 D	35.3%	64.6%	35.3%	64.7%
TOTAL	1,691,815	638,495	1,050,424	2,896	411,929 D	37.7%	62.1%	37.8%	62.2%

WISCONSIN

OTHER VOTE COMPOSITION:

1920	80,635 Socialist; 8,648 Prohibition.
1924	453,678 Progressive; 3,773 Communist; 2,918 Prohibition; 458 Socialist Labor; 271 Commonwealth Land.
1928	18,213 Socialist; 2,245 Prohibition; 1,528 Communist; 381 Socialist Labor.
1932	53,379 Socialist; 3,105 Communist; 2,672 Prohibition; 494 Socialist Labor; 13 scattered.
1936	60,297 Union; 10,626 Socialist; 2,197 Communist; 1,071 Prohibition; 557 Socialist Labor.
1940	15,071 Socialist; 2,394 Communist; 2,148 Prohibition; 1,882 Socialist Labor.
1944	13,205 Socialist; 1,002 Socialist Labor.
1948	25,282 Progressive; 12,547 Socialist; 399 Socialist Labor; 303 Socialist Workers.
1952	2,174 Progressive; 1,350 Socialist Workers; 1,157 Socialist; 770 Socialist Labor.
1956	6,918 States Rights; 754 Socialist; 710 Socialist Labor; 564 Socialist Workers.
1960	1,792 Socialist Workers; 1,310 Socialist Labor.
1964	1,692 Socialist Workers; 1,204 Socialist Labor.

SPECIAL CASES:

1920	Socialist candidates ran second in several counties.
1924	Progressive candidates carried the state, leading or running second in all counties.
1964	Menominee county organized in 1961.

WYOMING

PRESIDENT 1920

County	Total Vote	Republican	Democratic	Other	Rep.-Dem. Plurality	Total Vote Rep.	Total Vote Dem.	Major Vote Rep.	Major Vote Dem.
ALBANY	2,990	1,769	1,145	76	624 R	59.2%	38.3%	60.7%	39.3%
BIG HORN	3,278	2,157	1,082	39	1,075 R	65.8%	33.0%	66.6%	33.4%
CAMPBELL	1,540	1,027	493	20	534 R	66.7%	32.0%	67.6%	32.4%
CARBON	3,085	1,871	1,039	175	832 R	60.6%	33.7%	64.3%	35.7%
CONVERSE	2,249	1,561	679	9	882 R	69.4%	30.2%	69.7%	30.3%
CROOK	1,389	934	451	4	483 R	67.2%	32.5%	67.4%	32.6%
FREMONT	3,245	2,194	994	57	1,200 R	67.6%	30.6%	68.8%	31.2%
GOSHEN	2,057	1,496	552	9	944 R	72.7%	26.8%	73.0%	27.0%
HOT SPRINGS	1,876	1,212	529	135	683 R	64.6%	28.2%	69.6%	30.4%
JOHNSON	1,733	1,202	525	6	677 R	69.4%	30.3%	69.6%	30.4%
LARAMIE	5,430	3,399	1,810	221	1,589 R	62.6%	33.3%	65.3%	34.7%
LINCOLN	3,346	2,043	1,154	149	889 R	61.1%	34.5%	63.9%	36.1%
NATRONA	4,467	2,957	1,153	357	1,804 R	66.2%	25.8%	71.9%	28.1%
NIOBRARA	1,318	969	345	4	624 R	73.5%	26.2%	73.7%	26.3%
PARK	2,311	1,630	666	15	964 R	70.5%	28.8%	71.0%	29.0%
PLATTE	2,139	1,405	694	40	711 R	65.7%	32.4%	66.9%	33.1%
SHERIDAN	4,377	2,645	1,192	540	1,453 R	60.4%	27.2%	68.9%	31.1%
SUBLETTE									
SWEETWATER	3,221	1,744	1,216	261	528 R	54.1%	37.8%	58.9%	41.1%
TETON									
UINTA	2,139	1,194	914	31	280 R	55.8%	42.7%	56.6%	43.4%
WASHAKIE	947	609	333	5	276 R	64.3%	35.2%	64.6%	35.4%
WESTON	1,563	1,073	463	27	610 R	68.7%	29.6%	69.9%	30.1%
TOTAL	56,253	35,091	17,429	3,733	17,662 R	62.4%	31.0%	66.8%	33.2%

PRESIDENT 1924

County	Total Vote	Republican	Democratic	Other	Rep.-Dem. Plurality	Total Vote Rep.	Total Vote Dem.	Major Vote Rep.	Major Vote Dem.
ALBANY	4,535	2,164	743	1,628	1,421 R	47.7%	16.4%	74.4%	25.6%
BIG HORN	3,715	2,023	459	1,233	1,564 R	54.5%	12.4%	81.5%	18.5%
CAMPBELL	2,141	1,121	577	443	544 R	52.4%	27.0%	66.0%	34.0%
CARBON	4,395	2,398	733	1,264	1,665 R	54.6%	16.7%	76.6%	23.4%
CONVERSE	3,007	1,758	524	725	1,234 R	58.5%	17.4%	77.0%	23.0%
CROOK	1,795	978	468	349	510 R	54.5%	26.1%	67.6%	32.4%
FREMONT	3,839	1,986	561	1,292	1,425 R	51.7%	14.6%	78.0%	22.0%
GOSHEN	2,855	1,603	464	788	1,139 R	56.1%	16.3%	77.6%	22.4%
HOT SPRINGS	2,211	1,011	231	969	780 R	45.7%	10.4%	81.4%	18.6%
JOHNSON	1,891	1,097	501	293	596 R	58.0%	26.5%	68.6%	31.4%
LARAMIE	7,442	3,944	1,120	2,378	2,824 R	53.0%	15.0%	77.9%	22.1%
LINCOLN	3,094	1,493	576	1,025	917 R	48.3%	18.6%	72.2%	27.8%
NATRONA	13,755	8,267	1,631	3,857	6,636 R	60.1%	11.9%	83.5%	16.5%
NIOBRARA	1,693	820	202	671	618 R	48.4%	11.9%	80.2%	19.8%
PARK	2,897	1,607	530	760	1,077 R	55.5%	18.3%	75.2%	24.8%
PLATTE	2,791	1,383	436	972	947 R	49.6%	15.6%	76.0%	24.0%
SHERIDAN	5,917	2,530	1,115	2,272	1,415 R	42.8%	18.8%	69.4%	30.6%
SUBLETTE	846	570	183	93	387 R	67.4%	21.6%	75.7%	24.3%
SWEETWATER	5,026	2,119	688	2,219	1,431 R	42.2%	13.7%	75.5%	24.5%
TETON	626	342	173	111	169 R	54.6%	27.6%	66.4%	33.6%
UINTA	2,474	1,126	427	921	699 R	45.5%	17.3%	72.5%	27.5%
WASHAKIE	1,204	724	209	271	515 R	60.1%	17.4%	77.6%	22.4%
WESTON	1,751	794	317	640	477 R	45.3%	18.1%	71.5%	28.5%
TOTAL	79,900	41,858	12,868	25,174	28,990 R	52.4%	16.1%	76.5%	23.5%

WYOMING

PRESIDENT 1928

County	Total Vote	Republican	Democratic	Other	Rep.-Dem. Plurality	Percentage Total Vote Rep.	Total Vote Dem.	Major Vote Rep.	Major Vote Dem.
ALBANY	4,586	2,941	1,618	27	1,323 R	64.1%	35.3%	64.5%	35.5%
BIG HORN	3,596	2,646	933	17	1,713 R	73.5%	25.9%	73.9%	26.1%
CAMPBELL	2,297	1,528	744	25	784 R	66.5%	32.4%	67.3%	32.7%
CARBON	4,655	3,019	1,609	27	1,410 R	64.9%	34.6%	65.2%	34.8%
CONVERSE	2,893	2,040	845	8	1,195 R	70.5%	29.2%	70.7%	29.3%
CROOK	2,053	1,466	582	5	884 R	71.4%	28.3%	71.6%	28.4%
FREMONT	3,738	2,267	1,449	22	818 R	60.6%	38.8%	61.0%	39.0%
GOSHEN	3,298	2,483	777	38	1,706 R	75.3%	23.6%	76.2%	23.8%
HOT SPRINGS	2,205	1,220	940	45	280 R	55.3%	42.6%	56.5%	43.5%
JOHNSON	1,977	1,369	590	18	779 R	69.2%	29.8%	69.9%	30.1%
LARAMIE	8,973	5,862	3,029	82	2,833 R	65.3%	33.8%	65.9%	34.1%
LINCOLN	3,919	2,217	1,687	15	530 R	56.6%	43.0%	56.8%	43.2%
NATRONA	11,023	7,141	3,818	64	3,323 R	64.8%	34.6%	65.2%	34.8%
NIOBRARA	1,919	1,424	469	26	955 R	74.2%	24.4%	75.2%	24.8%
PARK	3,260	2,175	1,062	23	1,113 R	66.7%	32.6%	67.2%	32.8%
PLATTE	3,256	2,206	932	118	1,274 R	67.8%	28.6%	70.3%	29.7%
SHERIDAN	6,250	3,616	2,563	71	1,053 R	57.9%	41.0%	58.5%	41.5%
SUBLETTE	895	573	316	6	257 R	64.0%	35.3%	64.5%	35.5%
SWEETWATER	5,599	2,528	2,974	97	446 D	45.2%	53.1%	45.9%	54.1%
TETON	770	495	270	5	225 R	64.3%	35.1%	64.7%	35.3%
UINTA	2,468	1,439	1,012	17	427 R	58.3%	41.0%	58.7%	41.3%
WASHAKIE	1,366	966	392	8	574 R	70.7%	28.7%	71.1%	28.9%
WESTON	1,839	1,127	688	24	439 R	61.3%	37.4%	62.1%	37.9%
TOTAL	82,835	52,748	29,299	788	23,449 R	63.7%	35.4%	64.3%	35.7%

PRESIDENT 1932

County	Total Vote	Republican	Democratic	Other	Rep.-Dem. Plurality	Percentage Total Vote Rep.	Total Vote Dem.	Major Vote Rep.	Major Vote Dem.
ALBANY	5,289	2,281	2,665	343	384 D	43.1%	50.4%	46.1%	53.9%
BIG HORN	4,563	2,334	2,155	74	179 R	51.2%	47.2%	52.0%	48.0%
CAMPBELL	2,980	1,161	1,728	91	567 D	39.0%	58.0%	40.2%	59.8%
CARBON	5,073	2,088	2,836	149	748 D	41.2%	55.9%	42.4%	57.6%
CONVERSE	3,477	1,569	1,860	48	291 D	45.1%	53.5%	45.8%	54.2%
CROOK	2,413	1,062	1,317	34	255 D	44.0%	54.6%	44.6%	55.4%
FREMONT	4,374	1,696	2,612	66	916 D	38.8%	59.7%	39.4%	60.6%
GOSHEN	4,590	1,954	2,545	91	591 D	42.6%	55.4%	43.4%	56.6%
HOT SPRINGS	2,353	742	1,466	145	724 D	31.5%	62.3%	33.6%	66.4%
JOHNSON	2,340	1,101	1,171	68	70 D	47.1%	50.0%	48.5%	51.5%
LARAMIE	10,938	5,116	5,435	387	319 D	46.8%	49.7%	48.5%	51.5%
LINCOLN	4,006	1,673	2,275	58	602 D	41.8%	56.8%	42.4%	57.6%
NATRONA	11,533	4,368	6,777	388	2,409 D	37.9%	58.8%	39.2%	60.8%
NIOBRARA	2,185	908	1,237	40	329 D	41.6%	56.6%	42.3%	57.7%
PARK	3,757	1,600	2,043	114	443 D	42.6%	54.4%	43.9%	56.1%
PLATTE	3,624	1,430	1,893	301	463 D	39.5%	52.2%	43.0%	57.0%
SHERIDAN	7,142	2,738	4,260	144	1,522 D	38.3%	59.6%	39.1%	60.9%
SUBLETTE	1,172	512	633	27	121 D	43.7%	54.0%	44.7%	55.3%
SWEETWATER	6,983	2,043	4,637	303	2,594 D	29.3%	66.4%	30.6%	69.4%
TETON	1,115	406	699	10	293 D	36.4%	62.7%	36.7%	63.3%
UINTA	2,958	1,250	1,658	50	408 D	42.3%	56.1%	43.0%	57.0%
WASHAKIE	1,751	711	1,009	31	298 D	40.6%	57.6%	41.3%	58.7%
WESTON	2,346	840	1,459	47	619 D	35.8%	62.2%	36.5%	63.5%
TOTAL	96,962	39,583	54,370	3,009	14,787 D	40.8%	56.1%	42.1%	57.9%

WYOMING

PRESIDENT 1936

County	Total Vote	Republican	Democratic	Other	Rep.-Dem. Plurality	Total Vote Rep.	Total Vote Dem.	Major Vote Rep.	Major Vote Dem.
ALBANY	5,539	1,777	3,685	77	1,908 D	32.1%	66.5%	32.5%	67.5%
BIG HORN	5,236	1,996	3,156	84	1,160 D	38.1%	60.3%	38.7%	61.3%
CAMPBELL	2,784	1,322	1,435	27	113 D	47.5%	51.5%	48.0%	52.0%
CARBON	5,373	2,041	3,257	75	1,216 D	38.0%	60.6%	38.5%	61.5%
CONVERSE	3,251	1,556	1,639	56	83 D	47.9%	50.4%	48.7%	51.3%
CROOK	2,350	1,218	1,088	44	130 R	51.8%	46.3%	52.8%	47.2%
FREMONT	5,533	2,357	3,050	126	693 D	42.6%	55.1%	43.6%	56.4%
GOSHEN	4,751	2,047	2,639	65	592 D	43.1%	55.5%	43.7%	56.3%
HOT SPRINGS	2,319	796	1,419	104	623 D	34.3%	61.2%	35.9%	64.1%
JOHNSON	2,333	1,266	949	118	317 R	54.3%	40.7%	57.2%	42.8%
LARAMIE	12,140	4,356	7,594	190	3,238 D	35.9%	62.6%	36.5%	63.5%
LINCOLN	4,160	1,376	2,747	37	1,371 D	33.1%	66.0%	33.4%	66.6%
NATRONA	11,907	3,810	7,819	278	4,009 D	32.0%	65.7%	32.8%	67.2%
NIOBRARA	2,245	1,086	1,124	35	38 D	48.4%	50.1%	49.1%	50.9%
PARK	4,315	1,618	2,594	103	976 D	37.5%	60.1%	38.4%	61.6%
PLATTE	3,406	1,546	1,730	130	184 D	45.4%	50.8%	47.2%	52.8%
SHERIDAN	7,680	2,726	4,731	223	2,005 D	35.5%	61.6%	36.6%	63.4%
SUBLETTE	1,338	638	667	33	29 D	47.7%	49.9%	48.9%	51.1%
SWEETWATER	8,097	1,797	6,232	68	4,435 D	22.2%	77.0%	22.4%	77.6%
TETON	1,352	501	795	56	294 D	37.1%	58.8%	38.7%	61.3%
UINTA	3,015	1,015	1,972	28	957 D	33.7%	65.4%	34.0%	66.0%
WASHAKIE	1,963	810	1,109	44	299 D	41.3%	56.5%	42.2%	57.8%
WESTON	2,295	1,084	1,193	18	109 D	47.2%	52.0%	47.6%	52.4%
TOTAL	103,382	38,739	62,624	2,019	23,885 D	37.5%	60.6%	38.2%	61.8%

PRESIDENT 1940

County	Total Vote	Republican	Democratic	Other	Rep.-Dem. Plurality	Total Vote Rep.	Total Vote Dem.	Major Vote Rep.	Major Vote Dem.
ALBANY	6,804	2,756	4,018	30	1,262 D	40.5%	59.1%	40.7%	59.3%
BIG HORN	5,475	2,859	2,594	22	265 R	52.2%	47.4%	52.4%	47.6%
CAMPBELL	2,675	1,540	1,128	7	412 R	57.6%	42.2%	57.7%	42.3%
CARBON	6,320	2,882	3,429	9	547 D	45.6%	54.3%	45.7%	54.3%
CONVERSE	3,286	1,889	1,395	2	494 R	57.5%	42.5%	57.5%	42.5%
CROOK	2,233	1,359	869	5	490 R	60.9%	38.9%	61.0%	39.0%
FREMONT	6,453	3,788	2,644	21	1,144 R	58.7%	41.0%	58.9%	41.1%
GOSHEN	4,858	2,861	1,982	15	879 R	58.9%	40.8%	59.1%	40.9%
HOT SPRINGS	2,194	913	1,266	15	353 D	41.6%	57.7%	41.9%	58.1%
JOHNSON	2,247	1,460	781	6	679 R	65.0%	34.8%	65.1%	34.9%
LARAMIE	13,820	5,955	7,808	57	1,853 D	43.1%	56.5%	43.3%	56.7%
LINCOLN	4,605	1,765	2,839	1	1,074 D	38.3%	61.7%	38.3%	61.7%
NATRONA	11,949	5,555	6,373	21	818 D	46.5%	53.3%	46.6%	53.4%
NIOBRARA	2,632	1,427	1,200	5	227 R	54.2%	45.6%	54.3%	45.7%
PARK	5,282	2,512	2,747	23	235 D	47.6%	52.0%	47.8%	52.2%
PLATTE	3,622	1,758	1,849	15	91 D	48.5%	51.0%	48.7%	51.3%
SHERIDAN	8,268	3,814	4,439	15	625 D	46.1%	53.7%	46.2%	53.8%
SUBLETTE	1,402	771	627	4	144 R	55.0%	44.7%	55.2%	44.8%
SWEETWATER	9,094	2,439	6,637	18	4,198 D	26.8%	73.0%	26.9%	73.1%
TETON	1,353	623	728	2	105 D	46.0%	53.8%	46.1%	53.9%
UINTA	3,351	1,335	2,007	9	672 D	39.8%	59.9%	39.9%	60.1%
WASHAKIE	2,033	1,080	942	11	138 R	53.1%	46.3%	53.4%	46.6%
WESTON	2,284	1,292	985	7	307 R	56.6%	43.1%	56.7%	43.3%
TOTAL	112,240	52,633	59,287	320	6,654 D	46.9%	52.8%	47.0%	53.0%

WYOMING

PRESIDENT 1944

County	Total Vote	Republican	Democratic	Other	Rep.-Dem. Plurality	Total Vote Rep.	Total Vote Dem.	Major Vote Rep.	Major Vote Dem.
ALBANY	6,199	2,970	3,229		259 D	47.9%	52.1%	47.9%	52.1%
BIG HORN	4,973	2,659	2,314		345 R	53.5%	46.5%	53.5%	46.5%
CAMPBELL	2,408	1,514	894		620 R	62.9%	37.1%	62.9%	37.1%
CARBON	5,681	2,698	2,983		285 D	47.5%	52.5%	47.5%	52.5%
CONVERSE	2,580	1,601	979		622 R	62.1%	37.9%	62.1%	37.9%
CROOK	1,934	1,244	690		554 R	64.3%	35.7%	64.3%	35.7%
FREMONT	5,370	3,193	2,177		1,016 R	59.5%	40.5%	59.5%	40.5%
GOSHEN	4,188	2,674	1,514		1,160 R	63.8%	36.2%	63.8%	36.2%
HOT SPRINGS	1,846	877	969		92 D	47.5%	52.5%	47.5%	52.5%
JOHNSON	2,140	1,384	756		628 R	64.7%	35.3%	64.7%	35.3%
LARAMIE	14,868	7,326	7,542		216 D	49.3%	50.7%	49.3%	50.7%
LINCOLN	3,789	1,649	2,140		491 D	43.5%	56.5%	43.5%	56.5%
NATRONA	10,086	5,196	4,890		306 R	51.5%	48.5%	51.5%	48.5%
NIOBRARA	2,138	1,312	826		486 R	61.4%	38.6%	61.4%	38.6%
PARK	4,828	2,571	2,257		314 R	53.3%	46.7%	53.3%	46.7%
PLATTE	3,320	1,776	1,544		232 R	53.5%	46.5%	53.5%	46.5%
SHERIDAN	7,654	3,802	3,862		60 D	49.6%	50.4%	49.6%	50.4%
SUBLETTE	1,153	683	470		213 R	59.2%	40.8%	59.2%	40.8%
SWEETWATER	8,222	2,623	5,599		2,976 D	31.9%	68.1%	31.9%	68.1%
TETON	1,136	637	499		138 R	56.1%	43.9%	56.1%	43.9%
UINTA	3,059	1,305	1,754		449 D	42.7%	57.3%	42.7%	57.3%
WASHAKIE	1,907	1,130	777		353 R	59.3%	40.7%	59.3%	40.7%
WESTON	1,851	1,097	754		343 R	59.3%	40.7%	59.3%	40.7%
TOTAL	101,340	51,921	49,419		2,502 R	51.2%	48.8%	51.2%	48.8%

PRESIDENT 1948

County	Total Vote	Republican	Democratic	Other	Rep.-Dem. Plurality	Total Vote Rep.	Total Vote Dem.	Major Vote Rep.	Major Vote Dem.
ALBANY	6,045	2,856	3,141	46	283 D	47.3%	52.0%	47.6%	52.4%
BIG HORN	4,823	2,429	2,370	24	59 R	50.4%	49.1%	50.6%	49.4%
CAMPBELL	2,071	1,201	856	14	345 R	58.0%	41.3%	58.4%	41.6%
CARBON	5,813	2,319	3,439	55	1,120 D	39.9%	59.2%	40.3%	59.7%
CONVERSE	2,338	1,327	996	15	331 R	56.8%	42.6%	57.1%	42.9%
CROOK	1,892	1,166	712	14	454 R	61.6%	37.6%	62.1%	37.9%
FREMONT	6,400	3,357	3,019	24	338 R	52.5%	47.2%	52.7%	47.3%
GOSHEN	3,909	2,029	1,843	37	186 R	51.9%	47.1%	52.4%	47.6%
HOT SPRINGS	1,764	791	928	45	137 D	44.8%	52.6%	46.0%	54.0%
JOHNSON	2,045	1,351	682	12	669 R	66.1%	33.3%	66.5%	33.5%
LARAMIE	14,524	6,200	8,226	98	2,026 D	42.7%	56.6%	43.0%	57.0%
LINCOLN	3,738	1,730	1,925	83	195 D	46.3%	51.5%	47.3%	52.7%
NATRONA	11,608	5,341	6,183	84	842 D	46.0%	53.3%	46.3%	53.7%
NIOBRARA	1,745	975	753	17	222 R	55.9%	43.2%	56.4%	43.6%
PARK	5,145	2,655	2,461	29	194 R	51.6%	47.8%	51.9%	48.1%
PLATTE	2,853	1,366	1,465	22	99 D	47.9%	51.3%	48.3%	51.7%
SHERIDAN	7,601	3,698	3,852	51	154 D	48.7%	50.7%	49.0%	51.0%
SUBLETTE	1,126	622	496	8	126 R	55.2%	44.0%	55.6%	44.4%
SWEETWATER	8,085	2,538	5,146	401	2,608 D	31.4%	63.6%	33.0%	67.0%
TETON	1,289	719	556	14	163 R	55.8%	43.1%	56.4%	43.6%
UINTA	2,698	1,239	1,632	27	393 D	42.8%	56.3%	43.2%	56.8%
WASHAKIE	1,925	1,074	851		223 R	55.8%	44.2%	55.8%	44.2%
WESTON	1,788	962	822	4	140 R	53.8%	46.0%	53.9%	46.1%
TOTAL	101,425	47,947	52,354	1,124	4,407 D	47.3%	51.6%	47.8%	52.2%

WYOMING

PRESIDENT 1952

County	Total Vote	Republican	Democratic	Other	Rep.-Dem. Plurality	Total Vote Percentage Rep.	Total Vote Percentage Dem.	Major Vote Rep.	Major Vote Dem.
ALBANY	7,652	4,560	3,082	10	1,478 R	59.6%	40.3%	59.7%	40.3%
BIG HORN	5,620	3,859	1,755	6	2,104 R	68.7%	31.2%	68.7%	31.3%
CAMPBELL	2,494	1,823	666	5	1,157 R	73.1%	26.7%	73.2%	26.8%
CARBON	6,661	3,403	3,242	16	161 R	51.1%	48.7%	51.2%	48.8%
CONVERSE	2,916	2,056	850	10	1,206 R	70.5%	29.1%	70.8%	29.2%
CROOK	2,173	1,734	423	16	1,311 R	79.8%	19.5%	80.4%	19.6%
FREMONT	8,063	5,881	2,161	21	3,720 R	72.9%	26.8%	73.1%	26.9%
GOSHEN	5,058	3,396	1,648	14	1,748 R	67.1%	32.6%	67.3%	32.7%
HOT SPRINGS	2,432	1,573	856	3	717 R	64.7%	35.2%	64.8%	35.2%
JOHNSON	2,524	1,980	543	1	1,437 R	78.4%	21.5%	78.5%	21.5%
LARAMIE	19,051	10,785	8,187	79	2,598 R	56.6%	43.0%	56.8%	43.2%
LINCOLN	4,030	2,321	1,709		612 R	57.6%	42.4%	57.6%	42.4%
NATRONA	16,695	10,663	6,021	11	4,642 R	63.9%	36.1%	63.9%	36.1%
NIOBRARA	2,259	1,652	588	19	1,064 R	73.1%	26.0%	73.8%	26.2%
PARK	7,175	5,067	2,084	24	2,983 R	70.6%	29.0%	70.9%	29.1%
PLATTE	3,524	2,148	1,364	12	784 R	61.0%	38.7%	61.2%	38.8%
SHERIDAN	9,655	6,522	3,124	9	3,398 R	67.6%	32.4%	67.6%	32.4%
SUBLETTE	1,359	1,013	344	2	669 R	74.5%	25.3%	74.6%	25.4%
SWEETWATER	9,374	3,567	5,807		2,240 D	38.1%	61.9%	38.1%	61.9%
TETON	1,483	1,166	317		849 R	78.6%	21.4%	78.6%	21.4%
UINTA	3,248	1,801	1,444	3	357 R	55.4%	44.5%	55.5%	44.5%
WASHAKIE	3,033	2,148	880	5	1,268 R	70.8%	29.0%	70.9%	29.1%
WESTON	2,774	1,931	839	4	1,092 R	69.6%	30.2%	69.7%	30.3%
TOTAL	129,253	81,049	47,934	270	33,115 R	62.7%	37.1%	62.8%	37.2%

PRESIDENT 1956

County	Total Vote	Republican	Democratic	Other	Rep.-Dem. Plurality	Total Vote Percentage Rep.	Total Vote Percentage Dem.	Major Vote Rep.	Major Vote Dem.
ALBANY	7,722	4,315	3,407		908 R	55.9%	44.1%	55.9%	44.1%
BIG HORN	5,182	3,369	1,813		1,556 R	65.0%	35.0%	65.0%	35.0%
CAMPBELL	2,129	1,473	656		817 R	69.2%	30.8%	69.2%	30.8%
CARBON	6,554	3,336	3,218		118 R	50.9%	49.1%	50.9%	49.1%
CONVERSE	2,606	1,855	751		1,104 R	71.2%	28.8%	71.2%	28.8%
CROOK	1,565	1,139	426		713 R	72.8%	27.2%	72.8%	27.2%
FREMONT	7,456	4,887	2,569		2,318 R	65.5%	34.5%	65.5%	34.5%
GOSHEN	4,955	2,825	2,130		695 R	57.0%	43.0%	57.0%	43.0%
HOT SPRINGS	2,640	1,663	977		686 R	63.0%	37.0%	63.0%	37.0%
JOHNSON	2,420	1,842	578		1,264 R	76.1%	23.9%	76.1%	23.9%
LARAMIE	19,653	10,581	9,072		1,509 R	53.8%	46.2%	53.8%	46.2%
LINCOLN	3,827	2,264	1,563		701 R	59.2%	40.8%	59.2%	40.8%
NATRONA	17,258	10,796	6,462		4,334 R	62.6%	37.4%	62.6%	37.4%
NIOBRARA	1,766	1,248	518		730 R	70.7%	29.3%	70.7%	29.3%
PARK	6,357	4,397	1,960		2,437 R	69.2%	30.8%	69.2%	30.8%
PLATTE	3,347	1,848	1,499		349 R	55.2%	44.8%	55.2%	44.8%
SHERIDAN	8,750	5,546	3,204		2,342 R	63.4%	36.6%	63.4%	36.6%
SUBLETTE	1,252	901	351		550 R	72.0%	28.0%	72.0%	28.0%
SWEETWATER	8,102	3,355	4,747		1,392 D	41.4%	58.6%	41.4%	58.6%
TETON	1,401	1,089	312		777 R	77.7%	22.3%	77.7%	22.3%
UINTA	3,063	1,742	1,321		421 R	56.9%	43.1%	56.9%	43.1%
WASHAKIE	3,254	2,265	989		1,276 R	69.6%	30.4%	69.6%	30.4%
WESTON	2,868	1,837	1,031		806 R	64.1%	35.9%	64.1%	35.9%
TOTAL	124,127	74,573	49,554		25,019 R	60.1%	39.9%	60.1%	39.9%

WYOMING

PRESIDENT 1960

County	Total Vote	Republican	Democratic	Other	Rep.-Dem. Plurality	Percentage Total Vote Rep.	Total Vote Dem.	Major Vote Rep.	Major Vote Dem.
ALBANY	8,638	4,356	4,282		74 R	50.4%	49.6%	50.4%	49.6%
BIG HORN	5,493	3,449	2,044		1,405 R	62.8%	37.2%	62.8%	37.2%
CAMPBELL	2,436	1,575	861		714 R	64.7%	35.3%	64.7%	35.3%
CARBON	6,975	3,147	3,828		681 D	45.1%	54.9%	45.1%	54.9%
CONVERSE	2,859	1,933	926		1,007 R	67.6%	32.4%	67.6%	32.4%
CROOK	2,110	1,537	573		964 R	72.8%	27.2%	72.8%	27.2%
FREMONT	9,936	5,738	4,248		1,490 R	57.5%	42.5%	57.5%	42.5%
GOSHEN	5,592	3,178	2,414		764 R	56.8%	43.2%	56.8%	43.2%
HOT SPRINGS	2,603	1,659	1,144		515 R	59.2%	40.8%	59.2%	40.8%
JOHNSON	2,604	1,806	798		1,008 R	69.4%	30.6%	69.4%	30.6%
LARAMIE	23,723	11,637	12,086		449 D	49.1%	50.9%	49.1%	50.9%
LINCOLN	3,958	2,010	1,948		62 R	50.8%	49.2%	50.8%	49.2%
NATRONA	20,811	11,809	9,002		2,807 R	56.7%	43.3%	56.7%	43.3%
NIOBRARA	1,930	1,362	568		794 R	70.6%	29.4%	70.6%	29.4%
PARK	7,006	4,510	2,496		2,014 R	64.4%	35.6%	64.4%	35.6%
PLATTE	3,329	1,771	1,558		213 R	53.2%	46.8%	53.2%	46.8%
SHERIDAN	9,476	5,690	3,786		1,904 R	60.0%	40.0%	60.0%	40.0%
SUBLETTE	1,624	978	646		332 R	60.2%	39.8%	60.2%	39.8%
SWEETWATER	7,943	2,545	5,398		2,853 D	32.0%	68.0%	32.0%	68.0%
TETON	1,741	1,158	583		575 R	66.5%	33.5%	66.5%	33.5%
UINTA	3,206	1,606	1,600		6 R	50.1%	49.9%	50.1%	49.9%
WASHAKIE	3,595	2,254	1,341		913 R	62.7%	37.3%	62.7%	37.3%
WESTON	2,944	1,743	1,201		542 R	59.2%	40.8%	59.2%	40.8%
TOTAL	140,782	77,451	53,331		14,120 R	55.0%	45.0%	55.0%	45.0%

PRESIDENT 1964

County	Total Vote	Republican	Democratic	Other	Rep.-Dem. Plurality	Percentage Total Vote Rep.	Total Vote Dem.	Major Vote Rep.	Major Vote Dem.
ALBANY	8,942	2,923	6,019		3,096 D	32.7%	67.3%	32.7%	67.3%
BIG HORN	5,353	2,668	2,690		22 D	49.8%	50.2%	49.8%	50.2%
CAMPBELL	2,802	1,606	1,196		410 R	57.3%	42.7%	57.3%	42.7%
CARBON	6,482	2,160	4,322		2,162 D	33.3%	66.7%	33.3%	66.7%
CONVERSE	2,809	1,559	1,250		309 R	55.5%	44.5%	55.5%	44.5%
CROOK	1,994	1,214	780		434 R	60.9%	39.1%	60.9%	39.1%
FREMONT	10,794	4,809	5,985		1,176 D	44.6%	55.4%	44.6%	55.4%
GOSHEN	5,353	2,604	2,749		145 D	48.6%	51.4%	48.6%	51.4%
HOT SPRINGS	2,608	1,228	1,380		152 D	47.1%	52.9%	47.1%	52.9%
JOHNSON	2,492	1,640	852		788 R	65.8%	34.2%	65.8%	34.2%
LARAMIE	24,622	8,563	16,059		7,496 D	34.8%	65.2%	34.8%	65.2%
LINCOLN	4,384	1,811	2,273		462 D	44.3%	55.7%	44.3%	55.7%
NATRONA	21,302	10,135	11,167		1,032 D	47.6%	52.4%	47.6%	52.4%
NIOBRARA	1,965	1,122	843		279 R	57.1%	42.9%	57.1%	42.9%
PARK	7,443	3,698	3,745		47 D	49.7%	50.3%	49.7%	50.3%
PLATTE	3,360	1,470	1,890		420 D	43.8%	56.2%	43.8%	56.2%
SHERIDAN	9,238	4,491	4,747		256 D	48.6%	51.4%	48.6%	51.4%
SUBLETTE	1,691	900	791		109 R	53.2%	46.8%	53.2%	46.8%
SWEETWATER	7,913	1,944	5,969		4,025 D	24.6%	75.4%	24.6%	75.4%
TETON	2,049	1,081	968		113 R	52.8%	47.2%	52.8%	47.2%
UINTA	3,115	1,186	1,929		743 D	38.1%	61.9%	38.1%	61.9%
WASHAKIE	3,408	1,713	1,695		18 R	50.3%	49.7%	50.3%	49.7%
WESTON	2,692	1,473	1,419		54 R	50.9%	49.1%	50.9%	49.1%
TOTAL	142,716	61,998	80,718		18,720 D	43.4%	56.6%	43.4%	56.6%

WYOMING

OTHER VOTE COMPOSITION:

1920   2,180 Farmer-Labor; 1,288 Socialist; 265 Prohibition. The county-by-county
figures include only the Farmer-Labor vote; the state-wide total also includes
the Socialist and Prohibition vote.

1924   Progressive.

1928   Socialist.

1932   2,829 Socialist; 180 Communist.

1936   1,653 Union; 200 Socialist; 91 Communist; 75 Prohibition.

1940   172 Prohibition; 148 Socialist.

1944

1948   931 Progressive; 137 Socialist; 56 Socialist Labor.

1952   194 Prohibition; 40 Socialist; 36 Socialist Labor.

1956

1960

1964

SPECIAL CASES:

1924   Progressive candidates carried one county and ran second in a number of
others. Sublette and Teton counties organized in 1923.

DISTRICT OF COLUMBIA

In April, 1961, under provisions of the 23rd Amendment to the Constitution, the District of Columbia was authorized to choose Presidential and Vice-Presidential electors.

Three electors were chosen in 1964, the total vote being 198,597, of which 28,801 (14.5%) was Republican and 169,796 (85.5%) Democratic. There was no other vote cast and the Democratic margin was 140,995.

No major administrative sub-divisions of the District were used for the election, returns being reported only by individual voting precincts.

DISTRICT OF COLUMBIA